D0406995

Merriam-Webster's Spanish-English Dictionary

Merriam-Webster's Spanish-English Dictionary

MERRIAM-WEBSTER, INCORPORATED
Springfield, Massachusetts, U.S.A.

A GENUINE MERRIAM-WEBSTER

The name *Webster* alone is no guarantee of excellence. It is used by a number of publishers and may serve mainly to mislead an unwary buyer.

Merriam-Webster™ is the name you should look for when you consider the purchase of dictionaries or other fine reference books. It carries the reputation of a company that has been publishing since 1831 and is your assurance of quality and authority.

Library of Congress Cataloging in Publication Data
Main entry under title:

Merriam-Webster's Spanish-English dictionary.
p. cm.
ISBN 0-87779-165-1 (alk. paper)
1. Spanish language—Dictionaries—English. 2. English language—Dictionaries—Spanish. I. Merriam-Webster, Inc.
PC4640.M47 1998
463′.21—dc21

98-5887
CIP

MADE IN THE UNITED STATES OF AMERICA

05 04 03 RRD 10 9 8 7 6 5

Contents | Índice

Preface

MERRIAM-WEBSTER'S SPANISH-ENGLISH DICTIONARY is a completely new dictionary designed to meet the needs of English and Spanish speakers in a time of ever-expanding communication among the countries of the Western Hemisphere. It is intended for language learners, teachers, office workers, tourists, business travelers—anyone who needs to communicate effectively in the Spanish and English languages as they are spoken and written in the Americas. This new dictionary provides accurate and up-to-date coverage of current vocabulary in both languages, as well as abundant examples of words used in context to illustrate idiomatic usage. The selection of Spanish words and idioms was based on evidence drawn from a wide variety of modern Latin-American sources and interpreted by trained Merriam-Webster bilingual lexicographers. The English entries were chosen by Merriam-Webster editors from the most recent Merriam-Webster dictionaries, and they represent the current basic vocabulary of American English.

All of this material is presented in a format which is based firmly upon and, in many important ways, is similar to the traditional styling found in the Merriam-Webster monolingual dictionaries. The reader who is familiar with Merriam-Webster dictionaries will immediately recognize this style, with its emphasis on convenience and ease of use, clarity and conciseness of the information presented, precise discrimination of senses, and frequent inclusion of example phrases showing words in actual use. Also included are pronunciations (in the International Phonetic Alphabet) for all English words, full coverage of irregular verbs in both languages, a section on basic Spanish grammar, a table of the most common Spanish abbreviations, and a detailed Explanatory Notes section which answers any questions the reader might have concerning the use of this book.

Merriam-Webster's Spanish-English Dictionary represents the combined efforts of many members of the Merriam-Webster Editorial Department, along with advice and assistance from consultants outside the company. The primary defining work was done by Charlene M. Chateauneuf, Seán O'Mannion-Espejo, Karen L. Wilkinson, and Jocelyn Woods; early contributions to the text were also submitted by Cèsar Alegre, Hilton Alers, Marién Díaz, Anne Gatschet, and María D. Guijarro, with Victoria E. Neufeldt, Ph.D. and James L. Rader providing helpful suggestions regarding style. Proofreading was done by Susan L. Brady, Daniel B. Brandon, Charlene M. Chateauneuf, Deanna Chiasson, Seán O'Mannion-Espejo, James L. Rader, Donna L. Rickerby, Adrienne M. Scholz, Amy West, Karen L. Wilkinson, and Linda Picard Wood. Brian M. Sietsema, Ph.D. provided the pronunciations. Cross-reference services were provided by Donna L. Rickerby. Karen L. Levister assisted in inputting revisions. Carol Fugiel contributed many hours of clerical assistance and other valuable support. The editorial work relating to typesetting and production was begun by Jennifer S. Goss and continued by Susan L. Brady, who also offered helpful suggestions regarding format. Madeline L. Novak provided guidance on typographic matters. John M. Morse was responsible for the conception of this book as well as for numerous ideas and continued support along the way.

Eileen M. Haraty
Editor

Explanatory Notes

Entries

1. Main Entries

A boldface letter, word, or phrase appearing flush with the left-hand margin of each column of type is a main entry or entry word. The main entry may consist of letters set solid, of letters joined by a hyphen, or of letters separated by a space:

> **cafetalero**[1], **-ra** *adj*. . .
> **eye–opener**. . . *n*. . .
> **walk out** *vi* . . .

The main entry, together with the material that follows it on the same line and succeeding indented lines, constitutes a dictionary entry.

2. Order of Main Entries

Alphabetical order throughout the book follows the order of the English alphabet, with one exception: words beginning with the Spanish letter *ñ* follow all entries for the letter *n*. The main entries follow one another alphabetically letter by letter without regard to intervening spaces or hyphens; for example, *shake-up* follows *shaker.*

Homographs (words with the same spelling) having different parts of speech are usually given separate dictionary entries. These entries are distinguished by superscript numerals following the entry word:

> **hail**[1]. . . *vt*. . .
>
> **hail**[2] *n*. . .
>
> **hail**[3] *interj*. . .
>
> **madrileño**[1], **-ña** *adj*. . .
>
> **madrileño**[2], **-ña** *n*. . .

Numbered homograph entries are listed in the following order: verb, adverb, adjective, noun, conjunction, preposition, pronoun, interjection, article.

Homographs having the same part of speech are normally included at the same dictionary entry, without regard to their different semantic origins. On the English-to-Spanish side, however, separate entries are made if the homographs have distinct inflected forms or if they have distinct pronunciations.

3. Guide Words

A pair of guide words is printed at the top of each page, indicating the first and last main entries that appear on that page:

fregar • fuego

4. Variants

When a main entry is followed by the word *or* and another spelling, the two spellings are variants. Both are standard, and either one may be used according to personal inclination:

jailer *or* **jailor**. . . *n*. . .
quizá *or* **quizás** *adv*. . .

Occasionally, a variant spelling is used only for a particular sense of a word. In these cases, the variant spelling is listed after the sense number of the sense to which it pertains:

electric. . . *adj* **1** *or* **electrical**. . .

Sometimes the entry word is used interchangeably with a longer phrase containing the entry word. For the purposes of this dictionary, such phrases are considered variants of the headword:

bunk[2] *n* **1** *or* **bunk bed**. . .

angina *nf* **1** *or* **angina de pecho** : angina . . .

Variant wordings of boldface phrases may also be shown:

> **madera** *nf*. . . **3 madera dura** *or* **madera noble**. . .
>
> **atención**[1] *nf*. . . **2 poner atención** *or* **prestar atención**. . .

5. Run-On Entries

A main entry may be followed by one or more derivatives or by a homograph with a different functional label. These are run-on entries. Each is introduced by a boldface dash and each has a functional label. They are not defined, however, since their equivalents can be readily derived by adding the corresponding foreign-language suffix to the terms used to define the entry word or, in the case of homographs, simply substituting the appropriate part of speech:

> **illegal**. . . *adj* **:** ilegal **— illegally** *adv*
> (the Spanish adverb is *ilegalmente*)
>
> **transferir**. . . *vt* TRASLADAR **:** to transfer **— transferible** *adj*
> (the English adjective is **transferable**)
>
> **Bosnian** *n* **:** bosnio *m*, -nia *f* **— Bosnian** *adj*
> (the Spanish adjective is *bosnio, -nia*)

On the Spanish side of the book, reflexive verbs are sometimes run on undefined:

> **enrollar** *vt* **:** to roll up, to coil **— enrollarse** *vr*

The absence of a definition means that *enrollarse* has the simple reflexive meaning "to become rolled up or coiled," "to roll itself up."

6. Bold Notes

A main entry may be followed by one or more phrases containing the entry word or an inflected form of the entry word. These are bold notes. Each bold note is defined at its own numbered sense:

> **álamo** *nm* **1 :** poplar **2 álamo temblón :** aspen
>
> **hold**[1]. . . *vi*. . . **4 to hold to :**. . . **5 to hold with :**. . .

If the bold note consists only of the entry word and a single preposition, the entry word is represented by a boldface swung dash **~**.

> **pegar** . . . *vi* . . . **3 ~ con :** to match, to go with . . .

The same bold note phrase may appear at two or more senses if it has more than one distinct meaning:

> **wear**[1]. . . *vt*. . . **3 to wear out :** gastar <he wore out his shoes. . . > **4 to wear out** EXHAUST **:** agotar, fatigar <to wear oneself out . . .> . . .
>
> **estar** . . . *vi* . . . **15 ~ por :** to be in favor of **16 ~ por :** to be about to <está por cerrar . . .> . . .

If the use of the entry word is commonly restricted to one particular phrase, then a bold note may be given as the entry word's only sense:

> **ward**[1]. . . *vt* **to ward off :**. . .

Pronunciation

1. Pronunciation of English Entry Words

The matter between a pair of brackets [ ] following the entry word of an English-to-Spanish entry indicates the pronunciation. The symbols used are explained in the International Phonetic Alphabet chart on page 25a.

The presence of variant pronunciations indicates that not all educated speakers pronounce words the same way. A second-place variant is not to be regarded as less acceptable than the pronunciation that is given first. It may, in fact, be used by as many educated speakers as the first variant, but the requirements of the printed page are such that one must precede the other:

tomato [tə'meɪt̬o, -'mɑ-] . . .

When a compound word has less than a full pronunciation, the missing part is to be supplied from the pronunciation at the entry for the unpronounced element of the compound:

gamma ray ['gæmə]. . .

ray ['reɪ]. . .

smoke[1] ['smo:k]. . .

smoke detector [dɪ'tɛktər]. . .

In general, no pronunciation is given for open compounds consisting of two or more English words that are main entries at their own alphabetical place:

water lily *n* **:** nenúfar *m*

Only the first entry in a series of numbered homographs is given a pronunciation if their pronunciations are the same:

dab[1] ['dæb] *vt*. . .

dab[2] *n*. . .

No pronunciation is shown for principal parts of verbs that are formed by regular suffixation, nor for other derivative words formed by common suffixes.

2. Pronunciation of Spanish Entry Words

Spanish pronunciation is highly regular, so no pronunciations are given for most Spanish-to-English entries. Exceptions have been made for certain words (such as foreign borrowings) whose Spanish pronunciations are not evident from their spellings:

pizza ['pitsa, 'pisa] . . .

footing ['fu,tɪŋ]. . .

Functional Labels

An italic label indicating a part of speech or some other functional classification follows the pronunciation or, if no pronunciation is given, the main entry. The eight traditional parts of speech, adjective, adverb, conjunction, interjection, noun, preposition, pronoun, and verb, are indicated as follows:

daily[2] *adj*. . .

vagamente *adv*. . .

and. . . *conj*. . .

huy *interj*. . .

jackal. . . *n*. . .

para *prep*. . .

neither[3] *pron*. . .

leer. . . *v*. . .

Verbs that are intransitive are labeled *vi,* and verbs that are transitive are labeled *vt.* Entries for verbs that are both transitive and intransitive are labeled *v;* if such an entry includes irregular verb inflections, it is labeled *v* immediately after the main entry, with the labels *vi* and *vt* serving to introduce transitive and intransitive subdivisions when both are present:

deliberar *vi* **:** to deliberate

necessitate. . . *vt* **-tated; -tating :** necesitar, requerir

satisfy. . . *v* **-fied; -fying** *vt*. . . — *vi*. . .

Two other labels are used to indicate functional classifications of verbs: *v aux* (auxiliary verb) and *v impers* (impersonal verb).

may. . . *v aux, past* **might**. . .

haber[1]. . . *v aux* **1 :** have. . . — *v impers*
1 hay : there is, there are. . .

Gender Labels

In Spanish-to-English noun entries, the gender of the entry word is indicated by an italic *m* (masculine), *f* (feminine), or *mf* (masculine or feminine), immediately following the functional label:

magnesio *nm*. . .

galaxia *nf*. . .

turista *nmf*. . .

If both the masculine and feminine forms are shown for a noun referring to a person, the label is simply *n:*

director, -tora *n*. . .

Spanish noun equivalents of English entry words are also labeled for gender:

amnesia. . . *n* **:** amnesia *f*

earache. . . *n* **:** dolor *m* de oído

gamekeeper. . . *n* **:** guardabosque *mf*

Inflected Forms

1. Nouns

The plurals of nouns are shown in this dictionary when they are irregular, when plural suffixation brings about a change in accentuation or in the spelling of the root word, when an English noun ends in a consonant plus *-o* or in *-ey,* when an English noun ends in *-oo,* when an English noun is a compound that pluralizes any element but the last, when a noun has variant plurals, or whenever the dictionary user might have reasonable doubts regarding the spelling of a plural:

> **tooth**. . . *n, pl* **teeth**. . .
>
> **garrafón** *nm, pl* **-fones**. . .
>
> **potato**. . . *n, pl* **-toes**. . .
>
> **abbey**. . . *n, pl* **-beys**. . .
>
> **cuckoo**[2] *n, pl* **-oos**. . .
>
> **brother–in–law**. . . *n, pl* **brothers–in–law** . . .
>
> **quail**[2] *n, pl* **quail** *or* **quails**. . .
>
> **hábitat** *nm, pl* **-tats**. . .
>
> **tahúr** *nm, pl* **tahúres**. . .

Cutback inflected forms are used for most nouns on the English-to-Spanish side, regardless of the number of syllables. On the Spanish-to-English side, cutback inflections are given for nouns that have three or more syllables; plurals for shorter words are written out in full:

> **shampoo**[2] *n, pl* **-poos**. . .
>
> **calamity** . . . *n, pl* **-ties**. . .
>
> **mouse** . . . *n, pl* **mice**. . .
>
> **sartén** *nmf, pl* **sartenes**. . .
>
> **hámster** *nm, pl* **hámsters**. . .
>
> **federación** *nf, pl* **-ciones**. . .

If only one gender form has a plural which is irregular, that plural form will be given with the appropriate label:

> **campeón, -ona** *n, mpl* **-ones :** champion

The plurals of nouns are usually not shown when the base word is unchanged by the addition of the regular plural suffix or when the noun is unlikely to occur in the plural:

apple. . . *n* **:** manzana *f*

inglés[3] *nm* **:** English (language)

Nouns that are plural in form and that regularly occur in plural constructions are labeled as *npl* (for English nouns), *nmpl* (for Spanish masculine nouns), or *nfpl* (for Spanish feminine nouns):

knickers. . . *npl*. . .

enseres *nmpl*. . .

mancuernas *nfpl*. . .

Entry words that are unchanged in the plural are labeled *ns & pl* (for English nouns), *nms & pl* (for Spanish masculine nouns), *nfs & pl* (for Spanish feminine nouns), and *nmfs & pl* (for Spanish gender-variable nouns):

deer. . . *ns & pl* . . .

lavaplatos *nms & pl*. . .

tesis *nfs & pl* . . .

rompehuelgas *nmfs & pl* . . .

2. Verbs

ENGLISH VERBS

The principal parts of verbs are shown in English-to-Spanish entries when they are irregular, when suffixation brings about a change in spelling of the root word, when the verb ends in *-ey*, when there are variant inflected forms, or whenever it is believed that the dictionary user might have reasonable doubts about the spelling of an inflected form:

break[1]. . . *v* **broke**. . . ; **broken**. . . ; **breaking**. . .

drag[1]. . . *v* **dragged; dragging**. . .

monkey[1]. . . *vi* **-keyed; -keying**. . .

label[1]. . . *vt* **-beled** *or* **-belled; -beling** *or* **-belling. . .**

imagine. . . *vt* **-ined; -ining. . .**

Cutback inflected forms are usually used when the verb has two or more syllables:

multiply. . . *v* **-plied; -plying. . .**

bevel[1]. . . *v* **-eled** *or* **-elled; -eling** *or* **-elling. . .**

forgo *or* **forego. . .** *vt* **-went; -gone; -going. . .**

commit . . . *vt* **-mitted; -mitting . . .**

The principal parts of an English verb are not shown when the base word is unchanged by suffixation:

delay[1]. . . *vt*

pitch[1]. . . *vt*

SPANISH VERBS

Entries for irregular Spanish verbs are cross-referenced by number to the model conjugations appearing in the Conjugation of Spanish Verbs section:

abnegarse {49} *vr. . .*

volver {89} *vi. . .*

Entries for Spanish verbs with regular conjugations are not cross-referenced; however, model conjugations for regular Spanish verbs are included in the Conjugation of Spanish Verbs section beginning on page 44a.

Adverbs and Adjectives

The comparative and superlative forms of English adjective and adverb main entries are shown when suffixation brings about a change in spelling of the root word, when the inflection is irregular, and when there are variant inflected forms:

wet[2] *adj* **wetter; wettest**. . .

good[2] *adj* **better**. . . ; **best**. . .

evil[1]. . . *adj* **eviler** *or* **eviller; evilest** *or* **evillest**. . .

The superlative forms of adjectives and adverbs of two or more syllables are usually cut back; the superlative is shown in full, however, when it is desirable to indicate the pronunciation of the inflected form:

early[1]. . . *adv* **earlier; -est**. . .

gaudy. . . *adj* **gaudier; -est**. . .

secure[2] *adj* **-curer; -est**. . .

but

young[1]. . . *adj* **younger** [ˈjʌŋgər]; **youngest** [-gəst]. . .

At a few entries only the superlative form is shown:

mere *adj, superlative* **merest**. . .

The absence of the comparative form indicates that there is no evidence of its use.

The comparative and superlative forms of adjectives and adverbs are usually not shown when the base word is unchanged by suffixation:

quiet[3] *adj* **1**. . .

Usage

1. Usage Labels

Two types of usage labels are used in this dictionary—regional and stylistic. Spanish words that are limited in use to a specific area or areas of Latin America, or to Spain, are given labels indicating the countries in which they are most commonly used:

> **guarachear** *vi Cuba, PRi fam*. . .
>
> **bucket**. . . *n* **:**. . . cubeta *f Mex*

The following regional labels are used in this book: *Arg* (Argentina), *Bol* (Bolivia), *CA* (Central America), *Car* (Caribbean), *Chile* (Chile), *Col* (Colombia), *CoRi* (Costa Rica), *Cuba* (Cuba), *DomRep* (Dominican Republic), *Ecua* (Ecuador), *Sal* (El Salvador), *Guat* (Guatemala), *Hond* (Honduras), *Mex* (Mexico), *Nic* (Nicaragua), *Pan* (Panama), *Par* (Paraguay), *Peru* (Peru), *PRi* (Puerto Rico), *Spain* (Spain), *Uru* (Uruguay), *Ven* (Venezuela).

Since this book focuses on the Spanish spoken in Latin America, only the most common regionalisms from Spain have been included in order to allow for more thorough coverage of Latin-American forms.

A number of Spanish words are given a *fam* (familiar) label as well, indicating that these words are suitable for informal contexts but would not normally be used in formal writing or speaking. The stylistic label *usu considered vulgar* is added for a word which is usually considered vulgar or offensive but whose widespread use justifies its inclusion in this book. The label is intended to warn the reader that the word in question may be inappropriate in polite conversation.

2. Usage Notes

Definitions are sometimes preceded by parenthetical usage notes that give supplementary semantic information:

> **not**. . . *adv* **1** (*used to form a negative*) **:** no. . .
>
> **within**[2] *prep* . . . **2** (*in expressions of distance*) **:**. . . **3** (*in expressions of time*) **:** . . .

e[2] *conj* (*used instead of* **y** *before words beginning with i or hi*) **:**. . .

poder[1]. . . *v aux*. . . **2** (*expressing possibility*) **:**. . . **3** (*expressing permission*) **:**. . .

Additional semantic orientation is also sometimes given in the form of parenthetical notes appearing within the definition:

calibrate. . . *vt*. . . **:** calibrar (armas), graduar (termómetros)

palco *nm* **:** box (in a theater or stadium)

Occasionally a usage note is used in place of a definition. This is usually done when the entry word has no single foreign-language equivalent. This type of usage note will be accompanied by examples of common use:

shall. . . *v aux*. . . **1** (*used to express a command*) <you shall do as I say **:** harás lo que te digo> . . .

3. Illustrations of Usage

Definitions are sometimes followed by verbal illustrations that show a typical use of the word in context or a common idiomatic usage. These verbal illustrations include a translation and are enclosed in angle brackets:

lejos *adv* **1 :** far away, distant <a lo lejos **:** in the distance, far off> . . .

make[1]. . . **9** . . .**:** ganar <to make a living **:** ganarse la vida> . . .

Sense Division

A boldface colon is used to introduce a definition:

fable. . . *n* **:** fábula *f*

Boldface Arabic numerals separate the senses of a word that has more than one sense:

laguna *nf* **1 :** lagoon **2 :** lacuna, gap

Whenever some information (such as a synonym, a boldface word or phrase, a usage note, a cross-reference, or a label) follows a sense number, it applies only to that specific numbered sense and not to any other boldface numbered senses:

abanico *nm*. . . **2** GAMA **:**. . .

tonic² *n*. . . **2** *or* **tonic water :**. . .

grillo *nm*. . . **2 grillos** *nmpl* **:**. . .

fairy. . . *n, pl* **fairies**. . . **2 fairy tale :**. . .

myself. . . *pron* **1** (*used reflexively*) **:**. . .

pike. . . *n*. . . **3** → **turnpike**

atado² *nm*. . . **2** *Arg* **:**. . .

Cross-References

Three different kinds of cross-references are used in this dictionary: synonymous, cognate, and inflectional. In each instance the cross-reference is readily recognized by the boldface arrow following the entry word.

Synonymous and cognate cross-references indicate that a definition at the entry cross-referred to can be substituted for the entry word:

scapula. . . → **shoulder blade**

amuck. . . → **amok**

An inflectional cross-reference is used to identify the entry word as an inflected form of another word (as a noun or verb):

fue, etc. → **ir, ser**

mice → **mouse**

Synonyms

At many entries or senses in this book, a synonym in small capital letters is provided before the boldface colon and the following defining text. These synonyms are all main entries or bold notes elsewhere in the book. They serve as a helpful guide to the meaning of the entry or sense and also give the reader an additional term that might be substituted in a similar context. On the English-to-Spanish side synonyms are particularly abundant, since special care has been taken to guide the English speaker—by means of synonyms, verbal illustrations, or usage notes—to the meaning of the Spanish terms at each sense of a multisense entry.

Abbreviations in this Work

adj	adjective
adv	adverb
Arg	Argentina
Bol	Bolivia
Brit	British
CA	Central America
Car	Caribbean region
Col	Colombia
conj	conjuction
CoRi	Costa Rica
DomRep	Dominican Republic
Ecua	Ecuador
esp	especially
f	feminine
fam	familiar or colloquial
fpl	feminine plural
Guat	Guatemala
Hond	Honduras
interj	interjection
m	masculine
Mex	Mexico
mf	masculine or feminine
mpl	masculine plural
n	noun
nf	feminine noun
nfpl	feminine plural noun
nfs & pl	invariable singular or plural feminine noun
Nic	Nicaragua
nm	masculine noun
nmf	masculine or feminine noun
nmfpl	plural noun invariable for gender
nmfs & pl	noun invariable for both gender and number
nmpl	masculine plural noun
nms & pl	invariable singular or plural masculine noun
npl	plural noun
ns & pl	noun invariable for plural
Pan	Panama
Par	Paraguay
pl	plural
pp	past participle
prep	preposition
PRi	Puerto Rico
pron	pronoun
s	singular
Sal	El Salvador
Uru	Uruguay
usu	usually
v	verb (transitive and intransitive)
v aux	auxiliary verb
Ven	Venezuela
vi	intransitive verb
v impers	impersonal verb
vr	reflexive verb
vt	transitive verb

Pronunciation Symbols

VOWELS

æ	**a**sk, b**a**t, gl**a**d
ɑ	c**o**t, b**o**mb
a	*New England* **au**nt, *British* **a**sk, gl**a**ss, *Spanish* c**a**sa
e	*Spanish* p**e**so, j**e**fe
ɛ	**e**gg, b**e**t, f**e**d
ə	**a**bout, jav**e**lin, Alabam**a**
ə	when italicized as in *ə*l, *ə*m, *ə*n, indicates a syllabic pronunciation of the consonant as in bott**le**, pri**sm**, butt**on**
i	ver**y**, an**y**, thirt**y**, *Spanish* p**i**ña
iː	**ea**t, b**ea**d, b**ee**
ɪ	**i**d, b**i**d, p**i**t
o	**O**hio, yell**o**wer, potat**o**, *Spanish* **ó**val**o**
oː	**oa**ts, **ow**n, z**o**ne, bl**ow**
ɔ	**aw**l, m**au**l, c**au**ght, p**aw**
ʊ	s**u**re, sh**ou**ld, c**ou**ld
u	*Spanish* **u**va, c**u**lpa
uː	b**oo**t, f**ew**, c**oo**
ʌ	**u**nder, p**u**tt, b**u**d
eɪ	**ei**ght, w**a**de, b**ay**
aɪ	**i**ce, b**i**te, t**ie**
aʊ	**ou**t, g**ow**n, pl**ow**
ɔɪ	**oy**ster, c**oi**l, b**oy**
ɒ	*British* b**o**nd, g**o**d
ø	*French* d**eu**x, *German* H**öh**le
œ	*French* b**œu**f, *German* H**ö**lle
y	*French* l**u**ne, *German* f**üh**len
ʏ	*German* f**ü**llt
~	(tilde as in ã, ɔ̃, ɛ̃) *French* v**in**, b**on**, bi**en**
ː	indicates that the preceding vowel is long. Long vowels are almost always diphthongs in English, but not in Spanish.

STRESS MARKS

ˈ	high stress	**pen**manship
ˌ	low stress	penman**ship**

CONSONANTS

b	**b**a**b**y, la**b**or, ca**b**
β	*Spanish* ca**b**o, ó**v**alo
d	**d**ay, rea**d**y, ki**d**
dʒ	**j**ust, ba**dg**er, fu**dg**e
ð	**th**en, ei**th**er, ba**th**e
f	**f**oe, tou**gh**, bu**ff**
g	**g**o, bi**gg**er, ba**g**
ɣ	*Spanish* tra**g**ar, da**g**a
h	**h**ot, a**h**a
j	**y**es, vine**y**ard
ʲ	marks palatalization as in *French* digne [dinʲ]
k	**c**at, **k**eep, la**cqu**er, flo**ck**
l	**l**aw, ho**ll**ow, boi**l**
m	**m**at, he**m**p, ha**mm**er, ri**m**
n	**n**ew, te**n**t, te**n**or, ru**n**
ŋ	ru**ng**, ha**ng**, swi**ng**er
ɲ	*Spanish* caba**ñ**a, pi**ñ**a
p	**p**ay, la**p**se, to**p**
r	**r**ope, bu**r**n, ta**r**
s	**s**ad, mi**s**t, ki**ss**
ʃ	**sh**oe, mi**ss**ion, slu**sh**
t	**t**oe, bu**tt**on, ma**t**
t̬	indicates that some speakers of English pronounce this as a voiced alveolar flap [ɾ], as in la**t**er, ca**tt**y, ba**tt**le
tʃ	**ch**oose, ba**tch**
θ	**th**in, e**th**er, ba**th**
v	**v**at, ne**v**er, ca**v**e
w	**w**et, soft**w**are
x	*German* Ba**ch**, *Scots* lo**ch**, *Spanish* **g**ente, **j**efe
z	**z**oo, ea**s**y, bu**zz**
ʒ	**j**aborandi, a**z**ure, bei**g**e
ʔ	indicates a glottal stop, the sound beginning the syllables in **uh-oh**
h, k, p, t	when italicized indicate sounds which are present in the pronunciation of some speakers of English but absent in that of others, so that *whence* [ˈ*h*wɛn*t*s] can be pronounced as [ˈwɛns], [ˈhwɛns], [ˈwɛnts], or [ˈhwɛnts]

Spanish Grammar

Accentuation

Spanish word stress is generally determined according to the following rules:

- Words ending in a vowel, or in *-n* or *-s,* are stressed on the penultimate syllable (*za**pa**to,* ***lla**man*).
- Words ending in a consonant other than *-n* or *-s* are stressed on the last syllable (*per**diz**, curiosi**dad***).

Exceptions to these rules have a written accent mark over the stressed vowel (***fá**cil, habla**rá**, **úl**timo*). There are also a few words which take accent marks in order to distinguish them from homonyms (*si, sí; que, qué; el, él;* etc.).

Adverbs ending in *-mente* have two stressed syllables since they retain both the stress of the root word and of the *-mente* suffix (***len**ta**men**te, di**fí**cil**men**te*). Many compounds also have two stressed syllables (***lim**piapara**bri**sas*).

Punctuation and Capitalization

Questions and exclamations in Spanish are preceded by an inverted question mark ¿ and an inverted exclamation mark ¡, respectively:

¿Cuándo llamó Ana?
Y tú, ¿qué piensas?

¡No hagas eso!
Pero, ¡qué lástima!

In Spanish, unlike English, the following words are not capitalized:

- Names of days, months, and languages (*jueves, octubre, español*).
- Spanish adjectives or nouns derived from proper nouns (*los nicaragüenses, una teoría marxista*).

Articles

1. Definite Article

Spanish has five forms of the definite article: *el* (masculine singular), *la* (feminine singular), *los* (masculine plural), *las* (feminine plural), and *lo* (neuter). The first four agree in gender and number with the nouns they limit (*el carro,* the car; *las tijeras,* the scissors), although the form *el* is used with feminine singular nouns beginning with a stressed *a-* or *ha-* (*el águila, el hambre*).

The neuter article *lo* is used with the masculine singular form of an adjective to express an abstract concept (*lo mejor de este método,* the best thing about this method; *lo meticuloso de su trabajo,* the meticulousness of her work; *lo mismo para mí,* the same for me).

Whenever the masculine article *el* immediately follows the words *de* or *a,* it combines with them to form the contractions *del* and *al,* respectively (*viene* ***del*** *campo, vi* ***al*** *hermano de Roberto*).

The use of *el, la, los,* and *las* in Spanish corresponds largely to the use of *the* in English; some exceptions are noted below.

The definite article is used:

- When referring to something as a class (*los gatos son ágiles,* cats are agile; *me gusta el café,* I like coffee).
- In references to meals and in most expressions of time (*¿comiste el almuerzo?,* did you eat lunch?; *vino el año pasado,* he came last year; *son las dos,* it's two o'clock; *prefiero el verano,* I prefer summer; *la reunión es el lunes,*

the meeting is on Monday; but: *hoy es lunes,* today is Monday).

- Before titles (except *don, doña, san, santo, santa, fray,* and *sor*) in third-person references to people (*la señora Rivera llamó,* Mrs. Rivera called; but: *hola, señora Rivera,* hello, Mrs. Rivera).
- In references to body parts and personal possessions (*me duele la cabeza,* my head hurts; *dejó el sombrero,* he left his hat).
- To mean "the one" or "the ones" when the subject is already understood (*la de madera,* the wooden one; *los que vi ayer,* the ones I saw yesterday).

The definite article is omitted:

- Before a noun in apposition, if the noun is not modified (*Caracas, capital de Venezuela;* but: *Pico Bolívar, la montaña más alta de Venezuela*).
- Before a number in a royal title (*Carlos Quinto,* Charles the Fifth).

2. Indefinite Article

The forms of the indefinite article in Spanish are *un* (masculine singular), *una* (feminine singular), *unos* (masculine plural), and *unas* (feminine plural). They agree in number and gender with the nouns they limit (*una mesa,* a table; *unos platos,* some plates), although the form *un* is used with feminine singular nouns beginning with a stressed *a-* or *ha-* (*un ala, un hacha*).

The use of *un, una, unos,* and *unas* in Spanish corresponds largely to the use of *a, an,* and *some* in English, with some exceptions:

- Indefinite articles are generally omitted before nouns identifying someone or something as a member of a class or category (*Paco es profesor/católico,* Paco is a professor/Catholic; *se llama páncreas,* it's called a pancreas).

- They are also often omitted in instances where quantity is understood from context (*vine sin chaqueta,* I came without a jacket; *no tengo carro,* I don't have a car).

Nouns

1. Gender

Nouns in Spanish are either masculine or feminine. A noun's gender can often be determined according to the following guidelines:

- Nouns ending in *-aje, -o,* or *-or* are usually masculine (*el traje, el libro, el sabor*), with some exceptions (*la mano, la foto, la labor,* etc.).
- Nouns ending in *-a, -dad, -ión, -tud,* or *-umbre* are usually feminine (*la alfombra, la capacidad, la excepción, la juventud, la certidumbre*). Exceptions include: *el día, el mapa,* and many learned borrowings ending in *-ma* (*el idioma, el tema*).

Most nouns referring to people or animals agree in gender with the subject (*el hombre, la mujer; el hermano, la hermana; el perro, la perra*). However, some nouns referring to people, including those ending in *-ista,* use the same form for both sexes (*el artista, la artista; el modelo, la modelo;* etc.).

A few names of animals exist in only one gender form (*la jirafa, el sapo,* etc.). In these instances, the adjectives *macho* and *hembra* are sometimes used to distinguish males and females (*una jirafa macho,* a male giraffe).

2. Pluralization

Plurals of Spanish nouns are formed as follows:

- Nouns ending in an unstressed vowel or an accented *-é* are pluralized by adding *-s* (*la vaca, las vacas; el café, los cafés*).

- Nouns ending in a consonant other than *-s,* or in a stressed vowel other than *-é,* are generally pluralized by adding *-es* (*el papel, los papeles; el rubí, los rubíes*). Exceptions include *papá* (*papás*) and *mamá* (*mamás*).

- Nouns with an unstressed final syllable ending in *-s* usually have a zero plural (*la crisis, las crisis; el jueves, los jueves*). Other nouns ending in *-s* add *-es* to form the plural (*el mes, los meses; el país, los países*).

- Nouns ending in *-z* are pluralized by changing the *-z* to *-c* and adding *-es* (*el lápiz, los lápices; la vez, las veces*).

- Many compound nouns have a zero plural (*el paraguas, los paraguas; el aguafiestas, los aguafiestas*).

- The plurals of *cualquiera* and *quienquiera* are *cualesquiera* and *quienesquiera,* respectively.

Adjectives

1. Gender and Number

Most adjectives agree in gender and number with the nouns they modify (un chico *alto,* una chica *alta,* unos chicos *altos,* unas chicas *altas*). Some adjectives, including those ending in *-e* and *-ista* (*fuerte, altruista*) and comparative adjectives ending in *-or* (*mayor, mejor*), vary only for number.

Adjectives whose masculine singular forms end in *-o* generally change the *-o* to *-a* to form the feminine (*pequeño* → *pequeña*). Masculine adjectives ending in *-án, -ón,* or *-dor,* and masculine adjectives of nationality which end in a consonant, usually add *-a* to form the feminine (*holgazán* → *holgazana*; *llorón* → *llorona*; *trabajador* → *trabajadora*; *irlandés* → *irlandesa*).

Adjectives are pluralized in much the same manner as nouns:

- The plurals of adjectives ending in an unstressed vowel or an accented *-é* are formed by adding an *-s* (un postre *rico,* unos postres *ricos;* una camisa *café,* unas camisas *cafés*).

- Adjectives ending in a consonant, or in a stressed vowel other than *-é,* are generally pluralized by adding *-es* (un niño *cortés,* unos niños *corteses;* una persona *iraní,* unas personas *iraníes*).
- Adjectives ending in *-z* are pluralized by changing the *-z* to *-c* and adding *-es* (una respuesta *sagaz,* unas respuestas *sagaces*).

2. Shortening

- The following masculine singular adjectives drop their final *-o* when they occur before a masculine singular noun: *bueno* (*buen*), *malo* (*mal*), *uno* (*un*), *alguno* (*algún*), *ninguno* (*ningún*), *primero* (*primer*), *tercero* (*tercer*).
- *Grande* shortens to *gran* before any singular noun.
- *Ciento* shortens to *cien* before any noun.
- The title *Santo* shortens to *San* before all masculine names except those beginning with *To-* or *Do-* (*San Juan, Santo Tomás*).

3. Position

Descriptive adjectives generally follow the nouns they modify (*una cosa útil, un actor famoso*). However, adjectives that express an inherent quality often precede the noun (*la blanca nieve*).

Some adjectives change meaning depending on whether they occur before or after the noun: *un pobre niño,* a poor (pitiable) child; *un niño pobre,* a poor (not rich) child; *un gran hombre,* a great man; *un hombre grande,* a big man; *el único libro,* the only book; *el libro único,* the unique book, etc.

4. Comparative and Superlative Forms

The comparative of Spanish adjectives is generally rendered as *más . . . que* (more . . . than) or *menos . . . que* (less . . . than): *soy más alta que él,* I'm taller than he; *son menos inteligentes que tú,* they're less intelligent than you.

The superlative of Spanish adjectives usually follows the formula *definite article* + (*noun* +) *más/menos* + *adjective: ella es la estudiante más trabajadora,* she is the hardest-working student; *él es el menos conocido,* he's the least known.

A few Spanish adjectives have irregular comparative and superlative forms:

Adjective	Comparative/Superlative
bueno (good)	**mejor** (better, best)
malo (bad)	**peor** (worse, worst)
grande[1] (big, great), **viejo** (old)	**mayor** (greater, older; greatest, oldest)
pequeño[1] (little), **joven** (young)	**menor** (lesser, younger; least, youngest)
mucho (much), **muchos** (many)	**más** (more, most)
poco (little), **pocos** (few)	**menos** (less, least)

[1]These words have regular comparative and superlative forms when used in reference to physical size: *él es más grande que yo; nuestra casa es la más pequeña.*

ABSOLUTE SUPERLATIVE

The absolute superlative is formed by placing *muy* before the adjective, or by adding the suffix *-ísimo* (*ella es muy simpática* or *ella es simpatiquísima,* she is very nice). The absolute superlative using *-ísimo* is formed according to the following rules:

- Adjectives ending in a consonant other than *-z* simply add the *-ísimo* ending (*fácil* → *facilísimo*).
- Adjectives ending in *-z* change this consonant to *-c* and add *-ísimo* (*feliz* → *felicísimo*).
- Adjectives ending in a vowel or diphthong drop the vowel or diphthong and add *-ísimo* (*claro* → *clarísimo; amplio* → *amplísimo*).

- Adjectives ending in *-co* or *-go* change these endings to *qu* and *gu*, respectively, and add *-ísimo* (*rico* → *riquísimo; largo* → *larguísimo*).
- Adjectives ending in *-ble* change this ending to *-bil* and add *-ísimo* (*notable* → *notabilísimo*).
- Adjectives containing the stressed diphthong *ie* or *ue* will sometimes change these to *e* and *o*, respectively (*ferviente* → *fervientísimo* or *ferventísimo; bueno* → *buenísimo* or *bonísimo*).

Adverbs

Adverbs can be formed by adding the adverbial suffix *-mente* to virtually any adjective (*fácil* → *fácilmente*). If the adjective varies for gender, the feminine form is used as the basis for forming the adverb (*rápido* → *rápidamente*).

Pronouns

1. Personal Pronouns

The personal pronouns in Spanish are:

Person	Singular		Plural	
FIRST	**yo**	I	**nosotros, nosotras**	we
SECOND	**tú**	you (familiar)	**vosotros**[2], **vosotras**[2]	you, all of you
	vos[1]	you		
	usted	you (formal)	**ustedes**[3]	you, all of you
THIRD	**él**	he	**ellos, ellas**	they
	ella	she		
	ello	it (neuter)		

1 Familiar form used in addition to *tú* in South and Central America.
2 Familiar form used in Spain.
3 Formal form used in Spain; familiar and formal form used in Latin America.

FAMILIAR VS. FORMAL

The second person personal pronouns exist in both familiar and formal forms. The familiar forms are generally used when addressing relatives, friends, and children, although usage varies considerably from region to region; the formal forms are used in other contexts to show courtesy, respect, or emotional distance.

In Spain and in the Caribbean, *tú* is used exclusively as the familiar singular "you." In South and Central America, however, *vos* either competes with *tú* to varying degrees or replaces it entirely. (For a more detailed explanation of *vos* and its corresponding verb forms, refer to the Conjugation of Spanish Verbs section.)

The plural familiar form *vosotros, -as* is used only in Spain, where *ustedes* is reserved for formal contexts. In Latin America, *vosotros, -as* is not used, and *ustedes* serves as the all-purpose plural "you."

It should be noted that while *usted* and *ustedes* are regarded as second person pronouns, they take the third person form of the verb.

USAGE

In Spanish, personal pronouns are generally omitted (*voy al cine,* I'm going to the movies; *¿llamaron?,* did they call?), although they are sometimes used for purposes of emphasis or clarity (*se lo diré yo,* I will tell them; *vino ella, pero él se quedó,* she came, but he stayed behind). The forms *usted* and *ustedes* are usually included out of courtesy (*¿cómo está usted?,* how are you?).

Personal pronouns are not generally used in reference to inanimate objects or living creatures other than humans; in these instances, the pronoun is most often omitted (*¿es nuevo? no, es viejo,* is it new? no, it's old).

The neuter third person pronoun *ello* is reserved for indefinite subjects (as abstract concepts): *todo ello implica . . . ,* all of this implies . . . ; *por si ello fuera poco . . . ,* as if that weren't enough . . . . It most commonly appears in formal writing and

speech. In less formal contexts, *ello* is often either omitted or replaced with *esto, eso,* or *aquello.*

2. Prepositional Pronouns

Prepositional pronouns are used as the objects of prepositions (*¿es para mí?,* is it for me?; *se lo dio a ellos,* he gave it to them).

The prepositional pronouns in Spanish are:

Singular		Plural	
mí	me	**nosotros, nosotras**	us
ti	you	**vosotros[1], vosotras[1]**	you
usted	you (formal)	**ustedes**	you
él	him	**ellos, ellas**	them
ella	her		
ello	it (neuter)		
sí	yourself, himself, herself, itself, oneself	**sí**	yourselves, themselves

[1]Used primarily in Spain.

When the preposition *con* is followed by *mí, ti,* or *sí,* both words are replaced by *conmigo, contigo,* and *consigo,* respectively (*¿vienes conmigo?,* are you coming with me?; *habló contigo,* he spoke with you; *no lo trajo consigo,* she didn't bring it with her).

3. Object Pronouns

DIRECT OBJECT PRONOUNS

Direct object pronouns represent the primary goal or result of the action of a verb. The direct object pronouns in Spanish are:

Singular		Plural	
me	me	**nos**	us
te	you	**os[1]**	you
le[2]	you, him	**les[2]**	you, them
lo	you, him, it	**los**	you, them
la	you, her, it	**las**	you, them

[1]Used only in Spain.
[2]Used mainly in Spain.

Agreement

The third person forms agree in both gender and number with the nouns they replace or the people they refer to (*pintó las paredes,* she painted the walls → *las pintó,* she painted them; *visitaron al señor Juárez,* they visited Mr. Juárez → *lo visitaron,* they visited him). The remaining forms vary only for number.

Position

Direct object pronouns are normally affixed to the end of an affirmative command, a simple infinitive, or a present participle (*¡hazlo!,* do it!; *es difícil hacerlo,* it's difficult to do it; *haciéndolo, aprenderás,* you'll learn by doing it). With constructions involving an auxiliary verb and an infinitive or present participle, the pronoun may occur either immediately before the construction or suffixed to it (*lo voy a hacer* or *voy a hacerlo,* I'm going to do it; *estoy haciéndolo* or *lo estoy haciendo,* I'm doing it). In all other cases, the pronoun immediately precedes the conjugated verb (*no lo haré,* I won't do it).

Regional Variation

In Spain and in a few areas of Latin America, *le* and *les* are used in place of *lo* and *los* when referring to or addressing people (*le vieron,* they saw him; *les vistió,* she dressed them). In most parts of Latin America, however, *los* and *las* are used for the second person plural in both formal and familiar contexts.

The second person plural familiar form *os* is restricted to Spain.

INDIRECT OBJECT PRONOUNS

Indirect object pronouns represent the secondary goal of the action of a verb (*me dio el regalo,* he gave me the gift; *les dije que no,* I told them no). The indirect object pronouns in Spanish are:

Singular		Plural	
me	(to, for, from) me	**nos**	(to, for, from) us
te	(to, for, from) you	**os**[1]	(to, for, from) you
le	(to, for, from) you, him, her, it	**les**	(to, for, from) you, them
se[2]		**se**[2]	

[1]Used only in Spain.
[2]See explanation below.

Position

Indirect object pronouns follow the same rules as direct object pronouns with regard to their position in relation to verbs. When they occur with direct object pronouns, the indirect object pronoun always precedes (*nos lo dio,* she gave it to us; *estoy trayéndotela,* I'm bringing it to you).

Use of *Se*

When the indirect object pronouns *le* or *les* occur before any direct object pronoun beginning with an *l-*, the indirect object pronouns *le* and *les* convert to *se* (*les mandé la carta,* I sent them the letter → *se la mandé,* I sent it to them; *vamos a comprarle los aretes,* let's buy her the earrings → *vamos a comprárselos,* let's buy them for her).

4. Reflexive Pronouns

Reflexive pronouns are used to refer back to the subject of the verb (*me hice daño,* I hurt myself; *se vistieron,* they got dressed, they dressed themselves; *nos lo compramos,* we bought it for ourselves).

The reflexive pronouns in Spanish are:

Singular		Plural	
me	myself	**nos**	ourselves
te	yourself	**os**[1]	yourselves
se	yourself, himself, herself, itself	**se**	yourselves, themselves

[1]Used only in Spain.

Reflexive pronouns are also used:

- When the verb describes an action performed to one's own body, clothing, etc. (*me quité los zapatos,* I took off my shoes; *se arregló el pelo,* he fixed his hair).

- In the plural, to indicate reciprocal action (*se hablan con frecuencia,* they speak with each other frequently).
- In the third person singular and plural, as an indefinite subject reference (*se dice que es verdad,* they say it's true; *nunca se sabe,* one never knows; *se escribieron miles de páginas,* thousands of pages were written).

It should be noted that many verbs which take reflexive pronouns in Spanish have intransitive equivalents in English (*ducharse,* to shower; *quejarse,* to complain; etc.).

5. Relative Pronouns

Relative pronouns introduce subordinate clauses acting as nouns or modifiers (*el libro que escribió . . . ,* the book that he wrote . . . ; *las chicas a quienes conociste . . . ,* the girls whom you met . . .). In Spanish, the relative pronouns are:

que (that, which, who, whom)

quien, quienes (who, whom, that, whoever, whomever)

el cual, la cual, los cuales, las cuales (which, who)

el que, la que, los que, las que (which, who, whoever)

lo cual (which)

lo que (what, which, whatever)

cuanto, cuanta, cuantos, cuantas (all those that, all that, whatever, whoever, as much as, as many as)

Relative pronouns are not omitted in Spanish as they often are in English: *el carro que vi ayer,* the car (that) I saw yesterday. When relative pronouns are used with prepositions, the preposition precedes the clause (*la película sobre la cual le hablé,* the film I spoke to you about).

The relative pronoun *que* can be used in reference to both people and things. Unlike other relative pronouns, *que* does not take the personal *a* when used as a direct object referring to a person (*el hombre que llamé,* the man that I called; but: *el hombre a quien llamé,* the man whom I called).

Quien is used only in reference to people. It varies in number with the explicit or implied antecedent (*las mujeres con quienes charlamos . . .,* the women we chatted with; *quien lo hizo pagará,* whoever did it will pay).

El cual and *el que* vary for both number and gender, and are therefore often used in situations where *que* or *quien(es)* might create ambiguity: *nos contó algunas cosas sobre los libros, las cuales eran interesantes,* he told us some things about the books which (the things) were interesting.

Lo cual and *lo que* are used to refer back to a whole clause, or to something indefinite (*dijo que iría, lo cual me alegró,* he said he would go, which made me happy; *pide lo que quieras,* ask for whatever you want).

Cuanto varies for both number and gender with the implied antecedent: *conté a cuantas (personas) pude,* I counted as many (people) as I could. If an indefinite mass quantity is referred to, the masculine singular form is used (*anoté cuanto decía,* I jotted down whatever he said).

Possessives

1. Possessive Adjectives

UNSTRESSED FORMS

Singular		Plural	
mi(s)	my	**nuestro(s), nuestra(s)**	our
tu(s)	your	**vuestro(s)**[1], **vuestra(s)**[1]	your
su(s)	your, his, her, its	**su(s)**	your, their

[1]Used only in Spain.

STRESSED FORMS

Singular		Plural	
mío(s), mía(s)	my, mine, of mine	**nuestro(s), nuestra(s)**	our, ours, of ours
tuyo(s), tuya(s)	your, yours, of yours	**vuestro(s)[1], vuestra(s)[1]**	your, yours, of yours
suyo(s), suya(s)	your, yours, of yours; his, of his; her, hers, of hers; its, of its	**suyo(s), suya(s)**	your, yours, of yours; their, theirs, of theirs

[1]Used only in Spain.

The unstressed forms of possessive adjectives precede the nouns they modify (*mis zapatos,* my shoes; *nuestra escuela,* our school).

The stressed forms occur after the noun and are often used for purposes of emphasis (*el carro tuyo,* your car; *la pluma es mía,* the pen is mine; *unos amigos nuestros,* some friends of ours).

All possessive adjectives agree with the noun in number. The stressed forms, as well as the unstressed forms *nuestro* and *vuestro,* also vary for gender.

2. Possessive Pronouns

The possessive pronouns have the same forms as the stressed possessive adjectives (see table above). They are always preceded by the definite article, and they agree in number and gender with the nouns they replace (*las llaves mías,* my keys → *las mías,* mine; *los guantes nuestros,* our gloves → *los nuestros,* ours).

Demonstratives

1. Demonstrative Adjectives

The demonstrative adjectives in Spanish are:

Singular		Plural	
este, esta	this	**estos, estas**	these
ese, esa	that	**esos, esas**	those
aquel, aquella	that	**aquellos, aquellas**	those

Demonstrative adjectives agree with the nouns they modify in gender and number (*esta chica, aquellos árboles*). They normally precede the noun, but may occasionally occur after for purposes of emphasis or to express contempt: *en la época aquella de cambio,* in that era of change; *el perro ese ha ladrado toda la noche,* that (awful, annoying, etc.) dog barked all night long.

The forms *aquel, aquella, aquellos,* and *aquellas* are generally used in reference to people and things that are relatively distant from the speaker in space or time: *ese libro,* that book (a few feet away); *aquel libro,* that book (way over there).

2. Demonstrative Pronouns

The demonstrative pronouns in Spanish are orthographically identical to the demonstrative adjectives except that they take an accent mark over the stressed vowel (*éste, ése, aquél,* etc.). In addition, there are three neuter forms—*esto, eso,* and *aquello*—which are used when referring to abstract ideas or unidentified things (*¿te dijo eso?,* he said that to you?; *¿qué es esto?,* what is this?; *tráeme todo aquello,* bring me all that stuff).

Except for the neuter forms, demonstrative pronouns agree in gender and number with the nouns they replace (*esta silla,* this chair → *ésta,* this one; *aquellos vasos,* those glasses → *aquéllos,* those ones).

Spanish Numbers

Cardinal Numbers

1	uno	33	treinta y tres
2	dos	34	treinta y cuatro
3	tres	35	treinta y cinco
4	cuatro	36	treinta y seis
5	cinco	37	treinta y siete
6	seis	38	treinta y ocho
7	siete	39	treinta y nueve
8	ocho	40	cuarenta
9	nueve	41	cuarenta y uno
10	diez	50	cincuenta
11	once	60	sesenta
12	doce	70	setenta
13	trece	80	ochenta
14	catorce	90	noventa
15	quince	100	cien
16	dieciséis	101	ciento uno
17	diecisiete	102	ciento dos
18	dieciocho	200	doscientos
19	diecinueve	300	trescientos
20	veinte	400	cuatrocientos
21	veintiuno	500	quinientos
22	veintidós	600	seiscientos
23	veintitrés	700	setecientos
24	veinticuatro	800	ochocientos
25	veinticinco	900	novecientos
26	veintiséis	1,000	mil
27	veintisiete	1,001	mil uno
28	veintiocho	2,000	dos mil
29	veintinueve	100,000	cien mil
30	treinta	1,000,000	un millón
31	treinta y uno	1,000,000,000	mil millones
32	treinta y dos		

Ordinal Numbers

1st	primero, -ra	18th	decimoctavo, -va
2nd	segundo, -da	19th	decimonoveno, -na; *or* decimonono, -na
3rd	tercero, -ra	20th	vigésimo, -ma
4th	cuarto, -ta	21st	vigésimoprimero, vigésimaprimera
5th	quinto, -ta	22nd	vigésimosegundo, vigésimasegunda
6th	sexto, -ta	30th	trigésimo, -ma
7th	séptimo, -ma	40th	cuadragésimo, -ma
8th	octavo, -va	50th	quincuagésimo, -ma
9th	noveno, -na	60th	sexagésimo, -ma
10th	décimo, -ma	70th	septuagésimo, -ma
11th	undécimo, -ma	80th	octogésimo, -ma
12th	duodécimo, -ma	90th	nonagésimo, -ma
13th	decimotercero, -ra	100th	centésimo, -ma
14th	decimocuarto, -ta		
15th	decimoquinto, -ta		
16th	decimosexto, -ta		
17th	decimoséptimo, -ma		

Conjugation of Spanish Verbs

Simple Tenses

TENSE	REGULAR VERBS ENDING IN -AR hablar	
PRESENT INDICATIVE	hablo hablas habla	hablamos habláis hablan
PRESENT SUBJUNCTIVE	hable hables hable	hablemos habléis hablen
PRETERIT INDICATIVE	hablé hablaste habló	hablamos hablasteis hablaron
IMPERFECT INDICATIVE	hablaba hablabas hablaba	hablábamos hablabais hablaban
IMPERFECT SUBJUNCTIVE	hablara hablaras hablara *or* hablase hablases hablase	habláramos hablarais hablaran hablásemos hablaseis hablasen
FUTURE INDICATIVE	hablaré hablarás hablará	hablaremos hablaréis hablarán
FUTURE SUBJUNCTIVE	hablare hablares hablare	habláremos hablareis hablaren
CONDITIONAL	hablaría hablarías hablaría	hablaríamos hablaríais hablarían
IMPERATIVE	 habla hable	hablemos hablad hablen
PRESENT PARTICIPLE (GERUND)	hablando	
PAST PARTICIPLE	hablado	

REGULAR VERBS ENDING IN **-ER** comer		REGULAR VERBS ENDING IN **-IR** vivir	
como	comemos	vivo	vivimos
comes	coméis	vives	vivís
come	comen	vive	viven
coma	comamos	viva	vivamos
comas	comáis	vivas	viváis
coma	coman	viva	vivan
comí	comimos	viví	vivimos
comiste	comisteis	viviste	vivisteis
comió	comieron	vivió	vivieron
comía	comíamos	vivía	vivíamos
comías	comíais	vivías	vivíais
comía	comían	vivía	vivían
comiera	comiéramos	viviera	viviéramos
comieras	comierais	vivieras	vivierais
comiera	comieran	viviera	vivieran
or		*or*	
comiese	comiésemos	viviese	viviésemos
comieses	comieseis	vivieses	vivieseis
comiese	comiesen	viviese	viviesen
comeré	comeremos	viviré	viviremos
comerás	comeréis	vivirás	viviréis
comerá	comerán	vivirá	vivirán
comiere	comiéremos	viviere	viviéremos
comieres	comiereis	vivieres	viviereis
comiere	comieren	viviere	vivieren
comería	comeríamos	viviría	viviríamos
comerías	comeríais	vivirías	viviríais
comería	comerían	viviría	vivirían
	comamos		vivamos
come	comed	vive	vivid
coma	coman	viva	vivan
comiendo		viviendo	
comido		vivido	

Compound Tenses

1. Perfect Tenses

The perfect tenses are formed with *haber* and the past participle:

PRESENT PERFECT

he hablado, etc. (*indicative*);
haya hablado, etc. (*subjunctive*)

PAST PERFECT

había hablado, etc. (*indicative*);
hubiera hablado, etc. (*subjuntive*)
or
hubiese hablado, etc. (*subjunctive*)

PRETERIT PERFECT

hube hablado, etc. (*indicative*)

FUTURE PERFECT

habré hablado, etc. (*indicative*)

CONDITIONAL PERFECT

habría hablado, etc. (*indicative*)

2. Progressive Tenses

The progressive tenses are formed with *estar* and the present participle:

PRESENT PROGRESSIVE

estoy llamando, etc. (*indicative*);
esté llamando, etc. (*subjunctive*)

IMPERFECT PROGRESSIVE

estaba llamando, etc. (*indicative*);
estuviera llamando, etc. (*subjunctive*)
or
estuviese llamando, etc. (*subjunctive*)

PRETERIT PROGRESSIVE

estuve llamando, etc. (*indicative*)

FUTURE PROGRESSIVE

estaré llamando, etc. (*indicative*)

CONDITIONAL PROGRESSIVE

estaría llamando, etc. (*indicative*)

PRESENT PERFECT PROGRESSIVE

he estado llamando, etc. (*indicative*);
haya estado llamando, etc. (*subjunctive*)

PAST PERFECT PROGRESSIVE

había estado llamando, etc. (*indicative*);
hubiera estado llamando, etc. (*subjunctive*)
or
hubiese estado llamando, etc. (*subjunctive*)

Use of *Vos*

In parts of South and Central America, *vos* often replaces or competes with *tú* as the second person familiar personal pronoun. It is particularly well established in the Río de la Plata region and much of Central America.

The pronoun *vos* often takes a distinct set of verb forms, usually in the present tense and the imperative. These vary widely from region to region; examples of the most common forms are shown below.

INFINITIVE FORM	hablar	comer	vivir
PRESENT INDICATIVE	vos hablás	vos comés	vos vivís
PRESENT SUBJUNCTIVE	vos hablés	vos comás	vos vivás
IMPERATIVE	hablá	comé	viví

In some areas, *vos* may take the *tú* or *vosotros* forms of the verb, while in others (as Uruguay), *tú* is combined with the *vos* verb forms.

Irregular Verbs

The *imperfect subjunctive,* the *future subjunctive,* the *conditional,* and the remaining forms of the *imperative* are not included in the model conjugations list, but can be derived as follows:

The *imperfect subjunctive* and the *future subjunctive* are formed from the third person plural form of the preterit tense by removing the last syllable (*-ron*) and adding the appropriate suffix:

PRETERIT INDICATIVE, THIRD PERSON PLURAL (querer)	quisieron
IMPERFECT SUBJUNCTIVE (querer)	quisiera, quisieras, etc. *or* quisiese, quisieses, etc.
FUTURE SUBJUNCTIVE (querer)	quisiere, quisieres, etc.

The conditional uses the same stem as the future indicative:

FUTURE INDICATIVE (poner)	pondré, pondrás, etc.
CONDITIONAL (poner)	pondría, pondrías, etc.

The third person singular, first person plural, and third person plural forms of the *imperative* are the same as the corresponding forms of the present subjunctive.

The second person plural *(vosotros)* form of the *imperative* is formed by removing the final *-r* of the infinitive form and adding a *-d* (ex.: *oír → oíd).*

Model Conjugations of Irregular Verbs

The model conjugations below include the following simple tenses: the *present indicative* (*IND*), the *present subjunctive* (*SUBJ*), the *preterit indicative* (*PRET*), the *imperfect indicative* (*IMPF*), the *future indicative* (*FUT*), the second person singular form of the *imperative* (*IMPER*), the *present participle* or *gerund* (*PRP*), and the *past participle* (*PP*). Each set of conjugations is preceded by the corresponding infinitive form of the verb, shown in bold type. Only tenses containing irregularities are listed, and the irregular verb forms within each tense are displayed in bold type.

Conjugation of Spanish Verbs

Each irregular verb entry in the Spanish-English section of this dictionary is cross-referred by number to one of the following model conjugations. These cross-reference numbers are shown in curly braces { } immediately following the entry's functional label.

1 **abolir** *(defective verb)* **:** IND abolimos, abolís *(other forms not used);* SUBJ *(not used);* IMPER *(only second person plural is used)*

2 **abrir :** PP abierto

3 **actuar :** IND **actúo, actúas, actúa**, actuamos, actuáis, **actúan;** SUBJ **actúe, actúes, actúe,** actuemos, actuéis, **actúen;** IMPER **actúa**

4 **adquirir :** IND **adquiero, adquieres, adquiere,** adquirimos, adquirís, **adquieren;** SUBJ **adquiera, adquieras, adquiera,** adquiramos, adquiráis, **adquieran;** IMPER **adquiere**

5 **airar :** IND **aíro, aíras, aíra,** airamos, airáis, **aíran;** SUBJ **aíre, aíres, aíre,** airemos, airéis, **aíren;** IMPER **aíra**

6 **andar :** PRET **anduve, anduviste, anduvo, anduvimos, anduvisteis, anduvieron**

7 **asir :** IND **asgo,** ases, ase, asimos, asís, asen; SUBJ **asga, asgas, asga, asgamos, asgáis, asgan**

8 **aunar :** IND **aúno, aúnas, aúna,** aunamos, aunáis, **aúnan;** SUBJ **aúne, aúnes, aúne,** aunemos, aunéis, **aúnen;** IMPER **aúna**

9 **avergonzar :** IND **avergüenzo, avergüenzas, avergüenza,** avergonzamos, avergonzáis, **avergüenzan;** SUBJ **avergüence, avergüences, avergüence, avergoncemos, avergoncéis, avergüencen;** PRET **avergoncé;** IMPER **avergüenza**

10 **averiguar :** SUBJ **averigüe, averigües, averigüe, averigüemos, averigüéis, averigüen;** PRET **averigüé,** averiguaste, averiguó, averiguamos, averiguasteis, averiguaron

11 **bendecir :** IND **bendigo, bendices, bendice,** bendecimos, bendecís, **bendicen;** SUBJ **bendiga, bendigas, bendiga, bendigamos, bendigáis, bendigan;** PRET **bendije, bendijiste, bendijo, bendijimos, bendijisteis, bendijeron;** IMPER **bendice**

12 **caber :** *IND* **quepo,** cabes, cabe, cabemos, cabéis, caben; *SUBJ* **quepa, quepas, quepa, quepamos, quepáis, quepan;** *PRET* **cupe, cupiste, cupo, cupimos, cupisteis, cupieron;** *FUT* **cabré, cabrás, cabrá, cabremos, cabréis, cabrán**

13 **caer :** *IND* **caigo,** caes, cae, caemos, caéis, caen; *SUBJ* **caiga, caigas, caiga, caigamos, caigáis, caigan;** *PRET* caí, **caíste, cayó, caímos, caísteis, cayeron;** *PRP* **cayendo;** *PP* **caído**

14 **cocer :** *IND* **cuezo, cueces, cuece,** cocemos, cocéis, **cuecen;** *SUBJ* **cueza, cuezas, cueza, cozamos, cozáis, cuezan;** *IMPER* **cuece**

15 **coger :** *IND* **cojo,** coges, coge, cogemos, cogéis, cogen; *SUBJ* **coja, cojas, coja, cojamos, cojáis, cojan**

16 **colgar :** *IND* **cuelgo, cuelgas, cuelga,** colgamos, colgáis, **cuelgan;** *SUBJ* **cuelgue, cuelgues, cuelgue, colguemos, colguéis, cuelguen;** *PRET* **colgué,** colgaste, colgó, colgamos, colgasteis, colgaron; *IMPER* **cuelga**

17 **concernir** *(defective verb; used only in the third person singular and plural of the present indicative, present subjunctive, and imperfect subjunctive) see* 25 **discernir**

18 **conocer :** *IND* **conozco,** conoces, conoce, conocemos, conocéis, conocen; *SUBJ* **conozca, conozcas, conozca, conozcamos, conozcáis, conozcan**

19 **contar :** *IND* **cuento, cuentas, cuenta,** contamos, contáis, **cuentan;** *SUBJ* **cuente, cuentes, cuente,** contemos, contéis, **cuenten;** *IMPER* **cuenta**

20 **creer :** *PRET* creí, **creíste, creyó, creímos, creísteis, creyeron;** *PRP* **creyendo;** *PP* **creído**

21 **cruzar :** *SUBJ* **cruce, cruces, cruce, crucemos, crucéis, crucen;** *PRET* **crucé,** cruzaste, cruzó, cruzamos, cruzasteis, cruzaron

22 **dar :** *IND* **doy,** das, da, damos, **dais,** dan; *SUBJ* **dé,** des, **dé,** demos, **deis,** den; *PRET* **di, diste, dio, dimos, disteis, dieron**

23 **decir :** *IND* **digo, dices, dice,** decimos, decís, **dicen;** *SUBJ* **diga, digas, diga, digamos, digáis, digan;** *PRET* **dije, dijiste, dijo,**

dijimos, dijisteis, dijeron; *FUT* **diré, dirás, dirá, diremos, diréis, dirán;** *IMPER* **di;** *PRP* **diciendo;** *PP* **dicho**

24 **delinquir :** *IND* **delinco,** delinques, delinque, delinquimos, delinquís, delinquen; *SUBJ* **delinca, delincas, delinca, delincamos, delincáis, delincan**

25 **discernir :** *IND* **discierno, disciernes, discierne,** discernimos, discernís, **disciernen;** *SUBJ* **discierna, disciernas, discierna,** discernamos, discernáis, **disciernan;** *IMPER* **discierne**

26 **distinguir :** *IND* **distingo,** distingues, distingue, distinguimos, distinguís, distinguen; *SUBJ* **distinga, distingas, distinga, distingamos, distingáis, distingan**

27 **dormir :** *IND* **duermo, duermes, duerme,** dormimos, dormís, **duermen;** *SUBJ* **duerma, duermas, duerma, durmamos, durmáis, duerman;** *PRET* dormí, dormiste, **durmió,** dormimos, dormisteis, **durmieron;** *IMPER* **duerme;** *PRP* **durmiendo**

28 **elegir :** *IND* **elijo, eliges, elige,** elegimos, elegís, **eligen;** *SUBJ* **elija, elijas, elija, elijamos, elijáis, elijan;** *PRET* elegí, elegiste, **eligió,** elegimos, elegisteis, **eligieron;** *IMPER* **elige;** *PRP* **eligiendo**

29 **empezar :** *IND* **empiezo, empiezas, empieza,** empezamos, empezáis, **empiezan;** *SUBJ* **empiece, empieces, empiece, empecemos, empecéis, empiecen;** *PRET* **empecé,** empezaste, empezó, empezamos, empezasteis, empezaron; *IMPER* **empieza**

30 **enraizar :** *IND* **enraízo, enraízas, enraíza,** enraizamos, enraizáis, **enraízan;** *SUBJ* **enraíce, enraíces, enraíce, enraicemos, enraicéis, enraícen;** *PRET* **enraicé,** enraizaste, enraizó, enraizamos, enraizasteis, enraizaron; *IMPER* **enraíza**

31 **erguir :** *IND* **irgo** *or* **yergo, irgues** *or* **yergues, irgue** *or* **yergue,** erguimos, erguís, **irguen** *or* **yerguen;** *SUBJ* **irga** *or* **yerga, irgas** *or* **yergas, irga** *or* **yerga, irgamos, irgáis, irgan** *or* **yergan;** *PRET* erguí, erguiste, **irguió,** erguimos, erguisteis, **irguieron;** *IMPER* **irgue** *or* **yergue;** *PRP* **irguiendo**

32 **errar :** *IND* **yerro, yerras, yerra,** erramos, erráis, **yerran;** *SUBJ* **yerre, yerres, yerre,** erremos, erréis, **yerren;** *IMPER* **yerra**

33 **escribir :** *PP* **escrito**

34 **estar :** *IND* **estoy, estás, está,** estamos, estáis, **están;** *SUBJ* **esté, estés, esté,** estemos, estéis, **estén;** *PRET* **estuve, estuviste, estuvo, estuvimos, estuvisteis, estuvieron;** *IMPER* **está**

35 **exigir :** *IND* **exijo,** exiges, exige, exigimos, exigís, exigen; *SUBJ* **exija, exijas, exija, exijamos, exijáis, exijan**

36 **forzar :** *IND* **fuerzo, fuerzas, fuerza,** forzamos, forzáis, **fuerzan;** *SUBJ* **fuerce, fuerces, fuerce, forcemos, forcéis, fuercen;** *PRET* **forcé,** forzaste, forzó, forzamos, forzasteis, forzaron; *IMPER* **fuerza**

37 **freír :** *IND* **frío, fríes, fríe, freímos,** freís, **fríen;** *SUBJ* **fría, frías, fría, friamos, friáis, frían;** *PRET* freí, **freíste, frió, freímos, freísteis, frieron;** *IMPER* **fríe;** *PRP* **friendo;** *PP* **frito**

38 **gruñir :** *PRET* gruñí, gruñiste, **gruñó,** gruñimos, gruñisteis, **gruñeron;** *PRP* **gruñendo**

39 **haber :** *IND* **he, has, ha, hemos,** habéis, **han;** *SUBJ* **haya, hayas, haya, hayamos, hayáis, hayan;** *PRET* **hube, hubiste, hubo, hubimos, hubisteis, hubieron;** *FUT* **habré, habrás, habrá, habremos, habréis, habrán;** *IMPER* **he**

40 **hacer :** *IND* **hago,** haces, hace, hacemos, hacéis, hacen; *SUBJ* **haga, hagas, haga, hagamos, hagáis, hagan;** *PRET* **hice, hiciste, hizo, hicimos, hicisteis, hicieron;** *FUT* **haré, harás, hará, haremos, haréis, harán;** *IMPER* **haz;** *PP* **hecho**

41 **huir :** *IND* **huyo, huyes, huye,** huimos, huís, **huyen;** *SUBJ* **huya, huyas, huya, huyamos, huyáis, huyan;** *PRET* huí, huiste, **huyó,** huimos, huisteis, **huyeron;** *IMPER* **huye;** *PRP* **huyendo**

42 **imprimir :** *PP* **impreso**

43 **ir :** *IND* **voy, vas, va, vamos, vais, van;** *SUBJ* **vaya, vayas, vaya, vayamos, vayáis, vayan;** *PRET* **fui, fuiste, fue, fuimos, fuisteis, fueron;** *IMPF* **iba, ibas, iba, íbamos, ibais, iban;** *IMPER* **ve;** *PRP* **yendo;** *PP* **ido**

44 **jugar :** *IND* **juego, juegas, juega,** jugamos, jugáis, **juegan;** *SUBJ* **juegue, juegues, juegue, juguemos, juguéis, jueguen;** *PRET* **jugué,** jugaste, jugó, jugamos, jugasteis, jugaron; *IMPER* **juega**

45 **lucir** : *IND* **luzco,** luces, luce, lucimos, lucís, lucen; *SUBJ* **luzca, luzcas, luzca, luzcamos, luzcáis, luzcan**

46 **morir** : *IND* **muero, mueres, muere,** morimos, morís, **mueren;** *SUBJ* **muera, mueras, muera, muramos, muráis, mueran;** *PRET* morí, moriste, **murió,** morimos, moristeis, **murieron;** *IMPER* **muere;** *PRP* **muriendo;** *PP* **muerto**

47 **mover** : *IND* **muevo, mueves, mueve,** movemos, movéis, **mueven;** *SUBJ* **mueva, muevas, mueva,** movamos, mováis, **muevan;** *IMPER* **mueve**

48 **nacer** : *IND* **nazco,** naces, nace, nacemos, nacéis, nacen; *SUBJ* **nazca, nazcas, nazca, nazcamos, nazcáis, nazcan**

49 **negar** : *IND* **niego, niegas, niega,** negamos, negáis, **niegan;** *SUBJ* **niegue, niegues, niegue, neguemos, neguéis, nieguen;** *PRET* **negué,** negaste, negó, negamos, negasteis, negaron; *IMPER* **niega**

50 **oír** : *IND* **oigo, oyes, oye, oímos,** oís, **oyen;** *SUBJ* **oiga, oigas, oiga, oigamos, oigáis, oigan;** *PRET* oí, **oíste, oyó, oímos, oísteis, oyeron;** *IMPER* **oye;** *PRP* **oyendo;** *PP* **oído**

51 **oler** : *IND* **huelo, hueles, huele,** olemos, oléis, **huelen;** *SUBJ* **huela, huelas, huela,** olamos, oláis, **huelan;** *IMPER* **huele**

52 **pagar** : *SUBJ* **pague, pagues, pague, paguemos, paguéis, paguen;** *PRET* **pagué,** pagaste, pagó, pagamos, pagasteis, pagaron

53 **parecer** : *IND* **parezco,** pareces, parece, parecemos, parecéis, parecen; *SUBJ* **parezca, parezcas, parezca, parezcamos, parezcáis, parezcan**

54 **pedir** : *IND* **pido, pides, pide,** pedimos, pedís, **piden;** *SUBJ* **pida, pidas, pida, pidamos, pidáis, pidan;** *PRET* pedí, pediste, **pidió,** pedimos, pedisteis, **pidieron;** *IMPER* **pide;** *PRP* **pidiendo**

55 **pensar** : *IND* **pienso, piensas, piensa,** pensamos, pensáis, **piensan;** *SUBJ* **piense, pienses, piense,** pensemos, penséis, **piensen;** *IMPER* **piensa**

56 **perder** : *IND* **pierdo, pierdes, pierde,** perdemos, perdéis, **pierden;** *SUBJ* **pierda, pierdas, pierda,** perdamos, perdáis, **pierdan;** *IMPER* **pierde**

57 **placer :** *IND* **plazco,** places, place, placemos, placéis, placen; *SUBJ* **plazca, plazcas, plazca, plazcamos, plazcáis, plazcan;** *PRET* plací, placiste, plació *or* **plugo,** placimos, placisteis, placieron *or* **pluguieron**

58 **poder :** *IND* **puedo, puedes, puede,** podemos, podéis, **pueden;** *SUBJ* **pueda, puedas, pueda,** podamos, podáis, **puedan;** *PRET* **pude, pudiste, pudo, pudimos, pudisteis, pudieron;** *FUT* **podré, podrás, podrá, podremos, podréis, podrán;** *IMPER* **puede;** *PRP* **pudiendo**

59 **podrir** *or* **pudrir :** *PP* **podrido** *(all other forms based on* pudrir*)*

60 **poner :** *IND* **pongo,** pones, pone, ponemos, ponéis, ponen; *SUBJ* **ponga, pongas, ponga, pongamos, pongáis, pongan;** *PRET* **puse, pusiste, puso, pusimos, pusisteis, pusieron;** *FUT* **pondré, pondrás, pondrá, pondremos, pondréis, pondrán;** *IMPER* **pon;** *PP* **puesto**

61 **producir :** *IND* **produzco,** produces, produce, producimos, producís, producen; *SUBJ* **produzca, produzcas, produzca, produzcamos, produzcáis, produzcan;** *PRET* **produje, produjiste, produjo, produjimos, produjisteis, produjeron**

62 **prohibir :** *IND* **prohíbo, prohíbes, prohíbe,** prohibimos, prohibís, **prohíben;** *SUBJ* **prohíba, prohíbas, prohíba,** prohibamos, prohibáis, **prohíban;** *IMPER* **prohíbe**

63 **proveer :** *PRET* proveí, **proveíste, proveyó, proveímos, proveísteis, proveyeron;** *PRP* **proveyendo;** *PP* **provisto**

64 **querer :** *IND* **quiero, quieres, quiere,** queremos, queréis, **quieren;** *SUBJ* **quiera, quieras, quiera,** queramos, queráis, **quieran;** *PRET* **quise, quisiste, quiso, quisimos, quisisteis, quisieron;** *FUT* **querré, querrás, querrá, querremos, querréis, querrán;** *IMPER* **quiere**

65 **raer :** *IND* rao *or* **raigo** *or* **rayo,** raes, rae, raemos, raéis, raen; *SUBJ* **raiga** *or* **raya, raigas** *or* **rayas, raiga** *or* **raya, raigamos** *or* **rayamos, raigáis** *or* **rayáis, raigan** *or* **rayan;** *PRET* **raí, raíste, rayó, raímos, raísteis, rayeron;** *PRP* **rayendo;** *PP* **raído**

66 **reír :** *IND* **río, ríes, ríe, reímos,** reís, **ríen;** *SUBJ* **ría, rías, ría, riamos, riáis, rían;** *PRET* reí, **reíste, rió, reímos, reísteis, rieron;** *IMPER* **ríe;** *PRP* **riendo;** *PP* **reído**

67 **reñir** : *IND* **riño, riñes, riñe,** reñimos, reñís, **riñen;** *SUBJ* **riña, riñas, riña, riñamos, riñáis, riñan;** *PRET* reñí, reñiste, **riñó,** reñimos, reñisteis, **riñeron;** *PRP* **riñendo**

68 **reunir** : *IND* **reúno, reúnes, reúne,** reunimos, reunís, **reúnen;** *SUBJ* **reúna, reúnas, reúna,** reunamos, reunáis, **reúnan;** *IMPER* **reúne**

69 **roer** : *IND* roo *or* **roigo** *or* **royo,** roes, roe, roemos, roéis, roen; *SUBJ* roa *or* **roiga** *or* **roya,** roas *or* **roigas** *or* **royas,** roa *or* **roiga** *or* **roya,** roamos *or* **roigamos** *or* **royamos,** roáis *or* **roigáis** *or* **royáis,** roan *or* **roigan** *or* **royan;** *PRET* roí, **roíste, royó, roímos, roísteis, royeron;** *PRP* **royendo;** *PP* **roído**

70 **romper** : *PP* **roto**

71 **saber** : *IND* **sé,** sabes, sabe, sabemos, sabéis, saben; *SUBJ* **sepa, sepas, sepa, sepamos, sepáis, sepan;** *PRET* **supe, supiste, supo, supimos, supisteis, supieron;** *FUT* **sabré, sabrás, sabrá, sabremos, sabréis, sabrán**

72 **sacar** : *SUBJ* **saque, saques, saque, saquemos, saquéis, saquen;** *PRET* **saqué,** sacaste, sacó, sacamos, sacasteis, sacaron

73 **salir** : *IND* **salgo,** sales, sale, salimos, salís, salen; *SUBJ* **salga, salgas, salga, salgamos, salgáis, salgan;** *FUT* **saldré, saldrás, saldrá, saldremos, saldréis, saldrán;** *IMPER* **sal**

74 **satisfacer** : *IND* **satisfago,** satisfaces, satisface, satisfacemos, satisfacéis, satisfacen; *SUBJ* **satisfaga, satisfagas, satisfaga, satisfagamos, satisfagáis, satisfagan;** *PRET* **satisfice, satisficiste, satisfizo, satisficimos, satificisteis, satisficieron;** *FUT* **satisfaré, satisfarás, satisfará, satisfaremos, satisfaréis, satisfarán;** *IMPER* **satisfaz** *or* **satisface;** *PP* **satisfecho**

75 **seguir** : *IND* **sigo, sigues, sigue,** seguimos, seguís, **siguen;** *SUBJ* **siga, sigas, siga, sigamos, sigáis, sigan;** *PRET* seguí, seguiste, **siguió,** seguimos, seguisteis, **siguieron;** *IMPER* **sigue;** *PRP* **siguiendo**

76 **sentir** : *IND* **siento, sientes, siente,** sentimos, sentís, **sienten;** *SUBJ* **sienta, sientas, sienta, sintamos, sintáis, sientan;** *PRET* sentí, sentiste, **sintió,** sentimos, sentisteis, **sintieron;** *IMPER* **siente;** *PRP* **sintiendo**

77 **ser :** *IND* **soy, eres, es, somos, sois, son;** *SUBJ* **sea, seas, sea, seamos, seáis, sean;** *PRET* **fui, fuiste, fue, fuimos, fuisteis, fueron;** *IMPF* **era, eras, era, éramos, erais, eran;** *IMPER* **sé;** *PRP* **siendo;** *PP* **sido**

78 **soler** *(defective verb; used only in the present, preterit, and imperfect indicative, and the present and imperfect subjunctive) see* 47 **mover**

79 **tañer :** *PRET* tañí, tañiste, **tañó,** tañimos, tañisteis, **tañeron;** *PRP* **tañendo**

80 **tener :** *IND* **tengo, tienes, tiene,** tenemos, tenéis, **tienen;** *SUBJ* **tenga, tengas, tenga, tengamos, tengáis, tengan;** *PRET* **tuve, tuviste, tuvo, tuvimos, tuvisteis, tuvieron;** *FUT* **tendré, tendrás, tendrá, tendremos, tendréis, tendrán;** *IMPER* **ten**

81 **traer :** *IND* **traigo,** traes, trae, traemos, traéis, traen; *SUBJ* **traiga, traigas, traiga, traigamos, traigáis, traigan;** *PRET* **traje, trajiste, trajo, trajimos, trajisteis, trajeron;** *PRP* **trayendo;** *PP* **traído**

82 **trocar :** *IND* **trueco, truecas, trueca,** trocamos, trocáis, **truecan;** *SUBJ* **trueque, trueques, trueque, troquemos, troquéis, truequen;** *PRET* **troqué,** trocaste, trocó, trocamos, trocasteis, trocaron; *IMPER* **trueca**

83 **uncir :** *IND* **unzo,** unces, unce, uncimos, uncís, uncen; *SUBJ* **unza, unzas, unza, unzamos, unzáis, unzan**

84 **valer :** *IND* **valgo,** vales, vale, valemos, valéis, valen; *SUBJ* **valga, valgas, valga, valgamos, valgáis, valgan;** *FUT* **valdré, valdrás, valdrá, valdremos, valdréis, valdrán**

85 **variar :** *IND* **varío, varías, varía,** variamos, variáis, **varían;** *SUBJ* **varíe, varíes, varíe,** variemos, variéis, **varíen;** *IMPER* **varía**

86 **vencer :** *IND* **venzo,** vences, vence, vencemos, vencéis, vencen; *SUBJ* **venza, venzas, venza, venzamos, venzáis, venzan**

87 **venir :** *IND* **vengo, vienes, viene,** venimos, venís, **vienen;** *SUBJ* **venga, vengas, venga, vengamos, vengáis, vengan;** *PRET* **vine, viniste, vino, vinimos, vinisteis, vinieron;** *FUT* **vendré, vendrás, vendrá, vendremos, vendréis, vendrán;** *IMPER* **ven;** *PRP* **viniendo**

88 **ver :** *IND* veo, **ves, ve, vemos, veis, ven;** *PRET* **vi, viste, vio, vimos, visteis, vieron;** *IMPER* **ve;** *PRP* **viendo;** *PP* **visto**

89 **volver :** *IND* **vuelvo, vuelves, vuelve,** volvemos, volvéis, **vuelven;** *SUBJ* **vuelva, vuelvas, vuelva,** volvamos, volváis, **vuelvan;** *IMPER* **vuelve;** *PP* **vuelto**

90 **yacer :** *IND* **yazco** *or* **yazgo** *or* **yago,** yaces, yace, yacemos, yacéis, yacen; *SUBJ* **yazca** *or* **yazga** *or* **yaga, yazcas** *or* **yazgas** *or* **yagas, yazca** *or* **yazga** *or* **yaga, yazcamos** *or* **yazgamos** *or* **yagamos, yazcáis** *or* **yazgáis** *or* **yagáis, yazcan** *or* **yazgan** *or* **yagan;** *IMPER* yace *or* **yaz**

Notas explicativas

Entradas

1. Entradas principales

Toda letra, palabra o frase en negrita que aparece alineada con el margen izquierdo de la columna de texto de la que forma parte es una entrada principal, o lema. La composición de la entrada principal puede constar de letras continuas, de letras unidas por un guión, o bien de letras separadas por un espacio:

cafetalero[1]**, -ra** *adj* . . .
eye–opener . . . *n* . . .
walk out *vi* . . .

La entrada principal, junto con el texto que la sigue tanto en la misma línea como en las líneas sangradas subsiguientes, constituye una entrada del diccionario.

2. Orden de las entradas principales

El orden alfabético del diccionario concuerda con el orden del alfabeto inglés, con la excepción de las entradas españolas que comienzan con la letra *ñ-*. Éstas aparecen después de las entradas que comienzan con *n-*. Las entradas principales se suceden alfabéticamente, letra por letra, sin tener en cuenta guiones o espacios intermediarios; por ejemplo, *shake-up* aparece después de *shaker.*

Los homógrafos (palabras que se escriben igual) que pertenecen a distintas categorías gramaticales por lo general aparecen en entradas individuales. A estas entradas se les identifica con un número volado:

hail[1]. . . *vt*. . .

hail[2] *n*. . .

hail[3] *interj*. . .

madrileño[1]**, -ña** *adj*. . .

madrileño[2]**, -ña** *n*. . .

Estas entradas numeradas se listan en el siguiente orden: verbo, adverbio, adjetivo, sustantivo, conjunción, preposición, pronombre, interjección, y por último, artículo.

Los homógrafos que se clasifican bajo una misma categoría gramatical son normalmente incluidos bajo la misma entrada del diccionario, sin tener en cuenta diferencias de origen semántico. Sin embargo, en la sección Inglés-Español se les asigna a cada uno de estos homógrafos una entrada individual si entre ellos existe alguna diferencia ya sea en la inflexión o en la pronunciación.

3. Palabras guía

En el margen superior de cada página aparecen dos palabras guía, que indican la primera y última entrada de la página correspondiente.

fregar • fuego

4. Variantes

Cuando una entrada principal aparece seguida de la palabra *or* y otra ortografía, las dos ortografías se consideran como variantes. Ambas ortografías son estándar, y cualquiera de las dos puede usarse según se prefiera:

jailer *or* **jailor** . . . *n* . . .
quizá *or* **quizás** *adv* . . .

Hay ocasiones en las que una variante ortográfica se emplea únicamente para una de las acepciones de una palabra. En tales casos, la variante ortográfica aparece después del número de la acepción a la cual corresponde:

electric . . . *adj* **1** *or* **electrical** . . .

En otros casos, el lema puede usarse intercambiablemente con una frase de la que forma parte. Para los fines de este diccionario, tales frases se consideran como variantes del lema:

bunk² *n* **1** *or* **bunk bed** . . .

angina *nf* **1** *or* **angina de pecho :** angina . . .

Las frases en negrita también pueden, a su vez, presentar variantes:

> **madera** *nf*. . . **3 madera dura** *or* **madera noble** . . .
>
> **atención**[1] *nf*. . . **2 poner atención** *or* **prestar atención** . . .

5. Entradas secundarias

Una entrada principal puede ser seguida de uno o más derivados del lema, o de un homógrafo de distinta categoría gramatical. Éstas son entradas secundarias. Cada una de estas entradas aparece después de un guión en negrita, y cada una posee su propio calificativo. Tales entradas aparecen sin definición, ya que sus equivalentes en el idioma extranjero pueden derivarse fácilmente al combinar la definición del lema con el sufijo correspondiente, o como sucede con los homógrafos, al sustituir la categoría gramatical por otra. Véase por ejemplo:

> **illegal** . . . *adj* **:** ilegal **— illegally** *adv*
> (el adverbio español es *ilegalmente*)
>
> **transferir** . . . *vt* TRASLADAR **:** to transfer **— transferible** *adj*
> (el adjetivo inglés es *transferable*)
>
> **Bosnian** *n* **:** bosnio *m,* -nia *f* **— Bosnian** *adj*
> (el adjetivo español es *bosnio, -nia*)

En la sección Español-Inglés, los verbos pronominales aparecen en ocasiones como entradas secundarias, sin definición:

> **enrollar** *vt* **:** to roll up, to coil **— enrollarse** *vr*

La ausencia de la definición en este caso comunica al lector de habla inglesa que el verbo *enrollarse* tiene una función expresamente reflexiva. Esto elimina la necesidad de agregar una definición que resultaría superflua como "to become rolled up or coiled," o "to roll itself up."

6. Frases en negrita

Una entrada principal puede aparecer acompañada de una o varias frases en negrita (generalmente locuciones o términos compuestos) que contienen ya sea el lema, o una inflexión de éste. Cada una de estas frases se presenta como una de las acepciones numeradas del lema:

> **álamo** *nm* **1 :** poplar **2 álamo temblón :** aspen
>
> **hold**[1] . . . *vi* . . . **4 to hold to :** . . . **5 to hold with :** . . .

Cuando la frase en negrita consta únicamente de una combinación del lema con una preposición, el lema se representa entonces por medio de una tilde en negrita **~**.

> **pegar** . . . *vi* . . . **3 ~ con :** to match, to go with . . .

Si la frase en cuestión tiene más de un sentido, entonces puede aparecer en dos o más acepciones de la misma entrada principal:

> **wear**[1] . . . *vt* . . . **3 to wear out :** gastar <he wore out his shoes . . . > **4 to wear out** EXHAUST **:** agotar, fatigar <to wear oneself out . . . > . . .
>
> **estar** . . . *vi* . . . **15 ~ por :** to be in favor of **16 ~ por :** to be about to <está por cerrar . . . > . . .

Si el uso común de una palabra es generalmente limitado a una frase determinada, la frase es presentada como la única acepción del lema:

> **ward**[1] . . . *vt* **to ward off :** . . .

Pronunciación

1. Pronunciación de los lemas ingleses

El texto que aparece entre corchetes [ ] inmediatamente después de un lema en la sección Inglés-Español indica la pronunciación del lema. Para una explicación de los símbolos empleados, véase la tabla titulada Pronunciation Symbols que aparece en la página 25a.

La presencia de variantes de pronunciación indica que no todos los hablantes educados del idioma pronuncian una palabra determinada de igual forma. El hecho de que una variante aparezca después de otra no significa que sea menos apropiada que la que aparece primero. De hecho, la segunda variante puede ser tan común como la primera, pero las restricciones de la página impresa exigen que una preceda a la otra.

tomato [tə'meɪt̬o, -'mɑ-] . . .

Cuando un término compuesto aparece con sólo una pronunciación parcial, la pronunciación del resto del término puede obtenerse bajo la entrada correspondiente a la palabra cuya pronunciación se ha omitido:

gamma ray ['gæmə] . . .

ray ['reɪ] . . .

smoke[1] ['smo:k] . . .

smoke detector [dɪ'tɛktər] . . .

En general, no se indica la pronunciación de términos compuestos cuando éstos están formados de dos o más palabras inglesas que aparecen en el diccionario como entradas principales:

water lily *n* : nenúfar *m*

Solamente la primera entrada en una serie de homógrafos numerados incluye la pronunciación si ésta es la misma para todos los otros homógrafos:

dab[1] ['dæb] *vt* . . .

dab[2] *n* . . .

No se indica la pronunciación de las partes principales de los verbos formados por sufijación regular, ni por otros derivados formados por sufijos comunes.

2. Pronunciación de los lemas españoles

Dada la alta regularidad de la pronunciación del español, no se indica la pronunciación de la mayor parte de las entradas que aparecen en la sección Español-Inglés. Sin embargo, se han hecho excepciones para ciertas palabras (tales como aquéllas que se han adaptado de otras lenguas) cuya pronunciación en español no puede derivarse naturalmente de su ortografía:

pizza ['pitsɑ, 'pisɑ] *nf* **:** pizza

footing ['fu,tɪŋ] . . .

Calificativos funcionales

Un calificativo en itálicas que indica la categoría gramatical u otra clasificación funcional del lema aparece inmediatamente después de la pronunciación, o si la pronunciación se ha omitido, después del lema. Las ocho categorías gramaticales tradicionales, el adjetivo, el adverbio, la conjunción, la interjección, el sustantivo, la preposición, el pronombre, y el verbo, se indican como sigue:

daily[2] *adj* . . .

vagamente *adv* . . .

and . . . *conj* . . .

huy *interj* . . .

jackal . . . *n* . . .

para *prep* . . .

neither[3] *pron* . . .

leer . . . *v* . . .

Los verbos intransitivos se identifican con el calificativo *vi,* y los transitivos, *vt.* Las entradas para aquellos verbos que son a la vez transitivos e intransitivos llevan el calificativo *v.* Si una de estas entradas incluye inflexiones irregulares, el calificativo *v* aparece inmediatamente después del lema, y las acepciones transitivas e intransitivas son introducidas con los calificativos *vt* y *vi* respectivamente.

> **deliberar** *vi* **:** to deliberate
>
> **necessitate** . . . *vt* **-tated; -tating :** necesitar, requerir
>
> **satisfy** . . . *v* **-fied; -fying** *vt* . . . — *vi* . . .

Por último, dos otros calificativos se emplean para indicar la clasificación funcional de los verbos: *v aux* (auxiliary verb) y *v impers* (impersonal verb).

> **may** . . . *v aux, past* **might** . . .
>
> **haber**[1] . . . *v aux* **1 :** have . . . — *v impers* **1 hay :** there is, there are . . .

Calificativos de género

En toda entrada cuyo lema es un sustantivo español, el género de éste se indica con los calificativos *m* (masculino), *f* (femenino), o *mf* (masculino o femenino), que aparecen inmediatamente después del calificativo funcional:

> **magnesio** *nm* . . .
>
> **galaxia** *nf* . . .
>
> **turista** *nmf* . . .

Si se dan las formas tanto masculina como femenina de un sustantivo que denota a una persona, se aplica el calificativo *n.*

> **director, -tora** *n* . . .

Todo sustantivo español que aparece como definición de un lema inglés es acompañado de un calificativo de género:

> **amnesia** . . . *n* **:** amnesia *f*
>
> **earache** . . . *n* **:** dolor *m* de oído
>
> **gamekeeper** . . . *n* **:** guardabosque *mf*

Inflexiones

1. Sustantivos

En este diccionario se indica el plural de un sustantivo en los siguientes casos: cuando el plural es irregular, cuando la sufijación del plural produce un cambio en la acentuación o la ortografía del vocablo raíz, cuando un sustantivo inglés termina en una consonante seguida de *-o* o de *-ey,* cuando un sustantivo inglés termina en *-oo,* cuando un sustantivo inglés es un término compuesto del cual el elemento a pluralizar no es el último, cuando un sustantivo tiene variantes en el plural, o cuando podría suscitarse una duda razonable en cuanto a la ortografía del plural:

tooth . . . *n, pl* **teeth** . . .

garrafón *nm, pl* **-fones** . . .

potato . . . *n, pl* **-toes** . . .

abbey . . . *n, pl* **-beys** . . .

cuckoo[2] *n, pl* **-oos** . . .

brother–in–law . . . *n, pl* **brothers–in–law** . . .

quail[2] *n, pl* **quail** *or* **quails** . . .

hábitat *nm, pl* **-tats** . . .

tahúr *nm, pl* **tahúres** . . .

En la sección Inglés-Español, la forma plural de la mayor parte de los sustantivos se indica por medio de una inflexión reducida, sin tener en cuenta el número de sílabas que el lema contenga. En la sección Español-Inglés, se dan inflexiones reducidas sólo para aquellos sustantivos que contengan tres o más sílabas, mientras que las formas plurales de sustantivos más breves se presentan enteras:

shampoo[2] *n, pl* **-poos** . . .

calamity . . . *n, pl* **-ties** . . .

mouse . . . *n, pl* **mice** . . .

sartén *nmf, pl* **sartenes** . . .

hámster *nm, pl* **hámsters** . . .

federación *nf, pl* **-ciones** . . .

Si se produce un plural irregular en sólo uno de los géneros, la forma plural se da con el calificativo correspondiente:

campeón, -ona *n, mpl* **-ones** : champion

La forma plural de un sustantivo generalmente no aparece si el vocablo raíz permanece inalterado por la adición del sufijo plural regular, o cuando no es probable que el sustantivo se use en el plural:

apple . . . *n* **:** manzana *f*

inglés[3] *nm* **:** English (language)

Aquellos sustantivos que son plurales en forma y que ocurren regularmente en construcciones plurales son clasificados *npl* (si son sustantivos ingleses), *nmpl* (si son sustantivos masculinos españoles), o *nfpl* (si son sustantivos femeninos españoles):

knickers . . . *npl* . . .

enseres *nmpl* . . .

mancuernas *nfpl* . . .

Toda entrada que permanece inalterada en el plural es clasificada *ns & pl* (sustantivos ingleses), *nms & pl* (sustantivos masculinos españoles), *nfs & pl* (sustantivos femeninos españoles), y *nmfs & pl* (sustantivos españoles de género variable):

deer . . . *ns & pl* . . .

lavaplatos *nms & pl* . . .

tesis *nfs & pl* . . .

rompehuelgas *nmfs & pl* . . .

2. Verbos

VERBOS INGLESES

En la sección Inglés-Español, las partes principales de los verbos se indican en los siguientes casos: cuando el verbo es irregular, cuando la sufijación produce un cambio en la ortografía del vocablo raíz, cuando el verbo termina en *-ey*, cuando una inflexión tiene

variantes, o cuando puede suscitarse una duda razonable en cuanto a la ortografía de una inflexión:

break[1] . . . *v* **broke** . . . ; **broken** . . . ; **breaking** . . .

drag[1] . . . *v* **dragged; dragging** . . .

monkey[1] . . . *vi* **-keyed; -keying** . . .

label[1] . . . *vt* **-beled** *or* **-belled; -beling** *or* **-belling** . . .

imagine . . . *vt* **-ined; -ining** . . .

Si el verbo consta de dos o más sílabas, se da generalmente una forma reducida de la inflexión:

multiply . . . *v* **-plied; -plying** . . .

bevel[1] . . . *v* **-eled** *or* **-elled; -eling** *or* **-elling** . . .

forgo *or* **forego** . . . *vt* **-went; -gone; -going** . . .

commit . . . *vt* **-mitted; -mitting** . . .

Las partes principales de un verbo inglés no aparecen cuando el vocablo raíz permanece inalterado por la sufijación.

delay[1] . . . *vt*

pitch[1] . . . *vt*

VERBOS ESPAÑOLES

En cada entrada correspondiente a un verbo irregular español aparece un número entre llaves que remite al lector a los modelos de conjugación que aparecen en la sección titulada Conjugation of Spanish Verbs:

abnegarse {49} *vr* . . .

volver {89} *vi* . . .

Aunque estas remisiones no aparecen en las entradas que corresponden a los verbos regulares españoles, los modelos de conjugación de estas formas pueden consultarse en la susodicha sección, que comienza en la página 44a.

Adverbios y adjetivos

Las entradas principales de adjetivos y adverbios ingleses incluyen las formas comparativas y superlativas cuando la sufijación produce un cambio en la ortografía del vocablo raíz, cuando la inflexión es de forma irregular, o cuando existen variantes de la inflexión:

wet[2] *adj* **wetter; wettest** . . .

good[2] *adj* **better** . . . ; **best** . . .

evil[1] . . . *adj* **eviler** *or* **eviller; evilest** *or* **evillest** . . .

Las formas superlativas de adjetivos y adverbios de dos o más sílabas son presentadas generalmente en forma reducida:

early[1] . . . *adv* **earlier; -est** . . .

gaudy . . . *adj* **gaudier; -est** . . .

secure[2] *adj* **-curer; -est** . . .

but

young[1] . . . *adj* **younger** [ˈjʌŋgər]; **youngest** [-gəst] . . .

En algunas entradas aparece únicamente la forma superlativa:

mere *adj, superlative* **merest** . . .

La ausencia de la forma comparativa indica que no existe evidencia suficiente de su uso.

Las formas comparativas y superlativas de los adjetivos y adverbios generalmente no se muestran si la sufijación no altera el vocablo raíz:

quiet[3] *adj* **1** . . .

Uso

1. Calificativos de uso

En este diccionario se emplean dos tipos de calificativo de uso: regional y estilístico. Las palabras españolas cuyo uso se limita a

ciertas regiones de Latinoamérica o a España, reciben calificativos que indican los países en que suelen usarse con más frecuencia:

guarachear *vi Cuba, PRi fam* . . .

bucket . . . *n* **:** . . . cubeta *f Mex*

Los siguientes calificativos regionales se han empleado en la redacción de este libro: *Arg* (Argentina), *Bol* (Bolivia), *CA* (Centroamérica), *Car* (el Caribe), *Chile* (Chile), *Col* (Colombia), *CoRi* (Costa Rica), *Cuba* (Cuba), *DomRep* (República Dominicana), *Ecua* (Ecuador), *Sal* (El Salvador), *Guat* (Guatemala), *Hond* (Honduras), *Mex* (México), *Nic* (Nicaragua), *Pan* (Panamá), *Par* (Paraguay), *Peru* (Perú), *PRi* (Puerto Rico), *Spain* (España), *Uru* (Uruguay), *Ven* (Venezuela).

Dado el foco primordialmente latinoamericano de este diccionario, la mayoría de los regionalismos que contiene provienen de América Latina. Sin embargo, se han incluido también algunos regionalismos comunes de España.

Varios vocablos en español reciben un calificativo de *fam* (familiar), lo cual indica que el uso de tales palabras es apropiado solamente en contextos informales. El calificativo estilístico *usu considered vulgar* se emplea para indicar que el uso de la palabra indicada puede considerarse como vulgar u ofensivo. Se han omitido la mayoría de este tipo de voces, pero hay algunas cuyo uso es tan común que el omitirlas resultaría negligente. El propósito de este calificativo es, pues, de servir de advertencia al lector.

2. Notas de uso

En algunos casos, una acepción puede venir precedida de una nota parentética que proporciona al lector información semántica suplementaria:

not . . . *adv* **1** (*used to form a negative*) **:** no . . .

within[2] *prep* . . . **2** (*in expressions of distance*) **:** . . . **3** (*in expressions of time*) **:** . . .

e[2] *conj* (*used instead of* **y** *before words beginning with i or hi*) **:** . . .

poder[1] . . . *v aux* . . . **2** (*expressing possibility*) **:** . . . **3** (*expressing permission*) **:** . . .

Este tipo de orientación semántica puede aparecer también entre paréntesis como parte de la definición:

calibrate . . . *vt* . . . **:** calibrar (armas), graduar (termómetros)

palco *nm* **:** box (in a theater or stadium)

En algunas ocasiones, una nota de uso aparece en lugar de una definición. Esto ocurre sólo cuando el lema carece de equivalente en el idioma extranjero. Estas notas de uso aparecen acompañadas de ejemplos que ilustran el uso común del lema:

shall . . . *v aux* . . . **1** (*used to express a command*) <you shall do as I say **:** harás lo que te digo> . . .

3. Ejemplos de uso

Varias definiciones vienen acompañadas de ejemplos de uso. Estos ejemplos sirven para ilustrar un empleo típico del lema en un contexto dado, o un uso idiomático común de la palabra. Los ejemplos de uso incluyen una traducción, y aparecen entre paréntesis angulares:

lejos *adv* **1 :** far away, distant <a lo lejos **:** in the distance, far off> . . .

make[1] . . . **9** . . . **:** ganar <to make a living **:** ganarse la vida> . . .

División de las acepciones

Se introduce una acepción o definición por medio de dos puntos en negrita:

fable . . . *n* **:** fábula *f*

Cuando una entrada principal tiene varias acepciones, éstas se indican con un número arábigo, compuesto también en negrita:

laguna *nf* **1 :** lagoon **2 :** lacuna, gap

Cuando alguna información (como un sinónimo, una palabra o frase en negrita, una nota de uso, una remisión, o un calificativo) aparece después de un número de acepción, ésta se aplica única y específicamente a dicha acepción, y no a otras que puedan aparecer bajo la misma entrada principal:

abanico *nm* . . . **2** GAMA **:** . . .

tonic[2] *n* . . . **2** *or* **tonic water :** . . .

grillo *nm* . . . **2 grillos** *nmpl* **:** . . .

fairy . . . *n, pl* **fairies** . . . **2 fairy tale :** . . .

myself . . . *pron* **1** (*used reflexively*) **:** . . .

pike . . . *n* . . . **3** → **turnpike**

atado[2] *nm* . . . **2** *Arg* **:** . . .

Remisiones

Las remisiones empleadas en este diccionario se clasifican en tres categorías: sinónima, cognada, e inflexional. Toda remisión puede identificarse inmediatamente por la flecha en negrita que aparece a continuación del lema.

Las remisiones de tipo sinónimo y cognado indican que la definición correspondiente al lema que precede a la flecha puede encontrarse en la entrada a la cual se remite:

scapula . . . → **shoulder blade**

amuck → **amok**

Las remisiones de tipo inflexional se utilizan para indicar que el lema que precede a la flecha es meramente una inflexión de la entrada a la cual se remite (generalmente un verbo o un sustantivo):

fue, etc. → **ir, ser**

mice → **mouse**

Sinónimos

En varias entradas y acepciones del diccionario se encuentra, entre los dos puntos en negrita y el texto de la definición, un sinónimo compuesto en mayúsculas pequeñas. Toda palabra empleada como sinónimo tiene su propia entrada en el diccionario, ya sea como entrada principal o como frase en negritas. El propósito de estos sinónimos es de orientar al lector y ayudarlo a elegir la acepción correcta, así como de proveer un término que podría usarse alternativamente en el mismo contexto.

Abreviaturas empleadas en este libro

Las abreviaturas empleadas en este diccionario son formas acortadas de las palabras inglesas que aparecen entre paréntesis.

adj	adjetivo (adjective)
adv	adverbio (adverb)
Arg	Argentina (Argentina)
Bol	Bolivia (Bolivia)
CA	Centroamérica (Central America)
Car	Región del Caribe (Caribbean region)
Col	Colombia (Colombia)
conj	conjunción (conjunction)
CoRi	Costa Rica (Costa Rica)
DomRep	República Dominicana (Dominican Republic)
Ecua	Ecuador (Ecuador)
f	femenino (feminine)
fam	familiar o coloquial (familiar or colloquial)
fpl	femenino plural (feminine plural)
Guat	Guatemala (Guatemala)
Hond	Honduras (Honduras)
interj	interjección (interjection)
m	masculino (masculine)
Mex	México (Mexico)
mf	masculino o femenino (masculine or feminine)
mpl	masculino plural (masculine plural)

n	sustantivo (noun)
nf	sustantivo femenino (feminine noun)
nfpl	sustantivo plural femenino (feminine plural noun)
nfs & pl	sustantivo plural femenino, invariable en cuanto a número (invariable singular or plural feminine noun)
Nic	Nicaragua (Nicaragua)
nm	sustantivo masculino (masculine noun)
nmf	sustantivo masculino o femenino (masculine or feminine noun)
nmfpl	sustantivo plural, invariable en cuanto a género (plural noun invariable for gender)
nmfs & pl	sustantivo invariable en cuanto a género y número (noun invariable for both gender and number)
nmpl	sustantivo plural masculino (masculine plural noun)
nms & pl	sustantivo masculino, invariable en cuanto a número (invariable singular or plural masculine noun)
npl	sustantivo plural (plural noun)
ns & pl	sustantivo invariable en cuanto a número (noun invariable for plural)
Pan	Panamá (Panama)
Par	Paraguay (Paraguay)
pl	plural (plural)
prep	preposition (preposición)
PRi	Puerto Rico (Puerto Rico)
pron	pronoun (pronombre)
Sal	El Salvador (El Salvador)
Uru	Uruguay (Uruguay)
usu	generalmente (usually)
v	verbo (verb)
v aux	verbo auxiliar (auxiliary verb)
Ven	Venezuela (Venezuela)
vi	verbo intransitivo (intransitive verb)
v impers	verbo impersonal (impersonal verb)
vr	verbo pronominal (reflexive verb)
vt	verbo transitivo (transitive verb)

Gramática inglesa

El adjetivo

El adjetivo inglés es invariable en cuanto a número o género, y suele preceder al sustantivo que modifica:

the tall woman	la mujer alta
the tall women	las mujeres altas
a happy child	un niño contento
happy children	niños contentos

1. Adjetivos positivos, comparativos, y superlativos

Las formas comparativas y superlativas del adjetivo inglés se pueden construir de tres maneras. Cuando el adjetivo positivo consta de una sola sílaba, la construcción más común es de añadir los sufijos *-er* o *-est* al vocablo raíz; si el adjetivo positivo consta de más de dos sílabas, suele entonces combinarse con los adverbios *more*, *most*, *less* o *least;* al adjetivo positivo de dos sílabas puede aplicarse cualquiera de las dos fórmulas; y por último, existen los adjetivos irregulares cuyas formas comparativas y superlativas son únicas.

Positivo	Comparativo	Superlativo
clean (limpio)	**cleaner** (más limpio)	**cleanest** (el más limpio)
narrow (angosto)	**narrower** (más angosto)	**narrowest** (el más angosto)
meaningful (significativo)	**more meaningful** (más significativo)	**most meaningful** (el más significativo)
	less meaningful (menos significativo)	**least meaningful** (el menos significativo)
good (bueno)	**better** (mejor)	**best** (el mejor)
bad (malo)	**worse** (peor)	**worst** (el peor)

2. Adjetivos demostrativos

El adjetivo demostrativo *this* o *that* corresponde al adjetivo español *este* o *ese*, y sirve esencialmente la misma función. Debe notarse que este tipo de adjetivo es el único que tiene forma plural:

Singular		Plural	
this	este, esta	**these**	estos, estas
that	ese, esa	**those**	esos, esas

3. Adjetivos descriptivos

Un adjetivo descriptivo describe o indica una cualidad, clase o condición (*a fascinating conversation,* una conversación fascinante; *a positive attitude,* una actitud positiva; *a fast computer,* una computadora rápida).

4. Adjetivos indefinidos

Un adjetivo indefinido se usa para designar personas o cosas no identificadas (*some children,* unos niños *o* algunos niños; *other hotels,* otros hoteles).

5. Adjetivos interrogativos

El adjetivo interrogativo se usa para formular preguntas:

Whose office is this? — ¿***De quién*** es esta oficina?
Which book do you want? — ¿***Cuál*** libro quieres?

6. El sustantivo empleado como adjetivo

Un sustantivo puede usarse para modificar otro sustantivo. De esta manera el sustantivo funciona igual que un adjetivo (*the Vietnam War,* la Guerra de Vietnam; *word processing,* procesamiento de textos).

7. Adjetivos posesivos

Llámase adjetivo posesivo a la forma posesiva del pronombre personal. A continuación se listan los adjetivos posesivos ingleses y algunos ejemplos de su uso:

Singular	Plural
my	our
your	your
his/her/its	their

Where's ***my*** watch?	¿Dónde está ***mi*** reloj?
Your cab's here.	Ha llegado ***su*** taxi; ha llegado ***tu*** taxi.
It was ***her*** idea.	Fue ***su*** idea.
They read ***his*** book.	Leyeron ***su*** libro.
The box and ***its*** contents.	La caja y ***su*** contenido.
We paid for ***their*** ticket.	Pagamos por ***su*** boleto.
Your tables are ready.	***Sus*** mesas están listas.

8. Adjetivos predicativos

Un adjetivo predicativo modifica el sujeto de un verbo copulativo (como *be, become, feel, taste, smell,* o *seem*):

She is ***happy*** with the outcome.	Está ***contenta*** con el resultado.
The milk tastes ***sour***.	La leche sabe ***agria***.
The student seems ***puzzled***.	El estudiante parece estar ***desconcertado***.

9. Adjetivos propios

Un adjetivo propio es derivado de un nombre propio y suele escribirse con mayúscula:

Victorian furniture	muebles ***victorianos***
a ***Puerto Rican*** product	un producto ***puertorriqueño***

10. Adjetivos relativos

Un adjetivo relativo (tal como *which, that, who, whom, whose, where*) se emplea para introducir una cláusula adjetival o sustantiva:

toward late April, by ***which*** time the report should be finished	para fines de abril, fecha para la cual deberá estar listo el reporte
not knowing ***whose*** advice she should follow	sin saber a quién escuchar

El adverbio

La mayor parte de los adverbios ingleses se forman a partir de un adjetivo al que se le agrega el sufijo *-ly*:

mad***ly***	loca***mente***
wonderful***ly***	maravillosa***mente***

Para formar un adverbio de un adjetivo que termina en *-y*, suele cambiarse primero esta terminación a una *-i*, y luego se añade el sufijo *-ly*:

happily	felizmente
daintily	delicadamente

La forma adverbial que corresponde a varios adjetivos que terminan en *-ic* recibe el sufijo *-ally*:

basically	básicamente
numerically	numéricamente

Si un adjetivo termina en *-ly*, el adverbio que le corresponde suele escribirse de la misma manera:

she called her mother ***daily***	llamaba a su madre ***todos los días***
the show started ***early***	la función empezó ***temprano***

Por último, hay adverbios que no terminan en *-ly*, por ejemplo:

again (otra vez)	now (de nuevo)
too (demasiado)	too (también)

1. Adverbios positivos, comparativos, y superlativos

Al igual que el adjetivo, la mayoría de los adverbios ingleses poseen tres grados de comparación: positivo, comparativo, y superlativo. Como regla general, a un adverbio monosilábico se le añade el sufijo *-er* cuando es comparativo, y *-est* cuando es superlativo. Si el adverbio consta de tres o más sílabas, las formas comparativas y superlativas se forman al combinarlo con los adverbios *more/most* o *less/least*. Las formas comparativas y superlativas de un adverbio de dos sílabas pueden obtenerse empleando uno u otro de los dos métodos:

Positivo	Comparativo	Superlativo
fast	faster	fastest
easy	easier	easiest
madly	more madly	most madly
happily	more happily	most happily

Finalmente, hay algunos adverbios, tales como *quite* y *very*, que no poseen comparativo.

2. Adverbios de énfasis

Adverbios tales como *just* y *only* suelen usarse para poner el énfasis en otras palabras. El énfasis producido puede cambiar según la posición del adverbio en la oración:

He ***just*** nodded to me as he passed.	***Sólo*** me saludó con la cabeza al pasar.
He nodded to me ***just*** as he passed.	Me saludó con la cabeza ***justamente*** cuando me pasó.

3. Adverbios relativos

Los adverbios relativos (tales como *when*, *where*, y *why*) se utilizan principalmente para introducir preguntas:

When will he return?	¿***Cuándo*** volverá?
Where have the children gone?	¿***A dónde*** fueron los niños?
Why did you do it?	¿***Por qué*** lo hiciste?

El artículo

1. El artículo definido

En inglés existe solamente una forma del artículo definido, *the.* Este artículo es invariable en cuanto a género o número.

The boys were expelled.	***Los*** chicos fueron expulsados.
The First Lady dined with ***the*** ambassador.	***La*** Primera Dama cenó con ***el*** embajador.

2. El artículo indefinido

El artículo indefinido *a* se usa con cualquier sustantivo o abreviatura que comience ya sea con una consonante, o con un *sonido* consonántico:

a door	a hat
a B.A. degree	a one
a union	a U.S. Senator

El artículo *a* se emplea también antes de un sustantivo cuya primera sílaba comienza con *h-,* y esta sílaba o no es acentuada, o tiene solamente una acentuación moderada (a historian, a heroic attempt, a hilarious performance). Sin embargo, en el inglés hablado, suele más usarse el artículo *an* en estos casos (an historian, an heroic attempt, an hilarious performance). Ambas formas son perfectamente aceptables.

El artículo indefinido *an* se usa con cualquier sustantivo o abreviatura que comience con un *sonido* vocal, sin tener en cuenta si la primera letra del sustantivo es vocal o consonante (an icicle, an nth degree, an honor, an FBI investigation).

La conjunción

Existen tres tipos principales de conjunciones: la conjunción coordinante, la correlativa, y la subordinante.

1. Conjunciones coordinantes

Las conjunciones coordinantes, tales como *and, because, but, for, or, nor, since, so,* y *yet,* se emplean para unir elementos gramaticales de igual valor. Estos elementos pueden ser palabras, frases, cláusulas subordinadas, cláusulas principales, u oraciones completas. Las conjunciones coordinantes se emplean para unir elementos similares, para excluir o contrastar, para indicar una alternativa, para indicar una razón, o para precisar un resultado.

Unión de elementos similares:	She ordered pencils, pens, ***and*** erasers.
Exclusión o contraste:	He is a brilliant ***but*** arrogant man.
	They offered a promising plan, ***but*** it had not yet been tested.
Alternativa:	She can wait here ***or*** go on ahead.
Razón:	The report is useless, ***for*** its information is no longer current.
Resultado:	His diction is excellent, ***so*** every word is clear.

2. Conjunciones correlativas

Las conjunciones correlativas se usan en pares, y sirven para unir alternativas y elementos de igual valor gramatical.

Either you go ***or*** you stay.	***O*** te vas ***o*** te quedas.
He had ***neither*** looks ***nor*** wit.	No tenía ***ni*** atractivo físico ***ni*** inteligencia.

3. Conjunciones subordinantes

Las conjunciones subordinantes se usan para unir una cláusula subordinada a una cláusula principal. Estas conjunciones pueden emplearse para expresar la causa, la condición o concesión, el modo, el propósito o resultado, el tiempo, el lugar o la circunstancia, así como las condiciones o posibilidades alternativas.

causa:	***Because*** she learns quickly, she is doing well in her new job.
condición o concesión:	Don't call ***unless*** you are coming.
modo:	We'll do it ***however*** you tell us to.
propósito o resultado:	He distributes the mail early ***so that*** they can read it.
tiempo:	She kept meetings to a minimum ***when*** she was president.

El sustantivo

A diferencia del sustantivo español, el sustantivo inglés generalmente carece de género. En algunos sustantivos, el género femenino se identifica por la presencia del sufijo *-ess* (empress, hostess); existen también aquellos sustantivos que sólo se aplican a miembros de uno u otro sexo, por ejemplo: *husband, wife, father, mother, brother, sister,* así como nombres de ciertos animales: *bull, cow, deer, doe,* etc. Sin embargo, la mayoría de los sustantivos ingleses son neutros. Cuando es preciso atribuirle un género a un sustantivo neutro, suele combinarse éste con palabras como *male, female, man, woman,* etc., por ejemplo:

a ***male*** parrot	un loro ***macho***
women writers	escritoras

1. Usos básicos

Los sustantivos ingleses suelen usarse como sujetos, objetos directos, objetos de una preposición, objetos indirectos, objetos retenidos, nominativos predicativos, complementos objetivos, construcciones apositivas, y en trato directo:

sujeto:	The ***office*** was quiet.
objeto directo:	He locked the ***office.***
objeto de una preposición:	The file is in the ***office.***
objeto indirecto:	He gave his ***client*** the papers.
objeto retenido:	His client was given the ***papers.***
nominativo predicativo:	Mrs. Adams is the managing ***partner.***
complemento objetivo:	They made Mrs. Adams managing ***partner.***

construcción apositiva:	Mrs. Adams, the managing ***partner,*** wrote that memo.
trato directo:	***Mrs. Adams,*** may I present Mr. Bonkowski.

2. El sustantivo empleado como adjetivo

Los sustantivos desempeñan una función adjetival cuando preceden a otros sustantivos:

olive oil	aceite de olivo
business management	administración de empresas
emergency room	sala de emergencias

3. La formación del plural

La mayoría de los sustantivos ingleses se pluralizan añadiendo *-s* al final del singular (book, books; cat, cats; dog, dogs; tree, trees).

Cuando el sustantivo singular termina en *-s, -x, -z, -ch,* o *-sh,* su forma plural se obtiene añadiendo *-es* al final (cross, crosses; fox, foxes; witch, witches; wish, wishes; fez, fezes).
Si el sustantivo singular termina en *-y* precedida de una consonante, la *-y* es convertida en *-i* y se le añade la terminación *-es* (fairy, fairies; pony, ponies; guppy, guppies).

No todos los sustantivos ingleses obedecen estas normas. Hay algunos sustantivos (generalmente nombres de animales) que no siempre cambian en el plural (fish, fish o fishes; caribou, caribou o caribous). Por último, hay algunos sustantivos que poseen una forma plural única (foot, feet; mouse, mice; knife, knives).

4. El posesivo

La forma posesiva del sustantivo singular generalmente se obtiene al añadir un apóstrofe seguido de una *-s* al final:

Jackie's passport	el pasaporte ***de Jackie***
this hat is ***Billy's***	este sombrero es ***de Billy***

Cuando el sustantivo termina en *-s,* suele añadirse únicamente el apóstrofe, como sigue:

the ***neighbors'*** dog	el perro ***de los vecinos***
Mr. ***Ross'*** briefcase	portafolios ***del Sr. Ross***

La preposición

La preposición inglesa se combina generalmente con un sustantivo, un pronombre, o el equivalente de un sustantivo (como una frase o cláusula) para formar una frase con función adjetival, adverbial, o sustantiva. Suele distinguirse dos tipos de preposiciones: la preposición simple, es decir, aquélla que consta de una sola palabra (p. ej., *against, from, near, of, on, out,* o *without*), y la compuesta, que consta de más de un elemento (como *according to, by means of,* o *in spite of*).

1. Usos básicos

La preposición se emplea generalmente para unir un sustantivo, un pronombre, o el equivalente de un sustantivo al resto de la oración. Una frase preposicional suele emplearse como adverbio o adjetivo.

She expected resistance ***on*** his part.
He sat down ***beside*** her.

2. La conjunción vs. la preposición

Las palabras inglesas *after, before, but, for,* y *since* pueden funcionar como preposiciones así como conjunciones. El papel que desempeñan estas palabras suele determinarse según su posición dentro de la oración. Las conjunciones generalmente sirven para unir dos elementos de igual valor gramatical, mientras que las preposiciones suelen preceder a un sustantivo, un pronombre, o una frase sustantiva.

conjunción:	I was a bit concerned ***but*** not panicky. [***but*** vincula dos adjetivos]
preposición:	I was left with nothing ***but*** hope. [***but*** precede a un sustantivo]

conjunción: The device conserves fuel, ***for*** it is battery-powered.
[***for*** vincula dos cláusulas]

preposición: The device conserves fuel ***for*** residual heating.
[***for*** precede a una frase sustantiva]

3. Posición

Una preposición puede aparecer antes de un sustantivo o un pronombre (*below* the desk, *beside* them), después de un adjetivo (antagonistic *to,* insufficient *in,* symbolic *of*), o después de un elemento verbal con el cual combina para formar una frase con función verbal (take *for,* take *over,* come *across*).

A diferencia de la preposición española, la preposición inglesa puede aparecer al final de una oración, lo cual sucede frecuentemente en el uso común, especialmente si la preposición forma parte de una frase con función verbal.

After Rourke left, Joyce took ***over***.
What does this all add up ***to***?

El pronombre

Los pronombres pueden poseer las características siguientes: caso (nominativo, posesivo, u objetivo); número (singular o plural); persona (primera, segunda, o tercera), y género (masculino, femenino, o neutro). Los pronombres ingleses se clasifican en siete categorías principales, de las cuales cada una juega un papel específico.

1. Pronombres demostrativos

Las palabras *this, that, these* y *those* se consideran como pronombres cuando funcionan como sustantivos. (Se les clasifica como adjetivos demostrativos cuando modifican un sustantivo.) El pronombre demostrativo indica a una persona o cosa para distinguirla de otras.

> ***These*** are the best designs we've seen to date.
>
> ***Those*** are strong words.

El pronombre demostrativo también se usa para distinguir a una persona o cosa cercana de otra que se encuentre a mayor distancia (*this* is my desk; *that* is yours).

2. Pronombres indefinidos

El pronombre indefinido se emplea para designar a una persona o cosa cuya identidad se desconoce o no se puede establecer de inmediato. Estos pronombres se usan generalmente como referencias en la tercera persona, y no se distinguen en cuanto a género. A continuación se listan ejemplos de pronombres indefinidos.

all	either	none
another	everybody	no one
any	everyone	one
anybody	everything	other
anyone	few	several
anything	many	some
both	much	somebody
each	neither	someone
each one	nobody	something

Los pronombres indefinidos deben concordar en cuanto a número con los verbos que les corresponden. Los siguientes pronombres son singulares y deben usarse con un verbo conjugado en singular: *another, anything, each one, everything, much, nobody, no one, one, other, someone, something.*

> ***Much*** is being done.
>
> ***No one*** *wants* to go.

Los pronombres indefinidos *both, few, many, several* entre otros son plurales, y por lo tanto deben emplearse con verbos conjugados en plural:

Many *were* called; ***few*** *were* chosen.

Algunos pronombres, tales como *all, any, none,* y *some,* pueden presentar un problema ya que pueden usarse tanto con verbos singulares como plurales. Como regla general, los pronombres que se usan con sustantivos no numerables emplean verbos singulares, mientras que aquéllos que se usan con sustantivos numerables suelen tomar un verbo plural.

con sustantivo no numerable:	***All*** of the ***property is*** affected. ***None*** of the ***soup was*** spilled. ***Some*** of the ***money was*** spent.
con sustantivo numerable:	***All*** of my ***shoes are*** black. ***None*** of the ***clerks were*** available. ***Some*** of your ***friends were*** there.

2. Pronombres interrogativos

Los pronombres interrogativos *what, which, who, whom,* y *whose,* así como las combinaciones de estos con el sufijo *-ever* (*whatever, whichever,* etc.) se usan para introducir una pregunta:

Who is she?	He asked me ***who*** she was.
Whoever can that be?	We wondered ***whoever*** that could be.

4. Pronombres personales

El pronombre personal refleja la persona, el número, y el género del ser u objeto que representa. La mayoría de los pronombres personales toman una forma distinta para cada uno de estos tres casos.

Persona	Nominativo	Posesivo	Objetivo
PRIMERA			
SINGULAR:	I	my, mine	me
PLURAL:	we	our, ours	us
SEGUNDA			
SINGULAR:	you	your, yours	you
PLURAL:	you	your, yours	you
TERCERA			
SINGULAR:	he	his, his	him
	she	her, hers	her
	it	its, its	it
PLURAL:	they	their, theirs	them

Nótese que los pronombres personales en el caso posesivo no llevan apóstrofe, y no deben confundirse con los homófonos *you're, they're, there's, it's.*

5. Pronombres recíprocos

Los pronombres recíprocos *each other* y *one another* se emplean para indicar una acción o relación mutua:

They do not quarrel with ***one another***.	No se pelean (el uno con el otro).
Lou and Andy saw ***each other*** at the party.	Lou y Andy se vieron en la fiesta.

Un pronombre recíproco puede usarse también en el caso posesivo:

They always borrowed ***one another's*** money.	Siempre se prestaban dinero.
The two companies depend on ***each other's*** success.	Cada una de las dos compañías depende del éxito de la otra.

6. Pronombres reflexivos

Los pronombres reflexivos se forman al combinar los pronombres personales *him, her, it, my, our, them* y *your* con *-self* o *-selves.* El pronombre reflexivo se usa generalmente para expresar una acción reflexiva, o bien para recalcar el sujeto de una oración, cláusula, o frase.

> She dressed ***herself***.
> He asked ***himself*** if it was worth it.
> I ***myself*** am not concerned.

7. Pronombres relativos

Los pronombres relativos son *that, what, which, who, whom,* y *whose,* así como las combinaciones de éstos con la terminación *-ever.* Estos pronombres se emplean para introducir oraciones subordinadas con función sustantiva o adjetival.

El pronombre relativo *who* se usa para referirse a personas y, en ciertas ocasiones, algunos animales. *Which* suele usarse para referirse a animales o cosas, y *that* puede usarse para personas, animales, o cosas.

> a man ***who*** sought success
>
> a woman ***whom*** we trust
>
> Kentucky Firebolt, ***who*** won yesterday's horse race
>
> a movie ***which*** was a big hit
>
> a dog ***which*** kept barking
>
> a boy ***that*** behaves well
>
> a movie ***that*** was a big hit
>
> a dog ***that*** kept barking

En ciertas ocasiones el pronombre relativo puede omitirse:

> The man [***whom***] I was talking to is the senator.

El verbo

El verbo inglés posee típicamente las siguientes características: inflexión (p. ej., *help, helps, helping, helped*), persona (primera, segunda, o tercera), número (singular o plural), tiempo (presente, pasado, futuro), aspecto (categorías temporales distintas a los tiempos simples de presente, pasado y futuro), voz (activa o pasiva), y modo (indicativo, subjuntivo e imperativo).

1. La inflexión

Los verbos regulares ingleses tienen cuatro inflexiones diferentes, las cuales se producen al añadir los sufijos *-s* o *-es, -ed,* e *-ing.* La mayoría de los verbos irregulares poseen cuatro o cinco inflexiones (p. ej., *see, sees, seeing, saw, seen*); y el verbo *be* tiene ocho (*be, is, am, are, being, was, were, been*).

Los verbos que terminan en una *-e* muda conservan por lo general la *-e* al añadírsele un sufijo que comienza con una consonante (como *-s*), pero esta *-e* desaparece si el sufijo comienza con una vocal (como sucede con *-ed* o *-ing*).

arrange; arranges; arranged; arranging
hope; hopes; hoped; hoping

Sin embargo, algunos de estos verbos conservan la *-e* final para no ser confundidos con otras palabras de ortografía igual, por ejemplo:

dye; dyes; dyed; dyeing [vs. ***dying***, del verbo ***die***]
singe; singes; singed; singeing [vs. ***singing***, del verbo ***sing***]

Si un verbo consta de una sílaba y termina en una sola consonante a la cual precede una sola vocal, la consonante final se repite en algunas inflexiones:

brag; bragged; bragging
grip; gripped; gripping

Cuando un verbo posee esta misma terminación, pero consta de dos o más sílabas, y la última de éstas es acentuada, se repite también la consonante final:

commit; committed; committing
occur; occurred; occurring

Los verbos que terminan en *-y*, precedida de una consonante, suelen cambiar esta *-y* en *-i* en toda inflexión excepto cuando el sufijo correspondiente es *-ing*.

carry; carried; carrying
study; studied; studying

Cuando un verbo termina en *-c*, se le añade una *-k* en inflexiones cuyos sufijos comienzan con *-e* o *-i*.

mimic; mimics; mimicked; mimicking
traffic; traffics; trafficked; trafficking

2. El tiempo y el aspecto

Los verbos ingleses exhiben generalmente su presente simple o pasado simple en una sola palabra, por ejemplo:

I do, I did	we write, we wrote

El tiempo futuro suele expresarse al combinar el verbo auxiliar *shall* o *will* con la forma presente simple o presente progresiva del verbo:

I ***shall do*** it.	Lo haré.
We ***will come*** tomorrow.	Vendremos mañana.

Llámase aspecto de un verbo a aquellos tiempos que difieren del presente simple, pasado simple, o futuro simple. A continuación se presentan cuatro de estos tiempos o aspectos: el progresivo, el presente perfecto, el pasado perfecto, y el futuro perfecto.

El tiempo progresivo expresa una acción que está teniendo lugar en el presente o en el futuro.

He ***is reading*** the paper.	***Está leyendo*** el periódico.

El presente perfecto se emplea para expresar una acción que ha comenzado en el pasado y que continúa en el presente, o también para expresar una acción que haya tenido lugar en un momento indefinido del pasado.

She ***has written*** a book. ***Ha escrito*** un libro.

El pasado perfecto expresa una acción que fue llevada a cabo antes de otra acción o evento en el pasado.

She ***had written*** many books previously. ***Había escrito*** muchos libros anteriormente.

El futuro perfecto indica una acción que será llevada a cabo antes de una acción o evento en el futuro.

We ***will have finished*** the project by then. A esas alturas ***habremos terminado*** el proyecto.

3. La voz

La voz (activa o pasiva) indica si el sujeto de la oración es el que desempeña la acción del verbo o si es el objeto de esta acción:

Voz activa: He ***respected*** his colleagues.
Respetaba a sus colegas.

Voz pasiva: He ***was respected*** by his colleagues.
Era respetado por sus colegas.

4. El modo

En inglés existen tres modos: indicativo, imperativo, y subjuntivo.

El modo indicativo se emplea ya sea para indicar un hecho, o para hacer una pregunta:

He ***is*** here. ***Está*** aquí.
Is he here? ¿***Está*** aquí?

El modo imperativo se usa para expresar una orden o una petición:

Come here. ***Ven*** aquí.
Please ***come*** here. ***Ven*** aquí, por favor.

El modo subjuntivo expresa una condición contraria a los hechos. El modo subjuntivo en inglés ha caído en desuso, pero suele aparecer en cláusulas introducidas por *if*, y después del verbo *wish*.

I wish he ***were*** here.	Quisiera que ***estuviera*** él aquí.
If she ***were*** there, she could answer that.	Si ***estuviera*** ella allá, podría haberlo contestado.

5. Verbos transitivos e intransitivos

Como en español, el verbo inglés puede ser transitivo o intransitivo. El verbo transitivo es el que puede llevar un complemento directo:

She ***sold*** her car.	***Vendió*** su coche.

El verbo intransitivo no lleva un complemento directo:

He ***talked*** all day.	***Habló*** todo el día.

Spanish–English Dictionary

A

a[1] *nf* **:** first letter of the Spanish alphabet

a[2] *prep* **1 :** to <nos vamos a México : we're going to Mexico> **2** (*used before direct or indirect objects referring to persons*) <¿llamaste a tu papá? : did you call your dad?> <como a usted le guste : as you wish> **3 :** in the manner of <papas a la francesa : french fries> **4 :** on, by means of <a pie : on foot> **5 :** per, each <tres pastillas al día : three pills per day> **6** (*with infinitive*) <enséñales a leer : teach them to read> <problemas a resolver : problems to be solved>

ábaco *nm* **:** abacus

abad *nm* **:** abbot

abadesa *nf* **:** abbess

abadía *nf* **:** abbey

abajo *adv* **1 :** down <póngalo más abajo : put it further down> <arriba y abajo : up and down> **2 :** downstairs **3 :** under, beneath <el abajo firmante : the undersigned> **4 :** down with <¡abajo la inflación! : down with inflation!> **5 ~ de :** under, beneath **6 de ~ :** bottom <el cajón de abajo : the bottom drawer> **7 hacia ~** *or* **para ~ :** downwards **8 cuesta abajo :** downhill **9 río abajo :** downstream

abalanzarse {21} *vr* **:** to hurl oneself, to rush

abanderado, -da *n* **:** standard-bearer

abandonado, -da *adj* **1 :** abandoned, deserted **2 :** neglected **3 :** slovenly, unkempt

abandonar *vt* **1** DEJAR **:** to abandon, to leave **2 :** to give up, to quit <abandonaron la búsqueda : they gave up the search> **— abandonarse** *vr* **1 :** to neglect oneself **2 ~ a :** to succumb to, to give oneself over to

abandono *nm* **1 :** abandonment **2 :** neglect **3 :** withdrawal <ganar por abandono : to win by default>

abanicar {72} *vt* **:** to fan **— abanicarse** *vr*

abanico *nm* **1 :** fan **2** GAMA **:** range, gamut

abaratamiento *nm* **:** price reduction

abaratar *vt* **:** to lower the price of **— abaratarse** *vr* **:** to go down in price

abarcar {72} *vt* **1 :** to cover, to include, to embrace **2 :** to undertake **3 :** to monopolize

abaritonado, -da *adj* **:** baritone

abarrotado, -da *adj* **:** packed, crammed

abarrotar *vt* **:** to fill up, to pack

abarrotería *nf CA, Mex* **:** grocery store

abarrotero, -ra *n Col, Mex* **:** grocer

abarrotes *nmpl* **1 :** groceries, supplies **2 tienda de abarrotes :** general store, grocery store

abastecedor, -dora *n* **:** supplier

abastecer {53} *vt* **:** to supply, to stock **— abastecerse** *vr* **:** to stock up

abastecimiento → abasto

abasto *nm* **:** supply, supplying <no da abasto : there isn't enough for all>

abatido, -da *adj* **:** dejected, depressed

abatimiento *nm* **1 :** drop, reduction **2 :** dejection, depression

abatir *vt* **1** DERRIBAR **:** to demolish, to knock down **2 :** to shoot down **3** DEPRIMIR **:** to depress, to bring low **— abatirse** *vr* **1** DEPRIMIRSE **:** to get depressed **2 ~ sobre :** to swoop down on

abdicación *nf, pl* **-ciones :** abdication

abdicar {72} *vt* **:** to relinquish, to abdicate

abdomen *nm, pl* **-dómenes :** abdomen

abdominal *adj* **:** abdominal

abecé *nm* **:** ABC

abecedario *nm* ALFABETO **:** alphabet

abedul *nm* **:** birch (tree)

abeja *nf* **:** bee

abejorro *nm* **:** bumblebee

aberración *nf, pl* **-ciones :** aberration

aberrante *adj* **:** aberrant, perverse

abertura *nf* **1 :** aperture, opening **2** AGUJERO **:** hole **3 :** slit (in a skirt, etc.) **4** GRIETA **:** crack

abeto *nm* **:** fir (tree)

abierto[1] *pp* **→ abrir**

abierto[2], **-ta** *adj* **1 :** open **2 :** candid, frank **3 :** generous **— abiertamente** *adv*

abigarrado, -da *adj* **:** multicolored, variegated

abigeato *nm* **:** rustling (of livestock)

abismal *adj* **:** abysmal, vast

abismo *nm* **:** abyss, chasm <al borde del abismo : on the brink of ruin>

abjurar *vi* **~ de :** to abjure **— abjuración** *nf*

ablandamiento *nm* **:** softening, moderation

ablandar *vt* **1** SUAVIZAR **:** to soften **2** CALMAR **:** to soothe, to appease **—** *vi* **:** to moderate, to get milder **— ablandarse** *vr* **1 :** to become soft, to soften **2** CEDER **:** to yield, to relent

ablución *nf, pl* **-ciones :** ablution

abnegación *nf, pl* **-ciones :** abnegation, self-denial

abnegado, -da *adj* **:** self-sacrificing, selfless

abnegarse {49} *vr* **:** to deny oneself

abobado, -da *adj* **1 :** silly, stupid **2 :** bewildered

abocarse {72} *vr* **1** DIRIGIRSE **:** to head, to direct oneself **2** DEDICARSE **:** to dedicate oneself

abochornar *vt* AVERGONZAR **:** to embarrass, to shame **— abochornarse** *vr*

abofetear *vt* **:** to slap

abogacía *nf* **:** law, legal profession

abogado, -da *n* **:** lawyer, attorney

abogar {52} *vi* **~ por :** to plead for, to defend, to advocate

abolengo *nm* LINAJE **:** lineage, ancestry

abolición *nf, pl* **-ciones :** abolition

abolir {1} *vt* DEROGAR **:** to abolish, to repeal

abolladura *nf* **:** dent

abollar *vt* **:** to dent

abombar *vt* **:** to warp, to cause to bulge — **abombarse** *vr* **:** to decompose, to go bad

abominable *adj* ABORRECIBLE **:** abominable

abominación *nf, pl* **-ciones :** abomination

abominar *vt* ABORRECER **:** to abominate, to abhor

abonado, -da *n* **:** subscriber

abonar *vt* **1 :** to pay **2** FERTILIZAR **:** to fertilize — **abonarse** *vr* **:** to subscribe

abono *nm* **1 :** payment, installment **2** FERTILIZANTE **:** fertilizer **3 :** season ticket

abordaje *nm* **:** boarding

abordar *vt* **1 :** to address, to broach **2 :** to accost, to waylay **3 :** to come on board

aborigen[1] *adj, pl* **-rígenes :** aboriginal, native

aborigen[2] *nmf, pl* **-rígenes :** aborigine, indigenous inhabitant

aborrecer {53} *vt* ABOMINAR, ODIAR **:** to abhor, to detest, to hate

aborrecible *adj* ABOMINABLE, ODIOSO **:** abominable, detestable

aborrecimiento *nm* **:** abhorrence, loathing

abortar *vi* **:** to have an abortion — *vt* **1 :** to abort **2 :** to quash, to suppress

abortista *nmf* **:** abortionist

abortivo, -va *adj* **:** abortive

aborto *nm* **1 :** abortion **2 :** miscarriage

abotonar *vt* **:** to button — **abotonarse** *vr* **:** to button up

abovedado, -da *adj* **:** vaulted

abrasador, -dora *adj* **:** burning, scorching

abrasar *vt* QUEMAR **:** to burn, to sear, to scorch

abrasivo[1]**, -va** *adj* **:** abrasive

abrasivo[2] *nm* **:** abrasive

abrazadera *nf* **:** clamp, brace

abrazar {21} *vt* **:** to hug, to embrace — **abrazarse** *vr*

abrazo *nm* **:** hug, embrace

abrebotellas *nms & pl* **:** bottle opener

abrelatas *nms & pl* **:** can opener

abrevadero *nm* BEBEDERO **:** watering trough

abreviación *nf, pl* **-ciones :** abbreviation

abreviar *vt* **1 :** to abbreviate **2 :** to shorten, to cut short

abreviatura *nf* → **abreviación**

abridor *nm* **:** bottle opener, can opener

abrigadero *nm* **:** shelter, windbreak

abrigado, -da *adj* **1 :** sheltered **2 :** warm, wrapped up (with clothing)

abrigar {52} *vt* **1 :** to shelter, to protect **2 :** to keep warm, to dress warmly **3 :** to cherish, to harbor <abrigar esperanzas : to cherish hopes> — **abrigarse** *vr* **:** to dress warmly

abrigo *nm* **1 :** coat, overcoat **2 :** shelter, refuge

abril *nm* **:** April

abrillantador *nm* **:** polish

abrillantar *vt* **:** to polish, to shine

abrir {2} *vt* **1 :** to open **2 :** to unlock, to undo **3 :** to turn on (a tap or faucet) — *vi* **:** to open, to open up — **abrirse** *vr* **1 :** to open up **2 :** to clear (of the skies)

abrochar *vt* **:** to button, to fasten — **abrocharse** *vr* **:** to fasten, to hook up

abrogación *nf, pl* **-ciones :** abrogation, annulment, repeal

abrogar {52} *vt* **:** to abrogate, to annul, to repeal

abrojo *nm* **:** bur (of a plant)

abrumador, -dora *adj* **:** crushing, overwhelming

abrumar *vt* **1** AGOBIAR **:** to overwhelm **2** OPRIMIR **:** to oppress, to burden

abrupto, -ta *adj* **1 :** abrupt **2** ESCARPADO **:** steep — **abruptamente** *adv*

absceso *nm* **:** abscess

absolución *nf, pl* **-ciones 1 :** absolution **2 :** acquittal

absolutismo *nm* **:** absolutism

absoluto, -ta *adj* **1 :** absolute, unconditional **2 en ~ :** not at all <no me gustó en absoluto : I did not like it at all> — **absolutamente** *adv*

absolver {89} *vt* **1 :** to absolve **2 :** to acquit

absorbente *adj* **1 :** absorbent **2 :** absorbing, engrossing

absorber *vt* **1 :** to absorb, to soak up **2 :** to occupy, to take up, to engross

absorción *nf, pl* **-ciones :** absorption

absorto, -ta *adj* **:** absorbed, engrossed

abstemio[1]**, -mia** *adj* **:** abstemious, teetotal

abstemio[2]**, -mia** *n* **:** teetotaler

abstención *nf, pl* **-ciones :** abstention

abstenerse {80} *vr* **:** to abstain, to refrain

abstinencia *nf* **:** abstinence

abstracción *nf, pl* **-ciones :** abstraction

abstracto, -ta *adj* **:** abstract

abstraer {81} *vt* **:** to abstract — **abstraerse** *vr* **:** to lose oneself in thought

abstraído, -da *adj* **:** preoccupied, withdrawn

abstruso, -sa *adj* **:** abstruse

abstuvo, etc. → **abstenerse**

absuelto *pp* → **absolver**

absurdo[1]**, -da** *adj* DISPARATADO, RIDÍCULO **:** absurd, ridiculous — **absurdamente** *adv*

absurdo[2] *nm* **:** absurdity

abuchear *vt* **:** to boo, to jeer

abucheo *nm* **:** booing, jeering

abuela *nf* **1 :** grandmother **2 :** old woman **3 ¡tu abuela!** *fam* **:** no way!, forget about it!

abuelo *nm* **1 :** grandfather **2 :** old man **3 abuelos** *nmpl* **:** grandparents, ancestors

abulia *nf* **:** apathy, lethargy

abúlico, -ca *adj* **:** lethargic, apathetic

abultado, -da *adj* **:** bulging, bulky

abultar *vi* **:** to bulge — *vt* **:** to enlarge, to expand

abundancia *nf* **:** abundance

abundante *adj* **:** abundant, plentiful — **abundantemente** *adv*

abundar *vi* **1 :** to abound, to be plentiful **2 ~ en :** to be in agreement with

aburrido, -da *adj* **1 :** bored, tired, fed up **2** TEDIOSO **:** boring, tedious

aburrimiento *nm* **:** boredom, weariness

aburrir *vt* **:** to bore, to tire — **aburrirse** *vr* **:** to get bored

abusado, -da *adj Mex fam* **:** sharp, on the ball

abusador, -dora *n* **:** abuser

abusar *vi* **1 :** to go too far, to do something to excess **2 ~ de :** to abuse (as drugs) **3 ~ de :** to take unfair advantage of

abusivo, -va *adj* **1 :** abusive **2 :** outrageous, excessive

abuso *nm* **1 :** abuse **2 :** injustice, outrage

abyecto, -ta *adj* **:** despicable, contemptible

acá *adv* AQUÍ **:** here, over here <¡ven acá! : come here!>

acabado[1], -da *adj* **1 :** finished, done, completed **2 :** old, worn-out

acabado[2] *nm* **:** finish <un acabado brillante : a glossy finish>

acabar *vi* **1** TERMINAR **:** to finish, to end **2 ~ de :** to have just (done something) <acabo de ver a tu hermano : I just saw your brother> **3 ~ con :** to put an end to, to stamp out — *vt* TERMINAR **:** to finish — **acabarse** *vr* TERMINARSE **:** to come to an end, to run out <se me acabó el dinero : I ran out of money>

academia *nf* **:** academy

académico[1], -ca *adj* **:** academic, scholastic — **académicamente** *adv*

académico[2], -ca *n* **:** academic, academician

acaecer {53} *vi* (*3rd person only*) **:** to happen, to take place

acalambrarse *vr* **:** to cramp up, to get a cramp

acallar *vt* **:** to quiet, to silence

acalorado, -da *adj* **:** emotional, heated

acaloramiento *nm* **1 :** heat **2 :** ardor, passion

acalorar *vt* **:** to heat up, to inflame — **acalorarse** *vr* **:** to get upset, to get worked up

acampada *nf* **:** camp, camping <ir de acampada : to go camping>

acampar *vi* **:** to camp

acanalar *vt* **1 :** to groove, to furrow **2 :** to corrugate

acantilado *nm* **:** cliff

acanto *nm* **:** acanthus

acantonar *vt* **:** to station, to quarter

acaparador, -dora *adj* **:** greedy, selfish

acaparar *vt* **1 :** to stockpile, to hoard **2 :** to monopolize

acápite *nm* **:** paragraph

acariciar *vt* **:** to caress, to stroke, to pet

ácaro *nm* **:** mite

acarrear *vt* **1 :** to haul, to carry **2 :** to bring, to give rise to <los problemas que acarrea : the problems that come along with it>

acarreo *nm* **:** transport, haulage

acartonarse *vr* **1 :** to stiffen **2 :** to become wizened

acaso *adv* **1 :** perhaps, by any chance **2 por si acaso :** just in case

acatamiento *nm* **:** compliance, observance

acatar *vt* **:** to comply with, to respect

acaudalado, -da *adj* RICO **:** wealthy, rich

acaudillar *vt* **:** to lead, to command

acceder *vi* **~ a 1 :** to accede to, to agree to **2 :** to assume (a position) **3 :** to gain access to

accesar *vt* **:** to access (on a computer)

accesibilidad *nf* **:** accessibility

accesible *adj* ASEQUIBLE **:** accessible, attainable

acceso *nm* **1 :** access **2 :** admittance, entrance

accesorio[1], -ria *adj* **1 :** accessory **2 :** incidental

accesorio[2] *nm* **1 :** accessory **2 :** prop (in the theater)

accidentado[1], -da *adj* **1 :** eventful, turbulent **2 :** rough, uneven **3 :** injured

accidentado[2], -da *n* **:** accident victim

accidental *adj* **:** accidental, unintentional — **accidentalmente** *adv*

accidentarse *vr* **:** to have an accident

accidente *nm* **1 :** accident **2 :** unevenness **3 accidente geográfico :** geographical feature

acción *nf, pl* **acciones 1 :** action **2** ACTO **:** act, deed **3 :** share, stock

accionamiento *nm* **:** activation

accionar *vt* **:** to put into motion, to activate — *vi* **:** to gesticulate

accionario, -ria *adj* **:** stock <mercado accionario : stock market>

accionista *nmf* **:** stockholder, shareholder

acebo *nm* **:** holly

acechar *vt* **1 :** to watch, to spy on **2 :** to stalk, to lie in wait for

acecho *nm* **al acecho :** lying in wait

acedera *nf* **:** sorrel (herb)

acéfalo, -la *adj* **:** leaderless

aceitar *vt* **:** to oil

aceite *nm* **1 :** oil **2 aceite de ricino :** castor oil **3 aceite de oliva :** olive oil

aceitera *nf* **1 :** cruet (for oil) **2 :** oilcan **3** *Mex* **:** oil refinery

aceitoso, -sa *adj* **:** oily

aceituna *nf* OLIVA **:** olive

aceituno *nm* OLIVO **:** olive tree

aceleración *nf, pl* **-ciones** : acceleration, speeding up
acelerado, -da *adj* : accelerated, speedy
acelerador *nm* : accelerator
aceleramiento *nm* → **aceleración**
acelerar *vt* **1** : to accelerate, to speed up **2** AGILIZAR : to expedite — *vi* : to accelerate (of an automobile) — **acelerarse** *vr* : to hasten, to hurry up
acelga *nf* : chard, Swiss chard
acendrado, -da *adj* : pure, unblemished
acendrar *vt* : to purify, to refine
acento *nm* **1** : accent **2** : stress, emphasis
acentuación *nf, pl* **-ciones** : accentuation
acentuado, -da *adj* : marked, pronounced
acentuar {3} *vt* **1** : to accent **2** : to emphasize, to stress — **acentuarse** *vr* : to become more pronounced
acepción *nf, pl* **-ciones** SIGNIFICADO : sense, meaning
aceptabilidad *nf* : acceptability
aceptable *adj* : acceptable
aceptación *nf, pl* **-ciones** **1** : acceptance **2** APROBACIÓN : approval
aceptar *vt* **1** : to accept **2** : to approve
acequia *nf* **1** : irrigation ditch **2** *Mex* : sewer
acera *nf* : sidewalk
acerado, -da *adj* **1** : made of steel **2** : steely, tough
acerbo, -ba *adj* **1** : harsh, cutting <comentarios acerbos : cutting remarks> **2** : bitter — **acerbamente** *adv*
acerca *prep* **~ de** : about, concerning
acercamiento *nm* : rapprochement, reconciliation
acercar {72} *vt* APROXIMAR, ARRIMAR : to bring near, to bring closer — **acercarse** *vr* APROXIMARSE, ARRIMARSE : to approach, to draw near
acería *nf* : steel mill
acerico *nm* : pincushion
acero *nm* : steel <acero inoxidable : stainless steel>
acérrimo, -ma *adj* **1** : staunch, steadfast **2** : bitter <un acérrimo enemigo : a bitter enemy>
acertado, -da *adj* CORRECTO : accurate, correct, on target — **acertadamente** *adv*
acertante[1] *adj* : winning
acertante[2] *nmf* : winner
acertar {55} *vt* : to guess correctly — *vi* ATINAR : to be accurate, to be on target
acertijo *nm* ADIVINANZA : riddle
acervo *nm* **1** : pile, heap **2** : wealth, heritage <el acervo artístico del instituto : the artistic treasures of the institute>
acetato *nm* : acetate
acético, -ca *adj* : acetic <ácido acético : acetic acid>
acetileno *nm* : acetylene
acetona *nf* **1** : acetone **2** : nail-polish remover
achacar {72} *vt* : to attribute, to impute <te achaca todos sus problemas : he blames all his problems on you>
achacoso, -sa *adj* : frail, sickly
achaparrado, -da *adj* : stunted, scrubby <árboles achaparrados : scrubby trees>
achaque *nm* DOLENCIA : ailment, malady, discomfort
achatar *vt* : to flatten
achicar {72} *vt* **1** REDUCIR : to make smaller, to reduce **2** : to intimidate **3** : to bail out (water) — **achicarse** *vr* : to become intimidated
achicharrar *vt* : to scorch, to burn to a crisp
achicoria *nf* : chicory
achispado, -da *adj fam* : tipsy
achote *or* **achiote** *nm* : annatto seed
achuchón *nm, pl* **-chones** **1** : push, shove **2** *fam* : squeeze, hug **3** *fam* : mild illness
aciago, -ga *adj* : fateful, unlucky
acicalar *vt* **1** PULIR : to polish **2** : to dress up, to adorn — **acicalarse** *vr* : to get dressed up
acicate *nm* **1** : spur **2** INCENTIVO : incentive, stimulus
acidez *nf, pl* **-deces** **1** : acidity **2** : sourness **3** **acidez estomacal** : heartburn
acidificar {72} *vt* : to acidify
ácido[1], **-da** *adj* AGRIO : acid, sour
ácido[2] *nm* : acid
acierto *nm* **1** : correct answer, right choice **2** : accuracy, skill, deftness
acimut *nm* : azimuth
acitronar *vt Mex* : to fry until crisp
aclamación *nf, pl* **-ciones** : acclaim, acclamation
aclamar *vt* : to acclaim, to cheer, to applaud
aclaración *nf, pl* **-ciones** CLARIFICACIÓN : clarification, explanation
aclarar *vt* **1** CLARIFICAR : to clarify, to explain, to resolve **2** : to lighten **3** **aclarar la voz** : to clear one's throat — *vi* **1** : to get light, to dawn **2** : to clear up — **aclararse** *vr* : to become clear
aclaratorio, -ria *adj* : explanatory
aclimatar *vt* : to acclimatize — **aclimatarse** *vr* **~ a** : to get used to — **aclimatación** *nf*
acné *nm* : acne
acobardar *vt* INTIMIDAR : to frighten, to intimidate — **acobardarse** *vr* : to be frightened, to cower
acodarse *vr* **~ en** : to lean (one's elbows) on
acogedor, -dora *adj* : cozy, warm, friendly
acoger {15} *vt* **1** REFUGIAR : to take in, to shelter **2** : to receive, to welcome — **acogerse** *vr* **1** REFUGIARSE : to take refuge **2** **~ a** : to resort to, to avail oneself of

acogida *nf* **1** AMPARO, REFUGIO **:** refuge, protection **2** RECIBIMIENTO **:** reception, welcome

acolchar *vt* **1 :** to pad (a wall, etc.) **2 :** to quilt

acólito *nm* **1** MONAGUILLO **:** altar boy **2 :** follower, helper, acolyte

acomedido, -da *adj* **:** helpful, obliging

acometer *vt* **1** ATACAR **:** to attack, to assail **2** EMPRENDER **:** to undertake, to begin — *vi* **~ contra :** to rush against

acometida *nf* ATAQUE **:** attack, assault

acomodado, -da *adj* **1 :** suitable, appropriate **2 :** well-to-do, prosperous

acomodador, -dora *n* **:** usher, usherette *f*

acomodar *vt* **1 :** to accommodate, to make room for **2 :** to adjust, to adapt — **acomodarse** *vr* **1 :** to settle in **2 ~ a :** to adapt to

acomodaticio, -cia *adj* **:** accommodating, obliging

acomodo *nm* **1 :** job, position **2 :** arrangement, placement **3 :** accommodation, lodging

acompañamiento *nm* **:** accompaniment

acompañante *nmf* **1** COMPAÑERO **:** companion **2 :** accompanist

acompañar *vt* **:** to accompany, to go with

acompasado, -da *adj* **:** rhythmic, regular, measured

acomplejado, -da *adj* **:** full of complexes, neurotic

acondicionado, -da *adj* **1 :** equipped, fitted-out **2 bien acondicionado :** in good shape, in a fit state

acondicionador *nm* **1 :** conditioner **2 acondicionador de aire :** air conditioner

acondicionar *vt* **1 :** to condition **2 :** to fit out, to furnish

acongojado, -da *adj* **:** distressed, upset

acongojarse *vr* **:** to grieve, to become distressed

aconsejable *adj* **:** advisable

aconsejar *vt* **:** to advise, to counsel

acontecer {53} *vi* (*3rd person only*) **:** to occur, to happen

acontecimiento *nm* SUCESO **:** event

acopiar *vt* **:** to gather, to collect, to stockpile

acopio *nm* **:** collection, stock

acoplamiento *nm* **:** connection, coupling

acoplar *vt* **:** to couple, to connect — **acoplarse** *vr* **:** to fit together

acoquinar *vt* **:** to intimidate

acorazado[1], -da *adj* BLINDADO **:** armored

acorazado[2] *nm* **:** battleship

acordado, -da *adj* **:** agreed upon

acordar {19} *vt* **1 :** to agree on **2** OTORGAR **:** to award, to bestow — **acordarse** *vr* RECORDAR **:** to remember, to recall

acorde[1] *adj* **1 :** in agreement, in accordance **2 ~ con :** in keeping with

acorde[2] *nm* **:** chord

acordeón *nm, pl* **-deones :** accordion — **acordeonista** *nmf*

acordonar *vt* **1 :** to cordon off **2 :** to lace up **3 :** to mill (coins)

acorralar *vt* ARRINCONAR **:** to corner, to hem in, to corral

acortar *vt* **:** to shorten, to cut short — **acortarse** *vr* **1 :** to become shorter **2 :** to end early

acosar *vt* PERSEGUIR **:** to pursue, to hound, to harass

acoso *nm* ASEDIO **:** harassment <acoso sexual : sexual harassment>

acostar {19} *vt* **1 :** to lay (something) down **2 :** to put to bed — **acostarse** *vr* **1 :** to lie down **2 :** to go to bed

acostumbrado, -da *adj* **1** HABITUADO **:** accustomed **2** HABITUAL **:** usual, customary

acostumbrar *vt* **:** to accustom — *vi* **:** to be accustomed, to be in the habit — **acostumbrarse** *vr*

acotación *nf, pl* **-ciones 1 :** marginal note **2 :** stage direction

acotado, -da *adj* **:** enclosed

acotamiento *nm Mex* **:** shoulder (of a road)

acotar *vt* **1** ANOTAR **:** to note, to annotate **2** DELIMITAR **:** to mark off (land), to demarcate

acre[1] *adj* **1 :** acrid, pungent **2** MORDAZ **:** caustic, biting

acre[2] *nm* **:** acre

acrecentamiento *nm* **:** growth, increase

acrecentar {55} *vt* AUMENTAR **:** to increase, to augment

acreditación *nf, pl* **-ciones :** accreditation

acreditado, -da *adj* **1 :** accredited, authorized **2 :** reputable

acreditar *vt* **1 :** to accredit, to authorize **2 :** to credit **3 :** to prove, to verify — **acreditarse** *vr* **:** to gain a reputation

acreedor[1], -dora *adj* **:** deserving, worthy

acreedor[2], -dora *n* **:** creditor

acribillar *vt* **1 :** to riddle, to pepper (with bullets, etc.) **2 :** to hound, to harass

acrílico *nm* **:** acrylic

acrimonia *nf* **1 :** pungency **2 :** acrimony

acrimonioso, -sa *adj* **:** acrimonious

acriollarse *vr* **:** to adopt local customs, to go native

acritud *nf* **1 :** pungency, bitterness **2 :** intensity, sharpness **3 :** harshness, asperity

acrobacia *nf* **:** acrobatics

acróbata *nmf* **:** acrobat

acrónimo *nm* **:** acronym

acta *nf* **1 :** document, certificate <acta de nacimiento : birth certificate> **2 actas** *nfpl* **:** minutes (of a meeting)

actitud *nf* **1 :** attitude **2 :** posture, position

activación *nf, pl* **-ciones 1 :** activation, stimulation **2** ACELERACIÓN **:** acceleration, speeding up
activar *vt* **1 :** to activate **2 :** to stimulate, to energize **3 :** to speed up
actividad *nf* **:** activity
activista *nmf* **:** activist
activo[1], **-va** *adj* **:** active — **activamente** *adv*
activo[2] *nm* **:** assets *pl* <activo y pasivo : assets and liabilities>
acto *nm* **1** ACCIÓN **:** act, deed **2 :** act (in a play) **3 el acto sexual :** sexual intercourse **4 en el acto :** right away, on the spot **5 acto seguido :** immediately after
actor *nm* ARTISTA **:** actor
actriz *nf, pl* **actrices** ARTISTA **:** actress
actuación *nf, pl* **-ciones 1 :** performance **2 actuaciones** *nfpl* DILIGENCIAS **:** proceedings
actual *adj* PRESENTE **:** present, current
actualidad *nf* **1 :** present time <en la actualidad : at present> **2 actualidades** *nfpl* **:** current affairs
actualización *nf, pl* **-ciones :** updating, modernization
actualizar {21} *vt* **:** to modernize, to bring up to date
actualmente *adv* **:** at present, nowadays
actuar {3} *vi* **:** to act, to perform
actuarial *adj* **:** actuarial
actuario, -ria *n* **:** actuary
acuarela *nf* **:** watercolor
acuario *nm* **:** aquarium
Acuario *nmf* **:** Aquarius, Aquarian
acuartelar *vt* **:** to quarter (troops)
acuático, -ca *adj* **:** aquatic, water
acuchillar *vt* APUÑALAR **:** to knife, to stab
acuciante *adj* **:** pressing, urgent
acucioso, -sa → **acuciante**
acudir *vi* **1 :** to go, to come (someplace for a specific purpose) <acudió a la puerta : he went to the door> <acudimos en su ayuda : we came to her aid> **2 :** to be present, to show up <acudí a la cita : I showed up for the appointment> **3 ~ a :** to turn to, to have recourse to <hay que acudir al médico : you must consult the doctor>
acueducto *nm* **:** aqueduct
acuerdo *nm* **1 :** agreement **2 estar de acuerdo :** to agree **3 de acuerdo con :** in accordance with **4 de ~ :** OK, all right
acuicultura *nf* **:** aquaculture
acullá *adv* **:** yonder, over there
acumulación *nf, pl* **-ciones :** accumulation
acumulador *nm* **:** storage battery
acumular *vt* **:** to accumulate, to amass — **acumularse** *vr* **:** to build up, to pile up
acumulativo, -va *adj* **:** cumulative — **acumulativamente** *adv*
acunar *vt* **:** to rock, to cradle
acuñar *vt* **:** to coin, to mint
acuoso, -sa *adj* **:** aqueous, watery
acupuntura *nf* **:** acupuncture
acurrucarse {72} *vr* **:** to cuddle, to nestle, to curl up
acusación *nf, pl* **-ciones 1 :** accusation, charge **2 la acusación :** the prosecution
acusado[1], **-da** *adj* **:** prominent, marked
acusado[2], **-da** *n* **:** defendant
acusador, -dora *n* **1 :** accuser **2** FISCAL **:** prosecutor
acusar *vt* **1 :** to accuse, to charge **2 :** to reveal, to betray <sus ojos acusaban la desconfianza : his eyes revealed distrust> — **acusarse** *vr* **:** to confess
acusatorio, -ria *adj* **:** accusatory
acuse *nm* **acuse de recibo :** acknowledgment of receipt
acústica *nf* **:** acoustics
acústico, -ca *adj* **:** acoustic
adagio *nm* **1** REFRÁN **:** adage, proverb **2 :** adagio
adalid *nm* **:** leader, champion
adaptable *adj* **:** adaptable — **adaptabilidad** *nf*
adaptación *nf, pl* **-ciones :** adaptation, adjustment
adaptado, -da *adj* **:** suited, adapted
adaptador *nm* **:** adapter (in electricity)
adaptar *vt* **1** MODIFICAR **:** to adapt **2 :** to adjust, to fit — **adaptarse** *vr* **:** to adapt oneself, to conform
adecentar *vt* **:** to tidy up
adecuación *nf, pl* **-ciones** ADAPTACIÓN **:** adaptation
adecuadamente *adv* **:** adequately
adecuado, -da *adj* **1** IDÓNEO **:** suitable, appropriate **2 :** adequate
adecuar {8} *vt* **:** to adapt, to make suitable — **adecuarse** *vr* **~ a :** to be appropriate for, to fit in with
adefesio *nm* **:** eyesore, monstrosity
adelantado, -da *adj* **1 :** advanced, ahead **2 :** fast (of a clock or watch) **3 por ~ :** in advance
adelantamiento *nm* **1 :** advancement **2 :** speeding up
adelantar *vt* **1 :** to advance, to move forward **2 :** to overtake, to pass **3 :** to reveal (information) in advance **4 :** to advance, to lend (money) — **adelantarse** *vr* **1 :** to advance, to get in front **2 ~ a :** to forestall, to preempt
adelante *adv* **1 :** ahead, in front, forward **2 más adelante :** further on, later on **3 ¡adelante! :** come in!
adelanto *nm* **1 :** advance, progress **2 :** advance payment **3 :** earliness <llevamos una hora de adelanto : we're running an hour ahead of time>
adelfa *nf* **:** oleander
adelgazar {21} *vt* **:** to thin, to reduce — *vi* **:** to lose weight
ademán *nm, pl* **-manes 1** GESTO **:** gesture **2 ademanes** *nmpl* **:** manners
además *adv* **1 :** besides, furthermore **2 ~ de :** in addition to, as well as

adenoides *nfpl* : adenoids

adentrarse *vr* **~ en** : to go into, to penetrate

adentro *adv* : inside, within

adentros *nmpl* **decirse para sus adentros** : to say to oneself <me dije para mis adentros que nunca regresaría : I told myself that I'd never go back>

adepto[1], -ta *adj* : supportive <ser adepto a : to be a follower of>

adepto[2], -ta *n* PARTIDARIO : follower, supporter

aderezar {21} *vt* **1** SAZONAR : to season, to dress (salad) **2** : to embellish, to adorn

aderezo *nm* **1** : dressing, seasoning **2** : adornment, embellishment

adeudar *vt* **1** : to debit **2** DEBER : to owe

adeudo *nm* **1** DÉBITO : debit **2** *Mex* : debt, indebtedness

adherencia *nf* **1** : adherence, adhesiveness **2** : appendage, accretion

adherente *adj* : adhesive, sticky

adherirse {76} *vr* : to adhere, to stick

adhesión *nf, pl* **-siones 1** : adhesion **2** : attachment, commitment (to a cause, etc.)

adhesivo[1], -va *adj* : adhesive

adhesivo[2] *nm* : adhesive

adicción *nf, pl* **-ciones** : addiction

adición *nf, pl* **-ciones** : addition

adicional *adj* : additional — **adicionalmente** *adv*

adicionar *vt* : to add

adicto[1], -ta *adj* **1** : addicted **2** : devoted, dedicated

adicto[2], -ta *n* **1** : addict **2** PARTIDARIO : supporter, advocate

adiestrador, -dora *n* : trainer

adiestramiento *nm* : training

adiestrar *vt* : to train

adinerado, -da *adj* : moneyed, wealthy

adiós *nm, pl* **adioses 1** DESPEDIDA : farewell, good-bye **2 ¡adiós!** : good-bye!

aditamento *nm* : attachment, accessory

aditivo *nm* : additive

adivinación *nf, pl* **-ciones 1** : guess **2** : divination, prediction

adivinanza *nf* ACERTIJO : riddle

adivinar *vt* **1** : to guess **2** : to foretell, to predict

adivino, -na *n* : fortune-teller

adjetivo[1], -va *adj* : adjectival

adjetivo[2] *nm* : adjective

adjudicación *nf, pl* **-ciones 1** : adjudication **2** : allocation, awarding, granting

adjudicar {72} *vt* **1** : to adjudge, to adjudicate **2** : to assign, to allocate <adjudicar la culpa : to assign the blame> **3** : to award, to grant

adjuntar *vt* : to enclose, to attach

adjunto[1], -ta *adj* : enclosed, attached

adjunto[2], -ta *n* : deputy, assistant

adjunto[3] *nm* : adjunct

administración *nf, pl* **-ciones 1** : administration, management **2 administración de empresas** : business administration

administrador, -dora *n* : administrator, manager

administrar *vt* : to administer, to manage, to run

administrativo, -va *adj* : administrative

admirable *adj* : admirable, impressive — **admirablemente** *adv*

admiración *nf, pl* **-ciones** : admiration

admirador, -dora *n* : admirer

admirar *vt* **1** : to admire **2** : to amaze, to astonish — **admirarse** *vr* : to be amazed

admirativo, -va *adj* : admiring

admisibilidad *nf* : admissibility

admisible *adj* : admissible, allowable

admisión *nf, pl* **-siones** : admission, admittance

admitir *vt* **1** : to admit, to let in **2** : to acknowledge, to concede **3** : to allow, to make room for <la ley no admite cambios : the law doesn't allow for changes>

admonición *nf, pl* **-ciones** : admonition, warning

admonitorio, -ria *adj* : admonitory

ADN *nm* : DNA

adobar *vt* : to marinate

adobe *nm* : adobe

adobo *nm* **1** : marinade, seasoning **2** *Mex* : spicy marinade used for cooking pork

adoctrinamiento *nm* : indoctrination

adoctrinar *vt* : to indoctrinate

adolecer {53} *vi* PADECER : to suffer <adolece de timidez : he suffers from shyness>

adolescencia *nf* : adolescence

adolescente[1] *adj* : adolescent, teenage

adolescente[2] *nmf* : adolescent, teenager

adonde *conj* : where <el lugar adonde vamos es bello : the place where we're going is beautiful>

adónde *adv* : where <¿adónde vamos? : where are we going?>

adondequiera *adv* : wherever, anywhere <adondequiera que vayas : anywhere you go>

adopción *nf, pl* **-ciones** : adoption

adoptar *vt* **1** : to adopt (a measure), to take (a decision) **2** : to adopt (children)

adoptivo, -va *adj* **1** : adopted (children, country) **2** : adoptive (parents)

adoquín *nm, pl* **-quines** : paving stone, cobblestone

adorable *adj* : adorable, lovable

adoración *nf, pl* **-ciones** : adoration, worship

adorador[1], -dora *adj* : adoring, worshipping

adorador[2], -dora *n* : worshipper

adorar *vt* : to adore, to worship

adormecer {53} *vt* **1** : to make sleepy, to lull to sleep **2** : to numb — **ador-**

mecerse *vr* **1 :** to doze off **2 :** to go numb
adormecimiento *nm* **1** SUEÑO **:** drowsiness, sleepiness **2** INSENSIBILIDAD **:** numbness
adormilarse *vr* **:** to doze, to drowse
adornar *vt* DECORAR **:** to decorate, to adorn
adorno *nm* **:** ornament, decoration
adquirido, -da *adj* **1 :** acquired **2 mal adquirido :** ill-gotten
adquirir {4} *vt* **1 :** to acquire, to gain **2** COMPRAR **:** to purchase
adquisición *nf, pl* **-ciones 1 :** acquisition **2** COMPRA **:** purchase
adquisitivo, -va *adj* **poder adquisitivo :** purchasing power
adrede *adv* **:** intentionally, on purpose
adrenalina *nf* **:** adrenaline
adscribir {33} *vt* **:** to assign, to appoint — **adscribirse** *vr* **~ a :** to become a member of
adscripción *nf, pl* **-ciones :** assignment, appointment
adscrito *pp* → **adscribir**
aduana *nf* **:** customs, customs office
aduanero¹, -ra *adj* **:** customs
aduanero², -ra *n* **:** customs officer
aducir {61} *vt* **:** to adduce, to offer as proof
adueñarse *vr* **~ de :** to take possession of, to take over
adulación *nf, pl* **-ciones :** adulation, flattery
adulador¹, -dora *adj* **:** flattering
adulador², -dora *n* **:** flatterer, toady
adular *vt* LISONJEAR **:** to flatter
adulteración *nf, pl* **-ciones :** adulteration
adulterar *vt* **:** to adulterate
adulterio *nm* **:** adultery
adúltero¹, -ra *adj* **:** adulterous
adúltero², -ra *n* **:** adulterer
adultez *nf* **:** adulthood
adulto, -ta *adj & n* **:** adult
adusto, -ta *adj* **:** harsh, severe
advenedizo, -za *n* **1 :** upstart, parvenu **2 :** newcomer
advenimiento *nm* **:** advent
adventicio, -cia *adj* **:** adventitious
adverbio *nm* **:** adverb — **adverbial** *adj*
adversario¹, -ria *adj* **:** opposing, contrary
adversario², -ria *n* OPOSITOR **:** adversary, opponent
adversidad *nf* **:** adversity
adverso, -sa *adj* DESFAVORABLE **:** adverse, unfavorable — **adversamente** *adv*
advertencia *nf* AVISO **:** warning
advertir {76} *vt* **1** AVISAR **:** to warn **2 :** to notice, to tell <no advertí que estuviera enojada : I couldn't tell she was angry>
adviento *nm* **:** Advent
adyacente *adj* **:** adjacent
aéreo, -rea *adj* **1 :** aerial, air **2 correo aéreo :** airmail
aeróbic *nm* **:** aerobics
aeróbico, -ca *adj* **:** aerobic
aerobio, -bia *adj* **:** aerobic
aerodinámica *nf* **:** aerodynamics
aerodinámico, -ca *adj* **:** aerodynamic, streamlined
aeródromo *nm* **:** airfield
aeroespacial *adj* **:** aerospace
aerolínea *nf* **:** airline
aeromozo, -za *n* **:** flight attendant, steward *m,* stewardess *f*
aeronáutica *nf* **:** aeronautics
aeronáutico, -ca *adj* **:** aeronautical
aeronave *nf* **:** aircraft
aeropostal *adj* **:** airmail
aeropuerto *nm* **:** airport
aerosol *nm* **:** aerosol, aerosol spray
aeróstata *nmf* **:** baloonist
aerotransportado, -da *adj* **:** airborne
aerotransportar *vt* **:** to airlift
afabilidad *nf* **:** affability
afable *adj* **:** affable — **afablemente** *adv*
afamado, -da *adj* **:** well-known, famous
afán *nm, pl* **afanes 1** ANHELO **:** eagerness, desire **2** EMPEÑO **:** effort, determination
afanador, -dora *n Mex* **:** cleaning person, cleaner
afanarse *vr* **:** to toil, to strive
afanosamente *adv* **:** zealously, industriously, busily
afanoso, -sa *adj* **1 :** eager, industrious **2 :** arduous, hard
afear *vt* **:** to make ugly, to disfigure
afección *nf, pl* **-ciones 1 :** fondness, affection **2 :** illness, complaint
afectación *nf, pl* **-ciones :** affectation
afectado, -da *adj* **1 :** affected, mannered **2 :** influenced **3 :** afflicted **4 :** feigned
afectar *vt* **1 :** to affect **2 :** to upset **3 :** to feign, to pretend
afectísimo, -ma *adj* **suyo afectísimo :** yours truly
afectivo, -va *adj* **:** emotional
afecto¹, -ta *adj* **1 :** affected, afflicted **2 :** fond, affectionate
afecto² *nm* CARIÑO **:** affection
afectuoso, -sa *adj* CARIÑOSO **:** affectionate, caring
afeitar *vt* RASURAR **:** to shave — **afeitarse** *vr*
afelpado, -da *adj* **:** plush
afeminado, -da *adj* **:** effeminate
aferrado, -da *adj* **:** obstinate, stubborn
aferrarse {55} *vr* **:** to cling, to hold on
AFI *nm* (*Alfabeto Fonético Internacional*) **:** IPA
affidávit *nm, pl* **-dávits :** affidavit
afgano, -na *adj & n* **:** Afghan
afianzar {21} *vt* **1 :** to secure, to strengthen **2 :** to guarantee, to vouch for — **afianzarse** *vr* ESTABLECERSE **:** to establish oneself
afiche *nm* **:** poster
afición *nf, pl* **-ciones 1 :** enthusiasm, penchant, fondness <afición al de-

porte : love of sports> **2** PASATIEMPO : hobby

aficionado[1], -da *adj* ENTUSIASTA : enthusiastic, keen

aficionado[2], -da *n* **1** ENTUSIASTA : enthusiast, fan **2** : amateur

áfido *nm* : aphid

afiebrado, -da *adj* : feverish

afilado, -da *adj* **1** : sharp **2** : long, pointed <una nariz afilada : a sharp nose>

afilador *nm* : sharpener

afilalápices *nms & pl* : pencil sharpener

afilar *vt* : to sharpen

afiliación *nf, pl* **-ciones** : affiliation

afiliado[1], -da *adj* : affiliated

afiliado[2], -da *n* : member

afiliarse *vr* : to become a member, to join, to affiliate

afín *adj, pl* **afines 1** PARECIDO : related, similar <la biología y disciplinas afines : biology and related disciplines> **2** PRÓXIMO : adjacent, nearby

afinación *nf, pl* **-ciones 1** : tune-up **2** : tuning (of an instrument)

afinador, -dora *n* : tuner (of musical instruments)

afinar *vt* **1** : to perfect, to refine **2** : to tune (an instrument) — *vi* : to sing or play in tune

afincarse {72} *vr* : to establish oneself, to settle in

afinidad *nf* : affinity, similarity

afirmación *nf, pl* **-ciones 1** : statement **2** : affirmation

afirmar *vt* **1** : to state, to affirm **2** REFORZAR : to make firm, to strengthen

afirmativo, -va *adj* : affirmative — **afirmativamente** *adj*

aflicción *nf, pl* **-ciones** DESCONSUELO, PESAR : grief, sorrow

afligido, -da *adj* : grief-stricken, sorrowful

afligir {35} *vt* **1** : to distress, to upset **2** : to afflict — **afligirse** *vr* : to grieve

aflojar *vt* **1** : to loosen, to slacken **2** *fam* : to pay up, to fork over — *vi* : to slacken, to ease up — **aflojarse** *vr* : to become loose, to slacken

afloramiento *nm* : outcropping, emergence

aflorar *vi* : to come to the surface, to emerge

afluencia *nf* **1** : flow, influx **2** : abundance, plenty

afluente *nm* : tributary

afluir {41} *vi* **1** : to flock <la gente afluía a la frontera : people were flocking to the border> **2** : to flow

aforismo *nm* : aphorism

aforo *nm* **1** : appraisal, assessment **2** : maximum capacity (of a theater, highway, etc.)

afortunado, -da *adj* : fortunate, lucky — **afortunadamente** *adv*

afrecho *nm* : bran, mash

afrenta *nf* : affront, insult

afrentar *vt* : to affront, to dishonor, to insult

africano, -na *adj & n* : African

afroamericano, -na *adj & n* : Afro-American

afrodisiaco *or* **afrodisíaco** *nm* : aphrodisiac

afrontamiento *nm* : confrontation

afrontar *vt* : to confront, to face up to

afrutado, -da *adj* : fruity

afuera *adv* **1** : out <¡afuera! : get out!> **2** : outside, outdoors

afueras *nfpl* ALEDAÑOS : outskirts

agachadiza *nf* : snipe (bird)

agachar *vt* : to lower (a part of the body) <agachar la cabeza : to bow one's head> — **agacharse** *vr* : to crouch, to stoop, to bend down

agalla *nf* **1** BRANQUIA : gill **2 tener agallas** *fam* : to have guts, to have courage

agarradera *nf* ASA, ASIDERO : handle, grip

agarrado, -da *adj fam* : cheap, stingy

agarrar *vt* **1** : to grab, to grasp **2** : to catch, to take — *vi* **agarrar y** *fam* : to do (something) abruptly <el día siguiente agarró y se fue : the next day he up and left> — **agarrarse** *vr* **1** : to hold on, to cling **2** *fam* : to get into a fight <se agarraron a golpes : they came to blows>

agarre *nm* : grip, grasp

agasajar *vt* : to fête, to wine and dine

agasajo *nm* : lavish attention

ágata *nf* : agate

agave *nm* : agave

agazaparse *vr* **1** AGACHARSE : to crouch **2** : to hide

agencia *nf* : agency, office

agenciar *vt* : to obtain, to procure — **agenciarse** *vr* : to manage, to get by

agenda *nf* **1** : agenda **2** : appointment book

agente *nmf* **1** : agent **2 agente de viajes** : travel agent **3 agente de bolsa** : stockbroker **4 agente de tráfico** : traffic officer

agigantado, -da *adj* GIGANTESCO : gigantic

agigantar *vt* **1** : to increase greatly, to enlarge **2** : to exaggerate

ágil *adj* **1** : agile, nimble **2** : sharp, lively (of a response, etc.) — **ágilmente** *adv*

agilidad *nf* : agility, nimbleness

agilizar {21} *vt* ACELERAR : to expedite, to speed up

agitación *nf, pl* **-ciones 1** : agitation **2** NERVIOSISMO : nervousness

agitado, -da *adj* **1** : agitated, excited **2** : choppy, rough, turbulent

agitador, -dora *n* PROVOCADOR : agitator

agitar *vt* **1** : to agitate, to shake **2** : to wave, to flap **3** : to stir up — **agitarse** *vr* **1** : to toss about, to flap around **2** : to get upset

aglomeración *nf, pl* **-ciones 1 :** conglomeration, mass **2** GENTÍO **:** crowd
aglomerar *vt* **:** to cluster, to amass — **aglomerarse** *vr* **:** to crowd together
aglutinar *vt* **:** to bring together, to bind
agnóstico, -ca *adj & n* **:** agnostic
agobiado, -da *adj* **:** weary, worn-out, weighted-down
agobiante *adj* **1 :** exhausting, overwhelming **2 :** stifling, oppressive
agobiar *vt* **1** OPRIMIR **:** to oppress, to burden **2** ABRUMAR **:** to overwhelm **3 :** to wear out, to exhaust
agonía *nf* **:** agony, death throes
agonizante *adj* **:** dying
agonizar {21} *vi* **1 :** to be dying **2 :** to be in agony **3 :** to dim, to fade
agorero, -ra *adj* **:** ominous
agostar *vt* **1 :** to parch **2 :** to wither — **agostarse** *vr*
agosto *nm* **1 :** August **2 hacer uno su agosto :** to make a fortune, to make a killing
agotado, -da *adj* **1 :** exhausted, used up **2 :** sold out **3** FATIGADO **:** worn-out, tired
agotador, -dora *adj* **:** exhausting
agotamiento *nm* FATIGA **:** exhaustion
agotar *vt* **1 :** to exhaust, to use up **2 :** to weary, to wear out — **agotarse** *vr*
agraciado[1], -da *adj* **1 :** attractive **2 :** fortunate
agraciado[2], -da *n* **:** winner
agradable *adj* GRATO, PLACENTERO **:** pleasant, agreeable — **agradablemente** *adv*
agradar *vi* **:** to be pleasing <nos agradó mucho el resultado : we were very pleased with the result>
agradecer {53} *vt* **1 :** to be grateful for **2 :** to thank
agradecido, -da *adj* **:** grateful, thankful
agradecimiento *nm* **:** gratitude, thankfulness
agrado *nm* **1** GUSTO **:** taste, liking <no es de su agrado : it's not to his liking> **2 :** graciousness, agreeableness **3 con ~ :** with pleasure, willingly <lo haré con agrado : I will be happy to do it>
agrandar *vt* **1 :** to exaggerate **2 :** to enlarge — **agrandarse** *vr*
agrario, -ria *adj* **:** agrarian, agricultural
agravación *nf, pl* **-ciones :** aggravation, worsening
agravante *adj* **:** aggravating
agravar *vt* **1 :** to increase (weight), to make heavier **2** EMPEORAR **:** to aggravate, to worsen — **agravarse** *vr*
agraviar *vt* INJURIAR, OFENDER **:** to offend, to insult
agravio *nm* INJURIA **:** affront, offense, insult
agredir {1} *vt* **:** to assail, to attack
agregado[1], -da *n* **1 :** attaché **2 :** assistant professor
agregado[2] *nm* **1 :** aggregate **2** AÑADIDURA **:** addition, something added
agregar {52} *vt* **1** AÑADIR **:** to add, to attach **2 :** to appoint — **agregarse** *vr* **:** to join
agresión *nf, pl* **-siones 1 :** aggression **2** ATAQUE **:** attack
agresividad *nf* **:** aggressiveness, aggression
agresivo, -va *adj* **:** aggressive — **agresivamente** *adv*
agresor[1], -sora *adj* **:** hostile, attacking
agresor[2], -sora *n* **1 :** aggressor **2 :** assailant, attacker
agreste *adj* **1** CAMPESTRE **:** rural **2 :** wild, untamed
agriar *vt* **1 :** to sour, to make sour **2 :** to embitter — **agriarse** *vr* **:** to turn sour
agrícola *adj* **:** agricultural
agricultor, -tora *n* **:** farmer, grower
agricultura *nf* **:** agriculture, farming
agridulce *adj* **1 :** bittersweet **2 :** sweet-and-sour
agrietar *vt* **:** to crack — **agrietarse** *vr* **1 :** to crack **2 :** to chap
agrimensor, -sora *n* **:** surveyor
agrimensura *nf* **:** surveying
agrio, agria *adj* **1** ÁCIDO **:** sour **2 :** caustic, acrimonious
agriparse *vr* **:** to catch the flu
agroindustria *nf* **:** agribusiness
agronomía *nf* **:** agronomy
agropecuario, -ria *adj* **:** pertaining to livestock and agriculture
agrupación *nf, pl* **-ciones** GRUPO **:** group, association
agrupamiento *nm* **:** grouping, concentration
agrupar *vt* **:** to group together
agua *nf* **1 :** water **2 agua oxigenada :** hydrogen peroxide **3 aguas negras** *or* **aguas residuales :** sewage **4 como agua para chocolate** *Mex fam* **:** furious **5 echar aguas** *Mex fam* **:** to keep an eye out, to be on the lookout
aguacate *nm* **:** avocado
aguacero *nm* **:** shower, downpour
aguado, -da *adj* **1** DILUIDO **:** watered-down, diluted **2** *CA, Col, Mex fam* **:** soft, flabby **3** *Mex, Peru fam* **:** dull, boring
aguafiestas *nmfs & pl* **:** killjoy, stick-in-the-mud, spoilsport
aguafuerte *nm* **:** etching
aguamanil *nm* **:** ewer, pitcher
aguanieve *nf* **:** sleet <caer aguanieve : to be sleeting>
aguantar *vt* **1** SOPORTAR **:** to bear, to tolerate, to withstand **2 :** to hold **3 aguantar las ganas :** to resist an urge <no pude aguantar las ganas de reír : I couldn't keep myself from laughing> — *vi* **:** to hold out, to last — **aguantarse** *vr* **1 :** to resign oneself **2 :** to restrain oneself
aguante *nm* **1** TOLERANCIA **:** tolerance, patience **2** RESISTENCIA **:** endurance, strength
aguar {10} *vt* **1 :** to water down, to dilute **2 aguar la fiesta** *fam* **:** to spoil the party

aguardar *vt* ESPERAR **:** to wait for, to await **—** *vi* **:** to be in store

aguardiente *nm* **:** clear brandy

aguarrás *nm* **:** turpentine

agudeza *nf* **1 :** keenness, sharpness **2 :** shrillness **3 :** witticism

agudizar {21} *vt* **:** to intensify, to heighten

agudo, -da *adj* **1 :** acute, sharp **2 :** shrill, high-pitched **3** PERSPICAZ **:** clever, shrewd

agüero *nm* AUGURIO, PRESAGIO **:** augury, omen

aguijón *nm, pl* **-jones 1 :** stinger (of a bee, etc.) **2 :** goad

aguijonear *vt* **:** to goad

águila *nf* **1 :** eagle **2 águila o sol** *Mex* **:** heads or tails

aguileño, -ña *adj* **:** aquiline

aguilera *nf* **:** aerie, eagle's nest

aguilón *nm, pl* **-lones :** gable

aguinaldo *nm* **1 :** Christmas bonus, year-end bonus **2** *PRi, Ven* **:** Christmas carol

agüitarse *vr Mex fam* **:** to have the blues, to feel discouraged

aguja *nf* **1 :** needle **2 :** steeple, spire

agujerear *vt* **:** to make a hole in, to pierce

agujero *nm* **1 :** hole **2 agujero negro :** black hole (in astronomy)

agujeta *nf* **1** *Mex* **:** shoelace **2 agujetas** *nfpl* **:** muscular soreness or stiffness

agusanado, -da *adj* **:** worm-eaten

aguzar {21} *vt* **1 :** to sharpen <aguzar el ingenio : to sharpen one's wits> **2 aguzar el oído :** to prick up one's ears

ahí *adv* **1 :** there <ahí está : there it is> **2 por ~ :** somewhere, thereabouts **3 de ahí que :** with the result that, so that

ahijado, -da *n* **:** godchild, godson *m*, goddaughter *f*

ahijar {5} *vt* **:** to adopt (a child)

ahínco *nm* **:** eagerness, zeal

ahogar {52} *vt* **1 :** to drown **2 :** to smother **3 :** to choke back, to stifle **— ahogarse** *vr*

ahogo *nm* **:** breathlessness, suffocation

ahondar *vt* **:** to deepen **—** *vi* **:** to elaborate, to go into detail

ahora *adv* **1 :** now **2 ahora mismo :** right now **3 hasta ~ :** so far **4 por ~ :** for the time being

ahorcar {72} *vt* **:** to hang, to kill by hanging **— ahorcarse** *vr*

ahorita *adv fam* **:** right now, right away

ahorquillado, -da *adj* **:** forked

ahorrador, -dora *adj* **:** thrifty

ahorrar *vt* **1 :** to save (money) **2 :** to spare, to conserve **—** *vi* **:** to save up **— ahorrarse** *vr* **:** to spare oneself

ahorrativo, -va *adj* **:** thrifty, frugal

ahorro *nm* **:** saving <cuenta de ahorros : savings account>

ahuecar {72} *vt* **1 :** to hollow out **2 :** to cup (one's hands) **3 :** to plump up, to fluff up

ahuizote *nm Mex fam* **:** annoying person, pain in the neck

ahumar {8} *vt* **:** to smoke, to cure

ahuyentar *vt* **1 :** to scare away, to chase away **2 :** to banish, to dispel <ahuyentar las dudas : to dispel doubts>

airado, -da *adj* FURIOSO **:** angry, irate

airar {5} *vt* **:** to make angry, to anger

aire *nm* **1 :** air **2 aire acondicionado :** air-conditioning **3 darse aires :** to give oneself airs

airear *vt* **:** to air, to air out **— airearse** *vr* **:** to get some fresh air

airoso, -sa *adj* **1 :** elegant, graceful **2 salir airoso :** to come out winning

aislacionismo *nm* **:** isolationism

aislacionista *adj & nmf* **:** isolationist

aislado, -da *adj* **:** isolated, alone

aislamiento *nm* **1 :** isolation **2 :** insulation

aislante *nm* **:** insulator, nonconductor

aislar {5} *vt* **1 :** to isolate **2 :** to insulate

ajado, -da *adj* **1 :** worn, shabby **2 :** wrinkled, crumpled

ajar *vt* **:** to wear out, to spoil

ajardinado, -da *adj* **:** landscaped

ajedrecista *nmf* **:** chess player

ajedrez *nm, pl* **-dreces 1 :** chess **2 :** chess set

ajeno, -na *adj* **1 :** alien **2 :** of another, of others <propiedad ajena : somebody else's property> **3 ~ a :** foreign to **4 ~ de :** devoid of, free from

ajetreado, -da *adj* **:** hectic, busy

ajetrearse *vr* **:** to bustle about, to rush around

ajetreo *nm* **:** hustle and bustle, fuss

ají *nm, pl* **ajíes :** chili pepper

ajo *nm* **:** garlic

ajonjolí *nm, pl* **-líes :** sesame

ajuar *nm* **:** trousseau

ajustable *adj* **:** adjustable

ajustado, -da *adj* **1** CEÑIDO **:** tight, tight-fitting **2 :** reasonable, fitting

ajustar *vt* **1 :** to adjust, to adapt **2 :** to take in (clothing) **3 :** to settle, to resolve **— ajustarse** *vr* **:** to fit, to conform

ajuste *nm* **1 :** adjustment **2 :** tightening

ajusticiar *vt* EJECUTAR **:** to execute, to put to death

al (*contraction of* **a** *and* **el**) → **a²**

ala *nf* **1 :** wing **2 :** brim (of a hat)

Alá *nm* **:** Allah

alabanza *nf* ELOGIO **:** praise

alabar *vt* **:** to praise **— alabarse** *vr* **:** to boast

alabastro *nm* **:** alabaster

alabear *vt* **:** to warp **— alabearse** *vr*

alabeo *nm* **:** warp, warping

alacena *nf* **:** cupboard, larder

alacrán *nm, pl* **-cranes** ESCORPIÓN **:** scorpion

alado, -da *adj* **:** winged

alambique *nm* **:** still (to distill alcohol)

alambre *nm* **1 :** wire **2 alambre de púas :** barbed wire

alameda *nf* **1 :** poplar grove **2 :** tree-lined avenue
álamo *nm* **1 :** poplar **2 álamo temblón :** aspen
alar *nm* **:** eaves *pl*
alarde *nm* **1 :** show, display **2 hacer alarde de :** to make show of, to boast about
alardear *vi* PRESUMIR **:** to boast, to brag
alargado, -da *adj* **:** elongated, slender
alargamiento *nm* **:** lengthening, extension, elongation
alargar {52} *vt* **1 :** to extend, to lengthen **2** PROLONGAR **:** to prolong — **alargarse** *vr*
alarido *nm* **:** howl, shriek
alarma *nf* **:** alarm
alarmante *adj* **:** alarming — **alarmantemente** *adv*
alarmar *vt* **:** to alarm
alazán *nm, pl* **-zanes :** sorrel (color or animal)
alba *nf* AMANECER **:** dawn, daybreak
albacea *nmf* TESTAMENTARIO **:** executor, executrix *f*
albahaca *nf* **:** basil
albanés, -nesa *adj & n, mpl* **-neses :** Albanian
albañil *nmf* **:** bricklayer, mason
albañilería *nf* **:** bricklaying, masonry
albaricoque *nm* **:** apricot
albatros *nm* **:** albatross
albedrío *nm* **:** will <libre albedrío : free will>
alberca *nf* **1 :** reservoir, tank **2** *Mex* **:** swimming pool
albergar {52} *vt* ALOJAR **:** to house, to lodge, to shelter
albergue *nm* **1 :** shelter, refuge **2 :** hostel
albino, -na *adj & n* **:** albino — **albinismo** *nm*
albóndiga *nf* **:** meatball
albor *nm* **1 :** dawning, beginning **2** BLANCURA **:** whiteness
alborada *nf* **:** dawn
alborear *v impers* **:** to dawn
alborotado, -da *adj* **1 :** excited, agitated **2 :** rowdy, unruly
alborotador[1], -dora *adj* **1 :** noisy, boisterous **2 :** rowdy, unruly
alborotador[2], -dora *n* **:** agitator, troublemaker, rioter
alborotar *vt* **1 :** to excite, to agitate **2 :** to incite, to stir up — **alborotarse** *vr* **:** to riot
alboroto *nm* **1 :** disturbance, ruckus **2** MOTÍN **:** riot
alborozado, -da *adj* **:** jubilant
alborozar {21} *vt* **:** to gladden, to cheer
alborozo *nm* **:** joy, elation
álbum *nm* **:** album <álbum de recortes : scrapbook>
albúmina *nf* **:** albumin
albur *nm* **1 :** chance, risk **2** *Mex* **:** pun
alca *nf* **:** auk
alcachofa *nf* **:** artichoke
alcahuete, -ta *n* CHISMOSO **:** gossip
alcaide *nm* **:** warden (in a prison)
alcalde, -desa *n* **:** mayor
alcaldía *nf* **1 :** mayoralty **2** AYUNTAMIENTO **:** city hall
álcali *nm* **:** alkali
alcalino, -na *adj* **:** alkaline — **alcalinidad** *nf*
alcance *nm* **1 :** reach **2 :** range, scope
alcancía *nf* **1 :** piggy bank, money box **2 :** collection box (for alms, etc.)
alcanfor *nm* **:** camphor
alcantarilla *nf* CLOACA **:** sewer, drain
alcanzar {21} *vt* **1 :** to reach **2 :** to catch up with **3** LOGRAR **:** to achieve, to attain — *vi* **1** DAR **:** to suffice, to be enough **2 ~ a :** to manage to
alcaparra *nf* **:** caper
alcapurria *nf PRi* **:** stuffed fritter made with taro and green banana
alcaravea *nf* **:** caraway
alcatraz *nm, pl* **-traces :** gannet
alcázar *nm* **:** fortress, castle
alce[1], etc. → **alzar**
alce[2] *nm* **:** moose, European elk
alcoba *nf* **:** bedroom
alcohol *nm* **:** alcohol
alcohólico, -ca *adj & n* **:** alcoholic
alcoholismo *nm* **:** alcoholism
alcoholizarse {21} *vr* **:** to become an alcoholic
alcornoque *nm* **1 :** cork oak **2** *fam* **:** idiot, fool
alcurnia *nf* **:** ancestry, lineage
aldaba *nf* **:** door knocker
aldea *nf* **:** village
aldeano[1], -na *adj* **:** village, rustic
aldeano[2], -na *n* **:** villager
aleación *nf, pl* **-ciones :** alloy
alear *vt* **:** to alloy
aleatorio, -ria *adj* **:** random, fortuitous — **aleatoriamente** *adv*
alebrestar *vt* **:** to excite, to make nervous — **alebrestarse** *vr*
aledaño, -ña *adj* **:** bordering, neighboring
aledaños *nmpl* AFUERAS **:** outskirts, surrounding area
alegar {52} *vt* **:** to assert, to allege — *vi* DISCUTIR **:** to argue
alegato *nm* **1 :** allegation, claim **2** *Mex* **:** argument, summation (in law) **3 :** argument, dispute
alegoría *nf* **:** allegory
alegórico, -ca *adj* **:** allegorical
alegrar *vt* **:** to make happy, to cheer up — **alegrarse** *vr* **:** to be glad, to rejoice
alegre *adj* **1 :** glad, cheerful **2 :** colorful, bright **3** *fam* **:** tipsy
alegremente *adv* **:** happily, cheerfully
alegría *nf* **:** joy, cheer, happiness
alejado, -da *adj* **:** remote
alejamiento *nm* **1 :** removal, separation **2 :** estrangement
alejar *vt* **1 :** to remove, to move away **2 :** to estrange, to alienate — **alejarse** *vr* **1 :** to move away, to stray **2 :** to drift apart
alelado, -da *adj* **1 :** bewildered, stupefied **2 :** foolish, stupid
aleluya *interj* **:** hallelujah!, alleluia!

alemán[1], -mana *adj & n, mpl* **-manes** : German

alemán[2] *nm* : German (language)

alentador, -dora *adj* : encouraging

alentar {55} *vt* : to encourage, to inspire — *vi* : to breathe

alerce *nm* : larch

alérgeno *nm* : allergen

alergia *nf* : allergy

alérgico, -ca *adj* : allergic

alergista *nmf* : allergist

alero *nm* **1** : eaves *pl* **2** : forward (in basketball)

alerón *nm, pl* **-rones** : aileron

alerta[1] *adv* : on the alert

alerta[2] *nf* : alert, alarm

alertar *vt* : to alert

alerto, -ta *adj* : alert, watchful

aleta *nf* **1** : fin **2** : flipper **3** : small wing

aletargado, -da *adj* : lethargic, sluggish, torpid

aletargarse {52} *vr* : to feel drowsy, to become lethargic

aleteo *nm* : flapping, flutter

alevosía *nf* **1** : treachery **2** : premeditation

alevoso, -sa *adj* : treacherous

alfabético, -ca *adj* : alphabetical — **alfabéticamente** *adv*

alfabetismo *nm* : literacy

alfabetizado, -da *adj* : literate

alfabetizar {21} *vt* : to alphabetize

alfabeto *nm* : alphabet

alfalfa *nf* : alfalfa

alfanje *nm* : cutlass, scimitar

alfarería *nf* : pottery

alfarero, -ra *n* : potter

alféizar *nm* : sill, windowsill

alfeñique *nm fam* : wimp, weakling

alférez *nmf, pl* **-reces 1** : second lieutenant **2** : ensign

alfiler *nm* **1** : pin **2** BROCHE : brooch

alfiletero *nm* : pincushion

alfombra *nf* : carpet, rug

alfombrado *nm* : carpeting

alfombrar *vt* : to carpet

alfombrilla *nf* : small rug, mat

alforfón *nm, pl* **-fones** : buckwheat

alforja *nf* : saddlebag

alforza *nf* : pleat, tuck

alga *nf* **1** : aquatic plant, alga **2** : seaweed

algáceo, -cea *adj* : algal

algarabía *nf* **1** : gibberish, babble **2** : hubbub, uproar

álgebra *nf* : algebra

algebraico, -ca *adj* : algebraic

álgido, -da *adj* **1** : critical, decisive **2** : icy cold

algo[1] *adv* : somewhat, rather <es simpático, pero algo tacaño : he's nice but rather stingy>

algo[2] *pron* **1** : something **2 ~ de** : some, a little <tengo algo de dinero : I've got some money>

algodón *nm, pl* **-dones** : cotton

algoritmo *nm* : algorithm

alguacil *nm* : constable

alguien *pron* : somebody, someone

alguno[1], -na *adj* (**algún** *before masculine singular nouns*) **1** : some, any <algún día : someday, one day> **2** (*in negative constructions*) : not any, not at all <no tengo noticia alguna : I have no news at all> **3 algunas veces** : sometimes

alguno[2], -na *pron* **1** : one, someone, somebody <alguno de ellos : one of them> **2 algunos, -nas** *pron pl* : some, a few <algunos quieren trabajar : some want to work>

alhaja *nf* : jewel, gem

alhajar *vt* : to adorn with jewels

alharaca *nf* : fuss

alhelí *nm* : wallflower

aliado[1], -da *adj* : allied

aliado[2], -da *n* : ally

alianza *nf* : alliance

aliarse {85} *vr* : to form an alliance, to ally oneself

alias *adv & nm* : alias

alicaído, -da *adj* : depressed, discouraged

alicates *nmpl* PINZAS : pliers

aliciente *nm* **1** INCENTIVO : incentive **2** ATRACCIÓN : attraction

alienación *nf, pl* **-ciones** : alienation, derangement

alienar *vt* ENAJENAR : to alienate

aliento *nm* **1** : breath **2** : courage, strength **3 dar aliento a** : to encourage

aligerar *vt* **1** : to lighten **2** ACELERAR : to hasten, to quicken

alijo *nm* : cache, consignment (of contraband)

alimaña *nf* : pest, vermin

alimentación *nf, pl* **-ciones** NUTRICIÓN : nutrition, nourishment

alimentar *vt* **1** NUTRIR : to feed, to nourish **2** MANTENER : to support (a family) **3** FOMENTAR : to nurture, to foster — **alimentarse** *vr* **~ con** : to live on

alimentario, -ria → **alimenticio**

alimenticio, -cia *adj* **1** : nutritional, food, dietary **2** : nutritious, nourishing

alimento *nm* : food, nourishment

alineación *nf, pl* **-ciones 1** : alignment **2** : lineup (in sports)

alineamiento *nm* : alignment

alinear *vt* **1** : to align **2** : to line up — **alinearse** *vr* **1** : to fall in, to line up **2 ~ con** : to align oneself with

aliño *nm* : seasoning, dressing

alipús *nm, pl* **-puses** *Mex fam* : booze, drink

alisar *vt* : to smooth

aliso *nm* : alder

alistamiento *nm* : enlistment, recruitment

alistar *vt* **1** : to recruit **2** : to make ready — **alistarse** *vr* : to join up, to enlist

aliteración *nf, pl* **-ciones** : alliteration

aliterado, -da *adj* : alliterative

aliviar *vt* MITIGAR : to relieve, to alleviate, to soothe — **aliviarse** *vr* : to recover, to get better

alivio *nm* : relief

aljaba *nf* : quiver (for arrows)

aljibe *nm* : cistern, well

allá *adv* **1** : there, over there **2 más allá** : farther away **3 más allá de** : beyond **4 allá tú** : that's up to you

allanamiento *nm* **1** : (police) raid **2 allanamiento de morada** : breaking and entering

allanar *vt* **1** : to raid, to search **2** : to resolve, to solve **3** : to smooth, to level out

allegado[1], **-da** *adj* : close, intimate

allegado[2], **-da** *n* : close friend, relation <parientes y allegados : friends and relations>

allegar {52} *vt* : to gather, to collect

allende[1] *adv* : beyond, on the other side

allende[2] *prep* : beyond <allende las montañas : beyond the mountains>

allí *adv* : there, over there <allí mismo : right there> <hasta allí : up to that point>

alma *nf* **1** : soul **2** : person, human being **3 no tener alma** : to be pitiless **4 tener el alma en un hilo** : to have one's heart in one's mouth

almacén *nm, pl* **-cenes 1** BODEGA : warehouse, storehouse **2** TIENDA : shop, store **3 gran almacén** *Spain* : department store

almacenaje → **almacenamiento**

almacenamiento *nm* : storage <almacenamiento de datos : data storage>

almacenar *vt* : to store, to put in storage

almacenero, -ra *n* : shopkeeper

almacenista *nm* MAYORISTA : wholesaler

almádena *nf* : sledgehammer

almanaque *nm* : almanac

almeja *nf* : clam

almendra *nf* **1** : almond **2** : kernel

almendro *nm* : almond tree

almiar *nm* : haystack

almíbar *nm* : syrup

almidón *nm, pl* **-dones** : starch

almidonar *vt* : to starch

alminar *nm* MINARETE : minaret

almirante *nm* : admiral

almizcle *nm* : musk

almohada *nf* : pillow

almohadilla *nf* **1** : small pillow, cushion **2** : bag, base (in baseball)

almohadón *nm, pl* **-dones** : bolster, cushion

almohazar {21} *vt* : to curry (a horse)

almoneda *nf* SUBASTA : auction

almorranas *nfpl* HEMORROIDES : hemorrhoids, piles

almorzar {36} *vi* : to have lunch — *vt* : to have for lunch

almuerzo *nm* : lunch

alocado, -da *adj* **1** : crazy **2** : wild, reckless **3** : silly, scatterbrained

alocución *nf, pl* **-ciones** : speech, address

áloe *or* **aloe** *nm* : aloe

alojamiento *nm* : lodging, accommodations *pl*

alojar *vt* ALBERGAR : to house, to lodge — **alojarse** *vr* : to lodge, to room

alondra *nf* : lark, skylark

alpaca *nf* : alpaca

alpinismo *nm* : mountain climbing, mountaineering

alpinista *nmf* : mountain climber

alpino, -na *adj* : Alpine, alpine

alpiste *nm* : birdseed

alquilar *vt* ARRENDAR : to rent, to lease

alquiler *nm* ARRENDAMIENTO : rent, rental

alquimia *nf* : alchemy

alquimista *nmf* : alchemist

alquitrán *nm, pl* **-tranes** BREA : tar

alquitranar *vt* : to tar, to cover with tar

alrededor[1] *adv* **1** : around, about <todo temblaba alrededor : all around things were shaking> **2 ~ de** : around, approximately <alrededor de quince personas : around fifteen people>

alrededor[2] *prep* **~ de** : around, about <corrió alrededor de la casa : she ran around the house> <llegaré alrededor de diciembre : I will get there around December>

alrededores *nmpl* ALEDAÑOS : surroundings, outskirts

alta *nf* **1** : admission, entry, enrollment **2 dar de alta** : to release, to discharge (a patient)

altanería *nf* ALTIVEZ, ARROGANCIA : arrogance, haughtiness

altanero, -ra *adj* ALTIVO, ARROGANTE : arrogant, haughty — **altaneramente** *adv*

altar *nm* : altar

altavoz *nm, pl* **-voces** ALTOPARLANTE : loudspeaker

alteración *nf, pl* **-ciones 1** MODIFICACIÓN : alteration, modification **2** PERTURBACIÓN : disturbance, disruption

alterado, -da *adj* : upset

alterar *vt* **1** MODIFICAR : to alter, to modify **2** PERTURBAR : to disturb, to disrupt — **alterarse** *vr* : to get upset, to get worked up

altercado *nm* DISCUSIÓN, DISPUTA : altercation, argument, dispute

alternador *nm* : alternator

alternancia *nf* : alternation, rotation

alternar *vi* **1** : to alternate **2** : to mix, to socialize — *vt* : to alternate — **alternarse** *vr* : to take turns

alternativa *nf* OPCIÓN : alternative, option

alternativo, -va *adj* **1** : alternating **2** : alternative — **alternativamente** *adv*

alterno, -na *adj* : alternate <corriente alterna : alternating current>

alteza *nf* **1** : loftiness, lofty height **2 Alteza** : Highness

altibajos *nmpl* **1 :** unevenness (of terrain) **2 :** ups and downs
altímetro *nm* **:** altimeter
altiplano *nm* **:** high plateau
altisonante *adj* **1 :** pompous, affected (of language) **2** *Mex* **:** rude, obscene (of language)
altitud *nf* **:** altitude
altivez *nf, pl* **-veces** ALTANERÍA, ARROGANCIA **:** arrogance, haughtiness
altivo, -va *adj* ALTANERO, ARROGANTE **:** arrogant, haughty
alto[1] *adv* **1 :** high **2 :** loud, loudly
alto[2]**, -ta** *adj* **1 :** tall, high **2 :** loud <en voz alta : aloud, out loud>
alto[3] *nm* **1** ALTURA **:** height, elevation **2 :** stop, halt **3 altos** *nmpl* **:** upper floors
alto[4] *interj* **:** halt!, stop!
altoparlante *nm* ALTAVOZ **:** loudspeaker
altozano *nm* **:** hillock
altruismo *nm* **:** altruism
altruista[1] *adj* **:** altruistic
altruista[2] *nmf* **:** altruist
altura *nf* **1 :** height **2 :** altitude **3 :** loftiness, nobleness **4 a la altura de :** near, up by <en la avenida San Antonio a la altura de la Calle Tres : on San Antonio Avenue up near Third Street> **5 a estas alturas :** at this point, at this stage of the game
alubia *nf* **:** kidney bean
alucinación *nf, pl* **-ciones :** hallucination
alucinante *adj* **:** hallucinatory
alucinar *vi* **:** to hallucinate
alucinógeno[1]**, -na** *adj* **:** hallucinogenic
alucinógeno[2] *nm* **:** hallucinogen
alud *nm* AVALANCHA **:** avalanche, landslide
aludido, -da *n* **1 :** person in question <el aludido : the aforesaid> **2 darse por aludido :** to take personally
aludir *vi* **:** to allude, to refer
alumbrado *nm* ILUMINACIÓN **:** lighting
alumbramiento *nm* **1 :** lighting **2 :** childbirth
alumbrar *vt* **1** ILUMINAR **:** to light, to illuminate **2 :** to give birth to
alumbre *nm* **:** alum
aluminio *nm* **:** aluminum
alumnado *nm* **:** student body
alumno, -na *n* **1 :** pupil, student **2 ex–alumno, -na :** alumnus, alumna *f* **3 ex–alumnos, -nas** *npl* **:** alumni, alumnae *f*
alusión *nf, pl* **-siones :** allusion, reference
alusivo, -va *adj* **1 :** allusive **2 ~ a :** in reference to, regarding
aluvión *nm, pl* **-viones :** flood, barrage
alza *nf* SUBIDA **:** rise <precios en alza : rising prices>
alzamiento *nm* LEVANTAMIENTO **:** uprising, insurrection
alzar {21} *vt* **1** ELEVAR, LEVANTAR **:** to lift, to raise **2 :** to erect — **alzarse** *vr* LEVANTARSE **:** to rise up
ama *nf* → **amo**
amabilidad *nf* **:** kindness
amable *adj* **:** kind, nice — **amablemente** *adv*
amado[1]**, -da** *adj* **:** beloved, darling
amado[2]**, -da** *n* **:** sweetheart, loved one
amaestrar *vt* **:** to train (animals)
amafiarse *vr Mex fam* **:** to conspire, to be in cahoots
amagar {52} *vt* **1 :** to show signs of (an illness, etc.) **2 :** to threaten — *vi* **1 :** to be imminent, to threaten **2 :** to feint, to dissemble
amago *nm* **1** AMENAZA **:** threat **2 :** sign, hint
amainar *vi* **:** to abate, to ease up, to die down
amalgama *nf* **:** amalgam
amalgamar *vt* **:** to amalgamate, to unite
amamantar *v* **:** to breast-feed, to nurse, to suckle
amanecer[1] {53} *v impers* **1 :** to dawn **2 :** to begin to show, to appear **3 :** to wake up (in the morning)
amanecer[2] *nm* ALBA **:** dawn, daybreak
amanerado, -da *adj* **:** affected, mannered
amansar *vt* **1 :** to tame **2 :** to soothe, to calm down — **amansarse** *vr*
amante[1] *adj* **:** loving, fond
amante[2] *nmf* **:** lover
amañar *vt* **:** to rig, to fix, to tamper with — **amañarse** *vr* **amañárselas :** to manage
amaño *nm* **1 :** skill, dexterity **2 :** trick, ruse
amapola *nf* **:** poppy
amar *vt* **:** to love — **amarse** *vr*
amargado, -da *adj* **:** embittered, bitter
amargar {52} *vt* **:** to make bitter, to embitter — *vi* **:** to taste bitter
amargo[1]**, -ga** *adj* **:** bitter — **amargamente** *adv*
amargo[2] *nm* **:** bitterness, tartness
amargura *nf* **1 :** bitterness **2 :** grief, sorrow
amarilis *nf* **:** amaryllis
amarillear *vi* **:** to yellow, to turn yellow
amarillento, -ta *adj* **:** yellowish
amarillismo *nm* **:** yellow journalism, sensationalism
amarillo[1]**, -lla** *adj* **:** yellow
amarillo[2] *nm* **:** yellow
amarra *nf* **1 :** mooring, mooring line **2 soltar las amarras de :** to loosen one's grip on
amarrar *vt* **1 :** to moor (a boat) **2** ATAR **:** to fasten, to tie up, to tie down
amartillar *vt* **:** to cock (a gun)
amasar *vt* **1 :** to amass **2 :** to knead **3 :** to mix, to prepare
amasijo *nm* **:** jumble, hodgepodge
amasio, -sia *n* **:** lover, paramour
amateur *adj & nmf* **:** amateur — **amateurismo** *nm*
amatista *nf* **:** amethyst
amatorio, -ria *adj* **:** amatory, love

amazona *nf* **1 :** Amazon (in mythology) **2 :** horsewoman
amazónico, -ca *adj* **:** amazonian
ambages *mpl* **sin ~ :** without hesitation, straight to the point
ámbar *nm* **1 :** amber **2 ámbar gris :** ambergris
ambición *nf, pl* **-ciones :** ambition
ambicionar *vt* **:** to aspire to, to seek
ambicioso, -sa *adj* **:** ambitious — **ambiciosamente** *adv*
ambidextro, -tra *adj* **:** ambidextrous
ambientación *nf, pl* **-ciones :** setting, atmosphere
ambiental *adj* **:** environmental — **ambientalmente** *adv*
ambientalista *nmf* **:** environmentalist
ambientar *vt* **:** to give atmosphere to, to set (in literature and drama) — **ambientarse** *vr* **:** to adjust, to get one's bearings
ambiente *nm* **1 :** atmosphere **2 :** environment **3 :** surroundings *pl*
ambigüedad *nf* **:** ambiguity
ambiguo, -gua *adj* **:** ambiguous
ámbito *nm* **:** domain, field, area
ambivalencia *nf* **:** ambivalence
ambivalente *adj* **:** ambivalent
ambos, -bas *adj & pron* **:** both
ambulancia *nf* **:** ambulance
ambulante *adj* **1 :** traveling, itinerant **2 vendedor ambulante :** street vendor
ameba *nf* **:** amoeba
amedrentar *vt* **:** to frighten, to intimidate — **amedrentarse** *vr*
amén *nm* **1 :** amen **2 ~ de :** in addition to, besides **3 en un decir amén :** in an instant
amenaza *nf* **:** threat, menace
amenazador, -dora *adj* **:** threatening, menacing
amenazante → **amenazador**
amenazar {21} *v* **:** to threaten
amenguar {10} *vt* **1 :** to diminish **2 :** to belittle, to dishonor
amenidad *nf* **:** pleasantness, amenity
amenizar {21} *vt* **1 :** to make pleasant **2 :** to brighten up, to add life to
ameno, -na *adj* **:** agreeable, pleasant
amento *nm* **:** catkin
americano, -na *adj & n* **:** American
amerindio, -dia *adj & n* **:** Amerindian
ameritar *vt* MERECER **:** to deserve
ametralladora *nf* **:** machine gun
amianto *nm* **:** asbestos
amiba *nf* → **ameba**
amigable *adj* **:** friendly, amicable — **amigablemente** *adv*
amígdala *nf* **:** tonsil
amigdalitis *nf* **:** tonsilitis
amigo[1], **-ga** *adj* **:** friendly, close
amigo[2], **-ga** *n* **:** friend
amigote *nm* **:** crony, pal
amilanar *vt* **1 :** to frighten **2 :** to daunt, to discourage — **amilanarse** *vr* **:** to lose heart
aminoácido *nm* **:** amino acid
aminorar *vt* **:** to reduce, to lessen — *vi* **:** to diminish
amistad *nf* **:** friendship
amistoso, -sa *adj* **:** friendly — **amistosamente** *adv*
amnesia *nf* **:** amnesia
amnésico, -ca *adj & n* **:** amnesiac, amnesic
amnistía *nf* **:** amnesty
amnistiar {85} *vt* **:** to grant amnesty to
amo, ama *n* **1 :** master *m*, mistress *f* **2 :** owner, keeper (of an animal) **3 ama de casa :** housewife **4 ama de llaves :** housekeeper
amodorrado, -da *adj* **:** drowsy
amolar {19} *vt* **1 :** to grind, to sharpen **2 :** to pester, to annoy
amoldable *adj* **:** adaptable
amoldar *vt* **1 :** to mold **2 :** to adapt, to adjust — **amoldarse** *vr*
amonestación *nf, pl* **-ciones 1** APERCIBIMIENTO **:** admonition, warning **2** AMONESTACIONES *nfpl* **:** banns
amonestar *vt* APERCIBIR **:** to admonish, to warn
amoníaco *or* **amoniaco** *nm* **:** ammonia
amontonamiento *nm* **:** accumulation, piling up
amontonar *vt* **1** APILAR **:** to pile up, to heap up **2 :** to collect, to gather **3 :** to hoard — **amontonarse** *vr*
amor *nm* **1 :** love **2 :** loved one, beloved **3 amor propio :** self-esteem **4 hacer el amor :** to make love
amoral *adj* **:** amoral
amoratado, -da *adj* **:** black-and-blue, bruised, livid
amordazar {21} *vt* **1 :** to gag, to muzzle **2 :** to silence
amorfo, -fa *adj* **:** shapeless, amorphous
amorío *nm* **:** love affair, fling
amoroso, -sa *adj* **1 :** loving, affectionate **2 :** amorous <una mirada amorosa : an amorous glance> **3 :** charming, cute — **amorosamente** *adv*
amortiguación *nf* **:** cushioning, absorption
amortiguador *nm* **:** shock absorber
amortiguar {10} *vt* **:** to soften (an impact)
amortizar {21} *vt* **:** to amortize, to pay off — **amortización** *nf*
amotinado[1], **-da** *adj* **:** rebellious, insurgent, mutinous
amotinado[2], **-da** *n* **:** rebel, insurgent, mutineer
amotinamiento *nm* **:** uprising, rebellion
amotinar *vt* **:** to incite (to riot), to agitate — **amotinarse** *vr* **1 :** to riot, to rebel **2 :** to mutiny
amparar *vt* **:** to safeguard, to protect — **ampararse** *vr* **1 ~ de :** to take shelter from **2 ~ en :** to have recourse to
amparo *nm* ACOGIDA, REFUGIO **:** protection, refuge
amperímetro *nm* **:** ammeter

amperio *nm* : ampere
ampliable *adj* : expandable, enlargeable, extendible
ampliación *nf, pl* **-ciones** : expansion, extension
ampliar {85} *vt* **1** : to expand, to extend **2** : to widen **3** : to enlarge (photographs) **4** : to elaborate on, to develop (ideas)
amplificador *nm* : amplifier
amplificar {72} *vt* : to amplify — **amplificación** *nf*
amplio, -plia *adj* : broad, wide, ample — **ampliamente** *adj*
amplitud *nf* **1** : breadth, extent **2** : spaciousness
ampolla *nf* **1** : blister **2** : vial, ampoule
ampollar *vt* : to blister — **ampollarse** *vr*
ampolleta *nf* **1** : small vial **2** : hourglass **3** *Chile* : light bulb
ampulosidad *nf* : pompousness, bombast
ampuloso, -sa *adj* GRANDILOCUENTE : pompous, bombastic — **ampulosamente** *adv*
amputar *vt* : to amputate — **amputación** *nf*
amueblar *vt* : to furnish
amuleto *nm* TALISMÁN : amulet, charm
amurallar *vt* : to wall in, to fortify
anacardo *nm* : cashew nut
anaconda *nf* : anaconda
anacrónico, -ca *adj* : anachronistic
anacronismo *nm* : anachronism
ánade *nmf* **1** : duck **2 ánade real** : mallard
anagrama *nm* : anagram
anal *adj* : anal
anales *nmpl* : annals
analfabetismo *nm* : illiteracy
analfabeto, -ta *adj & n* : illiterate
analgésico[1], -ca *adj* : analgesic, painkilling
analgésico[2] *nm* : painkiller, analgesic
análisis *nm* : analysis
analista *nmf* **1** : analyst **2** : annalist
analítico, -ca *adj* : analytical, analytic — **analíticamente** *adv*
analizar {21} *vt* : to analyze
analogía *nf* : analogy
analógico, -ca *adj* **1** : analogical **2** : analog <computadora analógica : analog computer>
análogo, -ga *adj* : analogous, similar
ananá *or* **ananás** *nm, pl* **-nás** : pineapple
anaquel *nm* REPISA : shelf
anaranjado[1], -da *adj* NARANJA : orange-colored
anaranjado[2] *nm* NARANJA : orange (color)
anarquía *nf* : anarchy
anárquico, -ca *adj* : anarchic
anarquismo *nm* : anarchism
anarquista *adj & nmf* : anarchist
anatema *nm* : anathema
anatomía *nf* : anatomy — **anatomista** *nmf*
anatómico, -ca *adj* : anatomical — **anatómicamente** *adv*
anca *nm* **1** : haunch, hindquarter **2 ancas de rana** : frogs' legs
ancestral *adj* **1** : ancient, traditional **2** : ancestral
ancestro *nm* ASCENDIENTE : ancestor, forefather *m*
ancho[1], -cha *adj* **1** : wide, broad **2** : ample, loose-fitting
ancho[2] *nm* : width, breadth
anchoa *nf* : anchovy
anchura *nf* : width, breadth
ancianidad *nf* SENECTUD : old age
anciano[1], -na *adj* : aged, old, elderly
anciano[2], -na *n* : elderly person
ancla *nf* : anchor
ancladero *nm* → **anclaje**
anclaje *nm* : anchorage
anclar *v* FONDEAR : to anchor
andadas *nfpl* **1** : tracks **2 volver a las andadas** : to go back to one's old ways, to backslide
andador[1] *nm* **1** : walker, baby walker **2** *Mex* : walkway
andador[2], -dora *n* : walker, one who walks
andadura *nf* : course, journey <su agotadora andadura al campeonato : his exhausting journey to the championship>
andaluz, -luza *adj & n, mpl* **-luces** : Andalusian
andamiaje *nm* **1** : scaffolding **2** ESTRUCTURA : structure, framework
andamio *nm* : scaffold
andanada *nf* **1** : volley, broadside **2 soltar una andanada a** : to reprimand
andanzas *nfpl* : adventures
andar[1] {6} *vi* **1** CAMINAR : to walk **2** IR : to go, to travel **3** FUNCIONAR : to run, to function <el auto anda bien : the car runs well> **4** : to ride <andar a caballo : to ride on horseback> **5** : to be <anda sin dinero : he's broke> — *vt* : to walk, to travel
andar[2] *nm* : walk, gait
andas *nfpl* : stand (for a coffin), bier
andén *nm, pl* **andenes 1** : (train) platform **2** *CA, Col* : sidewalk
andino, -na *adj* : Andean
andorrano, -na *adj & n* : Andorran
andrajos *nmpl* : rags, tatters
andrajoso, -sa *adj* : ragged, tattered
andrógino, -na *adj* : androgynous
andurriales *nmpl* : remote place
anea *nf* : cattail
anduvo, etc. → **andar**
anécdota *nf* : anecdote
anecdótico, -ca *adj* : anecdotal
anegar {52} *vt* **1** INUNDAR : to flood **2** AHOGAR : to drown **3** : to overwhelm — **anegarse** *vr* : to be flooded
anejo *nm* → **anexo[2]**
anemia *nf* : anemia
anémico, -ca *adj* : anemic
anémona *nf* : anemone
anestesia *nf* : anesthesia

anestesiar *vt* : to anesthetize
anestésico[1], -ca *adj* : anesthetic
anestésico[2] *nm* : anesthetic
anestesista *nmf* : anesthetist
aneurisma *nmf* : aneurism
anexar *vt* : to annex, to attach
anexión *nf, pl* **-xiones** : annexation
anexo[1], -xa *adj* : attached, joined, annexed
anexo[2] *nm* **1** : annex **2** : supplement (to a book), appendix
anfetamina *nf* : amphetamine
anfibio[1], -bia *adj* : amphibious
anfibio[2] *nm* : amphibian
anfiteatro *nm* **1** : amphitheater **2** : lecture hall
anfitrión, -triona *n, mpl* **-triones** : host, hostess *f*
ánfora *nf* **1** : amphora **2** *Mex, Peru* : ballot box
ángel *nm* : angel
angelical *adj* : angelic, angelical
angina *nf* **1** *or* **angina de pecho** : angina **2** *Mex* : tonsil
anglicano, -na *adj & n* : Anglican
angloparlante[1] *adj* : English-speaking
angloparlante[2] *nmf* : English speaker
anglosajón, -jona *adj & n, mpl* **-jones** : Anglo-Saxon
angoleño, -ña *adj & n* : Angolan
angora *nf* : angora
angostar *vt* : to narrow — **angostarse** *vr*
angosto, -ta *adj* : narrow
angostura *nf* : narrowness
anguila *nf* : eel
angular *adj* : angular — **angularidad** *nf*
ángulo *nm* **1** : angle **2** : corner **3 ángulo muerto** : blind spot
anguloso, -sa *adj* : angular, sharp <una cara angulosa : an angular face> — **angulosidad** *nf*
angustia *nf* **1** CONGOJA : anguish, distress **2** : anxiety, worry
angustiar *vt* **1** : to anguish, to distress **2** : to worry — **angustiarse** *vr*
angustioso, -sa *adj* **1** : anguished, distressed **2** : distressing, worrisome
anhelante *adj* : yearning, longing
anhelar *vt* : to yearn for, to crave
anhelo *nm* : longing, yearning
anidar *vi* **1** : to nest **2** : to make one's home, to dwell — *vt* : to shelter
anillo *nm* SORTIJA : ring
ánima *n* ALMA : soul
animación *nf, pl* **-ciones** **1** : animation **2** VIVEZA : liveliness
animado, -da *adj* **1** : animated, lively **2** : cheerful — **animadamente** *adv*
animador, -dora *n* **1** : (television) host **2** : cheerleader
animadversión *nf, pl* **-siones** ANIMOSIDAD : animosity, antagonism
animal[1] *adj* **1** : animal **2** ESTÚPIDO : stupid, idiotic **3** : rough, brutish
animal[2] *nm* : animal
animal[3] *nmf* **1** IDIOTA : idiot, fool **2** : brute, beastly person
animar *vt* **1** ALENTAR : to encourage, to inspire **2** : to animate, to enliven **3** : to brighten up, to cheer up — **animarse** *vr*
anímico, -ca *adj* : mental <estado anímico : state of mind>
ánimo *nm* **1** ALMA : spirit, soul **2** : mood, spirits *pl* **3** : encouragement **4** PROPÓSITO : intention, purpose <sociedad sin ánimo de lucro : nonprofit organization> **5** : energy, vitality
animosidad *nf* ANIMADVERSIÓN : animosity, ill will
animoso, -sa *adj* : brave, spirited
aniñado, -da *adj* : childlike
aniquilación *nf* → **aniquilamiento**
aniquilamiento *nm* : annihilation, extermination
aniquilar *vt* **1** : to annihilate, to wipe out **2** : to overwhelm, to bring to one's knees — **aniquilarse** *vr*
anís *nm* **1** : anise **2 semilla de anís** : aniseed
aniversario *nm* : anniversary
ano *nm* : anus
anoche *adv* : last night
anochecer[1] {53} *v impers* : to get dark
anochecer[2] *nm* : dusk, nightfall
anodino, -na *adj* : insipid, dull
ánodo *nm* : anode
anomalía *nf* : anomaly
anómalo, -la *adj* : anomalous
anonadado, -da *adj* : dumbfounded, speechless
anonadar *vt* : to dumbfound, to stun
anonimato *nm* : anonymity
anónimo, -ma *adj* : anonymous — **anónimamente** *adv*
anorexia *nf* : anorexia
anoréxico, -ca *adj* : anorexic
anormal *adj* : abnormal — **anormalmente** *adv*
anormalidad *nf* : abnormality
anotación *nf, pl* **-ciones** **1** : annotation, note **2** : scoring (in sports) <lograron una anotación : they managed to score a goal>
anotar *vt* **1** : to annotate **2** APUNTAR, ESCRIBIR : to write down, to jot down **3** : to score (in sports) — *vi* : to score
anquilosado, -da *adj* **1** : stiff-jointed **2** : stagnated, stale
anquilosamiento *nm* **1** : stiffness (of joints) **2** : stagnation, paralysis
anquilosarse *vr* **1** : to stagnate **2** : to become stiff or paralyzed
anquilostoma *nm* : hookworm
ánsar *nm* : goose
ansarino *nm* : gosling
ansia *nf* **1** INQUIETUD : apprehensiveness, uneasiness **2** ANGUSTIA : anguish, distress **3** ANHELO : longing, yearning
ansiar {85} *vt* : to long for, to yearn for
ansiedad *nf* : anxiety
ansioso, -sa *adj* **1** : anxious, worried **2** : eager — **ansiosamente** *adv*
antagónico, -ca *adj* : conflicting, opposing
antagonismo *nm* : antagonism

antagonista[1] *adj* : antagonistic

antagonista[2] *nmf* : antagonist, opponent

antaño *adv* : yesteryear, long ago

antártico, -ca *adj* **1** : antarctic **2 círculo antártico** : antarctic circle

ante[1] *nm* **1** : elk, moose **2** : suede

ante[2] *prep* **1** : before, in front of **2** : considering, in view of **3 ante todo** : first and foremost, above all

anteanoche *adv* : the night before last

anteayer *adv* : the day before yesterday

antebrazo *nm* : forearm

antecedente[1] *adj* : previous, prior

antecedente[2] *nm* **1** : precedent **2 antecedentes** *nmpl* : record, background

anteceder *v* : to precede

antecesor, -sora *n* **1** ANTEPASADO : ancestor **2** PREDECESOR : predecessor

antedicho, -cha *adj* : aforesaid, above

antelación *nf, pl* **-ciones 1** : advance notice **2 con ~** : in advance, beforehand

antemano *adv* **de ~** : in advance <se lo agradezco de antemano : I thank you in advance>

antena *nf* : antenna

antenoche → **anteanoche**

anteojera *nf* **1** : eyeglass case **2 anteojeras** *nfpl* : blinders

anteojos *nmpl* GAFAS : glasses, eyeglasses

antepasado[1], **-da** *adj* : before last <el domingo antepasado : the Sunday before last>

antepasado[2], **-da** *n* ANTECESOR : ancestor

antepecho *nm* **1** : guardrail **2** : ledge, sill

antepenúltimo, -ma *adj* : third from last

anteponer {60} *vt* **1** : to place before <anteponer al interés de la nación el interés de la comunidad : to place the interests of the community before national interest> **2** : to prefer

anteproyecto *nm* **1** : draft, proposal **2 anteproyecto de ley** : bill

antera *nf* : anther

anterior *adj* **1** : previous **2** : earlier <tiempos anteriores : earlier times> **3** : anterior, forward, front

anterioridad *nf* **1** : priority **2 con ~** : beforehand, in advance

anteriormente *adv* : previously, beforehand

antes *adv* **1** : before, earlier **2** : formerly, previously **3** : rather, sooner <antes prefiero morir : I'd rather die> **4 ~ de** : before, previous to <antes de hoy : before today> **5 antes que** : before <antes que llegue Luis : before Luis arrives> **6 cuanto antes** : as soon as possible **7 antes bien** : on the contrary

antesala *nf* **1** : anteroom, waiting room, lobby **2** : prelude, prologue

antiaborto, -ta *adj* : antiabortion

antiácido *nm* : antacid

antiadherente *adj* : nonstick

antiaéreo, -rea *adj* : antiaircraft

antiamericano, -na *adj* : anti-American

antibalas *adj* : bulletproof

antibiótico[1], **-ca** *adj* : antibiotic

antibiótico[2] *nm* : antibiotic

antichoque *adj* : shockproof

anticipación *nf, pl* **-ciones 1** : expectation, anticipation **2 con ~** : in advance

anticipado, -da *adj* **1** : advance, early **2 por ~** : in advance

anticipar *vt* **1** : to anticipate, to forestall, to deal with in advance **2** : to pay in advance — **anticiparse** *vr* **1** : to be early **2** ADELANTARSE : to get ahead

anticipo *nm* **1** : advance (payment) **2** : foretaste, preview

anticlerical *adj* : anticlerical

anticlimático, -ca : anticlimatic

anticlímax *nm* : anticlimax

anticomunismo *nm* : anticommunism

anticomunista *adj & nmf* : anticommunist

anticoncepción *nf, pl* **-ciones** : birth control, contraception

anticonceptivo *nm* : contraceptive

anticongelante *nm* : antifreeze

anticuado, -da *adj* : antiquated, outdated

anticuario[1], **-ria** *adj* : antique, antiquarian

anticuario[2], **-ria** *n* : antiquarian, antiquary

anticuario[3] *nm* : antique shop

anticuerpo *nm* : antibody

antidemocrático, -ca *adj* : antidemocratic

antideportivo, -va *adj* : unsportsmanlike

antidepresivo *nm* : antidepressant

antídoto *nm* : antidote

antidrogas *adj* : antidrug

antier → **anteayer**

antiestético, -ca *adj* : unsightly, unattractive

antifascista *adj & nmf* : antifascist

antifaz *nm, pl* **-faces** : mask

antifeminista *adj & nmf* : antifeminist

antífona *nf* : anthem

antígeno *nm* : antigen

antigualla *nf* **1** : antique **2** : relic, old thing

antiguamente *adv* **1** : formerly, once **2** : long ago

antigüedad *nf* **1** : antiquity **2** : seniority **3** : age <con siglos de antigüedad : centuries-old> **4 antigüedades** *nfpl* : antiques

antiguo, -gua *adj* **1** : ancient, old **2** : former **3** : old-fashioned <a la antigua : in the old-fashioned way>

antihigiénico, -ca *adj* INSALUBRE : unhygienic, unsanitary

antihistamínico *nm* : antihistamine

antiimperialismo *nm* : anti-imperialism

antiimperialista *adj & nmf* : anti-imperialist

antiinflacionario, -ria *adj* : anti-inflationary

antiinflamatorio, -ria *adj* : anti-inflammatory

antillano[1], -na *adj* CARIBEÑO : Caribbean, West Indian

antillano[2], -na *n* : West Indian

antílope *nm* : antelope

antimilitarismo *nm* : antimilitarism

antimilitarista *adj & nmf* : antimilitarist

antimonio *nm* : antimony

antimonopolista *adj* : antimonopoly, antitrust

antinatural *adj* : unnatural, perverse

antipatía *nf* : aversion, dislike

antipático, -ca *adj* : obnoxious, unpleasant

antipatriótico, -ca *adj* : unpatriotic

antirrábico, -ca *adj* : antirabies <vacuna antirrábica : rabies vaccine>

antirreglamentario, -ria *adj* **1** : unlawful, illegal **2** : foul (in sports)

antirrevolucionario, -ria *adj & n* : antirevolutionary

antirrobo, -ba *adj* : antitheft

antisemita *adj* : anti-Semitic

antisemitismo *nm* : anti-Semitism

antiséptico[1], -ca *adj* : antiseptic

antiséptico[2] *nm* : antiseptic

antisocial *adj* : antisocial

antitabaco *adj* : antismoking

antiterrorista *adj* : antiterrorist

antítesis *nf* : antithesis

antitoxina *nf* : antitoxin

antitranspirante *nm* : antiperspirant

antojadizo, -za *adj* CAPRICHOSO : capricious

antojarse *vr* **1** APETECER : to be appealing, to be desirable <se me antoja un helado : I feel like having ice cream> **2** : to seem, to appear <los árboles se antojaban fantasmas : the trees seemed like ghosts>

antojitos *nmpl Mex* : traditional Mexican snack foods

antojo *nm* **1** CAPRICHO : whim **2** : craving

antología *nf* **1** : anthology **2 de ~** *fam* : fantastic, incredible

antónimo *nm* : antonym

antonomasia *nf* **por ~** : par excellence

antorcha *nf* : torch

antracita *nf* : anthracite

antro *nm* **1** : cave, den **2** : dive, seedy nightclub

antropofagia *nf* CANIBALISMO : cannibalism

antropófago[1], -ga *adj* : cannibalistic

antropófago[2], -ga *n* CANÍBAL : cannibal

antropoide *adj & nmf* : anthropoid

antropología *nf* : anthropology

antropológico, -ca *adj* : anthropological

antropólogo, -ga *n* : anthropologist

anual *adj* : annual, yearly — **anualmente** *adv*

anualidad *nf* : annuity

anuario *nm* : yearbook, annual

anudar *vt* : to knot, to tie in a knot — **anudarse** *vr*

anuencia *nf* : consent

anulación *nf, pl* **-ciones** : annulment, nullification

anular *vt* : to annul, to cancel

anunciador, -dora *n* → **anunciante**

anunciante *nmf* : advertiser

anunciar *vt* **1** : to announce **2** : to advertise

anuncio *nm* **1** : announcement **2** : advertisement, commercial

anzuelo *nm* **1** : fishhook **2 morder el anzuelo** : to take the bait

añadido *nm* : addition

añadidura *nf* **1** : additive, addition **2 por ~** : in addition, furthermore

añadir *vt* **1** AGREGAR : to add **2** AUMENTAR : to increase

añejar *vt* : to age, to ripen

añejo, -ja *adj* **1** : aged, vintage **2** : age-old, musty, stale

añicos *nmpl* : smithereens, bits <hacer(se) añicos : to shatter>

añil *nm* **1** : indigo **2** : bluing

año *nm* **1** : year <en el año 1990 : in (the year) 1990> <tiene diez años : she is ten years old> **2** : grade <cuarto año : fourth grade> **3 año bisiesto** : leap year **4 año luz** : light-year **5 Año Nuevo** : New Year

añoranza *nf* : longing, yearning

añorar *vt* **1** DESEAR : to long for **2** : to grieve for, to miss — *vi* : to mourn, to grieve

añoso, -sa *adj* : aged, old

aorta *nf* : aorta

apabullante *adj* : overwhelming, crushing

apabullar *vt* : to overwhelm

apacentar {55} *vt* : to pasture, to put to pasture

apache *adj & nmf* : Apache

apachurrado, -da *adj fam* : depressed, down

apachurrar *vt* : to crush, to squash

apacible *adj* : gentle, mild, calm — **apaciblemente** *adv*

apaciguador, -dora *adj* : calming

apaciguamiento *nm* : appeasement

apaciguar {10} *vt* APLACAR : to appease, to pacify — **apaciguarse** *vr* : to calm down

apadrinar *vt* **1** : to be a godparent to **2** : to sponsor, to support

apagado, -da *adj* **1** : off, out <la luz está apagada : the light is off> **2** : dull, subdued

apagador *nm Mex* : switch

apagar {52} *vt* **1** : to turn off, to shut off **2** : to extinguish, to put out — **apagarse** *vr* **1** : to go out, to fade **2** : to wane, to die down

apagón *nm, pl* **-gones** : blackout (of power)

apalancamiento *nm* : leverage

apalancar {72} *vt* **1** : to jack up **2** : to pry open

apalear *vt* : to beat up, to thrash

apantallar *vt Mex* : to dazzle, to impress

apañar *vt* **1** : to seize, to grasp **2** : to repair, to mend — **apañarse** *vr* : to manage, to get along

apaño *nm fam* **1** : patch **2** HABILIDAD : skill, knack

apapachar *vt Mex fam* : to cuddle, to caress — **apapacharse** *vr*

aparador *nm* **1** : sideboard, cupboard **2** ESCAPARATE, VITRINA : shop window

aparato *nm* **1** : machine, appliance, apparatus <aparato auditivo : hearing aid> <aparato de televisión : television set> **2** : system <aparato digestivo : digestive system> **3** : display, ostentation <sin aparato : without ceremony> **4 aparatos** *nmpl* : braces (for the teeth)

aparatoso, -sa *adj* **1** : ostentatious **2** : spectacular

aparcamiento *nm Spain* **1** : parking **2** : parking lot

aparcar {72} *v Spain* : to park

aparcero, -ra *n* : sharecropper

aparear *vt* **1** : to mate (animals) **2** : to match up — **aparearse** *vr* : to mate

aparecer {53} *vi* **1** : to appear **2** PRESENTARSE : to show up **3** : to turn up, to be found — **aparecerse** *vr* : to appear

aparejado, -da *adj* **1 ir aparejado con** : to go hand in hand with **2 llevar aparejado** : to entail

aparejar *vt* **1** PREPARAR : to prepare, to make ready **2** : to harness (a horse) **3** : to fit out (a ship)

aparejo *nm* **1** : equipment, gear **2** : harness, saddle **3** : rig, rigging (of a ship)

aparentar *vt* **1** : to seem, to appear <no aparentas tu edad : you don't look your age> **2** FINGIR : to feign, to pretend

aparente *adj* **1** : apparent **2** : showy, striking — **aparentemente** *adv*

aparición *nf, pl* **-ciones 1** : appearance **2** PUBLICACIÓN : publication, release **3** FANTASMA : apparition, vision

apariencia *nf* **1** ASPECTO : appearance, look **2 en ~** : seemingly, apparently

apartado *nm* **1** : section, paragraph **2 apartado postal** : post office box

apartamento *nm* DEPARTAMENTO : apartment

apartar *vt* **1** ALEJAR : to move away, to put at a distance **2** : to put aside, to set aside, to separate — **apartarse** *vr* **1** : to step aside, to move away **2** DESVIARSE : to stray

aparte[1] *adv* **1** : apart, aside <modestia aparte : if I say so myself> **2** : separately **3 ~ de** : apart from, besides

aparte[2] *adj* : separate, special

aparte[3] *nm* : aside (in theater)

apartheid *nm* : apartheid

apasionado, -da *adj* : passionate, enthusiastic — **apasionadamente** *adv*

apasionante *adj* : fascinating, exciting

apasionar *vt* : to enthuse, to excite — **apasionarse** *vr*

apatía *nf* : apathy

apático, -ca *adj* : apathetic

apearse *vr* **1** DESMONTAR : to dismount **2** : to get out of or off (a vehicle)

apedrear *vt* : to stone, to throw stones at

apegado, -da *adj* : attached, close, devoted <es muy apegado a su familia : he is very devoted to his family>

apegarse {52} *vr* **~ a** : to become attached to, to grow fond of

apego *nm* AFICIÓN : attachment, fondness, inclination

apelación *nf, pl* **-ciones** : appeal (in court)

apelar *vi* **1** : to appeal **2 ~ a** : to resort to

apelativo *nm* APELLIDO : last name, surname

apellidarse *vr* : to have for a last name <¿cómo se apellida? : what is your last name?>

apellido *nm* : last name, surname

apelotonar *vt* : to roll into a ball, to bundle up

apenar *vt* : to aggrieve, to sadden — **apenarse** *vr* **1** : to be saddened **2** : to become embarrassed

apenas[1] *adv* : hardly, scarcely

apenas[2] *conj* : as soon as

apéndice *nm* **1** : appendix **2** : appendage

apendicectomía *nf* : appendectomy

apendicitis *nf* : appendicitis

apercibimiento *nm* **1** : preparation **2** AMONESTACIÓN : warning

apercibir *vt* **1** DISPONER : to prepare, to make ready **2** AMONESTAR : to warn **3** OBSERVAR : to observe, to perceive — **apercibirse** *vr* **1** : to get ready **2 ~ de** : to notice

aperitivo *nm* **1** : appetizer **2** : aperitif

apero *nm* : tool, implement

apertura *nf* **1** : opening, aperture **2** : commencement, beginning **3** : openness

apesadumbrar *vt* : to distress, to sadden — **apesadumbrarse** *vr* : to be weighed down

apestar *vt* **1** : to infect with the plague **2** : to corrupt — *vi* : to stink

apestoso, -sa *adj* : stinking, foul

apetecer {53} *vt* **1** : to crave, to long for <apeteció la fama : he longed for fame> **2** : to appeal to <me apetece un bistec : I feel like having a steak> <¿cuándo te apetece ir? : when do you want to go?> — *vi* : to be appealing

apetecible *adj* : appetizing, appealing

apetito *nm* : appetite

apetitoso, -sa *adj* : appetizing

apiario *nm* : apiary

ápice *nm* **1** : apex, summit **2** PIZCA : bit, smidgen

apicultor, -tora *n* : beekeeper
apicultura *nf* : beekeeping
apilar *vt* AMONTONAR : to heap up, to pile up — **apilarse** *vr*
apiñado, -da *adj* : jammed, crowded
apiñar *vt* : to pack, to cram — **apiñarse** *vr* : to crowd together, to huddle
apio *nm* : celery
apisonadora *nf* : steamroller
apisonar *vt* : to pack down, to tamp
aplacamiento *nm* : appeasement
aplacar {72} *vt* APACIGUAR : to appease, to placate — **aplacarse** *vr* : to calm down
aplanadora *nf* : steamroller
aplanar *vt* : to flatten, to level
aplastante *adj* : crushing, overwhelming
aplastar *vt* : to crush, to squash
aplaudir *v* : to applaud
aplauso *nm* **1** : applause, clapping **2** : praise, acclaim
aplazamiento *nm* : postponement
aplazar {21} *vt* : to postpone, to defer
aplicable *adj* : applicable — **aplicabilidad** *nf*
aplicación *nf, pl* **-ciones 1** : application **2** : diligence, dedication
aplicado, -da *adj* : diligent, industrious
aplicador *nm* : applicator
aplicar {72} *vt* : to apply — **aplicarse** *vr* : to apply oneself
aplique *or* **apliqué** *nm* : appliqué
aplomar *vt* : to plumb, to make vertical
aplomo *nm* : aplomb, composure
apocado, -da *adj* : timid
apocalipsis *nms & pl* : apocalypse <el Libro del Apocalipsis : the Book of Revelation>
apocalíptico, -ca *adj* : apocalyptic
apocamiento *nm* : timidity
apocarse {72} *vr* **1** : to shy away, to be intimidated **2** : to humble oneself, to sell oneself short
apócrifo, -fa *adj* : apocryphal
apodar *vt* : to nickname, to call — **apodarse** *vr*
apoderado, -da *n* : proxy, agent
apoderar *vt* : to authorize, to empower — **apoderarse** *vr* **~ de** : to seize, to take over
apodo *nm* SOBRENOMBRE : nickname
apogeo *nm* : acme, peak, zenith
apología *nf* : defense, apology
apoplejía *nf* : apoplexy, stroke
apoplético, -ca *adj* : apoplectic
aporrear *vt* : to bang on, to beat, to bludgeon
aportación *nf, pl* **-ciones** : contribution
aportar *vt* CONTRIBUIR : to contribute, to provide
aporte *nm* → **aportación**
apostador, -dora *n* : bettor, better
apostar {19} *v* : to bet, to wager <I bet he's not coming : apuesto que no viene>
apostasía *nf* : apostasy
apóstata *nmf* : apostate
apostilla *nf* : note
apostillar *vt* : to annotate
apóstol *nm* : apostle
apostólico, -ca *adj* : apostolic
apóstrofe *nmf* : apostrophe
apostura *nf* : elegance, gracefulness
apoyacabezas *nms & pl* : headrest
apoyapiés *nms & pl* : footrest
apoyar *vt* **1** : to support, to back **2** : to lean, to rest — **apoyarse** *vr* **1 ~ en** : to lean on **2 ~ en** : to be based on, to rest on
apoyo *nm* : support, backing
apreciable *adj* : appreciable, substantial, considerable
apreciación *nf, pl* **-ciones 1** : appreciation **2** : appraisal, evaluation
apreciar *vt* **1** ESTIMAR : to appreciate, to value **2** EVALUAR : to appraise, to assess — **apreciarse** *vr* : to appreciate, to increase in value
aprecio *nm* **1** ESTIMO : esteem, appreciation **2** EVALUACIÓN : appraisal, assessment
aprehender *vt* **1** : to apprehend, to capture **2** : to conceive of, to grasp
aprehensión *nf, pl* **-siones** : apprehension, capture, arrest
apremiante *adj* : pressing, urgent
apremiar *vt* INSTAR : to pressure, to urge — *vi* URGIR : to be urgent <el tiempo apremia : time is of the essence>
apremio *nm* : pressure, urgency
aprender *v* : to learn — **aprenderse** *vr*
aprendiz, -diza *n, mpl* **-dices** : apprentice, trainee
aprendizaje *nm* : apprenticeship
aprensión *nf, pl* **-siones** : apprehension, dread
aprensivo, -va *adj* : apprehensive, worried
apresamiento *nm* : seizure, capture
apresar *vt* : to capture, to seize
aprestar *vt* : to make ready, to prepare — **aprestarse** *vr* : to get ready
apresuradamente *adv* **1** : hurriedly **2** : hastily, too fast
apresurado, -da *adj* : hurried, in a rush
apresuramiento *nm* : hurry, haste
apresurar *vt* : to quicken, to speed up — **apresurarse** *vr* : to hurry up, to make haste
apretado, -da *adj* **1** : tight **2** *fam* : cheap, tightfisted — **apretadamente** *adv*
apretar {55} *vt* **1** : to press, to push (a button) **2** : to tighten **3** : to squeeze — *vi* **1** : to press, to push **2** : to fit tightly, to be too tight <los zapatos me aprietan : my shoes are tight>
apretón *nm, pl* **-tones 1** : squeeze **2** **apretón de manos** : handshake

apretujar *vt* : to squash, to squeeze — **apretujarse** *vr*
aprieto *nm* APURO : predicament, difficulty <estar en un aprieto : to be in a fix>
aprisa *adv* : quickly, hurriedly
aprisionar *vt* **1** : to imprison **2** : to trap, to box in
aprobación *nf, pl* **-ciones** : approval, endorsement
aprobar {19} *vt* **1** : to approve of **2** : to pass (a law, an exam) — *vi* : to pass (in school)
aprobatorio, -ria *adj* : approving
apropiación *nf, pl* **-ciones** : appropriation
apropiado, -da *adj* : appropriate, proper, suitable — **apropiadamente** *adv*
apropiarse *vr* **~ de** : to take possession of, to appropriate
aprovechable *adj* : usable
aprovechado[1], -da *adj* **1** : diligent, hardworking **2** : pushy, opportunistic
aprovechado[2], -da *n* : pushy person, opportunist
aprovechamiento *nm* : use, exploitation
aprovechar *vt* : to take advantage of, to make good use of — *vi* **1** : to be of use **2** : to progress, to improve — **aprovecharse** *vr* **~ de** : to take advantage of, to exploit
aprovisionamiento *nm* : provisions *pl*, supplies *pl*
aprovisionar *vt* : to provide, to supply (with provisions)
aproximación *nf, pl* **-ciones 1** : approximation, estimate **2** : rapprochement
aproximado, -da *adj* : approximate, estimated — **aproximadamente** *adv*
aproximar *vt* ACERCAR, ARRIMAR : to approximate, to bring closer — **aproximarse** *vr* ACERCARSE, ARRIMARSE : to approach, to move closer
aptitud *nf* : aptitude, capability
apto, -ta *adj* **1** : suitable, suited, fit **2** HÁBIL : capable, competent
apuesta *nf* : bet, wager
apuesto, -ta *adj* : elegant, good-looking
apuntador, -dora *n* : prompter
apuntalar *vt* : to prop up, to shore up
apuntar *vt* **1** : to aim, to point **2** ANOTAR : to write down, to jot down **3** INDICAR, SEÑALAR : to point to, to point out **4** : to prompt (in the theater) — *vi* **1** : to take aim **2** : to become evident — **apuntarse** *vr* **1** : to sign up, to enroll **2** : to score, to chalk up
apunte *nm* : note
apuñalar *vt* : to stab
apuradamente *adv* **1** : with difficulty **2** : hurriedly, hastily
apurado, -da *adj* **1** APRESURADO : rushed, pressured **2** : poor, needy **3** : difficult, awkward **4** : embarrassed
apurar *vt* **1** APRESURAR : to hurry, to rush **2** : to use up, to exhaust **3** : to trouble — **apurarse** *vr* **1** APRESURARSE : to hurry up **2** PREOCUPARSE : to worry
apuro *nm* **1** APRIETO : predicament, jam **2** : rush, hurry **3** : embarrassment
aquejar *vt* : to afflict
aquel, aquella *adj, mpl* **aquellos** : that, those
aquél, aquélla *pron, mpl* **aquéllos 1** : that (one), those (ones) **2** : the former
aquello *pron* (*neuter*) : that, that matter, that business <aquello fue algo serio : that was something serious>
aquí *adv* **1** : here **2** : now <de aquí en adelante : from now on> **3 por ~** : around here, hereabouts
aquiescencia *nf* : acquiescence, approval
aquietar *vt* : to allay, to calm — **aquietarse** *vr* : to calm down
aquilatar *vt* **1** : to assay **2** : to assess, to size up
ara *nf* **1** : altar **2 en aras de** : in the interests of, for the sake of
árabe[1] *adj & nmf* : Arab, Arabian
árabe[2] *nm* : Arabic (language)
arabesco *nm* : arabesque — **arabesco, -ca** *adj*
arábigo, -ga *adj* **1** : Arabic, Arabian **2 número arábigo** : Arabic numeral
arable *adj* : arable
arado *nm* : plow
aragonés, -nesa *adj & n, mpl* **-neses** : Aragonese
arancel *nm* : tariff, duty
arándano *nm* : blueberry
arandela *nf* : washer (for a faucet, etc.)
araña *nf* **1** : spider **2** : chandelier
arañar *v* : to scratch, to claw
arañazo *nm* : scratch
arar *v* : to plow
arbitraje *nm* **1** : arbitration **2** : refereeing (in sports)
arbitrar *v* **1** : to arbitrate **2** : to referee, to umpire
arbitrariedad *nf* **1** : arbitrariness **2** INJUSTICIA : injustice, wrong
arbitrario, -ria *adj* **1** : arbitrary **2** : unfair, unjust — **arbitrariamente** *adv*
arbitrio *nm* **1** ALBEDRÍO : will **2** JUICIO : judgment
árbitro, -tra *n* **1** : arbitrator, arbiter **2** : referee, umpire
árbol *nm* **1** : tree **2 árbol genealógico** : family tree
arbolado[1], -da *adj* : wooded
arbolado[2] *nm* : woodland
arboleda *nf* : grove, wood
arbóreo, -rea *adj* : arboreal
arbusto *nm* : shrub, bush, hedge
arca *nf* **1** : ark **2** : coffer, chest
arcada *nf* **1** : arcade, series of arches **2 arcadas** *nfpl* : retching <hacer arcadas : to retch>
arcaico, -ca *adj* : archaic
arcángel *nm* : archangel
arcano, -na *adj* : arcane

arce *nm* **:** maple tree

arcén *nm, pl* **arcenes :** hard shoulder, berm

archidiócesis *nfs & pl* **:** archdiocese

archipiélago *nm* **:** archipelago

archivador *nm* **:** filing cabinet

archivar *vt* **1 :** to file **2 :** to archive

archivista *nmf* **:** archivist

archivo *nm* **1 :** file **2 :** archive, archives *pl*

arcilla *nf* **:** clay

arco *nm* **1 :** arch, archway **2 :** bow (in archery) **3 :** arc **4 :** wicket (in croquet) **5** PORTERÍA **:** goal, goalposts *pl* **6 arco iris :** rainbow

arder *vi* **1 :** to burn <el bosque está ardiendo : the forest is in flames> <arder de ira : to burn with anger, to be seething> **2 :** to smart, to sting, to burn <le ardía el estómago : he had heartburn>

ardid *nm* **:** scheme, ruse

ardiente *adj* **1 :** burning **2 :** ardent, passionate — **ardientemente** *adv*

ardilla *nf* **1 :** squirrel **2** *or* **ardilla listada :** chipmunk

ardor *nm* **1 :** heat **2 :** passion, ardor

ardoroso, -sa *adj* **:** heated, impassioned

arduo, -dua *adj* **:** arduous, grueling — **arduamente** *adv*

área *nf* **:** area

arena *nf* **1 :** sand <arena movediza : quicksand> **2 :** arena

arenga *nf* **:** harangue, lecture

arengar {52} *vt* **:** to harangue, to lecture

arenilla *nf* **1 :** fine sand **2 arenillas** *nfpl* **:** kidney stones

arenisca *nf* **:** sandstone

arenoso, -sa *adj* **:** sandy, gritty

arenque *nm* **:** herring

arepa *nf* **:** cornmeal bread

arete *nm* **:** earring

argamasa *nf* **:** mortar (cement)

argelino, -na *adj & n* **:** Algerian

argentino, -na *adj & n* **:** Argentinian, Argentine

argolla *nf* **:** hoop, ring

argón *nm* **:** argon

argot *nm* **:** slang

argucia *nf* **:** sophistry, subtlety

argüir {41} *vi* **:** to argue — *vt* **1** ARGUMENTAR **:** to contend, to argue **2** INFERIR **:** to deduce **3** PROBAR **:** to prove

argumentación *nf, pl* **-ciones :** line of reasoning, argument

argumentar *vt* **:** to argue, to contend

argumento *nm* **1 :** argument, reasoning **2 :** plot, story line

aria *nf* **:** aria

aridez *nf, pl* **-deces :** aridity, dryness

árido, -da *adj* **:** arid, dry

Aries *nmf* **:** Aries

ariete *nm* **:** battering ram

arisco, -ca *adj* **:** surly, sullen, unsociable

arista *nf* **1 :** ridge, edge **2 :** beard (of a plant) **3 aristas** *nfpl* **:** rough edges, complications, problems

aristocracia *nf* **:** aristocracy

aristócrata *nmf* **:** aristocrat

aristocrático, -ca *adj* **:** aristocratic

aritmética *nf* **:** arithmetic

aritmético, -ca *adj* **:** arithmetic, arithmetical — **aritméticamente** *adv*

arlequín *nm, pl* **-quines :** harlequin

arma *nf* **1 :** weapon **2 armas** *nfpl* **:** armed forces **3 arma de fuego :** firearm

armada *nf* **:** navy, fleet

armadillo *nm* **:** armadillo

armado, -da *adj* **1 :** armed **2 :** assembled, put together **3** *PRi* **:** obstinate, stubborn

armador, -dora *n* **:** shipowner

armadura *nf* **1 :** armor **2** ARMAZÓN **:** skeleton, framework

armamento *nm* **:** armament, arms *pl*, weaponry

armar *vt* **1 :** to assemble, to put together **2 :** to create, to cause <armar un escándalo : to cause a scene> **3 :** to arm — **armarse** *vr* **armarse de valor :** to steel oneself

armario *nm* **1** CLÓSET, ROPERO **:** closet **2** ALACENA **:** cupboard

armatoste *nm fam* **:** monstrosity, contraption

armazón *nmf, pl* **-zones 1** ESQUELETO **:** framework, skeleton <armazón de acero : steel framework> **2 :** frames *pl* (of eyeglasses)

armenio, -nia *adj & n* **:** Armenian

armería *nf* **1 :** armory **2 :** arms museum **3 :** gunsmith's shop **4 :** gunsmith's craft

armiño *nm* **:** ermine

armisticio *nm* **:** armistice

armonía *nf* **:** harmony

armónica *nf* **:** harmonica

armónico, -ca *adj* **1 :** harmonic **2 :** harmonious — **armónicamente** *adv*

armonioso, -sa *adj* **:** harmonious — **armoniosamente** *adv*

armonizar {21} *vt* **1 :** to harmonize **2 :** to reconcile — *vi* **:** to harmonize, to blend together

arnés *nm, pl* **arneses :** harness

aro *nm* **1 :** hoop **2 :** napkin ring **3** *Arg, Chile, Uru* **:** earring

aroma *nm* **:** aroma, scent

aromático, -ca *adj* **:** aromatic

arpa *nf* **:** harp

arpegio *nm* **:** arpeggio

arpía *nf* **:** shrew, harpy

arpista *nmf* **:** harpist

arpón *nm, pl* **arpones :** harpoon — **arponear** *vt*

arquear *vt* **:** to arch, to bend — **arquearse** *vr* **:** to bend, to bow

arqueología *nf* **:** archaeology

arqueológico, -ca *adj* **:** archaeological

arqueólogo, -ga *n* **:** archaeologist

arquero, -ra *n* **1 :** archer **2** PORTERO **:** goalkeeper, goalie

arquetípico, -ca *adj* : archetypal

arquetipo *nm* : archetype

arquitecto, -ta *n* : architect

arquitectónico, -ca *adj* : architectural — **aquitectónicamente** *adv*

arquitectura *nf* : architecture

arrabal *nm* **1** : slum **2 arrabales** *nmpl* : outskirts, outlying area

arracada *nf* : hoop earring

arracimarse *vr* : to cluster together

arraigado, -da *adj* : deep-seated, ingrained

arraigar {52} *vi* : to take root, to become established — **arraigarse** *vr*

arraigo *nm* : roots *pl* <con mucho arraigo : deep-rooted>

arrancar {72} *vt* **1** : to pull out, to tear out **2** : to pick, to pluck (a flower) **3** : to start (an engine) **4** : to boot (a computer) — *vi* **1** : to start an engine **2** : to get going — **arrancarse** *vr* : to pull out, to pull off

arrancón *nm, pl* **-cones** *Mex* **1** : sudden loud start (of a car) **2 carrera de arrancones** : drag race

arranque *nm* **1** : starter (of a car) **2** ARREBATO : outburst, fit **3 punto de arranque** : beginning, starting point

arrasar *vt* **1** : to level, to smooth **2** : to devastate, to destroy **3** : to fill to the brim

arrastrar *vt* **1** : to drag, to tow **2** : to draw, to attract — *vi* : to hang down, to trail — **arrastrarse** *vr* **1** : to crawl **2** : to grovel

arrastre *nm* **1** : dragging **2** : pull, attraction **3 red de arrastre** : dragnet, trawling net

arrayán *nm, pl* **-yanes 1** MIRTO : myrtle **2 arrayán brabántico** : bayberry, wax myrtle

arrear *vt* : to urge on, to drive — *vi* : to hurry along

arrebatado, -da *adj* **1** PRECIPITADO : impetuous, hotheaded, rash **2** : flushed, blushing

arrebatar *vt* **1** : to snatch, to seize **2** CAUTIVAR : to captivate — **arrebatarse** *vr* : to get carried away (with anger, etc.)

arrebato *nm* ARRANQUE : fit, outburst

arreciar *vi* : to intensify, to worsen

arrecife *nm* : reef

arreglado, -da *adj* **1** : fixed, repaired **2** : settled, sorted out **3** : neat, tidy **4** : smart, dressed-up

arreglar *vt* **1** COMPONER : to repair, to fix **2** : to tidy up <arregla tu cuarto : pick up your room> **3** : to solve, to work out <quiero arreglar este asunto : I want to settle this matter> — **arreglarse** *vr* **1** : to get dressed (up) <arreglarse el pelo : to get one's hair done> **2 arreglárselas** *fam* : to get by, to manage

arreglo *nm* **1** : repair **2** : arrangement **3** : agreement, understanding

arrellanarse *vr* : to settle (in a chair)

arremangarse {52} *vr* : to roll up one's sleeves

arremeter *vi* EMBESTIR : to attack, to charge

arremetida *nf* EMBESTIDA : attack, onslaught

arremolinarse *vr* **1** : to crowd around, to mill about **2** : to swirl (about)

arrendador, -dora *n* **1** : landlord, landlady *f* **2** : tenant, lessee

arrendajo *nm* : jay

arrendamiento *nm* **1** ALQUILER : rental, leasing **2 contrato de arrendamiento** : lease

arrendar {55} *vt* ALQUILAR : to rent, to lease

arrendatario, -ria *n* : tenant, lessee, renter

arreos *nmpl* GUARNICIONES : tack, harness, trappings

arrepentido, -da *adj* : repentant, remorseful

arrepentimiento *nm* : regret, remorse, repentance

arrepentirse {76} *vr* **1** : to regret, to be sorry **2** : to repent

arrestar *vt* DETENER : to arrest, to detain

arresto *nm* **1** DETENCIÓN : arrest **2 arrestos** *nmpl* : boldness, daring

arriate *nm Mex, Spain* : bed (for plants), border

arriba *adv* **1** : up, upwards **2** : above, overhead **3** : upstairs **4 ~ de** : more than **5 de arriba abajo** : from top to bottom, from head to foot

arribar *vi* **1** : to arrive **2** : to dock, to put into port

arribista *nmf* : parvenu, upstart

arribo *nm* : arrival

arriendo *nm* ARRENDAMIENTO : rent, rental

arriero, -ra *n* : mule driver, muleteer

arriesgado, -da *adj* **1** : risky **2** : bold, daring

arriesgar {52} *vt* : to risk, to venture — **arriesgarse** *vr* : to take a chance

arrimado, -da *n Mex fam* : sponger, freeloader

arrimar *vt* ACERCAR, APROXIMAR : to bring closer, to draw near — **arrimarse** *vr* ACERCARSE, APROXIMARSE : to approach, to get close

arrinconar *vt* **1** ACORRALAR : to corner, to box in **2** : to push aside, to abandon

arroba *nf* : arroba (Spanish unit of measurement)

arrobamiento *nm* : rapture, ecstasy

arrobar *vt* : to enrapture, to enchant — **arrobarse** *vr*

arrocero[1]**, -ra** *adj* : rice

arrocero[2]**, -ra** *n* : rice grower

arrodillarse *vr* : to kneel (down)

arrogancia *nf* ALTANERÍA, ALTIVEZ : arrogance, haughtiness

arrogante *adj* ALTANERO, ALTIVO : arrogant, haughty

arrogarse {52} *vr* : to usurp, to arrogate

arrojado, -da *adj* : daring, fearless

arrojar *vt* **1 :** to hurl, to cast, to throw **2 :** to give off, to spew out **3 :** to yield, to produce **4** *fam* **:** to vomit — **arrojarse** *vr* PRECIPITARSE **:** to throw oneself, to leap

arrojo *nm* **:** boldness, fearlessness

arrollador, -dora *adj* **:** sweeping, overwhelming

arrollar *vt* **1 :** to sweep away, to carry away **2 :** to crush, to overwhelm **3 :** to run over (with a vehicle)

arropar *vt* **:** to clothe, to cover (up) — **arroparse** *vr*

arrostrar *vt* **:** to confront, to face (up to)

arroyo *nm* **1** RIACHUELO **:** brook, creek, stream **2 :** gutter

arroz *nm, pl* **arroces :** rice

arrozal *nm* **:** rice field, rice paddy

arruga *nf* **:** wrinkle, fold, crease

arrugado, -da *adj* **:** wrinkled, creased, lined

arrugar {52} *vt* **:** to wrinkle, to crease, to pucker — **arrugarse** *vr*

arruinar *vt* **:** to ruin, to wreck — **arruinarse** *vr* **1 :** to be ruined **2 :** to fall into ruin, to go bankrupt

arrullar *vt* **:** to lull to sleep — *vi* **:** to coo

arrullo *nm* **1 :** lullaby **2 :** coo (of a dove)

arrumaco *nm fam* **:** kissing, cuddling

arrumbar *vt* **1 :** to lay aside, to put away **2 :** to floor, to leave speechless

arsenal *nm* **:** arsenal

arsénico *nm* **:** arsenic

arte *nmf* (*usually m in singular, f in plural*) **1 :** art <artes y oficios : arts and crafts> <bellas artes : fine arts> **2** HABILIDAD **:** skill **3 :** cunning, cleverness

artefacto *nm* **1 :** artifact **2** DISPOSITIVO **:** device

artemisa *nf* **:** sagebrush

arteria *nf* **:** artery — **arterial** *adj*

arteriosclerosis *nf* **:** arteriosclerosis, hardening of the arteries

artero, -ra *adj* **:** wily, crafty

artesanal *adj* **:** pertaining to crafts or craftsmanship, handmade

artesanía *nm* **1 :** craftsmanship **2 :** handicrafts *pl*

artesano, -na *n* **:** artisan, craftsman *m*, craftsperson

artesiano, -na *adj* **:** artesian <pozo artesiano : artesian well>

ártico, -ca *adj* **:** arctic

articulación *nf, pl* **-ciones 1 :** articulation, pronunciation **2** COYUNTURA **:** joint

articular *vt* **1 :** to articulate, to utter **2 :** to connect with a joint **3 :** to coordinate, to orchestrate

articulista *nmf* **:** columnist

artículo *nm* **1 :** article, thing **2 :** item, feature, report **3 artículo de comercio :** commodity **4 artículos de primera necesidad :** essentials **5 artículos de tocador :** toiletries

artífice *nmf* **1** ARTESANO **:** artisan **2 :** mastermind, architect

artificial *adj* **1 :** artificial, man-made **2 :** feigned, false — **artificialmente** *adv*

artificio *nm* **1** HABILIDAD **:** skill **2** APARATO **:** device, appliance **3** ARDID **:** artifice, ruse

artificioso, -sa *adj* **1 :** skillful **2 :** cunning, deceptive

artillería *nf* **:** artillery

artillero, -ra *n* **:** artilleryman *m*, gunner

artilugio *nm* **:** gadget, contraption

artimaña *nf* **:** ruse, trick

artista *nmf* **1 :** artist **2** ACTOR, ACTRIZ **:** actor, actress *f*

artístico, -ca *adj* **:** artistic — **artísticamente** *adv*

artrítico, -ca *adj* **:** arthritic

artritis *nms & pl* **:** arthritis

artrópodo *nm* **:** arthropod

arveja *nf* GUISANTE **:** pea

arzobispado *nm* **:** archbishopric

arzobispo *nm* **:** archbishop

as *nm* **:** ace

asa *nf* AGARRADERA, ASIDERO **:** handle, grip

asado[1], -da *adj* **:** roasted, grilled, broiled

asado[2] *nm* **1 :** roast **2 :** barbecued meat **3 :** barbecue, cookout

asador *nm* **:** spit, rotisserie

asaduras *nfpl* **:** entrails, offal

asalariado[1], -da *adj* **:** wage-earning, salaried

asalariado[2], -da *n* **:** wage earner

asaltante *nmf* **1 :** mugger, robber **2 :** assailant

asaltar *vt* **1 :** to assault **2 :** to mug, to rob **3 asaltar al poder :** to seize power

asalto *nm* **1 :** assault **2 :** mugging, robbery **3 :** round (in boxing) **4 asalto al poder :** coup d'etat

asamblea *nf* **:** assembly, meeting

asambleísta *nmf* **:** assemblyman *m*, assemblywoman *f*

asar *vt* **:** to roast, to grill — **asarse** *vr fam* **:** to roast, to be dying from heat

asbesto *nm* **:** asbestos

ascendencia *nf* **1 :** ancestry, descent **2 ~ sobre :** influence over

ascendente *adj* **:** ascending, upward <un curso ascendente : an upward trend>

ascender {56} *vi* **1 :** to ascend, to rise up **2 :** to be promoted <ascendió a gerente : she was promoted to manager> **3 ~ a :** to amount to, to reach <las deudas ascienden a 20 millones de pesos : the debt amounts to 20 million pesos> — *vt* **:** to promote

ascendiente[1] *nmf* ANCESTRO **:** ancestor

ascendiente[2] *nm* INFLUENCIA **:** influence, ascendancy

ascensión *nf, pl* **-siones 1 :** ascent, rise **2 Fiesta de la Ascensión :** Ascension Day

ascenso *nm* **1 :** ascent, rise **2 :** promotion

ascensor *nm* ELEVADOR **:** elevator

asceta *nmf* **:** ascetic

ascético, -ca *adj* **:** ascetic

ascetismo *nm* **:** asceticism

asco *nm* **1 :** disgust <¡qué asco! : that's disgusting!, how revolting!> **2 darle asco (a alguien) :** to sicken, to revolt **3 estar hecho un asco :** to be filthy **4 hacerle ascos a :** to turn up one's nose at

ascua *nf* **1** BRASA **:** ember **2 estar en ascuas** *fam* **:** to be on edge

asear *vt* **1 :** to wash, to clean **2 :** to tidy up — **asearse** *vr*

asechanza *nf* **:** snare, trap

asechar *vt* **:** to set a trap for

asediar *vt* **1** SITIAR **:** to besiege **2** ACOSAR **:** to harass

asedio *nm* **1 :** siege **2** ACOSO **:** harassment

asegurador[1], -dora *adj* **1 :** insuring, assuring **2 :** pertaining to insurance

asegurador[2], -dora *n* **:** insurer, underwriter

aseguradora *nf* **:** insurance company

asegurar *vt* **1 :** to assure **2 :** to secure **3 :** to insure — **asegurarse** *vr* **1** CERCIORARSE **:** to make sure **2 :** to take out insurance, to insure oneself

asemejar *vt* **1 :** to make similar <ese bigote te asemeja a tu abuelo : that mustache makes you look like your grandfather> **2** *Mex* **:** to be similar to, to resemble — **asemejarse** *vr* **~ a :** to be look like, to resemble

asentaderas *nfpl fam* **:** bottom, buttocks *pl*

asentado, -da *adj* **:** settled, established

asentamiento *nm* **:** settlement

asentar {55} *vt* **1 :** to lay down, to set down, to place **2 :** to settle, to establish **3** *Mex* **:** to state, to affirm — **asentarse** *vr* **1 :** to settle **2** ESTABLECERSE **:** to settle down, to establish oneself

asentimiento *nm* **:** assent, consent

asentir {76} *vi* **:** to consent, to agree

aseo *nm* **:** cleanliness

aséptico, -ca *adj* **:** aseptic, germ-free

asequible *adj* ACCESIBLE **:** accessible, attainable

aserción *nf* → **aserto**

aserradero *nm* **:** sawmill

aserrar {55} *vt* **:** to saw

aserrín *nm, pl* **-rrines :** sawdust

aserto *nm* **:** assertion, affirmation

asesinar *vt* **1 :** to murder **2 :** to assassinate

asesinato *nm* **1 :** murder **2 :** assassination

asesino[1], -na *adj* **:** murderous, homicidal

asesino[2], -na *n* **1 :** murderer, killer **2 :** assassin

asesor, -sora *n* **:** advisor, consultant

asesoramiento *nm* **:** advice, counsel

asesorar *vt* **:** to advise, to counsel — **asesorarse** *vr* **~ de :** to consult

asesoría *nf* **1 :** consulting, advising **2 :** consultant's office

asestar {55} *vt* **1 :** to aim, to point (a weapon) **2 :** to deliver, to deal (a blow)

aseveración *nf, pl* **-ciones :** assertion, statement

aseverar *vt* **:** to assert, to state

asexual *adj* **:** asexual — **asexualmente** *adv*

asfaltado[1], -da *adj* **:** asphalted, paved

asfaltado[2] *nm* PAVIMENTO **:** pavement, asphalt

asfaltar *vt* **:** to pave, to blacktop

asfalto *nm* **:** asphalt

asfixia *nf* **:** asphyxia, asphyxiation, suffocation

asfixiar *vt* **:** to asphyxiate, to suffocate, to smother — **asfixiarse** *vr*

asga, etc. → **asir**

así[1] *adv* **1 :** like this, like that **2 :** so, thus <así sea : so be it> **3 ~ de :** so, about so <una caja así de grande : a box about so big> **4 así que :** so, therefore **5 ~ como :** as well as **6 así así :** so-so, fair

así[2] *adj* **:** such, such a <un talento así es inestimable : a talent like that is priceless>

así[3] *conj* AUNQUE **:** even if, even though <no irá, así le paguen : he won't go, even if they pay him>

asiático[1], -ca *adj* **:** Asian, Asiatic

asiático[2], -ca *n* **:** Asian

asidero *nm* **1** AGARRADA, ASA **:** grip, handle **2** AGARRE **:** grip, hold

asiduamente *adv* **:** regularly, frequently

asiduidad *nf* **1 :** assiduousness **2 :** regularity, frequency

asiduo, -dua *adj* **1 :** assiduous **2 :** frequent, regular

asiento *nm* **1 :** seat, chair <asiento trasero : back seat> **2 :** location, site

asignación *nf, pl* **-ciones 1 :** allocation **2 :** appointment, designation **3 :** allowance, pay **4** *PRi* **:** homework, assignment

asignar *vt* **1 :** to assign, to allocate **2 :** to appoint

asignatura *nf* MATERIA **:** subject, course

asilado, -da *n* **:** exile, refugee

asilo *nm* **:** asylum, refuge, shelter

asimetría *nf* **:** asymmetry

asimétrico, -ca *adj* **:** asymmetrical, asymmetric

asimilación *nf, pl* **-ciones :** assimilation

asimilar *vt* **:** to assimilate — **asimilarse** *vr* **~ a :** to be similar to, to resemble

asimismo *adv* **1** IGUALMENTE **:** similarly, likewise **2** TAMBIÉN **:** as well, also

asir {7} *vt* : to seize, to grasp — **asirse** *vr* ~ **a** : to cling to
asistencia *nf* **1** : attendance **2** : assistance **3** : assist (in sports)
asistente[1] *adj* : attending, in attendance
asistente[2] *nmf* **1** : assistant **2 los asistentes** : those present, those in attendance
asistir *vi* : to attend, to be present <asistir a clase : to attend class> — *vt* : to aid, to assist
asma *nf* : asthma
asmático, -ca *adj* : asthmatic
asno *nm* BURRO : ass, donkey
asociación *nf, pl* **-ciones 1** : association, relationship **2** : society, group, association
asociado[1], **-da** *adj* : associate, associated
asociado[2], **-da** *n* : associate, partner
asociar *vt* **1** : to associate, to connect **2** : to pool (resources) **3** : to take into partnership — **asociarse** *vr* **1** : to become partners **2** ~ **a** : to join, to become a member of
asolar {19} *vt* : to devastate, to destroy
asoleado, -da *adj* : sunny
asolear *vt* : to put in the sun — **asolearse** *vr* : to sunbathe
asomar *vt* : to show, to stick out — *vi* : to appear, to become visible — **asomarse** *vr* **1** : to show, to appear **2** : to lean out, to look out <se asomó por la ventana : he leaned out the window>
asombrar *vt* MARAVILLAR : to amaze, to astonish — **asombrarse** *vr* : to marvel, to be amazed
asombro *nm* : amazement, astonishment
asombroso, -sa *adj* : amazing, astonishing — **asombrosamente** *adv*
asomo *nm* **1** : hint, trace **2 ni por asomo** : by no means
aspa *nf* : blade (of a fan or propeller)
aspaviento *nm* : exaggerated movement, fuss, flounce
aspecto *nm* **1** : aspect **2** APARIENCIA : appearance, look
aspereza *nf* RUDEZA : roughness, coarseness
áspero, -ra *adj* : rough, coarse, abrasive — **ásperamente** *adv*
aspersión *nf, pl* **-siones** : sprinkling
aspersor *nm* : sprinkler
aspiración *nf, pl* **-ciones 1** : inhalation, breathing in **2** ANHELO : aspiration, desire
aspiradora *nf* : vacuum cleaner
aspirante *nmf* : applicant, candidate
aspirar *vi* ~ **a** : to aspire to — *vt* : to inhale, to breathe in
aspirina *nf* : aspirin
asquear *vt* : to sicken, to disgust
asquerosidad *nf* : filth, foulness
asqueroso, -sa *adj* : disgusting, sickening, repulsive — **asquerosamente** *adv*
asta *nf* **1** : flagpole <a media asta : at half-mast> **2** : horn, antler **3** : shaft (of a weapon)
ástaco *nm* : crayfish
astado, -da *adj* : horned
áster *nm* : aster
asterisco *nm* : asterisk
asteroide *nm* : asteroid
astigmatismo *nm* : astigmatism
astil *nm* : shaft (of an arrow or feather)
astilla *nf* **1** : splinter, chip **2 de tal palo, tal astilla** : like father, like son
astillar *vt* : to splinter — **astillarse** *vr*
astillero *nm* : dry dock, shipyard
astral *adj* : astral
astringente *adj & nm* : astringent — **astringencia** *nf*
astro *nm* **1** : heavenly body **2** : star
astrología *nf* : astrology
astrológico, -ca *adj* : astrological
astrólogo, -ga *n* : astrologer
astronauta *nmf* : astronaut
astronáutica *nf* : astronautics
astronautico, -ca *adj* : astronautic, astronautical
astronave *nf* : spaceship
astronomía *nf* : astronomy
astronómico, -ca *adj* : astronomical — **astronómicamente** *adv*
astrónomo, -ma *n* : astronomer
astroso, -sa *adj* DESALIÑADO : slovenly, untidy
astucia *nf* **1** : astuteness, shrewdness **2** : cunning, guile
astuto, -ta *adj* **1** : astute, shrewd **2** : crafty, tricky — **astutamente** *adv*
asueto *nm* : time off, break
asumir *vt* **1** : to assume, to take on <asumir el cargo : to take office> **2** SUPONER : to assume, to suppose
asunción *nf, pl* **-ciones** : assumption
asunto *nm* **1** CUESTIÓN, TEMA : affair, matter, subject **2 asuntos** *nmpl* : affairs, business
asustadizo, -za *adj* : nervous, jumpy, skittish
asustado, -da *adj* : frightened, afraid
asustar *vt* ESPANTAR : to scare, to frighten — **asustarse** *vr*
atacante *nmf* : assailant, attacker
atacar {72} *v* : to attack
atado[1], **-da** *adj* : shy, inhibited
atado[2] *nm* **1** : bundle, bunch **2** *Arg* : pack (of cigarettes)
atadura *nf* LIGADURA : tie, bond
atajar *vt* **1** IMPEDIR : to block, to stop **2** INTERRUMPIR : to interrupt, to cut off **3** CONTENER : to hold back, to restrain — *vi* ~ **por** : to take a shortcut through
atajo *nm* : shortcut
atalaya *nf* **1** : watchtower **2** : vantage point
atañer {79} *vi* (*3rd person only*) : to concern, to have to do with <eso no me atañe : that does not concern me>
ataque *nm* **1** : attack, assault **2** : fit <ataque de risa : fit of laughter> **3** **ataque de nervios** : nervous break-

down **4 ataque cardíaco** *or* **ataque al corazón** : heart attack

atar *vt* AMARRAR : to tie, to tie up, to tie down — **atarse** *vr*

atarantado, -da *adj fam* **1** : restless **2** : dazed, stunned

atarantar *vt fam* : to daze, to stun

atarazana *nf* : shipyard

atardecer[1] {53} *v impers* : to get dark

atardecer[2] *v impers* : late afternoon, dusk

atareado, -da *adj* : busy, overworked

atascar {72} *vt* **1** ATORAR : to block, to clog, to stop up **2** : to hinder — **atascarse** *vr* **1** : to become obstructed **2** : to get bogged down **3** PARARSE : to stall

atasco *nm* **1** : blockage **2** EMBOTELLAMIENTO : traffic jam

ataúd *nm* : coffin, casket

ataviar {85} *vt* : to dress, to clothe — **ataviarse** *vr* : to dress up

atavío *nm* ATUENDO : dress, attire

ateísmo *nm* : atheism

atemorizar {21} *vt* : to frighten, to intimidate — **atemorizarse** *vr*

atemperar *vt* : to temper, to moderate

atención[1] *nf, pl* **-ciones 1** : attention **2 poner atención** *or* **prestar atención** : to pay attention **3 llamar la atención** : to attract attention **4 en atención a** : in view of

atención[2] *interj* **1** : attention! **2** : watch out!

atender {56 } *vt* **1** : to help, to wait on **2** : to look after, to take care of **3** : to heed, to listen to — *vi* : to pay attention

atenerse {80} *vr* : to abide <tendrás que atenerte a las reglas : you will have to abide by the rules>

atentado *nm* : attack, assault

atentamente *adv* **1** : attentively, carefully **2** (*used in correspondence*) : sincerely, sincerely yours

atentar {55} *vi* **~ contra** : to make an attempt on, to threaten <atentaron contra su vida : they made an attempt on his life>

atento, -ta *adj* **1** : attentive, mindful **2** CORTÉS : courteous

atenuación *nf, pl* **-ciones 1** : lessening **2** : understatement

atenuante[1] *adj* : extenuating, mitigating

atenuante[2] *nmf* : extenuating circumstance, excuse

atenuar {3} *vt* **1** MITIGAR : to extenuate, to mitigate **2** : to dim (light), to tone down (colors) **3** : to minimize, to lessen

ateo[1], **atea** *adj* : atheistic

ateo[2], **atea** *n* : atheist

aterciopelado, -da *adj* : velvety, downy

aterido, -da *adj* : freezing, frozen

aterrador, -dora *adj* : terrifying

aterrar {55} *vt* : to terrify, to frighten

aterrizaje *nm* : landing (of a plane)

aterrizar {21} *vi* : to land, to touch down

aterrorizar {21} *vt* **1** : to terrify **2** : to terrorize — **aterrorizarse** *vr* : to be terrified

atesorar *vt* : to hoard, to amass

atestado, -da *adj* : crowded, packed

atestar {55} *vt* **1** ATIBORRAR : to crowd, to pack **2** : to witness, to testify to — *vi* : to testify

atestiguar {10} *vt* : to testify to, to bear witness to — *vi* DECLARAR : to testify

atiborrar *vt* : to pack, to crowd — **atiborrarse** *vr* : to stuff oneself

ático *nm* **1** : penthouse **2** BUHARDILLA, DESVÁN : attic

atigrado, -da *adj* : tabby (of cats), striped (of fur)

atildado, -da *adj* : smart, neat, dapper

atildar *vt* **1** : to put a tilde over **2** : to clean up, to smarten up — **atildarse** *vr* : to get spruced up

atinar *vi* ACERTAR : to be accurate, to be on target

atingencia *nf* : bearing, relevance

atípico, -ca *adj* : atypical

atiplado, -da *adj* : shrill, high-pitched

atirantar *vt* : to make taut, to tighten

atisbar *vt* **1** : to spy on, to watch **2** : to catch a glimpse of, to make out

atisbo *nm* : glimpse, sign, hint

atizador *nm* : poker (for a fire)

atizar {21} *vt* **1** : to poke, to stir, to stoke (a fire) **2** : to stir up, to rouse **3** *fam* : to give, to land (a blow)

atlántico, -ca *adj* : Atlantic

atlas *nm* : atlas

atleta *nmf* : athlete

atlético, -ca *adj* : athletic

atletismo *nm* : athletics

atmósfera *nf* : atmosphere

atmosférico, -ca *adj* : atmospheric

atole *nm Mex* **1** : thick hot beverage prepared with corn flour **2 darle atole con el dedo (a alguien)** : to string (someone) along

atollarse *vr* : to get stuck, to get bogged down

atolón *nm, pl* **-lones** : atoll

atolondrado, -da *adj* **1** ATURDIDO : bewildered, dazed **2** DESPISTADO : scatterbrained, absentminded

atómico, -ca *adj* : atomic

atomizador *nm* : atomizer

atomizar {21} *vt* FRAGMENTAR : to fragment, to break into bits

átomo *nm* : atom

atónito, -ta *adj* : astonished, amazed

atontar *vt* **1** : to stupefy **2** : to bewilder, to confuse

atorar *vt* ATASCAR : to block, to clog — **atorarse** *vr* **1** ATASCARSE : to get stuck **2** ATRAGANTARSE : to choke

atormentador, -dora *n* : tormenter

atormentar *vt* : to torment, to torture — **atormentarse** *vr* : to torment oneself, to agonize

atornillar *vt* : to screw (in, on, down)

atorrante *nmf Arg* **:** bum, loafer

atosigar {52} *vt* **:** to harass, to annoy

atracadero *nm* **:** dock, pier

atracador, -dora *n* **:** robber, mugger

atracar {72} *vi* **:** to dock, to land — *vt* **:** to hold up, to rob, to mug — **atracarse** *vr fam* **~ de :** to gorge oneself with

atracción *nf, pl* **-ciones :** attraction

atraco *nm* **:** holdup, robbery

atractivo[1], -va *adj* **:** attractive

atractivo[2] *nm* **:** attraction, appeal, charm

atraer {81} *vt* **:** to attract — **atraerse** *vr* **1 :** to attract (each other) **2** GANARSE **:** to gain, to win

atragantarse *vr* **:** to choke (on food)

atrancar {72} *vt* **:** to block, to bar — **atrancarse** *vr*

atrapada *nf* **:** catch

atrapar *vt* **:** to trap, to capture

atrás *adv* **1** DETRÁS **:** back, behind <se quedó atrás : he stayed behind> **2** ANTES **:** ago <mucho tiempo atrás : long ago> **3 para ~** *or* **hacia ~ :** backwards, toward the rear **4 ~ de :** in back of, behind

atrasado, -da *adj* **1 :** late, overdue **2 :** backwards **3 :** old-fashioned **4 :** slow (of a clock or watch)

atrasar *vt* **:** to delay, to put off — *vi* **:** to lose time — **atrasarse** *vr* **:** to fall behind

atraso *nm* **1** RETRASO **:** lateness, delay <llegó con 20 minutos de atraso : he was 20 minutes late> **2 :** backwardness **3 atrasos** *nmpl* **:** arrears

atravesar {55} *vt* **1** CRUZAR **:** to cross, to go across **2 :** to pierce **3 :** to lay across **4 :** to go through (a situation or crisis) — **atravesarse** *vr* **1 :** to be in the way <se me atravesó : it blocked my path> **2 :** to interfere, to meddle

atrayente *adj* **:** attractive

atreverse *vr* **1 :** to dare **2 :** to be insolent

atrevido, -da *adj* **1 :** bold, daring **2 :** insolent

atrevimiento *nm* **1 :** daring, boldness **2 :** insolence

atribución *nf, pl* **-ciones :** attribution

atribuible *adj* IMPUTABLE **:** attributable, ascribable

atribuir {41} *vt* **1 :** to attribute, to ascribe **2 :** to grant, to confer — **atribuirse** *vr* **:** to take credit for

atribular *vt* **:** to afflict, to trouble — **atribularse** *vr*

atributo *nm* **:** attribute

atril *nm* **:** lectern, stand

atrincherar *vt* **:** to entrench — **atrincherarse** *vr* **1 :** to dig in, to entrench oneself **2 ~ en :** to hide behind

atrio *nm* **1 :** atrium **2 :** portico

atrocidad *nf* **:** atrocity

atrofia *nf* **:** atrophy

atrofiar *v* **:** to atrophy

atronador, -dora *adj* **:** thunderous, deafening

atropellado, -da *adj* **1 :** rash, hasty **2 :** brusque, abrupt

atropellamiento *nm* → **atropello**

atropellar *vt* **1 :** to knock down, to run over **2 :** to violate, to abuse — **atropellarse** *vr* **:** to rush through (a task), to trip over one's words

atropello *nm* **:** abuse, violation, outrage

atroz *adj, pl* **atroces :** atrocious, appalling — **atrozamente** *adv*

atuendo *nm* ATAVÍO **:** attire, costume

atufar *vt* **:** to vex, to irritate — **atufarse** *vr* **1 :** to get angry **2 :** to smell bad, to stink

atún *nm, pl* **atunes :** tuna fish, tuna

aturdimiento *nm* **:** bewilderment, confusion

aturdir *vt* **1 :** to stun, to shock **2 :** to bewilder, to confuse, to stupefy

atuvo, etc. → **atenerse**

audacia *nf* OSADÍA **:** boldness, audacity

audaz *adj, pl* **audaces :** bold, audacious, daring — **audazmente** *adv*

audible *adj* **:** audible

audición *nf, pl* **-ciones 1 :** hearing **2 :** audition

audiencia *nf* **:** audience

audífono *nm* **1 :** hearing aid **2 audífonos** *nmpl* **:** headphones, earphones

audio *nm* **:** audio

audiovisual *adj* **:** audiovisual

auditar *vt* **:** to audit

auditivo, -va *adj* **:** auditory, hearing, aural <aparato auditivo : hearing aid>

auditor, -tora *n* **:** auditor

auditoría *nf* **:** audit

auditorio *nm* **1 :** auditorium **2 :** audience

auge *nm* **1 :** peak, height **2 :** boom, upturn

augurar *vt* **:** to predict, to foretell

augurio *nm* AGÜERO, PRESAGIO **:** augury, omen

augusto, -ta *adj* **:** august

aula *nf* **:** classroom

aullar {8} *vi* **:** to howl, to wail

aullido *nm* **:** howl, wail

aumentar *vt* ACRECENTAR **:** to increase, to raise — *vi* **:** to rise, to increase, to grow

aumento *nm* INCREMENTO **:** increase, rise

aun *adv* **1 :** even <ni aun en coche llegaría a tiempo : I wouldn't arrive on time even if I drove> **2 aun así :** even so **3 aun más :** even more

aún *adv* **1** TODAVÍA **:** still, yet <¿aún no ha llegado el correo? : the mail still hasn't come?> **2 más aún :** furthermore

aunar {8} *vt* **:** to join, to combine — **aunarse** *vr* **:** to unite

aunque *conj* **1 :** though, although, even if, even though **2 aunque sea :** at least

aura *nf* **1 :** aura **2 :** turkey buzzard

áureo, -rea *adj* **:** golden

aureola *nf* **1 :** halo **2 :** aura (of power, fame, etc.)
aurícula *nf* **:** auricle
auricular *nm* **:** telephone receiver
aurora *nf* **1 :** dawn **2 aurora boreal :** aurora borealis
ausencia *nf* **:** absence
ausentarse *vr* **1 :** to leave, to go away **2 ~ de :** to stay away from
ausente[1] *adj* **:** absent, missing
ausente[2] *nmf* **1 :** absentee **2 :** missing person
auspiciar *vt* **1** PATROCINAR **:** to sponsor **2** FOMENTAR **:** to foster, to promote
auspicios *nmpl* **:** sponsorship, auspices
austeridad *nf* **:** austerity
austero, -ra *adj* **:** austere
austral[1] *adj* **:** southern
austral[2] *nm* **:** former monetary unit of Argentina
australiano, -na *adj & n* **:** Australian
austriaco *or* **austríaco, -ca** *adj & n* **:** Austrian
autenticar {72} *vt* **:** to authenticate — **autenticación** *nf*
autenticidad *nf* **:** authenticity
auténtico, -ca *adj* **:** authentic — **auténticamente** *adv*
autentificar {72} *vt* **:** to authenticate — **autentificación** *nf*
autismo *nm* **:** autism
autista *adj* **:** autistic
auto *nm* **:** auto, car
autoayuda *nf* **:** self-help
autobiografía *nf* **:** autobiography
autobiográfico, -ca *adj* **:** autobiographical
autobús *nm, pl* **-buses :** bus
autocompasión *nf* **:** self-pity
autocontrol *nm* **:** self-control
autocracia *nf* **:** autocracy
autócrata *nmf* **:** autocrat
autocrático, -ca *adj* **:** autocratic
autóctono, -na *adj* **:** indigenous, native <arte autóctono : indigenous art>
autodefensa *nf* **:** self-defense
autodestrucción *nf* **:** self-destruction — **autodestructivo, -va** *adj*
autodeterminación *nf* **:** self-determination
autodidacta *adj* **:** self-taught
autodisciplina *nf* **:** self-discipline
autoestima *nf* **:** self-esteem
autogobierno *nm* **:** self-government
autografiar *vt* **:** to autograph
autógrafo *nm* **:** autograph
autoinfligido, -da *adj* **:** self-inflicted
automación *nf* → **automatización**
autómata *nm* **:** automaton
automático, -ca *adj* **:** automatic — **automáticamente** *adv*
automatización *nf* **:** automation
automatizar {21} *vt* **:** to automate
automotor, -tora *adj* **1 :** self-propelled **2 :** automotive, car
automotriz[1] *adj, pl* **-trices :** automotive, car
automotriz[2] *nf, pl* **-trices :** car dealership
automóvil *nm* **:** automobile
automovilista *nmf* **:** motorist
automovilístico, -ca *adj* **:** automobile, car <accidente automovilístico : automobile accident>
autonombrado, -da *adj* **:** self-appointed
autonomía *nf* **:** autonomy
autónomo, -ma *adj* **:** autonomous — **autónomamente** *adv*
autopista *nf* **:** expressway, highway
autopropulsado, -da *adj* **:** self-propelled
autopsia *nf* **:** autopsy
autor, -tora *n* **1 :** author **2 :** perpetrator
autoría *nf* **:** authorship
autoridad *nf* **:** authority
autoritario, -ria *adj* **:** authoritarian
autorización *nf, pl* **-ciones :** authorization
autorizado, -da *adj* **1 :** authorized **2 :** authoritative
autorizar {21} *vt* **:** to authorize, to approve
autorretrato *nm* **:** self-portrait
autoservicio *nm* **1 :** self-service restaurant **2** SUPERMERCADO **:** supermarket
autostop *nm* **1 :** hitchhiking **2 hacer autostop :** to hitchhike
autostopista *nmf* **:** hitchhiker
autosuficiencia *nf* **:** self-sufficiency — **autosuficiente** *adj*
auxiliar[1] *vt* **:** to aid, to assist
auxiliar[2] *adj* **:** assistant, auxiliary
auxiliar[3] *nmf* **1 :** assistant, helper **2 auxiliar de vuelo :** flight attendant
auxilio *nm* **1 :** aid, assistance **2 primeros auxilios :** first aid
aval *nm* **:** guarantee, endorsement
avalancha *nf* ALUD **:** avalanche
avalar *vt* **:** to guarantee, to endorse
avaluar {3} *vt* **:** to evaluate, to appraise
avalúo *nm* **:** appraisal, evaluation
avance *nm* ADELANTO **:** advance
avanzado, -da *adj* **1 :** advanced **2 :** progressive
avanzar {21} *v* **:** to advance, to move forward
avaricia *nf* CODICIA **:** greed, avarice
avaricioso, -sa *adj* **:** avaricious, greedy
avaro[1]**, -ra** *adj* **:** miserly, greedy
avaro[2]**, -ra** *n* **:** miser
avasallador, -dora *adj* **:** overwhelming
avasallamiento *nm* **:** subjugation, domination
avasallar *vt* **:** to overpower, to subjugate
ave *nf* **1 :** bird **2 aves de corral :** poultry **3 ave rapaz** *or* **ave de presa :** bird of prey
avecinarse *vr* **:** to approach, to come near
avecindarse *vr* **:** to settle, to take up residence
avellana *nf* **:** hazelnut, filbert
avena *nf* **1 :** oat, oats *pl* **2 :** oatmeal

avenencia *nf* : agreement, pact
avenida *nf* : avenue
avenir {87} *vt* : to reconcile, to harmonize — **avenirse** *vr* **1** : to agree, to come to terms **2** : to get along
aventajado, -da *adj* : outstanding
aventajar *vt* **1** : to be ahead of, to lead **2** : to surpass, to outdo
aventar {55} *vt* **1** : to fan **2** : to winnow **3** *Col, Mex* : to throw, to toss — **aventarse** *vr* **1** *Col, Mex* : to hurl oneself **2** *Mex fam* : to dare, to take a chance
aventón *nm, pl* **-tones** *Col, Mex fam* : ride, lift
aventura *nf* **1** : adventure **2** RIESGO : venture, risk **3** : love affair
aventurado, -da *adj* : hazardous, risky
aventurar *vt* : to venture, to risk — **aventurarse** *vr* : to take a risk
aventurero[1]**, -ra** *adj* : adventurous
aventurero[2]**, -ra** *n* : adventurer
avergonzado, -da *adj* **1** : ashamed **2** : embarrassed
avergonzar {9} *vt* APENAR : to shame, to embarrass — **avergonzarse** *vr* APENARSE : to be ashamed, to be embarrassed
avería *nf* **1** : damage **2** : breakdown, malfunction
averiado, -da *adj* **1** : damaged, faulty **2** : broken down
averiar {85} *vt* : to damage — **averiarse** *vr* : to break down
averiguación *nf, pl* **-ciones** : investigation, inquiry
averiguar {10} *vt* **1** : to find out, to ascertain **2** : to investigate
aversión *nf, pl* **-siones** : aversion, dislike
avestruz *nm, pl* **-truces** : ostrich
avezado, -da *adj* : seasoned, experienced
aviación *nf, pl* **-ciones** : aviation
aviador, -dora *n* : aviator, flyer
aviar {85} *vt* **1** : to prepare, to make ready **2** : to tidy up **3** : to equip, to supply
avicultor, -tora *n* : poultry farmer
avicultura *nf* : poultry farming
avidez *nf, pl* **-deces** : eagerness
ávido, -da *adj* : eager, avid — **ávidamente** *adv*
avieso, -sa *adj* **1** : twisted, distorted **2** : wicked, depraved
avinagrado, -da *adj* : vinegary, sour
avío *nm* **1** : preparation, provision **2** : loan (for agriculture or mining) **3** **avíos** *nmpl* : gear, equipment
avión *nm, pl* **aviones** : airplane
avioneta *nf* : light airplane
avisar *vt* **1** : to notify, to inform **2** : to advise, to warn
aviso *nm* **1** : notice **2** : advertisement, ad **3** ADVERTENCIA : warning **4** **estar sobre aviso** : to be on the alert
avispa *nf* : wasp
avispado, -da *adj fam* : clever, sharp
avispero *nm* : wasps' nest
avispón *nm, pl* **-pones** : hornet
avistar *vt* : to sight, to catch sight of
avituallar *vt* : to suppy with food, to provision
avivar *vt* **1** : to enliven, to brighten **2** : to strengthen, to intensify
avizorar *vt* **1** ACECHAR : to spy on, to watch **2** : to observe, to perceive <se avizoran dificultades : difficulties are expected>
axila *nf* : underarm, armpit
axioma *nm* : axiom
axiomático, -ca *adj* : axiomatic
ay *interj* **1** : oh! **2** : ouch!, ow!
ayer[1] *adv* : yesterday
ayer[2] *nm* ANTAÑO : yesteryear, days gone by
ayote *nm CA, Mex* : squash, pumpkin
ayuda *nf* **1** : help, assistance **2** **ayuda de cámara** : valet
ayudante *nmf* : helper, assistant
ayudar *vt* : to help, to assist — **ayudarse** *vr* **~ de** : to make use of
ayunar *vi* : to fast
ayunas *nfpl* **en ~** : fasting <este medicamento ha de tomarse en ayunas : this medication should be taken on an empty stomach>
ayuno *nm* : fast
ayuntamiento *nm* **1** : town hall, city hall **2** : town or city council
azabache *nm* : jet <negro azabache : jet black>
azada *nf* : hoe
azafata *nf* **1** : stewardess *f* **2** : hostess *f* (on a TV show)
azafrán *nm, pl* **-franes** **1** : saffron **2** : crocus
azahar *nm* : orange blossom
azalea *nf* : azalea
azar *nm* **1** : chance <juegos de azar : games of chance> **2** : accident, misfortune **3** **al azar** : at random, randomly
azaroso, -sa *adj* **1** : perilous, hazardous **2** : turbulent, eventful
azimut *nm* : azimuth
azogue *nm* : mercury, quicksilver
azorar *vt* **1** : to alarm, to startle **2** : to fluster, to embarrass — **azorarse** *vr* : to get embarrassed
azotar *vt* **1** : to whip, to flog **2** : to lash, to batter **3** : to devastate, to afflict
azote *nm* **1** LÁTIGO : whip, lash **2** *fam* : spanking, licking **3** : calamity, scourge
azotea *nf* : flat roof, terraced roof
azteca *adj & nmf* : Aztec
azúcar *nmf* : sugar — **azucarar** *vt*
azucarado, -da *adj* : sweetened, sugary
azucarera *nf* : sugar bowl
azucarero, -ra *adj* : sugar <industria azucarera : sugar industry>
azucena *nf* : white lily
azuela *nf* : adz
azufre *nm* : sulphur — **azufroso, -sa** *adj*

azul *adj & nm* : blue
azulado, -da *adj* : bluish
azulejo *nm* : ceramic tile, floor tile
azulete *nm* : bluing
azuloso, -sa *adj* : bluish
azur[1] *adj* CELESTE : azure
azur[2] *n* CELESTE : azure, sky blue
azuzar {21} *vt* : to incite, to egg on

B

b *nf* : second letter of the Spanish alphabet
baba *nf* **1** : spittle, saliva **2** : dribble, drool (of a baby) **3** : slime, ooze
babear *vi* **1** : to drool, to slobber **2** : to ooze
babel *nf* : babel, chaos, bedlam
babero *nm* : bib
babor *nm* : port, port side
babosa *nf* : slug (mollusk)
babosada *nf CA, Mex* : silly act or remark
baboso, -sa *adj* **1** : drooling, slobbering **2** : slimy **3** *CA, Mex fam* : silly, dumb
babucha *nf* : slipper
babuino *nm* : baboon
bacalao *nm* : cod (fish)
bache *nm* **1** : pothole **2** *PRi* : deep puddle **3** : bad period, rough time <bache económico : economic slump>
bachiller *nmf* : high school graduate
bachillerato *nm* : high school diploma
bacilo *nm* : bacillus
backgammon *nm* : backgammon
bacon *nm Spain* : bacon
bacteria *nf* : bacterium
bacteriano, -na *adj* : bacterial
bacteriología *nf* : bacteriology
bacteriológico, -ca *adj* : bacteriologic, bacteriological
bacteriólogo, -ga *n* : bacteriologist
báculo *nm* **1** : staff, stick **2** : comfort, support
badajo *nm* : clapper (of a bell)
badén *nm, pl* **badenes 1** : (paved) ford, channel **2** : dip, ditch (in a road)
bádminton *nm* : badminton
bafle *or* **baffle** *nm* **1** : baffle **2** : speaker, loudspeaker
bagaje *nm* **1** EQUIPAJE : baggage, luggage **2** : background <bagaje cultural : cultural baggage>
bagatela *nf* : trifle, trinket
bagre *nm* : catfish
bahía *nf* : bay
bailar *vt* : to dance — *vi* **1** : to dance **2** : to spin **3** : to be loose, to be too big
bailarín[1], **-rina** *adj, mpl* **-rines 1** : dancing **2** : fond of dancing
bailarín[2], **-rina** *n, mpl* **-rines 1** : dancer **2** : ballet dancer, ballerina *f*
baile *nm* **1** : dance **2** : dance party, ball **3 llevarse al baile a** *Mex fam* : to take for a ride, to take advantage of
baja *nf* **1** DESCENSO : fall, drop **2** : slump, recession **3** : loss, casualty **4 dar de baja** : to discharge, to dismiss **5 darse de baja** : to withdraw, to drop out
bajada *nf* **1** : descent **2** : dip, slope **3** : decrease, drop
bajar *vt* **1** DESCENDER : to lower, to let down, to take down **2** REDUCIR : to reduce (prices) 3 INCLINAR : to lower, to bow (the head) **4** : to go down, to descend **5 bajar de categoría** : to downgrade — *vi* **1** : to drop, to fall **2** : to come down, to go down **3** : to ebb (of tides) — **bajarse** *vr* **~ de** : to get off, to get out of (a vehicle)
bajeza *nf* **1** : low or despicable act **2** : baseness
bajío *nm* **1** : lowland **2** : shoal, sandbank, shallows
bajista *nmf* : bass player, bassist
bajo[1] *adv* **1** : down, low **2** : softly, quietly <habla más bajo : speak more softly>
bajo[2], **-ja** *adj* **1** : low **2** : short (of stature) **3** : soft, faint, deep (of sounds) **4** : lower <el bajo Amazonas : the lower Amazon> **5** : lowered <con la mirada baja : with lowered eyes> **6** : base, vile **7 los bajos fondos** : the underworld
bajo[3] *nm* **1** : bass (musical instrument) **2** : first floor, ground floor **3** : hemline
bajo[4] *prep* : under, beneath, below
bajón *nm, pl* **bajones** : sharp drop, slump
bajorrelieve *m* : bas-relief
bala *nf* **1** : bullet **2** : bale
balacera *nf* TIROTEO : shoot-out, gunfight
balada *nf* : ballad
balance *nm* **1** : balance **2** : balance sheet
balancear *vt* **1** : to balance **2** : to swing (one's arms, etc.) **3** : to rock (a boat) — **balancearse** *vr* **1** OSCILAR : to swing, to sway, to rock **2** VACILAR : to hesitate, to vacillate
balanceo *nm* **1** : swaying, rocking **2** : vacillation
balancín *nm, pl* **-cines 1** : rocking chair **2** SUBIBAJA : seesaw
balandra *nf* : sloop
balanza *nf* BÁSCULA : scales *pl,* balance
balar *vi* : to bleat
balaustrada *nf* : balustrade
balaustre *nm* : baluster
balazo *nm* **1** TIRO : shot, gunshot **2** : bullet wound
balboa *nf* : balboa (monetary unit of Panama)

balbucear *vi* **1 :** to mutter, to stammer **2 :** to prattle, to babble <los niños están balbuceando : the children are prattling away>
balbuceo *nm* **:** mumbling, stammering
balbucir → **balbucear**
balcánico, -ca *adj* **:** Balkan
balcón *nm, pl* **balcones :** balcony
balde *nm* **1** CUBO **:** bucket, pail **2 en ~ :** in vain, to no avail
baldío[1], -día *adj* **1 :** fallow, uncultivated **2 :** useless, vain
baldío[2] *nm* **1 :** wasteland **2** *Mex* **:** vacant lot
baldosa *nf* LOSETA **:** floor tile
balear *vt* **:** to shoot, to shoot at
balero *nm* **1** *Mex* **:** ball bearing **2** *Mex, PRi* **:** cup-and-ball toy
balido *nm* **:** bleat
balín *nm, pl* **balines :** pellet
balística *nf* **:** ballistics
balístico, -ca *adj* **:** ballistic
baliza *nf* **1 :** buoy **2 :** beacon (for aircraft)
ballena *nf* **:** whale
ballenero[1], -ra *adj* **:** whaling
ballenero[2], -ra *n* **:** whaler
ballenero[3] *nm* **:** whaleboat, whaler
ballesta *nf* **1 :** crossbow **2 :** spring (of an automobile)
ballet *nm* **:** ballet
balneario *nm* **:** spa, bathing resort
balompié *nm* FUTBOL **:** soccer
balón *nm, pl* **balones :** ball
baloncesto *nm* BASQUETBOL **:** basketball
balsa *nf* **1 :** raft **2 :** balsa
balsámico, -ca *adj* **:** soothing
bálsamo *nm* **:** balsam, balm
báltico, -ca *adj* **:** Baltic
baluarte *nm* BASTIÓN **:** bulwark, bastion
bambolear *vi* **1 :** to sway, to swing **2 :** to wobble — **bambolearse** *vr*
bamboleo *nm* **1 :** swaying, swinging **2 :** wobbling
bambú *nm, pl* **bambúes** *or* **bambús :** bamboo
banal *adj* **:** banal, trivial
banalidad *nf* **:** banality
banana *nf* **:** banana
bananero[1], -ra *adj* **:** banana
bananero[2] *nm* **:** banana tree
banano *nm* **1 :** banana tree **2** *CA,Col* **:** banana
banca *nf* **1 :** banking **2** BANCO **:** bench
bancada *nf* **1 :** group, faction **2 :** workbench
bancal *nm* **1 :** terrace (in agriculture) **2 :** plot (of land)
bancario, -ria *adj* **:** bank, banking
bancarrota *nf* QUIEBRA **:** bankruptcy
banco *nm* **1 :** bank <banco central : central bank> <banco de datos : data bank> <banco de arena : sandbank> <banco de sangre : blood bank> **2** BANCA **:** stool, bench **3 :** pew **4 :** school (of fish)
banda *nf* **1 :** band, strip **2** *Mex* **:** belt <banda transportadora : conveyor belt> **3 :** band (of musicians) **4 :** gang (of persons), flock (of birds) **5 banda de rodadura :** tread (of a tire, etc.) **6 banda sonora** *or* **banda de sonido :** sound track
bandada *nf* **:** flock (of birds), school (of fish)
bandazo *nm* **:** swerving, lurch
bandearse *vr* **:** to look after oneself, to cope
bandeja *nf* **:** tray, platter
bandera *nf* **:** flag, banner
banderazo *nm* **:** starting signal (in sports)
banderilla *nf* **:** banderilla, dart (in bullfighting)
banderín *nm, pl* **-rines :** pennant, small flag
bandidaje *nm* **:** banditry
bandido, -da *n* BANDOLERO **:** bandit, outlaw
bando *nm* **1** FACCIÓN **:** faction, side **2** EDICTO **:** proclamation
bandolerismo *nm* **:** banditry
bandolero, -ra *n* BANDIDO **:** bandit, outlaw
banjo *nm* **:** banjo
banquero, -ra *n* **:** banker
banqueta *nf* **1 :** footstool, stool, bench **2** *Mex* **:** sidewalk
banquete *nm* **:** banquet
banquetear *v* **:** to feast
banquillo *nm* **1 :** bench (in sports) **2 :** dock, defendant's seat
bañadera *nf* → **bañera**
bañar *vt* **1 :** to bathe, to wash **2 :** to immerse, to dip **3 :** to coat, to cover <bañado en lágrimas : bathed in tears> — **bañarse** *vr* **1 :** to take a bath, to bathe **2 :** to go for a swim
bañera *nf* TINA **:** bathtub
bañista *nmf* **:** bather
baño *nm* **1 :** bath **2 :** swim, dip **3 :** bathroom **4 baño María :** double-boiler
baqueta *nf* **1 :** ramrod **2 baquetas** *nfpl* **:** drumsticks
bar *nm* **:** bar, tavern
baraja *nf* **:** deck of cards
barajar *vt* **1 :** to shuffle (cards) **2 :** to consider, to toy with
baranda *nf* **:** rail, railing
barandal *nm* **1 :** rail, railing **2 :** bannister, handrail
barandilla *nf Spain* **:** bannister, handrail, railing
barata *nf* **1** *Mex* **:** sale, bargain **2** *Chile* **:** cockroach
baratija *nf* **:** bauble, trinket
baratillo *nm* **:** rummage sale, flea market
barato[1] *adv* **:** cheap, cheaply <te lo vendo barato : I'll sell it to you cheap>
barato[2], -ta *adj* **:** cheap, inexpensive
baratura *nf* **1 :** cheapness **2 :** cheap thing
barba *nf* **1 :** beard, stubble **2 :** chin
barbacoa *nf* **:** barbecue

bárbaramente *adv* : barbarously
barbaridad *nf* **1** : barbarity, atrocity **2 ¡qué barbaridad!** : that's outrageous!
barbarie *nf* : barbarism, savagery
bárbaro[1] *adv fam* : wildly <anoche lo pasamos bárbaro : we had a wild time last night>
bárbaro[2], **-ra** *adj* **1** : barbarous, wild, uncivilized **2** *fam* : great, fantastic
bárbaro[3], **-ra** *n* : barbarian
barbecho *nm* : fallow land <dejar en barbecho : to leave fallow>
barbero, -ra *n* : barber
barbilla *nf* MENTÓN : chin
barbitúrico *nm* : barbiturate
barbudo[1], **-da** *adj* : bearded
barbudo[2] *nm* : bearded man
barca *nf* **1** : boat **2 barca de pasaje** : ferryboat
barcaza *nf* : barge
barcia *nf* : chaff
barco *nm* **1** BARCA : boat **2** BUQUE, NAVE : ship
bardo *nm* : bard
bario *nm* : barium
barítono *nm* : baritone
barlovento *nm* : windward
barman *nm* : bartender
barniz *nm, pl* **barnices 1** LACA : varnish, lacquer **2** : glaze (on ceramics, etc.)
barnizar {21} *vt* **1** : to varnish **2** : to glaze
barométrico, -ca *adj* : barometric
barómetro *nm* : barometer
barón *nm, pl* **barones** : baron
baronesa *nf* : baroness
baronet *nm* : baronet
barquero, -ra : boatman *m*, boatwoman *f*
barquillo *nm* : wafer, thin cookie or cracker
barra *nf* : bar
barraca *nf* **1** CABAÑA, CHOZA : hut, cabin **2** : booth, stall
barracuda *nf* : barracuda
barranca *nf* **1** : hillside, slope **2** → **barranco**
barranco *nm* : ravine, gorge
barredora *nf* : street sweeper (machine)
barrena *nf* **1** TALADRO : drill, auger, gimlet **2** : tailspin
barrenar *vt* **1** : to drill **2** : to undermine
barrendero, -ra *n* : sweeper, street cleaner
barrer *v* : to sweep — **barrerse** *vr* : to slide (in sports)
barrera *nf* OBSTÁCULO : barrier, obstacle <barrera de sonido : sound barrier>
barreta *nf* : crowbar
barriada *nf* **1** : district, quarter **2** : slums *pl*
barrica *nf* BARRIL, TONEL : barrel, cask, keg
barricada *nf* : barricade
barrida *nf* **1** : sweep **2** : slide (in sports)
barrido *nm* : sweeping
barriga *nf* PANZA : belly, paunch
barrigón, -gona *adj, mpl* **-gones** *fam* : potbellied, paunchy
barril *nm* **1** BARRICA : barrel, keg **2 cerveza de barril** : draft beer
barrio *nm* **1** : neighborhood, district **2 barrios bajos** : slums *pl*
barro *nm* **1** LODO : mud **2** ARCILLA : clay **3** ESPINILLA, GRANO : pimple, blackhead
barroco, -ca *adj* : baroque
barroso, -sa *adj* ENLODADO : muddy
barrote *nm* : bar (on a window)
barrunto *nm* **1** SOSPECHA : suspicion **2** INDICIO : sign, indication, hint
bártulos *nmpl* : things, belongings <liar los bártulos : to pack one's things>
barullo *nm* BULLA : racket, ruckus
basa *nf* : base, pedestal
basalto *nm* : basalt
basar *vt* FUNDAR : to base — **basarse** *vr* FUNDARSE **~ en** : to be based on
báscula *nf* BALANZA : balance, scales *pl*
base *nf* **1** : base, bottom **2** : base (in baseball) **3** FUNDAMENTO : basis, foundation **4 base de datos** : database **5 a base de** : based on, by means of **6 en base a** : based on, on the basis of
básico, -ca *adj* FUNDAMENTAL : basic — **básicamente** *adv*
basílica *nf* : basilica
basquetbol *or* **básquetbol** *nm* BALONCESTO : basketball
basset *nm* : basset hound
bastante[1] *adv* **1** : enough, sufficiently <he trabajado bastante : I have worked enough> **2** : fairly, rather, quite <llegaron bastante temprano : they arrived quite early>
bastante[2] *adj* : enough, sufficient
bastante[3] *pron* : enough <hemos visto bastante : we have seen enough>
bastar *vi* : to be enough, to suffice
bastardilla *nf* CURSIVA : italic type, italics *pl*
bastardo, -da *adj & n* : bastard
bastidor *nm* **1** : framework, frame **2** : wing (in theater) <entre bastidores : backstage, behind the scenes>
bastilla *nf* : hem
bastión *nf, pl* **bastiones** BALUARTE : bastion, bulwark
basto, -ta *adj* : coarse, rough
bastón *nm, pl* **bastones 1** : cane, walking stick **2** : baton **3 bastón de mando** : staff (of authority)
basura *nf* DESECHOS : garbage, waste, refuse
basurero[1], **-ra** *n* : garbage collector
basurero[2] *nm Mex* : garbage can
bata *nf* **1** : bathrobe, housecoat **2** : smock, coverall, lab coat
batalla *nf* **1** : battle **2** : fight, struggle **3 de ~** : ordinary, everyday <mis

zapatos de batalla : my everyday shoes>
batallar *vi* LIDIAR, LUCHAR : to battle, to fight
batallón *nm, pl* **-llones** : battalion
batata *nf* : yam, sweet potato
batazo *nm* HIT : hit (in baseball)
bate *nm* : baseball bat
batea *nf* **1** : tray, pan **2** : flat-bottomed boat, punt
bateador, -dora *n* : batter, hitter
batear *vi* : to bat — *vt* : to hit
batería *nf* **1** PILA : battery **2** : drum kit, drums *pl* **3** : artillery **4 batería de cocina** : kitchen utensils *pl*
baterista *nmf* : drummer
batido *nm* LICUADO : milk shake
batidor *nm* : eggbeater, whisk, mixer
batidora *nf* : (electric) mixer
batir *vt* **1** GOLPEAR : to beat, to hit **2** VENCER : to defeat **3** REVOLVER : to mix, to beat **4** : to break (a record) — **batirse** *vr* : to fight
batista *nf* : batiste, cambric
batuta *nf* **1** : baton **2 llevar la batuta** : to be the leader, to call the tune
baúl *nm* : trunk, chest
bautismal *adj* : baptismal
bautismo *nm* : baptism, christening
bautista *adj & nmf* : Baptist
bautizar {21} *vt* : to baptize, to christen
bautizo *nm* → **bautismo**
bávaro, -ra *adj & n* : Bavarian
baya *nf* **1** : berry **2 baya de saúco** : elderberry
bayeta *nf* : cleaning cloth
bayoneta *nf* : bayonet
baza *nf* **1** : trick (in card games) **2 meter baza en** : to butt in on
bazar *nm* : bazaar
bazo *nm* : spleen
bazofia *nf* **1** : table scraps *pl* **2** : slop, swill **3** : hogwash, rubbish
bazuca *nf* : bazooka
beagle *nm* : beagle
beatificar {72} *vt* : to beatify — **beatificación** *nf*
beatífico, -ca *adj* : beatific
beatitud *nf* : beatitude
beato, -ta *adj* **1** : blessed **2** : pious, devout **3** : sanctimonious, overly devout
bebé *nm* : baby
bebedero *nm* **1** ABREVADERO : watering trough **2** *Mex* : drinking fountain
bebedor, -dora *n* : drinker
beber *v* TOMAR : to drink
bebida *nf* : drink, beverage
beca *nf* : grant, scholarship
becado, -da *n* : scholar, scholarship holder
becerro, -rra *n* : calf
begonia *nf* : begonia
beige *adj & nm* : beige
beisbol *or* **béisbol** *nm* : baseball
beisbolista *nmf* : baseball player
beldad *nf* BELLEZA, HERMOSURA : beauty
belén *nf, pl* **belenes** NACIMIENTO : Nativity scene
belga *adj & nmf* : Belgian
beliceño, -ña *adj & n* : Belizean
belicista[1] *adj* : militaristic
belicista[2] *nmf* : warmonger
bélico, -ca *adj* GUERRERO : war, fighting <esfuerzos bélicos : war efforts>
belicosidad *nf* : bellicosity
belicoso, -sa *adj* **1** : warlike, martial **2** : aggressive, belligerent
beligerancia *nf* : belligerence
beligerante *adj & nmf* : belligerent
bellaco[1], **-ca** *adj* : sly, cunning
bellaco[2], **-ca** *n* : rogue, scoundrel
belleza *nf* BELDAD, HERMOSURA : beauty
bello, -lla *adj* **1** HERMOSO : beautiful **2 bellas artes** : fine arts
bellota *nf* : acorn
bemol *nm* : flat (in music) — **bemol** *adj*
benceno *nm* : benzene
bendecir {11} *vt* **1** CONSAGRAR : to bless, to consecrate **2** ALABAR : to praise, to extol **3 bendecir la mesa** : to say grace
bendición *nf, pl* **-ciones** : benediction, blessing
bendiga, bendijo, etc. → **bendecir**
bendito, -ta *adj* **1** : blessed, holy **2** : fortunate **3** : silly, simple-minded
benedictino, -na *adj & n* : Benedictine
benefactor[1], **-tora** *adj* : beneficent
benefactor[2], **-tora** *n* : benefactor, benefactress *f*
beneficencia *nf* : beneficence, charity
beneficiar *vt* : to benefit, to be of assistance to — **beneficiarse** *vr* : to benefit, to profit
beneficiario, -ria *n* : beneficiary
beneficio *nm* **1** GANANCIA, PROVECHO : gain, profit **2** : benefit
beneficioso, -sa *adj* PROVECHOSO : beneficial
benéfico, -ca *adj* : charitable, beneficent
benemérito, -ta *adj* : meritorious, worthy
beneplácito *nm* : approval, consent
benevolencia *nf* BONDAD : benevolence, kindness
benévolo, -la *adj* BONDADOSO : benevolent, kind, good
bengala *nf* **luz de bengala 1** : flare (signal) **2** : sparkler
bengalí[1] *adj & nmf* : Bengali
bengalí[2] *nm* : Bengali (language)
benignidad *nf* : mildness, kindness
benigno, -na *adj* : benign, mild
beninés, -nesa *adj & n* : Beninese
benjamín, -mina *n, mpl* **-mines** : youngest child
beodo[1], **-da** *adj* : drunk, inebriated
beodo[2], **-da** *n* : drunkard
berberecho *nm* : cockle
berbiquí *nm* : brace (in carpentry)
berenjena *nf* : eggplant
bergantín *nm, pl* **-tines** : brig (ship)
berilo *nm* : beryl

bermudas *nfpl* : Bermuda shorts

berrear *vi* **1** : to bellow, to low **2** : to bawl, to howl

berrido *nm* **1** : bellowing **2** : howl, scream

berrinche *nm fam* : tantrum, conniption

berro *nm* : watercress

berza *nf* : cabbage

besar *vt* : to kiss

beso *nm* : kiss

bestia[1] *adj* **1** : ignorant, stupid **2** : boorish, rude

bestia[2] *nf* : beast, animal

bestia[3] *nmf* **1** IGNORANTE : ignoramus **2** : brute

bestial *adj* **1** : bestial, beastly **2** *fam* : huge, enormous <hace un frío bestial : it's terribly cold> **3** *fam* : great, fantastic

besuquear *vt fam* : to cover with kisses — **besuquearse** *vr fam* : to neck, to smooch

betabel *nm Mex* : beet

betún *nm, pl* **betunes** **1** : shoe polish **2** *Mex* : icing

bianual *adj* : biannual

biatlón *nm, pl* **-lones** : biathlon

biberón *nm, pl* **-rones** : baby's bottle

biblia *nf* **1** : bible **2** **la Biblia** : the Bible

bíblico, -ca *adj* : biblical

bibliografía *nf* : bibliography

bibliográfico, -ca *adj* : bibliographic, bibliographical

bibliógrafo, -fa *n* : bibliographer

biblioteca *nf* : library

bibliotecario, -ria *n* : librarian

bicameral *adj* : bicameral

bicarbonato *nm* **1** : bicarbonate **2** **bicarbonato de soda** : sodium bicarbonate, baking soda

bicentenario *nm* : bicentennial

bíceps *nms & pl* : biceps

bicho *nm* : small animal, bug, insect

bici *nf fam* : bike

bicicleta *nf* : bicycle

bicolor *adj* : two-tone

bicúspide *adj* : bicuspid

bidón *nm, pl* **bidones** : large can, (oil) drum

bien[1] *adv* **1** : well <¿dormiste bien? : did you sleep well?> **2** CORRECTAMENTE : correctly, properly, right <hay que hacerlo bien : it must be done correctly> **3** : very, quite <el libro era bien divertido : the book was very amusing> **4** : easily <bien puede acabarlo en un día : he can easily finish it in a day> **5** : willingly, readily <bien lo aceptaré : I'll gladly accept it> **6** **bien que** : although **7** **más bien** : rather

bien[2] *adj* **1** : well, OK, all right <¿te sientes bien? : are you feeling all right?> **2** : pleasant, agreeable <las flores huelen bien : the flowers smell very nice> **3** : satisfactory **4** : correct, right

bien[3] *nm* **1** : good <el bien y el mal : good and evil> **2** **bienes** *nmpl* : property, goods, possessions

bienal *adj & nf* : biennial — **bienalmente** *adv*

bienaventurado, -da *adj* **1** : blessed **2** : fortunate, happy

bienaventuranzas *nfpl* : Beatitudes

bienestar *nm* **1** : welfare, well-being **2** CONFORT : comfort

bienhechor[1], **-chora** *adj* : beneficent, benevolent

bienhechor[2], **-chora** *n* : benefactor, benefactress *f*

bienintencionado, -da *adj* : well-meaning

bienvenida *nf* **1** : welcome **2** **dar la bienvenida a** : to welcome

bienvenido, -da *adj* : welcome

bies *nm* : bias (in sewing)

bife *nm Arg, Chile, Uru* : steak

bífido, -da *adj* : forked

bifocal *adj* : bifocal

bifocales *nmpl* : bifocals

bifurcación *nf, pl* **-ciones** : fork (in a river or road)

bifurcarse {72} *vr* : to fork

bigamia *nf* : bigamy

bígamo, -ma *n* : bigamist

bigote *nm* **1** : mustache **2** : whisker (of an animal)

bigotudo, -da *adj* : mustached, having a big mustache

bikini *nm* : bikini

bilateral *adj* : bilateral — **bilateralmente** *adv*

bilingüe *adj* : bilingual

bilioso, -sa *adj* **1** : bilious **2** : irritable

bilis *nf* : bile

billar *nm* : pool, billiards

billete *nm* **1** : bill <un billete de cinco dólares : a five-dollar bill> **2** BOLETO : ticket <billete de ida y vuelta : round-trip ticket>

billetera *nf* : billfold, wallet

billón *nm, pl* **billones** **1** : billion (Great Britain) **2** : trillion (U.S.A.)

bimestral *adj* : bimonthly — **bimestralmente** *adv*

bimotor *adj* : twin-engined

binacional *adj* : binational

binario, -ria *adj* : binary

binocular *adj* : binocular

binoculares *nmpl* : binoculars

binomio *nm* : binomial

biodegradable *adj* : biodegradable

biodegradarse *vr* : to biodegrade

biodiversidad *nf* : biodiversity

biofísica *nf* : biophysics

biofísico[1], **-ca** *adj* : biophysical

biofísico[2], **-ca** *n* : biophysicist

biografía *nf* : biography

biográfico, -ca *adj* : biographical

biógrafo, -fa *n* : biographer

biología *nf* : biology

biológico, -ca *adj* : biological, biologic — **biológicamente** *adv*

biólogo, -ga *n* : biologist

biombo *nm* MAMPARA : folding screen, room divider
biomecánica *nf* : biomechanics
biopsia *nf* : biopsy
bioquímica *nf* : biochemistry
bioquímico[1], -ca *adj* : biochemical
bioquímico[2], -ca *n* : biochemist
biosfera *or* **biósfera** *nf* : biosphere
biotecnología *nf* : biotechnology
biótico, -ca *adj* : biotic
bipartidismo *nm* : two-party system
bipartidista *adj* : bipartisan
bípedo *nm* : biped
birlar *vt fam* : to swipe, to pinch
birmano, -na *adj & n* : Burmese
bis[1] *adv* **1** : twice, again (in music) **2** : a, A <artículo 47 bis : Article 47A> <calle Bolívar, número 70 bis : Bolívar Street, number 70A>
bis[2] *nm* : encore
bisabuelo, -la *n* : great-grandfather *m,* great-grandmother *f,* great-grandparent
bisagra *nf* : hinge
bisbisar *vt fam* : to mutter, to mumble
bisecar {72} *vt* : bisect — **bisección** *nf*
bisel *nm* : bevel
biselar *vt* : to bevel
bisexual *adj* : bisexual
bisiesto *adj* **año bisiesto** : leap year
bismuto *nm* : bismuth
bisnieto, -ta *n* : great-grandson *m,* great-granddaughter *f,* great-grandchild
bisonte *nm* : bison, buffalo
bisoñé *nm* : hairpiece, toupee
bisoño[1], -ña *adj* : inexperienced, green
bisoño[2], -ña *n* : rookie, greenhorn
bistec *nm* : steak, beefsteak
bisturí *nm* ESCALPELO : scalpel
bisutería *nf* : costume jewelry
bit *nm* : bit (unit of information)
bituminoso, -sa *adj* : bituminous
bivalvo *nm* : bivalve
bizarría *nf* **1** : courage, gallantry **2** : generosity
bizarro, -rra *adj* **1** VALIENTE : courageous, valiant **2** GENEROSO : generous
bizco, -ca *adj* : cross-eyed
bizcocho *nm* **1** : sponge cake **2** : biscuit **3** *Mex* : breadstick
bizquera *nf* : crossed eyes, squint
blanco[1], -ca *adj* : white
blanco[2], -ca *n* : white person
blanco[3] *nm* **1** : white **2** : target, bull's-eye <dar en el blanco : to hit the target, to hit the nail on the head> **3** : blank space, blank <un cheque en blanco : a blank check>
blancura *nf* : whiteness
blancuzco, -ca *adj* **1** : whitish, off-white **2** PÁLIDO : pale
blandir {1} *vt* : to wave, to brandish
blando, -da *adj* **1** SUAVE : soft, tender **2** : weak (in character) **3** : lenient
blandura *nf* **1** : softness, tenderness **2** : leniency
blanqueador *nm* : bleach, whitener
blanquear *vt* **1** : to whiten, to bleach **2** : to shut out (in sports) **3** : to launder (money) — *vi* : to turn white
blanquillo *nm CA, Mex* : egg
blasfemar *vi* : to blaspheme
blasfemia *nf* : blasphemy
blasfemo, -ma *adj* : blasphemous
blazer *nm* : blazer
bledo *nm* **no me importa un bledo** *fam* : I couldn't care less, I don't give a damn
blindado, -da *adj* ACORAZADO : armored
blindaje *nm* **1** : armor, armor plating **2** : shield (for cables, machinery, etc.)
bloc *nm, pl* **blocs** : writing pad, pad of paper
blof *nm Col, Mex* : bluff
blofear *vi Col, Mex* : to bluff
blondo, -da *adj* : blond, flaxen
bloque *nm* **1** : block **2** GRUPO : bloc <el bloque comunista : the Communist bloc>
bloquear *vt* **1** OBSTRUIR : to block, to obstruct **2** : to blockade
bloqueo *nm* **1** OBSTRUCCIÓN : blockage, obstruction **2** : blockade
blusa *nf* : blouse
blusón *nm, pl* **blusones** : loose shirt, smock
boa *nf* : boa
boato *nm* : ostentation, show
bobada *nf* : folly, nonsense
bobalicón, -cona *adj, mpl* **-cones** *fam* : silly, stupid
bobina *nf* CARRETE : bobbin, reel
bobo[1], -ba *adj* : silly, stupid
bobo[2], -ba *n* : fool, simpleton
boca *nf* **1** : mouth **2 boca arriba** : face up, on one's back **3 boca abajo** : face down, prone **4 boca de riego** : hydrant **5 en boca de** : according to
bocacalle *nf* : entrance to a street <gire a la última bocacalle : take the last turning>
bocadillo *nm Spain* : sandwich
bocado *nm* **1** : bite, mouthful **2** FRENO : bit (of a bridle)
bocajarro *nm* **a ~** : point-blank, directly
bocallave *nf* : keyhole
bocanada *nf* **1** : swig, swallow **2** : puff, mouthful (of smoke) **3** : gust (of air) **4** : stream (of people)
boceto *nm* : sketch, outline
bochinche *nm fam* : ruckus, uproar
bochorno *nm* **1** VERGÜENZA : embarrassment **2** : hot and humid weather **3** : hot flash
bochornoso, -sa *adj* **1** EMBARAZOSO : embarrassing **2** : hot and muggy
bocina *nf* **1** : horn, trumpet **2** : automobile horn **3** : mouthpiece (of a telephone) **4** *Mex* : loudspeaker
bocinazo *nm* : honk (of a horn)
bocio *nm* : goiter
bocón, -cona *n, mpl* **bocones** *fam* : blabbermouth, loudmouth
boda *nf* : wedding

bodega *nf* **1** : wine cellar **2** *Chile, Col, Mex* : storeroom, warehouse **3** (*in various countries*) : grocery store

bofetada *nf* CACHETADA : slap on the face

bofetear *vt* CACHETEAR : to slap

bofetón *nm* → **bofetada**

bofo, -fa *adj* : flabby

boga *nf* : fashion, vogue <estar en boga : to be in style>

bogotano[1], -na *adj* : of or from Bogotá

bogotano[2], -na *n* : person from Bogotá

bohemio, -mia *adj & n* : bohemian, Bohemian

boicot *nm, pl* **boicots** : boycott

boicotear *vt* : to boycott

boina *nf* : beret

boiserie *nf* : wood paneling, wainscoting

boj *nm, pl* **bojes** : box (plant), boxwood

bola *nf* **1** : ball <bola de nieve : snowball> **2** *fam* : lie, fib **3** *Mex fam* : bunch, group <una bola de rateros : a bunch of thieves> **4** *Mex* : uproar, tumult

bolear *vt Mex* : to polish (shoes)

bolera *nf* : bowling alley

bolero *nm* : bolero

boleta *nf* **1** : ballot **2** : ticket **3** : receipt

boletería *nf* TAQUILLA : box office, ticket office

boletín *nm, pl* **-tines 1** : bulletin **2** : journal, review **3 boletín de prensa** : press release

boleto *nm* BILLETE : ticket

boliche *nm* **1** BOLOS : bowling **2** *Arg* : bar, tavern

bolígrafo *nm* : ballpoint pen

bolillo *nm* **1** : bobbin **2** *Mex* : roll, bun

bolívar *nm* : bolivar (monetary unit of Venezuela)

boliviano[1], -na *adj & n* : Bolivian

boliviano[2] *nm* : boliviano (monetary unit of Bolivia)

bollo *nm* : bun, sweet roll

bolo *nm* : bowling pin, tenpin

bolos *nmpl* BOLICHE : bowling

bolsa *nf* **1** : bag, sack **2** *Mex* : pocketbook, purse **3** *Mex* : pocket **4 la Bolsa** : the stock market, the stock exchange **5 bolsa de trabajo** : employment agency

bolsear *vi Mex* : to pick pockets

bolsillo *nm* **1** : pocket **2 dinero de bolsillo** : pocket change, loose change

bolso *nm* : pocketbook, handbag

bomba *nf* **1** : bomb **2** : bubble **3** : pump <bomba de gasolina : gas pump>

bombachos *nmpl* : baggy pants, bloomers

bombardear *vt* **1** : to bomb **2** : to bombard

bombardeo *nm* **1** : bombing, shelling **2** : bombardment

bombardero *nm* : bomber (airplane)

bombástico, -ca *adj* : bombastic

bombear *vt* : to pump

bombero, -ra *n* : firefighter, fireman *m*

bombilla *nf* : lightbulb

bombillo *nm CA, Col, Ven* : lightbulb

bombo *nm* **1** : bass drum **2** *fam* : exaggerated praise, hype <con bombos y platillos : with great fanfare>

bombón *nm, pl* **bombones 1** : bonbon, chocolate **2** *Mex* : marshmallow

bonachón[1], -chona *adj, mpl* **-chones** *fam* : good-natured, kindhearted

bonachón[2], -chona *n, mpl* **-chones** *fam* BUENAZO : kindhearted person

bonaerense[1] *adj* : of or from Buenos Aires

bonaerense[2] *nmf* : person from Buenos Aires

bonanza *nf* **1** PROSPERIDAD : prosperity <bonanza económica : economic boom> **2** : calm weather **3** : rich ore deposit, bonanza

bondad *nf* BENEVOLENCIA : goodness, kindness <tener la bondad de hacer algo : to be kind enough to do something>

bondadoso, -sa *adj* BENÉVOLO : kind, kindly, good — **bondadosamente** *adv*

bonete *nm* : cap, mortarboard

boniato *nm* : sweet potato

bonificación *nf, pl* **-ciones 1** : discount **2** : bonus, extra

bonito[1] *adv* : nicely, well <¡qué bonito canta tu hermana! : your sister sings wonderfully!>

bonito[2], -ta *adj* LINDO : pretty, lovely <tiene un apartamento bonito : she has a nice apartment>

bonito[3] *nm* : bonito (tuna)

bono *nm* **1** : bond <bono bancario : bank bond> **2** : voucher

boqueada *nf* : gasp <to give one's last gasp : dar la última boqueada>

boquear *vi* **1** : to gasp **2** : to be dying

boquete *nm* : gap, opening, breach

boquiabierto, -ta *adj* : open-mouthed, speechless, agape

boquilla *nf* : mouthpiece (of a musical instrument)

borbollar *vi* : to bubble

borbotar *or* **borbotear** *vi* : to boil, to bubble, to gurgle

borboteo *nm* : bubbling, gurgling

borda *nf* : gunwale

bordado *nm* : embroidery, needlework

bordar *v* : to embroider

borde *nm* **1** : border, edge **2 al borde de** : on the verge of <estoy al borde de la locura : I'm about to go crazy>

bordear *vt* **1** : to border, to skirt <el Río Este bordea Manhattan : the East River borders Manhattan> **2** : to border on <bordea la irrealidad : it borders on unreality> **3** : to line <una calle bordeada de árboles : a street lined with trees>

bordillo *nm* : curb

bordo *nm* **a ~** : aboard, on board

boreal *adj* : northern

borgoña *nf* : burgundy

bórico, -ca *adj* **:** boric <ácido bórico : boric acid>

boricua *adj & nmf fam* **:** Puerto Rican

borinqueño, -ña → **boricua**

borla *nf* **1 :** pom-pom, tassel **2 :** powder puff

boro *nm* **:** boron

borrachera *nf* **:** drunkenness <agarró una borrachera : he got drunk>

borrachín, -china *n, mpl* **-chines** *fam* **:** lush, drunk

borracho[1], -cha *adj* EBRIO **:** drunk, intoxicated

borracho[2], -cha *n* **:** drunk, drunkard

borrador *nm* **1 :** rough copy, first draft <en borrador : in the rough> **2 :** eraser

borrar *vt* **:** to erase, to blot out — **borrarse** *vr* **1 :** to fade, to fade away **2 :** to resign, to drop out **3** *Mex fam* **:** to split, to leave <me borro : I'm out of here>

borrascoso, -sa *adj* **:** gusty, blustery

borrego, -ga *n* **1 :** lamb, sheep **2 :** simpleton, fool

borrico *nm* → **burro**

borrón *nm, pl* **borrones :** smudge, blot <borrón y cuenta nueva : let's start on a clean slate, let's start over again>

borronear *vt* **:** to smudge, to blot

borroso, -sa *adj* **1 :** blurry, smudgy **2** CONFUSO **:** unclear, confused

boscoso, -sa *adj* **:** wooded

bosnio, -nia *adj & n* **:** Bosnian

bosque *nm* **:** woods, forest

bosquecillo *nm* **:** grove, copse, thicket

bosquejar *vt* ESBOZAR **:** to outline, to sketch

bosquejo *nm* **1** TRAZADO **:** outline, sketch **2 :** draft

bostezar {21} *vi* **:** to yawn

bostezo *nm* **:** yawn

bota *nf* **1 :** boot **2 :** wineskin

botana *nf Mex* **:** snack, appetizer

botanear *vi Mex* **:** to have a snack

botánica *nf* **:** botany

botánico[1], -ca *adj* **:** botanical

botánico[2], -ca *n* **:** botanist

botar *vt* **1** ARROJAR **:** to throw, to fling, to hurl **2** TIRAR **:** to throw out, to throw away **3 :** to launch (a ship)

bote *nm* **1 :** small boat <bote de remos : rowboat> **2 :** can, jar **3 :** jump, bounce **4** *Mex fam* **:** jail

botella *nf* **:** bottle

botica *nf* FARMACIA **:** drugstore, pharmacy

boticario, -ria *n* FARMACÉUTICO **:** pharmacist, druggist

botín *nm, pl* **botines 1 :** baby's bootee **2 :** ankle boot **3 :** booty, plunder

botiquín *nm, pl* **-quines 1 :** medicine cabinet **2 :** first-aid kit

botón *nm, pl* **botones 1 :** button **2 :** bud **3** INSIGNIA **:** badge

botones *nmfs & pl* **:** bellhop

botulismo *nm* **:** botulism

boulevard [ˌbuleˈvar] *nm* → **bulevar**

bouquet *nm* **1 :** fragrance, bouquet (of wine) **2** RAMILLETE **:** bouquet (of flowers)

boutique *nf* **:** boutique

bóveda *nf* **1 :** vault, dome **2** CRIPTA **:** crypt

bovino, -na *adj* **:** bovine

box *nm, pl* **boxes 1 :** pit (in auto racing) **2** *Mex* **:** boxing

boxeador, -dora *n* **:** boxer

boxear *vi* **:** to box

boxeo *nm* **:** boxing

boya *nf* **:** buoy

boyante *adj* **1 :** buoyant **2 :** prosperous, thriving

bozal *nm* **1 :** muzzle **2 :** halter (for a horse)

bracear *vi* **1 :** to wave one's arms **2 :** to make strokes (in swimming)

bracero, -ra *n* **:** migrant worker, day laborer

braguero *nm* **:** truss (in medicine)

bragueta *nf* **:** fly, pants zipper

braille *adj & nm* **:** braille

bramante *nm* **:** twine, string

bramar *vi* **1** RUGIR **:** to roar, to bellow **2 :** to howl (of the wind)

bramido *nm* **:** bellowing, roar

brandy *nm* **:** brandy

branquia *nf* AGALLA **:** gill

brasa *nf* ASCUA **:** ember, live coal

brasero *nm* **:** brazier

brasier *nm Col, Mex* **:** brassiere, bra

brasileño, -ña *adj & n* **:** Brazilian

bravata *nf* **1** JACTANCIA **:** boast, bravado **2** AMENAZA **:** threat

bravo, -va *adj* **1** FEROZ **:** ferocious, fierce <un perro bravo : a ferocious dog> **2** EXCELENTE **:** excellent, great <¡bravo! : bravo!, well done!> **3 :** rough, rugged, wild **4 :** annoyed, angry

bravucón, -cona *n, mpl* **-cones :** bully

bravuconadas *nfpl* **:** bravado

bravura *nf* **1** FEROCIDAD **:** fierceness, ferocity **2** VALENTÍA **:** bravery

braza *nf* **1 :** breaststroke **2 :** fathom (unit of length)

brazada *nf* **:** stroke (in swimming)

brazalete *nm* PULSERA **:** bracelet, bangle

brazo *nm* **1 :** arm **2 brazo derecho :** right-hand man **3 brazos** *nmpl* **:** hands, laborers

brea *nf* ALQUITRÁN **:** tar, pitch

brebaje *nm* **:** potion, brew

brecha *nf* **1 :** gap, breach <estar siempre en la brecha : to be always there when needed, to stay in the thick of things> **2 :** gash

brécol *nm* **:** broccoli

brega *nf* **1** LUCHA **:** struggle, fight **2 :** hard work

bregar {52} *vi* **1** LUCHAR **:** to struggle **2 :** to toil, to work hard **3 ~ con :** to deal with

brete *nm* **:** jam, tight spot

breve *adj* **1** CORTO **:** brief, short **2 en ~ :** shortly, in short — **brevemente** *adv*

brevedad *nf* **:** brevity, shortness

breviario *nm* **:** breviary

brezal *nm* : heath, moor
brezo *nm* : heather
bribón, -bona *n, mpl* **bribones** : rascal, scamp
bricolaje *or* **bricolage** *nm* : do-it-yourself
brida *nf* : bridle
brigada *nf* **1** : brigade **2** : gang, team, squad
brigadier *nm* : brigadier
brillante[1] *adj* : brilliant, bright — **brillantemente** *adv*
brillante[2] *nm* DIAMANTE : diamond
brillantez *nf* : brilliance, brightness
brillar *vi* : to shine, to sparkle
brillo *nm* **1** LUSTRE : luster, shine **2** : brilliance
brilloso, -sa *adj* LUSTROSO : lustrous, shiny
brincar {72} *vi* **1** SALTAR : to jump around, to leap about **2** : to frolic, to gambol
brinco *nm* **1** SALTO : jump, leap, skip **2 pegar un brinco** : to give a start, to jump
brindar *vi* : to drink a toast <brindó por los vencedores : he toasted the victors> — *vt* OFRECER, PROPORCIONAR : to offer, to provide — **brindarse** *vr* : to offer one's assistance, to volunteer
brindis *nm* : toast, drink <hacer un brindis : to drink a toast>
brinque, etc. → **brincar**
brío *nm* **1** : force, determination **2** : spirit, verve
brioso, -sa *adj* : spirited, lively
briqueta *nf* : briquette
brisa *nf* : breeze
británico[1], **-ca** *adj* : British
británico[2], **-ca** *n* **1** : British person **2 los británicos** : the British
brizna *nf* **1** : strand, thread **2** : blade (of grass)
brocado *nm* : brocade
brocha *nf* : paintbrush
broche *nm* **1** ALFILER : brooch **2** : fastener, clasp **3 broche de oro** : finishing touch
brocheta *nf* : skewer
brócoli *nm* : broccoli
broma *nf* **1** CHISTE : joke, prank **2** : fun, merriment **3 en ~** : in jest, jokingly
bromear *vi* : to joke, to fool around <sólo estaba bromeando : I was only kidding>
bromista[1] *adj* : fun-loving, joking
bromista[2] *nmf* : joker, prankster
bromo *nm* : bromine
bronca *nf fam* : fight, quarrel, fuss
bronce *nm* : bronze
bronceado[1], **-da** *adj* **1** : tanned, suntanned **2** : bronze
bronceado[2] *nm* **1** : suntan, tan **2** : bronzing
broncearse *vr* : to get a suntan
bronco, -ca *adj* **1** : harsh, rough **2** : untamed, wild
bronquial *adj* : bronchial
bronquio *nm* : bronchial tube, bronchus
bronquitis *nf* : bronchitis
broqueta *nf* : skewer
brotar *vi* **1** : to bud, to sprout **2** : to spring up, to stream, to gush forth **3** : to break out, to appear
brote *nm* **1** : outbreak **2** : sprout, bud, shoot
broza *nf* **1** : brushwood **2** MALEZA : scrub, undergrowth
brujería *nf* HECHICERÍA : witchcraft, sorcery
brujo[1], **-ja** *adj* : bewitching
brujo[2], **-ja** *n* : warlock *m,* witch *f,* sorcerer
brújula *nf* : compass
bruma *nf* : haze, mist
brumoso, -sa *adj* : hazy, misty
bruñir {38} *vt* : to burnish, to polish (metals)
brusco, -ca *adj* **1** SÚBITO : sudden, abrupt **2** : curt, brusque — **bruscamente** *adv*
brusquedad *nf* **1** : abruptness, suddenness **2** : brusqueness
brutal *adj* **1** : brutal **2** *fam* : incredible, terrific — **brutalmente** *adv*
brutalidad *nf* CRUELDAD : brutality
brutalizar {21} *vt* : to brutalize, to maltreat
bruto[1], **-ta** *adj* **1** : gross <peso bruto : gross weight> <ingresos brutos : gross income> **2** : unrefined <petróleo bruto : crude oil> **3** : brutish, stupid
bruto[2], **-ta** *n* **1** : brute **2** : dunce, blockhead
bucal *adj* : oral
bucanero *nm* : buccaneer, pirate
buccino *nm* : whelk
buceador, -dora *n* : diver, scuba diver
bucear *vi* **1** : to dive, to swim underwater **2** : to explore, to delve
buceo *nm* **1** : diving, scuba diving **2** : exploration, searching
buche *nm* **1** : crop (of a bird) **2** *fam* : belly, gut **3** : mouthful <hacer buches : to rinse one's mouth>
bucle *nm* **1** : curl, ringlet **2** : loop
bucólico, -ca *adj* : bucolic
budín *nm, pl* **budines** : pudding
budismo *nm* : Buddhism
budista *adj & nmf* : Buddhist
buen → **bueno**[1]
buenamente *adv* **1** : easily **2** : willingly
buenaventura *nf* **1** : good luck **2** : fortune, future <le dijo la buenaventura : she told his fortune>
buenazo, -za *n fam* BONACHÓN : kindhearted person
bueno[1], **-na** *adj* (**buen** *before masculine singular nouns*) **1** : good <una buena idea : a good idea> **2** BONDADOSO : nice, kind **3** APROPIADO : proper, appropriate **4** SANO : well, healthy **5** : considerable, goodly <una buena cantidad : a lot> **6 buenos días**

: hello, good day **7 buenas tardes** : good afternoon **8 buenas noches** : good evening, good night
bueno[2] *interj* **1** : OK!, all right! **2** *Mex* : hello! (on the telephone)
buey *nm* : ox, steer
búfalo *nm* **1** : buffalo **2 búfalo de agua** : water buffalo
bufanda *nf* : scarf, muffler
bufar *vi* : to snort
bufet *or* **bufé** *nm* : buffet-style meal
bufete *nm* **1** : law firm, law office **2** : writing desk
bufido *nm* : snort
bufo, -fa *adj* : comic
bufón, -fona *n, mpl* **bufones** : clown, buffoon, jester
bufonada *nf* **1** : jest, buffoonery **2** : sarcasm
buhardilla *nf* **1** ÁTICO, DESVÁN : attic **2** : dormer window
búho *nm* **1** : owl **2** *fam* : hermit, recluse
buhonero, -ra *n* MERCACHIFLE : peddler
buitre *nm* : vulture
bujía *nf* : spark plug
bulbo *nm* : bulb
bulboso, -sa *adj* : bulbous
bulevar *nm* : boulevard
búlgaro, -ra *adj & n* : Bulgarian
bulla *nf* BARULLO : racket, rowdiness
bullicio *nm* **1** : ruckus, uproar **2** : hustle and bustle
bullicioso, -sa *adj* : noisy, busy, turbulent
bullir {38} *vi* **1** HERVIR : to boil **2** MOVERSE : to stir, to bustle about
bulto *nm* **1** : package, bundle **2** : piece of luggage, bag **3** : size, bulk, volume **4** : form, shape **5** : lump (on the body), swelling, bulge
bumerán *nm, pl* **-ranes** : boomerang
búnker *nm, pl* **búnkers** : bunker
búnquer *nm* → **búnker**
buñuelo *nm* : fried pastry
buque *nm* BARCO : ship, vessel
burbuja *nf* : bubble, blister (on a surface)
burbujear *vi* **1** : to bubble **2** : to fizz
burbujeo *nm* : bubbling
burdel *nm* : brothel, whorehouse
burdo, -da *adj* **1** : coarse, rough **2** : crude, clumsy <una burda mentira : a clumsy lie> — **burdamente** *adj*
burgués, -guesa *adj & n, mpl* **burgueses** : bourgeois
burguesía *nf* : bourgeoisie, middle class
burla *nf* **1** : mockery, ridicule **2** : joke, trick **3 hacer burla de** : to make fun of, to mock
burlar *vt* ENGAÑAR : to trick, to deceive — **burlarse** *vr* ~ **de** : to make fun of, to ridicule
burlesco, -ca *adj* : burlesque, comic
burlón[1], **-lona** *adj, mpl* **burlones** : joking, mocking
burlón[2], **-lona** *n, mpl* **burlones** : joker
burocracia *nf* : bureaucracy
burócrata *nmf* : bureaucrat
burocrático, -ca *adj* : bureaucratic
burrada *nf fam* : stupid act, nonsense
burrito *nm* : burrito
burro[1], **-rra** *adj fam* : dumb, stupid
burro[2], **-rra** *n* **1** ASNO : donkey, ass **2** *fam* : dunce, poor student
burro[3] *nm* **1** : sawhorse **2** *Mex* : ironing board **3** *Mex* : stepladder
bursátil *adj* : stock-market
burundés, -desa *adj & n* : Burundian
bus *nm* : bus
busca *nf* : search
buscador, -dora *n* : hunter (for treasure, etc.), prospector
buscapleitos *nmfs & pl* : troublemaker
buscar {72} *vt* **1** : to look for, to seek **2** : to pick up, to collect **3** : to provoke — *vi* : to look, to search <buscó en los bolsillos : he searched through his pockets>
buscavidas *nmfs & pl* **1** : busybody **2** : go-getter
busque, etc. → **buscar**
búsqueda *nf* : search
busto *nm* : bust
butaca *nf* **1** SILLÓN : armchair **2** : seat (in a theatre) **3** *Mex* : pupil's desk
butano *nm* : butane
buzo[1], **-za** *adj Mex fam* : smart, astute <¡ponte buzo! : get with it!, get on the ball!>
buzo[2] *nm* : diver, scuba diver
buzón *nm, pl* **buzones** : mailbox
byte *nm* : byte

C

c *nf* : third letter of the Spanish alphabet
cabal *adj* **1** : exact, correct **2** : complete **3** : upright, honest
cabales *nmpl* **no estar en sus cabales** : not to be in one's right mind
cabalgar {52} *vi* : to ride (on horseback)
cabalgata *nf* : cavalcade, procession
cabalidad *nf* **a** ~ : thoroughly, conscientiously
caballa *nf* : mackerel
caballada *nf* **1** : herd of horses **2** *fam* : nonsense, stupidity, outrageousness
caballar *adj* EQUINO : horse, equine
caballeresco, -ca *adj* : gallant, chivalrous
caballería *nf* **1** : cavalry **2** : horse, mount **3** : knighthood, chivalry
caballeriza *nf* : stable
caballero[1] → **caballeroso**
caballero[2] *nm* **1** : gentleman **2** : knight

caballerosidad *nf* : chivalry, gallantry
caballeroso, -sa *adj* : gentlemanly, chivalrous
caballete *nm* **1** : ridge **2** : easel **3** : trestle (for a table, etc.) **4** : bridge (of the nose) **5** : sawhorse
caballista *nmf* : horseman *m,* horsewoman *f*
caballito *nm* **1** : rocking horse **2 caballito de mar** : seahorse **3 caballitos** *nmpl* : merry-go-round
caballo *nm* **1** : horse **2** : knight (in chess) **3 caballo de fuerza** *or* **caballo de vapor** : horsepower
cabalmente *adv* : fully, exactly
cabaña *nf* CHOZA : cabin, hut
cabaret *nm, pl* **-rets** : nightclub, cabaret
cabecear *vt* : to head (in soccer) — *vi* **1** : to nod one's head **2** : to lurch, to pitch
cabecera *nf* **1** : headboard **2** : head <cabecera de la mesa : head of the table> **3** : heading, headline **4** : headwaters *pl* **5 médico de cabecera** : family doctor **6 cabecera municipal** *CA, Mex* : downtown area
cabecilla *nmf* : ringleader, kingpin
cabellera *nf* : head of hair, mane
cabello *nm* : hair
cabelludo, -da *adj* **1** : hairy **2 cuero cabelludo** : scalp
caber {12} *vi* **1** : to fit, to go <no sé si cabremos todos en el coche : I don't know if we'll all fit in the car> **2** : to be possible <no cabe duda alguna : there's no doubt about it> <cabe que llegue mañana : he may come tomorrow>
cabestro *nm* : halter (for an animal)
cabeza *nf* **1** : head **2 cabeza hueca** : scatterbrain **3 de ~** : head first **4 dolor de cabeza** : headache
cabezada *nf* **1** : butt, blow with the head **2** : nod <echar una cabezada : to take a nap, to doze off>
cabezal *nm* : bolster
cabezazo *nm* : butt, blow with the head
cabezón, -zona *adj, mpl* **-zones** *fam* **1** : having a big head **2** : pigheaded, stubborn
cabida *nf* **1** : room, space, capacity **2 dar cabida a** : to accomodate, to hold
cabildear *vi* : to lobby
cabildeo *nm* : lobbying
cabildero, -ra *n* : lobbyist
cabildo *nm* AYUNTAMIENTO **1** : town or city hall **2** : town or city council
cabina *nf* **1** : cabin **2** : booth **3** : cab (of a truck), cockpit (of an airplane)
cabizbajo, -ja *adj* : dejected, downcast
cable *nm* : cable
cableado *nm* : wiring
cabo *nm* **1** : end <al cabo de dos semanas : at the end of two weeks> **2** : stub, end piece **3** : corporal **4** : cape, headland <el Cabo Cañaveral : Cape Canaveral> **5 al fin y al cabo** : after all, in the end **6 llevar a cabo** : to carry out, to do
caboverdiano, -na *adj & n* : Cape Verdean
cabrá, etc. → **caber**
cabra *nf* : goat
cabrestante *nm* : windlass
cabrío, -ría *adj* : goat, caprine
cabriola *nf* **1** : skip, jump **2 hacer cabriolas** : to prance
cabriolar *vi* : to prance
cabrito *nm* : kid, baby goat
cabús *nm, pl* **cabuses** *Mex* : caboose
cacahuate *or* **cacahuete** *nm* : peanut
cacalote *nm Mex* : crow
cacao *nm* : cacao, cocoa bean
cacarear *vi* : to crow, to cackle, to cluck — *vt fam* : to boast about, to crow about <cacarear un huevo : to brag about an accomplishment>
cacatúa *nf* : cockatoo
cace, etc. → **cazar**
cacería *nf* **1** CAZA : hunt, hunting **2** : hunting party
cacerola *nf* : pan, saucepan
cacha *nf* : butt (of a gun)
cachar *vt fam* : to catch
cacharro *nm* **1** *fam* : thing, piece of junk **2** *fam* : jalopy **3 cacharros** *nmpl* : pots and pans
cache *nm* : cache, cache memory
cachear *vt* : to search, to frisk
cachemir *nm* : cashmere
cachetada *nf* BOFETADA : slap on the face
cachete *nm* : cheek
cachetear *vt* BOFETEAR : to slap
cachiporra *nf* : bludgeon, club, blackjack
cachirul *nm Mex fam* : cheating <hacer cachirul : to cheat>
cachivache *nm fam* : thing <mete tus cachivaches en el maletero : put your stuff in the trunk>
cacho *nm fam* : piece, bit
cachorro, -rra *n* **1** : cub **2** PERRITO : puppy
cachucha *nf Mex* : cap, baseball cap
cacique *nm* **1** : chief (of a tribe) **2** : boss (in politics)
cacofonía *nf* : cacophony
cacofónico, -ca *adj* : cacophonous
cacto *nm* : cactus
cactus *nm* → **cacto**
cada *adj* **1** : each <cuestan diez pesos cada una : they cost ten pesos each> **2** : every <cada vez : every time> **3** : such, some <sales con cada historia : you come up with such crazy stories> **4 cada vez más** : more and more, increasingly **5 cada vez menos** : less and less
cadalso *nm* : scaffold, gallows
cadáver *nm* : corpse, cadaver
cadavérico, -ca *adj* **1** : cadaverous **2** PÁLIDO : deathly pale
caddie *or* **caddy** *nmf, pl* **caddies** : caddy

cadena *nf* **1 :** chain **2 :** network, channel **3 cadena de montaje :** assembly line **4 cadena perpetua :** life sentence

cadencia *nf* **:** cadence, rhythm

cadencioso, -sa *adj* **:** rhythmic, rhythmical

cadera *nf* **:** hip

cadete *nmf* **:** cadet

cadmio *nm* **:** cadmium

caducar {72} *vi* **:** to expire

caducidad *nf* **:** expiration

caduco, -ca *adj* **1 :** outdated, obsolete **2 :** deciduous

caer {13} *vi* **1 :** to fall, to drop **2 :** to collapse **3 :** to hang (down) **4 caer bien** *fam* **:** to be pleasant, to be likeable <me caes bien : I like you> **5 caer mal** *or* **caer gordo** *fam* **:** to be unpleasant, to be unlikeable — **caerse** *vr* **:** to fall down

café[1] *adj* **:** brown <ojos cafés : brown eyes>

café[2] *nm* **1 :** coffee **2 :** café

cafeína *nf* **:** caffeine

cafetal *nm* **:** coffee plantation

cafetalero[1], **-ra** *adj* **:** coffee <cosecha cafetalera : coffee harvest>

cafetalero[2], **-ra** *n* **:** coffee grower

cafetera *nf* **:** coffeepot, coffeemaker

cafetería *nf* **1 :** coffee shop, café **2 :** lunchroom, cafeteria

cafetero[1], **-ra** *adj* **:** coffee-producing

cafetero[2], **-ra** *n* **:** coffee grower

cafeticultura *nf Mex* **:** coffee industry

caguama *nf* **1 :** large Caribbean turtle **2** *Mex* **:** large bottle of beer

caída *nf* **1** BAJA, DESCENSO **:** fall, drop **2 :** collapse, downfall

caiga, etc. → **caer**

caimán *nm, pl* **caimanes :** alligator, caiman

caimito *nm* **:** star apple

caja *nf* **1 :** box, case **2 :** cash register, checkout counter **3 :** bed (of a truck) **4** *fam* **:** coffin **5 caja fuerte** *or* **caja de caudales :** safe **6 caja de seguridad :** safe-deposit box **7 caja torácica :** rib cage

cajero, -ra *n* **1 :** cashier **2 :** teller **3 cajero automático :** automated teller machine, ATM

cajeta *nf Mex* **:** a sweet carmel-flavored spread

cajetilla *nf* **:** pack (of cigarettes)

cajón *nm, pl* **cajones 1 :** drawer, till **2 :** crate, case **3 cajón de estacionamiento** *Mex* **:** parking space

cajuela *nf Mex* **:** trunk (of a car)

cal *nf* **:** lime, quicklime

cala *nf* **:** cove, inlet

calabacín *nm, pl* **-cines :** zucchini

calabacita *nf Mex* **:** zucchini

calabaza *nf* **1 :** pumpkin, squash **2 :** gourd **3 dar calabazas a :** to give the brush-off to, to jilt

calabozo *nm* **1 :** prison **2 :** jail cell

calado[1], **-da** *adj* **1 :** drenched **2 :** openworked

calado[2] *nm* **1 :** draft (of a ship) **2 :** openwork

calafatear *vt* **:** to caulk

calamar *nm* **1 :** squid **2 calamares** *nmpl* **:** calamari

calambre *nm* **1** ESPASMO **:** cramp **2 :** electric shock, jolt

calamidad *nf* DESASTRE **:** calamity, disaster

calamina *nf* **:** calamine

calamitoso, -sa *adj* **:** calamitous, disastrous

calaña *nf* **:** ilk, kind, sort <una persona de mala calaña : a bad sort>

calar *vt* **1 :** to soak through **2 :** to pierce, to penetrate — *vi* **:** to catch on — **calarse** *vr* **:** to get drenched

calavera[1] *nf* **1 :** skull **2** *Mex* **:** taillight

calavera[2] *nm* **:** rake, rogue

calcar {72} *vt* **1 :** to trace **2 :** to copy, to imitate

calce, etc. → **calzar**

calceta *nf* **:** knee-high stocking

calcetería *nf* **:** hosiery

calcetín *nm, pl* **-tines :** sock

calcificar {72} *v* **:** to calcify — **calcificarse** *vr*

calcinar *vt* **:** to char, to burn

calcio *nm* **:** calcium

calco *nm* **1 :** transfer, tracing **2 :** copy, image

calcomanía *nf* **:** decal, transfer

calculador, -dora *adj* **:** calculating

calculadora *nf* **:** calculator

calcular *vt* **1 :** to calculate, to estimate **2 :** to plan, to scheme

cálculo *nm* **1 :** calculation, estimation **2 :** calculus **3 :** plan, scheme **4 cálculo biliar :** gallstone **5 hoja de cálculo :** spreadsheet

caldas *nfpl* **:** hot springs

caldear *vt* **:** to heat, to warm — **caldearse** *vr* **1 :** to heat up **2 :** to become heated, to get tense

caldera *nf* **1 :** cauldron **2 :** boiler

caldo *nm* **1** CONSOMÉ **:** broth, stock **2 caldo de cultivo :** culture medium, breeding ground

caldoso, -sa *adj* **:** watery

calefacción *nf, pl* **-ciones :** heating, heat

calefactor *nm* **:** heater

caleidoscopio *nm* → **calidoscopio**

calendario *nm* **1 :** calendar **2 :** timetable, schedule

caléndula *nf* **:** marigold

calentador *nm* **:** heater

calentamiento *nm* **1 :** heating, warming **2 :** warm-up (in sports)

calentar {55} *vt* **1 :** to heat, to warm **2** *fam* **:** to annoy, to anger **3** *fam* **:** to excite, to turn on — **calentarse** *vr* **1 :** to get warm, to heat up **2 :** to warm up (in sports) **3** *fam* **:** to become sexually aroused **4** *fam* **:** to get mad

calentura *nf* **1** FIEBRE **:** temperature, fever **2 :** cold sore

calibrador *nm* **:** gauge, calipers *pl*

calibrar *vt* : to calibrate — **calibración** *nf*
calibre *nm* **1** : caliber, gauge **2** : importance, excellence **3** : kind, sort <un problema de grueso calibre : a serious problem>
calidad *nf* **1** : quality, grade **2** : position, status **3 en calidad de** : as, in the capacity of
cálido, -da *adj* **1** : hot <un clima cálido : a hot climate> **2** : warm <una cálida bienvenida : a warm welcome>
calidoscopio *nm* : kaleidoscope
caliente *adj* **1** : hot, warm <mantenerse caliente : to stay warm> **2** : heated, fiery <una disputa caliente : a heated argument> **3** *fam* : sexually excited, horny
califa *nm* : caliph
calificación *nf, pl* **-ciones 1** NOTA : grade (for a course) **2** : rating, score **3** CLASIFICACIÓN : qualification, qualifying <ronda de calificación : qualifying round>
calificar {72} *vt* **1** : to grade **2** : to describe, to rate <la calificaron de buena alumna : they described her as a good student> **3** : to qualify, to modify (in grammar)
calificativo[1], -va *adj* : qualifying
calificativo[2] *nm* : qualifier, epithet
caligrafía *nf* **1** ESCRITURA : handwriting **2** : calligraphy
calistenia *nf* : calisthenics
cáliz *nm, pl* **cálices 1** : chalice, goblet **2** : calyx
caliza *nf* : limestone
callado, -da *adj* : quiet, silent — **calladamente** *adv*
callar *vi* : to keep quiet, to be silent — *vt* **1** : to silence, to hush <¡calla a los niños! : keep the children quiet!> **2** : to keep secret — **callarse** *vr* : to remain silent <¡cállate! : be quiet!, shut up!>
calle *nf* : street, road
callejear *vi* : to wander about the streets, to hang out
callejero, -ra *adj* : street <perro callejero : stray dog>
callejón *nm, pl* **-jones 1** : alley **2 callejón sin salida** : dead-end street
callo *nm* : callus, corn
calloso, -sa *adj* : callous
calma *nf* : calm, quiet
calmante[1] *adj* : calming, soothing
calmante[2] *nm* : tranquilizer, sedative
calmar *vt* TRANQUILIZAR : to calm, to soothe — **calmarse** *vr* : to calm down
calmo, -ma *adj* TRANQUILO : calm, tranquil
calmoso, -sa *adj* **1** TRANQUILO : calm, quiet **2** LENTO : slow, sluggish
calor *nm* **1** : heat <hace calor : it's hot outside> <tener calor : to feel hot> **2** : warmth, affection **3** : ardor, passion
caloría *nf* : calorie
calórico, -ca *adj* : caloric
calque, etc. → **calcar**
calumnia *nf* : slander, libel — **calumnioso, -sa** *adj*
calumniar *vt* : to slander, to libel
caluroso, -sa *adj* **1** : hot **2** : warm, enthusiastic
calva *nf* : bald spot, bald head
calvario *nm* **1** : Calvary **2** : Stations of the Cross *pl* **3 vivir un calvario** : to suffer great adversity
calvicie *nf* : baldness
calvo[1], -va *adj* : bald
calvo[2], -va *n* : bald person
calza *nf* : block, wedge
calzada *nf* : roadway, avenue
calzado *nm* : footwear
calzador *nm* : shoehorn
calzar {21} *vt* **1** : to wear (shoes) <¿de cuál calza? : what is your shoe size?> <siempre calzaban tenis : they always wore sneakers> **2** : to provide with shoes
calzo *nm* : chock, wedge
calzoncillos *nmpl* : underpants, briefs
calzones *nmpl* : underpants, panties
cama *nf* **1** : bed **2 cama elástica** : trampoline
camada *nf* : litter, brood
camafeo *nm* : cameo
camaleón *nm, pl* **-leones** : chameleon
cámara *nf* **1** : camera **2** : chamber, room **3** : house (in government) **4** : inner tube
camarada *nmf* **1** : comrade, companion **2** : colleague
camaradería *nf* : camaraderie
camarero, -ra *n* **1** MESERO : waiter, waitress *f* **2** : bellboy *m*, chambermaid *f* (in a hotel) **3** : steward *m*, stewardess *f* (on a ship, etc.)
camarilla *nf* : political clique
camarógrafo, -fa *n* : cameraman *m*, camerawoman *f*
camarón *nm, pl* **-rones 1** : shrimp **2** : prawn
camarote *nm* : cabin, stateroom
camastro *nm* : small hard bed, pallet
cambalache *nm fam* : swap
cambiante *adj* **1** : changing **2** VARIABLE : changeable, variable
cambiar *vt* **1** ALTERAR, MODIFICAR : to change **2** : to exchange, to trade — *vi* **1** : to change **2 cambiar de velocidad** : to shift gears — **cambiarse** *vr* **1** : to change (clothing) **2** MUDARSE : to move (to a new address)
cambio *nm* **1** : change, alteration **2** : exchange **3** : change (money) **4 en cambio** : instead **5 en cambio** : however, on the other hand
cambista *nmf* : exchange broker
camboyano, -na *adj & n* : Cambodian
cambur *nm Ven* : banana
camelia *nf* : camellia
camello *nm* : camel
camellón *nm, pl* **-llones** *Mex* : traffic island
camerino *nm* : dressing room
camerunés, -nesa *adj, mpl* **-neses** : Cameroonian

camilla *nf* : stretcher
camillero, -ra *n* : orderly (in a hospital)
caminante *nmf* : wayfarer, walker
caminar *vi* ANDAR : to walk, to move — *vt* : to walk, to cover (a distance)
caminata *nf* : hike, long walk
camino *nm* **1** : path, road **2** : journey <ponerse en camino : to set off> **3** : way <a medio camino : halfway there>
camión *nm, pl* **camiones 1** : truck **2** *Mex* : bus
camionero, -ra *n* **1** : truck driver **2** *Mex* : bus driver
camioneta *nm* : light truck, van
camisa *nf* **1** : shirt **2 camisa de fuerza** : straitjacket
camiseta *nf* **1** : T-shirt **2** : undershirt
camisón *nm, pl* **-sones** : nightshirt, nightgown
camorra *nf fam* : fight, trouble <buscar camorra : to pick a fight>
camote *nm* **1** : root vegetable similar to the sweet potato **2 hacerse camote** *Mex fam* : to get mixed up
campal *adj* : pitched, fierce <batalla campal : pitched battle>
campamento *nm* : camp
campana *nf* : bell
campanada *nf* TAÑIDO : stroke (of a bell), peal
campanario *nm* : bell tower, belfry
campanilla *nf* **1** : small bell, handbell **2** : uvula
campante *adj* : nonchalant, smug <seguir tan campante : to go on as if nothing had happened>
campaña *nf* **1** CAMPO : countryside, country **2** : campaign **3 tienda de campaña** : tent
campañol *nm* : vole
campechana *nf Mex* : puff pastry
campechanía *nf* : geniality
campechano, -na *adj* : open, cordial, friendly
campeón, -peona *n, mpl* **-peones** : champion
campeonato *nm* : championship
cámper *nm* : camper (vehicle)
campero, -ra *adj* : country, rural
campesino, -na *n* : peasant, farm laborer
campestre *adj* : rural, rustic
camping *nm* **1** : camping **2** : campsite
campiña *nf* CAMPO : countryside, country
campista *nmf* : camper
campo *nm* **1** CAMPAÑA : countryside, country **2** : field <campo de aviación : airfield> <su campo de responsabilidad : her field of responsibility>
camposanto *nm* : graveyard, cemetery
campus *nms & pl* : campus
camuflaje *nm* : camouflage
camuflajear *vt* : to camouflage
camuflar → **camuflajear**
can *nm* : hound, dog
cana *nf* **1** : gray hair **2 salirle canas** : to go gray, to get gray hair **3 echar una cana al aire** : to let one's hair down
canadiense *adj & nmf* : Canadian
canal[1] *nm* **1** : canal **2** : channel
canal[2] *nmf* : gutter, groove
canalé *nm* : rib, ribbing (in fabric)
canaleta *nf* : gutter
canalete *nm* : paddle
canalizar {21} *vt* : to channel
canalla[1] *adj fam* : low, rotten
canalla[2] *nmf fam* : bastard, swine
canapé *nm* **1** : hors d'oeuvre, canapé **2** SOFÁ : couch, sofa
canario[1], **-ria** *adj* : of or from the Canary Islands
canario[2], **-ria** *n* : Canarian, Canary Islander
canario[3] *nm* : canary
canasta *nf* **1** : basket **2** : canasta (card game)
cancel *nm* **1** : sliding door **2** : partition
cancelación *nf, pl* **-ciones 1** : cancellation **2** : payment in full
cancelar *vt* **1** : to cancel **2** : to pay off, to settle
cáncer *nm* : cancer
Cáncer *nmf* : Cancer
cancerígeno[1], **-na** *adj* : carcinogenic
cancerígeno[2] *nm* : carcinogen
canceroso, -sa *adj* : cancerous
cancha *nf* : court, field (for sports)
canciller *nm* : chancellor
cancillería *nf* : chancellery, ministry
canción *nf, pl* **canciones 1** : song **2 canción de cuna** : lullaby
cancionero[1] *nm* : songbook
cancionero[2], **-ra** *n Mex* : songster, songstress *f*
candado *nm* : padlock
candela *nf* **1** : flame, fire **2** : candle
candelabro *nm* : candelabra
candelero *nm* **1** : candlestick **2 estar en el candelero** : to be the center of attention
candente *adj* : red-hot
candidato, -ta *n* : candidate, applicant
candidatura *nf* : candidacy
candidez *nf* **1** : simplicity **2** INGENUIDAD : naïveté, ingenuousness
cándido, -da *adj* **1** : simple, unassuming **2** INGENUO : naive, ingenuous
candil *nm* : oil lamp
candilejas *nfpl* : footlights
candor *nm* : naïveté, innocence
candoroso, -sa *adj* : naive, innocent
canela *nf* : cinnamon
canesú *nm* : yoke (of clothing)
cangrejo *nm* JAIBA : crab
canguro *nm* **1** : kangaroo **2 hacer de canguro** *Spain* : to baby-sit
caníbal[1] *adj* : cannibalistic
caníbal[2] *nmf* ANTROPÓFAGO : cannibal
canibalismo *nm* ANTROPOFAGIA : cannibalism
canibalizar {21} *vt* : to cannibalize
canica *nf* **1** : marble **2 canicas** *nfpl* : marbles (toys)
caniche *nm* : poodle

canijo, -ja *adj* **1** *fam* : puny, weak **2** *Mex fam* : tough, hard <un examen muy canijo : a very tough exam>
canilla *nf* **1** : shin, shinbone **2** *Arg, Uru* : faucet
canino[1], -na *adj* : canine
canino[2] *nm* **1** COLMILLO : canine (tooth) **2** : dog, canine
canje *nm* INTERCAMBIO : exchange, trade
canjear *vt* INTERCAMBIAR : to exchange, to trade
cannabis *nm* : cannabis
cano, -na *adj* : gray <un hombre de pelo cano : a gray-haired man>
canoa *nf* : canoe
canon *nm, pl* **cánones** : canon
canónico, -ca *adj* **1** : canonical **2 derecho canónico** : canon law
canonizar {21} *vt* : to canonize — **canonización** *nf*
canoso, -sa → **cano**
cansado, -da *adj* **1** : tired <estar cansado : to be tired> **2** : tiresome, wearying <ser cansado : to be tiring>
cansancio *nm* FATIGA : fatigue, weariness
cansar *vt* FATIGAR : to wear out, to tire — *vi* : to be tiresome — **cansarse** *vr* **1** : to wear oneself out **2** : to get bored
cansino, -na *adj* : slow, weary, lethargic
cantaleta *nf fam* : nagging <la misma cantaleta : the same old story>
cantalupo *nm* : cantaloupe
cantante *nmf* : singer
cantar[1] *v* : to sing
cantar[2] *nm* : song, ballad
cántaro *nm* **1** : pitcher, jug **2 llover a cántaros** *fam* : to rain cats and dogs
cantata *nf* : cantata
cantera *nf* : quarry <cantera de piedra : stone quarry>
cántico *nm* : canticle, chant
cantidad[1] *adv fam* : really <ese carro me costó cantidad : that car cost me plenty>
cantidad[2] *nf* **1** : quantity **2** : sum, amount (of money) **3** *fam* : a lot, a great many <había cantidad de niños en el parque : there were tons of kids in the park>
cantimplora *nf* : canteen, water bottle
cantina *nf* **1** : tavern, bar **2** : canteen, mess, dining quarters *pl*
cantinero, -ra *n* : bartender
canto *nm* **1** : singing **2** : chant <canto gregoriano : Gregorian chant> **3** : song (of a bird) **4** : edge, end <de canto : on end, sideways> **5 canto rodado** : boulder
cantón *nm, pl* **cantones 1** : canton **2** *Mex fam* : place, home
cantor[1], -tora *adj* **1** : singing **2 pájaro cantor** : songbird
cantor[2], -tora *n* **1** : singer **2** : cantor
caña *nf* **1** : cane <caña de azúcar : sugarcane> **2** : reed **3 caña de pescar** : fishing rod **4 caña del timón** : tiller (of a boat)
cañada *nf* : ravine, gully
cáñamo *nm* : hemp
cañaveral *nm* : sugarcane field
cañería *nf* TUBERÍA : pipes *pl*, piping
caño *nm* **1** : pipe **2** : spout **3** : channel (for navigation)
cañón *nm, pl* **cañones 1** : cannon **2** : barrel (of a gun) **3** : canyon
cañonear *vt* : to shell, to bombard
cañoneo *nm* : shelling, bombardment
cañonero *nm* : gunboat
caoba *nf* : mahogany
caos *nm* : chaos
caótico, -ca *adj* : chaotic
capa *nf* **1** : cape, cloak **2** : coating **3** : layer, stratum **4** : (social) class, stratum
capacidad *nf* **1** : capacity **2** : capability, ability
capacitación *nf, pl* **-ciones** : training
capacitar *vt* : to train, to qualify
caparazón *nm, pl* **-zones** : shell, carapace
capataz *nmf, pl* **-taces** : foreman *m*, forewoman *f*
capaz *adj, pl* **capaces 1** APTO : capable, able **2** COMPETENTE : competent **3** : spacious <capaz para : with room for>
capcioso, -sa *adj* : cunning, deceptive <pregunta capciosa : trick question>
capea *nf* : amateur bullfight
capear *vt* **1** : to make a pass with the cape (in bullfighting) **2** : to dodge, to weather <capear el temporal : to ride out the storm>
capellán *nm, pl* **-llanes** : chaplain
capilar *nm* : capillary — **capilar** *adj*
capilla *nf* : chapel
capirotada *nf Mex* : traditional bread pudding
capirotazo *nm* : flip, flick
capital[1] *adj* **1** : capital **2** : chief, principal
capital[2] *nm* : capital <capital de riesgo : venture capital>
capital[3] *nf* : capital, capital city
capitalino[1], -na *adj* : of or from a capital city
capitalino[2], -na *n* : inhabitant of a capital city
capitalismo *nm* : capitalism
capitalista *adj & nmf* : capitalist
capitalizar {21} *vt* : to capitalize — **capitalización** *nf*
capitán, -tana *n, mpl* **-tanes** : captain
capitanear *vt* : to captain, to command
capitanía *nf* : captaincy
capitel *nm* : capital (of a column)
capitolio *nm* : capitol
capitulación *nf, pl* **-ciones** : capitulation
capitular *vi* : to capitulate, to surrender
capítulo *nm* **1** : chapter, section **2** : matter, subject
capó *nm* : hood (of a car)
capón *nm, pl* **capones** : capon

caporal *nm* **1 :** chief, leader **2 :** foreman (on a ranch)

capota *nf* **:** top (of a convertible)

capote *nm* **1 :** cloak, overcoat **2 :** bullfighter's cape **3** *Mex* COFRE **:** hood (of a car)

capricho *nm* ANTOJO **:** whim, caprice

caprichoso, -sa *adj* ANTOJADIZO **:** capricious, fickle

Capricornio *nmf* **:** Capricorn

cápsula *nf* **:** capsule

captar *vt* **1 :** to catch, to grasp **2 :** to gain, to attract **3 :** to harness, to collect (waters)

captor, -tora *n* **:** captor

captura *nf* **:** capture, seizure

capturar *vt* **:** to capture, to seize

capucha *nf* **:** hood, cowl

capuchina *nf* **:** nasturtium

capuchino *nm* **1 :** Capuchin (monk) **2 :** capuchin (monkey) **3 :** cappuccino

capullo *nm* **1 :** cocoon **2 :** bud (of a flower)

caqui *adj & nm* **:** khaki

cara *nf* **1 :** face **2** ASPECTO **:** look, appearance <¡qué buena cara tiene ese pastel! : that cake looks delicious!> **3** *fam* **:** nerve, gall **4 ~ a** *or* **de cara a :** facing **5 de cara a :** in view of, in the light of

carabina *nf* **:** carbine

caracol *nm* **1 :** snail **2** CONCHA **:** conch, seashell **3 :** cochlea **4 :** ringlet

caracola *nf* **:** conch

carácter *nm, pl* **caracteres 1** ÍNDOLE **:** character, kind, nature **2** TEMPERAMENTO **:** disposition, temperament **3 :** letter, symbol <caracteres chinos : Chinese characters>

característica *nf* RASGO **:** trait, feature, characteristic

característico, -ca *adj* **:** characteristic — **característicamente** *adv*

caracterizar {21} *vt* **:** to characterize — **caracterización** *nf*

caramba *interj* **:** darn!, heck!

carámbano *nm* **:** icicle

carambola *nf* **1 :** carom **2 :** ruse, trick <por carambola : by a lucky chance>

caramelo *nm* **1 :** caramel **2** DULCE **:** candy

caramillo *nm* **1 :** pipe, small flute **2 :** heap, pile

caraqueño[1], **-ña** *adj* **:** of or from Caracas

caraqueño[2], **-ña** *n* **:** person from Caracas

carátula *nf* **1 :** title page **2 :** cover, dust jacket **3** CARETA **:** mask **4** *Mex* **:** face, dial (of a clock or watch)

caravana *nf* **1 :** caravan **2 :** convoy, motorcade **3** REMOLQUE **:** trailer

caray → **caramba**

carbohidrato *nm* **:** carbohydrate

carbón *nm, pl* **carbones 1 :** coal **2 :** charcoal

carbonatado, -da *adj* **:** carbonated

carbonato *nm* **:** carbonate

carboncillo *nm* **:** charcoal

carbonera *nf* **:** coal cellar, coal bunker (on a ship)

carbonero, -ra *adj* **:** coal

carbonizar {21} *vt* **:** to carbonize, to char

carbono *nm* **:** carbon

carbunco *or* **carbunclo** *nm* **:** carbuncle

carburador *nm* **:** carburetor

carca *nmf fam* **:** old fogy

carcacha *nf fam* **:** jalopy, wreck

carcaj *nm* **:** quiver (for arrows)

carcajada *nf* **:** loud laugh, guffaw <reírse a carcajadas : to roar with laughter>

carcajearse *vr* **:** to roar with laughter, to be in stitches

cárcel *nf* PRISIÓN **:** jail, prison

carcelero, -ra *n* **:** jailer

carcinogénico, -ca *adj* **:** carcinogenic

carcinógeno *nm* CANCERÍGENO **:** carcinogen

carcinoma *nm* **:** carcinoma

carcomer *vt* **:** to eat away at, to consume

carcomido, -da *adj* **1 :** worm-eaten **2 :** decayed, rotten

cardán *nm, pl* **cardanes :** universal joint

cardar *vt* **:** to card, to comb

cardenal *nm* **1 :** cardinal (in religion) **2 :** bruise

cardíaco *or* **cardiaco, -ca** *adj* **:** cardiac, heart

cárdigan *nm, pl* **-gans :** cardigan

cardinal *adj* **:** cardinal

cardiología *nf* **:** cardiology

cardiólogo, -ga *n* **:** cardiologist

cardiovascular *adj* **:** cardiovascular

cardo *nm* **:** thistle

cardumen *nm* **:** school of fish

carear *vt* **:** to bring face-to-face

carecer {53} *vi* **~ de :** to lack <el cheque carecía de fondos : the check lacked funds>

carencia *nf* **1** FALTA **:** lack **2** ESCASEZ **:** shortage **3** DEFICIENCIA **:** deficiency

carente *adj* **~ de :** lacking (in)

carero, -ra *adj fam* **:** pricey

carestía *nf* **1 :** rise in cost <la carestía de la vida : the high cost of living> **2 :** dearth, scarcity

careta *nf* MÁSCARA **:** mask

carey *nm* **1 :** hawksbill turtle, sea turtle **2 :** tortoiseshell

carga *nf* **1 :** loading **2 :** freight, load, cargo **3 :** burden, responsibility **4 :** charge <carga eléctrica : electrical charge> **5 :** attack, charge

cargado, -da *adj* **1 :** loaded **2 :** bogged down, weighted down **3 :** close, stuffy **4 :** charged <cargado de tensión : charged with tension> **5** FUERTE **:** strong <café cargado : strong coffee> **6 cargado de hombros :** stoop-shouldered

cargador[1], **-dora** *n* **:** longshoreman *m*, longshorewoman *f*

cargador² *nm* **1 :** magazine (for a firearm) **2 :** charger (for batteries)
cargamento *nm* **:** cargo, load
cargar {52} *vt* **1 :** to carry **2 :** to load, to fill **3 :** to charge — *vi* **1 :** to load **2 :** to rest (in architecture) **3 ~ sobre :** to fall upon
cargo *nm* **1 :** burden, load **2 :** charge <a cargo de : in charge of> **3 :** position, office
cargue, etc. → **cargar**
carguero¹, -ra *adj* **:** freight, cargo <tren carguero : freight train>
carguero² *nm* **:** freighter, cargo ship
cariarse *vr* **:** to decay (of teeth)
caribe *adj* **:** Caribbean <el mar caribe : the Caribbean Sea>
caribeño, -ña *adj* **:** Caribbean
caribú *nm* **:** caribou
caricatura *nf* **1 :** caricature **2 :** cartoon
caricaturista *nmf* **:** caricaturist, cartoonist
caricaturizar {21} *vt* **:** to caricature
caricia *nf* **1 :** caress **2 hacer caricias :** to pet, to stroke
caridad *nf* **1 :** charity **2** LIMOSNA **:** alms *pl*
caries *nfs & pl* **:** cavity (in a tooth)
carillón *nm, pl* **-llones 1 :** carillon **2 :** glockenspiel
cariño *nm* AFECTO **:** affection, love
cariñoso, -sa *adj* AFECTUOSO **:** affectionate, loving — **cariñosamente** *adv*
carioca¹ *adj* **:** of or from Rio de Janeiro
carioca² *nmf* **:** person from Rio de Janeiro
carisma *nf* **:** charisma
carismático, -ca *adj* **:** charismatic
carita *adj Mex fam* **:** cute (said of a man) <tu primo se cree muy carita : your cousin thinks he's gorgeous>
caritativo, -va *adj* **:** charitable
cariz *nm, pl* **carices :** appearance, aspect
carmesí *adj & nm* **:** crimson
carmín *nm, pl* **carmines 1 :** carmine **2 carmín de labios :** lipstick
carnada *nf* CEBO **:** bait
carnal *adj* **1 :** carnal **2 primo carnal :** first cousin
carnaval *nm* **:** carnival
carnaza *nf* **:** bait
carne *nf* **1 :** meat <carne molida : ground beef> **2 :** flesh <carne de gallina : goose bumps>
carné *nm* → **carnet**
carnero *nm* **1 :** ram, sheep **2 :** mutton
carnet *nm* **1 :** identification card, ID **2 :** membership card **3 carnet de conducir** *Spain* **:** driver's license
carnicería *nf* **1 :** butcher shop **2** MATANZA **:** slaughter, carnage
carnicero, -ra *n* **:** butcher
carnívoro¹, -ra *adj* **:** carnivorous
carnívoro² *nm* **:** carnivore
carnoso, -sa *adj* **:** fleshy, meaty
caro¹ *adv* **:** dearly, a lot <pagué caro : I paid a high price>
caro², -ra *adj* **1 :** expensive, dear **2** QUERIDO **:** dear, beloved
carpa *nf* **1 :** carp **2 :** big top (of a circus) **3 :** tent
carpelo *nm* **:** carpel
carpeta *nf* **:** folder, binder, portfolio (of drawings, etc.)
carpetazo *nm* **dar carpetazo a :** to shelve, to defer
carpintería *nf* **1 :** carpentry **2 :** carpenter's workshop
carpintero, -ra *n* **:** carpenter
carraspear *vi* **:** to clear one's throat
carraspera *nf* **:** hoarseness <tener carraspera : to have a frog in one's throat>
carrera *nf* **1 :** run, running <a la carrera : at full speed> <de carrera : hastily> **2 :** race **3 :** course of study **4 :** career, profession **5 :** run (in baseball)
carreta *nf* **:** cart, wagon
carrete *nm* **1** BOBINA **:** reel, spool **2 :** roll of film
carretel *nm* → **carrete**
carretera *nf* **:** highway, road <carretera de peaje : turnpike>
carretero, -ra *adj* **:** highway <el sistema carretero nacional : the national highway system>
carretilla *nf* **1 :** wheelbarrow **2 carretilla elevadora :** forklift
carril *nm* **1 :** lane <carretera de doble carril : two-lane highway> **2 :** rail (on a railroad track)
carrillo *nm* **:** cheek, jowl
carrito *nm* **:** cart <carrito de compras : shopping cart>
carrizo *nm* JUNCO **:** reed
carro *nm* **1** COCHE **:** car **2 :** cart **3** *Chile, Mex* **:** coach (of a train) **4 carro alegórico :** float (in a parade)
carrocería *nf* **:** bodywork
carroña *nf* **:** carrion
carroñero, -ra *n* **:** scavenger (animal)
carroza *nf* **1 :** carriage **2 :** float (in a parade)
carruaje *nm* **:** carriage
carrusel *nm* **1 :** merry-go-round **2 :** carousel <carrusel de equipaje : luggage carousel>
carta *nf* **1 :** letter **2** NAIPE **:** playing card **3 :** charter, constitution **4** MENÚ **:** menu **5 :** map, chart **6 tomar cartas en :** to intervene in
cártamo *nm* **:** safflower
cartearse *vr* ESCRIBIRSE **:** to write to one another, to correspond
cartel *nm* **:** sign, poster
cártel *or* **cartel** *nm* **:** cartel
cartelera *nf* **1 :** billboard **2 :** marquee
cartera *nf* **1** BILLETERA **:** wallet, billfold **2** BOLSO **:** pocketbook, purse **3 :** portfolio <cartera de acciones : stock portfolio>
carterista *nmf* **:** pickpocket
cartero, -ra *n* **:** letter carrier, mailman *m*

cartilaginoso, -sa *adj* : cartilaginous, gristly
cartílago *nm* : cartilage
cartilla *nf* **1** : primer, reader **2** : booklet <cartilla de ahorros : bankbook>
cartografía *nf* : cartography
cartógrafo, -fa *n* : cartographer
cartón *nm, pl* **cartones 1** : cardboard <cartón madera : fiberboard> **2** : carton
cartucho *nm* : cartridge
cartulina *nf* : poster board, cardboard
carúncula *nf* : wattle (of a bird)
casa *nf* **1** : house, building **2** HOGAR : home **3** : household, family **4** : company, firm **5 echar la casa por la ventana** : to spare no expense
casaca *nf* : jacket
casado¹, -da *adj* : married
casado², -da *n* : married person
casamentero, -ra *n* : matchmaker
casamiento *nm* **1** : marriage **2** BODA : wedding
casar *vt* : to marry — *vi* : to go together, to match up — **casarse** *vr* **1** : to get married **2 ~ con** : to marry
casateniente *nmf Mex* : landlord, landlady *f*
cascabel¹ *nm* : small bell
cascabel² *nf* : rattlesnake
cascada *nf* CATARATA, SALTO : waterfall, cascade
cascajo *nm* **1** : pebble, rock fragment **2** *fam* : piece of junk
cascanueces *nms & pl* : nutcracker
cascar {72} *vt* : to crack (a shell) — **cascarse** *vr* : to crack, to chip
cáscara *nf* **1** : skin, peel, rind, husk **2** : shell (of a nut or egg)
cascarón *nm, pl* **-rones 1** : eggshell **2** *Mex* : shell filled with confetti
cascarrabias *nmfs & pl fam* : grouch, crab
casco *nm* **1** : helmet **2** : hull **3** : hoof **4** : fragment, shard **5** : center (of a town) **6** *Mex* : empty bottle **7 cascos** *nmpl* : headphones
caserío *nm* **1** : country house **2** : hamlet
casero¹, -ra *adj* **1** : domestic, household **2** : homemade
casero², -ra *n* DUEÑO : landlord *m,* landlady *f*
caseta *nf* : booth, stand, stall <caseta telefónica : telephone booth>
casete *nmf* → **cassette**
casi *adv* **1** : almost, nearly, virtually **2** (*in negative phrases*) : hardly <casi nunca : hardly ever>
casilla *nf* **1** : booth **2** : pigeonhole **3** : box (on a form)
casino *nm* **1** : casino **2** : (social) club
caso *nm* **1** : case **2 en caso de** : in case of, in the event of **3 hacer caso de** : to pay attention to, to notice **4 hacer caso omiso de** : to ignore, to take no notice of **5 no venir al caso** : to be beside the point
caspa *nf* : dandruff
casque, etc. → **cascar**
casquete *nm* **1** : skullcap **2 casquete glaciar** : ice cap **3 casquete corto** *Mex* : crew cut
cassette *nmf* : cassette
casta *nf* **1** : caste **2** : lineage, stock <de casta : thoroughbred, purebred> **3 sacar la casta** *Mex* : to come out ahead
castaña *nf* : chestnut
castañetear *vi* : to chatter (of teeth)
castaño¹, -ña *adj* : chestnut, brown
castaño², -ña *nm* **1** : chestnut tree **2** : chestnut, brown
castañuela *nf* : castanet
castellano¹, -na *adj & n* : Castilian
castellano² *nm* ESPAÑOL : Spanish, Castilian (language)
castidad *nf* : chastity
castigar {52} *vt* : to punish
castigo *nm* : punishment
castillo *nm* **1** : castle **2 castillo de proa** : forecastle
casto, -ta *adj* : chaste, pure — **castamente** *adv*
castor *nm* : beaver
castración *nf, pl* **-ciones** : castration
castrar *vt* **1** : to castrate, to spay, to neuter, to geld **2** DEBILITAR : to weaken, to debilitate
castrense *adj* : military
casual *adj* **1** FORTUITO : fortuitous, accidental **2** *Mex* : casual (of clothing)
casualidad *nf* **1** : chance **2 por ~** *or* **de ~** : by chance, by any chance
casualmente *adv* : accidentally, by chance
casucha *or* **casuca** *nf* : shanty, hovel
cataclismo *nm* : cataclysm
catacumbas *nfpl* : catacombs
catador, -dora *n* : wine taster
catalán¹, -lana *adj & n, mpl* **-lanes** : Catalan
catalán² *nm* : Catalan (language)
catálisis *nm* : catalysis
catalítico, -ca *adj* : catalytic
catalizador *nm* **1** : catalyst **2** : catalytic converter
catalogar {52} *vt* : to catalog, to classify
catálogo *nm* : catalog
catamarán *nm, pl* **-ranes** : catamaran
cataplasma *nf* : poultice
catapulta *nf* : catapult
catapultar *vt* : to catapult
catar *vt* **1** : to taste, to sample **2** : to look at, to examine
catarata *nf* **1** CASCADA, SALTO : waterfall **2** : cataract
catarro *nm* RESFRIADO : cold, catarrh
catarsis *nf* : catharsis
catártico, -ca *adj* : cathartic
catástrofe *nf* DESASTRE : catastrophe, disaster
catastrófico, -ca *adj* DESASTROSO : catastrophic, disastrous
catcher *nmf* : catcher (in baseball)
catecismo *nm* : catechism

cátedra *nf* **1** : chair, professorship **2** : subject, class **3 libertad de cátedra** : academic freedom
catedral *nf* : cathedral
catedrático, -ca *n* PROFESOR : professor
categoría *nf* **1** CLASE : category **2** RANGO : rank, standing **3 categoría gramatical** : part of speech **4 de ~** : first-rate, outstanding
categórico, -ca *adj* : categorical, unequivocal — **categóricamente** *adv*
catéter *nm* : catheter
cátodo *nm* : cathode
catolicismo *nm* : Catholicism
católico, -ca *adj & n* : Catholic
catorce *adj & nm* : fourteen
catorceavo *nm* : fourteenth
catre *nm* : cot
catsup *nm* : ketchup
caucásico, -ca *adj & n* : Caucasian
cauce *nm* **1** LECHO : riverbed **2** : means *pl,* channel
caucho *nm* **1** GOMA : rubber **2** : rubber tree **3** *Ven* : tire
caución *nf, pl* **cauciones** FIANZA : bail, security
caudal *nm* **1** : volume of water **2** RIQUEZA : capital, wealth **3** ABUNDANCIA : abundance
caudillaje *nm* : leadership
caudillo *nm* : leader, commander
causa *nf* **1** MOTIVO : cause, reason, motive <a causa de : because of> **2** IDEAL : cause <morir por una causa : to die for a cause> **3** : lawsuit
causal[1] *adj* : causal
causal[2] *nm* : cause, grounds *pl*
causalidad *nf* : causality
causante[1] *adj* **~ de** : causing, responsible for
causante[2] *nmf Mex* : taxpayer
causar *vt* **1** : to cause **2** : to provoke, to arouse <eso me causa gracia : that strikes me as being funny>
cáustico, -ca *adj* : caustic
cautela *nf* : caution, prudence
cautelar *adj* : precautionary, preventive
cauteloso, -sa *adj* : cautious, prudent — **cautelosamente** *adv*
cauterizar {21} *vt* : to cauterize
cautivador, -dora *adj* : captivating
cautivar *vt* HECHIZAR : to captivate, to charm
cautiverio *nm* : captivity
cautivo, -va *adj & n* : captive
cauto, -ta *adj* : cautious, careful
cavar *vt* : to dig — *vi* **~ en** : to delve into, to probe
caverna *nf* : cavern, cave
cavernoso, -sa *adj* **1** : cavernous **2** : deep, resounding
caviar *nm* : caviar
cavidad *nf* : cavity
cavilar *vi* : to ponder, to deliberate
cayado *nm* : crook, staff, crosier
cayena *nf* : cayenne pepper
cayó, etc. → **caer**
caza[1] *nf* **1** CACERÍA : hunt, hunting **2** : game
caza[2] *nm* : fighter plane
cazador, -dora *n* **1** : hunter **2 cazador furtivo** : poacher
cazar {21} *vt* **1** : to hunt **2** : to catch, to bag **3** *fam* : to land (a job, a spouse) — *vi* : to go hunting
cazatalentos *nmfs & pl* : talent scout
cazo *nm* **1** : saucepan, pot **2** CUCHARÓN : ladle
cazuela *nf* **1** : pan, saucepan **2** : casserole
cazurro, -ra *adj* : sullen, surly
CD *nm* : CD, compact disk
cebada *nf* : barley
cebar *vt* **1** : to bait **2** : to feed, to fatten **3** : to prime (a pump, etc.) — **cebarse** *vr* **~ en** : to take it out on
cebo *nm* **1** CARNADA : bait **2** : feed **3** : primer (for firearms)
cebolla *nf* : onion
cebolleta *nf* : scallion, green onion
cebollino *nm* **1** : chive **2** : scallion
cebra *nf* : zebra
cebú *nm, pl* **cebús** *or* **cebúes** : zebu (cattle)
cecear *vi* : to lisp
ceceo *nm* : lisp
cecina *nf* : dried beef, beef jerky
cedazo *nm* : sieve
ceder *vi* **1** : to yield, to give way **2** : to diminish, to abate **3** : to give in, to relent — *vt* : to cede, to hand over
cedro *nm* : cedar
cédula *nf* : document, certificate
céfiro *nm* : zephyr
cegador, -dora *adj* : blinding
cegar {49} *vt* **1** : to blind **2** : to block, to stop up — *vi* : to be blinded, to go blind
cegatón, -tona *adj, mpl* **-tones** *fam* : blind as a bat
ceguera *nf* : blindness
ceiba *nf* : ceiba, silk-cotton tree
ceja *nf* **1** : eyebrow <fruncir las cejas : to knit one's brows> **2** : flange, rim
cejar *vi* : to give in, to back down
celada *nf* : trap, ambush
celador, -dora *n* GUARDIA : guard, warden
celda *nf* : cell (of a jail)
celebración *nf, pl* **-ciones** : celebration
celebrado, -da *adj* CÉLEBRE, FAMOSO : famous, celebrated
celebrante *nmf* OFICIANTE : celebrant
celebrar *vt* **1** FESTEJAR : to celebrate **2** : to hold (a meeting) **3** : to say (Mass) **4** : to welcome, to be happy about — *vi* : to be glad — **celebrarse** *vr* **1** : to be celebrated, to fall **2** : to be held, to take place
célebre *adj* CELEBRADO, FAMOSO : celebrated, famous
celebridad *nf* **1** : celebrity **2** FAMA : fame, renown
celeridad *nf* : celerity, swiftness
celeste[1] *adj* **1** : celestial **2** : sky blue, azure

celeste[2] *nm* : sky blue

celestial *adj* : heavenly, celestial

celibato *nm* : celibacy

célibe *adj & nmf* : celibate

cello *nm* : cello

celo *nm* **1** : zeal, fervor **2** : heat (of females), rut (of males) **3 celos** *nmpl* : jealousy <tenerle celos a alguien : to be jealous of someone>

celofán *nm, pl* **-fanes** : cellophane

celosía *nf* **1** : lattice window **2** : latticework, trellis

celoso, -sa *adj* **1** : jealous **2** : zealous — **celosamente** *adv*

celta[1] *adj* : Celtic

celta[2] *nmf* : Celt

célula *nf* : cell

celular *adj* : cellular

celuloide *nm* **1** : celluloid **2** : film, cinema

celulosa *nf* : cellulose

cementar *vt* : to cement

cementerio *nm* : cemetery

cemento *nm* : cement

cena *nf* : supper, dinner

cenador *nm* : arbor

cenagal *nm* : bog, quagmire

cenagoso, -sa *adj* : swampy

cenar *vi* : to have dinner, to have supper — *vt* : to have for dinner or supper <anoche cenamos tamales : we had tamales for supper last night>

cencerro *nm* : cowbell

cenicero *nm* : ashtray

ceniciento, -ta *adj* : ashen

cenit *nm* : zenith, peak

ceniza *nf* **1** : ash **2 cenizas** *nfpl* : ashes (of a deceased person)

cenizo, -za *n* : jinx

cenote *nm Mex* : natural deposit of spring water

censar *vt* : to take a census of

censo *nm* : census

censor, -sora *n* : censor, critic

censura *nf* **1** : censorship **2** : censure, criticism

censurable *adj* : reprehensible, blameworthy

censurar *vt* **1** : to censor **2** : to censure, to criticize

centauro *nm* : centaur

centavo *nm* **1** : cent (in English-speaking countries) **2** : unit of currency in various Latin-American countries

centella *nf* **1** : lightning flash **2** : spark

centellear *vi* **1** : to twinkle **2** : to gleam, to sparkle

centelleo *nm* : twinkling, sparkle

centenar *nm* **1** : hundred **2 a centenares** : by the hundreds

centenario[1], **-ria** *adj & n* : centenarian

centenario[2] *nm* : centennial

centeno *nm* : rye

centésimo[1], **-ma** *adj* : hundredth

centésimo[2] *nm* : hundredth

centígrado *adj* : centigrade, Celsius

centigramo *nm* : centigram

centímetro *nm* : centimeter

centinela *nmf* : sentinel, sentry

central[1] *adj* **1** : central **2** PRINCIPAL : main, principal

central[2] *nf* **1** : main office, headquarters **2 central camionera** *Mex* : bus terminal

centralita *nf* : switchboard

centralizar {21} *vt* : to centralize — **centralización** *nf*

centrar *vt* **1** : to center **2** : to focus — **centrarse** *vr* **~ en** : to focus on, to concentrate on

céntrico, -ca *adj* : central

centrífugo, -ga *adj* : centrifugal

centrípeto, -ta *adj* : centripetal

centro[1] *nmf* : center (in sports)

centro[2] *nm* **1** MEDIO : center <centro de atención : center of attention> <centro de gravedad : center of gravity> **2** : downtown **3 centro de mesa** : centerpiece

centroamericano, -na *adj & n* : Central American

ceñido, -da *adj* AJUSTADO : tight, tight-fitting

ceñir {67} *vt* **1** : to encircle, to surround **2** : to hug, to cling to <me ciñe demasiado : it's too tight on me> — **ceñirse** *vr* **~ a** : to restrict oneself to, to stick to

ceño *nm* **1** : frown, scowl **2 fruncir el ceño** : to frown, to knit one's brows

cepa *nf* **1** : stump (of a tree) **2** : stock (of a vine) **3** LINAJE : ancestry, stock

cepillar *vt* **1** : to brush **2** : to plane (wood) — **cepillarse** *vr*

cepillo *nm* **1** : brush <cepillo de dientes : toothbrush> **2** : plane (for woodworking)

cepo *nm* : trap (for animals)

cera *nf* **1** : wax <cera de abejas : beeswax> **2** : polish

cerámica *nf* **1** : ceramics *pl* **2** : pottery

cerámico, -ca *adj* : ceramic

ceramista *nmf* ALFARERO : potter

cerca[1] *adv* **1** : close, near, nearby **2 ~ de** : nearly, almost

cerca[2] *nf* **1** : fence **2** : (stone) wall

cercado *nm* : enclosure

cercanía *nf* **1** PROXIMIDAD : proximity, closeness **2 cercanías** *nfpl* : outskirts, suburbs

cercano, -na *adj* : near, close

cercar {72} *vt* **1** : to fence in, to enclose **2** : to surround

cercenar *vt* **1** : to cut off, to amputate **2** : to diminish, to curtail

cerceta *nf* : teal (duck)

cerciorarse *vr* ASEGURARSE **~ de** : to make sure of, to verify

cerco *nm* **1** : siege **2** : cordon, circle **3** : fence

cerda *nf* **1** : bristle **2** : sow

cerdo *nm* **1** : pig, hog **2 carne de cerdo** : pork

cereal *nm* : cereal — **cereal** *adj*

cerebelo *nm* : cerebellum

cerebral *adj* : cerebral

cerebro *nm* : brain

ceremonia *nf* : ceremony — **ceremonial** *adj*
ceremonioso, -sa *adj* : ceremonious
cereza *nf* : cherry
cerezo *nm* : cherry tree
cerilla *nf* **1** : match **2** : earwax
cerillo *nm* (*in various countries*) : match
cerner {56} *vt* : to sift — **cernerse** *vr* **1** : to hover **2 ~ sobre** : to loom over, to threaten
cernidor *nm* : sieve
cernir → **cerner**
cero *nm* : zero
ceroso, -sa *adj* : waxy
cerque, etc. → **cercar**
cerquita *adv fam* : very close, very near
cerrado, -da *adj* **1** : closed, shut **2** : thick, broad <tiene un acento cerrado : she has a thick accent> **3** : cloudy, overcast **4** : quiet, reserved **5** : dense, stupid
cerradura *nf* : lock
cerrajería *nf* : locksmith's shop
cerrajero, -ra *n* : locksmith
cerrar {55} *vt* **1** : to close, to shut **2** : to turn off **3** : to bring to an end — *vi* **1** : to close up, to lock up **2** : to close down — **cerrarse** *vr* **1** : to close **2** : to fasten, to button up **3** : to conclude, to end
cerrazón *nf, pl* **-zones** : obstinacy, stubbornness
cerro *nm* COLINA, LOMA : hill
cerrojo *nm* PESTILLO : bolt, latch
certamen *nm, pl* **-támenes** : competition, contest
certero, -ra *adj* : accurate, precise — **certeramente** *adv*
certeza *nf* : certainty
certidumbre *nf* : certainty
certificable *adj* : certifiable
certificación *nf, pl* **-ciones** : certification
certificado[1], -da *adj* **1** : certified **2** : registered (of mail)
certificado[2] *nm* **1** : certificate **2** : registered letter
certificar {72} *vt* **1** : to certify **2** : to register (mail)
cervato *nm* : fawn
cervecería *nf* **1** : brewery **2** : beer hall, bar
cerveza *nf* : beer <cerveza de barril : draft beer>
cervical *adj* : cervical
cerviz *nf, pl* **cervices** : nape of the neck, cervix
cesación *nf, pl* **-ciones** : cessation, suspension
cesante *adj* : laid off, unemployed
cesantía *nf* : unemployment
cesar *vi* : to cease, to stop — *vt* : to dismiss, to lay off
cesárea *nf* : cesarean, C-section
cese *nm* **1** : cessation, stop <cese del fuego : cease-fire> **2** : dismissal
cesio *nm* : cesium
cesión *nf, pl* **cesiones** : transfer, assignment <cesión de bienes : transfer of property>
césped *nm* : lawn, grass
cesta *nf* **1** : basket **2** : jai alai racket
cesto *nm* **1** : hamper **2** : basket (in basketball) **3 cesto de (la) basura** : wastebasket
cetrería *nf* : falconry
cetrino, -na *adj* : sallow
cetro *nm* : scepter
chabacano[1], -na *adj* : tacky, tasteless
chabacano[2] *nm Mex* : apricot
chacal *nm* : jackal
cháchara *nf fam* **1** : small talk, chatter **2 cháchara**s *nfpl* : trinkets, junk
chacharear *vi fam* : to chatter, to gab
chacra *nf Arg, Chile, Peru* : small farm
chadiano, -na *adj & n* : Chadian
chal *nm* MANTÓN : shawl
chalado[1], -da *adj fam* : crazy, nuts
chalado[2], -da *n* : nut, crazy person
chalán *nm, pl* **chalanes** *Mex* : barge
chalé *nm* → **chalet**
chaleco *nm* : vest
chalet *nm Spain* : house
chalupa *nf* **1** : small boat **2** *Mex* : small stuffed tortilla
chamaco, -ca *n Mex fam* : kid, boy *m*, girl *f*
chamarra *nf* **1** : sheepskin jacket **2** : poncho, blanket
chamba *nf Mex, Peru fam* : job, work
chambear *vi Mex, Peru fam* : to work
chamo -ma *n Ven fam* **1** : kid, boy *m*, girl *f* **2** : buddy, pal
champaña *or* **champán** *nm* : champagne
champiñón *nm, pl* **-ñones** : mushroom
champú *nm, pl* **-pus** *or* **-púes** : shampoo
champurrado *nm Mex* : hot chocolate thickened with cornstarch
chamuco *nm Mex fam* : devil
chamuscar {72} *vt* : to singe, to scorch — **chamuscarse** *vr*
chamusquina *nf* : scorch
chance *nm* OPORTUNIDAD : chance, opportunity
chancho[1], -cha *adj fam* : dirty, filthy, gross
chancho[2], -cha *n* **1** : pig, hog **2** *fam* : slob
chanchullero, -ra *adj fam* : shady, crooked
chanchullo *nm fam* : shady deal, scam
chancla *nf* **1** : thong sandal, slipper **2** : old shoe
chancleta *nf* → **chancla**
chanclo *nm* **1** : clog **2 chanclos** *nmpl* : overshoes, galoshes, rubbers
chancro *nm* : chancre
changarro *nm Mex* : small shop, stall
chango, -ga *n Mex* : monkey
chantaje *nm* : blackmail
chantajear *vt* : to blackmail
chantajista *nmf* : blackmailer
chanza *nf* **1** : joke, jest **2** *Mex fam* : chance, opportunity

chapa *nf* **1** : sheet, panel, veneer **2** : lock **3** : badge

chapado, -da *adj* **1** : plated **2 chapado a la antigua** : old-fashioned

chapar *vt* **1** : to veneer **2** : to plate (metals)

chaparrón *nm, pl* **-rrones 1** : downpour **2** : great quantity, torrent

chapeado, -da *adj Col, Mex* : flushed

chapopote *nm Mex* : tar, blacktop

chapotear *vi* : to splash about

chapucero[1], -ra *adj* **1** : crude, shoddy **2** *Mex fam* : dishonest

chapucero[2], -ra *n* **1** : sloppy worker, bungler **2** *Mex fam* : cheat, swindler

chapulín *nm, pl* **-lines** *CA, Mex* : grasshopper, locust

chapuza *nf* **1** : botched job **2** *Mex fam* : fraud, trick <hacer chapuzas : to cheat>

chapuzón *nm, pl* **-zones** : dip, swim <darse un chapuzón : to go for a quick dip>

chaqueta *nf* : jacket

charada *nf* : charades (game)

charango *nm* : traditional Andean stringed instrument

charca *nf* : pond, pool

charco *nm* : puddle, pool

charcutería *nf* : delicatessen

charla *nf* : chat, talk

charlar *vi* : to chat, to talk

charlatán[1], -tana *adj* : talkative, chatty

charlatán[2], -tana *n, mpl* **-tanes 1** : chatterbox **2** FARSANTE : charlatan, phony

charlatanear *vi* : to chatter away

charol *nm* **1** : lacquer, varnish **2** : patent leather **3** : tray

charola *nf Bol, Mex, Peru* : tray

charreada *nf Mex* : charro show, rodeo

charretera *nf* : epaulet

charro[1], -rra *adj* **1** : gaudy, tacky **2** *Mex* : pertaining to charros

charro[2], -rra *n Mex* : charro (Mexican cowboy or cowgirl)

chascarrillo *nm fam* : joke, funny story

chasco *nm* **1** BROMA : trick, joke **2** DECEPCIÓN, DESILUSIÓN : disillusionment, disappointment

chasis *or* **chasís** *nm* : chassis

chasquear *vt* **1** : to click (the tongue, fingers, etc.) **2** : to snap (a whip)

chasquido *nm* **1** : click (of the tongue or fingers) **2** : snap, crack

chatarra *nf* : scrap metal

chato, -ta *adj* **1** : pug-nosed **2** : flat

chauvinismo *nm* : chauvinism

chauvinista[1] *adj* : chauvinistic

chauvinista[2] *nmf* : chauvinist

chaval, -vala *n fam* : kid, boy *m,* girl *f*

chavo[1], -va *adj Mex fam* : young

chavo[2], -va *n Mex fam* : kid, boy *m,* girl *f*

chavo[3] *nm fam* : cent, buck <no tengo un chavo : I'm broke>

chayote *nm* : chayote (plant, fruit)

checar {72} *vt Mex* : to check, to verify

checo[1], -ca *adj & n* : Czech

checo[2] *nm* : Czech (language)

checoslovaco, -ca *adj & n* : Czechoslovakian

chef *nm* : chef

chelín *nm, pl* **chelines** : shilling

cheque[1], etc. → **checar**

cheque[2] *nm* **1** : check **2 cheque de viajero** : traveler's check

chequear *vt* **1** : to check, to verify **2** : to check in (baggage)

chequeo *nm* **1** INSPECCIÓN : check, inspection **2** : checkup, examination

chequera *nf* : checkbook

chévere *adj fam* : great, fantastic

chic *adj & nm* : chic

chica → **chico**

chicano, -na *adj & n* : Chicano, Chicana *f*

chicha *nf* : fermented alcoholic beverage made from corn

chícharo *nm* : pea

chicharra *nf* **1** CIGARRA : cicada **2** : buzzer

chicharrón *nm, pl* **-rrones 1** : pork rind **2 darle chicharrón a** *Mex fam* : to get rid of

chichón *nm, pl* **chichones** : bump, swelling

chicle *nm* : chewing gum

chicloso *nm Mex* : taffy

chico[1], -ca *adj* **1** : little, small **2** : young

chico[2], -ca *n* **1** : child, boy *m,* girl *f* **2** : young man *m,* young woman *f*

chicote *nm* LÁTIGO : whip, lash

chiffon *nm* → **chifón**

chiflado[1], -da *adj fam* : nuts, crazy

chiflado[2], -da *n fam* : crazy person, lunatic

chiflar *vi* : to whistle — *vt* : to whistle at, to boo — **chiflarse** *vr fam* **~ por** : to be crazy about

chiflido *nm* : whistle, whistling

chiflón *nm, pl* **chiflones** : draft (of air)

chifón *nm, pl* **chifones** : chiffon

chilango[1], -ga *adj Mex fam* : of or from Mexico City

chilango[2], -ga *n Mex fam* : person from Mexico City

chilaquiles *nmpl Mex* : shredded tortillas in sauce

chile *nm* : chili pepper

chileno, -na *adj & n* : Chilean

chillar *vi* **1** : to squeal, to screech **2** : to scream, to yell **3** : to be gaudy, to clash

chillido *nm* **1** : scream, shout **2** : squeal, screech, cry (of an animal)

chillo *nm PRi* : red snapper

chillón, -llona *adj, mpl* **chillones 1** : piercing, shrill **2** : loud, gaudy

chilpayate *nmf Mex fam* : child, little kid

chimenea *nf* **1** : chimney **2** : fireplace

chimichurri *nm Arg* : traditional hot sauce

chimpancé *nm* **:** chimpanzee
china *nf* **1 :** pebble, small stone **2** *PRi* **:** orange
chinchar *vt fam* **:** to annoy, to pester — **chincharse** *vr fam* **:** to put up with something, to grin and bear it
chinchayote *nm Mex* **:** chayote root
chinche[1] *nf* **1 :** bedbug **2** *Ven* **:** ladybug **3 :** thumbtack
chinche[2] *nmf fam* **:** nuisance, pain in the neck
chinchilla *nf* **:** chinchilla
chino[1], **-na** *adj* **1 :** Chinese **2** *Mex* **:** curly, kinky
chino[2], **-na** *n* **:** Chinese person
chino[3] *nm* **:** Chinese (language)
chip *nm, pl* **chips :** chip <chip de memoria : memory chip>
chipote *nm Mex fam* **:** bump (on the head)
chipotle *nm Mex* **:** type of chili pepper
chipriota *adj & nmf* **:** Cypriot
chiquear *vt Mex* **:** to spoil, to indulge
chiquero *nm* POCILGA **:** pigpen, pigsty
chiquillada *nf* **:** childish prank
chiquillo[1], **-lla** *adj* **:** very young, little
chiquillo[2], **-lla** *n* **:** kid, youngster
chiquito[1], **-ta** *adj* **:** tiny
chiquito[2], **-ta** *n* **:** little one, baby
chiribita *nf* **1 :** spark **2 chiribitas** *nfpl* **:** spots before the eyes
chiribitil *nm* **1** DESVÁN **:** attic, garret **2 :** cubbyhole
chirigota *nf fam* **:** joke
chirimía *nf* **:** traditional reed pipe
chirimoya *nf* **:** cherimoya, custard apple
chiripa *nf* **1 :** fluke **2 de ~ :** by sheer luck
chirivía *nf* **:** parsnip
chirona *nf fam* **:** slammer, jail
chirriar {85} *vi* **1 :** to squeak, to creak **2 :** to screech — **chirriante** *adj*
chirrido *nm* **1 :** squeak, squeaking **2 :** screech, screeching
chirrión *nm, pl* **chirriones** *Mex* **:** whip, lash
chisme *nm* **1 :** gossip, tale **2** *Spain fam* **:** gadget, thingamajig
chismear *vi* **:** to gossip
chismoso[1], **-sa** *adj* **:** gossipy, gossiping
chismoso[2], **-sa** *n* **1 :** gossiper, gossip **2** *Mex fam* **:** tattletale
chispa[1] *adj* **1** *Mex fam* **:** lively, vivacious <un perrito chispa : a frisky puppy> **2** *Spain fam* **:** tipsy
chispa[2] *nf* **1 :** spark **2 echar chispas :** to be furious
chispeante *adj* **:** sparkling, scintillating
chispear *vi* **1 :** to give off sparks **2 :** to sparkle
chisporrotear *vi* **:** to crackle, to sizzle
chiste *nm* **1 :** joke, funny story **2 tener chiste :** to be funny **3 tener su chiste** *Mex* **:** to be tricky
chistoso[1], **-sa** *adj* **1 :** funny, humorous **2 :** witty
chistoso[2], **-sa** *n* **:** wit, joker
chivas *nfpl Mex fam* **:** stuff, odds and ends
chivo[1], **-va** *n* **1 :** kid, young goat **2 chivo expiatorio :** scapegoat
chivo[2] *nm* **1 :** billy goat **2 :** fit of anger
chocante *adj* **1 :** shocking **2 :** unpleasant, rude
chocar {72} *vi* **1 :** to crash, to collide **2 :** to clash, to conflict **3 :** to be shocking <le chocó : he was shocked> **4** *Mex, Ven fam* **:** to be unpleasant or obnoxious <me choca tu jefe : I can't stand your boss> — *vt* **1 :** to shake (hands) **2 :** to clink glasses
chochear *vi* **1 :** to be senile **2 ~ por :** to dote on, to be soft on
chochín *nm, pl* **-chines :** wren
chocho, -cha *adj* **1 :** senile **2 :** doting
choclo *nm* **1 :** ear of corn, corncob **2 :** corn **3 meter el choclo** *Mex fam* **:** to make a mistake
chocolate *nm* **1 :** chocolate **2 :** hot chocolate, cocoa
chofer *or* **chófer** *nm* **1 :** chauffeur **2 :** driver
choke *nm* **:** choke (of an automobile)
chole *interj Mex fam* **¡ya chole! :** enough!, cut it out!
cholo, -la *adj & n* **:** mestizo
cholla *nf fam* **:** head
chollo *nm Spain fam* **:** bargain
chongo *nm Mex* **1 :** bun (chignon) **2 chongos** *nmpl Mex* **:** dessert made with fried bread
choque[1], **etc. → chocar**
choque[2] *nm* **1 :** crash, collision **2 :** clash, conflict **3 :** shock
chorizo *nm* **:** chorizo, sausage
chorrear *vi* **1 :** to drip **2 :** to pour out, to gush out
chorrito *nm* **:** squirt, splash
chorro *nm* **1 :** flow, stream, jet **2** *Mex fam* **:** heap, ton
choteado, -da *adj Mex fam* **:** worn-out, stale <esa canción está bien choteada : that song's been played to death>
chotear *vt* **:** to make fun of
choteo *nm* **:** joking around, kidding
chovinismo, chovinista → chauvinismo, chauvinista
choza *nf* BARRACA, CABAÑA **:** hut, shack
chubasco *nm* **:** downpour, storm
chuchería *nf* **:** knickknack, trinket
chueco, -ca *adj* **1 :** crooked, bent **2** *Chile, Mex fam* **:** dishonest, shady
chulada *nf Mex, Spain fam* **:** cute or pretty thing <¡qué chulada de vestido! : what a lovely dress!>
chulear *vt Mex fam* **:** to compliment
chuleta *nf* **:** cutlet, chop
chulo[1], **-la** *adj* **1** *fam* **:** cute, pretty **2** *Spain fam* **:** cocky, arrogant
chulo[2] *nm Spain* **:** pimp
chupada *nf* **1 :** suck, sucking **2 :** puff, drag (on a cigarette)
chupado, -da *adj fam* **1 :** gaunt, skinny **2 :** plastered, drunk
chupaflor *nm* COLIBRÍ **:** hummingbird
chupamirto *nm Mex* **:** hummingbird

chupar *vt* **1 :** to suck **2 :** to absorb **3 :** to puff on **4** *fam* **:** to drink, to guzzle — *vi* **:** to suckle — **chuparse** *vr* **1 :** to waste away **2** *fam* **:** to put up with **3 ¡chúpate esa!** *fam* **:** take that!

chupete *nm* **1 :** pacifier **2** *Chile, Peru* **:** lollipop

chupetear *vt* **:** to suck (at)

chupón *nm, pl* **chupones 1 :** sucker (of a plant) **2 :** baby bottle, pacifier

churrasco *nm* **1 :** steak **2 :** barbecued meat

churro *nm* **1 :** fried dough **2** *fam* **:** botch, mess **3** *fam* **:** attractive person, looker

chusco, -ca *adj* **:** funny, amusing

chusma *nf* GENTUZA **:** riffraff, rabble

chutar *vi* **:** to shoot (in soccer)

chute *nm* **:** shot (in soccer)

cianuro *nm* **:** cyanide

cibernética *nf* **:** cybernetics

cicatriz *nf, pl* **-trices :** scar

cicatrizarse {21} *vr* **:** to form a scar, to heal

cíclico, -ca *adj* **:** cyclical

ciclismo *nm* **:** bicycling

ciclista *nmf* **:** bicyclist

ciclo *nm* **:** cycle

ciclomotor *nm* **:** moped

ciclón *nm, pl* **ciclones :** cyclone

cicuta *nf* **:** hemlock

cidra *nf* **:** citron (fruit)

ciega, ciegue, etc. → **cegar**

ciego[1], -ga *adj* **1** INVIDENTE **:** blind **2 a ciegas :** blindly **3 quedarse ciego :** to go blind — **ciegamente** *adv*

ciego[2], -ga *n* INVIDENTE **:** blind person

cielo *nm* **1 :** sky **2 :** heaven **3 :** ceiling

ciempiés *nms & pl* **:** centipede

cien[1] *adj* **1 :** a hundred, hundred <las primeras cien páginas : the first hundred pages> **2 cien por cien** *or* **cien por ciento :** a hundred percent, through and through, wholeheartedly

cien[2] *nm* **:** one hundred

ciénaga *nf* **:** swamp, bog

ciencia *nf* **1 :** science **2 :** learning, knowledge **3 a ciencia cierta :** for a fact, for certain

cieno *nm* **:** mire, mud, silt

científico[1], -ca *adj* **:** scientific — **científicamente** *adv*

científico[2], -ca *n* **:** scientist

ciento[1] *adj* (*used in compound numbers*) **:** one hundred <ciento uno : one hundred and one>

ciento[2] *nm* **1 :** hundred, group of a hundred **2 por ~ :** percent

cierne, etc. → **cerner**

cierra, etc. → **cerrar**

cierre *nm* **1 :** closing, closure **2 :** fastener, clasp, zipper

cierto, -ta *adj* **1 :** true, certain, definite <lo cierto es que... : the fact is that...> **2 :** certain, one <cierto día de verano : one summer day> <bajo ciertas circunstancias : under certain circumstances> **3 por ~ :** in fact, as a matter of fact — **ciertamente** *adv*

ciervo, -va *n* **:** deer, stag *m,* hind *f*

cifra *nf* **1 :** figure, number **2 :** quantity, amount **3** CLAVE **:** code, cipher

cifrar *vt* **1 :** to write in code **2 :** to place, to pin <cifró su esperanza en la lotería : he pinned his hopes on the lottery> — **cifrarse** *vr* **:** to amount <la multa se cifra en millares : the fine amounts to thousands>

cigarra *nf* CHICHARRA **:** cicada

cigarrera *nf* **:** cigarette case

cigarrillo *nm* **:** cigarrette

cigarro *nm* **1 :** cigarette **2** PURO **:** cigar

cigoto *nm* **:** zygote

cigüeña *nf* **:** stork

cilantro *nm* **:** cilantro, coriander

cilíndrico, -ca *adj* **:** cylindrical

cilindro *nm* **:** cylinder

cima *nf* CUMBRE **:** peak, summit, top

cimarrón, -rrona *adj, mpl* **-rrones :** untamed, wild

címbalo *nm* **:** cymbal

cimbel *nm* **:** decoy

cimbrar *vt* **:** to shake, to rock — **cimbrarse** *vr* **:** to sway, to swing

cimentar {55} *vt* **1 :** to lay the foundation of, to establish **2 :** to strengthen, to cement

cimientos *nmpl* **:** base, foundation(s)

cinc *nm* **:** zinc

cincel *nm* **:** chisel

cincelar *vt* **1 :** to chisel **2 :** to engrave

cincha *nf* **:** cinch, girth

cinchar *vt* **:** to cinch (a horse)

cinco *adj & nm* **:** five

cincuenta *adj & nm* **:** fifty

cincuentavo[1], -va *adj* **:** fiftieth

cincuentavo[2] *nm* **:** fiftieth (fraction)

cine *nm* **1 :** cinema, movies *pl* **2 :** movie theater

cineasta *nmf* **:** filmmaker

cinematográfico, -ca *adj* **:** movie, film, cinematic <la industria cinematográfica : the film industry>

cingalés[1], -lesa *adj & n* **:** Sinhalese

cingalés[2] *nm* **:** Sinhalese (language)

cínico[1], -ca *adj* **1 :** cynical **2 :** shameless, brazen — **cínicamente** *adv*

cínico[2], -ca *n* **:** cynic

cinismo *nm* **:** cynicism

cinta *nf* **1 :** ribbon **2 :** tape <cinta métrica : tape measure> **3 :** strap, belt <cinta transportadora : conveyor belt>

cinto *nm* **:** strap, belt

cintura *nf* **1 :** waist, waistline **2 meter en cintura** *fam* **:** to bring into line, to discipline

cinturón *nm, pl* **-rones 1 :** belt **2 cinturón de seguridad :** seat belt

ciñe, etc. → **ceñir**

ciprés *nm, pl* **cipreses :** cypress

circo *nm* **:** circus

circón *nm, pl* **circones :** zircon

circonio *nm* **:** zirconium

circuitería *nf* **:** circuitry

circuito *nm* **:** circuit

circulación *nf, pl* **-ciones 1 :** circulation **2 :** movement **3 :** traffic

circular[1] *vi* **1 :** to circulate **2 :** to move along **3 :** to drive
circular[2] *adj* **:** circular
circular[3] *nf* **:** circular, flier
circulatorio, -ria *adj* **:** circulatory
círculo *nm* **1 :** circle **2 :** club, group
circuncidar *vt* **:** to circumcise
circuncisión *nf, pl* **-siones :** circumcision
circundar *vt* **:** to surround — **circundante** *adj*
circunferencia *nf* **:** circumference
circunflejo, -ja *adj* **acento circunflejo :** circumflex
circunlocución *nf, pl* **-ciones :** circumlocution
circunloquio *nm* → **circunlocución**
circunnavegar {52} *vt* **:** to circumnavigate — **circunnavegación** *nf*
circunscribir {33} *vt* **:** to circumscribe, to constrict, to limit — **circunscribirse** *vr*
circunscripción *nf, pl* **-ciones 1 :** limitation, restriction **2 :** constituency
circunscrito *pp* → **circunscribir**
circunspección *nf, pl* **-ciones :** circumspection, prudence
circunspecto, -ta *adj* **:** circumspect, prudent
circunstancia *nf* **:** circumstance
circunstancial *adj* **:** circumstantial, incidental
circunstante *nmf* **1 :** onlooker, bystander **2 los circunstantes :** those present
circunvalación *nf, pl* **-ciones :** surrounding, encircling <carretera de circunvalación : bypass, beltway>
circunvecino, -na *adj* **:** surrounding, neighboring
cirio *nm* **:** large candle
cirro *nm* **:** cirrus (cloud)
cirrosis *nf* **:** cirrhosis
ciruela *nf* **1 :** plum **2 ciruela pasa :** prune
cirugía *nf* **:** surgery
cirujano, -na *n* **:** surgeon
cisma *nm* **:** schism, rift
cisne *nm* **:** swan
cisterna *nf* **:** cistern, tank
cita *nf* **1 :** quote, quotation **2 :** appointment, date
citable *adj* **:** quotable
citación *nf, pl* **-ciones** EMPLAZAMIENTO **:** summons, subpoena
citadino[1], **-na** *adj* **:** of the city, urban
citadino[2], **-na** *n* **:** city dweller
citado, -da *adj* **:** said, aforementioned
citar *vt* **1 :** to quote, to cite **2 :** to make an appointment with **3 :** to summon (to court), to subpoena — **citarse** *vr* **~ con :** to arrange to meet (someone)
cítara *nf* **:** zither
citatorio *nm* **:** subpoena
citoplasma *nm* **:** cytoplasm
cítrico[1], **-ca** *adj* **:** citric
cítrico[2] *nm* **:** citrus fruit
ciudad *nf* **1 :** city, town **2 ciudad universitaria :** college or university campus **3 ciudad perdida** *Mex* **:** shantytown
ciudadanía *nf* **1 :** citizenship **2 :** citizenry, citizens *pl*
ciudadano[1], **-na** *adj* **:** civic, city
ciudadano[2], **-na** *n* **1** NACIONAL **:** citizen **2** HABITANTE **:** resident, city dweller
ciudadela *nf* **:** citadel, fortress
cívico, -ca *adj* **1 :** civic **2 :** public-spirited
civil[1] *adj* **1 :** civil **2 :** civilian
civil[2] *nmf* **:** civilian
civilidad *nf* **:** civility, courtesy
civilización *nf, pl* **-ciones :** civilization
civilizar {21} *vt* **:** to civilize
civismo *nm* **:** community spirit, civic-mindedness, civics
cizaña *nf* **:** discord, rift
clamar *vi* **:** to clamor, to raise a protest — *vt* **:** to cry out for
clamor *nm* **:** clamor, outcry
clamoroso, -sa *adj* **:** clamorous, resounding, thunderous
clan *nm* **:** clan
clandestinidad *nf* **:** secrecy <en la clandestinidad : underground>
clandestino, -na *adj* **:** clandestine, secret
clara *nf* **:** egg white
claraboya *nf* **:** skylight
claramente *adv* **:** clearly
clarear *v impers* **1 :** to clear, to clear up **2 :** to get light, to dawn — *vi* **:** to go gray, to turn white
claridad *nf* **1** NITIDEZ **:** clarity, clearness **2 :** brightness, light
clarificación *nf, pl* **-ciones** ACLARACIÓN **:** clarification, explanation
clarificar {72} *vt* ACLARAR **:** to clarify, to explain
clarín *nm, pl* **clarines :** bugle
clarinete *nm* **:** clarinet
clarividencia *nf* **1 :** clairvoyance **2 :** perspicacity, discernment
clarividente[1] *adj* **1 :** clairvoyant **2 :** perspicacious, discerning
clarividente[2] *nmf* **:** clairvoyant
claro[1] *adv* **1 :** clearly <habla más claro : speak more clearly> **2 :** of course, surely <¡claro!, ¡claro que sí! : absolutely!, of course!> <claro que entendió : of course she understood>
claro[2], **-ra** *adj* **1 :** bright, clear **2 :** pale, fair, light **3 :** clear, evident
claro[3] *nm* **1 :** clearing **2 claro de luna :** moonlight
clase *nf* **1 :** class **2** ÍNDOLE, TIPO **:** sort, kind, type
clasicismo *nm* **:** classicism
clásico[1], **-ca** *adj* **1 :** classic **2 :** classical
clásico[2] *nm* **:** classic
clasificación *nf, pl* **-ciones 1 :** classification, sorting out **2 :** rating **3** CALIFICACIÓN **:** qualification (in competitions)
clasificado, -da *adj* **:** classified <aviso clasificado : classified ad>
clasificar {72} *vt* **1 :** to classify, to sort out **2 :** to rate, to rank — *vi* CALIFICAR

: to qualify (in competitions) — **clasificarse** *vr*
claudicación *nf, pl* **-ciones** : surrender, abandonment of one's principles
claudicar {72} *vi* : to back down, to abandon one's principles
claustro *nm* : cloister
claustrofobia *nf* : claustrophobia
claustrofóbico, -ca *adj* : claustrophobic
cláusula *nf* : clause
clausura *nf* **1** : closure, closing **2** : closing ceremony **3** : cloister
clausurar *vt* **1** : to close, to bring to a close **2** : to close down
clavadista *nmf* : diver
clavado[1], **-da** *adj* **1** : nailed, fixed, stuck **2** *fam* : punctual, on the dot **3** *fam* : identical <es clavado a su padre : he's the image of his father>
clavado[2] *nm* : dive
clavar *vt* **1** : to nail, to hammer **2** HINCAR : to plunge, to stick **3** : to fix (one's eyes) on — **clavarse** *vr* : to stick oneself (with a sharp object)
clave[1] *adj* : key, essential
clave[2] *nf* **1** CIFRA : code **2** : key <la clave del misterio : the key to the mystery> **3** : clef **4** : keystone
clavel *nm* : carnation
clavelito *nm* : pink (flower)
clavicémbalo *nm* : harpsichord
clavícula *nf* : collarbone
clavija *nf* **1** : plug **2** : peg, pin
clavo *nm* **1** : nail <clavo grande : spike> **2** : clove **3 dar en el clavo** : to hit the nail on the head
claxon *nm, pl* **cláxones** : horn (of an automobile)
clemencia *nf* : clemency, mercy
clemente *adj* : merciful
cleptomanía *nf* : kleptomania
cleptómano, -na *n* : kleptomaniac
clerecía *nf* : ministry, ministers *pl*
clerical *adj* : clerical
clérigo, -ga *n* : cleric, member of the clergy
clero *nm* : clergy
cliché *nm* **1** : cliché **2** : stencil **3** : negative (of a photograph)
cliente, -ta *n* : customer, client
clientela *nf* : clientele, customers *pl*
clima *nm* **1** : climate **2** AMBIENTE : atmosphere, ambience
climático, -ca *adj* : climatic
climatización *nf, pl* **-ciones** : air-conditioning
climatizar {21} *vt* : to air-condition — **climatizado, -da** *adj*
clímax *nm* : climax
clínica *nf* : clinic
clínico, -ca *adj* : clinical — **clínicamente** *adv*
clip *nm* **1** : clip **2** : paper clip
clítoris *nms & pl* : clitoris
cloaca *nf* ALCANTARILLA : sewer
clocar {82} *vi* : to cluck
cloche *nm CA, Car, Col, Ven* : clutch (of an automobile)
clon *nm* : clone
cloqué, etc. → **clocar**
cloquear *vi* : to cluck
clorar *vt* : to chlorinate — **cloración** *nf*
cloro *nm* : chlorine
clorofila *nf* : chlorophyll
cloroformo *nm* : chloroform
cloruro *nm* : chloride
clóset *nm, pl* **clósets** **1** : closet **2** : cupboard
club *nm* : club
clueca, clueque, etc. → **clocar**
coa *nf Mex* : hoe
coacción *nf, pl* **-ciones** : coercion, duress
coaccionar *vt* : to coerce
coactivo, -va *adj* : coercive
coagular *v* : to clot, to coagulate — **coagulación** *nf*
coágulo *nm* : clot
coalición *nf, pl* **-ciones** : coalition
coartada *nf* : alibi
coartar *vt* : to restrict, to limit
cobalto *nm* : cobalt
cobarde[1] *adj* : cowardly
cobarde[2] *nmf* : coward
cobardía *nf* : cowardice
cobaya *nf* : guinea pig
cobertizo *nm* : shed, shelter
cobertor *nm* COLCHA : bedspread, quilt
cobertura *nf* **1** : coverage **2** : cover, collateral
cobija *nf* FRAZADA, MANTA : blanket
cobijar *vt* : to shelter — **cobijarse** *vr* : to take shelter
cobra *nf* : cobra
cobrador, -dora *n* **1** : collector **2** : conductor (of a bus or train)
cobrar *vt* **1** : to charge **2** : to collect, to draw, to earn **3** : to acquire, to gain **4** : to recover, to retrieve **5** : to cash (a check) **6** : to claim, to take (a life) **7** : to shoot (game), to bag — *vi* **1** : to be paid **2 llamar por cobrar** *Mex* : to call collect
cobre *nm* : copper
cobro *nm* : collection (of money), cashing (of a check)
coca *nf* **1** : coca **2** *fam* : coke, cocaine
cocaína *nf* : cocaine
cocal *nm* : coca plantation
cocción *nf, pl* **cocciones** : cooking
cocear *vi* : to kick (of an animal)
cocer {14} *vt* **1** COCINAR : to cook **2** HERVIR : to boil
cochambre *nmf fam* : filth, grime
cochambroso, -sa *adj* : filthy, grimy
coche *nm* **1** : car, automobile **2** : coach, carriage **3 coche cama** : sleeping car **4 coche fúnebre** : hearse
cochecito *nm* : baby carriage, stroller
cochera *nf* : garage, carport
cochinada *nf fam* **1** : filthy language **2** : disgusting behavior **3** : dirty trick
cochinillo *nm* : suckling pig, piglet
cochino[1], **-na** *adj* **1** : dirty, filthy, disgusting **2** *fam* : rotten, lousy
cochino[2], **-na** *n* : pig, hog

cocido[1], -da *adj* **1 :** boiled, cooked **2 bien cocido :** well-done

cocido[2] *nm* ESTOFADO, GUISADO **:** stew

cociente *nm* **:** quotient

cocimiento *nm* **:** cooking, baking

cocina *nf* **1 :** kitchen **2 :** stove **3 :** cuisine, cooking

cocinar *v* **:** to cook

cocinero, -ra *n* **:** cook, chef

cocineta *nf Mex* **:** kitchenette

coco *nm* **1 :** coconut **2** *fam* **:** head **3** *fam* **:** bogeyman

cocoa *nf* **:** cocoa, hot chocolate

cocodrilo *nm* **:** crocodile

cocotero *nm* **:** coconut palm

coctel *or* **cóctel** *nm* **1 :** cocktail **2 :** cocktail party

coctelera *nf* **:** cocktail shaker

codazo *nm* **1 darle un codazo a :** to elbow, to nudge **2 abrirse paso a codazos :** to elbow one's way through

codearse *vr* **:** to rub elbows, to hobnob

códice *nm* **:** codex, manuscript

codicia *nf* AVARICIA **:** avarice, covetousness

codiciar *vt* **:** to covet

codicilo *nm* **:** codicil

codicioso, -sa *adj* **:** avaricious, covetous

codificación *nf, pl* **-ciones 1 :** codification **2 :** coding, encoding

codificar {72} *vt* **1 :** to codify **2 :** to code, to encode

código *nm* **1 :** code **2 código postal :** zip code **3 código morse :** Morse code

codo[1], -da *adj Mex* **:** cheap, stingy

codo[2], -da *n Mex* **:** tightwad, cheapskate

codo[3] *nm* **:** elbow

codorniz *nf, pl* **-nices :** quail

coeficiente *nm* **1 :** coefficient **2 coeficiente intelectual :** IQ, intelligence quotient

coexistir *vi* **:** to coexist — **coexistencia** *nf*

cofa *nm* **:** crow's nest

cofre *nm* **1** BAÚL **:** trunk, chest **2** *Mex* CAPOTE **:** hood (of a car)

coger {15} *vt* **1 :** to seize, to take hold of **2 :** to catch **3 :** to pick up **4 :** to gather, to pick **5 :** to gore — **cogerse** *vr* AGARRARSE **:** to hold on

cogida *nf* **1 :** gathering, harvest **2 :** goring

cognición *nf, pl* **-ciones :** cognition

cognitivo, -va *adj* **:** cognitive

cogollo *nm* **1 :** heart (of a vegetable) **2 :** bud, bulb **3 :** core, crux <el cogollo de la cuestión : the heart of the matter>

cogote *nm* **:** scruff, nape

cohabitar *vi* **:** to cohabit — **cohabitación** *nf*

cohechar *vt* SOBORNAR **:** to bribe

cohecho *nm* SOBORNO **:** bribe, bribery

coherencia *nf* **:** coherence — **coherente** *adj*

cohesión *nf, pl* **-siones :** cohesion

cohesivo, -va *adj* **:** cohesive

cohete *nm* **:** rocket

cohibición *nf, pl* **-ciones 1 :** (legal) restraint **2** INHIBICIÓN **:** inhibition

cohibido, -da *adj* **:** inhibited, shy

cohibir {62} *vt* **:** to inhibit, to make self-conscious — **cohibirse** *vr* **:** to feel shy or embarrassed

cohorte *nf* **:** cohort

coima *nf Arg, Chile, Peru* **:** bribe

coimear *vt Arg, Chile, Peru* **:** to bribe

coincidencia *nf* **:** coincidence

coincidir *vi* **1 :** to coincide **2 :** to agree

coito *nm* **:** sexual intercourse, coitus

coja, etc. → **coger**

cojear *vi* **1 :** to limp **2 :** to wobble, to rock **3 cojear del mismo pie :** to be two of a kind

cojera *nf* **:** limp

cojín *nm, pl* **cojines :** cushion, throw pillow

cojinete *nm* **1 :** bearing, bushing **2 cojinete de bola :** ball bearing

cojo[1], -ja *adj* **1 :** limping, lame **2 :** wobbly **3 :** weak, ineffectual

cojo[2], -ja *n* **:** lame person

cojones *nmpl usu considered vulgar* **1 :** testicles *pl* **2 :** guts *pl,* courage

col *nf* **1** REPOLLO **:** cabbage **2 col de Bruselas :** Brussels sprout **3 col rizada :** kale

cola *nf* **1** RABO **:** tail <cola de caballo : ponytail> **2** FILA **:** line (of people) <hacer cola : to wait in line> **3 :** cola, drink **4 :** train (of a dress) **5 :** tails *pl* (of a tuxedo) **6** PEGAMENTO **:** glue **7** *fam* **:** buttocks *pl,* rear end

colaboracionista *nmf* **:** collaborator, traitor

colaborador, -dora *n* **1 :** contributor (to a periodical) **2 :** collaborator

colaborar *vi* **:** to collaborate — **colaboración** *nf*

colación *nf, pl* **-ciones 1 :** light meal **2 :** comparison, collation <sacar a colación : to bring up, to broach> **3 :** conferral (of a degree)

colador *nm* **1 :** colander, strainer **2** *PRi* **:** small coffeepot

colapso *nm* **1 :** collapse **2 :** standstill

colar {19} *vt* **:** to strain, to filter — **colarse** *vr* **1 :** to sneak in, to cut in line, to gate-crash **2 :** to slip up, to make a mistake

colateral[1] *adj* **:** collateral — **colateralmente** *adv*

colateral[2] *nm* **:** collateral

colcha *nf* COBERTOR **:** bedspread, quilt

colchón *nm, pl* **colchones 1 :** mattress **2 :** cushion, padding, buffer

colchoneta *nf* **:** mat (for gymnastic sports)

colear *vi* **1 :** to wag its tail **2 vivito y coleando** *fam* **:** alive and kicking

colección *nf, pl* **-ciones :** collection

coleccionar *vt* **:** to collect, to keep a collection of

coleccionista *nmf* **:** collector

colecta *nf* **:** collection (of donations)

colectar *vt* : to collect
colectividad *nf* : community, group
colectivo1, -va *adj* : collective — **colectivamente** *adv*
colectivo2 *nm* **1** : collective **2** *Arg, Bol, Peru* : city bus
colector1, -tora *n* : collector <colector de impuestos : tax collector>
colector2 *nm* **1** : sewer **2** : manifold (of an engine)
colega *nmf* **1** : colleague **2** HOMÓLOGO : counterpart **3** *fam* : buddy
colegiado1, -da *adj* : collegiate
colegiado2, -da *n* **1** ÁRBITRO : referee **2** : member (of a professional association)
colegial1, -giala *adj* **1** : school, collegiate **2** *Mex fam* : green, inexperienced
colegial2, -giala *n* : schoolboy *m*, schoolgirl *f*
colegiatura *nf Mex* : tuition
colegio *nm* **1** : school **2** : college <colegio electoral : electoral college> **3** : professional association
colegir {28} *vt* **1** JUNTAR : to collect, to gather **2** INFERIR : to infer, to deduce
cólera1 *nm* : cholera
cólera2 *nf* FURIA, IRA : anger, rage
colérico, -ca *adj* **1** FURIOSO : angry **2** IRRITABLE : irritable
colesterol *nm* : cholesterol
coleta *nf* **1** : ponytail **2** : pigtail
coletazo *nm* : lash, flick (of a tail)
colgado, -da *adj* **1** : hanging, hanged **2** : pending **3 dejar colgado a** : to disappoint, to let down
colgante1 *adj* : hanging, dangling
colgante2 *nm* : pendant, charm (on a bracelet)
colgar {16} *vt* **1** : to hang (up), to put up **2** AHORCAR : to hang (someone) **3** : to hang up (a telephone) **4** *fam* : to fail (an exam) — **colgarse** *vr* **1** : to hang, to be suspended **2** AHORCARSE : to hang oneself **3** : to hang up a telephone
colibrí *nm* CHUPAFLOR : hummingbird
cólico *nm* : colic
coliflor *nf* : cauliflower
colilla *nf* : butt (of a cigarette)
colina *nf* CERRO, LOMA : hill
colindante *adj* CONTIGUO : adjacent, neighboring
colindar *vi* : to adjoin, to be adjacent
coliseo *nm* : coliseum
colisión *nf, pl* **-siones** : collision
colisionar *vi* : to collide
collage *nm* : collage
collar *nm* **1** : collar (for an animal) **2** : necklace <collar de perlas : string of pearls>
colmado, -da *adj* : heaping
colmar *vt* **1** : to fill to the brim **2** : to fulfill, to satisfy **3** : to heap, to shower <me colmaron de regalos : they showered me with gifts>
colmena *nf* : beehive
colmenar *nm* APIARIO : apiary
colmillo *nm* **1** CANINO : canine (tooth), fang **2** : tusk
colmilludo, -da *adj Mex, PRi* : astute, shrewd, crafty
colmo *nm* : height, extreme, limit <el colmo de la locura : the height of folly> <¡eso es el colmo! : that's the last straw!>
colocación *nf, pl* **-ciones 1** : placement, placing **2** : position, job **3** : investment
colocar {72} *vt* **1** PONER : to place, to put **2** : to find a job for **3** : to invest — **colocarse** *vr* **1** SITUARSE : to position oneself **2** : to get a job
colofón *nm, pl* **-fones 1** : ending, finale **2** : colophon
colofonia *nf* : rosin
colombiano, -na *adj & n* : Colombian
colon *nm* : (intestinal) colon
colón *nm, pl* **colones** : Costa Rican and Salvadoran unit of currency
colonia *nf* **1** : colony **2** : cologne **3** *Mex* : residential area, neighborhood
colonial *adj* : colonial
colonización *nf, pl* **-ciones** : colonization
colonizador1, -dora *adj* : colonizing
colonizador2, -dora *n* : colonizer, colonist
colonizar {21} *vt* : to colonize, to settle
colono, -na *n* **1** : settler, colonist **2** : tenant farmer
coloquial *adj* : colloquial
coloquio *nm* **1** : discussion, talk **2** : conference, symposium
color *nm* **1** : color **2** : paint, dye **3 colores** *nmpl* : colored pencils
coloración *nf, pl* **-ciones** : coloring, coloration
colorado1, -da *adj* **1** ROJO : red **2 ponerse colorado** : to blush **3 chiste colorado** *Mex* : off-color joke
colorado2 *nm* ROJO : red
colorante *nm* : coloring <colorante de alimentos : food coloring>
colorear *vt* : to color — *vi* **1** : to redden **2** : to ripen
colorete *nm* : rouge, blusher
colorido *nm* : color, coloring
colorín *nm, pl* **-rines 1** : bright color **2** : goldfinch
colosal *adj* : colossal
coloso *nm* : colossus
coludir *vi* : to be in collusion, to conspire
columna *nf* **1** : column **2 columna vertebral** : spine, backbone
columnata *nf* : colonnade
columnista *nmf* : columnist
columpiar *vt* : to push (on a swing) — **columpiarse** *vr* : to swing
columpio *nm* : swing
colusión *nf, pl* **-siones** : collusion
colza *nf* : rape (plant)
coma1 *nm* : coma
coma2 *nf* : comma
comadre *nf* **1** : godmother of one's child **2** : mother of one's godchild **3**

fam : neighbor, female friend **4** *fam* : gossip

comadrear *vi fam* : to gossip

comadreja *nf* : weasel

comadrona *nf* : midwife

comanche *nmf* : Comanche

comandancia *nf* **1** : command headquarters **2** : command

comandante *nmf* **1** : commander, commanding officer **2** : major

comandar *vt* : to command, to lead

comando *nm* **1** : commando **2** : command (for computers)

comarca *nf* REGIÓN : region

comarcal *adj* REGIONAL : regional, local

combar *vt* : to bend, to curve — **combarse** *vr* **1** : to bend, to buckle **2** : to warp, to bulge, to sag

combate *nm* **1** : combat **2** : fight, boxing match

combatiente *nmf* : combatant, fighter

combatir *vt* : to combat, to fight against — *vi* : to fight

combatividad *nf* : fighting spirit

combativo, -va *adj* : combative, spirited

combinación *nf, pl* **-ciones 1** : combination **2** : connection (in travel)

combinar *vt* **1** UNIR : to combine, to mix together **2** : to match, to put together — **combinarse** *vr* : to get together, to conspire

combo *nm* **1** : (musical) band **2** *Chile, Peru* : sledgehammer **3** *Chile, Peru* : punch

combustible[1] *adj* : combustible

combustible[2] *nm* : fuel

combustión *nf, pl* **-tiones** : combustion

comedero *nm* : trough, feeder

comedia *nf* : comedy

comediante *nmf* : actor, actress *f*

comedido, -da *adj* MESURADO : moderate, restrained

comediógrafo, -fa *n* : playwright

comedor *nm* : dining room

comején *nm, pl* **-jenes** : termite

comelón[1], -lona *adj, mpl* **-lones** *fam* : gluttonous

comelón[2] -lona *n, pl* **-lones** *fam* : big eater, glutton

comensal *nmf* : dinner guest

comentador, -dora *n* → **comentarista**

comentar *vt* **1** : to comment on, to discuss **2** : to mention, to remark

comentario *nm* **1** : comment, remark <sin comentarios : no comment> **2** : commentary

comentarista *nmf* : commentator

comenzar {29} *v* EMPEZAR : to begin, to start

comer[1] *vt* **1** : to eat **2** : to consume, to eat up, to eat into — *vi* **1** : to eat **2** CENAR : to have a meal **3 dar de comer** : to feed — **comerse** *vr* : to eat up

comer[2] *nm* : eating, dining

comercial *adj & nm* : commercial — **comercialmente** *adv*

comercializar {21} *vt* **1** : to commercialize **2** : to market

comerciante *nmf* : merchant, dealer

comerciar *vi* : to do business, to trade

comercio *nm* **1** : commerce, trade **2** NEGOCIO : business, place of business

comestible *adj* : edible

comestibles *nmpl* VÍVERES : groceries, food

cometa[1] *nm* : comet

cometa[2] *nf* : kite

cometer *vt* **1** : to commit **2 cometer un error** : to make a mistake

cometido *nm* : assignment, task

comezón *nf, pl* **-zones** PICAZÓN : itchiness, itching

comible *adj fam* : eatable, edible

comic *or* **cómic** *nm* : comic strip, comic book

comicastro, -tra *n* : second-rate actor, ham

comicidad *nf* HUMOR : humor, wit

comicios *nmpl* : elections, voting

cómico[1], -ca *adj* : comic, comical

cómico[2], -ca *n* HUMORISTA : comic, comedian, comedienne *f*

comida *nf* **1** : food **2** : meal **3** : dinner **4 comida basura** : junk food **5 comida rápida** : fast food

comidilla *nf* : talk, gossip

comienzo *nm* **1** : start, beginning **2 al comienzo** : at first **3 dar comienzo** : to begin

comillas *nfpl* : quotation marks <entre comillas : in quotes>

comilón, -lona → **comelón, -lona**

comilona *nf fam* : feast

comino *nm* **1** : cumin **2 me vale un comino** *fam* : not to matter to someone <no me importa un comino : I couldn't care less>

comisaría *nf* : police station

comisario, -ria *n* : commissioner

comisión *nf, pl* **-siones 1** : commission, committing **2** : committee **3** : percentage, commission <comisión sobre las ventas : sales commission>

comisionado[1], -da *adj* : commissioned, entrusted

comisionado[2], -da *n* → **comisario**

comisionar *vt* : to commission

comité *nm* : committee

comitiva *nf* : retinue, entourage

como[1] *adv* **1** : around, about <cuesta como 500 pesos : it costs around 500 pesos> **2** : kind of, like <tengo como mareos : I'm kind of dizzy>

como[2] *conj* **1** : how, as <hazlo como dijiste que lo harías : do it the way you said you would> **2** : since, given that <como estaba lloviendo, no salí : since it was raining, I didn't go out> **3** : if <como lo vuelva a hacer lo arrestarán : if he does that again he'll be arrested> **4 como quiera** : in any way

como[3] *prep* **1 :** like, as <ligero como una pluma : light as a feather> **2 así como :** as well as
cómo *adv* **:** how <¿cómo estás? : how are you?> <¿a cómo están las manzanas? : how much are the apples?> <¿cómo? : excuse me?, what was that?> <¿se puede? ¡cómo no! : may I? please do!>
cómoda *nf* **:** bureau, chest of drawers
comodidad *nf* **1 :** comfort **2 :** convenience
comodín *nm, pl* **-dines 1 :** joker, wild card **2 :** all-purpose word or thing **3 :** pretext, excuse
cómodo, -da *adj* **1** CONFORTABLE **:** comfortable **2 :** convenient — **cómodamente** *adv*
comodoro *nm* **:** commodore
comoquiera *adv* **1 :** in any way **2 comoquiera que :** in whatever way, however <comoquiera que sea eso : however that may be>
compa *nm fam* **:** buddy, pal
compactar *vt* **:** to compact, to compress
compacto, -ta *adj* **:** compact
compadecer {53} *vt* **:** to sympathize with, to feel sorry for — **compadecerse** *vr* **1 ~ de :** to take pity on, to commiserate with **2 ~ con :** to fit, to accord (with)
compadre *nm* **1 :** godfather of one's child **2 :** father of one's godchild **3** *fam* **:** buddy, pal
compaginar *vt* **1** COORDINAR **:** to combine, to coordinate **2 :** to collate
compañerismo *nm* **:** comradeship, camaraderie
compañero, -ñera *n* **:** companion, mate, partner
compañía *nf* **1 :** company <llegó en compañía de su madre : he arrived with his mother> **2** EMPRESA, FIRMA **:** firm, company
comparable *adj* **:** comparable
comparación *nf, pl* **-ciones :** comparison
comparado, -da *adj* **:** comparative <literatura comparada : comparative literature>
comparar *vt* **:** to compare
comparativo[1], **-va** *adj* **:** comparative, relative — **comparativamente** *adv*
comparativo[2] *nm* **:** comparative degree or form
comparecencia *nf* **1 :** appearance (in court) **2 orden de comparecencia :** subpoena, summons
comparecer {53} *vi* **:** to appear (in court)
compartimiento *or* **compartimento** *nm* **:** compartment
compartir *vt* **:** to share
compás *nm, pl* **-pases 1 :** beat, rhythm, time **2 :** compass
compasión *nf, pl* **-siones :** compassion, pity
compasivo, -va *adj* **:** compassionate, sympathetic
compatibilidad *nf* **:** compatibility
compatible *adj* **:** compatible
compatriota *nmf* PAISANO **:** compatriot, fellow countryman
compeler *vt* **:** to compel
compendiar *vt* **:** to summarize, to condense
compendio *nm* **:** summary
compenetración *nf, pl* **-ciones :** rapport, mutual understanding
compenetrarse *vr* **1 :** to understand each other **2 ~ con :** to identify oneself with
compensación *nf, pl* **-ciones :** compensation
compensar *vt* **:** to compensate for, to make up for — *vi* **:** to be worth one's while
compensatorio, -ria *adj* **:** compensatory
competencia *nf* **1 :** competition, rivalry **2 :** competence
competente *adj* **:** competent, able — **competentemente** *adv*
competición *nf, pl* **-ciones :** competition
competidor[1], **-dora** *adj* RIVAL **:** competing, rival
competidor[2], **-dora** *n* RIVAL **:** competitor, rival
competir {54} *vi* **:** to compete
competitividad *nf* **:** competitiveness
competitivo, -va *adj* **:** competitive — **competitivamente** *adv*
compilar *vt* **:** to compile — **compilación** *nf*
compinche *nmf fam* **1 :** buddy, pal **2 :** partner in crime, accomplice
complacencia *nf* **:** pleasure, satisfaction
complacer {57} *vt* **:** to please — **complacerse** *vr* **~ en :** to take pleasure in
complaciente *adj* **:** obliging, eager to please
complejidad *nf* **:** complexity
complejo[1], **-ja** *adj* **:** complex
complejo[2] *nm* **:** complex
complementar *vt* **:** to complement, to supplement — **complementarse** *vr*
complementario, -ria *adj* **:** complementary
complemento *nm* **1 :** complement, supplement **2 :** supplementary pay, allowance
completamente *adv* **:** completely, totally
completar *vt* TERMINAR **:** to complete, to finish
completo, -ta *adj* **1 :** complete **2 :** perfect, absolute **3 :** full, detailed — **completamente** *adv*
complexión *nf, pl* **-xiones :** (physical) constitution
complicación *nf, pl* **-ciones :** complication
complicado, -da *adj* **:** complicated

complicar {72} *vt* **1 :** to complicate **2 :** to involve — **complicarse** *vr*
cómplice *nmf* **:** accomplice
complicidad *nf* **:** complicity
complot *nm, pl* **complots** CONFABULACIÓN, CONSPIRACIÓN **:** conspiracy, plot
componenda *nf* **:** shady deal, scam
componente *adj & nm* **:** component, constituent
componer {60} *vt* **1** ARREGLAR **:** to fix, to repair **2** CONSTITUIR **:** to make up, to compose **3 :** to compose, to write **4 :** to set (a bone) — **componerse** *vr* **1 :** to improve, to get better **2 ~ de :** to consist of
comportamiento *nm* CONDUCTA **:** behavior, conduct
comportarse *vr* **:** to behave, to conduct oneself
composición *nf, pl* **-ciones 1** OBRA **:** composition, work **2 :** makeup, arrangement
compositor, -tora *n* **:** composer, songwriter
compostura *nf* **1 :** composure **2 :** mending, repair
compra *nf* **1 :** purchase **2 ir de compras :** to go shopping **3 orden de compra :** purchase order
comprador, -dora *n* **:** buyer, shopper
comprar *vt* **:** to buy, to purchase
compraventa *nf* **:** buying and selling
comprender *vt* **1** ENTENDER **:** to comprehend, to understand **2** ABARCAR **:** to cover, to include — *vi* **:** to understand <¡ya comprendo! : now I understand!>
comprensible *adj* **:** understandable — **comprensiblemente** *adv*
comprensión *nf, pl* **-siones 1 :** comprehension, understanding, grasp **2 :** understanding, sympathy
comprensivo, -va *adj* **:** understanding
compresa *nf* **1 :** compress **2** *or* **compresa higiénica :** sanitary napkin
compresión *nf, pl* **-siones :** compression
compresor *nm* **:** compressor
comprimido *nm* PÍLDORA, TABLETA **:** pill, tablet
comprimir *vt* **:** to compress
comprobable *adj* **:** verifiable, provable
comprobación *nf, pl* **-ciones :** verification, confirmation
comprobante *nm* **1 :** proof <comprobante de identidad : proof of identity> **2 :** voucher, receipt <comprobante de ventas : sales slip>
comprobar {19} *vt* **1 :** to verify, to check **2 :** to prove
comprometedor, -dora *adj* **:** compromising
comprometer *vt* **1 :** to compromise **2 :** to jeopardize **3 :** to commit, to put under obligation — **comprometerse** *vr* **1 :** to commit oneself **2 ~ con :** to get engaged to
comprometido, -da *adj* **1 :** compromising, awkward **2 :** committed, obliged **3 :** engaged (to be married)
compromiso *nm* **1 :** obligation, commitment **2 :** engagement <anillo de compromiso : engagement ring> **3 :** agreement **4 :** awkward situation, fix
compuerta *nf* **:** floodgate
compuesto[1] *pp* → **componer**
compuesto[2], **-ta** *adj* **1 :** fixed, repaired **2 :** compound, composite **3 :** decked out, spruced up **4 ~ de :** made up of, consisting of
compuesto[3] *nm* **:** compound
compulsión *nf, pl* **-siones :** compulsion
compulsivo, -va *adj* **1 :** compelling, urgent **2 :** compulsive — **compulsivamente** *adv*
compungido, -da *adj* **:** contrite, remorseful
compungirse {35} *vr* **:** to feel remorse
compuso, etc. → **componer**
computación *nf, pl* **-ciones :** computing, computers *pl*
computador *nm* → **computadora**
computadora *nf* **1 :** computer **2 computadora portátil :** laptop computer
computar *vt* **:** to compute, to calculate
computarizar {21} *vt* **:** to computerize
cómputo *nm* **:** computation, calculation
comulgar {52} *vi* **:** to receive Communion
común *adj, pl* **comunes 1 :** common **2 común y corriente :** ordinary, regular **3 por lo común :** generally, as a rule
comuna *nf* **:** commune
comunal *adj* **:** communal
comunicación *nf, pl* **-ciones 1 :** communication **2 :** access, link **3 :** message, report
comunicado *nm* **1 :** communiqué **2 comunicado de prensa :** press release
comunicar {72} *vt* **1 :** to communicate, to convey **2 :** to notify — **comunicarse** *vr* **~ con 1 :** to contact, to get in touch with **2 :** to be connected to
comunicativo, -va *adj* **:** communicative, talkative
comunidad *nf* **:** community
comunión *nf, pl* **-niones 1 :** communion, sharing **2 :** Communion
comunismo *nm* **:** communism, Communism
comúnmente *adv* **:** commonly
con *prep* **1 :** with <vengo con mi padre : I'm going with my father> <¿con quién hablas? : who are you speaking to?> **2 :** in spite of <con todo : in spite of it all> **3 :** to, towards <ella es amable con los niños : she is kind to the children> **4 :** by <con llegar temprano : by arriving early> **5 con (tal) que :** as long as, so long as
conato *nm* **:** attempt, effort <conato de robo : attempted robbery>

cóncavo, -va *adj* : concave
concebible *adj* : conceivable
concebir {54} *vt* **1** : to conceive **2** : to conceive of, to imagine — *vi* : to conceive, to become pregnant
conceder *vt* **1** : to grant, to bestow **2** : to concede, to admit
concejal, -jala *n* : councilman *m*, councilwoman *f*, alderman *m*, alderwoman *f*
concejo *nm* : council <concejo municipal : town council>
concentración *nf, pl* **-ciones** : concentration
concentrado *nm* : concentrate
concentrar *vt* : to concentrate — **concentrarse** *vr*
concéntrico, -ca *adj* : concentric
concepción *nf, pl* **-ciones** : conception
concepto *nm* NOCIÓN : concept, idea, opinion
conceptuar {3} *vt* : to regard, to judge
concernir {17} *vi* : to be of concern
concertar {55} *vt* **1** : to arrange, to set up **2** : to agree on, to settle **3** : to harmonize — *vi* : to be in harmony
concesión *nf, pl* **-siones 1** : concession **2** : awarding, granting
concha *nf* : conch, seashell
conciencia *nf* **1** : conscience **2** : consciousness, awareness
concientizar {21} *vt* : to make aware — **concientizarse** *vr* **~ de** : to realize, to become aware of
concienzudo, -da *adj* : conscientious
concierto *nm* **1** : concert **2** : agreement **3** : concerto
conciliador¹, -dora *adj* : conciliatory
conciliador², -dora *n* : arbitrator, peacemaker
conciliar *vt* : to conciliate, to reconcile — **conciliación** *nf*
concilio *nm* : (church) council
conciso, -sa *adj* : concise — **concisión** *nf*
conciudadano, -na *n* : fellow citizen
cónclave *nm* : conclave, private meeting
concluir {41} *vt* **1** TERMINAR : to conclude, to finish **2** DEDUCIR : to deduce, to infer — *vi* : to end, to conclude
conclusión *nf, pl* **-siones** : conclusion
concluyente *adj* : conclusive
concomitante *adj* : concomitant
concordancia *nf* : agreement, accordance
concordar {19} *vi* : to agree, to coincide — *vt* : to reconcile
concordia *nf* : concord, harmony
concretar *vt* **1** : to pinpoint, to specify **2** : to fulfill, to realize — **concretarse** *vr* : to become real, to take shape
concretizar → **concretar**
concreto¹, -ta *adj* **1** : concrete, actual **2** : definite, specific <en concreto : specifically> — **concretamente** *adv*
concreto² *nm* HORMIGÓN : concrete
concubina *nf* : concubine
concurrencia *nf* **1** : audience, turnout **2** : concurrence
concurrente *adj* : concurrent — **concurrentemente** *adv*
concurrido, -da *adj* : busy, crowded
concurrir *vi* **1** : to converge, to come together **2** : to concur, to agree **3** : to take part, to participate **4** : to attend, to be present <concurrir a una reunión : to attend a meeting> **5 ~ a** : to contribute to
concursante *nmf* : contestant, competitor
concursar *vt* : to compete in — *vi* : to compete, to participate
concurso *nm* **1** : contest, competition **2** : concurrance, coincidence **3** : crowd, gathering **4** : cooperation, assistance
condado *nm* **1** : county **2** : earldom
conde, -desa *n* : count *m*, earl *m*, countess *f*
condecoración *nf, pl* **-ciones** : decoration, medal
condecorar *vt* : to decorate, to award (a medal)
condena *nf* **1** REPROBACIÓN : disapproval, condemnation **2** SENTENCIA : sentence, conviction
condenación *nf, pl* **-ciones 1** : condemnation **2** : damnation
condenado¹, -da *adj* **1** : fated, doomed **2** : convicted, sentenced **3** *fam* : darn, damned
condenado², -da *n* : convict
condenar *vt* **1** : to condemn **2** : to sentence **3** : to board up, to wall up — **condenarse** *vr* : to be damned
condensación *nf, pl* **-ciones** : condensation
condensar *vt* : to condense
condesa *nf* → **conde**
condescendencia *nf* : condescension
condescender {56} *vi* **1** : to condescend **2** : to agree, to acquiesce
condición *nf, pl* **-ciones 1** : condition, state **2** : capacity, position **3 condiciones** *nfpl* : conditions, circumstances <condiciones de vida : living conditions>
condicional *adj* : conditional — **condicionalmente** *adv*
condicionamiento *nm* : conditioning
condicionar *vt* **1** : to condition, to determine **2 ~ a** : to be contingent on, to depend on
condimentar *vt* SAZONAR : to season, to spice
condimento *nm* : condiment, seasoning, spice
condolencia *nf* : condolence, sympathy
condolerse {47} *vr* : to sympathize
condominio *nm* : condominium, condo
condón *nm, pl* **condones** : condom
cóndor *nm* : condor
conducción *nf, pl* **-ciones 1** : conduction (of electricity, etc.) **2** DIRECCIÓN : management, direction

conducir {61} *vt* **1** DIRIGIR, GUIAR : to direct, to lead **2** MANEJAR : to drive (a vehicle) — *vi* **1** : to drive a vehicle **2 ~ a** : to lead to — **conducirse** *vr* PORTARSE : to behave, to conduct oneself

conducta *nf* COMPORTAMIENTO : conduct, behavior

conducto *nm* : conduit, channel, duct

conductor[1], -tora *adj* : conducting, leading

conductor[2], -tora *n* : driver

conductor[3] *nm* : conductor (of electricity, etc.)

conectar *vt* : to connect — *vi* **~ con** : to link up with, to communicate with

conector *nm* : connector

conejera *nf* : rabbit hutch

conejillo *nm* **conejillo de Indias** : guinea pig

conejo, -ja *n* : rabbit

conexión *nf, pl* **-xiones** : connection

confabulación *nf, pl* **-ciones** COMPLOT, CONSPIRACIÓN : plot, conspiracy

confabularse *vr* : to plot, to conspire

confección *nf, pl* **-ciones 1** : preparation **2** : tailoring, dressmaking

confeccionar *vt* : to make, to produce, to prepare

confederación *nf, pl* **-ciones** : confederation

confederarse *vr* : to confederate, to form a confederation

conferencia *nf* **1** REUNIÓN : conference, meeting **2** : lecture

conferenciante *nmf* : lecturer

conferencista *nmf* → **conferenciante**

conferir {76} *vt* : to confer, to bestow

confesar {55} *v* : to confess — **confesarse** *vr* : to go to confession

confesión *nf, pl* **-siones 1** : confession **2** : creed, denomination

confesionario *nm* : confessional

confesor *nm* : confessor

confeti *nm* : confetti

confiable *adj* : trustworthy, reliable

confiado, -da *adj* **1** : confident, self-confident **2** : trusting — **confiadamente** *adv*

confianza *nf* **1** : trust <de poca confiaza : untrustworthy> **2** : confidence, self-confidence

confianzudo, -da *adj* : forward, presumptuous

confiar {85} *vi* : to have trust, to be trusting — *vt* **1** : to confide **2** : to entrust — **confiarse** *vr* **1** : to be overconfident **2 ~ a** : to confide in

confidencia *nf* : confidence, secret

confidencial *adj* : confidential — **confidencialmente** *adv*

confidencialidad *nf* : confidentiality

confidente *nmf* **1** : confidant, confidante *f* **2** : informer

configuración *nf, pl* **-ciones** : configuration, shape

configurar *vt* : to shape, to form

confín *nm, pl* **confines** : boundary, limit

confinamiento *nm* : confinement

confinar *vt* **1** : to confine, to limit **2** : to exile — *vi* **~ con** : to border on

confirmación *nf, pl* **-ciones** : confirmation

confirmar *vt* : to confirm, to substantiate

confiscar {72} *vt* DECOMISAR : to confiscate, to seize

confitado, -da *adj* : candied

confite *nm* : comfit, candy

confitería *nm* **1** DULCERÍA : candy store, confectionery **2** : tearoom, café

confitero, -ra *n* : confectioner

confitura *nf* : preserves, jam

conflagración *nf, pl* **-ciones 1** : conflagration, fire **2** : war

conflictivo, -va *adj* **1** : troubled **2** : controversial

conflicto *nm* : conflict

confluencia *nf* : junction, confluence

confluir {41} *vi* **1** : to converge, to join **2** : to gather, to assemble

conformar *vt* **1** : to form, to create **2** : to constitute, to make up — **conformarse** *vr* **1** RESIGNARSE : to resign oneself **2** : to comply, to conform **3 ~ con** : to content oneself with, to be satisfied with

conforme[1] *adj* **1** : content, satisfied **2 ~ a** : in accordance with

conforme[2] *conj* : as <entreguen sus tareas conforme vayan saliendo : hand in your homework as you leave>

conformidad *nf* **1** : agreement, consent **2** : resignation

confort *nm* : comfort

confortable *adj* CÓMODO : comfortable

confortar *vt* CONSOLAR : to comfort, to console

confraternidad *nf* : brotherhood, fraternity

confrontación *nf, pl* **-ciones** : confrontation

confrontar *vt* **1** ENCARAR : to confront **2** : to compare **3** : to bring face-to-face — *vi* : to border — **confrontarse** *vr* **~ con** : to face up to

confundir *vt* : to confuse, to mix up — **confundirse** *vr* : to make a mistake, to be confused <confundirse de número : to get the wrong number>

confusión *nf, pl* **-siones** : confusion

confuso, -sa *adj* **1** : confused, mixed-up **2** : obscure, indistinct

congelación *nf, pl* **-ciones 1** : freezing **2** : frostbite

congelado, -da *adj* HELADO : frozen

congelador *nm* HELADORA : freezer

congelamiento *nm* → **congelación**

congelar *vt* : to freeze — **congelarse** *vr*

congeniar *vi* : to get along (with someone)

congénito, -ta *adj* : congenital

congestión *nf, pl* **-tiones** : congestion

congestionado, -da *adj* : congested

congestionamiento *nm* → **congestión**

congestionarse *vr* **1 :** to become flushed **2 :** to become congested
conglomerado[1], **-da** *adj* **:** conglomerate, mixed
conglomerado[2] *nm* **:** conglomerate, conglomeration
congoja *nf* ANGUSTIA **:** anguish, grief
congoleño, -ña *adj & n* **:** Congolese
congraciarse *vr* **:** to ingratiate oneself
congratular *vt* FELICITAR **:** to congratulate
congregación *nf, pl* **-ciones :** congregation, gathering
congregar {52} *vt* **:** to bring together — **congregarse** *vr* **:** to congregate, to assemble
congresista *nmf* **:** congressman *m,* congresswoman *f*
congreso *nm* **:** congress, conference
congruencia *nf* **1 :** congruence **2** COHERENCIA **:** coherence — **congruente** *adj*
cónico, -ca *adj* **:** conical, conic
conífera *nf* **:** conifer
conífero, -ra *adj* **:** coniferous
conjetura *nf* **:** conjecture, guess
conjeturar *vt* **:** to guess, to conjecture
conjugación *nf, pl* **-ciones :** conjugation
conjugar {52} *vt* **1 :** to conjugate **2 :** to combine
conjunción *nf, pl* **-ciones :** conjunction
conjuntivo, -va *adj* **:** connective <tejido conjuntivo : connective tissue>
conjunto[1], **-ta** *adj* **:** joint
conjunto[2] *nm* **1 :** collection, group **2 :** ensemble, outfit <conjunto musical : musical ensemble> **3 :** whole, entirety <en conjunto : as a whole, altogether>
conjurar *vt* **1 :** to exorcise **2 :** to avert, to ward off — *vi* CONSPIRAR **:** to conspire, to plot
conjuro *nm* **1 :** exorcism **2 :** spell
conllevar *vt* **1 :** to bear, to suffer **2** IMPLICAR **:** to entail, to involve
conmemorar *vt* **:** to commemorate — **conmemoración** *nf*
conmemorativo, -va *adj* **:** commemorative, memorial
conmigo *pron* **:** with me <habló conmigo : he talked with me>
conminar *vt* AMENAZAR **:** to threaten, to warn
conmiseración *nf, pl* **-ciones :** pity, conmiseration
conmoción *nf, pl* **-ciones 1 :** shock, upheaval **2** *or* **conmoción cerebral :** concussion
conmocionar *vt* **:** to shake, to shock
conmovedor, -dora *adj* EMOCIONANTE **:** moving, touching
conmover {47} *vt* **1** EMOCIONAR **:** to move, to touch **2 :** to shake up — **conmoverse** *vr*
conmutador *nm* **1 :** switch **2 :** switchboard
connivencia *nf* **:** connivance
connotación *nf, pl* **-ciones :** connotation
connotar *vt* **:** to connote, to imply
cono *nm* **:** cone
conocedor[1], **-dora** *adj* **:** knowledgeable
conocedor[2], **-dora** *n* **:** connoisseur, expert
conocer {18} *vt* **1 :** to know, to be acquainted with <ya la conocí : I've already met him> **2 :** to meet **3** RECONOCER **:** to recognize — **conocerse** *vr* **1 :** to know each other **2 :** to meet **3 :** to know oneself
conocido[1], **-da** *adj* **1 :** familiar **2 :** well-known, famous
conocido[2], **-da** *n* **:** acquaintance
conocimiento *nm* **1 :** knowledge **2** SENTIDO **:** consciousness
conque *conj* **:** so, so then, and so <¡ah, conque esas tenemos! : oh, so that's what's going on!>
conquista *nf* **:** conquest
conquistador[1], **-dora** *adj* **:** conquering
conquistador[2], **-dora** *n* **:** conqueror
conquistar *vt* **:** to conquer
consabido, -da *adj* **:** usual, typical
consagración *nf, pl* **-ciones :** consecration
consagrar *vt* **1 :** to consecrate **2** DEDICAR **:** to dedicate, to devote
consciencia *nf* → **conciencia**
consciente *adj* **:** conscious, aware — **conscientemente** *adv*
conscripción *nf, pl* **-ciones :** conscription, draft
conscripto, -ta *n* **:** conscript, inductee
consecución *nf, pl* **-ciones :** attainment
consecuencia *nf* **1 :** consequence, result <a consecuencia de : as a result of> **2 en ~ :** accordingly
consecuente *adj* **:** consistent — **consecuentemente** *adv*
consecutivo, -va *adj* **:** consecutive, successive — **consecutivamente** *adv*
conseguir {75} *vt* **1 :** to get, to obtain **2 :** to achieve, to attain **3 :** to manage to <consiguió acabar el trabajo : she managed to finish the job>
consejero, -ra *n* **:** adviser, counselor
consejo *nm* **1 :** advice, counsel **2 :** council <consejo de guerra : court-martial>
consenso *nm* **:** consensus
consentido, -da *adj* **:** spoiled, pampered
consentimiento *nm* **:** consent, permission
consentir {76} *vt* **1** PERMITIR **:** to consent to, to allow **2** MIMAR **:** to pamper, to spoil — *vi* **~ en :** to agree to, to approve of
conserje *nmf* **:** custodian, janitor, caretaker
conserva *nf* **1 :** preserve(s), jam **2 conservas** *nfpl* **:** canned goods
conservación *nf, pl* **-ciones :** conservation, preservation

conservacionista *nmf* : conservationist

conservador[1], **-dora** *adj & n* : conservative

conservador[2] *nm* : preservative

conservadurismo *nf* : conservatism

conservante *nm* : preservative

conservar *vt* **1** : to preserve **2** GUARDAR : to keep, to conserve

conservatorio *nm* : conservatory

considerable *adj* : considerable — **considerablemente** *adv*

consideración *nf, pl* **-ciones 1** : consideration **2** : respect **3 de ~** : considerable, important

considerado, -da *adj* **1** : considerate, thoughtful **2** : respected

considerar *vt* **1** : to consider, to think over **2** : to judge, to deem **3** : to treat with respect

consigna *nf* **1** ESLOGAN : slogan **2** : assignment, orders *pl* **3** : checkroom

consignar *vt* **1** : to consign **2** : to record, to write down **3** : to assign, to allocate

consigo *pron* : with her, with him, with you, with oneself <se llevó las llaves consigo : she took the keys with her>

consiguiente *adj* **1** : resulting, consequent **2 por ~** : consequently, as a result

consistencia *nf* : consistency

consistente *adj* **1** : firm, strong, sound **2** : consistent — **consistentemente** *adv*

consistir *vi* **1 ~ en** : to consist of **2 ~ en** : to lie in, to consist in

consola *nf* : console

consolación *nf, pl* **-ciones** : consolation <premio de consolación : consolation prize>

consolar {19} *vt* CONFORTAR : to console, to comfort

consolidar *vt* : to consolidate — **consolidación** *nf*

consomé *nm* CALDO : consommé, clear soup

consonancia *nf* **1** : consonance, harmony **2 en consonancia con** : in accordance with

consonante[1] *adj* : consonant, harmonious

consonante[2] *nf* : consonant

consorcio *nm* : consortium

consorte *nmf* : consort, spouse

conspicuo, -cua *adj* : eminent, famous

conspiración *nf, pl* **-ciones** COMPLOT, CONFABULACIÓN : conspiracy, plot

conspirador, -dora *n* : conspirator

conspirar *vi* CONJURAR : to conspire, to plot

constancia *nf* **1** PRUEBA : proof, certainty **2** : record, evidence <que quede constancia : for the record> **3** : perseverance, constancy

constante[1] *adj* : constant — **constantemente** *adv*

constante[2] *nm* : constant

constar *vi* **1** : to be evident, to be on record <que conste : believe me, have no doubt> **2 ~ de** : to consist of

constatación *nf, pl* **-ciones** : confirmation, proof

constatar *vt* **1** : to verify **2** : to state

constelación *nf, pl* **-ciones** : constellation

consternación *nf, pl* **-ciones** : consternation, dismay

consternar *vt* : to dismay, to appall

constipación *nf, pl* **-ciones** : constipation

constipado[1], **-da** *adj* **estar constipado** : to have a cold

constipado[2] *nm* RESFRIADO : cold

constiparse *vr* : to catch a cold

constitución *nf, pl* **-ciones** : constitution — **constitucional** *adj* — **constitucionalmente** *adv*

constitucionalidad *nf* : constitutionality

constituir {41} *vt* **1** FORMAR : to constitute, to make up, to form **2** FUNDAR : to establish, to set up — **constituirse** *vr* **~ en** : to set oneself up as, to become

constitutivo, -va *adj* : constituent, component

constituyente *adj & nmf* : constituent

constreñir {67} *vt* **1** FORZAR, OBLIGAR : to constrain, to oblige **2** LIMITAR : to restrict, to limit

construcción *nf, pl* **-ciones** : construction, building

constructivo, -va *adj* : constructive — **constructivamente** *adv*

constructor, -tora *n* : builder

constructora *nf* : construction company

construir {41} *vt* : to build, to construct

consuelo *nm* : consolation, comfort

consuetudinario, -ria *adj* **1** : customary, habitual **2 derecho consuetudinario** : common law

cónsul *nmf* : consul — **consular** *adj*

consulado *nm* : consulate

consulta *nf* **1** : consultation **2** : inquiry

consultar *vt* : to consult

consultor[1], **-tora** *adj* : consulting <firma consultora : consulting firm>

consultor[2], **-tora** *n* : consultant

consultorio *nm* : office (of a doctor or dentist)

consumación *nf, pl* **-ciones** : consummation

consumado, -da *adj* : consummate, perfect

consumar *vt* **1** : to consummate, to complete **2** : to commit, to carry out

consumible *adj* : consumable

consumición *nf, pl* **-ciones 1** : consumption **2** : drink (in a restaurant)

consumido, -da *adj* : thin, emaciated

consumidor, -dora *n* : consumer

consumir *vt* : to consume — **consumirse** *vr* : to waste away

consumo *nm* : consumption

contabilidad *nf* **1 :** accounting, bookkeeping **2 :** accountancy

contabilizar {21} *vt* **:** to enter, to record (in accounting)

contable[1] *adj* **:** countable

contable[2] *nmf Spain* **:** accountant, bookkeeper

contactar *vt* : to contact — *vi* **~ con** : to get in touch with, to contact

contacto *nm* : contact

contado[1], -da *adj* **1 :** counted <tenía los días contados : his days were numbered> **2 :** rare, scarce <en contadas ocasiones : on rare occasions>

contado[2] *nm* **al contado :** cash <pagar al contado : to pay in cash>

contador[1], -dora *n* **:** accountant

contador[2] *nm* **:** meter <contador de agua : water meter>

contaduría *nf* **1 :** accounting office **2** CONTABILIDAD **:** accountancy

contagiar *vt* **1 :** to infect **2 :** to transmit (a disease) — **contagiarse** *vr* **1 :** to be contagious **2 :** to become infected

contagio *nm* **:** contagion, infection

contagioso, -sa *adj* **:** contagious, catching

contaminación *nf, pl* **-ciones :** contamination, pollution

contaminante *nm* **:** pollutant, contaminant

contaminar *vt* **:** to contaminate, to pollute

contar {19} *vt* **1 :** to count **2 :** to tell **3 :** to include — *vi* **1 :** to count (up) **2 :** to matter, to be of concern <eso no cuenta : that doesn't matter> **3 ~ con :** to rely on, to count on — **contarse** *vr* **~ entre :** to be numbered among

contemplación *nf, pl* **-ciones :** contemplation — **contemplativo, -va** *adj*

contemplar *vt* **1 :** to contemplate, to ponder **2 :** to gaze at, to look at

contemporáneo, -nea *adj & n* **:** contemporary

contención *nf, pl* **-ciones :** containment, holding

contencioso, -sa *adj* **:** contentious

contender {56} *vi* **1 :** to contend, to compete **2 :** to fight

contendiente *nmf* **:** contender

contenedor *nm* **1 :** container, receptacle **2 :** Dumpster™

contener {80} *vt* **1 :** to contain, to hold **2** ATAJAR **:** to restrain, to hold back — **contenerse** *vr* **:** to restrain oneself

contenido[1], -da *adj* **:** restrained, reserved

contenido[2] *nm* **:** contents *pl,* content

contentar *vt* **:** to please, to make happy — **contentarse** *vr* **:** to be satisfied, to be pleased

contento[1], -ta *adj* **:** contented, glad, happy

contento[2] *nm* **:** joy, happiness

contestación *nf, pl* **-ciones 1 :** answer, reply **2 :** protest

contestar *vt* RESPONDER **:** to answer — *vi* **1** RESPONDER **:** to answer, to reply **2** REPLICAR **:** to answer back

contexto *nm* **:** context

contienda *nf* **1 :** dispute, conflict **2 :** contest, competition

contigo *pron* **:** with you <voy contigo : I'm going with you>

contiguo, -gua *adj* COLINDANTE **:** contiguous, adjacent

continencia *nf* **:** continence

continente *nm* **:** continent — **continental** *adj*

contingencia *nf* **:** contingency, eventuality

contingente *adj & nm* **:** contingent

continuación *nf, pl* **-ciones 1 :** continuation **2 a ~ :** next <lo demás sigue a continuación : the rest follows> **3 a continuación de :** after, following

continuar {3} *v* **:** to continue

continuidad *nf* **:** continuity

continuo, -nua *adj* **:** continuous, steady, constant — **continuamente** *adv*

contonearse *vr* **:** to sway one's hips

contoneo *nm* **:** swaying, wiggling (of the hips)

contorno *nm* **1 :** outline **2 contornos** *nmpl* **:** outskirts

contorsión *nf, pl* **-siones :** contortion

contra[1] *nf* **1** *fam* **:** difficulty, snag **2 llevar la contra a :** to oppose, to contradict

contra[2] *nm* **:** con <los pros y los contras : the pros and cons>

contra[3] *prep* **:** against

contraalmirante *nm* **:** rear admiral

contraatacar {72} *v* **:** to counterattack — **contraataque** *nm*

contrabajo *nm* **:** double bass

contrabalancear *vt* **:** to counterbalance — **contrabalanza** *nf*

contrabandear *v* **:** to smuggle

contrabandista *nmf* **:** smuggler, black marketeer

contrabando *nm* **1 :** smuggling **2 :** contraband

contracción *nf, pl* **-ciones :** contraction

contracepción *nf, pl* **-ciones :** contraception

contrachapado *nm* **:** plywood

contraconceptivo *nm* ANTICONCEPTIVO **:** contraceptive — **contracepción** *nf*

contracorriente *nf* **1 :** crosscurrent **2 ir a contracorriente :** to go against the tide

contractual *adj* **:** contractual

contradecir {11} *vt* DESMENTIR **:** to contradict — **contradecirse** *vr* DESDECIRSE **:** to contradict oneself

contradicción *nf, pl* **-ciones :** contradiction

contradictorio, -ria *adj* **:** contradictory

contraer {81} *vt* **1 :** to contract (a disease) **2 :** to establish by contract

<contraer matrimonio : to get married> **3** : to tighten, to contract — **contraerse** *vr* : to contract, to tighten up
contrafuerte *nm* : buttress
contragolpe *nm* **1** : counterblow **2** : backlash
contrahecho, -cha *adj* : deformed, hunchbacked
contraindicado, -da *adj* : contraindicated — **contraindicación** *nf*
contralor, -lora *n* : comptroller
contralto *nmf* : contralto
contramaestre *nm* **1** : boatswain **2** : foreman
contramandar *vt* : to countermand
contramano *nm* **a ~** : the wrong way (on a street)
contramedida *nf* : countermeasure
contraorden *nf* : countermand
contraparte *nf* **1** : counterpart **2 en ~** : on the other hand
contrapartida *nf* : compensation
contrapelo *nm* **a ~** : in the wrong direction, against the grain
contrapeso *nm* : counterbalance
contraponer {60} *vt* **1** : to counter, to oppose **2** : to contrast, to compare
contraposición *nf, pl* **-ciones** : comparison
contraproducente *adj* : counterproductive
contrapunto *nm* : counterpoint
contrariar {85} *vt* **1** : to contradict, to oppose **2** : to vex, to annoy
contrariedad *nf* **1** : setback, obstacle **2** : vexation, annoyance
contrario, -ria *adj* **1** : contrary, opposite <al contrario : on the contrary> **2** : conflicting, opposed
contrarrestar *vt* : to counteract
contrarrevolución *nf, pl* **-ciones** : counterrevolution — **contrarrevolucionario, -ria** *adj & n*
contrasentido *nm* : contradiction
contraseña *nf* : password
contrastante *adj* : contrasting
contrastar *vt* **1** : to resist **2** : to check, to confirm — *vi* : to contrast
contraste *nm* : contrast
contratar *vt* **1** : to contract for **2** : to hire, to engage
contratiempo *nm* **1** PERCANCE : mishap, accident **2** DIFICULTAD : setback, difficulty
contratista *nmf* : contractor
contrato *nm* : contract
contravenir {87} *vt* : to contravene, to infringe
contraventana *nf* : shutter
contribución *nf, pl* **-ciones** : contribution
contribuidor, -dora *n* : contributor
contribuir {41} *vt* **1** APORTAR : to contribute **2** : to pay (in taxes) — *vi* **1** : contribute, to help out **2** : to pay taxes
contribuyente[1] *adj* : contributing
contribuyente[2] *nmf* : taxpayer
contrición *nf, pl* **-ciones** : contrition
contrincante *nmf* : rival, opponent
contrito, -ta *adj* : contrite, repentant
control *nm* **1** : control **2** : inspection, check **3** : checkpoint, roadblock
controlador, -dora *n* : controller <controlador aéreo : air traffic controller>
controlar *vt* **1** : to control **2** : to monitor, to check
controversia *nf* : controversy
controversial → **controvertido**
controvertido, -da *adj* : controversial
controvertir {76} *vt* : to dispute, to argue about — *vi* : to argue, to debate
contubernio *nm* : conspiracy
contumacia *nf* : obstinacy, stubbornness
contumaz *adj, pl* **-maces** : obstinate, stubbornly disobedient
contundencia *nf* **1** : forcefulness, weight **2** : severity
contundente *adj* **1** : blunt <un objeto contundente : a blunt instrument> **2** : forceful, convincing — **contundentemente** *adv*
contusión *nf, pl* **-siones** : bruise, contusion
contuvo, etc. → **contener**
convalecencia *nf* : convalescence
convalecer {53} *vi* : to convalesce, to recover
convaleciente *adj & nmf* : convalescent
convección *nf, pl* **-ciones** : convection
convencer {86} *vt* : to convince, to persuade — **convencerse** *vr*
convencimiento *nm* : belief, conviction
convención *nf, pl* **-ciones 1** : convention, conference **2** : pact, agreement **3** : convention, custom
convencional *adj* : conventional — **convencionalmente** *adv*
convencionalismo *nm* : conventionality
conveniencia *nf* **1** : convenience **2** : fitness, suitability, advisability
conveniente *adj* **1** : convenient **2** : suitable, advisable
convenio *nm* PACTO : agreement, pact
convenir {87} *vi* **1** : to be suitable, to be advisable **2** : to agree
convento *nm* **1** : convent **2** : monastery
convergencia *nf* : convergence
convergente *adj* : convergent, converging
converger {15} *vi* **1** : to converge **2 ~ en** : to concur on
conversación *nf, pl* **-ciones** : conversation
conversador, -dora *n* : conversationalist, talker
conversar *vi* : to converse, to talk
conversión *nf, pl* **-siones** : conversion
converso, -sa *n* : convert
convertible *adj & nm* : convertible
convertidor *nm* : converter

convertir {76} *vt* **1 :** to convert **2 :** to transform, to change **3 :** to exchange (money) — **convertirse** *vr* **~ en :** to turn into
convexo, -xa *adj* **:** convex
convicción *nf, pl* **-ciones :** conviction
convicto¹, -ta *adj* **:** convicted
convicto², -ta *n* **:** convict, prisoner
convidado, -da *n* **:** guest
convidar *vt* **1** INVITAR **:** to invite **2 :** to offer
convincente *adj* **:** convincing — **convincentemente** *adv*
convivencia *nf* **1 :** coexistence **2 :** cohabitation
convivir *vi* **1 :** to coexist **2 :** to live together
convocación *nf, pl* **-ciones :** convocation
convocar {72} *vt* **:** to convoke, to call together
convocatoria *nf* **:** summons, call
convoy *nm* **:** convoy
convulsión *nf, pl* **-siones 1 :** convulsion **2 :** agitation, upheaval
convulsivo, -va *adj* **:** convulsive
conyugal *adj* **:** conjugal
cónyuge *nmf* **:** spouse, partner
coñac *nm* **:** cognac, brandy
cooperación *nf, pl* **-ciones :** cooperation
cooperador, -dora *adj* **:** cooperative
cooperar *vi* **:** to cooperate
cooperativa *nf* **:** cooperative, co-op
cooperativo, -va *adj* **:** cooperative
cooptar *vt* **:** to co-opt
coordenada *nf* **:** coordinate
coordinación *nf, pl* **-ciones :** coordination
coordinador, -dora *n* **:** coordinator
coordinar *vt* COMPAGINAR **:** to coordinate, to combine
copa *nf* **1 :** wineglass, goblet **2 :** drink <irse de copas : to go out drinking> **3 :** cup, trophy
copar *vt* **1 :** to take <ya está copado el puesto : the job is already taken> **2 :** to fill, to crowd
copartícipe *nmf* **:** joint partner
copete *nm* **1 :** tuft (of hair) **2 estar hasta el copete :** to be completely fed up
copia *nf* **1 :** copy **2 :** imitation, replica
copiadora *nf* **:** photocopier
copiar *vt* **:** to copy
copiloto *nmf* **:** copilot
copioso, -sa *adj* **:** copious, abundant
copla *nf* **1 :** popular song or ballad **2 :** couplet, stanza
copo *nm* **1 :** snowflake **2 copos de avena :** rolled oats **3 copos de maíz :** cornflakes
copra *nf* **:** copra
cópula *nf* **:** copulation
copular *vi* **:** to copulate
coque *nm* **:** coke (fuel)
coqueta *nf* **:** dressing table
coquetear *vi* **:** to flirt
coqueteo *nm* **:** flirting, coquetry
coqueto¹, -ta *adj* **:** flirtatious, coquettish
coqueto², -ta *n* **:** flirt
coraje *nm* **1** VALOR **:** valor, courage **2** IRA **:** anger <darle coraje a alguien : to make someone angry>
coral¹ *nm* **1 :** coral **2 :** chorale
coral² *nf* **:** choir
Corán *nm* **el Corán :** the Koran
coraza *nf* **1 :** armor, armor plating **2 :** shell (of an animal)
corazón *nm, pl* **-zones 1 :** heart <de todo corazón : wholeheartedly> <de buen corazón : kindhearted> **2 :** core **3 :** darling, sweetheart
corazonada *nf* **:** hunch, impulse
corbata *nf* **:** tie, necktie
corcel *nm* **:** steed, charger
corchete *nm* **1 :** hook and eye, clasp **2 :** square bracket
corcho *nm* **:** cork
corcholata *nf Mex* **:** cap, bottle top
corcovear *vi* **:** to buck
cordel *nm* **:** cord, string
cordero *nm* **:** lamb
cordial¹ *adj* **:** cordial, affable — **cordialmente** *adv*
cordial² *nm* **:** cordial (liqueur)
cordialidad *nf* **:** cordiality, warmth
cordillera *nf* **:** mountain range
córdoba *nf* **:** Nicaraguan unit of currency
cordón *nm, pl* **cordones 1 :** cord <cordón umbilical : umbilical cord> **2 :** cordon
cordura *nf* **1 :** sanity **2 :** prudence, good judgment
coreano¹, -na *adj & n* **:** Korean
coreano² *nm* **:** Korean (language)
corear *vt* **:** to chant, to chorus
coreografía *nf* **:** choreography
coreografiar {85} *vt* **:** to choreograph
coreográfico, -ca *adj* **:** choreographic
coreógrafo, -fa *n* **:** choreographer
cormorán *nm, pl* **-ranes :** cormorant
cornada *nf* **:** goring, butt (with the horns)
córnea *nf* **:** cornea
cornear *vt* **:** to gore
cornejo *nm* **:** dogwood (tree)
corneta *nf* **:** bugle, horn, cornet
cornisa *nf* **:** cornice
cornudo, -da *adj* **:** horned
coro *nm* **1 :** choir **2 :** chorus
corola *nf* **:** corolla
corolario *nm* **:** corollary
corona *nf* **1 :** crown **2 :** wreath, garland **3 :** corona (in astronomy)
coronación *nf, pl* **-ciones :** coronation
coronar *vt* **1 :** to crown **2 :** to reach the top of, to culminate
coronel, -nela *n* **:** colonel
coronilla *nf* **1 :** crown (of the head) **2 estar hasta la coronilla :** to be completely fed up
corpiño *nm* **1 :** bodice **2** *Arg* **:** brassiere, bra
corporación *nf, pl* **-ciones :** corporation

corporal *adj* : corporal, bodily
corporativo, -va *adj* : corporate
corpóreo, -rea *adj* : corporeal, physical
corpulencia *nf* : corpulence, stoutness, sturdiness
corpulento, -ta *adj* ROBUSTO : robust, stout, sturdy
corpúsculo *nm* : corpuscle
corral *nm* **1** : farmyard **2** : corral, pen, stockyard **3** *or* **corralito** : playpen
correa *nf* : strap, belt
correcaminos *nms & pl* : roadrunner
corrección *nf, pl* **-ciones 1** : correction **2** : correctness, propriety **3** : rebuke, reprimand **4 corrección de pruebas** : proofreading
correccional *nm* REFORMATORIO : reformatory
correctivo, -va *adj* : corrective <lentes correctivos : corrective lenses>
correcto, -ta *adj* **1** : correct, right **2** : courteous, polite — **correctamente** *adv*
corrector, -tora *n* : proofreader
corredizo, -za *adj* : sliding <puerta corrediza : sliding door>
corredor[1]**, -dora** *n* **1** : runner, racer **2** : agent, broker <corredor de bolsa : stockbroker>
corredor[2] *nm* PASILLO : corridor, hallway
correduría *nf* → **corretaje**
corregir {28} *vt* **1** ENMENDAR : to correct, to emend **2** : to reprimand **3 corregir pruebas** : to proofread — **corregirse** *vr* : to reform, to mend one's ways
correlación *nf, pl* **-ciones** : correlation
correo *nm* **1** : mail <correo aéreo : airmail> **2** : post office
correoso, -sa *adj* : leathery, rough
correr *vi* **1** : to run, to race **2** : to rush **3** : to flow — *vt* **1** : to travel over, to cover **2** : to move, to slide, to roll, to draw (curtains) **3 correr un riesgo** : to run a risk — **correrse** *vr* **1** : to move along **2** : to run, to spill over
correspondencia *nf* **1** : correspondence, mail **2** : equivalence **3** : connection, interchange
corresponder *vi* **1** : to correspond **2** : to pertain, to belong **3** : to be appropriate, to fit **4** : to reciprocate — **corresponderse** *vr* : to write to each other
correspondiente *adj* : corresponding, respective
corresponsal *nmf* : correspondent
corretaje *nm* : brokerage
corretear *vi* **1** VAGAR : to loiter, to wander about **2** : to run around, to scamper about — *vt* : to pursue, to chase
corrida *nf* **1** : run, dash **2** : bullfight
corrido[1]**, -da** *adj* **1** : straight, continuous **2** : wordly, experienced
corrido[2] *nm* : Mexican narrative folk song
corriente[1] *adj* **1** : common, everyday **2** : current, present **3** *Mex* : cheap, trashy **4 perro corriente** *Mex* : mutt
corriente[2] *nf* **1** : current <corriente alterna : alternating current> <direct current : corriente continua> **2** : draft **3** TENDENCIA : tendency, trend
corrillo *nm* : small group, clique
corro *nm* : ring, circle (of people)
corroborar *vt* : to corroborate
corroer {69} *vt* **1** : to corrode **2** : to erode, to wear away
corromper *vt* **1** : to corrupt **2** : to rot — **corromperse** *vr*
corrompido, -da *adj* CORRUPTO : corrupt, rotten
corrosión *nf, pl* **-siones** : corrosion
corrosivo, -va *adj* : corrosive
corrugar {52} *vt* : to corrugate — **corrugación** *nf*
corrupción *nf, pl* **-ciones 1** : decay **2** : corruption
corruptela *nf* : corruption, abuse of power
corrupto, -ta *adj* CORROMPIDO : corrupt
corsario *nm* : privateer
corsé *nm* : corset
cortada *nf* : cut, gash
cortador, -dora *n* : cutter
cortadora *nf* : cutter, slicer
cortadura *nm* : cut, slash
cortafuego *nm* : firebreak
cortante *adj* : cutting, sharp
cortar *vt* **1** : to cut, to slice, to trim **2** : to cut out, to omit **3** : to cut off, to interrupt **4** : to block, to close off **5** : to curdle (milk) — *vi* **1** : to cut **2** : to break up **3** : to hang up (the telephone) — **cortarse** *vr* **1** : to cut oneself <cortarse el pelo : to cut one's hair> **2** : to be cut off **3** : to sour (of milk)
cortauñas *nms & pl* : nail clippers
corte[1] *nm* **1** : cut, cutting <corte de pelo : haircut> **2** : style, fit
corte[2] *nf* **1** : court <corte suprema : supreme court> **2 hacer la corte a** : to court, to woo
cortejar *vt* GALANTEAR : to court, to woo
cortejo *nm* **1** GALANTEO : courtship **2** : retinue, entourage
cortés *adj* : courteous, polite — **cortésmente** *adv*
cortesano[1]**, -na** *adj* : courtly
cortesano[2]**, -na** *n* : courtier
cortesía *nf* **1** : courtesy, politeness **2 de ~** : complimentary, free
corteza *nf* **1** : bark **2** : crust **3** : peel, rind **4** : cortex <corteza cerebral : cerebral cortex>
cortijo *nm* : farmhouse
cortina *nm* : curtain
cortisona *nf* : cortisone
corto, -ta *adj* **1** : short (in length or duration) **2** : scarce **3** : timid, shy **4 corto de vista** : nearsighted
cortocircuito *nm* : short circuit
corvo, -va *adj* : curved, bent

cosa *nf* **1 :** thing, object **2 :** matter, affair **3 otra cosa :** anything else, something else

cosecha *nf* **:** harvest, crop

cosechador, -dora *n* **:** harvester, reaper

cosechadora *nf* **:** harvester (machine)

cosechar *vt* **1 :** to harvest, to reap **2 :** to win, to earn, to garner — *vi* **:** to harvest

coser *vt* **1 :** to sew **2 :** to stitch up — *vi* **:** to sew

cosmético[1], **-ca** *adj* **:** cosmetic

cosmético[2] *nm* **:** cosmetic

cósmico, -ca *adj* **:** cosmic

cosmonauta *nmf* **:** cosmonaut

cosmopolita *adj & nmf* **:** cosmopolitan

cosmos *nm* **:** cosmos

cosquillas *nfpl* **1 :** tickling **2 hacer cosquillas :** to tickle

cosquilleo *nm* **:** tickling sensation, tingle

cosquilloso, -sa *adj* **:** ticklish

costa *nf* **1 :** coast, shore **2 :** cost <a toda costa : at all costs>

costado *nm* **1 :** side **2 al costado :** alongside

costar {19} *v* **:** to cost <¿cuánto cuesta? : how much does it cost?>

costarricense *adj & nmf* **:** Costa Rican

costarriqueño, -ña → **costarricense**

coste *nm* → **costo**

costear *vt* **:** to pay for, to finance

costero, -ra *adj* **:** coastal, coast

costilla *nf* **1 :** rib **2 :** chop, cutlet **3** *fam* **:** better half, wife

costo *nm* **1 :** cost, price **2 costo de vida :** cost of living

costoso, -sa *adj* **:** costly, expensive

costra *nf* **1 :** crust **2** POSTILLA **:** scab

costumbre *nf* **1 :** custom **2** HÁBITO **:** habit

costura *nf* **1 :** seam **2 :** sewing, dressmaking **3 alta costura :** haute couture

costurera *nf* **:** seamstress *f*

cotejar *vt* **:** to compare, to collate

cotejo *nm* **:** comparison, collation

cotidiano, -na *adj* **:** daily, everyday <la vida cotidiana : daily life>

cotización *nf, pl* **-ciones 1 :** market price **2 :** quote, estimate

cotizado, -da *adj* **:** in demand, sought after

cotizar {21} *vt* **:** to quote, to value — **cotizarse** *vr* **:** to be worth

coto *nm* **1 :** enclosure, reserve **2 poner coto a :** to put a stop to

cotorra *nf* **1 :** small parrot **2** *fam* **:** chatterbox, windbag

cotorrear *vi fam* **:** to chatter, to gab, to blab

cotorreo *nm fam* **:** chatter, prattle

coyote *nm* **1 :** coyote **2** *Mex fam* **:** smuggler (of illegal immigrants)

coyuntura *nf* **1** ARTICULACIÓN **:** joint **2 :** occasion, moment

coz *nm, pl* **coces :** kick (of an animal)

crac *nm, pl* **cracs :** crash (of the stock market)

cozamos, etc. → **cocer**

craneal *adj* **:** cranial

cráneo *nf* **:** cranium, skull — **craneano, -na** *adj*

cráter *nm* **:** crater

creación *nf, pl* **-ciones :** creation

creador[1], **-dora** *adj* **:** creative, creating

creador[2], **-dora** *n* **:** creator

crear *vt* **1 :** to create, to cause **2 :** to originate

creatividad *nf* **:** creativity

creativo, -va *adj* **:** creative

crecer {53} *vi* **1 :** to grow **2 :** to increase

crecida *nf* **:** flooding, floodwater

crecido, -da *adj* **1 :** grown, grown-up **2 :** large (of numbers)

creciente *adj* **1 :** growing, increasing **2 luna creciente :** waxing moon

crecientemente *adv* **:** increasingly

crecimiento *nm* **1 :** growth **2 :** increase

credencial *adj* **cartas credenciales :** credentials

credenciales *nfpl* **:** documents, documentation, credentials

credibilidad *nf* **:** credibility

crédito *nm* **:** credit

credo *nm* **:** creed, credo

credulidad *nf* **:** credulity

crédulo, -la *adj* **:** credulous, gullible

creencia *nf* **:** belief

creer {20} *v* **1 :** to believe **2 :** to suppose, to think <creo que sí : I think so> — **creerse** *vr* **1 :** to believe, to think **2 :** to regard oneself as <se cree guapísimo : he thinks he's so handsome>

creíble *adj* **:** believable, credible

creído, -da *adj* **1** *fam* **:** conceited **2 :** confident, sure

crema *nf* **1 :** cream **2 la crema y nata :** the pick of the crop

cremación *nf, pl* **-ciones :** cremation

cremallera *nf* **:** zipper

cremar *vt* **:** to cremate

cremoso, -sa *adj* **:** creamy

crepa *nf Mex* **:** crepe (pancake)

crepe *or* **crep** *nmf* **:** crepe (pancake)

crepé *nm* **1** → **crespón 2 papel crepé :** crepe paper

crepitar *vi* **:** to crackle

crepúsculo *nm* **:** twilight

crescendo *nm* **:** crescendo

crespo, -pa *adj* **:** curly, frizzy

crespón *nm, pl* **crespones :** crepe (fabric)

cresta *nf* **1 :** crest **2 :** comb (of a rooster)

creta *nf* **:** chalk (mineral)

cretino, -na *n* **:** cretin

creyente *nmf* **:** believer

creyó, etc. → **creer**

crezca, etc. → **crecer**

cría *nf* **1 :** breeding, rearing **2 :** young **3 :** litter

criadero *nm* **:** hatchery

criado[1], **-da** *adj* **1 :** raised, brought up **2 bien criado :** well-bred

criado[2], **-da** *n* **:** servant, maid *f*

criador, -dora *n* **:** breeder

crianza *nf* : upbringing, rearing
criar {85} *vt* **1** : to breed **2** : to bring up, to raise
criatura *nf* **1** : baby, child **2** : creature
criba *nf* : sieve, screen
cribar *vt* : to sift
cric *nm, pl* **crics** : jack
crimen *nm, pl* **crímenes** : crime
criminal *adj & nmf* : criminal
crin *nf* **1** : mane **2** : horsehair
criollo[1], -lla *adj* **1** : Creole **2** : native, national <comida criolla : native cuisine>
criollo[2], -lla *n* : Creole
criollo[3] *nm* : Creole (language)
cripta *nf* : crypt
críptico, -ca *adj* **1** : cryptic, coded **2** : enigmatic, cryptic
criptón *nm* : krypton
críquet *nm* : cricket (game)
crisálida *nf* : chrysalis, pupa
crisantemo *nm* : chrysanthemum
crisis *nf* **1** : crisis **2 crisis nerviosa** : nervous breakdown
crisma *nf fam* : head <romperle la crisma a alguien : to knock someone's block off>
crisol *nm* **1** : crucible **2** : melting pot
crispar *vt* **1** : to cause to contract **2** : to irritate, to set on edge <eso me crispa : that gets on my nerves> — **crisparse** *vr* : to tense up
cristal *nm* **1** VIDRIO : glass, piece of glass **2** : crystal
cristalería *nf* **1** : glassware shop <como chivo en cristalería : like a bull in a china shop> **2** : glassware, crystal
cristalino[1], -na *adj* : crystalline, clear
cristalino[2] *nm* : lens (of the eye)
cristalizar {21} *vi* : to crystallize — **cristalización** *nf*
cristianismo *nm* : Christianity
cristiano, -na *adj & n* : Christian
criterio *nm* **1** : criterion **2** : judgment, sense
crítica *nf* **1** : criticism **2** : review, critique
criticar {72} *vt* : to criticize
crítico[1], -ca *adj* : critical — **críticamente** *adv*
crítico[2], -ca *n* : critic
criticón[1], -cona *adj, mpl* **-cones** *fam* : hypercritical, captious
criticón[2], -cona *n, mpl* **-cones** *fam* : faultfinder, critic
croar *vi* : to croak
croata *adj & nmf* : Croatian
crocante *adj* : crunchy
croché *or* **crochet** *nm* : crochet
cromático, -ca *adj* : chromatic
cromo *nm* **1** : chromium, chrome **2** : picture card, sports card
cromosoma *nm* : chromosome
crónica *nf* **1** : news report **2** : chronicle, history
crónico, -ca *adj* : chronic
cronista *nmf* **1** : reporter, newscaster **2** HISTORIADOR : chronicler, historian
cronología *nf* : chronology
cronológico, -ca *adj* : chronological — **cronológicamente** *adv*
cronometrador, -dora *n* : timekeeper
cronometrar *vt* : to time, to clock
cronómetro *nm* : chronometer
croquet *nm* : croquet
croqueta *nf* : croquette
croquis *nm* : rough sketch
cruce[1], etc. → **cruzar**
cruce[2] *nm* **1** : crossing, cross **2** : crossroads, intersection <cruce peatonal : crosswalk>
crucero *nm* **1** : cruise **2** : cruiser, warship **3** *Mex* : intersection
crucial *adj* : crucial — **crucialmente** *adv*
crucificar {72} *vt* : to crucify
crucifijo *nm* : crucifix
crucifixión *nf, pl* **-xiones** : crucifixion
crucigrama *nm* : crossword puzzle
crudo[1], -da *adj* **1** : raw **2** : crude, harsh
crudo[2] *nm* : crude oil
cruel *adj* : cruel — **cruelmente** *adv*
crueldad *nf* : cruelty
cruento, -ta *adj* : bloody
crujido *nm* **1** : rustling **2** : creaking **3** : crackling (of a fire) **4** : crunching
crujiente *adj* : crunchy, crisp
crujir *vi* **1** : to rustle **2** : to creak, to crack **3** : to crunch
crup *nm* : croup
crustáceo *nm* : crustacean
crutón *nm, pl* **crutones** : crouton
cruz *nf, pl* **cruces** : cross
cruza *nf* : cross (hybrid)
cruzada *nf* : crusade
cruzado[1], -da *adj* : crossed <espadas cruzadas : crossed swords>
cruzado[2] *nm* **1** : crusader **2** : Brazilian unit of currency
cruzar {21} *vt* **1** : to cross **2** : to exchange (words, greetings) **3** : to cross, to interbreed — **cruzarse** *vr* **1** : to intersect **2** : to meet, to pass each other
cuaderno *nm* LIBRETA : notebook
cuadra *nf* **1** : city block **2** : stable
cuadrado[1], -da *adj* : square
cuadrado[2] *nm* : square <elevar al cuadrado : to square (a number)>
cuadragésimo[1] *adj* : fortieth, forty-
cuadragésimo[2], -ma *n* : fortieth, forty- (in a series)
cuadrante *nm* **1** : quadrant **2** : dial
cuadrar *vi* : to conform, to agree — *vt* : to square — **cuadrarse** *vr* : to stand at attention
cuadriculado *nm* : grid (on a map, etc.)
cuadrilátero *nm* **1** : quadrilateral **2** : ring (in sports)
cuadrilla *nf* : gang, team, group
cuadro *nm* **1** : square <una blusa a cuadros : a checkered blouse> **2** : painting, picture **3** : baseball diamond, infield **4** : panel, board, cadre
cuadrúpedo *nm* : quadruped
cuadruple *adj* : quadruple

cuadruplicar {72} *vt* : to quadruple — **cuadruplicarse** *vr*
cuajada *nf* : curd
cuajar *vi* **1** : to curdle **2** COAGULAR : to clot, to coagulate **3** : to set, to jell **4** : to be accepted <su idea no cuajó : his idea didn't catch on> — *vt* **1** : to curdle **2** : to adorn
cual[1] *prep* : like, as
cual[2] *pron* **1 el cual, la cual, los cuales, las cuales** : who, whom, which <la razón por la cual lo dije : the reason I said it> **2 lo cual** : which <se rió, lo cual me dio rabia : he laughed, which made me mad> **3 cada cual** : everyone, everybody
cuál[1] *adj* : which, what <¿cuáles libros? : which books?>
cuál[2] *pron* **1** (*in questions*) : which (one), what (one) <¿cuál es el mejor? : which one is the best?> <¿cuál es tu apellido? : what is your last name?> **2 cuál más, cuál menos** : some more, some less
cualidad *nf* : quality, trait
cualitativo, -va *adj* : qualitative — **cualitativamente** *adv*
cualquier → **cualquiera**[1]
cualquiera[1] (**cualquier** *before nouns*) *adj, pl* **cualesquiera 1** : any, whichever <cualquier persona : any person> **2** : everyday, ordinary <un hombre cualquiera : an ordinary man>
cualquiera[2] *pron, pl* **cualesquiera 1** : anyone, anybody, whoever **2** : whatever, whichever
cuán *adv* : how <¡cuán risible fue todo eso! : how funny it all was!>
cuando[1] *conj* **1** : when <cuando llegó : when he arrived> **2** : since, if <cuando lo dices : if you say so> **3 cuando más** : at the most **4 de vez en cuando** : from time to time
cuando[2] *prep* : during, at the time of <cuando la guerra : during the war>
cuándo *adv & conj* **1** : when <¿cuándo llegará? : when will she arrive?> <no sabemos cuándo será : we don't know when it will be> **2 ¿de cuándo acá?** : since when?, how come?
cuantía *nf* **1** : quantity, extent **2** : significance, import
cuántico, -ca *adj* : quantum <teoría cuántica : quantum theory>
cuantioso, -sa *adj* **1** : abundant, considerable **2** : heavy, grave <cuantiosos daños : heavy damage>
cuantitativo, -va *adj* : quantitative — **cuantitativamente** *adv*
cuanto[1] *adv* **1** : as much as <come cuanto puedas : eat as much as you can> **2 cuanto antes** : as soon as possible **3 en ~** : as soon as **4 en cuanto a** : as for, as regards
cuanto[2], **-ta** *adj* : as many, whatever <llévate cuantas flores quieras : take as many flowers as you wish>
cuanto[3], **-ta** *pron* **1** : as much as, all that, everything <tengo cuanto deseo : I have all that I want> **2 unos cuantos, unas cuantas** : a few
cuánto[1] *adv* : how much, how many <¿a cuánto están las manzanas? : how much are the apples?> <no sé cuánto desean : I don't know how much they want>
cuánto[2], **-ta** *adj* : how much, how many <¿cuántos niños tiene? : how many children do you have?>
cuánto[3] *pron* : how much, how many <¿cuántos quieren participar? : how many want to take part?> <¿cuánto cuesta? : how much does it cost?>
cuarenta *adj & nm* : forty
cuarentavo[1] *adj* : fortieth
cuarentavo[2] *nm* : fortieth (fraction)
cuarentena *nf* **1** : group of forty **2** : quarantine
Cuaresma *nf* : Lent
cuartear *vt* **1** : to quarter **2** : to divide up — **cuartearse** *vr* AGRIETARSE : to crack, to split
cuartel *nm* **1** : barracks, headquarters **2** : mercy <una guerra sin cuartel : a merciless war>
cuartelazo *nm* : coup d'état
cuarteto *nm* : quartet
cuartilla *nf* : sheet (of paper)
cuarto[1], **-ta** *adj* : fourth
cuarto[2], **-ta** *n* : fourth (in a series)
cuarto[3] *nm* **1** : quarter, fourth <cuarto de galón : quart> **2** HABITACIÓN : room
cuarzo *nm* : quartz
cuate, -ta *n Mex* **1** : twin **2** *fam* : buddy, pal
cuatrero, -ra *n* : rustler
cuatrillizo, -za *n* : quadruplet
cuatro *adj & nm* : four
cuatrocientos[1], **-tas** *adj* : four hundred
cuatrocientos[2] *nms & pl* : four hundred
cuba *nf* BARRÍL : cask, barrel
cubano, -na *adj & n* : Cuban
cubertería *nf* : flatware, silverware
cubeta *nf* **1** : keg, cask **2** : bulb (of a thermometer) **3** *Mex* : bucket, pail
cúbico, -ca *adj* : cubic, cubed
cubículo *nm* : cubicle
cubierta *nf* **1** : covering **2** FORRO : cover, jacket (of a book) **3** : deck
cubierto[1] *pp* → **cubrir**
cubierto[2] *nm* **1** : cover, shelter <bajo cubierto : under cover> **2** : table setting **3** : utensil, piece of silverware
cubil *nm* : den, lair
cúbito *nm* : ulna
cubo *nm* **1** : cube **2** BALDE : pail, bucket, can <cubo de basura : garbage can> **3** : hub (of a wheel)
cubrecama *nm* COLCHA : bedspread
cubrir {2} *vt* : to cover — **cubrirse** *vr*
cucaracha *nf* : cockroach, roach
cuchara *nf* : spoon
cucharada *nf* : spoonful
cucharilla *or* **cucharita** *nf* : teaspoon
cucharón *nf, pl* **-rones** : ladle
cuchichear *vi* : to whisper
cuchicheo *nm* : whisper

cuchilla *nf* **1** : kitchen knife, cleaver **2** : blade <cuchilla de afeitar : razor blade> **3** : crest, ridge

cuchillada *nf* : stab, knife wound

cuchillo *nm* : knife

cuclillas *nfpl* **en ~** : squatting, crouching

cuco[1], -ca *adj fam* : pretty, cute

cuco[2] *nm* : cuckoo

cuece, cueza, etc. → cocer

cuela, etc. → colar

cuelga, cuelgue, etc. → colgar

cuello *nm* **1** : neck **2** : collar (of a shirt) **3 cuello del útero** : cervix

cuenca *nf* **1** : river basin **2** : eye socket

cuenco *nm* : bowl, basin

cuenta[1], etc. → contar

cuenta[2] *nf* **1** : calculation, count **2** : account **3** : check, bill **4 darse cuenta** : to realize **5 tener en cuenta** : to bear in mind

cuentagotas *nfs & pl* **1** : dropper **2 con ~** : little by little

cuentista *nmf* **1** : short story writer **2** *fam* : liar, fibber

cuento *nm* **1** : story, tale **2 cuento de hadas** : fairy tale **3 sin ~** : countless

cuerda *nf* **1** : cord, rope, string **2 cuerdas vocales** : vocal cords **3 darle cuerda a** : to wind up (a clock, a toy, etc.)

cuerdo, -da *adj* : sane, sensible

cuerno *nm* **1** : horn, antler **2** : cusp (of the moon) **3** : horn (musical instrument)

cuero *nm* **1** : leather, hide **2 cuero cabelludo** : scalp

cuerpo *nm* **1** : body **2** : corps

cuervo *nm* : crow, raven

cuesta[1], etc. → costar

cuesta[2] *nf* **1** : slope <cuesta arriba : uphill> **2 a cuestas** : on one's back

cuestión *nf, pl* **-tiones** ASUNTO, TEMA : matter, affair

cuestionable *adj* : questionable, dubious

cuestionar *vt* : to question

cuestionario *nm* **1** : questionnaire **2** : quiz

cueva *nf* : cave

cuidado *nm* **1** : care **2** : worry, concern **3 tener cuidado** : to be careful **4 ¡cuidado!** : watch out!, be careful!

cuidadoso, -sa *adj* : careful, attentive — **cuidadosamente** *adv*

cuidar *vt* **1** : to take care of, to look after **2** : to pay attention to — *vi* **1 ~ de** : to look after **2 cuidar de que** : to make sure that — **cuidarse** *vr* : to take care of oneself

culata *nf* : butt (of a gun)

culatazo *nf* : kick, recoil

culebra *nf* SERPIENTE : snake

culi *nmf* : coolie

culinario, -ria *adj* : culinary

culminante *adj* **punto culminante** : peak, high point, climax

culminar *vi* : to culminate — **culminación** *nf*

culo *nm* **1** *fam* : backside, behind **2** : bottom (of a glass)

culpa *nf* **1** : fault, blame <echarle la culpa a alguien : to blame someone> **2** : sin

culpabilidad *nf* : guilt

culpable[1] *adj* : guilty

culpable[2] *nmf* : culprit, guilty party

culpar *vt* : to blame

cultivado, -da *adj* **1** : cultivated, farmed **2** : cultured

cultivador, -dora *n* : cultivator

cultivar *vt* **1** : to cultivate **2** : to foster

cultivo *nm* **1** : cultivation, farming **2** : crop

culto[1], -ta *adj* : cultured, educated

culto[2] *nm* **1** : worship **2** : cult

cultura *nf* : culture

cultural *adj* : cultural — **culturalmente** *adv*

cumbre *nf* CIMA : top, peak, summit

cumpleaños *nms & pl* : birthday

cumplido[1], -da *adj* **1** : complete, full **2** : courteous, correct

cumplido[2] *nm* : compliment, courtesy <por cumplido : out of courtesy> <andarse con cumplidos : to stand on ceremony, to be formal>

cumplimentar *vt* **1** : to congratulate **2** : to carry out, to perform

cumplimiento *nm* **1** : completion, fulfillment **2** : performance

cumplir *vt* **1** : to accomplish, to carry out **2** : to comply with, to fulfill **3** : to attain, to reach <su hermana cumple los 21 el viernes : her sister will be 21 on Friday> — *vi* **1** : to expire, to fall due **2** : to fulfill one's obligations <cumplir con el deber : to do one's duty> <cumplir con la palabra : to keep one's word> — **cumplirse** *vr* **1** : to come true, to be fulfilled <se cumplieron sus sueños : her dreams came true> **2** : to run out, to expire

cúmulo *nm* **1** MONTÓN : heap, pile **2** : cumulus

cuna *nf* **1** : cradle **2** : birthplace <Puerto Rico es la cuna de la música salsa : Puerto Rico is the birthplace of salsa music>

cundir *vi* **1** : to propagate, to spread <cundió el pánico en el vecindario : panic spread throughout the neighborhood> **2** : to progress, to make headway

cuneta *nf* : ditch (in a road), gutter

cuña *nf* : wedge

cuñado, -da *n* : brother-in-law *m*, sister-in-law *f*

cuño *nm* : die (for stamping)

cuota *nf* **1** : fee, dues **2** : quota, share **3** : installment, payment

cupé *nm* : coupe

cupo[1], etc. → caber

cupo[2] *nm* **1** : quota, share **2** : capacity, room

cupón *nm, pl* **cupones 1** : coupon, voucher **2 cupón federal** : food stamp

cúpula *nf* : dome, cupola

cura[1] *nm* : priest
cura[2] *nf* **1** CURACIÓN, TRATAMIENTO : cure, treatment **2** : dressing, bandage
curación *nf, pl* **-ciones** CURA, TRATAMIENTO : cure, treatment
curandero, -ra *nm* **1** : witch doctor **2** : quack, charlatan
curar *vt* **1** : to cure, to heal **2** : to treat, to dress **3** CURTIR : to tan **4** : to cure (meat) — *vi* : to get well, to recover — **curarse** *vr*
curativo, -va *adj* : curative, healing
curiosear *vi* **1** : to snoop, to pry **2** : to browse — *vt* : to look over, to check
curiosidad *nf* **1** : curiosity **2** : curio
curioso, -sa *adj* **1** : curious, inquisitive **2** : strange, unusual, odd — **curiosamente** *adv*
currículo *nm* → **currículum**
currículum *nm, pl* **-lums** **1** : résumé, curriculum vitae **2** : curriculum, course of study
curry ['kurri] *nm, pl* **-rries** **1** : curry powder **2** : curry (dish)
cursar *vt* **1** : to attend (school), to take (a course) **2** : to dispatch, to pass on
cursi *adj fam* : affected, pretentious
cursilería *nf* **1** : vulgarity, poor taste **2** : pretentiousness
cursiva *nf* BASTARDILLA : italic type, italics *pl*
curso *nm* **1** : course, direction **2** : school year **3** : course, subject (in school)
cursor *nm* : cursor
curtido, -da *adj* : weather-beaten, leathery (of skin)
curtidor, -dora *n* : tanner
curtiduría *nf* : tannery
curtir *vt* **1** : to tan **2** : to harden, to weather — **curtirse** *vr*
curva *nf* : curve, bend
curvar *vt* : to bend
curvatura *nf* : curvature
curvilíneo, -nea *adj* : curvaceous, shapely
curvo, -va *adj* : curved, bent
cúspide *nf* : zenith, apex, peak
custodia *nf* : custody
custodiar *vt* : to guard, to look after
custodio, -dia *n* : keeper, guardian
cúter *nm* : cutter (boat)
cutícula *nf* : cuticle
cutis *nms & pl* : skin, complexion
cuyo, -ya *adj* **1** : whose, of whom, of which **2 en cuyo caso** : in which case

D

d *nf* : fourth letter of the Spanish alphabet
dable *adj* : feasible, possible
dactilar *adj* **huellas dactilares** : fingerprints
dádiva *nf* : gift, handout
dadivoso, -sa *adj* : generous
dado, -da *adj* **1** : given **2 dado que** : given that, since
dador, -dora *n* : giver, donor
dados *nmpl* : dice
daga *nf* : dagger
dalia *nf* : dahlia
dálmata *nm* : dalmatian
daltónico, -ca *adj* : color-blind
daltonismo *nm* : color blindness
dama *nf* **1** : lady **2 damas** *nfpl* : checkers
damasco *nm* : damask
damisela *nf* : damsel
damnificado, -da *n* : victim (of a disaster)
damnificar {72} *vt* : to damage, to injure
dance, etc. → **danzar**
dandi *nm* : dandy, fop
danés[1], **-nesa** *adj* : Danish
danés[2], **-nesa** *n, mpl* **daneses** : Dane, Danish person
danza *nf* : dance, dancing <danza folklórica : folk dance>
danzante, -ta *n* BAILARÍN : dancer
danzar {21} *v* BAILAR : to dance
dañar *vt* **1** : to damage, to spoil **2** : to harm, to hurt — **dañarse** *vr*
dañino, -na *adj* : harmful
daño *nm* **1** : damage **2** : harm, injury **3 hacer daño a** : to harm, to damage **4 daños y perjuicios** : damages
dar {22} *vt* **1** : to give **2** ENTREGAR : to deliver, to hand over **3** : to hit, to strike **4** : to yield, to produce **5** : to perform **6** : to give off, to emit **7 ~ como** *or* **~ por** : to regard as, to consider — *vi* **1** ALCANZAR : to suffice, to be enough <no me da para dos pasajes : I don't have enough for two fares> **2 ~ a** *or* **~ sobre** : to overlook, to look out on **3 ~ con** : to run into **4 ~ con** : to hit upon (an idea) **5 dar de sí** : to give, to stretch — **darse** *vr* **1** : to give in, to surrender **2** : to occur, to arise **3** : to grow, to come up **4 ~ con** *or* **~ contra** : to hit oneself against **5 dárselas de** : to boast about <se las da de muy listo : he thinks he's very smart>
dardo *nm* : dart
datar *vt* : to date — *vi* **~ de** : to date from, to date back to
dátil *nm* : date (fruit)
dato *nm* **1** : fact, piece of information **2 datos** *nmpl* : data, information
dé → **dar**
de *prep* **1** : of <la casa de Pepe : Pepe's house> <un niño de tres años : a three-year-old boy> **2** : from <es de Managua : she's from Managua> <salió del edificio : he left the building> **3** : in, at <a las tres de la mañana

: at three in the morning> <salen de noche : they go out at night> **4 :** than <más de tres : more than three>

deambular *vi* **:** to wander, to roam

debajo *adv* **1 :** underneath, below, on the bottom **2 ~ de :** under, underneath **3 por ~ :** below, beneath

debate *nm* **:** debate

debatir *vt* **:** to debate, to discuss — **debatirse** *vr* **:** to struggle

debe *nm* **:** debit column, debit

deber[1] *vt* **:** to owe — *v aux* **1 :** must, have to <debo ir a la oficina : I must go to the office> **2 :** should, ought to <deberías buscar trabajo : you ought to look for work> **3** (*expressing probability*) **:** must <debe ser mexicano : he must be Mexican> — **deberse** *vr* **~ a :** to be due to

deber[2] *nm* **1** OBLIGACIÓN **:** duty, obligation **2 deberes** *nmpl Spain* **:** homework

debidamente *adv* **:** properly, duly

debido, -da *adj* **1 :** right, proper, due **2 ~ a :** due to, owing to

débil *adj* **:** weak, feeble — **débilmente** *adv*

debilidad *nf* **:** weakness, debility, feebleness

debilitamiento *nm* **:** debilitation, weakening

debilitar *vt* **:** to debilitate, to weaken — **debilitarse** *vr*

debilucho[1], **-cha** *adj* **:** weak, frail

debilucho[2], **-cha** *n* **:** weakling

debitar *vt* **:** to debit

débito *nm* **1** DEUDA **:** debt **2 :** debit

debut [deˈbut] *nm, pl* **debuts :** debut

debutante[1] *nmf* **:** beginner, newcomer

debutante[2] *nf* **:** debutante *f*

debutar *vi* **:** to debut, to make a debut

década *nf* DECENIO **:** decade

decadencia *nf* **1 :** decadence **2 :** decline

decadente *adj* **1 :** decadent **2 :** declining

decaer {13} *vi* **1 :** to decline, to decay, to deteriorate **2** FLAQUEAR **:** to weaken, to flag

decaiga, etc. → **decaer**

decano, -na *n* **1 :** dean **2 :** senior member

decantar *vt* **:** to decant

decapitar *vt* **:** to decapitate, to behead

decayó, etc. → **decaer**

decena *nf* **:** group of ten

decencia *nf* **:** decency

decenio *nm* DÉCADA **:** decade

decente *adj* **:** decent — **decentemente** *adv*

decepción *nf, pl* **-ciones :** disappointment, letdown

decepcionante *adj* **:** disappointing

decepcionar *vt* **:** to disappoint, to let down — **decepcionarse** *vr*

deceso *nm* DEFUNCIÓN **:** death, passing

dechado *nm* **1 :** sampler (of embroidery) **2 :** model, paragon

decibelio *or* **decibel** *nm* **:** decibel

decidido, -da *adj* **:** decisive, determined, resolute — **decididamente** *adv*

decidir *vt* **1 :** to decide, to determine <no he decidido nada : I haven't made a decision> **2 :** to persuade, to decide <su padre lo decidió a estudiar : his father persuaded him to study> — *vi* **:** to decide — **decidirse** *vr* **:** to make up one's mind

decimal *adj* **:** decimal

décimo, -ma *adj* **:** tenth — **décimo, -ma** *n*

decimoctavo[1], **-va** *adj* **:** eighteenth

decimoctavo[2], **-va** *nm* **:** eighteenth (in a series)

decimocuarto[1], **-ta** *adj* **:** fourteenth

decimocuarto[2], **-ta** *nm* **:** fourteenth (in a series)

decimonoveno[1], **-na** *or* **decimonono, -na** *adj* **:** nineteenth

decimonoveno[2], **-na** *or* **decimonono, -na** *nm* **:** nineteenth (in a series)

decimoquinto[1], **-ta** *adj* **:** fifteenth

decimoquinto[2], **-ta** *nm* **:** fifteenth (in a series)

decimoséptimo[1], **-ma** *adj* **:** seventeenth

decimoséptimo[2], **-ma** *nm* **:** seventeenth (in a series)

decimosexto[1], **-ta** *adj* **:** sixteenth

decimosexto[2], **-ta** *nm* **:** sixteenth (in a series)

decimotercero[1], **-ra** *adj* **:** thirteenth

decimotercero[2], **-ra** *nm* **:** thirteenth (in a series)

decir[1] {23} *vt* **1 :** to say <dice que no quiere ir : she says she doesn't want to go> **2 :** to tell <dime lo que estás pensando : tell me what you're thinking> **3 :** to speak, to talk <no digas tonterías : don't talk nonsense> **4 :** to call <me dicen Rosy : they call me Rosy> **5 es decir :** that is to say **6 querer decir :** to mean — **decirse** *vr* **1 :** to say to oneself **2 :** to be said <¿cómo se dice "lápiz" en francés? : how do you say "pencil" in French?>

decir[2] *nm* DICHO **:** saying, expression

decisión *nf, pl* **-siones :** decision, choice

decisivo, -va *adj* **:** decisive, conclusive — **decisivamente** *adv*

declamar *vi* **:** to declaim — *vt* **:** to recite

declaración *nf, pl* **-ciones 1 :** declaration, statement **2** TESTIMONIO **:** deposition, testimony **3 declaración de derechos :** bill of rights **4 declaración jurada :** affidavit

declarado, -da *adj* **:** professed, open — **declaradamente** *adv*

declarar *vt* **:** to declare, to state — *vi* ATESTIGUAR **:** to testify — **declararse** *vr* **1 :** to declare oneself, to make a statement **2 :** to confess one's love **3**

: to plead (in court) <declararse inocente : to plead not guilty>

declinación *nf, pl* **-ciones 1** : drop, downward trend **2** : declination **3** : declension (in grammar)

declinar *vt* : to decline, to turn down — *vi* **1** : to draw to a close **2** : to diminish, to decline

declive *nm* **1** DECADENCIA : decline **2** : slope, incline

decodificador *nm* : decoder

decolar *vi Chile, Col, Ecua* : to take off (of an airplane)

decolorar *vt* : to bleach — **decolorarse** *vr* : to fade

decomisar *vt* CONFISCAR : to seize, to confiscate

decomiso *nm* : seizure, confiscation

decoración *nf, pl* **-ciones 1** : decoration **2** : decor **3** : stage set, scenery

decorado *nm* : stage set, scenery

decorador, -dora *n* : decorator

decorar *vt* ADORNAR : to decorate, to adorn

decorativo, -va *adj* : decorative, ornamental

decoro *nm* : decorum, propriety

decoroso, -sa *adj* : decent, proper, respectable

decrecer {53} *vi* : to decrease, to wane, to diminish — **decreciente** *adj*

decrecimiento *nm* : decrease, decline

decrépito, -ta *adj* : decrepit

decretar *vt* : to decree, to order

decreto *nm* : decree

decúbito *nm* : horizontal position <en decúbito prono : prone> <en decúbito supino : supine>

dedal *nm* : thimble

dedalera *nf* DIGITAL : foxglove

dedicación *nf, pl* **-ciones** : dedication, devotion

dedicar {72} *vt* CONSAGRAR : to dedicate, to devote — **dedicarse** *vr* **~ a** : to devote oneself to, to engage in

dedicatoria *nf* : dedication (of a book, song, etc.)

dedo *nm* **1** : finger <dedo meñique : little finger> **2 dedo del pie** : toe

deducción *nf, pl* **-ciones** : deduction

deducible *adj* **1** : deducible, inferable **2** : deductible

deducir {61} *vt* **1** INFERIR : to deduce **2** DESCONTAR : to deduct

defecar {72} *vi* : to defecate — **defecación** *nf*

defecto *nm* **1** : defect, flaw, shortcoming **2 en su defecto** : lacking that, in the absence of that

defectuoso, -sa *adj* : defective, faulty

defender {56} *vt* : to defend, to protect — **defenderse** *vr* **1** : to defend oneself **2** : to get by, to know the basics <su inglés no es perfecto pero se defiende : his English isn't perfect but he gets by>

defendible *adj* : defensible, tenable

defensa[1] *nf* : defense

defensa[2] *nmf* : defender, back (in sports)

defensiva *nf* : defensive, defense

defensivo, -va *adj* : defensive — **defensivamente** *adv*

defensor[1]**, -sora** *adj* : defending, defense

defensor[2]**, -sora** *n* **1** : defender, advocate **2** : defense counsel

defeño, -ña *n* : person from the Federal District (Mexico City)

deficiencia *nf* : deficiency, flaw

deficiente *adj* : deficient

déficit *nm, pl* **-cits 1** : deficit **2** : shortage, lack

definición *nf, pl* **-ciones** : definition

definido, -da *adj* : definite, well-defined

definir *vt* **1** : to define **2** : to determine

definitivamente *adv* **1** : finally **2** : permanently, for good **3** : definitely, absolutely

definitivo, -va *adj* **1** : definitive, conclusive **2 en definitiva** : all in all, on the whole **3 en definitiva** *Mex* : permanently, for good

deflación *nf, pl* **-ciones** : deflation

deforestación *nf, pl* **-ciones** : deforestation

deformación *nf, pl* **-ciones 1** : deformation **2** : distortion

deformar *vt* **1** : to deform, to disfigure **2** : to distort — **deformarse** *vr*

deforme *adj* : deformed, misshapen

deformidad *nf* : deformity

defraudación *nf, pl* **-ciones** : fraud

defraudar *vt* **1** ESTAFAR : to defraud, to cheat **2** : to disappoint

defunción *nf, pl* **-ciones** DECESO : death, passing

degeneración *nf, pl* **-ciones 1** : degeneration **2** : degeneracy, depravity

degenerado, -da *adj* DEPRAVADO : degenerate

degenerar *vi* : to degenerate

degenerativo, -va *adj* : degenerative

degollar {19} *vt* **1** : to slit the throat of, to slaughter **2** DECAPITAR : to behead **3** : to ruin, to destroy

degradación *nf, pl* **-ciones 1** : degradation **2** : demotion

degradar *vt* **1** : to degrade, to debase **2** : to demote

degustación *nf, pl* **-ciones** : tasting, sampling

degustar *vt* : to taste

deidad *nf* : deity

deificar {72} *vt* : to idolize, to deify

dejado, -da *adj* **1** : slovenly **2** : careless, lazy

dejar *vt* **1** : to leave **2** ABANDONAR : to abandon, to forsake **3** : to let be, to let go **4** PERMITIR : to allow, to permit — *vi* **~ de** : to stop, to quit <dejar de fumar : to quit smoking> — **dejarse** *vr* **1** : to let oneself be <se deja insultar : he lets himself be insulted> **2** : to forget, to leave <me dejé las llaves en el carro : I left the keys in

the car> **3 :** to neglect oneself, to let oneself go **4 :** to grow <nos estamos dejando el pelo largo : we're growing our hair long>
dejo *nm* **1 :** aftertaste **2 :** touch, hint **3 :** (regional) accent
delación *nf, pl* **-ciones :** denunciation, betrayal
delantal *nm* **1 :** apron **2 :** pinafore
delante *adv* **1** ENFRENTE **:** ahead, in front **2 ~ de :** before, in front of
delantera *nf* **1 :** front, front part, front row <tomar la delantera : to take the lead> **2 :** forward line (in sports)
delantero¹, -ra *adj* **1 :** front, forward **2 tracción delantera :** front-wheel drive
delantero², -ra *n* **:** forward (in sports)
delatar *vt* **1 :** to betray, to reveal **2 :** to denounce, to inform against
delegación *nf, pl* **-ciones :** delegation
delegado, -da *n* **:** delegate, representative
delegar {52} *vt* **:** to delegate
deleitar *vt* **:** to delight, to please — **deleitarse** *vr*
deleite *nm* **:** delight, pleasure
deletrear *vi* **:** to spell <¿como se deletrea? : how do you spell it?>
deleznable *adj* **1 :** brittle, crumbly **2 :** slippery **3 :** weak, fragile <una excusa deleznable : a weak excuse>
delfín *nm, pl* **delfines 1 :** dolphin **2 :** dauphin, heir apparent
delgadez *nf* **:** thinness, skinniness
delgado, -da *adj* **1** FLACO **:** thin, skinny **2** ESBELTO **:** slender, slim **3** DELICADO **:** delicate, fine **4** AGUDO **:** sharp, clever
deliberación *nf, pl* **-ciones :** deliberation
deliberado, -da *adj* **:** deliberate, intentional — **deliberadamente** *adv*
deliberar *vi* **:** to deliberate
deliberativo, -va *adj* **:** deliberative
delicadeza *nf* **1 :** delicacy, fineness **2 :** gentleness, softness **3 :** tact, discretion, consideration
delicado, -da *adj* **1 :** delicate, fine **2 :** sensitive, frail **3 :** difficult, tricky **4 :** fussy, hard to please **5 :** tactful, considerate
delicia *nf* **:** delight
delicioso, -sa *adj* **1** RICO **:** delicious **2 :** delightful
delictivo, -va *adj* **:** criminal
delictuoso, -sa → delictivo
delimitación *nf, pl* **-ciones 1 :** demarcation **2 :** defining, specifying
delimitar *vt* **1 :** to demarcate **2 :** to define, to specify
delincuencia *nf* **:** delinquency, crime
delincuente¹ *adj* **:** delinquent
delincuente² *nmf* CRIMINAL **:** delinquent, criminal
delinear *vt* **1 :** to delineate, to outline **2 :** to draft, to draw up
delinquir {24} *vi* **:** to break the law
delirante *adj* **:** delirious
delirar *vi* DESVARIAR **1 :** to be delirious **2 :** to rave, to talk nonsense
delirio *nm* **1** DESVARÍO **:** delirium **2** DISPARATE **:** nonsense, ravings *pl* <delirios de grandeza : delusions of grandeur> **3** FRENESÍ **:** mania, frenzy <¡fue el delirio! : it was wild!>
delito *nm* **:** crime, offense
delta *nm* **:** delta
demacrado, -da *adj* **:** emaciated, gaunt
demagogia *nf* **:** demagogy
demagógico, -ca *adj* **:** demagogic, demagogical
demagogo, -ga *n* **:** demagogue
demanda *nf* **1 :** demand <la oferta y la demanda : supply and demand> **2 :** petition, request **3 :** lawsuit
demandado, -da *n* **:** defendant
demandante *nmf* **:** plaintiff
demandar *vt* **1 :** to demand **2** REQUERIR **:** to call for, to require **3 :** to sue, to file a lawsuit against
demarcar {72} *vt* **:** to demarcate — **demarcación** *nf*
demás¹ *adj* **:** remaining <acabó las demás tareas : she finished the rest of the chores>
demás² *pron* **1 lo (la, los, las) demás :** the rest, everyone else, everything else <Pepe, Rosa, y los demás : Pepe, Rosa, and everybody else> **2 estar por demás :** to be of no use, to be pointless <no estaría por demás : it couldn't hurt, it's worth a try> **3 por demás :** extremely **4 por lo demás :** otherwise **5 y demás :** and so on, et cetera
demasía *nf* **en ~ :** excessively, in excess
demasiado¹ *adv* **1 :** too <vas demasiado aprisa : you're going too fast> **2 :** too much <estoy comiendo demasiado : I'm eating too much>
demasiado², -da *adj* **:** too much, too many, excessive
demencia *nf* **1 :** dementia **2** LOCURA **:** madness, insanity
demente¹ *adj* **:** insane, mad
demente² *nmf* **:** insane person
demeritar *vt* **1 :** to detract from **2 :** to discredit
demérito *nm* **1 :** fault **2 :** discredit, disrepute
democracia *nf* **:** democracy
demócrata¹ *adj* **:** democratic
demócrata² *nmf* **:** democrat
democrático, -ca *adj* **:** democratic — **democráticamente** *adv*
democratizar {21} *vt* **:** to democratize, to make democratic
demografía *nf* **:** demography
demográfico, -ca *adj* **:** demographic
demoledor, -dora *adj* **:** devastating
demoler {47} *vt* DERRIBAR, DERRUMBAR **:** to demolish, to destroy
demolición *nf, pl* **-ciones :** demolition
demonio *nm* DIABLO **:** devil, demon
demora *nf* **:** delay

demorar *vt* **1** RETRASAR : to delay **2** TARDAR : to take, to last <la reparación demorará varios días : the repair will take several days> — *vi* : to delay, to linger — **demorarse** *vr* **1** : to be slow, to take a long time **2** : to take too long
demostración *nf, pl* **-ciones** : demonstration
demostrar {19} *vt* : to demonstrate, to show
demostrativo, -va *adj* : demonstrative
demudar *vt* : to change, to alter — **demudarse** *vr* : to change one's expression
denegación *nf, pl* **-ciones** : denial, refusal
denegar {49} *vt* : to deny, to turn down
denigrante *adj* : degrading, humiliating
denigrar *vt* **1** DIFAMAR : to denigrate, to disparage **2** : to degrade, to humiliate
denodado, -da *adj* : bold, dauntless
denominación *nf, pl* **-ciones 1** : name, designation **2** : denomination (of money)
denominador *nm* : denominator
denominar *vt* : to designate, to name
denostar {19} *vt* : to revile
denotar *vt* : to denote, to show
densidad *nf* : density, thickness
denso, -sa *adj* : dense, thick — **densamente** *adv*
dentado, -da *adj* SERRADO : serrated, jagged
dentadura *nf* **1** : teeth *pl* **2 dentadura postiza** : dentures *pl*
dental *adj* : dental
dentellada *nf* **1** : bite **2** : tooth mark
dentera *nf* **1** : envy, jealousy **2 dar dentera** : to set one's teeth on edge
dentición *nf, pl* **-ciones 1** : teething **2** : dentition, set of teeth
dentífrico *nm* : toothpaste
dentista *nmf* : dentist
dentro *adv* **1** : in, inside **2** : indoors **3 ~ de** : within, inside, in **4 dentro de poco** : soon, shortly **5 dentro de todo** : all in all, all things considered **6 por ~** : inwardly, inside
denuedo *nm* : valor, courage
denuesto *nm* : insult
denuncia *nf* **1** : denunciation, condemnation **2** : police report
denunciante *nmf* : accuser (of a crime)
denunciar *vt* **1** : to denounce, to condemn **2** : to report (to the authorities)
deparar *vt* : to have in store for, to provide with <no sabemos lo que nos depara el destino : we don't know what fate has in store for us>
departamental *adj* **1** : departmental **2 tienda departamental** *Mex* : department store
departamento *nm* **1** : department **2** APARTAMENTO : apartment
departir *vi* : to converse
dependencia *nf* **1** : dependence, dependency <dependencia emocional : emotional dependence> <dependencia del alcohol : dependence on alcohol> **2** : agency, branch office
depender *vi* **1** : to depend **2 ~ de** : to depend on **3 ~ de** : to be subordinate to
dependiente[1] *adj* : dependent
dependiente[2], **-ta** *n* : clerk, salesperson
deplorable *adj* : deplorable
deplorar *vt* **1** : to deplore **2** LAMENTAR : to regret
deponer {60} *vt* **1** : to depose, to overthrow **2** : to abandon (an attitude or stance) **3 deponer las armas** : to lay down one's arms — *vi* **1** TESTIFICAR : to testify, to make a statement **2** EVACUAR : to defecate
deportación *nf, pl* **-ciones** : deportation
deportar *vt* : to deport
deporte *nm* : sport, sports *pl* <hacer deporte : to engage in sports>
deportista[1] *adj* **1** : fond of sports **2** : sporty
deportista[2] *nmf* **1** : sports fan **2** : athlete, sportsman *m*, sportswoman *f*
deportividad *nf Spain* : sportsmanship
deportivo, -va *adj* **1** : sports, sporting <artículos deportivos : sporting goods> **2** : sporty
deposición *nf, pl* **-ciones 1** : statement, testimony **2** : removal from office
depositante *nmf* : depositor
depositar *vt* **1** : to deposit, to place **2** : to store — **depositarse** *vr* : to settle
depósito *nm* **1** : deposit **2** : warehouse, storehouse
depravado, -da *adj* DEGENERADO : depraved, degenerate
depravar *vt* : to deprave, to corrupt
depreciación *nf, pl* **-ciones** : depreciation
depreciar *vt* : to depreciate, to reduce the value of — **depreciarse** *vr* : to lose value
depredación *nf* SAQUEO : depredation, plunder
depredador[1], **-dora** *adj* : predatory
depredador[2] *nm* **1** : predator **2** SAQUEADOR : plunderer
depresión *nf, pl* **-siones 1** : depression **2** : hollow, recess **3** : drop, fall **4** : slump, recession
depresivo[1], **-va** *adj* **1** : depressive **2** : depressant
depresivo[2] *nm* : depressant
deprimente *adj* : depressing
deprimir *vt* **1** : to depress **2** : to lower — **deprimirse** *vr* ABATIRSE : to get depressed
depuesto *pp* → **deponer**
depuración *nf, pl* **-ciones 1** PURIFICACIÓN : purification **2** PURGA : purge **3** : refinement, polish
depurar *vt* **1** PURIFICAR : to purify **2** PURGAR : to purge
depuso, etc. → **deponer**
derecha *nf* **1** : right **2** : right hand, right side **3** : right wing, right (in politics)

derechazo *nm* **1 :** pass with the cape on the right hand (in bullfighting) **2 :** right (in boxing) **3 :** forehand (in tennis)
derechista[1] *adj* **:** rightist, right-wing
derechista[2] *nmf* **:** right-winger
derecho[1] *adv* **1 :** straight **2 :** upright **3 :** directly
derecho[2], **-cha** *adj* **1 :** right **2 :** right-hand **3 :** RECTO **:** straight, upright, erect
derecho[3] *nm* **1 :** right <derechos humanos **:** human rights> **2 :** law <derecho civil **:** civil law> **3 :** right side (of cloth or clothing)
deriva *nf* **1 :** drift **2 a la deriva :** adrift
derivación *nf, pl* **-ciones :** derivation
derivar *vi* **1 :** to drift **2 ~ de :** to come from, to derive from **3 ~ en :** to result in — *vt* **:** to steer, to direct <derivó la discusión hacia la política **:** he steered the discussion over to politics> — **derivarse** *vr* **:** to be derived from, to arise from
dermatología *nf* **:** dermatology
dermatológico, -ca *adj* **:** dermatological
dermatólogo, -ga *n* **:** dermatologist
derogación *nf, pl* **-ciones :** abolition, repeal
derogar {52} *vt* ABOLIR **:** to abolish, to repeal
derramamiento *nm* **1 :** spilling, overflowing **2 derramamiento de sangre :** bloodshed
derramar *vt* **1 :** to spill **2 :** to shed (tears, blood) — **derramarse** *vr* **1 :** to spill over **2 :** to scatter
derrame *nm* **1 :** spilling, shedding **2 :** leakage, overflow **3 :** discharge, hemorrhage
derrapar *vi* **:** to skid
derrape *nm* **:** skid
derredor *nm* **al derredor** *or* **en derredor :** around, round about
derrengado, -da *adj* **1 :** bent, twisted **2 :** exhausted
derretir {54} *vt* **:** to melt, to thaw — **derretirse** *vr* **1 :** to melt, to thaw **2 ~ por** *fam* **:** to be crazy about
derribar *vt* **1** DEMOLER, DERRUMBAR **:** to demolish, to knock down **2 :** to shoot down, to bring down (an airplane) **3** DERROCAR **:** to overthrow
derribo *nm* **1 :** demolition, razing **2 :** shooting down **3 :** overthrow
derrocamiento *nm* **:** overthrow
derrocar {72} *vt* DERRIBAR **:** to overthrow, to topple
derrochador[1], **-dora** *adj* **:** extravagant, wasteful
derrochador[2], **-dora** *n* **:** spendthrift
derrochar *vt* **:** to waste, to squander
derroche *nm* **:** extravagance, waste
derrota *nf* **1 :** defeat, rout **2 :** course (at sea)
derrotar *vt* **:** to defeat
derrotero *nm* RUTA **:** course
derrotista *adj & nmf* **:** defeatist
derruir {41} *vt* **:** to demolish, to tear down
derrumbamiento *nm* **:** collapse
derrumbar *vt* **1** DEMOLER, DERRIBAR **:** to demolish, to knock down **2** DESPEÑAR **:** to cast down, to topple — **derrumbarse** *vr* DESPLOMARSE **:** to collapse, to break down
derrumbe *nm* **1** DESPLOME **:** collapse, fall <el derrumbe del comunismo **:** the fall of Communism> **2 :** landslide
desabastecimiento *nm* **:** shortage, scarcity
desabasto *nm Mex* **:** shortage, scarcity
desabrido, -da *adj* **:** tasteless, bland
desabrigar {52} *vt* **1 :** to undress **2 :** to uncover **3 :** to deprive of shelter
desabrochar *vt* **:** to unbutton, to undo — **desabrocharse** *vr* **:** to come undone
desacato *nm* **1 :** disrespect **2 :** contempt (of court)
desacelerar *vi* **:** to decelerate, to slow down
desacertado, -da *adj* **1 :** mistaken **2 :** unwise
desacertar {55} *vi* ERRAR **:** to err, to be mistaken
desacierto *nm* ERROR **:** error, mistake
desaconsejado, -da *adj* **:** ill-advised, unwise
desacorde *adj* **1 :** conflicting **2 :** discordant
desacostumbrado, -da *adj* **:** unaccustomed, unusual
desacreditar *vt* DESPRESTIGIAR **:** to discredit, to disgrace
desactivar *vt* **:** to deactivate, to defuse
desacuerdo *nm* **:** disagreement
desafiante *adj* **:** defiant
desafiar {85} *vt* RETAR **:** to defy, to challenge
desafilado, -da *adj* **:** blunt
desafinado, -da *adj* **:** out-of-tune, off-key
desafinarse *vr* **:** to go out of tune
desafío *nm* **1** RETO **:** challenge **2** RESISTENCIA **:** defiance
desafortunado, -da *adj* **:** unfortunate, unlucky — **desafortunadamente** *adv*
desafuero *nm* ABUSO **:** injustice, outrage
desagradable *adj* **:** unpleasant, disagreeable — **desagradablemente** *adv*
desagradar *vi* **:** to be unpleasant, to be disagreeable
desagradecido, -da *adj* **:** ungrateful
desagrado *nm* **1 :** displeasure **2 con ~ :** reluctantly
desagravio *nm* **1 :** apology **2 :** amends, reparation
desagregarse {52} *vr* **:** to break up, to disintegrate
desaguar {10} *vi* **:** to drain, to empty
desagüe *nm* **1 :** drain **2 :** drainage
desahogado, -da *adj* **1 :** well-off, comfortable **2 :** spacious, roomy

desahogar {52} *vt* **1 :** to relieve, to ease **2 :** to give vent to — **desahogarse** *vr* **1 :** to recover, to feel better **2 :** to unburden oneself, to let off steam

desahogo *nm* **1 :** relief, outlet **2 con ~ :** comfortably

desahuciar *vt* **1 :** to deprive of hope **2 :** to evict — **desahuciarse** *vr* **:** to lose all hope

desahucio *nm* **:** eviction

desairar {5} *vt* **:** to snub, to rebuff

desaire *nm* **:** rebuff, snub, slight

desajustar *vt* **1 :** to disarrange, to put out of order **2 :** to upset (plans)

desajuste *nm* **1 :** maladjustment **2 :** imbalance **3 :** upset, disruption

desalentar {55} *vt* DESANIMAR **:** to discourage, to dishearten — **desalentarse** *vr*

desaliento *nm* **:** discouragement

desaliñado, -da *adj* **:** slovenly, untidy

desalmado, -da *adj* **:** heartless, callous

desalojar *vt* **1 :** to remove, to clear **2** EVACUAR **:** to evacuate, to vacate **3 :** to evict

desalojo *nm* **1 :** removal, expulsion **2 :** evacuation **3 :** eviction

desamor *nm* **1** FRIALDAD **:** indifference **2** ENEMISTAD **:** dislike, enmity

desamparado, -da *adj* DESVALIDO **:** helpless, destitute

desamparar *vt* **:** to abandon, to forsake

desamparo *nm* **1 :** abandonment, neglect **2 :** helplessness

desamueblado, -da *adj* **:** unfurnished

desandar {6} *vt* **:** to go back, to return to the starting point

desangelado, -da *adj* **:** dull, lifeless

desangrar *vt* **:** to bleed, to bleed dry — **desangrarse** *vr* **1 :** to be bleeding **2 :** to bleed to death

desanimar *vt* DESALENTAR **:** to discourage, to dishearten — **desanimarse** *vr*

desánimo *nm* DESALIENTO **:** discouragement, dejection

desanudar *vt* **:** to untie, to disentangle

desapacible *adj* **:** unpleasant, disagreeable

desaparecer {53} *vt* **:** to cause to disappear — *vi* **:** to disappear, to vanish

desaparecido[1], -da *adj* **1 :** late, deceased **2 :** missing

desaparecido[2], -da *n* **:** missing person

desaparición *nf, pl* **-ciones :** disappearance

desapasionado, -da *adj* **:** dispassionate, impartial — **desapasionadamente** *adv*

desapego *nm* **:** coolness, indifference

desapercibido, -da *adj* **1 :** unnoticed **2** DESPREVENIDO **:** unprepared, off guard

desaprobación *nf, pl* **-ciones :** disapproval

desaprobar {19} *vt* REPROBAR **:** to disapprove of

desaprovechar *vt* MALGASTAR **:** to waste, to misuse — *vi* **:** to lose ground, to slip back

desarmador *nm Mex* **:** screwdriver

desarmar *vt* **1 :** to disarm **2** DESMONTAR **:** to disassemble, to take apart

desarme *nm* **:** disarmament

desarraigado, -da *adj* **:** rootless

desarraigar {52} *vt* **:** to uproot, to root out

desarreglado, -da *adj* **:** untidy, disorganized

desarreglar *vt* **1 :** to mess up **2 :** to upset, to disrupt

desarreglo *nm* **1 :** untidiness **2 :** disorder, confusion

desarrollar *vt* **:** to develop — **desarrollarse** *vr* **:** to take place

desarrollo *nm* **:** development

desarticulación *nf, pl* **-ciones 1 :** dislocation **2 :** breaking up, dismantling

desarticular *vt* **1** DISLOCAR **:** to dislocate **2 :** to break up, to dismantle

desaseado, -da *adj* **1 :** dirty **2 :** messy, untidy

desastre *nm* CATÁSTROFE **:** disaster

desastroso, -sa *adj* **:** disastrous, catastrophic

desatar *vt* **1 :** to undo, to untie **2 :** to unleash **3 :** to trigger, to precipitate — **desatarse** *vr* **:** to break out, to erupt

desatascar {72} *vt* **:** to unblock, to clear

desatención *nf, pl* **-ciones 1 :** absentmindedness, distraction **2 :** discourtesy

desatender {56} *vt* **1 :** to disregard **2 :** to neglect

desatento, -ta *adj* **1** DISTRAÍDO **:** absentminded **2** GROSERO **:** discourteous, rude

desatinado, -da *adj* **:** foolish, silly

desatino *nm* **:** folly, mistake

desautorizar {21} *vt* **:** to deprive of authority, to discredit

desavenencia *nf* DISCORDANCIA **:** disagreement, dispute

desayunar *vi* **:** to have breakfast — *vt* **:** to have for breakfast

desayuno *nm* **:** breakfast

desazón *nf, pl* **-zones** INQUIETUD **:** uneasiness, anxiety

desbalance *nm* **:** imbalance

desbancar {72} *vt* **:** to displace, to oust

desbandada *nf* **:** scattering, dispersal

desbarajuste *nm* DESORDEN **:** disarray, disorder, mess

desbaratar *vt* **1** ARRUINAR **:** to destroy, to ruin **2** DESCOMPONER **:** to break, to break down — **desbaratarse** *vr* **:** to fall apart

desbloquear *vt* **1 :** to open up, to clear, to break through **2 :** to free, to release

desbocado, -da *adj* **:** unbridled, rampant

desbocarse {72} *vr* **:** to run away, to bolt

desbordamiento *nm* **:** overflowing

desbordante *adj* **:** overflowing, bursting <desbordante de energía : bursting with energy>

desbordar *vt* **1 :** to overflow, to spill over **2 :** to surpass, to exceed **3 :** to

burst with, to brim with — **desbordarse** *vr*
descabellado, -da *adj* : outlandish, ridiculous
descafeinado, -da *adj* : decaffeinated
descalabrar *vt* : to hit on the head — **descalabrarse** *vr*
descalabro *nm* : setback, misfortune, loss
descalificar {72} *vt* : to disqualify — **descalificarse** *vr*
descalzarse {21} *vr* : take off one's shoes
descalzo, -za *adj* : barefoot
descansado, -da *adj* **1** : rested, refreshed **2** : restful, peaceful
descansar *vi* : to rest, to relax — *vt* : to rest <descansar la vista : to rest one's eyes>
descansillo *nm* : landing (of a staircase)
descanso *nm* **1** : rest, relaxation **2** : break **3** : landing (of a staircase) **4** : intermission
descapotable *adj & nm* : convertible
descarado, -da *adj* : brazen, impudent — **descaradamente** *adv*
descarga *nf* **1** : discharge **2** : unloading
descargar {52} *vt* **1** : to discharge **2** : to unload **3** : to release, to free **4** : to take out, to vent (anger, etc.) — **descargarse** *vr* **1** : to unburden oneself **2** : to quit **3** : to lose power
descargo *nm* **1** : unloading **2** : defense <testigo de descargo : witness for the defense>
descarnado, -da *adj* : scrawny, gaunt
descaro *nm* : audacity, nerve
descarriado, -da *adj* : lost, gone astray
descarrilar *vi* : to derail — **descarrilarse** *vr*
descartar *vt* : to rule out, to reject — **descartarse** *vr* : to discard
descascarar *vt* : to peel, to shell, to husk — **descascararse** *vr* : to peel off, to chip
descendencia *nf* **1** : descendants *pl* **2** LINAJE : descent, lineage
descendente *adj* : downward, descending
descender {56} *vt* **1** : to descend, to go down **2** BAJAR : to lower, to take down, to let down — *vi* **1** : to descend, to come down **2** : to drop, to fall **3** ~ **de** : to be a descendant of
descendiente *adj & nm* : descendant
descenso *nm* **1** : descent **2** BAJA, CAÍDA : drop, fall
descentralizar {21} *vt* : to decentralize — **descentralizarse** *vr* — **descentralización** *nf*
descifrable *adj* : decipherable
descifrar *vt* : to decipher, to decode
descolgar {16} *vt* **1** : to take down, to let down **2** : to pick up, to answer (the telephone)
descollar {19} *vi* SOBRESALIR : to stand out, to be outstanding, to excel
descolorarse *vr* : to fade
descolorido, -da *adj* : discolored, faded
descomponer {60} *vt* **1** : to rot, to decompose **2** DESBARATAR : to break, to break down — **descomponerse** *vr* **1** : to break down **2** : to decompose
descomposición *nf, pl* **-ciones 1** : breakdown, decomposition **2** : decay
descompresión *nf* : decompression
descompuesto[1] *pp* → **descomponer**
descompuesto[2], **-ta** *adj* **1** : broken down, out of order **2** : rotten, decomposed
descomunal *adj* **1** ENORME : enormous, huge **2** EXTRAORDINARIO : extraordinary
desconcertante *adj* : disconcerting
desconcertar {55} *vt* : to disconcert — **desconcertarse** *vr*
desconchar *vt* : to chip — **desconcharse** *vr* : to chip off, to peel
desconcierto *nm* : uncertainty, confusion
desconectar *vt* **1** : to disconnect, to switch off **2** : to unplug
desconfiado, -da *adj* : distrustful, suspicious
desconfianza *nf* RECELO : distrust, suspicion
desconfiar {85} *vi* ~ **de** : to distrust, to be suspicious of
descongelar *vt* **1** : to thaw **2** : to defrost **3** : to unfreeze (assets) — **descongelarse** *vr*
descongestionante *adj & nm* : decongestant
desconocer {18} *vt* **1** IGNORAR : to be unaware of **2** : to fail to recognize
desconocido[1], **-da** *adj* : unknown, unfamiliar
desconocido[2], **-da** *n* EXTRAÑO : stranger
desconocimiento *nm* : ignorance
desconsiderado, -da *adj* : inconsiderate, thoughtless — **desconsideradamente** *adj*
desconsolado, -da *adj* : disconsolate, heartbroken
desconsuelo *nm* AFLICCIÓN : grief, distress, despair
descontaminar *vt* : to decontaminate — **descontaminación** *nf*
descontar {19} *vt* **1** : to discount, to deduct **2** EXCEPTUAR : to except, to exclude
descontento[1], **-ta** *adj* : discontented, dissatisfied
descontento[2] *nm* : discontent, dissatisfaction
descontrol *nm* : lack of control, disorder, chaos
descontrolarse *vr* : to get out of control, to be out of hand
descorazonado, -da *adj* : disheartened, discouraged
descorrer *vt* : to draw back
descortés *adj, pl* **-teses** : discourteous, rude
descortesía *nf* : discourtesy, rudeness

descrédito *nm* DESPRESTIGIO **:** discredit

descremado, -da *adj* **:** nonfat, skim

describir {33} *vt* **:** to describe

descripción *nf, pl* **-ciones :** description

descriptivo, -va *adj* **:** descriptive

descrito *pp* → **describir**

descuartizar {21} *vt* **1 :** to cut up, to quarter **2 :** to tear to pieces

descubierto[1] *pp* → **descubrir**

descubierto[2], -ta *adj* **1 :** exposed, revealed **2 al descubierto :** out in the open

descubridor, -dora *n* **:** discoverer, explorer

descubrimiento *nm* **:** discovery

descubrir {2} *vt* **1** HALLAR **:** to discover, to find out **2** REVELAR **:** to uncover, to reveal — **descubrirse** *vr*

descuento *nm* REBAJA **:** discount

descuidado, -da *adj* **1 :** neglectful, careless **2 :** neglected, unkempt

descuidar *vt* **:** to neglect, to overlook — *vi* **:** to be careless — **descuidarse** *vr* **1 :** to be careless, to drop one's guard **2 :** to let oneself go

descuido *nm* **1 :** carelessness, negligence **2 :** slip, oversight

desde *prep* **1 :** from **2 :** since **3 desde ahora :** from now on **4 desde entonces :** since then **5 desde hace :** for, since (a time) <ha estado nevando desde hace dos días : it's been snowing for two days> **6 desde luego :** of course **7 desde que :** since, ever since **8 desde ya :** right now, immediately

desdecir {11} *vi* **~ de 1 :** to be unworthy of **2 :** to clash with — **desdecirse** *vr* **1** CONTRADECIRSE **:** to contradict oneself **2** RETRACTARSE **:** to go back on one's word

desdén *nm, pl* **desdenes** DESPRECIO **:** disdain, scorn

desdentado, -da *adj* **:** toothless

desdeñar *vt* DESPRECIAR **:** to disdain, to scorn, to despise

desdeñoso, -sa *adj* **:** disdainful, scornful — **desdeñosamente** *adv*

desdibujar *vt* **:** to blur — **desdibujarse** *vr*

desdicha *nf* **1 :** misery **2 :** misfortune

desdichado[1], -da *adj* **1 :** unfortunate **2 :** miserable, unhappy

desdichado[2], -da *n* **:** wretch

desdicho *pp* → **desdecir**

desdiga, desdijo, etc. → **desdecir**

desdoblar *vt* DESPLEGAR **:** to unfold

deseable *adj* **:** desirable

desear *vt* **1 :** to wish <te deseo buena suerte : I wish you good luck> **2** QUERER **:** to want, to desire

desechable *adj* **:** disposable

desechar *vt* **1 :** to discard, to throw away **2** RECHAZAR **:** to reject

desecho *nm* **1 :** reject **2 desechos** *nmpl* RESIDUOS **:** rubbish, waste

desembarazarse {21} *vr* **~ de :** to get rid of

desembarcadero *nm* **:** jetty, landing pier

desembarcar {72} *vi* **:** to disembark — *vt* **:** to unload

desembarco *nm* **1 :** landing, arrival **2 :** unloading

desembarque *nm* → **desembarco**

desembocadura *nf* **1 :** mouth (of a river) **2 :** opening, end (of a street)

desembocar {72} *vi* **~ en** *or* **~ a 1 :** to flow into, to join **2 :** to lead to, to result in

desembolsar *vt* PAGAR **:** to disburse, to pay out

desembolso *nm* PAGO **:** disbursement, payment

desempacar {72} *v* **:** to unpack

desempate *nm* **:** tiebreaker, play-off

desempeñar *vt* **1 :** to play (a role) **2 :** to fulfill, to carry out **3 :** to redeem (from a pawnshop) — **desempeñarse** *vr* **:** to function, to act

desempeño *nm* **1 :** fulfillment, carrying out **2 :** performance

desempleado[1], -da *adj* **:** unemployed

desempleado[2], -da *n* **:** unemployed person

desempleo *nm* **:** unemployment

desempolvar *vt* **1 :** to dust off **2 :** to resurrect, to revive

desencadenar *vt* **1 :** to unchain **2 :** to trigger, to unleash — **desencadenarse** *vr*

desencajar *vt* **1 :** to dislocate **2 :** to disconnect, to disengage

desencantar *vt* **:** to disenchant, to disillusion — **desencantarse** *vr*

desencanto *nm* **:** disenchantment, disillusionment

desenchufar *vt* **:** to disconnect, to unplug

desenfadado, -da *adj* **1 :** uninhibited, carefree **2 :** confident, self-assured

desenfado *nm* **1** DESENVOLTURA **:** self-assurance, confidence **2 :** naturalness, ease

desenfrenadamente *adv* **:** wildly, with abandon

desenfrenado, -da *adj* **:** unbridled, unrestrained

desenfreno *nm* **:** abandon, unrestraint

desenganchar *vt* **:** to unhitch, to uncouple

desengañar *vt* **:** to disillusion, to disenchant — **desengañarse** *vr*

desengaño *nm* **:** disenchantment, disillusionment

desenlace *nm* **:** ending, outcome

desenlazar {21} *vt* **1 :** to untie **2 :** to clear up, to resolve

desenmarañar *vt* **:** to disentangle, to unravel

desenmascarar *vt* **:** to unmask, to expose

desenredar *vt* **:** to untangle, to disentangle

desenrollar *vt* **:** to unroll, to unwind

desentenderse {56} *vr* **~ de 1 :** to want nothing to do with, to be uninterested in **2 :** to pretend ignorance of

desenterrar {55} *vt* **1** EXHUMAR **:** to exhume **2 :** to unearth, to dig up
desentonar *vi* **1 :** to clash, to conflict **2 :** to be out of tune, to sing off-key
desentrañar *vt* **:** to get to the bottom of, to unravel
desenvainar *vt* **:** to draw, to unsheathe (a sword)
desenvoltura *nf* **1** DESENFADO **:** confidence, self-assurance **2** ELOCUENCIA **:** eloquence, fluency
desenvolver {89} *vt* **:** to unwrap, to open — **desenvolverse** *vr* **1 :** to unfold, to develop **2 :** to manage, to cope
desenvuelto[1] *pp* → **desenvolver**
desenvuelto[2], **-ta** *adj* **:** confident, relaxed, self-assured
deseo *nm* **:** wish, desire
deseoso, -sa *adj* **:** eager, anxious
desequilibrar *vt* **:** to unbalance, to throw off balance — **desequilibrarse** *vr*
desequilibrio *nm* **:** imbalance
deserción *nf, pl* **-ciones :** desertion, defection
desertar *vi* **1 :** to desert, to defect **2 ~ de :** to abandon, to neglect
desertor, -tora *n* **:** deserter, defector
desesperación *nf, pl* **-ciones :** desperation, despair
desesperado, -da *adj* **:** desperate, despairing, hopeless — **desesperadamente** *adv*
desesperanza *nf* **:** despair, hopelessness
desesperar *vt* **:** to exasperate — *vi* **:** to despair, to lose hope — **desesperarse** *vr* **:** to become exasperated
desestimar *vt* **1 :** to reject, to disallow **2 :** to have a low opinion of
desfachatez *nf, pl* **-teces :** audacity, nerve, cheek
desfalcador, -dora *n* **:** embezzler
desfalcar {72} *vt* **:** to embezzle
desfalco *nm* **:** embezzlement
desfallecer {53} *vi* **1 :** to weaken **2 :** to faint
desfallecimiento *nm* **1 :** weakness **2 :** fainting
desfasado, -da *adj* **1 :** out of sync **2 :** out of step, behind the times
desfase *nm* **:** gap, lag <desfase horario **:** jet lag>
desfavorable *adj* **:** unfavorable, adverse — **desfavorablemente** *adv*
desfavorecido, -da *adj* **:** underprivileged
desfigurar *vt* **1 :** to disfigure, to mar **2 :** to distort, to misrepresent
desfiladero *nm* **:** narrow gorge, defile
desfilar *vi* **:** to parade, to march
desfile *nm* **:** parade, procession
desfogar {52} *vt* **1 :** to vent **2** *Mex* **:** to unclog, to unblock — **desfogarse** *vr* **:** to vent one's feelings, to let off steam
desforestación *nf, pl* **-ciones :** deforestation
desgajar *vt* **1 :** to tear off **2 :** to break apart — **desgajarse** *vr* **:** to come apart
desgana *nf* **1** INAPETENCIA **:** lack of appetite **2** APATÍA **:** apathy, unwillingness, reluctance
desgano *nm* → **desgana**
desgarbado, -da *adj* **:** ungainly
desgarrador, -dora *adj* **:** heartrending, heartbreaking
desgarradura *nf* **:** tear, rip
desgarrar *vt* **1 :** to tear, to rip **2 :** to break (one's heart) — **desgarrarse** *vr*
desgarre *nm* → **desgarro**
desgarro *nm* **:** tear
desgarrón *nm, pl* **-rrones :** rip, tear
desgastar *vt* **1 :** to use up **2 :** to wear away, to wear down
desgaste *nm* **:** deterioration, wear and tear
desglosar *vt* **:** to break down, to itemize
desglose *nm* **:** breakdown, itemization
desgobierno *nm* **:** anarchy, disorder
desgracia *nf* **1 :** misfortune **2 :** disgrace **3 por ~ :** unfortunately
desgraciadamente *adv* **:** unfortunately
desgraciado[1], **-da** *adj* **1 :** unfortunate, unlucky **2 :** vile, wretched
desgraciado[2], **-da** *n* **:** unfortunate person, wretch
desgranar *vt* **:** to shuck, to shell
deshabitado, -da *adj* **:** unoccupied, uninhabited
deshacer {40} *vt* **1 :** to destroy, to ruin **2** DESATAR **:** to undo, to untie **3 :** to break apart, to crumble **4 :** to dissolve, to melt **5 :** to break, to cancel — **deshacerse** *vr* **1 :** to fall apart, to come undone **2 ~ de :** to get rid of
deshecho[1] *pp* → **deshacer**
deshecho[2], **-cha** *adj* **1 :** destroyed, ruined **2 :** devastated, shattered **3 :** undone, untied
desherbar {55} *vt* **:** to weed
desheredado, -da *adj* MARGINADO **:** dispossessed, destitute
desheredar *vt* **:** to disinherit
deshicieron, etc. → **deshacer**
deshidratar *vt* **:** to dehydrate — **deshidratación** *nf*
deshielo *nm* **:** thaw, thawing
deshilachar *vt* **:** to fray — **deshilacharse** *vr*
deshizo → **deshacer**
deshonestidad *nf* **:** dishonesty
deshonesto, -ta *adj* **:** dishonest
deshonra *nf* **:** dishonor, disgrace
deshonrar *vt* **:** to dishonor, to disgrace
deshonroso, -sa *adj* **:** dishonorable, disgraceful
deshuesar *vt* **1 :** to pit (a fruit, etc.) **2 :** to bone, to debone
deshumanizar {21} *vt* **:** to dehumanize — **deshumanización** *nf*
desidia *nf* **1** APATÍA **:** apathy, indolence **2** NEGLIGENCIA **:** negligence, sloppiness
desierto[1], **-ta** *adj* **:** deserted, uninhabited

desierto[2] *nm* : desert
designación *nf, pl* **-ciones** NOMBRAMIENTO : appointment, naming (to an office, etc.)
designar *vt* NOMBRAR : to designate, to appoint, to name
designio *nm* : plan
desigual *adj* **1** : unequal **2** DISPAREJO : uneven
desigualdad *nf* **1** : inequality **2** : unevenness
desilusión *nf, pl* **-siones** DESENCANTO, DESENGAÑO : disillusionment, disenchantment
desilusionar *vt* DESENCANTAR, DESENGAÑAR : to disillusion, to disenchant — **desilusionarse** *vr*
desinfectante *adj & nm* : disinfectant
desinfectar *vt* : to disinfect — **desinfección** *nf*
desinflar *vt* : to deflate — **desinflarse** *vr*
desinhibido, -da *adj* : unihibited, unrestrained
desintegración *nf, pl* **-ciones** : disintegration
desintegrar *vt* : to disintegrate, to break up — **desintegrarse** *vr*
desinterés *nm* **1** : lack of interest, indifference **2** : unselfishness
desinteresado, -da *adj* GENEROSO : unselfish
desintoxicar {72} *vt* : to detoxify, to detox
desistir *vi* **1** : to desist, to stop **2** **~ de** : to give up, to relinquish
deslave *nm Mex* : landslide
desleal *adj* INFIEL : disloyal — **deslealmente** *adv*
deslealtad *nf* : disloyalty
desleír {66} *vt* : to dilute, to dissolve
desligar {52} *vt* **1** : to separate, to undo **2** : to free (from an obligation) — **desligarse** *vr* **~ de** : to extricate oneself from
deslindar *vt* **1** : to mark the limits of, to demarcate **2** : to define, to clarify
deslinde *nm* : demarcation
desliz *nm, pl* **deslices** : error, mistake, slip <desliz de la lengua : slip of the tongue>
deslizar {21} *vt* **1** : to slide, to slip **2** : to slip in — **deslizarse** *vr* **1** : to slide, to glide **2** : to slip away
deslucido, -da *adj* **1** : unimpressive, dull **2** : faded, dingy, tarnished
deslucir {45} *vt* **1** : to spoil **2** : to fade, to dull, to tarnish **3** : to discredit
deslumbrar *vt* : to dazzle — **deslumbrante** *adj*
deslustrado, -da *adj* : dull, lusterless
deslustrar *vt* : to tarnish, to dull
deslustre *nm* : tarnish
desmán *nm, pl* **desmanes** **1** : outrage, abuse **2** : misfortune
desmandarse *vr* : to behave badly, to get out of hand
desmantelar *vt* DESMONTAR : to dismantle
desmañado, -da *adj* : clumsy, awkward
desmayado, -da *adj* **1** : fainting, weak **2** : dull, pale
desmayar *vi* : to lose heart, to falter — **desmayarse** *vr* DESVANECERSE : to faint, to swoon
desmayo *nm* **1** : faint, fainting **2** **sufrir un desmayo** : to faint
desmedido, -da *adj* DESMESURADO : excessive, undue
desmejorar *vt* : to weaken, to make worse — *vi* : to decline (in health), to get worse
desmembramiento *nm* : dismemberment
desmembrar {55} *vt* **1** : to dismember **2** : to break up
desmemoriado, -da *adj* : absent-minded, forgetful
desmentido *nm* : denial
desmentir {76} *vt* **1** NEGAR : to deny, to refute **2** CONTRADECIR : to contradict
desmenuzar {21} *vt* **1** : to break down, to scrutinize **2** : to crumble, to shred — **desmenuzarse** *vr*
desmerecer {53} *vt* : to be unworthy of — *vi* **1** : to decline in value **2** **~ de** : to compare unfavorably with
desmesurado, -da *adj* DESMEDIDO : excessive, inordinate — **desmesuradamente** *adv*
desmigajar *vt* : to crumble — **desmigajarse** *vr*
desmilitarizado, -da *adj* : demilitarized
desmontar *vt* **1** : to clear, to level off **2** DESMANTELAR : to dismantle, to take apart — *vi* : to dismount
desmonte *nm* : clearing, leveling
desmoralizador, -dora *adj* : demoralizing
desmoralizar {21} *vt* DESALENTAR : to demoralize, to discourage
desmoronamiento *nm* : crumbling, falling apart
desmoronar *vt* : to wear away, to erode — **desmoronarse** *vr* : to crumble, to deteriorate, to fall apart
desmotadora *nf* : gin, cotton gin
desmovilizar {21} *vt* : to demobilize — **desmovilización** *nf*
desnaturalizar {21} *vt* **1** : to denature **2** : to distort, to alter
desnivel *nm* **1** : disparity, difference **2** : unevenness (of a surface) **3** **paso a desnivel** *Mex* : underpass
desnivelado, -da *adj* **1** : uneven **2** : unbalanced
desnudar *vt* **1** : to undress **2** : to strip, to lay bare — **desnudarse** *vr* : to undress, to strip off one's clothing
desnudez *nf, pl* **-deces** : nudity, nakedness
desnudismo *nm* → **nudismo**
desnudista → **nudista**
desnudo[1], **-da** *adj* : nude, naked, bare
desnudo[2] *nm* : nude

desnutrición *nf, pl* **-ciones** : MALNUTRICIÓN : malnutrition, undernourishment
desnutrido, -da *adj* MALNUTRIDO : malnourished, undernourished
desobedecer {53} *v* : to disobey
desobediencia *nf* : disobedience — **desobediente** *adj*
desocupación *nf, pl* **-ciones** : unemployment
desocupado, -da *adj* **1** : vacant, empty **2** : free, unoccupied **3** : unemployed
desocupar *vt* **1** : to empty **2** : to vacate, to move out of — **desocuparse** *vr* : to leave, to quit (a job)
desodorante *adj & nm* : deodorant
desolación *nf, pl* **-ciones** : desolation
desolado, -da *adj* **1** : desolate **2** : devastated, distressed
desolador, -dora *adj* **1** : devastating **2** : bleak, desolate
desollar *vt* : to skin, to flay
desorbitado, -da *adj* **1** : excessive, exorbitant **2 con los ojos desorbitados** : with eyes popping out of one's head
desorden *nm, pl* **desórdenes 1** DESBARAJUSTE : disorder, mess **2** : disorder, disturbance, upset
desordenado, -da *adj* **1** : untidy, messy **2** : disorderly, unruly
desorganización *nf, pl* **-ciones** : disorganization
desorganizar {21} *vt* : to disrupt, to disorganize
desorientación *nf, pl* **-ciones** : disorientation, confusion
desorientar *vt* : to disorient, to mislead, to confuse — **desorientarse** *vr* : to become disoriented, to lose one's way
desovar *vi* : to spawn
despachar *vt* **1** : to complete, to conclude **2** : to deal with, to take care of, to handle **3** : to dispatch, to send off **4** *fam* : to finish off, to kill — **despacharse** *vr fam* : to gulp down, to polish off
despacho *nm* **1** : dispatch, shipment **2** OFICINA : office, study
despacio *adv* LENTAMENTE, LENTO : slowly, slow <¡despacio! : take it easy!, easy does it!>
desparasitar *vt* : to worm (an animal), to delouse
desparpajo *nm* **1** *fam* : self-confidence, nerve **2** *CA fam* : confusion, muddle
desparramar *vt* **1** : to spill, to splatter **2** : to spread, to scatter
despatarrarse *vr* : to sprawl (out)
despavorido, -da *adj* : terrified, horrified
despecho *nm* **1** : spite **2 a despecho de** : despite, in spite of
despectivo, -va *adj* **1** : contemptuous, disparaging **2** : derogatory, pejorative
despedazar {21} *vt* : to cut to pieces, to tear apart
despedida *nf* **1** : farewell, good-bye **2 despedida de soltera** : bridal shower
despedir {54} *vt* **1** : to see off, to show out **2** : to dismiss, to fire **3** EMITIR : to give off, to emit <despedir un olor : to give off an odor> — **despedirse** *vr* : to take one's leave, to say good-bye
despegado, -da *adj* **1** : separated, detached **2** : cold, distant
despegar {52} *vt* : to remove, to detach — *vi* : to take off, to lift off, to blast off
despegue *nm* : takeoff, liftoff
despeinado, -da *adj* : disheveled, tousled <estoy despeinada : my hair's a mess>
despejado, -da *adj* **1** : clear, fair **2** : alert, clear-headed **3** : uncluttered, unobstructed
despejar *vt* **1** : to clear, to free **2** : to clarify — *vi* **1** : to clear up **2** : to punt (in sports)
despeje *nm* **1** : clearing **2** : punt (in sports)
despellejar *vt* : to skin (an animal)
despenalizar {21} *vt* : to legalize — **despenalización** *nf*
despensa *nf* **1** : pantry, larder **2** PROVISIONES : provisions *pl,* supplies *pl*
despeñar *vt* : to hurl down
despepitar *vt* : to seed, to remove the seeds from
desperdiciar *vt* **1** DESAPROVECHAR, MALGASTAR : to waste **2** : to miss, to miss out on
desperdicio *nm* **1** : waste **2 desperdicios** *nmpl* RESIDUOS : refuse, scraps, rubbish
desperdigar {52} *vt* DISPERSAR : to disperse, to scatter
desperfecto *nm* **1** DEFECTO : flaw, defect **2** : damage
despertador *nm* : alarm clock
despertar {55} *vi* : to awaken, to wake up — *vt* **1** : to arouse, to wake **2** EVOCAR : to elicit, to evoke — **despertarse** *vr* : to wake (oneself) up
despiadado, -da *adj* CRUEL : cruel, merciless, pitiless — **despiadadamente** *adv*
despido *nm* : dismissal, layoff
despierto, -ta *adj* **1** : awake, alert **2** LISTO : clever, sharp <con la mente despierta : with a sharp mind>
despilfarrador[1], -dora *adj* : extravagant, wasteful
despilfarrador[2], -dora *n* : spendthrift, prodigal
despilfarrar *vt* MALGASTAR : to squander, to waste
despilfarro *nm* : extravagance, wastefulness
despintar *vt* : to strip the paint from — **despintarse** *vr* : to fade, to wash off, to peel off
despistado[1], -da *adj* **1** DISTRAÍDO : absentminded, forgetful **2** CONFUSO : confused, bewildered

despistado², **-da** *n* : scatterbrain, absentminded person
despistar *vt* : to throw off the track, to confuse — **despistarse** *vr*
despiste *nm* **1** : absentmindedness **2** : mistake, slip
desplantador *nm* : garden trowel
desplante *nm* : insolence, rudeness
desplazamiento *nm* **1** : movement, displacement **2** : journey
desplazar {21} *vt* **1** : to replace, to displace **2** TRASLADAR : to move, to shift
desplegar {49} *vt* **1** : to display, to show, to manifest **2** DESDOBLAR : to unfold, to unfurl **3** : to spread (out) **4** : to deploy
despliegue *nm* **1** : display **2** : deployment
desplomarse *vr* **1** : to plummet, to fall **2** DERRUMBARSE : to collapse, to break down
desplome *nm* **1** : fall, drop **2** : collapse
desplumar *vt* : to pluck (a chicken, etc.)
despoblado¹, **-da** *adj* : uninhabited, deserted
despoblado² *nm* : open country, deserted area
despoblar {19} *vt* : to depopulate
despojar *vt* **1** : to strip, to clear **2** : to divest, to deprive — **despojarse** *vr* **1** **~ de** : to remove (clothing) **2** **~ de** : to relinquish, to renounce
despojos *nmpl* **1** : remains, scraps **2** : plunder, spoils
desportilladura *nf* : chip, nick
desportillar *vt* : to chip — **desportillarse** *vr*
desposeer {20} *vt* : to dispossess
déspota *nmf* : despot, tyrant
despotismo *nm* : despotism — **despótico, -ca** *adj*
despotricar {72} *vi* : to rant and rave, to complain excessively
despreciable *adj* **1** : despicable, contemptible **2** : negligible <nada despreciable : not inconsiderable, significant>
despreciar *vt* DESDEÑAR, MENOSPRECIAR : to despise, to scorn, to disdain
despreciativo, -va *adj* : scornful, disdainful
desprecio *nm* DESDÉN, MENOSPRECIO : disdain, contempt, scorn
desprender *vt* **1** SOLTAR : to detach, to loosen, to unfasten **2** EMITIR : to emit, to give off — **desprenderse** *vr* **1** : to come off, to come undone **2** : to be inferred, to follow **3** **~ de** : to part with, to get rid of
desprendido, -da *adj* : generous, unselfish, disinterested
desprendimiento *nm* **1** : detachment **2** GENEROSIDAD : generosity **3** **desprendimiento de tierras** : landslide
despreocupación *nf, pl* **-ciones** : indifference, lack of concern
despreocupado, -da *adj* : carefree, easygoing, unconcerned
desprestigiar *vt* DESACREDITAR : to discredit, to disgrace — **desprestigiarse** *vr* : to lose prestige
desprestigio *nm* DESCRÉDITO : discredit, disrepute
desprevenido, -da *adj* DESAPERCIBIDO : unprepared, off guard, unsuspecting
desproporción *nf, pl* **-ciones** : disproportion, disparity
desproporcionado, -da : out of proportion
despropósito *nm* : piece of nonsense, absurdity
desprotegido, -da *adj* : unprotected, vulnerable
desprovisto, -ta *adj* **~ de** : devoid of, lacking in
después *adv* **1** : afterward, later **2** : then, next **3** **~ de** : after, next after <después de comer : after eating> **4** **después (de) que** : after <después que lo acabé : after I finished it> **5** **después de todo** : after all **6** **poco después** : shortly after, soon thereafter
despuntado, -da *adj* : blunt, dull
despuntar *vt* : to blunt — *vi* **1** : to dawn **2** : to sprout **3** : to excel, to stand out
desquiciar *vt* **1** : to unhinge (a door) **2** : to drive crazy — **desquiciarse** *vr* : to go crazy
desquitarse *vr* **1** : to get even, to retaliate **2** **~ con** : to take it out on
desquite *nm* : revenge
desregulación *nf, pl* **-ciones** : deregulation
desregular *vt* : to deregulate
destacadamente *adv* : outstandingly, prominently
destacado, -da *adj* **1** : outstanding, prominent **2** : stationed, posted
destacar {72} *vt* **1** ENFATIZAR, SUBRAYAR : to emphasize, to highlight, to stress **2** : to station, to post — *vi* : to stand out
destajo *nm* **1** : piecework **2** **a ~** : by the item, by the job
destapador *nm* : bottle opener
destapar *vt* **1** : to open, to take the top off **2** DESCUBRIR : to reveal, to uncover **3** : to unblock, to unclog
destape *nm* : uncovering, revealing
destartalado, -da *adj* : dilapidated, tumbledown
destellar *vi* **1** : to sparkle, to flash, to glint **2** : to twinkle
destello *nm* **1** : flash, sparkle, twinkle **2** : glimmer, hint
destemplado, -da *adj* **1** : out of tune **2** : irritable, out of sorts **3** : unpleasant (of weather)
desteñir {67} *vi* : to run, to fade — **desteñirse** DESCOLORARSE : to fade
desterrado¹, **-da** *adj* : banished, exiled
desterrado², **-da** *n* : exile

desterrar {55} *vt* **1** EXILIAR **:** to banish, to exile **2** ERRADICAR **:** to eradicate, to do away with

destetar *vt* **:** to wean

destiempo *adv* **a ~ :** at the wrong time

destierro *nm* EXILIO **:** exile

destilación *nf, pl* **-ciones :** distillation

destilador, -dora *n* **:** distiller

destilar *vt* **1 :** to exude **2 :** to distill

destilería *nf* **:** distillery

destinación *nf, pl* **-ciones** DESTINO **:** destination

destinado, -da *adj* **:** destined, bound

destinar *vt* **1 :** to appoint, to assign **2** ASIGNAR **:** to earmark, to allot

destinatario, -ria *n* **1 :** addressee **2 :** payee

destino *nm* **1 :** destiny, fate **2** DESTINACIÓN **:** destination **3 :** use **4 :** assignment, post

destitución *nf, pl* **-ciones :** dismissal, removal from office

destituir {41} *vt* **:** to dismiss, to remove from office

destorcer {14} *vt* **:** to untwist

destornillador *nm* **:** screwdriver

destornillar *vt* **:** to unscrew

destrabar *vt* **1 :** to untie, to undo, to ease up **2 :** to separate

destreza *nf* HABILIDAD **:** dexterity, skill

destronar *vt* **:** to depose, to dethrone

destrozado, -da *adj* **1 :** ruined, destroyed **2 :** devastated, brokenhearted

destrozar {21} *vt* **1 :** to smash, to shatter **2 :** to destroy, to wreck — **destrozarse** *vr*

destrozo *nm* **1** DAÑO **:** damage **2 :** havoc, destruction

destrucción *nf, pl* **-ciones :** destruction

destructivo, -va *adj* **:** destructive

destructor[1]**, -tora** *adj* **:** destructive

destructor[2] *nm* **:** destroyer (ship)

destruir {41} *vt* **:** to destroy — **destruirse** *vr*

desubicado, -da *adj* **1 :** out of place **2 :** confused, disoriented

desunión *nf, pl* **-niones :** disunity

desunir *vt* **:** to split, to divide

desusado, -da *adj* **1** INSÓLITO **:** unusual **2** OBSOLETO **:** obsolete, disused, antiquated

desuso *nm* **:** disuse, obsolescence <caer en desuso : to fall into disuse>

desvaído, -da *adj* **1 :** pale, washed-out **2 :** vague, blurred

desvainar *vt* **:** to shell

desvalido, -da *adj* DESAMPARADO **:** destitute, helpless

desvalijar *vt* **1 :** to ransack **2 :** to rob

desvalorización *nf, pl* **-ciones 1** DEVALUACIÓN **:** devaluation **2 :** depreciation

desvalorizar {21} *vt* **:** to devalue

desván *nm, pl* **desvanes** ÁTICO, BUHARDILLA **:** attic

desvanecer {53} *vt* **1** DISIPAR **:** to make disappear, to dispel **2 :** to fade, to blur — **desvanecerse** *vr* **1 :** to vanish, to disappear **2 :** to fade **3** DESMAYARSE **:** to faint, to swoon

desvanecimiento *nm* **1 :** disappearance **2** DESMAYO **:** faint **3 :** fading

desvariar {85} *vi* **1** DELIRAR **:** to be delirious **2 :** to rave, to talk nonsense

desvarío *nm* DELIRIO **:** delirium

desvelado, -da *adj* **:** sleepless

desvelar *vt* **1 :** to keep awake **2** REVELAR **:** to reveal, to disclose — **desvelarse** *vr* **1 :** to stay awake **2 :** to do one's utmost

desvelo *nm* **1 :** sleeplessness **2 desvelos** *nmpl* **:** efforts, pains

desvencijado, -da *adj* **:** dilapidated, rickety

desventaja *nf* **:** disadvantage, drawback

desventajoso, -sa *adj* **:** disadvantageous, unfavorable

desventura *nf* INFORTUNIO **:** misfortune

desventurado, -da *adj* **:** unfortunate, ill-fated

desvergonzado, -da *adj* **:** shameless, impudent

desvergüenza *nf* **:** shamelessness, impudence

desvestir {54} *vt* **:** to undress — **desvestirse** *vr* **:** to get undressed

desviación *nf, pl* **-ciones 1 :** deviation, departure **2 :** detour, diversion

desviar {85} *vt* **1 :** to change the course of, to divert **2 :** to turn away, to deflect — **desviarse** *vr* **1 :** to branch off **2** APARTARSE **:** to stray

desvinculación *nf, pl* **-ciones :** dissociation

desvincular *vt* **~ de :** to separate from, to dissociate from — **desvincularse** *vr*

desvío *nm* **1 :** diversion, detour **2 :** deviation

desvirtuar {3} *vt* **1 :** to impair, to spoil **2 :** to detract from **3 :** to distort, to misrepresent

detalladamente *adv* **:** in detail, at great length

detallar *vt* **:** to detail

detalle *nm* **1 :** detail **2 al detalle :** retail

detallista[1] *adj* **1 :** meticulous **2 :** retail

detallista[2] *nmf* **1 :** perfectionist **2 :** retailer

detección *nf, pl* **-ciones :** detection

detectar *vt* **:** to detect — **detectable** *adj*

detective *nmf* **:** detective

detector *nm* **:** detector <detector de mentiras : lie detector>

detención *nf, pl* **-ciones 1** ARRESTO **:** detention, arrest **2 :** stop, halt **3 :** delay, holdup

detener {80} *vt* **1** ARRESTAR **:** to arrest, to detain **2** PARAR **:** to stop, to halt **3 :** to keep, to hold back — **detenerse** *vr* **1 :** to stop **2 :** to delay, to linger

detenidamente *adv* **:** thoroughly, at length

detenimiento *nm* **con ~ :** carefully, in detail

detentar *vt* : to hold, to retain
detergente *nm* : detergent
deteriorado, -da *adj* : damaged, worn
deteriorar *vt* ESTROPEAR : to damage, to spoil — **deteriorarse** *vr* **1** : to get damaged, to wear out **2** : to deteriorate, to worsen
deterioro *nm* **1** : deterioration, wear **2** : worsening, decline
determinación *nf, pl* **-ciones 1** : determination, resolve **2 tomar una determinación** : to make a decision
determinado, -da *adj* **1** : certain, particular **2** : determined, resolute
determinante[1] *adj* : determining, deciding
determinante[2] *nm* : determinant
determinar *vt* **1** : to determine **2** : to cause, to bring about — **determinarse** *vr* : to make up one's mind, to decide
detestar *vt* : to detest — **detestable** *adj*
detonación *nf, pl* **-ciones** : detonation
detonador *nm* : detonator
detonante[1] *adj* : detonating, explosive
detonante[2] *nm* **1** → **detonador 2** : catalyst, cause
detonar *vi* : to detonate, to explode
detractor, -tora *n* : detractor, critic
detrás *adv* **1** : behind **2 ~ de** : in back of **3 por ~** : from behind
detuvo, etc. → **detener**
deuda *nf* **1** DÉBITO : debt **2 en deuda con** : indebted to
deudo, -da *n* : relative
deudor[1], **-dora** *adj* : indebted
deudor[2], **-dora** *n* : debtor
devaluación *nf, pl* **-ciones** DESVALORIZACIÓN : devaluation
devaluar {3} *vt* : to devalue — **devaluarse** *vr* : to depreciate
devanarse *vr* **devanarse los sesos** : to rack one's brains
devaneo *nm* **1** : flirtation, fling **2** : idle pursuit
devastador, -dora *adj* : devastating
devastar *vt* : to devastate — **devastación** *nf*
devenir {87} *vi* **1** : to come about **2 ~ en** : to become, to turn into
devoción *nf, pl* **-ciones** : devotion
devolución *nf, pl* **-ciones** REEMBOLSO : return, refund
devolver {89} *vt* **1** : to return, to give back **2** REEMBOLSAR : to refund, to pay back **3** : to vomit, to bring up — *vi* : to vomit, to throw up — **devolverse** *vr* : to return, to come back, to go back
devorar *vt* **1** : to devour **2** : to consume
devoto[1], **-ta** *adj* : devout — **devotamente** *adv*
devoto[2], **-ta** *n* : devotee, admirer
di → **dar, decir**
día *nm* **1** : day <todos los días : every day> **2** : daytime, daylight <de día : by day, in the daytime> <en pleno día : in broad daylight> **3 al día** : up-to-date **4 en su día** : in due time
diabetes *nf* : diabetes
diabético, -ca *adj & n* : diabetic
diablillo *nm* : little devil, imp
diablo *nm* DEMONIO : devil
diablura *nf* **1** : prank **2 diabluras** *nfpl* : mischief
diabólico, -ca *adj* : diabolical, diabolic, devilish
diaconisa *nf* : deaconess
diácono *nm* : deacon
diadema *nf* : diadem, crown
diáfano, -na *adj* : diaphanous
diafragma *nm* : diaphragm
diagnosticar {72} *vt* : to diagnose
diagnóstico[1], **-ca** *adj* : diagnostic
diagnóstico[2] *nm* : diagnosis
diagonal *adj & nf* : diagonal — **diagonalmente** *adv*
diagrama *nm* **1** : diagram **2 diagrama de flujo** ORGANIGRAMA : flowchart
dialecto *nm* : dialect
dialogar {52} *vi* : to have a talk, to converse
diálogo *nm* : dialogue
diamante *nm* : diamond
diametral *adj* : diametric, diametrical — **diametralmente** *adv*
diámetro *nm* : diameter
diana *nf* **1** : target, bull's-eye **2** *or* **toque de diana** : reveille
diapositiva *nf* : slide, transparency
diario[1] *adv Mex* : every day, daily
diario[2], **-ria** *adj* : daily, everyday — **diariamente** *adv*
diario[3] *nm* **1** : diary **2** PERIÓDICO : newspaper
diarrea *nf* : diarrhea
diatriba *nf* : diatribe, tirade
dibujante *nmf* **1** : draftsman *m,* draftswoman *f* **2** CARICATURISTA : cartoonist
dibujar *vt* **1** : to draw, to sketch **2** : to portray, to depict
dibujo *nm* **1** : drawing **2** : design, pattern **3 dibujos animados** : (animated) cartoons
dicción *nf, pl* **-ciones** : diction
diccionario *nm* : dictionary
dícese → **decir**
dicha *nf* **1** SUERTE : good luck **2** FELICIDAD : happiness, joy
dicho[1] *pp* → **decir**
dicho[2], **-cha** *adj* : said, aforementioned
dicho[3] *nm* DECIR : saying, proverb
dichoso, -sa *adj* **1** : blessed **2** FELIZ : happy **3** AFORTUNADO : fortunate, lucky
diciembre *nm* : December
diciendo → **decir**
dictado *nm* : dictation
dictador, -dora *n* : dictator
dictadura *nf* : dictatorship
dictamen *nm, pl* **dictámenes 1** : report **2** : judgment, opinion
dictaminar *vt* : to report — *vi* : to give an opinion, to pass judgment
dictar *vt* **1** : to dictate **2** : to pronounce (a judgment) **3** : to give, to deliver <dictar una conferencia : to give a lecture>
dictatorial *adj* : dictatorial

didáctico, -ca *adj* : didactic
diecinueve *adj & nm* : nineteen
diecinueveavo[1], **-va** *adj* : nineteenth
diecinueveavo[2] *nm* : nineteenth (fraction)
dieciocho *adj & nm* : eighteen
dieciochoavo[1], **-va** *or* **dieciochavo, -va** *adj* : eighteenth
dieciochoavo[2] *or* **dieciochavo** *nm* : eighteenth (fraction)
dieciséis *adj & nm* : sixteen
dieciseisavo[1], **-va** *adj* : sixteenth
dieciseisavo[2] *nm* : sixteenth (fraction)
diecisietaeavo[1], **-va** *adj* : seventeenth
diecisietaeavo[2] *nm* : seventeenth (fraction)
diecisiete *adj & nm* : seventeen
diecisieteavo[1], **-va** *adj* : seventeenth
diecisieteavo[2] *nm* : seventeenth
diente *nm* **1** : tooth <diente canino : eyetooth, canine tooth> **2** : tusk, fang **3** : prong, tine **4 diente de león** : dandelion
dieron, etc. → **dar**
diesel ['disɛl] *nm* : diesel
diestra *nf* : right hand
diestramente *adv* : skillfully, adroitly
diestro[1], **-tra** *adj* **1** : right **2** : skillful, accomplished
diestro[2] *nm* : bullfighter, matador
dieta *nf* : diet
dietética *nf* : dietetics
dietético, -ca *adj* : dietetic
dietista *nmf* : dietitian
diez *adj & nm, pl* **dieces** : ten
difamación *nf, pl* **-ciones** : defamation, slander
difamar *vt* : to defame, to slander
difamatorio, -ria *adj* : slanderous, defamatory, libelous
diferencia *nf* **1** : difference **2 a diferencia de** : unlike, in contrast to
diferenciación *nf, pl* **-ciones** : differentiation
diferenciar *vt* : to differentiate between, to distinguish — **diferenciarse** *vr* : to differ
diferendo *nm* : dispute, conflict
diferente *adj* DISTINTO : different — **diferentemente** *adv*
diferir {76} *vt* DILATAR, POSPONER : to postpone, to put off — *vi* : to differ
difícil *adj* : difficult, hard
difícilmente *adv* **1** : with difficulty **2** : hardly
dificultad *nf* : difficulty
dificultar *vt* : to make difficult, to obstruct
dificultoso, -sa *adj* : difficult, hard
difteria *nf* : diphtheria
difundir *vt* **1** : to diffuse, to spread out **2** : to broadcast, to spread
difunto, -ta *adj & n* FALLECIDO : deceased
difusión *nf, pl* **-siones 1** : spreading **2** : diffusion (of heat, etc.) **3** : broadcast, broadcasting <los medios de difusión : the media>
difuso, -sa *adj* : diffuse, widespread
diga, etc. → **decir**
digerir {76} *vt* : to digest — **digerible** *adj*
digestión *nf, pl* **-tiones** : digestion
digestivo, -va *adj* : digestive
digital[1] *adj* : digital — **digitalmente** *adv*
digital[2] *nm* **1** DEDALERA : foxglove **2** : digitalis
dígito *nm* : digit
dignarse *vr* : to deign, to condescend <no se dignó contestar : he didn't deign to answer>
dignatario, -ria *n* : dignitary
dignidad *nf* **1** : dignity **2** : dignitary
dignificar {72} *vt* : to dignify
digno, -na *adj* **1** HONORABLE : honorable **2** : worthy — **dignamente** *adv*
digresión *nf, pl* **-ciones** : digression
dije *nm* : charm (on a bracelet)
dijo, etc. → **decir**
dilación *nf, pl* **-ciones** : delay
dilapidar *vt* : to waste, to squander
dilatar *vt* **1** : to dilate, to widen, to expand **2** DIFERIR, POSPONER : to put off, to postpone — **dilatarse** *vr* **1** : to expand (of gases, metals, etc.) **2** *Mex* : to take long, to be long
dilatorio, -ria *adj* : dilatory, delaying
dilema *nm* : dilemma
diligencia *nf* **1** : diligence, care **2** : promptness, speed **3** : action, step **4** : task, errand **5** : stagecoach **6 diligencias** *nfpl* : judicial procedures, formalities
diligente *adj* : diligent — **diligentemente** *adv*
dilucidar *vt* : to elucidate, to clarify
diluir {41} *vt* : to dilute
diluviar *v impers* : to pour (with rain), to pour down
diluvio *nm* **1** : flood **2** : downpour
dimensión *nf, pl* **-siones** : dimension — **dimensional** *adj*
dimensionar *vt* : to measure, to gauge
diminuto, -ta *adj* : minute, tiny
dimisión *nf, pl* **-siones** : resignation
dimitir *vi* : to resign, to step down
dimos → **dar**
dinámica *nf* : dynamics
dinámico, -ca *adj* : dynamic — **dinámicamente** *adv*
dinamita *nf* : dynamite
dinamitar *vt* : to dynamite
dínamo *or* **dinamo** *nm* : dynamo
dinastía *nf* : dynasty
dineral *nm* : fortune, large sum of money
dinero *nm* : money
dinosaurio *nm* : dinosaur
dintel *nm* : lintel
dio, etc. → **dar**
diocesano, -na *adj* : diocesan
diócesis *nfs & pl* : diocese
dios, diosa *n* : god, goddess *f*
Dios *nm* : God
diploma *nm* : diploma
diplomacia *nf* : diplomacy

diplomado[1], **-da** *adj* : qualified, trained
diplomado[2] *nm Mex* : seminar
diplomático[1], **-ca** *adj* : diplomatic — **diplomáticamente** *adv*
diplomático[2], **-ca** *n* : diplomat
diputación *nf, pl* **-ciones** : deputation, delegation
diputado, -da *n* : delegate, representative
dique *nm* : dike
dirá, etc. → **decir**
dirección *nf, pl* **-ciones 1** : address **2** : direction **3** : management, leadership **4** : steering (of an automobile)
direccional[1] *adj* : directional
direccional[2] *nf* : directional, turn signal
directa *nf* : high gear
directamente *adv* : straight, directly
directiva *nf* **1** ORDEN : directive **2** DIRECTORIO, JUNTA : board of directors
directivo[1], **-va** *adj* : executive, managerial
directivo[2], **-va** *n* : executive, director
directo, -ta *adj* **1** : direct, straight, immediate **2 en ~** : live (in broadcasting)
director, -tora *n* **1** : director, manager, head **2** : conductor (of an orchestra)
directorial *adj* : managing, executive
directorio *nm* **1** : directory **2** DIRECTIVA, JUNTA : board of directors
directriz *nf, pl* **-trices** : guideline
dirigencia *nf* : leaders *pl*, leadership
dirigente[1] *adj* : directing, leading
dirigente[2] *nmf* : director, leader
dirigible *nm* : dirigible, blimp
dirigir {35} *vt* **1** : to direct, to lead **2** : to address **3** : to aim, to point **4** : to conduct (music) — **dirigirse** *vr* **~ a 1** : to go towards **2** : to speak to, to address
dirimir *vt* **1** : to resolve, to settle **2** : to annul, to dissolve (a marriage)
discapacidad *nf* MINUSVALÍA : disability, handicap
discapacitado[1], **-da** *adj* : disabled, handicapped
discapacitado[2], **-da** *n* : disabled person, handicapped person
discernimiento *nm* : discernment
discernir {25} *v* : to discern, to distinguish
disciplina *nf* : discipline
disciplinar *vt* : to discipline — **disciplinario, -ria** *adj*
discípulo, -la *n* : disciple, follower
disc jockey [ˌdiskˈjoke, -ˈdʒo-] *nmf* : disc jockey
disco *nm* **1** : phonograph record **2** : disc, disk <disco compacto : compact disc> **3** : discus
díscolo, -la *adj* : unruly, disobedient
disconforme *adj* : in disagreement
discontinuidad *nf* : discontinuity
discontinuo, -nua *adj* : discontinuous
discordancia *nf* DESAVENENCIA : conflict, disagreement
discordante *adj* **1** : discordant **2** : conflicting
discordia *nf* : discord
discoteca *nf* **1** : disco, discotheque **2** *CA, Mex* : record store
discreción *nf, pl* **-ciones** : discretion
discrecional *adj* : discretionary
discrepancia *nf* : discrepancy
discrepar *vi* **1** : to disagree **2** : to differ
discreto, -ta *adj* : discreet — **discretamente** *adv*
discriminación *nf, pl* **-ciones** : discrimination
discriminar *vt* **1** : to discriminate against **2** : to distinguish, to differentiate
discriminatorio, -ria *adj* : discriminatory
disculpa *nf* **1** : apology **2** : excuse
disculpable *adj* : excusable
disculpar *vt* : to excuse, to pardon — **disculparse** *vr* : to apologize
discurrir *vi* **1** : to flow **2** : to pass, to go by **3** : to ponder, to reflect
discurso *nm* **1** ORACIÓN : speech, address **2** : discourse, treatise
discusión *nf, pl* **-siones 1** : discussion **2** ALTERCADO, DISPUTA : argument
discutible *adj* : arguable, debatable
discutidor, -dora *adj* : argumentative
discutir *vt* **1** : to discuss **2** : to dispute — *vi* ALTERCAR : to argue, to quarrel
disecar {72} *vt* **1** : to dissect **2** : to stuff (for preservation)
disección *nf, pl* **-ciones** : dissection
diseminación *nf, pl* **-ciones** : dissemination, spreading
diseminar *vt* : to disseminate, to spread
disensión *nf, pl* **-siones** : dissension, disagreement
disentería *nf* : dysentery
disentir {76} *vi* : to dissent, to disagree
diseñador, -dora *n* : designer
diseñar *vt* **1** : to design, to plan **2** : to lay out, to outline
diseño *nm* : design
disertación *nf, pl* **-ciones 1** : lecture, talk **2** : dissertation
disertar *vi* : to lecture, to give a talk
disfraz *nm, pl* **disfraces 1** : disguise **2** : costume **3** : front, pretense
disfrazar {21} *vt* **1** : to disguise **2** : to mask, to conceal — **disfrazarse** *vr* : to wear a costume, to be in disguise
disfrutar *vt* : to enjoy — *vi* : to enjoy oneself, to have a good time
disfrute *nm* : enjoyment
disfunción *nf, pl* **-ciones** : dysfunction — **disfuncional** *adj*
disgresión *nf* → **digresión**
disgustar *vt* : to upset, to displease, to make angry — **disgustarse** *vr*
disgusto *nm* **1** : annoyance, displeasure **2** : argument, quarrel **3** : trouble, misfortune
disidencia *nf* : dissidence, dissent
disidente *adj* & *nmf* : dissident
disímbolo, -la *adj Mex* : dissimilar

disímil *adj* : dissimilar
disimulado, -da *adj* **1** : concealed, disguised **2** : furtive, sly
disimular *vi* : to dissemble, to pretend — *vt* : to conceal, to hide
disimulo *nm* **1** : dissembling, pretense **2** : slyness, furtiveness **3** : tolerance
disipar *vt* **1** : to dissipate **2** : to dispel — **disiparse** *vr*
diskette [di'skɛt] *nm* : floppy disk, diskette
dislocar {72} *vt* : to dislocate — **dislocación** *nf*
disminución *nf, pl* **-ciones** : decrease, drop, fall
disminuir {41} *vt* REDUCIR : to reduce, to decrease, to lower — *vi* **1** : to lower **2** : to drop, to fall
disociación *nf, pl* **-ciones** : dissociation
disociar *vt* : to dissociate, to separate
disolución *nf, pl* **-ciones 1** : dissolution, dissolving **2** : breaking up **3** : dissipation
disoluto, -ta *adj* : dissolute, dissipated
disolver {89} *vt* **1** : to dissolve **2** : to break up — **disolverse** *vr*
disonancia *nf* : dissonance — **disonante** *adj*
disparado, -da *adj* **salir disparado** *fam* : to take off in a hurry, to rush away
disparar *vi* **1** : to fire (a gun) **2** *Mex fam* : to pay — *vt* **1** : to shoot **2** : to rush off **3** *Mex fam* : to treat to, to buy — **dispararse** *vr* : to shoot up, to skyrocket
disparatado, -da *adj* ABSURDO, RIDÍCULO : absurd, ridiculous, crazy
disparate *nm* : silliness, stupidity <decir disparates : to talk nonsense>
disparejo, -ja *adj* DESIGUAL : uneven
disparidad *nf* : disparity
disparo *nm* TIRO : shot
dispendio *nm* : wastefulness, extravagance
dispendioso, -sa *adj* : wasteful, extravagant
dispensa *nf* : dispensation
dispensable *adj* **1** : dispensable **2** : excusable
dispensar *vt* **1** : to dispense, to give, to grant **2** EXCUSAR : to excuse, to forgive **3** EXIMIR : to exempt
dispensario *nm* **1** : dispensary, clinic **2** *Mex* : dispenser
dispersar *vt* DESPERDIGAR : to disperse, to scatter
dispersión *nf, pl* **-siones** : dispersion
disperso, -sa *adj* : dispersed, scattered
displicencia *nf* : indifference, coldness, disdain
displicente *adj* : indifferent, cold, disdainful
disponer {60} *vt* **1** : to arrange, to lay out **2** : to stipulate, to order **3** : to prepare — *vi* **~ de** : to have at one's disposal — **disponerse** *vr* **~ a** : to prepare to, to be about to
disponibilidad *nf* : availability
disponible *adj* : available
disposición *nf, pl* **-ciones 1** : disposition **2** : aptitude, talent **3** : order, arrangement **4** : willingness, readiness **5 última disposición** : last will and testament
dispositivo *nm* **1** APARATO, MECANISMO : device, mechanism **2** : force, detachment
dispuesto[1] *pp* → **disponer**
dispuesto[2], **-ta** *adj* PREPARADO : ready, prepared, disposed
dispuso, etc. → **disponer**
disputa *nf* ALTERCADO, DISCUSIÓN : dispute, argument
disputar *vi* : to argue, to contend, to vie — *vt* : to dispute, to question — **disputarse** *vr* : to be in competition for <se disputan la corona : they're fighting for the crown>
disquera *nf* : record label, recording company
disquete *nm* → **diskette**
disquisición *nf, pl* **-ciones 1** : formal discourse **2 disquisiciones** *nfpl* : digressions
distancia *nf* : distance
distanciamiento *nm* **1** : distancing **2** : rift, estrangement
distanciar *vt* **1** : to space out **2** : to draw apart — **distanciarse** *vr* : to grow apart, to become estranged
distante *adj* **1** : distant, far-off **2** : aloof
distar *vi* **~ de** : to be far from <dista de ser perfecto : he is far from perfect>
diste → **dar**
distender {56} *vt* : to distend, to stretch
distensión *nf, pl* **-siones** : distension
distinción *nf, pl* **-ciones** : distinction
distinguido, -da *adj* : distinguished, refined
distinguir {26} *vt* **1** : to distinguish **2** : to honor — **distinguirse** *vr*
distintivo, -va *adj* : distinctive, distinguishing
distinto, -ta *adj* **1** DIFERENTE : different **2** CLARO : distinct, clear, evident
distorsión *nf, pl* **-siones** : distortion
distorsionar *vt* : to distort
distracción *nf, pl* **-ciones 1** : distraction, amusement **2** : forgetfulness **3** : oversight
distraer {81} *vt* **1** : to distract **2** ENTRETENER : to entertain, to amuse — **distraerse** *vr* **1** : to get distracted **2** : to amuse oneself
distraídamente *adv* : absentmindedly
distraído[1] *pp* → **distraer**
distraído[2], **-da** *adj* **1** : distracted, preoccupied **2** DESPISTADO : absentminded
distribución *nf, pl* **-ciones** : distribution
distribuidor, -dora *n* : distributor
distribuir {41} *vt* : to distribute
distrital *adj* : district, of the district

distrito *nm* : district
distrofia *nf* : dystrophy <distrofia muscular : muscular dystrophy>
disturbio *nm* : disturbance
disuadir *vt* : to dissuade, to discourage
disuasión *nf, pl* **-siones** : dissuasion
disuasorio, -ria *adj* : discouraging
disuelto *pp* → **disolver**
disyuntiva *nf* : dilemma
diurético[1], **-ca** *adj* : diuretic
diurético[2] *nm* : diuretic
diurno, -na *adj* : day, daytime
diva *nf* → **divo**
divagar {52} *vi* : to digress
diván *nm, pl* **divanes** : divan
divergencia *nf* : divergence, difference
divergente *adj* : divergent, differing
divergir {35} *vi* **1** : to diverge **2** : to differ, to disagree
diversidad *nf* : diversity, variety
diversificación *nf, pl* **-ciones** : diversification
diversificar {72} *vt* : to diversify
diversión *nf, pl* **-siones** ENTRETENIMIENTO : fun, amusement, diversion
diverso, -sa *adj* : diverse, various
divertido, -da *adj* **1** : amusing, funny **2** : entertaining, enjoyable
divertir {76} *vt* ENTRETENER : to amuse, to entertain — **divertirse** *vr* : to have fun, to have a good time
dividendo *nm* : dividend
dividir *vt* **1** : to divide, to split **2** : to distribute, to share out — **dividirse** *vr*
divieso *nm* : boil
divinidad *nf* : divinity
divino, -na *adj* : divine
divisa *nf* **1** : currency **2** LEMA : motto **3** : emblem, insignia
divisar *vt* : to discern, to make out
divisible *adj* : divisible
división *nf, pl* **-siones** : division
divisionismo *nm* : factionalism
divisivo, -va *adj* : divisive
divisor *nm* : denominator
divisorio, -ria *adj* : dividing
divo, -va *n* **1** : prima donna **2** : celebrity, star
divorciado[1], **-da** *adj* **1** : divorced **2** : split, divided
divorciado[2], **-da** *n* : divorcé *m*, divorcée *f*
divorciar *vt* : to divorce — **divorciarse** *vr* : to get a divorce
divorcio *nm* : divorce
divulgación *nf, pl* **-ciones** **1** : spreading, dissemination **2** : popularization
divulgar {52} *vt* **1** : to spread, to circulate **2** REVELAR : to divulge, to reveal **3** : to popularize — **divulgarse** *vr*
dizque *adv* : supposedly, apparently
dobladillar *vt* : to hem
dobladillo *nm* : hem
doblar *vt* **1** : to double **2** PLEGAR : to fold, to bend **3** : to turn <doblar la esquina : to turn the corner> **4** : to dub — *vi* **1** : to turn **2** : to toll, to ring — **doblarse** *vr* **1** : to fold up, to double over **2** : to give in, to yield
doble[1] *adj* : double — **doblemente** *adv*
doble[2] *nm* **1** : double **2** : toll (of a bell), knell
doble[3] *nmf* : stand-in, double
doblegar {52} *vt* **1** : to fold, to crease **2** : to force to yield — **doblegarse** *vr* : to yield, to bow
doblez[1] *nm, pl* **dobleces** : fold, crease
doblez[2] *nmf* : duplicity, deceitfulness
doce *adj & nm* : twelve
doceavo[1], **-va** *adj* : twelfth
doceavo[2] *nm* : twelfth (fraction)
docena *nf* **1** : dozen **2 docena de fraile** : baker's dozen
docencia *nf* : teaching
docente[1] *adj* : educational, teaching
docente[2] *n* : teacher, lecturer
dócil *adj* : docile — **dócilmente** *adv*
docilidad *nf* : docility
docto, -ta *adj* : learned, erudite
doctor, -tora *n* : doctor
doctorado *nm* : doctorate
doctrina *nf* : doctrine — **doctrinal** *adj*
documentación *nf, pl* **-ciones** : documentation
documental *adj & nm* : documentary
documentar *vt* : to document
documento *nm* : document
dogma *nm* : dogma
dogmático, -ca *adj* : dogmatic
dogmatismo *nm* : dogmatism
dólar *nm* : dollar
dolencia *nf* : ailment, malaise
doler {47} *vi* **1** : to hurt, to ache **2** : to grieve — **dolerse** *vr* **1** : to be distressed **2** : to complain
doliente *nmf* : mourner, bereaved
dolor *nm* **1** : pain, ache <dolor de cabeza : headache> **2** PENA, TRISTEZA : grief, sorrow
dolorido, -da *adj* **1** : sore, aching **2** : hurt, upset
doloroso, -sa *adj* **1** : painful **2** : distressing — **dolorosamente** *adv*
doloso, -sa *adj* : fraudulent — **dolosamente** *adv*
domador, -dora *n* : tamer
domar *vt* : to tame, to break in
domesticado, -da *adj* : domesticated, tame
domesticar {72} *vt* : to domesticate, to tame
doméstico, -ca *adj* : domestic, household
domiciliado, -da *adj* : residing
domiciliario, -ria *adj* **1** : home **2 arresto domiciliario** : house arrest
domiciliarse *vr* RESIDIR : to reside
domicilio *nm* : home, residence <cambio de domicilio : change of address>
dominación *nf, pl* **-ciones** : domination
dominancia *nf* : dominance
dominante *adj* **1** : dominant **2** : domineering

dominar *vt* **1** : to dominate **2** : to master, to be proficient at — *vi* : to predominate, to prevail — **dominarse** *vr* : to control oneself
domingo *nm* : Sunday
dominical *adj* : Sunday <periódico dominical : Sunday newspaper>
dominicano, -na *adj & n* : Dominican
dominio *nm* **1** : dominion, power **2** : mastery **3** : domain, field
dominó *nm, pl* **-nós 1** : domino (tile) **2** : dominoes *pl* (game)
domo *nm* : dome
don[1] *nm* **1** : gift, present **2** : talent
don[2] *nm* **1** : title of courtesy preceding a man's first name **2 don nadie** : nobody, insignificant person
dona *nf Mex* : doughnut, donut
donación *nf, pl* **-ciones** : donation
donador, -dora *n* : donor
donaire *nm* **1** GARBO : grace, poise **2** : witticism
donante *nf* → **donador**
donar *vt* : to donate
donativo *nm* : donation
doncella *nf* : maiden, damsel
doncellez *nf* : maidenhood
donde[1] *conj* : where, in which <el pueblo donde vivo : the town where I live>
donde[2] *prep* : over by <lo encontré donde la silla : I found it over by the chair>
dónde *adv* : where <¿dónde está su casa? : where is your house?>
dondequiera *adv* **1** : anywhere, no matter where **2 dondequiera que** : wherever, everywhere
doña *nf* : title of courtesy preceding a woman's first name
doquier *adv* **por ~** : everywhere, all over
dorado[1], -da *adj* : gold, golden
dorado[2], -da *nm* : gilt
dorar *vt* **1** : to gild **2** : to brown
dormido, -da *adj* **1** : asleep **2** : numb <tiene el pie dormido : her foot's numb, her foot's gone to sleep>
dormilón, -lona *n* : sleepyhead, late riser
dormir {27} *vt* : to put to sleep — *vi* : to sleep — **dormirse** *vr* : to fall asleep
dormitar *vi* : to snooze, to doze
dormitorio *nm* **1** : bedroom **2** : dormitory
dorsal[1] *adj* : dorsal
dorsal[2] *nm* : number (worn in sports)
dorso *nm* **1** : back <el dorso de la mano : the back of the hand> **2** *Mex* : backstroke
dos *adj & nm* : two
doscientos[1], -tas *adj* : two hundred
doscientos[2] *nms & pl* : two hundred
dosel *nm* : canopy
dosificación *nf, pl* **-ciones** : dosage
dosis *nfs & pl* **1** : dose **2** : amount, quantity
dotación *nf, pl* **-ciones 1** : endowment, funding **2** : staff, personnel
dotado, -da *adj* **1** : gifted **2 ~ de** : endowed with, equipped with
dotar *vt* **1** : to provide, to equip **2** : to endow
dote *nf* **1** : dowry **2 dotes** *nfpl* : talent, gift
doy → **dar**
draga *nf* : dredge
dragado *nm* : dredging
dragar {52} *vt* : to dredge
dragón *nm, pl* **dragones 1** : dragon **2** : snapdragon
drague, etc. → **dragar**
drama *nm* : drama
dramático, -ca *adj* : dramatic — **dramáticamente** *adv*
dramatizar {21} *vt* : to dramatize — **dramatización** *nf*
dramaturgo, -ga *n* : dramatist, playwright
drástico, -ca *adj* : drastic — **drásticamente** *adv*
drenaje *nm* : drainage
drenar *vt* : to drain
drene *nm Mex* : drain
driblar *vi* : to dribble (in basketball)
drible *nm* : dribble (in basketball)
droga *nf* : drug
drogadicción *nf, pl* **-ciones** : drug addiction
drogadicto, -ta *n* : drug addict
drogar {52} *vt* : to drug — **drogarse** *vr* : to take drugs
drogue, etc. → **drogar**
droguería *nf* FARMACIA : drugstore
dual *adj* : dual
dualidad *nf* : duality
dualismo *nm* : dualism
ducha *nf* : shower <darse una ducha : to take a shower>
ducharse *vr* : to take a shower
ducho, -cha *adj* : experienced, skilled, expert
ducto *nm* **1** : duct, shaft **2** : pipeline
duda *nf* : doubt <no cabe duda : there's no doubt about it>
dudar *vt* : to doubt — *vi* **~ en** : to hesitate to <no dudes en pedirme ayuda : don't hesitate to ask me for help>
dudoso, -sa *adj* **1** : doubtful **2** : dubious, questionable — **dudosamente** *adv*
duele, etc. → **doler**
duelo *nm* **1** : duel **2** LUTO : mourning
duende *nm* **1** : elf, goblin **2** ENCANTO : magic, charm <una bailarina que tiene duende : a dancer with a certain magic>
dueño, -na *nmf* **1** : owner, proprietor, proprietress *f* **2** : landlord, landlady *f*
duerme, etc. → **dormir**
dueto *nm* : duet
dulce[1] *adv* : sweetly, softly
dulce[2] *adj* **1** : sweet **2** : mild, gentle, mellow — **dulcemente** *adv*
dulce[3] *nm* : candy, sweet

dulcería *nf* : candy store
dulcificante *nm* : sweetener
dulzura *nf* **1** : sweetness **2** : gentleness, mellowness
duna *nf* : dune
dúo *nm* : duo, duet
duodécimo[1], **-ma** *adj* : twelfth
duodécimo[2], **-ma** *nm* : twelfth (in a series)
dúplex *nms & pl* : duplex apartment
duplicación *nf, pl* **-ciones** : duplication, copying
duplicado *nm* : duplicate, copy
duplicar {72} *vt* **1** : to double **2** : to duplicate, to copy
duplicidad *nf* : duplicity
duque *nm* : duke
duquesa *nf* : duchess
durabilidad *nf* : durability
durable → **duradero**
duración *nf, pl* **-ciones** : duration, length
duradero, -ra *adj* : durable, lasting
duramente *adv* **1** : harshly, severely **2** : hard
durante *prep* : during <durante todo el día : all day long> <trabajó durante tres horas : he worked for three hours>
durar *vi* : to last, to endure
durazno *nm* **1** : peach **2** : peach tree
dureza *nf* **1** : hardness, toughness **2** : severity, harshness
durmiente[1] *adj* : sleeping
durmiente[2] *nmf* : sleeper
durmió, etc. → **dormir**
duro[1] *adv* : hard <trabajé tan duro : I worked so hard>
duro[2], -ra *adj* **1** : hard, tough **2** : harsh, severe

E

e[1] *nf* : fifth letter of the Spanish alphabet
e[2] *conj* (*used instead of* **y** *before words beginning with i or hi*) : and
ebanista *nmf* : cabinetmaker
ebanistería *nf* : cabinetmaking
ébano *nm* : ebony
ebriedad *nf* EMBRIAGUEZ : inebriation, drunkenness
ebrio, -bria *adj* EMBRIAGADO : inebriated, drunk
ebullición *nf, pl* **-ciones** : boiling
eccéntrico → **excéntrico**
echar *vt* **1** LANZAR : to throw, to cast, to hurl **2** EXPULSAR : to throw out, to expel **3** EMITIR : to emit, give off **4** BROTAR : to sprout, to put forth **5** DESPEDIR : to fire, to dismiss **6** : to put in, to add **7 echar a perder** : to spoil, to ruin **8 echar de menos** : to miss <echan de menos a su madre : they miss their mother> — *vi* **1** : to start off **2 ~ a** : to begin to — **echarse** *vr* **1** : to throw oneself **2** : to lie down **3** : to put on **4 ~ a** : to start to **5 echarse a perder** : to go bad, to spoil **6 echárselas de** : to pose as
ecléctico, -ca *adj* : eclectic
eclesiástico[1], **-ca** *adj* : ecclesiastical, ecclesiastic
eclesiástico[2] *nm* CLÉRIGO : cleric, clergyman
eclipsar *vt* **1** : to eclipse **2** : to outshine, to surpass
eclipse *nm* : eclipse
eco *nm* : echo
ecografía *nf* : ultrasound scanning
ecología *nf* : ecology
ecológico, -ca *adj* : ecological — **ecológicamente** *adv*
ecologista *nmf* : ecologist, environmentalist
ecólogo, -ga *n* : ecologist
economía *nf* **1** : economy **2** : economics
económicamente *adv* : financially
económico, -ca *adj* : economic, economical
economista *nmf* : economist
economizar {21} *vt* : to save, to economize on — *vi* : to save up, to be frugal
ecosistema *nm* : ecosystem
ecuación *nf, pl* **-ciones** : equation
ecuador *nm* : equator
ecuánime *adj* **1** : even-tempered **2** : impartial
ecuanimidad *nf* **1** : equanimity **2** : impartiality
ecuatorial *adj* : equatorial
ecuatoriano, -na *adj & n* : Ecuadorian
ecuestre *adj* : equestrian
ecuménico, -ca *adj* : ecumenical
eczema *nm* : eczema
edad *nf* **1** : age <¿qué edad tiene? : how old is she?> **2** ÉPOCA, ERA : epoch, era
edema *nm* : edema
Edén *nm, pl* **Edenes** : Eden, paradise
edición *nf, pl* **-ciones 1** : edition **2** : publication, publishing
edicto *nm* : edict, proclamation
edificación *nf, pl* **-ciones 1** : edification **2** : construction, building
edificante *adj* : edifying
edificar {72} *vt* **1** : to edify **2** CONSTRUIR : to build, to construct
edificio *nm* : building, edifice
editar *vt* **1** : to edit **2** PUBLICAR : to publish
editor[1], **-tora** *adj* : publishing <casa editora : publishing house>
editor[2], **-tora** *n* **1** : editor **2** : publisher
editora *nf* : publisher, publishing company
editorial[1] *adj* **1** : publishing **2** : editorial
editorial[2] *nm* : editorial
editorial[3] *nf* : publishing house

editorializar {21} *vi* : to editorialize
edredón *nm, pl* **-dones** COBERTOR, COLCHA : comforter, eiderdown, quilt
educable *adj* : educable, teachable
educación *nf, pl* **-ciones 1** ENSEÑANZA : education **2** : manners *pl* — **educacional** *adj*
educado, -da *adj* : polite, well-mannered
educador, -dora *n* : educator
educando, -da *n* ALUMNO, PUPILO : pupil, student
educar {72} *vt* **1** : to educate **2** CRIAR : to bring up, to raise **3** : to train — **educarse** *vr* : to be educated
educativo, -va *adj* : educational
efectista *adj* : dramatic, sensational
efectivamente *adv* : really, actually
efectividad *nf* : effectiveness
efectivo[1], -va *adj* **1** : effective **2** : real, actual **3** : permanent, regular (of employment)
efectivo[2] *nm* : cash
efecto *nm* **1** : effect **2 en ~** : actually, in fact **3 efectos** *nmpl* : goods, property <efectos personales : personal effects>
efectuar {3} *vt* : to carry out, to bring about
efervescencia *nf* **1** : effervescence **2** : vivacity, high spirits *pl*
efervescente *adj* **1** : effervescent **2** : vivacious
eficacia *nf* **1** : effectiveness, efficacy **2** : efficiency
eficaz *adj, pl* **-caces 1** : effective **2** EFICIENTE : efficient — **eficazmente** *adv*
eficiencia *nf* : efficiency
eficiente *adj* EFICAZ : efficient — **eficientemente** *adv*
eficientizar {21} *vt Mex* : to streamline, to make more efficient
efigie *nf* : effigy
efímera *nf* : mayfly
efímero, -ra *adj* : ephemeral
efusión *nf, pl* **-siones 1** : effusion **2** : warmth, effusiveness **3 con ~** : effusively
efusivo, -va *adj* : effusive — **efusivamente** *adv*
egipcio, -cia *adj & n* : Egyptian
eglefino *nm* : haddock
ego *nm* : ego
egocéntrico, -ca *adj* : egocentric, self-centered
egoísmo *nm* : selfishness, egoism
egoísta[1] *adj* : selfish, egoistic
egoísta[2] *nmf* : egoist, selfish person
egotismo *nm* : egotism, conceit
egotista[1] *adj* : egotistic, egotistical, conceited
egotista[2] *nmf* : egotist, conceited person
egresado, -da *n* : graduate
egresar *vi* : to graduate
egreso *nm* **1** : graduation **2 ingresos y egresos** : income and expenditure
eje *nm* **1** : axle **2** : axis
ejecución *nf, pl* **-ciones** : execution
ejecutante *nmf* : performer
ejecutar *vt* **1** : to execute, to put to death **2** : to carry out, to perform
ejecutivo, -va *adj & n* : executive
ejecutor, -tora *n* : executor
ejemplar[1] *adj* : exemplary, model
ejemplar[2] *nm* **1** : copy (of a book, magazine, etc.) **2** : specimen, example
ejemplificar {72} *vt* : to exemplify, to illustrate
ejemplo *nm* **1** : example **2 por ~** : for example **3 dar ejemplo** : to set an example
ejercer {86} *vi* **~ de** : to practice as, to work as — *vt* **1** : to practice **2** : exercise (a right) **3** : to exert
ejercicio *nm* **1** : exercise **2** : practice
ejercitar *vt* **1** : to exercise **2** ADIESTRAR : to drill, to train
ejército *nm* : army
ejidal *adj Mex* : cooperative
ejido *nm* **1** : common land **2** *Mex* : cooperative
ejote *nm Mex* : green bean
el[1] *pron* (*referring to masculine nouns*) **1** : the one <tengo mi libro y el tuyo : I have my book and yours> <de los cantantes me gusta el de México : I prefer the singer from México> **2 el que** : he who, whoever, the one that <el que vino ayer : the one who came yesterday> <el que trabaja duro estará contento : he who works hard will be happy>
el[2], la *art, pl* **los, las** : the <los niños están en la casa : the boys are in the house> <me duele el pie : my foot hurts>
él *pron* : he, him <él es mi amigo : he's my friend> <hablaremos con él : we will speak with him>
elaboración *nf, pl* **-ciones 1** PRODUCCIÓN : production, making **2** : preparation, devising
elaborado, -da *adj* : elaborate
elaborar *vt* **1** : to make, to produce **2** : to devise, to draw up
elasticidad *nf* : elasticity
elástico[1], -ca *adj* **1** FLEXIBLE : flexible **2** : elastic
elástico[2] *nm* **1** : elastic (material) **2** : rubber band
elección *nf, pl* **-ciones 1** SELECCIÓN : choice, selection **2** : election
electivo, -va *adj* : elective
electo, -ta *adj* : elect <el presidente electo : the president-elect>
elector, -tora *n* : elector, voter
electorado *nm* : electorate
electoral *adj* : electoral, election
electricidad *nf* : electricity
electricista *nmf* : electrician
eléctrico, -ca *adj* : electric, electrical
electrificar {72} *vt* : to electrify — **electrificación** *nf*
electrizar {21} *vt* : to electrify, to thrill — **electrizante** *adj*

electrocardiógrafo *nm* : electrocardiograph
electrocardiograma *nm* : electrocardiogram
electrocutar *vt* : to electrocute — **electrocución** *nf*
electrodo *nm* : electrode
electrodoméstico *nm* : electric appliance
electroimán *nm, pl* **-manes** : electromagnet
electrólisis *nfs & pl* : electrolysis
electrolito *nm* : electrolyte
electromagnético, -ca *adj* : electromagnetic
electromagnetismo *nm* : electromagnetism
electrón *nm, pl* **-trones** : electron
electrónica *nf* : electronics
electrónico, -ca *adj* : electronic — **electrónicamente** *adv*
elefante, -ta *n* : elephant
elegancia *nf* : elegance
elegante *adj* : elegant, smart — **elegantemente** *adv*
elegía *nf* : elegy
elegíaco, -ca *adj* : elegiac
elegibilidad *nf* : eligibility
elegible *adj* : eligible
elegido, -da *adj* **1** : chosen, selected **2** : elected
elegir {28} *vt* **1** ESCOGER, SELECCIONAR : to choose, to select **2** : to elect
elemental *adj* **1** : elementary, basic **2** : fundamental, essential
elemento *nm* : element
elenco *nm* : cast (of actors)
elepé *nm* : long-playing record
elevación *nf, pl* **-ciones** : elevation, height
elevado, -da *adj* **1** : elevated, lofty **2** : high
elevador *nm* ASCENSOR : elevator
elevar *vt* **1** ALZAR : to raise, to lift **2** AUMENTAR : to raise, to increase **3** : to elevate (in a hierarchy), to promote **4** : to present, to submit — **elevarse** *vr* : to rise
elfo *nm* : elf
eliminación *nf, pl* **-ciones** : elimination, removal
eliminar *vt* **1** : to eliminate, to remove **2** : to do in, to kill
elipse *nf* : ellipse
elipsis *nf* : ellipsis
elíptico, -ca *adj* : elliptical, elliptic
elite *or* **élite** *nf* : elite
elixir *or* **elíxir** *nm* : elixir
ella *pron* : she, her <ella es mi amiga : she is my friend> <nos fuimos con ella : we left with her>
ello *pron* : it <es por ello que me voy : that's why I'm going>
ellos, ellas *pron pl* **1** : they, them **2 de ellos, de ellas** : theirs
elocución *nf, pl* **-ciones** : elocution
elocuencia *nf* : eloquence
elocuente *adj* : eloquent — **elocuentemente** *adv*
elogiar *vt* ENCOMIAR : to praise
elogio *nm* : praise
elote *nm* **1** *Mex* : corn, maize **2** *CA, Mex* : corncob
elucidación *nf, pl* **-ciones** ESCLARECIMIENTO : elucidation
elucidar *vt* ESCLARECER : to elucidate
eludir *vt* EVADIR : to evade, to avoid, to elude
emanación *nf, pl* **-ciones** : emanation
emanar *vi* **~ de** : to emanate from — *vt* : to exude
emancipar *vt* : to emancipate — **emancipación** *nf*
embadurnar *vt* EMBARRAR : to smear, to daub
embajada *nf* : embassy
embajador, -dora *n* : ambassador
embalaje *nm* : packing, packaging
embalar *vt* EMPAQUETAR : to pack
embaldosar *vt* : to tile, to pave with tiles
embalsamar *vt* : to embalm
embalsar *vt* : to dam, to dam up
embalse *nm* : dam, reservoir
embarazada *adj* ENCINTA, PREÑADA : pregnant, expecting
embarazar {21} *vt* **1** : to obstruct, to hamper **2** PREÑAR : to make pregnant
embarazo *nm* : pregnancy
embarazoso, -sa *adj* : embarrassing, awkward
embarcación *nf, pl* **-ciones** : boat, craft
embarcadero *nm* : wharf, pier, jetty
embarcar {72} *vi* : to embark, to board — *vt* : to load
embarco *nm* : embarkation
embargar {52} *vt* **1** : to seize, to impound **2** : to overwhelm
embargo *nm* **1** : seizure **2** : embargo **3 sin ~** : however, nevertheless
embarque *nm* **1** : embarkation **2** : shipment
embarrancar {72} *vi* **1** : to run aground **2** : to get bogged down
embarrar *vt* **1** : to cover with mud **2** EMBADURNAR : to smear
embarullar *vt fam* : to muddle, to confuse — **embarullarse** *vr fam* : to get mixed up
embate *nm* **1** : onslaught **2** : battering (of waves or wind)
embaucador, -dora *n* : swindler, deceiver
embaucar {72} *vt* : to trick, to swindle
embeber *vt* : to absorb, to soak up — *vi* : to shrink
embelesado, -da *adj* : spellbound
embelesar *vt* : to enchant, to captivate
embellecer {53} *vt* : to embellish, to beautify
embellecimiento *nm* : beautification, embellishment
embestida *nf* **1** : charge (of a bull) **2** ARREMETIDA : attack, onslaught
embestir {54} *vt* : to hit, to run into, to charge at — *vi* ARREMETER : to charge, to attack

emblanquecer {53} *vt* BLANQUEAR : to bleach, to whiten — **emblanquecerse** *vr* : to turn white
emblema *nm* : emblem
emblemático, -ca *adj* : emblematic
embolia *nf* : embolism
émbolo *nm* : piston
embolsarse *vr* **1** : to pocket (money) **2** : to collect (payment)
emborracharse *vr* EMBRIAGARSE : to get drunk
emborronar *vt* **1** : to blot, to smudge **2** GARABATEAR : to scribble
emboscada *nf* : ambush
emboscar {72} *vt* : to ambush — **emboscarse** *vr* : to lie in ambush
embotadura *nf* : bluntness, dullness
embotar *vt* **1** : to dull, to blunt **2** : to weaken, to enervate
embotellamiento *nm* ATASCO : traffic jam
embotellar *vt* ENVASAR : to bottle
embragar {52} *vi* : to engage the clutch
embrague *nm* : clutch
embravecerse {53} *vr* **1** : to get furious **2** : to get rough <el mar se embraveció : the sea became tempestuous>
embriagado, -da *adj* : inebriated, drunk
embriagador, -dora *adj* : intoxicating
embriagarse {52} *vr* EMBORRACHARSE : to get drunk
embriaguez *nf* EBRIEDAD : drunkenness, inebriation
embrión *nm, pl* **embriones** : embryo
embrionario, -ria *adj* : embryonic
embrollo *nm* ENREDO : imbroglio, confusion
embrujar *vt* HECHIZAR : to bewitch
embrujo *nm* : spell, curse
embudo *nm* : funnel
embuste *nm* **1** MENTIRA : lie, fib **2** ENGAÑO : trick, hoax
embustero[1], **-ra** *adj* : lying, deceitful
embustero[2], **-ra** *n* : liar, cheat
embutido *nm* **1** : sausage **2** : inlaid work
embutir *vt* **1** : to cram, to stuff, to jam **2** : to inlay
emergencia *nf* **1** : emergency **2** : emergence
emergente *adj* **1** : emergent **2** : consequent, resultant
emerger {15} *vi* : to emerge, to surface
emético[1], **-ca** *adj* : emetic
emético[2] *nm* : emetic
emigración *nf, pl* **-ciones 1** : emigration **2** : migration
emigrante *adj & nmf* : emigrant
emigrar *vi* **1** : to emigrate **2** : to migrate
eminencia *nf* : eminence
eminente *adj* : eminent, distinguished
eminentemente *adv* : basically, essentially
emisario[1], **-ria** *n* : emissary
emisario[2] *nm* : outlet (of a body of water)
emisión *nf, pl* **-siones 1** : emission **2** : broadcast **3** : issue <emisión de acciones : stock issue>
emisor *nm* TRANSMISOR : television or radio transmitter
emisora *nf* : radio station
emitir *vt* **1** : to emit, to give off **2** : to broadcast **3** : to issue **4** : to cast (a vote)
emoción *nf, pl* **-ciones** : emotion — **emocional** *adj* — **emocionalmente** *adv*
emocionado, -da *adj* **1** : moved, affected by emotion **2** ENTUSIASMADO : excited
emocionante *adj* **1** CONMOVEDOR : moving, touching **2** EXCITANTE : exciting, thrilling
emocionar *vt* **1** CONMOVER : to move, to touch **2** : to excite, to thrill — **emocionarse** *vr*
emotivo, -va *adj* : emotional, moving
empacador, -dora *n* : packer
empacar {72} *vt* **1** EMPAQUETAR : to pack **2** : to bale — *vi* : to pack — **empacarse** *vr* **1** : to balk, to refuse to budge **2** *Col, Mex fam* : to eat ravenously, to devour
empachar *vt* **1** ESTORBAR : to obstruct **2** : to give indigestion to **3** DISFRAZAR : to disguise, to mask — **empacharse** *vr* **1** INDIGESTARSE : to get indigestion **2** AVERGONZARSE : to be embarrassed
empacho *nm* **1** INDIGESTIÓN : indigestion **2** VERGÜENZA : embarrassment **3 no tener empacho en** : to have no qualms about
empadronarse *vr* : to register to vote
empalagar {52} *vt* **1** : to cloy, to surfeit **2** FASTIDIAR : to annoy, to bother
empalagoso, -sa *adj* MELOSO : cloying, excessively sweet
empalar *vt* : to impale
empalizada *nf* : palisade (fence)
empalmar *vt* **1** : to splice, to link **2** : to combine — *vi* : to meet, to converge
empalme *nm* **1** CONEXIÓN : connection, link **2** : junction
empanada *nf* : pie, turnover
empanadilla *nf* : meat or seafood pie
empanar *vt* : to bread
empantanado, -da *adj* : bogged down, delayed
empañar *vt* **1** : to steam up **2** : to tarnish, to sully
empapado, -da *adj* : soggy, sodden
empapar *vt* MOJAR : to soak, to drench — **empaparse** *vr* **1** : to get soaking wet **2 ~ de** : to absorb, to be imbued with
empapelar *vt* : to wallpaper
empaque *nm fam* **1** : presence, bearing **2** : pomposity **3** DESCARO : impudence, nerve
empaquetar *vt* EMBALAR : to pack, to package — **empaquetarse** *vr fam* : to dress up

emparedado *nm* **:** sandwich

emparedar *vt* **:** to wall in, to confine

emparejar *vt* **1 :** to pair, to match up **2 :** to make even — *vi* **:** to catch up — **emparejarse** *vr* **:** to pair up

emparentado, -da *adj* **:** related

emparentar {55} *vi* **:** to become related by marriage

emparrillado *nm Mex* **:** gridiron (in football)

empastar *vt* **1 :** to fill (a tooth) **2 :** to bind (a book)

empaste *nm* **:** filling (of a tooth)

empatar *vt* **:** to tie, to connect — *vi* **:** to result in a draw, to be tied — **empatarse** *vr Ven* **:** to hook up, to link together

empate *nm* **:** draw, tie

empatía *nf* **:** empathy

empecinado, -da *adj* TERCO **:** stubborn

empecinarse *vr* OBSTINARSE **:** to be stubborn, to persist

empedernido, -da *adj* INCORREGIBLE **:** hardened, inveterate

empedrado *nm* **:** paving, pavement

empedrar {55} *vt* **:** to pave (with stones)

empeine *nm* **:** instep

empellón *nm, pl* **-llones :** shove, push

empelotado, -da *adj* **1** *Mex fam* **:** madly in love **2** *fam* **:** stark naked

empeñado, -da *adj* **:** determined, committed

empeñar *vt* **1 :** to pawn **2 :** to pledge, to give (one's word) — **empeñarse** *vr* **1 :** to insist stubbornly **2 :** to make an effort

empeño *nm* **1 :** pledge, commitment **2 :** insistence **3** ESFUERZO **:** effort, determination **4 :** pawning <casa de empeños : pawnshop>

empeoramiento *nm* **:** worsening, deterioration

empeorar *vi* **:** to deteriorate, to get worse — *vt* **:** to make worse

empequeñecer {53} *vi* **:** to diminish, to become smaller — *vt* **:** to minimize, to make smaller

emperador *nm* **:** emperor

emperatriz *nf, pl* **-trices :** empress

empero *conj* **:** however, nevertheless

empezar {29} *v* COMENZAR **:** to start, to begin

empinado, -da *adj* **:** steep

empinar *vt* ELEVAR **:** to lift, to raise — **empinarse** *vr* **:** to stand on tiptoe

empírico, -ca *adj* **:** empirical — **empíricamente** *adv*

emplasto *nm* **:** poultice, dressing

emplazamiento *nm* **1 :** location, site **2** CITACIÓN **:** summons, subpoena

emplazar {21} *vt* **1** CONVOCAR **:** to convene, to summon **2 :** to subpoena **3** UBICAR **:** to place, to position

empleado, -da *n* **:** employee

empleador, -dora *n* PATRÓN **:** employer

emplear *vt* **1 :** to employ **2** USAR **:** to use — **emplearse** *vr* **1 :** to get a job **2 :** to occupy oneself

empleo *nm* **1** OCUPACIÓN **:** employment, occupation, job **2 :** use, usage

empobrecer {53} *vt* **:** to impoverish — *vi* **:** to become poor — **empobrecerse** *vr*

empobrecimiento *nm* **:** impoverishment

empollar *vi* **:** to brood eggs — *vt* **:** to incubate

empolvado, -da *adj* **1 :** dusty **2 :** powdered, powdery

empolvar *vt* **1 :** to cover with dust **2 :** to powder — **empolvarse** *vr* **1 :** to gather dust **2 :** to powder one's face

emporio *nm* **1 :** center, capital, empire <un emporio cultural : a cultural center> <un emporio financiero : a financial empire> **2 :** department store

empotrado, -da *adj* **:** built-in <armarios empotrados : built-in cabinets>

empotrar *vt* **:** to build into, to embed

emprendedor, -dora *adj* **:** enterprising

emprender *vt* **:** to undertake, to begin

empresa *nf* **1** COMPAÑÍA, FIRMA **:** company, corporation, firm **2 :** undertaking, venture

empresariado *nm* **1 :** business world **2 :** management, managers *pl*

empresarial *adj* **:** business, managerial, corporate

empresario, -ria *n* **1 :** manager **2 :** businessman *m,* businesswoman *f* **3 :** impresario

empujar *vi* **:** to push, to shove — *vt* **1 :** to push **2** PRESIONAR **:** to spur on, to press

empuje *nm* **:** impetus, drive

empujón *nm, pl* **-jones :** push, shove

empuñadura *nf* MANGO **:** hilt, handle

empuñar *vt* **1** ASIR **:** to grasp **2 empuñar las armas :** to take up arms

emú *nm* **:** emu

emular *vt* IMITAR **:** to emulate — **emulación** *nf*

emulsión *nf, pl* **-siones :** emulsion

emulsionante *nm* **:** emulsifier

emulsionar *vt* **:** to emulsify

en *prep* **1 :** in <en el bolsillo : in one's pocket> <en una semana : in a week> **2 :** on <en la mesa : on the table> **3 :** at <en casa : at home> <en el trabajo : at work> <en ese momento : at that moment>

enagua *nf* **:** petticoat, slip

enajenación *nf, pl* **-ciones 1 :** transfer (of property) **2 :** alienation **3 :** absentmindedness

enajenado, -da *adj* **:** out of one's mind

enajenar *vt* **1 :** to transfer (property) **2 :** to alienate **3 :** to enrapture — **enajenarse** *vr* **1 :** to become estranged **2 :** to go mad

enaltecer {53} *vt* **:** to praise, to extol

enamorado[1], -da *adj* **:** in love

enamorado[2], -da *n* **:** lover, sweetheart

enamoramiento *nm* **:** infatuation, crush

enamorar *vt* : to enamor, to win the love of — **enamorarse** *vr* : to fall in love
enamoriscarse {72} *vr fam* : to have a crush, to be infatuated
enamorizado, -da *adj* : amorous, passionate
enano[1], -na *adj* : tiny, minute
enano[2], -na *n* : dwarf, midget
enarbolar *vt* **1** : to hoist, to raise **2** : to brandish
enarcar {72} *vt* : to arch, to raise
enardecer {53} *vt* **1** : to arouse (anger, passions) **2** : to stir up, to excite — **enardecerse** *vr*
encabezado *nm Mex* : headline
encabezamiento *nm* **1** : heading **2** : salutation, opening
encabezar {21} *vt* **1** : to head, to lead **2** : to put a heading on
encabritarse *vr* **1** : to rear up **2** *fam* : to get angry
encadenar *vt* **1** : to chain **2** : to connect, to link **3** INMOVILIZAR : to immobilize
encajar *vi* : to fit, to fit together, to fit in — *vt* **1** : to insert, to stick **2** : to take, to cope with <encajó el golpe : he withstood the blow>
encaje *nm* **1** : lace **2** : financial reserve
encajonar *vt* **1** : to box, to crate **2** : to cram in
encalar *vt* : to whitewash
encallar *vi* **1** : to run aground **2** : to get stuck
encallecido, -da *adj* : callused
encamar *vt* : to confine to a bed
encaminado, -da *adj* **1** : on the right track **2** ~ **a** : aimed at, designed to
encaminar *vt* **1** : to direct, to channel **2** : to head in the right direction — **encaminarse** *vr* ~ **a** : to head for, to aim at
encandilar *vt* : to dazzle
encanecer {53} *vi* : to gray, to go gray
encantado, -da *adj* **1** : charmed, bewitched **2** : delighted
encantador[1], -dora *adj* : charming, delightful
encantador[2], -dora *n* : magician
encantamiento *nm* : enchantment, spell
encantar *vt* **1** : to enchant, to bewitch **2** : to charm, to delight <me encanta esta canción : I love this song>
encanto *nm* **1** : charm, fascination **2** HECHIZO : spell **3** : delightful person or thing
encañonar *vt* : to point (a gun) at, to hold up
encapotado, -da *adj* : cloudy, overcast
encapotarse *vr* : to cloud over, to become overcast
encaprichado, -da *adj* : infatuated
encaprichamiento *nm* : infatuation
encapuchado, -da *adj* : hooded
encarado, -da *adj* **estar mal encarado** *fam* : to be ugly-looking, to look mean
encaramar *vt* : to raise, to lift up — **encaramarse** *vr* : to perch
encarar *vt* CONFRONTAR : to face, to confront
encarcelación *nf* → **encarcelamiento**
encarcelamiento *nm* : incarceration, imprisonment
encarcelar *vt* : to incarcerate, to imprison
encarecer {53} *vt* **1** : to increase, to raise (price, value) **2** : to beseech, to entreat — **encarecerse** *vr* : to become more expensive
encarecidamente *adv* : insistently, urgently
encarecimiento *nm* : increase, rise (in price)
encargado[1], -da *adj* : in charge
encargado[2], -da *n* : manager, person in charge
encargar {52} *vt* **1** : to put in charge of **2** : to recommend, to advise **3** : to order, to request — **encargarse** *vr* ~ **de** : to take charge of
encargo *nm* **1** : errand **2** : job assignment **3** : order <hecho de encargo : custom-made, made to order>
encariñarse *vr* ~ **con** : to become fond of, to grow attached to
encarnación *nf, pl* **-ciones** : incarnation, embodiment
encarnado[1], -da *adj* **1** : incarnate **2** : flesh-colored **3** : red **4** : ingrown
encarnado[2] *nm* : red
encarnar *vt* : to incarnate, to embody — **encarnarse** *vr* **encarnarse una uña** : to have an ingrown nail
encarnizado, -da *adj* **1** : bloodshot, inflamed **2** : fierce, bloody
encarnizar {21} *vt* : to enrage, to infuriate — **encarnizarse** *vr* : to be brutal, to attack viciously
encarrilar *vt* : to guide, to put on the right track
encasillar *vt* CLASIFICAR : to classify, to pigeonhole, to categorize
encausar *vt* : to prosecute, to charge
encauzar {21} *vt* : to channel, to guide — **encauzarse** *vr*
encebollado, -da *adj* : cooked with onions
encefalitis *nms & pl* : encephalitis
encendedor *nm* : lighter
encender {56} *vi* : to light — *vt* **1** : to light, to set fire to **2** PRENDER : to switch on **3** : to start (a motor) **4** : to arouse, to kindle — **encenderse** *vr* **1** : to get excited **2** : to blush
encendido[1], -da *adj* **1** : burning **2** : flushed **3** : fiery, passionate
encendido[2] *nm* : ignition
encerado *nm* **1** : waxing, polishing **2** : blackboard
encerar *vt* : to wax, to polish
encerrar {55} *vt* **1** : to lock up, to shut away **2** : to contain, to include **3** : to involve, to entail
encerrona *nf* **1** TRAMPA : trap, setup **2** **prepararle una encerrona a alguien**

: to set a trap for someone, to set someone up

encestar *vi* : to make a basket (in basketball)

enchapado *nm* : plating, coating (of metal)

encharcamiento *nm* : flood, flooding

encharcar {72} *vt* : to flood, to swamp — **encharcarse** *vr*

enchilada *nf* : enchilada

enchilar *vt Mex* : to season with chili

enchuecar {72} *vt Chile, Mex fam* : to make crooked, to twist

enchufar *vt* **1** : to plug in **2** : to connect, to fit together

enchufe *nm* **1** : connection **2** : plug, socket

encía *nf* : gum (tissue)

encíclica *nf* : encyclical

enciclopedia *nf* : encyclopedia

enciclopédico, -ca *adj* : encyclopedic

encierro *nm* **1** : confinement **2** : enclosure

encima *adv* **1** : on top, above **2** ADEMÁS : as well, besides **3 ~ de** : on, on top of, over **4 por encima de** : above, beyond <por encima de la ley : above the law> **5 echarse encima** : to take upon oneself **6 estar encima de** *fam* : to nag, to criticize **7 quitarse de encima** : to get rid of

encina *nf* : evergreen oak

encinta *adj* EMBARAZADA, PREÑADA : pregnant, expecting

enclaustrado, -da *adj* : cloistered, shut away

enclavado, -da *adj* : buried

enclenque *adj* : weak, sickly

encoger {15} *vt* **1** : to shrink, to make smaller **2** : to intimidate — *vi* : to shrink, to contract — **encogerse** *vr* **1** : to shrink **2** : to be intimidated, to cower, to cringe **3 encogerse de hombros** : to shrug <one's shoulders>

encogido, -da *adj* **1** : shriveled, shrunken **2** TÍMIDO : shy, inhibited

encogimiento *nm* **1** : shrinking, shrinkage **2** : shrug **3** TIMIDEZ : shyness

encolar *vt* : to paste, to glue

encolerizar {21} *vt* ENFURECER : to enrage, to infuriate — **encolerizarse** *vr*

encomendar {55} *vt* CONFIAR : to entrust, to commend — **encomendarse** *vr*

encomiable *adj* : commendable, praiseworthy

encomiar *vt* ELOGIAR : to praise, to pay tribute to

encomienda *nf* **1** : charge, mission **2** : royal land grant **3** : parcel

encomio *nm* : praise, eulogy

encomioso, -sa *adj* : eulogistic, laudatory

enconar *vt* **1** : to irritate, to anger **2** : to inflame — **enconarse** *vr* **1** : to become heated **2** : to fester

encono *nm* **1** RENCOR : animosity, rancor **2** : inflamation, infection

encontrado, -da *adj* : contrary, opposing

encontrar {19} *vt* **1** HALLAR : to find **2** : to encounter, to meet — **encontrarse** *vr* **1** REUNIRSE : to meet **2** : to clash, to conflict **3** : to be <su abuelo se encuentra mejor : her grandfather is doing better>

encorvar *vt* : to bend, to curve — **encorvarse** *vr* : to hunch over, to stoop

encrespar *vt* **1** : to curl, to ruffle, to ripple **2** : to annoy, to irritate — **encresparse** *vr* **1** : to curl one's hair **2** : to become choppy **3** : to get annoyed

encrucijada *nf* : crossroads

encuadernación *nf, pl* **-ciones** : bookbinding

encuadernar *vt* EMPASTAR : to bind (a book)

encuadrar *vt* **1** ENMARCAR : to frame **2** ENCAJAR : to fit, to insert **3** COMPRENDER : to contain, to include

encubierto *pp* → **encubrir**

encubrimiento *nm* : cover-up

encubrir {2} *vt* : to cover up, to conceal

encuentro *nm* **1** : meeting, encounter **2** : conference, congress

encuerado, -da *adj fam* : naked

encuerar *vt fam* : to undress

encuesta *nf* **1** INVESTIGACIÓN, PESQUISA : inquiry, investigation **2** SONDEO : survey

encuestador, -dora *n* : pollster

encuestar *vt* : to poll, to take a survey of

encumbrado, -da *adj* **1** : lofty, high **2** : eminent, distinguished

encumbrar *vt* **1** : to exalt, to elevate **2** : to extol — **encumbrarse** *vr* : to reach the top

encurtir *vt* ESCABECHAR : to pickle

ende *adv* **por ~** : therefore, consequently

endeble *adj* : feeble, weak

endeblez *nf* : weakness, frailty

endémico, -ca *adj* : endemic

endemoniado, -da *adj* : fiendish, diabolical

endentecer {53} *vi* : to teethe

enderezar {21} *vt* **1** : to straighten (out) **2** : to stand on end, to put upright

endeudado, -da *adj* : in debt, indebted

endeudamiento *nm* : indebtedness

endeudarse *vr* **1** : to go into debt **2** : to feel obliged

endiabladamente *adv* : extremely, diabolically

endiablado, -da *adj* **1** : devilish, diabolical **2** : complicated, difficult

endibia *or* **endivia** *nm* : endive

endilgar {52} *vt fam* : to spring, to foist <me endilgó la responsabilidad : he saddled me with the responsibility>

endocrino, -na *adj* : endocrine

endogamia *nf* : inbreeding

endosar *vt* : to endorse
endoso *nm* : endorsement
endulzante *nm* : sweetener
endulzar {21} *vt* **1** : to sweeten **2** : to soften, to mellow — **endulzarse** *vr*
endurecer {53} *vt* : to harden, to toughen — **endurecerse** *vr*
enebro *nm* : juniper
eneldo *nm* : dill
enema *nm* : enema
enemigo, -ga *adj & n* : enemy
enemistad *nf* : enmity, hostility
enemistar *vt* : to make enemies of — **enemistarse** *vr* **~ con** : to fall out with
energía *nf* : energy
enérgico, -ca *adj* **1** : energetic, vigorous **2** : forceful, emphatic — **enérgicamente** *adv*
energúmeno, -na *n fam* : lunatic, crazy person
enero *nm* : January
enervar *vt* **1** : to enervate **2** *fam* : to annoy, to get on one's nerves — **enervante** *adj*
enésimo, -ma *adj* : umpteenth, nth
enfadar *vt* **1** : to annoy, to make angry **2** *Mex fam* : to bore — **enfadarse** *vr* : to get angry, to get annoyed
enfado *nm* : anger, annoyance
enfadoso, -sa *adj* : irritating, annoying
enfardar *vt* : to bale
énfasis *nms & pl* : emphasis
enfático, -ca *adj* : emphatic — **enfáticamente** *adv*
enfatizar {21} *vt* DESTACAR, SUBRAYAR : to emphasize
enfermar *vt* : to make sick — *vi* : to fall ill, to get sick — **enfermarse** *vr*
enfermedad *nf* **1** INDISPOSICIÓN : sickness, illness **2** : disease
enfermería *nf* : infirmary
enfermero, -ra *n* : nurse
enfermizo, -za *adj* : sickly
enfermo[1], -ma *adj* : sick, ill
enfermo[2], -ma *n* **1** : sick person, invalid **2** PACIENTE : patient
enfilar *vt* **1** : to take, to go along <enfiló la carretera de Montevideo : she went up the road to Montevideo> **2** : to line up, to put in a row **3** : to string, to thread **4** : to aim, to direct — *vi* : to make one's way
enflaquecer {53} *vi* : to lose weight, to become thin — *vt* : to emaciate
enfocar {72} *vt* **1** : to focus (on) **2** : to consider, to look at
enfoque *nm* : focus
enfrascamiento *nm* : immersion, absorption
enfrascarse {72} *vr* **~ en** : to immerse oneself in, to get caught up in
enfrentamiento *nm* : clash, confrontation
enfrentar *vt* : to confront, to face — **enfrentarse** *vr* **1 ~ con** : to clash with **2 ~ a** : to face up to
enfrente *adv* **1** DELANTE : in front **2** : opposite
enfriamiento *nm* **1** CATARRO : chill, cold **2** : cooling off, damper
enfriar {85} *vt* **1** : to chill, to cool **2** : to cool down, to dampen — *vi* : to get cold — **enfriarse** *vr* : to get chilled, to catch a cold
enfundar *vt* : to sheathe, to encase
enfurecer {53} *vt* ENCOLERIZAR : to infuriate — **enfurecerse** *vr* : to fly into a rage
enfurecido, -da *adj* : furious, raging
enfurruñarse *vr fam* : to sulk
engalanar *vt* : to decorate, to deck out — **engalanarse** *vr* : to dress up
enganchar *vt* **1** : to hook, to snag **2** : to attach, to hitch up — **engancharse** *vr* **1** : to get snagged, to get hooked **2** : to enlist
enganche *nm* **1** : hook **2** : coupling, hitch **3** *Mex* : down payment
engañar *vt* **1** EMBAUCAR : to trick, to deceive, to mislead **2** : to cheat on, to be unfaithful to — **engañarse** *vr* **1** : to be mistaken **2** : to deceive oneself
engaño *nm* **1** : deception, trick **2** : fake, feint (in sports)
engañoso, -sa *adj* **1** : deceitful **2** : misleading, deceptive
engarrotarse *vr* : to stiffen up, to go numb
engatusamiento *nm* : cajolery
engatusar *vt* : to coax, to cajole
engendrar *vt* **1** : to beget, to father **2** : to give rise to, to engender
engentarse *vr Mex* : to be in a daze
englobar *vt* : to include, to embrace
engomar *vt* : to glue
engordar *vt* : to fatten, to fatten up — *vi* : to gain weight
engorro *nm* : nuisance, bother
engorroso, -sa *adj* : bothersome
engranaje *nm* : gears *pl*, cogs *pl*
engranar *vt* : to mesh, to engage — *vi* : to mesh gears
engrandecer {53} *vt* **1** : to enlarge **2** : to exaggerate **3** : to exalt
engrandecimiento *nm* **1** : enlargement **2** : exaggeration **3** : exaltation
engrane *nm Mex* : cogwheel
engrapadora *nf* : stapler
engrapar *vt* : to staple
engrasar *vt* : to grease, to lubricate
engrase *nm* : greasing, lubrication
engreído, -da *adj* PRESUMIDO, VANIDOSO : vain, conceited, stuck-up
engreimiento *nm* ARROGANCIA : arrogance, conceit
engreír {66} *vt* ENVANECER : to make vain — **engreírse** *vr* : to become conceited
engrosar {19} *vt* : to enlarge, to increase, to swell — *vi* ENGORDAR : to gain weight
engrudo *nm* : paste
engullir {38} *vt* : to gulp down, to gobble up — **engullirse** *vr*
enharinar *vt* : to flour
enhebrar *vt* ENSARTAR : to string, to thread

enhiesto, -ta *adj* **1 :** erect, upright **2 :** lofty, towering
enhilar *vt* **:** to thread (a needle, etc.)
enhorabuena *nf* FELICIDADES **:** congratulations *pl*
enigma *nm* **:** enigma, mystery
enigmático, -ca *adj* **:** enigmatic — **enigmáticamente** *adv*
enjabonar *vt* **:** to soap up, to lather — **enjabonarse** *vr*
enjaezar {21} *vt* **:** to harness
enjalbegar {52} *vt* **:** to whitewash
enjambrar *vi* **:** to swarm
enjambre *nm* **1 :** swarm **2** MUCHEDUMBRE **:** crowd, mob
enjaular *vt* **1 :** to cage **2** *fam* **:** to jail, to lock up
enjuagar {52} *vt* **:** to rinse — **enjuagarse** *vr* **:** to rinse out
enjuague *nm* **1 :** rinse **2 enjuague bucal :** mouthwash
enjugar {52} *vt* **:** to wipe away (tears)
enjuiciar *vt* **1 :** to indict, to prosecute **2** JUZGAR **:** to try
enjundioso, -sa *adj* **:** substantial, weighty
enjuto, -ta *adj* **:** lean, gaunt
enlace *nm* **1 :** bond, link, connection **2 :** liaison
enladrillado *nm* **:** brick paving
enladrillar *vt* **:** to pave with bricks
enlatar *vt* ENVASAR **:** to can
enlazar {21} *v* **:** to join, to link, to fit together
enlistar *vt* **:** to list — **enlistarse** *vr* **:** to enlist
enlodado, -da *adj* BARROSO **:** muddy
enlodar *vt* **1 :** to cover with mud **2 :** to stain, to sully — **enlodarse** *vr*
enlodazar → **enlodar**
enloquecedor, -dora *adj* **:** maddening
enloquecer {53} *vt* ALOCAR **:** to drive crazy — **enloquecerse** *vr* **:** to go crazy
enlosado *nm* **:** flagstone pavement
enlosar *vt* **:** to pave with flagstone
enlutarse *vr* **:** to go into mourning
enmaderado *nm* **1 :** wood paneling **2 :** hardwood floor
enmarañar *vt* **1 :** to tangle **2 :** to complicate **3 :** to confuse, to mix up — **enmarañarse** *vr*
enmarcar {72} *vt* **1** ENCUADRAR **:** to frame **2 :** to provide the setting for
enmascarar *vt* **:** to mask, to disguise
enmasillar *vt* **:** to putty, to caulk
enmendar {55} *vt* **1 :** to amend **2** CORREGIR **:** to emend, to correct **3** COMPENSAR **:** to compensate for — **enmendarse** *vr* **:** to mend one's ways
enmienda *nf* **1 :** amendment **2 :** correction, emendation
enmohecerse {53} *vr* **1 :** to become moldy **2** OXIDARSE **:** to rust, to become rusty
enmudecer {53} *vt* **:** to mute, to silence — *vi* **:** to fall silent
enmugrar *vt* **:** to soil, to make dirty — **enmugrarse** *vr* **:** to get dirty
ennegrecer {53} *vt* **:** to blacken, to darken — **ennegrecerse** *vr*
ennoblecer {53} *vt* **1 :** to ennoble **2 :** to embellish
enojadizo, -za *adj* IRRITABLE **:** irritable, cranky
enojado, -da *adj* **1 :** annoyed **2 :** angry, mad
enojar *vt* **1 :** to anger **2 :** to annoy, to upset — **enojarse** *vr*
enojo *nm* **1** CÓLERA **:** anger **2 :** annoyance
enojón, -jona *adj, pl* **-jones** *Chile, Mex fam* **:** irritable, cranky
enojoso, -sa *adj* FASTIDIOSO, MOLESTOSO **:** annoying, irritating
enorgullecer {53} *vt* **:** to make proud — **enorgullecerse** *vr* **:** to pride oneself
enorme *adj* INMENSO **:** enormous, huge — **enormemente** *adv*
enormidad *nf* **1 :** enormity, seriousness **2 :** immensity, hugeness
enraizado, -da *adj* **:** deep-seated, deeply rooted
enraizar {30} *vi* **:** to take root
enramada *nf* **:** arbor, bower
enramar *vt* **:** to cover with branches
enrarecer {53} *vt* **:** to rarefy — **enrarecerse** *vr*
enredadera *nf* **:** climbing plant, vine
enredar *vt* **1 :** to tangle up, to entangle **2 :** to confuse, to complicate **3 :** to involve, to implicate — **enredarse** *vr*
enredo *nm* **1** EMBROLLO **:** muddle, confusion **2** MARAÑA **:** tangle
enredoso, -sa *adj* **:** complicated, tricky
enrejado *nm* **1 :** railing **2 :** grating, grille **3 :** trellis, lattice
enrevesado, -da *adj* **:** complicated, involved
enriquecer {53} *vt* **:** to enrich — **enriquecerse** *vr* **:** to get rich
enriquecido, -da *adj* **:** enriched
enriquecimiento *nm* **:** enrichment
enrojecer {53} *vt* **:** to make red, to redden — **enrojecerse** *vr* **:** to blush
enrolar *vt* RECLUTAR **:** to recruit — **enrolarse** *vr* INSCRIBIRSE **:** to enlist, to sign up
enrollar *vt* **:** to roll up, to coil — **enrollarse** *vr*
enronquecerse {53} *vr* **:** to become hoarse
enroscar {72} *vt* TORCER **:** to twist — **enroscarse** *vr* **:** to coil, to twine
ensacar {72} *vt* **:** to bag (up)
ensalada *nf* **:** salad
ensaladera *nf* **:** salad bowl
ensalmo *nm* **:** incantation, spell
ensalzar {21} *vt* **1 :** to praise, to extol **2** EXALTAR **:** to exalt
ensamblaje *nm* **:** assembly
ensamblar *vt* **1 :** to assemble **2 :** to join, to fit together
ensanchar *vt* **1 :** to widen **2 :** to expand, to extend — **ensancharse** *vr*
ensanche *nm* **1 :** widening **2 :** expansion, development

ensangrentado, -da *adj* : bloody, bloodstained

ensañarse *vr* : to act cruelly, to be merciless

ensartar *vt* **1** ENHEBRAR : to string, to thread **2** : to skewer, to pierce

ensayar *vi* : to rehearse — *vt* **1** : to try out, to test **2** : to assay

ensayista *nmf* : essayist

ensayo *nm* **1** : essay **2** : trial, test **3** : rehearsal **4** : assay (of metals)

enseguida *adv* INMEDIATAMENTE : right away, immediately, at once

ensenada *nf* : cove, inlet

enseña *nf* **1** INSIGNIA : emblem, insignia **2** : standard, banner

enseñanza *nf* **1** EDUCACIÓN : education **2** : teaching

enseñar *vt* **1** : to teach **2** MOSTRAR : to show, to display — **enseñarse** *vr* **~ a** : to learn to, to get used to

enseres *nmpl* : equipment, furnishings *pl* <enseres domésticos : household goods>

ensillar *vt* : to saddle (up)

ensimismado, -da *adj* : absorbed, engrossed

ensimismarse *vr* : to lose oneself in thought

ensoberbecerse {53} *vr* : to become haughty

ensombrecer {53} *vt* : to cast a shadow over, to darken — **ensombrecerse** *vr*

ensoñación *nf, pl* **-ciones** : fantasy

ensopar *vt* **1** : to drench **2** : to dunk, to dip

ensordecedor, -dora *adj* : deafening, thunderous

ensordecer {53} *vt* : to deafen — *vi* : to go deaf

ensuciar *vt* : to soil, to dirty — **ensuciarse** *vr*

ensueño *nm* **1** : daydream, revery **2** FANTASÍA : illusion, fantasy

entablar *vt* **1** : to cover with boards **2** : to initiate, to enter into, to start

entallar *vt* AJUSTAR : to tailor, to fit, to take in — *vi* QUEDAR : to fit

ente *nm* **1** : being, entity **2** : body, organization <ente rector : ruling body> **3** *fam* : eccentric, crackpot

enteco, -ca *adj* : gaunt, frail

entenado, -da *n Mex* : stepchild, stepson *m,* stepdaughter *f*

entender[1] {56} *vt* **1** COMPRENDER : to understand **2** OPINAR : to think, to believe **3** QUERER : to mean, to intend **4** DEDUCIR : to infer, to deduce — *vi* **1** : to understand <¡ya entiendo! : now I understand!> **2 ~ de** : to know about, to be good at **3 ~ en** : to be in charge of — **entenderse** *vr* **1** : to be understood **2** : to get along well, to understand each other **3 ~ con** : to deal with

entender[2] *nm* **a mi entender** : in my opinion

entendible *adj* : understandable

entendido[1], **-da** *adj* **1** : skilled, expert **2 tener entendido** : to understand, to be under the impression <teníamos entendido que vendrías : we were under the impression you would come> **3 darse por entendido** : to go without saying

entendido[2] *nm* : expert, authority, connoisseur

entendimiento *nm* **1** : intellect, mind **2** : understanding, agreement

enterado, -da *adj* : aware, well-informed <estar enterado de : to be privy to>

enteramente *adv* : entirely, completely

enterar *vt* INFORMAR : to inform — **enterarse** *vr* INFORMARSE : to find out, to learn

entereza *nf* **1** INTEGRIDAD : integrity **2** FORTALEZA : fortitude **3** FIRMEZA : resolve

enternecedor, -dora *adj* CONMOVEDOR : touching, moving

enternecer {53} *vt* CONMOVER : to move, to touch

entero[1], **-ra** *adj* **1** : entire, whole **2** : complete, absolute **3** : intact — **enteramente** *adv*

entero[2] *nm* **1** : integer, whole number **2** : point (in finance)

enterramiento *nm* : burial

enterrar {55} *vt* : to bury

entibiar *vt* : to cool (down) — **entibiarse** *vr* : to become lukewarm

entidad *nf* **1** ENTE : entity **2** : body, organization **3** : firm, company **4** : importance, significance

entierro *nm* **1** : burial **2** : funeral

entintar *vt* : to ink

entoldado *nm* : awning

entomología *nf* : entomology

entomólogo, -ga *n* : entomologist

entonación *nf, pl* **-ciones** : intonation

entonar *vi* : to be in tune — *vt* **1** : to intone **2** : to tone up

entonces *adv* **1** : then **2 desde ~** : since then **3 en aquel entonces** : in those days

entornado, -da *adj* ENTREABIERTO : half-closed, ajar

entornar *vt* ENTREABRIR : to leave ajar

entorno *nm* : surroundings *pl,* environment

entorpecer {53} *vt* **1** : to hinder, to obstruct **2** : to dull — **entorpecerse** *vr* : to dull the senses

entrada *nf* **1** : entrance, entry **2** : ticket, admission **3** : beginning, onset **4** : entrée **5** : cue (in music) **6 entradas** *nfpl* : income <entradas y salidas : income and expenditures> **7 tener entradas** : to have a receding hairline

entrado, -da *adj* **entrado en años** : elderly

entramado *nm* : framework

entrampar *vt* **1** ATRAPAR : to entrap, to ensnare **2** ENGAÑAR : to deceive, to trick

entrante *adj* **1 :** next, upcoming <el año entrante : next year> **2 :** incoming, new <el presidente entrante : the president elect>
entraña *nf* **1** MEOLLO **:** core, heart, crux **2 entrañas** *nfpl* VÍSCERAS **:** entrails
entrañable *adj* **:** close, intimate
entrañar *vt* **:** to entail, to involve
entrar *vi* **1 :** to enter, to go in, to come in **2 :** to begin — *vt* **1 :** to bring in, to introduce **2 :** to access
entre *prep* **1 :** between **2 :** among
entreabierto[1] *pp* → **entreabrir**
entreabierto[2], **-ta** *adj* ENTORNADO **:** half-open, ajar
entreabrir {2} *vt* ENTORNAR **:** to leave ajar
entreacto *nm* **:** intermission, interval
entrecano, -na *adj* **:** grayish, graying
entrecejo *nm* **fruncir el entrecejo :** to knit one's brows
entrecomillar *vt* **:** to place in quotation marks
entrecortado, -da *adj* **1 :** labored, difficult <respiración entrecortada : shortness of breath> **2 :** faltering, hesitant <con la voz entrecortada : with a catch in his voice>
entrecruzar {21} *vt* ENTRELAZAR **:** to interweave, to intertwine — **entrecruzarse** *vr*
entredicho *nm* **1** DUDA **:** doubt, question **2 :** prohibition
entrega *nf* **1 :** delivery **2 :** handing over, surrender **3 :** installment <entrega inicial : down payment>
entregar {52} *vt* **1 :** to deliver **2** DAR **:** to give, to present **3 :** to hand in, to hand over — **entregarse** *vr* **1 :** to surrender, to give in **2 :** to devote oneself
entrelazar {21} *vt* ENTRECRUZAR **:** to interweave, to intertwine
entremedias *adv* **1 :** in between, halfway **2 :** in the meantime
entremés *nm, pl* **-meses 1** APERITIVO **:** appetizer, hors d'oeuvre **2 :** interlude, short play
entremeterse → **entrometerse**
entremetido *nm* → **entrometido**
entremezclar *vt* **:** to intermingle
entrenador, -dora *n* **:** trainer, coach
entrenamiento *nm* **:** training, drill, practice
entrenar *vt* **:** to train, to drill, to practice — **entrenarse** *vr* **:** to train, to spar (in boxing)
entreoír {50} *vt* **:** to hear indistinctly
entrepierna *nf* **1 :** inner thigh **2 :** crotch **3 :** inseam
entrepiso *nm* ENTRESUELO **:** mezzanine
entresacar {72} *vt* **1** SELECCIONAR **:** to pick out, to select **2 :** to thin out
entresuelo *nm* ENTREPISO **:** mezzanine
entretanto[1] *adv* **:** meanwhile
entretanto[2] *nm* **en el entretanto :** in the meantime
entretejer *vt* **:** to interweave
entretela *nf* **:** facing (of a garment)
entretener {80} *vt* **1** DIVERTIR **:** to entertain, to amuse **2** DISTRAER **:** to distract **3** DEMORAR **:** to delay, to hold up — **entretenerse** *vr* **1 :** to amuse oneself **2 :** to dally
entretenido, -da *adj* DIVERTIDO **:** entertaining, amusing
entretenimiento *nm* **1 :** entertainment, pastime **2** DIVERSIÓN **:** fun, amusement
entrever {88} *vt* **1 :** to catch a glimpse of **2 :** to make out, to see indistinctly
entreverar *vt* **:** to mix, to intermingle
entrevero *nm* **:** confusion, disorder
entrevista *nf* **:** interview
entrevistador, -dora *n* **:** interviewer
entrevistar *vt* **:** to interview — **entrevistarse** *vr* REUNIRSE **~ con :** to meet with
entristecer {53} *vt* **:** to sadden
entrometerse *vr* **:** to interfere, to meddle
entrometido, -da *n* **:** meddler, busybody
entroncar {72} *vt* RELACIONAR **:** to establish a relationship between, to connect — *vi* **1 :** to be related **2 :** to link up, to be connected
entronque *nm* **1 :** kinship **2** VÍNCULO **:** link, connection
entuerto *nm* **:** wrong, injustice
entumecer {53} *vt* **:** to make numb, to be numb — **entumecerse** *vr* **:** to go numb, to fall asleep
entumecido, -da *adj* **1 :** numb **2 :** stiff (of muscles, joints, etc.)
entumecimiento *nm* **:** numbness
enturbiar *vt* **1 :** to cloud **2 :** to confuse — **enturbiarse** *vr*
entusiasmar *vt* **:** to excite, to fill with enthusiasm — **entusiasmarse** *vr* **:** to get excited
entusiasmo *nm* **:** enthusiasm
entusiasta[1] *adj* **:** enthusiastic
entusiasta[2] *nmf* AFICIONADO **:** enthusiast
enumerar *vt* **:** to enumerate — **enumeración** *nf*
enunciación *nf, pl* **-ciones :** enunciation, statement
enunciar *vt* **:** to enunciate, to state
envainar *vt* **:** to sheathe
envalentonar *vt* **:** to make bold, to encourage — **envalentonarse** *vr*
envanecer {53} *vt* ENGREÍR **:** to make vain — **envanecerse** *vr*
envasar *vt* **1** EMBOTELLAR **:** to bottle **2** ENLATAR **:** to can **3 :** to pack in a container
envase *nm* **1 :** packaging, packing **2 :** container **3** LATA **:** can **4 :** empty bottle
envejecer {53} *vt* **:** to age, to make look old — *vi* **:** to age, to grow old
envejecido, -da *adj* **:** aged, old-looking
envejecimiento *nm* **:** aging
envenenamiento *nm* **:** poisoning
envenenar *vt* **1 :** to poison **2 :** to embitter

envergadura *nf* **1 :** span, breadth, spread **2 :** importance, scope

envés *nm, pl* **enveses :** reverse, opposite side

enviado, -da *n* **:** envoy, correspondent

enviar {85} *vt* **1 :** to send **2 :** to ship

envidia *nf* **:** envy, jealousy

envidiar *vt* **:** to envy — **envidiable** *adj*

envidioso, -sa *adj* **:** envious, jealous

envilecer {53} *vt* **:** to degrade, to debase

envilecimiento *nm* **:** degradation, debasement

envío *nm* **1 :** shipment **2 :** remittance

enviudar *vi* **:** to be widowed, to become a widower

envoltorio *nm* **1 :** bundle, package **2 :** wrapping, wrapper

envoltura *nf* **:** wrapper, wrapping

envolver {89} *vt* **1 :** to wrap **2 :** to envelop, to surround **3 :** to entangle, to involve — **envolverse** *vr* **1 :** to become involved **2 :** to wrap oneself (up)

envuelto *pp* → **envolver**

enyerbar *vt Mex* **:** to bewitch

enyesar *vt* **1 :** to plaster **2** ESCAYOLAR **:** to put in a plaster cast

enzima *nf* **:** enzyme

éon *nm, pl* **eones :** aeon

eperlano *nm* **:** smelt (fish)

épico, -ca *adj* **:** epic

epicúreo[1], -rea *adj* **:** epicurean

epicúreo[2], -rea *n* **:** epicure

epidemia *nf* **:** epidemic

epidémico, -ca *adj* **:** epidemic

epidermis *nf* **:** epidermis

epifanía *nf* **:** feast of the Epiphany (January 6th)

epigrama *nm* **:** epigram

epilepsia *nf* **:** epilepsy

epiléptico, -ca *adj & n* **:** epileptic

epílogo *nm* **:** epilogue

episcopal *adj* **:** episcopal

episcopalista *adj & nmf* **:** Episcopalian

episódico, -ca *adj* **:** episodic

episodio *nm* **:** episode

epístola *nf* **:** epistle

epitafio *nm* **:** epitaph

epíteto *nm* **:** epithet, name

epítome *nm* **:** summary, abstract

época *nf* **1** EDAD, ERA, PERÍODO **:** epoch, age, period **2 :** time of year, season **3 de ~ :** vintage, antique

epopeya *nf* **:** epic poem

equidad *nf* JUSTICIA **:** equity, justice, fairness

equilátero, -ra *adj* **:** equilateral

equilibrado, -da *adj* **:** well-balanced

equilibrar *vt* **:** to balance — **equilibrarse** *vr*

equilibrio *nm* **1 :** balance, equilibrium <perder el equilibrio : to lose one's balance> <equilibrio político : balance of power> **2 :** poise, aplomb

equilibrista *nmf* ACRÓBATA, FUNÁMBULO **:** acrobat, tightrope walker

equino, -na *adj* **:** equine

equinoccio *nm* **:** equinox

equipaje *nm* BAGAJE **:** baggage, luggage

equipamiento *nm* **:** equipping, equipment

equipar *vt* **:** to equip — **equiparse** *vr*

equiparable *adj* **:** comparable

equiparar *vt* **1** IGUALAR **:** to put on a same level, to make equal **2** COMPARAR **:** to compare

equipo *nm* **1 :** team, crew **2 :** gear, equipment

equitación *nf, pl* **-ciones :** horseback riding, horsemanship

equitativo, -va *adj* JUSTO **:** equitable, fair, just — **equitativamente** *adv*

equivalencia *nf* **:** equivalence

equivalente *adj & nm* **:** equivalent

equivaler {84} *vi* **:** to be equivalent

equivocación *nf, pl* **-ciones** ERROR **:** error, mistake

equivocado, -da *adj* **:** mistaken, wrong — **equivocadamente** *adv*

equivocar {72} *vt* **:** to mistake, to confuse — **equivocarse** *vr* **:** to make a mistake, to be wrong

equívoco[1], -ca *adj* AMBIGUO **:** ambiguous, equivocal

equívoco[2] *nm* **:** misunderstanding

era[1], etc. → **ser**

era[2] *nf* EDAD, ÉPOCA **:** era, age

erario *nm* **:** public treasury

erección *nf, pl* **-ciones :** erection, raising

eremita *nmf* ERMITAÑO **:** hermit

ergonomía *nf* **:** ergonomic

erguido, -da *adj* **:** erect, upright

erguir {31} *vt* **:** to raise, to lift up — **erguirse** *vr* **:** to straighten up

erial *nm* **:** uncultivated land

erigir {35} *vt* **:** to build, to erect — **erigirse** *vr* **~ en :** to set oneself up as

erizado, -da : bristly

erizarse {21} *vr* **:** to bristle, to stand on end

erizo *nm* **1 :** hedgehog **2 erizo de mar :** sea urchin

ermitaño[1], -ña *n* EREMITA **:** hermit, recluse

ermitaño[2] *nm* **:** hermit crab

erogación *nf, pl* **-ciones :** expenditure

erogar {52} *vt* **1 :** to pay out **2 :** to distribute

erosión *nf, pl* **-siones :** erosion

erosionar *vt* **:** to erode

erótico, -ca *adj* **:** erotic

erotismo *nm* **:** eroticism

errabundo, -da *adj* ERRANTE, VAGABUNDO **:** wandering

erradicar {72} *vt* **:** to eradicate — **erradicación** *nf*

errado, -da *adj* **:** wrong, mistaken

errante *adj* ERRABUNDO, VAGABUNDO **:** errant, wandering

errar {32} *vt* FALLAR **:** to miss — *vi* **1** DESACERTAR **:** to be wrong, to be mistaken **2** VAGAR **:** to wander

errata *nf* **:** misprint, error

errático, -ca *adj* : erratic — **erráticamente** *adv*
erróneo, -nea *adj* EQUIVOCADO : erroneous, wrong — **erróneamente** *adv*
error *nm* EQUIVOCACIÓN : error, mistake
eructar *vi* : to belch, to burp
eructo *nm* : belch, burp
erudición *nf, pl* **-ciones** : erudition, learning
erudito[1], -ta *adj* LETRADO : erudite, learned
erudito[2], -ta *n* : scholar
erupción *nf, pl* **-ciones 1** : eruption **2** SARPULLIDO : rash
eruptivo, -va *adj* : eruptive
es → **ser**
esbelto, -ta *adj* DELGADO : slender, slim
esbirro *nm* : henchman
esbozar {21} *vt* BOSQUEJAR : to sketch, to outline
esbozo *nm* **1** : sketch **2** : rough draft
escabechar *vt* **1** ENCURTIR : to pickle **2** *fam* : to kill, to rub out
escabeche *nm* : brine (for pickling)
escabechina *nf* MASACRE : massacre, bloodbath
escabel *nm* : footstool
escabroso, -sa *adj* **1** : rugged, rough **2** : difficult, tough **3** : risqué
escabullirse {38} *vr* : to slip away, to escape
escala *nf* **1** : scale **2** ESCALERA : ladder **3** : stopover
escalada *nf* : ascent, climb
escalador, -dora *n* ALPINISTA : mountain climber
escalafón *nm, pl* **-fones 1** : list of personnel **2** : salary scale, rank
escalar *vt* : to climb, to scale — *vi* **1** : to go climbing **2** : to escalate
escaldar *vt* : to scald
escalera *nf* **1** : ladder <escalera de tijera : stepladder> **2** : stairs *pl,* staircase **3 escalera mecánica** : escalator
escalfador *nm* : chafing dish
escalfar *vt* : to poach (eggs)
escalinata *nf* : flight of stairs
escalofriante *adj* : horrifying, bloodcurdling
escalofrío *nm* : shiver, chill, shudder
escalón *nm, pl* **-lones 1** : echelon **2** : step, rung
escalonado, -da *adj* GRADUAL : gradual, staggered
escalonar *vt* **1** : to terrace **2** : to stagger, to alternate
escalpelo *nm* BISTURÍ : scalpel
escama *nf* **1** : scale (of fish or reptiles) **2** : flake (of skin)
escamar *vt* **1** : to scale (fish) **2** : to make suspicious
escamocha *nf Mex* : fruit salad
escamoso, -sa *adj* : scaly
escamotear *vt* **1** : to palm, to conceal **2** *fam* : to lift, to swipe **3** : to hide, to cover up
escandalizar {21} *vt* : to shock, to scandalize — *vi* : to make a fuss — **escandalizarse** *vr* : to be shocked
escándalo *nm* **1** : scandal **2** : scene, commotion
escandaloso, -sa *adj* **1** : shocking, scandalous **2** RUIDOSO : noisy, rowdy **3** : flagrant, outrageous — **escandalosamente** *adv*
escandinavo, -va *adj & n* : Scandinavian
escandir *vt* : to scan (poetry)
escáner *nm* : scanner, scan
escaño *nm* **1** : seat (in a legislative body) **2** BANCO : bench
escapada *nf* HUIDA : flight, escape
escapar *vi* HUIR : to escape, to flee, to run away — **escaparse** *vr* : to escape notice, to leak out
escaparate *nm* **1** : shop window **2** : showcase
escapatoria *nf* **1** : loophole, excuse, pretext <no tener escapatoria : to have no way out> **2** ESCAPADA : escape, flight
escape *nm* **1** FUGA : escape **2** : exhaust (from a vehicle)
escapismo *nm* : escapism
escápula *nm* OMÓPLATO : scapula, shoulder blade
escapulario *nm* : scapular
escarabajo *nm* : beetle
escaramuza *nf* **1** : skirmish **2** : scrimmage
escaramuzar {21} *vi* : to skirmish
escarapela *nf* : rosette (ornament)
escarbar *vt* **1** : to dig, to scratch up **2** : to poke, to pick **3 ~ en** : to investigate, to pry into
escarcha *nf* **1** : frost **2** *Mex, PRi* : glitter
escarchar *vt* **1** : to frost (a cake) **2** : to candy (fruit)
escardar *vt* **1** : to weed, to hoe **2** : to weed out
escariar *vt* : to ream
escarlata *adj & nf* : scarlet
escarlatina *nf* : scarlet fever
escarmentar {55} *vt* : to punish, to teach a lesson to — *vi* : to learn one's lesson
escarmiento *nm* **1** : lesson, warning **2** CASTIGO : punishment
escarnecer {53} *vt* RIDICULIZAR : to ridicule, to mock
escarnio *nm* : ridicule, mockery
escarola *nf* : escarole
escarpa *nf* : escarpment, steep slope
escarpado, -da *adj* : steep, sheer
escarpia *nf* : hook, spike
escasamente *adv* : scarcely, barely
escasear *vi* : to be scarce, to run short
escasez *nf, pl* **-seces** : shortage, scarcity
escaso, -sa *adj* **1** : scarce, scant **2 ~ de** : short of
escatimar *vt* : to skimp on, to be sparing with <no escatimar esfuerzos : to spare no effort>
escayola *nf* **1** : plaster (for casts) **2** : plaster cast
escayolar *vt* : to put in a plaster cast

escena *nf* **1 :** scene **2 :** stage
escenario *nm* **1** ESCENA **:** stage **2 :** setting, scene <el escenario del crimen : the scene of the crime>
escénico, -ca *adj* **1 :** scenic **2 :** stage
escenificar {72} *vt* **:** to stage, to dramatize
escepticismo *nm* **:** skepticism
escéptico[1], -ca *adj* **:** skeptical
escéptico[2], -ca *n* **:** skeptic
escindirse *vr* **1 :** to split **2 :** to break away
escisión *nf, pl* **-siones 1 :** split, division **2 :** excision
esclarecer {53} *vt* **1** ELUCIDAR **:** to elucidate, to clarify **2** ILUMINAR **:** to illuminate, to light up
esclarecimiento *nm* ELUCIDACIÓN **:** elucidation, clarification
esclavitud *nf* **:** slavery
esclavización *nf, pl* **-ciones :** enslavement
esclavizar {21} *vt* **:** to enslave
esclavo, -va *n* **:** slave
esclerosis *nf* **esclerosis múltiple :** multiple sclerosis
esclusa *nf* **:** floodgate, lock (of a canal)
escoba *nf* **:** broom
escobilla *nf* **:** small broom, brush, whisk broom
escobillón *nm, pl* **-llones :** swab
escocer {14} *vi* ARDER **:** to smart, to sting — **escocerse** *vr* **:** to be sore
escocés[1], -cesa *adj, mpl* **-ceses 1 :** Scottish **2 :** tartan, plaid
escocés[2], -cesa *n, mpl* **-ceses :** Scottish person, Scot
escocés[3] *nm* **1 :** Scots (language) **2** *pl* **-ceses :** Scotch (whiskey)
escofina *nf* **:** file, rasp
escoger {15} *vt* ELEGIR, SELECCIONAR **:** to choose, to select
escogido, -da *adj* **:** choice, select
escolar[1] *adj* **:** school
escolar[2] *nmf* **:** student, pupil
escolaridad *nf* **:** schooling <escolaridad obligatoria : compulsory education>
escolarización *nf, pl* **-ciones :** education, schooling
escollo *nm* **1 :** reef **2** OBSTÁCULO **:** obstacle
escolta *nmf* **:** escort
escoltar *vt* **:** to escort, to accompany
escombro *nm* **1 :** debris, rubbish **2 escombros** *nmpl* **:** ruins, rubble
esconder *vt* OCULTAR **:** to hide, to conceal
escondidas *nfpl* **1 :** hide-and-seek **2 a ~ :** secretly, in secret
escondimiento *nm* **:** concealment
escondite *nm* **1** ENCONDRIJO **:** hiding place **2** ESCONDIDAS **:** hide-and-seek
escondrijo *nm* ESCONDITE **:** hiding place
escopeta *nf* **:** shotgun
escoplear *vt* **:** to chisel (out)
escoplo *nm* **:** chisel
escora *nf* **:** list, heeling
escorar *vi* **:** to list, to heel (of a boat)
escorbuto *nm* **:** scurvy
escoria *nf* **1 :** slag, dross **2** HEZ **:** dregs *pl,* scum <la escoria de la sociedad : the dregs of society>
Escorpio *or* **Escorpión** *nmf* **:** Scorpio
escorpión *nm, pl* **-piones** ALACRÁN **:** scorpion
escote *nm* **1 :** low neckline **2 pagar a escote :** to go dutch
escotilla *nf* **:** hatch, hatchway
escotillón *nf, pl* **-llones :** trapdoor
escozor *nm* **:** smarting, stinging
escriba *nm* **:** scribe
escribano, -na *n* **1 :** court clerk **2** NOTARIO **:** notary public
escribir {33} *v* **1 :** to write **2 :** to spell — **escribirse** *vr* CARTEARSE **:** to write to one another, to correspond
escrito[1] *pp* → **escribir**
escrito[2], -ta *adj* **:** written
escrito[3] *nm* **1 :** written document **2 escritos** *nmpl* **:** writings, works
escritor, -tora *n* **:** writer
escritorio *nm* **:** desk
escritorzuelo, -la *n* **:** hack (writer)
escritura *nf* **1 :** writing, handwriting **2 :** deed
escroto *nm* **:** scrotum
escrúpulo *nm* **:** scruple
escrupuloso, -sa *adj* **1 :** scrupulous **2** METICULOSO **:** exact, meticulous — **escrupulosamente** *adv*
escrutador, -dora *adj* **:** penetrating, searching
escrutar *vt* ESCUDRIÑAR **:** to scrutinize, to examine closely
escrutinio *nm* **:** scrutiny
escuadra *nf* **1 :** square (instrument) **2 :** fleet, squadron
escuadrilla *nf* **:** squadron, formation, flight
escuadrón *nm, pl* **-drones :** squadron
escuálido, -da *adj* **1 :** skinny, scrawny **2** INMUNDO **:** filthy, squalid
escuchar *vt* **1 :** to listen to **2 :** to hear — *vi* **:** to listen — **escucharse** *vr*
escudar *vt* **:** to shield — **escudarse** *vr* **~ en :** to hide behind
escudero *nm* **:** squire
escudo *nm* **1 :** shield **2 escudo de armas :** coat of arms
escudriñar *vt* **1** ESCRUTAR **:** to scrutinize **2 :** to inquire into, to investigate
escuela *nf* **:** school
escueto, -ta *adj* **1 :** plain, simple **2 :** succinct, concise — **escuetamente** *adv*
escuincle, -cla *n Mex fam* **:** child, kid
esculcar {72} *vt* **:** to search
esculpir *vt* **1 :** to sculpt **2 :** to carve, to engrave — *vi* **:** to sculpt
escultor, -tora *n* **:** sculptor
escultórico, -ca *adj* **:** sculptural
escultura *nf* **:** sculpture
escultural *adj* **:** statuesque
escupidera *nf* **:** spittoon, cuspidor
escupir *v* **:** to spit
escupitajo *nm* **:** spit
escurridizo, -za *adj* **:** slippery, elusive

escurridor *nm* **1 :** dish rack **2 :** colander
escurrir *vt* **1 :** to wring out **2 :** to drain — *vi* **1 :** to drain **2 :** to drip, to drip-dry — **escurrirse** *vr* **:** to slip away
ese, esa *adj, mpl* **esos :** that, those
ése, ésa *pron, mpl* **ésos :** that one, those ones *pl*
esencia *nf* **:** essence
esencial *adj* **:** essential — **esencialmente** *adv*
esfera *nf* **1 :** sphere **2 :** face, dial (of a watch)
esférico[1], **-ca** *adj* **:** spherical
esférico[2] *nm* **:** ball (in sports)
esfinge *nf* **:** sphinx
esforzado, -da *adj* **1 :** energetic, vigorous **2** VALIENTE **:** courageous, brave
esforzar {36} *vt* **:** to strain — **esforzarse** *vr* **:** to make an effort
esfuerzo *nm* **1 :** effort **2** ÁNIMO, VIGOR **:** spirit, vigor **3 sin ~ :** effortlessly
esfumar *vt* **:** to tone down, to soften — **esfumarse** *vr* **1 :** to fade away, to vanish **2** *fam* **:** to take off, to leave
esgrima *nf* **:** fencing (sport)
esgrimidor, -dora *n* **:** fencer
esgrimir *vt* **1 :** to brandish, to wield **2 :** to use, to resort to — *vi* **:** to fence
esguince *nm* **:** sprain, strain (of a muscle)
eslabón *nm, pl* **-bones :** link
eslabonar *vt* **:** to link, to connect, to join
eslavo[1], **-va** *adj* **:** Slavic
eslavo[2], **-va** *n* **:** Slav
eslogan *nm, pl* **-lóganes :** slogan
eslovaco, -ca *adj & n* **:** Slovakian, Slovak
esloveno, -na *adj & nm* **:** Slovene, Slovenian
esmaltar *vt* **:** to enamel
esmalte *nm* **1 :** enamel **2 esmalte de uñas :** nail polish
esmerado, -da *adj* **:** careful, painstaking
esmeralda *nf* **:** emerald
esmerarse *vr* **:** to take great pains, to do one's utmost
esmeril *nm* **:** emery
esmero *nm* **:** meticulousness, great care
esmoquin *nm, pl* **-quins :** tuxedo
esnob[1] *adj, pl* **esnobs :** snobbish
esnob[2] *nmf, pl* **esnobs :** snob
esnobismo *nm* **:** snobbery, snobbishness
eso *pron* (*neuter*) **1 :** that <eso no me gusta : I don't like that> **2 ¡eso es! :** that's it!, that's right! **3 a eso de :** around <a eso de las tres : around three o'clock> **4 en ~ :** at that point, just then
esófago *nm* **:** esophagus
esos → **ese**
ésos → **ése**
esotérico, -ca *adj* **:** esoteric — **esotéricamente** *adv*
espabilado, -da *adj* **:** bright, smart
espabilarse *vr* **1 :** to awaken **2 :** to get a move on **3 :** to get smart, to wise up
espacial *adj* **1 :** space **2 :** spatial
espaciar *vt* DISTANCIAR **:** to space out, to spread out
espacio *nm* **1 :** space, room **2 :** period, length (of time) **3 espacio exterior :** outer space
espacioso, -sa *adj* **:** spacious, roomy
espada[1] *nf* **1 :** sword **2 espadas** *nfpl* **:** spades (in playing cards)
espada[2] *nm* MATADOR, TORERO **:** bullfighter, matador
espadaña *nf* **1 :** belfry **2 :** cattail
espadilla *nf* **:** scull, oar
espagueti *nm or* **espaguetis** *nmpl* **:** spaghetti
espalda *nf* **1 :** back **2 espaldas** *nfpl* **:** shoulders, back **3 por la espalda :** from behind
espaldarazo *nm* **1 :** recognition, support **2 :** slap on the back
espaldera *nf* **:** trellis
espantajo *nm* **:** scarecrow
espantapájaros *nms & pl* **:** scarecrow
espantar *vt* ASUSTAR **:** to scare, to frighten — **espantarse** *vr*
espanto *nm* **:** fright, fear, horror
espantoso, -sa *adj* **1 :** frightening, terrifying **2 :** frightful, dreadful
español[1], **-ñola** *adj* **:** Spanish
español[2], **-ñola** *n* **:** Spaniard
español[3] *nm* CASTELLANO **:** Spanish (language)
esparadrapo *nm* **:** adhesive bandage, Band-Aid™
esparcimiento *nm* **1** DIVERSIÓN, RECREO **:** entertainment, recreation **2** DESCANSO **:** relaxation **3** DISEMINACIÓN **:** dissemination, spreading
esparcir {83} *vt* DISPERSAR **:** to scatter, to spread — **esparcirse** *vr* **1 :** to spread out **2** DESCANSARSE **:** to take it easy **3** DIVERTIRSE **:** to amuse oneself
espárrago *nm* **:** asparagus
espartano, -na *adj* **:** severe, austere
espasmo *nm* **:** spasm
espasmódico, -ca *adj* **:** spasmodic
espástico, -ca *adj* **:** spastic
espátula *nf* **:** spatula
especia *nf* **:** spice
especial *adj & nm* **:** special
especialidad *nf* **:** specialty
especialista *nmf* **:** specialist, expert
especializarse {21} *vr* **:** to specialize
especialmente *adv* **:** especially, particularly
especie *nf* **1 :** species **2** CLASE, TIPO **:** type, kind, sort
especificación *nf, pl* **-ciones :** specification
especificar {72} *vt* **:** to specify
específico, -ca *adj* **:** specific — **específicamente** *adv*
espécimen *nm, pl* **especímenes :** specimen
especioso, -sa *adj* **:** specious
espectacular *adj* **:** spectacular — **espectacularmente** *adv*

espectáculo *nm* **1 :** spectacle, sight **2 :** show, performance
espectador, -dora *n* **:** spectator, onlooker
espectro *nm* **1 :** ghost, specter **2 :** spectrum
especulación *nf, pl* **-ciones :** speculation
especulador, -dora *n* **:** speculator
especular *vi* **:** to speculate
especulativo, -va *adj* **:** speculative
espejismo *nm* **1 :** mirage **2 :** illusion
espejo *nm* **:** mirror
espejuelos *nmpl* ANTEOJOS **:** spectacles, glasses
espeluznante *adj* **:** hair-raising, terrifying
espera *nf* **:** wait
esperanza *nf* **:** hope, expectation
esperanzado, -da *adj* **:** hopeful
esperanzador, -dora *adj* **:** encouraging, promising
esperanzar {21} *vt* **:** to give hope to
esperar *vt* **1** AGUARDAR **:** to wait for, to await **2 :** to expect **3 :** to hope <espero poder trabajar : I hope to be able to work> <espero que sí : I hope so> — *vi* **:** to wait — **esperarse** *vr* **1 :** to expect, to be hoped <como podría esperarse : as would be expected> **2 :** to hold on, to hang on <espérate un momento : hold on a minute>
esperma *nmf* **:** sperm
esperpéntico, -ca *adj* GROTESCO **:** grotesque
esperpento *nm fam* MAMARRACHO **:** sight, fright <voy hecha un esperpento : I really look a sight>
espesante *nm* **:** thickener
espesar *vt* **:** to thicken — **espesarse** *vr*
espeso, -sa *adj* **:** thick, heavy, dense
espesor *nm* **:** thickness, density
espesura *nf* **1 :** thickness **2 :** thicket
espetar *vt* **1 :** to blurt out **2 :** to skewer
espía *nmf* **:** spy
espiar {85} *vt* **:** to spy on, to observe — *vi* **:** to spy
espiga *nf* **1 :** ear (of wheat) **2 :** spike (of flowers)
espigado, -da *adj* **:** willowy, slender
espigar {52} *vt* **:** to glean, to gather — **espigarse** *vr* **:** to grow quickly, to shoot up
espigón *nm, pl* **-gones :** breakwater
espina *nf* **1 :** thorn **2 :** spine <espina dorsal : spinal column> **3 :** fish bone
espinaca *nf* **1 :** spinach (plant) **2 espinacas** *nfpl* **:** spinach (food)
espinal *adj* **:** spinal
espinazo *nm* **:** backbone
espineta *nf* **:** spinet
espinilla *nf* **1** BARRO, GRANO **:** pimple **2 :** shin
espino *nm* **:** hawthorn
espinoso, -sa *adj* **1 :** thorny, prickly **2 :** bony (of fish) **3 :** knotty, difficult
espionaje *nm* **:** espionage
espiración *nf, pl* **-ciones :** exhalation
espiral *adj & nf* **:** spiral
espirar *vt* EXHALAR **:** to breathe out, to give off — *vi* **:** to exhale
espiritismo *nm* **:** spiritualism
espiritista *nmf* **:** spiritualist
espíritu *nm* **1 :** spirit **2** ÁNIMO **:** state of mind, spirits *pl* **3 el Espíritu Santo :** the Holy Ghost
espiritual *adj* **:** spiritual — **espiritualmente** *adv*
espiritualidad *nf* **:** spirituality
espita *nf* **:** spigot, tap
esplendidez *nf, pl* **-deces** ESPLENDOR **:** magnificence, splendor
espléndido, -da *adj* **1 :** splendid, magnificent **2 :** generous, lavish — **espléndidamente** *adv*
esplendor *nm* ESPLENDIDEZ **:** splendor
esplendoroso, -sa *adj* MAGNÍFICO **:** magnificent, grand
espliego *nm* LAVANDA **:** lavender
espolear *vt* **:** to spur on
espoleta *nf* **1** DETONADOR **:** detonator, fuse **2 :** wishbone
espolón *nm, pl* **-lones :** spur (of poultry), fetlock (of a horse)
espolvorear *vt* **:** to sprinkle, to dust
esponja *nf* **1 :** sponge **2 tirar la esponja :** to throw in the towel
esponjado, -da *adj* **:** spongy
esponjoso, -sa *adj* **1 :** spongy **2 :** soft, fluffy
esponsales *nmpl* **:** betrothal, engagement
espontaneidad *nf* **:** spontaneity
espontáneo, -nea *adj* **:** spontaneous — **espontáneamente** *adv*
espora *nf* **:** spore
esporádico, -ca *adj* **:** sporadic — **esporádicamente** *adv*
esposar *vt* **:** to handcuff
esposas *nfpl* **:** handcuffs
esposo, -sa *n* **:** spouse, wife *f,* husband *m*
esprint *nm* **:** sprint
esprintar *vi* **:** to sprint
esprinter *nmf* **:** sprinter
espuela *nf* **:** spur
espuerta *nf* **:** two-handled basket
espulgar {52} *vt* **1 :** to delouse **2 :** to scrutinize
espuma *nf* **1 :** foam **2 :** lather **3 :** froth, head (on beer)
espumar *vi* **:** to foam, to froth — *vt* **:** to skim off
espumoso, -sa *adj* **:** foamy, frothy
espurio, -ria *adj* **:** spurious
esputar *v* **:** to expectorate, to spit
esputo *nm* **:** spit, sputum
esqueje *nm* **:** cutting (from a plant)
esquela *nf* **1 :** note **2 :** notice, announcement
esquelético, -ca *adj* **:** emaciated, skeletal
esqueleto *nm* **1 :** skeleton **2** ARMAZÓN **:** framework
esquema *nf* BOSQUEJO **:** outline, sketch, plan
esquemático, -ca *adj* **:** schematic

esquí *nm* **1 :** ski **2 esquí acuático :** water ski, waterskiing
esquiador, -dora *n* **:** skier
esquiar {85} *vi* **:** to ski
esquife *nm* **:** skiff
esquila *nf* **1** CENCERRO **:** cowbell **2 :** shearing
esquilar *vt* TRASQUILAR **:** to shear
esquimal *adj & nmf* **:** Eskimo
esquina *nf* **:** corner
esquinazo *nm* **1 :** corner **2 dar esquinazo a** *fam* **:** to stand up, to give the slip to
esquirla *nf* **:** splinter (of bone, glass, etc.)
esquirol *nm* ROMPEHUELGAS **:** strikebreaker, scab
esquisto *nm* **:** shale
esquivar *vt* **1** EVADIR **:** to dodge, to evade **2** EVITAR **:** to avoid
esquivez *nf, pl* **-veces 1 :** aloofness **2** TIMIDEZ **:** shyness
esquivo, -va *adj* **1** HURAÑO **:** aloof, unsociable **2 :** shy **3 :** elusive, evasive
esquizofrenia *nf* **:** schizophrenia
esquizofrénico, -ca *adj & n* **:** schizophrenic
esta → **este[1]**
ésta → **éste**
estabilidad *nf* **:** stability
estabilización *nf, pl* **-ciones :** stabilization
estabilizador *nm* **:** stabilizer
estabilizar {21} *vt* **:** to stabilize — **estabilizarse** *vr*
estable *adj* **:** stable, steady
establecer {53} *vt* FUNDAR, INSTITUIR **:** to establish, to found, to set up — **establecerse** *vr* INSTALARSE **:** to settle, to establish oneself
establecimiento *nm* **1 :** establishing **2 :** establishment, institution, office
establo *nm* **:** stable
estaca *nf* **:** stake, picket, post
estacada *nf* **1 :** picket fence **2 :** stockade
estacar {72} *vt* **1 :** to stake out **2 :** to fasten down with stakes — **estacarse** *vr* **:** to remain rigid
estación *nf, pl* **-ciones 1 :** station <estación de servicio : service station, gas station> **2 :** season
estacional *adj* **:** seasonal
estacionamiento *nm* **1 :** parking **2 :** parking lot
estacionar *vt* **1 :** to place, to station **2 :** to park — **estacionarse** *vr* **1 :** to park **2 :** to remain stationary
estacionario, -ria *adj* **1 :** stationary **2 :** stable
estada *nf* **:** stay
estadía *nf* ESTANCIA **:** stay, sojourn
estadio *nm* **1 :** stadium **2 :** phase, stage
estadista *nmf* **:** statesman
estadística *nf* **1 :** statistic, figure **2 :** statistics
estadístico[1], -ca *adj* **:** statistical — **estadísticamente** *adv*
estadístico[2], -ca *n* **:** statistician
estado *nm* **1 :** state **2 :** status <estado civil : marital status> **3** CONDICIÓN **:** condition
estadounidense *adj & nmf* AMERICANO, NORTEAMERICANO **:** American
estafa *nf* **:** swindle, fraud
estafador, -dora *n* **:** cheat, swindler
estafar *vt* DEFRAUDAR **:** to swindle, to defraud
estalactita *nf* **:** stalactite
estalagmita *nf* **:** stalagmite
estallar *vi* **1** REVENTAR **:** to burst, to explode, to erupt **2 :** to break out
estallido *nm* **1** EXPLOSIÓN **:** explosion **2 :** report (of a gun) **3 :** outbreak, outburst
estambre *nm* **1 :** worsted (fabric) **2 :** stamen
estampa *nf* **1** ILUSTRACIÓN, IMAGEN **:** printed image, illustration **2** ASPECTO **:** appearance, demeanor
estampado[1], -da *adj* **:** patterned, printed
estampado[2] *nm* **:** print, pattern
estampar *vt* **:** to stamp, to print, to engrave
estampida *nf* **:** stampede
estampilla *nf* **1 :** rubber stamp **2** SELLO, TIMBRE **:** postage stamp
estancado, -da *adj* **:** stagnant
estancamiento *nm* **:** stagnation
estancar {72} *vt* **1 :** to dam up, to hold back **2 :** to bring to a halt, to deadlock — **estancarse** *vr* **1 :** to stagnate **2 :** to be brought to a standstill, to be deadlocked
estancia *nf* **1** ESTADÍA **:** stay, sojourn **2 :** ranch, farm
estanciero, -ra *n* **:** rancher, farmer
estanco, -ca *adj* **:** watertight
estándar *adj & nm* **:** standard
estandarización *nf, pl* **-ciones :** standardization
estandarizar {21} *vt* **:** to standardize
estandarte *nm* **:** standard, banner
estanque *nm* **1 :** pool, pond **2 :** tank, reservoir
estante *nm* REPISA **:** shelf
estantería *nf* **:** shelves *pl,* bookcase
estaño *nm* **:** tin
estaquilla *nf* **1 :** peg **2** ESPIGA **:** spike
estar {34} *v aux* **:** to be <estoy aprendiendo inglés : I'm learning English> <está terminado : it's finished> — *vi* **1** (*indicating a state or condition*) **:** to be <está muy alto : he's so tall, he's gotten very tall><¿ya estás mejor? : are you feeling better now?> <estoy casado : I'm married> **2** (*indicating location*) **:** to be <están en la mesa : they're on the table> <estamos en la página 2 : we're on page 2> **3 :** to be at home <¿está María? : is Maria in?> **4 :** to remain <estaré aquí 5 días : I'll be here for 5 days> **5 :** to be ready, to be done <estará para las diez : it will be ready by ten o'clock> **6 :** to agree <¿estamos? : are we in agreement?> <estoy contigo : I'm with you> **7**

¿cómo estás? : how are you? **8 ¡está bien!** : all right!, that's fine! **9 ~ a** : to cost **10 ~ a** : to be <¿a qué dia estamos? : what's today's date?> **11 ~ con** to have <está con fiebre : she has a fever> **12 ~ de** : to be <estoy de vacaciones : I'm on vacation> <está de director hoy : he's acting as director today> **13 estar bien (mal)** : to be well (sick) **14 ~ para** : to be in the mood for **15 ~ por** : to be in favor of **16 ~ por** : to be about to <está por cerrar : it's on the verge of closing> **17 estar de más** : to be unnecessary **18 estar que** : to be (in a state or condition) <está que echa chispas : he's hopping mad> — **estarse** *vr* QUEDARSE : to stay, to remain <¡estáte quieto! : be still!>
estarcir {83} *vt* : to stencil
estatal *adj* : state, national
estática *nf* : static
estático, -ca *adj* : static
estatizar {21} *vt* : to nationalize — **estatización** *nf*
estatua *nf* : statue
estatuilla *nf* : statuette, figurine
estatura *nf* : height, stature <de mediana estatura : of medium height>
estatus *nm* : status, prestige
estatutario, -ria *adj* : statutory
estatuto *nm* : statute
este[1], esta *adj, mpl* **estos** : this, these
este[2] *adj* : eastern, east
este[3] *nm* **1** ORIENTE : east **2** : east wind **3 el Este** : the East, the Orient
éste, ésta *pron, mpl* **éstos 1** : this one, these ones *pl* **2** : the latter
estela *nf* **1** : wake (of a ship) **2** RASTRO : trail (of dust, smoke, etc.)
estelar *adj* : stellar
estelarizar {21} *vt Mex* : to star in, to be the star of
esténcil *nm* : stencil
estentóreo, -rea *adj* : loud, thundering
estepa *nf* : steppe
éster *nf* : ester
estera *nf* : mat
estercolero *nm* : dunghill
estéreo *adj & nm* : stereo
estereofónico, -ca *adj* : stereophonic
estereotipado, -da *adj* : stereotyped
estereotipar *vt* : to stereotype
estereotipo *nm* : stereotype
estéril *adj* **1** : sterile, germ-free **2** : infertile, barren **3** : futile, vain
esterilidad *nf* **1** : sterility **2** : infertility
esterilizar {21} *vt* **1** : to sterilize, to disinfect **2** : to sterilize (a person), to spay (an animal) — **esterilización** *nf*
esterlina *adj* : sterling
esternón *nm, pl* **-nones** : sternum
estero *nm* : estuary
estertor *nm* : death rattle
estética *nf* : aesthetics
estético, -ca *adj* : aesthetic — **estéticamente** *adv*
estetoscopio *nm* : stethoscope
estibador, -dora *n* : longshoreman, stevedore
estibar *vt* : to load (freight)
estiércol *nm* : dung, manure
estigma *nm* : stigma
estigmatizar {21} *vt* : to stigmatize, to brand
estilarse *vr* : to be in fashion
estilete *nm* : stiletto
estilista *nmf* : stylist
estilizar {21} *vt* : to stylize
estilo *nm* **1** : style **2** : fashion, manner **3** : stylus
estima *nf* ESTIMACIÓN : esteem, regard
estimable *adj* **1** : considerable **2** : estimable, esteemed
estimación *nf, pl* **-ciones 1** ESTIMA : esteem, regard **2** : estimate
estimado, -da *adj* : esteemed, dear <Estimado señor Ortiz : Dear Mr. Ortiz>
estimar *vt* **1** APRECIAR : to esteem, to respect **2** EVALUAR : to estimate, to appraise **3** OPINAR : to consider, to deem
estimulación *nf, pl* **-ciones** : stimulation
estimulante[1] *adj* : stimulating
estimulante[2] *nm* : stimulant
estimular *vt* **1** : to stimulate **2** : to encourage
estímulo *nm* **1** : stimulus **2** INCENTIVO : incentive, encouragement
estío *nm* : summertime
estipendio *nm* **1** : salary **2** : stipend, remuneration
estipular *vt* : to stipulate — **estipulación** *nf*
estirado, -da *adj* **1** : stretched, extended **2** PRESUMIDO : stuck-up, conceited
estiramiento *nm* **1** : stretching **2 estiramiento facial** : face-lift
estirar *vt* : to stretch (out), to extend — **estirarse** *vr*
estirón *nm, pl* **-rones 1** : pull, tug **2 dar un estirón** : to grow quickly, to shoot up
estirpe *nf* LINAJE : lineage, stock
estival *adj* VERANIEGO : summer
esto *pron* (*neuter*) **1** : this <¿qué es esto? : what is this?> **2 en ~** : at this point **3 por ~** : for this reason
estocada *nf* **1** : final thrust (in bullfighting) **2** : thrust, lunge (in fencing)
estofa *nf* CLASE : class, quality <de baja estofa : low-class, poor-quality>
estofado *nm* COCIDO, GUISADO : stew
estofar *vt* GUISAR : to stew
estoicismo *nm* : stoicism
estoico[1], -ca *adj* : stoic, stoical
estoico[2], -ca *n* : stoic
estola *nf* : stole
estomacal *adj* GÁSTRICO : stomach, gastric
estómago *nm* : stomach
estoniano, -na *adj & n* : Estonian
estopa *nf* **1** : tow (yarn or cloth) **2** : burlap

estopilla *nf* : cheesecloth

estoque *nm* : rapier, sword

estorbar *vt* OBSTRUIR : to obstruct, to hinder — *vi* : to get in the way

estorbo *nm* **1** : obstacle, hindrance **2** : nuisance

estornino *nm* : starling

estornudar *vi* : to sneeze

estornudo *nm* : sneeze

estos → **este**[1]

éstos → **éste**

estoy → **estar**

estrabismo *nm* : squint

estrado *nm* **1** : dais, platform, bench (of a judge) **2** ESTRADOS *nmpl* : courts of law

estrafalario, -ria *adj* ESTRAMBÓTICO, EXCÉNTRICO : eccentric, bizarre

estragar {52} *vt* DEVASTAR : to ruin, to devastate

estragón *nm* : tarragon

estragos *nmpl* **1** : ravages, destruction, devastation <los estragos de la guerra : the ravages of war> **2 hacer estragos en** *or* **causar estragos entre** : to play havoc with

estrambótico, -ca *adj* ESTRAFALARIO, EXCÉNTRICO : eccentric, bizarre

estrangulamiento *nm* : strangling, strangulation

estrangular *vt* AHOGAR : to strangle — **estrangulación** *nf*

estratagema *nf* ARTIMAÑA : stratagem, ruse

estratega *nmf* : strategist

estrategia *nf* : strategy

estratégico, -ca *adj* : strategic, tactical — **estratégicamente** *adv*

estratificación *nf, pl* **-ciones** : stratification

estratificado, -da *adj* : stratified

estrato *nm* : stratum, layer

estratosfera *nf* : stratosphere

estratosférico, -ca *adj* **1** : stratospheric **2** : astronomical, exorbitant

estrechamiento *nm* **1** : narrowing **2** : narrow point **3** : tightening, strengthening (of relations)

estrechar *vt* **1** : to narrow **2** : to tighten, to strengthen (a bond) **3** : to hug, to embrace **4 estrechar la mano de** : to shake hands with — **estrecharse** *vr*

estrechez *nf, pl* **-checes 1** : tightness, narrowness **2 estrecheces** *nfpl* : financial problems

estrecho[1], **-cha** *adj* **1** : tight, narrow **2** ÍNTIMO : close — **estrechamente** *adv*

estrecho[2] *nm* : strait, narrows

estrella *nf* **1** ASTRO : star <estrella fugaz : shooting star> **2** : destiny <tener buena estrella : to be born lucky> **3** : movie star **4 estrella de mar** : starfish

estrellado, -da *adj* **1** : starry **2** : star-shaped **3 huevos estrellados** : fried eggs

estrellamiento *nm* : crash, collision

estrellar *vt* : to smash, to crash — **estrellarse** *vr* : to crash, to collide

estrellato *nm* : stardom

estremecedor, -dora *adj* : horrifying

estremecer {53} *vt* : to cause to shake — *vi* : to tremble, to shake — **estremecerse** *vr* : to shudder, to shiver (with emotion)

estremecimiento *nm* : trembling, shaking, shivering

estrenar *vt* **1** : to use for the first time **2** : to premiere, to open — **estrenarse** *vr* : to make one's debut

estreno *nm* DEBUT : debut, premiere

estreñimiento *nm* : constipation

estreñirse {67} *vr* : to be constipated

estrépito *nm* ESTRUENDO : clamor, din

estrepitoso, -sa *adj* : clamorous, noisy — **estrepitosamente** *adv*

estrés *nm, pl* **estreses** : stress

estresante *adj* : stressful

estresar *vt* : to stress, to stress out

estría *nf* : fluting, groove

estribación *nf, pl* **-ciones 1** : spur, ridge **2 estribaciones** *nfpl* : foothills

estribar *vi* FUNDARSE **~ en** : to be due to, to stem from

estribillo *nm* : refrain, chorus

estribo *nm* **1** : stirrup **2** : abutment, buttress **3 perder los estribos** : to lose one's temper

estribor *nm* : starboard

estricnina *nf* : strychnine

estricto, -ta *adj* SEVERO : strict, severe — **estrictamente** *adv*

estridente *adj* : strident, shrill, loud — **estridentemente** *adv*

estrofa *nf* : stanza, verse

estrógeno *nm* : estrogen

estropajo *nm* : scouring pad

estropear *vt* **1** ARRUINAR : to ruin, to spoil **2** : to break, to damage — **estropearse** *vr* **1** : to spoil, to go bad **2** : to break down

estropicio *nm* DAÑO : damage, breakage

estructura *nf* : structure, framework

estructuración *nf, pl* **-ciones** : structuring, structure

estructural *adj* : structural — **estructuralmente** *adv*

estructurar *vt* : to structure, to organize

estruendo *nm* ESTRÉPITO : racket, din, roar

estruendoso, -sa *adj* : resounding, thunderous

estrujar *vt* APRETAR : to press, to squeeze

estuario *nm* : estuary

estuche *nm* : kit, case

estuco *nm* : stucco

estudiado, -da *adj* : affected, mannered

estudiantado *nm* : student body, students *pl*

estudiante *nmf* : student

estudiantil *adj* : student <la vida estudiantil : student life>

estudiar *v* : to study
estudio *nm* **1** : study **2** : studio **3 estudios** *nmpl* : studies, education
estudioso, -sa *adj* : studious
estufa *nf* **1** : stove, heater **2** *Col, Mex* : cooking stove, range
estupefacción *nf, pl* **-ciones** : stupefaction, astonishment
estupefaciente[1] *adj* : narcotic
estupefaciente[2] *nm* DROGA, NARCÓTICO : drug, narcotic
estupefacto, -ta *adj* : astonished, stunned
estupendo, -da *adj* MARAVILLOSO : stupendous, marvelous — **estupendamente** *adv*
estupidez *nf, pl* **-deces 1** : stupidity **2** : nonsense
estúpido[1], **-da** *adj* : stupid — **estúpidamente** *adj*
estúpido[2], **-da** *n* IDIOTA : idiot, fool
estupor *nm* **1** : stupor **2** : amazement
esturión *nm, pl* **-riones** : sturgeon
estuvo, etc. → **estar**
etano *nm* : ethane
etanol *nm* : ethanol
etapa *nf* FASE : stage, phase
etcétera[1] : et cetera, and so on
etcétera[2] *nmf* : etcetera
éter *nm* : ether
etéreo, -rea *adj* : ethereal, heavenly
eternidad *nf* : eternity
eternizar {21} *vt* PERPETUAR : to make eternal, to perpetuate — **eternizarse** *vr fam* : to take forever
eterno, -na *adj* : eternal, endless — **eternamente** *adv*
ética *nf* : ethics
ético, -ca *adj* : ethical — **éticamente** *adv*
etimología *nf* : etymology
etimológico, -ca *adj* : etymological
etimólogo, -ga *n* : etymologist
etíope *adj & nmf* : Ethiopian
etiqueta *nf* **1** : etiquette **2** : tag, label **3 de ~** : formal, dressy
etiquetar *vt* : to label
étnico, -ca *adj* : ethnic
etnología *nf* : ethnology
etnólogo, -ga *n* : ethnologist
eucalipto *nm* : eucalyptus
Eucaristía *nf* : Eucharist, communion
eucarístico, -ca *adj* : eucharistic
eufemismo *nm* : euphemism
eufemístico, -ca *adj* : euphemistic
eufonía *nf* : euphony
eufónico, -ca *adj* : euphonious
euforia *nf* : euphoria, joyousness
eufórico, -ca *adj* : euphoric, exuberant, joyous — **eufóricamente** *adv*
eunuco *nm* : eunuch
europeo, -pea *adj & n* : European
euskera *nm* : Basque (language)
eutanasia *nf* : euthanasia
evacuación *nf, pl* **-ciones** : evacuation
evacuar *vt* **1** : to evacuate, to vacate **2** : to carry out — *vi* : to have a bowel movement
evadir *vt* ELUDIR : to evade, to avoid — **evadirse** *vr* : to escape, to slip away
evaluación *nf, pl* **-ciones** : assessment, evaluation
evaluar {3} *vt* : to evaluate, to assess, to appraise
evangélico, -ca *adj* : evangelical — **evangélicamente** *adv*
evangelio *nm* : gospel
evangelismo *nm* : evangelism
evangelista *nm* : evangelist
evangelizador, -dora *n* : evangelist, missionary
evaporación *nf, pl* **-ciones** : evaporation
evaporar *vt* : to evaporate — **evaporarse** *vr* ESFUMARSE : to disappear, to vanish
evasión *nf, pl* **-siones 1** : escape, flight **2** : evasion, dodge
evasiva *nf* : excuse, pretext
evasivo, -va *adj* : evasive
evento *nm* : event
eventual *adj* **1** : possible **2** : temporary <trabajadores eventuales : temporary workers> — **eventualmente** *adv*
eventualidad *nf* : possibility, eventuality
evidencia *nf* **1** : evidence, proof **2 poner en evidencia** : to demonstrate, to make clear
evidenciar *vt* : to demonstrate, to show — **evidenciarse** *vr* : to be evident
evidente *adj* : evident, obvious, clear — **evidentemente** *adv*
eviscerar *vt* : to eviscerate
evitable *adj* : avoidable, preventable
evitar *vt* **1** : to avoid **2** PREVENIR : to prevent **3** ELUDIR : to escape, to elude
evocación *nf, pl* **-ciones** : evocation
evocador, -dora *adj* : evocative
evocar {72} *vt* **1** : to evoke **2** RECORDAR : to recall
evolución *nf, pl* **-ciones 1** : evolution **2** : development, progress
evolucionar *vi* **1** : to evolve **2** : to change, to develop
evolutivo, -va *adj* : evolutionary
exabrupto *nm* : pointed remark
exacción *nf, pl* **-ciones** : levying, exaction
exacerbar *vt* **1** : to exacerbate, to aggravate **2** : to irritate, to exasperate
exactamente *adv* : exactly
exactitud *nf* PRECISIÓN : accuracy, precision, exactitude
exacto, -ta *adj* PRECISO : accurate, precise, exact
exageración *nf, pl* **-ciones** : exaggeration
exagerado, -da *adj* **1** : exaggerated **2** : excessive — **exageradamente** *adv*
exagerar *v* : to exaggerate
exaltación *nf, pl* **-ciones 1** : exaltation **2** : excitement, agitation
exaltado[1], **-da** *adj* : excitable, hotheaded
exaltado[2], **-da** *n* : hothead

exaltar *vt* **1** ENSALZAR **:** to exalt, to extol **2 :** to excite, to agitate — **exaltarse** *vr* ACALORARSE **:** to get overexcited
ex–alumno → **alumno**
examen *nm, pl* **exámenes 1 :** examination, test **2 :** consideration, investigation
examinar *vt* **1 :** to examine **2** INSPECCIONAR **:** to inspect — **examinarse** *vr* **:** to take an exam
exánime *adj* **1 :** lifeless **2 :** exhausted
exasperar *vt* IRRITAR **:** to exasperate, to irritate — **exasperación** *nf*
excavación *nf, pl* **-ciones :** excavation
excavadora *nf* **:** excavator
excavar *v* **:** to excavate, to dig
excedente[1] *adj* **1 :** excessive **2 :** excess, surplus
excedente[2] *nm* **:** surplus, excess
exceder *vt* **:** to exceed, to surpass — **excederse** *vr* **:** to go too far
excelencia *nf* **1 :** excellence **2 :** excellency <Su Excelencia : His Excellency>
excelente *adj* **:** excellent — **excelentemente** *adv*
excelso, -sa *adj* **:** lofty, sublime
excentricidad *nf* **:** eccentricity
excéntrico, -ca *adj & n* **:** eccentric
excepción *nf, pl* **-ciones :** exception
excepcional *adj* EXTRAORDINARIO **:** exceptional, extraordinary, rare
excepto *prep* SALVO **:** except
exceptuar {3} *vt* EXCLUIR **:** to except, to exclude
excesivo, -va *adj* **:** excessive — **excesivamente** *adv*
exceso *nm* **1 :** excess **2 excesos** *nmpl* **:** excesses, abuses **3 exceso de velocidad :** speeding
excitabilidad *nf* **:** excitability
excitación *nf, pl* **-ciones :** excitement
excitante *adj* **:** exciting
excitar *vt* **:** to excite, to arouse — **excitarse** *vr*
exclamación *nf, pl* **-ciones :** exclamation
exclamar *v* **:** to exclaim
excluir {41} *vt* EXCEPTUAR **:** to exclude, to leave out
exclusión *nf, pl* **-siones :** exclusion
exclusividad *nf* **1 :** exclusiveness **2 :** exclusive rights *pl*
exclusivo, -va *adj* **:** exclusive — **exclusivamente** *adv*
excomulgar {52} *vt* **:** to excommunicate
excomunión *nf, pl* **-niones :** excommunication
excreción *nf, pl* **-ciones :** excretion
excremento *nm* **:** excrement
excretar *vt* **:** to excrete
exculpar *vt* **:** to exonerate, to exculpate — **exculpación** *nf*
excursión *nf, pl* **-siones :** excursion, outing
excursionista *nmf* **1 :** sightseer, tourist **2 :** hiker
excusa *nf* **1** PRETEXTO **:** excuse **2** DISCULPA **:** apology
excusar *vt* **1 :** to excuse **2 :** to exempt — **excusarse** *vr* **:** to apologize, to send one's regrets
execrable *adj* **:** detestable, abominable
exención *nf, pl* **-ciones :** exemption
exento, -ta *adj* **1 :** exempt, free **2 exento de impuestos :** tax-exempt
exequias *nfpl* FUNERALES **:** funeral rites
exhalar *vt* ESPIRAR **:** to exhale, to give off
exhaustivo, -va *adj* **:** exhaustive — **exhaustivamente** *adv*
exhausto, -ta *adj* AGOTADO **:** exhausted, worn-out
exhibición *nf, pl* **-ciones 1 :** exhibition, show **2 :** showing
exhibir *vt* **:** to exhibit, to show, to display — **exhibirse** *vr*
exhortación *nf, pl* **-ciones :** exhortation
exhortar *vt* **:** to exhort
exhumar *vt* DESENTERRAR **:** to exhume — **exhumación** *nf*
exigencia *nf* **:** demand, requirement
exigente *adj* **:** demanding, exacting
exigir {35} *vt* **1 :** to demand, to require **2 :** to exact, to levy
exiguo, -gua *adj* **:** meager
exiliado[1], -da *adj* **:** exiled, in exile
exiliado[2], -da *n* **:** exile
exiliar *vt* DESTERRAR **:** to exile, to banish — **exiliarse** *vr* **:** to go into exile
exilio *nm* DESTIERRO **:** exile
eximio, -mia *adj* **:** distinguished, eminent
eximir *vt* EXONERAR **:** to exempt
existencia *nf* **1 :** existence **2 existencias** *nfpl* MERCANCÍA **:** goods, stock
existente *adj* **1 :** existing, in existence **2 :** in stock
existir *vi* **:** to exist
éxito *nm* **1** TRIUNFO **:** success, hit **2 tener éxito :** to be successful
exitoso, -sa *adj* **:** successful — **exitosamente** *adv*
éxodo *nm* **:** exodus
exoneración *nf, pl* **-ciones** EXENCIÓN **:** exoneration, exemption
exonerar *vt* **1** EXIMIR **:** to exempt, to exonerate **2** DESPEDIR **:** to dismiss
exorbitante *adj* **:** exorbitant
exorcismo *nm* **:** exorcism — **exorcista** *nmf*
exorcizar {21} *vt* **:** to exorcize
exótico, -ca *adj* **:** exotic
expandir *vt* EXPANSIONAR **:** to expand — **expandirse** *vr* **:** to spread
expansión *nf, pl* **-siones 1 :** expansion, spread **2** DIVERSIÓN **:** recreation, relaxation
expansionar *vt* EXPANDIR **:** to expand — **expansionarse** *vr* **1 :** to expand **2** DIVERTIRSE **:** to amuse oneself, to relax
expansivo, -va *adj* **:** expansive
expatriado, -da *adj & n* **:** expatriate
expatriarse {85} *vr* **1** EMIGRAR **:** to emigrate **2 :** to go into exile

expectación *nf, pl* **-ciones** : expectation, anticipation

expectante *adj* : expectant

expectativa *nf* **1** : expectation, hope **2 expectativas** *nfpl* : prospects

expedición *nf, pl* **-ciones** : expedition

expediente *nm* **1** : expedient, means **2** ARCHIVO : file, dossier, record

expedir {54} *vt* **1** EMITIR : to issue **2** DESPACHAR : to dispatch, to send

expedito, -ta *adj* **1** : free, clear **2** : quick, easy

expeler *vt* : to expel, to eject

expendedor, -dora *n* : dealer, seller

expendio *nm* TIENDA : store, shop

expensas *nfpl* **1** : expenses, costs **2 a expensas de** : at the expense of

experiencia *nf* **1** : experience **2** EXPERIMENTO : experiment

experimentación *nf, pl* **-ciones** : experimentation

experimental *adj* : experimental

experimentar *vi* : to experiment — *vt* **1** : to experiment with, to test out **2** : to experience

experimento *nm* EXPERIENCIA : experiment

experto, -ta *adj & n* : expert

expiación *nf, pl* **-ciones** : expiation, atonement

expiar {85} *vt* : to expiate, to atone for

expiración *nf, pl* **-ciones** VENCIMIENTO : expiration

expirar *vi* **1** FALLECER, MORIR : to pass away, to die **2** : to expire

explanada *nf* : esplanade, promenade

explayar *vt* : to extend — **explayarse** *vr* : to expound, to speak at length

explicable *adj* : explicable, explainable

explicación *nf, pl* **-ciones** : explanation

explicar {72} *vt* : to explain — **explicarse** *vr* : to understand

explicativo, -va *adj* : explanatory

explicitar *vt* : to state explicitly, to specify

explícito, -ta *adj* : explicit — **explícitamente** *adv*

exploración *nf, pl* **-ciones** : exploration

explorador, -dora *n* : explorer, scout

explorar *vt* : to explore — **exploratorio, -ria** *adj*

explosión *nf, pl* **-siones 1** ESTALLIDO : explosion **2** : outburst <una explosión de ira : an outburst of anger>

explosivo, -va *adj* : explosive

explotación *nf, pl* **-ciones 1** : exploitation **2** : operation, running

explotar *vt* **1** : to exploit **2** : to operate, to run — *vi* ESTALLAR, REVENTAR : to explode

exponente *nm* : exponent

exponential *adj* : exponential — **exponentialmente** *adv*

exponer {60} *vt* **1** : to exhibit, to show, to display **2** : to explain, to present, to set forth **3** : to expose, to risk — *vi* : to exhibit

exportación *nf, pl* **-ciones 1** : exportation **2 exportaciones** *nfpl* : exports

exportador, -dora *n* : exporter

exportar *vt* : to export — **exportable** *adj*

exposición *nf, pl* **-ciones 1** EXHIBICIÓN : exposition, exhibition **2** : exposure **3** : presentation, statement

expositor, -tora *n* **1** : exhibitor **2** : exponent

exprés *nms & pl* **1** : express, express train **2** : espresso

expresamente *adv* : expressly, on purpose

expresar *vt* : to express — **expresarse** *vr*

expresión *nf, pl* **-siones** : expression

expresivo, -va *adj* **1** : expressive **2** CARIÑOSO : affectionate — **expresivamente** *adv*

expreso[1], **-sa** *adj* : express, specific

expreso[2] *nm* : express train, express

exprimidor *nm* : squeezer, juicer

exprimir *vt* **1** : to squeeze **2** : to exploit

expropiar *vt* : to expropriate, to commandeer — **expropiación** *nf*

expuesto[1] *pp* → **exponer**

expuesto[2], **-ta** *adj* **1** : exposed **2** : hazardous, risky

expulsar *vt* : to expel, to eject

expulsión *nf, pl* **-siones** : expulsion

expurgar {52} *vt* : to expurgate

expuso, etc. → **exponer**

exquisitez *nf, pl* **-teces 1** : exquisiteness, refinement **2** : delicacy, special dish

exquisito, -ta *adj* **1** : exquisite **2** : delicious

extasiarse {85} *vr* : to be in ecstasy, to be enraptured

éxtasis *nms & pl* : ecstasy, rapture

extático, -ta *adj* : ecstatic

extemporáneo, -nea *adj* **1** : unseasonable **2** : untimely

extender {56} *vt* **1** : to spread out, to stretch out **2** : to broaden, to expand <extender la influencia : to broaden one's influence> **3** : to draw up (a document), to write out (a check) — **extenderse** *vr* **1** : to spread **2** : to last

extendido, -da *adj* **1** : outstretched **2** : widespread

extensamente *adv* : extensively, at length

extensible *adj* : extensible, extendable

extensión *nf, pl* **-siones 1** : extension, stretching **2** : expanse, spread **3** : extent, range **4** : length, duration

extenso, -sa *adj* **1** : extensive, detailed **2** : spacious, vast

extenuar {3} *vt* : to exhaust, to tire out — **extenuarse** *vr* — **extenuante** *adj*

exterior[1] *adj* **1** : exterior, external **2** : foreign <asuntos exteriores : foreign affairs>

exterior[2] *nm* **1** : outside **2** : abroad

exteriorizar {21} *vt* : to express, to reveal

exteriormente *adv* : outwardly

exterminar *vt* : to exterminate — **exterminación** *nf*
exterminio *nm* : extermination
externar *vt Mex* : to express, to display
externo, -na *adj* : external, outward
extinción *nf, pl* **-ciones** : extinction
extinguidor *nm* : fire extinguisher
extinguir {26} *vt* **1** APAGAR : to extinguish, to put out **2** : to wipe out — **extinguirse** *vr* **1** APAGARSE : to go out, to fade out **2** : to die out, to become extinct
extinto, -ta *adj* : extinct
extintor *nm* : extinguisher
extirpación *n, pl* **-ciones** : removal, excision
extirpar *vt* : to eradicate, to remove, to excise — **extirparse** *vr*
extorsión *nf, pl* **-siones** **1** : extortion **2** : harm, trouble
extorsionar *vt* : to extort
extra[1] *adv* : extra
extra[2] *adj* **1** : additional, extra **2** : superior, top-quality
extra[3] *nmf* : extra (in movies)
extra[4] *nm* : extra expense <paga extra : bonus>
extracción *nf, pl* **-ciones** : extraction
extracto *nm* **1** : extract <extracto de vainilla : vanilla extract> **2** : abstract, summary
extradición *nf, pl* **-ciones** : extradition
extraditar *vt* : to extradite
extraer {81} *vt* : to extract
extraído *pp* → **extraer**
extrajudicial *adj* : out-of-court
extramatrimonial *adj* : extramarital
extranjerizante *adj* : foreign-sounding, foreign-looking
extranjero[1], **-ra** *adj* : foreign
extranjero[2], **-ra** *n* : foreigner
extranjero[3] *nm* : foreign countries *pl* <viajó al extranjero : he traveled abroad> <trabajan en el extranjero : they work overseas>
extrañamente *adv* : strangely, oddly
extrañamiento *nm* ASOMBRO : amazement, surprise, wonder
extrañar *vt* : to miss (someone) — **extrañarse** *vr* : to be surprised
extrañeza *nf* **1** : strangeness, oddness **2** : surprise
extraño[1], **-ña** *adj* **1** RARO : strange, odd **2** EXTRANJERO : foreign
extraño[2], **-ña** *n* DESCONOCIDO : stranger
extraoficial *adj* OFICIOSO : unofficial — **extraoficialmente** *adv*
extraordinario, -ria *adj* EXCEPCIONAL : extraordinary — **extraordinariamente** *adv*
extrasensorial *adj* : extrasensory <percepción extrasensorial : extrasensory perception>
extraterrestre *adj & nmf* : extraterrestrial, alien
extravagancia *nf* : extravagance, outlandishness, flamboyance
extravagante *adj* : extravagant, outrageous, flamboyant
extraviar {85} *vt* **1** : to mislead, to lead astray **2** : to misplace, to lose — **extraviarse** *vr* : to get lost, to go astray
extravío *nm* **1** PÉRDIDA : loss, misplacement **2** : misconduct
extremado, -da *adj* : extreme — **extremadamente** *adv*
extremar *vt* : to carry to extremes — **extremarse** *vr* : to do one's utmost
extremidad *nf* **1** : extremity, tip, edge **2** **extremidades** *nfpl* : extremities
extremista *adj & nmf* : extremist
extremo[1], **-ma** *adj* **1** : extreme, utmost **2** EXCESIVO : excessive **3 en caso extremo** : as a last resort
extremo[2] *nm* **1** : extreme, end **2 al extremo de** : to the point of **3 en ~** : in the extreme
extrovertido[1] **-da** *adj* : extroverted, outgoing
extrovertido[2], **-da** *n* : extrovert
extrudir *vt* : to extrude
exuberancia *nf* **1** : exuberance **2** : luxuriance, lushness
exuberante *adj* : exuberant, luxuriant — **exuberantemente** *adv*
exudar *vt* : to exude
exultación *nf, pl* **-ciones** : exultation, elation
exultante *adj* : exultant, elated — **exultantemente** *adv*
exultar *vi* : to exult, to rejoice
eyacular *vi* : to ejaculate — **eyaculación** *nf*
eyección *nf, pl* **-ciones** : ejection, expulsion
eyectar *vt* : to eject, to expel — **eyectarse** *vr*

F

f *nf* : sixth letter of the Spanish alphabet
fábrica *nf* FACTORÍA : factory
fabricación *nf, pl* **-ciones** : manufacture
fabricante *nmf* : manufacturer
fabricar {72} *vt* MANUFACTURAR : to manufacture, to make
fabril *adj* INDUSTRIAL : industrial, manufacturing
fábula *nf* **1** : fable **2** : fabrication, fib
fabuloso, -sa *adj* **1** : fabulous, fantastic **2** : mythical, fabled
facción *nf, pl* **facciones** **1** : faction **2** **facciones** *nfpl* RASGOS : features
faccioso, -sa *adj* : factious
faceta *nf* : facet
facha *nf* : appearance, look <estar hecho una facha : to look a sight>
fachada *nf* : facade

facial *adj* **:** facial
fácil *adj* **1 :** easy **2 :** likely, probable <es fácil que no pase : it probably won't happen>
facilidad *nf* **1 :** facility, ease **2 facilidades** *nfpl* **:** facilities, services **3 facilidades** *nfpl* **:** opportunities
facilitar *vt* **1 :** to facilitate **2 :** to provide, to supply
fácilmente *adv* **:** easily, readily
facsímil *or* **facsímile** *nm* **1 :** facsimile, copy **2 :** fax
facsimilar *adj* **:** facsimile
factibilidad *nf* **:** feasibility
factible *adj* **:** feasible, practicable
facticio, -cia *adj* **:** artificial, factitious
factor[1], **-tora** *n* **1 :** agent, factor **2 :** baggage clerk
factor[2] *nm* ELEMENTO **:** factor, element
factoría *nf* FÁBRICA **:** factory
factótum *nm* **:** factotum
factura *nf* **1 :** making, manufacturing **2 :** bill, invoice
facturación *nf, pl* **-ciones 1 :** invoicing, billing **2 :** check-in
facturar *vt* **1 :** to bill, to invoice **2 :** to register, to check in
facultad *nf* **1 :** faculty, ability <facultades mentales : mental faculties> **2 :** authority, power **3 :** school (of a university) <facultad de derecho : law school>
facultar *vt* **:** to authorize, to empower
facultativo, -va *adj* **1** OPTATIVO **:** voluntary, optional **2 :** medical <informe facultativo : medical report>
faena *nf* **:** task, job, work <faenas domésticas : housework>
faenar *vi* **1 :** to work, to labor **2** PESCAR **:** to fish
fagot *nm* **:** bassoon
faisán *nm, pl* **faisanes :** pheasant
faja *nf* **1 :** sash, belt **2 :** girdle **3 :** strip (of land)
fajar *vt* **1 :** to wrap (a sash or girdle) around **2 :** to hit, to thrash — **fajarse** *vr* **1 :** to put on a sash or girdle **2 :** to come to blows
fajo *nm* **:** bundle, sheaf <un fajo de billetes : a wad of cash>
falacia *nf* **:** fallacy
falaz, -laza *adj, mpl* **falaces** FALSO **:** fallacious, false
falda *nf* **1 :** skirt <falda escocesa : kilt> **2** REGAZO **:** lap (of the body) **3** VERTIENTE **:** side, slope
falible *adj* **:** fallible
fálico, -ca *adj* **:** phallic
falla *nf* **1 :** flaw, defect **2 :** (geological) fault **3 :** fault, failing
fallar *vi* **1** FRACASAR **:** to fail, to go wrong **2 :** to rule (in a court of law) — *vt* **1** ERRAR **:** to miss (a target) **2 :** to pronounce judgment on
fallecer {53} *vi* MORIR **:** to pass away, to die
fallecido, -da *adj & n* DIFUNTO **:** deceased
fallecimiento *nm* **:** demise, death
fallido, -da *adj* **:** failed, unsuccessful
fallo *nm* **1** SENTENCIA **:** sentence, judgment, verdict **2 :** error, fault
falo *nm* **:** phallus, penis
falsamente *adv* **:** falsely
falsear *vt* **1 :** to falsify, to fake **2 :** to distort — *vi* **1** CEDER **:** to give way **2 :** to be out of tune
falsedad *nf* **1 :** falseness, hypocrisy **2** MENTIRA **:** falsehood, lie
falsete *nm* **:** falsetto
falsificación *nf, pl* **-ciones 1 :** counterfeit, forgery **2 :** falsification
falsificador, -dora *n* **:** counterfeiter, forger
falsificar {72} *vt* **1 :** to counterfeit, to forge **2 :** to falsify
falso, -sa *adj* **1** FALAZ **:** false, untrue **2 :** counterfeit, forged
falta *nf* **1** CARENCIA **:** lack <hacer falta : to be lacking, to be needed> **2** DEFECTO **:** defect, fault, error **3 :** offense, misdemeanor **4 :** foul (in basketball), fault (in tennis)
faltar *vi* **1 :** to be lacking, to be needed <me falta ayuda : I need help> **2 :** to be absent, to be missing **3** QUEDAR **:** to remain, to be left <faltan pocos días para la fiesta : the party is just a few days away> **4 ¡no faltaba más! :** don't mention it!, you're welcome!
falto, -ta *adj* **~ de :** lacking (in), short of
fama *nf* **1 :** fame **2** REPUTACIÓN **:** reputation **3 de mala fama :** disreputable
famélico, -ca *adj* HAMBRIENTO **:** starving, famished
familia *nf* **1 :** family **2 familia política :** in-laws
familiar[1] *adj* **1** CONOCIDO **:** familiar **2 :** familial, family **3** INFORMAL **:** informal
familiar[2] *nmf* PARIENTE **:** relation, relative
familiaridad *nf* **1 :** familiarity **2 :** informality
familiarizarse {21} *vr* **~ con :** to familiarize oneself with
famoso[1], **-sa** *adj* CÉLEBRE **:** famous
famoso[2], **-sa** *n* **:** celebrity
fanal *nm* **1 :** beacon, signal light **2** *Mex* **:** headlight
fanático, -ca *adj & n* **:** fanatic
fanatismo *nm* **:** fanaticism
fandango *nm* **:** fandango
fanfarria *nf* **1 :** (musical) fanfare **2 :** pomp, ceremony
fanfarrón[1], **-rrona** *adj, mpl* **-rrones** *fam* **:** bragging, boastful
fanfarrón[2], **-rrona** *n, mpl* **-rrones** *fam* **:** braggart
fanfarronada *nf* **:** boast, bluster
fanfarronear *vi* **:** to brag, to boast
fango *nm* LODO **:** mud, mire
fangosidad *nf* **:** muddiness
fangoso, -sa *adj* LODOSO **:** muddy
fantasear *vi* **:** to fantasize, to daydream
fantasía *nf* **1 :** fantasy **2 :** imagination

fantasma *nm* : ghost, phantom
fantasmal *adj* : ghostly
fantástico, -ca *adj* **1** : fantastic, imaginary, unreal **2** *fam* : great, fantastic
faquir *nm* : fakir
farándula *nf* : show business, theater
faraón *nm, pl* **faraones** : pharaoh
fardo *nm* **1** : bale **2** : bundle
farfulla *nf* : jabbering
farfullar *v* : to jabber, to gabble
faringe *nf* : pharynx
faríngeo, -gea *adj* : pharyngeal
fariña *nf* : coarse manioc flour
farmacéutico[1], -ca *adj* : pharmaceutical
farmacéutico[2], -ca *n* : pharmacist
farmacia *nf* : drugstore, pharmacy
fármaco *nm* : medicine, drug
farmacodependencia *nf* : drug addiction
farmacología *nf* : pharmacology
faro *nm* **1** : lighthouse **2** : headlight
farol *nm* **1** : streetlight **2** : lantern, lamp **3** *fam* : bluff **4** *Mex* : headlight
farola *nf* **1** : lamppost **2** : streetlight
farolero, -ra *n fam* : bluffer
farra *nf* : spree, revelry
fárrago *nm* REVOLTIJO : hodgepodge, jumble
farsa *nf* **1** : farce **2** : fake, sham
farsante *nmf* CHARLATÁN : charlatan, fraud, phony
fascículo *nm* : fascicle, part (of a publication)
fascinación *nf, pl* **-ciones** : fascination
fascinante *adj* : fascinating
fascinar *vt* **1** : to fascinate **2** : to charm, to captivate
fascismo *nm* : fascism
fascista *adj & nmf* : fascist
fase *nf* : phase, stage
fastidiar *vt* **1** MOLESTAR : to annoy, to bother, to hassle **2** ABURRIR : to bore — *vi* : to be annoying or bothersome
fastidio *nm* **1** MOLESTIA : annoyance, nuisance, hassle **2** ABURRIMIENTO : boredom
fastidioso, -sa *adj* **1** MOLESTO : annoying, bothersome **2** ABURRIDO : boring
fatal *adj* **1** MORTAL : fatal **2** *fam* : awful, terrible **3** : fateful, unavoidable
fatalidad *nf* **1** : fatality **2** DESGRACIA : misfortune, bad luck
fatalismo *nm* : fatalism
fatalista[1] *adj* : fatalistic
fatalista[2] *nmf* : fatalist
fatalmente *adv* **1** : unavoidably **2** : unfortunately
fatídico, -ca *adj* : fateful, momentous
fatiga *nf* CANSANCIO : fatigue
fatigado, -da *adj* AGOTADO : weary, tired
fatigar {52} *vt* CANSAR : to fatigue, to tire — **fatigarse** *vr* : to wear oneself out
fatigoso, -sa *adj* : fatiguing, tiring
fatuidad *nf* **1** : fatuousness **2** VANIDAD : vanity, conceit
fatuo, -tua *adj* **1** : fatuous **2** PRESUMIDO : vain
fauces *nfpl* : jaws *pl*, maw
faul *nm, pl* **fauls** : foul, foul ball
fauna *nf* : fauna
fausto *nm* : splendor, magnificence
favor *nm* **1** : favor **2** **a favor de** : in favor of **3** **por ~** : please
favorable *adj* : favorable — **favorablemente** *adv*
favorecedor, -dora *adj* : becoming, flattering
favorecer {53} *vt* **1** : to favor **2** : to look well on, to suit
favorecido, -da *adj* **1** : flattering **2** : fortunate
favoritismo *nm* : favoritism
favorito, -ta *adj & n* : favorite
fax *nm* : fax, facsimile
fayuca *nf Mex* **1** : contraband **2** : black market
fayuquero *nm Mex* : smuggler, black marketeer
faz *nf* **1** : face, countenance <la faz de la tierra : the face of the earth> **2** : side (of coins, fabric, etc.)
fe *nf* **1** : faith **2** : assurance, testimony <dar fe de : to bear witness to> **3** : intention, will <de buena fe : bona fide, in good faith>
fealdad *nf* : ugliness
febrero *nm* : February
febril *adj* : feverish — **febrilmente** *adv*
fecal *adj* : fecal
fecha *nf* **1** : date **2** **fecha de caducidad** *or* **fecha de vencimiento** : expiration date **3** **fecha límite** : deadline
fechar *vt* : to date, to put a date on
fechoría *nf* : misdeed
fécula *nf* : starch
fecundar *vt* : to fertilize (an egg) — **fecundación** *nf*
fecundidad *nf* **1** : fecundity, fertility **2** : productiveness
fecundo, -da *adj* FÉRTIL : fertile, fecund
federación *nf, pl* **-ciones** : federation
federal *adj* : federal
federalismo *nm* : federalism
federalista *adj & nmf* : federalist
federar *vt* : to federate
fehaciente *adj* : reliable, irrefutable — **fehacientemente** *adv*
feldespato *nm* : feldspar
felicidad *nf* **1** : happiness **2** **¡felicidades!** : best wishes!, congratulations!, happy birthday!
felicitación *nf, pl* **-ciones** **1** : congratulation <¡felicitaciones! : congratulations!> **2** : greeting card
felicitar *vt* CONGRATULAR : to congratulate — **felicitarse** *vr* : to be glad about
feligrés, -gresa *n, mpl* **-greses** : parishioner
feligresía *nf* : parish
felino, -na *adj & n* : feline
feliz *adj, pl* **felices** **1** : happy **2** **Feliz Navidad** : Merry Christmas

felizmente *adv* **1 :** happily **2 :** fortunately, luckily
felonía *nf* **:** felony
felpa *nf* **1 :** terry cloth **2 :** plush
felpudo *nm* **:** doormat
femenil *adj* **:** women's, girls' <futbol femenil : women's soccer>
femenino, -na *adj* **1 :** feminine **2 :** women's <derechos femeninos : women's rights> **3 :** female
femineidad *nf* **:** femininity
feminidad *nf* **:** femininity
feminismo *nm* **:** feminism
feminista *adj & nmf* **:** feminist
femoral *adj* **:** femoral
fémur *nm* **:** femur, thighbone
fenecer {53} *vi* **1 :** to die, to pass away **2 :** to come to an end, to cease
fénix *nm* **:** phoenix
fenomenal *adj* **1 :** phenomenal **2** *fam* **:** fantastic, terrific — **fenomenalmente** *adv*
fenómeno *nm* **1 :** phenomenon **2 :** prodigy, genius
feo[1] *adv* **:** badly, bad
feo[2], **fea** *adj* **1 :** ugly **2 :** unpleasant, nasty
féretro *nm* ATAÚD **:** coffin, casket
feria *nf* **1 :** fair, market **2 :** festival, holiday **3** *Mex* **:** change (money)
feriado, -da *adj* **día feriado :** public holiday
ferial *nm* **:** fairground
fermentar *v* **:** to ferment — **fermentación** *nf*
fermento *nm* **:** ferment
ferocidad *nf* **:** ferocity, fierceness
feroz *adj, pl* **feroces** FIERO **:** ferocious, fierce — **ferozmente** *adv*
férreo, -rrea *adj* **1 :** iron **2 :** strong, steely <una voluntad férrea : an iron will> **3 :** strict, severe **4 vía férrea :** railroad track
ferretería *nf* **1 :** hardware store **2 :** hardware **3 :** foundry, ironworks
férrico, -ca *adj* **:** ferric
ferrocarril *nm* **:** railroad, railway
ferrocarrilero → **ferroviario**
ferroso, -sa *adj* **:** ferrous
ferroviario, -ria *adj* **:** rail, railroad
ferry *nm, pl* **ferrys :** ferry
fértil *adj* FECUNDO **:** fertile, fruitful
fertilidad *nf* **:** fertility
fertilizante[1] *adj* **:** fertilizing <droga fertilizante : fertility drug>
fertilizante[2] *nm* ABONO **:** fertilizer
fertilizar *vt* ABONAR **:** to fertilize — **fertilización** *nf*
ferviente *adj* FERVOROSO **:** fervent
fervor *nm* **:** fervor, zeal
fervoroso, -sa *adj* FERVIENTE **:** fervent, zealous
festejar *vt* **1** CELEBRAR **:** to celebrate **2** AGASAJAR **:** to entertain, to wine and dine **3** *Mex fam* **:** to thrash, to beat
festejo *nm* **:** celebration, festivity
festín *nm, pl* **festines :** banquet, feast
festinar *vt* **:** to hasten, to hurry up
festival *nm* **:** festival
festividad *nf* **1 :** festivity **2 :** (religious) feast, holiday
festivo, -va *adj* **1 :** festive **2 día festivo :** holiday — **festivamente** *adv*
fetal *adj* **:** fetal
fetiche *nm* **:** fetish
fétido, -da *adj* **:** fetid, foul
feto *nm* **:** fetus
feudal *adj* **:** feudal — **feudalismo** *nm*
feudo *nm* **1 :** fief **2 :** domain, territory
fiabilidad *nf* **:** reliability, trustworthiness
fiable *adj* **:** trustworthy, reliable
fiado, -da *adj* **:** on credit
fiador, -dora *n* **:** bondsman, guarantor
fiambrería *nf* **:** delicatessen
fiambres *nfpl* **:** cold cuts
fianza *nf* **1** CAUCIÓN **:** bail, bond **2 :** surety, deposit
fiar {85} *vt* **1 :** to sell on credit **2 :** to guarantee — **fiarse** *vr* **~ de :** to place trust in
fiasco *nm* FRACASO **:** fiasco, failure
fibra *nf* **1 :** fiber **2 fibra de vidrio :** fiberglass
fibrilar *vi* **:** to fibrillate — **fibrilación** *nf*
fibroso, -sa *adj* **:** fibrous
ficción *nf, pl* **ficciones 1 :** fiction **2 :** fabrication, lie
ficha *nf* **1 :** index card **2 :** file, record **3 :** token **4 :** domino, checker, counter, poker chip
fichar *vt* **1 :** to open a file on **2 :** to sign up — *vi* **:** to punch in, to punch out
fichero *nm* **1 :** card file **2 :** filing cabinet
ficticio, -cia *adj* **:** fictitious
fidedigno, -na *adj* FIABLE **:** reliable, trustworthy
fideicomisario, -ria *n* **:** trustee
fideicomiso *nm* **:** trusteeship, trust <guardar en fideicomiso : to hold in trust>
fidelidad *nf* **:** fidelity, faithfulness
fideo *nm* **:** noodle
fiduciario[1], **-ria** *adj* **:** fiduciary
fiduciario[2], **-ria** *n* **:** trustee
fiebre *nf* **1** CALENTURA **:** fever, temperature <fiebre amarilla : yellow fever> <fiebre palúdica : malaria> **2 :** fever, excitement
fiel[1] *adj* **1 :** faithful, loyal **2 :** accurate — **fielmente** *adv*
fiel[2] *nm* **1 :** pointer (of a scale) **2 los fieles :** the faithful
fieltro *nm* **:** felt
fiera *nf* **1 :** wild animal, beast **2 :** fiend, demon <una fiera para el trabajo : a demon for work>
fiero, -ra *adj* FEROZ **:** fierce, ferocious
fierro *nm* HIERRO **:** iron
fiesta *nf* **1 :** party, fiesta **2 :** holiday, feast day
figura *nf* **1 :** figure **2 :** shape, form **3 figura retórica :** figure of speech
figurado, -da *adj* **:** figurative — **figuradamente** *adv*

figurar *vi* **1 :** to figure, to be included <Rivera figura entre los más grandes pintores de México : Rivera is among Mexico's greatest painters> **2 :** to be prominent, to stand out — *vt* **:** to represent <esta línea figura el horizonte : this line represents the horizon> — **figurarse** *vr* **:** to imagine, to think <¡figúrate el lío en que se metió! : imagine the mess she got into!>
fijación *nf, pl* **-ciones 1 :** fixation, obsession **2 :** fixing, establishing **3 :** fastening, securing
fijador *nm* **1 :** fixative **2 :** hair spray
fijamente *adv* **:** fixedly
fijar *vt* **1 :** to fasten, to affix **2** ESTABLECER **:** to establish, to set up **3** CONCRETAR **:** to set, to fix <fijar la fecha : to set the date> — **fijarse** *vr* **1 :** to settle, to become fixed **2 ~ en :** to notice, to pay attention to
fijeza *nf* **1 :** firmness (of convictions) **2 :** persistence, constancy <mirar con fijeza a : to stare at>
fijiano, -na *adj & n* **:** Fijian
fijo, -ja *adj* **1 :** fixed, firm, steady **2** PERMANENTE **:** permanent
fila *nf* **1** HILERA **:** line, file <ponerse en fila : to get in line> **2 :** rank, row **3 filas** *nfpl* **:** ranks <cerrar filas : to close ranks>
filamento *nm* **:** filament
filantropía *nf* **:** philanthropy
filantrópico, -ca *adj* **:** philanthropic
filántropo, -pa *n* **:** philanthropist
filatelia *nf* **:** philately, stamp collecting
filatelista *nmf* **:** stamp collector, philatelist
filete *nm* **1 :** fillet **2** SOLOMILLO **:** sirloin **3 :** thread (of a screw)
filiación *nf, pl* **-ciones 1 :** affiliation, connection **2 :** particulars *pl,* (police) description
filial[1] *adj* **:** filial
filial[2] *nf* **:** affiliate, subsidiary
filibustero *nm* **:** freebooter, pirate
filigrana *nf* **1 :** filigree **2 :** watermark (on paper)
filipino, -na *adj & n* **:** Filipino
filmación *nf, pl* **-ciones :** filming, shooting
filmar *vt* **:** to film, to shoot
filme *or* **film** *nm* PELÍCULA **:** film, movie
filmina *nf* **:** slide, transparency
filo *nm* **1 :** cutting edge, blade **2 :** edge <al filo del escritorio : at the edge of the desk> <al filo de la medianoche : at the stroke of midnight>
filología *nf* **:** philology
filólogo, -ga *n* **:** philologist
filón *nm, pl* **filones 1 :** seam, vein (of minerals) **2** *fam* **:** successful business, gold mine
filoso, -sa *adj* **:** sharp
filosofar *vi* **:** to philosophize
filosofía *nf* **:** philosophy
filosófico, -ca *adj* **:** philosophic, philosophical — **filosóficamente** *adv*
filósofo, -fa *n* **:** philosopher
filtración *nf* **:** seepage, leaking
filtrar *v* **:** to filter — **filtrarse** *vr* **:** to seep through, to leak
filtro *nm* **:** filter
filudo, -da *adj* **:** sharp
fin *nm* **1 :** end **2 :** purpose, aim, objective **3 en ~ :** in short **4 fin de semana :** weekend **5 por ~ :** finally, at last
finado, -da *adj & n* DIFUNTO **:** deceased
final[1] *adj* **:** final, ultimate — **finalmente** *adv*
final[2] *nm* **1 :** end, conclusion, finale **2 finales** *nmpl* **:** play-offs
finalidad *nf* **1 :** purpose, aim **2 :** finality
finalista *nmf* **:** finalist
finalización *nf* **:** completion, end
finalizar {21} *v* **:** to finish, to end
financiación *nf, pl* **-ciones :** financing, funding
financiamiento *nm* → **financiación**
financiar *vt* **:** to finance, to fund
financiero[1], **-ra** *adj* **:** financial
financiero[2], **-ra** *n* **:** financier
financista *nmf* **:** financier
finanzas *nfpl* **:** finances, finance <altas finanzas : high finance>
finca *nf* **1 :** farm, ranch **2 :** country house
fineza *nf* FINURA, REFINAMIENTO **:** refinement
fingido, -da *adj* **:** false, feigned
fingimiento *nm* **:** pretense
fingir {35} *v* **:** to feign, to pretend
finiquitar *vt* **1 :** to settle (an account) **2 :** to conclude, to bring to an end
finiquito *nm* **:** settlement (of an account)
finito, -ta *adj* **:** finite
finja, etc. → **fingir**
finlandés, -desa *adj & n* **:** Finnish
fino, -na *adj* **1 :** fine, excellent **2 :** delicate, slender **3** REFINADO **:** refined **4 :** sharp, acute <olfato fino : keen sense of smell> **5 :** subtle
finta *nf* **:** feint
fintar *or* **fintear** *vi* **:** to feint
finura *nf* **1 :** fineness, high quality **2** FINEZA, REFINAMIENTO **:** refinement
fiordo *nm* **:** fjord
fique *nm* **:** sisal
firma *nf* **1 :** signature **2 :** signing **3** EMPRESA **:** firm, company
firmamento *nm* **:** firmament, sky
firmante *nmf* **:** signer, signatory
firmar *v* **:** to sign
firme *adj* **1 :** firm, resolute **2 :** steady, stable
firmemente *adv* **:** firmly
firmeza *nf* **1 :** firmness, stability **2 :** strength, resolve
firuletes *nmpl* **:** frills, adornments
fiscal[1] *adj* **:** fiscal — **fiscalmente** *adv*
fiscal[2] *nmf* **:** district attorney, prosecutor
fiscalizar {21} *vt* **1 :** to audit, to inspect **2 :** to oversee **3 :** to criticize
fisco *nm* **:** national treasury, exchequer

fisgar {52} *vt* HUSMEAR : to pry into, to snoop on
fisgón, -gona *n, mpl* **fisgones** : snoop, busybody
fisgonear *vi* : to snoop, to pry
fisgue, etc. → **fisgar**
física *nf* : physics
físico[1], **-ca** *adj* : physical — **físicamente** *adv*
físico[2], **-ca** *n* : physicist
físico[3] *nm* : physique, figure
fisiología *nf* : physiology
fisiológico, -ca *adj* : physiological, physiologic
fisiólogo, -ga *n* : physiologist
fisión *nf, pl* **fisiones** : fission — **fisionable** *adj*
fisionomía *nf* → **fisonomía**
fisioterapeuta *nmf* : physical therapist
fisioterapia *nf* : physical therapy
fisonomía *nf* : physiognomy, features *pl*
fistol *nm Mex* : tie clip
fisura *nf* : fissure, crevasse
fláccido, -da *or* **flácido, -da** *adj* : flaccid, flabby
flaco, -ca *adj* **1** DELGADO : thin, skinny **2** : feeble, weak <una excusa flaca : a feeble excuse>
flagelar *vt* : to flagellate — **flagelación** *nf*
flagelo *nm* **1** : scourge, whip **2** : calamity
flagrante *adj* : flagrant, glaring, blatant — **flagrantemente** *adv*
flama *nf* LLAMA : flame
flamante *adj* **1** : bright, brilliant **2** : brand-new
flamear *vi* **1** LLAMEAR : to flame, to blaze **2** ONDEAR : to flap, to flutter
flamenco[1], **-ca** *adj* **1** : flamenco **2** : Flemish
flamenco[2], **-ca** *n* : Fleming, Flemish person
flamenco[3] *nm* **1** : Flemish (language) **2** : flamingo **3** : flamenco (music or dance)
flanco *nm* : flank, side
flanquear *vt* : to flank
flaquear *vi* DECAER : to flag, to weaken
flaqueza *nf* **1** DEBILIDAD : frailty, feebleness **2** : thinness **3** : weakness, failing
flato *nm* : gloom, melancholy
flatulento, -ta *adj* : flatulent — **flatulencia** *nf*
flauta *nf* **1** : flute **2 flauta dulce** : recorder
flautín *nm, pl* **flautines** : piccolo
flautista *nmf* : flute player, flutist
flebitis *nf* : phlebitis
flecha *nf* : arrow
fleco *nm* **1** : bangs *pl* **2** : fringe
flema *nf* : phlegm
flemático, -ca *adj* : phlegmatic, stolid, impassive
flequillo *nm* : bangs *pl*
fletar *vt* **1** : to charter, to hire **2** : to load (freight)
flete *nm* **1** : charter fee **2** : shipping cost **3** : freight, cargo
fletero *nm* : shipper, carrier
flexibilidad *nf* : flexibility
flexibilizar {21} *vt* : to make more flexible
flexible[1] *adj* : flexible
flexible[2] *nm* **1** : flexible electrical cord **2** : soft hat
flirtear *vi* : to flirt
flojear *vi* **1** DEBILITARSE : to weaken, to flag **2** : to idle, to loaf around
flojedad *nf* : weakness
flojera *nf fam* **1** : lethargy, feeling of weakness **2** : laziness
flojo, -ja *adj* **1** SUELTO : loose, slack **2** : weak, poor <está flojo en las ciencias : he's weak in science> **3** PEREZOSO : lazy
flor *nf* **1** : flower **2 flor de Pascua** : poinsettia
flora *nf* : flora
floración *nf* : flowering <en plena floración : in full bloom>
floral *adj* : floral
floreado, -da *adj* : flowered, flowery
florear *vi* FLORECER : to flower, to bloom — *vt* **1** : to adorn with flowers **2** *Mex* : to flatter, to compliment
florecer {53} *vi* **1** : to bloom, to blossom **2** : to flourish, to thrive
floreciente *adj* **1** : flowering **2** PROSPERO : flourishing, thriving
florecimiento *nm* : flowering
floreo *nm* : flourish
florería *nf* : flower shop, florist's
florero[1], **-ra** *n* : florist
florero[2] *nm* JARRÓN : vase
floresta *nf* **1** : glade, grove **2** BOSQUE : woods
florido, -da *adj* **1** : full of flowers **2** : florid, flowery <escritos floridos : flowery prose>
florista *nmf* : florist
floritura *nf* : frill, embellishment
flota *nf* : fleet
flotabilidad *nf* : buoyancy
flotación *nf, pl* **-ciones** : flotation
flotador *nm* **1** : float **2** : life preserver
flotante *adj* : floating, buoyant
flotar *vi* : to float
flote *nm* **a ~** : afloat
flotilla *nf* : flotilla, fleet
fluctuar {3} *vi* **1** : to fluctuate **2** VACILAR : to vacillate — **fluctuación** *nf* — **fluctuante** *adj*
fluidez *nf* **1** : fluency **2** : fluidity
fluido[1], **-da** *adj* **1** : flowing **2** : fluent **3** : fluid
fluido[2] *nm* : fluid
fluir {41} *vi* : to flow
flujo *nm* **1** : flow **2** : discharge
flúor *nm* : fluorine
fluoración *nf, pl* **-ciones** : fluoridation
fluorescencia *nf* : fluorescence — **fluorescente** *adj*
fluorizar {21} *vt* : to fluoridate
fluoruro *nm* : fluoride
fluvial *adj* : fluvial, river

fluye, etc. → **fluir**
fobia *nf* : phobia
foca *nf* : seal (animal)
focal *adj* : focal
focha *nf* : coot
foco *nm* **1** : focus **2** : center, pocket **3** : lightbulb **4** : spotlight **5** : headlight
fofo, -fa *adj* **1** ESPONJOSO : soft, spongy **2** : flabby
fogaje *nm* **1** FUEGO : skin eruption, cold sore **2** BOCHORNO : hot and humid weather
fogata *nf* : bonfire
fogón *nm, pl* **fogones** : bonfire
fogonazo *nm* : flash, explosion
fogonero, -ra *n* : stoker (of a furnace), fireman
fogoso, -sa *adj* ARDIENTE : ardent
foguear *vt* : to inure, to accustom
foja *nf* : sheet (of paper)
folículo *nm* : follicle
folio *nm* : folio, leaf
folklore *nm* : folklore
folklórico, -ca *adj* : folk, traditional
follaje *nm* : foliage
folleto *nm* : pamphlet, leaflet, circular
fomentar *vt* **1** : to foment, to stir up **2** PROMOVER : to promote, to foster
fomento *nm* : promotion, encouragement
fonda *nf* **1** POSADA : inn **2** : small restaurant
fondeado, -da *adj fam* : rich, in the money
fondear *vt* **1** : to sound **2** : to sound out, to examine **3** *Mex* : to fund, to finance — *vi* ANCLAR : to anchor — **fondearse** *vr fam* : to get rich
fondeo *nm* **1** : anchoring **2** *Mex* : funding, financing
fondillos *mpl* : seat, bottom (of clothing)
fondo *nm* **1** : bottom **2** : rear, back, end **3** : depth **4** : background **5** : sea bed **6** : fund <fondo de inversiones : investment fund> **7** *Mex* : slip, petticoat **8 fondos** *nmpl* : funds, resources <cheque sin fondos : bounced check> **9 a ~** : thoroughly, in depth **10 en ~** : abreast
fonema *nm* : phoneme
fonética *nf* : phonetics
fonético, -ca *adj* : phonetic
fontanería *nf* PLOMERÍA : plumbing
fontanero, -ra *n* PLOMERO : plumber
footing [ˈfuˌtɪŋ] *nm* : jogging <hacer footing : to jog>
foque *nm* : jib
forajido, -da *n* : bandit, fugitive, outlaw
foráneo, -nea *adj* : foreign, strange
forastero, -ra *n* : stranger, outsider
forcejear *vi* : to struggle
forcejeo *nm* : struggle
fórceps *nms & pl* : forceps *pl*
forense *adj* : forensic, legal
forestal *adj* : forest
forja *nf* FRAGUA : forge
forjar *vt* **1** : to forge **2** : to shape, to create <forjar un compromiso : to hammer out a compromise> **3** : to invent, to concoct
forma *nf* **1** : form, shape **2** MANERA, MODO : manner, way **3** : fitness <estar en forma : to be fit, to be in shape> **4 formas** *nfpl* : appearances, conventions
formación *nf, pl* **-ciones 1** : formation **2** : training <formación profesional : vocational training>
formal *adj* **1** : formal **2** : serious, dignified **3** : dependable, reliable
formaldehído *nm* : formaldehyde
formalidad *nf* **1** : formality **2** : seriousness, dignity **3** : dependability, reliability
formalizar {21} *vt* : to formalize, to make official
formalmente *adv* : formally
formar *vt* **1** : to form, to make **2** CONSTITUIR : to constitute, to make up **3** : to train, to educate — **formarse** *vr* **1** DESARROLLARSE : to develop, to take shape **2** EDUCARSE : to be educated
formatear *vt* : to format
formativo, -va *adj* : formative
formato *nm* : format
formidable *adj* **1** : formidable, tremendous **2** *fam* : fantastic, terrific
formón *nm, pl* **formones** : chisel
fórmula *nf* : formula
formulación *nf, pl* **-ciones** : formulation
formular *vt* **1** : to formulate, to draw up **2** : to make, to lodge (a protest or complaint)
formulario *nm* : form <rellenar un formulario : to fill out a form>
fornicar {72} *vi* : to fornicate — **fornicación** *nf*
fornido, -da *adj* : well-built, burly, hefty
foro *nm* **1** : forum **2** : public assembly, open discussion
forraje *nm* **1** : forage, fodder **2** : foraging **3** *fam* : hodgepodge
forrajear *vi* : to forage
forrar *vt* **1** : to line (a garment) **2** : to cover (a book)
forro *nm* **1** : lining **2** CUBIERTA : book cover
forsitia *nf* : forsythia
fortachón, -chona *adj, pl* **-chones** *fam* : brawny, strong, tough
fortalecer {53} *vt* : to strengthen, to fortify — **fortalecerse** *vr*
fortalecimiento *nm* **1** : strengthening, fortifying **2** : fortifications
fortaleza *nf* **1** : fortress **2** FUERZA : strength **3** : resolution, fortitude
fortificación *nf, pl* **-ciones** : fortification
fortificar {72} *vt* **1** : to fortify **2** : to strengthen
fortín *nm, pl* **fortines** : small fort
fortuito, -ta *adj* : fortuitous

fortuna *nf* **1** SUERTE **:** fortune, luck **2** RIQUEZA **:** wealth, fortune
forzar {36} *vt* **1** OBLIGAR **:** to force, to compel **2 :** to force open **3 :** to strain <forzar los ojos : to strain one's eyes>
forzosamente *adv* **1 :** forcibly, by force **2 :** necessarily, inevitably <forzosamente tendrán que pagar : they'll have no choice but to pay>
forzoso, -sa *adj* **1 :** forced, compulsory **2 :** necessary, inevitable
fosa *nf* **1 :** ditch, pit <fosa séptica : septic tank> **2** TUMBA **:** grave **3 :** cavity <fosas nasales : nasal cavities, nostrils>
fosfato *nm* **:** phosphate
fosforescencia *nf* **:** phosphorescence — **fosforescente** *adj*
fósforo *nm* **1** CERILLA **:** match **2 :** phosphorus
fósil[1] *adj* **:** fossilized, fossil
fósil[2] *nm* **:** fossil
fosilizarse {21} *vr* **:** to fossilize, to become fossilized
foso *nm* **1** FOSA, ZANJA **:** ditch **2 :** pit (of a theater) **3 :** moat
foto *nf* **:** photo, picture
fotocopia *nf* **:** photocopy — **fotocopiar** *vt*
fotocopiadora *nf* COPIADORA **:** photocopier
fotoeléctrico, -ca *adj* **:** photoelectric
fotogénico, -ca *adj* **:** photogenic
fotografía *nf* **1 :** photograph **2 :** photography
fotografiar {85} *vt* **:** to photograph
fotográfico, -ca *adj* **:** photographic — **fotográficamente** *adv*
fotógrafo, -fa *n* **:** photographer
fotosíntesis *nf* **:** photosynthesis
fotosintético, -ca *adj* **:** photosynthetic
fracasado[1], **-da** *adj* **:** unsuccessful, failed
fracasado[2], **-da** *n* **:** failure
fracasar *vi* **1** FALLAR **:** to fail **2 :** to fall through
fracaso *nm* FIASCO **:** failure
fracción *nf, pl* **fracciones 1 :** fraction **2 :** part, fragment **3 :** faction, splinter group
fraccionamiento *nm* **1 :** division, breaking up **2** *Mex* **:** residential area, housing development
fraccionar *vt* **:** to divide, to break up
fractura *nf* **1 :** fracture **2 fractura complicada :** compound fracture
fracturarse *vr* QUEBRARSE, ROMPERSE **:** to fracture, to break <fracturarse el brazo : to break one's arm>
fragancia *nf* **:** fragrance, scent
fragante *adj* **:** fragrant
fragata *nf* **:** frigate
frágil *adj* **1 :** fragile **2 :** frail, delicate
fragilidad *nf* **1 :** fragility **2 :** frailty, delicacy
fragmentar *vt* **:** to fragment — **fragmentación** *nf*
fragmentario, -ria *adj* **:** fragmentary, sketchy
fragmento *nm* **1 :** fragment, shard **2 :** bit, snippet **3 :** excerpt, passage
fragor *nm* **:** clamor, din, roar
fragoroso, -sa *adj* **:** thunderous, deafening
fragoso, -sa *adj* **1 :** rough, uneven **2 :** thick, dense
fragua *nf* FORJA **:** forge
fraguar {10} *vt* **1 :** to forge **2 :** to conceive, to concoct, to hatch — *vi* **:** to set, to solidify
fraile *nm* **:** friar, monk
frambuesa *nf* **:** raspberry
francamente *adv* **1 :** frankly, candidly **2** REALMENTE **:** really <es francamente admirable : it's really impressive>
francés[1], **-cesa** *adj, mpl* **franceses :** French
francés[2], **-cesa** *n, mpl* **franceses :** French person, Frenchman *m*, Frenchwoman *f*
francés[3] *nm* **:** French (language)
franciscano, -na *adj & n* **:** Franciscan
francmasón, -sona *n, mpl* **-sones :** Freemason — **francmasonería** *nf*
franco[1], **-ca** *adj* **1** CÁNDIDO **:** frank, candid **2** PATENTE **:** clear, obvious **3 :** free <franco a bordo : free on board>
franco[2] *nm* **:** franc
francotirador, -dora *n* **:** sniper
franela *nf* **:** flannel
franja *nf* **1 :** stripe, band **2 :** border, fringe
franquear *vt* **1 :** to clear **2** ATRAVESAR **:** to cross, to go through **3 :** to pay the postage on
franqueo *nm* **:** postage
franqueza *nf* **:** frankness
franquicia *nf* **1** EXENCIÓN **:** exemption **2 :** franchise
frasco *nm* **:** small bottle, flask, vial
frase *nf* **1 :** phrase **2** ORACIÓN **:** sentence
frasear *vt* **:** to phrase
fraternal *adj* **:** fraternal, brotherly
fraternidad *nf* **1 :** brotherhood **2 :** fraternity
fraternizar {21} *vi* **:** to fraternize — **fraternización** *nf*
fraterno, -na *adj* **:** fraternal, brotherly
fratricida *adj* **:** fratricidal
fratricidio *nm* **:** fratricide
fraude *nm* **:** fraud
fraudulento, -ta *adj* **:** fraudulent — **fraudulentamente** *adv*
fray *nm* **:** brother (title of a friar) <Fray Bartolomé : Brother Bartholomew>
frazada *nf* COBIJA, MANTA **:** blanket
frecuencia *nf* **:** frequency
frecuentar *vt* **:** to frequent, to haunt
frecuente *adj* **:** frequent — **frecuentemente** *adv*
fregadera *nf fam* **:** hassle, pain in the neck
fregadero *nm* **:** kitchen sink
fregado[1], **-da** *adj fam* **:** annoying, bothersome
fregado[2] *nm* **1 :** scrubbing, scouring **2** *fam* **:** mess, muddle

fregar {49} *vt* **1 :** to scrub, to scour, to wash <fregar los trastes : to do the dishes> <fregar el suelo : to scrub the floor> **2** *fam* **:** to annoy — *vi* **1 :** to wash the dishes **2 :** to clean, to scrub **3** *fam* **:** to be annoying

freidera *nf Mex* **:** frying pan

freír {37} *vt* **:** to fry — **freírse** *vr*

frenar *vt* **1 :** to brake **2** DETENER **:** to curb, to check — *vi* **:** to apply the brakes — **frenarse** *vr* **:** to restrain oneself

frenesí *nm* **:** frenzy

frenético, -ca *adj* **:** frantic, frenzied — **frenéticamente** *adv*

freno *nm* **1 :** brake **2 :** bit (of a bridle) **3 :** check, restraint **4 frenos** *nmpl Mex* **:** braces (for teeth)

frente[1] *nm* **1 :** front <al frente de : at the head of> <en frente : in front, opposite> **2 :** facade **3 :** front line, sphere of activity **4 :** front (in meteorology) <frente frío : cold front> **5 hacer frente a :** to face up to, to brave

frente[2] *nf* **1 :** forehead, brow **2 frente a frente :** face to face

fresa *nf* **1 :** strawberry **2 :** drill (in dentistry)

fresco[1], **-ca** *adj* **1 :** fresh **2 :** cool **3** *fam* **:** insolent, nervy

fresco[2] *nm* **1 :** coolness **2 :** fresh air <al fresco : in the open air, outdoors> **3 :** fresco

frescor *nm* **:** cool air <el frescor de la noche : the cool of the evening>

frescura *nf* **1 :** freshness **2 :** coolness **3 :** calmness **4** DESCARO **:** nerve, audacity

fresno *nm* **:** ash (tree)

freza *nf* **:** spawn, roe

frezar {21} *vi* DESOVAR **:** to spawn

friable *adj* **:** friable

frialdad *nf* **1 :** coldness **2** INDIFERENCIA **:** indifference, unconcern

fríamente *adv* **:** coldly, indifferently

fricasé *nm* **:** fricassee

fricción *nf, pl* **fricciones 1 :** friction **2 :** rubbing, massage **3 :** discord, disagreement <fricción entre los hermanos : friction between the brothers>

friccionar *vt* **1** FROTAR **:** to rub **2 :** to massage

friega[1], **friegue, etc.** → **fregar**

friega[2] *nf* **1** FRICCIÓN **:** rubdown, massage **2 :** annoyance, bother

frigidez *nf* **:** (sexual) frigidity

frigorífico *nm Spain* **:** refrigerator

frijol *nm* **:** bean <frijoles refritos : refried beans>

frío[1], **fría** *adj* **1 :** cold **2** INDIFERENTE **:** cool, indifferent

frío[2] *nm* **1 :** cold <hace mucho frío esta noche : it's very cold tonight> **2** INDIFERENCIA **:** coldness, indifference **3 tener frío :** to feel cold <tengo frío : I'm cold> **4 tomar frío** RESFRIARSE **:** to catch a cold

friolento, -ta *adj* **:** sensitive to cold

friolera *nf* (*used ironically or humorously*) **:** trifling amount <una friolera de mil dólares : a mere thousand dollars>

friso *nm* **:** frieze

fritar *vt* **:** to fry

frito[1] *pp* → **freír**

frito[2], **-ta** *adj* **1 :** fried **2** *fam* **:** worn-out, fed up <tener frito a alguien : to get on someone's nerves> **3** *fam* **:** fast asleep <se quedó frito en el sofá : she fell asleep on the couch>

fritura *nf* **1 :** frying **2 :** fried food

frivolidad *nf* **:** frivolity

frívolo, -la *adj* **:** frivolous — **frívolamente** *adv*

fronda *nf* **1 :** frond **2 frondas** *nfpl* **:** foliage

frondoso, -sa *adj* **:** leafy, luxuriant

frontal *adj* **:** frontal, head-on <un choque frontal : a head-on collision>

frontalmente *adv* **:** head-on

frontera *nf* **:** border, frontier

fronterizo, -za *adj* **:** border, on the border <estados fronterizos : neighboring states>

frotar *vt* **1 :** to rub **2 :** to strike (a match) — **frotarse** *vr* **:** to rub (together)

frote *nm* **:** rubbing, rub

fructífero, -ra *adj* **:** fruitful, productive

fructificar {72} *vi* **1 :** to bear or produce fruit **2 :** to be productive

fructuoso, -sa *adj* **:** fruitful

frugal *adj* **:** frugal, thrifty — **frugalmente** *adv*

frugalidad *adj* **:** frugality

frunce *nm* **:** gather (in cloth), pucker

fruncido *nm* **:** gathering, shirring

fruncir {83} *vt* **1 :** to gather, to shirr **2 fruncir el ceño :** to knit one's brow, to frown **3 fruncir la boca :** to pucker up, to purse one's lips

frunza, etc. → **fruncir**

frustración *nf, pl* **-ciones :** frustration

frustrado, -da *adj* **1 :** frustrated **2 :** failed, unsuccessful

frustrante *adj* **:** frustrating

frustrar *vt* **:** to frustrate, to thwart — **frustrarse** *vr* FRACASAR **:** to fail, to come to nothing <se frustraron sus esperanzas : his hopes were dashed>

fruta *nf* **:** fruit

frutal[1] *adj* **:** fruit, fruit-bearing

frutal[2] *nm* **:** fruit tree

frutilla *nf* **:** South American strawberry

fruto *nm* **1 :** fruit, agricultural product <los frutos de la tierra : the fruits of the earth> **2 :** result, consequence <los frutos de su trabajo : the fruits of his labor>

fucsia *adj & nm* **:** fuchsia

fue, etc. → **ir, ser**

fuego *nm* **1 :** fire **2 :** light <¿tienes fuego? : have you got a light?> **3 :** flame, burner (on a stove) **4 :** ardor, passion **5** FOGAJE **:** skin eruption, cold sore **6 fuegos artificiales** *nmpl* : fireworks

fuelle *nm* : bellows

fuente *nf* **1** MANANTIAL : spring **2** : fountain **3** ORIGEN : source <fuentes informativas : sources of information> **4** : platter, serving dish

fuera *adv* **1** : outside, out **2** : abroad, away **3 ~ de** : outside of, out of, beyond **4 ~ de** : besides, in addition to <fuera de eso : aside from that> **5 fuera de lugar** : out of place, amiss

fuerce, fuerza, etc. → **forzar**

fuero *nm* **1** JURISDICCIÓN : jurisdiction **2** : privilege, exemption **3 fuero interno** : conscience, heart of hearts

fuerte[1] *adv* **1** : strongly, tightly, hard **2** : loudly **3** : abundantly

fuerte[2] *adj* **1** : strong **2** : intense <un fuerte dolor : an intense pain> **3** : loud **4** : extreme, excessive

fuerte[3] *nm* **1** : fort, stronghold **2** : forte, strong point

fuerza *nf* **1** : strength, vigor <fuerza de voluntad : willpower> **2** : force <fuerza bruta : brute force> **3** : power, might <fuerza de brazos : manpower> **4 fuerzas** *nfpl* : forces <fuerzas armadas : armed forces> **5 a fuerza de** : by, by dint of

fuetazo *nm* : lash

fuga *nf* **1** HUIDA : flight, escape **2** : fugue **3** : leak <fuga de gas : gas leak>

fugarse {52} *vr* **1** : to escape **2** HUIR : to flee, to run away **3** : to elope

fugaz *adj, pl* **fugaces** : brief, fleeting

fugitivo, -va *adj & n* : fugitive

fulana *nf* : hooker, slut

fulano, -na *n* : so-and-so, what's-his-name, what's-her-name <fulano, mengano, y zutano : Tom, Dick, and Harry> <señora fulana de tal : Mrs. so-and-so>

fulcro *nm* : fulcrum

fulgor *nm* : brilliance, splendor

fulgurar *vi* : to shine brightly, to gleam, to glow

fulminante *adj* **1** : fulminating, explosive **2** : devastating, terrible <una mirada fulminante : a withering look>

fulminar *vt* **1** : to strike with lightning **2** : to strike down <fulminar a alguien con la mirada : to look daggers at someone>

fumador, -dora *n* : smoker

fumar *v* : to smoke

fumble *nm* : fumble (in football)

fumblear *vt* : to fumble (in football)

fumigante *nm* : fumigant

fumigar {52} *vt* : to fumigate — **fumigación** *nf*

funámbulo, -la *n* EQUILIBRISTA : tightrope walker

función *nf, pl* **funciones 1** : function **2** : duty **3** : performance, show

funcional *adj* : functional — **funcionalmente** *adv*

funcionamiento *nm* **1** : functioning **2 en ~** : in operation

funcionar *vi* **1** : to function **2** : to run, to work

funcionario, -ria *n* : civil servant, official

funda *nf* **1** : case, cover, sheath **2** : pillowcase

fundación *nf, pl* **-ciones** : foundation, establishment

fundado, -da *adj* : well-founded, justified

fundador, -dora *n* : founder

fundamental *adj* BÁSICO : fundamental, basic — **fundamentalmente** *adv*

fundamentar *vt* **1** : to lay the foundations for **2** : to support, to back up **3** : to base, to found

fundamento *nm* : basis, foundation, groundwork

fundar *vt* **1** ESTABLECER, INSTITUIR : to found, to establish **2** BASAR : to base — **fundarse** *vr* **~ en** : to be based on, to stem from

fundición *nf, pl* **-ciones 1** : founding, smelting **2** : foundry

fundir *vt* **1** : to melt down, to smelt **2** : to fuse, to merge **3** : to burn out (a lightbulb) — **fundirse** *vr* **1** : to fuse together, to blend, to merge **2** : to melt, to thaw **3** : to fade (in television or movies)

fúnebre *adj* **1** : funeral, funereal **2** LÚGUBRE : gloomy, mournful

funeral[1] *adj* : funeral, funerary

funeral[2] *nm* **1** : funeral **2 funerales** *nmpl* EXEQUIAS : funeral rites

funeraria *nf* **1** : funeral home, funeral parlor **2 director de funeraria** : funeral director, undertaker

funerario, -ria *adj* : funeral

funesto, -ta *adj* : terrible, disastrous <consecuencias funestas : disastrous consequences>

fungicida[1] *adj* : fungicidal

fungicida[2] *nm* : fungicide

fungir {35} *vi* : to act, to function <fungir de asesor : to act as a consultant>

fungoso, -sa *adj* : fungous

funja, etc. → **fungir**

furgón *nm, pl* **furgones 1** : van, truck **2** : freight car, boxcar **3 furgón de cola** : caboose

furgoneta *nf* : van

furia *nf* **1** CÓLERA, IRA : fury, rage **2** : violence, fury <la furia de la tormenta : the fury of the storm>

furibundo, -da *adj* : furious

furiosamente *adv* : furiously, frantically

furioso, -sa *adj* **1** AIRADO : furious, irate **2** : intense, violent

furor *nm* **1** : fury, rage **2** : violence (of the elements) **3** : passion, frenzy **4** : enthusiasm <hacer furor : to be all the rage>

furtivo, -va *adj* : furtive — **furtivamente** *adv*

furúnculo *nm* DIVIESO : boil
fuselaje *nm* : fuselage
fusible *nm* : (electrical) fuse
fusil *nm* : rifle
fusilar *vt* **1** : to shoot, to execute (by firing squad) **2** *fam* : to plagiarize, to pirate
fusilería *nf* **1** : rifles *pl,* rifle fire **2** **descarga de fusilería** : fusillade
fusión *nf, pl* **fusiones** **1** : fusion **2** : union, merger
fusionar *vt* **1** : to fuse **2** : to merge, to amalgamate — **fusionarse** *vr*
fusta *nf* : riding crop
fustigar {52} *vt* **1** AZOTAR : to whip, to lash **2** : to upbraid, to berate
futbol *or* **fútbol** *nm* **1** : soccer **2** **futbol americano** : football
futbolista *nmf* : soccer player
futesa *nf* **1** : small thing, trifle **2** **futesas** *nfpl* : small talk
fútil *adj* : trifling, trivial
futurista *adj* : futuristic
futuro[1], **-ra** *adj* : future
futuro[2] *nm* PORVENIR : future

G

g *nf* : seventh letter of the Spanish alphabet
gabán *nm, pl* **gabanes** : topcoat, overcoat
gabardina *nf* **1** : gabardine **2** : trench coat, raincoat
gabarra *nf* : barge
gabinete *nm* **1** : cabinet (in government) **2** : study, office (in the home) **3** : (professional) office
gablete *nm* : gable
gabonés, -nesa *adj & n, mpl* **-neses** : Gabonese
gacela *nf* : gazelle
gaceta *nf* : gazette, newspaper
gachas *nfpl* : porridge
gacho, -cha *adj* **1** : drooping, turned downward **2** *Mex fam* : nasty, awful **3** **ir a gachas** *fam* : to go on all fours
gaélico[1], **-ca** *adj* : Gaelic
gaélico[2] *nm* : Gaelic (language)
gafas *nfpl* ANTEOJOS : eyeglasses, glasses
gaita *nf* : bagpipes *pl*
gajes *nmpl* **gajes del oficio** : occupational hazards
gajo *nm* **1** : broken branch (of a tree) **2** : cluster, bunch (of fruit) **3** : segment (of citrus fruit)
gala *nf* **1** : gala <vestido de gala : formal dress> <tener algo a gala : to be proud of something> **2** **galas** *nfpl* : finery, attire
galáctico, -ca *adj* : galactic
galán *nm, pl* **galanes** **1** : ladies' man, gallant **2** : leading man, hero **3** : boyfriend, suitor
galano, -na *adj* **1** : elegant **2** *Mex* : mottled
galante *adj* : gallant, attentive — **galantemente** *adv*
galantear *vt* **1** CORTEJAR : to court, to woo **2** : to flirt with
galanteo *nm* **1** CORTEJO : courtship **2** : flirtation, flirting
galantería *nf* **1** : gallantry, attentiveness **2** : compliment
galápago *nm* : aquatic turtle
galardón *nm, pl* **-dones** : award, prize
galardonado, -da *adj* : prize-winning
galardonar *vt* : to give an award to
galaxia *nf* : galaxy
galeno *nm fam* : physician, doctor
galeón *nm, pl* **galeones** : galleon
galera *nf* : galley
galería *nf* **1** : gallery, balcony (in a theater) <galería comercial : shopping mall> **2** : corridor, passage
galerón *nm, pl* **-rones** *Mex* : large hall
galés[1], **-lesa** *adj* : Welsh
galés[2], **-lesa** *n, mpl* **galeses** **1** : Welshman *m,* Welshwoman *f* **2** **los galeses** : the Welsh
galés[3] *nm* : Welsh (language)
galgo *nm* : greyhound
galimatías *nms & pl* : gibberish, nonsense
galio *nm* : gallium
gallardete *nm* : pennant, streamer
gallardía *nf* **1** VALENTÍA : bravery **2** APOSTURA : elegance, gracefulness
gallardo, -da *adj* **1** VALIENTE : brave **2** APUESTO : elegant, graceful
gallear *vi* : to show off, to strut around
gallego[1], **-ga** *adj* **1** : Galician **2** *fam* : Spanish
gallego[2], **-ga** *n* **1** : Galician **2** *fam* : Spaniard
galleta *nf* **1** : cookie **2** : cracker
gallina *nf* **1** : hen **2** **gallina de Guinea** : guinea fowl
gallinazo *nm* : vulture, buzzard
gallinero *nm* : chicken coop, henhouse
gallito, -ta *adj fam* : cocky, belligerent
gallo *nm* **1** : rooster, cock **2** *fam* : squeak or crack in the voice **3** *Mex* : serenade **4** **gallo de pelea** : gamecock
galo[1], **-la** *adj* **1** : Gaulish **2** : French
galo[2], **-la** *n* : Frenchman *m,* Frenchwoman *f*
galocha *nf* : galosh
galón *nm, pl* **galones** **1** : gallon **2** : stripe (military insignia)
galopada *nf* : gallop
galopante *adj* : galloping <inflación galopante : galloping inflation>
galopar *vi* : to gallop
galope *nm* : gallop

galpón *nm, pl* **galpones** : shed, storehouse
galvanizar {21} *vt* : to galvanize — **galvanización** *nf*
gama *nf* **1** : range, spectrum, gamut **2** → **gamo**
gamba *nf* : large shrimp, prawn
gameto *nm* : gamete
gamo, -ma *n* : fallow deer
gamuza *nf* **1** : suede **2** : chamois
gana *nf* **1** : desire, inclination **2 de buena gana** : willingly, readily, gladly **3 de mala gana** : reluctantly, half-heartedly **4 tener ganas de** : to feel like, to be in the mood for <tengo ganas de bailar : I feel like dancing> **5 ponerle ganas a algo** : to put effort into something
ganadería *nf* **1** : cattle raising, stockbreeding **2** : cattle ranch **3** GANADO : cattle *pl,* livestock
ganadero¹, -ra *adj* : cattle, ranching
ganadero², -ra *n* : rancher, stockbreeder
ganado *nm* **1** : cattle *pl,* livestock **2 ganado ovino** : sheep *pl* **3 ganado porcino** : swine *pl*
ganador¹, -dora *adj* : winning
ganador², -dora *n* : winner
ganancia *nf* **1** : profit **2 ganancias** *nfpl* : winnings, gains
ganancioso, -sa *adj* : profitable
ganar *vt* **1** : to win **2** : to gain <ganar tiempo : to buy time> **3** : to earn <ganar dinero : to make money> **4** : to acquire, to obtain — *vi* **1** : to win **2** : to profit <salir ganando : to come out ahead> — **ganarse** *vr* **1** : to gain, to win <ganarse a alguien : to win someone over> **2** : to earn <ganarse la vida : to make a living> **3** : to deserve
gancho *nm* **1** : hook **2** : clothes hanger **3** : hairpin, bobby pin **4** *Col* : safety pin
gandul¹ *nm CA, Car, Col* : pigeon pea
gandul², -dula *n fam* : idler, lazybones
gandulear *vi* : to idle, to loaf, to lounge about
ganga *nf* : bargain
ganglio *nm* **1** : ganglion **2** : gland
gangrena *nf* : gangrene — **gangrenoso, -sa** *adj*
gángster *nmf, pl* **gángsters** : gangster
gansada *nf* : silly thing, nonsense
ganso, -sa *n* **1** : goose, gander *m* **2** : idiot, fool
gañido *nm* : yelp (of a dog)
gañir {38} *vi* : to yelp
garabatear *v* : to scribble, to scrawl, to doodle
garabato *nm* **1** : doodle **2 garabatos** *nmpl* : scribble, scrawl
garaje *nm* : garage
garante *nmf* : guarantor
garantía *nf* **1** : guarantee, warranty **2** : security <garantía de trabajo : job security>
garantizar {21} *vt* : to guarantee
garapiña *nf* : pineapple drink
garapiñar *vt* : to candy
garbanzo *nm* : chickpea, garbanzo
garbo *nm* **1** DONAIRE : grace, poise **2** : jauntiness
garboso, -sa *adj* **1** : graceful **2** : elegant, stylish
garceta *nf* : egret
gardenia *nf* : gardenia
garfio *nm* : hook, gaff, grapnel
gargajo *nm* : phlegm
garganta *nf* **1** : throat **2** : neck (of a person or a bottle) **3** : ravine, narrow pass
gargantilla *nf* : choker, necklace
gárgara *nf* **1** : gargle, gargling **2 hacer gárgaras** : to gargle
gargarizar *vi* : to gargle
gárgola *nf* : gargoyle
garita *nf* **1** : cabin, hut **2** : sentry box, lookout post
garoso, -sa *adj Col, Ven* : gluttonous, greedy
garra *nf* **1** : claw **2** : hand, paw **3 garras** *nfpl* : claws, clutches <caer en las garras de alguien : to fall into someone's clutches>
garrafa *nf* : decanter, carafe
garrafal *adj* : terrible, monstrous
garrafón *nm, pl* **-fones** : large decanter, large bottle
garrapata *nf* : tick
garrobo *nm CA* : large lizard, iguana
garrocha *nf* **1** PICA : lance, pike **2** : pole <salto con garrocha : pole vault>
garrotazo *nm* : blow (with a club)
garrote *nm* **1** : club, stick **2** *Mex* : brake
garúa *nf* : drizzle
garuar {3} *v impers* LLOVIZNAR : to drizzle
garza *nf* : heron
gas *nm* : gas, vapor, fumes *pl* <gas lagrimógeno : tear gas>
gasa *nf* : gauze
gasear *vt* **1** : to gas **2** : to aerate (a liquid)
gaseosa *nf* REFRESCO : soda, soft drink
gaseoso, -sa *adj* **1** : gaseous **2** : carbonated, fizzy
gasoducto *nm* : gas pipeline
gasolina *nf* : gasoline, gas
gasolinera *nf* : gas station, service station
gastado, -da *adj* **1** : spent **2** : worn, worn-out
gastador¹, -dora *adj* : extravagant, spendthrift
gastador², -dora *n* : spendthrift
gastar *vt* **1** : to spend **2** CONSUMIR : to consume, to use up **3** : to squander, to waste **4** : to wear <gasta un bigote : he sports a mustache> — **gastarse** *vr* **1** : to spend, to expend **2** : to run down, to wear out
gasto *nm* **1** : expense, expenditure **2** DETERIORO : wear **3 gastos generales** *or* **gastos indirectos** : overhead
gástrico, -ca *adj* : gastric
gastritis *nf* : gastritis

gastronomía *nf* : gastronomy
gastronómico, -ca *adj* : gastronomic
gastrónomo, -ma *n* : gourmet
gatas *adv* **andar a gatas** : to crawl, to go on all fours
gatear *vi* **1** : to crawl **2** : to climb, to clamber (up)
gatillero *nm Mex* : gunman
gatillo *nm* : trigger
gatito, -ta *n* : kitten
gato[1]**, -ta** *n* : cat
gato[2] *nm* : jack (for an automobile)
gauchada *nf Arg, Uru* : favor, kindness
gaucho *nm* : gaucho
gaveta *nf* **1** CAJÓN : drawer **2** : till
gavilla *nf* **1** : gang, band **2** : sheaf
gaviota *nf* : gull, seagull
gay ['ge, 'gai] *adj* : gay (homosexual)
gaza *nf* : loop
gazapo *nm* **1** : young rabbit **2** : misprint, error
gazmoñería *nf* MOJIGATERÍA : prudery, primness
gazmoño[1]**, -ña** *adj* : prudish, prim
gazmoño[2]**, -ña** *n* MOJIGATO : prude, prig
gaznate *nm* : throat, gullet
gazpacho *nm* : gazpacho
géiser *or* **géyser** *nm* : geyser
gel *nm* : gel
gelatina *nf* : gelatin
gélido, -da *adj* : icy, freezing cold
gelificarse *vr* : to jell
gema *nf* : gem
gemelo[1]**, -la** *adj & n* MELLIZO : twin
gemelo[2] *nm* **1** : cuff link **2** **gemelos** *nmpl* BINOCULARES : binoculars
gemido *nm* : moan, groan, wail
Géminis *nmf* : Gemini
gemir {54} *vi* : to moan, to groan, to wail
gen *or* **gene** *nm* : gene
gendarme *nmf* POLICÍA : police officer, policeman *m*, policewoman *f*
gendarmería *nf* : police
genealogía *nf* : genealogy
genealógico, -ca *adj* : genealogical
generación *nf, pl* **-ciones** **1** : generation <tercera generación : third generation> **2** : generating, creating **3** : class <la generación del '97 : the class of '97>
generacional *adj* : generation, generational
generador *nm* : generator
general[1] *adj* **1** : general **2** **en ~** *or* **por lo general** : in general, generally
general[2] *nmf* **1** : general **2** **general de división** : major general
generalidad *nf* **1** : generality, generalization **2** : majority
generalización *nf, pl* **-ciones** **1** : generalization **2** : escalation, spread
generalizado, -da *adj* : generalized, widespread
generalizar {21} *vi* : to generalize — *vt* : to spread, to spread out — **generalizarse** *vr* : to become widespread
generalmente *adv* : usually, generally
generar *vt* : to generate — **generarse** *vr*
genérico, -ca *adj* : generic
género *nm* **1** : genre, class, kind <el género humano : the human race, mankind> **2** : gender (in grammar) **3** **géneros** *nmpl* : goods, commodities
generosidad *nf* : generosity
generoso, -sa *adj* **1** : generous, unselfish **2** : ample — **generosamente** *adv*
genética *nf* : genetics
genético, -ca *adj* : genetic — **genéticamente** *adv*
genetista *nmf* : geneticist
genial *adj* **1** AGRADABLE : genial, pleasant **2** : brilliant <una obra genial : a work of genius> **3** *fam* FORMIDABLE : fantastic, terrific
genialidad *nf* **1** : genius **2** : stroke of genius **3** : eccentricity
genio *nm* **1** : genius **2** : temper, disposition <de mal genio : bad-tempered> **3** : genie
genital *adj* : genital
genitales *nmpl* : genitals, genitalia
genocidio *nm* : genocide
genotipo *nm* : genotype
gente *nf* **1** : people **2** : relatives *pl*, folks *pl* **3** **gente menuda** *fam* : children, kids *pl* **4** **ser buena gente** : to be nice, to be kind
gentil[1] *adj* **1** AMABLE : kind **2** : gentile
gentil[2] *nmf* : gentile
gentileza *nf* **1** AMABILIDAD : kindness **2** CORTESÍA : courtesy
gentilicio, -cia *adj* **1** : national, tribal **2** : family
gentío *nm* MUCHEDUMBRE, MULTITUD : crowd, mob
gentuza *nf* CHUSMA : riffraff, rabble
genuflexión *nf, pl* **-xiones** **1** : genuflection **2** **hacer una genuflexión** : to genuflect
genuino, -na *adj* : genuine — **genuinamente** *adv*
geofísica *nf* : geophysics
geofísico, -ca *adj* : geophysical
geografía *nf* : geography
geográfico, -ca *adj* : geographic, geographical — **geográficamente** *adv*
geógrafo, -fa *n* : geographer
geología *nf* : geology
geológico, -ca *adj* : geologic, geological — **geológicamente** *adv*
geólogo, -ga *n* : geologist
geometría *nf* : geometry
geométrico, -ca *adj* : geometric, geometrical — **geométricamente** *adv*
geopolítica *nf* : geopolitics
geopolítico, -ca *adj* : geopolitical
georgiano, -na *adj & n* : Georgian
geranio *nm* : geranium
gerbo *nm* : gerbil
gerencia *nf* : management, administration
gerencial *adj* : managerial
gerente *nmf* : manager, director
geriatría *nf* : geriatrics

geriátrico, -ca *adj* : geriatric
germanio *nm* : germanium
germano, -na *adj* : Germanic, German
germen *nm, pl* **gérmenes** : germ
germicida *nf* : germicide
germinación *nf, pl* **-ciones** : germination
germinar *vi* : to germinate, to sprout
gerontología *nf* : gerontology
gerundio *nm* : gerund
gesta *nf* : deed, exploit
gestación *nf, pl* **-ciones** : gestation
gesticulación *nf, pl* **-ciones** : gesturing, gesticulation
gesticular *vi* : to gesticulate, to gesture
gestión *nf, pl* **gestiones 1** TRÁMITE : procedure, step **2** ADMINISTRACIÓN : management **3 gestiones** *nfpl* : negotiations
gestionar *vt* **1** : to negotiate, to work towards **2** ADMINISTRAR : to manage, to handle
gesto *nm* **1** ADEMÁN : gesture **2** : facial expression **3** MUECA : grimace
gestor[1], **-tora** *adj* : facilitating, negotiating, managing
gestor[2], **-tora** *n* : facilitator, manager
géyser *nm* → **géiser**
ghanés, -nesa *adj & n, mpl* **ghaneses** : Ghanaian
ghetto → **gueto**
giba *nf* **1** : hump (of an animal) **2** : hunchback (of a person)
gibón *nm, pl* **gibones** : gibbon
giboso[1], **-sa** *adj* : hunchbacked, humpbacked
giboso[2], **-sa** *n* : hunchback, humpback
gigante[1] *adj* : giant, gigantic
gigante[2], **-ta** *n* : giant
gigantesco, -ca *adj* : gigantic, huge
gime, etc. → **gemir**
gimnasia *nf* : gymnastics
gimnasio *nm* : gymnasium, gym
gimnasta *nmf* : gymnast
gimnástico, -ca *adj* : gymnastic
gimotear *vi* LLORIQUEAR : to whine, to whimper
gimoteo *nm* : whimpering
ginebra *nf* : gin
ginecología *nf* : gynecology
ginecológico, -ca *adj* : gynecologic, gynecological
ginecólogo, -ga *n* : gynecologist
gira *nf* : tour
giralda *nf* : weather vane
girar *vi* **1** : to turn around, to revolve **2** : to swing around, to swivel — *vt* **1** : to turn, to twist, to rotate **2** : to draft (checks) **3** : to transfer (funds)
girasol *nm* MIRASOL : sunflower
giratorio, -ria *adj* : revolving
giro *nm* **1** VUELTA : turn, rotation **2** : change of direction <giro de 180 grados : U-turn, about-face> **3 giro bancario** : bank draft **4 giro postal** : money order
giroscopio *or* **giróscopo** *nm* : gyroscope
gis *nm Mex* : chalk
gitano, -na *adj & n* : Gypsy
glacial *adj* : glacial, icy — **glacialmente** *adv*
glaciar *nm* : glacier
gladiador *nm* : gladiator
gladiolo *or* **gladíolo** *nm* : gladiolus
glándula *nf* : gland — **glandular** *adj*
glaseado *nm* : glaze, icing
glasear *vt* : to glaze
glaucoma *nm* : glaucoma
glicerina *nf* : glycerin, glycerol
glicinia *nf* : wisteria
global *adj* **1** : global, worldwide **2** : full, comprehensive **3** : total, overall
globalizar {21} *vt* **1** ABARCAR : to include, to encompass **2** : to extend worldwide
globalmente *adv* : globally, as a whole
globo *nm* **1** : globe, sphere **2** : balloon **3 globo ocular** : eyeball
glóbulo *nm* **1** : globule **2** : blood cell, corpuscle
gloria *nf* **1** : glory **2** : fame, renown **3** : delight, enjoyment **4** : star, legend <las glorias del cine : the great names in motion pictures>
glorieta *nf* **1** : rotary, traffic circle **2** : bower, arbor
glorificar {72} *vt* ALABAR : to glorify — **glorificación** *nf*
glorioso, -sa *adj* : glorious — **gloriosamente** *adv*
glosa *nf* **1** : gloss **2** : annotation, commentary
glosar *vt* **1** : to gloss **2** : to annotate, to comment on (a text)
glosario *nm* : glossary
glotis *nf* : glottis
glotón[1], **-tona** *adj, mpl* **glotones** : gluttonous
glotón[2], **-tona** *n, mpl* **glotones** : glutton
glotón[3] *nm, pl* **glotones** : wolverine
glotonería *nf* GULA : gluttony
glucosa *nf* : glucose
glutinoso, -sa *adj* : glutinous
gnomo *nm* : gnome
gobernación *nf, pl* **-ciones** : governing, government
gobernador, -dora *n* : governor
gobernante[1] *adj* : ruling, governing
gobernante[2] *nmf* : ruler, leader, governor
gobernar {55} *vt* **1** : to govern, to rule **2** : to steer, to sail (a ship) — *vi* **1** : to govern **2** : to steer
gobierno *nm* : government
goce[1], **etc.** → **gozar**
goce[2] *nm* **1** PLACER : enjoyment, pleasure **2** : use, possession
gol *nm* : goal (in soccer)
golear *vt* : to rout, to score many goals against (in soccer)
goleta *nf* : schooner
golf *nm* : golf
golfista *nmf* : golfer
golfo *nm* : gulf, bay
golondrina *nf* **1** : swallow (bird) **2 golondrina de mar** : tern

golosina *nf* **:** sweet, snack

goloso, -sa *adj* **:** fond of sweets <ser goloso : to have a sweet tooth>

golpazo *nm* **:** heavy blow, bang, thump

golpe *nm* **1 :** blow <caerle a golpes a alguien : to give someone a beating> **2 :** knock **3 de ~ :** suddenly **4 de un golpe :** all at once, in one fell swoop **5 golpe de estado :** coup, coup d'etat **6 golpe de suerte :** stroke of luck

golpeado, -da *adj* **1 :** beaten, hit **2 :** bruised (of fruit) **3 :** dented

golpear *vt* **1 :** to beat (up), to hit **2 :** to slam, to bang, to strike — *vi* **1 :** to knock (at a door) **2 :** to beat <la lluvia golpeaba contra el tejado : the rain beat against the roof> — **golpearse** *vr*

golpetear *v* **:** to knock, to rattle, to tap

golpeteo *nm* **:** banging, knocking, tapping

goma *nf* **1 :** gum <goma de mascar : chewing gum> **2** CAUCHO **:** rubber <goma espuma : foam rubber> **3** PEGAMENTO **:** glue **4 :** rubber band **5** *Arg* **:** tire **6** *or* **goma de borrar :** eraser

gomita *nf* **:** rubber band

gomoso, -sa *adj* **:** gummy, sticky

góndola *nf* **:** gondola

gong *nm* **:** gong

gonorrea *nf* **:** gonorrhea

gorda *nf Mex* **:** thick corn tortilla

gordinflón[1], -flona *adj, mpl* **-flones** *fam* **:** chubby, pudgy

gordinflón[2], -flona *n, mpl* **-flones** *fam* **:** chubby person

gordo[1], -da *adj* **1 :** fat **2 :** thick **3 :** fatty, greasy, oily **4 :** unpleasant <me cae gorda tu tía : I can't stand your aunt>

gordo[2], -da *n* **:** fat person

gordo[3] *nm* **1** GRASA **:** fat **2 :** jackpot

gordura *nf* **:** fatness, flab

gorgojo *nm* **:** weevil

gorgotear *vi* **:** to gurgle, to bubble

gorgoteo *nm* **:** gurgle

gorila *nm* **:** gorilla

gorjear *vi* **1 :** to chirp, to tweet, to warble **2 :** to gurgle

gorjeo *nm* **1 :** chirping, warbling **2 :** gurgling

gorra *nf* **1 :** bonnet **2 :** cap **3 de ~** *fam* **:** for free, at someone else's expense <vivir de gorra : to sponge, to freeload>

gorrear *vt fam* **:** to bum, to scrounge — *vi fam* **:** to freeload

gorrero, -ra *n fam* **:** freeloader, sponger

gorrión *nm, pl* **gorriones :** sparrow

gorro *nm* **1 :** cap **2 estar hasta el gorro :** to be fed up

gorrón, -rrona *n fam, mpl* **gorrones :** freeloader, scrounger

gorronear *vt fam* **:** to bum, to scrounge — *vi fam* **:** to freeload

gota *nf* **1 :** drop <una gota de sudor : a bead of sweat> <como dos gotas de agua : like two peas in a pod> <sudar la gota gorda : to sweat buckets, to work very hard> **2 :** gout

gotear *v* **1 :** to drip **2 :** to leak — *v impers* LLOVIZNAR **:** to drizzle

goteo *nm* **:** drip, dripping

gotera *nf* **1 :** leak **2 :** stain (from dripping water)

gotero *nm* **:** (medicine) dropper

gótico, -ca *adj* **:** Gothic

gourmet *nmf* **:** gourmet

gozar {21} *vi* **1 :** to enjoy oneself, to have a good time **2 ~ de :** to enjoy, to have, to possess <gozar de buena salud : to enjoy good health> **3 ~ con :** to take delight in

gozne *nm* BISAGRA **:** hinge

gozo *nm* **1 :** joy **2** PLACER **:** enjoyment, pleasure

gozoso, -sa *adj* **:** joyful

grabación *nf, pl* **-ciones :** recording

grabado *nm* **1 :** engraving **2 grabado al aguafuerte :** etching

grabador, -dora *n* **:** engraver

grabadora *nf* **:** tape recorder

grabar *vt* **1 :** to engrave **2 :** to record, to tape — *vi* **grabar al aguafuerte :** to etch — **grabarse** *vr* **grabársele a alguien en la memoria :** to become engraved on someone's mind

gracia *nf* **1 :** grace **2 :** favor, kindness **3 :** humor, wit <su comentario no me hizo gracia : I wasn't amused by his remark> **4 gracias** *nfpl* **:** thanks <¡gracias! : thank you!> <dar gracias : to give thanks>

grácil *adj* **1 :** graceful **2 :** delicate, slender, fine

gracilidad *nm* **:** gracefulness

gracioso, -sa *adj* **1** CHISTOSO **:** funny, amusing **2 :** cute, attractive

grada *nf* **1 :** harrow **2** PELDAÑO **:** step, stair **3 gradas** *nfpl* **:** bleachers, grandstand

gradación *nf, pl* **-ciones :** gradation, scale

gradar *vt* **:** to harrow, to hoe

gradería *nf* **:** tiers *pl,* stands *pl,* rows *pl* (in a theater)

gradiente *nf* **:** gradient, slope

grado *nm* **1 :** degree (in meteorology and mathematics) <grado centígrado : degree centigrade> **2 :** extent, level, degree <en grado sumo : greatly, to the highest degree> **3** RANGO **:** rank **4 :** year, class (in education) **5 de buen grado :** willingly, readily

graduable *adj* **:** adjustable

graduación *nf, pl* **-ciones 1 :** graduation (from a school) **2** GRADO **:** rank **3 :** alcohol content, proof

graduado[1], -da *adj* **1 :** graduated **2 lentes graduados :** prescription lenses

graduado[2], -da *n* **:** graduate

gradual *adj* **:** gradual — **gradualmente** *adv*

graduar {3} *v* **1 :** to regulate, to adjust **2** CALIBRAR **:** to calibrate, to gauge —

graduarse *vr* : to graduate (from a school)
gráfica *nf* → **gráfico[2]**
gráfico[1], -ca *adj* : graphic — **gráficamente** *adv*
gráfico[2] *nm* **1** : graph, chart **2** : graphic (for a computer, etc.) **3 gráfico de barras** : bar graph
grafismo *nm* : graphics *pl*
grafito *nm* : graphite
gragea *nf* **1** : coated pill or tablet **2 grageas** *nfpl* : sprinkles, jimmies
grajo *nm* : rook (bird)
grama *nf* : grass
gramática *nf* : grammar
gramatical *adj* : grammatical — **gramaticalmente** *adv*
gramo *nm* : gram
gran → **grande**
grana *nf* : scarlet, deep red
granada *nf* **1** : pomegranate **2** : grenade <granada de mano : hand grenade>
granadero *nm* **1** : grenadier **2 granaderos** *nmpl Mex* : riot squad
granadino, -na *adj & n* : Grenadian
granado, -da *adj* **1** DISTINGUIDO : distinguished **2** : choice, select
granate *nm* **1** : garnet **2** : deep red, maroon
grande *adj* (**gran** *before singular nouns*) **1** : large, big <un libro grande : a big book> **2** ALTO : tall **3** NOTABLE : great <un gran autor : a great writer> **4** (*indicating intensity*) : great <con gran placer : with great pleasure> **5** : old, grown-up <hijos grandes : grown children>
grandeza *nf* **1** MAGNITUD : greatness, size **2** : nobility **3** : generosity, graciousness **4** : grandeur, magnificence
grandilocuencia *nf* : grandiloquence — **grandilocuente** *adj*
grandiosidad *nf* : grandeur
grandioso, -sa *adj* **1** MAGNÍFICO : grand, magnificent **2** : grandiose
granel *adv* **1 a ~** : galore, in great quantities **2 a ~** : in bulk <vender a granel : to sell in bulk>
granero *nm* : barn, granary
granito *nm* : granite
granizada *nf* : hailstorm
granizar {21} *v impers* : to hail
granizo *nm* : hail
granja *nf* : farm
granjear *vt* : to earn, to win — **granjearse** *vr* : to gain, to earn
granjero, -ra *n* : farmer
grano *nm* **1** PARTÍCULA : grain, particle <un grano de arena : a grain of sand> **2** : grain (of rice, etc.), bean (of coffee), seed **3** : grain (of wood or rock) **4** BARRO, ESPINILLA : pimple **5 ir al grano** : to get to the point
granuja *nmf* PILLUELO : rascal, urchin
granular[1] *vt* : to granulate — **granularse** *vr* : to break out in spots
granular[2] *adj* : granular, grainy
granza *nf* : chaff
grapa *nf* **1** : staple **2** : clamp
grapadora *nf* ENGRAPADORA : stapler
grapar *vt* ENGRAPAR : to staple
grasa *nf* **1** : grease **2** : fat **3** *Mex* : shoe polish
grasiento, -ta *adj* : greasy, oily
graso, -sa *adj* **1** : fatty **2** : greasy, oily
grasoso, -sa *adj* GRASIENTO : greasy, oily
gratificación *nf, pl* **-ciones 1** SATISFACCIÓN : gratification **2** : bonus **3** RECOMPENSA : recompense, reward
gratificar {72} *vt* **1** SATISFACER : to satisfy, to gratify **2** RECOMPENSAR : to reward **3** : to give a bonus to
gratinado, -da *adj* : au gratin
gratis[1] *adv* GRATUITAMENTE : free, for free, gratis
gratis[2] *adj* GRATUITO : free, gratis
gratitud *nf* : gratitude
grato, -ta *adj* AGRADABLE, PLACENTERO : pleasant, agreeable — **gratamente** *adv*
gratuitamente *adv* **1** : gratuitously **2** GRATIS : free, for free, gratis
gratuito, -ta *adj* **1** : gratuitous, unwarranted **2** GRATIS : free, gratis
grava *nf* : gravel
gravamen *nm, pl* **-vámenes 1** : burden, obligation **2** : (property) tax
gravar *vt* **1** : to burden, to encumber **2** : to levy (a tax)
grave *adj* **1** : grave, important **2** : serious, somber **3** : serious (of an illness)
gravedad *nf* **1** : gravity <centro de gravedad : center of gravity> **2** : seriousness, severity
gravemente *adv* : gravely, seriously
gravilla *nf* : (fine) gravel
gravitación *nf, pl* **-ciones** : gravitation
gravitar *vi* **1** : to gravitate **2 ~ sobre** : to rest on **3 ~ sobre** : to loom over
gravoso, -sa *adj* **1** ONEROSO : burdensome, onerous **2** : costly
graznar *vi* : to caw, to honk, to quack, to squawk
graznido *nm* : cawing, honking, quacking, squawking
gregario, -ria *adj* : gregarious
gregoriano, -na *adj* : Gregorian
gremial *adj* SINDICAL : union, labor
gremio *nm* SINDICATO : union, guild
greña *nf* **1** : mat, tangle **2 greñas** *nfpl* MELENAS : shaggy hair, mop
greñudo, -da *n* HIPPIE, MELENUDO : longhair, hippie
grey *nf* : congregation, flock
griego[1], -ga *adj & n* : Greek
griego[2] *nm* : Greek (language)
grieta *nf* : crack, crevice
grifo *nm* **1** : faucet <agua del grifo : tap water> **2** : griffin
grillete *nm* : shackle
grillo *nm* **1** : cricket **2 grillos** *nmpl* : fetters, shackles
grima *nf* **1** : disgust, uneasiness **2 darle grima a alguien** : to get on someone's nerves

gringo, -ga *adj & n* YANQUI : Yankee, gringo

gripa *nf Col, Mex* : flu

gripe *nf* : flu

gris *adj* **1** : gray **2** : overcast, cloudy

grisáceo, -cea *adj* : grayish

gritar *v* : to shout, to scream, to cry

gritería *nf* : shouting, clamor

grito *nm* : shout, scream, cry <a grito pelado : at the top of one's voice>

groenlandés, -desa *adj & n* : Greenlander

grogui *adj fam* : dazed, groggy

grosella *nf* **1** : currant **2 grosella espinosa** : gooseberry

grosería *nf* **1** : insult, coarse language **2** : rudeness, discourtesy

grosero[1], -ra *adj* **1** : rude, fresh **2** : coarse, vulgar

grosero[2], -ra *n* : rude person

grosor *nm* : thickness

grosso *adj* **a grosso modo** : roughly, broadly, approximately

grotesco, -ca *adj* : grotesque, hideous

grúa *nf* **1** : crane (machine) **2** : tow truck

gruesa *nf* : gross

grueso[1], -sa *adj* **1** : thick, bulky **2** : heavy, big **3** : heavyset, stout

grueso[2] *nm* **1** : thickness **2** : main body, mass **3 en ~** : in bulk

grulla *nf* : crane (bird)

grumo *nm* : lump, glob

gruñido *nm* : growl, grunt

gruñir {38} *vi* **1** : to growl, to grunt **2** : to grumble

gruñón[1], -ñona *adj, mpl* **gruñones** *fam* : grumpy, crabby

gruñón[2], -ñona *n, mpl* **gruñones** *fam* : grumpy person, nag

grupa *nf* : rump, hindquarters *pl*

grupo *nm* : group

gruta *nf* : grotto, cave

guacal *nm Col, Mex, Ven* : crate

guacamayo *nm* : macaw

guacamole *or* **guacamol** *nm* : guacamole

guacamote *nm Mex* : yuca, cassava

guachinango → **huachinango**

guacho, -cha *adj* **1** *Arg, Col, Chile, Peru* : orphaned **2** *Chile, Peru* : odd, unmatched

guadaña *nf* : scythe

guagua *nf* **1** *Arg, Col, Chile, Peru* : baby **2** *Cuba, PRi* : bus

guaira *nf* **1** *CA* : traditional flute **2** *Peru* : smelting furnace

guajiro, -ra *n Cuba* : peasant

guajolote *nm Mex* : turkey

guanábana *nf* : guanabana, soursop (fruit)

guanaco *nm* : guanaco

guandú *nm CA, Car, Col* : pigeon pea

guango, -ga *adj Mex* **1** : loose-fitting, baggy **2** : slack, loose

guano *nm* : guano

guante *nm* **1** : glove <guante de boxeo : boxing glove> **2 arrojarle el guante (a alguien)** : to throw down the gauntlet (to someone)

guantelete *nm* : gauntlet

guapo, -pa *adj* **1** : handsome, good-looking, attractive **2** : elegant, smart **3** *fam* : bold, dashing

guapura *nf fam* : handsomeness, attractiveness, good looks *pl* <¡qué guapura! : what a vision!>

guarache → **huarache**

guarachear *vi Cuba, PRi fam* : to go on a spree, to go out on the town

guaraní[1] *adj & nmf* : Guarani

guaraní[2] *nm* : Guarani (language of Paraguay)

guarda *nmf* **1** GUARDIÁN : security guard **2** : keeper, custodian

guardabarros *nms & pl* : fender, mudguard

guardabosque *nmfs & pl* : forest ranger, gamekeeper

guardacostas[1] *nmfs & pl* : coastguardsman

guardacostas[2] *nms & pl* : coast guard vessel

guardaespaldas *nmfs & pl* : bodyguard

guardafangos *nms & pl* : fender, mudguard

guardameta *nmf* ARQUERO, PORTERO : goalkeeper, goalie

guardapelo *nm* : locket

guardapolvo *nm* **1** : dustcover **2** : duster, housecoat

guardar *vt* **1** : to guard **2** : to maintain, to preserve **3** CONSERVAR : to put away **4** RESERVAR : to save **5** : to keep (a secret or promise) — **guardarse** *vr* **1 ~ de** : to refrain from **2 ~ de** : to guard against, to be careful not to

guardarropa *nm* **1** : cloakroom, checkroom **2** ARMARIO : closet, wardrobe

guardería *nf* : nursery, day-care center

guardia[1] *nf* **1** : guard, defense **2** : guard duty, watch **3 en ~** : on guard

guardia[2] *nmf* **1** : sentry, guardsman, guard **2** : police officer, policeman *m*, policewoman *f*

guardián, -diana *n, mpl* **guardianes 1** GUARDA : security guard, watchman **2** : guardian, keeper **3 perro guardián** : watchdog

guarecer {53} *vt* : to shelter, to protect — **guarecerse** *vr* : to take shelter

guarida *nf* **1** : den, lair **2** : hideout

guarismo *nm* : figure, numeral

guarnecer {53} *vt* **1** : to adorn **2** : to garnish **3** : to garrison

guarnición *nf, pl* **-ciones 1** : garnish **2** : garrison **3** : decoration, trimming, setting (of a jewel)

guaro *nm CA* : liquor distilled from sugarcane

guasa *nf fam* **1** : joking, fooling around **2 de ~** : in jest, as a joke

guasón[1], -sona *adj, mpl* **guasones** *fam* : funny, witty

guasón², -sona *n, mpl* **guasones** *fam* : joker, clown
guatemalteco, -ca *adj & n* : Guatemalan
guau *interj* : wow!
guayaba *nf* : guava (fruit)
gubernamental *adj* : governmental
gubernativo, -va → **gubernamental**
gubernatura *nf Mex* : governing body
guepardo *nm* : cheetah
güero, -ra *adj Mex* : blond, fair
guerra *nf* **1** : war <declarar la guerra : to declare war> <guerra sin cuartel : all-out war> **2** : warfare **3** LUCHA : conflict, struggle
guerrear *vi* : to wage war
guerrero¹, -ra *adj* **1** : war, fighting **2** : warlike
guerrero², -ra *n* : warrior
guerrilla *nf* : guerrilla warfare
guerrillero, -ra *adj & n* : guerrilla
gueto *nm* : ghetto
guía¹ *nf* **1** : directory, guidebook **2** ORIENTACIÓN : guidance, direction <la conciencia me sirve como guía : conscience is my guide>
guía² *nmf* : guide, leader <guía de turismo : tour guide>
guiar {85} *vt* **1** : to guide, to lead **2** CONDUCIR : to manage — **guiarse** *vr* : to be guided by, to go by
guija *nf* : pebble
guijarro *nm* : pebble
guillotina *nf* : guillotine — **guillotinar** *vt*
guinda¹ *adj & nm Mex* : burgundy (color)
guinda² *nf* : morello (cherry)
guineo *nm Car* : banana
guinga *nf* : gingham
guiñada → **guiño**
guiñar *vi* : to wink
guiño *nm* : wink
guión *nm, pl* **guiones 1** : script, screenplay **2** : hyphen, dash **3** ESTANDARTE : standard, banner
guirnalda *nf* : garland
guisa *nf* **1** : manner, fashion **2 a guisa de** : like, by way of **3 de tal guisa** : in such a way
guisado ESTOFADO *nm* : stew
guisante *nm* : pea
guisar *vt* **1** ESTOFAR : to stew **2** *Spain* : to cook
guiso *nm* **1** : stew **2** : casserole
güisqui → **whisky**
guita *nf* : string, twine
guitarra *nf* : guitar
guitarrista *nmf* : guitarist
gula *nf* GLOTONERÍA : gluttony, greed
gusano *nm* **1** LOMBRIZ : worm, earthworm <gusano de seda : silkworm> **2** : caterpillar, maggot, grub
gustar *vt* **1** : to taste **2** : to like <¿gustan pasar? : would you like to come in?> — *vi* **1** : to be pleasing <me gustan los dulces : I like sweets> <a María le gusta Carlos : Maria is attracted to Carlos> <no me gusta que me griten : I don't like to be yelled at> **2 ~ de** : to like, to enjoy <no gusta de chismes : she doesn't like gossip> **3 como guste** : as you wish, as you like
gustativo, -va *adj* : taste <papilas gustativas : taste buds>
gusto *nm* **1** : flavor, taste **2** : taste, style **3** : pleasure, liking **4** : whim, fancy <a gusto : at will> **5 a ~** : comfortable, at ease **6 al gusto** : to taste, as one likes **7 mucho gusto** : pleased to meet you
gustosamente *adv* : gladly
gustoso, -sa *adj* **1** : willing, glad <nuestra empresa participará gustosa : our company will be pleased to participate> **2** : zesty, tasty
gutural *adj* : guttural

H

h *nf* : eighth letter of the Spanish alphabet
ha → **haber**
haba *nf* : broad bean
habanero¹, -ra *adj* : of or from Havana
habanero², -ra *n* : native or resident of Havana
haber¹ {39} *v aux* **1** : have, has <no ha llegado el envío : the shipment hasn't arrived> **2 ~ de** : must <ha de ser tarde : it must be late> — *v impers* **1 hay** : there is, there are <hay dos mensajes : there are two messages> <¿qué hay de nuevo? : what's new?> **2 hay que** : it is necessary <hay que trabajar más rápido : you have to work faster>
haber² *nm* **1** : assets *pl* **2** : credit, credit side **3 haberes** *nmpl* : salary, income, remuneration
habichuela *nf* **1** : bean, kidney bean **2** : green bean
hábil *adj* **1** : able, skillful **2** : working <días hábiles : working days>
habilidad *nf* CAPACIDAD : ability, skill
habilidoso, -sa *adj* : skillful, clever
habilitación *nf, pl* **-ciones 1** : authorization **2** : furnishing, equipping
habilitar *vt* **1** : to enable, to authorize, to empower **2** : to equip, to furnish
hábilmente *adv* : skillfully, expertly
habitable *adj* : habitable, inhabitable
habitación *nf, pl* **-ciones 1** CUARTO : room **2** DORMITORIO : bedroom **3** : habitation, occupancy

habitante *nmf* : inhabitant, resident
habitar *vt* : to inhabit — *vi* : to reside, to dwell
hábitat *nm, pl* **-tats** : habitat
hábito *nm* **1** : habit, custom **2** : habit (of a monk or nun)
habitual *adj* : habitual, customary — **habitualmente** *adv*
habituar {3} *vt* : to accustom, to habituate — **habituarse** *vr* **~ a** : to get used to, to grow accustomed to
habla *nf* **1** : speech **2** : language, dialect **3 de ~** : speaking <de habla inglesa : English-speaking>
hablado, -da *adj* **1** : spoken **2 mal hablado** : foulmouthed
hablador[1], -dora *adj* : talkative
hablador[2], -dora *n* : chatterbox
habladuría *nf* **1** : rumor **2 habladurías** *nfpl* : gossip, scandal
hablante *nmf* : speaker
hablar *vi* **1** : to speak, to talk <hablar en broma : to be joking> **2 ~ de** : to mention, to talk about **3 dar que hablar** : to make people talk — *vt* **1** : to speak (a language) **2** : to talk about, to discuss <háblalo con tu jefe : discuss it with your boss> — **hablarse** *vr* **1** : to speak to each other, to be on speaking terms **2 se habla inglés (etc.)** : English (etc.) spoken
habrá, etc. → **haber**
hacedor, -dora *n* : creator, maker, doer
hacendado, -da *n* : landowner
hacer {40} *vt* **1** : to make **2** : to do, to perform **3** : to force, to oblige <los hice esperar : I made them wait> — *vi* : to act <haces bien : you're doing the right thing> — *v impers* **1** (*referring to weather*) <hacer frío : to be cold> <hace viento : it's windy> **2 hace** : ago <hace mucho tiempo : a long time ago, for a long time> **3 no le hace** : it doesn't matter, it makes no difference **4 hacer falta** : to be necessary, to be needed — **hacerse** *vr* **1** : to become **2** : to pretend, to act, to play <hacerse el tonto : to play dumb> **3** : to seem <el examen se me hizo difícil : the exam seemed difficult to me> **4** : to get, to grow <se hace tarde : it's growing late>
hacha *nf* : hatchet, ax
hachazo *nm* : blow, chop (with an ax)
hachís *nm* : hashish
hacia *prep* **1** : toward, towards <hacia abajo : downward> <hacia adelante : forward> **2** : near, around, about <hacia las seis : about six o'clock>
hacienda *nf* **1** : estate, ranch, farm **2** : property **3** : livestock **4 la Hacienda** : department of revenue, tax office
hacinar *vt* **1** : to pile up, to stack **2** : to overcrowd — **hacinarse** *vr* : to crowd together
hada *nf* : fairy
hado *nm* : destiny, fate
haga, etc. → **hacer**
haitiano, -na *adj & n* : Haitian
halagador[1], -dora *adj* : flattering
halagador[2], -dora *n* : flatterer
halagar {52} *vt* : to flatter, to compliment
halago *nm* : flattery, praise
halagüeño, -ña *adj* **1** : flattering **2** : encouraging, promising
halcón *nm, pl* **halcones** : hawk, falcon
halibut *nm, pl* **-buts** : halibut
hálito *nm* **1** : breath **2** : gentle breeze
hallar *vt* **1** ENCONTRAR : to find **2** DESCUBRIR : to discover, to find out — **hallarse** *vr* **1** : to be situated, to find oneself **2** : to feel <no se halla bien : he doesn't feel comfortable, he feels out of place>
hallazgo *nm* **1** : discovery **2** : find <¡es un verdadero hallazgo! : it's a real find!>
halo *nm* **1** : halo **2** : aura
halógeno *nm* : halogen
hamaca *nf* : hammock
hambre *nf* **1** : hunger **2** : starvation **3 tener hambre** : to be hungry **4 dar hambre** : to make hungry
hambriento, -ta *adj* : hungry, starving
hambruna *nf* : famine
hamburguesa *nf* : hamburger
hampa *nf* : criminal underworld
hampón, -pona *n, mpl* **hampones** : criminal, thug
hámster *nm, pl* **hámsters** : hamster
han → **haber**
handicap *or* **hándicap** [ˈhandi,kap] *nm, pl* **-caps** : handicap (in sports)
hangar *nm* : hangar
hará, etc. → **hacer**
haragán[1], -gana *adj, mpl* **-ganes** : lazy, idle
haragán[2], -gana *n, mpl* **-ganes** HOLGAZÁN : slacker, good-for-nothing
haraganear *vi* : to be lazy, to waste one's time
haraganería *nf* : laziness
harapiento, -ta *adj* : ragged, tattered
harapos *nmpl* ANDRAJOS : rags, tatters
hardware [ˈhard,wɛr] *nm* : computer hardware
harén *nm, pl* **harenes** : harem
harina *nf* **1** : flour **2 harina de maíz** : cornmeal
hartar *vt* **1** : to glut, to satiate **2** FASTIDIAR : to tire, to irritate, to annoy — **hartarse** *vr* : to be weary, to get fed up
harto[1] *adv* : most, extremely, very
harto[2], -ta *adj* **1** : full, satiated **2** : fed up
hartura *nf* **1** : surfeit **2** : abundance, plenty
has → **haber**
hasta[1] *adv* : even
hasta[2] *prep* **1** : until, up until <hasta entonces : until then> <¡hasta luego! : see you later!> **2** : as far as <nos fuimos hasta Managua : we went all the way to Managua> **3** : up to <hasta cierto punto : up to a certain point> **4 hasta que** : until

hastiar {85} *vt* **1 :** to make weary, to bore **2 :** to disgust, to sicken — **hastiarse** *vr* **~ de :** to get tired of

hastío *nm* **1** TEDIO **:** tedium **2** REPUGNANCIA **:** disgust

hato *nm* **1 :** flock, herd **2 :** bundle (of possessions)

hawaiano, -na *adj & n* **:** Hawaiian

hay → **haber**

haya[1], **etc.** → **haber**

haya[2] *nf* **:** beech (tree and wood)

hayuco *nm* **:** beechnut

haz[1] → **hacer**

haz[2] *nm, pl* **haces 1** FARDO **:** bundle **2 :** beam (of light)

haz[3] *nf, pl* **haces 1 :** face **2 haz de la tierra :** surface of the earth

hazaña *nf* PROEZA **:** feat, exploit

hazmerreír *nm fam* **:** laughingstock

he[1] {39} → **haber**

he[2] *v impers* **he aquí :** here is, here are, behold

hebilla *nf* **:** buckle, clasp

hebra *nf* **:** strand, thread

hebreo[1], **-brea** *adj & n* **:** Hebrew

hebreo[2] *nm* **:** Hebrew (language)

hecatombe *nm* **1** MATANZA **:** massacre **2 :** disaster

heces → **hez**

hechicería *nf* **1** BRUJERÍA **:** sorcery, witchcraft **2 :** curse, spell

hechicero[1], **-ra** *adj* **:** bewitching, enchanting

hechicero[2], **-ra** *n* **:** sorcerer, sorceress *f*

hechizar {21} *vt* **1** EMBRUJAR **:** to bewitch **2** CAUTIVAR **:** to charm

hechizo *nm* **1** SORTILEGIO **:** spell, enchantment **2** ENCANTO **:** charm, fascination

hecho[1] *pp* → **hacer**

hecho[2], **-cha** *adj* **1 :** made, done **2 :** ready-to-wear **3 :** complete, finished <hecho y derecho : full-fledged>

hecho[3] *nm* **1 :** fact **2 :** event <hechos históricos : historic events> **3 :** act, action **4 de ~ :** in fact, in reality

hechura *nf* **1 :** style **2 :** craftsmanship, workmanship **3 :** product, creation

hectárea *nf* **:** hectare

heder {56} *vi* **:** to stink, to reek

hediondez *nf* **:** stink, stench

hediondo, -da *adj* MALOLIENTE **:** foul-smelling, stinking

hedor *nm* **:** stench, stink

hegemonía *nf* **1 :** dominance **2 :** hegemony (in politics)

helada *nf* **:** frost (in meteorology)

heladería *nf* **:** ice-cream parlor, ice-cream stand

helado[1], **-da** *adj* **1** GÉLIDO **:** icy, freezing cold **2** CONGELADO **:** frozen

helado[2] *nm* **:** ice cream

heladora *nf* CONGELADOR **:** freezer

helar {55} *v* CONGELAR **:** to freeze — *v impers* **:** to produce frost <anoche heló : there was frost last night> — **helarse** *vr*

helecho *nm* **:** fern, bracken

hélice *nf* **1 :** spiral, helix **2 :** propeller

helicóptero *nm* **:** helicopter

helio *nm* **:** helium

helipuerto *nm* **:** heliport

hembra *adj & nf* **:** female

hemisférico, -ca *adj* **:** hemispheric, hemispherical

hemisferio *nm* **:** hemisphere

hemofilia *nf* **:** hemophilia

hemofílico, -ca *adj & n* **:** hemophiliac

hemoglobina *nf* **:** hemoglobin

hemorragia *nf* **1 :** hemorrhage **2 hemorragia nasal :** nosebleed

hemorroides *nfpl* ALMORRANAS **:** hemorrhoids, piles

hemos → **haber**

henchido, -da *adj* **:** swollen, bloated

henchir {54} *vt* **1 :** to stuff, to fill **2 :** to swell, to swell up — **henchirse** *vr* **:** to stuff oneself **2** LLENARSE **:** to fill up, to be full

hender {56} *vt* **:** to cleave, to split

hendidura *nf* **:** crack, crevice, fissure

henequén *nm, pl* **-quenes :** sisal hemp

heno *nm* **:** hay

hepatitis *nf* **:** hepatitis

heráldica *nf* **:** heraldry

heráldico, -ca *adj* **:** heraldic

heraldo *nm* **:** herald

herbario, -ria *adj* **:** herbal

herbicida *nm* **:** herbicide, weed killer

herbívoro[1], **-ra** *adj* **:** herbivorous

herbívoro[2] *nm* **:** herbivore

herbolario, -ria *n* **:** herbalist

hercúleo, -lea *adj* **:** herculean

heredar *vt* **:** to inherit

heredero, -ra *n* **:** heir, heiress *f*

hereditario, -ria *adj* **:** hereditary

hereje *nmf* **:** heretic

herejía *nf* **:** heresy

herencia *nf* **1 :** inheritance **2 :** heritage **3 :** heredity

herético, -ca *adj* **:** heretical

herida *nf* **:** injury, wound

herido[1], **-da** *adj* **1 :** injured, wounded **2 :** hurt, offended

herido[2], **-da** *n* **:** injured person, casualty

herir {76} *vt* **1 :** to injure, to wound **2 :** to hurt, to offend

hermafrodita *nmf* **:** hermaphrodite

hermanar *vt* **1 :** to unite, to bring together **2 :** to match up, to twin (cities)

hermanastro, -tra *n* **:** half brother *m*, half sister *f*

hermandad *nf* **1** FRATERNIDAD **:** brotherhood <hermandad de mujeres : sisterhood, sorority> **2 :** association

hermano, -na *n* **:** sibling, brother *m*, sister *f*

hermético, -ca *adj* **:** hermetic, watertight — **herméticamente** *adv*

hermoso, -sa *adj* BELLO **:** beautiful, lovely — **hermosamente** *adv*

hermosura *nf* BELLEZA **:** beauty, loveliness

hernia *nf* **:** hernia

héroe *nm* **:** hero

heroicidad *nf* **:** heroism, heroic deed

heroico, -ca *adj* : heroic — **heroicamente** *adv*
heroína *nf* **1** : heroine **2** : heroin
heroísmo *nm* : heroism
herpes *nms & pl* **1** : herpes **2** : shingles
herradura *nf* : horseshoe
herraje *nm* : ironwork
herramienta *nf* : tool
herrar {55} *vt* : to shoe (a horse)
herrería *nf* : blacksmith's shop
herrero, -ra *n* : blacksmith
herrumbre *nf* ORÍN : rust
herrumbroso, -sa *adj* OXIDADO : rusty
hertzio *nm* : hertz
hervidero *nm* **1** : mass, swarm **2** : hotbed (of crime, etc.)
hervidor *nm* : kettle
hervir {76} *vi* **1** BULLIR : to boil, to bubble **2 ~ de** : to teem with, to be swarming with — *vt* : to boil
hervor *nm* **1** : boiling **2** : fervor, ardor
heterogeneidad *nf* : heterogeneity
heterogéneo, -nea *adj* : heterogeneous
heterosexual *adj & nmf* : heterosexual
heterosexualidad *nf* : heterosexuality
hexágono *nm* : hexagon — **hexagonal** *adj*
hez *nf, pl* **heces 1** ESCORIA : scum, dregs *pl* **2** : sediment, lees *pl* **3 heces** *nfpl* : feces, excrement
hiato *nm* : hiatus
hibernar *vi* : to hibernate — **hibernación** *nf*
híbrido[1], **-da** *adj* : hybrid
híbrido[2] *nm* : hybrid
hicieron, etc. → **hacer**
hidalgo, -ga *n* : nobleman *m,* noblewoman *f*
hidrante *nm CA, Col* : hydrant
hidratar *vt* : to moisturize — **hidratante** *adj*
hidrato *nm* **1** : hydrate **2 hidrato de carbono** : carbohydrate
hidráulico, -ca *adj* : hydraulic
hidroavión *nm, pl* **-viones** : seaplane
hidrocarburo *nm* : hydrocarbon
hidroeléctrico, -ca *adj* : hydroelectric
hidrofobia *nf* RABIA : hydrophobia, rabies
hidrófugo, -ga *adj* : water-repellent
hidrógeno *nm* : hydrogen
hidroplano *nm* : hydroplane
hiede, etc. → **heder**
hiedra *nf* **1** : ivy **2 hiedra venenosa** : poison ivy
hiel *nf* **1** BILIS : bile **2** : bitterness
hiela, etc. → **helar**
hielo *nm* **1** : ice **2** : coldness, reserve <romper el hielo : to break the ice>
hiena *nf* : hyena
hiende, etc. → **hender**
hierba *nf* **1** : herb **2** : grass **3 mala hierba** : weed
hierbabuena *nf* : mint, spearmint
hiere, etc. → **herir**
hierra, etc. → **herrar**
hierro *nm* **1** : iron <hierro fundido : cast iron> **2** : branding iron
hierve, etc. → **hervir**
hígado *nm* : liver
higiene *nf* : hygiene
higiénico, -ca *adj* : hygienic — **higiénicamente** *adv*
higienista *nmf* : hygienist
higo *nm* **1** : fig **2 higo chumbo** : prickly pear (fruit)
higrómetro *nm* : hygrometer
higuera *nf* : fig tree
hijastro, -tra *n* : stepson *m,* stepdaughter *f*
hijo, -ja *n* **1** : son *m,* daughter *f* **2 hijos** *nmpl* : children, offspring
híjole *interj Mex* : wow!, good grief!
hilacha *nf* **1** : ravel, loose thread **2 mostrar la hilacha** : to show one's true colors
hilado *nm* **1** : spinning **2** HILO : yarn, thread
hilar *vt* **1** : to spin (thread) **2** : to consider, to string together (ideas) — *vi* **1** : to spin **2 hilar delgado** : to split hairs
hilarante *adj* **1** : humorous, hilarious **2 gas hilarante** : laughing gas
hilaridad *nf* : hilarity
hilera *nf* FILA : file, row, line
hilo *nm* **1** : thread <colgar de un hilo : to hang by a thread> <hilo dental : dental floss> **2** LINO : linen **3** : (electric) wire **4** : theme, thread (of a discourse) **5** : trickle (of water, etc.)
hilvanar *vt* **1** : to baste, to tack **2** : to piece together
himnario *nm* : hymnal
himno *nm* **1** : hymn **2 himno nacional** : national anthem
hincapié *nm* **hacer hincapié en** : to emphasize, to stress
hincar {72} *vt* CLAVAR : to stick, to plunge — **hincarse** *vr* **hincarse de rodillas** : to kneel down, to fall to one's knees
hinchado, -da *adj* **1** : swollen, inflated **2** : pompous, overblown
hinchar *vt* **1** INFLAR : to inflate **2** : to exaggerate — **hincharse** *vr* **1** : to swell up **2** : to become conceited, to swell with pride
hinchazón *nf, pl* **-zones** : swelling
hinche, etc. → **henchir**
hindú *adj & nmf* : Hindu
hinduismo *nm* : Hinduism
hiniesta *nf* : broom (plant)
hinojo *nm* **1** : fennel **2 de hinojos** : on bended knee
hinque, etc. → **hincar**
hipar *vi* : to hiccup
hiperactividad *nf* : hyperactivity
hiperactivo, -va *adj* : hyperactive, overactive
hipérbole *nf* : hyperbole
hiperbólico, -ca *adj* : hyperbolic, exaggerated
hipercrítico, -ca *adj* : hypercritical
hipermetropía *nf* : farsightedness
hipersensibilidad *nf* : hypersensitivity
hipersensible *adj* : hypersensitive

hipertensión *nf, pl* **-siones** : hypertension, high blood pressure

hípico, -ca *adj* : equestrian <concurso hípico : horse show>

hipil *nm* → **huipil**

hipnosis *nfs & pl* : hypnosis

hipnótico, -ca *adj* : hypnotic

hipnotismo *nm* : hypnotism

hipnotizador[1], -dora *adj* **1** : hypnotic **2** : spellbinding, mesmerizing

hipnotizador[2], -dora *n* : hypnotist

hipnotizar {21} *vt* : to hypnotize

hipo *nm* : hiccup, hiccups *pl*

hipocampo *nm* : sea horse

hipocondría *nf* : hypochondria

hipocondríaco, -ca *adj & n* : hypochondriac

hipocresía *nf* : hypocrisy

hipócrita[1] *adj* : hypocritical — **hipócritamente** *adv*

hipócrita[2] *nmf* : hypocrite

hipodérmico, -ca *adj* **aguja hipodérmica** : hypodermic needle

hipódromo *nm* : racetrack

hipopótamo *nm* : hippopotamus

hipoteca *nf* : mortgage

hipotecar {72} *vt* **1** : to mortgage **2** : to compromise, to jeopardize

hipotecario, -ria *adj* : mortgage

hipotensión *nf* : low blood pressure

hipotenusa *nf* : hypotenuse

hipótesis *nfs & pl* : hypothesis

hipotético, -ca *adj* : hypothetical — **hipotéticamente** *adv*

hippie *or* **hippy** [ˈhipi] *nmf, pl* **hippies** [-pis] : hippie

hiriente *adj* : hurtful, offensive

hirió, etc. → **herir**

hirsuto, -ta *adj* **1** : hirsute, hairy **2** : bristly, wiry

hirviente *adj* : boiling

hirvió, etc. → **hervir**

hisopo *nm* **1** : hyssop **2** : cotton swab

hispánico, -ca *adj & n* : Hispanic

hispano[1], -na *adj* : Hispanic <de habla hispana : Spanish-speaking>

hispano[2], -na *n* : Hispanic (person)

hispanoamericano[1], -na *adj* LATINOAMERICANO : Latin-American

hispanoamericano[2], -na *n* LATINOAMERICANO : Latin American

hispanohablante[1] *adj* : Spanish-speaking

hispanohablante[2] *nmf* : Spanish speaker

histerectomía *nf* : hysterectomy

histeria *nf* **1** : hysteria **2** : hysterics

histérico, -ca *adj* : hysterical — **histéricamente** *adv*

histerismo *nm* **1** : hysteria **2** : hysterics

historia *nf* **1** : history **2** NARRACIÓN, RELATO : story

historiador, -dora *n* : historian

historial *nm* **1** : record, document **2** CURRÍCULUM : résumé, curriculum vitae

histórico, -ca *adj* **1** : historical **2** : historic, important — **históricamente** *adv*

historieta *nf* : comic strip

histrionismo *nm* : histrionics, acting

hit [ˈhit] *nm, pl* **hits 1** ÉXITO : hit, popular song **2** : hit (in baseball)

hito *nm* : milestone, landmark

hizo → **hacer**

hobby [ˈhɔbi] *nm, pl* **hobbies** [-bis] : hobby

hocico *nm* : snout, muzzle

hockey [ˈhɔke, -ki] *nm* : hockey

hogar *nm* **1** : home **2** : hearth, fireplace

hogareño, -ña *adj* **1** : home-loving **2** : domestic, homelike

hogaza *nf* : large loaf (of bread)

hoguera *nf* **1** FOGATA : bonfire **2 morir en la hoguera** : to burn at the stake

hoja *nf* **1** : leaf, petal, blade (of grass) **2** : sheet (of paper), page (of a book) <hoja de cálculo : spreadsheet> **3** FORMULARIO : form <hoja de pedido : order form> **4** : blade (of a knife) <hoja de afeitar : razor blade>

hojalata *nf* : tinplate

hojaldra *or* **hojaldre** *nm* : puff pastry

hojarasca *nf* : fallen leaves *pl*

hojear *vt* : to leaf through (a book or magazine)

hojuela *nf* **1** : leaflet, young leaf **2** : flake

hola *interj* : hello!, hi!

holandés[1], -desa *adj, mpl* **-deses** : Dutch

holandés[2], -desa *n, mpl* **-deses** : Dutch person, Dutchman *m,* Dutchwoman *f* <los holandeses : the Dutch>

holandés[3] *nm* : Dutch (language)

holgadamente *adv* : comfortably, easily <vivir holgadamente : to be well-off>

holgado, -da *adj* **1** : loose, baggy **2** : at ease, comfortable

holganza *nf* : leisure, idleness

holgazán[1], -zana *adj, mpl* **-zanes** : lazy

holgazán[2], -zana *n, mpl* **-zanes** HARAGÁN : slacker, idler

holgazanear *vi* HARAGANEAR : to laze around, to loaf

holgazanería *nf* PEREZA : idleness, laziness

holgura *nf* **1** : looseness **2** COMODIDAD : comfort, ease

holístico, -ca *adj* : holistic

hollar {19} *vt* : to tread on, to trample

hollín *nm, pl* **hollines** TIZNE : soot

holocausto *nm* : holocaust

holograma *nm* : hologram

hombre *nm* **1** : man <el hombre : man, mankind> **2 hombre de estado** : statesman **3 hombre de negocios** : businessman **4 hombre lobo** : werewolf

hombrera *nf* **1** : shoulder pad **2** : epaulet

hombría *nf* : manliness

hombro *nm* : shoulder <encogerse de hombros : to shrug one's shoulders>

hombruno, -na *adj* : mannish

homenaje *nm* : homage, tribute <rendir homenaje a : to pay tribute to>
homenajear *vt* : to pay homage to, to honor
homeopatía *nf* : homeopathy
homicida[1] *adj* : homicidal, murderous
homicida[2] *nmf* ASESINO : murderer
homicidio *nm* ASESINATO : homicide, murder
homilía *nf* : homily, sermon
homófono *nm* : homophone
homogeneidad *nf* : homogeneity
homogeneización *nf* : homogenization
homogeneizar {21} *vt* : to homogenize
homogéneo, -nea *adj* : homogeneous
homógrafo *nm* : homograph
homologación *nf, pl* **-ciones** **1** : sanctioning, approval **2** : parity
homologar {52} *vt* **1** : to sanction **2** : to bring into line
homólogo[1], -ga *adj* : homologous, equivalent
homólogo[2], -ga *n* : counterpart
homónimo[1], -ma *n* TOCAYO : namesake
homónimo[2] *nm* : homonym
homosexual *adj & nmf* : homosexual
homosexualidad *nf* : homosexuality
honda *nf* : sling
hondo[1] *adv* : deeply
hondo[2], -da *adj* PROFUNDO : deep <en lo más hondo de : in the depths of> — **hondamente** *adv*
hondonada *nf* **1** : hollow, depression **2** : ravine, gorge
hondura *nf* : depth
hondureño, -ña *adj & n* : Honduran
honestidad *nf* **1** : decency, modesty **2** : honesty, uprightness
honesto, -ta *adj* **1** : decent, virtuous **2** : honest, honorable — **honestamente** *adv*
hongo *nm* **1** : fungus **2** : mushroom
honor *nm* **1** : honor <en honor a la verdad : to be quite honest> **2 honores** *nmpl* : honors <hacer los honores : to do the honors>
honorable *adj* HONROSO : honorable — **honorablemente** *adv*
honorario, -ria *adj* : honorary
honorarios *nmpl* : payment, fees (for professional services)
honorífico, -ca *adj* : honorary <mención honorífica : honorable mention>
honra *nf* **1** : dignity, self-respect <tener a mucha honra : to take great pride in> **2** : good name, reputation
honradamente *adv* : honestly, decently
honradez *nf, pl* **-deces** : honesty, integrity, probity
honrado, -da *adj* **1** HONESTO : honest, upright **2** : honored
honrar *vt* **1** : to honor **2** : to be a credit to <su generosidad lo honra : his generosity does him credit>
honroso, -sa *adj* HONORABLE : honorable — **honrosamente** *adv*
hora *nf* **1** : hour <media hora : half an hour> <a la última hora : at the last minute> <a la hora en punto : on the dot> <horas de oficina : office hours> **2** : time <¿qué hora es? : what time is it?> **3** CITA : appointment
horario *nm* : schedule, timetable, hours *pl* <horario de visita : visiting hours>
horca *nf* **1** : gallows *pl* **2** : pitchfork
horcajadas *nfpl* **a ~** : astride, astraddle
horcón *nm, pl* **horcones** : wooden post, prop
horda *nf* : horde
horizontal *adj* : horizontal — **horizontalmente** *adv*
horizonte *nm* : horizon, skyline
horma *nf* **1** : shoe tree **2** : shoemaker's last
hormiga *nf* : ant
hormigón *nm, pl* **-gones** CONCRETO : concrete
hormigonera *nf* : cement mixer
hormigueo *nm* **1** : tingling, pins and needles *pl* **2** : uneasiness
hormiguero *nm* **1** : anthill **2** : swarm (of people)
hormona *nf* : hormone — **hormonal** *adj*
hornacina *nf* : niche, recess
hornada *nf* : batch
hornear *vt* : to bake
hornilla *nf* : burner (of a stove)
horno *nm* **1** : oven <horno crematorio : crematorium> <horno de microondas : microwave oven> **2** : kiln
horóscopo *nm* : horoscope
horqueta *nf* **1** : fork (in a river or road) **2** : crotch (in a tree) **3** : small pitchfork
horquilla *nf* **1** : hairpin, bobby pin **2** : pitchfork
horrendo, -da *adj* : horrendous, horrible
horrible *adj* : horrible, dreadful — **horriblemente** *adv*
horripilante *adj* : horrifying, hair-raising
horripilar *vt* : to horrify, to terrify
horror *nm* : horror, dread
horrorizado, -da *adj* : terrified
horrorizar {21} *vt* : to horrify, to terrify — **horrorizarse** *vr*
horroroso, -sa *adj* **1** : horrifying, terrifying **2** : dreadful, bad
hortaliza *nf* **1** : vegetable **2 hortalizas** *nfpl* : garden produce
hortera *adj Spain fam* : tacky, gaudy
hortícola *adj* : horticultural
horticultor, -ra *n* : horticulturist
horticultura *nf* : horticulture
hosco, -ca *adj* : sullen, gloomy
hospedaje *nm* : lodging, accomodations *pl*
hospedar *vt* : to provide with lodging, to put up — **hospedarse** *vr* : to stay, to lodge

hospicio *nm* : orphanage
hospital *nm* : hospital
hospitalario, -ria *adj* : hospitable
hospitalidad *nf* : hospitality
hospitalización *nf, pl* **-ciones** : hospitalization
hospitalizar {21} *vt* : to hospitalize — **hospitalizarse** *vr*
hostería *nf* POSADA : inn
hostia *nf* : host, Eucharist
hostigamiento *nm* : harassment
hostigar {52} *vt* ACOSAR, ASEDIAR : to harass, to pester
hostil *adj* : hostile
hostilidad *nf* **1** : hostility, antagonism **2 hostilidades** *nfpl* : (military) hostilities
hostilizar {21} *vt* : to harass
hotel *nm* : hotel
hotelero[1], **-ra** *adj* : hotel <la industria hotelera : the hotel business>
hotelero[2], **-ra** *n* : hotel manager, hotelier
hoy *adv* **1** : today <hoy mismo : right now, this very day> **2** : now, nowadays <de hoy en adelante : from now on>
hoyo *nm* AGUJERO : hole
hoyuelo *nm* : dimple
hoz *nf, pl* **hoces** : sickle
hozar {21} *vi* : to root (of a pig)
huachinango *nm Mex* : red snapper
huarache *nm* : huarache sandal
hubo, etc. → **haber**
hueco[1], **-ca** *adj* **1** : hollow, empty **2** : soft, spongy **3** : hollow-sounding, resonant **4** : proud, conceited **5** : superficial
hueco[2] *nm* **1** : hole, hollow, cavity **2** : gap, space **3** : recess, alcove
huele, etc. → **oler**
huelga *nf* **1** PARO : strike **2 hacer huelga** : to strike, to go on strike
huelguista *nmf* : striker
huella[1], **etc.** → **hollar**
huella[2] *nf* **1** : footprint <seguir las huellas de alguien : to follow in someone's footsteps> **2** : mark, impact <dejar huella : to leave one's mark> <sin dejar huella : without a trace> **3 huella digital** *or* **huella dactilar** : fingerprint
huérfano[1], **-na** *adj* **1** : orphan, orphaned **2** : defenseless **3 ~ de** : lacking, devoid of
huérfano[2], **-na** *n* : orphan
huerta *nf* **1** : large vegetable garden, truck farm **2** : orchard **3** : irrigated land
huerto *nm* **1** : vegetable garden **2** : orchard
hueso *nm* **1** : bone **2** : pit, stone (of a fruit)
huésped[1], **-peda** *n* INVITADO : guest
huésped[2] *nm* : host <organismo huésped : host organism>
huestes *nfpl* **1** : followers **2** : troops, army
huesudo, -da *adj* : bony
hueva *nf* : roe, spawn
huevo *nm* : egg <huevos revueltos : scrambled eggs>
huida *nf* : flight, escape
huidizo, -za *adj* **1** ESCURRIDIZO : elusive, slippery **2** : shy, evasive
huipil *nm CA, Mex* : traditional sleeveless blouse or dress
huir {41} *vi* **1** ESCAPAR : to escape, to flee **2 ~ de** : to avoid
huiro *nm Chile, Peru* : seaweed
huizache *nm* : huisache, acacia
hule *nm* **1** : oilcloth, oilskin **2** *Mex* : rubber **3 hule espuma** *Mex* : foam rubber
humanidad *nf* **1** : humanity, mankind **2** : humaneness **3 humanidades** *nfpl* : humanities *pl*
humanismo *nm* : humanism
humanista *nmf* : humanist
humanístico, -ca *adj* : humanistic
humanitario, -ria *adj & n* : humanitarian
humano[1], **-na** *adj* **1** : human **2** BENÉVOLO : humane , benevolent — **humanamente** *adv*
humano[2] *nm* : human being, human
humareda *nf* : cloud of smoke
humeante *adj* **1** : smoky **2** : smoking, steaming
humear *vi* **1** : to smoke **2** : to steam
humectante[1] *adj* : moisturizing
humectante[2] *nm* : moisturizer
humedad *nf* **1** : humidity **2** : dampness, moistness
humedecer {53} *vt* **1** : to humidify **2** : to moisten, to dampen
húmedo, -da *adj* **1** : humid **2** : moist, damp
humidificador *nm* : humidifier
humidificar {72} *vt* : to humidify
humildad *nf* **1** : humility **2** : lowliness
humilde *adj* **1** : humble **2** : lowly <gente humilde : poor people>
humildemente *adv* : meekly, humbly
humillación *nf, pl* **-ciones** : humiliation
humillante *adj* : humiliating
humillar *vt* : to humiliate — **humillarse** *vr* : to humble oneself <humillarse a hacer algo : to stoop to doing something>
humo *nm* **1** : smoke, steam, fumes **2 humos** *nmpl* : airs *pl,* conceit
humor *nm* **1** : humor **2** : mood, temper <está de buen humor : she's in a good mood>
humorada *nf* **1** BROMA : joke, witticism **2** : whim, caprice
humorismo *nm* : humor, wit
humorista *nmf* : humorist, comedian, comedienne *f*
humorístico, -ca *adj* : humorous — **humorísticamente** *adv*
humoso, -sa *adj* : smoky, steamy
humus *nm* : humus
hundido, -da *adj* **1** : sunken **2** : depressed

hundimiento *nm* **1 :** sinking **2 :** collapse, ruin
hundir *vt* **1 :** to sink **2 :** to destroy, to ruin — **hundirse** *vr* **1 :** to sink down **2 :** to cave in **3 :** to break down, to go to pieces
húngaro[1], -ra *adj & n* **:** Hungarian
húngaro[2] *nm* **:** Hungarian (language)
huracán *nm, pl* **-canes :** hurricane
huraño, -ña *adj* **1 :** unsociable, aloof **2 :** timid, skittish (of an animal)
hurgar {52} *vt* **:** to poke, to jab, to rake (a fire) — *vi* **~ en :** to rummage in, to poke through
hurgue, etc. → **hurgar**
hurón *nm, pl* **hurones :** ferret
huronear *vi* **:** to pry, to snoop
hurra *interj* **:** hurrah!, hooray!
hurtadillas *nfpl* **a ~ :** stealthily, on the sly
hurtar *vt* ROBAR **:** to steal
hurto *nm* **1 :** theft, robbery **2 :** stolen property, loot
husmear *vt* **1 :** to follow the scent of, to track **2 :** to sniff out, to pry into — *vi* **1 :** to pry, to snoop **2 :** to sniff around (of an animal)
huso *nm* **1 :** spindle **2 huso horario :** time zone
huy *interj* **:** ow!, ouch!
huye, etc. → **huir**

I

i *nf* **:** ninth letter of the Spanish alphabet
iba, etc. → **ir**
ibérico, -ca *adj* **:** Iberian
ibero, -ra *or* **íbero, -ra** *adj & n* **:** Iberian
iberoamericano, -na *adj* HISPANOAMERICANO, LATINOAMERICANO **:** Latin-American
ibis *nfs & pl* **:** ibis
ice, etc. → **izar**
iceberg *nm, pl* **icebergs :** iceberg
icono *nm* **:** icon
iconoclasia *nf* **:** iconoclasm
iconoclasta *nmf* **:** iconoclast
ictericia *nf* **:** jaundice
ida *nf* **1 :** going, departure **2 ida y vuelta :** round-trip **3 idas y venidas :** comings and goings
idea *nf* **1 :** idea, notion **2 :** opinion, belief **3** PROPÓSITO **:** intention
ideal *adj & nm* **:** ideal — **idealmente** *adv*
idealismo *nm* **:** idealism
idealista[1] *adj* **:** idealistic
idealista[2] *nmf* **:** idealist
idealizar {21} *vt* **:** to idealize — **idealización** *nf*
idear *vt* **:** to devise, to think up
ideario *nm* **:** ideology
ídem *nm* **:** idem, the same, ditto
idéntico, -ca *adj* **:** identical, alike — **idénticamente** *adv*
identidad *nf* **:** identity
identificable *adj* **:** identifiable
identificación *nf, pl* **-ciones 1 :** identification, identifying **2 :** identification document, ID
identificar {72} *vt* **:** to identify — **identificarse** *vr* **1 :** to identify oneself **2 ~ con :** to identify with
ideología *nf* **:** ideology — **ideológicamente** *adv*
ideológico, -ca *adj* **:** ideological
idílico, -ca *adj* **:** idyllic
idilio *nm* **:** idyll
idioma *nm* **:** language <el idioma inglés : the English language>
idiomático, -ca *adj* **:** idiomatic — **idiomáticamente** *adv*
idiosincrasia *nf* **:** idiosyncrasy
idiosincrásico, -ca *adj* **:** idiosyncratic
idiota[1] *adj* **:** idiotic, stupid, foolish
idiota[2] *nmf* **:** idiot, foolish person
idiotez *nf, pl* **-teces 1 :** idiocy **2 :** idiotic act or remark <¡no digas idioteces! : don't talk nonsense!>
ido *pp* → **ir**
idólatra[1] *adj* **:** idolatrous
idólatra[2] *nmf* **:** idolater
idolatrar *vt* **:** to idolize
idolatría *nf* **:** idolatry
ídolo *nm* **:** idol
idoneidad *nf* **:** suitability
idóneo, -nea *adj* ADECUADO **:** suitable, fitting
iglesia *nf* **:** church
iglú *nm* **:** igloo
ignición *nf, pl* **-ciones :** ignition
ignífugo, -ga *adj* **:** fire-resistant, fireproof
ignominia *nf* **:** ignominy, disgrace
ignominioso, -sa *adj* **:** ignominious, shameful
ignorancia *nf* **:** ignorance
ignorante[1] *adj* **:** ignorant
ignorante[2] *nmf* **:** ignorant person, ignoramus
ignorar *vt* **1 :** to ignore **2** DESCONOCER **:** to be unaware of <lo ignoramos por absoluto : we have no idea>
ignoto, -ta *adj* **:** unknown
igual[1] *adv* **1 :** in the same way **2 por ~ :** equally
igual[2] *adj* **1 :** equal **2** IDÉNTICO **:** the same, alike **3 :** even, smooth **4** SEMEJANTE **:** similar **5** CONSTANTE **:** constant
igual[3] *nmf* **:** equal, peer
igualación *nf* **1 :** equalization **2 :** leveling, smoothing **3 :** equating (in mathematics)
igualado, -da *adj* **1 :** even (of a score) **2 :** level **3** *Mex* **:** disrespectful
igualar *vt* **1 :** to equalize **2 :** to tie <igualar el marcador : to even the score>

igualdad *nf* **1** : equality **2** UNIFORMIDAD : evenness, uniformity
igualmente *adv* **1** : equally **2** ASIMISMO : likewise
iguana *nf* : iguana
ijada *nf* : flank, loin, side
ijar *nm* → **ijada**
ilegal[1] *adj* : illegal, unlawful — **ilegalmente** *adv*
ilegal[2] *nmf CA, Mex* : illegal alien
ilegalidad *nf* : illegality, unlawfulness
ilegibilidad *nf* : illegibility
ilegible *adj* : illegible — **ilegiblemente** *adv*
ilegitimidad *nf* : illegitimacy
ilegítimo, -ma *adj* : illegitimate, unlawful
ileso, -sa *adj* : uninjured, unharmed
ilícito, -ta *adj* : illicit — **ilícitamente** *adv*
ilimitado, -da *adj* : unlimited
ilógico, -ca *adj* : illogical — **ilógicamente** *adv*
iluminación *nf, pl* **-ciones 1** : illumination **2** ALUMBRADO : lighting
iluminado, -da *adj* : illuminated, lighted
iluminar *vt* **1** : to illuminate, to light (up) **2** : to enlighten
ilusión *nf, pl* **-siones 1** : illusion, delusion **2** ESPERANZA : hope <hacerse ilusiones : to get one's hopes up>
ilusionado, -da *adj* ESPERANZADO : hopeful, eager
ilusionar *vt* : to build up hope, to excite — **ilusionarse** *vr* : to get one's hopes up
iluso[1], **-sa** *adj* : naive, gullible
iluso[2], **-sa** *n* SOÑADOR : dreamer, visionary
ilusorio, -ria *adj* ENGAÑOSO : illusory, misleading
ilustración *nf, pl* **-ciones 1** : illustration **2** : erudition, learning <la Ilustración : the Enlightenment>
ilustrado, -da *adj* **1** : illustrated **2** DOCTO : learned, erudite
ilustrador, -dora *n* : illustrator
ilustrar *vt* **1** : to illustrate **2** ACLARAR, CLARIFICAR : to explain
ilustrativo, -va *adj* : illustrative
ilustre *adj* : illustrious, eminent
imagen *nf, pl* **imágenes** : image, picture
imaginable *adj* : imaginable, conceivable
imaginación *nf, pl* **-ciones** : imagination
imaginar *vt* : to imagine — **imaginarse** *vr* **1** : to suppose, to imagine **2** : to picture
imaginario, -ria *adj* : imaginary
imaginativo, -va *adj* : imaginative — **imaginativamente** *adv*
imán *nm, pl* **imanes** : magnet
imantar *vt* : to magnetize
imbatible *adj* : unbeatable
imbécil[1] *adj* : stupid, idiotic
imbécil[2] *nmf* **1** : imbecile **2** *fam* : idiot, dope
imborrable *adj* : indelible
imbuir {41} *vt* : to imbue — **imbuirse** *vr*
imitación *nf, pl* **-ciones 1** : imitation **2** : mimicry, impersonation
imitador[1], **-dora** *adj* : imitative
imitador[2], **-dora** *n* **1** : imitator **2** : mimic
imitar *vt* **1** : to imitate, to copy **2** : to mimic, to impersonate
impaciencia *nf* : impatience
impacientar *vt* : to make impatient, to exasperate — **impacientarse** *vr*
impaciente *adj* : impatient — **impacientemente** *adv*
impactado, -da *adj* : shocked, stunned
impactante *adj* **1** : shocking **2** : impressive, powerful
impactar *vt* **1** GOLPEAR : to hit **2** IMPRESIONAR : to impact, to affect — **impactarse** *vr*
impacto *nm* **1** : impact, effect **2** : shock, collision
impagable *adj* **1** : unpayable **2** : priceless
impago *nm* : nonpayment
impalpable *adj* INTANGIBLE : impalpable, intangible
impar[1] *adj* : odd <números impares : odd numbers>
impar[2] *nm* : odd number
imparable *adj* : unstoppable
imparcial *adj* : impartial — **imparcialmente** *adv*
imparcialidad *nf* : impartiality
impartir *vt* : to impart, to give
impasible *adj* : impassive, unmoved — **impasiblemente** *adv*
impasse *nm* : impasse
impávido, -da *adj* : undaunted, unperturbed
impecable *adj* INTACHABLE : impeccable, faultless — **impecablemente** *adv*
impedido, -da *adj* : disabled, crippled
impedimento *nm* **1** : impediment, obstacle **2** : disability
impedir {54} *vt* **1** : to prevent, to block **2** : to impede, to hinder
impeler *vt* **1** : to drive, to propel **2** : to impel
impenetrable *adj* : impenetrable — **impenetrabilidad** *nf*
impenitente *adj* : unrepentant, impenitent
impensable *adj* : unthinkable
impensado, -da *adj* : unforeseen, unexpected
imperante *adj* : prevailing
imperar *vi* **1** : to reign, to rule **2** PREDOMINAR : to prevail
imperativo[1], **-va** *adj* : imperative
imperativo[2] *nm* : imperative
imperceptible *adj* : imperceptible — **imperceptiblemente** *adv*
imperdible *Spain nm* : safety pin

imperdonable *adj* : unpardonable, unforgivable

imperecedero, -ra *adj* **1** : imperishable **2** INMORTAL : immortal, everlasting

imperfección *nf, pl* **-ciones 1** : imperfection **2** DEFECTO : defect, flaw

imperfecto[1], -ta *adj* : imperfect, flawed

imperfecto[2] *nm* : imperfect tense

imperial *adj* : imperial

imperialismo *nm* : imperialism

imperialista *adj & nmf* : imperialist

impericia *nf* : lack of skill, incompetence

imperio *nm* : empire

imperioso, -sa *adj* **1** : imperious **2** : pressing, urgent — **imperiosamente** *adv*

impermeabilizante *adj* : water-repellent

impermeabilizar {21} *vt* : to waterproof

impermeable[1] *adj* **1** : impervious **2** : impermeable, waterproof

impermeable[2] *nm* : raincoat

impersonal *adj* : impersonal — **impersonalmente** *adv*

impertinencia *nf* INSOLENCIA : impertinence, insolence

impertinente *adj* **1** INSOLENTE : impertinent, insolent **2** INOPORTUNO : inappropriate, uncalled-for **3** IRRELEVANTE : irrelevant

imperturbable *adj* : imperturbable, impassive, stolid

ímpetu *nm* **1** : impetus, momentum **2** : vigor, energy **3** : force, violence

impetuoso, -sa *adj* : impetuous, impulsive — **impetuosamente** *adv*

impiedad *nf* : impiety

impío, -pía *adj* : impious, ungodly

implacable *adj* : implacable, relentless — **implacablemente** *adv*

implantación *nf, pl* **-ciones 1** : implantation **2** ESTABLECIMIENTO : establishment, introduction

implantado, -da *adj* : well-established

implantar *vt* **1** : to implant **2** ESTABLECER : to establish, to introduce — **implantarse** *vr*

implante *nm* : implant

implementar *vt* : to implement — **implementarse** *vr* — **implementación** *nf*

implemento *nm* : implement, tool

implicación *nf, pl* **-ciones** : implication

implicar {72} *vt* **1** ENREDAR, ENVOLVER : to involve, to implicate **2** : to imply

implícito, -ta *adj* : implied, implicit — **implícitamente** *adv*

implorar *vt* : to implore

implosión *nf, pl* **-siones** : implosion — **implosivo, -va** *adj*

implosionar *vi* : to implode

imponderable *adj & nm* : imponderable

imponente *adj* : imposing, impressive

imponer {60} *vt* **1** : to impose **2** : to confer — *vi* : to be impressive, to command respect — **imponerse** *vr* **1** : to take on (a duty) **2** : to assert oneself **3** : to prevail

imponible *adj* : taxable

impopular *adj* : unpopular — **impopularidad** *nf*

importación *nf, pl* **-ciones 1** : importation **2 importaciones** *nfpl* : imports

importado, -da *adj* : imported

importador[1], -dora *adj* : importing

importador[2], -dora *n* : importer

importancia *nf* : importance

importante *adj* : important — **importantemente** *adv*

importar *vi* : to matter, to be important <no le importa lo que piensen : she doesn't care what they think> — *vt* : to import

importe *nm* **1** : price, cost **2** : sum, amount

importunar *vt* : to bother, to inconvenience — *vi* : to be inconvenient

importuno, -na *adj* **1** : inopportune, inconvenient **2** : bothersome, annoying

imposibilidad *nf* : impossibility

imposibilitado, -da *adj* **1** : disabled, crippled **2 verse imposibilitado** : to be unable (to do something)

imposibilitar *vt* **1** : to make impossible **2** : to disable, to incapacitate — **imposibilitarse** *vr* : to become disabled

imposible *adj* : impossible

imposición *nf, pl* **-ciones 1** : imposition **2** EXIGENCIA : demand, requirement **3** : tax **4** : deposit

impositivo, -va *adj* : tax <tasa impositiva : tax rate>

impostor, -tora *n* : impostor

impotencia *nf* **1** : impotence, powerlessness **2** : impotence (in medicine)

impotente *adj* **1** : powerless **2** : impotent

impracticable *adj* : impracticable

imprecisión *nf, pl* **-siones 1** : imprecision, vagueness **2** : inaccuracy

impreciso, -sa *adj* **1** : imprecise, vague **2** : inaccurate

impredecible *adj* : unpredictable

impregnar *vt* : to impregnate

imprenta *nf* **1** : printing **2** : printing shop, press

imprescindible *adj* : essential, indispensable

impresentable *adj* : unpresentable, unfit

impresión *nf, pl* **-siones 1** : print, printing **2** : impression, feeling

impresionable *adj* : impressionable

impresionante *adj* : impressive, incredible, amazing — **impresionantemente** *adv*

impresionar *vt* **1** : to impress, to strike **2** : to affect, to move — *vi* : to make an impression — **impresionarse** *vr* : to be affected, to be removed

impresionismo *nm* : impressionism

impresionista[1] *adj* : impressionist, impressionistic
impresionista[2] *nmf* : impressionist
impreso[1] *pp* → **imprimir**
impreso[2], **-sa** *adj* : printed
impreso[3] *nm* PUBLICACIÓN : printed matter, publication
impresor, -sora *n* : printer
impresora *nf* : (computer) printer
imprevisible *adj* : unforeseeable
imprevisión *nf, pl* **-siones** : lack of foresight, thoughtlessness
imprevisto[1], **-ta** *adj* : unexpected, unforeseen
imprevisto[2] *nm* : unexpected occurrence, contingency
imprimir {42} *vt* **1** : to print **2** : to imprint, to stamp, to impress
improbabilidad *nf* : improbability
improbable *adj* : improbable, unlikely
improcedente *adj* **1** : inadmissible **2** : inappropriate, improper
improductivo, -va *adj* : unproductive
improperio *nm* : affront, insult
impropio, -pia *adj* **1** : improper, incorrect **2** INADECUADO : unsuitable, inappropriate
improvisación *nf, pl* **-ciones** : improvisation, ad-lib
improvisado, -da *adj* : improvised, ad-lib
improvisar *v* : to improvise, to ad-lib
improviso *adj* **de ~** : all of a sudden, unexpectedly
imprudencia *nf* INDISCRECIÓN : imprudence, indiscretion
imprudente *adj* INDISCRETO : imprudent, indiscreet — **imprudentemente** *adv*
impúdico, -ca *adj* : shameless, indecent
impuesto[1] *pp* → **imponer**
impuesto[2] *nm* : tax
impugnar *vt* : to challenge, to contest
impulsar *vt* : to propel, to drive
impulsividad *nf* : impulsiveness
impulsivo, -va *adj* : impulsive — **impulsivamente** *adv*
impulso *nm* **1** : drive, thrust **2** : impulse, urge
impune *adj* : unpunished
impunemente *adv* : with impunity
impunidad *nf* : impunity
impureza *nf* : impurity
impuro, -ra *adj* : impure
impuso, etc. → **imponer**
imputable *adj* ATRIBUIBLE : attributable
imputación *nf, pl* **-ciones** **1** : attribution, imputation **2** : accusation
imputar *vt* ATRIBUIR : to impute, to attribute
inacabable *adj* : endless
inacabado, -da *adj* INCONCLUSO : unfinished
inaccesibilidad *nf* : inaccessibility
inaccesible *adj* **1** : inaccessible **2** : unattainable
inacción *nf, pl* **-ciones** : inactivity, inaction
inaceptable *adj* : unacceptable
inactividad *nf* : inactivity, idleness
inactivo, -va *adj* : inactive, idle
inadaptado[1], **-da** *adj* : maladjusted
inadaptado[2], **-da** *n* : misfit
inadecuación *nf, pl* **-ciones** : inadequacy
inadecuado, -da *adj* **1** : inadequate **2** IMPROPIO : inappropriate — **inadecuadamente** *adv*
inadmisible *adj* **1** : inadmissible **2** : unacceptable
inadvertencia *nf* : oversight
inadvertidamente *adv* : inadvertently
inadvertido, -da *adj* **1** : unnoticed <pasar inadvertido : to go unnoticed> **2** DESPISTADO, DISTRAÍDO : inattentive, distracted
inagotable *adj* : inexhaustible
inaguantable *adj* INSOPORTABLE : insufferable, unbearable
inalámbrico, -ca *adj* : wireless, cordless
inalcanzable *adj* : unreachable, unattainable
inalienable *adj* : inalienable
inalterable *adj* **1** : unalterable, unchangeable **2** : impassive **3** : colorfast
inamovible *adj* : immovable, fixed
inanición *nf, pl* **-ciones** : starvation
inanimado, -da *adj* : inanimate
inapelable *adj* : indisputable
inapetencia *nf* : lack of appetite
inaplicable *adj* : inapplicable
inapreciable *adj* **1** : imperceptible, negligible **2** : invaluable
inapropiado, -da *adj* : inappropriate, unsuitable
inarticulado, -da *adj* : inarticulate, unintelligible — **inarticuladamente** *adv*
inasequible *adj* : unattainable, inaccessible
inasistencia *nf* AUSENCIA : absence
inatacable *adj* : unassailable, indisputable
inaudible *adj* : inaudible
inaudito, -ta *adj* : unheard-of, unprecedented
inauguración *nf, pl* **-ciones** : inauguration
inaugural *adj* : inaugural, opening
inaugurar *vt* **1** : to inaugurate **2** : to open
inca *adj & nmf* : Inca
incalculable *adj* : incalculable
incalificable *adj* : indescribable
incandescencia *nf* : incandescence — **incandescente** *adj*
incansable *adj* INFATIGABLE : tireless — **incansablemente** *adv*
incapacidad *nf* **1** : inability, incapacity **2** : disability, handicap
incapacitado, -da *adj* **1** : disqualified **2** : disabled, handicapped
incapacitar *vt* **1** : to incapacitate, to disable **2** : to disqualify
incapaz *adj, pl* **-paces** **1** : incapable, unable **2** : incompetent, inept

incautación *nf, pl* **-ciones** : seizure, confiscation
incautar *vt* CONFISCAR : to confiscate, to seize — **incautarse** *vr*
incauto, -ta *adj* : unwary, unsuspecting
incendiar *vt* : to set fire to, to burn (down) — **incendiarse** *vr* : to catch fire
incendiario[1], -ria *adj* : incendiary, inflammatory
incendiario[2], -ria *n* : arsonist
incendio *nm* **1** : fire **2 incendio premeditado** : arson
incentivar *vt* : to encourage, to stimulate
incentivo *nm* : incentive
incertidumbre *nf* : uncertainty, suspense
incesante *adj* : incessant — **incesantemente** *adv*
incesto *nm* : incest
incidencia *nf* **1** : incident **2** : effect, impact **3 por ~** : by chance, accidentally
incidental *adj* : incidental
incidentalmente *adv* : by chance
incidente *nm* : incident, occurrence
incidir *vi* **1 ~ en** : to fall into, to enter into <incidimos en el mismo error : we fell into the same mistake> **2 ~ en** : to affect, to influence, to have a bearing on
incienso *nm* : incense
incierto, -ta *adj* **1** : uncertain **2** : untrue **3** : unsteady, insecure
incineración *nf, pl* **-ciones 1** : incineration **2** : cremation
incinerador *nm* : incinerator
incinerar *vt* **1** : to incinerate **2** : to cremate
incipiente *adj* : incipient
incisión *nf, pl* **-siones** : incision
incisivo[1], -va *adj* : incisive
incisivo[2] *nm* : incisor
inciso *nm* : digression, aside
incitación *nf, pl* **-ciones** : incitement
incitante *adj* : provocative
incitar *vt* : to incite, to rouse
incivilizado, -da *adj* : uncivilized
inclemencia *nf* : inclemency, severity
inclemente *adj* : inclement
inclinación *nf, pl* **-ciones 1** PROPENSIÓN : inclination, tendency **2** : incline, slope
inclinado, -da *adj* **1** : sloping **2** : inclined, apt
inclinar *vt* : to tilt, to lean, to incline <inclinar la cabeza : to bow one's head> — **inclinarse** *vr* **1** : to lean, to lean over **2 ~ a** : to be inclined to
incluir {41} *vt* : to include
inclusión *nf, pl* **-siones** : inclusion
inclusive *adv* : inclusively, up to and including
inclusivo, -va *adj* : inclusive
incluso *adv* **1** AUN : even, in fact <es importante e incluso crucial : it is important and even crucial> **2** : inclusively
incógnita *nf* **1** : unknown quantity (in mathematics) **2** : mystery
incógnito, -ta *adj* **1** : unknown **2 de incógnito** : incognito
incoherencia *nf* : incoherence
incoherente *adj* : incoherent — **incoherentemente** *adv*
incoloro, -ra *adj* : colorless
incombustible *adj* : fireproof
incomible *adj* : inedible
incomodar *vt* **1** : to make uncomfortable **2** : to inconvenience — **incomodarse** *vr* : to put oneself out, to take the trouble
incomodidad *nf* **1** : discomfort, awkwardness **2** MOLESTIA : inconvenience, bother
incómodo, -da *adj* **1** : uncomfortable, awkward **2** INCONVENIENTE : inconvenient
incomparable *adj* : incomparable
incompatibilidad *nf* : incompatibility
incompatible *adj* : incompatible, uncongenial
incompetencia *nf* : incompetence
incompetente *adj & nmf* : incompetent
incompleto, -ta *adj* : incomplete
incomprendido, -da *adj* : misunderstood
incomprensible *adj* : incomprehensible
incomprensión *nf, pl* **-siones** : lack of understanding, incomprehension
incomunicación *nf, pl* **-ciones** : lack of communication
incomunicado, -da *adj* **1** : cut off, isolated **2** : in solitary confinement
inconcebible *adj* : inconceivable, unthinkable — **inconcebiblemente** *adv*
inconcluso, -sa *adj* INACABADO : unfinished
incondicional *adj* : unconditional — **incondicionalmente** *adv*
inconexo, -xa *adj* : unconnected, disconnected
inconfesable *adj* : unspeakable, shameful
inconforme *adj & nmf* : nonconformist
inconformidad *nf* : nonconformity
inconformista *adj & nmf* : nonconformist
inconfundible *adj* : unmistakable, obvious — **inconfundiblemente** *adv*
incongruencia *nf* : incongruity
incongruente *adj* : incongruous
inconmensurable *adj* : vast, immeasurable
inconquistable *adj* : unyielding
inconsciencia *nf* **1** : unconsciousness, unawareness **2** : irresponsibility
inconsciente[1] *adj* **1** : unconscious, unaware **2** : reckless, needless — **inconscientemente** *adv*
inconsciente[2] *n* **el inconsciente** : the unconscious

inconsecuente *adj* **:** inconsistent — **inconsecuencia** *nf*

inconsiderado, -da *adj* **:** inconsiderate, thoughtless

inconsistencia *nf* **:** inconsistency

inconsistente *adj* **1 :** weak, flimsy **2 :** watery, runny (of a sauce, etc.) **3 :** inconsistent, weak (of an argument)

inconsolable *adj* **:** inconsolable — **inconsolablemente** *adv*

inconstancia *nf* **:** inconstancy

inconstante *adj* **:** inconstant, fickle, changeable

inconstitucional *adj* **:** unconstitutional

inconstitucionalidad *nf* **:** unconstitutionality

incontable *adj* INNUMERABLE **:** countless, innumerable

incontenible *adj* **:** uncontrollable, unstoppable

incontestable *adj* INCUESTIONABLE, INDISCUTIBLE **:** irrefutable, indisputable

incontinencia *nf* **:** incontinence — **incontinente** *adj*

incontrolable *adj* **:** uncontrollable

incontrolado, -da *adj* **:** uncontrolled, out of control

incontrovertible *adj* **:** indisputable

inconveniencia *nf* **1 :** inconvenience, trouble **2 :** unsuitability, inappropriateness **3 :** tactless remark

inconveniente[1] *adj* **1** INCÓMODO **:** inconvenient **2** INAPROPIADO **:** improper, unsuitable

inconveniente[2] *nm* **:** obstacle, problem, snag <no tengo inconveniente en hacerlo : I don't mind doing it>

incorporación *nf, pl* **-ciones :** incorporation

incorporar *vt* **1 :** to incorporate **2 :** to add, to include — **incorporarse** *vr* **1 :** to sit up **2 ~ a :** to join

incorpóreo, -rea *adj* **:** incorporeal, bodiless

incorrección *n, pl* **-ciones :** impropriety, improper word or action

incorrecto, -ta *adj* **:** incorrect — **incorrectamente** *adv*

incorregible *adj* **:** incorrigible — **incorregibilidad** *nf*

incorruptible *adj* **:** incorruptible

incredulidad *nf* **:** incredulity, skepticism

incrédulo[1]**, -la** *adj* **:** incredulous, skeptical

incrédulo[2]**, -la** *n* **:** skeptic

increíble *adj* **:** incredible, unbelievable — **increíblemente** *adv*

incrementar *vt* **:** to increase — **incrementarse** *vr*

incremento *nm* AUMENTO **:** increase

incriminar *vt* **:** to incriminate — **incriminación** *nf*

incruento, -ta *adj* **:** bloodless

incrustación *nf, pl* **-ciones :** inlay

incrustar *vt* **1 :** to embed **2 :** to inlay — **incrustarse** *vr* **:** to become embedded

incubación *nf, pl* **-ciones :** incubation

incubadora *nf* **:** incubator

incubar *v* **:** to incubate

incuestionable *adj* INCONTESTABLE, INDISCUTIBLE **:** unquestionable, indisputable — **incuestionablemente** *adv*

inculcar {72} *vt* **:** to inculcate, to instill

inculpar *vt* ACUSAR **:** to accuse, to charge

inculto, -ta *adj* **1 :** uncultured, ignorant **2 :** uncultivated, fallow

incumbencia *nf* **:** obligation, responsibility

incumbir *vi* (*3rd person only*) **~ a :** to be incumbent upon, to be of concern to <a mí no me incumbe : it's not my concern>

incumplido, -da *adj* **:** irresponsible, unreliable

incumplimiento *nm* **1 :** nonfulfillment, neglect **2 incumplimiento de contrato :** breach of contract

incumplir *vt* **:** to fail to carry out, to break (a promise, a contract)

incurable *adj* **:** incurable

incurrir *vi* **1 ~ en :** to incur <incurrir en gastos : to incur expenses> **2 ~ en :** to fall into, to commit <incurrió en un error : he made a mistake>

incursión *nf, pl* **-siones :** incursion, raid

incursionar *vi* **1 :** to raid **2 ~ en :** to go into, to enter <el actor incursionó en el baile : the actor worked in dance for a while>

indagación *nf, pl* **-ciones :** investigation, inquiry

indagar {52} *vt* **:** to inquire into, to investigate

indebido, -da *adj* **:** improper, undue — **indebidamente** *adv*

indecencia *nf* **:** indecency, obscenity

indecente *adj* **:** indecent, obscene

indecible *adj* **:** indescribable, inexpressible

indecisión *nf, pl* **-siones :** indecision

indeciso, -sa *adj* **1** IRRESOLUTO **:** indecisive **2 :** undecided

indeclinable *adj* **:** unavoidable

indecoro *nm* **:** impropriety, indecorousness

indecoroso, -sa *adj* **:** indecorous, unseemly

indefectible *adj* **:** unfailing, sure

indefendible *adj* **:** indefensible

indefenso, -sa *adj* **:** defenseless, helpless

indefinido, -da *adj* **1 :** undefined, vague **2** INDETERMINADO **:** indefinite — **indefinidamente** *adv*

indeleble *adj* **:** indelible — **indeleblemente** *adv*

indelicado, -da *adj* **:** indelicate, tactless

indemnización *nf, pl* **-ciones 1 :** indemnity **2 indemnización por despido :** severance pay

indemnizar {21} *vt* **:** to indemnify, to compensate

independencia *nf* **:** independence

independiente *adj* : independent — **independientemente** *adv*
independizarse {21} *vr* : to become independent, to gain independence
indescifrable *adj* : indecipherable
indescriptible *adj* : indescribable — **indescriptiblemente** *adv*
indeseable *adj & nmf* : undesirable
indestructible *adj* : indestructible
indeterminación *nf, pl* **-ciones** : indeterminacy
indeterminado, -da *adj* **1** INDEFINIDO : indefinite **2** : indeterminate
indexar *vt* INDICIAR : to index (wages, prices, etc.)
indicación *nf, pl* **-ciones 1** : sign, signal **2** : direction, instruction **3** : suggestion, hint
indicado, -da *adj* **1** APROPIADO : appropriate, suitable **2** : specified, indicated <al día indicado : on the specified day>
indicador *nm* **1** : gauge, dial, meter **2** : indicator <indicadores económicos : economic indicators>
indicar {72} *vt* **1** SEÑALAR : to indicate **2** ENSEÑAR, MOSTRAR : to show
indicativo[1], **-va** *adj* : indicative
indicativo[2] *nm* : indicative (mood)
índice *nm* **1** : index **2** : index finger, forefinger **3** INDICIO : indication
indiciar *vt* : to index (prices, wages, etc.)
indicio *nm* : indication, sign
indiferencia *nf* : indifference
indiferente *adj* **1** : indifferent, unconcerned **2 ser indiferente** : to be of no concern <me es indiferente : it doesn't matter to me>
indígena[1] *adj* : indigenous, native
indígena[2] *nmf* : native
indigencia *nf* MISERIA : poverty, destitution
indigente *adj & nmf* : indigent
indigestarse *vr* **1** EMPACHARSE : to have indigestion **2** *fam* : to nauseate, to disgust <ese tipo se me indigesta : that guy makes me sick>
indigestión *nf, pl* **-tiones** EMPACHO : indigestion
indigesto, -ta *adj* : indigestible, difficult to digest
indignación *nf, pl* **-ciones** : indignation
indignado, -da *adj* : indignant
indignante *adj* : outrageous, infuriating
indignar *vt* : to outrage, to infuriate — **indignarse** *vr*
indignidad *nf* : indignity
indigno, -na *adj* : unworthy
indio[1], **-dia** *adj* **1** : American Indian, Indian, Amerindian **2** : Indian (from India)
indio[2], **-dia** *n* **1** : American Indian **2** : Indian (from India)
indirecta *nf* **1** : hint, innuendo **2 echar indirectas** *or* **lanzar indirectas** : to drop a hint, to insinuate
indirecto, -ta *adj* : indirect — **indirectamente** *adv*
indisciplina *nf* : indiscipline, unruliness
indisciplinado, -da *adj* : undisciplined, unruly
indiscreción *nf, pl* **-ciones 1** IMPRUDENCIA : indiscretion **2** : tactless remark
indiscreto, -ta *adj* IMPRUDENTE : indiscreet, imprudent — **indiscretamente** *adv*
indiscriminado, -da *adj* : indiscriminate — **indiscriminadamente** *adv*
indiscutible *adj* INCONTESTABLE, INCUESTIONABLE : indisputable, unquestionable — **indiscutiblemente** *adv*
indispensable *adj* : indispensable — **indispensablemente** *adv*
indisponer {60} *vt* **1** : to spoil, to upset **2** : to make ill — **indisponerse** *vr* **1** : to become ill **2 ~ con** : to fall out with
indisposición *nf, pl* **-ciones** : indisposition, illness
indispuesto, -ta *adj* : unwell, indisposed
indistinguible *adj* : indistinguishable
indistintamente *adv* **1** : indistinctly **2** : indiscriminately
indistinto, -ta *adj* : indistinct, vague, faint
individual *adj* : individual — **individualmente** *adv*
individualidad *nf* : individuality
individualismo *nm* : individualism
individualista[1] *adj* : individualistic
individualista[2] *nmf* : individualist
individualizar {21} *vt* : to individualize
individuo *nm* : individual, person
indivisible *adj* : indivisible — **indivisibilidad** *nf*
indocumentado, -da *n* : illegal immigrant
índole *nf* **1** : nature, character **2** CLASE, TIPO : sort, kind
indolencia *nf* : indolence, laziness
indolente *adj* : indolent, lazy
indoloro, -ra *adj* : painless
indomable *adj* **1** : indomitable **2** : unruly, unmanageable
indómito, -ta *adj* : indomitable
indonesio, -sia *adj & n* : Indonesian
inducción *nf, pl* **-ciones** : induction
inducir {61} *vt* **1** : to induce, to cause **2** : to infer, to deduce
inductivo, -va *adj* : inductive
indudable *adj* : unquestionable, beyond doubt
indudablemente *adv* : undoubtedly, unquestionably
indulgencia *nf* **1** : indulgence, leniency **2** : indulgence (in religion)
indulgente *adj* : indulgent, lenient
indultar *vt* : to pardon, to reprieve
indulto *nm* : pardon, reprieve
indumentaria *nf* : clothing, attire
industria *nf* : industry
industrial[1] *adj* : industrial

industrial² *nmf* : industrialist, manufacturer
industrialización *nf, pl* **-ciones** : industrialization
industrializar {21} *vt* : to industrialize
industrioso, -sa *adj* : industrious
inédito, -ta *adj* **1** : unpublished **2** : unprecedented
inefable *adj* : ineffable
ineficacia *nf* **1** : inefficiency **2** : ineffectiveness
ineficaz *adj, pl* **-caces 1** : inefficient **2** : ineffective — **ineficazmente** *adv*
ineficiencia *nf* : inefficiency
ineficiente *adj* : inefficient — **ineficientemente** *adv*
inelegancia *nf* : inelegance — **inelegante** *adj*
inelegible *adj* : ineligible — **inelegibilidad** *nf*
ineludible *adj* : inescapable, unavoidable — **ineludiblemente** *adv*
ineptitud *nf* : ineptitude, incompetence
inepto, -ta *adj* : inept, incompetent
inequidad *nf* : inequity
inequitativo, -va *adj* : inequitable
inequívoco, -ca *adj* : unequivocal, unmistakable — **inequívocamente** *adv*
inercia *nf* **1** : inertia **2** : apathy, passivity **3 por ~** : out of habit
inerme *adj* : unarmed, defenseless
inerte *adj* : inert
inescrupuloso, -sa *adj* : unscrupulous
inescrutable *adj* : inscrutable
inesperado, -da *adj* : unexpected — **inesperadamente** *adv*
inestabilidad *nf* : instability, unsteadiness
inestable *adj* : unstable, unsteady
inestimable *adj* : inestimable, invaluable
inevitabilidad *nf* : inevitability
inevitable *adj* : inevitable, unavoidable — **inevitablemente** *adv*
inexactitud *nf* : inaccuracy
inexacto, -ta *adj* : inexact, inaccurate
inexcusable *adj* : inexcusable, unforgivable
inexistencia *nf* : lack, nonexistence
inexistente *adj* : nonexistent
inexorable *adj* : inexorable — **inexorablemente** *adv*
inexperiencia *nf* : inexperience
inexperto, -ta *adj* : inexperienced, unskilled
inexplicable *adj* : inexplicable — **inexplicablemente** *adv*
inexplorado, -da *adj* : unexplored
inexpresable *adj* : inexpressible
inexpresivo, -va *adj* : inexpressive, expressionless
inextinguible *adj* **1** : inextinguishable **2** : unquenchable
inextricable *adj* : inextricable — **inextricablemente** *adv*
infalible *adj* : infallible — **infaliblemente** *adv*
infame *adj* **1** : infamous **2** : loathsome, vile <tiempo infame : terrible weather>
infamia *nf* : infamy, disgrace
infancia *nf* **1** NIÑEZ : infancy, childhood **2** : children *pl* **3** : beginnings *pl*
infante *nm* **1** : infante, prince **2** : infantryman
infantería *nf* : infantry
infantil *adj* **1** : childish, infantile **2** : child's, children's
infarto *nm* : heart attack
infatigable *adj* : indefatigable, tireless — **infatigablemente** *adv*
infección *nf, pl* **-ciones** : infection
infeccioso, -sa *adj* : infectious
infectar *vt* : to infect — **infectarse** *vr*
infecto, -ta *adj* **1** : infected **2** : repulsive, sickening
infecundidad *nf* : infertility
infecundo, -da *adj* : infertile, barren
infelicidad *nf* : unhappiness
infeliz¹ *adj, pl* **-lices 1** : unhappy **2** : hapless, unfortunate, wretched
infeliz² *nmf, pl* **-lices** : wretch
inferior¹ *adj* : inferior, lower
inferior² *nmf* : inferior, underling
inferioridad *nf* : inferiority
inferir {76} *vt* **1** DEDUCIR : to infer, to deduce **2** : to cause (harm or injury), to inflict
infernal *adj* : infernal, hellish
infestación *n, pl* **-ciones** : infestation
infestar *vt* **1** : to infest **2** : to overrun, to invade
infición *nf, pl* **-ciones** *Mex* : pollution
infidelidad *nf* : unfaithfulness, infidelity
infiel¹ *adj* : unfaithful, disloyal
infiel² *nmf* : infidel, heathen
infierno *nm* **1** : hell **2 el quinto infierno** : the middle of nowhere
infiltrar *vt* : to infiltrate — **infiltrarse** *vr* — **infiltración** *nf*
infinidad *nf* **1** : infinity **2** SINFÍN : great number, huge quantity <una infinidad de veces : countless times>
infinitesimal *adj* : infinitesimal
infinitivo *nm* : infinitive
infinito¹ *adv* : infinitely, vastly
infinito², -ta *adj* **1** : infinite **2** : limitless, endless **3 hasta lo infinito** : ad infinitum — **infinitamente** *adv*
infinito³ *nm* : infinity
inflable *adj* : inflatable
inflación *nf, pl* **-ciones** : inflation
inflacionario, -ria *adj* : inflationary
inflamable *adj* : flammable
inflamación *nf, pl* **-ciones** : inflammation
inflamar *vt* : to inflame
inflamatorio, -ria *adj* : inflammatory
inflar *vt* HINCHAR : to inflate — **inflarse** *vr* **1** : to swell **2** : to become conceited
inflexibilidad *nf* : inflexibility
inflexible *adj* : inflexible, unyielding
inflexión *nf, pl* **-xiones** : inflection
infligir {35} *vt* : to inflict
influencia *nf* INFLUJO : influence

influenciable *adj* : easily influenced, suggestible
influenciar *vt* : to influence
influenza *nf* : influenza
influir {41} *vt* : to influence — *vi* **~ en** *or* **~ sobre** : to have an influence on, to affect
influjo *nm* INFLUENCIA : influence
influyente *adj* : influential
información *nf, pl* **-ciones 1** : information **2** INFORME : report, inquiry **3** NOTICIAS : news
informado, -da *adj* : informed <bien informado : well-informed>
informador, -dora *n* : informer, informant
informal *adj* **1** : unreliable (of persons) **2** : informal, casual — **informalmente** *adv*
informalidad *nf* : informality
informante *nmf* : informant
informar *vt* ENTERAR : to inform — *vi* : to report — **informarse** *vr* ENTERARSE : to get information, to find out
informática *nf* : computer science, computing
informativo¹, -va *adj* : informative
informativo² *nm* : news program, news
informatización *nf, pl* **-ciones** : computerization
informatizar {21} *vt* : to computerize
informe¹ *adj* AMORFO : shapeless, formless
informe² *nm* **1** : report **2** : reference (for employment) **3** INFORMES *nmpl* : information, data
infortunado, -da *adj* : unfortunate, unlucky
infortunio *nm* **1** DESGRACIA : misfortune **2** CONTRATIEMPO : mishap
infracción *nf, pl* **-ciones** : violation, offense, infraction
infractor, -tora *n* : offender
infraestructura *nf* : infrastructure
infrahumano, -na *adj* : subhuman
infranqueable *adj* **1** : impassable **2** : insurmountable
infrarrojo, -ja *adj* : infrared
infrecuente *adj* : infrequent
infringir {35} *vt* : to infringe, to breach
infructuoso, -sa *adj* : fruitless — **infructuosamente** *adv*
ínfulas *nfpl* **1** : conceit **2 darse ínfulas** : to put on airs
infundado, -da *adj* : unfounded, baseless
infundio *nm* : false story, lie, tall tale <todo eso son infundios : that's a pack of lies>
infundir *vt* **1** : to instill **2 infundir ánimo a** : to encourage **3 infundir miedo a** : to intimidate
infusión *nf, pl* **-siones** : infusion
ingeniar *vt* : to devise, to think up — **ingeniarse** *vr* : to manage, to find a way
ingeniería *nf* : engineering
ingeniero, -ra *n* : engineer
ingenio *nm* **1** : ingenuity **2** CHISPA : wit, wits **3** : device, apparatus **4 ingenio azucarero** : sugar refinery
ingenioso, -sa *adj* **1** : ingenious **2** : clever, witty — **ingeniosamente** *adv*
ingente *adj* : huge, enormous
ingenuidad *nf* : naïveté, ingenuousness
ingenuo¹, -nua *adj* CÁNDIDO : naive — **ingenuamente** *adv*
ingenuo², -nua *n* : naive person
ingerencia → **injerencia**
ingerir {76} *vt* : to ingest, to consume
ingestión *nf, pl* **-tiones** : ingestion
ingle *nf* : groin
inglés¹, -glesa *adj, mpl* **ingleses** : English
inglés², -glesa *n, mpl* **ingleses** : Englishman *m,* Englishwoman *f*
inglés³ *nm* : English (language)
inglete *nm* : miter joint
ingobernable *adj* : ungovernable, lawless
ingratitud *nf* : ingratitude
ingrato¹, -ta *adj* **1** : ungrateful **2** : thankless
ingrato², -ta *n* : ingrate
ingrediente *nm* : ingredient
ingresar *vt* **1** : to admit <ingresaron a Luis al hospital : Luis was admitted into the hospital> **2** : to deposit — *vi* **1** : to enter, to go in **2 ~ en** : to join, to enroll in
ingreso *nm* **1** : entrance, entry **2** : admission **3 ingresos** *nmpl* : income, earnings *pl*
íngrimo, -ma *adj* : all alone, all by oneself
inhábil *adj* : unskillful, clumsy
inhabilidad *nf* **1** : unskillfulness **2** : unfitness
inhabilitar *vt* **1** : to disqualify, to bar **2** : to disable
inhabitable *adj* : uninhabitable
inhabituado, -da *adj* **~ a** : unaccustomed to
inhalante *nm* : inhalant
inhalar *vt* : to inhale — **inhalación** *nf*
inherente *adj* : inherent
inhibición *nf, pl* **-ciones** COHIBICIÓN : inhibition
inhibir *vt* : to inhibit — **inhibirse** *vr*
inhóspito, -ta *adj* : inhospitable
inhumación *nf, pl* **-ciones** : interment, burial
inhumanidad *nf* : inhumanity
inhumano, -na *adj* : inhuman, cruel, inhumane
inhumar *vt* : to inter, to bury
iniciación *nf, pl* **-ciones 1** : initiation **2** : introduction
iniciado, -da *n* : initiate
iniciador¹, -dora *adj* : initiatory
iniciador², -dora *n* : initiator, originator
inicial¹ *adj* : initial, original — **inicialmente** *adv*
inicial² *nf* : initial (letter)

iniciar *vt* COMENZAR : to initiate, to begin — **iniciarse** *vr*
iniciativa *nf* : initiative
inicio *nm* COMIENZO : beginning
inicuo, -cua *adj* : iniquitous, wicked
inigualado, -da *adj* : unequaled
inimaginable *adj* : unimaginable
inimitable *adj* : inimitable
ininteligible *adj* : unintelligible
ininterrumpido, -da *adj* : uninterrupted, continuous — **ininterrumpidamente** *adv*
iniquidad *nf* : iniquity, wickedness
injerencia *nf* : interference
injerirse {76} *vr* ENTROMETERSE, INMISCUIRSE : to meddle, to interfere
injertar *vt* : to graft
injerto *nm* : graft <injerto de piel : skin graft>
injuria *nf* AGRAVIO : affront, insult
injuriar *vt* INSULTAR : to insult, to revile
injurioso, -sa *adj* : insulting, abusive
injusticia *nf* : injustice, unfairness
injustificable *adj* : unjustifiable
injustificadamente *adv* : unjustifiably, unfairly
injustificado, -da *adj* : unjustified, unwarranted
injusto, -ta *adj* : unfair, unjust — **injustamente** *adv*
inmaculado, -da *adj* : immaculate, spotless
inmadurez *nf, pl* **-reces** : immaturity
inmaduro, -ra *adj* **1** : immature **2** : unripe
inmediaciones *nfpl* : environs, surrounding area
inmediatamente *adv* ENSEGUIDA : immediately
inmediatez *nf, pl* **-teces** : immediacy
inmediato, -ta *adj* **1** : immediate **2** CONTIGUO : adjoining **3 de ~** : immediately, right away **4 ~ a** : next to, close to
inmejorable *adj* : excellent, unbeatable
inmensidad *nf* : immensity, vastness
inmenso, -sa *adj* ENORME : immense, huge, vast — **inmensamente** *adv*
inmensurable *adj* : boundless, immeasurable
inmerecido, -da *adj* : undeserved — **inmerecidamente** *adv*
inmersión *nf, pl* **-siones** : immersion
inmerso, -sa *adj* **1** : immersed **2** : involved, absorbed
inmigración *nf, pl* **-ciones** : immigration
inmigrado, -da *adj & n* : immigrant
inmigrante *adj & nmf* : immigrant
inmigrar *vi* : to immigrate
inminencia *nf* : imminence
inminente *adj* : imminent — **inminentemente** *adv*
inmiscuirse {41} *vr* ENTROMETERSE, INJERIRSE : to meddle, to interfere
inmobiliario, -ria *adj* : real estate, property
inmoderación *n, pl* **-ciones** : immoderation, intemperance
inmoderado, -da *adj* : immoderate, excessive — **inmoderamente** *adv*
inmodestia *nf* : immodesty — **inmodesto, -ta** *adj*
inmolar *vt* : to immolate — **inmolación** *nf*
inmoral *adj* : immoral
inmoralidad *nf* : immorality
inmortal *adj & nmf* : immortal
inmortalidad *nf* : immortality
inmortalizar {21} *vt* : to immortalize
inmotivado, -da *adj* **1** : unmotivated **2** : groundless
inmovible *adj* : immovable, fixed
inmóvil *adj* **1** : still, motionless **2** : steadfast
inmovilidad *nf* : immobility
inmovilizar {21} *vt* : to immobilize
inmueble *nm* : building, property
inmundicia *nf* : dirt, filth, trash
inmundo, -da *adj* : dirty, filthy, nasty
inmune *adj* : immune
inmunidad *nf* : immunity
inmunizar {21} *vt* : to immunize — **inmunización** *nf*
inmunología *nf* : immunology
inmunológico, -ca *adj* : immune <sistema inmunológico : immune system>
inmutabilidad *nf* : immutability
inmutable *adj* : immutable, unchangeable
innato, -ta *adj* : innate, inborn
innecesario, -ria *adj* : unnecessary — **innecesariamente** *adv*
innegable *adj* : undeniable
innoble *adj* : ignoble — **innoblemente** *adv*
innovación *nf, pl* **-ciones** : innovation
innovador, -dora *adj* : innovative
innovar *vt* : to introduce — *vi* : to innovate
innumerable *adj* INCONTABLE : innumerable, countless
inobjetable *adj* : indisputable, unobjectionable
inocencia *nf* : innocence
inocente[1] *adj* **1** : innocent **2** INGENUO : naive — **inocentemente** *adv*
inocente[2] *nmf* : innocent person
inocentón[1], **-tona** *adj, mpl* **-tones** : naive, gullible
inocentón[2], **-tona** *n, mpl* **-tones** : simpleton, dupe
inocuidad *nf* : harmlessness
inocular *vt* : to inoculate, to vaccinate — **inoculación** *nf*
inocuo, -cua *adj* : innocuous, harmless
inodoro[1], **-ra** *adj* : odorless
inodoro[2] *nm* : toilet
inofensivo, -va *adj* : inoffensive, harmless
inolvidable *adj* : unforgettable
inoperable *adj* : inoperable
inoperante *adj* : ineffective, inoperative

inopinado, -da *adj* : unexpected — **inopinadamente** *adv*
inoportuno, -na *adj* : untimely, inopportune, inappropriate
inorgánico, -ca *adj* : inorganic
inoxidable *adj* **1** : rustproof **2 acero inoxidable** : stainless steel
inquebrantable *adj* : unshakable, unwavering
inquietante *adj* : disturbing, worrisome
inquietar *vt* PREOCUPAR : to disturb, to upset, to worry — **inquietarse** *vr*
inquieto, -ta *adj* **1** : anxious, uneasy, worried **2** : restless
inquietud *nf* **1** : anxiety, uneasiness, worry **2** AGITACIÓN : restlessness
inquilinato *nm* : tenancy
inquilino, -na *n* : tenant, occupant
inquina *nf* **1** : aversion, dislike **2** : ill will <tener inquina a alguien : to have a grudge against someone>
inquirir {4} *vi* : to make inquiries — *vt* : to investigate
inquisición *nf, pl* **-ciones** : investigation, inquiry
inquisidor, -dora *adj* : inquisitive
inquisitivo, -va *adj* : inquisitive, curious — **inquisitivamente** *adv*
insaciable *adj* : insatiable
insalubre *adj* **1** : unhealthy **2** ANTIHIGIÉNICO : unsanitary
insalubridad *nf* : unhealthiness
insalvable *adj* : insuperable, insurmountable
insano, -na *adj* **1** LOCO : insane, mad **2** INSALUBRE : unhealthy
insatisfacción *nf, pl* **-ciones** : dissatisfaction
insatisfactorio *nm* : unsatisfactory
insatisfecho, -cha *adj* **1** : dissatisfied **2** : unsatisfied
inscribir {33} *vt* **1** MATRICULAR : to enroll, to register **2** GRABAR : to engrave — **inscribirse** *vr* : to register, to sign up
inscripción *nf, pl* **-ciones 1** MATRÍCULA : enrollment, registration **2** : inscription
inscrito *pp* → **inscribir**
insecticida[1] *adj* : insecticidal
insecticida[2] *nm* : insecticide
insecto *nm* : insect
inseguridad *nf* **1** : insecurity **2** : lack of safety **3** : uncertainty
inseguro, -ra *adj* **1** : insecure **2** : unsafe **3** : uncertain
inseminar *vt* : to inseminate — **inseminación** *nf*
insensatez *nf, pl* **-teces** : foolishness, stupidity
insensato[1], **-ta** *adj* : foolish, senseless
insensato[2], **-ta** *n* : fool
insensibilidad *nf* : insensitivity
insensible *adj* : insensitive, unfeeling
inseparable *adj* : inseparable — **inseparablemente** *adv*
inserción *nf, pl* **-ciones** : insertion
insertar *vt* : to insert
inservible *adj* INÚTIL : useless, unusable
insidia *nf* **1** : snare, trap **2** : malice
insidioso, -sa *adj* : insidious
insigne *adj* : noted, famous
insignia *nf* ENSEÑA : insignia, emblem, badge
insignificancia *nf* **1** : insignificance **2** NIMIEDAD : trifle, triviality
insignificante *adj* : insignificant
insincero, -ra *adj* : insincere — **insinceridad** *nf*
insinuación *nf, pl* **-ciones** : insinuation, hint
insinuante *adj* : suggestive
insinuar {3} *vt* : to insinuate, to hint at — **insinuarse** *vr* **1 ~ a** : to make advances to **2 ~ en** : to worm one's way into
insipidez *nf, pl* **-deces** : insipidness, blandness
insípido, -da *adj* : insipid, bland
insistencia *nf* : insistence
insistente *adj* : insistent — **insistentemente** *adv*
insistir *v* : to insist
insociable *adj* : unsociable
insolación *nf, pl* **-ciones** : sunstroke
insolencia *nf* IMPERTINENCIA : insolence
insolente *adj* IMPERTINENTE : insolent
insólito, -ta *adj* : rare, unusual
insoluble *adj* : insoluble — **insolubilidad** *nf*
insolvencia *nf* : insolvency, bankruptcy
insolvente *adj* : insolvent, bankrupt
insomne *adj & nmf* : insomniac
insomnio *nm* : insomnia
insondable *adj* : fathomless, deep
insonorizado, -da *adj* : soundproof
insoportable *adj* INAGUANTABLE : unbearable, intolerable
insoslayable *adj* : unavoidable, inescapable
insospechado, -da *adj* : unexpected, unforeseen
insostenible *adj* : untenable
inspección *nf, pl* **-ciones** : inspection
inspeccionar *vt* : to inspect
inspector, -tora *n* : inspector
inspiración *nf, pl* **-ciones 1** : inspiration **2** INHALACIÓN : inhalation
inspirador, -dora *adj* : inspiring
inspirar *vt* : to inspire — *vi* INHALAR : to inhale
instalación *nf, pl* **-ciones** : installation
instalar *vt* **1** : to install **2** : to instate — **instalarse** *vr* ESTABLECERSE : to settle, to establish oneself
instancia *nf* **1** : petition, request **2 en última instancia** : as a last resort
instantánea *nf* : snapshot
instantáneo, -nea *adj* : instantaneous — **instantáneamente** *adv*
instante *nm* **1** : instant, moment **2 al instante** : immediately **3 a cada instante** : frequently, all the time **4 por instantes** : constantly, incessantly

instar *vt* APREMIAR **:** to urge, to press — *vi* URGIR **:** to be urgent or pressing <insta que vayamos pronto **:** it is imperative that we leave soon>
instauración *nf, pl* **-ciones :** establishment
instaurar *vt* **:** to establish
instigador, -dora *n* **:** instigator
instigar {52} *vt* **:** to instigate, to incite
instintivo, -va *adj* **:** instinctive — **instintivamente** *adv*
instinto *nm* **:** instinct
institución *nf, pl* **-ciones :** institution
institucional *adj* **:** institutional — **institucionalmente** *adv*
institucionalización *nf, pl* **-ciones :** institutionalization
institucionalizar {21} *vt* **:** to institutionalize
instituir {41} *vt* ESTABLECER, FUNDAR **:** to institute, to establish, to found
instituto *nm* **:** institute
institutriz *nf, pl* **-trices :** governess *f*
instrucción *nf, pl* **-ciones 1** EDUCACIÓN **:** education **2 instrucciones** *nfpl* **:** instructions, directions
instructivo, -va *adj* **:** instructive, educational
instructor, -tora *n* **:** instructor
instruir {41} *vt* **1** ADIESTRAR **:** to instruct, to train **2** ENSEÑAR **:** to educate, to teach
instrumentación *nf, pl* **-ciones :** orchestration
instrumental *adj* **:** instrumental
instrumentar *vt* **:** to orchestrate
instrumentista *nmf* **:** instrumentalist
instrumento *nm* **:** instrument
insubordinado, -da *adj* **:** insubordinate — **insubordinación** *nf*
insubordinarse *vr* **:** to rebel
insuficiencia *nf* **1 :** insufficiency, inadequacy **2 insuficiencia cardíaca :** heart failure
insuficiente *adj* **:** insufficient, inadequate — **insuficientemente** *adv*
insufrible *adj* **:** insufferable
insular *adj* **:** insular
insulina *nf* **:** insulin
insulso, -sa *adj* **1** INSÍPIDO **:** insipid, bland **2 :** dull
insultante *adj* **:** insulting
insultar *vt* **:** to insult
insulto *nm* **:** insult
insumos *nmpl* **:** supplies <insumos agrícolas **:** agricultural supplies>
insuperable *adj* **:** insuperable, insurmountable
insurgente *adj & nmf* **:** insurgent — **insurgencia** *nf*
insurrección *nf, pl* **-ciones :** insurrection, uprising
insustancial *adj* **:** insubstantial, flimsy
insustituible *adj* **:** irreplaceable
intachable *adj* **:** irreproachable, faultless
intacto, -ta *adj* **:** intact
intangible *adj* IMPALPABLE **:** intangible, impalpable
integración *nf, pl* **-ciones :** integration
integral *adj* **1 :** integral, essential **2 pan integral :** whole grain bread
integrante[1] *adj* **:** integrating, integral
integrante[2] *nmf* **:** member
integrar *vt* **:** to make up, to compose — **integrarse** *vr* **:** to integrate, to fit in
integridad *nf* **1** RECTITUD **:** integrity, honesty **2 :** wholeness, completeness
integrismo *nm* **:** fundamentalism
integrista *adj & nmf* **:** fundamentalist
íntegro, -gra *adj* **1 :** honest, upright **2** ENTERO **:** whole, complete **3 :** unabridged
intelecto *nm* **:** intellect
intelectual *adj & nmf* **:** intellectual — **intelectualmente** *adv*
intelectualidad *nf* **:** intelligentsia
inteligencia *nf* **:** intelligence
inteligente *adj* **:** intelligent — **inteligentemente** *adv*
inteligible *adj* **:** intelligible — **inteligibilidad** *nf*
intemperancia *adj* **:** intemperance, excess
intemperie *nf* **1 :** bad weather, elements *pl* **2 a la intemperie :** in the open air, outside
intempestivo, -va *adj* **:** inopportune, untimely — **intempestivamente** *adv*
intención *nf, pl* **-ciones :** intention, plan
intencional *adj* **:** intentional — **intencionalmente** *adv*
intendencia *nf* **:** management, administration
intendente *nmf* **:** quartermaster
intensidad *nf* **:** intensity
intensificar {72} *vt* **:** to intensify — **intensificarse** *vr*
intensivo, -va *adj* **:** intensive — **intensivamente** *adv*
intenso, -sa *adj* **:** intense — **intensamente** *adv*
intentar *vt* **:** to attempt, to try
intento *nm* **1** PROPÓSITO **:** intent, intention **2** TENTATIVA **:** attempt, try
interacción *nf, pl* **-ciones :** interaction
interactivo, -va *adj* **:** interactive
interactuar {3} *vi* **:** to interact
intercalar *vt* **:** to intersperse, to insert
intercambiable *adj* **:** interchangeable
intercambiar *vt* CANJEAR **:** to exchange, to trade
intercambio *nm* CANJE **:** exchange, trade
interceder *vi* **:** to intercede
intercepción *nf, pl* **-ciones :** interception
interceptar *vt* **1 :** to intercept, to block **2 interceptar las líneas :** to wiretap
intercesión *nf, pl* **-siones :** intercession
intercomunicación *nf, pl* **-ciones :** intercommunication
interconexión *nf, pl* **-xiones :** interconnection
interconfesional *adj* **:** interdenominational

interdependencia *nf* **:** interdependence — **interdependiente** *adj*

interdicción *nf, pl* **-ciones :** interdiction, prohibition

interés *nm, pl* **-reses :** interest

interesado, -da *adj* **1 :** interested **2 :** selfish, self-seeking

interesante *adj* **:** interesting

interesar *vt* **:** to interest — *vi* **:** to be of interest, to be interesting — **interesarse** *vr*

interestatal *adj* **:** interstate <autopista interestatal : interstate highway>

interestelar *adj* **:** interstellar

interfaz *nf, pl* **-faces :** interface

interferencia *nf* **:** interference, static

interferir {76} *vi* **:** to interfere, to meddle — *vt* **:** to interfere with, to obstruct

interín[1] *or* **ínterin** *adv* **:** meanwhile

interín[2] *or* **ínterin** *nm, pl* **-rines :** meantime, interim <en el interín : in the meantime>

interinamente *adv* **:** temporarily

interino, -na *adj* **:** acting, temporary, interim

interior[1] *adj* **:** interior, inner

interior[2] *nm* **1 :** interior, inside **2 :** inland region

interiormente *adv* **:** inwardly

interjección *nf, pl* **-ciones :** interjection

interlocutor, -tora *n* **:** interlocutor, speaker

intermediario, -ria *adj & n* **:** intermediary, go-between

intermedio[1], **-dia** *adj* **:** intermediate

intermedio[2] *nm* **1 :** intermission **2 por intermedio de :** by means of

interminable *adj* **:** interminable, endless — **interminablemente** *adv*

intermisión *nf, pl* **-siones :** intermission, pause

intermitente[1] *adj* **1 :** intermittent **2 luz intermitente :** strobe light — **intermitentemente** *adv*

intermitente[2] *nm* **:** blinker, turn signal

internacional *adj* **:** international — **internacionalmente** *adv*

internacionalismo *nm* **:** internationalism

internacionalizar {21} *vt* **:** to internationalize

internado *nm* **:** boarding school

internar *vt* **:** to commit, to confine — **internarse** *vr* **1 :** to penetrate, to advance into **2 ~ en :** to go into, to enter

internista *nmf* **:** internist

interno[1], **-na** *adj* **:** internal — **internamente** *adv*

interno[2], **-na** *n* **1 :** intern **2 :** inmate, internee

interpelación *nf, pl* **-ciones :** appeal, plea

interpelar *vt* **:** to question (formally)

interpolar *vt* **:** to insert, to interpolate

interponer {60} *vt* **:** to interpose — **interponerse** *vr* **:** to intervene

interpretación *nf, pl* **-ciones :** interpretation

interpretar *vt* **1 :** to interpret **2 :** to play, to perform

interpretativo, -va *adj* **:** interpretive

intérprete *nmf* **1** TRADUCTOR **:** interpreter **2 :** performer

interpuesto *pp* → **interponer**

interracial *adj* **:** interracial

interrelación *nf, pl* **-ciones :** interrelationship

interrelacionar *vi* **:** to interrelate

interrogación *nf, pl* **-ciones 1 :** interrogation, questioning **2 signo de interrogación :** question mark

interrogador, -dora *n* **:** interrogator, questioner

interrogante[1] *adj* **:** questioning

interrogante[2] *nm* **1 :** question mark **2 :** query

interrogar {52} *vt* **:** to interrogate, to question

interrogativo, -va *adj* **:** interrogative

interrogatorio *nm* **:** interrogation, questioning

interrumpir *v* **:** to interrupt

interrupción *nf, pl* **-ciones :** interruption

interruptor *nm* **1 :** (electrical) switch **2 :** circuit breaker

intersección *nf, pl* **-ciones :** intersection

intersticio *nm* **:** interstice — **intersticial** *adj*

intervalo *nm* **:** interval

intervención *nf, pl* **-ciones 1 :** intervention **2 :** audit **3 intervención quirúrgica :** operation

intervencionista *adj & nmf* **:** interventionist

intervenir {87} *vi* **1 :** to take part **2** INTERCEDER **:** to intervene, to intercede — *vt* **1 :** to control, to supervise **2 :** to audit **3 :** to operate on **4 :** to tap (a telephone)

interventor, -tora *n* **1 :** inspector **2 :** auditor, comptroller

intestado, -da *adj* **:** intestate

intestinal *adj* **:** intestinal

intestino *nm* **:** intestine

intimar *vi* **~ con :** to become friendly with — *vt* **:** to require, to call on

intimidación *nf, pl* **-ciones :** intimidation

intimidad *nf* **1 :** intimacy **2 :** privacy, private life

intimidar *vt* ACOBARDAR **:** to intimidate

íntimo, -ma *adj* **1 :** intimate, close **2** PRIVADO **:** private — **íntimamente** *adv*

intitular *vt* **:** to entitle, to title

intocable *adj* **:** untouchable

intolerable *adj* **:** intolerable, unbearable

intolerancia *nf* **:** intolerance

intolerante[1] *adj* **:** intolerant

intolerante[2] *nmf* **:** intolerant person, bigot

intoxicación *nf, pl* **-ciones :** poisoning

intoxicante *nm* **:** poison

intoxicar {72} *vt* : to poison
intranquilidad *nf* PREOCUPACIÓN : worry, anxiety
intranquilizar {21} *vt* : to upset, to make uneasy — **intranquilizarse** *vr* : to get worried, to be anxious
intranquilo, -la *adj* PREOCUPADO : uneasy, worried
intransigencia *nf* : intransigence
intransigente *adj* : intransigent, unyielding
intransitable *adj* : impassable
intransitivo, -va *adj* : intransitive
intrascendente *adj* : unimportant, insignificant
intratable *adj* **1** : intractable **2** : awkward **3** : unsociable
intravenoso, -sa *adj* : intravenous
intrepidez *nf* : fearlessness
intrépido, -da *adj* : intrepid, fearless
intriga *nf* : intrigue
intrigante *nmf* : schemer
intrigar {52} *v* : to intrigue — **intrigante** *adj*
intrincado, -da *adj* : intricate, involved
intrínseco, -ca *adj* : intrinsic — **intrínsecamente** *adv*
introducción *nf, pl* **-ciones** : introduction
introducir {61} *vt* **1** : to introduce **2** : to bring in **3** : to insert **4** : to input, to enter — **introducirse** *vr* : to penetrate, to get into
introductorio, -ria *adj* : introductory
intromisión *nf, pl* **-siones** : interference, meddling
introspección *nf, pl* **-ciones** : introspection
introspectivo, -va *adj* : introspective
introvertido[1], **-da** *adj* : introverted
introvertido[2], **-da** *n* : introvert
intrusión *nf, pl* **-siones** : intrusion
intruso[1], **-sa** *adj* : intrusive
intruso[2], **-sa** *n* : intruder
intuición *nf, pl* **-ciones** : intuition
intuir {41} *vt* : to intuit, to sense
intuitivo, -va *adj* : intuitive — **intuitivamente** *adv*
inundación *nf, pl* **-ciones** : flood, inundation
inundar *vt* : to flood, to inundate
inusitado, -da *adj* : unusual, uncommon — **inusitadamente** *adv*
inusual *adj* : unusual, uncommon — **inusualmente** *adv*
inútil[1] *adj* INSERVIBLE : useless — **inútilmente** *adv*
inútil[2] *nmf* : good-for-nothing
inutilidad *nf* : uselessness
inutilizar {21} *vt* **1** : to make useless **2** INCAPACITAR : to disable, to put out of commission
invadir *vt* : to invade
invalidar *vt* : to nullify, to invalidate
invalidez *nf, pl* **-deces 1** : invalidity **2** : disablement
inválido, -da *adj & n* : invalid
invariable *adj* : invariable — **invariablemente** *adv*
invasión *nf, pl* **-siones** : invasion
invasivo, -va *adj* : invasive
invasor[1], **-sora** *adj* : invading
invasor[2], **-sora** *n* : invader
invectiva *nf* : invective, abuse
invencible *adj* **1** : invincible **2** : insurmountable
invención *nf, pl* **-ciones 1** INVENTO : invention **2** MENTIRA : fabrication, lie
inventar *vt* **1** : to invent **2** : to fabricate, to make up
inventariar {85} *vt* : to inventory
inventario *nm* : inventory
inventiva *nf* : ingenuity, inventiveness
inventivo, -va *adj* : inventive
invento *nm* INVENCIÓN : invention
inventor, -tora *n* : inventor
invernadero *nm* : greenhouse, hothouse
invernal *adj* : winter, wintry
invernar {55} *vi* **1** : to spend the winter **2** HIBERNAR : to hibernate
inverosímil *adj* : unlikely, farfetched
inversión *nf, pl* **-siones 1** : inversion **2** : investment
inversionista *nmf* : investor
inverso[1], **-sa** *adj* **1** : inverse, inverted **2** CONTRARIO : opposite **3 a la inversa** : on the contrary, vice versa **4 en orden inverso** : in reverse order — **inversamente** *adv*
inverso[2] *n* : inverse
inversor, -sora *n* : investor
invertebrado[1], **-da** *adj* : invertebrate
invertebrado[2] *nm* : invertebrate
invertir {76} *vt* **1** : to invert, to reverse **2** : to invest — *vi* : to make an investment — **invertirse** *vr* : to be reversed
investidura *nf* : investiture, inauguration
investigación *nf, pl* **-ciones 1** ENCUESTA, INDAGACIÓN : investigation, inquiry **2** : research
investigador[1], **-dora** *adj* : investigative
investigador[2], **-dora** *n* **1** : investigator **2** : researcher
investigar {52} *vt* **1** INDAGAR : to investigate **2** : to research — *vi* ~ **sobre** : to do research into
investir {54} *vt* **1** : to empower **2** : to swear in, to inaugurate
inveterado, -da *adj* : inveterate, deep-seated
invicto, -ta *adj* : undefeated
invidente[1] *adj* CIEGO : blind, sightless
invidente[2] *nmf* CIEGO : blind person
invierno *nm* : winter, wintertime
inviolable *adj* : inviolable — **inviolabilidad** *nf*
inviolado, -da *adj* : inviolate, pure
invisibilidad *nf* : invisibility
invisible *adj* : invisible — **invisiblemente** *adv*
invitación *nf, pl* **-ciones** : invitation
invitado, -da *n* : guest

invitar *vt* : to invite

invocación *nf, pl* **-ciones** : invocation

invocar {72} *vt* : to invoke, to call on

involucramiento *nm* : involvement

involucrar *vt* : to implicate, to involve — **involucrarse** *vr* : to get involved

involuntario, -ria *adj* : involuntary — **involuntariamente** *adv*

invulnerable *adj* : invulnerable

inyección *nf, pl* **-ciones** : injection, shot

inyectado, -da *adj* **ojos inyectados** : bloodshot eyes

inyectar *vt* : to inject

ion *nm* : ion

ionizar {21} *vt* : to ionize — **ionización** *nf*

ionosfera *nf* : ionosphere

ir {43} *vi* **1** : to go <ir a pie : to go on foot, to walk> <ir a caballo : to ride horseback> <ir a casa : to go home> **2** : to lead, to extend, to stretch <el camino va de Cali a Bogotá : the road goes from Cali to Bogotá> **3** FUNCIONAR : to work, to function <esta computadora ya no va : this computer doesn't work anymore> **4** : to get on, to get along <¿cómo te va? : how are you?, how's it going?> <el negocio no va bien : the business isn't doing well> **5** : to suit <ese vestido te va bien : that dress really suits you> **6 ~ con** : to be <ir con prisa : to be in a hurry> **7 ~ por** : to follow, to go along <fueron por la costa : they followed the shoreline> **8 dejarse ir** : to let oneself go **9 ir a parar** : to end up **10 vamos a ver** : let's see — *v aux* **1** (*with present participle*) <ir caminando : to walk> <¡voy corriendo! : I'll be right there!> **2 ~ a** : to be going to <voy a hacerlo : I'm going to do it> <el avión va a despegar : the plane is about to take off> — **irse** *vr* **1** : to leave, to go <¡vámonos! : let's go!> <todo el mundo se fue : everyone left> **2** ESCAPARSE : to leak **3** GASTARSE : to be used up, to be gone

ira *nf* CÓLERA, FURIA : wrath, anger

iracundo, -da *adj* : irate, angry

iraní *adj & nmf* : Iranian

iraquí *adj & nmf* : Iraqi

irascible *adj* : irascible, irritable — **irascibilidad** *nf*

irga, irgue, etc. → **erguir**

iridio *nm* : iridium

iridiscencia *nf* : iridescence — **iridiscente** *adj*

iris *nms & pl* **1** : iris **2 arco iris** : rainbow

irlandés[1], -desa *adj, mpl* **-deses** : Irish

irlandés[2], -desa *n, pl* **-deses** : Irish person, Irishman *m,* Irishwoman *f*

irlandés[3] *nm* : Irish (language)

ironía *nf* : irony

irónico, -ca *adj* : ironic, ironical — **irónicamente** *adv*

irracional *adj* : irrational — **irracionalmente** *adv*

irracionalidad *nf* : irrationality

irradiar *vt* : to radiate, to irradiate

irrazonable *adj* : unreasonable

irreal *adj* : unreal

irrebatible *adj* : unanswerable, irrefutable

irreconciliable *adj* : irreconcilable

irreconocible *adj* : unrecognizable

irrecuperable *adj* : irrecoverable, irretrievable

irredimible *adj* : irredeemable

irreductible *adj* : unyielding

irreemplazable *adj* : irreplaceable

irreflexión *nf, pl* **-xiones** : thoughtlessness, impetuosity

irreflexivo, -va *adj* : rash, unthinking — **irreflexivamente** *adv*

irrefrenable *adj* : uncontrollable, unstoppable <un impulso irrefrenable : an irresistible urge>

irrefutable *adj* : irrefutable

irregular *adj* : irregular — **irregularmente** *adv*

irregularidad *nf* : irregularity

irrelevante *adj* : irrelevant — **irrelevancia** *nf*

irreligioso, -sa *adj* : irreligious

irremediable *adj* : incurable — **irremediablemente** *adv*

irreparable *adj* : irreparable

irreprimible *adj* : irrepressible

irreprochable *adj* : irreproachable

irresistible adj : irresistible — **irresistiblemente** adv

irresolución *nf, pl* **-ciones** : indecision, hesitation

irresoluto, -ta *adj* INDECISO : undecided

irrespeto *nm* : disrespect

irrespetuoso, -sa *adj* : disrespectful — **irrespetuosamente** *adv*

irresponsabilidad *nf* : irresponsibility

irresponsable *adj* : irresponsible — **irresponsablemente** *adv*

irrestricto, -ta *adj* : unrestricted, unconditional <apoyo irrestricto : unconditional support>

irreverencia *nf* : disrespect

irreverente *adj* : disrespectful

irreversible *adj* : irreversible

irrevocable *adj* : irrevocable — **irrevocablemente** *adv*

irrigar {52} *vt* : to irrigate — **irrigación** *nf*

irrisible *adj* : laughable

irrisión *nf, pl* **-siones** : derision, ridicule

irrisorio, -ria *adj* RISIBLE : ridiculous, ludicrous

irritabilidad *nf* : irritability

irritable *adj* : irritable

irritación *nf, pl* **-ciones** : irritation

irritante *adj* : irritating

irritar *vt* : to irritate — **irritación** *nf*

irrompible *adj* : unbreakable

irrumpir *vi* **~ en** : to burst into

irrupción *nf, pl* **-ciones** **1** : irruption **2** : invasion

isla *nf* : island

islámico, -ca *adj* : Islamic, Muslim

islandés[1], -desa *adj, mpl* **-deses** : Icelandic

islandés[2], -desa *n, mpl* **-deses** : Icelander

islandés[3] *nm* : Icelandic (language)

isleño, -ña *n* : islander

islote *nm* : islet

isometría *nfs & pl* : isometrics

isométrico, -ca *adj* : isometric

isósceles *adj* : isosceles <triángulo isósceles : isosceles triangle>

isótopo *nm* : isotope

israelí *adj & nmf* : Israeli

istmo *nm* : isthmus

itacate *nm Mex* : pack, provisions *pl*

italiano[1], -na *adj & n* : Italian

italiano[2] *nm* : Italian (language)

iterbio *nm* : ytterbium

itinerante *adj* AMBULANTE : traveling, itinerant

itinerario *nm* : itinerary, route

itrio *nm* : yttrium

izar {21} *vt* : to hoist, to raise <izar la bandera : to raise the flag>

izquierda *nf* : left

izquierdista *adj & nmf* : leftist

izquierdo, -da *adj* : left

J

j *nf* : tenth letter of the Spanish alphabet

jabalí *nm* : wild boar

jabalina *nf* : javelin

jabón *nm, pl* **jabones** : soap

jabonar *vt* ENJABONAR : to soap up, to lather — **jabonarse** *vr*

jabonera *nf* : soap dish

jabonoso, -sa *adj* : soapy

jaca *nf* **1** : pony **2** YEGUA : mare

jacal *nm Mex* : shack, hut

jacinto *nm* : hyacinth

jactancia *nf* **1** : boastfulness **2** : boasting, bragging

jactancioso[1], -sa *adj* : boastful

jactancioso[2], -sa *n* : boaster, braggart

jactarse *vr* : to boast, to brag

jade *nm* : jade

jadear *vi* : to pant, to gasp, to puff — **jadeante** *adj*

jadeo *nm* : panting, gasping, puffing

jaez *nm, pl* **jaeces 1** : harness **2** : kind, sort, ilk **3 jaeces** *nmpl* : trappings

jaguar *nm* : jaguar

jai alai *nm* : jai alai

jaiba *nf* CANGREJO : crab

jalapeño *nm Mex* : jalapeño pepper

jalar *vt* **1** : to pull, to tug **2** *fam* : to attract, to draw in <las ideas nuevas lo jalan : new ideas appeal to him> — *vi* **1** : to pull, to pull together **2** *fam* : to hurry up, to get going **3** *Mex fam* : to be in working order <esta máquina no jala : this machine doesn't work>

jalbegue *nm* : whitewash

jalea *nf* : jelly

jalear *vt* : to encourage, to urge on

jaleo *nm fam* **1** : uproar, ruckus, racket **2** *fam* : confusion, hassle **3** : cheering and clapping (for a dance)

jalón *nm, pl* **jalones 1** : milestone, landmark **2** TIRÓN : pull, tug

jalonar *vt* : to mark, to stake out

jalonear *vt Mex, Peru fam* : to tug at — *vi* **1** *fam* : to pull, to tug **2** *CA fam* : to haggle

jamaica *nf* : hibiscus

jamaicano, -na → **jamaiquino**

jamaiquino, -na *adj & n* : Jamaican

jamás *adv* **1** NUNCA : never **2 nunca jamás** *or* **jamás de los jamases** : never ever **3 para siempre jamás** : for ever and ever

jamba *nf* : jamb

jamelgo *nm* : nag (horse)

jamón *nm, pl* **jamones** : ham

Januká *nmf* : Hanukkah

japonés, -nesa *adj & n, mpl* **-neses** : Japanese

jaque *nm* **1** : check (in chess) <jaque mate : checkmate> **2 tener en jaque** : to intimidate, to bully

jaqueca *nf* : headache, migraine

jarabe *nm* **1** : syrup **2** : Mexican folk dance

jarana *nf* **1** *fam* : revelry, partying, spree **2** *fam* : joking, fooling around **3** : small guitar

jaranear *vi fam* : to go on a spree, to party

jarcia *nf* **1** : rigging **2** : fishing tackle

jardín *nm, pl* **jardines 1** : garden **2 jardín de niños** : kindergarten **3 los jardines** *nmpl* : the outfield

jardinería *nf* : gardening

jardinero, -ra *n* **1** : gardener **2** : outfielder (in baseball)

jarra *nf* **1** : pitcher, jug **2** : stein, mug **3 de jarras** *or* **en jarras** : akimbo

jarrete *nm* **1** : back of the knee **2** : hock (of an animal)

jarro *nm* **1** : pitcher, jug **2** : mug

jarrón *nm, pl* **jarrones** FLORERO : vase

jaspe *nm* : jasper

jaspeado, -da *adj* **1** VETEADO : streaked, veined **2** : speckled, mottled

jaula *nf* : cage

jauría *nf* : pack of hounds

javanés, -nesa *adj & n* : Javanese

jazmín *nm, pl* **jazmines** : jasmine

jazz [ˈjas, ˈdʒas] *nm* : jazz

jeans [ˈjins, ˈdʒins] *nmpl* : jeans

jeep [ˈjip, ˈdʒip] *nm, pl* **jeeps** : jeep

jefatura *nf* **1** : leadership **2** : headquarters <jefatura de policía : police headquarters>

jefe, -fa *n* **1** : chief, head, leader <jefe de bomberos : fire chief> **2** : boss

Jehová *nm* : Jehovah

jején *nm, pl* **jejenes :** gnat, small mosquito
jengibre *nm* **:** ginger
jeque *nm* **:** sheikh, sheik
jerarca *nmf* **:** leader, chief
jerarquía *nf* **1 :** hierarchy **2** RANGO **:** rank
jerárquico, -ca *adj* **:** hierarchical
jerbo *nm* **:** gerbil
jerez *nm, pl* **jereces :** sherry
jerga *nf* **1 :** jargon, slang **2 :** coarse cloth
jerigonza *nf* GALIMATÍAS **:** mumbo jumbo, gibberish
jeringa *nf* **:** syringe
jeringar {52} *vt* **1 :** to inject **2** *fam* JOROBAR **:** to annoy, to pester — *vi fam* JOROBAR **:** to be annoying, to be a nuisance
jeringuear → **jeringar**
jeringuilla *nf* → **jeringa**
jeroglífico *nm* **:** hieroglyphic
jersey *nm, pl* **jerseys 1 :** jersey (fabric) **2** *Spain* **:** sweater
jesuita *adj & nm* **:** Jesuit
Jesús *nm* **:** Jesus
jeta *nf* **1 :** snout **2** *fam* **:** face, mug
jíbaro, -ra *adj* **1 :** Jivaro **2 :** rustic, rural
jibia *nf* **:** cuttlefish
jícama *nf* **:** jicama
jícara *nf Mex* **:** calabash
jilguero *nm* **:** European goldfinch
jinete *nmf* **:** horseman, horsewoman *f,* rider
jinetear *vt* **1 :** to ride, to perform (on horseback) **2** DOMAR **:** to break in (a horse) — *vi* CABALGAR **:** to ride horseback
jingoísmo [ˌjɪŋgoˈizmo, ˌdʒɪŋ-] *nm* **:** jingoism
jingoísta *adj* **:** jingoist, jingoistic
jiote *nm Mex* **:** rash
jira *nf* **:** outing, picnic
jirafa *nf* **1 :** giraffe **2 :** boom microphone
jirón *nm, pl* **jirones :** shred, rag <hecho jirones : in tatters>
jitomate *nm Mex* **:** tomato
jockey [ˈjɔki, ˈdʒɔ-] *nmf, pl* **jockeys** [-kis] **:** jockey
jocosidad *nf* **:** humor, jocularity
jocoso, -sa *adj* **:** playful, jocular — **jocosamente** *adv*
jofaina *nf* **:** washbowl
jogging [ˈjɔgɪŋ, ˈdʒɔ-] *nm* **:** jogging
jolgorio *nm* **:** merrymaking, fun
jonrón *nm, pl* **jonrones :** home run
jordano, -na *adj & n* **:** Jordanian
jornada *nf* **1 :** expedition, day's journey **2 jornada de trabajo :** working day **3 jornadas** *nfpl* **:** conference, congress
jornal *nm* **1 :** day's pay **2 a ~ :** by the day
jornalero, -ra *n* **:** day laborer
joroba *nf* **1** GIBA **:** hump **2** *fam* **:** nuisance, pain in the neck
jorobado[1], -da *adj* GIBOSO **:** hunchbacked, humpbacked
jorobado[2], -da *n* GIBOSO **:** hunchback, humpback
jorobar *vt fam* JERINGAR **:** to bother, to annoy — *vi fam* JERINGAR **:** to be annoying, to be a nuisance
jorongo *nm Mex* **:** full-length poncho
jota *nf* **1 :** jot, bit <no entiendo ni jota : I don't understand a word of it> <no se ve ni jota : you can't see a thing> **2 :** jack (in playing cards)
joven[1] *adj, pl* **jóvenes 1 :** young **2 :** youthful
joven[2] *nmf, pl* **jóvenes :** young man *m,* young woman *f,* young person
jovial *adj* **:** jovial, cheerful — **jovialmente** *adv*
jovialidad *nf* **:** joviality, cheerfulness
joya *nf* **1 :** jewel, piece of jewelry **2 :** treasure, gem <la nueva empleada es una joya : the new employee is a real gem>
joyería *nf* **1 :** jewelry store **2 :** jewelry **3 joyería de fantasía :** costume jewelry
joyero, -ra *n* **:** jeweler
juanete *nm* **:** bunion
jubilación *nf, pl* **-ciones 1 :** retirement **2** PENSIÓN **:** pension
jubilado[1], -da *adj* **:** retired, in retirement
jubilado[2], -da *nmf* **:** retired person, retiree
jubilar *vt* **1 :** to retire, to pension off **2** *fam* **:** to get rid of, to discard — **jubilarse** *vr* **:** to retire
jubileo *nm* **:** jubilee
júbilo *nm* **:** jubilation, joy
jubiloso, -sa *adj* **:** jubilant, joyous
judaico, -ca *adj* **:** Judaic, Jewish
judaísmo *nm* **:** Judaism
judía *nf* **1 :** bean **2** *or* **judía verde :** green bean, string bean
judicatura *nf* **1 :** judiciary, judges *pl* **2 :** office of judge
judicial *adj* **:** judicial — **judicialmente** *adv*
judío[1], -día *adj* **:** Jewish
judío[2], -día *n* **:** Jewish person, Jew
judo [ˈjuðo, ˈdʒu-] *nm* **:** judo
juega, juegue, etc. → **jugar**
juego *nm* **1 :** play, playing <poner en juego : to bring into play> **2 :** game, sport <juego de cartas : card game> <Juegos Olímpicos : Olympic Games> **3 :** gaming, gambling <estar en juego : to be at stake> **4 :** set <un juego de llaves : a set of keys> **5 hacer juego :** to go together, to match **6 juego de manos :** conjuring trick, sleight of hand
juerga *nf* **:** partying, binge <irse de juerga : to go on a spree>
juerguista *nmf* **:** reveler, carouser
jueves *nms & pl* **:** Thursday
juez *nmf, pl* **jueces 1 :** judge **2** ÁRBITRO **:** umpire, referee

jugada *nf* **1 :** play, move **2 :** trick <hacer una mala jugada : to play a dirty trick>
jugador, -dora *n* **1 :** player **2 :** gambler
jugar {44} *vi* **1 :** to play <jugar a la pelota : to play ball> **2** APOSTAR **:** to gamble, to bet **3 :** to joke, to kid — *vt* **1 :** to play <jugar un papel : to play a role> <jugar una carta : to play a card> **2 :** to bet — **jugarse** *vr* **1 :** to risk, to gamble away <jugarse la vida : to risk one's life> **2 jugarse el todo por el todo :** to risk everything
jugarreta *nf fam* **:** prank, dirty trick
juglar *nm* **:** minstrel
jugo *nm* **1 :** juice **2 :** substance, essence <sacarle el jugo a algo : to get the most out of something>
jugosidad *nf* **:** juiciness, succulence
jugoso, -sa *adj* **:** juicy
juguete *nm* **:** toy
juguetear *vi* **1 :** to play, to cavort, to frolic **2 :** to toy, to fiddle
juguetería *nf* **:** toy store
juguetón, -tona *adj, mpl* **-tones :** playful — **juguetonamente** *adv*
juicio *nm* **1 :** good judgment, reason, sense **2 :** opinion <a mi juicio : in my opinion> **3 :** trial <llevar a juicio : to take to court>
juicioso, -sa *adj* **:** judicious, wise — **juiciosamente** *adv*
julio *nm* **:** July
juncia *nf* **:** sedge
junco *nm* **1 :** reed, rush **2 :** junk (boat)
jungla *nf* **:** jungle
junio *nm* **:** June
junquillo *nm* **:** jonquil
junta *nf* **1 :** board, committee <junta directiva : board of directors> **2** REUNIÓN **:** meeting, session **3 :** junta **4 :** joint, gasket
juntamente *adv* **1 :** jointly, together <juntamente con : together with> **2 :** at the same time
juntar *vt* **1** UNIR **:** to unite, to combine, to put together **2** REUNIR **:** to collect, to gather together, to assemble **3 :** to close partway <juntar la puerta : to leave the door ajar> — **juntarse** *vr* **1 :** to join together **2 :** to socialize, to get together
junto, -ta *adj* **1** UNIDO **:** joined, united **2 :** close, adjacent <colgaron los dos retratos juntos : they hung the two paintings side by side> **3** (*used adverbially*) **:** together <llegamos juntos : we arrived together> **4 ~ a :** next to, alongside of **5 ~ con :** together with, along with
juntura *nf* **:** joint, coupling
Júpiter *nm* **:** Jupiter
jura *nf* **:** oath, pledge <jura de bandera : pledge of allegiance>
jurado[1] *nm* **:** jury
jurado[2]**, -da** *n* **:** juror
juramento *nm* **1 :** oath <juramento hipocrático : Hippocratic oath> **2 :** swearword, oath
jurar *vt* **1 :** to swear <jurar lealtad : to swear loyalty> **2 :** to take an oath <el alcalde juró su cargo : the mayor took the oath of office> — *vi* **:** to curse, to swear
jurídico, -ca *adj* **:** legal
jurisdicción *nf, pl* **-ciones :** jurisdiction
jurisdiccional *adj* **:** jurisdictional, territorial
jurisprudencia *nf* **:** jurisprudence, law
justa *nf* **1 :** joust **2** TORNEO **:** tournament, competition
justamente *adv* **1** PRECISAMENTE **:** precisely, exactly **2 :** justly, fairly
justar *vi* **:** to joust
justicia *nf* **1 :** justice, fairness <hacerle justicia a : to do justice to> <ser de justicia : to be only fair> **2 la justicia :** the law <tomarse la justicia por su mano : to take the law into one's own hands>
justiciero, -ra *adj* **:** righteous, avenging
justificable *adj* **:** justifiable
justificación *nf, pl* **-ciones :** justification
justificante *nm* **1 :** justification **2 :** proof, voucher
justificar {72} *vt* **1 :** to justify **2 :** to excuse, to vindicate
justo[1] *adv* **1 :** justly **2 :** right, exactly <justo a tiempo : just in time> **3 :** tightly
justo[2]**, -ta** *adj* **1 :** just, fair **2 :** right, exact **3 :** tight <estos zapatos me quedan muy justos : these shoes are too tight>
justo[3]**, -ta** *n* **:** just person <los justos : the just>
juvenil *adj* **1 :** juvenile, young, youthful **2** ADOLESCENTE **:** teenage
juventud *nf* **1 :** youth **2 :** young people
juzgado *nm* TRIBUNAL **:** court, tribunal
juzgar {52} *vt* **1 :** to try, to judge (a case in court) **2 :** to pass judgment on **3** CONSIDERAR **:** to consider, to deem
juzgue, etc. → **juzgar**

K

k *nf* **:** eleventh letter of the Spanish alphabet
kaki *adj & nm* → **caqui**
kaleidoscopio *nm* → **caleidoscopio**
kamikaze *adj & nm* **:** kamikaze
kampucheano, -na *adj & n* **:** Kampuchean
kan *nm* **:** khan
karaoke *nm* **:** karaoke
karate *or* **kárate** *nm* **:** karate

kayac *or* **kayak** *nm, pl* **kayacs** *or* **kayaks** : kayak
keniano, -na *adj & n* : Kenyan
kepí *nm* : kepi
kermesse *or* **kermés** [kɛrˈmɛs] *nf, pl* **kermesses** *or* **kermeses** [-ˈmɛsɛs] : charity fair, bazaar
kerosene *or* **kerosén** *or* **keroseno** *nm* : kerosene, paraffin
kilo *nm* **1** : kilo, kilogram **2** *fam* : large amount
kilobyte [ˌkiloˈbait] *nm* : kilobyte
kilociclo *nm* : kilocycle
kilogramo *nm* : kilogram
kilohertzio *nm* : kilohertz
kilometraje *nm* : distance in kilometers, mileage
kilométrico, -ca *adj fam* : endless, very long
kilómetro *nm* : kilometer
kilovatio *nm* : kilowatt
kimono *nm* : kimono
kinder [ˈkɪndɛr] *nm* → **kindergarten**
kindergarten [ˌkɪndɛrˈgartɛn] *nm, pl* **kindergartens** [-tɛns] : kindergarten, nursery school
kinesiología *nf* : physical therapy
kinesiólogo, -ga *n* : physical therapist
kiosco *nm* → **quiosco**
kit *nm, pl* **kits** : kit
kiwi [ˈkiwi] *nm* **1** : kiwi (bird) **2** : kiwifruit
klaxon *nm* → **claxon**
knockout [nɔˈkaut] *nm* → **nocaut**
koala *nm* : koala bear
kriptón *nm* : krypton
kurdo[1], -da *adj* : Kurdish
kurdo[2], -da *n* : Kurd
kuwaiti [kuˌwaiˈti] *adj & nmf* : Kuwaiti

L

l *nf* : twelfth letter of the Spanish alphabet
la[1] *pron* **1** : her, it <llámala hoy : call her today> <sacó la botella y la abrió : he took out the bottle and opened it> **2** (*formal*) : you <no la vi a usted, Señora Díaz : I didn't see you, Mrs. Díaz> **3** : the one <mi casa y la de la puerta roja : my house and the one with the red door> **4 la que** : the one who
la[2] *art* → **el[2]**
laberíntico, -ca *adj* : labyrinthine
laberinto *nm* : labyrinth, maze
labia *nf fam* : gift of gab <tu amigo tiene labia : your friend has a way with words>
labial *adj* : labial, lip <lápiz labial : lipstick>
labio *nm* **1** : lip **2 labio leporino** : harelip
labor *nf* : work, labor
laborable *adj* **1** : arable **2 día laborable** : workday, business day
laboral *adj* **1** : work, labor <costos laborales : labor costs> **2 estancia laboral** : workstation
laborar *vi* : to work
laboratorio *nm* : laboratory, lab
laboriosidad *nf* : industriousness, diligence
laborioso, -sa *adj* **1** : laborious, hard **2** : industrious, hard-working
labrado[1], -da *adj* **1** : cultivated, tilled **2** : carved, wrought
labrado[2] *nm* : cultivated field
labrador, -dora *n* : farmer
labranza *nf* : farming
labrar *vt* **1** : to carve, to work (metal) **2** : to cultivate, to till **3** : to cause, to bring about
laca *nf* **1** : lacquer, shellac **2** : hair spray **3 laca de uñas** : nail polish
lacayo *nm* : lackey
lace, etc. → **lazar**
lacear *vt* : to lasso
laceración *nf, pl* **-ciones** : laceration
lacerante *adj* : hurtful, wounding
lacerar *vt* **1** : to lacerate, to cut **2** : to hurt, to wound (one's feelings)
lacio, -cia *adj* **1** : limp, lank **2 pelo lacio** : straight hair
lacónico, -ca *adj* : laconic — **lacónicamente** *adv*
lacra *nf* **1** : scar, mark (on the skin) **2** : stigma, blemish
lacrar *vt* : to seal (with wax)
lacrimógeno, -na *adj* **gas lacrimógeno** : tear gas
lacrimoso, -sa *adj* : tearful, moving
lactancia *nf* **1** : lactation **2** : breastfeeding
lactante *nmf* : nursing infant, suckling
lactar *v* : to breast-feed
lácteo, -tea *adj* **1** : dairy **2 Vía Láctea** : Milky Way
láctico, -ca *adj* : lactic
lactosa *nf* : lactose
ladeado, -da *adj* : crooked, tilted, lopsided
ladear *vt* : to tilt, to tip — **ladearse** *vr* : to bend (over)
ladera *nf* : slope, hillside
ladino[1], -na *adj* **1** : cunning, shrewd **2** *CA, Mex* : mestizo
ladino[2], -na *n* **1** : trickster **2** *CA, Mex* : Spanish-speaking Indian **3** *CA, Mex* : mestizo
lado *nm* **1** : side **2** PARTE : place <miró por todos lados : he looked everywhere> **3 al lado de** : next to, beside **4 de ~** : tilted, sideways <está de lado : it's lying on its side> **5 hacerse a un lado** : to step aside **6 lado a lado** : side by side **7 por otro lado** : on the other hand
ladrar *vi* : to bark
ladrido *nm* : bark (of a dog), barking

ladrillo *nm* : brick

ladrón, -drona *n, mpl* **ladrones** : robber, thief, burglar

lagartija *nf* : small lizard

lagarto *nm* **1** : lizard **2 lagarto de Indias** : alligator

lago *nm* : lake

lágrima *nf* : tear, teardrop

lagrimear *vi* **1** : to water (of eyes) **2** : to weep easily

laguna *nf* **1** : lagoon **2** : lacuna, gap

laicado *nm* : laity

laico[1], -ca *adj* : lay, secular

laico[2], -ca *n* : layman *m,* laywoman *f*

laja *nf* : slab

lama[1] *nf* : slime, ooze

lama[2] *nm* : lama

lamber *vt* : to lick

lamentable *adj* **1** : unfortunate, lamentable **2** : pitiful, sad

lamentablemente *adv* : unfortunately, regrettably

lamentación *nf, pl* **-ciones** : lamentation, groaning, moaning

lamentar *vt* **1** : to lament **2** : to regret <lo lamento : I'm sorry> — **lamentarse** *vr* : to grumble, to complain

lamento *nm* : lament, groan, cry

lamer *vt* **1** : to lick **2** : to lap against

lamida *nf* : lick

lámina *nf* **1** PLANCHA : sheet, plate **2** : plate, illustration

laminado[1], -da *adj* : laminated

laminado[2] *nm* : laminate

laminar *vt* : to laminate — **laminación** *nf*

lámpara *nf* : lamp

lampiño, -ña *adj* : hairless

lamprea *nf* : lamprey

lana *nf* **1** : wool <lana de acero : steel wool> **2** *Mex fam* : money, dough

lance[1], etc. → **lanzar**

lance[2] *nm* **1** INCIDENTE : event, incident **2** RIÑA : quarrel **3** : throw, cast (of a net, etc.) **4** : move, play (in a game), throw (of dice)

lancear *vt* : to spear

lanceta *nf* : lancet

lancha *nf* **1** : small boat, launch **2 lancha motora** : motorboat, speedboat

langosta *nf* **1** : lobster **2** : locust

langostino *nm* : prawn, crayfish

languidecer {53} *vi* : to languish

languidez *nf, pl* **-deces** : languor, listlessness

lánguido, -da *adj* : languid, listless — **lánguidamente** *adv*

lanolina *nf* : lanolin

lanudo, -da *adj* : woolly

lanza *nf* : spear, lance

lanzadera *nf* **1** : shuttle (for weaving) **2 lanzadera espacial** : space shuttle

lanzado, -da *adj* **1** : impulsive, brazen **2** : forward, determined <ir lanzado : to hurtle along>

lanzador, -dora *n* : thrower, pitcher

lanzallamas *nms & pl* : flamethrower

lanzamiento *nm* **1** : throw **2** : pitch (in baseball) **3** : launching, launch

lanzar {21} *vt* **1** : to throw, to hurl **2** : to pitch **3** : to launch — **lanzarse** *vr* **1** : to throw oneself (at, into) **2 ~ a** : to embark upon, to undertake

laosiano, -na *adj & n* : Laotian

lapicero *nm* **1** : mechanical pencil **2** *CA, Peru* : ballpoint pen

lápida *nf* : marker, tombstone

lapidar *vt* APEDREAR : to stone

lapidario, -ria *adj & n* : lapidary

lápiz *nm, pl* **lápices 1** : pencil **2 lápiz de labios** *or* **lápiz labial** : lipstick

lapón, -pona *adj & n, mpl* **lapones** : Lapp

lapso *nm* : lapse, space (of time)

lapsus *nms & pl* : error, slip

laquear *vt* : to lacquer, to varnish, to shellac

largamente *adv* **1** : at length, extensively **2** : easily, comfortably **3** : generously

largar {52} *vt* **1** SOLTAR : to let loose, to release **2** AFLOJAR : to loosen, to slacken **3** *fam* : to give, to hand over **4** *fam* : to hurl, to let fly (insults, etc.) — **largarse** *vr fam* : to scram, to beat it

largo[1], -ga *adj* **1** : long **2 a lo largo** : lengthwise **3 a lo largo de** : along **4 a la larga** : in the long run

largo[2] *nm* : length <tres metros de largo : three meters long>

largometraje *nm* : feature film

largue, etc. → **largar**

larguero *nm* : crossbeam

largueza *nf* : generosity, largesse

larguirucho, -cha *adj fam* : lanky

largura *nf* : length

laringe *nf* : larynx

laringitis *nfs & pl* : laryngitis

larva *nf* : larva — **larval** *adj*

las → **el[2], los[1]**

lasaña *nf* : lasagna

lasca *nf* : chip, chipping

lascivia *nf* : lasciviousness, lewdness

lascivo, -va *adj* : lascivious, lewd — **lascivamente** *adv*

láser *nm* : laser

lasitud *nf* : lassitude, weariness

laso, -sa *adj* : languid, weary

lástima *nf* **1** : compassion, pity **2** PENA : shame, pity <¡qué lástima! : what a shame!>

lastimadura *nf* : injury, wound

lastimar *vt* **1** DAÑAR, HERIR : to hurt, to injure **2** AGRAVIAR : to offend — **lastimarse** *vr* : to hurt oneself

lastimero, -ra *adj* : pitiful, wretched

lastimoso, -sa *adj* **1** : shameful **2** : pitiful, terrible

lastrar *vt* **1** : to ballast **2** : to burden, to encumber

lastre *nm* **1** : burden **2** : ballast

lata *nf* **1** : tinplate **2** : tin can **3** *fam* : pest, bother, nuisance **4 dar lata** *fam* : to bother, to annoy

latencia *nf* : latency

latente *adj* : latent

lateral[1] *adj* **1 :** lateral, side **2 :** indirect — **lateralmente** *adv*

lateral[2] *nm* **:** end piece, side

látex *nms & pl* **:** latex

latido *nm* **:** beat, throb <latido del corazón : heartbeat>

latifundio *nm* **:** large estate

latigazo *nm* **:** lash (with a whip)

látigo *nm* AZOTE **:** whip

latín *nm* **:** Latin (language)

latino[1], **-na** *adj* **1 :** Latin **2** *fam* **:** Latin-American

latino[2], **-na** *n fam* **:** Latin American

latinoamericano[1], **-na** *adj* HISPANOAMERICANO **:** Latin American

latinoamericano, -na *n* **:** Latin American

latir *vi* **1 :** to beat, to throb **2 latirle a uno** *Mex fam* **:** to have a hunch <me late que no va a venir : I have a feeling he's not going to come>

latitud *nf* **1 :** latitude **2 :** breadth

lato, -ta *adj* **1 :** extended, lengthy **2 :** broad (in meaning)

latón *nm, pl* **latones :** brass

latoso[1], **-sa** *adj fam* **:** annoying, bothersome

latoso[2], **-sa** *n fam* **:** pest, nuisance

latrocinio *nm* **:** larceny

laúd *nm* **:** lute

laudable *adj* **:** laudable, praiseworthy

laudo *nm* **:** findings, decision

laureado, -da *adj & n* **:** laureate

laurear *vt* **:** to award, to honor

laurel *nm* **1 :** laurel **2 :** bay leaf **3 dormirse en sus laureles :** to rest on one's laurels

lava *nf* **:** lava

lavable *adj* **:** washable

lavabo *nm* **1** LAVAMANOS **:** sink, washbowl **2 :** lavatory, toilet

lavadero *nm* **:** laundry room

lavado *nm* **1 :** laundry, wash **2 :** laundering <lavado de dinero : money laundering>

lavadora *nf* **:** washing machine

lavamanos *nms & pl* LAVABO **:** sink, washbowl

lavanda *nf* ESPLIEGO **:** lavender

lavandería *nf* **:** laundry (service)

lavandero, -ra *n* **:** launderer, laundress *f*

lavaplatos *nms & pl* **1 :** dishwasher **2** *Chile, Col, Mex* **:** kitchen sink

lavar *vt* **1 :** to wash, to clean **2 :** to launder (money) **3 lavar en seco :** to dry-clean — **lavarse** *vr* **1 :** to wash oneself **2 lavarse las manos de :** to wash one's hands of

lavativa *nf* **:** enema

lavatorio *nm* **:** lavatory, washroom

lavavajillas *nms & pl* **:** dishwasher

laxante *adj & nm* **:** laxative

laxitud *nf* **:** laxity, slackness

laxo, -xa *adj* **:** lax, slack

lazada *nf* **:** bow, loop

lazar {21} *vt* **:** to rope, to lasso

lazo *nm* **1** VÍNCULO **:** link, bond **2 :** bow, ribbon **3 :** lasso, lariat

le *pron* **1 :** to her, to him, to it <¿qué le dijiste? : what did you tell him?> **2 :** from her, from him, from it <el ladrón le robó la cartera : the thief stole his wallet> **3 :** for her, for him, for it <cómprale flores a tu mamá : buy your mom some flowers> **4** (*formal*) **:** to you, for you <le traje un regalo : I brought you a gift>

leal *adj* **:** loyal, faithful — **lealmente** *adv*

lealtad *nf* **:** loyalty, allegiance

lebrel *nm* **:** hound

lección *nf, pl* **lecciones :** lesson

lechada *nf* **1 :** whitewash **2 :** grout

lechal *adj* **:** suckling, unweaned <cordero lechal : suckling lamb>

leche *nf* **1 :** milk <leche en polvo : powdered milk> <leche de magnesia : milk of magnesia> **2 :** milky sap

lechera *nf* **1 :** milk jug **2 :** dairymaid *f*

lechería *nf* **:** dairy store

lechero[1], **-ra** *adj* **:** dairy

lechero[2], **-ra** *n* **:** milkman *m,* milk dealer

lecho *nm* **1 :** bed <un lecho de rosas : a bed of roses> <lecho de muerte : deathbed> **2 :** riverbed **3 :** layer, stratum (in geology)

lechón, -chona *n, mpl* **lechones :** suckling pig

lechoso, -sa *adj* **:** milky

lechuga *nf* **:** lettuce

lechuza *nf* BÚHO **:** owl, barn owl

lectivo, -va *adj* **:** school <año lectivo : school year>

lector[1], **-tora** *adj* **:** reading <nivel lector : reading level>

lector[2], **-tora** *n* **:** reader

lector[3] *nm* **:** scanner, reader <lector óptico : optical scanner>

lectura *nf* **1 :** reading **2 :** reading matter

leer {20} *v* **:** to read

legación *nf, pl* **-ciones :** legation

legado *nm* **1 :** legacy, bequest **2 :** legate, emissary

legajo *nm* **:** dossier, file

legal *adj* **:** legal, lawful — **legalmente** *adv*

legalidad *nf* **:** legality, lawfulness

legalizar {21} *vt* **:** to legalize — **legalización** *nf*

legar {52} *vt* **1 :** to bequeath, to hand down **2** DELEGAR **:** to delegate

legendario, -ria *adj* **:** legendary

legible *adj* **:** legible

legión *nf, pl* **legiones :** legion

legionario, -ria *n* **:** legionnaire

legislación *nf* **1 :** legislation, lawmaking **2 :** laws *pl,* legislation

legislador[1], **-dora** *adj* **:** legislative

legislador[2], **-dora** *n* **:** legislator

legislar *vi* **:** to legislate

legislativo, -va *adj* **:** legislative

legislatura *nf* **1 :** legislature **2 :** term of office

legitimar *vt* **1 :** to legitimize **2 :** to authenticate — **legitimación** *nf*

legitimidad *nf* : legitimacy
legítimo, -ma *adj* **1** : legitimate **2** : genuine, authentic — **legítimamente** *adv*
lego[1], -ga *adj* **1** : secular, lay **2** : uniformed, ignorant
lego[2], -ga *n* : layperson, layman *m,* laywoman *f*
legua *nf* **1** : league **2 notarse a leguas** : to be very obvious <se notaba a leguas : you could tell from a mile away>
legue, etc. → **legar**
legumbre *nf* **1** HORTALIZA : vegetable **2** : legume
leíble *adj* : readable
leída *nf* : reading, read <de una leída : in one reading, at one go>
leído[1] *pp* → **leer**
leído[2], -da *adj* : well-read
lejanía *nf* : remoteness, distance
lejano, -na *adj* : remote, distant, far away
lejía *nf* **1** : lye **2** : bleach
lejos *adv* **1** : far away, distant <a lo lejos : in the distance, far off> <desde lejos : from a distance> **2** : long ago, a long way off <está lejos de los 50 años : he's a long way from 50 years old> **3 de ~** : by far <esta decisión fue de lejos la más fácil : this decision was by far the easiest> **4 ~ de** : far from <lejos de ser reprobado, recibió una nota de B : far from failing, he got a B>
lelo, -la *adj* : silly, stupid
lema *nm* : motto, slogan
lencería *nf* : lingerie
lengua *nf* **1** : tongue <morderse la lengua : to bite one's tongue> **2** IDIOMA : language <lengua materna : mother tongue, native language> <lengua muerta : dead language>
lenguado *nm* : sole, flounder
lenguaje *nm* **1** : language, speech **2 lenguaje gestual** *or* **lenguaje de gestos** : sign language **3 lenguaje de programación** : programming language
lengüeta *nf* **1** : tongue (of a shoe), tab, flap **2** : reed (of a musical instrument) **3** : barb, point
lengüetada *nf* **beber a lengüetadas** : to lap (up)
lenidad *nf* : leniency
lenitivo, -va *adj* : soothing
lente *nmf* **1** : lens <lentes de contacto : contact lenses> **2 lentes** *nmpl* ANTEOJOS : eyeglasses <lentes de sol : sunglasses>
lenteja *nf* : lentil
lentejuela *nf* : sequin, spangle
lentitud *nf* : slowness
lento[1] *adv* DESPACIO : slowly
lento[2], -ta *adj* **1** : slow **2** : slow-witted, dull — **lentamente** *adv*
leña *nf* : wood, firewood
leñador, -dora *n* : lumberjack, woodcutter
leñera *nf* : woodshed
leño *nm* : log
leñoso, -sa *adj* : woody
Leo *nmf* : Leo
león, -ona *n, mpl* **leones 1** : lion, lioness *f* **2** (*in various countries*) : puma, cougar
leonado, -da *adj* : tawny
leonino, -na *adj* **1** : leonine **2** : one-sided, unfair
leopardo *nm* : leopard
leotardo *nm* MALLA : leotard, tights *pl*
leperada *nf Mex* : obscenity
lépero, -ra *adj Mex* : vulgar, coarse
lepra *nf* : leprosy
leproso[1], -sa *adj* : leprous
leproso[2], -sa *n* : leper
lerdo, -da *adj* **1** : clumsy **2** : dull, oafish, slow-witted
les *pron* **1** : to them <dales una propina : give them a tip> **2** : from them <se les privó de su herencia : they were deprived of their inheritance> **3** : for them <les hice sus tareas : I did their homework for them> **4** : to you *pl*, for you *pl* <les compré un regalo : I bought you all a present>
lesbiana *nf* : lesbian — **lesbiano, -na** *adj*
lesbianismo *nm* : lesbianism
lesión *nf, pl* **lesiones** HERIDA : lesion, wound, injury <una lesión grave : a serious injury>
lesionado, -da *adj* HERIDO : injured, wounded
lesionar *vt* : to injure, to wound — **lesionarse** *vr* : to hurt oneself
lesivo, -va *adj* : harmful, damaging
letal *adj* MORTÍFERO : deadly, lethal — **letalmente** *adv*
letanía *nf* **1** : litany **2** *fam* : spiel, song and dance
letárgico, -ca *adj* : lethargic
letargo *nm* : lethargy, torpor
letón[1], -tona *adj & n, mpl* **letones** : Latvian
letón[2] *nm* : Latvian (language)
letra *nf* **1** : letter **2** CALIGRAFÍA : handwriting, lettering **3** : lyrics *pl* **4 al pie de la letra** : word for word, by the book **5 letras** *nfpl* : arts (in education)
letrado[1], -da *adj* ERUDITO : learned, erudite
letrado[2], -da *n* : attorney-at-law, lawyer
letrero *nm* RÓTULO : sign, notice
letrina *nf* : latrine
letrista *nmf* : lyricist, songwriter
leucemia *nf* : leukemia
levadizo, -za *adj* **1** : liftable **2 puente levadizo** : drawbridge
levadura *nf* **1** : yeast, leavening **2 levadura en polvo** : baking powder
levantamiento *nm* **1** ALZAMIENTO : uprising **2** : raising, lifting <levantamiento de pesas : weight lifting>
levantar *vt* **1** ALZAR : to lift, to raise **2** : to put up, to erect **3** : to call off, to adjourn **4** : to give rise to, to arouse

<levantar sospechas : to arouse suspicion> — **levantarse** *vr* **1 :** to rise, to stand up **2 :** to get out of bed

levar *vt* **levar anclas :** to weigh anchor

leve *adj* **1 :** light, slight **2 :** trivial, unimportant — **levemente** *adv*

levedad *nf* **:** lightness

levemente *adv* LIGERAMENTE **:** lightly, softly

léxico[1], -ca *adj* **:** lexical

léxico[2] *nm* **:** lexicon, glossary

lexicografía *nf* **:** lexicography

lexicográfico, -ca *adj* **:** lexicographical, lexicographic

lexicógrafo, -fa *n* **:** lexicographer

ley *nf* **1 :** law <fuera de la ley : outside the law> <la ley de gravedad : the law of gravity> **2 :** purity (of metals) <oro de ley : pure gold>

leyenda *nf* **1 :** legend **2 :** caption, inscription

leyó, etc. → **leer**

liar {85} *vt* **1** ATAR **:** to bind, to tie (up) **2 :** to roll (a cigarette) **3 :** to confuse — **liarse** *vr* **:** to get mixed up

libanés, -nesa *adj & n, mpl* **-neses :** Lebanese

libar *vt* **1 :** to suck (nectar) **2 :** to sip, to swig (liquor, etc.)

libelo *nm* **1 :** libel, lampoon **2 :** petition (in court)

libélula *nf* **:** dragonfly

liberación *nf, pl* **-ciones :** liberation, deliverance <liberación de la mujer : women's liberation>

liberado, -da *adj* **1 :** liberated <una mujer liberada : a liberated woman> **2 :** freed, delivered

liberal *adj & nmf* **:** liberal

liberalidad *nf* **:** generosity, liberality

liberalismo *nm* **:** liberalism

liberalizar {21} *vt* **:** to liberalize — **liberalización** *nf*

liberar *vt* **:** to liberate, to free — **liberarse** *vr* **:** to get free of

liberiano, -na *adj & n* **:** Liberian

libertad *nf* **1 :** freedom, liberty <tomarse la libertad de : to take the liberty of> **2 libertad bajo fianza :** bail **3 libertad condicional :** parole

libertador[1], -dora *adj* **:** liberating

libertador[2], -dora *n* **:** liberator

libertar *vt* LIBRAR **:** to set free

libertario, -ria *adj & n* **:** libertarian

libertinaje *nm* **:** licentiousness, dissipation

libertino[1], -na *adj* **:** licentious, dissolute

libertino[2], -na *n* **:** libertine

libidinoso, -sa *adj* **:** lustful, lewd

libido *nf* **:** libido

libio, -bia *adj & n* **:** Libyan

libra *nf* **1 :** pound **2 libra esterlina :** pound sterling

Libra *nmf* **:** Libra

libramiento *nm* **1 :** liberating, freeing **2** LIBRANZA **:** order of payment **3** *Mex* **:** beltway

libranza *nf* **:** order of payment

librar *vt* **1** LIBERTAR **:** to deliver, to set free **2 :** to wage <librar batalla : to do battle> **3 :** to issue <librar una orden : to issue an order> — **librarse** *vr* **~ de :** to free oneself from, to get out of

libre *adj* **1 :** free <un país libre : a free country> <libre de : free from, exempt from> <libre albedrío : free will> **2** DESOCUPADO **:** vacant **3 día libre :** day off

librea *nf* **:** livery

librecambio *nm* **:** free trade

libremente *adv* **:** freely

librería *nf* **:** bookstore

librero[1], -ra *n* **:** bookseller

librero[2] *nm Mex* **:** bookcase

libresco, -ca *adj* **:** bookish

libreta *nf* CUADERNO **:** notebook

libreto *nm* **:** libretto, script

libro *nm* **1 :** book <libro de texto : textbook> **2 libros** *nmpl* **:** books (in bookkeeping), accounts <llevar los libros : to keep the books>

licencia *nf* **1 :** permission **2 :** leave, leave of absence **3 :** permit, license <licencia de conducir : driver's license>

licenciado, -da *n* **1 :** university graduate **2** ABOGADO **:** lawyer

licenciar *vt* **1 :** to license, to permit, to allow **2 :** to discharge **3 :** to grant a university degree to — **licenciarse** *vr* **:** to graduate

licenciatura *nf* **1 :** college degree **2 :** course of study (at a college or university)

licencioso, -sa *adj* **:** licentious, lewd

liceo *nm* **:** secondary school, high school

licitación *nf, pl* **-ciones :** bid, bidding

licitar *vt* **:** to bid on

lícito, -ta *adj* **1 :** lawful, licit **2** JUSTO **:** just, fair

licor *nm* **1 :** liquor **2 :** liqueur

licorera *nf* **:** decanter

licuado *nm* BATIDO **:** milk shake

licuadora *nf* **:** blender

licuar {3} *vt* **:** to liquefy — **licuarse** *vr*

lid *nf* **1 :** fight, combat **2 :** argument, dispute **3 lides** *nfpl* **:** matters, affairs **4 en buena lid :** fair and square

líder[1] *adj* **:** leading, foremost

líder[2] *nmf* **:** leader

liderar *vt* DIRIGIR **:** to lead, to head

liderato *nm* **:** leadership, leading

liderazgo *nm* → **liderato**

lidiar *vt* **:** to fight — *vi* BATALLAR, LUCHAR **:** to struggle, to battle, to wrestle

liebre *nf* **:** hare

liendre *nf* **:** nit

lienzo *nm* **1 :** linen **2 :** canvas, painting **3 :** stretch of wall or fencing

liga *nf* **1** ASOCIACIÓN **:** league **2** GOMITA **:** rubber band **3 :** garter

ligado, -da *adj* **:** linked, connected

ligadura *nf* **1** ATADURA **:** tie, bond **2 :** ligature

ligamento *nm* **:** ligament

ligar {52} *vt* **:** to bind, to tie (up)

ligeramente *adv* **1 :** slightly **2** LEVEMENTE **:** lightly, gently **3 :** casually, flippantly
ligereza *nf* **1 :** lightness **2 :** flippancy **3 :** agility
ligero, -ra *adj* **1 :** light, lightweight **2 :** slight, minor **3 :** agile, quick **4 :** lighthearted, superficial
ligue, etc. → ligar
lija *nf or* **papel de lija :** sandpaper
lijar *vt* **:** to sand
lila[1] *adj* **:** lilac, light purple
lila[2] *nf* **:** lilac
lima *nf* **1 :** lime (fruit) **2 :** file <lima de uñas : nail file>
limadora *nf* **:** polisher
limar *vt* **1 :** to file **2 :** to polish, to put the final touch on **3 :** to smooth over <limar las diferencias : to iron out differences>
limbo *nm* **1 :** limbo **2 :** limb (in botany and astronomy)
limeño[1], -ña *adj* **:** of or from Lima, Peru
limeño[2], -ña *n* **:** person from Lima, Peru
limero *nm* **:** lime tree
limitación *nf, pl* **-ciones 1 :** limitation **2 :** limit, restriction <sin limitación : unlimited>
limitado, -da *adj* **1** RESTRINGIDO **:** limited **2 :** dull, slow-witted
limitar *vt* RESTRINGIR **:** to limit, to restrict — *vi* **~ con :** to border on — **limitarse** *vr* **~ a :** to limit oneself to
límite *nm* **1 :** boundary, border **2 :** limit <el límite de mi paciencia : the limit of my patience> <límite de velocidad : speed limit> **3 fecha límite :** deadline
limítrofe *adj* LINDANTE, LINDERO **:** bordering, adjoining
limo *nm* **:** slime, mud
limón *nm, pl* **limones 1 :** lemon **2 :** lemon tree **3 limón verde** *Mex* **:** lime
limonada *nf* **:** lemonade
limosna *nf* **:** alms, charity
limosnear *vi* **:** to beg (for alms)
limosnero, -ra *n* MENDIGO **:** beggar
limoso, -sa *adj* **:** slimy
limpiabotas *nmfs & pl* **:** bootblack
limpiador[1], -dora *adj* **:** cleaning
limpiador[2], -dora *n* **:** cleaning person, cleaner
limpiamente *adv* **:** cleanly, honestly, fairly
limpiaparabrisas *nms & pl* **:** windshield wiper
limpiar *vt* **1 :** to clean, to cleanse **2 :** to clean up, to remove defects **3** *fam* **:** to clean out (in a game) **4** *fam* **:** to swipe, to pinch — *vi* **:** to clean — **limpiarse** *vr*
limpiavidrios *nmfs & pl Mex* **:** windshield wiper
límpido, -da *adj* **:** limpid
limpieza *nf* **1 :** cleanliness, tidiness **2 :** cleaning **3** HONRADEZ **:** integrity, honesty **4** DESTREZA **:** skill, dexterity
limpio[1] *adv* **:** fairly
limpio[2], -pia *adj* **1 :** clean, neat **2 :** honest <un juego limpio : a fair game> **3 :** free <limpio de impurezas : pure, free from impurities> **4 :** clear, net <ganancia limpia : clear profit>
limusina *nf* **:** limousine
linaje *nm* ABOLENGO **:** lineage, ancestry
linaza *nf* **:** linseed
lince *nm* **:** lynx
linchamiento *nm* **:** lynching
linchar *vt* **:** to lynch
lindante *adj* LIMÍTROFE, LINDERO **:** bordering, adjoining
lindar *vi* **1 ~ con :** to border, to skirt **2 ~ con** BORDEAR **:** to border on, to verge on
linde *nmf* **:** boundary, limit
lindero[1], -ra *adj* LIMÍTROFE, LINDANTE **:** bordering, adjoining
lindero[2] *nm* **:** boundary, limit
lindeza *nf* **1 :** prettiness **2 :** clever remark **3 lindezas** *nfpl* (*used ironically*) **:** insults
lindo[1] *adv* **1 :** beautifully, wonderfully <canta lindo tu mujer : your wife sings beautifully> **2 de lo lindo :** a lot, a great deal <los zancudos nos picaban de lo lindo : the mosquitoes were biting away at us>
lindo[2], -da *adj* **1** BONITO **:** pretty, lovely **2** MONO **:** cute
línea *nf* **1 :** line <línea divisoria : dividing line> <línea de banda : sideline> **2 :** line, course, position <línea de conducta : course of action> <en líneas generales : in general terms, along general lines> **3 :** line, service <línea aérea : airline> <línea telefónica : telephone line>
lineal *adj* **:** linear
linfa *nf* **:** lymph
linfático, -ca *adj* **:** lymphatic
lingote *nm* **:** ingot
lingüista *nmf* **:** linguist
lingüística *nf* **:** linguistics
lingüístico, -ca *adj* **:** linguistic
linimento *nm* **:** liniment
lino *nm* **1 :** linen **2 :** flax
linóleo *nm* **:** linoleum
linterna *nf* **1 :** lantern **2 :** flashlight
lío *nm fam* **1 :** confusion, mess **2 :** hassle, trouble, jam <meterse en un lío : to get into a jam> **3 :** affair, liason
liofilizar {21} *vt* **:** to freeze-dry
lioso, -sa *adj fam* **1 :** confusing, muddled **2 :** troublemaking
liquen *nm* **:** lichen
liquidación *nf, pl* **-ciones 1 :** liquidation **2 :** clearance sale **3 :** settlement, payment
liquidar *vt* **1 :** to liquefy **2 :** to liquidate **3 :** to settle, to pay off **4** *fam* **:** to rub out, to kill
liquidez *nf, pl* **-deces :** liquidity

líquido[1], **-da** *adj* **1 :** liquid, fluid **2 :** net <ingresos líquidos : net income>
líquido[2] *nm* **1 :** liquid, fluid <líquido de frenos : brake fluid> **2 :** ready cash, liquid assets
lira *nf* **:** lyre
lírica *nf* **:** lyric poetry
lírico, -ca *adj* **:** lyric, lyrical
lirio *nm* **1 :** iris **2 lirio de los valles** MUGUETE **:** lily of the valley
lirismo *nm* **:** lyricism
lirón *nm, pl* **lirones :** dormouse
lisiado[1], **-da** *adj* **:** disabled, crippled
lisiado[2], **-da** *n* **:** disabled person, cripple
lisiar *vt* **:** to cripple, to disable — **lisiarse** *vr*
liso, -sa *adj* **1 :** smooth **2 :** flat **3 :** straight <pelo liso : straight hair> **4 :** plain, unadorned <liso y llano : plain and simple>
lisonja *nf* **:** flattery
lisonjear *vt* ADULAR **:** to flatter
lista *nf* **1 :** list **2 :** roster, roll <pasar lista : to take attendance> **3 :** stripe, strip **4 :** menu
listado[1], **-da** *adj* **:** striped
listado[2] *nm* **:** listing
listar *vt* **:** to list
listeza *nf* **:** smartness, alertness
listo, -ta *adj* **1** DISPUESTO, PREPARADO **:** ready <¿estás listo? : are you ready?> **2 :** clever, smart
listón *nm, pl* **listones 1 :** ribbon **2 :** strip (of wood), lath **3 :** high bar (in sports)
lisura *nf* **:** smoothness
litera *nf* **:** bunk bed, berth
literal *adj* **:** literal — **literalmente** *adv*
literario, -ria *adj* **:** literary
literato, -ta *n* **:** writer, author
literatura *nf* **:** literature
litigante *adj & nmf* **:** litigant
litigar {52} *vi* **:** to litigate, to be in litigation
litigio *nm* **1 :** litigation, lawsuit **2 en ~ :** in dispute
litigioso, -sa *adj* **:** litigious
litio *nm* **:** lithium
litografía *nf* **1 :** lithography **2 :** lithograph
litógrafo, -fa *n* **:** lithographer
litoral[1] *adj* **:** coastal
litoral[2] *nm* **:** shore, seaboard
litosfera *nf* **:** lithosphere
litro *nm* **:** liter
lituano[1], **-na** *adj & n* **:** Lithuanian
lituano[2] *nm* **:** Lithuanian (language)
liturgia *nf* **:** liturgy
litúrgico, -ca *adj* **:** liturgical — **litúrgicamente** *adv*
liviandad *nf* LIGEREZA **:** lightness
liviano, -na *adj* **1 :** light, slight **2** INCONSTANTE **:** fickle
lividez *nf* PALIDEZ **:** pallor
lívido, -da *adj* **1** AMORATADO **:** livid **2** PÁLIDO **:** pallid, extremely pale
living *nm* **:** living room
llaga *nf* **:** sore, wound
llama *nf* **1 :** flame **2 :** llama
llamada *nf* **:** call <llamada a larga distancia : long-distance call> <llamada al orden : call to order>
llamado[1], **-da** *adj* **:** named, called <una mujer llamada Rosa : a woman called Rosa>
llamado[2] → **llamamiento**
llamador *nm* **:** door knocker
llamamiento *nm* **:** call, appeal
llamar *vt* **1 :** to name, to call **2 :** to call, to summon **3 :** to phone, to call up — **llamarse** *vr* **:** to be called, to be named <¿cómo te llamas? : what's your name?>
llamarada *nf* **1 :** flare-up, sudden blaze **2 :** flushing (of the face)
llamativo, -va *adj* **:** flashy, showy, striking
llameante *adj* **:** flaming, blazing
llamear *vi* **:** to flame, to blaze
llana *nf* **1 :** trowel **2** → **llano**[2]
llanamente *adv* **:** simply, plainly, straightforwardly
llaneza *nf* **:** simplicity, naturalness
llano[1], **-na** *adj* **1 :** even, flat **2 :** frank, open **3** LISO **:** plain, simple
llano[2] *nm* **:** plain
llanta *nf* **1** NEUMÁTICO **:** tire **2 :** rim
llantén *nm, pl* **llantenes :** plantain (weed)
llanto *nm* **:** crying, weeping
llanura *nf* **:** plain, prairie
llave *nf* **1 :** key **2 :** faucet **3** INTERRUPTOR **:** switch **4 :** brace (punctuation mark) **5 llave inglesa :** monkey wrench
llavero *nm* **:** key chain, key ring
llegada *nf* **:** arrival
llegar {52} *vi* **1 :** to arrive, to come **2 ~ a :** to arrive at, to reach, to amount to **3 ~ a :** to manage to <llegó a terminar la novela : she managed to finish the novel> **4 llegar a ser :** to become <llegó a ser un miembro permanente : he became a permanent member>
llegue, etc. → **llegar**
llenar *vt* **1 :** to fill, to fill up, to fill in **2 :** to meet, to fulfill <los regalos no llenaron sus expectativas : the gifts did not meet her expectations> — **llenarse** *vr* **:** to fill up, to become full
llenito, -ta *adj fam* REGORDETE **:** chubby, plump
lleno[1], **-na** *adj* **1 :** full, filled **2 de ~ :** completely, fully **3 estar lleno de sí mismo :** to be full of oneself
lleno[2] *nm* **1** *fam* **:** plenty, abundance **2 :** full house, sellout
llevadero, -ra *adj* **:** bearable
llevar *vt* **1 :** to take away, to carry <me gusta, me lo llevo : I like it, I'll take it> **2 :** to wear **3 :** to take, to lead <llevamos a Pedro al cine : we took Pedro to the movies> **4 llevar a cabo :** to carry out **5 llevar adelante :** to carry on, to keep going — *vi* **:** to lead <un problema lleva al otro : one problem leads to another> — *v aux* **:** to

have <llevo mucho tiempo buscándolo : I've been looking for it for a long time> <lleva leído medio libro : he's halfway through the book> — **llevarse** *vr* **1 :** to take away, to carry off **2 :** to get along <siempre nos llevábamos bien : we always got along well>

llorar *vi* **:** to cry, to weep — *vt* **:** to mourn, to bewail

lloriquear *vi* **:** to whimper, to whine

lloriqueo *nm* **:** whimpering, whining

llorón, -rona *n, mpl* **llorones :** crybaby, whiner

lloroso, -sa *adj* **:** tearful, sad

llovedizo, -za *adj* **:** rain <agua llovediza : rainwater>

llover {47} *v impers* **:** to rain <está lloviendo : it's raining> <llover a cántaros : to rain cats and dogs> — *vi* **:** to rain down, to shower <le llovieron regalos : he was showered with gifts>

llovizna *nf* **:** drizzle, sprinkle

lloviznar *v impers* **:** to drizzle, to sprinkle

llueve, etc. → **llover**

lluvia *nf* **1 :** rain, rainfall **2 :** barrage, shower

lluvioso, -sa *adj* **:** rainy

lo[1] *pron* **1 :** him, it <lo vi ayer : I saw him yesterday> <lo entiendo : I understand it> <no lo creo : I don't believe so> **2** (*formal, masculine*) **:** you <disculpe, señor, no lo oí : excuse me sir, I didn't hear you> **3 lo que :** what, that which <eso es lo que más le gusta : that's what he likes the most>

lo[2] *art* **1 :** the <lo mejor : the best, the best thing> **2 :** how <sé lo bueno que eres : I know how good you are>

loa *nf* **:** praise

loable *adj* **:** laudable, praiseworthy — **loablemente** *adv*

loar *vt* **:** to praise, to laud

lobato, -ta *n* **:** wolf cub

lobby *nm* **:** lobby, pressure group

lobo, -ba *n* **:** wolf

lóbrego, -ga *adj* SOMBRÍO **:** gloomy, dark

lobulado, -da *adj* **:** lobed

lóbulo *nm* **:** lobe <lóbulo de la oreja : earlobe>

locación *nf, pl* **-ciones 1 :** location (in moviemaking) **2** *Mex* **:** place

local[1] *adj* **:** local — **localmente** *adv*

local[2] *nm* **:** premises *pl*

localidad *nf* **:** town, locality

localización *nf, pl* **-ciones 1 :** locating, localization **2 :** location

localizar {21} *vt* **1** UBICAR **:** to locate, to find **2 :** to localize — **localizarse** *vr* UBICARSE **:** to be located <se localiza en el séptimo piso : it is located on the seventh floor>

locatario, -ria *n* **:** tenant

loción *nf, pl* **lociones :** lotion

lócker *nm, pl* **lóckers :** locker

loco[1]**, -ca** *adj* **1** DEMENTE **:** crazy, insane, mad **2 a lo loco :** wildly, recklessly **3 volverse loco :** to go mad

loco[2]**, -ca** *n* **1 :** crazy person, lunatic **2 hacerse el loco :** to act the fool

locomoción *nf, pl* **-ciones :** locomotion

locomotor, -tora *adj* **:** locomotive

locomotora *nf* **1 :** locomotive **2 :** driving force

locuacidad *nf* **:** loquacity, talkativeness

locuaz *adj, pl* **locuaces :** loquacious, talkative

locución *nf, pl* **-ciones :** locution, phrase <locución adverbial : adverbial phrase>

locura *nf* **1 :** insanity, madness **2 :** crazy thing, folly

locutor, -tora *n* **:** announcer

lodazal *nm* **:** bog, quagmire

lodo *nm* BARRO **:** mud, mire

lodoso, -sa *adj* **:** muddy

logaritmo *nm* **:** logarithm

logia *nf* **:** lodge <logia masónica : Masonic lodge>

lógica *nf* **:** logic

lógico, -ca *adj* **:** logical — **lógicamente** *adv*

logística *nf* **:** logistics *pl*

logístico, -ca *adj* **:** logistic, logistical

logo *nm* → **logotipo**

logotipo *nm* **:** logo

logrado, -da *adj* **:** successful, well done

lograr *vt* **1 :** to get, to obtain **2 :** to achieve, to attain — **lograrse** *vr* **:** to be successful

logro *nm* **:** achievement, attainment

loma *nf* **:** hill, hillock

lombriz *nf, pl* **lombrices :** worm <lombriz de tierra : earthworm, night crawler> <lombriz solitaria : tapeworm> <tener lombrices : to have worms>

lomo *nm* **1 :** back (of an animal) **2 :** loin <lomo de cerdo : pork loin> **3 :** spine (of a book) **4 :** blunt edge (of a knife)

lona *nf* **:** canvas

loncha *nf* LONJA, REBANADA **:** slice

lonche *nm* **1** ALMUERZO **:** lunch **2** *Mex* **:** submarine sandwich

lonchería *nf Mex* **:** luncheonette

londinense[1] *adj* **:** of or from London

londinense[2] *nmf* **:** Londoner

longaniza *nf* **:** spicy pork sausage

longevidad *nf* **:** longevity

longevo, -va *adj* **:** long-lived

longitud *nf* **1** LARGO **:** length <longitud de onda : wavelength> **2 :** longitude

longitudinal *adj* **:** longitudinal

lonja *nf* LONCHA, REBANADA **:** slice

lontananza *nf* **:** background <en lontananza : in the distance, far away>

lord *nm, pl* **lores** (*title in England*) **:** lord

loro *nm* **:** parrot

los[1]**, las** *pron* **1 :** them <hice galletas y se las di a los nuevos vecinos : I made cookies and gave them to the

new neighbors> **2 :** you <voy a llevarlos a los dos : I am going to take both of you> **3 los que, las que :** those, who, the ones <los que van a cantar deben venir temprano : those who are singing must come early> **4** (*used with* **haber**) <los hay en varios colores : they come in various colors>
los[2] → **el[2]**
losa *nf* **:** flagstone, paving stone
loseta *nf* BALDOSA **:** floor tile
lote *nm* **1 :** part, share **2 :** batch, lot **3 :** plot of land, lot
lotería *nf* **:** lottery
loto *nm* **:** lotus
loza *nf* **1 :** crockery, earthenware **2 :** china
lozanía *nf* **1 :** healthiness, robustness **2 :** luxuriance, lushness
lozano, -na *adj* **1 :** robust, healthy-looking <un rostro lozano : a smooth, fresh face> **2 :** lush, luxuriant
lubricante[1] *adj* **:** lubricating
lubricante[2] *nm* **:** lubricant
lubricar {72} *vt* **:** to lubricate, to oil — **lubricación** *nf*
lucero *nm* **:** bright star <lucero del alba : morning star>
lucha *nf* **1 :** struggle, fight **2 :** wrestling
luchador, -dora *n* **1 :** fighter **2 :** wrestler
luchar *vi* **1 :** to fight, to struggle **2 :** to wrestle
luchón, -chona *adj, mpl* **luchones** *Mex* **:** industrious, hardworking
lucidez *nf, pl* **-deces :** lucidity, clarity
lucido, -da *adj* MAGNÍFICO **:** magnificent, splendid
lúcido, -da *adj* **:** lucid
luciérnaga *nf* **:** firefly, glowworm
lucimiento *nm* **1 :** brilliance, splendor, sparkle **2 :** triumph, success <salir con lucimiento : to succeed with flying colors>
lucio *nm* **:** pike (fish)
lucir {45} *vi* **1 :** to shine **2 :** to look good, to stand out **3 :** to seem, to appear <ahora luce contento : he looks happy now> — *vt* **1 :** to wear, to sport **2 :** to flaunt, to show off — **lucirse** *vr* **1 :** to distinguish oneself, to excel **2 :** to show off
lucrarse *vr* **:** to make a profit
lucrativo, -va *adj* **:** lucrative, profitable — **lucrativamente** *adv*
lucro *nm* GANANCIA **:** profit, gain
luctuoso, -sa *adj* **:** mournful, tragic
luego[1] *adv* **1** DESPUÉS **:** then, afterwards **2 :** later (on) **3 desde ~ :** of course **4 ¡hasta luego! :** see you later! **5 luego que :** as soon as **6 luego luego** *Mex fam* **:** right away, immediately
luego[2] *conj* **:** therefore <pienso, luego existo : I think, therefore I am>
lugar *nm* **1 :** place, position <se llevó el primer lugar en su división : she took first place in her division> **2** ESPACIO **:** space, room **3 dar lugar a :** to give rise to, to lead to **4 en lugar de :** instead of **5 lugar común :** cliché, platitude **6 tener lugar :** to take place
lugareño[1], -ña *adj* **:** village, rural
lugareño[2], -ña *n* **:** villager
lugarteniente *nmf* **:** lieutenant, deputy
lúgubre *adj* **:** gloomy, lugubrious
lujo *nm* **1 :** luxury **2 de ~ :** deluxe
lujoso, -sa *adj* **:** luxurious
lujuria *nf* **:** lust, lechery
lujurioso, -sa *adj* **:** lustful, lecherous
lumbar *adj* **:** lumbar
lumbre *nf* **1** FUEGO **:** fire **2 :** brilliance, splendor **3 poner en la lumbre :** to put on the stove, to warm up
lumbrera *nf* **1 :** skylight **2 :** vent, port **3 :** brilliant person, luminary
luminaria *nf* **1 :** altar lamp **2** LUMBRERA **:** luminary, celebrity
luminiscencia *nf* **:** luminescence — **luminiscente** *adj*
luminosidad *nf* **:** luminosity, brightness
luminoso, -sa *adj* **:** shining, luminous
luna *nf* **1 :** moon **2 luna de miel :** honeymoon
lunar[1] *adj* **:** lunar
lunar[2] *nm* **1 :** mole, beauty spot **2 :** defect, blemish **3 :** polka dot
lunático, -ca *adj & n* **:** lunatic
lunes *nms & pl* **:** Monday
luneta *nf* **1 :** lens (of eyeglasses) **2 :** windshield (of an automobile) **3 :** crescent
lupa *nf* **:** magnifying glass
lúpulo *nm* **:** hops (plant)
lustrar *vt* **:** to shine, to polish
lustre *nm* **1** BRILLO **:** luster, shine **2 :** glory, distinction
lustroso, -sa *adj* BRILLOSO **:** lustrous, shiny
luto *nm* **:** mourning <estar de luto : to be in mourning>
luz *nf, pl* **luces 1 :** light **2 :** lighting **3** *fam* **:** electricity **4 :** window, opening **5 :** light, lamp **6 :** span, spread (between supports) **7 a la luz de :** in light of **8 dar a luz :** to give birth **9 traje de luces :** matador's costume
luzca, etc. → **lucir**

M

m *nf* **:** thirteenth letter of the Spanish alphabet
macabro, -bra *adj* **:** macabre
macaco[1], -ca *adj* **:** ugly, misshapen
macaco[2], -ca *n* **:** macaque
macadán *nm, pl* **-danes :** macadam
macana *nf* **1 :** club, cudgel **2** *fam* **:** nonsense, silliness **3** *fam* **:** lie, fib
macanudo, -da *adj fam* **:** great, fantastic

macarrón *nm, pl* **-rrones 1 :** macaroon **2 macarrones** *nmpl* **:** macaroni
maceta *nf* **1 :** flowerpot **2 :** mallet **3** *Mex fam* **:** head
machacar {72} *vt* **1 :** to crush, to grind **2 :** to beat, to pound — *vi* **:** to insist, to go on (about)
machacón, -cona *adj, mpl* **-cones :** insistent, tiresome
machete *nm* **:** machete
machetear *vt* **:** to hack with a machete — *vi Mex fam* **:** to plod, to work tirelessly
machismo *nm* **1 :** machismo **2 :** male chauvinism
machista *nm* **:** male chauvinist
macho¹ *adj* **1 :** male **2 :** macho, virile, tough
macho² *nm* **1 :** male **2 :** he-man
machote *nm* **1** *fam* **:** tough guy, he-man **2** *CA, Mex* **:** rough draft, model **3** *Mex* **:** blank form
machucar {72} *vt* **1 :** to pound, to beat, to crush **2 :** to bruise
machucón *nm, pl* **-cones 1** MORETÓN **:** bruise **2 :** smashing, pounding
macilento, -ta *adj* **:** gaunt, wan
macis *nm* **:** mace (spice)
macizo, -za *adj* **1 :** solid <oro macizo : solid gold> **2 :** strong, strapping **3 :** massive
macrocosmo *nm* **:** macrocosm
mácula *nf* **:** blemish, stain
madeja *nf* **1 :** skein, hank **2 :** tangle (of hair)
madera *nf* **1 :** wood **2 :** lumber, timber **3 madera dura** *or* **madera noble :** hardwood
maderero, -ra *adj* **:** timber, lumber
madero *nm* **:** piece of lumber, plank
madrastra *nf* **:** stepmother
madrazo *nm Mex fam* **:** punch, blow <se agarraron a madrazos : they beat each other up>
madre *nf* **1 :** mother **2 madre política :** mother-in-law **3 la Madre Patria :** the mother country (said of Spain)
madrear *vt Mex fam* **:** to beat up
madreperla *nf* NÁCAR **:** mother-of-pearl
madreselva *nf* **:** honeysuckle
madriguera *nf* **:** burrow, den, lair
madrileño¹, -ña *adj* **:** of or from Madrid
madrileño², -ña *n* **:** person from Madrid
madrina *nf* **1 :** godmother **2 :** bridesmaid **3 :** sponsor
madrugada *nf* **1 :** early morning, wee hours **2** ALBA **:** dawn, daybreak
madrugador, -dora *n* **:** early riser
madrugar {52} *vi* **1 :** to get up early **2 :** to get a head start
madurar *v* **1 :** to ripen **2 :** to mature
madurez *nf, pl* **-reces 1 :** maturity **2 :** ripeness
maduro, -ra *adj* **1 :** mature **2 :** ripe
maestría *nf* **1 :** mastery, skill **2 :** master's degree
maestro¹, -tra *adj* **1 :** masterly, skilled **2 :** chief, main **3 :** trained <un elefante maestro : a trained elephant>
maestro², -tra *n* **1 :** teacher (in grammar school) **2 :** expert, master **3 :** maestro
Mafia *nf* **:** Mafia
mafioso, -sa *n* **:** mafioso, gangster
magdalena *nf* **:** bun, muffin
magenta *adj & n* **:** magenta
magia *nf* **:** magic
mágico, -ca *adj* **:** magic, magical — **mágicamente** *adv*
magisterio *nm* **1 :** teaching **2 :** teachers *pl*, teaching profession
magistrado, -da *n* **:** magistrate, judge
magistral *adj* **1 :** masterful, skillful **2 :** magisterial
magistralmente *adv* **:** masterfully, brilliantly
magistratura *nf* **:** judgeship, magistracy
magma *nm* **:** magma
magnanimidad *nf* **:** magnanimity
magnánimo, -ma *adj* GENEROSO **:** magnanimous — **magnánimamente** *adv*
magnate *nmf* **:** magnate, tycoon
magnesia *nf* **:** magnesia
magnesio *nm* **:** magnesium
magnético, -ca *adj* **:** magnetic
magnetismo *nm* **:** magnetism
magnetizar {21} *vt* **:** to magnetize
magnetófono *nm* **:** tape recorder
magnetofónico, -ca *adj* **cinta magnetofónica :** magnetic tape
magnificar {72} *vt* **1 :** to magnify **2** EXAGERAR **:** to exaggerate **3** ENSALZAR **:** to exalt, to extol, to praise highly
magnificencia *nf* **:** magnificence, splendor
magnífico, -ca *adj* ESPLENDOROSO **:** magnificent, splendid — **magníficamente** *adv*
magnitud *nf* **:** magnitude
magnolia *nf* **:** magnolia (flower)
magnolio *nm* **:** magnolia (tree)
mago, -ga *n* **1 :** magician **2 :** wizard (in folk tales, etc.) **3 los Reyes Magos :** the Magi
magro, -gra *adj* **1 :** lean (of meat) **2 :** meager
maguey *nm* **:** maguey
magulladura *nf* MORETÓN **:** bruise
magullar *vt* **:** to bruise — **magullarse** *vr*
mahometano¹, -na *adj* ISLÁMICO **:** Islamic, Muslim
mahometano², -na *n* **:** Muslim
mahonesa *nf* → **mayonesa**
maicena *nf* **:** cornstarch
maíz *nm* **:** corn, maize
maizal *nm* **:** cornfield
maja *nf* **:** pestle
majadería *nf* **1** TONTERÍA **:** stupidity, foolishness **2** *Mex* LEPERADA **:** insult, obscenity
majadero¹, -ra *adj* **1 :** foolish, silly **2** *Mex* LÉPERO **:** crude, vulgar

majadero[2], -ra *n* **1** TONTO **:** fool **2** *Mex* **:** rude person, boor
majar *vt* **:** to crush, to mash
majestad *nf* **:** majesty <Su Majestad : Your Majesty>
majestuosamente *adv* **:** majestically
majestuosidad *nf* **:** majesty, grandeur
majestuoso, -sa *adj* **:** majestic, stately
majo, -ja *adj Spain* **1 :** nice, likeable **2** GUAPO **:** attractive, good-looking
mal[1] *adv* **1 :** badly, poorly <baila muy mal : he dances very badly> **2 :** wrong, incorrectly <me entendió mal : she misunderstood me> **3 :** with difficulty, hardly <mal puedo oírte : I can hardly hear you> **4 de mal en peor :** from bad to worse **5 menos mal :** it could have been worse
mal[2] *adj* → **malo**
mal[3] *nm* **1 :** evil, wrong **2** DAÑO **:** harm, damage **3** DESGRACIA **:** misfortune **4** ENFERMEDAD **:** illness, sickness
malabar *adj* **juegos malabares :** juggling
malabarista *nmf* **:** juggler
malaconsejado, -da *adj* **:** ill-advised
malacostumbrado, -da *adj* CONSENTIDO **:** spoiled, pampered
malacostumbrar *vt* **:** to spoil
malagradecido, -da *adj* INGRATO **:** ungrateful
malaisio → **malasio**
malaquita *nf* **:** malachite
malaria *nf* PALUDISMO **:** malaria
malasio, -sia *adj & n* **:** Malaysian
malaventura *nf* **:** misadventure, misfortune
malaventurado, -da *adj* MALHADADO **:** ill-fated, unfortunate
malayo, -ya *adj & n* **:** Malay, Malayan
malbaratar *vt* **1** MALGASTAR **:** to squander **2 :** to undersell
malcriado[1], -da *adj* **1 :** ill-bred, bad-mannered **2 :** spoiled, pampered
malcriado[2], -da *n* **:** spoiled brat
maldad *nf* **1 :** evil, wickedness **2 :** evil deed
maldecir {11} *vt* **:** to curse, to damn — *vi* **1 :** to curse, to swear **2 ~ de :** to speak ill of, to slander, to defame
maldición *nf, pl* **-ciones :** curse
maldiga, maldijo, etc. → **maldecir**
maldito, -ta *adj* **1 :** cursed, damned <¡maldita sea! : damn it all!> **2 :** wicked
maldoso, -sa *adj Mex* **:** mischievous
maleable *adj* **:** malleable
maleante *nmf* **:** crook, thug
malecón *nm, pl* **-cones :** jetty, breakwater
maleducado, -da *adj* **:** ill-mannered, rude
maleficio *nm* **:** curse, hex
maléfico, -ca *adj* **:** evil, harmful
malentender {56} *vt* **:** to misunderstand
malentendido *nm* **:** misunderstanding
malestar *nm* **1 :** discomfort **2** IRRITACIÓN **:** annoyance **3** INQUIETUD **:** uneasiness, unrest
maleta *nf* **:** suitcase, bag <haz tus maletas : pack your bags>
maletero[1], -ra *n* **:** porter
maletero[2] *nm* **:** trunk (of an automobile)
maletín *nm, pl* **-tines 1** PORTAFOLIO **:** briefcase **2 :** overnight bag, satchel
malevolencia *nf* **:** malevolence, wickedness
malévolo, -la *adj* **:** malevolent, wicked
maleza *nf* **1 :** thicket, underbrush **2 :** weeds *pl*
malformación *nf, pl* **-ciones :** malformation
malgache *adj & nmf* **:** Madagascan
malgastar *vt* **:** to squander (resources), to waste (time, effort)
malhablado, -da *adj* **:** foul-mouthed
malhadado, -da *adj* MALAVENTURADO **:** ill-fated
malhechor, -chora *n* **:** criminal, delinquent, wrongdoer
malherir {76} *vt* **:** to injure seriously
malhumor *nm* **:** bad mood, sullenness
malhumorado, -da *adj* **:** bad-tempered, cross
malicia *nf* **1 :** wickedness, malice **2 :** mischief, naughtiness **3 :** cunning, craftiness
malicioso, -sa *adj* **1 :** malicious **2** PÍCARO **:** mischievous
malignidad *nf* **1 :** malignancy **2** MALDAD **:** evil
maligno, -na *adj* **1 :** malignant <un tumor maligno : a malignant tumor> **2 :** evil, harmful, malign
malinchismo *nm Mex* **:** preference for foreign goods or people — **malinchista** *adj*
malintencionado, -da *adj* **:** malicious, spiteful
malinterpretar *vt* **:** to misinterpret
malla *nf* **1 :** mesh **2** LEOTARDO **:** leotard, tights *pl* **3 malla de baño :** bathing suit
mallorquín, -quina *adj & n* **:** Majorcan
malnutrición *nf, pl* **-ciones** DESNUTRICIÓN **:** malnutrition
malnutrido, -da *adj* DESNUTRIDO **:** malnourished, undernourished
malo[1], -la *adj* (**mal** *before masculine singular nouns*) **1 :** bad <mala suerte : bad luck> **2 :** wicked, naughty **3 :** cheap, poor (quality) **4 :** harmful <malo para la salud : bad for one's health> **5** (*using the form* **mal**) **:** unwell <estar mal del corazón : to have heart trouble> **6 estar de malas :** to be in a bad mood
malo[2], -la *n* **:** villain, bad guy (in novels, movies, etc.)
malogrado, -da *adj* **:** failed, unsuccessful
malograr *vt* **1 :** to spoil, to ruin **2 :** to waste (an opportunity, time) — **mal-**

ograrse *vr* **1** FRACASAR : to fail **2** : to die young
malogro *nm* **1** : untimely death **2** FRACASO : failure
maloliente *adj* HEDIONDO : foul-smelling, smelly
malparado, -da *adj* **salir malparado** *or* **quedar malparado** : to come out of (something) badly, to end up in a bad state
malpensado, -da *adj* : distrustful, suspicious, nasty-minded
malquerencia *nf* AVERSIÓN : ill will, dislike
malquerer {64} *vt* : to dislike
malquiso, etc. → **malquerer**
malsano, -na *adj* : unhealthy
malsonante *adj* : rude, offensive <palabras malsonantes : foul language>
malta *nf* : malt
malteada *nf* : malted milk <malteada de chocolate : chocolate malt>
maltés, -tesa *adj & n, mpl* **malteses** : Maltese
maltratar *vt* **1** : to mistreat, to abuse **2** : to damage, to spoil
maltrato *nm* : mistreatment, abuse
maltrecho, -cha *adj* : battered, damaged
malucho, -cha *adj fam* : sick, under the weather
malva *adj & nm* : mauve
malvado[1], -da *adj* : evil, wicked
malvado[2], -da *n* : evildoer, wicked person
malvavisco *nm* : marshmallow
malvender *vt* : to sell at a loss
malversación *nf, pl* **-ciones** : misappropriation (of funds), embezzlement
malversador, -dora *n* : embezzler
malversar *vt* : to embezzle
malvivir *vi* : to live badly, to just scrape by
mamá *nf fam* : mom, mama
mamar *vi* **1** : to suckle **2 darle de mamar a** : to breast-feed — *vt* **1** : to suckle, to nurse **2** : to learn from childhood, to grow up with — **mamarse** *vr fam* : to get drunk
mamario, -ria *adj* : mammary
mamarracho *nm fam* **1** ESPERPENTO : mess, sight **2** : laughingstock, fool **3** : rubbish, junk
mambo *nm* : mambo
mami *nf fam* : mommy
mamífero[1], -ra *adj* : mammalian
mamífero[2] *nm* : mammal
mamila *nf* **1** : nipple **2** *Mex* : baby bottle, pacifier
mamografía *nf* : mammogram
mamola *nf* : pat, chuck under the chin
mamotreto *nm fam* **1** : huge book, tome **2** ARMATOSTE : hulk, monstrosity
mampara *nf* BIOMBO : screen, room divider
mamparo *nm* : bulkhead
mampostería *nf* : masonry, stonemasonery
mampostero *nm* : mason, stonemason
mamut *nm, pl* **mamuts** : mammoth
maná *nm* : manna
manada *nf* **1** : flock, herd, pack **2** *fam* : horde, mob <llegaron en manada : they came in droves>
manantial *nm* **1** FUENTE : spring **2** : source
manar *vi* **1** : to flow **2** : to abound
manatí *nm* : manatee
mancha *nf* **1** : stain, spot, mark <mancha de sangre : bloodstain> **2** : blemish, blot <una mancha en su reputación : a blemish on his reputation> **3** : patch
manchado, -da *adj* : stained
manchar *vt* **1** ENSUCIAR : to stain, to soil **2** DESHONRAR : to sully, to tarnish — **mancharse** *vr* : to get dirty
mancillar vt : to sully, to besmirch
manco, -ca *adj* : one-armed, one-handed
mancomunar *vt* : to combine, to pool — **mancomunarse** *vr* : to unite, to join together
mancomunidad *nf* **1** : commonwealth **2** : association, confederation
mancuernas *nfpl* : cuff links
mancuernillas *nf Mex* : cuff links
mandadero, -ra *n* : errand boy *m*, errand girl *f*, messenger
mandado *nm* **1** : order, command **2** : errand <hacer los mandados : to run errands, to go shopping>
mandamás *nmf, pl* **-mases** *fam* : boss, bigwig, honcho
mandamiento *nm* **1** : commandment **2** : command, order, warrant <mandamiento judicial : warrant, court order>
mandar *vt* **1** ORDENAR : to command, to order **2** ENVIAR : to send <te manda saludos : he sends you his regards> **3** ECHAR : to hurl, to throw **4 ¿mande?** *Mex* : yes?, pardon? — *vi* : to be the boss, to be in charge — **mandarse** *vr Mex* : to take liberties, to take advantage
mandarina *nf* : mandarin orange, tangerine
mandatario, -ria *n* **1** : leader (in politics) <primer mandatario : head of state> **2** : agent (in law)
mandato *nm* **1** : term of office **2** : mandate
mandíbula *nf* **1** : jaw **2** : mandible
mandil *nm* **1** DELANTAL : apron **2** : horse blanket
mandilón *nm, pl* **-lones** *fam* : wimp, coward
mandioca *nf* **1** : manioc, cassava **2** : tapioca
mando *nm* **1** : command, leadership **2** : control (for a device) <mando a distancia : remote control> **3 al mando de** : in charge of **4 al mando de** : under the command of
mandolina *nf* : mandolin
mandón, -dona *adj, mpl* **mandones** : bossy, domineering

mandonear *vt fam* MANGONEAR **:** to boss around
mandrágora *nf* **:** mandrake
manecilla *nf* **:** hand (of a clock), pointer
manejable *adj* **1 :** manageable **2 :** docile, easily led
manejar *vt* **1** CONDUCIR **:** to drive (a car) **2** OPERAR **:** to handle, to operate **3 :** to manage **4 :** to manipulate (a person) — *vi* **:** to drive — **manejarse** *vr* **1** COMPORTARSE **:** to behave **2 :** to get along, to manage
manejo *nm* **1 :** handling, operation **2 :** management
manera *nf* **1** MODO **:** way, manner, fashion **2 de cualquier manera** *or* **de todas maneras :** anyway, anyhow **3 de manera que :** so, in order that **4 de ninguna manera :** by no means, absolutely not **5 manera de ser :** personality, demeanor
manga *nf* **1 :** sleeve **2** MANGUERA **:** hose
manganeso *nm* **:** manganese
mangle *nm* **:** mangrove
mango *nm* **1 :** hilt, handle **2 :** mango
mangonear *vt fam* **:** to boss around, to bully — *vi* **1 :** to be bossy **2 :** to loaf, to fool around
mangosta *nf* **:** mongoose
manguera *nf* **:** hose
maní *nm, pl* **maníes :** peanut
manía *nf* **1** OBSESIÓN **:** mania, obsession **2 :** craze, fad **3 :** odd habit, peculiarity **4 :** dislike, aversion
maníaco[1], -ca *adj* **:** maniacal
maníaco[2], -ca *n* **:** maniac
maniatar *vt* **:** to tie the hands of, to manacle
maniático[1], -ca *adj* **1** MANÍACO **:** maniacal **2 :** obsessive **3 :** fussy, finicky
maniático[2], -ca *n* **1** MANÍACO **:** maniac, lunatic **2 :** obsessive person, fanatic **3 :** eccentric, crank
manicomio *nm* **:** insane asylum, madhouse
manicura *nf* **:** manicure
manicuro, -ra *n* **:** manicurist
manido, -da *adj* **:** hackneyed, stale, trite
manifestación *nf, pl* **-ciones 1 :** manifestation, sign **2 :** demonstration, rally
manifestante *nmf* **:** demonstrator
manifestar {55} *vt* **1 :** to demonstrate, to show **2 :** to declare — **manifestarse** *vr* **1 :** to be or become evident **2 :** to state one's position <se han manifestado a favor del acuerdo : they have declared their support for the agreement> **3 :** to demonstrate, to rally
manifiesto[1], -ta *adj* **:** manifest, evident, clear — **manifiestamente** *adv*
manifiesto[2] *nm* **:** manifesto
manija *nf* MANGO **:** handle
manilla *nf* → **manecilla**
manillar *nm* **:** handlebars *pl*
maniobra *nf* **:** maneuver, stratagem
maniobrar *v* **:** to maneuver
manipulación *nf, pl* **-ciones :** manipulation
manipulador[1], -dora *adj* **:** manipulating, manipulative
manipulador[2], -dora *n* **:** manipulator
manipular *vt* **1 :** to manipulate **2** MANEJAR **:** to handle
maniquí[1] *nmf, pl* **-quíes :** mannequin, model
maniquí[2] *nm, pl* **-quíes :** mannequin, dummy
manirroto[1], -ta *adj* **:** extravagant
manirroto[2], -ta *n* **:** spendthrift
manivela *nf* **:** crank
manjar *nm* **:** delicacy, special dish
mano[1] *nf* **1 :** hand **2 :** coat (of paint or varnish) **3 a ~ :** by hand **4 a ~** *or* **a la mano :** handy, at hand, nearby **5 darse la mano :** to shake hands **6 de la mano :** hand in hand <la política y la economía van de la mano : politics and economics go hand in hand> **7 de primera mano :** firsthand, at firsthand **8 de segunda mano :** secondhand <ropa de segunda mano : secondhand clothing> **9 mano a mano :** one-on-one **10 mano de obra :** labor, manpower **11 mano de mortero :** pestle **12 echar una mano :** to lend a hand **13** *Mex fam* **mano negra :** shady dealings *pl*
mano[2], -na *n Mex fam* **:** buddy, pal <¡oye, mano! : hey man!>
manojo *nm* PUÑADO **:** handful, bunch
manopla *nf* **1 :** mitten, mitt **2 :** brass knuckles *pl*
manosear *vt* **1 :** to handle or touch excessively **2** ACARICIAR **:** to fondle, to caress
manotazo *nm* **:** slap, smack, swipe
manotear *vi* **:** to wave one's hands, to gesticulate
mansalva *adv* **a ~ :** at close range
mansarda *nf* BUHARDILLA **:** attic
mansedumbre *nf* **1 :** gentleness, meekness **2 :** tameness
mansión *nf, pl* **-siones :** mansion
manso, -sa *adj* **1 :** gentle, meek **2 :** tame — **mansamente** *adv*
manta *nf* **1** COBIJA, FRAZADA **:** blanket **2 :** poncho **3** *Mex* **:** coarse cotton fabric
manteca *nf* **1** GRASA **:** lard, fat **2 :** butter
mantecoso, -sa *adj* **:** buttery
mantel *nm* **1 :** tablecloth **2 :** altar cloth
mantelería *nf* **:** table linen
mantener {80} *vt* **1** SUSTENTAR **:** to support, to feed <mantener uno su familia : to support one's family> **2** CONSERVAR **:** to keep, to preserve **3** CONTINUAR **:** to keep up, to sustain <mantener una correspondencia : to keep up a correspondence> **4** AFIRMAR **:** to maintain, to affirm — **mantenerse** *vr* **1 :** to support oneself, to subsist **2 mantenerse firme :** to hold one's ground
mantenimiento *nm* **1 :** maintenance, upkeep **2 :** sustenance, food **3 :** preservation

mantequera *nf* **1** : churn **2** : butter dish
mantequería *nf* **1** : creamery, dairy **2** : grocery store
mantequilla *nf* : butter
mantilla *nf* : mantilla
manto *nm* **1** : cloak **2** : mantle (in geology)
mantón *nm, pl* **-tones** CHAL : shawl
mantuvo, etc. → **mantener**
manual[1] *adj* **1** : manual <trabajo manual : manual labor> **2** : handy, manageable — **manualmente** *adv*
manual[2] *nm* : manual, handbook
manualidades *nfpl* : handicrafts (in schools)
manubrio *nm* **1** : handle, crank **2** : handlebars *pl*
manufactura *nf* **1** FABRICACIÓN : manufacture **2** : manufactured item, product **3** FÁBRICA : factory
manufacturar *vt* FABRICAR : to manufacture
manufacturero[1], **-ra** *adj* : manufacturing
manufacturero[2], **-ra** *n* FABRICANTE : manufacturer
manuscrito[1], **-ta** *adj* : handwritten
manuscrito[2] *nm* : manuscript
manutención *nf, pl* **-ciones** : maintenance, support
manzana *nf* **1** : apple **2** CUADRA : block (enclosed by streets or buildings) **3** *or* **manzana de Adán** : Adam's apple
manzanal *nm* **1** : apple orchard **2** MANZANO : apple tree
manzanar *nm* : apple orchard
manzanilla *nf* **1** : chamomile **2** : chamomile tea
manzano *nm* : apple tree
maña *nf* **1** : dexterity, skill **2** : cunning, guile **3 mañas** *or* **malas mañas** *nfpl* : bad habits, vices
mañana *nf* **1** : morning **2** : tomorrow
mañanero, -ra *adj* MATUTINO : morning <rocío mañanero : morning dew>
mañanitas *nfpl Mex* : birthday serenade
mañoso, -sa *adj* **1** HÁBIL : skillful **2** ASTUTO : cunning, crafty **3** : fussy, finicky
mapa *nm* CARTA : map
mapache *nm* : raccoon
mapamundi *nm* : map of the world
maqueta *nf* : model, mock-up
maquillador, -dora *n* : makeup artist
maquillaje *nm* : makeup
maquillarse *vr* : to put on makeup, to make oneself up
máquina *nf* **1** : machine <máquina de coser : sewing machine> <máquina de escribir : typewriter> **2** LOCOMOTORA : engine, locomotive **3** : machine (in politics) **4 a toda máquina** : at full speed
maquinación *nf, pl* **-ciones** : machination, scheme, plot
maquinal *adj* : mechanical, automatic — **maquinalmente** *adv*
maquinar *vt* : to plot, to scheme
maquinaria *nf* **1** : machinery **2** : mechanism, works *pl*
maquinilla *nf* **1** : small machine or device **2** *CA, Car* : typewriter
maquinista *nmf* **1** : machinist **2** : railroad engineer
mar *nmf* **1** : sea <un mar agitado : a rough sea> <hacerse a la mar : to set sail> **2 alta mar** : high seas
maraca *nf* : maraca
maraña *nf* **1** : thicket **2** ENREDO : tangle, mess
marasmo *nm* : paralysis, stagnation
maratón *nm, pl* **-tones** : marathon
maravilla *nf* **1** : wonder, marvel <a las mil maravillas : wonderfully, marvelously> <hacer maravillas : to work wonders> **2** : marigold
maravillar *vt* ASOMBRAR : to astonish, to amaze — **maravillarse** *vr* : to be amazed, to marvel
maravilloso, -sa *adj* ESTUPENDO : wonderful, marvelous — **maravillosamente** *adv*
marbete *nm* **1** ETIQUETA : label, tag **2** *PRi* : registration sticker (of a car)
marca *nf* **1** : mark **2** : brand, make **3** : trademark <marca registrada : registered trademark> **4** : record (in sports) <batir la marca : to beat the record>
marcado, -da *adj* : marked <un marcado contraste : a marked contrast>
marcador *nm* **1** TANTEADOR : scoreboard **2** : marker, felt-tipped pen **3 marcador de libros** : bookmark
marcaje *nm* **1** : scoring (in sports) **2** : guarding (in sports)
marcapasos *nms & pl* : pacemaker
marcar {72} *vt* **1** : to mark **2** : to brand (livestock) **3** : to indicate, to show **4** RESALTAR : to emphasize **5** : to dial (a telephone) **6** : to guard (an opponent) **7** ANOTAR : to score (a goal, a point) — *vi* **1** ANOTAR : to score **2** : to dial
marcha *nf* **1** : march **2** : hike, walk <ir de marcha : to go hiking> **3** : pace, speed <a toda marcha : at top speed> **4** : gear (of an automobile) <marcha atrás : reverse, reverse gear> **5 en ~** : in motion, in gear, under way
marchar *vi* **1** IR : to go, to travel **2** ANDAR : to walk **3** FUNCIONAR : to work, to go **4** : to march — **marcharse** *vr* : to leave
marchitar *vi* : to make wither, to wilt — **marchitarse** *vr* **1** : to wither, to shrivel up, to wilt **2** : to languish, to fade away
marchito, -ta *adj* : withered, faded
marcial *adj* : martial, military
marco *nm* **1** : frame, framework **2** : goalposts *pl* **3** AMBIENTE : setting, atmosphere **4** : mark (unit of currency)
marea *nf* : tide
mareado, -da *adj* **1** : dizzy, lightheaded **2** : queasy, nauseous **3** : seasick

marear *vt* **1 :** to make sick <los gases me marearon : the fumes made me sick> **2 :** to bother, to annoy — **marearse** *vr* **1 :** to get sick, to become nauseated **2 :** to feel dizzy **3 :** to get tipsy
marejada *nf* **1 :** surge, swell (of the sea) **2 :** undercurrent, ferment, unrest
maremoto *nm* **:** tidal wave
mareo *nm* **1 :** dizzy spell **2 :** nausea **3 :** seasickness, motion sickness **4 :** annoyance, vexation
marfil *nm* **:** ivory
margarina *nf* **:** margarine
margarita *nf* **1 :** daisy **2 :** margarita (cocktail)
margen[1] *nf, pl* **márgenes :** bank (of a river), side (of a street)
margen[2] *nm, pl* **márgenes 1 :** edge, border **2 :** margin <margen de ganancia : profit margin>
marginación *nf, pl* **-ciones :** marginalization, exclusion
marginado[1], **-da** *adj* **1** DESHEREDADO **:** outcast, alienated, dispossessed **2 clases marginadas :** underclass
marginado[2], **-da** *n* **:** outcast, misfit
marginal *adj* **:** marginal, fringe
marginalidad *nf* **:** marginality
marginar *vt* **:** to ostracize, to exclude
mariachi *nm* **:** mariachi musician or band
maridaje *nm* **:** marriage, union
maridar *vt* UNIR **:** to marry, to unite
marido *nm* ESPOSO **:** husband
marihuana *or* **mariguana** *or* **marijuana** *nf* **:** marihuana
marimacho *nmf fam* **1 :** mannish woman **2 :** tomboy
marimba *nf* **:** marimba
marina *nf* **1 :** coast, coastal area **2 :** navy, fleet <marina mercante : merchant marine>
marinada *nf* **:** marinade
marinar *vt* **:** to marinate
marinero[1], **-ra** *adj* **1 :** seaworthy **2 :** sea, marine
marinero[2] *nm* **:** sailor
marino[1], **-na** *adj* **:** marine, sea
marino[2] *nm* **:** sailor, seaman
marioneta *nf* TÍTERE **:** puppet, marionette
mariposa *nf* **1 :** butterfly **2 mariposa nocturna :** moth
mariquita[1] *nf* **:** ladybug
mariquita[2] *nm fam* **:** sissy, wimp
mariscal *nm* **1 :** marshal **2 mariscal de campo :** field marshal (in the military), quarterback (in football)
marisco *nm* **1 :** shellfish **2 mariscos** *nmpl* **:** seafood
marisma *nf* **:** marsh, salt marsh
marital *adj* **:** marital, married <la vida marital : married life>
marítimo, -ma *adj* **:** maritime, shipping <la industria marítima : the shipping industry>
marmita *nf* **:** (cooking) pot
mármol *nm* **:** marble
marmóreo, -rea *adj* **:** marble, marmoreal
marmota *nf* **1 :** marmot **2 marmota de América :** woodchuck, groundhog
maroma *nf* **1 :** rope **2 :** acrobatic stunt **3** *Mex* **:** somersault
marque, etc. → **marcar**
marqués, -quesa *n, mpl* **marqueses :** marquis *m,* marquess *m,* marquise *f,* marchioness *f*
marquesina *nf* **:** marquee, canopy
marqueta *nf Mex* **:** block (of chocolate), lump (of sugar or salt)
marranada *nf* **1 :** disgusting thing **2 :** dirty trick
marrano[1], **-na** *adj* **:** filthy, disgusting
marrano[2], **-na** *n* **1** CERDO **:** pig, hog **2 :** dirty pig, slob
marrar *vt* **:** to miss (a target) — *vi* **:** to fail, to go wrong
marras *adv* **1 :** long ago **2 de ~ :** said, aforementioned <el individuo de marras : the individual in question>
marrasquino *nm* **:** maraschino
marrón *adj & nm, pl* **marrones** CASTAÑO **:** brown
marroquí *adj & nmf, pl* **-quíes :** Moroccan
marsopa *nf* **:** porpoise
marsupial *nm* **:** marsupial
marta *nf* **1 :** marten **2 marta cebellina :** sable (animal)
Marte *nm* **:** Mars
martes *nms & pl* **:** Tuesday
martillar *v* **:** to hammer
martillazo *nm* **:** blow with a hammer
martillo *nm* **1 :** hammer **2 martillo neumático :** jackhammer
martinete *nm* **1 :** heron **2 :** pile driver
mártir *nmf* **:** martyr
martirio *nm* **1 :** martyrdom **2 :** ordeal, torment
martirizar {21} *vt* **1 :** to martyr **2** ATORMENTAR **:** to torment
marxismo *nm* **:** Marxism
marxista *adj & nmf* **:** Marxist
marzo *nm* **:** March
mas *conj* PERO **:** but
más[1] *adv* **1 :** more <¿hay algo más grande? : is there anything bigger?> **2 :** most <Luis es el más alto : Luis is the tallest> **3 :** longer <el sabor dura más : the flavor lasts longer> **4 :** rather <más querría andar : I would rather walk> **5 a ~ :** besides, in addition **6 más allá :** further **7 qué . . . más . . . :** what . . ., what a . . . <¡qué día más bonito! : what a beautiful day!>
más[2] *adj* **1 :** more <dáme dos kilos más : give me two more kilos> **2 :** most <la que ganó más dinero : the one who earned the most money> **3 :** else <¿quién más quiere vino? : who else wants wine?>
más[3] *n* **:** plus sign
más[4] *prep* **:** plus <tres más dos es igual a cinco : three plus two equals five>

más[5] *pron* **1** : more <¿tienes más? : do you have more?> **2 a lo más** : at most **3 de ~** : extra, excess **4 más o menos** : more or less, approximately **5 por más que** : no matter how much <por más que corras no llegarás a tiempo : no matter how fast you run you won't arrive on time>
masa *nf* **1** : mass, volume <masa atómica : atomic mass> <producción en masa : mass production> **2** : dough, batter **3 masas** *nfpl* : people, masses <las masas populares : the common people> **4 masa harina** *Mex* : corn flour (for tortillas, etc.)
masacrar *vt* : to massacre
masacre *nf* : massacre
masaje *nm* : massage
masajear *vt* : to massage
masajista *nmf* : masseur *m,* masseuse *f*
mascar {72} *v* MASTICAR : to chew
máscara *nf* **1** CARETA : mask **2** : appearance, pretense
mascarada *nf* : masquerade
mascarilla *nf* **1** : mask (in medicine) <mascarilla de oxígeno : oxygen mask> **2** : facial mask (in cosmetology)
mascota *nf* : mascot
masculinidad *nf* : masculinity
masculino, -na *adj* **1** : masculine, male **2** : manly **3** : masculine (in grammar)
mascullar *v* : to mumble, to mutter
masificado, -da *adj* : overcrowded
masilla *nf* : putty
masivamente *adv* : en masse
masivo, -va *adj* : mass <comunicación masiva : mass communication>
masón *nm, pl* **masones** FRANCMASÓN : Mason, Freemason
masonería *nf* FRANCMASONERÍA : Masonry, Freemasonry
masónico, -ca *adj* : Masonic
masoquismo *nm* : masochism
masoquista[1] *adj* : masochistic
masoquista[2] *nmf* : masochist
masque, etc. → **mascar**
masticar {72} *v* MASCAR : to chew, to masticate
mástil *nm* **1** : mast **2** ASTA : flagpole **3** : neck (of a stringed instrument)
mastín *nm, pl* **mastines** : mastiff
mástique *nm* : putty, filler
mastodonte *nm* : mastodon
masturbación *nf, pl* **-ciones** : masturbation
masturbarse *vr* : to masturbate
mata *nf* **1** ARBUSTO : bush, shrub **2** : plant <mata de tomate : tomato plant> **3** : sprig, tuft **4 mata de pelo** : mop of hair
matadero *nm* : slaughterhouse, abattoir
matado, -da *adj Mex* : strenuous, exhausting
matador *nm* TORERO : matador, bullfighter
matamoscas *nms & pl* : flyswatter
matanza *nf* MASACRE : slaughter, butchering
matar *vt* **1** : to kill **2** : to slaughter, to butcher **3** APAGAR : to extinguish, to put out (fire, light) **4** : to tone down (colors) **5** : to pass, to waste (time) **6** : to trump (in card games) — *vi* : to kill — **matarse** *vr* **1** : to be killed **2** SUICIDARSE : to commit suicide **3** *fam* : to exhaust oneself <se mató tratando de terminarlo : he knocked himself out trying to finish it>
matasanos *nms & pl fam* : quack
matasellar *vt* : to cancel (a stamp), to postmark
matasellos *nms & pl* : postmark
matatena *nf Mex* : jacks
mate[1] *adj* : matte, dull
mate[2] *nm* **1** : maté **2 jaque mate** : checkmate <darle mate a *or* darle jaque mate a : to checkmate>
matemática → **matemáticas**
matemáticas *nfpl* : mathematics, math
matemático[1], **-ca** *adj* : mathematical — **matemáticamente** *adv*
matemático[2], **-ca** *n* : mathematician
materia *nf* **1** : matter <materia gris : gray matter> **2** : material <materia prima : raw material> **3** : (academic) subject **4 en materia de** : on the subject of, concerning
material[1] *adj* **1** : material, physical, real **2 daños materiales** : property damage
material[2] *nm* **1** : material <material de construcción : building material> **2** EQUIPO : equipment, gear
materialismo *nm* : materialism
materialista[1] *adj* : materialistic
materialista[2] *nmf* **1** : materialist **2** *Mex* : truck driver
materializar {21} *vt* : to bring to fruition, to realize — **materializarse** *vr* : to materialize, to come into being
materialmente *adv* **1** : materially, physically <materialmente imposible : physically impossible> **2** : really, absolutely
maternal *adj* : maternal, motherly
maternidad *nf* **1** : maternity, motherhood **2** : maternity hospital, maternity ward
materno, -na *adj* : maternal
matinal *adj* MATUTINO : morning <la pálida luz matinal : the pale morning light>
matinée *or* **matiné** *nf* : matinee
matiz *nm, pl* **matices** **1** : hue, shade **2** : nuance
matización *nf, pl* **-ciones** **1** : tinting, toning, shading **2** : clarification (of a statement)
matizar {21} *vt* **1** : to tinge, to tint (colors) **2** : to vary, to modulate (sounds) **3** : to qualify (statements)
matón *nm, pl* **matones** : thug, bully
matorral *nm* **1** : thicket **2** : scrub, scrubland

matraca *nf* **1 :** rattle, noisemaker **2 dar la matraca a :** to pester, to nag

matriarca *nf* **:** matriarch

matriarcado *nm* **:** matriarchy

matrícula *nf* **1 :** list, roll, register **2** INSCRIPCIÓN **:** registration, enrollment **3 :** license plate, registration number

matriculación *nf, pl* **-ciones :** matriculation, registration

matricular *vt* **1** INSCRIBIR **:** to enroll, to register (a person) **2 :** to register (a vehicle) — **matricularse** *vr* **:** to matriculate

matrimonial *adj* **:** marital, matrimonial <la vida matrimonial : married life>

matrimonio *nm* **1 :** marriage, matrimony **2 :** married couple

matriz *nf, pl* **matrices 1 :** uterus, womb **2 :** original, master copy **3 :** main office, headquarters **4 :** stub (of a check) **5 :** matrix <matriz de puntos : dot matrix>

matrona *nf* **:** matron

matronal *adj* **:** matronly

matutino[1], -na *adj* **:** morning <la edición matutina : the morning edition>

matutino[2] *nm* **:** morning paper

maullar {8} *vi* **:** to meow

maullido *nm* **:** meow

mauritano, -na *adj & n* **:** Mauritanian

mausoleo *nm* **:** mausoleum

maxilar *nm* **:** jaw, jawbone

máxima *nf* **:** maxim

máxime *adv* ESPECIALMENTE **:** especially, principally

maximizar {21} *vt* **:** to maximize

máximo[1], -ma *adj* **:** maximum, greatest, highest

máximo[2] *nm* **1 :** maximum **2 al máximo :** to the utmost **3 como ~ :** at the most, at the latest

maya[1] *adj & nmf* **:** Mayan

maya[2] *nmf* **:** Maya, Mayan

mayo *nm* **:** May

mayonesa *nf* **:** mayonnaise

mayor[1] *adj* **1** (*comparative of* **grande**) **:** bigger, larger, greater, elder, older **2** (*superlative of* **grande**) **:** biggest, largest, greatest, eldest, oldest **3 :** grown-up, mature **4 :** main, major **5 mayor de edad :** of (legal) age **6 al por mayor** *or* **por ~ :** wholesale

mayor[2] *nmf* **1 :** major (in the military) **2 :** adult

mayoral *nm* CAPATAZ **:** foreman, overseer

mayordomo *nm* **:** butler, majordomo

mayoreo *nm* **:** wholesale

mayores *nmpl* **:** grown-ups, elders

mayoría *nf* **1 :** majority **2 en su mayoría :** on the whole

mayorista[1] *adj* ALMACENISTA **:** wholesale

mayorista[2] *nmf* **:** wholesaler

mayoritariamente *adv* **:** primarily, chiefly

mayoritario, -ria *adj & n* **:** majority <un consenso mayoritario : a majority consensus>

mayormente *adv* **:** primarily, chiefly

mayúscula *nf* **:** capital letter

mayúsculo, -la *adj* **1 :** capital, uppercase **2 :** huge, terrible <un problema mayúsculo : a huge problem>

maza *nf* **1 :** mace (weapon) **2 :** drumstick **3** *fam* **:** bore, pest

mazacote *nm* **1 :** concrete **2 :** lumpy mess (of food) **3 :** eyesore, crude work of art

mazapán *nm, pl* **-panes :** marzipan

mazmorra *nf* CALABOZO **:** dungeon

mazo *nm* **1 :** mallet **2 :** pestle **3** MANOJO **:** handful, bunch

mazorca *nf* **1** CHOCLO **:** cob, ear of corn **2 pelar la mazorca** *Mex fam* **:** to smile from ear to ear

me *pron* **1 :** me <me vieron : they saw me> **2 :** to me, for me, from me <dame el libro : give me the book> <me lo compró : he bought it for me> <me robaron la cartera : they stole my pocketbook> **3 :** myself, to myself, for myself, from myself <me preparé una buena comida : I cooked myself a good dinner> <me equivoqué : I made a mistake>

mecánica *nf* **:** mechanics

mecánico[1], -ca *adj* **:** mechanical — **mecánicamente** *adv*

mecánico[2], -ca *n* **1 :** mechanic **2 :** technician <mecánico dental : dental technician>

mecanismo *nm* **:** mechanism

mecanización *nf, pl* **-ciones :** mechanization

mecanizar {21} *vt* **:** to mechanize

mecanografía *nf* **:** typing

mecanografiar {85} *vt* **:** to type

mecanógrafo, -fa *n* **:** typist

mecate *nm CA, Mex, Ven* **:** rope, twine, cord

mecedor *nm* **:** glider (seat)

mecedora *nf* **:** rocking chair

mecenas *nmfs & pl* **:** patron (of the arts), sponsor

mecenazgo *nm* PATROCINIO **:** sponsorship, patronage

mecer {86} *vt* **1 :** to rock **2** COLUMPIAR **:** to push (on a swing) — **mecerse** *vr* **:** to rock, to swing, to sway

mecha *nf* **1 :** fuse **2 :** wick **3 mechas** *nfpl* **:** highlights (in hair)

mechero *nm* **1 :** burner **2** *Spain* **:** lighter

mechón *nm, pl* **mechones :** lock (of hair)

medalla *nf* **:** medal, medallion

medallista *nmf* **:** medalist

medallón *nm, pl* **-llones 1 :** medallion **2 :** locket

media *nf* **1** CALCETÍN **:** sock **2 :** average, mean **3 medias** *nfpl* **:** stockings, hose, tights **4 a medias :** by halves, half and half, halfway <ir a medias : to go

halves> <verdad a medias : half-truth>

mediación *nf, pl* **-ciones** : mediation

mediado, -da *adj* **1** : half full, half empty, half over **2** : halfway through <mediada la tarea : halfway through the job>

mediador, -dora *n* : mediator

mediados *nmpl* **a mediados de** : halfway through, in the middle of <a mediados del mes : towards the middle of the month, mid-month>

medialuna *nf* **1** : crescent **2** : croissant, crescent roll

medianamente *adv* : fairly, moderately

medianero, -ra *adj* **1** : dividing **2** : mediating

medianía *nf* **1** : middle position **2** : mediocre person, mediocrity

mediano, -na *adj* **1** : medium, average <la mediana edad : middle age> **2** : mediocre

medianoche *nf* : midnight

mediante *prep* : through, by means of <Dios mediante : God willing>

mediar *vi* **1** : to mediate **2** : to be in the middle, to be halfway through **3** : to elapse, to pass <mediaron cinco años entre el inicio de la guerra y el armisticio : five years passed between the start of the war and the armistice> **4** : to be a consideration <media el hecho de que cuesta mucho : one must take into account that it is costly> **5** : to come up, to happen <medió algo urgente : something pressing came up>

mediatizar {21} *vt* : to influence, to interfere with

medicación *nf, pl* **-ciones** : medication, treatment

medicamento *nm* : medication, medicine, drug

medicar {72} *vt* : to medicate — **medicarse** *vr* : to take medicine

medicina *nf* : medicine

medicinal *adj* **1** : medicinal **2** : medicated

medicinar *vt* : to give medication to, to dose

medición *nf, pl* **-ciones** : measuring, measurement

médico[1], -ca *adj* : medical <una receta médica : a doctor's prescription>

médico[2], -ca *n* DOCTOR : doctor, physician

medida *nf* **1** : measurement, measure <hecho a medida : custom-made> **2** : measure, step <tomar medidas : to take steps> **3** : moderation, prudence <sin medida : immoderately> **4** : extent, degree <en gran medida : to a great extent>

medidor *nm* : meter, gauge

medieval *adj* : medieval — **medievalista** *nmf*

medievo *nm* → **medioevo**

medio[1] *adv* **1** : half <está medio dormida : she's half asleep> **2** : rather, kind of <está medio aburrida esta fiesta : this party is rather boring>

medio[2], -dia *adj* **1** : half <una media hora : half an hour> <medio hermano : half brother> <a media luz : in the half-light> <son las tres y media : it's half past three, it's three-thirty> **2** : midway, halfway <a medio camino : halfway there> **3** : middle <la clase media : the middle class> **4** : average <la temperatura media : the average temperature>

medio[3] *nm* **1** CENTRO : middle, center <en medio de : in the middle of, amid> **2** AMBIENTE : milieu, environment **3** : medium, spiritualist **4** : means *pl,* way <por medio de : by means of> <los medios de comunicación : the media> **5 medios** *nmpl* : means, resources

mediocre *adj* : mediocre, average

mediocridad *nf* : mediocrity

mediodía *nm* : noon, midday

medioevo *nm* : Middle Ages

medir {54} *vt* **1** : to measure **2** : to weigh, to consider <medir los riesgos : to weigh the risks> — *vi* : to measure — **medirse** *vr* : to be moderate, to exercise restraint

meditabundo, -da *adj* PENSATIVO : pensive, thoughtful

meditación *nf, pl* **-ciones** : meditation, thought

meditar *vi* : to meditate, to think <meditar sobre la vida : to contemplate life> — *vt* **1** : to think over, to consider **2** : to plan, to work out

meditativo, -va *adj* : pensive

mediterráneo, -nea *adj* : Mediterranean

medrar *vi* **1** PROSPERAR : to prosper, to thrive **2** AUMENTAR : to increase, to grow

medro *nm* PROSPERIDAD : prosperity, growth

medroso, -sa *adj* : fainthearted, fearful

médula *nf* **1** : marrow, pith **2 médula espinal** : spinal cord

medular *adj* : fundamental, core <el punto medular : the crux of the matter>

medusa *nf* : jellyfish, medusa

megabyte *nm* : megabyte

megáfono *nm* : megaphone

megahertzio *nm* : megahertz

megatón *nm, pl* **-tones** : megaton

megavatio *nm* : megawatt

mejicano → **mexicano**

mejilla *nf* : cheek

mejillón *nm, pl* **-llones** : mussel

mejor[1] *adv* **1** : better <Carla cocina mejor que Ana : Carla cooks better than Ana> **2** : best <ella es la que lo hace mejor : she's the one who does it best> **3** : rather <mejor morir que rendirme : I'd rather die than give up> **4** : it's better that . . . <mejor te

vas : you'd better go> **5 a lo mejor** : maybe, perhaps

mejor[2] *adj* **1** (*comparative of* **bueno**) : better <a falta de algo mejor : for lack of something better> **2** (*comparative of* **bien**) : better <está mucho mejor : he's much better> **3** (*superlative of* **bueno**) : best, the better <mi mejor amigo : my best friend> **4** (*superlative of* **bien**) : best, the better <duermo mejor en un clima seco : I sleep best in a dry climate> **5** PREFERIBLE : preferable, better **6 lo mejor** : the best thing, the best part

mejor[3] *nmf* (*with definite article*) : the better (one), the best (one)

mejora *nf* : improvement

mejoramiento *nm* : improvement

mejorana *nf* : marjoram

mejorar *vt* : to improve, to make better — *vi* : to improve, to get better — **mejorarse** *vr*

mejoría *nf* : improvement, betterment

mejunje *nm* : concoction, brew

melancolía *nf* : melancholy, sadness

melancólico, -ca *adj* : melancholy, sad

melanoma *nm* : melanoma

melaza *nf* : molasses

maleficio *nm* : curse, spell

melena *nf* **1** : mane **2** : long hair **3 melenas** *nfpl* GREÑAS : shaggy hair, mop

melenudo[1], **-da** *adj fam* : longhaired

melenudo[2], **-da** *n* GREÑUDO : longhair, hippie

melindres *nmpl* **1** : affectation, airs *pl* **2** : finickiness

melindroso[1], **-sa** *adj* **1** : affected **2** : fussy, finicky

melindroso[2], **-sa** *n* : finicky person, fussbudget

melisa *nf* : lemon balm

mella *nf* **1** : dent, nick **2 hacer mella en** : to have an effect on, to make an impression on

mellado, -da *adj* **1** : chipped, dented **2** : gap-toothed

mellar *vt* : to dent, to nick

mellizo, -za *adj & n* GEMELO : twin

melocotón *nm, pl* **-tones** : peach

melodía *nf* : melody, tune

melódico, -ca *adj* : melodic

melodioso, -sa *adj* : melodious

melodrama *nm* : melodrama

melodramático, -ca *adj* : melodramatic

melón *nm, pl* **melones** : melon, cantaloupe

meloso, -sa *adj* **1** : honeyed, sweet **2** EMPALAGOSO : cloying, saccharine

membrana *nf* **1** : membrane **2 membrana interdigital** : web, webbing (of a bird's foot) — **membranoso, -sa** *adj*

membresía *nf* : membership, members *pl*

membrete *nm* : letterhead, heading

membrillo *nm* : quince

membrudo, -da *adj* FORNIDO : muscular, well-built

memez *nf, pl* **memeces** : stupid thing

memo, -ma *adj* : silly, stupid

memorabilia *nf* : memorabilia

memorable *adj* : memorable

memorándum *or* **memorando** *nm, pl* **-dums** *or* **-dos 1** : memorandum, memo **2** : memo book, appointment book

memoria *nf* **1** : memory <de memoria : by heart> <hacer memoria : to try to remember> <traer a la memoria : to call to mind> **2** RECUERDO : remembrance, memory <su memoria perdurará para siempre : his memory will live forever> **3** : report <memoria anual : annual report> **4 memorias** *nfpl* : memoirs

memorizar {21} *vt* : to memorize — **memorización** *nf*

mena *nf* : ore

menaje *nm* : household goods *pl,* furnishings *pl*

mención *nf, pl* **-ciones** : mention

mencionar *vt* : to mention, to refer to

mendaz *adj, pl* **mendaces** : mendacious, lying

mendicidad *nf* : begging

mendigar {52} *vi* : to beg — *vt* : to beg for

mendigo, -ga *n* LIMOSNERO : beggar

mendrugo *nm* : crust (of bread)

menear *vt* **1** : to shake (one's head) **2** : to sway, to wiggle (one's hips) **3** : to wag (a tail) **4** : to stir (a liquid) — **menearse** *vr* **1** : to wiggle one's hips **2** : to fidget

meneo *nm* **1** : movement **2** : shake, toss **3** : swaying, wagging, wiggling **4** : stir, stirring

menester *nm* **1** : activity, occupation, duties *pl* **2 ser menester** : to be necessary <es menester que vengas : you must come>

mengano, -na *n* → **fulano**

mengua *nf* **1** : decrease, decline **2** : lack, want **3** : discredit, dishonor

menguar *vt* : to diminish, to lessen — *vi* **1** : to decline, to decrease **2** : to wane — **menguante** *adj*

meningitis *nf* : meningitis

menisco *nm* : meniscus, cartilage

menjurje *nm* → **mejunje**

menopausia *nf* : menopause

menor[1] *adj* **1** (*comparative of* **pequeño**) : smaller, lesser, younger **2** (*superlative of* **pequeño**) : smallest, least, youngest **3** : minor **4 al por menor** : retail **5 ser menor de edad** : to be a minor, to be underage

menor[2] *nmf* : minor, juvenile

menos[1] *adv* **1** : less <llueve menos en agosto : it rains less in August> **2** : least <el coche menos caro : the least expensive car> **3 ~ de** : less than, fewer than

menos[2] *adj* **1** : less, fewer <tengo más trabajo y menos tiempo : I have more

work and less time> **2** : least, fewest <la clase que tiene menos estudiantes : the class that has the fewest students>

menos[3] *prep* **1** SALVO, EXCEPTO : except **2** : minus <quince menos cuatro son once : fifteen minus four is eleven>

menos[4] *pron* **1** : less, fewer <no deberías aceptar menos : you shouldn't accept less> **2 al menos** *or* **por lo menos** : at least **3 a menos que** : unless

menoscabar *vt* **1** : to lessen, to diminish **2** : to disgrace, to discredit **3** PERJUDICAR : to harm, to damage

menoscabo *nm* **1** : lessening, diminishing **2** : disgrace, discredit **3** : harm, damage

menospreciar *vt* **1** DESPRECIAR : to scorn, to look down on **2** : to underestimate, to undervalue

menosprecio *nm* DESPRECIO : contempt, scorn

mensaje *nm* : message

mensajero, -ra *n* : messenger

menso, -sa *adj Mex fam* : foolish, stupid

menstrual *adj* : menstrual

menstruar {3} *vi* : to menstruate — **menstruación** *nf*

mensual *adj* : monthly

mensualidad *nf* **1** : monthly payment, installment **2** : monthly salary

mensualmente *adv* : every month, monthly

mensurable *adj* : measurable

menta *nf* **1** : mint, peppermint **2 menta verde** : spearmint

mentado, -da *adj* **1** : aforementioned **2** FAMOSO : renowned, famous

mental *adj* : mental, intellectual — **mentalmente** *adv*

mentalidad *nf* : mentality

mentar {55} *vt* **1** : to mention, to name **2 mentar la madre a** *fam* : to insult, to swear at

mente *nf* : mind <tener en mente : to have in mind>

mentecato[1], **-ta** *adj* : foolish, simple

mentecato[2], **-ta** *n* : fool, idiot

mentir {76} *vi* : to lie

mentira *nf* : lie

mentiroso[1], **-sa** *adj* EMBUSTERO : lying, untruthful

mentiroso[2], **-sa** *n* EMBUSTERO : liar

mentís *nm, pl* **mentises** : denial, repudiation <dar el mentís a : to deny, to refute>

mentol *nm* : menthol

mentón *nm, pl* **mentones** BARBILLA : chin

mentor *nm* : mentor, counselor

menú *nm, pl* **menús** : menu

menudear *vi* : to occur frequently — *vt* : to do repeatedly

menudencia *nf* **1** : trifle **2 menudencias** *nfpl* : giblets

menudeo *nm* : retail, retailing

menudillos *nmpl* : giblets

menudo[1], **-da** *adj* **1** : minute, small **2 a ~** FRECUENTEMENTE : often, frequently

menudo[2] *nm* **1** *Mex* : tripe stew **2 menudos** *nmpl* : giblets

meñique *nm or* **dedo meñique** : little finger, pinkie

meollo *nm* **1** MÉDULA : marrow **2** SESO : brains *pl* **3** ENTRAÑA : essence, core <el meollo del asunto : the heart of the matter>

mequetrefe *nm fam* : good-for-nothing

mercachifle *nm* : peddler, hawker

mercadeo *nm* : marketing

mercadería *nf* : merchandise, goods *pl*

mercado *nm* : market <mercado de trabajo *or* mercado laboral : labor market> <mercado de valores *or* mercado bursátil : stock market>

mercadotecnia *nf* : marketing

mercancía *nf* : merchandise, goods *pl*

mercante *nmf* : merchant, dealer

mercantil *adj* COMERCIAL : commercial, mercantile

merced *nf* **1** : favor **2 ~ a** : thanks to, due to **3 a merced de** : at the mercy of

mercenario, -ria *adj & n* : mercenary

mercería *nf* : notions store

mercurio *nm* : mercury

Mercurio *nm* : Mercury (planet)

merecedor, -dora *adj* : deserving, worthy

merecer {53} *vt* : to deserve, to merit — *vi* : to be worthy

merecidamente *adv* : rightfully, deservedly

merecido *nm* : something merited, due <recibieron su merecido : they got their just deserts>

merecimiento *nm* : merit, worth

merendar {55} *vi* : to have an afternoon snack — *vt* : to have as an afternoon snack

merendero *nm* **1** : lunchroom, snack bar **2** : picnic area

merengue *nm* **1** : meringue **2** : merengue (dance)

meridiano[1], **-na** *adj* **1** : midday **2** : crystal clear

meridiano[2] *nm* : meridian

meridional *adj* SUREÑO : southern

merienda *nf* : afternoon snack, tea

mérito *nm* : merit

meritorio[1], **-ria** *adj* : deserving, meritorious

meritorio[2], **-ria** *n* : intern, trainee

merluza *nf* : hake

merma *nf* **1** : decrease, cut **2** : waste, loss

mermar *vi* : to decrease, to diminish — *vt* : to reduce, to cut down

mermelada *nf* : marmalade, jam

mero[1], **-ra** *adv Mex fam* **1** : nearly, almost <ya mero me caí : I almost fell> **2** : just, exactly <aquí mero : right here>

mero[2], -ra *adj* **1 :** mere, simple **2** *Mex fam* (*used as an intensifier*) **:** very <en el mero centro : in the very center of town>
mero[3] *nm* **:** grouper
merodeador, -dora *n* **1 :** marauder **2 :** prowler
merodear *vi* **1 :** to maraud, to pillage **2 :** to prowl around, to skulk
mes *nm* **:** month
mesa *nf* **1 :** table **2 :** committee, board
mesada *nf* **:** allowance, pocket money
mesarse *vr* **:** to pull at <mesarse los cabellos : to tear one's hair>
mesero, -ra *n* CAMARERO **:** waiter, waitress *f*
meseta *nf* **:** plateau, tableland
Mesías *nm* **:** Messiah
mesón *nm, pl* **mesones :** inn
mesonero, -ra *nm* **:** innkeeper
mestizo[1], -za *adj* **1 :** of mixed ancestry **2** HÍBRIDO **:** hybrid
mestizo[2], -za *n* **:** person of mixed ancestry
mesura *nf* **1** MODERACIÓN **:** moderation, discretion **2** CORTESÍA **:** courtesy **3** GRAVEDAD **:** seriousness, dignity
mesurado, -da *adj* COMEDIDO **:** moderate, restrained
mesurar *vt* **:** to moderate, to restrain, to temper — **mesurarse** *vr* **:** to restrain oneself
meta *nf* **:** goal, objective
metabólico, -ca *adj* **:** metabolic
metabolismo *nm* **:** metabolism
metabolizar {21} *vt* **:** to metabolize
metafísica *nf* **:** metaphysics
metafísico, -ca *adj* **:** metaphysical
metáfora *nf* **:** metaphor
metafórico, -ca *adj* **:** metaphoric, metaphorical
metal *nm* **1 :** metal **2 :** brass section (in an orchestra)
metálico, -ca *adj* **:** metallic, metal
metalistería *nf* **:** metalworking
metalurgia *nf* **:** metallurgy
metalúrgico[1], -ca *adj* **:** metallurgical
metalúrgico[2], -ca *n* **:** metallurgist
metamorfosis *nfs & pl* **:** metamorphosis
metano *nm* **:** methane
meteórico, -ca *adj* **:** meteoric
meteorito *nm* **:** meteorite
meteoro *nm* **:** meteor
meteorología *nf* **:** meteorology
meteorológico, -ca *adj* **:** meteorologic, meteorological
meteorólogo, -ga *n* **:** meteorologist
meter *vt* **1 :** to put (in) <metieron su dinero en el banco : they put their money in the bank> **2 :** to fit, to squeeze <puedes meter dos líneas más en esa página : you can fit two more lines on that page> **3 :** to place (in a job) <lo metieron de barrendero : they got him a job as a street sweeper> **4 :** to involve <lo metió en un buen lío : she got him in an awful mess> **5 :** to make, to cause <meten demasiado ruido : they make too much noise> **6 :** to spread (a rumor) **7 :** to strike (a blow) **8 :** to take up, to take in (clothing) **9 a todo meter :** at top speed — **meterse** *vr* **1 :** to get into, to enter **2** *fam* **:** to meddle <no te metas en lo que no te importa : mind your own business> **3 ~ con** *fam* **:** to pick a fight with, to provoke <no te metas conmigo : don't mess with me>
metiche[1] *adj Mex fam* **:** nosy
metiche[2] *nmf Mex fam* **:** busybody
meticulosidad *nf* **:** thoroughness, meticulousness
meticuloso, -sa *adj* **:** meticulous, thorough — **meticulosamente** *adv*
metida *nf* **metida de pata** *fam* **:** blunder, gaffe, blooper
metódico, -ca *adj* **:** methodical — **metódicamente** *adv*
metodista *adj & nmf* **:** Methodist
método *nm* **:** method
metodología *nf* **:** methodology
metomentodo *nmf fam* **:** busybody
metralla *nf* **:** shrapnel
metralleta *nf* **:** submachine gun
métrico, -ca *adj* **1 :** metric **2 cinta métrica :** tape measure
metro *nm* **1 :** meter **2 :** subway
metrónomo *nm* **:** metronome
metrópoli *nf or* **metrópolis** *nfs & pl* **:** metropolis
metropolitano, -na *adj* **:** metropolitan
mexicanismo *nm* **:** Mexican word or expression
mexicano, -na *adj & n* **:** Mexican
mexicoamericano, -na *adj & n* **:** Mexican-American
meza, etc. → **mecer**
mezcla *nf* **1 :** mixing **2 :** mixture, blend **3 :** mortar (masonry material)
mezclar *vt* **1 :** to mix, to blend **2 :** to mix up, to muddle **3** INVOLUCRAR **:** to involve — **mezclarse** *vr* **1 :** to get mixed up (in) **2 :** to mix, to mingle (socially)
mezclilla *nf Chile, Mex* **:** denim <pantalones de mezclilla : jeans>
mezcolanza *nf* **:** jumble, hodgepodge
mezquindad *nf* **1 :** meanness, stinginess **2 :** petty deed, mean action
mezquino[1], -na *adj* **1 :** mean, petty **2 :** stingy **3 :** paltry
mezquino[2] *nm Mex* **:** wart
mezquita *nf* **:** mosque
mezquite *nm* **:** mesquite
mi *adj* **:** my
mí *pron* **1 :** me <es para mí : it's for me> <a mí no me importa : it doesn't matter to me> **2 mí mismo, mí misma :** myself
miasma *nm* **:** miasma
miau *nm* **:** meow
mica *nf* **:** mica
mico *nm* **:** monkey, long-tailed monkey
micra *nf* **:** micron
microbio *nm* **:** microbe, germ
microbiología *nf* **:** microbiology

microbiólogico, -ca *adj* : microbiological
microbús *nm, pl* **-buses** : minibus
microcomputadora *nf* : microcomputer
microcosmos *nms & pl* : microcosm
microficha *nf* : microfiche
microfilm *nm, pl* **-films** : microfilm
micrófono *nm* : microphone
micrómetro *nm* : micrometer
microonda *nf* : microwave
microondas *nms & pl* : microwave, microwave oven
microordenador *nm Spain* : microcomputer
microorganismo *nm* : microorganism
microprocesador *nm* : microprocessor
microscópico, -ca *adj* : microscopic
microscopio *nm* : microscope
mide, etc. → **medir**
miedo *nm* **1** TEMOR : fear <le tiene miedo al perro : he's scared of the dog> <tenían miedo de hablar : they were afraid to speak> **2 dar miedo** : to frighten
miedoso, -sa *adj* TEMEROSO : fearful
miel *nf* : honey
miembro *nm* **1** : member **2** EXTREMIDAD : limb, extremity
mienta, etc. → **mentar**
miente, etc. → **mentir**
mientras[1] *adv* **1** *or* **mientras tanto** : meanwhile, in the meantime **2 mientras más** : the more <mientras más como, más quiero : the more I eat, the more I want>
mientras[2] *conj* **1** : while, as <roncaba mientras dormía : he snored while he was sleeping> **2** : as long as <luchará mientras pueda : he will fight as long as he is able> **3 mientras que** : while, whereas <él es alto mientras que ella es muy baja : he is tall, whereas she is very short>
miércoles *nms & pl* : Wednesday
miga *nf* **1** : crumb **2 hacer buenas (malas) migas con** : to get along well (poorly) with
migaja *nf* **1** : crumb **2 migajas** *nfpl* SOBRAS : leftovers, scraps
migración *nf, pl* **-ciones** : migration
migrante *nmf* : migrant
migraña *nf* : migraine
migratorio, -ria *adj* : migratory
mijo *nm* : millet
mil[1] *adj* : thousand
mil[2] *nm* : one thousand, a thousand
milagro *nm* : miracle <de milagro : miraculously>
milagroso, -sa *adj* : miraculous, marvelous — **milagrosamente** *adv*
milenio *nm* : millennium
milésimo, -ma *adj* : thousandth — **milésimo** *n*
milicia *nf* **1** : militia **2** : military service
miligramo *nm* : milligram
mililitro *nm* : milliliter
milímetro *nm* : millimeter
militancia *nf* : militancy
militante[1] *adj* : militant
militante[2] *nmf* : militant, activist
militar[1] *vi* **1** : to serve (in the military) **2** : to be active (in politics)
militar[2] *adj* : military
militar[3] *nmf* SOLDADO : soldier
militarizar {21} *vt* : to militarize
milla *nf* : mile
millar *nm* : thousand
millón *nm, pl* **millones** : million
millonario, -ria *n* : millionaire
millonésimo[1], **-ma** *adj* : millionth
millonésimo[2] *nm* : millionth
mil millones *nms & pl* : billion
milpa *nf CA, Mex* : cornfield
milpiés *nms & pl* : millipede
mimar *vt* CONSENTIR : to pamper, to spoil
mimbre *nm* : wicker
mimeógrafo *nm* : mimeograph
mímica *nf* **1** : mime, sign language **2** IMITACIÓN : mimicry
mimo *nm* **1** : pampering, indulgence <hacerle mimos a alguien : to pamper someone> **2** : mime
mimoso, -sa *adj* **1** : fussy, finicky **2** : affectionate, clinging
mina *nf* **1** : mine **2** : lead (for pencils)
minar *vt* **1** : to mine **2** DEBILITAR : to undermine
minarete *nm* ALMINAR : minaret
mineral *adj & nm* : mineral
minería *nf* : mining
minero[1], **-ra** *adj* : mining
minero[2], **-ra** *n* : miner, mine worker
miniatura *nf* : miniature
minicomputadora *nf* : minicomputer
minifalda *nf* : miniskirt
minifundio *nm* : small farm
minimizar {21} *vt* : to minimize
mínimo[1], **-ma** *adj* **1** : minimum <salario mínimo : minimum wage> **2** : least, smallest **3** : very small, minute
mínimo[2] *nm* **1** : minimum, least amount **2** : modicum, small amount **3 como ~** : at least
minino, -na *n fam* : pussy, pussycat
miniserie *nf* : miniseries
ministerial *adj* : ministerial
ministerio *nm* : ministry, department
ministro, -tra *n* : minister, secretary <primer ministro : prime minister> <Ministro de Defensa : Secretary of Defense>
minivan [ˌminiˈban, -ˈvan] *nf, pl* **-vanes** : minivan
minoría *nf* : minority
minorista[1] *adj* : retail
minorista[2] *nmf* : retailer
minoritario, -ria *adj* : minority
mintió, etc. → **mentir**
minuciosamente *adv* **1** : minutely **2** : in great detail **3** : thoroughly, meticulously
minucioso, -sa *adj* **1** : minute **2** DETALLADO : detailed **3** : thorough, meticulous
minué *nm* : minuet

minúsculo, -la *adj* DIMINUTO : tiny, miniscule

minusvalía *nf* : disability, handicap

minusválido[1], -da *adj* : handicapped, disabled

minusválido[2], -da *n* : handicapped person

minuta *nf* **1** BORRADOR : rough draft **2** : bill, fee

minutero *nm* : minute hand

minuto *nm* : minute

mío[1], mía *adj* **1** : my, of mine <¡Dios mío! : my God!, good heavens!> <una amiga mía : a friend of mine> **2** : mine <es mío : it's mine>

mío[2], mía *pron* (*with definite article*) : mine, my own <tus zapatos son iguales a los míos : your shoes are just like mine>

miope *adj* : nearsighted, myopic

miopía *nf* : myopia, nearsightedness

mira *nf* **1** : sight (of a firearm or instrument) **2** : aim, objective <con miras a : with the intention of, with a view to> <de amplias miras : broad-minded> <poner la mira en : to aim at, to aspire to>

mirada *nf* **1** : look, glance, gaze **2** EXPRESIÓN : look, expression <una mirada de sorpresa : a look of surprise>

mirado, -da *adj* **1** : cautious, careful **2** : considerate **3 bien mirado** : well thought of **4 mal mirado** : disliked, disapproved of

mirador *nm* : balcony, lookout, vantage point

miramiento *nm* **1** CONSIDERACIÓN : consideration, respect **2 sin miramientos** : without due consideration, carelessly

mirar *vt* **1** : to look at **2** OBSERVAR : to watch **3** REFLEXIONAR : to consider, to think over — *vi* **1** : to look **2** : to face, to overlook **3 ~ por** : to look after, to look out for — **mirarse** *vr* **1** : to look at oneself **2** : to look at each other

mirasol *nm* GIRASOL : sunflower

miríada *nf* : myriad

mirlo *nm* : blackbird

mirra *nf* : myrrh

mirto *nm* ARRAYÁN : myrtle

misa *nf* : Mass

misantropía *nf* : misanthropy

misantrópico, -ca *adj* : misanthropic

misántropo, -pa *n* : misanthrope

miscelánea *nf* : miscellany

misceláneo, -nea *adj* : miscellaneous

miserable *adj* **1** LASTIMOSO : miserable, wretched **2** : paltry, meager **3** MEZQUINO : stingy, miserly **4** : despicable, vile

miseria *nf* **1** POBREZA : poverty **2** : misery, suffering **3** : pittance, meager amount

misericordia *nf* COMPASIÓN : mercy, compassion

misericordioso, -sa *adj* : merciful

mísero, -ra *adj* **1** : wretched, miserable **2** : stingy **3** : paltry, meager

misil *nm* : missile

misión *nf, pl* **misiones** : mission

misionero, -ra *adj & n* : missionary

misiva *nf* : missive, letter

mismísimo, -ma *adj* (*used as an intensifier*) : very, selfsame <el mismísimo día : that very same day>

mismo[1] *adv* (*used as an intensifier*) : right, exactly <hazlo ahora mismo : do it right now> <te llamará hoy mismo : he'll definitely call you today>

mismo[2], -ma *adj* **1** : same **2** (*used as an intensifier*) : very <en ese mismo momento : at that very moment> **3** : oneself <lo hizo ella misma : she made it herself> **4 por lo mismo** : for that reason

misoginia *nf* : misogyny

misógino *nm* : misogynist

misterio *nm* : mystery

misterioso, -sa *adj* : mysterious — **misteriosamente** *adv*

misticismo *nm* : mysticism

místico[1], -ca *adj* : mystic, mystical

místico[2], -ca *n* : mystic

mitad *nf* **1** : half <mitad y mitad : half and half> **2** MEDIO : middle <a mitad de : halfway through> <por la mitad : in half>

mítico, -ca *adj* : mythical, mythic

mitigar {52} *vt* ALIVIAR : to mitigate, to alleviate — **mitigación** *nf*

mitin *nm, pl* **mítines** : (political) meeting, rally

mito *nm* LEYENDA : myth, legend

mitología *nm* : mythology

mitológico, -ca *adj* : mythological

mitosis *nfs & pl* : mitosis

mitra *nf* : miter (bishop's hat)

mixto, -ta *adj* **1** : mixed, joint **2** : coeducational

mixtura *nf* : mixture, blend

mnemónico, -ca *adj* : mnemonic

mobiliario *nm* : furniture

mocasín *nm, pl* **-sines** : moccasin

mocedad *nf* **1** JUVENTUD : youth **2** : youthful prank

mochila *nf* MORRAL : backpack, knapsack

moción *nf, pl* **-ciones 1** MOVIMIENTO : motion, movement **2** : motion (to a court or assembly)

moco *nm* **1** : mucus **2** *fam* : snot <limpiarse los mocos : to wipe one's (runny) nose>

mocoso, -sa *n* : kid, brat

moda *nf* **1** : fashion, style **2 a la moda** *or* **de ~** : in style, fashionable **3 moda pasajera** : fad

modales *nmpl* : manners

modalidad *nf* **1** CLASE : kind, type **2** MANERA : way, manner

modelar *vt* : to model, to mold — **modelarse** *vr* : to model oneself after, to emulate

modelo[1] *adj* : model <una casa modelo : a model home>
modelo[2] *nm* : model, example, pattern
modelo[3] *nmf* : model, mannequin
módem *or* **modem** [ˈmoðɛm] *nm* : modem
moderación *nf, pl* **-ciones** MESURA : moderation
moderado, -da *adj & n* : moderate — **moderadamente** *adv*
moderador, -dora *n* : moderator, chair
moderar *vt* **1** TEMPERAR : to temper, to moderate **2** : to curb, to reduce <moderar gastos : to curb spending> **3** PRESIDIR : to chair (a meeting) — **moderarse** *vr* **1** : to restrain oneself **2** : to diminish, to calm down
modernidad *nf* **1** : modernity, modernness **2** : modern age
modernismo *nm* : modernism
modernista[1] *adj* : modernist, modernistic
modernista[2] *nmf* : modernist
modernizar {21} *vt* : to modernize — **modernización** *nf*
moderno, -na *adj* : modern, up-to-date
modestia *nf* : modesty
modesto, -ta *adj* : modest — **modestamente** *adv*
modificación *nf, pl* **-ciones** : alteration
modificante *nm* : modifier
modificar {72} *vt* ALTERAR : to modify, to alter, to adapt
modismo *nm* : idiom
modista *nmf* **1** : dressmaker **2** : fashion designer
modo *nm* **1** MANERA : way, manner, mode <de un modo u otro : one way or another> <a mi modo de ver : to my way of thinking> **2** : mood (in grammar) **3** : mode (in music) **4 a modo de** : by way of, in the manner of, like <a modo de ejemplo : by way of example> **5 de cualquier modo** : in any case, anyway **6 de modo que** : so, in such a way that **7 de todos modos** : in any case, anyway **8 en cierto modo** : in a way, to a certain extent
modorra *nf* : drowsiness, lethargy
modular[1] *v* : to modulate — **modulación** *nf*
modular[2] *adj* : modular
módulo *nm* : module, unit
mofa *nf* **1** : mockery, ridicule **2 hacer mofa de** : to make fun of, to ridicule
mofarse *vr* **~ de** : to scoff at, to make fun of
mofeta *nf* ZORRILLO : skunk
mofle *nm CA, Mex* : muffler (of a car)
moflete *nm fam* : fat cheek
mofletudo, -da *adj fam* : fat-cheeked, chubby
mohín *nm, pl* **mohines** : grimace, face
mohino, -na *adj* : gloomy, melancholy
moho *nm* **1** : mold, mildew **2** : rust
mohoso, -sa *adj* **1** : moldy **2** : rusty
moisés *nm, pl* **moiseses** : bassinet, cradle
mojado[1], **-da** *adj* : wet
mojado[2], **-da** *n Mex fam* : illegal immigrant
mojar *vt* **1** : to wet, to moisten **2** : to dunk — **mojarse** *vr* : to get wet
mojigatería *nf* **1** : hypocrisy **2** GAZMOÑERÍA : primness, prudery
mojigato[1], **-ta** *adj* : prudish, prim — **mojigatamente** *adv*
mojigato[2], **-ta** *n* : prude, prig
mojón *nm, pl* **mojones** : boundary stone, marker
molar *nm* MUELA : molar
molcajete *nm Mex* : mortar
molde *nm* **1** : mold, form **2 letras de molde** : printing, block lettering
moldear *vt* **1** FORMAR : to mold, to shape **2** : to cast
moldura *nf* : molding
mole[1] *nm Mex* **1** : spicy sauce made with chilies and usually chocolate **2** : meat served with mole sauce
mole[2] *nf* : mass, bulk
molécula *nf* : molecule — **molecular** *adj*
moler {47} *vt* **1** : to grind, to crush **2** CANSAR : to exhaust, to wear out
molestar *vt* **1** FASTIDIAR : to annoy, to bother **2** : to disturb, to disrupt — *vi* : to be a nuisance — **molestarse** *vr* **~ en** : to take the trouble to
molestia *nf* **1** FASTIDIO : annoyance, bother, nuisance **2** : trouble <se tomó la molestia de investigar : she took the trouble to investigate> **3** MALESTAR : discomfort
molesto, -ta *adj* **1** ENOJADO : bothered, annoyed **2** FASTIDIOSO : bothersome, annoying
molestoso, -sa *adj* : bothersome, annoying
molido, -da *adj* **1** MACHACADO : ground, crushed **2 estar molido** : to be exhausted
molinero, -ra *n* : miller
molinillo *nm* : grinder, mill <molinillo de café : coffee grinder>
molino *nm* **1** : mill **2 molino de viento** : windmill
molla *nf* : soft fleshy part, flesh (of fruit), lean part (of meat)
molleja *nf* : gizzard
molusco *nm* : mollusk
momentáneamente *adv* : momentarily
momentáneo, -nea *adj* **1** : momentary **2** TEMPORARIO : temporary
momento *nm* **1** : moment, instant <espera un momentito : wait just a moment> **2** : time, period of time <momentos difíciles : hard times> **3** : present, moment <los atletas del momento : the athletes of the moment, today's popular athletes> **4** : momentum **5 al momento** : right away, at once **6 de ~** : at the moment, for the moment **7 de un momento a otro** : any time now **8 por momentos** : at times

momia *nf* : mummy
monaguillo *nm* ACÓLITO : altar boy
monarca *nmf* : monarch
monarquía *nf* : monarchy
monárquico, -ca *n* : monarchist
monasterio *nm* : monastery
monástico, -ca *adj* : monastic
mondadientes *nms & pl* PALILLO : toothpick
mondar *vt* : to peel
mondongo *nm* ENTRAÑAS : innards *pl,* insides *pl,* guts *pl*
moneda *nf* **1** : coin **2** : money, currency
monedero *nm* : change purse
monetario, -ria *adj* : monetary, financial
mongol, -gola *adj & n* : Mongol, Mongolian
monitor[1]**, -tora** *n* : instructor (in sports)
monitor[2] *nm* : monitor <monitor de televisión : television monitor>
monitorear *vt* : to monitor
monja *nf* : nun
monje *nm* : monk
mono[1]**, -na** *adj fam* : lovely, pretty, cute, darling
mono[2]**, -na** *n* : monkey
monóculo *nm* : monocle
monogamia *nf* : monogamy
monógamo -ma *adj* : monogamous
monografía *nf* : monograph
monograma *nm* : monogram
monolingüe *adj* : monolingual
monolítico, -ca *adj* : monolithic
monolito *nm* : monolith
monólogo *nm* : monologue
monomanía *nf* : obsession
monopatín *nm, pl* **-tines** : scooter
monopolio *nm* : monopoly
monopolizar {21} *vt* : to monopolize — **monopolización** *nf*
monosilábico, -ca *adj* : monosyllabic
monosílabo *nm* : monosyllable
monoteísmo *nm* : monotheism
monoteísta[1] *adj* : monotheistic
monoteísta[2] *nmf* : monotheist
monotonía *nf* **1** : monotony **2** : monotone
monótono, -na *adj* : monotonous — **monótonamente** *adv*
monóxido *nm* : monoxide <monóxido de carbono : carbon monoxide>
monserga *nf* : gibberish, drivel
monstruo *nm* : monster
monstruosidad *nf* : monstrosity
monstruoso, -sa *adj* : monstrous — **monstruosamente** *adv*
monta *nf* **1** : sum, total **2** : importance, value <de poca monta : unimportant, insignificant>
montaje *nm* **1** : assembling, assembly **2** : montage
montante *nm* : transom, fanlight
montaña *nf* **1** MONTE : mountain **2 montaña rusa** : roller coaster
montañero, -ra *n* : mountaineer, mountain climber
montañoso, -sa *adj* : mountainous
montar *vt* **1** : to mount **2** ESTABLECER : to set up, to establish **3** ARMAR : to assemble, to put together **4** : to edit (a film) **5** : to stage, to put on (a show) **6** : to cock (a gun) **7 montar en bicicleta** : to get on a bicycle **8 montar a caballo** CABALGAR : to ride horseback
monte *nm* **1** MONTAÑA : mountain, mount **2** : woodland, scrubland <monte bajo : underbrush> **3** : outskirts (of a town), surrounding country **4 monte de piedad** : pawnshop
montés *adj, pl* **monteses** : wild (of animals or plants)
montículo *nm* **1** : mound, heap **2** : hillock, knoll
monto *nm* : amount, total
montón *nm, pl* **-tones 1** : heap, pile **2** *fam* : ton, load <un montón de preguntas : a ton of questions> <montones de gente : loads of people>
montura *nf* **1** : mount (horse) **2** : saddle, tack **3** : setting, mounting (of jewelry) **4** : frame (of glasses)
monumental *adj fam* **1** : tremendous, terrific **2** : massive, huge
monumento *nm* : monument
monzón *nm, pl* **monzones** : monsoon
moño *nm* **1** : bun (chignon) **2** LAZO : bow, knot <corbata de moño : bow tie>
moquear *vi* : to snivel
moquillo *nm* : distemper
mora *nf* **1** : blackberry **2** : mulberry
morada *nf* RESIDENCIA : dwelling, abode
morado[1]**, -da** *adj* : purple
morado[2] *nm* : purple
morador, -dora *n* : dweller, inhabitant
moral[1] *adj* : moral — **moralmente** *adv*
moral[2] *nf* **1** MORALIDAD : ethics, morality, morals *pl* **2** ÁNIMO : morale, spirits *pl*
moraleja *nf* : moral (of a story)
moralidad *nf* : morality
moralista[1] *adj* : moralistic
moralista[2] *nmf* : moralist
morar *vi* : to dwell, to reside
moratoria *nf* : moratorium
morboso, -sa *adj* : morbid — **morbosidad** *nf*
morcilla *nf* : blood sausage, blood pudding
mordacidad *nf* : bite, sharpness
mordaz *adj* : caustic, scathing
mordaza *nf* **1** : gag **2** : clamp
mordedura *nf* : bite (of an animal)
morder {47} *v* : to bite
mordida *nf* **1** : bite **2** *CA, Mex* : bribe, payoff
mordisco *nm* : bite, nibble
mordisquear *vt* : to nibble (on), to bite
morena *nf* **1** : moraine **2** : moray (eel)
moreno[1]**, -na** *adj* **1** : brunette **2** : dark, dark-skinned
moreno[2]**, -na** *n* **1** : brunette **2** : dark-skinned person

moretón *nm, pl* **-tones** : bruise

morfina *nf* : morphine

morfología *nf* : morphology

morgue *nf* : morgue

moribundo[1], **-da** *adj* : dying, moribund

moribundo[2], **-da** *n* : dying person

morillo *nm* : andiron

morir {46} *vi* **1** FALLECER : to die **2** APAGARSE : to die out, to go out

mormón, -mona *adj & n, pl* **mormones** : Mormon

moro[1], **-ra** *adj* : Moorish

moro[2], **-ra** *n* **1** : Moor **2** : Muslim

morosidad *nf* **1** : delinquency (in payment) **2** : slowness

moroso, -sa *adj* **1** : delinquent, in arrears <cuentas morosas : delinquent accounts> **2** : slow, sluggish

morral *nm* MOCHILA : backpack, knapsack

morralla *nf* **1** : small fish **2** : trash, riffraff **3** *Mex* : small change

morriña *nf* : homesickness

morro *nm* HOCICO : snout

morsa *nf* : walrus

morse *nm* : Morse code

mortaja *nf* SUDARIO : shroud

mortal[1] *adj* **1** : mortal **2** FATAL : fatal, deadly — **mortalmente** *adv*

mortal[2] *nmf* : mortal

mortalidad *nf* : mortality

mortandad *nf* **1** : loss of life, death toll **2** : carnage, slaughter

mortero *nm* : mortar (bowl, cannon, or building material)

mortífero, -ra *adj* LETAL : deadly, fatal

mortificación *nf, pl* **-ciones 1** : mortification **2** TORMENTO : anguish, torment

mortificar {72} *vt* **1** : to mortify **2** TORTURAR : to trouble, to torment — **mortificarse** *vr* : to be mortified, to feel embarrassed

mosaico *nm* : mosaic

mosca *nf* **1** : fly **2 mosca común** : housefly

moscada *adj* **nuez moscada** : nutmeg

moscovita *adj & nmf* : Muscovite

mosquearse *vr* **1** : to become suspicious **2** : to take offense

mosquete *nm* : musket

mosquetero *nm* : musketeer

mosquitero *nm* : mosquito net

mosquito *nm* ZANCUDO : mosquito

mostachón *nm, pl* **-chones** : macaroon

mostaza *nf* : mustard

mostrador *nm* : counter (in a store)

mostrar {19} *vt* **1** : to show **2** EXHIBIR : to exhibit, to display — **mostrarse** *vr* : to show oneself, to appear

mota *nf* **1** : fleck, speck **2** : defect, blemish

mote *nm* SOBRENOMBRE : nickname

moteado, -da *adj* : dotted, spotted, dappled

motel *nm* : motel

motín *nm, pl* **motines 1** : riot **2** : rebellion, mutiny

motivación *nf, pl* **-ciones** : motivation — **motivacional** *adj*

motivar *vt* **1** CAUSAR : to cause **2** IMPULSAR : to motivate

motivo *nm* **1** MÓVIL : motive **2** CAUSA : cause, reason **3** TEMA : theme, motif

moto *nf* : motorcycle, motorbike

motocicleta *nf* : motorcycle

motociclismo *nm* : motorcycling

motociclista *nmf* : motorcyclist

motor[1], **-ra** *adj* MOTRIZ : motor

motor[2] *nm* **1** : motor, engine **2** : driving force, cause

motorista *nmf* : motorist

motriz *adj, pl* **motrices** : driving

motu proprio *adv* **de motu proprio** [de'motu'proprio] : voluntarily, of one's own accord

mousse ['mus] *nm* : mousse

mover {47} *vt* **1** TRASLADAR : to move, to shift **2** AGITAR : to shake, to nod (the head) **3** ACCIONAR : to power, to drive **4** INDUCIR : to provoke, to cause **5** : to excite, to stir — **moverse** *vr* **1** : to move, to move over **2** : to hurry, to get a move on **3** : to get moving, to make an effort

movible *adj* : movable

movida *nf* : move (in a game)

móvil[1] *adj* : mobile

móvil[2] *nm* **1** MOTIVO : motive **2** : mobile

movilidad *nf* : mobility

movilizar {21} *vt* : to mobilize — **movilización** *nf*

movimiento *nm* : movement, motion <movimiento del cuerpo : bodily movement> <movimiento sindicalista : labor movement>

mozo[1], **-za** *adj* : young, youthful

mozo[2], **-za** *n* **1** JOVEN : young man *m*, young woman *f*, youth **2** : helper, servant

mucamo, -ma *n* : servant, maid *f*

muchacha *nf* : maid

muchacho, -cha *n* **1** : kid, boy *m*, girl *f* **2** JOVEN : young man *m*, young woman *f*

muchedumbre *nf* MULTITUD : crowd, multitude

mucho[1] *adv* **1** : much, a lot <mucho más : much more> <le gusta mucho : he likes it a lot> **2** : long, a long time <tardó mucho en venir : he was a long time getting here> **3 por mucho que** : no matter how much

mucho[2], **-cha** *adj* **1** : a lot of, many, much <mucha gente : a lot of people> <hace mucho tiempo que no lo veo : I haven't seen him in ages> **2 muchas veces** : often

mucho[3], **-cha** *pron* **1** : a lot, many, much <hay mucho que hacer : there is a lot to do> <muchas no vinieron : many didn't come> **2 cuando ~** *or* **como ~** : at most **3 con ~** : by far **4 ni mucho menos** : not at all, far from it

mucílago *nm* : mucilage

mucosidad *nf* : mucus

mucoso, -sa *adj* **:** mucous, slimy
muda *nf* **1 :** change <muda de ropa : change of clothes> **2 :** molt, molting
mudanza *nf* **1** CAMBIO **:** change **2** TRASLADO **:** move, moving
mudar *v* **1** CAMBIAR **:** to change **2 :** to molt, to shed — **mudarse** *vr* **1** TRASLADARSE **:** to move (one's residence) **2 :** to change (clothes)
mudo[1], -da *adj* **1** SILENCIOSO **:** silent <el cine mudo : silent films> **2 :** mute, dumb
mudo[2], -da *n* **:** mute
mueble *nm* **1 :** piece of furniture **2 muebles** *nmpl* **:** furniture, furnishings
mueblería *nf* **:** furniture store
mueca *nf* **:** grimace, face
muela *nf* **1 :** tooth, molar <dolor de muelas : toothache> <muela de juicio : wisdom tooth> **2 :** millstone **3 :** whetstone
muele, etc. → **moler**
muelle[1] *adj* **:** soft, comfortable, easy
muelle[2] *nm* **1 :** wharf, dock **2** RESORTE **:** spring
muérdago *nm* **:** mistletoe
muerde, etc. → **morder**
muere, etc. → **morir**
muerte *nf* **:** death
muerto[1] *pp* → **morir**
muerto[2], -ta *adj* **1 :** dead **2 :** lifeless, flat, dull **3 ~ de :** dying of <estoy muerto de hambre : I'm dying of hunger>
muerto[3], -ta *nm* DIFUNTO **:** dead person, deceased
muesca *nf* **:** nick, notch
muestra[1], etc. → **mostrar**
muestra[2] *nf* **1 :** sample **2** SEÑAL **:** sign, show <una muestra de respeto : a show of respect> **3** EXPOSICIÓN **:** exhibition, exposition **4 :** pattern, model
mueve, etc. → **mover**
mugido *nm* **:** moo, lowing, bellow
mugir {35} *vi* **:** to moo, to low, to bellow
mugre *nf* SUCIEDAD **:** grime, filth
mugriento, -ta *adj* **:** filthy
muguete *nm* **:** lily of the valley
muja, etc. → **mugir**
mujer *nf* **1 :** woman **2** ESPOSA **:** wife
mulato, -ta *adj & n* **:** mulatto
muleta *nf* **:** crutch
mullido, -da *adj* **1 :** soft, fluffy **2 :** spongy, springy
mulo, -la *n* **:** mule
multa *nf* **:** fine
multicolor *adj* **:** multicolored
multicultural *adj* **:** multicultural
multidisciplinario, -ria *adj* **:** multidisciplinary
multifacético, -ca *adj* **:** multifaceted
multifamiliar *adj* **:** multifamily
multilateral *adj* **:** multilateral
multimedia *nf* **:** multimedia
multimillonario, -ria *n* **:** multimillionaire
multinacional *adj* **:** multinational
múltiple *adj* **:** multiple
multiplicación *nf, pl* **-ciones :** multiplication
multiplicar {72} *v* **1 :** to multiply **2 :** to increase — **multiplicarse** *vr* **:** to multiply, to reproduce
multiplicidad *nf* **:** multiplicity
múltiplo *nm* **:** multiple
multitud *nf* MUCHEDUMBRE **:** crowd, multitude
multiuso, -sa *adj* **:** multipurpose
multivitamínico, -ca *adj* **:** multivitamin
mundano, -na *adj* **:** worldly, earthly
mundial *adj* **:** world, worldwide
mundialmente *adv* **:** worldwide, all over the world
mundo *nm* **1 :** world **2 todo el mundo :** everyone, everybody
municiones *nfpl* **:** ammunition, munitions
municipal *adj* **:** municipal
municipio *nm* **1 :** municipality **2** AYUNTAMIENTO **:** town council
muñeca *nf* **1 :** doll **2** MANIQUÍ **:** mannequin **3 :** wrist
muñeco *nm* **1 :** doll, boy doll **2** MARIONETA **:** puppet
muñon *nm, pl* **muñones :** stump (of an arm or leg)
mural *adj & nm* **:** mural
muralista *nmf* **:** muralist
muralla *nf* **:** rampart, wall
murciélago *nm* **:** bat (animal)
murga *nf* **:** band of street musicians
murió, etc. → **morir**
murmullo *nm* **1 :** murmur, murmuring **2 :** rustling, rustle <el murmullo de las hojas : the rustling of the leaves>
murmurar *vt* **1 :** to murmur, to mutter **2 :** to whisper (gossip) — *vi* **1 :** to murmur **2** CHISMEAR **:** to gossip
muro *nm* **:** wall
musa *nf* **:** muse
musaraña *nf* **:** shrew
muscular *adj* **:** muscular
musculatura *nf* **:** muscles *pl,* musculature
músculo *nm* **:** muscle
musculoso, -sa *adj* **:** muscular, brawny
muselina *nf* **:** muslin
museo *nm* **:** museum
musgo *nm* **:** moss
musgoso, -sa *adj* **:** mossy
música *nf* **:** music
musical *adj* **:** musical — **musicalmente** *adv*
músico[1], -ca *adj* **:** musical
músico[2], -ca *n* **:** musician
musitar *vt* **:** to mumble, to murmur
muslo *nm* **:** thigh
musulmán, -mana *adj & n, mpl* **-manes :** Muslim
mutación *nf, pl* **-ciones :** mutation
mutante *adj & nm* **:** mutant
mutar *v* **:** to mutate
mutilar *vt* **:** to mutilate — **mutilación** *nf*
mutis *nm* **1 :** exit (in theater) **2 :** silence
mutual *adj* **:** mutual

mutuo, -tua *adj* **:** mutual, reciprocal — **mutuamente** *adv*

muy *adv* **1 :** very, quite <es muy inteligente : she's very intelligent> <muy bien : very well, fine> <eso es muy americano : that's typically American> **2 :** too <es muy grande para él : it's too big for him>

N

n *nf* **:** fourteenth letter of the Spanish alphabet

nabo *nm* **:** turnip

nácar *nm* MADREPERLA **:** nacre, mother-of-pearl

nacarado, -da *adj* **:** pearly

nacer {48} *vi* **1 :** to be born <nací en Guatemala : I was born in Guatemala> <no nació ayer : he wasn't born yesterday> **2 :** to hatch **3 :** to bud, to sprout **4 :** to rise, to originate **5 nacer para algo :** to be born to be something **6 volver a nacer :** to have a lucky escape

nacido[1], -da *adj* **1 :** born **2 recién nacido :** newborn

nacido[2], -da *n* **1 los nacidos :** those born (at a particular time) **2 recién nacido :** newborn baby

naciente *adj* **1 :** newfound, growing **2 :** rising <el sol naciente : the rising sun>

nacimiento *nm* **1 :** birth **2 :** source (of a river) **3 :** beginning, origin **4** BELÉN **:** Nativity scene, crèche

nación *nf, pl* **naciones :** nation, country, people (of a country)

nacional[1] *adj* **:** national

nacional[2] *nmf* CIUDADANO **:** national, citizen

nacionalidad *nf* **:** nationality

nacionalismo *nm* **:** nationalism

nacionalista[1] *adj* **:** nationalist, nationalistic

nacionalista[2] *nmf* **:** nationalist

nacionalización *nf, pl* **-ciones 1 :** nationalization **2 :** naturalization

nacionalizar {21} *vt* **1 :** to nationalize **2 :** to naturalize (as a citizen) — **nacionalizarse** *vr*

naco, -ca *adj Mex* **:** trashy, vulgar, common

nada[1] *adv* **:** not at all, not in the least <no estamos nada cansados : we are not at all tired>

nada[2] *nf* **1 :** nothingness **2 :** smidgen, bit <una nada le disgusta : the slightest thing upsets him>

nada[3] *pron* **1 :** nothing <no estoy haciendo nada : I'm not doing anything> **2 casi nada :** next to nothing **3 de ~ :** you're welcome **4 dentro de nada :** very soon, in no time **5 nada más :** nothing else, nothing more

nadador, -dora *n* **:** swimmer

nadar *vi* **1 :** to swim **2 ~ en :** to be swimming in, to be rolling in — *vt* **:** to swim

nadería *nf* **:** small thing, trifle

nadie *pron* **:** nobody, no one <no vi a nadie : I didn't see anyone>

nadir *nm* **:** nadir

nado *nm* **1** *Mex* **:** swimming **2 a ~ :** swimming <cruzó el río a nado : he swam across the river>

nafta *nf* **1 :** naphtha **2** (*in various countries*) **:** gasoline

naftalina *nf* **:** naphthalene, mothballs *pl*

náhuatl[1] *adj & nmf, pl* **nahuas :** Nahuatl

náhuatl[2] *nm* **:** Nahuatl (language)

nailon → **nilón**

naipe *nm* **:** playing card

nalga *nf* **1 :** buttock **2 nalgas** *nfpl* **:** buttocks, bottom

nalgada *nf* **:** smack on the bottom, spanking

namibio, -bia *adj & n* **:** Namibian

nana *nf* **1 :** lullaby **2** *fam* **:** grandma **3** *CA, Col, Mex, Ven* **:** nanny

nanay *interj fam* **:** no way!, not likely!

naranja[1] *adj & nm* **:** orange (color)

naranja[2] *nf* **:** orange (fruit)

naranjal *nm* **:** orange grove

naranjo *nm* **:** orange tree

narcisismo *nm* **:** narcissism

narcisista[1] *adj* **:** narcissistic

narcisista[2] *nmf* **:** narcissist

narciso *nm* **:** narcissus, daffodil

narcótico[1], -ca *adj* **:** narcotic

narcótico[2] *nm* **:** narcotic

narcotizar {21} *vt* **:** to drug, to dope

narcotraficante *nmf* **:** drug trafficker

narcotráfico *nm* **:** drug trafficking

narigón, -gona *adj, mpl* **-gones :** big-nosed

narigudo → **narigón**

nariz *nf, pl* **narices 1 :** nose <sonar(se) la nariz : to blow one's nose> **2 :** sense of smell

narración *nf, pl* **-ciones :** narration, account

narrador, -dora *n* **:** narrator

narrar *vt* **:** to narrate, to tell

narrativa *nf* **:** narrative, story

narrativo, -va *adj* **:** narrative

narval *nm* **:** narwhal

nasa *nf* **:** creel

nasal *adj* **:** nasal

nata *nf* **1 :** cream <nata batida : whipped cream> **2 :** skin (on boiled milk)

natación *nf, pl* **-ciones :** swimming

natal *adj* **:** native, natal

natalicio *nm* **:** birthday <el natalicio de George Washington : George Washington's birthday>

natalidad *nf* **:** birthrate

natillas *nfpl* : custard
natividad *nf* : birth, nativity
nativo, -va *adj & n* : native
natural[1] *adj* **1** : natural **2** : normal <como es natural : naturally, as expected> **3 ~ de** : native of, from **4 de tamaño natural** : life-size
natural[2] *nm* **1** CARÁCTER : disposition, temperament **2** : native <un natural de Venezuela : a native of Venezuela>
naturaleza *nf* **1** : nature <la madre naturaleza : mother nature> **2** ÍNDOLE : nature, disposition, constitution <la naturaleza humana : human nature> **3 naturaleza muerta** : still life
naturalidad *nf* : simplicity, naturalness
naturalismo *nm* : naturalism
naturalista[1] *adj* : naturalistic
naturalista[2] *nmf* : naturalist
naturalización *nf, pl* **-ciones** : naturalization
naturalizar {21} *vt* : to naturalize — **naturalizarse** *vr* NACIONALIZARSE : to become naturalized
naturalmente *adv* **1** : naturally, inherently **2** : of course
naufragar {52} *vi* **1** : to be shipwrecked **2** FRACASAR : to fail, to collapse
naufragio *nm* **1** : shipwreck **2** FRACASO : failure, collapse
náufrago[1], **-ga** *adj* : shipwrecked, castaway
náufrago[2], **-ga** *n* : shipwrecked person, castaway
náusea *nf* **1** : nausea **2 dar náuseas** : to nauseate, to disgust **3 náuseas matutinas** : morning sickness
nauseabundo, -da *adj* : nauseating, sickening
náutica *nf* : navigation
náutico, -ca *adj* : nautical
nautilo *nm* : nautilus
navaja *nf* **1** : pocketknife, penknife <navaja de muelle : switchblade> **2 navaja de afeitar** : straight razor, razor blade
navajo, -ja *adj & n* : Navajo
naval *adj* : naval
nave *nf* **1** : ship <nave capitana : flagship> <nave espacial : spaceship> **2** : nave <nave lateral : aisle> **3 quemar uno sus naves** : to burn one's bridges
navegabilidad *nf* : navigability
navegable *adj* : navigable
navegación *nf, pl* **-ciones** : navigation
navegante[1] *adj* : sailing, seafaring
navegante[2] *nmf* : navigator
navegar {52} *v* : to navigate, to sail
Navidad *nf* : Christmas, Christmastime <Feliz Navidad : Merry Christmas>
navideño, -ña *adj* : Christmas
naviero, -ra *adj* : shipping
náyade *nf* : naiad
nazca, etc. → **nacer**
nazi *adj & nmf* : Nazi
nazismo *nm* : Nazism
nébeda *nf* : catnip
neblina *nf* : light fog, mist
neblinoso, -sa *adj* : misty, foggy
nebulosa *nf* : nebula
nebulosidad *nf* : mistiness, haziness
nebuloso, -sa *adj* **1** : hazy, misty **2** : nebulous, vague
necedad *nf* : stupidity, foolishness <decir necedades : to talk nonsense>
necesariamente *adv* : necessarily
necesario, -ria *adj* **1** : necessary **2 si es necesario** : if need be **3 hacerse necesario** : to be required
neceser *nm* : toilet kit, vanity case
necesidad *nf* **1** : need, necessity **2** : poverty, want **3 necesidades** *nfpl* : hardships **4 hacer sus necesidades** : to relieve oneself
necesitado, -da *adj* : needy
necesitar *vt* **1** : to need **2** : to necessitate, to require — *vi* **~ de** : to have need of
necio[1], **-cia** *adj* **1** : foolish, silly, dumb **2** *fam* : naughty
necio[2], **-cia** *n* ESTÚPIDO : fool, idiot
necrología *nf* : obituary
necrópolis *nfs & pl* : cemetery
néctar *nm* : nectar
nectarina *nf* : nectarine
neerlandés[1], **-desa** *adj, mpl* **-deses** HOLANDÉS : Dutch
neerlandés[2], **-desa** *n, mpl* **-deses** HOLANDÉS : Dutch person, Dutchman *m*
nefando, -da *adj* : unspeakable, heinous
nefario, -ria *adj* : nefarious
nefasto, -ta *adj* **1** : ill-fated, unlucky **2** : disastrous, terrible
negación *nf, pl* **-ciones** **1** : negation, denial **2** : negative (in grammar)
negar {49} *vt* **1** : to deny **2** REHUSAR : to refuse **3** : to disown — **negarse** *vr* **1** : to refuse **2** : to deny oneself
negativa *nf* **1** : denial **2** : refusal
negativo[1], **-va** *adj* : negative
negativo[2] *nm* : negative (of a photograph)
negligé *nm* : negligee
negligencia *nf* : negligence
negligente *adj* : neglectful, negligent — **negligentemente** *adv*
negociable *adj* : negotiable
negociación *nf, pl* **-ciones** **1** : negotiation **2 negociación colectiva** : collective bargaining
negociador, -dora *n* : negotiator
negociante *nmf* : businessman *m*, businesswoman *f*
negociar *vt* : to negotiate — *vi* : to deal, to do business
negocio *nm* **1** : business, place of business **2** : deal, transaction **3 negocios** *nmpl* : commerce, trade, business
negrero, -ra *n* **1** : slave trader **2** *fam* : slave driver, brutal boss
negrita *nf* : boldface (type)

negro[1], **-gra** *adj* **1** : black, dark **2** BRONCEADO : suntanned **3** : gloomy, awful, desperate <la cosa se está poniendo negra : things are looking bad> **4 mercado negro** : black market
negro[2], **-gra** *n* **1** : dark-skinned person, black person **2** *fam* : darling, dear
negro[3] *nm* : black (color)
negrura *nf* : blackness
negruzco, -ca *adj* : blackish
nene, -na *n* : baby, small child
nenúfar *nm* : water lily
neocelandés → **neozelandés**
neoclasicismo *nm* : neoclassicism
neoclásico, -ca *adj* : neoclassical
neófito, -ta *n* : neophyte, novice
neologismo *nm* : neologism
neón *nm, pl* **neones** : neon
neoyorquino[1], **-na** *adj* : of or from New York
neoyorquino[2], **-na** *n* : New Yorker
neozelandés[1], **-desa** *adj, mpl* **-deses** : of or from New Zealand
neozelandés[2], **-desa** *n, mpl* **-deses** : New Zealander
nepalés, -lesa *adj & n, mpl* **-leses** : Nepali
nepotismo *nm* : nepotism
neptunio *nm* : neptunium
Neptuno *nm* : Neptune
nervio *nm* **1** : nerve **2** : tendon, sinew, gristle (in meat) **3** : energy, drive **4** : rib (of a vault) **5 nervios** *nmpl* : nerves <estar mal de los nervios : to be a bundle of nerves> <ataque de nervios : nervous breakdown>
nerviosamente *adv* : nervously
nerviosidad *nf* → **nerviosismo**
nerviosismo *nf* : nervousness, anxiety
nervioso, -sa *adj* **1** : nervous, nerve <sistema nervioso : nervous system> **2** : high-strung, restless, anxious <ponerse nervioso : to get nervous> **3** : vigorous, energetic
nervudo, -da *adj* : sinewy, wiry
neta *nf Mex fam* : truth <la neta es que me cae mal : the truth is, I don't like her>
netamente *adv* : clearly, obviously
neto, -ta *adj* **1** : net <peso neto : net weight> **2** : clear, distinct
neumático[1], **-ca** *adj* : pneumatic
neumático[2] *nm* LLANTA : tire
neumonía *nf* PULMONÍA : pneumonia
neural *adj* : neural
neuralgia *nf* : neuralgia
neuritis *nf* : neuritis
neurología *nf* : neurology
neurológico, -ca *adj* : neurological, neurologic
neurólogo, -ga *n* : neurologist
neurosis *nfs & pl* : neurosis
neurótico, -ca *adj & n* : neurotic
neutral *adj* : neutral
neutralidad *nf* : neutrality
neutralizar {21} *vt* : to neutralize — **neutralización** *nf*
neutro, -tra *adj* **1** : neutral **2** : neuter
neutrón *nm, pl* **neutrones** : neutron
nevada *nf* : snowfall
nevado, -da *adj* **1** : snowcapped **2** : snow-white
nevar {55} *v impers* : to snow
nevasca *nf* : snowstorm, blizzard
nevera *nf* REFRIGERADOR : refrigerator
nevería *nf Mex* : ice cream parlor
nevisca *nf* : light snowfall, flurry
nevoso, -sa *adj* : snowy
nexo *nm* VÍNCULO : link, connection, nexus
ni *conj* **1** : neither, nor <afuera no hace ni frío ni calor : it's neither cold nor hot outside> **2 ni que** : not even if, not as if <ni que me pagaran : not even if they paid me> <ni que fuera (yo) su madre : it's not as if I were his mother> **3 ni siquiera** : not even <ni siquiera nos llamaron : they didn't even call us>
nicaragüense *adj & nmf* : Nicaraguan
nicho *nm* : niche
nicotina *nf* : nicotine
nido *nm* **1** : nest **2** : hiding place, den
niebla *nf* : fog, mist
niega, niegue, etc. → **negar**
nieto, -ta *n* **1** : grandson *m*, granddaughter *f* **2 nietos** *nmpl* : grandchildren
nieva, etc. → **nevar**
nieve *nf* **1** : snow **2** *Cuba, Mex, PRi* : sherbet
nigeriano, -na *adj & n* : Nigerian
nigua *nf* : sand flea, chigger
nihilismo *nm* : nihilism
nilón *or* **nilon** *nm, pl* **nilones** : nylon
nimbo *nm* **1** : halo **2** : nimbus
nimiedad *nf* INSIGNIFICANCIA : trifle, triviality
nimio, -mia *adj* INSIGNIFICANTE : insignificant, trivial
ninfa *nf* : nymph
ningunear *vt Mex fam* : to disrespect
ninguno[1], **-na** (**ningún** *before masculine singular nouns*) *adj, mpl* **ningunos** : no, none <no es ninguna tonta : she's no fool> <no debe hacerse en ningún momento : that should never be done>
ninguno[2], **-na** *pron* **1** : neither, none <ninguno de los dos ha vuelto aún : neither one has returned yet> **2** : no one, no other <te quiero más que a ninguna : I love you more than any other>
niña *nf* **1** PUPILA : pupil (of the eye) **2 la niña de los ojos** : the apple of one's eye
niñada *nf* **1** : childishness **2** : trifle, silly thing
niñería *nf* → **niñada**
niñero, -ra *n* : baby-sitter, nanny
niñez *nf, pl* **niñeces** INFANCIA : childhood
niño, -ña *n* : child, boy *m*, girl *f*
niobio *nm* : niobium
nipón, -pona *adj & n, mpl* **nipones** JAPONÉS : Japanese
níquel *nm* : nickel

nitidez *nf, pl* **-deces** CLARIDAD : clarity, vividness, sharpness

nítido, -da *adj* CLARO : clear, vivid, sharp

nitrato *nm* : nitrate

nítrico, -ca *adj* **ácido nítrico** : nitric acid

nitrito *nm* : nitrite

nitrógeno *nm* : nitrogen

nitroglicerina *nf* : nitroglycerin

nivel *nm* **1** : level, height <nivel del mar : sea level> **2** : level, standard <nivel de vida : standard of living>

nivelar *vt* : to level (out)

nixtamal *nm Mex* : limed corn used for tortillas

no *adv* **1** : no <¿quieres ir al mercado? no, voy más tarde : do you want to go shopping? no, I'm going later> **2** : not <¡no hagas eso! : don't do that!> <creo que no : I don't think so> **3** : non- <no fumador : non-smoker> **4** **¡como no!** : of course! **5 no bien** : as soon as, no sooner

nobelio *nm* : nobelium

noble[1] *adj* : noble — **noblemente** *adv*

noble[2] *nmf* : nobleman *m,* noblewoman *f*

nobleza *nf* **1** : nobility **2** HONRADEZ : honesty, integrity

nocaut *nm* : knockout, KO

noche *nf* **1** : night, nighttime, evening **2 buenas noches** : good evening, good night **3 de noche** *or* **por la noche** : at night **4 hacerse de noche** : to get dark

Nochebuena *nf* : Christmas Eve

nochecita *nf* : dusk

Nochevieja *nf* : New Year's Eve

noción *nf, pl* **nociones 1** CONCEPTO : notion, concept **2 nociones** *nfpl* : smattering, rudiments *pl*

nocivo, -va *adj* DAÑINO : harmful, noxious

noctámbulo, -la *n* **1** : sleepwalker **2** : night owl

nocturno[1]**, -na** *adj* : night, nocturnal

nocturno[2] *nm* : nocturne

nodriza *nf* : wet nurse

nódulo *nm* : nodule

nogal *nm* **1** : walnut tree **2** *Mex* : pecan tree **3 nogal americano** : hickory

nómada[1] *adj* : nomadic

nómada[2] *nmf* : nomad

nomás *adv* : only, just <lo hice nomás porque sí : I did it just because> <nomás de recordarlo me enojo : I get angry just remembering it> <nomás faltan dos semanas para Navidad : there are only two weeks left till Christmas>

nombradía *nf* RENOMBRE : fame, renown

nombrado, -da *adj* : famous, well-known

nombramiento *nm* : appointment, nomination

nombrar *vt* **1** : to appoint **2** : to mention, to name

nombre *nm* **1** : name <nombre de pluma : pseudonym, pen name> <en nombre : on behalf of> <sin nombre : nameless> **2** : noun <nombre propio : proper noun> **3** : fame, renown

nomenclatura *nf* : nomenclature

nomeolvides *nmfs & pl* : forget-me-not

nómina *nf* : payroll

nominación *nf, pl* **-ciones** : nomination

nominal *adj* : nominal — **nominalmente** *adv*

nominar *vt* : to nominate

nominativo[1]**, -va** *adj* : nominative

nominativo[2] *nm* : nominative (case)

nomo *nm* : gnome

non[1] *adj* IMPAR : odd, not even

non[2] *nm* : odd number

nonagésimo[1]**, -ma** *adj* : ninetieth, ninety-

nonagésimo[2]**, -ma** *n* : ninetieth, ninety- (in a series)

nono, -na *adj* : ninth — **nono** *nm*

nopal *nm* : nopal, cactus

nopalitos *nmpl Mex* : pickled cactus leaves

noquear *vt* : to knock out, to KO

norcoreano, -na *adj & n* : North Korean

nordeste[1] *or* **noreste** *adj* **1** : northeastern **2** : northeasterly

nordeste[2] *or* **noreste** *nm* : northeast

nórdico, -ca *adj & n* ESCANDINAVO : Scandinavian

noreste → **nordeste**

noria *nf* **1** : waterwheel **2** : Ferris wheel

norirlandés[1]**, -desa** *adj, mpl* **-deses** : Northern Irish

norirlandés[2]**, -desa** *n, mpl* **-deses** : person from Northern Ireland

norma *nf* **1** : rule, regulation **2** : norm, standard

normal *adj* **1** : normal, usual **2** : standard **3 escuela normal** : teacher-training college

normalidad *nf* : normality, normalcy

normalización *nf, pl* **-ciones** *nf* **1** REGULARIZACIÓN : normalization **2** ESTANDARIZACIÓN : standardization

normalizar {21} *vt* **1** REGULARIZAR : to normalize **2** ESTANDARIZAR : to standardize — **normalizarse** *vr* : to return to normal

normalmente *adv* GENERALMENTE : ordinarily, generally

noroeste[1] *adj* **1** : northwestern **2** : northwesterly

noroeste[2] *nm* : northwest

norte[1] *adj* : north, northern

norte[2] *nm* **1** : north **2** : north wind **3** META : aim, objective

norteamericano, -na *adj & n* **1** : North American **2** AMERICANO, ESTADOUNIDENSE : American, native or inhabitant of the United States

norteño[1]**, -ña** *adj* : northern

norteño[2]**, -ña** *n* : Northerner

noruego[1], **-ga** *adj & n* : Norwegian

noruego[2] *nm* : Norwegian (language)

nos *pron* **1** : us <nos enviaron a la frontera : they sent us to the border> **2** : ourselves <nos divertimos muchísimo : we enjoyed ourselves a great deal> **3** : each other, one another <nos vimos desde lejos : we saw each other from far away> **4** : to us, for us, from us <nos lo dio : he gave it to us> <nos lo compraron : they bought it from us>

nosotros, -tras *pron* **1** : we <nosotros llegamos ayer : we arrived yesterday> **2** : us <ven con nosotros : come with us> **3 nosotros mismos** : ourselves <lo arreglamos nosotros mismos : we fixed it ourselves>

nostalgia *nf* **1** : nostalgia, longing **2** : homesickness

nostálgico, -ca *adj* **1** : nostalgic **2** : homesick

nota *nf* **1** : note, message **2** : announcement <nota de prensa : press release> **3** : grade, mark (in school) **4** : characteristic, feature, touch **5** : note (in music) **6** : bill, check (in a restaraunt)

notable *adj* **1** : notable, noteworthy **2** : outstanding

notar *vt* **1** : to notice <hacer notar algo : to point out something> **2** : to tell <la diferencia se nota inmediatamente : you can tell the difference right away> — **notarse** *vr* **1** : to be evident, to show **2** : to feel, to seem

notario, -ria *n* : notary, notary public

noticia *nf* **1** : news item, piece of news **2 noticias** *nfpl* : news

noticiero *nm* : news program, newscast

noticioso, -sa *adj* : news <agencia noticiosa : news agency>

notificación *nf, pl* **-ciones** : notification

notificar {72} *vt* : to notify, to inform

notoriedad *nf* **1** : knowledge, obviousness **2** : fame, notoriety

notorio, -ria *adj* **1** OBVIO : obvious, evident **2** CONOCIDO : well-known

novato[1], **-ta** *adj* : inexperienced, new

novato[2], **-ta** *n* : beginner, novice

novecientos[1], **-tas** *adj* : nine hundred

novecientos[2] *nms & pl* : nine hundred

novedad *nf* **1** : newness, novelty **2** : innovation

novedoso, -sa *adj* : original, novel

novel *adj* NOVATO : inexperienced, new

novela *nf* **1** : novel **2** : soap opera

novelar *vt* : to fictionalize, to make a novel out of

novelesco, -ca *adj* **1** : fictional **2** : fantastic, fabulous

novelista *nmf* : novelist

novena *nf* : novena

noveno, -na *adj* : ninth — **noveno, -na** *n*

noventa *adj & nm* : ninety

noventavo[1], **-va** *adj* : ninetieth

noventavo[2] *nm* : ninetieth (fraction)

noviazgo *nm* **1** : courtship, relationship **2** : engagement, betrothal

novicio, -cia *n* **1** : novice (in religion) **2** PRINCIPIANTE : novice, beginner

noviembre *nm* : November

novilla *nf* : heifer

novillada *nf* : bullfight featuring young bulls

novillero, -ra *n* : apprentice bullfighter

novillo *nm* : young bull

novio, -via *n* **1** : boyfriend *m,* girlfriend *f* **2** PROMETIDO : fiancé *m,* fiancée *f* **3** : bridegroom *m,* bride *f*

novocaína *nf* : novocaine

nubarrón *nm, pl* **-rrones** : storm cloud

nube *nf* **1** : cloud <andar en las nubes : to have one's head in the clouds> <por las nubes : sky-high> **2** : cloud (of dust), swarm (of insects, etc.)

nublado[1], **-da** *adj* **1** NUBOSO : cloudy, overcast **2** : clouded, dim

nublado[2] *nm* **1** : storm cloud **2** AMENAZA : menace, threat

nublar *vt* **1** : to cloud **2** OSCURECER : to obscure — **nublarse** *vr* : to get cloudy

nubosidad *nf* : cloudiness

nuboso, -sa *adj* NUBLADO : cloudy

nuca *nf* : nape, back of the neck

nuclear *adj* : nuclear

núcleo *nm* **1** : nucleus **2** : center, heart, core

nudillo *nm* : knuckle

nudismo *nm* : nudism

nudista *adj & nmf* : nudist

nudo *nm* **1** : knot <square knot : nudo de rizo> <un nudo en la garganta : a lump in one's throat> **2** : node **3** : junction, hub <nudo de comunicaciones : communication center> **4** : crux, heart (of a problem, etc.)

nudoso, -sa *adj* : knotty, gnarled

nuera *nf* : daughter-in-law

nuestro[1], **-tra** *adj* : our

nuestro[2], **-tra** *pron* (*with definite article*) : ours, our own <el nuestro es más grande : ours is bigger> <es de los nuestros : it's one of ours>

nuevamente *adv* : again, anew

nuevas *nfpl* : tidings *pl*

nueve *adj & nm* : nine

nuevecito, -ta *adj* : brand-new

nuevo, -va *adj* **1** : new <una casa nueva : a new house> <¿qué hay de nuevo? : what's new?> **2 de ~** : again, once more

nuez *nf, pl* **nueces 1** : nut **2** : walnut **3** *Mex* : pecan **4 nuez de Adán** : Adam's apple **5 nuez moscada** : nutmeg

nulidad *nf* **1** : nullity **2** : incompetent person <¡es una nulidad! : he's hopeless!>

nulo, -la *adj* **1** : null, null and void **2** INEPTO : useless, inept <es nula para la cocina : she's hopeless at cooking>

numen *nm* : poetic muse, inspiration

numerable *adj* : countable

numeración *nf, pl* **-ciones 1 :** numbering **2 :** numbers *pl,* numerals *pl* <numeración romana : Roman numerals>
numerador *nm* **:** numerator
numeral *adj* **:** numeral
numerar *vt* **:** to number
numerario, -ria *adj* **:** long-standing, permanent <profesor numerario : tenured professor>
numérico, -ca *adj* **:** numerical — **numéricamente** *adv*
número *nm* **1 :** number <número impar : odd number> <número ordinal : ordinal number> <número arábico : Arabic numeral> <número quebrado : fraction> **2 :** issue (of a publication) **3 sin ~ :** countless
numeroso, -sa *adj* **:** numerous
numismática *nf* **:** numismatics
nunca *adv* **1 :** never, ever <nunca es tarde : it's never too late> <no trabaja casi nunca : he hardly ever works> **2 nunca más :** never again **3 nunca jamás :** never ever
nuncio *nm* **:** harbinger, herald
nupcial *adj* **:** nuptial, wedding
nupcias *nfpl* **:** nuptials *pl,* wedding
nutria *nf* **1 :** otter **2 :** nutria
nutrición *nf, pl* **-ciones :** nutrition, nourishment
nutrido, -da *adj* **1 :** nourished <mal nutrido : undernourished, malnourished> **2 :** considerable, abundant <de nutrido : full of, abounding in>
nutriente *nm* **:** nutrient
nutrimento *nm* **:** nutriment
nutrir *vt* **1** ALIMENTAR **:** to feed, to nourish **2 :** to foster, to provide
nutritivo, -va *adj* **:** nourishing, nutritious
nylon *nm* → **nilón**

ñ *nf* **:** fifteenth letter of the Spanish alphabet
ñame *nm* **:** yam
ñandú *nm* **:** rhea
ñapa *nf* **:** extra amount <de ñapa : for good measure>
ñoñear *vi fam* **:** to whine
ñoño, -ña *adj fam* **:** whiny, fussy <no seas tan ñoño : don't be such a wimp>
ñoquis *nmpl* **:** gnocchi *pl*
ñu *nm* **:** gnu, wildebeest

O

o[1] *nf* **:** sixteenth letter of the Spanish alphabet
o[2] *conj* (**u** *before words beginning with o- or ho-*) **1 :** or <¿vienes con nosotros o te quedas? : are you coming with us or staying?> **2 :** either <o vienes con nosotros o te quedas : either you come with us or you stay> **3 o sea :** that is to say, in other words
oasis *nms & pl* **:** oasis
obcecado, -da *adj* **1 :** blinded <obcecado por la ira : blinded by rage> **2 :** stubborn, obstinate
obcecar {72} *vt* **:** to blind (by emotions) — **obcecarse** *vr* **:** to become stubborn
obedecer {53} *vt* **:** to obey <obedecer órdenes : to obey orders> <obedece a tus padres : obey your parents> — *vi* **1 :** to obey **2 ~ a :** to respond to **3 ~ a :** to be due to, to result from
obediencia *nf* **:** obedience
obediente *adj* **:** obedient — **obedientemente** *adv*
obelisco *nm* **:** obelisk
obertura *nf* **:** overture
obesidad *nf* **:** obesity
obeso, -sa *adj* **:** obese
óbice *nm* **:** obstacle, impediment
obispado *nm* DIÓCESIS **:** bishopric, diocese
obispo *nm* **:** bishop
obituario *nm* **:** obituary
objeción *nf, pl* **-ciones :** objection <ponerle objeciones a algo : to object to something>
objetar *v* **:** to object <no tengo nada que objetar : I have no objections>
objetividad *nf* **:** objectivity
objetivo[1]**, -va** *adj* **:** objective — **objetivamente** *adv*
objetivo[2] *nm* **1** META **:** objective, goal, target **2 :** lens
objeto *nm* **1** COSA **:** object, thing **2** OBJETIVO **:** objective, purpose <con objeto de : in order to, with the aim of> **3 objeto volador no identificado :** unidentified flying object
objetor, -tora *n* **:** objector <objetor de conciencia : conscientious objector>
oblea *nf* **1 :** wafer **2 hecho una oblea** *fam* **:** skinny as a rail
oblicuo, -cua *adj* **:** oblique — **oblicuamente** *adv*
obligación *nf, pl* **-ciones 1** DEBER **:** obligation, duty **2 :** bond, debenture
obligado, -da *adj* **1 :** obliged **2 :** obligatory, compulsory **3 :** customary
obligar {52} *vt* **:** to force, to require, to oblige — **obligarse** *vr* **:** to commit

oneself, to undertake (to do something)

obligatorio, -ria *adj* : mandatory, required, compulsory

obliterar *vt* : to obliterate, to destroy — **obliteración** *nf*

oblongo, -ga *adj* : oblong

obnubilación *nf, pl* **-ciones** : bewilderment, confusion

obnubilar *vt* : to daze, to bewilder

oboe[1] *nm* : oboe

oboe[2] *nmf* : oboist

obra *nf* **1** : work <obra de arte : work of art> <obra de teatro : play> <obra de consulta : reference work> **2** : deed <una buena obra : a good deed> **3** : construction work **4 obra maestra** : masterpiece **5 obras públicas** : public works **6 por obra de** : thanks to, because of

obrar *vt* : to work, to produce <obrar milagros : to work miracles> — *vi* **1** : to act, to behave <obrar con cautela : to act with caution> **2 obrar en poder de** : to be in possession of

obrero[1], **-ra** *adj* : working <la clase obrera : the working class>

obrero[2], **-ra** *n* : worker, laborer

obscenidad *nf* : obscenity

obsceno, -na *adj* : obscene

obscurecer, obscuridad, obscuro → **oscurecer, oscuridad, oscuro**

obsequiar *vt* REGALAR : to give, to present <lo obsequiaron con una placa : they presented him with a plaque>

obsequio *nm* REGALO : gift, present

obsequiosidad *nf* : attentiveness, deference

obsequioso, -sa *adj* : obliging, attentive

observación *nf, pl* **-ciones 1** : observation, watching **2** : remark, comment

observador[1], **-dora** *adj* : observant

observador[2], **-dora** *n* : observer, watcher

observancia *nf* : observance

observar *vt* **1** : to observe, to watch <estábamos observando a los niños : we were watching the children> **2** NOTAR : to notice **3** ACATAR : to obey, to abide by **4** COMENTAR : to remark, to comment

observatorio *nm* : observatory

obsesión *nf, pl* **-siones** : obsession

obsesionar *vt* : to obsess, to preoccupy excessively — **obsesionarse** *vr*

obsesivo, -va *adj* : obsessive

obseso, -sa *adj* : obsessed

obsolescencia *nf* DESUSO : obsolescence — **obsolescente** *adj*

obsoleto, -ta *adj* DESUSADO : obsolete

obstaculizar {21} *vt* IMPEDIR : to obstruct, to hinder

obstáculo *nm* IMPEDIMENTO : obstacle

obstante[1] *conj* **no obstante** : nevertheless, however

obstante[2] *prep* **no obstante** : in spite of, despite <mantuvo su inocencia no obstante la evidencia : he maintained his innocence in spite of the evidence>

obstar *v impers* **~ a** *or* **~ para** : to hinder, to prevent <eso no obsta para que me vaya : that doesn't prevent me from leaving>

obstetra *nmf* TOCÓLOGO : obstetrician

obstetricia *nf* : obstetrics

obstétrico, -ca *adj* : obstetric, obstetrical

obstinación *nf, pl* **-ciones 1** TERQUEDAD : obstinacy, stubbornness **2** : perseverance, tenacity

obstinado, -da *adj* **1** TERCO : obstinate, stubborn **2** : persistent — **obstinadamente** *adv*

obstinarse *vr* EMPECINARSE : to be obstinate, to be stubborn

obstrucción *nf, pl* **-ciones** : obstruction, blockage

obstruccionismo *nm* : obstructionism, filibustering

obstructor, -tora *adj* : obstructive

obstruir {41} *vt* BLOQUEAR : to obstruct, to block, to clog — **obstruirse** *vr*

obtención *nf* : obtaining, procurement

obtener {80} *vt* : to obtain, to secure, to get — **obtenible** *adj*

obturador *nm* : shutter (of a camera)

obtuso, -sa *adj* : obtuse

obtuvo, etc. → **obtener**

obviar *vt* : to get around (a difficulty), to avoid

obvio, -via *adj* : obvious — **obviamente** *adv*

oca *nf* : goose

ocasión *nf, pl* **-siones 1** : occasion, time **2** : opportunity, chance **3** : bargain **4 de ~** : secondhand **5 aviso de ocasión** *Mex* : classified ad

ocasional *adj* **1** : occasional **2** : chance, fortuitous

ocasionalmente *adv* **1** : occasionally **2** : by chance

ocasionar *vt* CAUSAR : to cause, to occasion

ocaso *nm* **1** ANOCHECER : sunset, sundown **2** DECADENCIA : decline, fall

occidental *adj* : western, occidental

occidente *nm* **1** OESTE, PONIENTE : west **2 el Occidente** : the West

oceánico, -ca *adj* : oceanic

océano *nm* : ocean

oceanografía *nf* : oceanography

oceanográfico, -ca *adj* : oceanographic

ocelote *nm* : ocelot

ochenta *adj & nm* : eighty

ochentavo[1], **-va** *adj* : eightieth

ochentavo[2] *nm* : eightieth (fraction)

ocho *adj & nm* : eight

ochocientos[1], **-tas** *adj* : eight hundred

ochocientos[2] *nms & pl* : eight hundred

ocio *nm* **1** : free time, leisure **2** : idleness

ociosidad *nf* : idleness, inactivity

ocioso, -sa *adj* **1** INACTIVO **:** idle, inactive **2** INÚTIL **:** pointless, useless

ocre *nm* **:** ocher

octágono *nm* **:** octagon — **octagonal** *adj*

octava *nf* **:** octave

octavo, -va *adj* **:** eighth — **octavo, -va** *n*

octeto *nm* **1 :** octet **2 :** byte

octogésimo[1]**, -ma** *adj* **:** eightieth, eighty-

octogésimo[2]**, -ma** *n* **:** eightieth, eighty- (in a series)

octubre *nm* **:** October

ocular *adj* **1 :** ocular, eye <músculos oculares : eye muscles> **2 testigo ocular :** eyewitness

oculista *nmf* **:** oculist, opthalmologist

ocultación *nf, pl* **-ciones :** concealment

ocultar *vt* ESCONDER **:** to conceal, to hide — **ocultarse** *vr*

oculto, -ta *adj* **1** ESCONDIDO **:** hidden, concealed **2 :** occult

ocupación *nf, pl* **-ciones 1 :** occupation, activity **2 :** occupancy **3** EMPLEO **:** employment, job

ocupacional *adj* **:** occupational, job-related

ocupado, -da *adj* **1 :** busy **2 :** taken <este asiento está ocupado : this seat is taken> **3 :** occupied <territorios ocupados : occupied territories> **4 señal de ocupado :** busy signal

ocupante *nmf* **:** occupant

ocupar *vt* **1 :** to occupy, to take possession of **2 :** to hold (a position) **3 :** to employ, to keep busy **4 :** to fill (space, time) **5 :** to inhabit (a dwelling) **6 :** to bother, to concern — **ocuparse** *vr* **~ de 1 :** to be concerned with **2 :** to take care of

ocurrencia *nf* **1 :** occurrence, event **2 :** witticism **3 :** bright idea

ocurrente *adj* **1 :** witty **2 :** clever, sharp

ocurrir *vi* **:** to occur, to happen — **ocurrirse** *vr* **~ a :** to occur to, to strike <se me ocurrió una mejor idea : a better idea occurred to me>

oda *nf* **:** ode

odiar *vt* ABOMINAR, ABORRECER **:** to hate

odio *nm* **:** hate, hatred

odioso, -sa *adj* ABOMINABLE, ABORRECIBLE **:** hateful, detestable

odisea *nf* **:** odyssey

odontología *nf* **:** dentistry, dental surgery

odontólogo, -ga *n* **:** dentist, dental surgeon

oeste[1] *adj* **1 :** west, western <la región oeste : the western region> **2 :** westerly

oeste[2] *nm* **1 :** west, West **2 :** west wind

ofender *vt* AGRAVIAR **:** to offend, to insult — *vi* **:** to offend, to be insulting — **ofenderse** *vr* **:** to take offense

ofensa *nf* **:** offense, insult

ofensiva *nf* **:** offensive <pasar a la ofensiva : to go on the offensive>

ofensivo, -va *adj* **:** offensive, insulting

ofensor, -sora *n* **:** offender

oferente *nmf* **1 :** supplier **2** FUENTE **:** source <un oferente no identificado : an unidentified source>

oferta *nf* **1 :** offer **2 :** sale, bargain <las camisas están en oferta : the shirts are on sale> **3 oferta y demanda :** supply and demand

ofertar *vt* OFRECER **:** to offer

oficial[1] *adj* **:** official — **oficialmente** *adv*

oficial[2] *nmf* **1 :** officer, police officer, commissioned officer (in the military) **2 :** skilled worker

oficializar {21} *vt* **:** to make official

oficiante *nmf* **:** celebrant

oficiar *vt* **1 :** to inform officially **2 :** to officiate at, to celebrate (Mass) — *vi* **~ de :** to act as

oficina *nf* **:** office

oficinista *nmf* **:** office worker

oficio *nm* **1 :** trade, profession <es electricista de oficio : he's an electrician by trade> **2 :** function, role **3 :** official communication **4 :** experience <tener oficio : to be experienced> **5 :** religious ceremony

oficioso, -sa *adj* **1** EXTRAOFICIAL **:** unofficial **2 :** officious — **oficiosamente** *adv*

ofrecer {53} *vt* **1 :** to offer **2 :** to provide, to give **3 :** to present (an appearance, etc.) — **ofrecerse** *vr* **1 :** to offer oneself, to volunteer **2 :** to open up, to present itself

ofrecimiento *nm* **:** offer, offering

ofrenda *nf* **:** offering

oftalmología *nf* **:** ophthalmology

oftalmólogo, -ga *n* **:** ophthalmologist

ofuscación *nf, pl* **-ciones :** blindness, confusion

ofuscar {72} *vt* **1 :** to blind, to dazzle **2** CONFUNDIR **:** to bewilder, to confuse — **ofuscarse** *vr* **~ con :** to be blinded by

ogro *nm* **:** ogre

ohm *nm, pl* **ohms :** ohm

ohmio *nm* → **ohm**

oídas *nfpl* **de ~ :** by hearsay

oído *nm* **1 :** ear <oído interno : inner ear> **2 :** hearing <duro de oído : hard of hearing> **3 tocar de oído :** to play by ear

oiga, etc. → **oír**

oír {50} *vi* **:** to hear — *vt* **1 :** to hear **2** ESCUCHAR **:** to listen to **3 :** to pay attention to, to heed **4 ¡oye!** *or* **¡oiga! :** listen!, excuse me!, look here!

ojal *nm* **:** buttonhole

ojalá *interj* **1 :** I hope so!, if only!, God willing! **2 :** I hope, I wish, hopefully <¡ojalá que le vaya bien! : I hope things go well for her!> <¡ojalá no llueva! : hopefully it won't rain!>

ojeada *nf* **:** glimpse, glance <echar una ojeada : to have a quick look>

ojear *vt* **:** to eye, to have a look at

ojete *nm* **:** eyelet

ojiva *nf* **:** warhead

ojo *nm* **1 :** eye **2 :** judgment, sharpness <tener buen ojo para : to be a good judge of, to have a good eye for> **3 :** hole (in cheese), eye (in a needle), center (of a storm) **4 :** span (of a bridge) **5 a ojos vistas :** openly, publicly **6 andar con ojo :** to be careful **7 ojo de agua** *Mex* **:** spring, source **8 ¡ojo! :** look out!, pay attention!

ola *nf* **1 :** wave **2 ola de calor :** heat wave

oleada *nf* **:** swell, wave <una oleada de protestas : a wave of protests>

oleaje *nm* **:** waves *pl*, surf

óleo *nm* **1 :** oil **2 :** oil painting

oleoducto *nm* **:** oil pipeline

oleoso, -sa *adj* **:** oily

oler {51} *vt* **1 :** to smell **2** INQUIRIR **:** to pry into, to investigate **3** AVERIGUAR **:** to smell out, to uncover — *vi* **1 :** to smell <huele mal : it smells bad> **2 ~ a :** to smell like, to smell of <huele a pino : it smells like pine> — **olerse** *vr* **:** to have a hunch, to suspect

olfatear *vt* **1 :** to sniff **2 :** to sense, to sniff out

olfativo, -va *adj* **:** olfactory

olfato *nm* **1 :** sense of smell **2 :** nose, instinct

oligarquía *nf* **:** oligarchy

olimpiada *or* **olimpíada** *nf* **:** Olympics *pl*, Olympic Games *pl*

olímpico, -ca *adj* **:** Olympic

olisquear *vt* **:** to sniff at

oliva *nf* ACEITUNA **:** olive <aceite de oliva : olive oil>

olivo *nm* **:** olive tree

olla *nf* **1 :** pot <olla de presión : pressure cooker> **2 olla podrida :** Spanish stew

olmeca *adj & nmf* **:** Olmec

olmo *nm* **:** elm

olor *nm* **:** smell, odor

oloroso, -sa *adj* **:** scented, fragrant

olote *nm Mex* **:** cob, corncob

olvidadizo, -za *adj* **:** forgetful, absent-minded

olvidar *vt* **1 :** to forget, to forget about <olvida lo que pasó : forget about what happened> **2 :** to leave behind <olvidé mi chequera en la casa : I left my checkbook at home> — **olvidarse** *vr* **:** to forget <se me olvidó mi cuaderno : I forgot my notebook> <se le olvidó llamarme : he forgot to call me>

olvido *nm* **1 :** forgetfulness **2 :** oblivion **3** DESCUIDO **:** oversight

omaní *adj & nmf* **:** Omani

ombligo *nm* **:** navel, belly button

ombudsman *nmfs & pl* **:** ombudsman

omelette *nmf* **:** omelet

ominoso, -sa *adj* **:** ominous — **ominosamente** *adv*

omisión *nf, pl* **-siones :** omission, neglect

omiso, -sa *adj* **1** NEGLIGENTE **:** neglectful **2 hacer caso omiso de :** to ignore

omitir *vt* **1 :** to omit, to leave out **2 :** to fail to <omitió dar su nombre : he failed to give his name>

ómnibus *n, pl* **-bus** *or* **-buses :** bus, coach

omnipotencia *nf* **:** omnipotence

omnipotente *adj* TODOPODEROSO **:** omnipotent, almighty

omnipresencia *nf* **:** ubiquity, omnipresence

omnipresente *adj* **:** ubiquitous, omnipresent

omnisciente *adj* **:** omniscient — **omnisciencia** *nf*

omnívoro, -ra *adj* **:** omnivorous

omóplato *or* **omoplato** *nm* **:** shoulder blade

once *adj & nm* **:** eleven

onceavo[1]**, -va** *adj* **:** eleventh

onceavo[2] *nm* **:** eleventh (fraction)

onda *nf* **1 :** wave, ripple, undulation <onda sonora : sound wave> **2 :** wave (in hair) **3 :** scallop (on clothing) **4** *fam* **:** wavelength, understanding <agarrar la onda : to get the point> <en la onda : on the ball, with it> **5 ¿qué onda?** *fam* **:** what's happening?, what's up?

ondear *vi* **:** to ripple, to undulate, to flutter

ondulación *nf, pl* **-ciones :** undulation

ondulado, -da *adj* **1 :** wavy <pelo ondulado : wavy hair> **2 :** undulating

ondular *vt* **:** to wave (hair) — *vi* **:** to undulate, to ripple

oneroso, -sa *adj* GRAVOSO **:** onerous, burdensome

ónix *nm* **:** onyx

onza *nf* **:** ounce

opacar {72} *vt* **1 :** to make opaque or dull **2 :** to outshine, to overshadow

opacidad *nf* **1 :** opacity **2 :** dullness

opaco, -ca *adj* **1 :** opaque **2 :** dull

ópalo *nm* **:** opal

opción *nf, pl* **opciones 1** ALTERNATIVA **:** option, choice **2 :** right, chance <tener opción a : to be eligible for>

opcional *adj* **:** optional — **opcionalmente** *adv*

ópera *nf* **:** opera

operación *nf, pl* **-ciones 1 :** operation **2 :** transaction, deal

operacional *adj* **:** operational

operador, -dora *n* **1 :** operator **2 :** cameraman, projectionist

operante *adj* **:** operating, working

operar *vt* **1 :** to produce, to bring about **2** INTERVENIR **:** to operate on **3** *Mex* **:** to operate, to run (a machine) — *vi* **1 :** to operate, to function **2 :** to deal, to do business — **operarse** *vr* **1 :** to come about, to take place **2 :** to have an operation

operario, -ria *n* **:** laborer, worker

operático, -ca → **operístico**

operativo[1]**, -va** *adj* **1 :** operating <capacidad operativa : operating capacity> **2 :** operative

operativo[2] *nm* : operation <operativo militar : military operation>
opereta *nf* : operetta
operístico, -ca *adj* : operatic
opiato *nm* : opiate
opinable *adj* : arguable
opinar *vi* **1** : to think, to have an opinion **2** : to express an opinion **3 opinar bien de** : to think highly of — *vt* : to think <opinamos lo mismo : we're of the same opinion, we're in agreement>
opinión *nf, pl* **-niones** : opinion, belief
opio *nm* : opium
oponente *nmf* : opponent
oponer {60} *vt* **1** CONTRAPONER : to oppose, to place against **2 oponer resistencia** : to resist, to put up a fight — **oponerse** *vr* **~ a** : to object to, to be against
oporto *nm* : port (wine)
oportunamente *adv* **1** : at the right time, opportunely **2** : appropriately
oportunidad *nf* : opportunity, chance
oportunismo *nm* : opportunism
oportunista[1] *adj* : opportunistic
oportunista[2] *nmf* : opportunist
oportuno, -na *adj* **1** : opportune, timely **2** : suitable, appropriate
oposición *nf, pl* **-ciones** : opposition
opositor, -tora *n* ADVERSARIO : opponent
oposum *nm* ZARIGÜEYA : opossum
opresión *nf, pl* **-siones 1** : oppression **2 opresión de pecho** : tightness in the chest
opresivo, -va *adj* : oppressive
opresor[1], **-sora** *adj* : oppressive
opresor[2], **-sora** *n* : oppressor
oprimir *vt* **1** : to oppress **2** : to press, to squeeze <oprima el botón : push the button>
oprobio *nm* : opprobrium, shame
optar *vi* **1 ~ por** : to opt for, to choose **2 ~ a** : to aspire to, to apply for <dos candidatos optan a la presidencia : two candidates are running for president>
optativo, -va *adj* FACULTATIVO : optional
óptica *nf* **1** : optics **2** : optician's shop **3** : viewpoint
óptico[1], **-ca** *adj* : optical, optic
óptico[2], **-ca** *n* : optician
optimismo *nm* : optimism
optimista[1] *adj* : optimistic
optimista[2] *nmf* : optimist
óptimo, -ma *adj* : optimum, optimal
optometría *nf* : optometry — **optometrista** *nmf*
opuesto[1] *pp* → **oponer**
opuesto[2] *adj* **1** : opposite, contrary **2** : opposed
opulencia *nf* : opulence — **opulento, -ta** *adj*
opus *nm* : opus
opuso, etc. → **oponer**
ora *conj* : now <los matices eran variados, ora verdes, ora ocres : the hues were varied, now green, now ocher>
oración *nf, pl* **-ciones 1** DISCURSO : oration, speech **2** PLEGARIA : prayer **3** FRASE : sentence, clause
oráculo *nm* : oracle
orador, -dora *n* : speaker, orator
oral *adj* : oral — **oralmente** *adv*
órale *interj Mex fam* **1** : sure!, OK! <¿los dos por cinco pesos? ¡órale! : both for five pesos? you've got a deal!> **2** : come on! <¡órale, vámonos! : come on, let's go!>
orangután *nm, pl* **-tanes** : orangutan
orar *vi* REZAR : to pray
oratoria *nf* : oratory
oratorio *nm* **1** CAPILLA : oratory, chapel **2** : oratorio
orbe *nm* **1** : orb, sphere **2** GLOBO : globe, world
órbita *nf* **1** : orbit **2** : eye socket **3** ÁMBITO : sphere, field
orbitador *nm* : space shuttle, orbiter
orbital *adj* : orbital
orden[1] *nm, pl* **órdenes 1** : order <todo está en orden : everything's in order> <por orden cronológico : in chronological order> **2 orden del día** : agenda (at a meeting) **3 orden público** : law and order
orden[2] *nf, pl* **órdenes 1** : order <una orden religiosa : a religious order> <una orden de tacos : an order of tacos> **2 orden de compra** : purchase order **3 estar a la orden del día** : to be the order of the day, to be prevalent
ordenación *nf, pl* **-ciones 1** : ordination **2** : ordering, organizing
ordenadamente *adv* : in an orderly fashion, neatly
ordenado, -da *adj* : orderly, neat
ordenador *nm Spain* : computer
ordenamiento *nm* **1** : ordering, organizing **2** : code (of laws)
ordenanza[1] *nf* REGLAMENTO : ordinance, regulation
ordenanza[2] *nm* : orderly (in the armed forces)
ordenar *vt* **1** MANDAR : to order, to command **2** ARREGLAR : to put in order, to arrange **3** : to ordain (a priest)
ordeñar *vt* : to milk
ordeño *nm* : milking
ordinal *nm* : ordinal (number)
ordinariamente *adv* **1** : usually **2** : coarsely
ordinariez *nf* : coarseness, vulgarity
ordinario, -ria *adj* **1** : ordinary **2** : coarse, common, vulgar **3 de ~** : usually
orear *vt* : to air
orégano *nm* : oregano
oreja *nf* : ear
orfanato *nm* : orphanage
orfanatorio *nm Mex* : orphanage
orfebre *nmf* : goldsmith, silversmith
orfebrería *nf* : articles of gold or silver

orfelinato *nm* : orphanage
orgánico, -ca *adj* : organic — **orgánicamente** *adv*
organigrama *nm* : organization chart, flowchart
organismo *nm* **1** : organism **2** : agency, organization
organista *nmf* : organist
organización *nf, pl* **-ciones** : organization
organizador¹, -dora *adj* : organizing
organizador², -dora *n* : organizer
organizar {21} *vt* : to organize, to arrange — **organizarse** *vr* : to get organized
organizativo, -va *adj* : organizational
órgano *nm* : organ
orgasmo *nm* : orgasm
orgía *nf* : orgy
orgullo *nm* : pride
orgulloso, -sa *adj* : proud — **orgullosamente** *adv*
orientación *nf, pl* **-ciones 1** : orientation **2** DIRECCIÓN : direction, course **3** GUÍA : guidance, direction
oriental¹ *adj* **1** : eastern **2** : oriental **3** *Arg, Uru* : Uruguayan
oriental² *nmf* **1** : Easterner **2** : Oriental **3** *Arg, Uru* : Uruguayan
orientar *vt* **1** : to orient, to position **2** : to guide, to direct — **orientarse** *vr* **1** : to orient oneself, to get one's bearings **2 ~ hacia** : to turn towards, to lean towards
oriente *nm* **1** : east, East **2 el Oriente** : the Orient
orífice *nmf* : goldsmith
orificio *nm* : orifice, opening
origen *nm, pl* **orígenes 1** : origin **2** : lineage, birth **3 dar origen a** : to give rise to **4 en su origen** : originally
original *adj & nm* : original — **originalmente** *adv*
originalidad *nf* : originality
originar *vt* : to originate, to give rise to — **originarse** *vr* : to originate, to begin
originario, -ria *adj* **~ de** : native of
originariamente *adv* : originally
orilla *nf* **1** BORDE : border, edge **2** : bank (of a river) **3** : shore
orillar *vt* **1** : to skirt, to go around **2** : to trim, to edge (cloth) **3** : to settle, to wind up **4** *Mex* : to pull over (a vehicle)
orín *nm* **1** HERRUMBRE : rust **2 orines** *nmpl* : urine
orina *nf* : urine
orinación *nf* : urination
orinal *nm* : urinal (vessel)
orinar *vi* : to urinate — **orinarse** *vr* : to wet oneself
oriol *nm* OROPÉNDOLA : oriole
oriundo, -da *adj* **~ de** : native of
orla *nf* : border, edging
orlar *vt* : to edge, to trim
ornamentación *nf, pl* **-ciones** : ornamentation
ornamental *adj* : ornamental
ornamentar *vt* ADORNAR : to ornament, to adorn
ornamento *nm* : ornament, adornment
ornar *vt* : to adorn, to decorate
ornitología *nf* : ornithology
ornitólogo, -ga *n* : ornithologist
ornitorrinco *nm* : platypus
oro *nm* : gold
orondo, -da *adj* **1** : rounded, potbellied (of a container) **2** *fam* : smug, self-satisfied
oropel *nm* : glitz, glitter, tinsel
oropéndola *nf* : oriole
orquesta *nf* : orchestra — **orquestal** *adj*
orquestar *vt* : to orchestrate — **orquestación** *nf*
orquídea *nf* : orchid
ortiga *nf* : nettle
ortodoncia *nf* : orthodontics
ortodoncista *nmf* : orthodontist
ortodoxia *nf* : orthodoxy
ortodoxo, -xa *adj* : orthodox
ortografía *nf* : orthography, spelling
ortográfico, -ca *adj* : orthographic, spelling
ortopedia *nf* : orthopedics
ortopedista *nmf* : orthopedist
oruga *nf* **1** : caterpillar **2** : track (of a tank, etc.)
orzuelo *nm* : sty, stye (in the eye)
os *pron pl* (*objective form of* **vosotros**) *Spain* **1** : you, to you **2** : yourselves, to yourselves **3** : each other, to each other
osa *nf* → **oso**
osadía *nf* **1** VALOR : boldness, daring **2** AUDACIA : audacity, nerve
osado, -da *adj* **1** : bold, daring **2** : audacious, impudent — **osadamente** *adv*
osamenta *nf* : skeletal remains *pl*, bones *pl*
osar *vi* : to dare
oscilación *nf, pl* **-ciones 1** : oscillation **2** : fluctuation **3** : vacillation, wavering
oscilar *vi* **1** BALANCEARSE : to swing, to sway, to oscillate **2** FLUCTUAR : to fluctuate **3** : to vacillate, to waver
oscuramente *adv* : obscurely
oscurecer {53} *vt* **1** : to darken **2** : to obscure, to confuse, to cloud **3 al oscurecer** : at dusk, at nightfall — *v impers* : to grow dark, to get dark — **oscurecerse** *vr* : to darken, to dim
oscuridad *nf* **1** : darkness **2** : obscurity
oscuro, -ra *adj* **1** : dark **2** : obscure **3 a oscuras** : in the dark, in darkness
óseo, ósea *adj* : skeletal, bony
ósmosis *or* **osmosis** *nf* : osmosis
oso, osa *n* **1** : bear **2 Osa Mayor** : Big Dipper **3 Osa Menor** : Little Dipper **4 oso blanco** : polar bear **5 oso hormiguero** : anteater **6 oso de peluche** : teddy bear
ostensible *adj* : ostensible, apparent — **ostensiblemente** *adv*
ostentación *nf, pl* **-ciones** : ostentation, display

ostentar *vt* **1 :** to display, to flaunt **2** POSEER **:** to have, to hold <ostenta el récord mundial : he holds the world record>
ostentoso, -sa *adj* **:** ostentatious, showy — **ostentosamente** *adv*
osteópata *nmf* **:** osteopath
osteopatía *n* **:** osteopathy
osteoporosis *nf* **:** osteoporosis
ostión *nm, pl* **ostiones 1** *Mex* **:** oyster **2** *Chile* **:** scallop
ostra *nf* **:** oyster
ostracismo *nm* **:** ostracism
otear *vt* **:** to scan, to survey, to look over
otero *nm* **:** knoll, hillock
otomana *nf* **:** ottoman
otoñal *adj* **:** autumn, autumnal
otoño *nm* **:** autumn, fall
otorgamiento *nm* **:** granting, awarding
otorgar {52} *vt* **1 :** to grant, to award **2 :** to draw up, to frame (a legal document)
otro[1], otra *adj* **1 :** other **2 :** another <en otro juego, ellos ganaron : in another game, they won> **3 otra vez :** again **4 de otra manera :** otherwise **5 otra parte :** elsewhere **6 en otro tiempo :** once, formerly
otro[2], otra *pron* **1 :** another one <dame otro : give me another> **2 :** other one <el uno o el otro : one or the other> **3 los otros, las otras :** the others, the rest <me dio una y se quedó con las otras : he gave me one and kept the rest>
ovación *nf, pl* **-ciones :** ovation
ovacionar *vt* **:** to cheer, to applaud
oval → **ovalado**
ovalado, -da *adj* **:** oval
óvalo *nm* **:** oval
ovárico, -ca *adj* **:** ovarian
ovario *nm* **:** ovary
oveja *nf* **1 :** sheep, ewe **2 oveja negra :** black sheep
overol *nm* **:** overalls *pl*
ovillar *vt* **:** to roll into a ball
ovillo *nm* **1 :** ball (of yarn) **2 :** tangle
ovni *or* **OVNI** *nm* (*objeto volador no identificado*) **:** UFO
ovoide *adj* **:** ovoid, ovoidal
ovulación *nf, pl* **-ciones :** ovulation
ovular *vi* **:** to ovulate
óvulo *nm* **:** ovum
oxidación *nf, pl* **-ciones 1 :** oxidation **2 :** rusting
oxidado, -da *adj* **:** rusty
oxidar *vt* **1 :** to cause to rust **2 :** to oxidize — **oxidarse** *vr* **:** to rust, to become rusty
óxido *nm* **1** HERRUMBRE, ORÍN **:** rust **2 :** oxide
oxigenar *vt* **1 :** to oxygenate **2 :** to bleach (hair)
oxígeno *nm* **:** oxygen
oxiuro *nm* **:** pinworm
oye, etc. → **oír**
oyente *nmf* **1 :** listener **2 :** auditor, auditing student
ozono *nm* **:** ozone

P

p *nf* **:** seventeenth letter of the Spanish alphabet
pabellón *nm, pl* **-llones 1 :** pavilion **2 :** summerhouse, lodge **3 :** flag (of a vessel)
pabilo *nm* MECHA **:** wick
paca *nf* FARDO **:** bale
pacana *nf* **:** pecan
pacer {48} *v* **:** to graze, to pasture
paces → **paz**
pachanga *nf fam* **:** party, bash
paciencia *nf* **:** patience
paciente *adj & nmf* **:** patient — **pacientemente** *adv*
pacificación *nf, pl* **-ciones :** pacification
pacíficamente *adv* **:** peacefully, peaceably
pacificar {72} *vt* **:** to pacify, to calm — **pacificarse** *vr* **:** to calm down, to abate
pacífico, -ca *adj* **:** peaceful, pacific
pacifismo *nm* **:** pacifism
pacifista *adj & nmf* **:** pacifist
pacotilla *nf* **de ~ :** shoddy, trashy
pactar *vt* **:** to agree on — *vi* **:** to come to an agreement
pacto *nm* CONVENIO **:** pact, agreement
padecer {53} *vt* **:** to suffer, to endure — *vi* ADOLECER **~ de :** to suffer from
padecimiento *nm* **1 :** suffering **2 :** ailment, condition
padrastro *nm* **1 :** stepfather **2 :** hangnail
padre[1] *adj Mex fam* **:** fantastic, great
padre[2] *nm* **1 :** father **2 padres** *nmpl* **:** parents
padrenuestro *nm* **:** Lord's Prayer, paternoster
padrino *nm* **1 :** godfather **2 :** best man **3 :** sponsor, patron
padrón *nm, pl* **padrones :** register, roll <padrón municipal : city register>
paella *nf* **:** paella
paga *nf* **1 :** payment **2 :** pay, wages *pl*
pagadero, -ra *adj* **:** payable
pagado, -da *adj* **1 :** paid **2 pagado de sí mismo :** self-satisfied, smug
pagador, -dora *n* **:** payer
paganismo *nm* **:** paganism
pagano, -na *adj & n* **:** pagan
pagar {52} *vt* **:** to pay, to pay for, to repay — *vi* **:** to pay
pagaré *nm* VALE **:** promissory note, IOU
página *nf* **:** page

pago *nm* **1 :** payment **2 en pago de :** in return for
pagoda *nf* **:** pagoda
pague, etc. → **pagar**
país *nm* **1** NACIÓN **:** country, nation **2** REGIÓN **:** region, territory
paisaje *nm* **:** scenery, landscape
paisano, -na *n* COMPATRIOTA **:** compatriot, fellow countryman
paja *nf* **1 :** straw **2** *fam* **:** trash, tripe
pajar *nm* **:** hayloft, haystack
pajarera *nf* **:** aviary
pájaro *nm* **:** bird <pájaro cantor : songbird> <pájaro bobo : penguin> <pájaro carpintero : woodpecker>
pajita *nf* **:** (drinking) straw
pajote *nm* **:** straw, mulch
pala *nf* **1 :** shovel, spade **2 :** blade (of an oar or a rotor) **3 :** paddle, racket
palabra *nf* **1** VOCABLO **:** word **2** PROMESA **:** word, promise <un hombre de palabra : a man of his word> **3** HABLA **:** speech **4 :** right to speak <tener la palabra : to have the floor>
palabrería *nf* **:** empty talk
palabrota *nf* **:** swearword
palacio *nm* **1 :** palace, mansion **2 palacio de justicia :** courthouse
paladar *nm* **1 :** palate **2** GUSTO **:** taste
paladear *vt* SABOREAR **:** to savor
paladín *nm, pl* **-dines :** champion, defender
palanca *nf* **1 :** lever, crowbar **2** *fam* **:** leverage, influence **3 palanca de cambio** *or* **palanca de velocidad :** gearshift
palangana *nf* **:** washbowl
palanqueta *nf* **:** jimmy, small crowbar
palco *nm* **:** box (in a theater or stadium)
palear *vt* **1 :** to shovel **2 :** to paddle
palenque *nm* **1** ESTACADA **:** stockade, palisade **2 :** arena, ring
paleontología *nf* **:** paleontology
paleontólogo, -ga *n* **:** paleontologist
palestino, -na *adj & n* **:** Palestinian
palestra *nf* **:** arena <salir a la palestra : to join the fray>
paleta *nf* **1 :** palette **2 :** trowel **3 :** spatula **4 :** blade, vane **5 :** paddle **6** *CA, Mex* **:** lollipop, Popsicle—
paletilla *nf* **:** shoulder blade
paliar *vt* MITIGAR **:** to alleviate, to palliate
paliativo[1], -va *adj* **:** palliative
paliativo[2] *nm* **:** palliative
palidecer {53} *vi* **:** to turn pale
palidez *nf, pl* **-deces :** paleness, pallor
pálido, -da *adj* **:** pale
palillo *nm* **1** MONDADIENTES **:** toothpick **2 palillos** *nmpl* **:** chopsticks **3 palillo de tambor :** drumstick
paliza *nf* **:** beating, pummeling <darle una paliza a : to beat, to thrash>
palma *nf* **1 :** palm (of the hand) **2 :** palm (tree or leaf) **3 batir palmas :** to clap, to applaud **4 llevarse la palma** *fam* **:** to take the cake
palmada *nf* **1 :** pat **2 :** slap **3 :** clap
palmarés *nm* **:** record (of achievements)
palmario, -ria *adj* MANIFIESTO **:** clear, manifest
palmeado, -da *adj* **:** webbed
palmear *vt* **:** to slap on the back — *vi* **:** to clap, to applaud
palmera *nf* **:** palm tree
palmo *nm* **1 :** span, small amount **2 palmo a palmo :** bit by bit, inch by inch **3 dejar con un palmo de narices :** to disappoint
palmotear *vi* **:** to applaud
palmoteo *nm* **:** clapping, applause
palo *nm* **1 :** stick, pole, post **2 :** shaft, handle <palo de escoba : broomstick> **3 :** mast, spar **4 :** wood **5 :** blow (with a stick) **6 :** suit (of cards)
paloma *nf* **1 :** pigeon, dove **2 paloma mensajera :** carrier pigeon
palomilla *nf* **:** moth
palomitas *nfpl* **:** popcorn
palpable *adj* **:** palpable, tangible
palpar *vt* **:** to feel, to touch
palpitación *nf, pl* **-ciones :** palpitation
palpitar *vi* **:** to palpitate, to throb — **palpitante** *adj*
palta *nf* **:** avocado
paludismo *nm* MALARIA **:** malaria
palurdo, -da *n* **:** boor, yokel, bumpkin
pampa *nf* **:** pampa
pampeano, -na *adj* **:** pampean, pampas
pampero → **pampeano**
pan *nm* **1 :** bread **2 :** loaf of bread **3 :** cake, bar <pan de jabón : bar of soap> **4 pan dulce** *CA, Mex* **:** traditional pastry **5 pan tostado :** toast **6 ser pan comido** *fam* **:** to be a piece of cake, to be a cinch
pana *nf* **:** corduroy
panacea *nf* **:** panacea
panadería *nf* **:** bakery, bread shop
panadero, -ra *n* **:** baker
panal *nm* **:** honeycomb
panameño, -ña *adj & n* **:** Panamanian
pancarta *nf* **:** placard, sign
pancita *nf Mex* **:** tripe
páncreas *nms & pl* **:** pancreas
panda *nmf* **:** panda
pandeado, -da *adj* **:** warped
pandearse *vr* **1 :** to warp **2 :** to bulge, to sag
pandemonio *or* **pandemónium** *nm* **:** pandemonium
pandereta *nf* **:** tambourine
pandero *nm* **:** tambourine
pandilla *nf* **1 :** group, clique **2 :** gang
panecito *nm* **:** roll, bread roll
panegírico[1], -ca *adj* **:** eulogistic, panegyrical
panegírico[2] *nm* **:** eulogy, panegyric
panel *nm* **:** panel — **panelista** *nmf*
panera *nf* **:** bread box
panfleto *nm* **:** pamphlet
pánico *nm* **:** panic
panorama *nm* **1** VISTA **:** panorama, view **2 :** scene, situation <el pa-

norama nacional : the national scene> 3 PERSPECTIVA : outlook

panorámico, -ca *adj* : panoramic

panqueque *nm* : pancake

pantaletas *nfpl* : panties

pantalla *nf* **1** : screen, monitor **2** : lampshade **3** : fan

pantalón *nm, pl* **-lones 1** : pants *pl,* trousers *pl* **2 pantalones vaqueros** : jeans **3 pantalones de mezclilla** *Chile, Mex* : jeans **4 pantalones de montar** : jodhpurs

pantano *nm* **1** : swamp, marsh, bayou **2** : reservoir **3** : obstacle, difficulty

pantanoso, -sa *adj* **1** : marshy, swampy **2** : difficult, thorny

panteón *nm, pl* **-teones 1** CEMENTERIO : cemetery **2** : pantheon, mausoleum

pantera *nf* : panther

pantimedias *nfpl Mex* : panty hose

pantomima *nf* : pantomime

pantorrilla *nf* : calf (of the leg)

pantufla *nf* ZAPATILLA : slipper

panza *nf* BARRIGA : belly, paunch

panzón, -zona *adj, mpl* **panzones** : potbellied, paunchy

pañal *nm* : diaper

pañería *nf* **1** : cloth, material **2** : fabric store

pañito *nm* : doily

paño *nm* **1** : cloth **2** : rag, dust cloth **3 paño de cocina** : dishcloth **4 paño higiénico** : sanitary napkin

pañuelo *nm* **1** : handkerchief **2** : scarf

papa[1] *nm* : pope

papa[2] *nf* **1** : potato **2 papa dulce** : sweet potato **3 papas fritas** : potato chips, french fries **4 papas a la francesa** *Mex* : french fries

papá *nm fam* **1** : dad, pop **2 papás** *nmpl* : parents, folks

papada *nf* **1** : double chin, jowl **2** : dewlap

papagayo *nm* LORO : parrot

papal *adj* : papal

papalote *nm Mex* : kite

papaya *nf* : papaya

papel *nm* **1** : paper, piece of paper **2** : role, part **3 papel de estaño** : tinfoil **4 papel de empapelar** *or* **papel pintado** : wallpaper **5 papel higiénico** : toilet paper **6 papel de lija** : sandpaper

papeleo *nm* : paperwork, red tape

papelera *nf* : wastebasket

papelería *nf* : stationery store

papelero, -ra *adj* : paper

papeleta *nf* **1** : ballot **2** : ticket, slip

paperas *nfpl* : mumps

papi *nm fam* : daddy, papa

papilla *nf* **1** : pap, mash **2 hacer papilla** : to beat to a pulp

papiro *nm* : papyrus

paquete *nm* BULTO : package, parcel

paquistaní *adj & nmf* : Pakistani

par[1] *adj* : even (in number)

par[2] *nm* **1** : pair, couple **2** : equal, peer <sin par : matchless, peerless> **3** : par (in golf) **4** : rafter **5 de par en par** : wide open

par[3] *nf* **1** : par <por encima de la par : above par> **2 a la par que** : at the same time as, as well as <interesante a la par que instructivo : both interesting and informative>

para *prep* **1** : for <para ti : for you> <alta para su edad : tall for her age> <una cita para el lunes : an appointment for Monday> **2** : to, towards <para la derecha : to the right> <van para el río : they're heading towards the river> **3** : to, in order to <lo hace para molestarte : he does it to annoy you> **4** : around, by (a time) <para mañana estarán listos : they'll be ready by tomorrow> **5 para adelante** : forwards **6 para atrás** : backwards **7 para que** : so, so that, in order that <te lo digo para que sepas : I'm telling you so you'll know>

parabién *nm, pl* **-bienes** : congratulations *pl*

parábola *nf* **1** : parable **2** : parabola

parabrisas *nms & pl* : windshield

paracaídas *nms & pl* : parachute

paracaidista *nmf* **1** : parachutist **2** : paratrooper

parachoques *nms & pl* : bumper

parada *nf* **1** : stop <parada de autobús : bus stop> **2** : catch, save, parry (in sports) **3** DESFILE : parade

paradero *nm* : whereabouts

paradigma *nm* : paradigm

parado, -da *adj* **1** : motionless, idle, stopped **2** : standing (up) **3** : confused, bewildered **4 bien (mal) parado** : in good (bad) shape <salió bien parado : it turned out well for him>

paradoja *nf* : paradox

paradójico, -ca *adj* : paradoxical

parafernalia *nf* : paraphernalia

parafina *nf* : paraffin

parafrasear *vt* : to paraphrase

paráfrasis *nfs & pl* : paraphrase

paraguas *nms & pl* : umbrella

paraguayo, -ya *adj & n* : Paraguayan

paraíso *nm* **1** : paradise, heaven **2 paraíso fiscal** : tax shelter

paraje *nm* : spot, place

paralelismo *nm* : parallelism, similarity

paralelo[1], -la *adj* : parallel

paralelo[2] *nm* : parallel

paralelogramo *nm* : parallelogram

parálisis *nfs & pl* **1** : paralysis **2** : standstill **3 parálisis cerebral** : cerebral palsy

paralítico, -ca *adj & n* : paralytic

paralizar {21} *vt* **1** : to paralyze **2** : to bring to a standstill — **paralizarse** *vr*

parámetro *nm* : parameter

páramo *nm* : barren plateau, moor

parangón *nm, pl* **-gones 1** : comparison **2 sin ~** : incomparable

paraninfo *nm* : auditorium, assembly hall

paranoia *nf* : paranoia

paranoico, -ca *adj & n* : paranoid

parapeto *nm* : parapet, rampart

parapléjico, -ca *adj & n* : paraplegic

parar *vt* **1** DETENER : to stop **2** : to stand, to prop — *vi* **1** CESAR : to stop **2** : to stay, to put up **3 ir a parar** : to end up, to wind up — **pararse** *vr* **1** : to stop **2** ATASCARSE : to stall (out) **3** : to stand up, to get up

pararrayos *nms & pl* : lightning rod

parasitario, -ria *adj* : parasitic

parasitismo *nm* : parasitism

parásito *nm* : parasite

parasol *nm* SOMBRILLA : parasol

parcela *nf* : parcel, tract of land

parcelar *vt* : to parcel (land)

parchar *vt* : to patch, to patch up

parche *nm* : patch

parcial *adj* : partial — **parcialmente** *adv*

parcialidad *nf* : partiality, bias

parco, -ca *adj* **1** : sparing, frugal **2** : moderate, temperate

pardo, -da *adj* : brownish grey

pardusco → **pardo**

parecer[1] {53} *vi* **1** : to seem, to look, to appear to be <parece bien fácil : it looks very easy> <así parece : so it seems> <pareces una princesa : you look like a princess> **2** : to think, to have an opinion <me parece que sí : I think so> **3** : to like, to be in agreement <si te parece : if you like, if it's all right with you> — **parecerse** *vr* **~ a** : to resemble

parecer[2] *nm* **1** OPINIÓN : opinion **2** ASPECTO : appearance <al parecer : apparently>

parecido[1], **-da** *adj* **1** : similar, alike **2 bien parecido** : good-looking

parecido[2] *nm* : resemblance, similarity

pared *nf* : wall

pareja *nf* **1** : couple, pair **2** : partner, mate

parejo, -ja *adj* **1** : even, smooth, level **2** : equal, similar

parentela *nf* : relations *pl*, kinfolk

parentesco *nm* : relationship, kinship

paréntesis *nms & pl* **1** : parenthesis **2** : digression

parentético, -ca *adj* : parenthetic, parenthetical

paria *nmf* : pariah, outcast

paridad *nf* : parity, equality

pariente *nmf* : relative, relation

parir *vi* : to give birth — *vt* : to give birth to, to bear

parking *nm* : parking lot

parlamentar *vi* : to talk, to parley

parlamentario[1], **-ria** *adj* : parliamentary

parlamentario[2], **-ria** *n* : member of parliament

parlamento *nm* **1** : parliament **2** : negotiations *pl*, talks *pl*

parlanchín[1], **-china** *adj, mpl* **-chines** : chatty, talkative

parlanchín[2], **-china** *n, mpl* **-chines** : chatterbox

parlante *nm* ALTOPARLANTE : loudspeaker

parlotear *vi fam* : to gab, to chat, to prattle

parloteo *nm fam* : prattle, chatter

paro *nm* **1** HUELGA : strike **2** : stoppage, stopping **3 paro forzoso** : layoff

parodia *nf* : parody

parodiar *vt* : to parody

parpadear *vi* **1** : to blink **2** : to flicker

parpadeo *nm* **1** : blink, blinking **2** : flickering

párpado *nm* : eyelid

parque *nm* **1** : park **2 parque de atracciones** : amusement park

parquear *vt* : to park — **parquearse** *vr*

parqueo *nm* : parking

parquet *or* **parqué** *nm* : parquet

parquímetro *nm* : parking meter

parra *nf* : vine, grapevine

párrafo *nm* : paragraph

parranda *nf fam* : party, spree

parrilla *nf* **1** : broiler, grill **2** : grate

parrillada *nf* BARBACOA : barbecue

párroco *nm* : parish priest

parroquia *nf* **1** : parish **2** : parish church **3** : customers *pl*, clientele

parroquial *adj* : parochial

parroquiano, -na *nm* **1** : parishioner **2** : customer, patron

parsimonia *nf* **1** : calm **2** : parsimony, thrift

parsimonioso, -sa *adj* **1** : calm, unhurried **2** : parsimonious, thrifty

parte[1] *nm* : report, dispatch

parte[2] *nf* **1** : part, share **2** : part, place <en alguna parte : somewhere> <por todas partes : everywhere> **3** : party (in negotiations, etc.) **4 de parte de** : on behalf of **5 ¿de parte de quién?** : may I ask who's calling? **6 tomar parte** : to take part

partero, -ra *n* : midwife

partición *nf, pl* **-ciones** : division, sharing

participación *nf, pl* **-ciones** **1** : participation **2** : share, interest **3** : announcement, notice

participante *nmf* **1** : participant **2** : competitor, entrant

participar *vi* **1** : to participate, to take part **2 ~ en** : to have a share in — *vt* : to announce, to notify

partícipe *nmf* : participant

participio *nm* : participle

partícula *nf* : particle

particular[1] *adj* **1** : particular, specific **2** : private, personal **3** : special, unique

particular[2] *nm* **1** : matter, detail **2** : individual

particularidad *nf* : characteristic, peculiarity

particularizar {21} *vt* **1** : to distinguish, to characterize **2** : to specify

partida *nf* **1 :** departure **2 :** item, entry **3 :** certificate <partida de nacimiento : birth certificate> **4 :** game, match, hand **5 :** party, group

partidario, -ria *n* **:** follower, supporter

partido *nm* **1 :** (political) party **2 :** game, match <partido de futbol : soccer game> **3** APOYO **:** support, following **4** PROVECHO **:** profit, advantage <sacar partido de : to profit from>

partir *vt* **1 :** to cut, to split **2 :** to break, to crack **3 :** to share (out), to divide — *vi* **1 :** to leave, to depart **2 ~ de :** to start from **3 a partir de :** as of, from <a partir de hoy : as of today> — **partirse** *vr* **1 :** to smash, to split open **2 :** to chap

partisano, -na *adj & n* **:** partisan

partitura *nf* **:** (musical) score

parto *nm* **1 :** childbirth, delivery, labor <estar de parto : to be in labor> **2 :** product, creation, brainchild

parvulario *nm* **:** nursery school

párvulo, -la *n* **:** toddler, preschooler

pasa *nf* **1 :** raisin **2 pasa de Corinto :** currant

pasable *adj* **:** passable, tolerable — **pasablemente** *adv*

pasada *nf* **1 :** passage, passing **2 :** pass, wipe, coat (of paint) **3 de ~ :** in passing **4 mala pasada :** dirty trick

pasadizo *nm* **:** passageway, corridor

pasado[1], -da *adj* **1 :** past <el año pasado : last year> <pasado mañana : the day after tomorrow> <pasadas las siete : after seven o'clock> **2 :** stale, bad, overripe **3 :** old-fashioned, out-of-date **4 :** overripe, slightly spoiled

pasado[2] *nm* **:** past

pasador *nm* **1 :** bolt, latch **2 :** barrette **3** *Mex* **:** bobby pin

pasaje *nm* **1 :** ticket (for travel) **2** TARIFA **:** fare **3 :** passageway **4 :** passengers *pl*

pasajero[1], -ra *adj* **:** passing, fleeting

pasajero[2], -ra *n* **:** passenger

pasamanos *nms & pl* **1 :** handrail **2 :** banister

pasante *nmf* **:** assistant

pasaporte *nm* **:** passport

pasar *vi* **1 :** to pass, to go by, to come by **2 :** to come in, to enter <¿se puede pasar? : may we come in?> **3 :** to happen <¿qué pasa? : what's happening?, what's going on?> **4 :** to manage, to get by **5 :** to be over, to end **6 ~ de :** to exceed, to go beyond **7 ~ por :** to pretend to be — *vt* **1 :** to pass, to give <¿me pasas la sal? : would you pass me the salt?> **2 :** to pass (a test) **3 :** to go over, to cross **4 :** to spend (time) **5 :** to tolerate **6 :** to go through, to suffer **7 :** to show (a movie, etc.) **8 :** to overtake, to pass, to surpass **9 :** to pass over, to wipe up **10 pasarlo bien** *or* **pasarla bien :** to have a good time **11 pasarlo mal** *or* **pasarla mal :** to have a bad time, to have a hard time **12 pasar por alto :** to overlook, to omit — **pasarse** *vr* **1 :** to move, to pass, to go away **2 :** to slip one's mind, to forget **3 :** to go too far

pasarela *nf* **1 :** gangplank **2 :** footbridge **3 :** runway, catwalk

pasatiempo *nm* **:** pastime, hobby

Pascua *nf* **1 :** Easter **2 :** Passover **3 :** Christmas **4 Pascuas** *nfpl* **:** Christmas season

pase *nm* **1** PERMISO **:** pass, permit **2 pase de abordar** *Mex* **:** boarding pass

pasear *vi* **:** to take a walk, to go for a ride — *vt* **1 :** to take for a walk **2 :** to parade around, to show off — **pasearse** *vr* **:** to walk around

paseo *nm* **1 :** walk, stroll **2 :** ride **3** EXCURSIÓN **:** outing, trip

pasiflora *nf* **:** passionflower

pasillo *nm* CORREDOR **:** hallway, corridor, aisle

pasión *nf, pl* **pasiones :** passion

pasional *adj* **:** passionate <crimen pasional : crime of passion>

pasionaria *nf* → **pasiflora**

pasivo[1], -va *adj* **:** passive — **pasivamente** *adv*

pasivo[2] *nm* **1 :** liability <activos y pasivos : assets and liabilities> **2 :** debit side (of an account)

pasmado, -da *adj* **:** stunned, flabbergasted

pasmar *vt* **:** to amaze, to stun — **pasmarse** *vr*

pasmo *nm* **1 :** shock, astonishment **2 :** wonder, marvel

pasmoso, -sa *adj* **:** incredible, amazing — **pasmosamente** *adv*

paso[1], -sa *adj* **:** dried <ciruela pasa : prune>

paso[2] *nm* **1 :** passage, passing <de paso : in passing, on the way> **2 :** way, path <abrirse paso : to make one's way> **3 :** crossing <paso de peatones : crosswalk> <paso a desnivel : underpass> <paso elevado : overpass> **4 :** step <paso a paso : step by step> **5 :** pace, gait <a buen paso : quickly, at a good rate>

pasta *nf* **1 :** paste <pasta de dientes *or* pasta dental : toothpaste> **2 :** pasta **3 :** pastry dough **4 libro en pasta dura :** hardcover book **5 tener pasta de :** to have the makings of

pastar *vi* **:** to graze — *vt* **:** to put to pasture

pastel[1] *adj* **:** pastel

pastel[2] *nm* **1 :** cake <pastel de cumpleaños : birthday cake> **2 :** pie, turnover **3 :** pastel

pastelería *nf* **:** pastry shop

pasteurización *nf, pl* **-ciones :** pasteurization

pasteurizar {21} *vt* **:** to pasteurize

pastilla *nf* **1** COMPRIMIDO, PÍLDORA **:** pill, tablet **2 :** lozenge <pastilla para la tos

: cough drop> **3** : cake (of soap), bar (of chocolate)
pastizal *nm* : pasture, grazing land
pasto *nm* **1** : pasture **2** HIERBA : grass, lawn
pastor, -tora *n* **1** : shepherd, shepherdess *f* **2** : minister, pastor
pastoral *adj & nf* : pastoral
pastorear *vt* : to shepherd, to tend
pastorela *nf* **1** : pastoral, pastourelle **2** *Mex* : a traditional Christmas play
pastoso, -sa *adj* **1** : pasty, doughy **2** : smooth, mellow (of sounds)
pata *nf* **1** : paw, leg (of an animal) **2** : foot, leg (of furniture) **3 patas de gallo** : crow's-feet **4 meter la pata** *fam* : to put one's foot in it, to make a blunder
patada *nf* **1** PUNTAPIÉ : kick **2** : stamp (of the foot)
patalear *vi* **1** : to kick **2** : to stamp one's feet
pataleta *nf fam* : tantrum
patán[1] *adj, pl* **patanes** : boorish, crude
patán[2] *nm, pl* **patanes** : boor, lout
patata *nf Spain* : potato
patear *vt* : to kick — *vi* : to stamp one's foot
patentar *vt* : to patent
patente[1] *adj* EVIDENTE : obvious, patent — **patentemente** *adv*
patente[2] *nf* : patent
paternal *adj* : fatherly, paternal
paternidad *nf* **1** : fatherhood, paternity **2** : parenthood **3** : authorship
paterno, -na *adj* : paternal <abuela paterna : paternal grandmother>
patético, -ca *adj* : pathetic, moving
patetismo *nm* : pathos
patíbulo *nm* : gallows, scaffold
patillas *nfpl* : sideburns
patín *nm, pl* **patines** : skate <patín de ruedas : roller skate>
patinador, -dora *n* : skater
patinaje *nm* : skating
patinar *vi* **1** : to skate **2** : to skid, to slip **3** *fam* : to slip up, to blunder
patinazo *nm* **1** : skid **2** *fam* : blunder, slipup
patineta *nf* **1** : scooter **2** : skateboard
patinete *nm* : scooter
patio *nm* **1** : courtyard, patio **2 patio de recreo** : playground
patito, -ta *n* : duckling
pato, -ta *n* **1** : duck **2 pato real** : mallard **3 pagar el pato** *fam* : to take the blame
patología *nf* : pathology
patológico, -ca *adj* : pathological
patólogo, -ga *n* : pathologist
patraña *nf* : tall tale, humbug, nonsense
patria *nf* : native land
patriarca *nm* : patriarch — **patriarcal** *adj*
patriarcado *nm* : patriarchy
patrimonio *nm* : patrimony, legacy
patrio, -tria *adj* **1** : native, home <suelo patrio : native soil> **2** : paternal
patriota[1] *adj* : patriotic
patriota[2] *nmf* : patriot
patriotería *nf* : jingoism, chauvinism
patriotero[1], **-ra** *adj* : jingoistic, chauvinistic
patriotero[2], **-ra** *n* : jingoist, chauvinist
patriótico, -ca *adj* : patriotic
patriotismo *nm* : patriotism
patrocinador, -dora *n* : sponsor, patron
patrocinar *vt* : to sponsor
patrocinio *nm* : sponsorship, patronage
patrón[1], **-trona** *n, mpl* **patrones 1** JEFE : boss **2** : patron saint
patrón[2] *nm, pl* **patrones 1** : standard **2** : pattern (in sewing)
patronal *adj* **1** : management, employers' <sindicato patronal : employers' association> **2** : pertaining to a patron saint <fiesta patronal : patron saint's day>
patronato *nm* **1** : board, council **2** : foundation, trust
patrono, -na *n* **1** : employer **2** : patron saint
patrulla *nf* **1** : patrol **2** : police car, cruiser
patrullar *v* : to patrol
patrullero *nm* **1** : police car **2** : patrol boat
paulatino, -na *adj* : gradual
paupérrimo, -ma *adj* : destitute, poverty-stricken
pausa *nf* : pause, break
pausado[1] *adv* : slowly, deliberately <habla más pausado : speak more slowly>
pausado[2], **-da** *adj* : slow, deliberate — **pausadamente** *adv*
pauta *nf* **1** : rule, guideline **2** : lines *pl* (on paper)
pava *nf Arg, Bol, Chile* : kettle
pavimentar *vt* : pave
pavimento *nm* : pavement
pavo, -va *n* **1** : turkey **2 pavo real** : peacock **3 comer pavo** : to be a wallflower
pavón *nm, pl* **pavones** : peacock
pavonearse *vr* : to strut, to swagger
pavoneo *nm* : strut, swagger
pavor *nm* TERROR : dread, terror
pavoroso, -sa *adj* ATERRADOR : dreadful, terrifying
payasada *nf* BUFONADA : antic, buffoonery
payasear *vi* : to clown around
payaso, -sa *n* : clown
paz *nf, pl* **paces 1** : peace **2 dejar en paz** : to leave alone **3 hacer las paces** : to make up, to reconcile
pazca, etc. → **pacer**
PC *nmf* : PC, personal computer
peaje *nm* : toll
peatón *nm, pl* **-tones** : pedestrian
peca *nf* : freckle

pecado *nm* : sin
pecador[1], **-dora** *adj* : sinful, sinning
pecador[2], **-dora** *n* : sinner
pecaminoso, -sa *adj* : sinful
pecar {72} *vi* **1** : to sin **2 ~ de** : to be too much (something) <no pecan de amabilidad : they're not overly friendly>
pécari *or* **pecarí** *nm* : peccary
pececillo *nm* : small fish
pecera *nf* : fishbowl, fish tank
pecho *nm* **1** : chest **2** SENO : breast, bosom **3** : heart, courage **4 dar el pecho** : to breast-feed **5 tomar a pecho** : to take to heart
pechuga *nf* : breast (of fowl)
pecoso, -sa *adj* : freckled
pectoral *adj* : pectoral
peculado *nm* : embezzlement
peculiar *adj* **1** CARACTERÍSTICO : particular, characteristic **2** RARO : peculiar, uncommon
peculiaridad *nf* : peculiarity
pecuniario, -ria *adj* : pecuniary
pedagogía *nf* : pedagogy
pedagógico, -ca *adj* : pedagogic, pedagogical
pedagogo, -ga *n* : educator, pedagogue
pedal *nm* : pedal
pedalear *vi* : to pedal
pedante[1] *adj* : pedantic
pedante[2] *nmf* : pedant
pedantería *nf* : pedantry
pedazo *nm* TROZO : piece, bit, chunk <caerse a pedazos : to fall to pieces> <hacer pedazos : to tear into shreds, to smash to pieces>
pedernal *nm* : flint
pedestal *nm* : pedestal
pedestre *adj* : commonplace, pedestrian
pediatra *nmf* : pediatrician
pediatría *nf* : pediatrics
pediátrico, -ca *adj* : pediatric
pedido *nm* **1** : order (of merchandise) **2** : request
pedigrí *nm* : pedigree
pedir {54} *vt* **1** : to ask for, to request <le pedí un préstamo a Claudia : I asked Claudia for a loan> **2** : to order (food, merchandise) **3 pedir disculpas** *or* **pedir perdón** : to apologize — *vi* **1** : to order **2** : to beg
pedrada *nf* **1** : blow (with a rock or stone) <la ventana se quebró de una pedrada : the window was broken by a rock> **2** *fam* : cutting remark, dig
pedregal *nm* : rocky ground
pedregoso, -sa *adj* : rocky, stony
pedrera *nf* CANTERA : quarry
pedrería *nf* : precious stones *pl*, gems *pl*
pegado, -da *adj* **1** : glued, stuck, stuck together **2 ~ a** : right next to
pegajoso, -sa *adj* **1** : sticky, gluey **2** : catchy <una tonada pegajosa : a catchy tune>
pegamento *nm* : adhesive, glue
pegar {52} *vt* **1** : to glue, to stick, to paste **2** : to attach, to sew on **3** : to infect with, to give <me pegó el resfriado : he gave me his cold> **4** GOLPEAR : to hit, to deal, to strike <me pegaron un puntapié : they gave me a kick> **5** : to give (out with) <pegó un grito : she let out a yell> — *vi* **1** : to adhere, to stick **2 ~ en** : to hit, to strike (against) **3 ~ con** : to match, to go with — **pegarse** *vr* **1** GOLPEARSE : to hit oneself, to hit each other **2** : to stick, to take hold **3** : to be contagious **4** *fam* : to tag along, to stick around
pegote *nm* **1** : sticky mess **2** *Mex* : sticker, adhesive label
pegue, etc. → **pegar**
peinado *nm* : hairstyle, hairdo
peinador, -dora *n* : hairdresser
peinar *vt* : to comb — **peinarse** *vr*
peine *nm* : comb
peineta *nf* : ornamental comb
peladez *nf, pl* **-deces** *Mex fam* : obscenity, bad language
pelado, -da *adj* **1** : bald, hairless **2** : peeled **3** : bare, barren **4** : broke, penniless **5** *Mex fam* : coarse, crude
pelador *nm* : peeler
pelagra *nf* : pellagra
pelaje *nm* : coat (of an animal), fur
pelar *vt* **1** : to peel, to shell **2** : to skin **3** : to pluck **4** : to remove hair from **5** *fam* : to clean out (of money) — **pelarse** *vr* **1** : to peel **2** *fam* : to get a haircut **3** *Mex fam* : to split, to leave
peldaño *nm* **1** : step, stair **2** : rung
pelea *nf* **1** LUCHA : fight **2** : quarrel
pelear *vi* **1** LUCHAR : to fight **2** DISPUTAR : to quarrel — **pelearse** *vr*
peleón, -ona *adj, mpl* **-ones** *Spain* : quarrelsome, argumentative
peleonero, -ra *adj Mex* : quarrelsome
peletería *nf* **1** : fur shop **2** : fur trade
peletero, -ra *n* : furrier
peliagudo, -da *adj* : tricky, difficult, ticklish
pelícano *nm* : pelican
película *nf* **1** : movie, film **2** : (photographic) film **3** : thin covering, layer
peligrar *vi* : to be in danger
peligro *nm* **1** : danger, peril **2** : risk <correr peligro de : to run the risk of>
peligroso, -sa *adj* : dangerous, hazardous
pelirrojo[1], **-ja** *adj* : red-haired, redheaded
pelirrojo[2], **-ja** *n* : redhead
pellejo *nm* **1** : hide, skin **2 salvar el pellejo** : to save one's neck
pellizcar {72} *vt* **1** : to pinch **2** : to nibble on
pellizco *nm* : pinch
pelo *nm* **1** : hair **2** : fur **3** : pile, nap **4 a pelo** : bareback **5 con pelos y señales** : in great detail **6 no tener pelos en la lengua** : to not mince words, to be blunt **7 tomarle el pelo a alguien** : to tease someone, to pull someone's leg

pelón, -lona *adj, mpl* **pelones 1 :** bald **2** *fam* **:** broke **3** *Mex fam* **:** tough, difficult

pelota *nf* **1 :** ball **2** *fam* **:** head **3 en pelotas** *fam* **:** naked **4 pelota vasca :** jai alai **5 pasar la pelota** *fam* **:** to pass the buck

pelotón *nm, pl* **-tones :** squad, detachment

peltre *nm* **:** pewter

peluca *nf* **:** wig

peluche *nm* **:** plush (fabric)

peludo, -da *adj* **:** hairy, shaggy, bushy

peluquería *nf* **1 :** hairdresser's, barber shop **2 :** hairdressing

peluquero, -ra *n* **:** barber, hairdresser

peluquín *nm, pl* **-quines** TUPÉ **:** hairpiece, toupee

pelusa *nf* **:** lint, fuzz

pélvico, -ca *adj* **:** pelvic

pelvis *nfs & pl* **:** pelvis

pena *nf* **1** CASTIGO **:** punishment, penalty <pena de muerte : death penalty> **2** AFLICCIÓN **:** sorrow, grief <morir de pena : to die of a broken heart> <¡que pena! : what a shame!, how sad!> **3** DOLOR **:** pain, suffering **4** DIFICULTAD **:** difficulty, trouble <a duras penas : with great difficulty> **5** VERGÜENZA **:** shame, embarrassment **6 valer la pena :** to be worthwhile

penacho *nm* **1 :** crest, tuft **2 :** plume (of feathers)

penal[1] *adj* **:** penal

penal[2] *nm* CÁRCEL **:** prison, penitentiary

penalidad *nf* **1 :** hardship **2 :** penalty, punishment

penalizar {21} *vt* **:** to penalize

penalty *nm* **:** penalty (in sports)

penar *vt* **:** to punish, to penalize — *vi* **:** to suffer, to grieve

pendenciero, -ra *adj* **:** argumentative, quarrelsome

pender *vi* **1 :** to hang **2 :** to be pending

pendiente[1] *adj* **1 :** pending **2 estar pendiente de :** to be watchful of, to be on the lookout for

pendiente[2] *nm Spain* **:** earring

pendiente[3] *nf* **:** slope, incline

pendón *nm, pl* **pendones :** banner

péndulo *nm* **:** pendulum

pene *nm* **:** penis

penetración *nf, pl* **-ciones 1 :** penetration **2 :** insight

penetrante *adj* **1 :** penetrating, piercing **2 :** sharp, acute **3 :** deep (of a wound)

penetrar *vi* **1 :** to penetrate, to sink in **2 ~ por** *or* **~ en :** to pierce, to go in, to enter into <el frío penetra por la ventana : the cold comes right in through the window> — *vt* **1 :** to penetrate, to permeate **2 :** to pierce <el dolor penetró su corazón : sorrow pierced her heart> **3 :** to fathom, to understand

penicilina *nf* **:** penicillin

península *nf* **:** peninsula — **peninsular** *adj*

penitencia *nf* **:** penance, penitence

penitenciaría *nf* **:** penitentiary

penitente *adj & nmf* **:** penitent

penol *nm* **:** yardarm

penoso, -sa *adj* **1 :** painful, distressing **2 :** difficult, arduous **3 :** shy, bashful

pensado, -da *adj* **1 bien pensado :** well thought-out **2 en el momento menos pensado :** when least expected **3 poco pensado :** badly thought-out **4 mal pensado :** evil-minded

pensador, -dora *n* **:** thinker

pensamiento *nm* **1 :** thought **2 :** thinking **3 :** pansy

pensar {55} *vi* **1 :** to think **2 ~ en :** to think about — *vt* **1 :** to think **2 :** to think about **3 :** to intend, to plan on — **pensarse** *vr* **:** to think over

pensativo, -va *adj* **:** pensive, thoughtful

pensión *nf, pl* **pensiones 1** JUBILACIÓN **:** pension **2 :** boarding house **3 pensión alimenticia :** alimony

pensionado, -da *n* **→ pensionista**

pensionista *nmf* **1** JUBILADO **:** pensioner, retiree **2 :** boarder, lodger

pentágono *nm* **:** pentagon — **pentagonal** *adj*

pentagrama *nm* **:** staff (in music)

penúltimo, -ma *adj* **:** next to last, penultimate

penumbra *nf* **:** semidarkness

penuria *nf* **1** ESCASEZ **:** shortage, scarcity **2 :** poverty

peña *nf* **:** rock, crag

peñasco *nm* **:** crag, large rock

peñón *nm* **→ peñasco**

peón *nm, pl* **peones 1 :** laborer, peon **2 :** pawn (in chess)

peonía *nf* **:** peony

peor[1] *adv* **1** (*comparative of* **mal**) **:** worse <se llevan peor que antes : they get along worse than before> **2** (*superlative of* **mal**) **:** worst <me fue peor que a nadie : I did the worst of all>

peor[2] *adj* **1** (*comparative of* **malo**) **:** worse <es peor que el original : it's worse than the original> **2** (*superlative of* **malo**) **:** worst <el peor de todos : the worst of all>

pepa *nf* **:** seed, pit (of a fruit)

pepenador, -dora *n CA, Mex* **:** scavenger

pepenar *vt CA, Mex* **:** to scavenge, to scrounge

pepinillo *nm* **:** pickle, gherkin

pepino *nm* **:** cucumber

pepita *nf* **1 :** seed, pip **2 :** nugget **3** *Mex* **:** dried pumpkin seed

peque, etc. → pecar

pequeñez *nf, pl* **-ñeces 1 :** smallness **2 :** trifle, triviality **3 pequeñez de espíritu :** pettiness

pequeño[1], **-ña** *adj* **1 :** small, little <un libro pequeño : a small book> **2 :** young **3** BAJO **:** short

pequeño[2], **-ña** *n* **:** child, little one

pera *nf* : pear
peraltar *vt* : to bank (a road)
perca *nf* : perch (fish)
percal *nm* : percale
percance *nm* : mishap, misfortune
percatarse *vr* ~ **de** : to notice, to become aware of
percebe *nm* : barnacle
percepción *nf, pl* **-ciones 1** : perception **2** : idea, notion **3** COBRO : receipt (of payment), collection
perceptible *adj* : perceptible, noticeable — **perceptiblemente** *adv*
percha *nf* **1** : perch **2** : coat hanger **3** : coatrack, coat hook
perchero *nm* : coatrack
percibir *vt* **1** : to perceive, to notice, to sense **2** : to earn, to draw (a salary)
percudido, -da *adj* : grimy
percudir *vt* : to make grimy — **percudirse** *vr*
percusión *nf, pl* **-siones** : percussion
percusor *or* **percutor** *nm* : hammer (of a firearm)
perdedor¹, -dora *adj* : losing
perdedor², -dora *n* : loser
perder {56} *vt* **1** : to lose **2** : to miss <perdimos la oportunidad : we missed the opportunity> **3** : to waste (time) — *vi* : to lose — **perderse** *vr* EXTRAVIARSE : to get lost, to stray
perdición *nf, pl* **-ciones** : perdition, damnation
pérdida *nf* **1** : loss **2 pérdida de tiempo** : waste of time
perdidamente *adv* : hopelessly
perdido, -da *adj* **1** : lost **2** : inveterate, incorrigible <es un caso perdido : he's a hopeless case> **3** : in trouble, done for **4 de** ~ *Mex fam* : at least
perdigón *nm, pl* **-gones** : shot, pellet
perdiz *nf, pl* **perdices** : partridge
perdón¹ *nm, pl* **perdones** : forgiveness, pardon
perdón² *interj* : excuse me!, sorry!
perdonable *adj* : forgivable
perdonar *vt* **1** DISCULPAR : to forgive, to pardon **2** : to exempt, to excuse
perdurable *adj* : lasting
perdurar *vi* : to last, to endure, to survive
perecedero, -ra *adj* : perishable
perecer {53} *vi* : to perish, to die
peregrinación *nf, pl* **-ciones** : pilgrimage
peregrinaje *nm* → **peregrinación**
peregrino¹, -na *adj* **1** : unusual, odd **2** MIGRATORIO : migratory
peregrino², -na *n* : pilgrim
perejil *nm* : parsley
perenne *adj* : perennial
pereza *nf* FLOJERA, HOLGAZANERÍA : laziness, idleness
perezoso¹, -sa *adj* FLOJO, HOLGAZÁN : lazy
perezoso² *nm* : sloth (animal)
perfección *nf, pl* **-ciones** : perfection
perfeccionamiento *nm* : perfecting, refinement
perfeccionar *vt* : to perfect, to refine
perfeccionismo *nm* : perfectionism
perfeccionista *nmf* : perfectionist
perfecto, -ta *adj* : perfect — **perfectamente** *adv*
perfidia *nf* : perfidy, treachery
pérfido, -da *adj* : perfidious
perfil *nm* **1** : profile **2 de** ~ : sideways, from the side **3 perfiles** *nmpl* RASGOS : features, characteristics
perfilar *vt* : to outline, to define — **perfilarse** *vr* **1** : to be outlined, to be silhouetted **2** : to take shape
perforación *nf, pl* **-ciones 1** : perforation **2** : drilling
perforar *vt* **1** : to perforate, to pierce **2** : to drill, to bore
perfumar *vt* : to perfume, to scent — **perfumarse** *vr*
perfume *nm* : perfume, scent
pergamino *nm* : parchment
pérgola *nf* : pergola, arbor
pericia *nf* : skill, expertise
pericial *adj* : expert <testigo pericial : expert witness>
perico *nm* COTORRA : small parrot
periferia *nf* : periphery
periférico¹, -ca *adj* : peripheral
periférico² *nm* **1** *CA, Mex* : beltway **2** : peripheral
perilla *nf* **1** : goatee **2** : pommel (on a saddle) **3** *Col, Mex* : knob, handle **4 perilla de la oreja** : earlobe **5 de perillas** *fam* : handy, just right
perímetro *nm* : perimeter
periódico¹, -ca *adj* : periodic — **periódicamente** *adv*
periódico² *nm* DIARIO : newspaper
periodismo *nm* : journalism
periodista *nmf* : journalist
periodístico, -ca *adj* : journalistic, news
período *or* **periodo** *nm* : period
peripecia *nf* VICISITUD : vicissitude, reversal <las peripecias de su carrera : the ups and downs of her career>
periquito *nm* **1** : parakeet **2 periquito australiano** : budgerigar
periscopio *nm* : periscope
perito, -ta *adj & n* : expert
perjudicar {72} *vt* : to harm, to be detrimental to
perjudicial *adj* : harmful, detrimental
perjuicio *nm* **1** : harm, damage **2 en perjuicio de** : to the detriment of
perjurar *vi* : to perjure oneself
perjurio *nm* : perjury
perjuro, -ra *n* : perjurer
perla *nf* **1** : pearl **2 de perlas** *fam* : wonderfully <me viene de perlas : it suits me just fine>
permanecer {53} *vi* **1** QUEDARSE : to remain, to stay **2** SEGUIR : to remain, to continue to be
permanencia *nf* **1** : permanence, continuance **2** ESTANCIA : stay
permanente¹ *adj* **1** : permanent **2** : constant — **permanentemente** *adv*
permanente² *nf* : permanent (wave)

permeabilidad *nf* : permeability
permeable *adj* : permeable
permisible *adj* : permissible, allowable
permisividad *nf* : permissiveness
permisivo, -va *adv* : permissive
permiso *nm* **1** : permission **2** : permit, license **3** : leave, furlough **4 con ~** : excuse me, pardon me
permitir *vt* : to permit, to allow — **permitirse** *vr*
permuta *nf* : exchange
permutar *vt* INTERCAMBIAR : to exchange
pernicioso, -sa *adj* : pernicious, destructive
pernil *nm* **1** : haunch (of an animal) **2** : leg (of meat), ham **3** : trouser leg
perno *nm* : bolt, pin
pernoctar *vi* : to stay overnight, to spend the night
pero[1] *nm* **1** : fault, defect <ponerle peros a : to find fault with> **2** : objection
pero[2] *conj* : but
perogrullada *nf* : truism, platitude, cliché
peroné *nm* : fibula
perorar *vi* : to deliver a speech
perorata *nf* : oration, long-winded speech
peróxido *nm* : peroxide
perpendicular *adj & nf* : perpendicular
perpetrar *vt* : to perpetrate
perpetuar {3} *vt* ETERNIZAR : to perpetuate
perpetuidad *nf* : perpetuity
perpetuo, -tua *adj* : perpetual — **perpetuamente** *adv*
perplejidad *nf* : perplexity
perplejo, -ja *adj* : perplexed, puzzled
perrada *nf fam* : dirty trick
perrera *nf* : kennel, dog pound
perrero, -ra *n* : dogcatcher
perrito, -ta *n* CACHORRO : puppy, small dog
perro, -rra *n* **1** : dog, bitch *f* **2 perro caliente** : hot dog **3 perro salchicha** : dachsund **4 perro faldero** : lapdog **5 perro cobrador** : retriever
persa *adj & nmf* : Persian
persecución *nf, pl* **-ciones 1** : pursuit, chase **2** : persecution
perseguidor, -dora *n* **1** : pursuer **2** : persecutor
perseguir {75} *vt* **1** : to pursue, to chase **2** : to persecute **3** : to pester, to annoy
perseverancia *nf* : perseverance
perseverar *vi* : to persevere
persiana *nf* : blind, venetian blind
persignarse *vr* SANTIGUARSE : to cross oneself, to make the sign of the cross
persistir *vi* : to persist — **persistencia** *nf* — **persistente** *adj*
persona *nf* : person
personaje *nm* **1** : character (in drama or literature) **2** : personage, celebrity
personal[1] *adj* : personal — **personalmente** *adv*
personal[2] *nm* : personnel, staff
personalidad *nf* : personality
personalizar {21} *vt* : to personalize
personificar {72} *vi* : to personify — **personificación** *nf*
perspectiva *nf* **1** : perspective, view **2** : prospect, outlook
perspicacia *nf* : shrewdness, perspicacity, insight
perspicaz *adj, pl* **-caces** : shrewd, perspicacious
persuadir *vt* : to persuade — **persuadirse** *vr* : to become convinced
persuasión *nf, pl* **-siones** : persuasion
persuasivo, -va *adj* : persuasive
pertenecer {53} *vi* : to belong
perteneciente *adj* **~ a** : belonging to
pertenencia *nf* **1** : membership **2** : ownership **3 pertenencias** *nfpl* : belongings, possessions
pértiga *nf* GARROCHA : pole <salto de pértiga : pole vault>
pertinaz *adj, pl* **-naces 1** OBSTINADO : obstinate **2** PERSISTENTE : persistent
pertinencia *nf* : pertinence, relevance — **pertinente** *adj*
pertrechos *nmpl* : equipment, gear
perturbación *nf, pl* **-ciones** : disturbance, disruption
perturbador, -dora *adj* **1** INQUIETANTE : disturbing, troubling **2** : disruptive
perturbar *vt* **1** : to disturb, to trouble **2** : to disrupt
peruano, -na *adj & n* : Peruvian
perversidad *nf* : perversity, depravity
perversión *nf, pl* **-siones** : perversion
perverso, -sa *adj* : wicked, depraved
pervertido[1], **-da** *adj* DEPRAVADO : perverted, depraved
pervertido[2], **-da** *n* : pervert
pervertir {76} *vt* : to pervert, to corrupt
pesa *nf* **1** : weight **2 levantamiento de pesas** : weightlifting
pesadamente *adv* **1** : heavily **2** : slowly, clumsily
pesadez *nf, pl* **-deces 1** : heaviness **2** : slowness **3** : tediousness
pesadilla *nf* : nightmare
pesado[1], **-da** *adj* **1** : heavy **2** : slow **3** : irritating, annoying **4** : tedious, boring **5** : tough, difficult
pesado[2], **-da** *n fam* : bore, pest
pesadumbre *nf* AFLICCIÓN : grief, sorrow, sadness
pésame *nm* : condolences *pl* <mi más sentido pésame : my heartfelt condolences>
pesar[1] *vt* **1** : to weigh **2** EXAMINAR : to consider, to think over — *vi* **1** : to weigh <¿cuánto pesa? : how much does it weigh?> **2** : to be heavy **3** : to weigh heavily, to be a burden <no le pesa : it's not a burden on him> <pesa sobre mi corazón : it weighs upon my heart> **4** INFLUIR : to carry weight, to have bearing **5** (*with personal pro-*

nouns) : to grieve, to sadden <me pesa mucho : I'm very sorry> **6 pese a** : in spite of, despite
pesar² *nm* **1** AFLICCIÓN, PENA : sorrow, grief **2** REMORDIMIENTO : remorse **3 a pesar de** : in spite of, despite
pesaroso, -sa *adj* **1** : sad, mournful **2** ARREPENTIDO : sorry, regretful
pesca *nf* : fishing
pescadería *nf* : fish market
pescado *nm* : fish (as food)
pescador, -dora *n* : fisherman *m*, fisherwoman *f*
pescar {72} *vt* **1** : to fish for **2** : to catch **3** *fam* : to get a hold of, to land — *vi* : to fish, to go fishing
pescuezo *nm* : neck
pesebre *nm* : manger
pesera *nf Mex* : minibus
peseta *nf* : peseta (Spanish unit of currency)
pesimismo *nm* : pessimism
pesimista¹ *adj* : pessimistic
pesimista² *nmf* : pessimist
pésimo, -ma *adj* : dreadful, abominable
peso *nm* **1** : weight, heaviness **2** : burden, responsibility **3** : weight (in sports) **4** BÁSCULA : scales *pl* **5** : peso
pesque, etc. → **pescar**
pesquería *nf* : fishery
pesquero¹, -ra *adj* : fishing <pueblo pesquero : fishing village>
pesquero² *nm* : fishing boat
pesquisa *nf* INVESTIGACIÓN : inquiry, investigation
pestaña *nf* **1** : eyelash **2** : flange, rim
pestañear *vi* : to blink
pestañeo *nm* : blink
peste *nf* **1** : plague, pestilence **2** : stench, stink **3** : nuisance, pest
pesticida *nm* : pesticide
pestilencia *nf* **1** : stench, foul odor **2** : pestilence
pestilente *adj* **1** : foul, smelly **2** : pestilent
pestillo *nm* CERROJO : bolt, latch
petaca *nf* **1** *Mex* : suitcase **2 petacas** *nfpl Mex fam* : bottom, behind
pétalo *nm* : petal
petardear *vi* : to backfire
petardeo *nm* : backfiring
petardo *nm* : firecracker
petate *nm Mex* : mat
petición *nf, pl* **-ciones** : petition, request
peticionar *vt* : to petition
peticionario, -ria *n* : petitioner
petirrojo *nm* : robin
peto *nm* : bib (of clothing)
pétreo, -trea *adj* : stone, stony
petrificar {72} *vt* : to petrify
petróleo *nm* : oil, petroleum
petrolero¹, -ra *adj* : oil <industria petrolera : oil industry>
petrolero² *nm* : oil tanker
petulancia *nf* INSOLENCIA : insolence, petulance
petulante *adj* INSOLENTE : insolent, petulant — **petulantemente** *adv*
petunia *nf* : petunia
peyorativo, -va *adj* : pejorative
pez¹ *nm, pl* **peces 1** : fish **2 pez de colores** : goldfish **3 pez espada** : swordfish **4 pez gordo** : big shot
pez² *nf, pl* **peces** : pitch, tar
pezón *nm, pl* **pezones** : nipple
pezuña *nf* : hoof <pezuña hendida : cloven hoof>
pi *nf* : pi
piadoso, -sa *adj* **1** : compassionate, merciful **2** DEVOTO : pious, devout
pianista *nmf* : pianist, piano player
piano *nm* : piano
piar {85} *vi* : to chirp, to cheep, to tweet
pibe, -ba *n Arg, Uru fam* : kid, child
pica *nf* **1** : pike, lance **2** : goad (in bullfighting) **3** : spade (in playing cards)
picada *nf* **1** : bite, sting (of an insect) **2** : sharp descent
picadillo *nm* **1** : minced meat, hash **2 hacer picadillo a** : to beat to a pulp
picado, -da *adj* **1** : perforated **2** : minced, chopped **3** : decayed (of teeth) **4** : choppy, rough **5** *fam* : annoyed, miffed
picador *nm* : picador
picadura *nf* **1** : sting, bite **2** : prick, puncture **3** : decay, cavity
picaflor *nm* COLIBRÍ : hummingbird
picana *nf* : goad, prod
picante¹ *adj* **1** : hot, spicy **2** : sharp, cutting **3** : racy, risqué
picante² *nm* **1** : spiciness **2** : hot spices *pl*, hot sauce
picaporte *nm* **1** : latch **2** : door handle **3** ALDABA : door knocker
picar {72} *vt* **1** : to sting, to bite **2** : to peck at **3** : to nibble on **4** : to prick, to puncture, to punch (a ticket) **5** : to grind, to chop **6** : to goad, to incite **7** : to pique, to provoke — *vi* **1** : to itch **2** : to sting **3** : to be spicy **4** : to nibble **5** : to take the bait **6 ~ en** : to dabble in **7 picar muy alto** : to aim too high — **picarse** *vr* **1** : to get a cavity, to decay **2** : to get annoyed, to take offense
picardía *nf* **1** : cunning, craftiness **2** : prank, dirty trick
picaresco, -ca *adj* **1** : picaresque **2** : rascally, roguish
pícaro¹, -ra *adj* **1** : mischievous **2** : cunning, sly **3** : off-color, risqué
pícaro², -ra *n* **1** : rogue, scoundrel **2** : rascal
picazón *nf, pl* **-zones** COMEZÓN : itch
picea *nf* : spruce (tree)
pichel *nm* : pitcher, jug
pichón, -chona *n, mpl* **pichones 1** : young pigeon, squab **2** *Mex fam* : novice, greenhorn
picnic *nm* : picnic
pico *nm* **1** : peak **2** : point, spike **3** : beak, bill **4** : pick, pickax **5 y pico**

: and a little, and a bit <las siete y pico : a little after seven> <dos metros y pico : a bit over two meters>

picor *nm* : itch, irritation

picoso, -sa *adj Mex* : very hot, spicy

picota *nf* **1** : pillory, stock **2 poner a alguien en la picota** : to put someone on the spot

picotada *nf* → **picotazo**

picotazo *nm* : peck (of a bird)

picotear *vt* : to peck — *vi* : to nibble, to pick

pictórico, -ca *adj* : pictorial

picudo, -da *adj* **1** : pointy, sharp **2 ~ para** *Mex fam* : clever at, good at

pide, etc. → **pedir**

pie *nm* **1** : foot <a pie : on foot> <de pie : on one's feet, standing> **2** : base, bottom, stem, foot <pie de la cama : foot of the bed> <pie de una lámpera : base of a lamp> <pie de la escalera : bottom of the stairs> <pie de una copa : stem of a glass> **3** : foot (in measurement) <pie cuadrado : square foot> **4** : cue (in theater) **5 dar pie a** : to give cause for, to give rise to **6 en pie de igualidad** : on equal footing

piedad *nf* **1** COMPASIÓN : mercy, pity **2** DEVOCIÓN : piety, devotion

piedra *nf* **1** : stone **2** : flint (of a lighter) **3** : hailstone **4 piedra de afilar** : whetstone, grindstone **5 piedra angular** : cornerstone **6 piedra arenisca** : sandstone **7 piedra caliza** : limestone **8 piedra imán** : lodestone **9 piedra de molino** : millstone **10 piedra de toque** : touchstone

piel *nf* **1** : skin **2** CUERO : leather, hide <piel de venado : deerskin> **3** : fur, pelt **4** CÁSCARA : peel, skin **5 piel de gallina** : goose bumps *pl* <me pone la piel de gallina : it gives me goose bumps>

piélago *nm* **el piélago** : the deep, the ocean

piensa, etc. → **pensar**

pienso *nm* : feed, fodder

pierde, etc. → **perder**

pierna *nf* : leg

pieza *nf* **1** ELEMENTO : piece, part, component <vestido de dos piezas : two-piece dress> <pieza de recambio : spare part> <pieza clave : key element> **2** : piece (in chess) **3** OBRA : piece, work <pieza de teatro : play> **4** : room, bedroom

pifia *nf fam* : goof, blunder

pigargo *nm* : osprey

pigmentación *nf, pl* **-ciones** : pigmentation

pigmento *nm* : pigment

pigmeo, -mea *adj & n* : pygmy, Pygmy

pijama *nm* : pajamas *pl*

pila *nf* **1** BATERÍA : battery <pila de linterna : flashlight battery> **2** MONTÓN : pile, heap **3** : sink, basin, font <pila bautismal : baptismal font> <pila para pájaros : birdbath>

pilar *nm* **1** : pillar, column **2** : support, mainstay

píldora *nf* PASTILLA : pill

pillaje *nm* : pillage, plunder

pillar *vt fam* **1** : to catch <¡cuidado! ¡nos pillarán! : watch out! they'll catch us!> **2** : to grasp, to catch on <¿no lo pillas? : don't you get it?>

pillo¹, -lla *adj* : cunning, crafty

pillo², -lla *n* **1** : rascal, brat **2** : rogue, scoundrel

pilluelo, -la *n* : urchin

pilotar *vt* : to pilot, to drive

pilote *nm* : pile (stake)

pilotear → **pilotar**

piloto *nm* **1** : pilot, driver **2** : pilot light

piltrafa *nf* **1** : poor quality meat **2** : wretch **3 piltrafas** *nfpl* : food scraps

pimentero *nm* : pepper shaker

pimentón *nm, pl* **-tones 1** : paprika **2** : cayenne pepper

pimienta *nf* **1** : pepper (condiment) **2 pimienta de Jamaica** : allspice

pimiento *nm* : pepper (fruit) <pimiento verde : green pepper>

pináculo *nm* **1** : pinnacle (of a building) **2** : peak, acme

pincel *nm* : paintbrush

pincelada *nf* **1** : brushstroke **2 últimas pinceladas** : final touches

pinchar *vt* **1** PICAR : to puncture (a tire) **2** : to prick, to stick **3** : to goad, to tease, to needle — *vi* **1** : to be prickly **2** : to get a flat tire **3** *fam* : to get beaten, to lose out — **pincharse** *vr* : to give oneself an injection

pinchazo *nm* **1** : prick, jab **2** : puncture, flat tire

pingüe *adj* **1** : rich, huge (of profits) **2** : lucrative

pingüino *nm* : penguin

pininos *or* **pinitos** *nmpl* : first steps <hacer pininos : to take one's first steps, to toddle>

pino *nm* : pine, pine tree

pinta *nf* **1** : dot, spot **2** : pint **3** *fam* : aspect, appearance <las peras tienen buena pinta : the pears look good> **4 pintas** *nfpl Mex* : graffiti

pintadas *nfpl* : graffiti

pintar *vt* **1** : to paint **2** : to draw, to mark **3** : to describe, to depict — *vi* **1** : to paint, to draw **2** : to look <no pinta bien : it doesn't look good> **3** *fam* : to count <aquí no pinta nada : he has no say here> — **pintarse** *vr* **1** MAQUILLARSE : to put on makeup **2 pintárselas solo** *fam* : to manage by oneself, to know it all

pintarrajear *vt* : to daub (with paint)

pinto, -ta *adj* : speckled, spotted

pintor, -tora *n* **1** : painter **2 pintor de brocha gorda** : housepainter, dauber

pintoresco, -ca *adj* : picturesque, quaint

pintura *nf* **1** : paint **2** : painting (art, work of art)

pinza *nf* **1 :** clothespin **2 :** claw, pincer **3 :** pleat, dart **4 pinzas** *nfpl* **:** tweezers **5 pinzas** *nfpl* ALICATES **:** pliers, pincers

pinzón *nm, pl* **pinzones :** finch

piña *nf* **1 :** pineapple **2 :** pine cone

piñata *nf* **:** piñata

piñón *nm, pl* **piñones 1 :** pine nut **2 :** pinion

pío[1], pía *adj* **1** DEVOTO **:** pious, devout **2 :** piebald, pied, dappled

pío[2] *nm* **:** peep, tweet, cheep

piocha *nf* **1 :** pickax **2** *Mex* **:** goatee

piojo *nm* **:** louse

piojoso, -sa *adj* **1 :** lousy **2 :** filthy

pionero[1], -ra *adj* **:** pioneering

pionero[2], -ra *n* **:** pioneer

pipa *nf* **:** pipe (for smoking)

pipián *nm, pl* **pipianes** *Mex* **:** a spicy sauce or stew

pipiolo, -la *n fam* **1 :** greenhorn, novice **2 :** kid, youngster

pique[1], etc. → picar

pique[2] *nm* **1 :** pique, resentment **2 :** rivalry, competition **3 a pique de :** about to, on the verge of **4 irse a pique :** to sink, to founder

piqueta *nf* **:** pickax

piquete *nm* **1 :** picketers *pl*, picket line **2 :** squad, detachment **3** *Mex* **:** prick, jab

piquetear *vt* **1 :** to picket **2** *Mex* **:** to prick, to jab

pira *nf* **:** pyre

piragua *nf* **:** canoe — **piragüista** *nmf*

pirámide *nf* **:** pyramid

piraña *nf* **:** piranha

pirata[1] *adj* **:** bootleg, pirated

pirata[2] *nmf* **1 :** pirate **2 :** bootlegger **3 pirata aéreo :** hijacker

piratear *vt* **1 :** to hijack, to commandeer **2 :** to bootleg, to pirate

piratería *nf* **:** piracy, bootlegging

piromanía *nf* **:** pyromania

pirómano, -na *n* **:** pyromaniac

piropo *nm* **:** flirtatious compliment

pirotecnia *nf* **:** fireworks *pl*, pyrotechnics *pl*

pirotécnico, -ca *adj* **:** fireworks, pyrotechnic

pírrico, -ca *adj* **:** Pyrrhic

pirueta *nf* **:** pirouette

pirulí *nm* **:** cone-shaped lollipop

pisada *nf* **1 :** footstep **2** HUELLA **:** footprint

pisapapeles *nms & pl* **:** paperweight

pisar *vt* **1 :** to step on, to set foot in **2 :** to walk all over, to mistreat — *vi* **:** to step, to walk, to tread

piscina *nf* **1 :** swimming pool **2 :** fish pond

Piscis *nmf* **:** Pisces

piso *nm* **1** PLANTA **:** floor, story **2** SUELO **:** floor **3** *Spain* **:** apartment

pisotear *vt* **1 :** to stamp on, to trample **2** PISAR **:** to walk all over **3 :** to flout, to disregard

pisotón *nm, pl* **-tones :** stamp, step <sufrieron empujones y pisotones : they were pushed and stepped on>

pista *nf* **1** RASTRO **:** trail, track <siguen la pista de los sospechosos : they're on the trail of the suspects> **2 :** clue **3** CAMINO **:** road, trail **4 :** track, racetrack **5 :** ring, arena, rink **6 pista de aterrizaje :** runway, airstrip **7 pista de baile :** dance floor

pistacho *nm* **:** pistachio

pistilo *nm* **:** pistil

pistola *nf* **1 :** pistol, handgun **2 :** spray gun

pistolera *nf* **:** holster

pistolero *nm* **:** gunman

pistón *nm, pl* **pistones :** piston

pita *nf* **1 :** agave **2 :** pita fiber **3 :** twine

pitar *vi* **1 :** to blow a whistle **2 :** to whistle, to boo **3 :** to beep, to honk, to toot — *vt* **:** to whistle at, to boo

pitido *nm* **1 :** whistle, whistling **2 :** beep, honk, toot

pito *nm* **1** SILBATO **:** whistle **2 no me importa un pito** *fam* **:** I don't give a damn

pitón *nm, pl* **pitones** *nm* **1 :** python **2 :** point of a bull's horn

pituitario, -ria *adj* **:** pituitary

pívot *nmf, pl* **pívots :** center (in basketball)

pivote *nm* **:** pivot

piyama *nmf* **:** pajamas *pl*

pizarra *nf* **1 :** slate **2 :** blackboard **3 :** scoreboard

pizarrón *nm, pl* **-rrones :** blackboard, chalkboard

pizca *nf* **1 :** pinch <una pizca de canela : a pinch of cinnamon> **2 :** speck, trace <ni pizca : not a bit> **3** *Mex* **:** harvest

pizcar {72} *vt Mex* **:** to harvest

pizque, etc. → pizcar

pizza [ˈpitsa, ˈpisa] *nf* **:** pizza

pizzería *nf* **:** pizzeria, pizza parlor

placa *nf* **1 :** sheet, plate **2 :** plaque, nameplate **3 :** plate (in photography) **4 :** badge, insignia **5 placa de matrícula :** license plate, tag **6 placa dental :** plaque, tartar

placebo *nm* **:** placebo

placenta *nf* **:** placenta, afterbirth

placentero, -ra *adj* AGRADABLE, GRATO **:** pleasant, agreeable

placer[1] {57} *vi* GUSTAR **:** to be pleasing <hazlo como te plazca : do it however you please>

placer[2] *nm* **1 :** pleasure, enjoyment **2 a ~ :** as much as one wants

plácido, -da *adj* TRANQUILO **:** placid, calm

plaga *nf* **1 :** plague, infestation, blight **2** CALAMIDAD **:** disaster, scourge

plagado, -da *adj* **~ de :** filled with, covered with

plagar {52} *vt* **:** to plague

plagiar *vt* **1 :** to plagiarize **2** SECUESTRAR **:** to kidnap, to abduct

plagiario, -ria *n* **1 :** plagiarist **2** SECUESTRADOR **:** kidnapper, abductor

plagio *nm* **1 :** plagiarism **2** SECUESTRO **:** kidnapping, abduction

plague, etc. → **plagar**

plan *nm* **1 :** plan, strategy, program <plan de inversiones : investment plan> <plan de estudios : curriculum> **2** PLANO **:** plan, diagram **3 :** attitude, intent, purpose <ponte en plan serio : be serious> <estamos en plan de divertirnos : we're looking to have some fun>

plana *nf* **1 :** page <noticias en primera plana : front-page news> **2 plana mayor :** staff (in the military)

plancha *nf* **1 :** iron, ironing **2 :** grill, griddle <a la plancha : grilled> **3 :** sheet, plate <plancha para hornear : baking sheet> **4** *fam* **:** blunder, blooper

planchada *nf* **:** ironing, pressing

planchado *nm* → **planchada**

planchar *v* **:** to iron

planchazo *nm fam* **:** goof, blunder

plancton *nm* **:** plankton

planeación *nf* → **planeamiento**

planeador *nm* **:** glider (aircraft)

planeamiento *nm* **:** plan, planning

planear *vt* **:** to plan — *vi* **:** to glide (in the air)

planeo *nm* **:** gliding, soaring

planeta *nm* **:** planet

planetario[1], -ria *adj* **1 :** planetary **2 :** global, worldwide

planetario[2] *nm* **:** planetarium

planicie *nf* **:** plain

planificación *nf* **:** planning <planificación familiar : family planning>

planificar {72} *vt* **:** to plan

planilla *nf* **1** LISTA **:** list **2** NÓMINA **:** payroll **3** TABLA **:** chart, table **4** *Mex* **:** slate, ticket (of candidates) **5 planilla de cálculo** *Arg, Chile* **:** spreadsheet

plano[1], -na *adj* **:** flat, level, plane

plano[2] *nm* **1** PLAN **:** map, plan **2 :** plane (surface) **3** NIVEL **:** level <en un plano personal : on a personal level> **4 :** shot (in photography) **5 de ~ :** flatly, outright, directly <se negó de plano : he flatly refused>

planta *nf* **1 :** plant <planta de interior : houseplant> **2** FÁBRICA **:** plant, factory **3** PISO **:** floor, story **4 :** staff, employees *pl* **5 :** sole (of the foot)

plantación *nf, pl* **-ciones 1 :** plantation **2 :** planting

plantar *vt* **1 :** to plant, to sow **2 :** to put in, to place **3** *fam* **:** to plant, to land <plantar un beso : to plant a kiss> **4** *fam* **:** to leave, to jilt — **plantarse** *vr* **1 :** to stand firm **2** *fam* **:** to arrive, to show up **3** *fam* **:** to balk

planteamiento *nm* **1 :** approach, position <el planteamiento feminista : the feminist viewpoint> **2 :** explanation, exposition **3 :** proposal, suggestion, plan

plantear *vt* **1 :** to set forth, to bring up, to suggest **2 :** to establish, to set up **3 :** to create, to pose (a problem) — **plantearse** *vr* **1 :** to think about **2 :** to arise

plantel *nm* **1 :** educational institution **2 :** staff, team

planteo *nm* → **planteamiento**

plantilla *nf* **1 :** insole **2 :** pattern, template, stencil **3** *Mex, Spain* **:** staff, roster of employees

plantío *nm* **:** field (planted with a crop)

plantón *nm, pl* **plantones 1 :** seedling **2 :** long wait <darle a alguien un plantón : to stand someone up>

plañidero[1], -ra *adj* **:** mournful

plañidero[2], -ra *nf* **:** hired mourner

plañir {38} *v* **:** to mourn, to lament

plasma *nm* **:** plasma

plasmar *vt* **:** to express, to give form to — **plasmarse** *vr*

plasta *nf* **:** soft mass, lump

plástica *nf* **:** modeling, sculpture

plasticidad *nf* **:** plasticity

plástico[1], -ca *adj* **:** plastic

plástico[2] *nm* **:** plastic

plastificar {72} *vt* **:** to laminate

plata *nf* **1 :** silver **2 :** money

plataforma *nf* **1** ESTRADO, TARIMA **:** platform, dais **2 :** platform (in politics) **3 :** springboard, stepping stone **4 plataforma continental :** continental shelf **5 plataforma de lanzamiento :** launchpad **6 plataforma petrolífera :** oil rig (at sea)

platal *nm* **:** large sum of money, fortune

platanal *nm* **:** banana plantation

platanero[1], -ra *adj* **:** banana, banana-producing

platanero[2], -ra *n* **:** banana grower

plátano *nm* **1 :** banana **2 :** plantain **3 plátano macho** *Mex* **:** plantain

platea *nf* **:** orchestra, pit (in a theater)

plateado, -da *adj* **1 :** silver, silvery **2 :** silver-plated

plática *nf* **1 :** talk, lecture **2 :** chat, conversation

platicar {72} *vi* **:** to talk, to chat — *vt Mex* **:** to tell, to say

platija *nf* **:** flatfish, flounder

platillo *nm* **1 :** saucer <platillo volador : flying saucer> **2 :** cymbal **3** *Mex* **:** dish <platillos típicos : local dishes>

platino *nm* **:** platinum

plato *nm* **1 :** plate, dish <lavar los platos : to do the dishes> **2 :** serving, helping **3 :** course (of a meal) **4 :** dish <plato típico : typical dish> **5 :** home plate (in baseball) **6 plato hondo :** soup bowl

plató *nm* **:** set (in the movies)

platónico, -ca *adj* **:** platonic

playa *nf* **:** beach, seashore

playera *nf* **1 :** canvas sneaker **2** *CA, Mex* **:** T-shirt

plaza *nf* **1 :** square, plaza **2 :** marketplace **3 :** room, space, seat (in a vehicle) **4 :** post, position **5 plaza fuerte**

: stronghold, fortified city **6 plaza de toros** : bullring

plazca, etc. → **placer**

plazo *nm* **1** : period, term <un plazo de cinco días : a period of five days> <a largo plazo : long-term> **2** ABONO : installment <pagar a plazos : to pay in installments>

pleamar *nf* : high tide

plebe *nf* : common people, masses *pl*

plebeyo[1], -ya *adj* : plebeian

plebeyo[2], -ya *n* : plebeian, commoner

plegable *adj* : folding, collapsible

plegadizo → **plegable**

plegar {49} *vt* DOBLAR : to fold, to bend — **plegarse** *vr* : to give in, to yield

plegaria *nf* ORACIÓN : prayer

pleito *nm* **1** : lawsuit **2** : fight, argument, dispute

plenamente *adv* COMPLETAMENTE : fully, completely

plenario, -ria *adj* : plenary, full

plenilunio *nm* : full moon

plenipotenciario, -ria *n* : plenipotentiary

plenitud *nf* : fullness, abundance

pleno, -na *adj* COMPLETO (*often used as an intensifier*) : full, complete <en pleno uso de sus facultades : in full command of his faculties> <en plena noche : in the middle of the night> <en pleno corazón de la ciudad : right in the heart of the city>

plétora *nf* : plethora

pleuresía *nf* : pleurisy

pliega, pliegue, etc. → **plegar**

pliego *nm* **1** HOJA : sheet of paper **2** : sealed document

pliegue *nm* **1** DOBLEZ : crease, fold **2** : pleat

plisar *vt* : to pleat

plomada *nf* **1** : plumb line **2** : sinker

plomería *nf* FONTANERÍA : plumbing

plomero, -ra *n* FONTANERO : plumber

plomizo, -za *adj* : leaden

plomo *nm* **1** : lead **2** : plumb line **3** : fuse **4** *fam* : bore, drag **5 a ~** : plumb, straight

plugo, etc. → **placer**

pluma *nf* **1** : feather **2** : pen **3 pluma fuente** : fountain pen

plumaje *nm* : plumage

plumero *nm* : feather duster

plumilla *nf* : nib

plumón *nm, pl* **plumones** : down

plumoso, -sa *adj* : feathery, downy

plural *adj & nm* : plural

pluralidad *nf* : plurality

pluralizar {21} *vt* : to pluralize

pluriempleado, -da *adj* : holding more than one job

pluriempleo *nm* : moonlighting

plus *nm* : bonus

plusvalía *nf* : appreciation, capital gain

Plutón *nm* : Pluto

plutocracia *nf* : plutocracy

plutonio *nm* : plutonium

población *nf, pl* **-ciones 1** : population **2** : city, town, village

poblado[1], -da *adj* **1** : inhabited, populated **2** : full, thick <cejas pobladas : bushy eyebrows>

poblado[2] *nm* : village, settlement

poblador, -dora *n* : settler

poblar {19} *vt* **1** : to populate, to inhabit **2** : to settle, to colonize **3 ~ de** : to stock with, to plant with — **poblarse** *vr* : to fill up, to become crowded

pobre[1] *adj* **1** : poor, impoverished **2** : unfortunate <¡pobre de mí! : poor me!> **3** : weak, deficient <una dieta pobre : a poor diet>

pobre[2] *nmf* : poor person <los pobres : the poor> <¡pobre! : poor thing!>

pobremente *adv* : poorly

pobreza *nf* : poverty

pocilga *nf* CHIQUERO : pigsty, pigpen

pocillo *nm* : small coffee cup, demitasse

poción *nf, pl* **pociones** : potion

poco[1] *adv* **1** : little, not much <poco probable : not very likely> <come poco : he doesn't eat much> **2** : a short time, a while <tardaremos poco : we won't be very long> **3 poco antes** : shortly before **4 poco después** : shortly after

poco[2], -ca *adj* **1** : little, not much, (a) few <tengo poco dinero : I don't have much money> <en no pocas ocasiones : on more than a few occasions> <poca gente : few people> **2 pocas veces** : rarely

poco[3], -ca *pron* **1** : little, few <le falta poco para terminar : he's almost finished> <uno de los pocos que quedan : one of the remaining few> **2 un poco** : a little, a bit <un poco de vino : a little wine> <un poco extraño : a bit strange> **3 a ~** *Mex* (*used to express disbelief*) <¿a poco no se te hizo difícil? : you mean you didn't find it difficult?> **4 de a poco** : little by little **5 hace poco** : not long ago **6 poco a poco** : little by little **7 dentro de poco** : shortly, in a little while **8 por ~** : nearly, almost

podar *vt* : to prune, to trim

poder[1] {58} *v aux* **1** : to be able to, can <no puede hablar : he can't speak> **2** (*expressing possibility*) : might, may <puede llover : it may rain at any moment> <¿cómo puede ser? : how can that be?> **3** (*expressing permission*) : can, may <¿puedo ir a la fiesta? : can I go to the party?> <¿se puede? : may I come in?> — *vi* **1** : to beat, to defeat <cree que le puede a cualquiera : he thinks he can beat anyone> **2** : to be possible <¿crees que vendrán? — puede (que sí) : do you think they'll come? — maybe> **3 ~ con** : to cope with, to manage <¡no puedo con estos niños! : I can't handle these children!> **4 no poder más** : to have had enough <no puede más : she can't take anymore> **5 no poder menos**

que : to not be able to help <no pudo menos que asombrarse : she couldn't help but be amazed>

poder[2] *nm* **1** : control, power <poder adquisitivo : purchasing power> **2** : authority <el poder legislativo : the legislature> **3** : possession <está en mi poder : it's in my hands> **4** : strength, force <poder militar : military might>

poderío *nm* **1** : power **2** : wealth, influence

poderoso, -sa *adj* **1** : powerful **2** : wealthy, influential **3** : effective

podiatría *nf* : podiatry

podio *nm* : podium

pódium *nm* → **podio**

podología *nf* : podiatry, chiropody

podólogo, -ga *n* : podiatrist, chiropodist

podrá, etc. → **poder**

podredumbre *nf* **1** : decay, rottenness **2** : corruption

podrido, -da *adj* **1** : rotten, decayed **2** : corrupt

podrir → **pudrir**

poema *nm* : poem

poesía *nf* **1** : poetry **2** POEMA : poem

poeta *nmf* : poet

poético, -ca *adj* : poetic, poetical

pogrom *nm* : pogrom

póker *or* **poker** *nm* : poker (card game)

polaco[1], **-ca** *adj* : Polish

polaco[2], **-ca** *n* : Pole, Polish person

polaco[3] *nm* : Polish (language)

polar *adj* : polar

polarizar {21} *vt* : to polarize — **polarizarse** *vr* — **polarización** *nf*

polea *nf* : pulley

polémica *nf* CONTROVERSIA : controversy, polemics

polémico, -ca *adj* CONTROVERTIDO : controversial, polemical

polen *nm, pl* **pólenes** : pollen

policía[1] *nf* : police

policía[2] *nmf* : police officer, policeman *m*, policewoman *f*

policíaco, -ca *or* **policiaco, -ca** *adj* : police <novela policíaca : detective story>

policial *adj* : police

poliéster *nm* : polyester

poligamia *nf* : polygamy

polígamo[1], **-ma** *adj* : polygamous

polígamo[2], **-ma** *n* : polygamist

polígono *nm* : polygon — **polígonal** *adj*

poliinsaturado, -da *adj* : polyunsaturated

polilla *nf* : moth

polimerizar {21} *vt* : to polymerize

polímero *nm* : polymer

polinesio, -sia *adj & n* : Polynesian

polinizar {21} *vt* : to pollinate — **polinización** *nf*

polio *nf* : polio

poliomielitis *nf* : poliomyelitis, polio

polisón *nm, pl* **-sones** : bustle (on clothing)

politécnico, -ca *adj* : polytechnic

politeísmo *nm* : polytheism — **politeísta** *adj & nmf*

política *nf* **1** : politics **2** : policy

políticamente *adv* : politically

político[1], **-ca** *adj* **1** : political **2** : tactful, politic **3** : by marriage <padre político : father-in-law>

político[2], **-ca** *n* : politician

póliza *nf* : policy <póliza de seguros : insurance policy>

polizón *nm, pl* **-zones** : stowaway <viajar de polizón : to stow away>

polla *nf* APUESTA : bet

pollera *nf* **1** : chicken coop **2** : skirt

pollero, -ra *n* **1** : poulterer **2** : poultry farm **3** *Mex fam* COYOTE : smuggler of illegal immigrants

pollito, -ta *n* : chick, young bird, fledgling

pollo, -lla *n* **1** : chicken **2** POLLITO : chick **3** JOVEN : young man *m*, young lady *f*

polluelo *nm* → **pollito**

polo *nm* **1** : pole <el Polo Norte : the North Pole> <polo negativo : negative pole> **2** : polo (sport) **3** : polo shirt **4** : focal point, center **5 polo opuesto** : exact opposite

polución *nf, pl* **-ciones** CONTAMINACIÓN : pollution

polvareda *nf* **1** : cloud of dust **2** : uproar, fuss

polvera *nf* : compact (for face powder)

polvo *nm* **1** : dust **2** : powder **3 polvos** *nmpl* : face powder **4 polvos de hornear** : baking powder **5 hacer polvo** *fam* : to crush, to shatter <vas a hacer polvo el reloj : you're going to destroy your watch>

pólvora *nf* **1** : gunpowder **2** : fireworks *pl*

polvoriento, -ta *adj* : dusty, powdery

polvorín *nm, pl* **-rines** : magazine, storehouse (for explosives)

pomada *nf* : ointment, cream

pomelo *nm* : grapefruit

pómez *nm or* **piedra pómez** : pumice

pomo *nm* **1** : pommel (on a sword) **2** : knob, handle **3** : perfume bottle

pompa *nf* **1** : bubble **2** : pomp, splendor **3 pompas fúnebres** : funeral

pompón *nm, pl* **pompones** BORLA : pom-pom

pomposidad *nf* **1** : pomp, splendor **2** : pomposity, ostentation

pomposo, -sa *adj* : pompous — **pomposamente** *adv*

pómulo *nm* : cheekbone

pon → **poner**

ponchadura *nf Mex* : puncture, flat (tire)

ponchar *vt* **1** : to strike out (in baseball) **2** *Mex* : to puncture — **poncharse** *vr* **1** *Col, Ven* : to strike out (in baseball) **2** *Mex* : to blow out (of a tire)

ponche *nm* **1 :** punch (drink) **2 ponche de huevo :** eggnog

poncho *nm* **:** poncho

ponderación *nf, pl* **-ciones 1 :** consideration, deliberation **2 :** high praise

ponderar *vt* **1 :** to weigh, to consider **2 :** to speak highly of

pondrá, etc. → **poner**

ponencia *nf* **1** DISCURSO **:** paper, presentation, address **2** INFORME **:** report

ponente *nmf* **:** speaker, presenter

poner {60} *vt* **1** COLOCAR **:** to put, to place <pon el libro en la mesa : put the book on the table> **2** AGREGAR, AÑADIR **:** to put in, to add **3 :** to put on (clothes) **4** CONTRIBUIR **:** to contribute **5** ESCRIBIR **:** to put in writing <no le puso su nombre : he didn't put his name on it> **6** IMPONER **:** to set, to impose **7** EXPONER **:** to put, to expose <lo puso en peligro : she put him in danger> **8 :** to prepare, to arrange <poner la mesa : to set the table> **9 :** to name <le pusimos Ana : we called her Ana> **10** ESTABLECER **:** to set up, to establish <puso un restaurante : he opened up a restaurant> **11** INSTALAR **:** to install, to put in **12** (*with an adjective or adverb*) **:** to make <siempre lo pones de mal humor : you always put him in a bad mood> **13 :** to turn on, to switch on **14** SUPONER **:** to suppose <pongamos que no viene : supposing he doesn't come> **15 :** to lay (eggs) **16 ~ a :** to start (someone doing something) <lo puse a trabajar : I put him to work> **17 ~ de :** to place as <la pusieron de directora : they made her director> **18 ~ en :** to put in (a state or condition) <poner en duda : to call into question — *vi* **1 :** to contribute **2 :** to lay eggs — **ponerse** *vr* **1 :** to move (into a position) <ponerse de pie : to stand up> **2 :** to put on, to wear **3 :** to become, to turn <se puso colorado : he turned red> **4 :** to set (of the sun or moon)

poni *or* **poney** *nm* **:** pony

ponga, etc. → **poner**

poniente *nm* **1** OCCIDENTE **:** west **2 :** west wind

ponqué *nm Col, Ven* **:** cake

pontifical *adj* **:** pontifical

pontificar {72} *vi* **:** to pontificate

pontífice *nm* **:** pontiff, pope

pontón *nm, pl* **pontones :** pontoon

ponzoña *nf* VENENO **:** poison — **ponzoñoso, -sa** *adj*

popa *nf* **1 :** stern **2 a ~ :** astern, abaft, aft

popelín *nm, pl* **-lines :** poplin

popelina *nf* **:** poplin

popote *nm Mex* **:** (drinking) straw

populachero, -ra *adj* **:** common, popular, vulgar

populacho *nm* **:** rabble, masses *pl*

popular *adj* **1 :** popular **2 :** traditional **3 :** colloquial

popularidad *nf* **:** popularity

popularizar {21} *vt* **:** to popularize — **popularizarse** *vr*

populista *adj & nmf* **:** populist — **populismo** *nm*

populoso, -sa *adj* **:** populous

popurrí *nm* **:** potpourri

por *prep* **1 :** for, during <se quedaron allí por la semana : they stayed there during the week> <por el momento : for now, at the moment> **2 :** around, during <por noviembre empieza a nevar : around November it starts to snow> <por la mañana : in the morning> **3 :** around (a place) <debe estar por allí : it must be over there> <por todas partes : everywhere> **4 :** by, through, along <por la puerta : through the door> <pasé por tu casa : I stopped by your house> <por la costa : along the coast> **5 :** for, for the sake of <lo hizo por su madre : he did it for his mother> <¡por Dios! : for heaven's sake!> **6 :** because of, on account of <llegué tarde por el tráfico : I arrived late because of the traffic> <dejar por imposible : to give up as impossible> **7 :** per <60 millas por hora : 60 miles per hour> <por docena : by the dozen> **8 :** for, in exchange for, instead of <su hermana habló por él : his sister spoke on his behalf> **9 :** by means of <hablar por teléfono : to talk on the phone> <por escrito : in writing> **10 :** as for <por mí : as far as I'm concerned> **11 :** times <tres por dos son seis : three times two is six> **12** SEGÚN **:** from, according to <por lo que dices : judging from what you're telling me> **13 :** as, for <por ejemplo : for example> **14 :** by <hecho por mi abuela : made by my grandmother> <por correo : by mail> **15 :** for, in order to <lucha por ganar su respeto : he struggles to win her respect> **16 estar por :** to be about to **17 por ciento :** percent **18 por favor :** please **19 por lo tanto :** therefore, consequently **20 ¿por qué? :** why? **21 por que** → **porque 22 por . . . que :** no matter how <por mucho que intente : no matter how hard I try> **23 por si** *or* **por si acaso :** just in case

porcelana *nf* **:** china, porcelain

porcentaje *nm* **:** percentage

porche *nm* **:** porch

porción *nf, pl* **porciones 1 :** portion **2** PARTE **:** part, share **3** RACIÓN **:** serving, helping

pordiosear *vi* MENDIGAR **:** beg

pordiosero, -ra *n* MENDIGO **:** beggar

porfiado, -da *adj* OBSTINADO, TERCO **:** obstinate, stubborn — **: porfiadamente** *adv*

porfiar {85} *vi* **:** to insist, to persist

pormenor *nm* DETALLE **:** detail

pormenorizar {21} *vi* **:** to go into detail — *vt* **:** to tell in detail

pornografía *nf* **:** pornography

pornográfico, -ca *adj* : pornographic
poro *nm* : pore
poroso, -sa *adj* : porous — **porosidad** *nf*
poroto *nm Arg, Chile, Uru* : bean
porque *conj* **1** : because **2** *or* **por que** : in order that
porqué *nm* : reason, cause
porquería *nf* **1** SUCIEDAD : dirt, filth **2** : nastiness, vulgarity **3** : worthless thing, trifle **4** : junk food
porra *nf* **1** : nightstick, club **2** *Mex* : cheer, yell <los aficionados le echaban porras : the fans cheered him on>
porrazo *nm* **1** : blow, whack **2 de golpe y porrazo** : suddenly
porrista *nmf* **1** : cheerleader **2** : fan, supporter
portaaviones *nms & pl* : aircraft carrier
portada *nf* **1** : title page **2** : cover **3** : facade, front
portador, -dora *n* : carrier, bearer
portafolio *or* **portafolios** *nm, pl* **-lios 1** MALETÍN : briefcase **2** : portfolio (of investments)
portal *nm* **1** : portal, doorway **2** VESTÍBULO : vestibule, hall
portar *vt* **1** : to carry, to bear **2** : to wear — **portarse** *vr* CONDUCIRSE : to behave <pórtate bien : behave yourself>
portátil *adj* : portable
portaviandas *nms & pl* : lunch box
portaviones *nm* → **portaaviones**
portavoz *nmf, pl* **-voces** : spokesperson, spokesman *m*, spokeswoman *f*
portazo *nm* : slam (of a door)
porte *nm* **1** ASPECTO : bearing, demeanor **2** TRANSPORTE : transport, carrying <porte pagado : postage paid>
portento *nm* MARAVILLA : marvel, wonder
portentoso, -sa *adj* MARAVILLOSO : marvelous, wonderful
porteño, -ña *adj* : of or from Buenos Aires
portería *nf* **1** ARCO : goal, goalposts *pl* **2** : superintendent's office
portero, -ra *n* **1** ARQUERO : goalkeeper, goalie **2** : doorman *m* **3** : janitor, superintendent
pórtico *nm* : portico
portilla *nf* : porthole
portón *nm, pl* **portones 1** : main door **2** : gate
portugués[1], -guesa *adj & n, mpl* **-gueses** : Portuguese
portugués[2] *nm* : Portuguese (language)
porvenir *nm* FUTURO : future
pos *adv* **en pos de** : in pursuit of
posada *nf* **1** : inn **2** *Mex* : Advent celebration
posadero, -ra *n* : innkeeper
posar *vi* : to pose — *vt* : to place, to lay — **posarse** *vr* **1** : to land, to light, to perch **2** : to settle, to rest
posavasos *nms & pl* : coaster (for drinks)
posdata *nf* → **postdata**
pose *nf* : pose
poseedor, -dora *n* : possessor, holder
poseer {20} *vt* : to possess, to hold, to have
poseído, -da *adj* : possessed
posesión *nf, pl* **-siones** : possession
posesionarse *vr* **~ de** : to take possession of, to take over
posesivo[1], -va *adj* : possessive
posesivo[2] *nm* : possessive case
posguerra *nf* : postwar period
posibilidad *nf* **1** : possibility **2 posibilidades** *nfpl* : means, income
posibilitar *vt* : to make possible, to permit
posible *adj* : possible — **posiblemente** *adv*
posición *nf, pl* **-ciones 1** : position, place **2** : status, standing **3** : attitude, stance
posicionar *vt* **1** : to position, to place **2** : to establish — **posicionarse** *vr*
positivo[1], -va *adj* : positive
positivo[2] *nm* : print (in photography)
poso *nm* **1** : sediment, dregs *pl* **2** : grounds *pl* (of coffee)
posoperatorio, -ria *adj* : postoperative
posponer {60} *vt* **1** : to postpone **2** : to put behind, to subordinate
pospuso, etc. → **posponer**
posta *nf* : relay race
postal[1] *adj* : postal
postal[2] *nm* : postcard
postdata *nf* : postscript
poste *nm* : post, pole <poste de teléfonos : telephone pole>
póster *or* **poster** *nm, pl* **pósters** *or* **posters** : poster, placard
postergación *nf, pl* **-ciones** : postponement, deferring
postergar {52} *vt* **1** : to delay, to postpone **2** : to pass over (an employee)
posteridad *nf* : posterity
posterior *adj* **1** ULTERIOR : later, subsequent **2** TRASERO : back, rear
postgrado *nm* : graduate course
postgraduado, -da *n* : graduate student, postgraduate
postigo *nm* **1** CONTRAVENTANA : shutter **2** : small door, wicket gate
postilla *nf* : scab
postizo, -za *adj* : artificial, false <dentadura postiza : dentures>
postnatal *adj* : postnatal
postor, -tora *n* : bidder <mejor postor : highest bidder>
postración *nf, pl* **-ciones 1** : prostration **2** ABATIMIENTO : depression
postrado, -da *adj* **1** : prostrate **2 postrado en cama** : bedridden
postrar *vt* DEBILITAR : to debilitate, to weaken — **postrarse** *vr* : to prostrate oneself
postre *nm* : dessert

postrero, -ra *adj* (**postrer** *before masculine singular nouns*) ÚLTIMO : last

postulación *nf, pl* **-ciones 1** : collection **2** : nomination (of a candidate)

postulado *nm* : postulate, assumption

postulante, -ta *n* **1** : postulant **2** : candidate, applicant

postular *vt* **1** : to postulate **2** : to nominate **3** : to propose — **postularse** *vr* : to run, to be a candidate

póstumo, -ma *adj* : posthumous — **póstumamente** *adv*

postura *nf* **1** : posture, position (of the body) **2** ACTITUD, POSICIÓN : position, stance

potable *adj* : drinkable, potable

potaje *nm* : thick vegetable soup, pottage

potasa *nf* : potash

potasio *nm* : potassium

pote *nm* **1** OLLA : pot **2** : jar, container

potencia *nf* **1** : power <potencias extranjeras : foreign powers> <elevado a la tercera potencia : raised to the third power> **2** : capacity, potency

potencial *adj & nm* : potential

potenciar *vt* : to promote, to foster

potenciómetro *nm* : dimmer, dimmer switch

potentado, -da *n* **1** SOBERANO : potentate, sovereign **2** MAGNATE : tycoon, magnate

potente *adj* **1** : powerful, strong **2** : potent, virile

potestad *nf* **1** AUTORIDAD : authority, jurisdiction **2 patria potestad** : custody, guardianship

potrero *nm* **1** : field, pasture **2** : cattle ranch

potro[1], -tra *n* : colt *m*, filly *f*

potro[2] *nm* **1** : rack (for torture) **2** : horse (in gymnastics)

pozo *nm* **1** : well <pozo de petróleo : oil well> **2** : deep pool (in a river) **3** : mine shaft **4** *Arg, Par, Uru* : pothole **5 pozo séptico** : cesspool

pozole *nm Mex* : spicy stew made with pork and hominy

práctica *nf* **1** : practice, experience **2** EJERCICIO : exercising <la práctica de la medicina : the practice of medicine> **3** APLICACIÓN : application, practice <poner en práctica : to put into practice> **4 prácticas** *nfpl* : training

practicable *adj* : practicable, feasible

prácticamente *adv* : practically

practicante[1] *adj* : practicing <católicos practicantes : practicing Catholics>

practicante[2] *nmf* : practicer, practitioner

practicar {72} *vt* **1** : to practice **2** : to perform, to carry out **3** : to exercise (a profession) — *vi* : to practice

práctico, -ca *adj* : practical, useful

pradera *nf* : grassland, prairie

prado *nm* **1** CAMPO : field, meadow **2** : park

pragmático, -ca *adj* : pragmatic — **pragmáticamente** *adv*

pragmatismo *nm* : pragmatism

preámbulo *nm* **1** INTRODUCCIÓN : preamble, introduction **2** RODEO : evasion <gastar preámbulos : to beat around the bush>

prebélico, -ca *adj* : antebellum

prebenda *nf* : privilege, perquisite

precalentar {55} *vt* : to preheat

precariedad *nf* : precariousness

precario, -ria *adj* : precarious — **precariamente** *adv*

precaución *nf, pl* **-ciones 1** : precaution <medidas de precaución : precautionary measures> **2** PRUDENCIA : caution, care <con precaución : cautiously>

precautorio, -ria *adj* : precautionary

precaver *vt* PREVENIR : to prevent, to guard against — **precaverse** *vr* PREVENIRSE : to take precautions, to be on guard

precavido, -da *adj* CAUTELOSO : cautious, prudent

precedencia *nf* : precedence, priority

precedente[1] *adj* : preceding, previous

precedente[2] *nm* : precedent

preceder *v* : to precede

precepto *nm* : rule, precept

preciado, -da *adj* : esteemed, prized, valuable

preciarse *vr* **1** JACTARSE : to boast, to brag **2 ~ de** : to pride oneself on

precinto *nm* : seal

precio *nm* **1** : price **2** : cost, sacrifice <a cualquier precio : whatever the cost>

preciosidad *nf* : beautiful thing <este vestido es una preciosidad : this dress is lovely>

precioso, -sa *adj* **1** HERMOSO : beautiful, exquisite **2** VALIOSO : precious, valuable

precipicio *nm* **1** : precipice **2** RUINA : ruin

precipitación *nf, pl* **-ciones 1** PRISA : haste, hurry, rush **2** : precipitation, rain, snow

precipitado, -da *adj* **1** : hasty, sudden **2** : rash — **precipitadamente** *adv*

precipitar *vt* **1** APRESURAR : to hasten, to speed up **2** ARROJAR : to hurl, to throw — **precipitarse** *vr* **1** APRESURARSE : to rush **2** : to act rashly **3** ARROJARSE : to throw oneself

precisamente *adv* JUSTAMENTE : precisely, exactly

precisar *vt* **1** : to specify, to determine exactly **2** NECESITAR : to need, to require — *vi* : to be necessary

precisión *nf, pl* **-siones 1** EXACTITUD : precision, accuracy **2** CLARIDAD : clarity (of style, etc.) **3** NECESIDAD : necessity <tener precisión de : to have need of>

preciso, -sa *adj* **1** EXACTO : precise **2** : very, exact <en ese preciso instante : at that very instant> **3** NECESARIO : necessary

precocidad *nf* **:** precocity
precocinar *vt* **:** to precook
preconcebir {54} *vt* **:** to preconceive
precondición *nf, pl* **-ciones :** precondition
preconizar {21} *vt* **1 :** to recommend, to advocate **2 :** to extol
precoz *adj, pl* **precoces 1 :** precocious **2 :** early, premature — **precozmente** *adv*
precursor, -sora *n* **:** forerunner, precursor
predecesor, -sora *n* ANTECESOR **:** predecessor
predecir {11} *vt* **:** to foretell, to predict
predestinado, -da *adj* **:** predestined, fated
predestinar *vt* **:** to predestine — **predestinación** *nf*
predeterminar *vt* **:** to predetermine
prédica *nf* SERMÓN **:** sermon
predicado *nm* **:** predicate
predicador, -dora *n* **:** preacher
predicar {72} *v* **:** to preach
predicción *nf, pl* **-ciones 1 :** prediction **2** PRONÓSTICO **:** forecast <predicción del tiempo : weather forecast>
prediga, predijo, etc. → **predecir**
predilección *nf, pl* **-ciones :** predilection, preference
predilecto, -ta *adj* **:** favorite
predio *nm* **:** property, piece of land
predisponer {60} *vt* **1 :** to predispose, to incline **2 :** to prejudice, to bias
predisposición *nf, pl* **-ciones 1 :** predisposition, tendency **2 :** prejudice, bias
predominante *adj* **:** predominant — **predominantemente** *adv*
predominar *vi* PREVALECER **:** to predominate, to prevail
predominio *nm* **:** predominance, prevalence
preeminente *adj* **:** preeminent — **preeminencia** *nf*
preescolar *adj & nm* **:** preschool
preestreno *nm* **:** preview
prefabricado, -da *adj* **:** prefabricated
prefacio *nm* **:** preface
prefecto *nm* **:** prefect
preferencia *nf* **1 :** preference **2** PRIORIDAD **:** priority **3 de ~ :** preferably
preferencial *adj* **:** preferential
preferente *adj* **:** preferential, special <trato preferente : special treatment>
preferentemente *adv* **:** preferably
preferible *adj* **:** preferable
preferido, -da *adj & n* **:** favorite
preferir {76} *vt* **:** to prefer
prefijo *nm* **:** prefix
pregonar *vt* **1 :** to proclaim, to announce **2 :** to hawk (merchandise) **3 :** to extol **4 :** to reveal, to disclose
pregunta *nf* **1 :** question **2 hacer una pregunta :** to ask a question
preguntar *vt* **:** to ask, to question — *vi* **:** to ask, to inquire — **preguntarse** *vr* **:** to wonder
preguntón, -tona *adj, mpl* **-tones :** inquisitive
prehistórico, -ca *adj* **:** prehistoric
prejuicio *nm* **:** prejudice
prejuzgar {52} *vt* **:** to prejudge
prelado *nm* **:** prelate
preliminar *adj & nm* **:** preliminary
preludio *nm* **:** prelude
prematrimonial *adj* **:** premarital
prematuro, -ra *adj* **:** premature
premeditación *nf, pl* **-ciones :** premeditation
premeditar *vt* **:** to premeditate, to plan
premenstrual *adj* **:** premenstrual
premiado, -da *adj* **:** winning, prizewinning
premiar *vt* **1 :** to award a prize to **2 :** to reward
premier *nmf* **:** premier, prime minister
premio *nm* **1 :** prize <premio gordo : grand prize, jackpot> **2 :** reward **3 :** premium
premisa *nf* **:** premise, basis
premolar *nm* **:** bicuspid (tooth)
premonición *nf, pl* **-ciones :** premonition
premura *nf* **:** haste, urgency
prenatal *adj* **:** prenatal
prenda *nf* **1 :** piece of clothing **2 :** security, pledge
prendar *vt* **1 :** to charm, to captivate **2 :** to pawn, to pledge — **prendarse** *vr* **~ de :** to fall in love with
prendedor *nm* **:** brooch, pin
prender *vt* **1** SUJETAR **:** to pin, to fasten **2** APRESAR **:** to catch, to apprehend **3 :** to light (a cigarette, a match) **4 :** to turn on <prende la luz : turn on the light> **5 prender fuego a :** to set fire to — *vi* **1 :** to take root **2 :** to catch fire **3 :** to catch on
prensa *nf* **1 :** printing press **2 :** press <conferencia de prensa : press conference>
prensar *vt* **:** to press
prensil *adj* **:** prehensile
preñado, -da *adj* **1 :** pregnant **2 ~ de :** filled with
preñar *vt* EMBARAZAR **:** to make pregnant
preñez *nf, pl* **preñeces :** pregnancy
preocupación *nf, pl* **-ciones** INQUIETUD **:** worry, concern
preocupante *adj* **:** worrisome
preocupar *vt* INQUIETAR **:** to worry, to concern — **preocuparse** *vr* APURARSE **:** to worry, to be concerned
preparación *nf, pl* **-ciones 1 :** preparation, readiness **2 :** education, training **3 :** (medicinal) preparation
preparado[1], -da *adj* **1 :** ready, prepared **2 :** trained
preparado[2] *nm* **:** preparation, mixture
preparar *vt* **1 :** to prepare, to make ready **2 :** to teach, to train, to coach — **prepararse** *vr*
preparativos *nmpl* **:** preparations
preparatoria *nf Mex* **:** high school
preparatorio, -ria *adj* **:** preparatory

preponderante *adj* : preponderant, predominant — **preponderancia** *nf* — **preponderantemente** *adv*
preposición *nf, pl* **-ciones** : preposition — **preposicional** *adj*
prepotente *adj* : arrogant, domineering, overbearing — **prepotencia** *nf*
prerrogativa *nf* : prerogative, privilege
presa *nf* **1** : capture, seizure <hacer presa de : to seize> **2** : catch, prey <presa de : prey to, seized with> **3** : claw, fang **4** DIQUE : dam **5** : morsel, piece (of food)
presagiar *vt* : to presage, to portend
presagio *nm* : omen, portent
presbiterio *nm* : presbytery, sanctuary (of a church)
presbítero *nm* : presbyter
presciencia *nf* : prescience
prescindir *vi* **~ de 1** : to do without, to dispense with **2** DESATENDER : to ignore, to disregard **3** OMITIR : to omit, to skip
prescribir {33} *vt* : to prescribe
prescripción *nf, pl* **-ciones** : prescription
prescrito *pp* → **prescribir**
presencia *nf* **1** : presence **2** ASPECTO : appearance
presenciar *vt* : to be present at, to witness
presentación *nf, pl* **-ciones 1** : presentation **2** : introduction **3** : appearance
presentador, -dora *n* : newscaster, anchorman *m,* anchorwoman *f*
presentar *vt* **1** : to present, to show **2** : to offer, to give **3** : to submit (a document), to launch (a product) **4** : to introduce (a person) — **presentarse** *vr* **1** : to show up, to appear **2** : to arise, to come up **3** : to introduce oneself
presente[1] *adj* **1** : present, in attendance **2** : present, current **3 tener presente** : to keep in mind
presente[2] *nm* **1** : present (time, tense) **2** : one present <entre los presentes se encontraban . . . : those present included . . .>
presentimiento *nm* : premonition, hunch, feeling
presentir {76} *vt* : to sense, to intuit <presentía lo que iba a pasar : he sensed what was going to happen>
preservación *nf, pl* **-ciones** : preservation
preservar *vt* **1** : to preserve **2** : to protect
preservativo *nm* CONDÓN : condom
presidencia *nf* **1** : presidency **2** : chairmanship
presidencial *adj* : presidential
presidente, -ta *n* **1** : president **2** : chair, chairperson **3** : presiding judge
presidiario, -ria *n* : convict, prisoner
presidio *nm* : prison, penitentiary
presidir *vt* **1** MODERAR : to preside over, to chair **2** : to dominate, to rule over
presilla *nf* : eye, loop, fastener
presión *nf, pl* **presiones 1** : pressure **2 presión arterial** : blood pressure
presionar *vt* **1** : to pressure **2** : to press, to push — *vi* : to put on the pressure
preso[1], **-sa** *adj* : imprisoned
preso[2], **-sa** *n* : prisoner
prestado, -da *adj* **1** : borrowed, on loan **2 pedir prestado** : to borrow
prestamista *nmf* : moneylender, pawnbroker
préstamo *nm* : loan
prestar *vt* **1** : to lend, to loan **2** : to render (a service), to give (aid) **3 prestar atención** : to pay attention **4 prestar juramento** : to take an oath — **prestarse** *vr* : to lend oneself <se presta a confusiones : it lends itself to confusion>
prestatario, -ria *n* : borrower
presteza *nf* : promptness, speed
prestidigitación *nf, pl* **-ciones** : sleight of hand, prestidigitation
prestidigitador, -dora *n* : conjurer, magician
prestigio *nm* : prestige — **prestigioso, -sa** *adj*
presto[1] *adv* : promptly, at once
presto[2], **-ta** *adj* **1** : quick, prompt **2** DISPUESTO, PREPARADO : ready
presumido, -da *adj* VANIDOSO : conceited, vain
presumir *vt* SUPONER : to presume, to suppose — *vi* **1** ALARDEAR : to boast, to show off **2 ~ de** : to consider oneself <presume de inteligente : he thinks he's intelligent>
presunción *nf, pl* **-ciones 1** SUPOSICIÓN : presumption, supposition **2** VANIDAD : conceit, vanity
presunto, -ta *adj* : presumed, supposed, alleged — **presuntamente** *adv*
presuntuoso, -sa *adj* : conceited
presuponer {60} *vt* : to presuppose
presupuestal *adj* : budget, budgetary
presupuestar *vi* : to budget — *vt* : to budget for
presupuestario, -ria *adj* : budget, budgetary
presupuesto *nm* **1** : budget, estimate **2** : assumption, supposition
presurizar {21} *vt* : to pressurize
presuroso, -sa *adj* : hasty, quick
pretencioso, -sa *adj* : pretentious
pretender *vt* **1** INTENTAR : to attempt, to try <pretendo estudiar : I'm trying to study> **2** AFIRMAR : to claim <pretende ser pobre : he claims he's poor> **3** : to seek, to aspire to <¿qué pretendes tú? : what are you after?> **4** CORTEJAR : to court **5 pretender que** : to expect <¿pretendes que lo crea? : do you expect me to believe you?>
pretendiente[1] *nmf* **1** : candidate, applicant **2** : pretender, claimant (to a throne, etc.)
pretendiente[2] *nm* : suitor

pretensión *nf, pl* **-siones 1 :** intention, hope, plan **2 :** pretension <sin pretensiones : unpretentious>
pretexto *nm* EXCUSA **:** pretext, excuse
pretil *nm* **:** parapet, railing
prevalecer {53} *vi* **:** to prevail, to triumph
prevaleciente *adj* **:** prevailing, prevalent
prevalerse {84} *vr* **~ de :** to avail oneself of, to take advantage of
prevención *nf, pl* **-ciones 1 :** prevention **2 :** preparation, readiness **3 :** precautionary measure **4 :** prejudice, bias
prevenido, -da *adj* **1** PREPARADO **:** prepared, ready **2** ADVERTIDO **:** forewarned **3** CAUTELOSO **:** cautious
prevenir {87} *vt* **1 :** to prevent **2 :** to warn — **prevenirse** *vr* **~ contra** *or* **~ de :** to take precautions against
preventivo, -va *adj* **:** preventive, precautionary
prever {88} *vt* ANTICIPAR **:** to foresee, to anticipate
previo, -via *adj* **1 :** previous, prior **2 :** after, upon <previo pago : after paying, upon payment>
previsible *adj* **:** foreseeable
previsión *nf, pl* **-siones 1 :** foresight **2 :** prediction, forecast **3 :** precaution
previsor, -sora *adj* **:** farsighted, prudent
prieto, -ta *adj* **1 :** blackish, dark **2 :** dark-skinned, swarthy **3 :** tight, compressed
prima *nf* **1 :** premium **2 :** bonus **3 →** **primo**
primacía *nf* **1 :** precedence, priority **2 :** superiority, supremacy
primado *nm* **:** primate (bishop)
primario, -ria *adj* **:** primary
primate *nm* **:** primate
primavera *nf* **1 :** spring (season) **2** PRÍMULA **:** primrose
primaveral *adj* **:** spring, springlike
primero[1] *adv* **1 :** first **2 :** rather, sooner
primero[2]**, -ra** *adj* (**primer** *before masculine singular nouns*) **1 :** first **2 :** top, leading **3 :** fundamental, basic **4 de primera :** first-rate
primero[3]**, -ra** *n* **:** first
primicia *nf* **1 :** first fruits **2 :** scoop, exclusive
primigenio, -nia *adj* **:** original, primary
primitivo, -va *adj* **1 :** primitive **2** ORIGINAL **:** original
primo, -ma *n* **:** cousin
primogénito, -ta *adj & n* **:** firstborn
primor *nm* **1 :** skill, care **2 :** beauty, elegance
primordial *adj* **1 :** primordial **2 :** basic, fundamental
primoroso, -sa *adj* **1 :** exquisite, fine, delicate **2 :** skillful
prímula *nf* **:** primrose
princesa *nf* **:** princess
principado *nm* **:** principality
principal[1] *adj* **1 :** main, principal **2 :** foremost, leading
principal[2] *nm* **:** capital, principal
príncipe *nm* **:** prince
prinipesco, -ca *adj* **:** princely
principiante[1] *adj* **:** beginning
principiante[2] *nmf* **:** beginner, novice
principiar *vt* EMPEZAR **:** to begin
principio *nm* **1** COMIENZO **:** beginning **2 :** principle **3 al principio :** at first **4 a principios de :** at the beginning of <a principios de agosto : at the beginning of August> **5 en ~ :** in principle
pringar {52} *vt* **1 :** to dip (in grease) **2 :** to soil, to spatter (with grease) — **pringarse** *vr*
pringoso, -sa *adj* **:** greasy
pringue[1]**, etc. → pringar**
pringue[2] *nm* **:** grease, drippings *pl*
prior, priora *n* **:** prior *m,* prioress *f*
priorato *nm* **:** priory
prioridad *nf* **:** priority, precedence
prisa *nf* **1 :** hurry, rush **2 a ~** *or* **de ~ :** quickly, fast **3 a toda prisa :** as fast as possible **4 darse prisa :** to hurry **5 tener prisa :** to be in a hurry
prisión *nf, pl* **prisiones 1** CÁRCEL **:** prison, jail **2** ENCARCELAMIENTO **:** imprisonment
prisionero, -ra *n* **:** prisoner
prisma *nf* **:** prism
prismáticos *nmpl* **:** binoculars
prístino, -na *adj* **:** pristine
privacidad *nf* **:** privacy
privación *nf, pl* **-ciones 1 :** deprivation **2 :** privation, want
privado, -da *adj* **:** private — **privadamente** *adv*
privar *vt* **1** DESPOJAR **:** to deprive **2 :** to stun, to knock out — **privarse** *vr* **:** to deprive oneself
privativo, -va *adj* **:** exclusive, particular
privilegiado, -da *adj* **:** privileged
privilegiar *vt* **:** to grant a privilege to, to favor
privilegio *nm* **:** privilege
pro[1] *nm* **1 :** pro, advantage <los pros y contras : the pros and cons> **2 en pro de :** for, in favor of
pro[2] *prep* **:** for, in favor of <grupos pro derechos humanos : groups supporting human rights>
proa *nf* **:** bow, prow
probabilidad *nf* **:** probability
probable *adj* **:** probable, likely
probablemente *adv* **:** probably
probar {19} *vt* **1 :** to demonstrate, to prove **2 :** to test, to try out **3 :** to try on (clothing) **4 :** to taste, to sample — *vi* **:** to try — **probarse** *vr* **:** to try on (clothing)
probeta *nf* **:** test tube
probidad *nf* **:** probity
problema *nm* **:** problem
problemática *nf* **:** set of problems <la problemática que debemos enfrentar : the problems we must face>
probóscide *nf* **:** proboscis

problemático, -ca *adj* : problematic

procaz *adj, pl* **procaces 1** : insolent, impudent **2** : indecent

procedencia *nf* : origin, source

procedente *adj* **1** : proper, fitting **2** ~ **de** : coming from

proceder *vi* **1** AVANZAR : to proceed **2** : to act, to behave **3** : to be appropriate, to be fitting **4** ~ **de** : to originate from, to come from

procedimiento *nm* : procedure, process

prócer *nmf* : eminent person, leader

procesado, -da *n* : accused, defendant

procesador *nm* : processor <procesador de textos : word processor>

procesamiento *nm* : processing <procesamiento de datos : data processing>

procesar *vt* **1** : to prosecute, to try **2** : to process

procesión *nf, pl* **-siones** : procession

proceso *nm* **1** : process **2** : trial, proceedings *pl*

proclama *nf* : proclamation

proclamación *nf, pl* **-ciones** : proclamation

proclamar *vt* : to proclaim — **proclamarse** *vr*

proclive *adj* ~ **a** : inclined to, prone to

proclividad *nf* : proclivity, inclination

procrear *vi* : to procreate — **procreación** *nf*

procurador, -dora *n* ABOGADO : attorney

procurar *vt* **1** INTENTAR : to try, to endeavor **2** CONSEGUIR : to obtain, to procure **3 procurar hacer** : to manage to do

prodigar {52} *vt* : to lavish, to be generous with

prodigio *nm* : wonder, marvel

prodigioso, -sa *adj* : prodigious, marvelous

pródigo[1], -ga *adj* **1** : generous, lavish **2** : wasteful, prodigal

pródigo[2], -ga *n* : spendthrift, prodigal

producción *nf, pl* **-ciones 1** : production **2 producción en serie** : mass production

producir {61} *vt* **1** : to produce, to make, to manufacture **2** : to cause, to bring about **3** : to bear (interest) — **producirse** *vr* : to take place, to occur

productividad *nf* : productivity

productivo, -va *adj* **1** : productive **2** LUCRATIVO : profitable

producto *nm* **1** : product **2** : proceeds *pl*, yield

productor, -tora *n* : producer

proeza *nf* HAZAÑA : feat, exploit

profanar *vt* : to profane, to desecrate — **profanación** *nf*

profano[1], -na *adj* **1** : profane **2** : worldly, secular

profano[2], -na *n* : nonspecialist

profecía *nf* : prophecy

proferir {76} *vt* **1** : to utter **2** : to hurl (insults)

profesar *vt* **1** : to profess, to declare **2** : to practice, to exercise

profesión *nf, pl* **-siones** : profession

profesional *adj & nmf* : professional — **profesionalmente** *adv*

profesionalismo *nm* : professionalism

profesionalizar {21} *vt* : to professionalize

profesionista *nmf Mex* : professional

profesor, -sora *n* **1** MAESTRO : teacher **2** : professor

profesorado *nm* **1** : faculty **2** : teaching profession

profeta *nm* : prophet

profético, -ca *adj* : prophetic

profetisa *nf* : prophetess, prophet

profetizar {21} *vt* : to prophesy

prófugo, -ga *adj & n* : fugitive

profundidad *nf* : depth, profundity

profundizar {21} *vt* **1** : to deepen **2** : to study in depth — *vi* ~ **en** : to go deeply into, to study in depth

profundo, -da *adj* **1** HONDO : deep **2** : profound — **profundamente** *adv*

profusión *nf, pl* **-siones** : abundance, profusion

profuso, -sa *adj* : profuse, abundant, extensive

progenie *nf* : progeny, offspring

progenitor, -tora *n* ANTEPASADO : ancestor, progenitor

prognóstico *nm* : prognosis

programa *nm* **1** : program **2** : plan **3 programa de estudios** : curriculum

programable *adj* : programmable

programación *nf, pl* **-ciones 1** : programming **2** : planning

programador, -dora *n* : programmer

programar *vt* **1** : to schedule, to plan **2** : to program (a computer, etc.)

progresar *vi* : to progress, to make progress

progresista *adj & nmf* : progressive

progresivo, -va *adj* : progressive, gradual

progreso *nm* : progress

prohibición *nf, pl* **-ciones** : ban, prohibition

prohibir {62} *vt* : to prohibit, to ban, to forbid

prohibitivo, -va *adj* : prohibitive

prohijar {5} *vt* ADOPTAR : to adopt

prójimo *nm* : neighbor, fellow man

prole *nf* : offspring, progeny

proletariado *nm* : proletariat, working class

proletario, -ria *adj & n* : proletarian

proliferar *vi* : to proliferate — **proliferación** *nf*

prolífico, -ca *adj* : prolific

prolijo, -ja *adj* : wordy, long-winded

prólogo *nm* : prologue, preface, foreword

prolongación *nf, pl* **-ciones** : extension, lengthening

prolongar {52} *vt* **1** : to prolong **2** : to extend, to lengthen — **prolongarse** *vr* CONTINUAR : to last, to continue
promediar *vt* **1** : to average **2** : to divide in half — *vi* : to be half over
promedio *nm* **1** : average **2** : middle, mid-point
promesa *nf* : promise
prometedor, -dora *adj* : promising, hopeful
prometer *vt* : to promise — *vi* : to show promise — **prometerse** *vr* COMPROMETERSE : to get engaged
prometido[1], **-da** *adj* : engaged
prometido[2], **-da** *n* NOVIO : fiancé *m*, fiancée *f*
prominente *adj* : prominent — **prominencia** *nf*
promiscuo, -cua *adj* : promiscuous — **promiscuidad** *nf*
promisorio, -ria *adj* **1** : promising **2** : promissory
promoción *nf, pl* **-ciones 1** : promotion **2** : class, year **3** : play-off (in soccer)
promocionar *vt* : to promote — **promocional** *adj*
promontorio *nm* : promontory, headland
promotor, -tora *n* : promoter
promover {47} *vt* **1** : to promote, to advance **2** FOMENTAR : to foster, to encourage **3** PROVOCAR : to provoke, to cause
promulgación *nf, pl* **-ciones 1** : enactment **2** : proclamation, enactment
promulgar {52} *vt* **1** : to promulgate, to proclaim **2** : to enact (a law or decree)
prono, -na *adj* : prone
pronombre *nm* : pronoun
pronosticar {72} *vt* : to predict, to forecast
pronóstico *nm* **1** PREDICCIÓN : forecast, prediction **2** : prognosis
prontitud *nf* **1** PRESTEZA : promptness, speed **2 con ~** : promptly, quickly
pronto[1] *adv* **1** : quickly, promptly **2** : soon **3 de ~** : suddenly **4 lo más pronto posible** : as soon as possible **5 tan pronto como** : as soon as
pronto[2], **-ta** *adj* **1** RÁPIDO : quick, speedy, prompt **2** PREPARADO : ready
pronunciación *nf, pl* **-ciones** : pronunciation
pronunciado, -da *adj* **1** : pronounced, sharp, steep **2** : marked, noticeable
pronunciar *vt* **1** : to pronounce, to say **2** : to give, to deliver (a speech) **3 pronunciar un fallo** : to pronounce sentence — **pronunciarse** *vr* : to declare oneself
propagación *nf, pl* **-ciones** : propagation, spreading
propaganda *nf* **1** : propaganda **2** PUBLICIDAD : advertising
propagar {52} *vt* **1** : to propagate **2** : to spread, to disseminate — **propagarse** *vr*
propalar *vt* **1** : to divulge **2** : to spread
propano *nm* : propane
propasarse *vr* : to go too far, to overstep one's bounds
propensión *nf, pl* **-siones** INCLINACIÓN : inclination, propensity
propenso, -sa *adj* : prone, susceptible
propiamente *adv* **1** : properly, correctly **2** : exactly, precisely <propiamente dicho : strictly speaking>
propiciar *vt* **1** : to propitiate **2** : to favor, to foster
propicio, -cia *adj* : favorable, propitious
propiedad *nf* **1** : property <propiedad privada : private property> **2** : ownership **3** CUALIDAD : property, quality **4** : suitability, appropriateness
propietario[1], **-ria** *adj* : proprietary
propietario[2], **-ria** *n* DUEÑO : owner, proprietor
propina *nf* : tip, gratuity
propinar *vt* : to give, to strike <propinar una paliza : to give a beating>
propio, -pia *adj* **1** : own <su propia casa : his own house> <sus recursos propios : their own resources> **2** APROPIADO : appropriate, suitable **3** CARACTERÍSTICO : characteristic, typical **4** MISMO : oneself <el propio director : the director himself>
proponer {60} *vt* **1** : to propose, to suggest **2** : to nominate — **proponerse** *vr* : to intend, to plan, to set out <lo que se propone lo cumple : he does what he sets out to do>
proporción *nf, pl* **-ciones 1** : proportion **2** : ratio (in mathematics) **3 proporciones** *nfpl* : proportions, size <de grandes proporciones : very large>
proporcionado, -da *adj* **1** : proportionate **2** : proportioned <bien proporcionado : well-proportioned> — **proporcionadamente** *adv*
proporcional *adj* : proportional — **proporcionalmente** *adv*
proporcionar *vt* **1** : to provide, to give **2** : to proportion, to adapt
proposición *nf, pl* **-ciones** : proposal, proposition
propósito *nm* **1** INTENCIÓN : purpose, intention **2 a ~** : by the way **3 a ~** : on purpose, intentionally
propuesta *nf* PROPOSICIÓN : proposal
propulsar *vt* **1** IMPULSAR : to propel, to drive **2** PROMOVER : to promote, to encourage
propulsión *nf, pl* **-siones** : propulsion
propulsor *nm* : propellant
propuso, etc. → **proponer**
prorrata *nf* **1** : share, quota **2 a ~** : pro rata, proportionately
prórroga *nf* **1** : extension, deferment **2** : overtime (in sports)
prorrogar {52} *vt* **1** : to extend (a deadline) **2** : to postpone
prorrumpir *vi* : to burst forth, to break out <prorrumpí en lágrimas : I burst into tears>
prosa *nf* : prose

prosaico, -ca *adj* : prosaic, mundane

proscribir {33} *v* **1** PROHIBIR : to prohibit, to ban, to proscribe **2** DESTERRAR : to banish, to exile

proscripción *nf, pl* **-ciones** **1** PROHIBICIÓN : ban, proscription **2** DESTIERRO : banishment

proscrito[1] *pp* → **proscribir**

proscrito[2], -ta *n* **1** DESTERRADO : exile **2** : outlaw

prosecución *nf, pl* **-ciones** **1** : continuation **2** : pursuit

proseguir {75} *vt* **1** CONTINUAR : to continue **2** : to pursue (studies, goals) — *vi* : to continue, to go on

prosélito, -ta *n* : proselyte

prospección *nf, pl* **-ciones** : prospecting, exploration

prospectar *vi* : to prospect

prospecto *nm* : prospectus, leaflet, brochure

prosperar *vi* : to prosper, to thrive

prosperidad *nf* : prosperity

próspero, -ra *adj* : prosperous, flourishing

próstata *nf* : prostate

prostitución *nf, pl* **-ciones** : prostitution

prostituir {41} *vt* : to prostitute — **prostituirse** *vr* : to prostitute oneself

prostituto, -ta *n* : prostitute

protagonista *nmf* **1** : protagonist, main character **2** : leader

protagonizar {21} *vt* : to star in

protección *nf, pl* **-ciones** : protection

protector[1], -tora *adj* : protective

protector[2], -tora *n* **1** : protector, guardian **2** : patron

protector[3] *nm* : protector, guard <chaleco protector : chest protector>

protectorado *nm* : protectorate

proteger {15} *vt* : to protect, to defend — **protegerse** *vr*

protegido, -da *n* : protégé

proteína *nf* : protein

prótesis *nfs & pl* : prosthesis

protesta *nf* **1** : protest **2** *Mex* : promise, oath

protestante *adj & nmf* : Protestant

protestantismo *nm* : Protestantism

protestar *vi* : to protest, to object — *vt* **1** : to protest, to object to **2** : to declare, to profess

protocolo *nm* : protocol

protón *nm, pl* **protones** : proton

protoplasma *nm* : protoplasm

prototipo *nm* : prototype

protozoario *or* **protozoo** *nm* : protozoan

protuberancia *nf* : protuberance — **protuberante** *adj*

provecho *nm* : benefit, advantage

provechoso, -sa *adj* BENEFICIOSO : beneficial, profitable, useful — **provechosamente** *adv*

proveedor, -dora *n* : provider, supplier

proveer {63} *vt* : to provide, to supply — **proveerse** *vr* ~ **de** : to obtain, to supply oneself with

provenir {87} *vi* ~ **de** : to come from

provenzal[1] *adj* : Provençal

provenzal[2] *nmf* : Provençal

provenzal[3] *nm* : Provençal (language)

proverbio *nm* REFRÁN : proverb — **proverbial** *adj*

providencia *nf* **1** : providence, foresight **2** : Providence, God **3** **providencias** *nfpl* : steps, measures

providencial *adj* : providential

provincia *nf* : province — **provincial** *adj*

provinciano, -na *adj* : provincial, unsophisticated

provisión *nf, pl* **-siones** : provision

provisional *adj* : provisional, temporary

provisionalmente *adv* : provisionally, tentatively

provisorio, -ria *adj* : provisional, temporary

provisto *pp* → **proveer**

provocación *nf, pl* **-ciones** : provocation

provocador[1], -dora *adj* : provocative, provoking

provocador[2], -dora *n* AGITADOR : agitator

provocar {72} *vt* **1** CAUSAR : to provoke, to cause **2** IRRITAR : to provoke, to pique

provocativo, -va *adj* : provocative

proxeneta *nmf* : pimp *m*

próximamente *adv* : shortly, soon

proximidad *nf* **1** : nearness, proximity **2** **proximidades** *nfpl* : vicinity

próximo, -ma *adj* **1** : near, close <la Navidad está próxima : Christmas is almost here> **2** SIGUIENTE : next, following <la próxima semana : the following week>

proyección *nf, pl* **-ciones** **1** : projection **2** : showing, screening (of a film) **3** : range, influence, diffusion

proyectar *vt* **1** : to plan **2** LANZAR : to throw, to hurl **3** : to project, to cast (light or shadow) **4** : to show, to screen (a film)

proyectil *nm* : projectile, missile

proyecto *nm* **1** : plan, project **2** **proyecto de ley** : bill

proyector *nm* **1** : projector **2** : spotlight

prudencia *nf* : prudence, care, discretion

prudente *adj* : prudent, sensible, reasonable

prueba[1], etc. → **probar**

prueba[2] *nf* **1** : proof, evidence **2** : trial, test **3** : proof (in printing or photography) **4** : event, qualifying round (in sports) **5** **a prueba de agua** : waterproof **6** **prueba de fuego** : acid test **7** **poner a prueba** : to put to the test

prurito *nm* **1** : itching **2** : desire, urge

psicoanálisis *nm* : psychoanalysis — **psicoanalista** *nmf*

psicoanalítico, -ca *adj* : psychoanalytic
psicoanalizar {21} *vt* : to psychoanalyze
psicología *nf* : psychology
psicológico, -ca *adj* : psychological — **psicológicamente** *adv*
psicólogo, -ga *n* : psychologist
psicópata *nmf* : psychopath
psicopático, -ca *adj* : psycopathic
psicosis *nfs & pl* : psychosis
psicosomático, -ca *adj* : psychosomatic
psicoterapeuta *nmf* : psychotherapist
psicoterapia *nf* : psychotherapy
psicótico, -ca *adj & n* : psychotic
psique *nf* : psyche
psiquiatra *nmf* : psychiatrist
psiquiatría *nf* : psychiatry
psiquiátrico[1], -ca *adj* : psychiatric
psiquiátrico[2] *nm* : mental hospital
psíquico, -ca *adj* : psychic
psiquis *nfs & pl* : psyche
psoriasis *nf* : psoriasis
ptomaína *nf* : ptomaine
púa *nf* **1** : barb <alambre de púas : barbed wire> **2** : tooth (of a comb) **3** : quill, spine
pubertad *nf* : puberty
pubiano → **púbico**
púbico, -ca *adj* : pubic
publicación *nf, pl* **-ciones** : publication
publicar {72} *vt* **1** : to publish **2** DIVULGAR : to divulge, to disclose
publicidad *nf* **1** : publicity **2** : advertising
publicista *nmf* : publicist
publicitar *vt* **1** : to publicize **2** : to advertise
publicitario, -ria *adj* : advertising, publicity <agencia publicitaria : advertising agency>
público[1], -ca *adj* : public — **públicamente** *adv*
público[2] *nm* **1** : public **2** : audience, spectators *pl*
puchero *nm* **1** : pot **2** : stew **3** : pout <hacer pucheros : to pout>
pucho *nm* **1** : waste, residue **2** : cigarette butt **3 a puchos** : little by little, bit by bit
púdico, -ca *adj* : chaste, modest
pudiente *adj* **1** : powerful **2** : rich, wealthy
pudín *nm, pl* **pudines** BUDÍN : pudding
pudo, etc. → **poder**
pudor *nm* : modesty, reserve
pudoroso, -sa *adj* : modest, reserved, shy
pudrir {59} *vt* **1** : to rot **2** *fam* : to annoy, to upset — **pudrirse** *vr* **1** : to rot **2** : to languish
pueblerino, -na *adj* : provincial, countrified
puebla, etc. → **poblar**
pueblo *nm* **1** NACIÓN : people **2** : common people **3** ALDEA, POBLADO : town, village
puede, etc. → **poder**
puente *nm* **1** : bridge <puente levadizo : drawbridge> **2** : denture, bridge **3 puente aéreo** : airlift
puerco[1], -ca *adj* : dirty, filthy
puerco[2], -ca *n* **1** CERDO, MARRANO : pig, hog **2** : pig, dirty or greedy person **3 puerco espín** : porcupine
pueril *adj* : childish, puerile
puerro *nm* : leek
puerta *nf* **1** : door, entrance, gate **2 a puerta cerrada** : behind closed doors
puerto *nm* **1** : port, harbor **2** : mountain pass **3 puerto marítimo** : seaport
puertorriqueño, -ña *adj & n* : Puerto Rican
pues *conj* **1** : since, because, for <no puedo ir, pues no tengo plata : I can't go, since I don't have any money> <lo hace, pues a él le gusta : he does it because he likes to> **2** (*used interjectionally*) : well, then <¡pues claro que sí! : well, of course!> <¡pues no voy! : well then, I'm not going!>
puesta *nf* **1** : setting <puesta del sol : sunset> **2** : laying (of eggs) **3 puesta a punto** : tune-up **4 puesta en marcha** : start, starting up
puestero, -ra *n* : seller, vendor
puesto[1] *pp* → **poner**
puesto[2], -ta *adj* : dressed <bien puesto : well-dressed>
puesto[3] *nm* **1** LUGAR, SITIO : place, position **2** : position, job **3** : kiosk, stand, stall **4 puesto que** : since, given that
pugilato *nm* BOXEO : boxing, pugilism
pugilista *nm* BOXEADOR : boxer, pugilist
pugna *nf* **1** CONFLICTO, LUCHA : conflict, struggle **2 en ~** : at odds, in conflict
pugnar *vi* LUCHAR : to fight, to strive, to struggle
pugnaz *adj* : pugnacious
pujante *adj* : mighty, powerful
pujanza *nf* : strength, vigor <pujanza económica : economic strength>
pulcritud *nf* **1** : neatness, tidiness **2** ESMERO : meticulousness
pulcro, -cra *adj* **1** : clean, neat **2** : exquisite, delicate, refined
pulga *nf* **1** : flea **2 tener malas pulgas** : to be bad-tempered
pulgada *nf* : inch
pulgar *nm* **1** : thumb **2** : big toe
pulir *vt* **1** : to polish, to shine **2** REFINAR : to refine, to perfect
pulla *nf* **1** : cutting remark, dig, gibe **2** : obscenity
pulmón *nm, pl* **pulmones** : lung
pulmonar *adj* : pulmonary
pulmonía *nf* NEUMONÍA : pneumonia
pulpa *nf* : pulp, flesh
pulpería *nf* : small grocery store
púlpito *nm* : pulpit
pulpo *nm* : octopus
pulsación *nf, pl* **-ciones** **1** : beat, pulsation, throb **2** : keystroke
pulsar *vt* **1** APRETAR : to press, to push **2** : to strike (a key) **3** : to assess — *vi* : to beat, to throb

pulsera *nf* : bracelet

pulso *nm* **1** : pulse <tomarle el pulso a alguien : to take someone's pulse> <tomarle el pulso a la opinión : to sound out opinion> **2** : steadiness (of hand) <dibujo a pulso : freehand sketch>

pulular *vi* ABUNDAR : to abound, to swarm <en el río pululan los peces : the river is teeming with fish>

pulverizador *nm* **1** : atomizer, spray **2** : spray gun

pulverizar {21} *vt* **1** : to pulverize, to crush **2** : to spray

puma *nf* : cougar, puma

puna *nf* : bleak Andean tableland

punción *nf, pl* **punciones** : puncture

punible *adj* : punishable

punitivo, -va *adj* : punitive

punce, etc. → **punzar**

punta *nf* **1** : tip, end <punta del dedo : fingertip> <en la punta de la lengua : at the tip of one's tongue> **2** : point (of a weapon or pencil) <punta de lanza : spearhead> **3** : point, headland **4** : bunch, lot <una punta de ladrones : a bunch of thieves> **5 a punta de** : by, by dint of

puntada *nf* **1** : stitch (in sewing) **2** PUNZADA : sharp pain, stitch, twinge **3** *Mex* : witticism, quip

puntal *nm* **1** : prop, support **2** : stanchion

puntapié *nm* PATADA : kick

puntazo *nm* CORNADA : wound (from a goring)

puntear *vt* **1** : to pluck (a guitar) **2** : to lead (in sports)

puntería *nf* : aim, marksmanship

puntero *nm* **1** : pointer **2** : leader

puntiagudo, -da *adj* : sharp, pointed

puntilla *nf* **1** : lace edging **2** : dagger (in bullfighting) **3 de puntillas** : on tiptoe

puntilloso, -sa *adj* : punctilious

punto *nm* **1** : dot, point **2** : period (in punctuation) **3** : item, question **4** : spot, place **5** : moment, stage, degree **6** : point (in a score) **7** : stitch **8 en ~** : on the dot, sharp <a las dos en punto : at two o'clock sharp> **9 al punto** : at once **10 a punto fijo** : exactly, certainly **11 dos puntos** : colon **12 hasta cierto punto** : up to a point **13 punto decimal** : decimal point **14 punto de vista** : point of view **15 punto y coma** : semicolon **16 y punto** : period <es el mejor que hay y punto : it's the best there is, period> **17 puntos cardinales** : points of the compass

puntuación *nf, pl* **-ciones 1** : punctuation **2** : scoring, score, grade

puntual *adj* **1** : prompt, punctual **2** : exact, accurate — **puntualmente** *adv*

puntualidad *nf* **1** : promptness, punctuality **2** : exactness, accuracy

puntualizar {21} *vt* **1** : to specify, to state **2** : to point out

puntuar {3} *vt* : to punctuate — *vi* : to score points

punzada *nf* : sharp pain, twinge, stitch

punzante *adj* **1** : sharp **2** CÁUSTICO : biting, caustic

punzar {21} *vt* : to pierce, to puncture

punzón *nm, pl* **punzones 1** : awl **2** : hole punch

puñado *nm* **1** : handful **2 a puñados** : lots of, by the handful

puñal *nm* DAGA : dagger

puñalada *nf* : stab, stab wound

puñetazo *nm* : punch (with the fist)

puño *nm* **1** : fist **2** : handful, fistful **3** : cuff (of a shirt) **4** : handle, hilt

pupila *nf* : pupil (of the eye)

pupilo, -la *n* **1** : pupil, student **2** : ward, charge

pupitre *nm* : writing desk

puré *nm* : purée <puré de papas : mashed potatoes>

pureza *nf* : purity

purga *nf* **1** : laxative **2** : purge

purgante *adj & nm* : laxative, purgative

purgar {52} *vt* **1** : to purge, to cleanse **2** : to liquidate (in politics) **3** : to give a laxative to — **purgarse** *vr* **1** : to take a laxative **2 ~ de** : to purge oneself of

purgatorio *nm* : purgatory

purgue, etc. → **purgar**

purificador *nm* : purifier

purificar {72} *vt* : to purify — **purificación** *nf*

puritano[1], -na *adj* : puritanical, puritan

puritano[2], -na *n* **1** : Puritan **2** : puritan

puro[1] *adv* : sheer, much <de puro terco : out of sheer stubbornness>

puro[2], -ra *adj* **1** : pure <aire puro : fresh air> **2** : plain, simple, sheer <por pura curiosidad : from sheer curiosity> **3** : only, just <emplean puras mujeres : they only employ women> **4 pura sangre** : Thoroughbred horse

puro[3] *nm* : cigar

púrpura *nf* : purple

purpúreo, -rea *adj* : purple

purpurina *nf* : glitter (for decoration)

pus *nm* : pus

pusilánime *adj* COBARDE : pusillanimous, cowardly

puso, etc. → **poner**

pústula *nf* : pustule, pimple

puta *nf* : whore, slut

putrefacción *nf, pl* **-ciones** : putrefaction

putrefacto, -ta *adj* **1** PODRIDO : putrid, rotten **2** : decayed

pútrido, -da *adj* : putrid, rotten

puya *nf* **1** : point (of a lance) **2 lanzar una puya** : to gibe, to taunt

Q

q *nf* : eighteenth letter of the Spanish alphabet

que[1] *conj* **1** : that <dice que está listo : he says that he's ready> <espero que lo haga : I hope that he does it> **2** : than <más que nada : more than anything> **3** (*implying permission or desire*) <¡que entre! : send him in!> <¡que te vaya bien! : I wish you well!> **4** (*indicating a reason or cause*) <¡cuidado, que te caes! : be careful, you're about to fall!> <no provoques al perro, que te va a morder : don't provoke the dog or (else) he'll bite> **5 es que** : the thing is that, I'm afraid that **6 yo que tú** : if I were you

que[2] *pron* **1** : who, that <la niña que viene : the girl who is coming> **2** : whom, that <los alumnos que enseñé : the students that I taught> **3** : that, which <el carro que me gusta : the car that I like> **4 el (la, lo, las, los) que** → **el[1], la[1], lo[1], los[1]**

qué[1] *adv* : how, what <¡qué bonito! : how pretty!>

qué[2] *adj* : what, which <¿qué hora es? : what time is it?>

qué[3] *pron* : what <¿qué quieres? : what do you want?>

quebracho *nm* : quebracho (tree)

quebrada *nf* DESFILADERO : ravine, gorge

quebradizo, -za *adj* FRÁGIL : breakable, delicate, fragile

quebrado[1], -da *adj* **1** : bankrupt **2** : rough, uneven **3** ROTO : broken

quebrado[2] *nm* : fraction

quebrantamiento *nm* **1** : breaking **2** : deterioration, weakening

quebrantar *vt* **1** : to break, to split, to crack **2** : to weaken **3** : to violate (a law or contract)

quebranto *nm* **1** : break, breaking **2** AFLICCIÓN : affliction, grief **3** PÉRDIDA : loss

quebrar {55} *vt* **1** ROMPER : to break **2** DOBLAR : to bend, to twist — *vi* **1** : to go bankrupt **2** : to fall out, to break up — **quebrarse** *vr*

queda *nf* : curfew

quedar *vi* **1** PERMANECER : to remain, to stay **2** : to be <quedamos contentos con las mejoras : we were pleased with the improvements> **3** : to be situated <queda muy lejos : it's very far, it's too far away> **4** : to be left <quedan sólo dos alternativas : there are only two options left> **5** : to fit, to suit <estos zapatos no me quedan : these shoes don't fit> **6 quedar bien (mal)** : to turn out well (badly) **7 ~ en** : to agree, to arrange <¿en qué quedamos? : what's the arrangement, then?> — **quedarse** *vr* **1** : to stay <se quedó en casa : she stayed at home> **2** : to keep on <se quedó esperando : he kept on waiting> **3 quedarse atrás** : to stay behind <no quedarse atrás : to be no slouch> **4 ~ con** : to remain <me quedé con hambre después de comer : I was still hungry after I ate>

quedo[1] *adv* : softly, quietly

quedo[2], -da *adj* : quiet, still

quehacer *nm* **1** : work **2 quehaceres** *nmpl* : chores

queja *nf* : complaint

quejarse *vr* **1** : to complain **2** : to groan, to moan

quejido *nm* **1** : groan, moan **2** : whine, whimper

quejoso, -sa *adj* : complaining, whining

quejumbroso, -sa *adj* : querulous, whining

quema *nf* **1** FUEGO : fire **2** : burning

quemado, -da *adj* **1** : burned, burnt **2** : annoyed **3** : burned-out

quemador *nm* : burner

quemadura *nf* : burn

quemar *vt* : to burn, to set fire to — *vi* : to be burning hot — **quemarse** *vr*

quemarropa *nf* **a ~** : point-blank

quemazón *nf, pl* **-zones 1** : burning **2** : intense heat **3** : itch **4** : cutting remark

quena *nf* : Peruvian reed flute

quepa, etc. → **caber**

querella *nf* **1** : complaint **2** : lawsuit

querellante *nmf* : plaintiff

querellarse *vr* **~ contra** : to bring suit against, to sue

querer[1] {64} *vt* **1** DESEAR : to want, to desire <quiere ser profesor : he wants to be a teacher> <¿cuánto quieres por esta computadora? : how much do you want for this computer?> **2** : to love, to like, to be fond of <te quiero : I love you> **3** (*indicating a request*) <¿quieres pasarme la leche? : please pass the milk> **4 querer decir** : to mean **5 sin ~** : unintentionally — *vi* : like, want <si quieras : if you like>

querer[2] *nm* : love, affection

querido[1], -da *adj* : dear, beloved

querido[2], -da *n* : dear, sweetheart

queroseno *nm* : kerosene

querúbico, -ca *adj* : cherubic

querrá, etc. → **querer**

querubín *nm, pl* **-bines** : cherub

quesadilla *nf* : quesadilla

quesería *nf* : cheese shop

queso *nm* : cheese

quetzal *nm* **1** : quetzal (bird) **2** : monetary unit of Guatemala

quicio *nm* **1 estar fuera de quicio** : to be beside oneself **2 sacar de quicio** : to exasperate, to drive crazy

quid *nm* : crux, gist <el quid de la cuestión : the crux of the matter>

quiebra[1], etc. → **quebrar**

quiebra[2] *nf* **1 :** break, crack **2** BANCARROTA **:** failure, bankruptcy

quien *pron, pl* **quienes 1 :** who, whom <no sé quien ganará : I don't know who will win> <las personas con quienes trabajo : the people with whom I work> **2 :** whoever, whomever <quien quiere salir que salga : whoever wants to can leave> **3 :** anyone, some people <hay quienes no están de acuerdo : some people don't agree>

quién *pron, pl* **quiénes 1 :** who, whom <¿quién sabe? : who knows?> <¿con quién hablo? : with whom am I speaking?> **2 de ~ :** whose <¿de quién es este libro? : whose book is this?>

quienquiera *pron, pl* **quienesquiera :** whoever, whomever

quiere, etc. → querer

quieto, -ta *adj* **1 :** calm, quiet **2** INMÓVIL **:** still

quietud *nf* **1 :** calm, tranquility **2** INMOVILIDAD **:** stillness

quijada *nf* **:** jaw, jawbone

quijotesco, -ca *adj* **:** quixotic

quilate *nm* **:** karat

quilla *nf* **:** keel

quimera *nf* **:** chimera, illusion

quimérico, -ca *adj* **:** chimeric, fanciful

química *nf* **:** chemistry

químico[1], **-ca** *adj* **:** chemical

químico[2], **-ca** *n* **:** chemist

quimioterapia *nf* **:** chemotherapy

quimono *nm* **:** kimono

quince *adj & nm* **:** fifteen

quinceañero, -ra *n* **:** fifteen-year-old, teenager

quinceavo[1], **-va** *adj* **:** fifteenth

quinceavo[2] *nm* **:** fifteenth (fraction)

quincena *nf* **:** two week period, fortnight

quincenal *adj* **:** bimonthly, twice a month

quingombó *nm* **:** okra

quincuagésimo[1], **-ma** *adj* **:** fiftieth, fifty-

quincuagésimo[2], **-ma** *n* **:** fiftieth, fifty- (in a series)

quiniela *nf* **:** sports lottery

quinientos[1], **-tas** *adj* **:** five hundred

quinientos[2] *nms & pl* **:** five hundred

quinina *nf* **:** quinine

quino *nm* **:** cinchona

quinqué *nm* **:** oil lamp

quinquenal *adj* **:** five-year <un plan quinquenal : a five-year plan>

quinta *nf* **:** country house, villa

quintaesencia *nf* **:** quintessence — **quintaesencial** *adj*

quintal *nm* **:** hundredweight

quinteto *nm* **:** quintet

quintillizo, -za *n* **:** quintuplet

quinto, -ta *adj* **:** fifth — **quinto, -ta** *n*

quíntuplo, -la *adj* **:** quintuple, fivefold

quiosco *nm* **1 :** kiosk **2 :** newsstand **3 quiosco de música :** bandstand

quirófano *nm* **:** operating room

quiromancia *nf* **:** palmistry

quiropráctica *nf* **:** chiropractic

quiropráctico, -ca *n* **:** chiropractor

quirúrgico, -ca *adj* **:** surgical — **quirúrgicamente** *adv*

quiso, etc. → querer

quisquilloso[1], **-sa** *adj* **:** fastidious, fussy

quisquilloso[2], **-sa** *n* **:** fussy person, fussbudget

quiste *nm* **:** cyst

quitaesmalte *nm* **:** nail polish remover

quitamanchas *nms & pl* **:** stain remover

quitanieves *nms & pl* **:** snowplow

quitar *vt* **1 :** to remove, to take away **2 :** to take off (clothes) **3 :** to get rid of, to relieve — **quitarse** *vr* **1 :** to withdraw, to leave **2 :** to take off (one's clothes) **3 ~ de :** to give up (a habit) **4 quitar de encima :** to get rid of

quitasol *nm* **:** parasol

quiteño[1], **-ña** *adj* **:** of or from Quito

quiteño[2], **-ña** *n* **:** person from Quito

quizá *or* **quizás** *adv* **:** maybe, perhaps

quórum *nm, pl* **quórums :** quorum

R

r *nf* **:** nineteenth letter of the Spanish alphabet

rábano *nm* **1 :** radish **2 rábano picante :** horseradish

rabí *nmf, pl* **rabíes :** rabbi

rabia *nf* **1** HIDROFOBIA **:** rabies, hydrophobia **2 :** rage, anger

rabiar *vi* **1 :** to rage, to be furious **2 :** to be in great pain **3 a ~** *fam* **:** like crazy, like mad

rabieta *nf* BERRINCHE **:** tantrum

rabino, -na *n* **:** rabbi

rabioso, -sa *adj* **1 :** enraged, furious **2 :** rabid

rabo *nm* **1** COLA **:** tail **2 el rabo del ojo :** the corner of one's eye

racha *nf* **1 :** gust of wind **2 :** run, series, string <racha perdedora : losing streak>

racheado, -da *adj* **:** gusty, windy

racial *adj* **:** racial

racimo *nm* **:** bunch, cluster <un racimo de uvas : a bunch of grapes>

raciocinio *nm* **:** reason, reasoning

ración *nf, pl* **raciones 1 :** share, ration **2** PORCIÓN **:** portion, helping

racional *adj* **:** rational, reasonable — **racionalmente** *adv*

racionalidad *nf* **:** rationality

racionalización *nf, pl* **-ciones** : rationalization

racionalizar {21} *vt* **1** : to rationalize **2** : to streamline

racionamiento *nm* : rationing

racionar *vt* : to ration

racismo *nm* : racism

racista *adj & nmf* : racist

radar *nm* : radar

radiación *nf, pl* **-ciones** : radiation, irradiation

radiactividad *nf* : radioactivity

radiactivo, -va *adj* : radioactive

radiador *nm* : radiator

radial *adj* **1** : radial **2** : radio, broadcasting <emisora radial : radio transmitter>

radiante *adj* : radiant

radiar *vt* **1** : to radiate **2** : to irradiate **3** : to broadcast (on the radio)

radical[1] *adj* : radical, extreme — **radicalmente** *adv*

radical[2] *nmf* : radical

radicalismo *nm* : radicalism

radicar {72} *vi* **1** : to be found, to lie **2** ARRAIGAR : to take root — **radicarse** *vr* : to settle, to establish oneself

radio[1] *nm* **1** : radius **2** : radium

radio[2] *nmf* : radio

radioactividad *nf* : radioactivity

radioactivo, -va *adj* : radioactive

radioaficionado, -da *n* : ham radio operator

radiodifusión *nf, pl* **-siones** : radio broadcasting

radiodifusora *nf* : radio station

radioemisora *nf* : radio station

radiofaro *nm* : radio beacon

radiofónico, -ca *adj* : radio <estación radiofónica pública : public radio station>

radiofrecuencia *nf* : radio frequency

radiografía *nf* : X ray (photograph)

radiografiar {85} *vt* : to x-ray

radiología *nf* : radiology

radiólogo, -ga *n* : radiologist

radón *nm* : radon

raer {65} *vt* RASPAR : to scrape, to scrape off

ráfaga *nf* **1** : gust (of wind) **2** : flash, burst <una ráfaga de luz : a flash of light>

raid *nm CA, Mex fam* : lift, ride

raído, -da *adj* : worn, shabby

raiga, etc. → **raer**

raíz *nf, pl* **raíces** **1** : root **2** : origin, source **3** **a raíz de** : following, as a result of **4** **echar raíces** : to take root

raja *nf* **1** : crack, slit **2** : slice, wedge

rajá *nm* : raja

rajadura *nf* : crack, split

rajar *vt* HENDER : to crack, to split — *vi* **1** *fam* : to chatter **2** *fam* : to boast, to brag — **rajarse** *vr* **1** : to crack, to split open **2** *fam* : to back out

rajatabla *adv* **a ～** : strictly, to the letter

ralea *nf* : kind, sort, ilk <son de la misma valea : they're two of a kind>

ralentí *nm* **dejar al ralentí** : to leave (a motor) idling

rallado, -da *adj* **1** : grated **2** **pan rallado** : bread crumbs *pl*

rallador *nm* : grater

rallar *vt* : to grate

ralo, -la *adj* : sparse, thin

rama *nf* : branch

ramaje *nm* : branches *pl*

ramal *nm* **1** : branchline **2** : halter, strap

ramera *nf* : harlot, prostitute

ramificación *nf, pl* **-ciones** : ramification

ramificarse {72} *vr* : to branch out, to divide into branches

ramillete *nm* **1** RAMO : bouquet **2** : select group, cluster

ramo *nm* **1** : branch **2** RAMILLETE : bouquet **3** : division (of science or industry) **4** **Domingo de Ramos** : Palm Sunday

rampa *nf* : ramp, incline

rana *nf* **1** : frog **2** **rana toro** : bullfrog

ranchera *nf Mex* : traditional folk song

ranchería *nf* : settlement

ranchero, -ra *n* : rancher, farmer

rancho *nm* **1** : ranch, farm **2** : hut **3** : settlement, camp **4** : food, mess (for soldiers, etc.)

rancio, -cia *adj* **1** : aged, mellow (of wine) **2** : ancient, old **3** : rancid

rango *nm* **1** : rank, status **2** : high social standing **3** : pomp, splendor

ranúnculo *nm* : buttercup

ranura *nf* : groove, slot

rapacidad *nf* : rapacity

rapar *vt* **1** : to crop **2** : to shave

rapaz[1] *adj, pl* **rapaces** : rapacious, predatory

rapaz[2], **-paza** *n, mpl* **rapaces** : youngster, child

rape *nm* : close haircut

rapé *nm* : snuff

rapidez *nf* : rapidity, speed

rápido[1] *adv* : quickly, fast <¡manejas tan rápido! : you drive so fast!>

rápido[2], **-da** *adj* : rapid, quick — **rápidamente** *adv*

rápido[3] *nm* **1** : express train **2** **rápidos** *nmpl* : rapids

rapiña *nf* **1** : plunder, pillage **2** **ave de rapiña** : bird of prey

raposa *nf* : vixen (fox)

rapsodia *nf* : rhapsody

raptar *vt* SEQUESTRAR : to abduct, to kidnap

rapto *nm* **1** SECUESTRO : kidnapping, abduction **2** ARREBATO : fit, outburst

raptor, -tora *n* SECUESTRADOR : kidnapper

raque *nm* : beachcombing

raquero, -ra *n* : beachcomber

raqueta *nf* **1** : racket (in sports) **2** : snowshoe

raquítico, -ca *adj* **1** : scrawny, weak **2** : measly, skimpy

raquitismo *nm* : rickets

raramente *adv* : seldom, rarely

rareza *nf* **1 :** rarity **2 :** peculiarity, oddity
raro, -ra *adj* **1** EXTRAÑO **:** odd, strange, peculiar **2 :** unusual, rare **3 :** exceptional **4 rara vez :** seldom, rarely
ras *nm* **a ras de :** level with
rasar *vt* **1 :** to skim, to graze **2 :** to level
rascacielos *nms & pl* **:** skyscraper
rascar {72} *vt* **1 :** to scratch **2 :** to scrape — **rascarse** *vr* **:** to scratch an itch
rasgadura *nf* **:** tear, rip
rasgar {52} *vt* **:** to rip, to tear — **rasgarse** *vr*
rasgo *nm* **1 :** stroke (of a pen) <a grandes rasgos : in broad outlines> **2** CARACTERÍSTICA **:** trait, characteristic **3 :** gesture, deed **4 rasgos** *nmpl* FACCIONES **:** features
rasgón *nm, pl* **rasgones :** rip, tear
rasgue, etc. → **rasgar**
rasguear *vt* **:** to strum
rasguñar *vt* **1 :** to scratch **2 :** to sketch, to outline
rasguño *nm* **1 :** scratch **2 :** sketch
raso[1], -sa *adj* **1 :** level, flat **2 soldado raso :** private (in the army) <los soldados rasos : the ranks>
raso[2] *nm* **:** satin
raspadura *nf* **1 :** scratching, scraping **2 raspaduras** *nfpl* **:** scrapings
raspar *vt* **1 :** to scrape **2 :** to file down, to smooth — *vi* **:** to be rough
rasque, etc. → **rascar**
rastra *nf* **1 :** harrow **2 a rastras :** by dragging, unwillingly
rastrear *vt* **1 :** to track, to trace **2 :** to comb, to search **3 :** to trawl
rastrero, -ra *adj* **1 :** creeping, crawling **2 :** vile, despicable
rastrillar *vt* **:** to rake, to harrow
rastrillo *nm* **1 :** rake **2** *Mex* **:** razor
rastro *nm* **1** PISTA **:** trail, track **2** VESTIGIO **:** trace, sign
rastrojo *nm* **:** stubble (of plants)
rasurar *vt* AFEITAR **:** to shave — **rasurarse** *vr*
rata[1] *nm fam* **:** pickpocket, thief
rata[2] *nf* **1 :** rat **2** *Col, Pan, Peru* **:** rate, percentage
ratear *vt* **:** to pilfer, to steal
ratero, -ra *n* **:** petty thief
ratificación *nf, pl* **-ciones :** ratification
ratificar {72} *vt* **1 :** to ratify **2 :** to confirm
rato *nm* **1 :** while **2 pasar el rato :** to pass the time **3 a cada rato :** all the time, constantly <les sacaba dinero a cada rato : he was always taking money from them> **4 al poco rato :** later, shortly after
ratón[1], -tona *n, mpl* **ratones 1 :** mouse **2 ratón de biblioteca** *fam* **:** bookworm
ratón[2] *nm, pl* **ratones 1 :** (computer) mouse **2** *CoRi* **:** biceps
ratonera *nf* **:** mousetrap
raudal *nm* **1 :** torrent **2 a raudales :** in abundance
raya[1], etc. → **raer**
raya[2] *nf* **1 :** line **2 :** stripe **3 :** skate, ray **4 :** part (in the hair) **5 :** crease (in clothing)
rayar *vt* **1** ARAÑAR **:** to scratch **2 :** to scrawl on, to mark up <rayaron las paredes : they covered the walls with graffiti> — *vi* **1 :** to scratch **2** AMANECER **:** to dawn, to break <al rayar el alba : at break of day> **3 ~ con :** to be adjacent to, to be next to **4 ~ en :** to border on, to verge on <su respuesta raya en lo ridículo : his answer borders on the ridiculous> — **rayarse** *vr*
rayo *nm* **1 :** ray, beam <rayo láser : laser beam> <rayo de gamma : gamma ray> <rayo de sol : sunbeam> **2** RELÁMPAGO **:** lightning bolt **3 rayo X :** X ray
rayón *nm, pl* **rayones :** rayon
raza *nf* **1 :** race <raza humana : human race> **2 :** breed, strain **3 de ~ :** thoroughbred, pedigreed
razón *nf, pl* **razones 1** MOTIVO **:** reason, motive <en razón de : by reason of, because of> **2** JUSTICIA **:** rightness, justice <tener razón : to be right> **3 :** reasoning, sense <perder la razón : to lose one's mind> **4 :** ratio, proportion
razonable *adj* **:** reasonable — **razonablemente** *adv*
razonado, -da *adj* **:** itemized, detailed
razonamiento *nm* **:** reasoning
razonar *v* **:** to reason, to think
reabastecimiento *nm* **:** replenishment
reabierto *pp* → **reabrir**
reabrir {2} *vt* **:** to reopen — **reabrirse** *vr*
reacción *nf, pl* **-ciones 1 :** reaction **2 motor a reacción :** jet engine
reaccionar *vi* **:** to react, to respond
reaccionario, -ria *adj & n* **:** reactionary
reacio, -cia *adj* **:** resistant, opposed
reacondicionar *vt* **:** to recondition
reactor *nm* **1 :** reactor <reactor nuclear : nuclear reactor> **2 :** jet engine **3 :** jet airplane, jet
reafirmar *vt* **:** to reaffirm, to assert, to strengthen
reajustar *vt* **:** to readjust, to adjust
reajuste *nm* **:** readjustment <reajuste de precios : price increase>
real *adj* **1 :** real, true **2 :** royal
realce *nm* **1 :** embossing, relief **2 dar realce :** to highlight, to bring out
realeza *nf* **:** royalty
realidad *nf* **1 :** reality **2 en ~ :** in truth, actually
realinear *vt* **:** to realign
realismo *nm* **1 :** realism **2 :** royalism
realista[1] *adj* **1 :** realistic **2 :** realist **3 :** royalist
realista[2] *nmf* **1 :** realist **2 :** royalist
realización *nf, pl* **-ciones :** execution, realization
realizar {21} *vt* **1 :** to carry out, to execute **2 :** to produce, to direct (a

film or play) **3 :** to fulfill, to achieve **4 :** to realize (a profit) — **realizarse** *vr* **1 :** to come true **2 :** to fulfill oneself
realmente *adv* **:** really, in reality
realzar {21} *vt* **1 :** to heighten, to raise **2 :** to highlight, to enhance
reanimación *nf, pl* **-ciones :** revival, resuscitation
reanimar *vt* **1 :** to revive, to restore **2 :** to resuscitate — **reanimarse** *vr* **:** to come around, to recover
reanudar *vt* **:** to resume, to renew — **reanadarse** *vr* **:** to resume, to continue
reaparecer {53} *vi* **1 :** to reappear **2 :** to make a comeback
reaparición *nf, pl* **-ciones :** reappearance
reapertura *nf* **:** reopening
reata *nf* **1 :** rope **2** *Mex* **:** lasso, lariat **3 de ~ :** single file
reavivar *vt* **:** to revive, to reawaken
rebaja *nf* **1 :** reduction **2** DESCUENTO **:** discount **3 rebajas** *nfpl* **:** sale
rebajar *vt* **1 :** to reduce, to lower **2 :** to lessen, to diminish **3 :** to humiliate — **rebajarse** *vr* **: 1 :** to humble oneself **2 rebajarse a :** to stoop to
rebanada *nf* **:** slice
rebañar *vt* **:** to mop up, to sop up
rebaño *nm* **1 :** flock **2 :** herd
rebasar *vt* **1 :** to surpass, to exceed **2** *Mex* **:** to pass, to overtake
rebatiña *nf* **:** scramble, fight (over something)
rebatir *vt* REFUTAR **:** to refute
rebato *nm* **1 :** surprise attack **2 tocar a rebato :** to sound the alarm
rebelarse *vr* **:** to rebel
rebelde[1] *adj* **:** rebellious, unruly
rebelde[2] *nmf* **1 :** rebel **2 :** defaulter
rebeldía *nf* **1 :** rebelliousness **2 en ~ :** in default
rebelión *nf, pl* **-liones :** rebellion
rebobinar *vt* **:** to rewind
reborde *nm* **:** border, flange, rim
rebosante *adj* **:** brimming, overflowing <rebosante de salud : brimming with health>
rebosar *vi* **1 :** to overflow **2 ~ de :** to abound in, to be bursting with — *vt* **:** to radiate
rebotar *vi* **1 :** to bounce **2 :** to ricochet, to rebound
rebote *nm* **1 :** bounce **2 :** rebound, ricochet
rebozar {21} *vt* **:** to coat in batter
rebozo *nm* **1 :** shawl, wrap **2 sin ~ :** frankly, openly
rebullir {38} *v* **:** to move, to stir — **rebullirse** *vr*
rebuscado, -da *adj* **:** affected, pretentious
rebuscar {72} *vi* **:** to search thoroughly
rebuznar *vi* **:** to bray
rebuzno *nm* **:** bray, braying
recabar *vt* **1 :** to gather, to obtain, to collect **2 recabar fondos :** to raise money
recado *nm* **1 :** message <mandar recado : to send word> **2** *Spain* **:** errand
recaer {13} *vi* **1 :** to relapse **2 ~ en** *or* **~ sobre :** to fall on, to fall to
recaída *nf* **:** relapse
recaiga, etc. → recaer
recalar *vi* **:** to arrive
recalcar {72} *vt* **:** to emphasize, to stress
recalcitrante *adj* **:** recalcitrant
recalentar {55} *vt* **1 :** to reheat, to warm up **2 :** to overheat
recámara *nf* **1** *Col, Mex, Pan* **:** bedroom **2 :** chamber (of a firearm)
recamarera *nf Mex* **:** chambermaid
recambio *nm* **1 :** spare part **2 :** refill (for a pen, etc.)
recapacitar *vi* **1 :** to reconsider **2 ~ en :** to reflect on, to weigh
recapitular *v* **:** to recapitulate — **recapitulación** *nf*
recargable *adj* **:** rechargeable
recargado, -da *adj* **:** overly elaborate or ornate
recargar {52} *vt* **1 :** to recharge **2 :** to overload
recargo *nm* **:** surcharge
recatado, -da *adj* MODESTO **:** modest, demure
recato *nm* PUDOR **:** modesty
recaudación *nf, pl* **-ciones 1 :** collection **2 :** earnings *pl*, takings *pl*
recaudador, -dora *n* **recaudador de impuestos :** tax collector
recaudar *vt* **:** to collect
recaudo *nm* **:** safe place <a (buen) recaudo : in safe keeping>
recayó, etc. → recaer
rece, etc. → rezar
recelo *nm* **:** distrust, suspicion
receloso, -sa *adj* **:** distrustful, suspicious
recepción *nf, pl* **-ciones :** reception
recepcionista *nmf* **:** receptionist
receptáculo *nm* **:** receptacle
receptividad *nf* **:** receptivity, receptiveness
receptivo, -va *adj* **:** receptive
receptor[1], **-tora** *adj* **:** receiving
receptor[2], **-tora** *n* **1 :** recipient **2 :** catcher (in baseball), receiver (in football)
receptor[3] *nm* **:** receiver <receptor de televisión : television set>
recesión *nf, pl* **-siones :** recession
recesivo, -va *adj* **:** recessive
receso *nm* **:** recess, adjournment
receta *nf* **1 :** recipe **2 :** prescription
recetar *vt* **:** to prescribe (medications)
rechazar {21} *vt* **1 :** to reject **2 :** to turn down, to refuse
rechazo *nm* **:** rejection, refusal
rechifla *nf* **:** booing, jeering

rechinar *vi* **1 :** to squeak **2 :** to grind, to gnash <hacer rechinar los dientes : to grind one's teeth>

rechoncho, -cha *adj fam* **:** chubby, squat

recibidor *nm* **:** vestibule, entrance hall

recibimiento *nm* **:** reception, welcome

recibir *vt* **1 :** to receive, to get **2 :** to welcome — *vi* **:** to receive visitors — **recibirse** *vr* **~ de :** to qualify as

recibo *nm* **:** receipt

reciclable *adj* **:** recyclable

reciclado *nm* → **reciclaje**

reciclaje *nm* **1 :** recycling **2 :** retraining

reciclar *vt* **1 :** to recycle **2 :** to retrain

recién *adv* **1 :** newly, recently <recién nacido : newborn> <recién casados : newlyweds> <recién llegado : newcomer> **2 :** just, only just <recién ahora me acordé : I just now remembered>

reciente *adj* **:** recent — **recientemente** *adv*

recinto *nm* **1 :** enclosure **2 :** site, premises *pl*

recio[1] *adv* **1 :** strongly, hard **2 :** loudly, loud

recio[2]**, -cia** *adj* **1 :** severe, harsh **2 :** tough, strong

recipiente[1] *nm* **:** container, receptacle

recipiente[2] *nmf* **:** recipient

reciprocar {72} *vi* **:** to reciprocate

reciprocidad *nf* **:** reciprocity

recíproco, -ca *adj* **:** reciprocal, mutual

recitación *nf, pl* **-ciones :** recitation, recital

recital *nm* **:** recital

recitar *vt* **:** to recite

reclamación *nf, pl* **-ciones 1 :** claim, demand **2** QUEJA **:** complaint

reclamar *vt* **1** EXIGIR **:** to demand, to require **2 :** to claim — *vi* **:** to complain

reclamo *nm* **1 :** bird call, lure **2 :** lure, decoy **3 :** inducement, attraction **4 :** advertisement **5 :** complaint

reclinar *vt* **:** to rest, to lean — **reclinarse** *vr* **:** to recline, to lean back

recluir {41} *vt* **:** to confine, to lock up — **recluirse** *vr* **:** to shut oneself up, to withdraw

reclusión *nf, pl* **-siones :** imprisonment

recluso, -sa *n* **1 :** inmate, prisoner **2** SOLITARIO **:** recluse

recluta *nmf* **:** recruit, draftee

reclutamiento *nm* **:** recruitment, recruiting

reclutar *vt* ENROLAR **:** to recruit, to enlist

recobrar *vt* **:** to recover, to regain — **recobrarse** *vr* **:** to recover, to recuperate

recocer {14} *vt* **:** to overcook, to cook again

recodo *nm* **:** bend

recogedor *nm* **:** dustpan

recoger {15} *vt* **1 :** to collect, to gather **2 :** to get, to retrieve, to pick up **3 :** to clean up, to tidy (up)

recogido, -da *adj* **:** quiet, secluded

recogimiento *nm* **1 :** collecting, gathering **2 :** withdrawal **3 :** absorption, concentration

recolección *nf, pl* **-ciones 1 :** collection <recolección de basura : trash pickup> **2 :** harvest

recolectar *vt* **1 :** to gather, to collect **2 :** to harvest, to pick

recomendable *adj* **:** advisable, recommended

recomendación *nf, pl* **-ciones :** recommendation

recomendar {55} *vt* **1 :** to recommend **2** ACONSEJAR **:** to advise

recompensa *nf* **:** reward, recompense

recompensar *vt* **1** PREMIAR **:** to reward **2 :** to compensate

reconciliación *nf, pl* **-ciones :** reconciliation

reconciliar *vt* **:** to reconcile — **reconciliarse** *vr*

recóndito, -ta *adj* **1 :** remote, isolated **2 :** hidden, recondite **3 en lo más recóndito de :** in the depths of

reconfortar *vt* **:** to comfort — **reconfortante** *adj*

reconocer {18} *vt* **1 :** to recognize **2 :** to admit **3 :** to examine

reconocible *adj* **:** recognizable

reconocido, -da *adj* **1 :** recognized, accepted **2 :** grateful

reconocimiento *nm* **1 :** acknowledgment, recognition, avowal **2 :** (medical) examination **3 :** reconnaissance

reconsiderar *vt* **:** to reconsider — **reconsideración** *nf*

reconstrucción *nf, pl* **-ciones :** reconstruction

reconstruir {41} *vt* **:** to rebuild, to reconstruct

reconversión *nf, pl* **-siones :** restructuring

reconvertir {76} *vt* **1 :** to restructure **2 :** to retrain

recopilación *nf, pl* **-ciones 1 :** summary **2 :** collection, compilation

recopilar *vt* **:** to compile, to collect

récord *or* **record** [ˈrɛkɔr] *nm, pl* **récords** *or* **records** [-kɔrs] **:** record <record mundial : world record> — **récord** *or* **record** *adj*

recordar {19} *vt* **1 :** to recall, to remember **2 :** to remind — *vi* **1** ACORDARSE **:** to remember **2** DESPERTAR **:** to wake up

recordatorio[1]**, -ria** *adj* **:** commemorative

recordatorio[2] *nm* **:** reminder

recorrer *vt* **1 :** to travel through, to tour **2 :** to cover (a distance) **3 :** to go over, to look over

recorrido *nm* **1 :** journey, trip **2 :** path, route, course **3 :** round (in golf)

recortar *vt* **1 :** to cut, to reduce **2 :** to cut out **3 :** to trim, to cut off **4 :** to outline — **recortarse** *vr* **:** to stand out <los árboles se recortaban en el horizonte : the trees were silhouetted against the horizon>

recorte *nm* **1 :** cut, reduction **2 :** clipping <recortes de periódicos : newspaper clippings>
recostar {19} *vt* **:** to lean, to rest — **recostarse** *vr* **:** to lie down, recline
recoveco *nm* **1** VUELTA **:** bend, turn **2 :** nook, corner **3 recovecos** *nmpl* **:** intricacies, ins and outs
recreación *nf, pl* **-ciones 1 :** re-creation **2** DIVERSIÓN **:** recreation, entertainment
recrear *vt* **1 :** to re-create **2 :** to entertain, to amuse — **recrearse** *vr* **:** to enjoy oneself
recreativo, -va *adj* **:** recreational
recreo *nm* **1** DIVERSIÓN **:** entertainment, amusement **2 :** recess, break
recriminación *nf, pl* **-ciones :** reproach, recrimination
recriminar *vt* **:** to reproach — *vi* **:** to recriminate — **recriminarse** *vr*
recrudecer {53} *v* **:** to intensify, to worsen — **recrudecerse** *vr*
rectal *adj* **:** rectal
rectangular *adj* **:** rectangular
rectángulo *nm* **:** rectangle
rectificación *nf, pl* **-ciones :** rectification, correction
rectificar {72} *vt* **1 :** to rectify, to correct **2 :** to straighten (out)
rectitud *nf* **1 :** straightness **2 :** honesty, rectitude
recto[1] *adv* **:** straight
recto[2]**, -ta** *adj* **1 :** straight **2 :** upright, honorable **3 :** sound
recto[3] *nm* **:** rectum
rector[1]**, -tora** *adj* **:** governing, managing
rector[2]**, -tora** *n* **:** rector
rectoría *nf* **:** rectory
recubierto *pp* → **recubrir**
recubrir {2} *vt* **:** to cover, to coat
recuento *nm* **:** recount, count <un recuento de los votos : a recount of the votes>
recuerdo *nm* **1 :** memory **2 :** souvenir, memento **3 recuerdos** *nmpl* **:** regards
recuperación *nf, pl* **-ciones 1 :** recovery, recuperation **2 recuperación de datos :** data retrieval
recuperar *vt* **1 :** to recover, to get back, to retrieve **2 :** to recuperate **3 :** to make up for <recuperar el tiempo perdido : to make up for lost time> — **recuperarse** *vr* **~ de :** to recover from, to get over
recurrente *adj* **:** recurrent, recurring
recurrir *vi* **1 ~ a :** to turn to, to appeal to **2 ~ a :** to resort to **3 :** to appeal (in law)
recurso *nm* **1 :** recourse <el último recurso : the last resort> **2 :** appeal (in law) **3 recursos** *nmpl* **:** resources, means <recursos naturales : natural resources>
red *nf* **1 :** net, mesh **2 :** network, system, chain **3 :** trap, snare
redacción *nf, pl* **-ciones 1 :** writing, composition **2 :** editing
redactar *vt* **1 :** to write, to draft **2 :** to edit
redactor, -tora *n* **:** editor
redada *nf* **1 :** raid **2 :** catch, haul
redefinir *vt* **:** to redefine — **redefinición** *nf*
redención *nf, pl* **-ciones :** redemption
redentor[1]**, -tora** *adj* **:** redeeming
redentor[2]**, -tora** *n* **:** redeemer
redescubierto *pp* → **redescubrir**
redescubrir {2} *vt* **:** to rediscover
redicho, -cha *adj fam* **:** affected, pretentious
redil *nm* **1 :** sheepfold **2 volver al redil :** to return to the fold
redimir *vt* **:** to redeem, to deliver (from sin)
rediseñar *vt* **:** to redesign
redistribuir {41} *vt* **:** to redistribute — **redistribución** *nf*
rédito *nm* **:** return, yield
redituar {3} *vt* **:** to produce, to yield
redoblar *vt* **:** to redouble, to strengthen — **redoblado, -da** *adj*
redomado, -da *adj* **1 :** sly, crafty **2 :** utter, out-and-out
redonda *nf* **1 :** region, surrounding area **2 a la redonda** ALREDEDOR **:** around <de diez millas a la redonda : for ten miles around>
redondear *vt* **:** to round off, to round out
redondel *nm* **1 :** ring, circle **2 :** bullring, arena
redondez *nf* **:** roundness
redondo, -da *adj* **1 :** round <mesa redonda : round table> **2 :** great, perfect <un negocio redondo : an excellent deal> **3 :** straightforward, flat <un rechazo redondo : a flat refusal> **4** *Mex* **:** round-trip **5 en ~ :** around
reducción *nf, pl* **-ciones :** reduction, decrease
reducido, -da *adj* **1 :** reduced, limited **2 :** small
reducir {61} *vt* **1** DISMINUIR **:** to reduce, to decrease, to cut **2 :** to subdue **3 :** to boil down — **reducirse** *vr* **~ a :** to come down to, to be nothing more than
redundancia *nf* **:** reduncancy
redundante *adj* **:** redundant
reedición *nf, pl* **-ciones :** reprint
reelegir {28} *vt* **:** to reelect — **reelección** *nf*
reembolsable *adj* **:** refundable
reembolsar *vt* **1 :** to refund, to reimburse **2 :** to repay
reembolso *nm* **:** refund, reimbursement
reemplazable *adj* **:** replaceable
reemplazar {21} *vt* **:** to replace, to substitute
reemplazo *nm* **:** replacement, substitution
reencarnación *nf, pl* **-ciones :** reincarnation
reencuentro *nm* **:** reunion
reestablecer {53} *vt* **:** to reestablish

reestructurar *vt* : to restructure
reexaminar *vt* : to reexamine
refaccionar *vt* : to repair, to renovate
refacciones *nfpl* : repairs, renovations
referencia *nf* **1** : reference **2 hacer referencia a** : to refer to
referendo *nm* → **referéndum**
referéndum *nm, pl* **-dums** : referendum
referente *adj* **~ a** : concerning
réferi *or* **referi** [ˈrɛfɛri] *nmf* : referee
referir {76} *vt* **1** : to relate, to tell **2** : to refer <nos refirió al diccionario : she referred us to the dictionary> — **referirse** *vr* **1 ~ a** : to refer to **2 ~ a** : to be concerned, to be in reference to <en lo que se refiere a la educación : as far as education is concerned>
refinado[1], **-da** *adj* : refined
refinado[2] *nm* : refining
refinamiento *nm* **1** : refining **2** FINURA : refinement
refinanciar *vt* : to refinance
refinar *vt* : to refine
refinería *nf* : refinery
reflectante *adj* : reflective, reflecting
reflector[1], **-tora** *adj* : reflecting
reflector[2] *nm* **1** : spotlight, searchlight **2** : reflector
reflejar *vt* : to reflect — **reflejarse** *vr* : to be reflected <la decepción se refleja en su rostro : the disappointment shows on her face>
reflejo *nm* **1** : reflection **2** : reflex **3 reflejos** *nmpl* : highlights, streaks (in hair)
reflexión *nf, pl* **-xiones** : reflection, thought
reflexionar *vi* : to reflect, to think
reflexivo, -va *adj* **1** : reflective, thoughtful **2** : reflexive
reflujo *nm* : ebb, ebb tide
reforma *nf* **1** : reform **2** : alteration, renovation
reformador, -dora *n* : reformer
reformar *vt* **1** : to reform **2** : to change, to alter **3** : to renovate, to repair — **reformarse** *vr* : to mend one's ways
reformatorio *nm* : reformatory
reformular *vt* : to reformulate — **reformulación** *nf*
reforzar {36} *vt* **1** : to reinforce, to strengthen **2** : to encourage, to support
refracción *nf, pl* **-ciones** : refraction
refractar *vt* : to refract — **refractarse** *vr*
refractario, -ria *adj* : refractory, obstinate
refrán *nm, pl* **refranes** ADAGIO : proverb, saying
refregar {49} *vt* : to scrub
refrenar *vt* **1** : to rein in (a horse) **2** : to restrain, to check — **refrenarse** *vr* : to restrain oneself
refrendar *vt* **1** : to countersign, to endorse **2** : to stamp (a passport)
refrescante *adj* : refreshing
refrescar {72} *vt* **1** : to refresh, to cool **2** : to brush up (on) **3 refrescar la memoria** : to refresh one's memory — *vi* : to turn cooler
refresco *nm* : refreshment, soft drink
refriega *nf* : skirmish, scuffle
refrigeración *nf, pl* **-ciones 1** : refrigeration **2** : air-conditioning
refrigerador *nmf* NEVERA : refrigerator
refrigeradora *nf Col, Peru* : refrigerator
refrigerante *nm* : coolant
refrigerar *vt* **1** : to refrigerate **2** : to air-condition
refrigerio *nm* : snack, refreshments *pl*
refrito[1], **-ta** *adj* : refried
refrito[2] *nm* : rehash
refuerzo *nm* : reinforcement, support
refugiado, -da *n* : refugee
refugiar *vt* : to shelter — **refugiarse** *vr* ACOGERSE : to take refuge
refugio *nm* : refuge, shelter
refulgencia *nf* : brilliance, splendor
refulgir {35} *vi* : to shine brightly
refundir *vt* **1** : to recast (metals) **2** : to revise, to rewrite
refunfuñar *vi* : to grumble, to groan
refutar *vt* : to refute — **refutación** *nf*
regadera *nf* **1** : watering can **2** : shower head, shower **3** : sprinkler
regaderazo *nm Mex* : shower
regalar *vt* **1** OBSEQUIAR : to present (as a gift), to give away **2** : to regale, to entertain **3** : to flatter, to make a fuss over — **regalarse** *vr* : to pamper oneself
regalía *nf* : royalty, payment
regaliz *nm, pl* **-lices** : licorice
regalo *nm* **1** OBSEQUIO : gift, present **2** : pleasure, comfort **3** : treat
regañadientes *mpl* **a ~** : reluctantly, unwillingly
regañar *vt* : to scold, to give a talking to — *vi* **1** QUEJARSE : to grumble, to complain **2** REÑIR : to quarrel, to argue
regaño *nm fam* : scolding
regañon, -ñona *adj, mpl* **-ñones** *fam* : grumpy, irritable
regar {49} *vt* **1** : to irrigate **2** : to water **3** : to wash, to hose down **4** : to spill, to scatter
regata *nf* : regatta, yacht race
regate *nm* : dodge, feint
regatear *vt* **1** : to haggle over **2** ESCATIMAR : to skimp on, to be sparing with — *vi* : to bargain, to haggle
regateo *nm* : bargaining, haggling
regatón *nm, pl* **-tones** : ferrule, tip
regazo *nm* : lap (of a person)
regencia *nf* : regency
regenerar *vt* : to regenerate — **regenerarse** *vr* — **regeneración** *nf*
regentar *vt* : to run, to manage
regente *nmf* : regent
regidor, -dora *n* : town councillor
régimen *nm, pl* **regímenes 1** : regime **2** : diet **3** : regimen, rules *pl* <régimen de vida : lifestyle>
regimiento *nm* : regiment

regio, -gia *adj* **1** : great, magnificent **2** : regal, royal
región *nf, pl* **regiones** : region, area
regional *adj* : regional — **regionalmente** *adv*
regir {28} *vt* **1** : to rule **2** : to manage, to run **3** : to control, to govern <las costumbres que rigen la conducta : the customs which govern behavior> — *vi* : to apply, to be in force <las leyes rigen en los tres países : the laws apply in all three countries> — **regirse** *vr* **~ por** : to go by, to be guided by
registrador[1], -dora *adj* **caja registradora** : cash register
registrador[2], -dora *n* : registrar, recorder
registrar *vt* **1** : to register, to record **2** GRABAR : to record, to tape **3** : to search, to examine — **registrarse** *vr* **1** INSCRIBIRSE : to register **2** OCURRIR : to happen, to occur
registro *nm* **1** : register **2** : registration **3** : registry, record office **4** : range (of a voice or musical instrument) **5** : search
regla *nf* **1** NORMA : rule, regulation **2** : ruler <regla de cálculo : slide rule> **3** MENSTRUACIÓN : period, menstruation
reglamentación *nf, pl* **-ciones 1** : regulation **2** : rules *pl*
reglamentar *vt* : to regulate, to set rules for
reglamentario, -ria *adj* : regulation, official <equipo reglamentario : standard equipment>
reglamento *nm* : regulations *pl*, rules *pl* <reglamento de tráfico : traffic regulations>
regocijar *vt* : to gladden, to delight — **regocijarse** *vr* : to rejoice
regocijo *nm* : delight, rejoicing
regordete *adj fam* LLENITO : chubby
regresar *vt* DEVOLVER : to give back — *vi* : to return, to come back, to go back
regresión *nf, pl* **-siones** : regression, return
regresivo, -va *adj* : regressive
regreso *nm* **1** : return **2 estar de regreso** : to be back, to be home
reguero *nm* **1** : irrigation ditch **2** : trail, trace **3 propagarse como reguero de pólvora** : to spread like wildfire
regulable *adj* : adjustable
regulación *nf, pl* **-ciones** : regulation, control
regulador[1], -dora *adj* : regulating, regulatory
regulador[2] *nm* **1** : regulator, governor **2 regulador de tiro** : damper (in a chimney)
regular[1] *vt* : to regulate, to control
regular[2] *adj* **1** : regular **2** : fair, OK, so-so **3** : medium, average **4 por lo regular** : in general, generally
regularidad *nf* : regularity
regularización *nf, pl* **-ciones** NORMALIZACIÓN : normalization
regularizar {21} *vt* NORMALIZAR : to normalize, to make regular
regularmente *adv* : regularly
rehabilitar *vt* **1** : to rehabilitate **2** : to reinstate **3** : renovate, to restore — **rehabilitación** *nf*
rehacer {40} *vt* **1** : to redo **2** : to remake, to repair, to renew — **rehacerse** *vr* **1** : to recover **2 ~ de** : to get over
rehecho *pp* → **rehacer**
rehén *nm, pl* **rehenes** : hostage
rehicieron, etc. → **rehacer**
rehizo → **rehacer**
rehuir {41} *vt* : to avoid, to shun
rehusar {8} *v* : to refuse
reimprimir *vt* : to reprint
reina *nf* : queen
reinado *nm* : reign
reinante *adj* **1** : reigning **2** : prevailing, current
reinar *vi* **1** : to reign **2** : to prevail
reincidencia *nf* : recidivism, relapse
reincidente *nmf* : backslider, recidivist
reincidir *vi* : to backslide, to retrogress
reincorporar *vt* : to reinstate — **reincorporarse** *vr* **~ a** : to return to, to rejoin
reino *nm* : kingdom, realm <reino animal : animal kingdom>
reinstalar *vt* **1** : to reinstall **2** : to reinstate
reintegrar *vt* **1** : to reintegrate, reinstate **2** : to refund, to reimburse — **reintegrarse** *vr* **~ a** : to return to, to rejoin
reír {66} *vi* : to laugh — *vt* : to laugh at — **reírse** *vr*
reiteración *nf, pl* **-ciones** : reiteration, repetition
reiterado, -da *adj* : repeated <lo explicó en reiteradas ocasiones : he explained it repeatedly> — **reiteradamente** *adv*
reiterar *vt* : to reiterate, to repeat
reiterativo, -va *adj* : repetitive, repetitious
reivindicación *nf, pl* **-ciones 1** : demand, claim **2** : vindication
reivindicar {72} *vt* **1** : to vindicate **2** : to demand, to claim **3** : to restore
reja *nf* **1** : grill, grating <entre rejas : behind bars> **2** : plowshare
rejilla *nf* : grille, grate, screen
rejuvenecer {53} *vt* : to rejuvenate — *vi* : to be rejuvenated — **rejuvenecerse** *vr*
rejuvencimiento *m* : rejuvenation
relación *nf, pl* **-ciones 1** : relation, connection, relevance **2** : relationship **3** RELATO : account **4** LISTA : list **5 con relación a** *or* **en relación con** : in relation to, concerning **6 relaciones públicas** : public relations
relacionar *vt* : to relate, to connect — **relacionarse** *vr* **~ con** : to be connected to, to be linked with

relajación *nf, pl* **-ciones :** relaxation
relajado, -da *adj* **1 :** relaxed, loose **2 :** dissolute, depraved
relajar *vt* **:** to relax, to slacken — *vi* **:** to be relaxing — **relajarse** *vr*
relajo *nm* **1 :** commotion, ruckus **2 :** joke, laugh <lo hizo de relajo : he did it for a laugh>
relamerse *vr* **:** to smack one's lips, to lick one's chops
relámpago *nm* **:** flash of lightning
relampaguear *vi* **:** to flash
relanzar {21} *vt* **:** to relaunch
relatar *vt* **:** to relate, to tell
relativo, -va *adj* **1 :** relative **2 en lo relativo a :** with regard to, concerning — **relativamente** *adv*
relato *nm* **1 :** story, tale **2 :** account
releer {20} *vt* **:** to reread
relegar {52} *vt* **1 :** to relegate **2 relegar al olvido :** to consign to oblivion
relevante *adj* **:** outstanding, important
relevar *vt* **1 :** to relieve, to take over from **2 ~ de :** to exempt from — **relevarse** *vr* **:** to take turns
relevo *nm* **1 :** relief, replacement **2 :** relay <carrera de relevos : relay race>
relicario *nm* **1 :** reliquary **2 :** locket
relieve *nm* **1 :** relief, projection <mapa en relieve : relief map> <letras en relieve : embossed letters> **2 :** prominence, importance **3 poner en relieve :** to highlight, to emphasize
religión *nf, pl* **-giones :** religion
religiosamente *adv* **:** religiously, faithfully
religioso[1], -sa *adj* **:** religious
religioso[2], -sa *n* **:** monk *m,* nun *f*
relinchar *vi* **:** to neigh, to whinny
relincho *nm* **:** neigh, whinny
reliquia *nf* **1 :** relic **2 reliquia de familia :** family heirloom
rellenar *vt* **1 :** to refill **2 :** to stuff, to fill **3 :** to fill out
relleno[1], -na *adj* **:** stuffed, filled
relleno[2] *nm* **:** stuffing, filling
reloj *nm* **1 :** clock **2 :** watch **3 reloj de arena :** hourglass **4 reloj de pulsera :** wristwatch **5 como un reloj :** like clockwork
relojería *nf* **1 :** watchmaker's shop **2 :** watchmaking, clockmaking
reluciente *adj* **:** brilliant, shining
relucir {45} *vi* **1 :** to glitter, to shine **2 salir a relucir :** to come to the surface **3 sacar a relucir :** to bring up, to mention
relumbrante *adj* **:** dazzling
relumbrar *vi* **:** to shine brightly
relumbrón *nm, pl* **-brones 1 :** flash, glare **2 de ~ :** flashy, showy
remachar *vt* **1 :** to rivet **2 :** to clinch (a nail) **3 :** to stress, to drive home — *vi* **:** to smash, to spike (a ball)
remache *nm* **1 :** rivet **2 :** smash, spike (in sports)
remanente *nm* **1 :** remainder, balance **2 :** surplus
remanso *nm* **:** pool
remar *vi* **1 :** to row, to paddle **2 :** to struggle, to toil
remarcar {72} *vt* **:** to emphasize, to stress
rematado, -da *adj* **:** utter, complete
rematador, -dora *n* **:** auctioneer
rematar *vt* **1 :** to finish off **2 :** to auction — *vi* **1 :** to shoot **2 :** to end
remate *nm* **1 :** shot (in sports) **2 :** auction **3 :** end, conclusion **4 como ~ :** to top it off **5 de ~ :** completely, utterly
remecer {86} *vt* **:** to sway, to swing
remedar *vt* **1** IMITAR **:** to imitate, to copy **2 :** to mimic, to ape
remediar *vt* **1 :** to remedy, to repair **2 :** to help out, to assist **3** EVITAR **:** to prevent, to avoid
remedio *nm* **1 :** remedy, cure **2 :** solution **3 :** option <no me quedó más remedio : I had no other choice> <no hay remedio : it can't be helped> **4 poner remedio a :** to put a stop to **5 sin ~ :** unavoidable, inevitable
remedo *nm* **:** imitation
rememorar *vi* **:** to recall <rememorar los viejos tiempos : to reminisce>
remendar {55} *vt* **1 :** to mend, to patch, to darn **2 :** to correct
remero, -ra *n* **:** rower
remesa *nf* **1 :** remittance **2 :** shipment
remezón *nm, pl* **-zones :** mild earthquake, tremor
remiendo *nm* **1 :** patch **2 :** correction
remilgado, -da *adj* **1 :** prim, prudish **2 :** affected
remilgo *nm* **:** primness, affectation
reminiscencia *nf* **:** reminiscence
remisión *nf, pl* **-siones 1** ENVÍO **:** sending, delivery **2 :** remission **3 :** reference, cross-reference
remiso, -sa *adj* **1 :** lax, remiss **2 :** reluctant
remitente[1] *nm* **:** return address
remitente[2] *nmf* **:** sender (of a letter, etc.)
remitir *vt* **1 :** to send, to remit **2 ~ a :** to refer to, to direct to <nos remitió al diccionario : he referred us to the dictionary> — *vi* **:** to subside, to let up
remo *nm* **1 :** paddle, oar **2 :** rowing (sport)
remoción *nf, pl* **-ciones 1 :** removal **2 :** dismissal
remodelación *nf, pl* **-ciones 1 :** remodeling **2 :** reorganization, restructuring
remodelar *vt* **1 :** to remodel **2 :** to restructure
remojar *vt* **1 :** to soak, to steep **2 :** to dip, to dunk **3 :** to celebrate with a drink
remojo *nm* **1 :** soaking, steeping **2 poner en remojo :** to soak, to leave soaking
remolacha *nf* **:** beet
remolcador *nm* **:** tugboat
remolcar {72} *vt* **:** to tow, to haul

remolino *nm* **1 :** whirlwind **2 :** eddy, whirlpool **3 :** crowd, throng **4 :** cowlick

remolque *nm* **1 :** towing, tow **2 :** trailer **3 a ~ :** in tow

remontar *vt* **1 :** to overcome **2** SUBIR **:** to go up — **remontarse** *vr* **1 :** to soar **2 ~ a :** to date from, to go back to

rémora *nf* **:** obstacle, hindrance

remorder {47} *vt* INQUIETAR **:** to trouble, to distress

remordimiento *nm* **:** remorse

remotamente *adv* **:** remotely, vaguely

remoto, -ta *adj* **1 :** remote, unlikely <hay una posibilidad remota : there is a slim possibility> **2 :** distant, far-off

remover {47} *vt* **1 :** to stir **2 :** to move around, to turn over **3 :** to stir up **4 :** to remove **5 :** to dismiss

remozamiento *nm* **:** renovation

remozar {21} *vt* **1 :** to renew, to brighten up **2 :** to redo, to renovate

remuneración *nf, pl* **-ciones :** remuneration, pay

remunerar *vt* **:** to pay, to remunerate

remunerativo, -va *adj* **:** remunerative

renacer {48} *vi* **:** to be reborn, to revive

renacimiento *nm* **1 :** rebirth, revival **2 el Renacimiento :** the Renaissance

renacuajo *nm* **:** tadpole, pollywog

renal *adj* **:** renal, kidney

rencilla *nf* **:** quarrel

renco, -ca *adj* **:** lame

rencor *nm* **1 :** rancor, enmity, hostility **2 guardar rencor :** to hold a grudge

rencoroso, -sa *adj* **:** resentful, rancorous

rendición *nf, pl* **-ciones 1 :** surrender, submission **2 :** yield, return

rendido, -da *adj* **1 :** submissive **2 :** worn-out, exhausted **3 :** devoted

rendija *nf* GRIETA **:** crack, split

rendimiento *nm* **1 :** performance **2 :** yield

rendir {54} *vt* **1 :** to render, to give <rendir las gracias : to give thanks> <rendir homenaje a : to pay homage to> **2 :** to yield **3** CANSAR **:** to exhaust — *vi* **1** CUNDIR **:** to progress, to make headway **2 :** to last, to go a long way — **rendirse** *vr* **:** to surrender, to give up

renegado, -da *n* **:** renegade

renegar {49} *vi* **1 ~ de :** to renounce, to disown, to give up **2 ~ de :** to complain about — *vt* **1 :** to deny vigorously **2 :** to abhor, to hate

renegociar *vt* **:** to renegotiate — **renegociación** *nf*

renglón *nm, pl* **renglones 1 :** line (of writing) **2 :** merchandise, line (of products)

rengo, -ga *adj* **:** lame

renguear *vi* **:** to limp

reno *nm* **:** reindeer

renombrado, -da *adj* **:** renowned, famous

renombre *nm* NOMBRADÍA **:** renown, fame

renovable *adj* **:** renewable

renovación *nf, pl* **-ciones 1 :** renewal <renovación de un contrato : renewal of a contract> **2 :** change, renovation

renovar {19} *vt* **1 :** to renew, to restore **2 :** to renovate

renquear *vi* **:** to limp, to hobble

renquera *nf* COJERA **:** limp, lameness

renta *nf* **1 :** income **2 :** rent **3 impuesto sobre la renta :** income tax

rentable *adj* **:** profitable

rentar *vt* **1 :** to produce, to yield **2** ALQUILAR **:** to rent

renuencia *nf* **:** reluctance, unwillingness

renuente *adj* **:** reluctant, unwilling

renuncia *nf* **1 :** resignation **2 :** renunciation **3 :** waiver

renunciar *vi* **1 :** to resign **2 ~ a :** to renounce, to relinquish <renunció al título : he relinquished the title>

reñido, -da *adj* **1 :** tough, hard-fought **2 :** at odds, on bad terms

reñir {67} *vi* **1 :** to argue **2 ~ con :** to fall out with, to go up against — *vt* **:** to scold, to reprimand

reo, rea *n* **1 :** accused, defendant **2 :** offender, culprit

reojo *nm* **de ~ :** out of the corner of one's eye <una mirada de reojo : a sidelong glance>

reorganizar {21} *vt* **:** to reorganize — **reorganización** *nf*

repantigarse {52} *vr* **:** to slouch, to loll about

reparación *nf, pl* **-ciones 1 :** reparation, amends **2 :** repair

reparar *vt* **1 :** to repair, to fix, to mend **2 :** to make amends for **3 :** to correct **4 :** to restore, to refresh — *vi* **1 ~ en :** to observe, to take notice of **2 ~ en :** to consider, to think about

reparo *nm* **1 :** repair, restoration **2 :** reservation, qualm <no tuvieron reparos en decírmelo : they didn't hesitate to tell me> **3 poner reparos a :** to find fault with, to object to

repartición *nf, pl* **-ciones 1 :** distribution **2 :** department, division

repartidor[1], -dora *adj* **:** delivery <camión repartidor : delivery truck>

repartidor[2], -dora *n* **:** delivery person, distributor

repartimiento *nm* → **repartición**

repartir *vt* **1 :** to allocate **2** DISTRIBUIR **:** to distribute, to hand out **3 :** to spread

reparto *nm* **1 :** allocation **2 :** distribution **3 :** cast (of characters)

repasar *vt* **1 :** to pass by again **2 :** to review, to go over **3 :** to mend

repaso *nm* **1 :** review **2 :** mending **3 :** checkup, overhaul

repatriar {85} *vt* **:** to repatriate — **repatriación** *nf*

repavimentar *vt* **:** to resurface

repelente[1] *adj* **:** repellent, repulsive

repelente[2] *nm* : repellent <repelente de insectos : insect repellent>

repeler *vt* **1** : to repel, to resist, to repulse **2** : to reject **3** : to disgust <el sabor me repele : I find the taste repulsive>

repensar {55} *v* : to rethink, to reconsider

repente *nm* **1** : sudden movement, start <de repente : suddenly> **2** : fit, outburst <un repente de ira : a fit of anger>

repentino, -na *adj* : sudden — **repentinamente** *adv*

repercusión *nf, pl* **-siones** : repercussion

repercutir *vi* **1** : to reverberate, to echo **2 ~ en** : to have effects on, to have repercussions on

repertorio *nm* : repertoire

repetición *nf, pl* **-ciones 1** : repetition **2** : rerun, repeat

repetidamente *adv* : repeatedly

repetido, -da *adj* **1** : repeated, numerous **2 repetidas veces** : repeatedly, time and again

repetir {54} *vt* **1** : to repeat **2** : to have a second helping of — **repetirse** *vr* **1** : to repeat oneself **2** : to recur

repetitivo, -va *adj* : repetitive, repetitious

repicar {72} *vt* : to ring — *vi* : to ring out, to peal

repique *nm* : ringing, pealing

repisa *nf* : shelf, ledge <repisa de chimenea : mantelpiece> <repisa de ventana : windowsill>

replantear *vt* : to redefine, to restate — **replantearse** *vr* : to reconsider

replegar {49} *vt* : to fold — **replegarse** *vr* RETIRARSE : to retreat, to withdraw

repleto, -ta *adj* **1** : replete, full **2 ~ de** : packed with, crammed with

réplica *nf* **1** : reply **2** : replica, reproduction **3** *Chile, Mex* : aftershock

replicación *nf, pl* **-ciones** : replication

replicar {72} *vi* **1** : to reply, to retort **2** : to argue, to answer back

repliegue *nm* **1** : fold **2** : retreat, withdrawal

repollo *nm* COL : cabbage

reponer {60} *vt* **1** : to replace, to put back **2** : to reinstate **3** : to reply — **reponerse** *vr* : to recover

reportaje *nm* : article, story, report

reportar *vt* **1** : to check, to restrain **2** : to bring, to carry, to yield <me reportó numerosos beneficios : it brought me many benefits> **3** : to report — **reportarse** *vr* **1** CONTENERSE : to control oneself **2** PRESENTARSE : to report, to show up

reporte *nm* : report

reportear *vt* : to report on, to cover

reportero, -ra *n* **1** : reporter **2 reportero gráfico** : photojournalist

reposado, -da *adj* : calm

reposar *vi* **1** : to rest, to repose **2** : to stand, to settle <deje reposar la masa media hora : let the dough stand for half an hour> **3** : to lie, to be buried — **reposarse** *vr* : to settle

reposición *nf, pl* **-ciones 1** : replacement **2** : reinstatement **3** : revival

repositorio *nm* : repository

reposo *nm* : repose, rest

repostar *vi* **1** : to stock up **2** : to refuel

repostería *nf* **1** : confectioner's shop **2** : pastry-making

repostero, -ra *n* : confectioner

repreguntar *vt* : to cross-examine

repreguntas *nfpl* : cross-examination

reprender *vt* : to reprimand, to scold

reprensible *adj* : reprehensible

represa *nf* : dam

represalia *nf* **1** : reprisal, retaliation **2 tomar represalias** : to retaliate

represar *vt* : to dam

representación *nf, pl* **-ciones 1** : representation **2** : performance **3 en representación de** : on behalf of

representante *nmf* **1** : representative **2** : performer

representar *vt* **1** : to represent, to act for **2** : to perform **3** : to look, to appear as **4** : to symbolize, to stand for **5** : to signify, to mean — **representarse** *vr* : to imagine, to picture

representativo, -va *adj* : representative

represión *nf, pl* **-siones** : repression

represivo, -va *adj* : repressive

reprimenda *nf* : reprimand

reprimir *vt* **1** : to repress **2** : to suppress, to stifle

reprobable *adj* : reprehensible, culpable

reprobación *nf* : disapproval

reprobar {19} *vt* **1** DESAPROBAR : to condemn, to disapprove of **2** : to fail (a course)

reprobatorio, -ria *adj* : disapproving, admonitory

reprochar *vt* : to reproach — **reprocharse** *vr*

reproche *nm* : reproach

reproducción *nf, pl* **-ciones** : reproduction

reproducir {61} *vt* : to reproduce — **reproducirse** *vr* **1** : to breed, to reproduce **2** : to recur

reproductor, -tora *adj* : reproductive

reptar *vi* : to crawl, to slither

reptil[1] *adj* : reptilian

reptil[2] *nm* : reptile

república *nf* : republic

republicanismo *nm* : republicanism

republicano, -na *adj & n* : republican

repudiar *vt* : to repudiate — **repudiación** *nf*

repudio *nm* : repudiation

repuesto[1] *pp* → **reponer**

repuesto[2] *nm* **1** : spare part **2 de ~** : spare <rueda de repuesto : spare wheel>

repugnancia *nf* : repugnance

repugnante *adj* : repulsive, repugnant, revolting
repugnar *vt* : to cause repugnance, to disgust — **repugnarse** *vr*
repujar *vt* : to emboss
repulsivo, -va *adj* : repulsive
repuntar *vt Arg, Chile* : to round up (cattle) — *vi* : to begin to appear — **repuntarse** *vr* : to fall out, to quarrel
repuso, etc. → **reponer**
reputación *nf, pl* **-ciones** : reputation
reputar *vt* : to consider, to deem
requerir {76} *vt* **1** : to require, to call for **2** : to summon, to send for
requesón *nm, pl* **-sones** : curd cheese, cottage cheese
réquiem *nm* : requiem
requisa *nf* **1** : requisition **2** : seizure **3** : inspection
requisar *vt* **1** : to requisition **2** : to seize **3** INSPECCIONAR : to inspect
requisito *nm* **1** : requirement **2 requisito previo** : prerequisite
res *nf* **1** : beast, animal **2** *CA, Mex* : beef **3 reses** *nfpl* : cattle <60 reses : 60 head of cattle>
resabio *nm* **1** VICIO : bad habit, vice **2** DEJO : aftertaste
resaca *nf* **1** : undertow **2** : hangover
resaltar *vi* **1** SOBRESALIR : to stand out **2 hacer resaltar** : to bring out, to highlight — *vt* : to stress, to emphasize
resarcimiento *nm* **1** : compensation **2** : reimbursement
resarcir {83} *vt* : to compensate, to indemnify — **resarcirse** *vr* **~ de** : to make up for
resbaladizo, -za *adj* **1** RESBALOSO : slippery **2** : tricky, ticklish, delicate
resbalar *vi* **1** : to slip, to slide **2** : to slip up, to make a mistake **3** : to skid — **resbalarse** *vr*
resbalón *nm, pl* **-lones** : slip
resbaloso, -sa *adj* : slippery
rescatar *vt* **1** : to rescue, to save **2** : to recover, to get back
rescate *nm* **1** : rescue **2** : recovery **3** : ransom
rescindir *vt* : to rescind, to annul, to cancel
rescisión *nf, pl* **-siones** : annulment, cancelation
rescoldo *nm* : embers *pl*
resecar {72} *vt* : to make dry, to dry up — **resecarse** *vr* : to dry up
reseco, -ca *adj* : dry, dried-up
resentido, -da *adj* : resentful
resentimiento *nm* : resentment
resentirse {76} *vr* **1** : to suffer, to be weakened **2** OFENDERSE : to be upset <se resintió porque la insultaron : she got upset when they insulted her, she resented being insulted> **3 ~ de** : to feel the effects of
reseña *nf* **1** : report, summary, review **2** : description
reseñar *vt* **1** : to review **2** DESCRIBIR : to describe
reserva *nf* **1** : reservation **2** : reserve **3** : confidence, privacy <con la mayor reserva : in strictest confidence> **4 de ~** : spare, in reserve **5 reservas** *nfpl* : reservations, doubts
reservación *nf, pl* **-ciones** : reservation
reservado, -da *adj* **1** : reserved, reticent **2** : confidential
reservar *vt* : to reserve — **reservarse** *vr* **1** : to save oneself **2** : to conceal, to keep to oneself
reservorio *nm* : reservoir, reserve
resfriado *nm* CATARRO : cold
resfriar {85} *vt* : to cool — **resfriarse** *vr* **1** : to cool off **2** : to catch a cold
resfrío *nm* : cold
resguardar *vt* : to safeguard, to protect — **resguardarse** *vr*
resguardo *nm* **1** : safeguard, protection **2** : receipt, voucher **3** : border guard, coast guard
residencia *nf* **1** : residence **2** : boarding house
residencial *adj* : residential
residente *adj & nmf* : resident
residir *vi* **1** VIVIR : to reside, to dwell **2 ~ en** : to lie in, to consist of
residual *adj* : residual
residuo *nm* **1** : residue **2** : remainder **3 residuos** *nmpl* : waste <residuos nucleares : nuclear waste>
resignación *nf, pl* **-ciones** : resignation
resignar *vt* : to resign — **resignarse** *vr* **~ a** : to resign oneself to
resina *nf* **1** : resin **2 resina epoxídica** : epoxy
resistencia *nf* **1** : resistance **2** AGUANTE : endurance, strength, stamina
resistente *adj* **1** : resistant **2** : strong, tough
resistir *vt* **1** : to stand, to bear, to tolerate **2** : to withstand — *vi* : to resist <resistió hasta el último minuto : he held out until the last minute> — **resistirse** *vr* **~ a** : to be resistent to, to be reluctant
resollar {19} *vi* : to breathe heavily, to wheeze
resolución *nf, pl* **-ciones 1** : resolution, settlement **2** : decision **3** : determination, resolve
resolver {89} *vt* **1** : to resolve, to settle **2** : to decide — **resolverse** *vr* : to make up one's mind
resonancia *nf* **1** : resonance **2** : impact, repercussions *pl*
resonante *adj* **1** : resonant **2** : tremendous, resounding <un éxito resonante : a resounding success>
resonar {19} *vi* : to resound, to ring
resoplar *vi* **1** : to puff, to pant **2** : to snort
resoplo *nm* **1** : puffing, panting **2** : snort
resorte *nm* **1** MUELLE : spring **2** : elasticity **3** : influence, means *pl* <tocar resortes : to pull strings>
resortera *nf Mex* : slingshot

respaldar *vt* : to back, to support, to endorse — **respaldarse** *vr* : to lean back

respaldo *nm* **1** : back (of an object) **2** : support, backing

respectar *vt* : to concern, to relate to <por lo que a mí respecta : as far as I'm concerned>

respectivo, -va *adj* : respective — **respectivamente** *adv*

respecto *nm* **1 ~ a** : in regard to, concerning **2 al respecto** : on this matter, in this respect

respetable *adj* : respectable — **respetabilidad** *nf*

respetar *vt* : to respect

respeto *nm* **1** : respect, consideration **2 respetos** *nmpl* : respects <presentar sus respetos : to pay one's respects>

respetuosidad *nf* : respectfulness

respetuoso, -sa *adj* : respectful — **respetuosamente** *adv*

respingo *nm* : start, jump

respiración *nf, pl* **-ciones** : respiration, breathing

respiradero *nm* : vent, ventilation shaft

respirador *nm* : respirator

respirar *v* : to breathe

respiratorio, -ria *adj* : respiratory

respiro *nm* **1** : breath **2** : respite, break

resplandecer {53} *vi* **1** : to shine **2** : to stand out

resplandeciente *adj* **1** : resplendent, shining **2** : radiant

resplandor *nm* **1** : brightness, brilliance, radiance **2** : flash

responder *vt* : to answer — *vi* **1** : to answer, to reply, to respond **2 ~ a** : to respond to <responder al tratamiento : to respond to treatment> **3 ~ de** : to answer for, to vouch for (something) **4 ~ por** : to vouch for (someone)

responsabilidad *nf* : responsibility

responsable *adj* : responsible — **responsablemente** *adv*

respuesta *nf* : answer, response

resquebrajar *vt* : to split, to crack — **resquebrajarse** *vr*

resquemor *nm* : resentment, bitterness

resquicio *nm* **1** : crack **2** : opportunity, chance **3** : trace <sin un resquicio de remordimiento : without a trace of remorse> **4 resquicio legal** : loophole

resta *nf* SUSTRACCIÓN : subtraction

restablecer {53} *vt* : to reestablish, to restore — **restablecerse** *vr* : to recover

restablecimiento *nm* **1** : reestablishment, restoration **2** : recovery

restallar *vi* : to crack, to crackle, to click

restallido *nm* : crack, crackle

restante *adj* **1** : remaining **2 lo restante, los restantes** : the rest

restañar *vt* : to stanch

restar *vt* **1** : to deduct, to subtract <restar un punto : to deduct a point> **2** : to minimize, to play down — *vi* : to remain, to be left

restauración *nf, pl* **-ciones** **1** : restoration **2** : catering, food service

restaurante *nm* : restaurant

restaurar *vt* : to restore

restitución *nf, pl* **-ciones** : restitution, return

restituir {41} *vt* : to return, to restore, to reinstate

resto *nm* **1** : rest, remainder **2 restos** *nmpl* : remains <restos de comida : leftovers> <restos arqueológicos : archeological ruins> **3 restos mortales** : mortal remains

restorán *nm, pl* **-ranes** : restaurant

restregadura *nf* : scrub, scrubbing

restregar {49} *vt* **1** : to rub **2** : to scrub — **restregarse** *vr*

restricción *nf, pl* **-ciones** : restriction, limitation

restrictivo, -va *adj* : restrictive

restringido, -da *adj* LIMITADO : limited, restricted

restringir {35} *vt* LIMITAR : to restrict, to limit

restructuración *nf* : restructuring

restructurar *vt* : to restructure

resucitación *nf* : resuscitation <resucitación cardiopulmonar : CPR, cardiopulmonary resuscitation>

resucitar *vt* **1** : to resuscitate, to revive, to resurrect **2** : to revitalize

resuello *nm* **1** : puffing, heavy breathing, wheezing **2** : break, breather

resuelto[1] *pp* → **resolver**

resuelto[2], **-ta** *adj* : determined, resolved, resolute

resulta *nf* **1** : consequence, result **2 a resultas de** *or* **de resultas de** : as a result of

resultado *nm* : result, outcome

resultante *adj & nf* : resultant

resultar *vi* **1** : to work, to work out <mi idea no resultó : my idea didn't work out> **2** : to prove, to turn out to be <resultó bien simpático : he turned out to be very nice> **3 ~ en** : to lead to, to result in **4 ~ de** : to be the result of

resumen *nm, pl* **-súmenes** **1** : summary, summation **2 en ~** : in summary, in short

resumidero *nm* : drain

resumir *v* : to summarize, to sum up

resurgimiento *nm* : resurgence

resurgir {35} *vi* : to reappear, to revive

resurrección *nf, pl* **-ciones** : resurrection

retablo *nm* **1** : tableau **2** : altarpiece

retador, -dora *n* : challenger (in sports)

retaguardia *nf* : rear guard

retahíla *nf* : string, series <una retahíla de insultos : a volley of insults>

retaliación *nf, pl* **-ciones** : retaliation

retama *nf* : broom (plant)

retar *vt* DESAFIAR : to challenge, to defy

retardante *adj* : retardant

retardar *vt* **1** RETRASAR **:** to delay, to retard **2 :** to postpone
retazo *nm* **1 :** remnant, scrap **2 :** fragment, piece <retazos de su obra : bits and pieces from his writings>
retención *nf, pl* **-ciones 1 :** retention **2 :** deduction, withholding
retener {80} *vt* **1 :** to retain, to keep **2 :** to withhold **3 :** to detain
retentivo, -va *adj* **:** retentive
reticencia *nf* **1 :** reluctance, reticence **2 :** insinuation
reticente *adj* **1 :** reluctant, reticent **2 :** insinuating, misleading
retina *nf* **:** retina
retintín *nm, pl* **-tines 1 :** jingle, jangle **2 con ~ :** sarcastically
retirada *nf* **1 :** retreat <batirse en retirada : to withdraw, to beat a retreat> **2 :** withdrawl (of funds) **3 :** retirement **4 :** refuge, haven
retirado, -da *adj* **1 :** remote, distant, far off **2 :** secluded, quiet
retirar *vt* **1 :** to remove, to take away, to recall **2 :** to withdraw, to take out — **retirarse** *vr* **1** REPLEGARSE **:** to retreat, to withdraw **2** JUBILARSE **:** to retire
retiro *nm* **1** JUBILACIÓN **:** retirement **2 :** withdrawal, retreat **3 :** seclusion
reto *nm* DESAFÍO **:** challenge, dare
retocar {72} *vt* **:** to touch up
retoñar *vi* **:** to sprout
retoño *nm* **:** sprout, shoot
retoque *nm* **:** retouching
retorcer {14} *vt* **1 :** to twist **2 :** to wring — **retorcerse** *vr* **1 :** to get twisted, to get tangled up **2 :** to squirm, to writhe, to wiggle about
retorcijón *nm, pl* **-jones :** cramp, sharp pain
retorcimiento *nm* **1 :** twisting, wringing **2 :** deviousness
retórica *nf* **:** rhetoric
retórico, -ca *adj* **:** rhetorical — **retóricamente** *adv*
retornar *v* **:** to return
retorno *nm* **:** return
retozar {21} *vi* **:** to frolic, to romp
retozo *nm* **:** frolicking
retozón, -zona *adj, mpl* **-zones :** playful
retracción *nf, pl* **-ciones :** retraction, withdrawal
retractable *adj* **:** retractable
retractación *nf, pl* **-ciones :** retraction (of a statement, etc.)
retractarse *vr* **1 :** to withdraw, to back down **2 ~ de :** to take back, to retract
retraer {81} *vt* **1 :** to bring back **2 :** to dissuade — **retraerse** *vr* **1** RETIRARSE **:** to withdraw, to retire **2** REFUGIARSE **:** to take refuge
retraído, -da *adj* **:** withdrawn, retiring, shy
retraimiento *nm* **1 :** shyness, timidity **2 :** withdrawal
retrasado, -da *adj* **1 :** retarded, mentally slow **2 :** behind, in arrears **3 :** backward (of a country) **4 :** slow (of a watch)
retrasar *vt* **1** DEMORAR, RETARDAR **:** to delay, to hold up **2 :** to put off, to postpone — **retrasarse** *vr* **1 :** to be late **2 :** to fall behind
retraso *nm* **1** ATRASO **:** delay, lateness **2 retraso mental :** mental retardation
retratar *vt* **1 :** to portray, to depict **2 :** to photograph **3 :** to paint a portrait of
retrato *nm* **1 :** depiction, portrayal **2 :** portrait, photograph
retrete *nm* **:** restroom, toilet
retribución *nf, pl* **-ciones 1 :** pay, payment **2 :** reward
retribuir {41} *vt* **1 :** to pay **2 :** to reward
retroactivo, -va *adj* **:** retroactive — **retroactivamente** *adv*
retroalimentación *nf, pl* **-ciones :** feedback
retroceder *vi* **1 :** to move back, to turn back **2 :** to back off, to back down **3 :** to recoil (of a firearm)
retroceso *nm* **1 :** backward movement **2 :** backing down **3 :** setback, relapse **4 :** recoil
retrógrado, -da *adj* **1 :** reactionary **2 :** retrograde
retropropulsión *nf* **:** jet propulsion
retrospectiva *nf* **:** retrospective, hindsight
retrospectivo, -va *adj* **1 :** retrospective **2 mirada retrospectiva :** backward glance
retrovisor *nm* **:** rearview mirror
retruécano *nm* **:** pun, play on words
retumbar *vi* **1 :** to boom, to thunder **2 :** to resound, to reverberate
retumbo *nm* **:** booming, thundering, roll
retuvo, etc. → **retener**
reubicar {72} *vt* **:** to relocate — **reubicación** *nf*
reuma *or* **reúma** *nmf* → **reumatismo**
reumático, -ca *adj* **:** rheumatic
reumatismo *nm* **:** rheumatism
reunión *nf, pl* **-niones 1 :** meeting **2 :** gathering, reunion
reunir {68} *vt* **1 :** to unite, to join, to bring together **2 :** to have, to possess <reunieron los requisitos necesarios : they fulfilled the necessary requirements> **3 :** to gather, to collect, to raise (funds) — **reunirse** *vr* **:** to meet
reutilizable *adj* **:** reusable
reutilizar {21} *vt* **:** to recycle, to reuse
revalidar *vt* **1 :** to confirm, to ratify **2 :** to defend (a title)
revaluar {3} *vt* **:** to reevaluate — **revaluación** *n*
revancha *nf* **1** DESQUITE **:** revenge, requital **2 :** rematch
revelación *nf, pl* **-ciones :** revelation
revelado *nm* **:** developing (of film)
revelador[1]**, -dora** *adj* **:** revealing
revelador[2] *nm* **:** developer

revelar *vt* **1** : to reveal, to disclose **2** : to develop (film)

revendedor, -dora *n* **1** : scalper **2** DETALLISTA : retailer

revender *vt* **1** : to resell **2** : to scalp

reventa *nf* **1** : resale **2** : scalping

reventar {55} *vi* **1** ESTALLAR, EXPLOTAR : to burst, to blow up **2** **~ de** : to be bursting with — *vt* **1** : to burst **2** *fam* : to annoy, to rile

reventón *nm, pl* **-tones** **1** : burst, bursting **2** : blowout, flat tire **3** *Mex fam* : bash, party

reverberar *vi* : to reverberate — **reverberación** *nf*

reverdecer {53} *vi* **1** : to grow green again **2** : to revive

reverencia *nf* **1** : reverence **2** : bow, curtsy

reverenciar *vt* : to revere, to venerate

reverendo[1], -da *adj* **1** : reverend **2** *fam* : total, absolute <es un reverendo imbécil : he is a complete idiot>

reverendo[2], -da *n* : reverend

reverente *adj* : reverent

reversa *nf Col, Mex* : reverse (gear)

reversible *adj* : reversible

reversión *nf, pl* **-siones** : reversion

reverso *nm* **1** : back, other side **2** **el reverso de la medalla** : the complete opposite

revertir {76} *vi* **1** : to revert, to go back **2** **~ en** : to result in, to end up as

revés *nm, pl* **reveses** **1** : back, wrong side **2** : setback, reversal **3** : backhand (in sports) **4** **al revés** : the other way around, upside down, inside out **5** **al revés de** : contrary to

revestimiento *nm* : covering, facing (of a building)

revestir {54} *vt* **1** : to coat, to cover, to surface **2** : to conceal, to disguise **3** : to take on, to assume <la reunión revistió gravedad : the meeting took on a serious note>

revisar *vt* **1** : to examine, to inspect, to check **2** : to check over, to overhaul (machinery) **3** : to revise

revisión *nf, pl* **-siones** **1** : revision **2** : inspection, check

revisor, -sora *n* **1** : inspector **2** : conductor (on a train)

revista *nf* **1** : magazine, journal **2** : revue **3** **pasar revista** : to review, to inspect

revistar *vt* : to review, to inspect

revitalizar {21} *vt* : to revitalize — **revitalización** *nf*

revivir *vi* : to revive, to come alive again — *vt* : to relive

revocación *nf, pl* **-ciones** : revocation, repeal

revocar {72} *vt* **1** : to revoke, to repeal **2** : to plaster (a wall)

revolcar {82} *vt* : to knock over, to knock down — **revolcarse** *vr* : to roll around, to wallow

revolcón *nm, pl* **-cones** *fam* : tumble, fall

revolotear *vi* : to flutter around, to flit

revoloteo *nm* : fluttering, flitting

revoltijo *nm* **1** FÁRRAGO : mess, jumble **2** *Mex* : traditional seafood dish

revoltoso, -sa *adj* : unruly, rebellious

revolución *nf, pl* **-ciones** : revolution

revolucionar *vt* : to revolutionize

revolucionario, -ria *adj & n* : revolutionary

revolver {89} *vt* **1** : to move about, to mix, to shake, to stir **2** : to upset (one's stomach) **3** : to mess up, to rummage through <revolver la casa : to turn the house upside down> — **revolverse** *vr* **1** : to toss and turn **2** VOLVERSE : to turn around

revólver *nm* : revolver

revoque *nm* : plaster

revuelo *nm* **1** : fluttering **2** : commotion, stir

revuelta *nf* : uprising, revolt

revuelto[1] *pp* → **revolver**

revuelto[2], -ta *adj* **1** : choppy, rough <mar revuelto : rough sea> **2** : untidy **3** **huevos revueltos** : scrambled eggs

rey *nm* : king

reyerta *nf* : brawl, fight

rezagado, -da *n* : straggler, latecomer

rezagar {52} *vt* **1** : to leave behind **2** : to postpone — **rezagarse** *vr* : to fall behind, to lag

rezar {21} *vi* **1** : to pray **2** : to say <como reza el refrán : as the saying goes> **3** **~ con** : to concern, to have to do with — *vt* : to say, to recite <rezar un Ave María : to say a Hail Mary>

rezo *nm* : prayer, praying

rezongar {52} *vi* : to gripe, to grumble

rezumar *v* : to ooze, to leak

ría[1], etc. → **reír**

ría[2] *nf* : estuary

riachuelo *nm* ARROYO : brook, stream

riada *nf* : flood

ribera *nf* : bank, shore

ribete *nm* **1** : border, trim **2** : frill, adornment **3** **ribetes** *nmpl* : hint, touch <tiene sus ribetes de genio : there's a touch of genius in him>

ribetear *vt* : to border, to edge, to trim

ricamente *adv* : richly, splendidly

rice, etc. → **rizar**

rico[1], -ca *adj* **1** : rich, wealthy **2** : fertile **3** : luxurious, valuable **4** : delicious **5** : adorable, lovely **6** : great, wonderful

rico[2], -ca *n* : rich person

ridiculez *nf, pl* **-leces** : ridiculousness, absurdity

ridiculizar {21} *vt* : to ridicule

ridículo[1], -la *adj* ABSURDO, DISPARATADO : ridiculous, ludicrous — **ridículamente** *adv*

ridículo[2], -la *n* **1** **hacer el ridículo** : to make a fool of oneself **2** **poner en ridículo** : to ridicule

ríe, etc. → **reír**

riega, riegue, etc. → **regar**

riego *nm* : irrigation

riel *nm* : rail, track
rienda *nf* **1** : rein **2 dar rienda suelta a** : to give free rein to **3 llevar las riendas** : to be in charge **4 tomar las riendas** : to take control
riesgo *nm* : risk
riesgoso, -sa *adj* : risky
rifa *nf* : raffle
rifar *vt* : to raffle — *vi* : to quarrel, to fight
rifle *nm* : rifle
rige, rija, etc. → **regir**
rigidez *nf, pl* **-deces 1** : rigidity, stiffness <rigidez cadavérica : rigor mortis> **2** : inflexibility
rígido, -da *adj* **1** : rigid, stiff **2** : strict — **rígidamente** *adv*
rigor *nm* **1** : rigor, harshness **2** : precision, meticulousness **3 de ~** : usual <la respuesta de rigor : the standard reply> **4 de ~** : essential, obligatory **5 en ~** : strictly speaking, in reality
riguroso, -sa *adj* : rigorous — **rigurosamente** *adv*
rima *nf* **1** : rhyme **2 rimas** *nfpl* : verse, poetry
rimar *vi* : to rhyme
rimbombante *adj* **1** : grandiose, showy **2** : bombastic, pompous
rímel *or* **rimel** *nm* : mascara
rin *nm Col, Mex* : wheel, rim (of a tire)
rincón *nm, pl* **rincones** : corner, nook
rinde, etc. → **rendir**
rinoceronte *nm* : rhinoceros
riña *nf* **1** : fight, brawl **2** : dispute, quarrel
riñe, etc. → **reñir**
riñón *nm, pl* **riñones** : kidney
río[1] → **reír**
río[2] *nm* **1** : river **2** : torrent, stream <un río de lágrimas : a flood of tears>
ripio *nm* **1** : debris, rubble **2** : gravel
riqueza *nf* **1** : wealth, riches *pl* **2** : richness **3 riquezas naturales** : natural resources
risa *nf* **1** : laughter, laugh **2 dar risa** : to make laugh <me dio mucha risa : I found it very funny> **3** *fam* **morirse de la risa** : to die laughing, to crack up
risco *nm* : crag, cliff
risible *adj* IRRISORIO : ludicrous, laughable
risita *nf* : giggle, titter, snicker
risotada *nf* : guffaw
ristra *nf* : string, series *pl*
risueño, -ña *adj* **1** : cheerful, pleasant **2** : promising
rítmico, -ca *adj* : rhythmical, rhythmic — **rítmicamente** *adv*
ritmo *nm* **1** : rhythm **2** : pace, tempo <trabajó a ritmo lento : she worked at a slow pace>
rito *nm* : rite, ritual
ritual *adj & nm* : ritual — **ritualmente** *adv*
rival *adj & nmf* COMPETIDOR : rival
rivalidad *nf* : rivalry, competition
rivalizar {21} *vi* **~ con** : to rival, to compete with
rizado, -da *adj* **1** : curly **2** : ridged **3** : ripply, undulating
rizar {21} *vt* **1** : to curl **2** : to ripple, to ruffle (a surface) **3** : to crumple, to fold — **rizarse** *vr* **1** : to frizz **2** : to ripple
rizo *nm* **1** : curl **2** : loop (in aviation)
robalo *or* **róbalo** *nm* : sea bass
robar *vt* **1** : to steal **2** : to rob, to burglarize **3** SECUESTRAR : to abduct, to kidnap **4** : to captivate — *vi* **~ en** : to break into
roble *nm* : oak
robo *nm* : robbery, theft
robot *nm, pl* **robots** : robot
robótica *nf* : robotics
robustecer {53} *vt* : to grow stronger, to strengthen
robustez *nf* : sturdiness, robustness
robusto, -ta *adj* : robust, sturdy
roca *nf* : rock, boulder
roce[1], **etc.** → **rozar**
roce[2] *nm* **1** : rubbing, chafing **2** : brush, graze, touch **3** : close contact, familiarity **4** : friction, disagreement
rociador *nm* : sprinkler
rociar {85} *vt* : to spray, to sprinkle
rocío *nm* **1** : dew **2** : shower, light rain
rocola *nf* : jukebox
rocoso, -sa *adj* : rocky
rodada *nf* : track (of a tire), rut
rodado, -da *adj* **1** : wheeled **2** : dappled (of a horse)
rodaja *nf* : round, slice
rodaje *nm* **1** : filming, shooting **2** : breaking in (of a vehicle)
rodamiento *nm* **1** : bearing <rodamiento de bolas : ball bearings> **2** : rolling
rodar {19} *vi* **1** : to roll, to roll down, to roll along <rodé por la escalera : I tumbled down the stairs> <todo rodaba bien : everthing was going along well> **2** GIRAR : to turn, to go around **3** : to move about, to travel <andábamos rodando por todas partes : we drifted along from place to place> — *vt* **1** : to film, to shoot **2** : to break in (a new vehicle)
rodear *vt* **1** : to surround **2** : to round up (cattle) — *vi* **1** : to go around **2** : to beat around the bush — **rodearse** *vr* **~ de** : to surround oneself with
rodeo *nm* **1** : rodeo, roundup **2** DESVÍO : detour **3** : evasion <andar con rodeos : to beat around the bush> <sin rodeos : without reservations>
rodilla *nf* : knee
rodillo *nm* **1** : roller **2** : rolling pin
rododendro *nm* : rhododendron
roedor[1], **-dora** *adj* : gnawing
roedor[2] *nm* : rodent
roer {69} *vt* **1** : to gnaw **2** : to eat away at, to torment
rogar {16} *vt* : to beg, to request — *vi* **1** : to beg, to plead **2** : to pray
rojez *nf* : redness

roiga, etc. → **roer**

rojizo, -za *adj* : reddish

rojo[1], **-ja** *adj* **1** : red **2 ponerse rojo** : to blush

rojo[2] *nm* : red

rol *nm* **1** : role **2** : list, roll

rollo *nm* **1** : roll, coil <un rollo de cinta : a roll of tape> <en rollo : rolled up> **2** *fam* : roll of fat **3** *fam* : boring speech, lecture

romance *nm* **1** : Romance language **2** : ballad **3** : romance **4 en buen romance** : simply stated, simply put

romano, -na *adj & n* : Roman

romanticismo *nm* : romanticism

romántico, -ca *adj* : romantic — **románticamente** *adv*

rombo *nm* : rhombus

romería *nf* **1** : pilgrimage, procession **2** : crowd, gathering

romero[1], **-ra** *n* PEREGRINO : pilgrim

romero[2] *nm* : rosemary

romo, -ma *adj* : blunt, dull

rompecabezas *nms & pl* : puzzle, riddle

rompehielos *nms & pl* : icebreaker (ship)

rompehuelgas *nmfs & pl* ESQUIROL : strikebreaker, scab

rompenueces *nms & pl* : nutcracker

rompeolas *ns & pl* : breakwater, jetty

romper {70} *vt* **1** : to break, to smash **2** : to rip, to tear **3** : to break off (relations), to break (a contract) **4** : to break through, to break down **5** GASTAR : to wear out — *vi* **1** : to break <al romper del día : at the break of day> **2 ~ a** : to begin to, to burst out with <romper a llorar : to burst into tears> **3 ~ con** : to break off with

rompope *nm CA, Mex* : drink similar to eggnog

ron *nm* : rum

roncar {72} *vi* **1** : to snore **2** : to roar

ronco, -ca *adj* **1** : hoarse **2** : husky (of the voice) — **roncamente** *adv*

ronda *nf* **1** : beat, patrol **2** : round (of drinks, of negotiations, of a game)

rondar *vt* **1** : to patrol **2** : to hang around <siempre está rondando la calle : he's always hanging around the street> **3** : to be approximately <debe rondar los cincuenta : he must be about 50> — *vi* **1** : to be on patrol **2** : to prowl around, to roam about

ronque, etc. → **roncar**

ronquera *nf* : hoarseness

ronquido *nm* **1** : snore **2** : roar

ronronear *vi* : to purr

ronroneo *nm* : purr, purring

ronzal *nm* : halter (for an animal)

ronzar {21} *v* : to munch, to crunch

roña *nf* **1** : mange **2** : dirt, filth **3** *fam* : stinginess

roñoso, -sa *adj* **1** : mangy **2** : dirty **3** *fam* : stingy

ropa *nf* **1** : clothes *pl,* clothing **2 ropa interior** : underwear

ropaje *nm* : apparel, garments *pl,* regalia

ropero *nm* ARMARIO, CLÓSET : wardrobe, closet

rosa[1] *adj* : rose-colored, pink

rosa[2] *nm* : rose, pink (color)

rosa[3] *nf* : rose (flower)

rosáceo, -cea *adj* : pinkish

rosado[1], **-da** *adj* **1** : pink **2 vino rosado** : rosé

rosado[2] *nm* : pink (color)

rosal *nm* : rosebush

rosario *nm* **1** : rosary **2** : series <un rosario de islas : a string of islands>

rosbif *nm* : roast beef

rosca *nf* **1** : thread (of a screw) <una tapa a rosca : a screw top> **2** : ring, coil

roseta *nf* : rosette

rosquilla *nf* : ring-shaped pastry, doughnut

rostro *nm* : face, countenance

rotación *nf, pl* **-ciones** : rotation

rotar *vt* : to rotate, to turn — *vi* : to turn, to spin

rotativo[1], **-va** *adj* : rotary

rotativo[2] *nm* : newspaper

rotatorio, -ria → **rotativo**[1]

roto[1] *pp* → **romper**

roto[2], **-ta** *adj* **1** : broken **2** : ripped, torn

rotonda *nf* **1** : traffic circle, rotary **2** : rotunda

rotor *nm* : rotor

rótula *nf* : kneecap

rotular *vt* **1** : to head, to entitle **2** : to label

rótulo *nm* **1** : heading, title **2** : label, sign

rotundo, -da *adj* **1** REDONDO : round **2** : categorical, absolute <un éxito rotundo : a resounding success> — **rotundamente** *adv*

rotura *nf* : break, tear, fracture

roya *nf* : plant rust

roya, etc. → **roer**

rozado, -da *adj* GASTADO : worn

rozadura *nf* **1** : scratch, abrasion **2** : rubbed spot, sore

rozar {21} *vt* **1** : to chafe, to rub against **2** : to border on, to touch on **3** : to graze, to touch lightly — **rozarse** *vr* **~ con** *fam* : to rub shoulders with

ruandés, -desa *adj & n* : Rwandan

ruano, -na *adj* : roan

rubí *nm, pl* **rubíes** : ruby

rubio, -bia *adj & n* : blond

rublo *nm* : ruble

rubor *nm* **1** : flush, blush **2** : rouge, blusher

ruborizarse {21} *vr* : to blush

rubrica *nf* : title, heading

rubricar {72} *vt* **1** : sign with a flourish <firmado y rubricado : signed and sealed> **2** : to endorse, to sanction

rubro *nm* **1** : heading, title **2** : line, area (in business)

rudeza *nf* ASPEREZA : roughness, coarseness

rudimentario, -ria *adj* : rudimentary — **rudimentariamente** *adv*

rudimento *nm* : rudiment, basics *pl*

rudo, -da *adj* **1** : rough, harsh **2** : coarse, unpolished — **rudamente** *adv*

rueda[1], etc. → **rodar**

rueda[2] *nf* **1** : wheel **2** RODAJA : round slice **3** : circle, ring **4 rueda de andar** : treadmill **5 rueda de prensa** : press conference **6 ir sobre ruedas** : to go smoothly

ruedita *nf* : caster (on furniture)

ruedo *nm* **1** : bullring, arena **2** : rotation, turn **3** : hem

ruega, ruegue, etc. → **rogar**

ruego *nm* : request, appeal, plea

rugido *nm* : roar

rugir {35} *vi* : to roar

ruibarbo *nm* : rhubarb

ruido *nm* : noise, sound

ruidoso, -sa *adj* : loud, noisy — **ruidosamente** *adv*

ruin *adj* **1** : base, despicable **2** : mean, stingy

ruina *nf* **1** : ruin, destruction **2** : downfall, collapse **3 ruinas** *nfpl* : ruins, remains

ruinoso, -sa *adj* **1** : run-down, dilapidated **2** : ruinous, disasterous

ruiseñor *nm* : nightingale

ruja, etc. → **rugir**

ruleta *nf* : roulette

rulo *nm* : curler, roller

rumano, -na *n* : Romanian, Rumanian

rumbo *nm* **1** : direction, course <con rumbo a : bound for, heading for> <perder el rumbo : to go off course, to lose one's bearings> <sin rumbo : aimless, aimlessly> **2** : ostentation, pomp **3** : lavishness, generosity

rumiante *adj & nm* : ruminant

rumiar *vt* : to ponder, to mull over — *vi* **1** : to chew the cud **2** : to ruminate, to ponder

rumor *nm* **1** : rumor **2** : murmur

rumorearse *or* **rumorarse** *vr* : to be rumored <se rumorea que se va : rumor has it that she's leaving>

rumoroso, -sa *adj* : murmuring, babbling <un arroyo rumoroso : a babbling brook>

rupia *nf* : rupee

ruptura *nf* **1** : break **2** : breaking, breach (of a contract) **3** : breaking off, breakup

rural *adj* : rural

ruso[1], -sa *adj & n* : Russian

ruso[2] *nm* : Russian (language)

rústico[1], -ca *adj* : rural, rustic

rústico[2], -ca *n* : rustic, country dweller

ruta *nf* : route

rutina *nf* : routine, habit

rutinario, -ria *adj* : routine, ordinary <visita rutinaria : routine visit> — **rutinariamente** *adv*

S

s *nf* : twentieth letter of the Spanish alphabet

sábado *nm* **1** : Saturday **2** : Sabbath

sábalo *nm* : shad

sabana *nf* : savanna

sábana *nf* : sheet, bedsheet

sabandija *nf* BICHO : bug, small reptile, pesky creature

sabático, -ca *adj* : sabbatical

sabedor, -dora *adj* : aware, informed

sabelotodo *nmf fam* : know-it-all

saber[1] {71} *vt* **1** : to know **2** : to know how to, to be able to <sabe tocar el violín : she can play the violin> **3** : to learn, to find out **4 a ~** : to wit, namely — *vi* **1** : to know, to suppose **2** : to be informed <supimos del desastre : we heard about the disaster> **3** : to taste <esto no sabe bien : this doesn't taste right> **4 ~ a** : to taste like <sabe a naranja : it tastes like orange> — **saberse** *vr* : to know <ese chiste no me lo sé : I don't know that joke>

saber[2] *nm* : knowledge, learning

sabiamente *adv* : wisely

sabido, -da *adj* : well-known

sabiduría *nf* **1** : wisdom **2** : learning, knowledge

sabiendas *adv* **1 a ~** : knowingly **2 a sabiendas de que** : knowing full well that

sabio[1], -bia *adj* **1** PRUDENTE : wise, sensible **2** DOCTO : learned

sabio[2], -bia *n* **1** : wise person **2** : savant, learned person

sable *nm* : saber, cutlass

sablear *vt fam* : to scrounge, to cadge

sabor *nm* **1** : flavor, taste **2 sin ~** : flavorless

saborear *vt* **1** : to taste, to savor **2** : to enjoy, to relish

sabotaje *nm* : sabotage

saboteador, -dora *n* : saboteur

sabotear *vt* : to sabotage

sabrá, etc. → **saber**

sabroso, -sa *adj* **1** RICO : delicious, tasty **2** AGRADABLE : pleasant, nice, lovely

sabueso *nm* **1** : bloodhound **2** *fam* : detective, sleuth

sacacorchos *nms & pl* : corkscrew

sacapuntas *nms & pl* : pencil sharpener

sacar {72} *vt* **1** : to pull out, to take out <saca el pollo del congelador : take the chicken out of the freezer> **2** : to get, to obtain <saqué un 100 en el examen : I got 100 on the exam> **3** : to get out, to extract <le saqué la infor-

mación : I got the information from him> **4 :** to stick out <sacar la lengua : to stick out one's tongue> **5 :** to bring out, to introduce <sacar un libro : to publish a book> <sacaron una moda nueva : they introduced a new style> **6 :** to take (photos) **7 :** to make (copies) — *vi* **1 :** to kick off (in soccer or football) **2 :** to serve (in sports)

sacarina *nf* **:** saccharin

sacarosa *nf* **:** sucrose

sacerdocio *nm* **:** priesthood

sacerdotal *adj* **:** priestly

sacerdote, -tisa *n* **:** priest *m,* priestess *f*

saciar *vt* **1** HARTAR **:** to sate, to satiate **2** SATISFACER **:** to satisfy

saciedad *nf* **:** satiety

saco *nm* **1 :** bag, sack **2 :** sac **3 :** jacket, sport coat

sacramento *nm* **:** sacrament — **sacramental** *adj*

sacrificar {72} *vt* **:** to sacrifice — **sacrificarse** *vr* **:** to sacrifice oneself, to make sacrifices

sacrificio *nm* **:** sacrifice

sacrilegio *nm* **:** sacrilege

sacrílego, -ga *adj* **:** sacrilegious

sacristán *nm, pl* **-tanes :** sexton, sacristan

sacristía *nf* **:** sacristy, vestry

sacro, -cra *adj* SAGRADO **:** sacred <arte sacro : sacred art>

sacrosanto, -ta *adj* **:** sacrosanct

sacudida *nf* **1 :** shaking **2 :** jerk, jolt, shock **3 :** shake-up, upheaval

sacudir *vt* **1 :** to shake, to beat **2 :** to jerk, to jolt **3 :** to dust off **4** CONMOVER **:** to shake up, to shock — **sacudirse** *vr* **:** to shake off

sacudón *nm, pl* **-dones :** intense jolt or shake-up

sádico[1], -ca *adj* **:** sadistic

sádico[2], -ca *n* **:** sadist

sadismo *nm* **:** sadism

safari *nm* **:** safari

saga *nf* **:** saga

sagacidad *nf* **:** sagacity, shrewdness

sagaz *adj, pl* **sagaces** PERSPICAZ **:** shrewd, discerning, sagacious

Sagitario *nmf* **:** Sagittarius, Sagittarian

sagrado, -da *adj* **:** sacred, holy

sainete *nm* **:** comedy sketch, one-act farce <este proceso es un sainete : these proceedings are a farce>

sajar *vt* **:** to lance, to cut open

sal[1] → **salir**

sal[2] *nf* **1 :** salt **2** *CA, Mex* **:** misfortune, bad luck

sala *nf* **1 :** living room **2 :** room, hall <sala de conferencias : lecture hall> <sala de urgencias : emergency room> <sala de baile : ballroom>

salado, -da *adj* **1 :** salty **2 agua salada :** salt water

salamandra *nf* **:** salamander

salami *nm* **:** salami

salar *vt* **1 :** to salt **2 :** to spoil, to ruin **3** *CoRi, Mex* **:** to jinx, to bring bad luck

salarial *adj* **:** salary, salary-related

salario *nm* **1 :** salary **2 salario mínimo :** minimum wage

salaz *adj, pl* **salaces :** salacious, lecherous

salchicha *nf* **1 :** sausage **2 :** frankfurter, wiener

salchichón *nf, pl* **-chones :** a type of deli meat

salchichonería *nf Mex* **1 :** delicatessen **2 :** cold cuts *pl*

saldar *vt* **:** to settle, to pay off <saldar una cuenta : to settle an account>

saldo *nm* **1 :** settlement, payment **2 :** balance <saldo de cuenta : account balance> **3 :** remainder, leftover merchandise

saldrá, etc. → **salir**

salero *nm* **1 :** saltshaker **2 :** wit, charm

salga, etc. → **salir**

salida *nf* **1 :** exit <salida de emergencia : emergency exit> **2 :** leaving, departure **3** SOLUCIÓN **:** way out, solution **4 :** start (of a race) **5** OCURRENCIA **:** wisecrack, joke **6 salida del sol :** sunrise

saliente[1] *adj* **1 :** departing, outgoing **2 :** projecting **3** DESTACADO **:** salient, prominent

saliente[2] *nm* **1 :** projection, protrusion **2 ventana en saliente :** bay window

salinidad *nf* **:** salinity, saltiness

salino, -na *adj* **:** saline <solución salina : saline solution>

salir {73} *vi* **1 :** to go out, to come out, to get out <salimos todas las noches : we go out every night> <su libro acaba de salir : her book just came out> **2** PARTIR **:** to leave, to depart **3** APARECER **:** to appear <salió en todos los diarios : it came out in all the papers> **4 :** to project, to stick out **5 :** to cost, to come to **6** RESULTAR **:** to turn out, to prove **7 :** to come up, to occur <salga lo que salga : whatever happens> <salió una oportunidad : an opportunity came up> **8 ~ a :** to take after, to look like, to resemble **9 ~ con :** to go out with, to date — **salirse** *vr* **1 :** to escape, to get out, to leak out **2 :** to come loose, to come off **3 salirse con la suya :** to get one's own way

saliva *nf* **:** saliva

salivar *vi* **:** to salivate

salmo *nm* **:** psalm

salmón[1] *adj* **:** salmon-colored

salmón[2] *nm, pl* **salmones :** salmon

salmuera *nf* **:** brine

salobre *adj* **:** brackish, briny

salón *nm, pl* **salones 1 :** hall, large room <salón de clase : classroom> <salón de baile : ballroom> **2 :** salon <salón de belleza : beauty salon> **3 :** parlor, sitting room

salpicadera *nf Mex* **:** fender

salpicadura *nf* **:** spatter, splash

salpicar {72} *vt* **1 :** to spatter, to splash **2 :** to sprinkle, to scatter about

salpimentar {55} *vt* **1 :** to season (with salt and pepper) **2 :** to spice up

salsa *nf* **1 :** sauce <salsa picante : hot sauce> <salsa inglesa : Worcestershire sauce> <salsa tártara : tartar sauce> **2 :** gravy **3 :** salsa (music) **4 salsa mexicana :** salsa (sauce)

salsero, -ra *n* **:** salsa musician

saltador, -dora *n* **:** jumper

saltamontes *nms & pl* **:** grasshopper

saltar *vi* **1** BRINCAR **:** to jump, to leap **2 :** to bounce **3 :** to come off, to pop out **4 :** to shatter, to break **5 :** to explode, to blow up — *vt* **1 :** to jump, to jump over **2 :** to skip, to miss — **saltarse** *vr* OMITIR **:** to skip, to omit <me salté ese capítulo : I skipped that chapter>

saltarín, -rina *adj, mpl* **-rines :** leaping, hopping <frijol saltarín : jumping bean>

salteado, -da *adj* **1 :** sautéed **2 :** jumbled up <los episodios se transmitieron salteados : the episodes were broadcast in random order>

salteador *nm* **:** highwayman

saltear *vt* **1** SOFREÍR **:** to sauté **2 :** to skip around, to skip over

saltimbanqui *nmf* **:** acrobat

salto *nm* **1** BRINCO **:** jump, leap, skip **2 :** jump, dive (in sports) **3 :** gap, omission **4 dar saltos :** to jump up and down **5** *or* **salto de agua** CATARATA **:** waterfall

saltón, -tona *adj, mpl* **saltones :** bulging, protruding

salubre *adj* **:** healthful, salubrious

salubridad *nf* **:** healthfulness, health

salud *nf* **1 :** health <buena salud : good health> **2 ¡salud! :** bless you! (when someone sneezes) **3 ¡salud! :** cheers!, to your health!

saludable *adj* **1** SALUBRE **:** healthful **2** SANO **:** healthy, well

saludar *vt* **1 :** to greet, to say hello to **2 :** to salute — **saludarse** *vr*

saludo *nm* **1 :** greeting, regards *pl* **2 :** salute

salutación *nf, pl* **-ciones :** salutation

salva *nf* **1 :** salvo, volley **2 salva de aplausos :** round of applause

salvación *nf, pl* **-ciones 1 :** salvation **2** RESCATE **:** rescue

salvado *nm* **:** bran

salvador, -dora *n* **1 :** savior, rescuer **2 el Salvador :** the Savior

salvadoreño, -ña *adj & n* **:** Salvadoran, El Salvadoran

salvaguardar *vt* **:** to safeguard

salvaguardia *or* **salvaguarda** *nf* **:** safeguard, defense

salvajada *nf* ATROCIDAD **:** atrocity, act of savagery

salvaje[1] *adj* **1 :** wild <animales salvajes : wild animals> **2 :** savage, cruel **3 :** primitive, uncivilized

salvaje[2] *nmf* **:** savage

salvajismo *nm* **:** savagery

salvamento *nm* **1 :** rescuing, lifesaving **2 :** salvation **3 :** refuge

salvar *vt* **1 :** to save, to rescue **2 :** to cover (a distance) **3 :** to get around (an obstacle), to overcome (a difficulty) **4 :** to cross, to jump across **5 salvando :** except for, excluding — **salvarse** *vr* **1 :** to survive, to escape **2 :** to save one's soul

salvavidas[1] *nms & pl* **1 :** life preserver **2 bote salvavidas :** lifeboat

salvavidas[2] *nmf* **:** lifeguard

salvedad *nf* **1** EXCEPCIÓN **:** exception **2 :** proviso, stipulation

salvia *nf* **:** sage (plant)

salvo[1], **-va** *adj* **1 :** unharmed, sound <sano y salvo : safe and sound> **2 a ~ :** safe from danger

salvo[2] *prep* **1** EXCEPTO **:** except (for), save <todos asistirán salvo Jaime : all will attend except for Jaime> **2 salvo que :** unless <salvo que llueva : unless it rains>

salvoconducto *nm* **:** safe-conduct

samba *nf* **:** samba

San → **santo**[1]

sanar *vt* **:** to heal, to cure — *vi* **:** to get well, to recover

sanatorio *nm* **1 :** sanatorium **2 :** clinic, private hospital

sanción *nf, pl* **sanciones :** sanction

sancionar *vt* **1 :** to penalize, to impose a sanction on **2 :** to sanction, to approve

sancochar *vt* **:** to parboil

sandalia *nf* **:** sandal

sándalo *nm* **:** sandalwood

sandez *nf, pl* **sandeces** ESTUPIDEZ **:** nonsense, silly thing to say

sandía *nf* **:** watermelon

sandwich [ˈsandwitʃ, ˈsaŋgwitʃ] *nm, pl* **sandwiches** [-dwitʃɛs, -gwi-] EMPAREDADO **:** sandwich

saneamiento *nm* **1 :** cleaning up, sanitation **2 :** reorganizing, streamlining

sanear *vt* **1 :** to clean up, to sanitize **2 :** to reorganize, to streamline

sangrante *adj* **1 :** bleeding **2 :** flagrant, blatant

sangrar *vi* **:** to bleed — *vt* **:** to indent (a paragraph, etc.)

sangre *nf* **1 :** blood **2 a sangre fría :** in cold blood **3 a sangre y fuego :** by violent force **4 pura sangre :** thoroughbred

sangría *nf* **1 :** bloodletting **2 :** sangria (wine punch) **3 :** drain, draining <una sangría fiscal : a financial drain> **4 :** indentation, indenting

sangriento, -ta *adj* **1 :** bloody **2 :** cruel

sanguijuela *nf* **1 :** leech, bloodsucker **2 :** sponger, leech

sanguinario, -ria *adj* **:** bloodthirsty

sanguíneo, -nea *adj* **1 :** blood <vaso sanguíneo : blood vessel> **2 :** sanguine, ruddy

sanidad *nf* **1 :** health **2 :** public health, sanitation

sanitario[1], -ria *adj* **1 :** sanitary **2 :** health <centro sanitario : health center>
sanitario[2], -ria *n* **:** sanitation worker
sanitario[3] *nm Col, Mex, Ven* **:** toilet <los sanitarios : the toilets, the restroom>
sano, -na *adj* **1** SALUDABLE **:** healthy **2 :** wholesome **3 :** whole, intact
santiaguino, -na *adj* **:** of or from Santiago, Chile
santiamén *nm* **en un santiamén :** in no time at all
santidad *nf* **:** holiness, sanctity
santificar {72} *vt* **:** to sanctify, to consecrate, to hallow
santiguarse {10} *vr* PERSIGNARSE **:** to cross oneself
santo[1], -ta *adj* **1 :** holy, saintly <el Santo Padre : the Holy Father> <una vida santa : a saintly life> **2 Santo, Santa** (**San** *before names of masculine saints except those beginning with D or T*) **:** Saint <Santa Clara : Saint Claire> <Santo Tomás : Saint Thomas> <San Francisco : Saint Francis>
santo[2], -ta *n* **:** saint
santo[3] *nm* **1 :** saint's day **2** CUMPLEAÑOS **:** birthday
santuario *nm* **:** sanctuary
santurrón, -rrona *adj, mpl* **-rrones :** overly pious, sanctimonious — **santurronamente** *adv*
saña *nf* **1 :** fury, rage **2 :** viciousness <con saña : viciously>
sapo *nm* **:** toad
saque[1], etc. → sacar
saque[2] *nm* **1 :** kick-off (in soccer or football) **2 :** serve, service (in sports)
saqueador, -dora *n* DEPREDADOR **:** plunderer, looter
saquear *vt* **:** to sack, to plunder, to loot
saqueo *nm* DEPREDACIÓN **:** sacking, plunder, looting
sarampión *nm* **:** measles *pl*
sarape *nm CA, Mex* **:** serape, blanket
sarcasmo *nm* **:** sarcasm
sarcástico, -ca *adj* **:** sarcastic
sarcófago *nm* **:** sarcophagus
sardina *nf* **:** sardine
sardónico, -ca *adj* **:** sardonic
sarga *nf* **:** serge
sargento *nmf* **:** sergeant
sarna *nf* **:** mange
sarnoso, -sa *adj* **:** mangy
sarpullido *nm* ERUPCIÓN **:** rash
sarro *nm* **1 :** deposit, coating **2 :** tartar, plaque
sartén *nmf, pl* **sartenes 1 :** frying pan **2 tener la sartén por el mango :** to call the shots, to be in control
sasafrás *nm* **:** sassafras
sastre, -tra *n* **:** tailor
sastrería *nf* **1 :** tailoring **2 :** tailor's shop
Satanás *or* **Satán** *nm* **:** Satan, the devil
satánico, -ca *adj* **:** satanic
satélite *nm* **:** satellite
satín *or* **satén** *nm, pl* **satines** *or* **satenes :** satin
satinado, -da *adj* **:** satiny, glossy
sátira *nf* **:** satire
satírico, -ca *adj* **:** satirical, satiric
satirizar {21} *vt* **:** to satirize
sátiro *nm* **:** satyr
satisfacción *nf, pl* **-ciones :** satisfaction
satisfacer {74} *vt* **1 :** to satisfy **2 :** to fulfill, to meet **3 :** to pay, to settle — **satisfacerse** *vr* **1 :** to be satisfied **2 :** to take revenge
satisfactorio, -ria *adj* **:** satisfactory — **satisfactoriamente** *adv*
satisfecho, -cha *adj* **:** satisfied, content, pleased
saturación *nf, pl* **-ciones :** saturation
saturar *vt* **1 :** to saturate, to fill up **2 :** to satiate, to surfeit
saturnismo *nm* **:** lead poisoning
Saturno *nm* **:** Saturn
sauce *nm* **:** willow
saúco *nm* **:** elder (tree)
saudí *or* **saudita** *adj & nmf* **:** Saudi, Saudi Arabian
sauna *nmf* **:** sauna
savia *nf* **:** sap
saxofón *nm, pl* **-fones :** saxophone
sazón[1] *nf, pl* **sazones 1 :** flavor, seasoning **2 :** ripeness, maturity <en sazón : in season, ripe> **3 a la sazón :** at that time, then
sazón[2] *nmf, pl* **sazones** *Mex* **:** flavor, seasoning
sazonar *vt* CONDIMENTAR **:** to season, to spice
sé → saber, ser
se *pron* **1 :** to him, to her, to you, to them <se los daré a ella : I'll give them to her> **2 :** each other, one another <se abrazaron : they hugged each other> **3 :** himself, herself, itself, yourself, yourselves, themselves <se afeitó antes de salir : he shaved before leaving> **4** (*used in passive constructions*) <se dice que es hermosa : they say she's beautiful> <se habla inglés : English spoken>
sea, etc. → ser
sebo *nm* **1 :** grease, fat **2 :** tallow **3 :** suet
secado *nm* **:** drying
secador *nm* **:** hair dryer
secadora *nf* **1 :** dryer, clothes dryer **2** *Mex* **:** hair dryer
secante *nm* **:** blotting paper, blotter
secar {72} *v* **:** to dry — **secarse** *vr* **1 :** to get dry **2 :** to dry up
sección *nf, pl* **secciones 1 :** section <sección transversal : cross section> **2 :** department, division
seco, -ca *adj* **1 :** dry **2** DISECADO **:** dried <fruta seca : dried fruit> **3 :** thin, lean **4 :** curt, brusque **5 :** sharp <un golpe seco : a sharp blow> **6 a secas :** simply, just <se llama Chico, a secas : he's just called Chico> **7 en ~**

: abruptly, suddenly <frenar en seco : to make a sudden stop>

secoya *nf* : sequoia, redwood

secreción *nf, pl* **-ciones** : secretion

secretar *vt* : to secrete

secretaría *nf* **1** : secretariat, administrative department **2** *Mex* : ministry, cabinet office

secretariado *nm* **1** : secretariat **2** : secretarial profession

secretario, -ria *n* : secretary — **secretarial** *adj*

secreto[1], -ta *adj* **1** : secret **2** : secretive — **secretamente** *adv*

secreto[2] *nm* **1** : secret **2** : secrecy

secta *nf* : sect

sectario, -ria *adj & n* : sectarian

sector *nm* : sector

secuaz *nmf, pl* **secuaces** : follower, henchman, underling

secuela *nf* : consequence, sequel <las secuelas de la guerra : the aftermath of the war>

secuencia *nf* : sequence

secuestrador, -dora *n* **1** : kidnapper, abductor **2** : hijacker

secuestrar *vt* **1** RAPTAR : to kidnap, to abduct **2** : to hijack, to commandeer **3** CONFISCAR : to confiscate, to seize

secuestro *nm* **1** RAPTO : kidnapping, abduction **2** : hijacking **3** : seizure, confiscation

secular *adj* : secular — **secularismo** *nm* — **secularización** *nf*

secundar *vt* : to support, to second

secundaria *nf* **1** : secondary education, high school **2** *Mex* : junior high school, middle school

secundario, -ria *adj* : secondary

secuoya *nf* : sequoia

sed *nf* **1** : thirst <tener sed : to be thirsty> **2 tener sed de** : to hunger for, to thirst for

seda *nf* : silk

sedación *nf, pl* **-ciones** : sedation

sedal *nm* : fishing line

sedán *nm, pl* **sedanes** : sedan

sedante *adj & nm* CALMANTE : sedative

sedar *vt* : to sedate

sede *nf* **1** : seat, headquarters **2** : venue, site **3 la Santa Sede** : the Holy See

sedentario, -ria *adj* : sedentary

sedición *nf, pl* **-ciones** : sedition — **sedicioso, -sa** *adj*

sediento, -ta *adj* : thirsty, thirsting

sedimentación *nf, pl* **-ciones** : sedimentation

sedimentario, -ria *adj* : sedimentary

sedimento *nm* : sediment

sedoso, -sa *adj* : silky, silken

seducción *nf, pl* **-ciones** : seduction

seducir {61} *vt* **1** : to seduce **2** : to captivate, to charm

seductivo, -va *adj* : seductive

seductor[1], -tora *adj* **1** SEDUCTIVO : seductive **2** ENCANTADOR : charming, alluring

seductor[2], -tora *n* : seducer

segar {49} *vt* **1** : to reap, to harvest, to cut **2** : to sever abruptly <una vida segada por la enfermedad : a life cut short by illness>

seglar[1] *adj* LAICO : lay, secular

seglar[2] *nm* LAICO : layperson, layman *m,* laywoman *f*

segmentación *nm, pl* **-ciones** : segmentation

segmentado, -da *adj* : segmented

segmento *nm* : segment

segregar {52} *vt* **1** : to segregate **2** SECRETAR : to secrete

seguida *nf* **en ~** : right away, immediately <vuelvo en seguida : I'll be right back>

seguidamente *adv* **1** : next, immediately after **2** : without a break, continuously

seguido[1] *adv* **1** RECTO : straight, straight ahead **2** : often, frequently

seguido[2], -da *adj* **1** CONSECUTIVO : consecutive, successive <tres días seguidos : three days in a row> **2** : straight, unbroken **3 ~ por** *or* **~ de** : followed by

seguidor, -dora *n* : follower, supporter

seguimiento *nm* **1** : following, pursuit **2** : continuation **3** : tracking, monitoring

seguir {75} *vt* **1** : to follow <el sol sigue la lluvia : sunshine follows the rain> <seguiré tu consejo : I'll follow your advice> <me siguieron con la mirada : they followed me with their eyes> **2** : to go along, to keep on <seguimos toda la carretera panamericana : we continued along the Pan-American Highway> <siguió hablando : he kept on talking> <seguir el curso : to stay on course> **3** : to take (a course, a treatment) — *vi* **1** : to go on, to keep going <sigue adelante : keep going, carry on> **2** : to remain, to continue to be <¿todavía sigues aquí? : you're still here?> <sigue con vida : she's still alive> **3** : to follow, to come after <la frase que sigue : the following sentence>

según[1] *adv* : it depends <según y como : it all depends on>

según[2] *conj* **1** COMO, CONFORME : as, just as <según lo dejé : just as I left it> **2** : depending on how <según se vea : depending on how one sees it>

según[3] *prep* **1** : according to <según los rumores : according to the rumors> **2** : depending on <según los resultados : depending on the results>

segundo[1], -da *adj* : second <el segundo lugar : second place>

segundo[2], -da *n* **1** : second (in a series) **2** : second (person), second-in-command

segundo[3] *nm* : second <sesenta segundos : sixty seconds>

seguramente *adv* **1** : for sure, surely **2** : probably

seguridad *nf* **1 :** safety, security **2 :** (financial) security <seguridad social : Social Security> **3** CERTEZA **:** certainty, assurance <con toda seguridad : with complete certainty> **4 :** confidence, self-confidence

seguro[1] *adv* **:** certainly, definitely <va a llover, seguro : it's going to rain for sure> <¡seguro que sí! : of course!>

seguro[2], -ra *adj* **1 :** safe, secure **2 :** sure, certain <estoy segura que es él : I'm sure that's him> **3 :** reliable, trustworthy **4 :** self-assured

seguro[3] *nm* **1 :** insurance <seguro de vida : life insurance> **2 :** fastener, clasp **3** *Mex* **:** safety pin

seis *adj & nm* **:** six

seiscientos[1], -tas *adj* **:** six hundred

seiscientos[2] *nms & pl* **:** six hundred

selección *nf, pl* **-ciones 1** ELECCIÓN **:** selection, choice **2 selección natural :** natural selection

seleccionar *vt* ELEGIR **:** to select, to choose

selectivo, -va *adj* **:** selective — **selectivamente** *adv*

selecto, -ta *adj* **1 :** choice, select **2** EXCLUSIVO **:** exclusive

selenio *nm* **:** selenium

sellar *vt* **1 :** to seal **2 :** to stamp

sello *nm* **1 :** seal **2** ESTAMPILLA, TIMBRE **:** postage stamp **3 :** hallmark, characteristic

selva *nf* **1** BOSQUE **:** woods *pl,* forest <selva húmeda : rain forest> **2** JUNGLA **:** jungle

selvático, -ca *adj* **1 :** forest, jungle <sendero selvático : jungle path> **2 :** wild

semáforo *nm* **1 :** traffic light **2 :** stop signal

semana *nf* **:** week

semanal *adj* **:** weekly — **semanalmente** *adv*

semanario *nm* **:** weekly (publication)

semántica *nf* **:** semantics

semántico, -ca *adj* **:** semantic

semblante *nm* **1 :** countenance, face **2 :** appearance, look

semblanza *nf* **:** biographical sketch, profile

sembrado *nm* **:** cultivated field

sembrador, -dora *n* **:** planter, sower

sembradora *nf* **:** seeder (machine)

sembrar {55} *vt* **1 :** to plant, to sow **2 :** to scatter, to strew <sembrar el pánico : to spread panic>

semejante[1] *adj* **1** PARECIDO **:** similar, alike **2** TAL **:** such <nunca he visto cosa semejante : I have never seen such a thing>

semejante[2] *nm* PRÓJIMO **:** fellowman

semejanza *nf* PARECIDO **:** similarity, resemblance

semejar *vi* **:** to resemble, to look like — **semejarse** *vr* **:** to be similar, to look alike

semen *nm* **:** semen

semental *nm* **:** stud (animal) <caballo semental : stallion>

semestre *nm* **:** semester

semicírculo *nm* **:** semicircle, half circle

semiconductor *nm* **:** semiconductor

semidiós *nm, pl* **-dioses :** demigod *m*

semifinal *nf* **:** semifinal

semifinalista[1] *adj* **:** semifinal

semifinalista[2] *nmf* **:** semifinalist

semiformal *adj* **:** semiformal

semilla *nf* **:** seed

semillero *nm* **1 :** seedbed **2 :** hotbed, breeding ground

seminario *nm* **1 :** seminary **2 :** seminar, graduate course

seminarista *nm* **:** seminarian

semiprecioso, -sa *adj* **:** semiprecious

semita[1] *adj* **:** Semitic

semita[2] *nmf* **:** Semite

sémola *nf* **:** semolina

sempiterno, -na *adj* ETERNO **:** eternal, everlasting

senado *nm* **:** senate

senador, -dora *n* **:** senator

sencillamente *adv* **:** simply, plainly

sencillez *nf* **:** simplicity

sencillo[1], -lla *adj* **1 :** simple, easy **2 :** plain, unaffected **3 :** single

sencillo[2] *nm* **1 :** single (recording) **2 :** small change (coins) **3 :** one-way ticket

senda *nf* CAMINO, SENDERO **:** path, way

sendero *nm* CAMINO, SENDA **:** path, way

sendos, -das *adj pl* **:** each, both <llevaban sendos vestidos nuevos : they were each wearing a new dress>

senectud *nf* ANCIANIDAD **:** old age

senegalés, -lesa *adj & n, mpl* **-leses :** Senegalese

senil *adj* **:** senile — **senilidad** *nf*

seno *nm* **1 :** breast, bosom <los senos : the breasts> <el seno de la familia : the bosom of the family> **2 :** sinus **3 seno materno :** womb

sensación *nf, pl* **-ciones 1** IMPRESIÓN **:** feeling <tener la sensación : to have a feeling> **2 :** sensation <causar sensación : to cause a sensation>

sensacional *adj* **:** sensational

sensacionalista *adj* **:** sensationalistic, lurid

sensatez *nf* **1 :** good sense **2 con ~ :** sensibly

sensato, -ta *n* **:** sensible, sound — **sensatamente** *adv*

sensibilidad *nf* **1 :** sensitivity, sensibility **2** SENSACIÓN **:** feeling

sensibilizar {21} *vt* **:** to sensitize

sensible *adj* **1 :** sensitive **2** APRECIABLE **:** considerable, significant

sensiblemente *adv* **:** considerably, significantly

sensiblería *nf* **:** sentimentality, mush

sensiblero, -ra *adj* **:** mawkish, sentimental, mushy

sensitivo, -va *adj* **1 :** sense <órganos sensitivos : sense organs> **2 :** sentient, capable of feeling

sensor *nm* **:** sensor

sensorial *adj* : sensory

sensual *adj* : sensual, sensuous — **sensualmente** *adv*

sensualidad *nf* : sensuality

sentado, -da *adj* **1** : sitting, seated **2** : established, settled <dar por sentado : to take for granted> <dejar sentado : to make clear> **3** : sensible, steady, judicious

sentar {55} *vt* **1** : to seat, to sit **2** : to establish, to set — *vi* **1** : to suit <ese color te sienta : that color suits you> **2** : to agree with (of food or drink) <las cebollas no me sientan : onions don't agree with me> **3** : to please <le sentó mal el paseo : she didn't enjoy the trip> — **sentarse** *vr* : to sit, to sit down <siéntese, por favor : please have a seat>

sentencia *nf* **1** : sentence, judgment **2** : maxim, saying

sentenciar *vt* : to sentence

sentido[1], -da *adj* **1** : heartfelt, sincere <mi más sentido pésame : my sincerest condolences> **2** : touchy, sensitive **3** : offended, hurt

sentido[2] *nm* **1** : sense <sentido común : common sense> <los cinco sentidos : the five senses> <sin sentido : senseless> **2** CONOCIMIENTO : consciousness **3** SIGNIFICADO : meaning, sense <doble sentido : double entendre> **4** : direction <calle de sentido único : one-way street>

sentimental[1] *adj* **1** : sentimental **2** : love, romantic <vida sentimental : love life>

sentimental[2] *nmf* : sentimentalist

sentimentalismo *nm* : sentimentality, sentimentalism

sentimiento *nm* **1** : feeling, emotion **2** PESAR : regret, sorrow

sentir {76} *vt* **1** : to feel, to experience <no siento nada de dolor : I don't feel any pain> <sentía sed : he was feeling thirsty> <sentir amor : to feel love> **2** PERCIBIR : to perceive, to sense <sentir un ruido : to hear a noise> **3** LAMENTAR : to regret, to feel sorry for <lo siento mucho : I'm very sorry> — *vi* **1** : to have feeling, to feel **2 sin ~** : without noticing, inadvertently — **sentirse** *vr* **1** : to feel <¿te sientes mejor? : are you feeling better?> **2** *Chile, Mex* : to take offense

seña *nf* **1** : sign, signal **2 dar señas de** : to show signs of

señal *nf* **1** : signal **2** : sign <señal de tráfico : traffic sign> **3** INDICIO : indication <en señal de : as a token of> **4** VESTIGIO : trace, vestige **5** : scar, mark **6** : deposit, down payment

señalado, -da *adj* : distinguished, notable

señalador *nm* : marker <señalador de libros : bookmark>

señalar *vt* **1** INDICAR : to indicate, to show **2** : to mark **3** : to point out, to stress **4** : to fix, to set — **señalarse** *vr* : to distinguish oneself

señor, -ñora *n* **1** : gentleman *m,* man *m,* lady *f,* woman *f,* wife *f* **2** : Sir *m,* Madam *f* <estimados señores : Dear Sirs> **3** : Mr. *m,* Mrs. *f* **4** : lord *m,* lady *f* <el Señor : the Lord>

señoría *nf* **1** : lordship **2 Su Señoría** : Your Honor

señorial *adj* : stately, regal

señorío *nm* **1** : manor, estate **2** : dominion, power **3** : elegance, class

señorita *nf* **1** : young lady, young woman **2** : Miss

señuelo *nm* **1** : decoy **2** : bait

sépalo *nm* : sepal

sepa, etc. → **saber**

separación *nf, pl* **-ciones 1** : separation, division **2** : gap, space

separadamente *adv* : separately, apart

separado, -da *adj* **1** : separated **2** : separate <vidas separadas : separate lives> **3 por ~** : separately

separar *vt* **1** : to separate, to divide **2** : to split up, to pull apart — **separarse** *vr*

sepelio *nm* : interment, burial

sepia[1] *adj & nm* : sepia

sepia[2] *nf* : cuttlefish

septentrional *adj* : northern

séptico, -ca *adj* : septic

septiembre *nm* : September

séptimo[1], -ma *adj* : seventh

séptimo[2] *nm* : seventh

septuagésimo[1], -ma *adj* : seventieth

septuagésimo[2] *nm* : seventieth

sepulcral *adj* **1** : sepulcral **2** : dismal, gloomy

sepulcro *nm* TUMBA : tomb, sepulchre

sepultar *vt* ENTERRAR : to bury

sepultura *nf* **1** : burial **2** TUMBA : grave, tomb

seque, etc. → **secar**

sequedad *nf* **1** : dryness **2** : brusqueness, curtness

sequía *nf* : drought

séquito *nm* : retinue, entourage

ser[1] {77} *vi* **1** : to be <él es mi hermano : he is my brother> <Camila es linda : Camila is pretty> **2** : to exist, to live <ser, o no ser : to be or not to be> **3** : to take place, to occur <el concierto es el domingo : the concert is on Sunday> **4** (*used with expressions of time, date, season*) <son las diez : it's ten o'clock> <hoy es el 9 : today's the 9th> **5** : to cost, to come to <¿cuánto es? : how much is it?> **6** (*with the future tense*) : to be able to be <¿será posible? : can it be possible?> **7 ~ de** : to come from <somos de Managua : we're from Managua> **8 ~ de** : to belong to <ese lápiz es de Juan : that's Juan's pencil> **9 es que** : the thing is that <es que no lo conozco : it's just that I don't know him> **10 ¡sea!** : agreed!, all right! **11 sea . . . sea** : either . . . or — *v aux* (*used in passive constructions*) : to be <la cuenta

ha sido pagada : the bill has been paid> <él fue asesinado : he was murdered>
ser[2] *nm* : being <ser humano : human being>
seráfico, -ca *adj* : angelic, seraphic
serbio[1], **-bia** *adj & n* : Serb, Serbian
serbio[2] *nm* : Serbian (language)
serbocroata[1] *adj* : Serbo-Croatian
serbocroata[2] *nm* : Serbo-Croatian (language)
serenar *vt* : to calm, to soothe — **serenarse** *vr* CALMARSE : to calm down
serenata *nf* : serenade
serendipia *nf* : serendipity
serenidad *nf* : serenity, calmness
sereno[1], **-na** *adj* **1** SOSEGADO : serene, calm, composed **2** : fair, clear (of weather) **3** : calm, still (of the sea) — **serenamente** *adv*
sereno[2] *nm* : night watchman
seriado, -da *adj* : serial
serial *nm* : serial (on radio or television)
seriamente *adv* : seriously
serie *nf* **1** : series **2** SERIAL : serial **3** **fabricación en serie** : mass production **4** **fuera de serie** : extraordinary, amazing
seriedad *nf* **1** : seriousness, earnestness **2** : gravity, importance
serio, -ria *adj* **1** : serious, earnest **2** : reliable, responsible **3** : important **4** **en ~** : seriously, in earnest — **seriamente** *adv*
sermón *nm, pl* **sermones** **1** : sermon **2** *fam* : harangue, lecture
sermonear *vt fam* : to harangue, to lecture
serpentear *vi* : to twist, to wind — **serpenteante** *adj*
serpentina *nf* : paper streamer
serpiente *nf* : serpent, snake
serrado, -da *adj* DENTADO : serrated
serranía *nf* : mountainous area
serrano, -na *adj* : from the mountains
serrar {55} *vt* : to saw
serrín *nm, pl* **serrines** : sawdust
serruchar *vt* : to saw up
serrucho *nm* : saw, handsaw
servicentro *nm Peru* : gas station
servicial *adj* : obliging, helpful
servicio *nm* **1** : service **2** SAQUE : serve (in sports) **3** **servicios** *nmpl* : restroom
servidor, -dora *n* **1** : servant **2** **su seguro servidor** : yours truly (in correspondence)
servidumbre *nf* **1** : servitude **2** : help, servants *pl*
servil *adj* **1** : servile, subservient **2** : menial
servilismo *nm* : servility, subservience
servilleta *nf* : napkin
servir {54} *vt* **1** : to serve, to be of use to **2** : to serve, to wait **3** SURTIR : to fill (an order) — *vi* **1** : to work <mi radio no sirve : my radio isn't working> **2** : to be of use, to be helpful <esa computadora no sirve para nada : that computer's perfectly useless> — **servirse** *vr* **1** : to help oneself to **2** : to be kind enough <sírvase enviarnos un catálogo : please send us a catalog>
sésamo *nm* AJONJOLÍ : sesame, sesame seeds *pl*
sesenta *adj & nm* : sixty
sesentavo[1], **-va** *adj* : sixtieth
sesentavo[2] *n* : sixtieth (fraction)
sesgado, -da *adj* **1** : inclined, tilted **2** : slanted, biased
sesgar {52} *vt* **1** : to cut on the bias **2** : to tilt **3** : to bias, to slant
sesgo *nm* : bias
sesgue, etc. → **sesgar**
sesión *nf, pl* **sesiones** **1** : session **2** : showing, performance
sesionar *vi* REUNIRSE : to meet, to be in session
seso *nm* **1** : brains, intelligence **2** **sesos** *nmpl* : brains (as food)
sesudo, -da *adj* **1** : prudent, sensible **2** : brainy
set *nm, pl* **sets** : set (in tennis)
seta *nf* : mushroom
setecientos[1], **-tas** *adj* : seven hundred
setecientos[2] *nms & pl* : seven hundred
setenta *adj & nm* : seventy
setentavo[1], **-va** *adj* : seventieth
setentavo[2] *nm* : seventieth
setiembre *nm* → **septiembre**
seto *nm* **1** : fence, enclosure **2** **seto vivo** : hedge
seudónimo *nm* : pseudonym
severidad *nf* **1** : harshness, severity **2** : strictness
severo, -ra *adj* **1** : harsh, severe **2** ESTRICTO : strict — **severamente** *adv*
sexagésimo[1], **-ma** *adj* : sixtieth, sixty-
sexagésimo[2], **-ma** *n* : sixtieth, sixty- (in a series)
sexismo *nm* : sexism — **sexista** *adj & nmf*
sexo *nm* : sex
sextante *nm* : sextant
sexteto *nm* : sextet
sexto, -ta *adj* : sixth — **sexto, -ta** *n*
sexual *adj* : sexual, sex <educación sexual : sex education> — **sexualmente** *adv*
sexualidad *nf* : sexuality
sexy *adj, pl* **sexy** *or* **sexys** : sexy
shock [ˈʃɔk, ˈtʃɔk] *nm* : shock <estado de shock : state of shock>
short *nm, pl* **shorts** : shorts *pl*
show *nm, pl* **shows** : show
si *conj* **1** : if <lo haré si me pagan : I'll do it if they pay me> <si lo supiera te lo diría : if I knew it I would tell you> **2** : whether, if <no importa si funciona o no : it doesn't matter whether it works (or not)> **3** (*expressing desire, protest, or surprise*) <si supiera la verdad : if only I knew the truth> <¡si no quiero! : but I don't want to!> **4** **si bien** : although <si bien se ha progresado : although progress has been made> **5** **si no** : otherwise, or

else <si no, no voy : otherwise I won't go>

sí[1] *adv* **1 :** yes <sí, gracias : yes, please> <creo que sí : I think so> **2 sí que :** indeed, absolutely <esta vez sí que ganaré : this time I'm sure to win> **3 porque sí** *fam* **:** because, just because <lo hizo porque sí : she did it just because>

sí[2] *nm* **:** yes <dar el sí : to say yes, to express consent>

sí[3] *pron* **1 de por sí** *or* **en sí :** by itself, in itself, per se **2 fuera de sí :** beside oneself **3 para sí (mismo) :** to himself, to herself, for himself, for herself **4 entre ~ :** among themselves

siamés, -mesa *adj & n, mpl* **siameses :** Siamese

sibilante *adj & nf* **:** sibilant

siciliano, -na *adj & n* **:** Sicilian

sico- → **psico-**

sicomoro *or* **sicómoro** *nm* **:** sycamore

SIDA *or* **sida** *nm* **:** AIDS

siderurgia *nf* **:** iron and steel industry

siderúrgico, -ca *adj* **:** steel, iron <the steel industry : la industria siderúrgica>

sidra *nf* **:** hard cider

siega[1], **siegue, etc.** → **segar**

siega[2] *nf* **1 :** harvesting **2 :** harvest time **3 :** harvested crop

siembra[1], **etc.** → **sembrar**

siembra[2] *nf* **1 :** sowing **2 :** sowing season **3** SEMBRADO **:** cultivated field

siempre *adv* **1 :** always <siempre tienes hambre : you're always hungry> **2 :** still <¿siempre te vas? : are you still going?> **3** *Mex* **:** after all <siempre no fui : I didn't go after all> **4 siempre que :** whenever, every time <siempre que pasa : every time he walks by> **5 para ~ :** forever, for good **6 siempre y cuando :** provided that

sien *nf* **:** temple (on the forehead)

sienta, etc. → **sentar**

siente, etc. → **sentir**

sierpe *nf* **:** serpent, snake

sierra[1], **etc.** → **serrar**

sierra[2] *nf* **1 :** saw <sierra de vaivén : jigsaw> **2** CORDILLERA **:** mountain range **3 :** mountains *pl* <viven en la sierra : they live in the mountains>

siervo, -va *n* **1 :** slave **2 :** serf

siesta *nf* **:** nap, siesta

siete *adj & nm* **:** seven

sífilis *nf* **:** syphilis

sifón *nm, pl* **sifones :** siphon

siga, sigue, etc. → **seguir**

sigilo *nm* **:** secrecy, stealth

sigiloso, -sa *adj* FURTIVO **:** furtive, stealthy — **sigilosamente** *adv*

sigla *nf* **:** acronym, abbreviation

siglo *nm* **1 :** century **2 :** age <el Siglo de Oro : the Golden Age> <hace siglos que no te veo : I haven't seen you in ages> **3 :** world, secular life

signar *vt* **:** to sign (a treaty or agreement)

signatario, -ria *n* **:** signatory

significación *nf, pl* **-ciones 1 :** significance, importance **2 :** signification, meaning

significado *nm* **1 :** sense, meaning **2 :** significance

significante *adj* **:** significant

significar {72} *vt* **1 :** to mean, to signify **2 :** to express, to make known — **significarse** *vr* **1 :** to draw attention, to become known **2 :** to take a stance

significativo, -va *adj* **1 :** significant, important **2 :** meaningful — **significativamente** *adv*

signo *nm* **1 :** sign <signo de igual : equal sign> <un signo de alegría : a sign of happiness> **2 :** (punctuation) mark <signo de interrogación : question mark> <signo de admiración : exclamation point> <signo de intercalación : caret>

siguiente *adj* **:** next, following

sílaba *nf* **:** syllable

silábico, -ca *adj* **:** syllabic

silbar *v* **:** to whistle

silbato *nm* PITO **:** whistle

silbido *nm* **:** whistle, whistling

silenciador *nm* **1 :** muffler (of an automobile) **2 :** silencer

silenciar *vt* **1 :** to silence **2 :** to muffle

silencio *nm* **1 :** silence, quiet <¡silencio! : be quiet!> **2 :** rest (in music)

silencioso, -sa *adj* **:** silent, quiet — **silenciosamente** *adv*

sílice *nf* **:** silica

silicio *nm* **:** silicon

silla *nf* **1 :** chair **2 silla de ruedas :** wheelchair

sillón *nm, pl* **sillones :** armchair, easy chair

silo *nm* **:** silo

silueta *nf* **1 :** silhouette **2 :** figure, shape

silvestre *adj* **:** wild <flor silvestre : wildflower>

silvicultor, -tora *n* **:** forester

silvicultura *nf* **:** forestry

sima *nf* ABISMO **:** chasm, abyss

simbólico, -ca *adj* **:** symbolic — **simbólicamente** *adj*

simbolismo *nm* **:** symbolism

simbolizar {21} *vt* **:** to symbolize

símbolo *nm* **:** symbol

simetría *nf* **:** symmetry

simétrico, -ca *adj* **:** symmetrical, symmetric

simiente *nf* **:** seed

símil *nm* **1 :** simile **2 :** analogy, comparison

similar *adj* SEMEJANTE **:** similar, alike

similitud *nf* **:** similarity, resemblance

simio *nm* **:** ape

simpatía *nf* **1 :** liking, affection <tomarle simpatía a : to take a liking to> **2 :** warmth, friendliness **3 :** support, solidarity

simpático, -ca *adj* **:** nice, friendly, likeable

simpatizante *nf* **:** sympathizer, supporter

simpatizar {21} *vi* **1 :** to get along, to hit it off <simpaticé mucho con él : I really liked him> **2 ~ con :** to sympathize with, to support

simple[1] *adj* **1** SENCILLO **:** plain, simple, easy **2 :** pure, mere <por simple vanidad : out of pure vanity> **3 :** simpleminded, foolish

simple[2] *n* **:** fool, simpleton

simplemente *adv* **:** simply, merely, just

simpleza *nf* **1 :** foolishness, simpleness **2** NECEDAD **:** nonsense

simplicidad *nf* **:** simplicity

simplificar {72} *vt* **:** to simplify — **simplificación** *nf*

simposio *or* **simposium** *nm* **:** symposium

simulación *nf, pl* **-ciones :** simulation

simulacro *nm* **:** imitation, sham <simulacro de juicio : mock trial>

simular *vt* **1 :** to simulate **2 :** to feign, to pretend

simultáneo, -nea *adj* **:** simultaneous — **simultáneamente** *adv*

sin *prep* **1 :** without <sin querer : unintentionally> <sin refinar : unrefined> **2 sin que :** without <lo hicimos sin que él se diera cuenta : we did it without him noticing>

sinagoga *nf* **:** synagogue

sinceridad *nf* **:** sincerity

sincero, -ra *adj* **:** sincere, honest, true — **sinceramente** *adv*

síncopa *nf* **:** syncopation

sincopar *vt* **:** to syncopate

sincronizar {21} *vt* **:** to synchronize — **sincronización** *nf*

sindical *adj* GREMIAL **:** union, labor <representante sindical : union representative>

sindicalización *nf, pl* **-ciones :** unionizing, unionization

sindicalizar {21} *vt* **:** to unionize — **sindicalizarse** *vr* **1 :** to form a union **2 :** to join a union

sindicar → **sindicalizar**

sindicato *nm* GREMIO **:** union, guild

síndrome *nm* **:** syndrome

sinecura *nf* **:** sinecure

sinfín *nm* **:** endless number <un sinfín de problemas : no end of problems>

sinfonía *nf* **:** symphony

sinfónica *nf* **:** symphony orchestra

sinfónico, -ca *adj* **:** symphonic, symphony

singular[1] *adj* **1 :** singular, unique **2** PARTICULAR **:** peculiar, odd **3 :** singular (in grammar) — **singularmente** *adv*

singular[2] *nm* **:** singular

singularidad *nf* **:** uniqueness, singularity

singularizar {21} *vt* **:** to make unique or distinct — **singularizarse** *vr* **:** to stand out, to distinguish oneself

siniestrado, -da *adj* **:** damaged, wrecked <zona siniestrada : disaster zone>

siniestro[1], **-tra** *adj* **1** IZQUIERDO **:** left, left-hand **2** MALVADO **:** sinister, evil

siniestro[2] *nm* **:** accident, disaster

sinnúmero → **sinfín**

sino *conj* **1 :** but, rather <no será hoy, sino mañana : it won't be today, but tomorrow> **2** EXCEPTO **:** but, except <no hace sino despertar suspicacias : it does nothing but arouse suspicion>

sinónimo[1], **-ma** *adj* **:** synonymous

sinónimo[2] *nm* **:** synonym

sinopsis *nfs & pl* RESUMEN **:** synopsis, summary

sinrazón *nf, pl* **-zones :** wrong, injustice

sinsabores *nmpl* **:** woes, troubles

sinsonte *nm* **:** mockingbird

sintáctico, -ca *adj* **:** syntactic, syntactical

sintaxis *nfs & pl* **:** syntax

síntesis *nfs & pl* **1 :** synthesis, fusion **2** SINOPSIS **:** synopsis, summary

sintético, -ca *adj* **:** synthetic — **sintéticamente** *adv*

sintetizar {21} *vt* **1 :** to synthesize **2** RESUMIR **:** to summarize

sintió, etc. → **sentir**

síntoma *nm* **:** symptom

sintomático, -ca *adj* **:** symptomatic

sintonía *nf* **1 :** tuning in (of a radio) **2 en sintonía con :** in tune with, attuned to

sintonizador *nm* **:** tuner, knob for tuning (of a radio, etc.)

sintonizar {21} *vt* **:** to tune (in) to — *vi* **1 :** to tune in **2 ~ con :** to be in tune with, to empathize with

sinuosidad *nf* **:** sinuosity

sinuoso, -sa *adj* **1 :** winding, sinuous **2 :** devious

sinvergüenza[1] *adj* **1** DESCARADO **:** shameless, brazen, impudent **2** TRAVIESO **:** naughty

sinvergüenza[2] *nmf* **1 :** rogue, scoundrel **2 :** brat, rascal

sionista *adj & nmf* **:** Zionist — **sionismo** *nm*

siqui- → **psiqui-**

siquiera *adv* **1 :** at least <dame siquiera un poquito : at least give me a little bit> **2** (*in negative constructions*) **:** not even <ni siquiera nos saludaron : they didn't even say hello to us>

sirena *nf* **1 :** mermaid **2 :** siren <sirena de niebla : foghorn>

sirio, -ria *adj & n* **:** Syrian

sirope *nm* **:** syrup

sirve, etc. → **servir**

sirviente, -ta *n* **:** servant, maid *f*

sisal *nm* **:** sisal

sisear *vi* **:** to hiss

siseo *nm* **:** hiss

sísmico, -ca *adj* **:** seismic

sismo *nm* **1** TERREMOTO **:** earthquake **2** TEMBLOR **:** tremor

sismógrafo *nm* **:** seismograph

sistema *nm* **:** system

sistemático, -ca *adj* : systematic — **sistemáticamente** *adv*
sistematizar {21} *vt* : to systematize
sistémico, -ca *adj* : systemic
sitiar *vt* ASEDIAR : to besiege
sitio *nm* **1** LUGAR : place, site <vámonos a otro sitio : let's go somewhere else> **2** ESPACIO : room, space <hacer sitio a : to make room for> **3** : siege <estado de sitio : state of siege> **4** *Mex* : taxi stand
situación *nf, pl* **-ciones** : situation
situado, -da *adj* : situated, placed
situar {3} *vt* UBICAR : to situate, to place, to locate — **situarse** *vr* **1** : to be placed, to be located **2** : to make a place for oneself, to do well
sketch *nm* : sketch, skit
slip *nm* : briefs *pl*, underpants *pl*
smog *nm* : smog
smoking *nm* ESMOQUIN : tuxedo
snob → **esnob**
so *prep* : under <so pena de : under penalty of>
sobaco *nm* : armpit
sobado, -da *adj* **1** : worn, shabby **2** : well-worn, hackneyed
sobar *vt* **1** : to finger, to handle **2** : to knead **3** : to rub, to massage **4** *fam* : to beat, to pummel
soberanía *nf* : sovereignty
soberano, -na *adj & n* : sovereign
soberbia *nf* **1** ORGULLO : pride, arrogance **2** MAGNIFICENCIA : magnificence
soberbio, -bia *adj* **1** : proud, arrogant **2** : grand, magnificent
sobornable *adv* : venal, bribable
sobornar *vt* : to bribe
soborno *nm* **1** : bribery **2** : bribe
sobra *nf* **1** : excess, surplus **2 de ~** : extra, to spare **3 sobras** *nfpl* : leftovers, scraps
sobrado, -da *adj* : abundant, excessive, more than enough
sobrante[1] *adj* : remaining, superfluous
sobrante[2] *nm* : remainder, surplus
sobrar *vi* : to be in excess, to be superfluous <más vale que sobre a que falte : it's better to have too much than not enough>
sobre[1] *nm* **1** : envelope **2** : packet <un sobre de sazón : a packet of seasoning>
sobre[2] *prep* **1** : on, on top of <sobre la mesa : on the table> **2** : over, above **3** : about <¿tiene libros sobre Bolivia? : do you have books on Bolivia?> **4 sobre todo** : especially, above all
sobrealimentar *vt* : to overfeed
sobrecalentar {55} *vt* : to overheat — **sobrecalentarse** *vr*
sobrecama *nmf* : bedspread
sobrecargar {52} *vt* : to overload, to overburden, to weigh down
sobrecoger {15} *vt* **1** : to surprise, to startle **2** : to scare — **sobrecogerse** *vr*
sobrecubierta *nf* : dust jacket
sobredosis *nfs & pl* : overdose
sobreentender {56} *vt* : to infer, to understand
sobreestimar *vt* : to overestimate, to overrate
sobreexitado, -da *adj* : overexcited
sobreexponer {60} *vt* : to overexpose
sobregirar *vt* : to overdraw
sobregiro *nm* : overdraft
sobrehumano, -na *adj* : superhuman
sobrellevar *vt* : to endure, to bear
sobremanera *adv* : exceedingly
sobremesa *nf* : after-dinner conversation
sobrenatural *adj* : supernatural
sobrenombre *nm* APODO : nickname
sobrentender → **sobreentender**
sobrepasar *vt* : to exceed, to surpass — **sobrepasarse** *vr* PASARSE : to go too far
sobrepelliz *nf, pl* **-pellices** : surplice
sobrepeso *nm* **1** : excess weight **2** : overweight, obesity
sobrepoblación, sobrepoblado → **superpoblación, superpoblado**
sobreponer {60} *vt* **1** SUPERPONER : to superimpose **2** ANTEPONER : to put first, to give priority to — **sobreponerse** *vr* **1** : to pull oneself together **2 ~ a** : to overcome
sobreprecio *nm* : surcharge
sobreproducción *nf, pl* **-ciones** : overproduction
sobreproducir {61} *vt* : to overproduce
sobreprotector, -tora *adj* : overprotective
sobreproteger {15} *vt* : to overprotect
sobresaliente[1] *adj* **1** : protruding, projecting **2** : outstanding, noteworthy **3** : significant, salient
sobresaliente[2] *nmf* : understudy
sobresalir {73} *vi* **1** : to protrude, to jut out, to project **2** : to stand out, to excel
sobresaltar *vt* : to startle, to frighten — **sobresaltarse** *vr*
sobresalto *nm* : start, fright
sobresueldo *nm* : bonus, additional pay
sobretasa *nf* : surcharge <sobretasa a la gasolina : gas tax>
sobretodo *nm* : overcoat
sobrevalorar *or* **sobrevaluar** {3} *vt* : to overvalue, to overrate
sobrevender *vt* : to oversell
sobrevenir {87} *vi* ACAECER : to take place, to come about <podrían sobrevenir complicaciones : complications could occur>
sobrevivencia *nf* → **supervivencia**
sobreviviente → **superviviente**
sobrevivir *vi* : to survive — *vt* : to outlive, to outlast
sobrevolar {19} *vt* : to fly over, to overfly
sobriedad *nf* : sobriety, moderation
sobrino, -na *n* : nephew *m*, niece *f*
sobrio, -bria *adj* : sober — **sobriamente** *adv*

socarrón, -rrona *adj, mpl* **-rrones 1** : sly, cunning **2** : sarcastic

socavar *vt* : to undermine

sociabilidad *nf* : sociability

sociable *adj* : sociable

social *adj* : social — **socialmente** *adv*

socialista *adj & nmf* : socialist — **socialismo** *nm*

sociedad *nf* **1** : society **2** : company, enterprise **3 sociedad anónima** : incorporated company

socio, -cia *n* **1** : member **2** : partner

socioeconómico, -ca *adj* : socioeconomic

sociología *nf* : sociology

sociológico, -ca *adj* : sociological — **sociológicamente** *adv*

sociólogo, -ga *n* : sociologist

socorrer *vt* : to assist, to come to the aid of

socorrido, -da *adj* ÚTIL : handy, practical

socorrista *nmf* **1** : rescue worker **2** : lifeguard

socorro *nm* AUXILIO **1** : aid, help <equipo de socorro : rescue team> **2 ¡socorro!** : help!

soda *nf* : soda, soda water

sodio *nf* : sodium

soez *adj, pl* **soeces** GROSERO : rude, vulgar — **soezmente** *adv*

sofá *nm* : couch, sofa

sofistería *nf* : sophistry — **sofista** *nmf*

sofisticación *nf, pl* **-ciones** : sophistication

sofisticado, -da *adj* : sophisticated

sofocante *adj* : suffocating, stifling

sofocar {72} *vt* **1** AHOGAR : to suffocate, to smother **2** EXTINGUIR : to extinguish, to put out (a fire) **3** APLASTAR : to crush, to put down <sofocar una rebelión : to crush a rebellion> — **sofocarse** *vr* **1** : to suffocate **2** *fam* : to get upset, to get mad

sofreír {66} *vt* : to sauté

sofrito[1], -ta *adj* : sautéed

sofrito[2] *nm* : seasoning sauce

softbol *nm* : softball

software *nm* : software

soga *nf* : rope

soja *nf* → **soya**

sojuzgar *vt* : to subdue, to conquer, to subjugate

sol *nm* **1** : sun **2** : Peruvian unit of currency

solamente *adv* SÓLO : only, just

solapa *nf* **1** : lapel (of a jacket) **2** : flap (of an envelope)

solapado, -da *adj* : secret, underhanded

solapar *vt* : to cover up, to keep secret — **solaparse** *vr* : to overlap

solar[1] {19} *vt* : to floor, to tile

solar[2] *adj* : solar, sun

solar[3] *nm* **1** TERRENO : lot, piece of land, site **2** *Cuba, Peru* : tenement building

solariego, -ga *adj* : ancestral

solaz *nm, pl* **solaces 1** CONSUELO : solace, comfort **2** DESCANSO : relaxation, recreation

solazarse {21} *vr* : to relax, to enjoy oneself

soldado *nm* **1** : soldier **2 soldado raso** : private, enlisted man

soldador[1], -dora *n* : welder

soldador[2] *nm* : soldering iron

soldadura *nf* **1** : welding **2** : soldering, solder

soldar {19} *vt* **1** : to weld **2** : to solder

soleado, -da *adj* : sunny

soledad *nf* : loneliness, solitude

solemne *adj* : solemn — **solemnemente** *adv*

solemnidad *nf* : solemnity

soler {78} *vi* : to be in the habit of, to tend to <solía tomar café por la tarde : she usually drank coffee in the afternoon> <eso suele ocurrir : that frequently happens>

solera *nf* **1** : prop, support **2** : tradition

solicitante *nmf* : applicant

solicitar *vt* **1** : to request, to solicit **2** : to apply for <solicitar empleo : to apply for employment>

solícito, -ta *adj* : solicitous, attentive, obliging

solicitud *nf* **1** : solicitude, concern **2** : request **3** : application

solidaridad *nf* : solidarity

solidario, -ria *adj* : supportive, united in support <se declararon solidarios con la nueva ley : they declared their support for the new law> <espíritu solidario : spirit of solidarity>

solidarizar {21} *vi* : to be in solidarity <solidarizamos con la huelga : we support the strike>

solidez *nf* **1** : solidity, firmness **2** : soundness (of an argument, etc.)

solidificar {72} *vt* : to solidify, to make solid — **solidificarse** *vr* — **solidificación** *nf*

sólido[1], -da *adj* **1** : solid, firm **2** : sturdy, well-made **3** : sound, well-founded — **sólidamente** *adv*

sólido[2] *nm* : solid

soliloquio *nm* : soliloquy

solista *nmf* : soloist

solitaria *nf* TENIA : tapeworm

solitario[1], -ria *adj* **1** : lonely **2** : lone, solitary **3** DESIERTO : deserted, lonely <una calle solitaria : a deserted street>

solitario[2], -ria *n* : recluse, loner

solitario[3] *nm* : solitaire

sollozar {21} *vi* : to sob

sollozo *nm* : sob

solo[1], -la *adj* **1** : alone, by oneself **2** : lonely **3** ÚNICO : only, sole, unique <hay un solo problema : there's only one problem> **4 a solas** : alone

solo[2] *nm* : solo

sólo *adv* SOLAMENTE : just, only <sólo quieren comer : they just want to eat>

solomillo *nm* : sirloin, loin

solsticio *nm* : solstice

soltar {19} *vt* **1 :** to let go of, to drop **2 :** to release, to set free **3** AFLOJAR **:** to loosen, to slacken
soltería *nf* **:** bachelorhood, spinsterhood
soltero[1], -ra *adj* **:** single, unmarried
soltero[2], -ra *n* **1 :** bachelor *m,* single man *m,* single woman *f* **2 apellido de soltera :** maiden name
soltura *nf* **1 :** looseness, slackness **2 :** fluency (of language) **3 :** agility, ease of movement
soluble *adj* **:** soluble — **solubilidad** *nf*
solución *nf, pl* **-ciones 1 :** solution (in a liquid) **2 :** answer, solution
solucionar *vt* RESOLVER **:** to solve, to resolve — **solucionarse** *vr*
solvencia *nf* **1 :** solvency **2 :** settling, payment (of debts) **3 :** reliability <solvencia moral : trustworthiness>
solvente[1] *adj* **1 :** solvent **2 :** reliable, trustworthy
solvente[2] *nm* **:** solvent
somalí *adj & nmf* **:** Somalian
sombra *nf* **1 :** shadow **2 :** shade **3 sombras** *nfpl* **:** darkness, shadows *pl* **4 sin sombra de duda :** without a shadow of a doubt
sombreado, -da *adj* **1 :** shady **2 :** shaded, darkened
sombrear *vt* **:** to shade
sombrerero, -ra *n* **:** milliner, hatter
sombrero *nm* **1 :** hat **2 sin ~ :** bareheaded **3 sombrero hongo :** derby
sombrilla *nf* **:** parasol, umbrella
sombrío, -bría *adj* LÓBREGO **:** dark, somber, gloomy — **sombríamente** *adv*
someramente *adv* **:** cursorily, summarily
somero, -ra *adj* **:** superficial, cursory, shallow
someter *vt* **1 :** to subjugate, to conquer **2 :** to subordinate **3 :** to subject (to treatment or testing) **4 :** to submit, to present — **someterse** *vr* **1 :** to submit, to yield **2 :** to undergo
sometimiento *nm* **1 :** submission, subjection **2 :** presentation
somnífero[1], -ra *adj* **:** soporific
somnífero[2] *nm* **:** sleeping pill
somnolencia *nf* **:** drowsiness, sleepiness
somnoliento, -ta *adj* **:** drowsy, sleepy
somorgujo *or* **somormujo** *nm* **:** loon, grebe
somos → **ser**
son[1] → **ser**
son[2] *nm* **1 :** sound <al son de la trompeta : at the sound of the trumpet> **2 :** news, rumor **3 en son de :** as, in the manner of, by way of <en son de broma : as a joke> <en son de paz : in peace>
sonado, -da *adj* **:** celebrated, famous, much-discussed
sonaja *nf* **:** rattle
sonajero *nm* **:** rattle (toy)
sonámbulo, -la *n* **:** sleepwalker
sonar[1] {19} *vi* **1 :** to sound <suena bien : it sounds good> **2 :** to ring (bells) **3 :** to look or sound familiar <me suena ese nombre : that name rings a bell> **4 ~ a :** to sound like — *vt* **1 :** to ring **2 :** to blow (a trumpet, a nose) — **sonarse** *vr* **:** to blow one's nose
sonar[2] *nm* **:** sonar
sonata *nf* **:** sonata
sonda *nf* **1 :** sounding line **2 :** probe **3** CATÉTER **:** catheter
sondar *vt* **1 :** to sound, to probe (in medicine, drilling, etc.) **2 :** to probe, to explore (outer space)
sondear *vt* **1 :** to sound **2 :** to probe **3 :** to sound out, to test (opinions, markets)
sondeo *nm* **1 :** sounding, probing **2 :** drilling **3** ENCUESTA **:** survey, poll
soneto *nm* **:** sonnet
sónico, -ca *adj* **:** sonic
sonido *nm* **:** sound
sonoridad *nf* **:** sonority, resonance
sonoro, -ra *adj* **1 :** resonant, sonorous, voiced (in linguistics) **2 :** resounding, loud **3 banda sonora :** soundtrack
sonreír {66} *vi* **:** to smile
sonriente *adj* **:** smiling
sonrisa *nf* **:** smile
sonrojar *vt* **:** to cause to blush — **sonrojarse** *vr* **:** to blush
sonrojo *nm* RUBOR **:** blush
sonrosado, -da *adj* **:** rosy, pink
sonsacar {72} *vt* **:** to wheedle, to extract
sonsonete *nm* **1 :** tapping **2 :** drone **3 :** mocking tone
soñador[1], -dora *adj* **:** dreamy
soñador[2], -dora *n* **:** dreamer
soñar {19} *v* **1 :** to dream **2 ~ con :** to dream about **3 soñar despierto :** to daydream
soñoliento, -ta *adj* **:** sleepy, drowsy
sopa *nf* **1 :** soup **2 estar hecho una sopa :** to be soaked to the bone
sopera *nf* **:** soup tureen
sopesar *vt* **:** to weigh, to evaluate
soplar *vi* **:** to blow — *vt* **:** to blow on, to blow out, to blow off
soplete *nm* **:** blowtorch
soplido *nm* **:** puff
soplo *nm* **:** puff, gust
soplón, -plona *n, mpl* **soplones** *fam* **:** tattletale, sneak
sopor *nm* SOMNOLENCIA **:** drowsiness, sleepiness
soporífero, -ra *adj* **:** soporific
soportable *adj* **:** bearable, tolerable
soportar *vt* **1** SOSTENER **:** to support, to hold up **2** RESISTIR **:** to withstand, to resist **3** AGUANTAR **:** to bear, to tolerate
soporte *nm* **:** base, stand, support
soprano *nmf* **:** soprano
sor *nf* **:** Sister (religious title)
sorber *vt* **1 :** to sip, to suck in **2 :** to absorb, to soak up
sorbete *nm* **:** sherbet
sorbo *nm* **1 :** sip, gulp, swallow **2 beber a sorbos :** to sip

sordera *nf* : deafness

sordidez *nf, pl* **-deces** : sordidness, squalor

sórdido, -da *adj* : sordid, dirty, squalid

sordina *nf* : mute (for a musical instrument)

sordo, -da *adj* **1** : deaf **2** : muted, muffled

sordomudo, -da *n* : deaf-mute

sorgo *nm* : sorghum

soriasis *nfs & pl* : psoriasis

sorna *nf* : sarcasm, mocking tone

sorprendente *adj* : surprising — **sorprendentemente** *adv*

sorprender *vt* : to surprise — **sorprenderse** *vr*

sorpresa *nf* : surprise

sorpresivo, -va *adj* **1** : surprising, surprise **2** IMPREVISTO : sudden, unexpected

sortear *vt* **1** RIFAR : to raffle, to draw lots for **2** : to dodge, to avoid

sorteo *nm* : drawing, raffle

sortija *nf* **1** ANILLO : ring **2** : curl, ringlet

sortilegio *nm* **1** HECHIZO : spell, charm **2** HECHICERÍA : sorcery

SOS *nm* : SOS

sosegado, -da *adj* SERENO : calm, tranquil, serene

sosegar {49} *vt* : to calm, to pacify — **sosegarse** *vr*

sosiego *nm* : tranquillity, serenity, calm

soslayar *vt* ESQUIVAR : to dodge, to evade

soslayo *nm* **de ~** : obliquely, sideways <mirar de soslayo : to look askance>

soso, -sa *adj* **1** INSÍPIDO : bland, flavorless **2** ABURRIDO : dull, boring

sospecha *nf* : suspicion

sospechar *vt* : to suspect — *vi* : to be suspicious

sospechosamente *adv* : suspiciously

sospechoso[1], -sa *adj* : suspicious, suspect

sospechoso[2], -sa *n* : suspect

sostén *nm, pl* **sostenes 1** APOYO : support **2** : sustenance **3** : brassiere, bra

sostener {80} *vt* **1** : to support, to hold up **2** : to hold <sostenme la puerta : hold the door for me> <sostener una conversación : to hold a conversation> **3** : to sustain, to maintain — **sostenerse** *vr* **1** : to stand, to hold oneself up **2** : to continue, to remain

sostenible *adj* : sustainable, tenable

sostenido[1], -da *adj* **1** : sustained, prolonged **2** : sharp (in music)

sostenido[2] *nm* : sharp (in music)

sostuvo, etc. → **sostener**

sotana *nf* : cassock

sótano *nm* : basement

sotavento *nm* : lee <a sotavento : leeward>

soterrar {55} *vt* **1** : to bury **2** : to conceal, to hide away

soto *nm* : grove, copse

souvenir *nm, pl* **-nirs** RECUERDO : souvenir, memento

soviético, -ca *adj* : Soviet

soy → **ser**

soya *nf* : soy, soybean

spaghetti *nm* → **espagueti**

sport [ɛ'spor] *adj* : sport, casual

sprint [ɛ'sprin, -'sprint] *nm* : sprint — **sprinter** *nmf*

squash [ɛ'skwaʃ, -'skwatʃ] *nm* : squash (sport)

Sr. *nm* : Mr.

Sra. *nf* : Mrs., Ms.

Srta. *or* **Srita.** *nf* : Miss, Ms.

standard → **estándar**

stress *nm* → **estrés**

su *adj* **1** : his, her, its, their, one's <su libro : her book> <sus consecuencias : its consequences> **2** (*formal*) : your <tómese su medicina, señor : take your medicine, sir>

suave *adj* **1** BLANDO : soft **2** LISO : smooth **3** : gentle, mild **4** *Mex fam* : great, fantastic

suavemente *adj* : smoothly, gently, softly

suavidad *nf* : softness, smoothness, mellowness

suavizante *nm* : softener, fabric softener

suavizar {21} *vt* **1** : to soften, to smooth out **2** : to tone down — **suavizarse** *vr*

subacuático, -ca *adj* : underwater

subalterno[1], -na *adj* **1** SUBORDINADO : subordinate **2** SECUNDARIO : secondary

subalterno[2], -na *n* SUBORDINADO : subordinate

subarrendar {55} *vt* : to sublet

subasta *nf* : auction

subastador, -dora *n* : auctioneer

subastar *vt* : to auction, to auction off

subcampeón, -peona *n, mpl* **-peones** : runner-up

subcomité *nm* : subcommittee

subconsciente *adj & nm* : subconscious — **subconscientemente** *adv*

subcontratar *vt* : to subcontract

subcontratista *nmf* : subcontractor

subcultura *nf* : subculture

subdesarrollado, -da *adj* : underdeveloped

subdirector, -tora *n* : assistant manager

súbdito, -ta *n* : subject (of a monarch)

subdividir *vt* : to subdivide

subdivisión *nf, pl* **-siones** : subdivision

subestimar *vt* : to underestimate, to undervalue

subexponer {60} *vt* : to underexpose

subexposición *nf, pl* **-ciones** : underexposure

subgrupo *nm* : subgroup

subibaja *nm* : seesaw

subida *nf* **1** : ascent, climb **2** : rise, increase **3** : slope, hill <ir de subida : to go uphill>

subido, -da *adj* **1 :** intense, strong <amarillo subido : bright yellow> **2 subido de tono :** risqué

subir *vt* **1 :** to bring up, to take up **2 :** to climb, to go up **3 :** to raise — *vi* **1 :** to go up, to come up **2 :** to rise, to increase **3 :** to be promoted **4 ~ a :** to get on, to mount <subir a un tren : to get on a train> — **subirse** *vr* **1 :** to climb (up) **2 :** to pull up (clothing) **3 subirse a la cabeza :** to go to one's head

súbito, -ta *adj* **1** REPENTINO **:** sudden **2 de ~ :** all of a sudden, suddenly — **súbitamente** *adv*

subjetivo, -va *adj* **:** subjective — **subjetivamente** *adv* — **subjetividad** *nf*

subjuntivo[1]**, -va** *adj* **:** subjunctive

subjuntivo[2] *nm* **:** subjunctive

sublevación *nf, pl* **-ciones** ALZAMIENTO **:** uprising, rebellion

sublevar *vt* **:** to incite to rebellion — **sublevarse** *vr* **:** to rebel, to rise up

sublimar *vt* **:** to sublimate — **sublimación** *nf*

sublime *adj* **:** sublime

submarinismo *nm* **:** scuba diving

submarinista *nmf* **:** scuba diver

submarino[1]**, -na** *adj* **:** submarine, undersea

submarino[2] *nm* **:** submarine

suboficial *nmf* **:** noncommissioned officer, petty officer

subordinado, -da *adj & n* **:** subordinate

subordinar *vt* **:** to subordinate — **subordinarse** *vr* — **subordinación** *nf*

subproducto *nm* **:** by-product

subrayar *vt* **1 :** to underline, to underscore **2** ENFATIZAR **:** to highlight, to emphasize

subrepticio, -cia *adj* **:** surreptitious — **subrepticiamente** *adv*

subsahariano, -na *adj* **:** sub-Saharan

subsanar *vt* **1** RECTIFICAR **:** to rectify, to correct **2 :** to overlook, to excuse **3 :** to make up for

subscribir → suscribir

subsecretario, -ria *n* **:** undersecretary

subsecuente *adj* **:** subsequent — **subsecuentemente** *adv*

subsidiar *vt* **:** to subsidize

subsidiaria *nf* **:** subsidiary

subsidio *nm* **:** subsidy

subsiguiente *adj* **:** subsequent

subsistencia *nf* **1 :** subsistence **2 :** sustenance

subsistir *vi* **1 :** to subsist, to live **2 :** to endure, to survive

substancia *nf* **→ sustancia**

subteniente *nmf* **:** second lieutenant

subterfugio *nm* **:** subterfuge

subterráneo[1]**, -nea** *adj* **:** underground, subterranean

subterráneo[2] *nm* **1 :** underground passage, tunnel **2** *Arg, Uru* **:** subway

subtítulo *nm* **:** subtitle, subheading

subtotal *nm* **:** subtotal

suburbano, -na *adj* **:** suburban

suburbio *nm* **1 :** suburb **2 :** slum (outside a city)

subvención *nf, pl* **-ciones :** subsidy, grant

subvencionar *vt* **:** to subsidize

subversivo, -va *adj & n* **:** subversive — **subversión** *nf*

subvertir {76} *vt* **:** to subvert

subyacente *adj* **:** underlying

subyugar {52} *vt* **:** to subjugate — **subyugación** *nf*

succión *nf, pl* **succiones :** suction

succionar *vt* **:** to suck up, to draw in

sucedáneo *nm* **:** substitute <sucedáneo de azucar : sugar substitute>

suceder *vi* **1** OCURRIR **:** to happen, to occur <¿qué sucede? : what's going on?> <suceda lo que suceda : come what may> **2 ~ a :** to follow, to succeed <suceder al trono : to succeed to the throne> <a la primavera sucede el verano : summer follows sping>

sucesión *nf, pl* **-siones 1 :** succession **2 :** sequence, series **3 :** issue, heirs *pl*

sucesivamente *adv* **:** successively, consecutively <y así sucesivamente : and so on>

sucesivo, -va *adj* **:** successive <en los días sucesivos : in the days that followed>

suceso *nm* **1 :** event, happening, occurrence **2 :** incident, crime

sucesor, -sora *n* **:** successor

suciedad *nf* **1 :** dirtiness, filthiness **2** MUGRE **:** dirt, filth

sucinto, -ta *adj* CONCISO **:** succinct, concise — **sucintamente** *adv*

sucio, -cia *adj* **:** dirty, filthy

sucre *nm* **:** Ecuadoran unit of currency

suculento, -ta *adj* **:** succulent

sucumbir *vi* **:** to succumb

sucursal *nf* **:** branch (of a business)

sudadera *nf* **:** sweatshirt

sudado, -da → sudoroso

sudafricano, -na *adj & n* **:** South African

sudamericano, -na *adj & n* **:** South American

sudanés, -nesa *adj & n, mpl* **-neses :** Sudanese

sudar *vi* TRANSPIRAR **:** to sweat, to perspire

sudario *nm* **:** shroud

sudeste → sureste

sudoeste → suroeste

sudor *nm* TRANSPIRACIÓN **:** sweat, perspiration

sudoroso, -sa *adj* **:** sweaty

sueco[1]**, -ca** *adj* **:** Swedish

sueco[2]**, -ca** *n* **:** Swede

sueco[3] *nm* **:** Swedish (language)

suegro, -gra *n* **1 :** father-in-law *m,* mother-in-law *f* **2 suegros** *nmpl* **:** in-laws

suela *nf* **:** sole (of a shoe)

suelda, etc. → soldar

sueldo *nm* **:** salary, wage

suele, etc. → soler

suelo *nm* **1** : ground <caerse al suelo : to fall down, to hit the ground> **2** : floor, flooring **3** TIERRA : soil, land
suelta, etc. → **soltar**
suelto[1], -ta *adj* : loose, free, unattached
suelto[2] *nm* : loose change
suena, etc. → **sonar**
sueña, etc. → **soñar**
sueño *nm* **1** : dream **2** : sleep <perder el sueño : to lose sleep> **3** : sleepiness <tener sueño : to be sleepy>
suero *nm* **1** : serum **2** : whey
suerte *nf* **1** FORTUNA : luck, fortune <tener suerte : to be lucky> <por suerte : luckily> **2** DESTINO : fate, destiny, lot **3** CLASE, GÉNERO : sort, kind <toda suerte de cosas : all kinds of things>
suertudo, -da *adj fam* : lucky
suéter *nm* : sweater
suficiencia *nf* **1** : adequacy, sufficiency **2** : competence, fitness **3** : smugness, self-satisfaction
suficiente *adj* **1** BASTANTE : enough, sufficient <tener suficiente : to have enough> **2** : suitable, fit **3** : smug, complacent
suficientemente *adv* : sufficiently, enough
sufijo *nm* : suffix
suflé *nm* : soufflé
sufragar {52} *vt* **1** AYUDAR : to help out, to support **2** : to defray (costs) — *vi* : to vote
sufragio *nm* : suffrage, vote
sufrido, -da *adj* **1** : long-suffering, patient **2** : sturdy, serviceable (of clothing)
sufrimiento *nm* : suffering
sufrir *vt* **1** : to suffer <sufrir una pérdida : to suffer a loss> **2** : to tolerate, to put up with <ella no lo puede sufrir : she can't stand him> — *vi* : to suffer
sugerencia *nf* : suggestion
sugerir {76} *vt* **1** PROPONER, RECOMENDAR : to suggest, to recommend, to propose **2** : to suggest, to bring to mind
sugestión *nf, pl* **-tiones** : suggestion, prompting <poder de sugestión : power of suggestion>
sugestionable *adj* : suggestible, impressionable
sugestionar *vt* : to influence, to sway — **sugestionarse** *vr* **~ con** : to talk oneself into, to become convinced of
sugestivo, -va *adj* **1** : suggestive **2** : interesting, stimulating
suicida[1] *adj* : suicidal
suicida[2] *nmf* : suicide victim, suicide
suicidarse *vr* : to commit suicide
suicidio *nm* : suicide
suite *nf* : suite
suizo, -za *adj & n* : Swiss
sujeción *nf, pl* **-ciones** **1** : holding, fastening **2** : subjection
sujetador *nm* **1** : fastener **2** : holder <sujetador de tazas : cup holder>
sujetalibros *nms & pl* : bookend
sujetapapeles *nms & pl* CLIP : paper clip
sujetar *vt* **1** : to hold on to, to steady, to hold down **2** FIJAR : to fasten, to attach **3** DOMINAR : to subdue, to conquer — **sujetarse** *vr* **1** : to hold on, to hang on **2** **~ a** : to abide by
sujeto[1], -ta *adj* **1** : secure, fastened **2** **~ a** : subject to
sujeto[2] *nm* **1** INDIVIDUO : individual, character **2** : subject (in grammar)
sulfúrico, -ca *adj* : sulfuric
sulfuro *nm* : sulfur
sultán *nm, pl* **sultanes** : sultan
suma *nf* **1** CANTIDAD : sum, quantity **2** : addition
sumamente *adv* : extremely, exceedingly
sumar *vt* **1** : to add, to add up **2** : to add up to, to total — *vi* : to add up — **sumarse** *vr* **~ a** : to join
sumario[1], -ria *adj* SUCINTO : succinct, summary — **sumariamente** *adv*
sumario[2] *nm* : summary
sumergir {35} *vt* : to submerge, to immerse, to plunge — **sumergirse** *vr*
sumersión *nf, pl* **-siones** : submersion, immersion
sumidero *nm* : drain, sewer
suministrar *vt* : to supply, to provide
suministro *nm* : supply, provision
sumir *vt* SUMERGIR : to plunge, to immerse, to sink — **sumirse** *vr*
sumisión *nf, pl* **-siones** **1** : submission **2** : submissiveness
sumiso, -sa *adj* : submissive, acquiescent, docile
sumo, -ma *adj* **1** : extreme, great, high <la suma autoridad : the highest authority> **2** **a lo sumo** : at the most — **sumamente** *adv*
suntuoso, -sa *adj* : sumptuous, lavish — **suntuosamente** *adv*
supeditar *vt* SUBORDINAR : to subordinate — **supeditación** *nf*
super[1] *or* **súper** *adj fam* : super, great
super[2] *nm* SUPERMERCADO : market, supermarket
superable *adj* : surmountable
superabundancia *nf* : overabundance, superabundance — **superabundante** *adj*
superar *vt* **1** : to surpass, to exceed **2** : to overcome, to surmount — **superarse** *vr* : to improve oneself
superávit *nm, pl* **-vit** *or* **-vits** : surplus
superchería *nf* : trickery, fraud
superestructura *nf* : superstructure
superficial *adj* : superficial — **superficialmente** *adv*
superficialidad *nf* : superficiality
superficie *nf* **1** : surface **2** : area <el superficie de un triángulo : the area of a triangle>
superfluidad *nf* : superfluity
superfluo, -flua *adj* : superfluous
superintendente *nmf* : supervisor, superintendent

superior[1] *adj* **1 :** superior **2 :** upper <nivel superior : upper level> **3 :** higher <educación superior : higher education> **4 ~ a :** above, higher than, in excess of

superior[2] *nm* **:** superior

superioridad *nf* **:** superiority

superlativo[1], **-va** *adj* **:** superlative

superlativo[2] *nm* **:** superlative

supermercado *nm* **:** supermarket

superpoblación *nf, pl* **-ciones :** overpopulation

superpoblado, -da *adj* **:** overpopulated

superponer {60} *vt* **:** to superimpose

superpotencia *nf* **:** superpower

superproducción *nf* → **sobreproducción**

supersónico, -ca *adj* **:** supersonic

superstición *nf, pl* **-ciones :** superstition

supersticioso, -sa *adj* **:** superstitious

supervisar *vt* **:** to supervise, to oversee

supervisión *nf, pl* **-siones :** supervision

supervisor, -sora *n* **:** supervisor, overseer

supervivencia *nf* **:** survival

superviviente *nmf* **:** survivor

supino, -na *adj* **:** supine

suplantar *vt* **:** to supplant, to replace

suplemental → **suplementario**

suplementario, -ria *adj* **:** supplementary, additional, extra

suplemento *nm* **:** supplement

suplencia *nf* **:** substitution, replacement

suplente *adj & nmf* **:** substitute <equipo suplente : replacement team>

supletorio, -ria *adj* **:** extra, additional <teléfono supletorio : extension phone> <cama supletoria : spare bed>

súplica *nf* **:** plea, entreaty

suplicar {72} *vt* IMPLORAR, ROGAR **:** to entreat, to implore, to supplicate

suplicio *nm* TORMENTO **:** ordeal, torture

suplir *vt* **1** COMPENSAR **:** to make up for, to compensate for **2** REEMPLAZAR **:** to replace, to substitute

supo, etc. → **saber**

suponer {60} *vt* **1** PRESUMIR **:** to suppose, to assume <supongo que sí : I guess so, I suppose so> <se supone que van a llegar mañana : they're supposed to arrive tomorrow> **2 :** to imply, to suggest **3 :** to involve, to entail <el éxito supone mucho trabajo : success involves a lot of work>

suposición *nf, pl* **-ciones** PRESUNCIÓN **:** supposition, assumption

supositorio *nm* **:** suppository

supremacía *nf* **:** supremacy

supremo, -ma *adj* **:** supreme

supresión *nf, pl* **-siones 1 :** suppression, elimination **2 :** deletion

suprimir *vt* **1 :** to suppress, to eliminate **2 :** to delete

supuestamente *adv* **:** supposedly, allegedly

supuesto, -ta *adj* **1 :** supposed, alleged **2 por ~ :** of course, absolutely

supurar *vi* **:** to ooze, to discharge

supuso, etc. → **suponer**

sur[1] *adj* **:** southern, southerly, south

sur[2] *nm* **1 :** south, South **2 :** south wind

surafricano, -na → **sudafricano**

suramericano, -na → **sudamericano**

surcar {72} *vt* **1 :** to plow (through) **2 :** to groove, to score, to furrow

surco *nm* **:** groove, furrow, rut

sureño[1], **-ña** *adj* **:** southern, Southern

sureño[2], **-ña** *n* **:** Southerner

sureste[1] *adj* **1 :** southeast, southeastern **2 :** southeasterly

sureste[2] *nm* **:** southeast, Southeast

surf *nm* **:** surfing

surfear *vi* **:** to surf

surfing *nm* → **surf**

surfista *nmf* **:** surfer

surgimiento *nm* **:** rise, emergence

surgir {35} *vi* **:** to rise, to arise, to emerge

suroeste[1] *adj* **1 :** southwest, southwestern **2 :** southwesterly

suroeste[2] *nm* **:** southwest, Southwest

surtido[1], **-da** *adj* **1 :** assorted, varied **2 :** stocked, provisioned

surtido[2] *nm* **:** assortment, selection

surtidor *nm* **1 :** jet, spout **2** *Arg, Chile, Spain* **:** gas pump

surtir *vt* **1 :** to supply, to provide <surtir un pedido : to fill an order> **2 surtir efecto :** to have an effect — *vi* **:** to spout, to spurt up — **surtirse** *vr* **:** to stock up

susceptible *adj* **:** susceptible, sensitive — **susceptibilidad** *nf*

suscitar *vt* **:** to provoke, to give rise to

suscribir {33} *vt* **1 :** to sign (a formal document) **2 :** to endorse, to sanction — **suscribirse** *vr* **~ a :** to subscribe to

suscripción *nf, pl* **-ciones 1 :** subscription **2 :** endorsement, sanction **3 :** signing

suscriptor, -tora *n* **:** subscriber

susodicho, -cha *adj* **:** aforementioned, aforesaid

suspender *vt* **1** COLGAR **:** to suspend, to hang **2 :** to suspend, to discontinue **3 :** to suspend, to dismiss

suspensión *nf, pl* **-siones :** suspension

suspenso *nm* **:** suspense

suspicacia *nf* **:** suspicion, mistrust

suspicaz *adj, pl* **-caces** DESCONFIADO **:** suspicious, wary

suspirar *vi* **:** to sigh

suspiro *nm* **:** sigh

surque, etc. → **surcar**

suscrito *pp* → **suscribir**

sustancia *nf* **1 :** substance **2 sin ~ :** shallow, lacking substance

sustancial *adj* **1 :** substantial **2** ESENCIAL, FUNDAMENTAL **:** essential, fundamental — **sustancialmente** *adv*

sustancioso, -sa *adj* **1** NUTRITIVO **:** hearty, nutritious **2 :** substantial, solid
sustantivo *nm* **:** noun
sustentación *nf, pl* **-ciones** SOSTÉN **:** support
sustentar *vt* **1 :** to support, to hold up **2 :** to sustain, to nourish **3 :** to maintain, to hold (an opinion) — **sustentarse** *vr* **:** to support oneself
sustento *nm* **1 :** means of support, livelihood **2 :** sustenance, food
sustitución *nf, pl* **-ciones :** replacement, substitution
sustituir {41} *vt* **1 :** to replace, to substitute for **2 :** to stand in for
sustituto, -ta *n* **:** substitute, stand-in
susto *nm* **:** fright, scare
sustracción *nf, pl* **-ciones 1** RESTA **:** subtraction **2 :** theft
sustraer {81} *vt* **1 :** to remove, to take away **2** RESTAR **:** to subtract **3 :** to steal — **sustraerse** *vr* **~ a :** to avoid, to evade
susurrar *vi* **1 :** to whisper **2 :** to murmur **3 :** to rustle (leaves, etc.) — *vt* **:** to whisper
susurro *nm* **1 :** whisper **2 :** murmur **3 :** rustle, rustling
sutil *adj* **1 :** delicate, thin, fine **2 :** subtle
sutileza *nf* **1 :** delicacy **2 :** subtlety
sutura *nf* **:** suture
suturar *vt* **:** to suture
suyo[1], **-ya** *adj* **1 :** his, her, its, theirs <los libros suyos : his books> <un amigo suyo : a friend of hers> <esta casa es suya : this house is theirs> **2** (*formal*) **:** yours <¿este abrigo es suyo, señor? : is this your coat, sir?>
suyo[2], **-ya** *pron* **1 :** his, hers, theirs <mi guitarra y la suya : my guitar and hers> <ellos trajeron las suyas : they brought theirs, they brought their own> **2** (*formal*) **:** yours <usted olvidó la suya : you forgot yours>
switch *nm* **:** switch

T

t *nf* **:** twenty-first letter of the Spanish alphabet
taba *nf* **:** anklebone
tabacalero[1], **-ra** *adj* **:** tobacco <industria tabacalera : tobacco industry>
tabacalero[2], **-ra** *n* **:** tobacco grower
tabaco *nm* **:** tobacco
tábano *nm* **:** horsefly
taberna *nf* **:** tavern, bar
tabernáculo *nm* **:** tabernacle
tabicar {72} *vt* **:** to wall up
tabique *nm* **:** thin wall, partition
tabla *nf* **1 :** table, list <tabla de multiplicar : multiplication table> **2 :** board, plank, slab <tabla de planchar : ironing board> **3 :** plot, strip (of land) **4 tablas** *nfpl* **:** stage, boards *pl*
tablado *nm* **1 :** flooring, floorboards **2 :** platform, scaffold **3 :** stage
tablero *nm* **1 :** bulletin board **2 :** board (in games) <tablero de ajedrez : chessboard> <tablero de damas : checkerboard> **3** PIZARRA **:** blackboard **4 :** switchboard **5 tablero de instrumentos :** dashboard, instrument panel
tableta *nf* **1** COMPRIMIDO, PÍLDORA **:** tablet, pill **2 :** bar (of chocolate)
tabletear *vi* **:** to rattle, to clack
tableteo *nm* **:** clack, rattling
tablilla *nf* **1 :** small board or tablet **2 :** bulletin board **3 :** splint
tabloide *nm* **:** tabloid
tablón *nm, pl* **tablones 1 :** plank, beam **2 tablón de anuncios :** bulletin board
tabú[1] *adj* **:** taboo
tabú[2] *nm, pl* **tabúes** or **tabús :** taboo
tabulador *nm* **:** tabulator
tabular[1] *vt* **:** to tabulate
tabular[2] *adj* **:** tabular
taburete *nm* **:** footstool, stool
tacañería *nf* **:** miserliness, stinginess
tacaño[1], **-ña** *adj* MEZQUINO **:** stingy, miserly
tacaño[2], **-ña** *n* **:** miser, tightwad
tacha *nf* **1 :** flaw, blemish, defect **2 poner tacha a :** to find fault with **3 sin ~ :** flawless
tachadura *nf* **:** erasure, correction
tachar *vt* **1 :** to cross out, to delete **2 ~ de :** to accuse of, to label as <lo tacharon de mentiroso : they accused him of being a liar>
tachón *nm, pl* **tachones :** stud, hobnail
tachonar *vt* **:** to stud
tachuela *nf* **:** tack, hobnail, stud
tácito, -ta *adj* **:** tacit, implicit — **tácitamente** *adv*
taciturno, -na *adj* **1 :** taciturn **2 :** sullen, gloomy
tacle *nm* **:** tackle
taclear *vt* **:** to tackle (in football)
taco *nm* **1 :** wad, stopper, plug **2 :** pad (of paper) **3 :** cleat **4 :** heel (of a shoe) **5 :** cue (in billiards) **6 :** light snack, bite **7 :** taco
tacón *nm, pl* **tacones :** heel (of a shoe) <de tacón alto : high-heeled>
táctica *nf* **:** tactic, tactics *pl*
táctico[1], **-ca** *adj* **:** tactical
táctico[2], **-ca** *n* **:** tactician
táctil *adj* **:** tactile
tacto *nm* **1 :** touch, touching, feel **2** DELICADEZA **:** tact
tafetán *nm, pl* **-tanes :** taffeta
tahúr *nm, pl* **tahúres :** gambler
tailandés[1], **-desa** *adj & n, pl* **-deses :** Thai
tailandés[2] *nm* **:** Thai (language)

taimado, -da *adj* **1 :** crafty, sly **2** *Chile* **:** sullen, sulky
tajada *nf* **1 :** slice **2 sacar tajada** *fam* **:** to get one's share
tajante *adj* **1 :** cutting, sharp **2 :** decisive, categorical
tajantemente *adj* **:** emphatically, categorically
tajar *vt* **:** to cut, to slice
tajo *nm* **1 :** cut, slash, gash **2** ESCARPA **:** steep cliff
tal[1] *adv* **1 :** so, in such a way **2 tal como :** just as <tal como lo hice : just the way I did it> **3 con tal que :** provided that, as long as **4 ¿qué tal? :** how are you?, how's it going?
tal[2] *adj* **1 :** such, such a **2 tal vez :** maybe, perhaps
tal[3] *pron* **1 :** such a one, someone **2 :** such a thing, something **3 tal para cual :** two of a kind
tala *nf* **:** felling (of trees)
taladrar *vt* **:** to drill
taladro *nm* **:** drill, auger <taladro eléctrico : power drill>
talante *nm* **1** HUMOR **:** mood, disposition **2** VOLUNTAD **:** will, willingness
talar *vt* **1 :** to cut down, to fell **2** DEVASTAR **:** to devastate, to destroy
talco *nm* **1 :** talc **2 :** talcum powder
talego *nm* **:** sack
talento *nm* **:** talent, ability
talentoso, -sa *adj* **:** talented, gifted
talismán *nm, pl* **-manes** AMULETO **:** talisman, charm
talla *nf* **1** ESTATURA **:** height **2 :** size (in clothing) **3 :** stature, status **4 :** sculpture, carving
tallar *vt* **1 :** to sculpt, to carve **2 :** to measure (someone's height) **3 :** to deal (cards)
tallarín *nf, pl* **-rines :** noodle
talle *nm* **1 :** size **2 :** waist, waistline **3 :** figure, shape
taller *nm* **1 :** shop, workshop **2 :** studio (of an artist)
tallo *nm* **:** stalk, stem <tallo de maíz : cornstalk>
talón *nm, pl* **talones 1 :** heel (of the foot) **2 :** stub (of a check) **3 talón de Aquiles :** Achilles' heel
talud *nm* **:** slope, incline
tamal *nm* **:** tamale
tamaño[1], **-ña** *adj* **:** such a big <¿crees tamaña mentira? : do you believe such a lie?>
tamaño[2] *nm* **1 :** size **2 de tamaño natural :** life-size
tamarindo *nm* **:** tamarind
tambalearse *vr* **1 :** to teeter **2 :** to totter, to stagger, to sway — **tambaleante** *adj*
tambaleo *nm* **:** staggering, lurching, swaying
también *adv* **:** too, as well, also
tambor *nm* **:** drum
tamborilear *vi* **:** to drum, to tap
tamborileo *nm* **:** tapping, drumming
tamiz *nm* **:** sieve
tamizar {21} *vt* **:** to sift
tampoco *adv* **:** neither, not either <ni yo tampoco : me neither>
tampón *nm, pl* **tampones 1 :** ink pad **2 :** tampon
tam–tam *nm* **:** tom-tom
tan *adv* **1 :** so, so very <no es tan difícil : it is not that difficult> **2 :** as <tan pronto como : as soon as> **3 tan siquiera :** at least, at the least **4 tan sólo :** only, merely
tanda *nf* **1 :** turn, shift **2 :** batch, lot, series
tándem *nm* **1 :** tandem (bicycle) **2 :** duo, pair
tangente *adj & nf* **:** tangent — **tangencial** *adj*
tangible *adj* **:** tangible
tango *nm* **:** tango
tanino *nm* **:** tannin
tanque *nm* **1 :** tank, reservoir **2 :** tanker, tank (vehicle)
tanteador *nm* MARCADOR **:** scoreboard
tantear *vt* **1 :** to feel, to grope **2 :** to size up, to weigh — *vi* **1 :** to keep score **2 :** to feel one's way
tanteo *nm* **1 :** estimate, rough calculation **2 :** testing, sizing up **3 :** scoring
tanto[1] *adv* **1 :** so much <tanto mejor : so much the better> **2 :** so long <¿por qué te tardaste tanto? : why did you take so long?>
tanto[2], **-ta** *adj* **1 :** so much, so many, such <no hagas tantas preguntas : don't ask so many questions> <tiene tanto encanto : he has such charm, he's so charming> **2 :** as much, as many <come tantos dulces como yo : she eats as many sweets as I do> **3 :** odd, however many <cuarenta y tantos años : forty-odd years>
tanto[3] *nm* **1 :** certain amount **2 :** goal, point (in sports) **3 al tanto :** abreast, in the picture **4 un tanto :** somewhat, rather <un tanto cansado : rather tired>
tanto[4], **-ta** *pron* **1 :** so much, so many <tiene tanto que hacer : she has so much to do> <¡no me des tantos! : don't give me so many!> **2 entre ~ :** meanwhile **3 por lo tanto :** therefore
tañer {79} *vt* **1 :** to ring (a bell) **2 :** to play (a musical instrument)
tañido *nm* **1** CAMPANADA **:** ring, peal, toll **2 :** sound (of an instrument)
tapa *nf* **1 :** cover, top, lid **2** *Spain* **:** bar snack
tapacubos *nms & pl* **:** hubcap
tapadera *nf* **1 :** cover, lid **2 :** front, cover (for an organization or person)
tapar *vt* **1** CUBRIR **:** to cover, to cover up **2** OBSTRUIR **:** to block, to obstruct — **taparse** *vr*
tapete *nm* **1 :** small rug, mat **2 :** table cover **3 poner sobre el tapete :** to bring up for discussion
tapia *nf* **:** (adobe) wall, garden wall
tapiar *vt* **1 :** to wall in **2 :** to enclose, to block off

tapicería *nf* **1 :** upholstery **2** TAPIZ **:** tapestry
tapicero, -ra *n* **:** upholsterer
tapioca *nf* **:** tapioca
tapir *nm* **:** tapir
tapiz *nm, pl* **tapices :** tapestry
tapizar {21} *vt* **1 :** to upholster **2 :** to cover, to carpet
tapón *nm, pl* **tapones 1 :** cork **2 :** bottle cap **3 :** plug, stopper
tapujo *nm* **1 :** deceit, pretension **2 sin tapujos :** openly, frankly
taquigrafía *nf* **:** stenography, shorthand
taquigráfico, -ca *adj* **:** stenographic
taquígrafo, -fa *n* **:** stenographer
taquilla *nf* **1 :** box office, ticket office **2 :** earnings *pl*, take
taquillero, -ra *adj* **:** box-office, popular <un éxito taquillero : a box-office success>
tarántula *nf* **:** tarantula
tararear *vt* **:** to hum
tardanza *nf* **:** lateness, delay
tardar *vi* **1 :** to delay, to take a long time **2 :** to be late **3 a más tardar :** at the latest — *vt* DEMORAR **:** to take (time) <tarda una hora : it takes an hour>
tarde[1] *adv* **1 :** late **2 tarde o temprano :** sooner or later
tarde[2] *nf* **1 :** afternoon, evening **2 ¡buenas tardes! :** good afternoon!, good evening! **3 en la tarde** *or* **por la tarde :** in the afternoon, in the evening
tardío, -día *adj* **:** late, tardy
tardo, -da *adj* **:** slow
tarea *nf* **1 :** task, job **2 :** homework
tarifa *nf* **1 :** rate <tarifas postales : postal rates> **2 :** fare (for transportation) **3 :** price list **4** ARANCEL **:** duty
tarima *nf* PLATAFORMA **:** dais, platform, stage
tarjeta *nf* **:** card <tarjeta de crédito : credit card> <tarjeta postal : postcard>
tarro *nm* **1 :** jar, pot **2** *Arg, Chile* **:** can, tin
tarta *nf* **1 :** tart **2 :** cake
tartaleta *nf* **:** tart
tartamudear *vi* **:** to stammer, to stutter
tartamudeo *nm* **:** stutter, stammer
tartán *nm, pl* **tartanes :** tartan, plaid
tártaro *nm* **:** tartar <cream of tartar : crémor, tártaro>
tasa *nf* **1 :** rate <tasa de desempleo : unemployment rate> **2 :** tax, fee **3 :** appraisal, valuation
tasación *nf, pl* **-ciones :** appraisal, assessment
tasador, -dora *n* **:** assessor, appraiser
tasar *vt* **1** VALORAR **:** to appraise, to value **2 :** to set the price of **3 :** to ration, to limit
tasca *nf* **:** cheap bar, dive
tatuaje *nm* **:** tattoo, tattooing
tatuar {3} *vt* **:** to tattoo
taurino, -na *adj* **:** bull, bullfighting
Tauro *nmf* **:** Taurus
tauromaquia *nf* **:** (art of) bullfighting
taxi *nm, pl* **taxis :** taxi, taxicab
taxidermia *nf* **:** taxidermy
taxidermista *nmf* **:** taxidermist
taxímetro *nm* **:** taximeter
taxista *nmf* **:** taxi driver
taza *nf* **1 :** cup **2 :** cupful **3 :** (toilet) bowl **4 :** basin (of a fountain)
tazón *nm, pl* **tazones 1 :** bowl **2 :** large cup, mug
te *pron* **1 :** you <te quiero : I love you> **2 :** for you, to you, from you <me gustaría dártelo : I would like to give it to you> **3 :** yourself, for yourself, to yourself, from yourself <¡cálmate! : calm yourself!> <¿te guardaste uno? : did you keep one for yourself?> **4 :** thee
té *nm* **1 :** tea **2 :** tea party
tea *nf* **:** torch
teatral *adj* **:** theatrical — **teatralmente** *adv*
teatro *nm* **1 :** theater **2 hacer teatro :** to put on an act, to exaggerate
teca *nf* **:** teak
techado *nm* **1 :** roof **2 bajo techado :** under cover, indoors
techar *vt* **:** to roof, to shingle
techo *nm* **1** TEJADO **:** roof **2 :** ceiling **3 :** upper limit, ceiling
techumbre *nf* **:** roofing
tecla *nf* **1 :** key (of a musical instrument or a machine) **2 dar en la tecla :** to hit the nail on the head
teclado *nm* **:** keyboard
teclear *vt* **:** to type in, to enter
técnica *nf* **1 :** technique, skill **2 :** technology
técnico[1], **-ca** *adj* **:** technical — **técnicamente** *adv*
técnico[2], **-ca** *n* **:** technician, expert, engineer
tecnología *nf* **:** technology
tecnológico, -ca *adj* **:** technological — **tecnológicamente** *adv*
tecolote *nm Mex* **:** owl
tedio *nm* **:** tedium, boredom
tedioso, -sa *adj* **:** tedious, boring — **tediosamente** *adv*
teja *nf* **:** tile
tejado *nm* TECHO **:** roof
tejedor, -dora *n* **:** weaver
tejer *vt* **1 :** to knit, to crochet **2 :** to weave **3** FABRICAR **:** to concoct, to make up, to fabricate
tejido *nm* **1** TELA **:** fabric, cloth **2 :** weave, texture **3 :** tissue <tejido muscular : muscle tissue>
tejo *nm* **:** yew
tejón *nm, pl* **tejones :** badger
tela *nf* **1 :** fabric, cloth, material **2 tela de araña :** spiderweb **3 poner en tela de juicio :** to call into question, to doubt
telar *nm* **:** loom
telaraña *nf* **:** spiderweb, cobweb
tele *nf fam* **:** TV, television
telecomunicación *nf, pl* **-ciones :** telecommunication

teleconferencia *nf* **:** teleconference
teledifusión *nf, pl* **-siones :** television broadcasting
teledirigido, -da *adj* **:** remote-controlled
telefonear *v* **:** to telephone, to call
telefónico, -ca *adj* **:** phone, telephone <llamada telefónica : phone call>
telefonista *nmf* **:** telephone operator
teléfono *nm* **1 :** telephone **2 llamar por teléfono :** to telephone, to make a phone call
telegrafiar {85} *v* **:** to telegraph
telegráfico, -ca *adj* **:** telegraphic
telégrafo *nm* **:** telegaph
telegrama *nm* **:** telegram
telenovela *nf* **:** soap opera
telepatía *nf* **:** telepathy
telepático, -ca *adj* **:** telepathic — **telepáticamente** *adv*
telescópico, -ca *adj* **:** telescopic
telescopio *nm* **:** telescope
telespectador, -dora *n* **:** television viewer
telesquí *nm, pl* **-squís :** ski lift
televidente *nmf* **:** television viewer
televisar *vt* **:** to televise
televisión *nf, pl* **-siones :** television, TV
televisivo, -va *adj* **:** television <serie televisiva : television series>
televisor *nm* **:** television set
telón *nm, pl* **telones 1 :** curtain (in theater) **2 telón de fondo :** backdrop, background
tema *nm* **1** ASUNTO **:** theme, topic, subject **2** MOTIVO **:** motif, central theme
temario *nm* **1 :** set of topics (for study) **2 :** agenda
temática *nf* **:** subject matter
temático, -ca *adj* **:** thematic
temblar {55} *vi* **1 :** to tremble, to shake, to shiver <le temblaban las rodillas : his knees were shaking> **2 :** to shudder, to be afraid <tiemblo con sólo pensarlo : I shudder to think of it>
temblor *nm* **1 :** shaking, trembling **2 :** tremor, earthquake
tembloroso, -sa *adj* **:** tremulous, trembling, shaking <con la voz temblorosa : with a shaky voice>
temer *vt* **:** to fear, to dread — *vi* **:** to be afraid
temerario, -ria *adj* **:** reckless, rash — **temerariamente** *adv*
temeridad *nf* **1 :** temerity, recklessness, rashness **2 :** rash act
temeroso, -sa *adj* MIEDOSO **:** fearful, frightened
temible *adj* **:** fearsome, dreadful
temor *nm* MIEDO **:** fear, dread
témpano *nm* **:** ice floe
temperamento *nm* **:** temperament — **temperamental** *adj*
temperancia *nf* **:** temperance
temperar *vt* MODERAR **:** to temper, to moderate — *vi* **:** to have a change of air
temperatura *nf* **:** temperature
tempestad *nf* **1 :** storm, tempest **2 tempestad de arena :** sandstorm
tempestuoso, -sa *adj* **:** tempestuous, stormy
templado, -da *adj* **1 :** temperate, mild **2 :** moderate, restrained **3 :** warm, lukewarm **4** VALIENTE **:** courageous, bold
templanza *nf* **1 :** temperance, moderation **2 :** mildness (of weather)
templar *vt* **1 :** to temper (steel) **2 :** to restrain, to moderate **3 :** to tune (a musical instrument) **4 :** to warm up, to cool down — **templarse** *vr* **1 :** to be moderate **2 :** to warm up, to cool down
temple *nm* **1 :** temper (of steel, etc.) **2** HUMOR **:** mood <de buen temple : in a good mood> **3 :** tuning **4** VALOR **:** courage
templo *nm* **1 :** temple **2 :** church, chapel
tempo *nm* **:** tempo (in music)
temporada *nf* **1 :** season, time <temporada de béisbol : baseball season> **2 :** period, spell <por temporadas : on and off>
temporal[1] *adj* **1 :** temporal **2 :** temporary
temporal[2] *nm* **1 :** storm **2 capear el temporal :** to weather the storm
temporalmente *adv* **:** temporarily
temporario, -ria *adj* **:** temporary — **temporariamente** *adv*
temporero[1]**, -ra** *adj* **:** temporary, seasonal
temporero[2]**, -ra** *n* **:** temporary or seasonal worker
temporizador *nm* **:** timer
tempranero, -ra *adj* **1 :** early **2 :** early-rising
temprano[1] *adv* **:** early <lo más temprano posible : as soon as possible>
temprano[2]**, -na** *adj* **:** early <la parte temprana del siglo : the early part of the century>
ten → **tener**
tenacidad *nf* **:** tenacity, perseverance
tenaz *adj, pl* **tenaces 1 :** tenacious, persistent **2 :** strong, tough
tenaza *nf or* **tenazas** *nfpl* **1 :** pliers, pincers **2 :** tongs **3 :** claw (of a crustacean)
tenazmente *adv* **:** tenaciously
tendedero *nm* **:** clothesline
tendencia *nf* **1** PROPENSIÓN **:** tendency, inclination **2 :** trend
tendencioso, -sa *adj* **:** tendencious, biased
tendente → **tendiente**
tender {56} *vt* **1** EXTENDER **:** to spread out, to lay out **2 :** to hang out (clothes) **3 :** to lay (cables, etc.) **4 :** to set (a trap) — *vi* **~ a :** to tend to, to have a tendency towards — **tenderse** *vr* **:** to stretch out, to lie down
tendero, -ra *n* **:** shopkeeper, storekeeper

tendido *nm* **1 :** laying (of cables, etc.) **2 :** seats *pl*, section (at a bullfight)
tendiente *adj* **~ a :** aimed at, designed to
tendón *nm, pl* **tendones :** tendon
tenebrosidad *nf* **:** darkness, gloom
tendrá, etc. → tener
tenebroso, -sa *adj* **1** OSCURO **:** gloomy, dark **2** SINIESTRO **:** sinister
tenedor[1], -dora *n* **1 :** holder **2 tenedor de libros, tenedora de libros :** bookkeeper
tenedor[2] *nm* **:** table fork
tenencia *nf* **1 :** possession, holding **2 :** tenancy **3 :** tenure
tener {80} *vt* **1 :** to have <tiene ojos verdes : she has green eyes> <tengo mucho que hacer : I have a lot to do> <tiene veinte años : he's twenty years old> <tiene un metro de largo : it's one meter long> **2 :** to hold <ten esto un momento : hold this for a moment> **3 :** to feel, to make <tengo frío : I'm cold> <eso nos tiene contentos : that makes us happy> **4 ~ por :** to think, to consider <me tienes por loco : you think I'm crazy> — *v aux* **1 tener que :** to have to <tengo que salir : I have to leave> <tiene que estar aquí : it has to be here, it must be here> **2** (*with past participle*) <tenía pensado escribirte : I've been thinking of writing to you> — **tenerse** *vr* **1 :** to stand up **2 ~ por :** to consider oneself <me tengo por afortunado : I consider myself lucky>
tenería *nf* CURTIDURÍA **:** tannery
tenga, etc. → tener
tenia *nf* SOLITARIA **:** tapeworm
teniente *nmf* **1 :** lieutenant **2 teniente coronel :** lieutenant colonel
tenis *nms & pl* **1 :** tennis **2 tenis** *nmpl* **:** sneakers *pl*
tenista *nmf* **:** tennis player
tenor *nm* **1 :** tenor **2 :** tone, sense
tensar *vt* **1 :** to tense, to make taut **2 :** to draw (a bow) — **tensarse** *vr* **:** to become tense
tensión *nf, pl* **tensiones 1 :** tension, tautness **2 :** stress, strain **3 tensión arterial :** blood pressure
tenso, -sa *adj* **:** tense
tentación *nf, pl* **-ciones :** temptation
tentáculo *nm* **:** tentacle, feeler
tentador[1], -dora *adj* **:** tempting
tentador[2], -dora *n* **:** tempter, temptress *f*
tentar {55} *vt* **1** TOCAR **:** to feel, to touch **2** PROBAR **:** to test, to try **3** ATRAER **:** to tempt, to entice
tentativa *nf* **:** attempt, try
tentempié *nm fam* **:** snack, bite
tenue *adj* **1 :** tenuous **2 :** faint, weak, dim **3 :** light, fine **4 :** thin, slender
teñir {67} *vt* **1 :** to dye **2 :** to stain
teodolito *nm* **:** theodolite, transit (for surveying)
teología *nf* **:** theology
teológico, -ca *adj* **:** theological
teólogo, -ga *n* **:** theologian
teorema *nm* **:** theorem
teoría *nf* **:** theory
teórico[1], -ca *adj* **:** theoretical — **teóricamente** *adv*
teórico[2], -ca *n* **:** theorist
teorizar {21} *vi* **:** to theorize
tepe *nm* **:** sod, turf
teponaztle *nm Mex* **:** traditional drum
tequila *nm* **:** tequila
terapeuta *nmf* **:** therapist
terapéutica *nf* **:** therapeutics
terapéutico, -ca *adj* **:** therapeutic
terapia *nf* **1 :** therapy **2 terapia intensiva :** intensive care
tercer → tercero
tercermundista *adj* **:** third-world
tercero[1], -ra *adj* (**tercer** *before masculine singular nouns*) **1 :** third **2 el Tercer Mundo :** the Third World
tercero[2], -ra *n* **:** third (in a series)
terciar *vt* **1 :** to place diagonally **2 :** to divide into three parts — *vi* **1 :** to mediate **2 ~ en :** to take part in
terciario, -ria *adj* **:** tertiary
tercio[1], -cia → tercero
tercio[2] *nm* **:** third <dos tercios : two thirds>
terciopelo *nm* **:** velvet
terco, -ca *adj* OBSTINADO **:** obstinate, stubborn
tergiversación *nf, pl* **-ciones :** distortion
tergiversar *vt* **:** to distort, to twist
termal *adj* **:** thermal, hot
termas *nfpl* **:** hot springs
térmico, -ca *adj* **:** thermal, heat <energía térmica : thermal energy>
terminación *nf, pl* **-ciones :** termination, conclusion
terminal[1] *adj* **:** terminal — **terminalmente** *adv*
terminal[2] *nm* (*in some regions f*) **:** (electric or electronic) terminal
terminal[3] *nf* (*in some regions m*) **:** terminal, station
terminante *adj* **:** final, definitive, categorical — **terminantemente** *adv*
terminar *vt* **1** CONCLUIR **:** to end, to conclude **2** ACABAR **:** to complete, to finish off — *vi* **1 :** to finish **2 :** to stop, to end — **terminarse** *vr* **1 :** to run out **2 :** to come to an end
término *nm* **1** CONCLUSIÓN **:** end, conclusion **2 :** term, expression **3 :** period, term of office **4 término medio :** happy medium **5 términos** *nmpl* **:** terms, specifications <los términos del acuerdo : the terms of the agreement>
terminología *nf* **:** terminology
termita *nf* **:** termite
termo *nm* **:** thermos
termodinámica *nf* **:** thermodynamics
termómetro *nm* **:** thermometer
termóstato *nm* **:** thermostat
ternera *nf* **:** veal
ternero, -ra *n* **:** calf

terno *nm* **1** : set of three **2** : three-piece suit
ternura *nf* : tenderness
terquedad *nf* OBSTINACIÓN : obstinacy, stubbornness
terracota *nf* : terra-cotta
terraplén *nm, pl* **-plenes** : terrace, embankment
terráqueo, -quea *adj* **1** : earth **2 globo terráqueo** : the earth, globe (of the earth)
terrateniente *nmf* : landowner
terraza *nf* **1** : terrace, veranda **2** : balcony (in a theater) **3** : terrace (in agriculture)
terremoto *nm* : earthquake
terrenal *adj* : worldly, earthly
terreno *nm* **1** : terrain **2** SUELO : earth, ground **3** : plot, tract of land **4 perder terreno** : to lose ground **5 preparar el terreno** : to pave the way
terrestre *adj* : terrestrial
terrible *adj* : terrible, horrible — **terriblemente** *adv*
terrier *nmf* : terrier
territorial *adj* : territorial
territorio *nm* : territory
terrón *nm, pl* **terrones 1** : clod (of earth) **2 terrón de azúcar** : lump of sugar
terror *nm* : terror
terrorífico, -ca *adj* : horrific, terrifying
terrorismo *nm* : terrorism
terrorista *adj & nmf* : terrorist
terroso, -sa *adj* : earthy <colores terrosos : earthy colors>
terruño *nm* : native land, homeland
terso, -sa *adj* **1** : smooth **2** : glossy, shiny **3** : polished, flowing (of a style)
tersura *nf* **1** : smoothness **2** : shine
tertulia *nf* : gathering, group <tertulia literaria : literary circle>
tesauro *nm* : thesaurus
tesis *nfs & pl* : thesis
tesón *nm* : persistence, tenacity
tesonero, -ra *adj* : persistent, tenacious
tesorería *nf* : treasurer's office
tesorero, -ra *n* : treasurer
tesoro *nm* **1** : treasure **2** : thesaurus
testaferro *nm* : figurehead
testamentario[1], -ria *adj* : testamentary
testamentario[2], -ria *n* ALBACEA : executor, executrix *f*
testamento *nm* : testament, will
testar *vi* : to draw up a will
testarudo, -da *adj* : stubborn, pigheaded
testículo *nm* : testicle
testificar {72} *v* : to testify
testigo *nmf* : witness
testimonial *adj* **1** : testimonial **2** : token
testimoniar *vi* : to testify
testimonio *nm* : testimony, statement
teta *nf* : teat
tétano *or* **tétanos** *nm* : tetanus, lockjaw
tetera *nf* **1** : teapot **2** : teakettle
tetilla *nf* **1** : teat **2** : nipple
tetina *nf* : nipple (on a bottle)
tétrico, -ca *adj* : somber, gloomy
textil *adj & nm* : textile
texto *nm* : text
textual *adj* : literal, exact — **textualmente** *adv*
textura *nf* : texture
tez *nf, pl* **teces** : complexion, coloring
ti *pron* **1** : you <es para ti : it's for you> **2 ti mismo, ti misma** : yourself **3** : thee
tía → **tío**
tiamina *nf* : thiamine
tianguis *nm Mex* : open-air market
tibetano, -na *adj & n* : Tibetan
tibia *nf* : tibia
tibieza *nf* **1** : tepidness **2** : halfheartedness
tibio, -bia *adj* **1** : lukewarm, tepid **2** : cool, unenthusiastic
tiburón *nm, pl* **-rones 1** : shark **2** : raider (in finance)
tic *nm* **1** : click, tick **2 tic nervioso** : tic
tico, -ca *adj & n fam* : Costa Rican
tiembla, etc. → **temblar**
tiempo *nm* **1** : time <justo a tiempo : just in time> <perder tiempo : to waste time> <tiempo libre : spare time> **2** : period, age <en los tiempos que corren : nowadays> **3** : season, moment <antes de tiempo : prematurely> **4** : weather <hace buen tiempo : the weather is fine, it's nice outside> **5** : tempo (in music) **6** : half (in sports) **7** : tense (in grammar)
tienda *nf* **1** : store, shop **2** *or* **tienda de campaña** : tent
tiende, etc. → **tender**
tiene, etc. → **tener**
tienta[1], etc. → **tentar**
tienta[2] *nf* **andar a tientas** : to feel one's way, to grope around
tiernamente *adv* : tenderly
tierno, -na *adj* **1** : affectionate, tender **2** : tender, young
tierra *nf* **1** : land **2** SUELO : ground, earth **3** : country, homeland, soil **4 tierra natal** : native land **5 la Tierra** : the Earth
tieso, -sa *adj* **1** : stiff, rigid **2** : upright, erect
tiesto *nm* **1** : potsherd **2** MACETA : flowerpot
tiesura *nf* : stiffness, rigidity
tifoidea *nf* : typhoid
tifoideo, -dea *adj* : typhoid <fiebre tifoidea : typhoid fever>
tifón *nm, pl* **tifones** : typhoon
tifus *nm* : typhus
tigre, -gresa *n* **1** : tiger, tigress *f* **2** : jaguar
tijera *nf* **1** *or* **tijeras** *nfpl* : scissors **2 de ~** : folding <escalera de tijera : stepladder>
tijereta *nf* : earwig
tijeretada *nf or* **tijeretazo** *nm* : cut, snip

tildar *vt* **~ de** : to brand as, to call <lo tildaron de traidor : they branded him as a traitor>

tilde *nf* **1** : accent mark **2** : tilde (accent over *ñ*)

tilo *nm* : linden (tree)

timador, -dora *n* : swindler

timar *vt* : to swindle, to cheat

timbal *nm* **1** : kettledrum **2 timbales** *nmpl* : timpani

timbre *nm* **1** : bell <tocar el timbre : to ring the doorbell> **2** : tone, timbre **3** SELLO : seal, stamp **4** *CA, Mex* : postage stamp

timidez *nf* : timidity, shyness

tímido, -da *adj* : timid, shy — **tímidamente** *adv*

timo *nm fam* : swindle, trick, hoax

timón *nm, pl* **timones** : rudder <estar al timón : to beat the helm>

timonel *nm* : helmsman, coxwain

timorato, -ta *adj* **1** : timorous **2** : sanctimonious

tímpano *nm* **1** : eardrum **2 tímpanos** *nmpl* : timpani, kettledrums

tina *nf* **1** BAÑERA : tub, bathtub **2** : vat

tinaco *nm Mex* : water tank

tinieblas *nfpl* **1** OSCURIDAD : darkness **2** : ignorance

tino *nm* **1** : good judgment, sense **2** : tact, sensitivity, insight

tinta *nf* : ink

tinte *nm* **1** : dye, coloring **2** : overtone <tintes raciales : racial overtones>

tintero *nm* **1** : inkwell **2 quedarse en el tintero** : to remain unsaid

tintinear *vt* : to jingle, to clink, to tinkle

tintineo *nm* : clink, jingle, tinkle

tinto, -ta *adj* **1** : dyed, stained <tinto en sangre : bloodstained> **2** : red (of wine)

tintorería *nf* : dry cleaner (service)

tintura *nf* **1** : dye, tint **2** : tincture <tintura de yodo : tincture of iodine>

tiña *nf* : ringworm

tiñe, etc. → **teñir**

tío, tía *n* : uncle *m,* aunt *f*

tiovivo *nm* : merry-go-round

tipi *nm* : tepee

típico, -ca *adj* : typical — **típicamente** *adv*

tipificar {72} *vt* **1** : to classify, to categorize **2** : to typify

tiple *nm* : soprano

tipo[1] *nm* **1** CLASE : type, kind, sort **2** : figure, build, appearance **3** : rate <tipo de interés : interest rate> **4** : (printing) type, typeface **5** : style, model <un vestido tipo 60's : a 60's-style dress>

tipo[2], **-pa** *n fam* : guy *m,* gal *f,* character

tipografía *nf* : typography, printing

tipográfico, -ca *adj* : typographic, typographical

tipográfo, -fa *n* : printer, typographer

tique *or* **tiquet** *nm* **1** : ticket **2** : receipt

tira *nf* **1** : strip, strap **2 tira cómica** : comic, comic strip

tirabuzón *nf, pl* **-zones** : corkscrew

tirada *nf* **1** : throw **2** : distance, stretch **3** IMPRESIÓN : printing, issue

tiradero *nm Mex* **1** : dump **2** : mess, clutter

tirador[1] *nm* : handle, knob

tirador[2], **-dora** *n* : marksman *m,* markswoman *f*

tiragomas *nms & pl* : slingshot

tiranía *nf* : tyranny

tiránico, -ca *adj* : tyrannical

tiranizar {21} *vt* : to tyrannize

tirano[1], **-na** *adj* : tyrannical, despotic

tirano[2], **-na** *n* : tyrant

tirante[1] *adj* **1** : tense, strained **2** : taut

tirante[2] *nm* **1** : shoulder strap **2 tirantes** *nmpl* : suspenders

tirantez *nf* **1** : tautness **2** : tension, friction, strain

tirar *vt* **1** : to throw, to hurl, to toss **2** BOTAR : to throw away, to throw out, to waste **3** DERRIBAR : to knock down **4** : to shoot, to fire, to launch **5** : to take (a photo) **6** : to print, to run off — *vi* **1** : to pull, to draw **2** : to shoot **3** : to attract **4** : to get by, to manage <va tirando : he's getting along, he's managing> **5 ~ a** : to tend towards, to be rather <tira a picante : it's a bit spicy> — **tirarse** *vr* **1** : to throw oneself **2** *fam* : to spend (time)

tiritar *vi* : to shiver, to tremble

tiro *nm* **1** BALAZO, DISPARO : shot, gunshot **2** : shot, kick (in sports) **3** : flue **4** : team (of horses, etc.) **5 a ~** : within range **6 al tiro** : right away **7 tiro de gracia** : coup de grace, death blow

tiroideo, -dea *adj* : thyroid

tiroides *nmf* : thyroid, thyroid gland — **tiroides** *adj*

tirolés, -lesa *adj* : Tyrolean

tirón *nm, pl* **tirones 1** : pull, tug, yank **2 de un tirón** : all at once, in one go

tiroteo *nm* **1** : shooting **2** : gunfight, shoot-out

tirria *nf fam* **tener tirria a** : to have a grudge against

titánico, -ca *adj* : titanic, huge

titanio *nm* : titanium

títere *nm* : puppet

tití *nm* : marmoset

titilar *vi* : to twinkle, to flicker

titileo *nm* : twinkle, flickering

titiritero, -ra *n* **1** : puppeteer **2** : acrobat

titubear *vi* **1** : to hesitate **2** : to stutter, to stammer — **titubeante** *adj*

titubeo *nm* **1** : hesitation **2** : stammering

titulado, -da *adj* **1** : titled, entitled **2** : qualified

titular[1] *vt* : to title, to entitle — **titularse** *vr* **1** : to be called, to be entitled **2** : to receive a degree

titular[2] *adj* : titular, official

titular[3] *nm* : headline
titular[4] *nmf* **1** : owner, holder **2** : officeholder, incumbent
título *nm* **1** : title **2** : degree, qualification **3** : security, bond **4 a título de** : by way of, in the capacity of
tiza *nf* : chalk
tiznar *vt* : to blacken (with soot, etc.)
tizne *nm* HOLLÍN : soot
tiznón *nm, pl* **tiznones** : stain, smudge
tlapalería *nf Mex* : hardware store
TNT *nm* : TNT
toalla *nf* : towel
toallita *nf* : washcloth
tobillo *nm* : ankle
tobogán *nm, pl* **-ganes 1** : toboggan, sled **2** : slide, chute
tocadiscos *nms & pl* : record player, phonograph
tocado[1], **-da** *adj* **1** : bad, bruised (of fruit) **2** *fam* : touched, not all there
tocado[2] *nm* : headdress
tocador[1] *nm* **1** : dressing table, vanity table **2 artículos de tocador** : toiletries
tocador[2], **-dora** *n* : player (of music)
tocante *adj* **~ a** : with regard to, regarding
tocar {72} *vt* **1** : to touch, to feel, to handle **2** : to touch on, to refer to **3** : to concern, to affect **4** : to play (a musical instrument) — *vi* **1** : to knock, to ring <tocar a la puerta : to rap on the door> **2 ~ en** : to touch on, to border on <eso toca en lo ridículo : that's almost ludicrous> **3 tocarle a** : to fall to, to be up to, to be one's turn <¿a quién le toca manejar? : whose turn is it to drive?>
tocayo, -ya *n* : namesake
tocineta *nf Col, Ven* : bacon
tocino *nm* **1** : bacon **2** : salt pork
tocología *nf* OBSTETRICIA : obstetrics
tocólogo, -ga *n* OBSTETRA : obstetrician
tocón *nm, pl* **tocones** CEPA : stump (of a tree)
todavía *adv* **1** AÚN : still, yet <todavía puedes verlo : you can still see it> **2** : even <todavía más rápido : even faster> **3 todavía no** : not yet
todo[1], **-da** *adj* **1** : all, whole, entire <con toda sinceridad : with all sincerity> <toda la comunidad : the whole community> **2** : every, each <a todo nivel : at every level> **3** : maximum <a toda velocidad : at top speed> **4 todo el mundo** : everyone, everybody
todo[2] *nm* : whole
todo[3], **-da** *pron* **1** : everything, all, every bit <lo sabe todo : he knows it all> <es todo un soldado : he's every inch a soldier> **2 todos, -das** *pl* : everybody, everyone, all
todopoderoso, -sa *adj* OMNIPOTENTE : almighty, all-powerful
toga *nf* **1** : toga **2** : gown, robe (for magistrates, etc.)
toldo *nm* : awning, canopy
tolerable *adj* : tolerable — **tolerablemente** *adv*
tolerancia *nf* : tolerance, toleration
tolerante *adj* : tolerant — **tolerantemente** *adv*
tolerar *vt* : to tolerate
tolete *nm* : oarlock
tolva *nf* : hopper (container)
toma *nf* **1** : taking, seizure, capture **2** DOSIS : dose **3** : take, shot **4 toma de corriente** : wall socket, outlet **5 toma y daca** : give-and-take
tomar *vt* **1** : to take <tomé el libro : I took the book> <tomar un taxi : to take a taxi> <tomar una foto : to take a photo> <toma dos años : it takes two years> <tomaron medidas drásticas : they took drastic measures> **2** BEBER : to drink **3** CAPTURAR : to capture, to seize **4 tomar el sol** : to sunbathe **5 tomar tierra** : to land — *vi* : to drink (alcohol) — **tomarse** *vr* **1** : to take <tomarse la molestia de : to take the trouble to> **2** : to drink, to eat, to have
tomate *nm* : tomato
tomillo *nm* : thyme
tomo *nm* : volume, tome
ton *nm* **sin ton ni son** : without rhyme or reason
tonada *nf* **1** : tune, song **2** : accent
tonalidad *nf* : tonality
tonel *nm* BARRICA : barrel, cask
tonelada *nf* : ton
tonelaje *nm* : tonnage
tónica *nf* **1** : tonic (water) **2** : tonic (in music) **3** : trend, tone <dar la tónica : to set the tone>
tónico[1], **-ca** *adj* : tonic
tónico[2] *nm* : tonic <tónico capilar : hair tonic>
tono *nm* **1** : tone <tono muscular : muscle tone> **2** : shade (of colors) **3** : key (in music)
tontamente *adv* : foolishly, stupidly
tontear *vi* **1** : to fool around, to play the fool **2** : to flirt
tontería *nf* **1** : foolishness **2** : stupid remark or action **3 decir tonterías** : to talk nonsense
tonto[1], **-ta** *adj* **1** : dumb, stupid **2** : silly **3 a tontas y a locas** : without thinking, haphazardly
tonto[2], **-ta** *n* : fool, idiot
topacio *nm* : topaz
toparse *vr* **~ con** : to bump into, to run into, to come across <me topé con algunas dificultades : I ran into some problems>
tope *nm* **1** : limit, end <hasta el tope : to the limit, to the brim> **2** : stop, check, buffer <tope de puerta : doorstop> **3** : bump, collision **4** *Mex* : speed bump
tópico[1], **-ca** *adj* **1** : topical, external **2** : trite, commonplace
tópico[2] *nm* **1** : topic, subject **2** : cliché, trite expression

topo *nm* **1** : mole (animal) **2** *fam* : clumsy person, blunderer
topografía *nf* : topography
topográfico, -ca *adj* : topographic, topographical
topógrafo, -fa *n* : topographer
toque[1], **etc.** → **tocar**
toque[2] *nm* **1** : touch <el último toque : the finishing touch> <un toque de color : a touch of color> **2** : ringing, peal, chime **3** *Mex* : shock, jolt **4** **toque de queda** : curfew **5** **toque de diana** : reveille
toquetear *vt* : to touch, to handle, to finger
tórax *nm* : thorax
torbellino *nm* : whirlwind
torcedura *nf* **1** : twisting, buckling **2** : sprain
torcer {14} *vt* **1** : to bend, to twist **2** : to sprain **3** : to turn (a corner) **4** : to wring, to wring out **5** : to distort — *vi* : to turn — **torcerse** *vr*
torcido, -da *adj* **1** : twisted, crooked **2** : devious
tordo *nm* ZORZAL : thrush
torear *vt* **1** : to fight (bulls) **2** : to dodge, to sidestep
toreo *nm* : bullfighting
torero, -ra *n* MATADOR : bullfighter, matador
tormenta *nf* **1** : storm <tormenta de nieve : snowstorm> **2** : turmoil, frenzy
tormento *nm* **1** : torment, anguish **2** : torture
tormentoso, -sa *adj* : stormy, turbulent
tornado *nm* : tornado
tornamesa *nmf* : turntable
tornar *vt* **1** : to return, to give back **2** : to make, to render — *vi* : to go back — **tornarse** *vr* : to become, to turn into
tornasol *nm* **1** : reflected light **2** : sunflower **3** : litmus
tornear *vt* : to turn (in carpentry)
torneo *nm* : tournament
tornillo *nm* **1** : screw **2** **tornillo de banco** : vise
torniquete *nm* **1** : tourniquet **2** : turnstile
torno *nm* **1** : lathe **2** : winch **3** **torno de banco** : vise **4** **en torno a** : around, about <en torno a este asunto : about this issue> <en torno suyo : around him>
toro *nm* : bull
toronja *nf* : grapefruit
toronjil *nm* : balm, lemon balm
torpe *adj* **1** DESMAÑADO : clumsy, awkward **2** : stupid, dull — **torpemente** *adv*
torpedear *vt* : to torpedo
torpedo *nm* : torpedo
torpeza *nf* **1** : clumsiness, awkwardness **2** : stupidity **3** : blunder
torre *nf* **1** : tower <torre de perforación : oil rig> **2** : turret **3** : rook, castle (in chess)
torrencial *adj* : torrential — **torrencialmente** *adv*
torrente *nm* **1** : torrent **2** **torrente sanguíneo** : bloodstream
torreón *nm, pl* **-rreones** : tower (of a castle)
torreta *nf* : turret (of a tank, ship, etc.)
tórrido, -da *adj* : torrid
torsión *nf, pl* **torsiones** : torsion — **torsional** *adj*
torso *nm* : torso, trunk
torta *nf* **1** : torte, cake **2** *Mex* : sandwich
tortazo *nm fam* : blow, wallop
tortilla *nf* **1** : tortilla **2** *or* **tortilla de huevo** : omelet
tórtola *nf* : turtledove
tortuga *nf* **1** : turtle, tortoise **2** **tortuga de agua dulce** : terrapin **3** **tortuga boba** : loggerhead
tortuoso, -sa *adj* : tortuous, winding
tortura *nf* : torture
torturador, -dora *n* : torturer
torturar *vt* : to torture, to torment
torvo, -va *adj* : grim, stern, baleful
torzamos, etc. → **torcer**
tos *nf* **1** : cough **2** **tos ferina** : whooping cough
tosco, -ca *adj* : rough, coarse
toser *vi* : to cough
tosquedad *nf* : crudeness, coarseness, roughness
tostada *nf* **1** : piece of toast **2** : tostada
tostador *nm* **1** : toaster **2** : roaster (for coffee)
tostar {19} *vt* **1** : to toast **2** : to roast (coffee) **3** : to tan — **tostarse** *vr* : to get a tan
tostón *nm, pl* **tostones** *Car* : fried plantain chip
total[1] *adv* : in the end, so <total, que no fui : in short, I didn't go>
total[2] *adj & nm* : total — **totalmente** *adv*
totalidad *nf* : totality, whole
totalitario, -ria *adj & n* : totalitarian
totalitarismo *nm* : totalitarianism
totalizar {21} *vt* : total, to add up to
tótem *nm, pl* **tótems** : totem
totopo *nm CA, Mex* : tortilla chip
totuma *nf* : calabash
tour ['tur] *nm, pl* **tours** : tour, excursion
toxicidad *nf* : toxicity
tóxico[1], **-ca** *adj* : toxic, poisonous
tóxico[2] *nm* : poison
toxicomanía *nf* : drug addiction
toxicómano, -na *n* : drug addict
toxina *nf* : toxin
tozudez *nf* : stubbornness, obstinancy
tozudo, -da *adj* : stubborn, obstinate — **tozudamente** *adv*
traba *nf* **1** : tie, bond **2** : obstacle, hinderance
trabajador[1], **-dora** *adj* : hard-working
trabajador[2], **-dora** *n* : worker

trabajar *vi* **1 :** to work <trabaja mucho : he works hard> <trabajo de secretaria : I work as a secretary> **2 :** to strive <trabajan por mejores oportunidades : they're striving for better opportunities> **3 :** to act, to perform <trabajar en una película : to be in a movie> — *vt* **1 :** to work (metal) **2 :** to knead **3 :** to till **4 :** to work on <tienes que trabajar el español : you need to work on your Spanish>

trabajo *nm* **1 :** work, job **2** LABOR **:** labor, work <tengo mucho trabajo : I have a lot of work to do> **3** TAREA **:** task **4** ESFUERZA **:** effort **5 costar trabajo :** to be difficult **6 tomarse el trabajo :** to take the trouble **7 trabajo en equipo :** teamwork **8 trabajos** *nmpl* **:** hardships, difficulties

trabajoso, -sa *adj* LABORIOSO **:** laborious — **trabajosamente** *adv*

trabalenguas *nms & pl* **:** tongue twister

trabar *vt* **1 :** to join, to connect **2 :** to impede, to hold back **3 :** to strike up (a conversation), to form (a friendship) **4 :** to thicken (sauces) — **trabarse** *vr* **1 :** to jam **2 :** to become entangled **3 :** to be tongue-tied, to stammer

trabucar {72} *vt* **:** to confuse, to mix up

trabuco *nm* **:** blunderbuss

tracalero, -ra *adj Mex* **:** dishonest, tricky

tracción *nf* **:** traction

trace, etc. → **trazar**

tracto *nm* **:** tract

tractor *nm* **:** tractor

tradición *nf, pl* **-ciones :** tradition

tradicional *adj* **:** traditional — **tradicionalmente** *adv*

traducción *nf, pl* **-ciones :** translation

traducible *adj* **:** translatable

traducir {61} *vt* **1 :** to translate **2 :** to convey, to express — **traducirse** *vr* **~ en :** to result in

traductor, -dora *n* **:** translator

traer {81} *vt* **1 :** to bring <trae una ensalada : bring a salad> **2** CAUSAR **:** to cause, to bring about <el problema puede traer graves consecuencias : the problem could have serious consequences> **3 :** to carry, to have <todos los periódicos traían las mismas noticias : all of the newspapers carried the same news> **4** LLEVAR **:** to wear — **traerse** *vr* **1 :** to bring along **2 traérselas :** to be difficult

traficante *nmf* **:** dealer, trafficker

traficar {72} *vi* **1 :** to trade, to deal **2 ~ en :** to traffic in

tráfico *nm* **1 :** trade **2 :** traffic

tragaluz *nf, pl* **-luces :** skylight, fanlight

tragar {52} *v* **:** to swallow — **tragarse**

tragedia *nf* **:** tragedy

trágico, -ca *adj* **:** tragic — **trágicamente** *adv*

trago *nm* **1 :** swallow, swig **2 :** drink, liquor **3 trago amargo :** hard time

trague, etc. → **tragar**

traición *nf, pl* **traiciones 1 :** treason **2 :** betrayal, treachery

traicionar *vt* **:** to betray

traicionero, -ra → **traidor**

traidor[1], -dora *adj* **:** traitorous, treasonous

traidor[2], -dora *n* **:** traitor

traiga, etc. → **traer**

tráiler *or* **trailer** *nm* **:** trailer

traílla *nf* **1 :** leash **2 :** harrow

traje *nm* **1 :** suit **2 :** dress **3 :** costume **4 traje de baño :** bathing suit

trajín *nm, pl* **trajines 1 :** transport 2 *fam* **:** hustle and bustle

trajinar *vt* **:** to transport, to carry — *vi* **:** to rush around

trajo, etc. → **traer**

trama *nf* **1 :** plot **2 :** weave, weft (fabric)

tramar *vt* **1 :** to plot, to plan **2 :** to weave

tramitar *vt* **:** to transact, to negotiate, to handle

trámite *nm* **:** procedure, step

tramo *nm* **1 :** stretch, section **2 :** flight (of stairs)

trampa *nf* **1 :** trap **2 hacer trampas :** to cheat

trampear *vt* **:** to cheat

trampero, -ra *n* **:** trapper

trampilla *nf* **:** trapdoor

trampolín *nm, pl* **-lines 1 :** diving board **2 :** trampoline **3 :** springboard <un trampolín al éxito : a springboard to success>

tramposo[1], -sa *adj* **:** crooked, cheating

tramposo[2], -sa *n* **:** cheat, swindler

tranca *nf* **1 :** stick, club **2 :** bar, crossbar

trancar {72} *vt* **:** to bar (a door or window)

trancazo *nm* GOLPE **:** blow, hit

trance *nm* **1 :** critical juncture, tough time **2 :** trance **3 en trance de :** in the process of <en trance de extinción : on the verge of extinction>

tranco *nm* **1 :** stride **2** UMBRAL **:** threshold

tranque, etc. → **trancar**

tranquilidad *nf* **:** tranquility, peace

tranquilizador, -dora *adj* **1 :** soothing **2 :** reassuring

tranquilizante[1] *adj* **1 :** reassuring **2 :** tranquilizing

tranquilizante[2] *nm* **:** tranquilizer

tranquilizar {21} *vt* CALMAR **:** to calm down, to soothe <tranquilizar la conciencia : to ease the conscience> — **tranquilizarse** *vr*

tranquilo, -la *adj* CALMO **:** calm, tranquil <una vida tranquila : a quiet life> — **tranquilamente** *adv*

transacción *nf, pl* **-ciones :** transaction

transar *vi* TRANSIGIR **:** to give way, to compromise — *vt* **:** to buy and sell

transatlántico[1], -ca *adj* **:** transatlantic

transatlántico[2] *nm* : ocean liner
transbordador *nm* **1** : ferry **2 transbordador espacial** : space shuttle
transbordar *v* : to transfer
transbordo *nm* : transfer
transcendencia *nf* → **trascendencia**
transcender → **trascender**
transcribir {33} *vt* : to transcribe
transcrito *pp* → **transcribir**
transcripción *nf, pl* **-ciones** : transcription
transcurrir *vi* : to elapse, to pass
transcurso *nm* : course, progression <en el transcurso de cien años : over the course of a hundred years>
transeúnte *nmf* **1** : passerby **2** : transient
transferencia *nf* : transfer, transference
transferir {76} *vt* TRASLADAR : to transfer — **transferible** *adj*
transfigurar *vt* : to transfigure, to transform — **transfiguración** *nf*
transformación *nf, pl* **-ciones** : transformation, conversion
transformador *nm* : transformer
transformar *vt* **1** CONVERTIR : to convert **2** : to transform, to change, to alter — **transformarse** *vr*
transfusión *nf, pl* **-siones** : transfusion
transgredir {1} *vt* : to transgress — **transgresión** *nf*
transgresor, -sora *n* : transgressor
transición *nf, pl* **-ciones** : transition <período de transición : transition period>
transido, -da *adj* : overcome, beset <transido de dolor : racked with pain>
transigir {35} *vi* **1** : to give in, to compromise **2 ~ con** : to tolerate, to put up with
transistor *nm* : transistor
transitable *adj* : passable
transitar *vi* : to go, to pass, to travel <transitar por la ciudad : to travel through the city>
transitivo, -va *adj* : transitive
tránsito *nm* **1** TRÁFICO : traffic <hora de máximo tránsito : rush hour> **2** : transit, passage, movement **3** : death, passing
transitorio, -ria *adj* **1** : transitory **2** : provisional, temporary — **transitoriamente** *adv*
translúcido, -da *adj* : translucent
translucir → **traslucir**
transmisión *nf, pl* **-siones** **1** : transmission, broadcast **2** : transfer **3** : transmission (of an automobile)
transmisor *nm* : transmitter
transmitir *vt* **1** : to transmit, to broadcast **2** : to pass on, to transfer — *vi* : to transmit, to broadcast
transparencia *nf* : transparency
transparentar *vt* : to reveal, to betray — **transparentarse** *vr* **1** : to be transparent **2** : to show through
transparente[1] *adj* : transparent — **transparentemente** *adv*
transparente[2] *nm* : shade, blind
transpiración *nf, pl* **-ciones** SUDOR : perspiration, sweat
transpirado, -da *adj* : sweaty
transpirar *vi* **1** SUDAR : to perspire, to sweat **2** : to transpire
transplantar, transplante → **trasplantar, trasplante**
transponer {60} *vt* **1** : to transpose, to move about **2** TRASPLANTAR : to transplant — **transponerse** *vr* **1** OCULTARSE : to hide **2** PONERSE : to set, to go down (of the sun or moon) **3** DORMITAR : to doze off
transportación *nf, pl* **-ciones** : transportation
transportador *nm* **1** : protractor **2** : conveyor
transportar *vt* **1** : to transport, to carry **2** : to transmit **3** : to transpose (music) — **transportarse** *vr* : to get carried away
transporte *nm* : transport, transportation
transportista *nmf* : hauler, carrier, trucker
transpuso, etc. → **transponer**
transversal *adj* : transverse, cross <corte transversal : cross section>
transversalmente *adv* : obliquely
transverso, -sa *adj* : transverse
tranvía *nm* : streetcar, trolley
trapeador *nm* : mop
trapear *vt* : to mop
trapecio *nm* **1** : trapezoid **2** : trapeze
trapezoide *nm* : trapezoid
trapo *nm* **1** : cloth, rag <trapo de polvo : dust cloth> **2 soltar el trapo** : to burst into tears **3 trapos** *nmpl fam* : clothes
tráquea *nf* : trachea, windpipe
traquetear *vi* : to clatter, to jolt
traqueteo *nm* **1** : jolting **2** : clattering, clatter
tras *prep* **1** : after <día tras día : day after day> <uno tras otro : one after another> **2** : behind <tras la puerta : behind the door>
trasbordar, trasbordo → **transbordar, transbordo**
trascendencia *nf* **1** : importance, significance **2** : transcendence
trascendental *adj* **1** : transcendental **2** : important, momentous
trascendente *adj* **1** : important, significant **2** : transcendent
trascender {56} *vi* **1** : to leak out, to become known **2** : to spread, to have a wide effect **3 ~ a** : to smell of <la casa trascendía a flores : the house smelled of flowers> **4 ~ de** : to transcend, to go beyond — *vt* : to transcend
trasero[1], **-sa** *adj* POSTERIOR : rear, back
trasero[2] *nm* : buttocks
trasfondo *nm* **1** : background, backdrop **2** : undertone, undercurrent
trasformación *nf* → **transformación**
trasgo *nm* : goblin, imp

trasgredir → **transgredir**
trasladar *vt* **1** TRANSFERIR : to transfer, to move **2** POSPONER : to postpone **3** TRADUCIR : to translate **4** COPIAR : to copy, to transcribe — **trasladarse** *vr* MUDARSE : to move, to relocate
traslado *nm* **1** : transfer, move **2** : copy
traslapar *vt* : to overlap — **traslaparse** *vr*
traslapo *nm* : overlap
traslúcido, -da → **translúcido**
traslucir {45} *vi* : to reveal, to show — **traslucirse** *vr* : to show through
trasmano *nm* **a ~** : out of the way, out of reach
trasmisión, trasmitir → **transmisión, transmitir**
trasnochar *vi* : to stay up all night
trasparencia *nf,* **trasparente** → **transparencia, transparente**
traspasar *vt* **1** PERFORAR : to pierce, to go through **2** : to go beyond <traspasar los límites : to overstep the limits> **3** ATRAVESAR : to cross, to go across **4** : to sell, to transfer
traspaso *nm* : transfer, sale
traspié *nm* **1** : stumble **2** : blunder
traspiración *nf* → **transpiración**
trasplantar *vt* : to transplant
trasplante *nm* : transplant
trasponer → **transponer**
trasportar → **transportar**
trasquilar *vt* ESQUILAR : to shear
traste *nm* **1** : fret (on a guitar) **2** *CA, Mex, PRi* : kitchen utensil <lavar los trastes : to do the dishes> **3 dar al traste con** : to ruin, to destroy **4 irse al traste** : to fall through
trastornar *vt* : to disturb, to upset, to disrupt — **trastornarse** *vr*
trastorno *nm* **1** : disorder <trastorno mental : mental disorder> **2** : disturbance, upset
trastos *nmpl* **1** : implements, utensils **2** *fam* : pieces of junk, stuff
trasunto *nm* : image, likeness
tratable *adj* **1** : friendly, sociable **2** : treatable
tratado *nm* **1** : treatise **2** : treaty
tratamiento *nm* : treatment
tratante *nmf* : dealer, trader
tratar *vi* **1 ~ con** : to deal with, to have contact with <no trato mucho con los clientes : I don't have much contact with customers> **2 ~ de** : to try to <estoy tratando de comer : I am trying to eat> **3 ~ de** *or* **~ sobre** : to be about, to concern <el libro trata de las plantas : the book is about plants> **4 ~ en** : to deal in <trata en herramientas : he deals in tools> — *vt* **1** : to treat <tratan bien a sus empleados : they treat their employees well> **2** : to handle <trató el tema con delicadeza : he handled the subject tactfully> — **tratarse** *vr* **~ de** : to be about, to concern
trato *nm* **1** : deal, agreement **2** : relationship, dealings *pl* **3** : treatment <malos tratos : ill-treatment>
trauma *nm* : trauma
traumático, -ca *adj* : traumatic — **traumáticamente** *adv*
traumatismo *nm* : injury <traumatismo cervical : whiplash>
través *nm* **1 a través de** : across, through **2 al través** : crosswise, across **3 de través** : sideways
travesaño *nm* **1** : crossbar **2** : crossbeam, crosspiece, transom (of a window)
travesía *nf* : voyage, crossing (of the sea)
travesura *nf* **1** : prank, mischievous act **2 travesuras** *nfpl* : mischief
travieso, -sa *adj* : mischievous, naughty — **traviesamente** *adv*
trayecto *nm* **1** : journey **2** : route **3** : trajectory, path
trayectoria *nf* : course, path, trajectory
trayendo → **traer**
traza *nf* **1** DISEÑO : design, plan **2** : appearance
trazado *nm* **1** BOSQUEJO : outline, sketch **2** PLAN : plan, layout
trazar {21} *vt* **1** : to trace **2** : to draw up, to devise **3** : to outline, to sketch
trazo *nm* **1** : stroke, line **2** : sketch, outline
trébol *nm* **1** : clover, shamrock **2** : club (playing card)
trece *adj & nm* : thirteen
treceavo[1], -va *adj* : thirteenth
treceavo[2] *nm* : thirteenth (fraction)
trecho *nm* **1** : stretch, period <de trecho en trecho : at intervals> **2** : distance, space
tregua *nf* **1** : truce **2** : lull, respite **3 sin ~** : relentless, unrelenting
treinta *adj & nm* : thirty
treintavo[1], -va *adj* : thirtieth
treintavo[2] *nm* : thirtieth (fraction)
tremendo, -da *adj* **1** : tremendous, enormous **2** : terrible, dreadful **3** *fam* : great, super
trementina *nf* AGUARRÁS : turpentine
trémulo, -la *adj* **1** : trembling, shaky **2** : flickering
tren *nm* **1** : train **2** : set, assembly <tren de aterrizaje : landing gear> **3** : speed, pace <a todo tren : at top speed>
trence, etc. → **trenzar**
trenza *nf* : braid, pigtail
trenzar {21} *vt* : to braid — **trenzarse** *vr* : to get involved
trepador, -dora *adj* : climbing <rosal trepador : rambling rose>
trepadora *nf* **1** : climbing plant, climber **2** : nuthatch
trepar *vi* **1** : to climb <trepar a un árbol : to climb up a tree> **2** : to creep, to spread (of a plant)
trepidación *nf, pl* **-ciones** : vibration
trepidante *adj* **1** : vibrating **2** : fast, frantic

trepidar *vi* **1 :** to shake, to vibrate **2 :** to hesitate, to waver

tres *adj & nm* **:** three

trescientos[1], **-tas** *adj* **:** two hundred

trescientos[2] *nms & pl* **:** three hundred

treta *nf* **:** trick, ruse

tríada *nf* **:** triad

triángulo *nm* **:** triangle — **triangular** *adj*

tribal *adj* **:** tribal

tribu *nf* **:** tribe

tribulación *nf, pl* **-ciones :** tribulation

tribuna *nf* **1 :** dais, platform **2 :** stands *pl*, bleachers *pl*, grandstand

tribunal *nm* **:** court, tribunal

tributar *vt* **:** to pay, to render — *vi* **:** to pay taxes

tributario[1], **-ria** *adj* **:** tax <evasión tributaria **:** tax evasion>

tributario[2] *nm* **:** tributary

tributo *nm* **1 :** tax **2 :** tribute

triciclo *nm* **:** tricycle

tricolor *adj* **:** tricolor, tricolored

tridente *nm* **:** trident

tridimensional *adj* **:** three-dimensional, 3-D

trienal *adj* **:** triennial

trifulca *nf fam* **:** row, ruckus

trigésimo[1], **-ma** *adj* **:** thirtieth, thirty-

trigésimo[2], **-ma** *n* **:** thirtieth, thirty- (in a series)

trigo *nm* **1 :** wheat **2 trigo rubión :** buckwheat

trigonometría *nf* **:** trigonometry

trigueño, -ña *adj* **1 :** light brown (of hair) **2** MORENO **:** dark, olive-skinned

trillado, -da *adj* **:** trite, hackneyed

trilladora *nf* **:** thresher, threshing machine

trillar *vt* **:** to thresh

trillizo, -za *n* **:** triplet

trilogía *nf* **:** trilogy

trimestral *adj* **:** quarterly — **trimestralmente** *adv*

trinar *vi* **1 :** to thrill **2 :** to warble

trinchar *vt* **:** to carve, to cut up

trinchera *nf* **1 :** trench, ditch **2 :** trench coat

tridente *nm* **:** trident

trineo *nm* **:** sled, sleigh

trinidad *nf* **la Trinidad :** the Trinity

trino *nm* **:** trill, warble

trinquete *nm* **:** ratchet

trío *nm* **:** trio

tripa *nf* **1** INTESTINO **:** gut, intestine **2 tripas** *nfpl fam* **:** belly, tummy, insides *pl* <dolerle a uno las tripas **:** to have a stomach ache>

tripartito, -ta *adj* **:** tripartite

triple *adj & nm* **:** triple

triplicado *nm* **:** triplicate

triplicar {72} *vt* **:** to triple, to treble

trípode *nm* **:** tripod

tripulación *nf, pl* **-ciones :** crew

tripulante *nmf* **:** crew member

tripular *vt* **:** to man

tris *nm* **estar en un tris de :** to be within an inch of, to be very close to

triste *adj* **1 :** sad, gloomy <ponerse triste **:** to become sad> **2 :** desolate, dismal <una perspectiva triste **:** a dismal outlook> **3 :** sorry, sorry-looking <la triste verdad **:** the sorry truth>

tristeza *nf* DOLOR **:** sadness, grief

tristón, -tona *adj, mpl* **-tones :** melancholy, downhearted

tritón *nm, pl* **tritones :** newt

triturar *vt* **:** to crush, to grind

triunfal *adj* **:** triumphal, triumphant — **triunfalmente** *adv*

triunfante *adj* **:** triumphant, victorious

triunfar *vi* **:** to triumph, to win

triunfo *nm* **1 :** triumph, victory **2** ÉXITO **:** success **3 :** trump (in card games)

triunvirato *nm* **:** triumvirate

trivial *adj* **1 :** trivial **2 :** trite, commonplace

trivialidad *nf* **:** triviality

triza *nf* **1 :** shred, bit **2 hacer trizas :** to tear into shreds, to smash to pieces

trocar {82} *vt* **1** CAMBIAR **:** to exchange, to trade **2** CAMBIAR **:** to change, to alter, to transform **3** CONFUNDIR **:** to confuse, to mix up

trocha *nf* **:** path, trail

troce, etc. → **trozar**

trofeo *nm* **:** trophy

tromba *nf* **1 :** whirlwind **2 tromba de agua :** downpour, cloudburst

trombón *nm, pl* **trombones 1 :** trombone **2 :** trombonist — **trombonista** *nmf*

trombosis *nf* **:** thrombosis

trompa *nf* **1 :** trunk (of an elephant), proboscis (of an insect) **2 :** horn <trompa de caza **:** hunting horn> **3 :** tube, duct (in the body)

trompada *nf fam* **1 :** punch, blow **2 :** bump, collision (of persons)

trompeta *nf* **:** trumpet

trompetista *nmf* **:** trumpet player, trumpeter

trompo *nm* **:** spinning top

tronada *nf* **:** thunderstorm

tronar {19} *vi* **1 :** to thunder, to roar **2 :** to be furious, to rage **3** *CA, Mex fam* **:** to shoot — *v impers* **:** to thunder <está tronando **:** it's thundering>

tronchar *vt* **1 :** to snap, to break off **2 :** to cut off (relations)

tronco *nm* **1 :** trunk (of a tree) **2 :** log **3 :** torso

trono *nm* **1 :** throne **2** *fam* **:** toilet

tropa *nf* **1 :** troop, soldiers *pl* **2 :** crowd, mob **3 :** herd (of livestock)

tropel *nm* **:** mob, swarm

tropezar {29} *vi* **1 :** to trip, to stumble **2 :** to slip up, to blunder **3 ~ con :** to run into, to bump into **4 ~ con :** to come up against (a problem)

tropezón *nm, pl* **-zones 1 :** stumble **2 :** mistake, slip

tropical *adj* **:** tropical

trópico *nm* **1 :** tropic <trópico de Cáncer **:** tropic of Cancer> **2 el trópico :** the tropics

tropiezo *nm* **1** CONTRATIEMPO : snag, setback **2** EQUIVOCACIÓN : mistake, slip
troqué, etc. → **trocar**
troquel *nm* : die (for stamping)
trotamundos *nmf* : globe-trotter
trotar *vi* **1** : to trot **2** : to jog **3** *fam* : to rush about
trote *nm* **1** : trot **2** *fam* : rush, bustle **3** **de ~** : durable, for everyday use
trovador, -dora *n* : troubadour
trozar {21} *vt* : to cut up, to dice
trozo *nm* **1** PEDAZO : piece, bit, chunk **2** : passage, extract
trucha *nf* : trout
truco *nm* **1** : trick **2** : knack
truculento, -ta *adj* : horrifying, gruesome
trueca, trueque, etc. → **trocar**
truena, etc. → **tronar**
trueno *nm* : thunder
trueque *nm* : barter, exchange
trufa *nf* : truffle
truncar {72} *vt* **1** : to truncate, to cut short **2** : to thwart, to frustrate <truncó sus esperanzas : she shattered their hopes>
trunco, -ca *adj* **1** : truncated **2** : unfinished, incomplete
trunque, etc. → **truncar**
tu *adj* **1** : your <tu vestido : your dress> <toma tus vitaminas : take your vitamins> **2** : thy
tú *pron* **1** : you <tú eres mi hijo : you are my son> **2** : thou
tuba *nf* : tuba
tubérculo *nm* : tuber
tuberculosis *nf* : tuberculosis
tuberculoso, -sa *adj* : tuberculous, tubercular
tubería *nf* : pipes *pl*, tubing
tuberoso, -sa *adj* : tuberous
tubo *nm* **1** : tube <tubo de ensayo : test tube> **2** : pipe <tubo de desagüe : drainpipe> **3** **tubo digestivo** : alimentary canal
tubular *adj* : tubular
tuerca *nf* : nut <tuercas y tornillos : nuts and bolts>
tuerce, etc. → **torcer**
tuerto, -ta *adj* : one-eyed, blind in one eye
tuerza, etc. → **torcer**
tuesta, etc. → **tostar**
tuétano *nm* : marrow
tufo *nm* **1** : fume, vapor **2** *fam* : stench, stink
tugurio *nm* : hovel
tulipán *nm, pl* **-panes** : tulip
tumba *nf* **1** SEPULCRO : tomb **2** FOSA : grave **3** : felling of trees
tumbar *vt* **1** : to knock down **2** : to fell, to cut down — *vi* : to fall down — **tumbarse** *vr* ACOSTARSE : to lie down
tumbo *nm* **1** : tumble, fall **2** **dar tumbos** : to jolt, to bump around
tumor *nm* : tumor
túmulo *nm* : burial mound
tumulto *nm* **1** ALBOROTO : commotion, tumult **2** MOTÍN : riot **3** MULTITUD : crowd
tumultuoso, -sa *adj* : tumultuous
tuna *nf* : prickly pear (fruit)
tundra *nf* : tundra
tunecino, -na *adj & n* : Tunisian
túnel *nm* : tunnel
tungsteno *nm* : tungsten
túnica *nf* : tunic
tupé *nm* PELUQUÍN : toupee
tupido, -da *adj* **1** DENSO : dense, thick **2** OBSTRUIDO : obstructed, blocked up
turba *nf* **1** : peat **2** : mob, throng
turbación *nf, pl* **-ciones** **1** : disturbance **2** : alarm, concern **3** : confusion
turbante *nm* : turban
turbar *vt* **1** : to disturb, to disrupt **2** : to worry, to upset **3** : to confuse
turbina *nf* : turbine
turbio, -bia *adj* **1** : cloudy, murky, turbid **2** : dim, blurred **3** : shady, crooked
turbopropulsor *nm* : turboprop
turborreactor *nm* : turbojet
turbulencia *nf* : turbulence
turbulento, -ta *adj* : turbulent
turco[1]**, -ca** *adj* : Turkish
turco[2]**, -ca** *n* : Turk
turgente *adj* : turgid, swollen
turismo *nm* : tourism, tourist industry
turista *nmf* : tourist, vacationer
turístico, -ca *adj* : tourist, travel
turnar *vi* : to take turns, to alternate
turno *nm* **1** : turn <ya te tocará tu turno : you'll get your turn> **2** : shift, duty <turno de noche : night shift> **3** **por turno** : alternately
turón *nm, pl* **turones** : polecat
turquesa *nf* : turquoise
turrón *nm, pl* **turrones** : nougat
tusa *nf* : corn husk
tutear *vt* : to address as *tú*
tutela *nf* **1** : guardianship **2** : tutelage, protection
tuteo *nm* : addressing as *tú*
tutor, -tora *n* **1** : tutor **2** : guardian
tuvo, etc. → **tener**
tuyo[1]**, -ya** *adj* : yours, of yours <un amigo tuyo : a friend of yours> <¿es tuya esta casa? : is this house yours?>
tuyo[2]**, -ya** *pron* **1** : yours <ése es el tuyo : that one is yours> <trae la tuya : bring your own> **2** **los tuyos** : your relations, your friends <¿vendrán los tuyos? : are your folks coming?>
tweed ['twið] *nm* : tweed

U

u[1] *nf* : twenty-second letter of the Spanish alphabet

u[2] *conj* (*used instead of* **o** *before words beginning with o- or ho-*) : or

ualabí *nm* : wallaby

uapití *nm* : American elk, wapiti

ubicación *nf, pl* **-ciones** : location, position

ubicar {72} *vt* **1** SITUAR : to place, to put, to position **2** LOCALIZAR : to locate, to find — **ubicarse** *vr* **1** LOCALIZARSE : to be placed, to be located **2** SITUARSE : to position oneself

ubicuidad *nf* OMNIPRESENCIA : ubiquity

ubicuo, -cua *adj* OMNIPRESENTE : ubiquitous

ubre *nf* : udder

ucraniano, -na *adj & n* : Ukranian

Ud., Uds. → **usted**

ufanarse *vr* **~ de** : to boast about, to pride oneself on

ufano, -na *adj* **1** ORGULLOSO : proud **2** : self-satisfied, smug

ugandés, -desa *adj & n, mpl* **-deses** : Ugandan

ukelele *nm* : ukulele

úlcera *nf* : ulcer — **ulceroso, -sa** *adj*

ulcerar *vt* : to ulcerate — **ulcerarse** *vr* — **ulceración** *nf*

ulceroso, -sa *adj* : ulcerous

ulterior *adj* : later, subsequent — **ulteriormente** *adv*

últimamente *adv* : lately, recently

ultimar *vt* **1** CONCLUIR : to complete, to finish, to finalize **2** MATAR : to kill

ultimátum *nm, pl* **-tums** : ultimatum

último, -ma *adj* **1** : last, final <la última galleta : the last cookie> <en último caso : as a last resort> **2** : last, latest, most recent <su último viaje a España : her last trip to Spain> <en los últimos años : in recent years> **3 por ~** : finally

ultrajar *vt* INSULTAR : to offend, to outrage, to insult

ultraje *nm* INSULTO : outrage, insult

ultramar *nm* **de ~** *or* **en ~** : overseas, abroad

ultranza *nf* **a ~ 1** : to the extreme <lo defendió a ultranza : she defended him fiercely> **2** : extreme, out-and-out <perfeccionismo a ultranza : rabid perfectionism>

ultrarrojo, -ja *adj* : infrared

ultravioleta *adj* : ultraviolet

ulular *vi* **1** : to hoot **2** : to howl, to wail

ululato *nm* : hoot (of an owl), wail (of a person)

umbilical *adj* : umbilical <cordón umbilical : umbilical cord>

umbral *nm* : threshold, doorstep

un[1] → **uno**[1]

un[2], **una** *art, mpl* **unos 1** : a, an **2 unos** *or* **unas** *pl* : some, a few <hace unas semanas : a few weeks ago> **3 unos** *or* **unas** *pl* : about, approximately <unos veinte años antes : about twenty years before>

unánime *adj* : unanimous — **unánimemente** *adv*

unanimidad *nf* **1** : unanimity **2 por ~** : unanimously

unción *nf, pl* **-ciones** : unction

uncir {83} *vt* : to yoke

undécimo[1], **-ma** *adj* : eleventh

undécimo[2], **-ma** *n* : eleventh (in a series)

ungir {35} *vt* : to anoint

ungüento *nm* : ointment, salve

únicamente *adv* : only, solely

unicelular *adj* : unicellular

único[1], **-ca** *adj* **1** : only, sole **2** : unique, extraordinary

único[2], **-ca** *n* : only one <los únicos que vinieron : the only ones who showed up>

unicornio *nm* : unicorn

unidad *nf* **1** : unity **2** : unit

unidireccional *adj* : unidirectional

unido, -da *adj* **1** : joined, united **2** : close <unos amigos muy unidos : very close friends>

unificar {72} *vt* : to unify — **unificación** *nf*

uniformado, -da *adj* : uniformed

uniformar *vt* ESTANDARIZAR : to standardize, to make uniform

uniforme[1] *adj* : uniform — **uniformemente** *adv*

uniforme[2] *nm* : uniform

uniformidad *nf* : uniformity

unilateral *adj* : unilateral — **unilateralmente** *adv*

unión *nf, pl* **uniones 1** : union **2** JUNTURA : joint, coupling

unir *vt* **1** JUNTAR : to unite, to join, to link **2** COMBINAR : to combine, to blend — **unirse** *vr* **1** : to join together **2** : to combine, to mix together **3 ~ a** : to join <se unieron al grupo : they joined the group>

unísono *nm* : unison <al unísono : in unison>

unitario, -ria *adj* : unitary, unit <precio unitario : unit price>

universal *adj* : universal — **universalmente** *adv*

universidad *nf* : university

universitario[1], **-ria** *adj* : university, college

universitario[2], **-ria** *n* : university student, college student

universo *nm* : universe

unja, etc. → **ungir**

uno[1], **una** *adj* (**un** *before masculine singular nouns*) : one <una silla : one chair> <tiene treinta y un años : he's thirty-one years old> <el tomo uno : volume one>

uno[2] *nm* : one, number one

uno[3], **una** *pron* **1** : one (number) <uno por uno : one by one> <es la una : it's

one o'clock> **2** : one (person or thing) <una es mejor que las otras : one (of them) is better than the others> <hacerlo uno mismo : to do it oneself> **3 unos, unas** *pl* : some (ones), some people **4 uno y otro** : both **5 unos y otros** : all of them **6 el uno al otro** : one another, each other <se enseñaron los unos a los otros : they taught each other>

untar *vt* **1** : to anoint **2** : to smear, to grease **3** : to bribe

unza, etc. → **uncir**

uña *nf* **1** : fingernail, toenail **2** : claw, hoof, stinger

uranio *nm* : uranium

Urano *nm* : Uranus

urbanidad *nf* : urbanity, courtesy

urbanización *nf, pl* **-ciones** : housing development, residential area

urbano, -na *adj* **1** : urban **2** CORTÉS : urbane, polite

urbe *nf* : large city, metropolis

urdimbre *nf* : warp (in a loom)

uretra *nf* : urethra

urgencia *nf* **1** : urgency **2** EMERGENCIA : emergency

urgente *adj* : urgent — **urgentemente** *adv*

urgir {35} *v impers* : to be urgent, to be pressing <me urge localizarlo : I urgently need to find him> <el tiempo urge : time is running out>

urinario[1], -ria *adj* : urinary

urinario[2] *nm* : urinal (place)

urja, etc. → **urgir**

urna *nf* **1** : urn **2** : ballot box <acudir a las urnas : to go to the polls>

urogallo *nm* : grouse (bird)

urraca *nf* **1** : magpie **2 urraca de América** : blue jay

urticaria *nf* : hives

uruguayo, -ya *adj & n* : Uruguayan

usado, -da *adj* **1** : used, secondhand **2** : worn, worn-out

usanza *nf* : custom, usage

usar *vt* **1** EMPLEAR, UTILIZAR : to use, to make use of **2** CONSUMIR : to consume, to use (up) **3** LLEVAR : to wear **4 de usar y tirar** : disposable — **usarse 1** : to be used **2** : to be in fashion

uso *nm* **1** EMPLEO, UTILIZACIÓN : use <de uso personal : for personal use> <hacer uso de : to make use of> **2** : wear <uso y desgaste : wear and tear> **3** USANZA : custom, usage, habit <al uso de : in the manner of, in the style of>

usted *pron* **1** (*formal form of address in most countries; often written as* **Ud.** *or* **Vd.**) : you **2 ustedes** *pl* (*often written as* **Uds.** *or* **Vds.**) : you, all of you

usual *adj* : usual, common, normal <poco usual : not very common> — **usualmente** *adv*

usuario, -ria *n* : user

usura *nf* : usury — **usurario, -ria** *adj*

usurero, -ra *n* : usurer

usurpador, -dora *n* : usurper

usurpar *vt* : to usurp — **usurpación** *nf*

utensilio *nm* : utensil, tool

uterino, -na *adj* : uterine

útero *nm* : uterus, womb

útil *adj* : useful, handy, helpful

útiles *nmpl* : implements, tools

utilidad *nf* **1** : utility, usefulness **2 utilidades** *nfpl* : profits

utilitario, -ria *adj* : utilitarian

utilizable *adj* : usable, fit for use

utilización *nf, pl* **-ciones** : utilization, use

utilizar {21} *vt* : to use, to utilize

útilmente *adv* : usefully

utopía *nf* : utopia

utópico, -ca *adj* : utopian

uva *nf* : grape

uvular *adj* : uvular

V

v *nf* : twenty-third letter of the Spanish alphabet

va → **ir**

vaca *nf* : cow

vacación *nf, pl* **-ciones 1** : vacation <dos semanas de vacaciones : two weeks of vacation> **2 estar de vacaciones** : to be on vacation **3 irse de vacaciones** : to go on vacation

vacacionar *vi Mex* : to vacation

vacacionista *nmf CA, Mex* : vacationer

vacante[1] *adj* : vacant, empty

vacante[2] *nf* : vacancy (for a job)

vaciado *nm* : cast, casting <vaciado de yeso : plaster cast>

vaciar {85} *vt* **1** : to empty, to empty out, to drain **2** AHUECAR : to hollow out **3** : to cast (in a mold) — *vi* **~ en** : to flow into, to empty into

vacilación *nf, pl* **-ciones** : hesitation, vacillation

vacilante *adj* **1** : hesitant, unsure **2** : shaky, unsteady **3** : flickering

vacilar *vi* **1** : to hesitate, to vacillate, to waver **2** : to be unsteady, to wobble **3** : to flicker **4** *fam* : to joke, to fool around

vacío[1], -cía *adj* **1** : vacant **2** : empty **3** : meaningless

vacío[2] *nm* **1** : emptiness, void **2** : space, gap **3** : vacuum **4 hacerle el vacío a alguien** : to ostracize someone, to give someone the cold shoulder

vacuidad *nf* : vacuity, vacuousness

vacuna *nf* : vaccine

vacunación *nf, pl* **-ciones** INOCULACIÓN : vaccination, inoculation

vacunar *vt* INOCULAR **:** to vaccinate, to inoculate

vacuno[1], **-na** *adj* **:** bovine <ganado vacuno : beef cattle>

vacuno[2] *nm* **:** bovine

vacuo, -cua *adj* **:** empty, shallow, inane

vadear *vt* **:** to ford, to wade across

vado *nm* **:** ford

vagabundear *vi* **:** to wander, to roam about

vagabundo[1], **-da** *adj* **1** ERRANTE **:** wandering **2 :** stray

vagabundo[2], **-da** *n* **:** vagrant, bum, vagabond

vagamente *adv* **:** vaguely

vagancia *nf* **1 :** vagrancy **2** PEREZA **:** laziness, idleness

vagar {52} *vi* ERRAR **:** to roam, to wander

vagina *nf* **:** vagina — **vaginal** *adj*

vago[1], **-ga** *adj* **1 :** vague **2** PEREZOSO **:** lazy, idle

vago[2], **-ga** *n* **1 :** idler, loafer **2** VAGABUNDO **:** vagrant, bum

vagón *nm, pl* **vagones :** car (of a train)

vague, etc. → **vagar**

vaguear *vi* **1 :** to loaf, to lounge around **2** VAGAR **:** to wander

vaguedad *nf* **:** vagueness

vahído *nm* **:** dizzy spell

vaho *nm* **1 :** breath **2 :** vapor, steam (on glass, etc.)

vaina *nf* **1 :** sheath, scabbard **2 :** pod (of a pea or bean) **3** *fam* **:** nuisance, bother

vainilla *nf* **:** vanilla

vaivén *nm, pl* **vaivenes 1 :** swinging, swaying, rocking **2 :** change, fluctuation <los vaivenes de la vida : life's ups and downs>

vajilla *nf* **:** dishes *pl*, set of dishes

valdrá, etc. → **valer**

vale *nm* **1 :** voucher **2** PAGARÉ **:** promissary note, IOU

valedero, -ra *adj* **:** valid

valentía *nf* **:** courage, valor

valer {84} *vt* **1 :** to be worth <valen una fortuna : they're worth a fortune> <no vale protestar : there's no point in protesting> <valer la pena : to be worth the trouble> **2 :** to cost <¿cuánto vale? : how much does it cost?> **3 :** to earn, to gain <le valió una reprimenda : it earned him a reprimand> **4 :** to protect, to aid <¡válgame Dios! : God help me!> **5 :** to be equal to — *vi* **1 :** to have value <sus consejos no valen para nada : his advice is worthless> **2 :** to be valid, to count <¡eso no vale! : that doesn't count!> **3 hacerse valer :** to assert oneself **4 más vale :** it's better <más vale que te vayas : you'd better go> — **valerse** *vr* **1 ~ de :** to take advantage of **2 valerse solo** *or* **valerse por sí mismo :** to look after oneself **3** *Mex* **:** to be fair <no se vale : it's not fair>

valeroso, -sa *adj* **:** brave, valiant

valet ['balɛt, -'le] *nm* **:** jack (in playing cards)

valga, etc. → **valer**

valía *nf* **:** value, worth

validar *vt* **:** to validate — **validación** *nf*

validez *nf* **:** validity

válido, -da *adj* **:** valid

valiente *adj* **1 :** brave, valiant **2** (*used ironically*) **:** fine, great <¡valiente amiga! : what a fine friend!> — **valientemente** *adv*

valija *nf* **:** suitcase, valise

valioso, -sa *adj* PRECIOSO **:** valuable, precious

valla *nf* **1 :** fence, barricade **2 :** hurdle (in sports) **3 :** obstacle, hindrance

vallar *vt* **:** to fence, to put a fence around

valle *nm* **:** valley, vale

valor *nm* **1 :** value, worth, importance **2** CORAJE **:** courage, valor **3 valores** *nmpl* **:** values, principles **4 valores** *nmpl* **:** securities, bonds **5 sin ~ :** worthless

valoración *nf, pl* **-ciones 1** EVALUACIÓN **:** valuation, appraisal, assessment **2** APRECIACIÓN **:** appreciation

valorar *vt* **1** EVALUAR **:** to evaluate, to appraise, to assess **2** APRECIAR **:** to value, to appreciate

valorizarse {21} *vr* **:** to appreciate, to increase in value — **valorización** *nf*

vals *nm* **:** waltz

valsar *vi* **:** to waltz

valuación *nf, pl* **-ciones :** valuation, appraisal

valuar {3} *vt* **:** to value, to appraise, to assess

válvula *nf* **1 :** valve **2 válvula reguladora :** throttle

vamos → **ir**

vampiro *nm* **:** vampire

van → **ir**

vanadio *nm* **:** vanadium

vanagloriarse *vr* **:** to boast, to brag

vanamente *adv* **:** vainly, in vain

vandalismo : vandalism

vándalo *nm* **:** vandal — **vandalismo** *nm*

vanguardia *nf* **1 :** vanguard **2 :** avante-garde **3 a la vanguardia :** at the forefront

vanidad *nf* **:** vanity

vanidoso, -sa *adj* PRESUMIDO **:** vain, conceited

vano, -na *adj* **1** INÚTIL **:** vain, useless **2 :** vain, worthless <vanas promesas : empty promises> **3 en ~ :** in vain, of no avail

vapor *nm* **1 :** vapor, steam **2 :** steamer, steamship **3 al vapor :** steamed

vaporizador *nm* **:** vaporizer

vaporizar {21} *vt* **:** to vaporize — **vaporizarse** *vr* — **vaporización** *nf*

vaporoso, -sa *adj* **1 :** vaporous **2 :** sheer, airy

vapulear *vt* **:** to beat, to thrash

vaquero[1], -ra *adj* : cowboy <pantalón vaquero : jeans>

vaquero[2], -ra *n* : cowboy *m,* cowgirl *f*

vaqueros *nmpl* JEANS : jeans

vaquilla *nf* : heifer

vara *nf* **1** : pole, stick, rod **2** : staff (of office) **3** : lance, pike (in bullfighting) **4** : yardstick **5 vara de oro** : goldenrod

varado, -da *adj* **1** : beached, aground **2** : stranded

varar *vt* : to beach (a ship), to strand — *vi* : to run aground

variable *adj & nf* : variable — **variabilidad** *nf*

variación *nf, pl* **-ciones** : variation

variado, -da *adj* : varied, diverse

variante *adj & nf* : variant

varianza *nf* : variance

variar {85} *vt* **1** : to change, to alter **2** : to diversify — *vi* **1** : to vary, to change **2 variar de opinión** : to change one's mind

varicela *nf* : chicken pox

varices *or* **várices** *nfpl* : varicose veins

varicoso, -sa *adj* : varicose

variedad *nf* DIVERSIDAD : variety, diversity

varilla *nf* **1** : rod, bar **2** : spoke (of a wheel) **3** : rib (of an umbrella)

vario, -ria *adj* **1** : varied, diverse **2** : variegated, motley **3** : changeable **4 varios, varias** *pl* : various, several

variopinto, -ta *adj* : diverse, assorted, motley

varita *nf* : wand <varita mágica : magic wand>

varón *nm, pl* **varones 1** HOMBRE : man, male **2** NIÑO : boy

varonil *adj* **1** : masculine, manly **2** : mannish

vas → **ir**

vasallo *nm* : vassal — **vasallaje** *nm*

vasco[1], -ca *adj & n* : Basque

vasco[2] *nm* : Basque (language)

vascular *adj* : vascular

vasija *nf* : container, vessel

vaso *nm* **1** : glass, tumbler **2** : glassful **3** : vessel <vaso sanguíneo : blood vessel>

vástago *nm* **1** : offspring, descendent **2** : shoot (of a plant)

vastedad *nf* : vastness, immensity

vasto, -ta *adj* : vast, immense

vataje *nm* : wattage

vaticinar *vt* : to predict, to foretell

vaticinio *nm* : prediction, prophecy

vatio *nm* : watt

vaya, etc. → **ir**

Vd., Vds. → **usted**

ve, etc. → **ir, ver**

vea, etc. → **ver**

vecinal *adj* : local

vecindad *nf* **1** : neighborhood, vicinity **2 casa de vecindad** : tenement

vecindario *nm* **1** : neighborhood, area **2** : residents *pl*

vecino, -na *n* **1** : neighbor **2** : resident, inhabitant

veda *nf* **1** PROHIBICIÓN : prohibition **2** : closed season (for hunting or fishing)

vedar *vt* **1** : to prohibit, to ban **2** IMPEDIR : to impede, to prevent

vega *nf* : fertile lowland

vegetación *nf, pl* **-ciones 1** : vegetation **2 vegetaciones** *nfpl* : adenoids

vegetal *adj & nm* : vegetable, plant

vegetar *vi* : to vegetate

vegetarianismo *nm* : vegetarianism

vegetariano, -na *adj & n* : vegetarian

vegetativo, -va *adj* : vegetative

vehemente *adj* : vehement — **vehemencia** *nf*

vehículo *nm* : vehicle — **vehicular** *adj*

veía, etc. → **ver**

veinte *adj & nm* : twenty

veinteavo[1], -va *adj* : twentieth

veinteavo[2] *nm* : twentieth (fraction)

veintena *nf* : group of twenty, score <una veintena de participantes : about twenty participants>

vejación *nf, pl* **-ciones** : ill-treatment, humiliation

vejar *vt* : to mistreat, to ridicule, to harass

vejete *nm* : old fellow, codger

vejez *nf* : old age

vejiga *nf* **1** : bladder **2** AMPOLLA : blister

vela *nf* **1** VIGILIA : wakefulness <pasé la noche en vela : I stayed awake all night> **2** : watch, vigil, wake **3** : candle **4** : sail

velada *nf* : evening party, soirée

velado, -da *adj* **1** : veiled, hidden **2** : blurred **3** : muffled

velador[1], -dora *n* : guard, night watchman

velador[2] *nm* **1** : candlestick **2** : night table

velar *vt* **1** : to hold a wake over **2** : to watch over, to sit up with **3** : to blur, to expose (a photo) **4** : to veil, to conceal — *vi* **1** : to stay awake **2 ~ por** : to watch over, to look after

velatorio *nm* VELORIO : wake (for the dead)

veleidad *nf* **1** : fickleness **2** : whim, caprice

veleidoso, -sa : fickle, capricious

velero *nm* **1** : sailing ship **2** : sailboat

veleta *nf* : weather vane

vello *nm* **1** : body hair **2** : down, fuzz

vellocino *nm* : fleece

vellón *nm, pl* **vellones 1** : fleece, sheepskin **2** *PRi* : nickel (coin)

vellosidad *nf* : downiness, hairiness

velloso, -sa *adj* : downy, fluffy, hairy

velo *nm* : veil

velocidad *nf* **1** : speed, velocity <velocidad máxima : speed limit> **2** MARCHA : gear (of an automobile)

velocímetro *nm* : speedometer

velocista *nmf* : sprinter

velorio *nm* VELATORIO : wake (for the dead)

velour *nm* : velour, velours

veloz *adj, pl* **veloces** : fast, quick, swift — **velozmente** *adv*
ven → **venir**
vena *nf* **1** : vein <vena yugular : jugular vein> **2** : vein, seam, lode **3** : grain (of wood) **4** : style <en vena lírica : in a lyrical vein> **5** : strain, touch <una vena de humor : a touch of humor> **6** : mood
venado *nm* **1** : deer **2** : venison
venal *adj* : venal — **venalidad** *nf*
vencedor, -dora *n* : winner, victor
vencejo *nm* : swift (bird)
vencer {86} *vt* **1** DERROTAR : to vanquish, to defeat **2** SUPERAR : to overcome, to surmount — *vi* **1** GANAR : to win, to triumph **2** CADUCAR : to expire <el plazo vence el jueves : the deadline is Thursday> **3** : to fall due, to mature — **vencerse** *vr* **1** DOMINARSE : to control oneself **2** : to break, to collapse
vencido, -da *adj* **1** : defeated **2** : expired **3** : due, payable **4 darse por vencido** : to give up
vencimiento *nm* **1** : defeat **2** : expiration **3** : maturity (of a loan)
venda *nf* : bandage
vendaje *nm* : bandage, dressing
vendar *vt* **1** : to bandage **2 vendar los ojos** : to blindfold
vendaval *nm* : gale, strong wind
vendedor, -dora *n* : salesperson, salesman *m,* saleswoman *f*
vender *vt* **1** : to sell **2** : to sell out, to betray — **venderse 1** : to be sold <se vende : for sale> **2** : to sell out
vendetta *nf* : vendetta
vendible *adj* : salable, marketable
vendimia *nf* : grape harvest
vendrá, etc. → **venir**
veneno *nm* **1** : poison **2** : venom
venenoso, -sa *adj* : poisonous, venomous
venerable *adj* : venerable
veneración *nf, pl* **-ciones** : veneration, reverence
venerar *vt* : to venerate, to revere
venéreo, -rea *adj* : venereal
venero *nm* **1** VENA : seam, lode, vein **2** MANANTIAL : spring **3** FUENTE : origin, source
venezolano, -na *adj & n* : Venezuelan
venga, etc. → **venir**
vengador, -dora *n* : avenger
venganza *nf* : vengeance, revenge
vengar {52} *vt* : to avenge — **vengarse** *vr* : to get even, to revenge oneself
vengativo, -va *adj* : vindictive, vengeful
vengue, etc. → **vengar**
venia *nf* **1** PERMISO : permission, leave **2** PERDÓN : pardon **3** : bow (of the head)
venial *adj* : venial
venida *nf* **1** LLEGADA : arrival, coming **2** REGRESO : return **3 idas y venidas** : comings and goings
venidero, -ra *adj* : coming, future
venir {87} *vi* **1** : to come <lo vi venir : I saw him coming> <¡venga! : come on!> **2** : to arrive <vinieron en coche : they came by car> **3** : to come, to originate <sus zapatos vienen de Italia : her shoes are from Italy> **4** : to come, to be available <viene envuelto en plástico : it comes wrapped in plastic> **5** : to come back, to return **6** : to affect, to overcome <me vino un vahído : a dizzy spell came over me> **7** : to fit <te viene un poco grande : it's a little big for you> **8** (*with the present participle*) : to have been <viene entrenando diariamente : he's been training daily> **9 ~ a** (*with the infinitive*) : to end up, to turn out <viene a ser lo mismo : it comes out the same> **10 que viene** : coming, next <el año que viene : next year> **11 venir bien** : to be suitable, to be just right — **venirse** *vr* **1** : to come, to arrive **2** : to come back **3 venirse abajo** : to fall apart, to collapse
venta *nf* **1** : sale **2 venta al por menor** *or* **venta al detalle** : retail sales
ventaja *nf* **1** : advantage **2** : lead, head start **3 ventajas** *nfpl* : perks, extras
ventajoso, -sa *adj* **1** : advantageous **2** : profitable — **ventajosamente** *adv*
ventana *nf* **1** : window (of a building) **2 ventana de la nariz** : nostril
ventanal *nm* : large window
ventanilla *nf* **1** : window (of a vehicle or airplane) **2** : ticket window, box office
ventero, -ra *n* : innkeeper
ventilación *nf, pl* **-ciones** : ventilation
ventilador *nm* **1** : ventilator **2** : fan
ventilar *vt* **1** : to ventilate, to air out **2** : to air, to discuss **3** : to make public, to reveal — **ventilarse** *vr* : to get some air
ventisca *nf* : snowstorm, blizzard
ventisquero *nm* : snowdrift
ventosear *vi* : to break wind
ventosidad *nf* : wind, flatulence
ventoso, -sa *adj* : windy
ventrículo *nm* : ventricle
ventrílocuo, -cua *n* : ventriloquist
ventriloquia *nf* : ventriloquism
ventura *nf* **1** : fortune, luck, chance **2** : happiness **3 a la ventura** : at random, as it comes
venturoso, -sa *adj* **1** AFORTUNADO : fortunate, lucky **2** : successful
Venus *nm* : Venus
venza, etc. → **vencer**
ver[1] {88} *vt* **1** : to see <vimos la película : we saw the movie> **2** ENTENDER : to understand <ya lo veo : now I get it> **3** EXAMINAR : to examine, to look into <lo veré : I'll take a look at it> **4** JUZGAR : to see, to judge <a mi manera de ver : to my way of thinking> **5** VISITAR : to meet with, to visit **6** AVERIGUAR : to find out **7 a ver** *or* **vamos a ver** : let's see — *vi* **1** : to see **2** ENTERARSE : to learn, to find out **3**

ENTENDER : to understand — **verse** *vr* **1** HALLARSE : to find oneself **2** PARECER : to look, to appear **3** ENCONTRARSE : to see each other, to meet

ver[2] *nm* **1** : looks *pl*, appearance **2** : opinion <a mi ver : in my view>

vera *nf* : side <a la vera del camino : alongside the road>

veracidad *nf* : truthfulness, veracity

veranda *nf* : veranda

veraneante *nmf* : summer vacationer

veranear *vi* : to spend the summer

veraniego, -ga *adj* **1** ESTIVAL : summer <el sol veraniego : the summer sun> **2** : summery

verano *nm* : summer

veras *nfpl* **de ~** : really, truly

veraz *adj, pl* **veraces** : truthful, veracious

verbal *adj* : verbal — **verbalmente** *adv*

verbalizar {21} *vt* : to verbalize, to express

verbena *nf* **1** FIESTA : festival, fair **2** : verbena, vervain

verbigracia *adv* : for example

verbo *nm* : verb

verborrea *nf* : verbiage

verbosidad *nf* : verbosity, wordiness

verboso, -sa *adj* : verbose, wordy

verdad *nf* **1** : truth **2 de ~** : really, truly **3 ¿verdad?** : right?, isn't that so?

verdaderamente *adv* : really, truly

verdadero, -dera *adj* **1** REAL, VERÍDICO : true, real **2** AUTÉNTICO : genuine

verde[1] *adj* **1** : green (in color) **2** : green, unripe **3** : inexperienced, green **4** : dirty, risqué

verde[2] *nm* : green

verdear *vi* : to turn green, to become verdant

verdín *nm, pl* **verdines** : slime, scum

verdor *nm* **1** : greenness **2** : verdure

verdoso, -sa *adj* : greenish

verdugo *nm* **1** : executioner, hangman **2** : tyrant

verdugón *nm, pl* **-gones** : welt, wheal

verdura *nf* : vegetable(s), green(s)

vereda *nf* **1** SENDA : path, trail **2** : sidewalk, pavement

veredicto *nm* : verdict

verga *nf* : spar, yard (of a ship)

vergonzoso, -sa *adj* **1** : disgraceful, shameful **2** : bashful, shy — **vergonzosamente** *adv*

vergüenza *nf* **1** : disgrace, shame **2** : embarrassment **3** : bashfulness, shyness

vericueto *nm* : rough terrain

verídico, -ca *adj* **1** REAL, VERDADERO : true, real **2** VERAZ : truthful

verificación *nf, pl* **-ciones** **1** : verification **2** : testing, checking

verificador, -dora *n* : inspector, tester

verificar {72} *vt* **1** : to verify, to confirm **2** : to test, to check **3** : to carry out, to conduct — **verificarse** *vr* **1** : to take place, to occur **2** : to come true

verja *nf* **1** : rails *pl* (of a fence) **2** : grating, grille **3** : gate

vermut *nm, pl* **vermuts** : vermouth

vernáculo, -la *adj* : vernacular

vernal *adj* : vernal, spring

verosímil *adj* **1** : probable, likely **2** : credible, realistic

verosimilitud *nf* **1** : probability, likeliness **2** : verisimilitude

verraco *nm* : boar

verruga *nf* : wart

versado, -da *adj* **~ en** : versed in, knowledgeable about

versar *vi* **~ sobre** : to deal with, to be about

versátil *adj* **1** : versatile **2** : fickle

versatilidad *nf* **1** : versatility **2** : fickleness

versículo *nm* : verse (in the Bible)

versión *nf, pl* **versiones** **1** : version **2** : translation

verso *nm* : verse

versus *prep* : versus, against

vértebra *nf* : vertebra — **vertebral** *adj*

vertebrado[1], -da *adj* : vertebrate

vertebrado[2] *nm* : vertebrate

vertedero *nm* **1** : garbage dump **2** DESAGÜE : drain, outlet

verter {56} *vt* **1** : to pour **2** : to spill, to shed **3** : to empty out **4** : to express, to voice **5** : to translate, to render — *vi* : to flow

vertical *adj & nf* : vertical — **verticalmente** *adv*

vértice *nm* : vertex, apex

vertido *nm* : spilling, spill

vertiente *nf* **1** : slope **2** : aspect, side, element

vertiginoso, -sa *adj* : vertiginous — **vertiginosamente** *adv*

vértigo *nm* : vertigo, dizziness

vesícula *nf* **1** : vesicle **2 vesícula biliar** : gallbladder

vesicular *adj* : vesicular

vestíbulo *nm* : vestibule, hall, lobby, foyer

vestido *nm* **1** : dress, costume, clothes *pl* **2** : dress (garment)

vestidor *nm* : dressing room

vestiduras *nfpl* **1** : clothing, raiment, regalia **2** *or* **vestiduras sacerdotales** : vestments

vestigio *nm* : vestige, sign, trace

vestimenta *nf* ROPA : clothing, clothes *pl*

vestir {54} *vt* **1** : to dress, to clothe **2** LLEVAR : to wear **3** ADORNAR : to decorate, to dress up — *vi* **1** : to dress <vestir bien : to dress well> **2** : to look good, to suit the occasion — **vestirse** *vr* **1** : to get dressed **2 ~ de** : to dress up as <se vistieron de soldados : they dressed up as soldiers> **3 ~ de** : to wear, to dress in

vestuario *nm* **1** : wardrobe **2** : dressing room, locker room

veta *nf* **1** : grain (in wood) **2** : vein, seam, lode **3** : trace, streak <una veta de terco : a stubborn streak>

vetar *vt* : to veto
veteado, -da *adj* : streaked, veined
veterano, -na *adj & n* : veteran
veterinaria *nf* : veterinary medicine
veterinario[1], -ria *adj* : veterinary
veterinario[2], -ria *n* : veterinarian
veto *nm* : veto
vetusto, -ta *adj* ANTIGUO : ancient, very old
vez *nf, pl* **veces 1** : time, occasion <a la vez : at the same time> <a veces : at times, occasionally> <de vez en cuando : from time to time> **2** (*with numbers*) : time <una vez : once> <de una vez : all at once> <de una vez para siempre : once and for all> <dos veces : twice> **3** : turn <a su vez : in turn> <en vez de : instead of> <hacer las veces de : to act as, to stand in for>
vía[1] *nf* **1** RUTA, CAMINO : road, route, way <Vía Láctea : Milky Way> **2** MEDIO : means, way <por vía oficial : through official channels> **3** : track, line (of a railroad) **4** : tract, passage <por vía oral : orally> **5 en vías de** : in the process of <en vías de solución : on the road to a solution> **6 por ~** : by (in transportation) <por vía aérea : by air, airmail>
vía[2] *prep* : via
viable *adj* : viable, feasible — **viabilidad** *nf*
viaducto *nm* : viaduct
viajante *mf* : traveling salesman, traveling saleswoman
viajar *vi* : to travel, to journey
viaje *nm* : trip, journey <viaje de negocios : business trip>
viajero[1], -ra *adj* : traveling
viajero[2], -ra *n* **1** : traveler **2** PASAJERO : passenger
vial *adj* : road, traffic
viático *nm* : travel allowance, travel expenses *pl*
víbora *nf* : viper
vibración *nf, pl* **-ciones** : vibration
vibrador *nm* : vibrator
vibrante *adj* **1** : vibrant **2** : vibrating
vibrar *vi* : to vibrate
vibratorio, -ria *adj* : vibratory
vicario, -ria *n* : vicar
vicealmirante *nmf* : vice admiral
vicepresidente, -ta *n* : vice president — **vicepresidencia** *nf*
viceversa *adv* : vice versa, conversely
viciado, -da *adj* : stuffy, close
viciar *vt* **1** : to corrupt **2** : to invalidate **3** FALSEAR : to distort **4** : to pollute, to adulterate
vicio *nm* **1** : vice, depravity **2** : bad habit **3** : defect, blemish
vicioso, -sa *adj* : depraved, corrupt
vicisitud *nf* : vicissitude
víctima *nf* : victim
victimario, -ria *n* ASESINO : killer, murderer
victimizar {21} *vt Arg, Mex* : to victimize
victoria *nf* : victory — **victorioso, -sa** *adj* — **victoriosamente** *adv*
victoriano, -na *adj* : Victorian
vid *nf* : vine, grapevine
vida *nf* **1** : life <la vida cotidiana : everyday life> **2** : life span, lifetime **3** BIOGRAFÍA : biography, life **4** : way of life, lifestyle **5** : livelihood <ganarse la vida : to earn one's living> **6** VIVEZA : liveliness **7 media vida** : half-life
vidente *nmf* **1** : psychic, clairvoyant **2** : sighted person
video *or* **vídeo** *nm* : video
videocasete *or* **videocasette** *nm* : videocassette
videocasetera *or* **videocasettera** *nf* : videocassette recorder, VCR
videocinta *nf* : videotape
videograbar *vt* : to videotape
vidriado *nm* : glaze
vidriar *vt* : to glaze (pottery, tile, etc.)
vidriera *nf* **1** : stained-glass window **2** : glass door or window **3** : store window
vidriero, -ra *n* : glazier
vidrio *nm* **1** : glass, piece of glass **2** : windowpane
vidrioso, -sa *adj* **1** : brittle, fragile **2** : slippery **3** : glassy, glazed (of eyes) **4** : touchy, delicate
vieira *nf* **1** : scallop **2** : scallop shell
viejo[1], -ja *adj* **1** ANCIANO : old, elderly **2** ANTIGUO : former, longstanding <viejas tradiciones : old traditions> <viejos amigos : old friends> **3** GASTADO : old, worn, worn-out
viejo[2], -ja *n* ANCIANO : old man *m,* old woman *f*
viene, etc. → **venir**
viento *nm* **1** : wind **2 hacer viento** : to be windy **3 contra viento y marea** : against all odds **4 viento en popa** : splendidly, successfully
vientre *nm* **1** : abdomen, belly **2** : womb **3** : bowels *pl*
viernes *nms & pl* : Friday
vierte, etc. → **verter**
vietnamita *adj & nmf* : Vietnamese
viga *nf* **1** : beam, rafter, girder **2 viga voladiza** : cantilever
vigencia *nf* **1** : validity **2** : force, effect <entrar en vigencia : to go into effect>
vigente *adj* : valid, in force
vigésimo[1], -ma *adj* : twentieth, twenty- <la vigésima segunda edición : the twenty-second edition>
vigésimo[2], -ma *n* : twentieth, twenty- (in a series)
vigía *nmf* : lookout
vigilancia *nf* : vigilance, watchfulness <bajo vigilancia : under surveillance>
vigilante[1] *adj* : vigilant, watchful
vigilante[2] *nmf* : watchman, guard
vigilar *vt* **1** CUIDAR : to look after, to keep an eye on **2** GUARDAR : to watch over, to guard — *vi* **1** : to be watchful **2** : to keep watch

vigilia *nf* **1** VELA **:** wakefulness **2 :** night work **3 :** vigil (in religion)
vigor *nm* **1 :** vigor, energy, strength **2** VIGENCIA **:** force, effect
vigorizante *adj* **:** envigorating
vigorizar {21} *vt* **:** to strengthen, to invigorate
vigoroso, -sa *adj* **:** vigorous — **vigorosamente** *adv*
VIH *nm* **:** HIV
vil *adj* **:** vile, dispicable
vileza *nf* **1 :** vileness **2 :** despicable action, villainy
vilipendiar *vt* **:** to vilify, to revile
villa *nf* **1 :** town, village **2 :** villa
villancico *nm* **:** carol, Christmas carol
villano, -na *n* **1 :** villain **2 :** peasant
vilo *nm* **en ~ 1 :** in the air **2 :** uncertain, in suspense
vinagre *nm* **:** vinegar
vinagrera *nf* **:** cruet (for vinegar)
vinatería *nf* **:** wine shop
vinculación *nf, pl* **-ciones 1 :** linking **2** RELACIÓN **:** bond, link, connection
vincular *vt* CONECTAR, RELACIONAR **:** to tie, to link, to connect
vínculo *nm* LAZO **:** tie, link, bond
vindicación *nf, pl* **-ciones :** vindication
vindicar *vt* **1 :** to vindicate **2 :** to avenge
vinilo *nm* **:** vinyl
vino[1], etc. → **venir**
vino[2] *nm* **:** wine
viña *nf* **:** vineyard
viñedo *nm* **:** vineyard
vio, etc. → **ver**
viola *nf* **:** viola
violación *nf, pl* **-ciones 1 :** violation, offense **2 :** rape
violador[1], -dora *n* **:** violator, offender
violador[2] *nm* **:** rapist
violar *vt* **1 :** to rape **2 :** to violate (a law or right) **3** PROFANAR **:** to desecrate
violencia *nf* **:** violence
violentamente *adv* **:** by force, violently
violentar *vt* **1** FORZAR **:** to break open, to force **2 :** to distort (words or ideas) — **violentarse** *vr* **:** to force oneself
violento, -ta *adj* **1 :** violent **2** EMBARAZOSO, INCÓMODO **:** awkward, embarassing
violeta[1] *adj & nm* **:** violet (color)
violeta[2] *nf* **:** violet (flower)
violín *nm, pl* **-lines :** violin
violinista *nmf* **:** violinist
violonchelista *nmf* **:** cellist
violonchelo *nm* **:** cello, violoncello
VIP *nmf, pl* **VIPs :** VIP
vira *nf* **:** welt (of a shoe)
virago *nf* **:** virago, shrew
viraje *nm* **1 :** turn, swerve **2 :** change
viral *adj* **:** viral
virar *vi* **:** to tack, to turn, to veer
virgen[1] *adj* **:** virgin <lana virgen : virgin wool>
virgen[2] *nmf, pl* **vírgenes :** virgin <la Santísima Virgen : the Blessed Virgin>
virginal *adj* **:** virginal, chaste
virginidad *nf* **:** virginity
Virgo *nmf* **:** Virgo
vírico, -ca *adj* **:** viral
viril *adj* **:** virile — **virilidad** *nf*
virrey, -rreina *n* **:** viceroy *m,* vicereine *f*
virtual *adj* **:** virtual — **virtualmente** *adv*
virtud *nf* **1 :** virtue **2 en virtud de :** by virtue of
virtuosismo *nm* **:** virtuosity
virtuoso[1], -sa *adj* **:** virtuous — **virtuosamente** *adv*
virtuoso[2], -sa *n* **:** virtuoso
viruela *nf* **1 :** smallpox **2 :** pockmark
virulencia *nf* **:** virulence
virulento, -ta *adj* **:** virulent
virus *nm* **:** virus
viruta *nf* **:** shaving
visa *nf* **:** visa
visado *nm Spain* **:** visa
visaje *nm* **:** face, grimace <hacer visajes : to make faces>
visceral *adj* **:** visceral
vísceras *nfpl* **:** viscera, entrails
visconde, -desa *n* **:** viscount *m,* viscountess *f*
viscosidad *nf* **:** viscosity
viscoso, -sa *adj* **:** viscous
visera *nf* **:** visor
visibilidad *nf* **:** visibility
visible *adj* **:** visible — **visiblemente** *adv*
visión *nf, pl* **visiones 1 :** vision, eyesight **2 :** view, perspective **3 :** vision, illusion <ver visiones : to be seeing things>
visionario, -ria *adj & n* **:** visionary
visita *nf* **1 :** visit, call **2 :** visitor **3 ir de visita :** to go visiting
visitador, -dora *n* **:** visitor, frequent caller
visitante[1] *adj* **:** visiting
visitante[2] *nmf* **:** visitor
visitar *vt* **:** to visit
vislumbrar *vt* **1 :** to discern, to make out **2 :** to begin to see, to have an inkling of
vislumbre *nf* **:** glimmer, gleam
viso *nm* **1** APARIENCIA **:** appearance <tener visos de : to seem, to show signs of> **2** DESTELLO **:** glint, gleam **3 :** sheen, iridescence
visón *nm, pl* **visones :** mink
víspera *nf* **1 :** eve, day before **2 vísperas** *nfpl* **:** vespers
vista *nf* **1** VISIÓN **:** vision, eyesight **2** MIRADA **:** look, gaze, glance **3** PANORAMA **:** view, vista, panorama **4 :** hearing (in court) **5 a primera vista :** at first sight **6 en vista de :** in view of **7 hacer la vista gorda :** to turn a blind eye **8 ¡hasta la vista! :** so long!, see you! **9 perder de vista :** to lose sight of **10 punto de vista :** point of view
vistazo *nm* **:** glance, look
viste, etc. → **ver, vestir**

visto¹ *pp* → **ver**
visto², -ta *adj* **1** : obvious, clear **2** : in view of, considering **3 estar bien visto** : to be approved of **4 estar mal visto** : to be frowned upon **5 por lo visto** : apparently **6 nunca visto** : unheard-of **7 visto que** : since, given that
visto³ *nm* **visto bueno** : approval
vistoso, -sa *adj* : colorful, bright
visual *adj* : visual — **visualmente** *adv*
visualización *nf, pl* **-ciones** : visualization
visualizar {21} *vt* **1** : to visualize **2** : to display (on a screen)
vital *adj* **1** : vital **2** : lively, dynamic
vitalicio, -cia *adj* : life, lifetime
vitalidad *nf* : vitality
vitamina *nf* : vitamin
vitamínico, -ca *adj* : vitamin <complejos vitamínicos : vitamin compounds>
vitorear *vt* : to cheer, to acclaim
vitral *nm* : stained-glass window
vítreo, -rea *adj* : vitreous, glassy
vitrina *nf* **1** : showcase, display case **2** : store window
vitriolo *nm* : vitriol
vituperar *vt* : to condemn, to vituperate against
vituperio *nm* : vituperation, censure
viudez *nf* : widowerhood, widowhood
viudo, -da *n* : widower *m,* widow *f*
vivacidad *nf* VIVEZA : vivacity, liveliness
vivamente *adv* **1** : in a lively manner **2** : vividly **3** : strongly, acutely <lo recomendamos vivamente : we strongly recommend it>
vivaque *nm* : bivouac
vivaquear *vi* : to bivouac
vivar *vi* : to cheer
vivaz *adj, pl* **vivaces 1** : lively, vivacious **2** : clever, sharp **3** : perennial
víveres *nmpl* : provisions, supplies, food
vivero *nm* **1** : nursery (for plants) **2** : hatchery, fish farm
viveza *nf* **1** VIVACIDAD : liveliness **2** BRILLO : vividness, brightness **3** ASTUCIA : cleverness, sharpness
vívido, -da *adj* : vivid, lively
vividor, -dora *n* : sponger, parasite
vivienda *nf* **1** : housing **2** MORADA : dwelling, home
viviente *adj* : living
vivificar {72} *vt* : to vivify, to give life to
vivir¹ *vi* **1** : to live, to be alive **2** SUBSISTIR : to subsist, to make a living **3** RESIDIR : to reside **4** : to spend one's life <vive para trabajar : she lives to work> **5 ~ de** : to live on — *vt* **1** : to live <vivir su vida : to live one's life> **2** EXPERIMENTAR : to go through, to experience
vivir² *nm* **1** : life, lifestyle **2 de mal vivir** : disreputable
vivisección *nf, pl* **-ciones** : vivisection
vivo, -va *adj* **1** : alive **2** INTENSO : vivid, bright, intense **3** ANIMADO : lively, vivacious **4** ASTUTO : sharp, clever **5 en ~** : live <transmisión en vivo : live broadcast> **6 al rojo vivo** : red-hot
vizconde, -desa *n* : viscount *m,* viscountess *f*
vocablo *nm* PALABRA : word
vocabulario *nm* : vocabulary
vocación *nf, pl* **-ciones** : vocation
vocacional *adj* : vocational
vocal¹ *adj* : vocal
vocal² *nmf* : member (of a committee, board, etc.)
vocal³ *nf* : vowel
vocalista *nmf* CANTANTE : singer, vocalist
vocalizar {21} *vi* : to vocalize
vocear *v* : to shout
vocerío *nm* : clamor, shouting
vocero, -ra *n* PORTAVOZ : spokesperson, spokesman *m,* spokeswoman *f*
vociferante *adj* : vociferous
vociferar *vi* GRITAR : to shout, to yell
vodevil *nm* : vaudeville
vodka *nm* : vodka
voladizo¹, -za *adj* : projecting
voladizo² *nm* : projection
volador, -dora *adj* : flying
volando *adv* : quickly, in a hurry
volante¹ *adj* : flying
volante² *nm* **1** : steering wheel **2** FOLLETO : flier, circular **3** : shuttlecock **4** : flywheel **5** : balance wheel (of a watch) **6** : ruffle, flounce
volar {19} *vi* **1** : to fly **2** CORRER : to hurry, to rush <el tiempo vuela : time flies> <pasar volando : to fly past> **3** DIVULGARSE : to spread <unos rumores volaban : rumors were spreading around> **4** DESAPARECER : to disappear <el dinero ya voló : the money's already gone> — *vt* **1** : to blow up, to demolish **2** : to irritate
volátil *adj* : volatile — **volatilidad** *nf*
volatilizar {21} *vt* : to volatize — **volatilizarse** *vr*
volcán *nm, pl* **volcanes** : volcano
volcánico, -ca *adj* : volcanic
volcar {82} *vt, pl* **volcanes 1** : to upset, to knock over, to turn over **2** : to empty out **3** : to make dizzy **4** : to cause a change of mind in **5** : to irritate — *vi* **1** : to overturn, to tip over **2** : to capsize — **volcarse** *vr* **1** : to overturn **2** : to do one's utmost
volea *nf* : volley (in sports)
volear *vi* : to volley (in sports)
voleibol *nm* : volleyball
voleo *nm* **al voleo** : haphazardly, at random
volframio *nm* : wolfram, tungsten
volición *nf, pl* **-ciones** : volition
volqué, etc. → **volcar**
voltaje *nm* : voltage
voltear *vt* **1** : to turn over, to turn upside down **2** : to reverse, to turn inside out **3** : to turn <voltear la cara : to turn one's head> **4** : to knock

down — *vi* **1** : to roll over, to do somersaults **2** : to turn <volteó a la izquierda : he turned left> — **voltearse** *vr* **1** : to turn around **2** : to change one's allegiance
voltereta *nf* : somersault, tumble
voltio *nm* : volt
volubilidad *nf* : fickleness, changeableness
voluble *adj* : fickle, changeable
volumen *nm, pl* **-lúmenes 1** TOMO : volume, book **2** : capacity, size, bulk **3** CANTIDAD : amount <el volumen de ventas : the volume of sales> **4** : volume, loudness
voluminoso, -sa *adj* : voluminous, massive, bulky
voluntad *nf* **1** : will, volition **2** DESEO : desire, wish **3** INTENCIÓN : intention **4 a voluntad** : at will **5 buena voluntad** : good will **6 mala voluntad** : ill will **7 fuerza de voluntad** : willpower
voluntario[1], -ria *adj* : voluntary — **voluntariamente** *adv*
voluntario[2], -ria *n* : volunteer
voluntarioso, -sa *adj* **1** : stubborn **2** : willing, eager
voluptuosidad *nf* : voluptuousness
voluptuoso, -sa *adj* : voluptuous — **voluptuosamente** *adv*
voluta *nf* : spiral, column (of smoke)
volver {89} *vi* **1** : to return, to come or go back <volver a casa : to return home> **2** : to revert <volver al tema : to get back to the subject> **3 ~ a** : to do again <volvieron a llamar : they called again> **4 volver en sí** : to come to, to regain consciousness — *vt* **1** : to turn, to turn over, to turn inside out **2** : to return, to repay, to restore **3** : to cause, to make <la volvía loca : it was driving her crazy> — **volverse** *vr* **1** : to become <se volvió deprimido : he became depressed> **2** : to turn around
vomitar *vi* : to vomit — *vt* **1** : to vomit **2** : to spew out (lava, etc.)
vómito *nm* **1** : vomiting **2** : vomit
voracidad *nf* : voracity
vorágine *nf* : whirlpool, maelstrom
voraz *adj, pl* **voraces** : voracious — **vorazmente** *adv*
vórtice *nm* **1** : whirlpool, vortex **2** TORBELLINO : whirlwind
vos *pron* (*in some regions of Latin America*) : you
vosear *vt* : to address as *vos*
vosotros, -tras *pron pl Spain* **1** : you, yourselves **2** : ye
votación *nf, pl* **-ciones** : vote, voting
votante *nmf* : voter
votar *vi* : to vote — *vt* : to vote for
votivo, -va *adj* : votive
voto *nm* **1** : vote **2** : vow (in religion) **3 votos** *nmpl* : good wishes
voy → **ir**
voz *nf, pl* **voces 1** : voice **2** : opinion, say **3** GRITO : shout, yell **4** : sound **5** VOCABLO : word, term **6** : rumor **7 a voz en cuello** : at the top of one's lungs **8 dar voces** : to shout **9 en voz alta** : aloud, in a loud voice **10 en voz baja** : softly, in a low voice
vudú *nm* : voodoo
vuelco *nm* : upset, overturning <me dio un vuelco el corazón : my heart skipped a beat>
vuela, etc. → **volar**
vuelca, vuelque, etc. → **volcar**
vuelo *nm* **1** : flight, flying <alzar el vuelo : to take flight> **2** : flight (of an aircraft) <vuelo espacial : space flight> **3** : flare, fullness (of clothing) **4 al vuelo** : on the wing
vuelta *nf* **1** GIRO : turn <se dio la vuelta : he turned around> **2** REVOLUCIÓN : circle, revolution <dio la vuelta al mundo : she went around the world> <las ruedas daban vueltas : the wheels were spinning> **3** : flip, turn <le dio la vuelta : she flipped it over> **4** : bend, curve <a la vuelta de la esquina : around the corner> **5** REGRESO : return <de ida y vuelta : round trip> <a vuelta de correo : return mail> **6** : round, lap (in sports or games) **7** PASEO : walk, drive, ride <dio una vuelta : he went for a walk> **8** DORSO, REVÉS : back, other side <a la vuelta : on the back> **9** : cuff (of pants) **10 darle vueltas** : to think over **11 estar de vuelta** : to be back
vuelto *pp* → **volver**
vuelve, etc. → **volver**
vuestro[1], -stra *adj Spain* : your, of yours <vuestros coches : your cars> <una amiga vuestra : a friend of yours>
vuestro[2], -stra *pron Spain* (*with definite article*) : yours <la vuestra es más grande : yours is bigger> <esos son los vuestros : those are yours>
vulcanizar {21} *vt* : to vulcanize
vulgar *adj* **1** : common **2** : vulgar
vulgaridad *nf* : vulgarity
vulgarismo *nm* : vulgarism
vulgarizar {21} *vt* : to vulgarize, to popularize
vulgarmente *adv* : vulgarly, popularly
vulgo *nm* **el vulgo** : the masses, common people
vulnerable *adj* : vulnerable — **vulnerabilidad** *nf*
vulnerar *vt* **1** : to injure, to damage (one's reputation or honor) **2** : to violate, to break (a law or contract)

W

w *nf* **:** twenty-fourth letter of the Spanish alphabet
wafle *nm* **:** waffle
waflera *nf* **:** waffle iron
wapití *nm* **:** wapiti, elk
whisky *nm, pl* **whiskys** *or* **whiskies** **:** whiskey
wigwam *nm* **:** wigwam

X

x *nf* **:** twenty-fifth letter of the Spanish alphabet
xenofobia *nf* **:** xenophobia
xenófobo[1], -ba *adj* **:** xenophobic
xenófobo[2], -ba *n* **:** xenophobe
xenón *nm* **:** xenon
xerocopiar *vt* **:** to photocopy, to xerox
xilófono *nm* **:** xylophone

Y

y[1] *nf* **:** twenty-sixth letter of the Spanish alphabet
y[2] *conj* **1 :** and <mi hermano y yo : my brother and I> <¿y los demás? : and (what about) the others?> **2** (*used in numbers*) <cincuenta y cinco : fifty-five> **3** *fam* **:** well <y por supuesto : well, of course>
ya[1] *adv* **1 :** already <ya terminó : she's finished already> **2 :** now, right now <¡hazlo ya! : do it now!> <ya mismo : right away> **3 :** later, soon <ya iremos : we'll go later on> **4 :** no longer, anymore <ya no fuma : he no longer smokes> **5** (*used for emphasis*) **:** <¡ya lo sé! : I know!> <ya lo creo : of course> **6 no ya :** not only <no ya lloran sino gritan : they're not only crying but screaming> **7 ya que :** now that, since <ya que sabe la verdad : now that she knows the truth>
ya[2] *conj* **ya . . . ya :** whether . . . or, first . . . then <ya le gusta, ya no : first he likes it, then he doesn't>
yac *nm* **:** yak
yacer {90} *vi* **:** to lie <en esta tumba yacen sus abuelos : his grandparents lie in this grave>
yacimiento *nm* **:** bed, deposit <yacimiento petrolífero : oil field>
yaga, etc. → **yacer**
yanqui *adj & nmf* **:** Yankee
yarda *nf* **:** yard
yate *nm* **:** yacht
yaz, yazca, yazga, etc. → **yacer**
yedra *nf* **:** ivy
yegua *nf* **:** mare
yelmo *nm* **:** helmet
yema *nf* **1 :** bud, shoot **2 :** yolk (of an egg) **3 yema del dedo :** fingertip
yemenita *adj & nmf* **:** Yemenite
yendo → **ir**
yerba *nf* **1** *or* **yerba mate :** maté **2** → **hierba**
yerga, yergue, etc. → **erguir**
yermo[1], -ma *adj* **:** barren, deserted
yermo[2] *nm* **:** wasteland
yerno *nm* **:** son-in-law
yerra, etc. → **errar**
yerro *nm* **:** blunder, mistake
yerto, -ta *adj* **:** rigid, stiff
yesca *nf* **:** tinder
yeso *nm* **1 :** plaster **2 :** gypsum
yo[1] *nm* **:** ego, self
yo[2] *pron* **1 :** I **2 :** me <todos menos yo : everyone except me> <tan bajo como yo : as short as me> **3 soy yo :** it is I, it's me
yodado, -da *adj* **:** iodized
yodo *nm* **:** iodine
yoduro *nm* **:** iodide
yoga *nm* **:** yoga
yogui *nm* **:** yogi
yogurt *or* **yogur** *nm* **:** yogurt
yola *nf* **:** yawl
yoyo *or* **yoyó** *nm* **:** yo-yo
yuca *nf* **1 :** yucca (plant) **2 :** cassava, manioc
yucateco[1], -ca *adj* **:** of or from the Yucatán
yucateco[2], -ca *n* **:** person from the Yucatán
yudo → **judo**
yugo *nm* **:** yoke
yugoslavo, -va *adj & n* **:** Yugoslavian
yugular *adj* **:** jugular <vena yugular : jugular vein>
yungas *nfpl Bol, Chile, Peru* **:** warm tropical valleys
yunque *nm* **:** anvil
yunta *nf* **:** yoke, team (of oxen)
yute *nm* **:** jute
yuxtaponer {60} *vt* **:** to juxtapose — **yuxtaposición** *nf*

Z

z *nf* **:** twenty-seventh letter of the Spanish alphabet
zacate *nm CA, Mex* **1 :** grass, forage **2 :** hay
zafacón *nm, pl* **-cones :** wastebasket
zafar *vt* **:** to loosen, to untie — **zafarse** *vr* **1 :** to loosen up, to come undone **2 :** to get free of
zafio, -fia *adj* **:** coarse, crude
zafiro *nm* **:** sapphire
zaga *nf* **1 :** defense (in sports) **2 a la zaga** *or* **en ~ :** behind, in the rear
zagual *nm* **:** paddle (of a canoe)
zaguán *nm, pl* **zaguanes :** front hall, vestibule
zaherir {76} *vt* **1 :** to criticize sharply **2 :** to wound, to mortify
zahones *nmpl* **:** chaps
zaino, -na *adj* **:** chestnut (color)
zalamería *nf* **:** flattery, sweet talk
zalamero[1], -ra *adj* **:** flattering, fawning
zalamero[2], -ra *n* **:** flatterer
zambiano, -na *adj & nmf* **:** Zambian
zambullida *nf* **:** dive, plunge
zambullirse {38} *vr* **:** to dive, to plunge
zanahoria *nf* **:** carrot
zancada *nf* **:** stride, step
zancadilla *nf* **1 :** trip, stumble **2** *fam* **:** trick, ruse
zancos *nmpl* **:** stilts
zancuda *nf* **:** wading bird
zancudo *nm* MOSQUITO **:** mosquito
zángano *nm* **:** drone, male bee
zanja *nf* **:** ditch, trench
zanjar *vt* ACLARAR **:** to settle, to clear up, to resolve
zapallo *nm Arg, Chile, Peru, Uru* **:** pumpkin
zapapico *nm* **:** pickax
zapata *nf* **:** brake shoe
zapatería *nf* **1 :** shoemaker's, shoe factory **2 :** shoe store
zapatero[1], -ra *adj* **:** dry, tough, poorly cooked
zapatero[2], -ra *n* **:** shoemaker, cobbler
zapatilla *nf* **1** PANTUFLA **:** slipper **2** *or* **zapatilla de deporte :** sneaker
zapato *nm* **:** shoe
zar, zarina *n* **:** czar *m*, czarina *f*
zarandear *vt* **1 :** to sift, to sieve **2 :** to shake, to jostle, to jiggle
zarapito *nm* **:** curlew
zarcillo *nm* **1 :** earring **2 :** tendril (of a plant)
zarigüeya *nf* **:** opossum
zarista *adj & nmf* **:** czarist
zarpa *nf* **:** paw
zarpar *vi* **:** to set sail, to raise anchor
zarza *nf* **:** bramble, blackberry bush
zarzamora *nf* **1 :** blackberry **2 :** bramble, blackberry bush
zarzaparrilla *nf* **:** sarsaparilla
zepelín *nm, pl* **-lines :** zeppelin
zigoto *nm* **:** zygote
zigzag *nm, pl* **zigzags** *or* **zigzagues :** zigzag
zigzaguear *vi* **:** to zigzag
zimbabuense *adj & nmf* **:** Zimbabwean
zinc *nm* **:** zinc
zinnia *nf* **:** zinnia
zíper *nm CA, Mex* **:** zipper
zircón *nm, pl* **zircones :** zircon
zócalo *nm Mex* **:** main square
zodíaco *nm* **:** zodiac — **zodíacal** *adj*
zombi *or* **zombie** *nmf* **:** zombie
zona *nf* **:** zone, district, area
zonzo[1], -za *adj* **:** stupid, silly
zonzo[2], -za *n* **:** idiot, nitwit
zoo *nm* **:** zoo
zoología *nf* **:** zoology
zoológico[1], -ca *adj* **:** zoological
zoológico[2] *nm* **:** zoo
zoólogo, -ga *n* **:** zoologist
zoom *nm* **:** zoom lens
zopilote *nm CA, Mex* **:** buzzard
zoquete *nmf fam* **:** oaf, blockhead
zorrillo *nm* MOFETA **:** skunk
zorro[1], -rra *adj* **:** sly, crafty
zorro[2], -rra *n* **1 :** fox, vixen **2 :** sly crafty person
zorzal *nm* **:** thrush
zozobra *nf* **:** anxiety, worry
zozobrar *vi* **:** to capsize
zueco *nm* **:** clog (shoe)
zulú[1] *adj & nmf* **:** Zulu
zulú[2] *nm* **:** Zulu (language)
zumaque *nm* **:** sumac
zumbar *vi* **:** to buzz, to hum — *vt fam* **1 :** to hit, to thrash **2 :** to make fun of
zumbido *nm* **:** buzzing, humming
zumo *nf* JUGO **:** juice
zurcir {83} *vt* **:** to darn, to mend
zurdo[1], -da *adj* **:** left-handed
zurdo[2], -da *n* **:** left-handed person
zurza, etc. → **zurcir**
zutano, -na → **fulano**

English–Spanish Dictionary

A

a[1] [ˈeɪ] *n, pl* **a's** *or* **as** [ˈeɪz] : primera letra del alfabeto inglés

a[2] [ə, ˈeɪ] *art* (**an** [ən, ˈæn] *before vowel or silent h*) **1** : un *m,* una *f* <a house : una casa> <half an hour : media hora> <what a surprise! : ¡qué sorpresa!> **2** PER : por, a la, al <30 kilometers an hour : 30 kilómetros por hora> <twice a month : dos veces al mes>

aardvark [ˈɑrd͵vɑrk] *n* : oso *m* hormiguero

aback [əˈbæk] *adv* **1** : por sorpresa **2 to be taken aback** : quedarse desconcertado

abacus [ˈæbəkəs] *n, pl* **abaci** [ˈæbə͵saɪ, -͵kiː] *or* **abacuses** : ábaco *m*

abaft [əˈbæft] *adv* : a popa

abalone [͵æbəˈloːni] *n* : abulón *m,* oreja *f* marina

abandon[1] [əˈbændən] *vt* **1** DESERT, FORSAKE : abandonar, desamparar (a alguien), desertar de (algo) **2** GIVE UP, SUSPEND : renunciar a, suspender <he abandoned the search : suspendió la búsqueda> **3** EVACUATE, LEAVE : abandonar, evacuar, dejar <to abandon ship : abandonar el buque> **4 to abandon oneself** : entregarse, abandonarse

abandon[2] *n* : desenfreno *m* <with wild abandon : desenfrenadamente>

abandoned [əˈbændənd] *adj* **1** DESERTED : abandonado **2** UNRESTRAINED : desenfrenado, desinhibido

abandonment [əˈbændənmənt] *n* : abandono *m,* desamparo *m*

abase [əˈbeɪs] *vt* **abased; abasing** : degradar, humillar, rebajar

abash [əˈbæʃ] *vt* : avergonzar, abochornar

abashed [əˈbæʃt] *adj* : avergonzado

abate [əˈbeɪt] *vi* **abated; abating** : amainar, menguar, disminuir

abattoir [ˈæbə͵twɑr] *n* : matadero *m*

abbess [ˈæbɪs, -͵bɛs, -bəs] *n* : abadesa *f*

abbey [ˈæbi] *n, pl* **-beys** : abadía *f*

abbot [ˈæbət] *n* : abad *m*

abbreviate [əˈbriːvi͵eɪt] *vt* **-ated; -ating** : abreviar

abbreviation [ə͵briːviˈeɪʃən] *n* : abreviación *f,* abreviatura *f*

abdicate [ˈæbdɪ͵keɪt] *v* **-cated; -cating** : abdicar

abdication [͵æbdɪˈkeɪʃən] *n* : abdicación *f*

abdomen [ˈæbdəmən, æbˈdoːmən] *n* : abdomen *m,* vientre *m*

abdominal [æbˈdɑmənəl] *adj* : abdominal — **abdominally** *adv*

abduct [æbˈdʌkt] *vt* : raptar, secuestrar

abduction [æbˈdʌkʃən] *n* : rapto *m,* secuestro *m*

abductor [æbˈdʌktər] *n* : raptor *m,* -tora *f;* secuestrador *m,* -dora *f*

abed [əˈbɛd] *adv & adj* : en cama

aberrant [æˈbɛrənt, ˈæbərənt] *adj* **1** ABNORMAL : anormal, aberrante **2** ATYPICAL : anómalo, atípico

aberration [͵æbəˈreɪʃən] *n* **1** : aberración *f* **2** DERANGEMENT : perturbación *f* mental

abet [əˈbɛt] *vt* **abetted; abetting** ASSIST : ayudar <to aid and abet : ser cómplice de>

abeyance [əˈbeɪənts] *n* : desuso *m,* suspensión *f*

abhor [əbˈhɔr, æb-] *vt* **-horred; -horring** : abominar, aborrecer

abhorrence [əbˈhɔrənts, æb-] *n* : aborrecimiento *m,* odio *m*

abhorrent [əbˈhɔrənt, æb-] *adj* : abominable, aborrecible, odioso

abide [əˈbaɪd] *v* **abode** [əˈboːd] *or* **abided; abiding** *vt* STAND : soportar, tolerar <I can't abide them : no los puedo ver> — *vi* **1** ENDURE : quedar, permanecer **2** DWELL : morar, residir **3 to abide by** : atenerse a

ability [əˈbɪləti] *n, pl* **-ties 1** CAPABILITY : aptitud *f,* capacidad *f,* facultad *f* **2** COMPETENCE : competencia *f* **3** TALENT : talento *m,* don *m,* habilidad *f*

abject [ˈæb͵dʒɛkt, æbˈ-] *adj* **1** WRETCHED : miserable, desdichado **2** HOPELESS : abatido, desesperado **3** SERVILE : servil <abject flattery : halagos serviles> — **abjectly** *adv*

ablaze [əˈbleɪz] *adj* **1** BURNING : ardiendo, en llamas **2** RADIANT : resplandeciente, radiante

able [ˈeɪbəl] *adj* **abler; ablest 1** CAPABLE : capaz, hábil **2** COMPETENT : competente

ablution [əˈbluːʃən] *n* : ablución *f* <to perform one's ablutions : lavarse>

ably [ˈeɪbəli] *adv* : hábilmente, eficientemente

abnormal [æbˈnɔrməl] *adj* : anormal — **abnormally** *adv*

abnormality [͵æbnərˈmæləti, -nɔr-] *n, pl* **-ties** : anormalidad *f*

aboard[1] [əˈbord] *adv* : a bordo

aboard[2] *prep* : a bordo de

abode[1] → **abide**

abode[2] [əˈboːd] *n* : morada *f,* residencia *f,* vivienda *f*

abolish [əˈbɑlɪʃ] *vt* : abolir, suprimir

abolition [͵æbəˈlɪʃən] *n* : abolición *f,* supresión *f*

abominable [əˈbɑmənəbəl] *adj* DETESTABLE : abominable, aborrecible, espantoso

abominate [əˈbɑmə͵neɪt] *vt* **-nated; -nating** : abominar, aborrecer

abomination [ə͵bɑməˈneɪʃən] *n* : abominación *f*

aboriginal [͵æbəˈrɪdʒənəl] *adj* : aborigen, indígena

aborigine [ˌæbəˈrɪdʒəni] *n* NATIVE : aborigen *mf,* indígena *mf*
abort [əˈbɔrt] *vt* **1** : abortar (en medicina) **2** CALL OFF : suspender, abandonar — *vi* : abortar, hacerse un aborto
abortion [əˈbɔrʃən] *n* : aborto *m*
abortive [əˈbɔrt̬ɪv] *adj* UNSUCCESSFUL : fracasado, frustrado, malogrado
abound [əˈbaʊnd] *vi* **to abound in** : abundar en, estar lleno de
about[1] [əˈbaʊt] *adv* **1** APPROXIMATELY : aproximadamente, casi, más o menos **2** AROUND : por todas partes, alrededor <the children are running about : los niños están corriendo por todas partes> **3 to be about to** : estar a punto de **4 to be up and about** : estar levantado
about[2] *prep* **1** AROUND : alrededor de **2** CONCERNING : de, acerca de, sobre <he always talks about politics : siempre habla de política>
above[1] [əˈbʌv] *adv* **1** OVERHEAD : por encima, arriba **2** : más arriba <as stated above : como se indica más arriba>
above[2] *adj* : anterior, antedicho <for the above reasons : por las razones antedichas>
above[3] *prep* **1** OVER : encima de, arriba de, sobre **2** : superior a, por encima de <he's above those things : él está por encima de esas cosas> **3** : más de, superior a <he earns above $50,000 : gana más de $50,000> <a number above 10 : un número superior a 10> **4 above all** : sobre todo
aboveboard[1] [əˈbʌvˈbord, -ˌbord] *adv* **open and aboveboard** : sin tapujos
aboveboard[2] *adj* : legítimo, sincero
abrade [əˈbreɪd] *vt* **abraded; abrading 1** ERODE : erosionar, corroer **2** SCRAPE : escoriar, raspar
abrasion [əˈbreɪʒən] *n* **1** SCRAPE, SCRATCH : raspadura *f,* rasguño *m* **2** EROSION : erosión *f*
abrasive[1] [əˈbreɪsɪv] *adj* **1** ROUGH : abrasivo, áspero **2** BRUSQUE, IRRITATING : brusco, irritante
abrasive[2] *n* : abrasivo *m*
abreast [əˈbrɛst] *adv* **1** : en fondo, al lado <to march three abreast : marchar de tres en fondo> **2 to keep abreast** : mantenerse al día
abridge [əˈbrɪdʒ] *vt* **abridged; abridging** : compendiar, resumir
abridgment *or* **abridgement** [əˈbrɪdʒmənt] *n* : compendio *m,* resumen *m*
abroad [əˈbrɔd] *adv* **1** ABOUT, WIDELY : por todas partes, en todas direcciones <the news spread abroad : la noticia corrió por todas partes> **2** OVERSEAS : en el extranjero, en el exterior
abrupt [əˈbrʌpt] *adj* **1** SUDDEN : abrupto, repentino, súbito **2** BRUSQUE, CURT : brusco, cortante — **abruptly** *adv*
abscess [ˈæbˌsɛs] *n* : absceso *m*
abscond [æbˈskɑnd] *vi* : huir, fugarse
absence [ˈæbsənts] *n* **1** : ausencia *f* (de una persona) **2** LACK : falta *f,* carencia *f*
absent[1] [æbˈsɛnt] *vt* **to absent oneself** : ausentarse
absent[2] [ˈæbsənt] *adj* : ausente
absentee [ˌæbsənˈtiː] *n* : ausente *mf*
absentminded [ˌæbsəntˈmaɪndəd] *adj* : distraído, despistado
absentmindedly [ˌæbsəntˈmaɪndədli] *adv* : distraídamente
absentmindedness [ˌæbsəntˈmaɪndədnəs] *n* : distracción *f,* despiste *m*
absolute [ˈæbsəˌluːt, ˌæbsəˈluːt] *adj* **1** COMPLETE, PERFECT : completo, pleno, perfecto **2** UNCONDITIONAL : absoluto, incondicional **3** DEFINITE : categórico, definitivo
absolutely [ˈæbsəˌluːtli, ˌæbsəˈluːtli] *adv* **1** COMPLETELY : completamente, absolutamente **2** CERTAINLY : desde luego <do you agree? absolutely! : ¿estás de acuerdo? ¡desde luego!>
absolution [ˌæbsəˈluːʃən] *n* : absolución *f*
absolve [əbˈzɑlv, æb-, -ˈsɑlv] *vt* **-solved; -solving** : absolver, perdonar
absorb [əbˈzɔrb, æb-, -ˈsɔrb] *vt* **1** : absorber, embeber (un líquido), amortiguar (un golpe, la luz) **2** ENGROSS : absorber **3** ASSIMILATE : asimilar
absorbed [əbˈzɔrbd, æb-, -ˈsɔrbd] *adj* ENGROSSED : absorto, ensimismado
absorbency [əbˈzɔrbəntsi, æb-, -ˈsɔr-] *n* : absorbencia *f*
absorbent [əbˈzɔrbənt, æb-, -ˈsɔr-] *adj* : absorbente
absorbing [əbˈzɔrbɪŋ, æb-, -ˈsɔr-] *adj* : absorbente, fascinante
absorption [əbˈzɔrpʃən, æb-, -ˈsɔrp-] *n* **1** : absorción *f* **2** CONCENTRATION : concentración *f*
abstain [əbˈsteɪn, æb-] *vi* : abstenerse
abstainer [əbˈsteɪnər, æb-] *n* : abstemio *m,* -mia *f*
abstemious [æbˈstiːmiəs] *adj* : abstemio, sobrio — **abstemiously** *adv*
abstention [əbˈstɛntʃən, æb-] *n* : abstención *f*
abstinence [ˈæbstənənts] *n* : abstinencia *f*
abstract[1] [æbˈstrækt, ˈæbˌ-] *vt* **1** EXTRACT : abstraer, extraer **2** SUMMARIZE : compendiar, resumir
abstract[2] *adj* : abstracto — **abstractly** [æbˈstræktli, ˈæbˌ-] *adv*
abstract[3] [ˈæbˌstrækt] *n* : resumen *m,* compendio *m,* sumario *m*
abstraction [æbˈstrækʃən] *n* **1** : abstracción *f,* idea *f* abstracta **2** ABSENTMINDEDNESS : distracción *f*
abstruse [əbˈstruːs, æb-] *adj* : abstruso, recóndito — **abstrusely** *adv*
absurd [əbˈsərd, -ˈzərd] *adj* : absurdo, ridículo, disparatado — **absurdly** *adv*
absurdity [əbˈsərdət̬i, -ˈzər-] *n, pl* **-ties 1** : absurdo *m* **2** NONSENSE : disparate *m,* despropósito *m*

abundance [ə'bʌndənts] *n* : abundancia *f*

abundant [ə'bʌndənt] *adj* : abundante, cuantioso, copioso

abundantly [ə'bʌndəntli] *adv* : abundantemente, en abundancia

abuse[1] [ə'bjuːz] *vt* **abused; abusing 1** MISUSE : abusar de **2** MISTREAT : maltratar **3** REVILE : insultar, injuriar, denostar

abuse[2] [ə'bjuːs] *n* **1** MISUSE : abuso *m* **2** MISTREATMENT : abuso *m,* maltrato *m* **3** INSULTS : insultos *mpl,* improperios *mpl* <a string of abuse : una serie de improperios>

abuser [ə'bjuːzər] *n* : abusador *m,* -dora *f*

abusive [ə'bjuːsɪv] *adj* **1** ABUSING : abusivo **2** INSULTING : ofensivo, injurioso, insultante — **abusively** *adv*

abut [ə'bʌt] *v* **abutted; abutting** *vt* : bordear — *vi* **to abut on** : colindar con

abutment [ə'bʌtmənt] *n* **1** BUTTRESS : contrafuerte *m,* estribo *m* **2** CLOSENESS : contigüidad *f*

abysmal [ə'bɪzməl] *adj* **1** DEEP : abismal, insondable **2** TERRIBLE : atroz, desastroso

abysmally [ə'bɪzməli] *adv* : desastrosamente, terriblemente

abyss [ə'bɪs, 'æbɪs] *n* : abismo *m,* sima *f*

acacia [ə'keɪʃə] *n* : acacia *f*

academic[1] [ˌækə'dɛmɪk] *adj* **1** : académico **2** THEORETICAL : teórico — **academically** [-mɪkli] *adv*

academic[2] *n* : académico *m,* -ca *f*

academy [ə'kædəmi] *n, pl* **-mies** : academia *f*

accede [æk'siːd] *vi* **-ceded; -ceding 1** AGREE : acceder, consentir **2** ASCEND : subir, acceder <he acceded to the throne : subió al trono>

accelerate [ɪk'sɛləˌreɪt, æk-] *v* **-ated; -ating** *vt* : acelerar, apresurar — *vi* : acelerar (dícese de un carro)

acceleration [ɪkˌsɛlə'reɪʃən, æk-] *n* : aceleración *f*

accelerator [ɪk'sɛləˌreɪt̬ər, æk-] *n* : acelerador *m*

accent[1] ['ækˌsɛnt, æk'sɛnt] *vt* : acentuar

accent[2] ['ækˌsɛnt, -sənt] *n* **1** : acento *m* **2** EMPHASIS, STRESS : énfasis *m,* acento *m*

accentuate [ɪk'sɛntʃʊˌeɪt, æk-] *vt* **-ated; -ating** : acentuar, poner énfasis en

accept [ɪk'sɛpt, æk-] *vt* **1** : aceptar **2** ACKNOWLEDGE : admitir, reconocer

acceptability [ɪkˌsɛptə'bɪlət̬i, æk-] *n* : aceptabilidad *f*

acceptable [ɪk'sɛptəbəl, æk-] *adj* : aceptable, admisible — **acceptably** [-bli] *adv*

acceptance [ɪk'sɛptənts, æk-] *n* : aceptación *f,* aprobación *f*

access[1] ['ækˌsɛs] *vt* : obtener acceso a, entrar a

access[2] *n* : acceso *m*

accessible [ɪk'sɛsəbəl, æk-] *adj* : accesible, asequible

accession [ɪk'sɛʃən, æk-] *n* **1** : ascenso *f,* subida *f* (al trono, etc.) **2** ACQUISITION : adquisición *f*

accessory[1] [ɪk'sɛsəri, æk-] *adj* : auxiliar

accessory[2] *n, pl* **-ries 1** : accesorio *m,* complemento *m* **2** ACCOMPLICE : cómplice *mf*

accident ['æksədənt] *n* **1** MISHAP : accidente *m* **2** CHANCE : casualidad *f*

accidental [ˌæksə'dɛntəl] *adj* : accidental, casual, imprevisto, fortuito

accidentally [ˌæksə'dɛntəli, -'dɛntli] *adv* **1** BY CHANCE : por casualidad **2** UNINTENTIONALLY : sin querer, involuntariamente

acclaim[1] [ə'kleɪm] *vt* : aclamar, elogiar

acclaim[2] *n* : aclamación *f,* elogio *m*

acclamation [ˌæklə'meɪʃən] *n* : aclamación *f*

acclimate ['ækləˌmeɪt, ə'klaɪmət] → **acclimatize**

acclimatize [ə'klaɪməˌtaɪz] *v* **-tized; -tizing** *vt* **1** : aclimatar **2 to acclimatize oneself** : aclimatarse

accolade ['ækəˌleɪd, -ˌlɑd] *n* **1** PRAISE : elogio *m* **2** AWARD : galardón *m*

accommodate [ə'kɑməˌdeɪt] *vt* **-dated; -dating 1** ADAPT : acomodar, adaptar **2** SATISFY : tener en cuenta, satisfacer **3** HOLD : dar cabida a, tener cabida para

accommodation [əˌkɑmə'deɪʃən] *n* **1** : adaptación *f,* adecuación *f* **2 accommodations** *npl* LODGING : alojamiento *m,* hospedaje *m*

accompaniment [ə'kʌmpənəmənt, -'kɑm-] *n* : acompañamiento *m*

accompanist [ə'kʌmpənɪst, -'kɑm-] *n* : acompañante *mf*

accompany [ə'kʌmpəni, -'kɑm-] *vt* **-nied; -nying** : acompañar

accomplice [ə'kɑmpləs, -'kʌm-] *n* : cómplice *mf*

accomplish [ə'kɑmplɪʃ, -'kʌm-] *vt* : efectuar, realizar, lograr, llevar a cabo

accomplished [ə'kɑmplɪʃt, -'kʌm-] *adj* : consumado, logrado

accomplishment [ə'kɑmplɪʃmənt, -'kʌm-] *n* **1** ACHIEVEMENT : logro *m,* éxito *m* **2** SKILL : destreza *f,* habilidad *f*

accord[1] [ə'kɔrd] *vt* GRANT : conceder, otorgar — *vi* **to accord with** : concordar con, conformarse con

accord[2] *n* **1** AGREEMENT : acuerdo *m,* convenio *m* **2** VOLITION : voluntad *f* <on one's own accord : voluntariamente, de motu proprio>

accordance [ə'kɔrdənts] *n* **1** ACCORD : acuerdo *m,* conformidad *f* **2 in ac-**

cordance with : conforme a, según, de acuerdo con

accordingly [ə'kɔrdɪŋli] *adv* **1** CORRESPONDINGLY : en consecuencia **2** CONSEQUENTLY : por consiguiente, por lo tanto

according to [ə'kɔrdɪŋ] *prep* : según, de acuerdo con, conforme a

accordion [ə'kɔrdiən] *n* : acordeón *m*

accordionist [ə'kɔrdiənɪst] *n* : acordeonista *mf*

accost [ə'kɔst] *vt* : abordar, dirigirse a

account[1] [ə'kaʊnt] *vt* : considerar, estimar <he accounts himself lucky : se considera afortunado> — *vi* **to account for** : dar cuenta de, explicar

account[2] *n* **1** : cuenta *f* <savings account : cuenta de ahorros> **2** EXPLANATION : versión *f,* explicación *f* **3** REPORT : relato *m,* informe *m* **4** IMPORTANCE : importancia *f* <to be of no account : no tener importancia> **5 on account of** BECAUSE OF : a causa de, debido a, por **6 on no account** : de ninguna manera

accountability [əˌkaʊntə'bɪləṭi] *n* : responsabilidad *f*

accountable [ə'kaʊntəbəl] *adj* : responsable

accountant [ə'kaʊntənt] *n* : contador *m,* -dora *f;* contable *mf Spain*

accounting [ə'kaʊntɪŋ] *n* : contabilidad *f*

accoutrements *or* **accouterments** [ə'kuːtrəmənts, -'kuːṭər-] *npl* **1** EQUIPMENT : equipo *m,* avíos *mpl* **2** ACCESSORIES : accesorios *mpl* **3** TRAPPINGS : símbolos *mpl* <the accoutrements of power : los símbolos del poder>

accredit [ə'krɛdət] *vt* : acreditar, autorizar

accreditation [əˌkrɛdə'teɪʃən] *n* : acreditación *f,* homologación *f*

accrual [ə'kruːəl] *n* : incremento *m,* acumulación *f*

accrue [ə'kruː] *vi* **-crued; -cruing** : acumularse, aumentarse

accumulate [ə'kjuːmjəˌleɪt] *v* **-lated; -lating** *vt* : acumular, amontonar — *vi* : acumularse, amontonarse

accumulation [əˌkjuːmjə'leɪʃən] *n* : acumulación *f,* amontonamiento *m*

accuracy ['ækjərəsi] *n* : exactitud *f,* precisión *f*

accurate ['ækjərət] *adj* : exacto, correcto, fiel, preciso — **accurately** *adv*

accusation [ˌækjə'zeɪʃən] *n* : acusación *f*

accuse [ə'kjuːz] *vt* **-cused; -cusing** : acusar, delatar, denunciar

accused [ə'kjuːzd] *ns & pl* DEFENDANT : acusado *m,* -da *f*

accuser [ə'kjuːzər] *n* : acusador *m,* -dora *f*

accustom [ə'kʌstəm] *vt* : acostumbrar, habituar

ace ['eɪs] *n* : as *m*

acerbic [ə'sərbɪk, æ-] *adj* : acerbo, mordaz

acetate ['æsəˌteɪt] *n* : acetato *m*

acetylene [ə'sɛṭələn, -ṭəˌliːn] *n* : acetileno *m*

ache[1] ['eɪk] *vi* **ached; aching 1** : doler **2 to ache for** : anhelar, ansiar

ache[2] *n* : dolor *m*

achieve [ə'tʃiːv] *vt* **achieved; achieving** : lograr, alcanzar, conseguir, realizar

achievement [ə'tʃiːvmənt] *n* : logro *m,* éxito *m,* realización *f*

acid[1] ['æsəd] *adj* **1** SOUR : ácido, agrio **2** CAUSTIC, SHARP : acerbo, mordaz — **acidly** *adv*

acid[2] *n* : ácido *m*

acidic [ə'sɪdɪk, æ-] *adj* : ácido

acidity [ə'sɪdəṭi, æ-] *n, pl* **-ties** : acidez *f*

acknowledge [ɪk'nɑlɪdʒ, æk-] *vt* **-edged; -edging 1** ADMIT : reconocer, admitir **2** RECOGNIZE : reconocer **3 to acknowledge receipt of** : acusar recibo de

acknowledgment [ɪk'nɑlɪdʒmənt, æk-] *n* **1** RECOGNITION : reconocimiento *m* **2** THANKS : agradecimiento *m*

acme ['ækmi] *n* : colmo *m,* apogeo *m,* cúspide *f*

acne ['ækni] *n* : acné *m*

acorn ['eɪˌkɔrn, -kərn] *n* : bellota *f*

acoustic [ə'kuːstɪk] *or* **acoustical** [-stɪkəl] *adj* : acústico — **acoustically** *adv*

acoustics [ə'kuːstɪks] *ns & pl* : acústica *f*

acquaint [ə'kweɪnt] *vt* **1** INFORM : enterar, informar **2** FAMILIARIZE : familiarizar **3 to be acquainted with** : conocer a (una persona), estar al tanto de (un hecho)

acquaintance [ə'kweɪntənts] *n* **1** KNOWLEDGE : conocimiento *m* **2** : conocido *m,* -da *f* <friends and acquaintances : amigos y conocidos>

acquiesce [ˌækwi'ɛs] *vi* **-esced; -escing** : consentir, conformarse

acquiescence [ˌækwi'ɛsənts] *n* : consentimiento *m,* aquiescencia *f*

acquire [ə'kwaɪr] *vt* **-quired; -quiring** : adquirir, obtener

acquisition [ˌækwə'zɪʃən] *n* : adquisición *f*

acquisitive [ə'kwɪzəṭɪv] *adj* : adquisitivo, codicioso

acquit [ə'kwɪt] *vt* **-quitted; -quitting 1** : absolver, exculpar **2 to acquit oneself** : comportarse, defenderse

acquittal [ə'kwɪṭəl] *n* : absolución *f,* exculpación *f*

acre ['eɪkər] *n* : acre *m*

acreage ['eɪkərɪdʒ] *n* : superficie *f* en acres

acrid ['ækrəd] *adj* **1** BITTER : acre **2** CAUSTIC : acre, mordaz — **acridly** *adv*

acrimonious [ˌækrə'moːniəs] *adj* : áspero, cáustico, sarcástico

acrimony ['ækrəˌmoːni] *n, pl* **-nies** : acrimonia *f*

acrobat ['ækrə,bæt] *n* : acróbata *mf,* satimbanqui *mf*
acrobatic [,ækrə'bæṭɪk] *adj* : acrobático
acronym ['ækrə,nɪm] *n* : acrónimo *m*
across[1] [ə'krɔs] *adv* **1** CROSSWISE : al través **2** : a través, del otro lado <he's already across : ya está del otro lado> **3** : de ancho <40 feet across : 40 pies de ancho>
across[2] *prep* **1** : al otro lado de <across the street : al otro lado de la calle> **2** : a través de <a log across the road : un tronco a través del camino>
acrylic [ə'krɪlɪk] *n* : acrílico *m*
act[1] ['ækt] *vi* **1** PERFORM : actuar, interpretar **2** FEIGN, PRETEND : fingir, simular **3** BEHAVE : comportarse **4** FUNCTION : actuar, servir, funcionar **5** : tomar medidas <he acted to save the business : tomó medidas para salvar el negocio> **6 to act as** : servir de, hacer de
act[2] *n* **1** DEED : acto *m,* hecho *m,* acción *f* **2** DECREE : ley *f,* decreto *m* **3** : acto *m* (en una obra de teatro), número *m* (en un espectáculo) **4** PRETENSE : fingimiento *m*
action ['ækʃən] *n* **1** DEED : acción *f,* acto *m,* hecho *m* **2** BEHAVIOR : actuación *f,* comportamiento *m* **3** LAWSUIT : demanda *f* **4** MOVEMENT : movimiento *m* **5** COMBAT : combate *m* **6** PLOT : acción *f,* trama *f* **7** MECHANISM : mecanismo *m*
activate ['æktə,veɪt] *vt* **-vated; -vating** : activar
active ['æktɪv] *adj* **1** MOVING : activo, en movimiento **2** LIVELY : vigoroso, enérgico **3** : en actividad <an active volcano : un volcán en actividad> **4** OPERATIVE : vigente
actively ['æktɪvli] *adv* : activamente, enérgicamente
activity [æk'tɪvəṭi] *n, pl* **-ties 1** MOVEMENT : actividad *f,* movimiento *m* **2** VIGOR : vigor *m,* energía *f* **3** OCCUPATION : actividad *f,* ocupación *f*
actor ['æktər] *n* : actor *m,* artista *mf*
actress ['æktrəs] *n* : actriz *f*
actual ['æktʃʊəl] *adj* : real, verdadero
actuality [,æktʃʊ'ælǝti] *n, pl* **-ties** : realidad *f*
actually ['æktʃʊəli, -ʃəli] *adv* : realmente, en realidad
actuary ['æktʃʊ,ɛri] *n, pl* **-aries** : actuario *m,* -ria *f* de seguros
acumen [ə'kju:mən] *n* : perspicacia *f*
acupuncture ['ækjʊ,pʌŋktʃər] *n* : acupuntura *f*
acute [ə'kju:t] *adj* **acuter; acutest 1** SHARP : agudo **2** PERCEPTIVE : perspicaz, sagaz **3** KEEN : fino, muy desarrollado, agudo <an acute sense of smell : un fino olfato> **4** SEVERE : grave **5 acute angle** : ángulo *m* agudo
acutely [ə'kju:tli] *adv* : intensamente <to be acutely aware : estar perfectamente consciente>
acuteness [ə'kju:tnəs] *n* : agudeza *f*
ad ['æd] → **advertisement**
adage ['ædɪdʒ] *n* : adagio *m,* refrán *m,* dicho *m*
adamant ['ædəmənt, -,mænt] *adj* : firme, categórico, inflexible — **adamantly** *adv*
Adam's apple ['ædəmz] *n* : nuez *f* de Adán
adapt [ə'dæpt] *vt* : adaptar, ajustar — *vi* : adaptarse
adaptability [ə,dæptə'bɪləṭi] *n* : adaptabilidad *f,* flexibilidad *f*
adaptable [ə'dæptəbəl] *adj* : adaptable, amoldable
adaptation [,æ,dæp'teɪʃən, -dəp-] *n* **1** : adaptación *f,* modificación *f* **2** VERSION : versión *f*
adapter [ə'dæptər] *n* : adaptador *m*
add ['æd] *vt* **1** : añadir, agregar <to add a comment : añadir una observación> **2** : sumar <add these numbers : suma estos números> — *vi* : sumar (en total)
adder ['ædər] *n* : víbora *f*
addict[1] [ə'dɪkt] *vt* : causar adicción en
addict[2] ['ædɪkt] *n* **1** : adicto *m,* -ta *f* **2 drug addict** : drogadicto *m,* -ta *f;* toxicómano *m,* -na *f*
addiction [ə'dɪkʃən] *n* **1** : adicción *f,* dependencia *f* **2 drug addiction** : drogadicción *f*
addictive [ə'dɪktɪv] *adj* : adictivo
addition [ə'dɪʃən] *n* **1** : adición *f,* añadidura *f* **2 in ~** : además, también
additional [ə'dɪʃənəl] *adj* : extra, adicional, de más
additionally [ə'dɪʃənəli] *adv* : además, adicionalmente
additive ['ædəṭɪv] *n* : aditivo *m*
addle ['ædəl] *vt* **-dled; -dling** : confundir, enturbiar
address[1] [ə'drɛs] *vt* **1** : dirigirse a, pronunciar un discurso ante <to address a jury : dirigirse a un jurado> **2** : dirigir, ponerle la dirección a <to address a letter : dirigir una carta>
address[2] [ə'drɛs, 'æ,drɛs] *n* **1** SPEECH : discurso *m,* alocución *f* **2** : dirección *f* (de una residencia, etc.)
adenoids ['æd,nɔɪd, -dən,ɔɪd] *npl* : adenoides *fpl*
adept [ə'dɛpt] *adj* : experto, hábil — **adeptly** *adv*
adequacy ['ædɪkwəsi] *n, pl* **-cies** : cantidad *f* suficiente
adequate ['ædɪkwət] *adj* **1** SUFFICIENT : adecuado, suficiente **2** ACCEPTABLE, PASSABLE : adecuado, aceptable
adequately ['ædɪkwətli] *adv* : suficientemente, apropiadamente
adhere [æd'hɪr, əd-] *vi* **-hered; -hering 1** STICK : pegarse, adherirse **2 to adhere to** : adherirse a (una política, etc.), cumplir con (una promesa)

adherence [æd'hɪrənts, əd-] *n* : adhesión *f*, adherencia *f*, observancia *f* (de una ley, etc.)
adherent[1] [æd'hɪrənt, əd-] *adj* : adherente, adhesivo, pegajoso
adherent[2] *n* : adepto *m*, -ta *f*; partidario *m*, -ria *f*
adhesive[1] [æd'hi:sɪv, əd-, -zɪv] *adj* : adhesivo
adhesive[2] *n* : adhesivo *m*, pegamento *m*
adjacent [ə'dʒeɪsənt] *adj* : adyacente, colindante, contiguo
adjective ['ædʒɪktɪv] *n* : adjetivo *m* — **adjectival** [,ædʒɪk'taɪvəl] *adj*
adjoin [ə'dʒɔɪn] *vt* : lindar con, colindar con
adjoining [ə'dʒɔɪnɪŋ] *adj* : contiguo, colindante
adjourn [ə'dʒərn] *vt* : levantar, suspender <the meeting is adjourned : se levanta la sesión> — *vi* : aplazarse
adjournment [ə'dʒərnmənt] *n* : suspensión *f*, aplazamiento *m*
adjudicate [ə'dʒu:dɪ,keɪt] *vt* **-cated; -cating** : juzgar, arbitrar
adjunct ['æ,dʒʌŋkt] *n* : adjunto *m*, complemento *m*
adjust [ə'dʒʌst] *vt* : ajustar, arreglar, regular — *vi* **to adjust to** : adaptarse a
adjustable [ə'dʒʌstəbəl] *adj* : ajustable, regulable, graduable
adjustment [ə'dʒʌstmənt] *n* : ajuste *m*, modificación *f*
ad-lib[1] ['æd'lɪb] *v* **-libbed; -libbing** : improvisar
ad-lib[2] *adj* : improvisado
administer [æd'mɪnəstər, əd-] *vt* : administrar
administration [æd,mɪnə'streɪʃən, əd-] *n* **1** MANAGING : administración *f*, dirección *f* **2** GOVERNMENT, MANAGEMENT : administración *f*, gobierno *m*
administrative [æd'mɪnə,streɪtɪv, əd-] *adj* : administrativo — **administratively** *adv*
administrator [æd'mɪnə,streɪtər, əd-] *n* : administrador *m*, -dora *f*
admirable ['ædmərəbəl] *adj* : admirable, loable — **admirably** *adv*
admiral ['ædmərəl] *n* : almirante *mf*
admiration [,ædmə'reɪʃən] *n* : admiración *f*
admire [æd'maɪr] *vt* **-mired; -miring** : admirar
admirer [æd'maɪrər] *n* : admirador *m*, -dora *f*
admiring [æd'maɪrɪŋ] *adj* : admirativo, de admiración
admiringly [æd'maɪrɪŋli] *adv* : con admiración
admissible [æd'mɪsəbəl] *adj* : admisible, aceptable
admission [æd'mɪʃən] *n* **1** ADMITTANCE : entrada *f*, admisión *f* **2** ACKNOWLEDGMENT : reconocimiento *m*, admisión *f*
admit [æd'mɪt, əd-] *vt* **-mitted; -mitting 1** : admitir, dejar entrar <the museum admits children : el museo deja entrar a los niños> **2** ACKNOWLEDGE : reconocer, admitir
admittance [æd'mɪtənts, əd-] *n* : admisión *f*, entrada *f*, acceso *m*
admittedly [æd'mɪtədli, əd-] *adv* : la verdad es que, lo cierto es que <admittedly we went too fast : la verdad es que fuimos demasiado de prisa>
admonish [æd'mɑnɪʃ, əd-] *vt* : amonestar, reprender
admonition [,ædmə'nɪʃən] *n* : admonición *f*
ado [ə'du:] *n* **1** FUSS : ruido *m*, alboroto *m* **2** TROUBLE : dificultad *f*, lío *m* **3 without further ado** : sin más preámbulos
adobe [ə'do:bi] *n* : adobe *m*
adolescence [,ædəl'ɛsənts] *n* : adolescencia *f*
adolescent[1] [,ædəl'ɛsənt] *adj* : adolescente, de adolescencia
adolescent[2] *n* : adolescente *mf*
adopt [ə'dɑpt] *vt* : adoptar
adoption [ə'dɑpʃən] *n* : adopción *f*
adorable [ə'dorəbəl] *adj* : adorable, encantador
adorably [ə'dorəbli] *adv* : de manera adorable
adoration [,ædə'reɪʃən] *n* : adoración *f*
adore [ə'dor] *vt* **adored; adoring 1** WORSHIP : adorar **2** LOVE : querer, adorar **3** LIKE : encantarle (algo a uno), gustarle mucho (algo a uno) <I adore your new dress : me encanta tu vestido nuevo>
adorn [ə'dɔrn] *vt* : adornar, ornar, engalanar
adornment [ə'dɔrnmənt] *n* : adorno *m*, decoración *f*
adrift [ə'drɪft] *adj & adv* : a la deriva
adroit [ə'drɔɪt] *adj* : diestro, hábil — **adroitly** *adv*
adroitness [ə'drɔɪtnəs] *n* : destreza *f*, habilidad *f*
adult[1] [ə'dʌlt, 'æ,dʌlt] *adj* : adulto
adult[2] *n* : adulto *m*, -ta *f*
adulterate [ə'dʌltə,reɪt] *vt* **-ated; -ating** : adulterar
adulterous [ə'dʌltərəs] *adj* : adúltero
adultery [ə'dʌltəri] *n, pl* **-teries** : adulterio *m*
adulthood [ə'dʌlt,hʊd] *n* : adultez *f*, edad *f* adulta
advance[1] [æd'vænts, əd-] *v* **-vanced; -vancing** *vt* **1** : avanzar, adelantar <to advance troops : avanzar las tropas> **2** PROMOTE : ascender, promover **3** PROPOSE : proponer, presentar **4** : adelantar, anticipar <they advanced me next month's salary : me adelantaron el sueldo del próximo mes> — *vi* **1** PROCEED : avanzar, adelantarse **2** PROGRESS : progresar
advance[2] *adj* : anticipado <advance notice : previo aviso>
advance[3] *n* **1** PROGRESSION : avance *m* **2** PROGRESS : adelanto *m*, mejora *f*, pro-

greso *m* **3** RISE : aumento *m,* alza *f* **4** LOAN : anticipo *m,* préstamo *m* **5 in ~** : por adelantado
advanced [æd'vænʦt, əd-] *adj* **1** DEVELOPED : avanzado, desarrollado **2** PRECOCIOUS : adelantado, precoz **3** HIGHER : superior
advancement [æd'vænʦmənt, əd-] *n* **1** FURTHERANCE : fomento *m,* adelantamiento *m,* progreso *m* **2** PROMOTION : ascenso *m*
advantage [əd'væntɪʤ, æd-] *n* **1** SUPERIORITY : ventaja *f,* superioridad *f* **2** GAIN : provecho *m,* partido *m* **3 to take advantage of** : aprovecharse de
advantageous [ˌædˌvæn'teɪʤəs, -vən-] *adj* : ventajoso, provechoso — **advantageously** *adv*
advent ['ædˌvɛnt] *n* **1 Advent** : Adviento *m* **2** ARRIVAL : advenimiento *m,* venida *f*
adventure [æd'vɛnʧər, əd-] *n* : aventura *f*
adventurer [æd'vɛnʧərər, əd-] *n* : aventurero *m,* -ra *f*
adventurous [æd'vɛnʧərəs, əd-] *adj* **1** : intrépido, aventurero <an adventurous traveler : un viajero intrépido> **2** RISKY : arriesgado, aventurado
adverb ['ædˌvərb] *n* : adverbio *m* — **adverbial** [æd'vərbiəl] *adj*
adversary ['ædvərˌsɛri] *n, pl* **-saries** : adversario *m,* -ria *f*
adverse [æd'vərs, 'æd-ˌ] *adj* **1** OPPOSING : opuesto, contrario **2** UNFAVORABLE : adverso, desfavorable — **adversely** *adv*
adversity [æd'vərsəṭi, əd-] *n, pl* **-ties** : adversidad *f*
advertise ['ædvərˌtaɪz] *v* **-tised; -tising** *vt* : anunciar, hacerle publicidad a — *vi* : hacer publicidad, hacer propaganda
advertisement ['ædvərˌtaɪzmənt; æd'vərtəzmənt] *n* : anuncio *m*
advertiser ['ædvərˌtaɪzər] *n* : anunciante *mf*
advertising ['ædvərˌtaɪzɪŋ] *n* : publicidad *f,* propaganda *f*
advice [æd'vaɪs] *n* : consejo *m,* recomendación *f* <take my advice : sigue mis consejos>
advisability [ædˌvaɪzə'bɪləṭi, əd-] *n* : conveniencia *f*
advisable [æd'vaɪzəbəl, əd-] *adj* : aconsejable, recomendable, conveniente
advise [æd'vaɪz, əd-] *v* **-vised; -vising** *vt* **1** COUNSEL : aconsejar, asesorar **2** RECOMMEND : recomendar **3** INFORM : informar, notificar — *vi* : dar consejo
adviser *or* **advisor** [æd'vaɪzər, əd-] *n* : consejero *m,* -ra *f;* asesor *m,* -sora *f*
advisory [æd'vaɪzəri, əd-] *adj* **1** : consultivo **2 in an advisory capacity** : como asesor
advocacy ['ædvəkəsi] *n* : promoción *f,* apoyo *m*
advocate[1] ['ædvəˌkeɪt] *vt* **-cated; -cating** : recomendar, abogar por, ser partidario de
advocate[2] ['ædvəkət] *n* : defensor *m,* -sora *f;* partidario *m,* -ria *f*
adze ['ædz] *n* : azuela *f*
aeon ['iːən, 'iːˌɑn] *n* : eón *m,* siglo *m,* eternidad *f*
aerate ['ærˌeɪt] *vt* **-ated; -ating** : gasear (un líquido), oxigenar (la sangre)
aerial[1] ['æriəl] *adj* : aéreo
aerial[2] *n* : antena *f*
aerie ['æri, 'ɪri, 'eɪəri] *n* : aguilera *f*
aerobic [ˌær'oːbɪk] *adj* : aerobio, aeróbico <aerobic exercises : ejercicios aeróbicos>
aerobics [ˌær'oːbɪks] *ns & pl* : aeróbic *m*
aerodynamic [ˌæroːdaɪ'næmɪk] *adj* : aerodinámico — **aerodynamically** [-mikli] *adv*
aerodynamics [ˌæroːdaɪ'næmɪks] *n* : aerodinámica *f*
aeronautical [ˌærə'nɔṭɪkəl] *adj* : aeronáutico
aeronautics [ˌærə'nɔṭɪks] *n* : aeronáutica *f*
aerosol ['ærəˌsɔl] *n* : aerosol *m*
aerospace[1] ['æroˌspeɪs] *adj* : aeroespacial
aerospace[2] *n* : espacio *m*
aesthetic [ɛs'θɛṭɪk] *adj* : estético — **aesthetically** [-ṭɪkli] *adv*
aesthetics [ɛs'θɛṭɪks] *n* : estética *f*
afar [ə'fɑr] *adv* : lejos, a lo lejos
affability [ˌæfə'bɪləṭi] *n* : afabilidad *f*
affable ['æfəbəl] *adj* : afable — **affably** *adv*
affair [ə'fær] *n* **1** MATTER : asunto *m,* cuestión *f,* caso *m* **2** EVENT : ocasión *f,* acontecimiento *m* **3** LIAISON : amorío *m,* aventura *f* **4 business affairs** : negocios *mpl* **5 current affairs** : actualidades *fpl*
affect [ə'fɛkt, æ-] *vt* **1** INFLUENCE, TOUCH : afectar, tocar **2** FEIGN : fingir
affectation [ˌæˌfɛk'teɪʃən] *n* : afectación *f*
affected [ə'fɛktəd, æ-] *adj* **1** FEIGNED : afectado, fingido **2** MOVED : conmovido
affecting [ə'fɛktɪŋ, æ-] *adj* : conmovedor
affection [ə'fɛkʃən] *n* : afecto *m,* cariño *m*
affectionate [ə'fɛkʃənət] *adj* : afectuoso, cariñoso — **affectionately** *adv*
affidavit [ˌæfə'deɪvət, 'æfəˌ-] *n* : declaración *f* jurada, affidávit *m*
affiliate[1] [ə'fɪliˌeɪt] *v* **-ated; -ating** *vt* : afiliar, asociar <to be affiliated with : estar afiliado a>
affiliate[2] [ə'fɪliət] *n* : afiliado *m,* -da *f* (persona), filial *f* (organización)
affiliation [əˌfɪli'eɪʃən] *n* : afiliación *f,* filiación *f*
affinity [ə'fɪnəṭi] *n, pl* **-ties** : afinidad *f*

affirm [ə'fərm] *vt* : afirmar, aseverar, declarar

affirmation [ˌæfər'meɪʃən] *n* : afirmación *f,* aserto *m,* declaración *f*

affirmative[1] [ə'fərmət̬ɪv] *adj* : afirmativo <affirmative action : acción afirmativa>

affirmative[2] *n* **1** : afirmativa *f* **2 to answer in the affirmative** : responder afirmativamente, dar una respuesta afirmativa

affix [ə'fɪks] *vt* : fijar, poner, pegar

afflict [ə'flɪkt] *vt* **1** : afligir, aquejar **2 to be afflicted with** : padecer de, sufrir de

affliction [ə'flɪkʃən] *n* **1** TRIBULATION : aflicción *f,* tribulación *f* **2** AILMENT : enfermedad *f,* padecimiento *m*

affluence ['æˌfluːənts; æ'fluː-, ə-] *n* : afluencia *f,* abundancia *f,* prosperidad *f*

affluent ['æˌfluːənt; æ'fluː-, ə-] *adj* : próspero, adinerado

afford [ə'ford] *vt* **1** : tener los recursos para, permitirse el lujo de <I can afford it : puedo permitírmelo, tengo con que comprarlo> **2** PROVIDE : ofrecer, proporcionar, dar

affront[1] [ə'frʌnt] *vt* : afrentar, insultar, ofender

affront[2] *n* : afrenta *f,* insulto *m,* ofensa *f*

Afghan ['æfˌgæn, -gən] *n* : afgano *m,* -na *f* — **Afghan** *adj*

afire [ə'faɪr] *adj* : ardiendo, en llamas

aflame [ə'fleɪm] *adj* : llameante, en llamas

afloat [ə'floːt] *adv & adj* : a flote

afoot [ə'fʊt] *adj* **1** WALKING : a pie, andando **2** UNDER WAY : en marcha <something suspicious is afoot : algo sospechoso se está tramando>

aforesaid [ə'forˌsɛd] *adj* : antes mencionado, antedicho

afraid [ə'freɪd] *adj* **1 to be afraid** : tener miedo **2 to be afraid that** : temerse que <I'm afraid not : me temo que no>

afresh [ə'frɛʃ] *adv* **1** : de nuevo, otra vez **2 to start afresh** : volver a empezar

African ['æfrɪkən] *n* : africano *m,* -na *f* — **African** *adj*

Afro–American[1] [ˌæfroə'mɛrɪkən] *adj* : afroamericano *m,* -na *f*

Afro–American[2] *n* : afroamericano

aft ['æft] *adv* : a popa

after[1] ['æftər] *adv* **1** AFTERWARD : después **2** BEHIND : detrás, atrás

after[2] *adj* : posterior, siguiente <in after years : en los años posteriores>

after[3] *conj* : después de, después de que <after we ate : después de que comimos, después de comer>

after[4] *prep* **1** FOLLOWING : después de, tras <after Saturday : después del sábado> <day after day : día tras día> **2** BEHIND : tras de, después de <I ran after the dog : corrí tras del perro> **3** CONCERNING : por <they asked after you : preguntaron por ti> **4 after all** : después de todo

aftereffect ['æftərɪˌfɛkt] *n* : efecto *m* secundario

afterlife ['æftərˌlaɪf] *n* : vida *f* venidera, vida *f* después de la muerte

aftermath ['æftərˌmæθ] *n* : consecuencias *fpl,* resultados *mpl*

afternoon [ˌæftər'nuːn] *n* : tarde *f*

afterthought ['æftərˌθɔt] *n* : ocurrencia *f* tardía, idea *f* tardía

afterward ['æftərwərd] *or* **afterwards** [-wərdz] *adv* : después, luego <soon afterward : poco después>

again [ə'gɛn, -'gɪn] *adv* **1** ANEW, OVER : de nuevo, otra vez **2** BESIDES : además **3 then again** : por otra parte <I may stay, then again I may not : puede ser que me quede, por otra parte, puede que no>

against [ə'gɛntst, -'gɪntst] *prep* **1** TOUCHING : contra <against the wall : contra la pared> **2** OPPOSING : contra, en contra de <I will vote against the proposal : votaré en contra de la propuesta> <against the grain : a contrapelo>

agape [ə'geɪp] *adj* : boquiabierto

agate ['ægət] *n* : ágata *f*

age[1] ['eɪdʒ] *vi* **aged; aging** : envejecer, madurar

age[2] *n* **1** : edad *f* <ten years of age : diez años de edad> <to be of age : ser mayor de edad> **2** PERIOD : era *f,* siglo *m,* época *f* **3 old age** : vejez *f* **4 ages** *npl* : siglos *mpl,* eternidad *f*

aged *adj* **1** ['eɪdʒəd, 'eɪdʒd] OLD : anciano, viejo, vetusto **2** ['eɪdʒd] (*indicating a specified age*) <a girl aged 10 : una niña de 10 años de edad>

ageless ['eɪdʒləs] *adj* **1** YOUTHFUL : eternamente joven **2** TIMELESS : eterno, perenne

agency ['eɪdʒəntsi] *n, pl* **-cies 1** : agencia *f,* oficina *f* <travel agency : agencia de viajes> **2 through the agency of** : a través de, por medio de

agenda [ə'dʒɛndə] *n* : agenda *f,* orden *m* del día

agent ['eɪdʒənt] *n* **1** MEANS : agente *m,* medio *m,* instrumento *m* **2** REPRESENTATIVE : agente *mf,* representante *mf*

aggravate ['ægrəˌveɪt] *vt* **-vated; -vating 1** WORSEN : agravar, empeorar **2** ANNOY : irritar, exasperar

aggravation [ˌægrə'veɪʃən] *n* **1** WORSENING : empeoramiento *m* **2** ANNOYANCE : molestia *f,* irritación *f,* exasperación *f*

aggregate[1] ['ægrɪˌgeɪt] *vt* **-gated; -gating** : juntar, sumar

aggregate[2] ['ægrɪgət] *adj* : total, global, conjunto

aggregate[3] ['ægrɪgət] *n* **1** CONGLOMERATE : agregado *m,* conglomerado *m* **2** WHOLE : total *m,* conjunto *m*

aggression [ə'grɛʃən] *n* **1** ATTACK : agresión *f* **2** AGGRESSIVENESS : agresividad *f*

aggressive [ə'grɛsɪv] *adj* : agresivo — **aggressively** *adv*

aggressiveness [ə'grɛsɪvnəs] *n* : agresividad *f*

aggressor [ə'grɛsər] *n* : agresor *m*, -sora *f*

aggrieved [ə'griːvd] *adj* : ofendido, herido

aghast [ə'gæst] *adj* : espantado, aterrado, horrorizado

agile ['ædʒəl] *adj* : ágil

agility [ə'dʒɪləṭi] *n, pl* **-ties** : agilidad *f*

agitate ['ædʒəˌteɪt] *v* **-tated; -tating** *vt* **1** SHAKE : agitar **2** UPSET : inquietar, perturbar — *vi* **to agitate against** : hacer campaña en contra de

agitation [ˌædʒə'teɪʃən] *n* : agitación *f*, inquietud *f*

agitator ['ædʒəˌteɪṭər] *n* : agitador *m*, -dora *f*

agnostic [æg'nɑstɪk] *n* : agnóstico *m*, -ca *f*

ago [ə'goː] *adv* : hace <two years ago : hace dos años> <long ago : hace tiempo, hace mucho tiempo>

agog [ə'gɑg] *adj* : ansioso, curioso

agonize ['ægəˌnaɪz] *vi* **-nized; -nizing** : tormentarse, angustiarse

agonizing ['ægəˌnaɪzɪŋ] *adj* : angustioso, terrible — **agonizingly** [-zɪŋli] *adv*

agony ['ægəni] *n, pl* **-nies 1** PAIN : dolor *m* **2** ANGUISH : angustia *f*

agrarian [ə'grɛriən] *adj* : agrario

agree [ə'griː] *v* **agreed; agreeing** *vt* ACKNOWLEDGE : estar de acuerdo <he agreed that I was right : estuvo de acuerdo en que tenía razón> — *vi* **1** CONCUR : estar de acuerdo **2** CONSENT : ponerse de acuerdo **3** TALLY : concordar **4 to agree with** : sentarle bien (a alguien) <this climate agrees with me : este clima me sienta bien>

agreeable [ə'griːəbəl] *adj* **1** PLEASING : agradable, simpático **2** WILLING : dispuesto **3** AGREEING : de acuerdo, conforme

agreeably [ə'griːəbli] *adv* : agradablemente

agreement [ə'griːmənt] *n* **1** : acuerdo *m*, conformidad *f* <in agreement with : de acuerdo con> **2** CONTRACT, PACT : acuerdo *m*, pacto *m*, convenio *m* **3** CONCORD, HARMONY : concordia *f*

agriculture ['ægrɪˌkʌltʃər] *n* : agricultura *f* — **agricultural** [ˌægrɪ'kʌltʃərəl] *adj*

aground [ə'graʊnd] *adj* : encallado, varado

ahead [ə'hɛd] *adv* **1** : al frente, delante, adelante <he walked ahead : caminó delante> **2** BEFOREHAND : por adelantado, con antelación **3** LEADING : a la delantera **4 to get ahead** : adelantar, progresar

ahead of *prep* **1** : al frente de, delante de, antes de **2 to get ahead of** : adelantarse a

ahoy [ə'hɔɪ] *interj* **ship ahoy!** : ¡barco a la vista!

aid¹ ['eɪd] *vt* : ayudar, auxiliar

aid² *n* **1** HELP : ayuda *f*, asistencia *f* **2** ASSISTANT : asistente *mf*

aide ['eɪd] *n* : ayudante *mf*

AIDS ['eɪdz] *n* : SIDA *m*, sida *m*

ail ['eɪl] *vt* : molestar, afligir — *vi* : sufrir, estar enfermo

aileron ['eɪləˌrɑn] *n* : alerón *m*

ailment ['eɪlmənt] *n* : enfermedad *f*, dolencia *f*, achaque *m*

aim¹ ['eɪm] *vt* **1** : apuntar (un arma), dirigir (una observación) **2** INTEND : proponerse, querer <he aims to do it tonight : se propone hacerlo esta noche> — *vi* **1** POINT : apuntar **2 to aim at** : aspirar a

aim² *n* **1** MARKSMANSHIP : puntería *f* **2** GOAL : propósito *m*, objetivo *m*, fin *m*

aimless ['eɪmləs] *adj* : sin rumbo, sin objeto

aimlessly ['eɪmləsli] *adv* : sin rumbo, sin objeto

air¹ ['ær] *vt* **1** : airear, ventilar <to air out a mattress : airear un colchón> **2** EXPRESS : airear, manifestar, comunicar **3** BROADCAST : transmitir, emitir

air² *n* **1** : aire *m* **2** MELODY : aire *m* **3** APPEARANCE : aire *m*, aspecto *m* **4 airs** *npl* : aires *mpl*, afectación *f* **5 by ~** : por avión (dícese de una carta), en avión (dícese de una persona) **6 to be on the air** : estar en el aire, estar emitiendo

airborne ['ærˌborn] *adj* **1** : aerotransportado <airborne troops : tropas aerotransportadas> **2** FLYING : volando, en el aire

air–condition [ˌærkən'dɪʃən] *vt* : climatizar, condicionar con el aire

air conditioner [ˌærkən'dɪʃənər] *n* : acondicionador *m* de aire

air–conditioning [ˌærkən'dɪʃənɪŋ] *n* : aire *m* acondicionado

aircraft ['ærˌkræft] *ns & pl* **1** : avión *m*, aeronave *f* **2 aircraft carrier** : portaaviones *m*

airfield ['ærˌfiːld] *n* : aeródromo *m*, campo *m* de aviación

air force *n* : fuerza *f* aérea

airlift ['ærˌlɪft] *n* : puente *m* aéreo, transporte *m* aéreo

airline ['ærˌlaɪn] *n* : aerolínea *f*, línea *f* aérea

airliner ['ærˌlaɪnər] *n* : avión *m* de pasajeros

airmail¹ ['ærˌmeɪl] *vt* : enviar por vía aérea

airmail² *n* : correo *m* aéreo

airman ['ærmən] *n, pl* **-men** [-mən, -ˌmɛn] **1** AVIATOR : aviador *m*, -dora *f* **2** : soldado *m* de la fuerza aérea

airplane ['ærˌpleɪn] *n* : avión *m*

airport ['ærˌport] *n* : aeropuerto *m*

airship [ˈær,ʃɪp] *n* : dirigible *m*, zepelín *m*
airstrip [ˈær,strɪp] *n* : pista *f* de aterrizaje
airtight [ˈærˈtaɪt] *adj* : hermético, herméticamente cerrado
airwaves [ˈær,weɪvz] *npl* : radio *m*, televisión *f*
airy [ˈæri] *adj* **airier** [-iər]; **-est 1** DELICATE, LIGHT : delicado, ligero **2** BREEZY : aireado, bien ventilado
aisle [ˈaɪl] *n* : pasillo *m*, nave *f* lateral (de una iglesia)
ajar [əˈdʒɑr] *adj* : entreabierto, entornado
akimbo [əˈkɪmbo] *adj & adv* : en jarras
akin [əˈkɪn] *adj* **1** RELATED : emparentado **2** SIMILAR : semejante, parecido
alabaster [ˈælə,bæstər] *n* : alabastro *m*
alacrity [əˈlækrət̬i] *n* : presteza *f*, prontitud *f*
alarm[1] [əˈlɑrm] *vt* **1** WARN : alarmar, alertar **2** FRIGHTEN : asustar
alarm[2] *n* **1** WARNING : alarma *f*, alerta *f* **2** APPREHENSION, FEAR : aprensión *f*, inquietud *f*, temor *m* **3 alarm clock** : despertador *m*
alas [əˈlæs] *interj* : ¡ay!
Albanian [ælˈbeɪniən] *n* : albanés *m*, -nesa *f* — **Albanian** *adj*
albatross [ˈælbə,trɔs] *n, pl* **-tross** *or* **-trosses** : albatros *m*
albeit [ɔlˈbiːət, æl-] *conj* : aunque
albino [ælˈbaɪno] *n, pl* **-nos** : albino *m*, -na *f*
album [ˈælbəm] *n* : álbum *m*
albumen [ælˈbjuːmən] *n* **1** : clara *f* de huevo **2** → **albumin**
albumin [ælˈbjuːmən] *n* : albúmina *f*
alcohol [ˈælkə,hɔl] *n* **1** ETHANOL : alcohol *m*, etanol *m* **2** LIQUOR : alcohol *m*, bebidas *fpl* alcohólicas
alcoholic[1] [,ælkəˈhɔlɪk] *adj* : alcohólico
alcoholic[2] *n* : alcohólico *m*, -ca *f*
alcoholism [ˈælkəhɔ,lɪzəm] *n* : alcoholismo *m*
alcove [ˈæl,koːv] *n* : nicho *m*, hueco *m*
alderman [ˈɔldərmən] *n, pl* **-men** [-mən, -,mɛn] : concejal *mf*
ale [ˈeɪl] *n* : cerveza *f*
alert[1] [əˈlərt] *vt* : alertar, poner sobre aviso
alert[2] *adj* **1** WATCHFUL : alerta, vigilante **2** QUICK : listo, vivo
alert[3] *n* : alerta *f*, alarma *f*
alertly [əˈlərtli] *adv* : con listeza
alertness [əˈlərtnəs] *n* **1** WATCHFULNESS : vigilancia *f* **2** ASTUTENESS : listeza *f*, viveza *f*
alfalfa [ælˈfælfə] *n* : alfalfa *f*
alga [ˈælgə] *n, pl* **-gae** [ˈæl,dʒiː] : alga *f*
algebra [ˈældʒəbrə] *n* : álgebra *m*
algebraic [,ældʒəˈbreɪɪk] *adj* : algebraico — **algebraically** [-ɪkli] *adv*
Algerian [ælˈdʒɪriən] *n* : argelino *m*, -na *f* — **Algerian** *adj*
alias[1] [ˈeɪliəs] *adv* : alias
alias[2] *n* : alias *m*
alibi[1] [ˈælə,baɪ] *vi* : ofrecer una coartada
alibi[2] *n* **1** : coartada *f* **2** EXCUSE : pretexto *m*, excusa *f*
alien[1] [ˈeɪliən] *adj* **1** STRANGE : ajeno, extraño **2** FOREIGN : extranjero, foráneo **3** EXTRATERRESTRIAL : extraterrestre
alien[2] *n* **1** FOREIGNER : extranjero *m*, -ra *f*; forastero *m*, -ra *f* **2** EXTRATERRESTRIAL : extraterrestre *mf*
alienate [ˈeɪliə,neɪt] *vt* **-ated; -ating 1** ESTRANGE : alienar, enajenar **2 to alienate oneself** : alejarse, distanciarse
alienation [,eɪliəˈneɪʃən] *n* : alienación *f*, enajenación *f*
alight [əˈlaɪt] *vi* **1** DISMOUNT : bajarse, apearse **2** LAND : posarse, aterrizar
align [əˈlaɪn] *vt* : alinear
alignment [əˈlaɪnmənt] *n* : alineación *f*, alineamiento *m*
alike[1] [əˈlaɪk] *adv* : igual, del mismo modo
alike[2] *adj* : igual, semejante, parecido
alimentary [,æləˈmɛntəri] *adj* **1** : alimenticio **2 alimentary canal** : tubo *m* digestivo
alimony [ˈælə,moːni] *n, pl* **-nies** : pensión *f* alimenticia
alive [əˈlaɪv] *adj* **1** LIVING : vivo, viviente **2** LIVELY : animado, activo **3** ACTIVE : vigente, en uso **4** AWARE : consciente <alive to the danger : consciente del peligro>
alkali [ˈælkə,laɪ] *n, pl* **-lies** [-,laɪz] *or* **-lis** [-,laɪz] : álcali *m*
alkaline [ˈælkələn, -,laɪn] *adj* : alcalino
all[1] [ˈɔl] *adv* **1** COMPLETELY : todo, completamente **2** : igual <the score is 14 all : es 14 iguales, están empatados a 14> **3 all the better** : tanto mejor **4 all the more** : aún más, todavía más
all[2] *adj* : todo <all the children : todos los niños> <in all likelihood : con toda probabilidad, con la mayor probabilidad>
all[3] *pron* **1** : todo, -da <they ate it all : lo comieron todo> <that's all : eso es todo> <enough for all : suficiente para todos> **2 all in all** : en general **3 not at all** (*in negative constructions*) : en absoluto, para nada
Allah [ˈɑlɑ, ɑˈlɑ] *n* : Alá *m*
all–around [,ɔləˈraʊnd] *adj* : completo, amplio
allay [əˈleɪ] *vt* **1** ALLEVIATE : aliviar, mitigar **2** CALM : aquietar, calmar
allegation [,ælɪˈgeɪʃən] *n* : alegato *m*, acusación *f*
allege [əˈlɛdʒ] *vt* **-leged; -leging 1** : alegar, afirmar **2 to be alleged** : decirse, pretenderse <she is alleged

to be wealthy : se dice que es adinerada>

alleged [əˈlɛdʒd, əˈlɛdʒəd] *adj* : presunto, supuesto

allegedly [əˈlɛdʒədli] : *adv* : supuestamente, según se alega

allegiance [əˈliːdʒənts] *n* : lealtad *f*, fidelidad *f*

allegorical [ˌæləˈgɔrɪkəl] *adj* : alegórico

allegory [ˈæləˌgori] *n, pl* **-ries** : alegoría *f*

alleluia [ˌɑləˈluːjə, ˌæ-] → **hallelujah**

allergic [əˈlərdʒɪk] *adj* : alérgico

allergy [ˈælərdʒi] *n, pl* **-gies** : alergia *f*

alleviate [əˈliːviˌeɪt] *vt* **-ated; -ating** : aliviar, mitigar, paliar

alleviation [əˌliːviˈeɪʃən] *n* : alivio *m*

alley [ˈæli] *n, pl* **-leys 1** : callejón *m* **2 bowling alley** : bolera *f*

alliance [əˈlaɪənts] *n* : alianza *f*, coalición *f*

alligator [ˈæləˌgeɪt̬ər] *n* : caimán *m*

alliteration [əˌlɪt̬əˈreɪʃən] *n* : aliteración *f*

allocate [ˈæləˌkeɪt] *vt* **-cated; -cating** : asignar, adjudicar

allocation [ˌæləˈkeɪʃən] *n* : asignación *f*, reparto *m*, distribución *f*

allot [əˈlɑt] *vt* **-lotted; -lotting** : repartir, distribuir, asignar

allotment [əˈlɑtmənt] *n* : reparto *m*, asignación *f*, distribución *f*

allow [əˈlaʊ] *vt* **1** PERMIT : permitir, dejar **2** ALLOT : conceder, dar **3** ADMIT, CONCEDE : admitir, conceder — *vi* **to allow for** : tener en cuenta

allowable [əˈlaʊəbəl] *adj* **1** PERMISSIBLE : permisible, lícito **2** : deducible <allowable expenditure : gasto deducible>

allowance [əˈlaʊənts] *n* **1** : complemento *m* (para gastos, etc.), mesada *f* (para niños) **2 to make allowance(s)** : tener en cuenta, disculpar

alloy [ˈæˌlɔɪ] *n* : aleación *f*

all right[1] *adv* **1** YES : sí, por supuesto **2** WELL : bien <I did all right : me fue bien> **3** DEFINITELY : bien, ciertamente, sin duda <he's sick all right : está bien enfermo>

all right[2] *adj* **1** OK : bien <are you all right? : ¿estás bien?> **2** SATISFACTORY : bien, bueno <your work is all right : tu trabajo es bueno>

all–round [ˌɔlˈraʊnd] → **all–around**

allspice [ˈɔlspaɪs] *n* : pimienta *f* de Jamaica

allude [əˈluːd] *vi* **-luded; -luding** : aludir, referirse

allure[1] [əˈlʊr] *vt* **-lured; -luring** : cautivar, atraer

allure[2] *n* : atractivo *m*, encanto *m*

allusion [əˈluːʒən] *n* : alusión *f*

ally[1] [əˈlaɪ, ˈæˌlaɪ] *vi* **-lied; -lying** : aliarse

ally[2] [ˈæˌlaɪ, əˈlaɪ] *n* : aliado *m*, -da *f*

almanac [ˈɔlməˌnæk, ˈæl-] *n* : almanaque *m*

almighty [ɔlˈmaɪt̬i] *adj* : omnipotente, todopoderoso

almond [ˈɑmənd, ˈɑl-, ˈæ-, ˈæl-] *n* : almendra *f*

almost [ˈɔlˌmoːst, ɔlˈmoːst] *adv* : casi, prácticamente

alms [ˈɑmz, ˈɑlmz, ˈælmz] *ns & pl* : limosna *f*, caridad *f*

aloft [əˈlɔft] *adv* : en alto, en el aire

alone[1] [əˈloːn] *adv* : sólo, solamente, únicamente

alone[2] *adj* : solo <they're alone in the house : están solos en la casa>

along[1] [əˈlɔŋ] *adv* **1** FORWARD : adelante <farther along : más adelante> <move along! : ¡circulen, por favor!> **2 to bring along** : traer **3 ~ with** : con, junto con **4 all along** : desde el principio

along[2] *prep* **1** : por, a lo largo de <along the coast : a lo largo de la costa> **2** : en, en el curso de, por <along the way : en el curso del viaje>

alongside[1] [əˌlɔŋˈsaɪd] *adv* : al costado, al lado

alongside[2] *or* **alongside of** *prep* : junto a, al lado de

aloof [əˈluːf] *adj* : distante, reservado

aloofness [əˈluːfnəs] *n* : reserva *f*, actitud *f* distante

aloud [əˈlaʊd] *adv* : en voz alta

alpaca [ælˈpækə] *n* : alpaca *f*

alphabet [ˈælfəˌbɛt] *n* : alfabeto *m*

alphabetical [ˌælfəˈbɛt̬ɪkəl] *or* **alphabetic** [-ˈbɛtɪk] *adj* : alfabético — **alphabetically** [-tɪkli] *adv*

alphabetize [ˈælfəbəˌtaɪz] *vt* **-ized; -izing** : alfabetizar, poner en orden alfabético

already [ɔlˈrɛdi] *adv* : ya

also [ˈɔlˌsoː] *adv* : también, además

altar [ˈɔltər] *n* : altar *m*

alter [ˈɔltər] *vt* : alterar, cambiar, modificar

alteration [ˌɔltəˈreɪʃən] *n* : alteración *f*, cambio *m*, modificación *f*

altercation [ˌɔltərˈkeɪʃən] *n* : altercado *m*, disputa *f*

alternate[1] [ˈɔltərˌneɪt] *v* **-nated; -nating** : alternar

alternate[2] [ˈɔltərnət] *adj* **1** : alterno <alternate cycles of inflation and depression : ciclos alternos de inflación y depresión> **2** : uno sí y uno no <he cooks on alternate days : cocina un día sí y otro no>

alternate[3] [ˈɔltərnət] *n* : suplente *mf;* sustituto *m*, -ta *f*

alternately [ˈɔltərnətli] *adv* : alternativamente, por turno

alternating current [ˈɔltərˌneɪt̬ɪŋ] *n* : corriente *f* alterna

alternation [ˌɔltərˈneɪʃən] *n* : alternancia *f*, rotación *f*

alternative[1] [ɔlˈtərnət̬ɪv] *adj* : alternativo

alternative[2] *n* : alternativa *f*
alternator ['ɔltər,neɪt̬ər] *n* : alternador *m*
although [ɔl'ðo:] *conj* : aunque, a pesar de que
altitude ['æltə,tu:d, -,tju:d] *n* : altitud *f*, altura *f*
alto ['æl,to:] *n, pl* **-tos** : alto *mf*, contralto *mf*
altogether [,ɔltə'gɛðər] *adv* **1** COMPLETELY : completamente, totalmente, del todo **2** ON THE WHOLE : en suma, en general
altruism ['æltrʊ,ɪzəm] *n* : altruismo *m*
altruistic [,æltrʊ'ɪstɪk] *adj* : altruista — **altruistically** [-tɪkli] *adv*
alum ['æləm] *n* : alumbre *m*
aluminum [ə'lu:mənəm] *n* : aluminio *m*
alumna [ə'lʌmnə] *n, pl* **-nae** [-,ni:] : ex-alumna *f*
alumnus [ə'lʌmnəs] *n, pl* **-ni** [-,naɪ] : ex-alumno *m*
always ['ɔlwiz, -,weɪz] *adv* **1** INVARIABLY : siempre, invariablemente **2** FOREVER : para siempre
am → **be**
amalgam [ə'mælgəm] *n* : amalgama *f*
amalgamate [ə'mælgə,meɪt] *vt* **-ated; -ating** : amalgamar, unir, fusionar
amalgamation [ə,mælgə'meɪʃən] *n* : fusión *f*, unión *f*
amaryllis [,æmə'rɪləs] *n* : amarilis *f*
amass [ə'mæs] *vt* : amasar, acumular
amateur ['æmətʃər, -tər, -,tʊr, -,tjʊr] *n* **1** : amateur *mf* **2** BEGINNER : principiante *mf*; aficionado *m*, -da *f*
amateurish ['æmə,tʃərɪʃ, -,tər-, -,tʊr-, -,tjʊr-] *adj* : amateur, inexperto
amaze [ə'meɪz] *vt* **amazed; amazing** : asombrar, maravillar, pasmar
amazement [ə'meɪzmənt] *n* : asombro *m*, sorpresa *f*
amazing [ə'meɪzɪŋ] *adj* : asombroso, sorprendente — **amazingly** [-zɪŋli] *adv*
ambassador [æm'bæsədər] *n* : embajador *m*, -dora *f*
amber ['æmbər] *n* : ámbar *m*
ambergris ['æmbər,grɪs, -,gri:s] *n* : ámbar *m* gris
ambidextrous [,æmbɪ'dɛkstrəs] *adj* : ambidextro — **ambidextrously** *adv*
ambience *or* **ambiance** ['æmbiənts, 'ɑmbi,ɑnts] *n* : ambiente *m*, atmósfera *f*
ambiguity [,æmbə'gju:ət̬i] *n, pl* **-ties** : ambigüedad *f*
ambiguous [æm'bɪgjʊəs] *adj* : ambiguo
ambition [æm'bɪʃən] *n* : ambición *f*
ambitious [æm'bɪʃəs] *adj* : ambicioso — **ambitiously** *adv*
ambivalence [æm'bɪvələnts] *n* : ambivalencia *f*
ambivalent [æm'bɪvələnt] *adj* : ambivalente
amble[1] ['æmbəl] *vi* **-bled; -bling** : ir tranquilamente, pasearse despreocupadamente
amble[2] *n* : paseo *m* tranquilo
ambulance ['æmbjələnts] *n* : ambulancia *f*
ambush[1] ['æm,bʊʃ] *vt* : emboscar
ambush[2] *n* : emboscada *f*, celada *f*
ameliorate [ə'mi:ljə,reɪt] *v* **-rated; -rating** IMPROVE : mejorar
amelioration [ə,mi:ljə'reɪʃən] *n* : mejora *f*
amen ['eɪ'mɛn, 'ɑ-] *interj* : amén
amenable [ə'mi:nəbəl, -'mɛ-] *adj* RESPONSIVE : susceptible, receptivo, sensible
amend [ə'mɛnd] *vt* **1** IMPROVE : mejorar, enmendar **2** CORRECT : enmendar, corregir
amendment [ə'mɛndmənt] *n* : enmienda *f*
amends [ə'mɛndz] *ns & pl* : compensación *f*, reparación *f*, desagravio *m*
amenity [ə'mɛnət̬i, -'mi:-] *n, pl* **-ties** **1** PLEASANTNESS : lo agradable, amenidad *f* **2 amenities** *npl* : servicios *mpl*, comodidades *fpl*
American [ə'mɛrɪkən] *n* : americano *m*, -na *f* — **American** *adj*
American Indian *n* : indio *m* (americano), india *f* (americana)
amethyst ['æməθəst] *n* : amatista *f*
amiability [,eɪmi:ə'bɪlət̬i] *n* : amabilidad *f*, afabilidad *f*
amiable ['eɪmi:əbəl] *adj* : amable, afable — **amiably** [-bli] *adv*
amicable ['æmɪkəbəl] *adj* : amigable, amistoso, cordial — **amicably** [-bli] *adv*
amid [ə'mɪd] *or* **amidst** [ə'mɪdst] *prep* : en medio de, entre
amino acid [ə'mi:no] *n* : aminoácido *m*
amiss[1] [ə'mɪs] *adv* : mal, fuera de lugar <to take amiss : tomar a mal, llevar a mal>
amiss[2] *adj* **1** WRONG : malo, inoportuno **2 there's something amiss** : pasa algo, algo anda mal
ammeter ['æ,mi:t̬ər] *n* : amperímetro *m*
ammonia [ə'mo:njə] *n* : amoníaco *m*
ammunition [,æmjə'nɪʃən] *n* **1** : municiones *fpl* **2** ARGUMENTS : argumentos *mpl*
amnesia [æm'ni:ʒə] *n* : amnesia *f*
amnesty ['æmnəsti] *n, pl* **-ties** : amnistía *f*
amoeba [ə'mi:bə] *n, pl* **-bas** *or* **-bae** [-,bi:] : ameba *f*
amoebic [ə'mi:bɪk] *adj* : amébico
amok [ə'mʌk, -'mɑk] *adv* **to run amok** : correr a ciegas, enloquecerse, desbocarse (dícese de la economía, etc.)
among [ə'mʌŋ] *prep* : entre
amorous ['æmərəs] *adj* **1** PASSIONATE : enamoradizo, apasionado **2** ENAM-

ORED : enamorado **3** LOVING : amoroso, cariñoso

amorously ['æmərəsli] *adv* : con cariño

amorphous [ə'mɔrfəs] *adj* : amorfo, informe

amortize ['æmər,taɪz, ə'mɔr-] *vt* **-tized; -tizing** : amortizar

amount[1] [ə'maʊnt] *vi* **to amount to 1** : equivaler a, significar <that amounts to treason : eso equivale a la traición> **2** : ascender (a) <my debts amount to $2000 : mis deudas ascienden a $2000>

amount[2] *n* : cantidad *f,* suma *f*

ampere ['æm,pɪr] *n* : amperio *m*

ampersand ['æmpər,sænd] *n* : el signo *&*

amphibian [æm'fɪbiən] *n* : anfibio *m*

amphibious [æm'fɪbiəs] *adj* : anfibio

amphitheater ['æmfə,θiːət̬ər] *n* : anfiteatro *m*

ample ['æmpəl] *adj* **-pler; -plest 1** LARGE, SPACIOUS : amplio, extenso, grande **2** ABUNDANT : abundante, generoso

amplifier ['æmplə,faɪər] *n* : amplificador *m*

amplify ['æmplə,faɪ] *vt* **-fied; -fying** : amplificar

amply ['æmpli] *adv* : ampliamente, abundantemente, suficientemente

amputate ['æmpjə,teɪt] *vt* **-tated; -tating** : amputar

amputation [,æmpjə'teɪʃən] *n* : amputación *f*

amuck [ə'mʌk] → **amok**

amulet ['æmjələt] *n* : amuleto *m,* talismán *m*

amuse [ə'mjuːz] *vt* **amused; amusing 1** ENTERTAIN : entretener, distraer **2** : hacer reír, divertir <the joke amused us : la broma nos hizo reír>

amusement [ə'mjuːzmənt] *n* **1** ENTERTAINMENT : diversión *f,* entretenimiento *m,* pasatiempo *m* **2** LAUGHTER : risa *f*

an → **a**[2]

anachronism [ə'nækrə,nɪzəm] *n* : anacronismo *m*

anachronistic [ə,nækrə'nɪstɪk] *adj* : anacrónico

anaconda [,ænə'kɑndə] *n* : anaconda *f*

anagram ['ænə,græm] *n* : anagrama *m*

anal ['eɪnəl] *adj* : anal

analgesic [,ænəl'dʒiːzɪk, -sɪk] *n* : analgésico *m*

analogical [,ænə'lɑdʒɪkəl] *adj* : analógico — **analogically** [-kli] *adv*

analogous [ə'næləgəs] *adj* : análogo

analogy [ə'nælədʒi] *n, pl* **-gies** : analogía *f*

analysis [ə'næləsəs] *n, pl* **-yses** [-,siːz] **1** : análisis *m* **2** PSYCHOANALYSIS : psicoanálisis *m*

analyst ['ænəlɪst] *n* **1** : analista *mf* **2** PSYCHOANALYST : psicoanalista *mf*

analytic [,ænə'lɪt̬ɪk] *or* **analytical** [-tɪkəl] *adj* : analítico — **analytically** [-t̬ɪkli] *adv*

analyze ['ænə,laɪz] *vt* **-lyzed; -lyzing** : analizar

anarchic [æ'nɑrkɪk] *adj* : anárquico — **anarchically** [-kɪkli] *adv*

anarchism ['ænər,kɪzəm, -nɑr-] *n* : anarquismo *m*

anarchist ['ænərkɪst, -nɑr-] *n* : anarquista *mf*

anarchy ['ænərki, -nɑr-] *n* : anarquía *f*

anathema [ə'næθəmə] *n* : anatema *m*

anatomic [,ænə'tɑmɪk] *or* **anatomical** [-mɪkəl] *adj* : anatómico — **anatomically** [-mɪkli] *adv*

anatomy [ə'næt̬əmi] *n, pl* **-mies** : anatomía *f*

ancestor ['æn,sɛstər] *n* : antepasado *m,* -da *f;* antecesor *m,* -sora *f*

ancestral [æn'sɛstrəl] *adj* : ancestral, de los antepasados

ancestry ['æn,sɛstri] *n* **1** DESCENT : ascendencia *f,* linaje *m,* abolengo *m* **2** ANCESTORS : antepasados *mpl,* -das *fpl*

anchor[1] ['æŋkər] *vt* **1** MOOR : anclar, fondear **2** FASTEN : sujetar, asegurar, fijar

anchor[2] *n* **1** : ancla *f* **2** : presentador *m,* -dora *f* (en televisión)

anchorage ['æŋkərɪdʒ] *n* : anclaje *m*

anchovy ['æn,tʃoːvi, æn'tʃoː-] *n, pl* **-vies** *or* **-vy** : anchoa *f*

ancient ['eɪntʃənt] *adj* **1** : antiguo <ancient history : historia antigua> **2** OLD : viejo

ancients ['eɪntʃənts] *npl* : los antiguos *mpl*

and ['ænd] *conj* **1** : y (e *before words beginning with i- or hi-*) **2** : con <ham and eggs : huevos con jamón> **3** : a <go and see : ve a ver> **4** : de <try and finish it soon : trata de terminarlo pronto>

andiron ['æn,daɪərn] *n* : morillo *m*

Andorran [æn'dɔrən] *n* : andorrano *m,* -na *f* — **Andorran** *adj*

androgynous [æn'drɑdʒənəs] *adj* : andrógino

anecdotal [,ænɪk'doːt̬əl] *adj* : anecdótico

anecdote ['ænɪk,doːt] *n* : anécdota *f*

anemia [ə'niːmiə] *n* : anemia *f*

anemic [ə'niːmɪk] *adj* : anémico

anemone [ə'nɛməni] *n* : anémona *f*

anesthesia [,ænəs'θiːʒə] *n* : anestesia *f*

anesthetic[1] [,ænəs'θɛt̬ɪk] *adj* : anestésico

anesthetic[2] *n* : anestésico *m*

anesthetist [ə'nɛsθətɪst] *n* : anestesista *mf*

anesthetize [ə'nɛsθə,taɪz] *vt* **-tize; -tized** : anestesiar

anew [ə'nuː, -'njuː] *adv* : de nuevo, otra vez, nuevamente

angel ['eɪndʒəl] *n* : ángel *m*

angelic [æn'dʒɛlɪk] *or* **angelical** [-lɪkəl] *adj* : angélico — **angelically** [-lɪkli] *adv*

anger[1] ['æŋgər] *vt* : enojar, enfadar

anger[2] *n* : enojo *m,* enfado *m,* ira *f,* cólera *f,* rabia *f*

angina [æn'dʒaɪnə] *n* : angina *f*

angle[1] ['æŋgəl] *v* **angled; angling** *vt* DIRECT, SLANT : orientar, dirigir — *vi* FISH : pescar (con caña)

angle[2] *n* **1** : ángulo *m* **2** POINT OF VIEW : perspectiva *f,* punto *m* de vista

angler ['æŋglər] *n* : pescador *m,* -dora *f*

Anglo–Saxon[1] [ˌæŋglo'sæksən] *adj* : anglosajón

Anglo–Saxon[2] *n* : anglosajón *m,* -jona *f*

Angolan [æŋ'go:lən, æn-] *n* : angoleño *m,* -ña *f* — **Angolan** *adj*

angora [æŋ'gorə, æn-] *n* : angora *f*

angrily ['æŋgrəli] *adv* : furiosamente, con ira

angry ['æŋgri] *adj* **-grier; -est** : enojado, enfadado, furioso

anguish ['æŋgwɪʃ] *n* : angustia *f,* congoja *f*

anguished ['æŋgwɪʃt] *adj* : angustiado, acongojado

angular ['æŋgjələr] *adj* : angular (dícese de las formas), anguloso (dícese de las caras)

animal ['ænəməl] *n* **1** : animal *m* **2** BRUTE : bruto *m,* -ta *f*

animate[1] ['ænəˌmeɪt] *vt* **-mated; -mating** : animar

animate[2] ['ænəmət] *adj* : animado

animated ['ænəˌmeɪṭəd] *adj* **1** LIVELY : animado, vivo, vivaz **2 animated cartoon** : dibujos *mpl* animados

animation [ˌænə'meɪʃən] *n* : animación *f*

animosity [ˌænə'mɑsəṭi] *n, pl* **-ties** : animosidad *f,* animadversión *f*

anise ['ænəs] *n* : anís *m*

aniseed ['ænəsˌsi:d] *n* : anís *m,* semilla *f* de anís

ankle ['æŋkəl] *n* : tobillo *m*

anklebone ['æŋkəlˌbo:n] *n* : taba *f*

annals ['ænəlz] *npl* : anales *mpl,* crónica *f*

anneal [ə'ni:l] *vt* **1** TEMPER : templar **2** STRENGTHEN : fortalecer

annex[1] [ə'nɛks, 'æˌnɛks] *vt* : anexar

annex[2] ['æˌnɛks, -nɪks] *n* : anexo *m,* anejo *m*

annexation [ˌæˌnɛk'seɪʃən] *n* : anexión *f*

annihilate [ə'naɪəˌleɪt] *vt* **-lated; -lating** : aniquilar

annihilation [əˌnaɪə'leɪʃən] *n* : aniquilación *f,* aniquilamiento *m*

anniversary [ˌænə'vərsəri] *n, pl* **-ries** : aniversario *m*

annotate ['ænəˌteɪt] *vt* **-tated; -tating** : anotar

annotation [ˌænə'teɪʃən] *n* : anotación *f*

announce [ə'naʊnts] *vt* **-nounced; -nouncing** : anunciar

announcement [ə'naʊntsmənt] *n* : anuncio *m*

announcer [ə'naʊntsər] *n* : anunciador *m,* -dora *f;* comentarista *mf;* locutor *m,* -tora *f*

annoy [ə'nɔɪ] *vt* : molestar, fastidiar, irritar

annoyance [ə'nɔɪənts] *n* **1** IRRITATION : irritación *f,* fastidio *m* **2** NUISANCE : molestia *f,* fastidio *m*

annoying [ə'nɔɪɪŋ] *adj* : molesto, fastidioso, engorroso — **annoyingly** [-ɪŋli] *adv*

annual[1] ['ænjʊəl] *adj* : anual — **annually** *adv*

annual[2] *n* **1** : planta *f* anual **2** YEARBOOK : anuario *m*

annuity [ə'nu:əṭi] *n, pl* **-ties** : anualidad *f*

annul [ə'nʌl] *vt* **annulled; annulling** : anular, invalidar

annulment [ə'nʌlmənt] *n* : anulación *f*

anode ['æˌno:d] *n* : ánodo

anoint [ə'nɔɪnt] *vt* : ungir

anomalous [ə'nɑmələs] *adj* : anómalo

anomaly [ə'nɑməli] *n, pl* **-lies** : anomalía *f*

anonymity [ˌænə'nɪməṭi] *n* : anonimato *m*

anonymous [ə'nɑnəməs] *adj* : anónimo — **anonymously** *adv*

another[1] [ə'nʌðər] *adj* : otro

another[2] *pron* : otro, otra

answer[1] ['æntsər] *vt* **1** : contestar (a), responder (a) <to answer the telephone : contestar el teléfono> **2** FULFILL : satisfacer **3 to answer for** : ser responsable de, pagar por <she'll answer for that mistake : pagará por ese error> — *vi* : contestar, responder

answer[2] *n* **1** REPLY : respuesta *f,* contestación *f* **2** SOLUTION : solución *f*

answerable ['æntsərəbəl] *adj* : responsable

ant ['ænt] *n* : hormiga *f*

antagonism [æn'tægəˌnɪzəm] *n* : antagonismo *m,* hostilidad *f*

antagonist [æn'tægənɪst] *n* : antagonista *mf*

antagonistic [ænˌtægə'nɪstɪk] *adj* : antagonista, hostil

antagonize [æn'tægəˌnaɪz] *vt* **-nized; -nizing** : antagonizar

antarctic [ænt'ɑrktɪk, -'ɑrṭɪk] *adj* : antártico

antarctic circle *n* : círculo *m* antártico

antebellum [ˌæntɪ'bɛləm] *adj* : prebélico

antecedent[1] [ˌæntə'si:dənt] *adj* : antecedente, precedente

antecedent[2] *n* : antecedente *mf;* precursor *m,* -sora *f*

antelope ['æntəlˌo:p] *n, pl* **-lope** *or* **-lopes** : antílope *m*

antenna [æn'tɛnə] *n, pl* **-nae** [-ˌni:, -ˌnaɪ] *or* **-nas** : antena *f*

anterior [æn'tɪriər] *adj* : anterior

anthem ['ænθəm] *n* : himno *m* <national anthem : himno nacional>

anther [ˈænθər] *n* : antera *f*
anthill [ˈænt,hɪl] *n* : hormiguero *m*
anthology [ænˈθɑlədʒi] *n, pl* **-gies** : antología *f*
anthracite [ˈænθrə,saɪt] *n* : antracita *f*
anthropoid[1] [ˈænθrə,pɔɪd] *adj* : antropoide
anthropoid[2] *n* : antropoide *mf*
anthropological [,ænθrəpəˈlɑdʒɪkəl] *adj* : antropológico
anthropologist [,ænθrəˈpɑlədʒɪst] *n* : antropólogo *m*, -ga *f*
anthropology [,ænθrəˈpɑlədʒi] *n* : antropología *f*
antiabortion [,æntiəˈbɔrʃən, ,æntaɪ-] *adj* : antiaborto
antiaircraft [,æntiˈær,kræft, ,æntaɪ-] *adj* : antiaéreo
anti–American [,æntiəˈmɛrɪkən, ,æntaɪ-] *adj* : antiamericano
antibiotic[1] [,æntibaɪˈɑt̬ɪk, ,æntaɪ-, -bi-] *adj* : antibiótico
antibiotic[2] *n* : antibiótico *m*
antibody [ˈænti,bɑdi] *n, pl* **-bodies** : anticuerpo *m*
antic[1] [ˈæntɪk] *adj* : extravagante, juguetón
antic[2] *n* : payasada *f*, travesura *f*
anticipate [ænˈtɪsə,peɪt] *vt* **-pated; -pating 1** FORESEE : anticipar, prever **2** EXPECT : esperar, contar con
anticipation [æn,tɪsəˈpeɪʃən] *n* **1** FORESIGHT : previsión *f* **2** EXPECTATION : anticipación *f*, expectación *f*, esperanza *f*
anticipatory [ænˈtɪsəpə,tori] *adj* : en anticipación, en previsión
anticlimactic [,æntiklaɪˈmæktɪk] *adj* : anticlimático, decepcionante
anticlimax [,æntiˈklaɪ,mæks] *n* : anticlímax *m*
anticommunism [,æntiˈkɑmjə,nɪzəm, ,æntaɪ-] *n* : anticomunismo *m*
anticommunist[1] [,æntiˈkɑmjənɪst, ,æntaɪ-] *adj* : anticomunista
anticommunist[2] *n* : anticomunista *mf*
antidemocratic [,ænti,dɛməˈkræt̬ɪk, ,æntaɪ-] *adj* : antidemocrático
antidote [ˈæntɪ,doːt] *n* : antídoto *m*
antidrug [,æntiˈdrʌg, ,æntaɪ-; ˈænti,drʌg, ˈæntaɪ-] *adj* : antidrogas
antifascist [,æntiˈfæʃɪst, ,æntaɪ-] *adj* : antifascista
antifeminist [,æntiˈfɛmənɪst, ,æntaɪ-] *adj* : antifeminista
antifreeze [ˈænti,friːz] *n* : anticongelante *m*
anti–imperialism [,æntiɪmˈpɪriə,lɪzəm, ,æntaɪ-] *n* : antiimperialismo *m*
anti–imperialist [,æntiɪmˈpɪriəlɪst, ,æntaɪ-] *adj* : antiimperialista
anti–inflationary [,æntiɪnˈfleɪʃə,nɛri, ,æntaɪ-] *adj* : antiinflacionario
antimony [ˈæntə,moːni] *n* : antimonio *m*
antipathy [ænˈtɪpəθi] *n, pl* **-thies** : antipatía *f*, aversión *f*
antiperspirant [,æntiˈpərspərənt, ,æntaɪ-] *n* : antitranspirante *m*
antiquarian[1] [,æntəˈkwɛriən] *adj* : antiguo, anticuario <an antiquarian book : un libro antiguo>
antiquarian[2] *n* : anticuario *m*, -ria *f*
antiquary [ˈæntə,kwɛri] → **antiquarian**[2]
antiquated [ˈæntə,kweɪt̬əd] *adj* : anticuado, pasado de moda
antique[1] [ænˈtiːk] *adj* **1** OLD : antiguo, de época <an antique mirror : un espejo antiguo> **2** OLD-FASHIONED : anticuado, pasado de moda
antique[2] *n* : antigüedad *f*
antiquity [ænˈtɪkwət̬i] *n, pl* **-ties** : antigüedad
antirevolutionary [,ænti,rɛvəˈluːʃə,nɛri, ,æntaɪ-] *adj* : antirrevolucionario
anti–Semitic [,æntisəˈmɪt̬ɪk, ,æntaɪ-] *adj* : antisemita
anti–Semitism [,æntiˈsɛmə,tɪzəm, ,æntaɪ-] *n* : antisemitismo *m*
antiseptic[1] [,æntəˈsɛptɪk] *adj* : antiséptico — **antiseptically** [-tɪkli] *adv*
antiseptic[2] *n* : antiséptico *m*
antismoking [,æntiˈsmoːkɪŋ, ,æntaɪ-] *adj* : antitabaco
antisocial [,æntiˈsoːʃəl, ,æntaɪ-] *adj* **1** : antisocial **2** UNSOCIABLE : poco sociable
antitheft [,æntiˈθɛft, ,æntaɪ-] *adj* : antirrobo
antithesis [ænˈtɪθəsɪs] *n, pl* **-eses** [-,siːz] : antítesis *f*
antitoxin [,æntiˈtɑksən, ,æntaɪ-] *n* : antitoxina *f*
antitrust [,æntiˈtrʌst, ,æntaɪ-] *adj* : antimonopolista
antler [ˈæntlər] *n* : asta *f*, cuerno *m*
antonym [ˈæntə,nɪm] *n* : antónimo *m*
anus [ˈeɪnəs] *n* : ano *m*
anvil [ˈænvəl, -vɪl] *n* : yunque *m*
anxiety [æŋ*k*ˈzaɪət̬i] *n, pl* **-eties 1** UNEASINESS : inquietud *f*, preocupación *f*, ansiedad *f* **2** APPREHENSION : ansiedad *f*, angustia *f*
anxious [ˈæŋ*k*ʃəs] *adj* **1** WORRIED : inquieto, preocupado, ansioso **2** WORRISOME : preocupante, inquietante **3** EAGER : ansioso, deseoso
anxiously [ˈæŋ*k*ʃəsli] *adv* : con inquietud, con ansiedad
any[1] [ˈɛni] *adv* **1** : algo <is it any better? : ¿está (algo) mejor?> **2** : para nada <it is not any good : no sirve para nada>
any[2] *adj* **1** : alguno <is there any doubt? : ¿hay alguna duda?> <call me if you have any questions : llámeme si tiene alguna pregunta> **2** : cualquier <I can answer any question : puedo responder a cualquier pregunta> **3** : todo <in any case : en todo caso> **4** : ningún <he would not accept it under any circumstances : no lo aceptaría bajo ninguna circunstancia>
any[3] *pron* **1** : alguno *m*, -na *f* <are there any left? : ¿queda alguno?> **2** : nin-

guno *m,* -na *f* <I don't want any : no quiero ninguno>
anybody [ˈɛni͵bʌdi, -͵bɑ-] → **anyone**
anyhow [ˈɛni͵haʊ] *adv* **1** HAPHAZARDLY : de cualquier manera **2** IN ANY CASE : de todos modos, en todo caso
anymore [͵ɛniˈmor] *adv* **1** : ya, ya más <he doesn't dance anymore : ya no baila más> **2** : todavía <do they sing anymore? : ¿cantan todavía?>
anyone [ˈɛni͵wʌn] *pron* **1** : alguien <is anyone here? : ¿hay alguien aquí?> <if anyone wants to come : si alguno quiere venir> **2** : cualquiera <anyone can play : cualquiera puede jugar> **3** : nadie <I don't want anyone here : no quiero a nadie aquí>
anyplace [ˈɛni͵pleɪs] → **anywhere**
anything [ˈɛni͵θɪŋ] *pron* **1** : algo, alguna cosa <do you want anything? : ¿quieres algo?, ¿quieres alguna cosa?> **2** : nada <hardly anything : casi nada> **3** : cualquier cosa <I eat anything : como de todo>
anytime [ˈɛni͵taɪm] *adv* : en cualquier momento, a cualquier hora, cuando sea
anyway [ˈɛni͵weɪ] → **anyhow**
anywhere [ˈɛni͵*h*wɛr] *adv* **1** : en algún sitio, en alguna parte <do you see it anywhere? : ¿lo ves en alguna parte?> **2** : en ningún sitio, por ninguna parte <I can't find it anywhere : no puedo encontrarlo por ninguna parte> **3** : en cualquier parte, dondequiera, donde sea <put it anywhere : ponlo dondequiera>
aorta [eɪˈɔrt̬ə] *n, pl* **-tas** *or* **-tae** [-t̬i, -͵taɪ] : aorta *f*
apart [əˈpɑrt] *adv* **1** SEPARATELY : aparte, separadamente **2** ASIDE : aparte, a un lado **3 to fall apart** : deshacerse, hacerse pedazos **4 to take apart** : desmontar, desmantelar
apartheid [əˈpɑr͵teɪt, -͵taɪt] *n* : apartheid *m*
apartment [əˈpɑrtmənt] *n* : apartamento *m,* departamento *m,* piso *m Spain*
apathetic [͵æpəˈθɛt̬ɪk] *adj* : apático, indiferente — **apathetically** [-t̬ɪkli] *adv*
apathy [ˈæpəθi] *n* : apatía *f,* indiferencia *f*
ape[1] [ˈeɪp] *vt* **aped; aping** : imitar, remedar
ape[2] *n* : simio *m;* mono *m,* -na *f*
aperture [ˈæpərtʃər, -͵tʃʊr] *n* : abertura *f,* rendija *f,* apertura *f* (en fotografía)
apex [ˈeɪ͵pɛks] *n, pl* **apexes** *or* **apices** [ˈeɪpə͵siːz, ˈæ-] : ápice *m,* cúspide *f,* cima *f*
aphid [ˈeɪfɪd, ˈæ-] *n* : áfido *m*
aphorism [ˈæfə͵rɪzəm] *n* : aforismo *m*
aphoristic [͵æfəˈrɪstɪk] *adj* : aforístico
aphrodisiac [͵æfrəˈdiːzi͵æk, -ˈdɪ-] *n* : afrodisíaco *m*
apiary [ˈeɪpi͵ɛri] *n, pl* **-aries** : apiario *m,* colmenar *m*
apiece [əˈpiːs] *adv* : cada uno
aplenty [əˈplɛnti] *adj* : en abundancia
aplomb [əˈplɑm, -ˈplʌm] *n* : aplomo *m*
apocalypse [əˈpɑkə͵lɪps] *n* : apocalipsis *m*
apocalyptic [ə͵pɑkəˈlɪptɪk] *adj* : apocalíptico
apocrypha [əˈpɑkrəfə] *n* : textos *mpl* apócrifos
apocryphal [əˈpɑkrəfəl] *adj* : apócrifo
apologetic [ə͵pɑləˈdʒɛt̬ɪk] *adj* : lleno de disculpas
apologetically [ə͵pɑləˈdʒɛt̬ɪkli] *adv* : disculpándose, con aire de disculpas
apologize [əˈpɑlə͵dʒaɪz] *vi* **-gized; -gizing** : disculparse, pedir perdón
apology [əˈpɑlədʒi] *n, pl* **-gies** : disculpa *f,* excusa *f*
apoplectic [͵æpəˈplɛktɪk] *adj* : apopléticο
apoplexy [ˈæpə͵plɛksi] *n* : apoplejía *f*
apostasy [əˈpɑstəsi] *n, pl* **-sies** : apostasía *f*
apostate [əˈpɑs͵teɪt] *n* : apóstata *mf*
apostle [əˈpɑsəl] *n* : apóstol *m*
apostleship [əˈpɑsəlʃɪp] *n* : apostolado *m*
apostolic [͵æpəˈstɑlɪk] *adj* : apostólico
apostrophe [əˈpɑstrə͵fiː] *n* : apóstrofo *m*
apothecary [əˈpɑθə͵kɛri] *n, pl* **-caries** : boticario *m,* -ria *f*
appall [əˈpɔl] *vt* : consternar, horrorizar
apparatus [͵æpəˈræt̬əs, -ˈreɪ-] *n, pl* **-tuses** *or* **-tus** : aparato *m,* equipo *m*
apparel [əˈpærəl] *n* : atavío *m,* ropa *f*
apparent [əˈpærənt] *adj* **1** VISIBLE : visible **2** OBVIOUS : claro, evidente, manifiesto **3** SEEMING : aparente, ostensible
apparently [əˈpærəntli] *adv* : aparentemente, al parecer
apparition [͵æpəˈrɪʃən] *n* : aparición *f,* visión *f*
appeal[1] [əˈpiːl] *vt* **1** : apelar <to appeal a decision : apelar contra una decisión> — *vi* **1 to appeal for** : pedir, solicitar **2 to appeal to** : atraer a <that doesn't appeal to me : eso no me atrae>
appeal[2] *n* **1** : apelación *f* (en derecho) **2** PLEA : ruego *m,* súplica *f* **3** ATTRACTION : atracción *f,* atractivo *m,* interés *m*
appear [əˈpɪr] *vi* **1** : aparecer, aparecerse, presentarse <he suddenly appeared : apareció de repente> **2** COME OUT : aparecer, salir, publicarse **3** : comparecer (ante el tribunal), actuar (en el teatro) **4** SEEM : parecer
appearance [əˈpɪrən*t*s] *n* **1** APPEARING : aparición *f,* presentación *f,* comparecencia *f* (ante un tribunal), publicación *f* (de un libro) **2** LOOK : apariencia *f,* aspecto *m*

appease [ə'pi:z] *vt* **-peased; -peasing 1** CALM, PACIFY **:** aplacar, apaciguar, sosegar **2** SATISFY **:** satisfacer, mitigar
appeasement [ə'pi:zmənt] *n* **:** aplacamiento *m,* apaciguamiento *m*
append [ə'pɛnd] *vt* **:** agregar, añadir, adjuntar
appendage [ə'pɛndɪdʒ] *n* **1** ADDITION **:** apéndice *m,* añadidura *f* **2** LIMB **:** miembro *m,* extremidad *f*
appendectomy [ˌæpən'dɛktəmi] *n, pl* **-mies :** apendicectomía *f*
appendicitis [əˌpɛndə'saɪt̬əs] *n* **:** apendicitis *f*
appendix [ə'pɛndɪks] *n, pl* **-dixes** *or* **-dices** [-dəˌsi:z] **:** apéndice *m*
appetite ['æpəˌtaɪt] *n* **1** CRAVING **:** apetito *m,* deseo *m,* ganas *fpl* **2** PREFERENCE **:** gusto *m,* preferencia *f* <the cultural appetites of today : los gustos culturales de hoy>
appetizer ['æpəˌtaɪzər] *n* **:** aperitivo *m,* entremés *m,* botana *f Mex,* tapa *f Spain*
appetizing ['æpəˌtaɪzɪŋ] *adj* **:** apetecible, apetitoso — **appetizingly** [-zɪŋli] *adv*
applaud [ə'plɔd] *v* **:** aplaudir
applause [ə'plɔz] *n* **:** aplauso *m*
apple ['æpəl] *n* **:** manzana *f*
appliance [ə'plaɪənts] *n* **1 :** aparato *m* **2 household appliance :** electrodoméstico *m,* aparato *m* electrodoméstico
applicability [ˌæplɪkə'bɪlət̬i, əˌplɪkə-] *n* **:** aplicabilidad *f*
applicable ['æplɪkəbəl, ə'plɪkə-] *adj* **:** aplicable, pertinente
applicant ['æplɪkənt] *n* **:** solicitante *mf,* aspirante *mf,* postulante *mf;* candidato *m,* -ta *f*
application [ˌæplə'keɪʃən] *n* **1** USE **:** aplicación *f,* empleo *m,* uso *m* **2** DILIGENCE **:** aplicación *f,* diligencia *f,* dedicación *f* **3** REQUEST **:** solicitud *f,* petición *f,* demanda *f*
applicator ['æpləˌkeɪt̬ər] *n* **:** aplicador *m*
appliqué¹ [ˌæplə'keɪ] *vt* **:** decorar con apliques
appliqué² *n* **:** aplique *m*
apply [ə'plaɪ] *v* **-plied; -plying** *vt* **1 :** aplicar (una sustancia, los frenos, el conocimiento) **2 to apply oneself :** dedicarse, aplicarse — *vi* **1 :** aplicarse, referirse <the rules apply to everyone : las reglas se aplican a todos> **2 to apply for :** solicitar, pedir
appoint [ə'pɔɪnt] *vt* **1** NAME **:** nombrar, designar **2** FIX, SET **:** fijar, señalar, designar <to appoint a date : fijar una fecha> **3** EQUIP **:** equipar <a well-appointed office : una oficina bien equipada>
appointee [əˌpɔɪn'ti:, ˌæ-] *n* **:** persona *f* designada
appointment [ə'pɔɪntmənt] *n* **1** APPOINTING **:** nombramiento *m,* designación *f* **2** ENGAGEMENT **:** cita *f,* hora *f* **3** POST **:** puesto *m*
apportion [ə'porʃən] *vt* **:** distribuir, repartir
apportionment [ə'porʃənmənt] *n* **:** distribución *f,* repartición *f,* reparto *m*
apposite ['æpəzət] *adj* **:** apropiado, oportuno, pertinente — **appositely** *adv*
appraisal [ə'preɪzəl] *n* **:** evaluación *f,* valoración *f,* tasación *f,* apreciación *f*
appraise [ə'preɪz] *vt* **-praised; -praising :** evaluar, valorar, tasar, apreciar
appraiser [ə'preɪzər] *n* **:** tasador *m,* -dora *f*
appreciable [ə'pri:ʃəbəl, -'prɪʃiə-] *adj* **:** apreciable, sensible, considerable — **appreciably** [-bli] *adv*
appreciate [ə'pri:ʃiˌeɪt, -'prɪ-] *v* **-ated; -ating** *vt* **1** VALUE **:** apreciar, valorar **2 :** agradecer <we appreciate his frankness : agradecemos su franqueza> **3** UNDERSTAND **:** darse cuenta de, entender — *vi* **:** apreciarse, valorizarse
appreciation [əˌpri:ʃi'eɪʃən, -ˌprɪ-] *n* **1** GRATITUDE **:** agradecimiento *m,* reconocimiento *m* **2** VALUING **:** apreciación *f,* valoración *f,* estimación *f* <art appreciation : apreciación artística> **3** UNDERSTANDING **:** comprensión *f,* entendimiento *m*
appreciative [ə'pri:ʃət̬ɪv, -'prɪ-; ə'pri:ʃiˌeɪ-] *adj* **1 :** apreciativo <an appreciative audience : un público apreciativo> **2** GRATEFUL **:** agradecido **3** ADMIRING **:** de admiración
apprehend [ˌæprɪ'hɛnd] *vt* **1** ARREST **:** aprehender, detener, arrestar **2** DREAD **:** temer **3** COMPREHEND **:** comprender, entender
apprehension [ˌæprɪ'hɛntʃən] *n* **1** ARREST **:** arresto *m,* detención *f,* aprehensión *f* **2** ANXIETY **:** aprensión *f,* ansiedad *f,* temor *m* **3** UNDERSTANDING **:** comprensión *f,* percepción *f*
apprehensive [ˌæprɪ'hɛntsɪv] *adj* **:** aprensivo, inquieto — **apprehensively** *adv*
apprentice¹ [ə'prɛntɪs] *vt* **-ticed; -ticing :** colocar de aprendiz
apprentice² *n* **:** aprendiz *m,* -diza *f*
apprenticeship [ə'prɛntɪsˌʃɪp] *n* **:** aprendizaje *f*
apprise [ə'praɪz] *vt* **-prised; -prising :** informar, avisar
approach¹ [ə'pro:tʃ] *vt* **1** NEAR **:** acercarse a **2** APPROXIMATE **:** aproximarse a **3 :** abordar, dirigirse a <I approached my boss with the proposal : me dirigí a mi jefe con la propuesta> **4** TACKLE **:** abordar, enfocar, considerar — *vi* **:** acercarse, aproximarse
approach² *n* **1** NEARING **:** acercamiento *m,* aproximación *f* **2** POSITION **:** enfoque *m,* planteamiento *m* **3** OFFER **:** propuesta *f,* oferta *f* **4** ACCESS **:** acceso *m,* vía *f* de acceso
approachable [ə'pro:tʃəbəl] *adj* **:** accesible, asequible

approbation [ˌæprəˈbeɪʃən] *n* : aprobación *f*
appropriate[1] [əˈproːpriˌeɪt] *vt* **-ated; -ating 1** SEIZE : apropiarse de **2** ALLOCATE : destinar, asignar
appropriate[2] [əˈproːpriət] *adj* : apropiado, adecuado, idóneo — **appropriately** *adv*
appropriateness [əˈproːpriətnəs] *n* : idoneidad *f,* propiedad *f*
appropriation [əˌproːpriˈeɪʃən] *n* **1** SEIZURE : apropiación *f* **2** ALLOCATION : asignación *f*
approval [əˈpruːvəl] *n* **1** : aprobación *f,* visto *m* bueno **2 on approval** : a prueba
approve [əˈpruːv] *vt* **-proved; -proving 1** : aprobar, sancionar, darle el visto bueno a **2 to approve of** : consentir en, aprobar <he doesn't approve of smoking : está en contra del tabaco>
approximate[1] [əˈprɑksəˌmeɪt] *vt* **-mated; -mating** : aproximarse a, acercarse a
approximate[2] [əˈprɑksəmət] *adj* : aproximado
approximately [əˈprɑksəmətli] *adv* : aproximadamente, más o menos
approximation [əˌprɑksəˈmeɪʃən] *n* : aproximación *f*
appurtenance [əˈpərtənənts] *n* : accesorio *m*
apricot [ˈæprəˌkɑt, ˈeɪ-] *n* : albaricoque *m,* chabacano *m Mex*
April [ˈeɪprəl] *n* : abril *m*
apron [ˈeɪprən] *n* : delantal *m,* mandil *m*
apropos[1] [ˌæprəˈpoː, ˈæprəˌpoː] *adv* : a propósito
apropos[2] *adj* : pertinente, oportuno, acertado
apropos of *prep* : a propósito de
apt [ˈæpt] *adj* **1** FITTING : apto, apropiado, acertado, oportuno **2** LIABLE : propenso, inclinado **3** CLEVER, QUICK : listo, despierto
aptitude [ˈæptəˌtuːd, -ˌtjuːd] *n* **1** : aptitud *f,* capacidad *f* <aptitude test : prueba de aptitud> **2** TALENT : talento *m,* facilidad *f*
aptly [ˈæptli] *adv* : acertadamente
aqua [ˈækwə, ˈɑ-] *n* : color *m* aguamarina
aquarium [əˈkwæriəm] *n, pl* **-iums** *or* **-ia** [-iə] : acuario *m*
Aquarius [əˈkwæriəs] *n* : Acuario *mf*
aquatic [əˈkwɑṭɪk, -ˈkwæ-] *adj* : acuático
aqueduct [ˈækwəˌdʌkt] *n* : acueducto *m*
aquiline [ˈækwəˌlaɪn, -lən] *adj* : aguileño
Arab[1] [ˈærəb] *adj* : árabe
Arab[2] *n* : árabe *mf*
arabesque [ˌærəˈbɛsk] *n* : arabesco *m*
Arabian[1] [əˈreɪbiən] *adj* : árabe
Arabian[2] *n* → **Arab**[2]
Arabic[1] [ˈærəbɪk] *adj* : árabe
Arabic[2] *n* : árabe *m* (idioma)
arable [ˈærəbəl] *adj* : arable, cultivable
arbiter [ˈɑrbəṭər] *n* : árbitro *m,* -tra *f*
arbitrary [ˈɑrbəˌtrɛri] *adj* : arbitrario — **arbitrarily** [ˌɑrbəˈtrɛrəli] *adv*
arbitrate [ˈɑrbəˌtreɪt] *v* **-trated; -trating** : arbitrar
arbitration [ˌɑrbəˈtreɪʃən] *n* : arbitraje *m*
arbitrator [ˈɑrbəˌtreɪṭər] *n* : árbitro *m,* -tra *f*
arbor [ˈɑrbər] *n* : cenador *m,* pérgola *f*
arboreal [ɑrˈboriəl] *adj* : arbóreo
arc[1] [ˈɑrk] *vi* **arced; arcing** : formar un arco
arc[2] *n* : arco *m*
arcade [ɑrˈkeɪd] *n* **1** ARCHES : arcada *f* **2** MALL : galería *f* comercial
arcane [ɑrˈkeɪn] *adj* : arcano, secreto, misterioso
arch[1] [ˈɑrtʃ] *vt* : arquear, enarcar — *vi* : formar un arco, arquearse
arch[2] *adj* **1** CHIEF : principal **2** MISCHIEVOUS : malicioso, pícaro
arch[3] *n* : arco *m*
archaeological [ˌɑrkiəˈlɑdʒɪkəl] *adj* : arqueológico
archaeologist [ˌɑrkiˈɑlədʒɪst] *n* : arqueólogo *m,* -ga *f*
archaeology *or* **archeology** [ˌɑrkiˈɑlədʒi] *n* : arqueología *f*
archaic [ɑrˈkeɪɪk] *adj* : arcaico — **archaically** [-ɪkli] *adv*
archangel [ˈɑrkˌeɪndʒəl] *n* : arcángel *m*
archbishop [ɑrtʃˈbɪʃəp] *n* : arzobispo *m*
archdiocese [ɑrtʃˈdaɪəsəs, -ˌsiːz, -ˌsiːs] *n* : archidiócesis *f*
archer [ˈɑrtʃər] *n* : arquero *m,* -ra *f*
archery [ˈɑrtʃəri] *n* : tiro *m* al arco
archetype [ˈɑrkɪˌtaɪp] *n* : arquetipo *m*
archipelago [ˌɑrkəˈpɛləˌgoː, ˌɑrtʃə-] *n, pl* **-goes** *or* **-gos** [-goːz] : archipiélago *m*
architect [ˈɑrkəˌtɛkt] *n* : arquitecto *m,* -ta *f*
architectural [ˌɑrkəˈtɛktʃərəl] *adj* : arquitectónico — **architecturally** *adv*
architecture [ˈɑrkəˌtɛktʃər] *n* : arquitectura *f*
archives [ˈɑrˌkaɪvz] *npl* : archivo *m*
archivist [ˈɑrkəvɪst, -ˌkaɪ-] *n* : archivero *m,* -ra *f;* archivista *mf*
archway [ˈɑrtʃˌweɪ] *n* : arco *m,* pasadizo *m* abovedado
arctic [ˈɑrktɪk, ˈɑrṭ-] *adj* **1** : ártico <arctic regions : zonas árticas> **2** FRIGID : glacial
arctic circle *n* : círculo *m* ártico
ardent [ˈɑrdənt] *adj* **1** PASSIONATE : ardiente, fogoso, apasionado **2** FERVENT : ferviente, fervoroso — **ardently** *adv*
ardor [ˈɑrdər] *n* : ardor *m,* pasión *f,* fervor *m*
arduous [ˈɑrdʒʊəs] *adj* : arduo, duro, riguroso — **arduously** *adv*

arduousness [ˈɑrdʒʊəsnəs] *n* **:** dureza *f,* rigor *m*

are → **be**

area [ˈæriə] *n* **1** SURFACE **:** área *f,* superficie *f* **2** REGION **:** área *f,* región *f,* zona *f* **3** FIELD **:** área *f,* terreno *m,* campo *m* (de conocimiento)

area code *n* **:** código *m* de la zona, prefijo *m Spain*

arena [əˈriːnə] *n* **1 :** arena *f,* estadio *m* <sports arena : estadio deportivo> **2 :** arena *f,* ruedo *m* <the political arena : el ruedo político>

Argentine [ˈɑrdʒənˌtaɪn, -ˌtiːn] *or* **Argentinean** *or* **Argentinian** [ˌɑrdʒənˈtɪniən] *n* **:** argentino *m,* -na *f* — **Argentine** *or* **Argentinean** *or* **Argentinian** *adj*

argon [ˈɑrˌgɑn] *n* **:** argón *m*

argot [ˈɑrgət, -ˌgoː] *n* **:** argot *m*

arguable [ˈɑrgjʊəbəl] *adj* **:** discutible

argue [ˈɑrˌgjuː] *v* **-gued; -guing** *vi* **1** REASON **:** argüir, argumentar, razonar **2** DISPUTE **:** discutir, pelear(se), alegar — *vt* **1** SUGGEST **:** sugerir **2** MAINTAIN **:** alegar, argüir, sostener **3** DISCUSS **:** discutir, debatir

argument [ˈɑrgjəmənt] *n* **1** REASONING **:** argumento *m,* razonamiento *m* **2** DISCUSSION **:** discusión *f,* debate *m* **3** QUARREL **:** pelea *f,* riña *f,* disputa *f*

argumentative [ˌɑrgjəˈmɛntət̬ɪv] *adj* **:** discutidor

argyle [ˈɑrˌgaɪl] *n* **:** diseño *m* de rombos

aria [ˈɑriə] *n* **:** aria *f*

arid [ˈærəd] *adj* **:** árido

aridity [əˈrɪdət̬i, æ-] *n* **:** aridez *f*

Aries [ˈɛriːz, -iˌiːz] *n* **:** Aries *mf*

arise [əˈraɪz] *vi* **arose** [əˈroːz]; **arisen** [əˈrɪzən]; **arising 1** ASCEND **:** ascender, subir, elevarse **2** ORIGINATE **:** originarse, surgir, presentarse **3** GET UP **:** levantarse

aristocracy [ˌærəˈstɑkrəsi] *n, pl* **-cies :** aristocracia *f*

aristocrat [əˈrɪstəˌkræt] *n* **:** aristócrata *mf*

aristocratic [əˌrɪstəˈkræt̬ɪk] *adj* **:** aristocrático, noble

arithmetic[1] [ˌærɪθˈmɛt̬ɪk] *or* **arithmetical** [-t̬ɪkəl] *adj* **:** aritmético

arithmetic[2] [əˈrɪθməˌtɪk] *n* **:** aritmética

ark [ˈɑrk] *n* **:** arca *f*

arm[1] [ˈɑrm] *vt* **:** armar — *vi* **:** armarse

arm[2] *n* **1 :** brazo *m* (del cuerpo o de un sillón), manga *f* (de una prenda) **2** BRANCH **:** rama *f,* sección *f* **3** WEAPON **:** arma *f* <to take up arms : tomar las armas> **4 coat of arms :** escudo *m* de armas

armada [ɑrˈmɑdə, -ˈmeɪ-] *n* **:** armada *f,* flota *f*

armadillo [ˌɑrməˈdɪlo] *n, pl* **-los :** armadillo *m*

armament [ˈɑrməmənt] *n* **:** armamento *m*

armed [ˈɑrmd] *adj* **1 :** armado <armed robbery : robo a mano armada> **2 armed forces :** fuerzas *fpl* armadas

Armenian [ɑrˈmiːniən] *n* **:** armenio *m,* -nia *f* — **Armenian** *adj*

armistice [ˈɑrməstɪs] *n* **:** armisticio *m*

armor [ˈɑrmər] *n* **:** armadura *f,* coraza *f*

armored [ˈɑrmərd] *adj* **:** blindado, acorazado

armory [ˈɑrməri] *n, pl* **-mories :** arsenal *m* (almacén), armería *f* (museo), fábrica *f* de armas

armpit [ˈɑrmˌpɪt] *n* **:** axila *f,* sobaco *m*

army [ˈɑrmi] *n, pl* **-mies 1 :** ejército *m* (militar) **2** MULTITUDE **:** legión *f,* multitud *f,* ejército *m*

aroma [əˈroːmə] *n* **:** aroma *f*

aromatic [ˌærəˈmæt̬ɪk] *adj* **:** aromático

around[1] [əˈraʊnd] *adv* **1 :** de circunferencia <a tree three feet around : un árbol de tres pies de circunferencia> **2 :** alrededor, a la redonda <for miles around : por millas a la redonda> <all around : por todos lados, todo alrededor> **3 :** por ahí <they're somewhere around : deben estar por ahí> **4** APPROXIMATELY **:** más o menos, aproximadamente <around 5 o'clock : a eso de las 5> **5 to turn around :** darse la vuelta, voltearse

around[2] *prep* **1** SURROUNDING **:** alrededor de, en torno a **2** THROUGH **:** por, en <he traveled around Mexico : viajó por México> <around the house : en casa> **3 :** a la vuelta de <around the corner : a la vuelta de la esquina> **4** NEAR **:** alrededor de, cerca de

arousal [əˈraʊzəl] *n* **:** excitación *f*

arouse [əˈraʊz] *vt* **aroused; arousing 1** AWAKE **:** despertar **2** EXCITE **:** despertar, suscitar, excitar

arraign [əˈreɪn] *vt* **:** hacer comparecer (ante un tribunal)

arraignment [əˈreɪnmənt] *n* **:** orden *m* de comparecencia, acusación *f*

arrange [əˈreɪndʒ] *vt* **-ranged; -ranging 1** ORDER **:** arreglar, poner en orden, disponer **2** SETTLE **:** arreglar, fijar, concertar **3** ADAPT **:** arreglar, adaptar

arrangement [əˈreɪndʒmənt] *n* **1** ORDER **:** arreglo *m,* orden *m* **2** ARRANGING **:** disposición *f* <floral arrangement : arreglo floral> **3** AGREEMENT **:** arreglo *m,* acuerdo *m,* convenio *m* **4 arrangements** *npl* **:** preparativos *mpl,* planes *mpl*

array[1] [əˈreɪ] *vt* **1** ORDER **:** poner en orden, presentar, formar **2** GARB **:** vestir, ataviar, engalanar

array[2] *n* **1** ORDER **:** orden *m,* formación *f* **2** ATTIRE **:** atavío *m,* galas *mpl* **3** RANGE, SELECTION **:** selección *f,* serie *f,* gama *f* <an array of problems : una serie de problemas>

arrears [əˈrɪrz] *npl* **:** atrasos *mpl* <to be in arrears : estar atrasado en los pagos>

arrest[1] [ə'rɛst] *vt* **1** APPREHEND : arrestar, detener **2** CHECK, STOP : detener, parar
arrest[2] *n* **1** APPREHENSION : arresto *m,* detención *f* <under arrest : detenido> **2** STOPPING : paro *m*
arrival [ə'raɪvəl] *n* : llegada *f,* venida *f,* arribo *m*
arrive [ə'raɪv] *vi* **-rived; -riving 1** COME : llegar, arribar **2** SUCCEED : triunfar, tener éxito
arrogance ['ærəgənts] *n* : arrogancia *f,* soberbia *f,* altanería *f,* altivez *f*
arrogant ['ærəgənt] *adj* : arrogante, soberbio, altanero, altivo — **arrogantly** *adv*
arrogate ['ærə,geɪt] *vt* **-gated; -gating to arrogate to oneself** : arrogarse
arrow ['æro] *n* : flecha *f*
arrowhead ['æro,hɛd] *n* : punta *f* de flecha
arroyo [ə'rɔɪo] *n* : arroyo *m*
arsenal ['ɑrsənəl] *n* : arsenal *m*
arsenic ['ɑrsənɪk] *n* : arsénico *m*
arson ['ɑrsən] *n* : incendio *m* premeditado
arsonist *n* ['ɑrsənɪst] : incendiario *m,* -ria *f;* pirómano *m,* -na *f*
art ['ɑrt] *n* **1** : arte *m* **2** SKILL : destreza *f,* habilidad *f,* maña *f* **3 arts** *npl* : letras *fpl* (en la educación) **4 fine arts** : bellas artes *fpl*
arterial [ɑr'tɪriəl] *adj* : arterial
arteriosclerosis [ɑr,tɪriosklə'ro:sɪs] *n* : arteriosclerosis *f*
artery ['ɑrtəri] *n, pl* **-teries 1** : arteria *f* **2** THOROUGHFARE : carretera *f* principal, arteria *f*
artesian well [ɑr'ti:ʒən] *n* : pozo *m* artesiano
artful ['ɑrtfəl] *adj* **1** INGENIOUS : ingenioso, diestro **2** CRAFTY : astuto, taimado, ladino, artero — **artfully** *adv*
arthritic [ɑr'θrɪtɪk] *adj* : artrítico
arthritis [ɑr'θraɪtəs] *n, pl* **-tides** [ɑr'θrɪtə,di:z] : artritis *f*
arthropod ['ɑrθrə,pɑd] *n* : artrópodo *m*
artichoke ['ɑrtə,tʃo:k] *n* : alcachofa *f*
article ['ɑrtɪkəl] *n* **1** ITEM : artículo *m,* objeto *m* **2** ESSAY : artículo *m* **3** CLAUSE : artículo *m,* cláusula *f* **4** : artículo *m* <definite article : artículo determinado>
articulate[1] [ɑr'tɪkjə,leɪt] *vt* **-lated; -lating 1** UTTER : articular, enunciar, expresar **2** CONNECT : articular (en anatomía)
articulate[2] [ɑr'tɪkjələt] *adj* **to be articulate** : poder articular palabras, expresarse bien
articulately [ɑr'tɪkjələtli] *adv* : elocuentemente, con fluidez
articulateness [ɑr'tɪkjələtnəs] *n* : elocuencia *f,* fluidez *f*
articulation [ɑr,tɪkjə'leɪʃən] *n* **1** JOINT : articulación *f* **2** UTTERANCE : articulación *f,* declaración *f* **3** ENUNCIATION : articulación *f,* pronunciación *f*
artifact ['ɑrtə,fækt] *n* : artefacto *m*
artifice ['ɑrtəfəs] *n* : artificio *m*
artificial [,ɑrtə'fɪʃəl] *adj* **1** SYNTHETIC : artificial, sintético **2** FEIGNED : artificial, falso, afectado
artificially [,ɑrtə'fɪʃəli] *adv* : artificialmente, con afectación
artillery [ɑr'tɪləri] *n, pl* **-leries** : artillería *f*
artisan ['ɑrtəzən, -sən] *n* : artesano *m,* -na *f*
artist ['ɑrtɪst] *n* : artista *mf*
artistic [ɑr'tɪstɪk] *adj* : artístico — **artistically** [-tɪkli] *adv*
artistry ['ɑrtəstri] *n* : maestría *f,* arte *m*
artless ['ɑrtləs] *adj* : sencillo, natural, ingenuo, cándido — **artlessly** *adv*
artlessness ['ɑrtləsnəs] *n* : ingenuidad *f,* candidez *f*
arty ['ɑrti] *adj* **artier; -est** : pretenciosamente artístico
as[1] ['æz] *adv* **1** : tan, tanto <this one's not as difficult : éste no es tan difícil> **2** : como <some trees, as oak and pine : algunos árboles, como el roble y el pino>
as[2] *conj* **1** LIKE : como, igual que **2** WHEN, WHILE : cuando, mientras, a la vez que **3** BECAUSE : porque **4** THOUGH : aunque, por más que <strange as it may appear : por extraño que parezca> **5 as is** : tal como está
as[3] *prep* **1** : de <I met her as a child : la conocí de pequeña> **2** LIKE : como <behave as a man : compórtate como un hombre>
as[4] *pron* : que <in the same building as my brother : en el mismo edificio que mi hermano>
asbestos [æz'bɛstəs, æs-] *n* : asbesto *m,* amianto *m*
ascend [ə'sɛnd] *vi* : ascender, subir — *vt* : subir, subir a, escalar
ascendancy [ə'sɛndəntsi] *n* : ascendiente *m,* predominio *m*
ascendant[1] [ə'sɛndənt] *adj* **1** RISING : ascendente **2** DOMINANT : superior, dominante
ascendant[2] *n* **to be in the ascendant** : estar en alza, ir ganando predominio
ascension [ə'sɛntʃən] *n* : ascensión *f*
ascent [ə'sɛnt] *n* **1** RISE : ascensión, *f,* subida *f,* ascenso *m* **2** SLOPE : cuesta *f,* pendiente *f*
ascertain [,æsər'teɪn] *vt* : determinar, establecer, averiguar
ascertainable [,æsər'teɪnəbəl] *adj* : determinable, averiguable
ascetic[1] [ə'sɛtɪk] *adj* : ascético
ascetic[2] *n* : asceta *mf*
asceticism [ə'sɛtə,sɪzəm] *n* : ascetismo *m*
ascribable [ə'skraɪbəbəl] *adj* : atribuible, imputable
ascribe [ə'skraɪb] *vt* **-cribed; -cribing** : atribuir, imputar
aseptic [eɪ'sɛptɪk] *adj* : aséptico
as for *prep* CONCERNING : en cuanto a, respecto a, para

ash [ˈæʃ] *n* **1 :** ceniza *f* <to reduce to ashes : reducir a cenizas> **2 :** fresno *m* (árbol)

ashamed [əˈʃeɪmd] *adj* **:** avergonzado, abochornado, apenado — **ashamedly** [əˈʃeɪmədli] *adv*

ashen [ˈæʃən] *adj* **:** lívido, ceniciento, pálido

ashore [əˈʃor] *adv* **1 :** en tierra **2 to go ashore :** desembarcar

ashtray [ˈæʃˌtreɪ] *n* **:** cenicero *m*

Asian[1] [ˈeɪʒən, -ʃən] *adj* **:** asiático

Asian[2] *n* **:** asiático *m,* -ca *f*

aside [əˈsaɪd] *adv* **1 :** a un lado <to step aside : hacerse a un lado> **2 :** de lado, aparte <jesting aside : bromas aparte> **3 to set aside :** guardar, apartar, reservar

aside from *prep* **1** BESIDES **:** además de **2** EXCEPT **:** aparte de, menos

as if *conj* **:** como si

asinine [ˈæsənˌaɪn] *adj* **:** necio, estúpido

ask [ˈæsk] *vt* **1 :** preguntar <ask him if he's coming : pregúntale si viene> **2** REQUEST **:** pedir, solicitar <to ask a favor : pedir un favor> **3** INVITE **:** invitar — *vi* **1** INQUIRE **:** preguntar <I asked about her children : pregunté por sus niños> **2** REQUEST **:** pedir <we asked for help : pedimos ayuda>

askance [əˈskæn*t*s] *adv* **1** SIDELONG **:** de reojo, de soslayo **2** SUSPICIOUSLY **:** con recelo, con desconfianza

askew [əˈskjuː] *adj* **:** torcido, ladeado

asleep [əˈsliːp] *adj* **1 :** dormido, durmiendo **2 to fall asleep :** quedarse dormido

as of *prep* **:** desde, a partir de

asparagus [əˈspærəgəs] *n* **:** espárrago *m*

aspect [ˈæˌspɛkt] *n* **:** aspecto *m*

aspen [ˈæspən] *n* **:** álamo *m* temblón

asperity [æˈspɛrət̬i, ə-] *n, pl* **-ties :** aspereza *f*

aspersion [əˈspərʒən] *n* **:** difamación *f,* calumnia *f*

asphalt [ˈæsˌfɔlt] *n* **:** asfalto *m*

asphyxia [æˈsfɪksiə, ə-] *n* **:** asfixia *f*

asphyxiate [æˈsfɪksiˌeɪt] *v* **-ated; -ating** *vt* **:** asfixiar — *vi* **:** asfixiarse

asphyxiation [æˌsfɪksiˈeɪʃən] *n* **:** asfixia *f*

aspirant [ˈæspərənt, əˈspaɪrənt] *n* **:** aspirante *mf,* pretendiente *mf*

aspiration [ˌæspəˈreɪʃən] *n* **1** DESIRE **:** aspiración *f,* anhelo *m,* ambición *f* **2** BREATHING **:** aspiración *f*

aspire [əˈspaɪr] *vi* **-pired; -piring :** aspirar

aspirin [ˈæsprən, ˈæspə-] *n, pl* **aspirin** *or* **aspirins :** aspirina *f*

ass [ˈæs] *n* **1 :** asno *m* **2** IDIOT **:** imbécil *mf,* idiota *mf*

assail [əˈseɪl] *vt* **:** atacar, asaltar

assailant [əˈseɪlənt] *n* **:** asaltante *mf,* atacante *mf*

assassin [əˈsæsən] *n* **:** asesino *m,* -na *f*

assassinate [əˈsæsənˌeɪt] *vt* **-nated; -nating :** asesinar

assassination [əˌsæsənˈeɪʃən] *n* **:** asesinato *m*

assault[1] [əˈsɔlt] *vt* **:** atacar, asaltar, agredir

assault[2] *n* **:** ataque *m,* asalto *m,* agresión *f*

assay[1] [æˈseɪ, ˈæˌseɪ] *vt* **:** ensayar

assay[2] [ˈæˌseɪ, æˈseɪ] *n* **:** ensayo *m*

assemble [əˈsɛmbəl] *v* **-bled; -bling** *vt* **1** GATHER **:** reunir, recoger, juntar **2** CONSTRUCT **:** ensamblar, montar, construir — *vi* **:** reunirse, congregarse

assembly [əˈsɛmbli] *n, pl* **-blies 1** MEETING **:** reunión *f* **2** CONSTRUCTING **:** ensamblaje *m,* montaje *m*

assemblyman [əˈsɛmblimən] *n, pl* **-men** [-mən, -ˌmɛn] **:** asambleísta *m*

assemblywoman [əˈsɛmbliˌwʊmən] *n, pl* **-women** [-ˌwɪmən] **:** asambleísta *f*

assent[1] [əˈsɛnt] *vi* **:** asentir, consentir

assent[2] *n* **:** asentimiento *m,* aprobación *f*

assert [əˈsərt] *vt* **1** AFFIRM **:** afirmar, aseverar, mantener **2 to assert oneself :** imponerse, hacerse valer

assertion [əˈsərʃən] *n* **:** afirmación *f,* aseveración *f,* aserto *m*

assertive [əˈsərt̬ɪv] *adj* **:** firme, enérgico

assertiveness [əˈsərt̬ɪvnəs] *n* **:** seguridad *f* en sí mismo

assess [əˈsɛs] *vt* **1** IMPOSE **:** gravar (un impuesto), imponer **2** EVALUATE **:** evaluar, valorar, aquilatar

assessment [əˈsɛsmənt] *n* **:** evaluación *f,* valoración *f*

assessor [əˈsɛsər] *n* **:** evaluador *m,* -dora *f;* tasador *m,* -dora *f*

asset [ˈæˌsɛt] *n* **1 :** ventaja *f,* recurso *m* **2 assets** *npl* **:** bienes *mpl,* activo *m* <assets and liabilities : activo y pasivo>

assiduous [əˈsɪdʒʊəs] *adj* **:** diligente, aplicado, asiduo — **assiduously** *adv*

assign [əˈsaɪn] *vt* **1** APPOINT **:** designar, nombrar **2** ALLOT **:** asignar, señalar **3** ATTRIBUTE **:** atribuir, dar, conceder

assignment [əˈsaɪnmənt] *n* **1** TASK **:** función *f,* tarea *f,* misión *f* **2** HOMEWORK **:** tarea *f,* asignación *f PRi,* deberes *mpl Spain* **3** APPOINTMENT **:** nombramiento *m* **4** ALLOCATION **:** asignación *f*

assimilate [əˈsɪməˌleɪt] *v* **-lated; -lating** *vt* **:** asimilar — *vi* **:** adaptarse, integrarse

assimilation [əˌsɪməˈleɪʃən] *n* **:** asimilación *f*

assist[1] [əˈsɪst] *vt* **:** asistir, ayudar

assist[2] *n* **:** asistencia *f,* contribución *f*

assistance [əˈsɪstən*t*s] *n* **:** asistencia *f,* ayuda *f,* auxilio *m*

assistant [əˈsɪstənt] *n* **:** ayudante *mf,* asistente *mf*

associate[1] [əˈsoːʃiˌeɪt, -si-] *v* **-ated; -ating** *vt* **1** CONNECT, RELATE **:** asociar, relacionar **2 to be associated with**

: estar relacionado con, estar vinculado a — *vi* **to associate with** : relacionarse con, frecuentar

associate[2] [ə'soːʃiət, -siət] *n* : asociado *m*, -da *f*; colega *mf*; socio *m*, -cia *f*

association [əˌsoːʃi'eɪʃən, -si-] *n* **1** ORGANIZATION : asociación *f*, sociedad *f* **2** RELATIONSHIP : asociación *f*, relación *f*

as soon as *conj* : en cuanto, tan pronto como

assorted [ə'sɔrt̬əd] *adj* : surtido

assortment [ə'sɔrtmənt] *n* : surtido *m*, variedad *f*, colección *f*

assuage [ə'sweɪdʒ] *vt* **-suaged; -suaging 1** EASE : aliviar, mitigar **2** CALM : calmar, aplacar **3** SATISFY : saciar, satisfacer

assume [ə'suːm] *vt* **-sumed; -suming 1** SUPPOSE : suponer, asumir **2** UNDERTAKE : asumir, encargarse de **3** TAKE ON : adquirir, adoptar, tomar <to assume importance : tomar importancia> **4** FEIGN : adoptar, afectar, simular

assumption [ə'sʌmpʃən] *n* : asunción *f*, presunción *f*

assurance [ə'ʃʊrənts] *n* **1** CERTAINTY : certidumbre *f*, certeza *f* **2** CONFIDENCE : confianza *f*, aplomo *m*, seguridad *f*

assure [ə'ʃʊr] *vt* **-sured; -suring** : asegurar, garantizar <I assure you that I'll do it : te aseguro que lo haré>

assured [ə'ʃʊrd] *adj* **1** CERTAIN : seguro, asegurado **2** CONFIDENT : confiado, seguro de sí mismo

aster ['æstər] *n* : áster *m*

asterisk ['æstəˌrɪsk] *n* : asterisco *m*

astern [ə'stərn] *adv* **1** BEHIND : detrás, a popa **2** BACKWARDS : hacia atrás

asteroid ['æstəˌrɔɪd] *n* : asteroide *m*

asthma ['æzmə] *n* : asma *m*

asthmatic [æz'mæt̬ɪk] *adj* : asmático

as though → **as if**

astigmatism [ə'stɪgməˌtɪzəm] *n* : astigmatismo *m*

as to *prep* **1** ABOUT : sobre, acerca de **2** → **according to**

astonish [ə'stɑnɪʃ] *vt* : asombrar, sorprender, pasmar

astonishing [ə'stɑnɪʃɪŋ] *adj* : asombroso, sorprendente, increíble — **astonishingly** *adv*

astonishment [ə'stɑnɪʃmənt] *n* : asombro *m*, estupefacción *f*, sorpresa *f*

astound [ə'staʊnd] *vt* : asombrar, pasmar, dejar estupefacto

astounding [ə'staʊndɪŋ] *adj* : asombroso, pasmoso — **astoundingly** *adv*

astraddle [ə'strædəl] *adv* : a horcajadas

astral ['æstrəl] *adj* : astral

astray [ə'streɪ] *adv & adj* : perdido, extraviado, descarriado

astride [ə'straɪd] *adv* : a horcajadas

astringency [ə'strɪndʒəntsi] *n* : astringencia *f*

astringent[1] [ə'strɪndʒənt] *adj* : astringente

astringent[2] *n* : astringente *m*

astrologer [ə'strɑlədʒər] *n* : astrólogo *m*, -ga *f*

astrological [ˌæstrə'lɑdʒɪkəl] *adj* : astrológico

astrology [ə'strɑlədʒi] *n* : astrología *f*

astronaut ['æstrəˌnɔt] *n* : astronauta *mf*

astronautic [ˌæstrə'nɔt̬ɪk] *or* **astronautical** [-t̬ɪkəl] *adj* : astronáutico

astronautics [ˌæstrə'nɔt̬ɪks] *ns & pl* : astronáutica *f*

astronomer [ə'strɑnəmər] *n* : astrónomo *m*, -ma *f*

astronomical [ˌæstrə'nɑmɪkəl] *adj* **1** : astronómico **2** ENORMOUS : astronómico, enorme, gigantesco

astronomy [ə'strɑnəmi] *n, pl* **-mies** : astronomía *f*

astute [ə'stuːt, -'stjuːt] *adj* : astuto, sagaz, perspicaz — **astutely** *adv*

astuteness [ə'stuːtnəs, -'stjuːt-] *n* : astucia *f*, sagacidad *f*, perspicacia *f*

asunder [ə'sʌndər] *adv* : en dos, en pedazos <to tear asunder : hacer pedazos>

as well as[1] *conj* : tanto como

as well as[2] *prep* BESIDES : además de, aparte de

as yet *adv* : aún, todavía

asylum [ə'saɪləm] *n* **1** REFUGE : refugio *m*, santuario *m*, asilo *m* **2 insane asylum** : manicomio *m*

asymmetrical [ˌeɪsə'mɛtrɪkəl] *or* **asymmetric** [-'mɛtrɪk] *adj* : asimétrico

asymmetry [ˌeɪ'sɪmətri] *n* : asimetría *f*

at ['æt] *prep* **1** : en <at the top : en lo alto> <at peace : en paz> <at Ana's house : en casa de Ana> **2** : a <at the rear : al fondo> <at 10 o'clock : a las diez> **3** : por <at last : por fin> <to be surprised at something : sorprenderse por algo> **4** : de <he's laughing at you : está riéndose de ti> **5** : para <you're good at this : eres bueno para esto>

at all *adv* : en absoluto, para nada

ate → **eat**

atheism *n* ['eɪθiˌɪzəm] : ateísmo *m*

atheist ['eɪθiɪst] *n* : ateo *m*, atea *f*

atheistic [ˌeɪθi'ɪstɪk] *adj* : ateo

athlete ['æθˌliːt] *n* : atleta *mf*

athletic [æθ'lɛt̬ɪk] *adj* : atlético

athletics [æθ'lɛt̬ɪks] *ns & pl* : atletismo *m*

atlas ['ætləs] *n* : atlas *m*

atmosphere ['ætməˌsfɪr] *n* **1** AIR : atmósfera *f*, aire *m* **2** AMBIENCE : ambiente *m*, atmósfera *f*, clima *m*

atmospheric [ˌætmə'sfɪrɪk, -'sfɛr-] *adj* : atmosférico — **atmospherically** [-ɪkli] *adv*

atoll ['æˌtɔl, 'eɪ-, -ˌtɑl] *n* : atolón *m*

atom ['æt̬əm] *n* **1** : átomo *m* **2** SPECK : ápice *m*, pizca *f*

atomic [ə'tɑmɪk] *adj* : atómico

atomic bomb *n* **:** bomba *f* atómica
atomizer [ˈætə,maɪzər] *n* **:** atomizador *m,* pulverizador *m*
atone [əˈtoːn] *vt* **atoned; atoning to atone for :** expiar
atonement [əˈtoːnmənt] *n* **:** expiación *f,* desagravio *m*
atop[1] [əˈtɑp] *adj* **:** encima
atop[2] *prep* **:** encima de, sobre
atrium [ˈeɪtriəm] *n, pl* **atria** [-triə] *or* **atriums 1 :** atrio *m* **2 :** aurícula *f* (del corazón)
atrocious [əˈtroːʃəs] *adj* **:** atroz — **atrociously** *adv*
atrocity [əˈtrɑsət̬i] *n, pl* **-ties :** atrocidad *f*
atrophy[1] [ˈætrəfi] *vt* **-phied; -phying :** atrofiar
atrophy[2] *n, pl* **-phies :** atrofia *f*
atropine [ˈætrə,piːn] *n* **:** atropina *f*
attach [əˈtætʃ] *vt* **1** FASTEN **:** sujetar, atar, amarrar, pegar **2** JOIN **:** juntar, adjuntar **3** ATTRIBUTE **:** dar, atribuir <I attached little importance to it : le di poca importancia> **4** SEIZE **:** embargar **5 to become attached to someone :** encariñarse con alguien
attaché [,æt̬əˈʃeɪ, ,æ,tæ-, ə,tæ-] *n* **:** agregado *m,* -da *f*
attachment [əˈtætʃmənt] *n* **1** ACCESSORY **:** accesorio *m* **2** CONNECTION **:** conexión *f,* acoplamiento *m* **3** FONDNESS **:** apego *m,* cariño *m,* afición *f*
attack[1] [əˈtæk] *vt* **1** ASSAULT **:** atacar, asaltar, agredir **2** TACKLE **:** acometer, combatir, enfrentarse con
attack[2] *n* **1 :** ataque *m,* asalto *m,* acometida *f* <to launch an attack : lanzar un ataque> **2 :** ataque *m,* crisis *f* <heart attack : ataque cardíaco, infarto> <attack of nerves : crisis nerviosa>
attacker [əˈtækər] *n* **:** asaltante *mf*
attain [əˈteɪn] *vt* **1** ACHIEVE **:** lograr, conseguir, alcanzar, realizar **2** REACH **:** alcanzar, llegar a
attainable [əˈteɪnəbəl] *adj* **:** alcanzable, realizable, asequible
attainment [əˈteɪnmənt] *n* **:** logro *m,* consecución *f,* realización *f*
attempt[1] [əˈtɛmpt] *vt* **:** intentar, tratar de
attempt[2] *n* **:** intento *m,* tentativa *f*
attend [əˈtɛnd] *vt* **1 :** asistir a <to attend a meeting : asistir a una reunión> **2 :** atender, ocuparse de, cuidar <to attend a patient : atender a un paciente> **3** HEED **:** atender a, hacer caso de **4** ACCOMPANY **:** acompañar
attendance [əˈtɛndən*t*s] *n* **1** ATTENDING **:** asistencia *f* **2** TURNOUT **:** concurrencia *f*
attendant[1] [əˈtɛndənt] *adj* **:** concomitante, inherente
attendant[2] *n* **:** asistente *mf,* acompañante *mf,* guarda *mf*
attention [əˈtɛntʃən] *n* **1 :** atención *f* **2 to pay attention :** prestar atención, hacer caso **3 to stand at attention :** estar firme
attentive [əˈtɛntɪv] *adj* **:** atento — **attentively** *adv*
attentiveness [əˈtɛntɪvnəs] *n* **1** THOUGHTFULNESS **:** cortesía *f,* consideración *f* **2** CONCENTRATION **:** atención *f,* concentración *f*
attest [əˈtɛst] *vt* **:** atestiguar, dar fe de
attestation [,æ,tɛsˈteɪʃən] *n* **:** testimonio *m*
attic [ˈætɪk] *n* **:** ático *m,* desván *m,* buhardilla *f*
attire[1] [əˈtaɪr] *vt* **-tired; -tiring :** ataviar
attire[2] *n* **:** atuendo *m,* atavío *m*
attitude [ˈæt̬ə,tuːd, -,tjuːd] *n* **1** FEELING **:** actitud *f* **2** POSTURE **:** postura *f*
attorney [əˈtərni] *n, pl* **-neys :** abogado *m,* -da *f*
attract [əˈtrækt] *vt* **1 :** atraer **2 to attract attention :** llamar la atención
attraction [əˈtrækʃən] *n* **:** atracción *f,* atractivo *m*
attractive [əˈtræktɪv] *adj* **:** atractivo, atrayente
attractively [əˈtræktɪvli] *adv* **:** de manera atractiva, de buen gusto, hermosamente
attractiveness [əˈtræktɪvnəs] *n* **:** atractivo *m*
attributable [əˈtrɪbjʊt̬əbəl] *adj* **:** atribuible, imputable
attribute[1] [əˈtrɪ,bjuːt] *vt* **-tributed; -tributing :** atribuir
attribute[2] [ˈætrə,bjuːt] *n* **:** atributo *m,* cualidad *f*
attribution [,ætrəˈbjuːʃən] *n* **:** atribución *f*
attune [əˈtuːn, -ˈtjuːn] *vt* **-tuned; -tuning 1** ADAPT **:** adaptar, adecuar **2 to be attuned to :** estar en armonía con
auburn [ˈɔbərn] *adj* **:** castaño rojizo
auction[1] [ˈɔkʃən] *vt* **:** subastar, rematar
auction[2] *n* **:** subasta *f,* remate *m*
auctioneer [,ɔkʃəˈnɪr] *n* **:** subastador *m,* -dora *f;* rematador *m,* -dora *f*
audacious [ɔˈdeɪʃəs] *adj* **:** audaz, atrevido
audacity [ɔˈdæsət̬i] *n, pl* **-ties :** audacia *f,* atrevimiento *m,* descaro *m*
audible [ˈɔdəbəl] *adj* **:** audible — **audibly** [-bli] *adv*
audience [ˈɔdiən*t*s] *n* **1** INTERVIEW **:** audiencia *f* **2** PUBLIC **:** audiencia *f,* público *m,* auditorio *m,* espectadores *mpl*
audio[1] [ˈɔdi,oː] *adj* **:** de sonido, de audio
audio[2] *n* **:** audio *m*
audiovisual [,ɔdioˈvɪʒʊəl] *adj* **:** audiovisual
audit[1] [ˈɔdət] *vt* **1 :** auditar (finanzas) **2 :** asistir como oyente a (una clase o un curso)
audit[2] *n* **:** auditoría *f*
audition[1] [ɔˈdɪʃən] *vi* **:** hacer una audición
audition[2] *n* **:** audición *f*

auditor [ˈɔdət̬ər] *n* **1 :** auditor *m,* -tora *f* (de finanzas) **2** STUDENT **:** oyente *mf*
auditorium [ˌɔdəˈtoriəm] *n, pl* **-riums** *or* **-ria** [-riə] **:** auditorio *m,* sala *f*
auditory [ˈɔdəˌtori] *adj* **:** auditivo
auger [ˈɔgər] *n* **:** taladro *m,* barrena *f*
augment [ɔgˈmɛnt] *vt* **:** aumentar, incrementar
augmentation [ˌɔgmənˈteɪʃən] *n* **:** aumento *m,* incremento *m*
augur[1] [ˈɔgər] *vt* **:** augurar, presagiar — *vi* **to augur well :** ser de buen agüero
augur[2] *n* **:** augur *m*
augury [ˈɔgjʊri, -gər-] *n, pl* **-ries :** augurio *m,* presagio *m,* agüero *m*
august [ɔˈgʌst] *adj* **:** augusto
August [ˈɔgəst] *n* **:** agosto *m*
auk [ˈɔk] *n* **:** alca *f*
aunt [ˈænt, ˈant] *n* **:** tía *f*
aura [ˈɔrə] *n* **:** aura *f*
aural [ˈɔrəl] *adj* **:** auditivo
auricle [ˈɔrɪkəl] *n* **:** aurícula *f*
aurora borealis [əˈrorəˌboriˈæləs] *n* **:** aurora *f* boreal
auspices [ˈɔspəsəz, -ˌsiːz] *npl* **:** auspicios *mpl*
auspicious [ɔˈspɪʃəs] *adj* **:** prometedor, propicio, de buen augurio
austere [ɔˈstɪr] *adj* **:** austero, severo, adusto — **austerely** *adv*
austerity [ɔˈstɛrət̬i] *n, pl* **-ties :** austeridad *f*
Australian [ɔˈstreɪljən] *n* **:** australiano *m,* -na *f* — **Australian** *adj*
Austrian [ˈɔstriən] *n* **:** austriaco *m,* -ca *f* — **Austrian** *adj*
authentic [əˈθɛntɪk, ɔ-] *adj* **:** auténtico, genuino — **authentically** [-tɪkli] *adv*
authenticate [əˈθɛntɪˌkeɪt, ɔ-] *vt* **-cated; -cating :** autenticar, autentificar
authenticity [ɔˌθɛnˈtɪsət̬i] *n* **:** autenticidad *f*
author [ˈɔθər] *n* **1** WRITER **:** escritor *m,* -tora *f;* autor *m,* -tora *f* **2** CREATOR **:** autor *m,* -tora *f;* creador *m,* -dora *f;* artífice *mf*
authoritarian [ɔˌθɔrəˈtɛriən, ə-] *adj* **:** autoritario
authoritative [əˈθɔrəˌteɪt̬ɪv, ɔ-] *adj* **1** RELIABLE **:** fidedigno, autorizado **2** DICTATORIAL **:** autoritario, dictatorial, imperioso
authoritatively [əˈθɔrəˌteɪt̬ɪvli, ɔ-] *adv* **1** RELIABLY **:** con autoridad **2** DICTATORIALLY **:** de manera autoritaria
authority [əˈθɔrət̬i, ɔ-] *n, pl* **-ties 1** EXPERT **:** autoridad *f;* experto *m,* -ta *f* **2** POWER **:** autoridad *f,* poder *m* **3** AUTHORIZATION **:** autorización *f,* licencia *f* **4 the authorities :** las autoridades *fpl* **5 on good authority :** de buena fuente
authorization [ˌɔθərəˈzeɪʃən] *n* **:** autorización *f*
authorize [ˈɔθəˌraɪz] *vt* **-rized; -rizing :** autorizar, facultar
authorship [ˈɔθərˌʃɪp] *n* **:** autoría *f*
auto [ˈɔt̬o] → **automobile**
autobiographical [ˌɔt̬oˌbaɪəˈgræfɪkəl] *adj* **:** autobiográfico
autobiography [ˌɔt̬obaɪˈagrəfi] *n, pl* **-phies :** autobiografía *f*
autocracy [ɔˈtakrəsi] *n, pl* **-cies :** autocracia *f*
autocrat [ˈɔt̬əˌkræt] *n* **:** autócrata *mf*
autocratic [ˌɔt̬əˈkræt̬ɪk] *adj* **:** autocrático — **autocratically** [-tɪkli] *adv*
autograph[1] [ˈɔt̬əˌgræf] *vt* **:** autografiar
autograph[2] *n* **:** autógrafo *m*
automate [ˈɔt̬əˌmeɪt] *vt* **-mated; -mating :** automatizar
automatic [ˌɔt̬əˈmæt̬ɪk] *adj* **:** automático — **automatically** [-tɪkli] *adv*
automation [ˌɔt̬əˈmeɪʃən] *n* **:** automatización *f*
automaton [ɔˈtaməˌtan] *n, pl* **-atons** *or* **-ata** [-tə, -ˌta] **:** autómata *m*
automobile [ˌɔt̬əmoˈbiːl, -ˈmoːˌbiːl] *n* **:** automóvil *m,* auto *m,* carro *m,* coche *m*
automotive [ˌɔt̬əˈmoːt̬ɪv] *adj* **:** automotor
autonomous [ɔˈtanəməs] *adj* **:** autónomo — **autonomously** *adv*
autonomy [ɔˈtanəmi] *n, pl* **-mies :** autonomía *f*
autopsy [ˈɔˌtapsi, -təp-] *n, pl* **-sies :** autopsia *f*
autumn [ˈɔt̬əm] *n* **:** otoño *m*
autumnal [ɔˈtʌmnəl] *adj* **:** otoñal
auxiliary[1] [ɔgˈzɪljəri, -ˈzɪləri] *adj* **:** auxiliar
auxiliary[2] *n, pl* **-ries :** auxiliar *mf,* ayudante *mf*
avail[1] [əˈveɪl] *vt* **to avail oneself :** aprovecharse, valerse
avail[2] *n* **1 :** provecho *m,* utilidad *f* **2 to no avail :** en vano **3 to be of no avail :** no servir de nada, ser inútil
availability [əˌveɪləˈbɪlət̬i] *n, pl* **-ties :** disponibilidad *f*
available [əˈveɪləbəl] *adj* **:** disponible
avalanche [ˈævəˌlæntʃ] *n* **:** avalancha *f,* alud *m*
avarice [ˈævərəs] *n* **:** avaricia *f,* codicia *f*
avaricious [ˌævəˈrɪʃəs] *adj* **:** avaricioso, codicioso
avenge [əˈvɛndʒ] *vt* **avenged; avenging :** vengar
avenger [əˈvɛndʒər] *n* **:** vengador *m,* -dora *f*
avenue [ˈævəˌnuː, -ˌnjuː] *n* **1 :** avenida *f* **2** MEANS **:** vía *f,* camino *m*
average[1] [ˈævrɪdʒ, ˈævə-] *vt* **-aged; -aging 1 :** hacer un promedio de <he averages 8 hours a day : hace un promedio de 8 horas diarias> **2 :** calcular el promedio de, promediar (en matemáticas)
average[2] *adj* **1** MEAN **:** medio <the average temperature : la temperatura media> **2** ORDINARY **:** común, ordinario <the average man : el hombre común>

average[3] *n* : promedio *m*
averse [ə'vərs] *adj* : reacio, opuesto
aversion [ə'vərʒən] *n* : aversión *f*
avert [ə'vərt] *vt* **1** : apartar, desviar <he averted his eyes from the scene : apartó los ojos de la escena> **2** AVOID, PREVENT : evitar, prevenir
aviary ['eɪvi,ɛri] *n, pl* **-aries** : pajarera *f*
aviation [,eɪvi'eɪʃən] *n* : aviación *f*
aviator ['eɪvi,eɪt̬ər] *n* : aviador *m*, -dora *f*
avid ['ævɪd] *adj* **1** GREEDY : ávido, codicioso **2** ENTHUSIASTIC : ávido, entusiasta, ferviente — **avidly** *adv*
avocado [,ævə'kɑdo, ,ɑvə-] *n, pl* **-dos** : aguacate *m*, palta *f*
avocation [,ævə'keɪʃən] *n* : pasatiempo *m*, afición *f*
avoid [ə'vɔɪd] *vt* **1** SHUN : evitar, eludir **2** FORGO : evitar, abstenerse de <I always avoided gossip : siempre evitaba los chismes> **3** EVADE : evitar <if I can avoid it : si puedo evitarlo>
avoidable [ə'vɔɪdəbəl] *adj* : evitable
avoidance [ə'vɔɪdənts] *n* : el evitar
avoirdupois [,ævərdə'pɔɪz] *n* : sistema *m* inglés de pesos y medidas
avow [ə'vaʊ] *vt* : reconocer, confesar
avowal [ə'vaʊəl] *n* : reconocimiento *m*, confesión *f*
await [ə'weɪt] *vt* : esperar
awake[1] [ə'weɪk] *v* **awoke** [ə'wo:k]; **awoken** [ə'wo:kən] *or* **awaked**; **awaking** : despertar
awake[2] *adj* : despierto
awaken [ə'weɪkən] → **awake**[1]
award[1] [ə'wɔrd] *vt* : otorgar, conceder, conferir
award[2] *n* **1** PRIZE : premio *m*, galardón *m* **2** MEDAL : condecoración *f*
aware [ə'wær] *adj* : consciente <to be aware of : darse cuenta de, estar consciente de>
awareness [ə'wærnəs] *n* : conciencia *f*, conocimiento *m*
awash [ə'wɔʃ] *adj* : inundado
away[1] [ə'weɪ] *adv* **1** : de aquí <go away! : ¡fuera de aquí!, ¡vete!> **2** : de distancia <10 miles away : 10 millas de distancia, queda a 10 millas> **3 far away** : lejos, a lo lejos **4 right away** : en seguida, ahora mismo **5 to be away** : estar ausente, estar de viaje **6 to give away** : regalar (una posesión), revelar (un secreto) **7 to go away** : irse, largarse **8 to put away** : guardar **9 to turn away** : volver la cara
away[2] *adj* **1** ABSENT : ausente <away for the week : ausente por la semana> **2 away game** : partido *m* que se juega fuera
awe[1] ['ɔ] *vt* **awed; awing** : abrumar, asombrar, impresionar
awe[2] *n* : asombro *m*
awesome ['ɔsəm] *adj* **1** IMPOSING : imponente, formidable **2** AMAZING : asombroso
awestruck ['ɔ,strʌk] *adj* : asombrado
awful ['ɔfəl] *adj* **1** AWESOME : asombroso **2** DREADFUL : horrible, terrible, atroz **3** ENORMOUS : enorme, tremendo <an awful lot of people : muchísima gente, la mar de gente>
awfully ['ɔfəli] *adv* **1** EXTREMELY : terriblemente, extremadamente **2** BADLY : muy mal, espantosamente
awhile [ə'hwaɪl] *adv* : un rato, algún tiempo
awkward ['ɔkwərd] *adj* **1** CLUMSY : torpe, desmañado **2** EMBARRASSING : embarazoso, delicado — **awkwardly** *adv*
awkwardness ['ɔkwərdnəs] *n* **1** CLUMSINESS : torpeza *f* **2** INCONVENIENCE : incomodidad *f*
awl ['ɔl] *n* : punzón *m*
awning ['ɔnɪŋ] *n* : toldo *m*
awry [ə'raɪ] *adj* 1 ASKEW : torcido **2 to go awry** : salir mal, fracasar
ax *or* **axe** ['æks] *n* : hacha *m*
axiom ['æksiəm] *n* : axioma *m*
axiomatic [,æksiə'mæt̬ɪk] *adj* : axiomático
axis ['æksɪs] *n, pl* **axes** [-,si:z] : eje *m*
axle ['æksəl] *n* : eje *m*
aye[1] ['aɪ] *adv* : sí
aye[2] *n* : sí *m*
azalea [ə'zeɪljə] *n* : azalea *f*
azimuth ['æzəməθ] *n* : azimut *m*, acimut *m*
azure[1] ['æʒər] *adj* : azur, celeste
azure[2] *n* : azur *m*

B

b ['bi:] *n, pl* **b's** *or* **bs** ['bi:z] : segunda letra del alfabeto inglés
babble[1] ['bæbəl] *vi* **-bled; -bling 1** PRATTLE : balbucear **2** CHATTER : charlatanear, parlotear *fam* **3** MURMUR : murmurar
babble[2] *n* : balbuceo *m* (de bebé), parloteo *m* (de adultos), murmullo *m* (de voces, de un arroyo)
babe ['beɪb] → **baby**[3]
babel ['beɪbəl, 'bæ-] *n* : babel *f*, caos *m*
baboon [bæ'bu:n] *n* : babuino *m*
baby[1] ['beɪbi] *vt* **-bied; -bying** : mimar, consentir
baby[2] *adj* **1** : de niño <a baby carriage : un cochecito> <baby talk : habla infantil> **2** TINY : pequeño, minúsculo
baby[3] *n, pl* **-bies** : bebé *m*; niño *m*, -ña *f*
babyhood ['beɪbi,hʊd] *n* : niñez *f*, primera infancia *f*
babyish ['beɪbiɪʃ] *adj* : infantil, pueril

baby–sit [ˈbeɪbiˌsɪt] *vi* **-sat** [-ˌsæt]; **-sitting** : cuidar niños, hacer de canguro *Spain*

baby–sitter [ˈbeɪbiˌsɪtər] *n* : niñero *m,* -ra *f;* canguro *mf Spain*

baccalaureate [ˌbækəˈlɔriət] *n* : licenciatura *f*

bachelor [ˈbætʃələr] *n* **1** : soltero *m* **2** : licenciado *m,* -da *f* <bachelor of arts degree : licenciatura en filosofía y letras>

bacillus [bəˈsɪləs] *n, pl* **-li** [-ˌlaɪ] : bacilo *m*

back[1] [ˈbæk] *vt* **1** *or* **to back up** SUPPORT : apoyar, respaldar **2** *or* **to back up** REVERSE : darle marcha atrás a (un vehículo) **3** : estar detrás de, formar el fondo de <trees back the garden : unos árboles están detrás del jardín> — *vi* **1** *or* **to back up** : retroceder **2** **to back away** : echarse atrás **3** **to back down** *or* **to back out** : volverse atrás, echarse para atrás

back[2] *adv* **1** : atrás, hacia atrás, detrás <to move back : moverse atrás> <back and forth : de acá para allá> **2** AGO : atrás, antes, ya <some years back : unos años atrás, ya unos años> <10 months back : hace diez meses> **3** : de vuelta, de regreso <we're back : estamos de vuelta> <she ran back : volvió corriendo> <to call back : llamar de nuevo>

back[3] *adj* **1** REAR : de atrás, posterior, trasero **2** OVERDUE : atrasado **3** **back pay** : atrasos *mpl*

back[4] *n* **1** : espalda *f* (de un ser humano), lomo *m* (de un animal) **2** : respaldo *m* (de una silla), espalda *f* (de ropa) **3** REVERSE : reverso *m,* dorso *m,* revés *m* **4** REAR : fondo *m,* parte *f* de atrás **5** : defensa *mf* (en deportes)

backache [ˈbækˌeɪk] *n* : dolor *m* de espalda

backbite [ˈbækˌbaɪt] *v* **-bit** [-ˌbɪt]; **-bitten** [-ˌbɪtən]; **-biting** *vt* : calumniar, hablar mal de — *vi* : murmurar

backbiter [ˈbækˌbaɪtər] *n* : calumniador *m,* -dora *f*

backbone [ˈbækˌboːn] *n* **1** : columna *f* vertebral **2** FIRMNESS : firmeza *f,* carácter *m*

backdrop [ˈbækˌdrɑp] *n* : telón *m* de fondo

backer [ˈbækər] *n* **1** SUPPORTER : partidario *m,* -ria *f* **2** SPONSOR : patrocinador *m,* -dora *f*

backfire[1] [ˈbækˌfaɪr] *vi* **-fired; -firing** **1** : petardear (dícese de un automóvil) **2** FAIL : fallar, salir el tiro por la culata

backfire[2] *n* : petardeo *m,* explosión *f*

background [ˈbækˌgraʊnd] *n* **1** : fondo *m* (de un cuadro, etc.), antecedentes *mpl* (de una situación) **2** EXPERIENCE, TRAINING : experiencia *f* profesional, formación *f*

backhand[1] [ˈbækˌhænd] *adv* : de revés, con el revés

backhand[2] *n* : revés *m*

backhanded [ˈbækˌhændəd] *adj* **1** : dado con el revés, de revés **2** INDIRECT : indirecto, ambiguo

backing [ˈbækɪŋ] *n* **1** SUPPORT : apoyo *m,* respaldo *m* **2** REINFORCEMENT : refuerzo *m* **3** SUPPORTERS : partidarios *mpl,* -rias *fpl*

backlash [ˈbækˌlæʃ] *n* : reacción *f* violenta

backlog [ˈbækˌlɔg] *n* : atraso *m,* trabajo *m* acumulado

backpack[1] [ˈbækˌpæk] *vi* : viajar con mochila

backpack[2] *n* : mochila *f*

backrest [ˈbækˌrɛst] *n* : respaldo *m*

backslide [ˈbækˌslaɪd] *vi* **-slid** [-ˌslɪd]; **-slid** *or* **-slidden** [-ˌslɪdən]; **-sliding** : recaer, reincidir

backstage [ˌbækˈsteɪdʒ, ˈbækˌ-] *adv & adj* : entre bastidores

backtrack [ˈbækˌtræk] *vi* : dar marcha atrás, volverse atrás

backup [ˈbækˌʌp] *n* **1** SUPPORT : respaldo *m,* apoyo *m* **2** : copia *f* de seguridad (para computadoras)

backward[1] [ˈbækwərd] *or* **backwards** [-wərdz] *adv* **1** : hacia atrás **2** : de espaldas <he fell backwards : se cayó de espaldas> **3** : al revés <you're doing it backwards : lo estás haciendo al revés> **4** **to bend over backwards** : hacer todo lo posible

backward[2] *adj* **1** : hacia atrás <a backward glance : una mirada hacia atrás> **2** RETARDED : retrasado **3** SHY : tímido **4** UNDERDEVELOPED : atrasado

backwardness [ˈbækwərdnəs] *n* : atraso *m* (dícese de una región), retraso *m* (dícese de una persona)

backwoods [ˌbækˈwʊdz] *npl* : monte *m,* región *f* alejada

bacon [ˈbeɪkən] *n* : tocino *m,* tocineta *f Col, Ven,* bacon *m Spain*

bacterial [bækˈtɪriəl] *adj* : bacteriano

bacteriologist [bækˌtɪriˈɑlədʒɪst] *n* : bacteriólogo *m,* -ga *f*

bacteriology [bækˌtɪriˈɑlədʒi] *n* : bacteriología *f*

bacterium [bækˈtɪriəm] *n, pl* **-ria** [-iə] : bacteria *f*

bad[1] [ˈbæd] *adv* → **badly**

bad[2] *adj* **1** : malo **2** ROTTEN : podrido **3** SERIOUS, SEVERE : grave **4** DEFECTIVE : defectuoso <a bad check : un cheque sin fondos> **5** HARMFUL : perjudicial **6** CORRUPT, EVIL : malo, corrompido **7** NAUGHTY : travieso **8** **from bad to worse** : de mal en peor **9** **too bad!** : ¡qué lástima!

bad[3] *n* : lo malo <the good and the bad : lo bueno y lo malo>

bade → **bid**

badge [ˈbædʒ] *n* : insignia *f,* botón *m,* chapa *f*

badger[1] [ˈbædʒər] *vt* : fastidiar, acosar, importunar

badger[2] *n* : tejón *m*

badly ['bædli] *adv* **1** : mal **2** URGENTLY : mucho, con urgencia **3** SEVERELY : gravemente
badminton ['bæd,mɪntən, -,mɪt-] *n* : bádminton *m*
badness ['bædnəs] *n* : maldad *f*
baffle¹ ['bæfəl] *vi* **-fled; -fling 1** PERPLEX : desconcertar, confundir **2** FRUSTRATE : frustrar
baffle² *n* : deflector *m,* bafle *m* (acústico)
bafflement ['bæfəlmənt] *n* : desconcierto *m,* confusión *f*
bag¹ ['bæg] *v* **bagged; bagging** *vi* SAG : formar bolsas — *vt* **1** : ensacar, poner en una bolsa **2** : cobrar (en la caza), cazar
bag² *n* **1** : bolsa *f,* saco *m* **2** HANDBAG : cartera *f,* bolso *m,* bolsa *f Mex* **3** SUITCASE : maleta *f,* valija *f*
bagatelle [,bægə'tɛl] *n* : bagatela *f*
bagel ['beɪgəl] *n* : rosquilla *f* de pan
baggage ['bægɪdʒ] *n* : equipaje *m*
baggy ['bægi] *adj* **-gier; -est** : holgado, ancho
bagpipe ['bæg,paɪp] *n* : gaita *f*
bail¹ ['beɪl] *vt* **1** : achicar (agua de un bote) **2 to bail out** : poner en libertad (de una cárcel) bajo fianza **3 to bail out** EXTRICATE : sacar de apuros
bail² *n* : fianza *f,* caución *f*
bailiff ['beɪləf] *n* : aguacil *mf*
bailiwick ['beɪli,wɪk] *n* : dominio *m*
bailout ['beɪl,aʊt] *n* : rescate *m* (financial)
bait¹ ['beɪt] *vt* **1** : cebar (un anzuelo o cepo) **2** HARASS : acosar
bait² *n* : cebo *m,* carnada *f*
bake¹ ['beɪk] *vt* **baked; baking** : hornear, hacer al horno
bake² *n* : fiesta con platos hechos al horno
baker ['beɪkər] *n* : panadero *m,* -ra *f*
baker's dozen *n* : docena *f* de fraile
bakery ['beɪkəri] *n, pl* **-ries** : panadería *f*
bakeshop ['beɪk,ʃɑp] *n* : pastelería *f,* panadería *f*
baking powder *n* : levadura *f* en polvo
baking soda → **sodium bicarbonate**
balance¹ ['bæləntsl] *v* **-anced; -ancing** *vt* **1** : hacer el balance de (una cuenta) <to balance the books : cuadrar las cuentas> **2** EQUALIZE : balancear, equilibrar **3** HARMONIZE : armonizar — *vi* : balancearse
balance² *n* **1** SCALES : balanza *f,* báscula *f* **2** COUNTERBALANCE : contrapeso *m* **3** EQUILIBRIUM : equilibrio *m* **4** REMAINDER : balance *m,* resto *m*
balanced ['bæləntst] *adj* : equilibrado, balanceado
balcony ['bælkəni] *n, pl* **-nies 1** : balcón *m,* terraza *f* (de un edificio) **2** : galería *f* (de un teatro)
bald ['bɔld] *adj* **1** : calvo, pelado, pelón **2** PLAIN : simple, puro <the bald truth : la pura verdad>
balding ['bɔldɪŋ] *adj* : quedándose calvo
baldly ['bɔldli] *adv* : sin reparos, sin rodeos, francamente
baldness ['bɔldnəs] *n* : calvicie *f*
bale¹ ['beɪl] *vt* **baled; baling** : empacar, hacer balas de
bale² *n* : bala *f,* fardo *m,* paca *f*
baleful ['beɪlfəl] *adj* **1** DEADLY : mortífero **2** SINISTER : siniestro, funesto, torvo <a baleful glance : una mirada torva>
balk¹ ['bɔk] *vt* : obstaculizar, impedir — *vi* **1** : plantarse *fam* (dícese de un caballo, etc.) **2 to balk at** : resistarse a, mostrarse reacio a
balk² *n* : obstáculo *m*
Balkan ['bɔlkən] *adj* : balcánico
balky ['bɔki] *adj* **balkier; -est** : reacio, obstinado, terco
ball¹ ['bɔl] *vt* : apelotonar, ovillar
ball² *n* **1** : pelota *f,* bola *f,* balón *m,* ovillo *m* (de lana) **2** : juego *m* con pelota o bola **3** DANCE : baile *m,* baile *m* de etiqueta
ballad ['bæləd] *n* : romance *m,* balada *f*
balladeer [,bælə'dɪr] *n* : cantante *mf* de baladas
ballast¹ ['bæləst] *vt* : lastrear
ballast² *n* : lastre *m*
ball bearing *n* : cojinete *m* de bola
ballerina [,bælə'riːnə] *n* : bailarina *f*
ballet [bæ'leɪ, 'bæ,leɪ] *n* : ballet *m*
ballistic [bə'lɪstɪk] *adj* : balístico
ballistics [bə'lɪstɪks] *ns & pl* : balística *f*
balloon¹ [bə'luːn] *vi* **1** : viajar en globo **2** SWELL : hincharse, inflarse
balloon² *n* : globo *m*
balloonist [bə'luːnɪst] *n* : aeróstata *mf*
ballot¹ ['bælət] *vi* : votar
ballot² *n* **1** : papeleta *f* (de voto) **2** BALLOTING : votación *f* **3** VOTE : voto *m*
ballpoint pen ['bɔl,pɔɪnt] *n* : bolígrafo *m*
ballroom ['bɔl,ruːm, -,rʊm] *n* : sala *f* de baile
ballyhoo ['bæli,huː] *n* : propaganda *f,* publicidad *f,* bombo *m fam*
balm ['bɑm, 'bɑlm] *n* : bálsamo *m,* ungüento *m*
balmy ['bɑmi, 'bɑl-] *adj* **balmier; -est 1** MILD : templado, agradable **2** SOOTHING : balsámico **3** CRAZY : chiflado *fam,* chalado *fam*
baloney [bə'loːni] *n* NONSENSE : tonterías *fpl,* estupideces *fpl*
balsa ['bɔlsə] *n* : balsa *f*
balsam ['bɔlsəm] *n* **1** : bálsamo *m* **2** *or* **balsam fir** : abeto *m* balsámico
baluster ['bæləstər] *n* : balaustre *m*
balustrade ['bælə,streɪd] *n* : balaustrada *f*
bamboo [bæm'buː] *n* : bambú *m*
bamboozle [bæm'buːzəl] *vt* **-zled; -zling** : engañar, embaucar
ban¹ ['bæn] *vt* **banned; banning** : prohibir, proscribir

ban[2] *n* **:** prohibición *f,* proscripción *f*

banal [bə'nɑl, bə'næl, 'beɪnəl] *adj* **:** banal, trivial

banality [bə'næləti] *n, pl* **-ties :** banalidad *f,* trivialidad *f*

banana [bə'nænə] *n* **:** banano *m,* plátano *m,* banana *f,* cambur *m Ven,* guineo *m Car*

band[1] ['bænd] *vt* **1** BIND **:** fajar, atar **2 to band together :** unirse, juntarse

band[2] *n* **1** STRIP **:** banda *f,* cinta *f* (de un sombrero, etc.) **2** STRIPE **:** franja *f* **3 :** banda *f* (de radiofrecuencia) **4** RING **:** anillo *m* **5** GROUP **:** banda *f,* grupo *m,* conjunto *m* <jazz band : conjunto de jazz>

bandage[1] ['bændɪdʒ] *vt* **-daged; -daging :** vendar

bandage[2] *n* **:** vendaje *m,* venda *f*

bandanna *or* **bandana** [bæn'dænə] *n* **:** pañuelo *m* (de colores)

bandit ['bændət] *n* **:** bandido *m,* -da *f;* bandolero *m,* -ra *f*

banditry ['bændətri] *n* **:** bandolerismo *m,* bandidaje *m*

bandstand ['bænd,stænd] *n* **:** quiosco *m* de música

bandwagon ['bænd,wægən] *n* **1 :** carroza *f* de músicos **2 to jump on the bandwagon :** subirse al carro, seguir la moda

bandy[1] ['bændi] *vt* **-died; -dying 1** EXCHANGE **:** intercambiar **2 to bandy about :** circular, propagar

bandy[2] *adj* **:** arqueado, torcido <bandy-legged : de piernas arqueadas>

bane ['beɪn] *n* **1** POISON **:** veneno *m* **2** RUIN **:** ruina *f,* pesadilla *f*

baneful ['beɪnfəl] *adj* **:** nefasto, funesto

bang[1] ['bæŋ] *vt* **1** STRIKE **:** golpear, darse <he banged his elbow against the door : se dio con el codo en la puerta> **2** SLAM **:** cerrar (la puerta) con un portazo — *vi* **1** SLAM **:** cerrarse de un golpe **2 to bang on :** aporrear, golpear <she was banging on the table : aporreaba la mesa>

bang[2] *adv* **:** directamente, exactamente

bang[3] *n* **1** BLOW **:** golpe *m,* porrazo *m,* trancazo *m* **2** EXPLOSION **:** explosión *f,* estallido *m* **3** SLAM **:** portazo *m* **4 bangs** *npl* **:** flequilla *f,* fleco *m*

Bangladeshi [,bɑŋglə'dɛʃi, ,bæŋ-, ,bʌŋ-, -'deɪ-] *n* **:** bangladesí *mf* — **Bangladeshi** *adj*

bangle ['bæŋgəl] *n* **:** brazalete *m,* pulsera *f*

banish ['bænɪʃ] *vt* **1** EXILE **:** desterrar, exiliar **2** EXPEL **:** expulsar

banishment ['bænɪʃmənt] *n* **1** EXILE **:** destierro *m,* exilio *m* **2** EXPULSION **:** expulsión *f*

banister ['bænəstər] *n* **1** BALUSTER **:** balaustre *m* **2** HANDRAIL **:** pasamanos *m,* barandilla *f,* barandal *m*

banjo ['bæn,dʒoː] *n, pl* **-jos :** banjo *m*

bank[1] ['bæŋk] *vt* **1** TILT **:** peraltar (una carretera), ladear (un avión) **2** HEAP **:** amontonar **3 :** cubrir (un fuego) **4 :** depositar (dinero en un banco) — *vi* **1 :** ladearse (dícese de un avión) **2 :** tener una cuenta (en un banco) **3 to bank on :** contar con

bank[2] *n* **1** MASS **:** montón *m,* montículo *m,* masa *f* **2 :** orilla *f,* ribera *f* (de un río) **3 :** peralte *m* (de una carretera) **4 :** banco *m* <World Bank : Banco Mundial> <banco de sangre : blood bank>

bankbook ['bæŋk,bʊk] *n* **:** libreta *f* bancaria, libreta *f* de ahorros

banker ['bæŋkər] *n* **:** banquero *m,* -ra *f*

bankrupt[1] ['bæŋ,krʌpt] *vt* **:** hacer quebrar, llevar a la quiebra, arruinar

bankrupt[2] *adj* **1 :** en bancarrota, en quiebra **2 ~ of** LACKING **:** carente de, falto de

bankrupt[3] *n* **:** fallido *m,* -da *f;* quebrado *m,* -da *f*

bankruptcy ['bæŋ,krʌptsi] *n, pl* **-cies :** ruina *f,* quiebra *f,* bancarrota *f*

banner[1] ['bænər] *adj* **:** excelente

banner[2] *n* **:** estandarte *m,* bandera *f*

banns ['bænz] *npl* **:** amonestaciones *fpl*

banquet[1] ['bæŋkwət] *vi* **:** celebrar un banquete

banquet[2] *n* **:** banquete *m*

banter[1] ['bæntər] *vi* **:** bromear, hacer bromas

banter[2] *n* **:** bromas *fpl*

baptism ['bæp,tɪzəm] *n* **:** bautismo *m*

baptismal [bæp'tɪzməl] *adj* **:** bautismal

baptize [bæp'taɪz, 'bæp,taɪz] *vt* **-tized; -tizing :** bautizar

bar[1] ['bɑr] *vt* **barred; barring 1** OBSTRUCT **:** obstruir, bloquear **2** EXCLUDE **:** excluir **3** PROHIBIT **:** prohibir **4** SECURE **:** atrancar, asegurar <bar the door! : ¡atranca la puerta!>

bar[2] *n* **1 :** barra *f,* barrote *m* (de una ventana), tranca *f* (de una puerta) **2** BARRIER **:** barrera *f,* obstáculo *m* **3** LAW **:** abogacía *f* **4** STRIPE **:** franja *f* **5** COUNTER **:** mostrador *m,* barra *f* **6** TAVERN **:** bar *m,* taberna *f*

bar[3] *prep* **1 :** excepto, con excepción de **2 bar none :** sin excepción

barb ['bɑrb] *n* **1** POINT **:** púa *f,* lengüeta *f* **2** GIBE **:** pulla *f*

barbarian[1] [bɑr'bæriən] *adj* **1 :** bárbaro **2** CRUDE **:** tosco, bruto

barbarian[2] *n* **:** bárbaro *m,* -ra *f*

barbaric [bɑr'bærɪk] *adj* **1** PRIMITIVE **:** primitivo **2** CRUEL **:** brutal, cruel

barbarity [bɑr'bærəti] *n, pl* **-ties :** barbaridad *f*

barbarous ['bɑrbərəs] *adj* **1** UNCIVILIZED **:** bárbaro **2** MERCILESS **:** despiadado, cruel

barbarously ['bɑrbərəsli] *adv* **:** bárbaramente

barbecue[1] [ˈbɑrbɪˌkjuː] *vt* **-cued; -cuing :** asar a la parrilla
barbecue[2] *n* **:** barbacoa *f,* parrillada *f*
barber [ˈbɑrbər] *n* **:** barbero *m,* -ra *f*
barbiturate [bɑrˈbɪtʃərət] *n* **:** barbitúrico *m*
bard [ˈbɑrd] *n* **:** bardo *m*
bare[1] [ˈbær] *vt* **bared; baring :** desnudar
bare[2] *adj* **1** NAKED **:** desnudo **2** EXPOSED **:** descubierto, sin protección **3** EMPTY **:** desprovisto, vacío **4** MINIMUM **:** mero, mínimo <the bare necessities : las necesidades mínimas> **5** PLAIN **:** puro, sencillo
bareback [ˈbærˌbæk] *or* **barebacked** [-ˌbækt] *adv & adj* **:** a pelo
barefaced [ˈbærˌfeɪst] *adj* **:** descarado
barefoot [ˈbærˌfʊt] *or* **barefooted** [-ˌfʊtəd] *adv & adj* **:** descalzo
bareheaded [ˈbærˈhɛdəd] *adv & adj* **:** sin sombrero, con la cabeza descubierta
barely [ˈbærli] *adv* **:** apenas, por poco
bareness [ˈbærnəs] *n* **:** desnudez *f*
bargain[1] [ˈbɑrgən] *vi* HAGGLE **:** regatear, negociar — *vt* BARTER **:** trocar, cambiar
bargain[2] *n* **1** AGREEMENT **:** acuerdo *m,* convenio *m* <to strike a bargain : cerrar un trato> **2 :** ganga *f* <bargain price : precio de ganga>
barge[1] [ˈbɑrdʒ] *vi* **barged; barging 1 :** mover con torpeza **2 to barge in :** entrometerse, interrumpir
barge[2] *n* **:** barcaza *f,* gabarra *f*
bar graph *n* **:** gráfico *m* de barras
baritone [ˈbærəˌtoːn] *n* **:** barítono *m*
barium [ˈbæriəm] *n* **:** bario *m*
bark[1] [ˈbɑrk] *vi* **:** ladrar — *vt or* **to bark out :** gritar <to bark out an order : dar una orden a gritos>
bark[2] *n* **1 :** ladrido *m* (de un perro) **2 :** corteza *f* (de un árbol) **3** *or* **barque :** tipo de embarcación con velas de proa y popa
barley [ˈbɑrli] *n* **:** cebada *f*
barn [ˈbɑrn] *n* **:** granero *m* (para cosechas), establo *m* (para ganado)
barnacle [ˈbɑrnɪkəl] *n* **:** percebe *m*
barnyard [ˈbɑrnˌjɑrd] *n* **:** corral *m*
barometer [bəˈrɑmətər] *n* **:** barómetro *m*
barometric [ˌbærəˈmɛtrɪk] *adj* **:** barométrico
baron [ˈbærən] *n* **1 :** barón *m* **2** TYCOON **:** magnate *mf*
baroness [ˈbærənɪs, -nəs, -ˌnɛs] *n* **:** baronesa *f*
baronet [ˌbærəˈnɛt, ˈbærənət] *n* **:** baronet *m*
baronial [bəˈroːniəl] *adj* **1 :** de barón **2** STATELY **:** señorial, majestuoso
baroque [bəˈroːk, -ˈrɑk] *adj* **:** barroco
barracks [ˈbærəks] *ns & pl* **:** cuartel *m*
barracuda [ˌbærəˈkuːdə] *n, pl* **-da** *or* **-das :** barracuda *f*
barrage [bəˈrɑʒ, -ˈrɑdʒ] *n* **1 :** descarga *f* (de artillería) **2** DELUGE **:** aluvión *m* <a barrage of questions : un aluvión de preguntas>
barred [ˈbɑrd] *adj* **:** excluido, prohibido
barrel[1] [ˈbærəl] *v* **-reled** *or* **-relled; -reling** *or* **-relling** *vt* **:** embarrilar — *vi* **:** ir disparado
barrel[2] *n* **1 :** barril *m,* tonel *m* **2 :** cañón *m* (de un arma de fuego), cilindro *m* (de una cerradura)
barren [ˈbærən] *adj* **1** STERILE **:** estéril (dícese de las plantas o la mujer), árido (dícese del suelo) **2** DESERTED **:** yermo, desierto
barrette [bɑˈrɛt, bə-] *n* **:** pasador *m,* broche *m* para el cabello
barricade[1] [ˈbærəˌkeɪd, ˌbærəˈ-] *vt* **-caded; -cading :** cerrar con barricadas
barricade[2] *n* **:** barricada *f*
barrier [ˈbæriər] *n* **1 :** barrera *f* **2** OBSTACLE **:** obstáculo *m,* impedimento *m*
barring [ˈbɑrɪŋ] *prep* **:** excepto, salvo, a excepción de
barrio [ˈbɑrio, ˈbær-] *n* **:** barrio *m*
barroom [ˈbɑrˌruːm, -ˌrʊm] *n* **:** bar *m*
barrow [ˈbærˌoː] → **wheelbarrow**
bartender [ˈbɑrˌtɛndər] *n* **:** camarero *m,* -ra *f;* barman *m*
barter[1] [ˈbɑrtər] *vt* **:** cambiar, trocar
barter[2] *n* **:** trueque *m,* permuta *f*
basalt [bəˈsɔlt, ˈbeɪˌ-] *n* **:** basalto *m*
base[1] [ˈbeɪs] *vt* **based; basing :** basar, fundamentar, establecer
base[2] *adj* **baser; basest 1 :** de baja ley (dícese de un metal) **2** CONTEMPTIBLE **:** vil, despreciable
base[3] *n, pl* **bases :** base *f*
baseball [ˈbeɪsˌbɔl] *n* **:** beisbol *m,* béisbol *m*
baseless [ˈbeɪsləs] *adj* **:** infundado
basely [ˈbeɪsli] *adv* **:** vilmente
basement [ˈbeɪsmənt] *n* **:** sótano *m*
baseness [ˈbeɪsnəs] *n* **:** vileza *f,* bajeza *f*
bash[1] [ˈbæʃ] *vt* **:** golpear violentamente
bash[2] *n* **1** BLOW **:** golpe *m,* porrazo *m,* madrazo *m Mex fam* **2** PARTY**:** fiesta *f,* juerga *f fam*
bashful [ˈbæʃfəl] *adj* **:** tímido, vergonzoso, penoso
bashfulness [ˈbæʃfəlnəs] *n* **:** timidez *f*
basic [ˈbeɪsɪk] *adj* **1** FUNDAMENTAL **:** básico, fundamental **2** RUDIMENTARY **:** básico, elemental **3 :** básico (en química)
basically [ˈbeɪsɪkli] *adv* **:** fundamentalmente
basil [ˈbeɪzəl, ˈbæzəl] *n* **:** albahaca *f*
basilica [bəˈsɪlɪkə] *n* **:** basílica *f*
basin [ˈbeɪsən] *n* **1** WASHBOWL **:** palangana *f,* lavamanos *m,* lavabo *m* **2 :** cuenca *f* (de un río)
basis [ˈbeɪsəs] *n, pl* **bases** [-ˌsiːz] **1** BASE **:** base *f,* pilar *m* **2** FOUNDATION **:** fundamento *m,* base *f* **3 on a weekly basis :** semanalmente

bask [ˈbæsk] *vi* : disfrutar, deleitarse <to bask in the sun : disfrutar del sol>

basket [ˈbæskət] *n* : cesta *f,* cesto *m,* canasta *f*

basketball [ˈbæskətˌbɔl] *n* : baloncesto *m,* basquetbol *m*

bas–relief [ˌbɑrɪˈliːf] *n* : bajorrelieve *m*

bass[1] [ˈbæs] *n, pl* **bass** *or* **basses** : róbalo *m* (pesca)

bass[2] [ˈbeɪs] *n* : bajo *m* (tono, voz, cantante)

bass drum *n* : bombo *m*

basset hound [ˈbæsətˌhaʊnd] *n* : basset *m*

bassinet [ˌbæsəˈnɛt] *n* : moisés *m,* cuna *f*

bassoon [bəˈsuːn, bæ-] *n* : fagot *m*

bass viol [ˈbeɪsˈvaɪəl, -ˌoːl] → **double bass**

bastard[1] [ˈbæstərd] *adj* : bastardo

bastard[2] *n* : bastardo *m,* -da *f*

bastardize [ˈbæstərˌdaɪz] *vt* **-ized; -izing** DEBASE : degradar, envilecer

baste [ˈbeɪst] *vt* **basted; basting 1** STITCH : hilvanar **2** : bañar (con su jugo durante la cocción)

bastion [ˈbæstʃən] *n* : bastión *m,* baluarte *m*

bat[1] [ˈbæt] *vt* **batted; batting 1** HIT : batear **2 without batting an eye** : sin pestañear

bat[2] *n* **1** : murciélago *m* (animal) **2** : bate *m* <baseball bat : bate de beisbol>

batch [ˈbætʃ] *n* : hornada *f,* tanda *f,* grupo *m,* cantidad *f*

bate [ˈbeɪt] *vt* **bated; bating 1** : aminorar, reducir **2 with bated breath** : con ansiedad, aguantando la respiración

bath [ˈbæθ, ˈbaθ] *n, pl* **baths** [ˈbæðz, ˈbæθs, ˈbaðz, ˈbaθs] **1** BATHING : baño *m* <to take a bath : bañarse> **2** : baño *m* (en fotografía, etc.) **3** BATHROOM : baño *m,* cuarto *m* de baño **4** SPA : balneario *m* **5** LOSS : pérdida *f*

bathe [ˈbeɪð] *v* **bathed; bathing** *vt* **1** WASH : bañar, lavar **2** SOAK : poner en remojo **3** FLOOD : inundar <to bathe with light : inundar de luz> — *vi* : bañarse, ducharse

bather [ˈbeɪðər] *n* : bañista *mf*

bathrobe [ˈbæθˌroːb] *n* : bata *f* (de baño)

bathroom [ˈbæθˌruːm, -ˌrʊm] *n* : baño *m,* cuarto *m* de baño

bathtub [ˈbæθˌtʌb] *n* : bañera *f,* tina *f* (de baño)

batiste [bəˈtiːst] *n* : batista *f*

baton [bəˈtɑn] *n* : batuta *f,* bastón *m*

battalion [bəˈtæljən] *n* : batallón *m*

batten [ˈbætən] *vt* **to batten down the hatches** : cerrar las escotillas

batter[1] [ˈbætər] *vt* **1** BEAT : aporrear, golpear **2** MISTREAT : maltratar

batter[2] *n* **1** : masa *f* para rebozar **2** HITTER : bateador *m,* -dora *f*

battering ram *n* : ariete *m*

battery [ˈbætəri] *n, pl* **-teries 1** : lesiones *fpl* <assault and battery : agresión con lesiones> **2** ARTILLERY : batería *f* **3** : batería *f,* pila *f* (de electricidad) **4** SERIES : serie *f*

batting [ˈbætɪŋ] *n* **1** *or* **cotton batting** : algodón *m* en láminas **2** : bateo *m* (en beisbol)

battle[1] [ˈbætəl] *vi* **-tled; -tling** : luchar, pelear

battle[2] *n* : batalla *f,* lucha *f,* pelea *f*

battle–ax [ˈbætəlˌæks] *n* : hacha *f* de guerra

battlefield [ˈbætəlˌfɪːld] *n* : campo *m* de batalla

battlements [ˈbætəlmənts] *npl* : almenas *fpl*

battleship [ˈbætəlˌʃɪp] *n* : acorazado *m*

batty [ˈbæti] *adj* **-tier; -est** : chiflado *fam,* chalado *fam*

bauble [ˈbɔbəl] *n* : chuchería *f,* baratija *f*

bawdiness [ˈbɔdinəs] *n* : picardía *f*

bawdy [ˈbɔdi] *adj* **bawdier; -est** : subido de tono, verde, colorado *Mex*

bawl[1] [ˈbɔl] *vi* : llorar a gritos

bawl[2] *n* : grito *m,* alarido *m*

bawl out *vt* SCOLD : regañar

bay[1] [ˈbeɪ] *vi* HOWL : aullar

bay[2] *adj* : castaño, zaino (dícese de los caballos)

bay[3] *n* **1** : bahía *f* <Bay of Campeche : Bahía de Campeche> **2** *or* **bay horse** : caballo *m* castaño **3** LAUREL : laurel *m* **4** HOWL : aullido *m* **5** : saliente *m* <bay window : ventana en saliente> **6** COMPARTMENT : área *f,* compartimento *m* **7 at ~** : acorralado

bayberry [ˈbeɪˌbɛri] *n, pl* **-ries** : arrayán *m* brabántico

bayonet[1] [ˌbeɪəˈnɛt, ˈbeɪəˌnɛt] *vt* **-neted; -neting** : herir (*o* matar) con bayoneta

bayonet[2] *n* : bayoneta *f*

bayou [ˈbaɪˌuː, -ˌoː] *n* : pantano *m*

bazaar [bəˈzɑr] *n* **1** : bazar *m* **2** SALE : venta *f* benéfica

bazooka [bəˈzuːkə] *n* : bazuca *f*

BB [ˈbiːbi] *n* : balín *m*

be [ˈbiː] *v* **was** [ˈwəz, ˈwɑz], **were** [ˈwər]; **been** [ˈbɪn]; **being; am** [ˈæm], **is** [ˈɪz], **are** [ˈɑr] *vi* **1** (*expressing equality*) : ser <José is a doctor : José es doctor> <I'm Ana's sister : soy la hermana de Ana> **2** (*expressing quality*) : ser <the tree is tall : el árbol es alto> <you're silly! : ¡eres tonto!> **3** (*expressing origin or possession*) : ser <she's from Managua : es de Managua> <it's mine : es mío> **4** (*expressing location*) : estar <my mother is at home : mi madre está en casa> <the cups are on the table : las tazas están en la mesa> **5** (*expressing existence*) : ser, existir <to be or not to be : ser, o no ser> <I think, therefore I am : pienso, luego existo> **6** (*expressing a state of being*)

: estar, tener <how are you? : ¿cómo estás?> <I'm cold : tengo frío> <she's 10 years old : tiene 10 años> <they're both sick : están enfermos los dos> — *v impers* **1** (*indicating time*) : ser <it's eight o'clock : son las ocho> <it's Friday : hoy es viernes> **2** (*indicating a condition*) : hacer, estar <it's sunny : hace sol> <it's very dark outside : está bien oscuro afuera> — *v aux* **1** (*expressing progression*) : estar <what are you doing? —I'm working : ¿qué haces? —estoy trabajando> **2** (*expressing occurrence*) : ser <it was finished yesterday : fue acabado ayer, se acabó ayer> <it was cooked in the oven : se cocinó en el horno> **3** (*expressing possibility*) : poderse <can she be trusted? : ¿se puede confiar en ella?> **4** (*expressing obligation*) : deber <you are to stay here : debes quedarte aquí> <he was to come yesterday : se esperaba que viniese ayer>

beach[1] [ˈbiːtʃ] *vt* : hacer embarrancar, hacer varar, hacer encallar

beach[2] *n* : playa *f*

beachcomber [ˈbiːtʃˌkoːmər] *n* : raquero *m*, -ra *f*

beachhead [ˈbiːtʃˌhɛd] *n* : cabeza *f* de playa

beacon [ˈbiːkən] *n* : faro *m*

bead[1] [ˈbiːd] *vi* : formarse en gotas

bead[2] *n* **1** : cuenta *f* **2** DROP : gota *f* **3 beads** *npl* NECKLACE : collar *m*

beady [ˈbiːdi] *adj* **beadier; -est 1** : de forma de cuenta **2 beady eyes** : ojos *mpl* pequeños y brillantes

beagle [ˈbiːgəl] *n* : beagle *m*

beak [ˈbiːk] *n* : pico *m*

beaker [ˈbiːkər] *n* **1** CUP : taza *f* alta **2** : vaso *m* de precipitados (en un laboratorio)

beam[1] [ˈbiːm] *vi* **1** SHINE : brillar **2** SMILE : sonreír radiantemente — *vt* BROADCAST : transmitir, emitir

beam[2] *n* **1** : viga *f*, barra *f* **2** RAY : rayo *m*, haz *m* de luz **3** : haz *m* de radiofaro (para guiar pilotos, etc.)

bean [ˈbiːn] *n* **1** : habichuela *f*, frijol *m* **2 broad bean** : haba *f* **3 string bean** : judía *f*

bear[1] [ˈbær] *v* **bore** [ˈbor]; **borne** [ˈbɔrn]; **bearing** *vt* **1** CARRY : llevar, portar **2** : dar a luz a (un niño) **3** PRODUCE : dar (frutas, cosechas) **4** ENDURE, SUPPORT : soportar, resistir, aguantar — *vi* **1** TURN : doblar, dar la vuelta <bear right : doble a la derecha> **2 to bear up** : resistir

bear[2] *n, pl* **bears** *or* **bear** : oso *m*, osa *f*

bearable [ˈbærəbəl] *adj* : soportable

beard [ˈbɪrd] *n* **1** : barba *f* **2** : arista *f* (de plantas)

bearded [ˈbɪrdəd] *adj* : barbudo, de barba

bearer [ˈbærər] *n* : portador *m*, -dora *f*

bearing [ˈbærɪŋ] *n* **1** CONDUCT, MANNERS : comportamiento *m*, modales *mpl* **2** SUPPORT : soporte *f* **3** SIGNIFICANCE : relacíon *f*, importancia *f* <to have no bearing on : no tener nada que ver con> **4** : cojinete *m*, rodamiento *m* (de una máquina) **5** COURSE, DIRECTION : dirección *f*, rumbo *m* <to get one's bearings : orientarse>

beast [ˈbiːst] *n* **1** : bestia *f*, fiera *f* <beast of burden : animal de carga> **2** BRUTE : bruto *m*, -ta *f*; bestia *mf*

beastly [ˈbiːstli] *adj* : detestable, repugnante

beat[1] [ˈbiːt] *v* **beat; beaten** [ˈbiːtən] *or* **beat; beating** *vt* **1** STRIKE : golpear, pegar, darle una paliza (a alguien) **2** DEFEAT : vencer, derrotar **3** AVOID : anticiparse a, evitar <to beat the crowd : evitar el gentío> **4** MASH, WHIP : batir — *vi* THROB : palpitar, latir

beat[2] *adj* EXHAUSTED : derrengado, muy cansado <I'm beat! : ¡estoy molido!>

beat[3] *n* **1** : golpe *m*, redoble *m* (de un tambor), latido *m* (del corazón) **2** RHYTHM : ritmo *m*, tiempo *m*

beater [ˈbiːt̬ər] *n* **1** : batidor *m*, -dora *f* **2** EGGBEATER : batidor *m*

beatific [ˌbiːəˈtɪfɪk] *adj* : beatífico

beatitude [biˈætəˌtuːd] *n* **1** : beatitud *f* **2 the Beatitudes** : las bienaventuranzas

beau [ˈboː] *n, pl* **beaux** *or* **beaus** : pretendiente *m*, galán *m*

beautification [ˌbjuːt̬əfəˈkeɪʃən] *n* : embellecimiento *m*

beautiful [ˈbjuːtɪfəl] *adj* : hermoso, bello, lindo, precioso

beautifully [ˈbjuːtɪfəli] *adv* **1** ATTRACTIVELY : hermosamente **2** EXCELLENTLY : maravillosamente, excelentemente

beauty [ˈbjuːt̬i] *n, pl* **-ties** : belleza *f*, hermosura *f*, beldad *f*

beauty shop *or* **beauty salon** *n* : salón *m* de belleza

beaver [ˈbiːvər] *n* : castor *m*

because [bɪˈkʌz, -ˈkɔz] *conj* : porque

because of *prep* : por, a causa de, debido a

beck [ˈbɛk] *n* **to be at the beck and call of** : estar a la entera disposición de, estar sometido a la voluntad de

beckon [ˈbɛkən] *vi* **to beckon to someone** : hacerle señas a alguien

become [bɪˈkʌm] *v* **-came** [-ˈkeɪm]; **-come; -coming** *vi* : hacerse, volverse, ponerse <he became famous : se hizo famoso> <to become sad : ponerse triste> <to become accustomed to : acostumbrarse a> — *vt* **1** BEFIT : ser apropiado para **2** SUIT : favorecer, quedarle bien (a alguien) <that dress becomes you : ese vestido te favorece>

becoming [bɪˈkʌmɪŋ] *adj* **1** SUITABLE : apropiado **2** FLATTERING : favorecedor

bed[1] [ˈbɛd] *v* **bedded; bedding** *vt* : acostar — *vi* : acostarse

bed[2] *n* **1** : cama *f*, lecho *m* **2** : cauce *m* (de un río), fondo *m* (del mar) **3**

: arriate *m* (para plantas) **4** LAYER, STRATUM : estrato *m,* capa *f*
bedbug [ˈbɛd,bʌg] *n* : chinche *f*
bedclothes [ˈbɛd,kloːðz, -,kloːz] *npl* : ropa *f* de cama, sábanas *fpl*
bedding [ˈbɛdɪŋ] *n* **1** → **bedclothes 2** : cama *f* (para animales)
bedeck [bɪˈdɛk] *vt* : adornar, engalanar
bedevil [bɪˈdɛvəl] *vt* **-iled** *or* **-illed; -iling** *or* **-illing** : acosar, plagar
bedlam [ˈbɛdləm] *n* : locura *f,* caos *m,* alboroto *m*
bedraggled [bɪˈdrægəld] *adj* : desaliñado, despeinado
bedridden [ˈbɛd,rɪdən] *adj* : postrado en cama
bedrock [ˈbɛd,rɑk] *n* : lecho *m* de roca
bedroom [ˈbɛd,ruːm, -,rʊm] *n* : dormitorio *m,* habitación *f,* pieza *f,* recámara *f Col, Mex, Pan*
bedspread [ˈbɛd,sprɛd] *n* : cubrecama *m,* colcha *f,* cobertor *m*
bee [ˈbiː] *n* **1** : abeja *f* (insecto) **2** GATHERING : círculo *m,* reunión *f*
beech [ˈbiːtʃ] *n, pl* **beeches** *or* **beech** : haya *f*
beechnut [ˈbiːtʃ,nʌt] *n* : hayuco *m*
beef[1] [ˈbiːf] *vt* **to beef up** : fortalecer, reforzar — *vi* COMPLAIN : quejarse
beef[2] *n, pl* **beefs** [ˈbiːfs] *or* **beeves** [ˈbiːvz] : carne *f* de vaca, carne *f* de res *CA, Mex*
beefsteak [ˈbiːf,steɪk] *n* : filete *m,* bistec *m*
beehive [ˈbiː,haɪv] *n* : colmena *f*
beekeeper [ˈbiː,kiːpər] *n* : apicultor *m,* -tora *f*
beeline [ˈbiː,laɪn] *n* **to make a beeline for** : ir derecho a, ir directo hacia
been → **be**
beep[1] [ˈbiːp] *v* : pitar
beep[2] *n* : pitido *m*
beeper [ˈbiːpər] *n* : busca *m,* buscapersonas *m*
beer [ˈbɪr] *n* : cerveza *f*
beeswax [ˈbiːz,wæks] *n* : cera *f* de abejas
beet [ˈbiːt] *n* : remolacha *f,* betabel *m Mex*
beetle [ˈbiːtəl] *n* : escarabajo *m*
befall [bɪˈfɔl] *v* **-fell** [-ˈfɛl]; **-fallen** [-ˈfɔlən] *vt* : sucederle a, acontecerle a — *vi* : acontecer
befit [bɪˈfɪt] *vt* **-fitted; -fitting** : convenir a, ser apropiado para
before[1] [bɪˈfor] *adv* **1** : antes <before and after : antes y después> **2** : anterior <the month before : el mes anterior>
before[2] *conj* : antes que <he would die before surrendering : moriría antes que rendirse>
before[3] *prep* **1** : antes de <before eating : antes de comer> **2** : delante de, ante <I stood before the house : estaba parada delante de la casa> <before the judge : ante el juez>
beforehand [bɪˈfor,hænd] *adv* : antes, por adelantado, de antemano, con anticipación
befriend [bɪˈfrɛnd] *vt* : hacerse amigo de
befuddle [bɪˈfʌdəl] *vt* **-dled; -dling** : aturdir, ofuscar, confundir
beg [ˈbɛg] *v* **begged; begging** *vt* : pedir, mendigar, suplicar <I begged him to go : le supliqué que fuera> — *vi* : mendigar, pedir limosna
beget [bɪˈgɛt] *vt* **-got** [-ˈgɑt]; **-gotten** [-ˈgɑtən] *or* **-got; -getting** : engendrar
beggar [ˈbɛgər] *n* : mendigo *m,* -ga *f;* pordiosero *m,* -ra *f*
begin [bɪˈgɪn] *v* **-gan** [-ˈgæn]; **-gun** [-ˈgʌn]; **-ginning** *vt* : empezar, comenzar, iniciar — *vi* **1** START : empezar, comenzar, iniciarse **2** ORIGINATE : nacer, originarse **3 to begin with** : en primer lugar, para empezar
beginner [bɪˈgɪnər] *n* : principiante *mf*
beginning [bɪˈgɪnɪŋ] *n* : principio *m,* comienzo *m*
begone [biˈgɔn] *interj* : ¡fuera de aquí!
begonia [bɪˈgoːnjə] *n* : begonia *f*
begrudge [bɪˈgrʌdʒ] *vt* **-grudged; -grudging 1** : dar de mala gana **2** ENVY : envidiar, resentir
beguile [bɪˈgaɪl] *vt* **-guiled; -guiling 1** DECEIVE : engañar **2** AMUSE : divertir, entretener
behalf [bɪˈhæf, -ˈhaf] *n* **1** : favor *m,* beneficio *m,* parte *f* **2 on behalf of** *or* **in behalf of** : de parte de, en nombre de
behave [bɪˈheɪv] *vi* **-haved; -having** : comportarse, portarse
behavior [bɪˈheɪvjər] *n* : comportamiento *m,* conducta *f*
behead [bɪˈhɛd] *vt* : decapitar
behest [bɪˈhɛst] *n* **1** : mandato *m,* orden *f* **2 at the behest of** : a instancia de
behind[1] [bɪˈhaɪnd] *adv* : atrás, detrás <to fall behind : quedarse atrás>
behind[2] *prep* **1** : atrás de, detrás de, tras <behind the house : detrás de la casa> <one behind another : uno tras otro> **2** : atrasado con, después de <behind schedule : atrasado con el trabajo> <I arrived behind the others : llegué después de los otros> **3** SUPPORTING : en apoyo de, detrás
behold [bɪˈhoːld] *vt* **-held; -holding** : contemplar
beholder [bɪˈhoːldər] *n* : observador *m,* -dora *f*
behoove [bɪˈhuːv] *vt* **-hooved; -hooving** : convenirle a, corresponderle a <it behooves us to help him : nos conviene ayudarlo>
beige[1] [ˈbeɪʒ] *adj* : beige
beige[2] *n* : beige *m*
being [ˈbiːɪŋ] *n* **1** EXISTENCE : ser *m,* existencia *f* **2** CREATURE : ser *m,* ente *m*
belabor [bɪˈleɪbər] *vt* **to belabor the point** : extenderse sobre el tema

belated [bɪˈleɪt̬əd] *adj* : tardío, retrasado

belch[1] [ˈbɛltʃ] *vi* **1** BURP : eructar **2** EXPEL : expulsar, arrojar

belch[2] *n* : eructo *m*

beleaguer [bɪˈliːgər] *vt* **1** BESIEGE : asediar, sitiar **2** HARASS : fastidiar, molestar

belfry [ˈbɛlfri] *n, pl* **-fries** : campanario *m*

Belgian [ˈbɛldʒən] *n* : belga *mf* — **Belgian** *adj*

belie [bɪˈlaɪ] *vt* **-lied; -lying 1** MISREPRESENT : falsear, ocultar **2** CONTRADICT : contradecir, desmentir

belief [bəˈliːf] *n* **1** TRUST : confianza *f* **2** CONVICTION : creencia *f,* convicción *f* **3** FAITH : fe *f*

believable [bəˈliːvəbəl] *adj* : verosímil, creíble

believe [bəˈliːv] *v* **-lieved; -lieving** : creer

believer [bəˈliːvər] *n* **1** : creyente *mf* **2** : partidario *m,* -ria *f;* entusiasta *mf* <she's a great believer in vitamins : ella es una gran partidaria de las vitaminas>

belittle [bɪˈlɪt̬əl] *vt* **-littled; -littling 1** DISPARAGE : menospreciar, denigrar, rebajar **2** MINIMIZE : minimizar, quitar importancia a

Belizean [bəˈliːziən] *n* : beliceño *m,* -ña *f* — **Belizean** *adj*

bell[1] [ˈbɛl] *vt* : ponerle un cascabel a

bell[2] *n* : campana *f,* cencerro *m* (para una vaca o cabra), cascabel *m* (para un gato), timbre *m* (de teléfono, de la puerta)

belladonna [ˌbɛləˈdɑnə] *n* : belladona *f*

belle [ˈbɛl] *n* : belleza *f,* beldad *f*

bellhop [ˈbɛlˌhɑp] *n* : botones *m*

bellicose [ˈbɛlɪˌkoːs] *adj* : belicoso *m* — **bellicosity** [ˌbɛlɪˈkɑsət̬i] *n*

belligerence [bəˈlɪdʒərənts] *n* : agresividad *f,* beligerancia *f*

belligerent[1] [bəˈlɪdʒərənt] *adj* : agresivo, beligerante

belligerent[2] *n* : beligerante *mf*

bellow[1] [ˈbɛˌloː] *vi* : bramar, mugir — *vt* : gritar

bellow[2] *n* : bramido *m,* grito *m*

bellows [ˈbɛˌloːz] *ns & pl* : fuelle *m*

bellwether [ˈbɛlˌwɛðər] *n* : líder *mf*

belly[1] [ˈbɛli] *vi* **-lied; -lying** SWELL : hincharse, inflarse

belly[2] *n, pl* **-lies** : abdomen *m,* vientre *m,* barriga *f,* panza *f*

belong [bɪˈlɔŋ] *vi* **1** : pertenecer (a), ser propiedad (de) <it belongs to her : pertenece a ella, es suyo, es de ella> **2** : ser parte (de), ser miembro (de) <he belongs to the club : es miembro del club> **3** : deber estar, ir <your coat belongs in the closet : tu abrigo va en el ropero>

belongings [bɪˈlɔŋɪŋz] *npl* : pertenencias *fpl,* efectos *mpl* personales

beloved[1] [bɪˈlʌvəd, -ˈlʌvd] *adj* : querido, amado

beloved[2] *n* : amado *m,* -da *f;* enamorado *m,* -da *f;* amor *m*

below[1] [bɪˈloː] *adv* : abajo

below[2] *prep* **1** : abajo de, debajo de <below the window : debajo de la ventana> **2** : por debajo de, bajo <below average : por debajo del promedio> <5 degrees below zero : 5 grados bajo cero>

belt[1] [ˈbɛlt] *vt* **1** : ceñir con un cinturón, ponerle un cinturón a **2** THRASH : darle una paliza a, darle un trancazo a

belt[2] *n* **1** : cinturón *m,* cinto *m* (para el talle) **2** BAND, STRAP : cinta *f,* correa *f,* banda *f Mex* **3** AREA : frente *m,* zona *f*

bemoan [bɪˈmoːn] *vt* : lamentarse de

bemuse [bɪˈmjuːz] *vt* **-mused; -musing 1** BEWILDER : confundir, desconcertar **2** ENGROSS : absorber

bench [ˈbɛntʃ] *n* **1** SEAT : banco *m,* escaño *m,* banca *f* **2** : estrado *m* (de un juez) **3** COURT : tribunal *m*

bend[1] [ˈbɛnd] *v* **bent** [ˈbɛnt]; **bending** *vt* : torcer, doblar, curvar, flexionar — *vi* **1** : torcerse, agacharse <to bend over : inclinarse> **2** TURN : torcer, hacer una curva

bend[2] *n* **1** TURN : vuelta *f,* recodo *m* **2** CURVE : curva *f,* ángulo *m,* codo *m*

beneath[1] [bɪˈniːθ] *adv* : bajo, abajo, debajo

beneath[2] *prep* : bajo de, abajo de, por debajo de

benediction [ˌbɛnəˈdɪkʃən] *n* : bendición *f*

benefactor [ˈbɛnəˌfæktər] *n* : benefactor *m,* -tora *f*

beneficence [bəˈnɛfəsənts] *n* : beneficencia *f*

beneficent [bəˈnɛfəsənt] *adj* : benéfico, caritativo

beneficial [ˌbɛnəˈfɪʃəl] *adj* : beneficioso, provechoso — **beneficially** *adv*

beneficiary [ˌbɛnəˈfɪʃiˌɛri, -ˈfɪʃəri] *n, pl* **-ries** : beneficiario *m,* -ria *f*

benefit[1] [ˈbɛnəfɪt] *vt* : beneficiar — *vi* : beneficiarse

benefit[2] *n* **1** ADVANTAGE : beneficio *m,* ventaja *f,* provecho *m* **2** AID : asistencia *f,* beneficio *m* **3** : función *f* benéfica (para recaudar fondos)

benevolence [bəˈnɛvələnts] *n* : bondad *f,* benevolencia *f*

benevolent [bəˈnɛvələnt] *adj* : benévolo, bondadoso — **benevolently** *adv*

Bengali [bɛnˈgɔli, bɛŋ-] *n* **1** : bengalí *mf* **2** : bengalí *m* (idioma) — **Bengali** *adj*

benign [bɪˈnaɪn] *adj* **1** GENTLE, KIND : benévolo, amable **2** FAVORABLE : propicio, favorable **3** MILD : benigno <a benign tumor : un tumor benigno>

Beninese [bəˌnɪ'niːz, -ˌniː-, -'niːs; ˌbɛnɪ'-] *n* : beninés *m,* -nesa *f* — **Beninese** *adj*

bent ['bɛnt] *n* : aptitud *f,* inclinación *f*

benumb [bɪ'nʌm] *vt* : entumecer

benzene ['bɛnˌziːn] *n* : benceno *m*

bequeath [bɪ'kwiːθ, -'kwiːð] *vt* : legar, dejar en testamento

bequest [bɪ'kwɛst] *n* : legado *m*

berate [bɪ'reɪt] *vt* **-rated; -rating** : reprender, regañar

bereaved[1] [bɪ'riːvd] *adj* : que está de luto, afligido (por la muerte de alguien)

bereaved[2] *n* **the bereaved** : los deudos del difunto (o de la difunta)

bereavement [bɪ'riːvmənt] *n* **1** SORROW : dolor *m,* pesar *m* **2** LOSS : pérdida *f*

bereft [bɪ'rɛft] *adj* : privado, desprovisto

beret [bə'reɪ] *n* : boina *f*

beriberi [ˌbɛri'bɛri] *n* : beriberi *m*

berm ['bərm] *n* : arcén *m*

berry ['bɛri] *n, pl* **-ries** : baya *f*

berserk [bər'sərk, -'zərk] *adj* **1** : enloquecido **2 to go beserk** : volverse loco

berth[1] ['bərθ] *vi* : atracar

berth[2] *n* **1** DOCK : atracadero *m* **2** ACCOMMODATION : litera *f,* camarote *m* **3** POSITION : trabajo *m,* puesto *m*

beryl ['bɛrəl] *n* : berilo *m*

beseech [bɪ'siːtʃ] *vt* **-sought** [-'sɔt] *or* **-seeched; -seeching** : suplicar, implorar, rogar

beset [bɪ'sɛt] *vt* **-set; -setting 1** HARASS : acosar **2** SURROUND : rodear

beside [bɪ'saɪd] *prep* : al lado de, junto a

besides[1] [bɪ'saɪdz] *adv* **1** ALSO : además, también, aparte **2** MOREOVER : además, por otra parte

besides[2] *prep* **1** : además de, aparte de <six others besides you : seis otros además de ti> **2** EXCEPT : excepto, fuera de, aparte de

besiege [bɪ'siːdʒ] *vt* **-sieged; -sieging** : asediar, sitiar, cercar

besmirch [bɪ'smərtʃ] *vt* : ensuciar, mancillar

best[1] ['bɛst] *vt* : superar, ganar a

best[2] *adv* (*superlative of* **well**) : mejor <as best I can : lo mejor que puedo>

best[3] *adj* (*superlative of* **good**) : mejor <my best friend : mi mejor amigo>

best[4] *n* **1 the best** : lo mejor, el mejor, la mejor, los mejores, las mejores **2 at ~** : a lo más **3 to do one's best** : hacer todo lo posible

bestial ['bɛstʃəl, 'biːs-] *adj* **1** : bestial **2** BRUTISH : brutal, salvaje

best man *n* : padrino *m*

bestow [bɪ'stoː] *vt* : conferir, otorgar, conceder

bestowal [bɪ'stoːəl] *n* : concesión *f,* otorgamiento *m*

bet[1] ['bɛt] *v* **bet; betting** *vt* : apostar — *vi* **to bet on** : apostarle a

bet[2] *n* : apuesta *f*

betoken [bɪ'toːkən] *vt* : denotar, ser indicio de

betray [bɪ'treɪ] *vt* **1** : traicionar <to betray one's country : traicionar uno a su patria> **2** DIVULGE, REVEAL : delatar, revelar <to betray a secret : revelar un secreto>

betrayal [bɪ'treɪəl] *n* : traición *f,* delación *f,* revelación *f* <betrayal of trust : abuso de confianza>

betrothal [bɪ'troːðəl, -'trɔ-] *n* : esponsales *mpl,* compromiso *m*

betrothed [bɪ'troːðd, -'trɔθt] *n* FIANCÉ : prometido *m,* -da *f*

better[1] ['bɛt̬ər] *vt* **1** IMPROVE : mejorar **2** SURPASS : superar

better[2] *adv* (*comparative of* **well**) **1** : mejor **2** MORE : más <better than 50 miles : más de 50 millas>

better[3] *adj* (*comparative of* **good**) **1** : mejor <the weather is better today : hace mejor tiempo hoy> <I was sick, but now I'm better : estuve enfermo, pero ahora estoy mejor> **2** : mayor <the better part of a month : la mayor parte de un mes>

better[4] *n* **1** : el mejor, la mejor <the better of the two : el mejor de los dos> **2 to get the better of** : vencer a, quedar por encima de, superar

betterment ['bɛt̬ərmənt] *n* : mejoramiento *m,* mejora *f*

bettor *or* **better** ['bɛt̬ər] *n* : apostador *m,* -dora *f*

between[1] [bɪ'twiːn] *adv* **1** : en medio, por lo medio **2 in ~** : intermedio

between[2] *prep* : entre

bevel[1] ['bɛvəl] *v* **-eled** *or* **-elled; -eling** *or* **-elling** *vt* : biselar — *vi* INCLINE : inclinarse

bevel[2] *n* : bisel *m*

beverage ['bɛvrɪdʒ, 'bɛvə-] *n* : bebida *f*

bevy ['bɛvi] *n, pl* **bevies** : grupo *m* (de personas), bandada *f* (de pájaros)

bewail [bɪ'weɪl] *vt* : lamentarse de, llorar

beware [bɪ'wær] *vi* **to beware of** : tener cuidado con <beware of the dog! : ¡cuidado con el perro!> — *vt* : guardarse de, cuidarse de

bewilder [bɪ'wɪldər] *vt* : desconcertar, dejar perplejo

bewilderment [bɪ'wɪldərmənt] *n* : desconcierto *m,* perplejidad *f*

bewitch [bɪ'wɪtʃ] *vt* **1** : hechizar, embrujar **2** CHARM : cautivar, encantar

bewitchment [bɪ'wɪtʃmənt] *n* : hechizo *m*

beyond[1] [bi'jɑnd] *adv* **1** FARTHER, LATER : más allá, más lejos (en el espacio), más adelante (en el tiempo) **2** MORE : más <$50 and beyond : $50 o más>

beyond[2] *n* **the beyond** : el más allá, lo desconocido

beyond[3] *prep* **1** : más allá de <beyond the frontier : más allá de la frontera>

2 : fuera de <beyond one's reach : fuera de su alcance> 3 BESIDES : además de

biannual [ˌbaɪˈænjʊəl] *adj* : bianual — **biannually** *adv*

bias[1] [ˈbaɪəs] *vt* **-ased** *or* **-assed; -asing** *or* **-assing 1** : predisponer, sesgar, influir en, afectar **2 to be biased against** : tener prejuicio contra

bias[2] *n* **1** : sesgo *m,* bies *m* (en la costura) **2** PREJUDICE : prejuicio *m* **3** TENDENCY : inclinación *f,* tendencia *f*

biased [ˈbaɪəst] *adj* : tendencioso, parcial

bib [ˈbɪb] *n* **1** : peto *m* **2** : babero *m* (para niños)

Bible [ˈbaɪbəl] *n* : Biblia *f*

biblical [ˈbɪblɪkəl] *adj* : bíblico

bibliographer [ˌbɪbliˈɑgrəfər] *n* : bibliógrafo *m,* -fa *f*

bibliographic [ˌbɪbliəˈgræfɪk] *adj* : bibliográfico

bibliography [ˌbɪbliˈɑgrəfi] *n, pl* **-phies** : bibliografía *f*

bicameral [ˌbaɪˈkæmərəl] *adj* : bicameral

bicarbonate [ˌbaɪˈkɑrbənət, -ˌneɪt] *n* : bicarbonato *m*

bicentennial [ˌbaɪsɛnˈtɛniəl] *n* : bicentenario *m*

biceps [ˈbaɪˌsɛps] *ns & pl* : bíceps *m*

bicker[1] [ˈbɪkər] *vi* : pelear, discutir, reñir

bicker[2] *n* : pelea *f,* riña *f,* discusión *f*

bicuspid [baɪˈkʌspɪd] *n* : premolar *m,* diente *m* bicúspide

bicycle[1] [ˈbaɪsɪkəl, -ˌsɪ-] *vi* **-cled; -cling** : ir en bicicleta

bicycle[2] *n* : bicicleta *f*

bicycling [ˈbaɪsɪkəlɪŋ] *n* : ciclismo *m*

bicyclist [ˈbaɪsɪkəlɪst] *n* : ciclista *mf*

bid[1] [ˈbɪd] *vt* **bade** [ˈbæd, ˈbeɪd] *or* **bid; bidden** [ˈbɪdən] *or* **bid; bidding 1** ORDER : pedir, mandar **2** INVITE : invitar **3** SAY : dar, decir <to bid good evening : dar las buenas noches> <to bid farewell to : decir adiós a> **4** : ofrecer (en una subasta), declarar (en juegos de cartas)

bid[2] *n* **1** OFFER : oferta *f* (en una subasta), declaración *f* (en juegos de cartas) **2** INVITATION : invitación *f* **3** ATTEMPT : intento *m,* tentativa *f*

bidder [ˈbɪdər] *n* : postor *m,* -tora *f*

bide [ˈbaɪd] *v* **bode** [ˈboːd] *or* **bided; bided; biding** *vt* : esperar, aguardar <to bide one's time : esperar el momento oportuno> — *vi* DWELL : morar, vivir

biennial [baɪˈɛniəl] *adj* : bienal — **biennially** *adv*

bier [ˈbɪr] *n* **1** STAND : andas *fpl* **2** COFFIN : ataúd *m,* féretro *m*

bifocals [ˈbaɪˌfoːkəlz] *npl* : lentes *mpl* bifocales, bifocales *mpl*

big [ˈbɪg] *adj* **bigger; biggest 1** LARGE : grande **2** PREGNANT : embarazada **3** IMPORTANT, MAJOR : importante, grande <a big decision : una gran decisión> **4** POPULAR : popular, famoso, conocido

bigamist [ˈbɪgəmɪst] *n* : bígamo *m,* -ma *f*

bigamous [ˈbɪgəməs] *adj* : bígamo

bigamy [ˈbɪgəmi] *n* : bigamia *f*

Big Dipper → **dipper**

bighorn [ˈbɪgˌhɔrn] *n, pl* **-horn** *or* **-horns** *or* **bighorn sheep** : oveja *f* salvaje de las montañas

bight [ˈbaɪt] *n* : bahía *f,* ensenada *f,* golfo *m*

bigot [ˈbɪgət] *n* : intolerante *mf*

bigoted [ˈbɪgət̬əd] *adj* : intolerante, prejuiciado, fanático

bigotry [ˈbɪgətri] *n, pl* **-tries** : intolerancia *f,* fanaticismo *m*

big shot *n* : pez *m* gordo *fam,* mandamás *mf*

bigwig [ˈbɪgˌwɪg] → **big shot**

bike [ˈbaɪk] *n* **1** : bicicleta *f,* bici *f fam* **2** : motocicleta *f,* moto *f*

bikini [bəˈkiːni] *n* : bikini *m*

bilateral [baɪˈlæt̬ərəl] *adj* : bilateral — **bilaterally** *adv*

bile [ˈbaɪl] *n* **1** : bilis *f* **2** IRRITABILITY : mal genio *m*

bilingual [baɪˈlɪŋgwəl] *adj* : bilingüe

bilious [ˈbɪliəs] *adj* **1** : bilioso **2** IRRITABLE : bilioso, colérico

bilk [ˈbɪlk] *vt* : burlar, estafar, defraudar

bill[1] [ˈbɪl] *vt* : pasarle la cuenta a — *vi* : acariciar <to bill and coo : acariciarse>

bill[2] *n* **1** LAW : proyecto *m* de ley, ley *f* **2** INVOICE : cuenta *f,* factura *f* **3** POSTER : cartel *m* **4** PROGRAM : programa *m* (del teatro) **5** : billete *m* <a five-dollar bill : un billete de cinco dólares> **6** BEAK : pico *m*

billboard [ˈbɪlˌbord] *n* : cartelera *f*

billet[1] [ˈbɪlət] *vt* : acuartelar, alojar

billet[2] *n* : alojamiento *m*

billfold [ˈbɪlˌfoːld] *n* : billetera *f,* cartera *f*

billiards [ˈbɪljərdz] *n* : billar *m*

billion [ˈbɪljən] *n, pl* **billions** *or* **billion** : mil millones *mpl*

billow[1] [ˈbɪlo] *vi* : hincharse, inflarse

billow[2] *n* **1** WAVE : ola *f* **2** CLOUD : nube *f* <a billow of smoke : un nube de humo>

billowy [ˈbɪlowi] *adj* : ondulante

billy goat [ˈbɪliˌgoːt] *n* : macho *m* cabrío

bin [ˈbɪn] *n* : cubo *m,* cajón *m*

binary [ˈbaɪnəri, -ˌnɛri] *adj* : binario *m*

bind [ˈbaɪnd] *vt* **bound** [ˈbaʊnd]; **binding 1** TIE : atar, amarrar **2** OBLIGATE : obligar **3** UNITE : aglutinar, ligar, unir **4** BANDAGE : vendar **5** : encuadernar (un libro)

binder [ˈbaɪndər] *n* **1** FOLDER : carpeta *f* **2** : encuadernador *m,* -dora *f* (de libros)

binding [ˈbaɪndɪŋ] *n* **1** : encuadernación *f* (de libros) **2** COVER : cubierta *f,* forro *m*

binge [ˈbɪndʒ] *n* **:** juerga *f*, parranda *f fam*

bingo [ˈbɪŋˌgoː] *n, pl* **-gos :** bingo *m*

binocular [baɪˈnɑkjələr, bə-] *adj* **:** binocular

binoculars [bəˈnɑkjələrz, baɪ-] *npl* **:** binoculares *mpl*

biochemical[1] [ˌbaɪoˈkɛmɪkəl] *adj* **:** bioquímico

biochemical[2] *n* **:** bioquímico *m*

biochemist [ˌbaɪoˈkɛmɪst] *n* **:** bioquímico *m*, -ca *f*

biochemistry [ˌbaɪoˈkɛməstri] *n* **:** bioquímica *f*

biodegradable [ˌbaɪodɪˈgreɪdəbəl] *adj* **:** biodegradable

biodegradation [ˌbaɪodɛgrəˈdeɪʃən] *n* **:** biodegradación *f*

biodegrade [ˌbaɪodɪˈgreɪd] *vi* **-graded; -grading :** biodegradarse

biographer [baɪˈɑgrəfər] *n* **:** biógrafo *m*, -fa *f*

biographical [ˌbaɪəˈgræfɪkəl] *adj* **:** biográfico

biography [baɪˈɑgrəfi, biː-] *n, pl* **-phies :** biografía *f*

biologic [ˌbaɪəˈlɑdʒɪk] *or* **biological** [-dʒɪkəl] *adj* **:** biológico

biologist [baɪˈɑlədʒɪst] *n* **:** biólogo *m*, -ga *f*

biology [baɪˈɑlədʒi] *n* **:** biología *f*

biophysical [ˌbaɪoˈfɪzɪkəl] *adj* **:** biofísico

biophysicist [ˌbaɪoˈfɪzəsɪst] *n* **:** biofísico *m*, -ca *f*

biophysics [ˌbaɪoˈfɪzɪks] *ns & pl* **:** biofísica *f*

biopsy [ˈbaɪˌɑpsi] *n, pl* **-sies :** biopsia *f*

biotechnology [ˌbaɪotɛkˈnɑlədʒi] *n* **:** biotecnología *f*

biotic [baɪˈɑtɪk] *adj* **:** biótico

bipartisan [baɪˈpɑrtəzən, -sən] *adj* **:** bipartidista, de dos partidas

biped [ˈbaɪˌpɛd] *n* **:** bípedo *m*

birch [ˈbərtʃ] *n* **:** abedul *m*

bird [ˈbərd] *n* **:** pájaro *m* (pequeño), ave *f* (grande)

birdbath [ˈbərdˌbæθ, -ˌbaθ] *n* **:** pila *f* para pájaros

bird dog *n* **:** perro *m*, -rra *f* de caza

bird of prey *n* **:** ave *f* rapaz, ave *f* de presa

birdseed [ˈbərdˌsiːd] *n* **:** alpiste *m*

bird's–eye [ˈbərdzˌaɪ] *adj* **1 :** visto desde arriba <bird's-eye view : vista aérea> **2** CURSORY **:** rápido, somero

birth [ˈbərθ] *n* **1 :** nacimiento *m*, parto *m* **2** ORIGIN **:** origen *m*, nacimiento *m*

birthday [ˈbərθˌdeɪ] *n* **:** cumpleaños *m*, aniversario *m*

birthmark [ˈbərθˌmɑrk] *n* **:** mancha *f* de nacimiento

birthplace [ˈbərθˌpleɪs] *n* **:** lugar *m* de nacimiento

birthrate [ˈbərθˌreɪt] *n* **:** índice *m* de natalidad

birthright [ˈbərθˌraɪt] *n* **:** derecho *m* de nacimiento

biscuit [ˈbɪskət] *n* **:** bizcocho *m*

bisect [ˈbaɪˌsɛkt, ˌbaɪˈ-] *vt* **:** bisecar

bisector [ˈbaɪˌsɛktər, ˌbaɪˈ-] *n* **:** bisectriz *f*

bishop [ˈbɪʃəp] *n* **:** obispo *m*

bismuth [ˈbɪzməθ] *n* **:** bismuto *m*

bison [ˈbaɪzən, -sən] *ns & pl* **:** bisonte *m*

bistro [ˈbiːstro, ˈbɪs-] *n, pl* **-tros :** bar *m*, restaurante *m* pequeño

bit [ˈbɪt] *n* **1** FRAGMENT, PIECE **:** pedazo *m*, trozo *m* <a bit of luck : un poco de suerte> **2 :** freno *m*, bocado *m* (de una brida) **3 :** broca *f* (de un taladro) **4 :** bit *m* (de información)

bitch[1] [ˈbɪtʃ] *vi* COMPLAIN **:** quejarse, reclamar

bitch[2] *n* **:** perra *f*

bite[1] [ˈbaɪt] *v* **bit** [ˈbɪt]; **bitten** [ˈbɪtən]; **biting** *vt* **1 :** morder **2** STING **:** picar **3** PUNCTURE **:** punzar, pinchar **4** GRIP **:** agarrar — *vi* **1 :** morder <that dog bites : ese perro muerde> **2** STING **:** picar (dícese de un insecto), cortar (dícese del viento) **3 :** picar <the fish are biting now : ya están picando los peces> **4** GRAB **:** agarrarse

bite[2] *n* **1** BITING **:** mordisco *m*, dentellada *f* **2** SNACK **:** bocado *m* <a bite to eat : algo de comer> **3 :** picadura *f* (de un insecto), mordedura *f* (de un animal) **4** SHARPNESS **:** mordacidad *f*, penetración *f*

biting *adj* **1** PENETRATING **:** cortante, penetrante **2** CAUSTIC **:** mordaz, sarcástico

bitter [ˈbɪtər] *adj* **1** ACRID **:** amargo, acre **2** PENETRATING **:** cortante, penetrante <bitter cold : frío glacial> **3** HARSH **:** duro, amargo <to the bitter end : hasta el final> **4** INTENSE, RELENTLESS **:** intenso, extremo, implacable <bitter hatred : odio implacable>

bitterly [ˈbɪtərli] *adv* **:** amargamente

bittern [ˈbɪtərn] *n* **:** avetoro *m* común

bitterness [ˈbɪtərnəs] *n* **:** amargura *f*

bituminous coal [bəˈtuːmənəs, -ˈtjuː-] *n* **:** carbón *m* bituminoso

bivalve [ˈbaɪˌvælv] *n* **:** bivalvo *m* — **bivalve** *adj*

bivouac[1] [ˈbɪvəˌwæk, ˈbɪvˌwæk] *vi* **-ouacked; -ouacking :** acampar, vivaquear

bivouac[2] *n* **:** vivaque *m*

bizarre [bəˈzɑr] *adj* **:** extraño, singular, estrafalario, estrambótico — **bizarrely** *adv*

blab [ˈblæb] *vi* **blabbed; blabbing :** parlotear *fam*, cotorrear *fam*

black[1] [ˈblæk] *vt* **:** ennegrecer

black[2] *adj* **1 :** negro (color, raza) **2** SOILED **:** sucio **3** DARK **:** oscuro, negro **4** WICKED **:** malvado, perverso, malo **5** GLOOMY **:** negro, sombrío, deprimente

black[3] *n* **1 :** negro *m* (color) **2 :** negro *m*, -gra *f* (persona)

black–and–blue [ˌblækənˈbluː] *adj* **:** amoratado

blackball [ˈblæk,bɔl] *vt* **1** OSTRACIZE : hacerle el vacío a, aislar **2** BOYCOTT : boicotear
blackberry [ˈblæk,bɛri] *n, pl* **-ries** : mora *f*
blackbird [ˈblæk,bərd] *n* : mirlo *m*
blackboard [ˈblæk,bɔrd] *n* : pizarra *f,* pizarrón *m*
blacken [ˈblækən] *vt* **1** BLACK : ennegrecer **2** DEFAME : deshonrar, difamar, manchar
blackhead [ˈblæk,hɛd] *n* : espinilla *f,* punto *m* negro
black hole *n* : agujero *m* negro
blackjack [ˈblæk,jæk] *n* **1** : cachiporra *f* (arma) **2** : veintiuna *f* (juego de cartas)
blacklist¹ [ˈblæk,lɪst] *vt* : poner en la lista negra
blacklist² *n* : lista *f* negra
blackmail¹ [ˈblæk,meɪl] *vt* : chantajear, hacer chantaje a
blackmail² *n* : chantaje *m*
blackmailer [ˈblæk,meɪlər] *n* : chantajista *mf*
blackout [ˈblæk,aʊt] *n* **1** : apagón *m* (de poder eléctrico) **2** FAINT : desmayo *m,* desvanecimiento *m*
black out *vt* : dejar sin luz — *vi* FAINT : perder el conocimiento, desmayarse
blacksmith [ˈblæk,smɪθ] *n* : herrero *m*
blacktop [ˈblæk,tɑp] *n* : asfalto *m*
bladder [ˈblædər] *n* : vejiga *f*
blade [ˈbleɪd] *n* : hoja *f* (de un cuchillo), cuchilla *f* (de un patín), pala *f* (de un remo o una hélice), brizna *f* (de hierba)
blamable [ˈbleɪməbəl] *adj* : culpable
blame¹ [ˈbleɪm] *vt* **blamed; blaming** : culpar, echar la culpa a
blame² *n* : culpa *f*
blameless [ˈbleɪmləs] *adj* : intachable, sin culpa, inocente — **blamelessly** *adv*
blameworthiness [ˈbleɪm,wərðinəs] *n* : culpa *f,* culpabilidad *f*
blameworthy [ˈbleɪm,wərði] *adj* : culpable, reprochable, censurable
blanch [ˈblæntʃ] *vt* WHITEN : blanquear — *vi* PALE : palidecer
bland [ˈblænd] *adj* : soso, insulso, desabrido <a bland smile : una sonrisa insulsa> <a bland diet : una dieta fácil de digerir>
blandishments [ˈblændɪʃmənts] *npl* : lisonjas *fpl,* halagos *mpl*
blandly [ˈblændli] *adv* : de manera insulsa
blandness [ˈblændnəs] *n* : lo insulso, lo desabrido
blank¹ [ˈblæŋk] *vt* OBLITERATE : borrar
blank² *adj* **1** DAZED : perplejo, desconcertado **2** EXPRESSIONLESS : sin expresión, inexpresivo **3** : en blanco (dícese de un papel), liso (dícese de una pared) **4** EMPTY : vacío, en blanco <a blank stare : una mirada vacía> <his mind went blank : se quedó en blanco>
blank³ *n* **1** SPACE : espacio *m* en blanco **2** FORM : formulario *m* **3** CARTRIDGE : cartucho *m* de fogueo **4** *or* **blank key** : llave *f* ciega
blanket¹ [blæŋkət] *vt* : cubrir
blanket² *adj* : global
blanket³ *n* : manta *f,* cobija *f,* frazada *f*
blankly [ˈblænkli] *adv* : sin comprender
blankness [ˈblænknəs] *n* **1** PERPLEXITY : desconcierto *m,* perplejidad *f* **2** EMPTINESS : vacío *m,* vacuidad *f*
blare¹ [ˈblær] *vi* **blared; blaring** : resonar
blare² *n* : estruendo *m*
blarney [ˈblɑrni] *n* : labia *f fam*
blasé [blɑˈzeɪ] *adj* : displicente, indiferente
blaspheme [blæsˈfiːm, ˈblæs,-] *vi* **-phemed; -pheming** : blasfemar
blasphemer [blæsˈfiːmər, ˈblæs,-] *n* : blasfemo *m,* -ma *f*
blasphemous [ˈblæsfəməs] *adj* : blasfemo
blasphemy [ˈblæsfəmi] *n, pl* **-mies** : blasfemia *f*
blast¹ [ˈblæst] *vt* **1** BLOW UP : volar, hacer volar **2** ATTACK : atacar, arremeter contra
blast² *n* **1** GUST : ráfaga *f* **2** EXPLOSION : explosión *f*
blast-off [ˈblæst,ɔf] *n* : despegue *m*
blast off *vi* : despegar
blatant [ˈbleɪtənt] *adj* : descarado — **blatantly** [ˈbleɪtəntli] *adv*
blaze¹ [ˈbleɪz] *v* **blazed; blazing** *vi* SHINE : arder, brillar, resplandecer — *vt* MARK : marcar, señalar <to blaze a trail : abrir un camino>
blaze² *n* **1** FIRE : fuego *m* **2** BRIGHTNESS : resplandor *m,* brillantez *f* **3** OUTBURST : arranque *m* <a blaze of anger : un arranque de cólera> **4** DISPLAY : alarde *m,* llamarada *f* <a blaze of color : un derroche de color>
blazer [ˈbleɪzər] *n* : chaqueta *f* deportiva, blazer *m*
bleach¹ [ˈbliːtʃ] *vt* : blanquear, decolorar
bleach² *n* : lejía *f,* blanqueador *m*
bleachers [ˈbliːtʃərz] *ns & pl* : gradas *fpl,* tribuna *f* descubierta
bleak [ˈbliːk] *adj* **1** DESOLATE : inhóspito, sombrío, desolado **2** DEPRESSING : deprimente, triste, sombrío
bleakly [ˈbliːkli] *adv* : sombríamente
bleakness [ˈbliːknəs] *n* : lo inhóspito, lo sombrío
blear [ˈblɪr] *adj* : empañado, nublado
bleary [ˈblɪri] *adj* **1** : adormilado, fatigado **2** **bleary–eyed** : con los ojos nublados
bleat¹ [ˈbliːt] *vi* : balar
bleat² *n* : balido *m*
bleed [ˈbliːd] *v* **bled** [ˈblɛd]; **bleeding** *vi* **1** : sangrar **2** GRIEVE : sufrir, afligirse **3** EXUDE : exudar (dícese de una planta), correrse (dícese de los colo-

res) — *vt* **1** : sangrar (a una persona), purgar (frenos) **2 to bleed someone dry** : sacarle todo el dinero a alguien

blemish[1] [ˈblɛmɪʃ] *vt* : manchar, marcar

blemish[2] *n* : imperfección *f,* mancha *f,* marca *f*

blend[1] [ˈblɛnd] *vt* **1** MIX : mezclar **2** COMBINE : combinar, aunar

blend[2] *n* : mezcla *f,* combinación *f*

blender [ˈblɛndər] *n* : licuadora *f*

bless [ˈblɛs] *vt* **blessed** [ˈblɛst]; **blessing 1** CONSECRATE : bendecir, consagrar **2** : bendecir <may God bless you! : ¡que Dios te bendiga!> **3 to bless with** : dotar de **4 to bless oneself** : santiguarse

blessed [ˈblɛsəd] *or* **blest** [ˈblɛst] *adj* : bienaventurado, bendito, dichoso

blessedly [ˈblɛsədli] *adv* : felizmente, alegremente, afortunadamente

blessing [ˈblɛsɪŋ] *n* **1** : bendición *f* **2** APPROVAL : aprobación *f,* consentimiento *m*

blew → **blow**

blight[1] [ˈblaɪt] *vt* : arruinar, infestar

blight[2] *n* **1** : añublo *m* **2** PLAGUE : peste *f,* plaga *f* **3** DECAY : deterioro *m,* ruina *f*

blimp [ˈblɪmp] *n* : dirigible *m*

blind[1] [ˈblaɪnd] *vt* **1** : cegar, dejar ciego **2** DAZZLE : deslumbrar

blind[2] *adj* **1** SIGHTLESS : ciego **2** INSENSITIVE : ciego, insensible, sin razón **3** CLOSED : sin salida <blind alley : callejón sin salida>

blind[3] *n* **1** : persiana *f* (para una ventana) **2** COVER : escondite *m,* escondrijo *m*

blindfold[1] [ˈblaɪnd,foːld] *vt* : vendar los ojos

blindfold[2] *n* : venda *f* (para los ojos)

blindly [ˈblaɪndli] *adv* : a ciegas, ciegamente

blindness [ˈblaɪndnəs] *n* : ceguera *f*

blink[1] [ˈblɪŋk] *vi* **1** WINK : pestañear, parpadear **2** : brillar intermitentemente

blink[2] *n* : pestañeo *m,* parpadeo *m*

blinker [ˈblɪŋkər] *n* : intermitente *m,* direccional *f*

bliss [ˈblɪs] *n* **1** HAPPINESS : dicha *f,* felicidad *f* absoluta **2** PARADISE : paraíso *m*

blissful [ˈblɪsfəl] *adj* : dichoso, feliz — **blissfully** *adv*

blister[1] [ˈblɪstər] *vi* : ampollarse

blister[2] *n* : ampolla *f* (en la piel o una superficie), burbuja *f* (en una superficie)

blithe [ˈblaɪθ, ˈblaɪð] *adj* **blither; blithest 1** CAREFREE : despreocupado **2** CHEERFUL : alegre, risueño — **blithely** *adv*

blitz[1] [ˈblɪts] *vt* **1** BOMBARD : bombardear **2** : atacar con rapidez

blitz[2] *n* **1** : bombardeo *m* aéreo **2** CAMPAIGN : ataque *m,* acometida *f*

blizzard [ˈblɪzərd] *n* : tormenta *f* de nieve, ventisca *f*

bloat [ˈbloːt] *vi* : hincharse, inflarse

blob [ˈblɑb] *n* : gota *f,* mancha *f,* borrón *m*

bloc [ˈblɑk] *n* : bloque *m*

block[1] [ˈblɑk] *vt* **1** OBSTRUCT : obstruir, bloquear **2** CLOG : atascar, atorar

block[2] *n* **1** PIECE : bloque *m* <building blocks : cubos de construcción> <auction block : plataforma de subastas> <starting block : taco de salida> **2** OBSTRUCTION : obstrucción *f,* bloqueo *m* **3** : cuadra *f,* manzana *f* (de edificios) <to go around the block : dar la vuelta a la cuadra> **4** BUILDING : edificio *m* (de apartamentos, oficinas, etc.) **5** GROUP, SERIES : serie *f,* grupo *m* <a block of tickets : una serie de entradas> **6 block and tackle** : aparejo *m* de poleas

blockade[1] [blɑˈkeɪd] *vt* **-aded; -ading** : bloquear

blockade[2] *n* : bloqueo *m*

blockage [ˈblɑkɪdʒ] *n* : bloqueo *m,* obstrucción *f*

blockhead [ˈblɑk,hɛd] *n* : bruto *m,* -ta *f;* estúpido *m,* -da *f*

blond[1] *or* **blonde** [ˈblɑnd] *adj* : rubio, güero *Mex,* claro (dícese de la madera)

blond[2] *or* **blonde** *n* : rubio *m,* -bia *f;* güero *m,* -ra *f Mex*

blood [ˈblʌd] *n* **1** : sangre *f* **2** LIFEBLOOD : vida *f,* alma *f* **3** LINEAGE : linaje *m,* sangre *f*

blood bank *n* : banco *m* de sangre

bloodcurdling [ˈblʌd,kərdəlɪŋ] *adj* : espeluznante, aterrador

blooded [ˈblʌdəd] *adj* : de sangre <cold-blooded animal : animal de sangre fría>

bloodhound [ˈblʌd,haʊnd] *n* : sabueso *m*

bloodless [ˈblʌdləs] *adj* **1** : incruento, sin derramamiento de sangre **2** LIFELESS : desanimado, insípido, sin vida

bloodmobile [ˈblʌdmo,biːl] *n* : unidad *f* móvil para donantes de sangre

blood pressure *n* : tensión *f,* presión *f* (arterial)

bloodshed [ˈblʌd,ʃɛd] *n* : derramamiento *m* de sangre

bloodshot [ˈblʌd,ʃɑt] *adj* : inyectado de sangre

bloodstain [ˈblʌd,steɪn] *n* : mancha *f* de sangre

bloodstained [ˈblʌd,steɪnd] *adj* : manchado de sangre

bloodstream [ˈblʌd,striːm] *n* : torrente *m* sanguíneo, corriente *f* sanguínea

bloodsucker [ˈblʌd,sʌkər] *n* : sanguijuela *f*

bloodthirsty [ˈblʌd,θərsti] *adj* : sanguinario

blood vessel *n* : vaso *m* sanguíneo

bloody [ˈblʌdi] *adj* **bloodier; -est** : ensangrentado, sangriento

bloom[1] [ˈbluːm] *vi* **1** FLOWER : florecer **2** MATURE : madurar
bloom[2] *n* **1** FLOWER : flor *f* <to be in bloom : estar en flor> **2** FLOWERING : floración *f* <in full bloom : en plena floración> **3** : rubor *m* (de la tez) <in the bloom of youth : en plena juventud, en la flor de la vida>
bloomers [ˈbluːmərz] *npl* : bombachos *mpl*
blooper [ˈbluːpər] *n* : metedura *f* de pata *fam*
blossom[1] [ˈblɑsəm] *vi* : florecer, dar flor
blossom[2] *n* : flor *f*
blot[1] [ˈblɑt] *vt* **blotted; blotting 1** SPOT : emborronar, borronear **2** DRY : secar
blot[2] *n* **1** STAIN : mancha *f,* borrón *m* **2** BLEMISH : mancha *f,* tacha *f*
blotch[1] [ˈblɑtʃ] *vt* : emborronar, borronear
blotch[2] *n* : mancha *f,* borrón *m*
blotchy [ˈblɑtʃi] *adj* **blotchier; -est** : lleno de manchas
blotter [ˈblɑtər] *n* : hoja *f* de papel secante, secante *m*
blouse [ˈblaʊs, ˈblaʊz] *n* : blusa *f*
blow[1] [ˈbloː] *v* **blew** [ˈbluː]; **blown** [ˈbloːn]; **blowing** *vi* **1** : soplar, volar <the wind is blowing hard : el viento está soplando con fuerza> <it blew out the door : voló por la puerta> <the window blew shut : se cerró la ventana> **2** SOUND : sonar <the whistle blew : sonó el silbato> **3 to blow out** : fundirse (dícese de un fusible eléctrico), reventarse (dícese de una llanta) — *vt* **1** : soplar, echar <to blow smoke : echar humo> **2** SOUND : tocar, sonar **3** SHAPE : soplar, dar forma a <to blow glass : soplar vidrio> **4** BUNGLE : echar a perder
blow[2] *n* **1** PUFF : soplo *m,* soplido *m* **2** GALE : vendaval *f* **3** HIT, STROKE : golpe *m* **4** CALAMITY : golpe *m,* desastre *m* **5 to come to blows** : llegar a las manos
blower [ˈbloːər] *n* FAN : ventilador *m*
blowout [ˈbloːˌaʊt] *n* : reventón *m*
blowtorch [ˈbloːˌtɔrtʃ] *n* : soplete *m*
blow up *vi* EXPLODE : estallar, hacer explosión — *vt* BLAST : volar, hacer volar
blubber[1] [ˈblʌbər] *vi* : lloriquear
blubber[2] *n* : esperma *f* de ballena
bludgeon [ˈblʌdʒən] *vt* : aporrear
blue[1] [ˈbluː] *adj* **bluer; bluest 1** : azul **2** MELANCHOLY : melancólico, triste
blue[2] *n* : azul *m*
blueberry [ˈbluːˌbɛri] *n, pl* **-ries** : arándano *m*
bluebird [ˈbluːˌbərd] *n* : azulejo *m*
blue cheese *n* : queso *m* azul
blueprint [ˈbluːˌprɪnt] *n* **1** : plano *m,* proyecto *m,* cianotipo *m* **2** PLAN : anteproyecto *m,* programa *m*
blues [ˈbluːz] *npl* **1** DEPRESSION : depresión *f,* melancolía *f* **2** : blues *m* <to sing the blues : cantar blues>
bluff[1] [ˈblʌf] *vi* : hacer un farol, blofear *Col, Mex*
bluff[2] *adj* **1** STEEP : escarpado **2** FRANK : campechano, franco, directo
bluff[3] *n* **1** : farol *m,* blof *m Col, Mex* **2** CLIFF : acantilado *m,* risco *m*
bluffer [ˈblʌfər] *n* : farolero *m,* -ra *f fam;* blofeador *m,* -dora *f Col, Mex*
bluing *or* **blueing** [ˈbluːɪŋ] *n* : añil *m,* azulete *m*
bluish [ˈbluːɪʃ] *adj* : azulado
blunder[1] [ˈblʌndər] *vi* **1** STUMBLE : tropezar, dar traspiés **2** ERR : cometer un error, tropezar, meter la pata *fam*
blunder[2] *n* : error *m,* fallo *m* garrafal, metedura *f* de pata *fam*
blunderbuss [ˈblʌndərˌbʌs] *n* : trabuco *m*
blunt[1] [ˈblʌnt] *vt* : despuntar (aguja o lápiz), desafilar (cuchillo o tijeras), suavizar (crítica)
blunt[2] *adj* **1** DULL : desafilado, despuntado **2** DIRECT : directo, franco, categórico
bluntly [ˈblʌntli] *adv* : sin rodeos, francamente, bruscamente
bluntness [ˈblʌntnəs] *n* **1** DULLNESS : falta *f* de filo, embotadura *f* **2** FRANKNESS : franqueza *f*
blur[1] [ˈblər] *vt* **blurred; blurring** : desdibujar, hacer borroso
blur[2] *n* **1** SMEAR : mancha *f,* borrón *m* **2** : aspecto *m* borroso <everything was just a blur : todo se volvió borroso>
blurb [ˈblərb] *n* : propaganda *f,* nota *f* publicitaria
blurt [ˈblərt] *vt* : espetar, decir impulsivamente
blush[1] [ˈblʌʃ] *vi* : ruborizarse, sonrojarse, hacerse colorado
blush[2] *n* : rubor *m,* sonrojo *m*
bluster[1] [ˈblʌstər] *vi* **1** BLOW : soplar con fuerza **2** BOAST : fanfarronear, echar bravatas
bluster[2] *n* : fanfarronada *f,* bravata *f*
blustery [ˈblʌstəri] *adj* : borrascoso, tempestuoso
boa [ˈboːə] *n* : boa *f*
boar [ˈbor] *n* : cerdo *m* macho, verraco *m*
board[1] [ˈbord] *vt* **1** : embarcarse en, subir a bordo de (una nave o un avión), subir a (un tren o carro) **2** LODGE : hospedar, dar hospedaje con comidas a **3 to board up** : cerrar con tablas
board[2] *n* **1** PLANK : tabla *f,* tablón *m* **2** : tablero *m* <chessboard : tablero de ajedrez> **3** MEALS : comida *f* <board and lodging : comida y alojamiento> **4** COMMITTEE, COUNCIL : junta *f,* consejo *m*
boarder [ˈbordər] *n* LODGER : huésped *m,* -peda *f*
boardinghouse [ˈbordɪŋˌhaʊs] *n* : casa *f* de huéspedes
boarding school *n* : internado *m*

boardwalk [ˈbordˌwɔk] *n* : paseo *m* marítimo entablado

boast[1] [ˈboːst] *vi* : alardear, presumir, jactarse

boast[2] *n* : jactancia *f,* alarde *m*

boaster [ˈboːstər] *n* : presumido *m,* -da *f;* fanfarrón *m,* -rrona *f fam*

boastful [ˈboːstfəl] *adj* : jactancioso, fanfarrón *fam*

boastfully [ˈboːstfəli] *adv* : de manera jactanciosa

boat[1] [ˈboːt] *vt* : transportar en barco, poner a bordo

boat[2] *n* : barco *m,* embarcación *f,* bote *m,* barca *f*

boatman [ˈboːtmən] *n, pl* **-men** [-mən, -ˌmɛn] : barquero *m*

boatswain [ˈboːsən] *n* : contramaestre *m*

bob[1] [ˈbɑb] *v* **bobbed; bobbing** *vi* **1** : balancearse, mecerse <to bob up and down : subir y bajar> **2** *or* **to bob up** APPEAR : presentarse, surgir — *vt* **1** : inclinar (la cabeza o el cuerpo) **2** CUT : cortar, recortar <she bobbed her hair : se cortó el pelo>

bob[2] *n* **1** : inclinación *f* (de la cabeza, del cuerpo), sacudida *f* **2** FLOAT : flotador *m,* corcho *m* (de pesca) **3** : pelo *m* corto

bobbin [ˈbɑbən] *n* : bobina *f,* carrete *m*

bobby pin [ˈbɑbiˌpɪn] *n* : horquilla *f*

bobcat [ˈbɑbˌkæt] *n* : lince *m* rojo

bobolink [ˈbɑbəˌlɪŋk] *n* : tordo *m* arrocero

bobsled [ˈbɑbˌslɛd] *n* : bobsleigh *m*

bobwhite [ˈbɑbˈ*h*waɪt] *n* : codorniz *m* (del Nuevo Mundo)

bode[1] [ˈboːd] *v* **boded; boding** *vt* : presagiar, augurar — *vi* **to bode well** : ser de buen agüero

bode[2] → **bide**

bodice [ˈbɑdəs] *n* : corpiño *m*

bodied [ˈbɑdid] *adj* : de cuerpo <lean-bodied : de cuerpo delgado> <able-bodied : no discapacitado>

bodiless [ˈbɑdiləs, ˈbɑdələs] *adj* : incorpóreo

bodily[1] [ˈbɑdəli] *adv* : en peso <to lift someone bodily : levantar a alguien en peso>

bodily[2] *adj* : corporal, del cuerpo <bodily harm : daños corporales>

body [ˈbɑdi] *n, pl* **bodies 1** : cuerpo *m,* organismo *m* **2** CORPSE : cadáver *m* **3** PERSON : persona *f,* ser *m* humano **4** : nave *f* (de una iglesia), carrocería (de un automóvil), fuselaje *m* (de un avión), casco *m* (de una nave) **5** COLLECTION, MASS : conjunto *m,* grupo *m,* masa *f* <in a body : todos juntos, en masa> **6** ORGANIZATION : organismo *m,* organización *f*

bodyguard [ˈbɑdiˌgɑrd] *n* : guardaespaldas *mf*

bog[1] [ˈbɑg, ˈbɔg] *vt* **bogged; bogging** : empantanar, inundar <to get bogged down : empantanarse>

bog[2] *n* : lodazal *m,* ciénaga *f,* cenagal *m*

bogey [ˈbʊgi, ˈboː-] *n, pl* **-geys** : terror *m,* coco *m fam*

boggle [ˈbɑgəl] *vi* **-gled; -gling** : quedarse atónito, quedarse pasmado <the mind boggles! : ¡es increíble!>

boggy [ˈbɑgi, ˈbɔ-] *adj* **boggier; -est** : cenagoso

bogus [ˈboːgəs] *adj* : falso, fingido, falaz

bohemian [boːˈhiːmiən] *n* : bohemio *m,* -mia *f* — **bohemian** *adj*

boil[1] [ˈbɔɪl] *vi* **1** : hervir **2 to make one's blood boil** : hervirle la sangre a uno — *vt* **1** : hervir, hacer hervir <to boil water : hervir agua> **2** : cocer, hervir <to boil potatoes : cocer papas>

boil[2] *n* **1** BOILING : hervor *m* **2** : furúnculo *m,* divieso *m* (in medicine)

boiler [ˈbɔɪlər] *n* : caldera *f*

boisterous [ˈbɔɪstərəs] *adj* : bullicioso, escandaloso — **boisterously** *adv*

bold [ˈboːld] *adj* **1** COURAGEOUS : valiente **2** INSOLENT : insolente, descarado **3** DARING : atrevido, audaz — **boldly** *adv*

boldface [ˈboːldˌfeɪs] *n or* **boldface type** : negrita *f*

boldness [ˈboːldnəs] *n* **1** COURAGE : valor *m,* coraje *m* **2** INSOLENCE : atrevimiento *m,* insolencia *f,* descaro *m* **3** DARING : audacia *f*

bolero [bəˈlɛro] *n, pl* **-ros** : bolero *m*

Bolivian [bəˈlɪviən] *n* : boliviano *m,* -na *f* — **Bolivian** *adj*

boll [ˈboːl] *n* : cápsula *f* (del algodón)

boll weevil *n* : gorgojo *m* del algodón

bologna [bəˈloːni] *n* : salchicha *f* ahumada

bolster[1] [ˈboːlstər] *vt* **-stered; -stering** : reforzar, reafirmar <to bolster morale : levantar la moral>

bolster[2] *n* : cabezal *m,* almohadón *m*

bolt[1] [ˈboːlt] *vt* **1** atornillar, sujetar con pernos <bolted to the floor : sujetado con pernos al suelo> **2** : cerrar con pestillo, echar el cerrojo a <to bolt the door : echar el cerrojo a la puerta> **3 to bolt down** : engullir <she bolted down her dinner : engulló su comida> — *vi* : echar a correr, salir corriendo <he bolted from the room : salió corriendo de la sala>

bolt[2] *n* **1** LATCH : pestillo *m,* cerrojo *m* **2** : tornillo *m,* perno *m* <nuts and bolts : tuercas y tornillos> **3** : rollo *m* <a bolt of cloth : un rollo de tela> **4 lightning bolt** : relámpago *m,* rayo *m*

bomb[1] [ˈbɑm] *vt* : bombardear

bomb[2] *n* : bomba *f*

bombard [bɑmˈbɑrd, bəm-] *vt* : bombardear

bombardier [ˌbɑmbəˈdɪr] *n* : bombardero *m,* -ra *f*

bombardment [bɑmˈbɑrdmənt] *n* : bombardeo *m*

bombast [ˈbɑmˌbæst] *n* : grandilocuencia *f,* ampulosidad *f*

bombastic [bɑmˈbæstɪk] *adj* : grandilocuente, ampuloso, bombástico

bomber [ˈbɑmər] *n* : bombardero *m*

bombproof [ˈbɑmˌpruːf] *adj* : a prueba de bombas

bombshell [ˈbɑmˌʃɛl] *n* : bomba *f* <a political bombshell : una bomba política>

bona fide [ˈboːnəˌfaɪd, ˈbɑ-; ˌboːnəˈfaɪdi] *adj* **1** : de buena fe <a bona fide offer : una oferta de buena fe> **2** GENUINE : genuino, auténtico

bonanza [bəˈnænzə] *n* : bonanza *f*

bonbon [ˈbɑnˌbɑn] *n* : bombón *m*

bond[1] [ˈbɑnd] *vt* **1** INSURE : dar fianza a, asegurar **2** STICK : adherir, pegar — *vi* : adherirse, pegarse

bond[2] *n* **1** LINK, TIE : vínculo *m,* lazo *m* **2** BAIL : fianza *f,* caución *f* **3** : bono *m* <stocks and bonds : acciones y bonos> **4 bonds** *npl* FETTERS : cadenas *fpl*

bondage [ˈbɑndɪdʒ] *n* : esclavitud *f*

bondholder [ˈbɑndˌhoːldər] *n* : tenedor *m,* -dora *f* de bonos

bondsman [ˈbɑndzmən] *n, pl* **-men** [-mən, -ˌmɛn] **1** SLAVE : esclavo *m* **2** SURETY : fiador *m,* -dora *f*

bone[1] [ˈboːn] *vt* **boned; boning** : deshuesar

bone[2] *n* : hueso *m*

boneless [ˈboːnləs] *adj* : sin huesos, sin espinas

boner [ˈboːnər] *n* : metedura *f* de pata, metida *f* de pata

bonfire [ˈbɑnˌfaɪr] *n* : hoguera *f,* fogata *f,* fogón *m*

bonito [bəˈniːt̬o] *n, pl* **-tos** *or* **-to** : bonito *m*

bonnet [ˈbɑnət] *n* : sombrero *m* (de mujer), gorra *f* (de niño)

bonus [ˈboːnəs] *n* **1** : prima *f,* bonificación *f* (pagado al empleado) **2** ADVANTAGE, BENEFIT : beneficio *m,* provecho *m*

bony [ˈboːni] *adj* **bonier; -est** : huesudo, osudo

boo[1] [ˈbuː] *vt* : abuchear

boo[2] *n, pl* **boos** : abucheo *m*

booby [ˈbuːbi] *n, pl* **-bies** : bobo *m,* -ba *f;* tonto *m,* -ta *f*

book[1] [ˈbʊk] *vt* : reservar <to book a flight : reservar un vuelo>

book[2] *n* **1** : libro *m* **2 the Book** : la Biblia **3 by the book** : según las reglas

bookcase [ˈbʊkˌkeɪs] *n* : estantería *f,* librero *m Mex*

bookend [ˈbʊkˌɛnd] *n* : sujetalibros *m*

bookie [ˈbʊki] → **bookmaker**

bookish [ˈbʊkɪʃ] *adj* : libresco

bookkeeper [ˈbʊkˌkiːpər] *n* : tenedor *m,* -dora *f* de libros; contable *mf Spain*

bookkeeping [ˈbʊkˌkiːpɪŋ] *n* : contabilidad *f,* teneduría *f* de libros

booklet [ˈbʊklət] *n* : folleto *m*

bookmaker [ˈbʊkˌmeɪkər] *n* : corredor *m,* -dora *f* de apuestas

bookmark [ˈbʊkˌmɑrk] *n* : señalador *m* de libros, marcador *m* de libros

bookseller [ˈbʊkˌsɛlər] *n* : librero *m,* -ra *f*

bookshelf [ˈbʊkˌʃɛlf] *n, pl* **-shelves 1** : estante *m* **2 bookshelves** *npl* : estantería *f*

bookstore [ˈbʊkˌstor] *n* : librería *f*

bookworm [ˈbʊkˌwərm] *n* : ratón *m* de biblioteca *fam*

boom[1] [ˈbuːm] *vi* **1** THUNDER : tronar, resonar **2** FLOURISH, PROSPER : estar en auge, prosperar

boom[2] *n* **1** BOOMING : bramido *m,* estruendo *m* **2** FLOURISHING : auge *m* <population boom : auge de población>

boomerang [ˈbuːməˌræŋ] *n* : bumerán *m*

boon[1] [ˈbuːn] *adj* **boon companion** : amigo *m,* -ga *f* del alma

boon[2] *n* : ayuda *f,* beneficio *m,* adelanto *m*

boondocks [ˈbuːnˌdɑks] *npl* : area *f* rural remota, región *f* alejada

boor [ˈbʊr] *n* : grosero *m,* -ra *f*

boorish [ˈbʊrɪʃ] *adj* : grosero

boost[1] [ˈbuːst] *vt* **1** LIFT : levantar, alzar **2** INCREASE : aumentar, incrementar **3** PROMOTE : promover, fomentar, hacer publicidad por

boost[2] *n* **1** THRUST : impulso *m,* empujón *m* **2** ENCOURAGEMENT : estímulo *m,* aliento *m* **3** INCREASE : aumento *m,* incremento *m*

booster [ˈbuːstər] *n* **1** SUPPORTER : partidario *m,* -ria *f* **2 booster rocket** : cohete *m* propulsor **3 booster shot** : vacuna *f* de refuerzo

boot[1] [ˈbuːt] *vt* KICK : dar una patada a, patear

boot[2] *n* **1** : bota *f,* botín *m* **2** KICK : puntapié *m,* patada *f*

bootee *or* **bootie** [ˈbuːt̬i] *n* : botita *f,* botín *m*

booth [ˈbuːθ] *n, pl* **booths** [ˈbuːðz, ˈbuːθs] : cabina *f* (de teléfono, de votar), caseta *f* (de información), barraca *f* (a una feria)

bootlegger [ˈbuːtˌlɛgər] *n* : contrabandista *mf* del alcohol

booty [ˈbuːt̬i] *n, pl* **-ties** : botín *m*

booze [ˈbuːz] *n* : trago *m,* bebida *f* (alcohólica)

borax [ˈbɔrˌæks] *n* : bórax *m*

border[1] [ˈbɔrdər] *vt* **1** EDGE : ribetear, bordear **2** BOUND : limitar con, lindar con — *vi* VERGE : rayar, lindar <that borders on absurdity : eso raya en el absurdo>

border[2] *n* **1** EDGE : borde *m,* orilla *f* **2** TRIM : ribete *m* **3** FRONTIER : frontera *f*

bore[1] [ˈbor] *vt* **bored; boring 1** PIERCE : taladrar, perforar <to bore metals : taladrar metales> **2** OPEN : hacer, abrir <to bore a tunnel : abrir un túnel> **3** WEARY : aburrir

bore[2] → **bear**[1]
bore[3] *n* **1 :** pesado *m,* -da *f* (persona aburrida) **2** TEDIOUSNESS **:** pesadez *f,* lo aburrido **3** DIAMETER **:** calibre *m*
boredom [ˈbordəm] *n* **:** aburrimiento *m*
boring [ˈborɪŋ] *adj* **:** aburrido, pesado
born [ˈbɔrn] *adj* **1 :** nacido **2 :** nato <she's a born singer : es una cantante nata> <he's a born leader : nació para mandar>
borne → **bear**[1]
boron [ˈborˌɑn] *n* **:** boro *m*
borough [ˈbəro] *n* **:** distrito *m* municipal
borrow [ˈbɑro] *vt* **1 :** pedir prestado, tomar prestado **2** APPROPRIATE **:** apropiarse de, adoptar
Bosnian [ˈbɑzniən, ˈbɔz-] *n* **:** bosnio *m,* -nia *f* — **Bosnian** *adj*
bosom[1] [ˈbʊzəm, ˈbuː-] *adj* **:** íntimo
bosom[2] *n* **1** CHEST **:** pecho *m* **2** BREAST **:** pecho *m,* seno *m* **3** CLOSENESS **:** seno *m* <in the bosom of her family : en el seno de su familia>
bosomed [ˈbʊzəmd, ˈbuː-] *adj* **:** con busto <big-bosomed : con mucho busto>
boss[1] [ˈbɔs] *vt* **1** SUPERVISE **:** dirigir, supervisar **2 to boss around :** mandonear *fam,* mangonear *fam*
boss[2] *n* **:** jefe *m,* -fa *f;* patrón *m,* -trona *f*
bossy [ˈbɔsi] *adj* **bossier; -est :** mandón *fam,* autoritario, dominante
botanist [ˈbɑtənɪst] *n* **:** botánico *m,* -ca *f*
botany [ˈbɑtəni] *n* **:** botánica *f* — **botanical** [bəˈtænɪkəl] *adj*
botch[1] [ˈbɑtʃ] *vt* **:** hacer una chapuza de, estropear
botch[2] *n* **:** chapuza *f*
both[1] [ˈboːθ] *adj* **:** ambos, los dos, las dos <both books : ambos libros, los dos libros>
both[2] *conj* **:** tanto como <both Ana and her mother are tall : tanto Ana como su madre son altas>
both[3] *pron* **:** ambos *m,* -bas *f;* los dos, las dos
bother[1] [ˈbɑðər] *vt* **1** IRK **:** preocupar <nothing's bothering me : nada me preocupa> <what's bothering him? : ¿qué le pasa?> **2** PESTER **:** molestar, fastidiar — *vi* **to bother to :** molestarse en, tomar la molestia de
bother[2] *n* **1** TROUBLE **:** molestia *f,* problemas *mpl* **2** ANNOYANCE **:** molestia *f,* fastidio *m*
bothersome [ˈbɑðərsəm] *adj* **:** molesto, fastidioso
bottle[1] [ˈbɑtəl] *vt* **bottled; bottling :** embotellar, envasar
bottle[2] *n* **:** botella *f,* frasco *m*
bottleneck [ˈbɑtəlˌnɛk] *n* **1 :** cuello *m* de botello (en un camino) **2 :** embotellamiento *m,* atasco *m* (de tráfico) **3** OBSTACLE **:** obstáculo *m*
bottom[1] [ˈbɑtəm] *adj* **:** más bajo, inferior, de abajo
bottom[2] *n* **1 :** fondo *m* (de una caja, de una taza, del mar), pie *m* (de una escalera, una página, una montaña), asiento *m* (de una silla), parte *f* de abajo (de una pila) **2** CAUSE **:** origen *m,* causa *f* <to get to the bottom of : llegar al fondo de> **3** BUTTOCKS **:** trasero *m,* nalgas *fpl*
bottomless [ˈbɑtəmləs] *adj* **:** sin fondo, sin límites
botulism [ˈbɑtʃəˌlɪzəm] *n* **:** botulismo *m*
boudoir [bəˈdwɑr, bʊ-; ˈbuːˌ-, ˈbʊ-] *n* **:** tocador *m*
bough [ˈbaʊ] *n* **:** rama *f*
bought → **buy**[1]
bouillon [ˈbuːˌjɑn; ˈbʊlˌjɑn, -jən] *n* **:** caldo *m*
boulder [ˈboːldər] *n* **:** canto *m* rodado, roca *f* grande
boulevard [ˈbʊləˌvɑrd, ˈbuː-] *n* **:** bulevar *m,* boulevard *m*
bounce[1] [ˈbaʊnts] *v* **bounced; bouncing** *vt* **:** hacer rebotar — *vi* **:** rebotar
bounce[2] *n* **:** rebote *m*
bouncy [ˈbaʊntsi] *adj* **bouncier; -est 1** LIVELY **:** vivo, exuberante, animado **2** RESILIENT **:** elástico, flexible **3 :** que rebota (dícese de una pelota)
bound[1] [ˈbaʊnd] *vt* **:** delimitar, rodear — *vi* LEAP **:** saltar, dar brincos
bound[2] *adj* **1** OBLIGED **:** obligado **2 :** encuadernado, empastado <a book bound in leather : un libro encuadernado en cuero> **3** DETERMINED **:** decidido, empeñado **4 to be bound to :** ser seguro que, tener que, no caber duda que <it was bound to happen : tenía que suceder> **5 bound for :** con rumbo a <bound for Chicago : con rumbo a Chicago> <to be homeward bound : ir camino a casa>
bound[3] *n* **1** LIMIT **:** límite *m* **2** LEAP **:** salto *m,* brinco *m*
boundary [ˈbaʊndri, -dəri] *n, pl* **-aries :** límite *m,* línea *f* divisoria, linde *mf*
boundless [ˈbaʊndləs] *adj* **:** sin límites, infinito
bounteous [ˈbaʊntiəs] *adj* **1** GENEROUS **:** generoso **2** ABUNDANT **:** copioso, abundante — **bounteously** *adv*
bountiful [ˈbaʊntɪfəl] *adj* **1** GENEROUS, LIBERAL **:** munificente, pródigo, generoso **2** ABUNDANT **:** copioso, abundante
bounty [ˈbaʊnti] *n, pl* **-ties 1** GENEROSITY **:** generosidad *f,* munificiencia *f* **2** REWARD **:** recompensa *f*
bouquet [boːˈkeɪ, buː-] *n* **1 :** ramo *m,* ramillete *m* **2** FRAGRANCE **:** bouquet *m,* aroma *m*
bourbon [ˈbərbən, ˈbʊr-] *n* **:** bourbon *m,* whiskey *m* americano
bourgeois[1] [ˈbʊrʒˌwɑ, bʊrʒˈwɑ] *adj* **:** burgués
bourgeois[2] *n* **:** burgués *m,* -guesa *f*
bourgeoisie [ˌbʊrʒˌwɑˈzi] *n* **:** burguesía *f*

bout [ˈbaʊt] *n* **1** : encuentro *m,* combate *m* (en deportes) **2** ATTACK : ataque *m* (de una enfermedad) **3** PERIOD, SPELL : período *m* (de actividad)
boutique [buːˈtiːk] *n* : boutique *f*
bovine[1] [ˈboːˌvaɪn, -ˌviːn] *adj* : bovino, vacuno
bovine[2] *n* : bovino *m*
bow[1] [ˈbaʊ] *vi* **1** : hacer una reverencia, inclinarse **2** SUBMIT : ceder, resignarse, someterse — *vt* **1** LOWER : inclinar, bajar **2** BEND : doblar
bow[2] [ˈbaʊː] *n* **1** BOWING : reverencia *f,* inclinación *f* **2** : proa *f* (de un barco)
bow[3] [ˈboː] *vi* CURVE : arquearse, doblarse
bow[4] [ˈboː] *n* **1** ARCH, CURVE : arco *m,* curva *f* **2** : arco *m* (arma o vara para tocar varios instrumentos de música) **3** : lazo *m,* moño *m* <to tie a bow : hacer un moño>
bowels [ˈbaʊəls] *npl* **1** INTESTINES : intestinos *mpl* **2** : entrañas *fpl* <in the bowels of the earth : en las entrañas de la tierra>
bower [ˈbaʊər] *n* : enramada *f*
bowl[1] [ˈboːl] *vi* : jugar a los bolos
bowl[2] *n* : tazón *m,* cuenco *m*
bowler [ˈboːlər] *n* : jugador *m,* -dora *f* de bolos
bowling [ˈboːlɪŋ] *n* : bolos *mpl*
box[1] [ˈbɑks] *vt* **1** PACK : empaquetar, embalar, encajonar **2** SLAP : bofetear, cachetear — *vi* : boxear
box[2] *n* **1** CONTAINER : caja *f,* cajón *m* **2** COMPARTMENT : compartimento *m,* palco *m* (en el teatro) **3** SLAP : bofetada *f,* cachetada *f* **4** : boj *m* (planta)
boxcar [ˈbɑksˌkɑr] *n* : vagón *m* de carga, furgón *m*
boxer [ˈbɑksər] *n* : boxeador *m,* -dora *f*
boxing [ˈbɑksɪŋ] *n* : boxeo *m*
box office *n* : taquilla *f,* boletería *f*
boxwood [ˈbɑksˌwʊd] *n* : boj *m*
boy [ˈbɔɪ] *n* : niño *m,* chico *m*
boycott[1] [ˈbɔɪˌkɑt] *vt* : boicotear
boycott[2] *n* : boicot *m*
boyfriend [ˈbɔɪˌfrɛnd] *n* **1** FRIEND : amigo *m* **2** SWEETHEART : novio *m*
boyhood [ˈbɔɪˌhʊd] *n* : niñez *f*
boyish [ˈbɔɪɪʃ] *adj* : de niño, juvenil
bra [ˈbrɑ] → **brassiere**
brace[1] [ˈbreɪs] *v* **braced; bracing** *vt* **1** PROP UP, SUPPORT : apuntalar, apoyar, sostener **2** INVIGORATE : vigorizar **3** REINFORCE : reforzar — *vi* **to brace oneself** PREPARE : prepararse
brace[2] *n* **1** : berbiquí *m* <brace and bit : berbiquí y barrena> **2** CLAMP, REINFORCEMENT : abrazadera *f,* refuerzo *m* **3** : llave *f* (signo de puntuación) **4 braces** *npl* : aparatos *mpl* (de ortodoncia), frenos *mpl Mex*
bracelet [ˈbreɪslət] *n* : brazalete *m,* pulsera *f*
bracken [ˈbrækən] *n* : helecho *m*
bracket[1] [ˈbrækət] *vt* **1** SUPPORT : asegurar, apuntalar **2** : poner entre corchetes **3** CATEGORIZE, GROUP : catalogar, agrupar
bracket[2] *n* **1** SUPPORT : soporte *m* **2** : corchete *m* (marca de puntuación) **3** CATEGORY, CLASS : clase *f,* categoría *f*
brackish [ˈbrækɪʃ] *adj* : salobre
brad [ˈbræd] *n* : clavo *m* con cabeza pequeña, clavito *m*
brag[1] [ˈbræg] *vi* **bragged; bragging** : alardear, fanfarronear, jactarse
brag[2] *n* : alarde *m,* jactancia *f,* fanfarronada *f*
braggart [ˈbrægərt] *n* : fanfarrón *m,* -rrona *f fam;* jactancioso *m,* -sa *f*
braid[1] [ˈbreɪd] *vt* : trenzar
braid[2] *n* : trenza *f*
braille [ˈbreɪl] *n* : braille *m*
brain[1] [ˈbreɪn] *vt* : romper la crisma a, aplastar el cráneo a
brain[2] *n* **1** : cerebro *m* **2 brains** *npl* INTELLECT : inteligencia *f,* sesos *mpl*
brainless [ˈbreɪnləs] *adj* : estúpido, tonto
brainstorm [ˈbreɪnˌstɔrm] *n* : idea *f* brillante, idea *f* genial
brainy [ˈbreɪni] *adj* **brainier; -est** : inteligente, listo
braise [ˈbreɪz] *vt* **braised; braising** : cocer a fuego lento, estofar
brake[1] [ˈbreɪk] *v* **braked; braking** : frenar
brake[2] *n* : freno *m*
bramble [ˈbræmbəl] *n* : zarza *f,* zarzamora *f*
bran [ˈbræn] *n* : salvado *m*
branch[1] [ˈbræntʃ] *vi* **1** : echar ramas (dícese de una planta) **2** DIVERGE : ramificarse, separarse
branch[2] *n* **1** : rama *f* (de una planta) **2** EXTENSION : ramal *m* (de un camino, un ferrocarril, un río), rama *f* (de una familia o un campo de estudiar), sucursal *f* (de una empresa), agencia *f* (del gobierno)
brand[1] [ˈbrænd] *vt* **1** : marcar (ganado) **2** LABEL : tachar, tildar <they branded him as a liar : lo tacharon de mentiroso>
brand[2] *n* **1** : marca *f* (de ganado) **2** STIGMA : estigma *m* **3** MAKE : marca *f* <brand name : marca de fábrica>
brandish [ˈbrændɪʃ] *vt* : blandir
brand–new [ˈbrændˈnuː, -ˈnjuː] *adj* : nuevo, flamante
brandy [ˈbrændi] *n, pl* **-dies** : brandy *m*
brash [ˈbræʃ] *adj* **1** IMPULSIVE : impulsivo, impetuoso **2** BRAZEN : excesivamente desenvuelto, descarado
brass [ˈbræs] *n* **1** : latón *m* **2** GALL, NERVE : descaro *m,* cara *f fam* **3** OFFICERS : mandamases *mpl fam*
brassiere [brəˈzɪr, brɑ-] *n* : sostén *m,* brasier *m Col, Mex*
brassy [ˈbræsi] *adj* **brassier; -est** : dorado
brat [ˈbræt] *n* : mocoso *m,* -sa *f;* niño *m* mimado, niña *f* mimada

bravado [brəˈvɑdo] *n, pl* **-does** *or* **-dos** : bravuconadas *fpl*, bravatas *fpl*

brave[1] [ˈbreɪv] *vt* **braved; braving** : afrontar, hacer frente a

brave[2] *adj* **braver; bravest** : valiente, valeroso — **bravely** *adv*

brave[3] *n* : guerrero *m* indio

bravery [ˈbreɪvəri] *n* : valor *m*, valentía *f*

bravo [ˈbrɑˌvoː] *n, pl* **-vos** : bravo *m*

brawl[1] [ˈbrɔl] *vi* : pelearse, pegarse

brawl[2] *n* : pelea *f*, reyerta *f*

brawn [ˈbrɔn] *n* : fuerza *f* muscular

brawny [ˈbrɔni] *adj* **brawnier; -est** : musculoso

bray[1] [ˈbreɪ] *vi* : rebuznar

bray[2] *n* : rebuzno *m*

brazen [ˈbreɪzən] *adj* **1** : de latón **2** BOLD : descarado, directo

brazenly [ˈbreɪzənli] *adv* : descaradamente, insolentemente

brazenness [ˈbreɪzənnəs] *n* : descaro *m*, atrevimiento *m*

brazier [ˈbreɪʒər] *n* : brasero *m*

Brazilian [brəˈzɪljən] *n* : brasileño *m*, -ña *f* — **Brazilian** *adj*

Brazil nut [brəˈzɪlˌnʌt] *n* : nuez *f* de Brasil

breach[1] [ˈbriːtʃ] *vt* **1** PENETRATE : abrir una brecha en, penetrar **2** VIOLATE : infringir, violar

breach[2] *n* **1** VIOLATION : infracción *f*, violación *f* <breach of trust : abuso de confianza> **2** GAP, OPENING : brecha *f*

bread[1] [ˈbrɛd] *vt* : empanar

bread[2] *n* : pan *m*

breadth [ˈbrɛtθ] *n* : ancho *m*, anchura *f*

breadwinner [ˈbrɛdˌwɪnər] *n* : sostén *m* de la familia

break[1] [ˈbreɪk] *v* **broke** [ˈbroːk]; **broken** [ˈbroːkən]; **breaking** *vt* **1** SMASH : romper, quebrar **2** VIOLATE : infringir, violar, romper **3** SURPASS : batir, superar **4** CRUSH, RUIN : arruinar, deshacer, destrozar <to break one's spirit : quebrantar su espíritu> **5** : dar, comunicar <to break the news : dar las noticias> **6** INTERRUPT : cortar, interrumpir — *vi* **1** : romperse, quebrarse <my calculator broke : se me rompió la calculadora> **2** DISPERSE : dispersarse, despejarse **3** : estallar (dícese de una tormenta), romper (dícese del día) **4** CHANGE : cambiar (dícese del tiempo o de la voz) **5** DECREASE : bajar <my fever broke : me bajó la fiebre> **6** : divulgarse, revelarse <the news broke : la noticia se divulgó> **7 to break into** : forzar, abrir **8 to break out of** : escaparse de **9 to break through** : penetrar

break[2] *n* **1** : ruptura *f*, rotura *f*, fractura *f* (de un hueso), claro *m* (entre las nubes), cambio *m* (del tiempo) **2** CHANCE : oportunidad *f* <a lucky break : un golpe de suerte> **3** REST : descanso *m* <to take a break : tomar(se) un descanso>

breakable [ˈbreɪkəbəl] *adj* : quebradizo, frágil

breakage [ˈbreɪkɪdʒ] *n* **1** BREAKING : rotura *f* **2** DAMAGE : destrozos *mpl*, daños *mpl*

breakdown [ˈbreɪkˌdaʊn] *n* **1** : avería *f* (de máquinas), interrupción *f* (de comunicaciones), fracaso *m* (de negociaciones) **2** ANALYSIS : análisis *m*, desglose *m* **3** *or* **nervous breakdown** : crisis *f* nerviosa

break down *vi* **1** : estropearse, descomponerse <the machine broke down : la máquina se descompuso> **2** FAIL : fracasar **3** CRY : echarse a llorar — *vt* **1** DESTROY : derribar, echar abajo **2** OVERCOME : vencer (la resistencia), disipar (sospechas) **3** ANALYZE : analizar, descomponer

breaker [ˈbreɪkər] *n* **1** WAVE : ola *f* grande **2** : interruptor *m* automático (de electricidad)

breakfast[1] [ˈbrɛkfəst] *vi* : desayunar

breakfast[2] *n* : desayuno *m*

breakneck [ˈbreɪkˌnɛk] *adj* **at breakneck speed** : a una velocidad vertiginosa

break out *vi* **1** : salirse <she broke out in spots : le salieron granos> **2** ERUPT : estallar (dícese de una guerra, la violencia, etc.) **3** ESCAPE : fugarse, escaparse

break up *vt* **1** DIVIDE : dividir **2** : disolver (una muchedumbre, una pelea, etc.) — *vi* **1** BREAK : romperse **2** SEPARATE : deshacerse, separarse <I broke up with him : terminé con él>

breast [ˈbrɛst] *n* **1** : pecho *m*, seno *m* (de una mujer) **2** CHEST : pecho *m*

breastbone [ˈbrɛstˌboːn] *n* : esternón *m*

breast–feed [ˈbrɛstˌfiːd] *vt* **-fed** [-ˌfɛd]; **-feeding** : amamantar, darle de mamar (a un niño)

breath [ˈbrɛθ] *n* **1** BREATHING : aliento *m* <to hold one's breath : aguantar la respiración>**2** BREEZE : soplo *m* <a breath of fresh air : un soplo de aire fresco>

breathe [ˈbriːð] *v* **breathed; breathing** *vi* **1** : respirar **2** LIVE : vivir, respirar — *vt* **1** : respirar, aspirar <to breathe fresh air : respirar el aire fresco> **2** UTTER : decir <I won't breathe a word of this : no diré nada de esto>

breathless [ˈbrɛθləs] *adj* : sin aliento, jadeante

breathlessly [ˈbrɛθləsli] *adv* : entrecortadamente, jadeando

breathlessness [ˈbrɛθləsnəs] *n* : dificultad *f* al respirar

breathtaking [ˈbrɛθˌteɪkɪŋ] *adj* IMPRESSIVE : impresionante, imponente

breeches [ˈbrɪtʃəz, ˈbriː-] *npl* : pantalones *mpl*, calzones *mpl*, bombachos *mpl*

breed[1] [ˈbriːd] *v* **bred** [ˈbrɛd]; **breeding** *vt* **1** : criar (animales) **2** ENGENDER

: engendrar, producir <familiarity breeds contempt : la confianza hace perder el respeto> **3** RAISE, REAR : criar, educar — *vi* REPRODUCE : reproducirse

breed[2] *n* **1** : variedad *f* (de plantas), raza *f* (de animales) **2** CLASS : clase *f,* tipo *m*

breeder [ˈbriːdər] *n* : criador *m,* -dora *f* (de animales); cultivador *m,* -dora *f* (de plantas)

breeze[1] [ˈbriːz] *vi* **breezed; breezing** : pasar con ligereza <to breeze in : entrar como si nada>

breeze[2] *n* : brisa *f,* soplo *m* (de aire)

breezy [ˈbriːzi] *adj* **breezier; -est 1** AIRY, WINDY : aireado, ventoso **2** LIVELY : animado, alegre **3** NONCHALANT : despreocupado

brethren → **brother**

brevity [ˈbrɛvəṭi] *n, pl* **-ties** : brevedad *f,* concisión *f*

brew[1] [ˈbruː] *vt* **1** : fabricar, elaborar (cerveza) **2** FOMENT : tramar, maquinar, fomentar — *vi* **1** : fabricar cerveza **2** : amenazar <a storm is brewing : una tormenta amenaza>

brew[2] *n* **1** BEER : cerveza *f* **2** POTION : brebaje *m*

brewer [ˈbruːər] *n* : cervecero *m,* -ra *f*

brewery [ˈbruːəri, ˈbrʊri] *n, pl* **-eries** : cervecería *f*

briar [ˈbraɪər] → **brier**

bribe[1] [ˈbraɪb] *vt* **bribed; bribing** : sobornar, cohechar, coimear *Arg, Chile, Peru*

bribe[2] *n* : soborno *m,* cohecho *m,* coima *f Arg, Chile, Peru,* mordida *f CA, Mex*

bribery [ˈbraɪbəri] *n, pl* **-eries** : soborno *m,* cohecho *m,* coima *f,* mordida *f CA, Mex*

bric–a–brac [ˈbrɪkəˌbræk] *npl* : baratijas *fpl,* chucherías *fpl*

brick[1] [ˈbrɪk] *vt* **to brick up** : tabicar, tapiar

brick[2] *n* : ladrillo *m*

bricklayer [ˈbrɪkˌleɪər] *n* : albañil *mf*

bricklaying [ˈbrɪkˌleɪɪŋ] *n* : albañilería *f*

bridal [ˈbraɪdəl] *adj* : nupcial, de novia

bride [ˈbraɪd] *n* : novia *f*

bridegroom [ˈbraɪdˌgruːm] *n* : novio *m*

bridesmaid [ˈbraɪdzˌmeɪd] *n* : dama *f* de honor

bridge[1] [ˈbrɪdʒ] *vt* **bridged; bridging 1** : tender un puente sobre **2 to bridge the gap** : salvar las diferencias

bridge[2] *n* **1** : puente *m* **2** : caballete *m* (de la nariz) **3** : puente *m* de mando (de un barco) **4** DENTURE : puente *m* (dental) **5** : bridge *m* (juego de naipes)

bridle[1] [ˈbraɪdəl] *v* **-dled; -dling** *vt* **1** : embridar (un caballo) **2** RESTRAIN : refrenar, dominar, contener — *vi* **to bridle at** : molestarse por, picarse por

bridle[2] *n* : brida *f*

brief[1] [ˈbriːf] *vt* : dar órdenes a, instruir

brief[2] *adj* : breve, sucinto, conciso

brief[3] *n* : resumen *m,* sumario *m*

briefcase [ˈbriːfˌkeɪs] *n* : portafolio *m,* maletín *m*

briefly [ˈbriːfli] *adv* : brevemente, por poco tiempo <to speak briefly : discursar en pocas palabras>

brier [ˈbraɪər] *n* **1** BRAMBLE : zarza *f,* rosal *m* silvestre **2** HEATH : brezo *m* veteado

brig [ˈbrɪg] *n* **1** : bergantín *m* (barco) **2** : calabozo *m* (en un barco)

brigade [brɪˈgeɪd] *n* : brigada *f*

brigadier general [ˌbrɪgəˈdɪr] *n* : general *m* de brigada

brigand [ˈbrɪgənd] *n* : bandolero *m,* -ra *f;* forajido *m,* -da *f*

bright [ˈbraɪt] *adj* **1** : brillante (dícese del sol, de los ojos), vivo (dícese de un color), claro, fuerte **2** CHEERFUL : alegre, animado <bright and early : muy temprano> **3** INTELLIGENT : listo, inteligente <a bright idea : una idea luminosa>

brighten [ˈbraɪtən] *vt* **1** ILLUMINATE : iluminar **2** ENLIVEN : alegrar, animar — *vi* **1** : hacerse más brillante **2 to brighten up** : animarse, alegrarse, mejorar

brightly [ˈbraɪtli] *adv* : vivamente, intensamente, alegremente

brightness [ˈbraɪtnəs] *n* **1** LUMINOSITY : luminosidad *f,* brillantez *f,* resplandor *m,* brillo *m* **2** CHEERFULNESS : alegría *f,* ánimo *m*

brilliance [ˈbrɪljən*t*s] *n* **1** BRIGHTNESS : resplandor *m,* fulgor *m,* brillo *m,* brillantez *f* **2** INTELLIGENCE : inteligencia *f,* brillantez *f*

brilliancy [ˈbrɪljən*t*si] → **brilliance**

brilliant [ˈbrɪljənt] *adj* : brillante

brilliantly [ˈbrɪljəntli] *adv* : brillantemente, con brillantez

brim[1] [ˈbrɪm] *vi* **brimmed; brimming 1** *or* **to brim over** : desbordarse, rebosar **2 to brim with tears** : llenarse de lágrimas

brim[2] *n* **1** : ala *f* (de un sombrero) **2** : borde *m* (de una taza o un vaso)

brimful [ˈbrɪmˈfʊl] *adj* : lleno hasta el borde, repleto, rebosante

brimless [ˈbrɪmləs] *adj* : sin ala

brimstone [ˈbrɪmˌstoːn] *n* : azufre *m*

brindled [ˈbrɪndəld] *adj* : manchado, pinto

brine [ˈbraɪn] *n* **1** : salmuera *f,* escabeche *m* (para encurtir) **2** OCEAN : océano *m,* mar *m*

bring [ˈbrɪŋ] *vt* **brought** [ˈbrɔt]; **bringing 1** CARRY : traer <bring me some coffee : tráigame un café> **2** PRODUCE : traer, producir, conseguir <his efforts will bring him success : sus esfuerzos le conseguirán el éxito> **3** PERSUADE : convencer, persuadir **4** YIELD : rendir, alcanzar, venderse por <to bring a good price : alcanzar un

precio alto> **5 to bring to an end** : terminar (con) **6 to bring to light** : sacar a la luz
bring about *vt* : ocasionar, provocar, determinar
bring forth *vt* PRODUCE : producir
bring out *vt* : sacar, publicar (un libro, etc.)
bring to *vt* REVIVE : resucitar
bring up *vt* **1** REAR : criar **2** MENTION : sacar, mencionar
brininess [ˈbraɪninəs] *n* : salinidad *f*
brink [ˈbrɪŋk] *n* : borde *m*
briny [ˈbraɪni] *adj* **brinier; -est** : salobre
briquette *or* **briquet** [brɪˈkɛt] *n* : briqueta *f*
brisk [ˈbrɪsk] *adj* **1** LIVELY : rápido, enérgico, brioso **2** INVIGORATING : fresco, estimulante
brisket [ˈbrɪskət] *n* : falda *f*
briskly [ˈbrɪskli] *adv* : rápidamente, enérgicamente, con brío
briskness [ˈbrɪsknəs] *n* : brío *m,* rapidez *f*
bristle[1] [ˈbrɪsəl] *vi* **-tled; -tling 1** : erizarse, ponerse de punta **2** : enfurecerse, enojarse <she bristled at the suggestion : se enfureció ante tal sugerencia> **3** : estar plagado, estar repleto <a city bristling with tourists : una ciudad repleta de turistas>
bristle[2] *n* : cerda *f* (de un animal), pelo *m* (de una planta)
bristly [ˈbrɪsəli] *adj* **bristlier; -est** : erizado, cerdoso, hirsuto
British[1] [ˈbrɪtɪʃ] *adj* : británico
British[2] *n* **the British** *npl* : los británicos
brittle [ˈbrɪtəl] *adj* **-tler; -tlest** : frágil, quebradizo
brittleness [ˈbrɪtəlnəs] *n* : fragilidad *f*
broach [ˈbroːtʃ] *vt* BRING UP : mencionar, abordar, sacar
broad [ˈbrɔd] *adj* **1** WIDE : ancho **2** SPACIOUS : amplio, extenso **3** FULL : pleno <in broad daylight : en pleno día> **4** OBVIOUS : claro, evidente **5** TOLERANT : tolerante, liberal **6** GENERAL : general **7** ESSENTIAL : principal, esencial <the broad outline : los rasgos esenciales>
broadcast[1] [ˈbrɔd,kæst] *vt* **-cast; -casting 1** SCATTER : esparcir, diseminar **2** CIRCULATE, SPREAD : divulgar, difundir, propagar **3** TRANSMIT : transmitir, emitir
broadcast[2] *n* **1** TRANSMISSION : transmisión *f,* emisión *f* **2** PROGRAM : programa *m,* emisión *f*
broadcaster [ˈbrɔd,kæstər] *n* : presentador *m,* -dora *f;* locutor *m,* -tora *f*
broadcloth [ˈbrɔd,klɔθ] *n* : paño *m* fino
broaden [ˈbrɔdən] *vt* : ampliar, ensanchar — *vi* : ampliarse, ensancharse
broadloom [ˈbrɔd,luːm] *adj* : tejido en telar ancho
broadly [ˈbrɔdli] *adv* **1** GENERALLY : en general, aproximadamente **2** WIDELY : extensivamente
broad–minded [ˈbrɔdˈmaɪndəd] *adj* : tolerante, de amplias miras
broad–mindedness [brɔdˈmaɪndədnəs] *n* : tolerancia *f*
broadside [ˈbrɔd,saɪd] *n* **1** VOLLEY : andanada *f* **2** ATTACK : ataque *m,* invectiva *f,* andanada *f*
brocade [broˈkeɪd] *n* : brocado *m*
broccoli [ˈbrɑkəli] *n* : brócoli *m,* brécol *m*
brochure [broˈʃʊr] *n* : folleto *m*
brogue [ˈbroːg] *n* : acento *m* irlandés
broil[1] [ˈbrɔɪl] *vt* : asar a la parrilla
broil[2] *n* : asado *m*
broiler [ˈbrɔɪlər] *n* **1** GRILL : parrilla *f* **2** : pollo *m* para asar
broke[1] [ˈbroːk] → **break**[1]
broke[2] *adj* : pelado, arruinado <to go broke : arruinarse, quebrar>
broken [ˈbroːkən] *adj* **1** DAMAGED, SHATTERED : roto, quebrado, fracturado **2** IRREGULAR, UNEVEN : accidentado, irregular, recortado **3** VIOLATED : roto, quebrantado **4** INTERRUPTED : interrumpido, descontinuo **5** CRUSHED : abatido, quebrantado <a broken man : un hombre destrozado> **6** IMPERFECT : mal <to speak broken English : hablar el inglés con dificultad>
brokenhearted [,broːkənˈhɑrt̬əd] *adj* : descorazonado, desconsolado
broker[1] [ˈbroːkər] *vt* : hacer corretaje de
broker[2] *n* **1** : agente *mf;* corredor *m,* -dora *f* **2** → **stockbroker**
brokerage [ˈbroːkərɪdʒ] *n* : corretage *m,* agencia *f* de corredores
bromine [ˈbroː,miːn] *n* : bromo *m*
bronchitis [brɑnˈkaɪt̬əs, brɑŋ-] *n* : bronquitis *f*
bronze[1] [ˈbrɑnz] *vt* **bronzed; bronzing** : broncear
bronze[2] *n* : bronce *m*
brooch [ˈbroːtʃ, ˈbruːtʃ] *n* : broche *m,* prendedor *m*
brood[1] [ˈbruːd] *vt* **1** INCUBATE : empollar, incubar **2** PONDER : sopesar, considerar — *vi* **1** INCUBATE : empollar **2** REFLECT : rumiar, reflexionar **3** WORRY : ponerse melancólico, inquietarse
brood[2] *adj* : de cría
brood[3] *n* : nidada *f* (de pájaros), camada *f* (de mamíferos)
brooder [ˈbruːdər] *n* **1** THINKER : pensador *m,* -dora *f* **2** INCUBATOR : incubadora *f*
brook[1] [ˈbrʊk] *vt* TOLERATE : tolerar, admitir
brook[2] *n* : arroyo *m*
broom [ˈbruːm, ˈbrʊm] *n* **1** : retama *f,* hiniesta *f* **2** : escoba *f* (para barrer)
broomstick [ˈbruːm,stɪk, ˈbrʊm-] *n* : palo *m* de escoba
broth [ˈbrɔθ] *n, pl* **broths** [ˈbrɔθs, ˈbrɔðz] : caldo *m*

brothel [ˈbrɑθəl, ˈbrɔ-] *n* : burdel *m*

brother [ˈbrʌðər] *n, pl* **brothers** *also* **brethren** [ˈbrɛðrən, -ðərn] **1** : hermano *m* **2** KINSMAN : pariente *m,* familiar *m*

brotherhood [ˈbrʌðərˌhʊd] *n* **1** FELLOWSHIP : fraternidad *f* **2** ASSOCIATION : hermandad *f*

brother–in–law [ˈbrʌðərɪnˌlɔ] *n, pl* **brothers–in–law:** cuñado *m*

brotherly [ˈbrʌðərli] *adj* : fraternal

brought → **bring**

brow [ˈbraʊ] *n* **1** EYEBROW : ceja *f* **2** FOREHEAD : frente *f* **3** : cima *f* <the brow of a hill : la cima de una colina>

browbeat [ˈbraʊˌbiːt] *vt* **-beat; -beaten** [-ˌbiːtən] *or* **-beat; -beating** : intimidar

brown[1] [ˈbraʊn] *vt* **1** : dorar (en cocinar) **2** TAN : broncear — *vi* **1** : dorarse (en cocinar) **2** TAN : broncearse

brown[2] *adj* : marrón, café, castaño (dícese del pelo), moreno (dícese de la piel)

brown[3] *n* : marrón *m,* café *m*

brownish [ˈbraʊnɪʃ] *adj* : pardo

browse [ˈbraʊz] *vi* **browsed; browsing** **1** GRAZE : pacer **2** LOOK : mirar, echar un vistazo

bruin [ˈbruːɪn] *n* BEAR : oso *m*

bruise[1] [ˈbruːz] *vt* **bruised; bruising** **1** : contusionar, machucar, magullar (a una persona) **2** DAMAGE : magullar, dañar (frutas) **3** CRUSH : majar **4** HURT : herir (los sentimientos)

bruise[2] *n* : moretón *m,* cardenal *m,* magulladura *f* (dícese de frutas)

brunch [ˈbrʌntʃ] *n* : combinación *f* de desayuno y almuerzo

brunet[1] *or* **brunette** [bruːˈnɛt] *adj* : moreno

brunet[2] *or* **brunette** *n* : moreno *m,* -na *f*

brunt [ˈbrʌnt] *n* **to bear the brunt of** : llevar el peso de, aguantar el mayor impacto de

brush[1] [ˈbrʌʃ] *vt* **1** : cepillar <to brush one's teeth : cepillarse uno los dientes> **2** SWEEP : barrer, quitar con un cepillo **3** GRAZE : rozar **4** **to brush off** DISREGARD : hacer caso omiso de, ignorar — *vi* **to brush up on** : repasar, refrescar, dar un repaso a

brush[2] *n* **1** *or* **brushwood** [ˈbrʌʃˌwʊd] : broza *f* **2** SCRUB, UNDERBRUSH : maleza *f* **3** : cepillo *m,* pincel *m* (de artista), brocha *f* (de pintor) **4** TOUCH : roce *m* **5** SKIRMISH : escaramuza *f*

brush–off [ˈbrʌʃˌɔf] *n* **to give the brush–off to** : dar calabazas a

brusque [ˈbrʌsk] *adj* : brusco — **brusquely** *adv*

brussels sprout [ˈbrʌsəlzˌspraʊt] *n* : col *f* de Bruselas

brutal [ˈbruːtəl] *adj* : brutal, cruel, salvaje — **brutally** *adv*

brutality [bruːˈtæləṭi] *n, pl* **-ties** : brutalidad *f*

brutalize [ˈbruːtəlˌaɪz] *vt* **-ized; -izing** : brutalizar, maltratar

brute[1] [ˈbruːt] *adj* : bruto <brute force : fuerza bruta>

brute[2] *n* **1** BEAST : bestia *f,* animal *m* **2** : bruto *m,* -ta *f;* bestia *mf* (persona)

brutish [ˈbruːṭɪʃ] *adj* **1** : de animal **2** CRUEL : brutal, salvaje **3** STUPID : bruto, estúpido

bubble[1] [ˈbʌbəl] *vi* **-bled; -bling** : burbujear <to bubble over with joy : rebosar de alegría>

bubble[2] *n* : burbuja *f*

bubbly [ˈbʌbəli] *adj* **bubblier; -est** **1** BUBBLING : burbujeante **2** LIVELY : vivaz, lleno de vida

bubonic plague [buːˈbɑnɪk, ˈbjuː-] *n* : peste *f* bubónica

buccaneer [ˌbʌkəˈnɪr] *n* : bucanero *m*

buck[1] [ˈbʌk] *vi* **1** : corcovear (dícese de un caballo o un burro) **2** JOLT : dar sacudidas **3** **to buck against** : resistirse a, rebelarse contra **4** **to buck up** : animarse, levantar el ánimo — *vt* OPPOSE : oponerse a, ir en contra de

buck[2] *n, pl* **buck** *or* **bucks** **1** : animal *m* macho, ciervo *m* (macho) **2** DOLLAR : dólar *m* **3** **to pass the buck** *fam* : pasar la pelota *fam*

bucket [ˈbʌkət] *n* : balde *m,* cubo *m,* cubeta *f Mex*

bucketful [ˈbʌkətˌfʊl] *n* : balde *m* lleno

buckle[1] [ˈbʌkəl] *v* **-led; -ling** *vt* **1** FASTEN : abrochar **2** BEND, TWIST : combar, torcer — *vi* **1** BEND, TWIST : combarse, torcerse, doblarse (dícese de las rodillas) **2** **to buckle down** : ponerse a trabajar con esmero **3** **to buckle up** : abrocharse

buckle[2] *n* **1** : hebilla *f* **2** TWISTING : torcedura *f*

buckshot [ˈbʌkˌʃɑt] *n* : perdigón *m*

buckskin [ˈbʌkˌskɪn] *n* : gamuza *f*

bucktooth [ˈbʌkˌtuːθ] *n* : diente *m* saliente, diente *m* salido

buckwheat [ˈbʌkˌ*h*wiːt] *n* : trigo *m* rubión, alforfón *m*

bucolic [bjuːˈkɑlɪk] *adj* : bucólico

bud[1] [ˈbʌd] *v* **budded; budding** *vt* GRAFT : injertar — *vi* : brotar, hacer brotes

bud[2] *n* : brote *m,* yema *f,* capullo *m* (de una flor)

Buddhism [ˈbuːˌdɪzəm, ˈbʊ-] *n* : Budismo *m*

Buddhist [ˈbuːdɪst, ˈbʊ-] *n* : budista *mf* — **Buddhist** *adj*

buddy [ˈbʌdi] *n, pl* **-dies** : amigo *m,* -ga *f;* compinche *mf fam;* cuate *m,* -ta *f Mex fam*

budge [ˈbʌdʒ] *vi* **budged; budging** **1** MOVE : moverse, desplazarse **2** YIELD : ceder

budget[1] [ˈbʌdʒət] *vt* : presupuestar (gastos), asignar (dinero) — *vi* : presupuestar, planear el presupuesto

budget[2] *n* : presupuesto

budgetary [ˈbʌdʒəˌtɛri] *adj* : presupuestario

buff¹ [ˈbʌf] *vt* POLISH : pulir, sacar brillo a, lustrar

buff² *adj* : beige, amarillento

buff³ *n* **1** : beige *m,* amarillento *m* **2** ENTHUSIAST : aficionado *m,* -da *f;* entusiasta *mf*

buffalo [ˈbʌfəˌloː] *n, pl* **-lo** *or* **-loes 1** : búfalo *m* **2** BISON : bisonte *m*

buffer [ˈbʌfər] *n* **1** BARRIER : barrera *f* <buffer state : estado tapón> **2** SHOCK ABSORBER : amortiguador *m*

buffet¹ [ˈbʌfət] *vt* : golpear, zarandear, sacudir

buffet² *n* BLOW : golpe *m*

buffet³ [ˌbʌˈfeɪ, ˌbuː-] *n* **1** : bufete *m,* bufé *m* (comida) **2** SIDEBOARD : aparador *m*

buffoon [ˌbʌˈfuːn] *n* : bufón *m,* -fona *f;* payaso *m,* -sa *f*

buffoonery [ˌbʌˈfuːnəri] *n, pl* **-eries** : bufonada *f,* payasada *f*

bug¹ [ˈbʌg] *vt* **bugged; bugging 1** PESTER : fastidiar, molestar **2** : ocultar micrófonos en

bug² *n* **1** INSECT : bicho *m,* insecto *m* **2** DEFECT : defecto *m,* falla *f,* problema *m* **3** GERM : microbio *m,* virus *m* **4** MICROPHONE : micrófono *m*

bugaboo [ˈbʌgəˌbuː] → **bogey**

bugbear [ˈbʌgˌbær] *n* : pesadilla *f,* coco *m*

buggy [ˈbʌgi] *n, pl* **-gies** : calesa *f* (tirada por caballos), cochecito *m* (para niños)

bugle [ˈbjuːgəl] *n* : clarín *m,* corneta *f*

bugler [ˈbjuːgələr] *n* : corneta *mf*

build¹ [ˈbɪld] *v* **built** [ˈbɪlt]; **building** *vt* **1** CONSTRUCT : construir, edificar, ensamblar, levantar **2** DEVELOP : desarrollar, elaborar, forjar **3** INCREASE : incrementar, aumentar — *vi* **to build up** : aumentar, intensificar

build² *n* PHYSIQUE : físico *m,* complexión *f*

builder [ˈbɪldər] *n* : constructor *m,* -tora *f;* contratista *mf*

building [ˈbɪldɪŋ] *n* **1** EDIFICE : edificio *m* **2** CONSTRUCTION : construcción *f*

built-in [ˈbɪltˈɪn] *adj* **1** : empotrado <built-in cabinets : armarios empotrados> **2** INHERENT : incorporado, intrínseco

bulb [ˈbʌlb] *n* **1** : bulbo *m* (de una planta), cabeza *f* (de ajo), cubeta *f* (de un termómetro) **2** LIGHTBULB : bombilla *f,* foco *m,* bombillo *m CA, Col, Ven*

bulbous [ˈbʌlbəs] *adj* : bulboso

Bulgarian [bʌlˈgæriən, bʊl-] *n* **1** : búlgaro *m,* -ra *f* **2** : búlgaro *m* (idioma) — **Bulgarian**

bulge¹ [ˈbʌldʒ] *vi* **bulged; bulging** : abultar, sobresalir

bulge² *n* : bulto *m,* protuberancia *f*

bulk¹ [ˈbʌlk] *vt* : hinchar — *vi* EXPAND, SWELL : ampliarse, hincharse

bulk² *n* **1** SIZE, VOLUME : volumen *m,* tamaño *m* **2** FIBER : fibra *f* **3** MASS : mole *f* **4 the bulk of** : la mayor parte de **5 in ~** : en grandes cantidades

bulkhead [ˈbʌlkˌhɛd] *n* : mamparo *m*

bulky [ˈbʌlki] *adj* **bulkier; -est** : voluminoso, grande

bull¹ [ˈbʊl] *adj* : macho

bull² *n* **1** : toro *m,* macho *m* (de ciertas especies) **2** : bula *f* (papal) **3** DECREE : decreto *m,* edicto *m*

bulldog [ˈbʊlˌdɔg] *n* : buldog *m*

bulldoze [ˈbʊlˌdoːz] *vt* **-dozed; -dozing 1** LEVEL : nivelar (el terreno), derribar (un edificio) **2** FORCE : forzar <he bulldozed his way through : se abrió paso a codazos>

bulldozer [ˈbʊlˌdoːzər] *n* : bulldozer *m*

bullet [ˈbʊlət] *n* : bala *f*

bulletin [ˈbʊlətən, -lətən] *n* **1** NOTICE : comunicado *m,* anuncio *m,* boletín *m* **2** NEWSLETTER : boletín *m* (informativo)

bulletin board *n* : tablón *m* de anuncios

bulletproof [ˈbʊlətˌpruːf] *adj* : antibalas, a prueba de balas

bullfight [ˈbʊlˌfaɪt] *n* : corrida *f* (de toros)

bullfighter [ˈbʊlˌfaɪtər] *n* : torero *m,* -ra *f;* matador *m*

bullfrog [ˈbʊlˌfrɔg] *n* : rana *f* toro

bullheaded [ˈbʊlˈhɛdəd] *adj* : testarudo

bullion [ˈbʊljən] *n* : oro *m* en lingotes, plata *f* en lingotes

bullock [ˈbʊlək] *n* **1** STEER : buey *m,* toro *m* castrado **2** : toro *m* joven, novillo *m*

bull's–eye [ˈbʊlzˌaɪ] *n, pl* **bull's–eyes** : diana *f,* blanco *m*

bully¹ [ˈbʊli] *vt* **-lied; -lying** : intimidar, amendrentar, mangonear

bully² *n, pl* **-lies** : matón *m;* bravucón *m,* -cona *f*

bulrush [ˈbʊlˌrʌʃ] *n* : especie *f* de junco

bulwark [ˈbʊlˌwərk, -ˌwɔrk; ˈbʌlˌwərk] *n* : baluarte *m,* bastión *f*

bum¹ [ˈbʌm] *v* **bummed; bumming** *vi* **to bum around** : vagabundear, vagar — *vt* : gorronear *fam,* sablear *fam*

bum² *adj* : inútil, malo <a bum rap : una acusación falsa>

bum³ *n* **1** LOAFER : vago *m,* -ga *f* **2** HOBO, TRAMP : vagabundo *m,* -da *f*

bumblebee [ˈbʌmbəlˌbiː] *n* : abejorro *m*

bump¹ [ˈbʌmp] *vt* : chocar contra, golpear contra, dar <to bump one's head : darse (un golpe) en la cabeza> — *vi* **to bump into** MEET : encontrarse con, tropezarse con

bump² *n* **1** BULGE : bulto *m,* protuberancia *f* **2** IMPACT : golpe *m,* choque *m* **3** JOLT : sacudida *f*

bumper¹ [ˈbʌmpər] *adj* : extraordinario, récord <a bumper crop : una cosecha abundante>

bumper[2] *n* : parachoques *mpl*

bumpkin [ˈbʌmpkən] *n* : palurdo *m*, -da *f*

bumpy [ˈbʌmpi] *adj* **bumpier; -est** : desigual, lleno de baches (dícese de un camino), agitado (dícese de un vuelo en avión)

bun [ˈbʌn] *n* : bollo *m*

bunch[1] [ˈbʌntʃ] *vt* : agrupar, amontonar — *vi* **to bunch up** : amontonarse, agruparse, fruncirse (dícese de una tela)

bunch[2] *n* : grupo *m*, montón *m*, ramo *m* (de flores)

bundle[1] [ˈbʌndəl] *vt* **-dled; -dling** : liar, atar

bundle[2] *n* **1** : fardo *m*, atado *m*, bulto *m*, haz *m* (de palos) **2** PARCEL : paquete *m* **3** LOAD : montón *m* <a bundle of money : un montón de dinero>

bungalow [ˈbʌŋgəˌloː] *n* : tipo de casa de un solo piso

bungle[1] [ˈbʌŋgəl] *vt* **-gled; -gling** : echar a perder, malograr

bungle[2] *n* : chapuza *f*, desatino *m*

bungler [ˈbʌŋgələr] *n* : chapucero *m*, -ra *f*; inepto *m*, -ta *f*

bunion [ˈbʌnjən] *n* : juanete *m*

bunk[1] [ˈbʌŋk] *vi* : dormir (en una litera)

bunk[2] *n* **1** *or* **bunk bed** : litera *f* **2** NONSENSE : tonterías *fpl*, bobadas *fpl*

bunker [ˈbʌŋkər] *n* **1** : carbonera *f* (en un barco) **2** SHELTER : búnker *m*

bunny [ˈbʌni] *n, pl* **-nies** : conejo *m*, -ja *f*

buoy[1] [ˈbuːi, ˈbɔɪ] *vt* **to buoy up 1** : mantener a flote **2** CHEER, HEARTEN : animar, levantar el ánimo a

buoy[2] *n* : boya *f*

buoyancy [ˈbɔɪən*t*si, ˈbuːjən-] *n* **1** : flotabilidad *f* **2** OPTIMISM : confianza *f*, optimismo *m*

buoyant [ˈbɔɪənt, ˈbuːjənt] *adj* : boyante, flotante

bur *or* **burr** [ˈbər] *n* : abrojo *m* (de una planta)

burden[1] [ˈbərdən] *vt* : cargar, oprimir

burden[2] *n* : carga *f*, peso *m*

burdensome [ˈbərdənsəm] *adj* : oneroso

burdock [ˈbərˌdɑk] *n* : bardana *f*

bureau [ˈbjʊro] *n* **1** CHEST OF DRAWERS : cómoda *f* **2** DEPARTMENT : departamento *m* (del gobierno) **3** AGENCY : agencia *f* <travel bureau : agencia de viajes>

bureaucracy [bjʊˈrɑkrəsi] *n, pl* **-cies** : burocracia *f*

bureaucrat [ˈbjʊrəˌkræt] *n* : burócrata *mf*

bureaucratic [ˌbjʊrəˈkræt̬ɪk] *adj* : burocrático

burgeon [ˈbərdʒən] *vi* : florecer, retoñar, crecer

burglar [ˈbərglər] *n* : ladrón *m*, -drona *f*

burglarize [ˈbərgləˌraɪz] *vt* **-ized; -izing** : robar

burglary [ˈbərgləri] *n, pl* **-glaries** : robo *m*

burgle [ˈbərgəl] *vt* **-gled; -gling** : robar

burgundy [ˈbərgəndi] *n, pl* **-dies** : borgoña *m*, vino *m* de Borgoña

burial [ˈbɛriəl] *n* : entierro *m*, sepelio *m*

burlap [ˈbərˌlæp] *n* : arpillera *f*

burlesque[1] [bərˈlɛsk] *vt* **-lesqued; -lesquing** : parodiar

burlesque[2] *n* **1** PARODY : parodia *f* **2** REVUE : revista *f* (musical)

burly [ˈbərli] *adj* **-lier; -liest** : fornido, corpulento, musculoso

burn[1] [ˈbərn] *v* **burned** [ˈbərnd, ˈbərnt] *or* **burnt** [ˈbərnt]; **burning** *vt* **1** : quemar, incendiar <to burn a building : incendiar un edificio> <I burned my hand : me quemé la mano> **2** CONSUME : usar, gastar, consumir — *vi* **1** : arder (dícese de un fuego o un edificio), quemarse (dícese de la comida, etc.) **2** : estar prendido, estar encendido <we left the lights burning : dejamos las luces encendidas> **3 to burn out** : consumirse, apagarse **4 to burn with** : arder de <he was burning with jealousy : ardía de celos>

burn[2] *n* : quemadura *f*

burner [ˈbərnər] *n* : quemador *m*

burnish [ˈbərnɪʃ] *vt* : bruñir

burp[1] [ˈbərp] *vi* : eructar — *vt* : hacer eructar

burp[2] *n* : eructo *m*

burr → **bur**

burro [ˈbəro, ˈbʊr-] *n, pl* **-os** : burro *m*

burrow[1] [ˈbəro] *vi* **1** : cavar, hacer una madriguera **2 to burrow into** : hurgar en — *vt* : cavar, excavar

burrow[2] *n* : madriguera *f*, conejera *f* (de un conejo)

bursar [ˈbərsər] *n* : administrador *m*, -dora *f*

bursitis [bərˈsaɪt̬əs] *n* : bursitis *f*

burst[1] [ˈbərst] *v* **burst** *or* **bursted; bursting** *vi* **1** : reventarse (dícese de una llanta o un globo), estallar (dícese de obuses o fuegos artificiales), romperse (dícese de un dique) **2 to burst in** : irrumpir en **3 to burst into** : empezar a, echar a <to burst into tears : echarse a llorar> — *vt* : reventar

burst[2] *n* **1** EXPLOSION : estallido *m*, explosión *f*, reventón *m* (de una llanta) **2** OUTBURST : arranque *m* (de actividad, de velocidad), arrebato *m* (de ira), salva *f* (de aplausos)

Burundian [bʊˈruːndiən, -ˈrʊn-] *n* : burundés *m*, -desa *f* — **Burundian** *adj*

bury [ˈbɛri] *vt* **buried; burying 1** INTER : enterrar, sepultar **2** HIDE : esconder, ocultar **3 to bury oneself in** : enfrascarse en

bus[1] [ˈbʌs] *v* **bused** *or* **bussed** [ˈbʌst]; **busing** *or* **bussing** [ˈbʌsɪŋ] *vt* : transportar en autobús — *vi* : viajar en autobús

bus[2] *n* : autobús *m,* bus *m,* camión *m Mex,* colectivo *m Arg, Bol, Peru*

busboy [ˈbʌsˌbɔɪ] *n* : ayudante *mf* de camarero

bush [ˈbʊʃ] *n* **1** SHRUB : arbusto *m,* mata *f* **2** THICKET : maleza *f,* matorral *m*

bushel [ˈbʊʃəl] *n* : medida de áridos igual a 35.24 litros

bushing [ˈbʊʃɪŋ] *n* : cojinete *m*

bushy [ˈbʊʃi] *adj* **bushier; -est** : espeso, poblado <bushy eyebrows : cejas pobladas>

busily [ˈbɪzəli] *adv* : afanosamente, diligentemente

business [ˈbɪznəs, -nəz] *n* **1** OCCUPATION : ocupación *f,* oficio *m* **2** DUTY, MISSION : misión *f,* deber *m,* responsabilidad *f* **3** ESTABLISHMENT, FIRM : empresa *f,* firma *f,* negocio *m,* comercio *m* **4** COMMERCE : negocios *mpl,* comercio *m* **5** AFFAIR, MATTER : asunto *m,* cuestión *f,* cosa *f* <it's none of your business : no es asunto tuyo>

businessman [ˈbɪznəsˌmæn, -nəz-] *n, pl* **-men** [-mən, -ˌmɛn] : empresario *m,* hombre *m* de negocios

businesswoman [ˈbɪznəsˌwʊmən, -nəz-] *n, pl* **-women** [-ˌwɪmən] : empresaria *f,* mujer *f* de negocios

bust[1] [ˈbʌst] *vt* **1** BREAK, SMASH : romper, estropear, destrozar **2** TAME : domar, amansar (un caballo) — *vi* : romperse, estropearse

bust[2] *n* **1** : busto *m* (en la escultura) **2** BREASTS : pecho *m,* senos *mpl,* busto *m*

bustle[1] [ˈbʌsəl] *vi* **-tled; -tling to bustle about** : ir y venir, trajinar, ajetrearse

bustle[2] *n* **1** *or* **hustle and bustle** : bullicio *m,* ajetreo *m* **2** : polisón *m* (en la ropa femenina)

busy[1] [ˈbɪzi] *vt* **busied; busying to busy oneself with** : ocuparse con, ponerse a, entretenerse con

busy[2] *adj* **busier; -est 1** OCCUPIED : ocupado, atareado <he's busy working : está ocupado en su trabajo> <the telephone was busy : el teléfono estaba ocupado> **2** BUSTLING : concurrido, animado <a busy street : una calle concurrida, una calle con mucho tránsito>

busybody [ˈbɪziˌbɑdi] *n, pl* **-bodies** : entrometido *m,* -da *f;* metiche *mf fam;* metomentodo *mf*

but[1] [ˈbʌt] *conj* **1** THAT : que <there is no doubt but he is lazy : no cabe duda que sea perezoso> **2** WITHOUT : sin que **3** NEVERTHELESS : pero, no obstante, sin embargo <I called her but she didn't answer : la llamé pero no contestó> **4** YET : pero <he was poor but proud : era pobre pero orgulloso>

but[2] *prep* EXCEPT : excepto, menos <everyone but Carlos : todos menos Carlos> <the last but one : el penúltimo>

butcher[1] [ˈbʊtʃər] *vt* **1** SLAUGHTER : matar (animales) **2** KILL : matar, asesinar, masacrar **3** BOTCH : estropear, hacer una chapuza

butcher[2] *n* **1** : carnicero *m,* -ra *f* **2** KILLER : asesino *m,* -na *f* **3** BUNGLER : chapucero *m,* -ra *f*

butler [ˈbʌtlər] *n* : mayordomo *m*

butt[1] [ˈbʌt] *vt* **1** : embestir (con los cuernos), darle un cabezazo a **2** ABUT : colindar con, bordear — *vi* **to butt in 1** INTERRUPT : interrumpir **2** MEDDLE : entrometerse, meterse

butt[2] *n* **1** BUTTING : embestida *f* (de cuernos), cabezazo *m* **2** TARGET : blanco *m* <the butt of their jokes : el blanco de sus bromas> **3** BOTTOM, END : extremo *m,* culata *f* (de un rifle), colilla *f* (de un cigarillo)

butte [ˈbjuːt] *n* : colina *f* empinada y aislada

butter[1] [ˈbʌt̬ər] *vt* **1** : untar con mantequilla **2 to butter up** : halagar

butter[2] *n* : mantequilla *f*

buttercup [ˈbʌt̬ərˌkʌp] *n* : ranúnculo *m*

butterfat [ˈbʌt̬ərˌfæt] *n* : grasa *f* de la leche

butterfly [ˈbʌt̬ərˌflaɪ] *n, pl* **-flies** : mariposa *f*

buttermilk [ˈbʌt̬ərˌmɪlk] *n* : suero *m* de la leche

butternut [ˈbʌt̬ərˌnʌt] *n* : nogal *m* ceniciento (árbol)

butterscotch [ˈbʌt̬ərˌskɑtʃ] *n* : caramelo *m* duro hecho con mantequilla

buttery [ˈbʌt̬əri] *adj* : mantecoso

buttocks [ˈbʌt̬əks, -ˌtɑks] *npl* : nalgas *fpl,* trasero *m*

button[1] [ˈbʌtən] *vt* : abrochar, abotonar — *vi* : abrocharse, abotonarse

button[2] *n* : botón *m*

buttonhole[1] [ˈbʌtənˌhoːl] *vt* **-holed; -holing** : acorralar

buttonhole[2] *n* : ojal *m*

buttress[1] [ˈbʌtrəs] *vt* : apoyar, reforzar

buttress[2] *n* **1** : contrafuerte *m* (en la arquitectura) **2** SUPPORT : apoyo *m,* sostén *m*

buxom [ˈbʌksəm] *adj* : con mucho busto, con mucho pecho

buy[1] [ˈbaɪ] *vt* **bought** [ˈbɔt]; **buying** : comprar

buy[2] *n* BARGAIN : compra *f,* ganga *f*

buyer [ˈbaɪər] *n* : comprador *m,* -dora *f*

buzz[1] [ˈbʌz] *vi* : zumbar (dícese de un insecto), sonar (dícese de un teléfono o un despertador)

buzz[2] *n* **1** : zumbido *m* (de insectos) **2** : murmullo *m,* rumor *m* (de voces)

buzzard [ˈbʌzərd] *n* VULTURE : buitre *m,* zopilote *m CA, Mex*

buzzer [ˈbʌzər] *n* : timbre *m,* chicharra *f*

buzzword [ˈbʌzˌwərd] *n* : palabra *f* de moda

by[1] [ˈbaɪ] *adv* **1** NEAR : cerca <he lives close by : vive muy cerca> **2 to stop**

by : pasar por casa, hacer una visita **3 to go by** : pasar <they rushed by : pasaron corriendo> **4 to put by** : reservar, poner a un lado **5 by and by** : poco después, dentro de poco **6 by and large** : en general

by[2] *prep* **1** NEAR : cerca de, al lado de, junto a **2** VIA : por <she left by the door : salió por la puerta> **3** PAST : por, por delante de <they walked by him : pasaron por delante de él> **4** DURING : de, durante <by night : de noche> **5** (*in expressions of time*) : para <we'll be there by ten : estaremos allí para las diez> <by then : para entonces> **6** (*indicating cause or agent*) : por, de, a <built by the Romans : construido por los romanos> <a book by Borges : un libro de Borges> <made by hand : hecho a mano>

by and by *adv* : dentro de poco

bygone[1] [ˈbaɪˌgɔn] *adj* : pasado

bygone[2] *n* **let bygones be bygones** : lo pasado, pasado está

bylaw *or* **byelaw** [ˈbaɪˌlɔ] *n* : norma *f*, reglamento *m*

by–line [ˈbaɪˌlaɪn] *n* : data *f*

bypass[1] [ˈbaɪˌpæs] *vt* : evitar

bypass[2] *n* : carretera *f* de circunvalación, desvío *m*

by–product [ˈbaɪˌprɑdəkt] *n* : subproducto *m*, producto *m* derivado

bystander [ˈbaɪˌstændər] *n* : espectador *m*, -dora *f*

byway [ˈbaɪˌweɪ] *n* : camino *m* (apartado), carretera *f* secundaria

byword [ˈbaɪˌwərd] *n* **1** PROVERB : proverbio *m*, refrán *m* **2 to be a byword for** : estar sinónimo de

C

c [ˈsiː] *n*, *pl* **c's** *or* **cs** : tercera letra del alfabeto inglés

cab [ˈkæb] *n* **1** TAXI : taxi *m* **2** : cabina *f* (de un camión o una locomotora) **3** CARRIAGE : coche *m* de caballos

cabal [kəˈbɑl, -ˈbæl] *n* **1** INTRIGUE, PLOT : conspiración *f*, complot *m*, intriga *f* **2** : grupo *m* de conspiradores

cabaret [ˌkæbəˈreɪ] *n* : cabaret *m*

cabbage [ˈkæbɪdʒ] *n* : col *f*, repollo *m*

cabbie *or* **cabby** [ˈkæbi] *n* : taxista *mf*

cabin [ˈkæbən] *n* **1** HUT : cabaña *f*, choza *f*, barraca *f* **2** STATEROOM : camarote *m* **3** : cabina *f* (de un automóvil o avión)

cabinet [ˈkæbnət] *n* **1** CUPBOARD : armario *m* **2** : gabinete *m*, consejo *m* de ministros **3 medicine cabinet** : botiquín *m*

cabinetmaker [ˈkæbnətˌmeɪkər] *n* : ebanista *mf*

cabinetmaking [ˈkæbnətˌmeɪkɪŋ] *n* : ebanistería *f*

cable[1] [ˈkeɪbəl] *vt* **-bled; -bling** : enviar un cable, telegrafiar

cable[2] *n* **1** : cable *m* (para colgar o sostener algo) **2** : cable *m* eléctrico **3** → **cablegram**

cablegram [ˈkeɪbəlˌgræm] *n* : telegrama *m*, cable *m*

caboose [kəˈbuːs] *n* : furgón *m* de cola, cabús *m Mex*

cabstand [ˈkæbˌstænd] *n* : parada *f* de taxis

cacao [kəˈkaʊ, -ˈkeɪo] *n*, *pl* **cacaos** : cacao *m*

cache[1] [ˈkæʃ] *vt* **cached; caching** : esconder, guardar en un escondrijo

cache[2] *n* **1** : escondite *m*, escondrijo *m* <cache of weapons : escondite de armas> **2** : cache *m* <cache memory : memoria cache>

cachet [kæˈʃeɪ] *n* : caché *m*, prestigio *m*

cackle[1] [ˈkækəl] *vi* **-led; -ling 1** CLUCK : cacarear **2** : reírse o carcajearse estridentemente <he was cackling with delight : estaba carcajeándose de gusto>

cackle[2] *n* **1** : cacareo *m* (de una polla) **2** LAUGH : risa *f* estridente

cacophony [kæˈkɑfəni, -ˈkɔ-] *n*, *pl* **-nies** : cacofonía *f*

cactus [ˈkæktəs] *n*, *pl* **cacti** [-ˌtaɪ] *or* **-tuses** : cacto *m*, cactus *m*

cadaver [kəˈdævər] *n* : cadáver *m*

cadaverous [kəˈdævərəs] *adj* : cadavérico

caddie[1] *or* **caddy** [ˈkædi] *vi* **caddied; caddying** : trabajar de caddie, hacer de caddie

caddie[2] *or* **caddy** *n*, *pl* **-dies** : caddie *mf*

caddy [ˈkædi] *n*, *pl* **-dies** : cajita *f* para té

cadence [ˈkeɪdənts] *n* : cadencia *f*, ritmo *m*

cadenced [ˈkeɪdəntst] *adj* : cadencioso, rítmico

cadet [kəˈdɛt] *n* : cadete *mf*

cadmium [ˈkædmiəm] *n* : cadmio *m*

cadre [ˈkæˌdreɪ, ˈkɑ-, -ˌdriː] *n* : cuadro *m* (de expertos)

café [kæˈfeɪ, kə-] *n* : café *m*, cafetería *f*

cafeteria [ˌkæfəˈtɪriə] *n* : cafetería *f*, restaurante *m* de autoservicio

caffeine [kæˈfiːn] *n* : cafeína *f*

cage[1] [ˈkeɪdʒ] *vt* **caged; caging** : enjaular

cage[2] *n* : jaula *f*

cagey [ˈkeɪdʒi] *adj* **-gier; -est 1** CAUTIOUS : cauteloso, reservado **2** SHREWD : astuto, vivo — **cagily** [-dʒəli] *adv*

caisson [ˈkeɪˌsɑn, -sən] *n* **1 :** cajón *m* de municiones **2 :** cajón *m* hidráulico
cajole [kəˈdʒoːl] *vt* **-joled; -joling :** engatusar
cajolery [kəˈdʒoːləri] *n* **:** engatusamiento *m*
cake¹ [ˈkeɪk] *v* **caked; caking** *vt* **:** cubrir <caked with mud : cubierto de barro> — *vi* **:** endurecerse
cake² *n* **1 :** torta *f,* bizcocho *m,* pastel *m* **2 :** pastilla *f* (de jabón) **3 to take the cake :** llevarse la palma, ser el colmo
calabash [ˈkæləˌbæʃ] *n* **:** calabaza *f*
calamine [ˈkæləˌmaɪn] *n* **:** calamina *f* <calamine lotion : loción de calamina>
calamitous [kəˈlæmət̬əs] *adj* **:** desastroso, catastrófico, calamitoso — **calamitously** *adv*
calamity [kəˈlæmət̬i] *n, pl* **-ties :** desastre *m,* desgracia *f,* calamidad *f*
calcium [ˈkælsiəm] *n* **:** calcio *m*
calcium carbonate [ˈkɑrbəˌneɪt, -nət] *n* **:** carbonato *m* de calcio
calculable [ˈkælkjələbəl] *adj* **:** calculable, computable
calculate [ˈkælkjəˌleɪt] *v* **-lated; -lating** *vt* **1** COMPUTE **:** calcular, computar **2** ESTIMATE **:** calcular, creer **3** INTEND **:** planear, tener la intención de <I calculated on spending $100 : planeaba gastar $100> — *vi* **:** calcular, hacer cálculos
calculated [ˈkælkjəˌleɪt̬əd] *adj* **1** ESTIMATED **:** calculado **2** DELIBERATE **:** intencional, premeditado, deliberado
calculating [ˈkælkjəˌleɪt̬ɪŋ] *adj* SHREWD **:** calculador, astuto
calculation [ˌkælkjəˈleɪʃən] *n* **:** cálculo *m*
calculator [ˈkælkjəˌleɪt̬ər] *n* **:** calculadora *f*
calculus [ˈkælkjələs] *n, pl* **-li** [-ˌlaɪ] **1 :** cálculo *m* <differential calculus : cálculo diferencial> **2** TARTAR **:** sarro *m* (dental)
caldron [ˈkɔldrən] → **cauldron**
calendar [ˈkæləndər] *n* **1 :** calendario *m* **2** SCHEDULE **:** calendario *m,* programa *m,* agenda *f*
calf [ˈkæf, ˈkɑf] *n, pl* **calves** [ˈkævz, ˈkɑvz] **1 :** becerro *m,* -rra *f;* ternero *m,* -ra *f* (de vacunos) **2 :** cría *f* (de otros mamíferos) **3 :** pantorrilla *f* (de la pierna)
calfskin [ˈkæfˌskɪn] *n* **:** piel *f* de becerro
caliber *or* **calibre** [ˈkæləbər] *n* **1 :** calibre *m* <a .38 caliber gun : una pistola de calibre .38> **2** ABILITY **:** calibre *m,* valor *m,* capacidad *f*
calibrate [ˈkæləˌbreɪt] *vt* **-brated; -brating :** calibrar (armas), graduar (termómetros)
calibration [ˌkæləˈbreɪʃən] *n* **:** calibrado *m,* calibración *f*
calico [ˈkælɪˌkoː] *n, pl* **-coes** *or* **-cos 1 :** calicó *m,* percal *m* **2** *or* **calico cat :** gato *m* manchado
calipers [ˈkæləpərz] *npl* **:** calibrador *m*
caliph *or* **calif** [ˈkeɪləf, ˈkæ-] *n* **:** califa *m*
calisthenics [ˌkæləsˈθɛnɪks] *ns & pl* **:** calistenia *f*
calk [ˈkɔk] → **caulk**
call¹ [ˈkɔl] *vi* **1** CRY, SHOUT **:** gritar, vociferar **2** VISIT **:** hacer (una) visita, visitar **3 to call for :** exigir, requerir, necesitar <it calls for patience : requiere mucha paciencia> — *vt* **1** SUMMON **:** llamar, convocar **2** TELEPHONE **:** llamar por teléfono, telefonear **3** NAME **:** llamar, apodar
call² *n* **1** SHOUT **:** grito *m,* llamada *f* **2 :** grito *m* (de un animal), reclamo *m* (de un pájaro) **3** SUMMONS **:** llamada *f* **4** DEMAND **:** llamado *m,* petición *f* **5** VISIT **:** visita *f* **6** DECISION **:** decisión *f* (en deportes) **7** *or* **telephone call :** llamada *f* (telefónica)
call down *vt* REPRIMAND **:** reprender, reñir
caller [ˈkɔlər] *n* **1** VISITOR **:** visita *f* **2 :** persona *f* que llama (por teléfono)
calling [ˈkɔlɪŋ] *n* **:** vocación *f,* profesión *f*
calliope [kəˈlaɪəˌpiː, ˈkæliˌoːp] *n* **:** órgano *m* de vapor
call off *vt* CANCEL **:** cancelar, suspender
callous¹ [ˈkæləs] *vt* **:** encallecer
callous² *adj* **1** CALLUSED **:** calloso, encallecido **2** UNFEELING **:** insensible, desalmado, cruel
callously [ˈkæləsli] *adv* **:** cruelmente, insensiblemente
callousness [ˈkæləsnəs] *n* **:** insensibilidad *f,* crueldad *f*
callow [ˈkælo] *adj* **:** inexperto, inmaduro
callus [ˈkæləs] *n* **:** callo m
callused [ˈkæləst] *adj* **:** encallecido, calloso
calm¹ [ˈkɑm, ˈkɑlm] *vt* **:** tranquilizar, calmar, sosegar — *vi* **:** tranquilizarse, calmarse <calm down! : ¡tranquilízate!>
calm² *adj* **1** TRANQUIL **:** calmo, tranquilo, sereno, ecuánime **2** STILL **:** en calma (dícese del mar), sin viento (dícese del aire)
calm³ *n* **:** tranquilidad *f,* calma *f*
calmly [ˈkɑmli, ˈkɑlm-] *adv* **:** con calma, tranquilamente
calmness [ˈkɑmnəs, ˈkɑlm-] *n* **:** calma *f,* tranquilidad *f*
caloric [kəˈlɔrɪk] *adj* **:** calórico (dícese de los alimentos), calorífico (dícese de la energía)
calorie [ˈkæləri] *n* **:** caloría *f*
calumniate [kəˈlʌmniˌeɪt] *vt* **-ated; -ating :** calumniar, difamar
calumny [ˈkæləmni] *n, pl* **-nies :** calumnia *f,* difamación *f*
calve [ˈkæv, ˈkɑv] *vi* **calved; calving :** parir (dícese de los mamíferos)
calves → **calf**
calypso [kəˈlɪpˌsoː] *n, pl* **-sos :** calipso *m*

calyx [ˈkeɪlɪks, ˈkæ-] *n, pl* **-lyxes** *or* **-lyces** [-ləˌsiːz] : cáliz *m*

cam [ˈkæm] *n* : leva *f*

camaraderie [ˌkɑmˈrɑdəri, ˌkæm-; ˌkɑməˈrɑ-] *n* : compañerismo *m,* camaradería *f*

Cambodian [kæmˈboːdiən] *n* : camboyano *m,* -na *f* — **Cambodian** *adj*

came → **come**

camel [ˈkæməl] *n* : camello *m*

camellia [kəˈmiːljə] *n* : camelia *f*

cameo [ˈkæmiˌoː] *n, pl* **-eos 1** : camafeo *m* **2** *or* **cameo performance** : actuación *f* especial

camera [ˈkæmrə, ˈkæmərə] *n* : cámara *f,* máquina *f* fotográfica

Cameroonian [ˌkæməˈruːniən] *n* : camerunés *m,* -nesa *f*

camouflage[1] [ˈkæməˌflɑʒ, -ˌflɑdʒ] *vt* **-flaged; -flaging** : camuflajear, camuflar

camouflage[2] *n* : camuflaje *m*

camp[1] [ˈkæmp] *vi* : acampar, ir de camping

camp[2] *n* **1** : campamento *m* **2** FACTION : campo *m,* bando *m* <in the same camp : del mismo bando> **3 to pitch camp** : acampar, poner el campamento **4 to break camp** : levantar el campamento

campaign[1] [kæmˈpeɪn] *vi* : hacer (una) campaña

campaign[2] *n* : campaña *f*

campanile [ˌkæmpəˈniːˌliː, -ˈniːl] *n, pl* **-niles** *or* **-nili** [-ˈniːˌliː] : campanario *m*

camper [ˈkæmpər] *n* **1** : campista *mf* (persona) **2** : cámper *m* (vehículo)

campground [ˈkæmpˌgraʊnd] *n* : campamento *m,* camping *m*

camphor [ˈkæmpfər] *n* : alcanfor *m*

campsite [ˈkæmpˌsaɪt] *n* : campamento *m,* camping *m*

campus [ˈkæmpəs] *n* : campus *m,* recinto *m* universitario

can[1] [ˈkæn] *v aux, past* **could** [ˈkʊd]; *present s & pl* **can 1** : poder <could you help me? : ¿podría ayudarme?> **2** : saber <she can't drive yet : todavía no sabe manejar> **3** MAY : poder, tener permiso para <can I sit down? : ¿puedo sentarme?> **4** : poder <it can't be! : ¡no puede ser!> <where can they be? : ¿dónde estarán?>

can[2] [ˈkæn] *vt* **canned; canning 1** : enlatar, envasar <to can tomatoes : enlatar tomates> **2** DISMISS, FIRE : despedir, echar

can[3] *n* : lata *f,* envase *m,* cubo *m* <a can of beer : una lata de cerveza> <garbage can : cubo de basura>

Canadian [kəˈneɪdiən] *n* : canadiense *mf* — **Canadian** *adj*

canal [kəˈnæl] *n* **1** : canal *m,* tubo *m* <alimentary canal : tubo digestivo> **2** : canal *m* <Panama Canal : Canal de Panamá>

canapé [ˈkænəpi, -ˌpeɪ] *n* : canapé *m*

canary [kəˈnɛri] *n, pl* **-naries** : canario *m*

cancel [ˈkæntsəl] *vt* **-celed** *or* **-celled; -celing** *or* **-celling** : cancelar

cancellation [ˌkæntsəˈleɪʃən] *n* : cancelación *f*

cancer [ˈkæntsər] *n* : cáncer *m*

Cancer *n* : Cáncer *mf*

cancerous [ˈkæntsərəs] *adj* : canceroso

candelabrum [ˌkændəˈlɑbrəm, -ˈlæ-] *or* **candelabra** [-brə] *n, pl* **-bra** *or* **-bras** : candelabro *m*

candid [ˈkændɪd] *adj* **1** FRANK : franco, sincero, abierto **2** : natural, espontáneo (en la fotografía)

candidacy [ˈkændədəsi] *n, pl* **-cies** : candidatura *f*

candidate [ˈkændəˌdeɪt, -dət] *n* : candidato *m,* -ta *f*

candidly [ˈkændɪdli] *adv* : con franqueza

candied [ˈkændid] *adj* : confitado

candle [ˈkændəl] *n* : vela *f,* candela *f,* cirio *m* (ceremonial)

candlestick [ˈkændəlˌstɪk] *n* : candelero *m*

candor [ˈkændər] *n* : franqueza *f*

candy [ˈkændi] *n, pl* **-dies** : dulce *m,* caramelo *m*

cane[1] [ˈkeɪn] *vt* **caned; caning 1** : tapizar (muebles) con mimbre **2** FLOG : azotar con una vara

cane[2] *n* **1** : bastón *m* (para andar), vara *f* (para castigar) **2** REED : caña *f,* mimbre *m* (para muebles)

canine[1] [ˈkeɪˌnaɪn] *adj* : canino

canine[2] *n* **1** DOG : canino *m;* perro *m,* -rra *f* **2** *or* **canine tooth** : colmillo *m,* diente *m* canino

canister [ˈkænəstər] *n* : lata *f,* bote *m*

canker [ˈkæŋkər] *n* : úlcera *f* bucal

cannery [ˈkænəri] *n, pl* **-ries** : fábrica *f* de conservas

cannibal [ˈkænəbəl] *n* : caníbal *mf;* antropófago *m,* -ga *f*

cannibalism [ˈkænəbəˌlɪzəm] *n* : canibalismo *m,* antropofagia *f*

cannily [ˈkænəbəˌlaɪz] *adv* : astutamente, sagazmente

cannon [ˈkænən] *n, pl* **-nons** *or* **-non** : cañón *m*

cannot (can not) [ˈkænˌɑt, kəˈnɑt] → **can**[1]

canny [ˈkæni] *adj* **-nier; -est** SHREWD : astuto, sagaz

canoe[1] [kəˈnuː] *vt* **-noed; -noeing** : ir en canoa

canoe[2] *n* : canoa *f,* piragua *f*

canon [ˈkænən] *n* **1** : canon *m* <canon law : derecho canónico> **2** WORKS : canon *m* <the canon of American literature : el canon de la literatura americana> **3** : canónigo *m* (de una catedral) **4** STANDARD : canon *m,* norma *f*

canonize [ˈkænəˌnaɪz] *vt* **-ized; -izing** : canonizar

canopy [ˈkænəpi] *n, pl* **-pies** : dosel *m,* toldo *m*

cant[1] [ˈkænt] *vt* TILT : ladear, inclinar — *vi* **1** SLANT : ladearse, inclinarse, escorar (dícese de un barco) **2** : hablar insinceramente

cant[2] *n* **1** SLANT : plano *m* inclinado **2** JARGON : jerga *f* **3** : palabras *fpl* insinceras

can't [ˈkænt, ˈkant] (*contraction of* **can not**) → **can**[1]

cantaloupe [ˈkæntəl͵oːp] *n* : melón *m,* cantalupo *m*

cantankerous [kænˈtæŋkərəs] *adj* : irritable, irascible — **cantankerously** *adv*

cantankerousness [kænˈtæŋkərəsnəs] *n* : irritabilidad *f,* irascibilidad *f*

cantata [kənˈtɑt̬ə] *n* : cantata *f*

canteen [kænˈtiːn] *n* **1** FLASK : cantimplora *f* **2** CAFETERIA : cantina *f,* comedor *m* **3** : club *m* para actividades sociales y recreativas

canter[1] [ˈkæntər] *vi* : ir a medio galope

canter[2] *n* : medio galope *m*

cantilever [ˈkæntə͵liːvər, -͵lɛvər] *n* **1** : viga *f* voladiza **2 cantilever bridge** : puente *m* voladizo

canto [ˈkæn͵toː] *n, pl* **-tos** : canto *m*

cantor [ˈkæntər] *n* : solista *mf*

canvas [ˈkænvəs] *n* **1** : lona *f* **2** SAILS : velas *fpl* (de un barco) **3** : lienzo *m,* tela *f* (de pintar) **4** PAINTING : pintura *f,* óleo *m,* cuadro *m*

canvass[1] [ˈkænvəs] *vt* **1** SOLICIT : solicitar votos o pedidos de, hacer campaña entre **2** SOUND OUT : sondear (opiniones, etc.)

canvass[2] *n* SURVEY : sondeo *m,* encuesta *f*

canyon [ˈkænjən] *n* : cañón *m*

cap[1] [ˈkæp] *vt* **capped; capping 1** COVER : tapar (un recipiente), enfundar (un diente), cubrir (una montaña) **2** CLIMAX : coronar, ser el punto culminante de <to cap it all off : para colmo> **3** LIMIT : limitar, poner un tope a

cap[2] *n* **1** : gorra *f,* gorro *m,* cachucha *f Mex* <baseball cap : gorra de béisbol> **2** COVER, TOP : tapa *f,* tapón *m* (de botellas), corcholata *f Mex* **3** LIMIT : tope *m,* límite *m*

capability [͵keɪpəˈbɪlət̬i] *n, pl* **-ties** : capacidad *f,* habilidad *f,* competencia *f*

capable [ˈkeɪpəbəl] *adj* : competente, capaz, hábil — **capably** [-bli] *adv*

capacious [kəˈpeɪʃəs] *adj* : amplio, espacioso, de gran capacidad *f*

capacity[1] [kəˈpæsət̬i] *adj* : completo, total <a capacity crowd : un lleno completo>

capacity[2] *n, pl* **-ties 1** ROOM, SPACE : capacidad *f,* cabida *f,* espacio *m* **2** CAPABILITY : habilidad *f,* competencia *f* **3** FUNCTION, ROLE : calidad *f,* función *f* <in his capacity as ambassador : en su calidad de embajador>

cape [ˈkeɪp] *n* **1** : capa *f* **2** : cabo *m* <Cape Horn : el Cabo de Hornos>

caper[1] [ˈkeɪpər] *vi* : dar saltos, correr y brincar

caper[2] *n* **1** : alcaparra *f* <olives and capers : aceitunas y alcaparras> **2** ANTIC, PRANK : broma *f,* travesura *f* **3** LEAP : brinco *m,* salto *m*

Cape Verdean [ˈkeɪpˈvərdiən] *n* : caboverdiano *m,* -na *f* — **Cape Verdean** *adj*

capful [ˈkæp͵fʊl] *n* : tapa *f,* tapita *f*

capillary[1] [ˈkæpə͵lɛri] *adj* : capilar

capillary[2] *n, pl* **-ries** : capilar *m*

capital[1] [ˈkæpət̬əl] *adj* **1** : capital <capital punishment : pena capital> **2** : mayúsculo (dícese de las letras) **3** : de capital <capital assets : activo fijo> <capital gain : ganancia de capital, plusvalía> **4** EXCELLENT : excelente, estupendo

capital[2] *n* **1** *or* **capital city** : capital *f,* sede *f* del gobierno **2** WEALTH : capital *m* **3** *or* **capital letter** : mayúscula *f* **4** : capitel *m* (de una columna)

capitalism [ˈkæpət̬əl͵ɪzəm] *n* : capitalismo *m*

capitalist[1] [ˈkæpət̬əlɪst] *or* **capitalistic** [͵kæpət̬əlˈɪstɪk] *adj* : capitalista

capitalist[2] *n* : capitalista *mf*

capitalization [͵kæpət̬ələˈzeɪʃən] *n* : capitalización *f*

capitalize [ˈkæpət̬əl͵aɪz] *v* **-ized; -izing** *vt* **1** FINANCE : capitalizar, financiar **2** : escribir con mayúscula — *vi* **to capitalize on** : sacar partido de, aprovechar

capitol [ˈkæpət̬əl] *n* : capitolio *m*

capitulate [kəˈpɪtʃə͵leɪt] *vi* **-lated; -lating** : capitular

capitulation [kə͵pɪtʃəˈleɪʃən] *n* : capitulación *f*

capon [ˈkeɪ͵pɑn, -pən] *n* : capón *m*

caprice [kəˈpriːs] *n* : capricho *m,* antojo *m*

capricious [kəˈprɪʃəs, -ˈpriː-] *adj* : caprichoso — **capriciously** *adv*

Capricorn [ˈkæprɪ͵kɔrn] *n* : Capricornio *mf*

capsize [ˈkæp͵saɪz, kæpˈsaɪz] *v* **-sized; -sizing** *vi* : volcar, volcarse — *vt* : hacer volcar

capstan [ˈkæpstən, -͵stæn] *n* : cabrestante *m*

capsule [ˈkæpsəl, -͵suːl] *n* **1** : cápsula *f* (en la farmacéutica y botánica) **2 space capsule** : cápsula *f* espacial

captain[1] [ˈkæptən] *vt* : capitanear

captain[2] *n* **1** : capitán *m,* -tana *f* **2** HEADWAITER : jefe *m,* -fa *f* de comedor **3 captain of industry** : magnate *mf*

caption[1] [ˈkæpʃən] *vt* : ponerle una leyenda a (una ilustración), titular (un artículo), subtitular (una película)

caption[2] *n* **1** HEADING : titular *m,* encabezamiento *m* **2** : leyenda *f* (al pie de una ilustración) **3** SUBTITLE : subtítulo *m*

captivate [ˈkæptəˌveɪt] *vt* **-vated; -vating** CHARM : cautivar, hechizar, encantar
captivating [ˈkæptəˌveɪt̬ɪŋ] *adj* : cautivador, hechicero, encantador
captive[1] [ˈkæptɪv] *adj* : cautivo
captive[2] *n* : cautivo *m*, -va *f*
captivity [kæpˈtɪvət̬i] *n* : cautiverio *m*
captor [ˈkæptər] *n* : captor *m*, -tora *f*
capture[1] [ˈkæpʃər] *vt* **-tured; -turing** **1** SEIZE : capturar, apresar **2** CATCH : captar <to capture one's interest : captar el interés de uno>
capture[2] *n* : captura *f*, apresamiento *m*
car [ˈkɑr] *n* **1** AUTOMOBILE : automóvil *m*, coche *m*, carro *m* **2** : vagón *m*, coche *m* (de un tren) **3** : cabina *f* (de un ascensor)
carafe [kəˈræf, -ˈrɑf] *n* : garrafa *f*
caramel [ˈkɑrməl; ˈkærəməl, -ˌmɛl] *n* **1** : caramelo *m*, azúcar *f* quemada **2** *or* **caramel candy** : caramelo *m*, dulce *m* de leche
carat [ˈkærət] *n* : quilate *m*
caravan [ˈkærəˌvæn] *n* : caravana *f*
caraway [ˈkærəˌweɪ] *n* : alcaravea *f*
carbine [ˈkɑrˌbaɪn, -ˌbiːn] *n* : carabina *f*
carbohydrate [ˌkɑrboˈhaɪˌdreɪt, -drət] *n* : carbohidrato *m*, hidrato *m* de carbono
carbon [ˈkɑrbən] *n* **1** : carbono *m* **2** → **carbon paper** **3** → **carbon copy**
carbonated [ˈkɑrbəˌneɪt̬əd] *adj* : carbonatado (dícese del agua), gaseoso (dícese de las bebidas)
carbon copy *n* **1** : copia *f* al carbón **2** DUPLICATE : duplicado *m*, copia *f* exacta
carbon paper *n* : papel *m* carbón
carbuncle [ˈkɑrˌbʌŋkəl] *n* : carbunco *m*
carburetor [ˈkɑrbəˌreɪt̬ər, -bjə-] *n* : carburador *m*
carcass [ˈkɑrkəs] *n* : cuerpo *m* (de un animal muerto)
carcinogen [kɑrˈsɪnəd͡ʒən, ˈkɑrsənəˌd͡ʒɛn] *n* : carcinógeno *m*, cancerígeno *m*
carcinogenic [ˌkɑrsənoˈd͡ʒɛnɪk] *adj* : carcinogénico
card[1] [ˈkɑrd] *vt* : cardar (fibras)
card[2] *n* **1** : carta *f*, naipe *m* <to play cards : jugar a las cartas> <a deck of cards : una baraja> **2** : tarjeta *f* <birthday card : tarjeta de cumpleaños> <business card : tarjeta (de visita)> **3** : carda *f* (para cardar fibras)
cardboard [ˈkɑrdˌbord] *n* : cartón *m*, cartulina *f*
cardiac [ˈkɑrdiˌæk] *adj* : cardíaco, cardiaco
cardigan [ˈkɑrdɪgən] *n* : cárdigan *m*, chaqueta *f* de punto
cardinal[1] [ˈkɑrdənəl] *adj* FUNDAMENTAL : cardinal, fundamental
cardinal[2] *n* : cardenal *m*
cardinal number *n* : número *m* cardinal
cardinal point *n* : punto *m* cardinal
cardiologist [ˌkɑrdiˈɑləd͡ʒɪst] *n* : cardiólogo *m*, -ga *f*
cardiology [ˌkɑrdiˈɑləd͡ʒi] *n* : cardiología *f*
cardiovascular [ˌkɑrdioˈvæskjələr] *adj* : cardiovascular
care[1] [ˈkær] *v* **cared; caring** *vi* **1** : importarle a uno <they don't care : no les importa> **2** : preocuparse, inquietarse <she cares about the poor : se preocupa por los pobres> **3 to care for** TEND : cuidar (de), atender, encargarse de **4 to care for** CHERISH : querer, sentir cariño por **5 to care for** LIKE : gustarle (algo a uno) <I don't care for your attitude : tu actitud no me agrada> — *vt* WISH : desear, querer <if you care to go : si deseas ir>
care[2] *n* **1** ANXIETY : inquietud *f*, preocupación *f* **2** CAREFULNESS : cuidado *m*, atención *f* <handle with care : manejar con cuidado> **3** CHARGE : cargo *m*, cuidado *m* **4 to take care of** : cuidar (de), atender, encargarse de
careen [kəˈriːn] *vi* **1** SWAY : oscilar, balancearse **2** CAREER : ir a toda velocidad
career[1] [kəˈrɪr] *vi* : ir a toda velocidad
career[2] *n* VOCATION : vocación *f*, profesión *f*, carrera *f*
carefree [ˈkærˌfriː, ˌkærˈ-] *adj* : despreocupado
careful [ˈkærfəl] *adj* **1** CAUTIOUS : cuidadoso, cauteloso **2** PAINSTAKING : cuidadoso, esmerado, meticuloso
carefully [ˈkærfəli] *adv* : con cuidado, cuidadosamente
carefulness [ˈkærfəlnəs] *n* **1** CAUTION : cuidado *m*, cautela *f* **2** METICULOUSNESS : esmero *m*, meticulosidad *f*
caregiver [ˈkærˌgɪvər] *n* : persona *f* que cuida a niños o enfermos
careless [ˈkærləs] *adj* : descuidado, negligente — **carelessly** *adv*
carelessness [ˈkærləsnəs] *n* : descuido *m*, negligencia *f*
caress[1] [kəˈrɛs] *vt* : acariciar
caress[2] *n* : caricia *f*
caret [ˈkærət] *n* : signo *m* de intercalación
caretaker [ˈkɛrˌteɪkər] *n* : conserje *mf*; velador *m*, -dora *f*
cargo [ˈkɑrˌgoː] *n, pl* **-goes** *or* **-gos** : cargamento *m*, carga *f*
caribou [ˈkærəˌbuː] *n, pl* **-bou** *or* **-bous** : caribú *m*
caricature[1] [ˈkærɪkəˌtʃʊr] *vt* **-tured; -turing** : caricaturizar
caricature[2] *n* : caricatura *f*
caricaturist [ˈkærɪkəˌtʃʊrɪst] *n* : caricaturista *mf*
caries [ˈkærˌiːz] *n, pl* **caries** : caries *f*
carillon [ˈkærəˌlɑn] *n* : carillón *m*
carmine [ˈkɑrmən, -ˌmaɪn] *n* : carmín *m*
carnage [ˈkɑrnɪd͡ʒ] *n* : matanza *f*, carnicería *f*

carnal [ˈkɑrnəl] *adj* : carnal

carnation [kɑrˈneɪʃən] *n* : clavel *m*

carnival [ˈkɑrnəvəl] *n* : carnaval *m,* feria *f*

carnivore [ˈkɑrnəˌvor] *n* : carnívoro *m*

carnivorous [kɑrˈnɪvərəs] *adj* : carnívoro

carol[1] [ˈkærəl] *vi* **-oled** *or* **-olled; -oling** *or* **-olling** : cantar villancicos

carol[2] *n* : villancico *m*

caroler *or* **caroller** [ˈkærələr] *n* : persona *f* que canta villancicos

carom[1] [ˈkærəm] *vi* **1** REBOUND : rebotar <the bullet caromed off the wall : la bala rebotó contra el muro> **2** : hacer carambola (en billar)

carom[2] *n* : carambola *f*

carouse [kəˈraʊz] *vt* **-roused; -rousing** : irse de parranda, irse de juerga

carousel *or* **carrousel** [ˌkærəˈsɛl, ˈkærəˌ-] *n* : carrusel *m,* tiovivo *m*

carouser [kəˈraʊzər] *n* : juerguista *mf*

carp[1] [ˈkɑrp] *vi* **1** COMPLAIN : quejarse **2 to carp at** : criticar

carp[2] *n, pl* **carp** *or* **carps** : carpa *f*

carpel [ˈkɑrpəl] *n* : carpelo *m*

carpenter [ˈkɑrpəntər] *n* : carpintero *m,* -ra *f*

carpentry [ˈkɑrpəntri] *n* : carpintería *f*

carpet[1] [ˈkɑrpət] *vt* : alfombrar

carpet[2] *n* : alfombra *f*

carpeting [ˈkɑrpət̬ɪŋ] *n* : alfombrado *m*

carport [ˈkɑrˌpɔrt] *n* : cochera *f,* garaje *m* abierto

carriage [ˈkærɪdʒ] *n* **1** TRANSPORT : transporte *m* **2** POSTURE : porte *m,* postura *f* **3 horse–drawn carriage** : carruaje *m,* coche *m* **4 baby carriage** : cochecito *m*

carrier [ˈkæriər] *n* **1** : transportista *mf,* empresa *f* de transportes **2** : portador *m,* -dora *f* (de una enfermedad) **3 aircraft carrier** : portaaviones *m*

carrier pigeon : paloma *f* mensajera

carrion [ˈkæriən] *n* : carroña *f*

carrot [ˈkærət] *n* : zanahoria *f*

carry [ˈkæri] *v* **-ried; -rying** *vt* **1** TRANSPORT : llevar, cargar, transportar (cargamento), conducir (electricidad), portar (un virus) <to carry a bag : cargar una bolsa> <to carry money : llevar dinero encima, traer dinero consigo> **2** BEAR : soportar, aguantar, resistir (peso) **3** STOCK : vender, tener en abasto **4** ENTAIL : llevar, implicar, acarrear **5** WIN : ganar (una elección o competición), aprobar (una moción) **6 to carry oneself** : portarse, comportarse <he carried himself honorably : se comportó dignamente> — *vi* : oírse, proyectarse <her voice carries well : su voz se puede oír desde lejos>

carryall [ˈkæriˌɔl] *n* : bolsa *f* de viaje

carry away *vt* **to get carried away** : exaltarse, entusiasmarse

carry on *vt* CONDUCT : realizar, ejercer, mantener <to carry on research : realizar investigaciones> <to carry on a correspondence : mantener una correspondencia> — *vi* **1** : portarse de manera escandalosa o inapropiada <it's embarrassing how he carries on : su manera de comportarse da vergüenza> **2** CONTINUE : seguir, continuar

carry out *vt* **1** PERFORM : llevar a cabo, realizar **2** FULFILL : cumplir

cart[1] [ˈkɑrt] *vt* : acarrear, llevar

cart[2] *n* : carreta *f,* carro *m*

cartel [kɑrˈtɛl] *n* : cártel *m*

cartilage [ˈkɑrt̬əlɪdʒ] *n* : cartílago *m*

cartilaginous [ˌkɑrt̬əlˈædʒənəs] *adj* : cartilaginoso

cartographer [kɑrˈtɑgrəfər] *n* : cartógrafo *m,* -fa *f*

cartography [kɑrˈtɑgrəfi] *n* : cartografía *f*

carton [ˈkɑrtən] *n* : caja *f* de cartón

cartoon [kɑrˈtuːn] *n* **1** : chiste *m* (gráfico), caricatura *f* <a political cartoon : un chiste político> **2** COMIC STRIP : tira *f* cómica, historieta *f* **3** *or* **animated cartoon** : dibujo *m* animado

cartoonist [kɑrˈtuːnɪst] *n* : caricaturista *mf,* dibujante *mf* (de chistes)

cartridge [ˈkɑrtrɪdʒ] *n* : cartucho *m*

carve [ˈkɑrv] *vt* **carved; carving 1** : tallar (madera), esculpir (piedra), grabar <he carved his name in the bark : grabó su nombre en la corteza> **2** SLICE : cortar, trinchar (carne)

cascade[1] [kæsˈkeɪd] *vi* **-caded; -cading** : caer en cascada

cascade[2] *n* : cascada *f,* salto *m* de agua

case[1] [ˈkeɪs] *vt* **cased; casing 1** BOX, PACK : embalar, encajonar **2** INSPECT : observar, inspeccionar (antes de cometer un delito)

case[2] *n* **1** : caso *m* <an unusual case : un caso insólito> <ablative case : caso ablativo> <a case of the flu : un caso de gripe> **2** BOX : caja *f* **3** CONTAINER : funda *f,* estuche *m* **4 in any case** : de todos modos, en cualquier caso **5 in case** : como precaución <just in case : por si acaso> **6 in case of** : en caso de

casement [ˈkeɪsmənt] *n* : ventana *f* con bisagras

cash[1] [ˈkæʃ] *vt* : convertir en efectivo, cobrar, cambiar (un cheque)

cash[2] *n* : efectivo *m,* dinero *m* en efectivo

cashew [ˈkæˌʃuː, kəˈʃuː] *n* : anacardo *m*

cashier[1] [kæˈʃɪr] *vt* : destituir, despedir

cashier[2] *n* : cajero *m,* -ra *f*

cashmere [ˈkæʒˌmɪr, ˈkæʃ-] *n* : cachemir *m*

casino [kəˈsiːˌnoː] *n, pl* **-nos** : casino *m*

cask [ˈkæsk] *n* : tonel *m,* barrica *f,* barril *m*

casket [ˈkæskət] *n* COFFIN : ataúd *m,* féretro *m*

casserole [ˈkæsəˌroːl] *n* **1** : cazuela *f* **2** : guiso *m,* guisado *m* <tuna casserole : guiso de atún>
cassette [kəˈsɛt, kæ-] *n* : cassette *mf*
cassock [ˈkæsək] *n* : sotana *f*
cast[1] [ˈkæst] *vt* **cast; casting 1** THROW : tirar, echar, arrojar <the die is cast : la suerte está echada> **2** : depositar (un voto) **3** : asignar (papeles en una obra de teatro) **4** MOLD : moldear, fundir, vaciar **5 to cast off** ABANDON : desamparar, abandonar
cast[2] *n* **1** THROW : lance *m,* lanzamiento *m* **2** APPEARANCE : aspecto *m,* forma *f* **3** : elenco *m,* reparto *m* (de una obra de teatro) **4 plaster cast** : molde *m* de yeso, escayola *f*
castanets [ˌkæstəˈnɛts] *npl* : castañuelas *fpl*
castaway[1] [ˈkæstəˌweɪ] *adj* : náufrago
castaway[2] *n* : náufrago *m,* -ga *f*
caste [ˈkæst] *n* : casta *f*
caster [ˈkæstər] *n* : ruedita *f* (de un mueble)
castigate [ˈkæstəˌgeɪt] *vt* **-gated; -gating** : castigar severamente, censurar, reprobar
cast iron *n* : hierro *m* fundido
castle [ˈkæsəl] *n* **1** : castillo *m* **2** : torre *f* (en ajedrez)
cast–off [ˈkæstˌɔf] *adj* : desechado
castoff [ˈkæstˌɔf] *n* : desecho *m*
castrate [ˈkæsˌtreɪt] *vt* **-trated; -trating** : castrar
castration [kæˈstreɪʃən] *n* : castración *f*
casual [ˈkæʒʊəl] *adj* **1** FORTUITOUS : casual, fortuito **2** INDIFFERENT : indiferente, despreocupado **3** INFORMAL : informal — **casually** [ˈkæʒʊəli, ˈkæʒəli] *adv*
casualness [ˈkæʒʊəlnəs] *n* **1** FORTUITOUSNESS : casualidad *f* **2** INDIFFERENCE : indiferencia *f,* despreocupación *f* **3** INFORMALITY : informalidad *f*
casualty [ˈkæʒʊəlti, ˈkæʒəl-] *n, pl* **-ties 1** ACCIDENT : accidente *m* serio, desastre *m* **2** VICTIM : víctima *f;* baja *f;* herido *m,* -da *f*
cat [ˈkæt] *n* : gato *m,* -ta *f*
cataclysm [ˈkæt̬əˌklɪzəm] *n* : cataclismo *m*
cataclysmal [ˌkæt̬əˈklɪzməl] *or* **cataclysmic** [ˌkæt̬əˈklɪzmɪk] *adj* : catastrófico
catacombs [ˈkæt̬əˌkoːmz] *npl* : catacumbas *fpl*
catalog[1] *or* **catalogue** [ˈkæt̬əˌlɔg] *vt* **-loged** *or* **-logued; -loging** *or* **-loguing** : catalogar
catalog[2] *n* : catálogo *m*
catalpa [kəˈtælpə, -ˈtɔl-] *n* : catalpa *f*
catalyst [ˈkæt̬ələst] *n* : catalizador *m*
catalytic [ˌkæt̬əlˈɪtɪk] *adj* : catalítico
catamaran [ˌkæt̬əməˈræn, ˈkæt̬əməˌræn] *n* : catamarán *m*
catapult[1] [ˈkæt̬əˌpʌlt, -ˌpʊlt] *vt* : catapultar
catapult[2] *n* : catapulta *f*
cataract [ˈkæt̬əˌrækt] *n* : catarata *f*
catarrh [kəˈtɑr] *n* : catarro *m*
catastrophe [kəˈtæstrəˌfiː] *n* : catástrofe *f*
catastrophic [ˌkæt̬əˈstrɑfɪk] *adj* : catastrófico — **catastrophically** [-fɪkli] *adv*
catcall [ˈkætˌkɔl] *n* : rechifla *f,* abucheo *m*
catch[1] [ˈkætʃ, ˈkɛtʃ] *v* **caught** [ˈkɔt]; **catching** *vt* **1** CAPTURE, TRAP : capturar, agarrar, atrapar, coger **2** : agarrar, pillar *fam,* tomar de sorpresa <they caught him red-handed : lo pillaron con las manos en la masa> **3** GRASP : agarrar, captar **4** ENTANGLE : enganchar, enredar **5** : tomar (un tren, etc.) **6** : contagiarse de <to catch a cold : contagiarse de un resfriado, resfriarse> — *vi* **1** GRASP : agarrar **2** HOOK : engancharse **3** IGNITE : prender, agarrar
catch[2] *n* **1** CATCHING : captura *f,* atrapada *f,* parada *f* (de una pelota) **2** : redada *f* (de pescado), presa *f* (de caza) <he's a good catch : es un buen partido> **3** LATCH : pestillo *m,* pasador *m* **4** DIFFICULTY, TRICK : problema *m,* trampa *f,* truco *m*
catcher [ˈkætʃər, ˈkɛ-] *n* : catcher *mf;* receptor *m* , -tora *f* (en béisbol)
catching [ˈkætʃɪŋ, ˈkɛ-] *adj* : contagioso
catchup [ˈkætʃəp, ˈkɛ-] → **ketchup**
catchword [ˈkætʃˌwərd, ˈkɛtʃ-] *n* : eslogan *m,* lema *m*
catchy [ˈkætʃi, ˈkɛ-] *adj* **catchier; -est** : pegajoso <a catchy song : una canción pegajosa>
catechism [ˈkæt̬əˌkɪzəm] *n* : catecismo *m*
categorical [ˌkæt̬əˈgɔrɪkəl] *adj* : categórico, absoluto, rotundo — **categorically** [-kli] *adv*
categorize [ˈkæt̬ɪgəˌraɪz] *vt* **-rized; -rizing** : clasificar, catalogar
category [ˈkæt̬əˌgori] *n, pl* **-ries** : categoría *f,* género *m,* clase *f*
cater [ˈkeɪt̬ər] *vi* **1** : proveer alimentos (para fiestas, bodas, etc.) **2 to cater to** : atender a <to cater to all tastes : atender a todos los gustos>
catercorner[1] [ˈkæt̬iˌkɔrnər, ˈkæt̬ə-, ˈkɪt̬i-] *or* **cater–cornered** [-ˌkɔrnərd] *adv* : diagonalmente, en diagonal
catercorner[2] *or* **cater–cornered** *adj* : diagonal
caterer [ˈkeɪt̬ərər] *n* : proveedor *m,* -dora *f* de comida
caterpillar [ˈkætərˌpɪlər] *n* : oruga *f*
catfish [ˈkætˌfɪʃ] *n* : bagre *m*
catgut [ˈkætˌgʌt] *n* : cuerda *f* de tripa
catharsis [kəˈθɑrsɪs] *n, pl* **catharses** [-ˌsiːz] : catarsis *f*
cathartic[1] [kəˈθɑrt̬ɪk] *adj* : catártico
cathartic[2] *n* : purgante *m*
cathedral [kəˈθiːdrəl] *n* : catedral *f*
catheter [ˈkæθət̬ər] *n* : catéter *m,* sonda *f*

cathode [ˈkæˌθoːd] *n* : cátodo *m*

catholic [ˈkæθəlɪk] *adj* **1** BROAD, UNIVERSAL : liberal, universal **2 Catholic** : católico

Catholic *n* : católico *m*, -ca *f*

Catholicism [kəˈθɑləˌsɪzəm] *n* : catolicismo *m*

catkin [ˈkætkɪn] *n* : amento *m*, candelilla *f*

catlike [ˈkætˌlaɪk] *adj* : gatuno, felino

catnap[1] [ˈkætˌnæp] *vi* **-napped; -napping** : tomarse una siestecita

catnap[2] *n* : siesta *f* breve, siestecita *f*

catnip [ˈkætˌnɪp] *n* : nébeda *f*

catsup [ˈkɛtʃəp, ˈkætsəp] → **ketchup**

cattail [ˈkætˌteɪl] *n* : espadaña *f*, anea *f*

cattiness [ˈkæt̬inəs] *n* : malicia *f*

cattle [ˈkæt̬əl] *npl* : ganado *m*, reses *mpl*

cattleman [ˈkæt̬əlmən, -ˌmæn] *n, pl* **-men** [-mən, -ˌmɛn] : ganadero *m*

catty [ˈkæt̬i] *adj* **-tier; -est** : malicioso, malintencionado

catwalk [ˈkætˌwɔk] *n* : pasarela *f*

Caucasian[1] [kɔˈkeɪʒən] *adj* : caucásico

Caucasian[2] *n* : caucásico *m*, -ca *f*

caucus [ˈkɔkəs] *n* : junta *f* de políticos

caught → **catch**

cauldron [ˈkɔldrən] *n* : caldera *f*

cauliflower [ˈkɑlɪˌflaʊər, ˈkɔ-] *n* : coliflor *f*

caulk[1] [ˈkɔk] *vt* : calafatear (un barco), enmasillar (una grieta)

caulk[2] *n* : masilla *f*

causal [ˈkɔzəl] *adj* : causal

cause[1] [ˈkɔz] *vt* **caused; causing** : causar, provocar, ocasionar

cause[2] *n* **1** ORIGIN : causa *f*, origen *m* **2** REASON : causa *f*, razón *f*, motivo *m* **3** LAWSUIT : litigio *m*, pleito *m* **4** MOVEMENT : causa *f*, movimiento *m*

causeless [ˈkɔzləs] *adj* : sin causa

causeway [ˈkɔzˌweɪ] *n* : camino *m* elevado

caustic [ˈkɔstɪk] *adj* **1** CORROSIVE : cáustico, corrosivo **2** BITING : mordaz, sarcástico

cauterize [ˈkɔt̬əˌraɪz] *vt* **-ized; -izing** : cauterizar

caution[1] [ˈkɔʃən] *vt* : advertir

caution[2] *n* **1** WARNING : advertencia *f*, aviso *m* **2** CARE, PRUDENCE : precaución *f*, cuidado *m*, cautela *f*

cautionary [ˈkɔʃəˌnɛri] *adv* : admonitorio <cautionary tale : cuento moral>

cautious [ˈkɔʃəs] *adj* : cauteloso, cuidadoso, precavido

cautiously [ˈkɔʃəsli] *adv* : cautelosamente, con precaución

cautiousness [ˈkɔʃəsnəs] *n* : cautela *f*, precaución *f*

cavalcade [ˌkævəlˈkeɪd, ˈkævəlˌ-] *n* **1** : cabalgata *f* **2** SERIES : serie *f*

cavalier[1] [ˌkævəˈlɪr] *adj* : altivo, desdeñoso — **cavalierly** *adv*

cavalier[2] *n* : caballero *m*

cavalry [ˈkævəlri] *n, pl* **-ries** : caballería *f*

cave[1] [ˈkeɪv] *vi* **caved; caving** *or* **to cave in** : derrumbarse

cave[2] *n* : cueva *f*

cavern [ˈkævərn] *n* : caverna *f*

cavernous [ˈkævərnəs] *adj* : cavernoso — **cavernously** *adv*

caviar *or* **caviare** [ˈkæviˌɑr, ˈkɑ-] *n* : caviar *m*

cavity [ˈkævət̬i] *n, pl* **-ties 1** HOLE : cavidad *f*, hueco *m* **2** CARIES : caries *f*

cavort [kəˈvɔrt] *vi* : brincar, hacer cabriolas

caw[1] [ˈkɔ] *vi* : graznar

caw[2] *n* : graznido *m*

cayenne pepper [ˌkaɪˈɛn, ˌkeɪ-] *n* : pimienta *f* cayena, pimentón *m*

CD [ˌsiːˈdiː] *n* : CD *m*, disco *m* compacto

cease [ˈsiːs] *v* **ceased; ceasing** *vt* : dejar de <they ceased bickering : dejaron de discutir> — *vi* : cesar, pasarse

ceaseless [ˈsiːsləs] *adj* : incesante, continuo

cedar [ˈsiːdər] *n* : cedro *m*

cede [ˈsiːd] *vt* **ceded; ceding** : ceder, conceder

ceiling [ˈsiːlɪŋ] *n* **1** : techo *m*, cielo *m* **2** LIMIT : límite *m*, tope *m*

celebrant [ˈsɛləbrənt] *n* : celebrante *mf*, oficiante *mf*

celebrate [ˈsɛləˌbreɪt] *v* **-brated; -brating** *vt* **1** : celebrar, oficiar <to celebrate Mass : celebrar la misa> **2** : celebrar, festejar <we're celebrating our anniversary : estamos celebrando nuestro aniversario> **3** EXTOL : alabar, ensalzar, exaltar — *vi* : estar de fiesta, divertirse

celebrated [ˈsɛləˌbreɪt̬əd] *adj* : célebre, famoso, renombrado

celebration [ˌsɛləˈbreɪʃən] *n* : celebración *f*, festejos *mpl*

celebrity [səˈlɛbrət̬i] *n, pl* **-ties 1** RENOWN : fama *f*, renombre *m*, celebridad *f* **2** PERSONALITY : celebridad *f*, personaje *m*

celery [ˈsɛləri] *n, pl* **-eries** : apio *m*

celestial [səˈlɛstʃəl, -ˈlɛstiəl] *adj* **1** : celeste **2** HEAVENLY : celestial, paradisiaco

celibacy [ˈsɛləbəsi] *n* : celibato *m*

celibate[1] [ˈsɛləbət] *adj* : célibe

celibate[2] *n* : célibe *mf*

cell [ˈsɛl] *n* **1** : célula *f* (de un organismo) **2** : celda *f* (en una cárcel, etc.) **3** : elemento *m* (de una pila)

cellar [ˈsɛlər] *n* **1** BASEMENT : sótano *m* **2** : bodega *f* (de vinos)

cellist [ˈtʃɛlɪst] *n* : violonchelista *mf*

cello [ˈtʃɛˌloː] *n, pl* **-los** : violonchelo *m*

cellophane [ˈsɛləˌfeɪn] *n* : celofán *m*

cellular [ˈsɛljələr] *adj* : celular

cellulose [ˈsɛljəˌloːs] *n* : celulosa *f*

Celsius [ˈsɛlsiəs] *adj* : centígrado <100 degrees Celsius : 100 grados centígrados>

Celt [ˈkɛlt, ˈsɛlt] *n* : celta *mf*

Celtic[1] [ˈkɛltɪk, ˈsɛl-] *adj* : celta

Celtic[2] *n* : celta *m* (idioma)

cement[1] [sɪˈmɛnt] *vi* : unir o cubrir algo con cemento, cementar

cement[2] *n* **1** : cemento *m* **2** GLUE : pegamento *m*

cemetery [ˈsɛməˌtɛri] *n, pl* **-teries** : cementerio *m*, panteón *m*

censer [ˈsɛntsər] *n* : incensario *m*

censor[1] [ˈsɛntsər] *vt* : censurar

censor[2] *n* : censor *m*, -sora *f*

censorious [sɛnˈsoriəs] *adj* : de censura, crítico

censorship [ˈsɛntsərˌʃɪp] *n* : censura *f*

censure[1] [ˈsɛntʃər] *vt* **-sured; -suring** : censurar, criticar, reprobar — **censurable** [-tʃərəbəl] *adj*

censure[2] *n* : censura *f*, reproche *f* oficial

census [ˈsɛntsəs] *n* : censo *m*

cent [ˈsɛnt] *n* : centavo *m*

centaur [ˈsɛnˌtɔr] *n* : centauro *m*

centennial[1] [sɛnˈtɛniəl] *adj* : del centenario

centennial[2] *n* : centenario *m*

center[1] [ˈsɛntər] *vt* **1** : centrar **2** CONCENTRATE : concentrar, fijar, enfocar — *vi* : centrarse, enfocarse

center[2] *n* **1** : centro *m* <center of gravity : centro de gravedad> **2** : centro *mf* (en futbol americano), pívot *mf* (en basquetbol)

centerpiece [ˈsɛntərˌpiːs] *n* : centro *m* de mesa

centigrade [ˈsɛntəˌgreɪd, ˈsɑn-] *adj* : centígrado

centigram [ˈsɛntəˌgræm, ˈsɑn-] *n* : centigramo *m*

centimeter [ˈsɛntəˌmiːtər, ˈsɑn-] *n* : centímetro *m*

centipede [ˈsɛntəˌpiːd] *n* : ciempiés *m*

central [ˈsɛntrəl] *adj* **1** : céntrico, central <in a central location : en un lugar céntrico> **2** MAIN, PRINCIPAL : central, fundamental, principal

Central American[1] *adj* : centroamericano

Central American[2] *n* : centroamericano *m*, -na *f*

centralization [ˌsɛntrələˈzeɪʃən] *n* : centralización *f*

centralize [ˈsɛntrəˌlaɪz] *vt* **-ized; -izing** : centralizar

centrally [ˈsɛntrəli] *adv* **1 centrally heated** : con calefacción central **2 centrally located** : céntrico, en un lugar céntrico

centre [ˈsɛntər] → **center**

centrifugal force [sɛnˈtrɪfjəgəl, -ˈtrɪfɪgəl] *n* : fuerza *f* centrífuga

century [ˈsɛntʃəri] *n, pl* **-ries** : siglo *m*

ceramic[1] [səˈræmɪk] *adj* : de cerámica

ceramic[2] *n* **1** : objeto *m* de cerámica, cerámica *f* **2 ceramics** *npl* : cerámica *f*

cereal[1] [ˈsɪriəl] *adj* : cereal

cereal[2] *n* : cereal *m*

cerebellum [ˌsɛrəˈbɛləm] *n, pl* **-bellums** *or* **-bella** [-ˈbɛlə] : cerebelo *m*

cerebral [səˈriːbrəl, ˈsɛrə-] *adj* : cerebral

cerebral palsy *n* : parálisis *f* cerebral

cerebrum [səˈriːbrəm, ˈsɛrə-] *n, pl* **-brums** *or* **-bra** [-brə] : cerebro *m*

ceremonial[1] [ˌsɛrəˈmoːniəl] *adj* : ceremonial

ceremonial[2] *n* : ceremonial *m*

ceremonious [ˌsɛrəˈmoːniəs] *adj* **1** FORMAL : ceremonioso, formal **2** CEREMONIAL : ceremonial

ceremony [ˈsɛrəˌmoːni] *n, pl* **-nies** : ceremonia *f*

cerise [səˈriːs] *n* : rojo *m* cereza

certain[1] [ˈsərtən] *adj* **1** DEFINITE : cierto, determinado <a certain percentage : un porcentaje determinado> **2** TRUE : cierto, con certeza <I don't know for certain : no sé exactamente> **3** : cierto, alguno <it has a certain charm : tiene cierta gracia> **4** INEVITABLE : seguro, inevitable **5** ASSURED : seguro, asegurado <she's certain to do well : seguro que le irá bien>

certain[2] *pron* : ciertos *pl*, algunos *pl* <certain of my friends : algunos de mis amigos>

certainly [ˈsərtənli] *adv* **1** DEFINITELY : ciertamente, seguramente **2** OF COURSE : por supuesto

certainty [ˈsərtənti] *n, pl* **-ties** : certeza *f*, certidumbre *f*, seguridad *f*

certifiable [ˌsərt̬əˈfaɪəbəl] *adj* : certificable

certificate [sərˈtɪfɪkət] *n* : certificado *m*, acta *f* <birth certificate : acta de nacimiento>

certification [ˌsərt̬əfəˈkeɪʃən] *n* : certificación *f*

certify [ˈsərt̬əˌfaɪ] *vt* **-fied; -fying 1** VERIFY : certificar, verificar, confirmar **2** ENDORSE : endosar, aprobar oficialmente

certitude [ˈsərt̬əˌtuːd, -ˌtjuːd] *n* : certeza *f*, certidumbre *f*

cervical [ˈsərvɪkəl] *adj* **1** : cervical (dícese del cuello) **2** : del cuello del útero

cervix [ˈsərvɪks] *n, pl* **-vices** [-vəˌsiːz] *or* **-vixes 1** NECK : cerviz *f* **2** *or* **uterine cervix** : cuello *m* del útero

cesarean[1] [sɪˈzæriən] *adj* : cesáreo

cesarean[2] *n* : cesárea *f*

cesium [ˈsiːziəm] *n* : cesio *m*

cessation [sɛˈseɪʃən] *n* : cesación *f*, cese *m*

cesspool [ˈsɛsˌpuːl] *n* : pozo *m* séptico

Chadian [ˈtʃædiən] *n* : chadiano *m*, -na *f* — **Chadian** *adj*

chafe [ˈtʃeɪf] *v* **chafed; chafing** *vi* : enojarse, irritarse — *vt* : rozar

chaff [ˈtʃæf] *n* **1** : barcia *f*, granzas *fpl* **2 to separate the wheat from the chaff** : separar el grano de la paja

chafing dish [ˈtʃeɪfɪŋˌdɪʃ] *n* : escalfador *m*
chagrin[1] [ʃəˈgrɪn] *vt* : desilusionar, avergonzar
chagrin[2] *n* : desilusión *f,* disgusto *m*
chain[1] [ˈtʃeɪn] *vt* : encadenar
chain[2] *n* **1** : cadena *f* <steel chain : cadena de acero> <restaurant chain : cadena de restaurantes> **2** SERIES : serie *f* <chain of events : serie de eventos> **3 chains** *npl* FETTERS : grillos *mpl*
chair[1] [ˈtʃɛr] *vt* : presidir, moderar
chair[2] *n* **1** : silla *f* **2** CHAIRMANSHIP : presidencia *f* **3** → **chairman, chairwoman**
chairman [ˈtʃɛrmən] *n, pl* **-men** [-mən, -ˌmɛn] : presidente *m*
chairmanship [ˈtʃɛrmənˌʃɪp] *n* : presidencia *f*
chairwoman [ˈtʃɛrˌwʊmən] *n, pl* **-women** [-ˌwɪmən] : presidenta *f*
chaise longue [ˈʃeɪzˈlɔŋ] *n, pl* **chaise longues** [-lɔŋ, -ˈlɔŋz] : chaise longue *f*
chalet [ʃæˈleɪ] *n* : chalet *m,* chalé *m*
chalice [ˈtʃælɪs] *n* : cáliz *m*
chalk[1] [ˈtʃɔk] *vt* : escribir con tiza
chalk[2] *n* **1** LIMESTONE : creta *f,* caliza *f* **2** : tiza *f,* gis *m Mex* (para escribir)
chalkboard [ˈtʃɔkˌbord] → **blackboard**
chalk up *vt* **1** ASCRIBE : atribuir, adscribir **2** SCORE : apuntarse, anotarse (una victoria, etc.)
chalky [ˈtʃɔki] *adj* **chalkier; -est** : calcáreo
challenge[1] [ˈtʃælɪndʒ] *vt* **-lenged; -lenging 1** DISPUTE : disputar, cuestionar, poner en duda **2** DARE : desafiar, retar **3** STIMULATE : estimular, incentivar
challenge[2] *n* : reto *m,* desafío *m*
challenger [ˈtʃælɪndʒər] *n* : retador *m,* -dora *f;* contendiente *mf*
chamber [ˈtʃeɪmbər] *n* **1** ROOM : cámara *f,* sala *f* <the senate chamber : la cámara del senado> **2** : recámara *f* (de un arma de fuego), cámara *f* (de combustión) **3** : cámara *f* <chamber of commerce : cámara de comercio> **4 chambers** *npl or* **judge's chambers** : despacho *m* del juez
chambermaid [ˈtʃeɪmbərˌmeɪd] *n* : camarera *f*
chamber music *n* : música *f* de cámara
chameleon [kəˈmiːljən, -liən] *n* : camaleón *m*
chamois [ˈʃæmi] *n, pl* **chamois** [-mi, -miz] : gamuza *f*
champ[1] [ˈtʃæmp, ˈtʃɑmp] *vi* **1** : masticar ruidosamente **2 to champ at the bit** : impacientarse, comerle a uno la impaciencia
champ[2] [ˈtʃæmp] *n* : campeón *m,* -peona *f*
champagne [ʃæmˈpeɪn] *n* : champaña *m,* champán *m*
champion[1] [ˈtʃæmpiən] *vt* : defender, luchar por (una causa)
champion[2] *n* **1** ADVOCATE, DEFENDER : paladín *m;* campeón *m,* -peona *f;* defensor *m,* -sora *f* **2** WINNER : campeón *m,* -peona *f* <world champion : campeón mundial>
championship [ˈtʃæmpiənˌʃɪp] *n* : campeonato *m*
chance[1] [ˈtʃænts] *v* **chanced; chancing** *vi* **1** HAPPEN : ocurrir por casualidad **2 to chance upon** : encontrar por casualidad — *vt* RISK : arriesgar
chance[2] *adj* : fortuito, casual <a chance encounter : un encuentro casual>
chance[3] *n* **1** FATE, LUCK : azar *m,* suerte *f,* fortuna *f* **2** OPPORTUNITY : oportunidad *f,* ocasión *f* **3** PROBABILITY : probabilidad *f,* posibilidad *f* **4** RISK : riesgo *m* **5** : boleto *m* (de una rifa o lotería) **6 by chance** : por casualidad
chancellor [ˈtʃæntsələr] *n* **1** : canciller *m* **2** : rector *m,* -tora *f* (de una universidad)
chancre [ˈʃæŋkər] *n* : chancro *m*
chancy [ˈtʃæntsi] *adj* **chancier; -est** : riesgoso, arriesgado
chandelier [ˌʃændəˈlɪr] *n* : araña *f* de luces
change[1] [ˈtʃeɪndʒ] *v* **changed; changing** *vt* **1** ALTER : cambiar, alterar, modificar **2** EXCHANGE : cambiar de, intercambiar <to change places : cambiar de sitio> — *vi* **1** VARY : cambiar, variar, transformarse <you haven't changed : no has cambiado> **2** *or* **to change clothes** : cambiarse (de ropa)
change[2] *n* **1** ALTERATION : cambio *m* **2** : cambio *m,* vuelto *m* <two dollars change : dos dólares de vuelto> **3** COINS : cambio *m,* monedas *fpl*
changeable [ˈtʃeɪndʒəbəl] *adj* : cambiante, variable
changeless [ˈtʃeɪndʒləs] *adj* : invariable, constante
changer [ˈtʃeɪndʒər] *n* **1** : cambiador *m* <record changer : cambiador de discos> **2** *or* **money changer** : cambista *mf* (de dinero)
channel[1] [ˈtʃænəl] *vt* **-neled** *or* **-nelled; -neling** *or* **-nelling** : encauzar, canalizar
channel[2] *n* **1** RIVERBED : cauce *m* **2** STRAIT : canal *m,* estrecho *m* <English Channel : Canal de la Mancha> **3** COURSE, MEANS : vía *f,* conducto *m* <the usual channels : las vías normales> **4** : canal *m* (de televisión)
chant[1] [ˈtʃænt] *v* : salmodiar, cantar
chant[2] *n* : **1** : salmodia *f* **2 Gregorian chant** : canto *m* gregoriano
Chanukah [ˈxɑnəkə, ˈhɑ-] → **Hanukkah**
chaos [ˈkeɪˌɑs] *n* : caos *m*
chaotic [keɪˈɑtɪk] *adj* : caótico — **chaotically** [-tɪkli] *adv*
chap[1] [ˈtʃæp] *vi* **chapped; chapping** : partirse, agrietarse
chap[2] *n* FELLOW : tipo *m,* hombre *m*
chapel [ˈtʃæpəl] *n* : capilla *f*

chaperon[1] *or* **chaperone** [ˈʃæpəˌroːn] *vt* **-oned; -oning :** ir de chaperón, acompañar

chaperon[2] *or* **chaperone** *n* **:** chaperón *m,* -rona *f;* acompañante *mf*

chaplain [ˈtʃæplɪn] *n* **:** capellán *m*

chapter [ˈtʃæptər] *n* **1 :** capítulo *m* (de un libro) **2** BRANCH **:** sección *f,* división *f* (de una organización)

char [ˈtʃɑr] *vt* **charred; charring 1** BURN **:** carbonizar **2** SCORCH **:** chamuscar

character [ˈkærɪktər] *n* **1** LETTER, SYMBOL **:** carácter *m* <Chinese characters : caracteres chinos> **2** DISPOSITION **:** carácter *m,* personalidad *f* <of good character : de buena reputación> **3 :** tipo *m,* personaje *m* peculiar <he's quite a character! : ¡él es algo serio!> **4 :** personaje *m* (ficticio)

characteristic[1] [ˌkærɪktəˈrɪstɪk] *adj* **:** característico, típico — **characteristically** [-tɪkli] *adv*

characteristic[2] *n* **:** característica *f*

characterization [ˌkærɪktərəˈzeɪʃən] *n* **:** caracterización *f*

characterize [ˈkærɪktəˌraɪz] *vt* **-ized; -izing :** caracterizar

charades [ʃəˈreɪdz] *ns & pl* **:** charada *f*

charcoal [ˈtʃɑrˌkoːl] *n* **:** carbón *m*

chard [ˈtʃɑrd] → **Swiss chard**

charge[1] [ˈtʃɑrdʒ] *v* **charged; charging** *vt* **1 :** cargar <to charge the batteries : cargar las pilas> **2** ENTRUST **:** encomendar, encargar **3** COMMAND **:** ordenar, mandar **4** ACCUSE **:** acusar <charged with robbery : acusado de robo> **5 :** cargar a una cuenta, comprar a crédito — *vi* **1 :** cargar (contra el enemigo) <charge! : ¡a la carga!> **2 :** cobrar <they charge too much : cobran demasiado>

charge[2] *n* **1 :** carga *f* (eléctrica) **2** BURDEN **:** carga *f,* peso *m* **3** RESPONSIBILITY **:** cargo *m,* responsabilidad *f* <to take charge of : hacerse cargo de> **4** ACCUSATION **:** cargo *m,* acusación *f* **5** COST **:** costo *m,* cargo *m,* precio *m* **6** ATTACK **:** carga *f,* ataque *m*

charge card → **credit card**

chargeable [ˈtʃɑrdʒəbəl] *adj* **1 :** acusable, perseguible (dícese de un delito) **2 ~ to :** a cargo de (una cuenta)

charger [ˈtʃɑrdʒər] *n* **:** corcel *m,* caballo *m* (de guerra)

chariot [ˈtʃæriət] *n* **:** carro *m* (de guerra)

charisma [kəˈrɪzmə] *n* **:** carisma *m*

charismatic [ˌkærəzˈmætɪk] *adj* **:** carismático

charitable [ˈtʃærətəbəl] *adj* **1** GENEROUS **:** caritativo <a charitable organization : una organización benéfica> **2** KIND, UNDERSTANDING **:** generoso, benévolo, comprensivo — **charitably** [-bli] *adv*

charitableness [ˈtʃærəṭəbəlnəs] *n* **:** caridad *f*

charity [ˈtʃærəti] *n, pl* **-ties 1** GENEROSITY **:** caridad *f* **2** ALMS **:** caridad *f,* limosna *f* **3 :** organización *f* benéfica, obra *f* de beneficencia

charlatan [ˈʃɑrlətən] *n* **:** charlatán *m,* -tana *f;* farsante *mf*

charley horse [ˈtʃɑrliˌhɔrs] *n* **:** calambre *m*

charm[1] [ˈtʃɑrm] *vt* **:** encantar, cautivar, fascinar

charm[2] *n* **1** AMULET **:** amuleto *m,* talismán *m* **2** ATTRACTION **:** encanto *m,* atractivo *m* <it has a certain charm : tiene cierto atractivo> **3 :** dije *m,* colgante *m* <charm bracelet : pulsera de dijes>

charmer [ˈtʃɑrmər] *n* **:** persona *f* encantadora

charming [ˈtʃɑrmɪŋ] *adj* **:** encantador, fascinante

chart[1] [ˈtʃɑrt] *vt* **1 :** trazar un mapa de, hacer un gráfico de **2** PLAN **:** trazar, planear <to chart a course : trazar un derrotero>

chart[2] *n* **1** MAP **:** carta *f,* mapa *m* **2** DIAGRAM **:** gráfico *m,* cuadro *m,* tabla *f*

charter[1] [ˈtʃɑrtər] *vt* **1 :** establecer los estatutos de (una organización) **2** RENT **:** alquilar, fletar

charter[2] *n* **1** STATUTES **:** estatutos *mpl* **2** CONSTITUTION **:** carta *f,* constitución *f*

chartreuse [ʃɑrˈtruːz, -ˈtruːs] *n* **:** color *m* verde-amarillo intenso

chary [ˈtʃæri] *adj* **charier; -est 1** WARY **:** cauteloso, precavido **2** SPARING **:** parco

chase[1] [ˈtʃeɪs] *vt* **chased; chasing 1** PURSUE **:** perseguir, ir a la caza de **2** DRIVE **:** ahuyentar, echar <he chased the dog from the garden : ahuyentó al perro del jardín> **3 :** grabar (metales)

chase[2] *n* **1** PURSUIT **:** persecución *f,* caza *f* **2 the chase** HUNTING **:** caza *f*

chaser [ˈtʃeɪsər] *n* **1** PURSUER **:** perseguidor *m,* -dora *f* **2 :** bebida *f* que se toma después de un trago de licor

chasm [ˈkæzəm] *n* **:** abismo *m,* sima *f*

chassis [ˈtʃæsi, ˈʃæsi] *n, pl* **chassis** [-siz] **:** chasis *m,* armazón *m*

chaste [ˈtʃeɪst] *adj* **chaster; -est 1 :** casto **2** MODEST **:** modesto, puro **3** AUSTERE **:** austero, sobrio

chastely [ˈtʃeɪstli] *adv* **:** castamente

chasten [ˈtʃeɪsən] *vt* **:** castigar, sancionar

chasteness [ˈtʃeɪstnəs] *n* **1** MODESTY **:** modestia *f,* castidad *f* **2** AUSTERITY **:** sobriedad *f,* austeridad *f*

chastise [ˈtʃæsˌtaɪz, tʃæsˈ-] *vt* **-tised; -tising 1** REPRIMAND **:** reprender, corregir, reprobar **2** PUNISH **:** castigar

chastisement [ˈtʃæsˌtaɪzmənt, tʃæsˈtaɪz-, ˈtʃæstəz-] *n* **:** castigo *m,* corrección *f*

chastity [ˈtʃæstəṭi] *n* **:** castidad *f,* decencia *f,* modestia *f*

chat[1] [ˈtʃæt] *vi* **chatted; chatting :** charlar, platicar

chat² *n* : charla *f,* plática *f*
château [ʃæ'toː] *n, pl* **-teaus** [-'toː, -'toːz] *or* **-teaux** [-'toːz] : mansión *f* campestre
chattel ['tʃætəl] *n* : bienes *fpl* muebles, enseres *mpl*
chatter¹ ['tʃætər] *vi* **1** : castañetear (dícese de los dientes) **2** GAB : parlotear *fam,* cotorrear *fam*
chatter² *n* **1** CHATTERING : castañeteo *m* (de dientes) **2** GABBING : parloteo *m fam,* cotorreo *m fam,* cháchara *f fam*
chatterbox ['tʃætər,bɑks] *n* : parlanchín *m,* -china *f;* charlatán *m,* -tana *f;* hablador *m,* -dora *f*
chatty ['tʃæti] *adj* **chattier; chattiest** **1** TALKATIVE : parlanchín, charlatán **2** CONVERSATIONAL : familiar, conversador <a chatty letter : una carta llena de noticias>
chauffeur¹ ['ʃoːfər, ʃo'fər] *vi* : trabajar de chofer privado — *vt* : hacer de chofer para
chauffeur² *n* : chofer *m* privado
chauvinism ['ʃoːvə,nɪzəm] *n* : chauvinismo *m,* patriotería *f*
chauvinist ['ʃoːvənɪst] *n* : chauvinista *mf;* patriotero *m,* -ta *f*
chauvinistic [,ʃoːvə'nɪstɪk] *adj* : chauvinista, patriotero
cheap¹ ['tʃiːp] *adv* : barato <to sell cheap : vender barato>
cheap² *adj* **1** INEXPENSIVE : barato, económico **2** SHODDY : barato, mal hecho **3** STINGY : tacaño, agarrado *fam,* codo *Mex*
cheapen ['tʃiːpən] *vt* : degradar, rebajar
cheaply ['tʃiːpli] *adv* : barato, a precio bajo
cheapness ['tʃiːpnəs] *n* **1** : baratura *f,* precio *m* bajo **2** STINGINESS : tacañería *f*
cheapskate ['tʃiːp,skeɪt] *n* : tacaño *m,* -ña *f;* codo *m,* -da *f Mex*
cheat¹ ['tʃiːt] *vt* : defraudar, estafar, engañar — *vi* : hacer trampa
cheat² *n* **1** CHEATING : engaño *m,* fraude *m,* trampa *f* **2** → **cheater**
cheater ['tʃiːtər] *n* : estafador *m,* -dora *f;* tramposo *m,* -sa *f*
check¹ ['tʃɛk] *vt* **1** HALT : frenar, parar, detener **2** RESTRAIN : refrenar, contener, reprimir **3** VERIFY : verificar, comprobar **4** INSPECT : revisar, chequear, inspeccionar **5** MARK : marcar, señalar **6** : chequear, facturar (maletas, equipaje) **7** CHECKER : marcar con cuadros **8 to check in** : registrarse en un hotel **9 to check out** : irse de un hotel
check² *n* **1** HALT : detención *f* súbita, parada *f* **2** RESTRAINT : control *m,* freno *m* **3** INSPECTION : inspección *f,* verificación *f,* chequeo *m* **4** : cheque *m* <to pay by check : pagar con cheque> **5** VOUCHER : resguardo *m,* comprobante *m* **6** BILL : cuenta *f* (en un restaurante) **7** SQUARE : cuadro *m* **8** MARK : marca *f* **9** : jaque *m* (en ajedrez)
checker¹ ['tʃɛkər] *vt* : marcar con cuadros
checker² *n* **1** : pieza *f* (en el juego de damas) **2** : verificador *m,* -dora *f;* revisador *m,* -dora *f*
checkerboard ['tʃɛkər,bord] *n* : tablero *m* de damas
checkers ['tʃɛkərz] *n* : damas *fpl*
checkmate¹ ['tʃɛk,meɪt] *vt* **-mated; -mating** **1** : dar jaque mate a (en ajedrez) **2** THWART : frustrar, arruinar
checkmate² *n* : jaque mate *m*
checkpoint ['tʃɛk,pɔɪnt] *n* : puesto *m* de control
checkup ['tʃɛk,ʌp] *n* : examen *m* médico, chequeo *m*
cheddar ['tʃɛdər] *n* : queso *m* Cheddar
cheek ['tʃiːk] *n* **1** : mejilla *f,* cachete *m* **2** IMPUDENCE : insolencia *f,* descaro *m*
cheeky ['tʃiːki] *adj* **cheekier; -est** : descarado, insolente, atrevido
cheep¹ ['tʃiːp] *vi* : piar
cheep² *n* : pío *m*
cheer¹ ['tʃɪr] *vt* **1** ENCOURAGE : alentar, animar **2** GLADDEN : alegrar, levantar el ánimo a **3** ACCLAIM : aclamar, vitorear, echar porras a
cheer² *n* **1** CHEERFULNESS : alegría *f,* buen humor *m,* jovialidad *f* **2** APPLAUSE : aclamación *f,* ovación *f,* aplausos *mpl* <three cheers for the chief! : ¡viva el jefe!> **3 cheers!** : ¡salud!
cheerful ['tʃɪrfəl] *adj* : alegre, de buen humor
cheerfully ['tʃɪrfəli] *adv* : alegremente, jovialmente
cheerfulness ['tʃɪrfəlnəs] *n* : buen humor *m,* alegría *f*
cheerily ['tʃɪrəli] *adv* : alegremente
cheeriness ['tʃɪrinəs] *n* : buen humor *m,* alegría *f*
cheerleader ['tʃɪr,liːdər] *n* : porrista *mf*
cheerless ['tʃɪrləs] *adj* BLEAK : triste, sombrío
cheerlessly ['tʃɪrləsli] *adv* : desanimadamente
cheery ['tʃɪri] *adj* **cheerier; -est** : alegre, de buen humor
cheese ['tʃiːz] *n* : queso *m*
cheesecloth ['tʃiːz,klɔθ] *n* : estopilla *f*
cheesy ['tʃiːzi] *adj* **cheesier; -est** **1** : a queso **2** : que contiene queso **3** CHEAP : barato, de mala calidad
cheetah ['tʃiːtə] *n* : guepardo *m*
chef ['ʃɛf] *n* : chef *m*
chemical¹ ['kɛmɪkəl] *adj* : químico — **chemically** [-mɪkli] *adv*
chemical² *n* : sustancia *f* química
chemise [ʃə'miːz] *n* **1** : camiseta *f,* prenda *f* interior de una pieza **2** : vestido *m* holgado
chemist ['kɛmɪst] *n* : químico *m,* -ca *f*
chemistry ['kɛmɪstri] *n, pl* **-tries** : química *f*
chemotherapy [,kiːmo'θɛrəpi, ,kɛmo-] *n, pl* **-pies** : quimioterapia *f*

chenille [ʃə'niːl] *n* : felpilla *f*
cherish ['tʃɛrɪʃ] *vt* **1** VALUE : apreciar, valorar **2** HARBOR : abrigar, albergar
cherry ['tʃɛri] *n, pl* **-ries 1** : cereza *f* (fruta) **2** : cerezo *m* (árbol)
cherub ['tʃɛrəb] *n* **1** *pl* **-ubim** ['tʃɛrə,bɪm, 'tʃɛrjə-] ANGEL : ángel *m,* querubín *m* **2** *pl* **-ubs** : niño *m* regordete, niña *f* regordeta
cherubic [tʃə'ruːbɪk] *adj* : querúbico, angelical
chess ['tʃɛs] *n* : ajedrez *m*
chessboard ['tʃɛs,bord] *n* : tablero *m* de ajedrez
chessman ['tʃɛsmən, -,mæn] *n, pl* **-men** [-mən, -,mɛn] : pieza *f* de ajedrez
chest ['tʃɛst] *n* **1** : cofre *m,* baúl *m* **2** : pecho *m* <chest pains : dolores de pecho>
chestnut ['tʃɛst,nʌt] *n* **1** : castaña *f* (fruto) **2** : castaño *m* (árbol)
chest of drawers *n* : cómoda *f*
chevron ['ʃɛvrən] *n* : galón *m* (de un oficial militar)
chew[1] ['tʃuː] *vt* : masticar, mascar
chew[2] *n* : algo que se masca (como tabaco)
chewable ['tʃuːəbəl] *adj* : masticable
chewing gum *n* : goma *f* de mascar, chicle *m*
chewy ['tʃuːi] *adj* **chewier; -est 1** : fibroso (dícese de las carnes o los vegetales) **2** : pegajoso, chicloso (dícese de los los dulces)
chic[1] ['ʃiːk] *adj* : chic, elegante, de moda
chic[2] *n* : chic *m,* elegancia *f*
Chicano [tʃɪ'kɑno] *n* : chicano *m,* -na *f* — **Chicano** *adj*
chick ['tʃɪk] *n* : pollito *m,* -ta *f;* polluelo *m,* -la *f*
chicken ['tʃɪkən] *n* **1** FOWL : pollo *m* **2** COWARD : cobarde *mf*
chickenhearted ['tʃɪkən,hɑrṭəd] *n* : miedoso, cobarde
chicken pox *n* : varicela *f*
chicle ['tʃɪkəl] *n* : chicle *m* (resina)
chicory ['tʃɪkəri] *n, pl* **-ries 1** : endibia *f* (para ensaladas) **2** : achicoria *f* (aditivo de café)
chide ['tʃaɪd] *vt* **chid** ['tʃɪd] *or* **chided; chid** *or* **chidden** ['tʃɪdən] *or* **chided; chiding** ['tʃaɪdɪŋ] : regañar, reprender
chief[1] ['tʃiːf] *adj* : principal, capital <chief negotiator : negociador en jefe> — **chiefly** *adv*
chief[2] *n* : jefe *m,* -fa *f*
chieftain ['tʃiːftən] *n* : jefe *m,* -fa *f* (de una tribu)
chiffon [ʃɪ'fɑn, 'ʃɪ,-] *n* : chifón *m*
chigger ['tʃɪgər] *n* : nigua *f*
chignon ['ʃiːn,jɑn, -,jɔn] *n* : moño *m,* chongo *m Mex*
chilblain ['tʃɪl,bleɪn] *n* : sabañón *m*
child ['tʃaɪld] *n, pl* **children** ['tʃɪldrən] **1** BABY, YOUNGSTER : niño *m,* -ña *f;* criatura *f* **2** OFFSPRING : hijo *m,* -ja *f;* progenie *f*
childbearing[1] ['tʃaɪlbɛrɪŋ] *adj* : relativo al parto <of childbearing age : en edad fértil>
childbearing[2] → **childbirth**
childbirth ['tʃaɪld,bərθ] *n* : parto *m*
childhood ['tʃaɪld,hʊd] *n* : infancia *f,* niñez *f*
childish ['tʃaɪldɪʃ] *adj* : infantil, inmaduro — **childishly** *adv*
childishness ['tʃaɪldɪʃnəs] *n* : infantilismo *m,* inmadurez *f*
childless ['tʃaɪldləs] *adj* : sin hijos
childlike ['tʃaɪld,laɪk] *adj* : infantil, inocente <a childlike imagination : una imaginación infantil>
childproof ['tʃaɪld,pruːf] *adj* : a prueba de niños
Chilean ['tʃɪliən, tʃɪ'leɪən] : chileno *m,* -na *f* — **Chilean** *adj*
chili *or* **chile** *or* **chilli** ['tʃɪli] *n, pl* **chilies** *or* **chiles** *or* **chillies 1** *or* **chili pepper** : chile *m,* ají *m* **2** : chile *m* con carne
chill[1] ['tʃɪl] *v* : enfriar
chill[2] *adj* : frío, gélido <a chill wind : un viento frío>
chill[3] *n* **1** CHILLINESS : fresco *m,* frío *m* **2** SHIVER : escalofrío *m* **3** DAMPER : enfriamiento *m,* frío *m* <to cast a chill over : enfriar>
chilliness ['tʃɪlinəs] *n* : frío *m,* fresco *m*
chilly ['tʃɪli] *adj* **chillier; -est** : frío <it's chilly tonight : hace frío esta noche>
chime[1] ['tʃaɪm] *v* **chimed; chiming** *vt* : hacer sonar (una campana) — *vi* : sonar una campana, dar campanadas
chime[2] *n* **1** BELLS : juego *m* de campanitas sintonizadas, carillón *m* **2** PEAL : tañido *m,* campanada *f*
chime in *vi* : meterse en una conversación
chimera *or* **chimaera** [kaɪ'mɪrə, kə-] *n* : quimera *f*
chimney ['tʃɪmni] *n, pl* **-neys** : chimenea *f*
chimney sweep *n* : deshollinador *m,* -dora *f*
chimp ['tʃɪmp, 'ʃɪmp] → **chimpanzee**
chimpanzee [,tʃɪm,pæn'ziː, ,ʃɪm-; tʃɪm'pænzi, ʃɪm-] *n* : chimpancé *m*
chin ['tʃɪn] *n* : barbilla *f,* mentón *m,* barba *f*
china ['tʃaɪnə] *n* **1** PORCELAIN : porcelana *f,* loza *f* **2** CROCKERY, TABLEWARE : loza *f,* vajilla *f*
chinchilla [tʃɪn'tʃɪlə] *n* : chinchilla *f*
Chinese ['tʃaɪ'niːz, -'niːs] *n* **1** : chino *m,* -na *f* **2** : chino *m* (idioma) — **Chinese** *adj*
chink ['tʃɪŋk] *n* : grieta *f,* abertura *f*
chintz ['tʃɪnts] *n* : chintz *m,* chinz *m*
chip[1] ['tʃɪp] *v* **chipped; chipping** *vt* : desportillar, desconchar, astillar (madera) — *vi* : desportillarse, desconcharse, descascararse (dícese de la pintura, etc.)
chip[2] *n* **1** : astilla *f* (de madera o vidrio), lasca *f* (de piedra) <he's a chip

off the old block : de tal palo, tal astilla> **2** : bocado *m* pequeño (en rodajas o rebanadas) <tortilla chips : totopos, tortillitas tostadas> **3** : ficha *f* (de póker, etc.) **4** NICK : desportilladura *f*, mella *f* **5** : chip *m* <memory chip : chip de memoria>
chip in *v* CONTRIBUTE : contribuir
chipmunk [ˈtʃɪp,mʌŋk] *n* : ardilla *f* listada
chipper [ˈtʃɪpər] *adj* : alegre y vivaz
chiropodist [kəˈrɑpədɪst, ʃə-] *n* : podólogo *m*, -ga *f*
chiropody [kəˈrɑpədi, ʃə-] *n* : podología *f*
chiropractic [ˈkaɪrə,præktɪk] *n* : quiropráctica *f*
chiropractor [ˈkaɪrə,præktər] *n* : quiropráctico *m*, -ca *f*
chirp[1] [ˈtʃərp] *vi* : gorjear (dícese de los pájaros), chirriar (dícese de los grillos)
chirp[2] *n* : gorjeo *m* (de un pájaro), chirrido *m* (de un grillo)
chisel[1] [ˈtʃɪzəl] *vt* **-eled** *or* **-elled; -eling** *or* **-elling 1** : cincelar, tallar, labrar **2** CHEAT : estafar, defraudar
chisel[2] *n* : cincel *m* (para piedras y metales), escoplo *m* (para madera), formón *m*
chiseler [ˈtʃɪzələr] *n* SWINDLER : estafador *m*, -dora *f*; fraude *mf*
chit [ˈtʃɪt] *n* : resguardo *m*, recibo *m*
chitchat [ˈtʃɪt,tʃæt] *n* : cotorreo *m*, charla *f*
chivalric [ʃəˈvælrɪk] → **chivalrous**
chivalrous [ˈʃɪvəlrəs] *adj* **1** KNIGHTLY : caballeresco, relativo a la caballería **2** GENTLEMANLY : caballeroso, honesto, cortés
chivalrousness [ˈʃɪvəlrəsnəs] *n* : caballerosidad *f*, cortesía *f*
chivalry [ˈʃɪvəlri] *n, pl* **-ries 1** KNIGHTHOOD : caballería *f* **2** CHIVALROUSNESS : caballerosidad *f*, nobleza *f*, cortesía *f*
chive [ˈtʃaɪv] *n* : cebollino *m*
chloride [ˈklor,aɪd] *n* : cloruro *m*
chlorinate [ˈklorə,neɪt] *vt* **-nated; -nating** : clorar
chlorination [,klorəˈneɪʃən] *n* : cloración *f*
chlorine [ˈklor,iːn] *n* : cloro *m*
chloroform[1] [ˈklorə,fɔrm] *vt* : cloroformizar
chloroform[2] *n* : cloroformo *m*
chlorophyll [ˈklorə,fɪl] *n* : clorofila *f*
chock–full [ˈtʃɑkˈfʊl, ˈtʃʌk-] *adj* : colmado, repleto
chocolate [ˈtʃɑkələt, ˈtʃɔk-] *n* **1** : chocolate *m* **2** BONBON : bombón *m* **3** : color *m* chocolate, marrón *m*
choice[1] [ˈtʃɔɪs] *adj* **choicer; -est** : selecto, escogido, de primera calidad
choice[2] *n* **1** CHOOSING : elección *f*, selección *f* **2** OPTION : elección *f*, opción *f* <I have no choice : no tengo alternativa> **3** PREFERENCE : preferencia *f*, elección *f* **4** VARIETY : surtido *m*, selección *f* <a wide choice : un gran surtido>
choir [ˈkwaɪr] *n* : coro *m*
choirboy [ˈkwaɪr,bɔɪ] *n* : niño *m* de coro
choke[1] [ˈtʃoːk] *v* **choked; choking** *vt* **1** ASPHYXIATE, STRANGLE : sofocar, asfixiar, ahogar, estrangular **2** BLOCK : tapar, obstruir — *vi* **1** SUFFOCATE : asfixiarse, sofocarse, ahogarse, atragantarse (con comida) **2** CLOG : taparse, obstruirse
choke[2] *n* **1** CHOKING : estrangulación *f* **2** : choke *m* (de un motor)
choker [ˈtʃoːkər] *n* : gargantilla *f*
cholera [ˈkɑlərə] *n* : cólera *m*
cholesterol [kəˈlɛstə,rɔl] *n* : colesterol *m*
choose [ˈtʃuːz] *v* **chose** [ˈtʃoːz]; **chosen** [ˈtʃoːzən]; **choosing** *vt* **1** SELECT : escoger, elegir <choose only one : escoja sólo uno> **2** DECIDE : decidir <he chose to leave : decidió irse> **3** PREFER : preferir <which one do you choose? : ¿cuál prefiere?> — *vi* : escoger <much to choose from : mucho de donde escoger>
choosy *or* **choosey** [ˈtʃuːzi] *adj* **choosier; -est** : exigente, remilgado
chop[1] [ˈtʃɑp] *vt* **chopped; chopping 1** MINCE : picar, cortar, moler (carne) **2 to chop down** : cortar, talar (un árbol)
chop[2] *n* **1** CUT : hachazo *m* (con una hacha), tajo *m* (con una cuchilla) **2** BLOW : golpe *m* (penetrante) <karate chop : golpe de karate> **3** : chuleta *f* <pork chops : chuletas de cerdo>
chopper [ˈtʃɑpər] → **helicopter**
choppy [ˈtʃɑpi] *adj* **choppier; -est 1** : agitado, picado (dícese del mar) **2** DISCONNECTED : incoherente, inconexo
chops [ˈtʃɑps] *npl* **1** : quijada *f*, mandíbula *f*, boca *f* (de una persona) **2 to lick one's chops** : relamerse
chopsticks [ˈtʃɑp,stɪks] *npl* : palillos *mpl*
choral [ˈkorəl] *adj* : coral
chorale [kəˈræl, -ˈrɑl] *n* **1** : coral *f* (composición musical vocal) **2** CHOIR, CHORUS : coral *f*, coro *m*
chord [ˈkɔrd] *n* **1** : acorde *m* (en música) **2** : cuerda *f* (en anatomía o geometría)
chore [ˈtʃor] *n* **1** TASK : tarea *f* rutinaria **2** BOTHER, NUISANCE : lata *f fam*, fastidio *m* **3 chores** *npl* WORK : quehaceres *mpl*, faenas *fpl*
choreograph [ˈkoriə,græf] *vt* : coreografiar
choreographer [,koriˈɑgrəfər] *n* : coreógrafo *m*, -fa *f*
choreographic [,koriəˈgræfɪk] *adj* : coreográfico
choreography [,koriˈɑgrəfi] *n, pl* **-phies** : coreografía *f*
chorister [ˈkorəstər] *n* : corista *mf*
chortle[1] [ˈtʃɔrtəl] *vi* **-tled; -tling** : reírse (con satisfacción o júbilo)

chortle[2] *n* : risa *f* (de satisfacción o júbilo)
chorus[1] [ˈkorəs] *vt* : corear
chorus[2] *n* **1** : coro *m* (grupo o composición musical) **2** REFRAIN : coro *m,* estribillo *m*
chose *pp* → **choose**
chosen [ˈtʃoːzən] *adj* : elegido, selecto
chow [ˈtʃaʊ] *n* **1** FOOD : comida *f* **2** : chow-chow *m* (perro)
chowder [ˈtʃaʊdər] *n* : sopa *f* de pescado
christen [ˈkrɪsən] *vt* **1** BAPTIZE : bautizar **2** NAME : bautizar con el nombre de
Christendom [ˈkrɪsəndəm] *n* : cristiandad *f*
christening [ˈkrɪsənɪŋ] *n* : bautismo *m,* bautizo *m*
Christian[1] [ˈkrɪstʃən] *adj* : cristiano
Christian[2] *n* : cristiano *m,* -na *f*
Christianity [ˌkrɪstʃiˈænət̬i, ˌkrɪsˈtʃæ-] *n* : cristianismo *m*
Christian name *n* : nombre *m* de pila
Christmas [ˈkrɪsməs] *n* : Navidad *f* <Christmas season : las Navidades>
chromatic [kroːˈmæt̬ɪk] *adj* : cromático <chromatic scale : escala cromática>
chrome [ˈkroːm] *n* : cromo *m* (metal)
chromium [ˈkroːmiəm] *n* : cromo *m* (elemento)
chromosome [ˈkroːməˌsoːm, -ˌzoːm] *n* : cromosoma *m*
chronic [ˈkrɑnɪk] *adj* : crónico — **chronically** [-nɪkli] *adv*
chronicle[1] [ˈkrɑnɪkəl] *vt* **-cled; -cling** : escribir (una crónica o historia)
chronicle[2] *n* : crónica *f,* historia *f*
chronicler [ˈkrɑnɪklər] *n* : historiador *m,* -dora *f;* cronista *mf*
chronological [ˌkrɑnəlˈɑdʒɪkəl] *adj* : cronológico — **chronologically** [-kli] *adv*
chronology [krəˈnɑlədʒi] *n, pl* **-gies** : cronología *f*
chronometer [krəˈnɑmət̬ər] *n* : cronómetro *m*
chrysalis [ˈkrɪsələs] *n, pl* **chrysalides** [krɪˈsæləˌdiːz] *or* **chrysalises** : crisálida *f*
chrysanthemum [krɪˈsænṯθəməm] *n* : crisantemo *m*
chubbiness [ˈtʃʌbinəs] *n* : gordura *f*
chubby [ˈtʃʌbi] *adj* **-bier; -est** : gordito, regordete, rechoncho
chuck[1] [ˈtʃʌk] *vt* **1** TOSS : tirar, lanzar, aventar *Col, Mex* **2 to chuck under the chin** : hacer la mamola
chuck[2] *n* **1** PAT : mamola *f,* palmada *f* **2** TOSS : lanzamiento *m* **3** *or* **chuck steak** : corte *m* de carne de res
chuckle[1] [ˈtʃʌkəl] *vi* **-led; -ling** : reírse entre dientes
chuckle[2] *n* : risita *f,* risa *f* ahogada
chug[1] [ˈtʃʌg] *vi* **chugged; chugging** : resoplar, traquetear
chug[2] *n* : resoplido *m,* traqueteo *m*
chum[1] [ˈtʃʌm] *vi* **chummed; chumming** : ser camaradas, ser cuates *Mex fam*
chum[2] *n* : amigo *m,* -ga *f;* camarada *mf;* compinche *mf fam*
chummy [ˈtʃʌmi] *adj* **-mier; -est** : amistoso <they're very chummy : son muy amigos>
chump [ˈtʃʌmp] *n* : tonto *m,* -ta *f;* idiota *mf*
chunk [ˈtʃʌnk] *n* **1** PIECE : cacho *m,* pedazo *m,* trozo *m* **2** : cantidad *f* grande <a chunk of money : mucho dinero>
chunky [ˈtʃʌnki] *adj* **chunkier; -est 1** STOCKY : fornido, robusto **2** : que contiene pedazos
church [ˈtʃərtʃ] *n* **1** : iglesia *f* <to go to church : ir a la iglesia> **2** CHRISTIANS : iglesia *f,* conjunto *m* de fieles cristianos **3** DENOMINATION : confesión *f,* secta *f* **4** CONGREGATION : feligreses *mpl,* fieles *mpl*
churchgoer [ˈtʃərtʃˌgoːər] *n* : practicante *mf*
churchyard [ˈtʃərtʃˌjɑrd] *n* : cementerio *m* (junto a una iglesia)
churn[1] [ˈtʃərn] *vt* **1** : batir (crema), hacer (mantequilla) **2** : agitar con fuerza, revolver — *vi* : agitarse, arremolinarse
churn[2] *n* : mantequera *f*
chute [ˈʃuːt] *n* : conducto *m* inclinado, vertedero *m* (para basuras)
chutney [ˈtʃʌtni] *n, pl* **-neys** : chutney *m*
chutzpah [ˈhʊtspə, ˈxʊt-, -ˌspɑ] *n* : descaro *m,* frescura *f,* cara *f fam*
cicada [səˈkeɪdə, -ˈkɑ-] *n* : cigarra *f,* chicharra *f*
cider [ˈsaɪdər] *n* **1** : jugo *m* (de manzana, etc.) **2 hard cider** : sidra *f*
cigar [sɪˈgɑr] *n* : puro *m,* cigarro *m*
cigarette [ˌsɪgəˈrɛt, ˈsɪgəˌrɛt] *n* : cigarrillo *m,* cigarro *m*
cinch[1] [ˈsɪntʃ] *vt* **1** : cinchar (un caballo) **2** ASSURE : asegurar
cinch[2] *n* **1** : cincha *f* (para caballos) **2** : algo fácil o seguro <it's a cinch : es bien fácil, es pan comido>
cinchona [sɪŋˈkoːnə] *n* : quino *m*
cinder [ˈsɪndər] *n* **1** EMBER : brasa *f,* ascua *f* **2 cinders** *npl* ASHES : cenizas *fpl*
cinema [ˈsɪnəmə] *n* : cine *m*
cinematic [ˌsɪnəˈmæt̬ɪk] *adj* : cinematográfico
cinnamon [ˈsɪnəmən] *n* : canela *f*
cipher [ˈsaɪfər] *n* **1** ZERO : cero *m* **2** CODE : cifra *f,* clave *f*
circa [ˈsərkə] *prep* : alrededor de, hacia <circa 1800 : hacia el año 1800>
circle[1] [ˈsərkəl] *v* **-cled; -cling** *vt* **1** : encerrar en un círculo, poner un círculo alrededor de **2** : girar alrededor de, dar vueltas a <we circled the building twice : le dimos vueltas al edificio dos veces> — *vi* : dar vueltas

circle[2] *n* **1** : círculo *m* **2** CYCLE : ciclo *m* <to come full circle : volver al punto de partida> **3** GROUP : círculo *m,* grupo *m* (social)

circuit [ˈsərkət] *n* **1** BOUNDARY : circuito *m,* perímetro *m* (de una zona o un territorio) **2** TOUR : circuito *m,* recorrido *m,* tour *m* **3** : circuito *m* (eléctrico) <a short circuit : un cortocircuito>

circuitous [ˌsərˈkjuːətəs] *adj* : sinuoso, tortuoso

circuitry [ˈsərkətri] *n, pl* **-ries** : sistema *m* de circuitos

circular[1] [ˈsərkjələr] *adj* ROUND : circular, redondo

circular[2] *n* : circular *f*

circulate [ˈsərkjəˌleɪt] *v* **-lated; -lating** *vi* : circular — *vt* **1** : circular (noticias, etc.) **2** DISSEMINATE : hacer circular, divulgar

circulation [ˌsərkjəˈleɪʃən] *n* : circulación *f*

circulatory [ˈsərkjələˌtori] *adj* : circulatorio

circumcise [ˈsərkəmˌsaɪz] *vt* **-cised; -cising** : circuncidar

circumcision [ˌsərkəmˈsɪʒən, ˈsərkəmˌ-] *n* : circuncisión *f*

circumference [sərˈkʌmpfrənts] *n* : circunferencia *f*

circumflex [ˈsərkəmˌflɛks] *n* : acento *m* circunflejo

circumlocution [ˌsərkəmloˈkjuːʃən] *n* : circunlocución *f*

circumnavigate [ˌsərkəmˈnævəˌgeɪt] *vt* **-gated; -gating** : circunnavegar

circumscribe [ˈsərkəmˌskraɪb] *vt* **-scribed; -scribing 1** : circunscribir, trazar una figura alrededor de **2** LIMIT : circunscribir, limitar

circumspect [ˈsərkəmˌspɛkt] *adj* : circunspecto, prudente, cauto

circumspection [ˌsərkəmˈspɛkʃən] *n* : circunspección *f,* cautela *f*

circumstance [ˈsərkəmˌstænts] *n* **1** EVENT : circunstancia *f,* acontecimiento *m* **2 circumstances** *npl* SITUATION : circunstancias *fpl,* situación *f* <under the circumstances : dadas las circunstancias> <under no circumstances : de ninguna manera, bajo ningún concepto> **3 circumstances** *npl* : situación *f* económica

circumstantial [ˌsərkəmˈstæntʃəl] *adj* : circunstancial

circumvent [ˌsərkəmˈvɛnt] *vt* : evadir, burlar (una ley o regla), sortear (una responsabilidad o dificultad)

circumvention [ˌsərkəmˈvɛntʃən] *n* : evasión *f*

circus [ˈsərkəs] *n* : circo *m*

cirrhosis [səˈroːsɪs] *n* : cirrosis *f*

cirrus [ˈsɪrəs] *n, pl* **-ri** [ˈsɪrˌaɪ] : cirro *m*

cistern [ˈsɪstərn] *n* : cisterna *f,* aljibe *m*

citadel [ˈsɪtədəl, -ˌdɛl] *n* FORTRESS : ciudadela *f,* fortaleza *f*

citation [saɪˈteɪʃən] *n* **1** SUMMONS : emplazamiento *m,* citación *f,* convocatoria *f* (judicial) **2** QUOTATION : cita *f* **3** COMMENDATION : elogio *m,* mención *f* (de honor)

cite [ˈsaɪt] *vt* **cited; citing 1** ARRAIGN, SUBPOENA : emplazar, citar, hacer comparecer (ante un tribunal) **2** QUOTE : citar **3** COMMEND : elogiar, honrar (oficialmente)

citizen [ˈsɪtəzən] *n* : ciudadano *m,* -na *f*

citizenry [ˈsɪtəzənri] *n, pl* **-ries** : ciudadanía *f,* conjunto *m* de ciudadanos

citizenship [ˈsɪtəzənˌʃɪp] *n* : ciudadanía *f* <Nicaraguan citizenship : ciudadanía nicaragüense>

citron [ˈsɪtrən] *n* : cidra *f*

citrus [ˈsɪtrəs] *n, pl* **-rus** *or* **-ruses** : cítrico *m*

city [ˈsɪti] *n, pl* **cities** : ciudad *f*

civic [ˈsɪvɪk] *adj* : cívico

civics [ˈsɪvɪks] *ns & pl* : civismo *m*

civil [ˈsɪvəl] *adj* **1** : civil <civil law : derecho civil> **2** POLITE : civil, cortés

civilian [səˈvɪljən] *n* : civil *mf* <soldiers and civilians : soldados y civiles>

civility [səˈvɪləti] *n, pl* **-ties** : cortesía *f,* educación *f*

civilization [ˌsɪvələˈzeɪʃən] *n* : civilización *f*

civilize [ˈsɪvəˌlaɪz] *vt* **-lized; -lizing** : civilizar — **civilized** *adj*

civil liberties *npl* : derechos *mpl* civiles

civilly [ˈsɪvəli] *adv* : cortésmente

civil rights *npl* : derechos *mpl* civiles

civil service *n* : administración *f* pública

civil war *n* : guerra *f* civil

clack[1] [ˈklæk] *vi* : tabletear

clack[2] *n* : tableteo *m*

clad [ˈklæd] *adj* **1** CLOTHED : vestido **2** COVERED : cubierto

claim[1] [ˈkleɪm] *vt* **1** DEMAND : reclamar, reivindicar <she claimed her rights : reclamó sus derechos> **2** MAINTAIN : afirmar, sostener <they claim it's theirs : sostienen que es suyo>

claim[2] *n* **1** DEMAND : demanda *f,* reclamación *f* **2** DECLARATION : declaración *f,* afirmación *f* **3 to stake a claim** : reclamar, reivindicar

claimant [ˈkleɪmənt] *n* : demandante *mf* (ante un juez), pretendiente *mf* (al trono, etc.)

clairvoyance [klærˈvɔɪənts] *n* : clarividencia *f*

clairvoyant[1] [klærˈvɔɪənt] *adj* : clarividente

clairvoyant[2] *n* : clarividente *mf*

clam [ˈklæm] *n* : almeja *f*

clamber [ˈklæmbər] *vi* : treparse o subirse torpemente

clammy [ˈklæmi] *adj* **-mier; -est** : húmedo y algo frío

clamor[1] [ˈklæmər] *vi* : gritar, clamar

clamor[2] *n* : clamor *m*

clamorous [ˈklæmərəs] *adj* : clamoroso, ruidoso, estrepitoso

clamp[1] [ˈklæmp] *vt* : sujetar con abrazaderas

clamp[2] *n* : abrazadera *f*

clan [ˈklæn] *n* : clan *m*

clandestine [klænˈdɛstɪn] *adj* : clandestino, secreto

clang[1] [ˈklæŋ] *vi* : hacer resonar (dícese de un objeto metálico)

clang[2] *n* : ruido *m* metálico fuerte

clangor [ˈklæŋər, -gər] *n* : estruendo *m* metálico

clank[1] [ˈklæŋk] *vi* : producir un ruido metálico seco

clank[2] *n* : ruido *m* metálico seco

clannish [ˈklænɪʃ] *adj* : exclusivista

clap[1] [ˈklæp] *v* **clapped; clapping** *vt* **1** SLAP, STRIKE : golpear ruidosamente, dar una palmada <to clap one's hands : batir palmas, dar palmadas> **2** APPLAUD : aplaudir — *vi* APPLAUD : aplaudir

clap[2] *n* **1** SLAP : palmada *f,* golpecito *m* **2** NOISE : ruido *m* seco <a clap of thunder : un trueno>

clapboard [ˈklæbərd, ˈklæp,bord] *n* : tabla *f* de madera (para revestir muros)

clapper [ˈklæpər] *n* : badajo *m* (de una campana)

clarification [,klærəfəˈkeɪʃən] *n* : clarificación *f*

clarify [ˈklærə,faɪ] *vt* **-fied; -fying 1** EXPLAIN : aclarar **2** : clarificar (un líquido)

clarinet [,klærəˈnɛt] *n* : clarinete *m*

clarinetist *or* **clarinettist** [,klærəˈnɛtɪst] *n* : clarinetista *mf*

clarion [ˈklæriən] *adj* : claro y sonoro

clarity [ˈklærəṭi] *n* : claridad *f,* nitidez *f*

clash[1] [ˈklæʃ] *vi* **1** : sonar, chocarse <the cymbals clashed : los platillos sonaron> **2** : chocar, enfrentarse <the students clashed with the police : los estudiantes se enfrentaron con la policía> **3** CONFLICT : estar en conflicto, oponerse **4** : desentonar (dícese de los colores), coincidir (dícese de los datos)

clash[2] *n* **1** : ruido *m* (producido por un choque) **2** CONFLICT, CONFRONTATION : enfrentamiento *m,* conflicto *m,* choque *m* **3** : desentono *m* (de colores), coincidencia *f* (de datos)

clasp[1] [ˈklæsp] *vt* **1** FASTEN : sujetar, abrochar **2** EMBRACE, GRASP : agarrar, sujetar, abrazar

clasp[2] *n* **1** FASTENING : broche *m,* cierre *m* **2** EMBRACE, SQUEEZE : apretón *m,* abrazo *m*

class[1] [ˈklæs] *vt* : clasificar, catalogar

class[2] *n* **1** KIND, TYPE : clase *f,* tipo *m,* especie *f* **2** : clase *f,* rango *m* social <the working class : la clase obrera> **3** LESSON : clase *f,* curso *m* <English class : clase de inglés> **4** : conjunto *m* de estudiantes, clase *f* <the class of '97 : la promoción del 97>

classic[1] [ˈklæsɪk] *adj* : clásico

classic[2] *n* : clásico *m,* obra *f* clásica

classical [ˈklæsɪkəl] *adj* : clásico — **classically** [-kli] *adv*

classicism [ˈklæsə,sɪzəm] *n* : clasicismo *m*

classification [,klæsəfəˈkeɪʃən] *n* : clasificación *f*

classified [ˈklæsə,faɪd] *adj* **1** : clasificado <classified ads : avisos clasificados> **2** RESTRICTED : confidencial, secreto <classified documents : documentos secretos>

classify [ˈklæsə,faɪ] *vt* **-fied; -fying** : clasificar, catalogar

classless [ˈklæsləs] *adj* : sin clases

classmate [ˈklæs,meɪt] *n* : compañero *m,* -ra *f* de clase

classroom [ˈklæs,ruːm] *n* : aula *f,* salón *m* de clase

clatter[1] [ˈklæṭər] *vi* : traquetear, hacer ruido

clatter[2] *n* : traqueteo *m,* ruido *m,* estrépito *m*

clause [ˈklɔz] *n* : cláusula *f*

claustrophobia [,klɔstrəˈfoːbiə] *n* : claustrofobia *f*

clavicle [ˈklævɪkəl] *n* : clavícula *f*

claw[1] [ˈklɔ] *v* : arañar

claw[2] *n* : garra *f,* uña *f* (de un gato), pinza *f* (de un crustáceo)

clay [ˈkleɪ] *n* : arcilla *f,* barro *m*

clayey [ˈkleɪi] *adj* : arcilloso

clean[1] [ˈkliːn] *vt* : limpiar, lavar, asear

clean[2] *adv* : limpio, limpiamente <to play clean : jugar limpio>

clean[3] *adj* **1** : limpio **2** UNADULTERATED : puro **3** IRREPROACHABLE : intachable, sin mancha <to have a clean record : no tener antecedentes penales> **4** DECENT : decente **5** COMPLETE : completo, absoluto <a clean break with the past : un corte radical con el pasado>

cleaner [ˈkliːnər] *n* **1** : limpiador *m,* -dora *f* **2** : producto *m* de limpieza **3** DRY CLEANER : tintorería *f* (servicio)

cleanliness [ˈklɛnlinəs] *n* : limpieza *f,* aseo *m*

cleanly[1] [ˈkliːnli] *adv* : limpiamente, con limpieza

cleanly[2] [ˈklɛnli] *adj* **-lier; -est** : limpio, pulcro

cleanness [ˈkliːnnəs] *n* : limpieza *f*

cleanse [ˈklɛnz] *vt* **cleansed; cleansing** : limpiar, purificar

cleanser [ˈklɛnzər] *n* : limpiador *m,* purificador *m*

clear[1] [ˈklɪr] *vt* **1** CLARIFY : aclarar, clarificar (un líquido) **2** : despejar (una superficie), desatascar (un tubo), desmontar (una selva) <to clear the table : levantar la mesa> <to clear one's throat : carraspear, aclararse la voz> **3** EXONERATE : absolver, limpiar el nombre de **4** EARN : ganar, sacar (una ganancia de) **5** : pasar sin tocar

<he cleared the hurdle : saltó por encima de la valla> **6 to clear up** RESOLVE : aclarar, resolver, esclarecer — *vi* **1** DISPERSE : irse, despejarse, disiparse **2** : ser compensado (dícese de un cheque) **3 to clear up** : despejar (dícese del tiempo), mejorarse (dícese de una enfermedad)
clear[2] *adv* : claro, claramente
clear[3] *adj* **1** BRIGHT : claro, lúcido **2** FAIR : claro, despejado **3** TRANSPARENT : transparente, translúcido **4** EVIDENT, UNMISTAKABLE : evidente, claro, obvio **5** CERTAIN : seguro **6** UNOBSTRUCTED : despejado, libre
clear[4] *n* **1 in the clear** : inocente, libre de toda sospecha **2 in the clear** SAFE : fuera de peligro
clearance [ˈklɪrən*t*s] *n* **1** CLEARING : despeje *m* **2** SPACE : espacio *m* (libre), margen *m* **3** AUTHORIZATION : autorización *f,* despacho *m* (de la aduana)
clearing [ˈklɪrɪŋ] *n* : claro *m* (de un bosque)
clearly [ˈklɪrli] *adv* **1** DISTINCTLY : claramente, directamente **2** OBVIOUSLY : obviamente, evidentemente
cleat [ˈkliːt] *n* **1** : taco *m* **2 cleats** *npl* : zapatos *mpl* deportivos (con tacos)
cleavage [ˈkliːvɪdʒ] *n* **1** CLEFT : hendidura *f,* raja *f* **2** : escote *m* (del busto)
cleave[1] [ˈkliːv] *vi* **cleaved** [ˈkliːvd] *or* **clove** [ˈkloːv]; **cleaving** ADHERE : adherirse, unirse
cleave[2] *vt* **cleaved; cleaving** SPLIT : hender, dividir, partir
cleaver [ˈkliːvər] *n* : cuchilla *f* de carnicero
clef [ˈklɛf] *n* : clave *f*
cleft [ˈklɛft] *n* : hendidura *f,* raja *f,* grieta *f*
clemency [ˈklɛmən*t*si] *n* : clemencia *f*
clement [ˈklɛmənt] *adj* **1** MERCIFUL : clemente, piadoso **2** MILD : clemente, apacible
clench [ˈklɛntʃ] *vt* **1** CLUTCH : agarrar **2** TIGHTEN : apretar (el puño, los dientes)
clergy [ˈklərdʒi] *n, pl* **-gies** : clero *m*
clergyman [ˈklərdʒimən] *n, pl* **-men** [-mən, -ˌmɛn] : clérigo *m*
cleric [ˈklɛrɪk] *n* : clérigo *m,* -ga *f*
clerical [ˈklɛrɪkəl] *adj* **1** : clerical <a clerical collar : un alzacuello> **2** : de oficina <clerical staff : personal de oficina>
clerk[1] [ˈklərk, *Brit* ˈklɑrk] *vi* : trabajar de oficinista, trabajar de dependiente
clerk[2] *n* **1** : funcionario *m,* -ria *f* (de una oficina gubernamental) **2** : oficinista *mf,* empleado *m,* -da *f* de oficina **3** SALESPERSON : dependiente *m,* -ta *f*
clever [ˈklɛvər] *adj* **1** SKILLFUL : ingenioso, hábil **2** SMART : listo, inteligente, astuto
cleverly [ˈklɛvərli] *adv* **1** SKILLFULLY : ingeniosamente, hábilmente **2** INTELLIGENTLY : inteligentemente
cleverness [ˈklɛvərnəs] *n* **1** SKILL : ingenio *m,* habilidad *f* **2** INTELLIGENCE : inteligencia *f*
clew [ˈkluː] → **clue**
cliché [kliˈʃeɪ] *n* : cliché *m,* tópico *m*
click[1] [ˈklɪk] *vt* : chasquear (la lengua, los dedos) — *vi* **1** : chasquear **2** SUCCEED : tener éxito **3** GET ALONG : congeniar, llevarse bien
click[2] *n* : chasquido *m*
client [ˈklaɪənt] *n* : cliente *m,* -ta *f*
clientele [ˌklaɪənˈtɛl, ˌkliː-] *n* : clientela *f*
cliff [ˈklɪf] *n* : acantilado *m,* precipicio *m,* risco *m*
climate [ˈklaɪmət] *n* : clima *m*
climax[1] [ˈklaɪˌmæks] *vi* : llegar al punto culminante, culminar — *vt* : ser el punto culminante de
climax[2] *n* : clímax *m,* punto *m* culminante
climb[1] [ˈklaɪm] *vt* : escalar, trepar a, subir a <to climb a mountain : escalar una montaña> — *vi* **1** RISE : subir, ascender <prices are climbing : los precios están subiendo> **2** subirse, treparse <to climb up a tree : treparse a un árbol>
climb[2] *n* : ascenso *m,* subida *f*
climber [ˈklaɪmər] *n* **1** : escalador *m,* -dora *f* <a mountain climber : un alpinista> **2** : trepadora *f* (planta)
clinch[1] [ˈklɪntʃ] *vt* **1** FASTEN, SECURE : remachar (un clavo), afianzar, abrochar **2** SETTLE : decidir, cerrar <to clinch the title : ganar el título>
clinch[2] *n* : abrazo *m,* clinch *m* (en el boxeo)
clincher [ˈklɪntʃər] *n* : argumento *m* decisivo
cling [ˈklɪŋ] *vi* **clung** [ˈklʌŋ]; **clinging 1** STICK : adherirse, pegarse **2** : aferrarse, agarrarse <he clung to the railing : se aferró a la barandilla>
clinic [ˈklɪnɪk] *n* : clínica *f*
clinical [ˈklɪnɪkəl] *adj* : clínico — **clinically** [-kli] *adv*
clink[1] [ˈklɪŋk] *vi* : tintinear
clink[2] *n* : tintineo *m*
clip[1] [ˈklɪp] *vt* **clipped; clipping 1** CUT : cortar, recortar **2** HIT : golpear, dar un puñetazo a **3** FASTEN : sujetar (con un clip)
clip[2] *n* **1** → **clippers 2** BLOW : golpe *m,* puñetazo *m* **3** PACE : paso *m* rápido **4** FASTENER : clip *m* <a paper clip : un sujetapapeles>
clipper [ˈklɪpər] *n* **1** : clíper *m* (buque de vela) **2 clippers** *npl* : tijeras *fpl* <nail clippers : cortauñas>
clique [ˈkliːk, ˈklɪk] *n* : grupo *m* exclusivo, camarilla *f* (de políticos)
clitoris [ˈklɪtərəs, klɪˈtɔrəs] *n, pl* **clitorides** [-ˈtɔrəˌdiːz] : clítoris *m*
cloak[1] [ˈkloːk] *vt* : encubrir, envolver (en un manto de)
cloak[2] *n* : capa *f,* capote *m,* manto *m* <under the cloak of darkness : al amparo de la oscuridad>

clobber ['klɑbər] *vt* : dar una paliza a

clock[1] ['klɑk] *vt* : cronometrar

clock[2] *n* **1** : reloj *m* (de pared), cronómetro *m* (en deportes o competencias) **2 around the clock** : las veinticuatro horas

clockwise ['klɑk,waɪz] *adv & adj* : en la dirección de las manecillas del reloj

clockwork ['klɑk,wərk] *n* : mecanismo *m* de relojería

clod ['klɑd] *n* **1** : terrón *m* **2** OAF : zoquete *mf*

clog[1] ['klɑg] *v* **clogged; clogging** *vt* **1** HINDER : estorbar, impedir **2** BLOCK : atascar, tapar — *vi* : atascarse, taparse

clog[2] *n* **1** OBSTACLE : traba *f*, impedimento *m*, estorbo *m* **2** : zueco *m* (zapato)

cloister[1] ['klɔɪstər] *vt* : enclaustrar

cloister[2] *n* : claustro *m*

clone ['klo:n] *n* **1** : clon *m* (de un organismo) **2** COPY : copia *f*, reproducción *f*

close[1] ['klo:z] *v* **closed; closing** *vt* : cerrar — *vi* **1** : cerrarse, cerrar **2** TERMINATE : concluirse, terminar **3 to close in** APPROACH : acercarse, aproximarse

close[2] ['klo:s] *adv* : cerca, de cerca

close[3] *adj* **closer; closest 1** CONFINING : restrictivo, estrecho **2** SECRETIVE : reservado **3** STRICT : estricto, detallado **4** STUFFY : cargado, bochornoso (dícese del tiempo) **5** TIGHT : apretado, entallado, ceñido <it's a close fit : es muy apretado> **6** NEAR : cercano, próximo **7** INTIMATE : íntimo <close friends : amigos íntimos> **8** ACCURATE : fiel, exacto **9** : reñido <a close election : una elección muy reñida>

close[4] ['klo:z] *n* : fin *m*, final *m*, conclusión *f*

closely ['klo:sli] *adv* : cerca, de cerca

closeness ['klo:snəs] *n* **1** NEARNESS : cercanía *f*, proximidad *f* **2** INTIMACY : intimidad *f*

closet[1] ['klɑzət] *vt* **to be closeted with** : estar encerrado con

closet[2] *n* : armario *m*, guardarropa *f*, clóset *m*

closure ['klo:ʒər] *n* **1** CLOSING, END : cierre *m*, clausura *f*, fin *m* **2** FASTENER : cierre *m*

clot[1] ['klɑt] *v* **clotted; clotting** *vt* : coagular, cuajar — *vi* : cuajarse, coagularse

clot[2] *n* : coágulo *m*

cloth ['klɔθ] *n, pl* **cloths** ['klɔðz, 'klɔθs] **1** FABRIC : tela *f* **2** RAG : trapo *m* **3** TABLECLOTH : mantel *m*

clothe ['klo:ð] *vt* **clothed** *or* **clad** ['klæd]; **clothing** DRESS : vestir, arropar, ataviar

clothes ['klo:z, 'klo:ðz] *npl* **1** CLOTHING : ropa *f* **2** BEDCLOTHES : ropa *f* de cama

clothespin ['klo:z,pɪn] *n* : pinza *f* (para la ropa)

clothing ['klo:ðɪŋ] *n* : ropa *f*, indumentaria *f*

cloud[1] ['klaʊd] *vt* : nublar, oscurecer — *vi* **to cloud over** : nublarse

cloud[2] *n* : nube *f*

cloudburst ['klaʊd,bərst] *n* : chaparrón *m*, aguacero *m*

cloudless ['klaʊdləs] *adj* : despejado, claro

cloudy ['klaʊdi] *adj* **cloudier; -est** : nublado, nuboso

clout[1] ['klaʊt] *vt* : bofetear, dar un tortazo a

clout[2] *n* **1** BLOW : golpe *m*, tortazo *m fam* **2** INFLUENCE : influencia *f*, palanca *f fam*

clove[1] ['klo:v] *n* **1** : diente *m* (de ajo) **2** : clavo *m* (especia)

clove[2] → **cleave**

cloven hoof ['klo:vən] : pezuña *f* hendida

clover ['klo:vər] *n* : trébol *m*

cloverleaf ['klo:vər,li:f] *n, pl* **-leafs** *or* **-leaves** [-,li:vz] : intersección *f* en trébol

clown[1] ['klaʊn] *vi* : payasear, bromear <stop clowning around : déjate de payasadas>

clown[2] *n* : payaso *m*, -sa *f*

clownish ['klaʊnɪʃ] *adj* **1** : de payaso **2** BOORISH : grosero — **clownishly** *adv*

cloying ['klɔɪɪŋ] *adj* : empalagoso, meloso

club[1] ['klʌb] *vt* **clubbed; clubbing** : aporrear, dar garrotazos a

club[2] *n* **1** CUDGEL : garrote *m*, porra *f* **2** : palo *m* <golf club : palo de golf> **3** : trébol *m* (naipe) **4** ASSOCIATION : club *m*

clubfoot ['klʌb,fʊt] *n, pl* **-feet** : pie *m* deforme

clubhouse ['klʌb,haʊs] *n* : sede *f* de un club

cluck[1] ['klʌk] *vi* : cloquear, cacarear

cluck[2] *n* : cloqueo *m*, cacareo *m*

clue[1] ['klu:] *vt* **clued; clueing** *or* **cluing** *or* **to clue in** : dar una pista a, informar

clue[2] *n* : pista *f*, indicio *m*

clump[1] ['klʌmp] *vi* **1** : caminar con pisadas fuertes **2** LUMP : agruparse, aglutinarse — *vt* : amontonar

clump[2] *n* **1** : grupo *m* (de arbustos o árboles), terrón *m* (de tierra) **2** : pisada *f* fuerte

clumsily ['klʌmzəli] *adv* : torpemente, sin gracia

clumsiness ['klʌmzinəs] *n* : torpeza *f*

clumsy ['klʌmzi] *adj* **-sier; -est 1** AWKWARD : torpe, desmañado **2** TACTLESS : carente de tacto, poco delicado

clung → **cling**

cluster[1] ['klʌstər] *vt* : agrupar, juntar — *vi* : agruparse, apiñarse, arracimarse

cluster[2] *n* : grupo *m*, conjunto *m*, racimo *m* (de uvas)

clutch[1] ['klʌtʃ] *vt* : agarrar, asir — *vi* **to clutch at** : tratar de agarrar

clutch[2] *n* **1** GRASP, GRIP **:** agarre *m,* apretón *m* **2 :** embrague *m,* clutch *m* (de una máquina) **3 clutches** *npl* **:** garras *fpl* <he fell into their clutches : cayó en sus garras>

clutter[1] ['klʌtər] *vt* **:** atiborrar o atestar de cosas, llenar desordenadamente

clutter[2] *n* **:** desorden *m,* revoltijo *m*

coach[1] ['ko:tʃ] *vt* **:** entrenar (atletas, artistas), preparar (alumnos)

coach[2] *n* **1** CARRIAGE **:** coche *m,* carruaje *m,* carroza *f* **2 :** vagón *m* de pasajeros (de un tren) **3** BUS **:** autobús *m,* ómnibus *m* **4 :** pasaje *m* aéreo de segunda clase **5** TRAINER **:** entrenador *m,* -dora *f*

coagulate [ko'ægjə,leɪt] *v* **-lated; -lating** *vt* **:** coagular, cuajar — *vi* **:** coagularse, cuajarse

coal ['ko:l] *n* **1** EMBER **:** ascua *f,* brasa *f* **2 :** carbón *m* <a coal mine : una mina de carbón>

coalesce [,ko:ə'lɛs] *vi* **-alesced; -alescing :** unirse

coalition [,ko:ə'lɪʃən] *n* **:** coalición *f*

coarse ['kors] *adj* **coarser; -est 1 :** grueso (dícese de la arena o la sal), basto (dícese de las telas), áspero (dícese de la piel) **2** CRUDE, ROUGH **:** basto, tosco, ordinario **3** VULGAR **:** grosero — **coarsely** *adv*

coarsen ['korsən] *vt* **:** hacer áspero o basto — *vi* **:** volverse áspero o basto

coarseness ['korsnəs] *n* **:** aspereza *f,* tosquedad *f*

coast[1] ['ko:st] *vi* **:** deslizarse, rodar sin impulso

coast[2] *n* **:** costa *f,* litoral *m*

coastal ['ko:stəl] *adj* **:** costero

coaster ['ko:stər] *n* **:** posavasos *m*

coast guard *n* **:** guardia *f* costera, guardacostas *mpl*

coastline ['ko:st,laɪn] *n* **:** costa *f*

coat[1] ['ko:t] *vt* **:** cubrir, revestir, bañar (en un líquido)

coat[2] *n* **1 :** abrigo *m* <a sport coat : una chaqueta, un saco> **2 :** pelaje *m* (de animales) **3** LAYER **:** capa *f,* mano *f* (de pintura)

coating ['ko:t̬ɪŋ] *n* **:** capa *f*

coat of arms *n* **:** escudo *m* de armas

coax ['ko:ks] *vt* **:** engatusar, persuadir

cob ['kɑb] → **corncob**

cobalt ['ko:,bɔlt] *n* **:** cobalto *m*

cobble ['kɑbəl] *vt* **cobbled; cobbling 1 :** fabricar o remendar (zapatos) **2 to cobble together :** improvisar, hacer apresuradamente

cobbler ['kɑblər] *n* **1** SHOEMAKER **:** zapatero *m,* -ra *f* **2 fruit cobbler :** tarta *f* de fruta

cobblestone ['kɑbəl,sto:n] *n* **:** adoquín *m*

cobra ['ko:brə] *n* **:** cobra *f*

cobweb ['kɑb,wɛb] *n* **:** telaraña *f*

cocaine [ko:'keɪn, 'ko:,keɪn] *n* **:** cocaína *f*

cock[1] ['kɑk] *vt* **1 :** ladear <to cock one's head : ladear la cabeza> **2 :** montar, amartillar (un arma de fuego)

cock[2] *n* **1** ROOSTER **:** gallo *m* **2** FAUCET **:** grifo *m,* llave *f* **3 :** martillo *m* (de un arma de fuego)

cockatoo ['kɑkə,tu:] *n, pl* **-toos :** cacatúa *f*

cockeyed ['kɑk,aɪd] *adj* **1** ASKEW **:** ladeado, torcido, chueco **2** ABSURD **:** disparatado, absurdo

cockfight ['kɑk,faɪt] *n* **:** pelea *f* de gallos

cockiness ['kɑkinəs] *n* **:** arrogancia *f*

cockle ['kɑkəl] *n* **:** berberecho *m*

cockpit ['kɑk,pɪt] *n* **:** cabina *f*

cockroach ['kɑk,ro:tʃ] *n* **:** cucaracha *f*

cocktail ['kɑk,teɪl] *n* **1 :** coctel *m,* cóctel *m* **2** APPETIZER **:** aperitivo *m*

cocky ['kɑki] *adj* **cockier; -est :** creído, engreído

cocoa ['ko:,ko:] *n* **1** CACAO **:** cacao *m* **2 :** cocoa *f,* chocolate *m* (bebida)

coconut ['ko:kə,nʌt] *n* **:** coco *m*

cocoon [kə'ku:n] *n* **:** capullo *m*

cod ['kɑd] *n, pl* **cod :** bacalao *m*

coddle ['kɑdəl] *vt* **-dled; -dling :** mimar, consentir

code ['ko:d] *n* **1 :** código *m* <civil code : código civil> **2 :** código *m,* clave *f* <secret code : clave secreta>

codeine ['ko:,di:n] *n* **:** codeína *f*

codger ['kɑdʒər] *n* **:** viejo *m,* vejete *m*

codify ['kɑdə,faɪ, 'ko:-] *vt* **-fied; -fying :** codificar

coeducation [,ko:,ɛdʒə'keɪʃən] *n* **:** coeducación *f,* enseñanza *f* mixta

coeducational [,ko:,ɛdʒə'keɪʃənəl] *adj* **:** mixto

coefficient [,ko:ə'fɪʃənt] *n* **:** coeficiente *m*

coerce [ko'ərs] *vt* **-erced; -ercing :** coaccionar, forzar, obligar

coercion [ko'ərʒən, -ʃən] *n* **:** coacción *f*

coercive [ko'ərsɪv] *adj* **:** coactivo

coexist [,ko:ɪg'zɪst] *vi* **:** coexistir

coexistence [,ko:ɪg'zɪstənts] *n* **:** coexistencia *f*

coffee ['kɔfi] *n* **:** café *m*

coffeepot ['kɔfi,pɑt] *n* **:** cafetera *f*

coffer ['kɔfər] *n* **:** cofre *m*

coffin ['kɔfən] *n* **:** ataúd *m,* féretro *m*

cog ['kɑg] *n* **:** diente *m* (de una rueda dentada)

cogent ['ko:dʒənt] *adj* **:** convincente, persuasivo

cogitate ['kɑdʒə,teɪt] *vi* **-tated; -tating :** reflexionar, meditar, discurrir

cogitation [,kɑdʒə'teɪʃən] *n* **:** reflexión *f,* meditación *f*

cognac ['ko:n,jæk] *n* **:** coñac *m*

cognate ['kɑg,neɪt] *adj* **:** relacionado, afín

cogwheel ['kɑg,hwi:l] *n* **:** rueda *f* dentada

cohabit [,ko:'hæbət] *vi* **:** cohabitar

cohere [ko'hɪr] *vi* **-hered; -hering 1** ADHERE **:** adherirse, pegarse **2 :** ser coherente o congruente

coherence [ko'hɪrən*t*s] *n* : coherencia *f,* congruencia *f*
coherent [ko'hɪrənt] *adj* : coherente, congruente — **coherently** *adv*
cohesion [ko'hiːʒən] *n* : cohesión *f*
cohort ['koː,hɔrt] *n* **1** : cohorte *f* (de soldados) **2** COMPANION : compañero *m,* -ra *f;* colega *mf*
coiffure [kwɑ'fjʊr] *n* : peinado *m*
coil[1] ['kɔɪl] *vt* : enrollar — *vi* : enrollarse, enroscarse
coil[2] *n* : rollo *m* (de cuerda, etc.), espiral *f* (de humo)
coin[1] ['kɔɪn] *vt* **1** MINT : acuñar (moneda) **2** INVENT : acuñar, crear, inventar <to coin a phrase : como se suele decir>
coin[2] *n* : moneda *f*
coincide [,koːɪn'saɪd, 'koːɪn,saɪd] *vi* **-cided; -ciding** : coincidir
coincidence [ko'ɪn*t*sədən*t*s] *n* : coincidencia *f,* casualidad *f* <what a coincidence! : ¡qué casualidad!>
coincident [ko'ɪn*t*sədənt] *adj* : coincidente, concurrente
coincidental [ko,ɪn*t*sə'dɛntəl] *adj* : casual, accidental, fortuito
coitus ['koːət̬əs] *n* : coito *m*
coke ['koːk] *n* : coque *m*
colander ['kɑləndər, 'kʌ-] *n* : colador *m*
cold[1] ['koːld] *adj* : frío <it's cold out : hace frío> <a cold reception : una fría recepción> <in cold blood : a sangre fría>
cold[2] *n* **1** : frío *m* <to feel the cold : sentir frío> **2** : resfriado *m,* catarro *m* <to catch a cold : resfriarse>
cold-blooded ['koːld'blʌdəd] *adj* **1** CRUEL : cruel, despiadado **2** : de sangre fría (dícese de los reptiles, etc.)
coldly ['koːldli] *adv* : fríamente, con frialdad
coldness ['koːldnəs] *n* : frialdad *f* (de una persona o una actitud), frío *m* (de la temperatura)
coleslaw ['koːl,slɔ] *n* : ensalada *f* de col
colic ['kɑlɪk] *n* : cólico *m*
coliseum [,kɑlə'siːəm] *n* : coliseo *m,* arena *f*
collaborate [kə'læbə,reɪt] *vi* **-rated; -rating** : colaborar
collaboration [kə,læbə'reɪʃən] *n* : colaboración *f*
collaborator [kə'læbə,reɪt̬ər] *n* **1** COLLEAGUE : colaborador *m,* -dora *f* **2** TRAITOR : colaboracionista *mf*
collapse[1] [kə'læps] *vi* **-lapsed; -lapsing 1** : derrumbarse, desplomarse, hundirse <the building collapsed : el edificio se derrumbó> **2** FALL : desplomarse, caerse <he collapsed on the bed : se desplomó en la cama> <to collapse with laughter : morirse de risa> **3** FAIL : fracasar, quebrar, arruinarse **4** FOLD : plegarse
collapse[2] *n* **1** FALL : derrumbe *m,* desplome *m* **2** BREAKDOWN, FAILURE : fracaso *m,* colapso *m* (físico), quiebra *f* (económica)
collapsible [kə'læpsəbəl] *adj* : plegable
collar[1] ['kɑlər] *vt* : agarrar, atrapar
collar[2] *n* : cuello *m*
collarbone ['kɑlər,boːn] *n* : clavícula *f*
collate [kə'leɪt; 'kɑ,leɪt, 'koː-] *vt* **-lated; -lating 1** COMPARE : cotejar, comparar **2** : ordenar, recopilar (páginas)
collateral[1] [kə'læt̬ərəl] *adj* : colateral
collateral[2] *n* : garantía *f,* fianza *f,* prenda *f*
colleague ['kɑ,liːg] *n* : colega *mf;* compañero *m,* -ra *f*
collect[1] [kə'lɛkt] *vt* **1** GATHER : recopilar, reunir, recoger <she collected her thoughts : puso en orden sus ideas> **2** : coleccionar, juntar <to collect stamps : coleccionar timbres> **3** : cobrar (una deuda), recaudar (un impuesto) **4** DRAW : cobrar, percibir (un sueldo, etc.) — *vi* **1** ACCUMULATE : acumularse, juntarse **2** CONGREGATE : congregarse, reunirse
collect[2] *adv & adj* : por cobrar, a cobro revertido
collectible *or* **collectable** [kə'lɛktəbəl] *adj* : coleccionable
collection [kə'lɛkʃən] *n* **1** COLLECTING : colecta *f* (de contribuciones), cobro *m* (de deudas), recaudación *f* (de impuestos) **2** GROUP : colección *f* (de objetos), grupo *m* (de personas)
collective[1] [kə'lɛktɪv] *adj* : colectivo — **collectively** *adv*
collective[2] *n* : colectivo *m*
collector [kə'lɛktər] *n* **1** : coleccionista *mf* (de objetos) **2** : cobrador *m,* -dora *f* (de deudas)
college ['kɑlɪdʒ] *n* **1** : universidad *f* **2** : colegio *m* (de electores o profesionales)
collegiate [kə'liːdʒət] *adj* : universitario
collide [kə'laɪd] *vi* **-lided; -liding** : chocar, colisionar, estrellarse
collie ['kɑli] *n* : collie *mf*
collision [kə'lɪʒən] *n* : choque *m,* colisión *f*
colloquial [kə'loːkwiəl] *adj* : coloquial
colloquialism [kə'loːkwiə,lɪzəm] *n* : expresión *f* coloquial
collusion [kə'luːʒən] *n* : colusión *f*
cologne [kə'loːn] *n* : colonia *f*
Colombian [kə'lʌmbiən] *n* : colombiano *m,* -na *f* — **Colombian** *adj*
colon[1] ['koːlən] *n, pl* **colons** *or* **cola** [-lə] : colon *m* (de los intestinos)
colon[2] *n, pl* **colons** : dos puntos *mpl* (signo ortográfico)
colonel ['kərnəl] *n* : coronel *m*
colonial[1] [kə'loːniəl] *adj* : colonial
colonial[2] *n* : colono *m,* -na *f*
colonist ['kɑlənɪst] *n* : colono *m,* -na *f;* colonizador *m,* -dora *f*

colonization [ˌkɑlənəˈzeɪʃən] *n* : colonización *f*

colonize [ˈkɑləˌnaɪz] *vt* **-nized; -nizing** **1** : establecer una colonia en **2** SETTLE : colonizar

colonnade [ˌkɑləˈneɪd] *n* : columnata *f*

colony [ˈkɑləni] *n, pl* **-nies** : colonia *f*

color[1] [ˈkʌlər] *vt* **1** : colorear, pintar **2** INFLUENCE : influir en, influenciar — *vi* BLUSH : sonrojarse, ruborizarse

color[2] *n* **1** : color *m* <primary colors : colores primarios> **2** INTEREST, VIVIDNESS : color *m,* colorido *m* <local color : color local>

color–blind [ˈkʌlərˌblaɪnd] *adj* : daltónico

color blindness *n* : daltonismo *m*

colored [ˈkʌlərd] *adj* **1** : de color (dícese de los objetos) **2** : de color, negro (dícese de las personas)

colorfast [ˈkʌlərˌfæst] *adj* : que no se destiñe

colorful [ˈkʌlərfəl] *adj* **1** : lleno de colorido, de colores vivos **2** PICTURESQUE, STRIKING : pintoresco, llamativo

colorless [ˈkʌlərləs] *adj* **1** : incoloro, sin color **2** DULL : soso, aburrido

colossal [kəˈlɑsəl] *adj* : colosal

colossus [kəˈlɑsəs] *n, pl* **-si** [-ˌsaɪ] : coloso *m*

colt [ˈkoːlt] *n* : potro *m*

column [ˈkɑləm] *n* : columna *f*

columnist [ˈkɑləmnɪst, -ləmɪst] *n* : columnista *mf*

coma [ˈkoːmə] *n* : coma *m,* estado *m* de coma

comatose [ˈkoːməˌtoːs, ˈkɑ-] *adj* : comatoso, en estado de coma

comb[1] [ˈkoːm] *vt* **1** : peinar (el pelo) **2** SEARCH : peinar, rastrear, registrar a fondo

comb[2] *n* **1** : peine *m* **2** : cresta *f* (de un gallo)

combat[1] [kəmˈbæt, ˈkɑmˌbæt] *vt* **-bated** *or* **-batted; -bating** *or* **-batting** : combatir, luchar contra

combat[2] [ˈkɑmˌbæt] *n* : combate *m,* lucha *f*

combatant [kəmˈbætənt] *n* : combatiente *mf*

combative [kəmˈbæt̬ɪv] *adj* : combativo

combination [ˌkɑmbəˈneɪʃən] *n* : combinación *f*

combine[1] [kəmˈbaɪn] *v* **-bined; -bining** *vt* : combinar, aunar — *vi* : combinarse, mezclarse

combine[2] [ˈkɑmˌbaɪn] *n* **1** ALLIANCE : alianza *f* comercial o política **2** HARVESTER : cosechadora *f*

combustible [kəmˈbʌstəbəl] *adj* : inflamable, combustible

combustion [kəmˈbʌstʃən] *n* : combustión *f*

come [ˈkʌm] *vi* **came** [ˈkeɪm]; **come; coming** **1** APPROACH : venir, aproximarse <here they come : acá vienen> **2** ARRIVE : venir, llegar, alcanzar <they came yesterday : vinieron ayer> **3** ORIGINATE : venir, provenir <this wine comes from France : este vino viene de Francia> **4** AMOUNT : llegar, ascender <the investment came to two million : la inversión llegó a dos millones> **5 to come clean** : confesar, desahogar la conciencia **6 to come into** ACQUIRE : adquirir <to come into a fortune : heredar una fortuna> **7 to come off** SUCCEED : tener éxito, ser un éxito **8 to come out** : salir, aparecer, publicarse **9 to come to** REVIVE : recobrar el conocimiento, volver en sí **10 to come to pass** HAPPEN : acontecer **11 to come to terms** : llegar a un acuerdo

comeback [ˈkʌmˌbæk] *n* **1** RETORT : réplica *f,* respuesta *f* **2** RETURN : retorno *m,* regreso *m* <the champion announced his comeback : el campeón anunció su regreso>

come back *vi* **1** RETORT : replicar, contestar **2** RETURN : volver <come back here! : ¡vuelve acá!> <that style's coming back : ese estilo está volviendo>

comedian [kəˈmiːdiən] *n* : cómico *m,* -ca *f;* humorista *mf*

comedienne [kəˌmiːdiˈɛn] *n* : cómica *f,* humorista *f*

comedy [ˈkɑmədi] *n, pl* **-dies** : comedia *f*

comely [ˈkʌmli] *adj* **-lier; -est** : bello, bonito

comet [ˈkɑmət] *n* : cometa *m*

comfort[1] [ˈkʌmpfərt] *vt* **1** CHEER : confortar, alentar **2** CONSOLE : consolar

comfort[2] *n* **1** CONSOLATION : consuelo *m* **2** WELL-BEING : confort *m,* bienestar *m* **3** CONVENIENCE : comodidad *f* <the comforts of home : las comodidades del hogar>

comfortable [ˈkʌmpfərt̬əbəl, ˈkʌmpftə-] *adj* : cómodo, confortable — **comfortably** [ˈkʌmpfərt̬əbli, ˈkʌmpftə-] *adv*

comforter [ˈkʌmpfərtər] *n* **1** : confortador *m,* -dora *f* **2** QUILT : edredón *m,* cobertor *m*

comic[1] [ˈkɑmɪk] *adj* : cómico, humorístico

comic[2] *n* **1** COMEDIAN : cómico *m,* -ca *f;* humorista *mf* **2** *or* **comic book** : historieta *f,* cómic *m*

comical [ˈkɑmɪkəl] *adj* : cómico, gracioso, chistoso

comic strip *n* : tira *f* cómica, historieta *f*

coming [ˈkʌmɪŋ] *adj* : siguiente, próximo, que viene

comma [ˈkɑmə] *n* : coma *f*

command[1] [kəˈmænd] *vt* **1** ORDER : ordenar, mandar **2** CONTROL, DIRECT : comandar, tener el mando de — *vi* **1** : dar órdenes **2** GOVERN : estar al mando *m,* gobernar

command² *n* **1** CONTROL, LEADERSHIP : mando *m,* control *m,* dirección *f* **2** ORDER : orden *f,* mandato *m* **3** MASTERY : maestría *f,* destreza *f,* dominio *m* **4** : tropa *f* asignada a un comandante
commandant [ˈkɑmənˌdɑnt, -ˌdænt] *n* : comandante *mf*
commandeer [ˌkɑmənˈdɪr] *vt* : piratear, secuestrar (un vehículo, etc.)
commander [kəˈmændər] *n* : comandante *mf*
commandment [kəˈmændmənt] *n* : mandamiento *m,* orden *f* <the Ten Commandments : los diez mandamientos>
commemorate [kəˈmɛməˌreɪt] *vt* **-rated; -rating** : conmemorar
commemoration [kəˌmɛməˈreɪʃən] *n* : conmemoración *f*
commemorative [kəˈmɛmrət̬ɪv, -ˈmɛməˌreɪt̬ɪv] *adj* : conmemorativo
commence [kəˈmɛnts] *v* **-menced; -mencing** *vt* : iniciar, comenzar — *vi* : iniciarse, comenzar
commencement [kəˈmɛntsmənt] *n* **1** BEGINNING : inicio *m,* comienzo *m* **2** : ceremonia *f* de graduación
commend [kəˈmɛnd] *vt* **1** ENTRUST : encomendar **2** RECOMMEND : recomendar **3** PRAISE : elogiar, alabar
commendable [kəˈmɛndəbəl] *adj* : loable, meritorio, encomiable
commendation [ˌkɑmənˈdeɪʃən, -ˌmɛn-] *n* : elogio *m,* encomio *m*
commensurate [kəˈmɛntsərət, -ˈmɛntʃʊrət] *adj* : proporcionado <commensurate with : en proporción a>
comment¹ [ˈkɑˌmɛnt] *vi* **1** : hacer comentarios **2 to comment on** : comentar, hacer observaciones sobre
comment² *n* : comentario *m,* observación *f*
commentary [ˈkɑmənˌtɛri] *n, pl* **-taries** : comentario *m,* crónica *f* (deportiva)
commentator [ˈkɑmənˌteɪt̬ər] *n* : comentarista *mf,* cronista *mf* (de deportes)
commerce [ˈkɑmərs] *n* : comercio *m*
commercial¹ [kəˈmərʃəl] *adj* : comercial — **commercially** *adv*
commercial² *n* : comercial *m*
commercialize [kəˈmərʃəˌlaɪz] *vt* **-ized; -izing** : comercializar
commiserate [kəˈmɪzəˌreɪt] *vi* **-ated; -ating** : compadecerse, consolarse
commiseration [kəˌmɪzəˈreɪʃən] *n* : conmiseración *f*
commission¹ [kəˈmɪʃən] *vt* **1** : nombrar (un oficial) **2** : comisionar, encargar <to commission a painting : encargar una pintura>
commission² *n* **1** : nombramiento *m* (al grado de oficial) **2** COMMITTEE : comisión *f,* comité *m* **3** COMMITTING : comisión *f,* realización *f* (de un acto) **4** PERCENTAGE : comisión *f* <sales commissions : comisiones de venta>
commissioned officer *n* : oficial *mf*
commissioner [kəˈmɪʃənər] *n* **1** : comisionado *m,* -da *f;* miembro *m* de una comisión **2** : comisario *m,* -ria *f* (de policía, etc.)
commit [kəˈmɪt] *vt* **-mitted; -mitting** **1** ENTRUST : encomendar, confiar **2** CONFINE : internar (en un hospital), encarcelar (en una prisión) **3** PERPETRATE : cometer <to commit a crime : cometer un crimen> **4 to commit oneself** : comprometerse
commitment [kəˈmɪtmənt] *n* **1** RESPONSIBILITY : compromiso *m,* responsabilidad *f* **2** DEDICATION : dedicación *f,* devoción *f* <commitment to the cause : devoción a la causa>
committee [kəˈmɪt̬i] *n* : comité *m*
commodious [kəˈmoːdiəs] *adj* SPACIOUS : amplio, espacioso
commodity [kəˈmɑdət̬i] *n, pl* **-ties** : artículo *m* de comercio, mercancía *f,* mercadería *f*
commodore [ˈkɑməˌdor] *n* : comodoro *m*
common¹ [ˈkɑmən] *adj* **1** PUBLIC : común, público <the common good : el bien común> **2** SHARED : común <a common interest : un interés común> **3** GENERAL : común, general <it's common knowledge : todo el mundo lo sabe> **4** ORDINARY : ordinario, común y corriente <the common man : el hombre medio, el hombre de la calle>
common² *n* **1** : tierra *f* comunal **2 in ~** : en común
common cold *n* : resfriado *m* común
common denominator *n* : denominador *m* común
commoner [ˈkɑmənər] *n* : plebeyo *m,* -ya *f*
commonly [ˈkɑmənli] *adv* **1** FREQUENTLY : comúnmente, frecuentemente **2** USUALLY : normalmente
common noun *n* : nombre *m* común
commonplace¹ [ˈkɑmənˌpleɪs] *adj* : común, ordinario
commonplace² *n* : cliché *m,* tópico *m*
common sense *n* : sentido *m* común
commonwealth [ˈkɑmənˌwɛlθ] *n* : entidad *f* política <the British Commonwealth : la Mancomunidad Británica>
commotion [kəˈmoːʃən] *n* **1** RUCKUS : alboroto *m,* jaleo *m,* escándalo *m* **2** STIR, UPSET : revuelo *m,* conmoción *f*
communal [kəˈmjuːnəl] *adj* : communal
commune¹ [kəˈmjuːn] *vi* **-muned; -muning** : estar en comunión *f*
commune² [ˈkɑˌmjuːn, kəˈmjuːn] *n* : comuna *f*
communicable [kəˈmjuːnɪkəbəl] *adj* CONTAGIOUS : transmisible, contagioso
communicate [kəˈmjuːnəˌkeɪt] *v* **-cated; -cating** *vt* **1** CONVEY : comunicar, expresar, hacer saber **2** TRANSMIT : transmitir (una enfermedad), contagiar — *vi* : comunicarse, expresarse

communication [kə,mju:nə'keɪʃən] *n* : comunicación *f*

communicative [kə'mju:nɪ,keɪt̬ɪv, -kət̬ɪv] *adj* : comunicativo

communion [kə'mju:njən] *n* **1** SHARING : comunión *f* **2 Communion** : comunión *f,* eucaristía *f*

communiqué [kə'mju:nə,keɪ, -,mju:nə-'keɪ] *n* : comunicado *m*

communism *or* **Communism** ['kamjə-,nɪzəm] *n* : comunismo *m*

communist[1] *or* **Communist** ['kamjə-,nɪst] *adj* : comunista <the Communist Party : el Partido Comunista>

communist[2] *or* **Communist** *n* : comunista *mf*

communistic *or* **Communistic** [,kamjə-'nɪstɪk] *adj* : comunista

community [kə'mju:nət̬i] *n, pl* **-ties** : comunidad *f*

commute [kə'mju:t] *v* **-muted; -muting** *vt* REDUCE : conmutar, reducir (una sentencia) — *vi* : viajar de la residencia al trabajo

commuter [kə'mju:t̬ər] *n* : persona *f* que viaja diariamente al trabajo

compact[1] [kəm'pækt, 'kam,pækt] *vt* : compactar, consolidar, comprimir

compact[2] [kəm'pækt, 'kam,pækt] *adj* **1** DENSE, SOLID : compacto, macizo, denso **2** CONCISE : breve, conciso

compact[3] ['kam,pækt] *n* **1** AGREEMENT : acuerdo *m,* pacto *m* **2** : polvera *f,* estuche *m* de maquillaje **3** *or* **compact car** : auto *m* compacto

compact disc ['kam,pækt'dɪsk] *n* : disco *m* compacto, compact disc *m*

compactly [kəm'pæktli, 'kam,pækt-] *adv* **1** DENSELY : densamente, macizamente **2** CONCISELY : concisamente, brevemente

companion [kəm'pænjən] *n* **1** COMRADE : compañero *m,* -ra *f;* acompañante *mf* **2** MATE : pareja *f* (de un zapato, etc.)

companionable [kəm'pænjənəbəl] *adj* : sociable, amigable

companionship [kəm'pænjən,ʃɪp] *n* : compañerismo *m,* camaradería *f*

company ['kʌmpəni] *n, pl* **-nies 1** FIRM : compañía *f,* empresa *f* **2** GROUP : compañía *f* (de actores o soldados) **3** GUESTS : visita *f* <we have company : tenemos visita>

comparable ['kampərəbəl] *adj* : comparable, parecido

comparative[1] [kəm'pærət̬ɪv] *adj* RELATIVE : comparativo, relativo — **comparatively** *adv*

comparative[2] *n* : comparativo *m*

compare[1] [kəm'pær] *v* **-pared; -paring** *vt* : comparar — *vi* **to compare with** : poder comparar con, tener comparación con

compare[2] *n* : comparación *f* <beyond compare : sin igual, sin par>

comparison [kəm'pærəsən] *n* : comparación *f*

compartment [kəm'partmənt] *n* : compartimento *m,* compartimiento *m*

compass ['kʌmpəs, 'kam-] *n* **1** RANGE, SCOPE : alcance *m,* extensión *f,* límites *mpl* **2** : compás *m* (para trazar circunferencias) **3** : compás *m,* brújula *f* <the points of the compass : los puntos cardinales>

compassion [kəm'pæʃən] *n* : compasión *f,* piedad *f,* misericordia *f*

compassionate [kəm'pæʃənət] *adj* : compasivo

compatibility [kəm,pæt̬ə'bɪlət̬i] *n* : compatibilidad *f*

compatible [kəm'pæt̬əbəl] *adj* : compatible, afín

compatriot [kəm'peɪtriət, -'pæ-] *n* : compatriota *mf;* paisano *m,* -na *f*

compel [kəm'pɛl] *vt* **-pelled; -pelling** : obligar, compeler

compendium [kəm'pɛndiəm] *n, pl* **-diums** *or* **-dia** [-diə] : compendio *m*

compensate ['kampən,seɪt] *v* **-sated; -sating** *vi* **to compensate for** : compensar — *vt* : indemnizar, compensar

compensation [,kampən'seɪʃən] *n* : compensación *f,* indemnización *f*

compensatory [kəm'pɛntsə,tori] *adj* : compensatorio

compete [kəm'pi:t] *vi* **-peted; -peting** : competir, contender, rivalizar

competence ['kampətənts] *n* : competencia *f,* aptitud *f*

competency ['kampətəntsi] → **competence**

competent ['kampətənt] *adj* : competente, capaz

competition [,kampə'tɪʃən] *n* : competencia *f,* concurso *m*

competitive [kəm'pɛt̬ət̬ɪv] *adj* : competitivo

competitor [kəm'pɛt̬ət̬ər] *n* : competidor *m,* -dora *f*

compile [kəm'paɪl] *vt* **-piled; -piling** : compilar, recopilar

complacency [kəm'pleɪsəntsi] *n* : satisfacción *f* consigo mismo, suficiencia *f*

complacent [kəm'pleɪsənt] *adj* : satisfecho de sí mismo, suficiente

complain [kəm'pleɪn] *vi* **1** GRIPE : quejarse, regañar, rezongar **2** PROTEST : reclamar, protestar

complaint [kəm'pleɪnt] *n* **1** GRIPE : queja *f* **2** AILMENT : afección *f,* dolencia *f* **3** ACCUSATION : reclamo *m,* acusación *f*

complement[1] ['kamplə,mɛnt] *vt* : complementar

complement[2] ['kampləmənt] *n* : complemento *m*

complementary [,kamplə'mɛntəri] *adj* : complementario

complete[1] [kəm'pli:t] *vt* **-pleted; -pleting 1** : completar, hacer entero <this piece completes the collection : esta pieza completa la colección> **2** FINISH : completar, acabar, terminar

<she completed her studies : completó sus estudios>

complete[2] *adj* **-pleter; -est 1** WHOLE : completo, entero, íntegro **2** FINISHED : terminado, acabado **3** TOTAL : completo, total, absoluto

completely [kəm'pli:tli] *adv* : completamente, totalmente

completion [kəm'pli:ʃən] *n* : finalización *f,* cumplimiento *m*

complex[1] [kɑm'plɛks, kəm-; 'kɑm‚plɛks] *adj* : complejo, complicado

complex[2] ['kɑm‚plɛks] *n* : complejo *m*

complexion [kəm'plɛkʃən] *n* : cutis *m,* tez *f* <of dark complexion : de tez morena>

complexity [kəm'plɛksəṭi, kɑm-] *n, pl* **-ties** : complejidad *f*

compliance [kəm'plaɪənts] *n* : conformidad *f* <in compliance with the law : conforme a la ley>

compliant [kəm'plaɪənt] *adj* : dócil, sumiso

complicate ['kɑmplə‚keɪt] *vt* **-cated; -cating** : complicar

complicated ['kɑmplə‚keɪṭəd] *adj* : complicado

complication [‚kɑmplə'keɪʃən] *n* : complicación *f*

complicity [kəm'plɪsəṭi] *n, pl* **-ties** : complicidad *f*

compliment[1] ['kɑmplə‚mɛnt] *vt* : halagar, florear *Mex*

compliment[2] ['kɑmpləmənt] *n* **1** : halago *m,* cumplido *m* **2 compliments** *npl* : saludos *mpl* <give them my compliments : déles saludos de mi parte>

complimentary [‚kɑmplə'mɛntəri] *adj* **1** FLATTERING : halagador, halagüeño **2** FREE : de cortesía, gratis

comply [kəm'plaɪ] *vi* **-plied; -plying** : cumplir, acceder, obedecer

component[1] [kəm'po:nənt, 'kɑm‚po:-] *adj* : componente

component[2] *n* : componente *m,* elemento *m,* pieza *f*

compose [kəm'po:z] *vt* **-posed; -posing 1** : componer, crear <to compose a melody : componer una melodía > **2** CALM : calmar, serenar <to compose oneself : serenarse> **3** CONSTITUTE : constar, componer <to be composed of : constar de> **4** : componer (un texto a imprimirse)

composer [kəm'po:zər] *n* : compositor *m,* -tora *f*

composite[1] [kɑm'pɑzət, kəm-; 'kɑmpəzət] *adj* : compuesto (de varias partes)

composite[2] *n* : compuesto *m,* mezcla *f*

composition [‚kɑmpə'zɪʃən] *n* **1** MAKEUP : composición *f* **2** ESSAY : ensayo *m,* trabajo *m*

compost ['kɑm‚po:st] *n* : abono *m* vegetal

composure [kəm'po:ʒər] *n* : compostura *f,* serenidad *f*

compound[1] [kɑm'paʊnd, kəm-; 'kɑm‚paʊnd] *vt* **1** COMBINE, COMPOSE : combinar, componer **2** AUGMENT : agravar, aumentar <to compound a problem : agravar un problema>

compound[2] ['kɑm‚paʊnd; kɑm'paʊnd, kəm-] *adj* : compuesto <compound interest : interés compuesto>

compound[3] ['kɑm‚paʊnd] *n* **1** MIXTURE : compuesto *m,* mezcla *f* **2** ENCLOSURE : recinto *m* (de residencias, etc.)

compound fracture *n* : fractura *f* complicada

comprehend [‚kɑmprɪ'hɛnd] *vt* **1** UNDERSTAND : comprender, entender **2** INCLUDE : comprender, incluir, abarcar

comprehensible [‚kɑmprɪ'hɛntsəbəl] *adj* : comprensible

comprehension [‚kɑmprɪ'hɛntʃən] *n* : comprensión *f*

comprehensive [‚kɑmprɪ'hɛntsɪv] *adj* **1** INCLUSIVE : inclusivo, exhaustivo **2** BROAD : extenso, amplio

compress[1] [kəm'prɛs] *vt* : comprimir

compress[2] ['kɑm‚prɛs] *n* : compresa *f*

compression [kəm'prɛʃən] *n* : compresión *f*

comprise [kəm'praɪz] *vt* **-prised; -prising 1** INCLUDE : comprender, incluir **2** : componerse de, constar de <the installation comprises several buildings : la instalación está compuesta de varios edificios>

compromise[1] ['kɑmprə‚maɪz] *v* **-mised; -mising** *vi* : transigir, avenirse — *vt* JEOPARDIZE : comprometer, poner en peligro

compromise[2] *n* : acuerdo *m* mutuo, compromiso *m*

comptroller [kən'tro:lər, 'kɑmp‚tro:-] *n* : contralor *m,* -lora *f;* interventor *m,* -tora *f*

compulsion [kəm'pʌlʃən] *n* **1** COERCION : coacción *f* **2** URGE : compulsión *f,* impulso *m*

compulsive [kəm'pʌlsɪv] *adj* : compulsivo

compulsory [kəm'pʌlsəri] *adj* : obligatorio

compunction [kəm'pʌŋkʃən] *n* **1** QUALM : reparo *m,* escrúpulo *m* **2** REMORSE : remordimiento *m*

computation [‚kɑmpjʊ'teɪʃən] *n* : cálculo *m,* cómputo *m*

compute [kəm'pju:t] *vt* **-puted; -puting** : computar, calcular

computer [kəm'pju:ṭər] *n* : computadora *f,* computador *m,* ordenador *m Spain*

computerize [kəm'pju:ṭə‚raɪz] *vt* **-ized; -izing** : computarizar, informatizar

comrade ['kɑm‚ræd] *n* : camarada *mf;* compañero *m,* -ra *f*

con[1] ['kɑn] *vt* **conned; conning** SWINDLE : estafar, timar

con[2] *adv* : contra

con[3] *n* : contra *m* <the pros and cons : los pros y los contras>

concave [kɑnˈkeɪv, ˈkɑn,keɪv] *adj* : cóncavo

conceal [kənˈsiːl] *vt* : esconder, ocultar, disimular

concealment [kənˈsiːlmənt] *n* : escondimiento *m,* ocultación *f*

concede [kənˈsiːd] *vt* **-ceded; -ceding 1** ALLOW, GRANT : conceder **2** ADMIT : conceder, reconocer <to concede defeat : reconocer la derrota>

conceit [kənˈsiːt] *n* : engreimiento *m,* presunción *f*

conceited [kənˈsiːt̬əd] *adj* : presumido, engreído, presuntuoso

conceivable [kənˈsiːvəbəl] *adj* : concebible, imaginable

conceivably [kənˈsiːvəbli] *adv* : posiblemente, de manera concebible

conceive [kənˈsiːv] *v* **-ceived; -ceiving** *vi* : concebir, embarazarse — *vt* IMAGINE : concebir, imaginar

concentrate[1] [ˈkɑntsən,treɪt] *v* **-trated; -trating** *vt* : concentrar — *vi* : concentrarse

concentrate[2] *n* : concentrado *m*

concentration [,kɑntsənˈtreɪʃən] *n* : concentración *f*

concentric [kənˈsɛntrɪk] *adj* : concéntrico

concept [ˈkɑn,sɛpt] *n* : concepto *m,* idea *f*

conception [kənˈsɛpʃən] *n* **1** : concepción *f* (de un bebé) **2** IDEA : concepto *m,* idea *f*

concern[1] [kənˈsərn] *vt* **1** : tratarse de, tener que ver con <the novel concerns a sailor : la novela se trata de un marinero> **2** INVOLVE : concernir, incumbir a, afectar <that does not concern me : eso no me incumbe>

concern[2] *n* **1** AFFAIR : asunto *m* **2** WORRY : inquietud *f,* preocupación *f* **3** BUSINESS : negocio *m*

concerned [kənˈsərnd] *adj* **1** ANXIOUS : preocupado, ansioso **2** INTERESTED, INVOLVED : interesado, afectado

concerning [kənˈsərnɪŋ] *prep* REGARDING : con respecto a, acerca de, sobre

concert [ˈkɑn,sərt] *n* **1** AGREEMENT : concierto *m,* acuerdo *m* **2** : concierto *m* (musical)

concerted [kənˈsərt̬əd] *adj* : concertado, coordinado <to make a concerted effort : coordinar los esfuerzos>

concertina [,kɑntsərˈtiːnə] *n* : concertina *f*

concerto [kənˈtʃɛrtoː] *n, pl* **-ti** [-ti, -,tiː] *or* **-tos** : concierto *m* <violin concerto : concierto para violín>

concession [kənˈsɛʃən] *n* : concesión *f*

conch [ˈkɑŋk, ˈkɑntʃ] *n, pl* **conchs** [ˈkɑŋks] *or* **conches** [ˈkɑntʃəz] : caracol *m* (animal), caracola *f* (concha)

conciliatory [kənˈsɪliə,tori] *adj* : conciliador, conciliatorio

concise [kənˈsaɪs] *adj* : conciso, breve — **concisely** *adv*

conclave [ˈkɑn,kleɪv] *n* : cónclave *m*

conclude [kənˈkluːd] *v* **-cluded; -cluding** *vt* **1** END : concluir, finalizar <to conclude a meeting : concluir una reunión> **2** DECIDE : concluir, llegar a la conclusión de — *vi* END : concluir, terminar

conclusion [kənˈkluːʒən] *n* **1** INFERENCE : conclusión *f* **2** END : fin *m,* final *m*

conclusive [kənˈkluːsɪv] *adj* : concluyente, decisivo — **conclusively** *adv*

concoct [kənˈkɑkt, kɑn-] *vt* **1** PREPARE : preparar, confeccionar **2** DEVISE : inventar, tramar

concoction [kənˈkɑkʃən] *n* : invención *f,* mejunje *m,* brebaje *m*

concord [ˈkɑn,kɔrd, ˈkɑŋ-] *n* **1** HARMONY : concordia *f,* armonía *f* **2** AGREEMENT : acuerdo *m*

concordance [kənˈkɔrdənts] *n* : concordancia *f*

concourse [ˈkɑn,kors] *n* : explanada *f,* salón *m* (para pasajeros)

concrete[1] [kɑnˈkriːt, ˈkɑn,kriːt] *adj* **1** REAL : concreto <concrete objects : objetos concretos> **2** SPECIFIC : determinado, específico **3** : de concreto, de hormigón <concrete walls : paredes de concreto>

concrete[2] [ˈkɑn,kriːt, kɑnˈkriːt] *n* : concreto *m,* hormigón *m*

concur [kənˈkər] *vi* **concurred; concurring 1** COINCIDE : concurrir, coincidir **2** AGREE : concurrir, estar de acuerdo

concurrent [kənˈkərənt] *adj* : concurrente, simultáneo

concussion [kənˈkʌʃən] *n* : conmoción *f* cerebral

condemn [kənˈdɛm] *vt* **1** CENSURE : condenar, reprobar, censurar **2** : declarar insalubre (alimentos), declarar ruinoso (un edificio) **3** SENTENCE : condenar <condemned to death : condenado a muerte>

condemnation [,kɑn,dɛmˈneɪʃən] *n* : condena *f,* reprobación *f*

condensation [,kɑn,dɛnˈseɪʃən, -dən-] *n* : condensación *f*

condense [kənˈdɛnts] *v* **-densed; -densing** *vt* **1** ABRIDGE : condensar, resumir **2** : condensar (vapor, etc.) — *vi* : condensarse

condescend [,kɑndɪˈsɛnd] *vi* **1** DEIGN : condescender, dignarse **2 to condescend to someone** : tratar a alguien con condescendencia

condescension [,kɑndɪˈsɛntʃən] *n* : condescendencia *f*

condiment [ˈkɑndəmənt] *n* : condimento *m*

condition[1] [kənˈdɪʃən] *vt* **1** DETERMINE : condicionar, determinar **2** : acondicionar (el pelo o el aire), poner en forma (el cuerpo)

condition[2] *n* **1** STIPULATION : condición *f,* estipulación *f* <on the condition that : a condición de que> **2** STATE : condición *f,* estado *m* <in poor condition : en malas condiciones> **3 conditions** *npl* : condiciones *fpl,* situación *f* <working conditions : condiciones del trabajo>

conditional [kənˈdɪʃənəl] *adj* : condicional — **conditionally** *adv*

condolence [kənˈdoːlənts] *n* **1** SYMPATHY : condolencia *f* **2 condolences** *npl* : pésame *m*

condominium [ˌkɑndəˈmɪniəm] *n, pl* **-ums** : condominio *m*

condone [kənˈdoːn] *vt* **-doned; -doning** : aprobar, perdonar, tolerar

condor [ˈkɑndər, -ˌdɔr] *n* : cóndor *m*

conducive [kənˈduːsɪv, -ˈdjuː-] *adj* : propicio, favorable

conduct[1] [kənˈdʌkt] *vt* **1** GUIDE : guiar, conducir <to conduct a tour : guiar una visita> **2** DIRECT : conducir, dirigir <to conduct an orchestra : dirigir una orquesta> **3** CARRY OUT : realizar, llevar a cabo <to conduct an investigation : llevar a cabo una investigación> **4** TRANSMIT : conducir, transmitir (calor, electricidad, etc.) **5 to conduct oneself** BEHAVE : conducirse, comportarse

conduct[2] [ˈkɑnˌdʌkt] *n* **1** MANAGEMENT : conducción *f,* dirección *f,* manejo *m* <the conduct of foreign affairs : la conducción de asuntos exteriores> **2** BEHAVIOR : conducta *f,* comportamiento *m*

conduction [kənˈdʌkʃən] *n* : conducción *f*

conductivity [ˌkɑnˌdʌkˈtɪvəṭi] *n, pl* **-ties** : conductividad *f*

conductor [kənˈdʌktər] *n* **1** : conductor *m,* -tora *f;* revisor *m,* -sora *f* (en un tren); cobrador *m,* -dora *f* (en un bus); director *m,* -tora *f* (de una orquesta) **2** : conductor *m* (de electricidad, etc.)

conduit [ˈkɑnˌduːət, -ˌdjuː-] *n* : conducto *m,* canal *m,* vía *f*

cone [ˈkoːn] *n* **1** : piña *f* (fruto de las coníferas) **2** : cono *m* (en geometría) **3 ice–cream cone** : cono *m,* barquillo *m,* cucurucho *m*

confection [kənˈfɛkʃən] *n* : dulce *m*

confectioner [kənˈfɛkʃənər] *n* : confitero *m,* -ra *f*

confederacy [kənˈfɛdərəsi] *n, pl* **-cies** : confederación *f*

confederate[1] [kənˈfɛdəˌreɪt] *v* **-ated; -ating** *vt* : unir, confederar — *vi* : confederarse, aliarse

confederate[2] [kənˈfɛdərət] *adj* : confederado

confederate[3] *n* : cómplice *mf;* aliado *m,* -da *f*

confederation [kənˌfɛdəˈreɪʃən] *n* : confederación *f,* alianza *f*

confer [kənˈfər] *v* **-ferred; -ferring** *vt* : conferir, otorgar — *vi* **to confer with** : consultar

conference [ˈkɑnfrənts, -fərənts] *n* : conferencia *f* <press conference : conferencia de prensa>

confess [kənˈfɛs] *vt* : confesar — *vi* **1** : confesar <the prisoner confessed : el detenido confesó> **2** : confesarse (en religión)

confession [kənˈfɛʃən] *n* : confesión *f*

confessional [kənˈfɛʃənəl] *n* : confesionario *m*

confetti [kənˈfɛṭi] *n* : confeti *m*

confidant [ˈkɑnfəˌdɑnt, -ˌdænt] *n* : confidente *mf*

confide [kənˈfaɪd] *v* **-fided; -fiding** : confiar

confidence [ˈkɑnfədənts] *n* **1** TRUST : confianza *f* **2** SELF-ASSURANCE : confianza *f* en sí mismo, seguridad *f* en sí mismo **3** SECRET : confidencia *f,* secreto *m*

confident [ˈkɑnfədənt] *adj* **1** SURE : seguro **2** SELF-ASSURED : confiado, seguro de sí mismo

confidential [ˌkɑnfəˈdɛntʃəl] *adj* : confidencial — **confidentially** [ˌkɑnfəˈdɛntʃəli] *adv*

confidently [ˈkɑnfədəntli] *adv* : con seguridad, con confianza

configuration [kənˌfɪgjəˈreɪʃən] *n* : configuración *f*

confine [kənˈfaɪn] *vt* **-fined; -fining 1** LIMIT : confinar, restringir, limitar **2** IMPRISON : recluir, encarcelar, encerrar

confinement [kənˈfaɪnmənt] *n* : confinamiento *m,* reclusión *f,* encierro *m*

confines [ˈkɑnˌfaɪnz] *npl* : límites *mpl,* confines *mpl*

confirm [kənˈfərm] *vt* **1** RATIFY : ratificar **2** VERIFY : confirmar, verificar **3** : confirmar (en religión)

confirmation [ˌkɑnfərˈmeɪʃən] *n* : confirmación *f*

confiscate [ˈkɑnfəˌskeɪt] *vt* **-cated; -cating** : confiscar, incautar, decomisar

confiscation [ˌkɑnfəˈskeɪʃən] *n* : confiscación *f,* incautación *f,* decomiso *m*

conflagration [ˌkɑnfləˈgreɪʃən] *n* : conflagración *f*

conflict[1] [kənˈflɪkt] *vi* : estar en conflicto, oponerse

conflict[2] [ˈkɑnˌflɪkt] *n* : conflicto *m* <to be in conflict : estar en desacuerdo>

conform [kənˈfɔrm] *vi* **1** ACCORD, COMPLY : ajustarse, adaptarse, conformarse <it conforms with our standards : se ajusta a nuestras normas> **2** CORRESPOND : corresponder, encajar <to conform to the truth : corresponder a la verdad>

conformity [kənˈfɔrməṭi] *n, pl* **-ties** : conformidad *f*

confound [kənˈfaʊnd, kɑn-] *vt* : confundir, desconcertar

confront [kənˈfrʌnt] *vt* : afrontar, enfrentarse a, encarar

confrontation [ˌkɑnfrənˈteɪʃən] *n* : enfrentamiento *m,* confrontación *f*

confuse [kən'fju:z] *vt* **-fused; -fusing 1** PUZZLE : confundir, enturbiar **2** COMPLICATE : confundir, enredar, complicar <to confuse the issue : complicar las cosas>
confusion [kən'fju:ʒən] *n* **1** PERPLEXITY : confusión *f* **2** MESS, TURMOIL : confusión *f,* embrollo *m,* lío *m fam*
congeal [kən'dʒi:l] *vi* **1** FREEZE : congelarse **2** COAGULATE, CURDLE : coagularse, cuajarse
congenial [kən'dʒi:niəl] *adj* : agradable, simpático
congenital [kən'dʒɛnət̬əl] *adj* : congénito
congest [kən'dʒɛst] *vt* **1** : congestionar (en la medicina) **2** OVERCROWD : abarrotar, atestar, congestionar (el tráfico) — *vi* : congestionarse
congestion [kən'dʒɛstʃən] *n* : congestión *f*
conglomerate[1] [kən'glɑmərət] *adj* : conglomerado
conglomerate[2] [kən'glɑmərət] *n* : conglomerado *m*
conglomeration [kən,glɑmə'reɪʃən] *n* : conglomerado *m,* acumulación *f*
Congolese [,kɑŋgə'li:z, -'li:s] *n* : congoleño *m,* -ña *f* — **Congolese** *adj*
congratulate [kən'grædʒə,leɪt, -'grætʃə-] *vt* **-lated; -lating** : felicitar
congratulation [kən,grædʒə'leɪʃən, -,grætʃə-] *n* : felicitación *f* <congratulations! : ¡felicidades!, ¡enhorabuena!>
congregate ['kɑŋgrɪ,geɪt] *v* **-gated; -gating** *vt* : congregar, reunir — *vi* : congregarse, reunirse
congregation [,kɑŋgrɪ'geɪʃən] *n* **1** GATHERING : congregación *f,* fieles *mpl* (a un servicio religioso) **2** PARISHIONERS : feligreses *mpl*
congress ['kɑŋgrəs] *n* : congreso *m*
congressional [kən'grɛʃənəl, kɑn-] *adj* : del congreso
congressman ['kɑŋgrəsmən] *n, pl* **-men** [-mən, -,mɛn] : congresista *m,* diputado *m*
congresswoman ['kɑŋgrəs,wʊmən] *n, pl* **-women** [-,wɪmən] : congresista *f,* diputada *f*
congruence [kən'gru:ənts, 'kɑŋgrʊənts] *n* : congruencia *f*
congruent [kən'gru:ənt, 'kɑŋgrʊənt] *adj* : congruente
conic ['kɑnɪk]→ **conical**
conical ['kɑnɪkəl] *adj* : cónico
conifer ['kɑnəfər, 'ko:-] *n* : conífera *f*
coniferous [ko:'nɪfərəs, kə-] *adj* : conífero
conjecture[1] [kən'dʒɛktʃər] *v* **-tured; -turing** : conjeturar
conjecture[2] *n* : conjetura *f,* presunción *f*
conjugal ['kɑndʒɪgəl, kən'dʒu:-] *adj* : conyugal
conjugate ['kɑndʒə,geɪt] *vt* **-gated; -gating** : conjugar
conjugation [,kɑndʒə'geɪʃən] *n* : conjugación *f*
conjunction [kən'dʒʌŋkʃən] *n* : conjunción *f* <in conjunction with : en combinación con>
conjure ['kɑndʒər, 'kʌn-] *v* **-jured; -juring** *vt* **1** ENTREAT : rogar, suplicar **2 to conjure up** : hacer aparecer (apariciones), evocar (memorias, etc.) — *vi* : practicar la magia
conjurer *or* **conjuror** ['kɑndʒərər, 'kʌn-] *n* : mago *m,* -ga *f;* prestidigitador *m,* -dora *f*
connect [kə'nɛkt] *vi* : conectar, enlazar, empalmar, comunicarse — *vt* **1** JOIN, LINK : conectar, unir, juntar, vincular **2** RELATE : relacionar, asociar (ideas)
connection [kən'nɛkʃən] *n* : conexión *f,* enlace *m* <professional connections : relaciones profesionales>
connective [kə'nɛktɪv] *adj* : conectivo, conjuntivo <connective tissue : tejido conjuntivo>
connector [kə'nɛktər] *n* : conector *m*
connivance [kə'naɪvənts] *n* : connivencia *f,* complicidad *f*
connive [kə'naɪv] *vi* **-nived; -niving** CONSPIRE, PLOT : actuar en connivencia, confabularse, conspirar
connoisseur [,kɑnə'sər, -'sʊr] *n* : conocedor *m,* -dora *f;* entendido *m,* -da *f*
connotation [,kɑnə'teɪʃən] *n* : connotación *f*
connote [kə'no:t] *vt* **-noted; -noting** : connotar
conquer ['kɑŋkər] *vt* : conquistar, vencer
conqueror ['kɑŋkərər] *n* : conquistador *m,* -dora *f*
conquest ['kɑn,kwɛst, 'kɑŋ-] *n* : conquista *f*
conscience ['kɑntʃənts] *n* : conciencia *f,* consciencia *f* <to have a clear conscience : tener la conciencia limpia>
conscientious [,kɑntʃi'ɛntʃəs] *adj* : concienzudo — **conscientiously** *adv*
conscious ['kɑntʃəs] *adj* **1** AWARE : consciente <to become conscious of : darse cuenta de> **2** ALERT, AWAKE : consciente **3** INTENTIONAL : intencional, deliberado
consciously ['kɑntʃəsli] *adv* INTENTIONALLY : intencionalmente, deliberadamente, a propósito
consciousness ['kɑntʃəsnəs] *n* **1** AWARENESS : conciencia *f,* consciencia *f* **2** conocimiento *m* <to lose consciousness : perder el conocimiento>
conscript[1] [kən'skrɪpt] *vt* : reclutar, alistar, enrolar
conscript[2] ['kɑn,skrɪpt] *n* : conscripto *m,* -ta *f;* recluta *mf*
consecrate ['kɑntsə,kreɪt] *vt* **-crated; -crating** : consagrar
consecration [,kɑntsə'kreɪʃən] *n* : consagración *f,* dedicación *f*

consecutive [kən'sɛkjət̬ɪv] *adj* : consecutivo, seguido <on five consecutive days : cinco días seguidos>
consecutively [kən'sɛkjət̬ɪvli] *adv* : consecutivamente
consensus [kən'sɛn*t*səs] *n* : consenso *m*
consent[1] [kən'sɛnt] *vi* **1** AGREE : acceder, ponerse de acuerdo **2 to consent to do something** : consentir en hacer algo
consent[2] *n* : consentimiento *m,* permiso *m* <by common consent : de común acuerdo>
consequence ['kɑn*t*sə,kwɛn*t*s, -kwən*t*s] *n* **1** RESULT : consecuencia *f,* secuela *f* **2** IMPORTANCE : importancia *f,* trascendencia *f*
consequent ['kɑn*t*səkwənt, -,kwɛnt] *adj* : consiguiente
consequential [,kɑn*t*sə'kwɛntʃəl] *adj* **1** CONSEQUENT : consiguiente **2** IMPORTANT : importante, trascendente, trascendental
consequently ['kɑn*t*səkwəntli, -,kwɛnt-] *adv* : por consiguiente, por ende, por lo tanto
conservation [,kɑn*t*sər'veɪʃən] *n* : conservación *f,* protección *f*
conservationist [,kɑn*t*sər'veɪʃənɪst] *n* : conservacionista *mf*
conservatism [kən'sərvə,tɪzəm] *n* : conservadurismo *m*
conservative[1] [kən'sərvət̬ɪv] *adj* **1** : conservador **2** CAUTIOUS : moderado, cauteloso <a conservative estimate : un cálculo moderado>
conservative[2] *n* : conservador *m,* -dora *f*
conservatory [kən'sərvə,tori] *n, pl* **-ries** : conservatorio *m*
conserve[1] [kən'sərv] *vt* **-served; -serving** : conservar, preservar
conserve[2] ['kɑn,sərv] *n* PRESERVES : confitura *f*
consider [kən'sɪdər] *vt* **1** CONTEMPLATE : considerar, pensar en <we'd considered attending : habíamos pensado en asistir> **2** : considerar, tener en cuenta <consider the consequences : considera las consecuencias> **3** JUDGE, REGARD : considerar, estimar
considerable [kən'sɪdərəbəl] *adj* : considerable — **considerably** [-bli] *adv*
considerate [kən'sɪdərət] *adj* : considerado, atento
consideration [kən,sɪdə'reɪʃən] *n* : consideración *f* <to take into consideration : tener en cuenta>
considering [kən'sɪdərɪŋ] *prep* : teniendo en cuenta, visto
consign [kən'saɪn] *vt* **1** COMMIT, ENTRUST : confiar, encomendar **2** TRANSFER : consignar, transferir **3** SEND : consignar, enviar (mercancía)
consignment [kən'saɪnmənt] *n* **1** : envío *m,* remesa *f* **2 on ~** : en consignación
consist [kən'sɪst] *vi* **1** LIE : consistir <success consists in hard work : el éxito consiste en trabajar duro> **2** : constar, componerse <the set consists of 5 pieces : el juego se compone de 5 piezas>
consistency [kən'sɪstən*t*si] *n, pl* **-cies 1** : consistencia *f* (de una mezcla o sustancia) **2** COHERENCE : coherencia *f* **3** UNIFORMITY : regularidad *f,* uniformidad *f*
consistent [kən'sɪstənt] *adj* **1** COMPATIBLE : compatible, coincidente <consistent with policy : coincidente con la política> **2** UNIFORM : uniforme, constante, regular — **consistently** [kən'sɪstəntli] *adv*
consolation [,kɑn*t*sə'leɪʃən] *n* **1** : consuelo *m* **2 consolation prize** : premio *m* de consolación
console[1] [kən'so:l] *vt* **-soled; -soling** : consolar
console[2] ['kɑn,so:l] *n* : consola *f*
consolidate [kən'sɑlə,deɪt] *vt* **-dated; -dating** : consolidar, unir
consolidation [kən,sɑlə'deɪʃən] *n* : consolidación *f*
consommé [,kɑn*t*sə'meɪ] *n* : consomé *m*
consonant ['kɑn*t*sənənt] *n* : consonante *m*
consort[1] [kən'sɔrt] *vi* : asociarse, relacionarse, tener trato <to consort with criminals : tener trato con criminales>
consort[2] ['kɑn,sɔrt] *n* : consorte *mf*
conspicuous [kən'spɪkjʊəs] *adj* **1** OBVIOUS : visible, evidente **2** STRIKING : llamativo
conspicuously [kən'spɪkjʊəsli] *adv* : de manera llamativa
conspiracy [kən'spɪrəsi] *n, pl* **-cies** : conspiración *f,* complot *m,* confabulación *f*
conspirator [kən'spɪrət̬ər] *n* : conspirador *m,* -dora *f*
conspire [kən'spaɪr] *vi* **-spired; -spiring** : conspirar, confabularse
constable ['kɑn*t*stəbəl, 'kʌn*t*stə-] *n* : agente *mf* de policía (en un pueblo)
constancy ['kɑn*t*stən*t*si] *n, pl* **-cies** : constancia *f*
constant[1] ['kɑn*t*stənt] *adj* **1** FAITHFUL : leal, fiel **2** INVARIABLE : constante, invariable **3** CONTINUAL : constante, continuo
constant[2] *n* : constante *f*
constantly ['kɑn*t*stəntli] *adv* : constantemente, continuamente
constellation [,kɑn*t*stə'leɪʃən] *n* : constelación *f*
consternation [,kɑn*t*stər'neɪʃən] *n* : consternación *f*
constipate ['kɑn*t*stə,peɪt] *vt* **-pated; -pating** : estreñir
constipation ['kɑn*t*stə'peɪʃən] *n* : estreñimiento *m,* constipación *f* (de vientre)

constituency [kən'stɪtʃʊəntsi] *n, pl* **-cies 1** : distrito *m* electoral **2** : residentes *mpl* de un distrito electoral

constituent[1] [kən'stɪtʃʊənt] *adj* **1** COMPONENT : constituyente, componente **2** : constituyente, constitutivo <a constituent assembly : una asamblea constituyente>

constituent[2] *n* **1** COMPONENT : componente *m* **2** ELECTOR, VOTER : elector *m,* -tora *f;* votante *mf*

constitute ['kɑntstə,tu:t, -,tju:t] *vt* **-tuted; -tuting 1** ESTABLISH : constituir, establecer **2** COMPOSE, FORM : constituir, componer

constitution [,kɑntstə'tu:ʃən, -'tju:-] *n* : constitución *f*

constitutional [,kɑntstə'tu:ʃənəl, -'tju:-] *adj* : constitucional

constitutionality [,kɑntstə,tu:ʃə 'næləti, -,tju:-] *n* : constitucionalidad *f*

constrain [kən'streɪn] *vt* **1** COMPEL : constreñir, obligar **2** CONFINE : constreñir, limitar, restringir **3** RESTRAIN : contener, refrenar

constraint [kən'streɪnt] *n* : restricción *f,* limitación *f*

constrict [kən'strɪkt] *vt* : estrechar, apretar, comprimir

constriction [kən'strɪkʃən] *n* : estrechamiento *m,* compresión *f*

construct [kən'strʌkt] *vt* : construir

construction [kən'strʌkʃən] *n* : construcción *f*

constructive [kən'strʌktɪv] *adj* : constructivo

construe [kən'stru:] *vt* **-strued; -struing** : interpretar

consul ['kɑntsəl] *n* : cónsul *mf*

consular ['kɑntsələr] *adj* : consular

consulate ['kɑntsələt] *n* : consulado *m*

consult [kən'sʌlt] *vt* : consultar — *vi* **to consult with** : consultar con, solicitar la opinión de

consultant [kən'sʌltənt] *n* : consultor *m,* -tora *f;* asesor *m,* -sora *f*

consultation [,kɑntsəl'teɪʃən] *n* : consulta *f*

consumable [kən'su:məbəl] *adj* : consumible

consume [kən'su:m] *vt* **-sumed; -suming** : consumir, usar, gastar

consumer [kən'su:mər] *n* : consumidor *m,* -dora *f*

consummate[1] ['kɑntsə,meɪt] *vt* **-mated; -mating** : consumar

consummate[2] [kən'sʌmət, 'kɑntsəmət] *adj* : consumado, perfecto

consummation [,kɑntsə'meɪʃən] *n* : consumación *f*

consumption [kən'sʌmpʃən] *n* **1** USE : consumo *m,* uso *m* <consumption of electricity : consumo de electricidad> **2** TUBERCULOSIS : tisis *f,* consunción *f*

contact[1] ['kɑn,tækt, kən'-] *vt* : ponerse en contacto con, contactar (con)

contact[2] ['kɑn,tækt] *n* **1** TOUCHING : contacto *m,* tocamiento *m* <to come into contact with : entrar en contacto con> **2** TOUCH : contacto *m,* comunicación *f* <to lose contact with : perder contacto con> **3** CONNECTION : contacto *m* (en negocios) **4** → **contact lens**

contact lens ['kɑn,tækt'lɛnz] *n* : lente *mf* de contacto, pupilente *m Mex*

contagion [kən'teɪdʒən] *n* : contagio *m*

contagious [kən'teɪdʒəs] *adj* : contagioso

contain [kən'teɪn] *vt* **1** : contener **2 to contain oneself** : contenerse

container [kən'teɪnər] *n* : recipiente *m,* envase *m*

contaminate [kən'tæmə,neɪt] *vt* **-nated; -nating** : contaminar

contamination [kən,tæmə'neɪʃən] *n* : contaminación *f*

contemplate ['kɑntəm,pleɪt] *v* **-plated; -plating** *vt* **1** VIEW : contemplar **2** PONDER : contemplar, considerar **3** CONSIDER, PROPOSE : proponerse, proyectar, pensar en <to contemplate a trip : pensar en viajar> — *vi* MEDITATE : meditar

contemplation [,kɑntəm'pleɪʃən] *n* : contemplación *f*

contemplative [kən'tɛmplətɪv, 'kɑntəm,pleɪtɪv] *adj* : contemplativo

contemporaneous [kən,tɛmpə'reɪniəs] → **contemporary[1]**

contemporary[1] [kən'tɛmpə,rɛri] *adj* : contemporáneo

contemporary[2] *n, pl* **-raries** : contemporáneo *m,* -nea *f*

contempt [kən'tɛmpt] *n* **1** DISDAIN : desprecio *m,* desdén *m* <to hold in contempt : despreciar> **2** : desacato *m* (ante un tribunal)

contemptible [kən'tɛmptəbəl] *adj* : despreciable, vil

contemptuous [kən'tɛmptʃʊəs] *adj* : despectivo, despreciativo, desdeñoso

contemptuously [kən'tɛmptʃʊəsli] *adv* : despectivamente, con desprecio

contend [kən'tɛnd] *vi* **1** STRUGGLE : luchar, lidiar, contender <to contend with a problem : lidiar con un problema> **2** COMPETE : competir <to contend for a position : competir por un puesto> — *vt* **1** ARGUE, MAINTAIN : argüir, sostener, afirmar <he contended that he was right : afirmó que tenía razón> **2** CONTEST : protestar contra (una decisión, etc.), disputar

contender [kən'tɛndər] *n* : contendiente *mf;* aspirante *mf;* competidor *m,* -dora *f*

content[1] [kən'tɛnt] *vt* SATISFY : contentar, satisfacer

content[2] *adj* : conforme, contento, satisfecho

content[3] *n* CONTENTMENT : contento *m,* satisfacción *f* <to one's heart's content : hasta quedar satisfecho, a más no poder>

content[4] [ˈkɑn,tɛnt] *n* **1** MEANING : contenido *m,* significado *m* **2** PROPORTION : contenido *m,* proporción *f* <fat content : contenido de grasa> **3 contents** *npl* : contenido *m,* sumario *m* (de un libro) <table of contents : índice de materias>
contented [kənˈtɛntəd] *adj* : conforme, satisfecho <a contented smile : una sonrisa de satisfacción>
contentedly [kənˈtɛntədli] *adv* : con satisfacción
contention [kənˈtɛntʃən] *n* **1** DISPUTE : disputa *f,* discusión *f* **2** COMPETITION : competencia *f,* contienda *f* **3** OPINION : argumento *m,* opinión *f*
contentious [kənˈtɛntʃəs] *adj* : disputador, pugnaz, combativo
contentment [kənˈtɛntmənt] *n* : satisfacción *f,* contento *m*
contest[1] [kənˈtɛst] *vt* : disputar, cuestionar, impugnar <to contest a will : impugnar un testamento>
contest[2] [ˈkɑn,tɛst] *n* **1** STRUGGLE : lucha *f,* contienda *f* **2** GAME : concurso *m,* competencia *f*
contestable [kənˈtɛstəbəl] *adj* : discutible, cuestionable
contestant [kənˈtɛstənt] *n* : concursante *mf;* competidor *m,* -dora *f*
context [ˈkɑn,tɛkst] *n* : contexto *m*
contiguous [kənˈtɪgjʊəs] *adj* : contiguo
continence [ˈkɑntənənts] *n* : continencia *f*
continent[1] [ˈkɑntənənt] *adj* : continente
continent[2] *n* : continente *m* — **continental** [,kɑntənˈɛntəl] *adj*
contingency [kənˈtɪndʒəntsi] *n, pl* **-cies** : contingencia *f,* eventualidad *f*
contingent[1] [kənˈtɪndʒənt] *adj* **1** POSSIBLE : contingente, eventual **2** ACCIDENTAL : fortuito, accidental **3 to be contingent on** : depender de, estar sujeto a
contingent[2] *n* : contingente *m*
continual [kənˈtɪnjʊəl] *adj* : continuo, constante — **continually** [kənˈtɪnjʊəli, -ˈtɪnjəli] *adv*
continuance [kənˈtɪnjʊənts] *n* **1** CONTINUATION : continuación *f* **2** DURATION : duración *f* **3** : aplazamiento *m* (de un proceso)
continuation [kən,tɪnjʊˈeɪʃən] *n* : continuación *f,* prolongación *f*
continue [kənˈtɪnju:] *v* **-tinued; -tinuing** *vi* **1** CARRY ON : continuar, seguir, proseguir <please continue : continúe, por favor> **2** ENDURE, LAST : continuar, prolongarse, durar **3** RESUME : continuar, reanudarse — *vt* **1** : continuar, seguir <she continued writing : continuó escribiendo> **2** RESUME : continuar, reanudar **3** EXTEND, PROLONG : continuar, prolongar
continuity [,kɑntənˈu:əṭi, -ˈju:-] *n, pl* **-ties** : continuidad *f*
continuous [kənˈtɪnjʊəs] *adj* : continuo — **continuously** *adv*
contort [kənˈtɔrt] *vt* : torcer, retorcer, contraer (el rostro) — *vi* : contraerse, demudarse
contortion [kənˈtɔrʃən] *n* : contorsión *f*
contour [ˈkɑn,tʊr] *n* **1** OUTLINE : contorno *m* **2 contours** *npl* SHAPE : forma *f,* curvas *fpl* **3 contour map** : mapa *m* topográfico
contraband [ˈkɑntrə,bænd] *n* : contrabando *m*
contraception [,kɑntrəˈsɛpʃən] *n* : anticoncepción *f,* contracepción *f*
contraceptive[1] [,kɑntrəˈsɛptɪv] *adj* : anticonceptivo, contraceptivo
contraceptive[2] *n* : anticonceptivo *m,* contraceptivo *m*
contract[1] [kənˈtrækt, 1 *usu* ˈkɑn,trækt] *vt* **1** : contratar (servicios profesionales) **2** : contraer (una enfermedad, una deuda) **3** TIGHTEN : contraer (un músculo) **4** SHORTEN : contraer (una palabra) — *vi* : contraerse, reducirse
contract[2] [ˈkɑn,trækt] *n* : contrato *m*
contraction [kənˈtrækʃən] *n* : contracción *f*
contractor [ˈkɑn,træktər, kənˈtræk-] *n* : contratista *mf*
contractual [kənˈtræktʃʊəl] *adj* : contractual — **contractually** *adv*
contradict [,kɑntrəˈdɪkt] *vt* : contradecir, desmentir
contradiction [,kɑntrəˈdɪkʃən] *n* : contradicción *f*
contradictory [,kɑntrəˈdɪktəri] *adj* : contradictorio
contralto [kənˈtræl,to:] *n, pl* **-tos** : contralto *m* (voz), contralto *mf* (vocalista)
contraption [kənˈtræpʃən] *n* DEVICE : aparato *m,* artefacto *m*
contrary[1] [ˈkɑn,trɛri, 2 *often* kənˈtrɛri] *adj* **1** OPPOSITE : contrario, opuesto **2** BALKY, STUBBORN : terco, testarudo **3 contrary to** : al contrario de, en contra de <contrary to the facts : en contra de los hechos>
contrary[2] [ˈkɑn,trɛri] *n, pl* **-traries 1** OPPOSITE : lo contrario, lo opuesto **2 on the contrary** : al contrario, todo lo contrario
contrast[1] [kənˈtræst] *vi* DIFFER : contrastar, diferir — *vt* COMPARE : contrastar, comparar
contrast[2] [ˈkɑn,træst] *n* : contraste *m*
contravene [,kɑntrəˈvi:n] *vt* **-vened; -vening** : contravenir, infringir
contribute [kənˈtrɪbjət] *v* **-uted; -uting** *vt* : contribuir, aportar (dinero, bienes, etc.) — *vi* : contribuir
contribution [,kɑntrəˈbju:ʃən] *n* : contribución *f*
contributor [kənˈtrɪbjəṭər] *n* : contribuidor *m,* -dora *f;* colaborador *m,* -dora *f* (en periodismo)

contrite [ˈkɑnˌtraɪt, kənˈtraɪt] *adj* REPENTANT : contrito, arrepentido

contrition [kənˈtrɪʃən] *n* : contrición *f,* arrepentimiento *m*

contrivance [kənˈtraɪvənts] *n* **1** DEVICE : aparato *m,* artefacto *m* **2** SCHEME : artimaña *f,* treta *f,* ardid *m*

contrive [kənˈtraɪv] *vt* **-trived; -triving 1** DEVISE : idear, ingeniar, maquinar **2** MANAGE : lograr, ingeniárselas para <she contrived a way out of the mess : se las ingenió para salir del enredo>

control[1] [kənˈtroːl] *vt* **-trolled; -trolling** : controlar, dominar

control[2] *n* **1** : control *m,* dominio *m,* mando *m* <to be under control : estar bajo control> **2** RESTRAINT : control *m,* limitación *f* <birth control : control natal> **3** : control *m,* dispositivo *m* de mando <remote control : control remoto>

controllable [kənˈtroːləbəl] *adj* : controlable

controller [kənˈtroːlər, ˈkɑnˌ-] *n* **1** → **comptroller 2** : controlador *m,* -dora *f* <air traffic controller : controlador aéreo>

controversial [ˌkɑntrəˈvərʃəl, -siəl] *adj* : controvertido <a controversial decision : una decisión controvertida>

controversy [ˈkɑntrəˌvərsi] *n, pl* **-sies** : controversia *f*

controvert [ˈkɑntrəˌvərt, ˌkɑntrəˈ-] *vt* : controvertir, contradecir

contusion [kənˈtuːʒən, -tjuː-] *n* BRUISE : contusión *f,* moretón *m*

conundrum [kəˈnʌndrəm] *n* RIDDLE : acertijo *m,* adivinanza *f*

convalesce [ˌkɑnvəˈlɛs] *vi* **-lesced; -lescing** : convalecer

convalescence [ˌkɑnvəˈlɛsənts] *n* : convalecencia *f*

convalescent[1] [ˌkɑnvəˈlɛsənt] *adj* : convaleciente

convalescent[2] *n* : convaleciente *mf*

convection [kənˈvɛkʃən] *n* : convección *f*

convene [kənˈviːn] *v* **-vened; -vening** *vt* : convocar — *vi* : reunirse

convenience [kənˈviːnjənts] *n* **1** : conveniencia *f* <at your convenience : cuando le resulte conveniente> **2** AMENITY : comodidad *f* <modern conveniences : comodidades modernas>

convenient [kənˈviːnjənt] *adj* : conveniente, cómodo — **conveniently** *adv*

convent [ˈkɑnvənt, -ˌvɛnt] *n* : convento *m*

convention [kənˈvɛntʃən] *n* **1** PACT : convención *f,* convenio *m,* pacto *m* <the Geneva Convention : la Convención de Ginebra> **2** MEETING : convención *f,* congreso *m* **3** CUSTOM : convención *f,* convencionalismo *m*

conventional [kənˈvɛntʃənəl] *adj* : convencional — **conventionally** *adv*

converge [kənˈvərdʒ] *vi* **-verged; -verging** : converger, convergir

conversant [kənˈvərsənt] *adj* **conversant with** : versado con, experto en

conversation [ˌkɑnvərˈseɪʃən] *n* : conversación *f*

conversational [ˌkɑnvərˈseɪʃənəl] *adj* : familiar <a conversational style : un estilo familiar>

converse[1] [kənˈvərs] *vi* **-versed; -versing** : conversar

converse[2] [kənˈvərs, ˈkɑnˌvɛrs] *adj* : contrario, opuesto, inverso

conversely [kənˈvərsli, ˈkɑnˌvɛrs-] *adv* : a la inversa

conversion [kənˈvərʒən] *n* **1** CHANGE : conversión *f,* transformación *f,* cambio *m* **2** : conversión *f* (a una religión)

convert[1] [kənˈvərt] *vt* **1** : convertir (a una religión o un partido) **2** CHANGE : convertir, cambiar — *vi* : convertirse

convert[2] [ˈkɑnˌvərt] *n* : converso *m,* -sa *f*

converter *or* **convertor** [kənˈvərt̬ər] *n* : convertidor *m*

convertible[1] [kənˈvərt̬əbəl] *adj* : convertible

convertible[2] *n* : convertible *m,* descapotable *m*

convex [kɑnˈvɛks, ˈkɑnˌ-, kənˈ-] *adj* : convexo

convey [kənˈveɪ] *vt* **1** TRANSPORT : transportar, conducir **2** TRANSMIT : transmitir, comunicar, expresar (noticias, ideas, etc.)

conveyance [kənˈveɪənts] *n* **1** TRANSPORT : transporte *m,* transportación *f* **2** COMMUNICATION : transmisión *f,* comunicación *f* **3** TRANSFER : transferencia *f,* traspaso *m* (de una propiedad)

conveyor [kənˈveɪər] *n* : transportador *m,* -dora *f* <conveyor belt : cinta transportadora>

convict[1] [kənˈvɪkt] *vt* : declarar culpable

convict[2] [ˈkɑnˌvɪkt] *n* : preso *m,* -sa *f;* presidiario *m,* -ria *f;* recluso *m,* -sa *f*

conviction [kənˈvɪkʃən] *n* **1** : condena *f* (de un acusado) **2** BELIEF : convicción *f,* creencia *f*

convince [kənˈvɪnts] *vt* **-vinced; -vincing** : convencer

convincing [kənˈvɪntsɪŋ] *adj* : convincente, persuasivo

convincingly [kənˈvɪntsɪŋli] *adv* : de forma convincente

convivial [kənˈvɪvjəl, -ˈvɪviəl] *adj* : jovial, festivo, alegre

conviviality [kənˌvɪviˈæləṭi] *n, pl* **-ties** : jovialidad *f*

convoke [kənˈvoːk] *vt* **-voked; -voking** : convocar

convoluted [ˈkɑnvəˌluːt̬əd] *adj* : intrincado, complicado

convoy [ˈkɑnˌvɔɪ] *n* : convoy *m*

convulse [kənˈvʌls] *v* **-vulsed; -vulsing** *vt* : convulsionar <convulsed with laughter : muerto de risa> — *vi* : sufrir convulsiones

convulsion [kən'vʌlʃən] *n* : convulsión *f*

convulsive [kən'vʌlsɪv] *adj* : convulsivo — **convulsively** *adv*

coo[1] ['ku:] *vi* : arrullar

coo[2] *n* : arrullo *m* (de una paloma)

cook[1] ['kʊk] *vi* : cocinar — *vt* **1** : preparar (comida) **2 to cook up** CONCOCT : inventar, tramar

cook[2] *n* : cocinero *m*, -ra *f*

cookbook ['kʊk,bʊk] *n* : libro *m* de cocina

cookery ['kʊkəri] *n, pl* **-eries** : cocina *f*

cookie *or* **cooky** ['kʊki] *n, pl* **-ies** : galleta *f* (dulce)

cookout ['kʊk,aʊt] *n* : comida *f* al aire libre

cool[1] ['ku:l] *vt* : refrescar, enfriar — *vi* **1** : refrescarse, enfriarse <the pie is cooling : el pastel se está enfriando> **2** : calmarse, tranquilizarse <his anger cooled : su ira se calmó>

cool[2] *adj* **1** : fresco, frío <cool weather : tiempo fresco> **2** CALM : tranquilo, sereno **3** ALOOF : frío, distante

cool[3] *n* **1** : fresco *m* <the cool of the evening : el fresco de la tarde> **2** COMPOSURE : calma *f*, serenidad *f*

coolant ['ku:lənt] *n* : refrigerante *m*

cooler ['ku:lər] *n* : nevera *f* portátil

coolie ['ku:li] *n* : culi *m*

coolly ['ku:lli] *adv* **1** CALMLY : con calma, tranquilamente **2** COLDLY : fríamente, con frialdad

coolness ['ku:lnəs] *n* **1** : frescura *f*, frescor *m* <the coolness of the evening : el frescor de la noche> **2** CALMNESS : tranquilidad *f*, serenidad *f* **3** COLDNESS, INDIFFERENCE : frialdad *f*, indiferencia

coop[1] ['ku:p, 'kʊp] *vt or* **to coop up** : encerrar <cooped up in the house : encerrado en la casa>

coop[2] *n* : gallinero *m*

co–op ['ko:,ɑp] → **cooperative[2]**

cooperate [ko'ɑpə,reɪt] *vi* **-ated; -ating** : cooperar, colaborar

cooperation [ko,ɑpə'reɪʃən] *n* : cooperación *f*, colaboración *f*

cooperative[1] [ko'ɑpərəṭiv, -'ɑpə,reɪṭiv] *adj* : cooperativo

cooperative[2] [ko'ɑpərəṭiv] *n* : cooperativa *f*

co–opt [ko'ɑpt] *vt* **1** : nombrar como miembro, cooptar **2** APPROPRIATE : apropiarse de

coordinate[1] [ko'ɔrdən,eɪt] *v* **-nated; -nating** *vt* : coordinar — *vi* : coordinarse, combinar, acordar

coordinate[2] [ko'ɔrdənət] *adj* **1** COORDINATED : coordinado **2** EQUAL : igual, semejante

coordinate[3] [ko'ɔrdənət] *n* : coordenada *f*

coordination [ko,ɔrdən'eɪʃən] *n* : coordinación *f*

coordinator [ko'ɔrdən,eɪṭər] *n* : coordinador *m*, -dora *f*

cop ['kɑp] → **police officer**

cope ['ko:p] *vi* **coped; coping 1** : arreglárselas **2 to cope with** : hacer frente a, poder con <I can't cope with all this! : ¡no puedo con todo esto!>

copier ['kɑpiər] *n* : copiadora *f*, fotocopiadora *f*

copilot ['ko:,paɪlət] *n* : copiloto *m*

copious ['ko:piəs] *adj* : copioso, abundante — **copiously** *adv*

copiousness ['ko:piəsnəs] *n* : abundancia *f*

copper ['kɑpər] *n* : cobre *m*

coppery ['kɑpəri] *adj* : cobrizo

copra ['ko:prə, 'kɑ-] *n* : copra *f*

copse ['kɑps] *n* THICKET : soto *m*, matorral *m*

copulate ['kɑpjə,leɪt] *vi* **-lated; -lating** : copular

copulation [,kɑpjə'leɪʃən] *n* : cópula *f*, relaciones *fpl* sexuales

copy[1] ['kɑpi] *vt* **copied; copying 1** DUPLICATE : hacer una copia de, duplicar, reproducir **2** IMITATE : copiar, imitar

copy[2] *n, pl* **copies 1** : copia *f*, duplicado *m* (de un documento), reproducción *f* (de una obra de arte) **2** : ejemplar *m* (de un libro), número *m* (de una revista) **3** TEXT : manuscrito *m*, texto *m*

copyright[1] ['kɑpi,raɪt] *vt* : registrar los derechos de

copyright[2] *n* : derechos *mpl* de autor

coral[1] ['kɔrəl] *adj* : de coral <a coral reef : un arrecife de coral>

coral[2] *n* : coral *m*

coral snake *n* : serpiente *f* de coral

cord ['kɔrd] *n* **1** ROPE, STRING : cuerda *f*, cordón *m*, cordel *m* **2** : cuerda *f*, cordón *m*, médula *f* (en la anatomía) <vocal cords : cuerdas vocales> **3** : cuerda *f* <a cord of firewood : una cuerda de leña> **4** *or* **electric cord** : cable *m* eléctrico

cordial[1] ['kɔrdʒəl] *adj* : cordial — **cordially** *adv*

cordial[2] *n* : cordial *m*

cordiality [,kɔrdʒi'æləṭi] *n* : cordialidad *f*

cordon[1] ['kɔrdən] *vt* **to cordon off** : acordonar

cordon[2] *n* : cordón *m*

corduroy ['kɔrdə,rɔɪ] *n* **1** : pana *f* **2 corduroys** *npl* : pantalones *mpl* de pana

core[1] ['kor] *vt* **cored; coring** : quitar el corazón a (una fruta)

core[2] *n* **1** : corazón *m*, centro *m* (de algunas frutas) **2** CENTER : núcleo *m*, centro *m* **3** ESSENCE : núcleo *m*, meollo *m* <to the core : hasta la médula>

cork[1] ['kɔrk] *vt* : ponerle un corcho a

cork[2] *n* : corcho *m*

corkscrew ['kɔrk,skru:] *n* : tirabuzón *m*, sacacorchos *m*

cormorant ['kɔrmərənt, -,rænt] *n* : cormorán *m*

corn[1] ['kɔrn] *vt* : conservar en salmuera <corned beef : carne en conserva>

corn[2] *n* **1** GRAIN : grano *m* **2** : maíz *m,* elote *m Mex* <corn tortillas : tortillas de maíz> **3** : callo *m* <corn plaster : emplasto para callos>

corncob [ˈkɔrn,kɑb] *n* : mazorca *f* (de maíz), choclo *m,* elote *m CA, Mex*

cornea [ˈkɔrniə] *n* : córnea *f*

corner[1] [ˈkɔrnər] *vt* **1** TRAP : acorralar, arrinconar **2** MONOPOLIZE : monopolizar, acaparar (un mercado) — *vi* : tomar una curva, doblar una esquina (en un automóvil)

corner[2] *n* **1** ANGLE : rincón *m,* esquina *f,* ángulo *m* <the corner of a room : el rincón de una sala> <all corners of the world : todos los rincones del mundo> <to cut corners : atajar, economizar esfuerzos> **2** INTERSECTION : esquina *f* **3** IMPASSE, PREDICAMENT : aprieto *m,* impasse *m* <to be backed into a corner : estar acorralado>

cornerstone [ˈkɔrnər,sto:n] *n* : piedra *f* angular

cornet [kɔrˈnɛt] *n* : corneta *f*

cornice [ˈkɔrnɪs] *n* : cornisa *f*

cornmeal [ˈkɔrn,mi:l] *n* : harina *f* de maíz

cornstalk [ˈkɔrn,stɔk] *n* : tallo *m* del maíz

cornstarch [ˈkɔrn,stɑrtʃ] *n* : maicena *f,* almidón *m* de maíz

cornucopia [,kɔrnəˈko:piə, -njə-] *n* : cornucopia *f*

corolla [kəˈrɑlə] *n* : corola *f*

corollary [ˈkɔrə,lɛri] *n, pl* **-laries** : corolario *m*

corona [kəˈro:nə] *n* : corona *f* (del sol)

coronary[1] [ˈkɔrə,nɛri] *adj* : coronario

coronary[2] *n, pl* **-naries 1** : trombosis *f* coronaria **2** HEART ATTACK : infarto *m,* ataque *m* al corazón

coronation [,kɔrəˈneɪʃən] *n* : coronación *f*

coroner [ˈkɔrənər] *n* : médico *m* forense

corporal[1] [ˈkɔrpərəl] *adj* : corporal <corporal punishment : castigos corporales>

corporal[2] *n* : cabo *m*

corporate [ˈkɔrpərət] *adj* : corporativo, empresarial

corporation [,kɔrpəˈreɪʃən] *n* : sociedad *f* anónima, corporación *f,* empresa *f*

corporeal [kɔrˈporiəl] *adj* **1** PHYSICAL : corpóreo **2** MATERIAL : material, tangible — **corporeally** *adv*

corps [ˈkor] *n, pl* **corps** [ˈkorz] : cuerpo *m* <medical corps : cuerpo médico> <diplomatic corps : cuerpo diplomático>

corpse [ˈkɔrps] *n* : cadáver *m*

corpulence [ˈkɔrpjələnts] *n* : obesidad *f,* gordura *f*

corpulent [ˈkɔrpjələnt] *adj* : obeso, gordo

corpuscle [ˈkɔr,pʌsəl] *n* : corpúsculo *m,* glóbulo *m* (sanguíneo)

corral[1] [kəˈræl] *vt* **-ralled; -ralling** : acorralar, encorralar (ganado)

corral[2] *n* : corral *m*

correct[1] [kəˈrɛkt] *vt* **1** RECTIFY : corregir, rectificar **2** REPRIMAND : corregir, reprender

correct[2] *adj* **1** ACCURATE, RIGHT : correcto, exacto <to be correct : estar en lo cierto> **2** PROPER : correcto, apropiado

correction [kəˈrɛkʃən] *n* : corrección *f*

corrective [kəˈrɛktɪv] *adj* : correctivo

correctly [kəˈrɛktli] *adv* : correctamente

correlate [ˈkɔrə,leɪt] *vt* **-lated; -lating** : relacionar, poner en correlación

correlation [,kɔrəˈleɪʃən] *n* : correlación *f*

correspond [,kɔrəˈspɑnd] *vi* **1** MATCH : corresponder, concordar, coincidir **2** WRITE : corresponderse, escribirse

correspondence [,kɔrəˈspɑndənts] *n* : correspondencia *f*

correspondent [,kɔrəˈspɑndənt] *n* : corresponsal *mf*

correspondingly [,kɔrəˈspɑndɪŋli] *adv* : en consecuencia, de la misma manera

corridor [ˈkɔrədər, -,dɔr] *n* : corredor *m,* pasillo *m*

corroborate [kəˈrɑbə,reɪt] *vt* **-rated; -rating** : corroborar

corroboration [kə,rɑbəˈreɪʃən] *n* : corroboración *f*

corrode [kəˈro:d] *v* **-roded; -roding** *vt* : corroer — *vi* : corroerse

corrosion [kəˈro:ʒən] *n* : corrosión *f*

corrosive [kəˈro:sɪv] *adj* : corrosivo

corrugate [ˈkɔrə,geɪt] *vt* **-gated; -gating** : ondular, acanalar, corrugar

corrugated [ˈkɔrə,geɪṭəd] *adj* : ondulado, acanalado <corrugated cardboard : cartón ondulado>

corrupt[1] [kəˈrʌpt] *vt* **1** PERVERT : corromper, pervertir, degradar (información) **2** BRIBE : sobornar

corrupt[2] *adj* : corrupto, corrompido

corruptible [kəˈrʌptəbəl] *adj* : corruptible

corruption [kəˈrʌpʃən] *n* : corrupción *f*

corsage [kɔrˈsɑʒ, -ˈsɑdʒ] *n* : ramillete *m* que se lleva como adorno

corset [ˈkɔrsət] *n* : corsé *m*

cortex [ˈkɔr,tɛks] *n, pl* **-tices** [ˈkɔrṭə,si:z] *or* **-texes** : corteza *f* <cerebral cortex : corteza cerebral>

cortisone [ˈkɔrṭə,so:n, -zo:n] *n* : cortisona *f*

cosmetic[1] [kɑzˈmɛtɪk] *adj* : cosmético

cosmetic[2] *n* : cosmético *m*

cosmic [ˈkɑzmɪk] *adj* **1** : cósmico <cosmic ray : rayo cósmico> **2** VAST : grandioso, inmenso, vasto

cosmonaut [ˈkɑzmə,nɔt] *n* : cosmonauta *mf*

cosmopolitan[1] [,kɑzməˈpɑlətən] *adj* : cosmopolita

cosmopolitan[2] *n* : cosmopolita *mf*

cosmos [ˈkɑzməs, -ˌmoːs, -ˌmɑs] *n* : cosmos *m,* universo *m*
cost¹ [ˈkɔst] *v* **cost; costing** *vt* : costar <how much does it cost? : ¿cuánto cuesta?, ¿cuánto vale?> — *vi* : costar <these cost more : éstos cuestan más>
cost² *n* : costo *m,* precio *m,* coste *m* <cost of living : costo de vida> <victory at all costs : victoria a toda costa>
Costa Rican¹ [ˌkɔstəˈriːkən] *adj* : costarricense
Costa Rican² *n* : costarricense *mf*
costly [ˈkɔstli] *adj* : costoso, caro
costume [ˈkɑsˌtuːm, -ˌtjuːm] *n* **1** : traje *m* <national costume : traje típico> **2** : disfraz *m* <costume party : fiesta de disfraces> **3** OUTFIT : vestimenta *f,* traje *m,* conjunto *m*
cosy [ˈkoːzi] → **cozy**
cot [ˈkɑt] *n* : catre *m*
coterie [ˈkoːt̬əˌri, ˌkoːt̬əˈ-] *n* : tertulia *f,* círculo *m* (social)
cottage [ˈkɑt̬ɪdʒ] *n* : casita *f* (de campo)
cottage cheese *n* : requesón *m*
cotton [ˈkɑtən] *n* : algodón *m*
cottonmouth [ˈkɑtənˌmaʊθ] → **moccasin**
cottonseed [ˈkɑtənˌsiːd] *n* : semilla *f* de algodón
cotton swab → **swab**
cottontail [ˈkɑtənˌteɪl] *n* : conejo *m* de cola blanca
couch¹ [ˈkaʊtʃ] *vt* : expresar, formular <couched in strong language : expresado en lenguaje enérgico>
couch² *n* SOFA : sofá *m*
cougar [ˈkuːgər] *n* : puma *m*
cough¹ [ˈkɔf] *vi* : toser
cough² *n* : tos *f*
could [ˈkʊd] → **can**
council [ˈkaʊntsəl] *n* **1** : concejo *m* <city council : concejo municipal, ayuntamiento> **2** MEETING : concejo *m,* junta *f* **3** BOARD : consejo *m* **4** : concilio *m* (eclesiástico)
councillor *or* **councilor** [ˈkaʊntsələr] *n* : concejal *m,* -jala *f*
councilman [ˈkaʊntsəlmən] *n, pl* **-men** [-mən, -ˌmɛn] : concejal *m*
councilwoman [ˈkaʊntsəlˌwʊmən] *n, pl* **-women** [-ˌwɪmən] : concejala *f*
counsel¹ [ˈkaʊntsəl] *v* **-seled** *or* **-selled; -seling** *or* **-selling** *vt* ADVISE : aconsejar, asesorar, recomendar — *vi* CONSULT : consultar
counsel² *n* **1** ADVICE : consejo *m,* recomendación *f* **2** CONSULTATION : consulta *f* **3 counsel** *ns & pl* LAWYER : abogado *m,* -da *f*
counselor *or* **counsellor** [ˈkaʊntsələr] *n* : consejero *m,* -ra *f;* consultor *m,* -tora *f;* asesor *m,* -sora *f*
count¹ [ˈkaʊnt] *vt* : contar, enumerar — *vi* **1** : contar <to count out loud : contar en voz alta> **2** MATTER : contar, valer, importar <that's what counts : eso es lo que cuenta> **3 to count on** : contar con
count² *n* **1** COMPUTATION : cómputo *m,* recuento *m,* cuenta *f* <to lose count : perder la cuenta> **2** CHARGE : cargo *m* <two counts of robbery : dos cargos de robo> **3** : conde *m* (noble)
countable [ˈkaʊntəbəl] *adj* : numerable
countdown [ˈkaʊntˌdaʊn] *n* : cuenta *f* atrás
countenance¹ [ˈkaʊntənənts] *vt* **-nanced; -nancing** : permitir, tolerar
countenance² *n* FACE : semblante *m,* rostro *m*
counter¹ [ˈkaʊntər] *vt* **1** → **counteract** **2** OPPOSE : oponerse a, resistir — *vi* RETALIATE : responder, contraatacar
counter² *adv* **counter to** : contrario a, en contra de
counter³ *adj* : contrario, opuesto
counter⁴ *n* **1** PIECE : ficha *f* (de un juego) **2** : mostrador *m* (de un negocio), ventanilla *f* (en un banco) **3** : contador *m* (aparato) **4** COUNTERBALANCE : fuerza *f* opuesta, contrapeso *m*
counteract [ˌkaʊntərˈækt] *vt* : contrarrestar
counterattack [ˈkaʊntərəˌtæk] *n* : contraataque *m*
counterbalance¹ [ˌkaʊntərˈbæləntsl] *vt* **-anced; -ancing** : contrapesar
counterbalance² [ˈkaʊntərˌbæləntsl] *n* : contrapeso *m*
counterclockwise [ˌkaʊntərˈklɑkˌwaɪz] *adv & adj* : en el sentido opuesto al de las manecillas del reloj
counterfeit¹ [ˈkaʊntərˌfɪt] *vt* **1** : falsificar (dinero) **2** PRETEND : fingir, aparentar
counterfeit² *adj* : falso, inauténtico
counterfeit³ *n* : falsificación *f*
counterfeiter [ˈkaʊntərˌfɪt̬ər] *n* : falsificador *m,* -dora *f*
countermand [ˈkaʊntərˌmænd, ˌkaʊntərˈ-] *vt* : contramandar
countermeasure [ˈkaʊntərˌmɛʒər] *n* : contramedida *f*
counterpart [ˈkaʊntərˌpɑrt] *n* : homólogo *m,* contraparte *f Mex*
counterpoint [ˈkaʊntərˌpɔɪnt] *n* : contrapunto *m*
counterproductive [ˌkaʊntərprəˈdʌktɪv] *adj* : contraproducente
counterrevolution [ˌkaʊntərˌrɛvəˈluːʃən] *n* : contrarrevolución *f*
counterrevolutionary¹ [ˌkaʊntərˌrɛvəˈluːʃənˌɛri] *adj* : contrarrevolucionario
counterrevolutionary² *n, pl* **-ries** : contrarrevolucionario *m,* -ria *f*
countersign [ˈkaʊntərˌsaɪn] *n* : contraseña *f*
countess [ˈkaʊntɪs] *n* : condesa *f*
countless [ˈkaʊntləs] *adj* : incontable, innumerable
country¹ [ˈkʌntri] *adj* : campestre, rural
country² *n, pl* **-tries** **1** NATION : país *m,* nación *f,* patria *f* <country of origin : país de origen> <love of one's country : amor a la patria> **2** : campo *m*

<they left the city for the country : se fueron de la ciudad al campo>
countryman [ˈkʌntrimən] *n, pl* **-men** [-mən, -ˌmɛn] : compatriota *mf;* paisano *m,* -na *f*
countryside [ˈkʌntriˌsaɪd] *n* : campo *m,* campiña *f*
county [ˈkaʊnti] *n, pl* **-ties** : condado *m*
coup [ˈkuː] *n, pl* **coups** [ˈkuːz] **1** : golpe *m* maestro **2** *or* **coup d'etat** : golpe *m* (de estado), cuartelazo *m*
coupe [ˈkuːp] *n* : cupé *m*
couple[1] [ˈkʌpəl] *vt* **-pled; -pling** : acoplar, enganchar, conectar
couple[2] *n* **1** PAIR : par *m* <a couple of hours : un par de horas, unas dos horas> **2** : pareja *f* <a young couple : una pareja joven>
coupling [ˈkʌplɪŋ] *n* : acoplamiento *m*
coupon [ˈkuːˌpɑn, ˈkjuː-] *n* : cupón *m*
courage [ˈkərɪdʒ] *n* : valor *m,* valentía *f,* coraje *m*
courageous [kəˈreɪdʒəs] *adj* : valiente, valeroso
courier [ˈkʊriər, ˈkəriər] *n* : mensajero *m,* -ra *f*
course[1] [ˈkors] *vi* **coursed; coursing** : correr (a toda velocidad)
course[2] *n* **1** PROGRESS : curso *m,* transcurso *m* <to run its course : seguir su curso> **2** DIRECTION : rumbo *m* (de un avión), derrota *f,* derrotero *m* (de un barco) **3** PATH, WAY : camino *m,* vía *f* <course of action : línea de conducta> **4** : plato *m* (de una cena) <the main course : el plato principal> **5** : curso *m* (académico) **6 of course** : desde luego, por supuesto <yes, of course! : ¡claro que sí!>
court[1] [ˈkort] *vt* WOO : cortejar, galantear
court[2] *n* **1** PALACE : palacio *m* **2** RETINUE : corte *f,* séquito *m* **3** COURTYARD : patio *m* **4** : cancha *f* (de tenis, baloncesto, etc.) **5** TRIBUNAL : corte *f,* tribunal *m* <the Supreme Court : la Corte Suprema>
courteous [ˈkərt̬iəs] *adj* : cortés, atento, educado — **courteously** *adv*
courtesan [ˈkort̬əzən, ˈkər-] *n* : cortesana *f*
courtesy [ˈkərt̬əsi] *n, pl* **-sies** : cortesía *f*
courthouse [ˈkortˌhaʊs] *n* : palacio *m* de justicia, juzgado *m*
courtier [ˈkort̬iər, ˈkortjər] *n* : cortesano *m,* -na *f*
courtly [ˈkortli] *adj* **-lier; -est** : distinguido, elegante, cortés
court–martial[1] [ˈkortˌmɑrʃəl] *vt* : someter a consejo de guerra
court–martial[2] *n, pl* **courts–martial** [ˈkortsˌmɑrʃəl] : consejo *m* de guerra
court order *n* : mandamiento *m* judicial
courtroom [ˈkortˌruːm] *n* : tribunal *m,* corte *f*
courtship [ˈkortˌʃɪp] *n* : cortejo *m,* noviazgo *m*
courtyard [ˈkortˌjɑrd] *n* : patio *m*
cousin [ˈkʌzən] *n* : primo *m,* -ma *f*
cove [ˈkoːv] *n* : ensenada *f,* cala *f*
covenant [ˈkʌvənənt] *n* : pacto *m,* contrato *m*
cover[1] [ˈkʌvər] *vt* **1** : cubrir, tapar <cover your head : tápate la cabeza> <covered with mud : cubierto de lodo> **2** HIDE, PROTECT : encubrir, proteger **3** TREAT : tratar **4** INSURE : asegurar, cubrir
cover[2] *n* **1** SHELTER : cubierta *f,* abrigo *m,* refugio *m* <to take cover : ponerse a cubierto> <under cover of darkness : al amparo de la oscuridad> **2** LID, TOP : cubierta *f,* tapa *f* **3** : cubierta *f* (de un libro), portada *f* (de una revista) **4 covers** *npl* BEDCLOTHES : ropa *f* de cama, cobijas *fpl,* mantas *fpl*
coverage [ˈkʌvərɪdʒ] *n* : cobertura *f*
coverlet [ˈkʌvərlət] *n* : cobertor *m*
covert[1] [ˈkoːˌvərt, ˈkʌvərt] *adj* : encubierto, secreto <covert operations : operaciones encubiertas>
covert[2] [ˈkʌvərt, ˈkoː-] *n* THICKET : espesura *f,* maleza *f*
cover–up [ˈkʌvərˌʌp] *n* : encubrimiento
covet [ˈkʌvət] *vt* : codiciar
covetous [ˈkʌvət̬əs] *adj* : codicioso
covey [ˈkʌvi] *n, pl* **-eys 1** : bandada *f* pequeña (de codornices, etc.) **2** GROUP : grupo *m*
cow[1] [ˈkaʊ] *vt* : intimidar, acobardar
cow[2] *n* : vaca *f,* hembra *f* (de ciertas especies)
coward [ˈkaʊərd] *n* : cobarde *mf*
cowardice [ˈkaʊərdɪs] *n* : cobardía *f*
cowardly [ˈkaʊərdli] *adj* : cobarde
cowboy [ˈkaʊˌbɔɪ] *n* : vaquero *m,* cowboy *m*
cower [ˈkaʊər] *vi* : encogerse (de miedo), acobardarse
cowgirl [ˈkaʊˌgərl] *n* : vaquera *f*
cowherd [ˈkaʊˌhərd] *n* : vaquero *m,* -ra *f*
cowhide [ˈkaʊˌhaɪd] *n* : cuero *m,* piel *f* de vaca
cowl [ˈkaʊl] *n* : capucha *f* (de un monje)
cowlick [ˈkaʊˌlɪk] *n* : remolino *m*
cowpuncher [ˈkaʊˌpʌntʃər] → **cowboy**
cowslip [ˈkaʊˌslɪp] *n* : prímula *f,* primavera *f*
coxswain [ˈkɑksən, -ˌsweɪn] *n* : timonel *m*
coy [ˈkɔɪ] *adj* **1** SHY : tímido, cohibido **2** COQUETTISH : coqueto
coyote [kaɪˈoːt̬i, ˈkaɪˌoːt] *n, pl* **coyotes** *or* **coyote** : coyote *m*
cozy [ˈkoːzi] *adj* **-zier; -est** : acogedor, cómodo
crab [ˈkræb] *n* : cangrejo *m,* jaiba *f*
crabby [ˈkræbi] *adj* **-bier; -est** : gruñón, malhumorado
crabgrass [ˈkræbˌgræs] *n* : garranchuelo *m*

crack[1] [ˈkræk] *vi* **1** : chasquear, restallar <the whip cracked : el látigo restalló> **2** SPLIT : rajarse, resquebrajarse, agrietarse **3** : quebrarse (dícese de la voz) — *vt* **1** : restallar, chasquear (un látigo, etc.) **2** SPLIT : rajar, agrietar, resquebrajar **3** BREAK : romper (un huevo), cascar (nueces), forzar (una caja fuerte) **4** SOLVE : resolver, descifrar (un código)

crack[2] *adj* FIRST-RATE : buenísimo, de primera

crack[3] *n* **1** : chasquido *m,* restallido *m,* estallido *m* (de un arma de fuego), crujido *m* (de huesos) <a crack of thunder : un trueno> **2** WISECRACK : chiste *m,* ocurrencia *f,* salida *f* **3** CREVICE : raja *f,* grieta *f,* fisura *f* **4** BLOW : golpe *m* **5** ATTEMPT : intento *m*

crackdown [ˈkræk,daʊn] *n* : medidas *fpl* enérgicas

crack down *vt* : tomar medidas enérgicas

cracker [ˈkrækər] *n* : galleta *f* (de soda, etc.)

crackle[1] [ˈkrækəl] *vi* **-led; -ling** : crepitar, chisporrotear

crackle[2] *n* : crujido *m,* chisporroteo *m*

crackpot [ˈkræk,pɑt] *n* : excéntrico *m,* -ca *f;* chiflado *m,* -da *f*

crack–up [ˈkræk,ʌp] *n* **1** CRASH : choque *m,* estrellamiento *m* **2** BREAKDOWN : crisis *f* nerviosa

crack up *vt* WRECK : estrellar (un vehículo) — *vi* : sufrir una crisis nerviosa

cradle[1] [ˈkreɪdəl] *vt* **-dled; -dling** : acunar, mecer (a un niño)

cradle[2] *n* : cuna *f*

craft [ˈkræft] *n* **1** TRADE : oficio *m* <the craft of carpentry : el oficio de carpintero> **2** CRAFTSMANSHIP, SKILL : arte *m,* artesanía *f,* destreza *f* **3** CRAFTINESS : astucia *f,* maña *f* **4** *pl usually* **craft** BOAT : barco *m,* embarcación *f* **5** *pl usually* **craft** AIRCRAFT : avión *m,* aeronave *f*

craftiness [ˈkræftinəs] *n* : astucia *f,* maña *f*

craftsman [ˈkræftsmən] *n, pl* **-men** [-mən, -,mɛn] : artesano *m,* -na *f*

craftsmanship [ˈkræftsmən,ʃɪp] *n* : artesanía *f,* destreza *f*

crafty [ˈkræfti] *adj* **craftier; -est** : astuto, taimado

crag [ˈkræg] *n* : peñasco *m*

craggy [ˈkrægi] *adj* **-gier; -est** : peñascoso

cram [ˈkræm] *v* **crammed; cramming** *vt* **1** JAM : embutir, meter **2** STUFF : atiborrar, abarrotar <crammed with people : atiborrado de gente> — *vi* : estudiar a última hora, memorizar (para un examen)

cramp[1] [ˈkræmp] *vt* **1** : dar calambre en **2** RESTRICT : limitar, restringir, entorpecer <to cramp someone's style : cortarle el vuelo a alguien> — *vi or* **to cramp up** : acalambrarse

cramp[2] *n* **1** SPASM : calambre *m,* espasmo *m* (de los músculos) **2 cramps** *npl* : retorcijones *mpl* <stomach cramps : retorcijones de estómago>

cranberry [ˈkræn,bɛri] *n, pl* **-berries** : arándano *m* (rojo y agrio)

crane[1] [ˈkreɪn] *vi* **craned; craning** : estirar <to crane one's neck : estirar el cuello>

crane[2] *n* **1** : grulla *f* (ave) **2** : grúa *f* (máquina)

cranial [ˈkreɪniəl] *adj* : craneal, craneano

cranium [ˈkreɪniəm] *n, pl* **-niums** *or* **-nia** [-niə]: cráneo *m*

crank[1] [ˈkræŋk] *vt or* **to crank up** : arrancar (con una manivela)

crank[2] *n* **1** : manivela *f,* manubrio *m* **2** ECCENTRIC : excéntrico *m,* -ca *f*

cranky [ˈkræŋki] *adj* **crankier; -est** : irritable, malhumorado, enojadizo

cranny [ˈkræni] *n, pl* **-nies** : grieta *f* <every nook and cranny : todos los rincones>

crash[1] [ˈkræʃ] *vi* **1** SMASH : caerse con estrépito, estrellarse **2** COLLIDE : estrellarse, chocar **3** BOOM, RESOUND : retumbar, resonar — *vt* **1** SMASH : estrellar **2 to crash one's car** : tener un accidente

crash[2] *n* **1** DIN : estrépito *m* **2** COLLISION : choque *m,* colisión *f* <car crash : accidente automovilístico> **3** FAILURE : quiebra *f* (de un negocio), crac *m* (de la bolsa)

crass [ˈkræs] *adj* : grosero, de mal gusto

crate[1] [ˈkreɪt] *vt* **crated; crating** : empacar en un cajón

crate[2] *n* : cajón *m* (de madera)

crater [ˈkreɪt̬ər] *n* : cráter *m*

cravat [krəˈvæt] *n* : corbata *f*

crave [ˈkreɪv] *vt* **craved; craving** : ansiar, apetecer, tener muchas ganas de

craven [ˈkreɪvən] *adj* : cobarde, pusilánime

craving [ˈkreɪvɪŋ] *n* : ansia *f,* antojo *m,* deseo *m*

crawfish [ˈkrɔ,fɪʃ] → **crayfish**

crawl[1] [ˈkrɔl] *vi* **1** CREEP : arrastrarse, gatear (dícese de un bebé) **2** TEEM : estar plagado

crawl[2] *n* : paso *m* lento

crayfish [ˈkreɪ,fɪʃ] *n* **1** : ástaco *m* (de agua dulce) **2** : langostino *m* (de mar)

crayon [ˈkreɪ,ɑn, -ən] *n* : crayón *m*

craze [ˈkreɪz] *n* : moda *f* pasajera, manía *f*

crazed [ˈkreɪzd] *adj* : enloquecido

crazily [ˈkreɪzəli] *adv* : locamente, erráticamente, insensatamente

craziness [ˈkreɪzinəs] *n* : locura *f,* demencia *f*

crazy [ˈkreɪzi] *adj* **-zier; -est 1** INSANE : loco, demente <to go crazy : volverse loco> **2** ABSURD, FOOLISH : loco, insensato, absurdo **3 to be crazy about** : estar loco por

creak[1] [ˈkriːk] *vi* **:** chirriar, rechinar, crujir
creak[2] *n* **:** chirrido *m,* crujido *m*
creaky [ˈkriːki] *adj* **creakier; -est :** chirriante, que cruje
cream[1] [ˈkriːm] *vt* **1** BEAT, MIX **:** batir, mezclar (azúcar y mantequilla, etc.) **2 :** preparar (alimentos) con crema
cream[2] *n* **1 :** crema *f* (de leche) **2** LOTION **:** crema *f,* loción *f* **3** ELITE **:** crema *f,* elite *f* <the cream of the crop : la crema y nata, lo mejor>
creamery [ˈkriːməri] *n, pl* **-eries :** fábrica *f* de productos lácteos
creamy [ˈkriːmi] *adj* **creamier; -est :** cremoso
crease[1] [ˈkriːs] *vt* **creased; creasing 1 :** plegar, poner una raya en (pantalones) **2** WRINKLE **:** arrugar
crease[2] *n* **:** pliegue *m,* doblez *m,* raya *f* (de pantalones)
create [kriˈeɪt] *vt* **-ated; -ating :** crear, hacer
creation [kriˈeɪʃən] *n* **:** creación *f*
creative [kriˈeɪtɪv] *adj* **:** creativo, original <creative people : personas creativas> <a creative work : un obra original>
creatively [kriˈeɪtɪvli] *adv* **:** creativamente, con originalidad
creativity [ˌkriːeɪˈtɪvəti] *n* **:** creatividad *f*
creator [kriˈeɪtər] *n* **:** creador *m,* -dora *f*
creature [ˈkriːtʃər] *n* **:** ser *m* viviente, criatura *f,* animal *m*
credence [ˈkriːdənts] *n* **:** crédito *m*
credentials [krɪˈdɛntʃəlz] *npl* **:** referencias *fpl* oficiales, cartas *fpl* credenciales
credibility [ˌkrɛdəˈbɪləti] *n* **:** credibilidad *f*
credible [ˈkrɛdəbəl] *adj* **:** creíble
credit[1] [ˈkrɛdɪt] *vt* **1** BELIEVE **:** creer, dar crédito a **2 :** ingresar, abonar <to credit $100 to an account : ingresar $100 en (una) cuenta> **3** ATTRIBUTE **:** atribuir <they credit the invention to him : a él se le atribuye el invento>
credit[2] *n* **1 :** saldo *m* positivo, saldo *m* a favor (de una cuenta) **2 :** crédito *m* <to buy on credit : comprar a crédito> <credit card : tarjeta de crédito> **3** CREDENCE **:** crédito *m* <I gave credit to everything he said : di crédito a todo lo que dijo> **4** RECOGNITION **:** reconocimiento *m* **5 :** orgullo *m,* honor *m* <she's a credit to the school : ella es el orgullo de la escuela>
creditable [ˈkrɛdɪtəbəl] *adj* **:** encomiable, loable — **creditably** [-bli] *adv*
credit card *n* **:** tarjeta de crédito
creditor [ˈkrɛdɪtər] *n* **:** acreedor *m,* -dora *f*
credulity [krɪˈduːləti, -ˈdjuː-] *n* **:** credulidad *f*
credulous [ˈkrɛdʒələs] *adj* **:** crédulo
creed [ˈkriːd] *n* **:** credo *m*
creek [ˈkriːk, ˈkrɪk] *n* **:** arroyo *m,* riachuelo *m*
creel [ˈkriːl] *n* **:** nasa *f,* cesta *f* (de pescador)
creep[1] [ˈkriːp] *vi* **crept** [ˈkrɛpt]; **creeping 1** CRAWL **:** arrastrarse, gatear **2 :** moverse lentamente o sigilosamente <he crept out of the house : salió sigilosamente de la casa> **3** SPREAD **:** trepar (dícese de una planta)
creep[2] *n* **1** CRAWL **:** paso *m* lento **2 creeps** *npl* **:** escalofríos *mpl* <that gives me the creeps : eso me da escalofríos>
creeper [ˈkriːpər] *n* **:** planta *f* trepadora, trepadora *f*
cremate [ˈkriːˌmeɪt] *vt* **-mated; -mating :** cremar
cremation [krɪˈmeɪʃən] *n* **:** cremación *f*
creosote [ˈkriːəˌsoːt] *n* **:** creosota *f*
crepe *or* **crêpe** [ˈkreɪp] *n* **1 :** crespón *m* (tela) **2** PANCAKE **:** crepe *mf,* crepa *f Mex*
crescendo [krɪˈʃɛnˌdoː] *n, pl* **-dos** *or* **-does :** crescendo *m*
crescent [ˈkrɛsənt] *n* **:** creciente *m*
crest [ˈkrɛst] *n* **1 :** cresta *f,* penacho *m* (de un ave) **2** PEAK, TOP **:** cresta *f* (de una ola), cima *f* (de una colina) **3 :** emblema *m* (sobre un escudo de armas)
crestfallen [ˈkrɛstˌfɔlən] *adj* **:** alicaído, abatido
cretin [ˈkriːtən] *n* **:** cretino *m,* -na *f*
crevasse [krɪˈvæs] *n* **:** grieta *f,* fisura *f*
crevice [ˈkrɛvɪs] *n* **:** grieta *f,* hendidura *f*
crew [ˈkruː] *n* **1 :** tripulación *f* (de una nave) **2** TEAM **:** equipo *m* (de trabajadores o atletas)
crib [ˈkrɪb] *n* **1** MANGER **:** pesebre *m* **2** GRANARY **:** granero *m* **3 :** cuna *f* (de un bebé)
crick [ˈkrɪk] *n* **:** calambre *m,* espasmo *m* muscular
cricket [ˈkrɪkət] *n* **1 :** grillo *m* (insecto) **2 :** críquet *m* (juego)
crime [ˈkraɪm] *n* **1 :** crimen *m,* delito *m* <to commit a crime : cometer un delito> **2 :** crimen *m,* delincuencia *f* <organized crime : crimen organizado>
criminal[1] [ˈkrɪmənəl] *adj* **:** criminal
criminal[2] *n* **:** criminal *mf,* delincuente *mf*
crimp [ˈkrɪmp] *vt* **:** ondular, rizar (el pelo), arrugar (una tela, etc.)
crimson [ˈkrɪmzən] *n* **:** carmesí *m*
cringe [ˈkrɪndʒ] *vi* **cringed; cringing :** encogerse
crinkle[1] [ˈkrɪŋkəl] *v* **-kled; -kling** *vt* **:** arrugar — *vi* **:** arrugarse
crinkle[2] *n* **:** arruga *f*
crinkly [ˈkrɪŋkəli] *adj* **:** arrugado
cripple[1] [ˈkrɪpəl] *vt* **-pled; -pling 1** DISABLE **:** lisiar, dejar inválido **2** INCAPACITATE **:** inutilizar, incapacitar
cripple[2] *n* **:** lisiado *m,* -da *f*

crisis ['kraɪsɪs] *n, pl* **crises** [-ˌsiːz] : crisis *f*
crisp[1] ['krɪsp] *vt* : tostar, hacer crujiente
crisp[2] *adj* **1** CRUNCHY : crujiente, crocante **2** FIRM, FRESH : firme, fresco <crisp lettuce : lechuga fresca> **3** LIVELY : vivaz, alegre <a crisp tempo : un ritmo alegre> **4** INVIGORATING : fresco, vigorizante <the crisp autumn air : el fresco aire otoñal> — **crisply** *adv*
crispy ['krɪspi] *adj* **crispier; -est** : crujiente <crispy potato chips : papitas crujientes>
crisscross ['krɪsˌkrɔs] *vt* : entrecruzar
criterion [kraɪ'tɪriən] *n, pl* **-ria** [-iə] : criterio *m*
critic ['krɪtɪk] *n* **1** : crítico *m,* -ca *f* (de las artes) **2** FAULTFINDER : detractor *m,* -tora *f;* criticón *m,* -cona *f*
critical ['krɪtɪkəl] *adj* : crítico
critically ['krɪtɪkli] *adv* : críticamente <critically ill : gravemente enfermo>
criticism ['krɪtəˌsɪzəm] *n* : crítica *f*
criticize ['krɪtəˌsaɪz] *vt* **-cized; -cizing** **1** EVALUATE, JUDGE : criticar, analizar, evaluar **2** CENSURE : criticar, reprobar
critique [krɪ'tiːk] *n* : crítica *f,* evaluación *f*
croak[1] ['kroːk] *vi* : croar
croak[2] *n* : croar *m,* canto *m* (de la rana)
Croatian [kro'eɪʃən] *n* : croata *mf* — **Croatian** *adj*
crochet[1] [kroː'ʃeɪ] *v* : tejer al croché
crochet[2] *n* : croché *m,* crochet *m*
crock ['krɑk] *n* : vasija *f* de barro
crockery ['krɑkəri] *n* : vajilla *f* (de barro)
crocodile ['krɑkəˌdaɪl] *n* : cocodrilo *m*
crocus ['kroːkəs] *n, pl* **-cuses** : azafrán *m*
crone ['kroːn] *n* : vieja *f* arpía, vieja *f* bruja
crony ['kroːni] *n, pl* **-nies** : amigote *m fam;* compinche *mf fam*
crook[1] ['krʊk] *vt* : doblar (el brazo o el dedo)
crook[2] *n* **1** STAFF : cayado *m* (de pastor), báculo *m* (de obispo) **2** THIEF : ratero *m,* -ra *f;* ladrón *m,* -drona *f*
crooked ['krʊkəd] *adj* **1** BENT : chueco, torcido **2** DISHONEST : deshonesto
crookedness ['krʊkədnəs] *n* **1** : lo torcido, lo chueco **2** DISHONESTY : falta *f* de honradez
croon ['kruːn] *v* : cantar suavemente
crop[1] ['krɑp] *v* **cropped; cropping** *vt* TRIM : recortar, cortar — *vi* **to crop up** : aparecer, surgir <these problems keep cropping up : estos problemas no cesan de surgir>
crop[2] *n* **1** : buche *m* (de un ave o insecto) **2** WHIP : fusta *f* (de jinete) **3** HARVEST : cosecha *f,* cultivo *m*
croquet [ˌkroː'keɪ] *n* : croquet *m*
croquette [ˌkroː'kɛt] *n* : croqueta *f*
cross[1] ['krɔs] *vt* **1** : cruzar, atravesar <to cross the street : cruzar la calle> <several canals cross the city : varios canales atraviesan la ciudad> **2** CANCEL : tachar, cancelar <he crossed his name off the list : tachó su nombre de la planilla> **3** INTERBREED : cruzar (en genética)
cross[2] *adj* **1** : que atraviesa <cross ventilation : ventilación que atraviesa un cuarto> **2** CONTRARY : contrario, opuesto <cross purposes : objetivos opuestos> **3** ANGRY : enojado, de mal humor
cross[3] *n* **1** : cruz *f* <the sign of the cross : la señal de la cruz> **2** : cruza *f* (en biología)
crossbones ['krɔsˌboːnz] *npl* **1** : huesos *mpl* cruzados **2** → **skull**
crossbow ['krɔsˌboː] *n* : ballesta *f*
crossbreed ['krɔsˌbriːd] *vt* **-bred** [-+bred]; **-breeding** : cruzar
cross–examination [ˌkrɔsɪgˌzæmə'neɪʃən] *n* : repreguntas *fpl,* interrogatorio *m*
cross–examine [ˌkrɔsɪg'zæmən] *vt* **-ined; -ining** : repreguntar
cross–eyed ['krɔsˌaɪd] *adj* : bizco
crossing ['krɔsɪŋ] *n* **1** INTERSECTION : cruce *m,* paso *m* <pedestrian crossing : paso de peatones> **2** VOYAGE : travesía *f* (del mar)
crossly ['krɔsli] *adv* : con enojo, con enfado
cross–reference [ˌkrɔs'rɛfrən*t*s, -'rɛfərən*t*s] *n* : referencia *f,* remisión *f*
crossroads ['krɔsˌroːdz] *n* : cruce *m,* encrucijada *f,* crucero *m Mex*
cross section *n* **1** SECTION : corte *m* transversal **2** SAMPLE : muestra *f* representativa <a cross section of the population : una muestra representativa de la población>
crosswalk ['krɔsˌwɔk] *n* : cruce *m* peatonal, paso *m* de peatones
crossways ['krɔsˌweɪz] → **crosswise**
crosswise[1] ['krɔsˌwaɪz] *adv* : transversalmente, diagonalmente
crosswise[2] *adj* : transversal, diagonal
crossword puzzle ['krɔsˌwərd] *n* : crucigrama *m*
crotch ['krɑtʃ] *n* : entrepierna *f*
crotchety ['krɑtʃəti] *adj* CRANKY : malhumorado, irritable, enojadizo
crouch ['kraʊtʃ] *vi* : agacharse, ponerse de cuclillas
croup ['kruːp] *n* : crup *m*
crouton ['kruːˌtɑn] *n* : crutón *m*
crow[1] ['kroː] *vi* **1** : cacarear, cantar (como un cuervo) **2** BRAG : alardear, presumir
crow[2] *n* **1** : cuervo *m* (ave) **2** : cantar *m* (del gallo)
crowbar ['kroːˌbɑr] *n* : palanca *f*
crowd[1] ['kraʊd] *vi* : aglomerarse, amontonarse — *vt* : atestar, atiborrar, llenar
crowd[2] *n* : multitud *f,* muchedumbre *f,* gentío *m*
crown[1] ['kraʊn] *vt* : coronar
crown[2] *n* : corona *f*

crow's nest *n* : cofa *f*
crucial ['kruːʃəl] *adj* : crucial, decisivo
crucible ['kruːsəbəl] *n* : crisol *m*
crucifix ['kruːsə,fɪks] *n* : crucifijo *m*
crucifixion [,kruːsə'fɪkʃən] *n* : crucifixión *f*
crucify ['kruːsə,faɪ] *vt* **-fied; -fying** : crucificar
crude ['kruːd] *adj* **cruder; -est 1** RAW, UNREFINED : crudo, sin refinar <crude oil : petróleo crudo> **2** VULGAR : grosero, de mal gusto **3** ROUGH : tosco, burdo, rudo
crudely ['kruːdli] *adv* **1** VULGARLY : groseramente **2** ROUGHLY : burdamente, de manera rudimentaria
crudity ['kruːdəṭi] *n, pl* **-ties 1** VULGARITY : grosería *f* **2** COARSENESS, ROUGHNESS : tosquedad *f,* rudeza *f*
cruel ['kruːəl] *adj* **-eler** *or* **-eller; -elest** *or* **-ellest** : cruel
cruelly ['kruːəli] *adv* : cruelmente
cruelty ['kruːəlti] *n, pl* **-ties** : crueldad *f*
cruet ['kruːɪt] *n* : vinagrera *f,* aceitera *f*
cruise¹ ['kruːz] *vi* **cruised; cruising 1** : hacer un crucero **2** : navegar o conducir a una velocidad constante <cruising speed : velocidad de crucero>
cruise² *n* : crucero *m*
cruiser ['kruːzər] *n* **1** WARSHIP : crucero *m,* buque *m* de guerra **2** : patrulla *f* (de policía)
crumb ['krʌm] *n* : miga *f,* migaja *f*
crumble ['krʌmbəl] *v* **-bled; -bling** *vt* : desmigajar, desmenuzar — *vi* : desmigajarse, desmoronarse, desmenuzarse
crumbly ['krʌmbli] *adj* : que se desmenuza fácilmente, friable
crumple ['krʌmpəl] *v* **-pled; -pling** *vt* RUMPLE : arrugar — *vi* **1** WRINKLE : arrugarse **2** COLLAPSE : desplomarse
crunch¹ ['krʌntʃ] *vt* **1** : ronzar (con los dientes) **2** : hacer crujir (con los pies, etc.) — *vi* : crujir
crunch² *n* : crujido *m*
crunchy ['krʌntʃi] *adj* **crunchier; -est** : crujiente
crusade¹ [kruː'seɪd] *vi* **-saded; -sading** : hacer una campaña (a favor de o contra algo)
crusade² *n* **1** : campaña *f* (de reforma, etc.) **2 Crusade** : cruzada *f*
crusader [kruː'seɪdər] *n* **1** : cruzado *m* (en la Edad Media) **2** : campeón *m,* -peona *f* (de una causa)
crush¹ ['krʌʃ] *vt* **1** SQUASH : aplastar, apachurrar **2** GRIND, PULVERIZE : triturar, machacar **3** SUPPRESS : aplastar, suprimir
crush² *n* **1** CROWD, MOB : gentío *m,* multitud *f,* aglomeración *f* **2** INFATUATION : enamoramiento *m*
crushing ['krʌʃɪŋ] *adj* : aplastante, abrumador
crust ['krʌst] *n* **1** : corteza *f,* costra *f* (de pan) **2** : tapa *f* de masa, pasta *f* (de un pastel) **3** LAYER : capa *f,* corteza *f* <the earth's crust : la corteza terrestre>
crustacean [,krʌs'teɪʃən] *n* : crustáceo *m*
crusty ['krʌsti] *adj* **crustier; -est 1** : de corteza dura **2** CROSS, GRUMPY : enojado, malhumorado
crutch ['krʌtʃ] *n* : muleta *f*
crux ['krʌks, 'krʊks] *n, pl* **cruxes** : quid *m,* esencia *f,* meollo *m* <the crux of the problem : el quid del problema>
cry¹ ['kraɪ] *vi* **cried; crying 1** SHOUT : gritar <they cried for more : a gritos pidieron más> **2** WEEP : llorar
cry² *n, pl* **cries 1** SHOUT : grito *m* **2** WEEPING : llanto *m* **3** : chillido *m* (de un animal)
crybaby ['kraɪ,beɪbi] *n, pl* **-bies** : llorón *m,* -rona *f*
crypt ['krɪpt] *n* : cripta *f*
cryptic ['krɪptɪk] *adj* : enigmático, críptico
crystal ['krɪstəl] *n* : cristal *m*
crystalline ['krɪstəlɪn] *adj* : cristalino
crystallize ['krɪstə,laɪz] *v* **-lized; -lizing** *vt* : cristalizar, materializar <to crystallize one's thoughts : cristalizar uno sus pensamientos> — *vi* : cristalizarse
cub ['kʌb] *n* : cachorro *m*
Cuban ['kjuːbən] *n* : cubano *m,* -na *f* — **Cuban** *adj*
cubbyhole ['kʌbi,hoːl] *n* : chiribitil *m*
cube¹ ['kjuːb] *vt* **cubed; cubing 1** : elevar (un número) al cubo **2** : cortar en cubos
cube² *n* **1** : cubo *m* **2 ice cube** : cubito *m* de hielo **3 sugar cube** : terrón *m* de azúcar
cubic ['kjuːbɪk] *adj* : cúbico
cubicle ['kjuːbɪkəl] *n* : cubículo *m*
cuckoo¹ ['kuː,kuː, 'kʊ-] *adj* : loco, chiflado
cuckoo² *n, pl* **-oos** : cuco *m,* cuclillo *m*
cucumber ['kjuː,kʌmbər] *n* : pepino *m*
cud ['kʌd] *n* **to chew the cud** : rumiar
cuddle ['kʌdəl] *v* **-dled; -dling** *vi* : abrazarse tiernamente, acurrucarse — *vt* : abrazar
cudgel¹ ['kʌdʒəl] *vt* **-geled** *or* **-gelled; -geling** *or* **-gelling** : apalear, aporrear
cudgel² *n* : garrote *m,* porra *f*
cue¹ ['kjuː] *vt* **cued; cuing** *or* **cueing** : darle el pie a, darle la señal a
cue² *n* **1** SIGNAL : señal *f,* pie *m* (en teatro), entrada *f* (en música) **2** : taco *m* (de billar)
cuff¹ ['kʌf] *vt* : bofetear, cachetear
cuff² *n* **1** : puño *m* (de una camisa), vuelta *f* (de pantalones) **2** SLAP : bofetada *f,* cachetada *f* **3 cuffs** *npl* HANDCUFFS : esposas *fpl*
cuisine [kwɪ'ziːn] *n* : cocina *f* <Mexican cuisine : la cocina mexicana>

culinary [ˈkʌləˌnɛri, ˈkjuːlə-] *adj* : culinario

cull [ˈkʌl] *vt* : seleccionar, entresacar

culminate [ˈkʌlməˌneɪt] *vi* **-nated; -nating** : culminar

culmination [ˌkʌlməˈneɪʃən] *n* : culminación *f,* punto *m* culminante

culpable [ˈkʌlpəbəl] *adj* : culpable

culprit [ˈkʌlprɪt] *n* : culpable *mf*

cult [ˈkʌlt] *n* : culto *m*

cultivate [ˈkʌltəˌveɪt] *vt* **-vated; -vating 1** TILL : cultivar, labrar **2** FOSTER : cultivar, fomentar **3** REFINE : cultivar, refinar <to cultivate the mind : cultivar la mente>

cultivation [ˌkʌltəˈveɪʃən] *n* **1** : cultivo *m* <under cultivation : en cultivo> **2** CULTURE, REFINEMENT : cultura *f,* refinamiento *m*

cultural [ˈkʌltʃərəl] *adj* : cultural — **culturally** *adv*

culture [ˈkʌltʃər] *n* **1** CULTIVATION : cultivo *m* **2** REFINEMENT : cultura *f,* educación *f,* refinamiento *m* **3** CIVILIZATION : cultura *f,* civilización *f* <the Incan culture : la cultura inca>

cultured [ˈkʌltʃərd] *adj* **1** EDUCATED, REFINED : culto, educado, refinado **2** : de cultivo, cultivado <cultured pearls : perlas de cultivo>

culvert [ˈkʌlvərt] *n* : alcantarilla *f*

cumbersome [ˈkʌmbərsəm] *adj* : torpe y pesado, difícil de manejar

cumulative [ˈkjuːmjələt̬ɪv, -ˌleɪt̬ɪv] *adj* : acumulativo

cumulus [ˈkjuːmjələs] *n, pl* **-li** [-ˌlaɪ, -ˌliː] : cúmulo *n*

cunning¹ [ˈkʌnɪŋ] *adj* **1** CRAFTY : astuto, taimado **2** CLEVER : ingenioso, hábil **3** CUTE : mono, gracioso, lindo

cunning² *n* **1** SKILL : habilidad *f* **2** CRAFTINESS : astucia *f,* maña *f*

cup¹ [ˈkʌp] *vt* **cupped; cupping** : ahuecar (las manos)

cup² *n* **1** : taza *f* <a cup of coffee : una taza de café> **2** CUPFUL : taza *f* **3** : media pinta *f* (unidad de medida) **4** GOBLET : copa *f* **5** TROPHY : copa *f,* trofeo *m*

cupboard [ˈkʌbərd] *n* : alacena *f,* armario *m*

cupcake [ˈkʌpˌkeɪk] *n* : pastelito *m*

cupful [ˈkʌpˌfʊl] *n* : taza *f*

cupola [ˈkjuːpələ, -ˌloː] *n* : cúpula *f*

cur [ˈkər] *n* : perro *m* callejero, perro *m* corriente *Mex*

curate [ˈkjʊrət] *n* : cura *m,* párroco *m*

curator [ˈkjʊrˌeɪt̬ər, kjʊˈreɪt̬ər] *n* : conservador *m,* -dora *f* (de un museo); director *m,* -tora *f* (de un zoológico)

curb¹ [ˈkərb] *vt* : refrenar, restringir, controlar

curb² *n* **1** RESTRAINT : freno *m,* control *m* **2** : borde *m* de la acera

curd [ˈkərd] *n* : cuajada *f*

curdle [ˈkərdəl] *v* **-dled; -dling** *vi* : cuajarse — *vt* : cuajar <to curdle one's blood : helarle la sangre a uno>

cure¹ [ˈkjʊr] *vt* **cured; curing 1** HEAL : curar, sanar **2** REMEDY : remediar **3** PROCESS : curar (alimentos, etc.)

cure² *n* **1** RECOVERY : curación *f,* recuperación *f* **2** REMEDY : cura *f,* remedio *m*

curfew [ˈkərˌfjuː] *n* : toque *m* de queda

curio [ˈkjʊriˌoː] *n, pl* **-rios** : curiosidad *f,* objeto *m* curioso

curiosity [ˌkjʊriˈɑsət̬i] *n, pl* **-ties** : curiosidad *f*

curious [ˈkjʊriəs] *adj* **1** INQUISITIVE : curioso **2** STRANGE : curioso, raro

curl¹ [ˈkərl] *vt* **1** : rizar, ondular (el pelo) **2** COIL : enrollar **3** TWIST : torcer <to curl one's lip : hacer una mueca> — *vi* **1** : rizarse, ondularse **2 to curl up** : acurrucarse (con un libro, etc.)

curl² *n* **1** RINGLET : rizo *m* **2** COIL : espiral *f,* rosca *f*

curler [ˈkərlər] *n* : rulo *m*

curlew [ˈkərˌluː, ˈkərlˌjuː] *n, pl* **-lews** *or* **-lew** : zarapito *m*

curly [ˈkərli] *adj* **curlier; -est** : rizado, crespo

currant [ˈkərənt] *n* **1** : grosella *f* (fruta) **2** RAISIN : pasa *f* de Corinto

currency [ˈkərəntsi] *n, pl* **-cies 1** PREVALENCE, USE : uso *m,* aceptación *f,* difusión *f* <to be in currency : estar en uso> **2** MONEY : moneda *f,* dinero *m*

current¹ [ˈkərənt] *adj* **1** PRESENT : actual <current events : actualidades> **2** PREVALENT : corriente, común — **currently** *adv*

current² *n* : corriente *f*

curriculum [kəˈrɪkjələm] *n, pl* **-la** [-lə] : currículum *m,* currículo *m,* programa *m* de estudio

curriculum vitae [ˈviːˌtaɪ, ˈvaɪt̬i] *n, pl* **curricula vitae** : currículum *m,* currículo *m*

curry¹ [ˈkəri] *vt* **-ried; -rying 1** GROOM : almohazar (un caballo) **2** : condimentar con curry **3 to curry favor** : congraciarse (con alguien)

curry² *n, pl* **-ries** : curry *m*

curse¹ [ˈkərs] *v* **cursed; cursing** *vt* **1** DAMN : maldecir **2** INSULT : injuriar, insultar, decir malas palabras a **3** AFFLICT : afligir — *vi* : maldecir, decir malas palabras

curse² *n* **1** : maldición *f* <to put a curse on someone : echarle una maldición a alguien> **2** AFFLICTION : maldición *f,* aflicción *f,* cruz *f*

cursor [ˈkərsər] *n* : cursor *m*

cursory [ˈkərsəri] *adj* : rápido, superficial, somero

curt [ˈkərt] *adj* : cortante, brusco, seco — **curtly** *adv*

curtail [kərˈteɪl] *vt* : acortar, limitar, restringir

curtailment [kərˈteɪlmənt] *n* : restricción *f,* limitación *f*

curtain [ˈkərtən] *n* : cortina *f* (de una ventana), telón *m* (en un teatro)

curtness [ˈkərtnəs] *n* : brusquedad *f,* sequedad *f*

curtsy[1] *or* **curtsey** [ˈkərtsi] *vt* **-sied** *or* **-seyed; -sying** *or* **-seying :** hacer una reverencia
curtsy[2] *or* **curtsey** *n, pl* **-sies** *or* **-seys :** reverencia *f*
curvature [ˈkərvəˌtʃʊr] *n* **:** curvatura *f*
curve[1] [ˈkərv] *v* **curved; curving** *vi* **:** torcerse, describir una curva — *vt* **:** encorvar
curve[2] *n* **:** curva *f*
cushion[1] [ˈkʊʃən] *vt* **1 :** poner cojines o almohadones a **2** SOFTEN **:** amortiguar, mitigar, suavizar <to cushion a blow : amortiguar un golpe>
cushion[2] *n* **1 :** cojín *m,* almohadón *m* **2** PROTECTION **:** colchón *m,* protección *f*
cusp [ˈkʌsp] *n* **:** cúspide *f* (de un diente), cuerno *m* (de la luna)
cuspid [ˈkʌspɪd] *n* **:** diente *m* canino, colmillo *m*
custard [ˈkʌstərd] *n* **:** natillas *fpl*
custodian [ˌkʌˈstoːdiən] *n* **:** custodio *m,* -dia *f;* guardián, -diana *f*
custody [ˈkʌstədi] *n, pl* **-dies :** custodia *f,* cuidado *m* <to be in custody : estar detenido>
custom[1] [ˈkʌstəm] *adj* **:** a la medida, a la orden
custom[2] *n* **1 :** costumbre *f,* tradición *f* **2 customs** *npl* **:** aduana *f*
customarily [ˌkʌstəˈmɛrəli] *adv* **:** habitualmente, normalmente, de costumbre
customary [ˈkʌstəˌmɛri] *adj* **1** TRADITIONAL **:** tradicional **2** USUAL **:** habitual, de costumbre
customer [ˈkʌstəmər] *n* **:** cliente *m,* -ta *f*
custom–made [ˈkʌstəmˈmeɪd] *adj* **:** hecho a la medida
cut[1] [ˈkʌt] *v* **cut; cutting** *vt* **1 :** cortar <to cut paper : cortar papel> **2 :** cortarse <to cut one's finger : cortarse uno el dedo> **3** TRIM **:** cortar, recortar <to have one's hair cut : cortarse el pelo> **4** INTERSECT **:** cruzar, atravesar **5** SHORTEN **:** acortar, abreviar **6** REDUCE **:** reducir, rebajar <to cut prices : rebajar los precios> **7 to cut one's teeth :** salirle los dientes a uno — *vi* **1 :** cortar, cortarse **2 to cut in :** entrometerse
cut[2] *n* **1 :** corte *m* <a cut of meat : un corte de carne> **2** SLASH **:** tajo *m,* corte *m,* cortadura *f* **3** REDUCTION **:** rebaja *f,* reducción *f* <a cut in the rates : una rebaja en las tarifas>
cute [ˈkjuːt] *adj* **cuter; -est :** mono *fam,* lindo
cuticle [ˈkjuːtɪkəl] *n* **:** cutícula *f*
cutlass [ˈkʌtləs] *n* **:** alfanje *m*
cutlery [ˈkʌtləri] *n* **:** cubiertos *mpl*
cutlet [ˈkʌtlət] *n* **:** chuleta *f*
cutter [ˈkʌtər] *n* **1 :** cortadora *f* (implemento) **2 :** cortador *m,* -dora *f* (persona) **3 :** cúter *m* (embarcación)
cutthroat [ˈkʌtˌθroːt] *adj* **:** despiadado, desalmado <cutthroat competition : competencia feroz>
cutting[1] [ˈkʌtɪŋ] *adj* **1 :** cortante <a cutting wind : un viento cortante> **2** CAUSTIC **:** mordaz
cutting[2] *n* **:** esqueje *m* (de una planta)
cuttlefish [ˈkʌtəlˌfɪʃ] *n, pl* **-fish** *or* **-fishes :** jibia *f,* sepia *f*
cyanide [ˈsaɪəˌnaɪd, -nɪd] *n* **:** cianuro *m*
cycle[1] [ˈsaɪkəl] *vi* **-cled; -cling :** andar en bicicleta, ir en bicicleta
cycle[2] *n* **1 :** ciclo *m* <life cycle : ciclo de vida, ciclo vital> **2** BICYCLE **:** bicicleta *f* **3** MOTORCYCLE **:** motocicleta *f*
cyclic [ˈsaɪklɪk, ˈsɪ-] *or* **cyclical** [-klɪkəl] *adj* **:** cíclico
cyclist [ˈsaɪklɪst] *n* **:** ciclista *mf*
cyclone [ˈsaɪˌkloːn] *n* **1 :** ciclón *m* **2** TORNADO **:** tornado *m*
cyclopedia *or* **cyclopaedia** [ˌsaɪkləˈpiːdiə] → **encyclopedia**
cylinder [ˈsɪləndər] *n* **:** cilindro *m*
cylindrical [səˈlɪndrɪkəl] *adj* **:** cilíndrico
cymbal [ˈsɪmbəl] *n* **:** platillo *m,* címbalo *m*
cynic [ˈsɪnɪk] *n* **:** cínico *m,* -ca *f*
cynical [ˈsɪnɪkəl] *adj* **:** cínico
cynicism [ˈsɪnəˌsɪzəm] *n* **:** cinismo *m*
cypress [ˈsaɪprəs] *n* **:** ciprés *m*
Cypriot [ˈsɪpriət, -ˌɑt] *n* **:** chipriota *mf* — **Cypriot** *adj*
cyst [ˈsɪst] *n* **:** quiste *m*
cytoplasm [ˈsaɪtoˌplæzəm] *n* **:** citoplasma *m*
czar [ˈzɑr, ˈsɑr] *n* **:** zar *m*
czarina [zɑˈriːnə, sɑ-] *n* **:** zarina *f*
Czech [ˈtʃɛk] *n* **1 :** checo *m,* -ca *f* **2 :** checo *m* (idioma) — **Czech** *adj*
Czechoslovak [ˌtʃɛkoˈsloːˌvɑk, -ˌvæk] *or* **Czechoslovakian** [-sloˈvɑkiən, -ˈvæ-] *n* **:** checoslovaco *m,* -ca *f* — **Czechoslovak** *or* **Czechoslovakian** *adj*

D

d [ˈdiː] *n, pl* **d's** *or* **ds** [ˈdiːz] **:** cuarta letra del alfabeto inglés
dab[1] [ˈdæb] *vt* **dabbed; dabbing :** darle toques ligeros a, aplicar suavemente
dab[2] *n* **1** BIT **:** toque *m,* pizca *f,* poco *m* <a dab of ointment : un toque de ungüento> **2** PAT **:** toque *m* ligero, golpecito *m*
dabble [ˈdæbəl] *v* **-bled; -bling** *vt* SPATTER **:** salpicar — *vi* **1** SPLASH **:** chapotear **2** TRIFLE **:** jugar, interesarse superficialmente

dabbler [ˈdæbələr] *n* **:** diletante *mf*
dachshund [ˈdɑksˌhʊnt, -ˌhʊnd; ˈdɑksənt, -sənd] *n* **:** perro *m* salchicha
dad [ˈdæd] *n* **:** papá *m fam*
daddy [ˈdædi] *n, pl* **-dies :** papi *m fam*
daffodil [ˈdæfəˌdɪl] *n* **:** narciso *m*
daft [ˈdæft] *adj* **:** tonto, bobo
dagger [ˈdægər] *n* **:** daga *f,* puñal *m*
dahlia [ˈdæljə, ˈdɑl-, ˈdeɪl-] *n* **:** dalia *f*
daily[1] [ˈdeɪli] *adv* **:** a diario, diariamente
daily[2] *adj* **:** diario, cotidiano
daily[3] *n, pl* **-lies :** diario *m,* periódico *m*
daintily [ˈdeɪntəli] *adv* **:** delicadamente, con delicadeza
daintiness [ˈdeɪntinəs] *n* **:** delicadeza *f,* finura *f*
dainty[1] [ˈdeɪnti] *adj* **-tier; -est 1** DELICATE **:** delicado **2** FASTIDIOUS **:** remilgado, melindroso **3** DELICIOUS **:** exquisito, sabroso
dainty[2] *n, pl* **-ties** DELICACY **:** exquisitez *f,* manjar *m*
dairy [ˈdæri] *n, pl* **-ies 1** *or* **dairy store :** lechería *f* **2** *or* **dairy farm :** granja *f* lechera
dairymaid [ˈdæriˌmeɪd] *n* **:** lechera *f*
dairyman [ˈdærimən, -ˌmæn] *n, pl* **-men** [-mən, -ˌmɛn] **:** lechero *m*
dais [ˈdeɪəs] *n* **:** tarima *f,* estrado *m*
daisy [ˈdeɪzi] *n, pl* **-sies :** margarita *f*
dale [ˈdeɪl] *n* **:** valle *m*
dally [ˈdæli] *vi* **-lied; -lying 1** TRIFLE **:** juguetear **2** DAWDLE **:** entretenerse, perder tiempo
dalmatian [dælˈmeɪʃən, dɔl-] *n* **:** dálmata *m*
dam[1] [ˈdæm] *vt* **dammed; damming :** represar, embalsar
dam[2] *n* **1 :** represa *f,* dique *m* **2 :** madre *f* (de animales domésticos)
damage[1] [ˈdæmɪdʒ] *vt* **-aged; -aging :** dañar (un objeto o una máquina), perjudicar (la salud o una reputación)
damage[2] *n* **1 :** daño *m,* perjuicio *m* **2 damages** *npl* **:** daños y perjuicios *mpl*
damask [ˈdæməsk] *n* **:** damasco *m*
dame [ˈdeɪm] *n* LADY **:** dama *f,* señora *f*
damn[1] [ˈdæm] *vt* **1** CONDEMN **:** condenar **2** CURSE **:** maldecir
damn[2] *or* **damned** [ˈdæmd] *adj* **:** condenado *fam,* maldito *fam*
damn[3] *n* **:** pito *m,* bledo *m,* comino *m* <it's not worth a damn : no vale un pito> <I don't give a damn : me importa un comino>
damnable [ˈdæmnəbəl] *adj* **:** condenable, detestable
damnation [dæmˈneɪʃən] *n* **:** condenación *f*
damned[1] [ˈdæmd] *adv* VERY **:** muy
damned[2] *adj* **1** → **damnable 2** REMARKABLE **:** extraordinario
damp[1] [ˈdæmp] *vt* → **dampen**
damp[2] *adj* **:** húmedo
damp[3] *n* MOISTURE **:** humedad *f*
dampen [ˈdæmpən] *vt* **1** MOISTEN **:** humedecer **2** DISCOURAGE **:** desalentar, desanimar
damper [ˈdæmpər] *n* **1 :** regulador *m* de tiro (de una chimenea) **2 :** sordina *f* (de un piano) **3 to put a damper on :** desanimar, apagar (el entusiasmo), enfriar
dampness [ˈdæmpnəs] *n* **:** humedad *f*
damsel [ˈdæmzəl] *n* **:** damisela *f*
dance[1] [ˈdænts] *v* **danced; dancing :** bailar
dance[2] *n* **:** baile *m*
dancer [ˈdæntsər] *n* **:** bailarín *m,* -rina *f*
dandelion [ˈdændəlˌaɪən] *n* **:** diente *m* de león
dandruff [ˈdændrəf] *n* **:** caspa *f*
dandy[1] [ˈdændi] *adj* **-dier; -est :** excelente, magnífico, macanudo *fam*
dandy[2] *n, pl* **-dies 1** FOP **:** dandi *m* **2 :** algo *m* excelente <this new program is a dandy : este programa nuevo es algo excelente>
Dane [ˈdeɪn] *n* **:** danés *m,* -nesa *f*
Danish[1] [ˈdeɪnɪʃ] *adj* **:** danés
Danish[2] *n* **:** danés *m* (idioma)
danger [ˈdeɪndʒər] *n* **:** peligro *m*
dangerous [ˈdeɪndʒərəs] *adj* **:** peligroso
dangle [ˈdæŋgəl] *v* **-gled; -gling** *vi* HANG **:** colgar, pender — *vt* **1** SWING **:** hacer oscilar **2** PROFFER **:** ofrecer (como incentivo) **3 to keep someone dangling :** dejar a alguien en suspenso
dank [ˈdæŋk] *adj* **:** frío y húmedo
dapper [ˈdæpər] *adj* **:** pulcro, atildado
dappled [ˈdæpəld] *adj* **:** moteado <a dappled horse : un caballo rodado>
dare[1] [ˈdær] *v* **dared; daring** *vi* **:** osar, atreverse <how dare you! : ¡cómo te atreves!> — *vt* **1** CHALLENGE **:** desafiar, retar **2 to dare to do something :** atreverse a hacer algo, osar hacer algo
dare[2] *n* **:** desafío *m,* reto *m*
daredevil [ˈdærˌdɛvəl] *n* **:** persona *f* temeraria
daring[1] [ˈdærɪŋ] *adj* **:** osado, atrevido, audaz
daring[2] *n* **:** arrojo *m,* coraje *m,* audacia *f*
dark [ˈdɑrk] *adj* **1 :** oscuro (dícese del ambiente o de los colores), moreno (dícese del pelo o de la piel) **2** SOMBER **:** sombrío, triste
darken [ˈdɑrkən] *vt* **1** DIM **:** oscurecer **2** SADDEN **:** entristecer — *vi* **:** ensombrecerse, nublarse
darkly [ˈdɑrkli] *adv* **1** DIMLY **:** oscuramente **2** GLOOMILY **:** tristemente **3** MYSTERIOUSLY **:** misteriosamente, enigmáticamente
darkness [ˈdɑrknəs] *n* **:** oscuridad *f,* tinieblas *f*
darling[1] [ˈdɑrlɪŋ] *adj* **1** BELOVED **:** querido, amado **2** CHARMING **:** encantador, mono *fam*

darling[2] *n* **1** BELOVED : querido *m,* -da *f;* amado *m,* -da *f;* cariño *m,* -ña *f* **2** FAVORITE : preferido *m,* -da *f;* favorito *m,* -ta *f*

darn[1] ['dɑrn] *vt* : zurcir

darn[2] *n* **1** : zurcido *m* **2** → **damn**[3]

dart[1] ['dɑrt] *vt* THROW : lanzar, tirar — *vi* DASH : lanzarse, precipitarse

dart[2] *n* **1** : dardo *m* **2 darts** *npl* : juego *m* de dardos

dash[1] ['dæʃ] *vt* **1** SMASH : romper, estrellar **2** HURL : arrojar, lanzar **3** SPLASH : salpicar **4** FRUSTRATE : frustrar **5 to dash off** : hacer (algo) rápidamente — *vi* **1** SMASH : romperse, estrellarse **2** DART : lanzarse, irse apresuradamente

dash[2] *n* **1** BURST, SPLASH : arranque *m,* salpicadura *f* (de aguas) **2** : guión *m* largo (signo de puntuación) **3** DROP : gota *f,* pizca *f* **4** VERVE : brío *m* **5** RACE : carrera *f* <a 100-meter dash : una carrera de 100 metros> **6 to make a dash for it** : precipitarse (hacia), echarse a correr **7** → **dashboard**

dashboard ['dæʃ,bord] *n* : tablero *m* de instrumentos

dashing ['dæʃɪŋ] *adj* : gallardo, apuesto

data ['deɪtə, 'dæ-, 'dɑ-] *ns & pl* : datos *mpl,* información *f*

database ['deɪtə,beɪs, 'dæ-, 'dɑ-] *n* : base *f* de datos

date[1] ['deɪt] *v* **dated; dating** *vt* **1** : fechar (una carta, etc.), datar (un objeto) <it was dated June 9 : estaba fechada el 9 de junio> **2** : salir con <she's dating my brother : sale con mi hermano> — *vi* : datar

date[2] *n* **1** : fecha *f* <to date : hasta la fecha> **2** EPOCH, PERIOD : época *f,* período *m* **3** APPOINTMENT : cita *f* **4** COMPANION : acompañante *mf* **5** : dátil *m* (fruta)

dated ['deɪt̬əd] *adj* OUT-OF-DATE : anticuado, pasado de moda

datum ['deɪt̬əm, 'dæ-, 'dɑ-] *n, pl* **-ta** [-t̬ə] *or* **-tums** : dato *m*

daub[1] ['dɔb] *vt* : embadurnar

daub[2] *n* : mancha *f*

daughter ['dɔt̬ər] *n* : hija *f*

daughter-in-law ['dɔt̬ərɪn,lɔ] *n, pl* **daughters-in-law** : nuera *f,* hija *f* política

daunt ['dɔnt] *vt* : amilanar, acobardar, intimidar

dauntless ['dɔntləs] *adj* : intrépido, impávido

davenport ['dævən,port] *n* : sofá *m*

dawdle ['dɔdəl] *vi* **-dled; -dling 1** DALLY : demorarse, entretenerse, perder tiempo **2** LOITER : vagar, holgazanear, haraganear

dawn[1] ['dɔn] *vi* **1** : amanecer, alborear, despuntar <Saturday dawned clear and bright : el sábado amaneció claro y luminoso> **2 to dawn on** : hacerse obvio <it dawned on me that she was right : me di cuenta de que tenía razón>

dawn[2] *n* **1** DAYBREAK : amanecer *m,* alba *f* **2** BEGINNING : albor *m,* comienzo *m* <the dawn of history : los albores de la historia> **3 from dawn to dusk** : de sol a sol

day ['deɪ] *n* **1** : día *m* **2** DATE : fecha *f* **3** TIME : día *m,* tiempo *m* <in olden days : antaño> **4** WORKDAY : jornada *f* laboral

daybreak ['deɪ,breɪk] *n* : alba *f,* amanecer *m*

day care *n* : servicio *m* de guardería infantil

daydream[1] ['deɪ,dri:m] *vi* : soñar despierto, fantasear

daydream[2] *n* : ensueño *m,* ensoñación *f,* fantasía *f*

daylight ['deɪ,laɪt] *n* **1** : luz *f* del día <in broad daylight : a plena luz del día> **2** → **daybreak 3** → **daytime**

daylight saving time *n* : hora *f* de verano

daytime ['deɪ,taɪm] *n* : horas *fpl* diurnas, día *m*

daze[1] ['deɪz] *vt* **dazed; dazing 1** STUN : aturdir **2** DAZZLE : deslumbrar, ofuscar

daze[2] *n* **1** : aturdimiento *m* **2 in a daze** : aturdido, atonado

dazzle[1] ['dæzəl] *vt* **-zled; -zling** : deslumbrar, ofuscar

dazzle[2] *n* : resplandor *m,* brillo *m*

DDT [,di:,di:'ti:] *n* : DDT *m*

deacon ['di:kən] *n* : diácono *m*

dead[1] ['dɛd] *adv* **1** ABRUPTLY : repentinamente, súbitamente <to stop dead : parar en seco> **2** ABSOLUTELY : absolutamente <I'm dead certain : estoy absolutamente seguro> **3** DIRECTLY : justo <dead ahead : justo adelante>

dead[2] *adj* **1** LIFELESS : muerto **2** NUMB : entumecido **3** INDIFFERENT : indiferente, frío **4** INACTIVE : inactivo <a dead volcano : un volcán inactivo> **5** : desconectado (dícese del teléfono), descargado (dícese de una batería) **6** EXHAUSTED : agotado, derrengado, muerto **7** OBSOLETE : obsoleto, muerto <a dead language : una lengua muerta> **8** EXACT : exacto <in the dead center : justo en el blanco>

dead[3] *n* **1 the dead** : los muertos **2 in the dead of night** : a las altas horas de la noche **3 in the dead of winter** : en pleno invierno

deadbeat ['dɛd,bi:t] *n* **1** LOAFER : vago *m,* -ga *f;* holgazán *m,* -zana *f* **2** FREELOADER : gorrón *m,* -rrona *f fam;* gorrero *m,* -ra *f fam*

deaden ['dɛdən] *vt* **1** : atenuar (un dolor), entorpecer (sensaciones) **2** DULL : deslustrar **3** DISPIRIT : desanimar **4** MUFFLE : amortiguar, reducir (sonidos)

dead-end ['dɛd'ɛnd] *adj* **1** : sin salida <dead-end street : calle sin salida> **2** : sin futuro <a dead-end job : un trabajo sin porvenir>

dead end *n* : callejón *m* sin salida

dead heat *n* **:** empate *m*
deadline [ˈdɛdˌlaɪn] *n* **:** fecha *f* límite, fecha *f* tope, plazo *m* (determinado)
deadlock[1] [ˈdɛdˌlɑk] *vt* **:** estancar — *vi* **:** estancarse, llegar a punto muerto
deadlock[2] *n* **:** punto *m* muerto, impasse *m*
deadly[1] [ˈdɛdli] *adv* **:** extremadamente, sumamente <deadly serious : muy en serio>
deadly[2] *adj* **-lier; -est 1** LETHAL **:** mortal, letal, mortífero **2** ACCURATE **:** certero, preciso <a deadly aim : una puntería infalible> **3** CAPITAL **:** capital <the seven deadly sins : los siete pecados capitales> **4** DULL **:** funesto, aburrido **5** EXTREME **:** extremo, absoluto <a deadly calm : una calma absoluta>
deadpan[1] [ˈdɛdˌpæn] *adv* **:** de manera inexpresiva, sin expresión
deadpan[2] *adj* **:** inexpresivo, impasible
deaf [ˈdɛf] *adj* **:** sordo
deafen [ˈdɛfən] *vt* **-ened; -ening :** ensordecer
deaf–mute [ˈdɛfˈmjuːt] *n* **:** sordomudo *m*, -da *f*
deafness [ˈdɛfnəs] *n* **:** sordera *f*
deal[1] [ˈdiːl] *v* **dealt; dealing** *vt* **1** APPORTION **:** repartir <to deal justice : repartir la justicia> **2** DISTRIBUTE **:** repartir, dar (naipes) **3** DELIVER **:** asestar, propinar <to deal a blow : asestar un golpe> — *vi* **1 :** dar, repartir (en juegos de naipes) **2 to deal in :** comerciar en, traficar con (drogas) **3 to deal with** CONCERN **:** tratar de, tener que ver con <the book deals with poverty : el libro trata de la pobreza> **4 to deal with** HANDLE **:** tratar (con), encargarse de **5 to deal with** TREAT **:** tratar <the judge dealt with him severely : el juez lo trató con severidad> **6 to deal with** ACCEPT **:** aceptar (una situación o desgracia)
deal[2] *n* **1 :** reparto *m* (de naipes) **2** AGREEMENT, TRANSACTION **:** trato *m*, acuerdo *m*, transacción *f* **3** TREATMENT **:** trato *m* <he got a raw deal : le hicieron una injusticia> **4** BARGAIN **:** ganga *f*, oferta *f* **5 a good deal** *or* **a great deal :** mucho, una gran cantidad
dealer [ˈdiːlər] *n* **:** comerciante *mf*, traficante *mf*
dealings [ˈdiːlɪŋz] *npl* **1 :** relaciones *fpl* (personales) **2** TRANSACTIONS **:** negocios *mpl*, transacciones *fpl*
dean [ˈdiːn] *n* **1 :** deán *m* (del clero) **2 :** decano *m*, -na *f* (de una facultad o profesión)
dear[1] [ˈdɪr] *adj* **1** ESTEEMED, LOVED **:** querido, estimado <a dear friend : un amigo querido> <Dear Sir : Estimado Señor> **2** COSTLY **:** caro, costoso
dear[2] *n* **:** querido *m*, -da *f*; amado *m*, -da *f*
dearly [ˈdɪrli] *adv* **1 :** mucho <I love them dearly : los quiero mucho> **2 :** caro <to pay dearly : pagar caro>
dearth [ˈdərθ] *n* **:** escasez *f*, carestía *f*
death [ˈdɛθ] *n* **1 :** muerte *f*, fallecimiento *m* <to be the death of : matar> **2** FATALITY **:** víctima *f* (mortal); muerto *m*, -ta *f* **3** END **:** fin *m* <the death of civilization : el fin de la civilización>
deathbed [ˈdɛθˌbɛd] *n* **:** lecho *m* de muerte
deathblow [ˈdɛθˌbloː] *n* **:** golpe *m* mortal
deathless [ˈdɛθləs] *adj* **:** eterno, inmortal
deathly [ˈdɛθli] *adj* **:** de muerte, sepulcral (dícese del silencio), cadavérico (dícese de la palidez)
debacle [dɪˈbɑkəl, -ˈbæ-] *n* **:** desastre *m*, debacle *m*, fiasco *m*
debar [diˈbɑr] *vt* **-barred; -barring :** excluir, prohibir
debase [diˈbeɪs] *vt* **-based; -basing :** degradar, envilecer
debasement [diˈbeɪsmənt] *n* **:** degradación *f*, envilecimiento *m*
debatable [diˈbeɪtəbəl] *adj* **:** discutible
debate[1] [diˈbeɪt] *vt* **-bated; -bating :** debatir, discutir
debate[2] *n* **:** debate *m*, discusión *f*
debauch [diˈbɔtʃ] *vt* **:** pervertir, corromper
debauchery [diˈbɔtʃəri] *n, pl* **-eries :** libertinaje *m*, disipación *f*, intemperancia *f*
debilitate [diˈbɪləˌteɪt] *vt* **-tated; -tating :** debilitar
debility [diˈbɪləti] *n, pl* **-ties :** debilidad *f*
debit[1] [ˈdɛbɪt] *vt* **:** adeudar, cargar, debitar
debit[2] *n* **:** débito *m*, cargo *m*, debe *m*
debonair [ˌdɛbəˈnær] *adj* **:** elegante y desenvuelto, apuesto
debris [dəˈbriː, deɪ-; ˈdeɪˌbriː] *n, pl* **-bris** [-ˈbriːz, -ˌbriːz] **1** RUBBLE, RUINS **:** escombros *mpl*, ruinas *fpl*, restos *mpl* **2** RUBBISH **:** basura *f*, deshechos *mpl*
debt [ˈdɛt] *n* **1 :** deuda *f* <to pay a debt : saldar una deuda> **2** INDEBTEDNESS **:** endeudamiento *m*
debtor [ˈdɛtər] *n* **:** deudor *m*, -dora *f*
debunk [diˈbʌŋk] *vt* DISCREDIT **:** desacreditar, desprestigiar
debut[1] [deɪˈbjuː, ˈdeɪˌbjuː] *vi* **:** debutar
debut[2] *n* **1 :** debut *m* (de un actor), estreno *m* (de una obra) **2 :** debut *m*, presentación *f* (en sociedad)
debutante [ˈdɛbjʊˌtɑnt] *n* **:** debutante *f*
decade [ˈdɛˌkeɪd, dɛˈkeɪd] *n* **:** década *f*
decadence [ˈdɛkədənts] *n* **:** decadencia *f*
decadent [ˈdɛkədənt] *adj* **:** decadente
decal [ˈdiːˌkæl, diˈkæl] *n* **:** calcomanía *f*

decamp [di'kæmp] *vi* : irse, largarse *fam*

decant [di'kænt] *vt* : decantar

decanter [di'kæntər] *n* : licorera *f,* garrafa *f*

decapitate [di'kæpə,teɪt] *vt* **-tated; -tating** : decapitar

decay[1] [di'keɪ] *vi* **1** DECOMPOSE : descomponerse, pudrirse **2** DETERIORATE : deteriorarse **3** : cariarse (dícese de los dientes)

decay[2] *n* **1** DECOMPOSITION : descomposición *f* **2** DECLINE, DETERIORATION : decadencia *f,* deterioro *m* **3** : caries *f* (de los dientes)

decease[1] [di'si:s] *vi* **-ceased; -ceasing** : morir, fallecer

decease[2] *n* : fallecimiento *m,* defunción *f,* deceso *m*

deceit [di'si:t] *n* **1** DECEPTION : engaño *m* **2** DISHONESTY : deshonestidad *f*

deceitful [di'si:tfəl] *adj* : falso, embustero, engañoso, mentiroso

deceitfully [di'si:tfəli] *adv* : con engaño, con falsedad

deceitfulness [di'si:tfəlnəs] *n* : falsedad *f,* engaño *m*

deceive [di'si:v] *vt* **-ceived; -ceiving** : engañar, burlar

deceiver [di'si:vər] *n* : impostor *m,* -tora *f*

decelerate [di'sɛlə,reɪt] *vi* **-ated; -ating** : reducir la velocidad, desacelerar

December [di'sɛmbər] *n* : diciembre *m*

decency ['disəntsi] *n, pl* **-cies** : decencia *f,* decoro *m*

decent ['di:sənt] *adj* **1** CORRECT, PROPER : decente, decoroso, correcto **2** CLOTHED : vestido, presentable **3** MODEST : púdico, modesto **4** ADEQUATE : decente, adecuado <decent wages : paga adecuada>

decently ['di:səntli] *adv* : decentemente

deception [di'sɛpʃən] *n* : engaño *m*

deceptive [di'sɛptɪv] *adj* : engañoso, falaz — **deceptively** *adv*

decibel ['dɛsəbəl, -,bɛl] *n* : decibelio *m*

decide [di'saɪd] *v* **-cided; -ciding** *vt* **1** CONCLUDE : decidir, llegar a la conclusión de <he decided what to do : decidió qué iba a hacer> **2** DETERMINE : decidir, determinar <one blow decided the fight : un solo golpe determinó la pelea> **3** CONVINCE : decidir <her pleas decided me to help : sus súplicas me decidieron a ayudarla> **4** RESOLVE : resolver — *vi* : decidirse

decided [di'saɪdəd] *adj* **1** UNQUESTIONABLE : indudable **2** RESOLUTE : decidido, resuelto — **decidedly** *adv*

deciduous [di'sɪdʒʊəs] *adj* : caduco, de hoja caduca

decimal[1] ['dɛsəməl] *adj* : decimal

decimal[2] *n* : número *m* decimal

decipher [di'saɪfər] *vt* : descifrar — **decipherable** [-əbəl] *adj*

decision [dɪ'sɪʒən] *n* : decisión *f,* determinación *f* <to make a decision : tomar una decisión>

decisive [dɪ'saɪsɪv] *adj* **1** DECIDING : decisivo <the decisive vote : el voto decisivo> **2** CONCLUSIVE : decisivo, concluyente, contundente <a decisive victory : una victoria contundente> **3** RESOLUTE : decidido, resuelto, firme

decisively [dɪ'saɪsɪvli] *adv* : con decisión, de manera decisiva

decisiveness [dɪ'saɪsɪvnəs] *n* **1** FORCEFULNESS : contundencia *f* **2** RESOLUTION : firmeza *f,* decisión *f,* determinación *f*

deck[1] ['dɛk] *vt* **1** FLOOR : tumbar, derribar <she decked him with one blow : lo tumbó de un solo golpe> **2 to deck out** : adornar, engalanar

deck[2] *n* **1** : cubierta *f* (de un barco) **2** *or* **deck of cards** : baraja *f* (de naipes)

declaim [di'kleɪm] *v* : declamar

declaration [,dɛklə'reɪʃən] *n* : declaración *f,* pronunciamiento *m* (oficial)

declare [di'klær] *vt* **-clared; -claring** : declarar, manifestar <to declare war : declarar la guerra> <they declared their support : manifestaron su apoyo>

decline[1] [di'klaɪn] *v* **-clined; -clining** *vi* **1** DESCEND : descender **2** DETERIORATE : deteriorarse, decaer <her health is declining : su salud se está deteriorando> **3** DECREASE : disminuir, decrecer, decaer **4** REFUSE : rehusar — *vt* **1** INFLECT : declinar **2** REFUSE, TURN DOWN : declinar, rehusar

decline[2] *n* **1** DETERIORATION : decadencia *f,* deterioro *m* **2** DECREASE : disminución *f,* descenso *m* **3** SLOPE : declive *m,* pendiente *f*

decode [di'ko:d] *vt* **-coded; -coding** : descifrar (un mensaje), descodificar (una señal)

decompose [,di:kəm'po:z] *v* **-posed; -posing** *vt* **1** BREAK DOWN : descomponer **2** ROT : descomponer, pudrir — *vi* : descomponerse, pudrirse

decomposition [,di:,kɑmpə'zɪʃən] *n* : descomposición *f*

decongestant [,di:kən'dʒɛstənt] *n* : descongestionante *m*

decor *or* **décor** [deɪ'kɔr, 'deɪ,kɔr] *n* : decoración *f*

decorate ['dɛkə,reɪt] *vt* **-rated; -rating 1** ADORN : decorar, adornar **2** : condecorar <he was decorated for bravery : lo condecoraron por valor>

decoration [,dɛkə'reɪʃən] *n* **1** ADORNMENT : decoración *f,* adorno *m* **2** : condecoración *f* (de honor)

decorative ['dɛkərət̬ɪv, -,reɪ-] *adj* : decorativo, ornamental, de adorno

decorator ['dɛkə,reɪt̬ər] *n* : decorador *m,* -dora *f*

decorum [di'korəm] *n* : decoro *m*

decoy[1] ['diː,kɔɪ, di'-] *vt* : atraer (con señuelo)

decoy[2] *n* : señuelo *m,* reclamo *m,* cimbel *m*

decrease[1] [di'kriːs] *v* **-creased; -creasing** *vi* : decrecer, disminuir, bajar — *vt* : reducir, disminuir

decrease[2] ['diː,kriːs] *n* : disminución *f,* descenso *m,* bajada *f*

decree[1] [di'kriː] *vt* **-creed; -creeing** : decretar

decree[2] *n* : decreto *m*

decrepit [di'krɛpɪt] *adj* **1** FEEBLE : decrépito, débil **2** DILAPIDATED : deteriorado, ruinoso

decry [di'kraɪ] *vt* **-cried; -crying** : censurar, criticar

dedicate ['dɛdɪ,keɪt] *vt* **-cated; -cating 1** : dedicar <she dedicated the book to Carlos : le dedicó el libro a Carlos> **2** : consagrar, dedicar <to dedicate one's life : consagrar uno su vida>

dedication [,dɛdɪ'keɪʃən] *n* **1** DEVOTION : dedicación *f,* devoción *f* **2** : dedicatoria *f* (de un libro, una canción, etc.) **3** CONSECRATION : dedicación *f*

deduce [di'duːs, -'djuːs] *vt* **-duced; -ducing** : deducir, inferir

deduct [di'dʌkt] *vt* : deducir, descontar, restar

deductible [di'dʌktəbəl] *adj* : deducible

deduction [di'dʌkʃən] *n* : deducción *f*

deed[1] ['diːd] *vt* : ceder, transferir

deed[2] *n* **1** ACT : acto *m,* acción *f,* hecho *m* <a good deed : una buena acción> **2** FEAT : hazaña *f,* proeza *f* **3** TITLE : escritura *f,* título *m*

deem ['diːm] *vt* : considerar, juzgar

deep[1] ['diːp] *adv* : hondo, profundamente <to dig deep : cavar hondo>

deep[2] *adj* **1** : hondo, profundo <the deep end : la parte honda> <a deep wound : una herida profunda> **2** WIDE : ancho **3** INTENSE : profundo, intenso **4** DARK : intenso, subido <deep red : rojo subido> **5** LOW : profundo <a deep tone : un tono profundo> **6** ABSORBED : absorto <deep in thought : absorto en la meditación>

deep[3] *n* **1 the deep** : lo profundo, el piélago **2 the deep of night** : lo más profundo de la noche

deepen ['diːpən] *vt* **1** : ahondar, profundizar **2** INTENSIFY : intensificar — *vi* **1** : hacerse más profundo **2** INTENSIFY : intensificarse

deeply ['diːpli] *adv* : hondo, profundamente <I'm deeply sorry : lo siento sinceramente>

deep–seated ['diːp'siːt̬əd] *adj* : profundamente arraigado, enraizado

deer ['dɪr] *ns & pl* : ciervo *m,* venado *m*

deerskin ['dɪr,skɪn] *n* : piel *f* de venado

deface [di'feɪs] *vt* **-faced; -facing** MAR : desfigurar

defacement [di'feɪsmənt] *n* : desfiguración *f*

defamation [,dɛfə'meɪʃən] *n* : difamación *f*

defamatory [di'fæmə,tori] *adj* : difamatorio

defame [di'feɪm] *vt* **-famed; -faming** : difamar, calumniar

default[1] [di'fɔlt, 'diː,fɔlt] *vi* **1** : no cumplir (con una obligación), no pagar **2** : no presentarse (en un tribunal)

default[2] *n* **1** NEGLECT : omisión *f,* negligencia *f* **2** NONPAYMENT : impago *m,* falta *f* de pago **3 to win by default** : ganar por abandono

defaulter [di'fɔltər] *n* : moroso *m,* -sa *f;* rebelde *mf* (en un tribunal)

defeat[1] [di'fiːt] *vt* **1** FRUSTRATE : frustrar **2** BEAT : vencer, derrotar

defeat[2] *n* : derrota *f,* rechazo *m* (de legislación), fracaso *m* (de planes, etc.)

defecate ['dɛfɪ,keɪt] *vi* **-cated; -cating** : defecar

defect[1] [di'fɛkt] *vi* : desertar

defect[2] ['diː,fɛkt, di'fɛkt] *n* : defecto *m*

defection [di'fɛkʃən] *n* : deserción *f,* defección *f*

defective [di'fɛktɪv] *adj* **1** FAULTY : defectuoso **2** DEFICIENT : deficiente

defector [di'fɛktər] *n* : desertor *m,* -tora *f*

defend [di'fɛnd] *vt* : defender

defendant [di'fɛndənt] *n* : acusado *m,* -da *f;* demandado *m,* -da *f*

defender [di'fɛndər] *n* **1** ADVOCATE : defensor *m,* -sora *f* **2** : defensa *mf* (en deportes)

defense [di'fɛnts, 'diː,fɛnts] *n* : defensa *f*

defenseless [di'fɛntsləs] *adj* : indefenso

defensive[1] [di'fɛntsɪv] *adj* : defensivo

defensive[2] *n* **on the defensive** : a la defensiva

defer [di'fər] *v* **-ferred; -ferring** *vt* POSTPONE : diferir, aplazar, posponer — *vi* **to defer to** : deferir a

deference ['dɛfərənts] *n* : deferencia *f*

deferential [,dɛfə'rɛntʃəl] *adj* : respetuoso

deferment [di'fərmənt] *n* : aplazamiento *m*

defiance [di'faɪənts] *n* : desafío *m*

defiant [di'faɪənt] *adj* : desafiante, insolente

deficiency [di'fɪʃəntsi] *n, pl* **-cies** : deficiencia *f,* carencia *f*

deficient [di'fɪʃənt] *adj* : deficiente, carente

deficit ['dɛfəsɪt] *n* : déficit *m*

defile [di'faɪl] *vt* **-filed; -filing 1** DIRTY : ensuciar, manchar **2** CORRUPT : corromper **3** DESECRATE, PROFANE : profanar **4** DISHONOR : deshonrar

defilement [di'faɪlmənt] *n* **1** DESECRATION : profanación *f* **2** CORRUPTION

: corrupción *f* 3 CONTAMINATION : contaminación *f*
define [di'faɪn] *vt* **-fined; -fining** 1 BOUND : delimitar, demarcar 2 CLARIFY : aclarar, definir 3 : definir <to define a word : definir una palabra>
definite ['dɛfənɪt] *adj* 1 CERTAIN : definido, determinado 2 CLEAR : claro, explícito 3 UNQUESTIONABLE : seguro, incuestionable
definite article *n* : artículo *m* definido
definitely ['dɛfənɪtli] *adv* 1 DOUBTLESSLY : indudablemente, sin duda 2 DEFINITIVELY : definitivamente, seguramente
definition [,dɛfə'nɪʃən] *n* : definición *f*
definitive [di'fɪnət̬ɪv] *adj* 1 CONCLUSIVE : definitivo, decisivo 2 AUTHORITATIVE : de autoridad, autorizado
deflate [di'fleɪt] *v* **-flated; -flating** *vt* 1 : desinflar (una llanta, etc.) 2 REDUCE : rebajar <to deflate one's ego : bajarle los humos a uno> — *vi* : desinflarse
deflect [di'flɛkt] *vt* : desviar — *vi* : desviarse
defoliant [di'foːliənt] *n* : defoliante *m*
deform [di'fɔrm] *vt* : deformar
deformed [di'fɔrmd] *adj* : deforme
deformity [di'fɔrmət̬i] *n, pl* **-ties** : deformidad *f*
defraud [di'frɔd] *vt* : estafar, defraudar
defray [di'freɪ] *vt* : sufragar, costear
defrost [di'frɔst] *vt* : descongelar, deshelar — *vi* : descongelarse, deshelarse
deft ['dɛft] *adj* : hábil, diestro — **deftly** *adv*
defunct [di'fʌŋkt] *adj* 1 DECEASED : difunto, fallecido 2 EXTINCT : extinto, fenecido
defy [di'faɪ] *vt* **-fied; -fying** 1 CHALLENGE : desafiar, retar 2 DISOBEY : desobedecer 3 RESIST : resistir, hacer imposible, hacer inútil
degenerate¹ [di'dʒɛnə,reɪt] *vi* **-ated; -ating** : degenerar
degenerate² [di'dʒɛnərət] *adj* : degenerado
degeneration [di,dʒɛnə'reɪʃən] *n* : degeneración *f*
degradation [,dɛgrə'deɪʃən] *n* : degradación *f*
degrade [di'greɪd] *vt* **-graded; -grading** 1 : degradar, envilecer 2 **to degrade oneself** : rebajarse
degree [di'griː] *n* 1 EXTENT : grado *m* <a third degree burn : una quemadura de tercer grado> 2 : título *m* (de enseñanza superior) 3 : grado *m* (de un círculo, de la temperatura) 4 **by degrees** : gradualmente, poco a poco
dehydrate [di'haɪ,dreɪt] *v* **-drated; -drating** *vt* : deshidratar — *vi* : deshidratarse
dehydration [,diːhaɪ'dreɪʃən] *n* : deshidratación *f*
deice [,diː'aɪs] *vt* **-iced; -icing** : deshelar, descongelar
deify ['diːə,faɪ, 'deɪ-] *vt* **-fied; -fying** : deificar
deign ['deɪn] *vi* : dignarse, condescender
deity ['diːət̬i, 'deɪ-] *n, pl* **-ties** 1 **the Deity** : Dios *m* 2 GOD, GODDESS : deidad *f;* dios *m,* diosa *f*
dejected [di'dʒɛktəd] *adj* : abatido, desalentado, desanimado
dejection [di'dʒɛkʃən] *n* : abatimiento *m,* desaliento *m,* desánimo *m*
delay¹ [di'leɪ] *vt* 1 POSTPONE : posponer, postergar 2 HOLD UP : retrasar, demorar — *vi* : tardar, demorar
delay² *n* 1 LATENESS : tardanza *f* 2 HOLDUP : demora *f,* retraso *m*
delectable [di'lɛktəbəl] *adj* 1 DELICIOUS : delicioso, exquisito 2 DELIGHTFUL : encantador
delegate¹ ['dɛlɪ,geɪt] *v* **-gated; -gating** : delegar
delegate² ['dɛlɪgət, -,geɪt] *n* : delegado *m,* -da *f*
delegation [,dɛlɪ'geɪʃən] *n* : delegación *f*
delete [di'liːt] *vt* **-leted; -leting** : suprimir, tachar, eliminar
deletion [di'liːʃən] *n* : supresión *f,* tachadura *f,* eliminación *f*
deliberate¹ [dɪ'lɪbə,reɪt] *v* **-ated; -ating** *vt* : deliberar sobre, reflexionar sobre, considerar — *vi* : deliberar
deliberate² [dɪ'lɪbərət] *adj* 1 CONSIDERED : reflexionado, premeditado 2 INTENTIONAL : deliberado, intencional 3 SLOW : lento, pausado
deliberately [dɪ'lɪbərətli] *adv* 1 INTENTIONALLY : adrede, a propósito 2 SLOWLY : pausadamente, lentamente
deliberation [dɪ,lɪbə'reɪʃən] *n* 1 CONSIDERATION : deliberación *f,* consideración *f* 2 SLOWNESS : lentitud *f*
delicacy ['dɛlɪkəsi] *n, pl* **-cies** 1 : manjar *m,* exquisitez *f* <caviar is a real delicacy : el caviar es un verdadero manjar> 2 FINENESS : delicadeza *f* 3 FRAGILITY : fragilidad *f*
delicate ['dɛlɪkət] *adj* 1 SUBTLE : delicado <a delicate fragrance : una fragancia delicada> 2 DAINTY : delicado, primoroso, fino 3 FRAGILE : frágil 4 SENSITIVE : delicado <a delicate matter : un asunto delicado>
delicately ['dɛlɪkətli] *adv* : delicadamente, con delicadeza
delicatessen [,dɛlɪkə'tɛsən] *n* : charcutería *f,* fiambrería *f,* salchichonería *f Mex*
delicious [di'lɪʃəs] *adj* : delicioso, exquisito, rico — **deliciously** *adv*
delight¹ [dɪ'laɪt] *vt* : deleitar, encantar — *vi* **to delight in** : deleitarse con, complacerse en
delight² *n* 1 JOY : placer *m,* deleite *m,* gozo *m* 2 : encanto *m* <your garden is a delight : su jardín es un encanto>

delightful [dɪˈlaɪtfəl] *adj* : delicioso, encantador
delightfully [dɪˈlaɪtfəli] *adv* : de manera encantadora, de maravilla
delineate [diˈlɪni,eɪt] *vt* **-eated; -eating** : delinear, trazar, bosquejar
delinquency [diˈlɪŋkwən*t*si] *n, pl* **-cies** : delincuencia *f*
delinquent¹ [diˈlɪŋkwənt] *adj* **1** : delincuente **2** OVERDUE : vencido y sin pagar, moroso
delinquent² *n* : delincuente *mf* <juvenile delinquent : delincuente juvenil>
delirious [diˈlɪriəs] *adj* : delirante <delirious with joy : loco de alegría>
delirium [diˈlɪriəm] *n* : delirio *m,* desvarío *m*
deliver [diˈlɪvər] *vt* **1** FREE : liberar, librar **2** DISTRIBUTE, HAND : entregar, repartir **3** : asistir en el parto de (un niño) **4** : pronunciar <to deliver a speech : pronunciar un discurso> **5** PROJECT : despachar, lanzar <he delivered a fast ball : lanzó un pelota rápida> **6** DEAL : propinar, asestar <to deliver a blow : asestar un golpe>
deliverance [diˈlɪvərən*t*s] *n* : liberación *f,* rescate *m,* salvación *f*
deliverer [diˈlɪvərər] *n* RESCUER : libertador *m,* -dora *f;* salvador *m,* -dora *f*
delivery [diˈlɪvəri] *n, pl* **-eries 1** LIBERATION : liberación *f* **2** : entrega *f,* reparto *m* <cash on delivery : entrega contra reembolso> <home delivery : servicio a domicilio> **3** CHILDBIRTH : parto *m,* alumbramiento *m* **4** SPEECH : expresión *f* oral, modo *m* de hablar **5** THROW : lanzamiento *m*
dell [ˈdɛl] *n* : hondonada *f,* valle *m* pequeño
delta [ˈdɛltə] *n* : delta *m*
delude [diˈluːd] *vt* **-luded; -luding 1** : engañar **2 to delude oneself** : engañarse
deluge¹ [ˈdɛl,juːdʒ, -,juːʒ] *vt* **-uged; -uging 1** FLOOD : inundar **2** OVERWHELM : abrumar <deluged with requests : abrumado de pedidos>
deluge² *n* **1** FLOOD : inundación *f* **2** DOWNPOUR : aguacero *m* **3** BARRAGE : aluvión *m*
delusion [diˈluːʒən] *n* **1** : ilusión *f* (falsa) **2 delusions of grandeur** : delirios *mpl* de grandeza
deluxe [diˈlʌks, -ˈlʊks] *adj* : de lujo
delve [ˈdɛlv] *vi* **delved; delving 1** DIG : escarbar **2 to delve into** PROBE : cavar en, ahondar en
demand¹ [diˈmænd] *vt* : demandar, exigir, reclamar
demand² *n* **1** REQUEST : petición *f,* pedido *m,* demanda *f* <by popular demand : a petición del público> **2** CLAIM : reclamación *f,* exigencia *f* **3** MARKET : demanda *f* <supply and demand : la oferta y la demanda>
demarcation [,diː,mɑrˈkeɪʃən] *n* : demarcación *f,* deslinde *m*
demean [diˈmiːn] *vt* : degradar, rebajar
demeanor [diˈmiːnər] *n* : comportamiento *m,* conducta *f*
demented [diˈmɛntəd] *adj* : demente, loco
demerit [diˈmɛrət] *n* : demérito *m*
demigod [ˈdɛmi,gɑd, -,gɔd] *n* : semidiós *m*
demise [dɪˈmaɪz] *n* **1** DEATH : fallecimiento *m,* deceso *m* **2** END : hundimiento *m,* desaparición *f* (de una institución, etc.)
demitasse [ˈdɛmi,tæs, -,tɑs] *n* : taza *f* pequeña (de café)
demobilization [di,moːbələˈzeɪʃən] *n* : desmovilización *f*
demobilize [diˈmoːbə,laɪz] *vt* **-lized; -lizing** : desmovilizar
democracy [diˈmɑkrəsi] *n, pl* **-cies** : democracia *f*
democrat [ˈdɛmə,kræt] *n* : demócrata *mf*
democratic [,dɛməˈkræt̬ɪk] *adj* : democrático — **democratically** [-t̬ɪkli] *adv*
demolish [diˈmɑlɪʃ] *vt* **1** RAZE : demoler, derribar, arrasar **2** DESTROY : destruir, destrozar
demolition [,dɛməˈlɪʃən, ,diː-] *n* : demolición *f,* derribo *m*
demon [ˈdiːmən] *n* : demonio *m,* diablo *m*
demonstrably [diˈmɑn*t*strəbli] *adv* : manifiestamente, claramente
demonstrate [ˈdɛmən,streɪt] *vt* **-strated; -strating 1** SHOW : demostrar **2** PROVE : probar, demostrar **3** EXPLAIN : explicar, ilustrar
demonstration [,dɛmənˈstreɪʃən] *n* **1** SHOW : muestra *f,* demostración *f* **2** RALLY : manifestación *f*
demonstrative [diˈmɑn*t*strət̬ɪv] *adj* **1** EFFUSIVE : efusivo, expresivo, demostrativo **2** : demostrativo (en lingüística) <demonstrative pronoun : pronombre demostrativo>
demonstrator [ˈdɛmən,streɪt̬ər] *n* **1** : demostrador *m,* -dora *f* (de productos) **2** PROTESTER : manifestante *mf*
demoralize [diˈmɔrə,laɪz] *vt* **-ized; -izing** : desmoralizar
demote [diˈmoːt] *vt* **-moted; -moting** : degradar, bajar de categoría
demotion [diˈmoːʃən] *n* : degradación *f,* descenso *m* de categoría
demur [diˈmər] *vi* **-murred; -murring 1** OBJECT : oponerse **2 to demur at** : ponerle objeciones a (algo)
demure [diˈmjʊr] *adj* : recatado, modesto — **demurely** *adv*
den [ˈdɛn] *n* **1** LAIR : cubil *m,* madriguera *f* **2** HIDEOUT : guarida *f* **3** STUDY : estudio *m,* gabinete *m*
denature [diˈneɪtʃər] *vt* **-tured; -turing** : desnaturalizar
denial [diˈnaɪəl] *n* **1** REFUSAL : rechazo *m,* denegación *f,* negativa *f* **2** REPUDIATION : negación *f* (de una creencia, etc.), rechazo *m*

denim [ˈdɛnəm] *n* **1** : tela *f* vaquera, mezclilla *f Chile, Mex* **2 denims** *npl* → **jeans**

denizen [ˈdɛnəzən] *n* : habitante *mf;* morador *m,* -dora *f*

denomination [dɪˌnɑməˈneɪʃən] *n* **1** FAITH : confesión *f,* fe *f* **2** VALUE : denominación *f,* valor *m* (de una moneda)

denominator [dɪˈnɑməˌneɪt̬ər] *n* : denominador *m*

denote [diˈnoːt] *vt* **-noted; -noting 1** INDICATE, MARK : indicar, denotar, señalar **2** MEAN : significar

denouement [ˌdeɪˌnuːˈmɑ] *n* : desenlace *m*

denounce [diˈnaʊnts] *vt* **-nounced; -nouncing 1** CENSURE : denunciar, censurar **2** ACCUSE : denunciar, acusar, delatar

dense [ˈdɛnts] *adj* **denser; -est 1** THICK : espeso, denso <dense vegetation : vegetación densa> <a dense fog : una niebla espesa> **2** STUPID : estúpido, burro *fam*

densely [ˈdɛntsli] *adv* **1** THICKLY : densamente **2** STUPIDLY : torpemente

denseness [ˈdɛntsnəs] *n* **1** → **density 2** STUPIDITY : estupidez *f*

density [ˈdɛntsət̬i] *n, pl* **-ties** : densidad *f*

dent[1] [ˈdɛnt] *vt* : abollar, mellar

dent[2] *n* : abolladura *f,* mella *f*

dental [ˈdɛntəl] *adj* : dental

dental floss *n* : hilo *m* dental

dentifrice [ˈdɛntəfrɪs] *n* : dentífrico *m,* pasta *f* de dientes

dentist [ˈdɛntɪst] *n* : dentista *mf*

dentistry [ˈdɛntɪstri] *n* : odontología *f*

dentures [ˈdɛntʃərz] *npl* : dentadura *f* postiza

denude [diˈnuːd, -ˈnjuːd] *vt* **-nuded; -nuding** STRIP : desnudar, despojar

denunciation [diˌnʌntsiˈeɪʃən] *n* : denuncia *f,* acusación *f*

deny [diˈnaɪ] *vt* **-nied; -nying 1** REFUTE : desmentir, negar **2** DISOWN, REPUDIATE : negar, renegar de **3** REFUSE : denegar **4 to deny oneself** : privarse, sacrificarse

deodorant [diˈoːdərənt] *n* : desodorante *m*

deodorize [diˈoːdəˌraɪz] *vt* **-ized; -izing** : desodorizar

depart [diˈpɑrt] *vt* : salirse de — *vi* **1** LEAVE : salir, partir, irse **2** DIE : morir

department [diˈpɑrtmənt] *n* **1** DIVISION : sección *f* (de una tienda, una organización, etc.), departamento *m* (de una empresa, una universidad, etc.), ministerio *m* (del gobierno) **2** PROVINCE, SPHERE : esfera *f,* campo *m,* competencia *f*

departmental [diˌpɑrtˈmɛntəl, ˌdiː-] *adj* : departamental

department store *n* : grandes almacenes *mpl*

departure [diˈpɑrtʃər] *n* **1** LEAVING : salida *f,* partida *f* **2** DEVIATION : desviación *f*

depend [diˈpɛnd] *vi* **1** RELY : contar (con), confiar (en) <depend on me! : ¡cuenta conmigo!> **2 to depend on** : depender de <success depends on hard work : el éxito depende de trabajar duro> **3 that depends** : según, eso depende

dependable [diˈpɛndəbəl] *adj* : responsable, digno de confianza, fiable

dependence [diˈpɛndənts] *n* : dependencia *f*

dependency [diˈpɛndəntsi] *n, pl* **-cies 1** → **dependence 2** : posesión *f* (de una unidad política)

dependent[1] [diˈpɛndənt] *adj* : dependiente

dependent[2] *n* : persona *f* a cargo de alguien

depict [diˈpɪkt] *vt* **1** PORTRAY : representar **2** DESCRIBE : describir

depiction [diˈpɪkʃən] *n* : representación *f,* descripción *f*

deplete [diˈpliːt] *vt* **-pleted; -pleting 1** EXHAUST : agotar **2** REDUCE : reducir

depletion [diˈpliːʃən] *n* **1** EXHAUSTION : agotamiento *m* **2** REDUCTION : reducción *f,* disminución *f*

deplorable [diˈplorəbəl] *adj* **1** CONTEMPTIBLE : deplorable, despreciable **2** LAMENTABLE : lamentable

deplore [diˈplor] *vt* **-plored; -ploring 1** REGRET : deplorar, lamentar **2** CONDEMN : condenar, deplorar

deploy [diˈplɔɪ] *vt* : desplegar

deployment [diˈplɔɪmənt] *n* : despliegue *m*

deport [diˈport] *vt* **1** EXPEL : deportar, expulsar (de un país) **2 to deport oneself** BEHAVE : comportarse

deportment [diˈportmənt] *n* : conducta *f,* comportamiento *f*

depose [diˈpoːz] *v* **-posed; -posing** *vt* : deponer

deposit[1] [diˈpɑzət] *vt* **-ited; -iting** : depositar

deposit[2] *n* **1** : depósito *m* (en el banco) **2** DOWN PAYMENT : entrega *f* inicial **3** : depósito *m,* yacimiento *m* (en geología)

depositor [diˈpɑzət̬ər] *n* : depositante *mf*

depository [diˈpɑzəˌtori] *n, pl* **-ries** : almacén *m,* depósito *m*

depot [*in sense 1 usu* ˈdɛˌpoː, *2 usu* ˈdiː-] *n* **1** STOREHOUSE : almacén *m,* depósito *m* **2** STATION, TERMINAL : terminal *mf,* estación *f* (de autobuses, ferrocarriles, etc.)

deprave [diˈpreɪv] *vt* **-praved; -praving** : depravar, pervertir

depraved [diˈpreɪvd] *adj* : depravado, degenerado

depravity [diˈprævət̬i] *n, pl* **-ties** : depravación *f*

depreciate [diˈpriːʃiˌeɪt] *v* **-ated; -ating** *vt* **1** DEVALUE : depreciar, devaluar 2 DISPARAGE : menospreciar, despreciar — *vi* : depreciarse, devaluarse

depreciation [diˌpriːʃiˈeɪʃən] *n* : depreciación *f,* devaluación *f*

depress [diˈprɛs] *vt* **1** PRESS, PUSH : apretar, presionar, pulsar **2** REDUCE : reducir, hacer bajar (precios, ventas, etc.) **3** SADDEN : deprimir, abatir, entristecer **4** DEVALUE : depreciar

depressant¹ [diˈprɛsənt] *adj* : depresivo

depressant² *n* : depresivo *m*

depressed [diˈprɛst] *adj* **1** DEJECTED : deprimido, abatido **2** : deprimido, en crisis (dícese de la economía)

depressing [diˈprɛsɪŋ] *adj* : deprimente, triste

depression [diˈprɛʃən] *n* **1** DESPONDENCY : depresión *f,* abatimiento *m* **2** : depresión (en una superficie) **3** RECESSION : depresión *f* económica, crisis *f*

deprivation [ˌdɛprəˈveɪʃən] *n* : privación *f*

deprive [diˈpraɪv] *vt* **-prived; -priving** : privar

depth [ˈdɛpθ] *n, pl* **depths** [ˈdɛpθs, ˈdɛps] : profundidad *f,* fondo *m* <to study in depth : estudiar a fondo> <in the depths of winter : en pleno invierno>

deputize [ˈdɛpjʊˌtaɪz] *vt* **-tized; -tizing** : nombrar como segundo

deputy [ˈdɛpjʊt̬i] *n, pl* **-ties** : suplente *mf;* sustituto *m,* -ta *f*

derail [diˈreɪl] *v* : descarrilar

derailment [diˈreɪlmənt] *n* : descarrilamiento *m*

derange [diˈreɪndʒ] *vt* **-ranged; -ranging 1** DISARRANGE : desarreglar, desordenar **2** DISTURB, UPSET : trastornar, perturbar **3** MADDEN : enloquecer, volver loco

derangement [diˈreɪndʒmənt] *n* **1** DISTURBANCE, UPSET : trastorno *m* **2** INSANITY : locura *f,* perturbación *f* mental

derby [ˈdərbi] *n, pl* **-bies 1** : derby *m* <the Kentucky Derby : el Derby de Kentucky> **2** : sombrero *m* hongo

deregulate [diˈrɛgjʊˌleɪt] *vt* **-lated; -lating** : desregular

deregulation [diˌrɛgjʊˈleɪʃən] *n* : desregularización *f*

derelict¹ [ˈdɛrəˌlɪkt] *adj* **1** ABANDONED : abandonado, en ruinas **2** REMISS : negligente, remiso

derelict² *n* **1** : propiedad *f* abandonada **2** VAGRANT : vagabundo *m,* -da *f*

deride [diˈraɪd] *vt* **-rided; -riding** : ridiculizar, burlarse de

derision [diˈrɪʒən] *n* : escarnio *m,* irrisión *f,* mofa *f*

derisive [diˈraɪsɪv] *adj* : burlón

derivative¹ [diˈrɪvət̬ɪv] *adj* **1** DERIVED : derivado **2** BANAL : carente de originalidad, banal

derivative² *n* : derivado *m*

derive [diˈraɪv] *v* **-rived; -riving** *vt* **1** OBTAIN : obtener, sacar **2** DEDUCE : deducir, inferir — *vi* : provenir, derivar, proceder

dermatologist [ˌdərməˈtɑlədʒɪst] *n* : dermatólogo *m,* -ga *f*

dermatology [ˌdərməˈtɑlədʒi] *n* : dermatología *f*

derogatory [diˈrɑgəˌtori] *adj* : despectivo, despreciativo

derrick [ˈdɛrɪk] *n* **1** CRANE : grúa *f* **2** : torre *f* de perforación (sobre un pozo de petróleo)

descend [diˈsɛnd] *vt* : descender, bajar — *vi* **1** : descender, bajar <he descended from the platform : descendió del estrado> **2** DERIVE : descender, provenir **3** STOOP : rebajarse <I descended to his level : me rebajé a su nivel> **4 to descend upon** : caer sobre, invadir

descendant¹ [diˈsɛndənt] *adj* : descendente

descendant² *n* : descendiente *mf*

descent [diˈsɛnt] *n* **1** : bajada *f,* descenso *m* <the descent from the mountain : el descenso de la montaña> **2** ANCESTRY : ascendencia *f,* linaje *f* **3** SLOPE : pendiente *f,* cuesta *f* **4** FALL : caída *f* **5** ATTACK : incursión *f,* ataque *m*

describe [diˈskraɪb] *vt* **-scribed; -scribing** : describir

description [diˈskrɪpʃən] *n* : descripción *f*

descriptive [diˈskrɪptɪv] *adj* : descriptivo <descriptive adjective : adjetivo calificativo>

desecrate [ˈdɛsɪˌkreɪt] *vt* **-crated; -crating** : profanar

desecration [ˌdɛsɪˈkreɪʃən] *n* : profanación *f*

desegregate [diˈsɛgrəˌgeɪt] *vt* **-gated; -gating** : eliminar la segregación racial de

desegregation [diˌsɛgrəˈgeɪʃən] *n* : eliminación *f* de la segregación racial

desert¹ [diˈzərt] *vt* : abandonar (una persona o un lugar), desertar de (una causa, etc.) — *vi* : desertar

desert² [ˈdɛzərt] *adj* : desierto <a desert island : una isla desierta>

desert³ *n* **1** [ˈdɛzərt] : desierto *m* (en geografía) **2** [diˈzərt] → **deserts**

deserter [diˈzərt̬ər] *n* : desertor *m,* -tora *f*

desertion [diˈzərʃən] *n* : abandono *m,* deserción *f* (militar)

deserts [diˈzərts] *npl* : merecido *m* <to get one's just deserts : llevarse uno su merecido>

deserve [diˈzərv] *vt* **-served; -serving** : merecer, ser digno de

desiccate [ˈdɛsɪˌkeɪt] *vt* **-cated; -cating** : desecar, deshidratar

design¹ [diˈzaɪn] *vt* **1** DEVISE : diseñar, concebir, idear **2** PLAN : proyectar **3** SKETCH : trazar, bosquejar

design[2] *n* **1** PLAN, SCHEME : plan *m,* proyecto *m* <by design : a propósito, intencionalmente> **2** SKETCH : diseño *m,* bosquejo *m* **3** PATTERN, STYLE : diseño *m,* estilo *m* **4 designs** *npl* INTENTIONS : propósitos *mpl,* designios *mpl*
designate [ˈdɛzɪɡˌneɪt] *vt* **-nated; -nating 1** INDICATE, SPECIFY : indicar, especificar **2** APPOINT : nombrar, designar
designation [ˌdɛzɪɡˈneɪʃən] *n* **1** NAMING : designación *f* **2** NAME : denominación *f,* nombre *m* **3** APPOINTMENT : designación *f,* nombramiento *m*
designer [diˈzaɪnər] *n* : diseñador *m,* -dora *f*
desirability [diˌzaɪrəˈbɪləṭi] *n, pl* **-ties 1** ADVISABILITY : conveniencia *f* **2** ATTRACTIVENESS : atractivo *m*
desirable [diˈzaɪrəbəl] *adj* **1** ADVISABLE : conveniente, aconsejable **2** ATTRACTIVE : deseable, atractivo
desire[1] [diˈzaɪr] *vt* **-sired; -siring 1** WANT : desear **2** REQUEST : rogar, solicitar
desire[2] *n* : deseo *m,* anhelo *m,* ansia *m*
desist [diˈsɪst, -ˈzɪst] *vi* **to desist from** : desistir de, abstenerse de
desk [ˈdɛsk] *n* : escritorio *m,* pupitre *m* (en la escuela)
desolate[1] [ˈdɛsəˌleɪt, -zə-] *vt* **-lated; -lating** : devastar, desolar
desolate[2] [ˈdɛsələt, -zə-] *adj* **1** BARREN : desolado, desierto, yermo **2** DISCONSOLATE : desconsolado, desolado
desolation [ˌdɛsəˈleɪʃən, -zə-] *n* : desolación *f*
despair[1] [diˈspær] *vi* : desesperar, perder las esperanzas
despair[2] *n* : desesperación *f,* desesperanza *f*
desperate [ˈdɛspərət] *adj* **1** HOPELESS : desesperado, sin esperanzas **2** RASH : desesperado, precipitado **3** SERIOUS, URGENT : grave, urgente, apremiante <a desperate need : una necesidad apremiante>
desperately [ˈdɛspərətli] *adv* : desesperadamente, urgentemente
desperation [ˌdɛspəˈreɪʃən] *n* : desesperación *f*
despicable [diˈspɪkəbəl, ˈdɛspɪ-] *adj* : vil, despreciable, infame
despise [diˈspaɪz] *vt* **-spised; -spising** : despreciar
despite [dəˈspaɪt] *prep* : a pesar de, aún con
despoil [diˈspɔɪl] *vt* : saquear
despondency [diˈspɑndəntsi] *n* : desaliento *m,* desánimo *m,* depresión *f*
despondent [diˈspɑndənt] *adj* : desalentado, desanimado
despot [ˈdɛspət, -ˌpɑt] *n* : déspota *mf;* tirano *m,* -na *f*
despotic [dɛsˈpɑṭɪk] *adj* : despótico
despotism [ˈdɛspəˌtɪzəm] *n* : despotismo *m*
dessert [diˈzərt] *n* : postre *m*
destination [ˌdɛstəˈneɪʃən] *n* : destino *m,* destinación *f*
destined [ˈdɛstənd] *adj* **1** FATED : predestinado **2** BOUND : destinado, con destino (a), con rumbo (a)
destiny [ˈdɛstəni] *n, pl* **-nies** : destino *m*
destitute [ˈdɛstəˌtuːt, -ˌtjuːt] *adj* **1** LACKING : carente, desprovisto **2** POOR : indigente, en miseria
destitution [ˌdɛstəˈtuːʃən, -ˈtjuː-] *n* : indigencia *f,* miseria *f*
destroy [diˈstrɔɪ] *vt* **1** KILL : matar **2** DEMOLISH : destruir, destrozar
destroyer [diˈstrɔɪər] *n* : destructor *m* (buque)
destructible [diˈstrʌktəbəl] *adj* : destructible
destruction [diˈstrʌkʃən] *n* : destrucción *f,* ruina *f*
destructive [diˈstrʌktɪv] *adj* : destructor, destructivo
desultory [ˈdɛsəlˌtori] *adj* **1** AIMLESS : sin rumbo, sin objeto **2** DISCONNECTED : inconexo
detach [diˈtætʃ] *vt* : separar, quitar, desprender
detached [diˈtætʃt] *adj* **1** SEPARATE : separado, suelto **2** ALOOF : distante, indiferente **3** IMPARTIAL : imparcial, objetivo
detachment [diˈtætʃmənt] *n* **1** SEPARATION : separación *f* **2** DETAIL : destacamento *m* (de tropas) **3** ALOOFNESS : reserva *f,* indiferencia *f* **4** IMPARTIALITY : imparcialidad *f*
detail[1] [diˈteɪl, ˈdiːˌteɪl] *vt* : detallar, exponer en detalle
detail[2] *n* **1** : detalle *m,* pormenor *m* **2** : destacamento *m* (de tropas)
detailed [diˈteɪld, ˈdiːˌteɪld] *adj* : detallado, minucioso
detain [diˈteɪn] *vt* **1** HOLD : detener **2** DELAY : entretener, demorar, retrasar
detect [diˈtɛkt] *vt* : detectar, descubrir
detection [diˈtɛkʃən] *n* : descubrimiento *m*
detective [diˈtɛktɪv] *n* : detective *mf* <private detective : detective privado>
detention [diˈtɛntʃən] *n* : detención *m*
deter [diˈtər] *vt* **-terred; -terring** : disuadir, impedir
detergent [diˈtərdʒənt] *n* : detergente *m*
deteriorate [diˈtɪriəˌreɪt] *vi* **-rated; -rating** : deteriorarse, empeorar
deterioration [diˌtɪriəˈreɪʃən] *n* : deterioro *m,* empeoramiento *m*
determination [dɪˌtərməˈneɪʃən] *n* **1** DECISION : determinación *f,* decisión *f* **2** RESOLUTION : resolución *f,* determinación *f* <with grim determination : con una firme resolución>
determine [diˈtərmən] *vt* **-mined; -mining 1** ESTABLISH : determinar, establecer **2** SETTLE : decidir **3** FIND OUT : averiguar **4** BRING ABOUT : determinar

determined [di'tərmənd] *adj* RESOLUTE : decidido, resuelto

deterrent [di'tərənt] *n* : medida *f* disuasiva

detest [di'tɛst] *vt* : detestar, odiar, aborrecer

detestable [di'tɛstəbəl] *adj* : detestable, odioso, aborrecible

dethrone [di'θroːn] *vt* **-throned; -throning** : destronar

detonate ['dɛtən,eɪt] *v* **-nated; -nating** *vt* : hacer detonar — *vi* : detonar, estallar

detonator ['dɛtən,eɪt̬ər] *n* : detonador *m*

detour[1] ['diː,tʊr, di'tʊr] *vi* : desviarse

detour[2] *n* : desvío *m,* rodeo *m*

detract [di'trækt] *vi* **to detract from** : restarle valor a, quitarle méritos a

detriment ['dɛtrəmənt] *n* : detrimento *m,* perjuicio *m*

detrimental [,dɛtrə'mɛntəl] *adj* : perjudicial — **detrimentally** *adv*

devaluation [di,væljʊ'eɪʃən] *n* : devaluación *f*

devalue [di'væl,juː] *vt* **-ued; -uing** : devaluar, depreciar

devastate ['dɛvə,steɪt] *vt* **-tated; -tating** : devastar, arrasar, asolar

devastation [,dɛvə'steɪʃən] *n* : devastación *f,* estragos *mpl*

develop [di'vɛləp] *vt* **1** FORM, MAKE : desarrollar, elaborar, formar **2** : revelar (en fotografía) **3** FOSTER : desarrollar, fomentar **4** EXPLOIT : explotar (recursos), urbanizar (un área) **5** ACQUIRE : adquirir <to develop an interest : adquirir un interés> **6** CONTRACT : contraer (una enfermedad) — *vi* **1** GROW : desarrollarse **2** ARISE : aparecer, surgir

developed [di'vɛləpt] *adj* : avanzado, desarrollado

development [di'vɛləpmənt] *n* **1** : desarrollo *m* <physical development : desarrollo físico> **2** : urbanización *f* (de un área), explotación *f* (de recursos), creación *f* (de inventos) **3** EVENT : acontecimiento *m,* suceso *m* <to await developments : esperar acontecimientos>

deviant ['diːviənt] *adj* : desviado, anormal

deviate ['diːvi,eɪt] *v* **-ated; -ating** *vi* : desviarse, apartarse — *vt* : desviar

deviation [,diːvi'eɪʃən] *n* : desviación *f*

device [di'vaɪs] *n* **1** MECHANISM : dispositivo *m,* aparato *m,* mecanismo *m* **2** EMBLEM : emblema *m*

devil[1] ['dɛvəl] *vt* **-iled** *or* **-illed; -iling** *or* **-illing 1** : sazonar con picante y especias **2** PESTER : molestar

devil[2] *n* **1** SATAN : el diablo, Satanás *m* **2** DEMON : diablo *m,* demonio *m* **3** FIEND : persona *f* diabólica; malvado *m,* -da *f*

devilish ['dɛvəlɪʃ] *adj* : diabólico

devilry ['dɛvəlri] *n, pl* **-ries** : diabluras *fpl,* travesuras *fpl*

devious ['diːviəs] *adj* **1** CRAFTY : taimado, artero **2** WINDING : tortuoso, sinuoso

devise [di'vaɪz] *vt* **-vised; -vising 1** INVENT : idear, concebir, inventar **2** PLOT : tramar

devoid [di'vɔɪd] *adj* **~ of** : carente de, desprovisto de

devote [di'voːt] *vt* **-voted; -voting 1** DEDICATE : consagrar, dedicar <to devote one's life : dedicar uno su vida> **2 to devote oneself** : dedicarse

devoted [di'voːt̬əd] *adj* **1** FAITHFUL : leal, fiel **2 to be devoted to someone** : tenerle mucho cariño a alguien

devotee [,dɛvə'tiː, -'teɪ] *n* : devoto *m,* -ta *f*

devotion [di'voːʃən] *n* **1** DEDICATION : dedicación *f,* devoción *f* **2 devotions** PRAYERS : oraciones *fpl,* devociones *fpl*

devour [di'vaʊər] *vt* : devorar

devout [di'vaʊt] *adj* **1** PIOUS : devoto, piadoso **2** EARNEST, SINCERE : sincero, ferviente — **devoutly** *adv*

devoutness [di'vaʊtnəs] *n* : devoción *f,* piedad *f*

dew ['duː, 'djuː] *n* : rocío *m*

dewlap ['du,læp, 'dju-] *n* : papada *f*

dew point *n* : punto *m* de condensación

dewy ['duːi, 'djuːi] *adj* **dewier; -est** : cubierto de rocío

dexterity [dɛk'stɛrət̬i] *n, pl* **-ties** : destreza *f,* habilidad *f*

dexterous ['dɛkstrəs] *adj* : diestro, hábil

dexterously ['dɛkstrəsli] *adv* : con destreza, con habilidad, hábilmente

dextrose ['dɛk,stroːs] *n* : dextrosa *f*

diabetes [,daɪə'biːtiz] *n* : diabetes *f*

diabetic[1] [,daɪə'bɛt̬ɪk] *adj* : diabético

diabetic[2] *n* : diabético *m,* -ca *f*

diabolic [,daɪə'bɑlɪk] *or* **diabolical** [-lɪkəl] *adj* : diabólico, satánico

diacritical mark [,daɪə'krɪt̬ɪkəl] *n* : signo *m* diacrítico

diadem ['daɪə,dɛm, -dəm] *n* : diadema *f*

diagnose ['daɪɪg,noːs, ,daɪɪg'noːs] *vt* **-nosed; -nosing** : diagnosticar

diagnosis [,daɪɪg'noːsɪs] *n, pl* **-noses** [-'noː,siːz] : diagnóstico *m*

diagnostic [,daɪɪg'nɑstɪk] *adj* : diagnóstico

diagonal[1] [daɪ'ægənəl] *adj* : diagonal, en diagonal

diagonal[2] *n* : diagonal *f*

diagonally [daɪ'ægənəli] *adv* : diagonalmente, en diagonal

diagram[1] ['daɪə,græm] *vt* **-gramed** *or* **-grammed; -graming** *or* **-gramming** : hacer un diagrama de

diagram[2] *n* : diagrama *m,* gráfico *m,* esquema *m*

dial[1] ['daɪl] *v* **dialed** *or* **dialled; dialing** *or* **dialling** : marcar, discar

dial[2] *n* : esfera *f* (de un reloj), dial *m* (de un radio), disco *m* (de un teléfono)
dialect ['daɪə,lɛkt] *n* : dialecto *m*
dialogue ['daɪə,lɔg] *n* : diálogo *m*
diameter [daɪ'æmət̬ər] *n* : diámetro *m*
diamond ['daɪmənd, 'daɪə-] *n* **1** : diamante *m,* brillante *m* <a diamond necklace : un collar de brillantes> **2** : rombo *m,* forma *f* de rombo **3** : diamante *m* (en naipes) **4** INFIELD : cuadro *m,* diamante *m* (en béisbol)
diaper ['daɪpər, 'daɪə-] *n* : pañal *m*
diaphragm ['daɪə,fræm] *n* : diafragma *m*
diarrhea [,daɪə'ri:ə] *n* : diarrea *f*
diary ['daɪəri] *n, pl* **-ries:** diario *m*
diatribe ['daɪə,traɪb] *n* : diatriba *f*
dice[1] ['daɪs] *vt* **diced; dicing** : cortar en cubos
dice[2] *ns & pl* **1** → **die**[2] **2** : dados *mpl* (juego)
dicker ['dɪkər] *vt* : regatear
dictate[1] ['dɪk,teɪt, dɪk'teɪt] *v* **-tated; -tating** *vt* **1** : dictar <to dictate a letter : dictar una carta> **2** ORDER : mandar, ordenar — *vi* : dar órdenes
dictate[2] ['dɪk,teɪt] *n* **1** : mandato *m,* orden *f* **2 dictates** *npl* : dictados *mpl* <the dictates of conscience : los dictados de la conciencia>
dictation [dɪk'teɪʃən] *n* : dictado *m*
dictator ['dɪk,teɪt̬ər] *n* : dictador *m,* -dora *f*
dictatorial [,dɪktə'toriəl] *adj* : dictatorial — **dictatorially** *adv*
dictatorship [dɪk'teɪt̬ər,ʃɪp, 'dɪk,-] *n* : dictadura *f*
diction ['dɪkʃən] *n* **1** : lenguaje *m,* estilo *m* **2** ENUNCIATION : dicción *f,* articulación *f*
dictionary ['dɪkʃə,nɛri] *n, pl* **-naries** : diccionario *m*
did → **do**
didactic [daɪ'dæktɪk] *adj* : didáctico
die[1] ['daɪ] *vi* **died** ['daɪd]; **dying** ['daɪɪŋ] **1** : morir **2** CEASE : morir, morirse <a dying civilization : una civilización moribunda> **3** STOP : apagarse, dejar de funcionar <the motor died : el motor se apagó> **4 to die down** SUBSIDE : amainar, disminuir **5 to die out** : extinguirse **6 to be dying for** *or* **to be dying to** : morirse por <I'm dying to leave : me muero por irme>
die[2] ['daɪ] *n, pl* **dice** ['daɪs] : dado *m*
die[3] *n, pl* **dies** ['daɪz] **1** STAMP : troquel *m,* cuño *m* **2** MOLD : matriz *f,* molde *m*
diesel ['di:zəl, -səl] *n* : diesel *m*
diet[1] ['daɪət] *vi* : ponerse a régimen, hacer dieta
diet[2] *n* : régimen *m,* dieta *f*
dietary ['daɪə,tɛri] *adj* : alimenticio, dietético
dietitian *or* **dietician** [,daɪə'tɪʃən] *n* : dietista *mf*
differ ['dɪfər] *vi* **-ferred; -ferring 1** : diferir, diferenciarse **2** VARY : variar **3** DISAGREE : discrepar, diferir, no estar de acuerdo
difference ['dɪfrənts, 'dɪfərənts] *n* : diferencia *f*
different ['dɪfrənt, 'dɪfərənt] *adj* : distinto, diferente
differentiate [,dɪfə'rɛntʃi,eɪt] *v* **-ated; -ating** *vt* **1** : hacer diferente **2** DISTINGUISH : distinguir, diferenciar — *vi* : distinguir
differentiation [,dɪfə,rɛntʃi'eɪʃən] *n* : diferenciación *f*
differently ['dɪfrəntli, 'dɪfərənt-] *adv* : de otra manera, de otro modo, distintamente
difficult ['dɪfɪ,kʌlt] *adj* : difícil
difficulty ['dɪfɪ,kʌlti] *n, pl* **-ties 1** : dificultad *f* **2** PROBLEM : problema *f,* dificultad *f*
diffidence ['dɪfədənts] *n* **1** SHYNESS : retraimiento *m,* timidez *f,* apocamiento *m* **2** RETICENCE : reticencia *f*
diffident ['dɪfədənt] *adj* **1** SHY : tímido, apocado, inseguro **2** RESERVED : reservado
diffuse[1] [dɪ'fju:z] *v* **-fused; -fusing** *vt* : difundir, esparcir — *vi* : difundirse, esparcirse
diffuse[2] [dɪ'fju:s] *adj* **1** WORDY : prolijo, verboso **2** WIDESPREAD : difuso
diffusion [dɪ'ju:ʒən] *n* : difusión *f*
dig[1] ['dɪg] *v* **dug** ['dʌg]; **digging** *vt* **1** : cavar, excavar <to dig a hole : cavar un hoyo> **2** EXTRACT : sacar <to dig up potatoes : sacar papas del suelo> **3** POKE, THRUST : clavar, hincar <he dug me in the ribs : me dio un codazo en las costillas> **4 to dig up** DISCOVER : descubrir, sacar a luz — *vi* : cavar, excavar
dig[2] *n* **1** POKE : codazo *m* **2** GIBE : pulla *f* **3** EXCAVATION : excavación *f*
digest[1] [daɪ'dʒɛst, dɪ-] *vt* **1** ASSIMILATE : digerir, asimilar **2** : digerir (comida) **3** SUMMARIZE : compendiar, resumir
digest[2] ['daɪ,dʒɛst] *n* : compendio *m,* resumen *m*
digestible [daɪ'dʒɛstəbəl, dɪ-] *adj* : digerible
digestion [daɪ'dʒɛstʃən, dɪ-] *n* : digestión *f*
digestive [daɪ'dʒɛstɪv, dɪ-] *adj* : digestivo <the digestive system : el sistema digestivo>
digit ['dɪdʒət] *n* **1** NUMERAL : dígito *m,* número *m* **2** FINGER, TOE : dedo *m*
digital ['dɪdʒət̬əl] *adj* : digital — **digitally** *adv*
dignified ['dɪgnə,faɪd] *adj* : digno, decoroso
dignify ['dɪgnə,faɪ] *vt* **-fied; -fying** : dignificar, honrar
dignitary ['dɪgnə,tɛri] *n, pl* **-taries** : dignatario *m,* -ria *f*
dignity ['dɪgnət̬i] *n, pl* **-ties** : dignidad *f*
digress [daɪ'grɛs, də-] *vi* : desviarse del tema, divagar

digression [daɪˈgrɛʃən, də-] *n* : digresión *f*

dike *or* **dyke** [ˈdaɪk] *n* : dique *m*

dilapidated [dəˈlæpəˌdeɪtəd] *adj* : ruinoso, desvencijado, destartalado

dilapidation [dəˌlæpəˈdeɪʃən] *n* : deterioro *m,* estado *m* ruinoso

dilate [daɪˈleɪt, ˈdaɪˌleɪt] *v* **-lated; -lating** *vt* : dilatar — *vi* : dilatarse

dilemma [dɪˈlɛmə] *n* : dilema *m*

dilettante [ˈdɪləˌtɑnt, -ˌtænt] *n, pl* **-tantes** [-ˌtɑnts, -ˌtænts] *or* **-tanti** [ˌdɪləˈtɑnti, -ˈtæn-] : diletante *mf*

diligence [ˈdɪlədʒənts] *n* : diligencia *f,* aplicación *f*

diligent [ˈdɪlədʒənt] *adj* : diligente <a diligent search : una búsqueda minuciosa> — **diligently** *adv*

dill [ˈdɪl] *n* : eneldo *m*

dillydally [ˈdɪliˌdæli] *vi* **-lied; lying** : demorarse, perder tiempo

dilute [daɪˈluːt, də-] *vt* **-luted; -luting** : diluir, aguar

dilution [daɪˈluːʃən, də-] *n* : dilución *f*

dim[1] [ˈdɪm] *v* **dimmed; dimming** *vt* : atenuar (la luz), nublar (la vista), borrar (la memoria), opacar (una superficie) — *vi* : oscurecerse, apagarse

dim[2] *adj* **dimmer; dimmest 1** FAINT : oscuro, tenue (dícese de la luz), nublado (dícese de la vista), borrado (dícese de la memoria) **2** DULL : deslustrado **3** STUPID : tonto, torpe

dime [ˈdaɪm] *n* : moneda *f* de diez centavos

dimension [dəˈmɛntʃən, daɪ-] *n* **1** : dimensión *f* **2 dimensions** *npl* EXTENT, SCOPE : dimensiones *fpl,* extensión *f,* medida *f*

diminish [dəˈmɪnɪʃ] *vt* LESSEN : disminuir, reducir, amainar — *vi* DWINDLE, WANE : menguar, reducirse

diminutive [dəˈmɪnjʊtɪv] *adj* : diminutivo, minúsculo

dimly [ˈdɪmli] *adv* : indistintamente, débilmente

dimmer [ˈdɪmər] *n* : potenciómetro *m,* conmutador *m* de luces (en automóviles)

dimness [ˈdɪmnəs] *n* : oscuridad *f,* debilidad *f* (de la vista), imprecisión *f* (de la memoria)

dimple [ˈdɪmpəl] *n* : hoyuelo *m*

din [ˈdɪn] *n* : estrépito *m,* estruendo *m*

dine [ˈdaɪn] *vi* **dined; dining** : cenar

diner [ˈdaɪnər] *n* **1** : comensal *mf* (persona) **2** : vagón *m* restaurante (en un tren) **3** : cafetería *f,* restaurante *m* barato

dinghy [ˈdɪŋi, ˈdɪŋgi, ˈdɪŋki] *n, pl* **-ghies** : bote *m*

dinginess [ˈdɪndʒinəs] *n* **1** DIRTINESS : suciedad *f* **2** SHABBINESS : lo gastado, lo deslucido

dingy [ˈdɪndʒi] *adj* **-gier; -est 1** DIRTY : sucio **2** SHABBY : gastado, deslucido

dinner [ˈdɪnər] *n* : cena *f,* comida *f*

dinosaur [ˈdaɪnəˌsɔr] *n* : dinosaurio *m*

dint [ˈdɪnt] *n* **by dint of** : a fuerza de

diocese [ˈdaɪəsəs, -ˌsiːz, -ˌsiːs] *n, pl* **-ceses** [ˈdaɪəsəsəz] : diócesis *f*

dip[1] [ˈdɪp] *v* **dipped; dipping** *vt* **1** DUNK, PLUNGE : sumergir, mojar, meter **2** LADLE : servir con cucharón **3** LOWER : bajar, arriar (una bandera) — *vi* **1** DESCEND, DROP : bajar en picada, descender **2** SLOPE : bajar, inclinarse

dip[2] *n* **1** SWIM : chapuzón *m* **2** DROP : descenso *m,* caída *f* **3** SLOPE : cuesta *f,* declive *m* **4** SAUCE : salsa *f*

diphtheria [dɪfˈθɪriə] *n* : difteria *f*

diphthong [ˈdɪfˌθɔŋ] *n* : diptongo *m*

diploma [dəˈploːmə] *n, pl* **-mas** : diploma *m*

diplomacy [dəˈploːməsi] *n* **1** : diplomacia *f* **2** TACT : tacto *m,* discreción *f*

diplomat [ˈdɪpləˌmæt] *n* **1** : diplomático *m,* -ca *f* (en relaciones internacionales) **2** : persona *f* diplomática

diplomatic [ˌdɪpləˈmætɪk] *adj* : diplomático <diplomatic immunity : inmunidad diplomática>

dipper [ˈdɪpər] *n* **1** LADLE : cucharón *m,* cazo *m* **2 Big Dipper** : Osa *f* Mayor **3 Little Dipper** : Osa *f* Menor

dire [ˈdaɪr] *adj* **direr; direst 1** HORRIBLE : espantoso, terrible, horrendo **2** EXTREME : extremo <dire poverty : pobreza extrema>

direct[1] [dəˈrɛkt, daɪ-] *vt* **1** ADDRESS : dirigir, mandar **2** AIM, POINT : dirigir **3** GUIDE : indicarle el camino (a alguien), orientar **4** MANAGE : dirigir <to direct a film : dirigir una película> **5** COMMAND : ordenar, mandar

direct[2] *adv* : directamente

direct[3] *adj* **1** STRAIGHT : directo **2** FRANK : franco

direct current *n* : corriente *f* continua

direction [dəˈrɛkʃən, daɪ-] *n* **1** SUPERVISION : dirección *f* **2** INSTRUCTION, ORDER : instrucción *f,* orden *f* **3** COURSE : dirección *f,* rumbo *m* <to change direction : cambiar de dirección> **4 to ask directions** : pedir indicaciones

directly [dəˈrɛktli, daɪ-] *adv* **1** STRAIGHT : directamente <directly north : directamente al norte> **2** FRANKLY : francamente **3** EXACTLY : exactamente, justo <directly opposite : justo enfrente> **4** IMMEDIATELY : en seguida, inmediatamente

directness [dəˈrɛktnəs, daɪ-] *n* : franqueza *f*

director [dəˈrɛktər, daɪ-] *n* **1** : director *m,* -tora *f* **2 board of directors** : junta *f* directiva, directorio *m*

directory [dəˈrɛktəri, daɪ-] *n, pl* **-ries** : guía *f,* directorio *m* <telephone directory : directorio telefónico>

dirge [ˈdərdʒ] *n* : canto *m* fúnebre

dirigible [ˈdɪrədʒəbəl, dəˈrɪdʒə-] *n* : dirigible *m,* zepelín *m*

dirt [ˈdərt] *n* **1** FILTH : suciedad *f,* mugre *f,* porquería *f* **2** SOIL : tierra *f*

dirtiness [ˈdərtinəs] *n* : suciedad *f*

dirty[1] [ˈdərti] *vt* **dirtied; dirtying** : ensuciar, manchar

dirty² *adj* **dirtier; -est 1** SOILED, STAINED : sucio, manchado **2** DISHONEST : sucio, deshonesto <a dirty player : un jugador tramposo> <a dirty trick : una mala pasada> **3** INDECENT : indecente, cochino <a dirty joke : un chiste verde>
disability [ˌdɪsəˈbɪləṭi] *n, pl* **-ties** : minusvalía *f,* discapacidad *f,* invalidez *f*
disable [dɪsˈeɪbəl] *vt* **-abled; -abling** : dejar inválido, inutilizar, incapacitar
disabled [dɪsˈeɪbəld] *adj* : minusválido, discapacitado
disabuse [ˌdɪsəˈbjuːz] *vt* **-bused; -busing** : desengañar, sacar del error
disadvantage [ˌdɪsədˈvæntɪdʒ] *n* : desventaja *f*
disadvantageous [ˌdɪsˌædˌvænˈteɪdʒəs] *adj* : desventajoso, desfavorable
disagree [ˌdɪsəˈgriː] *vi* **1** DIFFER : discrepar, no coincidir **2** DISSENT : disentir, discrepar, no estar de acuerdo
disagreeable [ˌdɪsəˈgriːəbəl] *adj* : desagradable
disagreement [ˌdɪsəˈgriːmənt] *n* **1** : desacuerdo *m* **2** DISCREPANCY : discrepancia *f* **3** ARGUMENT : discusión *f,* altercado *m,* disputa *f*
disappear [ˌdɪsəˈpɪr] *vi* : desaparecer, desvanecerse <to disappear from view : perderse de vista>
disappearance [ˌdɪsəˈpɪrən*t*s] *n* : desaparición *f*
disappoint [ˌdɪsəˈpɔɪnt] *vt* : decepcionar, defraudar, fallar
disappointment [ˌdɪsəˈpɔɪntmənt] *n* : decepción *f,* desilusión *f,* chasco *m*
disapproval [ˌdɪsəˈpruːvəl] *n* : desaprobación *f*
disapprove [ˌdɪsəˈpruːv] *vi* **-proved; -proving** : desaprobar, estar en contra
disapprovingly [ˌdɪsəˈpruːvɪŋli] *adv* : con desaprobación
disarm [dɪsˈɑrm] *vt* : desarmar
disarmament [dɪsˈɑrməmənt] *n* : desarme *m* <nuclear disarmament : desarme nuclear>
disarrange [ˌdɪsəˈreɪndʒ] *vt* **-ranged; -ranging** : desarreglar, desordenar
disarray [ˌdɪsəˈreɪ] *n* : desorden *m,* confusión *f,* desorganización *f*
disaster [dɪˈzæstər] *n* : desastre *m,* catástrofe *f*
disastrous [dɪˈzæstrəs] *adj* : desastroso
disband [dɪsˈbænd] *vt* : disolver — *vi* : disolverse, dispersarse
disbar [dɪsˈbɑr] *vt* **-barred; -barring** : prohibir de ejercer la abogacía
disbelief [ˌdɪsbɪˈliːf] *n* : incredulidad *f*
disbelieve [ˌdɪsbɪˈliːv] *v* **-lieved; -lieving** : no creer, dudar
disburse [dɪsˈbərs] *vt* **-bursed; -bursing** : desembolsar
disbursement [dɪsˈbərsmənt] *n* : desembolso *m*
disc → **disk**
discard [dɪsˈkɑrd, ˈdɪsˌkɑrd] *vt* : desechar, deshacerse de, botar — *vi* : descartarse (en juegos de naipes)
discern [dɪˈsərn, -ˈzərn] *vt* : discernir, distinguir, percibir
discernible [dɪˈsərnəbəl, -ˈzər-] *adj* : perceptible, visible
discernment [dɪˈsərnmənt, -ˈzərn-] *n* : discernimiento *m,* criterio *m*
discharge¹ [dɪsˈtʃɑrdʒ, ˈdɪsˌ-] *v* **-charged; -charging 1** UNLOAD : descargar (carga), desembarcar (pasajeros) **2** SHOOT : descargar, disparar **3** FREE : liberar, poner en libertad **4** DISMISS : despedir **5** EMIT : despedir (humo, etc.), descargar (electricidad) **6** : cumplir con (una obligación), saldar (una deuda) — *vi* **1** : descargarse (dícese de una batería) **2** OOZE : supurar
discharge² [ˈdɪsˌtʃɑrdʒ, dɪsˈ-] *n* **1** EMISSION : descarga *f* (de electricidad), emisión *f* (de gases) **2** DISMISSAL : despido *m* (del empleo), baja *f* (del ejército) **3** SECRETION : secreción *f*
disciple [dɪˈsaɪpəl] *n* : discípulo *m,* -la *f*
discipline¹ [ˈdɪsəplən] *vt* **-plined; -plining 1** PUNISH : castigar, sancionar (a los empleados) **2** CONTROL : disciplinar **3 to discipline oneself** : disciplinarse
discipline² *n* **1** FIELD : disciplina *f,* campo *m* **2** TRAINING : disciplina *f* **3** PUNISHMENT : castigo *m* **4** SELF-CONTROL : dominio *m* de sí mismo
disc jockey *n* : disc jockey *mf*
disclaim [dɪsˈkleɪm] *vt* DENY : negar
disclose [dɪsˈkloːz] *vt* **-closed; -closing** : revelar, poner en evidencia
disclosure [dɪsˈkloːʒər] *n* : revelación *f*
discolor [dɪsˈkʌlər] *vt* **1** BLEACH : decolorar **2** FADE : desteñir **3** STAIN : manchar — *vi* : decolorarse, desteñirse
discoloration [dɪsˌkʌləˈreɪʃən] *n* **1** FADING : decoloración *f* **2** STAIN : mancha *f*
discomfort [dɪsˈkʌmfərt] *n* **1** PAIN : molestia *f,* malestar *m* **2** UNEASINESS : inquietud *f*
disconcert [ˌdɪskənˈsərt] *vt* : desconcertar
disconnect [ˌdɪskəˈnɛkt] *vt* : desconectar
disconnected [ˌdɪskəˈnɛktəd] *adj* : inconexo
disconsolate [dɪsˈkɑn*t*sələt] *adj* : desconsolado
discontent [ˌdɪskənˈtɛnt] *n* : descontento *m*
discontented [ˌdɪskənˈtɛntəd] *adj* : descontento
discontinue [ˌdɪskənˈtɪnˌjuː] *vt* **-ued; -uing** : suspender, descontinuar
discord [ˈdɪsˌkɔrd] *n* **1** STRIFE : discordia *f,* discordancia *f* **2** : disonancia *f* (en música)

discordant [dɪs'kɔrdənt] *adj* : discordante, discorde — **discordantly** *adv*
discount[1] ['dɪs,kaʊnt, dɪs'-] *vt* **1** REDUCE : descontar, rebajar (precios) **2** DISREGARD : descartar, ignorar
discount[2] ['dɪs,kaʊnt] *n* : descuento *m,* rebaja *f*
discourage [dɪs'kərɪdʒ] *vt* **-aged; -aging 1** DISHEARTEN : desalentar, desanimar **2** DISSUADE : disuadir
discouragement [dɪs'kərɪdʒmənt] *n* : desánimo *m,* desaliento *m*
discourse[1] [dɪs'kors] *vi* **-coursed; -coursing** : disertar, conversar
discourse[2] ['dɪs,kors] *n* **1** TALK : conversación *f* **2** SPEECH, TREATISE : discurso *m,* tratado *m*
discourteous [dɪs'kərt̬iəs] *adj* : descortés — **discourteously** *adv*
discourtesy [dɪs'kərt̬əsi] *n, pl* **-sies** : descortesía *f*
discover [dɪs'kʌvər] *vt* : descubrir
discoverer [dɪs'kʌvərər] *n* : descubridor *m,* -dora *f*
discovery [dɪs'kʌvəri] *n, pl* **-ries** : descubrimiento *m*
discredit[1] [dɪs'krɛdət] *vt* **1** DISBELIEVE : no creer, dudar **2** : desacreditar, desprestigiar, poner en duda <they discredited his research : desacreditaron sus investigaciones>
discredit[2] *n* **1** DISREPUTE : descrédito *m,* desprestigio *m* **2** DOUBT : duda *f*
discreet [dɪs'kri:t] *adj* : discreto — **discreetly** *adv*
discrepancy [dɪs'krɛpəntsi] *n, pl* **-cies** : discrepancia *f*
discretion [dɪs'krɛʃən] *n* **1** CIRCUMSPECTION : discreción *f,* circunspección *f* **2** JUDGMENT : discernimiento *m,* criterio *m*
discriminate [dɪs'krɪmə,neɪt] *v* **-nated; -nating** *vt* DISTINGUISH : distinguir, discriminar, diferenciar — *vi* : discriminar <to discriminate against women : discriminar a las mujeres>
discrimination [dɪs,krɪmə'neɪʃən] *n* **1** PREJUDICE : discriminación *f* **2** DISCERNMENT : discernimiento *m*
discriminatory [dɪs'krɪmənə,tori] *adj* : discriminatorio
discus ['dɪskəs] *n, pl* **-cuses** [-kəsəz] : disco *m*
discuss [dɪs'kʌs] *vt* : hablar de, discutir, tratar (de)
discussion [dɪs'kʌʃən] *n* : discusión *f,* debate *m,* conversación *f*
disdain[1] [dɪs'deɪn] *vt* : desdeñar, despreciar <they disdained to reply : no se dignaron a responder>
disdain[2] *n* : desdén *m*
disdainful [dɪs'deɪnfəl] *adj* : desdeñoso — **disdainfully** *adv*
disease [dɪ'zi:z] *n* : enfermedad *f,* mal *m,* dolencia *f*
diseased [dɪ'zi:zd] *adj* : enfermo
disembark [,dɪsɪm'bɑrk] *v* : desembarcar
disembarkation [dɪs,ɛm,bɑr'keɪʃən] *n* : desembarco *m,* desembarque *m*
disembodied [,dɪsɪm'bɑdid] *adj* : incorpóreo
disenchant [,dɪsɪn'tʃænt] *vt* : desilusionar, desencantar, desengañar
disenchantment [,dɪsɪn'tʃæntmənt] *n* : desencanto *m,* desilusión *f*
disengage [,dɪsɪn'geɪdʒ] *vt* **-gaged; -gaging 1** : soltar, desconectar (un mecanismo) **2 to disengage the clutch** : desembragar
disentangle [,dɪsɪn'tæŋgəl] *vt* **-gled; -gling** UNTANGLE : desenredar, desenmarañar
disfavor [dɪs'feɪvər] *n* : desaprobación *f*
disfigure [dɪs'fɪgjər] *vt* **-ured; -uring** : desfigurar (a una persona), afear (un edificio, un área)
disfigurement [dɪs'fɪgjərmənt] *n* : desfiguración *f,* afeamiento *m*
disfranchise [dɪs'fræn,tʃaɪz] *vt* **-chised; -chising** : privar del derecho a votar
disgrace[1] [dɪ'skreɪs] *vt* **-graced; -gracing** : deshonrar
disgrace[2] *n* **1** DISHONOR : desgracia *f,* deshonra *f* **2** SHAME : vergüenza *f* <he's a disgrace to his family : es una vergüenza para su familia>
disgraceful [dɪ'skreɪsfəl] *adj* : vergonzoso, deshonroso, ignominioso
disgracefully [dɪ'skreɪsfəli] *adv* : vergonzosamente
disgruntle [dɪs'grʌntəl] *vt* **-tled; -tling** : enfadar, contrariar
disguise[1] [dɪ'skaɪz] *vt* **-guised; -guising 1** : disfrazar, enmascarar (el aspecto) **2** CONCEAL : encubrir, disimular
disguise[2] *n* : disfraz *m*
disgust[1] [dɪ'skʌst] *vt* : darle asco (a alguien), asquear, repugnar <eso me da asco : that disgusts me>
disgust[2] *n* : asco *m,* repugnancia *f*
disgusting [dɪ'skʌstɪŋ] *adj* : asqueroso, repugnante — **disgustingly** *adv*
dish[1] ['dɪʃ] *vt* SERVE : servir
dish[2] *n* **1** : plato *m* <the national dish : el plato nacional> **2** PLATE : plato *m* <to wash the dishes : lavar los platos> **3 serving dish** : fuente *f*
dishcloth ['dɪʃ,klɔθ] *n* : paño *m* de cocina (para secar), trapo *m* de fregar (para lavar)
dishearten [dɪs'hɑrtən] *vt* : desanimar, desalentar
dishevel [dɪ'ʃɛvəl] *vt* **-eled** *or* **-elled; -eling** *or* **-elling** : desarreglar, despeinar (el pelo)
disheveled *or* **dishevelled** [dɪ'ʃɛvəld] *adj* : despeinado (dícese del pelo), desarreglado, desaliñado
dishonest [dɪ'sɑnəst] *adj* : deshonesto, fraudulento — **dishonestly** *adv*
dishonesty [dɪ'sɑnəsti] *n, pl* **-ties** : deshonestidad *f,* falta *f* de honradez
dishonor[1] [dɪ'sɑnər] *vt* : deshonrar

dishonor[2] *n* : deshonra *f*
dishonorable [dɪˈsɑnərəbəl] *adj* : deshonroso — **dishonorably** [-bli] *adv*
dishrag [ˈdɪʃˌræg] → **dishcloth**
dishwasher [ˈdɪʃˌwɔʃər] *n* : lavaplatos *m*, lavavajillas *m*
disillusion [ˌdɪsəˈluːʒən] *vt* : desilusionar, desencantar, desengañar
disillusionment [ˌdɪsəˈluːʒənmənt] *n* : desilusión *f*, desencanto *m*
disinclination [dɪsˌɪnkləˈneɪʃən, -ˌɪŋ-] *n* : aversión *f*
disinclined [ˌdɪsɪnˈklaɪnd] *adv* : poco dispuesto
disinfect [ˌdɪsɪnˈfɛkt] *vt* : desinfectar
disinfectant[1] [ˌdɪsɪnˈfɛktənt] *adj* : desinfectante
disinfectant[2] *n* : desinfectante *m*
disinherit [ˌdɪsɪnˈhɛrət] *vt* : desheredar
disintegrate [dɪsˈɪntəˌgreɪt] *v* **-grated; -grating** *vt* : desintegrar, deshacer — *vi* : desintegrarse, deshacerse
disintegration [dɪsˌɪntəˈgreɪʃən] *n* : desintegración *f*
disinterested [dɪsˈɪntərəstəd, -ˌrɛs-] *adj* **1** INDIFFERENT : indiferente **2** IMPARTIAL : imparcial, desinteresado
disinterestedness [dɪsˈɪntərəstədnəs, -ˌrɛs-] *n* : desinterés *m*
disjointed [dɪsˈdʒɔɪntəd] *adj* : inconexo, incoherente
disk *or* **disc** [ˈdɪsk] *n* : disco *m*
dislike[1] [dɪsˈlaɪk] *vt* **-liked; -liking** : tenerle aversión a (algo), tenerle antipatía (a alguien), no gustarle (algo a uno)
dislike[2] *n* : aversión *f*, antipatía *f*
dislocate [ˈdɪsloˌkeɪt, dɪsˈloː-] *vt* **-cated; -cating** : dislocar
dislocation [ˌdɪsloˈkeɪʃən] *n* : dislocación *f*
dislodge [dɪsˈlɑdʒ] *vt* **-lodged; -lodging** : sacar, desalojar, desplazar
disloyal [dɪsˈlɔɪəl] *adj* : desleal
disloyalty [dɪsˈlɔɪəlti] *n, pl* **-ties** : deslealtad *f*
dismal [ˈdɪzməl] *adj* **1** GLOOMY : sombrío, lúgubre, tétrico **2** DEPRESSING : deprimente, triste
dismantle [dɪsˈmæntəl] *vt* **-tled; -tling** : desmantelar, desmontar, desarmar
dismay[1] [dɪsˈmeɪ] *vt* : consternar
dismay[2] *n* : consternación *f*
dismember [dɪsˈmɛmbər] *vt* : desmembrar
dismiss [dɪsˈmɪs] *vt* **1** : dejar salir, darle permiso (a alguien) para retirarse **2** DISCHARGE : despedir, destituir **3** REJECT : descartar, desechar, rechazar
dismissal [dɪsˈmɪsəl] *n* **1** : permiso *m* para retirarse **2** DISCHARGE : despido *m* (de un empleado), destitución *f* (de un funcionario) **3** REJECTION : rechazo *m*
dismount [dɪsˈmaʊnt] *vi* : desmontar, bajarse, apearse
disobedience [ˌdɪsəˈbiːdiənts] *n* : desobediencia *f* — **disobedient** [-ənt] *adj*
disobey [ˌdɪsəˈbeɪ] *v* : desobedecer
disorder[1] [dɪsˈɔrdər] *vt* : desordenar, desarreglar
disorder[2] *n* **1** DISARRAY : desorden *m* **2** UNREST : disturbios *mpl*, desórdenes *mpl* **3** AILMENT : afección *f*, indisposición *f*, dolencia *f*
disorderly [dɪsˈɔrdərli] *adj* **1** UNTIDY : desordenado, desarreglado **2** UNRULY : indisciplinado, alborotado **3 disorderly conduct** : conducta *f* escandalosa
disorganization [dɪsˌɔrgənəˈzeɪʃən] *n* : desorganización *f*
disorganize [dɪsˈɔrgəˌnaɪz] *vt* **-nized; -nizing** : desorganizar
disown [dɪsˈoːn] *vt* : renegar de, repudiar
disparage [dɪsˈpærɪdʒ] *vt* **-aged; -aging** : menospreciar, denigrar
disparagement [dɪsˈpærɪdʒmənt] *n* : menosprecio *m*
disparate [ˈdɪspərət, dɪsˈpærət] *adj* : dispar, diferente
disparity [dɪsˈpærəṭi] *n, pl* **-ties** : disparidad *f*
dispassionate [dɪsˈpæʃənət] *adj* : desapasionado, imparcial — **dispassionately** *adv*
dispatch[1] [dɪsˈpætʃ] *vt* **1** SEND : despachar, enviar **2** KILL : despachar, matar **3** HANDLE : despachar
dispatch[2] *n* **1** SENDING : envío *m*, despacho *m* **2** MESSAGE : despacho *m*, reportaje *m* (de un periodista), parte *m* (en el ejército) **3** PROMPTNESS : prontitud *f*, rapidez *f*
dispel [dɪsˈpɛl] *vt* **-pelled; -pelling** : disipar, desvanecer
dispensation [ˌdɪspɛnˈseɪʃən] *n* EXEMPTION : exención *m*, dispensa *f*
dispense [dɪsˈpɛnts] *v* **-pensed; -pensing** *vt* **1** DISTRIBUTE : repartir, distribuir, dar **2** ADMINISTER, BESTOW : administrar (justicia), conceder (favores, etc.) **3** : preparar y despachar (medicamentos) — *vi* **to dispense with** : prescindir de
dispenser [dɪsˈpɛntsər] *n* : dispensador *m*, distibuidor *m* automático
dispersal [dɪsˈpərsəl] *n* : dispersión *f*
disperse [dɪsˈpərs] *v* **-persed; -persing** *vt* : dispersar, diseminar — *vi* : dispersarse
dispirit [dɪˈspɪrət] *vt* : desalentar, desanimar
displace [dɪsˈpleɪs] *vt* **-placed; -placing 1** : desplazar (un líquido, etc.) **2** REPLACE : reemplazar
displacement [dɪsˈpleɪsmənt] *n* **1** : desplazamiento *m* (de personas) **2** REPLACEMENT : sustitución *f*, reemplazo *m*
display[1] [dɪsˈpleɪ] *vt* : exponer, exhibir, mostrar
display[2] *n* : muestra *f*, exposición *m*, alarde *m*

displease [dɪs'pli:z] *vt* **-pleased; -pleasing** : desagradar a, disgustar, contrariar

displeasure [dɪs'plɛʒər] *n* : desagrado *m*

disposable [dɪs'po:zəbəl] *adj* **1** : desechable <disposable diapers : pañales desechables> **2** AVAILABLE : disponible

disposal [dɪs'po:zəl] *n* **1** PLACEMENT : disposición *f*, colocación *f* **2** REMOVAL : eliminación *f* **3 to have at one's disposal** : disponer de, tener a su disposición

dispose [dɪs'po:z] *v* **-posed; -posing** *vt* **1** ARRANGE : disponer, colocar **2** INCLINE : predisponer — *vi* **1 to dispose of** DISCARD : desechar, deshacerse de **2 to dispose of** HANDLE : despachar

disposition [ˌdɪspə'zɪʃən] *n* **1** ARRANGEMENT : disposición *f* **2** TENDENCY : predisposición *f*, inclinación *f* **3** TEMPERAMENT : temperamento *m*, carácter *m*

disproportion [ˌdɪsprə'porʃən] *n* : desproporción *f*

disproportionate [ˌdɪsprə'porʃənət] *adj* : desproporcionado — **disproportionately** *adv*

disprove [dɪs'pru:v] *vt* **-proved; -proving** : rebatir, refutar

disputable [dɪs'pju:təbəl, 'dɪspjʊtəbəl] *adj* : disputable, discutible

dispute¹ [dɪs'pju:t] *v* **-puted; -puting** *vt* **1** QUESTION : discutir, cuestionar **2** OPPOSE : combatir, resistir — *vi* ARGUE, DEBATE : discutir

dispute² *n* **1** DEBATE : debate *m*, discusión *f* **2** QUARREL : disputa *f*, discusión *f*

disqualification [dɪsˌkwɑləfə'keɪʃən] *n* : descalificación *f*

disqualify [dɪs'kwɑləˌfaɪ] *vt* **-fied; -fying** : descalificar, inhabilitar

disquiet¹ *vt* [dɪs'kwaɪət] : inquietar

disquiet² *n* : ansiedad *f*, inquietud *f*

disregard¹ [ˌdɪsrɪ'gɑrd] *vt* : ignorar, no prestar atención a

disregard² *n* : indiferencia *f*

disrepair [ˌdɪsrɪ'pær] *n* : mal estado *m*

disreputable [dɪs'rɛpjʊtəbəl] *adj* : de mala fama (dícese de una persona o un lugar), vergonzoso (dícese de la conducta)

disreputably [dɪs'rɛpjʊtəbli] *adv* : vergonzosamente

disrepute [ˌdɪsrɪ'pju:t] *n* : descrédito *m*, mala fama *f*, deshonra *f*

disrespect [ˌdɪsrɪ'spɛkt] *n* : falta *f* de respeto

disrespectful [ˌdɪsrɪ'spɛktfəl] *adj* : irrespetuoso — **disrespectfully** *adv*

disrobe [dɪs'ro:b] *v* **-robed; -robing** *vt* : desvestir, desnudar — *vi* : desvestirse, desnudarse

disrupt [dɪs'rʌpt] *vt* : trastornar, perturbar

disruption [dɪs'rʌpʃən] *n* : trastorno *m*

disruptive [dɪs'rʌptɪv] *adj* : perjudicial, perturbador — **disruptively** *adv*

dissatisfaction [dɪsˌsætəs'fækʃən] *n* : descontento *m*, insatisfacción *f*

dissatisfied [dɪs'sætəsˌfaɪd] *adj* : descontento, insatisfecho

dissatisfy [dɪs'sætəsˌfaɪ] *vt* **-fied; -fying** : no contentar, no satisfacer

dissect [dɪ'sɛkt] *vt* : disecar

dissemble [dɪ'sɛmbəl] *v* **-bled; -bling** *vt* HIDE : ocultar, disimular — *vi* PRETEND : fingir, disimular

disseminate [dɪ'sɛməˌneɪt] *vt* **-nated; -nating** : diseminar, difundir, divulgar

dissemination [dɪˌsɛmə'neɪʃən] *n* : diseminación *f*, difusión *f*

dissension [dɪ'sɛntʃən] *n* : disensión *f*, desacuerdo *m*

dissent¹ [dɪ'sɛnt] *vi* : disentir

dissent² *n* : disentimiento *m*, disensión *f*

dissertation [ˌdɪsər'teɪʃən] *n* **1** DISCOURSE : disertación *f*, discurso *m* **2** THESIS : tesis *f*

disservice [dɪs'sərvɪs] *n* : perjuicio *m*

dissident¹ ['dɪsədənt] *adj* : disidente

dissident² *n* : disidente *mf*

dissimilar [dɪ'sɪmələr] *adj* : distinto, diferente, disímil

dissipate ['dɪsəˌpeɪt] *vt* **-pated; -pating 1** DISPERSE : disipar, dispersar **2** SQUANDER : malgastar, desperdiciar, derrochar, disipar

dissipation [ˌdɪsə'peɪʃən] *n* : disipación *f*, libertinaje *m*

dissolute ['dɪsəˌlu:t] *adj* : disoluto

dissolution [ˌdɪsə'lu:ʃən] *n* : disolución *f*

dissolve [dɪ'zɑlv] *v* **-solved; -solving** *vt* : disolver — *vi* : disolverse

dissonance ['dɪsənənts] *n* : disonancia *f*

dissuade [dɪ'sweɪd] *vt* **-suaded; -suading** : disuadir

distance ['dɪstənts] *n* **1** : distancia *f* <the distance between two points : la distancia entre dos puntos> <in the distance : a lo lejos> **2** RESERVE : actitud *f* distante, reserva *f* <to keep one's distance : guardar las distancias>

distant ['dɪstənt] *adj* **1** FAR : distante, lejano **2** REMOTE : distante, lejano, remoto **3** ALOOF : distante, frío

distantly ['dɪstəntli] *adv* **1** LOOSELY : aproximadamente, vagamente **2** COLDLY : fríamente, con frialdad

distaste [dɪs'teɪst] *n* : desagrado *m*, aversión *f*

distasteful [dɪs'teɪstfəl] *adj* : desagradable, de mal gusto

distemper [dɪs'tɛmpər] *n* : moquillo *m*

distend [dɪs'tɛnd] *vt* : dilatar, hinchar — *vi* : dilatarse, hincharse

distill [dɪ'stɪl] *vt* : destilar

distillation [ˌdɪstə'leɪʃən] *n* : destilación *f*

distiller [dɪˈstɪlər] *n* : destilador *m,* -dora *f*

distinct [dɪˈstɪŋkt] *adj* **1** DIFFERENT : distinto, diferente **2** CLEAR, UNMISTAKABLE : marcado, claro, evidente <a distinct possibility : una clara posibilidad>

distinction [dɪˈstɪŋkʃən] *n* **1** DIFFERENTIATION : distinción *f* **2** DIFFERENCE : diferencia *f* **3** EXCELLENCE : distinción *f,* excelencia *f* <a writer of distinction : un escritor destacado>

distinctive [dɪˈstɪŋktɪv] *adj* : distintivo, característico — **distinctively** *adv*

distinctiveness [dɪˈstɪŋktɪvnəs] *n* : peculiaridad *f*

distinctly [dɪˈstɪŋktli] *adv* : claramente, con claridad

distinguish [dɪsˈtɪŋgwɪʃ] *vt* **1** DIFFERENTIATE : distinguir, diferenciar **2** DISCERN : distinguir <he distinguished the sound of the piano : distinguió el sonido del piano> **3 to distinguish oneself** : señalarse, distinguirse — *vi* DISCRIMINATE : distinguir

distinguishable [dɪsˈtɪŋgwɪʃəbəl] *adj* : distinguible

distinguished [dɪsˈtɪŋgwɪʃt] *adj* : distinguido

distort [dɪˈstɔrt] *vt* **1** MISREPRESENT : distorsionar, tergiversar **2** DEFORM : distorsionar, deformar

distortion [dɪˈstɔrʃən] *n* : distorsión *f,* deformación *f,* tergiversación *f*

distract [dɪˈstrækt] *vt* : distraer, entretener

distracted [dɪˈstræktəd] *adj* : distraído

distraction [dɪˈstrækʃən] *n* **1** INTERRUPTION : distracción *f,* interrupción *f* **2** CONFUSION : confusión *f* **3** AMUSEMENT : diversión *f,* entretenimiento *m,* distracción *f*

distraught [dɪˈstrɔt] *adj* : afligido, turbado

distress[1] [dɪˈstrɛs] *vt* : afligir, darle pena (a alguien), hacer sufrir

distress[2] *n* **1** SORROW : dolor *m,* angustia *f,* aflicción *f* **2** PAIN : dolor *m* **3 in ~** : en peligro

distressful [dɪˈstrɛsfəl] *adj* : doloroso, penoso

distribute [dɪˈstrɪˌbjuːt, -bjʊt] *vt* **-uted; -uting** : distribuir, repartir

distribution [ˌdɪstrəˈbjuːʃən] *n* : distribución *f,* reparto *m*

distributive [dɪˈstrɪbjʊ̬tɪv] *adj* : distributivo

distributor [dɪˈstrɪbjʊ̬tər] *n* : distribuidor *m,* -dora *f*

district [ˈdɪsˌtrɪkt] *n* **1** REGION : región *f,* zona *f,* barrio *m* (de una ciudad) **2** : distrito *m* (zona política)

distrust[1] [dɪsˈtrʌst] *vt* : desconfiar de

distrust[2] *n* : desconfianza *f,* recelo *m*

distrustful [dɪsˈtrʌstfəl] *adj* : desconfiado, receloso, suspicaz

disturb [dɪˈstərb] *vt* **1** BOTHER : molestar, perturbar <sorry to disturb you : perdone la molestia> **2** DISARRANGE : desordenar **3** WORRY : inquietar, preocupar **4 to disturb the peace** : alterar el orden público

disturbance [dɪˈstərbənts] *n* **1** COMMOTION : alboroto *m,* disturbio *m* **2** INTERRUPTION : interrupción *f*

disuse [dɪsˈjuːs] *n* : desuso *m*

ditch[1] [ˈdɪtʃ] *vt* **1** : cavar zanjas en **2** DISCARD : deshacerse de, botar

ditch[2] *n* : zanja *f,* fosa *f,* cuneta *f* (en una carretera)

dither [ˈdɪðər] *n* **to be in a dither** : estar nervioso, ponerse como loco

ditto [ˈdɪtoː] *n, pl* **-tos 1** : lo mismo, ídem *m* **2 ditto marks** : comillas *fpl*

ditty [ˈdɪ̬ti] *n, pl* **-ties** : canción *f* corta y simple

diurnal [daɪˈərnəl] *adj* **1** DAILY : diario, cotidiano **2** : diurno <a diurnal animal : un animal diurno>

divan [ˈdaɪˌvæn, dɪˈ-] *n* : diván *m*

dive[1] [ˈdaɪv] *vi* **dived** *or* **dove** [ˈdoːv]; **dived; diving 1** PLUNGE : tirarse al agua, zambullirse, dar un clavado **2** SUBMERGE : sumergirse **3** DROP : bajar en picada (dícese de un avión), caer en picada

dive[2] *n* **1** PLUNGE : zambullida *f,* clavado *m* (en el agua) **2** DESCENT : descenso *m* en picada **3** BAR, JOINT : antro *m*

diver [ˈdaɪvər] *n* : saltador *m,* -dora *f;* clavadista *mf*

diverge [dəˈvərdʒ, daɪ-] *vi* **-verged; -verging 1** SEPARATE : divergir, separarse **2** DIFFER : divergir, discrepar

divergence [dəˈvərdʒənts, daɪ-] *n* : divergencia *f* — **divergent** [-ənt] *adj*

diverse [daɪˈvərs, də-, ˈdaɪˌvərs] *adj* : diverso, variado

diversify [daɪˈvərsəˌfaɪ, də-] *vt* **-fied; -fying** : diversificar, variar

diversion [daɪˈvərʒən, də-] *n* **1** DEVIATION : desviación *f* **2** AMUSEMENT, DISTRACTION : diversión *f,* distracción *f,* entretenimiento *m*

diversity [daɪˈvərsəṯi, də-] *n, pl* **-ties** : diversidad *f*

divert [dəˈvərt, daɪ-] *vt* **1** DEVIATE : desviar **2** DISTRACT : distraer **3** AMUSE : divertir, entretener

divest [daɪˈvɛst, də-] *vt* **1** UNDRESS : desnudar, desvestir **2 to divest of** : despojar de

divide [dəˈvaɪd] *v* **-vided; -viding** *vt* **1** HALVE : dividir, partir por la mitad **2** SHARE : repartir, dividir **3** : dividir (números) — *vi* : dividirse, dividir (en matemáticas)

dividend [ˈdɪvəˌdɛnd, -dənd] *n* **1** : dividendo *m* (en finanzas) **2** BONUS : benefício *m,* provecho *m* **3** : dividendo *m* (en matemáticas)

divider [dɪˈvaɪdər] *n* **1** : separador *m* (para ficheros, etc.) **2** *or* **room divider** : mampara *f,* biombo *m*

divine[1] [də'vaɪn] *adj* **-viner; -est 1** : divino **2** SUPERB : divino, espléndido — **divinely** *adv*

divine[2] *n* : clérigo *m,* eclesiástico *m*

divinity [də'vɪnəṭi] *n, pl* **-ties** : divinidad *f*

divisible [dɪ'vɪzəbəl] *adj* : divisible

division [dɪ'vɪʒən] *n* **1** DISTRIBUTION : división *f,* reparto *m* <division of labor : distribución del trabajo> **2** PART : división *f,* sección *f* **3** : división *f* (en matemáticas)

divisor [dɪ'vaɪzər] *n* : divisor *m*

divorce[1] [də'vors] *v* **-vorced; -vorcing** *vt* : divorciar — *vi* : divorciarse

divorce[2] *n* : divorcio *m*

divorcé [dɪˌvor'seɪ, -'siː; -'vorˌ-] *n* : divorciado *m*

divorcée [dɪˌvor'seɪ, -'siː; -'vorˌ-] *n* : divorciada *f*

divulge [də'vʌldʒ, daɪ-] *vt* **-vulged; -vulging** : revelar, divulgar

dizzily ['dɪzəli] *adv* : vertiginosamente

dizziness ['dɪzinəs] *n* : mareo *m,* vahído *m,* vértigo *m*

dizzy ['dɪzi] *adj* **dizzier; -est 1** : mareado <I feel dizzy : estoy mareado> **2** : vertiginoso <a dizzy speed : una velocidad vertiginosa>

DNA [ˌdiːˌɛn'eɪ] *n* : AND *m*

do ['duː] *v* **did** ['dɪd]; **done** ['dʌn]; **doing; does** ['dʌz] *vt* **1** CARRY OUT, PERFORM : hacer, realizar, llevar a cabo <she did her best : hizo todo lo posible> **2** PREPARE : preparar, hacer <do your homework : haz tu tarea> **3** ARRANGE : arreglar, peinar (el pelo) **4 to do in** RUIN : estropear, arruinar **5 to do in** KILL : matar, liquidar *fam* — *vi* **1** : hacer <you did well : hiciste bien> **2** FARE : estar, ir, andar <how are you doing? : ¿cómo estás?, ¿cómo te va?> **3** FINISH : terminar <now I'm done : ya terminé> **4** SERVE : servir, ser suficiente, alcanzar <this will do for now : esto servirá por el momento> **5 to do away with** ABOLISH : abolir, suprimir **6 to do away with** KILL : eliminar, matar **7 to do by** TREAT : tratar <he does well by her : él la trata bien> — *v aux* **1** (*used in interrogative sentences and negative statements*) <do you know her? : ¿la conoces?> <I don't like that : a mí no me gusta eso> **2** (*used for emphasis*) <I do hope you'll come : espero que vengas> **3** (*used as a substitute verb to avoid repetition*) <do you speak English? yes, I do : ¿habla inglés? sí>

docile ['dɑsəl] *adj* : dócil, sumiso

dock[1] ['dɑk] *vt* **1** CUT : cortar **2** : descontar dinero de (un sueldo) — *vi* ANCHOR, LAND : fondear, atracar

dock[2] *n* **1** PIER : atracadero *m* **2** WHARF : muelle *m* **3** : banquillo *m* de los acusados (en un tribunal)

doctor[1] ['dɑktər] *vt* **1** TREAT : tratar, curar **2** ALTER : adulterar, alterar, falsificar (un documento)

doctor[2] *n* **1** : doctor *m,* -tora *f* <Doctor of Philosophy : doctor en filosofía> **2** PHYSICIAN : médico *m,* -ca *f;* doctor *m,* -tora *f*

doctrine ['dɑktrɪn] *n* : doctrina *f*

document[1] ['dɑkjʊˌmɛnt] *vt* : documentar

document[2] ['dɑkjʊmənt] *n* : documento *m*

documentary[1] [ˌdɑkjʊ'mɛntəri] *adj* : documental

documentary[2] *n, pl* **-ries** : documental *m*

documentation [ˌdɑkjʊmən'teɪʃən] *n* : documentación *f*

dodge[1] ['dɑdʒ] *v* **dodged; dodging** *vt* : esquivar, eludir, evadir (impuestos) — *vi* : echarse a un lado

dodge[2] *n* **1** RUSE : truco *m,* treta *f,* artimaña *f* **2** EVASION : regate *m,* evasión *f*

dodo ['doːˌdoː] *n, pl* **-does** *or* **-dos** : dodo *m*

doe ['doː] *n, pl* **does** *or* **doe** : gama *f,* cierva *f*

doer ['duːər] *n* : hacedor *m,* -dora *f*

does → **do**

doff ['dɑf, 'dɔf] *vt* : quitarse <to doff one's hat : quitarse el sombrero>

dog[1] ['dɔg, 'dɑg] *vt* **dogged; dogging** : seguir de cerca, perseguir, acosar <to dog someone's footsteps : seguir los pasos de alguien> <dogged by bad luck : perseguido por la mala suerte>

dog[2] *n* : perro *m,* -rra *f*

dogcatcher ['dɔgˌkætʃər] *n* : perrero *m,* -ra *f*

dog–eared ['dɔgˌɪrd] *adj* : con las esquinas dobladas

dogged ['dɔgəd] *adj* : tenaz, terco, obstinado

doggy ['dɔgi] *n, pl* **doggies** : perrito *m,* -ta *f*

doghouse ['dɔgˌhaʊs] *n* : casita *f* de perro

dogma ['dɔgmə] *n* : dogma *m*

dogmatic [dɔg'mæṭɪk] *adj* : dogmático

dogmatism ['dɔgməˌtɪzəm] *n* : dogmatismo *m*

dogwood ['dɔgˌwʊd] *n* : cornejo *m*

doily ['dɔɪli] *n, pl* **-lies** : pañito *m*

doings ['duːɪŋz] *npl* : eventos *mpl,* actividades *fpl*

doldrums ['doːldrəmz, 'dɑl-] *npl* **1** : zona *f* de las calmas ecuatoriales **2 to be in the doldrums** : estar abatido (dícese de una persona), estar estancado (dícese de una empresa)

dole ['doːl] *n* **1** ALMS : distribución *f* a los necesitados, limosna *f* **2** : subsidios *mpl* de desempleo

doleful ['doːlfəl] *adj* : triste, lúgubre

dolefully ['doːlfəli] *adv* : con pesar, de manera triste

dole out *vt* **doled out; doling out** : repartir

doll ['dɑl, 'dɔl] *n* : muñeco *m,* -ca *f*

dollar ['dɑlər] *n* : dólar *m*

dolly [ˈdɑli] *n, pl* **-lies 1 → doll 2** : plataforma *f* rodante

dolphin [ˈdɑlfən, ˈdɔl-] *n* : delfín *m*

dolt [ˈdoːlt] *n* : imbécil *mf;* tonto *m,* -ta *f*

domain [doˈmeɪn, də-] *n* **1** TERRITORY : dominio *m,* territorio *m* **2** FIELD : campo *m,* esfera *f,* ámbito *m* <the domain of art : el ámbito de las artes>

dome [ˈdoːm] *n* : cúpula *f,* bóveda *f*

domestic[1] [dəˈmɛstɪk] *adj* **1** HOUSEHOLD : doméstico, casero **2** : nacional, interno <domestic policy : política interna> **3** TAME : domesticado

domestic[2] *n* : empleado *m* doméstico, empleada *f* doméstica

domestically [dəˈmɛstɪkli] *adv* : domésticamente

domesticate [dəˈmɛstɪˌkeɪt] *vt* **-cated; -cating** : domesticar

domicile [ˈdɑməˌsaɪl, ˈdoː-; ˈdɑməsɪl] *n* : domicilio *m*

dominance [ˈdɑmənənts] *n* : dominio *m,* dominación *f*

dominant [ˈdɑmənənt] *adj* : dominante

dominate [ˈdɑməˌneɪt] *v* **-nated; -nating** : dominar

domination [ˌdɑməˈneɪʃən] *n* : dominación *f*

domineer [ˌdɑməˈnɪr] *vt* : dominar sobre, avasallar, tiranizar

Dominican [dəˈmɪnɪkən] *n* : dominicano *m,* -na *f* — **Dominican** *adj*

dominion [dəˈmɪnjən] *n* **1** POWER : dominio *m* **2** DOMAIN, TERRITORY : dominio *m,* territorio *m*

domino [ˈdɑməˌnoː] *n, pl* **-noes** *or* **-nos 1** : dominó *m* **2 dominoes** *npl* : dominó *m* (juego)

don [ˈdɑn] *vt* **donned; donning** : ponerse

donate [ˈdoːˌneɪt, doːˈ-] *vt* **-nated; -nating** : donar, hacer un donativo de

donation [doːˈneɪʃən] *n* : donación *f,* donativo *m*

done[1] [ˈdʌn] **→ do**

done[2] *adj* **1** FINISHED : terminado, acabado, concluido **2** COOKED : cocinado

donkey [ˈdɑŋki, ˈdʌŋ-] *n, pl* **-keys** : burro *m,* asno *m*

donor [ˈdoːnər] *n* : donante *mf;* donador *m,* -dora *f*

doodle[1] [ˈduːdəl] *v* **-dled; -dling** : garabatear

doodle[2] *n* : garabato *m*

doom[1] [ˈduːm] *vt* : condenar

doom[2] *n* **1** JUDGMENT : sentencia *f,* condena *f* **2** DEATH : muerte *f* **3** FATE : destino *m* **4** RUIN : perdición *f,* ruina *f*

door [ˈdor] *n* : puerta *f*

doorbell [ˈdorˌbɛl] *n* : timbre *m*

doorknob [ˈdorˌnɑb] *n* : pomo *m,* perilla *f*

doorman [ˈdormən] *n, pl* **-men** [-mən, -ˌmɛn] : portero *m*

doormat [ˈdorˌmæt] *n* : felpudo *m*

doorstep [ˈdorˌstɛp] *n* : umbral *m*

doorway [ˈdorˌweɪ] *n* : entrada *f,* portal *m*

dope[1] [ˈdoːp] *vt* **doped; doping** : drogar, narcotizar

dope[2] *n* **1** DRUG : droga *f,* estupefaciente *m,* narcótico *m* **2** IDIOT : idiota *mf;* tonto *m,* -ta *f* **3** INFORMATION : información *f*

dormant [ˈdɔrmənt] *adj* : inactivo, latente

dormer [ˈdɔrmər] *n* : buhardilla *f*

dormitory [ˈdɔrməˌtori] *n, pl* **-ries** : dormitorio *m,* residencia *f* de estudiantes

dormouse [ˈdɔrˌmaʊs] *n* : lirón *m*

dorsal [ˈdɔrsəl] *adj* : dorsal — **dorsally** *adv*

dory [ˈdori] *n, pl* **-ries** : bote *m* de fondo plano

dosage [ˈdoːsɪdʒ] *n* : dosis *f*

dose[1] [ˈdoːs] *vt* **dosed; dosing** : medicinar

dose[2] *n* : dosis *f*

dot[1] [ˈdɑt] *vt* **dotted; dotting 1** : poner el punto sobre (una letra) **2** SCATTER : esparcir, salpicar

dot[2] *n* : punto *m* <at six on the dot : a las seis en punto> <dots and dashes : puntos y rayas>

dote [ˈdoːt] *vi* **doted; doting** : chochear

double[1] [ˈdʌbəl] *v* **-bled; -bling** *vt* **1** : doblar, duplicar (una cantidad), redoblar (esfuerzos) **2** FOLD : doblar, plegar **3 to double one's fist** : apretar el puño — *vi* **1** : doblarse, duplicarse **2 to double over** : retorcerse

double[2] *adj* : doble — **doubly** *adv*

double[3] *n* : doble *mf*

double bass *n* : contrabajo *m*

double–cross [ˌdʌbəlˈkrɔs] *vt* : traicionar

double–crosser [ˌdʌbəlˈkrɔsər] *n* : traidor *m,* -dora *f*

double–jointed [ˌdʌbəlˈdʒɔintəd] *adj* : con articulaciones dobles

double–talk [ˈdʌbəlˌtɔk] *n* : ambigüedades *fpl,* lenguaje *m* con doble sentido

doubt[1] [ˈdaʊt] *vt* **1** QUESTION : dudar de, cuestionar **2** DISTRUST : desconfiar de **3** : dudar, creer poco probable <I doubt it very much : lo dudo mucho>

doubt[2] *n* **1** UNCERTAINTY : duda *f,* incertidumbre *f* **2** DISTRUST : desconfianza *f* **3** SKEPTICISM : duda *f,* escepticismo *m*

doubtful [ˈdaʊtfəl] *adj* **1** QUESTIONABLE : dudoso **2** UNCERTAIN : dudoso, incierto

doubtfully [ˈdaʊtfəli] *adv* : dudosamente, sin estar convencido

doubtless [ˈdaʊtləs] *or* **doubtlessly** *adv* : sin duda

douche[1] [ˈduːʃ] *vt* **douched; douching** : irrigar

douche[2] *n* : ducha *f,* irrigación *f*

dough [ˈdoː] *n* : masa *f*

doughnut [ˈdoːˌnʌt] *n* : rosquilla *f*, dona *f Mex*
doughty [ˈdaʊt̬i] *adj* **-tier; -est** : fuerte, valiente
dour [ˈdaʊər, ˈdʊr] *adj* **1** STERN : severo, adusto **2** SULLEN : hosco, taciturno — **dourly** *adv*
douse [ˈdaʊs, ˈdaʊz] *vt* **doused; dousing 1** DRENCH : empapar, mojar **2** EXTINGUISH : extinguir, apagar
dove[1] [ˈdoːv] → **dive**
dove[2] [ˈdʌv] *n* : paloma *f*
dovetail [ˈdʌvˌteɪl] *vi* : encajar, enlazar
dowdy [ˈdaʊdi] *adj* **dowdier; -est** : sin gracia, poco elegante
dowel [ˈdaʊəl] *n* : clavija *f*
down[1] [ˈdaʊn] *vt* **1** FELL : tumbar, derribar, abatir **2** DEFEAT : derrotar
down[2] *adv* **1** DOWNWARD : hacia abajo **2 to lie down** : acostarse, echarse **3 to put down (money)** : pagar un depósito (de dinero) **4 to sit down** : sentarse **5 to take down, to write down** : apuntar, anotar
down[3] *adj* **1** DESCENDING : de bajada <the down elevator : el ascensor de bajada> **2** REDUCED : reducido, rebajado <attendance is down : la concurrencia ha disminuido> **3** DOWNCAST : abatido, deprimido
down[4] *n* : plumón *m*
down[5] *prep* **1** : (hacia) abajo <down the mountain : montaña abajo> <I walked down the stairs : bajé por la escalera> **2** ALONG : por, a lo largo de <we ran down the beach : corrimos por la playa> **3** : a través de <down the years : a través de los años>
downcast [ˈdaʊnˌkæst] *adj* **1** SAD : triste, abatido **2 with downcast eyes** : con los ojos bajos, con los ojos mirando al suelo
downfall [ˈdaʊnˌfɔl] *n* : ruina *f*, perdición *f*
downgrade[1] [ˈdaʊnˌgreɪd] *vt* **-graded; -grading** : bajar de categoría
downgrade[2] *n* : bajada *f*
downhearted [ˈdaʊnˌhɑrt̬əd] *adj* : desanimado, descorazonado
downhill [ˈdaʊnˈhɪl] *adv & adj* : cuesta abajo
down payment *n* : entrega *f* inicial
downpour [ˈdaʊnˌpor] *n* : aguacero *m*, chaparrón *m*
downright[1] [ˈdaʊnˌraɪt] *adv* THOROUGHLY : absolutamente, completamente
downright[2] *adj* : patente, manifiesto, absoluto <a downright refusal : un rechazo categórico>
downstairs[1] [ˈdaʊnˈstærz] *adv* : abajo
downstairs[2] [ˈdaʊnˌstærz] *adj* : del piso de abajo
downstairs[3] [ˈdaʊnˈstærz, -ˌstærz] *n* : planta *f* baja
downstream [ˈdaʊnˈstriːm] *adv* : río abajo
down–to–earth [ˌdaʊntuˈərth] *adj* : práctico, realista
downtown[1] [ˌdaʊnˈtaʊn] *adv* : hacia el centro, al centro, en el centro (de la ciudad)
downtown[2] *adj* : del centro (de la ciudad) <downtown Chicago : el centro de Chicago>
downtown[3] [ˌdaʊnˈtaʊn, ˈdaʊnˌtaʊn] *n* : centro *m* (de la ciudad)
downtrodden [ˈdaʊnˌtrɑdən] *adj* : oprimido
downward [ˈdaʊnwərd] *or* **downwards** [-wərdz] *adv & adj* : hacia abajo
downwind [ˈdaʊnˈwɪnd] *adv & adj* : en la dirección del viento
downy [ˈdaʊni] *adj* **downier; -est 1** : cubierto de plumón, plumoso **2** VELVETY : aterciopelado, velloso
dowry [ˈdaʊri] *n, pl* **-ries** : dote *f*
doze[1] [ˈdoːz] *vi* **dozed; dozing** : dormitar
doze[2] *n* : sueño *m* ligero, cabezada *f*
dozen [ˈdʌzən] *n, pl* **dozens** *or* **dozen** : docena *f*
drab [ˈdræb] *adj* **drabber; drabbest 1** BROWNISH : pardo **2** DULL, LACKLUSTER : monótono, gris, deslustrado
draft[1] [ˈdræft, ˈdraft] *vt* **1** CONSCRIPT : reclutar **2** COMPOSE, SKETCH : hacer el borrador de, redactar
draft[2] *adj* **1** : de barril <draft beer : cerveza de barril> **2** : de tiro <draft horses : caballos de tiro>
draft[3] *n* **1** HAULAGE : tiro *m* **2** DRINK, GULP : trago *m* **3** OUTLINE, SKETCH : bosquejo *m*, borrador *m*, versión *f* **4** : corriente *f* de aire, chiflón *m*, tiro *m* (de una chimenea) **5** CONSCRIPTION : conscripción *f* **6 bank draft** : giro *m* bancario, letra *f* de cambio
draftee [dræfˈtiː] *n* : recluta *mf*
draftsman [ˈdræftsmən] *n, pl* **-men** [-mən, -ˌmɛn] : dibujante *mf*
drafty [ˈdræfti] *adj* **draftier; -est** : con corrientes de aire
drag[1] [ˈdræg] *v* **dragged; dragging** *vt* **1** HAUL : arrastrar, jalar **2** DREDGE : dragar — *vi* **1** TRAIL : arrastrarse **2** LAG : rezagarse **3** : hacerse pesado, hacerse largo <the day dragged on : el día se hizo largo>
drag[2] *n* **1** RESISTANCE : resistencia *f* (aerodinámica) **2** HINDRANCE : traba *f*, estorbo *m* **3** BORE : pesadez *f*, plomo *m fam*
dragnet [ˈdrægˌnɛt] *n* **1** : red *f* barredera (en pesca) **2** : operativo *m* policial de captura
dragon [ˈdrægən] *n* : dragón *m*
dragonfly [ˈdrægənˌflaɪ] *n, pl* **-flies** : libélula *f*
drain[1] [ˈdreɪn] *vt* **1** EMPTY : vaciar, drenar **2** EXHAUST : agotar, consumir — *vi* **1** : escurrir, escurrirse <the dishes are draining : los platos están escurriéndose> **2** EMPTY : desaguar **3 to drain away** : irse agotando

drain² *n* **1** : desagüe *m* **2** SEWER : alcantarilla *f* **3** GRATING : sumidero *m,* resumidero *m,* rejilla *f* **4** EXHAUSTION : agotamiento *m,* disminución *f* (de energía, etc.) <to be a drain on : agotar, consumir> **5** **to throw down the drain** : tirar por la ventana

drainage [ˈdreɪnɪdʒ] *n* : desagüe *m,* drenaje *m*

drainpipe [ˈdreɪn͵paɪp] *n* : tubo *m* de desagüe, caño *m*

drake [ˈdreɪk] *n* : pato *m* (macho)

drama [ˈdrɑmə, ˈdræ-] *n* **1** THEATER : drama *m,* teatro *m* **2** PLAY : obra *f* de teatro, drama *m*

dramatic [drəˈmætɪk] *adj* : dramático — **dramatically** [-tɪkli] *adv*

dramatist [ˈdræmətɪst, ˈdrɑ-] *n* : dramaturgo *m,* -ga *f*

dramatization [͵dræmət̬əˈzeɪʃən, ͵drɑ-] *n* : dramatización *f*

dramatize [ˈdræmə͵taɪz, ˈdrɑ-] *vt* **-tized; -tizing** : dramatizar

drank → **drink**

drape¹ [ˈdreɪp] *vt* **draped; draping** **1** COVER : cubrir (con tela) **2** HANG : drapear, disponer los pliegues de

drape² *n* **1** HANG : caída *f* **2** **drapes** *npl* : cortinas *fpl*

drapery [ˈdreɪpəri] *n, pl* **-eries** **1** CLOTH : pañería *f,* tela *f* para cortinas **2** **draperies** *npl* : cortinas *fpl*

drastic [ˈdræstɪk] *adj* **1** HARSH, SEVERE : drástico, severo **2** EXTREME : radical, excepcional — **drastically** [-tɪkli] *adv*

draught [ˈdræft, ˈdraft] → **draft³**

draughty [ˈdrafti] → **drafty**

draw¹ [ˈdrɔ] *v* **drew** [ˈdruː]; **drawn** [ˈdrɔn]; **drawing** *vt* **1** PULL : tirar de, jalar, correr (cortinas) **2** ATTRACT : atraer **3** PROVOKE : provocar, suscitar **4** INHALE : aspirar <to draw breath : respirar> **5** EXTRACT : sacar, extraer **6** TAKE : sacar <to draw a number : sacar un número> **7** COLLECT : cobrar, percibir (un sueldo, etc.) **8** BEND : tensar (un arco) **9** TIE : empatar (en deportes) **10** SKETCH : dibujar, trazar **11** FORMULATE : sacar, formular, llegar a <to draw a conclusion : llegar a una conclusión> **12** **to draw out** : hacer hablar (sobre algo), hacer salir de sí mismo **13** **to draw up** DRAFT : redactar — *vi* **1** SKETCH : dibujar **2** TUG : tirar, jalar **3** **to draw near** : acercarse **4** **to draw to a close** : terminar, finalizar **5** **to draw up** STOP : parar

draw² *n* **1** DRAWING, RAFFLE : sorteo *m* **2** TIE : empate *m* **3** ATTRACTION : atracción *f* **4** PUFF : chupada *f* (de un cigarrillo, etc.)

drawback [ˈdrɔ͵bæk] *n* : desventaja *f,* inconveniente *m*

drawbridge [ˈdrɔ͵bridʒ] *n* : puente *m* levadizo

drawer [ˈdrɔr, ˈdrɔər] *n* **1** ILLUSTRATOR : dibujante *mf* **2** : gaveta *f,* cajón *m* (en un mueble) **3** **drawers** *npl* UNDERPANTS : calzones *mpl*

drawing [ˈdrɔɪŋ] *n* **1** LOTTERY : sorteo *m,* lotería *f* **2** SKETCH : dibujo *m,* bosquejo *m*

drawl¹ [ˈdrɔl] *vi* : hablar arrastrando las palabras

drawl² *n* : habla *f* lenta y con vocales prolongadas

dread¹ [ˈdrɛd] *vt* : tenerle pavor a, temer

dread² *adj* : pavoroso, aterrado

dread³ *n* : pavor *m,* temor *m*

dreadful [ˈdrɛdfəl] *adj* **1** DREAD : pavoroso **2** TERRIBLE : espantoso, atroz, terrible — **dreadfully** *adv*

dream¹ [ˈdriːm] *v* **dreamed** [ˈdrɛmpt, ˈdriːmd] *or* **dreamt** [ˈdrɛmpt]; **dreaming** *vi* **1** : soñar <to dream about : soñar con> **2** FANTASIZE : fantasear — *vt* **1** : soñar **2** IMAGINE : imaginarse **3** **to dream up** : inventar, idear

dream² *n* **1** : sueño *m,* ensueño *m* **2** **bad dream** NIGHTMARE : pesadilla *f*

dreamer [ˈdriːmər] *n* : soñador *m,* -dora *f*

dreamlike [ˈdriːm͵laɪk] *adj* : de ensueño

dreamy [ˈdriːmi] *adj* **dreamier; -est** **1** DISTRACTED : soñador, distraído **2** DREAMLIKE : de ensueño **3** MARVELOUS : maravilloso

drearily [ˈdrɪrəli] *adv* : sombríamente

dreary [ˈdrɪri] *adj* **-rier; -est** : deprimente, lóbrego, sombrío

dredge¹ [ˈdrɛdʒ] *vt* **dredged; dredging** **1** DIG : dragar **2** COAT : espolvorear, enharinar

dredge² *n* : draga *f*

dredger [ˈdrɛdʒər] *n* : draga *f*

dregs [ˈdrɛgz] *npl* **1** LEES : posos *mpl,* heces *fpl* (de un líquido) **2** : heces *fpl,* escoria *f* <the dregs of society : la escoria de la sociedad>

drench [ˈdrɛntʃ] *vt* : empapar, mojar, calar

dress¹ [ˈdrɛs] *vt* **1** CLOTHE : vestir **2** DECORATE : decorar, adornar **3** : preparar (pollo o pescado), aliñar (ensalada) **4** : curar, vendar (una herida) **5** FERTILIZE : abonar (la tierra) — *vi* **1** : vestirse **2** **to dress up** : ataviarse, engalanarse, ponerse de etiqueta

dress² *n* **1** APPAREL : indumentaria *f,* ropa *f* **2** : vestido *m,* traje *m* (de mujer)

dresser [ˈdrɛsər] *n* : cómoda *f* con espejo

dressing [ˈdrɛsɪŋ] *n* **1** : vestirse *m* **2** : aderezo *m,* aliño *m* (de ensalada), relleno *m* (de pollo) **3** BANDAGE : vendaje *m,* gasa *f*

dressmaker [ˈdrɛs͵meɪkər] *n* : modista *mf*

dressmaking [ˈdrɛs͵meɪkɪŋ] *n* : costura *f*

dressy [ˈdrɛsi] *adj* **dressier; -est** : de mucho vestir, elegante

drew → **draw**

dribble[1] [ˈdrɪbəl] *vi* **-bled; -bling 1** DRIP : gotear **2** DROOL : babear **3** : driblar (en basquetbol)
dribble[2] *n* **1** TRICKLE : goteo *m,* hilo *m* **2** DROOL : baba *f* **3** : drible *m* (en basquetbol)
drier → **dry**[2], **dryer**
driest → **dry**[2]
drift[1] [ˈdrɪft] *vi* **1** : dejarse llevar por la corriente, ir a la deriva (dícese de un bote), ir sin rumbo (dícese de una persona) **2** ACCUMULATE : amontonarse, acumularse, apilarse
drift[2] *n* **1** DRIFTING : deriva *f* **2** HEAP, MASS : montón *m* (de arena, etc.), ventisquero *m* (de nieve) **3** MEANING : sentido *m*
drifter [ˈdrɪftər] *n* : vagabundo *m,* -da *f*
driftwood [ˈdrɪft,wʊd] *n* : madera *f* flotante
drill[1] [ˈdrɪl] *vt* **1** BORE : perforar, taladrar **2** INSTRUCT : instruir por repetición — *vi* **1** TRAIN : entrenarse **2 to drill for oil** : perforar en busca de petróleo
drill[2] *n* **1** : taladro *m,* barrena *f* **2** EXERCISE, PRACTICE : ejercicio *m,* instrucción *f*
drily → **dryly**
drink[1] [ˈdrɪŋk] *v* **drank** [ˈdræŋk]; **drunk** [ˈdrʌŋk] *or* **drank; drinking** *vt* **1** IMBIBE : beber, tomar **2 to drink up** ABSORB : absorber — *vi* **1** : beber **2** : beber alcohol, tomar
drink[2] *n* **1** : bebida *f* **2** : bebida *f* alcohólica
drinkable [ˈdrɪŋkəbəl] *adj* : potable
drinker [ˈdrɪŋkər] *n* : bebedor *m,* -dora *f*
drip[1] [ˈdrɪp] *vi* **dripped; dripping** : gotear, chorrear
drip[2] *n* **1** DROP : gota *f* **2** DRIPPING : goteo *m*
drive[1] [ˈdraɪv] *v* **drove** [ˈdroːv]; **driven** [ˈdrɪvən]; **driving** *vt* **1** IMPEL : impeler, impulsar **2** OPERATE : guiar, conducir, manejar (un vehículo) **3** COMPEL : obligar, forzar **4** : clavar, hincar <to drive a stake : clavar una estaca> **5** *or* **to drive away** : ahuyentar, echar **6 to drive crazy** : volver loco — *vi* : manejar, conducir <do you know how to drive? : ¿sabes manejar?>
drive[2] *n* **1** RIDE : paseo *m* en coche **2** CAMPAIGN : campaña *f* <fund-raising drive : campaña para recaudar fondos> **3** DRIVEWAY : camino *m* de entrada, entrada *f* **4** TRANSMISSION : transmisión *f* <front-wheel drive : tracción delantera> **5** ENERGY : dinamismo *m,* energía *f* **6** INSTINCT, NEED : instinto *m,* necesidad *f* básica
drivel [ˈdrɪvəl] *n* : tontería *f,* estupidez *f*
driver [ˈdraɪvər] *n* : conductor *m,* -tora *f;* chofer *m*
driveway [ˈdraɪv,weɪ] *n* : camino *m* de entrada, entrada *f* (para coches)
drizzle[1] [ˈdrɪzəl] *vi* **-zled; -zling** : lloviznar, garuar
drizzle[2] *n* : llovizna *f,* garúa *f*
droll [ˈdroːl] *adj* : cómico, gracioso, chistoso — **drolly** *adv*
dromedary [ˈdrɑmə,dɛri] *n, pl* **-daries** : dromedario *m*
drone[1] [ˈdroːn] *vi* **droned; droning 1** BUZZ : zumbar **2** MURMUR : hablar con monotonía, murmurar
drone[2] *n* **1** : zángano *m* (abeja) **2** FREELOADER : gorrón *m,* -rrona *f fam;* parásito *m,* -ta *f* **3** BUZZ, HUM : zumbido *m,* murmullo *m*
drool[1] [ˈdruːl] *vi* : babear
drool[2] *n* : baba *f*
droop[1] [ˈdruːp] *vi* **1** HANG : inclinarse (dícese de la cabeza), encorvarse (dícese de los escombros), marchitarse (dícese de las flores) **2** FLAG : decaer, flaquear <his spirits drooped : se desanimó>
droop[2] *n* : inclinación *f,* caída *f*
drop[1] [ˈdrɑp] *v* **dropped; dropping** *vt* **1** : dejar caer, soltar <she dropped the glass : se le cayó el vaso> <to drop a hint : dejar caer una indirecta> **2** SEND : mandar <drop me a line : mándame unas líneas> **3** ABANDON : abandonar, dejar <to drop the subject : cambiar de tema> **4** LOWER : bajar <he dropped his voice : bajó la voz> **5** OMIT : omitir **6 to drop off** : dejar — *vi* **1** DRIP : gotear **2** FALL : caer(se) **3** DECREASE, DESCEND : bajar, descender <the wind dropped : amainó el viento> **4 to drop back** *or* **to drop behind** : rezagarse, quedarse atrás **5 to drop by** *or* **to drop in** : pasar
drop[2] *n* **1** : gota *f* (de líquido) **2** DECLINE : caída *f,* bajada *f,* descenso *m* **3** INCLINE : caída *f,* pendiente *f* <a 20-foot drop : una caída de 20 pies> **4** SWEET : pastilla *f,* dulce *m* **5 drops** *npl* : gotas *fpl* (de medicina)
droplet [ˈdrɑplət] *n* : gotita *f*
dropper [ˈdrɑpər] *n* : gotero *m,* cuentagotas *m*
dross [ˈdrɑs, ˈdrɔs] *n* : escoria *f*
drought [ˈdraʊt] *n* : sequía *f*
drove[1] → **drive**
drove[2] [ˈdroːv] *n* : multitud *f,* gentío *m,* manada *f* (de ganado) <in droves : en manada>
drown [ˈdraʊn] *vt* **1** : ahogar **2** INUNDATE : anegar, inundar **3 to drown out** : ahogar — *vi* : ahogarse
drowse[1] [ˈdraʊz] *vi* **drowsed; drowsing** DOZE : dormitar
drowse[2] *n* : sueño *m* ligero, cabezada *f*
drowsiness [ˈdraʊzinəs] *n* : somnolencia *f,* adormecimiento *m*
drowsy [ˈdraʊzi] *adj* **drowsier; -est** : somnoliento, soñoliento

drub [ˈdrʌb] *vt* **drubbed; drubbing 1** BEAT, THRASH **:** golpear, apalear **2** DEFEAT **:** derrotar por completo

drudge[1] [ˈdrʌdʒ] *vi* **drudged; drudging :** trabajar como esclavo, trabajar duro

drudge[2] *n* **:** esclavo *m,* -va *f* del trabajo

drudgery [ˈdrʌdʒəri] *n, pl* **-eries :** trabajo *m* pesado

drug[1] [ˈdrʌg] *vt* **drugged; drugging :** drogar, narcotizar

drug[2] *n* **1** MEDICATION **:** droga *f,* medicina *f,* medicamento *m* **2** NARCOTIC **:** narcótico *m,* estupefaciente *m,* droga *f*

druggist [ˈdrʌgɪst] *n* **:** farmacéutico *m,* -ca *f*

drugstore [ˈdrʌgˌstor] *n* **:** farmacia *f,* botica *f,* droguería *f*

drum[1] [ˈdrʌm] *v* **drummed; drumming** *vt* **:** meter a fuerza <he drummed it into my head : me lo metió en la cabeza a fuerza> — *vi* **:** tocar el tambor

drum[2] *n* **1 :** tambor *m* **2 :** bidón *m* <oil drum : bidón de petróleo>

drummer [ˈdrʌmər] *n* **:** baterista *mf*

drumstick [ˈdrʌmˌstɪk] *n* **1 :** palillo *m* (de tambor), baqueta *f* **2 :** muslo *m* de pollo

drunk[1] *pp* → **drink**

drunk[2] [ˈdrʌŋk] *adj* **:** borracho, embriagado, ebrio

drunk[3] *n* **:** borracho *m,* -cha *f*

drunkard [ˈdrʌŋkərd] *n* **:** borracho *m,* -cha *f*

drunken [ˈdrʌŋkən] *adj* **:** borracho, ebrio <drunken driver : conductor ebrio> <drunken brawl : pleito de borrachos>

drunkenly [ˈdrʌŋkənli] *adv* **:** como un borracho

drunkenness [ˈdrʌŋkənnəs] *n* **:** borrachera *f,* embriaguez *f,* ebriedad *f*

dry[1] [ˈdraɪ] *v* **dried; drying** *vt* **:** secar — *vi* **:** secarse

dry[2] *adj* **drier; driest 1 :** seco **2** THIRSTY **:** sediento **3 :** donde la venta de bebidas alcohólicas está prohibida <a dry county : un condado seco> **4** DULL **:** aburrido, árido **5 :** seco (dícese del vino), brut (dícese de la champaña)

dry–clean [ˈdraɪˌkliːn] *v* **:** limpiar en seco

dry cleaner *n* **:** tintorería *f* (servicio)

dry cleaning *n* **:** limpieza *f* en seco

dryer [ˈdraɪər] *n* **1 hair dryer :** secador *m* **2 clothes dryer :** secadora *f*

dry goods *npl* **:** artículos *mpl* de confección

dry ice *n* **:** hielo *m* seco

dryly [ˈdraɪli] *adv* **:** secamente

dryness [ˈdraɪnəs] *n* **:** sequedad *f,* aridez *f*

dual [ˈduːəl, ˈdjuː-] *adj* **:** doble

dub [ˈdʌb] *vt* **dubbed; dubbing 1** CALL **:** apodar **2 :** doblar (una película), mezclar (una grabación)

dubious [ˈduːbiəs, ˈdjuː-] *adj* **1** UNCERTAIN **:** dudoso, indeciso **2** QUESTIONABLE **:** sospechoso, dudoso, discutible

dubiously [ˈduːbiəsli, ˈdjuː-] *adv* **1** UNCERTAINLY **:** dudosamente, con desconfianza **2** SUSPICIOUSLY **:** de modo sospechoso, con recelo

duchess [ˈdʌtʃəs] *n* **:** duquesa *f*

duck[1] [ˈdʌk] *vt* **1** LOWER **:** agachar, bajar (la cabeza) **2** PLUNGE **:** zambullir **3** EVADE **:** eludir, evadir — *vi* **to duck down :** agacharse

duck[2] *n, pl* **duck** *or* **ducks :** pato *m,* -ta *f*

duckling [ˈdʌklɪŋ] *n* **:** patito *m,* -ta *f*

duct [ˈdʌkt] *n* **:** conducto *m*

ductile [ˈdʌktəl] *adj* **:** dúctil

dude [ˈduːd, ˈdjuːd] *n* **1** DANDY **:** dandi *m,* dandy *m* **2** GUY **:** tipo *m*

due[1] [ˈduː, ˈdjuː] *adv* **:** justo a, derecho hacia <due north : derecho hacia el norte>

due[2] *adj* **1** PAYABLE **:** pagadero, sin pagar **2** APPROPRIATE **:** debido, apropiado <after due consideration : con las debidas consideraciones> **3** EXPECTED **:** esperado <the train is due soon : esperamos el tren muy pronto, el tren debe llegar pronto> **4 due to :** debido a, por

due[3] *n* **1 to give someone his (her) due :** darle a alguien su merecido **2 dues** *npl* **:** cuota *f*

duel[1] [ˈduːəl, ˈdjuː-] *vi* **:** batirse en duelo

duel[2] *n* **:** duelo *m*

duet [duˈɛt, dju-] *n* **:** dúo *m*

due to *prep* **:** debido a

dug *pp* → **dig**

dugout [ˈdʌgˌaʊt] *n* **1** CANOE **:** piragua *f* **2** SHELTER **:** refugio *m* subterráneo

duke [ˈduːk, ˈdjuːk] *n* **:** duque *m*

dull[1] [ˈdʌl] *vt* **1** DIM **:** opacar, quitar el brillo a, deslustrar **2** BLUNT **:** embotar (un filo), entorpecer (los sentidos), aliviar (el dolor), amortiguar (sonidos)

dull[2] *adj* **1** STUPID **:** torpe, lerdo, lento **2** BLUNT **:** desafilado, despuntado **3** LACKLUSTER **:** sin brillo, deslustrado **4** BORING **:** aburrido, soso, pesado — **dully** *adv*

dullness [ˈdʌlnəs] *n* **1** STUPIDITY **:** estupidez *f* **2 :** embotamiento *m* (de los sentidos) **3** MONOTONY **:** monotonía *f,* insipidez *f* **4 :** falta *f* de brillo **5** BLUNTNESS **:** falta *f* de filo, embotadura *f*

duly [ˈduːli, ˈdjuː-] *adv* PROPERLY **:** debidamente, a su debido tiempo

dumb [ˈdʌm] *adj* **1** MUTE **:** mudo **2** STUPID **:** estúpido, tonto, bobo — **dumbly** *adv*

dumbbell [ˈdʌmˌbɛl] *n* **1** WEIGHT **:** pesa *f* **2 :** estúpido *m,* -da *f*

dumbfound *or* **dumfound** [ˌdʌmˈfaʊnd] *vt* **:** dejar atónito, dejar sin habla

dummy [ˈdʌmi] *n, pl* **-mies 1** SHAM **:** imitación *f,* sustituto *m* **2** PUPPET

: muñeco *m* 3 MANNEQUIN : maniquí *m* 4 IDIOT : tonto *m,* -ta *f;* idiota *mf*
dump[1] [ˈdʌmp] *vt* : descargar, verter
dump[2] *n* **1** : vertedero *m,* tiradero *m Mex* **2 down in the dumps** : triste, deprimido
dumpling [ˈdʌmplɪŋ] *n* : bola *f* de masa hervida
dumpy [ˈdʌmpi] *adj* **dumpier; -est** : rechoncho, regordete
dun[1] [ˈdʌn] *vt* **dunned; dunning** : apremiar (a un deudor)
dun[2] *adj* : pardo (color)
dunce [ˈdʌnts] *n* : estúpido *m,* -da *f;* burro *m,* -rra *f fam*
dune [ˈduːn, ˈdjuːn] *n* : duna *f*
dung [ˈdʌŋ] *n* **1** FECES : excrementos *mpl* **2** MANURE : estiércol *m*
dungaree [ˌdʌŋgəˈriː] *n* **1** DENIM : tela *f* vaquera, mezclilla *f Chile, Mex* **2 dungarees** *npl* : pantalones *mpl* de trabajo hechos de tela vaquera
dungeon [ˈdʌndʒən] *n* : mazmorra *f,* calabozo *m*
dunk [ˈdʌŋk] *vt* : mojar, ensopar
duo [ˈduːoː, ˈdjuː-] *n, pl* **duos** : dúo *m,* par *m*
dupe[1] [ˈduːp, djuːp] *vt* **duped; duping** : engañar, embaucar
dupe[2] *n* : inocentón *m,* -tona *f;* simple *mf*
duplex[1] [ˈduːˌplɛks, ˈdjuː-] *adj* : doble
duplex[2] *n* : casa *f* de dos viviendas, dúplex *m*
duplicate[1] [ˈduːplɪˌkeɪt, ˈdjuː-] *vt* **-cated; -cating 1** COPY : duplicar, hacer copias de **2** REPEAT : repetir, reproducir
duplicate[2] [ˈduːplɪkət, ˈdjuː-] *adj* : duplicado <a duplicate invoice : una factura por duplicado>
duplicate[3] [ˈduːplɪkət, ˈdjuː-] *n* : duplicado *m,* copia *f*
duplication [ˌduːplɪˈkeɪʃən, ˌdjuː-] *n* **1** DUPLICATING : duplicación *f,* repetición *f* (de esfuerzos) **2** DUPLICATE : copia *f,* duplicado *m*
duplicity [dʊˈplɪsət̬i, ˌdjuː-] *n, pl* **-ties** : duplicidad *f*
durability [ˌdʊrəˈbɪlət̬i, ˌdjʊr-] *n* : durabilidad *f* (de un producto), permanencia *f*
durable [ˈdʊrəbəl, ˈdjʊr-] *adj* : duradero
duration [dʊˈreɪʃən, djʊ-] *n* : duración *f*
duress [dʊˈrɛs, djʊ-] *n* : coacción *f*
during [ˈdʊrɪŋ, ˈdjʊr-] *prep* : durante
dusk [ˈdʌsk] *n* : anochecer *m,* crepúsculo *m*
dusky [ˈdʌski] *adj* **duskier; -est** : oscuro (dícese de los colores)
dust[1] [ˈdʌst] *vt* **1** : quitar el polvo de **2** SPRINKLE : espolvorear
dust[2] *n* : polvo *m*
duster [ˈdʌstər] *n* **1** *or* **dust cloth** : trapo *m* de polvo **2** HOUSECOAT : guardapolvo *m* **3 feather duster** : plumero *m*
dustpan [ˈdʌstˌpæn] *n* : recogedor *m*
dusty [ˈdʌsti] *adj* **dustier; -est** : cubierto de polvo, polvoriento
Dutch[1] [ˈdʌtʃ] *adj* : holandés
Dutch[2] *n* **1** : holandés *m* (idioma) **2 the Dutch** *npl* : los holandeses
Dutch treat *n* : invitación *f* o pago *m* a escote
dutiful [ˈduːt̬ɪfəl, ˈdjuː-] *adj* : motivado por sus deberes, responsable
duty [ˈduːt̬i, ˈdjuː-] *n, pl* **-ties 1** OBLIGATION : deber *m,* obligación *f,* responsabilidad *f* **2** TAX : impuesto *m,* arancel *m*
dwarf[1] [ˈdwɔrf] *vt* **1** STUNT : arrestar el crecimiento de **2** : hacer parecer pequeño
dwarf[2] *n, pl* **dwarfs** [ˈdwɔrfs] *or* **dwarves** [ˈdwɔrvz] : enano *m,* -na *f*
dwell [ˈdwɛl] *vi* **dwelled** *or* **dwelt** [ˈdwɛlt]; **dwelling 1** RESIDE : residir, morar, vivir **2 to dwell on** : pensar demasiado en, insistir en
dweller [ˈdwɛlər] *n* : habitante *mf*
dwelling [ˈdwɛlɪŋ] *n* : morada *f,* vivienda *f,* residencia *f*
dwindle [ˈdwɪndəl] *vi* **-dled; -dling** : menguar, reducirse, disminuir
dye[1] [ˈdaɪ] *vt* **dyed; dyeing** : teñir
dye[2] *n* : tintura *f,* tinte *m*
dying → **die**
dyke → **dike**
dynamic [daɪˈnæmɪk] *adj* : dinámico
dynamite[1] [ˈdaɪnəˌmaɪt] *vt* **-mited; -miting** : dinamitar
dynamite[2] *n* : dinamita *f*
dynamo [ˈdaɪnəˌmoː] *n, pl* **-mos** : dínamo *m,* generador *m* de electricidad
dynasty [ˈdaɪnəsti, -ˌnæs-] *n, pl* **-ties** : dinastía *f*
dysentery [ˈdɪsənˌtɛri] *n, pl* **-teries** : disentería *f*
dystrophy [ˈdɪstrəfi] *n, pl* **-phies 1** : distrofia *f* **2** → **muscular dystrophy**

E

e [ˈiː] *n, pl* **e's** *or* **es** [ˈiːz] : quinta letra del alfabeto inglés
each[1] [ˈiːtʃ] *adv* : cada uno, por persona <they cost $10 each : costaron $10 cada uno>
each[2] *adj* : cada <each student : cada estudiante> <each and every one : todos sin excepción>
each[3] *pron* **1** : cada uno *m,* cada una *f* <each of us : cada uno de nosotros>

2 **each other** : el uno al otro, mutuamente <we are helping each other : nos ayudamos el uno al otro> <they love each other : se aman>
eager ['i:gər] *adj* **1** ENTHUSIASTIC : entusiasta, ávido, deseoso **2** ANXIOUS : ansioso, impaciente
eagerly ['i:gərli] *adv* : con entusiasmo, ansiosamente
eagerness ['i:gərnəs] *n* : entusiasmo *m*, deseo *m*, impaciencia *f*
eagle ['i:gəl] *n* : águila *f*
ear ['ɪr] *n* **1** : oído *m*, oreja *f* <inner ear : oído interno> <big ears : orejas grandes> **2 ear of corn** : mazorca *f*, choclo *m*
earache ['ɪr,eɪk] *n* : dolor *m* de oído
eardrum ['ɪr,drʌm] *n* : tímpano *m*
earl ['ərl] *n* : conde *m*
earlobe ['ɪr,lo:b] *n* : lóbulo *m* de la oreja, perilla *f* de la oreja
early[1] ['ərli] *adv* **earlier; -est** : temprano, pronto <he arrived early : llegó temprano> <as early as possible : lo más pronto posible, cuanto antes> <ten minutes early : diez minutos de adelanto>
early[2] *adj* **earlier; -est 1** (*referring to a beginning*) : primero <the early stages : las primeras etapas> <in early May : a principios de mayo> **2** (*referring to antiquity*) : primitivo, antiguo <early man : el hombre primitivo> <early painting : la pintura antigua> **3** (*referring to a designated time*) : temprano, antes de la hora, prematuro <he was early : llegó temprano> <early fruit : frutas tempraneras> <an early death : una muerte prematura>
earmark ['ɪr,mɑrk] *vt* : destinar <earmarked funds : fondos destinados>
earn ['ərn] *vt* **1** : ganar <to earn money : ganar dinero> **2** DESERVE : ganarse, merecer
earnest[1] ['ərnəst] *adj* : serio, sincero
earnest[2] *n* **in ~** : en serio, de verdad <we began in earnest : empezamos de verdad>
earnestly ['ərnəstli] *adv* **1** SERIOUSLY : con seriedad, en serio **2** FERVENTLY : de todo corazón
earnestness ['ərnəstnəs] *n* : seriedad *f*, sinceridad *f*
earnings ['ərnɪŋz] *npl* : ingresos *mpl*, ganancias *fpl*, utilidades *fpl*
earphone ['ɪr,fo:n] *n* : audífono *m*
earring ['ɪr,rɪŋ] *n* : zarcillo *m*, arete *m*, aro *m Arg, Chile, Uru*, pendiente *m Spain*
earshot ['ɪr,ʃɑt] *n* : alcance *m* del oído
earth ['ərθ] *n* **1** LAND, SOIL : tierra *f*, suelo *m* **2 the Earth** : la Tierra
earthen ['ərθən, -ðən] *adj* : de tierra, de barro
earthenware ['ərθən,wær, -ðən-] *n* : loza *f*, vajillas *fpl* de barro
earthly ['ərθli] *adj* : terrenal, mundano
earthquake ['ərθ,kweɪk] *n* : terremoto *m*, temblor *m*
earthworm ['ərθ,wərm] *n* : lombriz *f* (de tierra)
earthy ['ərθi] *adj* **earthier; -est 1** : terroso <earthy colors : colores terrosos> **2** DOWN-TO- EARTH : realista, práctico, llano **3** COARSE, CRUDE : basto, grosero, tosco <earthy jokes : chistes groseros>
earwax ['ɪr,wæks] → **wax**[2]
earwig ['ɪr,wɪg] *n* : tijereta *f*
ease[1] ['i:z] *v* **eased; easing** *vt* **1** ALLEVIATE : aliviar, calmar, hacer disminuir **2** LOOSEN, RELAX : aflojar (una cuerda), relajar (restricciones), descargar (tensiones) **3** FACILITATE : facilitar — *vi* : calmarse, relajarse
ease[2] *n* **1** CALM, RELIEF : tranquilidad *f*, comodidad *f*, desahogo *m* **2** FACILITY : facilidad *f* **3 at ~** : relajado, cómodo <to put someone at ease : tranquilizar a alguien>
easel ['i:zəl] *n* : caballete *m*
easily ['i:zəli] *adv* **1** : fácilmente, con facilidad **2** UNQUESTIONABLY : con mucho, de lejos
easiness ['i:zinəs] *n* : facilidad *f*, soltura *f*
east[1] ['i:st] *adv* : al este
east[2] *adj* : este, del este, oriental <east winds : vientos del este>
east[3] *n* **1** : este *m* **2 the East** : el Oriente
Easter ['i:stər] *n* : Pascua *f* (de Resurrección)
easterly ['i:stərli] *adv & adj* : del este
eastern ['i:stərn] *adj* **1** : Oriental, del Este <Eastern Europe : Europa del Este> **2** : oriental, este
Easterner ['i:stərnər] *n* : habitante *mf* del este
eastward ['i:stwərd] *adv & adj* : hacia el este
easy ['i:zi] *adj* **easier; -est 1** : fácil **2** LENIENT : indulgente
easygoing [,i:zi'go:ɪŋ] *adj* : acomodaticio, tolerante, poco exigente
eat ['i:t] *v* **ate** ['eɪt]; **eaten** ['i:tən]; **eating** *vt* **1** : comer **2** CONSUME : consumir, gastar, devorar <expenses ate up profits : los gastos devoraron las ganancias> **3** CORRODE : corroer — *vi* **1** : comer **2 to eat away at** *or* **to eat into** : comerse **3 to eat out** : comer fuera
eatable[1] ['i:t̬əbəl] *adj* : comestible, comible *fam*
eatable[2] *n* **1** : algo para comer **2 eatables** *npl* : comestibles *mpl*, alimentos *mpl*
eater ['i:t̬ər] *n* : comedor *m*, -dora *f*
eaves ['i:vz] *npl* : alero *m*
eavesdrop ['i:vz,drɑp] *vi* **-dropped; -dropping** : escuchar a escondidas
eavesdropper ['i:vz,drɑpər] *n* : persona *f* que escucha a escondidas
ebb[1] ['ɛb] *vi* **1** : bajar, menguar (dícese de la marea) **2** DECLINE : decaer, disminuir

ebb[2] *n* **1** : reflujo *m* (de una marea) **2** DECLINE : decadencia *f,* declive *m,* disminución *f*

ebony[1] [ˈɛbəni] *adj* **1** : de ébano **2** BLACK : de color ébano, negro

ebony[2] *n, pl* **-nies** : ébano *m*

ebullience [ɪˈbʊljənts, -ˈbʌl-] *n* : efervescencia *f,* vivacidad *f*

ebullient [ɪˈbʊljənt, -ˈbʌl-] *adj* : efervescente, vivaz

eccentric[1] [ɪkˈsɛntrɪk] *adj* **1** : excéntrico <an eccentric wheel : una rueda excéntrica> **2** ODD, SINGULAR : excéntrico, extraño, raro — **eccentrically** [-trɪkli] *adv*

eccentric[2] *n* : ecéntrico *m,* -ca *f*

eccentricity [ˌɛkˌsɛnˈtrɪsəṭi] *n, pl* **-ties** : excentricidad *f*

ecclesiastic [ɪˌkliːziˈæstɪk] *n* : eclesiástico *m,* clérigo *m*

ecclesiastical [ɪˌkliːziˈæstɪkəl] *or* **ecclesiastic** *adj* : eclesiástico — **ecclesiastically** *adv*

echelon [ˈɛʃəˌlɑn] *n* **1** : escalón *m* (de tropas o aviones) **2** LEVEL : nivel *m,* esfera *f,* estrato *m*

echo[1] [ˈɛˌkoː] *v* **echoed; echoing** *vi* : hacer eco, resonar — *vt* : repetir

echo[2] *n, pl* **echoes** : eco *m*

éclair [eɪˈklær, i-] *n* : pastel *m* relleno de crema

eclectic [ɛˈklɛktɪk, ɪ-] *adj* : ecléctico

eclipse[1] [ɪˈklɪps] *vt* **eclipsed; eclipsing** : eclipsar

eclipse[2] *n* : eclipse *m*

ecological *adj* [ˌiːkəˈlɑdʒɪkəl, ˌɛkə-] : ecológico — **ecologically** *adv*

ecologist [iˈkɑlədʒɪst, ɛ-] *n* : ecólogo *m,* -ga *f*

ecology [iˈkɑlədʒi, ɛ-] *n, pl* **-gies** : ecología *f*

economic [ˌiːkəˈnɑmɪk, ˌɛkə-] *adj* : económico

economical [ˌiːkəˈnɑmɪkəl, ˌɛkə-] *adj* : económico — **economically** *adv*

economics [ˌiːkəˈnɑmɪks, ˌɛkə-] *n* : economía *f*

economist [iˈkɑnəmɪst] *n* : economista *mf*

economize [iˈkɑnəˌmaɪz] *v* **-mized; -mizing** : economizar, ahorrar

economy [iˈkɑnəmi] *n, pl* **-mies** **1** : economía *f,* sistema *m* económico **2** THRIFT : economía *f,* ahorro *m*

ecosystem [ˈiːkoˌsɪstəm] *n* : ecosistema *m*

ecru [ˈɛˌkruː, ˈeɪ-] *n* : color *m* crudo

ecstasy [ˈɛkstəsi] *n, pl* **-sies** : éxtasis *m*

ecstatic [ɛkˈstæṭɪk, ɪk-] *adj* : extático

ecstatically [ɛkˈstæṭɪkli, ɪk-] *adv* : con éxtasis, con gran entusiasmo

Ecuadoran [ˌɛkwəˈdorən] *or* **Ecuadorean** *or* **Ecuadorian** [-ˈdoriən] *n* : ecuatoriano *m,* -na *f* — **Ecuadorean** *or* **Ecuadorian** *adj*

ecumenical [ˌɛkjʊˈmɛnɪkəl] *adj* : ecuménico

eczema [ɪgˈziːmə, ˈɛgzəmə, ˈɛksə-] *n* : eczema *m*

eddy[1] [ˈɛdi] *vi* **eddied; eddying** : arremolinarse, hacer remolinos

eddy[2] *n, pl* **-dies** : remolino *m*

edema [ɪˈdiːmə] *n* : edema *m*

Eden [ˈiːdən] *n* : Edén *m*

edge[1] [ˈɛdʒ] *v* **edged; edging** *vt* **1** BORDER : bordear, ribetear, orlar **2** SHARPEN : afilar, aguzar **3** *or* **to edge one's way** : avanzar poco a poco **4 to edge out** : derrotar por muy poco — *vi* ADVANCE : ir avanzando (poco a poco)

edge[2] *n* **1** : filo *m* (de un cuchillo) **2** BORDER : borde *m,* orilla *f,* margen *m* **3** ADVANTAGE : ventaja *f*

edger [ˈɛdʒər] *n* : cortabordes *m*

edgewise [ˈɛdʒˌwaɪz] *adv* SIDEWAYS : de lado, de canto

edginess [ˈɛdʒinəs] *n* : tensión *f,* nerviosismo *m*

edgy [ˈɛdʒi] *adj* **edgier; -est** : tenso, nervioso

edible [ˈɛdəbəl] *adj* : comestible

edict [ˈiːˌdɪkt] *n* : edicto *m,* mandato *m,* orden *f*

edification [ˌɛdəfəˈkeɪʃən] *n* : edificación *f,* instrucción *f*

edifice [ˈɛdəfɪs] *n* : edificio *m*

edify [ˈɛdəˌfaɪ] *vt* **-fied; -fying** : edificar

edit [ˈɛdɪt] *vt* **1** : editar, redactar, corregir **2** *or* **to edit out** DELETE : recortar, cortar

edition [ɪˈdɪʃən] *n* : edición *f*

editor [ˈɛdɪṭər] *n* : editor *m,* **-tora** *f;* redactor *m,* -tora *f*

editorial[1] [ˌɛdɪˈtoriəl] *adj* **1** : de redacción **2** : editorial <an editorial comment : un comentario editorial>

editorial[2] *n* : editorial *m*

editorship [ˈɛdəṭərˌʃɪp] *n* : dirección *f*

educable [ˈɛdʒəkəbəl] *adj* : educable

educate [ˈɛdʒəˌkeɪt] *vt* **-cated; -cating** **1** TEACH : educar, enseñar **2** INSTRUCT : formar, educar, instruir **3** INFORM : informar, concientizar

education [ˌɛdʒəˈkeɪʃən] *n* : educación *f*

educational [ˌɛdʒəˈkeɪʃənəl] *adj* **1** : docente, de enseñanza <an educational institution : una institución docente> **2** PEDAGOGICAL : pedagógico **3** INSTRUCTIONAL : educativo, instructivo

educator [ˈɛdʒəˌkeɪṭər] *n* : educador *m,* -dora *f*

eel [ˈiːl] *n* : anguila *f*

eerie [ˈɪri] *adj* **-rier; -est** : extraño, misterioso, fantasmagórico

eerily [ˈɪrəli] *adv* : de manera extraña y misteriosa

efface [ɪˈfeɪs, ɛ-] *vt* **-faced; -facing** : borrar

effect[1] [ɪˈfɛkt] *vt* **1** CARRY OUT : efectuar, llevar a cabo **2** ACHIEVE : lograr, realizar

effect[2] *n* **1** RESULT : efecto *m,* resultado *m,* consecuencia *f* <to no effect : sin resultado> **2** MEANING : sentido *m* <something to that effect : algo por el estilo> **3** INFLUENCE : efecto *m,* influencia *f* **4 effects** *npl* BELONGINGS : efectos *mpl*, pertenencias *fpl* **5 to go into effect** : entrar en vigor **6 in ~** REALLY : en realidad, efectivamente

effective [ɪˈfɛktɪv] *adj* **1** EFFECTUAL : efectivo, eficaz **2** OPERATIVE : vigente — **effectively** *adv*

effectiveness [ɪˈfɛktɪvnəs] *n* : eficacia *f*, efectividad *f*

effectual [ɪˈfɛktʃʊəl] *adj* : eficaz, efectivo — **effectually** *adv*

effeminate [əˈfɛmənət] *adj* : afeminado

effervesce [ˌɛfərˈvɛs] *vi* **-vesced; -vescing 1** : estar en efervescencia, burbujear (dícese de líquidos) **2** : estar eufórico, estar muy animado (dícese de las personas)

effervescence [ˌɛfərˈvɛsənts] *n* **1** : efervescencia *f* **2** LIVELINESS : vivacidad *f*

effervescent [ˌɛfərˈvɛsənt] *adj* **1** : efervescente **2** LIVELY, VIVACIOUS : vivaz, animado

effete [ɛˈfiːt, ɪ-] *adj* **1** WORN- OUT : desgastado, agotado **2** DECADENT : decadente **3** EFFEMINATE : afeminado

efficacious [ˌɛfəˈkeɪʃəs] *adj* : eficaz, efectivo

efficacy [ˈɛfɪkəsi] *n, pl* **-cies** : eficacia *f*

efficiency [ɪˈfɪʃəntsi] *n, pl* **-cies** : eficiencia *f*

efficient [ɪˈfɪʃənt] *adj* : eficiente — **efficiently** *adv*

effigy [ˈɛfədʒi] *n, pl* **-gies** : efigie *f*

effluent [ˈɛˌfluːənt, ɛˈfluː-] *n* : efluente *m* — **effluent** *adj*

effort [ˈɛfərt] *n* **1** EXERTION : esfuerzo *m* **2** ATTEMPT : tentativa *f*, intento *m* <it's not worth the effort : no vale la pena>

effortless [ˈɛfərtləs] *adj* : fácil, sin esfuerzo

effortlessly [ˈɛfərtləsli] *adv* : sin esfuerzo, fácilmente

effrontery [ɪˈfrʌntəri] *n, pl* **-teries** : insolencia *f*, desfachatez *f*, descaro *m*

effusion [ɪˈfjuːʒən, ɛ-] *n* : efusión *f*

effusive [ɪˈfjuːsɪv, ɛ-] *adj* : efusivo — **effusively** *adv*

egg[1] [ˈɛg] *vt* **to egg on** : incitar, azuzar, provocar

egg[2] *n* **1** : huevo *m* **2** OVUM : óvulo *m*

eggbeater [ˈɛgˌbiːt̬ər] *n* : batidor *m* (de huevos)

eggnog [ˈɛgˌnɑg] *n* : ponche *m* de huevo, rompope *m CA, Mex*

eggplant [ˈɛgˌplænt] *n* : berenjena *f*

eggshell [ˈɛgˌʃɛl] *n* : cascarón *m*

ego [ˈiːˌgoː] *n, pl* **egos 1** SELF-ESTEEM : amor *m* propio **2** SELF : ego *m*, yo *m*

egocentric [ˌiːgoˈsɛntrɪk] *adj* : egocéntrico

egoism [ˈiːgoˌwɪzəm] *n* : egoísmo *m*

egoist [ˈiːgowɪst] *n* : egoísta *mf*

egoistic [ˌiːˌgoˈwɪstɪk] *adj* : egoísta

egotism [ˈiːgəˌtɪzəm] *n* : egotismo *m*

egotist [ˈiːgətɪst] *n* : egotista *mf*

egotistic [ˌiːgəˈtɪstɪk] *or* **egotistical** [-ˈtɪstɪkəl] *adj* : egotista — **egotistically** *adv*

egregious [ɪˈgriːdʒəs] *adj* : atroz, flagrante, mayúsculo — **egregiously** *adv*

egress [ˈiːˌgrɛs] *n* : salida *f*

egret [ˈiːgrət, -ˌgrɛt] *n* : garceta *f*

eiderdown [ˈaɪdərˌdaʊn] *n* **1** : plumón *m* **2** COMFORTER : edredón *m*

eight[1] *adj* [ˈeɪt] : ocho

eight[2] *n* : ocho *m*

eight hundred[1] *adj* : ochocientos

eight hundred[2] *n* : ochocientos *m*

eighteen[1] [eitˈtiːn] *adj* : dieciocho

eighteen[2] *n* : dieciocho *m*

eighteenth[1] [eɪtˈtiːnθ] *adj* : decimoctavo

eighteenth[2] *n* **1** : decimoctavo *m*, -va *f* (en una serie) **2** : dieciochoavo *m*, dieciochoava parte *f*

eighth[1] [ˈeɪtθ] *adj* : octavo

eighth[2] *n* **1** : octavo *m*, -va *f* (en una serie) **2** : octavo *m*, octava parte *f*

eightieth[1] [ˈeɪt̬iəθ] *adj* : octagésimo

eightieth[2] *n* **1** : octogésimo *m*, -ma *f* (en una serie) **2** : ochentavo *m*, ochentava parte *f*

eighty[1] [ˈeɪt̬i] *adj* : ochenta

eighty[2] *n, pl* **eighties 1** : ochenta *m* **2 the eighties** : los ochenta *mpl*

either[1] [ˈiːðər, ˈaɪ-] *adj* **1** : cualquiera (de los dos) <we can watch either movie : podemos ver cualquiera de las dos películas> **2** : ninguno de los dos <she wasn't in either room : no estaba en ninguna de las dos salas> **3** EACH : cada <on either side of the street : a cada lado de la calle>

either[2] *pron* **1** : cualquiera *mf* (de los dos) <either is fine : cualquiera de los dos está bien> **2** : ninguno *m*, -na *f* (de los dos) <I don't like either : no me gusta ninguno> **3** : algún *m*, alguna *f* <is either of you interested? : ¿está alguno de ustedes (dos) interesado?>

either[3] *conj* **1** : o, u <either David or Daniel could go : puede ir (o) David o Daniel> **2** : ni <we won't watch either this movie or the other : no veremos ni esta película ni la otra>

ejaculate [iˈdʒækjəˌleɪt] *v* **-lated; -lating** *vt* **1** : eyacular **2** EXCLAIM : exclamar — *vi* : eyacular

ejaculation [iˌdʒækjəˈleɪʃən] *n* **1** : eyaculación *f* (en fisiología) **2** EXCLAMATION : exclamación *f*

eject [iˈdʒɛkt] *vt* : expulsar, expeler

ejection [iˈdʒɛkʃən] *n* : expulsión *f*

eke [ˈiːk] *vt* **eked; eking** *or* **to eke out** : ganar a duras penas

elaborate[1] [iˈlæbəˌreɪt] *v* **-rated; -rating** *vt* : elaborar, idear, desarrollar — *vi* **to elaborate on** : ampliar, entrar en detalles

elaborate[2] [iˈlæbərət] *adj* **1** DETAILED : detallado, minucioso, elaborado **2** COMPLICATED : complicado, intrincado, elaborado — **elaborately** *adv*

elaboration [i,læbə'reɪʃən] *n* : elaboración *f*

elapse [i'læps] *vi* **elapsed; elapsing** : transcurrir, pasar

elastic[1] [i'læstɪk] *adj* : elástico

elastic[2] *n* **1** : elástico *m* **2** RUBBER BAND : goma *f,* gomita *f,* elástico *m,* liga *f*

elasticity [i,læs'tɪsəti, ,i:,læs-] *n, pl* **-ties** : elasticidad *f*

elate [i'leɪt] *vt* **elated; elating** : alborozar, regocijar

elation [i'leɪʃən] *n* : euforia *f,* júbilo *m,* alborozo *m*

elbow[1] ['ɛl,bo:] *vt* : darle un codazo a

elbow[2] *n* : codo *m*

elder[1] ['ɛldər] *adj* : mayor

elder[2] *n* **1 to be someone's elder** : ser mayor que alguien **2** : anciano *m,* -na *f* (de un pueblo o una tribu) **3** : miembro *m* del consejo (en varias religiones)

elderberry ['ɛldər,bɛri] *n, pl* **-berries** : baya *f* de saúco (fruta), saúco *m* (árbol)

elderly ['ɛldərli] *adj* : mayor, de edad, anciano

eldest ['ɛldəst] *adj* : mayor, de más edad

elect[1] [i'lɛkt] *vt* : elegir

elect[2] *adj* : electo <the president-elect : el presidente electo>

elect[3] *npl* **the elect** : los elegidos *mpl*

election [i'lɛkʃən] *n* : elección *f*

elective[1] [i'lɛktɪv] *adj* **1** : electivo **2** OPTIONAL : facultativo, optativo

elective[2] *n* : asignatura *f* electiva

elector [i'lɛktər] *n* : elector *m,* -tora *f*

electoral [i'lɛktərəl] *adj* : electoral

electorate [i'lɛktərət] *n* : electorado *m*

electric [i'lɛktrɪk] *adj* **1** *or* **electrical** [-trɪkəl] : eléctrico **2** THRILLING : electrizante, emocionante

electrician [i,lɛk'trɪʃən] *n* : electricista *mf*

electricity [i,lɛk'trɪsəti] *n, pl* **-ties 1** : electricidad *f* **2** CURRENT : corriente *m* eléctrica

electrification [i,lɛktrəfə'keɪʃən] *n* : electrificación *f*

electrify [i'lɛktrə,faɪ] *vt* **-fied; -fying 1** : electrificar **2** THRILL : electrizar, emocionar

electrocardiogram [i,lɛktro'kardiə,græm] *n* : electrocardiograma *m*

electrocardiograph [i,lɛktro'kardiə,græf] *n* : electrocardiógrafo *m*

electrocute [i'lɛktrə,kju:t] *vt* **-cuted; -cuting** : electrocutar

electrocution [i,lɛktrə'kju:ʃən] *n* : electrocución *f*

electrode [i'lɛk,tro:d] *n* : electrodo *m*

electrolysis [i,lɛk'traləsɪs] *n* : electrólisis *f*

electrolyte [i'lɛktrə,laɪt] *n* : electrolito *m*

electromagnet [i,lɛktro'mægnət] *n* : electroimán *m*

electromagnetic [i,lɛktromæg'nɛtɪk] *adj* : electromagnético — **electromagnetically** [-tɪkli] *adv*

electromagnetism [i,lɛktro'mægnə,tɪzəm] *n* : electromagnetismo *m*

electron [i'lɛk,tran] *n* : electrón *m*

electronic [i,lɛk'tranɪk] *adj* : electrónico — **electronically** [-nɪkli] *adv*

electronic mail *n* : correo *m* electrónico

electronics [i,lɛk'tranɪks] *n* : electrónica *f*

electroplate [i'lɛktrə,pleɪt] *vt* **-plated; -plating** : galvanizar mediante electrólisis

elegance ['ɛlɪgənts] *n* : elegancia *f*

elegant ['ɛlɪgənt] *adj* : elegante — **elegantly** *adv*

elegy ['ɛlədʒi] *n, pl* **-gies** : elegía *f*

element ['ɛləmənt] *n* **1** COMPONENT : elemento *m,* factor *m* **2** : elemento *m* (en la química) **3** MILIEU : elemento *m,* medio *m* <to be in one's element : estar en su elemento> **4 elements** *npl* RUDIMENTS : elementos *mpl,* rudimentos *mpl,* bases *fpl* **5 the elements** WEATHER : los elementos *mpl*

elemental [,ɛlə'mɛntəl] *adj* **1** BASIC : elemental, primario **2** : elemental (dícese de los elementos químicos)

elementary [,ɛlə'mɛntri] *adj* **1** SIMPLE : elemental, simple, fundamental **2** : de enseñanza primaria

elementary school *n* : escuela *f* primaria

elephant ['ɛləfənt] *n* : elefante *m,* -ta *f*

elevate ['ɛlə,veɪt] *vt* **-vated; -vating 1** RAISE : elevar, levantar, alzar **2** EXALT, PROMOTE : elevar, exaltar, ascender **3** ELATE : alborozar, regocijar

elevation [,ɛlə'veɪʃən] *n* **1** : elevación *f* **2** ALTITUDE : altura *f,* altitud *f* **3** PROMOTION : ascenso *m*

elevator ['ɛlə,veɪtər] *n* : ascensor *m,* elevador *m*

eleven[1] [ɪ'lɛvən] *adj* : once *m*

eleven[2] *n* : once *m*

eleventh[1] [ɪlɛvəntθ] *adj* : undécimo

eleventh[2] *n* **1** : undécimo *m,* -ma *f* (en una serie) **2** : onceavo *m,* onceava parte *f*

elf ['ɛlf] *n, pl* **elves** ['ɛlvz] : elfo *m,* geniecillo *m,* duende *m*

elfin ['ɛlfən] *adj* **1** : de elfo, menudo **2** ENCHANTING, MAGIC : mágico, encantador

elfish ['ɛlfɪʃ] *adj* **1** : de elfo **2** MISCHIEVOUS : travieso

elicit [ɪ'lɪsət] *vt* : provocar

eligibility [,ɛlədʒə'bɪləti] *n, pl* **-ties** : elegibilidad *f*

eligible ['ɛlədʒəbəl] *adj* **1** QUALIFIED : elegible **2** SUITABLE : idóneo

eliminate [ɪ'lɪmə,neɪt] *vt* **-nated; -nating** : eliminar

elimination [ɪ,lɪmə'neɪʃən] *n* : eliminación *f*

elite [eɪ'li:t, i-] *n* : elite *f*

elixir [iˈlɪksər] *n* **:** elixir *m*

elk [ˈɛlk] *n* **:** alce *m* (de Europa), uapití *m* (de América)

ellipse [ɪˈlɪps, ɛ-] *n* **:** elipse *f*

ellipsis [ɪˈlɪpsəs, ɛ-] *n, pl* **-lipses** [-ˌsiːz] **1 :** elipsis *f* **2 :** puntos *mpl* suspensivos (en la puntuación)

elliptical [ɪˈlɪptɪkəl, ɛ-] *or* **elliptic** [-tɪk] *adj* **:** elíptico

elm [ˈɛlm] *n* **:** olmo *m*

elocution [ˌɛləˈkjuːʃən] *n* **:** elocución *f*

elongate [iˈlɔŋˌgeɪt] *vt* **-gated; -gating :** alargar

elongation [ˌiːˌlɔŋˈgeɪʃən] *n* **:** alargamiento *m*

elope [iˈloːp] *vi* **eloped; eloping :** fugarse

elopement [iˈloːpmənt] *n* **:** fuga *f*

eloquence [ˈɛləkwənts] *n* **:** elocuencia *f*

eloquent [ˈɛləkwənt] *adj* **:** elocuente — **eloquently** *adv*

El Salvadoran [ˌɛlˌsælvəˈdorən] *n* **:** salvadoreño *m,* -ña *f* — **El Salvadoran** *adj*

else[1] [ˈɛls] *adv* **1** DIFFERENTLY **:** de otro modo, de otra manera <how else? **:** ¿de qué otro modo?> **2** ELSEWHERE **:** de otro sitio, de otro lugar <where else? **:** ¿en qué otro sitio?> **3 or else** OTHERWISE **:** si no, de lo contrario

else[2] *adj* **1** OTHER **:** otro <anyone else **:** cualquier otro> <everyone else **:** todos los demás> <nobody else **:** ningún otro, nadie más> <somebody else **:** otra persona> **2** MORE **:** más <nothing else **:** nada más> <what else? **:** ¿qué más?>

elsewhere [ˈɛlsˌhwɛr] *adv* **:** en otra parte, en otro sitio, en otro lugar

elucidate [iˈluːsəˌdeɪt] *vt* **-dated; -dating :** dilucidar, elucidar, esclarecer

elucidation [iˌluːsəˈdeɪʃən] *n* **:** elucidación *f,* esclarecimiento *m*

elude [iˈluːd] *vt* **eluded; eluding :** eludir, evadir

elusive [iˈluːsɪv] *adj* **1** EVASIVE **:** evasivo, esquivo **2** SLIPPERY **:** huidizo, escurridizo **3** FLEETING, INTANGIBLE **:** impalpable, fugaz

elusively [iˈluːsɪvli] *adv* **:** de manera esquiva

elves → **elf**

emaciate [iˈmeɪʃiˌeɪt] *vt* **-ated; -ating :** enflaquecer

emaciation [iˌmeɪsiˈeɪʃən, -ʃi-] *n* **:** enflaquecimiento *m,* escualidez *f,* delgadez *f* extrema

E–mail [ˈiːˌmeɪl] → **electronic mail**

emanate [ˈɛməˌneɪt] *v* **-nated; -nating** *vi* **:** emanar, provenir, proceder — *vt* **:** emanar

emanation [ˌɛməˈneɪʃən] *n* **:** emanación *f*

emancipate [iˈmæntsəˌpeɪt] *vt* **-pated; -pating :** emancipar

emancipation [iˌmæntsəˈpeɪʃən] *n* **:** emancipación *f*

emasculate [iˈmæskjəˌleɪt] *vt* **-lated; -lating 1** CASTRATE **:** castrar, emascular **2** WEAKEN **:** debilitar

embalm [ɪmˈbɑm, ɛm-, -ˈbɑlm] *vt* **:** embalsamar

embankment [ɪmˈbæŋkmənt, ɛm-] *n* **:** terraplén *m,* muro *m* de contención

embargo[1] [ɪmˈbɑrgo, ɛm-] *vt* **-goed; -going :** imponer un embargo sobre

embargo[2] *n, pl* **-goes :** embargo *m*

embark [ɪmˈbɑrk, ɛm-] *vt* **:** embarcar — *vi* **1 :** embarcarse **2 to embark on** START **:** emprender, embarcarse en

embarkation [ˌɛmˌbɑrˈkeɪʃən] *n* **:** embarque *m,* embarco *m*

embarrass [ɪmˈbærəs, ɛm-] *vt* **:** avergonzar, abochornar

embarrassing [ɪmˈbærəsɪŋ, ɛm-] *adj* **:** embarazoso, violento

embarrassment [ɪmˈbærəsmənt, ɛm-] *n* **:** vergüenza *f,* pena *f*

embassy [ˈɛmbəsi] *n, pl* **-sies :** embajada *f*

embed [ɪmˈbɛd, ɛm-] *vt* **-bedded; -bedding :** incrustar, empotrar, grabar (en la memoria)

embellish [ɪmˈbɛlɪʃ, ɛm-] *vt* **:** adornar, embellecer

embellishment [ɪmˈbɛlɪʃmənt, ɛm-] *n* **:** adorno *m*

ember [ˈɛmbər] *n* **:** ascua *f,* brasa *f*

embezzle [ɪmˈbɛzəl, ɛm-] *vt* **-zled; -zling :** desfalcar, malversar

embezzlement [ɪmˈbɛzəlmənt, ɛm-] *n* **:** desfalco *m,* malversación *f*

embezzler [ɪmˈbɛzələr, ɛm-] *n* **:** desfacador *m,* **-dora** *f;* malversador *m,* -dora *f*

embitter [ɪmˈbɪtər, ɛm-] *vt* **:** amargar

emblem [ˈɛmbləm] *n* **:** emblema *m,* símbolo *m*

emblematic [ˌɛmbləˈmætɪk] *adj* **:** emblemático, simbólico

embodiment [ɪmˈbɑdɪmənt, ɛm-] *n* **:** encarnación *f,* personificación *f*

embody [ɪmˈbɑdi, ɛm-] *vt* **-bodied; -bodying :** encarnar, personificar

emboss [ɪmˈbɑs, ɛm-, -ˈbɔs] *vt* **:** repujar, grabar en relieve

embrace[1] [ɪmˈbreɪs, ɛm-] *vt* **-braced; -bracing 1** HUG **:** abrazar **2** ADOPT, TAKE ON **:** adoptar, aceptar **3** INCLUDE **:** abarcar, incluir

embrace[2] *n* **:** abrazo *m*

embroider [ɪmˈbrɔɪdər, ɛm-] *vt* **:** bordar (una tela), adornar (una historia)

embroidery [ɪmˈbrɔɪdəri, ɛm-] *n, pl* **-deries :** bordado *m*

embroil [ɪmˈbrɔɪl, ɛm-] *vt* **:** embrollar, enredar

embryo [ˈɛmbriˌoː] *n, pl* **embryos :** embrión *m*

embryonic [ˌɛmbriˈɑnɪk] *adj* **:** embrionario

emend [iˈmɛnd] *vt* **:** enmendar, corregir

emendation [ˌiːˌmɛnˈdeɪʃən] *n* : enmienda *f*
emerald[1] [ˈɛmrəld, ˈɛmə-] *adj* : verde esmeralda
emerald[2] *n* : esmeralda *f*
emerge [iˈmərdʒ] *vi* **emerged; emerging** : emerger, salir, aparecer, surgir
emergence [iˈmərdʒən*t*s] *n* : aparición *f*, surgimiento *m*
emergency [iˈmərdʒən*t*si] *n, pl* **-cies** : emergencia *f*
emergent [iˈmərdʒənt] *adj* : emergente
emery [ˈɛməri] *n, pl* **-eries** : esmeril *m*
emetic[1] [iˈmɛt̬ɪk] *adj* : vomitivo, emético
emetic[2] *n* : vomitivo *m*, emético *m*
emigrant [ˈɛmɪgrənt] *n* : emigrante *mf*
emigrate [ˈɛməˌgreɪt] *vi* **-grated; -grating** : emigrar
emigration [ˌɛməˈgreɪʃən] *n* : emigración *f*
eminence [ˈɛmənən*t*s] *n* **1** PROMINENCE : eminencia *f*, prestigio *m*, renombre *m* **2** DIGNITARY : eminencia *f*; dignatario *m*, -ria *f* <Your Eminence : Su Eminencia>
eminent [ˈɛmənənt] *adj* : eminente, ilustre
eminently [ˈɛmənəntli] *adv* : sumamente
emissary [ˈɛməˌsɛri] *n, pl* **-saries** : emisario *m*, -ria *f*
emission [iˈmɪʃən] *n* : emisión *f*
emit [iˈmɪt] *vt* **emitted; emitting** : emitir, despedir, producir
emote [iˈmoːt] *vi* **emoted; emoting** : exteriorizar las emociones
emotion [iˈmoːʃən] *n* : emoción *f*, sentimiento *m*
emotional [iˈmoːʃənəl] *adj* **1** : emocional, afectivo <an emotional reaction : una reacción emocional> **2** MOVING : emocionante, emotivo, conmovedor
emotionally [iˈmoːʃənəli] *adv* : emocionalmente
emperor [ˈɛmpərər] *n* : emperador *m*
emphasis [ˈɛmfəsɪs] *n, pl* **-phases** [-ˌsiːz] : énfasis *m*, hincapié *m*
emphasize [ˈɛmfəˌsaɪz] *vt* **-sized; -sizing** : enfatizar, destacar, subrayar, hacer hincapié en
emphatic [ɪmˈfætɪk, ɛm-] *adj* : enfático, enérgico, categórico — **emphatically** [-ɪkli] *adv*
empire [ˈɛmˌpaɪr] *n* : imperio *m*
empirical [ɪmˈpɪrɪkəl, ɛm-] *adj* : empírico — **empirically** [-ɪkli] *adv*
employ[1] [ɪmˈplɔɪ, ɛm-] *vt* **1** USE : usar, utilizar **2** HIRE : contratar, emplear **3** OCCUPY : ocupar, dedicar, emplear
employ[2] [ɪmˈplɔɪ, ɛm-; ˈɪm,-, ˈɛm,-] *n* **1** : puesto *m*, cargo *m*, ocupación *f* **2 to be in the employ of** : estar al servicio de, trabajar para
employee [ɪmˌplɔɪˈiː, ɛm-, -ˈplɔɪˌiː] *n* : empleado *m*, -da *f*
employer [ɪmˈplɔɪər, ɛm-] *n* : patrón *m*, -trona *f*; empleador *m*, -dora *f*
employment [ɪmˈplɔɪmənt, ɛm-] *n* : trabajo *m*, empleo *m*
empower [ɪmˈpaʊər, ɛm-] *vt* : facultar, autorizar, conferirle poder a
empowerment [ɪmˈpaʊərmənt, ɛm-] *n* : autorización *f*
empress [ˈɛmprəs] *n* : emperatriz *f*
emptiness [ˈɛmptinəs] *n* : vacío *m*, vacuidad *f*
empty[1] [ˈɛmpti] *v* **-tied; -tying** *vt* : vaciar — *vi* : desaguar (dícese de un río)
empty[2] *adj* **emptier; -est 1** : vacío **2** VACANT : desocupado, libre **3** MEANINGLESS : vacío, hueco, vano
empty–handed [ˌɛmptiˈhændəd] *adj* : con las manos vacías
empty–headed [ˌɛmptiˈhɛdəd] *adj* : cabeza hueca, tonto
emu [ˈiːˌmjuː] *n* : emú *m*
emulate [ˈɛmjəˌleɪt] *vt* **-lated; -lating** : emular
emulation [ˌɛmjəˈleɪʃən] *n* : emulación *f*
emulsifier [ɪˈmʌlsəˌfaɪər] *n* : emulsionante *m*
emulsify [ɪˈmʌlsəˌfaɪ] *vt* **-fied; -fying** : emulsionar
emulsion [ɪˈmʌlʃən] *n* : emulsión *f*
enable [ɪˈneɪbəl, ɛ-] *vt* **-abled; -abling 1** EMPOWER : habilitar, autorizar, facultar **2** PERMIT : hacer posible, posibilitar, permitar
enact [ɪˈnækt, ɛ-] *vt* **1** : promulgar (un ley o decreto) **2** : representar (un papel en el teatro)
enactment [ɪˈnæktmənt, ɛ-] *n* : promulgación *f*
enamel[1] [ɪˈnæməl] *vt* **-eled** *or* **-elled; -eling** *or* **-elling** : esmaltar
enamel[2] *n* : esmalte *m*
enamor [ɪˈnæmər] *vt* **1** : enamorar **2 to be enamored of** : estar enamorado de (una persona), estar entusiasmado con (algo)
encamp [ɪnˈkæmp, ɛn-] *vi* : acampar
encampment [ɪnˈkæmpmənt, ɛn-] *n* : campamento *m*
encase [ɪnˈkeɪs, ɛn-] *vt* **-cased; -casing** : encerrar, revestir
encephalitis [ɪnˌsɛfəˈlaɪtəs, ɛn-] *n, pl* **-litides** [-ˈlɪtəˌdiːz] : encefalitis *f*
enchant [ɪnˈtʃænt, ɛn-] *vt* **1** BEWITCH : hechizar, encantar, embrujar **2** CHARM, FASCINATE : cautivar, fascinar, encantar
enchanting [ɪnˈtʃæntɪŋ, ɛn-] *adj* : encantador
enchanter [ɪnˈtʃæntər, ɛn-] *n* SORCERER : mago *m*, encantador *m*
enchantment [ɪnˈtʃæntmənt, ɛn-] *n* **1** SPELL : encanto *m*, hechizo *m* **2** CHARM : encanto *m*
enchantress [ɪnˈtʃæntrəs, ɛn-] *n* **1** SORCERESS : maga *f*, hechicera *f* **2** CHARMER : mujer *f* cautivadora
encircle [ɪnˈsərkəl, ɛn-] *vt* **-cled; -cling** : rodear, ceñir, cercar
enclose [ɪnˈkloːz, ɛn-] *vt* **-closed; -closing 1** SURROUND : encerrar, cer-

car, rodear **2** INCLUDE : incluir, adjuntar, acompañar <please find enclosed : le enviamos adjunto>
enclosure [ɪn'klo:ʒər, ɛn-] *n* **1** ENCLOSING : encierro *m* **2** : cercado *m* (de terreno), recinto *m* <an enclosure for the press : un recinto para la prensa> **3** ADJUNCT : anexo *m* (con una carta), documento *m* adjunto
encompass [ɪn'kʌmpəs, ɛn-, -'kɑm-] *vt* **1** SURROUND : circundar, rodear **2** INCLUDE : abarcar, comprender
encore ['ɑn,kor] *n* : bis *m*, repetición *f*
encounter[1] [ɪn'kaʊntər, ɛn-] *vt* **1** MEET : encontrar, encontrarse con, toparse con, tropezar con **2** FIGHT : combatir, luchar contra
encounter[2] *n* : encuentro *m*
encourage [ɪn'kərɪdʒ, ɛn-] *vt* **-aged; -aging 1** HEARTEN, INSPIRE : animar, alentar **2** FOSTER : fomentar, promover
encouragement [ɪn'kərɪdʒmənt, ɛn-] *n* : ánimo *m*, aliento *m*
encroach [ɪn'kro:tʃ, ɛn-] *vi* **to encroach on** : invadir, abusar (derechos), quitar (tiempo)
encroachment [ɪn'kro:tʃmənt, ɛn-] *n* : invasión *f*, usurpación *f*
encrust [ɪn'krʌst, ɛn-] *vt* **1** : recubrir con una costra **2** INLAY : incrustar <encrusted with gems : incrustado de gemas>
encumber [ɪn'kʌmbər, ɛn-] *vt* **1** BLOCK : obstruir, estorbar **2** BURDEN : cargar, gravar
encumbrance [ɪn'kʌmbrən*t*s, ɛn-] *n* : estorbo *m*, carga *f*, gravamen *m*
encyclopedia [ɪn,saɪklə'pi:diə, ɛn-] *n* : enciclopedia *f*
encyclopedic [ɪn,saɪklə'pi:dɪk, ɛn-] *adj* : enciclopédico
end[1] ['ɛnd] *vt* **1** STOP : terminar, poner fin a **2** CONCLUDE : concluir, terminar — *vi* : terminar(se), acabar, concluir(se)
end[2] *n* **1** EXTREMITY : extremo *m*, final *m*, punta *f* **2** CONCLUSION : fin *m*, final *m* **3** AIM : fin *m*
endanger [ɪn'deɪndʒər, ɛn-] *vt* : poner en peligro
endear [ɪn'dɪr, ɛn-] *vt* **to endear oneself to** : ganarse la simpatía de, granjearse el cariño de
endearment [ɪn'dɪrmənt, ɛn-] *n* : expresión *f* de cariño
endeavor[1] [ɪn'dɛvər, ɛn-] *vt* : intentar, esforzarse por <he endeavored to improve his work : intentó por mejorar su trabajo>
endeavor[2] *n* : intento *m*, esfuerzo *m*
ending ['ɛndɪŋ] *n* **1** CONCLUSION : final *m*, desenlace *m* **2** SUFFIX : sufijo *m*, terminación *f*
endive ['ɛn,daɪv, ,ɑn'di:v] *n* : endibia *f*, endivia *f*
endless ['ɛndləs] *adj* **1** INTERMINABLE : interminable, inacabable, sin fin **2** INNUMERABLE : innumerable, incontable
endlessly ['ɛndləsli] *adv* : interminablemente, eternamente, sin parar
endocrine ['ɛndəkrən, -,kraɪn, -,kri:n] *adj* : endocrino
endorse [ɪn'dɔrs, ɛn-] *vt* **-dorsed; -dorsing 1** SIGN : endosar, firmar **2** APPROVE : aprobar, sancionar
endorsement [ɪn'dɔrsmənt, ɛn-] *n* **1** SIGNATURE : endoso *m*, firma *f* **2** APPROVAL : aprobación *f*, aval *m*
endow [ɪn'daʊ, ɛn-] *vt* : dotar
endowment [ɪn'daʊmənt, ɛn-] *n* **1** FUNDING : dotación *f* **2** DONATION : donación *f*, legado *m* **3** ATTRIBUTE, GIFT : atributo *m*, dotes *fpl*
endurable [ɪn'dʊrəbəl, ɛn-, -'djʊr-] *adj* : tolerable, soportable
endurance [ɪn'dʊrən*t*s, ɛn-, -'djʊr-] *n* : resistencia *f*, aguante *m*
endure [ɪn'dʊr, ɛn-, -'djʊr] *v* **-dured; -during** *vt* **1** BEAR : resistir, soportar, aguantar **2** TOLERATE : tolerar, soportar — *vi* LAST : durar, perdurar
enema ['ɛnəmə] *n* : enema *m*, lavativa *f*
enemy ['ɛnəmi] *n*, *pl* **-mies** : enemigo *m*, -ga *f*
energetic [,ɛnər'dʒɛt̬ɪk] *adj* : enérgico, vigoroso — **energetically** [-t̬ɪkli] *adv*
energize ['ɛnər,dʒaɪz] *vt* **-gized; -gizing 1** ACTIVATE : activar **2** INVIGORATE : vigorizar
energy ['ɛnərdʒi] *n*, *pl* **-gies 1** VITALITY : energía *f*, vitalidad *f* **2** EFFORT : esfuerzo *m*, energías *fpl* **3** POWER : energía *f* <atomic energy : energía atómica>
enervate ['ɛnər,veɪt] *vt* **-vated; -vating** : enervar, debilitar
enervation [,ɛnər'veɪʃən] *n* : enervación *f*, debilidad *f*
enfold [ɪn'fo:ld, ɛn-] *vt* : envolver
enforce [ɪn'fors, ɛn-] *vt* **-forced; -forcing 1** : hacer respetar, hacer cumplir (una ley, etc.) **2** IMPOSE : imponer <to enforce obedience : imponer la obediencia>
enforcement [ɪn'forsmənt, ɛn-] *n* : imposición *f*
enfranchise [ɪn'fræn,tʃaɪz, ɛn-] *vt* **-chised; -chising** : conceder el voto a
enfranchisement [ɪn'fræn,tʃaɪzmənt, ɛn-] *n* : concesión *f* del voto
engage [ɪn'geɪdʒ, ɛn-] *v* **-gaged; -gaging** *vt* **1** ATTRACT : captar, atraer, llamar <to engage one's attention : captar la atención> **2** MESH : engranar <to engage the clutch : embragar> **3** COMMIT : comprometer <to get engaged : comprometerse> **4** HIRE : contratar **5** : entablar combate con (un enemigo) — *vi* **1** PARTICIPATE : participar **2 to engage in combat** : entrar en combate

engagement [ɪn'geɪdʒmənt, ɛn-] *n* **1** APPOINTMENT : cita *f,* hora *f* **2** BETROTHAL : compromiso *m*
engaging [ɪn'geɪdʒɪŋ, ɛn-] *adj* : atractivo, encantador, interesante
engender [ɪn'dʒɛndər, ɛn-] *vt* **-dered; -dering** : engendrar
engine ['ɛndʒən] *n* **1** MOTOR : motor *m* **2** LOCOMOTIVE : locomotora *f,* máquina *f*
engineer[1] [ˌɛndʒə'nɪr] *vt* **1** : diseñar, construir (un sistema, un mecanismo, etc.) **2** CONTRIVE : maquinar, tramar, fraguar
engineer[2] *n* **1** : ingeniero *m,* -ra *f* **2** : maquinista *mf* (de locomotoras)
engineering [ˌɛndʒə'nɪrɪŋ] *n* : ingeniería *f*
English[1] ['ɪŋglɪʃ, 'ɪŋlɪʃ] *adj* : inglés
English[2] *n* **1** : inglés *m* (idioma) **2 the English** : los ingleses
Englishman ['ɪŋglɪʃmən, 'ɪŋlɪʃ-] *n, pl* **-men** [-mən, -ˌmɛn] : inglés *m*
Englishwoman ['ɪŋglɪʃˌwʊmən, 'ɪŋlɪʃ-] *n, pl* **-women** [-ˌwɪmən] : inglesa *f*
engrave [ɪn'greɪv, ɛn-] *vt* **-graved; -graving** : grabar
engraver [ɪn'greɪvər, ɛn-] *n* : grabador *m,* -dora *f*
engraving [ɪn'greɪvɪŋ, ɛn-] *n* : grabado *m*
engross [ɪn'groːs, ɛn-] *vt* : absorber
engrossed [ɪn'groːst, ɛn-] *adj* : absorto
engulf [ɪn'gʌlf, ɛn-] *vt* : envolver, sepultar
enhance [ɪn'hænts, ɛn-] *vt* **-hanced; -hancing** : realzar, aumentar, mejorar
enhancement [ɪn'hæntsmənt, ɛn-] *n* : mejora *f,* realce *m,* aumento *m*
enigma [ɪ'nɪgmə] *n* : enigma *m*
enigmatic [ˌɛnɪg'mæt̬ɪk, ˌiːnɪg-] *adj* : enigmático — **enigmatically** [-t̬ɪkli] *adv*
enjoin [ɪn'dʒɔɪn, ɛn-] *vt* **1** COMMAND : ordenar, imponer **2** FORBID : prohibir, vedar
enjoy [ɪn'dʒɔɪ, ɛn-] *vt* **1** : disfrutar, gozar de <did you enjoy the book? : ¿te gustó el libro?> <to enjoy good health : gozar de buena salud> **2 to enjoy oneself** : divertirse, pasarlo bien
enjoyable [ɪn'dʒɔɪəbəl, ɛn-] *adj* : agradable, placentero, divertido
enjoyment [ɪn'dʒɔɪmənt, ɛn-] *n* : placer *m,* goce *m,* disfrute *m,* deleite *m*
enlarge [ɪn'lɑrdʒ, ɛn-] *v* **-larged; -larging** *vt* : extender, agrandar, ampliar — *vi* **1** : ampliarse **2 to enlarge upon** : extenderse sobre, entrar en detalles sobre
enlargement [ɪn'lɑrdʒmənt, ɛn-] *n* : expansión *f,* ampliación *f* (dícese de fotografías)
enlarger [ɪn'lɑrdʒər, ɛn-] *n* : ampliadora *f*
enlighten [ɪn'laɪtən, ɛn-] *vt* : iluminar, aclarar
enlightenment [ɪn'laɪtənmənt, ɛn-] *n* **1** : ilustración *f* <the Enlightenment : la Ilustración> **2** CLARIFICATION : aclaración *f*
enlist [ɪn'lɪst, ɛn-] *vt* **1** ENROLL : alistar, reclutar **2** SECURE : conseguir <to enlist the support of : conseguir el apoyo de> — *vi* : alistarse
enlisted man [ɪn'lɪstəd, ɛn-] *n* : soldado *m* raso
enlistment [ɪn'lɪstmənt, ɛn-] *n* : alistamiento *m,* reclutamiento *m*
enliven [ɪn'laɪvən, ɛn-] *vt* : animar, alegrar, darle vida a
enmity ['ɛnmət̬i] *n, pl* **-ties** : enemistad *f,* animadversión *f*
ennoble [ɪ'noːbəl, ɛ-] *vt* **-bled; -bling** : ennoblecer
ennui [ˌɑn'wiː] *n* : hastío *m,* tedio *m,* fastidio *m,* aburrimiento *m*
enormity [ɪ'nɔrmət̬i] *n, pl* **-ties 1** ATROCITY : atrocidad *f,* barbaridad *f* **2** IMMENSITY : enormidad *f,* inmensidad *f*
enormous [ɪ'nɔrməs] *adj* : enorme, inmenso, tremendo — **enormously** *adv*
enough[1] [ɪ'nʌf] *adv* **1** : bastante, suficientemente **2 fair enough!** : ¡está bien!, ¡de acuerdo! **3 strangely enough** : por extraño que parezca **4 sure enough** : en efecto, sin duda alguna **5 well enough** : muy bien, bastante bien
enough[2] *adj* : bastante, suficiente <do we have enough chairs? : ¿tenemos suficientes sillas?>
enough[3] *pron* : (lo) suficiente, (lo) bastante <enough to eat : lo suficiente para comer> <it's not enough : no basta> <I've had enough! : ¡estoy harto!, ¡está bueno ya!>
enquire [ɪn'kwaɪr, ɛn-], **enquiry** ['ɪnˌkwaɪri, 'ɛn-, -kwəri; ɪn'kwaɪri, ɛn'-] → **inquire**, **inquiry**
enrage [ɪn'reɪdʒ, ɛn-] *vt* **-raged; -raging** : enfurecer, encolerizar
enraged [ɪn'reɪdʒd, ɛn-] *adj* : enfurecido, furioso
enrich [ɪn'rɪtʃ, ɛn-] *vt* : enriquecer
enrichment [ɪn'rɪtʃmənt, ɛn-] *n* : enriquecimiento *m*
enroll *or* **enrol** [ɪn'roːl, ɛn-] *v* **-rolled; -rolling** *vt* : matricular, inscribir — *vi* : matricularse, inscribirse
enrollment [ɪn'roːlmənt, ɛn-] *n* : matrícula *f,* inscripción *f*
en route [ɑ'ruːt, ɛn'raʊt] *adv* : de camino, por el camino
ensconce [ɪn'skɑnts, ɛn-] *vt* **-sconced; -sconcing** : acomodar, instalar, establecer cómodamente
ensemble [ɑn'sɑmbəl] *n* : conjunto *m*
enshrine [ɪn'ʃraɪn, ɛn-] *vt* **-shrined; -shrining** : conservar religiosamente, preservar
ensign ['ɛntsən, 'ɛnˌsaɪn] *n* **1** FLAG : enseña *f,* pabellón *m* **2** : alférez *mf* (de fragata)

enslave [ɪnˈsleɪv, ɛn-] *vt* **-slaved; -slaving** : esclavizar
enslavement [ɪnˈsleɪvmənt, ɛn-] *n* : esclavización *f*
ensnare [ɪnˈsnær, ɛn-] *vt* **-snared; -snaring** : atrapar
ensue [ɪnˈsuː, ɛn-] *vi* **-sued; -suing** : seguir, resultar
ensure [ɪnˈʃʊr, ɛn-] *vt* **-sured; -suring** : asegurar, garantizar
entail [ɪnˈteɪl, ɛn-] *vt* : implicar, suponer, conllevar
entangle [ɪnˈtæŋgəl, ɛn-] *vt* **-gled; -gling** : enredar
entanglement [ɪnˈtæŋgəlmənt, ɛn-] *n* : enredo *m*
enter [ˈɛntər] *vt* **1** : entrar en, entrar a **2** BEGIN : entrar en, comenzar, iniciar **3** RECORD : anotar, inscribir, dar entrada a **4** JOIN : entrar en, alistarse en, hacerse socio de — *vi* **1** : entrar **2 to enter into** : entrar en, firmar (un acuerdo), entablar (negociaciones, etc.)
enterprise [ˈɛntər,praɪz] *n* **1** UNDERTAKING : empresa *f* **2** BUSINESS : empresa *f*, firma *f* **3** INITIATIVE : iniciativa *f*, empuje *m*
enterprising [ˈɛntər,praɪzɪŋ] *adj* : emprendedor
entertain [,ɛntərˈteɪn] *vt* **1** : recibir, agasajar <to entertain guests : tener invitados> **2** CONSIDER : considerar, contemplar **3** AMUSE : entretener, divertir
entertainer [,ɛntərˈteɪnər] *n* : artista *mf*
entertainment [,ɛntərˈteɪnmənt] *n* : entretenimiento *m*, diversión *f*
enthrall *or* **enthral** [ɪnˈθrɔl, ɛn-] *vt* **-thralled; -thralling** : cautivar, embelesar
enthusiasm [ɪnˈθuːzi,æzəm, ɛn-, -ˈθjuː-] *n* : entusiasmo *m*
enthusiast [ɪnˈθuːzi,æst, ɛn-, -ˈθjuː-, -əst] *n* : entusiasta *mf*; aficionado *m*, -da *f*
enthusiastic [ɪn,θuːziˈæstɪk, ɛn-, -,θjuː-] *adj* : entusiasta, aficionado
enthusiastically [ɪn,θuːziˈæstɪkli, ɛn-, -,θjuː-] *adv* : con entusiasmo
entice [ɪnˈtaɪs, ɛn-] *vt* **-ticed; -ticing** : atraer, tentar
enticement [ɪnˈtaɪsmənt, ɛn-] *n* : tentación *f*, atracción *f*, señuelo *m*
entire [ɪnˈtaɪr, ɛn-] *adj* : entero, completo
entirely [ɪnˈtaɪrli, ɛn-] *adv* : completamente, totalmente
entirety [ɪnˈtaɪrti, ɛn-, -ˈtaɪrəṱi] *n, pl* **-ties** : totalidad *f*
entitle [ɪnˈtaɪṱəl, ɛn-] *vt* **-tled; -tling 1** NAME : titular, intitular **2** : dar derecho a <it entitles you to enter free : le da derecho a entrar gratis> **3 to be entitled to** : tener derecho a
entitlement [ɪnˈtaɪṱəlmənt, ɛn-] *n* RIGHT : derecho *m*
entity [ˈɛntəṱi] *n, pl* **-ties** : entidad *f*, ente *m*
entomologist [,ɛntəˈmɑlədʒɪst] *n* : entomólogo *m*, -ga *f*
entomology [,ɛntəˈmɑlədʒi] *n* : entomología *f*
entourage [,ɑntʊˈrɑʒ] *n* : séquito *m*
entrails [ˈɛn,treɪlz, -trəlz] *npl* : entrañas *fpl*, vísceras *fpl*
entrance[1] [ɪnˈtræn*t*s, ɛn-] *vt* **-tranced; -trancing** : encantar, embelesar, fascinar
entrance[2] [ˈɛntrən*t*s] *n* **1** ENTERING : entrada *f* <to make an entrance : entrar en escena> **2** ENTRY : entrada *f*, puerta *f* **3** ADMISSION : entrada *f*, ingreso *m* <entrance examination : examen de ingreso>
entrant [ˈɛntrənt] *n* : candidato *m*, -ta *f* (en un examen); participante *mf* (en un concurso)
entrap [ɪnˈtræp, ɛn-] *vt* **-trapped; -trapping** : atrapar, entrampar, hacer caer en una trampa
entrapment [ɪnˈtræpmənt, ɛn-] *n* : captura *f*
entreat [ɪnˈtriːt, ɛn-] *vt* : suplicar, rogar
entreaty [ɪnˈtriːṱi, ɛn-] *n, pl* **-treaties** : ruego *m*, súplica *f*
entrée *or* **entree** [ˈɑn,treɪ, ,ɑnˈ-] *n* : plato *m* principal
entrench [ɪnˈtrɛntʃ, ɛn-] *vt* **1** FORTIFY : atrincherar (una posición militar) **2** : consolidar, afianzar <firmly entrenched in his job : afianzado en su puesto>
entrepreneur [,ɑntrəprəˈnər, -ˈnjʊr] *n* : empresario *m*, -ria *f*
entrust [ɪnˈtrʌst, ɛn-] *vt* : confiar, encomendar
entry [ˈɛntri] *n, pl* **-tries 1** ENTRANCE : entrada *f* **2** NOTATION : entrada *f*, anotación *f*
entwine [ɪnˈtwaɪn, ɛn-] *vt* **-twined; -twining** : entrelazar, entretejer, entrecruzar
enumerate [ɪˈnuːmə,reɪt, ɛ-, -ˈnjuː-] *vt* **-ated; -ating 1** LIST : enumerar **2** COUNT : contar, enumerar
enumeration [ɪ,nuːməˈreɪʃən, ɛ-, -,njuː-] *n* : enumeración *f*, lista *f*
enunciate [iˈnʌn*t*si,eɪt, ɛ-] *vt* **-ated; -ating 1** STATE : enunciar, decir **2** PRONOUNCE : articular, pronunciar
enunciation [i,nʌn*t*siˈeɪʃən, ɛ-] *n* **1** STATEMENT : enunciación *f*, declaración *f* **2** ARTICULATION : articulación *f*, pronunciación *f*, dicción *f*
envelop [ɪnˈvɛləp, ɛn-] *vt* : envolver, cubrir
envelope [ˈɛnvə,loːp, ˈɑn-] *n* : sobre *m*
enviable [ˈɛnviəbəl] *adj* : envidiable
envious [ˈɛnviəs] *adj* : envidioso — **enviously** *adv*
environment [ɪnˈvaɪrənmənt, ɛn-, -ˈvaɪərn-] *n* : medio *m* (ambiente), ambiente *m*, entorno *m*
environmental [ɪn,vaɪrənˈmɛntəl, ɛn-, -,vaɪərn-] *adj* : ambiental

environmentalist [ɪnˌvaɪrənˈmɛntəlɪst, ɛn-, -ˌvaɪərn-] *n* : ecologista *mf*
environs [ɪnˈvaɪrənz, ɛn-, -ˈvaɪərnz] *npl* : alrededores *mpl*, entorno *m*, inmediaciones *fpl*
envisage [ɪnˈvɪzɪdʒ, ɛn-] *vt* **-aged; -aging 1** IMAGINE : imaginarse, concebir **2** FORESEE : prever
envision [ɪnˈvɪʒən, ɛn-] *vt* : imaginar
envoy [ˈɛnˌvɔɪ, ˈɑn-] *n* : enviado *m*, -da *f*
envy[1] [ˈɛnvi] *vt* **-vied; -vying** : envidiar
envy[2] *n, pl* **envies** : envidia *f*
enzyme [ˈɛnˌzaɪm] *n* : enzima *f*
eon [ˈiːən, iːˌɑn] → **aeon**
epaulet [ˌɛpəˈlɛt] *n* : charretera *f*
ephemeral [ɪˈfɛmərəl, -ˈfiː-] *adj* : efímero, fugaz
epic[1] [ˈɛpɪk] *adj* : épico
epic[2] *n* : poema *m* épico, epopeya *f*
epicure [ˈɛpɪˌkjʊr] *n* : epicúreo *m*, -rea *f*; gastrónomo *m*, -ma *f*
epicurean [ˌɛpɪkjʊˈriːən, -ˈkjʊriən] *adj* : epicúreo
epidemic[1] [ˌɛpəˈdɛmɪk] *adj* : epidémico
epidemic[2] *n* : epidemia *f*
epidermis [ˌɛpəˈdərməs] *n* : epidermis *f*
epigram [ˈɛpəˌgræm] *n* : epigrama *m*
epilepsy [ˈɛpəˌlɛpsi] *n, pl* **-sies** : epilepsia *f*
epileptic[1] [ˌɛpəˈlɛptɪk] *adj* : epiléptico
epileptic[2] *n* : epiléptico *m*, -ca *f*
episcopal [ɪˈpɪskəpəl] *adj* : episcopal
episode [ˈɛpəˌsoːd] *n* : episodio *m*
episodic [ˌɛpəˈsɑdɪk] *adj* : episódico
epistle [ɪˈpɪsəl] *n* : epístola *f*, carta *f*
epitaph [ˈɛpəˌtæf] *n* : epitafio *m*
epithet [ˈɛpəˌθɛt, -θət] *n* : epíteto *m*
epitome [ɪˈpɪtəmi] *n* **1** SUMMARY : epítome *m*, resumen *m* **2** EMBODIMENT : personificación *f*
epitomize [ɪˈpɪtəˌmaɪz] *vt* **-mized; -mizing 1** SUMMARIZE : resumir **2** EMBODY : ser la personificación de, personificar
epoch [ˈɛpək, ˈɛˌpɑk, ˈiːˌpɑk] *n* : época *f*, era *f*
equable [ˈɛkwəbəl, ˈiː-] *adj* **1** CALM, STEADY : ecuánime **2** UNIFORM : estable (dícese de la temperatura), constante (dícese del clima), uniforme
equably [ˈɛkwəbli, ˈiː-] *adv* : con ecuanimidad
equal[1] [ˈiːkwəl] *vt* **equaled** *or* **equalled; equaling** *or* **equalling 1** : ser igual a <two plus three equals five : dos más tres es igual a cinco> **2** MATCH : igualar
equal[2] *adj* **1** SAME : igual **2** ADEQUATE : adecuado, capaz
equal[3] *n* : igual *mf*
equality [ɪˈkwɑləṭi] *n, pl* **-ties** : igualdad *f*
equalize [ˈiːkwəˌlaɪz] *vt* **-ized; -izing** : igualar, equiparar
equally [ˈiːkwəli] *adv* : igualmente, por igual
equanimity [ˌiːkwəˈnɪməṭi, ˌɛ-] *n, pl* **-ties** : ecuanimidad *f*
equate [ɪˈkweɪt] *vt* **equated; equating** : equiparar, identificar
equation [ɪˈkweɪʒən] *n* : ecuación *f*
equator [ɪˈkweɪṭər] *n* : ecuador *m*
equatorial [ˌiːkwəˈtoriəl, ˌɛ-] *adj* : ecuatorial
equestrian[1] [ɪˈkwɛstriən, ɛ-] *adj* : ecuestre
equestrian[2] *n* : jinete *mf*, caballista *mf*
equilateral [ˌiːkwəˈlæṭərəl, ˌɛ-] *adj* : equilátero
equilibrium [ˌiːkwəˈlɪbriəm, ˌɛ-] *n, pl* **-riums** *or* **-ria** [-briə] : equilibrio *m*
equine [ˈiːˌkwaɪn, ˈɛ-] *adj* : equino, hípico
equinox [ˈiːkwəˌnɑks, ˈɛ-] *n* : equinoccio *m*
equip [ɪˈkwɪp] *vt* **equipped; equipping 1** FURNISH : equipar **2** PREPARE : preparar
equipment [ɪˈkwɪpmənt] *n* : equipo *m*
equitable [ˈɛkwəṭəbəl] *adj* : equitativo, justo, imparcial
equity [ˈɛkwəṭi] *n, pl* **-ties 1** FAIRNESS : equidad *f*, imparcialidad *f* **2** VALUE : valor *m* líquido
equivalence [ɪˈkwɪvələnts] *n* : equivalencia *f*
equivalent[1] [ɪˈkwɪvələnt] *adj* : equivalente
equivalent[2] *n* : equivalente *m*
equivocal [ɪˈkwɪvəkəl] *adj* **1** AMBIGUOUS : equívoco, ambiguo **2** QUESTIONABLE : incierto, dudoso, sospechoso
equivocate [ɪˈkwɪvəˌkeɪt] *vi* **-cated; -cating** : usar lenguaje equívoco, andarse con evasivas
equivocation [ɪˌkwɪvəˈkeɪʃən] *n* : evasiva *f*, subterfugio *m*
era [ˈɪrə, ˈɛrə, ˈiːrə] *n* : era *f*, época *f*
eradicate [ɪˈrædəˌkeɪt] *vt* **-cated; -cating** : erradicar
erase [ɪˈreɪs] *vt* **erased; erasing** : borrar
eraser [ɪˈreɪsər] *n* : goma *f* de borrar, borrador *m*
erasure [ɪˈreɪʃər] *n* : tachadura *f*
ere[1] [ˈɛr] *conj* : antes de que
ere[2] *prep* **1** : antes de **2 ere long** : dentro de poco
erect[1] [ɪˈrɛkt] *vt* **1** CONSTRUCT : erigir, construir **2** RAISE : levantar **3** ESTABLISH : establecer
erect[2] *adj* : erguido, derecho, erecto
erection [ɪˈrɛkʃən] *n* **1** : erección *f* (en fisiología) **2** BUILDING : construcción *f*
ermine [ˈərmən] *n* : armiño *m*
erode [ɪˈroːd] *vt* **eroded; eroding** : erosionar (el suelo), corroer (metales)
erosion [ɪˈroːʒən] *n* : erosión *f*, corrosión *f*
erotic [ɪˈrɑṭɪk] *adj* : erótico — **erotically** [-ṭɪkli] *adv*

eroticism [ɪˈrɑt̬əˌsɪzəm] *n* : erotismo *m*

err [ˈɛr, ˈər] *vi* : cometer un error, equivocarse, errar

errand [ˈɛrənd] *n* : mandado *m,* encargo *m,* recado *m Spain* <an errand of mercy : una misión de caridad>

errant [ˈɛrənt] *adj* **1** WANDERING : errante **2** ASTRAY : descarriado

erratic [ɪˈræt̬ɪk] *adj* **1** INCONSISTENT : errático, irregular, inconsistente **2** ECCENTRIC : excéntrico, raro

erratically [ɪˈræt̬ɪkli] *adv* : erráticamente, de manera irregular

erroneous [ɪˈroːniəs, ɛ-] *adj* : erróneo — **erroneously** *adv*

error [ˈɛrər] *n* : error *m,* equivocación *f* <to be in error : estar equivocado>

ersatz [ˈɛrˌsɑts, ˈərˌsæts] *adj* : artificial, sustituto

erstwhile [ˈərstˌhwaɪl] *adj* : antiguo

erudite [ˈɛrəˌdaɪt, ˈɛrjʊ-] *adj* : erudito, letrado

erudition [ˌɛrəˈdɪʃən, ˌɛrjʊ-] *n* : erudición *f*

erupt [ɪˈrʌpt] *vi* **1** : hacer erupción (dícese de un volcán o un sarpullido) **2** : estallar (dícese de la cólera o la violencia)

eruption [ɪˈrʌpʃən] *n* : erupción *f,* estallido *m*

eruptive [ɪˈrʌptɪv] *adj* : eruptivo

escalate [ˈɛskəˌleɪt] *v* **-lated; -lating** *vt* : intensificar (un conflicto), aumentar (precios) — *vi* : intensificarse, aumentarse

escalation [ˌɛskəˈleɪʃən] *n* : intensificación *f,* escalada *f,* aumento *m,* subida *f*

escalator [ˈɛskəˌleɪtər] *n* : escalera *f* mecánica

escapade [ˈɛskəˌpeɪd] *n* : aventura *f*

escape[1] [ɪˈskeɪp, ɛ-] *v* **-caped; -caping** *vt* : escaparse de, librarse de, evitar — *vi* : escaparse, fugarse, huir

escape[2] *n* **1** FLIGHT : fuga *f,* huida *f,* escapada *f* **2** LEAKAGE : escape *m,* fuga *f* **3** : escapatoria *f,* evasión *f* <to have no escape : no tener escapatoria> <escape from reality : evasión de la realidad>

escapee [ɪˌskeɪˈpiː, ˌɛ-] *n* : fugitivo *m,* -va *f*

escarole [ˈɛskəˌroːl] *n* : escarola *f*

escarpment [ɪsˈkɑrpmənt, ɛs-] *n* : escarpa *f,* escarpadura *f*

eschew [ɛˈʃuː, ɪsˈtʃuː] *vt* : evitar, rehuir, abstenerse de

escort[1] [ɪˈskɔrt, ɛ-] *vt* **1** : escoltar <to escort a ship : escoltar un barco> **2** ACCOMPANY : acompañar

escort[2] [ˈɛsˌkɔrt] *n* **1** : escolta *f* <armed escort : escolta armada> **2** COMPANION : acompañante *mf;* compañero *m,* -ra *f*

escrow [ˈɛsˌkroː] *n* **in escrow** : en depósito, en custodia de un tercero

esophagus [ɪˈsɑfəgəs, iː-] *n, pl* **-gi** [-ˌgaɪ, -ˌdʒaɪ] : esófago *m*

esoteric [ˌɛsəˈtɛrɪk] *adj* : esotérico, hermético

especially [ɪˈspɛʃəli] *adv* : especialmente, particularmente

espionage [ˈɛspiəˌnɑʒ, -ˌnɑdʒ] *n* : espionaje *m*

espouse [ɪˈspaʊz, ɛ-] *vt* **espoused; espousing** **1** MARRY : casarse con **2** ADOPT, ADVOCATE : apoyar, adherirse a, adoptar

espresso [ɛˈsprɛˌsoː] *n, pl* **-sos** : café *m* exprés

essay[1] [ɛˈseɪ, ˈɛˌseɪ] *vt* : intentar, tratar

essay[2] [ˈɛˌseɪ] *n* **1** COMPOSITION : ensayo *m,* trabajo *m* **2** ATTEMPT : intento *m*

essayist [ˈɛˌseɪɪst] *n* : ensayista *mf*

essence [ˈɛsənts] *n* **1** CORE : esencia *f,* núcleo *m,* meollo *m* <in essence : esencialmente> **2** EXTRACT : esencia *f,* extracto *m* **3** PERFUME : esencia *f,* perfume *m*

essential[1] [ɪˈsɛntʃəl] *adj* : esencial, imprescindible, fundamental — **essentially** *adv*

essential[2] *n* : elemento *m* esencial, lo imprescindible

establish [ɪˈstæblɪʃ, ɛ-] *vt* **1** FOUND : establecer, fundar **2** SET UP : establecer, instaurar, instituir **3** PROVE : demostrar, probar

establishment [ɪˈstæblɪʃmənt, ɛ-] *n* **1** ESTABLISHING : establecimiento *m,* fundación *f,* instauración *f* **2** BUSINESS : negocio *m,* establecimiento *m* **3 the Establishment** : la clase dirigente

estate [ɪˈsteɪt, ɛ-] *n* **1** POSSESSIONS : bienes *mpl,* propiedad *f,* patrimonio *m* **2** PROPERTY : hacienda *f,* finca *f,* propiedad *f*

esteem[1] [ɪˈstiːm, ɛ-] *vt* : estimar, apreciar

esteem[2] *n* : estima *f,* aprecio *m*

ester [ˈɛstər] *n* : éster *m*

esthetic [ɛsˈθɛt̬ɪk] → **aesthetic**

estimable [ˈɛstəməbəl] *adj* : estimable

estimate[1] [ˈɛstəˌmeɪt] *vt* **-mated; -mating** : calcular, estimar

estimate[2] [ˈɛstəmət] *n* **1** : cálculo *m* aproximado <to make an estimate : hacer un cálculo> **2** ASSESSMENT : valoración *f,* estimación *f*

estimation [ˌɛstəˈmeɪʃən] *n* **1** JUDGMENT : juicio *m,* opinión *f* <in my estimation : en mi opinión, según mis cálculos> **2** ESTEEM : estima *f,* aprecio *m*

estimator [ˈɛstəˌmeɪt̬ər] *n* : tasador *m,* -dora *f*

Estonian [ɛˈstoːniən] *n* : estonio *m,* -nia *f* — **Estonian** *adj*

estrange [ɪˈstreɪndʒ, ɛ-] *vt* **-tranged; -tranging** : enajenar, apartar, alejar

estrangement [ɪˈstreɪndʒmənt, ɛ-] *n* : alejamiento *m,* distanciamiento *m*

estrogen [ˈɛstrədʒən] *n* : estrógeno *m*

estrus [ˈɛstrəs] *n* : celo *m*

estuary [ˈɛstʃʊˌwɛri] *n, pl* **-aries** : estuario *m,* -ria *f*

et cetera [ɛtˈsɛt̬ərə, -ˈsɛtrə] **:** etcétera

etch [ˈɛtʃ] *v* **:** grabar al aguafuerte

etching [ˈɛtʃɪŋ] *n* **:** aguafuerte *m,* grabado *m* al aguafuerte

eternal [ɪˈtərnəl, iː-] *adj* **1** EVERLASTING **:** eterno **2** INTERMINABLE **:** constante, incesante

eternally [ɪˈtərnəli, iː-] *adv* **:** eternamente, para siempre

eternity [ɪˈtərnət̬i, iː-] *n, pl* **-ties :** eternidad *f*

ethane [ˈɛˌθeɪn] *n* **:** etano *m*

ethanol [ˈɛθəˌnɔl, -ˌnoːl] *n* **:** etanol *m*

ether [ˈiːθər] *n* **:** éter *m*

ethereal [ɪˈθɪriəl, iː-] *adj* **1** CELESTIAL **:** etéreo, celeste **2** DELICATE **:** delicado

ethical [ˈɛθɪkəl] *adj* **:** ético **— ethically** *adv*

ethics [ˈɛθɪks] *ns & pl* **1 :** ética *f* **2** MORALITY **:** ética *f,* moral *f,* moralidad *f*

Ethiopian [ˌiːθiˈoːpiən] *n* **:** etíope *mf* **— Ethiopian** *adj*

ethnic [ˈɛθnɪk] *adj* **:** étnico

ethnologist [ɛθˈnɑlədʒɪst] *n* **:** etnólogo *m,* -ga *f*

ethnology [ɛθˈnɑlədʒi] *n* **:** etnología *f*

etiquette [ˈɛt̬ɪkət, -ˌkɛt] *n* **:** etiqueta *f,* protocolo *m*

etymological [ˌɛt̬əməˈlɑdʒɪkəl] *adj* **:** etimológico

etymology [ˌɛt̬əˈmɑlədʒi] *n, pl* **-gies :** etimología *f*

eucalyptus [ˌjuːkəˈlɪptəs] *n, pl* **-ti** [-ˌtaɪ] *or* **-tuses** [-təsəz] **:** eucalipto *m*

Eucharist [ˈjuːkərɪst] *n* **:** Eucaristía *f*

eulogize [ˈjuːləˌdʒaɪz] *vt* **-gized; -gizing :** elogiar, encomiar

eulogy [ˈjuːlədʒi] *n, pl* **-gies :** elogio *m,* encomio *m,* panegírico *m*

eunuch [ˈjuːnək] *n* **:** eunuco *m*

euphemism [ˈjuːfəˌmɪzəm] *n* **:** eufemismo *m*

euphemistic [ˌjuːfəˈmɪstɪk] *adj* **:** eufemístico

euphony [ˈjuːfəni] *n, pl* **-nies :** eufonía *f*

euphoria [jʊˈforiə] *n* **:** euforia *f*

euphoric [jʊˈforɪk] *adj* **:** eufórico

euthanasia [ˌjuːθəˈneɪʒə, -ʒiə] *n* **:** eutanasia *f*

evacuate [ɪˈvækjʊˌeɪt] *v* **-ated; -ating** *vt* VACATE **:** evacuar, desalojar **—** *vi* WITHDRAW **:** retirarse

evacuation [ɪˌvækjʊˈeɪʃən] *n* **:** evacuación *f,* desalojo *m*

evade [ɪˈveɪd] *vt* **evaded; evading :** evadir, eludir, esquivar

evaluate [ɪˈvæljʊˌeɪt] *vt* **-ated; -ating :** evaluar, valorar, tasar

evaluation [ɪˌvæljʊˈeɪʃən] *n* **:** evaluación *f,* valoración *f,* tasación *f*

evangelical [ˌiːˌvænˈdʒɛlɪkəl, ˌɛvən-] *adj* **:** evangélico

evangelist [ɪˈvændʒəlɪst] *n* **1 :** evangelista *m* **2** PREACHER **:** predicador *m,* -dora *f*

evaporate [ɪˈvæpəˌreɪt] *vi* **-rated; -rating 1** VAPORIZE **:** evaporarse **2** VANISH **:** evaporarse, desvanecerse, esfumarse

evaporation [ɪˌvæpəˈreɪʃən] *n* **:** evaporación *f*

evasion [ɪˈveɪʒən] *n* **:** evasión *f*

evasive [ɪˈveɪsɪv] *adj* **:** evasivo

evasiveness [ɪˈveɪsɪvnəs] *n* **:** carácter *m* evasivo

eve [ˈiːv] *n* **1 :** víspera *f* <on the eve of the festivities : en vísperas de las festividades> **2 → evening**

even[1] [ˈiːvən] *vt* **1** LEVEL **:** allanar, nivelar, emparejar **2** EQUALIZE **:** igualar, equilibrar **—** *vi* **to even out :** nivelarse, emparejarse

even[2] *adv* **1 :** hasta, incluso <even a child can do it : hasta un niño puede hacerlo> <he looked content, even happy : se le veía satisfecho, incluso feliz> **2** (*in negative constructions*) **:** ni siquiera <he didn't even try : ni siquiera lo intentó> **3** (*in comparisons*) **:** aún, todavía <even better : aún mejor, todavía mejor> **4 even if :** aunque **5 even so :** aun así **6 even though :** aun cuando, a pesar de que

even[3] *adj* **1** SMOOTH **:** uniforme, liso, parejo **2** FLAT **:** plano, llano **3** EQUAL **:** igual, igualado <an even score : un marcador igualado> **4** REGULAR **:** regular, constante <an even pace : un ritmo constante> **5** EXACT **:** exacto, justo **6 :** par <even number : número par> **7 to be even :** estar en paz, estar a mano **8 to get even :** desquitarse, vengarse

evening [ˈiːvnɪŋ] *n* **:** tarde *f,* noche *f* <in the evening : por la noche>

evenly [ˈiːvənli] *adv* **1** UNIFORMLY **:** de modo uniforme, de manera constante **2** FAIRLY **:** igualmente, equitativamente

evenness [ˈiːvənnəs] *n* **:** uniformidad *f,* igualdad *f,* regularidad *f*

event [ɪˈvɛnt] *n* **1 :** acontecimiento *m,* suceso *m,* prueba *f* (en deportes) **2 in the event that :** en caso de que

eventful [ɪˈvɛntfəl] *adj* **:** lleno de incidentes, memorable

eventual [ɪˈvɛntʃʊəl] *adj* **:** final, consiguiente

eventuality [ɪˌvɛntʃʊˈælət̬i] *n, pl* **-ties :** eventualidad *f*

eventually [ɪˈvɛntʃʊəli] *adv* **:** al fin, con el tiempo, algún día

ever [ˈɛvər] *adv* **1** ALWAYS **:** siempre <as ever : como siempre> <ever since : desde entonces> **2** (*in questions*) **:** alguna vez, algún día <have you ever been to Mexico? : ¿has estado en México alguna vez?> **3** (*in negative constructions*) **:** nunca <doesn't he ever work? : ¿es que nunca trabaja?> <nobody ever helps me : nadie nunca me ayuda> **4** (*in comparisons*) **:** nunca <better than ever : mejor que nunca> **5** (*as intensifier*) <I'm ever so happy! : ¡estoy tan y tan feliz!> <he

looks ever so angry : parece estar muy enojado>
evergreen[1] [ˈɛvər,griːn] *adj* : de hoja perenne
evergreen[2] *n* : planta *f* de hoja perenne
everlasting [,ɛvərˈlæstɪŋ] *adj* : eterno, perpetuo, imperecedero
evermore [,ɛvərˈmor] *adv* : eternamente
every [ˈɛvri] *adj* **1** EACH : cada <every time : cada vez> <every other house : cada dos casas> **2** ALL : todo <every month : todos los meses> <every woman : toda mujer, todas las mujeres> **3** COMPLETE : pleno, entero <to have every confidence : tener plena confianza>
everybody [ˈɛvri,bʌdi, -,bɑ-] *pron* : todos *mpl*, -das *fpl*; todo el mundo
everyday [,ɛvriˈdeɪ, ˈɛvri,-] *adj* : cotidiano, diario, corriente <everyday clothes : ropa de todos los días>
everyone [ˈɛvri ,wʌn] → **everybody**
everything [ˈɛvri,θɪŋ] *pron* : todo
everywhere [ˈɛvri,*h*wɛr] *adv* : en todas partes, por todas partes, dondequiera <I looked everywhere : busqué en todas partes> <everywhere we go : dondequiera que vayamos>
evict [ɪˈvɪkt] *vt* : desalojar, desahuciar
eviction [ɪˈvɪkʃən] *n* : desalojo *m*, desahucio *m*
evidence [ˈɛvədən*t*s] *n* **1** INDICATION : indicio *m*, señal *m* <to be in evidence : estar a la vista> **2** PROOF : evidencia *f*, prueba *f* **3** TESTIMONY : testimonio *m*, declaración *f* <to give evidence : declarar como testigo, prestar declaración>
evident [ˈɛvidənt] *adj* : evidente, patente, manifiesto
evidently [ˈɛvidəntli, ,ɛviˈdɛntli] *adv* **1** CLEARLY : claramente, obviamente **2** APPARENTLY : aparentemente, evidentemente, al parecer
evil[1] [ˈiːvəl, -vɪl] *adj* **eviler** *or* **eviller; evilest** *or* **evillest 1** WICKED : malvado, malo, maligno **2** HARMFUL : nocivo, dañino, pernicioso **3** UNPLEASANT : desagradable <an evil odor : un olor horrible>
evil[2] *n* **1** WICKEDNESS : mal *m*, maldad *f* **2** MISFORTUNE : desgracia *f*, mal *m*
evildoer [,iːvəlˈduːər, ,iːvɪl-] *n* : malvado *m*, -da *f*
evince [ɪˈvɪn*t*s] *vt* **evinced; evincing** : mostrar, manifestar, revelar
eviscerate [ɪˈvɪsə,reɪt] *vt* **-ated; -ating** : eviscerar, destripar (un pollo, etc.)
evocation [,iːvoˈkeɪʃən, ,ɛ-] *n* : evocación *f*
evocative [iˈvɑkət̬ɪv] *adj* : evocador
evoke [iˈvoːk] *vt* **evoked; evoking** : evocar, provocar
evolution [,ɛvəˈluːʃən, ,iː-] *n* : evolución *f*, desarrollo *m*
evolutionary [,ɛvəˈluːʃə,nɛri, ,iː-] *adj* : evolutivo
evolve [iˈvɑlv] *vi* **evolved; evolving** : evolucionar, desarrollarse
ewe [ˈjuː] *n* : oveja *f*
exact[1] [ɪgˈzækt, ɛ-] *vt* : exigir, imponer, arrancar
exact[2] *adj* : exacto, preciso — **exactly** *adv*
exacting [ɪˈzæktɪŋ, ɛg-] *adj* : exigente, riguroso
exactitude [ɪgˈzæktə,tuːd, ɛg-, -,tjuːd] *n* : exactitud *f*, precisión *f*
exaggerate [ɪgˈzædʒə,reɪt, ɛg-] *v* **-ated; -ating** : exagerar
exaggerated [ɪgˈzædʒə,reɪt̬əd, ɛg-] *adj* : exagerado — **exaggeratedly** *adv*
exaggeration [ɪg,zædʒəˈreɪʃən, ɛg-] *n* : exageración *f*
exalt [ɪgˈzɔlt, ɛg-] *vt* : exaltar, ensalzar, glorificar
exaltation [,ɛg,zɔlˈteɪʃən, ,ɛk,sɔl-] *n* : exaltación *f*
exam [ɪgˈzæm, ɛg-] → **examination**
examination [ɪg,zæməˈneɪʃən, ɛg-] *n* **1** TEST : examen *m* **2** INSPECTION : inspección *f*, revisión *f* **3** INVESTIGATION : examen *m*, estudio *m*
examine [ɪgˈzæmən, ɛg-] *vt* **-ined; -ining 1** TEST : examinar **2** INSPECT : inspeccionar, revisar **3** STUDY : examinar
example [ɪgˈzæmpəl, ɛg-] *n* : ejemplo *m* <for example : por ejemplo> <to set an example : dar ejemplo>
exasperate [ɪgˈzæspə,reɪt, ɛg-] *vt* **-ated; -ating** : exasperar, sacar de quicio
exasperation [ɪg,zæspəˈreɪʃən, ɛg-] *n* : exasperación *f*
excavate [ˈɛkskə,veɪt] *vt* **-vated; -vating** : excavar
excavation [,ɛkskəˈveɪʃən] *n* : excavación *f*
exceed [ɪkˈsiːd, ɛk-] *vt* **1** SURPASS : exceder, rebasar, sobrepasar **2** : exceder de, sobrepasar <not exceeding two months : que no exceda de dos meses>
exceedingly [ɪkˈsiːdɪŋli, ɛk-] *adv* : extremadamente, sumamente
excel [ɪkˈsɛl, ɛk-] *v* **-celled; -celling** *vi* : sobresalir, descollar, lucirse — *vt* : superar
excellence [ˈɛksələn*t*s] *n* : excelencia *f*
excellency [ˈɛksələn*t*si] *n, pl* **-cies** : excelencia *f* <His Excellency : Su Excelencia>
excellent [ˈɛksələnt] *adj* : excelente, sobresaliente — **excellently** *adv*
except[1] [ɪkˈsɛpt] *vt* : exceptuar, excluir
except[2] *conj* : pero, si no fuera por
except[3] *prep* : excepto, menos, salvo <everyone except Carlos : todos menos Carlos>
exception [ɪkˈsɛpʃən] *n* **1** : excepción *f* **2 to take exception to** : ofenderse por, objetar a
exceptional [ɪkˈsɛpʃənəl] *adj* : excepcional, extraordinario — **exceptionally** *adv*

excerpt[1] [ɛk'sərpt, ɛg'zərpt, 'ɛk,-, 'ɛg,-] *vt* : escoger, seleccionar
excerpt[2] ['ɛk,sərpt, 'ɛg,zərpt] *n* : pasaje *m,* selección *f*
excess[1] ['ɛk,sɛs, ɪk'sɛs] *adj* **1** : excesivo, de sobra **2 excess baggage** : exceso *m* de equipaje
excess[2] [ɪk'sɛs, 'ɛk,sɛs] *n* **1** SUPERFLUITY : exceso *m,* superfluidad *f* <an excess of energy : un exceso de energía> **2** SURPLUS : excedente *m,* sobrante *m* <in excess of : superior a>
excessive [ɪk'sɛsɪv, ɛk-] *adj* : excesivo, exagerado, desmesurado — **excessively** *adv*
exchange[1] [ɪks'tʃeɪndʒ, ɛks-; 'ɛks,tʃeɪndʒ] *vt* **-changed; -changing** : cambiar, intercambiar, canjear
exchange[2] *n* **1** : cambio *m,* intercambio *m,* canje *m* **2 stock exchange** : bolsa *f* (de valores)
exchangeable [ɪks'tʃeɪndʒəbəl, ɛks-] *adj* : canjeable
excise[1] [ɪk'saɪz, ɛk-] *vt* **-cised; -cising** : extirpar
excise[2] ['ɛk,saɪz] *n* **excise tax** : impuesto *m* interno, impuesto *m* sobre el consumo
excision [ɪk'sɪʒən, ɛk-] *n* : extirpación *f,* excisión *f*
excitability [ɪk,saɪtə'bɪləṱi, ɛk-] *n* : excitabilidad *f*
excitable [ɪk'saɪṱəbəl, ɛk-] *adj* : excitable
excitation [,ɛk,saɪ'teɪʃən] *n* : excitación *f*
excite [ɪk'saɪt, ɛk-] *vt* **-cited; -citing 1** AROUSE, STIMULATE : excitar, mover, estimular **2** ANIMATE : entusiasmar, animar **3** EVOKE, PROVOKE : provocar, despertar, suscitar <to excite curiousity : despertar la curiosidad>
excited [ɪk'saɪṱəd, ɛk-] *adj* **1** STIMULATED : excitado, estimulado **2** ENTHUSIASTIC : entusiasmado, emocionado
excitedly [ɪk'saɪṱədli, ɛk-] *adv* : con excitación, con entusiasmo
excitement [ɪk'saɪtmənt, ɛk-] *n* **1** ENTHUSIASM : entusiasmo *m,* emoción *f* **2** AGITATION : agitación *f,* alboroto *m,* conmoción *f* **3** AROUSAL : excitación *f*
exclaim [ɪks'kleɪm, ɛk-] *v* : exclamar
exclamation [,ɛksklə'meɪʃən] *n* : exclamación *f*
exclamation point *n* : signo *m* de admiración
exclamatory [ɪks'klæmə,tori, ɛks-] *adj* : exclamativo
exclude [ɪks'klu:d, ɛks-] *vt* **-cluded; -cluding 1** BAR : excluir, descartar, no admitir **2** EXPEL : expeler, expulsar
exclusion [ɪks'klu:ʒən, ɛks-] *n* : exclusión *f*
exclusive[1] [ɪks'klu:sɪv, ɛks-] *adj* **1** SOLE : exclusivo, único **2** SELECT : exclusivo, selecto
exclusive[2] *n* : exclusiva *f*
exclusively [ɪks'klu:sɪvli, ɛks-] *adv* : exclusivamente, únicamente
exclusiveness [ɪks'klu:sɪvnəs, ɛks-] *n* : exclusividad *f*
excommunicate [,ɛkskə'mju:nə,keɪt] *vt* **-cated; -cating** : excomulgar
excommunication [,ɛkskə,mju:nə'keɪʃən] *n* : excomunión *f*
excrement ['ɛkskrəmənt] *n* : excremento *m*
excrete [ɪk'skri:t, ɛk-] *vt* **-creted; -creting** : excretar
excretion [ɪk'skri:ʃən, ɛk-] *n* : excreción *f*
excruciating [ɪk'skru:ʃi,eɪṱɪŋ, ɛk-] *adj* : insoportable, atroz, terrible — **excruciatingly** *adv*
exculpate ['ɛkskəl,peɪt] *vt* **-pated; -pating** : exculpar
excursion [ɪk'skərʒən, ɛk-] *n* **1** OUTING : excursión *f,* paseo *m* **2** DIGRESSION : digresión *f*
excuse[1] [ɪk'skju:z, ɛk-] *vt* **-cused; -cusing 1** PARDON : disculpar, perdonar <excuse me : con permiso, perdóneme, perdón> **2** EXEMPT : eximir, disculpar **3** JUSTIFY : excusar, justificar
excuse[2] [ɪk'skju:s, ɛk-] *n* **1** JUSTIFICATION : excusa *f,* justificación *f* **2** PRETEXT : pretexto *m* **3 to make one's excuses to someone** : pedirle disculpas a alguien
execute ['ɛksɪ,kju:t] *vt* **-cuted; -cuting 1** CARRY OUT : ejecutar, llevar a cabo, desempeñar **2** ENFORCE : ejecutar, cumplir (un testamento, etc.) **3** KILL : ejecutar, ajusticiar
execution [,ɛksɪ'kju:ʃən] *n* **1** PERFORMANCE : ejecución *f,* desempeño *m* **2** IMPLEMENTATION : cumplimiento *m* **3** : ejecución *f* (por un delito)
executioner [,ɛksɪ'kju:ʃənər] *n* : verdugo *m*
executive[1] [ɪg'zɛkjəṱɪv, ɛg-] *adj* : ejecutivo
executive[2] *n* : ejecutivo *m,* -va *f*
executor [ɪg'zɛkjəṱər, ɛg-] *n* : albacea *m,* testamentario *m*
executrix [ɪg'zɛkjə,trɪks, ɛg-] *n, pl* **executrices** [-,zɛkjə'traɪ,si:z] *or* **executrixes** [-'zɛkjə,trɪksəz] : albacea *f,* testamentaria *f*
exemplary [ɪg'zɛmpləri, ɛg-] *adj* : ejemplar
exemplify [ɪg'zɛmplə,faɪ, ɛg-] *vt* **-fied; -fying** : ejemplificar, ilustrar, demostrar
exempt[1] [ɪg'zɛmpt, ɛg-] *vt* : eximir, dispensar, exonerar
exempt[2] *adj* : exento, eximido
exemption [ɪg'zɛmpʃən, ɛg-] *n* : exención *f*
exercise[1] ['ɛksər,saɪz] *v* **-cised; -cising** *vt* **1** : ejercitar (el cuerpo) **2** USE : ejercer, hacer uso de — *vi* : hacer ejercicio
exercise[2] *n* **1** : ejercicio *m* **2 exercises** *npl* WORKOUT : ejercicios *mpl* físicos **3 exercises** *npl* CEREMONY : ceremonia *f*
exert [ɪg'zərt, ɛg-] *vt* **1** : ejercer, emplear **2 to exert oneself** : esforzarse

exertion [ɪg'zərʃən, ɛg-] *n* **1** USE : ejercicio *m* (de autoridad, etc.), uso *m* (de fuerza, etc.) **2** EFFORT : esfuerzo *m,* empeño *m*

exhalation [ˌɛksə'leɪʃən, ˌɛkshə-] *n* : exhalación *f,* espiración *f*

exhale [ɛks'heɪl] *v* **-haled; -haling** *vt* **1** : exhalar, espirar **2** EMIT : exhalar, despedir, emitir — *vi* : espirar

exhaust[1] [ɪg'zɔst, ɛg-] *vt* **1** DEPLETE : agotar **2** TIRE : cansar, fatigar, agotar **3** EMPTY : vaciar

exhaust[2] *n* **1 exhaust fumes** : gases *mpl* de escape **2 exhaust pipe** : tubo *m* de escape **3 exhaust system** : sistema *m* de escape

exhausted [ɪg'zɔstəd, ɛg-] *adj* : agotado, derrengado

exhausting [ɪg'zɔstɪŋ, ɛg-] *adj* : extenuante, agotador

exhaustion [ɪg'zɔstʃən, ɛg-] *n* : agotamiento *m*

exhaustive [ɪg'zɔstɪv, ɛg-] *adj* : exhaustivo

exhibit[1] [ɪg'zɪbət, ɛg-] *vt* **1** DISPLAY : exhibir, exponer **2** PRODUCE, SHOW : mostrar, presentar

exhibit[2] *n* **1** OBJECT : objeto *m* expuesto **2** EXHIBITION : exposición *f,* exhibición *f* **3** EVIDENCE : prueba *f* instrumental

exhibition [ˌɛksə'bɪʃən] *n* **1** : exposición *f,* exhibición *f* **2 to make an exhibition of oneself** : dar el espectáculo, hacer el ridículo

exhilarate [ɪg'zɪləˌreɪt, ɛg-] *vt* **-rated; -rating** : alegrar, levantar el ánimo de

exhilaration [ɪgˌzɪlə'reɪʃən, ɛg-] *n* : alegría *f,* regocijo *m,* júbilo *m*

exhort [ɪg'zɔrt, ɛg-] *vt* : exhortar

exhortation [ˌɛkˌsɔr'teɪʃən, -sər-; ˌɛgˌzɔr-] *n* : exhortación *f*

exhumation [ˌɛksju'meɪʃən, -hju-; ˌɛgzu-, -zju-] *n* : exhumación *f*

exhume [ɪg'zuːm, -'zjuːm; ɪks'juːm, -'hjuːm] *vt* **-humed; -huming** : exhumar, desenterrar

exigencies ['ɛksɪdʒən*t*siz, ɪg'zɪdʒənˌsiːz] *npl* : exigencias *fpl*

exile[1] ['ɛgˌzaɪl, 'ɛkˌsaɪl] *vt* **exiled; exiling** : exiliar, desterrar

exile[2] *n* **1** BANISHMENT : exilio *m,* destierro *m* **2** OUTCAST : exiliado *m,* **-da** *f;* desterrado *m,* **-da** *f*

exist [ɪg'zɪst, ɛg-] *vi* **1** BE : existir **2** LIVE : subsistir, vivir

existence [ɪg'zɪstən*t*s, ɛg-] *n* : existencia *f*

existent [ɪg'zɪstənt, ɛg-] *adj* : existente

exit[1] ['ɛgzət, 'ɛksət] *vi* : salir, hacer mutis (en el teatro) — *vt* : salir de

exit[2] *n* **1** DEPARTURE : salida *f,* partida *f* **2** EGRESS : salida *f* <emergency exit : salida de emergencia>

exodus ['ɛksədəs] *n* : éxodo *m*

exonerate [ɪg'zɑnəˌreɪt, ɛg-] *vt* **-ated; -ating** : exonerar, disculpar, absolver

exoneration [ɪgˌzɑnə'reɪʃən, ɛg-] *n* : exoneración *f*

exorbitant [ɪg'zɔrbətənt, ɛg-] *adj* : exorbitante, excesivo

exorcise ['ɛkˌsɔrˌsaɪz, -sər-] *vt* **-cised; -cising** : exorcizar

exorcism ['ɛksərˌsɪzəm] *n* : exorcismo *m*

exotic[1] [ɪg'zɑtɪk, ɛg-] *adj* : exótico — **exotically** [-ɪkli] *adv*

exotic[2] *n* : planta *f* exótica

expand [ɪk'spænd, ɛk-] *vt* **1** ENLARGE : expandir, dilatar, aumentar, ampliar **2** EXTEND : extender — *vi* **1** ENLARGE : ampliarse, extenderse **2** : expandirse, dilatarse (dícese de los metales, gases, etc.)

expanse [ɪk'spæn*t*s, ɛk-] *n* : extensión *f*

expansion [ɪk'spæntʃən, ɛk-] *n* **1** ENLARGEMENT : expansión *f,* ampliación *f* **2** EXPANSE : extensión *f*

expansive [ɪk'spæn*t*sɪv, ɛk-] *adj* **1** : expansivo **2** OUTGOING : expansivo, comunicativo **3** AMPLE : ancho, amplio — **expansively** *adv*

expansiveness [ɪk'spæn*t*sɪvnəs, ɛk-] *n* : expansibilidad *f*

expatriate[1] [ɛks'peɪtriˌeɪt] *vt* **-ated; -ating** : expatriar

expatriate[2] [ɛks'peɪtriət, -ˌeɪt] *adj* : expatriado

expatriate[3] [ɛks'peɪtriət, -ˌeɪt] *n* : expatriado *m,* **-da** *f*

expect [ɪk'spɛkt, ɛk-] *vt* **1** SUPPOSE : suponer, imaginarse **2** ANTICIPATE : esperar **3** COUNT ON, REQUIRE : contar con, esperar — *vi* **to be expecting** : estar embarazada

expectancy [ɪk'spɛktən*t*si, ɛk-] *n, pl* **-cies** : expectativa *f,* esperanza *f*

expectant [ɪk'spɛktənt, ɛk-] *adj* **1** ANTICIPATING : expectante **2** EXPECTING : futuro <expectant mother : futura madre>

expectantly [ɪk'spɛktəntli, ɛk-] *adv* : con expectación

expectation [ˌɛkˌspɛk'teɪʃən] *n* **1** ANTICIPATION : expectación *f* **2** EXPECTANCY : expectativa *f*

expedient[1] [ɪk'spiːdiənt, ɛk-] *adj* : conveniente, oportuno

expedient[2] *n* : expediente *m,* recurso *m*

expedite ['ɛkspəˌdaɪt] *vt* **-dited; -diting 1** FACILITATE : facilitar, dar curso a **2** HASTEN : acelerar

expedition [ˌɛkspə'dɪʃən] *n* : expedición *f*

expeditious [ˌɛkspə'dɪʃəs] *adj* : pronto, rápido

expel [ɪk'spɛl, ɛk-] *vt* **-pelled; -pelling** : expulsar, expeler

expend [ɪk'spɛnd, ɛk-] *vt* **1** DISBURSE : gastar, desembolsar **2** CONSUME : consumir, agotar

expendable [ɪk'spɛndəbəl, ɛk-] *adj* : prescindible

expenditure [ɪk'spɛndɪtʃər, ɛk-, -ˌtʃʊr] *n* : gasto *m*

expense [ɪk'spɛn*t*s, ɛk-] *n* **1** COST : gasto *m* **2 expenses** *npl* : gastos *mpl,*

expensas *fpl* **3 at the expense of :** a expensas de
expensive [ɪk'spɛntsɪv, ɛk-] *adj* : costoso, caro — **expensively** *adv*
experience¹ [ɪk'spɪriənts, ɛk-] *vt* **-enced; -encing :** experimentar (sentimientos), tener (dificultades), sufrir (una pérdida)
experience² *n* : experiencia *f*
experiment¹ [ɪk'spɛrəmənt, ɛk-, -'spɪr-] *vi* : experimentar, hacer experimentos
experiment² *n* : experimento *m*
experimental [ɪk,spɛrə'mɛntəl, ɛk-, -,spɪr-] *adj* : experimental — **experimentally** *adv*
experimentation [ɪk,spɛrəmən'teɪʃən, ɛk-, -,spɪr-] *n* : experimentación *f*
expert¹ ['ɛk,spərt, ɪk'spərt] *adj* : experto, de experto, pericial (dícese de un testigo) — **expertly** *adv*
expert² ['ɛk,spərt] *n* : experto *m*, -ta *f*; perito *m*, -ta *f*; especialista *mf*
expertise [,ɛkspər'ti:z] *n* : pericia *f*, competencia *f*
expiate ['ɛkspi,eɪt] *vt* **-ated; -ating** : expiar
expiation [,ɛkspi'eɪʃən] *n* : expiación *f*
expiration [,ɛkspə'reɪʃən] *n* **1** EXHALATION : exhalación *f*, espiración *f* **2** DEATH : muerte *f* **3** TERMINATION : vencimiento *m*, caducidad *f*
expire [ɪk'spaɪr, ɛk-] *vi* **-pired; -piring 1** EXHALE : espirar **2** DIE : expirar, morir **3** TERMINATE : caducar, vencer
explain [ɪk'spleɪn, ɛk-] *vt* : explicar
explanation [,ɛksplə'neɪʃən] *n* : explicación *f*
explanatory [ɪk'splænə,tori, ɛk-] *adj* : explicativo, aclaratorio
expletive ['ɛkspləṭɪv] *n* : improperio *m*, palabrota *f fam*, grosería *f*
explicable [ɛk'splɪkəbəl, 'ɛksplɪ-] *adj* : explicable
explicit [ɪk'splɪsət, ɛk-] *adj* : explícito, claro, categórico, rotundo — **explicitly** *adv*
explicitness [ɪk'splɪsətnəs, ɛk-] *n* : claridad *f*, carácter *m* explícito
explode [ɪk'splo:d, ɛk-] *v* **-ploded; -ploding** *vt* **1** BURST : explosionar, hacer explotar **2** REFUTE : rebatir, refutar, desmentir — *vi* **1** BURST : explotar, estallar, reventar **2** SKYROCKET : dispararse
exploit¹ [ɪk'splɔɪt, ɛk-] *vt* : explotar, aprovecharse de
exploit² ['ɛk,splɔɪt] *n* : hazaña *f*, proeza *f*
exploitation [,ɛk,splɔɪ'teɪʃən] *n* : explotación *f*
exploration [,ɛksplə'reɪʃən] *n* : exploración *f*
exploratory [ɪk'splorə,tori, ɛk-] *adj* : exploratorio
explore [ɪk'splor, ɛk-] *vt* **-plored; -ploring :** explorar, investigar, examinar
explorer [ɪk'splorər, ɛk-] *n* : explorador *m*, -dora *f*
explosion [ɪk'splo:ʒən, ɛk-] *n* : explosión *f*, estallido *m*
explosive¹ [ɪk'splo:sɪv, ɛk-] *adj* : explosivo, fulminante — **explosively** *adv*
explosive² *n* : explosivo *m*
exponent [ɪk'spo:nənt, 'ɛk,spo:-] *n* **1** : exponente *m* **2** ADVOCATE : defensor *m*, -sora *f*; partidario *m*, -ria *f*
exponential [,ɛkspə'nɛntʃəl] *adj* : exponencial — **exponentially** *adv*
export¹ [ɛk'sport, 'ɛk,sport] *vt* : exportar
export² ['ɛk,sport] *n* **1** : artículo *m* de exportación **2** → **exportation**
exportation [,ɛk,spor'teɪʃən] *n* : exportación *f*
exporter [ɛk'sportər, 'ɛk,spor-] *n* : exportador *m*, -dora *f*
expose [ɪk'spo:z, ɛk-] *vt* **-posed; -posing 1** : exponer (al peligro, a los elementos, a una enfermedad) **2** : exponer (una película a la luz) **3** DISCLOSE : descubrir, revelar, poner en evidencia **4** UNMASK : desenmascarar
exposé *or* **expose** [,ɛkspo'zeɪ] *n* : exposición *f* (de hechos), relevación *f* (de un escándalo)
exposed [ɪk'spo:zd, ɛk-] *adj* : descubierto, sin protección
exposition [,ɛkspə'zɪʃən] *n* : exposición *f*
exposure [ɪk'spo:ʒər, ɛk-] *n* **1** : exposición *f* **2** CONTACT : exposición *f*, experiencia *f*, contacto *m* **3** UNMASKING : desenmascaramiento *m* **4** ORIENTATION : orientación *f* <a room with a northern exposure : una sala orientada al norte>
expound [ɪk'spaʊnd, ɛk-] *vt* : exponer, explicar — *vi* : hacer comentarios detallados
express¹ [ɪk'sprɛs, ɛk-] *vt* **1** SAY : expresar, comunicar **2** SHOW : expresar, manifestar, externar *Mex* **3** SQUEEZE : exprimir <to express the juice from a lemon : exprimir el jugo de un limón>
express² *adv* : por correo exprés, por correo urgente
express³ *adj* **1** EXPLICIT : expreso, manifiesto **2** SPECIFIC : específico <for that express purpose : con ese fin específico> **3** RAPID : expreso, rápido
express⁴ *n* **1** : correo *m* exprés, correo *m* urgente **2** : expreso *m* (tren)
expression [ɪk'sprɛʃən, ɛk-] *n* **1** UTTERANCE : expresión *f* <freedom of expression : libertad de expresión> **2** : expresión *f* (en la matemática) **3** PHRASE : frase *f*, expresión *f* **4** LOOK : expresión *f*, cara *f*, gesto *m* <with a sad expression : con un gesto de tristeza>
expressionless [ɪk'sprɛʃənləs, ɛk-] *adj* : inexpresivo

expressive [ɪkˈsprɛsɪv, ɛk-] *adj* : expresivo

expressway [ɪkˈsprɛsˌweɪ, ɛk-] *n* : autopista *f*

expulsion [ɪkˈspʌlʃən, ɛk-] *n* : expulsión *f*

expurgate [ˈɛkspərˌgeɪt] *vt* **-gated; -gating** : expurgar

exquisite [ɛkˈskwɪzət, ˈɛkˌskwɪ-] *adj* **1** FINE : exquisito, delicado, primoroso **2** INTENSE : intenso, extremo

extant [ˈɛkstənt, ɛkˈstænt] *adj* : existente

extemporaneous [ɛkˌstɛmpəˈreɪniəs] *adj* : improvisado — **extemporaneously** *adv*

extend [ɪkˈstɛnd, ɛk-] *vt* **1** STRETCH : extender, tender **2** PROLONG : prolongar, prorrogar **3** ENLARGE : agrandar, ampliar, aumentar **4** PROFFER : extender, dar, ofrecer — *vi* : extenderse

extended [ɪkˈstɛndəd, ɛk-] *adj* LENGTHY : prolongado, largo

extension [ɪkˈstɛntʃən, ɛk-] *n* **1** EXTENDING : extensión *f,* ampliación *f,* prórroga *f,* prolongación *f* **2** ANNEX : ampliación *f,* anexo *m* **3** : extensión *f* (de teléfono)

extensive [ɪkˈstɛntsɪv, ɛk-] *adj* : extenso, vasto, amplio — **extensively** *adv*

extent [ɪkˈstɛnt, ɛk-] *n* **1** SIZE : extensión *f,* magnitud *f* **2** DEGREE, SCOPE : alcance *m,* grado *m* <to a certain extent : hasta cierto punto>

extenuate [ɪkˈstɛnjəˌweɪt, ɛk-] *vt* **-ated; -ating** : atenuar, aminorar, mitigar <extenuating circumstances : circunstancias atenuantes>

extenuation [ɪkˌstɛnjəˈweɪʃən, ɛk-] *n* : atenuación *f,* aminoración *f*

exterior¹ [ɛkˈstɪriər] *adj* : exterior

exterior² *n* : exterior *m*

exterminate [ɪkˈstərməˌneɪt, ɛk-] *vt* **-nated; -nating** : exterminar

extermination [ɪkˌstərməˈneɪʃən, ɛk-] *n* : exterminación *f,* exterminio *m*

exterminator [ɪkˈstərməˌneɪtər, ɛk-] *n* : exterminador *m,* -dora *f*

external [ɪkˈstərnəl, ɛk-] *adj* : externo, exterior — **externally** *adv*

extinct [ɪkˈstɪŋkt, ɛk-] *adj* : extinto

extinction [ɪkˈstɪŋkʃən, ɛk-] *n* : extinción *f*

extinguish [ɪkˈstɪŋgwɪʃ, ɛk-] *vt* : extinguir, apagar

extinguisher [ɪkˈstɪŋgwɪʃər, ɛk-] *n* : extinguidor *m,* extintor *m*

extirpate [ˈɛkstərˌpeɪt] *vt* **-pated; -pating** : extirpar, exterminar

extol [ɪkˈstoːl, ɛk-] *vt* **-tolled; -tolling** : exaltar, ensalzar, alabar

extort [ɪkˈstɔrt, ɛk-] *vt* : extorsionar

extortion [ɪkˈstɔrʃən, ɛk-] *n* : extorsión *f*

extra¹ [ˈɛkstrə] *adv* : extra, más, extremadamente, super <extra special : super especial>

extra² *adj* **1** ADDITIONAL : adicional, suplementario, de más **2** SUPERIOR : superior

extra³ *n* : extra *m*

extract¹ [ɪkˈstrækt, ɛk-] *vt* : extraer, sacar

extract² [ˈɛkˌstrækt] *n* **1** EXCERPT : pasaje *m,* selección *f,* trozo *m* **2** : extracto *m* <vanilla extract : extracto de vainilla>

extraction [ɪkˈstrækʃən, ɛk-] *n* : extracción *f*

extractor [ɪkˈstræktər, ɛk-] *n* : extractor *m*

extracurricular [ˌɛkstrəkəˈrɪkjələr] *adj* : extracurricular

extradite [ˈɛkstrəˌdaɪt] *vt* **-dited; -diting** : extraditar

extradition [ˌɛkstrəˈdɪʃən] *n* : extradición *f*

extramarital [ˌɛkstrəˈmærət̬əl] *adj* : extramatrimonial

extraneous [ɛkˈstreɪniəs] *adj* **1** OUTSIDE : extrínseco, externo **2** SUPERFLUOUS : superfluo, ajeno — **extraneously** *adv*

extraordinary [ɪkˈstrɔrdənˌɛri, ˌɛkstrəˈɔrd-] *adj* : extraordinario, excepcional — **extraordinarily** [ɪkˌstrɔrdənˈɛrəli, ˌɛkstrəˌɔrd-] *adv*

extrasensory [ˌɛkstrəˈsɛntsəri] *adj* : extrasensorial

extraterrestrial¹ [ˌɛkstrətəˈrɛstriəl] *adj* : extraterrestre

extraterrestrial² *n* : extraterrestre *mf*

extravagance [ɪkˈstrævɪgənts, ɛk-] *n* **1** EXCESS : exceso *m,* extravagancia *f* **2** WASTEFULNESS : derroche *m,* despilfarro *m* **3** LUXURY : lujo *m*

extravagant [ɪkˈstrævɪgənt, ɛk-] *adj* **1** EXCESSIVE : excesivo, extravagante **2** WASTEFUL : despilfarrador, derrochador, gastador **3** EXORBITANT : costoso, exorbitante

extravagantly [ɪkˈstrævɪgəntli, ɛk-] *adv* **1** LAVISHLY : a lo grande **2** EXCESSIVELY : exageradamente, desmesuradamente

extravaganza [ɪkˌstrævəˈgænzə, ɛk-] *n* : gran espectáculo *m*

extreme¹ [ɪkˈstriːm, ɛk-] *adj* **1** UTMOST : extremo, sumo <of extreme importance : de suma importancia> **2** INTENSE : intenso, extremado <extreme cold : frío extremado> **3** EXCESSIVE : excesivo, extremo <extreme views : opiniones extremas> <extreme measures : medidas excepcionales, medidas drásticas> **4** OUTERMOST : extremo <the extreme north : el norte extremo>

extreme² *n* **1** : extremo *m* **2 in the extreme** : en extremo, en sumo grado

extremely [ɪkˈstriːmli, ɛk-] *adv* : sumamente, extremadamente, terriblemente

extremity [ɪkˈstrɛmət̬i, ɛk-] *n, pl* **-ties** **1** EXTREME : extremo *m* **2 extremities** *npl* LIMBS : extremidades *fpl*

extricate [ˈɛkstrəˌkeɪt] *vt* **-cated; -cating :** librar, sacar
extrinsic [ɪkˈstrɪnzɪk, -ˈstrɪntsɪk] *adj* **:** extrínseco
extrovert [ˈɛkstrəˌvərt] *n* **:** extrovertido *m,* -da *f*
extroverted [ˈɛkstrəˌvərt̬əd] *adj* **:** extrovertido
extrude [ɪkˈstruːd, ɛk-] *vt* **-truded; -truding :** extrudir, expulsar
exuberance [ɪgˈzuːbərənts, ɛg-] *n* **1** JOYOUSNESS **:** euforia *f,* exaltación *f* **2** VIGOR **:** exuberancia *f,* vigor *m*
exuberant [ɪgˈzuːbərənt, ɛg-] *adj* **1** JOYOUS **:** eufórico **2** LUSH **:** exuberante **— exuberantly** *adv*
exude [ɪgˈzuːd, ɛg-] *vt* **-uded; -uding 1** OOZE **:** rezumar, exudar **2** EMANATE **:** emanar, irradiar
exult [ɪgˈzʌlt, ɛg-] *vi* **:** exultar, regocijarse
exultant [ɪgˈzʌltənt, ɛg-] *adj* **:** exultante, jubiloso **— exultantly** *adv*
exultation [ˌɛksəlˈteɪʃən, ˌɛgzəl-] *n* **:** exultación *f,* júbilo *m,* alborozo *m*
eye[1] [ˈaɪ] *vt* **eyed; eyeing** *or* **eying :** mirar, observar
eye[2] *n* **1 :** ojo *m* **2** VISION **:** visión *f,* vista *f,* ojo *m* <a good eye for bargains : un buen ojo para las gangas> **3** GLANCE **:** mirada *f,* ojeada *f* **4** ATTENTION **:** atención *f* <to catch one's eye : llamar la atención> **5** POINT OF VIEW **:** punto *m* de vista <in the eyes of the law : según la ley> **6 :** ojo *m* (de una aguja, una papa, una tormenta)
eyeball [ˈaɪˌbɔl] *n* **:** globo *m* ocular
eyebrow [ˈaɪˌbraʊ] *n* **:** ceja *f*
eyedropper [ˈaɪˌdrɑpər] *n* **:** cuentagotas *f*
eyeglasses [ˈaɪˌglæsəz] *npl* **:** anteojos *mpl,* lentes *mpl,* espejuelos *mpl,* gafas *fpl*
eyelash [ˈaɪˌlæʃ] *n* **:** pestaña *f*
eyelet [ˈaɪlət] *n* **:** ojete *m*
eyelid [ˈaɪˌlɪd] *n* **:** párpado *m*
eye–opener [ˈaɪˌoːpənər] *n* **:** revelación *f,* sorpresa *f*
eye–opening [ˈaɪˌoːpənɪŋ] *adj* **:** revelador
eyepiece [ˈaɪˌpiːs] *n* **:** ocular *m*
eyesight [ˈaɪˌsaɪt] *n* **:** vista *f,* visión *f*
eyesore [ˈaɪˌsor] *n* **:** monstruosidad *f,* adefesio *m*
eyestrain [ˈaɪˌstreɪn] *n* **:** fatiga *f* visual, vista *f* cansada
eyetooth [ˈaɪˌtuːθ] *n* **:** colmillo *m*
eyewitness [ˈaɪˈwɪtnəs] *n* **:** testigo *mf* ocular, testigo *mf* presencial
eyrie [ˈaɪri] → **aerie**

F

f [ˈɛf] *n, pl* **f's** *or* **fs** [ˈɛfs] **:** sexta letra del alfabeto inglés
fable [ˈfeɪbəl] *n* **:** fábula *f*
fabled [ˈfeɪbəld] *adj* **:** legendario, fabuloso
fabric [ˈfæbrɪk] *n* **1** MATERIAL **:** tela *f,* tejido *m* **2** STRUCTURE **:** estructura *f* <the fabric of society : la estructura de la sociedad>
fabricate [ˈfæbrɪˌkeɪt] *vt* **-cated; -cating 1** CONSTRUCT, MANUFACTURE **:** construir, fabricar **2** INVENT **:** inventar (excusas o mentiras)
fabrication [ˌfæbrɪˈkeɪʃən] *n* **1** LIE **:** mentira *f,* invención *f* **2** MANUFACTURE **:** fabricación *f*
fabulous [ˈfæbjələs] *adj* **1** LEGENDARY **:** fabuloso, legendario **2** INCREDIBLE **:** increíble, fabuloso <fabulous wealth : riqueza fabulosa> **3** WONDERFUL **:** magnífico, estupendo, fabuloso **— fabulously** *adv*
facade [fəˈsɑd] *n* **:** fachada *f*
face[1] [ˈfeɪs] *v* **faced; facing** *vt* **1** LINE **:** recubrir (una superficie), forrar (ropa) **2** CONFRONT **:** enfrentarse a, afrontar, hacer frente a <to face the music : afrontar las consecuencias> <to face the facts : aceptar la realidad> **3 :** estar de cara a, estar enfrente de <she's facing her brother : está de cara a su hermano> **4** OVERLOOK **:** dar a **—** *vi* **:** mirar (hacia), estar orientado (a)
face[2] *n* **1 :** cara *f,* rostro *m* <he told me to my face : me lo dijo a la cara> **2** EXPRESSION **:** cara *f,* expresión *f* <to pull a long face : poner mala cara> **3** GRIMACE **:** mueca *f* <to make faces : hacer muecas> **4** APPEARANCE **:** fisonomía *f,* aspecto *m* <the face of society : la fisonomía de la sociedad> **5** EFFRONTERY **:** desfachatez *f* **6** PRESTIGE **:** prestigio *m* <to lose face : desprestigiarse> **7** FRONT, SIDE **:** cara *f* (de una moneda), esfera *f* (de un reloj), fachada *f* (de un edificio), pared *f* (de una montaña) **8** SURFACE **:** superficie *f,* faz *f* (de la tierra), cara *f* (de la luna) **9 in the face of** DESPITE **:** en medio de, en visto de, ante
facedown [ˈfeɪsˌdaʊn] *adv* **:** boca abajo
faceless [ˈfeɪsləs] *adj* ANONYMOUS **:** anónimo
face–lift [ˈfeɪsˌlɪft] *n* **1 :** estiramiento *m* facial **2** RENOVATION **:** renovación *f,* remozamiento *m*
facet [ˈfæsət] *n* **1 :** faceta *f* (de una piedra) **2** ASPECT **:** faceta *f,* aspecto *m*
facetious [fəˈsiːʃəs] *adj* **:** gracioso, burlón, bromista
facetiously [fəˈsiːʃəsli] *adv* **:** en tono de burla
facetiousness [fəˈsiːʃəsnəs] *n* **:** jocosidad *f*
face–to–face *adv & adj* **:** cara a cara
faceup [ˈfeɪsˈʌp] *adv* **:** boca arriba

face value *n* : valor *m* nominal

facial[1] [ˈfeɪʃəl] *adj* : de la cara, facial

facial[2] *n* : tratamiento *m* facial, limpieza *f* de cutis

facile [ˈfæsəl] *adj* SUPERFICIAL : superficial, simplista

facilitate [fəˈsɪləˌteɪt] *vt* **-tated; -tating** : facilitar

facility [fəˈsɪləṭi] *n, pl* **-ties 1** EASE : facilidad *f* **2** CENTER, COMPLEX : centro *m,* complejo *m* **3 facilities** *npl* AMENITIES : comodidades *fpl*, servicios *mpl*

facing [ˈfeɪsɪŋ] *n* **1** LINING : entretela *f* (de una prenda) **2** : revestimiento *m* (de un edificio)

facsimile [fækˈsɪməli] *n* : facsímile *m,* facsímil *m*

fact [ˈfækt] *n* **1** : hecho *m* <as a matter of fact : de hecho> **2** INFORMATION : información *f,* datos *mpl* <facts and figures : datos y cifras> **3** REALITY : realidad *f* <in fact : en realidad>

faction [ˈfækʃən] *n* : facción *m,* bando *m*

factional [ˈfækʃənəl] *adj* : entre facciones

factious [ˈfækʃəs] *adj* : faccioso, contencioso

factitious [fækˈtɪʃəs] *adj* : artificial, facticio

factor [ˈfæktər] *n* : factor *m*

factory [ˈfæktəri] *n, pl* **-ries** : fábrica *f*

factual [ˈfæktʃʊəl] *adj* : basado en hechos, objetivo

factually [ˈfæktʃʊəli] *adv* : en cuanto a los hechos

faculty [ˈfækəlti] *n, pl* **-ties 1** : facultad *f* <the faculty of sight : las facultades visuales, el sentido de la vista> **2** APTITUDE : aptitud *f,* facilidad *f* **3** TEACHERS : cuerpo *m* docente

fad [ˈfæd] *n* : moda *f* pasajera, manía *f*

fade [ˈfeɪd] *v* **faded; fading** *vi* **1** WITHER : debilitarse (dícese de las personas), marchitarse (dícese de las flores y las plantas) **2** DISCOLOR : desteñirse, decolorarse **3** DIM : apagarse (dícese de la luz), perderse (dícese de los sonidos), fundirse (dícese de las imágenes) **4** VANISH : desvanecerse, decaer — *vt* DISCOLOR : desteñir

fag [ˈfæg] *vt* **fagged; fagging** EXHAUST : cansar, fatigar

fagot *or* **faggot** [ˈfægət] *n* : haz *m* de leña

Fahrenheit [ˈfærənˌhaɪt] *adj* : Fahrenheit

fail[1] [ˈfeɪl] *vi* **1** WEAKEN : fallar, deteriorarse **2** STOP : fallar, detenerse <his heart failed : le falló el corazón> **3** : fracasar, fallar <her plan failed : su plan fracasó> <the crops failed : se perdió la cosecha> **4** : quebrar <a business about to fail : una empresa a punto de quebrar> **5 to fail in** : faltar a, no cumplir con <to fail in one's duties : faltar a sus deberes> — *vt* **1** FLUNK : reprobar (un examen) **2** : fallar <words fail me : las palabras me fallan, no encuentro palabras> **3** DISAPPOINT : fallar, decepcionar <don't fail me! : ¡no me falles!>

fail[2] *n* : fracaso *m*

failing [ˈfeɪlɪŋ] *n* : defecto *m*

failure [ˈfeɪljər] *n* **1** : fracaso *m,* malogro *m* <crop failure : pérdida de la cosecha> <heart failure : insuficiencia cardíaca> <engine failure : falla mecánica> **2** BANKRUPTCY : bancarrota *f,* quiebra *f* **3** : fracaso *m* (persona) <he was a failure as a manager : como gerente, fue un fracaso>

faint[1] [ˈfeɪnt] *vi* : desmayarse

faint[2] *adj* **1** COWARDLY, TIMID : cobarde, tímido **2** DIZZY : mareado <faint with hunger : desfallecido de hambre> **3** SLIGHT : leve, ligero, vago <I haven't the faintest idea : no tengo la más mínima idea> **4** INDISTINCT : tenue, indistinto, apenas perceptible

faint[3] *n* : desmayo *m*

fainthearted [ˈfeɪntˈhɑrṭəd] *adj* : cobarde, pusilánime

faintly [ˈfeɪntli] *adv* : débilmente, ligeramente, levemente

faintness [ˈfeɪntnəs] *n* **1** INDISTINCTNESS : lo débil, falta *f* de claridad **2** FAINTING : desmayo *m,* desfallecimiento *m*

fair[1] [ˈfær] *adj* **1** ATTRACTIVE, BEAUTIFUL : bello, hermoso, atractivo **2** (*relating to weather*) : bueno, despejado <fair weather : tiempo despejado> **3** JUST : justo, imparcial **4** ALLOWABLE : permisible **5** BLOND, LIGHT : rubio (dícese del pelo), blanco (dícese de la tez) **6** ADEQUATE : bastante, adecuado <fair to middling : mediano, regular> **7 fair game** : presa *f* fácil **8 to play fair** : jugar limpio

fair[2] *n* : feria *f*

fairground [ˈfærˌgraʊnd] *n* : parque *m* de diversiones

fairly [ˈfærli] *adv* **1** IMPARTIALLY : imparcialmente, limpiamente, equitativamente **2** QUITE : bastante **3** MODERATELY : medianamente

fairness [ˈfærnəs] *n* **1** IMPARTIALITY : imparcialidad *f,* justicia *f* **2** LIGHTNESS : blancura *f* (de la piel), lo rubio (del pelo)

fairy [ˈfæri] *n, pl* **fairies 1** : hada *f* **2 fairy tale** : cuento *m* de hadas

fairyland [ˈfæriˌlænd] *n* **1** : país *m* de las hadas **2** : lugar *m* encantador

faith [ˈfeɪθ] *n, pl* **faiths** [ˈfeɪθs, ˈfeɪðz] **1** BELIEF : fe *f* **2** ALLEGIANCE : lealtad *f* **3** CONFIDENCE, TRUST : confianza *f,* fe *f* **4** RELIGION : religión *f*

faithful [ˈfeɪθfəl] *adj* : fiel — **faithfully** *adv*

faithfulness [ˈfeɪθfəlnəs] *n* : fidelidad *f*

faithless [ˈfeɪθləs] *adj* **1** DISLOYAL : desleal **2** : infiel (en la religión) — **faithlessly** *adv*

faithlessness [ˈfeɪθləsnəs] *n* : deslealtad *f*

fake[1] [ˈfeɪk] *v* **faked; faking** *vt* **1** FALSIFY : falsificar, falsear **2** FEIGN : fingir — *vi* **1** PRETEND : fingir **2** : hacer un engaño, hacer una finta (en deportes)

fake[2] *adj* : falso, fingido, postizo

fake[3] *n* **1** IMITATION : imitación *f,* falsificación *f* **2** IMPOSTOR : impostor *m,* -tora *f;* charlatán *m,* -tana *f;* farsante *mf* **3** FEINT : engaño *m,* finta *f* (en deportes)

faker [ˈfeɪkər] *n* : impostor *m,* -tora *f;* charlatán *m,* -tana *f;* farsante *mf*

fakir [fəˈkɪr, ˈfeɪkər] *n* : faquir *m*

falcon [ˈfælkən, ˈfɔl-] *n* : halcón *m*

falconry [ˈfælkənri, ˈfɔl-] *n* : cetrería *f*

fall[1] [ˈfɔl] *vi* **fell** [ˈfɛl]; **fallen** [fɔlən]; **falling 1** : caer, caerse <to fall out of bed : caer de la cama> <to fall down : caerse> **2** HANG : caer **3** DESCEND : caer (dícese de la lluvia o de la noche), bajar (dícese de los precios), descender (dícese de la temperatura) **4** : caer (a un enemigo), rendirse <the city fell : la ciudad se rindió> **5** OCCUR : caer <Christmas falls on a Friday : la Navidad cae en viernes> **6 to fall asleep** : dormirse, quedarse dormido **7 to fall from grace** SIN : perder la gracia **8 to fall sick** : caer enfermo, enfermarse **9 to fall through** : fracasar, caer en la nada **10 to fall to** : tocar a, corresponder a <the task fell to him : le tocó hacerlo>

fall[2] *n* **1** TUMBLE : caída *f* <to break one's fall : frenar uno su caída> <a fall of three feet : una caída de tres pies> **2** FALLING : derrumbe *m* (de rocas), aguacero *m* (de lluvia), nevada *f* (de nieve), bajada *f* (de precios), disminución *f* (de cantidades) **3** AUTUMN : otoño *m* **4** DOWNFALL : caída *f,* ruina *f* **5 falls** *npl* WATERFALL : cascada *f,* catarata *f*

fallacious [fəˈleɪʃəs] *adj* : erróneo, engañoso, falaz

fallacy [ˈfæləsi] *n, pl* **-cies** : falacia *f*

fall back *vi* **1** RETREAT : retirarse, replegarse **2 to fall back on** : recurrir a

fall guy *n* SCAPEGOAT : chivo *m* expiatorio

fallible [ˈfæləbəl] *adj* : falible

fallout [ˈfɔlˌaʊt] *n* **1** : lluvia *f* radioactiva **2** CONSEQUENCES : secuelas *fpl,* consecuencias *fpl*

fallow[1] [ˈfælo] *vt* : barbechar

fallow[2] *adj* **to lie fallow** : estar en barbecho

fallow[3] *n* : barbecho *m*

false [ˈfɔls] *adj* **falser; falsest 1** UNTRUE : falso **2** ERRONEOUS : erróneo, equivocado **3** FAKE : falso, postizo **4** UNFAITHFUL : infiel **5** FRAUDULENT : fraudulento <under false pretenses : por fraude>

falsehood [ˈfɔlsˌhʊd] *n* : mentira *f,* falsedad *f*

falsely [ˈfɔlsli] *adv* : falsamente, con falsedad

falseness [ˈfɔlsnəs] *n* : falsedad *f*

falsetto [fɔlˈsɛtoː] *n, pl* **-tos** : falsete *m*

falsification [ˌfɔlsəfəˈkeɪʃən] *n* : falsificación *f,* falseamiento *m*

falsify [ˈfɔlsəˌfaɪ] *vt* **-fied; fying** : falsificar, falsear

falsity [ˈfɔlsət̬i] *n, pl* **-ties** : falsedad *f*

falter [ˈfɔltər] *vi* **-tered; -tering 1** TOTTER : tambalearse **2** STAMMER : titubear, tartamudear **3** WAVER : vacilar

faltering [ˈfɔltərɪŋ] *adj* : titubeante, vacilante

fame [ˈfeɪm] *n* : fama *f*

famed [ˈfeɪmd] *adj* : famoso, célebre, afamado

familial [fəˈmɪljəl, -liəl] *adj* : familiar

familiar[1] [fəˈmɪljər] *adj* **1** KNOWN : familiar, conocido <to be familiar with : estar familiarizado con> **2** INFORMAL : familiar, informal **3** INTIMATE : íntimo, de confianza **4** FORWARD : confianzudo, atrevido — **familiarly** *adv*

familiar[2] *n* : espíritu *m* guardián

familiarity [fəˌmɪliˈærət̬i, -ˌmɪlˈjær-] *n, pl* **-ties 1** KNOWLEDGE : conocimiento *m,* familiaridad *f* **2** INFORMALITY, INTIMACY : confianza *f,* familiaridad *f* **3** FORWARDNESS : exceso *m* de confianza, descaro *m*

familiarize [fəˈmɪljəˌraɪz] *vt* **-ized; -izing 1** : familiarizar **2 to familiarize oneself** : familiarizarse

family [ˈfæmli, ˈfæmə-] *n, pl* **-lies** : familia *f*

family tree *n* : árbol *m* genealógico

famine [ˈfæmən] *n* : hambre *f,* hambruna *f*

famish [ˈfæmɪʃ] *vi* **to be famished** : estar famélico, estar hambriento, morir de hambre *fam*

famous [ˈfeɪməs] *adj* : famoso

famously [ˈfeɪməsli] *adv* **to get on famously** : llevarse de maravilla

fan[1] [ˈfæn] *vt* **fanned; fanning 1** : abanicar (a una persona), avivar (un fuego) **2** STIMULATE : avivar, estimular

fan[2] *n* **1** : ventilador *m,* abanico *m* **2** ADMIRER, ENTHUSIAST : aficionado *m,* -da *f;* entusiasta *mf;* admirador *m,* -dora *f*

fanatic[1] [fəˈnæt̬ɪk] *or* **fanatical** [-tɪkəl] *adj* : fanático

fanatic[2] *n* : fanático *m,* -ca *f*

fanaticism [fəˈnæt̬əˌsɪzəm] *n* : fanatismo *m*

fanciful [ˈfæntsɪfəl] *adj* **1** CAPRICIOUS : caprichoso, fantástico, extravagante **2** IMAGINATIVE : imaginativo — **fancifully** *adv*

fancy[1] [ˈfæntsi] *vt* **-cied; -cying 1** IMAGINE : imaginarse, figurarse <fancy that! : ¡figúrate!, ¡imagínate!> **2** CRAVE : apetecer, tener ganas de

fancy[2] *adj* **-cier; -est 1** ELABORATE : elaborado **2** LUXURIOUS : lujoso, elegante — **fancily** [ˈfæntsəli] *adv*

fancy[3] *n, pl* **-cies 1** LIKING : gusto *m,* afición *f* **2** WHIM : antojo *m,* capricho *m* **3** IMAGINATION : fantasía *f,* imaginación *f*

fandango [fæn'dæŋgo] *n, pl* **-gos** : fandango *m*

fanfare ['fæn,fær] *n* : fanfarria *f*

fang ['fæŋ] *n* : colmillo *m* (de un animal), diente *m* (de una serpiente)

fanlight ['fæn,laɪt] *n* : tragaluz *m*

fantasia [fæn'teɪʒə, -ziə; ,fæntə'ziːə] *n* : fantasía *f*

fantasize ['fæntə,saɪz] *vi* **-sized; -sizing** : fantasear

fantastic [fæn'tæstɪk] *adj* **1** UNBELIEVABLE : fantástico, increíble, extraño **2** ENORMOUS : fabuloso, inmenso <fantastic sums : sumas fabulosas> **3** WONDERFUL : estupendo, fantástico, bárbaro *fam,* macanudo *fam* — **fantastically** [-tɪkli] *adv*

fantasy ['fæntəsi] *n, pl* **-sies** : fantasía *f*

far[1] ['fɑr] *adv* **farther** ['fɑrðər] *or* **further** ['fər-]; **farthest** *or* **furthest** [-ðəst] **1** : lejos <far from here : lejos de aquí> <to go far : llegar lejos> <as far as Chicago : hasta Chicago> <far away : a lo lejos> **2** MUCH : muy, mucho <far bigger : mucho más grande> <far superior : muy superior> <it's by far the best : es con mucho el mejor> **3** (*expressing degree or extent*) <the results are far off : salieron muy inexactos los resultados> <to go so far as : decir tanto como> <to go far enough : tener el alcance necesario> **4** (*expressing progress*) <the work is far advanced : el trabajo está muy avanzado> <to take (something) too far : llevar (algo) demasiado lejos> **5 far and wide** : por todas partes **6 far from it!** : ¡todo lo contrario! **7 so far** : hasta ahora, todavía

far[2] *adj* **farther** *or* **further; farthest** *or* **furthest 1** REMOTE : lejano, remoto <the Far East : el Lejano Oriente, el Extremo Oriente> <a far country : un país lejano> **2** LONG : largo <a far journey : un viaje largo> **3** EXTREME : extremo <the far right : la extrema derecha> <at the far end of the room : en el otro extremo de la sala>

faraway ['fɑrə,weɪ] *adj* : remoto, lejano

farce ['fɑrs] *n* : farsa *f*

farcical ['fɑrsɪkəl] *adj* : absurdo, ridículo

fare[1] ['fær] *vi* **fared; faring** : ir, salir <how did you fare? : ¿cómo te fue?>

fare[2] *n* **1** : pasaje *m,* billete *m,* boleto *m* <half fare : medio pasaje> **2** FOOD : comida *f*

farewell[1] [fær'wɛl] *adj* : de despedida

farewell[2] *n* : despedida *f*

far–fetched ['fɑr'fɛtʃt] *adj* : improbable, exagerado

farina [fə'riːnə] *n* : harina *f*

farm[1] ['fɑrm] *vt* **1** : cultivar, labrar **2** : criar (animales) — *vi* : ser agricultor

farm[2] *n* : granja *f,* hacienda *f,* finca *f,* estancia *f*

farmer ['fɑrmər] *n* : agricultor *m,* granjero *m*

farmhand ['fɑrm,hænd] *n* : peón *m*

farmhouse ['fɑrm,haʊs] *n* : granja *f,* vivienda *f* del granjero, casa *f* de hacienda

farming ['fɑrmɪŋ] *n* : labranza *f,* cultivo *m,* crianza *f* (de animales)

farmland ['fɑrm,lænd] *n* : tierras *fpl* de labranza

farmyard ['fɑrm,jɑrd] *n* : corral *m*

far–off ['fɑr,ɔf, -'ɔf] *adj* : remoto, distante, lejano

far–reaching ['fɑr'riːtʃɪŋ] *adj* : de gran alcance

farsighted ['fɑr,saɪtəd] *adj* **1** : hipermétrope **2** JUDICIOUS : con visión de futuro, previsor, precavido

farsightedness ['fɑr,saɪtədnəs] *n* **1** : hipermetropía *f* **2** PRUDENCE : previsión *f*

farther[1] ['fɑrðər] *adv* **1** AHEAD : más lejos (en el espacio), más adelante (en el tiempo) **2** MORE : más

farther[2] *adj* : más lejano, más remoto

farthermost ['fɑrðər,moːst] *adj* : (el) más lejano

farthest[1] ['fɑrðəst] *adv* **1** : lo más lejos <I jumped farthest : salté lo más lejos> **2** : lo más avanzado <he progressed farthest : progresó al punto más avanzado> **3** : más <the farthest developed plan : el plan más desarrollado>

farthest[2] *adj* : más lejano

fascicle ['fæsɪkəl] *n* : fascículo *m*

fascinate ['fæsən,eɪt] *vt* **-nated; -nating** : fascinar, cautivar

fascination [,fæsən'eɪʃən] *n* : fascinación *f*

fascism ['fæʃ,ɪzəm] *n* : fascismo *m*

fascist[1] ['fæʃɪst] *adj* : fascista

fascist[2] *n* : fascista *mf*

fashion[1] ['fæʃən] *vt* : formar, moldear

fashion[2] *n* **1** MANNER : manera *f,* modo *m* **2** CUSTOM : costumbre *f* **3** STYLE : moda *f*

fashionable ['fæʃənəbəl] *adj* : de moda, chic

fashionably ['fæʃənəbli] *adv* : a la moda

fast[1] ['fæst] *vi* : ayunar

fast[2] *adv* **1** SECURELY : firmemente, seguramente <to hold fast : agarrarse bien> **2** RAPIDLY : rápidamente, rápido, de prisa **3** SOUNDLY : profundamente <fast asleep : profundamente dormido>

fast[3] *adj* **1** SECURE : firme, seguro <to make fast : amarrar (un barco)> **2** FAITHFUL : leal <fast friends : amigos leales> **3** RAPID : rápido, veloz **4** : adelantado <10 minutes fast : 10 minutos adelantado> **5** DEEP : profundo <a fast sleep : un sueño pro-

fundo> 6 COLORFAST : inalterable, que no destiñe 7 DISSOLUTE : extravagante, disipado, disoluto
fast⁴ *n* : ayuno *m*
fasten ['fæsən] *vt* **1** ATTACH : sujetar, atar **2** FIX : fijar <to fasten one's eyes on : fijar los ojos en> **3** SECURE : abrochar (ropa o cinturones), atar (cordones), cerrar (una maleta) — *vi* : abrocharse, cerrar
fastener ['fæsənər] *n* : cierre *m*, sujetador *m*
fastening ['fæsənɪŋ] *n* : cierre *m*, sujetador *m*
fastidious [fæs'tɪdiəs] *adj* : quisquilloso, exigente — **fastidiously** *adv*
fat¹ ['fæt] *adj* **fatter; fattest 1** OBESE : gordo, obeso **2** THICK : grueso
fat² *n* : grasa *f*
fatal ['feɪtəl] *adj* **1** DEADLY : mortal **2** ILL-FATED : malhadado, fatal **3** MOMENTOUS : fatídico
fatalism ['feɪtəl,ɪzəm] *n* : fatalismo *m*
fatalist ['feɪtəlɪst] *n* : fatalista *mf*
fatalistic [,feɪtəl'ɪstɪk] *adj* : fatalista
fatality [feɪ'tæləti, fə-] *n, pl* **-ties** : víctima *f* mortal
fatally ['feɪtəli] *adv* : mortalmente
fate ['feɪt] *n* **1** DESTINY : destino *m* **2** END, LOT : final *m*, suerte *f*
fated ['feɪtəd] *adj* : predestinado
fateful ['feɪtfəl] *adj* **1** MOMENTOUS : fatídico, aciago **2** PROPHETIC : profético — **fatefully** *adv*
father¹ ['fɑðər] *vt* : engendrar
father² *n* **1** : padre *m* <my father and my mother : mi padre y mi madre> <Father Smith : el padre Smith> **2 the Father** GOD : el Padre, Dios *m*
fatherhood ['fɑðər,hʊd] *n* : paternidad *f*
father-in-law ['fɑðərɪn,lɔ] *n, pl* **fathers-in-law** : suegro *m*
fatherland ['fɑðər,lænd] *n* : patria *f*
fatherless ['fɑðərləs] *adj* : huérfano de padre, sin padre
fatherly ['fɑðərli] *adj* : paternal
fathom¹ ['fæðəm] *vt* UNDERSTAND : entender, comprender
fathom² *n* : braza *f*
fatigue¹ [fə'ti:g] *vt* **-tigued; -tiguing** : fatigar, cansar
fatigue² *n* : fatiga *f*
fatness ['fætnəs] *n* : gordura *f* (de una persona o un animal), grosor *m* (de un objeto)
fatten ['fætən] *vt* : engordar, cebar
fatty ['fæti] *adj* **fattier; -est** : graso, grasoso, adiposo (dícese de los tejidos)
fatuous ['fætʃʊəs] *adj* : necio, fatuo — **fatuously** *adv*
faucet ['fɔsət] *n* : llave *f*, canilla *f Arg, Uru*, grifo *m*
fault¹ ['fɔlt] *vt* : encontrar defectos a
fault² *n* **1** SHORTCOMING : defecto *m*, falta *f* **2** DEFECT : falta *f*, defecto *m*, falla *f* **3** BLAME : culpa *f* **4** FRACTURE : falla *f* (geológica)
faultfinder ['fɔlt,faɪndər] *n* : criticón *m*, -cona *f*
faultfinding ['fɔlt,faɪndɪŋ] *n* : crítica *f*
faultless ['fɔltləs] *adj* : sin culpa, sin imperfecciones, impecable
faultlessly ['fɔltləsli] *adv* : impecablemente, perfectamente
faulty ['fɔlti] *adj* **faultier; -est** : defectuoso, imperfecto — **faultily** ['fɔltəli] *adv*
fauna ['fɔnə] *n* : fauna *f*
faux pas [,fo:'pɑ] *n, pl* **faux pas** [*same or* -'pɑz] : metedura *f* de pata *fam*
favor¹ ['feɪvər] *vt* **1** SUPPORT : estar a favor de, ser partidario de, apoyar **2** OBLIGE : hacerle un favor a **3** PREFER : preferir **4** RESEMBLE : parecerse a, salir a
favor² *n* : favor *m* <in favor of : a favor de> <an error in his favor : un error a su favor>
favorable ['feɪvərəbəl] *adj* : favorable, propicio
favorably ['feɪvərəbli] *adv* : favorablemente, bien
favorite¹ ['feɪvərət] *adj* : favorito, preferido
favorite² *n* : favorito *m*, -ta *f*; preferido *m*, -da *f*
favoritism ['feɪvərə,tɪzəm] *n* : favoritismo *m*
fawn¹ ['fɔn] *vi* : adular, lisonjear
fawn² *n* : cervato *m*
fax ['fæks] *n* : facsímil *m*, facsímile *m*
faze ['feɪz] *vt* **fazed; fazing** : desconcertar, perturbar
fear¹ ['fɪr] *vt* : temer, tener miedo de — *vi* : temer
fear² *n* : miedo *m*, temor *m* <for fear of : por temor a>
fearful ['fɪrfəl] *adj* **1** FRIGHTENING : espantoso, aterrador, horrible **2** FRIGHTENED : temeroso, miedoso
fearfully ['fɪrfəli] *adv* **1** EXTREMELY : extremadamente, terriblemente **2** TIMIDLY : con temor
fearless ['fɪrləs] *adj* : intrépido, impávido
fearlessly ['fɪrləsli] *adv* : sin temor
fearlessness ['fɪrləsnəs] *n* : intrepidez *f*, impavidez *f*
fearsome ['fɪrsəm] *adj* : aterrador
feasibility [,fi:zə'bɪləti] *n* : viabilidad *f*, factibilidad *f*
feasible ['fi:zəbəl] *adj* : viable, factible, realizable
feast¹ ['fi:st] *vi* : banquetear — *vt* **1** : agasajar, festejar **2 to feast one's eyes on** : regalarse la vista con
feast² *n* **1** BANQUET : banquete *m*, festín *m* **2** FESTIVAL : fiesta *f*
feat ['fi:t] *n* : proeza *f*, hazaña *f*
feather¹ ['fɛðər] *vt* **1** : emplumar **2 to feather one's nest** : hacer su agosto
feather² *n* **1** : pluma *f* **2 a feather in one's cap** : un triunfo personal
feathered ['fɛðərd] *adj* : con plumas
feathery ['fɛðəri] *adj* **1** DOWNY : plumoso **2** LIGHT : liviano

feature[1] [ˈfiːtʃər] *v* **-tured; -turing** *vt* **1** IMAGINE **:** imaginarse **2** PRESENT **:** presentar — *vi* **:** figurar
feature[2] *n* **1** CHARACTERISTIC **:** característica *f,* rasgo *m* **2 :** largometraje *m* (en el cine), artículo *m* (en un periódico), documental *m* (en la televisión) **3 features** *npl* **:** rasgos *mpl,* facciones *fpl* <delicate features **:** facciones delicadas>
February [ˈfɛbjʊˌɛri, ˈfɛbʊ-, ˈfɛbrʊ-] *n* **:** febrero *m*
fecal [ˈfiːkəl] *adj* **:** fecal
feces [ˈfiːˌsiːz] *npl* **:** heces *fpl,* excrementos *mpl*
feckless [ˈfɛkləs] *adj* **:** irresponsable
fecund [ˈfɛkənd, ˈfiː-] *adj* **:** fecundo
fecundity [fɪˈkʌndəṱi, fɛ-] *n* **:** fecundidad *f*
federal [ˈfɛdrəl, -dərəl] *adj* **:** federal
federalism [ˈfɛdrəˌlɪzəm, -dərə-] *n* **:** federalismo *m*
federalist[1] [ˈfɛdrəlɪst, -dərə-] *adj* **:** federalista
federalist[2] *n* **:** federalista *mf*
federate [ˈfɛdəˌreɪt] *vt* **-ated; -ating :** federar
federation [ˌfɛdəˈreɪʃən] *n* **:** federación *f*
fedora [fɪˈdorə] *n* **:** sombrero *m* flexible de fieltro
fed up *adj* **:** harto
fee [ˈfiː] *n* **1 :** honorarios *mpl* (a un médico, un abogado, etc.) **2 entrance fee :** entrada *f*
feeble [ˈfiːbəl] *adj* **-bler; -blest 1** WEAK **:** débil, endeble **2** INEFFECTIVE **:** flojo, pobre, poco convincente
feebleminded [ˌfiːbəlˈmaɪndəd] *adj* **1 :** débil mental **2** FOOLISH, STUPID **:** imbécil, tonto
feebleness [ˈfiːbəlnəs] *n* **:** debilidad *f*
feebly [ˈfiːbli] *adv* **:** débilmente
feed[1] [ˈfiːd] *v* **fed** [ˈfɛd]; **feeding** *vt* **1 :** dar de comer a, nutrir, alimentar (a una persona) **2 :** alimentar (un fuego o una máquina), proveer (información), introducir (datos) — *vi* **:** comer, alimentarse
feed[2] *n* **1** NOURISHMENT **:** alimento *m* **2** FODDER **:** pienso *m*
feel[1] [ˈfiːl] *v* **felt** [ˈfɛlt]; **feeling** *vi* **1 :** sentirse, encontrarse <I feel tired **:** me siento cansada> <he feels hungry **:** tiene hambre> <she feels like a fool **:** se siente como una idiota> <to feel like doing something **:** tener ganas de hacer algo> **2** SEEM **:** parecer <it feels like spring **:** parece primavera> **3** THINK **:** parecerse, opinar, pensar <how does he feel about that? **:** ¿qué opina él de eso?> — *vt* **1** TOUCH **:** tocar, palpar **2** SENSE **:** sentir <to feel the cold **:** sentir el frío> **3** CONSIDER **:** sentir, creer, considerar <to feel (it) necessary **:** creer necesario>
feel[2] *n* **1** SENSATION, TOUCH **:** sensación *f,* tacto *m* **2** ATMOSPHERE **:** ambiente *m,* atmósfera *f* **3 to have a feel for :** tener un talento especial para
feeler [ˈfiːlər] *n* **:** antena *f,* tentáculo *m*
feeling [ˈfiːlɪŋ] *n* **1** SENSATION **:** sensación *f,* sensibilidad *f* **2** EMOTION **:** sentimiento *m* **3** OPINION **:** opinión *f* **4 feelings** *npl* SENSIBILITIES **:** sentimientos *mpl* <to hurt someone's feelings **:** herir los sentimientos de alguien>
feet → **foot**
feign [ˈfeɪn] *vt* **:** simular, aparentar, fingir
feint[1] [ˈfeɪnt] *vi* **:** fintar, fintear
feint[2] *n* **:** finta *f*
felicitate [fɪˈlɪsəˌteɪt] *vt* **-tated; -tating :** felicitar, congratular
felicitation [fɪˌlɪsəˈteɪʃən] *n* **:** felicitación *f*
felicitous [fɪˈlɪsəṱəs] *adj* **:** acertado, oportuno
feline[1] [ˈfiːˌlaɪn] *adj* **:** felino
feline[2] *n* **:** felino *m,* -na *f*
fell[1] [ˈfɛl] *vt* **:** talar (un árbol), derribar (a una persona)
fell[2] → **fall**
fellow [ˈfɛˌloː] *n* **1** COMPANION **:** compañero *m,* -ra *f;* camarada *mf* **2** ASSOCIATE **:** socio *m,* -cia *f* **3** MAN **:** tipo *m,* hombre *m*
fellowman [ˌfɛloˈmæn] *n, pl* **-men :** prójimo *m,* semejante *m*
fellowship [ˈfɛloˌʃɪp] *n* **1** COMPANIONSHIP **:** camaradería *f,* compañerismo *m* **2** ASSOCIATION **:** fraternidad *f* **3** GRANT **:** beca *f* (de investigación)
felon [ˈfɛlən] *n* **:** malhechor *m,* -chora *f;* criminal *mf*
felonious [fəˈloːniəs] *adj* **:** criminal
felony [ˈfɛləni] *n, pl* **-nies :** delito *m* grave
felt[1] [ˈfɛlt] *n* **:** fieltro *m*
felt[2] → **feel**
female[1] [ˈfiːˌmeɪl] *adj* **:** femenino
female[2] *n* **1 :** hembra *f* (de animal) **2** WOMAN **:** mujer *f*
feminine [ˈfɛmənən] *adj* **:** femenino
femininity [ˌfɛməˈnɪnəṱi] *n* **:** feminidad *f,* femineidad *f*
feminism [ˈfɛməˌnɪzəm] *n* **:** feminismo *m*
feminist[1] [ˈfɛmənɪst] *adj* **:** feminista
feminist[2] *n* **:** feminista *mf*
femoral [ˈfɛmərəl] *adj* **:** femoral
femur [ˈfiːmər] *n, pl* **femurs** *or* **femora** [ˈfɛmərə] **:** fémur *m*
fence[1] [ˈfɛnts] *v* **fenced; fencing** *vt* **:** vallar, cercar — *vi* **:** hacer esgrima
fence[2] *n* **:** cerca *f,* valla *f,* cerco *m*
fencer [ˈfɛntsər] *n* **:** esgrimista *mf;* esgrimidor *m,* -dora *f*
fencing [ˈfɛntsɪŋ] *n* **1 :** esgrima *m* (deporte) **2 :** materiales *mpl* para cercas **3** ENCLOSURE **:** cercado *m*
fend [ˈfɛnd] *vt* **to fend off :** rechazar (un enemigo), parar (un golpe), eludir (una pregunta) — *vi* **to fend for oneself :** arreglárselas sólo, valerse por sí mismo

fender [ˈfɛndər] *n* **:** guardabarros *mpl,* salpicadera *f Mex*
fennel [ˈfɛnəl] *n* **:** hinojo *m*
ferment[1] [fərˈmɛnt] *v* **:** fermentar
ferment[2] [ˈfərˌmɛnt] *n* **1 :** fermento *m* (en la química) **2** TURMOIL **:** agitación *f,* conmoción *f*
fermentation [ˌfərmənˈteɪʃən, -ˌmɛn-] *n* **:** fermentación *f*
fern [ˈfərn] *n* **:** helecho *m*
ferocious [fəˈroːʃəs] *adj* **:** feroz — **ferociously** *adv*
ferociousness [fəˈroːʃəsnəs] *n* **:** ferocidad *f*
ferocity [fəˈrɑsəṭi] *n* **:** ferocidad *f*
ferret[1] [ˈfɛrət] *vi* SNOOP **:** hurgar, husmear — *vt* **to ferret out :** descubrir
ferret[2] *n* **:** hurón *m*
ferric [ˈfɛrɪk] *or* **ferrous** [ˈfɛrəs] *adj* **:** férrico
Ferris wheel [ˈfɛrɪs] *n* **:** noria *f*
ferry[1] [ˈfɛri] *vt* **-ried; -rying :** llevar, transportar
ferry[2] *n, pl* **-ries :** transbordador *m,* ferry *m*
ferryboat [ˈfɛriˌboːt] *n* **:** transbordador *m,* ferry *m*
fertile [ˈfərṭəl] *adj* **:** fértil, fecundo
fertility [fərˈtɪləṭi] *n* **:** fertilidad *f*
fertilization [ˌfərṭələˈzeɪʃən] *n* **:** fertilización *f* (del suelo), fecundación (de un huevo)
fertilize [ˈfərṭəlˌaɪz] *vt* **-ized; -izing 1 :** fecundar (un huevo) **2 :** fertilizar, abonar (el suelo)
fertilizer [ˈfərṭəlˌaɪzər] *n* **:** fertilizante *m,* abono *m*
fervent [ˈfərvənt] *adj* **:** ferviente, fervoroso, ardiente — **fervently** *adv*
fervid [ˈfərvɪd] *adj* **:** ardiente, apasionado — **fervidly** *adv*
fervor [ˈfərvər] *n* **:** fervor *m,* ardor *m*
fester [ˈfɛstər] *vi* **:** enconarse, supurar
festival [ˈfɛstəvəl] *n* **:** fiesta *f,* festividad *f,* festival *m*
festive [ˈfɛstɪv] *adj* **:** festivo — **festively** *adv*
festivity [fɛsˈtɪvəṭi] *n, pl* **-ties :** festividad *f,* celebración *f*
festoon[1] [fɛsˈtuːn] *vt* **:** adornar, engalanar
festoon[2] *n* GARLAND **:** guirnalda *f*
fetal [ˈfiːṭəl] *adj* **:** fetal
fetch [ˈfɛtʃ] *vt* **1** BRING **:** traer, recoger, ir a buscar **2** REALIZE **:** realizar, venderse por <the jewelry fetched $10,000 : las joyas se vendieron por $10,000>
fetching [ˈfɛtʃɪŋ] *adj* **:** atractivo, encantador
fête[1] [ˈfeɪt, ˈfɛt] *vt* **fêted; fêting :** festejar, agasajar
fête[2] *n* **:** fiesta *f*
fetid [ˈfɛṭəd] *adj* **:** fétido
fetish [ˈfɛṭɪʃ] *n* **:** fetiche *m*
fetlock [ˈfɛtˌlɑk] *n* **:** espolón *m*
fetter [ˈfɛṭər] *vt* **:** encadenar, poner grillos a
fetters [ˈfɛṭərz] *npl* **:** grillos *mpl,* grilletes *mpl,* cadenas *fpl*
fettle [ˈfɛṭəl] *n* **in fine fettle :** en buena forma, en plena forma
fetus [ˈfiːṭəs] *n* **:** feto *m*
feud[1] [ˈfjuːd] *vi* **:** pelear, contender
feud[2] *n* **:** contienda *f,* enemistad *f* (heredada)
feudal [ˈfjuːdəl] *adj* **:** feudal
feudalism [ˈfjuːdəlˌɪzəm] *n* **:** feudalismo *m*
fever [ˈfiːvər] *n* **:** fiebre *f,* calentura *f*
feverish [ˈfiːvərɪʃ] *adj* **1 :** afiebrado, con fiebre, febril **2** FRANTIC **:** febril, frenético
few[1] [ˈfjuː] *adj* **:** pocos <with few exceptions : con pocas excepciones> <a few times : varias veces>
few[2] *pron* **1 :** pocos <few (of them) were ready : pocos estaban listos> **2 a few :** algunos, unos cuantos **3 few and far between :** contados
fewer [ˈfjuːər] *pron* **:** menos <the fewer the better : cuantos menos mejor>
fez [ˈfɛz] *n, pl* **fezzes :** fez *m*
fiancé [ˌfiːˌɑnˈseɪ, ˌfiːˈɑnˌseɪ] *n* **:** prometido *m,* novio *m*
fiancée [ˌfiːˌɑnˈseɪ, ˌfiːˈɑnˌseɪ] *n* **:** prometida *f,* novia *f*
fiasco [fiˈæsˌkoː] *n, pl* **-coes :** fiasco *m,* fracaso *m*
fiat [ˈfiːˌɑt, -ˌæt, -ət; ˈfaɪət, -ˌæt] *n* **:** decreto *m,* orden *m*
fib[1] [ˈfɪb] *vi* **fibbed; fibbing :** decir mentirillas
fib[2] *n* **:** mentirilla *f,* bola *f fam*
fibber [ˈfɪbər] *n* **:** mentirosillo *m,* -lla *f;* cuentista *mf fam*
fiber *or* **fibre** [ˈfaɪbər] *n* **:** fibra *f*
fiberboard [ˈfaɪbərˌbord] *n* **:** cartón *m* madera
fiberglass [ˈfaɪbərˌglæs] *n* **:** fibra *f* de vidrio
fibrillate [ˈfɪbrəˌleɪt, ˈfaɪ-] *vi* **-lated; -lating :** fibrilar
fibrillation [ˌfɪbrəˈleɪʃən, ˌfaɪ-] *n* **:** fibrilación *f*
fibrous [ˈfaɪbrəs] *adj* **:** fibroso
fibula [ˈfɪbjələ] *n, pl* **-lae** [-ˌliː, -ˌlaɪ] *or* **-las :** peroné *m*
fickle [ˈfɪkəl] *adj* **:** inconstante, voluble, veleidoso
fickleness [ˈfɪkəlnəs] *n* **:** volubilidad *f,* inconstancia *f,* veleidad *f*
fiction [ˈfɪkʃən] *n* **:** ficción *f*
fictional [ˈfɪkʃənəl] *adj* **:** ficticio
fictitious [fɪkˈtɪʃəs] *adj* **1** IMAGINARY **:** ficticio, imaginario **2** FALSE **:** falso, ficticio
fiddle[1] [ˈfɪdəl] *vi* **-dled; -dling 1 :** tocar el violín **2 to fiddle with :** juguetear con, toquetear
fiddle[2] *n* **:** violín *m*
fiddler [ˈfɪdlər, ˈfɪdələr] *n* **:** violinista *mf*
fiddlesticks [ˈfɪdəlˌstɪks] *interj* **:** ¡tonterías!
fidelity [fəˈdɛləṭi, faɪ-] *n, pl* **-ties :** fidelidad *f*

fidget[1] [ˈfɪdʒət] *vi* **1 :** moverse, estarse inquieto **2 to fidget with :** juguetear con

fidget[2] *n* **1 :** persona *f* inquieta **2 fidgets** *npl* RESTLESSNESS **:** inquietud *f*

fidgety [ˈfɪdʒəti] *adj* **:** inquieto

fiduciary[1] [fəˈduːʃiˌɛri, -ˈdjuː-, -ʃəri] *adj* **:** fiduciario

fiduciary[2] *n, pl* **-ries :** fiduciario *m*, -ria *f*

field[1] [ˈfiːld] *vt* **:** interceptar y devolver (una pelota), presentar (un candidato), sortear (una pregunta)

field[2] *adj* **:** de campaña, de campo <field hospital : hospital de campaña> <field goal : gol de campo> <field trip : viaje de estudio>

field[3] *n* **1 :** campo *m* (de cosechas, de batalla, de magnetismo) **2 :** campo *m*, cancha *f* (en deportes) **3 :** campo *m* (de trabajo), esfera *f* (de actividades)

fielder [ˈfiːldər] *n* **:** jugador *m*, -dora *f* de campo; fildeador *m*, -dora *f*

field glasses *n* **:** binoculares *mpl*, gemelos *mpl*

fiend [ˈfiːnd] *n* **1** DEMON **:** demonio *m* **2** EVILDOER **:** persona *f* maligna; malvado *m*, -da *f* **3** FANATIC **:** fanático *m*, -ca *f*

fiendish [ˈfiːndɪʃ] *adj* **:** diabólico — **fiendishly** *adv*

fierce [ˈfɪrs] *adj* **fiercer; -est 1** FEROCIOUS **:** fiero, feroz **2** HEATED **:** acalorado **3** INTENSE **:** intenso, violento, fuerte — **fiercely** *adv*

fierceness [ˈfɪrsnəs] *n* **1** FEROCITY **:** ferocidad *f*, fiereza *f* **2** INTENSITY **:** intensidad *f*, violencia *f*

fieriness [ˈfaɪərinəs] *n* **:** pasión *f*, ardor *m*

fiery [ˈfaɪəri] *adj* **fierier; -est 1** BURNING **:** ardiente, llameante **2** GLOWING **:** encendido **3** PASSIONATE **:** acalorado, ardiente, fogoso

fiesta [fiˈɛstə] *n* **:** fiesta *f*

fife [ˈfaɪf] *n* **:** pífano *m*

fifteen[1] [fɪfˈtiːn] *adj* **:** quince

fifteen[2] *n* **:** quince *m*

fifteenth[1] [fɪfˈtiːnθ] *adj* **:** decimoquinto

fifteenth[2] *n* **1 :** decimoquinto *m*, -ta *f* (en una serie) **2 :** quinceavo *m*, quinceava parte *f*

fifth[1] [ˈfɪfθ] *adj* **:** quinto

fifth[2] *n* **1 :** quinto *m*, -ta *f* (en una serie) **2 :** quinto *m*, quinta parte *f* **3 :** quinta *f* (en la música)

fiftieth[1] [ˈfɪftiəθ] *adj* **:** quincuagésimo

fiftieth[2] *n* **1 :** quincuagésimo *m*, -ma *f* (en una serie) **2 :** cincuentavo *m*, cincuentava parte *f*

fifty[1] [ˈfɪfti] *adj* **:** cincuenta

fifty[2] *n, pl* **-ties :** cincuenta *m*

fifty–fifty[1] [ˌfɪftiˈfɪfti] *adv* **:** a medias, mitad y mitad

fifty–fifty[2] *adj* **to have a fifty–fifty chance :** tener un cincuenta por ciento de posibilidades

fig [ˈfɪg] *n* **:** higo *m*

fight[1] [ˈfaɪt] *v* **fought** [ˈfɔt]; **fighting** *vi* **:** luchar, combatir, pelear — *vt* **:** luchar contra, combatir contra

fight[2] *n* **1** COMBAT **:** lucha *f*, pelea *f*, combate *m* **2** MATCH **:** pelea *f*, combate *m* (en boxeo) **3** QUARREL **:** disputa *f*, pelea *f*, pleito *m*

fighter [ˈfaɪt̬ər] *n* **1** COMBATANT **:** luchador *m*, -dora *f*; combatiente *mf* **2** BOXER **:** boxeador *m*, -dora *f*

figment [ˈfɪgmənt] *n* **figment of the imagination :** producto *m* de la imaginación

figurative [ˈfɪgjərət̬ɪv, -gə-] *adj* **:** figurado, metafórico

figuratively [ˈfɪgjərət̬ɪvli, -gə-] *adv* **:** en sentido figurado, de manera metafórica

figure[1] [ˈfɪgjər, -gər] *v* **-ured; -uring** *vt* **1** CALCULATE **:** calcular **2** ESTIMATE **:** figurarse, calcular <he figured it was possible : se figuró que era posible> — *vi* **1** FEATURE, STAND OUT **:** figurar, destacar **2 that figures! :** ¡obvio!, ¡no me extraña nada!

figure[2] *n* **1** DIGIT **:** número *m*, cifra *f* **2** PRICE **:** precio *m*, cifra *f* **3** PERSONAGE **:** figura *f*, personaje *m* **4 :** figura *f*, tipo *m*, físico *m* <to have a good figure : tener buen tipo, tener un buen físico> **5** DESIGN, OUTLINE **:** figura *f* **6 figures** *npl* **:** aritmética *f*

figurehead [ˈfɪgjərˌhɛd, -gər-] *n* **:** testaferro *m*, líder *mf* sin poder

figure of speech *n* **:** figura *f* retórica, figura *f* de hablar

figure out *vt* **1** UNDERSTAND **:** entender **2** RESOLVE **:** resolver (un problema, etc.)

figurine [ˌfɪgjəˈriːn] *n* **:** estatuilla *f*

Fijian [ˈfiːdʒiən, fɪˈjiːən] *n* **:** fijiano *m*, -na *f* — **Fijian** *adj*

filament [ˈfɪləmənt] *n* **:** filamento *m*

filbert [ˈfɪlbərt] *n* **:** avellana *f*

filch [ˈfɪltʃ] *vt* **:** hurtar, birlar *fam*

file[1] [ˈfaɪl] *v* **filed; filing** *vt* **1** CLASSIFY **:** clasificar **2 :** archivar (documentos) **3** SUBMIT **:** presentar <to file charges : presentar cargos> **4** SMOOTH **:** limar — *vi* **:** desfilar, entrar (o salir) en fila

file[2] *n* **1 :** lima *f* <nail file : lima de uñas> **2** DOCUMENTS **:** archivo *m* **3** LINE **:** fila *f*

filial [ˈfɪliəl, ˈfɪljəl] *adj* **:** filial

filibuster[1] [ˈfɪləˌbʌstər] *vi* **:** practicar el obstruccionismo

filibuster[2] *n* **:** obstruccionismo *m*

filibusterer [ˈfɪləˌbʌstərər] *n* **:** obstruccionista *mf*

filigree [ˈfɪləˌgriː] *n* **:** filigrana *f*

Filipino [ˌfɪləˈpiːnoː] *n* **:** filipino *m*, -na *f* — **Filipino** *adj*

fill[1] [ˈfɪl] *vt* **1 :** llenar, ocupar <to fill a cup : llenar una taza> <to fill a room : ocupar una sala> **2** STUFF **:** rellenar **3** PLUG **:** tapar, rellenar, empastar (un diente) **4** SATISFY **:** cumplir con, satisfacer **5** *or* **to fill out :** llenar, rellenar <to fill out a form : rellenar un formulario>

fill[2] *n* **1** FILLING, STUFFING : relleno *m* **2 to eat one's fill** : comer lo suficiente **3 to have one's fill of** : estar harto de

filler [ˈfɪlər] *n* : relleno *m*

fillet[1] [ˈfɪlət, fɪˈleɪ, ˈfɪˌleɪ] *vt* : cortar en filetes

fillet[2] *n* : filete *m*

fill in *vt* INFORM : informar, poner al corriente — *vi* **to fill in for** : reemplazar a

filling [ˈfɪlɪŋ] *n* **1** : relleno *m* **2** : empaste *m* (de un diente)

filling station → **service station**

filly [ˈfɪli] *n, pl* **-lies** : potra *f,* potranca *f*

film[1] [ˈfɪlm] *vt* : filmar — *vi* : rodar

film[2] *n* **1** COATING : capa *f,* película *f* **2** : película *f* (fotográfica) **3** MOVIE : película *f,* filme *m*

filmy [ˈfɪlmi] *adj* **filmier; -est 1** GAUZY : diáfano, vaporoso **2** : cubierto de una película

filter[1] [ˈfɪltər] *vt* : filtrar

filter[2] *n* : filtro *m*

filth [ˈfɪlθ] *n* : mugre *f,* porquería *f,* roña *f*

filthiness [ˈfɪlθinəs] *n* : suciedad *f*

filthy [ˈfɪlθi] *adj* **filthier; -est 1** DIRTY : mugriento, sucio **2** OBSCENE : obsceno, indecente

filtration [fɪlˈtreɪʃən] *n* : filtración *f*

fin [ˈfɪn] *n* **1** : aleta *f* **2** : alerón *m* (de un automóvil o un avión)

finagle [fəˈneɪgəl] *vt* **-gled; -gling** : arreglárselas para conseguir

final[1] [ˈfaɪnəl] *adj* **1** DEFINITIVE : definitivo, final, inapelable **2** ULTIMATE : final **3** LAST : último, final

final[2] *n* **1** : final *f* (en deportes) **2 finals** *npl* : exámenes *mpl* finales

finale [fɪˈnæli, -ˈnɑ-] *n* : final *m* <grand finale : final triunfal>

finalist [ˈfaɪnəlɪst] *n* : finalista *mf*

finality [faɪˈnæləṭi, fə-] *n, pl* **-ties** : finalidad *f*

finalize [ˈfaɪnəlˌaɪz] *vt* **-ized; -izing** : finalizar

finally [ˈfaɪnəli] *adv* **1** LASTLY : por último, finalmente **2** EVENTUALLY : por fin, al final **3** DEFINITIVELY : definitivamente

finance[1] [fəˈnænts, ˈfaɪˌnænts] *vt* **-nanced; -nancing** : financiar

finance[2] *n* **1** : finanzas *fpl* **2 finances** *npl* RESOURCES : recursos *mpl* financieros

financial [fəˈnæntʃəl, faɪ-] *adj* : financiero, económico

financially [fəˈnæntʃəli, faɪ-] *adv* : económicamente

financier [ˌfɪnənˈsɪr, ˌfaɪˌnæn-] *n* : financiero *m,* -ra *f;* financista *mf*

finch [ˈfɪntʃ] *n* : pinzón *m*

find[1] [ˈfaɪnd] *vt* **found** [ˈfaʊnd]; **finding 1** LOCATE : encontrar, hallar <I can't find it : no lo encuentro> <to find one's way : encontrar el camino, orientarse> **2** DISCOVER, REALIZE : descubrir, darse cuenta de <he found it difficult : descubrió que era difícil> **3** DECLARE : declarar, hallar <they found him guilty : lo declararon culpable>

find[2] *n* : hallazgo *m*

finder [ˈfaɪndər] *n* : descubridor *m,* -dora *f*

finding [ˈfaɪndɪŋ] *n* **1** FIND : hallazgo *m* **2 findings** *npl* : conclusiones *fpl*

find out *vt* DISCOVER : descubrir, averiguar — *vi* LEARN : enterarse

fine[1] [ˈfaɪn] *vt* **fined; fining** : multar

fine[2] *adj* **finer; -est 1** PURE : puro (dícese del oro y de la plata) **2** THIN : fino, delgado **3** : fino <fine sand : arena fina> **4** SMALL : pequeño, minúsculo <fine print : letras minúsculas> **5** SUBTLE : sutil, delicado **6** EXCELLENT : excelente, magnífico, selecto **7** FAIR : bueno <it's a fine day : hace buen tiempo> **8** EXQUISITE : exquisito, delicado, fino **9 fine arts** : bellas artes *fpl*

fine[3] *n* : multa *f*

finely [ˈfaɪnli] *adv* **1** EXCELLENTLY : con arte **2** ELEGANTLY : elegantemente **3** PRECISELY : con precisión **4 to chop finely** : picar muy fino, picar en trozos pequeños

fineness [ˈfaɪnnəs] *n* **1** EXCELLENCE : excelencia *f* **2** ELEGANCE : elegancia *f,* refinamiento *m* **3** DELICACY : delicadeza *f,* lo fino **4** PRECISION : precisión *f* **5** SUBTLETY : sutileza *f* **6** PURITY : ley *f* (de oro y plata)

finery [ˈfaɪnəri] *n* : galas *fpl,* adornos *mpl*

finesse[1] [fəˈnɛs] *vt* **-nessed; -nessing** : ingeniar

finesse[2] *n* **1** REFINEMENT : refinamiento *m,* finura *f* **2** TACT : delicadeza *f,* tacto *m,* diplomacia *f* **3** CRAFTINESS : astucia *f*

finger[1] [ˈfɪŋgər] *vt* **1** HANDLE : tocar, toquetear **2** ACCUSE : acusar, delatar

finger[2] *n* : dedo *m*

fingerling [ˈfɪŋgərlɪŋ] *n* : pez *m* pequeño y joven

fingernail [ˈfɪŋgərˌneɪl] *n* : uña *f*

fingerprint[1] [ˈfɪŋgərˌprɪnt] *vt* : tomar las huellas digitales a

fingerprint[2] *n* : huella *f* digital

fingertip [ˈfɪŋgərˌtɪp] *n* : punta *f* del dedo, yema *f* del dedo

finicky [ˈfɪnɪki] *adj* : maniático, melindroso, mañoso

finish[1] [ˈfɪnɪʃ] *vt* **1** COMPLETE : acabar, terminar **2** : aplicar un acabado a (muebles, etc.)

finish[2] *n* **1** END : fin *m,* final *m* **2** REFINEMENT : refinamiento *m* **3** : acabado *m* <a glossy finish : un acabado brillante>

finite [ˈfaɪˌnaɪt] *adj* : finito

fink [ˈfɪŋk] *n* : mequetrefe *mf fam*

Finn [ˈfɪn] *n* : finlandés *m,* -desa *f*

Finnish[1] [ˈfɪnɪʃ] *adj* : finlandés

Finnish[2] *n* : finlandés *m* (idioma)

fiord [fiˈɔrd] → **fjord**

fir [ˈfər] *n* : abeto *m*
fire[1] [ˈfaɪr] *vt* **fired; firing 1** IGNITE, KINDLE : encender **2** ENLIVEN : animar, avivar **3** DISMISS : despedir **4** SHOOT : disparar **5** BAKE : cocer (cerámica)
fire[2] *n* **1** : fuego *m* **2** BURNING : incendio *m* <fire alarm : alarma contra incendios> <to be on fire : estar en llamas> **3** ENTHUSIASM : ardor *m,* entusiasmo *m* **4** SHOOTING : disparos *mpl,* fuego *m*
firearm [ˈfaɪrˌɑrm] *n* : arma *f* de fuego
fireball [ˈfaɪrˌbɔl] *n* **1** : bola *f* de fuego **2** METEOR : bólido *m*
firebreak [ˈfaɪrˌbreɪk] *n* : cortafuegos *m*
firebug [ˈfaɪrˌbʌg] *n* : pirómano *m,* -na *f;* incendiario *m,* -ria *f*
firecracker [ˈfaɪrˌkrækər] *n* : petardo *m*
fire escape *n* : escalera *f* de incendios
firefighter [ˈfaɪrˌfaɪt̬ər] *n* : bombero *m,* -ra *f*
firefly [ˈfaɪrˌflaɪ] *n, pl* **-flies** : luciérnaga *f*
fireman [ˈfaɪrmən] *n, pl* **-men** [-mən, -ˌmɛn] **1** FIREFIGHTER : bombero *m,* -ra *f* **2** STOKER : fogonero *m,* -ra *f*
fireplace [ˈfaɪrˌpleɪs] *n* : hogar *m,* chimenea *f*
fireproof[1] [ˈfaɪrˌpruːf] *vt* : hacer incombustible
fireproof[2] *adj* : incombustible, ignífugo
fireside[1] [ˈfaɪrˌsaɪd] *adj* : informal <fireside chat : charla informal>
fireside[2] *n* **1** HEARTH : chimenea *f,* hogar *m* **2** HOME : hogar *m,* casa *f*
firewood [ˈfaɪrˌwʊd] *n* : leña *f*
fireworks [ˈfaɪrˌwərks] *npl* : fuegos *mpl* artificiales, pirotecnia *f*
firm[1] [ˈfərm] *vi* : endurecer
firm[2] *adj* **1** VIGOROUS : fuerte, vigoroso **2** SOLID, UNYIELDING : firme, duro, sólido **3** UNCHANGING : firme, inalterable **4** RESOLUTE : firme, resuelto
firm[3] *n* : empresa *f,* firma *f,* compañía *f*
firmament [ˈfərməmənt] *n* : firmamento *m*
firmly [ˈfərmli] *adv* : firmemente
firmness [ˈfərmnəs] *n* : firmeza *f*
first[1] [ˈfərst] *adv* **1** : primero <finish your homework first : primero termina tu tarea> <first and foremost : ante todo> <first of all : en primer lugar> **2** : por primera vez <I saw it first in Boston : lo vi por primera vez en Boston>
first[2] *adj* **1** : primero <the first time : la primera vez> <at first sight : a primera vista> <in the first place : en primer lugar> <the first ten applicants : los diez primeros candidatos> **2** FOREMOST : principal, primero <first tenor : tenor principal>
first[3] *n* **1** : primero *m,* -ra *f* (en una serie) **2** : primero *m,* primera parte *f* **3** *or* **first gear** : primera *f* **4 at ~** : al principio
first aid *n* : primeros auxilios *mpl*
first-class[1] [ˈfərstˈklæs] *adv* : en primera <to travel first-class : viajar en primera>
first-class[2] *adj* : de primera
first class *n* : primera clase *f*
firsthand[1] [ˈfərstˈhænd] *adv* : directamente
firsthand[2] *adj* : de primera mano
first lieutenant *n* : teniente *mf;* teniente primero *m,* teniente primera *f*
firstly [ˈfərstli] *adv* : primeramente, principalmente, en primer lugar
first-rate[1] [ˈfərstˈreɪt] *adv* : muy bien
first-rate[2] *adj* : de primera, de primera clase
first sergeant *n* : sargento *mf*
firth [ˈfərθ] *n* : estuario *m*
fiscal [ˈfɪskəl] *adj* : fiscal — **fiscally** *adv*
fish[1] [ˈfɪʃ] *vi* **1** : pescar **2 to fish for** SEEK : buscar, rebuscar <to fish for compliments : andar a la caza de cumplidos> — *vt* : pescar
fish[2] *n, pl* **fish** *or* **fishes** : pez *m* (vivo), pescado *m* (para comer)
fisherman [ˈfɪʃərmən] *n, pl* **-men** [-mən, -ˌmɛn] : pescador *m,* -dora *f*
fishery [ˈfɪʃəri] *n, pl* **-eries 1 → fishing 2** : zona *f* pesquera, pesquería *f*
fishhook [ˈfɪʃˌhʊk] *n* : anzuelo *m*
fishing [ˈfɪʃɪŋ] *n* : pesca *f,* industria *f* pesquera
fishing pole *n* : caña *f* de pescar
fish market *n* : pescadería *f*
fishy [ˈfɪʃi] *adj* **fishier; -est 1** : a pescado <a fishy taste : un sabor a pescado> **2** QUESTIONABLE : dudoso, sospechoso <there's something fishy going on : aquí hay gato encerrado>
fission [ˈfɪʃən, -ʒən] *n* : fisión *f*
fissure [ˈfɪʃər] *n* : fisura *f,* hendidura *f*
fist [ˈfɪst] *n* : puño *m*
fistful [ˈfɪstˌfʊl] *n* : puñado *m*
fisticuffs [ˈfɪstɪˌkʌfs] *npl* : lucha *f* a puñetazos
fit[1] [ˈfɪt] *v* **fitted; fitting** *vt* **1** MATCH : corresponder a, coincidir con <the punishment fits the crime : el castigo corresponde al crimen> **2** : quedar <the dress doesn't fit me : el vestido no me queda> **3** GO : caber, encajar en <her key fits the lock : su llave encaja en la cerradura> **4** INSERT, INSTALL : poner, colocar **5** ADAPT : adecuar, ajustar, adaptar **6** *or* **to fit out** EQUIP : equipar — *vi* **1** : quedar, entallar <these pants don't fit : estos pantalones no me quedan> **2** CONFORM : encajar, cuadrar **3 to fit in** : encajar, estar integrado
fit[2] *adj* **fitter; fittest 1** SUITABLE : adecuado, apropiado, conveniente **2** QUALIFIED : calificado, competente **3** HEALTHY : sano, en forma
fit[3] *n* **1** ATTACK : ataque *m,* acceso *m,* arranque *m* **2 to be a good fit** : quedar bien **3 to be a tight fit** : ser muy

entallado (de ropa), estar apretado (de espacios)

fitful [ˈfɪtfəl] *adj* : irregular, intermitente — **fitfully** *adv*

fitness [ˈfɪtnəs] *n* **1** HEALTH : salud *f,* buena forma *f* (física) **2** SUITABILITY : idoneidad *f*

fitting[1] [ˈfɪṭɪŋ] *adj* : adecuado, apropiado

fitting[2] *n* : accesorio *m*

five[1] [ˈfaɪv] *adj* : cinco

five[2] *n* : cinco *m*

five hundred[1] *adj* : quinientos

five hundred[2] *n* : quinientos *m*

fix[1] [ˈfɪks] *vt* **1** ATTACH, SECURE : sujetar, asegurar, fijar **2** ESTABLISH : fijar, concretar, establecer **3** REPAIR : arreglar, reparar **4** PREPARE : preparar <to fix dinner : preparar la cena> **5** : arreglar, amañar <to fix a race : arreglar una carrera> **6** RIVET : fijar (los ojos, la mirada, etc.)

fix[2] *n* **1** PREDICAMENT : aprieto *m,* apuro *m* **2** : posición *f* <to get a fix on : establecer la posición de>

fixate [ˈfɪkˌseɪt] *vi* **-ated; -ating** : obsesionarse

fixation [fɪkˈseɪʃən] *n* : fijación *f,* obsesión *f*

fixed [ˈfɪkst] *adj* **1** STATIONARY : estacionario, inmóvil **2** UNCHANGING : fijo, inalterable **3** INTENT : fijo <a fixed stare : una mirada fija> **4 to be comfortably fixed** : estar en posición acomodada

fixedly [ˈfɪksədli] *adv* : fijamente

fixedness [ˈfɪksədnəs, ˈfikst-] *n* : rigidez *f*

fixture [ˈfɪkstʃər] *n* **1** : parte *f* integrante, elemento *m* fijo **2 fixtures** *npl* : instalaciones *fpl* (de una casa)

fizz[1] [ˈfɪz] *vi* : burbujear

fizz[2] *n* : efervescencia *f,* burbujeo *m*

fizzle[1] [ˈfɪzəl] *vi* **-zled; -zling 1** FIZZ : burbujear **2** FAIL : fracasar

fizzle[2] *n* : fracaso *m,* fiasco *m*

fjord [fiˈɔrd] *n* : fiordo *m*

flab [ˈflæb] *n* : gordura *f*

flabbergast [ˈflæbərˌgæst] *vt* : asombrar, pasmar, dejar atónito

flabby [ˈflæbi] *adj* **-bier; -est** : blando, fofo, aguado *CA, Col, Mex*

flaccid [ˈflæksəd, ˈflæsəd] *adj* : fláccido

flag[1] [ˈflæg] *vi* **flagged; flagging 1** : hacer señales con banderas **2** WEAKEN : flaquear, desfallecer

flag[2] *n* : bandera *f,* pabellón *m,* estandarte *m*

flagon [ˈflægən] *n* : jarra *f* grande

flagpole [ˈflægˌpoːl] *n* : asta *f,* mástil *m*

flagrant [ˈfleɪgrənt] *adj* : flagrante — **flagrantly** *adv*

flagship [ˈflægˌʃɪp] *n* : buque *m* insignia

flagstaff [ˈflægˌstæf] → **flagpole**

flagstone [ˈflægˌstoːn] *n* : losa *f,* piedra *f*

flail[1] [ˈfleɪl] *vt* **1** : trillar (grano) **2** : sacudir, agitar (los brazos)

flail[2] *n* : mayal *m*

flair [ˈflær] *n* : don *m,* facilidad *f*

flak [ˈflæk] *ns & pl* **flak 1** : fuego *m* antiaéreo **2** CRITICISM : críticas *fpl*

flake[1] [ˈfleɪk] *vi* **flaked; flaking** : desmenuzarse, pelarse (dícese de la piel)

flake[2] *n* : copo *m* (de nieve), escama *f* (de la piel), astilla *f* (de madera)

flamboyance [flæmˈbɔɪənts] *n* : extravagancia *f,* rimbombancia *f*

flamboyant [flæmˈbɔɪənt] *adj* : exuberante, extravagante, rimbombante

flame[1] [ˈfleɪm] *vi* **flamed; flaming 1** BLAZE : arder, llamear **2** GLOW : brillar, encenderse

flame[2] *n* BLAZE : llama *f* <to burst into flames : estallar en llamas> <to go up in flame : incendiarse>

flamethrower [ˈfleɪmˌθroːər] *n* : lanzallamas *m*

flamingo [fləˈmɪŋgo] *n, pl* **-gos** : flamenco *m*

flammable [ˈflæməbəl] *adj* : inflamable, flamable

flange [ˈflændʒ] *n* : reborde *m,* pestaña *f*

flank[1] [ˈflæŋk] *vt* **1** : flanquear (para defender o atacar) **2** BORDER, LINE : bordear

flank[2] *n* : ijada *f* (de un animal), costado *m* (de una persona), falda *f* (de una colina), flanco *m* (de un cuerpo de soldados)

flannel [ˈflænəl] *n* : franela *f*

flap[1] [ˈflæp] *v* **flapped; flapping** *vi* **1** : aletear <the bird was flapping (its wings) : el pájaro aleteaba> **2** FLUTTER : ondear, agitarse — *vt* : batir, agitar

flap[2] *n* **1** FLAPPING : aleteo *m,* aletazo *m* (de alas) **2** : soplada *f* (de un sobre), hoja *f* (de una mesa), faldón *m* (de una chaqueta)

flapjack [ˈflæpˌdʒæk] → **pancake**

flare[1] [ˈflær] *vi* **flared; flaring 1** FLAME, SHINE : llamear, brillar **2 to flare up** : estallar, explotar (de cólera)

flare[2] *n* **1** FLASH : destello *m* **2** SIGNAL : (luz *f* de) bengala *f* **3 solar flare** : erupción *f* solar

flash[1] [ˈflæʃ] *vi* **1** SHINE, SPARKLE : destellar, brillar, relampaguear **2** : pasar como un relámpago <an idea flashed through my mind : una idea me cruzó la mente como un relámpago> — *vt* : despedir, lanzar (una luz), transmitir (un mensaje)

flash[2] *adj* SUDDEN : repentino

flash[3] *n* **1** : destello *m* (de luz), fogonazo *m* (de una explosión) **2 flash of lightning** : relámpago *m* **3 in a flash** : de repente, de un abrir y cerrar los ojos

flashiness [ˈflæʃinəs] *n* : ostentación *f*

flashlight [ˈflæʃˌlaɪt] *n* : linterna *f*

flashy [ˈflæʃi] *adj* **flashier; -est** : llamativo, ostentoso

flask [ˈflæsk] *n* : frasco *m*

flat[1] [ˈflæt] *vt* **flatted; flatting 1** FLATTEN : aplanar, achatar **2** : bajar de tono (en música)

flat[2] *adv* **1** EXACTLY : exactamente <in ten minutes flat : en diez minutos exactos> **2** : desafinado, demasiado bajo (en la música)

flat[3] *adj* **flatter; flattest 1** EVEN, LEVEL : plano, llano **2** SMOOTH : liso **3** DEFINITE : categórico, rotundo, explícito <a flat refusal : una negativa categórica> **4** DULL : aburrido, soso, monótono (dícese la voz) **5** DEFLATED : desinflado, pinchado, ponchado *Mex* **6** : bemol (en música) <to sing flat : cantar desafinado>

flat[4] *n* **1** PLAIN : llano *m,* terreno *m* llano **2** : bemol *m* (en la música) **3** APARTMENT : apartamento *m,* departamento *m* **4** *or* **flat tire** : pinchazo *m,* ponchadura *f Mex*

flatbed [ˈflæt,bɛd] *n* : camión *m* de plataforma

flatcar [ˈflæt,kɑr] *n* : vagón *m* abierto

flatfish [ˈflæt,fɪʃ] *n* : platija *f*

flat–footed [ˈflæt,fʊt̬əd, ,flætˈ-] *adj* : de pies planos

flatly [ˈflætli] *adv* DEFINITELY : categóricamente, rotundamente

flatness [ˈflætnəs] *n* **1** EVENNESS : lo llano, lisura *f,* uniformidad *f* **2** DULLNESS : monotonía *f*

flat–out [ˈflætˈaʊt] *adj* **1** : frenético, a toda máquina <a flat-out effort : un esfuerzo frenético> **2** CATEGORICAL : descarado, rotundo, categórico

flatten [ˈflætən] *vt* : aplanar, achatar

flatter [ˈflæt̬ər] *vt* **1** OVERPRAISE : adular **2** COMPLIMENT : halagar **3** : favorecer <the photo flatters you : la foto te favorece>

flatterer [ˈflæt̬ərər] *n* : adulador *m,* -dora *f*

flattering [ˈflæt̬ərɪŋ] *adj* **1** COMPLIMENTARY : halagador **2** BECOMING : favorecedor

flattery [ˈflæt̬əri] *n, pl* **-ries** : halagos *mpl*

flatulence [ˈflætʃələnts] *n* : flatulencia *f,* ventosidad *f*

flatulent [ˈflætʃələnt] *adj* : flatulento

flatware [ˈflæt,wær] *n* : cubertería *f,* cubiertos *mpl*

flaunt[1] [ˈflɔnt] *vt* : alardear, hacer alarde de

flaunt[2] *n* : alarde *m,* ostentación *f*

flavor[1] [ˈfleɪvər] *vt* : dar sabor a, sazonar

flavor[2] *n* **1** : gusto *m,* sabor *m* **2** FLAVORING : sazón *f,* condimento *m*

flavorful [ˈfleɪvərfəl] *adj* : sabroso

flavoring [ˈfleɪvərɪŋ] *n* : condimento *m,* sazón *f*

flavorless [ˈfleɪvərləs] *adj* : sin sabor

flaw [ˈflɔ] *n* : falla *f,* defecto *m,* imperfección *f*

flawless [ˈflɔləs] *adj* : impecable, perfecto — **flawlessly** *adv*

flax [ˈflæks] *n* : lino *m*

flaxen [ˈflæksən] *adj* : rubio, blondo (dícese del pelo)

flay [ˈfleɪ] *vt* **1** SKIN : desollar, despellejar **2** VILIFY : criticar con dureza, vilipendiar

flea [ˈfliː] *n* : pulga *f*

fleck[1] [ˈflɛk] *vt* : salpicar

fleck[2] *n* : mota *f,* pinta *f*

fledgling [ˈflɛdʒlɪŋ] *n* : polluelo *m,* pollito *m*

flee [ˈfliː] *v* **fled** [ˈflɛd]; **fleeing** *vi* : huir, escapar(se) — *vt* : huir de

fleece[1] [ˈfliːs] *vt* **fleeced; fleecing 1** SHEAR : esquilar, trasquilar **2** SWINDLE : estafar, defraudar

fleece[2] *n* : lana *f,* vellón *m*

fleet[1] [ˈfliːt] *vi* : moverse con rapidez

fleet[2] *adj* SWIFT : rápido, veloz

fleet[3] *n* : flota *f*

fleet admiral *n* : almirante *mf*

fleeting [ˈfliːt̬ɪŋ] *adj* : fugaz, breve

flesh [ˈflɛʃ] *n* **1** : carne *f* (de seres humanos y animales) **2** : pulpa *f* (de frutas)

flesh out *vt* : desarrollar, darle cuerpo a

fleshy [ˈflɛʃi] *adj* **fleshier; -est** : gordo (dícese de las personas), carnoso (dícese de la fruta)

flew → **fly**

flex [ˈflɛks] *vt* : doblar, flexionar

flexibility [,flɛksəˈbɪlət̬i] *n, pl* **-ties** : flexibilidad *f,* elasticidad *f*

flexible [ˈflɛksəbəl] *adj* : flexible — **flexibly** [-bli] *adv*

flick[1] [ˈflɪk] *vt* : dar un capirotazo a (con el dedo) <to flick a switch : darle al interruptor> — *vi* **1** FLIT : revolotear **2 to flick through** : hojear (un libro)

flick[2] *n* : coletazo *m* (de una cola), capirotazo *m* (de un dedo)

flicker[1] [ˈflɪkər] *vi* **1** FLUTTER : revolotear, aletear **2** BLINK, TWINKLE : parpadear, titilar

flicker[2] *n* **1** : parpadeo *m,* titileo *m* **2** HINT, TRACE : indicio *m,* rastro *m* <a flicker of hope : un rayo de esperanza>

flier [ˈflaɪər] *n* **1** AVIATOR : aviador *m,* -dora *f* **2** CIRCULAR : folleto *m* publicitario, circular *f*

flight [ˈflaɪt] *n* **1** : vuelo *m* (de aves o aviones), trayectoria *f* (de proyectiles) **2** TRIP : vuelo *m* **3** FLOCK, SQUADRON : bandada *f* (de pájaros), escuadrilla *f* (de aviones) **4** ESCAPE : huida *f,* fuga *f* **5 flight of fancy** : ilusiones *fpl,* fantasía *f* **6 flight of stairs** : tramo *m*

flightless [ˈflaɪtləs] *adj* : no volador

flighty [ˈflaɪt̬i] *adj* **flightier; -est** : caprichoso, frívolo

flimsy [flɪmzi] *adj* **flimsier; -est 1** LIGHT, THIN : ligero, fino **2** WEAK : endeble, poco sólido **3** IMPLAUSIBLE : pobre, flojo, poco convincente <a flimsy excuse : una excusa floja>

flinch [ˈflɪntʃ] *vi* **1** WINCE : estremecerse **2** RECOIL : recular, retroceder

fling[1] [ˈflɪŋ] *vt* **flung** [ˈflʌŋ]; **flinging 1** THROW : lanzar, tirar, arrojar **2 to fling oneself** : lanzarse, tirarse, precipitarse

fling[2] *n* **1** THROW : lanzamiento *m* **2** ATTEMPT : intento *m* **3** AFFAIR : aventura *f* **4** BINGE : juerga *f*

flint [ˈflɪnt] *n* : pedernal *m*

flinty [ˈflɪnti] *adj* **flintier; -est 1** : de pedernal **2** STERN, UNYIELDING : severo, inflexible

flip[1] [ˈflɪp] *v* **flipped; flipping** *vt* **1** TOSS : tirar <to flip a coin : echar a cara o cruz> **2** OVERTURN : dar la vuelta a, voltear — *vi* **1** : moverse bruscamente **2 to flip through** : hojear (un libro)

flip[2] *adj* : insolente, descarado

flip[3] *n* **1** FLICK : capirotazo *m*, golpe *m* ligero **2** SOMERSAULT : voltereta *f*

flippancy [ˈflɪpəntsi] *n, pl* **-cies** : ligereza *f*, falta *f* de seriedad

flippant [ˈflɪpənt] *adj* : ligero, frívolo, poco serio

flipper [ˈflɪpər] *n* : aleta *f*

flirt[1] [ˈflərt] *vi* **1** : coquetear, flirtear **2** TRIFLE : jugar <to flirt with death : jugar con la muerte>

flirt[2] *n* : coqueto *m*, -ta *f*

flirtation [ˌflərˈteɪʃən] *n* : devaneo *m*, coqueteo *m*

flirtatious [ˌflərˈteɪʃəs] *adj* : insinuante, coqueto

flit [ˈflɪt] *vi* **flitted; flitting 1** : revolotear **2 to flit about** : ir y venir rápidamente

float[1] [ˈfloːt] *vi* **1** : flotar **2** WANDER : vagar, errar — *vt* **1** : poner a flote, hacer flotar (un barco) **2** LAUNCH : hacer flotar (una empresa) **3** ISSUE : emitir (acciones en la bolsa)

float[2] *n* **1** : flotador *m*, corcho *m* (para pescar) **2** BUOY : boya *f* **3** : carroza *f* (en un desfile)

flock[1] [ˈflɑk] *vi* **1** : moverse en rebaño **2** CONGREGATE : congregarse, reunirse

flock[2] *n* : rebaño *m* (de ovejas), bandada *f* (de pájaros)

floe [ˈfloː] *n* : témpano *m* de hielo

flog [ˈflɑg] *vt* **flogged; flogging** : azotar, fustigar

flood[1] [ˈflʌd] *vt* : inundar, anegar

flood[2] *n* **1** INUNDATION : inundación *f* **2** TORRENT : avalancha *f*, diluvio *m*, torrente *m* <a flood of tears : un mar de lágrimas>

floodlight [ˈflʌdˌlaɪt] *n* : foco *m*

floodwater [ˈflʌdˌwɔt̬ər] *n* : crecida *f*, creciente *f*

floor[1] [ˈflor] *vt* **1** : solar, poner suelo a (una casa o una sala) **2** KNOCK DOWN : derribar, echar al suelo **3** NONPLUS : desconcertar, confundir, dejar perplejo

floor[2] *n* **1** : suelo *m*, piso *m* <dance floor : pista de baile> **2** STORY : piso *m*, planta *f* <ground floor : planta baja> <second floor : primer piso> **3** : mínimo *m* (de sueldos, precios, etc.)

floorboard [ˈflorˌbord] *n* : tabla *f* del suelo, suelo *m*, piso *m*

flop[1] [ˈflɑp] *vi* **flopped; flopping 1** FLAP : golpearse, agitarse **2** COLLAPSE : dejarse caer, desplomarse **3** FAIL : fracasar

flop[2] *n* **1** FAILURE : fracaso *m* **2 to take a flop** : caerse

floppy [ˈflɑpi] *adj* **-pier; -est 1** : blando, flexible **2 floppy disk** : diskette *m*, disquete *m*

flora [ˈflorə] *n* : flora *f*

floral [ˈflorəl] *adj* : floral, floreado

florid [ˈflorɪd] *adj* **1** FLOWERY : florido **2** REDDISH : rojizo

florist [ˈflorɪst] *n* : florista *mf*

floss[1] [ˈflɔs] *vi* : limpiarse los dientes con hilo dental

floss[2] *n* **1** : hilo *m* de seda (de brodar) **2** → **dental floss**

flotation [floˈteɪʃən] *n* : flotación *f*

flotilla [floˈtɪlə] *n* : flotilla *f*

flotsam [ˈflɑtsəm] *n* **1** : restos *mpl* flotantes (en el mar) **2 flotsam and jetsam** : desechos *mpl*, restos *mpl*

flounce[1] [ˈflaʊnts] *vi* **flounced; flouncing** : moverse haciendo aspavientos <she flounced into the room : entró en la sala haciendo aspavientos>

flounce[2] *n* **1** RUFFLE : volante *m* **2** FLOURISH : aspaviento *m*

flounder[1] [ˈflaʊndər] *vi* **1** STRUGGLE : forcejear **2** STUMBLE : no saber qué hacer o decir, perder el hilo (en un discurso)

flounder[2] *n, pl* **flounder** *or* **flounders** : platija *f*

flour[1] [ˈflaʊər] *vt* : enharinar

flour[2] *n* : harina *f*

flourish[1] [ˈflərɪʃ] *vi* THRIVE : florecer, prosperar, crecer (dícese de las plantas) — *vt* BRANDISH : blandir

flourish[2] *n* : floritura *f*, floreo *m*

flourishing [ˈflərɪʃɪŋ] *adj* : floreciente, próspero

flout [ˈflaʊt] *vt* : desacatar, burlarse de

flow[1] [ˈfloː] *vi* **1** COURSE : fluir, manar, correr **2** CIRCULATE : circular, correr <traffic is flowing smoothly : el tránsito está circulando con fluidez>

flow[2] *n* **1** FLOWING : flujo *m*, circulación *f* **2** STREAM : corriente *f*, chorro *m*

flower[1] [ˈflaʊər] *vi* : florecer, florear

flower[2] *n* : flor *f*

flowered [ˈflaʊərd] *adj* : florido, floreado

floweriness [ˈflaʊərinəs] *n* : floritura *f*

flowering[1] [ˈflaʊərɪŋ] *adj* : floreciente

flowering[2] *n* : floración *f*, florecimiento *m*

flowerpot [ˈflaʊərˌpɑt] *n* : maceta *f*, tiesto *m*, macetero *m*

flowery [ˈflaʊəri] *adj* **1** : florido **2** FLOWERED : floreado, de flores

flowing [ˈfloːɪŋ] *adj* : fluido, corriente

flown → **fly**

flu [ˈfluː] *n* : gripe *f*, gripa *f Col, Mex*

fluctuate [ˈflʌktʃʊˌeɪt] *vi* **-ated; -ating** : fluctuar
fluctuation [ˌflʌktʃʊˈeɪʃən] *n* : fluctuación *f*
flue [ˈfluː] *n* : tiro *m,* salida *f* de humos
fluency [ˈfluːəntsi] *n* : fluidez *f,* soltura *f*
fluent [ˈfluːənt] *adj* : fluido
fluently [ˈfluːəntli] *adv* : con soltura, con fluidez
fluff[1] [ˈflʌf] *vt* **1** : mullir <to fluff up the pillows : mullir las almohadas> **2** BUNGLE : echar a perder, equivocarse
fluff[2] *n* **1** FUZZ : pelusa *f* **2** DOWN : plumón *m*
fluffy [ˈflʌfi] *adj* **fluffier; -est 1** DOWNY : lleno de pelusa, velloso **2** SPONGY : esponjoso
fluid[1] [ˈfluːɪd] *adj* : fluido
fluid[2] *n* : fluido *m,* líquido *m*
fluidity [fluˈɪdət̬i] *n* : fluidez *f*
fluid ounce *n* : onza *f* líquida (29.57 mililitros)
fluke [ˈfluːk] *n* : golpe *m* de suerte, chiripa *f,* casualidad *f*
flung → **fling**
flunk [ˈflʌŋk] *vt* FAIL : reprobar — *vi* : salir reprobando
fluorescence [ˌflʊrˈɛsənts, ˌflɔr-] *n* : fluorescencia *f*
fluorescent [ˌflʊrˈɛsənt, ˌflɔr-] *adj* : fluorescente
fluoridate [ˈflɔrəˌdeɪt, ˈflʊr-] *vt* **-dated; -dating** : fluorizar
fluoridation [ˌflɔrəˈdeɪʃən, ˌflʊr-] *n* : fluorización *f,* fluoración *f*
fluoride [ˈflɔrˌaɪd, ˈflʊr-] *n* : fluoruro *m*
fluorine [ˈflʊrˌiːn] *n* : flúor *m*
fluorocarbon [ˌflɔroˈkɑrbən, ˌflʊr-] *n* : fluorocarbono *m*
flurry [ˈfləri] *n, pl* **-ries 1** GUST : ráfaga *f* **2** SNOWFALL : nevisca *f* **3** BUSTLE : frenesí *m,* bullicio *m* **4** BARRAGE : aluvión *m,* oleada *f* <a flurry of questions : un aluvión de preguntas>
flush[1] [ˈflʌʃ] *vt* **1** : limpiar con agua <to flush the toilet : jalar la cadena> **2** RAISE : hacer salir, levantar (en la caza) — *vi* BLUSH : ruborizarse, sonrojarse
flush[2] *adv* : al mismo nivel, a ras
flush[3] *adj* **1** *or* **flushed** [ˈflʌʃt] : colorado, rojo, encendido (dícese de la cara) **2** FILLED : lleno a rebosar **3** ABUNDANT : copioso, abundante **4** AFFLUENT : adinerado **5** ALIGNED, SMOOTH : alineado, liso **6 flush against** : pegado a, contra
flush[4] *n* **1** FLOW, JET : chorro *m,* flujo *m* rápido **2** SURGE : arrebato *m,* arranque *m* <a flush of anger : un arrebato de cólera> **3** BLUSH : rubor *m,* sonrojo *m* **4** GLOW : resplandor *m,* flor *f* <the flush of youth : la flor de la juventud> <in the flush of victory : en la euforia del triunfo>
fluster[1] [ˈflʌstər] *vt* : poner nervioso, aturdir
fluster[2] *n* : agitación *f,* confusión *f*
flute [ˈfluːt] *n* : flauta *f*
fluted [ˈfluːt̬əd] *adj* **1** GROOVED : estriado, acanalado **2** WAVY : ondulado
fluting [ˈfluːt̬ɪŋ] *n* : estrías *fpl*
flutist [ˈfluːt̬ɪst] *n* : flautista *mf*
flutter[1] [ˈflʌt̬ər] *vi* **1** : revolotear (dícese de un pájaro), ondear (dícese de una bandera), palpitar con fuerza (dícese del corazón) **2 to flutter about** : ir y venir, revoltear — *vt* : sacudir, batir
flutter[2] *n* **1** FLUTTERING : revoloteo *m,* aleteo *m* **2** COMMOTION, STIR : revuelo *m,* agitación *f*
flux [ˈflʌks] *n* **1** : flujo *m* (en física y medicina) **2** CHANGE : cambio *m* <to be in a state of flux : estar cambiando continuamente>
fly[1] [ˈflaɪ] *v* **flew** [ˈfluː]; **flown** [ˈfloːn]; **flying** *vi* **1** : volar (dícese de los pájaros, etc.) **2** TRAVEL : volar (dícese de los aviones), ir en avión (dícese de los pasajeros) **3** FLOAT : flotar, ondear **4** FLEE : huir, escapar **5** RUSH : correr, irse volando **6** PASS : pasar (volando) <how time flies! : ¡cómo pasa el tiempo!> **7 to fly open** : abrir de golpe — *vt* : pilotar (un avión), hacer volar (una cometa)
fly[2] *n, pl* **flies 1** : mosca *f* <to drop like flies : caer como moscas> **2** : bragueta *f* (de pantalones, etc.)
flyer → **flier**
flying saucer → **UFO**
flypaper [ˈflaɪˌpeɪpər] *n* : papel *m* matamoscas
flyspeck [ˈflaɪˌspɛk] *n* **1** : excremento *m* de mosca **2** SPECK : motita *f,* puntito *m*
flyswatter [ˈflaɪˌswɑt̬ər] *n* : matamoscas *m*
flywheel [ˈflaɪˌhwiːl] *n* : volante *m*
foal[1] [ˈfoːl] *vi* : parir
foal[2] *n* : potro *m,* -tra *f*
foam[1] [ˈfoːm] *vi* : hacer espuma
foam[2] *n* : espuma *f*
foamy [ˈfoːmi] *adj* **foamier; -est** : espumoso
focal [ˈfoːkəl] *adj* **1** : focal, central **2 focal point** : foco *m,* punto *m* de referencia
fo'c'sle [ˈfoːksəl] → **forecastle**
focus[1] [ˈfoːkəs] *v* **-cused** *or* **-cussed; -cusing** *or* **-cussing** *vt* **1** : enfocar (un instrumento) **2** CONCENTRATE : concentrar, centrar — *vi* : enfocar, fijar la vista
focus[2] *n, pl* **-ci** [ˈfoːˌsaɪ, -ˌkaɪ] **1** : foco *m* <to be in focus : estar enfocado> **2** FOCUSING : enfoque *m* **3** CENTER : centro *m,* foco *m*
fodder [ˈfɑdər] *n* : pienso *m,* forraje *m*
foe [ˈfoː] *n* : enemigo *m,* -ga *f*
fog[1] [ˈfɔg, ˈfɑg] *v* **fogged; fogging** *vt* : empañar — *vi* **to fog up** : empañarse
fog[2] *n* : niebla *f,* neblina *f*
foggy [ˈfɔgi, ˈfɑ-] *adj* **foggier; -est** : nebuloso, brumoso

foghorn [ˈfɔg,hɔrn, ˈfɑg-] *n* **:** sirena *f* de niebla

fogy [ˈfoːgi] *n, pl* **-gies :** carca *mf fam,* persona *f* chapada a la antigua

foible [ˈfɔɪbəl] *n* **:** flaqueza *f,* debilidad *f*

foil[1] [ˈfɔɪl] *vt* **:** frustrar, hacer fracasar

foil[2] *n* **1 :** lámina *f* de metal, papel *m* de aluminio **2** CONTRAST **:** contraste *m,* complemento *m* **3** SWORD **:** florete *m* (en esgrima)

foist [ˈfɔɪst] *vt* **:** encajar, endilgar *fam,* colocar

fold[1] [ˈfoːld] *vt* **1** BEND **:** doblar, plegar **2** CLASP **:** cruzar (brazos), enlazar (manos), plegar (alas) **3** EMBRACE **:** estrechar, abrazar **—** *vi* **1** FAIL **:** fracasar **2 to fold up :** doblarse, plegarse

fold[2] *n* **1** SHEEPFOLD **:** redil *m* (para ovejas) **2** FLOCK **:** rebaño *m* <to return to the fold **:** volver al redil> **3** CREASE **:** pliegue *m,* doblez *m*

folder [ˈfoːldər] *n* **1** CIRCULAR **:** circular *f,* folleto *m* **2** BINDER **:** carpeta *f*

foliage [ˈfoːliɪdʒ, -lɪdʒ] *n* **:** follaje *m*

folio [ˈfoːli,oː] *n, pl* **-lios :** folio *m*

folk[1] [ˈfoːk] *adj* **:** popular, folklórico <folk customs **:** costumbres populares> <folk dance **:** danza folklórica>

folk[2] *n, pl* **folk** *or* **folks 1** PEOPLE **:** gente *f* **2 folks** *npl* **:** familia *f,* padres *mpl*

folklore [ˈfoːk,lor] *n* **:** folklore *m*

folklorist [ˈfoːk,lorɪst] *n* **:** folklorista *mf*

folksy [ˈfoːksi] *adj* **folksier; -est :** campechano

follicle [ˈfɑlɪkəl] *n* **:** folículo *m*

follow [ˈfɑlo] *vt* **1 :** seguir <follow the guide **:** siga al guía> <she followed the road **:** siguió el camino, continuó por el camino> **2** PURSUE **:** perseguir, seguir **3** OBEY **:** seguir, cumplir, observar **4** UNDERSTAND **:** entender **—** *vi* **1 :** seguir **2** UNDERSTAND **:** entender **3 it follows that... :** se deduce que...

follower [ˈfɑloər] *n* **:** seguidor *m,* -dora *f*

following[1] [ˈfɑloɪŋ] *adj* NEXT **:** siguiente

following[2] *n* FOLLOWERS **:** seguidores *mpl*

following[3] *prep* AFTER **:** después de

follow through *vi* **to follow through with :** continuar con, realizar

follow up *vt* **:** seguir (una sugerencia, etc.), investigar (una huella)

folly [ˈfɑli] *n, pl* **-lies :** locura *f,* desatino *m*

foment [foˈmɛnt] *vt* **:** fomentar

fond [ˈfɑnd] *adj* **1** LOVING **:** cariñoso, tierno **2** PARTIAL **:** aficionado **3** FERVENT **:** ferviente, fervoroso

fondle [ˈfɑndəl] *vt* **-dled; -dling :** acariciar

fondly [ˈfɑndli] *adv* **:** cariñosamente, afectuosamente

fondness [ˈfɑndnəs] *n* **1** LOVE **:** cariño *m* **2** LIKING **:** afición *f*

fondue [fɑnˈduː, -ˈdjuː] *n* **:** fondue *f*

font [ˈfɑnt] *n* **1** *or* **baptismal font :** pila *f* bautismal **2** FOUNTAIN **:** fuente *f*

food [ˈfuːd] *n* **:** comida *f,* alimento *m*

food chain *n* **:** cadena *f* alimenticia

foodstuffs [ˈfuːd,stʌfs] *npl* **:** comestibles *mpl*

fool[1] [ˈfuːl] *vi* **1** JOKE **:** bromear, hacer el tonto **2** TOY **:** jugar, juguetear <don't fool with the computer **:** no juegues con la computadora> **3 to fool around :** perder el tiempo <he fools around instead of working **:** pierde el tiempo en vez de trabajar> **—** *vt* DECEIVE **:** engañar, burlar

fool[2] *n* **1** IDIOT **:** idiota *mf;* tonto *m,* -ta *f;* bobo *m,* -ba *f* **2** JESTER **:** bufón *m,* -fona *f*

foolhardiness [ˈfuːl,hɑrdinəs] *n* **:** imprudencia *f*

foolhardy [ˈfuːl,hɑrdi] *adj* RASH **:** imprudente, temerario, precipitado

foolish [ˈfuːlɪʃ] *adj* **1** STUPID **:** insensato, estúpido **2** SILLY **:** idiota, tonto

foolishly [ˈfuːlɪʃli] *adv* **:** tontamente

foolishness [ˈfuːlɪʃnəs] *n* **:** insensatez *f,* estupidez *f,* tontería *f*

foolproof [ˈfuːl,pruːf] *adj* **:** infalible

foot [ˈfʊt] *n, pl* **feet** [ˈfiːt] **:** pie *m*

footage [ˈfʊtɪdʒ] *n* **:** medida *f* en pies, metraje *m* (en el cine)

football [ˈfʊt,bɔl] *n* **:** futbol *m* americano, fútbol *m* americano

footbridge [ˈfʊt,brɪdʒ] *n* **:** pasarela *f,* puente *m* peatonal

foothills [ˈfʊt,hɪlz] *npl* **:** estribaciones *fpl*

foothold [ˈfʊt,hoːld] *n* **1 :** punto *m* de apoyo **2 to gain a foothold :** afianzarse en una posición

footing [ˈfʊtɪŋ] *n* **1** BALANCE **:** equilibrio *m* **2** FOOTHOLD **:** punto *m* de apoyo **3** BASIS **:** base *f* <on an equal footing **:** en igualdad>

footlights [ˈfʊt,laɪts] *npl* **:** candilejas *fpl*

footlocker [ˈfʊt,lɑkər] *n* **:** baúl *m* pequeño, cofre *m*

footloose [ˈfʊt,luːs] *adj* **:** libre y sin compromiso

footman [ˈfʊtmən] *n, pl* **-men** [-mən, -,mɛn] **:** lacayo *m*

footnote [ˈfʊt,noːt] *n* **:** nota *f* al pie de la página

footpath [ˈfʊt,pæθ] *n* **:** sendero *m,* senda *f,* vereda *f*

footprint [ˈfʊt,prɪnt] *n* **:** huella *f*

footrace [ˈfʊt,reɪs] *n* **:** carrera *f* pedestre

footrest [ˈfʊt,rɛst] *n* **:** apoyapiés *m,* reposapiés *m*

footstep [ˈfʊt,stɛp] *n* **1** STEP **:** paso *m* **2** FOOTPRINT **:** huella *f*

footstool [ˈfʊt,stuːl] *n* **:** taburete *m,* escabel *m*

footwear [ˈfʊt,wær] *n* **:** calzado *m*

footwork [ˈfʊt,wərk] *n* **:** juego *m* de piernas, juego *m* de pies

fop [ˈfɑp] *n* **:** petimetre *m,* dandi *m*

for[1] [ˈfɔr] *conj* : puesto que, porque

for[2] *prep* **1** (*indicating purpose*) : para, de <clothes for children : ropa para niños> <it's time for dinner : es la hora de comer> **2** BECAUSE OF : por <for fear of : por miedo de> **3** (*indicating a recipient*) : para, por <a gift for you : un regalo para ti> **4** (*indicating support*) : por <he fought for his country : luchó por su patria> **5** (*indicating a goal*) : por, para <a cure for cancer : una cura para el cáncer> <for your own good : por tu propio bien> **6** (*indicating correspondence or exchange*) : por, para <I bought it for $5 : lo compré por $5> <a lot of trouble for nothing : mucha molestia para nada> **7** AS FOR : para, con respecto a **8** (*indicating duration*) : durante, por <he's going for two years : se va por dos años> <I spoke for ten minutes : hablé (durante) diez minutos> <she has known it for three months : lo sabe desde hace tres meses>

forage[1] [ˈfɔrɪdʒ] *v* **-aged; -aging** *vi* : hurgar (en busca de alimento) — *vt* : buscar (provisiones)

forage[2] *n* : forraje *m*

foray [ˈfɔr,eɪ] *n* : incursión *f*

forbear[1] [fɔrˈbær] *vi* **-bore** [-ˈbor]; **-borne** [-ˈborn]; **-bearing 1** ABSTAIN : abstenerse **2** : tener paciencia

forbear[2] → **forebear**

forbearance [fɔrˈbærənts] *n* **1** ABSTAINING : abstención *f* **2** PATIENCE : paciencia *f*

forbid [fərˈbɪd] *vt* **-bade** [-ˈbæd, -ˈbeɪd] *or* **-bad** [-ˈbæd]; **-bidden** [-ˈbɪdən]; **-bidding 1** PROHIBIT : prohibir **2** PREVENT : impedir

forbidding [fərˈbɪdɪŋ] *adj* **1** IMPOSING : imponente **2** DISAGREEABLE : desagradable, ingrato **3** GRIM : severo

force[1] [ˈfors] *vt* **forced; forcing 1** COMPEL : obligar, forzar **2** : forzar <to force open the window : forzar la ventana> <to force a lock : forzar una cerradura> **3** IMPOSE : imponer, obligar

force[2] *n* **1** : fuerza *f* **2 by force** : por la fuerza **3 in force** : en vigor, en vigencia

forced [ˈforst] *adj* : forzado, forzoso

forceful [ˈforsfəl] *adj* : fuerte, energético, contundente

forcefully [ˈforsfəli] *adv* : con energía, con fuerza

forcefulness [ˈforsfəlnəs] *n* : contundencia *f*, fuerza *f*

forceps [ˈfɔrsəps, -,sɛps] *ns & pl* : fórceps *m*

forcible [ˈforsəbəl] *adj* **1** FORCED : forzoso **2** CONVINCING : contundente, convincente — **forcibly** [-bli] *adv*

ford[1] [ˈford] *vt* : vadear

ford[2] *n* : vado *m*

fore[1] [ˈfor] *adv* **1** FORWARD : hacia adelante **2 fore and aft** : de popa a proa

fore[2] *adj* **1** FORWARD : delantero, de adelante **2** FORMER : anterior

fore[3] *n* **1** : frente *m*, delantera *f* **2 to come to the fore** : empezar a destacar, saltar a primera plana

fore–and–aft [ˈforənˈæft, -ənd-] *adj* : longitudinal

forearm [ˈfor,ɑrm] *n* : antebrazo *m*

forebear [ˈfor,bær] *n* : antepasado *m*, -da *f*

foreboding [forˈboːdɪŋ] *n* : premonición *f*, presentimiento *m*

forecast[1] [ˈfor,kæst] *vt* **-cast; -casting** : pronosticar, predecir

forecast[2] *n* : predicción *f*, pronóstico *m*

forecastle [ˈfoːksəl] *n* : castillo *m* de proa

foreclose [forˈkloːz] *vt* **-closed; -closing** : ejecutar (una hipoteca)

forefather [ˈfor,fɑðər] *n* : antepasado *m*, ancestro *m*

forefinger [ˈfor,fɪŋgər] *n* : índice *m*, dedo *m* índice

forefoot [ˈfor,fʊt] *n* : pata *f* delantera

forefront [ˈfor,frʌnt] *n* : frente *m*, vanguardia *f* <in the forefront : a la vanguardia>

forego [forˈgoː] *vt* **-went; -gone; -going 1** PRECEDE : preceder **2** → **forgo**

foregoing [forˈgoːɪŋ] *adj* : precedente, anterior

foregone [forˈgɔn] *adj* : previsto <a foregone conclusion : un resultado inevitable>

foreground [ˈfor,graʊnd] *n* : primer plano *m*

forehand[1] [ˈfor,hænd] *adj* : directo, derecho

forehand[2] *n* : golpe *m* del derecho

forehead [ˈfɔrəd, ˈfor,hɛd] *n* : frente *f*

foreign [ˈfɔrən] *adj* **1** : extranjero, exterior <foreign countries : países extranjeros> <foreign trade : comercio exterior> **2** ALIEN : ajeno, extraño <foreign to their nature : ajeno a su carácter> <a foreign body : un cuerpo extraño>

foreigner [ˈfɔrənər] *n* : extranjero *m*, -ra *f*

foreknowledge [forˈnɑlɪdʒ] *n* : conocimiento *m* previo

foreleg [ˈfor,lɛg] *n* : pata *f* delantera

foreman [ˈformən] *n*, *pl* **-men** [-mən, -,mɛn] : capataz *mf* <foreman of the jury : presidente del jurado>

foremost[1] [ˈfor,moːst] *adv* : en primer lugar

foremost[2] *adj* : más importante, principal, grande

forenoon [ˈfor,nuːn] *n* : mañana *m*

forensic [fəˈrɛntsɪk] *adj* **1** RHETORICAL : retórico, de argumentación **2** : forense <forensic medicine : medicina forense>

foreordain [ˌforɔr'deɪn] *vt* **:** predestinar, predeterminar
forequarter ['forˌkwɔrt̬ər] *n* **:** cuarto *m* delantero
forerunner ['forˌrʌnər] *n* **:** precursor *m,* -sora *f*
foresee [for'siː] *vt* **-saw; -seen; -seeing :** prever
foreseeable [for'siːəbəl] *adj* **:** previsible <in the foreseeable future : en el futuro inmediato>
foreshadow [for'ʃædoː] *vt* **:** anunciar, prefigurar
foresight ['forˌsaɪt] *n* **:** previsión *f*
foresighted ['forˌsaɪt̬əd] *adj* **:** previsto
forest ['fɔrəst] *n* **:** bosque *m* (en zonas templadas), selva *f* (en zonas tropicales)
forestall [for'stɔl] *vt* **1** PREVENT **:** prevenir, impedir **2** PREEMPT **:** adelantarse a
forested ['fɔrəstəd] *adj* **:** arbolado
forester ['fɔrəstər] *n* **:** silvicultor *m,* -tora *f*
forestland ['fɔrəstˌlænd] *n* **:** zona *f* boscosa
forest ranger → **ranger**
forestry ['fɔrəstri] *n* **:** silvicultura *f,* ingeniería *f* forestal
foreswear → **forswear**
foretaste[1] ['forˌteɪst] *vt* **-tasted; -tasting :** anticipar
foretaste[2] *n* **:** anticipo *m*
foretell [for'tɛl] *vt* **-told; -telling :** predecir, pronosticar, profetizar
forethought ['forˌθɔt] *n* **:** previsión *f,* reflexión *f* previa
forever [fɔr'ɛvər] *adv* **1** PERPETUALLY **:** para siempre, eternamente **2** CONTINUALLY **:** siempre, constantemente
forevermore [fɔrˌɛvər'mor] *adv* **:** por siempre jamás
forewarn [for'wɔrn] *vt* **:** prevenir, advertir
foreword ['forwərd] *n* **:** prólogo *m*
forfeit[1] ['fɔrfət] *vt* **:** perder el derecho a
forfeit[2] *n* **1** FINE, PENALTY **:** multa *f* **2 :** prenda *f* (en un juego)
forge[1] ['fordʒ] *v* **forged; forging** *vt* **1 :** forjar (metal o un plan) **2** COUNTERFEIT **:** falsificar — *vi* **to forge ahead :** avanzar, seguir adelante
forge[2] *n* **:** forja *f*
forger ['fordʒər] *n* **:** falsificador *m,* -dora *f*
forgery ['fordʒəri] *n, pl* **-eries :** falsificación *f*
forget [fər'gɛt] *v* **-got** [-'gɑt]; **-gotten** [-'gɑtən] *or* **-got; -getting** *vt* **:** olvidar — *vi* **to forget about :** olvidarse de, no acordarse de
forgetful [fər'gɛtfəl] *adj* **:** olvidadizo
forget–me–not [fər'gɛtmiˌnɑt] *n* **:** nomeolvides *mf*
forgettable [fər'gɛt̬əbəl] *adj* **:** poco memorable
forgivable [fər'gɪvəbəl] *adj* **:** perdonable
forgive [fər'gɪv] *vt* **-gave** [-'geɪv]; **-given** [-'gɪvən]; **-giving :** perdonar
forgiveness [fər'gɪvnəs] *n* **:** perdón *m*
forgiving [fər'gɪvɪŋ] *adj* **:** indulgente, comprensivo, clemente
forgo *or* **forego** [for'goː] *vt* **-went; -gone; -going :** privarse de, renunciar a
fork[1] ['fɔrk] *vi* **:** ramificarse, bifurcarse — *vt* **1 :** levantar (con un tenedor, una horca, etc.) **2 to fork over :** desembolsar
fork[2] *n* **1 :** tenedor *m* (utensilio de cocina) **2** PITCHFORK **:** horca *f,* horquilla *f* **3 :** bifurcación *f* (de un río o camino), horqueta *f* (de un árbol)
forked ['fɔrkt, 'fɔrkəd] *adj* **:** bífido, ahorquillado
forklift ['fɔrkˌlɪft] *n* **:** carretilla *f* elevadora
forlorn [fɔr'lɔrn] *adj* **1** DESOLATE **:** abandonado, desolado, desamparado **2** SAD **:** triste **3** DESPERATE **:** desesperado
forlornly [fɔr'lɔrnli] *adv* **1** SADLY **:** con tristeza **2** HALFHEARTEDLY **:** sin ánimo
form[1] ['fɔrm] *vt* **1** FASHION, MAKE **:** formar **2** DEVELOP **:** moldear, desarrollar **3** CONSTITUTE **:** constituir, formar **4** ACQUIRE **:** adquirir (un hábito), formar (una idea) — *vi* **:** tomar forma, formarse
form[2] *n* **1** SHAPE **:** forma *f,* figura *f* **2** MANNER **:** manera *f,* forma *f* **3** DOCUMENT **:** formulario *m* **4 :** forma *f* <in good form : en buena forma> <true to form : en forma consecuente> **5** MOLD **:** molde *m* **6** KIND, VARIETY **:** clase *f,* tipo *m* **7 :** forma *f* (en gramática) <plural forms : formas plurales>
formal[1] ['fɔrməl] *adj* **1** CEREMONIOUS **:** formal, de etiqueta, ceremonioso **2** OFFICIAL **:** formal, oficial, de forma
formal[2] *n* **1** BALL **:** baile *m* formal, baile *m* de etiqueta **2** *or* **formal dress :** traje *m* de etiqueta
formaldehyde [fɔr'mældəˌhaɪd] *n* **:** formaldehído *m*
formality [fɔr'mæləţi] *n, pl* **-ties :** formalidad *f*
formalize ['fɔrməˌlaɪz] *vt* **-ized; -izing :** formalizar
formally ['fɔrməli] *adv* **:** formalmente
format[1] ['fɔrˌmæt] *vt* **-matted; -matting :** formatear
format[2] *n* **:** formato *m*
formation [fɔr'meɪʃən] *n* **1** FORMING **:** formación *f* **2** SHAPE **:** forma *f* **3 in formation :** en formación
formative ['fɔrməţɪv] *adj* **:** formativo
former ['fɔrmər] *adj* **1** PREVIOUS **:** antiguo, anterior <the former president : el antiguo presidente> **2 :** primero (de dos)
formerly ['fɔrmərli] *adv* **:** anteriormente, antes
formidable ['fɔrmədəbəl, fɔr'mɪdə-] *adj* **:** formidable — **formidably** *adv*

formless [ˈfɔrmləs] *adj* : informe, amorfo
formula [ˈfɔrmjələ] *n, pl* **-las** *or* **-lae** [-ˌliː, -ˌlaɪ] **1** : fórmula *f* **2 baby formula** : preparado *m* para biberón
formulate [ˈfɔrmjəˌleɪt] *vt* **-lated; -lating** : formular, hacer
formulation [ˌfɔrmjəˈleɪʃən] *n* : formulación *f*
fornicate [ˈfɔrnəˌkeɪt] *vi* **-cated; -cating** : fornicar
fornication [ˌfɔrnəˈkeɪʃən] *n* : fornicación *f*
forsake [fərˈseɪk] *vt* **-sook** [-ˈsʊk]; **-saken** [-ˈseɪkən]; **-saking 1** ABANDON : abandonar, desamparar **2** RELINQUISH : renunciar a
forswear [fɔrˈswær] *v* **-swore; -sworn; -swearing** *vt* RENOUNCE : renunciar a — *vi* : perjurar
forsythia [fərˈsɪθiə] *n* : forsitia *f*
fort [ˈfort] *n* **1** STRONGHOLD : fuerte *m,* fortaleza *f,* fortín *m* **2** BASE : base *f* militar
forte [ˈfort, ˈforˌteɪ] *n* : fuerte *m*
forth [ˈforθ] *adv* **1** : adelante <from this day forth : de hoy en adelante> **2 and so forth** : etcétera
forthcoming [forθˈkʌmɪŋ, ˈforθˌ-] *adj* **1** COMING : próximo **2** DIRECT, OPEN : directo, franco, comunicativo
forthright [ˈforθˌraɪt] *adj* : directo, franco — **forthrightly** *adv*
forthrightness [ˈforθˌraɪtnəs] *n* : franqueza *f*
forthwith [forθˈwɪθ, -ˈwɪð] *adv* : inmediatamente, en el acto, enseguida
fortieth[1] [ˈfɔrtiəθ] *adj* : cuadragésimo
fortieth[2] *n* **1** : cuadragésimo *m,* -ma *f* (en una serie) **2** : cuarentavo *m,* cuarentava parte *f*
fortification [ˌfɔrt̬əfəˈkeɪʃən] *n* : fortificación *f*
fortify [ˈfɔrt̬əˌfaɪ] *vt* **-fied; -fying** : fortificar
fortitude [ˈfɔrt̬əˌtuːd, -ˌtjuːd] *n* : fortaleza *f,* valor *m*
fortnight [ˈfortˌnaɪt] *n* : quince días *mpl,* dos semanas *fpl*
fortnightly[1] [ˈfortˌnaɪtli] *adv* : cada quince días
fortnightly[2] *adj* : quincenal
fortress [ˈfɔrtrəs] *n* : fortaleza *f*
fortuitous [fɔrˈtuːət̬əs, -ˈtjuː-] *adj* : fortuito, accidental
fortunate [ˈfɔrtʃənət] *adj* : afortunado
fortunately [ˈfɔrtʃənətli] *adv* : afortunadamente, con suerte
fortune [ˈfɔrtʃən] *n* **1** : fortuna *f* <to seek one's fortune : buscar uno su fortuna> **2** LUCK : suerte *f,* fortuna *f* **3** DESTINY, FUTURE : destino *m,* buenaventura *f* **4** : dineral *m,* platal *m* <she spent a fortune : se gastó un dineral>
fortune–teller [ˈfɔrtʃənˌtɛlər] *n* : adivino *m,* -na *f*
fortune–telling [ˈfɔrtʃənˌtɛlɪŋ] *n* : adivinación *f*
forty[1] [ˈfɔrti] *adj* : cuarenta
forty[2] *n, pl* **forties** : cuarenta *m*
forum [ˈforəm] *n, pl* **-rums** : foro *m*
forward[1] [ˈfɔrwərd] *vt* **1** PROMOTE : promover, adelantar, fomentar **2** SEND : remitir, enviar
forward[2] *adv* **1** : adelante, hacia adelante <to go forward : irse adelante> **2 from this day forward** : de aquí en adelante
forward[3] *adj* **1** : hacia adelante, delantero **2** BRASH : atrevido, descarado
forward[4] *n* : delantero *m,* -ra *f* (en deportes)
forwarder [ˈfɔrwərdər] *n* : agencia *f* de transportes, agente *mf* expedidor
forwardness [ˈfɔrwərdnəs] *n* : atrevimiento *m,* descaro *m*
forwards [ˈfɔrwərdz] → **forward[2]**
fossil[1] [ˈfɑsəl] *adj* : fósil
fossil[2] *n* : fósil *m*
fossilize [ˈfɑsəˌlaɪz] *vt* **-ized; -izing** : fosilizar — *vi* : fosilizarse
foster[1] [ˈfɔstər] *vt* : promover, fomentar
foster[2] *adj* : adoptivo <foster child : niño adoptivo>
fought → **fight**
foul[1] [ˈfaʊl] *vi* : cometer faltas (en deportes) — *vt* **1** DIRTY, POLLUTE : contaminar, ensuciar **2** TANGLE : enredar
foul[2] *adv* **1** → **foully 2** : contra las reglas
foul[3] *adj* **1** REPULSIVE : asqueroso, repugnante **2** CLOGGED : atascado, obstruido **3** TANGLED : enredado **4** OBSCENE : obsceno **5** BAD : malo <foul weather : mal tiempo> **6** : antirreglamentario (en deportes)
foul[4] *n* : falta *f,* faul *m*
foully [ˈfaʊli] *adv* : asquerosamente
foulmouthed [ˈfaʊlˌmæuːðd, -ˌmaʊθt] *adj* : malhablado
foulness [ˈfaʊlnəs] *n* **1** DIRTINESS : suciedad *f* **2** INCLEMENCY : inclemencia *f* **3** OBSCENITY : obscenidad *f,* grosería *f*
foul play *n* : actos *mpl* criminales
foul–up [ˈfaʊlˌʌp] *n* : lío *m,* confusión *f,* desastre *m*
foul up *vt* SPOIL : estropear, arruinar — *vi* BUNGLE : echar todo a perder
found[1] → **find**
found[2] [ˈfaʊnd] *vt* : fundar, establecer
foundation [faʊnˈdeɪʃən] *n* **1** FOUNDING : fundación *f* **2** BASIS : fundamento *m,* base *f* **3** INSTITUTION : fundación *f* **4** : cimientos *mpl* (de un edificio)
founder[1] [ˈfaʊndər] *vi* SINK : hundirse, irse a pique
founder[2] *n* : fundador *m,* -dora *f*
foundling [ˈfaʊndlɪŋ] *n* : expósito *m,* -ta *f*
foundry [ˈfaʊndri] *n, pl* **-dries** : fundición *f*
fount [ˈfaʊnt] *n* SOURCE : fuente *f,* origen *m*

fountain ['faʊntən] *n* 1 SPRING : fuente *f*, manantial *m* 2 SOURCE : fuente *f*, origen *m* 3 JET : chorro *m* (de agua), surtidor *m*
fountain pen *n* : pluma *f* fuente
four[1] ['for] *adj* : cuatro
four[2] *n* : cuatro *m*
fourfold ['for,fo:ld, -'fo:ld] *adj* : cuadruple
four hundred[1] *adj* : cuatrocientos
four hundred[2] *n* : cuatrocientos *m*
fourscore ['for'skor] *adj* EIGHTY : ochenta *m*
fourteen[1] [for'ti:n] *adj* : catorce
fourteen[2] *n* : catorce *m*
fourteenth[1] [for'ti:nθ] *adj* : decimocuarto
fourteenth[2] *n* 1 : decimocuarto *m*, -ta *f* (en una serie) 2 : catorceavo *m*, catorceava parte *f*
fourth[1] ['forθ] *adj* : cuarto
fourth[2] *n* 1 : cuarto *m*, -ta *f* (en una serie) 2 : cuarto *m*, cuarta parte *f*
fowl ['faʊl] *n, pl* **fowl** *or* **fowls** 1 BIRD : ave *f* 2 CHICKEN : pollo *m*
fox[1] ['faks] *vt* 1 TRICK : engañar 2 BAFFLE : confundir
fox[2] *n, pl* **foxes** : zorro *m*, -ra *f*
foxglove ['faks,glʌv] *n* : dedalera *f*, digital *f*
foxhole ['faks,ho:l] *n* : hoyo *m* para atrincherarse, trinchera *f* individual
foxy ['faksi] *adj* **foxier; -est** SHREWD : astuto
foyer ['fɔɪər, 'fɔɪ,jeɪ] *n* : vestíbulo *m*
fracas ['freɪkəs, 'fræ-] *n, pl* **-cases** [-kəsəz] : altercado *m*, pelea *f*, reyerta *f*
fraction ['frækʃən] *n* 1 : fracción *f*, quebrado *m* 2 PORTION : porción *f*, parte *f*
fractional ['frækʃənəl] *adj* 1 : fraccionario 2 TINY : minúsculo, mínimo, insignificante
fractious ['frækʃəs] *adj* 1 UNRULY : rebelde 2 IRRITABLE : malhumorado, irritable
fracture[1] ['fræktʃər] *vt* **-tured; -turing** : fracturar
fracture[2] *n* 1 : fractura *f* (de un hueso) 2 CRACK : fisura *f*, grieta *f*, falla *f* (geológica)
fragile ['frædʒəl, -,dʒaɪl] *adj* : frágil
fragility [frə'dʒɪləṭi] *n, pl* **-ties** : fragilidad *f*
fragment[1] ['fræg,mɛnt] *vt* : fragmentar — *vi* : fragmentarse, hacerse añicos
fragment[2] ['frægmənt] *n* : fragmento *m*, trozo *m*, pedazo *m*
fragmentary ['frægmən,tɛri] *adj* : fragmentario, incompleto
fragmentation [,frægmən'teɪʃən, -,mɛn-] *n* : fragmentación *f*
fragrance ['freɪgrənts] *n* : fragancia *f*, aroma *m*
fragrant ['freɪgrənt] *adj* : fragante, aromático — **fragrantly** *adv*
frail ['freɪl] *adj* : débil, delicado
frailty ['freɪlti] *n, pl* **-ties** : debilidad *f*, flaqueza *f*
frame[1] ['freɪm] *vt* **framed; framing** 1 FORMULATE : formular, elaborar 2 BORDER : enmarcar, encuadrar 3 INCRIMINATE : incriminar
frame[2] *n* 1 BODY : cuerpo *m* 2 : armazón *f* (de un edificio, un barco, o un avión), bastidor *m* (de un automóvil), cuadro *m* (de una bicicleta), marco *m* (de un cuadro, una ventana, una puerta, etc.) 3 **frames** *npl* : armazón *mf*, montura *f* (para anteojos) 4 **frame of mind** : estado *m* de ánimo
framework ['freɪm,wərk] *n* 1 SKELETON, STRUCTURE : armazón *f*, estructura *f* 2 BASIS : marco *m*
franc ['fræŋk] *n* : franco *m*
franchise ['fræn,tʃaɪz] *n* 1 LICENSE : licencia *f* exclusiva, concesión *f* (en comercio) 2 SUFFRAGE : sufragio *m*
franchisee [,fræn,tʃaɪ'zi:, -tʃə-] *n* : concesionario *m*, -ria *f*
frank[1] ['fræŋk] *vt* : franquear
frank[2] *adj* : franco, sincero, cándido — **frankly** *adv*
frank[3] *n* : franqueo *m* (de correo)
frankfurter ['fræŋkfərṭər, -,fər-] *or* **frankfurt** [-fərt] *n* : salchicha *f* (de Frankfurt, de Viena), perro *m* caliente
frankincense ['fræŋkən,sɛnts] *n* : incienso *m*
frankness ['fræŋknəs] *n* : franqueza *f*, sinceridad *f*, candidez *f*
frantic ['fræntɪk] *adj* : frenético, desesperado — **frantically** *adv*
fraternal [frə'tərnəl] *adj* : fraterno, fraternal
fraternity [frə'tərnəṭi] *n, pl* **-ties** : fraternidad *f*
fraternization [,frætərnə'zeɪʃən] *n* : fraternización *f*, confraternización *f*
fraternize ['frætər,naɪz] *vi* **-nized; -nizing** : fraternizar, confraternizar
fratricidal [,frætrə'saɪdəl] *adj* : fratricida
fratricide ['frætrə,saɪd] *n* : fratricidio *m*
fraud ['frɔd] *n* 1 DECEPTION, SWINDLE : fraude *m*, estafa *f*, engaño *m* 2 IMPOSTOR : impostor *m*, -tora *f*; farsante *mf*
fraudulent ['frɔdʒələnt] *adj* : fraudulento — **fraudulently** *adv*
fraught ['frɔt] *adj* **fraught with** : lleno de, cargado de
fray[1] ['freɪ] *vt* 1 WEAR : desgastar, deshilachar 2 IRRITATE : crispar, irritar (los nervios) — *vi* : desgastarse, deshilacharse
fray[2] *n* : pelea *f*, lucha *f*, refriega *f*
frazzle[1] ['fræzəl] *vt* **-zled; -zling** 1 FRAY : desgastar, deshilachar 2 EXHAUST : agotar, fatigar
frazzle[2] *n* EXHAUSTION : agotamiento *m*
freak ['fri:k] *n* 1 ODDITY : ejemplar *m* anormal, fenómeno *m*, rareza *f* 2 ENTHUSIAST : entusiasta *mf*

freakish ['fri:kɪʃ] *adj* : extraño, estrafalario, raro
freckle[1] ['frɛkəl] *vi* **-led; -ling** : cubrirse de pecas
freckle[2] *n* : peca *f*
free[1] ['fri:] *vt* **freed; freeing 1** LIBERATE : libertar, liberar, poner en libertad **2** RELIEVE, RID : librar, eximir **3** RELEASE, UNTIE : desatar, soltar **4** UNCLOG : desatascar, destapar
free[2] *adv* **1** FREELY : libremente **2** GRATIS : gratuitamente, gratis
free[3] *adj* **freer; freest 1** : libre <free as a bird : libre como un pájaro> **2** EXEMPT : libre <tax-free : libre de impuestos> **3** GRATIS : gratuito, gratis **4** VOLUNTARY : espontáneo, voluntario, libre **5** UNOCCUPIED : desocupado, libre **6** LOOSE : suelto
freebooter ['fri:ˌbu:t̬ər] *n* : pirata *mf*
freeborn ['fri:'bɔrn] *adj* : nacido libre
freedom ['fri:dəm] *n* : libertad *f*
free–for–all ['fri:fərˌɔl] *n* : pelea *f*, batalla *f* campal
freelance[1] ['fri:ˌlænts] *vi* **-lanced; -lancing** : trabajar por cuenta propia
freelance[2] *adj* : por cuenta propia, independiente
freeload ['fri:ˌlo:d] *vi* : gorronear *fam*, gorrear *fam*
freeloader ['fri:ˌlo:dər] *n* : gorrón *m*, -rrona *f;* gorrero *m*, -ra *f;* vividor *m*, -dora *f*
freely ['fri:li] *adv* **1** FREE : libremente **2** GRATIS : gratis, gratuitamente
freestanding ['fri:'stændɪŋ] *adj* : de pie, no empotrado, independiente
freeway ['fri:ˌweɪ] *n* : autopista *f*
freewill ['fri:ˌwɪl] *adj* : de propia voluntad
free will *n* : libre albedrío *m*, propia voluntad *f*
freeze[1] ['fri:z] *v* **froze** ['fro:z]; **frozen** ['fro:zən]; **freezing** *vi* **1** : congelarse, helarse <the water froze in the lake : el agua se congeló en el lago> <my blood froze : se me heló la sangre> <I'm freezing : me estoy helando> **2** STOP : quedarse inmóvil — *vt* : helar, congelar (líquidos), congelar (alimentos, precios, activos)
freeze[2] *n* **1** FROST : helada *f* **2** FREEZING : congelación *f*, congelamiento *m*
freeze–dried ['fri:z'draɪd] *adj* : liofilizado
freeze–dry ['fri:z'draɪ] *vt* **-dried; -drying** : liofilizar
freezer ['fri:zər] *n* : congelador *m*
freezing ['fri:zɪŋ] *adj* : helando <it's freezing! : ¡hace un frío espantoso!>
freezing point *n* : punto *m* de congelación
freight[1] ['freɪt] *vt* : enviar como carga
freight[2] *n* **1** SHIPPING, TRANSPORT : transporte *m*, porte *m*, flete *m* **2** GOODS : mercancías *fpl*, carga *f*
freighter ['freɪt̬ər] *n* : carguero *m*, buque *m* de carga
French[1] ['frɛntʃ] *adj* : francés
French[2] *n* **1** : francés *m* (idioma) **2 the French** *npl* : los franceses
Frenchman ['frɛntʃmən] *n, pl* **-men** [-mən, -ˌmɛn] : francés *m*
Frenchwoman ['frɛntʃˌwʊmən] *n, pl* **-women** [-ˌwɪmən] : francesa *f*
french fries ['frɛntʃˌfraɪz] *npl* : papas *fpl* fritas
frenetic [frɪ'nɛt̬ɪk] *adj* : frenético — **frenetically** [-t̬ɪkli] *adv*
frenzied ['frɛnzid] *adj* : frenético
frenzy ['frɛnzi] *n, pl* **-zies** : frenesí *m*
frequency ['fri:kwəntsi] *n, pl* **-cies** : frecuencia *f*
frequent[1] [fri'kwɛnt, 'fri:kwənt] *vt* : frecuentar
frequent[2] ['fri:kwənt] *adj* : frecuente — **frequently** *adv*
fresco ['frɛsˌko:] *n, pl* **-coes** : fresco *m*
fresh ['frɛʃ] *adj* **1** : dulce <freshwater : agua dulce> **2** PURE : puro **3** : fresco <fresh fruits : frutas frescas> **4** CLEAN, NEW : limpio, nuevo <fresh clothes : ropa limpia> <fresh evidence : evidencia nueva> **5** REFRESHED : fresco, descansado **6** IMPERTINENT : descarado, impertinente
freshen ['frɛʃən] *vt* : refrescar, arreglar — *vi* **to freshen up** : arreglarse, lavarse
freshet ['frɛʃət] *n* : arroyo *m* desbordado
freshly ['frɛʃli] *adv* : recientemente, recién
freshman ['frɛʃmən] *n, pl* **-men** [-mən, -ˌmɛn] : estudiante *mf* de primer año universitario
freshness ['frɛʃnəs] *n* : frescura *f*
freshwater ['frɛʃˌwɔt̬ər] *n* : agua *f* dulce
fret[1] ['frɛt] *vi* **fretted; fretting** : preocuparse, inquietarse
fret[2] *n* **1** VEXATION : irritación *f*, molestia *f* **2** WORRY : preocupación *f* **3** : traste *m* (de un instrumento musical)
fretful ['frɛtfəl] *adj* : fastidioso, quejoso, neurótico
fretfully ['frɛtfəli] *adv* : ansiosamente, fastidiosamente, inquieto
fretfulness ['frɛtfəlnəs] *n* : inquietud *f*, irritabilidad *f*
friable ['fraɪəbəl] *adj* : friable, pulverizable
friar ['fraɪər] *n* : fraile *m*
fricassee[1] ['frɪkəˌsi:, ˌfrɪkə'si:] *vt* **-seed; -seeing** : cocinar al fricasé
fricassee[2] *n* : fricasé *m*
friction ['frɪkʃən] *n* **1** RUBBING : fricción *f* **2** CONFLICT : fricción *f*, roce *m*
Friday ['fraɪˌdeɪ, -di] *n* : viernes *m*
fridge ['frɪdʒ] → **refrigerator**
friend ['frɛnd] *n* : amigo *m*, -ga *f*
friendless ['frɛndləs] *adj* : sin amigos
friendliness ['frɛndlinəs] *n* : simpatía *f*, amabilidad *f*
friendly ['frɛndli] *adj* **-lier; -est 1** : simpático, amable, de amigo <a friendly child : un niño simpático> <friendly advice : consejo de amigo>

2 : agradable, acogedor <a friendly atmosphere : un ambiente agradable> 3 GOOD-NATURED : amigable, amistoso <friendly competition : competencia amistosa>

friendship [frɛnd,ʃɪp] *n* : amistad *f*

frieze [ˈfriːz] *n* : friso *m*

frigate [ˈfrɪgət] *n* : fragata *f*

fright [ˈfraɪt] *n* : miedo *m,* susto *m*

frighten [ˈfraitən] *vt* : asustar, espantar

frightened [ˈfraitənd] *adj* : asustado, temeroso

frightening [ˈfraitənɪŋ] *adj* : espantoso, aterrador

frightful [ˈfraɪtfəl] *adj* **1** → **frightening** **2** TREMENDOUS : espantoso, tremendo

frightfully [ˈfraɪtfəli] *adv* : terriblemente, tremendamente

frigid [ˈfrɪdʒɪd] *adj* : glacial, extremadamente frío

frigidity [frɪˈdʒɪdəti] *n* **1** COLDNESS : frialdad *f* **2** : frigidez *f* (sexual)

frill [ˈfrɪl] *n* **1** RUFFLE : volante *m* **2** EMBELLISHMENT : floritura *f,* adorno *m*

frilly [ˈfrɪli] *adj* **frillier; -est** **1** RUFFLY : con volantes **2** OVERDONE : recargado

fringe[1] [ˈfrɪndʒ] *vt* **fringed; fringing** : orlar, bordear

fringe[2] *n* **1** BORDER : fleco *m,* orla *f* **2** EDGE : periferia *f,* margen *m* **3 fringe benefits** : incentivos *mpl*, extras *mpl*

frisk [ˈfrɪsk] *vi* FROLIC : retozar, juguetear — *vt* SEARCH : cachear, registrar

friskiness [ˈfrɪskinəs] *n* : vivacidad *f*

frisky [ˈfrɪski] *adj* **friskier; -est** : retozón, juguetón

fritter[1] [ˈfrɪtər] *vt* : desperdiciar, malgastar <I frittered away the money : malgasté el dinero>

fritter[2] *n* : buñuelo *m*

frivolity [frɪˈvɑləti] *n, pl* **-ties** : frivolidad *f*

frivolous [ˈfrɪvələs] *adj* : frívolo, de poca importancia

frivolously [ˈfrɪvələsli] *adv* : frívolamente, a la ligera

frizz[1] [ˈfrɪz] *vi* : rizarse, encresparse, ponerse chino *Mex*

frizz[2] *n* : rizos *mpl* muy apretados

frizzy [ˈfrɪzi] *adj* **frizzier; -est** : rizado, crespo, chino *Mex*

fro [ˈfroː] *adv* **to and fro** : de aquí para allá, de un lado para otro

frock [ˈfrɑk] *n* DRESS : vestido *m*

frog [ˈfrɔg, ˈfrɑg] *n* **1** : rana *f* **2** FASTENER : alamar *m* 3 **to have a frog in one's throat** : tener carraspera

frogman [ˈfrɔg,mæn, ˈfrɑg-, -mən] *n, pl* **-men** [-mən, -,mɛn] : hombre *m* rana, submarinista *mf*

frolic[1] [ˈfrɑlɪk] *vi* **-icked; -icking** : retozar, juguetear

frolic[2] *n* FUN : diversión *f*

frolicsome [ˈfrɑlɪksəm] *adj* : juguetón

from [ˈfrʌm, ˈfrɑm] *prep* **1** (*indicating a starting point*) : desde, de, a partir de <from Cali to Bogota : de Cali a Bogotá> <where are you from? : ¿de dónde eres?> <from that time onward : desde entonces> <from tomorrow : a partir de mañana> **2** (*indicating a source or sender*) : de <a letter from my friend : una carta de mi amiga> <a quote from Shakespeare : una cita de Shakespeare> **3** (*indicating distance*) : de <10 feet from the entrance : a 10 pies de la entrada> **4** (*indicating a cause*) : de <red from crying : rojos de llorar> <he died from the cold : murió del frío> **5** OFF, OUT OF : de <she took it from the drawer : lo sacó del cajón> **6** (*with adverbs or adverbial phrases*) : de, desde <from above : desde arriba> <from among : de entre>

frond [ˈfrɑnd] *n* : fronda *f,* hoja *f*

front[1] [ˈfrʌnt] *vi* **1** FACE : dar, estar orientado <the house fronts north : la casa da al norte> **2** : servir de pantalla <he fronts for his boss : sirve de pantalla para su jefe>

front[2] *adj* : delantero, de adelante, primero <the front row : la primera fila>

front[3] *n* **1** : frente *m,* parte *f* de adelante, delantera *f* <the front of the class : el frente de la clase> <at the front of the train : en la parte delantera del tren> **2** AREA, ZONE : frente *m,* zona *f* <the Eastern front : el frente oriental> <on the educational front : en el frente de la enseñanza> **3** FACADE : fachada *f* (de un edificio o una persona> **4** : frente *m* (en meteorología)

frontage [ˈfrʌntɪdʒ] *n* : fachada *f,* frente *m*

frontal [ˈfrʌntəl] *adj* : frontal, de frente

frontier [,frʌnˈtɪr] *n* : frontera *f*

frontiersman [,frʌnˈtɪrzmən] *n, pl* **-men** [-mən, -,mɛn] : hombre *m* de la frontera

frontispiece [ˈfrʌntəs,piːs] *n* : frontispicio *m*

frost[1] [ˈfrɔst] *vt* **1** FREEZE : helar **2** ICE : escarchar (pasteles)

frost[2] *n* **1** : helada *f* (en meteorología) **2** : escarcha *f* <frost on the window : escarcha en la ventana>

frostbite [ˈfrɔst,baɪt] *n* : congelación *f*

frostbitten [ˈfrɔst,bɪtən] *adj* : congelado (dícese de una persona), quemado (dícese de una planta)

frosting [ˈfrɔstɪŋ] *n* ICING : glaseado *m,* betún *m Mex*

frosty [ˈfrɔsti] *adj* **frostier; -est** **1** CHILLY : helado, frío **2** COOL, UNFRIENDLY : frío, glacial

froth [ˈfrɔθ] *n, pl* **froths** [ˈfrɔθs, ˈfrɔðz] : espuma *f*

frothy [ˈfrɔθi] *adj* **frothier; -est** : espumoso

frown[1] [ˈfraʊn] *vi* **1** : fruncir el ceño, fruncir el entrecejo **2 to frown at**

: mirar (algo) con ceño, mirar (a alguien) con ceño
frown[2] *n* : ceño *m* (fruncido)
frowsy *or* **frowzy** [ˈfraʊzi] *adj* **frowsier** *or* **frowzier; -est** : desaliñado, desaseado
froze → **freeze**
frozen → **freeze**
frugal [ˈfruːgəl] *adj* : frugal, ahorrativo, parco — **frugally** *adv*
frugality [fruˈgæləṭi] *n* : frugalidad *f*
fruit[1] [ˈfruːt] *vi* : dar fruto
fruit[2] *n* **1** : fruta *f* (término genérico), fruto *m* (término particular) **2 fruits** *npl* REWARDS : frutos *mpl* <the fruits of his labor : los frutos de su trabajo>
fruitcake [ˈfruːtˌkeɪk] *n* : pastel *m* de frutas
fruitful [ˈfruːtfəl] *adj* : fructífero, provechoso
fruition [fruˈɪʃən] *n* **1** : cumplimiento *m*, realización *f* **2 to bring to fruition** : realizar
fruitless [ˈfruːtləs] *adj* : infructuoso, inútil — **fruitlessly** *adv*
fruity [ˈfruːṭi] *adj* **fruitier; -est** : (con sabor) a fruta
frumpy [ˈfrʌmpi] *adj* **frumpier; -est** : anticuado y sin atractivo
frustrate [ˈfrʌsˌtreɪt] *vt* **-trated; -trating** : frustrar
frustrating [ˈfrʌsˌtreɪṭɪŋ] *adj* : frustrante — **frustratingly** *adv*
frustration [ˌfrʌsˈtreɪʃən] *n* : frustración *f*
fry[1] [ˈfraɪ] *vt* **fried; frying** : freír
fry[2] *n, pl* **fries 1** : fritura *f*, plato *m* frito **2** : fiesta *f* en que se sirven frituras **3** *pl* **fry** : alevín *m* (pez)
fuddle [ˈfʌdəl] *vt* **-dled; -dling** : confundir, atontar
fuddy–duddy [ˈfʌdiˌdʌdi] *n, pl* **-dies** : persona *f* chapada a la antigua, carca *mf*
fudge[1] [ˈfʌdʒ] *vt* **fudged; fudging 1** FALSIFY : amañar, falsificar **2** DODGE : esquivar
fudge[2] *n* : dulce *m* blando de chocolate y leche
fuel[1] [ˈfjuːəl] *vt* **-eled** *or* **-elled; -eling** *or* **-elling 1** : abastecer de combustible **2** STIMULATE : estimular
fuel[2] *n* : combustible *m*, carburante *m* (para motores)
fugitive[1] [ˈfjuːdʒəṭɪv] *adj* **1** RUNAWAY : fugitivo **2** FLEETING : efímero, pasajero, fugaz
fugitive[2] *n* : fugitivo *m*, -va *f*
fulcrum [ˈfʊlkrəm, ˈfʌl-] *n, pl* **-crums** *or* **-cra** [-krə] : fulcro *m*
fulfill *or* **fulfil** [fʊlˈfɪl] *vt* **-filled; -filling 1** PERFORM : cumplir con, realizar, llevar a cabo **2** SATISFY : satisfacer
fulfillment [fʊlˈfɪlmənt] *n* **1** PERFORMANCE : cumplimiento *m*, ejecución *f* **2** SATISFACTION : satisfacción *f*, realización *f*
full[1] [ˈfʊl, ˈfʌl] *adv* **1** VERY : muy <full well : muy bien, perfectamente> **2** ENTIRELY : completamente <she swung full around : giró completamente> **3** DIRECTLY : de lleno, directamente <he looked me full in the face : me miró directamente a la cara>
full[2] *adj* **1** FILLED : lleno **2** COMPLETE : completo, detallado **3** MAXIMUM : todo, pleno <at full speed : a toda velocidad> <in full bloom : en plena flor> **4** PLUMP : redondo, llenito *fam*, regordete *fam* <a full face : una cara redonda> <a full figure : un cuerpo llenito> **5** AMPLE : amplio <a full skirt : una falda amplia>
full[3] *n* **1 to pay in full** : pagar en su totalidad **2 to the full** : al máximo
full–fledged [ˈfʊlˈflɛdʒd] *adj* : hecho y derecho
fullness [ˈfʊlnəs] *n* **1** ABUNDANCE : plenitud *f*, abundancia *f* **2** : amplitud *f* (de una falda)
fully [ˈfʊli] *adv* **1** COMPLETELY : completamente, totalmente **2** : al menos, por lo menos <fully half of them : al menos la mitad de ellos>
fulsome [ˈfʊlsəm] *adj* : excesivo, exagerado, efusivo
fumble[1] [ˈfʌmbəl] *v* **-bled; -bling** *vt* **1** : dejar caer, fumblear **2 to fumble one's way** : ir a tientas — *vi* **1** GROPE : hurgar, tantear **2 to fumble with** : manejar con torpeza
fumble[2] *n* : fumble *m* (en futbol americano)
fume[1] [ˈfjuːm] *vi* **fumed; fuming 1** SMOKE : echar humo, humear **2** : enfadarse, enojarse
fume[2] *n* : gas *m*, humo *m*, vapor *m*
fumigate [ˈfjuːməˌgeɪt] *vt* **-gated; -gating** : fumigar
fumigation [ˌfjuːməˈgeɪʃən] *n* : fumigación *m*
fun[1] [ˈfʌn] *adj* : divertido, entretenido
fun[2] *n* **1** AMUSEMENT : diversión *f*, entretenimiento *m* **2** ENJOYMENT : disfrute *m* **3 to have fun** : divertirse **4 to make fun of** : reírse de, burlarse de
function[1] [ˈfʌŋkʃən] *vi* : funcionar, desempeñarse, servir
function[2] *n* **1** PURPOSE : función *f* **2** GATHERING : reunión *f* social, recepción *f* **3** CEREMONY : ceremonia *f*, acto *m*
functional [ˈfʌŋkʃənəl] *adj* : funcional — **functionally** *adv*
functionary [ˈfʌŋkʃəˌnɛri] *n, pl* **-aries** : funcionario *m*, -ria *f*
fund[1] [ˈfʌnd] *vt* : financiar
fund[2] *n* **1** SUPPLY : reserva *f*, cúmulo *m* **2** : fondo *m* <investment fund : fondo de inversiones> **3 funds** *npl* RESOURCES : fondos *mpl*
fundamental[1] [ˌfʌndəˈmɛntəl] *adj* **1** BASIC : fundamental, básico **2** PRINCIPAL : esencial, principal **3** INNATE : innato, intrínseco
fundamental[2] *n* : fundamento *m*

fundamentally [ˌfʌndəˈmɛntəli] *adv* : fundamentalmente, básicamente

funding [ˈfʌndɪŋ] *n* : financiación *f*

funeral[1] [ˈfjuːnərəl] *adj* **1** : funeral, funerario, fúnebre <funeral procession : cortejo fúnebre> **2 funeral home** : funeraria *f*

funeral[2] *n* : funeral *m,* funerales *mpl*

funereal [fjuːˈnɪriəl] *adj* : fúnebre

fungal [ˈfʌŋgəl] *adj* : de hongos, micótico

fungicidal [ˌfʌndʒəˈsaɪdəl, ˌfʌŋgə-] *adj* : fungicida

fungicide [ˈfʌndʒəˌsaɪd, ˈfʌŋgə-] *n* : fungicida *m*

fungous [ˈfʌŋgəs] *adj* : fungoso

fungus [ˈfʌŋgəs] *n, pl* **fungi** [ˈfʌnˌdʒaɪ, ˈfʌŋˌgaɪ] : hongo *m*

funk [ˈfʌŋk] *n* **1** FEAR : miedo *m* **2** DEPRESSION : depresión *f*

funky [ˈfʌŋki] *adj* **funkier; -est** ODD, QUAINT : raro, extraño, original

funnel[1] [ˈfʌnəl] *vt* **-neled; -neling** CHANNEL : canalizar, encauzar

funnel[2] *n* **1** : embudo *m* **2** SMOKESTACK : chimenea *f* (de un barco o vapor)

funnies [ˈfʌniz] *npl* : tiras *fpl* cómicas

funny [ˈfʌni] *adj* **funnier; -est 1** AMUSING : divertido, cómico **2** STRANGE : extraño, raro

fur[1] [ˈfər] *adj* : de piel

fur[2] *n* **1** : pelaje *m,* piel *f* **2** : prenda *f* de piel

furbish [ˈfərbɪʃ] *vt* : pulir, limpiar

furious [ˈfjʊriəs] *adj* **1** ANGRY : furioso **2** FRANTIC : violento, frenético, vertiginoso (dícese de la velocidad)

furiously [ˈfjʊriəsli] *adv* **1** ANGRILY : furiosamente **2** FRANTICALLY : frenéticamente

furlong [ˈfərˌlɔŋ] *n* : estadio *m* (201.2 m)

furlough[1] [ˈfərˌloː] *vt* : dar permiso a, dar licencia a

furlough[2] *n* LEAVE : permiso *m,* licencia *f*

furnace [ˈfərnəs] *n* : horno *m*

furnish [ˈfərnɪʃ] *vt* **1** SUPPLY : proveer, suministrar **2** : amueblar <furnished apartment : departamento amueblado>

furnishings [ˈfərnɪʃɪŋz] *npl* **1** ACCESSORIES : accesorios *mpl* **2** FURNITURE : muebles *mpl,* mobiliario *m*

furniture [ˈfərnɪtʃər] *n* : muebles *mpl,* mobiliario *m*

furor [ˈfjʊrˌɔr, -ər] *n* **1** RAGE : furia *f,* rabia *f* **2** UPROAR : escándalo *m,* jaleo *m,* alboroto *m*

furrier [ˈfəriər] *n* : peletero *m,* -ra *f*

furrow[1] [ˈfəroː] *vt* **1** : surcar **2 to furrow one's brow** : fruncir el ceño

furrow[2] *n* **1** GROOVE : surco *m* **2** WRINKLE : arruga *f,* surco *m*

furry [ˈfəri] *adj* **furrier; -est** : peludo (dícese de un animal), peluche (dícese de un objeto)

further[1] [ˈfərðər] *vt* : promover, fomentar

further[2] *adv* **1** FARTHER : más lejos, más adelante **2** MOREOVER : además **3** MORE : más <I'll consider it further in the morning : lo consideraré más en la mañana>

further[3] *adj* **1** FARTHER : más lejano **2** ADDITIONAL : adicional, más

furtherance [ˈfərðərənts] *n* : promoción *f,* fomento *m,* adelantamiento *m*

furthermore [ˈfərðərˌmor] *adv* : además

furthermost [ˈfərðərˌmoːst] *adj* : más lejano, más distante

furthest [ˈfərðəst] → **farthest**[1], **farthest**[2]

furtive [ˈfərt̬ɪv] *adj* : furtivo, sigiloso — **furtively** *adv*

furtiveness [ˈfərt̬ɪvnəs] *n* STEALTH : sigilo *m*

fury [ˈfjʊri] *n, pl* **-ries 1** RAGE : furia *f,* ira *f* **2** VIOLENCE : furia *f,* furor *m*

fuse[1] [ˈfjuːz] *or* **fuze** *vt* **fused** *or* **fuzed; fusing** *or* **fuzing** : equipar con un fusible

fuse[2] *v* **fused; fusing** *vt* **1** SMELT : fundir **2** MERGE : fusionar, fundir — *vi* : fundirse, fusionarse

fuse[3] *n* : fusible *m*

fuselage [ˈfjuːsəˌlɑʒ, -zə-] *n* : fuselage *m*

fusillade [ˈfjuːsəˌlɑd, -ˌleɪd, ˌfjuːsəˈ-, -zə-] *n* : descarga *f* de fusilería

fusion [ˈfjuːʒən] *n* : fusión *f*

fuss[1] [ˈfʌs] *vi* **1** WORRY : preocuparse **2 to fuss with** : juguetear con, toquetear **3 to fuss over** : mimar

fuss[2] *n* **1** COMMOTION : alboroto *m,* escándalo *m* **2** ATTENTION : atenciones *fpl* **3** COMPLAINT : quejas *fpl*

fussbudget [ˈfʌsˌbʌdʒət] *n* : quisquilloso *m,* -sa *f;* melindroso *m,* -sa *f*

fussiness [ˈfʌsinəs] *n* **1** IRRITABILITY : irritabilidad *f* **2** ORNATENESS : lo recargado **3** METICULOUSNESS : meticulosidad *f*

fussy [ˈfʌsi] *adj* **fussier; -est 1** IRRITABLE : irritable, nervioso **2** OVERELABORATE : recargado **3** METICULOUS : meticuloso **4** FASTIDIOUS : quisquilloso, exigente

futile [ˈfjuːt̬əl, ˈfjuːˌtaɪl] *adj* : inútil, vano

futility [fjuˈtɪlət̬i] *n, pl* **-ties** : inutilidad *f*

future[1] [ˈfjuːtʃər] *adj* : futuro

future[2] *n* : futuro *m*

futuristic [ˌfjuːtʃəˈrɪstɪk] *adj* : futurista

fuze → **fuse**[1]

fuzz [ˈfʌz] *n* : pelusa *f*

fuzziness [ˈfʌzinəs] *n* **1** DOWNINESS : vellosidad *f* **2** INDISTINCTNESS : falta *f* de claridad

fuzzy [ˈfʌzi] *adj* **fuzzier; -est 1** FLUFFY, FURRY : con pelusa, peludo **2** INDISTINCT : indistinto, borroso

G

g [ˈdʒiː] *n, pl* **g's** *or* **gs** [ˈdʒiːz] : séptima letra del alfabeto inglés

gab[1] [ˈgæb] *vi* **gabbed; gabbing** : charlar, cotorrear *fam,* parlotear *fam*

gab[2] *n* CHATTER : cotorreo *m fam,* parloteo *m fam*

gabardine [ˈgæbərˌdiːn] *n* : gabardina *f*

gabby [ˈgæbi] *adj* **gabbier; -est** : hablador, parlanchín

gable [ˈgeɪbəl] *n* : hastial *m,* aguilón *m*

Gabonese [ˌgæbəˈnɪːz, -ˈnɪːs] *n* : gabonés *m,* -nesa *f* — **Gabonese** *adj*

gad [ˈgæd] *vi* **gadded; gadding** WANDER : deambular, vagar, callejear

gadfly [ˈgædˌflaɪ] *n, pl* **-flies 1** : tábano *m* (insecto) **2** FAULTFINDER : criticón *m,* -cona *f fam*

gadget [ˈgædʒət] *n* : artilugio *m,* aparato *m*

gadgetry [ˈgædʒətri] *n* : artilugios *mpl,* aparatos *mpl*

gaff [ˈgæf] *n* **1** : garfio *m* **2** → **gaffe**

gaffe [ˈgæf] *n* : metedura *f* de pata *fam*

gag[1] [ˈgæg] *v* **gagged; gagging** *vt* : amordazar <to tie up and gag : atar y amordazar> — *vi* **1** CHOKE : atragantarse **2** RETCH : hacer arcadas

gag[2] *n* **1** : mordaza *f* (para la boca) **2** JOKE : chiste *m*

gage → **gauge**

gaggle [ˈgægəl] *n* : bandada *f,* manada *f* (de gansos)

gaiety [ˈgeɪəti] *n, pl* **-eties 1** MERRYMAKING : juerga *f* **2** MERRIMENT : alegría *f,* regocijo *m*

gaily [ˈgeɪli] *adv* : alegremente

gain[1] [ˈgeɪn] *vt* **1** ACQUIRE, OBTAIN : ganar, obtener, adquirir, conseguir <to gain knowledge : adquirir conocimientos> <to gain a victory : obtener una victoria> **2** REACH : alcanzar, llegar a **3** INCREASE : ganar, aumentar <to gain weight : aumentar de peso> **4** : adelantarse, ganar <the watch gains two minutes a day : el reloj se adelanta dos minutos por día> — *vi* **1** PROFIT : beneficiarse **2** INCREASE : aumentar

gain[2] *n* **1** PROFIT : beneficio *m,* ganancia *f,* lucro *m,* provecho *m* **2** INCREASE : aumento *m*

gainful [ˈgeɪnfəl] *adj* : lucrativo, beneficioso, provechoso <gainful employment : trabajo remunerado>

gait [ˈgeɪt] *n* : paso *m,* andar *m,* manera *f* de caminar

gal [ˈgæl] *n* : muchacha *f*

gala[1] [ˈgeɪlə, ˈgæ-, ˈgɑ-] *adj* : de gala

gala[2] *n* : gala *f,* fiesta *f*

galactic [gəˈlæktɪk] *adj* : galáctico

galaxy [ˈgæləksi] *n, pl* **-axies** : galaxia *f*

gale [ˈgeɪl] *n* **1** WIND : vendaval *f,* viento *m* fuerte **2 gales of laughter** : carcajadas *fpl*

gall[1] [ˈgɔl] *vt* **1** CHAFE : rozar **2** IRRITATE, VEX : irritar, molestar

gall[2] *n* **1** BILE : bilis *f,* hiel *f* **2** INSOLENCE : audacidad *f,* insolencia *f,* descaro *m* **3** SORE : rozadura *f* (de un caballo) **4** : agalla *f* (de una planta)

gallant [ˈgælənt] *adj* **1** BRAVE : valiente, gallardo **2** CHIVALROUS, POLITE : galante, cortés

gallantry [ˈgæləntri] *n, pl* **-ries** : galantería *f,* caballerosidad *f*

gallbladder [ˈgɔlˌblædər] *n* : vesícula *f* biliar

galleon [ˈgæljən] *n* : galeón *m*

gallery [ˈgæləri] *n, pl* **-leries 1** BALCONY : galería *f* (para espectadores) **2** CORRIDOR : pasillo *m,* galería *f,* corredor *m* **3** : galería *f* (para exposiciones)

galley [ˈgæli] *n, pl* **-leys** : galera *f*

gallium [ˈgæliəm] *n* : galio *m*

gallivant [ˈgæləˌvænt] *vi* : callejear

gallon [ˈgælən] *n* : galón *m*

gallop[1] [ˈgæləp] *vi* : galopar

gallop[2] *n* : galope *m*

gallows [ˈgæˌloːz] *n, pl* **-lows** *or* **-lowses** [-ˌloːzəz] : horca *f*

gallstone [ˈgɔlˌstoːn] *n* : cálculo *m* biliar

galore [gəˈlor] *adj* : en abundancia <bargains galore : muchísimas gangas>

galoshes [gəˈlɑʃəz] *n* : galochas *fpl,* chanclos *mpl*

galvanize [ˈgælvənˌaɪz] *vt* **-nized; -nizing 1** STIMULATE : estimular, excitar, impulsar **2** : galvanizar (metales)

Gambian [ˈgæmbiən] *n* : gambiano *m,* -na *f* — **Gambian** *adj*

gambit [ˈgæmbɪt] *n* **1** : gambito *m* (en ajedrez) **2** STRATAGEM : estratagema *f,* táctica *f*

gamble[1] [ˈgæmbəl] *v* **-bled; -bling** *vi* : jugar, arriesgarse — *vt* **1** BET, WAGER : apostar, jugarse **2** RISK : arriesgar

gamble[2] *n* **1** BET : apuesta *f* **2** RISK : riesga *f*

gambler [ˈgæmbələr] *n* : jugador *m,* -dora *f*

gambol [ˈgæmbəl] *vi* **-boled** *or* **-bolled; -boling** *or* **-bolling** FROLIC : retozar, juguetear

game[1] [ˈgeɪm] *adj* **1** READY : listo, dispuesto <we're game for anything : estamos listos para lo que sea> **2** LAME : cojo

game[2] *n* **1** AMUSEMENT : juego *m,* diversión *f* **2** CONTEST : juego *m,* partido *m,* concurso *m* **3** : caza *f* <big game : caza mayor>

gamecock [ˈgeɪmˌkɑk] *n* : gallo *m* de pelea

gamekeeper [ˈgeɪmˌkiːpər] *n* : guardabosque *mf*

gamely [ˈgeɪmli] *adv* : animosamente

gamma ray [ˈgæmə] *n* : rayo *m* gamma

gamut [ˈgæmət] *n* : gama *f,* espectro *m* <to run the gamut : pasar por toda la gama>

gamy *or* **gamey** [ˈgeɪmi] *adj* **gamier; -est** : con sabor de animal de caza, fuerte

gander [ˈgændər] *n* **1** : ganso *m* (animal) **2** GLANCE : mirada *f,* vistazo *m,* ojeada *f*

gang[1] [ˈgæŋ] *vi* **to gang up** : agruparse, unirse

gang[2] *n* : banda *f,* pandilla *f*

gangling [ˈgæŋglɪŋ] *adj* LANKY : larguirucho *fam*

ganglion [ˈgæŋgliən] *n, pl* **-glia** [-gliə] : ganglio *m*

gangplank [ˈgæŋˌplæŋk] *n* : pasarela *f*

gangrene [ˈgæŋˌgriːn, ˈgæn-; gæŋˈ-, gænˈ-] *n* : gangrena *f*

gangrenous [ˈgæŋgrənəs] *adj* : gangrenoso

gangster [ˈgæŋstər] *n* : gángster *mf*

gangway [ˈgæŋˌweɪ] *n* **1** : pasarela *f* **2 gangway!** : ¡abran paso!

gap [ˈgæp] *n* **1** BREACH, OPENING : espacio *m,* brecha *f,* abertura *f* **2** GORGE : desfiladero *m,* barranco *m* **3** : laguna *f* <a gap in my education : una laguna en mi educación> **4** INTERVAL : pausa *f,* intervalo *m* **5** DISPARITY : brecha *f,* disparidad *f*

gape[1] [ˈgeɪp] *vi* **gaped; gaping 1** OPEN : abrirse, estar abierto **2** STARE : mirar fijamente con la boca abierta, mirar boquiabierto

gape[2] *n* **1** OPENING : abertura *f,* brecha *f* **2** STARE : mirada *f* boquiabierta

garage[1] [gəˈrɑʒ, -ˈrɑdʒ] *vt* **-raged; -raging** : dejar en un garaje

garage[2] *n* : garaje *m,* cochera *f*

garb[1] [ˈgɑrb] *vt* : vestir, ataviar

garb[2] *n* : vestimenta *f,* atuendo *f*

garbage [ˈgɑrbɪdʒ] *n* : basura *f,* desechos *mpl*

garbageman [ˈgɑrbɪdʒmən] *n, pl* **-men** [-mən, -ˌmɛn] : basurero *m*

garble [ˈgɑrbəl] *vt* **-bled; -bling** : tergiversar, distorsionar

garbled [ˈgɑrbəld] *adj* : incoherente, incomprensible

garden[1] [ˈgɑrdən] *vi* : trabajar en el jardín

garden[2] *n* : jardín *m*

gardener [ˈgɑrdənər] *n* : jardinero *m,* -ra *f*

gardenia [gɑrˈdiːnjə] *n* : gardenia *f*

gargantuan [gɑrˈgæntʃʊən] *adj* : gigantesco, colosal

gargle[1] [ˈgɑrgəl] *vi* **-gled; -gling** : hacer gárgaras, gargarizar

gargle[2] *n* : gárgara *f*

gargoyle [ˈgɑrˌgɔɪl] *n* : gárgola *f*

garish [ˈgærɪʃ] *adj* GAUDY : llamativo, chillón, charro — **garishly** *adv*

garland[1] [ˈgɑrlənd] *vt* : adornar con guirnaldas

garland[2] *n* : guirnalda *f*

garlic [ˈgɑrlɪk] *n* : ajo *m*

garment [ˈgɑrmənt] *n* : prenda *f*

garner [ˈgɑrnər] *vt* : recoger, cosechar

garnet [ˈgɑrnət] *n* : granate *m*

garnish[1] [ˈgɑrnɪʃ] *vt* : aderezar, guarnecer

garnish[2] *n* : aderezo *m,* guarnición *f*

garret [ˈgærət] *n* : buhardilla *f,* desván *m*

garrison[1] [ˈgærəsən] *vt* **1** QUARTER : acuartelar (tropas) **2** OCCUPY : guarnecer, ocupar (con tropas)

garrison[2] *n* **1** : guarnición *f* (ciudad) **2** FORT : fortaleza *f,* poste *m* militar

garrulous [ˈgærələs] *adj* : charlatán, parlanchín, garlero *Col fam*

garter [ˈgɑrtər] *n* : liga *f*

gas[1] [ˈgæs] *v* **gassed; gassing** *vt* : gasear — *vi* **to gas up** : llenar el tanque con gasolina

gas[2] *n, pl* **gases** [ˈgæsəz] **1** : gas *m* <tear gas : gas lacrimógeno> **2** GASOLINE : gasolina *f*

gaseous [ˈgæʃəs, ˈgæsiəs] *adj* : gaseoso

gash[1] [ˈgæʃ] *vt* : hacer un tajo en, cortar

gash[2] *n* : cuchillada *f,* tajo *m*

gasket [ˈgæskət] *n* : junta *f*

gas mask *n* : máscara *f* antigás

gasoline [ˈgæsəˌliːn, ˌgæsəˈ-] *n* : gasolina *f,* nafta *f*

gasp[1] [ˈgæsp] *vi* **1** : boquear <to gasp with surprise : gritar de asombro> **2** PANT : jadear, respirar con dificultad

gasp[2] *n* **1** : boqueada *f* <a gasp of surprise : un grito sofocado> **2** PANTING : jadeo *m*

gas station → **service station**

gastric [ˈgæstrɪk] *adj* : gástrico <gastric juice : jugo gástrico>

gastronomic [ˌgæstrəˈnɑmɪk] *adj* : gastronómico

gastronomy [gæsˈtrɑnəmi] *n* : gastronomía *f*

gate [ˈgeɪt] *n* : portón *m,* verja *f,* puerta *f*

gatekeeper [ˈgeɪtˌkiːpər] *n* : guarda *mf;* guardián *m,* -diana *f*

gateway [ˈgeɪtˌweɪ] *n* : puerta *f* (de acceso), entrada *f*

gather [ˈgæðər] *vt* **1** ASSEMBLE : juntar, recoger, reunir **2** HARVEST : recoger, cosechar **3** : fruncir (una tela) **4** INFER : deducir, suponer

gathering [ˈgæðərɪŋ] *n* : reunión *f*

gauche [ˈgoːʃ] *adj* : torpe, falto de tacto

gaudy [ˈgɔdi] *adj* **gaudier; -est** : chillón, llamativo

gauge[1] [ˈgeɪdʒ] *vt* **gauged; gauging 1** MEASURE : medir **2** ESTIMATE, JUDGE : estimar, evaluar, juzgar

gauge[2] *n* **1** : indicador *m* <pressure gauge : indicador de presión> **2** CALIBER : calibre *m* **3** INDICATION : indicio *m,* muestra *f*

gaunt ['gɔnt] *adj* : demacrado, enjuto, descarnado
gauntlet ['gɔntlət] *n* : guante *m* <to run the gauntlet of : exponerse a>
gauze ['gɔz] *n* : gasa *f*
gauzy ['gɔzi] *adj* **gauzier; -est** : diáfano, vaporoso
gave → **give**
gavel ['gævəl] *n* : martillo *m* (de un juez, un subastador, etc.)
gawk ['gɔk] *vi* GAPE : mirar boquiabierto
gawky ['gɔki] *adj* **gawkier; -est** : desmañado, torpe, desgarbado
gay ['geɪ] *adj* **1** MERRY : alegre **2** BRIGHT, COLORFUL : vistoso, vivo **3** HOMOSEXUAL : homosexual
gaze[1] ['geɪz] *vi* **gazed; gazing** : mirar (fijamente)
gaze[2] *n* : mirada *f* (fija)
gazelle [gə'zɛl] *n* : gacela *f*
gazette [gə'zɛt] *n* : gaceta *f*
gazetteer [ˌgæzə'tɪr] *n* : diccionario *m* geográfico
gear[1] ['gɪr] *vt* ADAPT, ORIENT : adaptar, ajustar, orientar <a book geared to children : un libro adaptado a los niños> — *vi* **to gear up** : prepararse
gear[2] *n* **1** CLOTHING : ropa *f* **2** BELONGINGS : efectos *mpl* personales **3** EQUIPMENT, TOOLS : equipo *m*, aparejo *m*, herramientas *fpl* <fishing gear : aparejo de pescar> <landing gear : tren de aterrizaje> **4** COGWHEEL : rueda *f* dentada **5** : marcha *f*, velocidad *f* (de un vehículo) <to put in gear : poner en marcha> <to change gear(s) : cambiar de velocidad>
gearshift ['gɪrˌʃɪft] *n* : palanca *f* de cambio, palanca *f* de velocidad
geese → **goose**
Geiger counter ['gaɪgərˌkaʊntər] *n* : contador *m* Geiger
gelatin ['dʒɛlətən] *n* : gelatina *f*
gem ['dʒɛm] *n* : joya *f*, gema *f*, alhaja *f*
Gemini ['dʒɛməˌnaɪ] *n* : Géminis *mf*
gemstone ['dʒɛmˌsto:n] *n* : piedra *f* (semipreciosa o preciosa), gema *f*
gender ['dʒɛndər] *n* **1** SEX : sexo *m* **2** : género *m* (en la gramática)
gene ['dʒi:n] *n* : gen *m*, gene *m*
genealogical [ˌdʒi:niə'lɑdʒɪkəl] *adj* : genealógico
genealogy [ˌdʒi:ni'ɑlədʒi, ˌdʒɛ-, -'æ-] *n, pl* **-gies** : genealogía *f*
genera → **genus**
general[1] ['dʒɛnrəl, 'dʒɛnə-] *adj* : general <in general : en general, por lo general>
general[2] *n* : general *mf*
generality [ˌdʒɛnə'rælət̬i] *n, pl* **-ties** : generalidad *f*
generalization [ˌdʒɛnrələ'zeɪʃən, ˌdʒɛnərə-] *n* : generalización *f*
generalize ['dʒɛnrəˌlaɪz, 'dʒɛnərə-] *v* **-ized; -izing** : generalizar
generally ['dʒɛnrəli, 'dʒɛnərə-] *adv* : generalmente, por lo general, en general
generate ['dʒɛnəˌreɪt] *vt* **-ated; -ating** : generar, producir
generation [ˌdʒɛnə'reɪʃən] *n* : generación *f*
generator ['dʒɛnəˌreɪt̬ər] *n* : generador *m*
generic [dʒə'nɛrɪk] *adj* : genérico
generosity [ˌdʒɛnə'rɑsət̬i] *n, pl* **-ties** : generosidad *f*
generous ['dʒɛnərəs] *adj* **1** OPENHANDED : generoso, dadivoso, desprendido **2** ABUNDANT, AMPLE : abundante, amplio, generoso — **generously** *adv*
genetic [dʒə'nɛtɪk] *adj* : genético — **genetically** [-t̬ɪkli] *adv*
geneticist [dʒə'nɛt̬əsɪst] *n* : genetista *mf*
genetics [dʒə'nɛtɪks] *n* : genética *f*
genial ['dʒi:niəl] *adj* GRACIOUS : simpático, cordial, afable — **genially** *adv*
geniality [ˌdʒi:ni'ælət̬i] *n* : simpatía *f*, afabilidad *f*
genie ['dʒi:ni] *n* : genio *m*
genital ['dʒɛnət̬əl] *adj* : genital
genitals ['dʒɛnət̬əlz] *npl* : genitales *mpl*
genius ['dʒi:njəs] *n* : genio *m*
genocide ['dʒɛnəˌsaɪd] *n* : genocidio *m*
genre ['ʒɑnrə, 'ʒɑr] *n* : género *m*
genteel [dʒɛn'ti:l] *adj* : cortés, fino, refinado
gentile[1] ['dʒɛnˌtaɪl] *adj* : gentil
gentile[2] *n* : gentil *mf*
gentility [dʒɛn'tɪlət̬i] *n, pl* **-ties 1** : nobleza *f* (de nacimiento) **2** POLITENESS, REFINEMENT : cortesía *f*, refinamiento *m*
gentle ['dʒɛntəl] *adj* **-tler; -tlest 1** NOBLE : bien nacido, noble **2** DOCILE : dócil, manso **3** KINDLY : bondadoso, amable **4** MILD : suave, apacible <a gentle breeze : una brisa suave> **5** SOFT : suave (dícese de un sonido), ligero (dícese del tacto) **6** MODERATE : moderado, gradual <a gentle slope : una cuesta gradual>
gentleman ['dʒɛntəlmən] *n, pl* **-men** [-mən, -ˌmɛn] : caballero *m*, señor *m*
gentlemanly ['dʒɛntəlmənli] *adj* : caballeroso
gentleness ['dʒɛntəlnəs] *n* : delicadeza *f*, suavidad *f*, ternura *f*
gentlewoman ['dʒɛntəlˌwʊmən] *n, pl* **-women** [-ˌwɪmən] : dama *f*, señora *f*
gently ['dʒɛntli] *adv* **1** CAREFULLY, SOFTLY : con cuidado, suavemente, ligeramente **2** KINDLY : amablemente, con delicadeza
gentry ['dʒɛntri] *n, pl* **-tries** : aristocracia *f*
genuflect ['dʒɛnjʊˌflɛkt] *vi* : doblar la rodilla, hacer una genuflexión
genuflection [ˌdʒɛnjʊ'flɛkʃən] *n* : genuflexión *f*

genuine ['dʒɛnjʊwən] *adj* **1** AUTHENTIC, REAL : genuino, verdadero, auténtico **2** SINCERE : sincero — **genuinely** *adv*
genus ['dʒi:nəs] *n, pl* **genera** ['dʒɛnərə] : género *m*
geographer [dʒi'ɑgrəfər] *n* : geógrafo *m,* -fa *f*
geographical [,dʒi:ə'græfɪkəl] *or* **geographic** [-fɪk] *adj* : geográfico — **geographically** [-fɪkli] *adv*
geography [dʒi'ɑgrəfi] *n, pl* **-phies** : geografía *f*
geologic [,dʒi:ə'lɑdʒɪk] *or* **geological** [-dʒɪkəl] *adj* : geológico — **geologically** [-dʒɪkli] *adv*
geologist [dʒi'ɑlədʒɪst] *n* : geólogo *m,* -ga *f*
geology [dʒi'ɑlədʒi] *n* : geología *f*
geometric [,dʒi:ə'mɛtrɪk] *or* **geometrical** [-trɪkəl] *adj* : geométrico
geometry [dʒi'ɑmətri] *n, pl* **-tries** : geometría *f*
geranium [dʒə'reɪniəm] *n* : geranio *m*
gerbil ['dʒərbəl] *n* : jerbo *m,* gerbo *m*
geriatric [,dʒɛri'ætrɪk] *adj* : geriátrico
geriatrics [,dʒɛri'ætrɪks] *n* : geriatría *f*
germ ['dʒərm] *n* **1** MICROORGANISM : microbio *m,* germen *m* **2** BEGINNING : germen *m,* principio *m* <the germ of a plan : el germen de un plan>
German ['dʒərmən] *n* **1** : alemán *m,* -mana *f* **2** : alemán *m* (idioma) — **German** *adj*
germane [dʒər'meɪn] *adj* : relevante, pertinente
germanium [dʒər'meɪniəm] *n* : germanio *m*
germ cell *n* : célula *f* germen
germicide ['dʒərmə,saɪd] *n* : germicida *m*
germinate ['dʒərmə,neɪt] *v* **-nated; -nating** *vi* : germinar — *vt* : hacer germinar
germination [,dʒərmə'neɪʃən] *n* : germinación *f*
gerund ['dʒɛrənd] *n* : gerundio *m*
gestation [dʒɛ'steɪʃən] *n* : gestación *f*
gesture¹ ['dʒɛstʃər] *vi* **-tured; -turing** : gesticular, hacer gestos
gesture² *n* **1** : gesto *m,* ademán *m* **2** SIGN, TOKEN : gesto *m,* señal *f* <a gesture of friendship : una señal de amistad>
get ['gɛt] *v* **got** ['gɑt]; **got** *or* **gotten** ['gɑtən]; **getting** *vt* **1** OBTAIN : conseguir, obtener, adquirir **2** RECEIVE : recibir <to get a letter : recibir una carta> **3** EARN : ganar <he gets $10 an hour : gana $10 por hora> **4** FETCH : traer <get me my book : tráigame el libro> **5** CATCH : tomar (un tren, etc.), agarrar (una pelota, una persona, etc.) **6** CONTRACT : contagiarse de, contraer <she got the measles : le dio el sarampión> **7** PREPARE : preparar (una comida) **8** PERSUADE : persuadir, mandar a hacer <I got him to agree : logré convencerlo> **9** (*to cause to be*) <to get one's hair cut : cortarse el pelo> **10** UNDERSTAND : entender <now I get it! : ¡ya entiendo!> **11 to have got** : tener <I've got a headache : tengo un dolor de cabeza> **12 to have got to** : tener que <you've got to come : tienes que venir> — *vi* **1** BECOME : ponerse, volverse, hacerse <to get angry : ponerse furioso, enojarse> **2** GO, MOVE : ir, avanzar <he didn't get far : no avanzó mucho> **3** ARRIVE : llegar <to get home : llegar a casa> **4 to get to be** : llegar a ser <she got to be the director : llegó a ser directora> **5 to get ahead** : adelantarse, progresar **6 to get along** : llevarse bien (con alguien), congeniar **7 to get by** MANAGE : arreglárselas **8 to get over** OVERCOME : superar, consolarse de **9 to get together** MEET : reunirse **10 to get up** : levantarse
getaway ['gɛt̬ə,weɪ] *n* ESCAPE : fuga *f,* huida *f,* escapada *f*
geyser ['gaɪzər] *n* : géiser *m*
Ghanaian ['gɑniən, 'gæ-] *n* : ghanés *m,* -nesa *f* — **Ghanaian** *adj*
ghastly ['gæstli] *adj* **-lier; -est 1** HORRIBLE : horrible, espantoso **2** PALE : pálido, cadavérico
gherkin ['gərkən] *n* : pepinillo *m*
ghetto ['gɛt̬o:] *n, pl* **-tos** *or* **-toes** : gueto *m*
ghost ['go:st] *n* **1** : fantasma *f,* espectro *m* **2 the Holy Ghost** : el Espíritu Santo
ghostly ['go:stli] *adv* : fantasmal
ghoul ['gu:l] *n* **1** : demonio *m* necrófago **2** : persona *f* de gustos macabros
GI [,dʒi:'aɪ] *n, pl* **GI's** *or* **GIs** : soldado *m* estadounidense
giant¹ ['dʒaɪənt] *adj* : gigante, gigantesco, enorme
giant² *n* : gigante *m,* -ta *f*
gibberish ['dʒɪbərɪʃ] *n* : galimatías *m,* jerigonza *f*
gibbon ['gɪbən] *n* : gibón *m*
gibe¹ ['dʒaɪb] *vi* **gibed; gibing** : mofarse, burlarse
gibe² *n* : pulla *f,* burla *f,* mofa *f*
giblets ['dʒɪbləts] *npl* : menudos *mpl,* menudencias *fpl*
giddiness ['gɪdinəs] *n* **1** DIZZINESS : vértigo *m,* mareo *m* **2** SILLINESS : frivolidad *f,* estupidez *f*
giddy ['gɪdi] *adj* **-dier; -est 1** DIZZY : mareado, vertiginoso **2** FRIVOLOUS, SILLY : frívolo, tonto
gift ['gɪft] *n* **1** TALENT : don *m,* talento *m,* dotes *fpl* **2** PRESENT : regalo *m,* obsequio *m*
gifted ['gɪftəd] *adj* TALENTED : talentoso
gigantic [dʒaɪ'gæntɪk] *adj* : gigantesco, enorme, colosal
giggle¹ ['gɪgəl] *vi* **-gled; -gling** : reírse tontamente
giggle² *n* : risita *f,* risa *f* tonta
gild ['gɪld] *vt* **gilded** *or* **gilt** ['gɪlt]; **gilding** : dorar
gill ['gɪl] *n* : agalla *f,* branquia *f*

gilt[1] [ˈgɪlt] *adj* : dorado

gilt[2] *n* : dorado *m*

gimlet [ˈgɪmlət] *n* **1** : barrena *f* (herramiento) **2** : bebida *f* de vodka o ginebra y limón

gimmick [ˈgɪmɪk] *n* **1** GADGET : artilugio *m* **2** CATCH : engaño *m,* trampa *f* **3** SCHEME, TRICK : ardid *m,* truco *m*

gin[1] [ˈdʒɪn] *vt* **ginned; ginning** : desmotar (algodón)

gin[2] *n* **1** : desmotadora *f* (de algodón) **2** : ginebra *f* (bebida alcohólica)

ginger [ˈdʒɪndʒər] *n* : jengibre *m*

ginger ale *n* : ginger ale *m,* gaseosa *f* de jengibre

gingerbread [ˈdʒɪndʒərˌbrɛd] *n* : pan *m* de jengibre

gingerly [ˈdʒɪndʒərli] *adv* : con cuidado, cautelosamente

gingham [ˈgɪŋəm] *n* : guinga *f*

ginseng [ˈdʒɪnˌsɪŋ, -ˌsɛŋ] *n* : ginseng *m*

giraffe [dʒəˈræf] *n* : jirafa *f*

gird [ˈgərd] *vt* **girded** *or* **girt** [ˈgərt]; **girding 1** BIND : ceñir, atar **2** ENCIRCLE : rodear **3 to gird oneself** : prepararse

girder [ˈgərdər] *n* : viga *f*

girdle[1] [ˈgərdəl] *vt* **-dled; -dling 1** GIRD : ceñir, atar **2** SURROUND : rodear, circundar

girdle[2] *n* : faja *f*

girl [ˈgərl] *n* **1** : niña *f,* muchacha *f,* chica *f* **2** SWEETHEART : novia *f* **3** DAUGHTER : hija *f*

girlfriend [ˈgərlˌfrɛnd] *n* : novia *f,* amiga *f*

girlhood [ˈgərlˌhʊd] *n* : niñez *f,* juventud *f* (de una muchacha)

girlish [ˈgərlɪʃ] *adj* : de niña

girth [ˈgərθ] *n* **1** : circunferencia *f* (de un árbol, etc.), cintura *f* (de una persona) **2** CINCH : cincha *f* (para caballos, etc.)

gist [ˈdʒɪst] *n* : quid *m,* meollo *m*

give[1] [ˈgɪv] *v* **gave** [ˈgeɪv]; **given** [ˈgɪvən]; **giving** *vt* **1** HAND, PRESENT : dar, regalar, obsequiar <give it to me : dámelo> <they gave him a gold watch : le regalaron un reloj de oro> **2** PAY : dar, pagar <I'll give you $10 for this one : te daré $10 por éste> **3** UTTER : dar, pronunciar <to give a shout : dar un grito> <to give a speech : pronunciar un discurso> <to give a verdict : dictar sentencia> **4** PROVIDE : dar <to give one's word : dar uno su palabra> <to give a party : dar una fiesta> **5** CAUSE : dar, causar, ocasionar <to give trouble : causar problemas> <to give someone to understand : darle a entender a alguien> **6** GRANT : dar, otorgar <to give permission : dar permiso> — *vi* **1** : hacer regalos **2** YIELD : ceder, romperse <it gave under the weight of the crowd : cedió bajo el peso de la muchedumbre> **3 to give in** *or* **to give up** SURRENDER : rendirse, entregarse **4 to give out** : agotarse, acabarse <the supplies gave out : las provisiones se agotaron>

give[2] *n* FLEXIBILITY : flexibilidad *f,* elasticidad *f*

giveaway [ˈgɪvəˌweɪ] *n* **1** : revelación *f* involuntaria **2** GIFT : regalo *m,* obsequio *m*

given [ˈgɪvən] *adj* **1** INCLINED : dado, inclinado <he's given to quarreling : es muy dado a discutir> **2** SPECIFIC : dado, determinado <at a given time : en un momento dado>

given name *n* : nombre *m* de pila

give up *vt* : dejar, renunciar a, abandonar <to give up smoking : dejar de fumar>

gizzard [ˈgɪzərd] *n* : molleja *f*

glacial [ˈgleɪʃəl] *adj* : glacial — **glacially** *adv*

glacier [ˈgleɪʃər] *n* : glaciar *m*

glad [ˈglæd] *adj* **gladder; gladdest 1** PLEASED : alegre, contento <she was glad I came : se alegró de que haya venido> <glad to meet you! : ¡mucho gusto!> **2** HAPPY, PLEASING : feliz, agradable <glad tidings : buenas nuevas> **3** WILLING : dispuesto, gustoso <I'll be glad to do it : lo haré con mucho gusto>

gladden [ˈglædən] *vt* : alegrar

glade [ˈgleɪd] *n* : claro *m*

gladiator [ˈglædiˌeɪt̬ər] *n* : gladiador *m*

gladiolus [ˌglædiˈoːləs] *n, pl* **-li** [-li, -ˌlaɪ] : gladiolo *m,* gladíolo *m*

gladly [ˈglædli] *adv* : con mucho gusto

gladness [ˈglædnəs] *n* : alegría *f,* gozo *m*

glamor *or* **glamour** [ˈglæmər] *n* : atractivo *m,* hechizo *m,* encanto *m*

glamorous [ˈglæmərəs] *adj* : atractivo, encantador

glance[1] [ˈglænts] *vi* **glanced; glancing 1** RICOCHET : rebotar <it glanced off the wall : rebotó en la pared> **2 to glance at** : mirar, echar un vistazo a **3 to glance away** : apartar los ojos

glance[2] *n* : mirada *f,* vistazo *m,* ojeada *f*

gland [ˈglænd] *n* : glándula *f*

glandular [ˈglændʒʊlər] *adj* : glandular

glare[1] [ˈglær] *vi* **glared; glaring 1** SHINE : brillar, relumbrar **2** STARE : mirar con ira, lanzar una mirada feroz

glare[2] *n* **1** BRIGHTNESS : resplandor *m,* luz *f* deslumbrante **2** : mirada *f* feroz

glaring [ˈglærɪŋ] *adj* **1** BRIGHT : deslumbrante, brillante **2** FLAGRANT, OBVIOUS : flagrante, manifiesto <a glaring error : un error que salta a la vista>

glass [ˈglæs] *n* **1** : vidrio *m,* cristal *m* <stained glass : vidrio de color> **2** : vaso *m* <a glass of milk : un vaso de leche> **3 glasses** *npl* SPECTACLES : gafas *fpl,* anteojos *mpl,* lentes *mpl,* espejuelos *mpl*

glassblowing [ˈglæs͵bloːɪŋ] *n* : soplado *m* del vidrio
glassful [ˈglæs͵fʊl] *n* : vaso *m,* copa *f*
glassware [ˈglæs͵wær] *n* : cristalería *f*
glassy [ˈglæsi] *adj* **glassier; -est 1** VITREOUS : vítreo **2** : vidrioso <glassy eyes : ojos vidriosos>
glaze[1] [ˈgleɪz] *vt* **glazed; glazing 1** : ponerle vidrios a (una ventana, etc.) **2** : vidriar (cerámica) **3** : glasear (papel, verduras, etc.)
glaze[2] *n* : vidriado *m,* glaseado *m,* barniz *m*
glazier [ˈgleɪʒər] *n* : vidriero *m,* -ra *f*
gleam[1] [ˈgliːm] *vi* : brillar, destellar, relucir
gleam[2] *n* **1** LIGHT : luz *f* (oscura) **2** GLINT : destello *m* **3** GLIMMER : rayo *m,* vislumbre *f* <a gleam of hope : un rayo de esperanza>
glean [ˈgliːn] *vt* : recoger, espigar
glee [ˈgliː] *n* : alegría *f,* júbilo *m,* regocijo *m*
gleeful [ˈgliːfəl] *adj* : lleno de alegría
glen [ˈglɛn] *n* : cañada *f*
glib [ˈglɪb] *adj* **glibber; glibbest 1** : simplista <a glib reply : una respuesta simplista> **2** : con mucha labia (dícese de una persona)
glibly [ˈglɪbli] *adv* : con mucha labia
glide[1] [ˈglaɪd] *vi* **glided; gliding** : deslizarse (en una superficie), planear (en el aire)
glide[2] *n* : planeo *m*
glider [ˈglaɪdər] *n* **1** : planeador *m* (aeronave) **2** : mecedor *m* (tipo de columpio)
glimmer[1] [ˈglɪmər] *vi* : brillar con luz trémula
glimmer[2] *n* **1** : luz *f* trémula, luz *f* tenue **2** GLEAM : rayo *m,* vislumbre *f* <a glimmer of understanding : un rayo de entendimiento>
glimpse[1] [ˈglɪmps] *vt* **glimpsed; glimpsing** : vislumbrar, entrever
glimpse[2] *n* : mirada *f* breve <to catch a glimpse of : alcanzar a ver, vislumbrar>
glint[1] [ˈglɪnt] *vi* GLEAM, SPARKLE : destellar, fulgurar
glint[2] *n* **1** SPARKLE : destello *m,* centelleo *m* **2 to have a glint in one's eye** : chispearle los ojos a uno
glisten[1] [ˈglɪsən] *vi* : brillar, centellear
glisten[2] *n* : brillo *m,* centelleo *m*
glitter[1] [ˈglɪtər] *vi* **1** SPARKLE : destellar, relucir, brillar **2** FLASH : relampaguear <his eyes glittered in anger : le relampagueaban los ojos de ira>
glitter[2] *n* **1** BRIGHTNESS : brillo *m* **2** : purpurina *f* (para decoración)
gloat [ˈgloːt] *vi* **to gloat over** : regodearse en
glob [ˈglɑb] *n* : plasta *f,* masa *f,* grumo *m*
global [ˈgloːbəl] *adj* **1** SPHERICAL : esférico **2** WORLDWIDE : global, mundial — **globally** *adv*
globe [ˈgloːb] *n* **1** SPHERE : esfera *f,* globo *m* **2** EARTH : globo *m,* Tierra *f* **3** : globo *m* terráqueo (modelo de la Tierra)
globe–trotter [ˈgloːb͵trɑt̬ər] *n* : trotamundos *mf*
globular [ˈglɑbjʊlər] *adj* : globular
globule [ˈglɑ͵bjuːl] *n* : glóbulo *m*
gloom [ˈgluːm] *n* **1** DARKNESS : penumbra *f,* oscuridad *f* **2** MELANCHOLY : melancolía *f,* tristeza *f*
gloomily [ˈgluːməli] *adv* : tristemente
gloomy [ˈgluːmi] *adj* **gloomier; -est 1** DARK : oscuro, tenebroso <gloomy weather : tiempo gris> **2** MELANCHOLY : melancólico **3** PESSIMISTIC : pesimista **4** DEPRESSING : deprimente, lúgubre
glorification [͵glorəfəˈkeɪʃən] *n* : glorificación *f*
glorify [ˈglorə͵faɪ] *vt* **-fied; -fying** : glorificar
glorious [ˈgloriəs] *adj* **1** ILLUSTRIOUS : glorioso, ilustre **2** MAGNIFICENT : magnífico, espléndido, maravilloso — **gloriously** *adv*
glory[1] [ˈglori] *vi* **-ried; -rying** EXULT : exultar, regocijarse
glory[2] *n, pl* **-ries 1** RENOWN : gloria *f,* fama *f,* honor *m* **2** PRAISE : gloria *f* <glory to God : gloria a Dios> **3** MAGNIFICENCE : magnificencia *f,* esplendor *m,* gloria *f* **4 to be in one's glory** : estar uno en su gloria
gloss[1] [ˈglɔs, ˈglɑs] *vt* **1** EXPLAIN : glosar, explicar **2** POLISH : lustrar, pulir **3 to gloss over** : quitarle importancia a, minimizar
gloss[2] *n* **1** SHINE : lustre *m,* brillo *m* **2** EXPLANATION : glosa *f,* explicación *f* breve **3** → **glossary**
glossary [ˈglɔsəri, ˈglɑ-] *n, pl* **-ries** : glosario *m*
glossy [ˈglɔsi, ˈglɑ-] *adj* **glossier; -est** : brillante, lustroso, satinado (dícese del papel)
glove [ˈglʌv] *n* : guante *m*
glow[1] [ˈgloː] *vi* **1** SHINE : brillar, resplandecer **2** BRIM : rebosar <to glow with health : rebosar de salud>
glow[2] *n* **1** BRIGHTNESS : resplandor *m,* brillo *m,* luminosidad *f* **2** FEELING : sensación *f* (de bienestar), oleada *f* (de sentimiento) **3** INCANDESCENCE : incandescencia *f*
glower [ˈglaʊər] *vi* : fruncir el ceño
glowworm [ˈgloː͵wərm] *n* : luciérnaga *f*
glucose [ˈgluː͵koːs] *n* : glucosa *f*
glue[1] [ˈgluː] *vt* **glued; gluing** *or* **glueing** : pegar, encolar
glue[2] *n* : pegamento *m,* cola *f*
gluey [ˈgluːi] *adj* **gluier; -est** : pegajoso
glum [ˈglʌm] *adj* **glummer; glummest 1** SULLEN : hosco, sombrío **2** DREARY, GLOOMY : sombrío, triste, melancólico

glut¹ [ˈglʌt] *vt* **glutted; glutting** **1** SATIATE : saciar, hartar **2** : inundar (el mercado)
glut² *n* : exceso *m,* superabundancia *f*
glutinous [ˈgluːtənəs] *adj* STICKY : pegajoso, glutinoso
glutton [ˈglʌtən] *n* : glotón *m,* -tona *f*
gluttonous [ˈglʌtənəs] *adj* : glotón
gluttony [ˈglʌtəni] *n, pl* **-tonies** : glotonería *f,* gula *f*
gnarled [ˈnɑrld] *adj* **1** KNOTTY : nudoso **2** TWISTED : retorcido
gnash [ˈnæʃ] *vt* : hacer rechinar (los dientes)
gnat [ˈnæt] *n* : jején *m*
gnaw [ˈnɔ] *vt* : roer
gnome [ˈnoːm] *n* : gnomo *m*
gnu [ˈnuː, ˈnjuː] *n, pl* **gnu** *or* **gnus** : ñu *m*
go¹ [ˈgoː] *v* **went** [ˈwɛnt]; **gone** [ˈgɔn, ˈgɑn]; **going; goes** [ˈgoːz] *vi* **1** PROCEED : ir <to go slow : ir despacio> <to go shopping : ir de compras> **2** LEAVE : irse, marcharse, salir <let's go! : ¡vámonos!> <the train went on time : el tren salió a tiempo> **3** DISAPPEAR : desaparecer, pasarse, irse <her fear is gone : se le ha pasado el miedo> <my pen is gone! : ¡mi pluma desapareció!> **4** EXTEND : ir, extenderse, llegar <this road goes to the river : este camino se extiende hasta el río> <to go from top to bottom : ir de arriba abajo> **5** FUNCTION : funcionar, marchar <the car won't go : el coche no funciona> <to get something going : poner algo en marcha> **6** SELL : venderse <it goes for $15 : se vende por $15> **7** PROGRESS : ir, andar, seguir <my exam went well : me fue bien en el examen> <how did the meeting go? : ¿qué tal la reunión?> **8** BECOME : volverse, quedarse <he's going crazy : está volviéndose loco> <the tire went flat : la llanta se desinfló> **9** FIT : caber <it will go through the door : cabe por la puerta> **10 anything goes!** : ¡todo vale! **11 to go** : faltar <only 10 days to go : faltan sólo 10 días> **12 to go back on** : faltar uno a (su promesa) **13 to go bad** SPOIL : estropearse, echarse a perder **14 to go for** : interesarse uno en, gustarle a uno (algo, alguien) <I don't go for that : eso no me interesa> **15 to go off** EXPLODE : estallar **16 to go with** MATCH : armonizar con, hacer juego con — *v aux* **to be going to** : ir a <I'm going to write a letter : voy a escribir una carta> <it's not going to last : no va a durar>
go² *n, pl* **goes** **1** ATTEMPT : intento *m* <to have a go at : intentar, probar> **2** SUCCESS : éxito *m* **3** ENERGY : energía *f,* empuje *m* <to be on the go : no parar, no descansar>
goad¹ [ˈgoːd] *vt* : aguijonear (un animal), incitar (a una persona)
goad² *n* : aguijón *m*
goal [ˈgoːl] *n* **1** : gol *m* (en deportes) <to score a goal : anotar un gol> **2** *or* **goalposts** : portería *f* **3** AIM, OBJECTIVE : meta *m,* objetivo *m*
goalie [ˈgoːli] → **goalkeeper**
goalkeeper [ˈgoːlˌkiːpər] *n* : portero *m,* -ra *f;* guardameta *mf;* arquero *m,* -ra *f*
goaltender [ˈgoːlˌtɛndər] → **goalkeeper**
goat [ˈgoːt] *n* **1** : cabra *f* (hembra) **2 billy goat** : macho *m* cabrío, chivo *m*
goatee [goːˈtiː] *n* : barbita *f* de chivo, piocha *f Mex*
goatskin [ˈgoːtˌskɪn] *n* : piel *f* de cabra
gob [ˈgɑb] *n* : masa *f,* grumo *m*
gobble [ˈgɑbəl] *v* **-bled; -bling** *vt* **to gobble up** : tragar, engullir — *vi* : hacer ruidos de pavo
gobbledygook [ˈgɑbəldiˌgʊk, -ˌguːk] *n* GIBBERISH : jerigonza *f*
go–between [ˈgoːbɪˌtwiːn] *n* : intermediario *m,* -ria *f;* mediador *m,* -dora *f*
goblet [ˈgɑblət] *n* : copa *f*
goblin [ˈgɑblən] *n* : duende *m,* trasgo *m*
god [ˈgɑd, ˈgɔd] *n* **1** : dios *m* **2 God** : Dios *m*
godchild [ˈgɑdˌtʃaɪld, ˈgɔd-] *n, pl* **-children** : ahijado *m,* -da *f*
goddess [ˈgɑdəs, ˈgɔ-] *n* : diosa *f*
godfather [ˈgɑdˌfɑðər, ˈgɔd-] *n* : padrino *m*
godless [ˈgɑdləs, ˈgɔd-] *adj* : ateo
godlike [ˈgɑdˌlaɪk, ˈgɔd-] *adj* : divino
godly [ˈgɑdli, ˈgɔd-] *adj* **-lier; -est** **1** DIVINE : divino **2** DEVOUT, PIOUS : piadoso, devoto, beato
godmother [ˈgɑdˌmʌðər, ˈgɔd-] *n* : madrina *f*
godparents [ˈgɑdˌpærənts, ˈgɔd-] *npl* : padrinos *mpl*
godsend [ˈgɑdˌsɛnd, ˈgɔd-] *n* : bendición *f,* regalo *m* divino
goes → **go**
go–getter [ˈgoːˌgɛt̬ər] *n* : persona *f* ambiciosa, buscavidas *mf fam*
goggle [ˈgɑgəl] *vi* **-gled; -gling** : mirar con ojos desorbitados
goggles [ˈgɑgəlz] *npl* : gafas *fpl* (protectoras), anteojos *mpl*
goings–on [ˌgoːɪŋzˈɑn, -ˈɔn] *npl* : sucesos *mpl,* ocurrencias *fpl*
goiter [ˈgɔɪt̬ər] *n* : bocio *m*
gold [ˈgoːld] *n* : oro *m*
golden [ˈgoːldən] *adj* **1** : (hecho) de oro **2** : dorado, de color oro <golden hair : pelo rubio> **3** FLOURISHING, PROSPEROUS : dorado, próspero <golden years : años dorados> **4** FAVORABLE : favorable, excelente <a golden opportunity : una excelente oportunidad>
goldenrod [ˈgoːldənˌrɑd] *n* : vara *f* de oro
golden rule *n* : regla *f* de oro
goldfinch [ˈgoːldˌfɪntʃ] *n* : jilguero *m*

goldfish [ˈgoːldˌfɪʃ] *n* : pez *m* de colores

goldsmith [ˈgoːldˌsmɪθ] *n* : orífice *mf,* orfebre *mf*

golf[1] [ˈgɑlf, ˈgɔlf] *vi* : jugar (al) golf

golf[2] *n* : golf *m*

golfer [ˈgɑlfər, ˈgɔl-] *n* : golfista *mf*

gondola [ˈgɑndələ, gɑnˈdoːlə] *n* : góndola *f*

gone [ˈgɔn] *adj* **1** DEAD : muerto **2** PAST : pasado, ido **3** LOST : perdido, desaparecido **4 to be far gone :** estar muy avanzado **5 to be gone on :** estar loco por

goner [ˈgɔnər] *n* **to be a goner :** estar en las últimas

gong [ˈgɔŋ, ˈgɑŋ] *n* : gong *m*

gonorrhea [ˌgɑnəˈriːə] *n* : gonorrea *f*

good[1] [ˈgʊd] *adv* **1** (*used as an intensifier*) : bien <a good strong rope : una cuerda bien fuerte> **2** WELL : bien

good[2] *adj* **better** [ˈbɛt̬ər]; **best** [ˈbɛst] **1** PLEASANT : bueno, agradable <good news : buenas noticias> <to have a good time : divertirse> **2** BENEFICIAL : bueno, beneficioso <good for a cold : beneficioso para los resfriados> <it's good for you : es bueno para uno> **3** FULL : completo, entero <a good hour : una hora entera> **4** CONSIDERABLE : bueno, bastante <a good many people : muchísima gente, un buen número de gente> **5** ATTRACTIVE, DESIRABLE : bueno, bien <a good salary : un buen sueldo> <to look good : quedar bien> **6** KIND, VIRTUOUS : bueno, amable <she's a good person : es buena gente> <that's good of you! : ¡qué amable!> <good deeds : buenas obras> **7** SKILLED : bueno, hábil <to be good at : tener facilidad para> **8** SOUND : bueno, sensato <good advice : buenos consejos> **9** (*in greetings*) : bueno <good morning : buenos días> <good afternoon (evening) : buenas tardes> <good night : buenas noches>

good[3] *n* **1** RIGHT : bien *m* <to do good : hacer el bien> **2** GOODNESS : bondad *f* **3** BENEFIT : bien *m,* provecho *m* <it's for your own good : es por tu propio bien> **4 goods** *npl* PROPERTY : efectos *mpl* personales, posesiones *fpl* **5 goods** *npl* WARES : mercancía *f,* mercadería *f,* artículos *mpl* **6 for ~ :** para siempre

good–bye *or* **good–by** [gʊdˈbaɪ] *n* : adiós *m*

good–for–nothing [ˈgʊdfərˌnʌθɪŋ] *n* : inútil *mf;* haragán *m,* -gana *f;* holgazán *m,* -zana *f*

Good Friday *n* : Viernes *m* Santo

good–hearted [ˈgʊdˈhɑrt̬əd] *adj* : bondadoso, benévolo, de buen corazón

good–looking [ˈgʊdˈlʊkɪŋ] *adj* : bello, bonito, guapo

goodly [ˈgʊdli] *adj* **-lier; -est :** considerable, importante <a goodly number : un número considerable>

good–natured [ˈgʊdˈneɪtʃərd] *adj* : amigable, amistoso, bonachón *fam*

goodness [ˈgʊdnəs] *n* **1** : bondad *f* **2 thank goodness! :** ¡gracias a Dios!, ¡menos mal!

good–tempered [ˈgʊdˈtɛmpərd] *adj* : de buen genio

goodwill [ˌgʊdˈwɪl] *n* **1** BENEVOLENCE : benevolencia *f,* buena voluntad *f* **2** : buen nombre *m* (de comercios), renombre *m* comercial

goody [ˈgʊdi] *n, pl* **goodies :** cosa *f* rica para comer, golosina *f*

gooey [ˈguːi] *adj* **gooier; gooiest :** pegajoso

goof[1] [ˈguːf] *vi* **1 to goof off :** holgazanear **2 to goof around :** hacer tonterías **3 to goof up** BLUNDER : cometer un error

goof[2] *n* **1** : bobo *m,* -ba *f;* tonto *m,* -ta *f* **2** BLUNDER : error *m,* planchazo *m fam*

goofy [ˈguːfi] *adj* **goofier; -est** SILLY : tonto, bobo

goose [ˈguːs] *n, pl* **geese** [ˈgiːs] : ganso *m,* -sa *f;* ánsar *m;* oca *f*

gooseberry [ˈguːsˌbɛriː, ˈguːz-] *n, pl* **-berries :** grosella *f* espinosa

goose bumps *npl* : carne *f* de gallina

gooseflesh [ˈguːsˌflɛʃ] → **goose bumps**

goose pimples → **goose bumps**

gopher [ˈgoːfər] *n* : taltuza *f*

gore[1] [ˈgor] *vt* **gored; goring :** cornear

gore[2] *n* BLOOD : sangre *f*

gorge[1] [ˈgɔrdʒ] *vt* **gorged; gorging 1** SATIATE : saciar, hartar **2 to gorge oneself :** hartarse, atiborrarse, atracarse *fam*

gorge[2] *n* RAVINE : desfiladero *m*

gorgeous [ˈgɔrdʒəs] *adj* : hermoso, espléndido, magnífico

gorilla [gəˈrɪlə] *n* : gorila *m*

gory [ˈgori] *adj* **gorier; -est** BLOODY : sangriento

gosling [ˈgɑzlɪŋ, ˈgɔz-] *n* : ansarino *m*

gospel [ˈgɑspəl] *n* **1** *or* **Gospel :** evangelio *m* <the four Gospels : los cuatro evangelios> **2 the gospel truth :** el evangelio, la pura verdad

gossamer [ˈgɑsəmər, ˈgɑzə-] *adj* : tenue, sutil <gossamer wings : alas tenues>

gossip[1] [ˈgɑsɪp] *vi* : chismear, contar chismes

gossip[2] *n* **1** : chismoso *m,* -sa *f* (persona) **2** RUMOR : chisme *m,* rumor *m*

gossipy [ˈgɑsɪpi] *adj* : chismoso

got → **get**

Gothic [ˈgɑθɪk] *adj* : gótico

gotten → **get**

gouge[1] [ˈgaʊdʒ] *vt* **gouged; gouging 1** : excavar, escoplear (con una gubia) **2** SWINDLE : estafar, extorsionar

gouge[2] *n* **1** CHISEL : gubia *f,* formón *m* **2** GROOVE : ranura *f,* hoyo *m* (hecho por un formón)

goulash ['gu:ˌlɑʃ, -ˌlæʃ] *n* : estofado *m,* guiso *m* al estilo húngaro

gourd ['gord, 'gʊrd] *n* : calabaza *f*

gourmand ['gʊrˌmɑnd] *n* **1** GLUTTON : glotón *m,* -tona *f* **2** → **gourmet**

gourmet ['gʊrˌmeɪ, gʊr'meɪ] *n* : gourmet *mf;* gastrónomo *m,* -ma *f*

gout ['gaʊt] *n* : gota *f*

govern ['gʌvərn] *vt* **1** RULE : gobernar **2** CONTROL, DETERMINE : determinar, controlar, guiar **3** RESTRAIN : dominar (las emociones, etc.) — *vi* : gobernar

governess ['gʌvərnəs] *n* : institutriz *f*

government ['gʌvərmənt] *n* : gobierno *m*

governmental [ˌgʌvər'mɛntəl] *adj* : gubernamental, gubernativo

governor ['gʌvənər, 'gʌvərnər] *n* **1** : gobernador *m,* -dora *f* (de un estado, etc.) **2** : regulador *m* (de una máquina)

governorship ['gʌvənərˌʃɪp, 'gʌvərnər-] *n* : cargo *m* de gobernador

gown ['gaʊn] *n* **1** : vestido *m* <evening gown : traje de fiesta> **2** : toga *f* (de magistrados, clérigos, etc.)

grab[1] ['græb] *v* **grabbed; grabbing** *vt* SNATCH : agarrar, arrebatar — *vi* : agarrarse

grab[2] *n* **1 to make a grab for** : tratar de agarrar **2 up for grabs** : disponible, libre

grace[1] ['greɪs] *vt* **graced; gracing 1** HONOR : honrar **2** ADORN : adornar, embellecer

grace[2] *n* **1** : gracia *f* <by the grace of God : por la gracia de Dios> **2** BLESSING : bendición *f* (de la mesa) **3** RESPITE : plazo *m,* gracia *f* <a five days' grace (period) : un plazo de cinco días> **4** GRACIOUSNESS : gentileza *f,* cortesía *f* **5** ELEGANCE : elegancia *f,* gracia *f* **6 to be in the good graces of** : estar en buenas relaciones con **7 with good grace** : de buena gana

graceful ['greɪsfəl] *adj* : lleno de gracia, garboso, grácil

gracefully ['greɪsfəli] *adv* : con gracia, con garbo

gracefulness ['greɪsfəlnəs] *n* : gracilidad *f,* apostura *f,* gallardía *f*

graceless ['greɪsləs] *adj* **1** DISCOURTEOUS : descortés **2** CLUMSY, INELEGANT : torpe, desgarbado, poco elegante

gracious ['greɪʃəs] *adj* : cortés, gentil, cordial

graciously ['greɪʃəsli] *adv* : gentilmente

graciousness ['greɪʃəsnəs] *n* : gentileza *f*

gradation [greɪ'deɪʃən, grə-] *n* : gradación *f*

grade[1] ['greɪd] *vt* **graded; grading 1** SORT : clasificar **2** LEVEL : nivelar **3** : calificar (exámenes, alumnos)

grade[2] *n* **1** QUALITY : categoría *f,* calidad *f* **2** RANK : grado *m,* rango *m* (militar) **3** YEAR : grado *m,* curso *m,* año *m* <sixth grade : el sexto grado> **4** MARK : nota *f,* calificación *f* (en educación) **5** SLOPE : cuesta *f,* pendiente *f,* gradiente *f*

grade school → **elementary school**

gradual ['grædʒʊəl] *adj* : gradual, paulatino

gradually ['grædʒʊəli, 'grædʒəli] *adv* : gradualmente, poco a poco

graduate[1] ['grædʒʊˌeɪt] *v* **-ated; -ating** *vi* : graduarse, licenciarse — *vt* : graduar <a graduated thermometer : un termómetro graduado>

graduate[2] ['grædʒʊət] *adj* : de postgrado <graduate course : curso de postgrado>

graduate[3] *n* **1** : licenciado *m,* -da *f;* graduado *m,* -da *f* (de la universidad) **2** : bachiller *mf* (de la escuela secundaria)

graduate student *n* : postgraduado *m,* -da *f*

graduation [ˌgrædʒʊ'eɪʃən] *n* : graduación *f*

graffiti [grə'fi:ti, græ-] *npl* : pintadas *fpl,* graffiti *mpl*

graft[1] ['græft] *vt* : injertar

graft[2] *n* **1** : injerto *m* <skin graft : injerto cutáneo> **2** CORRUPTION : soborno *m* (político), ganancia *f* ilegal

grain ['greɪn] *n* **1** : grano *m* <a grain of corn : un grano de maíz> <like a grain of sand : como grano de arena> **2** CEREALS : cereales *mpl* **3** : veta *f,* vena *f,* grano *m* (de madera) **4** SPECK, TRACE : pizca *f,* ápice *m* <a grain of truth : una pizca de verdad> **5** : grano *m* (unidad de peso)

gram ['græm] *n* : gramo *m*

grammar ['græmər] *n* : gramática *f*

grammar school → **elementary school**

grammatical [grə'mætɪkəl] *adj* : gramatical — **grammatically** [-kli] *adv*

granary ['greɪnəri, 'græ-] *n, pl* **-ries** : granero *m*

grand ['grænd] *adj* **1** FOREMOST : grande **2** IMPRESSIVE : impresionante, magnífico <a grand view : una vista magnífica> **3** LAVISH : grandioso, suntuoso, lujoso <to live in a grand manner : vivir a lo grande> **4** FABULOUS : fabuloso, magnífico <to have a grand time : pasarlo estupendamente, pasarlo en grande> **5 grand total** : total *m,* suma *f* total

grandchild ['grændˌtʃaɪld] *n, pl* **-children** : nieto *m,* -ta *f*

granddaughter ['grændˌdɔtər] *n* : nieta *f*

grandeur ['grændʒər] *n* : grandiosidad *f,* esplendor *m*

grandfather ['grændˌfɑðər] *n* : abuelo *m*

grandiose ['grændiˌo:s, ˌgrændi'-] *adj* **1** IMPOSING : imponente, grandioso **2** POMPOUS : pomposo, presuntuoso

grandmother [ˈgrænd͵mʌðər] *n* : abuela *f*
grandparents [ˈgrænd͵pærənts] *npl* : abuelos *mpl*
grandson [ˈgrænd͵sʌn] *n* : nieto *m*
grandstand [ˈgrænd͵stænd] *n* : tribuna *f*
granite [ˈgrænɪt] *n* : granito *m*
grant[1] [ˈgrænt] *vt* **1** ALLOW : conceder <to grant a request : conceder una petición> **2** BESTOW : conceder, dar, otorgar <to grant a favor : otorgar un favor> **3** ADMIT : reconocer, admitir <I'll grant that he's clever : reconozco que es listo> **4 to take for granted** : dar (algo) por sentado
grant[2] *n* **1** GRANTING : concesión *f,* otorgamiento *m* **2** SCHOLARSHIP : beca *f* **3** SUBSIDY : subvención *f*
granular [ˈgrænjʊlər] *adj* : granular
granulated [ˈgrænjʊ͵leɪt̬əd] *adj* : granulado
grape [ˈgreɪp] *n* : uva *f*
grapefruit [ˈgreɪp͵fruːt] *n* : toronja *f,* pomelo *m*
grapevine [ˈgreɪp͵vaɪn] *n* **1** : vid *f,* parra *f* **2 through the grapevine** : por vías secretas <I heard it through the grapevine : me lo contaron>
graph [ˈgræf] *n* : gráfica *f,* gráfico *m*
graphic [ˈgræfɪk] *adj* **1** VIVID : vívido, gráfico **2 graphic arts** : artes gráficas
graphically [ˈgræfɪkli] *adv* : gráficamente
graphite [ˈgræ͵faɪt] *n* : grafito *m*
grapnel [ˈgræpnəl] *n* : rezón *m*
grapple [ˈgræpəl] *vi* **-pled; -pling 1** GRIP : agarrar (con un garfio) **2** STRUGGLE : forcejear, luchar (con un problema, etc.)
grasp[1] [ˈgræsp] *vt* **1** GRIP, SEIZE : agarrar, asir **2** COMPREHEND : entender, comprender — *vi* **to grasp at** : aprovechar
grasp[2] *n* **1** GRIP : agarre *m* **2** CONTROL : control *m,* garras *fpl* **3** REACH : alcance *m* <within your grasp : a su alcance> **4** UNDERSTANDING : comprensión *f,* entendimiento *m*
grass [ˈgræs] *n* **1** : hierba *f* (planta) **2** PASTURE : pasto *m,* zacate *m CA, Mex* **3** LAWN : césped *m,* pasto *m*
grasshopper [ˈgræs͵hɑpər] *n* : saltamontes *m*
grassland [ˈgræs͵lænd] *n* : pradera *f*
grassy [ˈgræsi] *adj* **grassier; -est** : cubierto de hierba
grate[1] [ˈgreɪt] *v* **grated; -ing** *vt* **1** : rallar (en cocina) **2** SCRAPE : rascar **3 to grate one's teeth** : hacer rechinar los dientes — *vi* **1** RASP, SQUEAK : chirriar **2** IRRITATE : irritar <to grate on one's nerves : crisparle los nervios a uno>
grate[2] *n* **1** : parrilla *f* (para cocinar) **2** GRATING : reja *f,* rejilla *f,* verja *f* (en una ventana)
grateful [ˈgreɪtfəl] *adj* : agradecido
gratefully [ˈgreɪtfəli] *adv* : con agradecimiento
gratefulness [ˈgreɪtfəlnəs] *n* : gratitud *f,* agradecimiento *m*
grater [ˈgreɪt̬ər] *n* : rallador *m*
gratification [͵græt̬əfəˈkeɪʃən] *n* : gratificación *f*
gratify [ˈgræt̬ə͵faɪ] *vt* **-fied; -fying 1** PLEASE : complacer **2** SATISFY : satisfacer, gratificar
grating [ˈgreɪt̬ɪŋ] *n* : reja *f,* rejilla *f*
gratis[1] [ˈgræt̬əs, ˈgreɪ-] *adv* : gratis, gratuitamente
gratis[2] *adj* : gratis, gratuito
gratitude [ˈgræt̬ə͵tuːd, -͵tjuːd] *n* : gratitud *f,* agradecimiento *m*
gratuitous [grəˈtuːət̬əs] *adj* : gratuito
gratuity [grəˈtuːət̬i] *n, pl* **-ities** TIP : propina *f*
grave[1] [ˈgreɪv] *adj* **graver; -est 1** IMPORTANT : grave, de mucha gravedad **2** SERIOUS, SOLEMN : grave, serio
grave[2] *n* : tumba *f,* sepultura *f*
gravel [ˈgrævəl] *n* : grava *f,* gravilla *f*
gravelly [ˈgrævəli] *adj* **1** : de grava **2** HARSH : áspero (dícese de la voz)
gravely [ˈgreɪvli] *adv* : gravemente
gravestone [ˈgreɪv͵stoːn] *n* : lápida *f*
graveyard [ˈgreɪv͵jɑrd] *n* CEMETERY : cementerio *m,* panteón *m,* camposanto *m*
gravitate [ˈgrævə͵teɪt] *vi* **-tated; -tating** : gravitar
gravitation [͵grævəˈteɪʃən] *n* : gravitación *f*
gravitational [͵grævəˈteɪʃənəl] *adj* : gravitacional
gravity [ˈgrævət̬i] *n, pl* **-ties 1** SERIOUSNESS : gravedad *f,* seriedad *f* **2** : gravedad *f* <the law of gravity : la ley de la gravedad>
gravy [ˈgreɪvi] *n, pl* **-vies** : salsa *f* (preparada con el jugo de la carne asada)
gray[1] [ˈgreɪ] *vt* : hacer gris — *vi* : encanecer, ponerse gris
gray[2] *adj* **1** : gris (dícese del color) **2** : cano, canoso <gray hair : pelo canoso> <to go gray : volverse cano> **3** DISMAL, GLOOMY : gris, triste
gray[3] *n* : gris *m*
grayish [ˈgreɪɪʃ] *adj* : grisáceo
graze [ˈgreɪz] *v* **grazed; grazing** *vi* : pastar, pacer — *vt* **1** : pastorear (ganado) **2** BRUSH : rozar **3** SCRATCH : raspar
grease[1] [ˈgriːs, ˈgriːz] *vt* **greased; greasing** : engrasar, lubricar
grease[2] [ˈgriːs] *n* : grasa *f*
greasy [ˈgriːsi, -zi] *adj* **greasier; -est 1** : grasiento **2** OILY : graso, grasoso
great [ˈgreɪt] *adj* **1** LARGE : grande <a great mountain : una montaña grande> <a great crowd : una gran muchedumbre> **2** INTENSE : intenso, fuerte, grande <great pain : gran dolor> **3** EMINENT : grande, eminente, distinguido <a great poet : un gran poeta> **4** EXCELLENT, TERRIFIC : excelente, estupendo, fabuloso <to have a

great time : pasarlo en grande> **5 a great while :** mucho tiempo

great-aunt [ˌgreɪtˈænt, -ˈɑnt] *n* : tía *f* abuela

greater [ˈgreɪt̬ər] (*comparative of* **great**) : mayor

greatest [ˈgreɪt̬əst] (*superlative of* **great**) : el mayor, la mayor

great–grandchild [ˌgreɪtˈgrændˌtʃaɪld] *n, pl* **-children** [-ˌtʃɪldrən] : bisnieto *m*, -ta *f*

great–grandfather [ˌgreɪtˈgrændˌfɑðər] *n* : bisabuelo *m*

great–grandmother [ˌgreɪtˈgrændˌmʌðər] *n* : bisabuela *f*

greatly [ˈgreɪtli] *adv* **1** MUCH : mucho, sumamente <to be greatly improved : haber mejorado mucho> **2** VERY : muy <greatly superior : muy superior>

greatness [ˈgreɪtnəs] *n* : grandeza *f*

great–uncle [ˌgreɪtˈʌŋkəl] *n* : tío *m* abuelo

grebe [ˈgri:b] *n* : somorgujo *m*

greed [ˈgri:d] *n* **1** AVARICE : avaricia *f*, codicia *f* **2** GLUTTONY : glotonería *f*, gula *f*

greedily [ˈgri:dəli] *adv* : con avaricia, con gula

greediness [ˈgri:dinəs] → **greed**

greedy [ˈgri:di] *adj* **greedier; -est 1** AVARICIOUS : codicioso, avaricioso **2** GLUTTONOUS : glotón

Greek [ˈgri:k] *n* **1 :** griego *m*, -ga *f* **2** : griego *m* (idioma) — **Greek** *adj*

green[1] [ˈgri:n] *adj* **1 :** verde (dícese del color) **2** UNRIPE : verde, inmaduro **3** INEXPERIENCED : verde, novato

green[2] *n* **1** : verde *m* **2 greens** *npl* VEGETABLES : verduras *fpl*

greenery [ˈgri:nəri] *n, pl* **-eries :** plantas *fpl* verdes, vegetación *f*

greenhorn [ˈgri:nˌhɔrn] *n* : novato *m*, -ta *f*

greenhouse [ˈgri:nˌhaʊs] *n* : invernadero *m*

greenhouse effect : efecto *m* invernadero

greenish [ˈgri:nɪʃ] *adj* : verdoso

Greenlander [ˈgri:nləndər, -ˌlæn-] *n* : groenlandés *m*, -desa *f*

greenness [ˈgri:nnəs] *n* **1** : verdor *m* **2** INEXPERIENCE : inexperiencia *f*

green thumb *n* **to have a green thumb** : tener buena mano para las plantas

greet [ˈgri:t] *vt* **1 :** saludar <to greet a friend : saludar a un amigo> **2** : acoger, recibir <they greeted him with boos : lo recibieron con abucheos>

greeting [ˈgri:t̬ɪŋ] *n* **1** : saludo *m* **2 greetings** *npl* REGARDS : saludos *mpl*, recuerdos *mpl*

gregarious [grɪˈgæriəs] *adj* : gregario (dícese de los animales), sociable (dícese de las personas) — **gregariously** *adv*

gregariousness [grɪˈgæriəsnəs] *n* : sociabilidad *f*

gremlin [ˈgrɛmlən] *n* : duende *m*

grenade [grəˈneɪd] *n* : granada *f*

Grenadian [grəˈneɪdiən] *n* : granadino *m*, -na *f* — **Grenadian** *adj*

grew → **grow**

grey → **gray**

greyhound [ˈgreɪˌhaʊnd] *n* : galgo *m*

grid [ˈgrɪd] *n* **1** GRATING : rejilla *f* **2** NETWORK : red *f* (de electricidad, etc.) **3** : cuadriculado *m* (de un mapa)

griddle [ˈgrɪdəl] *n* : plancha *f*

griddle cake → **pancake**

gridiron [ˈgrɪdˌaɪərn] *n* **1** GRILL : parrilla *f* **2** : campo *m* de futbol americano

grief [ˈgri:f] *n* **1** SORROW : dolor *m*, pena *f* **2** ANNOYANCE, TROUBLE : problemas *mpl*, molestia *f*

grievance [ˈgri:vənts] *n* COMPLAINT : queja *f*

grieve [ˈgri:v] *v* **grieved; grieving** *vt* DISTRESS : afligir, entristecer, apenar — *vi* **1** : sufrir, afligirse **2 to grieve for** *or* **to grieve over** : llorar, lamentar

grievous [ˈgri:vəs] *adj* **1** OPPRESSIVE : gravoso, opresivo, severo **2** GRAVE, SERIOUS : grave, severo, doloroso

grievously [ˈgri:vəsli] *adv* : gravemente, de gravedad

grill[1] [ˈgrɪl] *vt* **1** : asar (a la parrilla) **2** INTERROGATE : interrogar

grill[2] *n* **1** : parrilla *f* (para cocinar) **2** : parrillada *f* (comida) **3** RESTAURANT : grill *m*

grille *or* **grill** [ˈgrɪl] *n* : reja *f*, enrejado *m*

grim [ˈgrɪm] *adj* **grimmer; grimmest 1** CRUEL : cruel, feroz **2** STERN : adusto, severo <a grim expression : un gesto severo> **3** GLOOMY : sombrío, deprimente **4** SINISTER : macabro, siniestro **5** UNYIELDING : inflexible, persistente <with grim determination : con una voluntad de hierro>

grimace[1] [ˈgrɪməs, grɪˈmeɪs] *vi* **-maced; -macing :** hacer muecas

grimace[2] *n* : mueca *f*

grime [ˈgraɪm] *n* : mugre *f*, suciedad *f*

grimly [ˈgrɪmli] *adv* **1** STERNLY : severamente **2** RESOLUTELY : inexorablemente

grimy [ˈgraɪmi] *adj* **grimier; -est** : mugriento, sucio

grin[1] [ˈgrɪn] *vi* **grinned; grinning** : sonreír abiertamente

grin[2] *n* : sonrisa *f* abierta

grind[1] [ˈgraɪnd] *v* **ground** [ˈgraʊnd]; **grinding** *vt* **1** CRUSH : moler, machacar, triturar **2** SHARPEN : afilar **3** POLISH : pulir, esmerilar (lentes, espejos) **4 to grind one's teeth** : rechinarle los dientes a uno **5 to grind down** OPPRESS : oprimir, agobiar — *vi* **1** : funcionar con dificultad, rechinar <to grind to a halt : pararse

poco a poco, llegar a un punto muerto> **2** STUDY : estudiar mucho
grind[2] *n* : trabajo *m* pesado <the daily grind : la rutina diaria>
grinder [ˈgraɪndər] *n* : molinillo *m* <coffee grinder : molinillo de café>
grindstone [ˈgraɪnd,sto:n] *n* : piedra *m* de afilar
grip[1] [ˈgrɪp] *vt* **gripped; gripping** **1** GRASP : agarrar, asir **2** HOLD, INTEREST : captar el interés de
grip[2] *n* **1** GRASP : agarre *m,* asidero *m* <to have a firm grip on something : agarrarse bien de algo> **2** CONTROL, HOLD : control *m,* dominio *m* <to lose one's grip on : perder el control de> <inflation tightened its grip on the economy : la inflación se afianzó en su dominio de la economía> **3** UNDERSTANDING : comprensión *f,* entendimiento *m* <to come to grips with : llegar a entender> **4** HANDLE : asidero *m,* empuñadura *f* (de un arma)
gripe[1] [ˈgraɪp] *v* **griped; griping** *vt* IRRITATE, VEX : irritar, fastidiar, molestar — *vi* COMPLAIN : quejarse, rezongar
gripe[2] *n* : queja *f*
grippe [ˈgrɪp] *n* : influenza *f,* gripe *f,* gripa *f Col, Mex*
grisly [ˈgrɪzli] *adj* **-lier; -est** : horripilante, horroroso, truculento
grist [ˈgrɪst] *n* : molienda *f* <it's all grist for the mill : todo ayuda, todo es provechoso>
gristle [ˈgrɪsəl] *n* : cartílago *m*
gristly [ˈgrɪsli] *adj* **-tlier; -est** : cartilaginoso
grit[1] [ˈgrɪt] *vt* **gritted; gritting** : hacer rechinar (los dientes, etc.)
grit[2] *n* **1** SAND : arena *f* **2** GRAVEL : grava *f* **3** COURAGE : valor *m,* coraje *m* **4 grits** *npl* : sémola *f* de maíz
gritty [ˈgrɪṭi] *adj* **-tier; -est** **1** : arenoso <a gritty surface : una superficie arenosa> **2** PLUCKY : valiente
grizzled [ˈgrɪzəld] *adj* : entrecano
grizzly bear [ˈgrɪzli] *n* : oso *m* pardo
groan[1] [ˈgro:n] *vi* **1** MOAN : gemir, quejarse **2** CREAK : crujir
groan[2] *n* **1** MOAN : gemido *m,* quejido *m* **2** CREAK : crujido *m*
grocer [ˈgro:sər] *n* : tendero *m,* -ra *f*
grocery [ˈgro:səri, -ʃəri] *n, pl* **-ceries** **1** *or* **grocery store** : tienda *f* de comestibles, tienda *f* de abarrotes **2 groceries** *npl* : comestibles *mpl,* abarrotes *mpl*
groggy [ˈgrɑgi] *adj* **-gier; -est** : atontado, grogui, tambaleante
groin [ˈgrɔɪn] *n* : ingle *f*
grommet [ˈgrɑmət, ˈgrʌ-] *n* : arandela *f*
groom[1] [ˈgru:m, ˈgrʊm] *vt* **1** : cepillar, almohazar (un animal) **2** : arreglar, cuidar <well-groomed : bien arreglado> **3** PREPARE : preparar
groom[2] *n* **1** : mozo *m,* -za *f* de cuadra **2** BRIDEGROOM : novio *m*
groove[1] [ˈgru:v] *vt* **grooved; grooving** : acanalar, hacer ranuras en, surcar
groove[2] *n* **1** FURROW, SLOT : ranura *f,* surco *m* **2** RUT : rutina *f*
grope [ˈgro:p] *v* **groped; groping** *vi* : andar a tientas, tantear <he groped for the switch : buscó el interruptor a tientas> — *vt* **to grope one's way** : avanzar a tientas
gross[1] [ˈgro:s] *vt* : tener entrada bruta de, recaudar en bruto
gross[2] *adj* **1** FLAGRANT : flagrante, grave <a gross error : un error flagrante> <a gross injustice : una injusticia grave> **2** FAT : muy gordo, obeso **3** : bruto <gross national product : producto nacional bruto> **4** COARSE, VULGAR : grosero, basto
gross[3] *n* **1** *pl* **gross** : gruesa *f* (12 docenas) **2** *or* **gross income** : ingresos *mpl* brutos
grossly [ˈgro:sli] *adv* **1** EXTREMELY : extremadamente <grossly unfair : totalmente injusto> **2** CRUDELY : groseramente
grotesque [gro:ˈtɛsk] *adj* : grotesco
grotesquely [gro:ˈtɛskli] *adv* : de forma grotesca
grotto [ˈgrɑṭo:] *n, pl* **-toes** : gruta *f*
grouch[1] [ˈgraʊtʃ] *vi* : refunfuñar, rezongar
grouch[2] *n* **1** COMPLAINT : queja *f* **2** GRUMBLER : gruñón *m,* -ñona *f;* cascarrabias *mf fam*
grouchy [ˈgraʊtʃi] *adj* **grouchier; -est** : malhumorado, gruñón
ground[1] [ˈgraʊnd] *vt* **1** BASE : fundar, basar **2** INSTRUCT : enseñar los conocimientos básicos a <to be well grounded in : ser muy entendido en> **3** : conectar a tierra (un aparato eléctrico) **4** : varar, hacer encallar (un barco) **5** : restringir (un avión o un piloto) a la tierra
ground[2] *n* **1** EARTH, SOIL : suelo *m,* tierra *f* <to dig (in) the ground : cavar la tierra> <to fall to the ground : caerse al suelo> **2** LAND, TERRAIN : terreno *m* <hilly ground : terreno alto> <to lose ground : perder terreno> **3** BASIS, REASON : razón *f,* motivo *m* <grounds for complaint : motivos de queja> **4** BACKGROUND : fondo *m* **5** FIELD : campo *m,* plaza *f* <parade ground : plaza de armas> **6** : tierra *f* (para electricidad) **7 grounds** *npl* PREMISES : recinto *m,* terreno *m* **8 grounds** *npl* DREGS : posos *mpl* (de café)
ground[3] → **grind**
groundhog [ˈgraʊnd,hɔg] *n* : marmota *f* (de América)
groundless [ˈgraʊndləs] *adj* : infundado
groundwork [ˈgraʊnd,wərk] *n* **1** FOUNDATION : fundamento *m,* base *f* **2** PREPARATION : trabajo *m* preparatorio
group[1] [ˈgru:p] *vt* : agrupar
group[2] *n* : grupo *m,* agrupación *f,* conjunto *m,* compañía *f*

grouper [ˈgruːpər] *n* : mero *m*
grouse[1] [ˈgraʊs] *vi* **groused; grousing** : quejarse, rezongar, refunfuñar
grouse[2] *n, pl* **grouse** *or* **grouses** : urogallo *m* (ave)
grout [ˈgraʊt] *n* : lechada *f*
grove [ˈgroːv] *n* : bosquecillo *m,* arboleda *f,* soto *m*
grovel [ˈgrɑvəl, ˈgrʌ-] *vi* **-eled** *or* **-elled; -eling** *or* **-elling 1** CRAWL : arrastrarse **2** : humillarse, postrarse <to grovel before someone : postrarse ante alguien>
grow [ˈgroː] *v* **grew** [ˈgruː]; **grown** [ˈgroːn]; **growing** *vi* **1** : crecer <palm trees grow on the islands : las palmas crecen en las islas> <my hair grows very fast : mi pelo crece muy rápido> **2** DEVELOP, MATURE : desarrollarse, madurar **3** INCREASE : crecer, aumentar **4** BECOME : hacerse, volverse, ponerse <she was growing angry : se estaba poniendo furiosa> <to grow dark : oscurecerse> **5 to grow up** : hacerse mayor <grow up! : ¡no seas niño!> — *vt* **1** CULTIVATE, RAISE : cultivar **2** : dejar crecer <to grow one's hair : dejarse crecer el pelo>
grower [ˈgroːər] *n* : cultivador *m,* -dora *f*
growl[1] [ˈgraʊl] *vi* : gruñir (dícese de un animal), refunfuñar (dícese de una persona)
growl[2] *n* : gruñido *m*
grown–up[1] [ˈgroːnˌəp] *adj* : adulto, mayor
grown–up[2] *n* : adulto *m,* -ta *f;* persona *f* mayor
growth [ˈgroːθ] *n* **1** : crecimiento *m* <to stunt one's growth : detener el crecimiento> **2** INCREASE : aumento *m,* crecimiento *m,* expansión *f* **3** DEVELOPMENT : desarrollo *m* <economic growth : desarrollo económico> <a five days' growth of beard : una barba de cinco días> **4** LUMP, TUMOR : bulto *m,* tumor *m*
grub[1] [ˈgrʌb] *vi* **grubbed; grubbing 1** DIG : escarbar **2** RUMMAGE : hurgar, buscar **3** DRUDGE : trabajar duro
grub[2] *n* **1** : larva *f* <beetle grub : larva del escarabajo> **2** DRUDGE : esclavo *m,* -va *f* del trabajo **3** FOOD : comida *f*
grubby [ˈgrʌbi] *adj* **grubbier; -est** : mugriento, sucio
grudge[1] [ˈgrʌdʒ] *vt* **grudged; grudging** : resentir, envidiar
grudge[2] *n* : rencor *m,* resentimiento *m* <to hold a grudge : guardar rencor>
grueling *or* **gruelling** [ˈgruːlɪŋ, ˈgruːə-] *adj* : extenuante, agotador, duro
gruesome [ˈgruːsəm] *adj* : horripilante, truculento, horroroso
gruff [ˈgrʌf] *adj* **1** BRUSQUE : brusco <a gruff reply : una respuesta brusca> **2** HOARSE : ronco — **gruffly** *adv*
grumble[1] [ˈgrʌmbəl] *vi* **-bled; -bling 1** COMPLAIN : refunfuñar, rezongar, quejarse **2** RUMBLE : hacer un ruido sordo, retumbar (dícese del trueno)
grumble[2] *n* **1** COMPLAINT : queja *f* **2** RUMBLE : ruido *m* sordo, estruendo *m*
grumbler [ˈgrʌmbələr] *n* : gruñón *m,* -ñona *f*
grumpy [ˈgrʌmpi] *adj* **grumpier; -est** : malhumorado, gruñón
grunt[1] [ˈgrʌnt] *vi* : gruñir
grunt[2] *n* : gruñido *m*
guacamole [ˌgwɑkəˈmoːli] *n* : guacamole *m,* guacamol *m*
guarantee[1] [ˌgærənˈtiː] *vt* **-teed; -teeing 1** PROMISE : asegurar, prometer **2** : poner bajo garantía, garantizar (un producto o servicio)
guarantee[2] *n* **1** PROMISE : garantía *f,* promesa *f* <lifetime guarantee : garantía de por vida> **2** → **guarantor**
guarantor [ˌgærənˈtɔr] *n* : garante *mf;* fiador *m,* -dora *f*
guaranty [ˌgærənˈtiː] → **guarantee**
guard[1] [ˈgɑrd] *vt* **1** DEFEND, PROTECT : defender, proteger **2** : guardar, vigilar, custodiar <to guard the frontier : vigilar la frontera> <she guarded my secret well : guardó bien mi secreto> — *vi* **to guard against** : protegerse contra, evitar
guard[2] *n* **1** WATCHMAN : guarda *mf* <security guard : guarda de seguridad> **2** VIGILANCE : guardia *f,* vigilancia *f* <to be on guard : estar en guardia> <to let one's guard down : bajar la guardia> **3** SAFEGUARD : salvaguardia *f,* dispositivo *m* de seguridad (en una máquina) **4** PRECAUTION : precaución *f,* protección *f*
guardhouse [ˈgɑrdˌhaʊs] *n* : cuartel *m* de la guardia
guardian [ˈgɑrdiən] *n* **1** PROTECTOR : guardián *m,* -diana *f;* custodio *m,* -dia *f* **2** : tutor *m,* -tora *f* (de un niño)
guardianship [ˈgɑrdiənˌʃɪp] *n* : custodia *f,* tutela *f*
Guatemalan [ˌgwɑtəˈmɑlən] *n* : guatemalteco *m,* -ca *f* — **Guatemalan** *adj*
guava [ˈgwɑvə] *n* : guayaba *f*
gubernatorial [ˌguːbənəˈtoriːəl, ˌgjuː-] *adj* : del gobernador
guerrilla *or* **guerilla** [gəˈrɪlə] *n* : guerrillero *m,* -ra *f*
guess[1] [ˈgɛs] *vt* **1** CONJECTURE : adivinar, conjeturar <guess what happened! : ¡adivina lo que pasó!> **2** SUPPOSE : pensar, creer, suponer <I guess so : supongo que sí> **3** : adivinar correctamente, acertar <to guess the answer : acertar la respuesta> — *vi* : adivinar
guess[2] *n* : conjetura *f,* suposición *f*
guesswork [ˈgɛsˌwərk] *n* : suposiciones *fpl,* conjeturas *fpl*
guest [ˈgɛst] *n* : huésped *mf;* invitado *m,* -da *f*
guffaw[1] [gəˈfɔ] *vi* : reírse a carcajadas, carcajearse *fam*

guffaw² [gə'fɔ, 'gʌˌfɔ] *n* **:** carcajada *f,* risotada *f*

guidance ['gaɪdənts] *n* **:** orientación *f,* consejos *mpl*

guide¹ ['gaɪd] *vt* **guided; guiding 1** DIRECT, LEAD **:** guiar, dirigir, conducir **2** ADVISE, COUNSEL **:** aconsejar, orientar

guide² *n* **:** guía *f*

guidebook ['gaɪdˌbʊk] *n* **:** guía *f* (para viajeros)

guideline ['gaɪdˌlaɪn] *n* **:** pauta *f,* directriz *f*

guild ['gɪld] *n* **:** gremio *m,* sindicato *m,* asociación *f*

guile ['gaɪl] *n* **:** astucia *f,* engaño *m*

guileless ['gaɪlləs] *adj* **:** inocente, cándido, sin malicia

guillotine¹ ['gɪləˌtiːn, 'giːjəˌ-] *vt* **-tined; -tining :** guillotinar

guillotine² *n* **:** guillotina *f*

guilt ['gɪlt] *n* **:** culpa *f,* culpabilidad *f*

guilty ['gɪlti] *adj* **guiltier; -est :** culpable

guinea fowl ['gɪni] *n* **:** gallina *f* de Guinea

guinea pig *n* **:** conejillo *m* de Indias, cobaya *f*

guise ['gaɪz] *n* **:** apariencia *f,* aspecto *m,* forma *f*

guitar [gə'tɑr, gɪ-] *n* **:** guitarra *f*

gulch ['gʌltʃ] *n* **:** barranco *m,* quebrada *f*

gulf ['gʌlf] *n* **1 :** golfo *m* <the Gulf of Mexico : el Golfo de México> **2** GAP **:** brecha *f* <the gulf between generations : la brecha entre las generaciones> **3** CHASM **:** abismo *m*

gull ['gʌl] *n* **:** gaviota *f*

gullet ['gʌlət] *n* **:** garganta *f*

gullible ['gʌlɪbəl] *adj* **:** crédulo

gully ['gʌli] *n, pl* **-lies :** barranco *m,* hondonada *f*

gulp¹ ['gʌlp] *vt* **1 :** engullir, tragar <he gulped down the whiskey : engulló el whisky> **2** SUPPRESS **:** suprimir, reprimir, tragar <to gulp down a sob : reprimir un sollozo> **—** *vi* **:** tragar saliva, tener un nudo en la garganta

gulp² *n* **:** trago *m*

gum ['gʌm] *n* **1** CHEWING GUM **:** goma *f* de mascar, chicle *m* **2 gums** *npl* **:** encías *fpl*

gumbo ['gʌmˌboː] *n* **:** sopa *f* de quingombó

gumdrop ['gʌmˌdrɑp] *n* **:** pastilla *f* de goma

gummy ['gʌmi] *adj* **gummier; -est :** gomoso

gumption ['gʌmpʃən] *n* **:** iniciativa *f,* agallas *fpl fam*

gun¹ ['gʌn] *vt* **gunned; gunning 1** *or* **to gun down :** matar a tiros, asesinar **2 :** acelerar (rápidamente) <to gun the engine : acelerar el motor>

gun² *n* **1** CANNON **:** cañón *m* **2** FIREARM **:** arma *f* de fuego **3** SPRAY GUN **:** pistola *f* **4 to jump the gun :** adelantarse, salir antes de tiempo

gunboat ['gʌnˌboːt] *n* **:** cañonero *m*

gunfight ['gʌnˌfaɪt] *n* **:** tiroteo *m,* balacera *f*

gunfire ['gʌnˌfaɪr] *n* **:** disparos *mpl*

gunman ['gʌnmən] *n, pl* **-men** [-mən, -ˌmɛn] **:** pistolero *m,* gatillero *m Mex*

gunner ['gʌnər] *n* **:** artillero *m,* -ra *f*

gunnysack ['gʌniˌsæk] *n* **:** saco *m* de yute

gunpowder ['gʌnˌpaʊdər] *n* **:** pólvora *f*

gunshot ['gʌnˌʃɑt] *n* **:** disparo *m,* tiro *m,* balazo *m*

gunwale ['gʌnəl] *n* **:** borda *f*

guppy ['gʌpi] *n, pl* **-pies :** lebistes *m*

gurgle¹ ['gərgəl] *vi* **-gled; -gling 1 :** borbotar, gorgotear (dícese de un líquido) **2 :** gorjear (dícese de un niño)

gurgle² *n* **1 :** borboteo *m,* gorgoteo *m* (de un líquido) **2 :** gorjeo *m* (de un niño)

gush ['gʌʃ] *vi* **1** SPOUT **:** surgir, salir a chorros, chorrear **2 :** hablar con entusiasmo efusivo <she gushed with praise : se deshizo en elogios>

gust ['gʌst] *n* **:** ráfaga *f,* racha *f*

gusto ['gʌsˌtoː] *n, pl* **gustoes :** entusiasmo *m* <with gusto : con deleite, con ganas>

gusty ['gʌsti] *adj* **gustier; -est :** racheado

gut¹ ['gʌt] *vt* **gutted; gutting 1** EVISCERATE **:** destripar (un pollo, etc.), limpiar (un pescado) **2 :** destruir el interior de (un edificio)

gut² *n* **1** INTESTINE **:** intestino *m* **2 guts** *npl* INNARDS **:** tripas *fpl fam,* entrañas *fpl* **3 guts** *npl* COURAGE **:** valentía *f,* agallas *fpl*

gutter ['gʌt̬ər] *n* **1 :** canal *mf,* canaleta *f* (de un techo) **2 :** cuneta *f,* arroyo *m* (de una calle)

guttural ['gʌt̬ərəl] *adj* **:** gutural

guy ['gaɪ] *n* **1** *or* **guyline :** cuerda *f* tensora, cable *m* **2** FELLOW **:** tipo *m,* hombre *m*

guzzle ['gʌzəl] *vt* **-zled; -zling :** chupar, tragarse

gym ['dʒɪm] → **gymnasium**

gymnasium [dʒɪm'neɪziəm, -ʒəm] *n, pl* **-siums** *or* **-sia** [-ziːə, -ʒə] **:** gimnasio *m*

gymnast ['dʒɪmnəst, -ˌnæst] *n* **:** gimnasta *mf*

gymnastic [dʒɪm'næstɪk] *adj* **:** gimnástico

gymnastics [dʒɪm'næstɪks] *ns & pl* **:** gimnasia *f*

gynecologist [ˌgaɪnə'kɑlədʒɪst, ˌdʒɪnə-] *n* **:** ginecólogo *m,* -ga *f*

gynecology [ˌgaɪnə'kɑlədʒi, ˌdʒɪnə-] *n* **:** ginecología *f*

gyp¹ ['dʒɪp] *vt* **gypped; gypping :** estafar, timar

gyp² *n* **1** SWINDLER **:** estafador *m,* -dora *f* **2** FRAUD, SWINDLE **:** estafa *f,* timo *m fam*

gypsum ['dʒɪpsəm] *n* **:** yeso *m*

Gypsy [ˈdʒɪpsi] *n, pl* **-sies** : gitano *m,* -na *f*

gyrate [ˈdʒaɪˌreɪt] *vi* **-rated; -rating** : girar, rotar

gyration [dʒaɪˈreɪʃən] *n* : giro *m,* rotación *f*

gyroscope [ˈdʒaɪrəˌskoːp] *n* : giroscopio *m,* giróscopo *m*

H

h [ˈeɪtʃ] *n, pl* **h's** *or* **hs** [ˈeɪtʃəz] : octava letra del alfabeto inglés

haberdashery [ˈhæbərˌdæʃəri] *n, pl* **-eries** : tienda *f* de ropa para caballeros

habit [ˈhæbɪt] *n* **1** CUSTOM : hábito *m,* costumbre *f* **2** : hábito *m* (de un monje o una religiosa) **3** ADDICTION : dependencia *f,* adicción *f*

habitable [ˈhæbɪtəbəl] *adj* : habitable

habitat [ˈhæbɪˌtæt] *n* : hábitat *m*

habitation [ˌhæbɪˈteɪʃən] *n* **1** OCCUPANCY : habitación *f* **2** RESIDENCE : residencia *f,* morada *f*

habit-forming [ˈhæbɪtˌfɔrmɪŋ] *adj* : que crea dependencia

habitual [həˈbɪtʃʊəl] *adj* **1** CUSTOMARY : habitual, acostumbrado **2** INVETERATE : incorregible, empedernido — **habitually** *adv*

habituate [həˈbɪtʃʊˌeɪt] *vt* **-ated; -ating** : habituar, acostumbrar

hack[1] [ˈhæk] *vt* : cortar, tajar <to hack one's way : abrirse paso> — *vi* **1** : hacer tajos **2** COUGH : toser

hack[2] *n* **1** CHOP : hachazo *m,* tajo *m* **2** HORSE : caballo *m* de alquiler **3** WRITER : escritor *m,* -tora *f* a sueldo; escritorzuelo *m,* -la *f* **4** COUGH : tos *f* seca

hackles [ˈhækəlz] *npl* **1** : pluma *f* erizada (de un ave), pelo *m* erizado (de un perro, etc.) **2 to get one's hackles up** : ponerse furioso

hackney [ˈhækni] *n, pl* **-neys** : caballo *m* de silla, caballo *m* de tiro

hackneyed [ˈhæknid] *adj* TRITE : trillado, gastado

hacksaw [ˈhækˌsɔ] *n* : sierra *f* para metales

had → **have**

haddock [ˈhædək] *ns & pl* : eglefino *m*

hadn't [ˈhædənt] (*contraction of* **had not**) → **have**

haft [ˈhæft] *n* : mango *m,* empuñadura *f*

hag [ˈhæg] *n* **1** WITCH : bruja *f,* hechicera *f* **2** CRONE : vieja *f* fea

haggard [ˈhægərd] *adj* : demacrado, macilento — **haggardly** *adv*

haggle [ˈhægəl] *vi* **-gled; -gling** : regatear

ha-ha [ˌhɑˈhɑ, ˈhɑˈhɑ] *interj* : ¡ja, ja!

hail[1] [ˈheɪl] *vt* **1** GREET : saludar **2** SUMMON : llamar <to hail a taxi : llamar un taxi> — *vi* : granizar (en meteorología)

hail[2] *n* **1** : granizo *m* **2** BARRAGE : aluvión *m,* lluvia *f*

hail[3] *interj* : ¡salve!

hailstone [ˈheɪlˌstoːn] *n* : granizo *m,* piedra *f* de granizo

hailstorm [ˈheɪlˌstɔrm] *n* : granizada *f*

hair [ˈhær] *n* **1** : pelo *m,* cabello *m* <to get one's hair cut : cortarse el pelo> **2** : vello *m* (en las piernas, etc.)

hairbreadth [ˈhærˌbrɛdθ] *or* **hairsbreadth** [ˈhærz-] *n* **by a hairbreadth** : por un pelo

hairbrush [ˈhærˌbrʌʃ] *n* : cepillo *m* (del pelo)

haircut [ˈhærˌkʌt] *n* : corte *m* de pelo

hairdo [ˈhærˌduː] *n, pl* **-dos** : peinado *m*

hairdresser [ˈhærˌdrɛsər] *n* : peluquero *m,* -ra *f*

hairiness [ˈhærinəs] *n* : vellosidad *f*

hairless [ˈhærləs] *adj* : sin pelo, calvo, pelón

hairline [ˈhærˌlaɪn] *n* **1** : línea *f* delgada **2** : nacimiento *m* del pelo <to have a receding hairline : tener entradas>

hairpin [ˈhærˌpɪn] *n* : horquilla *f*

hair-raising [ˈhærˌreɪzɪŋ] *adj* : espeluznante

hairy [ˈhæri] *adj* **hairier; -est** : peludo, velludo

Haitian [ˈheɪʃən, ˈheɪtiən] *n* : haitiano *m,* -na *f* — **Haitian** *adj*

hake [ˈheɪk] *n* : merluza *f*

hale[1] [ˈheɪl] *vt* **haled; haling** : arrastrar, halar <to hale to court : arrastrar al tribunal>

hale[2] *adj* : saludable, robusto

half[1] [ˈhæf, ˈhaf] *adv* : medio, a medias <half cooked : medio cocido>

half[2] *adj* : medio, a medias <a half hour : una media hora> <a half truth : una verdad a medias>

half[3] *n, pl* **halves** [ˈhævz, ˈhavz] **1** : mitad *f* <half of my friends : la mitad de mis amigos> <in half : por la mitad> **2** : tiempo *m* (en deportes)

half brother *n* : medio hermano *m,* hermanastro *m*

halfhearted [ˈhæfˈhɑrtəd] *adj* : sin ánimo, poco entusiasta

halfheartedly [ˈhæfˈhɑrtədli] *adv* : con poco entusiasmo, sin ánimo

half-life [ˈhæfˌlaɪf] *n, pl* **half-lives** : media vida *f*

half sister *n* : media hermana *f,* hermanastra *f*

halfway[1] [ˈhæfˈweɪ] *adv* : a medio camino, a mitad de camino

halfway[2] *adj* : medio, intermedio <a halfway point : un punto intermedio>

half-wit [ˈhæfˌwɪt] *n* : tonto *m,* -ta *f;* imbécil *mf*

half–witted [ˈhæfˌwɪt̬əd] *adj* : estúpido

halibut [ˈhælɪbət] *ns & pl* : halibut *m*

hall [ˈhɔl] *n* **1** BUILDING : residencia *f* estudiantil, facultad *f* (de una universidad) **2** VESTIBULE : entrada *f,* vestíbulo *m,* zaguán *m* **3** CORRIDOR : corredor *m,* pasillo *m* **4** AUDITORIUM : sala *f,* salón *m* <concert hall : sala de conciertos> **5 city hall** : ayuntamiento *m*

hallelujah [ˌhæləˈluːjə, ˌhɑ-] *interj* : ¡aleluya!

hallmark [ˈhɔlˌmɑrk] *n* : sello *m* (distintivo)

hallow [ˈhæˌloː] *vt* : santificar, consagrar

hallowed [ˈhæˌloːd, ˈhæˌloːəd, ˈhɑˌloːd] *adj* : sagrado

Halloween [ˌhæləˈwiːn, ˌhɑ-] *n* : víspera *f* de Todos los Santos

hallucinate [həˈluːsənˌeɪt] *vi* **-nated; -nating** : alucinar

hallucination [həˌluːsənˈeɪʃən] *n* : alucinación *f*

hallucinatory [həˈluːsənəˌtori] *adj* : alucinante

hallucinogen [həˈluːsənədʒən] *n* : alucinógeno *m*

hallucinogenic [həˌluːsənəˈdʒɛnɪk] *adj* : alucinógeno

hallway [ˈhɔlˌweɪ] *n* **1** ENTRANCE : entrada *f* **2** CORRIDOR : corredor *m,* pasillo *m*

halo [ˈheɪˌloː] *n, pl* **-los** *or* **-loes** : aureola *f,* halo *m*

halt[1] [ˈhɔlt] *vi* : detenerse, pararse — *vt* **1** STOP : detener, parar (a una persona) **2** INTERRUPT : interrumpir (una actividad)

halt[2] *n* **1** : alto *m,* parada *f* **2 to come to a halt** : pararse, detenerse

halter [ˈhɔltər] *n* **1** : cabestro *m,* ronzal *m* (para un animal) **2** : blusa *f* sin espalda

halting [ˈhɔltɪŋ] *adj* HESITANT : vacilante, titubeante — **haltingly** *adv*

halve [ˈhæv, ˈhav] *vt* **halved; halving 1** DIVIDE : partir por la mitad **2** REDUCE : reducir a la mitad

halves → **half**

ham [ˈhæm] *n* **1** : jamón *m* **2** *or* **ham actor** : comicastro *m,* -tra *f* **3** *or* **ham radio operator** : radioaficionado *m,* -da *f* **4 hams** *npl* HAUNCHES : ancas *fpl*

hamburger [ˈhæmˌbərgər] *or* **hamburg** [-ˌbərg] *n* **1** : carne *f* molida **2** : hamburguesa *f* (emparedado)

hamlet [ˈhæmlət] *n* VILLAGE : aldea *f,* poblado *m*

hammer[1] [ˈhæmər] *vt* **1** STRIKE : clavar, golpear **2** NAIL : clavar, martillar **3 to hammer out** NEGOTIATE : elaborar, negociar, llegar a — *vi* : martillar, golpear

hammer[2] *n* **1** : martillo *m* **2** : percusor *m,* percutor *m* (de un arma de fuego)

hammock [ˈhæmək] *n* : hamaca *f*

hamper[1] [ˈhæmpər] *vt* : obstaculizar, dificultar

hamper[2] *n* : cesto *m,* canasta *f*

hamster [ˈhæmpstər] *n* : hámster *m*

hamstring [ˈhæmˌstrɪŋ] *vt* **-strung** [-ˌstrʌŋ]; **-stringing 1** : cortarle el tendón del corvejón a (un animal) **2** INCAPACITATE : incapacitar, inutilizar

hand[1] [ˈhænd] *vt* : pasar, dar, entregar

hand[2] *n* **1** : mano *f* <made by hand : hecho a mano> **2** POINTER : manecilla *f,* aguja *f* (de un reloj o instrumento) **3** SIDE : lado *m* <on the other hand : por otro lado> **4** HANDWRITING : letra *f,* escritura *f* **5** APPLAUSE : aplauso *m* **6** : mano *f,* cartas *fpl* (en juegos de naipes) **7** WORKER : obrero *m,* -ra *f;* trabajador *m,* -dora *f* **8 to ask for someone's hand (in marriage)** : pedir la mano de alguien **9 to lend a hand** : echar una mano

handbag [ˈhændˌbæg] *n* : cartera *f,* bolso *m,* bolsa *f Mex*

handball [ˈhændˌbɔl] *n* : frontón *m*

handbill [ˈhændˌbɪl] *n* : folleto *m,* volante *m*

handbook [ˈhændˌbʊk] *n* : manual *m*

handcuff [ˈhændˌkʌf] *vt* : esposar, ponerle esposas (a alguien)

handcuffs [ˈhændˌkʌfs] *npl* : esposas *fpl*

handful [ˈhændˌfʊl] *n* : puñado *m*

handgun [ˈhændˌgʌn] *n* : pistola *f,* revólver *m*

handicap[1] [ˈhændiˌkæp] *vt* **-capped; -capping 1** : asignar un handicap a (en deportes) **2** HAMPER : obstaculizar, poner en desventaja

handicap[2] *n* **1** DISABILITY : minusvalía *f,* discapacidad *f* **2** DISADVANTAGE : desventaja *f,* handicap *m* (en deportes)

handicapped [ˈhændiˌkæpt] *adj* DISABLED : minusválido, discapacitado

handicraft [ˈhændiˌkræft] *n* : artesanía *f*

handily [ˈhændəli] *adv* EASILY : fácilmente, con facilidad

handiwork [ˈhændiˌwərk] *n* **1** WORK : trabajo *m* **2** CRAFTS : artesanías *fpl*

handkerchief [ˈhæŋkərtʃəf, -ˌtʃiːf] *n, pl* **-chiefs** : pañuelo *m*

handle[1] [ˈhændəl] *v* **-dled; -dling** *vt* **1** TOUCH : tocar **2** MANAGE : tratar, manejar, despachar **3** SELL : comerciar con, vender — *vi* : responder, conducirse (dícese de un vehículo)

handle[2] *n* : asa *m,* asidero *m,* mango *m* (de un cuchillo, etc.), pomo *m* (de una puerta), tirador *m* (de un cajón)

handlebars [ˈhændəlˌbɑrz] *npl* : manubrio *m,* manillar *m*

handler [ˈhændələr] *n* : cuidador *m,* -dora *f*

handmade [ˈhændˌmeɪd] *adj* : hecho a mano

hand–me–downs [ˈhændmiˌdaʊnz] *npl* : ropa *f* usada

handout [ˈhændˌaʊt] *n* **1** AID : dádiva *f,* limosna *f* **2** LEAFLET : folleto *m*

handpick [ˈhændˈpɪk] *vt* : seleccionar con cuidado

handrail [ˈhændˌreɪl] *n* : pasamanos *m,* barandilla *f,* barandal *m*

handsaw [ˈhændˌsɔ] *n* : serrucho *m*

hands down *adv* **1** EASILY : con facilidad **2** UNQUESTIONABLY : con mucho, de lejos

handshake [ˈhændˌʃeɪk] *n* : apretón *m* de manos

handsome [ˈhæn*t*səm] *adj* **-somer; -est 1** ATTRACTIVE : apuesto, guapo, atractivo **2** GENEROUS : generoso **3** SIZABLE : considerable

handsomely [ˈhæn*t*səmli] *adv* **1** ELEGANTLY : elegantemente **2** GENEROUSLY : con generosidad

handspring [ˈhændˌsprɪŋ] *n* : voltereta *f*

handstand [ˈhændˌstænd] *n* **to do a handstand** : pararse de manos

hand–to–hand [ˈhænd*d*təˈhænd] *adj* : cuerpo a cuerpo

handwriting [ˈhændˌraɪt̬ɪŋ] *n* : letra *f,* escritura *f*

handwritten [ˈhændˌrɪtən] *adj* : escrito a mano

handy [ˈhændi] *adj* **handier; -est 1** NEARBY : a mano, cercano **2** USEFUL : útil, práctico **3** DEXTEROUS : hábil

hang[1] [ˈhæŋ] *v* **hung** [ˈhʌŋ]; **hanging** *vt* **1** SUSPEND : colgar, tender, suspender **2** (*past tense often* **hanged**) EXECUTE : colgar, ahorcar **3 to hang one's head** : bajar la cabeza — *vi* **1** FALL : caer (dícese de las telas y la ropa) **2** DANGLE : colgar **3** HOVER : flotar, sostenerse en el aire **4** : ser ahorcado **5** DROOP : inclinarse **6 to hang up** : colgar <he hung up on me : me colgó>

hang[2] *n* **1** DRAPE : caída *f* **2 to get the hang of something** : colgarle el truco a algo, lograr entender algo

hangar [ˈhæŋər, ˈhæŋgər] *n* : hangar *m*

hanger [ˈhæŋər] *n* : percha *f,* gancho *m* (para ropa)

hangman [ˈhæŋmən] *n, pl* **-men** [-mən, -ˌmɛn] : verdugo *m*

hangnail [ˈhæŋˌneɪl] *n* : padrastro *m*

hangout [ˈhæŋˌaʊt] *n* : lugar *m* popular, sitio *m* muy frecuentado

hangover [ˈhæŋˌoːvər] *n* : resaca *f*

hank [ˈhæŋk] *n* : madeja *f*

hanker [ˈhæŋkər] *vi* **to hanker for** : ansiar, anhelar, tener ganas de

hankering [ˈhæŋkərɪŋ] *n* : ansia *f,* anhelo *m*

hansom [ˈhæn*t*səm] *n* : coche *m* de caballos

Hanukkah [ˈxɑnəkə, ˈhɑ-] *n* : Janucá, Hanukkah

haphazard [hæpˈhæzərd] *adj* : casual, fortuito, al azar — **haphazardly** *adv*

hapless [ˈhæpləs] *adj* UNFORTUNATE : desafortunado, desventurado — **haplessly**

happen [ˈhæpən] *vi* **1** OCCUR : pasar, ocurrir, suceder, tener lugar **2** BEFALL : pasar, acontecer <what happened to her? : ¿qué le ha pasado?> **3** CHANCE : resultar, ocurrir por casualidad <it happened that I wasn't home : resulta que estaba fuera de casa> <he happens to be right : da la casualidad de que tiene razón>

happening [ˈhæpənɪŋ] *n* : suceso *m,* acontecimiento *m*

happiness [ˈhæpinəs] *n* : felicidad *f,* dicha *f*

happy [ˈhæpi] *adj* **-pier; -est 1** JOYFUL : feliz, contento, alegre **2** FORTUNATE : afortunado, feliz — **happily** [-pəli] *adv*

happy–go–lucky [ˈhæpigoːˈlʌki] *adj* : despreocupado

harangue[1] [həˈræŋ] *vt* **-rangued; -ranguing** : arengar

harangue[2] *n* : arenga *f*

harass [həˈræs, ˈhærəs] *vt* **1** BESIEGE, HOUND : acosar, asediar, hostigar **2** ANNOY : molestar

harassment [həˈræsmənt, ˈhærəsmənt] *n* : acoso *m,* hostigamiento *m* <sexual harrassment : acoso sexual>

harbinger [ˈhɑrbɪndʒər] *n* **1** HERALD : heraldo *m,* precursor *m* **2** OMEN : presagio *m*

harbor[1] [ˈhɑrbər] *vt* **1** SHELTER : dar refugio a, albergar **2** CHERISH, KEEP : abrigar, guardar, albergar <to harbor doubts : guardar dudas>

harbor[2] *n* **1** REFUGE : refugio *m* **2** PORT : puerto *m*

hard[1] [ˈhɑrd] *adv* **1** FORCEFULLY : fuerte, con fuerza <the wind blew hard : el viento sopló fuerte> **2** STRENUOUSLY : duro, mucho <to work hard : trabajar duro> **3 to take something hard** : tomarse algo muy mal, estar muy afectado por algo

hard[2] *adj* **1** FIRM, SOLID : duro, firme, sólido **2** DIFFICULT : difícil, arduo **3** SEVERE : severo, duro <a hard winter : un invierno severo> **4** UNFEELING : insensible, duro **5** DILIGENT : diligente <to be a hard worker : ser muy trabajador> **6 hard liquor** : bebidas *fpl* fuertes **7 hard water** : agua *f* dura

harden [ˈhɑrdən] *vt* : endurecer

hardheaded [ˌhɑrdˈhɛdəd] *adj* **1** STUBBORN : testarudo, terco **2** REALISTIC : realista, práctico — **hardheadedly** *adv*

hard–hearted [ˌhɑrdˈhɑrt̬əd] *adj* : despiadado, insensible — **hard–heartedly** *adv*

hard–heartedness [ˌhɑrdˈhɑrt̬ədnəs] *n* : dureza *f* de corazón

hardly [ˈhɑrdli] *adv* **1** SCARCELY : apenas, casi <I hardly knew her : apenas la conocía> <hardly ever : casi nunca> **2** NOT : difícilmente, poco, no <they can hardly blame me! : ¡difícilmente pueden echarme la culpa!> <it's hardly likely : es poco probable>

hardness ['hardnəs] *n* **1** FIRMNESS : dureza *f* **2** DIFFICULTY : dificultad *f* **3** SEVERITY : severidad *f*

hardship ['hard,ʃɪp] *n* : dificultad *f,* privación *f*

hardware ['hard,wær] *n* **1** TOOLS : ferretería *f* **2** : hardware *m* (de una computadora)

hardwood ['hard,wʊd] *n* : madera *f* dura, madera *f* noble

hardy ['hardi] *adj* **-dier; -est** : fuerte, robusto, resistente (dícese de las plantas) — **hardily** [-dəli] *adv*

hare ['hær] *n, pl* **hare** *or* **hares** : liebre *f*

harebrained ['hær,breɪnd] *adj* : estúpido, absurdo, disparatado

harelip ['hær,lɪp] *n* : labio *m* leporino

harem ['hærəm] *n* : harén *m*

hark ['hark] *vi* **1** (*used only in the imperative*) LISTEN : escuchar **2 hark back** RETURN : volver **3 hark back** RECALL : recordar

harlequin ['harlɪkən, -kwən] *n* : arlequín *m*

harm[1] ['harm] *vt* : hacerle daño a, perjudicar

harm[2] *n* : daño *m,* perjuicio *m*

harmful ['harmfəl] *adj* : dañino, perjudicial — **harmfully** *adv*

harmless ['harmləs] *adj* : inofensivo, inocuo — **harmlessly** *adv*

harmlessness ['harmləsnəs] *n* : inocuidad *f*

harmonic [har'manɪk] *adj* : armónico — **harmonically** [-nɪkli] *adv*

harmonica [har'manɪkə] *n* : armónica *f*

harmonious [har'mo:niəs] *adj* : armonioso — **harmoniously** *adv*

harmonize ['harmə,naɪz] *v* **-nized; -nizing** : armonizar

harmony ['harməni] *n, pl* **-nies** : armonía *f*

harness[1] ['harnəs] *vt* **1** : enjaezar (un animal) **2** UTILIZE : utilizar, aprovechar

harness[2] *n* : arreos *mpl,* guarniciones *fpl,* arnés *m*

harp[1] ['harp] *vi* **to harp on** : insistir sobre, machacar sobre

harp[2] *n* : arpa *m*

harpist ['harpɪst] *n* : arpista *mf*

harpoon[1] [har'pu:n] *vt* : arponear

harpoon[2] *n* : arpón *m*

harpsichord ['harpsɪ,kɔrd] *n* : clavicémbalo *m*

harrow[1] ['hær,o:] *vt* **1** CULTIVATE : gradar, labrar (la tierra) **2** TORMENT : atormentar

harrow[2] *n* : grada *f,* rastra *f*

harry ['hæri] *vt* **-ried; -rying** HARASS : acosar, hostigar

harsh ['harʃ] *adj* **1** ROUGH : áspero **2** SEVERE : duro, severo **3** : discordante (dícese de los sonidos) — **harshly** *adv*

harshness ['harʃnəs] *n* **1** ROUGHNESS : aspereza *f* **2** SEVERITY : dureza *f,* severidad *f*

harvest[1] ['harvəst] *v* : cosechar

harvest[2] *n* **1** HARVESTING : siega *f,* recolección *f* **2** CROP : cosecha *f*

harvester ['harvəstər] *n* : segador *m,* -dora *f;* cosechadora *f* (máquina)

has → **have**

hash[1] ['hæʃ] *vt* **1** MINCE : picar **2 to hash over** DISCUSS : discutir, repasar

hash[2] *n* **1** : picadillo *m* (comida) **2** JUMBLE : revoltijo *m,* fárrago *m*

hasn't ['hæzənt] (*contraction of* **has not**) → **has**

hasp ['hæsp] *n* : picaporte *m,* pestillo *m*

hassle[1] ['hæsəl] *vt* **-sled; -sling** : fastidiar, molestar

hassle[2] *n* **1** ARGUMENT : discusión *f,* disputa *f,* bronca *f* **2** FIGHT : pelea *f,* riña *f* **3** BOTHER, TROUBLE : problemas *mpl,* lío *m*

hassock ['hæsək] *n* **1** CUSHION : almohadón *m,* cojín *m* **2** FOOTSTOOL : escabel *m*

haste ['heɪst] *n* **1** : prisa *f,* apuro *m* **2 to make haste** : darse prisa, apurarse

hasten ['heɪsən] *vt* : acelerar, precipitar — *vi* : apresurarse, apurarse

hasty ['heɪsti] *adj* **hastier; -est 1** HURRIED, QUICK : rápido, apresurado, apurado **2** RASH : precipitado — **hastily** [-təli] *adv*

hat ['hæt] *n* : sombrero *m*

hatch[1] ['hætʃ] *vt* **1** : incubar, empollar (huevos) **2** DEVISE : idear, tramar — *vi* : salir del cascarón

hatch[2] *n* : escotilla *f*

hatchery ['hætʃəri] *n, pl* **-ries** : criadero *m*

hatchet ['hætʃət] *n* : hacha *f*

hatchway ['hætʃ,weɪ] *n* : escotilla *f*

hate[1] ['heɪt] *vt* **hated; hating** : odiar, aborrecer, detestar

hate[2] *n* : odio *m*

hateful ['heɪtfəl] *adj* : odioso, aborrecible, detestable — **hatefully** *adv*

hatred ['heɪtrəd] *n* : odio *m*

hatter ['hæt̬ər] *n* : sombrerero *m,* -ra *f*

haughtiness ['hɔt̬inəs] *n* : altanería *f,* altivez *f*

haughty ['hɔt̬i] *adj* **-tier; -est** : altanero, altivo — **haughtily** [-t̬əli] *adv*

haul[1] ['hɔl] *vt* **1** DRAG, PULL : arrastrar, jalar **2** TRANSPORT : transportar

haul[2] *n* **1** PULL : tirón *m,* jalón *m* **2** CATCH : redada *f* **3** JOURNEY : viaje *m,* trayecto *m* <it's a long haul : es un trayecto largo>

haulage ['hɔlɪdʒ] *n* : transporte *m,* tiro *m*

hauler ['hɔlər] *n* : transportista *mf*

haunch [ˈhɔntʃ] *n* **1** HIP : cadera *f* **2** **haunches** *npl* HINDQUARTERS : ancas *fpl*, cuartos *mpl* traseros

haunt[1] [ˈhɔnt] *vt* **1** : aparecer en (dícese de un fantasma) **2** FREQUENT : frecuentar, rondar **3** PREOCCUPY : perseguir, obsesionar

haunt[2] *n* : guarida *f* (de animales o ladrones), lugar *m* predilecto

haunting [ˈhɔntɪŋ] *adj* : obsesionante, evocador — **hauntingly** *adv*

have [ˈhæv, *in sense 3 as an auxiliary verb usu* ˈhæf] *v* **had** [ˈhæd]; **having; has** [ˈhæz, *in sense 3 as an auxiliary verb usu* ˈhæs] *vt* **1** POSSESS : tener <do you have change? : ¿tienes cambio?> **2** EXPERIENCE, UNDERGO : tener, experimentar, sufrir <I have a toothache : tengo un dolor de muelas> **3** INCLUDE : tener, incluir <April has 30 days : abril tiene 30 días> **4** CONSUME : comer, tomar **5** RECEIVE : tener, recibir <he had my permission : tenía mi permiso> **6** ALLOW : permitir, dejar <I won't have it! : ¡no lo permitiré!> **7** HOLD : hacer <to have a party : dar una fiesta> <to have a meeting : convocar una reunión> **8** HOLD : tener <he had me in his power : me tenía en su poder> **9** BEAR : tener (niños) **10** (*indicating causation*) <she had a dress made : mandó hacer un vestido> <to have one's hair cut : cortarse el pelo> — *v aux* **1** : haber <she has been very busy : ha estado muy ocupada> <I've lived here three years : hace tres años que vivo aquí> **2** (*used in tags*) <you've finished, haven't you? : ha terminado, ¿no?> **3 to have to** : deber, tener que <we have to leave : tenemos que salir>

haven [ˈheɪvən] *n* : refugio *m*

havoc [ˈhævək] *n* **1** DESTRUCTION : estragos *mpl*, destrucción *f* **2** CHAOS, DISORDER : desorden *m*, caos *m*

Hawaiian[1] [həˈwaɪən] *adj* : hawaiano

Hawaiian[2] *n* : hawaiano *m*, -na *f*

hawk[1] [ˈhɔk] *vt* : pregonar, vender (mercancías) en la calle

hawk[2] *n* : halcón *m*

hawker [ˈhɔkər] *n* : vendedor *m*, -dora *f* ambulante

hawthorn [ˈhɔˌθɔrn] *n* : espino *m*

hay [ˈheɪ] *n* : heno *m*

hay fever *n* : fiebre *f* del heno

hayloft [ˈheɪˌlɔft] *n* : pajar *m*

hayseed [ˈheɪˌsiːd] *n* : palurdo *m*, -da *f*

haystack [ˈheɪˌstæk] *n* : almiar *m*

haywire [ˈheɪˌwaɪr] *adj* : descompuesto, desbaratado <to go haywire : estropearse>

hazard[1] [ˈhæzərd] *vt* : arriesgar, aventurar

hazard[2] *n* **1** DANGER : peligro *m*, riesgo *m* **2** CHANCE : azar *m*

hazardous [ˈhæzərdəs] *adj* : arriesgado, peligroso

haze[1] [ˈheɪz] *vt* **hazed; hazing** : abrumar, acosar

haze[2] *n* : bruma *f*, neblina *f*

hazel [ˈheɪzəl] *n* **1** : avellano *m* (árbol) **2** : color *m* avellana

hazelnut [ˈheɪzəlˌnʌt] *n* : avellana *f*

haziness [ˈheɪzinəs] *n* **1** MISTINESS : nebulosidad *f* **2** VAGUENESS : vaguedad *f*

hazy [ˈheɪzi] *adj* **hazier; -est** **1** MISTY : brumoso, neblinoso, nebuloso **2** VAGUE : vago, confuso

he [ˈhiː] *pron* : él

head[1] [ˈhɛd] *vt* **1** LEAD : encabezar **2** DIRECT : dirigir — *vi* : dirigirse

head[2] *adj* MAIN : principal <the head office : la oficina central, la sede>

head[3] *n* **1** : cabeza *f* <from head to foot : de pies a cabeza> **2** MIND : mente *f*, cabeza *f* **3** TIP, TOP : cabeza *f* (de un clavo, un martillo, etc.), cabecera *f* (de una mesa o un río), punta *f* (de una flecha), flor *m* (de un repollo, etc.), encabezamiento *m* (de una carta, etc.), espuma *f* (de cerveza) **4** DIRECTOR, LEADER : director *m*, -tora *f*; jefe *m*, -fa *f*; cabeza *f* (de una familia) **5** : cara *f* (de una moneda) <heads or tails : cara o cruz> **6** : cabeza *f* <500 head of cattle : 500 cabezas de ganado> <$10 a head : $10 por cabeza> **7 to come to a head** : llegar a un punto crítico

headache [ˈhɛdˌeɪk] *n* : dolor *m* de cabeza, jaqueca *f*

headband [ˈhɛdˌbænd] *n* : cinta *f* del pelo

headdress [ˈhɛdˌdrɛs] *n* : tocado *m*

headfirst [ˈhɛdˈfərst] *adv* : de cabeza

headgear [ˈhɛdˌgɪr] *n* : gorro *m*, casco *m*, sombrero *m*

heading [ˈhɛdɪŋ] *n* **1** DIRECTION : dirección *f* **2** TITLE : encabezamiento *m*, título *m* **3** : membrete *m* (de una carta)

headland [ˈhɛdlənd, -ˌlænd] *n* : cabo *m*

headlight [ˈhɛdˌlaɪt] *n* : faro *m*, foco *m*, farol *m Mex*

headline [ˈhɛdˌlaɪn] *n* : titular *m*

headlong[1] [ˈhɛdˈlɔŋ] *adv* **1** HEADFIRST : de cabeza **2** HASTILY : precipitadamente

headlong[2] [ˈhɛdˌlɔŋ] *adj* : precipitado

headmaster [ˈhɛdˌmæstər] *n* : director *m*

headmistress [ˈhɛdˌmɪstrəs, -ˈmɪs-] *n* : directora *f*

head–on [ˈhɛdˈɑn, -ˈɔn] *adv & adj* : de frente

headphones [ˈhɛdˌfoːnz] *npl* : audífonos *mpl*, cascos *mpl*

headquarters [ˈhɛdˌkwɔrtərz] *ns & pl* **1** SEAT : oficina *f* central, sede *f* **2** : cuartel *m* general (de los militares)

headrest [ˈhɛdˌrɛst] *n* : apoyacabezas *m*

headship [ˈhɛdˌʃɪp] *n* : dirección *f*

head start *n* : ventaja *f*

headstone [ˈhɛdˌstoːn] *n* : lápida *f*

headstrong [ˈhɛdˈstrɔŋ] *adj* : testarudo, obstinado, empecinado

headwaiter [ˈhɛdˈweɪt̬ər] *n* : jefe *m*, -fa *f* de comedor

headwaters [ˈhɛd,wɔt̬ərz, -,wɑ-] *npl* : cabecera *f*

headway [ˈhɛd,weɪ] *n* : progreso *m* <to make headway against : avanzar contra>

heady [ˈhɛdi] *adj* **headier; -est** **1** INTOXICATING : embriagador, excitante **2** SHREWD : astuto, sagaz

heal [ˈhiːl] *vt* : curar, sanar — *vi* **1** : sanar, curarse **2 to heal up** : cicatrizarse

healer [ˈhiːlər] *n* : curador *m*, -dora *f*

health [ˈhɛlθ] *n* : salud *f*

healthful [ˈhɛlθfəl] *adj* : saludable, salubre — **healthfully** *adv*

healthy [ˈhɛlθi] *adj* **healthier; -est** : sano, bien — **healthily** [-θəli] *adv*

heap[1] [ˈhiːp] *vt* **1** PILE : amontonar, apilar **2** SHOWER : colmar

heap[2] *n* : montón *m*, pila *f*

hear [ˈhɪr] *v* **heard** [ˈhərd]; **hearing** *vt* **1** : oír <do you hear me? : ¿me oyes?> **2** HEED : oír, prestar atención a **3** LEARN : oír, enterarse de — *vi* **1** : oír <to hear about : oír hablar de> **2 to hear from** : tener noticias de

hearing [ˈhɪrɪŋ] *n* **1** : oído *m* <hard of hearing : duro de oído> **2** : vista *f* (en un tribunal) **3** ATTENTION : consideración *f*, oportunidad *f* de expresarse **4** EARSHOT : alcance *m* del oído

hearing aid *n* : audífono *m*

hearken [ˈhɑrkən] *vt* : escuchar

hearsay [ˈhɪr,seɪ] *n* : rumores *mpl*

hearse [ˈhərs] *n* : coche *m* fúnebre

heart [ˈhɑrt] *n* **1** : corazón *m* **2** CENTER, CORE : corazón *m*, centro *m* <the heart of the matter : el meollo del asunto> **3** FEELINGS : corazón *m*, sentimientos *mpl* <a broken heart : un corazón destrozado> <to have a good heart : tener buen corazón> <to take something to heart : tomarse algo a pecho> **4** COURAGE : valor *m*, corazón *m* <to take heart : animarse, cobrar ánimos> **5 hearts** *npl* : corazones *mpl* (en juegos de naipes) **6 by heart** : de memoria

heartache [ˈhɑrt,eɪk] *n* : pena *f*, angustia *f*

heart attack *n* : infarto *m*, ataque *m* al corazón

heartbeat [ˈhɑrt,biːt] *n* : latido *m* (del corazón)

heartbreak [ˈhɑrt,breɪk] *n* : congoja *f*, angustia *f*

heartbreaking [ˈhɑrt,breɪkɪŋ] *adj* : desgarrador, que parte el corazón

heartbroken [ˈhɑrt,broːkən] *adj* : desconsolado, destrozado

heartburn [ˈhɑrt,bərn] *n* : acidez *f* estomacal

hearten [ˈhɑrtən] *vt* : alentar, animar

hearth [ˈhɑrθ] *n* : hogar *m*, chimenea *f*

heartily [ˈhɑrt̬əli] *adv* **1** ENTHUSIASTICALLY : de buena gana, con entusiasmo **2** TOTALLY : totalmente, completamente

heartless [ˈhɑrtləs] *adj* : desalmado, despiadado, cruel

heartsick [ˈhɑrt,sɪk] *adj* : abatido, desconsolado

heartstrings [ˈhɑrt,strɪŋz] *npl* : fibras *fpl* del corazón

heartwarming [ˈhɑrt,wɔrmɪŋ] *adj* : conmovedor, emocionante

hearty [ˈhɑrt̬i] *adj* **heartier; -est** **1** CORDIAL, WARM : cordial, caluroso **2** STRONG : fuerte <to have a hearty appetite : ser de buen comer> **3** SUBSTANTIAL : abundante, sustancioso <a hearty breakfast : un desayuno abundante>

heat[1] [ˈhiːt] *vt* : calentar

heat[2] *n* **1** WARMTH : calor *m* **2** HEATING : calefacción *f* **3** EXCITEMENT : calor *m*, entusiasmo *m* <in the heat of the moment : en el calor del momento> **4** ESTRUS : celo *m*

heated [ˈhiːt̬əd] *adj* **1** WARMED : calentado **2** IMPASSIONED : acalorado, apasionado

heater [ˈhiːt̬ər] *n* : calentador *m*, estufa *f*, calefactor *m*

heath [ˈhiːθ] *n* **1** MOOR : brezal *m*, páramo *m* **2** HEATHER : brezo *m*

heathen[1] [ˈhiːðən] *adj* : pagano

heathen[2] *n*, *pl* **-thens** *or* **-then** : pagano *m*, -na *f*; infiel *mf*

heather [ˈhɛðər] *n* : brezo *m*

heave[1] [ˈhiːv] *v* **heaved** *or* **hove** [ˈhoːv]; **heaving** *vt* **1** LIFT, RAISE : levantar con esfuerzo **2** HURL : lanzar, tirar **3 to heave a sigh** : echar un suspiro, suspirar — *vi* **1** : subir y bajar, palpitar (dícese del pecho) **2 to heave up** RISE : levantarse

heave[2] *n* **1** EFFORT : gran esfuerzo *m* (para levantar algo) **2** THROW : lanzamiento *m*

heaven [ˈhɛvən] *n* **1** : cielo *m* <for heaven's sake : por Dios> **2 heavens** *npl* SKY : cielo *m* <the heavens opened up : empezó a llover a cántaros>

heavenly [ˈhɛvənli] *adj* **1** : celestial, celeste **2** DELIGHTFUL : divino, encantador

heavily [ˈhɛvəli] *adv* **1** : pesadamente, con mucho peso **2** LABORIOUSLY : trabajosamente, penosamente **3** : mucho

heaviness [ˈhɛvinəs] *n* : peso *m*, pesadez *f*

heavy [ˈhɛvi] *adj* **heavier; -est** **1** WEIGHTY : pesado **2** DENSE, THICK : denso, espeso, grueso **3** BURDENSOME : oneroso, gravoso **4** PROFOUND : profundo **5** SLUGGISH : lento, tardo **6** STOUT : corpulento **7** SEVERE : severo, duro, fuerte

heavy–duty [ˈhɛviˈduːt̬i, -ˈdjuː-] *adj* : muy resistente, fuerte

heavyweight [ˈhɛvi,weɪt] *n* : peso *m* pesado (en deportes)

Hebrew[1] [ˈhiːˌbruː] *adj* **:** hebreo

Hebrew[2] *n* **1 :** hebreo *m,* -brea *f* **2 :** hebreo *m* (idioma)

heckle [ˈhɛkəl] *vt* **-led; -ling :** interrumpir (a un orador)

hectic [ˈhɛktɪk] *adj* **:** agitado, ajetreado — **hectically** [-tɪkli] *adv*

he'd [ˈhiːd] (*contraction of* **he had** *or* **he would**) → **have, would**

hedge[1] [ˈhɛdʒ] *v* **hedged; hedging** *vt* **1 :** cercar con un seto **2 to hedge one's bet :** cubrirse — *vi* **1 :** dar rodeos, contestar con evasivas **2 to hedge against :** cubrirse contra, protegerse contra

hedge[2] *n* **1 :** seto *m* vivo **2** SAFEGUARD **:** salvaguardia *f,* protección *f*

hedgehog [ˈhɛdʒˌhɔg, -hɑg] *n* **:** erizo *m*

heed[1] [ˈhiːd] *vt* **:** prestar atención a, hacer caso de

heed[2] *n* **:** atención *f*

heedless [ˈhiːdləs] *adj* **:** descuidado, despreocupado, inconsciente <to be heedless of : hacer caso omiso de> — **heedlessly** *adv*

heel[1] [ˈhiːl] *vi* **:** inclinarse

heel[2] *n* **:** talón *m* (del pie), tacón *m* (de calzado)

heft [ˈhɛft] *vt* **:** sopesar

hefty [ˈhɛfti] *adj* **heftier; -est :** robusto, fornido, pesado

heifer [ˈhɛfər] *n* **:** novilla *f*

height [ˈhaɪt] *n* **1** PEAK **:** cumbre *f,* cima *f,* punto *m* alto <at the height of her career : en la cumbre de su carrera> <the height of stupidity : el colmo de la estupidez> **2** TALLNESS **:** estatura *f* (de una persona), altura *f* (de un objeto) **3** ALTITUDE **:** altura *f*

heighten [ˈhaɪtən] *vt* **1 :** hacer más alto **2** INTENSIFY **:** aumentar, intensificar — *vi* **:** aumentarse, intensificarse

heinous [ˈheɪnəs] *adj* **:** atroz, abominable, nefando

heir [ˈær] *n* **:** heredero *m,* -ra *f*

heiress [ˈærəs] *n* **:** heredera *f*

heirloom [ˈærˌluːm] *n* **:** reliquia *f* de familia

held → **hold**

helicopter [ˈhɛləˌkɑptər] *n* **:** helicóptero *m*

helium [ˈhiːliəm] *n* **:** helio *m*

hell [ˈhɛl] *n* **:** infierno *m*

he'll [ˈhiːl, ˈhɪl] (*contraction of* **he shall** *or* **he will**) → **shall, will**

hellish [ˈhɛlɪʃ] *adj* **:** horroroso, infernal

hello [həˈloː, hɛ-] *interj* **:** ¡hola!

helm [ˈhɛlm] *n* **1 :** timón *m* **2 to take the helm :** tomar el mando

helmet [ˈhɛlmət] *n* **:** casco *m*

help[1] [ˈhɛlp] *vt* **1** AID, ASSIST **:** ayudar, auxiliar, socorrer, asistir **2** ALLEVIATE **:** aliviar **3** SERVE **:** servir <help yourself! : ¡sírvete!> **4** AVOID **:** evitar <it can't be helped : no lo podemos evitar, no hay más remedio> <I couldn't help smiling : no pude menos que sonreír>

help[2] *n* **1** ASSISTANCE **:** ayuda *f* <help! : ¡socorro!, ¡auxilio!> **2** STAFF **:** personal *m* (en una oficina), servicio *m* doméstico

helper [ˈhɛlpər] *n* **:** ayudante *mf*

helpful [ˈhɛlpfəl] *adj* **1** OBLIGING **:** servicial, amable, atento **2** USEFUL **:** útil, práctico — **helpfully** *adv*

helpfulness [ˈhɛlpfəlnəs] *n* **1** KINDNESS **:** bondad *f,* amabilidad *f* **2** USEFULNESS **:** utilidad *f*

helping [ˈhɛlpɪŋ] *n* **:** porción *f*

helpless [ˈhɛlpləs] *adj* **1** POWERLESS **:** incapaz, impotente **2** DEFENSELESS **:** indefenso

helplessly [ˈhɛlpləsli] *adv* **:** en vano, inútilmente

helplessness [ˈhɛlpləsnəs] *n* POWERLESSNESS **:** incapacidad *f,* impotencia *f*

helter–skelter [ˌhɛltərˈskɛltər] *adv* **:** atropelladamente, precipitadamente

hem[1] [ˈhɛm] *vt* **hemmed; hemming 1 :** dobladillar **2 to hem in :** encerrar

hem[2] *n* **:** dobladillo *m,* bastilla *f*

hemisphere [ˈhɛməˌsfɪr] *n* **:** hemisferio *m*

hemispheric [ˌhɛməˈsfɪrɪk, -ˈsfɛr-] *or* **hemispherical** [-ɪkəl] *adj* **:** hemisférico

hemlock [ˈhɛmˌlɑk] *n* **:** cicuta *f*

hemoglobin [ˈhiːməˌgloːbən] *n* **:** hemoglobina *f*

hemophilia [ˌhiːməˈfɪliə] *n* **:** hemofilia *f*

hemorrhage[1] [ˈhɛmərɪdʒ] *vi* **-rhaged; -rhaging :** sufrir una hemorragia

hemorrhage[2] *n* **:** hemorragia *f*

hemorrhoids [ˈhɛməˌrɔɪdz, ˈhɛmˌrɔɪdz] *npl* **:** hemorroides *fpl,* almorranas *fpl*

hemp [ˈhɛmp] *n* **:** cáñamo *m*

hen [ˈhɛn] *n* **:** gallina *f*

hence [ˈhɛnts] *adv* **1 :** de aquí, de ahí <10 years hence : de aquí a 10 años> <a dog bit me, hence my dislike of animals : un perro me mordió, de ahí mi aversión a los animales> **2** THEREFORE **:** por lo tanto, por consiguiente

henceforth [ˈhɛntsˌforθ, ˌhɛntsˈ-] *adv* **:** de ahora en adelante

henchman [ˈhɛntʃmən] *n, pl* **-men** [-mən, -ˌmɛn] **:** secuaz *mf,* esbirro *m*

henpeck [ˈhɛnˌpɛk] *vt* **:** dominar (al marido)

hepatitis [ˌhɛpəˈtaɪtəs] *n, pl* **-titides** [-ˈtɪtəˌdiːz] **:** hepatitis *f*

her[1] [ˈhər] *adj* **:** su, sus, de ella <her house : su casa, la casa de ella>

her[2] [ˈhər, ər] *pron* **1** (*used as direct object*) **:** la <I saw her yesterday : la vi ayer> **2** (*used as indirect object*) **:** le, se <he gave her the book : le dio el libro> <he sent it to her : se lo mandó> **3** (*used as object of a preposition*) **:** ella <we did it for her : lo hicimos por ella> <taller than her : más alto que ella>

herald[1] [ˈhɛrəld] *vt* ANNOUNCE : anunciar, proclamar
herald[2] *n* **1** MESSENGER : heraldo *m* **2** HARBINGER : precursor *m*
heraldic [hɛˈrældɪk, hə-] *adj* : heráldico
heraldry [ˈhɛrəldri] *n, pl* **-ries** : heráldica *f*
herb [ˈərb, ˈhərb] *n* : hierba *f*
herbal [ˈərbəl, ˈhər-] *adj* : herbario
herbicide [ˈərbə,saɪd, ˈhər-] *n* : herbicida *m*
herbivore [ˈərbə,vor, ˈhər-] *n* : herbívoro *m*
herbivorous [,ərˈbɪvərəs, ,hər-] *adj* : herbívoro
herculean [,hərkjəˈliːən, ,hərˈkjuːliən] *adj* : hercúleo, sobrehumano
herd[1] [ˈhərd] *vt* : reunir en manada, conducir en manada — *vi* : ir en manada (dícese de los animales), apiñarse (dícese de la gente)
herd[2] *n* : manada *f*
herder [ˈhərdər] → **herdsman**
herdsman [ˈhərdzmən] *n, pl* **-men** [-mən, -,mɛn] : vaquero *m* (de ganado), pastor *m* (de ovejas)
here [ˈhɪr] *adv* **1** : aquí, acá <come here! : ¡ven acá!> <right here : aquí mismo> **2** NOW : en este momento, ahora, ya <here he comes : ya viene> <here it's three o'clock (already) : ahora son las tres> **3** : en este punto <here we agree : estamos de acuerdo en este punto> **4 here you are!** : ¡toma!
hereabouts [ˈhɪrə,baʊts] *or* **hereabout** [-,baʊt] *adv* : por aquí (cerca)
hereafter[1] [hɪrˈæftər] *adv* **1** : de aquí en adelante, a continuación **2** : en el futuro
hereafter[2] *n* **the hereafter** : el más allá
hereby [hɪrˈbaɪ] *adv* : por este medio
hereditary [həˈrɛdə,tɛri] *adj* : hereditario
heredity [həˈrɛdəti] *n* : herencia *f*
herein [hɪrˈɪn] *adv* : aquí
hereof [hɪrˈʌv] *adv* : de aquí
hereon [hɪrˈɑn, -ˈɔn] *adv* : sobre esto
heresy [ˈhɛrəsi] *n, pl* **-sies** : herejía *f*
heretic [ˈhɛrə,tɪk] *n* : hereje *mf*
heretical [həˈrɛtɪkəl] *adj* : herético
hereto [hɪrˈtuː] *adv* : a esto
heretofore [ˈhɪrtə,for] *adv* HITHERTO : hasta ahora
hereunder [hɪrˈʌndər] *adv* : a continuación, abajo
hereupon [hɪrəˈpɑn, -ˈpɔn] *adv* : con esto, en ese momento
herewith [hɪrˈwɪθ] *adv* : adjunto
heritage [ˈhɛrətɪdʒ] *n* : patrimonio *m* (nacional)
hermaphrodite [hərˈmæfrə,daɪt] *n* : hermafrodita *mf*
hermetic [hərˈmɛtɪk] *adj* : hermético — **hermetically** [-tɪkli] *adv*
hermit [ˈhərmət] *n* : ermitaño *m*, -ña *f*; eremita *mf*
hernia [ˈhərniə] *n, pl* **-nias** *or* **-niae** [-ni,iː, -ni,aɪ] : hernia *f*
hero [ˈhiː,roː, ˈhɪr,oː] *n, pl* **-roes** **1** : héroe *m* **2** PROTAGONIST : protagonista *mf*
heroic [hɪˈroːɪk] *adj* : heroico — **heroically** [-ɪkli] *adv*
heroics [hɪˈroːɪks] *npl* : actos *mpl* heroicos
heroin [ˈhɛroən] *n* : heroína *f*
heroine [ˈhɛroən] *n* **1** : heroína *f* **2** PROTAGONIST : protagonista *f*
heroism [ˈhɛro,ɪzəm] *n* : heroísmo *m*
heron [ˈhɛrən] *n* : garza *f*
herpes [ˈhər,piːz] *n* : herpes *m*
herpetology [,hərpəˈtɑlədʒi] *n* : herpetología *f*
herring [ˈhɛrɪŋ] *n, pl* **-ring** *or* **-rings** : arenque *m*
hers [ˈhərz] *pron* : suyo, -ya; suyos, -yas; de ella <these shoes are hers : estos zapatos son suyos> <hers are bigger : los de ella son más grandes>
herself [hərˈsɛlf] *pron* **1** (*used reflexively*) : se <she dressed herself : se vistió> **2** (*used emphatically*) : ella misma <she fixed it herself : lo arregló ella misma, lo arregló por sí sola>
hertz [ˈhərts, ˈhɛrts] *ns & pl* : hercio *m*
he's [ˈhiːz] (*contraction of* **he is** *or* **he has**) → **be, have**
hesitancy [ˈhɛzətəntsi] *n, pl* **-cies** : vacilación *f*, titubeo *m*, indecisión *f*
hesitant [ˈhɛzətənt] *adj* : titubeante, vacilante — **hesitantly** *adv*
hesitate [ˈhɛzə,teɪt] *vi* **-tated; -tating** : vacilar, titubear
hesitation [,hɛzəˈteɪʃən] *n* : vacilación *f*, indecisión *f*, titubeo *m*
heterogeneous [,hɛtərəˈdʒiːniəs, -njəs] *adj* : heterogéneo
heterosexual[1] [,hɛtəroˈsɛkʃʊəl] *adj* : heterosexual
heterosexual[2] *n* : heterosexual *mf*
heterosexuality [,hɛtəro,sɛkʃʊˈæləti] *n* : heterosexualidad *f*
hew [ˈhjuː] *v* **hewed; hewed** *or* **hewn** [ˈhjuːn]; **hewing** *vt* **1** CUT : cortar, talar (árboles) **2** SHAPE : labrar, tallar — *vi* CONFORM : conformarse, ceñirse
hex[1] [ˈhɛks] *vt* : hacerle un maleficio (a alguien)
hex[2] *n* : maleficio *m*
hexagon [ˈhɛksə,gɑn] *n* : hexágono *m*
hexagonal [hɛkˈsægənəl] *adj* : hexagonal
hey [ˈheɪ] *interj* : ¡eh!, ¡oye!
heyday [ˈheɪ,deɪ] *n* : auge *m*, apogeo *m*
hi [ˈhaɪ] *interj* : ¡hola!
hiatus [haɪˈeɪtəs] *n* **1** : hiato *m* **2** PAUSE : pausa *f*
hibernate [ˈhaɪbər,neɪt] *vi* **-nated; -nating** : hibernar, invernar
hibernation [,haɪbərˈneɪʃən] *n* : hibernación *f*
hiccup[1] [ˈhɪkəp] *vi* **-cuped; -cuping** : hipar, tener hipo

hiccup[2] *n* : hipo *m* <to have the hiccups : tener hipo>

hick [ˈhɪk] *n* BUMPKIN : palurdo *m,* -da *f*

hickory [ˈhɪkəri] *n, pl* **-ries** : nogal *m* americano

hidden [ˈhɪdən] *adj* : oculto

hide[1] [ˈhaɪd] *v* **hid** [ˈhɪd]; **hidden** [ˈhɪdən] *or* **hid; hiding** *vt* **1** CONCEAL : esconder **2** ocultar <to hide one's motives : ocultar uno sus motivos> **3** SCREEN : tapar, no dejar ver — *vi* : esconderse

hide[2] *n* : piel *f,* cuero *m* <to save one's hide : salvar el pellejo>

hide–and–seek [ˈhaɪdən*d*ˈsiːk] *n* **to play hide–and–seek** : jugar a las escondidas

hidebound [ˈhaɪd,baʊnd] *adj* : rígido, conservador

hideous [ˈhɪdiəs] *adj* : horrible, horroroso, espantoso — **hideously** *adv*

hideout [ˈhaɪd,aʊt] *n* : guarida *f,* escondrijo *m*

hierarchical [,haɪəˈrɑrkɪkəl] *adj* : jerárquico

hierarchy [ˈhaɪə,rɑrki] *n, pl* **-chies** : jerarquía *f*

hieroglyphic [,haɪərəˈglɪfɪk] *n* : jeroglífico *m*

hi–fi [ˈhaɪˈfaɪ] *n* **1** → **high fidelity** **2** : equipo *m* de alta fidelidad

high[1] [ˈhaɪ] *adv* : alto

high[2] *adj* **1** TALL : alto <a high wall : una pared alta> **2** ELEVATED : alto, elevado <high prices : precios elevados> <high blood pressure : presión alta> **3** GREAT, IMPORTANT : grande, importante, alto <a high number : un número grande> <high society : alta sociedad> <high hopes : grandes esperanzas> **4** : alto (en música) **5** INTOXICATED : borracho, drogado

high[3] *n* **1** : récord *m,* punto *m* máximo <to reach an all-time high : batir el récord> **2** : zona *f* de alta presión (en meteorología) **3** *or* **high gear** : directa *f* **4 on high** : en las alturas

highbrow [ˈhaɪ,braʊ] *n* : intelectual *mf*

higher [ˈhaɪər] *adj* : superior

high fidelity *n* : alta fidelidad *f*

high–flown [ˈhaɪˈfloːn] *adj* : altisonante

high–handed [ˈhaɪˈhændəd] *adj* : arbitrario

highlands [ˈhaɪləndz] *npl* : tierras *fpl* altas, altiplano *m*

highlight[1] [ˈhaɪ,laɪt] *vt* **1** EMPHASIZE : destacar, poner en relieve, subrayar **2** : ser el punto culminante de

highlight[2] *n* : punto *m* culminante

highly [ˈhaɪli] *adv* **1** VERY : muy, sumamente **2** FAVORABLY : muy bien <to speak highly of : hablar muy bien de> <to think highly of : tener en mucho a>

highness [ˈhaɪnəs] *n* **1** HEIGHT : altura *f* **2 Highness** : Alteza *f* <Your Royal Highness : Su Alteza Real>

high–rise [ˈhaɪ,raɪz] *adj* : alto, de muchas plantas

high school *n* : escuela *f* superior, escuela *f* secundaria

high seas *npl* : alta mar *f*

high–spirited [ˈhaɪˈspɪrət̬əd] *adj* : vivaz, muy animado, brioso

high–strung [,haɪˈstrʌŋ] *adj* : nervioso, excitable

highway [ˈhaɪ,weɪ] *n* : carretera *f*

highwayman [ˈhaɪ,weɪmən] *n, pl* **-men** [- mən, -,mɛn] : salteador *m* (de caminos), bandido *m*

hijack[1] [ˈhaɪ,dʒæk] *vt* : secuestrar

hijack[2] *n* : secuestro *m*

hijacker [ˈhaɪ,dʒækər] *n* : secuestrador *m,* -dora *f*

hike[1] [ˈhaɪk] *v* **hiked; hiking** *vi* : hacer una caminata — *vt* RAISE : subir

hike[2] *n* **1** : caminata *f,* excursión *f* **2** INCREASE : subida *f* (de precios)

hiker [ˈhaɪkər] *n* : excursionista *mf*

hilarious [hɪˈlæriəs, haɪˈ-] *adj* : muy divertido, hilarante

hilarity [hɪˈlærət̬i, haɪ-] *n* : hilaridad *f*

hill [ˈhɪl] *n* **1** : colina *f,* cerro *m* **2** SLOPE : cuesta *f,* pendiente *f*

hillbilly [ˈhɪl,bɪli] *n, pl* **-lies** : palurdo *m,* -da *f* (de las montañas)

hillock [ˈhɪlək] *n* : loma *f,* altozano *m,* otero *m*

hillside [ˈhɪl,saɪd] *n* : ladera *f,* cuesta *f*

hilltop [ˈhɪl,tɑp] *n* : cima *f,* cumbre *f*

hilly [ˈhɪli] *adj* **hillier; -est** : montañoso, accidentado

hilt [ˈhɪlt] *n* : puño *m,* empuñadura *f*

him [ˈhɪm, əm] *pron* **1** (*used as direct object*) : lo <I found him : lo encontré> **2** (*used as indirect object*) : le, se <we gave him a present : le dimos un regalo> <I sent it to him : se lo mandé> **3** (*used as object of a preposition*) : él <she was thinking of him : pensaba en él> <younger than him : más joven que él>

himself [hɪmˈsɛlf] *pron* **1** (*used reflexively*) : se <he washed himself : se lavó> **2** (*used emphatically*) : él mismo <he did it himself : lo hizo él mismo, lo hizo por sí solo>

hind[1] [ˈhaɪnd] *adj* : trasero, posterior <hind legs : patas traseras>

hind[2] *n* : cierva *f*

hinder [ˈhɪndər] *vt* : dificultar, impedir, estorbar

hindquarters [ˈhaɪnd,kwɔrt̬ərz] *npl* : cuartos *mpl* traseros

hindrance [ˈhɪndrən*t*s] *n* : estorbo *m,* obstáculo *m,* impedimento *m*

hindsight [ˈhaɪnd,saɪt] *n* : retrospectiva *f* <with the benefit of hindsight : en retrospectiva, con la perspectiva que da la experiencia>

Hindu[1] [ˈhɪn,duː] *adj* : hindú

Hindu[2] *n* : hindú *mf*

Hinduism [ˈhɪnduː,ɪzəm] *n* : hinduismo *m*

hinge[1] [ˈhɪndʒ] *v* **hinged; hinging** *vt* : unir con bisagras — *vi* **to hinge on** : depender de

hinge[2] *n* : bisagra *f,* gozne *m*

hint[1] [ˈhɪnt] *vt* : insinuar, dar a entender — *vi* : soltar indirectas

hint[2] *n* **1** INSINUATION : insinuación *f,* indirecta *f* **2** TIP : consejo *m,* sugerencia *f* **3** TRACE : pizca *f,* indicio *m*

hinterland [ˈhɪntər,lænd, -lənd] *n* : interior *m* (de un país)

hip [ˈhɪp] *n* : cadera *f*

hippopotamus [,hɪpəˈpɑtəməs] *n, pl* **-muses** *or* **-mi** [-,maɪ] : hipopótamo *m*

hippo [ˈhɪpoː] *n, pl* **hippos** → **hippopotamus**

hire[1] [ˈhaɪr] *vt* **hired; hiring 1** EMPLOY : contratar, emplear **2** RENT : alquilar, arrendar

hire[2] *n* **1** RENT : alquiler *m* <for hire : se alquila> **2** WAGES : paga *f,* sueldo *m* **3** EMPLOYEE : empleado *m,* -da *f*

his[1] [ˈhɪz, ɪz] *adj* : su, sus, de él <his hat : su sombrero, el sombrero de él>

his[2] *pron* : suyo, -ya; suyos, suyas; de él <the decision is his : la decisión es suya> <it's his, not hers : es de él, no de ella>

Hispanic[1] [hɪˈspænɪk] *adj* : hispano, hispánico

Hispanic[2] *n* : hispano *m,* -na *f;* hispánico *m,* -ca *f*

hiss[1] [ˈhɪs] *vi* : sisear, silbar — *vt* : decir entre dientes

hiss[2] *n* : siseo *m,* silbido *m*

historian [hɪˈstɔriən] *n* : historiador *m,* -dora *f*

historic [hɪˈstɔrɪk] *or* **historical** [-ɪkəl] *adj* : histórico — **historically** [-ɪkli] *adv*

history [ˈhɪstəri] *n, pl* **-ries 1** : historia *f* **2** RECORD : historial *m*

histrionics [,hɪstriˈɑnɪks] *ns & pl* : histrionismo *m*

hit[1] [ˈhɪt] *v* **hit; hitting** *vt* **1** STRIKE : golpear, pegar, batear (una pelota) <he hit the dog : le pegó al perro> **2** : chocar contra, dar con, dar en (el blanco) <the car hit a tree : el coche chocó contra un árbol> **3** AFFECT : afectar <the news hit us hard : la noticia nos afectó mucho> **4** ENCOUNTER : tropezar con, toparse con <to hit a snag : tropezar con un obstáculo> **5** REACH : llegar a, alcanzar <the price hit $10 a pound : el precio alcanzó los $10 dólares por libra> <to hit town : llegar a la ciudad> <to hit the headlines : ser noticia> **6 to hit on** *or* **to hit upon** : dar con — *vi* : golpear

hit[2] *n* **1** BLOW : golpe *m* **2** : impacto *m* (de un arma) **3** SUCCESS : éxito *m*

hitch[1] [ˈhɪtʃ] *vt* **1** : mover con sacudidas **2** ATTACH : enganchar, atar, amarriar **3** → **hitchhike 4 to hitch up** : subirse (los pantalones, etc.)

hitch[2] *n* **1** JERK : tirón *m,* jalón *m* **2** OBSTACLE : obstáculo *m,* impedimento *m,* tropiezo *m*

hitchhike [ˈhɪtʃ,haɪk] *vi* **-hiked; -hiking** : hacer autostop, ir de aventón *Col, Mex fam*

hitchhiker [ˈhɪtʃ,haɪkər] *n* : autostopista *mf*

hither [ˈhɪðər] *adv* : acá, por aquí

hitherto [ˈhɪðər,tuː, ,hɪðərˈ-] *adv* : hasta ahora

hitter [ˈhɪtər] *n* BATTER : bateador *m,* -dora *f*

HIV [,ɛɪtʃ,aɪˈviː] *n* : VIH *m,* virus *m* del sida

hive [ˈhaɪv] *n* **1** : colmena *f* **2** SWARM : enjambre *m* **3** : lugar *m* muy activo <a hive of activity : un hervidero de actividad>

hives [ˈhaɪvz] *ns & pl* : urticaria *f*

hoard[1] [ˈhord] *vt* : acumular, atesorar

hoard[2] *n* : tesoro *m,* reserva *f,* provisión *f*

hoarfrost [ˈhor,frɔst] *n* : escarcha *f*

hoarse [ˈhors] *adj* **hoarser; -est** : ronco — **hoarsely** *adv*

hoarseness [ˈhorsnəs] *n* : ronquera *f*

hoary [ˈhori] *adj* **hoarier; -est 1** : cano, canoso **2** OLD : vetusto, antiguo

hoax[1] [ˈhoːks] *vt* : engañar, embaucar, bromar

hoax[2] *n* : engaño *m,* broma *f*

hobble[1] [ˈhɑbəl] *v* **-bled; -bling** *vi* LIMP : cojear, renguear — *vt* : manear (un animal)

hobble[2] *n* **1** LIMP : cojera *f,* rengo *m* **2** : maniota *f* (para un animal)

hobby [ˈhɑbi] *n, pl* **-bies** : pasatiempo *m,* afición *f*

hobgoblin [ˈhɑb,gɑblən] *n* : duende *m*

hobnail [ˈhɑb,neɪl] *n* : tachuela *f*

hobnob [ˈhɑb,nɑb] *vi* **-nobbed; -nobbing** : codearse

hobo [ˈhoː,boː] *n, pl* **-boes** : vagabundo *m,* -da *f*

hock[1] [ˈhɑk] *vt* PAWN : empeñar

hock[2] *n* **in hock** : empeñado

hockey [ˈhɑki] *n* : hockey *m*

hod [ˈhɑd] *n* : capacho *m* (de albañil)

hodgepodge [ˈhɑdʒ,pɑdʒ] *n* : mezcolanza *f*

hoe[1] [ˈhoː] *vt* **hoed; hoeing** : azadonar

hoe[2] *n* : azada *f,* azadón *m*

hog[1] [ˈhɔg, ˈhɑg] *vt* **hogged; hogging** : acaparar, monopolizar

hog[2] *n* **1** PIG : cerdo *m,* -da *f* **2** GLUTTON : glotón *m,* -tona *f*

hogshead [ˈhɔgz,hɛd, ˈhɑgz-] *n* : tonel *m*

hoist[1] [ˈhɔɪst] *vt* : levantar, alzar, izar (una bandera, una vela)

hoist[2] *n* : grúa *f*

hold[1] [ˈhoːld] *v* **held** [ˈhɛld]; **holding** *vt* **1** POSSESS : tener <to hold office : ocupar un puesto> **2** RESTRAIN : detener, controlar <to hold one's temper : controlar su mal genio> **3** CLASP, GRASP : agarrar, coger <to hold hands : agarrarse de la mano> **4** : sujetar, mantener fijo <hold this nail for me : sujétame este clavo> 5 CONTAIN : contener, dar cabida a 6 SUPPORT : aguantar, sostener 7 REGARD : considerar, tener <he held me responsible : me consideró responsable> 8 CONDUCT : celebrar (una reunión), realizar (un evento), mantener (una conversación) — *vi* 1 : aguantar, resistir <the rope will hold : la cuerda resistirá> 2 : ser válido, valer <my offer still holds : mi oferta todavía es válida> 3 **to hold forth** : perorar, arengar 4 **to hold to** : mantenerse firme en 5 **to hold with** : estar de acuerdo con

hold[2] *n* 1 GRIP : agarre *m,* llave *f* (en deportes) 2 CONTROL : control *m,* dominio *m* <to get hold of oneself : controlarse> 3 DELAY : demora *f* <to put on hold : suspender temporalmente> 4 : bodega *f* (en un barco o un avión) 5 **to get hold of** : conseguir, localizar

holder [ˈhoːldər] *n* : poseedor *m,* -dora *f;* titular *mf*

holdings [ˈhoːldɪŋz] *npl* : propiedades *fpl*

hold out *vi* 1 LAST : aguantar, durar 2 RESIST : resistir

holdup [ˈhoːld,ʌp] *n* 1 ROBBERY : atraco *m* 2 DELAY : retraso *m,* demora *f*

hold up *vt* 1 ROB : robarle (a alguien), atracar, asaltar 2 DELAY : retrasar

hole [ˈhoːl] *n* : agujero *m,* hoyo *m*

holiday [ˈhɑlə,deɪ] *n* 1 : día *m* feriado, fiesta *f* 2 VACATION : vacaciones *fpl*

holiness [ˈhoːlinəs] *n* 1 : santidad *f* 2 **His Holiness** : Su Santidad

holistic [hoːˈlɪstɪk] *adj* : holístico

holler[1] [ˈhɑlər] *vi* : gritar, chillar

holler[2] *n* : grito *m,* chillido *m*

hollow[1] [ˈhɑ,loː] *vt or* **to hollow out** : ahuecar

hollow[2] *adj* **-lower; -est** 1 : hueco, hundido (dícese de las mejillas, etc.), cavernoso (dícese de un sonido) 2 EMPTY, FALSE : vacío, falso

hollow[3] *n* 1 CAVITY : hueco *m,* depresión *f,* cavidad *f* 2 VALLEY : hondonada *f,* valle *m*

hollowness [ˈhɑ,loːnəs] *n* 1 HOLLOW : hueco *m,* cavidad *f* 2 FALSENESS : falsedad *f* 3 EMPTINESS : vacuidad *f*

holly [ˈhɑli] *n, pl* **-lies** : acebo *m*

hollyhock [ˈhɑli,hɑk] *n* : malvarrosa *f*

holocaust [ˈhɑlə,kɔst, ˈhoː-, ˈhɔ-] *n* : holocausto *m*

holster [ˈhoːlstər] *n* : pistolera *f*

holy [ˈhoːli] *adj* **-lier; -est** : santo, sagrado

Holy Ghost → **Holy Spirit**

Holy Spirit *n* **the Holy Spirit** : el Espíritu Santo

homage [ˈɑmɪdʒ, ˈhɑ-] *n* : homenaje *m*

home [ˈhoːm] *n* 1 : casa *f,* hogar *m,* domicilio *m* <to feel at home : sentirse en casa> 2 INSTITUTION : residencia *f,* asilo *m*

homecoming [ˈhoːm,kʌmɪŋ] *n* : regreso *m* (a casa)

homegrown [ˈhoːmˈgroːn] *adj* 1 : de cosecha propia 2 LOCAL : local

homeland [ˈhoːm,lænd] *n* : patria *f,* tierra *f* natal, terruño *m*

homeless [ˈhoːmləs] *adj* : sin hogar, sin techo

homely [ˈhoːmli] *adj* **-lier; -est** 1 DOMESTIC : casero, hogareño 2 UGLY : feo, poco atractivo

homemade [ˈhoːmˈmeɪd] *adj* : casero, hecho en casa

homemaker [ˈhoːm,meɪkər] *n* : ama *f* de casa, persona *f* que se ocupa de la casa

home plate *n* : base *f* del bateador

home run *n* : jonrón *m*

homesick [ˈhoːm,sɪk] *adj* : nostálgico <to be homesick : echar de menos a la familia>

homesickness [ˈhoːm,sɪknəs] *n* : nostalgia *f,* morriña *f*

homespun [ˈhoːm,spʌn] *adj* : simple, sencillo

homestead [ˈhoːm,stɛd] *n* : estancia *f,* hacienda *f*

homeward[1] [ˈhoːmwərd] *or* **homewards** [-wərdz] *adv* : de vuelta a casa, hacia casa

homeward[2] *adj* : de vuelta, de regreso

homework [ˈhoːm,wərk] *n* : tarea *f,* deberes *mpl Spain*, asignación *f PRi*

homey [ˈhoːmi] *adj* **homier; -est** : hogareño

homicidal [,hɑməˈsaɪdəl, ,hoː-] *adj* : homicida

homicide [ˈhɑmə,saɪd, ˈhoː-] *n* : homicidio *m*

hominy [ˈhɑməni] *n* : maíz *m* descascarillado

homogeneous [,hoːməˈdʒiːniəs, -njəs] *adj* : homogéneo — **homogeneously** *adv*

homogenize [hoːˈmɑdʒə,naɪz, hə-] *vt* **-nized; -nizing** : homogeneizar

homograph [ˈhɑmə,græf, ˈhoː-] *n* : homógrafo *m*

homonym [ˈhɑmə,nɪm, ˈhoː-] *n* : homónimo *m*

homophone [ˈhɑmə,foːn, ˈhoː-] *n* : homófono *m*

homosexual[1] [,hoːməˈsɛkʃʊəl] *adj* : homosexual

homosexual[2] *n* : homosexual *mf*

homosexuality [,hoːmə,sɛkʃʊˈæləṭi] *n* : homosexualidad *f*

Honduran [hɑnˈdʊrən, -ˈdjʊr-] *n* : hondureño *m,* -ña *f* — **Honduran** *adj*

hone [ˈhoːn] *vt* **honed; honing** : afilar

honest [ˈɑnəst] *adj* : honesto, honrado — **honestly** *adv*

honesty [ˈɑnəsti] *n, pl* **-ties** : honestidad *f,* honradez *f*

honey [ˈhʌni] *n, pl* **-eys** : miel *f*

honeybee [ˈhʌni,biː] *n* : abeja *f*

honeycomb [ˈhʌni,koːm] *n* : panal *m*

honeymoon[1] [ˈhʌni,muːn] *vi* : pasar la luna de miel
honeymoon[2] *n* : luna *f* de miel
honeysuckle [ˈhʌni,sʌkəl] *n* : madreselva *f*
honk[1] [ˈhɑŋk, ˈhɔŋk] *vi* **1** : graznar (dícese del ganso) **2** : tocar la bocina (dícese de un vehículo), pitar
honk[2] *n* : graznido *m* (del ganso), bocinazo *m* (de un vehículo)
honor[1] [ˈɑnər] *vt* **1** RESPECT : honrar **2** : cumplir con <to honor one's word : cumplir con su palabra> **3** : aceptar (un cheque, etc.)
honor[2] *n* **1** : honor *m* <in honor of : en honor de> **2 honors** *npl* AWARDS : honores *mpl*, condecoraciones *fpl* **3 Your Honor** : Su Señoría
honorable [ˈɑnərəbəl] *adj* : honorable, honroso — **honorably** [-bli] *adv*
honorary [ˈɑnə,rɛri] *adj* : honorario
hood [ˈhʊd] *n* **1** : capucha *f* **2** : capó *m*, bonete *m Car* (de un automóvil)
hooded [ˈhʊdəd] *adj* : encapuchado
hoodlum [ˈhʊdləm, ˈhuːd-] *n* THUG : maleante *mf*, matón *m*
hoodwink [ˈhʊd,wɪŋk] *vt* : engañar
hoof [ˈhʊf, ˈhuːf] *n*, *pl* **hooves** [ˈhʊvz, ˈhuːvz] *or* **hoofs** : pezuña *f*, casco *m*
hoofed [ˈhʊft, ˈhuːft] *adj* : ungulado
hook[1] [ˈhʊk] *vt* : enganchar — *vi* : abrocharse, engancharse
hook[2] *n* : gancho *m*, percha *f*
hookworm [ˈhʊk,wərm] *n* : anquilostoma *m*
hooligan [ˈhuːlɪgən] *n* : gamberro *m*, -rra *f*
hoop [ˈhuːp] *n* : aro *m*
hooray [hʊˈreɪ] → **hurrah**
hoot[1] [ˈhuːt] *vi* **1** SHOUT : gritar <to hoot with laughter : morirse de risa, reírse a carcajadas> **2** : ulular (dícese de un búho), tocar la bocina (dícese de un vehículo), silbar (dícese de un tren o un barco)
hoot[2] *n* **1** : ululato *m* (de un búho), silbido *m* (de un tren), bocinazo *m* (de un vehículo) **2** GUFFAW : carcajada *f*, risotada *f* **3 I don't give a hoot** : me vale un comino, me importa un pito
hop[1] [ˈhɑp] *vi* **hopped; hopping** : brincar, saltar
hop[2] *n* **1** LEAP : salto *m*, brinco *m* **2** FLIGHT : vuelo *m* corto **3** : lúpulo *m* (planta)
hope[1] [ˈhoːp] *v* **hoped; hoping** *vi* : esperar — *vt* : esperar que <we hope she comes : esperamos que venga> <I hope not : espero que no>
hope[2] *n* : esperanza *f*
hopeful [ˈhoːpfəl] *adj* : esperanzado — **hopefully** *adv*
hopeless [ˈhoːpləs] *adj* **1** DESPAIRING : desesperado **2** IMPOSSIBLE : imposible <a hopeless case : un caso perdido>
hopelessly [ˈhoːpləsli] *adv* **1** : sin esperanzas, desesperadamente **2** COMPLETELY : totalmente, completamente **3** IMPOSSIBLY : imposiblemente
hopelessness [ˈhoːpləsnəs] *n* : desesperanza *f*
hopper [ˈhɑpər] *n* : tolva *f*
hopscotch [ˈhɑp,skɑtʃ] *n* : tejo *m*
horde [ˈhord] *n* : horda *f*, multitud *f*
horizon [həˈraɪzən] *n* : horizonte *m*
horizontal [,hɔrəˈzɑntəl] *adj* : horizontal — **horizontally** *adv*
hormone [ˈhɔr,moːn] *n* : hormona *f* — **hormonal** [hɔrˈmoːnəl] *adj*
horn [ˈhɔrn] *n* **1** : cuerno *m* (de un toro, una vaca, etc.) **2** : cuerno *m*, trompa *f* (instrumento musical) **3** : bocina *f*, claxon *m* (de un vehículo)
horned [ˈhɔrnd, ˈhɔrnəd] *adj* : cornudo, astado, con cuernos
hornet [ˈhɔrnət] *n* : avispón *m*
horn of plenty → **cornucopia**
horny [ˈhɔrni] *adj* **hornier; -est** CALLOUS : calloso
horoscope [ˈhɔrə,skoːp] *n* : horóscopo *m*
horrendous [hɔˈrɛndəs] *adj* : horrendo, horroroso, atroz
horrible [ˈhɔrəbəl] *adj* : horrible, espantoso, horroroso — **horribly** [-bli] *adv*
horrid [ˈhɔrɪd] *adj* : horroroso, horrible — **horridly** *adv*
horrify [ˈhɔrə,faɪ] *vt* **-fied; -fying** : horrorizar
horrifying [ˈhɔrə,faɪɪŋ] *adj* : horripilante, horroroso
horror [ˈhɔrər] *n* : horror *m*
hors d'oeuvre [ɔrˈdərv] *n*, *pl* **hors d'oeuvres** [-ˈdərvz] : entremés *m*
horse [ˈhɔrs] *n* : caballo *m*
horseback [ˈhɔrs,bæk] *n* **on ~** : a caballo
horse chestnut *n* : castaña *f* de Indias
horsefly [ˈhɔrs,flaɪ] *n*, *pl* **-flies** : tábano *m*
horsehair [ˈhɔrs,hær] *n* : crin *f*
horseman [ˈhɔrsmən] *n*, *pl* **-men** [-mən, -,mɛn] : jinete *m*, caballista *m*
horsemanship [ˈhɔrsmən,ʃɪp] *n* : equitación *f*
horseplay [ˈhɔrs,pleɪ] *n* : payasadas *fpl*
horsepower [ˈhɔrs,paʊər] *n* : caballo *m* de fuerza
horseradish [ˈhɔrs,rædɪʃ] *n* : rábano *m* picante
horseshoe [ˈhɔrs,ʃuː] *n* : herradura *f*
horsewhip [ˈhɔrs,*h*wɪp] *vt* **-whipped; -whipping** : azotar, darle fuetazos (a alguien)
horsewoman [ˈhɔrs,wʊmən] *n*, *pl* **-women** [-,wɪmən] : amazona *f*, jinete *f*, caballista *f*
horsey *or* **horsy** [ˈhɔrsi] *adj* **horsier; -est** : relacionado a los caballos, caballar
horticultural [,hɔrt̬əˈkʌltʃərəl] *adj* : hortícola
horticulture [ˈhɔrt̬ə,kʌltʃər] *n* : horticultura *f*

hose[1] [ˈhoːz] *vt* **hosed; hosing :** regar o lavar con manguera

hose[2] *n* **1** *pl* **hose** SOCKS **:** calcetines *mpl*, medias *fpl* **2** *pl* **hose** STOCKINGS **:** medias *fpl* **3** *pl* **hoses :** manguera *f*, manga *f*

hosiery [ˈhoːʒəri, ˈhoːzə-] *n* **:** calcetería *f*, medias *fpl*

hospice [ˈhɑspəs] *n* **:** hospicio *m*

hospitable [hɑˈspɪt̬əbəl, ˈhɑs,pɪ-] *adj* **:** hospitalario **— hospitably** [-bli] *adv*

hospital [ˈhɑs,pɪt̬əl] *n* **:** hospital *m*

hospitality [,hɑspəˈtæləti] *n*, *pl* **-ties :** hospitalidad *f*

hospitalization [,hɑs,pɪt̬ələˈzeɪʃən] *n* **:** hospitalización *f*

hospitalize [ˈhɑs,pɪt̬əl,aɪz] *vt* **-ized; -izing :** hospitalizar

host[1] [ˈhoːst] *vt* **:** presentar (un programa de televisión, etc.)

host[2] *n* **1 :** anfitrión *m*, -triona *f* (en la casa, a un evento); presentador *m*, -dora *f* (de un programa de televisión, etc.) **2** *or* **host organism :** huésped *m* **3** TROOPS **:** huestes *fpl* **4** MULTITUDE **:** multitud *f* <for a host of reasons : por muchas razones> **5** EUCHARIST **:** hostia *f*, Eucaristía *f*

hostage [ˈhɑstɪdʒ] *n* **:** rehén *m*

hostel [ˈhɑstəl] *n* **:** albergue *m* juvenil

hostess [ˈhoːstɪs] *n* **:** anfitriona *f* (en la casa), presentadora *f* (de un programa)

hostile [ˈhɑstəl, -,taɪl] *adj* **:** hostil **— hostilely** *adv*

hostility [hɑsˈtɪləti] *n*, *pl* **-ties :** hostilidad *f*

hot [ˈhɑt] *adj* **hotter; hottest 1 :** caliente, cálido, caluroso <hot water : agua caliente> <a hot climate : un clima cálido> <a hot day : un día caluroso> **2** ARDENT, FIERY **:** ardiente, acalorado <to have a hot temper : tener mal genio> **3** SPICY **:** picante **4** FRESH **:** reciente, nuevo <hot news : noticias de última hora> **5** EAGER **:** ávido **6** STOLEN **:** robado

hot air *n* **:** palabrería *f*

hotbed [ˈhɑt,bɛd] *n* **1 :** semillero *m* (de plantas) **2 :** hervidero *m*, semillero *m* (de crimen, etc.)

hot dog *n* **:** perro *m* caliente

hotel [hoːˈtɛl] *n* **:** hotel *m*

hothead [ˈhɑt,hɛd] *n* **:** exaltado *m*, -da *f*

hotheaded [ˈhɑtˈhɛdəd] *adj* **:** exaltado

hothouse [ˈhɑt,haʊs] *n* **:** invernadero *m*

hot plate *n* **:** placa *f* (de cocina)

hot rod *n* **:** coche *m* con motor modificado

hot water *n* **to get into hot water :** meterse en un lío

hound[1] [ˈhaʊnd] *vt* **:** acosar, perseguir

hound[2] *n* **:** perro *m* (de caza)

hour [ˈaʊər] *n* **:** hora *f*

hourglass [ˈaʊər,glæs] *n* **:** reloj *m* de arena

hourly [ˈaʊərli] *adv & adj* **:** cada hora, por hora

house[1] [ˈhaʊz] *vt* **housed; housing :** albergar, alojar, hospedar

house[2] [ˈhaʊs] *n*, *pl* **houses** [ˈhaʊzəz, -səz] **1** HOME **:** casa *f* **2 :** cámara *f* (del gobierno) **3** BUSINESS **:** casa *f*, empresa *f*

houseboat [ˈhaʊs,boːt] *n* **:** casa *f* flotante

housebroken [ˈhaʊs,broːkən] *adj* **:** enseñado

housefly [ˈhaʊs,flaɪ] *n*, *pl* **-flies :** mosca *f* común

household[1] [ˈhaʊs,hoːld] *adj* **1** DOMESTIC **:** doméstico, de la casa **2** FAMILIAR **:** conocido por todos

household[2] *n* **:** casa *f*, familia *f*

householder [ˈhaʊs,hoːldər] *n* **:** dueño *m*, -ña *f* de casa

housekeeper [ˈhaʊs,kiːpər] *n* **:** ama *f* de llaves

housekeeping [ˈhaʊs,kiːpɪŋ] *n* **:** gobierno *m* de la casa, quehaceres *mpl* domésticos

housemaid [ˈhaʊs,meɪd] *n* **:** criada *f*, mucama *f*, muchacha *f*, sirvienta *f*

housewarming [ˈhaʊs,wɔrmɪŋ] *n* **:** fiesta *f* de estreno de una casa

housewife [ˈhaʊs,waɪf] *n*, *pl* **-wives :** ama *f* de casa

housework [ˈhaʊs,wərk] *n* **:** faenas *fpl* domésticas, quehaceres *mpl* domésticos

housing [ˈhaʊzɪŋ] *n* **1** HOUSES **:** vivienda *f* **2** COVERING **:** caja *f* protectora

hove → **heave**

hovel [ˈhʌvəl, ˈhɑ-] *n* **:** casucha *f*, tugurio *m*

hover [ˈhʌvər, ˈhɑ-] *vi* **1 :** cernerse, sostenerse en el aire **2 to hover about :** rondar

how [ˈhaʊ] *adv* **1 :** cómo <how are you? : ¿cómo estas?> <I don't know how to fix it : no se cómo arreglarlo> **2 :** qué <how beautiful! : ¡qué bonito!> **3 :** cuánto <how old are you? : ¿cuántos años tienes?> **4 how about...? :** ¿qué te parece...?

however[1] [haʊˈɛvər] *adv* **1 :** por mucho que, por más que <however hot it is : por mucho calor que haga> **2** NEVERTHELESS **:** sin embargo, no obstante

however[2] *conj* **:** comoquiera que, de cualquier manera que

howl[1] [ˈhaʊl] *vi* **:** aullar

howl[2] *n* **:** aullido *m*, alarido *m*

hub [ˈhʌb] *n* **1** CENTER **:** centro *m* **2 :** cubo *m* (de una rueda)

hubbub [ˈhʌ,bʌb] *n* **:** algarabía *f*, alboroto *m*, jaleo *m*

hubcap [ˈhʌb,kæp] *n* **:** tapacubos *m*

huckster [ˈhʌkstər] *n* **:** buhonero *m*, -ra *f*; vendedor *m*, -dora *f* ambulante

huddle[1] [ˈhʌdəl] *vi* **-dled; -dling 1 :** apiñarse, amontonarse **2 to huddle together :** acurrucarse

huddle[2] *n* : grupo *m* (cerrado) <to go into a huddle : conferenciar en secreto>

hue [ˈhjuː] *n* : color *m,* tono *m*

huff [ˈhʌf] *n* : enojo *m,* enfado *m* <to be in a huff : estar enojado>

huffy [ˈhʌfi] *adj* **huffier; -est** : enojado, enfadado

hug[1] [ˈhʌg] *vt* **hugged; hugging 1** EMBRACE : abrazar **2** : ir pegado a <the road hugs the river : el camino está pegado al río>

hug[2] *n* : abrazo *m*

huge [ˈhjuːdʒ] *adj* **huger; hugest** : inmenso, enorme — **hugely** *adv*

hulk [ˈhʌlk] *n* **1** : persona *f* fornida **2** : casco *m* (barco), armatoste *m* (edificio, etc.)

hulking [ˈhʌlkɪŋ] *adj* : grandote *fam,* pesado

hull[1] [ˈhʌl] *vt* : pelar

hull[2] *n* **1** HUSK : cáscara *f* **2** : casco *m* (de un barco, un avión, etc.)

hullabaloo [ˈhʌləbəˌluː] *n, pl* **-loos** : alboroto *m,* jaleo *m*

hum[1] [ˈhʌm] *v* **hummed; humming** *vi* **1** BUZZ : zumbar **2** : estar muy activo, moverse <to hum with activity : bullir de actividad> — *vt* : tararear (una melodía)

hum[2] *n* : zumbido *m,* murmullo *m*

human[1] [ˈhjuːmən, ˈjuː-] *adj* : humano — **humanly** *adv*

human[2] *n* : ser *m* humano

humane [hjuːˈmeɪn, ˌjuː-] *adj* : humano, humanitario — **humanely** *adv*

humanism [ˈhjuːməˌnɪzəm, ˈjuː-] *n* : humanismo *m*

humanist [ˈhjuːmənɪst, ˈjuː-] *n* : humanista *mf*

humanitarian[1] [hjuːˌmænəˈtɛriən, juː-] *adj* : humanitario

humanitarian[2] *n* : humanitario *m,* -ria *f*

humanity [hjuːˈmænət̬i, juː-] *n, pl* **-ties** : humanidad *f*

humankind [ˈhjuːmənˈkaɪnd, ˈjuː-] *n* : género *m* humano

humble[1] [ˈhʌmbəl] *vt* **-bled; -bling 1** : humillar **2 to humble oneself** : humillarse

humble[2] *adj* **-bler; -blest** : humilde, modesto — **humbly** [ˈhʌmbli] *adv*

humbug [ˈhʌmˌbʌg] *n* **1** FRAUD : charlatán *m,* -tana *f;* farsante *mf* **2** NONSENSE : patrañas *fpl,* tonterías *fpl*

humdrum [ˈhʌmˌdrʌm] *adj* : monótono, rutinario

humid [ˈhjuːməd, ˈjuː-] *adj* : húmedo

humidifier [hjuːˈmɪdəˌfaɪər, juː-] *n* : humidificador *m*

humidify [hjuːˈmɪdəˌfaɪ, juː-] *vt* **-fied; -fying** : humidificar

humidity [hjuːˈmɪdət̬i, juː-] *n, pl* **-ties** : humedad *f*

humiliate [hjuːˈmɪliˌeɪt, juː-] *vt* **-ated; -ating** : humillar

humiliating [hjuːˈmɪliˌeɪt̬ɪŋ, juː-] *adj* : humillante

humiliation [hjuːˌmɪliˈeɪʃən, juː-] *n* : humillación *f*

humility [hjuːˈmɪlət̬i, juː-] *n* : humildad *f*

hummingbird [ˈhʌmɪŋˌbərd] *n* : colibrí *m,* picaflor *m*

hummock [ˈhʌmək] *n* : montículo *m*

humor[1] [ˈhjuːmər, ˈjuː-] *vt* : seguir el humor a, complacer

humor[2] *n* : humor *m*

humorist [ˈhjuːmərɪst, ˈjuː-] *n* : humorista *mf*

humorless [ˈhjuːmərləs, ˈjuː-] *adj* : sin sentido del humor <a humorless smile : una sonrisa forzada>

humorous [ˈhjuːmərəs, ˈjuː-] *adj* : humorístico, cómico — **humorously** *adv*

hump [ˈhʌmp] *n* : joroba *f,* giba *f*

humpback [ˈhʌmpˌbæk] *n* **1** HUMP : joroba *f,* giba *f* **2** HUNCHBACK : jorobado *m,* -da *f;* giboso *m,* -sa *f*

humpbacked [ˈhʌmpˌbækt] *adj* : jorobado, giboso

humus [ˈhjuːməs, ˈjuː-] *n* : humus *m*

hunch[1] [ˈhʌntʃ] *vt* : encorvar — *vi or* **to hunch up** : encorvarse

hunch[2] *n* PREMONITION : presentimiento *m*

hunchback [ˈhʌntʃˌbæk] *n* **1** HUMP : joroba *f,* giba *f* **2** HUMPBACK : jorobado *m,* -da *f;* giboso *m,* -sa *f*

hunchbacked [ˈhʌntʃˌbækt] *adj* : jorobado, giboso

hundred[1] [ˈhʌndrəd] *adj* : cien, ciento

hundred[2] *n, pl* **-dreds** *or* **-dred** : ciento *m*

hundredth[1] [ˈhʌndrədθ] *adj* : centésimo

hundredth[2] *n* **1** : centésimo *m,* -ma *f* (en una serie) **2** : centésimo *m,* centésima parte *f*

hung → **hang**

Hungarian [hʌŋˈgæriən] *n* **1** : húngaro *m,* -ra *f* **2** : húngaro *m* (idioma) — **Hungarian** *adj*

hunger[1] [ˈhʌŋgər] *vi* **1** : tener hambre **2 to hunger for** : ansiar, anhelar

hunger[2] *n* : hambre *m*

hungrily [ˈhʌŋgrəli] *adv* : ávidamente

hungry [ˈhʌŋgri] *adj* **-grier; -est 1** : hambriento **2 to be hungry** : tener hambre

hunk [ˈhʌŋk] *n* : trozo *m,* pedazo *m*

hunt[1] [ˈhʌnt] *vt* **1** PURSUE : cazar **2 to hunt for** : buscar

hunt[2] *n* **1** PURSUIT : caza *f,* cacería *f* **2** SEARCH : búsqueda *f,* busca *f*

hunter [ˈhʌntər] *n* : cazador *m,* -dora *f*

hunting [ˈhʌntɪŋ] *n* : caza *f* <to go hunting : ir de caza>

hurdle[1] [ˈhərdəl] *vt* **-dled; -dling** : saltar, salvar (un obstáculo)

hurdle[2] *n* : valla *f* (en deportes), obstáculo *m*

hurl [ˈhərl] *vt* : arrojar, tirar, lanzar

hurrah [hʊˈrɑ, -ˈrɔ] *interj* : ¡hurra!

hurricane [ˈhərəˌkeɪn] *n* : huracán *m*

hurried ['hərid] *adj* **:** apresurado, precipitado
hurriedly ['hərədli] *adv* **:** apresuradamente, de prisa
hurry[1] ['həri] *v* **-ried; -rying** *vi* **:** apurarse, darse prisa, apresurarse — *vt* **:** apurar, darle prisa (a alguien)
hurry[2] *n* **:** prisa *f,* apuro *f*
hurt[1] ['hərt] *v* **hurt; hurting** *vt* **1** INJURE **:** hacer daño a, herir, lastimar <to hurt oneself : hacerse daño> **2** DISTRESS, OFFEND **:** hacer sufrir, ofender, herir — *vi* **:** doler <my foot hurts : me duele el pie>
hurt[2] *n* **1** INJURY **:** herida *f* **2** DISTRESS, PAIN **:** dolor *m,* pena *f*
hurtful ['hərtfəl] *adj* **:** hiriente, doloroso
hurtle ['hərtəl] *vi* **-tled; -tling :** lanzarse, precipitarse
husband[1] ['hʌzbənd] *vt* **:** economizar, bien administrar
husband[2] *n* **:** esposo *m,* marido *m*
husbandry ['hʌzbəndri] *n* **1** MANAGEMENT, THRIFT **:** economía *f,* buena administración *f* **2** AGRICULTURE **:** agricultura *f* <animal husbandry : cría de animales>
hush[1] ['hʌʃ] *vt* **1** SILENCE **:** hacer callar, acallar **2** CALM **:** calmar, apaciguar
hush[2] *n* **:** silencio *m*
hush–hush ['hʌʃ,hʌʃ, ,hʌʃ'hʌʃ] *adj* **:** muy secreto, confidencial
husk[1] ['hʌsk] *vt* **:** descascarar
husk[2] *n* **:** cáscara *f*
huskily ['hʌskəli] *adv* **:** con voz ronca
husky[1] ['hʌski] *adj* **-kier; -est 1** HOARSE **:** ronco **2** BURLY **:** fornido
husky[2] *n, pl* **-kies :** perro *m,* -rra *f* esquimal
hustle[1] ['həsəl] *v* **-tled; -tling** *vt* **:** darle prisa (a alguien), apurar <they hustled me in : me hicieron entrar a empujones> — *vi* **:** apurarse, ajetrearse
hustle[2] *n* BUSTLE **:** ajetreo *m*
hut ['hʌt] *n* **:** cabaña *f,* choza *f,* barraca *f*
hutch ['hʌtʃ] *n* **1** CUPBOARD **:** alacena *f* **2 rabbit hutch :** conejera *f*
hyacinth ['haɪə,sɪnθ] *n* **:** jacinto *m*
hybrid[1] ['haɪbrɪd] *adj* **:** híbrido
hybrid[2] *n* **:** híbrido *m*
hydrant ['haɪdrənt] *n* **:** boca *f* de riego, hidrante *m CA, Col* <fire hydrant : boca de incendios>
hydraulic [haɪ'drɔlɪk] *adj* **:** hidráulico — **hydraulically** *adv*
hydrocarbon [,haɪdro'kɑrbən] *n* **:** hidrocarburo *m*
hydrochloric acid [,haɪdro'klorɪk] *n* **:** ácido *m* clorohídrico
hydroelectric [,haɪdroɪ'lɛktrɪk] *adj* **:** hidroeléctrico
hydrogen ['haɪdrədʒən] *n* **:** hidrógeno *m*
hydrogen bomb *n* **:** bomba *f* de hidrógeno
hydrogen peroxide *n* **:** agua *f* oxigenada, peróxido *m* de hidrógeno
hydrophobia [,haɪdrə'fo:biə] *n* **:** hidrofobia *f,* rabia *f*
hydroplane ['haɪdrə,pleɪn] *n* **:** hidroplano *m*
hyena [haɪ'i:nə] *n* **:** hiena *f*
hygiene ['haɪ,dʒi:n] *n* **:** higiene *f*
hygienic [haɪ'dʒɛnɪk, -'dʒi:-; ,haɪdʒi'ɛnɪk] *adj* **:** higiénico — **hygienically** [-nɪkli] *adv*
hygienist [haɪ'dʒi:nɪst, -'dʒɛ-; 'haɪ,dʒi:-] *n* **:** higienista *mf*
hygrometer [haɪ'grɑmət̬ər] *n* **:** higrómetro *m*
hymn ['hɪm] *n* **:** himno *m*
hymnal ['hɪmnəl] *n* **:** himnario *m*
hype ['haɪp] *n* **:** bombo *m* publicitario
hyperactive [,haɪpər'æktɪv] *adj* **:** hiperactivo
hyperbole [haɪ'pərbəli] *n* **:** hipérbole *f*
hypercritical [,haɪpər'krɪt̬əkəl] *adj* **:** hipercrítico
hypersensitivity [,haɪpər,sɛntsə'tɪvət̬i] *n* **:** hipersensibilidad *f*
hypertension ['haɪpər,tɛntʃən] *n* **:** hipertensión *f*
hyphen ['haɪfən] *n* **:** guión *m*
hyphenate ['haɪfən,eɪt] *vt* **-ated; -ating :** escribir con guión
hypnosis [hɪp'no:sɪs] *n, pl* **-noses** [-,si:z] **:** hipnosis *f*
hypnotic [hɪp'nɑt̬ɪk] *adj* **:** hipnótico, hipnotizador
hypnotism ['hɪpnə,tɪzəm] *n* **:** hipnotismo *m*
hypnotize ['hɪpnə,taɪz] *vt* **-tized; -tizing :** hipnotizar
hypochondria [,haɪpə'kɑndriə] *n* **:** hipocondría *f*
hypochondriac [,haɪpə'kɑndri,æk] *n* **:** hipocondríaco *m,* -ca *f*
hypocrisy [hɪp'ɑkrəsi] *n, pl* **-sies :** hipocresía *f*
hypocrite ['hɪpə,krɪt] *n* **:** hipócrita *mf*
hypocritical [,hɪpə'krɪt̬ɪkəl] *adj* **:** hipócrita
hypodermic[1] [,haɪpə'dərmɪk] *adj* **:** hipodérmico
hypodermic[2] *n* **:** aguja *f* hipodérmica
hypotenuse [haɪ'pɑtən,u:s, -,u:z, -,ju:s, -,ju:z] *n* **:** hipotenusa *f*
hypothesis [haɪ'pɑθəsɪs] *n, pl* **-eses** [-,si:z] **:** hipótesis *f*
hypothetical [,haɪpə'θɛt̬ɪkəl] *adj* **:** hipotético — **hypothetically** [-t̬ɪkli] *adv*
hysteria [hɪs'tɛriə, -tɪr-] *n* **:** histeria *f,* histerismo *m*
hysterical [hɪs'tɛrɪkəl] *adj* **:** histérico — **hysterically** [-ɪkli] *adv*
hysterics [hɪs'tɛrɪks] *n* **:** histeria *f,* histerismo *m*

I

i ['aɪ] *n, pl* **i's** *or* **is** ['aɪz] : novena letra del alfabeto inglés
I ['aɪ] *pron* : yo
ibis ['aɪbəs] *n, pl* **ibis** *or* **ibises** : ibis *f*
ice[1] ['aɪs] *v* **iced; icing** *vt* **1** FREEZE : congelar, helar **2** CHILL : enfriar **3 to ice a cake** : escarchar un pastel — *vi* : helarse, congelarse
ice[2] *n* **1** : hielo *m* **2** SHERBET : sorbete *m,* nieve *f Cuba, Mex, PRi*
iceberg ['aɪs,bərg] *n* : iceberg *m*
icebox ['aɪs,bɑks] → **refrigerator**
icebreaker ['aɪs,breɪkər] *n* : rompehielos *m*
ice cap *n* : casquete *m* glaciar
ice–cold ['aɪs'ko:ld] *adj* : helado
ice cream *n* : helado *m,* mantecado *m PRi*
Icelander ['aɪs,lændər, -lən-] *n* : islandés *m,* -desa *f*
Icelandic[1] [aɪs'lændɪk] *adj* : islandés
Icelandic[2] *n* : islandés *m* (idioma)
ice–skate ['aɪs,skeɪt] *vi* **-skated; -skating** : patinar
ice skater *n* : patinador *m,* -dora *f*
ichthyology [,ɪkthi'ɑləd͡ʒi] *n* : ictiología *f*
icicle ['aɪ,sɪkəl] *n* : carámbano *m*
icily ['aɪsəli] *adv* : fríamente, con frialdad <he stared at me icily : me fijó la mirada con mucha frialdad>
icing ['aɪsɪŋ] *n* : glaseado *m,* betún *m Mex*
icon ['aɪ,kɑn, -kən] *n* : icono *m*
iconoclasm [aɪ'kɑnə,klæzəm] *n* : iconoclasia *f*
iconoclast [aɪ'kɑnə,klæst] *n* : iconoclasta *mf*
icy ['aɪsi] *adj* **icier; -est 1** : cubierto de hielo <an icy road : una carretera cubierta de hielo> **2** FREEZING : helado, gélido, glacial **3** ALOOF : frío, distante
id ['ɪd] *n* : id *m*
I'd ['aɪd] (*contraction of* **I should** *or* **I would**) → **should, would**
idea [aɪ'di:ə] *n* : idea *f*
ideal[1] [aɪ'di:əl] *adj* : ideal
ideal[2] *n* : ideal *m*
idealism [aɪ'di:ə,lɪzəm] *n* : idealismo *m*
idealist [aɪ'di:əlɪst] *n* : idealista *mf*
idealistic [aɪ,di:ə'lɪstɪk] *adj* : idealista
idealistically [aɪ,di:ə'lɪstɪkli] *adv* : con idealismo
idealization [aɪ,di:ələ'zeɪʃən] *n* : idealización *f*
idealize [aɪ'di:ə,laɪz] *vt* **-ized; -izing** : idealizar
ideally [aɪ'di:əli] *adv* : perfectamente
identical [aɪ'dɛntɪkəl] *adj* : idéntico — **identically** [-tɪkli] *adv*
identifiable [aɪ,dɛntə'faɪəbəl] *adj* : identificable
identification [aɪ,dɛntəfə'keɪʃən] *n* **1** : identificación *f* **2 identification card** : carnet *m,* cédula *f* de identidad, identificación *f*
identify [aɪ'dɛntə,faɪ] *v* **-fied; -fying** *vt* : identificar — *vi* **to identify with** : identificarse con
identity [aɪ'dɛntət̬i] *n, pl* **-ties** : identidad *f*
ideological [,aɪdiə'lɑd͡ʒɪkəl, ,ɪ-] *adj* : ideológico — **ideologically** [-d͡ʒɪkli] *adv*
ideology [,aɪdi'ɑləd͡ʒi, ,ɪ-] *n, pl* **-gies** : ideología *f*
idiocy ['ɪdiəsi] *n, pl* **-cies 1** : idiotez *f* **2** NONSENSE : estupidez *f,* tontería *f*
idiom ['ɪdiəm] *n* **1** LANGUAGE : lenguaje *m* **2** EXPRESSION : modismo *m,* expresión *f* idiomática
idiomatic [,ɪdiə'mæt̬ɪk] *adj* : idiomático
idiosyncrasy [,ɪdio'sɪŋkrəsi] *n, pl* **-sies** : idiosincrasia *f*
idiosyncratic [,ɪdiosɪn'kræt̬ɪk] *adj* : idiosincrásico — **idiosyncratically** [-t̬ɪkli] *adv*
idiot ['ɪdiət] *n* **1** : idiota *mf* (en medicina) **2** FOOL : idiota *mf;* tonto *m,* -ta *f;* imbécil *mf fam*
idiotic [,ɪdi'ɑt̬ɪk] *adj* : estúpido, idiota
idiotically [,ɪdi'ɑt̬ɪkli] *adv* : estúpidamente
idle[1] ['aɪdəl] *v* **idled; idling** *vi* **1** LOAF : holgazanear, flojear, haraganear **2** : andar al ralentí (dícese de un automóvil), marchar en vacío (dícese de una máquina) — *vt* : dejar sin trabajo
idle[2] *adj* **idler; idlest 1** VAIN : frívolo, vano, infundado <idle curiosity : pura curiosidad> **2** INACTIVE : inactivo, parado, desocupado **3** LAZY : holgazán, haragán, perezoso
idleness ['aɪdəlnəs] *n* **1** INACTIVITY : inactividad *f,* ociosidad *f* **2** LAZINESS : holgazanería *f,* flojera *f,* pereza *f*
idler ['aɪdələr] *n* : haragán *m,* -gana *f;* holgazán *m,* -zana *f*
idly ['aɪdəli] *adv* : ociosamente
idol ['aɪdəl] *n* : ídolo *m*
idolater *or* **idolator** [aɪ'dɑlət̬ər] *n* : idólatra *mf*
idolatrous [aɪ'dɑlətrəs] *adj* : idólatra
idolatry [aɪ'dɑlətri] *n, pl* **-tries** : idolatría *f*
idolize ['aɪdəlaɪz] *vt* **-ized; -izing** : idolatrar
idyll ['aɪdəl] *n* : idilio *m*
idyllic [aɪ'dɪlɪk] *adj* : idílico
if ['ɪf] *conj* **1** : si <I would do it if I could : lo haría si pudiera> <if so : si es así> <as if : como si> <if I were you : yo que tú> **2** WHETHER : si <I don't know if they're ready : no sé si están listos> **3** THOUGH : aunque, si bien <it's pretty, if somewhat old-fashioned : es lindo aunque algo anticuado>
igloo ['ɪ,glu:] *n, pl* **-loos** : iglú *m*

ignite [ɪg'naɪt] *v* **-nited; -niting** *vt* : prenderle fuego a, encender — *vi* : prender, encenderse
ignition [ɪg'nɪʃən] *n* **1** IGNITING : ignición *f*, encendido *m* **2** *or* **ignition switch** : encendido *m*, arranque *m* <to turn on the ignition : arrancar el motor>
ignoble [ɪg'noːbəl] *adj* : innoble — **ignobly** *adv*
ignominious [ˌɪgnə'mɪniəs] *adj* : ignominioso, deshonroso — **ignominiously** *adv*
ignominy ['ɪgnəˌmɪni] *n, pl* **-nies** : ignominia *f*
ignoramus [ˌɪgnə'reɪməs] *n* : ignorante *mf;* bestia *mf;* bruto *m*, -ta *f*
ignorance ['ɪgnərən*t*s] *n* : ignorancia *f*
ignorant ['ɪgnərənt] *adj* **1** : ignorante **2 to be ignorant of** : no ser consciente de, desconocer, ignorar
ignorantly ['ɪgnərəntli] *adv* : ignorantemente, con ignorancia
ignore [ɪg'nor] *vt* **-nored; -noring** : ignorar, hacer caso omiso de, no hacer caso de
iguana [ɪ'gwɑnə] *n* : iguana *f*, garrobo *f CA*
ilk ['ɪlk] *n* : tipo *m*, clase *f*, índole *f*
ill[1] ['ɪl] *adv* **worse** ['wərs]; **worst** ['wərst] : mal <to speak ill of : hablar mal de> <he can ill afford to fail : mal puede permitirse el lujo de fracasar>
ill[2] *adj* **worse; worst 1** SICK : enfermo **2** BAD : malo <ill luck : mala suerte>
ill[3] *n* **1** EVIL : mal *m* **2** MISFORTUNE : mal *m*, desgracia *f* **3** AILMENT : enfermedad *f*
I'll ['aɪl] (*contraction of* **I shall** *or* **I will**) → **shall, will**
illegal [ɪl'liːgəl] *adj* : ilegal — **illegally** *adv*
illegality [ɪli'gæləṭi] *n* : ilegalidad *f*
illegibility [ɪlˌlɛdʒə'bɪləṭi] *n, pl* **-ties** : ilegibilidad *f*
illegible [ɪl'lɛdʒəbəl] *adj* : ilegible — **illegibly** [-bli] *adv*
illegitimacy [ˌɪlɪ'dʒɪṭəməsi] *n* : ilegitimidad *f*
illegitimate [ˌɪlɪ'dʒɪṭəmət] *adj* **1** BASTARD : ilegítimo, bastardo **2** UNLAWFUL : ilegítimo, ilegal — **illegitimately** *adv*
ill–fated ['ɪl'feɪṭəd] *adj* : malhadado, infortunado, desventurado
illicit [ɪl'lɪsət] *adj* : ilícito — **illicitly** *adv*
illiteracy [ɪl'lɪṭərəsi] *n, pl* **-cies** : analfabetismo *m*
illiterate[1] [ɪl'lɪṭərət] *adj* : analfabeto
illiterate[2] *n* : analfabeto *m*, -ta *f*
ill–mannered [ˌɪl'manərd] *adj* : descortés, maleducado
ill–natured [ˌɪl'neɪtʃərd] *adj* : desagradable, de mal genio
ill–naturedly [ˌɪl'neɪtʃərdli] *adv* : desagradablemente
illness ['ɪlnəs] *n* : enfermedad *f*
illogical [ɪl'lɑdʒɪkəl] *adj* : ilógico — **illogically** [-kli] *adv*
ill–tempered [ˌɪl'tempərd] → **ill–natured**
ill–treat [ˌɪl'triːt] *vt* : maltratar
ill–treatment [ˌɪl'triːtmənt] *n* : maltrato *m*
illuminate [ɪ'luːməˌneɪt] *vt* **-nated; -nating 1** : iluminar, alumbrar **2** ELUCIDATE : esclarecer, elucidar
illumination [ɪˌluːmə'neɪʃən] *n* **1** LIGHTING : iluminación *f*, luz *f* **2** ELUCIDATION : esclarecimiento *m*, elucidación *f*
ill–use ['ɪl'juːz] → **ill–treat**
illusion [ɪ'luːʒən] *n* : ilusión *f*
illusory [ɪ'luːsəri, -zəri] *adj* : engañoso, ilusorio
illustrate ['ɪləsˌtreɪt] *v* **-trated; -trating** : ilustrar
illustration [ˌɪlə'streɪʃən] *n* **1** PICTURE : ilustración *f* **2** EXAMPLE : ejemplo *m*, ilustración *f*
illustrative [ɪ'lʌstrəṭɪv, 'ɪləˌstreɪṭɪv] *adj* : ilustrativo — **illustratively** *adv*
illustrator ['ɪləˌstreɪṭər] *n* : ilustrador *m*, -dora *f;* dibujante *mf*
illustrious [ɪ'lʌstriəs] *adj* : ilustre, eminente, glorioso
illustriousness [ɪ'lʌstriəsnəs] *n* : eminencia *f*, prestigio *m*
ill will *n* : animosidad *f*, malquerencia *f*, mala voluntad *f*
I'm ['aɪm] (*contraction of* **I am**) → **be**
image[1] ['ɪmɪdʒ] *vt* **-aged; -aging** : imaginar, crear una imagen de
image[2] *n* : imagen *f*
imagery ['ɪmɪdʒri] *n, pl* **-eries 1** IMAGES : imágenes *fpl* **2** : imaginería *f* (en el arte)
imaginable [ɪ'mædʒənəbəl] *adj* : imaginable — **imaginably** [-bli] *adv*
imaginary [ɪ'mædʒəˌnɛri] *adj* : imaginario
imagination [ɪˌmædʒə'neɪʃən] *n* : imaginación *f*
imaginative [ɪ'mædʒənəṭɪv, -əˌneɪṭɪv] *adj* : imaginativo — **imaginatively** *adv*
imagine [ɪ'mædʒən] *vt* **-ined; -ining** : imaginar(se)
imbalance [ɪm'bælən*t*s] *n* : desajuste *m*, desbalance *m*, desequilibrio *m*
imbecile[1] ['ɪmbəsəl, -ˌsɪl] *or* **imbecilic** [ˌɪmbə'sɪlɪk] *adj* : imbécil, estúpido
imbecile[2] *n* **1** : imbécil *mf* (en medicina) **2** FOOL : idiota *mf;* imbécil *mf fam;* estúpido *m*, -da *f*
imbecility [ˌɪmbə'sɪləṭi] *n, pl* **-ties** : imbecilidad *f*
imbibe [ɪm'baɪb] *v* **-bibed; -bibing** *vt* **1** DRINK : beber **2** ABSORB : absorber, embeber — *vi* : beber
imbue [ɪm'bjuː] *vt* **-bued; -buing** : imbuir
imitate ['ɪməˌteɪt] *vt* **-tated; -tating** : imitar, remedar

imitation[1] [ˌɪməˈteɪʃən] *adj* : de imitación, artificial
imitation[2] *n* : imitación *f*
imitative [ˈɪməˌteɪtɪv] *adj* : imitativo, imitador, poco original
imitator [ˈɪməˌteɪt̬ər] *n* : imitador *m*, -dora *f*
immaculate [ɪˈmækjələt] *adj* **1** PURE : inmaculado, puro **2** FLAWLESS : impecable, intachable — **immaculately** *adv*
immaterial [ˌɪməˈtɪriəl] *adj* **1** INCORPOREAL : incorpóreo **2** UNIMPORTANT : irrelevante, sin importancia
immature [ˌɪməˈtʃʊr, -ˈtjʊr, -ˈtʊr] *adj* : inmaduro, verde (dícese de la fruta)
immaturity [ˌɪməˈtʃʊrət̬i, -ˈtjʊr-, -ˈtʊr-] *n, pl* **-ties** : inmadurez *f*, falta *f* de madurez
immeasurable [ɪˈmɛʒərəbəl] *adj* : inconmensurable, incalculable — **immeasurably** [-bli] *adv*
immediate [ɪˈmiːdiət] *adj* **1** INSTANT : inmediato, instantáneo <immediate relief : alivio instantáneo> **2** DIRECT : inmediato, directo <the immediate cause of death : la causa directa de la muerte> **3** URGENT : urgente, apremiante **4** CLOSE : cercano, próximo, inmediato <her immediate family : sus familiares más cercanos> <in the immediate vicinity : en los alrededores, en las inmediaciones>
immediately [ɪˈmiːdiətli] *adv* : inmediatamente, enseguida
immemorial [ˌɪməˈmoriəl] *adj* : inmemorial
immense [ɪˈmɛnts] *adj* : inmenso, enorme — **immensely** *adv*
immensity [ɪˈmɛntsət̬i] *n, pl* **-ties** : inmensidad *f*
immerse [ɪˈmərs] *vt* **-mersed; -mersing 1** SUBMERGE : sumergir **2 to immerse oneself in** : enfrascarse en
immersion [ɪˈmərʒən] *n* **1** : inmersión *f* (en un líquido) **2** : enfrascamiento *m* (en una actividad)
immigrant [ˈɪmɪgrənt] *n* : inmigrante *mf*
immigrate [ˈɪməˌgreɪt] *vi* **-grated; -grating** : inmigrar
immigration [ˌɪməˈgreɪʃən] *n* : inmigración *f*
imminence [ˈɪmənənts] *n* : inminencia *f*
imminent [ˈɪmənənt] *adj* : inminente — **imminently** *adv*
immobile [ɪmˈoːbəl] *adj* **1** FIXED, IMMOVABLE : inmovible, fijo **2** MOTIONLESS : inmóvil
immobility [ˌɪmoˈbɪlət̬i] *n, pl* **-ties** : inmovilidad *f*
immobilize [ɪˈmoːbəˌlaɪz] *vt* **-lized; -lizing** : inmovilizar, paralizar
immoderate [ɪˈmɑdərət] *adj* : inmoderado, desmesurado, desmedido, excesivo — **immoderately** *adv*
immodest [ɪˈmɑdəst] *adj* **1** INDECENT : inmodesto, indecente, impúdico **2** CONCEITED : inmodesto, presuntuoso, engreído — **immodestly** *adv*
immodesty [ɪˈmɑdəsti] *n* : inmodestia *f*
immoral [ɪˈmɔrəl] *adj* : inmoral
immorality [ˌɪmɔˈrælət̬i, ˌɪmə-] *n, pl* **-ties** : inmoralidad *f*
immorally [ɪˈmɔrəli] *adv* : de manera inmoral
immortal[1] [ɪˈmɔrtəl] *adj* : inmortal
immortal[2] *n* : inmortal *mf*
immortality [ˌɪˌmɔrˈtælət̬i] *n* : inmortalidad *f*
immortalize [ɪˈmɔrtəlˌaɪz] *vt* **-ized; -izing** : inmortalizar
immovable [ɪˈmuːvəbəl] *adj* **1** FIXED : fijo, inmovible **2** UNYIELDING : inflexible
immune [ɪˈmjuːn] *adj* **1** : inmune <immune to smallpox : inmune a la viruela> **2** EXEMPT : exento, inmune
immune system *n* : sistema *m* inmunológico
immunity [ɪˈmjuːnət̬i] *n, pl* **-ties 1** : inmunidad *f* **2** EXEMPTION : exención *f*
immunization [ˌɪmjʊnəˈzeɪʃən] *n* : inmunización *f*
immunize [ˈɪmjʊˌnaɪz] *vt* **-nized; -nizing** : inmunizar
immunology [ˌɪmjʊˈnɑlədʒi] *n* : inmunología *f*
immutable [ɪˈmjuːt̬əbəl] *adj* : inmutable
imp [ˈɪmp] *n* RASCAL : diablillo *m*; pillo *m*, -lla *f*
impact[1] [ɪmˈpækt] *vt* **1** STRIKE : chocar con, impactar **2** AFFECT : afectar, impactar, impresionar — *vi* **1** STRIKE : hacer impacto, golpear **2 to impact on** : tener un impacto sobre
impact[2] [ˈɪmˌpækt] *n* **1** COLLISION : impacto *m*, choque *m*, colisión *f* **2** EFFECT : efecto *m*, impacto *m*, consecuencias *fpl*
impacted [ɪmˈpæktəd] *adj* : impactado, incrustado (dícese de los dientes)
impair [ɪmˈpær] *vt* : perjudicar, dañar, afectar
impairment [ɪmˈpærmənt] *n* : perjuicio *m*, daño *m*
impala [ɪmˈpɑlə, -ˈpæ-] *n, pl* **impalas** *or* **impala** : impala *m*
impale [ɪmˈpeɪl] *vt* **-paled; -paling** : empalar
impanel [ɪmˈpænəl] *vt* **-eled** *or* **-elled; eling** *or* **-elling** : elegir (un jurado)
impart [ɪmˈpɑrt] *vt* **1** CONVEY : impartir, dar, conferir **2** DISCLOSE : revelar, divulgar
impartial [ɪmˈpɑrʃəl] *adj* : imparcial — **impartially** *adv*
impartiality [ɪmˌpɑrʃiˈælət̬i] *n, pl* **-ties** : imparcialidad *f*
impassable [ɪmˈpæsəbəl] *adj* : infranqueable, intransitable — **impassably** [-bli] *adv*

impasse ['ɪm,pæs] *n* **1** DEADLOCK : impasse *m,* punto *m* muerto **2** DEAD END : callejón *m* sin salida

impassioned [ɪm'pæʃənd] *adj* : apasionado, vehemente

impassive [ɪm'pæsɪv] *adj* : impasible, indiferente

impassively [ɪm'pæsɪvli] *adv* : impasiblemente, sin emoción

impatience [ɪm'peɪʃənts] *n* : impaciencia *f*

impatient [ɪm'peɪʃənt] *adj* : impaciente — **impatiently** *adv*

impeach [ɪm'pi:tʃ] *vt* : destituir (a un funcionario) de su cargo

impeachment [ɪm'pi:tʃmənt] *n* **1** ACCUSATION : acusación *f* **2** DISMISSAL : destitución *f*

impeccable [ɪm'pɛkəbəl] *adj* : impecable — **impeccably** [-bli] *adv*

impecunious [,ɪmpɪ'kju:niəs] *adj* : falto de dinero

impede [ɪm'pi:d] *vt* **-peded; -peding** : impedir, dificultar, obstaculizar

impediment [ɪm'pɛdəmənt] *n* **1** HINDRANCE : impedimento *m,* obstáculo *m* **2 speech impediment** : defecto *m* del habla

impel [ɪm'pɛl] *vt* **-pelled; -pelling** : impeler

impend [ɪm'pɛnd] *vi* : ser inminente

impenetrable [ɪm'pɛnətrəbəl] *adj* **1** : impenetrable <an impenetrable forest : una selva impenetrable> **2** INSCRUTABLE : incomprensible, inescrutable, impenetrable — **impenetrably** [-bli] *adv*

impenitent [ɪm'pɛnətənt] *adj* : impenitente

imperative¹ [ɪm'pɛrət̬ɪv] *adj* **1** AUTHORITATIVE : imperativo, imperioso **2** NECESSARY : imprescindible — **imperatively** *adv*

imperative² *n* : imperativo *m*

imperceptible [,ɪmpər'sɛptəbəl] *adj* : imperceptible — **imperceptibly** [-bli] *adv*

imperfect [ɪm'pərfɪkt] *adj* : imperfecto, defectuoso — **imperfectly** *adv*

imperfection [ɪm,pər'fɛkʃən] *n* : imperfección *f,* defecto *m*

imperial [ɪm'pɪriəl] *adj* **1** : imperial **2** SOVEREIGN : soberano **3** IMPERIOUS : imperioso, señorial

imperialism [ɪm'pɪriə,lɪzəm] *n* : imperialismo *m*

imperialist¹ [ɪm'pɪriəlɪst] *adj* : imperialista

imperialist² *n* : imperialista *mf*

imperialistic [ɪm,pɪri:ə'lɪstɪk] *adj* : imperialista

imperil [ɪm'pɛrəl] *vt* **-iled** *or* **-illed; -iling** *or* **-illing** : poner en peligro

imperious [ɪm'pɪriəs] *adj* : imperioso — **imperiously** *adv*

imperishable [ɪm'pɛrɪʃəbəl] *adj* : imperecedero

impermanent [ɪm'pərmənənt] *adj* : pasajero, inestable, efímero — **impermanently** *adv*

impermeable [ɪm'pərmiəbəl] *adj* : impermeable

impersonal [ɪm'pərsənəl] *adj* : impersonal — **impersonally** *adv*

impersonate [ɪm'pərsən,eɪt] *vt* **-ated; -ating** : hacerse pasar por, imitar

impersonation [ɪm,pərsən'eɪʃən] *n* : imitación *f*

impersonator [ɪm'pərsən,eɪt̬ər] *n* : imitador *m,* -dora *f*

impertinence [ɪm'pərtənənts] *n* : impertinencia *f*

impertinent [ɪm'pərtənənt] *adj* **1** IRRELEVANT : impertinente, irrelevante **2** INSOLENT : impertinente, insolente

impertinently [ɪm'pərtənəntli] *adv* : con impertinencia, impertinentemente

imperturbable [,ɪmpər'tərbəbəl] *adj* : imperturbable

impervious [ɪm'pərviəs] *adj* **1** IMPENETRABLE : impermeable **2** INSENSITIVE : insensible <impervious to criticism : insensible a la crítica>

impetuosity [ɪm,pɛtʃʊ'ɑsət̬i] *n, pl* **-ties** : impetuosidad *f*

impetuous [ɪm'pɛtʃʊəs] *adj* : impetuoso, impulsivo

impetuously [ɪm'pɛtʃʊəsli] *adv* : de manera impulsiva, impetuosamente

impetus ['ɪmpət̬əs] *n* : ímpetu *m,* impulso *m*

impiety [ɪm'paɪət̬i] *n, pl* **-ties** : impiedad *f*

impinge [ɪm'pɪndʒ] *vi* **-pinged; -pinging 1 to impinge on** AFFECT : afectar a, incidir en **2 to impinge on** VIOLATE : violar, vulnerar

impious ['ɪmpiəs, ɪm'paɪəs] *adj* : impío, irreverente

impish ['ɪmpɪʃ] *adj* MISCHIEVOUS : pícaro, travieso

impishly ['ɪmpɪʃli] *adv* : con picardía

implacable [ɪm'plækəbəl] *adj* : implacable — **implacably** [-bli] *adv*

implant¹ [ɪm'plænt] *vt* **1** INCULCATE, INSTILL : inculcar, implantar **2** INSERT : implantar, insertar

implant² ['ɪm,plænt] *n* : implante *m* (de pelo), injerto *m* (de piel)

implantation [,ɪm,plæn'teɪʃən] *n* : implantación *f*

implausibility [ɪm,plɔzə'bɪlət̬i] *n, pl* **-ties** : inverosimilitud *f*

implausible [ɪm'plɔzəbəl] *adj* : inverosímil, poco convincente

implement¹ ['ɪmplə,mɛnt] *vt* : poner en práctica, implementar

implement² ['ɪmpləmənt] *n* : utensilio *m,* instrumento *m,* implemento *m*

implementation [,ɪmpləmən'teɪʃən] *n* : implementación *f,* ejecución *f,* cumplimiento *m*

implicate ['ɪmplə,keɪt] *vt* **-cated; -cating** : implicar, involucrar

implication [ˌɪmpləˈkeɪʃən] *n* **1** CONSEQUENCE **:** implicación *f,* consecuencia *f* **2** INFERENCE **:** insinuación *f,* inferencia *f*
implicit [ɪmˈplɪsət] *adj* **1** IMPLIED **:** implícito, tácito **2** ABSOLUTE **:** absoluto, completo <implicit faith : fe ciega> **— implicitly** *adv*
implied [ɪmˈplaɪd] *adj* **:** implícito, tácito
implode [ɪmˈploːd] *vi* **-ploded; -ploding :** implosionar
implore [ɪmˈplor] *vt* **-plored; -ploring :** implorar, suplicar
imply [ɪmˈplaɪ] *vt* **-plied; -plying 1** SUGGEST **:** insinuar, dar a entender **2** INVOLVE **:** implicar, suponer <rights imply obligations : los derechos implican unas obligaciones>
impolite [ˌɪmpəˈlaɪt] *adj* **:** descortés, maleducado
impoliteness [ˌɪmpəˈlaɪtnəs] *n* **:** descortesía *f,* falta *f* de educación
impolitic [ɪmˈpɑləˌtɪk] *adj* **:** imprudente, poco político
imponderable[1] [ɪmˈpɑndərəbəl] *adj* **:** imponderable
imponderable[2] *n* **:** imponderable *m*
import[1] [ɪmˈport] *vt* **1** SIGNIFY **:** significar **2 :** importar <to import foreign cars : importar autos extranjeros>
import[2] [ˈɪmˌport] *n* **1** SIGNIFICANCE **:** importancia *f,* significación *f* **2 → importation**
importance [ɪmˈportənts] *n* **:** importancia *f*
important [ɪmˈpɔrtənt] *adj* **:** importante
importantly [ɪmˈpɔrtəntli] *adv* **1 :** con importancia **2 more importantly :** lo que es más importante
importation [ˌɪmˌpɔrˈteɪʃən] *n* **:** importación *f*
importer [ɪmˈportər] *n* **:** importador *m,* -dora *f*
importunate [ɪmˈpɔrtʃənət] *adj* **:** importuno, insistente
importune [ˌɪmpərˈtuːn, -ˈtjuːn; ɪmˈpɔrtʃən] *vt* **-tuned; -tuning :** importunar, implorar
impose [ɪmˈpoːz] *v* **-posed; -posing** *vt* **:** imponer <to impose a tax : imponer un impuesto> **—** *vi* **to impose on :** abusar de, molestar <to impose on her kindness : abusar de su bondad>
imposing [ɪmˈpoːzɪŋ] *adj* **:** imponente, impresionante
imposition [ˌɪmpəˈzɪʃən] *n* **:** imposición *f*
impossibility [ɪmˌpɑsəˈbɪləṱi] *n, pl* **-ties :** imposibilidad *f*
impossible [ɪmˈpɑsəbəl] *adj* **1 :** imposible <an impossible task : una tarea imposible> <to make life impossible for : hacerle la vida imposible a> **2** UNACCEPTABLE **:** inaceptable
impossibly [ɪmˈpɑsəbli] *adv* **:** imposiblemente, increíblemente
impostor *or* **imposter** [ɪmˈpɑstər] *n* **:** impostor *m,* -tora *f*
imposture [ɪmˈpɑstʃər] *n* **:** impostura *f*
impotence [ˈɪmpətənts] *n* **:** impotencia *f*
impotency [ˈɪmpətəntsi] **→ impotence**
impotent [ˈɪmpətənt] *adj* **:** impotente
impound [ɪmˈpaʊnd] *vt* **:** incautar, embargar, confiscar
impoverish [ɪmˈpɑvərɪʃ] *vt* **:** empobrecer
impoverishment [ɪmˈpɑvərɪʃmənt] *n* **:** empobrecimiento *m*
impracticable [ɪmˈpræktɪkəbəl] *adj* **:** impracticable
impractical [ɪmˈpræktɪkəl] *adj* **:** poco práctico
imprecise [ˌɪmprɪˈsaɪs] *adj* **:** impreciso
imprecisely [ˌɪmprɪˈsaɪsli] *adv* **:** con imprecisión
impreciseness [ˌɪmprɪˈsaɪsnəs] **→ imprecision**
imprecision [ˌɪmprɪˈsɪʒən] *n* **:** imprecisión *f,* falta de precisión *f*
impregnable [ɪmˈprɛgnəbəl] *adj* **:** inexpugnable, impenetrable, inconquistable
impregnate [ɪmˈprɛgˌneɪt] *vt* **-nated; -nating 1** FERTILIZE **:** fecundar **2** PERMEATE, SATURATE **:** impregnar, empapar, saturar
impresario [ˌɪmprəˈsɑriˌo, -ˈsær-] *n, pl* **-rios :** empresario *m,* -ria *f*
impress [ɪmˈprɛs] *vt* **1** IMPRINT **:** imprimir, estampar **2 :** impresionar, causar impresión a <I was not impressed : no me hizo buena impresión> **3 to impress (something) on someone :** recalcarle (algo) a alguien **—** *vi* **:** impresionar, hacer una impresión
impression [ɪmˈprɛʃən] *n* **1** IMPRINT **:** marca *f,* huella *f,* molde *m* (de los dientes) **2** EFFECT **:** impresión *f,* efecto *m,* impacto *m* **3** PRINTING **:** impresión *f* **4** NOTION **:** impresión *f,* noción *f*
impressionable [ɪmˈprɛʃənəbəl] *adj* **:** impresionable
impressive [ɪmˈprɛsɪv] *adj* **:** impresionante **— impressively** *adv*
impressiveness [ɪmˈprɛsɪvnəs] *n* **:** calidad de ser impresionante
imprint[1] [ɪmˈprɪnt, ˈɪmˌ-] *vt* **:** imprimir, estampar
imprint[2] [ˈɪmˌprɪnt] *n* **:** marca *f,* huella *f*
imprison [ɪmˈprɪzən] *vt* **1** JAIL **:** encarcelar, aprisionar **2** CONFINE **:** recluir, encerrar
imprisonment [ɪmˈprɪzənmənt] *n* **:** encarcelamiento *m*
improbability [ɪmˌprɑbəˈbɪləṱi] *n, pl* **-ties :** improbabilidad *f,* inverosimilitud *f*
improbable [ɪmˈprɑbəbəl] *adj* **:** improbable, inverosímil

impromptu[1] [ɪm'prɑmp,tu:, -,tju:] *adv* : sin preparación, espontáneamente
impromptu[2] *adj* : espontáneo, improvisado
impromptu[3] *n* : improvisación *f*
improper [ɪm'prɑpər] *adj* **1** INCORRECT : incorrecto, impropio **2** INDECOROUS : indecoroso
improperly [ɪm'prɑpərli] *adv* : incorrectamente, indebidamente
impropriety [,ɪmprə'praɪəti] *n, pl* **-eties 1** INDECOROUSNESS : indecoro *m,* falta *f* de decoro **2** ERROR : impropiedad *f,* incorrección *f*
improve [ɪm'pru:v] *v* **-proved; -proving** : mejorar
improvement [ɪm'pru:vmənt] *n* : mejoramiento *m,* mejora *f*
improvidence [ɪm'prɑvədənts] *n* : imprevisión *f*
improvident [ɪm'prɑvədənt] *adj* : sin previsión, imprevisor
improvisation [ɪm,prɑvə'zeɪʃən, ,ɪmprəvə-] *n* : improvisación *f*
improvise ['ɪmprə,vaɪz] *v* **-vised; -vising** : improvisar
imprudence [ɪm'pru:dənts] *n* : imprudencia *f,* indiscreción *f*
imprudent [ɪm'pru:dənt] *adj* : imprudente, indiscreto
impudence ['ɪmpjədənts] *n* : insolencia *f,* descaro *m*
impudent ['ɪmpjədənt] *adj* : insolente, descarado — **impudently** *adv*
impugn [ɪm'pju:n] *vt* : impugnar
impulse ['ɪm,pʌls] *n* **1** : impulso *m* **2 on impulse** : sin reflexionar
impulsive [ɪm'pʌlsɪv] *adj* : impulsivo — **impulsively** *adv*
impulsiveness [ɪm'pʌlsɪvnəs] *n* : impulsividad *f*
impunity [ɪm'pju:nəti] *n* **1** : impunidad *f* **2 with impunity** : impunemente
impure [ɪm'pjʊr] *adj* **1** : impuro <impure thoughts : pensamientos impuros> **2** CONTAMINATED : con impurezas, impuro
impurity [ɪm'pjʊrəti] *n, pl* **-ties** : impureza *f*
impute [ɪm'pju:t] *vt* **-puted; -puting** ATTRIBUTE : imputar, atribuir
in[1] ['ɪn] *adv* **1** INSIDE : dentro, adentro <let's go in : vamos adentro> **2** HARVESTED : recogido <the crops are in : las cosechas ya están recogidas> **3 to be in** : estar <is Linda in? : ¿está Linda?> **4 to be in** : estar en poder <the Democrats are in : los demócratas están en el poder> **5 to be in for** : ser objeto de, estar a punto de <they're in for a treat : los van a agasajar> <he's in for a surprise : se va a llevar una sorpresa> **6 to be in on** : participar en, tomar parte en
in[2] *adj* **1** INSIDE : interior <the in part : la parte interior> **2** FASHIONABLE : de moda
in[3] *prep* **1** (*indicating location or position*) <in the lake : en el lago> <a pain in the leg : un dolor en la pierna> <in the sun : al sol> <in the rain : bajo la lluvia> <the best restaurant in Buenos Aires : el mejor restaurante de Buenos Aires> **2** INTO : en, a <he broke it in pieces : lo rompió en pedazos> <she went in the house : se metió a la casa> **3** DURING : por, durante <in the afternoon : por la tarde> **4** WITHIN : dentro de <I'll be back in a week : vuelvo dentro de una semana> **5** (*indicating manner*) : en, con, de <in Spanish : en español> <written in pencil : escrito con lápiz> <in this way : de esta manera> **6** (*indicating states or circumstances*) <to be in luck : tener suerte> <to be in love : estar enamorado> <to be in a hurry : tener prisa> **7** (*indicating purpose*) : en <in reply : en respuesta, como réplica>
inability [,ɪnə'bɪləti] *n, pl* **-ties** : incapacidad *f*
inaccessibility [,ɪnɪk,sɛsə'bɪləti] *n, pl* **-ties** : inaccesibilidad *f*
inaccessible [,ɪnɪk'sɛsəbəl] *adj* : inaccesible
inaccuracy [ɪn'ækjərəsi] *n, pl* **-cies 1** : inexactitud *f* **2** MISTAKE : error *m*
inaccurate [ɪn'ækjərət] *n* : inexacto, erróneo, incorrecto
inaccurately [ɪn'ækjərətli] *adv* : incorrectamente, con inexactitud
inaction [ɪn'ækʃən] *n* : inactividad *f,* inacción *f*
inactive [ɪn'æktɪv] *n* : inactivo
inactivity [,ɪn,æk'tɪvəti] *n, pl* **-ties** : inactividad *f,* ociosidad *f*
inadequacy [ɪn'ædɪkwəsi] *n, pl* **-cies 1** INSUFFICIENCY : insuficiencia *f* **2** INCOMPETENCE : ineptitud *f,* incompetencia *f*
inadequate [ɪn'ædɪkwət] *adj* **1** INSUFFICIENT : insuficiente, inadecuado **2** INCOMPETENT : inepto, incompetente
inadmissible [,ɪnæd'mɪsəbəl] *adj* : inadmisible
inadvertent [,ɪnəd'vərtənt] *adj* : inadvertido, involuntario — **inadvertently** *adv*
inadvisable [,ɪnæd'vaɪzəbəl] *adj* : desaconsejable
inalienable [ɪn'eɪljənəbəl, -'eɪliənə-] *adj* : inalienable
inane [ɪ'neɪn] *adj* **inaner; -est** : estúpido, idiota, necio
inanimate [ɪn'ænəmət] *adj* : inanimado, exánime
inanity [ɪ'nænəti] *n, pl* **-ties 1** STUPIDITY : estupidez *f* **2** NONSENSE : idiotez *f,* disparate *m*
inapplicable [ɪn'æplɪkəbəl, ,ɪnə'plɪkəbəl] *adj* IRRELEVANT : inaplicable, irrelevante
inappreciable [,ɪnə'pri:ʃəbəl] *adj* : inapreciable, imperceptible
inappropriate [,ɪnə'pro:priət] *adj* : inapropiado, inadecuado, impropio

inappropriateness [ˌɪnəˈproːpriətnəs] *n* **:** lo inapropiado, impropiedad *f*

inapt [ɪnˈæpt] *adj* **1** UNSUITABLE **:** inadecuado, inapropiado **2** INEPT **:** inepto

inarticulate [ˌɪnɑrˈtɪkjələt] *adj* **:** inarticulado, incapaz de expresarse

inarticulately [ˌɪnɑrˈtɪkjələtli] *adv* **:** inarticuladamente

inasmuch as [ˌɪnæzˈmʌtʃæz] *conj* **:** ya que, dado que, puesto que

inattention [ˌɪnəˈtɛntʃən] *n* **:** falta *f* de atención, distracción *f*

inattentive [ˌɪnəˈtɛntɪv] *adj* **:** distraído, despistado

inattentively [ˌɪnəˈtɛntɪvli] *adv* **:** distraídamente, sin prestar atención

inaudible [ɪnˈɔdəbəl] *adj* **:** inaudible

inaudibly [ɪnˈɔdəbli] *adv* **:** de forma inaudible

inaugural[1] [ɪˈnɔgjərəl, -gərəl] *adj* **:** inaugural, de investidura

inaugural[2] *n* **1** *or* **inaugural address :** discurso *m* de investidura **2** INAUGURATION **:** investidura *f* (de una persona)

inaugurate [ɪˈnɔgjəˌreɪt, -gə-] *vt* **-rated; -rating 1** BEGIN **:** inaugurar **2** INDUCT **:** investir <to inaugurate the president : investir al presidente>

inauguration [ɪˌnɔgjəˈreɪʃən, -gə-] *n* **1 :** inauguración *f* (de un edificio, un sistema, etc.) **2 :** investidura *f* (de una persona)

inauspicious [ˌɪnɔˈspɪʃəs] *adj* **:** desfavorable, poco propicio

inborn [ˈɪnˌbɔrn] *adj* **1** CONGENITAL, INNATE **:** innato, congénito **2** HEREDITARY **:** hereditario

inbred [ˈɪnˌbrɛd] *adj* **1 :** engendrado por endogamia **2** INNATE **:** innato

inbreed [ˈɪnˌbriːd] *vt* **-bred; -breeding :** engendrar por endogamia

inbreeding [ˈɪnˌbriːdɪŋ] *n* **:** endogamia *f*

incalculable [ɪnˈkælkjələbəl] *adj* **:** incalculable — **incalculably** [-bli] *adv*

incandescence [ˌɪnkənˈdɛsənts] *n* **:** incandescencia *f*

incandescent [ˌɪnkənˈdɛsənt] *adj* **1 :** incandescente **2** BRILLIANT **:** brillante

incantation [ˌɪnˌkænˈteɪʃən] *n* **:** conjuro *m*, ensalmo *m*

incapable [ɪnˈkeɪpəbəl] *adj* **:** incapaz

incapacitate [ˌɪnkəˈpæsəˌteɪt] *vt* **-tated; -tating :** incapacitar

incapacity [ˌɪnkəˈpæsəti] *n, pl* **-ties :** incapacidad *f*

incarcerate [ɪnˈkɑrsəˌreɪt] *vt* **-ated; -ating :** encarcelar

incarceration [ɪnˌkɑrsəˈreɪʃən] *n* **:** encarcelamiento *m*, encarcelación *f*

incarnate[1] [ɪnˈkɑrˌneɪt] *vt* **-nated; -nating :** encarnar

incarnate[2] [ɪnˈkɑrnət, -ˌneɪt] *adj* **:** encarnado

incarnation [ˌɪnˌkɑrˈneɪʃən] *n* **:** encarnación *f*

incendiary[1] [ɪnˈsɛndiˌɛri] *adj* **:** incendiario

incendiary[2] *n, pl* **-aries :** incendiario *m*, -ria *f*; pirómano *m*, -na *f*

incense[1] [ɪnˈsɛnts] *vt* **-censed; -censing :** indignar, enfadar, enfurecer

incense[2] [ˈɪnˌsɛnts] *n* **:** incienso *m*

incentive [ɪnˈsɛntɪv] *n* **:** incentivo *m*, aliciente *m*, motivación *f*, acicate *m*

inception [ɪnˈsɛpʃən] *n* **:** comienzo *m*, principio *m*

incessant [ɪnˈsɛsənt] *adj* **:** incesante, continuo — **incessantly** *adv*

incest [ˈɪnˌsɛst] *n* **:** incesto *m*

incestuous [ɪnˈsɛstʃʊəs] *adj* **:** incestuoso

inch[1] [ˈɪntʃ] *v* **:** avanzar poco a poco

inch[2] *n* **1 :** pulgada *f* **2 every inch :** absoluto, seguro <every inch a winner : un seguro ganador> **3 within an inch of :** a punto de

incidence [ˈɪntsədənts] *n* **1** FREQUENCY **:** frecuencia *f*, índice *m* <a high incidence of crime : un alto índice de crímenes> **2 angle of incidence :** ángulo *m* de incidencia

incident[1] [ˈɪntsədənt] *adj* **:** incidente

incident[2] *n* **:** incidente *m*, incidencia *f*, episodio *m* (en una obra de ficción)

incidental[1] [ˌɪntsəˈdɛntəl] *adj* **1** SECONDARY **:** incidental, secundario **2** ACCIDENTAL **:** casual, fortuito

incidental[2] *n* **1 :** algo incidental **2 incidentals** *npl* **:** imprevistos *mpl*

incidentally [ˌɪntsəˈdɛntəli, -ˈdɛntli] *adv* **1** BY CHANCE **:** incidentalmente, casualmente **2** BY THE WAY **:** a propósito, por cierto

incinerate [ɪnˈsɪnəˌreɪt] *vt* **-ated; -ating :** incinerar

incinerator [ɪnˈsɪnəˌreɪtər] *n* **:** incinerador *m*

incipient [ɪnˈsɪpiənt] *adj* **:** incipiente, naciente

incise [ɪnˈsaɪz] *vt* **-cised; -cising 1** ENGRAVE **:** grabar, cincelar, inscribir **2 :** hacer una incisión en

incision [ɪnˈsɪʒən] *n* **:** incisión *f*

incisive [ɪnˈsaɪsɪv] *adj* **:** incisivo, penetrante

incisively [ɪnˈsaɪsɪvli] *adv* **:** con agudeza

incisor [ɪnˈsaɪzər] *n* **:** incisivo *m*

incite [ɪnˈsaɪt] *vt* **-cited; -citing :** incitar, instigar

incitement [ɪnˈsaɪtmənt] *n* **:** incitación *f*

inclemency [ɪnˈklɛməntsi] *n, pl* **-cies :** inclemencia *f*

inclement [ɪnˈklɛmənt] *adj* **:** inclemente, tormentuoso

inclination [ˌɪnkləˈneɪʃən] *n* **1** PROPENSITY **:** inclinación *f*, tendencia *f* **2** DESIRE **:** deseo *m*, ganas *fpl* **3** BOW **:** inclinación *f*

incline[1] [ɪnˈklaɪn] *v* **-clined; -clining** *vi* **1** SLOPE **:** inclinarse **2** TEND **:** inclinarse, tender <he is inclined to be late : tiende a llegar tarde> — *vt* **1** LOWER **:** inclinar, bajar <to incline one's head

: bajar la cabeza> **2** SLANT : inclinar **3** PREDISPOSE : predisponer
incline² [ˈɪnˌklaɪn] *n* : inclinación *f*, pendiente *f*
inclined [ɪnˈklaɪnd] *adj* **1** SLOPING : inclinado **2** PRONE : prono, dispuesto, dado
inclose, inclosure → **enclose, enclosure**
include [ɪnˈkluːd] *vt* **-cluded; -cluding** : incluir, comprender
inclusion [ɪnˈkluːʒən] *n* : inclusión *f*
inclusive [ɪnˈkluːsɪv] *adj* : inclusivo
incognito [ˌɪnˌkɑgˈniːt̬o, ɪnˈkɑgnəˌtoː] *adv & adj* : de incógnito
incoherence [ˌɪnkoˈhɪrənts, -ˈhɛr-] *n* : incoherencia *f*
incoherent [ˌɪnkoˈhɪrənt, -ˈhɛr-] *adj* : incoherente — **incoherently** *adv*
incombustible [ˌɪnkəmˈbʌstəbəl] *adj* : incombustible
income [ˈɪnˌkʌm] *n* : ingresos *mpl*, entradas *fpl*
income tax *n* : impuesto *m* sobre la renta
incoming [ˈɪnˌkʌmɪŋ] *adj* **1** ARRIVING : que se recibe (dícese del correo), que llega (dícese de las personas), ascendente (dícese de la marea) **2** NEW : nuevo, entrante <the incoming president : el nuevo presidente> <the incoming year : el año entrante>
incommunicado [ˌɪnkəˌmjuːnəˈkɑdo] *adj* : incomunicado
incomparable [ɪnˈkɑmpərəbəl] *adj* : incomparable, sin igual
incompatible [ˌɪnkəmˈpæt̬əbəl] *adj* : incompatible
incompetence [ɪnˈkɑmpət̬ənts] *n* : incompetencia *f*, impericia *f*, ineptitud *f*
incompetent [ɪnˈkɑmpət̬ənt] *adj* : incompetente, inepto, incapaz
incomplete [ˌɪnkəmˈpliːt] *adj* : incompleto — **incompletely** *adv*
incomprehensible [ˌɪnˌkɑmpriˈhɛntsəbəl] *adj* : incomprensible
inconceivable [ˌɪnkənˈsiːvəbəl] *adj* **1** INCOMPREHENSIBLE : incomprensible **2** UNBELIEVABLE : inconcebible, increíble
inconceivably [ˌɪnkənˈsiːvəbli] *adv* : inconcebiblemente, increíblemente
inconclusive [ˌɪnkənˈkluːsɪv] *adj* : inconcluyente, no decisivo
incongruity [ˌɪnkənˈgruːət̬i, -ˌkɑn-] *n, pl* **-ties** : incongruencia *f*
incongruous [ɪnˈkɑŋgrʊəs] *adj* : incongruente, inapropiado, fuera de lugar
incongruously [ɪnˈkɑŋgrʊəsli] *adv* : de manera incongruente, inapropiadamente
inconsequential [ˌɪnˌkɑnsəˈkwɛntʃəl] *adj* : intrascendente, de poco importancia
inconsiderable [ˌɪnkənˈsɪdərəbəl] *adj* : insignificante
inconsiderate [ˌɪnkənˈsɪdərət] *adj* : desconsiderado, sin consideración — **inconsiderately** *adv*
inconsistency [ˌɪnkənˈsɪstəntsi] *n, pl* **-cies** : inconsecuencia *f*, inconsistencia *f*
inconsistent [ˌɪnkənˈsɪstənt] *adj* : inconsecuente, inconsistente
inconsolable [ˌɪnkənˈsoːləbəl] *adj* : inconsolable — **inconsolably** [-bli] *adv*
inconspicuous [ˌɪnkənˈspɪkjʊəs] *adj* : discreto, no conspicuo, que no llama la atención
inconspicuously [ˌɪnkənˈspɪkjʊəsli] *adv* : discretamente, sin llamar la atención
incontestable [ˌɪnkənˈtɛstəbəl] *adj* : incontestable, indiscutible — **incontestably** [-bli] *adv*
incontinence [ɪnˈkɑntənənts] *n* : incontinencia *f*
incontinent [ɪnˈkɑntənənt] *adj* : incontinente
inconvenience¹ [ˌɪnkənˈviːnjənts] **-nienced; -niencing** *vt* : importunar, incomodar, molestar
inconvenience² *n* : incomodidad *f*, molestia *f*
inconvenient [ˌɪnkənˈviːnjənt] *adj* : inconveniente, importuno, incómodo — **inconveniently** *adv*
incorporate [ɪnˈkɔrpəˌreɪt] *vt* **-rated; -rating 1** INCLUDE : incorporar, incluir **2** : incorporar, constituir en sociedad (dícese de un negocio)
incorporation [ɪnˌkɔrpəˈreɪʃən] *n* : incorporación *f*
incorporeal [ˌɪnˌkɔrˈporiəl] *adj* : incorpóreo
incorrect [ˌɪnkəˈrɛkt] *adj* **1** INACCURATE : incorrecto **2** WRONG : equivocado, erróneo **3** IMPROPER : impropio — **incorrectly** *adv*
incorrigible [ɪnˈkɔrədʒəbəl] *adj* : incorregible
incorruptible [ˌɪnkəˈrʌptəbəl] *adj* : incorruptible
increase¹ [ɪnˈkriːs, ˈɪnˌkriːs] *v* **-creased; -creasing** *vi* GROW : aumentar, crecer, subir (dícese de los precios) — *vt* AUGMENT : aumentar, acrecentar
increase² [ˈɪnˌkriːs, ɪnˈkriːs] *n* : aumento *m*, incremento *m*, subida *f* (de precios)
increasing [ɪnˈkriːsɪŋ, ˈɪnˌkriːsɪŋ] *adj* : creciente
increasingly [ɪnˈkriːsɪŋli] *adv* : cada vez más
incredible [ɪnˈkrɛdəbəl] *adj* : increíble — **incredibly** [-bli] *adv*
incredulity [ˌɪnkrɪˈduːlət̬i, -ˈdjuː-] *n* : incredulidad *f*
incredulous [ɪnˈkrɛdʒələs] *adj* : incrédulo, escéptico
incredulously [ɪnˈkrɛdʒələsli] *adv* : con incredulidad
increment [ˈɪŋkrəmənt, ˈɪn-] *n* : incremento *m*, aumento *m*
incremental [ˌɪŋkrəˈmɛntəl, ˌɪn-] *adj* : de incremento

incriminate [ɪn'krɪmə,neɪt] *vt* **-nated; -nating** : incriminar
incrimination [ɪn,krɪmə'neɪʃən] *n* : incriminación *f*
incriminatory [ɪn'krɪmənə,tori] *adj* : incriminatorio
incubate ['ɪŋkjʊ,beɪt, 'ɪn-] *v* **-bated; -bating** *vt* : incubar, empollar — *vi* : incubar(se), empollar
incubation [,ɪŋkjʊ'beɪʃən, ,ɪn-] *n* : incubación *f*
incubator ['ɪŋkjʊ,beɪṭər, 'ɪn-] *n* : incubadora *f*
inculcate [ɪn'kʌl,keɪt, 'ɪn,kʌl-] *vt* **-cated; -cating** : inculcar
incumbency [ɪn'kʌmbəntsi] *n, pl* **-cies** **1** OBLIGATION : incumbencia *f* **2** : mandato *m* (en la política)
incumbent[1] [ɪn'kʌmbənt] *adj* : obligatorio
incumbent[2] *n* : titular *mf*
incur [ɪn'kər] *vt* **incurred; incurring** : provocar (al enojo), incurrir en (gastos, obligaciones)
incurable [ɪn'kjʊrəbəl] *adj* : incurable, sin remedio
incursion [ɪn'kərʒən] *n* : incursión *f*
indebted [ɪn'dɛṭəd] *adj* **1** : endeudado **2 to be indebted to** : estar en deuda con, estarle agracido a
indebtedness [ɪn'dɛṭədnəs] *n* : endeudamiento *m*
indecency [ɪn'diːsəntsi] *n, pl* **-cies** : indecencia *f*
indecent [ɪn'diːsənt] *adj* : indecente — **indecently** *adv*
indecipherable [,ɪndɪ'saɪfərəbəl] *adj* : indescifrable
indecision [,ɪndɪ'sɪʒən] *n* : indecisión *f*, irresolución *f*
indecisive [,ɪndɪ'saɪsɪv] *adj* **1** INCONCLUSIVE : indeciso, que no es decisivo **2** IRRESOLUTE : indeciso, irresoluto, vacilante **3** INDEFINITE : indefinido — **indecisively** *adv*
indecorous [ɪn'dɛkərəs, ,ɪndɪ'korəs] *adj* : indecoroso — **indecorously** *adv*
indecorousness [ɪn'dɛkərəsnəs, ,ɪndɪ'korəs-] *n* : indecoro *m*
indeed [ɪn'diːd] *adv* **1** TRULY : verdaderamente, de veras **2** (*used as intensifier*) <thank you very much indeed : muchísimas gracias> **3** OF COURSE : claro, por supuesto
indefatigable [,ɪndɪ'fæṭɪgəbəl] *adj* : incansable, infatigable — **indefatigably** [-bli] *adv*
indefensible [,ɪndɪ'fɛntsəbəl] *adj* **1** VULNERABLE : indefendible, vulnerable **2** INEXCUSABLE : inexcusable
indefinable [,ɪndɪ'faɪnəbəl] *adj* : indefinible
indefinite [ɪn'dɛfənət] *adj* **1** : indefinido, indeterminado <indefinite pronouns : pronombres indefinidos> **2** VAGUE : vago, impreciso
indefinitely [ɪn'dɛfənətli] *adv* : indefinidamente, por un tiempo indefinido
indelible [ɪn'dɛləbəl] *adj* : indeleble, imborrable — **indelibly** [-bli] *adv*
indelicacy [ɪn'dɛləkəsi] *n* : falta *f* de delicadeza
indelicate [ɪn'dɛlɪkət] *adj* **1** IMPROPER : indelicado, indecoroso **2** TACTLESS : indiscreto, falto de tacto
indemnify [ɪn'dɛmnə,faɪ] *vt* **-fied; -fying** **1** INSURE : asegurar **2** COMPENSATE : indemnizar, compensar
indemnity [ɪn'dɛmnəṭi] *n, pl* **-ties** **1** INSURANCE : indemnidad *f* **2** COMPENSATION : indemnización *f*
indent [ɪn'dɛnt] *vt* : sangrar (un párrafo)
indentation [,ɪn,dɛn'teɪʃən] *n* **1** NOTCH : muesca *f*, mella *f* **2** INDENTING : sangría *f* (de un párrafo)
indenture[1] [ɪn'dɛntʃər] *vt* **-tured; -turing** : ligar por contrato
indenture[2] *n* : contrato de aprendizaje
independence [,ɪndə'pɛndənts] *n* : independencia *f*
Independence Day *n* : día *m* de la Independencia (4 de julio en los EE.UU.)
independent[1] [,ɪndə'pɛndənt] *adj* : independiente — **independently** *adv*
independent[2] *n* : independiente *mf*
indescribable [,ɪndɪ'skraɪbəbəl] *adj* : indescriptible, incalificable — **indescribably** [-bli] *adv*
indestructibility [,ɪndɪ,strʌktə'bɪləṭi] *n* : indestructibilidad *f*
indestructible [,ɪndɪ'strʌktəbəl] *adj* : indestructible
indeterminate [,ɪndɪ'tərmənət] *adj* **1** VAGUE : vago, impreciso, indeterminado **2** INDEFINITE : indeterminado, indefinido
index[1] ['ɪn,dɛks] *vt* **1** : ponerle un índice a (un libro o una revista) **2** : incluir en un índice <all proper names are indexed : todos los nombres propios están incluidos en el índice> **3** INDICATE : indicar, señalar **4** REGULATE : indexar, indiciar <to index prices : indiciar los precios>
index[2] *n, pl* **-dexes** *or* **-dices** ['ɪndə,siːz] **1** : índice *m* (de un libro, de precios) **2** INDICATION : indicio *m*, índice *m*, señal *f* <an index of her character : una señal de su carácter>
index finger *n* FOREFINGER : dedo *m* índice
Indian ['ɪndiən] *n* **1** : indio *m*, -dia *f* **2** → **American Indian** — **Indian** *adj*
indicate ['ɪndə,keɪt] *vt* **-cated; -cating** **1** POINT OUT : indicar, señalar **2** SHOW, SUGGEST : ser indicio de, ser señal de **3** EXPRESS : expresar, señalar **4** REGISTER : marcar, poner (una medida, etc.)
indication [,ɪndə'keɪʃən] *n* : indicio *m*, señal *f*
indicative [ɪn'dɪkəṭɪv] *adj* : indicativo

indicator [ˈɪndəˌkeɪt̬ər] *n* : indicador *m*
indict [ɪnˈdaɪt] *vt* : acusar, procesar (por un crímen)
indictment [ɪnˈdaɪtmənt] *n* : acusación *f*
indifference [ɪnˈdɪfrənts, -ˈdɪfə-] *n* : indiferencia *f*
indifferent [ɪnˈdɪfrənt, -ˈdɪfə-] *adj* **1** UNCONCERNED : indiferente **2** MEDIOCRE : mediocre
indifferently [ɪnˈdɪfrəntli, -ˈdɪfə-] *adv* **1** : con indiferencia, indiferentemente **2** SO-SO : de modo regular, más o menos
indigence [ˈɪndɪdʒənts] *n* : indigencia *f*
indigenous [ɪnˈdɪdʒənəs] *adj* : indígena, nativo
indigent [ˈɪndɪdʒənt] *adj* : indigente, pobre
indigestible [ˌɪndaɪˈdʒɛstəbəl, -dɪ-] *adj* : difícil de digerir
indigestion [ˌɪndaɪˈdʒɛstʃən, -dɪ-] *n* : indigestión *f*, empacho *m*
indignant [ɪnˈdɪgnənt] *adj* : indignado
indignantly [ɪnˈdɪgnəntli] *adv* : con indignación
indignation [ˌɪndɪgˈneɪʃən] *n* : indignación *f*
indignity [ɪnˈdɪgnət̬i] *n, pl* **-ties** : indignidad *f*
indigo [ˈɪndɪˌgoː] *n, pl* **-gos** *or* **-goes** : añil *m*, índigo *m*
indirect [ˌɪndəˈrɛkt, -daɪ-] *adj* : indirecto — **indirectly** *adv*
indiscernible [ˌɪndɪˈsərnəbəl, -ˈzər-] *adj* : imperceptible
indiscreet [ˌɪndɪˈskriːt] *adj* : indiscreto, imprudente — **indiscreetly** *adv*
indiscretion [ˌɪndɪˈskrɛʃən] *n* : indiscreción *f*, imprudencia *f*
indiscriminate [ˌɪndɪˈskrɪmənət] *adj* : indiscriminado
indiscriminately [ˌɪndɪˈskrɪmənətli] *adv* : sin discriminación, sin discernimiento
indispensable [ˌɪndɪˈspɛntsəbəl] *adj* : indispensable, necesario, imprescindible — **indispensably** [-bli] *adv*
indisposed [ˌɪndɪˈspoːzd] *adj* **1** ILL : indispuesto, enfermo **2** AVERSE, DISINCLINED : opuesto, reacio <to be indisposed toward working : no tener ganas de trabajar>
indisputable [ˌɪndɪˈspjuːt̬əbəl, ɪnˈdɪspjʊt̬ə-] *adj* : indiscutible, incuestionable, incontestable — **indisputably** [-bli] *adv*
indistinct [ˌɪndɪˈstɪŋkt] *adj* : indistinto — **indistinctly** *adv*
indistinctness [ˌɪndɪˈstɪŋktnəs] *n* : falta *f* de claridad
individual¹ [ˌɪndəˈvɪdʒʊəl] *adj* **1** PERSONAL : individual, personal <individual traits : características personales> **2** SEPARATE : individual, separado **3** PARTICULAR : particular, propio
individual² *n* : individuo *m*
individualist [ˌɪndəˈvɪdʒʊəlɪst] *n* : individualista *mf*
individuality [ˌɪndəˌvɪdʒʊˈælət̬i] *n, pl* **-ties** : individualidad *f*
individually [ˌɪndəˈvɪdʒʊəli, -dʒəli] *adv* : individualmente
indivisible [ˌɪndɪˈvɪzəbəl] *adj* : indivisible
indoctrinate [ɪnˈdɑktrəˌneɪt] *vt* **-nated; -nating 1** TEACH : enseñar, instruir **2** PROPAGANDIZE : adoctrinar
indoctrination [ɪnˌdɑktrəˈneɪʃən] *n* : adoctrinamiento *m*
indolence [ˈɪndələnts] *n* : indolencia *f*
indolent [ˈɪndələnt] *adj* : indolente
indomitable [ɪnˈdɑmət̬əbəl] *adj* : invencible, indomable, indómito — **indomitably** [-bli] *adv*
Indonesian [ˌɪndoˈniːʒən, -ʃən] *n* : indonesio *m*, -sia *f* — **Indonesian** *adj*
indoor [ˈɪnˈdor] *adj* : interior (dícese de las plantas), para estar en casa (dícese de la ropa), cubierto (dícese de las piscinas, etc.), bajo techo (dícese de los deportes)
indoors [ˈɪnˈdorz] *adv* : adentro, dentro
indubitable [ɪnˈduːbət̬əbəl, -ˈdjuː-] *adj* : indudable, incuestionable, indiscutible
indubitably [ɪnˈduːbət̬əbli, -ˈdjuː-] *adv* : indudablemente
induce [ɪnˈduːs, -ˈdjuːs] *vt* **-duced; -ducing 1** PERSUADE : persuadir, inducir **2** CAUSE : inducir, provocar <to induce labor : provocar un parto>
inducement [ɪnˈduːsmənt, -ˈdjuːs-] *n* **1** INCENTIVE : incentivo *m*, aliciente *m* **2** : inducción *f*, provocación *f* (de un parto)
induct [ɪnˈdʌkt] *vt* **1** INSTALL : instalar, investir **2** ADMIT : admitir (como miembro) **3** CONSCRIPT : reclutar (al servicio militar)
inductee [ˌɪnˌdʌkˈtiː] *n* : recluta *mf*, conscripto *m*, -ta *f*
induction [ɪnˈdʌkʃən] *n* **1** INTRODUCTION : iniciación *f*, introducción *f* **2** : inducción *f* (en la lógica o la electricidad)
inductive [ɪnˈdʌktɪv] *adj* : inductivo
indulge [ɪnˈdʌldʒ] *v* **-dulged; -dulging** *vt* **1** GRATIFY : gratificar, satisfacer **2** SPOIL : consentir, mimar — *vi* **to indulge in** : permitirse
indulgence [ɪnˈdʌldʒənts] *n* **1** SATISFYING : satisfacción *f*, gratificación *f* **2** HUMORING : complacencia *f*, indulgencia *f* **3** SPOILING : consentimiento *m* **4** : indulgencia *f* (en la religión)
indulgent [ɪŋˈdʌldʒənt] *adj* : indulgente, consentido — **indulgently** *adv*
industrial [ɪnˈdʌstriəl] *adj* : industrial — **industrially** *adv*
industrialist [ɪnˈdʌstriəlɪst] *n* : industrial *mf*

industrialization [ɪn,dʌstriələ'zeɪʃən] *n* : industrialización *f*
industrialize [ɪn'dʌstriə,laɪz] *vt* **-ized; -izing** : industrializar
industrious [ɪn'dʌstriəs] *adj* : diligente, industrioso, trabajador
industriously [ɪn'dʌstriəsli] *adv* : con diligencia, con aplicación
industriousness [ɪn'dʌstriəsnəs] *n* : diligencia *f,* aplicación *f*
industry ['ɪndəstri] *n, pl* **-tries 1** DILIGENCE : diligencia *f,* aplicación *f* **2** : industria *f* <the steel industry : la industria siderúrgica>
inebriated [ɪ'niːbri,eɪt̬əd] *adj* : ebrio, embriagado
inebriation [ɪ,niːbri'eɪʃən] *n* : ebriedad *f,* embriaguez *f*
ineffable [ɪn'ɛfəbəl] *adj* : inefable — **ineffably** [-bli] *adv*
ineffective [,ɪnɪ'fɛktɪv] *adj* **1** INEFFECTUAL : ineficaz, inútil **2** INCAPABLE : incompetente, ineficiente, incapaz
ineffectively [,ɪnɪ'fɛktɪvli] *adv* : ineficazmente, infructuosamente
ineffectual [,ɪnɪ'fɛktʃʊəl] *adj* : inútil, ineficaz — **ineffectually** *adv*
inefficiency [,ɪnɪ'fɪʃəntsi] *n, pl* **-cies** : ineficiencia *f,* ineficacia *f*
inefficient [,ɪnɪ'fɪʃənt] *adj* **1** : ineficiente, ineficaz **2** INCAPABLE, INCOMPETENT : incompetente, incapaz — **inefficiently** *adv*
inelegance [ɪn'ɛləgənts] *n* : inelegancia *f*
inelegant [ɪn'ɛləgənt] *adj* : inelegante, poco elegante
ineligibility [ɪn,ɛlədʒə'bɪlət̬i] *n* : inelegibilidad *f*
ineligible [ɪn'ɛlədʒəbəl] *adj* : inelegible
inept [ɪ'nɛpt] *adj* : inepto <inept at : incapaz para>
ineptitude [ɪ'nɛptə,tuːd, -,tjuːd] *n* : ineptitud *f,* incompetencia *f,* incapacidad *f*
inequality [,ɪnɪ'kwɑlət̬i] *n, pl* **-ties** : desigualdad *f*
inert [ɪ'nərt] *adj* **1** INACTIVE : inerte, inactivo **2** SLUGGISH : lento
inertia [ɪ'nərʃə] *n* : inercia *f*
inescapable [,ɪnɪ'skeɪpəbəl] *adj* : inevitable, ineludible — **inescapably** [-bli] *adv*
inessential [,ɪnɪ'sɛntʃəl] *adj* : que no es esencial, innecesario
inestimable [ɪn'ɛstəməbəl] *adj* : inestimable, inapreciable
inevitability [ɪn,ɛvət̬ə'bɪlət̬i] *n, pl* **-ties** : inevitabilidad *f*
inevitable [ɪn'ɛvət̬əbəl] *adj* : inevitable — **inevitably** [-bli] *adv*
inexact [,ɪnɪg'zækt] *adj* : inexacto
inexactly [,ɪnɪg'zæktli] *adv* : sin exactitud
inexcusable [,ɪnɪk'skjuːzəbəl] *adj* : inexcusable, imperdonable — **inexcusably** [-bli] *adv*
inexhaustible [,ɪnɪg'zɔstəbəl] *adj* **1** INDEFATIGABLE : infatigable, incansable **2** ENDLESS : inagotable — **inexhaustibly** [-bli] *adv*
inexorable [ɪn'ɛksərəbəl] *adj* : inexorable — **inexorably** [-bli] *adv*
inexpensive [,ɪnɪk'spɛntsɪv] *adj* : barato, económico
inexperience [,ɪnɪk'spɪriənts] *n* : inexperiencia *f*
inexperienced [,ɪnɪk'spɪriəntst] *adj* : inexperto, novato
inexplicable [,ɪnɪk'splɪkəbəl] *adj* : inexplicable — **inexplicably** [-bli] *adv*
inexpressible [,ɪnɪk'sprɛsəbəl] *adj* : inexpresable, inefable
inextricable [,ɪnɪk'strɪkəbəl, ɪ'nɛk,strɪ-] *adj* : inextricable — **inextricably** [-bli] *adv*
infallibility [ɪn,fælə'bɪlət̬i] *n* : infalibilidad *f*
infallible [ɪn'fæləbəl] *adj* : infalible — **infallibly** [-bli] *adv*
infamous ['ɪnfəməs] *adj* : infame — **infamously** *adv*
infamy ['ɪnfəmi] *n, pl* **-mies** : infamia *f*
infancy ['ɪnfəntsi] *n, pl* **-cies** : infancia *f*
infant ['ɪnfənt] *n* : bebé *m;* niño *m,* -ña *f*
infantile ['ɪnfən,taɪl, -təl, -,tiːl] *adj* : infantil, pueril
infantile paralysis → **poliomyelitis**
infantry ['ɪnfəntri] *n, pl* **-tries** : infantería *f*
infatuated [ɪn'fætʃʊ,eɪt̬əd] *adj* **to be infatuated with** : estar encaprichado con
infatuation [ɪn,fætʃʊ'eɪʃən] *n* : encaprichamiento *m,* enamoramiento *m*
infect [ɪn'fɛkt] *vt* : infectar, contagiar
infection [ɪn'fɛkʃən] *n* : infección *f,* contagio *m*
infectious [ɪn'fɛkʃəs] *adj* : infeccioso, contagioso
infer [ɪn'fər] *vt* **inferred; inferring 1** DEDUCE : deducir, inferir **2** SURMISE : concluir, suponer, tener entendido **3** IMPLY : sugerir, insinuar
inference ['ɪnfərənts] *n* : deducción *f,* inferencia *f,* conclusión *f*
inferior[1] [ɪn'fɪriər] *adj* : inferior, malo
inferior[2] *n* : inferior *mf*
inferiority [ɪn,fɪri'ɔrət̬i] *n, pl* **-ties** : inferioridad *f* <inferiority complex : complejo de inferioridad>
infernal [ɪn'fərnəl] *adj* **1** : infernal <infernal fires : fuegos infernales> **2** DIABOLICAL : infernal, diabólico **3** DAMNABLE : maldito, condenado
inferno [ɪn'fər,noː] *n, pl* **-nos** : infierno *m*
infertile [ɪn'fərt̬əl, -,taɪl] *adj* : estéril, infecundo
infertility [,ɪnfər'tɪlət̬i] *n* : esterilidad *f,* infecundidad *f*
infest [ɪn'fɛst] *vt* : infestar, plagar
infidel ['ɪnfədəl, -,dɛl] *n* : infiel *mf*

infidelity [ˌɪnfəˈdɛlət̬i, -faɪ-] *n, pl* **-ties** **1** UNFAITHFULNESS : infidelidad *f* **2** DISLOYALTY : deslealtad *f*

infield [ˈɪnˌfiːld] *n* : cuadro *m,* diamante *m*

infiltrate [ɪnˈfɪlˌtreɪt, ˈɪnfɪl-] *v* **-trated; -trating** *vt* : infiltrar — *vi* : infiltrarse

infiltration [ˌɪnfɪlˈtreɪʃən] *n* : infiltración *f*

infinite [ˈɪnfənət] *adj* **1** LIMITLESS : infinito, sin límites **2** VAST : infinito, vasto, extenso

infinitely [ˈɪnfənətli] *adv* : infinitamente

infinitesimal [ˌɪnˌfɪnəˈtɛsəməl] *adj* : infinitésimo, infinitesimal — **infinitesimally** *adv*

infinitive [ɪnˈfɪnət̬ɪv] *n* : infinitivo *m*

infinitude [ɪnˈfɪnəˌtuːd, -tjuːd] *n* : infinitud *f*

infinity [ɪnˈfɪnət̬i] *n, pl* **-ties** **1** : infinito *m* (en matemáticas, etc.) **2** : infinidad *f* <an infinity of stars : una infinidad de estrellas>

infirm [ɪnˈfərm] *adj* **1** FEEBLE : enfermizo, endeble **2** INSECURE : inseguro

infirmary [ɪnˈfərməri] *n, pl* **-ries** : enfermería *f,* hospital *m*

infirmity [ɪnˈfərmət̬i] *n, pl* **-ties** **1** FRAILTY : debilidad *f,* endeblez *f* **2** AILMENT : enfermedad *f,* dolencia *f* <the infirmities of age : los achaques de la vejez>

inflame [ɪnˈfleɪm] *v* **-flamed; -flaming** *vt* **1** KINDLE : inflamar, encender **2** : inflamar (una herida) **3** STIR UP : encender, provocar, inflamar — *vi* : inflamarse

inflammable [ɪnˈflæməbəl] *adj* **1** FLAMMABLE : inflamable **2** IRASCIBLE : irascible, explosivo

inflammation [ˌɪnfləˈmeɪʃən] *n* : inflamación *f*

inflammatory [ɪnˈflæməˌtori] *adj* : inflamatorio, incendiario

inflatable [ɪnˈfleɪt̬əbəl] *adj* : inflable

inflate [ɪnˈfleɪt] *vt* **-flated; -flating** : inflar, hinchar

inflation [ɪnˈfleɪʃən] *n* : inflación *f*

inflationary [ɪnˈfleɪʃəˌnɛri] *adj* : inflacionario, inflacionista

inflect [ɪnˈflɛkt] *vt* **1** CONJUGATE, DECLINE : conjugar, declinar **2** MODULATE : modular (la voz)

inflection [ɪnˈflɛkʃən] *n* : inflexión *f*

inflexibility [ɪnˌflɛksəˈbɪlət̬i] *n, pl* **-ties** : inflexibilidad *f*

inflexible [ɪnˈflɛksɪbəl] *adj* : inflexible

inflict [ɪnˈflɪkt] *vt* **1** : infligir, causar, imponer **2** **to inflict oneself on** : imponer uno su presencia (a alguien)

infliction [ɪnˈflɪkʃən] *n* : imposición *f*

influence¹ [ˈɪnˌfluːən*t*s, ɪnˈfluːən*t*s] *vt* **-enced; -encing** : influenciar, influir en

influence² *n* **1** : influencia *f,* influjo *m* <to exert influence over : ejercer influencia sobre> <the influence of gravity : el influjo de la gravidad> **2** **under the influence** : bajo la influencia del alcohol, embriagado

influential [ˌɪnfluˈɛntʃəl] *adj* : influyente

influenza [ˌɪnfluˈɛnzə] *n* : gripe *f,* influenza *f,* gripa *f Col, Mex*

influx [ˈɪnˌflʌks] *n* : afluencia *f* (de gente), entrada *f* (de mercancías), llegada *f* (de ideas)

inform [ɪnˈfɔrm] *vt* : informar, notificar, avisar — *vi* **to inform on** : delatar, denunciar

informal [ɪnˈfɔrməl] *adj* **1** UNCEREMONIOUS : sin ceremonia, sin etiqueta **2** CASUAL : informal, familiar (dícese del lenguaje) **3** UNOFFICIAL : extraoficial

informality [ˌɪnfɔrˈmælət̬i, -fər-] *n, pl* **-ties** : informalidad *f,* familiaridad *f,* falta *f* de ceremonia

informally [ɪnˈfɔrməli] *adv* : sin ceremonias, de manera informal, informalmente

informant [ɪnˈfɔrmənt] *n* : informante *mf;* informador *m,* -dora *f*

information [ˌɪnfərˈmeɪʃən] *n* : información *f*

informative [ɪnˈfɔrmət̬ɪv] *adj* : informativo, instructivo

informer [ɪnˈfɔrmər] *n* : informante *mf;* informador *m,* -dora *f*

infraction [ɪnˈfrækʃən] *n* : infracción *f,* violación *f,* transgresión *f*

infrared [ˌɪnfrəˈrɛd] *adj* : infrarrojo

infrastructure [ˈɪnfrəˌstrʌktʃər] *n* : infraestructura *f*

infrequent [ɪnˈfriːkwənt] *adj* : infrecuente, raro

infrequently [ɪnˈfriːkwəntli] *adv* : raramente, con poca frecuencia

infringe [ɪnˈfrɪndʒ] *v* **-fringed; -fringing** *vt* : infringir, violar — *vi* **to infringe on** : abusar de, violar

infringement [ɪnˈfrɪndʒmənt] *n* **1** VIOLATION : violación *f* (de la ley), incumplimiento *m* (de un contrato) **2** ENCROACHMENT : usurpación *f* (de derechos, etc.)

infuriate [ɪnˈfjʊriˌeɪt] *vt* **-ated; -ating** : enfurecer, poner furioso

infuriating [ɪnˈfjʊriˌeɪt̬ɪŋ] *adj* : indignante, exasperante

infuse [ɪnˈfjuːz] *vt* **-fused; -fusing** **1** INSTILL : infundir **2** STEEP : hacer una infusión de

infusion [ɪnˈfjuːʒən] *n* : infusión *f*

ingenious [ɪnˈdʒiːnjəs] *adj* : ingenioso — **ingeniously** *adv*

ingenue *or* **ingénue** [ˈɑndʒəˌnuː, ˈæn-; ˈæʒə-, ˈɑ-] *n* : ingenua *f*

ingenuity [ˌɪndʒəˈnuːət̬i, -ˈnjuː-] *n, pl* **-ities** : ingenio

ingenuous [ɪnˈdʒɛnjʊəs] *adj* **1** FRANK : cándido, franco **2** NAIVE : ingenuo — **ingenuously** *adv*

ingenuousness [ɪnˈdʒɛnjʊəsnəs] *n* **1** FRANKNESS : candidez *f,* candor *m* **2** NAÏVETÉ : ingenuidad *f*

ingest [ɪn'dʒɛst] *vt* : ingerir
inglorious [ɪn'gloriəs] *adj* : deshonroso, ignominioso
ingot ['ɪŋgət] *n* : lingote *m*
ingrained [ɪn'greɪnd] *adj* : arraigado
ingrate ['ɪn,greɪt] *n* : ingrato *m*, -ta *f*
ingratiate [ɪn'greɪʃi,eɪt] *vt* **-ated; -ating** : conseguir la benevolencia de <to ingratiate oneself with someone : congraciarse con alguien>
ingratiating [ɪn'greɪʃi,eɪt̬ɪŋ] *adj* : halagador, zalamero, obsequioso
ingratitude [ɪn'grætə,tu:d, -,tju:d] *n* : ingratitud *f*
ingredient [ɪn'gri:diənt] *n* : ingrediente *m*, componente *m*
ingrown ['ɪn,gro:n] *adj* **1** : crecido hacia adentro **2 ingrown toenail** : uña *f* encarnada
inhabit [ɪn'hæbət] *vt* : vivir en, habitar, ocupar
inhabitable [ɪn'hæbət̬əbəl] *adj* : habitable
inhabitant [ɪn'hæbət̬ənt] *n* : habitante *mf*
inhalant [ɪn'heɪlənt] *n* : inhalante *m*
inhalation [,ɪnhə'leɪʃən, ,ɪnə-] *n* : inhalación *f*
inhale [ɪn'heɪl] *v* **-haled; -haling** *vt* : inhalar, aspirar — *vi* : inspirar
inhaler [ɪn'heɪlər] *n* : inhalador *m*
inhere [ɪn'hɪr] *vi* **-hered; -hering** : ser inherente
inherent [ɪn'hɪrənt, -'hɛr-] *adj* : inherente, intrínseco — **inherently** *adv*
inherit [ɪn'hɛrət] *vt* : heredar
inheritance [ɪn'hɛrət̬ənts] *n* : herencia *f*
inheritor [ɪn'hɛrət̬ər] *n* : heredero *m*, -da *f*
inhibit [ɪn'hɪbət] *vt* IMPEDE : inhibir, impedir
inhibition [,ɪnhə'bɪʃən, ,ɪnə-] *n* : inhibición *f*, cohibición *f*
inhuman [ɪn'hju:mən, -'ju:-] *adj* : inhumano, cruel — **inhumanly** *adv*
inhumane [,ɪnhju'meɪn, -ju-] *adj* INHUMAN : inhumano, cruel
inhumanity [,ɪnhju'mænət̬i, -ju-] *n, pl* **-ties** : inhumanidad *f*, crueldad *f*
inimical [ɪ'nɪmɪkəl] *adj* **1** UNFAVORABLE : adverso, desfavorable **2** HOSTILE : hostil — **inimically** *adv*
inimitable [ɪ'nɪmət̬əbəl] *adj* : inimitable
iniquitous [ɪ'nɪkwət̬əs] *adj* : inicuo, malvado
iniquity [ɪ'nɪkwət̬i] *n, pl* **-ties** : iniquidad *f*
initial[1] [ɪ'nɪʃəl] *vt* **-tialed** *or* **-tialled; -tialing** *or* **-tialling** : poner las iniciales a, firmar con las iniciales
initial[2] *adj* : inicial, primero — **initially** *adv*
initial[3] *n* : inicial *f*
initiate[1] [ɪ'nɪʃi,eɪt] *vt* **-ated; -ating 1** BEGIN : comenzar, iniciar **2** INDUCT : instruir **3** INTRODUCE : introducir, instruir
initiate[2] [ɪ'nɪʃiət] *n* : iniciado *m*, -da *f*
initiation [ɪ,nɪʃi'eɪʃən] *n* : iniciación *f*
initiative [ɪ'nɪʃət̬ɪv] *n* : iniciativa *f*
initiatory [ɪ'nɪʃiə,tori] *adj* **1** INTRODUCTORY : introductorio **2** : de iniciación <initiatory rites : ritos de iniciación>
inject [ɪn'dʒɛkt] *vt* : inyectar
injection [ɪn'dʒɛkʃən] *n* : inyección *f*
injudicious [,ɪndʒʊ'dɪʃəs] *adj* : imprudente, indiscreto, poco juicioso
injunction [ɪn'dʒʌŋkʃən] *n* **1** ORDER : orden *f*, mandato *m* **2** COURT ORDER : mandamiento *m* judicial
injure ['ɪndʒər] *vt* **-jured; -juring 1** WOUND : herir, lesionar **2** HURT : lastimar, dañar, herir **3 to injure oneself** : hacerse daño
injurious [ɪn'dʒʊriəs] *adj* : perjudicial <injurious to one's health : perjudicial a la salud>
injury ['ɪndʒəri] *n, pl* **-ries 1** WRONG : mal *m*, injusticia *f* **2** DAMAGE, HARM : herida *f*, daño *m*, perjuicio *m*
injustice [ɪn'dʒʌstəs] *n* : injusticia *f*
ink[1] ['ɪŋk] *vt* : entintar
ink[2] *n* : tinta *f*
inkling ['ɪŋklɪŋ] *n* : presentimiento *m*, indicio *m*, sospecho *m*
inkwell ['ɪŋk,wɛl] *n* : tintero *m*
inky ['ɪŋki] *adj* **1** : manchado de tinta **2** BLACK : negro, impenetrable <inky darkness : negra oscuridad>
inland[1] ['ɪn,lænd, -lənd] *adv* : hacia el interior, tierra adentro
inland[2] *adj* : interior
inland[3] *n* : interior *m*
in–law ['ɪn,lɔ] *n* **1** : pariente *m* político **2 in–laws** *npl* : suegros *mpl*
inlay[1] [ɪn'leɪ, 'ɪn,leɪ] *vt* **-laid** [-'leɪd, -,leɪd]; **-laying** : incrustar, taracear
inlay[2] ['ɪn,leɪ] *n* **1** : incrustación *f* **2** : empaste *m* (de un diente)
inlet ['ɪn,lɛt, -lət] *n* : cala *f*, ensenada *f*
inmate ['ɪn,meɪt] *n* : paciente *mf* (en un hospital); preso *m*, -sa *f* (en una prisión); interno *m*, -na *f* (en un asilo)
in memoriam [,ɪnmə'moriəm] *prep* : en memoria de
inmost ['ɪn,mo:st] → **innermost**
inn ['ɪn] *n* **1** : posada *f*, hostería *f*, fonda *f* **2** TAVERN : taberna *f*
innards ['ɪnərdz] *npl* : entrañas *fpl*, tripas *fpl fam*
innate [ɪ'neɪt] *adj* **1** INBORN : innato **2** INHERENT : inherente
inner ['ɪnər] *adj* : interior, interno
innermost ['ɪnər,mo:st] *adj* : más íntimo, más profundo
innersole ['ɪnər'so:l] → **insole**
inning ['ɪnɪŋ] *n* : entrada *f*
innkeeper ['ɪn,ki:pər] *n* : posadero *m*, -ra *f*
innocence ['ɪnəsənts] *n* : inocencia *f*
innocent[1] ['ɪnəsənt] *adj* : inocente — **innocently** *adv*
innocent[2] *n* : inocente *mf*

innocuous [ɪ'nɑkjəwəs] *adj* **1** HARMLESS : inocuo **2** INOFFENSIVE : inofensivo

innovate ['ɪnə,veɪt] *vi* **-vated; -vating** : innovar

innovation [,ɪnə'veɪʃən] *n* : innovación *f,* novedad *f*

innovative ['ɪnə,veɪt̬ɪv] *adj* : innovador

innovator ['ɪnə,veɪt̬ər] *n* : innovador *m,* -dora *f*

innuendo [,ɪnjʊ'ɛndo] *n, pl* **-dos** *or* **-does** : insinuación *f,* indirecta *f*

innumerable [ɪ'nu:mərəbəl, -'nju:-] *adj* : innumerable

inoculate [ɪ'nɑkjə,leɪt] *vt* **-lated; -lating** : inocular

inoculation [ɪ,nɑkjə'leɪʃən] *n* : inoculación *f*

inoffensive [,ɪnə'fɛntsɪv] *adj* : inofensivo

inoperable [ɪn'ɑpərəbəl] *adj* : inoperable

inoperative [ɪn'ɑpərət̬ɪv, -,reɪ-] *adj* : inoperante

inopportune [ɪn,ɑpər'tu:n, -'tju:n] *adj* : inoportuno — **inopportunely** *adv*

inordinate [ɪn'ɔrdənət] *adj* : excesivo, inmoderado, desmesurado — **inordinately** *adv*

inorganic [,ɪn,ɔr'gænɪk] *adj* : inorgánico

inpatient ['ɪn,peɪʃənt] *n* : paciente *mf* hospitalizado

input[1] ['ɪn,pʊt] *vt* **inputted** *or* **input; inputting** : entrar (datos, información)

input[2] *n* **1** CONTRIBUTION : aportación *f,* contribución *f* **2** ENTRY : entrada *f* (de datos) **3** ADVICE, OPINION : consejos *mpl,* opinión *f*

inquest ['ɪn,kwɛst] *n* INQUIRY, INVESTIGATION : investigación *f,* averiguación *f,* pesquisa *f* (judicial)

inquire [ɪn'kwaɪr] *v* **-quired; -quiring** *vt* : preguntar, informarse de, inquirir <he inquired how to get in : preguntó como entrar> — *vi* **1** ASK : preguntar, informarse <to inquire about : informarse sobre> <to inquire after (someone) : preguntar por (alguien)> **2 to inquire into** INVESTIGATE : investigar, inquirir sobre

inquirer [ɪn'kwaɪrər] *n* : inquiridor *m,* -dora *f;* investigador *m,* -dora *f*

inquiringly [ɪn'kwaɪrɪŋli] *adv* : inquisitivamente

inquiry ['ɪn,kwaɪri, ɪn'kwaɪri; 'ɪnkwəri, 'ɪŋ-] *n, pl* **-ries 1** QUESTION : pregunta *f* <to make inquiries about : pedir información sobre> **2** INVESTIGATION : investigación *f,* inquisición *f,* pesquisa *f*

inquisition [,ɪnkwə'zɪʃən, ,ɪŋ-] *n* **1** : inquisición *f,* interrogatorio *m,* investigación *f* **2 the Inquisition** : la Inquisición *f*

inquisitive [ɪn'kwɪzət̬ɪv] *adj* : inquisidor, inquisitivo, curioso — **inquisitively** *adv*

inquisitiveness [ɪn'kwɪzət̬ɪvnəs] *n* : curiosidad *f*

inquisitor [ɪn'kwɪzət̬ər] *n* : inquisidor *m,* -dora *f;* interrogador *m,* -dora *f*

inroad ['ɪn,ro:d] *n* **1** ENCROACHMENT, INVASION : invasión *f,* incursión *f* **2 to make inroads into** : ocupar parte de (un tiempo), agotar parte de (ahorros, recursos), invadir (un territorio)

insane [ɪn'seɪn] *adj* **1** MAD : loco, demente <to go insane : volverse loco> **2** ABSURD : absurdo, insensato <an insane scheme : un proyecto insensato>

insanely [ɪn'seɪnli] *adv* : como un loco <insanely suspicious : loco de recelo>

insanity [ɪn'sænət̬i] *n, pl* **-ties 1** MADNESS : locura *f* **2** FOLLY : locura *f,* insensatez *f*

insatiable [ɪn'seɪʃəbəl] *adj* : insaciable — **insatiably** [-bli] *adv*

inscribe [ɪn'skraɪb] *vt* **-scribed; -scribing 1** ENGRAVE : inscribir, grabar **2** ENROLL : inscribir **3** DEDICATE : dedicar (un libro)

inscription [ɪn'skrɪpʃən] *n* : inscripción *f* (en un monumento), dedicación *f* (en un libro), leyenda *f* (de una ilustración, etc.)

inscrutable [ɪn'skru:t̬əbəl] *adj* : inescrutable, misterioso — **inscrutably** [-bli] *adv*

inseam ['ɪn,si:m] *n* : entrepierna *f*

insect ['ɪn,sɛkt] *n* : insecto *m*

insecticidal [ɪn,sɛktə'saɪdəl] *adj* : insecticida

insecticide [ɪn'sɛktə,saɪd] *n* : insecticida *m*

insecure [,ɪnsɪ'kjʊr] *adj* : inseguro, poco seguro — **insecurely** *adv*

insecurely [,ɪnsɪ'kjʊrli] *adv* : inseguramente

insecurity [,ɪnsɪ'kjʊrət̬i] *n, pl* **-ties** : inseguridad *f*

inseminate [ɪn'sɛmə,neɪt] *vt* **-nated; -nating** : inseminar

insemination [ɪn,sɛmə'neɪʃən] *n* : inseminación *f*

insensibility [ɪn,sɛntsə'bɪlət̬i] *n, pl* **-ties** : insensibilidad *f*

insensible [ɪn'sɛntsəbəl] *adj* **1** UNCONSCIOUS : inconsciente, sin conocimiento **2** NUMB : insensible, entumecido **3** UNAWARE : inconsciente

insensitive [ɪn'sɛntsət̬ɪv] *adj* : insensible

insensitivity [ɪn,sɛntsə'tɪvət̬i] *n, pl* **-ties** : insensibilidad *f*

inseparable [ɪn'sɛpərəbəl] *adj* : inseparable

insert[1] [ɪn'sərt] *vt* **1** : insertar, introducir, poner, meter <insert your key in the lock : mete tu llave en la cerradura> **2** INTERPOLATE : interpolar, intercalar

insert[2] [ˈɪn,sərt] *n* **:** inserción *f,* hoja *f* insertada (en una revista, etc.)

insertion [ɪnˈsərʃən] *n* **:** inserción *f*

inset [ˈɪn,sɛt] *n* **:** página *f* intercalada (en un libro), entredós *m* (de encaje en la ropa)

inshore[1] [ˈɪnˈʃor] *adv* **:** hacia la costa

inshore[2] *adj* **:** cercano a la costa, costero <inshore fishing : pesca costera>

inside[1] [ɪnˈsaɪd, ˈɪn,saɪd] *adv* **:** adentro, dentro <to run inside : correr para adentro> <inside and out : por dentro y por fuera>

inside[2] *adj* **1 :** interior, de adentro, de dentro <the inside lane : el carril interior> **2 :** confidencial <inside information : información confidencial>

inside[3] *n* **1 :** interior *m,* parte *f* de adentro **2 insides** *npl* BELLY, GUTS **:** tripas *fpl fam* **3 inside out :** al revés

inside[4] *prep* **1** INTO **:** al interior de **2** WITHIN **:** dentro de **3** (*referring to time*) **:** en menos de <inside an hour : en menos de una hora>

inside of *prep* INSIDE **:** dentro de

insider [ɪnˈsaɪdər] *n* **:** persona *f* enterada

insidious [ɪnˈsɪdiəs] *adj* **:** insidioso — **insidiously** *adv*

insidiousness [ɪnˈsɪdiəsnəs] *n* **:** insidia *f*

insight [ˈɪn,saɪt] *n* **:** perspicacia *f,* penetración *f*

insightful [ɪnˈsaɪtfəl] *adj* **:** perspicaz

insignia [ɪnˈsɪgniə] *or* **insigne** [-,ni:] *n, pl* **-nia** *or* **-nias :** insignia *f,* enseña *f*

insignificance [,ɪnsɪgˈnɪfɪkənts] *n* **:** insignificancia *f*

insignificant [,ɪnsɪgˈnɪfɪkənt] *adj* **:** insignificante

insincere [,ɪnsɪnˈsɪr] *adj* **:** insincero, poco sincero

insincerely [,ɪnsɪnˈsɪrli] *adv* **:** con poca sinceridad

insincerity [,ɪnsɪnˈsɛrəṭi, -ˈsɪr-] *n, pl* **-ties :** insinceridad *f*

insinuate [ɪnˈsɪnjʊ,eɪt] *vt* **-ated; -ating :** insinuar

insinuation [ɪn,sɪnjʊˈeɪʃən] *n* **:** insinuación *f*

insipid [ɪnˈsɪpəd] *adj* **:** insípido

insist [ɪnˈsɪst] *v* **:** insistir

insistence [ɪnˈsɪstənts] *n* **:** insistencia *f*

insistent [ɪnˈsɪstənt] *adj* **:** insistente — **insistently** *adv*

insofar as [,ɪnsoˈfɑræz] *conj* **:** en la medida en que, en tanto que, en cuanto a

insole [ˈɪn,so:l] *n* **:** plantilla *f*

insolence [ˈɪntsələnts] *n* **:** insolencia *f*

insolent [ˈɪntsələnt] *adj* **:** insolente

insolubility [ɪn,sɑljʊˈbɪləṭi] *n* **:** insolubilidad *f*

insoluble [ɪnˈsɑljʊbəl] *adj* **:** insoluble

insolvency [ɪnˈsɑlvəntsi] *n, pl* **-cies :** insolvencia *f*

insolvent [ɪnˈsɑlvənt] *adj* **:** insolvente

insomnia [ɪnˈsɑmniə] *n* **:** insomnio *m*

insomuch as [,ɪnsoˈmʌtʃæz] → **inasmuch as**

insomuch that *conj* so **:** así que, de manera que

inspect [ɪnˈspɛkt] *vt* **:** inspeccionar, examinar, revisar

inspection [ɪnˈspɛkʃən] *n* **:** inspección *f,* examen *m,* revisión *f,* revista *f* (de tropas)

inspector [ɪnˈspɛktər] *n* **:** inspector *m,* -tora *f*

inspiration [,ɪntspəˈreɪʃən] *n* **:** inspiración *f*

inspirational [,ɪntspəˈreɪʃənəl] *adj* **:** inspirador

inspire [ɪnˈspaɪr] *v* **-spired; -spiring** *vt* **1** INHALE **:** inhalar, aspirar **2** STIMULATE **:** estimular, animar, inspirar **3** INSTILL **:** inspirar, infundir — *vi* **:** inspirar

instability [,ɪntstəˈbɪləṭi] *n, pl* **-ties :** inestabilidad *f*

install [ɪnˈstɔl] *vt* **-stalled; -stalling 1 :** instalar <to install the new president : instalar el presidente nuevo> <to install a fan : montar un abanico> **2 to install oneself :** instalarse

installation [,ɪntstəˈleɪʃən] *n* **:** instalación *f*

installment [ɪnˈstɔlmənt] *n* **1 :** plazo *m,* cuota *f* <to pay in four installments : pagar a cuatro plazos> **2 :** entrega *f* (de una publicación o telenovela) **3** INSTALLATION **:** instalación *f*

instance [ˈɪntstənts] *n* **1** INSTIGATION **:** instancia *f* **2** EXAMPLE **:** ejemplo *m* <for instance : por ejemplo> **3** OCCASION **:** instancia *f,* caso *m,* ocasión *f* <he prefers, in this instance, to remain anonymous : en este caso prefiere quedarse anónimo>

instant[1] [ˈɪntstənt] *adj* **1** IMMEDIATE **:** inmediato, instantáneo <an instant reply : una respuesta inmediata> **2 :** instantáneo <instant coffee : café instantáneo>

instant[2] *n* **:** momento *m,* instante *m*

instantaneous [,ɪntstənˈteɪniəs] *adj* **:** instantáneo

instantaneously [,ɪntstənˈteɪniəsli] *adv* **:** instantáneamente, al instante

instantly [ˈɪntstəntli] *adv* **:** al instante, instantáneamente

instead [ɪnˈstɛd] *adv* **1 :** en cambio, en lugar de eso, en su lugar <Dad was going, but Mom went instead : papá iba a ir, pero mamá fue en su lugar> **2** RATHER **:** al contrario

instead of *prep* **:** en vez de, en lugar de

instep [ˈɪn,stɛp] *n* **:** empeine *m*

instigate [ˈɪntstə,geɪt] *vt* **-gated; -gating** INCITE, PROVOKE **:** instigar, incitar, provocar, fomentar

instigation [,ɪntstəˈgeɪʃən] *n* **:** instancia *f,* incitación *f*

instigator [ˈɪntstə,geɪṭər] *n* **:** instigador *m,* -dora *f;* incitador *m,* -dora *f*

instill [ɪn'stɪl] *vt* **-stilled; -stilling :** inculcar, infundir

instinct ['ɪn,stɪŋkt] *n* **1** TALENT **:** instinto *m,* don *m* <an instinct for the right word : un don para escoger la palabra apropiada> **2 :** instinto *m* <maternal instincts : instintos maternales>

instinctive [ɪn'stɪŋktɪv] *adj* **:** instintivo

instinctively [ɪn'stɪŋktɪvli] *adv* **:** instintivamente, por instinto

instinctual [ɪn'stɪŋktʃʊəl] *adj* **:** instintivo

institute[1] ['ɪntstə,tu:t, -,tju:t] *vt* **-tuted; -tuting 1** ESTABLISH**:** establecer, instituir, fundar **2** INITIATE **:** iniciar, empezar, entablar

institute[2] *n* **:** instituto *m*

institution [,ɪntstə'tu:ʃən, -'tju:-] *n* **1** ESTABLISHING **:** institución *f,* establecimiento *m* **2** CUSTOM **:** institución *f,* tradición *f* <the institution of marriage : la institución del matrimonio> **3** ORGANIZATION **:** institución *f,* organismo *m* **4** ASYLUM **:** asilo *m*

institutional [,ɪntstə'tu:ʃənəl, -'tju:-] *adj* **:** institucional

institutionalize [,ɪntstə'tu:ʃənə,laɪz, -'tju:-] *vt* **-ized; -izing 1 :** institucionalizar <institutionalized values : valores institucionalizados> **2 :** internar <institutionalized orphans : huérfanos internados>

instruct [ɪn'strʌkt] *vt* **1** TEACH, TRAIN **:** instruir, adiestrar, enseñar **2** COMMAND **:** mandar, ordenar, dar instrucciones a

instruction [ɪn'strʌkʃən] *n* **1** TEACHING **:** instrucción *f,* enseñanza *f* **2** COMMAND **:** orden *f,* instrucción *f* **3 instructions** *npl* DIRECTIONS **:** instrucciones *fpl,* modo *m* de empleo

instructional [ɪn'strʌkʃənəl] *adj* **:** instructivo, educativo

instructive [ɪn'strʌktɪv] *adj* **:** instructivo

instructor [ɪn'strʌktər] *n* **:** instructor *m,* -tora *f*

instrument ['ɪntstrəmənt] *n* **:** instrumento *m*

instrumental [,ɪntstrə'mɛntəl] *adj* **:** instrumental

instrumentalist [,ɪntstrə'mɛntəlɪst] *n* **:** instrumentista *mf*

insubordinate [,ɪnsə'bɔrdənət] *adj* **:** insubordinado

insubordination [,ɪnsə,bɔrdən'eɪʃən] *n* **:** insubordinación *f*

insubstantial [,ɪnsəb'stæntʃəl] *adj* **:** insustancial, poco nutritivo (dícese de una comida), poco sólido (dícese de una estructura o un argumento)

insufferable [ɪn'sʌfərəbəl] *adj* UNBEARABLE **:** insufrible, intolerable, inaguantable, insoportable — **insufferably** [-bli] *adv*

insufficiency [,ɪnsə'fɪʃəntsi] *n, pl* **-cies :** insuficiencia *f*

insufficient [,ɪnsə'fɪʃənt] *adj* **:** insuficiente — **insufficiently** *adv*

insular ['ɪntsʊlər, -sjʊ-] *adj* **1 :** isleño (dícese de la gente), insular (dícese del clima) <insular residents : residentes de la isla> **2** NARROW-MINDED **:** de miras estrechas

insularity [,ɪntsʊ'lærət̬i, -sjʊ-] *n* **:** insularidad *f*

insulate ['ɪntsə,leɪt] *vt* **-lated; -lating :** aislar

insulation [,ɪntsə'leɪʃən] *n* **:** aislamiento *m*

insulator ['ɪntsə,leɪt̬ər] *n* **:** aislante *m,* aislador *m*

insulin ['ɪntsələn] *n* **:** insulina *f*

insult[1] [ɪn'sʌlt] *vt* **:** insultar, ofender, injuriar

insult[2] ['ɪn,sʌlt] *n* **:** insulto *m,* injuria *f,* agravio *m*

insulting [ɪn'sʌltɪŋ] *adj* **:** ofensivo, injurioso, insultante

insultingly [ɪn'sʌltɪŋli] *adv* **:** ofensivamente, de manera insultante

insuperable [ɪn'su:pərəbəl] *adj* **:** insuperable — **insuperably** [-bli] *adv*

insurable [ɪn'ʃʊrəbəl] *adj* **:** asegurable

insurance [ɪn'ʃʊrənts, 'ɪn,ʃʊr-] *n* **:** seguro *m* <life insurance : seguro de vida> <insurance company : compañía de seguros>

insure [ɪn'ʃʊr] *vt* **-sured; -suring 1** UNDERWRITE **:** asegurar **2** ENSURE **:** asegurar, garantizar

insured [ɪn'ʃʊrd] *n* **:** asegurado *m,* -da *f*

insurer [ɪn'ʃʊrər] *n* **:** asegurador *m,* -dora *f*

insurgent[1] [ɪn'sərdʒənt] *adj* **:** insurgente

insurgent[2] *n* **:** insurgente *mf*

insurmountable [,ɪnsər'maʊntəbəl] *adj* **:** insuperable, insalvable — **insurmountably** [-bli] *adv*

insurrection [,ɪnsə'rɛkʃən] *n* **:** insurrección *f,* levantamiento *m,* alzamiento *m*

intact [ɪn'tækt] *adj* **:** intacto

intake ['ɪn,teɪk] *n* **1** OPENING **:** entrada *f,* toma *f* <fuel intake : toma de combustible> **2 :** entrada *f* (de agua o aire), consumo *m* (de sustancias nutritivas) **3 intake of breath :** inhalación *f*

intangible [ɪn'tændʒəbəl] *adj* **:** intangible, impalpable — **intangibly** [-bli] *adv*

integer ['ɪntɪdʒər] *n* **:** entero *m*

integral ['ɪntɪgrəl] *adj* **:** integral, esencial

integrate ['ɪntə,greɪt] *v* **-grated; -grating** *vt* **1** UNITE **:** integrar, unir **2** DESEGREGATE **:** eliminar la segregación de — *vi* **:** integrarse

integration [,ɪntə'greɪʃən] *n* **:** integración *f*

integrity [ɪn'tɛgrət̬i] *n* **:** integridad *f*

intellect ['ɪntəl,ɛkt] *n* **:** intelecto *m,* inteligencia *f,* capacidad *f* intelectual

intellectual[1] [ˌɪntəˈlɛktʃʊəl] *adj* : intelectual — **intellectually** *adv*
intellectual[2] *n* : intelectual *mf*
intellectualism [ˌɪntəˈlɛktʃʊəˌlɪzəm] *n* : intelectualismo *m*
intelligence [ɪnˈtɛlədʒənts] *n* **1** : inteligencia *f* **2** INFORMATION, NEWS : inteligencia *f,* información *f,* noticias *fpl*
intelligent [ɪnˈtɛlədʒənt] *adj* : inteligente — **intelligently** *adv*
intelligibility [ɪnˌtɛlədʒəˈbɪləṭi] *n* : inteligibilidad *f*
intelligible [ɪnˈtɛlədʒəbəl] *adj* : inteligible, comprensible — **intelligibly** [-bli] *adv*
intemperance [ɪnˈtɛmpərənts] *n* : inmoderación *f,* intemperancia *f*
intemperate [ɪnˈtɛmpərət] *adj* : excesivo, inmoderado, desmedido
intend [ɪnˈtɛnd] *vt* **1** MEAN : querer decir <that's not what I intended : eso no es lo que quería decir> **2** PLAN : tener planeado, proyectar, proponerse <I intend to finish by Thursday : me propongo acabar para el jueves>
intended [ɪnˈtɛndəd] *adj* **1** PLANNED : previsto, proyectado **2** INTENTIONAL : intencional, deliberado
intense [ɪnˈtɛnts] *adj* **1** EXTREME : intenso, extremo <intense pain : dolor intenso> **2** : profundo, intenso <to my intense relief : para mi alivio profundo> <intense enthusiasm : entusiasmo ardiente>
intensely [ɪnˈtɛntsli] *adv* : sumamente, profundamente, intensamente
intensification [ɪnˌtɛntsəfəˈkeɪʃən] *n* : intensificación *f*
intensify [ɪnˈtɛntsəˌfaɪ] *v* **-fied; -fying** *vt* **1** STRENGTHEN : intensificar, redoblar <to intensify one's efforts : redoblar uno sus esfuerzos> **2** SHARPEN : intensificar, agudizar (dolor, ansiedad) — *vi* : intensificarse, hacerse más intenso
intensity [ɪnˈtɛntsəṭi] *n, pl* **-ties** : intensidad *f*
intensive [ɪnˈtɛntsɪv] *adj* : intensivo — **intensively** *adv*
intent[1] [ɪnˈtɛnt] *adj* **1** FIXED : concentrado, fijo <an intent stare : una mirada fija> **2 intent on** *or* **intent upon** : resuelto a, atento a
intent[2] *n* **1** PURPOSE : intención *f,* propósito *m* **2 for all intents and purposes** : a todos los efectos, prácticamente
intention [ɪnˈtɛntʃən] *n* : intención *f,* propósito *m*
intentional [ɪnˈtɛntʃənəl] *adj* : intencional, deliberado
intentionally [ɪnˈtɛntʃənəli] *adv* : a propósito, adrede
intently [ɪnˈtɛntli] *adv* : atentamente, fijamente
inter [ɪnˈtər] *vt* **-terred; -terring** : enterrar, inhumar
interact [ˌɪntərˈækt] *vi* : interactuar, actuar recíprocamente, relacionarse
interaction [ˌɪntərˈækʃən] *n* : interacción *f,* interrelación *f*
interactive [ˌɪntərˈæktɪv] *adj* : interactivo
interbreed [ˌɪntərˈbriːd] *v* **-bred** [-ˈbrɛd]; **-breeding** *vt* : cruzar — *vi* : cruzarse
intercalate [ɪnˈtərkəˌleɪt] *vt* **-lated; -lating** : intercalar
intercede [ˌɪntərˈsiːd] *vi* **-ceded; -ceding** : interceder
intercept [ˌɪntərˈsɛpt] *vt* : interceptar
interception [ˌɪntərˈsɛpʃən] *n* : intercepción *f*
intercession [ˌɪntərˈsɛʃən] *n* : intercesión *f*
interchange[1] [ˌɪntərˈtʃeɪndʒ] *vt* **-changed; -changing** : intercambiar
interchange[2] [ˈɪntərˌtʃeɪndʒ] *n* **1** EXCHANGE : intercambio *m,* cambio *m* **2** JUNCTION : empalme *m,* enlace *m* de carreteras
interchangeable [ˌɪntərˈtʃeɪndʒəəl] *adj* : intercambiable
intercity [ˈɪntərˈsɪṭi] *adj* : interurbano
intercollegiate [ˌɪntərkəˈliːdʒət, -dʒiət] *adj* : interuniversitario
intercontinental [ˌɪntərˌkɑntənˈɛntəl] *adj* : intercontinental
intercourse [ˈɪntərˌkors] *n* **1** RELATIONS : relaciones *fpl,* trato *m* **2** COPULATION : acto *m* sexual, relaciones *fpl* sexuales, coito *m*
interdenominational [ˌɪntərdɪˌnɑməˈneɪʃənəl] *adj* : interconfesional
interdepartmental [ˌɪntərdɪˌpɑrtˈmɛntəl, -ˌdiː-] *adj* : interdepartamental
interdependence [ˌɪntərdɪˈpɛndənts] *n* : interdependencia *f*
interdependent [ˌɪntərdɪˈpɛndənt] *adj* : interdependiente
interdict [ˌɪntərˈdɪkt] *vt* **1** PROHIBIT : prohibir **2** : cortar (las líneas de comunicación o provisión del enemigo)
interest[1] [ˈɪntrəst, -təˌrɛst] *vt* : interesar
interest[2] *n* **1** SHARE, STAKE : interés *m,* participación *f* **2** BENEFIT : provecho *m,* beneficio *m,* interés *m* <in the public interest : en el interés público> **3** CHARGE : interés *m,* cargo *m* <compound interest : interés compuesto> **4** CURIOSITY : interés *m,* curiosidad *f* **5** COLOR : color *m,* interés *m* <places of local interest : lugares de color local> **6** HOBBY : afición *f*
interesting [ˈɪntrəstɪŋ, -təˌrɛstɪŋ] *adj* : interesante — **interestingly** *adv*
interface [ˈɪntərˌfeɪs] *n* **1** : punto *m* de contacto <oil-water interface : punto de contacto entre el agua y el aceite> **2** : interfase *f,* interfaz *f* (de una computadora)
interfere [ˌɪntərˈfɪr] *vi* **-fered; -fering** **1** INTERPOSE : interponerse, hacer in-

terferencia <to interfere with a play : obstruir una jugada> **2** MEDDLE : entrometerse, interferir, intervenir **3 to interfere with** DISRUPT : afectar (una actividad), interferir (la radiotransmisión) **4 to interfere with** TOUCH : tocar <someone interfered with my papers : alguien tocó mis papeles>

interference [ˌɪntərˈfɪrənts] *n* : interferencia *f,* intromisión *f*

intergalactic [ˌɪntərgəˈlæktɪk] *adj* : intergaláctico

intergovernmental [ˌɪntərˌgʌvərˈmɛntəl, -vərn-] *adj* : intergubernamental

interim[1] [ˈɪntərəm] *adj* : interino, provisional

interim[2] *n* 1 : interín *m,* intervalo *m* **2 in the interim** : en el interín, mientras tanto

interior[1] [ɪnˈtɪriər] *adj* : interior

interior[2] *n* : interior *m*

interject [ˌɪntərˈdʒɛkt] *vt* : interponer, agregar

interjection [ˌɪntərˈdʒɛkʃən] *n* **1** : interjección *f* (en lingüística) **2** EXCLAMATION : exclamación *f* **3** INTERPOSITION, INTERRUPTION : interposición *f,* interrupción *f*

interlace [ˌɪntərˈleɪs] *vt* **-laced; -lacing 1** INTERWEAVE : entrelazar **2** INTERSPERSE : intercalar

interlock [ˌɪntərˈlɑk] *vt* **1** UNITE : trabar, unir **2** ENGAGE, MESH : engranar — *vi* : entrelazarse, trabarse

interloper [ˌɪntərˈloːpər] *n* **1** INTRUDER : intruso *m,* -sa *f* **2** MEDDLER : entrometido *m,* -da *f*

interlude [ˈɪntərˌluːd] *n* **1** INTERVAL : intervalo *m,* intermedio *m* (en el teatro) **2** : interludio *m* (en música)

intermarriage [ˌɪntərˈmærɪdʒ] *n* **1** : matrimonio *m* mixto (entre miembros de distintas razas o religiones) **2** : matrimonio *m* entre miembros del mismo grupo

intermarry [ˌɪntərˈmæri] *vi* **-married; -marrying 1** : casarse (con miembros de otros grupos) **2** : casarse entre sí (con miembros del mismo grupo)

intermediary[1] [ˌɪntərˈmiːdiˌɛri] *adj* : intermediario

intermediary[2] *n, pl* **-aries** : intermediario *m,* -ria *f*

intermediate[1] [ˌɪntərˈmiːdiət] *adj* : intermedio

intermediate[2] *n* GO-BETWEEN : intermediario *m,* -ria *f;* mediador *m,* -dora *f*

interment [ɪnˈtərmənt] *n* : entierro *m*

interminable [ɪnˈtərmənəbəl] *adj* : interminable, constante — **interminably** [-bli] *adv*

intermingle [ˌɪntərˈmɪŋgəl] *vt* **-mingled; -mingling** : entremezclar, mezclar — *vi* : entremezclarse

intermission [ˌɪntərˈmɪʃən] *n* : intermisión *f,* intervalo *m,* intermedio *m*

intermittent [ˌɪntərˈmɪtənt] *adj* : intermitente — **intermittently** *adv*

intermix [ˌɪntərˈmɪks] *vt* : entremezclar

intern[1] [ˈɪnˌtərn, ɪnˈtərn] *vt* : confinar (durante la guerra) — *vi* : servir de interno, hacer las prácticas

intern[2] [ˈɪnˌtərn] *n* : interno *m,* -na *f*

internal [ɪnˈtərnəl] *adj* : interno, interior <internal bleeding : hemorragia interna> <internal affairs : asuntos interiores, asuntos domésticos> — **internally** *adv*

international [ˌɪntərˈnæʃənəl] *adj* : internacional — **internationally** *adv*

internationalize [ˌɪntərˈnæʃənəˌlaɪz] *vt* **-ized; -izing** : internacionalizar

internee [ˌɪnˌtərˈniː] *n* : interno *m,* -na *f*

internist [ˈɪnˌtərnɪst] *n* : internista *mf*

interpersonal [ˌɪntərˈpərsənəl] *adj* : interpersonal

interplay [ˈɪntərˌpleɪ] *n* : interacción *f,* juego *m*

interpolate [ɪnˈtərpəˌleɪt] *vt* **-lated; -lating** : interpolar

interpose [ˌɪntərˈpoːz] *v* **-posed; -posing** *vt* : interponer, interrumpir con — *vi* : interponerse

interposition [ˌɪntərpəˈzɪʃən] *n* : interposición *f*

interpret [ɪnˈtərprət] *vt* : interpretar

interpretation [ɪnˌtərprəˈteɪʃən] *n* : interpretación *f*

interpretative [ɪnˈtərprəˌteɪtɪv] *adj* : interpretativo

interpreter [ɪnˈtərprətər] *n* : intérprete *mf*

interpretive [ɪnˈtərprətɪv] *adj* : interpretativo

interracial [ˌɪntərˈreɪʃəl] *adj* : interracial

interrelate [ˌɪntərɪˈleɪt] *vi* **-related; -relating** : interelacionar

interrelationship [ˌɪntərɪˈleɪʃənˌʃɪp] *n* : interrelación *f*

interrogate [ɪnˈtɛrəˌgeɪt] *vt* **-gated; -gating** : interrogar, someter a un interrogatorio

interrogation [ɪnˌtɛrəˈgeɪʃən] *n* : interrogación *f*

interrogative[1] [ˌɪntəˈrɑgətɪv] *adj* : interrogativo

interrogative[2] *n* : interrogativo *m*

interrogator [ɪnˈtɛrəˌgeɪtər] *n* : interrogador *m,* -dora *f*

interrogatory [ˌɪntəˈrɑgəˌtɔri] → **interrogative**[1]

interrupt [ˌɪntəˈrʌpt] *v* : interrumpir

interruption [ˌɪntəˈrʌpʃən] *n* : interrupción *f*

intersect [ˌɪntərˈsɛkt] *vt* : cruzar, cortar — *vi* : cruzarse (dícese de los caminos), intersectarse (dícese de las líneas o figuras), cortarse

intersection [ˌɪntərˈsɛkʃən] *n* : intersección *f,* cruce *m*

intersperse [ˌɪntərˈspərs] *vt* **-spersed; -spersing** : intercalar, entremezclar

interstate [ˌɪntərˈsteɪt] *adj* : interestatal

interstellar [ˌɪntərˈstɛlər] *adj* : interestelar

interstice [ɪnˈtərstəs] *n, pl* **-stices** [-stəˌsiːz, -stəsəz] : intersticio *m*

intertwine [ˌɪntərˈtwaɪn] *vi* **-twined; -twining** : entrelazarse

interval [ˈɪntərvəl] *n* : intervalo *m*

intervene [ˌɪntərˈviːn] *vi* **-vened; -vening 1** ELAPSE : transcurrir, pasar <the intervening years : los años intermediarios> **2** INTERCEDE : intervenir, interceder, mediar

intervention [ˌɪntərˈvɛntʃən] *n* : intervención *f*

interview[1] [ˈɪntərˌvjuː] *vt* : entrevistar — *vi* : hacer entrevistas

interview[2] *n* : entrevista *f*

interviewer [ˈɪntərˌvjuːər] *n* : entrevistador *m*, -dora *f*

interweave [ˌɪntərˈwiːv] *v* **-wove** [-ˈwoːv]; **-woven** [-ˈwoːvən]; **-weaving** *vt* : entretejer, entrelazar — *vi* INTERTWINE : entrelazarse, entretejerse

interwoven [ˌɪntərˈwoːvən] *adj* : entretejido

intestate [ɪnˈtɛsˌteɪt, -tət] *adj* : intestado

intestinal [ɪnˈtɛstənəl] *adj* : intestinal

intestine [ɪnˈtɛstən] *n* **1** : intestino *m* **2 small intestine** : intestino *m* delgado **3 large intestine** : intestino *m* grueso

intimacy [ˈɪntəməsi] *n, pl* **-cies 1** CLOSENESS : intimidad *f* **2** FAMILIARITY : familiaridad *f*

intimate[1] [ˈɪntəˌmeɪt] *vt* **-mated; -mating** : insinuar, dar a entender

intimate[2] [ˈɪntəmət] *adj* **1** CLOSE : íntimo, de confianza <intimate friends : amigos íntimos> **2** PRIVATE : íntimo, privado <intimate clubs : clubes íntimos> **3** INNERMOST, SECRET : íntimo, secreto <intimate fantasies : fantasías secretas>

intimate[3] *n* : amigo *m* íntimo, amiga *f* íntima

intimidate [ɪnˈtɪməˌdeɪt] *vt* **-dated; -dating** : intimidar

intimidation [ɪnˌtɪməˈdeɪʃən] *n* : intimidación *f*

into [ˈɪnˌtuː] *prep* **1** (*indicating motion*) : en, a, contra, dentro de <she got into bed : se metió en la cama> <to get into a plane : subir a un avión> <he crashed into the wall : chocó contra la pared> <looking into the sun : mirando al sol> **2** (*indicating state or condition*) : a, en <to burst into tears : echarse a llorar> <the water turned into ice : el agua se convirtió en hielo> <to translate into English : traducir al inglés> **3** (*indicating time*) <far into the night : hasta bien entrada la noche> <he's well into his eighties : tiene los ochenta bien cumplidos> **4** (*in mathematics*) <3 into 12 is 4 : 12 dividido por 3 es 4>

intolerable [ɪnˈtɑlərəbəl] *adj* : intolerable — **intolerably** [-bli] *adv*

intolerance [ɪnˈtɑlərən*t*s] *n* : intolerancia *f*

intolerant [ɪnˈtɑlərənt] *adj* : intolerante

intonation [ˌɪntoˈneɪʃən] *n* : intonación *f*

intone [ɪnˈtoːn] *vt* **-toned; -toning** : entonar

intoxicant [ɪnˈtɑksɪkənt] *n* : bebida *f* alcohólica

intoxicate [ɪnˈtɑksəˌkeɪt] *vt* **-cated; -cating** : emborrachar, embriagar

intoxicated [ɪnˈtɑksəˌkeɪt̬əd] *adj* : borracho, embriagado

intoxicating [ɪnˈtɑksəˌkeɪt̬ɪŋ] *adj* : embriagador

intoxication [ɪnˌtɑksəˈkeɪʃən] *n* : embriaguez *f*

intractable [ɪnˈtræktəbəl] *adj* : obstinado, intratable

intramural [ˌɪntrəˈmjʊrəl] *adj* : interno, dentro de la universidad

intransigence [ɪnˈtræn*t*sədʒən*t*s, -ˈtrænzə-] *n* : intransigencia *f*

intransigent [ɪnˈtræn*t*sədʒənt, -ˈtrænzə-] *adj* : intransigente

intravenous [ˌɪntrəˈviːnəs] *adj* : intravenoso — **intravenously** *adv*

intrepid [ɪnˈtrɛpəd] *adj* : intrépido

intricacy [ˈɪntrɪkəsi] *n, pl* **-cies** : complejidad *f*, lo intrincado

intricate [ˈɪntrɪkət] *adj* : intrincado, complicado — **intricately** *adv*

intrigue[1] [ɪnˈtriːg] *v* **-trigued; -triguing** : intrigar

intrigue[2] [ˈɪnˌtriːg, ɪnˈtriːg] *n* : intriga *f*

intriguing [ɪnˈtriːgɪŋli] *adj* : intrigante, fascinante

intrinsic [ɪnˈtrɪnzɪk, -ˈtrɪn*t*sɪk] *adj* : intrínseco, esencial — **intrinsically** [-zɪkli, -sɪ-] *adv*

introduce [ˌɪntrəˈduːs, -ˈdjuːs] *vt* **-duced; -ducing 1** : presentar <let me introduce my father : permítame presentar a mi padre> **2** : introducir (algo nuevo), lanzar (un producto), presentar (una ley), proponer (una idea o un tema)

introduction [ˌɪntrəˈdʌkʃən] *n* : introducción *f*, presentación *f*

introductory [ˌɪntrəˈdʌktəri] *adj* : introductorio, preliminar, de introducción

introspection [ˌɪntrəˈspɛkʃən] *n* : introspección *f*

introspective [ˌɪntrəˈspɛktɪv] *adj* : introspectivo — **introspectively** *adv*

introvert [ˈɪntrəˌvərt] *n* : introvertido *m*, -da *f*

introverted [ˈɪntrəˌvərt̬əd] *adj* : introvertido

intrude [ɪnˈtruːd] *v* **-truded; -truding** *vi* **1** INTERFERE : inmiscuirse, entrometerse **2** DISTURB, INTERRUPT : molestar, estorbar, interrumpir — *vt* : introducir por fuerza

intruder [ɪnˈtruːdər] *n* : intruso *m*, -sa *f*
intrusion [ɪnˈtruːʒən] *n* : intrusión *f*
intrusive [ɪnˈtruːsɪv] *adj* : intruso
intuit [ɪnˈtuːɪt, -ˈtjuː-] *vt* : intuir
intuition [ˌɪntʊˈɪʃən, -tjʊ-] *n* : intuición *f*
intuitive [ɪnˈtuːət̬ɪv, -ˈtjuː-] *adj* : intuitivo — **intuitively** *adv*
inundate [ˈɪnənˌdeɪt] *vt* **-dated; -dating** : inundar
inundation [ˌɪnənˈdeɪʃən] *n* : inundación *f*
inure [ɪˈnʊr, -ˈnjʊr] *vt* **-ured; -uring** : acostumbrar, habituar
invade [ɪnˈveɪd] *vt* **-vaded; -vading** : invadir
invader [ɪnˈveɪdər] *n* : invasor *m*, -sora *f*
invalid[1] [ɪnˈvæləd] *adj* : inválido, nulo
invalid[2] [ˈɪnvələd] *adj* : inválido, discapacitado
invalid[3] [ˈɪnvələd] *n* : inválido *m*, -da *f*
invalidate [ɪnˈvæləˌdeɪt] *vt* **-dated; -dating** : invalidar
invalidity [ˌɪnvəˈlɪdət̬i] *n, pl* **-ties** : invalidez *f*, falta de validez *f*
invaluable [ɪnˈvæljəbəl, -ˈvæljʊə-] *adj* : invalorable, inestimable, inapreciable
invariable [ɪnˈværiəbəl] *adj* : invariable, constante — **invariably** [-bli] *adv*
invasion [ɪnˈveɪʒən] *n* : invasión *f*
invasive [ɪnˈveɪsɪv] *adj* : invasivo
invective [ɪnˈvɛktɪv] *n* : invectiva *f*, improperio *m*, vituperio *m*
inveigh [ɪnˈveɪ] *vi* **to inveigh against** : arremeter contra, lanzar invectivas contra
inveigle [ɪnˈveɪgəl, -ˈviː-] *vt* **-gled; -gling** : engatusar, embaucar, persuadir con engaños
invent [ɪnˈvɛnt] *vt* : inventar
invention [ɪnˈvɛntʃən] *n* : invención *f*, invento *m*
inventive [ɪnˈvɛntɪv] *adj* : inventivo
inventiveness [ɪnˈvɛntɪvnəs] *n* : ingenio *m*, inventiva *f*
inventor [ɪnˈvɛntər] *n* : inventor *m*, -tora *f*
inventory[1] [ˈɪnvənˌtɔri] *vt* **-ried; -rying** : inventariar
inventory[2] *n, pl* **-ries 1** LIST : inventario *m* **2** STOCK : existencias *fpl*
inverse[1] [ɪnˈvərs, ˈɪnˌvərs] *adj* : inverso — **inversely** *adv*
inverse[2] *n* : inverso *m*
inversion [ɪnˈvərʒən] *n* : inversión *f*
invert [ɪnˈvərt] *vt* : invertir
invertebrate[1] [ɪnˈvərt̬əbrət, -ˌbreɪt] *adj* : invertebrado
invertebrate[2] *n* : invertebrado *m*
invest [ɪnˈvɛst] *vt* **1** AUTHORIZE : investir, autorizar **2** CONFER : conferir **3** : invertir, dedicar <he invested his savings in stocks : invirtió sus ahorros en acciones> <to invest one's time : dedicar uno su tiempo>
investigate [ɪnˈvɛstəˌgeɪt] *v* **-gated; -gating** : investigar
investigation [ɪnˌvɛstəˈgeɪʃən] *n* : investigación *f*, estudio *m*
investigative [ɪnˈvɛstəˌgeɪt̬ɪv] *adj* : investigador
investigator [ɪnˈvɛstəˌgeɪt̬ər] *n* : investigador *m*, -dora *f*
investiture [ɪnˈvɛstəˌtʃʊr, -tʃər] *n* : investidura *f*
investment [ɪnˈvɛstmənt] *n* : inversión *f*
investor [ɪnˈvɛstər] *n* : inversor *m*, -sora *f*; inversionista *mf*
inveterate [ɪnˈvɛt̬ərət] *adj* **1** DEEP-SEATED : inveterado, enraizado **2** HABITUAL : empedernido, incorregible
invidious [ɪnˈvɪdiəs] *adj* **1** OBNOXIOUS : repugnante, odioso **2** UNJUST : injusto — **invidiously** *adv*
invigorate [ɪnˈvɪgəˌreɪt] *vt* **-rated; -rating** : vigorizar, animar
invigorating [ɪnˈvɪgəˌreɪt̬ɪŋ] *adj* : vigorizante, estimulante
invigoration [ɪnˌvɪgəˈreɪʃən] *n* : animación *f*
invincibility [ɪnˌvɪntsəˈbɪlət̬i] *n* : invencibilidad *f*
invincible [ɪnˈvɪntsəbəl] *adj* : invencible — **invincibly** [-bli] *adv*
inviolable [ɪnˈvaɪələbəl] *adj* : inviolable
inviolate [ɪnˈvaɪələt] *adj* : inviolado, puro
invisibility [ɪnˌvɪzəˈbɪlət̬i] *n* : invisibilidad *f*
invisible [ɪnˈvɪzəbəl] *adj* : invisible — **invisibly** [-bli] *adv*
invitation [ˌɪnvəˈteɪʃən] *n* : invitación *f*
invite [ɪnˈvaɪt] *vt* **-vited; -viting 1** ATTRACT : atraer, tentar <a book that invites interest : un libro que atrae el interés> **2** PROVOKE : provocar, buscar <to invite trouble : buscarse problemas> **3** ASK : invitar <we invited them for dinner : los invitamos a cenar> **4** SOLICIT : solicitar, buscar (preguntas, comentarios, etc.)
inviting [ɪnˈvaɪt̬ɪŋ] *adj* : atractivo, atrayente
invocation [ˌɪnvəˈkeɪʃən] *n* : invocación *f*
invoice[1] [ˈɪnˌvɔɪs] *vt* **-voiced; -voicing** : facturar
invoice[2] *n* : factura *f*
invoke [ɪnˈvoːk] *vt* **-voked; -voking 1** : invocar, apelar a <she invoked our aid : apeló a nuestra ayuda> **2** CITE : invocar, citar <to invoke a precedent : invocar un precedente> **3** CONJURE UP : hacer aparecer, invocar
involuntary [ɪnˈvɑlənˌtɛri] *adj* : involuntario — **involuntarily** [ɪnˌvɑlənˈtɛrəli] *adv*

involve [ɪn'vɑlv] *vt* **-volved; -volving 1** ENGAGE **:** ocupar <workers involved in construction **:** trabajadores ocupados con la construcción> **2** IMPLICATE **:** involucrar, enredar, implicar <to be involved in a crime **:** estar involucrado en un crimen> **3** CONCERN **:** concernir, afectar **4** CONNECT **:** conectar, relacionar **5** ENTAIL, INCLUDE **:** suponer, incluir, consistir en <what does the job involve? **:** ¿en qué consiste el trabajo?> **6 to be involved with someone :** tener una relación (amorosa) con alguien

involved [ɪn'vɑlvd] *adj* **1** COMPLEX, INTRICATE **:** complicado, complejo, enrevesado **2** CONCERNED **:** interesado, afectado

involvement [ɪn'vɑlvmənt] *n* **1** PARTICIPATION **:** participación *f,* complicidad *f* **2** RELATIONSHIP **:** relación *f*

invulnerable [ɪn'vʌlnərəbəl] *adj* **:** invulnerable

inward[1] ['ɪnwərd] *or* **inwards** [-wərdz] *adv* **:** hacia adentro, hacia el interior

inward[2] *adj* INSIDE **:** interior, interno

inwardly ['ɪnwərdli] *adv* **1** MENTALLY, SPIRITUALLY **:** por dentro **2** INTERNALLY **:** internamente, interiormente **3** PRIVATELY **:** para sus adentros, para sí

iodide ['aɪə,daɪd] *n* **:** yoduro *m*

iodine ['aɪə,daɪn, -dən] *n* **:** yodo *m,* tintura *f* de yodo

iodize ['aɪə,daɪz] *vt* **-dized; -dizing :** yodar

ion ['aɪən, 'aɪ,ɑn] *n* **:** ion *m*

ionic [aɪ'ɑnɪk] *adj* **:** iónico

ionize ['aɪə,naɪz] *v* **ionized; ionizing :** ionizar

ionosphere [aɪ'ɑnə,sfɪr] *n* **:** ionosfera *f*

iota [aɪ'oːt̬ə] *n* **:** pizca *f,* ápice *m*

IOU [,aɪ,o'juː] *n* **:** pagaré *m,* vale *m*

Iranian [ɪ'reɪniən, -'ræ-, -'rɑ-; aɪ'-] *n* **:** iraní *mf* — **Iranian** *adj*

Iraqi [ɪ'rakiː] *n* **:** iraquí *mf* — **Iraqi** *adj*

irascibility [ɪ,ræsə'bɪlət̬i] *n* **:** irascibilidad *f*

irascible [ɪ'ræsəbəl] *adj* **:** irascible

irate [aɪ'reɪt] *adj* **:** furioso, airado, iracundo — **irately** *adv*

ire ['aɪr] *n* **:** ira *f,* cólera *f*

iridescence [,ɪrə'dɛsənts] *n* **:** iridiscencia *f*

iridescent [,ɪrə'dɛsənt] *adj* **:** iridiscente

iris ['aɪrəs] *n, pl* **irises** *or* **irides** ['aɪrə,diːz, 'ɪr-] **1 :** iris *m* (del ojo) **2 :** lirio *m* (planta)

Irish[1] ['aɪrɪʃ] *adj* **:** irlandés

Irish[2] **1 :** irlandés *m* (idioma) **2 the Irish** *npl* **:** los irlandeses

Irishman ['aɪrɪʃmən] *n* **:** irlandés *m*

Irishwoman ['aɪrɪʃ,wʊmən] *n* **:** irlandesa *f*

irk ['ərk] *vt* **:** fastidiar, irritar, preocupar

irksome ['ərksəm] *adj* **:** irritante, fastidioso — **irksomely** *adv*

iron[1] ['aɪərn] *v* **:** planchar

iron[2] *n* **1 :** hierro *m,* fierro *m* <a will of iron **:** una voluntad de hierro, una voluntad férrea> **2 :** plancha *f* (para planchar la ropa)

ironclad ['aɪərn'klæd] *adj* **1 :** acorazado, blindado **2** STRICT **:** riguroso, estricto

ironic [aɪ'rɑnɪk] *or* **ironical** [-nɪkəl] *adj* **:** irónico — **ironically** [-kli] *adv*

ironing ['aɪərnɪŋ] *n* **1** PRESSING **:** planchada *f* **2 :** ropa *f* para planchar

ironing board *n* **:** tabla *f* (de planchar)

ironwork ['aɪərn,wərk] *n* **1 :** obra *f* de hierro **2 ironworks** *npl* **:** fundición *f*

ironworker ['aɪərn,wərkər] *n* **:** fundidor *m,* -dora *f*

irony ['aɪrəni] *n, pl* **-nies :** ironía *f*

irradiate [ɪ'reɪdi,eɪt] *vt* **-ated; -ating :** irradiar, radiar

irradiation [ɪ,reɪdi'eɪʃən] *n* **:** irradiación *f,* radiación *f*

irrational [ɪ'ræʃənəl] *adj* **:** irracional — **irrationally** *adv*

irrationality [ɪ,ræʃə'nælət̬i] *n, pl* **-ties :** irracionalidad *f*

irreconcilable [ɪ,rɛkən'saɪləbəl] *adj* **:** irreconciliable

irrecoverable [,ɪrɪ'kʌvərəbəl] *adj* **:** irrecuperable — **irrecoverably** [-bli] *adv*

irredeemable [,ɪrɪ'diːməbəl] *adj* **1 :** irredimible (dícese de un bono) **2** HOPELESS **:** irremediable, irreparable

irreducible [,ɪrɪ'duːsəbəl, -'djuː-] *adj* **:** irreducible — **irreducibly** [-bli] *adv*

irrefutable [,ɪrɪ'fjuːt̬əbəl, ɪr'ɛfjə-] *adj* **:** irrefutable

irregular[1] [ɪ'rɛgjələr] *adj* **:** irregular — **irregularly** *adv*

irregular[2] *n* **1 :** soldado *m* irregular **2 irregulars** *npl* **:** artículos *mpl* defectuosos

irregularity [ɪ,rɛgjə'lærət̬i] *n, pl* **-ties :** irregularidad *f*

irrelevance [ɪ'rɛləvənts] *n* **:** irrelevancia *f*

irrelevant [ɪ'rɛləvənt] *adj* **:** irrelevante

irreligious [,ɪrɪ'lɪdʒəs] *adj* **:** irreligioso

irreparable [ɪ'rɛpərəbəl] *adj* **:** irreparable

irreplaceable [,ɪrɪ'pleɪsəbəl] *adj* **:** irreemplazable, insustituible

irrepressible [,ɪrɪ'prɛsəbəl] *adj* **:** incontenible, incontrolable

irreproachable [ɪrɪ'proːtʃəbəl] *adj* **:** irreprochable, intachable

irresistible [,ɪrɪ'zɪstəbəl] *adj* **:** irresistible — **irresistibly** [-bli] *adv*

irresolute [ɪ'rɛzə,luːt] *adj* **:** irresoluto, indeciso

irresolutely [ɪ'rɛzə,luːtli, -,rɛzə'luːt-] *adv* **:** de manera indecisa

irresolution [ɪ,rɛzə'luːʃən] *n* **:** irresolución *f*

irrespective of [ˌɪrɪˈspɛktɪvəv] *prep* : sin tomar en consideración, sin tener en cuenta
irresponsibility [ˌɪrɪˌspɑntsəˈbɪləṭi] *n, pl* **-ties** : irresponsabilidad *f,* falta *f* de responsabilidad
irresponsible [ˌɪrɪˈspɑntsəbəl] *adj* : irresponsable — **irresponsibly** [-bli] *adv*
irretrievable [ˌɪrɪˈtriːvəbəl] *adj* IRRECOVERABLE : irrecuperable
irreverence [ɪˈrɛvərənts] *n* : irreverencia *f,* falta *f* de respeto
irreverent [ɪˈrɛvərənt] *adj* : irreverente, irrespetuoso
irreversible [ˌɪrɪˈvərsəbəl] *adj* : irreversible
irrevocable [ɪˈrɛvəkəbəl] *adj* : irrevocable — **irrevocably** [-bli] *adv*
irrigate [ˈɪrəˌgeɪt] *vt* **-gated; -gating** : irrigar, regar
irrigation [ˌɪrəˈgeɪʃən] *n* : irrigación *f,* riego *m*
irritability [ˌɪrəṭəˈbɪləṭi] *n, pl* **-ties** : irritabilidad *f*
irritable [ˈɪrəṭəbəl] *adj* : irritable, colérico
irritably [ˈɪrəṭəbli] *adv* : con irritación
irritant[1] [ˈɪrəṭənt] *adj* : irritante
irritant[2] *n* : agente *m* irritante
irritate [ˈɪrəˌteɪt] *vt* **-tated; -tating 1** ANNOY : irritar, molestar **2** : irritar (en medicina)
irritating [ˈɪrəˌteɪṭɪŋ] *adj* : irritante
irritatingly [ˈɪrəˌteɪṭɪŋli] *adv* : de modo irritante, fastidiosamente
irritation [ˌɪrəˈteɪʃən] *n* : irritación *f*
is → **be**
Islam [ɪsˈlɑm, ɪz-, -ˈlæm; ˈɪsˌlɑm, ˈɪz-, -ˌlæm] *n* : el Islam
Islamic [ɪsˈlɑmɪk, ɪz-, -ˈlæ-] *adj* : islámico
island [ˈaɪlənd] *n* : isla *f*
islander [ˈaɪləndər] *n* : isleño *m,* -ña *f*
isle [ˈaɪl] *n* : isla *f,* islote *m*
islet [ˈaɪlət] *n* : islote *m*
isolate [ˈaɪsəˌleɪt] *vt* **-lated; -lating** : aislar
isolated [ˈaɪsəˌleɪṭəd] *adj* : aislado, solo
isolation [ˌaɪsəˈleɪʃən] *n* : aislamiento *m*
isometric [ˌaɪsəˈmɛtrɪk] *adj* : isométrico
isometrics [ˌaɪsəˈmɛtrɪks] *ns & pl* : isometría *f*
isosceles [aɪˈsɑsəˌliːz] *adj* : isósceles
isotope [ˈaɪsəˌtoːp] *n* : isótopo *m*
Israeli [ɪzˈreɪli] *n* : israelí *mf* — **Israeli** *adj*
issue[1] [ˈɪˌʃuː] *v* **-sued; -suing** *vi* **1** EMERGE : emerger, salir, fluir **2** DESCEND : descender (dícese de los padres o antepasados específicos) **3** EMANATE, RESULT : emanar, surgir, resultar — *vt* **1** EMIT : emitir **2** DISTRIBUTE : emitir, distribuir <to issue a new stamp : emitir un sello nuevo> **3** PUBLISH : publicar
issue[2] *n* **1** EMERGENCE, FLOW : emergencia *f,* flujo *m* **2** PROGENY : descendencia *f,* progenie *f* **3** OUTCOME, RESULT : desenlace *m,* resultado *m,* consecuencia *f* **4** MATTER, QUESTION : asunto *m,* cuestión *f* **5** PUBLICATION : publicación *f,* distribución *f,* emisión *f* **6** : número *m* (de un periódico o una revista)
isthmus [ˈɪsməs] *n* : istmo *m*
it [ˈɪt] *pron* **1** (*as subject; generally omitted*) : él, ella, ello <it's a big building : es un edificio grande> <who was it? : ¿quién era?> **2** (*as indirect object*) : le <I'll give it some water : voy a darle agua> **3** (*as direct object*) : lo, la <give it to me : dámelo> **4** (*as object of a preposition; generally omitted*) : él, ella, ello <behind it : detrás, detrás de él> **5** (*in impersonal constructions*) <it's raining : está lloviendo> <it's 8 o'clock : son las ocho> **6** (*as the implied subject or object of a verb*) <it is necessary to study : es necesario estudiar> <to give it all one's got : dar lo mejor de sí>
Italian [ɪˈtæliən, aɪ-] *n* **1** : italiano *m,* -na *f* **2** : italiano *m* (idioma) — **Italian** *adj*
italic[1] [ɪˈtælɪk, aɪ-] *adj* : en cursiva, en bastardilla
italic[2] *n* : cursiva *f,* bastardilla *f*
italicize [ɪˈtæləˌsaɪz, aɪ-] *vt* **-cized; -cizing** : poner en cursiva
itch[1] [ˈɪtʃ] *vi* **1** : picar <her arm itched : le pica el brazo> **2** : morirse <they were itching to go outside : se morían por salir> — *vt* : dar picazón, hacer picar
itch[2] *n* **1** ITCHING : picazón *f,* picor *m,* comezón *f* **2** RASH : sarpullido *m,* erupción *f* **3** DESIRE : ansia *f,* deseo *m*
itchy [ˈɪtʃi] *adj* **itchier; -est** : que pica, que da comezón
it'd [ˈɪṭəd] (*contraction of* **it had** *or* **it would**) → **have, would**
item [ˈaɪṭəm] *n* **1** OBJECT : artículo *m,* pieza *f* <item of clothing : prenda de vestir> **2** : punto *m* (en una agenda), número *m* (en el teatro), ítem *m* (en un documento) **3 news item** : noticia *f*
itemize [ˈaɪṭəˌmaɪz] *vt* **-ized; -izing** : detallar, enumerar, listar
itinerant [aɪˈtɪnərənt] *adj* : itinerante, ambulante
itinerary [aɪˈtɪnəˌrɛri] *n, pl* **-aries** : itinerario *m*
it'll [ˈɪṭəl] (*contraction of* **it shall** *or* **it will**) → **shall, will**
its [ˈɪts] *adj* : su, sus <its kennel : su perrera> <a city and its inhabitants : una ciudad y sus habitantes>
it's [ˈɪts] (*contraction of* **it is** *or* **it has**) → **be, have**
itself [ɪtˈsɛlf] *pron* **1** (*used reflexively*) : se <the cat gave itself a bath : el gato se bañó> **2** (*used for emphasis*) : (él) mismo, (ella) misma, sí (mismo), solo <he is courtesy itself : es la misma cortesía> <in and of itself : por sí

mismo> <it opened by itself : se abrió solo>
I've ['aɪv] (*contraction of* **I have**) → **have**
ivory ['aɪvəri] *n, pl* **-ries 1 :** marfil *m* **2 :** color *m* de marfil
ivy ['aɪvi] *n, pl* **ivies 1 :** hiedra *f,* yedra *f* **2** → **poison ivy**

J

j ['dʒeɪ] *n, pl* **j's** *or* **js** ['dʒeɪz] **:** décima letra del alfabeto inglés
jab[1] ['dʒæb] *v* **jabbed; jabbing** *vt* **1** PUNCTURE **:** clavar, pinchar **2** POKE **:** dar, golpear (con la punta de algo) <he jabbed me in the ribs : me dio un codazo en las costillas> — *vi* **to jab at :** dar, golpear
jab[2] *n* **1** PRICK **:** pinchazo *m* **2** POKE **:** golpe *m* abrupto
jabber[1] ['dʒæbər] *v* **:** farfullar
jabber[2] *n* **:** galimatías *m,* farfulla *f*
jack[1] ['dʒæk] *vt* **to jack up 1 :** levantar (con un gato) **2** INCREASE **:** subir, aumentar
jack[2] *n* **1 :** gato *m,* cric *m* <hydraulic jack : gato hidráulico> **2** FLAG **:** pabellón *m* **3** SOCKET **:** enchufe *m* hembra **4 :** jota *f,* valet *m* <jack of hearts : jota de corazones> **5 jacks** *npl* **:** cantillos *mpl*
jackal ['dʒækəl] *n* **:** chacal *m*
jackass ['dʒæk,æs] *n* **:** asno *m,* burro *m*
jacket ['dʒækət] *n* **1 :** chaqueta *f* **2** COVER **:** sobrecubierta *f* (de un libro), carátula *f* (de un disco)
jackhammer ['dʒæk,hæmər] *n* **:** martillo *m* neumático
jack-in-the-box ['dʒækɪnðə,bɑks] *n* **:** caja *f* de sorpresa
jackknife[1] ['dʒæk,naɪf] *vi* **-knifed; -knifing :** doblarse como una navaja, plegarse
jackknife[2] *n* **:** navaja *f*
jack-of-all-trades *n* **:** persona *f* que sabe un poco de todo, persona *f* de muchos oficios
jack-o'-lantern ['dʒækə,læntərn] *n* **:** linterna *f* hecha de una calabaza
jackpot ['dʒæk,pɑt] *n* **1 :** primer premio *m,* gordo *m* **2 to hit the jackpot :** sacarse la lotería, sacarse el gordo
jackrabbit ['dʒæk,ræbət] *n* **:** liebre *f* grande de Norteamérica
jade ['dʒeɪd] *n* **:** jade *m*
jaded ['dʒeɪdəd] *adj* **1** TIRED **:** agotado **2** BORED **:** hastiado
jagged ['dʒægəd] *adj* **:** dentado, mellado
jaguar ['dʒæg,wɑr, 'dʒægjʊ,wɑr] *n* **:** jaguar *m*
jai alai ['haɪ,laɪ] *n* **:** jai alai *m,* pelota *f* vasca
jail[1] ['dʒeɪl] *vt* **:** encarcelar
jail[2] *n* **:** cárcel *f*
jailbreak ['dʒeɪl,breɪk] *n* **:** fuga *f,* huida *f* (de la cárcel)
jailer *or* **jailor** ['dʒeɪlər] *n* **:** carcelero *m,* -ra *f*
jalapeño [,hɑlə'peɪnjo, ,hæ-, -'pi:no] *n* **:** jalapeño *m*
jalopy [dʒə'lɑpi] *n, pl* **-lopies :** cacharro *m fam,* carro *m* destartalado
jalousie ['dʒæləsi] *n* **:** celosía *f*
jam[1] ['dʒæm] *v* **jammed; jamming** *vt* **1** CRAM **:** apiñar, embutir **2** BLOCK **:** atascar, atorar **3 to jam on the brakes :** frenar en seco — *vi* STICK **:** atascarse, atrancarse
jam[2] *n* **1** *or* **traffic jam :** atasco *m,* embotellamiento *m* (de tráfico) **2** PREDICAMENT **:** lío *m,* aprieto *m,* apuro *m* **3 :** mermelada *f* <strawberry jam : mermelada de fresa>
jamb ['dʒæm] *n* **:** jamba *f*
jamboree [,dʒæmbə'ri:] *n* **:** fiesta *f* grande
jangle[1] ['dʒæŋgəl] *v* **-gled; -gling** *vi* **:** hacer un ruido metálico — *vt* **1 :** hacer sonar **2 to jangle one's nerves :** irritar, crispar
jangle[2] *n* **:** ruido *m* metálico
janitor ['dʒænətər] *n* **:** portero *m,* -ra *f;* conserje *mf*
January ['dʒænjʊ,ɛri] *n* **:** enero *m*
Japanese [,dʒæpə'ni:z, -'ni:s] *n* **1 :** japonés *m,* -nesa *f* **2 :** japonés *m* (idioma) — **Japanese** *adj*
jar[1] ['dʒɑr] *v* **jarred; jarring** *vi* **1** GRATE **:** chirriar **2** CLASH **:** desentonar **3** SHAKE **:** sacudirse **4 to jar on :** crispar, enervar — *vt* JOLT **:** sacudir
jar[2] *n* **1** GRATING **:** chirrido *m* **2** JOLT **:** vibración *f,* sacudida *f* **3 :** tarro *m,* bote *m,* pote *m* <a jar of honey : un tarro de miel>
jargon ['dʒɑrgən] *n* **:** jerga *f*
jasmine ['dʒæzmən] *n* **:** jazmín *m*
jasper ['dʒæspər] *n* **:** jaspe *m*
jaundice ['dʒɔndɪs] *n* **:** ictericia *f*
jaundiced ['dʒɔndɪst] *adj* **1 :** ictérico **2** EMBITTERED, RESENTFUL **:** amargado, resentido, negativo <with a jaundiced eye : con una actitud de cinismo>
jaunt ['dʒɔnt] *n* **:** excursión *f,* paseo *m*
jauntily ['dʒɔntəli] *adv* **:** animadamente
jauntiness ['dʒɔntinəs] *n* **:** animación *f,* vivacidad *f*
jaunty ['dʒɔnti] *adj* **-tier; -est 1** SPRIGHTLY **:** animado, alegre **2** RAKISH **:** desenvuelto, desenfadado
javelin ['dʒævələn] *n* **:** jabalina *f*
jaw[1] ['dʒɔ] *vi* GAB **:** cotorrear *fam,* parlotear *fam*
jaw[2] *n* **1 :** mandíbula *f,* quijada *f* **2 :** mordaza *f* (de una herramienta) **3 the jaws of death :** las garras *f* de la muerte

jawbone [ˈdʒɔˌboːn] *n* **:** mandíbula *f*
jay [ˈdʒeɪ] *n* **:** arrendajo *m,* chara *f Mex,* azulejo *m Mex*
jaybird [ˈdʒeɪˌbərd] → **jay**
jaywalk [ˈdʒeɪˌwɔk] *vi* **:** cruzar la calle sin prudencia
jaywalker [ˈdʒeɪˌwɔkər] *n* **:** peatón *m* imprudente
jazz[1] [ˈdʒæz] *vt* **to jazz up :** animar, alegrar
jazz[2] *n* **:** jazz *m*
jazzy [ˈdʒæzi] *adj* **jazzier; -est 1 :** con ritmo de jazz **2** FLASHY, SHOWY **:** llamativo, ostentoso
jealous [ˈdʒɛləs] *adj* **:** celoso, envidioso — **jealously** *adv*
jealousy [ˈdʒɛləsi] *n* **:** celos *mpl,* envidia *f*
jeans [ˈdʒiːnz] *npl* **:** jeans *mpl,* vaqueros *mpl*
jeep [ˈdʒiːp] *n* **:** jeep *m*
jeer[1] [ˈdʒɪr] *vi* **1** BOO **:** abuchear **2** SCOFF **:** mofarse, burlarse — *vt* RIDICULE **:** mofarse de, burlarse de
jeer[2] *n* **1 :** abucheo *m* **2** TAUNT **:** mofa *f,* burla *f*
Jehovah [dʒɪˈhoːvə] *n* **:** Jehová *m*
jell [ˈdʒɛl] *vi* **1** SET **:** gelificarse, cuajar **2** FORM **:** cuajar, formarse (una idea, etc.)
jelly[1] [ˈdʒɛli] *v* **jellied; jellying** *vi* **1** JELL **:** gelificarse, cuajar **2 :** hacer jalea — *vt* **:** gelificar
jelly[2] *n, pl* **-lies 1 :** jalea *f* **2** GELATIN **:** gelatina *f*
jellyfish [ˈdʒɛliˌfɪʃ] *n* **:** medusa *f*
jeopardize [ˈdʒɛpərˌdaɪz] *vt* **-dized; -dizing :** arriesgar, poner en peligro
jeopardy [ˈdʒɛpərdi] *n* **:** peligro *m,* riesgo *m*
jerk[1] [ˈdʒərk] *vt* **1** JOLT **:** sacudir **2** TUG, YANK **:** darle un tirón a — *vi* JOLT **:** dar sacudidas <the train jerked along : el tren iba moviéndose a sacudidas>
jerk[2] *n* **1** TUG **:** tirón *m,* jalón *m* **2** JOLT **:** sacudida *f* brusca **3** FOOL **:** estúpido *m,* -da *f;* idiota *mf*
jerkin [ˈdʒərkən] *n* **:** chaqueta *f* sin mangas, chaleco *m*
jerky [ˈdʒərki] *adj* **jerkier; -est 1 :** espasmódico (dícese de los movimientos) **2** CHOPPY **:** inconexo (dícese de la prosa) — **jerkily** [-kəli] *adv*
jerry–built [ˈdʒɛriˌbɪlt] *adj* **:** mal construido, chapucero
jersey [ˈdʒərzi] *n, pl* **-seys :** jersey *m*
jest[1] [ˈdʒɛst] *vi* **:** bromear
jest[2] *n* **:** broma *f,* chiste *m*
jester [ˈdʒɛstər] *n* **:** bufón *m,* -fona *f*
Jesus [ˈdʒiːzəs, -zəz] *n* **:** Jesús *m*
jet[1] [ˈdʒɛt] *v* **jetted; jetting** *vt* SPOUT **:** arrojar a chorros — *vi* **1** GUSH **:** salir a chorros, chorrear **2** FLY **:** viajar en avión, volar
jet[2] *n* **1** STREAM **:** chorro *m* **2** *or* **jet airplane :** avión *m* a reacción, reactor *m* **3 :** azabache *m* (mineral) **4 jet engine :** reactor *m,* motor *m* a reacción **5 jet lag :** desajuste *m* de horario (debido a un vuelo largo)
jet–propelled *adj* **:** a reacción
jetsam [ˈdʒɛtsəm] *n* **flotsam and jetsam :** restos *mpl,* desechos *mpl*
jettison [ˈdʒɛtəsən] *vt* **1 :** echar al mar **2** DISCARD **:** desechar, deshacerse de
jetty [ˈdʒɛti] *n, pl* **-ties 1** PIER, WHARF **:** desembarcadero *m,* muelle *m* **2** BREAKWATER **:** malecón *m,* rompeolas *m*
Jew [ˈdʒuː] *n* **:** judío *m,* -día *f*
jewel [ˈdʒuːəl] *n* **1 :** joya *f,* alhaja *f* **2** GEM **:** piedra *f* preciosa, gema *f* **3 :** rubí *m* (de un reloj) **4** TREASURE **:** joya *f,* tesoro *m*
jeweler *or* **jeweller** [ˈdʒuːələr] *n* **:** joyero *m,* -ra *f*
jewelry [ˈdʒuːəlri] *n* **:** joyas *fpl,* alhajas *fpl*
Jewish [ˈdʒuːɪʃ] *adj* **:** judío
jib [ˈdʒɪb] *n* **:** foque *m* (de un barco)
jibe [ˈdʒaɪb] *vi* **jibed; jibing** AGREE **:** concordar
jiffy [ˈdʒɪfi] *n, pl* **-fies :** santiamén *m,* segundo *m,* momento *m*
jig[1] [ˈdʒɪg] *vi* **jigged; jigging :** bailar la giga
jig[2] *n* **1 :** giga *f* **2 the jig is up :** se acabó la fiesta
jigger [ˈdʒɪgər] *n* **:** medida de 1 a 2 onzas (para licores)
jiggle[1] [ˈdʒɪgəl] *v* **-gled; -gling** *vt* **:** agitar o sacudir ligeramente — *vi* **:** agitarse, vibrar
jiggle[2] *n* **:** sacudida *f,* vibración *f*
jigsaw [ˈdʒɪgˌsɔ] *n* **1 :** sierra *f* de vaivén **2 jigsaw puzzle :** rompecabezas *m*
jilt [ˈdʒɪlt] *vt* **:** dejar plantado, dar calabazas a
jimmy[1] [ˈdʒɪmi] *vt* **-mied; -mying :** forzar con una palanqueta
jimmy[2] *n, pl* **-mies :** palanqueta *f*
jingle[1] [ˈdʒɪŋgəl] *v* **-gled; -gling** *vi* **:** tintinear — *vt* **:** hacer sonar
jingle[2] *n* **1** TINKLE **:** tintineo *m,* retintín *m* **2 :** canción *f* rimada
jingoism [ˈdʒɪŋgoˌɪzəm] *n* **:** jingoísmo *m,* patriotería *f*
jingoistic [ˌdʒɪŋgoˈɪstɪk] *or* **jingoist** [ˈdʒɪŋgoɪst] *adj* **:** jingoísta, patriotero
jinx[1] [ˈdʒɪŋks] *vt* **:** traer mala suerte a, salar *CoRi, Mex*
jinx[2] *n* **1 :** cenizo *m,* -za *f* **2 to put a jinx on :** echarle el mal de ojo a
jitters [ˈdʒɪtərz] *npl* **:** nervios *mpl* <he got the jitters : se puso nervioso>
jittery [ˈdʒɪtəri] *adj* **:** nervioso
job [ˈdʒɑb] *n* **1 :** trabajo *m* <he did odd jobs for her : le hizo algunos trabajos> **2** CHORE, TASK **:** tarea *f,* quehacer *m* **3** EMPLOYMENT **:** trabajo *m,* empleo *m,* puesto *m*
jobber [ˈdʒɑbər] *n* MIDDLEMAN **:** intermediario *m,* -ria *f*
jockey[1] [ˈdʒɑki] *v* **-eyed; -eying** *vt* **1** MANIPULATE **:** manipular **2** MANEUVER

: maniobrar — *vi* **to jockey for position :** maniobrar para conseguir algo

jockey[2] *n, pl* **-eys :** jockey *mf*

jocose [dʒoˈkoːs] *adj* **:** jocoso

jocular [ˈdʒɑkjʊlər] *adj* **:** jocoso — **jocularly** *adv*

jocularity [ˌdʒɑkjʊˈlærəṱi] *n* **:** jocosidad *f*

jodhpurs [ˈdʒɑdpərz] *npl* **:** pantalones *mpl* de montar

jog[1] [ˈdʒɑg] *v* **jogged; jogging** *vt* **1** NUDGE **:** dar, empujar, codear **2 to jog one's memory :** refrescar la memoria — *vi* **1** RUN **:** correr despacio, trotar, hacer footing (como ejercicio) **2** TRUDGE **:** andar a trote corto

jog[2] *n* **1** PUSH, SHAKE **:** empujoncito *m,* sacudida *f* leve **2** TROT **:** trote *m* corto, footing *m* (en deportes) **3** TWIST **:** recodo *m,* vuelta *f,* curva *f*

jogger [ˈdʒɑgər] *n* **:** persona *f* que hace footing

join [ˈdʒɔɪn] *vt* **1** CONNECT, LINK **:** unir, juntar <to join in marriage : unir en matrimonio> **2** ADJOIN **:** lindar con, colindar con **3** MEET **:** reunirse con, encontrarse con <we joined them for lunch : nos reunimos con ellos para almorzar> **4 :** hacerse socio de (una organización), afiliarse a (un partido), entrar en (una empresa) — *vi* **1** UNITE **:** unirse **2** MERGE **:** empalmar (dícese de las carreteras), confluir (dícese de los ríos) **3 to join up :** hacerse socio, enrolarse

joiner [ˈdʒɔɪnər] *n* **1** CARPENTER **:** carpintero *m,* -ra *f* **2 :** persona *f* que se une a varios grupos

joint[1] [ˈdʒɔɪnt] *adj* **:** conjunto, colectivo, mutuo <a joint effort : un esfuerzo conjunto> — **jointly** *adv*

joint[2] *n* **1 :** articulación *f,* coyuntura *f* <out of joint : dislocado> **2** ROAST **:** asado *m* **3** JUNCTURE **:** juntura *f,* unión *f* **4** DIVE **:** antro *m,* tasca *f*

joist [ˈdʒɔɪst] *n* **:** viga *f*

joke[1] [ˈdʒoːk] *vi* **joked; joking :** bromear

joke[2] *n* **1** STORY **:** chiste *m* **2** PRANK **:** broma *f*

joker [ˈdʒoːkər] *n* **1** PRANKSTER **:** bromista *mf* **2 :** comodín *m* (en los naipes)

jokingly [ˈdʒoːkɪŋli] *adv* **:** en broma

jollity [ˈdʒɑləṱi] *n, pl* **-ties** MERRIMENT **:** alegría *f,* regocijo *m*

jolly [ˈdʒɑli] *adj* **-lier; -est :** alegre, jovial

jolt[1] [ˈdʒoːlt] *vi* JERK **:** dar tumbos, dar sacudidas — *vt* **:** sacudir

jolt[2] *n* **1** JERK **:** sacudida *f* brusca **2** SHOCK **:** golpe *m* (emocional)

jonquil [ˈdʒɑnkwɪl] *n* **:** junquillo *m*

Jordanian [dʒɔrˈdeɪniən] *n* **:** jordano *m,* -na *f* — **Jordanian** *adj*

josh [ˈdʒɑʃ] *vt* TEASE **:** tomarle el pelo (a alguien) — *vi* JOKE **:** bromear

jostle [ˈdʒɑsəl] *v* **-tled; -tling** *vi* **1** SHOVE **:** empujar, dar empellones **2** CONTEND **:** competir — *vt* **1** SHOVE **:** empujar **2 to jostle one's way :** abrirse paso a empellones

jot[1] [ˈdʒɑt] *vt* **jotted; jotting :** anotar, apuntar <jot it down : apúntalo>

jot[2] *n* BIT **:** ápice *m,* jota *f,* pizca *f*

jounce[1] [ˈdʒæʊnts] *v* **jounced; jouncing** *vt* JOLT **:** sacudir — *vi* **:** dar tumbos, dar sacudidas

jounce[2] *n* JOLT **:** sacudida *f,* tumbo *m*

journal [ˈdʒərnəl] *n* **1** DIARY **:** diario *m* **2** PERIODICAL **:** revista *f,* publicación *f* periódica **3** NEWSPAPER **:** periódico *m,* diario *m*

journalism [ˈdʒərnəlˌɪzəm] *n* **:** periodismo *m*

journalist [ˈdʒərnəlɪst] *n* **:** periodista *mf*

journalistic [ˌdʒərnəlˈɪstɪk] *adj* **:** periodístico

journey[1] [ˈdʒərni] *vi* **-neyed; -neying :** viajar

journey[2] *n, pl* **-neys :** viaje *m*

journeyman [ˈdʒərnimən] *n, pl* **-men** [-mən, -ˌmɛn] **:** oficial *m*

joust[1] [ˈdʒæʊst] *vi* **:** justar

joust[2] *n* **:** justa *f*

jovial [ˈdʒoːviəl] *adj* **:** jovial — **jovially** *adv*

joviality [ˌdʒoːviˈæləṱi] *n* **:** jovialidad *f*

jowl [ˈdʒæʊl] *n* **1** JAW **:** mandíbula *f* **2** CHEEK **:** mejilla *f,* cachete *m*

joy [ˈdʒɔɪ] *n* **1** HAPPINESS **:** gozo *m,* alegría *f,* felicidad *f* **2** DELIGHT **:** placer *m,* deleite *m* <the child is a real joy : el niño es un verdadero placer>

joyful [ˈdʒɔɪfəl] *adj* **:** gozoso, alegre, feliz — **joyfully** *adv*

joyless [ˈdʒɔɪləs] *adj* **:** sin alegría, triste

joyous [ˈdʒɔɪəs] *adj* **:** alegre, feliz, eufórico — **joyously** *adv*

joyousness [ˈdʒɔɪəsnəs] *n* **:** alegría *f,* felicidad *f,* euforia *f*

joyride [ˈdʒɔɪˌraɪd] *n* **:** paseo *m* temerario e irresponsable (en coche)

jubilant [ˈdʒuːbələnt] *adj* **:** jubiloso, alborozado — **jubilantly** *adv*

jubilation [ˌdʒuːbəˈleɪʃən] *n* **:** júbilo *m*

jubilee [ˈdʒuːbəˌliː] *n* **1 :** quincuagésimo aniversario *m* **2** CELEBRATION **:** celebración *f,* festejos *mpl*

Judaic [dʒʊˈdeɪɪk] *adj* **:** judaico

Judaism [ˈdʒuːdəˌɪzəm, ˈdʒuːdi-, ˈdʒuːˌdeɪ-] *n* **:** judaísmo *m*

judge[1] [ˈdʒʌdʒ] *vt* **judged; judging 1** ASSESS **:** evaluar, juzgar **2** DEEM **:** juzgar, considerar **3** TRY **:** juzgar (ante el tribuno) **4 judging by :** a juzgar por

judge[2] *n* **1 :** juez *mf,* jueza *f* **2 to be a good judge of :** saber juzgar a, entender mucho de

judgment *or* **judgement** [ˈdʒʌdʒmənt] *n* **1** RULING **:** fallo *m,* sentencia *f* **2** OPINION **:** opinión *f* **3** DISCERNMENT **:** juicio *m,* discernimiento *m*

judgmental [ˌdʒʌdʒˈmɛnṱəl] *adj* **:** crítico — **judgmentally** *adv*

judicature [ˈdʒuːdɪkəˌtʃʊr] *n* : judicatura *f*

judicial [dʒʊˈdɪʃəl] *adj* : judicial — **judicially** *adv*

judiciary[1] [dʒʊˈdɪʃiˌɛri, -ˈdɪʃəri] *adj* : judicial

judiciary[2] *n* **1** JUDICATURE : judicatura *f* **2** : poder *m* judicial

judicious [dʒʊˈdɪʃəs] *adj* SOUND, WISE : juicioso, sensato — **judiciously** *adv*

judo [ˈdʒuːˌdoː] *n* : judo *m*

jug [ˈdʒʌg] *n* **1** : jarra *f,* jarro *m,* cántaro *m* **2** JAIL : cárcel *f,* chirona *f fam*

juggernaut [ˈdʒʌgərˌnɔt] *n* : gigante *m,* fuerza *f* irresistible <a political juggernaut : un gigante político>

juggle [ˈdʒʌgəl] *v* **-gled; -gling** *vt* **1** : hacer juegos malabares con **2** MANIPULATE : manipular, jugar con — *vi* : hacer juegos malabares

juggler [ˈdʒʌgələr] *n* : malabarista *mf*

jugular [ˈdʒʌgjʊlər] *adj* : yugular <jugular vein : vena yugular>

juice [ˈdʒuːs] *n* **1** : jugo *m* (de carne, de frutas) *m,* zumo *m* (de frutas) **2** ELECTRICITY : electricidad *f,* luz *f*

juicer [ˈdʒuːsər] *n* : exprimidor *m*

juiciness [ˈdʒuːsinəs] *n* : jugosidad *f*

juicy [ˈdʒuːsi] *adj* **juicier; -est 1** SUCCULENT : jugoso, suculento **2** PROFITABLE : jugoso, lucrativo **3** RACY : picante

jukebox [ˈdʒuːkˌbɑks] *n* : rocola *f,* máquina *f* de discos

julep [ˈdʒuːləp] *n* : bebida *f* hecha con whisky americano y menta

July [dʒʊˈlaɪ] *n* : julio *m*

jumble[1] [ˈdʒʌmbəl] *vt* **-bled; -bling** : mezclar, revolver

jumble[2] *n* : revoltijo *m,* fárrago *m,* embrollo *m*

jumbo[1] [ˈdʒʌmˌboː] *adj* : gigante, enorme, de tamaño extra grande

jumbo[2] *n, pl* **-bos** : coloso *m,* cosa *f* de tamaño extra grande

jump[1] [ˈdʒʌmp] *vi* **1** LEAP : saltar, brincar **2** START : levantarse de un salto, sobresaltarse **3** MOVE, SHIFT : moverse, pasar <to jump from job to job : pasar de un empleo a otro> **4** INCREASE, RISE : dar un salto, aumentarse de golpe, subir bruscamente **5** BUSTLE : animarse, ajetrearse **6 to jump to conclusions** : sacar conclusiones precipitadas — *vt* **1** : saltar <to jump a fence : saltar una valla> **2** SKIP : saltarse **3** ATTACK : atacar, asaltar **4 to jump the gun** : precipitarse

jump[2] *n* **1** LEAP : salto *m* **2** START : sobresalto *m,* respingo *m* **3** INCREASE : subida *f* brusca, aumento *m* **4** ADVANTAGE : ventaja *f* <we got the jump on them : les llevamos la ventaja>

jumper [ˈdʒʌmpər] *n* **1** : saltador *m,* -dora *f* (en deportes) **2** : jumper *m,* vestido *m* sin mangas

jumpy [ˈdʒʌmpi] *adj* **jumpier; -est** : asustadizo, nervioso

junction [ˈdʒʌŋkʃən] *n* **1** JOINING : unión *f* **2** : cruce *m* (de calles), empalme *m* (de un ferrocarril), confluencia *f* (de ríos)

juncture [ˈdʒʌŋktʃər] *n* **1** UNION : juntura *f,* unión *f* **2** MOMENT, POINT : coyuntura *f* <at this juncture : en esta coyuntura, en este momento>

June [ˈdʒuːn] *n* : junio *m*

jungle [ˈdʒʌŋgəl] *n* : jungla *f,* selva *f*

junior[1] [ˈdʒuːnjər] *adj* **1** YOUNGER : más joven <John Smith, Junior : John Smith, hijo> **2** SUBORDINATE : subordinado, subalterno

junior[2] *n* **1** : persona *f* de menor edad <she's my junior : es menor que yo> **2** SUBORDINATE : subalterno *m,* -na *f;* subordinado *m,* -da *f* **3** : estudiante *mf* de penúltimo año

juniper [ˈdʒuːnəpər] *n* : enebro *m*

junk[1] [ˈdʒʌŋk] *vt* : echar a la basura

junk[2] *n* **1** RUBBISH : desechos *mpl,* desperdicios *mpl* **2** STUFF : trastos *mpl fam,* cachivaches *mpl fam* **3 piece of junk** : cacharro *m,* porquería *f*

junket [ˈdʒʌŋkət] *n* : viaje *m* (pagado con dinero público)

junta [ˈhʊntə, ˈdʒʌn-, ˈhʌn-] *n* : junta *f* militar

Jupiter [ˈdʒuːpətər] *n* : Júpiter *m*

jurisdiction [ˌdʒʊrəsˈdɪkʃən] *n* : jurisdicción *f*

jurisprudence [ˌdʒʊrəsˈpruːdən*t*s] *n* : jurisprudencia *f*

jurist [ˈdʒʊrɪst] *n* : jurista *mf;* magistrado *m,* -da *f*

juror [ˈdʒʊrər] *n* : jurado *m,* -da *f*

jury [ˈdʒʊri] *n, pl* **-ries** : jurado *m*

just[1] [ˈdʒʌst] *adv* **1** EXACTLY : justo, precisamente, exactamente **2** POSSIBLY : posiblemente <it just might work : tal vez resulte> **3** BARELY : justo, apenas <just in time : justo a tiempo> **4** ONLY : sólo, solamente, nada más <just us : sólo nosotros> **5** QUITE : muy, simplemente <it's just horrible! : ¡qué horrible!> **6 to have just (done something)** : acabar de (hacer algo) <he just called : acaba de llamar>

just[2] *adj* : justo — **justly** *adv*

justice [ˈdʒʌstɪs] *n* **1** : justicia *f* **2** JUDGE : juez *mf,* jueza *f*

justification [ˌdʒʌstəfəˈkeɪʃən] *n* : justificación *f*

justify [ˈdʒʌstəˌfaɪ] *vt* **-fied; -fying** : justificar — **justifiable** [ˌdʒʌstəˈfaɪəbəl] *adj*

jut [ˈdʒʌt] *vi* **jutted; jutting** : sobresalir

jute [ˈdʒuːt] *n* : yute *m*

juvenile[1] [ˈdʒuːvəˌnaɪl, -vənəl] *adj* **1** : juvenil <juvenile delinquent : delincuente juvenil> <juvenile court : tribunal de menores> **2** CHILDISH : infantil

juvenile[2] *n* : menor *mf*

juxtapose [ˈdʒʌkstəˌpoːz] *vt* **-posed; -posing** : yuxtaponer

juxtaposition [ˌdʒʌkstəpəˈzɪʃən] *n* : yuxtaposición *f*

K

k [ˈkeɪ] *n, pl* **k's** *or* **ks** [ˈkeɪz] : undécima letra del alfabeto inglés
kaiser [ˈkaɪzər] *n* : káiser *m*
kale [ˈkeɪl] *n* : col *f* rizada
kaleidoscope [kəˈlaɪdəˌskoːp] *n* : calidoscopio *m*
kangaroo [ˌkæŋgəˈruː] *n, pl* **-roos** : canguro *m*
kaolin [ˈkeɪələn] *n* : caolín *m*
karat [ˈkærət] *n* : quilate *m*
karate [kəˈrɑti] *n* : karate *m*
katydid [ˈkeɪt̬iˌdɪd] *n* : saltamontes *m*
kayak [ˈkaɪˌæk] *n* : kayac *m,* kayak *m*
keel[1] [ˈkiːl] *vi* **to keel over** : volcar (dícese de un barco), desplomarse (dícese de una persona)
keel[2] *n* : quilla *f*
keen [ˈkiːn] *adj* **1** SHARP : afilado, filoso <a keen blade : una hoja afilada> **2** PENETRATING : cortante, penetrante <a keen wind : un viento cortante> **3** ENTHUSIASTIC : entusiasta **4** ACUTE : agudo, fino <keen hearing : oído fino> <keen intelligence : inteligencia aguda>
keenly [ˈkiːnli] *adv* **1** ENTHUSIASTICALLY : con entusiasmo **2** INTENSELY : vivamente, profundamente <keenly aware of : muy consciente de>
keenness [ˈkiːnnəs] *n* **1** SHARPNESS : lo afilado, lo filoso **2** ENTHUSIASM : entusiasmo *m* **3** ACUTENESS : agudeza *f*
keep[1] [ˈkiːp] *v* **kept** [ˈkɛpt]; **keeping** *vt* **1** : cumplir (la palabra a uno), acudir a (una cita) **2** OBSERVE : observar (una fiesta) **3** GUARD : guardar, cuidar **4** CONTINUE : mantener <to keep silence : mantener silencio> **5** SUPPORT : mantener (una familia) **6** RAISE : criar (animales) **7** : llevar, escribir (un diario, etc.) **8** RETAIN : guardar, conservar, quedarse con **9** STORE : guardar **10** DETAIN : hacer quedar, detener **11** PRESERVE : guardar <to keep a secret : guardar un secreto> — *vi* **1** : conservarse (dícese de los alimentos) **2** CONTINUE : seguir, no dejar <he keeps on pestering us : no deja de molestarnos> **3 to keep from** : abstenerse de <I couldn't keep from laughing : no podía contener la risa>
keep[2] *n* **1** TOWER : torreón *m* (de un castillo), torre *f* del homenaje **2** SUSTENANCE : manutención *f,* sustento *m* **3 for keeps** : para siempre
keeper [ˈkiːpər] *n* **1** : guarda *mf* (en un zoológico); conservador *m,* -dora *f* (en un museo) **2** GAMEKEEPER : guardabosque *mf*
keeping [ˈkiːpɪŋ] *n* **1** CONFORMITY : conformidad *f,* acuerdo *m* <in keeping with : de acuerdo con> **2** CARE : cuidado *m* <in the keeping of : al cuidado de>
keepsake [ˈkiːpˌseɪk] *n* : recuerdo *m*
keep up *vt* CONTINUE, MAINTAIN : mantener, seguir con — *vi* **1** : mantenerse al corriente <he kept up with the news : se mantenía al tanto de las noticias> **2** CONTINUE : continuar **3 to keep up with someone** : mantener contacto con alguien
keg [ˈkɛg] *n* : barril *m*
kelp [ˈkɛlp] *n* : alga *f* marina
ken [ˈkɛn] *n* **1** SIGHT : vista *f,* alcance *m* de la vista **2** UNDERSTANDING : comprensión *f,* alcance *m* del conocimiento <it's beyond his ken : no lo puede entender>
kennel [ˈkɛnəl] *n* : caseta *f* para perros, perrera *f*
Kenyan [ˈkɛnjən, ˈkiːn-] *n* : keniano *m,* -na *f* — **Kenyan** *adj*
kept → **keep**
kerchief [ˈkərtʃəf, -ˌtʃiːf] *n* : pañuelo *m*
kernel [ˈkərnəl] *n* **1** : almendra *f* (de semillas y nueces) **2** : grano *m* (de cereales) **3** CORE : meollo *m* <a kernel of truth : un fondo de verdad>
kerosene *or* **kerosine** [ˈkɛrəˌsiːn, ˌkɛrəˈ-] *n* : queroseno *m,* kerosén *m,* kerosene *m*
ketchup [ˈkɛtʃəp, ˈkæ-] *n* : salsa *f* catsup
kettle [ˈkɛtəl] *n* **1** : hervidor *m,* pava *f Arg, Bol, Chile* **2** → **teakettle**
kettledrum [ˈkɛtəlˌdrʌm] *n* : timbal *m*
key[1] [ˈkiː] *vt* **1** ATTUNE : adaptar, adecuar **2 to key up** : poner nervioso, inquietar
key[2] *adj* : clave, fundamental
key[3] *n* **1** : llave *f* **2** SOLUTION : clave *f,* soluciones *fpl* **3** : tecla *f* (de un piano o una máquina) **4** : tono *m,* tonalidad *f* (en la música) **5** ISLET, REEF : cayo *m,* islote *m*
keyboard [ˈkiːˌbord] *n* : teclado *m*
keyhole [ˈkiːˌhoːl] *n* : bocallave *f,* ojo *m* (de una cerradura)
keynote[1] [ˈkiːˌnoːt] *vt* **-noted; -noting 1** : establecer la tónica de (en música) **2** : pronunciar el discurso principal de
keynote[2] *n* **1** : tónica *f* (en música) **2** : idea *f* fundamental
keystone [ˈkiːˌstoːn] *n* : clave *f,* dovela *f*
khaki [ˈkæki, ˈkɑ-] *n* : caqui *m*
khan [ˈkɑn, ˈkæn] *n* : kan *m*
kibbutz [kəˈbʊts, -ˈbuːts] *n, pl* **-butzim** [-ˌbʊtˈsiːm, -ˌbuːt-] : kibutz *m*
kibitz [ˈkɪbɪts] *vi* : dar consejos molestos
kibitzer [ˈkɪbɪtsər, kɪˈbɪt-] *n* : persona *f* que da consejos molestos
kick[1] [ˈkɪk] *vi* **1** : dar patadas (dícese de una persona), cocear (dícese de un animal) **2** PROTEST : patalear, protestar **3** RECOIL : dar un culatazo (dícese de

un arma de fuego) — *vt* : patear, darle una patada (a alguien)

kick[2] *n* **1** : patada *f,* puntapié *m,* coz *f* (de un animal) **2** RECOIL : culatazo *m* (de un arma de fuego) **3** : fuerza *f* <a drink with a kick : una bebida fuerte>

kicker [ˈkɪkər] *n* : pateador *m,* -dora *f* (en deportes)

kickoff [ˈkɪkˌɔf] *n* : saque *m* (inicial)

kick off *vi* **1** : hacer el saque inicial (en deportes) **2** BEGIN : empezar — *vt* : empezar

kid[1] [ˈkɪd] *v* **kidded; kidding** *vt* **1** FOOL : engañar **2** TEASE : tomarle el pelo (a alguien) — *vi* JOKE : bromear <I'm only kidding : lo digo en broma>

kid[2] *n* **1** : chivo *m,* -va *f;* cabrito *m,* -ta *f* **2** CHILD : chico *m,* -ca *f;* niño *m,* -ña *f*

kidder [ˈkɪdər] *n* : bromista *mf*

kiddingly [ˈkɪdɪŋli] *adv* : en broma

kidnap [ˈkɪdˌnæp] *vt* **-napped** *or* **-naped** [-ˌnæpt]; **-napping** *or* **-naping** [-ˌnæpɪŋ] : secuestrar, raptar

kidnapper *or* **kidnaper** [ˈkɪdˌnæpər] *n* : secuestrador *m,* -dora *f;* raptor *m,* -tora *f*

kidney [ˈkɪdni] *n, pl* **-neys** : riñón *m*

kidney bean *n* : frijol *m*

kill[1] [ˈkɪl] *vt* **1** : matar **2** END : acabar con, poner fin a **3 to kill time** : matar el tiempo

kill[2] *n* **1** KILLING : matanza *f* **2** PREY : presa *f*

killer [ˈkɪlər] *n* : asesino *m,* -na *f*

kiln [ˈkɪl, ˈkɪln] *n* : horno *m*

kilo [ˈkiːˌloː] *n, pl* **-los** : kilo *m*

kilocycle [ˈkɪləˌsaɪkəl] *n* : kilociclo *m*

kilogram [ˈkɪləˌgræm, ˈkiː-] *n* : kilogramo *m*

kilohertz [ˈkɪləˌhərts] *n* : kilohertzio *m*

kilometer [kɪˈlɑmət̬ər, ˈkɪləˌmiː-] *n* : kilómetro *m*

kilowatt [ˈkɪləˌwɑt] *n* : kilovatio *m*

kilt [ˈkɪlt] *n* : falda *f* escocesa

kilter [ˈkɪltər] *n* **1** ORDER : buen estado *m* **2 out of kilter** : descompuesto, estropeado

kimono [kəˈmoːno, -nə] *n, pl* **-nos** : kimono *m,* quimono *m*

kin [ˈkɪn] *n* : familiares *mpl,* parientes *mpl*

kind[1] [ˈkaɪnd] *adj* : amable, bondadoso, benévolo

kind[2] *n* **1** ESSENCE : esencia *f* <a difference in degree, not in kind : una diferencia cuantitativa y no cualitativa> **2** CATEGORY : especie *f,* género *m* **3** TYPE : clase *f,* tipo *m,* índole *f*

kindergarten [ˈkɪndərˌgɑrtən, -dən] *n* : kinder *m,* kindergarten *m,* jardín *m* de infantes, jardín *m* de niños *Mex*

kindhearted [ˌkaɪndˈhɑrt̬əd] *adj* : bondadoso, de buen corazón

kindle [ˈkɪndəl] *v* **-dled; -dling** *vt* **1** IGNITE : encender **2** AROUSE : despertar, suscitar — *vi* : encenderse

kindliness [ˈkaɪndlinəs] *n* : bondad *f*

kindling [ˈkɪndlɪŋ, ˈkɪndlən] *n* : astillas *fpl,* leña *f*

kindly[1] [ˈkaɪndli] *adv* **1** AMIABLY : amablemente, bondadosamente **2** COURTEOUSLY : cortésmente, con cortesía <we kindly ask you not smoke : les rogamos que no fumen> **3** PLEASE : por favor **4 to take kindly to** : aceptar de buena gana

kindly[2] *adj* **-lier; -est** : bondadoso, amable

kindness [ˈkaɪndnəs] *n* : bondad *f*

kind of *adv* SOMEWHAT : un tanto, algo

kindred[1] [ˈkɪndrəd] *adj* SIMILAR : similar, afín <kindred spirits : almas gemelas>

kindred[2] *n* **1** FAMILY : familia *f,* parentela *f* **2** → **kin**

kinfolk [ˈkɪnˌfoːk] *or* **kinfolks** [-ˌfoːks] *npl* → **kin**

king [ˈkɪŋ] *n* : rey *m*

kingdom [ˈkɪŋdəm] *n* : reino *m*

kingfisher [ˈkɪŋˌfɪʃər] *n* : martín *m* pescador

kingly [ˈkɪŋli] *adj* **-lier; -est** : regio, real

king–size [ˈkɪŋˌsaɪz] *or* **king–sized** [-ˌsaɪzd] *adj* : de tamaño muy grande, extra largo (dícese de cigarillos)

kink [ˈkɪŋk] *n* **1** : rizo *m* (en el pelo), vuelta *f* (en una cuerda) **2** CRAMP : calambre *m* <to have a kink in the neck : tener tortícolis>

kinky [ˈkɪŋki] *adj* **-kier; -est** : rizado (dícese del pelo), enroscado (dícese de una cuerda)

kinship [ˈkɪnˌʃɪp] *n* : parentesco *m*

kinsman [ˈkɪnzmən] *n, pl* **-men** [-mən, -ˌmɛn] : familiar *m,* pariente *m*

kinswoman [ˈkɪnzˌwʊmən] *n, pl* **-women** [-ˌwɪmən] : familiar *f,* pariente *f*

kipper [ˈkɪpər] *n* : arenque *m* ahumado

kiss[1] [ˈkɪs] *vt* : besar — *vi* : besarse

kiss[2] *n* : beso *m*

kit [ˈkɪt] *n* **1** SET : juego *m,* kit *m* **2** CASE : estuche *m,* caja *f* **3 first–aid kit** : botiquín *m* **4 tool kit** : caja *f* de herramientas **5 travel kit** : neceser *m*

kitchen [ˈkɪtʃən] *n* : cocina *f*

kite [ˈkaɪt] *n* **1** : milano *m* (ave) **2** : cometa *f,* papalote *m Mex* <to fly a kite : hacer volar una cometa>

kith [ˈkɪθ] *n* : amigos *mpl* <kith and kin : amigos y parientes>

kitten [ˈkɪtən] *n* : gatito *m,* -ta *f*

kitty [ˈkɪt̬i] *n, pl* **-ties 1** FUND, POOL : bote *m,* fondo *m* común **2** CAT : gato *m,* gatito *m*

kitty–corner [ˈkɪt̬iˌkɔrnər] *or* **kitty–cornered** [-nərd] → **catercorner**

kiwi [ˈkiːˌwiː] *n* : kiwi *m*

kleptomania [ˌklɛptəˈmeɪniə] *n* : cleptomanía *f*

kleptomaniac [ˌklɛptəˈmeɪniˌæk] *n* : cleptómano *m,* -na *f*

knack [ˈnæk] *n* : maña *f,* facilidad *f*

knapsack [ˈnæpˌsæk] *n* : mochila *f,* morral *m*

knave [ˈneɪv] *n* **:** bellaco *m,* pícaro *m*
knead [ˈniːd] *vt* **1 :** amasar, sobar **2** MASSAGE **:** masajear
knee [ˈniː] *n* **:** rodilla *f*
kneecap [ˈniːˌkæp] *n* **:** rótula *f*
kneel [ˈniːl] *vi* **knelt** [ˈnɛlt] *or* **kneeled** [ˈniːld]; **kneeling :** arrodillarse, ponerse de rodillas
knell [ˈnɛl] *n* **:** doble *m,* toque *m* <death knell : toque de difuntos>
knew → **know**
knickers [ˈnɪkərz] *npl* **:** pantalones *mpl* bombachos de media pierna
knickknack [ˈnɪkˌnæk] *n* **:** chuchería *f,* baratija *f*
knife[1] [ˈnaɪf] *vt* **knifed** [ˈnaɪft]; **knifing :** acuchillar, apuñalar
knife[2] *n, pl* **knives** [ˈnaɪvz] **:** cuchillo *m*
knight[1] [ˈnaɪt] *vt* **:** conceder el título de *Sir* a
knight[2] *n* **1 :** caballero *m* <knight errant : caballero andante> **2 :** caballo *m* (en ajedrez) **3 :** uno que tiene el título de *Sir*
knighthood [ˈnaɪtˌhʊd] *n* **1 :** caballería *f* **2 :** título *m* de *Sir*
knightly [ˈnaɪtli] *adj* **:** caballeresco
knit[1] [ˈnɪt] *v* **knit** *or* **knitted** [ˈnɪt̬əd]; **knitting** *vt* **1** UNITE **:** unir, enlazar **2 :** tejer <to knit a sweater : tejer un suéter> **3 to knit one's brows :** fruncir el ceño — *vi* **1 :** tejer **2 :** soldarse (dícese de los huesos)
knit[2] *n* **:** prenda *f* tejida
knitter [ˈnɪt̬ər] *n* **:** tejedor *m,* -dora *f*
knob [ˈnɑb] *n* **1** LUMP **:** bulto *m,* protuberancia *f* **2** HANDLE **:** perilla *f,* tirador *m,* botón *m*
knobbed [ˈnɑbd] *adj* **1** KNOTTY **:** nudoso **2 :** que tiene perilla o botón
knobby [ˈnɑbi] *adj* **knobbier; -est 1** KNOTTY **:** nudoso **2 knobby knees :** rodillas *fpl* huesudas
knock[1] [ˈnɑk] *vt* **1** HIT, RAP **:** golpear, golpetear **2 :** hacer chocar <they knocked heads : se dieron en la cabeza> **3** CRITICIZE **:** criticar — *vi* **1** RAP **:** dar un golpe, llamar (a la puerta) **2** COLLIDE **:** darse, chocar
knock[2] *n* **:** golpe *m,* llamada *f* (a la puerta), golpeteo *m* (de un motor)
knock down *vt* **:** derribar, echar al suelo
knocker [ˈnɑkər] *n* **:** aldaba *f,* llamador *m*
knock–kneed [ˈnɑkˈniːd] *adj* **:** patizambo
knock out *vt* **:** dejar sin sentido, poner fuera de combate (en el boxeo)
knoll [ˈnoːl] *n* **:** loma *f,* otero *m,* montículo *m*
knot[1] [ˈnɑt] *v* **knotted; knotting** *vt* **:** anudar — *vi* **:** anudarse
knot[2] *n* **1 :** nudo *m* (en cordel o madera), nódulo *m* (en los músculos) **2** CLUSTER **:** grupo *m* **3 :** nudo *m* (unidad de velocidad)
knotty [ˈnɑt̬i] *adj* **-tier; -est 1** GNARLED **:** nudoso **2** COMPLEX **:** espinoso, enredado, complejo
know [ˈnoː] *v* **knew** [ˈnuː, ˈnjuː]; **known** [ˈnoːn]; **knowing** *vt* **1 :** saber <he knows the answer : sabe la respuesta> **2 :** conocer (a una persona, un lugar) <do you know Julia? : ¿conoces a Julia?> **3** RECOGNIZE **:** reconocer **4** DISCERN, DISTINGUISH **:** distinguir, discernir **5 to know how to :** saber <I don't know how to dance : no sé bailar> — *vi* **:** saber
knowable [ˈnoːəbəl] *adj* **:** conocible
knowing [ˈnoːɪŋ] *adj* **1** KNOWLEDGEABLE **:** informado <a knowing look : una mirada de complicidad> **2** ASTUTE **:** astuto **3** DELIBERATE **:** deliberado, intencional
knowingly [ˈnoːɪŋli] *adv* **1 :** con complicidad <she smiled knowingly : sonrió con una mirada de complicidad> **2** DELIBERATELY **:** a sabiendas, adrede, a propósito
know–it–all [ˈnoːɪtˌɔl] *n* **:** sabelotodo *mf fam*
knowledge [ˈnɑlɪdʒ] *n* **1** AWARENESS **:** conocimiento *m* **2** LEARNING **:** conocimientos *mpl,* saber *m*
knowledgeable [ˈnɑlɪdʒəbəl] *adj* **:** informado, entendido, enterado
known [ˈnoːn] *adj* **:** conocido, familiar
knuckle [ˈnʌkəl] *n* **:** nudillo *m*
koala [koˈwɑlə] *n* **:** koala *m*
kohlrabi [ˌkoːlˈrɑbi, -ˈræ-] *n, pl* **-bies :** colinabo *m*
Koran [kəˈrɑn, -ˈræn] *n* **the Koran :** el Corán
Korean [kəˈriːən] *n* **:** coreano *m,* -na *f* — **Korean** *adj*
kosher [ˈkoːʃər] *adj* **:** aprobado por la ley judía
kowtow [ˌkaʊˈtaʊ, ˈkaʊˌtaʊ] *vi* **to kowtow to :** humillarse ante, doblegarse ante
krypton [ˈkrɪpˌtɑn] *n* **:** criptón *m*
kudos [ˈkjuːˌdɑs, ˈkuː-, -ˌdoːz] *n* **:** fama *f,* renombre *m*
kumquat [ˈkʌmˌkwɑt] *n* **:** naranjita *f* china
Kuwaiti [kʊˈweɪt̬i] *n* **:** kuwaití *mf* — **Kuwaiti** *adj*

L

l [ˈɛl] *n, pl* **l's** *or* **ls** [ˈɛlz] **:** duodécima letra del alfabeto inglés
lab [ˈlæb] → **laboratory**
label[1] [ˈleɪbəl] *vt* **-beled** *or* **-belled; -beling** *or* **-belling 1 :** etiquetar, poner etiqueta a **2** BRAND, CATEGORIZE

: calificar, tildar, tachar <they labeled him as a fraud : lo calificaron de farsante>
label[2] *n* **1** : etiqueta *f,* rótulo *m* **2** DESCRIPTION : calificación *f,* descripción *f* **3** BRAND : marca *f*
labial [ˈleɪbiəl] *adj* : labial
labor[1] [ˈleɪbər] *vi* **1** WORK : trabajar **2** STRUGGLE : avanzar penosamente (dícese de una persona), funcionar con dificultad (dícese de un motor) **3 to labor under a delusion** : hacerse ilusiones, tener una falsa impresión — *vt* BELABOR : insistir en, extenderse sobre
labor[2] *n* **1** EFFORT, WORK : trabajo *m,* esfuerzos *mpl* **2** : parto *m* <to be in labor : estar de parto> **3** TASK : tarea *f,* labor *m* **4** WORKERS : mano *f* de obra
laboratory [ˈlæbrəˌtori, ləˈbɔrə-] *n, pl* **-ries** : laboratorio *m*
Labor Day *n* : Día *m* del Trabajo
laborer [ˈleɪbərər] *n* : peón *m;* trabajador *m,* -dora *f*
laborious [ləˈboriəs] *adj* : laborioso, difícil
laboriously [ləˈboriəsli] *adv* : laboriosamente, trabajosamente
labor union → **union**
labyrinth [ˈlæbəˌrɪnθ] *n* : laberinto *m*
lace[1] [ˈleɪs] *vt* **laced; lacing 1** TIE : acordonar, atar los cordones de **2** : adornar de encaje <I laced the dress in white : adorné el vestido de encaje blanco> **3** SPIKE : echar licor a
lace[2] *n* **1** : encaje *m* **2** SHOELACE : cordón *m* (de zapatos), agujeta *f Mex*
lacerate [ˈlæsəˌreɪt] *vt* **-ated; -ating** : lacerar
laceration [ˌlæsəˈreɪʃən] *n* : laceración *f*
lack[1] [ˈlæk] *vt* : carecer de, no tener <she lacks patience : carece de paciencia> — *vi* : faltar <they lack for nothing : no les falta nada>
lack[2] *n* : falta *f,* carencia *f*
lackadaisical [ˌlækəˈdeɪzɪkəl] *adj* : apático, indiferente, lánguido — **lackadaisically** [-kli] *adv*
lackey [ˈlæki] *n, pl* **-eys 1** FOOTMAN : lacayo *m* **2** TOADY : adulador *m,* -dora *f*
lackluster [ˈlækˌlʌstər] *adj* **1** DULL : sin brillo, apagado, deslustrado **2** MEDIOCRE : deslucido, mediocre
laconic [ləˈkɑnɪk] *adj* : lacónico — **laconically** [-nɪkli] *adv*
lacquer[1] [ˈlækər] *vt* : laquear, pintar con laca
lacquer[2] *n* : laca *f*
lacrosse [ləˈkrɔs] *n* : lacrosse *f*
lactic acid [ˈlæktɪk] *n* : ácido *m* láctico
lacuna [ləˈkuːnə, -ˈkjuː-] *n, pl* **-nae** [-ˌniː, -ˌnaɪ] *or* **-nas** : laguna *f*
lacy [ˈleɪsi] *adj* **lacier; -est** : de encaje, como de encaje
lad [ˈlæd] *n* : muchacho *m,* niño *m*
ladder [ˈlædər] *n* : escalera *f*
laden [ˈleɪdən] *adj* : cargado
ladle[1] [ˈleɪdəl] *vt* **-dled; -dling** : servir con cucharón
ladle[2] *n* : cucharón *m,* cazo *m*
lady [ˈleɪdi] *n, pl* **-dies 1** : señora *f,* dama *f* **2** WOMAN : mujer *f*
ladybird [ˈleɪdiˌbərd] → **ladybug**
ladybug [ˈleɪdiˌbʌg] *n* : mariquita *f*
lag[1] [ˈlæg] *vi* **lagged; lagging** : quedarse atrás, retrasarse, rezagarse
lag[2] *n* **1** DELAY : retraso *m,* demora *f* **2** INTERVAL : lapso *m,* intervalo *m*
lager [ˈlɑgər] *n* : cerveza *f* rubia
laggard[1] [ˈlægərd] *adj* : retardado, retrasado
laggard[2] *n* : rezagado *m,* -da *f*
lagoon [ləˈguːn] *n* : laguna *f*
laid *pp* → **lay**
lain *pp* → **lie**
lair [ˈlær] *n* : guarida *f,* madriguera *f*
laissez-faire [ˌlɛˌseɪˈfær, ˌleɪˌzeɪ-] *n* : liberalismo *m* económico
laity [ˈleɪəti] *n* **the laity** : los laicos, el laicado
lake [ˈleɪk] *n* : lago *m*
lama [ˈlɑmə] *n* : lama *m*
lamb [ˈlæm] *n* **1** : cordero *m,* borrego *m* (animal) **2** : carne *f* de cordero
lambaste [læmˈbeɪst] *or* **lambast** [-ˈbæst] *vt* **-basted; -basting 1** BEAT, THRASH : golpear, azotar, darle una paliza (a alguien) **2** CENSURE : arremeter contre, censurar
lame[1] [ˈleɪm] *vt* **lamed; laming** : lisiar, hacer cojo
lame[2] *adj* **lamer; lamest 1** : cojo, renco, rengo **2** WEAK : pobre, débil, poco convincente <a lame excuse : una excusa débil>
lamé [lɑˈmeɪ, læ-] *n* : lamé *m*
lame duck *n* : persona *f* sin poder <a lame-duck President : un presidente saliente>
lamely [ˈleɪmli] *adv* : sin convicción
lameness [ˈleɪmnəs] *n* **1** : cojera *f,* renquera *f* **2** : falta *f* de convicción, debilidad *f,* pobreza *f* <the lameness of her response : la pobreza de su respuesta>
lament[1] [ləˈmɛnt] *vt* **1** MOURN : llorar, llorar por **2** DEPLORE : lamentar, deplorar — *vi* : llorar
lament[2] *n* : lamento *m*
lamentable [ˈlæməntəbəl, ləˈmɛntə-] *adj* : lamentable, deplorable — **lamentably** [-bli] *adv*
lamentation [ˌlæmənˈteɪʃən] *n* : lamentación *f,* lamento *m*
laminate[1] [ˈlæməˌneɪt] *vt* **-nated; -nating** : laminar
laminate[2] [ˈlæmənət] *n* : laminado *m*
laminated [ˈlæməˌneɪtəd] *adj* : laminado
lamp [ˈlæmp] *n* : lámpara *f*
lampoon[1] [læmˈpuːn] *vt* : satirizar
lampoon[2] *n* : sátira *f*
lamprey [ˈlæmpri] *n, pl* **-preys** : lamprea *f*
lance[1] [ˈlænts] *vt* **lanced; lancing** : abrir con lanceta, sajar

lance[2] *n* **:** lanza *f*

lance corporal *n* **:** cabo *m* interino, soldado *m* de primera clase

lancet [ˈlæntsət] *n* **:** lanceta *f*

land[1] [ˈlænd] *vt* **1 :** desembarcar (pasajeros de un barco), hacer aterrizar (un avión) **2** CATCH **:** pescar, sacar (un pez) del agua **3** GAIN, SECURE **:** conseguir, ganar <to land a job : conseguir empleo> **4** DELIVER **:** dar, asestar <he landed a punch : asestó un puñetazo> — *vi* **1 :** aterrizar, tomar tierra, atracar <the plane just landed : el avión acaba de aterrizar> <the ship landed an hour ago : el barco atracó hace una hora>**2** ALIGHT **:** posarse, aterrizar <to land on one's feet : caer de pie>

land[2] *n* **1** GROUND **:** tierra *f* <dry land : tierra firme> **2** TERRAIN **:** terreno *m* **3** NATION **:** país *m,* nación *f* **4** DOMAIN **:** mundo *m,* dominio *m* <the land of dreams : el mundo de los sueños>

landfill [ˈlændˌfɪl] *n* **:** vertadero *m* (de basuras)

landing [ˈlændɪŋ] *n* **1 :** aterrizaje *m* (de aviones), desembarco *m* (de barcos) **2 :** descansillo *m* (de una escalera)

landing field *n* **:** campo *m* de aterrizaje

landing strip → **airstrip**

landlady [ˈlændˌleɪdi] *n, pl* **-dies :** casera *f,* dueña *f,* arrendadora *f*

landless [ˈlændləs] *adj* **:** sin tierra

landlocked [ˈlændˌlɑkt] *adj* **:** sin salida al mar

landlord [ˈlændˌlɔrd] *n* **:** dueño *m,* casero *m,* arrendador *m*

landlubber [ˈlændˌlʌbər] *n* **:** marinero *m* de agua dulce

landmark [ˈlændˌmɑrk] *n* **1 :** señal *f* (geográfica), punto *m* de referencia **2** MILESTONE **:** hito *m* <a landmark in our history : un hito en nuestra historia> **3** MONUMENT **:** monumento *m* histórico

landowner [ˈlændˌoːnər] *n* **:** hacendado *m,* -da *f;* terrateniente *mf*

landscape[1] [ˈlændˌskeɪp] *vt* **-scaped; -scaping :** ajardinar

landscape[2] *n* **:** paisaje *m*

landslide [ˈlændˌslaɪd] *n* **1 :** desprendimiento *m* de tierras, derrumbe *m* **2 landslide victory :** victoria *f* arrolladora

landward [ˈlændwərd] *adv* **:** en dirección de la tierra, hacia tierra

lane [ˈleɪn] *n* **1** PATH, WAY **:** camino *m,* sendero *m* **2 :** carril *m* (de una carretera)

language [ˈlæŋgwɪdʒ] *n* **1 :** idioma *m,* lengua *f* <the English language : el idioma inglés> **2 :** lenguaje *m* <body language : lenguaje corporal>

languid [ˈlæŋgwɪd] *adj* **:** lánguido — **languidly** *adv*

languish [ˈlæŋgwɪʃ] *vi* **1** WEAKEN **:** languidecer, debilitarse **2** PINE **:** consumirse, suspirar (por) <to languish for love : suspirar por el amor> <he languished in prison : estuvo pudriéndose en la cárcel>

languor [ˈlæŋgər] *n* **:** languidez *f*

languorous [ˈlæŋgərəs] *adj* **:** lánguido — **languorously** *adv*

lank [ˈlæŋk] *adj* **1** THIN **:** delgado, larguirucho *fam* **2** LIMP **:** lacio

lanky [ˈlæŋki] *adj* **lankier; -est :** delgado, larguirucho *fam*

lanolin [ˈlænəlɪn] *n* **:** lanolina *f*

lantern [ˈlæntərn] *n* **:** linterna *f,* farol *m*

Laotian [leɪˈoːʃən, ˈlaʊʃən] *n* **:** laosiano *m,* -na *f* — **Laotian** *adj*

lap[1] [ˈlæp] *v* **lapped; lapping** *vt* **1** FOLD **:** plegar, doblar **2** WRAP **:** envolver **3 :** lamer, besar <waves were lapping the shore : las olas lamían la orilla> **4 to lap up :** beber a lengüetadas (como un gato) — *vi* OVERLAP **:** traslaparse

lap[2] *n* **1 :** falda *f,* regazo *m* (del cuerpo) **2** OVERLAP **:** traslapo *m* **3 :** vuelta *f* (en deportes) **4** STAGE **:** etapa *f* (de un viaje)

lapdog [ˈlæpˌdɔg] *n* **:** perro *m* faldero

lapel [ləˈpɛl] *n* **:** solapa *f*

Lapp [ˈlæp] *n* **:** lapón *m,* -pona *f* — **Lapp** *adj*

lapse[1] [ˈlæps] *vi* **lapsed; lapsing 1** FALL, SLIP **:** caer <to lapse into bad habits : caer en malos hábitos> <to lapse into unconsciousness : perder el conocimiento> <to lapse into silence : quedarse callado> **2** FADE **:** decaer, desvanecerse <her dedication lapsed : su dedicación se desvaneció> **3** CEASE **:** cancelarse, perderse **4** ELAPSE **:** transcurrir, pasar **5** EXPIRE **:** caducar

lapse[2] *n* **1** SLIP **:** lapsus *m,* deliz *m,* falla *f* <a lapse of memory : una falla de memoria> **2** INTERVAL **:** lapso *m,* intervalo *m,* período *m* **3** EXPIRATION **:** caducidad *f*

laptop [ˈlæpˌtɑp] *adj* **:** portátil, laptop

larboard [ˈlɑrbərd] *n* **:** babor *m*

larcenous [ˈlɑrsənəs] *adj* **:** de robo

larceny [ˈlɑrsəni] *n, pl* **-nies :** robo *m,* hurto *m*

larch [ˈlɑrtʃ] *n* **:** alerce *f*

lard [ˈlɑrd] *n* **:** manteca *f* de cerdo

larder [ˈlɑrdər] *n* **:** despensa *f,* alacena *f*

large [ˈlɑrdʒ] *adj* **larger; largest 1** BIG **:** grande **2** COMPREHENSIVE **:** amplio, extenso **3 by and large :** por lo general

largely [ˈlɑrdʒli] *adv* **:** en gran parte, en su mayoría

largeness [ˈlɑrdʒnəs] *n* **:** lo grande

largesse *or* **largess** [lɑrˈʒɛs, -ˈdʒɛs] *n* **:** generosidad *f,* largueza *f*

lariat [ˈlæriət] *n* **:** lazo *m*

lark [ˈlɑrk] *n* **1** FUN **:** diversión *f* <what a lark! : ¡qué divertido!> **2 :** alondra *f* (pájaro)

larva [ˈlɑrvə] *n, pl* **-vae** [-ˌviː, -ˌvaɪ] **:** larva *f* — **larval** [-vəl] *adj*

laryngitis [ˌlærənˈdʒaɪtəs] *n* **:** laringitis *f*

larynx [ˈlærɪŋks] *n, pl* **-rynges** [ləˈrɪnˌdʒiːz] *or* **-ynxes** [ˈlærɪŋksəz] : laringe *f*

lasagna [ləˈzɑnjə] *n* : lasaña *f*

lascivious [ləˈsɪviəs] *adj* : lascivo

lasciviousness [ləˈsɪviəsnəs] *n* : lascivia *f,* lujuria *f*

laser [ˈleɪzər] *n* : láser *m*

lash[1] [ˈlæʃ] *vt* **1** WHIP : azotar **2** BIND : atar, amarrar

lash[2] *n* **1** WHIP : látigo *m* **2** STROKE : latigazo *m* **3** EYELASH : pestaña *f*

lass [ˈlæs] *or* **lassie** [ˈlæsi] *n* : muchacha *f,* chica *f*

lassitude [ˈlæsəˌtuːd, -ˌtjuːd] *n* : lasitud *f*

lasso[1] [ˈlæˌsoː, læˈsuː] *vt* : lazar

lasso[2] *n, pl* **-sos** *or* **-soes** : lazo *m,* reata *f Mex*

last[1] [ˈlæst] *vi* **1** CONTINUE : durar <how long will it last? : ¿cuánto durará?> **2** ENDURE : aguantar, durar **3** SURVIVE : durar, sobrevivir **4** SUFFICE : durar, bastar — *vt* **1** : durar <it will last a lifetime : durará toda la vida> **2 to last out** : aguantar

last[2] *adv* **1** : en último lugar, al último <we came in last : llegamos en último lugar> **2** : por última vez, la última vez <I saw him last in Bogota : lo vi por última vez en Bogotá> **3** FINALLY : por último, en conclusión

last[3] *adj* **1** FINAL : último, final **2** PREVIOUS : pasado <last year : el año pasado>

last[4] *n* **1** : el último, la última, lo último <at last : por fin, al fin, finalmente> **2** : horma *f* (de zapatero)

lasting [ˈlæstɪŋ] *adj* : perdurable, duradero, estable

lastly [ˈlæstli] *adv* : por último, finalmente

latch[1] [ˈlætʃ] *vt* : cerrar con picaporte

latch[2] *n* : picaporte *m,* pestillo *m,* pasador *m*

late[1] [ˈleɪt] *adv* **later; latest 1** : tarde <to arrive late : llegar tarde> <to sleep late : dormir hasta tarde> **2** : a última hora, a finales <late in the month : a finales del mes> **3** RECENTLY : recién, últimamente <as late as last year : todavía en el año pasado>

late[2] *adj* **later; latest 1** TARDY : tardío, de retraso <to be late : llegar tarde> **2** : avanzado <because of the late hour : a causa de la hora avanzada> **3** DECEASED : difunto, fallecido **4** RECENT : reciente, último <our late quarrel : nuestra última pelea>

latecomer [ˈleɪtˌkʌmər] *n* : rezagado *m,* -da *f*

lately [ˈleɪtli] *adv* : recientemente, últimamente

lateness [ˈleɪtnəs] *n* **1** DELAY : retraso *m,* atraso *m,* tardanza *f* **2** : lo avanzado (de la hora)

latent [ˈleɪtənt] *adj* : latente — **latently** *adv*

lateral [ˈlæt̬ərəl] *adj* : lateral — **laterally** *adv*

latex [ˈleɪˌtɛks] *n, pl* **-tices** [ˈleɪt̬əˌsiːz, ˈlæt̬ə-] *or* **-texes** : látex *m*

lath [ˈlæθ, ˈlæð] *n, pl* **laths** *or* **lath** : listón *m*

lathe [ˈleɪð] *n* : torno *m*

lather[1] [ˈlæðər] *vt* : enjabonar — *vi* : espumar, hacer espuma

lather[2] *n* **1** : espuma *f* (de jabón) **2** : sudor *m* (de caballo) **3 to get into a lather** : ponerse histérico

Latin[1] *adj* : latino

Latin[2] *n* **1** : latín *m* (idioma) **2** → **Latin American**

Latin–American [ˈlætənəˈmɛrikən] *adj* : latinoamericano

Latin American *n* : latinoamericano *m,* -na *f*

latitude [ˈlæt̬əˌtuːd, -ˌtjuːd] *n* : latitud *f*

latrine [ləˈtriːn] *n* : letrina *f*

latter[1] [ˈlæt̬ər] *adj* **1** SECOND : segundo **2** LAST : último

latter[2] *pron* **the latter** : éste, ésta, éstos *pl,* éstas *pl*

lattice [ˈlæt̬əs] *n* : enrejado *m,* celosía *f*

Latvian [ˈlætviən] *n* : letón *m,* -tona *f* — **Latvian** *adj*

laud[1] [ˈlɔd] *vt* : alabar, loar

laud[2] *n* : alabanza *f,* loa *f*

laudable [ˈlɔdəbəl] *adj* : loable — **laudably** [-bli] *adv*

laugh[1] [ˈlæf] *vi* : reír, reírse

laugh[2] *n* **1** LAUGHTER : risa *f* **2** JOKE : chiste *m,* broma *f* <he did it for a laugh : lo hizo en broma, lo hizo para divertirse>

laughable [ˈlæfəbəl] *adj* : risible, de risa

laughingstock [ˈlæfɪŋˌstɑk] *n* : hazmerreír *m*

laughter [ˈlæftər] *n* : risa *f,* risas *fpl*

launch[1] [ˈlɔntʃ] *vt* **1** HURL : lanzar **2** : botar (un barco) **3** START : iniciar, empezar

launch[2] *n* **1** : lancha *f* (bote) **2** LAUNCHING : lanzamiento *m*

launder [ˈlɔndər] *vt* **1** : lavar y planchar (ropa) **2** : blanquear, lavar (dinero)

launderer [ˈlɔndərər] *n* : lavandero *m,* -ra *f*

laundress [ˈlɔndrəs] *n* : lavandera *f*

laundry [ˈlɔndri] *n, pl* **laundries 1** : ropa *f* sucia, ropa *f* para lavar <to do the laundry : lavar la ropa> **2** : lavandería *f* (servicio de lavar)

laureate [ˈlɔriət] *n* : laureado *m,* -da *f* <poet laureate : poeta laureado>

laurel [ˈlɔrəl] *n* **1** : laurel *m* (planta) **2 laurels** *npl* : laureles *mpl* <to rest on one's laurels : dormirse uno en sus laureles>

lava [ˈlɑvə, ˈlæ-] *n* : lava *f*

lavatory [ˈlævəˌtori] *n, pl* **-ries** : baño *m,* cuarto *m* de baño

lavender [ˈlævəndər] *n* **:** lavanda *f,* espliego *m*

lavish[1] [ˈlævɪʃ] *vt* **:** prodigar (a), colmar (de)

lavish[2] *adj* **1** EXTRAVAGANT **:** pródigo, generoso, derrochador **2** ABUNDANT **:** abundante **3** LUXURIOUS **:** lujoso, espléndido

lavishly [ˈlævɪʃli] *adv* **:** con generosidad, espléndidamente <to live lavishly : vivir a lo grande>

lavishness [ˈlævɪʃnəs] *n* **:** generosidad *f,* esplendidez *f*

law [ˈlɔ] *n* **1 :** ley *f* <to break the law : violar la ley> **2 :** derecho *m* <criminal law : derecho criminal> **3 :** abogacía *f* <to practice law : ejercer la abogacía>

law–abiding [ˈlɔəˌbaɪdɪŋ] *adj* **:** observante de la ley

lawbreaker [ˈlɔˌbreɪkər] *n* **:** infractor *m,* -tora *f* de la ley

lawful [ˈlɔfəl] *adj* **:** legal, legítimo, lícito — **lawfully** *adv*

lawgiver [ˈlɔˌgɪvər] *n* **:** legislador *m,* -dora *f*

lawless [ˈlɔləs] *adj* **:** anárquico, ingobernable — **lawlessly** *adv*

lawlessness [ˈlɔləsnəs] *n* **:** anarquía *f,* desorden *m*

lawmaker [ˈlɔˌmeɪkər] *n* **:** legislador *m,* -dora *f*

lawman [ˈlɔmən] *n, pl* **-men** [-mən, -ˌmɛn] **:** agente *m* del orden

lawn [ˈlɔn] *n* **:** césped *m,* pasto *m*

lawn mower *n* **:** cortadora *f* de césped

lawsuit [ˈlɔˌsuːt] *n* **:** pleito *m,* litigio *m,* demanda *f*

lawyer [ˈlɔɪər, ˈlɔjər] *n* **:** abogado *m,* -da *f*

lax [ˈlæks] *adj* **:** laxo, relajado — **laxly** *adv*

laxative [ˈlæksət̬ɪv] *n* **:** laxante *m*

laxity [ˈlæksət̬i] *n* **:** relajación *f,* descuido *m,* falta *f* de rigor

lay[1] [ˈleɪ] *vt* **laid** [ˈleɪd]; **laying 1** PLACE, PUT **:** poner, colocar <she laid it on the table : lo puso en la mesa> <to lay eggs : poner huevos> **2 :** hacer <to lay a bet : hacer una apuesta> **3** IMPOSE **:** imponer <to lay a tax : imponer un impuesto> <to lay the blame on : echarle la culpa a> **4 to lay out** PRESENT **:** presentar, exponer <he laid out his plan : presentó su proyecto> **5 to lay out** DESIGN **:** diseñar (el trazado de)

lay[2] *pp* → **lie**

lay[3] *adj* SECULAR **:** laico, lego

lay[4] *n* **1 :** disposición *f,* configuración *f* <the lay of the land : la configuración del terreno> **2** BALLAD **:** romance *m,* balada *f*

layer [ˈleɪər] *n* **1 :** capa *f* (de pintura, etc.), estrato *m* (de roca) **2 :** gallina *f* ponedora

layman [ˈleɪmən] *n, pl* **-men** [-mən, -ˌmɛn] **:** laico *m,* lego *m*

layoff [ˈleɪˌɔf] *n* **:** despido *m*

lay off *vt* **:** despedir

layout [ˈleɪˌaʊt] *n* **:** disposición *f,* distribución *f* (de una casa, etc.), trazado *m* (de una ciudad)

lay up *vt* **1** STORE **:** guardar, almacenar **2 to be laid up :** estar enfermo, tener que guardar cama

laywoman [ˈleɪˌwʊmən] *n, pl* **-women** [-ˌwɪmən] **:** laica *f,* lega *f*

laziness [ˈleɪzinəs] *n* **:** pereza *f,* flojera *f*

lazy [ˈleɪzi] *adj* **-zier; -est :** perezoso, holgazán — **lazily** [ˈleɪzəli] *adv*

leach [ˈliːtʃ] *vt* **:** filtrar

lead[1] [ˈliːd] *vt* **led** [ˈlɛd]; **leading 1** GUIDE **:** conducir, llevar, guiar **2** DIRECT **:** dirigir **3** HEAD **:** encabezar, ir al frente de **4 to lead to :** resultar en, llevar a <it only leads to trouble : sólo resulta en problemas>

lead[2] *n* **:** delantera *f,* primer lugar *m* <to take the lead : tomar la delantera>

lead[3] [ˈlɛd] *n* **1 :** plomo *m* (metal) **2 :** mina *f* (de lápiz) **3 lead poisoning :** saturnismo *m*

leaden [ˈlɛdən] *adj* **1 :** plomizo <a leaden sky : un ciel plomizo> **2** HEAVY **:** pesado

leader [ˈliːdər] *n* **:** jefe *m,* -fa *f;* líder *mf;* dirigente *mf;* gobernante *mf*

leadership [ˈliːdərˌʃɪp] *n* **:** mando *m,* dirección *f*

leaf[1] [ˈliːf] *vi* **1 :** echar hojas (dícese de un árbol) **2 to leaf through :** hojear (un libro)

leaf[2] *n, pl* **leaves** [ˈliːvz] **1 :** hoja *f* (de plantas o libros) **2 to turn over a new leaf :** hacer borrón y cuenta nueva

leafless [ˈliːfləs] *adj* **:** sin hojas, pelado

leaflet [ˈliːflət] *n* **:** folleto *m*

leafy [ˈliːfi] *adj* **leafier; -est :** frondoso

league[1] [ˈliːg] *v* **leagued; leaguing** *vt* **:** aliar, unir — *vi* **:** aliarse, unirse

league[2] *n* **1 :** legua *f* (medida de distancia) **2** ASSOCIATION **:** alianza *f,* sociedad *f,* liga *f*

leak[1] [ˈliːk] *vt* **1 :** perder, dejar escapar (un líquido o un gas) **2 :** filtrar (información) — *vi* **1 :** gotear, escaparse, fugarse (dícese de un líquido o un gas) **2 :** hacer agua (dícese de un bote) **3 :** filtrarse, divulgarse (dícese de información)

leak[2] *n* **1** HOLE **:** agujero *m* (en recipientes), gotera *f* (en un tejado) **2** ESCAPE **:** fuga *f,* escape *m* **3 :** filtración *f* (de información)

leakage [ˈliːkɪdʒ] *n* **:** escape *m,* fuga *f*

leaky [ˈliːki] *adj* **leakier; -est :** agujereado (dícese de un recipiente), que hace agua (dícese de un bote), con goteras (dícese de un tejado)

lean[1] [ˈliːn] *vi* **1** BEND **:** inclinarse, ladearse **2** RECLINE **:** reclinarse **3** RELY **:** apoyarse (en), depender (de) **4** INCLINE, TEND **:** inclinarse, tender — *vt* **:** apoyar

lean[2] *adj* **1** THIN **:** delgado, flaco **2 :** sin grasa, magro (dícese de la carne)

leanness [ˈliːnnəs] *n* **:** delgadez *f*

lean–to [ˈliːnˌtuː] *n* **:** cobertizo *m*

leap[1] [ˈliːp] *vi* **leapt** *or* **leaped** [ˈliːpt, ˈlɛpt]; **leaping :** saltar, brincar

leap[2] *n* **:** salto *m,* brinco *m*

leap year *n* **:** año *m* bisiesto

learn [ˈlərn] *vt* **1 :** aprender <to learn to sing : aprender a cantar> **2** MEMORIZE **:** aprender de memoria **3** DISCOVER **:** saber, enterarse de — *vi* **1 :** aprender <to learn from experience : aprender por experiencia> **2** FIND OUT **:** enterarse, saber

learned [ˈlərnəd] *adj* **:** erudito

learner [ˈlərnər] *n* **:** principiante *mf,* estudiante *mf*

learning [ˈlərnɪŋ] *n* **:** erudición *f,* saber *m*

lease[1] [ˈliːs] *vt* **leased; leasing :** arrendar

lease[2] *n* **:** contrato *m* de arrendamiento

leash[1] [ˈliːʃ] *vt* **:** atraillar (un animal)

leash[2] *n* **:** traílla *f*

least[1] [ˈliːst] *adv* **:** menos <when least expected : cuando menos se espera>

least[2] *adj* (*superlative of* **little**) **:** menor, más mínimo

least[3] *n* **1 :** lo menos <at least : por lo menos> **2 to say the least :** por no decir más

leather [ˈlɛðər] *n* **:** cuero *m*

leathery [ˈlɛðəri] *adj* **:** curtido (dícese de la piel), correoso (dícese de la carne)

leave[1] [ˈliːv] *v* **left** [ˈlɛft]; **leaving** *vt* **1** BEQUEATH **:** dejar, legar **2** DEPART **:** dejar, salir(se) de **3** ABANDON **:** abandonar, dejar **4** FORGET **:** dejar, olvidarse de <I left the books at the library : dejé los libros en la biblioteca> **5 to be left :** quedar <it's all I have left : es todo lo que me queda> **6 to be left over :** sobrar **7 to leave out :** omitir, excluir — *vi* **:** irse, salir, partir, marcharse <she left yesterday morning : se fue ayer por la mañana>

leave[2] *n* **1** PERMISSION **:** permiso *m* <by your leave : con su permiso> **2** *or* **leave of absence :** permiso *m,* licencia *f* <maternity leave : licencia por maternidad> **3 to take one's leave :** despedirse

leaven [ˈlɛvən] *n* **:** levadura *f*

leaves → **leaf**[2]

leaving [ˈliːvɪŋ] *n* **1 :** salida *f,* partida *f* **2 leavings** *npl* **:** restos *mpl,* sobras *fpl*

Lebanese [ˌlɛbəˈniːz, -ˈniːs] *n* **:** libanés *m,* -nesa *f* — **Lebanese** *adj*

lecherous [ˈlɛtʃərəs] *adj* **:** lascivo, libidinoso — **lecherously** *adv*

lechery [ˈlɛtʃəri] *n* **:** lascivia *f,* lujuria *f*

lecture[1] [ˈlɛktʃər] *v* **-tured; -turing** *vi* **:** dar clase, dictar clase, dar una conferencia — *vt* SCOLD **:** sermonear, echar una reprimenda a, regañar

lecture[2] *n* **1 :** conferencia *f* **2** REPRIMAND **:** reprimenda *f*

led *pp* → **lead**[1]

ledge [ˈlɛdʒ] *n* **:** repisa *f* (de una pared), antepecho *m* (de una ventana), saliente *m* (de una montaña)

ledger [ˈlɛdʒər] *n* **:** libro *m* mayor, libro *m* de contabilidad

lee[1] [ˈliː] *adj* **:** de sotavento

lee[2] *n* **:** sotavento *m*

leech [ˈliːtʃ] *n* **:** sanguijuela *f*

leek [ˈliːk] *n* **:** puerro *m*

leer[1] [ˈlɪr] *vi* **:** mirar con lascivia

leer[2] *n* **:** mirada *f* lasciva

leery [ˈlɪri] *adj* **:** receloso

lees [ˈliːz] *npl* **:** posos *mpl,* heces *fpl*

leeward[1] [ˈliːwərd, ˈluːərd] *adj* **:** de sotavento

leeward[2] *n* **:** sotavento *m*

leeway [ˈliːˌweɪ] *n* **:** libertad *f,* margen *m*

left[1] [ˈlɛft] *adv* **:** hacia la izquierda

left[2] *pp* → **leave**

left[3] *adj* **:** izquierdo

left[4] *n* **:** izquierda *f* <on the left : a la izquierda>

left–hand [ˈlɛftˈhænd] *adj* **1 :** de la izquierda **2** → **left–handed**

left–handed [ˈlɛftˈhændəd] *adj* **1 :** zurdo (dícese de una persona) **2 :** con doble sentido <a left-handed compliment : un cumplido a medias>

leftovers [ˈlɛftˌoːvərz] *npl* **:** restos *mpl,* sobras *fpl*

left wing *n* **the left wing :** la izquierda

left–winger [ˈlɛftˈwɪŋər] *n* **:** izquierdista *mf*

leg [ˈlɛg] *n* **1 :** pierna *f* (de una persona, de carne, de ropa), pata *f* (de un animal, de muebles) **2** STAGE **:** etapa *f* (de un viaje), vuelta *f* (de una carrera)

legacy [ˈlɛgəsi] *n, pl* **-cies :** legado *m,* herencia *f*

legal [ˈliːgəl] *adj* **1 :** legal, jurídico <legal advisor : asesor jurídico> <the legal profession : la abogacía> **2** LAWFUL **:** legítimo, legal

legalistic [ˌliːgəˈlɪstɪk] *adj* **:** legalista

legality [liˈgæləṱi] *n, pl* **-ties :** legalidad *f*

legalize [ˈliːgəˌlaɪz] *vt* **-ized; -izing :** legalizar

legally [ˈliːgəli] *adv* **:** legalmente

legate [ˈlɛgət] *n* **:** legado *m*

legation [lɪˈgeɪʃən] *n* **:** legación *f*

legend [ˈlɛdʒənd] *n* **1** STORY **:** leyenda *f* **2** INSCRIPTION **:** leyenda *f,* inscripción *f* **3 :** signos *mpl* convencionales (en un mapa)

legendary [ˈlɛdʒənˌdɛri] *adj* **:** lengendario

legerdemain [ˌlɛdʒərdəˈmeɪn] → **sleight of hand**

leggings [ˈlɛgɪŋz, ˈlɛgənz] *npl* **:** mallas *fpl*

legibility [ˌlɛdʒəˈbɪləṱi] *n* **:** legibilidad *f*

legible [ˈlɛdʒəbəl] *adj* **:** legible

legibly [ˈlɛdʒəbli] *adv* **:** de manera legible
legion [ˈliːdʒən] *n* **:** legión *f*
legionnaire [ˌliːdʒəˈnær] *n* **:** legionario *m,* -ria *f*
legislate [ˈlɛdʒəsˌleɪt] *vi* **-lated; -lating :** legislar
legislation [ˌlɛdʒəsˈleɪʃən] *n* **:** legislación *f*
legislative [ˈlɛdʒəsˌleɪt̬ɪv] *adj* **:** legislativo, legislador
legislator [ˈlɛdʒəsˌleɪt̬ər] *n* **:** legislador *m,* -dora *f*
legislature [ˈlɛdʒəsˌleɪtʃər] *n* **:** asamblea *f* legislativa
legitimacy [lɪˈdʒɪt̬əməsi] *n* **:** legitimidad *f*
legitimate [lɪˈdʒɪt̬əmət] *adj* **1** VALID **:** legítimo, válido, justificado **2** LAWFUL **:** legítimo, legal
legitimately [lɪˈdʒɪt̬əmətli] *adv* **:** legítimamente
legitimize [lɪˈdʒɪt̬əˌmaɪz] *vt* **-mized; -mizing :** legitimar, hacer legítimo
legume [ˈlɛˌgjuːm, lɪˈgjuːm] *n* **:** legumbre *f*
leisure [ˈliːʒər, ˈlɛ-] *n* **1 :** ocio *m,* tiempo *m* libre <a life of leisure : una vida de ocio>**2 to take one's leisure :** reposar **3 at your leisure :** cuando te venga bien, cuando tengas tiempo
leisurely [ˈliːʒərli, ˈlɛ-] *adj & adv* **:** lento, sin prisas
lemming [ˈlɛmɪŋ] *n* **:** lemming *m*
lemon [ˈlɛmən] *n* **:** limón *m*
lemonade [ˌlɛməˈneɪd] *n* **:** limonada *f*
lemony [ˈlɛməni] *adj* **:** a limón
lend [ˈlɛnd] *vt* **lent** [ˈlɛnt]; **lending 1 :** prestar <to lend money : prestar dinero> **2** GIVE **:** dar <it lends force to his criticism : da fuerza a su crítica> **3 to lend oneself to :** prestarse a
length [ˈlɛŋkθ] *n* **1 :** longitud *f,* largo *m* <10 feet in length : 10 pies de largo> **2** DURATION **:** duración *f* **3 :** trozo *m* (de madera), corte *m* (de tela) **4 to go to any lengths :** hacer todo lo posible **5 at ~ :** extensamente <to speak at length : hablar largo y tendido>
lengthen [ˈlɛŋkθən] *vt* **1 :** alargar <can they lengthen the dress? : ¿se puede alargar el vestido?> **2** EXTEND, PROLONG **:** prolongar, extender **—** *vi* **:** alargarse, crecer <the days are lengthening : los días están creciendo>
lengthways [ˈlɛŋkθˌweɪz] **→ lengthwise**
lengthwise [ˈlɛŋkθˌwaɪz] *adv* **:** a lo largo, longitudinalmente
lengthy [ˈlɛŋkθi] *adj* **lengthier; -est 1** OVERLONG **:** largo y pesado **2** EXTENDED **:** prolongado, largo
leniency [ˈliːniəntsi] *n, pl* **-cies :** lenidad *f,* indulgencia *f*
lenient [ˈliːniənt] *adj* **:** indulgente, poco severo
leniently [ˈliːniəntli] *adv* **:** con lenidad, con indulgencia
lens [ˈlɛnz] *n* **1 :** cristalino *m* (del ojo) **2 :** lente *mf* (de un instrumento o una cámara) **3 → contact lens**
lent → lend
Lent [ˈlɛnt] *n* **:** Cuaresma *f*
lentil [ˈlɛntəl] *n* **:** lenteja *f*
Leo [ˈliːoː] *n* **:** Leo *mf*
leopard [ˈlɛpərd] *n* **:** leopardo *m*
leotard [ˈliːəˌtard] *n* **:** leotardo *m,* malla *f*
leper [ˈlɛpər] *n* **:** leproso *m,* -sa *f*
leprechaun [ˈlɛprəˌkan] *n* **:** duende *m* (irlandés)
leprosy [ˈlɛprəsi] *n* **:** lepra *f* **— leprous** [ˈlɛprəs] *adj*
lesbian[1] [ˈlɛzbiən] *adj* **:** lesbiano
lesbian[2] *n* **:** lesbiana *f*
lesbianism [ˈlɛzbiəˌnɪzəm] *n* **:** lesbianismo *m*
lesion [ˈliːʒən] *n* **:** lesión *f*
less[1] [ˈlɛs] *adv* (*comparative of* **little**[1]) **:** menos <the less you know, the better : cuanto menos sepas, mejor> <less and less : cada vez menos>
less[2] *adj* (*comparative of* **little**[2]) **:** menos <less than three : menos de tres> <less money : menos dinero> <nothing less than perfection : nada menos que la perfección>
less[3] *pron* **:** menos <I'm earning less : estoy ganando menos>
less[4] *prep* **:** menos <one month less two days : un mes menos dos días>
lessee [lɛˈsiː] *n* **:** arrendatario *m,* -ria *f*
lessen [ˈlɛsən] *vt* **:** disminuir, reducir **—** *vi* **:** disminuir, reducirse
lesser [ˈlɛsər] *adj* **:** menor <to a lesser degree : en menor grado>
lesson [ˈlɛsən] *n* **1** CLASS **:** clase *f,* curso *m* **2 :** lección *f* <the lessons of history : las lecciones de la historia>
lessor [ˈlɛˌsɔr, lɛˈsɔr] *n* **:** arrendador *m,* -dora *f*
lest [ˈlɛst] *conj* **:** para (que) no <lest we forget : para que no olvidemos>
let [ˈlɛt] *vt* **let; letting 1** ALLOW **:** dejar, permitir <let me see it : déjame verlo> **2** MAKE **:** hacer <let me know : házmelo saber, avísame> <let them wait : que esperen, haz que esperen> **3** RENT **:** alquilar **4** (*used in the first person plural imperative*) <let's go! : ¡vamos!, ¡vámonos!> <let us pray : oremos> **5 to let down** DISAPPOINT **:** fallar **6 to let off** FORGIVE **:** perdonar **7 to let out** REVEAL **:** revelar **8 to let up** ABATE **:** amainar, disminuir <the pace never lets up : el ritmo nunca disminuye>
letdown *n* **:** chasco *m,* decepción *f*
lethal [ˈliːθəl] *adj* **:** letal **— lethally** *adv*
lethargic [lɪˈθardʒɪk] *adj* **:** letárgico
lethargy [ˈlɛθərdʒi] *n* **:** letargo *m*
let on *vi* **1** ADMIT **:** reconocer <don't let on! : ¡no digas nada!> **2** PRETEND **:** fingir
let's [ˈlɛts] (*contraction of* **let us**) **→ let**

letter[1] [ˈlɛt̬ər] *vt* : marcar con letras, inscribir letras en

letter[2] *n* **1** : letra *f* (del alfabeto) **2** : carta *f* <a letter to my mother : una carta a mi madre> **3 letters** *npl* ARTS : letras *fpl* **4 to the letter** : al pie de la letra

lettering [ˈlɛt̬ərɪŋ] *n* : letra *f*

lettuce [ˈlɛt̬əs] *n* : lechuga *f*

leukemia [luːˈkiːmiə] *n* : leucemia *f*

levee [ˈlɛvi] *n* : dique *m*

level[1] [ˈlɛvəl] *vt* **-eled** *or* **-elled; -eling** *or* **-elling 1** FLATTEN : nivelar, aplanar **2** AIM : apuntar (una pistola), dirigir (una acusación) **3** RAZE : rasar, arrasar

level[2] *adj* **1** EVEN : llano, plano, parejo **2** CALM : tranquilo <to keep a level head : no perder la cabeza>

level[3] *n* : nivel *m*

leveler [ˈlɛvələr] *n* : nivelador *m,* -dora *f*

levelheaded [ˈlɛvəlˈhɛdəd] *adj* : sensato, equilibrado

levelly [ˈlɛvəli] *adv* CALMLY : con ecuanimidad *f,* con calma

levelness [ˈlɛvəlnəs] *n* : uniformidad *f*

lever [ˈlɛvər, ˈliː-] *n* : palanca *f*

leverage [ˈlɛvərɪdʒ, ˈliː-] *n* **1** : apalancamiento *m* (en física) **2** INFLUENCE : influencia *f,* palanca *f fam*

leviathan [lɪˈvaɪəθən] *n* : leviatán *m,* gigante *m*

levity [ˈlɛvət̬i] *n* : ligereza *f,* frivolidad *f*

levy[1] [ˈlɛvi] *vt* **levied; levying 1** IMPOSE : imponer, exigir, gravar (un impuesto) **2** COLLECT : recaudar (un impuesto)

levy[2] *n, pl* **levies** : impuesto *m,* gravamen *m*

lewd [ˈluːd] *adj* : lascivo — **lewdly** *adv*

lewdness [ˈluːdnəs] *n* : lascivia *f*

lexicographer [ˌlɛksəˈkɑgrəfər] *n* : lexicógrafo *m,* -fa *f*

lexicographical [ˌlɛksəkoˈgræfɪkəl] *or* **lexicographic** [-ˈgræfɪk] *adj* : lexicográfico

lexicography [ˌlɛksəˈkɑgrəfi] *n* : lexicografía *f*

lexicon [ˈlɛksɪˌkɑn] *n, pl* **-ica** [-kə] *or* **-icons** : léxico *m,* lexicón *m*

liability [ˌlaɪəˈbɪlət̬i] *n, pl* **-ties 1** RESPONSIBILITY : responsabilidad *f* **2** SUSCEPTIBILITY : propensión *f* **3** DRAWBACK : desventaja *f* **4 liabilities** *npl* DEBTS : deudas *fpl,* pasivo *m*

liable [ˈlaɪəbəl] *adj* **1** RESPONSIBLE : responsable **2** SUSCEPTIBLE : propenso **3** PROBABLE : probable <it's liable to happen : es probable que suceda>

liaison [ˈliːəˌzɑn, liˈeɪ-] *n* **1** CONNECTION : enlace *m,* relación *f* **2** AFFAIR : amorío *m,* aventura *f*

liar [ˈlaɪər] *n* : mentiroso *m,* -sa *f;* embustero *m,* -ra *f*

libel[1] [ˈlaɪbəl] *vt* **-beled** *or* **-belled; -beling** *or* **-belling** : difamar, calumniar

libel[2] *n* : difamación *f,* calumnia *f*

libeler [ˈlaɪbələr] *n* : difamador *m,* -dora *f;* calumniador *m,* -dora *f;* libelista *mf*

libelous *or* **libellous** [ˈlaɪbələs] *adj* : difamatorio, calumnioso, injurioso

liberal[1] [ˈlɪbrəl, ˈlɪbərəl] *adj* **1** TOLERANT : liberal, tolerante **2** GENEROUS : generoso **3** ABUNDANT : abundante **4 liberal arts** : humanidades *fpl,* artes *fpl* liberales

liberal[2] *n* : liberal *mf*

liberalism [ˈlɪbrəˌlɪzəm, ˈlɪbərə-] *n* : liberalismo *m*

liberality [ˌlɪbəˈrælət̬i] *n, pl* **-ties** : liberalidad *f,* generosidad *f*

liberalize [ˈlɪbrəˌlaɪz, ˈlɪbərə-] *vt* **-ized; -izing** : liberalizar

liberally [ˈlɪbrəli, ˈlɪbərə-] *adv* **1** GENEROUSLY : generosamente **2** ABUNDANTLY : abundantemente **3** FREELY : libremente

liberate [ˈlɪbəˌreɪt] *vt* **-ated; -ating** : liberar, libertar

liberation [ˌlɪbəˈreɪʃən] *n* : liberación *f*

liberator [ˈlɪbəˌreɪt̬ər] *n* : libertador *m,* -dora *f*

Liberian [laɪˈbɪriən] *n* : liberiano *m,* -na *f* — **Liberian** *adj*

libertine [ˈlɪbərˌtiːn] *n* : libertino *m,* -na *f*

liberty [ˈlɪbərt̬i] *n, pl* **-ties 1** : libertad *f* **2 to take the liberty of** : tomarse la libertad de **3 to take liberties with** : tomarse confianzas con, tomarse libertades con

libido [ləˈbiːdoː, -ˈbaɪ-] *n, pl* **-dos** : libido *f* — **libidinous** [ləˈbɪdənəs] *adj*

Libra [ˈliːbrə] *n* : Libra *mf*

librarian [laɪˈbrɛriən] *n* : bibliotecario *m,* -ria *f*

library [ˈlaɪˌbrɛri] *n, pl* **-braries** : biblioteca *f*

librettist [lɪˈbrɛt̬ɪst] *n* : libretista *mf*

libretto [lɪˈbrɛt̬o] *n, pl* **-tos** *or* **-ti** [-tiː] : libreto *m*

Libyan [ˈlɪbiən] *n* : libio *m,* -bia *f* — **Libyan** *adj*

lice → **louse**

license[1] [ˈlaɪsənts] *vt* **licensed; licensing** : licenciar, autorizar, dar permiso a

license[2] *or* **licence** *n* **1** PERMISSION : licencia *f,* permiso *m* **2** PERMIT : licencia *f,* carnet *m Spain* <driver's license : licencia de conducir> **3** FREEDOM : libertad *f* **4** LICENTIOUSNESS : libertinaje *m*

licentious [laɪˈsɛntʃəs] *adj* : licencioso, disoluto — **licentiously** *adv*

licentiousness [laɪˈsɛntʃəsnəs] *n* : libertinaje *m*

lichen [ˈlaɪkən] *n* : liquen *m*

licit [ˈlɪsət] *adj* : lícito

lick[1] [ˈlɪk] *vt* **1** : lamer **2** BEAT : darle una paliza (a alguien)

lick[2] *n* **:** lamida *f,* lengüetada *f* <a lick of paint : una mano de pintura> **2** BIT **:** pizca *f,* ápice *m* **3 a lick and a promise :** una lavada a la carrera

licorice [ˈlɪkərɪʃ, -rəs] *n* **:** regaliz *m,* dulce *m* de regaliz

lid [ˈlɪd] *n* **1** COVER **:** tapa *f* **2** EYELID **:** párpado *m*

lie[1] [ˈlaɪ] *vi* **lay** [ˈleɪ]; **lain** [ˈleɪn]; **lying** [ˈlaɪɪŋ] **1 :** acostarse, echarse <I lay down : me acosté> **2 :** estar, estar situado, encontrarse <the book lay on the table : el libro estaba en la mesa> <the city lies to the south : la ciudad se encuentra al sur> **3** CONSIST **:** consistir **4 to lie in :** residir en <the power lies in the people : el poder reside en el pueblo>

lie[2] *vi* **lied; lying** [ˈlaɪɪŋ] **:** mentir

lie[3] *n* **1** UNTRUTH **:** mentira *f* <to tell lies : decir mentiras> **2** POSITION **:** posición *f*

liege [ˈliːdʒ] *n* **:** señor *m* feudal

lien [ˈliːn, ˈliːən] *n* **:** derecho *m* de retención

lieutenant [luːˈtɛnənt] *n* **:** teniente *mf*

lieutenant colonel *n* **:** teniente *mf* coronel

lieutenant commander *n* **:** capitán *m,* -tana *f* de corbeta

lieutenant general *n* **:** teniente *mf* general

life [ˈlaɪf] *n, pl* **lives** [ˈlaɪvz] **1 :** vida *f* <plant life : la vida vegetal> **2** EXISTENCE **:** vida *f,* existencia *f* **3** BIOGRAPHY **:** biografía *f,* vida *f* **4** DURATION **:** duración *f,* vida *f* **5** LIVELINESS **:** vivacidad *f,* animación *f*

lifeblood [ˈlaɪfˌblʌd] *n* **:** parte *f* vital, sustento *m*

lifeboat [ˈlaɪfˌboːt] *n* **:** bote *m* salvavidas

lifeguard [ˈlaɪfˌgɑrd] *n* **:** socorrista *mf,* salvavidas *mf*

lifeless [ˈlaɪfləs] *adj* **:** sin vida, muerto

lifelike [ˈlaɪfˌlaɪk] *adj* **:** que parece vivo, natural, verosímil

lifelong [ˈlaɪfˈlɔŋ] *adj* **:** de toda la vida <a lifelong friend : un amigo de toda la vida>

life preserver *n* **:** salvavidas *m*

lifesaver [ˈlaɪfˌseɪvər] *n* **1 :** salvación *f* **2** → **lifeguard**

lifesaving [ˈlaɪfˌseɪvɪŋ] *n* **:** socorrismo *m*

lifestyle [ˈlaɪfˌstaɪl] *n* **:** estilo *m* de vida

lifetime [ˈlaɪfˌtaɪm] *n* **:** vida *f,* curso *m* de la vida

lift[1] [ˈlɪft] *vt* **1** RAISE **:** levantar, alzar, subir **2** END **:** levantar <to lift a ban : levantar una prohibición> — *vi* **1** RISE **:** levantarse, alzarse **2** CLEAR UP **:** despejar <the fog lifted : se disipó la niebla>

lift[2] *n* **1** LIFTING **:** levantamiento *m,* alzamiento *m* **2** BOOST **:** impulso *m,* estímulo *m* **3 to give someone a lift :** llevar en coche a alguien

liftoff [ˈlɪftˌɔf] *n* **:** despegue *m*

ligament [ˈlɪgəmənt] *n* **:** ligamento *m*

ligature [ˈlɪgəˌtʃʊr, -tʃər] *n* **:** ligadura *f*

light[1] [ˈlaɪt] *v* **lit** [ˈlɪt] *or* **lighted; lighting** *vt* **1** ILLUMINATE **:** iluminar, alumbrar **2** IGNITE **:** encender, prenderle fuego a — *vi* **:** encenderse, prender

light[2] *vi* **lighted** *or* **lit** [ˈlɪt]; **lighting 1** LAND, SETTLE **:** posarse **2** DISMOUNT **:** bajarse, apearse

light[3] [ˈlaɪt] *adv* **1** LIGHTLY **:** suavemente, ligeramente **2 to travel light :** viajar con poco equipaje

light[4] *adj* **1** LIGHTWEIGHT **:** ligero, liviano, poco pesado **2** EASY **:** fácil, ligero, liviano <light reading : lectura fácil> <light work : trabajo liviano> **3** GENTLE, MILD **:** fino, suave, leve <a light breeze : una brisa suave> <a light rain : una lluvia fina> **4** FRIVOLOUS **:** de poca importancia, superficial **5** BRIGHT **:** bien iluminado, claro **6** PALE **:** claro (dícese de los colores), rubio (dícese del pelo)

light[5] *n* **1** ILLUMINATION **:** luz *f* **2** DAYLIGHT **:** luz *f* del día **3** DAWN **:** amanecer *m,* madrugada *f* **4** LAMP **:** lámpara *f* <to turn on off the light : apagar la luz> **5** ASPECT **:** aspecto *m* <in a new light : con otros ojos> <in the light of : en vista de, a la luz de> **6** MATCH **:** fósforo *m,* cerillo *m* **7 to bring to light :** sacar a (la) luz

lightbulb [ˈlaɪtˌbʌlb] *n* **:** bombilla *f,* foco *m,* bombillo *m CA, Col, Ven*

lighten [ˈlaɪtən] *vt* **1** ILLUMINATE **:** iluminar, dar más luz a **2 :** aclararse (el pelo) **3 :** aligerar (una carga, etc.) **4** RELIEVE **:** aliviar **5** GLADDEN **:** alegrar <it lightened his heart : alegró su corazón>

lighter [ˈlaɪtər] *n* **:** encendedor *m*

lighthearted [ˈlaɪtˈhɑrtəd] *adj* **:** alegre, despreocupado, desenfadado — **lightheartedly** *adv*

lightheartedness [ˈlaɪtˈhɑrtədnəs] *n* **:** desenfado *m,* alegría *f*

lighthouse [ˈlaɪtˌhaʊs] *n* **:** faro *m*

lighting [ˈlaɪtɪŋ] *n* **:** iluminación *f*

lightly [ˈlaɪtli] *adv* **1** GENTLY **:** suavemente **2** SLIGHTLY **:** ligeramente **3** FRIVOLOUSLY **:** a la ligera **4 to let off lightly :** tratar con indulgencia

lightness [ˈlaɪtnəs] *n* **1** BRIGHTNESS **:** luminosidad *f,* claridad *f* **2** GENTLENESS **:** ligereza *f,* suavidad *f,* delicadeza *f* **3 :** ligereza *f,* liviandad *f* (de peso)

lightning [ˈlaɪtnɪŋ] *n* **:** relámpago *m,* rayo *m*

lightning bug → **firefly**

lightproof [ˈlaɪtˌpruːf] *adj* **:** impenetrable por la luz, opaco

lightweight [ˈlaɪtˈweɪt] *adj* **:** ligero, liviano, de poco peso

light-year [ˈlaɪtˌjɪr] *n* **:** año *m* luz

lignite [ˈlɪgˌnaɪt] *n* **:** lignito *m*

likable *or* **likeable** [ˈlaɪkəbəl] *adj* **:** simpático, agradable

like[1] [ˈlaɪk] *v* **liked; liking** *vt* **1 :** agradar, gustarle (algo a uno) <he likes rice : le gusta el arroz> <she doesn't like flowers : a ella no le gustan las flores> <I like you : me caes bien> **2** WANT : querer, desear <I'd like a hamburger : quiero una hamburguesa> <he would like more help : le gustaría tener más ayuda> — *vi* **:** querer <do as you like : haz lo que quieras>

like[2] *adj* **:** parecido, semejante, similar

like[3] *n* **1** PREFERENCE **:** preferencia *f,* gusto *m* **2 the like :** cosa *f* parecida, cosas *fpl* por el estilo <I've never seen the like : nunca he visto cosa parecida>

like[4] *conj* **1** AS IF **:** como si <they looked at me like I was crazy : se me quedaron mirando como si estuviera loca> **2** AS **:** como, igual que <she doesn't love you like I do : ella no te quiere como yo>

like[5] *prep* **1 :** como, parecido a <she acts like my mother : se comporta como mi madre> <he looks like me : se parece a mí> **2 :** propio de, típico de <that's just like her : eso es muy típico de ella> **3 :** como <animals like cows : animales como vacas> **4 like this, like that :** así <do it like that : hazlo así>

likelihood [ˈlaɪkli͵hʊd] *n* **:** probabilidad *f* <in all likelihood : con toda probabilidad>

likely[1] [ˈlaɪkli] *adv* **:** probablemente <most likely he's sick : lo más probable es que esté enfermo> <they're likely to come : es probable que vengan>

likely[2] *adj* **-lier; -est 1** PROBABLE **:** probable <to be likely to : ser muy probable que> **2** SUITABLE **:** apropiado, adecuado **3** BELIEVABLE **:** verosímil, creíble **4** PROMISING **:** prometedor

liken [ˈlaɪkən] *vt* **:** comparar

likeness [ˈlaɪknəs] *n* **1** SIMILARITY **:** semejanza *f,* parecido *m* **2** PORTRAIT **:** retrato *m*

likewise [ˈlaɪk͵waɪz] *adv* **1** SIMILARLY **:** de la misma manera, asimismo **2** ALSO **:** también, además, asimismo

liking [ˈlaɪkɪŋ] *n* **1** FONDNESS **:** afición *f* (por una cosa), simpatía *f* (por una persona) **2** TASTE **:** gusto *m* <is it to your liking? : ¿te gusta?>

lilac [ˈlaɪlək, -͵læk, -͵lɑk] *n* **:** lila *f*

lilt [ˈlɪlt] *n* **:** cadencia *f,* ritmo *m* alegre

lily [ˈlɪli] *n, pl* **lilies 1 :** lirio *m,* azucena *f* **2 lily of the valley :** lirio *m* de los valles, muguete *m*

lima bean [ˈlaɪmə] *n* **:** frijol *m* de media luna

limb [ˈlɪm] *n* **1** APPENDAGE **:** miembro *m,* extremidad *f* **2** BRANCH **:** rama *f*

limber[1] [ˈlɪmbər] *vi or* **to limber up :** calentarse, prepararse

limber[2] *adj* **:** ágil (dícese de las personas), flexible (dícese de los objetos)

limbo [ˈlɪm͵boː] *n, pl* **-bos 1 :** limbo *m* (en la religión) **2** OBLIVION **:** olvido *m* <the project is in limbo : el proyecto ha caído en el olvido>

lime [ˈlaɪm] *n* **1 :** cal *f* (óxido) **2 :** lima *f* (fruta), limón *m* verde *Mex*

limelight [ˈlaɪm͵laɪt] *n* **to be in the limelight :** ser el centro de atención, estar en el candelero

limerick [ˈlɪmərɪk] *n* **:** poema *m* jocoso de cinco versos

limestone [ˈlaɪm͵stoːn] *n* **:** piedra *f* caliza, caliza *f*

limit[1] [ˈlɪmət] *vt* **:** limitar, restringir

limit[2] *n* **1** MAXIMUM **:** límite *m,* máximo *m* <speed limit : límite de velocidad> **2 limits** *npl* **:** límites *mpl,* confines *mpl* <city limits : límites de la ciudad> **3 that's the limit! :** ¡eso es el colmo!

limitation [͵lɪməˈteɪʃən] *n* **:** limitación *f,* restricción *f*

limited [ˈlɪmət̬əd] *adj* **:** limitado, restringido

limitless [ˈlɪmətləs] *adj* **:** ilimitado, sin límites

limousine [ˈlɪmə͵ziːn, ͵lɪməˈ-] *n* **:** limusina *f*

limp[1] [ˈlɪmp] *vi* **:** cojear

limp[2] *adj* **1** FLACCID **:** fláccido **2** LANK **:** lacio (dícese del pelo) **3** WEAK **:** débil <to feel limp : sentirse desfallecer, sentirse sin fuerzas>

limp[3] *n* **:** cojera *f*

limpid [ˈlɪmpəd] *adj* **:** límpido, claro

limply [ˈlɪmpli] *adv* **:** sin fuerzas

limpness [ˈlɪmpnəs] *n* **:** flaccidez *f,* debilidad *f*

linden [ˈlɪndən] *n* **:** tilo *m*

line[1] [ˈlaɪn] *v* **lined; lining** *vt* **1 :** forrar, cubrir <to line a dress : forrar un vestido> <to line the walls : cubrir las paredes> **2** MARK **:** rayar, trazar líneas en **3** BORDER **:** bordear **4** ALIGN **:** alinear — *vi* **to line up :** ponerse in fila, hacer cola

line[2] *n* **1** CORD, ROPE **:** cuerda *f* **2** WIRE **:** cable *m* <power line : cable eléctrico> **3 :** línea *f* (de teléfono) **4** ROW **:** fila *f,* hilera *f* **5** NOTE **:** nota *f,* líneas *fpl* <drop me a line : mándame unas líneas> **6** COURSE **:** línea *f* <line of inquiry : línea de investigación> **7** AGREEMENT **:** conformidad *f* <to be in line with : ser conforme a> <to fall into line : estar de acuerdo> **8** OCCUPATION **:** ocupación *f,* rama *f,* especialidad *f* **9** LIMIT **:** línea *f,* límite *m* <dividing line : línea divisoria> <to draw the line : fijar límites> **10** SERVICE **:** línea *f* <bus line : línea de autobuses> **11** MARK **:** línea *f,* arruga *f* (de la cara)

lineage [ˈlɪniɪdʒ] *n* **:** linaje *m,* abolengo *m*

lineal [ˈlɪniəl] *adj* **:** en línea directa

lineaments [ˈlɪniəmənts] *npl* **:** facciones *fpl* (de la cara), rasgos *mpl*

linear [ˈlɪniər] *adj* **:** lineal

linen [ˈlɪnən] *n* **:** lino *m*
liner [ˈlaɪnər] *n* **1** LINING **:** forro *m* **2** SHIP **:** buque *m,* transatlántico *m*
lineup [ˈlaɪn,əp] *n* **1 :** fila *f* de sospechosos **2 :** formación *f* (en deportes) **3** ALIGNMENT **:** alineación *f*
linger [ˈlɪŋgər] *vi* **1** TARRY **:** quedarse, entretenerse, rezagarse **2** PERSIST **:** persistir, sobrevivir
lingerie [,lɑndʒəˈreɪ, ,læʒəˈriː] *n* **:** ropa *f* íntima femenina, lencería *f*
lingo [ˈlɪŋgo] *n, pl* **-goes 1** LANGUAGE **:** idioma *m* **2** JARGON **:** jerga *f*
linguist [ˈlɪŋgwɪst] *n* **:** lingüista *mf*
linguistic [lɪŋˈgwɪstɪk] *adj* **:** lingüístico
linguistics [lɪŋˈgwɪstɪks] *n* **:** lingüística *f*
liniment [ˈlɪnəmənt] *n* **:** linimento *m*
lining [ˈlaɪnɪŋ] *n* **:** forro *m*
link[1] [ˈlɪŋk] *vt* **:** unir, enlazar, conectar — *vi* **to link up :** unirse, conectar
link[2] *n* **1 :** eslabón *m* (de una cadena) **2** BOND **:** conexión *f,* lazo *m,* vínculo *m*
linkage [ˈlɪŋkɪdʒ] *n* **:** conexión *f,* unión *f,* enlace *m*
linoleum [ləˈnoːliəm] *n* **:** linóleo *m*
linseed oil [ˈlɪn,siːd] *n* **:** aceite *m* de linaza
lint [ˈlɪnt] *n* **:** pelusa *f*
lintel [ˈlɪntəl] *n* **:** dintel *m*
lion [ˈlaɪən] *n* **:** león *m*
lioness [ˈlaɪənɪs] *n* **:** leona *f*
lionize [ˈlaɪə,naɪz] *vt* **-ized; -izing :** tratar a una persona como muy importante
lip [ˈlɪp] *n* **1 :** labio *m* **2** EDGE, RIM **:** pico *m* (de una jarra), borde *m* (de una taza)
lipreading [ˈlɪp,riːdɪŋ] *n* **:** lectura *f* de los labios
lipstick [ˈlɪp,stɪk] *n* **:** lápiz *m* de labios, barra *f* de labios
liquefy [ˈlɪkwə,faɪ] *v* **-fied; -fying** *vt* **:** licuar — *vi* **:** licuarse
liqueur [lɪˈkʊr, -ˈkər, -ˈkjʊr] *n* **:** licor *m*
liquid[1] [ˈlɪkwəd] *adj* **:** líquido
liquid[2] *n* **:** líquido *m*
liquidate [ˈlɪkwə,deɪt] *vt* **-dated; -dating :** liquidar
liquidation [,lɪkwəˈdeɪʃən] *n* **:** liquidación *f*
liquidity [lɪkˈwɪdəti] *n* **:** liquidez *f*
liquor [ˈlɪkər] *n* **:** alcohol *m,* bebidas *fpl* alcohólicas, licor *m*
lisp[1] [ˈlɪsp] *vi* **:** cecear
lisp[2] *n* **:** ceceo *m*
lissome [ˈlɪsəm] *adj* **1** FLEXIBLE **:** flexible **2** LITHE **:** ágil y grácil
list[1] [ˈlɪst] *vt* **1** ENUMERATE **:** hacer una lista de, enumerar **2** INCLUDE **:** poner en una lista, incluir — *vi* **:** escorar (dícese de un barco)
list[2] *n* **1** ENUMERATION **:** lista *f* **2** SLANT **:** escora *f,* inclinación *f*
listen [ˈlɪsən] *vi* **1 :** escuchar, oír **2 to listen to** HEED **:** prestar atención a, hacer caso de, escuchar **3 to listen to reason :** atender a razones
listener [ˈlɪsənər] *n* **:** oyente *mf,* persona *f* que sabe escuchar
listless [ˈlɪstləs] *adj* **:** lánguido, apático — **listlessly** *adv*
listlessness [ˈlɪstləsnəs] *n* **:** apatía *f,* languidez *f,* desgana *f*
lit [ˈlɪt] *pp* → **light**
litany [ˈlɪtəni] *n, pl* **-nies :** letanía *f*
liter [ˈliːtər] *n* **:** litro *m*
literacy [ˈlɪtərəsi] *n* **:** alfabetismo *m*
literal [ˈlɪtərəl] *adj* **:** literal — **literally** *adv*
literary [ˈlɪtə,rɛri] *adj* **:** literario
literate [ˈlɪtərət] *adj* **:** alfabetizado
literature [ˈlɪtərə,tʃʊr, -tʃər] *n* **:** literatura *f*
lithe [ˈlaɪð, ˈlaɪθ] *adj* **:** ágil y grácil
lithesome [ˈlaɪðsəm, ˈlaɪθ-] → **lissome**
lithograph [ˈlɪθə,græf] *n* **:** litografía *f*
lithographer [lɪˈθɑgrəfər, ˈlɪθə,græfər] *n* **:** litógrafo *m,* -fa *f*
lithography [lɪˈθɑgrəfi] *n* **:** litografía *f*
litigant [ˈlɪtɪgənt] *n* **:** litigante *mf*
litigate [ˈlɪtə,geɪt] *vi* **-gated; -gating :** litigar
litigation [,lɪtəˈgeɪʃən] *n* **:** litigio *m*
litmus paper [ˈlɪtməs] *n* **:** papel *m* de tornasol
litter[1] [ˈlɪtər] *vt* **:** tirar basura en, ensuciar — *vi* **:** tirar basura
litter[2] *n* **1 :** camada *f,* cría *f* <a litter of kittens **:** una cría de gatitos> **2** STRETCHER **:** camilla *f* **3** RUBBISH **:** basura *f* **4 :** arena *f* higiénica (para gatos)
little[1] [ˈlɪtəl] *adv* **less** [ˈlɛs]; **least** [ˈliːst] **1 :** poco <she sings very little **:** canta muy poco> **2 little did I know that... :** no tenía la menor idea de que ... **3 as little as possible :** lo menos posible
little[2] *adj* **littler** *or* **less** [ˈlɛs] *or* **lesser** [ˈlɛsər]; **littlest** *or* **least** [ˈliːst] **1** SMALL **:** pequeño **2 :** poco <they speak little Spanish **:** hablan poco español> <little by little **:** poco a poco> **3** TRIVIAL **:** sin importancia, trivial
little[3] *n* **1 :** poco *m* <little has changed **:** poco ha cambiado> **2 a little :** un poco, algo <it's a little surprising **:** es algo sorprendente>
Little Dipper → **dipper**
liturgical [ləˈtərdʒɪkəl] *adj* **:** litúrgico — **liturgically** [-kli] *adv*
liturgy [ˈlɪtərdʒi] *n, pl* **-gies :** liturgia *f*
livable [ˈlɪvəbəl] *adj* **:** habitable
live[1] [ˈlɪv] *vi* **lived; living 1** EXIST **:** vivir <as long as I live **:** mientras viva> <to live from day to day **:** vivir al día> **2 :** llevar una vida, vivir <he lived simply **:** llevó una vida sencilla> **3** SUBSIST **:** mantenerse, vivir **4** RESIDE **:** vivir, residir
live[2] [ˈlaɪv] *adj* **1** LIVING **:** vivo **2** BURNING **:** encendido <a live coal **:** una brasa> **3 :** con corriente <live wires

: cables con corriente> **4** : cargado, sin estallar <a live bomb : una bomba sin estallar> **5** CURRENT : de actualidad <a live issue : un asunto de actualidad> **6** : en vivo, en directo <a live interview : una entrevista en vivo>

livelihood [ˈlaɪvliˌhʊd] *n* : sustento *m,* vida *f,* medio *m* de vida

liveliness [ˈlaɪvlinəs] *n* : animación *f,* vivacidad *f*

livelong [ˈlɪvˈlɔŋ] *adj* : entero, completo

lively [ˈlaɪvli] *adj* **-lier; -est** : animado, vivaz, vivo, enérgico

liven [ˈlaɪvən] *vt* : animar — *vi* : animarse

liver [ˈlɪvər] *n* : hígado *m*

livery [ˈlɪvəri] *n, pl* **-eries** : librea *f*

lives → **life**

livestock [ˈlaɪvˌstɑk] *n* : ganado *m*

live wire *n* : persona *f* vivaz y muy activa

livid [ˈlɪvəd] *adj* **1** BLACK-AND-BLUE : amoratado **2** PALE : lívido **3** ENRAGED : furioso

living¹ [ˈlɪvɪŋ] *adj* : vivo

living² *n* **to make a living** : ganarse la vida

living room *n* : living *m,* sala *f* de estar

lizard [ˈlɪzərd] *n* : lagarto *m*

llama [ˈlɑmə, ˈjɑ-] *n* : llama *f*

load¹ [ˈloːd] *vt* : cargar, embarcar

load² *n* **1** CARGO : carga *f* **2** WEIGHT : peso *m* **3** BURDEN : carga *f,* peso *m* **4** **loads** *npl* : montón *m,* pila *f,* cantidad *f* <loads of work : un montón de trabajo>

loaf¹ [ˈloːf] *vi* : holgazanear, flojear, haraganear

loaf² *n, pl* **loaves** [ˈloːvz] **1** : pan *m,* pan *m* de molde, barra *f* de pan **2** **meat loaf** : pan *m* de carne

loafer [ˈloːfər] *n* : holgazán *m,* -zana *f;* haragán *m,* -gana *f;* vago *m,* -ga *f*

loam [ˈloːm] *n* : marga *f,* suelo *m*

loan¹ [ˈloːn] *vt* : prestar

loan² *n* : préstamo *m,* empréstito *m* (del banco)

loath [ˈloːθ, ˈloːð] *adj* : poco dispuesto <I am loath to say it : me resisto a decirlo>

loathe [ˈloːð] *vt* **loathed; loathing** : odiar, aborrecer

loathing [ˈloːðɪŋ] *n* : aversión *f,* odio *m,* aborrecimiento *m*

loathsome [ˈloːθsəm, ˈloːð-] *adj* : odioso, repugnante

lob¹ [ˈlɑb] *vt* **lobbed; lobbing** : hacerle un globo (a otro jugador)

lob² *n* : globo *m* (en deportes)

lobby¹ [ˈlɑbi] *v* **-bied; -bying** *vt* : presionar, ejercer presión sobre — *vi* **to lobby for** : presionar para (lograr algo)

lobby² *n, pl* **-bies** **1** FOYER : vestíbulo *m* **2** LOBBYISTS : grupo *m* de presión, lobby *m*

lobbyist [ˈlɑbiɪst] *n* : miembro *m* de un lobby

lobe [ˈloːb] *n* : lóbulo *m*

lobed [ˈloːbd] *adj* : lobulado

lobotomy [ləˈbɑt̬əmi, lo-] *n, pl* **-mies** : lobotomía *f*

lobster [ˈlɑbstər] *n* : langosta *f*

local¹ [ˈloːkəl] *adj* : local

local² *n* **1** : anestesia *f* local **2 the locals** : los vecinos del lugar, los habitantes

locale [loˈkæl] *n* : lugar *m,* escenario *m*

locality [loˈkæləti] *n, pl* **-ties** : localidad *f*

localize [ˈloːkəˌlaɪz] *vt* **-ized; -izing** : localizar

locally [ˈloːkəli] *adv* : en la localidad, en la zona

locate [ˈloːˌkeɪt, loˈkeɪt] *v* **-cated; -cating** *vt* **1** POSITION : situar, ubicar **2** FIND : localizar, ubicar — *vi* SETTLE : establecerse

location [loˈkeɪʃən] *n* **1** POSITION : posición *f,* emplazamiento *m,* ubicación *f* **2** PLACE : lugar *m,* sitio *m*

lock¹ [ˈlɑk] *vt* **1** FASTEN : cerrar **2** CONFINE : encerrar <they locked me in the room : me encerraron en la sala> **3** IMMOBILIZE : bloquear (una rueda) — *vi* **1** : cerrarse (dícese de una puerta) **2** : trabarse, bloquearse (dícese de una rueda)

lock² *n* **1** : mechón *m* (de pelo) **2** FASTENER : cerradura *f,* cerrojo *m,* chapa *f* **3** : esclusa *f* (de un canal)

locker [ˈlɑkər] *n* : armario *m,* cajón *m* con llave, lócker *m*

locket [ˈlɑkət] *n* : medallón *m,* guardapelo *m,* relicario *m*

lockjaw [ˈlɑkˌjɔ] *n* : tétano *m*

lockout [ˈlɑkˌaʊt] *n* : cierre *m* patronal, lockout *m*

locksmith [ˈlɑkˌsmɪθ] *n* : cerrajero *m,* -ra *f*

lockup [ˈlɑkˌʌp] *n* JAIL : cárcel *f*

locomotion [ˌloːkəˈmoːʃən] *n* : locomoción *f*

locomotive¹ [ˌloːkəˈmoːt̬ɪv] *adj* : locomotor

locomotive² *n* : locomotora *f*

locust [ˈloːkəst] *n* **1** : langosta *f,* chapulín *m CA, Mex* **2** CICADA : cigarra *f,* chicharra *f* **3** : acacia *f* blanca (árbol)

locution [loˈkjuːʃən] *n* : locución *f*

lode [ˈloːd] *n* : veta *f,* vena *f,* filón *m*

lodestar [ˈloːdˌstɑr] *n* : estrella *f* polar

lodestone [ˈloːdˌstoːn] *n* : piedra *f* imán

lodge¹ [ˈlɑdʒ] *v* **lodged; lodging** *vt* **1** HOUSE : hospedar, alojar **2** FILE : presentar <to lodge a complaint : presentar una demanda> — *vi* **1** : posarse, meterse <the bullet lodged in the door : la bala se incrustó en la puerta> **2** STAY : hospedarse, alojarse

lodge² *n* **1** : pabellón *m,* casa *f* de campo <hunting lodge : refugio de caza> **2** : madriguera *f* (de un castor) **3** : logia *f* <Masonic lodge : logia masónica>

lodger [ˈlɑʤər] *n* : inquilino *m*, -na *f*; huésped *m*, -peda *f*

lodging [ˈlɑʤɪŋ] *n* **1** : alojamiento *m* **2 lodgings** *npl* ROOMS : habitaciones *fpl*

loft [ˈlɔft] *n* **1** ATTIC : desván *m*, ático *m*, buhardilla *f* **2** : loft *m* (en un depósito comercial) **3** HAYLOFT : pajar *m* **4** : galería *f* <choir loft : galería del coro>

loftily [ˈlɔftəli] *adv* : altaneramente, con altivez

loftiness [ˈlɔftinəs] *n* **1** NOBILITY : nobleza *f* **2** ARROGANCE : altanería *f*, arrogancia *f* **3** HEIGHT : altura *f*, elevación *f*

lofty [ˈlɔfti] *adj* **loftier; -est 1** NOBLE : noble, elevado **2** HAUGHTY : altivo, arrogante, altanero **3** HIGH : majestuoso, elevado

log[1] [ˈlɔg, ˈlɑg] *vi* **logged; logging 1** : talar (árboles) **2** RECORD : registrar, anotar **3 to log on** : entrar (al sistema) **4 to log off** : salir (del sistema)

log[2] *n* **1** : tronco *m*, leño *m* **2** RECORD : diario *m*

logarithm [ˈlɔgəˌrɪðəm, ˈlɑ-] *n* : logaritmo *m*

logger [ˈlɔgər, ˈlɑ-] *n* : leñador *m*, -dora *f*

loggerhead [ˈlɔgərˌhɛd, ˈlɑ-] *n* **1** : tortuga *f* boba **2 to be at loggerheads** : estar en pugna, estar en desacuerdo

logic [ˈlɑʤɪk] *n* : lógica *f* — **logical** [ˈlɑʤɪkəl] *adj* — **logically** [-kli] *adv*

logistic [ləˈʤɪstɪk, lo-] *adj* : logístico

logistics [ləˈʤɪstɪks, lo-] *ns & pl* : logística *f*

logo [ˈloːˌgoː] *n, pl* **logos** [-ˌgoːz] : logotipo *m*

loin [ˈlɔɪn] *n* **1** : lomo *m* <pork loin : lomo de cerdo> **2 loins** *npl* : lomos *mpl* <to gird one's loins : prepararse para la lucha>

loiter [ˈlɔɪt̬ər] *vi* : vagar, perder el tiempo

loll [ˈlɑl] *vi* **1** SLOUCH : repantigarse **2** IDLE : holgazanear, hacer el vago

lollipop *or* **lollypop** [ˈlɑliˌpɑp] *n* : dulce *m* en palito, chupete *m Chile, Peru*, paleta *f CA, Mex*

lone [ˈloːn] *adj* **1** SOLITARY : solitario **2** ONLY : único

loneliness [ˈloːnlinəs] *n* : soledad *f*

lonely [ˈloːnli] *adj* **-lier; -est 1** SOLITARY : solitario, aislado **2** LONESOME : solo <to feel lonely : sentirse muy solo>

loner [ˈloːnər] *n* : solitario *m*, -ria *f*; recluso *m*, -sa *f*

lonesome [ˈloːnsəm] *adj* : solo, solitario

long[1] [ˈlɔŋ] *vi* **1 to long for** : añorar, desear, anhelar **2 to long to** : anhelar, estar deseando <they longed to see her : estaban deseando verla, tenían muchas ganas de verla>

long[2] *adv* **1** : mucho, mucho tiempo <it didn't take long : no llevó mucho tiempo> <will it last long? : ¿va a durar mucho?> **2 all day long** : todo el día **3 as long as** *or* **so long as** : mientras, con tal que **4 long before** : mucho antes **5 so long!** : ¡hasta luego!, ¡adiós!

long[3] *adj* **longer** [ˈlɔŋgər]; **longest** [ˈlɔŋgəst] **1** (*indicating length*) : largo <the dress is too long : el vestido es demasiado largo> <a long way from : bastante lejos de> <in the long run : a la larga> **2** (*indicating time*) : largo, prolongado <a long illness : una enfermedad prolongada> <a long walk : un paseo largo> <at long last : por fin> **3 to be long on** : estar cargado de

long[4] *n* **1 before long** : dentro de poco **2 the long and the short** : lo esencial, lo fundamental

longevity [lɑnˈʤɛvət̬i] *n* : longevidad *f*

longhand [ˈlɔŋˌhænd] *n* : escritura *f* a mano, escritura *f* cursiva

longhorn [ˈlɔŋˌhɔrn] *n* : longhorn *mf*

longing [ˈlɔŋɪŋ] *n* : vivo deseo *m*, ansia *f*, anhelo *m*

longingly [ˈlɔŋɪŋli] *adv* : ansiosamente, con ansia

longitude [ˈlɑnʤəˌtuːd, -ˌtjuːd] *n* : longitud *f*

longitudinal [ˌlɑnʤəˈtuːdənəl, -ˈtjuː-] *adj* : longitudinal — **longitudinally** *adv*

longshoreman [ˈlɔŋˈʃormən] *n, pl* **-men** [-mən, -ˌmɛn] : estibador *m*, -dora *f*

long-suffering [ˈlɔŋˈsʌfərɪŋ] *adj* : paciente, sufrido

look[1] [ˈlʊk] *vi* **1** GLANCE : mirar <to look out the window : mirar por la ventana> **2** INVESTIGATE : buscar, mirar <look in the closet : busca en el closet> <look before you leap : mira lo que haces> **3** SEEM : parecer <he looks happy : parece estar contento> <I look like my mother : me parezco a mi madre> **4 to look after** : cuidar, cuidar de **5 to look for** EXPECT : esperar **6 to look for** SEEK : buscar — *vt* : mirar

look[2] *n* **1** GLANCE : mirada *f* **2** EXPRESSION : cara *f* <a look of disapproval : una cara de desaprobación> **3** ASPECT : aspecto *m*, apariencia *f*, aire *m*

lookout [ˈlʊkˌaʊt] *n* **1** : centinela *mf*, vigía *mf* **2 to be on the lookout for** : estar al acecho de, andar a la caza de

loom[1] [ˈluːm] *vi* **1** : aparecer, surgir <the city loomed up in the distance : la ciudad surgió en la distancia> **2** IMPEND : amenazar, ser inminente **3 to loom large** : cobrar mucha importancia

loom[2] *n* : telar *m*

loon [ˈluːn] *n* : somorgujo *m*, somormujo *m*

loony *or* **looney** [ˈluːni] *adj* **-nier; -est** : loco, chiflado *fam*

loop[1] [ˈluːp] *vt* **1** : hacer lazadas con **2 to loop around** : pasar alrededor de — *vi* **1** : rizar el rizo (dícese de un avión) **2** : serpentear (dícese de una carretera)
loop[2] *n* **1** : lazada *f* (en hilo o cuerda) **2** BEND : curva *f* **3** CIRCUIT : circuito *m* cerrado **4** : rizo *m* (en la aviación) <to loop the loop : rizar el rizo>
loophole [ˈluːpˌhoːl] *n* : escapatoria *f*, pretexto *m*
loose[1] [ˈluːs] *vt* **loosed; loosing 1** RELEASE : poner en libertad, soltar **2** UNTIE : deshacer, desatar **3** DISCHARGE, UNLEASH : descargar, desatar
loose[2] → **loosely**
loose[3] *adj* **looser; -est 1** INSECURE : flojo, suelto, poco seguro <a loose tooth : un diente flojo> **2** ROOMY : suelto, holgado <loose clothing : ropa holgada> **3** OPEN : suelto, abierto <loose soil : suelo suelto> <a loose weave : una tejida abierta> **4** FREE : suelto <to break loose : soltarse> **5** SLACK : flojo, flexible **6** APPROXIMATE : libre, aproximado <a loose translation : una traducción aproximada>
loosely [ˈluːsli] *adv* **1** : sin apretar **2** ROUGHLY : aproximadamente, más o menos
loosen [ˈluːsən] *vt* : aflojar
loose–leaf [ˈluːsˈliːf] *adj* : de hojas sueltas
looseness [ˈluːsnəs] *n* **1** : aflojamiento *m*, holgura *f* (de ropa) **2** IMPRECISION : imprecisión *f*
loot[1] [ˈluːt] *vt* : saquear, robar
loot[2] *n* : botín *m*
looter [ˈluːt̬ər] *n* : saqueador *m*, -dora *f*
lop [ˈlɑp] *vt* **lopped; lopping** : cortar, podar
lope[1] [ˈloːp] *vi* **loped; loping** : correr a paso largo
lope[2] *n* : paso *m* largo
lopsided [ˈlɑpˌsaɪdəd] *adj* **1** CROOKED : torcido, chueco, ladeado **2** ASYMETRICAL : asimétrico
loquacious [loˈkweɪʃəs] *adj* : locuaz
lord [ˈlɔrd] *n* **1** : señor *m*, noble *m* **2** : lord *m* (en la Gran Bretaña) **3 the Lord** : el Señor **4 good Lord!** : ¡Dios mío!
lordly [ˈlɔrdli] *adj* **-lier; -est** HAUGHTY : arrogante, altanero
lordship [ˈlɔrdˌʃɪp] *n* : señoría *f*
Lord's Supper *n* : Eucaristía *f*
lore [ˈlor] *n* : saber *m* popular, tradición *f*
lose [ˈluːz] *v* **lost** [ˈlɔst]; **losing** [ˈluːzɪŋ] *vt* **1** : perder <I lost my umbrella : perdí mi paraguas> <to lose blood : perder sangre> <to lose one's voice : quedarse afónico> <to have nothing to lose : no tener nada que perder> <to lose no time : no perder tiempo> <to lose weight : perder peso, adelgazar> <to lose one's temper : perder los estribos, enojarse, enfadarse> <to lose sight of : perder de vista> **2** : costar, hacer perder <the errors lost him his job : los errores le costaron su empleo> **3** : atrasar <my watch loses 5 minutes a day : mi reloj atrasa 5 minutos por día> **4 to lose oneself** : perderse, ensimismarse — *vi* **1** : perder <we lost to the other team : perdimos contra el otro equipo> **2** : atrasarse <the clock loses time : el reloj se atrasa>
loser [ˈluːzər] *n* : perdedor *m*, -dora *f*
loss [ˈlɔs] *n* **1** LOSING : pérdida *f* <loss of memory : pérdida de memoria> <to sell at a loss : vender con pérdida> <to be at a loss to : no saber como> **2** DEFEAT : derrota *f*, juego *m* perdido **3 losses** *npl* DEATHS : muertos *mpl*
lost [ˈlɔst] *adj* **1** : perdido <a lost cause : una causa perdida> <lost in thought : absorto> **2 to get lost** : perderse **3 to make up for lost time** : recuperar el tiempo perdido
lot [ˈlɑt] *n* **1** DRAWING : sorteo *m* <by lot : por sorteo> **2** SHARE : parte *f*, porción *f* **3** FATE : suerte *f* **4** LAND, PLOT : terreno *m*, solar *m*, lote *m*, parcela *f* **5 a lot of** *or* **lots of** : mucho, un montón de, bastante <lots of books : un montón de libros, muchos libros> <a lot of people : mucha gente>
loth [ˈloːθ, ˈloːð] → **loath**
lotion [ˈloːʃən] *n* : loción *f*
lottery [ˈlɑt̬əri] *n, pl* **-teries** : lotería *f*
lotus [ˈloːt̬əs] *n* : loto *m*
loud[1] [ˈlaʊd] *adv* : alto, fuerte <out loud : en voz alta>
loud[2] *adj* **1** : alto, fuerte <a loud voice : una voz alta> **2** NOISY : ruidoso <a loud party : una fiesta ruidosa> **3** FLASHY : llamativo, chillón
loudly [ˈlaʊdli] *adv* : alto, fuerte, en voz alta
loudness [ˈlaʊdnəs] *n* : volumen *m*, fuerza *f* (del ruido)
loudspeaker [ˈlaʊdˌspiːkər] *n* : altavoz *m*, altoparlante *m*
lounge[1] [ˈlaʊndʒ] *vi* **lounged; lounging** : holgazanear, gandulear
lounge[2] *n* : salón *m*, sala *f* de estar
louse [ˈlaʊs] *n, pl* **lice** [ˈlaɪs] : piojo *m*
lousy [ˈlaʊzi] *adj* **lousier; -est 1** : piojoso, lleno de piojos **2** BAD : pésimo, muy malo
lout [ˈlaʊt] *n* : bruto *m*, patán *m*
louver *or* **louvre** [ˈluːvər] *n* : persiana *f*, listón *m* de persiana
lovable [ˈlʌvəbəl] *adj* : adorable, amoroso, encantador
love[1] [ˈlʌv] *v* **loved; loving** *vt* **1** : querer, amar <I love you : te quiero> **2** ENJOY : encantarle a alguien, ser (muy) aficionado a, gustarle mucho a uno (algo) <she loves flowers : le encantan las flores> <he loves golf : es muy aficionado al golf> <I'd love

to go with you : me gustaría mucho acompañarte> — *vi* : querer, amar

love[2] *n* **1** : amor *m,* cariño *m* <to be in love with : estar enamorado de> <to fall in love with : enamorarse de> **2** ENTHUSIASM, INTEREST : amor *m,* afición *m,* gusto *m* <love of music : afición a la música> **3** BELOVED : amor *m;* amado *m,* -da *f;* enamorado *m,* -da *f*

loveless [ˈlʌvləs] *adj* : sin amor

loveliness [ˈlʌvlinəs] *n* : belleza *f,* hermosura *f*

lovelorn [ˈlʌv,lɔrn] *adj* : herido de amor, perdidamente enamorado

lovely [ˈlʌvli] *adj* **-lier; -est** : hermoso, bello, lindo, precioso

lover [ˈlʌvər] *n* : amante *mf* (de personas); aficionado *m,* -da *f* (a alguna actividad)

loving [ˈlʌvɪŋ] *adj* : amoroso, cariñoso

lovingly [ˈlʌvɪŋli] *adv* : cariñosamente

low[1] [ˈloː] *vi* : mugir

low[2] *adv* : bajo, profundo <to aim low : apuntar bajo> <to lie low : mantenerse escondido> <to turn the lights down low : bajar las luces>

low[3] *adj* **lower** [ˈloːər]; **-est 1** : bajo <a low building : un edificio bajo> <a low bow : una profunda reverencia> **2** SOFT : bajo, suave <in a low voice : en voz baja> **3** SHALLOW : bajo, poco profundo **4** HUMBLE : humilde, modesto **5** DEPRESSED : deprimido, bajo de moral **6** INFERIOR : bajo, inferior **7** UNFAVORABLE : mal <to have a low opinion of him : tener un mal concepto de él> **8 to be low on** : tener poco de, estar escaso de

low[4] *n* **1** : punto *m* bajo <to reach an all-time low : estar más bajo que nunca> **2** *or* **low gear** : primera velocidad *f* **3** : mugido *m* (de una vaca)

lowbrow [ˈloː,braʊ] *n* : persona *f* inculta

lower[1] [ˈloːər] *vt* **1** DROP : bajar <to lower one's voice : bajar la voz> **2** : arriar, bajar <to lower the flag : arriar la bandera> **3** REDUCE : reducir, bajar **4 to lower oneself** : rebajarse

lower[2] [ˈloːər] *adj* : inferior, más bajo, de abajo

lowland [ˈloːlənd, -ˌlænd] *n* : tierras *fpl* bajas

lowly [ˈloːli] *adj* **-lier; -est** : humilde, modesto

loyal [ˈlɔɪəl] *adj* : leal, fiel — **loyally** *adv*

loyalist [ˈlɔɪəlɪst] *n* : partidario *m,* -ria *f* del régimen

loyalty [ˈlɔɪəlti] *n, pl* **-ties** : lealtad *f,* fidelidad *f*

lozenge [ˈlɑzəndʒ] *n* : pastilla *f*

LSD [ˌɛlˌɛsˈdiː] *n* : LSD *m*

lubricant [ˈluːbrɪkənt] *n* : lubricante *m*

lubricate [ˈluːbrɪˌkeɪt] *vt* **-cated; -cating** : lubricar — **lubrication** [ˌluːbrɪˈkeɪʃən] *n*

lucid [ˈluːsəd] *adj* : lúcido, claro — **lucidly** *adv*

lucidity [luːˈsɪdəti] *n* : lucidez *f*

luck [ˈlʌk] *n* **1** : suerte *f* **2 to have bad luck** : tener mala suerte **3 good luck!** : ¡(buena) suerte!

luckily [ˈlʌkəli] *adv* : afortunadamente, por suerte

luckless [ˈlʌkləs] *adj* : desafortunado

lucky [ˈlʌki] *adj* **luckier; -est 1** : afortunado, que tiene suerte <a lucky woman : una mujer afortunada **2** FORTUITOUS : fortuito, de suerte **3** OPPORTUNE : oportuno **4** : de (la) suerte <lucky number : número de la suerte>

lucrative [ˈluːkrət̬ɪv] *adj* : lucrativo, provechoso — **lucratively** *adv*

ludicrous [ˈluːdəkrəs] *adj* : ridículo, absurdo — **ludicrously** *adv*

ludicrousness [ˈluːdəkrəsnəs] *n* : ridiculez *f,* absurdo *m*

lug [ˈlʌg] *vt* **lugged; lugging** : arrastrar, transportar con dificultad

luggage [ˈlʌgɪdʒ] *n* : equipaje *m*

lugubrious [lʊˈguːbriəs] *adj* : lúgubre — **lugubriously** *adv*

lukewarm [ˈluːkˈwɔrm] *adj* **1** TEPID : tibio **2** HALFHEARTED : poco entusiasta

lull[1] [ˈlʌl] *vt* **1** CALM, SOOTHE : calmar, sosegar **2 to lull to sleep** : arrullar, adormecer

lull[2] *n* : calma *f,* pausa *f*

lullaby [ˈlʌləˌbaɪ] *n, pl* **-bies** : canción *f* de cuna, arrullo *m,* nana *f*

lumbago [ˌlʌmˈbeɪgo] *n* : lumbago *m*

lumber[1] [ˈlʌmbər] *vt* : aserrar (madera) — *vi* : moverse pesadamente

lumber[2] *n* : madera *f*

lumberjack [ˈlʌmbərˌdʒæk] *n* : leñador *m,* -dora *f*

lumberyard [ˈlʌmbərˌjɑrd] *n* : almacén *m* de maderas

luminary [ˈluːməˌnɛri] *n, pl* **-naries** : lumbrera *f,* luminaria *f*

luminescence [ˌluːməˈnɛsənts] *n* : luminiscencia *f* — **luminescent** [-ˈnɛsənt] *adj*

luminosity [ˌluːməˈnɑsət̬i] *n, pl* **-ties** : luminosidad *f*

luminous [ˈluːmənəs] *adj* : luminoso — **luminously** *adv*

lump[1] [ˈlʌmp] *vt or* **to lump together** : juntar, agrupar, amontonar — *vi* CLUMP : agruparse, aglutinarse

lump[2] *n* **1** GLOB : grumo *m* **2** PIECE : pedazo *m,* trozo *m,* terrón *m* <a lump of coal : un trozo de carbón> <a lump of sugar : un terrón de azúcar> **3** SWELLING : bulto *m,* hinchazón *f,* protuberancia *f* **4 to have a lump in one's throat** : tener un nudo en la garganta

lumpy [ˈlʌmpi] *adj* **lumpier; -est 1** : lleno de grumos (dícese de una salsa) **2** UNEVEN : desigual, disparejo

lunacy [ˈluːnəsi] *n, pl* **-cies** : locura *f*

lunar [ˈluːnər] *adj* : lunar

lunatic[1] [ˈluːnəˌtɪk] *adj* : lunático, loco

lunatic[2] *n* : loco *m,* -ca *f*
lunch[1] ['lʌntʃ] *vi* : almorzar, comer
lunch[2] *n* : almuerzo *m,* comida *f,* lonche *m*
luncheon ['lʌntʃən] *n* **1** : comida *f,* almuerzo *m* **2 luncheon meat** : fiambres *fpl*
lung ['lʌŋ] *n* : pulmón *m*
lunge[1] ['lʌndʒ] *vi* **lunged; lunging 1** THRUST : atacar (en la esgrima) **2 to lunge forward** : arremeter, lanzarse
lunge[2] *n* **1** : arremetida *f,* embestida *f* **2** : estocada *f* (en la esgrima)
lurch[1] ['lərtʃ] *vi* **1** PITCH : cabecear, dar bandazos, dar sacudidas **2** STAGGER : tambalearse
lurch[2] *n* **1** : sacudida *f,* bandazo *m* (de un vehículo) **2** : tambaleo *m* (de una persona)
lure[1] ['lʊr] *vt* **lured; luring** : atraer
lure[2] *n* **1** ATTRACTION : atractivo *m* **2** ENTICEMENT : señuelo *m,* aliciente *m* **3** BAIT : cebo *m* artificial (en la pesca)
lurid ['lʊrəd] *adj* **1** GRUESOME : espeluznante, horripilante **2** SENSATIONAL : sensacionalista, chocante **3** GAUDY : chillón
lurk ['lərk] *vi* : estar al acecho
luscious ['lʌʃəs] *adj* **1** DELICIOUS : delicioso, exquisito **2** SEDUCTIVE : seductor, cautivador
lush ['lʌʃ] *adj* **1** LUXURIANT : exuberante, lozano **2** LUXURIOUS : suntuoso, lujoso
lust[1] ['lʌst] *vi* **to lust after** : desear (a una persona), codiciar (riquezas, etc.)
lust[2] *n* **1** LASCIVIOUSNESS : lujuria *f,* lascivia *f* **2** CRAVING : deseo *m,* ansia *f,* anhelo *m*
luster *or* **lustre** ['lʌstər] *n* **1** GLOSS, SHEEN : lustre *m,* brillo *m* **2** SPLENDOR : lustre *m,* esplendor *m*
lusterless ['lʌstərləs] *adj* : deslustrado, sin brillo
lustful ['lʌstfəl] *adj* : lujurioso, lascivo, lleno de deseo
lustrous ['lʌstrəs] *adj* : brillante, brilloso, lustroso
lusty ['lʌsti] *adj* **lustier; -est** : fuerte, robusto, vigoroso — **lustily** ['lʌstəli] *adv*
lute ['lu:t] *n* : laúd *m*
luxuriant [ˌlʌg'ʒʊriənt, ˌlʌk'ʃʊr-] *adj* **1** : exuberante, lozano (dícese de las plantas) **2** : abundante y hermoso (dícese del pelo) — **luxuriantly** *adv*
luxuriate [ˌlʌg'ʒʊriˌeɪt, ˌlʌk'ʃʊr-] *vi* **-ated; -ating 1** : disfrutar **2 to luxuriate in** : deleitarse con
luxurious [ˌlʌg'ʒʊriəs, ˌlʌk'ʃʊr-] *adj* : lujoso, suntuoso — **luxuriously** *adv*
luxury ['lʌkʃəri, 'lʌgʒə-] *n, pl* **-ries** : lujo *m*
lye ['laɪ] *n* : lejía *f*
lying → **lie**[1], **lie**[2]
lymph ['lɪmpf] *n* : linfa *f*
lymphatic [lɪm'fæt̬ɪk] *adj* : linfático
lynch ['lɪntʃ] *vt* : linchar
lynx ['lɪŋks] *n, pl* **lynx** *or* **lynxes** : lince *m*
lyre ['laɪr] *n* : lira *f*
lyric[1] ['lɪrɪk] *adj* : lírico
lyric[2] *n* **1** : poema *m* lírico **2 lyrics** *npl* : letra *f* (de una canción)
lyrical ['lɪrɪkəl] *adj* : lírico, elocuente

M

m ['ɛm] *n, pl* **m's** *or* **ms** ['ɛmz] : decimotercera letra del alfabeto inglés
ma'am ['mæm] → **madam**
macabre [mə'kɑb, -'kɑbər, -'kɑbrə] *adj* : macabro
macadam [mə'kædəm] *n* : macadán *m*
macaroni [ˌmækə'ro:ni] *n* : macarrones *mpl*
macaroon [ˌmækə'ru:n] *n* : macarrón *m,* mostachón *m*
macaw [mə'kɔ] *n* : guacamayo *m*
mace ['meɪs] *n* **1** : maza *f* (arma o símbolo) **2** : macis *f* (especia)
machete [mə'ʃɛt̬i] *n* : machete *m*
machination [ˌmækə'neɪʃən, ˌmæʃə-] *n* : maquinación *f,* intriga *f*
machine[1] [mə'ʃi:n] *vt* **-chined; -chining** : trabajar a máquina
machine[2] *n* **1** : máquina *f* <machine shop : taller de máquinas> <machine language : lenguaje de la máquina> **2** : aparato *m,* maquinaria *f* (en política)
machine gun *n* : ametralladora *f*
machinery [mə'ʃi:nəri] *n, pl* **-eries 1** : maquinaria *f* **2** WORKS : mecanismo *m*
machinist [mə'ʃi:nɪst] *n* : maquinista *mf*
mackerel ['mækərəl] *n, pl* **-el** *or* **-els** : caballa *f*
mackinaw ['mækəˌnɔ] *n* : chaqueta *f* escocesa de lana
mad ['mæd] *adj* **madder; maddest 1** INSANE : loco, demente **2** RABID : rabioso **3** FOOLISH : tonto, insensato **4** ANGRY : enojado, furioso **5** CRAZY : loco <I'm mad about you : estoy loco por ti>
Madagascan [ˌmædə'gæskən] *n* : malgache *mf* — **Madagascan** *adj*
madam ['mædəm] *n, pl* **mesdames** [meɪ'dɑm, -'dæm] : señora *f*
madcap[1] ['mædˌkæp] *adj* ZANY : alocado, disparatado
madcap[2] *n* : alocado *m,* -da *f*
madden ['mædən] *vt* : enloquecer, enfurecer
maddeningly ['mædənɪŋli] *adv* : irritantemente <maddeningly vague : tan vago que te exaspera>

made → **make**[1]

madhouse ['mæd,haʊs] *n* : manicomio *m* <the office was a madhouse : la oficina parecía una casa de locos>

madly ['mædli] *adv* : como un loco, locamente

madman ['mæd,mæn, -mən] *n, pl* **-men** [-mən, -,mɛn] : loco *m,* demente *m*

madness ['mædnəs] *n* : locura *f,* demencia *f*

madwoman ['mæd,wʊmən] *n, pl* **-women** [-,wɪmən] : loca *f,* demente *f*

maelstrom ['meɪlstrəm] *n* : remolino *m,* vorágine *f*

maestro ['maɪ,stroː] *n, pl* **-stros** *or* **-stri** [-,striː] : maestro *m*

Mafia ['mɑfiə] *n* : Mafia *f*

magazine ['mægə,ziːn] *n* **1** STOREHOUSE : almacén *m,* polvorín *m* (de explosivos) **2** PERIODICAL : revista *f* **3** : cargador *m* (de un arma de fuego)

magenta [mə'dʒɛntə] *n* : magenta *f,* color *m* magenta

maggot ['mægət] *n* : gusano *m*

magic[1] ['mædʒɪk] *or* **magical** ['mædʒɪkəl] *adj* : mágico

magic[2] *n* : magia *f*

magically ['mædʒɪkli] *adv* : mágicamente <they magically appeared : aparecieron como por arte de magia>

magician [mə'dʒɪʃən] *n* **1** SORCERER : mago *m,* -ga *f* **2** CONJURER : prestidigitador *m,* -dora *f;* mago *m,* -ga *f*

magistrate ['mædʒə,streɪt] *n* : magistrado *m,* -da *f*

magma ['mægmə] *n* : magma *m*

magnanimity [,mægnə'nɪməṭi] *n, pl* **-ties** : magnanimidad *f*

magnanimous [mæg'nænəməs] *adj* : magnánimo, generoso — **magnanimously** *adv*

magnate ['mæg,neɪt, -nət] *n* : magnate *mf*

magnesium [mæg'niːziəm, -ʒəm] *n* : magnesio *m*

magnet ['mægnət] *n* : imán *m*

magnetic [mæg'nɛṭɪk] *adj* : magnético — **magnetically** [-ṭɪkli] *adv*

magnetic field *n* : campo *m* magnético

magnetism ['mægnə,tɪzəm] *n* : magnetismo *m*

magnetize ['mægnə,taɪz] *vt* **-tized; -tizing 1** : magnetizar, imantar **2** ATTRACT : magnetizar, atraer

magnification [,mægnəfə'keɪʃən] *n* : aumento *m,* ampliación *f*

magnificence [mæg'nɪfəsənts] *n* : magnificencia *f*

magnificent [mæg'nɪfəsənt] *adj* : magnífico — **magnificently** *adv*

magnify ['mægnə,faɪ] *vt* **-fied; -fying 1** ENLARGE : ampliar **2** EXAGGERATE : magnificar, exagerar

magnifying glass *n* : lupa *f*

magnitude ['mægnə,tuːd, -,tjuːd] *n* **1** GREATNESS : magnitud *f,* grandeza *f* **2** QUANTITY : cantidad *f* **3** IMPORTANCE : magnitud *f,* envergadura *f*

magnolia [mæg'noːljə] *n* : magnolia *f* (flor), magnolio *m* (árbol)

magpie ['mæg,paɪ] *n* : urraca *f*

mahogany [mə'hɑgəni] *n, pl* **-nies** : caoba *f*

maid ['meɪd] *n* **1** MAIDEN : doncella *f* **2** *or* **maidservant** ['meɪd,sərvənt] : sirvienta *f,* muchacha *f,* mucama *f,* criada *f*

maiden[1] ['meɪdən] *adj* **1** UNMARRIED : soltera **2** FIRST : primero <maiden voyage : primera travesía>

maiden[2] *n* : doncella *f*

maidenhood ['meɪdən,hʊd] *n* : doncellez *f*

maiden name *n* : nombre *m* de soltera

mail[1] ['meɪl] *vt* : enviar por correo, echar al correo

mail[2] *n* **1** : correo *m* <airmail : correo aéreo> **2** : malla *f* <coat of mail : cota de malla>

mailbox ['meɪl,bɑks] *n* : buzón *m*

mailman ['meɪl,mæn, -mən] *n, pl* **-men** [-mən, -,mɛn] : cartero *m*

maim ['meɪm] *vt* : mutilar, desfigurar, lisiar

main[1] ['meɪn] *adj* : principal, central <the main office : la oficina central>

main[2] *n* **1** HIGH SEAS : alta mar *f* **2** : tubería *f* principal (de agua o gas), cable *m* principal (de un circuito) **3 with might and main** : con todas sus fuerzas

mainframe ['meɪn,freɪm] *n* : mainframe *m,* computadora *f* central

mainland ['meɪn,lænd, -lənd] *n* : continente *m*

mainly ['meɪnli] *adv* **1** PRINCIPALLY : principalmente, en primer lugar **2** MOSTLY : principalmente, en la mayor parte

mainstay ['meɪn,steɪ] *n* : pilar *m,* sostén *m* principal

mainstream[1] ['meɪn,striːm] *adj* : dominante, corriente, convencional

mainstream[2] *n* : corriente *f* principal

maintain [meɪn'teɪn] *vt* **1** SERVICE : dar mantenimiento a (una máquina) **2** PRESERVE : mantener, conservar <to maintain silence : guardar silencio> **3** SUPPORT : mantener, sostener **4** ASSERT : mantener, sostener, afirmar

maintenance ['meɪntənənts] *n* : mantenimiento *m*

maize ['meɪz] *n* : maíz *m*

majestic [mə'dʒɛstɪk] *adj* : majestuoso — **majestically** [-tɪkli] *adv*

majesty ['mædʒəsti] *n, pl* **-ties 1** : majestad *f* <Your Majesty : su Majestad> **2** SPLENDOR : majestuosidad *f,* esplendor *m*

major[1] ['meɪdʒər] *vi* **-jored; -joring** : especializarse

major[2] *adj* **1** GREATER : mayor **2** NOTEWORTHY : mayor, notable **3** SERIOUS : grave **4** : mayor (en la música)

major[3] *n* **1** : mayor *mf,* comandante *mf* (en las fuerzas armadas) **2** : especialidad *f* (universitaria)

Majorcan [mɑˈdʒɔrkən, mə-, -ˈjɔr-] *n* : mallorquín *m,* -quina *f* — **Majorcan** *adj*

major general *n* : general *mf* de división

majority [məˈdʒɔrət̬i] *n, pl* **-ties 1** ADULTHOOD : mayoría *f* de edad **2** : mayoría *f,* mayor parte *f* <the vast majority : la inmensa mayoría>

make[1] [ˈmeɪk] *v* **made** [ˈmeɪd]; **making** *vt* **1** CREATE : hacer <to make noise : hacer ruido> **2** FASHION, MANUFACTURE : hacer, fabricar <she made a dress : hizo un vestido> **3** DEVISE, FORM : desarrollar, elaborar, formar **4** CONSTITUTE : hacer, constituir <made of stone : hecho de piedra> **5** PREPARE : hacer, preparar **6** RENDER : hacer, poner <it makes him nervous : lo pone nervioso> <to make someone happy : hacer feliz a alguien> <it made me sad : me dio pena> **7** PERFORM : hacer <to make a gesture : hacer un gesto> **8** COMPEL : hacer, forzar, obligar **9** EARN : ganar <to make a living : ganarse la vida> — *vi* **1** HEAD : ir, dirigirse <we made for home : nos fuimos a casa> **2 to make do** : arreglárselas **3 to make good** REPAY : pagar **4 to make good** SUCCEED : tener éxito

make[2] *n* BRAND : marca *f*

make–believe[1] [ˌmeɪkbəˈliːv] *adj* : imaginario

make–believe[2] *n* : fantasía *f,* invención *f* <a world of make-believe : un mundo de ensueño>

make out *vt* **1** WRITE : hacer (un cheque) **2** DISCERN : distinguir, divisar **3** UNDERSTAND : comprender, entender — *vi* : arreglárselas <how did you make out? : ¿qué tal te fue?>

maker [ˈmeɪkər] *n* : fabricante *mf*

makeshift [ˈmeɪkˌʃɪft] *adj* : provisional, improvisado

makeup [ˈmeɪkˌʌp] *n* **1** COMPOSITION : composición *f* **2** CHARACTER : carácter *m,* temperamento *m* **3** COSMETICS : maquillaje *m*

make up *vt* **1** INVENT : inventar **2** : recuperar <she made up the time : recuperó las horas perdidas> — *vi* RECONCILE : hacer las paces, reconciliarse

maladjusted [ˌmæləˈdʒʌstəd] *adj* : inadaptado

malady [ˈmælədi] *n, pl* **-dies** : dolencia *f,* enfermedad *f,* mal *m*

malaise [məˈleɪz, mæ-] *n* : malestar *m*

malapropism [ˈmæləˌprɑˌpɪzəm] *n* : uso *m* incorrecto y cómico de una palabra

malaria [məˈlɛriə] *n* : malaria *f,* paludismo *m*

malarkey [məˈlɑrki] *n* : tonterías *fpl,* estupideces *fpl*

Malawian [məˈlɑwiən] *n* : malauiano *m,* -na *f* — **Malawian** *adj*

Malay [məˈleɪ, ˈmeɪˌleɪ] *n* **1** *or* **Malayan** [məˈleɪən, meɪ-; ˈmeɪˌleɪən] : malayo *m,* -ya *f* **2** : malayo *m* (idioma) — **Malay** *or* **Malayan** *adj*

male[1] [ˈmeɪl] *adj* **1** : macho **2** MASCULINE : masculino

male[2] *n* : macho *m* (de animales o plantas), varón *m* (de personas)

malefactor [ˈmæləˌfæktər] *n* : malhechor *m,* -chora *f*

maleness [ˈmeɪlnəs] *n* : masculinidad *f*

malevolence [məˈlɛvələnts] *n* : malevolencia *f*

malevolent [məˈlɛvələnt] *adj* : malévolo

malformation [ˌmælfɔrˈmeɪʃən] *n* : malformación *f*

malformed [mælˈfɔrmd] *adj* : mal formado, deforme

malfunction[1] [mælˈfʌŋkʃən] *vi* : funcionar mal

malfunction[2] *n* : mal funcionamiento *m*

malice [ˈmælɪs] *n* **1** : malicia *f,* malevolencia *f* **2 with malice aforethought** : con premeditación

malicious [məˈlɪʃəs] *adj* : malicioso, malévolo — **maliciously** *adv*

malign[1] [məˈlaɪn] *vt* : calumniar, difamar

malign[2] *adj* : maligno

malignancy [məˈlɪgnəntsi] *n, pl* **-cies** : malignidad *f*

malignant [məˈlɪgnənt] *adj* : maligno

malinger [məˈlɪŋgər] *vi* : fingirse enfermo

malingerer [məˈlɪŋgərər] *n* : uno que se finge enfermo

mall [ˈmɔl] *n* **1** PROMENADE : alameda *f,* paseo *m* (arbolado) **2** : centro *m* comercial <shopping mall : galería comercial>

mallard [ˈmælərd] *n, pl* **-lard** *or* **-lards** : pato *m* real, ánade *mf* real

malleable [ˈmæliəbəl] *adj* : maleable

mallet [ˈmælət] *n* : mazo *m*

malnourished [mælˈnərɪʃt] *adj* : desnutrido, malnutrido

malnutrition [ˌmælnʊˈtrɪʃən, -njʊ-] *n* : desnutrición *f,* malnutrición *f*

malodorous [mælˈoːdərəs] *adj* : maloliente

malpractice [ˌmælˈpræktəs] *n* : mala práctica *f,* negligencia *f*

malt [ˈmɔlt] *n* : malta *f*

maltreat [mælˈtriːt] *vt* : maltratar

mama *or* **mamma** [ˈmɑmə] *n* : mamá *f*

mammal [ˈmæməl] *n* : mamífero *m*

mammalian [məˈmeɪliən, mæ-] *adj* : mamífero

mammary [ˈmæməri] *adj* **1** : mamario **2 mammary gland** : glándula mamaria

mammogram [ˈmæmə͵græm] *n* : mamografía *f*
mammoth[1] [ˈmæməθ] *adj* : colosal, gigantesco
mammoth[2] *n* : mamut *m*
man[1] [ˈmæn] *vt* **manned; manning** : tripular (un barco o avión), encargarse de (un servicio)
man[2] *n, pl* **men** [ˈmɛn] **1** PERSON : hombre *m,* persona *f* **2** MALE : hombre *m* **3** MANKIND : humanidad *f*
manacles [ˈmænɪkəlz] *npl* HANDCUFFS : esposas *fpl*
manage [ˈmænɪdʒ] *v* **-aged; -aging** *vt* **1** HANDLE : controlar, manejar **2** DIRECT : administrar, dirigir **3** CONTRIVE : lograr, ingeniárselas para — *vi* COPE : arreglárselas
manageable [ˈmænɪdʒəbəl] *adj* : manejable
management [ˈmænɪdʒmənt] *n* **1** DIRECTION : administración *f,* gestión *f,* dirección *f* **2** HANDLING : manejo *m* **3** MANAGERS : dirección *f,* gerencia *f*
manager [ˈmænɪdʒər] *n* : director *m,* -tora *f;* gerente *mf;* administrador *m,* -dora *f*
managerial [͵mænəˈdʒɪriəl] *adj* : directivo, gerencial
mandarin [ˈmændərən] *n* **1** : mandarín *m* **2** *or* **mandarin orange** : mandarina *f*
mandate [ˈmæn͵deɪt] *n* : mandato *m*
mandatory [ˈmændə͵tori] *adj* : obligatorio
mandible [ˈmændəbəl] *n* : mandíbula *f*
mandolin [͵mændəˈlɪn, ˈmændələn] *n* : mandolina *f*
mane [ˈmeɪn] *n* : crin *f* (de un caballo), melena *f* (de un león o una persona)
maneuver[1] [məˈnuːvər, -ˈnjuː-] *vt* **1** PLACE, POSITION : maniobrar, posicionar, colocar **2** MANIPULATE : manipular, maniobrar — *vi* : maniobrar
maneuver[2] *n* : maniobra *f*
manfully [ˈmænfəli] *adj* : valientemente
manganese [ˈmæŋgə͵niːz, -͵niːs] *n* : manganeso *m*
mange [ˈmeɪndʒ] *n* : sarna *f*
manger [ˈmeɪndʒər] *n* : pesebre *m*
mangle [ˈmæŋgəl] *vt* **-gled; -gling** **1** CRUSH, DESTROY : aplastar, despedazar, destrozar **2** MUTILATE : mutilar <to mangle a text : mutilar un texto>
mango [ˈmæŋ͵goː] *n, pl* **-goes** : mango *m*
mangrove [ˈmæn͵groːv, ˈmæŋ-] *n* : mangle *m*
mangy [ˈmeɪndʒi] *adj* **mangier; -est** **1** : sarnoso **2** SHABBY : gastoso
manhandle [ˈmæn͵hændəl] *vi* **-dled; -dling** : maltratar, tratar con poco cuidado
manhole [ˈmæn͵hoːl] *n* : boca *f* de alcantarilla
manhood [ˈmæn͵hʊd] *n* **1** : madurez *f* (de un hombre) **2** COURAGE, MANLINESS : hombría *f,* valor *m* **3** MEN : hombres *mpl*
manhunt [ˈmæn͵hʌnt] *n* : búsqueda *f* (de un criminal)
mania [ˈmeɪniə, -njə] *n* : manía *f*
maniac [ˈmeɪni͵æk] *n* : maníaco *m,* -ca *f;* maniático *m,* -ca *f*
maniacal [məˈnaɪəkəl] *adj* : maníaco, maniaco
manicure[1] [ˈmænə͵kjʊr] *vt* **-cured; -curing** **1** : hacer la manicura a **2** TRIM : recortar
manicure[2] *n* : manicura *f*
manicurist [ˈmænə͵kjʊrɪst] *n* : manicuro *m,* -ra *f*
manifest[1] [ˈmænə͵fɛst] *vt* : manifestar
manifest[2] *adj* : manifiesto, patente — **manifestly** *adv*
manifestation [͵mænəfəˈsteɪʃən] *n* : manifestación *f*
manifesto [͵mænəˈfɛs͵toː] *n, pl* **-tos** *or* **-toes** : manifiesto *m*
manifold[1] [ˈmænə͵foːld] *adj* : diverso, variado
manifold[2] *n* : colector *m* (de escape)
manipulate [məˈnɪpjə͵leɪt] *vt* **-lated; -lating** : manipular
manipulation [mə͵nɪpjəˈleɪʃən] *n* : manipulación *f*
manipulative [məˈnɪpjə͵leɪt̬ɪv, -lət̬ɪv] *adj* : manipulador
mankind [ˈmænˈkaɪnd, ͵kaɪnd] *n* : género *m* humano, humanidad *f*
manliness [ˈmænlinəs] *n* : hombría *f,* masculinidad *f*
manly [ˈmænli] *adj* **-lier; -est** : varonil, viril
man–made [ˈmænˈmeɪd] *adj* : artificial <man-made fabrics : telas sintéticas>
manna [ˈmænə] *n* : maná *m*
mannequin [ˈmænɪkən] *n* **1** DUMMY : maniquí *m* **2** MODEL : modelo *mf*
manner [ˈmænər] *n* **1** KIND, SORT : tipo *m,* clase *f* **2** WAY : manera *f,* modo *m* **3** STYLE : estilo *m* (artístico) **4 manners** *npl* CUSTOMS : costumbres *fpl* <Victorian manners : costumbres victorianas> **5 manners** *npl* ETIQUETTE : modales *mpl,* educación *f,* etiqueta *f* <good manners : buenos modales>
mannered [ˈmænərd] *adj* **1** AFFECTED, ARTIFICIAL : amanerado, afectado **2 well–mannered** : educado, cortés **3** → **ill–mannered**
mannerism [ˈmænə͵rɪzəm] *n* : peculiaridad *f,* gesto *m* particular
mannerly [ˈmænərli] *adj* : cortés, bien educado
mannish [ˈmænɪʃ] *adj* : masculino, hombruno
man–of–war [͵mænəˈwɔr, -əvˈwɔr] *n, pl* **men–of–war** [͵mɛn-] WARSHIP : buque *m* de guerra
manor [ˈmænər] *n* **1** : casa *f* solariega, casa *f* señorial **2** ESTATE : señorío *m*

manpower ['mæn,paʊər] *n* : personal *m,* mano *f* de obra
mansion ['mæntʃən] *n* : mansión *f*
manslaughter ['mæn,slɔtər] *n* : homicidio *m* sin premeditación
mantel ['mæntəl] *n* : repisa *f* de chimenea
mantelpiece ['mæntəl,piːs] → **mantel**
mantis ['mæntəs] *n, pl* **-tises** *or* **-tes** ['mæn,tiːz] : mantis *f* religiosa
mantle ['mæntəl] *n* : manto *m*
manual[1] ['mænjʊəl] *adj* : manual — **manually** *adv*
manual[2] *n* : manual *m*
manufacture[1] [,mænjə'fæktʃər] *vt* **-tured; -turing** : fabricar, manufacturar, confeccionar (ropa), elaborar (comestibles)
manufacture[2] *n* : manufactura *f,* fabricación *f,* confección *f* (de ropa), elaboración *f* (de comestibles)
manufacturer [,mænjə'fæktʃərər] *n* : fabricante *m;* manufacturero *m,* -ra *f*
manure [mə'nʊr, -'njʊr] *n* : estiércol *m*
manuscript ['mænjə,skrɪpt] *n* : manuscrito *m*
many[1] ['mɛni] *adj* **more** ['mor]; **most** ['moːst] : muchos
many[2] *pron* : muchos *pl,* -chas *pl*
map[1] ['mæp] *vt* **mapped; mapping 1** : trazar el mapa de **2** PLAN : planear, proyectar <to map out a program : planear un programa>
map[2] *n* : mapa *m*
maple ['meɪpəl] *n* : arce *m*
mar ['mɑr] *vt* **marred; marring 1** SPOIL : estropear, echar a perder **2** DEFACE : desfigurar
maraschino [,mærə'skiːnoː, -'ʃiː-] *n, pl* **-nos** : cereza *f* al marrasquino
marathon ['mærə,θɑn] *n* **1** RACE : maratón *m* **2** CONTEST : competencia *f* de resistencia
maraud [mə'rɔd] *vi* : merodear
marauder [mə'rɔdər] *n* : merodeador *m,* -dora *f*
marble ['mɑrbəl] *n* **1** : mármol *m* **2** : canica *f* <to play marbles : jugar a las canicas>
march[1] ['mɑrtʃ] *vi* **1** : marchar, desfilar <they marched past the grandstand : desfilaron ante la tribuna> **2** : caminar con resolución <she marched right up to him : se le acercó sin vacilación>
march[2] *n* **1** MARCHING : marcha *f* **2** PASSAGE : paso *m* (del tiempo) **3** PROGRESS : avance *m,* progreso *m* **4** : marcha *f* (en música)
March ['mɑrtʃ] *n* : marzo *m*
marchioness ['mɑrʃənɪs] *n* : marquesa *f*
Mardi Gras ['mɑrdi,grɑ] *n* : martes *m* de Carnaval
mare ['mær] *n* : yegua *f*
margarine ['mɑrdʒərən] *n* : margarina *f*
margin ['mɑrdʒən] *n* : margen *m*
marginal ['mɑrdʒənəl] *adj* **1** : marginal **2** MINIMAL : mínimo — **marginally** *adv*
marigold ['mærə,goːld] *n* : maravilla *f,* caléndula *f*
marijuana [,mærə'*h*wɑnə] *n* : marihuana *f*
marina [mə'riːnə] *n* : puerto *m* deportivo
marinate ['mærə,neɪt] *vt* **-nated; -nating** : marinar
marine[1] [mə'riːn] *adj* **1** : marino <marine life : vida marina> **2** NAUTICAL : náutico, marítimo **3** : de la infantería de marina
marine[2] *n* : soldado *m* de marina
mariner ['mærɪnər] *n* : marinero *m,* marino *m*
marionette [,mæriə'nɛt] *n* : marioneta *f,* títere *m*
marital ['mærətəl] *adj* **1** : matrimonial **2 marital status** : estado *m* civil
maritime ['mærə,taɪm] *adj* : marítimo
marjoram ['mɑrdʒərəm] *n* : mejorana *f*
mark[1] ['mɑrk] *vt* **1** : marcar **2** CHARACTERIZE : caracterizar **3** SIGNAL : señalar **4** NOTICE : prestar atención a, hacer caso de **5 to mark off** : demarcar, delimitar
mark[2] *n* **1** TARGET : blanco *m* **2** : marca *f,* señal *f* <put a mark where you left off : pon una señal donde terminaste> **3** INDICATION : señal *f,* indicio *m* **4** GRADE : nota *f* **5** IMPRINT : huella *f,* marca *f* **6** BLEMISH : marca *f,* imperfección *f*
marked ['mɑrkt] *adj* : marcado, notable — **markedly** ['mɑrkədli] *adv*
marker ['mɑrkər] *n* : marcador *m*
market[1] ['mɑrkət] *vt* : poner en venta, comercializar
market[2] *n* **1** MARKETPLACE : mercado *m* <the open market : el mercado libre> **2** DEMAND : demanda *f,* mercado *m* **3** STORE : tienda *f* **4** → **stock market**
marketable ['mɑrkətəbəl] *adj* : vendible
marketplace ['mɑrkət,pleɪs] *n* : mercado *m*
marksman ['mɑrksmən] *n, pl* **-men** [-mən, -,mɛn] : tirador *m*
marksmanship ['mɑrksmən,ʃɪp] *n* : puntería *f*
marlin ['mɑrlɪn] *n* : marlín *m*
marmalade ['mɑrmə,leɪd] *n* : mermelada *f*
marmoset ['mɑrmə,sɛt] *n* : tití *m*
marmot ['mɑrmət] *n* : marmota *f*
maroon[1] [mə'ruːn] *vt* : abandonar, aislar
maroon[2] *n* : rojo *m* oscuro, granate *m*
marquee [mɑr'kiː] *n* : marquesina *f*
marquess ['mɑrkwɪs] *or* **marquis** ['mɑrkwɪs, mɑr'kiː] *n, pl* **-quesses** *or* **-quises** [-'kiːz, -'kiːzəz] *or* **-quis** [-'kiː, -'kiːz] : marqués *m*
marquise [mɑr'kiːz] → **marchioness**

marriage [ˈmærɪdʒ] *n* **1** : matrimonio *m* **2** WEDDING : casamiento *m,* boda *f*

marriageable [ˈmærɪdʒəbəl] *adj* **of marriageable age** : de edad de casarse

married [ˈmærid] *adj* **1** : casado **2 to get married** : casarse

marrow [ˈmæroː] *n* : médula *f,* tuétano *m*

marry [ˈmæri] *vt* **-ried; -rying 1** : casar <the priest married them : el cura los casó> **2** : casarse con <she married John : se casó con John>

Mars [ˈmɑrz] *n* : Marte *m*

marsh [ˈmɑrʃ] *n* **1** : pantano *m* **2 salt marsh** : marisma *f*

marshal[1] [ˈmɑrʃəl] *vt* **-shaled** *or* **-shalled; -shaling** *or* **-shalling 1** : poner en orden, reunir **2** USHER : conducir

marshal[2] *n* **1** : maestro *m* de ceremonias **2** : mariscal *m* (en el ejército); jefe *m,* -fa *f* (de la policía, de los bomberos, etc.)

marshmallow [ˈmɑrʃˌmɛloː, -ˌmæloː] *n* : malvavisco *m*

marshy [ˈmɑrʃi] *adj* **marshier; -est** : pantanoso

marsupial [mɑrˈsuːpiəl] *n* : marsupial *m*

mart [ˈmɑrt] *n* MARKET : mercado *m*

marten [ˈmɑrtən] *n, pl* **-ten** *or* **-tens** : marta *f*

martial [ˈmɑrʃəl] *adj* : marcial

martin [ˈmɑrtən] *n* **1** SWALLOW : golondrina *f* **2** SWIFT : vencejo *m*

martyr[1] [ˈmɑrṭər] *vt* : martirizar

martyr[2] *n* : mártir *mf*

martyrdom [ˈmɑrṭərdəm] *n* : martirio *m*

marvel[1] [ˈmɑrvəl] *vi* **-veled** *or* **-velled; -veling** *or* **-velling** : maravillarse

marvel[2] *n* : maravilla *f*

marvelous [ˈmɑrvələs] *or* **marvellous** *adj* : maravilloso — **marvelously** *adv*

Marxism [ˈmɑrkˌsɪzəm] *n* : marxismo *m*

Marxist[1] [ˈmɑrksɪst] *adj* : marxista

Marxist[2] *n* : marxista *mf*

mascara [mæsˈkærə] *n* : rímel *m,* rimel *m*

mascot [ˈmæsˌkɑt, -kət] *n* : mascota *f*

masculine [ˈmæskjələn] *adj* : masculino

masculinity [ˌmæskjəˈlɪnəṭi] *n* : masculinidad *f*

mash[1] [ˈmæʃ] *vt* **1** : hacer puré de (papas, etc.) **2** CRUSH : aplastar, majar

mash[2] *n* **1** FEED : afrecho *m* **2** : malta *f* (para hacer bebidas alcohólicas) **3** PASTE, PULP : papilla *f,* pasta *f*

mask[1] [ˈmæsk] *vt* **1** CONCEAL, DISGUISE : enmascarar, ocultar **2** COVER : cubrir, tapar

mask[2] *n* : máscara *f,* careta *f,* mascarilla *f* (de un cirujano o dentista)

masochism [ˈmæsəˌkɪzəm, ˈmæzə-] *n* : masoquismo *m*

masochist [ˈmæsəˌkɪst, ˈmæzə-] *n* : masoquista *mf*

masochistic [ˌmæsəˈkɪstɪk, ˌmæzə-] *adj* : masoquista

mason [ˈmeɪsən] *n* **1** BRICKLAYER : albañil *mf* **2** *or* **stonemason** [ˈstoːnˌ-] : mampostero *m,* cantero *m*

masonry [ˈmeɪsənri] *n, pl* **-ries 1** BRICKLAYING : albañería *f* **2** *or* **stonemasonry** [ˈstoːnˌ-] : mampostería *f*

masquerade[1] [ˌmæskəˈreɪd] *vi* **-aded; -ading 1** : disfrazarse (de), hacerse pasar (por) **2** : asistir a una mascarada

masquerade[2] *n* **1** : mascarada *f,* baile *m* de disfraces **2** FACADE : farsa *f,* fachada *f*

mass[1] [ˈmæs] *vi* : concentrarse, juntarse en masa — *vt* : concentrar

mass[2] *n* **1** : masa *f* <atomic mass : masa atómica> **2** BULK : mole *f,* volumen *m* **3** MULTITUDE : cantidad *f,* montón *m* (de cosas), multitud *f* (de gente) **4 the masses** : las masas, el pueblo, el populacho

Mass [ˈmæs] *n* : misa *f*

massacre[1] [ˈmæsɪkər] *vt* **-cred; -cring** : masacrar

massacre[2] *n* : masacre *f*

massage[1] [məˈsɑʒ, -ˈsɑdʒ] *vt* **-saged; -saging** : masajear

massage[2] *n* : masaje *m*

masseur [mæˈsər] *n* : masajista *m*

masseuse [mæˈsøz, -ˈsuːz] *n* : masajista *f*

massive [ˈmæsɪv] *adj* **1** BULKY : voluminoso, macizo **2** HUGE : masivo, enorme — **massively** *adv*

mast [ˈmæst] *n* : mástil *m,* palo *m*

master[1] [ˈmæstər] *vt* **1** SUBDUE : dominar **2** : llegar a dominar <she mastered French : llegó a dominar el francés>

master[2] *n* **1** TEACHER : maestro *m,* profesor *m* **2** EXPERT : experto *m,* -ta *f;* maestro *m,* -tra *f* **3** : amo *m* (de animales o esclavos), señor *m* (de la casa) **4 master's degree** : maestría *f*

masterful [ˈmæstərfəl] *adj* **1** IMPERIOUS : autoritario, imperioso, dominante **2** SKILLFUL : magistral — **masterfully** *adv*

masterly [ˈmæstərli] *adj* : magistral

masterpiece [ˈmæstərˌpiːs] *n* : obra *f* maestra

masterwork [ˈmæstərˌwərk] → **masterpiece**

mastery [ˈmæstəri] *n* **1** DOMINION : dominio *m,* autoridad *f* **2** SUPERIORITY : superioridad *f* **3** EXPERTISE : maestría *f*

masticate [ˈmæstəˌkeɪt] *v* **-cated; -cating** : masticar

mastiff [ˈmæstɪf] *n* : mastín *m*

mastodon [ˈmæstəˌdɑn] *n* : mastodonte *m*

masturbate [ˈmæstərˌbeɪt] *v* **-bated; bating** *vi* : masturbarse — *vt* : masturbar

masturbation [ˌmæstərˈbeɪʃən] *n* : masturbación *f*

mat[1] ['mæt] *v* **matted; matting** *vt* TANGLE : enmarañar — *vi* : enmarañarse

mat[2] *n* **1** : estera *f* **2** TANGLE : maraña *f* **3** PAD : colchoneta *f* (de gimnasia) **4** *or* **matt** *or* **matte** ['mæt] FRAME : marco *m* (de cartón)

mat[3] → **matte**

matador ['mætə,dɔr] *n* : matador *m*

match[1] ['mætʃ] *vt* **1** PIT : enfrentar, oponer **2** EQUAL, FIT : igualar, corresponder a, coincidir con **3** : combinar con, hacer juego con <her shoes match her dress : sus zapatos hacen juego con su vestido> — *vi* **1** CORRESPOND : concordar, coincidir **2** : hacer juego <with a tie to match : con una corbata que hace juego>

match[2] *n* **1** EQUAL : igual *mf* <he's no match for her : no puede competir con ella> **2** FIGHT, GAME : partido *m,* combate *m* (en boxeo) **3** MARRIAGE : matrimonio *m,* casamiento *m* **4** : fósforo *m,* cerilla *f,* cerillo *m* (*in various countries*) <he lit a match : encendió un fósforo> **5 to be a good match** : hacer buena pareja (dícese de las personas), hacer juego (dícese de la ropa)

matchless ['mætʃləs] *adj* : sin igual, sin par

matchmaker ['mætʃ,meɪkər] *n* : casamentero *m,* -ra *f*

mate[1] ['meɪt] *v* **mated; mating** *vi* **1** FIT : encajar **2** PAIR : emparejarse **3** (*relating to animals*) : aparearse, copular — *vt* : aparear, acoplar (animales)

mate[2] *n* **1** COMPANION : compañero *m,* -ra *f;* camarada *mf* **2** : macho *m,* hembra *f* (de animales) **3** : oficial *mf* (de un barco) <first mate : primer oficial> **4** : compañero *m,* -ra *f;* pareja *f* (de un zapato, etc.)

material[1] [mə'tɪriəl] *adj* **1** PHYSICAL : material, físico <the material world : el mundo material> <material needs : necesidades materiales> **2** IMPORTANT : importante, esencial **3 material evidence** : prueba *f* sustancial

material[2] *n* **1** : material *m* **2** CLOTH : tejido *m,* tela *f*

materialism [mə'tɪriə,lɪzəm] *n* : materialismo *m*

materialist [mə'tɪriəlɪst] *n* : materialista *mf*

materialistic [mə,tɪriə'lɪstɪk] *adj* : materialista

materialize [mə'tɪriə,laɪz] *v* **-ized; -izing** *vt* : materializar, hacer aparecer — *vi* : materializarse, aparecer

maternal [mə'tərnəl] *adj* MOTHERLY : maternal — **maternally** *adv*

maternity[1] [mə'tərnət̬i] *adj* : de maternidad <maternity clothes : ropa de futura mamá> <maternity leave : licencia por maternidad>

maternity[2] *n, pl* **-ties** : maternidad *f*

math ['mæθ] → **mathematics**

mathematical [,mæθə'mætɪkəl] *adj* : matemático — **mathematically** *adv*

mathematician [,mæθəmə'tɪʃən] *n* : matemático *m,* -ca *f*

mathematics [,mæθə'mætɪks] *ns & pl* : matemáticas *fpl,* matemática *f*

matinee *or* **matinée** [,mætən'eɪ] *n* : matiné *f*

matriarch ['meɪtri,ɑrk] *n* : matriarca *f*

matriarchy ['meɪtri,ɑrki] *n, pl* **-chies** : matriarcado *m*

matriculate [mə'trɪkjə,leɪt] *v* **-lated; -lating** *vt* : matricular — *vi* : matricularse

matriculation [mə,trɪkjə'leɪʃən] *n* : matrícula *f,* matriculación *f*

matrimony ['mætrə,mo:ni] *n* : matrimonio *m* — **matrimonial** [,mætrə'mo:niəl] *adj*

matrix ['meɪtrɪks] *n, pl* **-trices** ['meɪtrə,si:z, 'mæ-] *or* **-trixes** ['meɪtrɪksəz] : matriz *f*

matron ['meɪtrən] *n* : matrona *f*

matronly ['meɪtrənli] *adj* : de matrona, matronal

matte ['mæt] *adj* : mate, de acabado mate

matter[1] ['mætər] *vi* : importar <it doesn't matter : no importa>

matter[2] *n* **1** QUESTION : asunto *m,* cuestión *f* <a matter of taste : una cuestión de gusto> **2** SUBSTANCE : materia *f,* sustancia *f* **3 matters** *npl* CIRCUMSTANCES : situación *f,* cosas *fpl* <to make matters worse : para colmo de males> **4 to be the matter** : pasar <what's the matter? : ¿qué pasa?> **5 as a matter of fact** : en efecto, en realidad **6 for that matter** : de hecho **7 no matter how much** : por mucho que

matter–of–fact ['mætərəv'fækt] *adj* : práctico, realista

mattress ['mætrəs] *n* : colchón *m*

mature[1] [mə'tʊr, -'tjʊr, -'tʃʊr] *vi* **-tured; -turing 1** : madurar **2** : vencer <when does the loan mature? : ¿cuándo vence el préstamo?>

mature[2] *adj* **-turer; -est 1** : maduro **2** DUE : vencido

maturity [mə'tʊrət̬i, -'tjʊr-, -'tʃʊr-] *n* : madurez *f*

maudlin ['mɔdlɪn] *adj* : sensiblero

maul[1] ['mɔl] *vt* **1** BEAT : golpear, pegar **2** MANGLE : mutilar **3** MANHANDLE : maltratar

maul[2] *n* MALLET : mazo *m*

Mauritanian [,mɔrə'teɪniən] *n* : mauritano *m,* -na *f* — **Mauritanian** *adj*

mausoleum [,mɔsə'li:əm, ,mɔzə-] *n, pl* **-leums** *or* **-lea** [-'li:ə] : mausoleo *m*

mauve ['mo:v, 'mɔv] *n* : malva *m*

maven *or* **mavin** ['meɪvən] *n* EXPERT : experto *m,* -ta *f*

maverick ['mævrɪk, 'mævə-] *n* **1** : ternero *m* sin marcar **2** NONCONFORMIST : inconformista *mf,* disidente *mf*

mawkish ['mɔkɪʃ] *adj* : sensiblero

maxim ['mæksəm] *n* : máxima *f*

maximize ['mæksə,maɪz] *vt* **-mized; -mizing** : maximizar, llevar al máximo

maximum[1] ['mæksəməm] *adj* : máximo

maximum[2] *n, pl* **-ma** ['mæksəmə] *or* **-mums** : máximo *m*

may ['meɪ] *v aux, past* **might** ['maɪt]; *present s & pl* **may 1** (*expressing permission*) : poder <you may go : puedes ir> **2** (*expressing possibility or probability*) : poder <you may be right : puede que tengas razón> <it may happen occasionally : puede pasar de vez en cuando> **3** (*expressing desires, intentions, or contingencies*) <may the best man win : que gane el mejor> <I laugh that I may not weep : me río para no llorar> <come what may : pase lo que pase>

May ['meɪ] *n* : mayo *m*

maybe ['meɪbi] *adv* PERHAPS : quizás, tal vez

mayfly ['meɪ,flaɪ] *n, pl* **-flies** : efímera *f*

mayhem ['meɪ,hɛm, 'meɪəm] *n* **1** MUTILATION : mutilación *f* **2** DEVASTATION : estragos *mpl*

mayonnaise ['meɪə,neɪz] *n* : mayonesa *f*

mayor ['meɪər, 'mɛr] *n* : alcalde *m*, -desa *f*

mayoral ['meɪərəl, 'mɛrəl] *adj* : de alcalde

maze ['meɪz] *n* : laberinto *m*

me ['mi:] *pron* **1** : me <she called me : me llamó> <give it to me : dámelo> **2** (*after a preposition*) : mí <for me : para mí> <with me : conmigo> **3** (*after conjunctions and verbs*) : yo <it's me : soy yo> <as big as me : tan grande como yo> **4** (*emphatic use*) : yo <me, too! : ¡yo también!> <who, me? : ¿quién, yo?>

meadow ['mɛdo:] *n* : prado *m*, pradera *f*

meadowland ['mɛdo,lænd] *n* : pradera *f*

meadowlark ['mɛdo,lɑrk] *n* : pájaro *m* cantor con el pecho amarillo

meager *or* **meagre** ['mi:gər] *adj* **1** THIN : magro, flaco **2** POOR, SCANTY : exiguo, escaso, pobre

meagerly ['mi:gərli] *adv* : pobremente

meagerness ['mi:gərnəs] *n* : escasez *f*, pobreza *f*

meal ['mi:l] *n* **1** : comida *f* <a hearty meal : una comida sustanciosa> **2** : harina *f* (de maíz, etc.)

mealtime ['mi:l,taɪm] *n* : hora *f* de comer

mean[1] ['mi:n] *vt* **meant** ['mɛnt]; **meaning 1** INTEND : querer, pensar, tener la intención de <I didn't mean to do it : lo hice sin querer> <what do you mean to do? : ¿qué piensas hacer?> **2** SIGNIFY : querer decir, significar <what does that mean? : ¿qué quiere decir eso?> **3** : importar <health means everything : lo que más importa es la salud>

mean[2] *adj* **1** HUMBLE : humilde **2** NEGLIGIBLE : despreciable <it's no mean feat : no es poca cosa> **3** STINGY : mezquino, tacaño **4** CRUEL : malo, cruel <to be mean to someone : tratar mal a alguien> **5** AVERAGE, MEDIAN : medio

mean[3] *n* **1** MIDPOINT : término *m* medio **2** AVERAGE : promedio *m*, media *f* aritmética **3 means** *npl* WAY : medio *m*, manera *f*, vía *f* **4 means** *npl* RESOURCES : medios *mpl*, recursos *mpl* **5 by all means** : por supuesto, cómo no **6 by means of** : por medio de **7 by no means** : de ninguna manera, de ningún modo

meander [mi'ændər] *vi* **-dered; -dering 1** WIND : serpentear **2** WANDER : vagar, andar sin rumbo fijo

meaning ['mi:nɪŋ] *n* **1** : significado *m*, sentido *m* <double meaning : doble sentido> **2** INTENT : intención *f*, propósito *m*

meaningful ['mi:nɪŋfəl] *adj* : significativo — **meaningfully** *adv*

meaningless ['mi:nɪŋləs] *adj* : sin sentido

meanness ['mi:nnəs] *n* **1** CRUELTY : crueldad *f*, mezquindad *f* **2** STINGINESS : tacañería *f*

meantime[1] ['mi:n,taɪm] *adv* → **meanwhile**[1]

meantime[2] *n* **1** : interín *m* **2 in the meantime** : entretanto, mientras tanto

meanwhile[1] ['mi:n,*h*waɪl] *adv* : entretanto, mientras tanto

meanwhile[2] *n* → **meantime**[2]

measles ['mi:zəlz] *ns & pl* : sarampión *m*

measly ['mi:zli] *adj* **-slier; -est** : miserable, mezquino

measurable ['mɛʒərəbəl, 'meɪ-] *adj* : mensurable — **measurably** [-bli] *adv*

measure[1] ['mɛʒər, 'meɪ-] *v* **-sured; -suring** : medir <he measured the table : midió la mesa> <it measures 15 feet tall : mide 15 pies de altura>

measure[2] *n* **1** AMOUNT : medida *f*, cantidad *f* <in large measure : en gran medida> <a full measure : una cantidad exacta> <a measure of proficiency : una cierta competencia> <for good measure : de ñapa, por añadidura> **2** DIMENSIONS, SIZE : medida *f*, tamaño *m* **3** RULER : regla *f* <tape measure : cinta métrica> **4** MEASUREMENT : medida *f* <cubic measure : medida de capacidad> **5** MEASURING : medición *f* **6 measures** *npl* : medidas *fpl* <security measures : medidas de seguridad>

measureless ['mɛʒərləs, 'meɪ-] *adj* : inmensurable

measurement ['mɛʒərmənt, 'meɪ-] *n* **1** MEASURING : medición *f* **2** DIMENSION : medida *f*

measure up *vi* **to measure up to** : estar a la altura de
meat [ˈmiːt] *n* **1** FOOD : comida *f* **2** : carne *f* <meat and fish : carne y pescado> **3** SUBSTANCE : sustancia *f*, esencia *f* <the meat of the story : la sustancia del cuento>
meatball [ˈmiːtˌbɔl] *n* : albóndiga *f*
meaty [ˈmiːti] *adj* **meatier; -est** : con mucha carne, carnoso
mechanic [mɪˈkænɪk] *n* : mecánico *m*, -ca *f*
mechanical [mɪˈkænɪkəl] *adj* : mecánico — **mechanically** *adv*
mechanics [mɪˈkænɪks] *ns & pl* **1** : mecánica *f* <fluid mechanics : la mecánica de fluidos> **2** MECHANISMS : mecanismos *mpl*, aspectos *mpl* prácticos
mechanism [ˈmɛkəˌnɪzəm] *n* : mecanismo *m*
mechanization [ˌmɛkənəˈzeɪʃən] *n* : mecanización *f*
mechanize [ˈmɛkəˌnaɪz] *vt* **-nized; -nizing** : mecanizar
medal [ˈmɛdəl] *n* : medalla *f*, condecoración *f*
medalist [ˈmɛdəlɪst] *or* **medallist** *n* : medallista *mf*
medallion [məˈdæljən] *n* : medallón *m*
meddle [ˈmɛdəl] *vi* **-dled; -dling** : meterse, entrometerse
meddler [ˈmɛdələr] *n* : entrometido *m*, -da *f*
meddlesome [ˈmɛdəlsəm] *adj* : entrometido
media [ˈmiːdiə] *npl* : medios *mpl* de comunicación
median[1] [ˈmiːdiən] *adj* : medio
median[2] *n* : valor *m* medio
mediate [ˈmiːdiˌeɪt] *vi* **-ated; -ating** : mediar
mediation [ˌmiːdiˈeɪʃən] *n* : mediación *f*
mediator [ˈmiːdiˌeɪṯər] *n* : mediador *m*, -dora *f*
medical [ˈmɛdɪkəl] *adj* : médico
medicate [ˈmɛdəˌkeɪt] *vt* **-cated; -cating** : medicar <medicated powder : polvos medicinales>
medication [ˌmɛdəˈkeɪʃən] *n* **1** TREATMENT : tratamiento *m*, medicación *f* **2** MEDICINE : medicamento *m* <to be on medication : estar medicado>
medicinal [məˈdɪsənəl] *adj* : medicinal
medicine [ˈmɛdəsən] *n* **1** MEDICATION : medicina *f*, medicamento *m* **2** : medicina *f* <he's studying medicine : estudia medicina>
medicine man *n* : hechicero *m*
medieval *or* **mediaeval** [mɪˈdiːvəl, ˌmiː-, ˌmɛ-, -diˈiːvəl] *adj* : medieval
mediocre [ˌmiːdiˈoːkər] *adj* : mediocre
mediocrity [ˌmiːdiˈɑkrəṯi] *n, pl* **-ties** : mediocridad *f*
meditate [ˈmɛdəˌteɪt] *vi* **-tated; -tating** : meditar
meditation [ˌmɛdəˈteɪʃən] *n* : meditación *f*
meditative [ˈmɛdəˌteɪṯɪv] *adj* : meditabundo
medium[1] [ˈmiːdiəm] *adj* : mediano <of medium height : de estatura mediana, de estatura regular>
medium[2] *n, pl* **-diums** *or* **-dia** [ˈmiːdiə] **1** MEAN : punto *m* medio, término *m* medio <happy medium : justo medio> **2** MEANS : medio *m* **3** SUBSTANCE : medio *m*, sustancia *f* <a viscous medium : un medio viscoso> **4** : medio *m* de comunicación **5** : medio *m* (artístico)
medley [ˈmɛdli] *n, pl* **-leys** : popurrí *m* (de canciones)
meek [ˈmiːk] *adj* **1** LONG-SUFFERING : paciente, sufrido **2** SUBMISSIVE : sumiso, dócil, manso
meekly [ˈmiːkli] *adv* : dócilmente
meekness [ˈmiːknəs] *n* : mansedumbre *f*, docilidad *f*
meet[1] [ˈmiːt] *v* **met** [ˈmɛt]; **meeting** *vt* **1** ENCOUNTER : encontrarse con **2** JOIN : unirse con **3** CONFRONT : enfrentarse a **4** SATISFY : satisfacer, cumplir con <to meet costs : pagar los gastos> **5** : conocer <I met his sister : conocí a su hermana> — *vi* ASSEMBLE : reunirse, congregarse
meet[2] *n* : encuentro *m*
meeting [ˈmiːṯɪŋ] *n* **1** : reunión *f* <to open the meeting : abrir la sesión> **2** ENCOUNTER : encuentro *m* **3** : entrevista *f* (formal)
meetinghouse [ˈmiːṯɪŋˌhaʊs] *n* : iglesia *f* (de ciertas confesiones protestantes)
megabyte [ˈmɛgəˌbaɪt] *n* : megabyte *m*
megahertz [ˈmɛgəˌhərts, -ˌhɛrts] *n* : megahercio *m*
megaphone [ˈmɛgəˌfoːn] *n* : megáfono *m*
melancholy[1] [ˈmɛlənˌkɑli] *adj* : melancólico, triste, sombrío
melancholy[2] *n, pl* **-cholies** : melancolía *f*
melanoma [ˌmɛləˈnoːmə] *n, pl* **-mas** : melanoma *m*
melee [ˈmeɪˌleɪ, meɪˈleɪ] *n* BRAWL : reyerta *f*, riña *f*, pelea *f*
meliorate [ˈmiːljəˌreɪt, ˈmiːliə-] → **ameliorate**
mellow[1] [ˈmɛloː] *vt* : suavizar, endulzar — *vi* : suavizarse, endulzarse
mellow[2] *adj* **1** RIPE : maduro **2** MILD : apacible <a mellow character : un carácter apacible> <mellow wines : vinos añejos> **3** : suave, dulce <mellow colors : colores suaves> <mellow tones : tonos dulces>
mellowness [ˈmɛlonəs] *n* : suavidad *f*, dulzura *f*
melodic [məˈlɑdɪk] *adj* : melódico — **melodically** [-dɪkli] *adv*
melodious [məˈloːdiəs] *adj* : melodioso — **melodiously** *adv*

melodiousness [mə'loːdiəsnəs] *n* : calidad *f* de melódico
melodrama ['mɛlə,drɑmə, -,dræ-] *n* : melodrama *m*
melodramatic [,mɛlədrə'mæṭɪk] *adj* : melodramático — **melodramatically** [-ṭɪkli] *adv*
melody ['mɛlədi] *n, pl* **-dies** : melodía *f,* tonada *f*
melon ['mɛlən] *n* : melón *m*
melt ['mɛlt] *vt* **1** : derretir, disolver **2** SOFTEN : ablandar <it melted his heart : ablandó su corazón> — *vi* **1** : derretirse, disolverse **2** SOFTEN : ablandarse **3** DISAPPEAR : desvanecerse, esfumarse <the clouds melted away : las nubes se desvanecieron>
melting point *n* : punto *m* de fusión
member ['mɛmbər] *n* **1** LIMB : miembro *m* **2** : miembro *m* (de un grupo); socio *m,* -cia *f* (de un club) **3** PART : miembro *m,* parte *f*
membership ['mɛmbər,ʃɪp] *n* **1** : membresía *f* <application for membership : solicitud de entrada> **2** MEMBERS : membresía *f,* miembros *mpl,* socios *mpl*
membrane ['mɛm,breɪn] *n* : membrana *f* — **membranous** ['mɛmbrənəs] *adj*
memento [mɪ'mɛn,toː] *n, pl* **-tos** *or* **-toes** : recuerdo *m*
memo ['mɛmoː] *n, pl* **memos** : memorándum *m*
memoirs ['mɛm,wɑrz] *npl* : memorias *fpl,* autobiografía *f*
memorabilia [,mɛmərə'biliə, -'bɪljə] *npl* **1** : objetos *mpl* de interés histórico **2** MEMENTOS : recuerdos *mpl*
memorable ['mɛmərəbəl] *adj* : memorable, notable — **memorably** [-bli] *adv*
memorandum [,mɛmə'rændəm] *n, pl* **-dums** *or* **-da** [-də] : memorándum *m*
memorial[1] [mə'moriəl] *adj* : conmemorativo
memorial[2] *n* : monumento *m* conmemorativo
Memorial Day *n* : el último lunes de mayo (observado en Estados Unidos como día feriado para conmemorar a los caídos en guerra)
memorialize [mə'moriə,laɪz] *vt* **-ized; -izing** COMMEMORATE : conmemorar
memorization [,mɛmərə'zeɪʃən] *n* : memorización *f*
memorize ['mɛmə,raɪz] *vt* **-rized; -rizing** : memorizar, aprender de memoria
memory ['mɛmri, 'mɛmə-] *n, pl* **-ries** **1** : memoria *f* <he has a good memory : tiene buena memoria> **2** RECOLLECTION : recuerdo *m* **3** COMMEMORATION : memoria *f,* conmemoración *f*
men → **man**[2]
menace[1] ['mɛnəs] *vt* **-aced; -acing** **1** THREATEN : amenazar **2** ENDANGER : poner en peligro
menace[2] *n* : amenaza *f*
menacing ['mɛnəsɪŋli] *adj* : amenazador, amenazante
menagerie [mə'nædʒəri, -'næʒəri] *n* : colección *f* de animales salvajes
mend[1] ['mɛnd] *vt* **1** CORRECT : enmendar, corregir <to mend one's ways : enmendarse> **2** REPAIR : remendar, arreglar, reparar — *vi* HEAL : curarse
mend[2] *n* : remiendo *m*
mendicant ['mɛndɪkənt] *n* BEGGAR : mendigo *m,* -ga *f*
menhaden [mɛn'heɪdən, mən-] *ns & pl* : pez *m* de la misma familia que los arenques
menial[1] ['miːniəl] *adj* : servil, bajo
menial[2] *n* : sirviente *m,* -ta *f*
meningitis [,mɛnən'dʒaɪṭəs] *n, pl* **-gitides** [-'dʒɪṭə,diːz] : meningitis *f*
menopause ['mɛnə,pɔz] *n* : menopausia *f*
menorah [mə'norə] *n* : candelabro *m* (usado en los oficios religiosos judíos)
menstrual ['mɛn*t*strʊəl] *adj* : menstrual
menstruate ['mɛn*t*strʊ,eɪt] *vi* **-ated; -ating** : menstruar
menstruation [,mɛn*t*strʊ'eɪʃən] *n* : menstruación *f*
mental ['mɛntəl] *adj* : mental <mental hospital : hospital psiquiátrico> — **mentally** *adv*
mentality [mɛn'tæləṭi] *n, pl* **-ties** : mentalidad *f*
menthol ['mɛn,θɔl, -,θoːl] *n* : mentol *m*
mentholated [,mɛn*t*θə,leɪṭəd] *adj* : mentolado
mention[1] ['mɛntʃən] *vt* : mencionar, mentar, referirse a <don't mention it! : ¡de nada!, ¡no hay de qué!>
mention[2] *n* : mención *f*
mentor ['mɛn,tɔr, 'mɛntər] *n* : mentor *m*
menu ['mɛn,juː] *n* **1** : menú *m,* carta *f* (en un restaurante) **2** : menú *m* (de computadoras)
meow[1] [miː'aʊ] *vi* : maullar
meow[2] *n* : maullido *m,* miau *m*
mercantile ['mərkən,tiːl, -,taɪl] *adj* : mercantil
mercenary[1] ['mərsən,ɛri] *adj* : mercenario
mercenary[2] *n, pl* **-naries** : mercenario *m,* -ria *f*
merchandise ['mərtʃən,daɪz, -,daɪs] *n* : mercancía *f,* mercadería *f*
merchandiser ['mərtʃən,daɪzər] *n* : comerciante *mf;* vendedor *m,* -dora *f*
merchant ['mərtʃənt] *n* : comerciante *mf*
merchant marine *n* : marina *f* mercante
merciful ['mərsɪfəl] *adj* : misericordioso, clemente
mercifully ['mərsɪfli] *adv* **1** : con misericordia, con compasión **2** FORTUNATELY : afortunadamente

merciless [ˈmərsɪləs] *adj* : despiadado — **mercilessly** *adv*
mercurial [ˌmərˈkjʊriəl] *adj* TEMPERAMENTAL : temperamental, volátil
mercury [ˈmərkjəri] *n, pl* **-ries** : mercurio *m*
Mercury *n* : Mercurio *m*
mercy [ˈmərsi] *n, pl* **-cies** **1** CLEMENCY : misericordia *f,* clemencia *f* **2** BLESSING : bendición *f*
mere [ˈmɪr] *adj, superlative* **merest** : mero, simple
merely [ˈmɪrli] *adv* : solamente, simplemente
merge [ˈmərdʒ] *v* **merged; merging** *vi* : unirse, fusionarse (dícese de las compañías), confluir (dícese de los ríos, las calles, etc.) — *vt* : unir, fusionar, combinar
merger [ˈmərdʒər] *n* : unión *f,* fusión *f*
meridian [məˈrɪdiən] *n* : meridiano *m*
meringue [məˈræŋ] *n* : merengue *m*
merino [məˈriːno] *n, pl* **-nos** **1** : merino *m,* -na *f* **2** *or* **merino wool** : lana *f* merino
merit[1] [ˈmɛrət] *vt* : merecer, ser digno de
merit[2] *n* : mérito *m,* valor *m*
meritorious [ˌmɛrəˈtoriəs] *adj* : meritorio
mermaid [ˈmərˌmeɪd] *n* : sirena *f*
merriment [ˈmɛrɪmənt] *n* : alegría *f,* júbilo *m,* regocijo *m*
merry [ˈmɛri] *adj* **-rier; -est** : alegre — **merrily** [ˈmɛrəli] *adv*
merry–go–round [ˈmɛrigoˌraʊnd] *n* : carrusel *m,* tiovivo *m*
merrymaker [ˈmɛriˌmeɪkər] *n* : juerguista *mf*
merrymaking [ˈmɛriˌmeɪkɪŋ] *n* : juerga *f*
mesa [ˈmeɪsə] *n* : mesa *f*
mesdames → **madam, Mrs.**
mesh[1] [ˈmɛʃ] *vi* **1** ENGAGE : engranar (dícese de las piezas mecánicas) **2** TANGLE : enredarse **3** COORDINATE : coordinarse, combinar
mesh[2] *n* **1** : malla *f* <wire mesh : malla metálica> **2** NETWORK : red *f* **3** MESHING : engranaje *m* <in mesh : engranado>
mesmerize [ˈmɛzməˌraɪz] *vt* **-ized; -izing** **1** HYPNOTIZE : hipnotizar **2** FASCINATE : cautivar, embelesar, fascinar
mess[1] [ˈmɛs] *vt* **1** SOIL : ensuciar **2 to mess up** DISARRANGE : desordenar, desarreglar **3 to mess up** BUNGLE : echar a perder — *vi* **1** PUTTER : entretenerse **2** INTERFERE : meterse, entrometerse <don't mess with me : no te metas conmigo>
mess[2] *n* **1** : rancho *m* (para soldados, etc.) **2** DISORDER : desorden *m* <your room is a mess : tienes el cuarto hecho un desastre> **3** CONFUSION, TURMOIL : confusión *f,* embrollo *m,* lío *m fam*
message [ˈmɛsɪdʒ] *n* : mensaje *m,* recado *m*
messenger [ˈmɛsəndʒər] *n* : mensajero *m,* -ra *f*
Messiah [məˈsaɪə] *n* : Mesías *m*
Messrs. → **Mr.**
messy [ˈmɛsi] *adj* **messier; -est** UNTIDY : desordenado, sucio
met → **meet**
metabolic [ˌmɛt̬əˈbɑlɪk] *adj* : metabólico
metabolism [məˈtæbəˌlɪzəm] *n* : metabolismo *m*
metabolize [məˈtæbəˌlaɪz] *vt* **-lized; -lizing** : metabolizar
metal [ˈmɛt̬əl] *n* : metal *m*
metallic [məˈtælɪk] *adj* : metálico
metallurgical [ˌmɛt̬əlˈərdʒɪkəl] *adj* : metalúrgico
metallurgy [ˈmɛt̬əlˌərdʒi] *n* : metalurgia *f*
metalwork [ˈmɛt̬əlˌwərk] *n* : objeto *m* de metal
metalworking [ˈmɛt̬əlˌwərkɪŋ] *n* : metalistería *f*
metamorphosis [ˌmɛt̬əˈmɔrfəsɪs] *n, pl* **-phoses** [-ˌsiːz] : metamorfosis *f*
metaphor [ˈmɛt̬əˌfɔr, -fər] *n* : metáfora *f*
metaphoric [ˌmɛt̬əˈfɔrɪk] *or* **metaphorical** [-ɪkəl] *adj* : metafórico
metaphysical [ˌmɛt̬əˈfɪzəkəl] *adj* : metafísico
metaphysics [ˌmɛt̬əˈfɪzɪks] *n* : metafísica *f*
mete [ˈmiːt] *vt* **meted; meting** ALLOT : repartir, distribuir <to mete out punishment : imponer castigos>
meteor [ˈmiːt̬iər, -tiːˌɔr] *n* : meteoro *m*
meteoric [ˌmiːt̬iˈɔrɪk] *adj* : meteórico
meteorite [ˈmiːt̬iəˌraɪt] *n* : meteorito *m*
meteorologic [ˌmiːt̬iˌɔrəˈlɑdʒɪk] *or* **meteorological** [-ˈlɑdʒɪkəl] *adj* : meteorológico
meteorologist [ˌmiːt̬iəˈrɑlədʒɪst] *n* : meteorólogo *m,* -ga *f*
meteorology [ˌmiːt̬iəˈrɑlədʒi] *n* : meteorología *f*
meter [ˈmiːt̬ər] *n* **1** : metro *m* <it measures 2 meters : mide 2 metros> **2** : contador *m,* medidor *m* (de electricidad, etc.) <parking meter : parquímetro> **3** : metro *m* (en literatura o música)
methane [ˈmɛˌθeɪn] *n* : metano *m*
method [ˈmɛθəd] *n* : método *m*
methodical [məˈθɑdɪkəl] *adj* : metódico — **methodically** *adv*
meticulous [məˈtɪkjələs] *adj* : meticuloso — **meticulously** *adv*
meticulousness [məˈtɪkjələsnəs] *n* : meticulosidad *f*
metric [ˈmɛtrɪk] *or* **metrical** [-trɪkəl] *adj* : métrico
metric system *n* : sistema *m* métrico
metronome [ˈmɛtrəˌnoːm] *n* : metrónomo *m*
metropolis [məˈtrɑpələs] *n* : metrópoli *f,* metrópolis *f*
metropolitan [ˌmɛtrəˈpɑlətən] *adj* : metropolitano

mettle [ˈmɛt̬əl] *n* **:** temple *m,* valor *m* <on one's mettle : dispuesto a mostrar su valía>
Mexican [ˈmɛksɪkən] *n* **:** mexicano *m,* -na *f* — **Mexican** *adj*
mezzanine [ˈmɛzəˌniːn, ˌmɛzəˈniːn] *n* **1 :** entrepiso *m,* entresuelo *m* **2 :** primer piso *m* (de un teatro)
miasma [maɪˈæzmə] *n* **:** miasma *m*
mica [ˈmaɪkə] *n* **:** mica *f*
mice → **mouse**
micro [ˈmaɪkro] *adj* **:** muy pequeño, microscópico
microbe [ˈmaɪˌkroːb] *n* **:** microbio *m*
microbiology [ˌmaɪkrobaɪˈɑlədʒi] *n* **:** microbiología *f*
microcomputer [ˈmaɪkrokəmˌpjuːt̬ər] *n* **:** microcomputadora *f*
microcosm [ˈmaɪkroˌkɑzəm] *n* **:** microcosmo *m*
microfilm [ˈmaɪkroˌfɪlm] *n* **:** microfilm *m*
micrometer [maɪˈkrɑmət̬ər] *n* **:** micrómetro *m*
micron [ˈmaɪˌkrɑn] *n* **:** micrón *m*
microorganism [ˌmaɪkroˈɔrgəˌnɪzəm] *n* **:** microorganismo *m,* microbio *m*
microphone [ˈmaɪkrəˌfoːn] *n* **:** micrófono *m*
microprocessor [ˈmaɪkroˌprɑˌsɛsər] *n* **:** microprocesador *m*
microscope [ˈmaɪkrəˌskoːp] *n* **:** microscopio *m*
microscopic [ˌmaɪkrəˈskɑpɪk] *adj* **:** microscópico
microscopy [maɪˈkrɑskəpi] *n* **:** microscopía *f*
microwave [ˈmaɪkrəˌweɪv] *n* **1 :** microonda *f* **2** *or* **microwave oven :** microondas *m*
mid [ˈmɪd] *adj* **:** medio <mid morning : a media mañana> <in mid-August : a mediados de agosto> <in mid ocean : en alta mar>
midair [ˈmɪdˈær] *n* **in ~ :** en el aire <to catch in midair : agarrar al vuelo>
midday [ˈmɪdˈdeɪ] *n* NOON **:** mediodía *m*
middle[1] [ˈmɪdəl] *adj* **1** CENTRAL **:** medio, del medio, de en medio **2** INTERMEDIATE **:** intermedio, mediano <middle age : la mediana edad>
middle[2] *n* **1** CENTER **:** medio *m,* centro *m* <fold it down the middle : dóblalo por la mitad> **2 in the middle of :** en medio de (un espacio), a mitad de (una actividad) <in the middle of the month : a mediados del mes>
Middle Ages *npl* **:** Edad *f* Media
middle class *n* **:** clase *f* media
middleman [ˈmɪdəlˌmæn] *n, pl* **-men** [-mən, -ˌmɛn] **:** intermediario *m,* -ria *f*
middling [ˈmɪdlɪŋ, -lən] *adj* **1** MEDIUM, MIDDLE **:** mediano **2** MEDIOCRE **:** mediocre, regular
midge [ˈmɪdʒ] *n* **:** mosca *f* pequeña
midget [ˈmɪdʒət] *n* **1 :** enano *m,* -na *f* (persona) **2 :** cosa *f* diminuta
midland [ˈmɪdlənd, -ˌlænd] *n* **:** región *f* central (de un país)
midnight [ˈmɪdˌnaɪt] *n* **:** medianoche *f*
midpoint [ˈmɪdˌpɔɪnt] *n* **:** punto *m* medio, término *m* medio
midriff [ˈmɪdˌrɪf] *n* **:** diafragma *m*
midshipman [ˈmɪdˌʃɪpmən, ˌmɪdˈʃɪp-] *n, pl* **-men** [-mən, -ˌmɛn] **:** guardiamarina *m*
midst[1] [ˈmɪdst] *n* **:** medio *m* <in our midst : entre nosotros> <in the midst of : en medio de>
midst[2] *prep* **:** entre
midstream [ˈmɪdˈstriːm, -ˌstriːm] *n* **:** medio *m* de la corriente <in the midstream of his career : en medio de su carrera>
midsummer [ˈmɪdˈsʌmər, -ˌsʌ-] *n* **:** pleno verano *m*
midtown [ˈmɪdˌtaʊn] *n* **:** centro *m* (de una ciudad)
midway [ˈmɪdˌweɪ] *adv* HALFWAY **:** a mitad de camino
midweek [ˈmɪdˌwiːk] *n* **:** medio *m* de la semana <in midweek : a media semana>
midwife [ˈmɪdˌwaɪf] *n, pl* **-wives** [-ˌwaɪvz] **:** partera *f,* comadrona *f*
midwinter [ˈmɪdˈwɪntər, -ˌwɪn-] *n* **:** pleno invierno *m*
midyear [ˈmɪdˌjɪr] *n* **:** medio *m* del año <at midyear : a mediados del año>
mien [ˈmiːn] *n* **:** aspecto *m,* porte *m,* semblante *m*
miff [ˈmɪf] *vt* **:** ofender
might[1] [ˈmaɪt] (*used to express permission or possibility or as a polite alternative to* **may**) → **may** <it might be true : podría ser verdad> <might I speak with Sarah? : ¿se puede hablar con Sarah?>
might[2] *n* **:** fuerza *f,* poder *m*
mightily [ˈmaɪt̬əli] *adv* **:** con mucha fuerza, poderosamente
mighty[1] [ˈmaɪt̬i] *adv* VERY **:** muy <mighty good : muy bueno, buenísimo>
mighty[2] *adj* **mightier; -est 1** POWERFUL **:** poderoso, potente **2** GREAT **:** grande, imponente
migraine [ˈmaɪˌgreɪn] *n* **:** jaqueca *f,* migraña *f*
migrant [ˈmaɪgrənt] *n* **:** trabajador *m,* -dora *f* ambulante
migrate [ˈmaɪˌgreɪt] *vi* **-grated; -grating :** emigrar
migration [maɪˈgreɪʃən] *n* **:** migración *f*
migratory [ˈmaɪgrəˌtori] *adj* **:** migratorio
mild [ˈmaɪld] *adj* **1** GENTLE **:** apacible, suave <a mild disposition : un temperamento suave> **2** LIGHT **:** leve, ligero <a mild punishment : un castigo leve, un castigo poco severo> **3** TEMPERATE **:** templado (dícese del clima) — **mildly** *adv*

mildew[1] ['mɪl,duː, -,djuː] *vi* : enmohecerse

mildew[2] *n* : moho *m*

mildness ['maɪldnəs] *n* : apacibilidad *f,* suavidad *f*

mile ['maɪl] *n* : milla *f*

mileage ['maɪlɪdʒ] *n* **1** ALLOWANCE : viáticos *mpl* (pagados por milla recorrida) **2** : distancia *f* recorrida (en millas), kilometraje *m*

milestone ['maɪl,stoːn] *n* LANDMARK : hito *m,* jalón *m* <a milestone in his life : un hito en su vida>

milieu [miːl'juː, -'jø] *n, pl* **-lieus** *or* **-lieux** [-'juːz, -'jø] SURROUNDINGS : entorno *m,* medio *m,* ambiente *m*

militant[1] ['mɪlətənt] *adj* : militante, combativo

militant[2] *n* : militante *mf*

militarism ['mɪlət̬ə,rɪzəm] *n* : militarismo *m*

militaristic [,mɪlət̬ə'rɪstɪk] *adj* : militarista

military[1] ['mɪlə,tɛri] *adj* : militar

military[2] *n* **the military** : las fuerzas armadas

militia [mə'lɪʃə] *n* : milicia *f*

milk[1] ['mɪlk] *vt* **1** : ordeñar (una vaca, etc.) **2** EXPLOIT : explotar

milk[2] *n* : leche *f*

milkman ['mɪlk,mæn, -mən] *n, pl* **-men** [-mən, -,mɛn] : lechero *m*

milk shake *n* : batido *m,* licuado *m*

milkweed ['mɪlk,wiːd] *n* : algodoncillo *m*

milky ['mɪlki] *adj* **milkier; -est** : lechoso

Milky Way *n* : Vía *f* Láctea

mill[1] ['mɪl] *vt* : moler (granos), fresar (metales), acordonar (monedas) — *vi* **to mill about** : arremolinarse

mill[2] *n* **1** : molino *m* (para moler granos) **2** FACTORY : fábrica *f* <textile mill : fábrica textil> **3** GRINDER : molinillo *m*

millennium [mə'lɛniəm] *n, pl* **-nia** [-niə] *or* **-niums** : milenio *m*

miller ['mɪlər] *n* : molinero *m,* -ra *f*

millet ['mɪlət] *n* : mijo *m*

milligram ['mɪlə,græm] *n* : miligramo *m*

milliliter ['mɪlə,liːt̬ər] *n* : mililitro *m*

millimeter ['mɪlə,miːt̬ər] *n* : milímetro *m*

milliner ['mɪlənər] *n* : sombrerero *m,* -ra *f* (de señoras)

millinery ['mɪlə,nɛri] *n* : sombreros *mpl* de señora

million[1] ['mɪljən] *adj* **a million** : un millón de

million[2] *n, pl* **millions** *or* **million** : millón *m*

millionaire [,mɪljə'nær, 'mɪljə,nær] *n* : millonario *m,* -ria *f*

millionth[1] ['mɪljənθ] *adj* : millonésimo

millionth[2] *n* : millonésimo *m*

millipede ['mɪlə,piːd] *n* : milpiés *m*

millstone ['mɪl,stoːn] *n* : rueda *f* de molino, muela *f*

mime[1] ['maɪm] *v* **mimed; miming** *vt* MIMIC : imitar, remedar — *vi* PANTOMIME : hacer la mímica

mime[2] *n* **1** : mimo *mf* **2** PANTOMIME : pantomima *f*

mimeograph ['mɪmiə,græf] *n* : mimeógrafo *m*

mimic[1] ['mɪmɪk] *vt* **-icked; -icking** : imitar, remedar

mimic[2] *n* : imitador *m,* -dora *f*

mimicry ['mɪmɪkri] *n, pl* **-ries** : mímica *f,* imitación *f*

minaret [,mɪnə'rɛt] *n* : alminar *m,* minarete *m*

mince ['mɪnts] *v* **minced; mincing** *vt* **1** CHOP : picar, moler (carne) **2 not to mince one's words** : no tener uno pelos en la lengua — *vi* : caminar de manera afectada

mincemeat ['mɪnts,miːt] *n* : mezcla *f* de fruta picada, sebo, y especias

mind[1] ['maɪnd] *vt* **1** TEND : cuidar, atender <mind the children : cuida a los niños> **2** OBEY : obedecer **3** : preocuparse por, sentirse molestado por <I don't mind his jokes : sus bromas no me molestan> **4** : tener cuidado con <mind the ladder! : ¡cuidado con la escalera!> — *vi* **1** OBEY : obedecer **2** CARE : importarle a uno <I don't mind : no me importa, me es igual>

mind[2] *n* **1** MEMORY : memoria *f,* recuerdo *m* <keep it in mind : téngalo en cuenta> **2** : mente *f* <the mind and the body : la mente y el cuerpo> **3** INTENTION : intención *f,* propósito *m* <to have a mind to do something : tener intención de hacer algo> **4** : razón *f* <he's out of his mind : está loco> **5** OPINION : opinión *f* <to change one's mind : cambiar de opinión> **6** INTELLECT : capacidad *f* intelectual

minded ['maɪndəd] *adj* **1** (*used in combination*) <narrow-minded : de mentalidad cerrada> <health-minded : preocupado por la salud> **2** INCLINED : inclinado

mindful ['maɪndfəl] *adj* AWARE : consciente — **mindfully** *adv*

mindless ['maɪndləs] *adj* **1** SENSELESS : estúpido, sin sentido <mindless violence : violencia sin sentido> **2** HEEDLESS : inconsciente

mindlessly ['maɪndləsli] *adv* **1** SENSELESSLY : sin sentido **2** HEEDLESSLY : inconscientemente

mine[1] ['maɪn] *vt* **mined; mining 1** : extraer (oro, etc.) **2** : minar (con artefactos explosivos)

mine[2] *n* : mina *f* <gold mine : mina de oro>

mine[3] *pron* : mío, mía <that one's mine : ése es el mío> <some friends of mine : unos amigos míos>

minefield ['maɪn,fiːld] *n* : campo *m* de minas

miner ['maɪnər] *n* : minero *m,* -ra *f*

mineral [ˈmɪnərəl] *n* : mineral *m* — **mineral** *adj*
mineralogy [ˌmɪnəˈrɑləʤi, -ˈræ-] *n* : mineralogía *f*
mingle [ˈmɪŋgəl] *v* **-gled; -gling** *vt* MIX : mezclar — *vi* **1** MIX : mezclarse **2** CIRCULATE : circular
miniature[1] [ˈmɪniəˌʧʊr, ˈmɪnɪˌʧʊr, -ʧər] *adj* : en miniatura, diminuto
miniature[2] *n* : miniatura *f*
minibus [ˈmɪniˌbʌs] *n* : microbús *m,* pesera *f Mex*
minicomputer [ˈmɪnikəmˌpjuːt̬ər] *n* : minicomputadora *f*
minimal [ˈmɪnəməl] *adj* : mínimo
minimally [ˈmɪnəməli] *adv* : en grado mínimo
minimize [ˈmɪnəˌmaɪz] *vt* **-mized; -mizing** : minimizar
minimum[1] [ˈmɪnəməm] *adj* : mínimo
minimum[2] *n, pl* **-ma** [ˈmɪnəmə] *or* **-mums** : mínimo *m*
miniskirt [ˈmɪniˌskərt] *n* : minifalda *f*
minister[1] [ˈmɪnəstər] *vi* **to minister to** : cuidar (de), atender a
minister[2] *n* **1** : pastor *m,* -tora *f* (de una iglesia) **2** : ministro *m,* -tra *f* (en política)
ministerial [ˌmɪnəˈstɪriəl] *adj* : ministerial
ministry [ˈmɪnəstri] *n, pl* **-tries** **1** : ministerio *m* (en política) **2** : sacerdocio *m* (en el catolicismo), clerecía *f* (en el protestantismo)
minivan [ˈmɪniˌvæn] *n* : minivan *f*
mink [ˈmɪŋk] *n, pl* **mink** *or* **minks** : visón *m*
minnow [ˈmɪnoː] *n, pl* **-nows** : pececillo *m* de agua dulce
minor[1] [ˈmaɪnər] *adj* : menor
minor[2] *n* **1** : menor *mf* (de edad) **2** : asignatura *f* secundaria (de estudios)
minority [məˈnɔrət̬i, maɪ-] *n, pl* **-ties** : minoría *f*
minstrel [ˈmɪn*t*strəl] *n* : juglar *m,* trovador *m* (en el medioevo)
mint[1] [ˈmɪnt] *vt* : acuñar
mint[2] *adj* : sin usar <in mint condition : como nuevo>
mint[3] *n* **1** : menta *f* <mint tea : té de menta> **2** : pastilla *f* de menta **3** : casa *f* de la moneda <the U.S. Mint : la casa de la moneda de los EE.UU.> **4** FORTUNE : dineral *m,* fortuna *f*
minuet [ˌmɪnjʊˈɛt] *n* : minué *m*
minus[1] [ˈmaɪnəs] *n* **1** : cantidad *f* negativa **2 minus sign** : signo *m* de menos
minus[2] *prep* **1** : menos <four minus two : cuatro menos dos> **2** WITHOUT : sin <minus his hat : sin su sombrero>
minuscule *or* **miniscule** [ˈmɪnəsˌkjuːl, mɪˈnʌs-] *adj* : minúsculo
minute[1] [maɪˈnuːt, mɪ-, -ˈnjuːt] *adj* **-nuter; -est** **1** TINY : diminuto, minúsculo **2** DETAILED : minucioso
minute[2] [ˈmɪnət] *n* **1** : minuto *m* <ten minutes late : diez minutos de retraso> **2** MOMENT : momento *m* **3 minutes** *npl* : actas *fpl* (de una reunión)
minutely [maɪˈnuːtli, mɪ-, -ˈnjuːt-] *adv* : minuciosamente
miracle [ˈmɪrɪkəl] *n* : milagro *m*
miraculous [məˈrækjələs] *adj* : milagroso — **miraculously** *adv*
mirage [mɪˈrɑʒ, *chiefly Brit* ˈmɪrˌɑʒ] *n* : espejismo *m*
mire[1] [ˈmaɪr] *vi* **mired; miring** : atascarse
mire[2] *n* : lodo *m,* barro *m,* fango *m*
mirror[1] [ˈmɪrər] *vt* : reflejar
mirror[2] *n* : espejo *m*
mirth [ˈmərθ] *n* : alegría *f,* regocijo *m*
mirthful [ˈmərθfəl] *adj* : alegre, regocijado
misanthrope [ˈmɪsənˌθroːp] *n* : misántropo *m,* -pa *f*
misanthropic [ˌmɪsənˈθrɑpɪk] *adj* : misantrópico
misanthropy [mɪˈsænθrəpi] *n* : misantropía *f*
misapprehend [ˌmɪsˌæprəˈhɛnd] *vt* : entender mal
misapprehension [ˌmɪsˌæprəˈhɛntʃən] *n* : malentendido *m*
misappropriate [ˌmɪsəˈproːpriˌeɪt] *vt* **-ated; -ating** : malversar
misbegotten [ˌmɪsbiˈgɑtən] *adj* **1** ILLEGITIMATE : ilegítimo **2** : mal concebido <misbegotten laws : leyes mal concebidas>
misbehave [ˌmɪsbiˈheɪv] *vi* **-haved; -having** : portarse mal
misbehavior [ˌmɪsbiˈheɪvjər] *n* : mala conducta *f*
miscalculate [mɪsˈkælkjəˌleɪt] *v* **-lated; -lating** : calcular mal
miscalculation [mɪsˌkælkjəˈleɪʃən] *n* : error *m* de cálculo, mal cálculo *m*
miscarriage [ˌmɪsˈkærɪʤ, ˈmɪsˌkærɪʤ] *n* **1** : aborto *m* **2** FAILURE : fracaso *m,* malogro *m* <a miscarriage of justice : una injusticia, un error judicial>
miscarry [ˌmɪsˈkæri, ˈmɪsˌkæri] *vi* **-ried; -rying** **1** ABORT : abortar **2** FAIL : malograrse, fracasar
miscellaneous [ˌmɪsəˈleɪniəs] *adj* : misceláneo
miscellany [ˈmɪsəˌleɪni] *n, pl* **-nies** : miscelánea *f*
mischance [mɪsˈʧæn*t*s] *n* : desgracia *f,* infortunio *m,* mala suerte *f*
mischief [ˈmɪsʧəf] *n* : diabluras *fpl,* travesuras *fpl*
mischievous [ˈmɪsʧəvəs] *adj* : travieso, pícaro
mischievously [ˈmɪsʧəvəsli] *adv* : de manera traviesa
misconception [ˌmɪskənˈsɛpʃən] *n* : concepto *m* erróneo, idea *f* falsa
misconduct [mɪsˈkɑndəkt] *n* : mala conducta *f*
misconstrue [ˌmɪskənˈstruː] *vt* **-strued; -struing** : malinterpretar
misdeed [mɪsˈdiːd] *n* : fechoría *f*

misdemeanor [ˌmɪsdɪˈmiːnər] *n* : delito *m* menor
miser [ˈmaɪzər] *n* : avaro *m*, -ra *f*; tacaño *m*, -ña *f*
miserable [ˈmɪzərəbəl] *adj* **1** UNHAPPY : triste, desdichado **2** WRETCHED : miserable, desgraciado <a miserable hut : una choza miserable> **3** UNPLEASANT : desagradable, malo <miserable weather : tiempo malísimo> **4** CONTEMPTIBLE : despreciable, mísero <for a miserable $10 : por unos míseros diez dólares>
miserably [ˈmɪzərəbli] *adv* **1** SADLY : tristemente **2** WRETCHEDLY : miserablemente, lamentablemente **3** UNFORTUNATELY : desgraciadamente
miserly [ˈmaɪzərli] *adj* : avaro, tacaño
misery [ˈmɪzəri] *n, pl* **-eries** : miseria *f*, sufrimiento *m*
misfire [mɪsˈfaɪr] *vi* **-fired; -firing** : fallar
misfit [ˈmɪsˌfɪt] *n* : inadaptado *m*, -da *f*
misfortune [mɪsˈfɔrtʃən] *n* : desgracia *f*, desventura *f*, infortunio *m*
misgiving [mɪsˈgɪvɪŋ] *n* : duda *f*, recelo *m*
misguided [mɪsˈgaɪdəd] *adj* : desacertado, equivocado, mal informado
mishap [ˈmɪsˌhæp] *n* : contratiempo *m*, percance *m*, accidente *m*
misinform [ˌmɪsɪnˈfɔrm] *vt* : informar mal
misinterpret [ˌmɪsɪnˈtərprət] *vt* : malinterpretar
misinterpretation [ˌmɪsɪnˌtərprəˈteɪʃən] *n* : mala interpretación *f*, malentendido *m*
misjudge [mɪsˈdʒʌdʒ] *vt* **-judged; -judging** : juzgar mal
mislay [mɪsˈleɪ] *vt* **-laid** [-leɪd]; **-laying** : extraviar, perder
mislead [mɪsˈliːd] *vt* **-led** [-ˈlɛd]; **-leading** : engañar
misleading [mɪsˈliːdɪŋ] *adj* : engañoso
mismanage [mɪsˈmænɪdʒ] *vt* **-aged; -aging** : administrar mal
mismanagement [mɪsˈmænɪdʒmənt] *n* : mala administración *f*
misnomer [mɪsˈnoːmər] *n* : nombre *m* inapropiado
misogynist [mɪˈsɑdʒənɪst] *n* : misógino *m*
misplace [mɪsˈpleɪs] *vt* **-placed; -placing** : extraviar, perder
misprint [ˈmɪsˌprɪnt, mɪsˈ-] *n* : errata *f*, error *m* de imprenta
mispronounce [ˌmɪsprəˈnaʊnts] *vt* **-nounced; -nouncing** : pronunciar mal
mispronunciation [ˌmɪsprəˌnʌntsiˈeɪʃən] *n* : pronunciación *f* incorrecta
misquote [mɪsˈkwoːt] *vt* **-quoted; -quoting** : citar incorrectamente
misread [mɪsˈriːd] *vt* **-read; -reading 1** : leer mal <she misread the sentence : leyó mal la frase> **2** MISUNDERSTAND : malinterpretar <they misread his intention : malinterpretaron su intención>
misrepresent [ˌmɪsˌrɛprɪˈzɛnt] *vt* : distorsionar, falsear, tergiversar
misrule[1] [mɪsˈruːl] *vt* **-ruled; -ruling** : gobernar mal
misrule[2] *n* : mal gobierno *m*
miss[1] [ˈmɪs] *vt* **1** : errar, faltar <to miss the target : no dar en el blanco> **2** : no encontrar, perder <they missed each other : no se encontraron> <I missed the plane : perdí el avión> **3** : echar de menos, extrañar <we miss him a lot : lo echamos mucho de menos> **4** OVERLOOK : pasar por alto, perder (una oportunidad, etc.) **5** AVOID : evitar <they just missed hitting the tree : por muy poco chocan contra el árbol> **6** OMIT : saltarse <he missed breakfast : se saltó el desayuno>
miss[2] *n* **1** : fallo *m* (de un tiro, etc.) **2** FAILURE : fracaso *m* **3** : señorita *f* <Miss Jones : la señorita Jones> <excuse me, miss : perdone, señorita>
missal [ˈmɪsəl] *n* : misal *m*
misshapen [mɪˈʃeɪpən] *adj* : deforme
missile [ˈmɪsəl] *n* **1** : misil *m* <guided missile : misil guiado> **2** PROJECTILE : proyectil *m*
missing [ˈmɪsɪŋ] *adj* **1** ABSENT : ausente <who's missing? : ¿quién falta?> **2** LOST : perdido, desaparecido <missing persons : los desaparecidos>
mission [ˈmɪʃən] *n* **1** : misión *f* (mandada por una iglesia) **2** DELEGATION : misión *f*, delegación *f*, embajada *f* **3** TASK : misión *f*
missionary[1] [ˈmɪʃəˌnɛri] *adj* : misionero
missionary[2] *n, pl* **-aries** : misionero *m*, -ra *f*
missive [ˈmɪsɪv] *n* : misiva *f*
misspell [mɪsˈspɛl] *vt* : escribir mal
misspelling [mɪsˈspɛlɪŋ] *n* : falta *f* de ortografía
misstep [ˈmɪsˌstɛp] *n* : traspié *m*, tropezón *m*
mist [ˈmɪst] *n* **1** HAZE : neblina *f*, niebla *f* **2** SPRAY : rocío *m*
mistake[1] [mɪˈsteɪk] *vt* **-took** [-ˈstʊk]; **-taken** [-ˈsteɪkən]; **-taking 1** MISINTERPRET : malinterpretar **2** CONFUSE : confundir <he mistook her for Clara : la confundió con Clara>
mistake[2] *n* **1** MISUNDERSTANDING : malentendido *m*, confusión *f* **2** ERROR : error *m* <I made a mistake : me equivoqué, cometí un error>
mistaken [mɪˈsteɪkən] *adj* WRONG : equivocado — **mistakenly** *adv*
mister [ˈmɪstər] *n* : señor *m* <watch out, mister : cuidado, señor>
mistiness [ˈmɪstinəs] *n* : nebulosidad *f*
mistletoe [ˈmɪsəlˌtoː] *n* : muérdago *m*
mistreat [mɪsˈtriːt] *vt* : maltratar
mistreatment [mɪsˈtriːtmənt] *n* : maltrato *m*, abuso *m*

mistress [ˈmɪstrəs] *n* **1** : dueña *f,* señora *f* (de una casa) **2** LOVER : amante *f*

mistrust[1] [mɪsˈtrʌst] *vt* : desconfiar de

mistrust[2] *n* : desconfianza *f*

mistrustful [mɪsˈtrʌstfəl] *adj* : desconfiado

misty [ˈmɪsti] *adj* **mistier; -est 1** : neblinoso, nebuloso **2** TEARFUL : lloroso

misunderstand [ˌmɪsˌʌndərˈstænd] *vt* **-stood** [-ˈstʊd]; **-standing 1** : entender mal **2** MISINTERPRET : malinterpretar <don't misunderstand me : no me malinterpretes>

misunderstanding [ˌmɪsˌʌndərˈstændɪŋ] *n* **1** MISINTERPRETATION : malentendido *m* **2** DISAGREEMENT, QUARREL : disputa *f,* discusión *f*

misuse[1] [mɪsˈjuːz] *vt* **-used; -using 1** : emplear mal **2** ABUSE, MISTREAT : abusar de, maltratar

misuse[2] [mɪsˈjuːs] *n* **1** : mal empleo *m,* mal uso *m* **2** WASTE : derroche *m,* despilfarro *m* **3** ABUSE : abuso *m*

mite [ˈmaɪt] *n* **1** : ácaro *m* **2** BIT : poco *m* <a mite tired : un poquito cansado>

miter *or* **mitre** [ˈmaɪtər] *n* **1** : mitra *f* (de un obispo) **2** *or* **miter joint** : inglete *m*

mitigate [ˈmɪt̬əˌgeɪt] *vt* **-gated; -gating** : mitigar, aliviar

mitigation [ˌmɪt̬əˈgeɪʃən] *n* : mitigación *f,* alivio *m*

mitosis [maɪˈtoːsɪs] *n, pl* **-toses** [-ˌsiːz] : mitosis *f*

mitt [ˈmɪt] *n* : manopla *f,* guante *m* (de béisbol)

mitten [ˈmɪtən] *n* : manopla *f,* mitón *m*

mix[1] [ˈmɪks] *vt* **1** COMBINE : mezclar **2** STIR : remover, revolver **3 to mix up** CONFUSE : confundir — *vi* : mezclarse

mix[2] *n* : mezcla *f*

mixer [ˈmɪksər] *n* **1** : batidora *f* (de la cocina) **2 cement mixer** : hormigonera *f*

mixture [ˈmɪkstʃər] *n* : mezcla *f*

mix–up [ˈmɪksˌʌp] *n* CONFUSION : confusión *f,* lío *m fam*

mnemonic [nɪˈmɑnɪk] *adj* : mnemónico

moan[1] [ˈmoːn] *vi* : gemir

moan[2] *n* : gemido *m*

moat [ˈmoːt] *n* : foso *m*

mob[1] [ˈmɑb] *vt* **mobbed; mobbing 1** ATTACK : atacar en masa **2** HOUND : acosar, rodear

mob[2] *n* **1** THRONG : multitud *f,* turba *f,* muchedumbre *f* **2** GANG : pandilla *f*

mobile[1] [ˈmoːbəl, -ˌbiːl, -ˌbaɪl] *adj* : móvil <mobile home : caravana, casa rodante>

mobile[2] [ˈmoˌbiːl] *n* : móvil *m*

mobility [moˈbɪlət̬i] *n* : movilidad *f*

mobilize [ˈmoːbəˌlaɪz] *vt* **-lized; -lizing** : movilizar

moccasin [ˈmɑkəsən] *n* **1** : mocasín *m* **2** *or* **water moccasin** : serpiente *f* venenosa de Norteamérica

mocha [ˈmoːkə] *n* **1** : mezcla *f* de café y chocolate **2** : color *m* chocolate

mock[1] [ˈmɑk, ˈmɔk] *vt* **1** RIDICULE : burlarse de, mofarse de **2** MIMIC : imitar, remedar (de manera burlona)

mock[2] *adj* **1** SIMULATED : simulado **2** PHONY : falso

mockery [ˈmɑkəri, ˈmɔ-] *n, pl* **-eries 1** JEER, TAUNT : burla *f,* mofa *f* <to make a mockery of : burlarse de> **2** FAKE : imitación *f* (burlona)

mockingbird [ˈmɑkɪŋˌbərd, ˈmɔ-] *n* : sinsonte *m*

mode [ˈmoːd] *n* **1** FORM : modo *m,* forma *f* **2** MANNER : modo *m,* manera *f,* estilo *m* **3** FASHION : moda *f*

model[1] [ˈmɑdəl] *v* **-eled** *or* **-elled; -eling** *or* **-elling** *vt* SHAPE : modelar — *vi* : trabajar de modelo

model[2] *adj* **1** EXEMPLARY : modelo, ejemplar <a model student : un estudiante modelo> **2** MINIATURE : en miniatura

model[3] *n* **1** PATTERN : modelo *m* **2** MINIATURE : modelo *m,* miniatura *f* **3** EXAMPLE : modelo *m,* ejemplo *m* **4** MANNEQUIN : modelo *mf* **5** DESIGN : modelo *m* <the '97 model : el modelo '97>

modem [ˈmoːdəm, -ˌdɛm] *n* : módem *m*

moderate[1] [ˈmɑdəˌreɪt] *v* **-ated; -ating** *vt* : moderar, temperar — *vi* **1** CALM : moderarse, calmarse **2** : fungir como moderador (en un debate, etc.)

moderate[2] [ˈmɑdərət] *adj* : moderado

moderate[3] [ˈmɑdərət] *n* : moderado *m,* -da *f*

moderately [ˈmɑdərətli] *adv* **1** : con moderación **2** FAIRLY : medianamente

moderation [ˌmɑdəˈreɪʃən] *n* : moderación *f*

moderator [ˈmɑdəˌreɪt̬ər] *n* : moderador *m,* -dora *f*

modern [ˈmɑdərn] *adj* : moderno

modernity [məˈdərnət̬i] *n* : modernidad *f*

modernization [ˌmɑdərnəˈzeɪʃən] *n* : modernización *f*

modernize [ˈmɑdərˌnaɪz] *v* **-ized; -izing** *vt* : modernizar — *vi* : modernizarse

modest [ˈmɑdəst] *adj* **1** HUMBLE : modesto **2** DEMURE : recatado, pudoroso **3** MODERATE : modesto, moderado — **modestly** *adv*

modesty [ˈmɑdəsti] *n* : modestia *f*

modicum [ˈmɑdɪkəm] *n* : mínimo *m,* pizca *f*

modification [ˌmɑdəfəˈkeɪʃən] *n* : modificación *f*

modifier [ˈmɑdəˌfaɪər] *n* : modificante *m,* modificador *m*

modify [ˈmɑdəˌfaɪ] *vt* **-fied; -fying** : modificar, calificar (en gramática)

modish [ˈmoːdɪʃ] *adj* STYLISH : a la moda, de moda

modular [ˈmɑdʒələr] *adj* : modular

modulate [ˈmɑdʒəˌleɪt] *vt* **-lated; -lating** : modular

modulation [ˌmɑdʒəˈleɪʃən] *n* : modulación *f*

module [ˈmɑˌdʒuːl] *n* : módulo *m*

mogul [ˈmoːgəl] *n* : magnate *mf;* potentado *m,* -da *f*

mohair [ˈmoːˌhær] *n* : mohair *m*

moist [ˈmɔɪst] *adj* : húmedo

moisten [ˈmɔɪsən] *vt* : humedecer

moistness [ˈmɔɪstnəs] *n* : humedad *f*

moisture [ˈmɔɪstʃər] *n* : humedad *f*

moisturize [ˈmɔɪstʃəˌraɪz] *vt* **-ized; -izing :** humedecer (el aire), humectar (la piel)

moisturizer [ˈmɔɪtʃəˌraɪzər] *n* : crema *f* hidratante, crema *f* humectante

molar [ˈmoːlər] *n* : muela *f,* molar *m*

molasses [məˈlæsəz] *n* : melaza *f*

mold[1] [ˈmoːld] *vt* : moldear, formar (carácter, etc.) — *vi* : enmohecerse <the bread will mold : el pan se enmohecerá>

mold[2] *n* **1** *or* **leaf mold :** mantillo *m* **2** FORM : molde *m* <to break the mold : romper el molde> **3** FUNGUS : moho *m*

molder [ˈmoːldər] *vi* CRUMBLE : desmoronarse

molding [ˈmoːldɪŋ] *n* : moldura *f* (en arquitectura)

moldy [ˈmoːldi] *adj* **moldier; -est** : mohoso

mole [ˈmoːl] *n* **1** : lunar *m* (en la piel) **2** : topo *m* (animal)

molecule [ˈmɑlɪˌkjuːl] *n* : molécula *f* — **molecular** [məˈlɛkjələr] *adj*

molehill [ˈmoːlˌhɪl] *n* : topera *f*

molest [məˈlɛst] *vt* **1** ANNOY, DISTURB : molestar **2** : abusar (sexualmente)

mollify [ˈmɑləˌfaɪ] *vt* **-fied; -fying** : apaciguar, aplacar

mollusk *or* **mollusc** [ˈmɑləsk] *n* : molusco *m*

mollycoddle [ˈmɑliˌkɑdəl] *vt* **-dled; -dling** PAMPER : consentir, mimar

molt [ˈmoːlt] *vi* : mudar, hacer la muda

molten [ˈmoːltən] *adj* : fundido

mom [ˈmɑm, ˈmʌm] *n* : mamá *f*

moment [ˈmoːmənt] *n* **1** INSTANT : momento *m* <one moment, please : un momento, por favor> **2** TIME : momento *m* <at the moment : de momento, actualmente> <from that moment : desde entonces> **3** IMPORTANCE : importancia *f* <of great moment : de gran importancia>

momentarily [ˌmoːmənˈtɛrəli] *adv* **1** : momentáneamente **2** SOON : dentro de poco, pronto

momentary [ˈmoːmənˌtɛri] *adj* : momentáneo

momentous [moˈmɛntəs] *adj* : de suma importancia, fatídico

momentum [moˈmɛntəm] *n, pl* **-ta** [-tə] *or* **-tums 1** : momento *m* (en física) **2** IMPETUS : ímpetu *m,* impulso *m*

monarch [ˈmɑˌnɑrk, -nərk] *n* : monarca *mf*

monarchism [ˈmɑˌnɑrˌkɪzəm, -nər-] *n* : monarquismo *m*

monarchist [ˈmɑˌnɑrkɪst, -nər-] *n* : monárquico *m,* -ca *f*

monarchy [ˈmɑˌnɑrki, -nər-] *n, pl* **-chies :** monarquía *f*

monastery [ˈmɑnəˌstɛri] *n, pl* **-teries** : monasterio *m*

monastic [məˈnæstɪk] *adj* : monástico — **monastically** [-tɪkli] *adv*

Monday [ˈmʌnˌdeɪ, -di] *n* : lunes *m*

monetary [ˈmɑnəˌtɛri, ˈmʌnə-] *adj* : monetario

money [ˈmʌni] *n, pl* **-eys** *or* **-ies** [ˈmʌniz] : dinero *m,* plata *f*

moneyed [ˈmʌnid] *adj* : adinerado

moneylender [ˈmʌniˌlɛndər] *n* : prestamista *mf*

money order *n* : giro *m* postal

Mongolian [mɑnˈgoːliən, mɑŋ-] *n* : mongol *m,* -gola *f* — **Mongolian** *adj*

mongoose [ˈmɑnˌguːs, ˈmɑŋ-] *n, pl* **-gooses** : mangosta *f*

mongrel [ˈmɑŋgrəl, ˈmʌŋ-] *n* **1** : perro *m* mestizo, perro *m* corriente *Mex* **2** HYBRID : híbrido *m*

monitor[1] [ˈmɑnət̬ər] *vt* : controlar, monitorear

monitor[2] *n* **1** : ayudante *mf* (en una escuela) **2** : monitor *m* (de una computadora, etc.)

monk [ˈmʌŋk] *n* : monje *m*

monkey[1] [ˈmʌŋki] *vi* **-keyed; -keying 1 to monkey around** : hacer payasadas, payasear **2 to monkey with** : juguetear con

monkey[2] *n, pl* **-keys** : mono *m,* -na *f*

monkeyshines [ˈmʌŋkiˌʃaɪnz] *npl* PRANKS : picardías *fpl,* travesuras *fpl*

monkey wrench *n* : llave *f* inglesa

monkshood [ˈmʌŋksˌhʊd] *n* : acónito *m*

monocle [ˈmɑnɪkəl] *n* : monóculo *m*

monogamous [məˈnɑgəməs] *adj* : monógamo

monogamy [məˈnɑgəmi] *n* : monogamia *f*

monogram[1] [ˈmɑnəˌgræm] *vt* **-grammed; -gramming :** marcar con monograma <monogrammed towels : toallas con monograma>

monogram[2] *n* : monograma *m*

monograph [ˈmɑnəˌgræf] *n* : monografía *f*

monolingual [ˌmɑnəˈlɪŋgwəl] *adj* : monolingüe

monolith [ˈmɑnəˌlɪθ] *n* : monolito *m*

monolithic [ˌmɑnəˈlɪθɪk] *adj* : monolítico

monologue [ˈmɑnəˌlɔg] *n* : monólogo *m*

monoplane [ˈmɑnəˌpleɪn] *n* : monoplano *m*

monopolize [məˈnɑpəˌlaɪz] *vt* **-lized; -lizing :** monopolizar

monopoly [məˈnɑpəli] *n, pl* **-lies** : monopolio *m*

monosyllabic [ˌmɑnosəˈlæbɪk] *adj* : monosilábico

monosyllable [ˈmɑnoˌsɪləbəl] *n* : monosílabo *m*
monotheism [ˈmɑnoθiːˌɪzəm] *n* : monoteísmo *m*
monotheistic [ˌmɑnoθiːˈɪstɪk] *adj* : monoteísta
monotone [ˈmɑnəˌtoːn] *n* : voz *f* monótona
monotonous [məˈnɑtənəs] *adj* : monótono — **monotonously** *adv*
monotony [məˈnɑtəni] *n* : monotonía *f*, uniformidad *f*
monoxide [məˈnɑkˌsaɪd] *n* : monóxido *m*
monsoon [mɑnˈsuːn] *n* : monzón *m*
monster [ˈmɑn*t*stər] *n* : monstruo *m*
monstrosity [mɑnˈstrɑsət̬i] *n, pl* **-ties** : monstruosidad *f*
monstrous [ˈmɑn*t*strəs] *adj* : monstruoso — **monstrously** *adv*
montage [mɑnˈtɑʒ] *n* : montaje *m*
month [ˈmʌnθ] *n* : mes *m*
monthly[1] [ˈmʌnθli] *adv* : mensualmente
monthly[2] *adj* : mensual
monthly[3] *n, pl* **-lies** : publicación *f* mensual
monument [ˈmɑnjəmənt] *n* : monumento *m*
monumental [ˌmɑnjəˈmɛntəl] *adj* : monumental — **monumentally** *adv*
moo[1] [ˈmuː] *vi* : mugir
moo[2] *n* : mugido *m*
mood [ˈmuːd] *n* : humor *m* <to be in a good mood : estar de buen humor> <to be in the mood for : tener ganas de> <to be in no mood for : no estar para>
moodiness [ˈmuːdinəs] *n* **1** SADNESS : melancolía *f*, tristeza *f* **2** : cambios *mpl* de humor, carácter *m* temperamental
moody [ˈmuːdi] *adj* **moodier; -est 1** GLOOMY : melancólico, deprimido **2** TEMPERAMENTAL : temperamental, de humor variable
moon [ˈmuːn] *n* : luna *f*
moonbeam [ˈmuːnˌbiːm] *n* : rayo *m* de luna
moonlight[1] [ˈmuːnˌlaɪt] *vi* : estar pluriempleado
moonlight[2] *n* : claro *m* de luna, luz *f* de la luna
moonlit [ˈmuːnˌlɪt] *adj* : iluminado por la luna <a moonlit night : una noche de luna>
moonshine [ˈmuːnˌʃaɪn] *n* **1** MOONLIGHT : luz *f* de la luna **2** NONSENSE : disparates *mpl*, tonterías *fpl* **3** : whiskey *m* destilado ilegalmente
moor[1] [ˈmʊr, ˈmɔr] *vt* : amarrar
moor[2] *n* : brezal *m*, páramo *m*
mooring [ˈmʊrɪŋ, ˈmɔr-] *n* DOCK : atracadero *m*
moose [ˈmuːs] *ns & pl* : alce *m* (norteamericano)
moot [ˈmuːt] *adj* DEBATABLE : discutible
mop[1] [ˈmɑp] *vt* **mopped; mopping** : trapear
mop[2] *n* : trapeador *m*
mope [ˈmoːp] *vi* **moped; moping** : andar deprimido, quedar abatido
moped [ˈmoːˌpɛd] *n* : ciclomotor *m*
moral[1] [ˈmɔrəl] *adj* : moral <moral judgment : juicio moral> <moral support : apoyo moral> — **morally** *adv*
moral[2] *n* **1** : moraleja *f* (de un cuento, etc.) **2 morals** *npl* : moral *f*, moralidad *f*
morale [məˈræl] *n* : moral *f*
morality [məˈrælət̬i] *n, pl* **-ties** : moralidad *f*
morass [məˈræs] *n* **1** SWAMP : ciénaga *f*, pantano *m* **2** CONFUSION, MESS : lío *m fam*, embrollo *m*
moratorium [ˌmɔrəˈtoriəm] *n, pl* **-riums** *or* **-ria** [-iə] : moratoria *f*
moray [ˈmɔrˌeɪ, məˈreɪ] *n* : morena *f*
morbid [ˈmɔrbɪd] *adj* **1** : mórbido, morboso (en medicina) **2** GRUESOME : morboso, horripilante
morbidity [mɔrˈbɪdət̬i] *n* : morbosidad *f*
more[1] [ˈmor] *adv* : más <what more can I say? : ¿qué más puedo decir?> <more important : más importante> <once more : una vez más>
more[2] *adj* : más <nothing more than that : nada más que eso> <more work : más trabajo>
more[3] *n* : más *m* <the more you eat, the more you want : cuanto más comes, tanto más quieres>
more[4] *pron* : más <more were found : se encontraron más>
moreover [morˈoːvər] *adv* : además
mores [ˈmɔrˌeɪz, -iːz] *npl* CUSTOMS : costumbres *fpl*, tradiciones *fpl*
morgue [ˈmɔrg] *n* : morgue *f*
moribund [ˈmɔrəˌbʌnd] *adj* : moribundo
morn [ˈmɔrn] → **morning**
morning [ˈmɔrnɪŋ] *n* : mañana *f* <good morning! : ¡buenos días!>
Moroccan [məˈrɑkən] *n* : marroquí *mf* — **Moroccan** *adj*
moron [ˈmorˌɑn] *n* **1** : retrasado *m*, -da *f* mental **2** DUNCE : estúpido *m*, -da *f*; tonto *m*, -ta *f*
morose [məˈroːs] *adj* : hosco, sombrío — **morosely** *adv*
moroseness [məˈroːsnəs] *n* : malhumor *m*
morphine [ˈmɔrˌfiːn] *n* : morfina *f*
morrow [ˈmɑroː] *n* : día *m* siguiente
Morse code [ˈmɔrs] *n* : código *m* morse
morsel [ˈmɔrsəl] *n* **1** BITE : bocado *m* **2** FRAGMENT : pedazo *m*
mortal[1] [ˈmɔrt̬əl] *adj* : mortal <mortal blow : golpe mortal> <mortal fear : miedo mortal> — **mortally** *adv*
mortal[2] *n* : mortal *mf*
mortality [mɔrˈtælət̬i] *n* : mortalidad *f*
mortar [ˈmɔrt̬ər] *n* **1** : mortero *m*, molcajete *m Mex* <mortar and pestle

: mortero y maja> 2 : mortero *m* <mortar shell : granada de mortero> 3 CEMENT : mortero *m,* argamasa *f*

mortgage¹ ['mɔrgɪdʒ] *vt* **-gaged; -gaging** : hipotecar

mortgage² *n* : hipoteca *f*

mortification [ˌmɔrṭəfə'keɪʃən] *n* 1 : mortificación *f* 2 HUMILIATION : humillación *f,* vergüenza *f*

mortify ['mɔrṭəˌfaɪ] *vt* **-fied; -fying** 1 : mortificar (en religión) 2 HUMILIATE : humillar, avergonzar

mortuary ['mɔrtʃəˌwɛri] *n, pl* **-aries** FUNERAL HOME : funeraria *f*

mosaic [mo'zeɪɪk] *n* : mosaico *m*

Moslem ['mɑzləm] → **Muslim**

mosque ['mɑsk] *n* : mezquita *f*

mosquito [mə'ski:to] *n, pl* **-toes** : mosquito *m,* zancudo *m*

moss ['mɔs] *n* : musgo *m*

mossy ['mɔsi] *adj* **-ier; -est** : musgoso

most¹ ['mo:st] *adv* : más <the most interesting book : el libro más interesante>

most² *adj* 1 : la mayoría de, la mayor parte de <most people : la mayoría de la gente> 2 GREATEST : más (dícese de los números), mayor (dícese de las cantidades) <the most ability : la mayor capacidad>

most³ *n* : más *m,* máximo *m* <the most I can do : lo más que puedo hacer> <three weeks at the most : tres semanas como máximo>

most⁴ *pron* : la mayoría, la mayor parte <most will go : la mayoría irá>

mostly ['mo:stli] *adv* MAINLY : en su mayor parte, principalmente

mote ['mo:t] *n* SPECK : mota *f*

motel [mo'tɛl] *n* : motel *m*

moth ['mɔθ] *n* : palomilla *f,* polilla *f*

mother¹ ['mʌðər] *vt* 1 BEAR : dar a luz a 2 PROTECT : cuidar de, proteger

mother² *n* : madre *f*

motherhood ['mʌðərˌhʊd] *n* : maternidad *f*

mother-in-law ['mʌðərɪnˌlɔ] *n, pl* **mothers-in-law** : suegra *f*

motherland ['mʌðərˌlænd] *n* : patria *f*

motherly ['mʌðərli] *adj* : maternal

mother-of-pearl [ˌmʌðərəv'pərl] *n* : nácar *m,* madreperla *f*

motif [mo'ti:f] *n* : motivo *m*

motion¹ ['mo:ʃən] *vt* : hacerle señas (a alguien) <she motioned us to come in : nos hizo señas para que entráramos>

motion² *n* 1 MOVEMENT : movimiento *m* <to set in motion : poner en marcha> 2 PROPOSAL : moción *f* <to second a motion : apoyar una moción>

motionless ['mo:ʃənləs] *adj* : inmóvil, quieto

motion picture *n* MOVIE : película *f*

motivate ['mo:ṭəˌveɪt] *vt* **-vated; -vating** : motivar, mover, inducir

motivation [ˌmo:ṭə'veɪʃən] *n* : motivación *f*

motive¹ ['mo:tɪv] *adj* : motor <motive power : fuerza motriz>

motive² *n* : motivo *m,* móvil *m*

motley ['mɑtli] *adj* : abigarrado, variopinto

motor¹ ['mo:ṭər] *vi* : viajar en coche

motor² *n* : motor *m*

motorbike ['mo:ṭərˌbaɪk] *n* : motocicleta *f* (pequeña), moto *f*

motorboat ['mo:ṭərˌbo:t] *n* : bote *m* a motor, lancha *f* motora

motorcar ['mo:ṭərˌkɑr] *n* : automóvil *m*

motorcycle ['mo:ṭərˌsaɪkəl] *n* : motocicleta *f*

motorcyclist ['mo:ṭərˌsaɪkəlɪst] *n* : motociclista *mf*

motorist ['mo:ṭərɪst] *n* : automovilista *mf,* motorista *mf*

mottle ['mɑṭəl] *vt* **-tled; -tling** : manchar, motear <mottled skin : piel manchada> <a mottled surface : una superficie moteada>

motto ['mɑto:] *n, pl* **-toes** : lema *m*

mould ['mo:ld] → **mold**

mound ['maʊnd] *n* 1 PILE : montón *m* 2 KNOLL : montículo *m* 3 **burial mound** : túmulo *m*

mount¹ ['maʊnt] *vt* 1 : montar a (un caballo), montar en (una bicicleta), subir a 2 : montar (artillería, etc.) — *vi* INCREASE : aumentar

mount² *n* 1 SUPPORT : soporte *m* 2 HORSE : caballería *f,* montura *f* 3 MOUNTAIN : monte *m,* montaña *f*

mountain ['maʊntən] *n* : montaña *f*

mountaineer [ˌmaʊntən'ɪr] *n* : alpinista *mf;* montañero *m,* -ra *f*

mountainous ['maʊntənəs] *adj* : montañoso

mountaintop ['maʊntənˌtɑp] *n* : cima *f,* cumbre *f*

mourn ['morn] *vt* : llorar (por), lamentar <to mourn the death of : llorar la muerte de> — *vi* : llorar, estar de luto

mourner ['mornər] *n* : doliente *mf*

mournful ['mornfəl] *adj* 1 SORROWFUL : lloroso, plañidero, triste 2 GLOOMY : deprimente, entristecedor — **mournfully** *adv*

mourning ['mornɪŋ] *n* : duelo *m,* luto *m*

mouse ['maʊs] *n, pl* **mice** ['maɪs] 1 : ratón *m,* -tona *f* 2 : ratón *m* (de una computadora)

mousetrap ['maʊsˌtræp] *n* : ratonera *f*

moustache ['mʌˌstæʃ, mə'stæʃ] → **mustache**

mouth¹ ['maʊð] *vt* 1 : decir con poca sinceridad, repetir sin comprensión 2 : articular en silencio <she mouthed the words : formó las palabras con los labios>

mouth² ['maʊθ] *n* : boca *f* (de una persona o un animal), entrada *f* (de un túnel), desembocadura *f* (de un río)

mouthful ['maʊθˌfʊl] *n* : bocado *m* (de comida), bocanada *f* (de líquido o humo)

mouthpiece [ˈmaʊθˌpiːs] *n* : boquilla *f* (de un instrumento musical)
movable [ˈmuːvəbəl] *or* **moveable** *adj* : movible, móvil
move[1] [ˈmuːv] *v* **moved; moving** *vi* **1** GO : ir **2** RELOCATE : mudarse, trasladarse **3** STIR : moverse <¡no te muevas! : don't move!> **4** ACT : actuar — *vt* **1** : mover <move it over there : ponlo allí> <he kept moving his feet : no dejaba de mover los pies> **2** INDUCE, PERSUADE : inducir, persuadir, mover **3** TOUCH : conmover <it moved him to tears : lo hizo llorar> **4** PROPOSE : proponer
move[2] *n* **1** MOVEMENT : movimiento *m* **2** RELOCATION : mudanza *f* (de casa), traslado *m* **3** STEP : paso *m* <a good move : un paso acertado>
movement [ˈmuːvmənt] *n* : movimiento *m*
mover [ˈmuːvər] *n* : persona *f* que hace mudanzas
movie [ˈmuːvi] *n* **1** : película *f* **2 movies** *npl* : cine *m*
moving [ˈmuːvɪŋ] *adj* **1** : en movimiento <a moving target : un blanco móvil> **2** TOUCHING : conmovedor, emocionante
mow[1] [ˈmoː] *vt* **mowed; mowed** *or* **mown** [ˈmoːn]; **mowing** : cortar (la hierba)
mow[2] [ˈmaʊ] *n* : pajar *m*
mower [ˈmoːər] → **lawn mower**
Mr. [ˈmɪstər] *n, pl* **Messrs.** [ˈmɛsərz] : señor *m*
Mrs. [ˈmɪsəz, -səs, *esp South* ˈmɪzəz, -zəs] *n, pl* **Mesdames** [meɪ-ˈdɑm, -ˈdæm] : señora *f*
Ms. [ˈmɪz] *n* : señora *f,* señorita *f*
much[1] [ˈmʌtʃ] *adv* **more** [ˈmor]; **most** [ˈmoːst] : mucho <I'm much happier : estoy mucho más contenta> <she talks as much as I do : habla tanto como yo>
much[2] *adj* **more; most** : mucho <it has much validity : tiene mucha validez> <too much time : demasiado tiempo>
much[3] *pron* : mucho, -cha <I don't need much : no necesito mucho>
mucilage [ˈmjuːsəlɪdʒ] *n* : mucílago *m*
muck [ˈmʌk] *n* **1** MANURE : estiércol *m* **2** DIRT, FILTH : mugre *f,* suciedad *f* **3** MIRE, MUD : barro *m,* fango *m,* lodo *m*
mucous [ˈmjuːkəs] *adj* : mucoso <mucous membrane : membrana mucosa>
mucus [ˈmjuːkəs] *n* : mucosidad *f*
mud [ˈmʌd] *n* : barro *m,* fango *m,* lodo *m*
muddle[1] [ˈmʌdəl] *v* **-dled; -dling** *vt* **1** CONFUSE : confundir **2** BUNGLE : echar a perder, malograr — *vi* : andar confundido <to muddle through : arreglárselas>
muddle[2] *n* : confusión *f,* embrollo *m,* lío *m*
muddleheaded [ˌmʌdəlˈhɛdəd, ˈmʌdəlˌ-] *adj* CONFUSED : confuso, despistado
muddy[1] [ˈmʌdi] *vt* **-died; -dying** : llenar de barro
muddy[2] *adj* **-dier; -est** : barroso, fangoso, lodoso, enlodado <you're all muddy : estás cubierto de barro>
muff[1] [ˈmʌf] *vt* BUNGLE : echar a perder, fallar (un tiro, etc.)
muff[2] *n* : manguito *m*
muffin [ˈmʌfən] *n* : magdalena *f,* mantecada *f Mex*
muffle [ˈmʌfəl] *vt* **-fled; -fling 1** ENVELOP : cubrir, tapar **2** DEADEN : amortiguar (un sonido)
muffler [ˈmʌflər] *n* **1** SCARF : bufanda *f* **2** : silenciador *m,* mofle *m CA, Mex* (de un automóvil)
mug[1] [ˈmʌg] *v* **mugged; mugging** *vi* : posar (con afectación), hacer muecas <mugging for the camera : haciendo muecas para la cámara> — *vt* ASSAULT : asaltar, atracar
mug[2] *n* CUP : tazón *m*
mugger [ˈmʌgər] *n* : atracador *m,* -dora *f*
mugginess [ˈmʌginəs] *n* : bochorno *m*
muggy [ˈmʌgi] *adj* **-gier; -est** : bochornoso
mulatto [mʊˈlɑṭo, -ˈlæ-] *n, pl* **-toes** *or* **-tos** : mulato *m,* -ta *f*
mulberry [ˈmʌlˌbɛri] *n, pl* **-ries** : morera *f* (árbol), mora *f* (fruta)
mulch[1] [ˈmʌltʃ] *vt* : cubrir con pajote
mulch[2] *n* : pajote *m*
mule [ˈmjuːl] *n* **1** : mula *f* **2** : obstinado *m,* -da *f;* terco *m,* -ca *f*
mulish [ˈmjuːlɪʃ] *adj* : obstinado, terco
mull [ˈmʌl] *vt* **to mull over** : reflexionar sobre
mullet [ˈmʌlət] *n, pl* **-let** *or* **-lets** : mújol *m,* múgil *m*
multicolored [ˌmʌltiˈkʌlərd, ˌmʌltaɪ-] *adj* : multicolor, abigarrado
multifaceted [ˌmʌltiˈfæsəṭəd, ˌmʌltaɪ-] *adj* : multifacético
multifamily [ˌmʌltiˈfæmli, ˌmʌltaɪ-] *adj* : multifamiliar
multifarious [ˌmʌltəˈfæriəs] *adj* DIVERSE : diverso, variado
multilateral [ˌmʌltiˈlæṭərəl, ˌmʌltaɪ-] *adj* : multilateral
multimedia [ˌmʌltiˈmiːdiə, ˌmʌltaɪ-] *adj* : multimedia
multimillionaire [ˌmʌltiˌmɪljəˈnær, ˌmʌltaɪ-, -ˈmɪljəˌnær] *adj* : multimillonario
multinational [ˌmʌltiˈnæʃənəl, ˌmʌltaɪ-] *adj* : multinacional
multiple[1] [ˈmʌltəpəl] *adj* : múltiple
multiple[2] *n* : múltiplo *m*
multiple sclerosis [skləˈroːsɪs] *n* : esclerosis *f* múltiple
multiplication [ˌmʌltəpləˈkeɪʃən] *n* : multiplicación *f*
multiplicity [ˌmʌltəˈplɪsəṭi] *n, pl* **-ties** : multiplicidad *f*
multiplier [ˈmʌltəˌplaɪər] *n* : multiplicador *m* (en matemáticas)

multiply [ˈmʌltəˌplaɪ] *v* **-plied; -plying** *vt* : multiplicar — *vi* : multiplicarse
multipurpose [ˌmʌltiˈpərpəs, ˌmʌltaɪ-] *adj* : multiuso
multitude [ˈmʌltəˌtuːd, -ˌtjuːd] *n* **1** CROWD : multitud *f,* muchedumbre *f* **2** HOST : multitud *f,* gran cantidad *f* <a multitude of ideas : numerosas ideas>
multivitamin [ˌmʌltiˈvaɪṯəmən, ˌmʌltaɪ-] *adj* : multivitamínico
mum¹ [ˈmʌm] *adj* SILENT : callado
mum² *n* → **chrysanthemum**
mumble¹ [ˈmʌmbəl] *v* **-bled; -bling** *vt* : mascullar, musitar — *vi* : mascullar, hablar entre dientes, murmurar
mumble² *n* **to speak in a mumble** : hablar entre dientes
mummy [ˈmʌmi] *n, pl* **-mies** : momia *f*
mumps [ˈmʌmps] *ns & pl* : paperas *fpl*
munch [ˈmʌntʃ] *v* : mascar, masticar
mundane [ˌmʌnˈdeɪn, ˈmʌnˌ-] *adj* **1** EARTHLY, WORLDLY : mundano, terrenal **2** COMMONPLACE : rutinario, ordinario
municipal [mjʊˈnɪsəpəl] *adj* : municipal
municipality [mjʊˌnɪsəˈpæləṯi] *n, pl* **-ties** : municipio *m*
munitions [mjʊˈnɪʃənz] *npl* : municiones *fpl*
mural¹ [ˈmjʊrəl] *adj* : mural
mural² [ˈmjʊrəlɪst] *n* : mural *m*
murder¹ [ˈmərdər] *vt* : asesinar, matar — *vi* : matar
murder² *n* : asesinato *m,* homicidio *m*
murderer [ˈmərdərər] *n* : asesino *m,* -na *f;* homicida *mf*
murderess [ˈmərdərɪs, -dəˌrɛs, -dərəs] *n* : asesina *f,* homicida *f*
murderous [ˈmərdərəs] *adj* : asesino, homicida
murk [ˈmərk] *n* DARKNESS : oscuridad *f,* tinieblas *fpl*
murkiness [ˈmərkinəs] *n* : oscuridad *f,* tenebrosidad *f*
murky [ˈmərki] *adj* **-kier; -est** : oscuro, tenebroso
murmur¹ [ˈmərmər] *vi* **1** DRONE : murmurar **2** GRUMBLE : refunfuñar, regañar, rezongar — *vt* MUMBLE : murmurar
murmur² *n* **1** COMPLAINT : queja *f* **2** DRONE : murmullo *m,* rumor *m*
muscle¹ [ˈmʌsəl] *vi* **-cled; -cling** : meterse <to muscle in on : meterse por la fuerza en, entrometerse en>
muscle² *n* **1** : músculo *m* **2** STRENGTH : fuerza *f*
muscular [ˈmʌskjələr] *adj* **1** : muscular <muscular tissue : tejido muscular> **2** BRAWNY : musculoso
muscular dystrophy *n* : distrofia *f* muscular
musculature [ˈmʌskjələˌtʃʊr, -tʃər] *n* : musculatura *f*
muse¹ [ˈmjuːz] *vi* **mused; musing** PONER, REFLECT : cavilar, meditar, reflexionar
muse² *n* : musa *f*
museum [mjʊˈziːəm] *n* : museo *m*
mush [ˈmʌʃ] *n* **1** : gachas *fpl* (de maíz) **2** SENTIMENTALITY : sensiblería *f*
mushroom¹ [ˈmʌʃˌruːm, -ˌrʊm] *vi* GROW, MULTIPLY : crecer rápidamente, multiplicarse
mushroom² *n* : hongo *m,* champiñón *m,* seta *f*
mushy [ˈmʌʃi] *adj* **mushier; -est** **1** SOFT : blando **2** MAWKISH : sensiblero
music [ˈmjuːzɪk] *n* : música *f*
musical¹ [ˈmjuːzɪkəl] *adj* : musical, de música — **musically** *adv*
musical² *n* : comedia *f* musical
music box *n* : cajita *f* de música
musician [mjʊˈzɪʃən] *n* : músico *m,* -ca *f*
musk [ˈmʌsk] *n* : almizcle *m*
musket [ˈmʌskət] *n* : mosquete *m*
musketeer [ˌmʌskəˈtɪr] *n* : mosquetero *m*
muskrat [ˈmʌskˌræt] *n, pl* **-rat** *or* **-rats** : rata *f* almizclera
Muslim¹ [ˈmʌzləm, ˈmʊs-, ˈmʊz-] *adj* : musulmán
Muslim² *n* : musulmán *m,* -mana *f*
muslin [ˈmʌzlən] *n* : muselina *f*
muss¹ [ˈmʌs] *vt* : desordenar, despeinar (el pelo)
muss² *n* : desorden *m*
mussel [ˈmʌsəl] *n* : mejillón *m*
must¹ [ˈmʌst] *v aux* **1** (*expressing obligation or necessity*) : deber, tener que <you must stop : debes parar> <we must obey : tenemos que obedecer> **2** (*expressing probability*) : deber (de), haber de <you must be tired : debes de estar cansado> <it must be late : ha de ser tarde>
must² *n* : necesidad *f* <exercise is a must : el ejercicio es imprescindible>
mustache [ˈmʌˌstæʃ, mʌˈstæʃ] *n* : bigote *m,* bigotes *mpl*
mustang [ˈmʌˌstæŋ] *n* : mustang *m*
mustard [ˈmʌstərd] *n* : mostaza *f*
muster¹ [ˈmʌstər] *vt* **1** ASSEMBLE : reunir **2 to muster up** : armarse de, cobrar (valor, fuerzas, etc.)
muster² *n* **1** INSPECTION : revista *f* (de tropas) <it didn't pass muster : no resistió un examen minucioso> **2** COLLECTION : colección *f*
mustiness [ˈmʌstinəs] *n* : lo mohoso
musty [ˈmʌsti] *adj* **mustier; -est** : mohoso, que huele a moho, que huele a encerrado
mutant¹ [ˈmjuːtənt] *adj* : mutante
mutant² *n* : mutante *m*
mutate [ˈmjuːˌteɪt] *vi* **-tated; -tating** **1** : mutar (genéticamente) **2** CHANGE : transformarse
mutation [mjuːˈteɪʃən] *n* : mutación *f* (genética)

mute[1] [ˈmjuːt] *vt* **muted; muting** MUFFLE : amortiguar, ponerle sordina a (un instrumento musical)
mute[2] *adj* **muter; mutest** : mudo — **mutely** *adv*
mute[3] *n* **1** : mudo *m*, -da *f* (persona) **2** : sordina *f* (para un instrumento musical)
mutilate [ˈmjuːt̬əˌleɪt] *vt* **-lated; -lating** : mutilar
mutilation [ˌmjuːt̬əˈleɪʃən] *n* : mutilación *f*
mutineer [ˌmjuːtənˈɪr] *n* : amotinado *m*, -da *f*
mutinous [ˈmjuːtənəs] *adj* : amotinado
mutiny[1] [ˈmjuːtəni] *vi* **-nied; -nying** : amotinarse
mutiny[2] *n, pl* **-nies** : amotinamiento *m*, motín *m*
mutt [ˈmʌt] *n* MONGREL : perro *m* mestizo, perro *m* corriente *Mex*
mutter [ˈmʌt̬ər] *vi* **1** MUMBLE : mascullar, hablar entre dientes, murmurar **2** GRUMBLE : refunfuñar, regañar, rezongar
mutton [ˈmʌtən] *n* : carne *f* de carnero
mutual [ˈmjuːtʃʊəl] *adj* **1** : mutuo <mutual respect : respeto mutuo> **2** COMMON : común <a mutual friend : un amigo común>
mutually [ˈmjuːtʃʊəli, -tʃəli] *adv* **1** : mutuamente <mutually beneficial : mutuamente beneficioso> **2** JOINTLY : conjuntamente
muzzle[1] [ˈmʌzəl] *vt* **-zled; -zling** : ponerle un bozal a (un animal), amordazar
muzzle[2] *n* **1** SNOUT : hocico *m* **2** : bozal *m* (para un perro, etc.) **3** : boca *f* (de un arma de fuego)
my[1] [ˈmaɪ] *adj* : mi <my parents : mis padres>
my[2] *interj* : ¡caramba!, ¡Dios mío!
myopia [maɪˈoːpiə] *n* : miopía *f*
myopic [maɪˈoːpɪk, -ˈɑ-] *adj* : miope
myriad[1] [ˈmɪriəd] *adj* INNUMERABLE : innumerable
myriad[2] *n* : miríada *f*
myrrh [ˈmər] *n* : mirra *f*
myrtle [ˈmərt̬əl] *n* : mirto *m*, arrayán *m*
myself [maɪˈsɛlf] *pron* **1** (*used reflexively*) : me <I washed myself : me lavé> **2** (*used for emphasis*) : yo mismo, yo misma <I did it myself : lo hice yo mismo>
mysterious [mɪˈstɪriəs] *adj* : misterioso — **mysteriously** *adv*
mysteriousness [mɪˈstɪriəsnəs] *n* : lo misterioso
mystery [ˈmɪstəri] *n, pl* **-teries** : misterio *m*
mystic[1] [ˈmɪstɪk] *adj* : místico
mystic[2] *n* : místico *m*, -ca *f*
mystical [ˈmɪstɪkəl] *adj* : místico — **mystically** *adv*
mysticism [ˈmɪstəˌsɪzəm] *n* : misticismo *m*
mystify [ˈmɪstəˌfaɪ] *vt* **-fied; -fying** : dejar perplejo, confundir
mystique [mɪˈstiːk] *n* : aura *f* de misterio
myth [ˈmɪθ] *n* : mito *m*
mythical [ˈmɪθɪkəl] *adj* : mítico
mythological [ˌmɪθəˈlɑdʒɪkəl] *adj* : mitológico
mythology [mɪˈθɑlədʒi] *n, pl* **-gies** : mitología *f*

N

n [ˈɛn] *n, pl* **n's** *or* **ns** [ˈɛnz] : decimocuarta letra del alfabeto inglés
nab [ˈnæb] *vt* **nabbed; nabbing** : prender, pillar *fam*, pescar *fam*
nadir [ˈneɪdər, ˈneɪˌdɪr] *n* : nadir *m*, punto *m* más bajo
nag[1] [ˈnæg] *v* **nagged; nagging** *vi* **1** COMPLAIN : quejarse, rezongar **2 to nag at** HASSLE : molestar, darle (la) lata (a alguien) — *vt* **1** PESTER : molestar, fastidiar **2** SCOLD : regañar, estarle encima a *fam*
nag[2] *n* **1** GRUMBLER : gruñón *m*, -ñona *f* **2** HORSE : jamelgo *m*
naiad [ˈneɪəd, ˈnaɪ-, -ˌæd] *n, pl* **-iads** *or* **-iades** [-əˌdiːz] : náyade *f*
nail[1] [ˈneɪl] *vt* : clavar, sujetar con clavos
nail[2] *n* **1** FINGERNAIL : uña *f* <nail file : lima (de uñas)> <nail polish : laca de uñas> **2** : clavo *m* <to hit the nail on the head : dar en el clavo>
naive *or* **naïve** [nɑˈiːv] *adj* **-iver; -est** **1** INGENUOUS : ingenuo, cándido **2** GULLIBLE : crédulo
naively [nɑˈiːvli] *adv* : ingenuamente
naïveté [ˌnɑˌiːvəˈteɪ, nɑˈiːvəˌ-] *n* : ingenuidad *f*
naked [ˈneɪkəd] *adj* **1** UNCLOTHED : desnudo **2** UNCOVERED : desenvainado (dícese de una espada), pelado (dícese de los árboles), expuesto al aire (dícese de una llama) **3** OBVIOUS, PLAIN : manifiesto, puro, desnudo <the naked truth : la pura verdad> **4 to the naked eye** : a simple vista
nakedly [ˈneɪkədli] *adv* : manifiestamente
nakedness [ˈneɪkədnəs] *n* : desnudez *f*
name[1] [ˈneɪm] *vt* **named; naming** **1** CALL : llamar, bautizar, ponerle nombre a **2** MENTION : mentar, mencionar, dar el nombre de <they have named a suspect : han dado el nombre de un

sospechoso> 3 APPOINT : nombrar **4 to name a price** : fijar un precio

name[2] *adj* **1** KNOWN : de nombre <name brand : marca conocida> **2** PROMINENT : de renombre, de prestigio

name[3] *n* **1** : nombre *m* <what is your name : ¿cómo se llama?> **2** SURNAME : apellido *m* **3** EPITHET : epíteto *m* <to call somebody names : llamar a alguien de todo> **4** REPUTATION : fama *f,* reputación *f* <to make a name for oneself : darse a conocer, hacerse famoso>

nameless [ˈneɪmləs] *adj* **1** ANONYMOUS : anónimo **2** INDESCRIBABLE : indecible, indescriptible

namelessly [ˈneɪmləsli] *adv* : anónimamente

namely [ˈneɪmli] *adv* : a saber

namesake [ˈneɪm,seɪk] *n* : tocayo *m,* -ya *f;* homónimo *m,* -ma *f*

Namibian [nəˈmɪbiən] *n* : namibio *m,* -bia *f* — **Namibian** *adj*

nap[1] [ˈnæp] *vi* **napped; napping 1** : dormir, dormir la siesta **2 to be caught napping** : estar desprevenido

nap[2] *n* **1** SLEEP : siesta *f* <to take a nap : echarse una siesta> **2** FUZZ, PILE : pelo *m,* pelusa *f* (de telas)

nape [ˈneɪp, ˈnæp] *n* : nuca *f,* cerviz *f,* cogote *m*

naphtha [ˈnæfθə] *n* : nafta *f*

napkin [ˈnæpkən] *n* : servilleta *f*

narcissism [ˈnɑrsə,sɪzəm] *n* : narcisismo *m*

narcissist [ˈnɑrsəsɪst] *n* : narcisista *mf*

narcissistic [,nɑrsəˈsɪstɪk] *adj* : narcisista

narcissus [nɑrˈsɪsəs] *n, pl* **-cissus** *or* **-cissuses** *or* **-cissi** [-ˈsɪ,saɪ, -,siː] : narciso *m*

narcotic[1] [nɑrˈkɑtɪk] *adj* : narcótico

narcotic[2] *n* : narcótico *m,* estupefaciente *m*

narrate [ˈnær,eɪt] *vt* **-rated; -rating** : narrar, relatar

narration [næˈreɪʃən] *n* : narración *f*

narrative[1] [ˈnærət̬ɪv] *adj* : narrativo

narrative[2] *n* : narración *f,* narrativa *f,* relato *m*

narrator [ˈnær,eɪt̬ər] *n* : narrador *m,* -dora *f*

narrow[1] [ˈnær,oː] *vi* : estrecharse, angostarse <the river narrowed : el río se estrechó> — *vt* **1** : estrechar, angostar **2** LIMIT : restringir, limitar <to narrow the search : limitar la búsqueda>

narrow[2] *adj* **1** : estrecho, angosto **2** LIMITED : estricto, limitado <in the narrowest sense of the word : en el sentido más estricto de la palabra> **3 to have a narrow escape** : escapar por un pelo

narrowly [ˈnæroli] *adv* **1** BARELY : por poco **2** CLOSELY : de cerca

narrow–minded [,næroˈmaɪndəd] *adj* : de miras estrechas

narrowness [ˈnæronəs] *n* : estrechez *f*

narrows [ˈnæroːz] *npl* STRAIT : estrecho *m*

narwhal [ˈnɑr,*h*wɑl, ˈnɑrwəl] *n* : narval *m*

nasal [ˈneɪzəl] *adj* : nasal, gangoso <a nasal voice : una voz gangosa>

nasally [ˈneɪzəli] *adv* **1** : por la nariz **2** : con voz gangosa

nastily [ˈnæstəli] *adv* : con maldad, cruelmente

nastiness [ˈnæstinəs] *n* : porquería *f*

nasturtium [nəˈstərʃəm, næ-] *n* : capuchina *f*

nasty [ˈnæsti] *adj* **-tier; -est 1** FILTHY : sucio, mugriento **2** OBSCENE : obsceno **3** MEAN, SPITEFUL : malo, malicioso **4** UNPLEASANT : desagradable, feo **5** REPUGNANT : asqueroso, repugnante <a nasty smell : un olor asqueroso>

natal [ˈneɪt̬əl] *adj* : natal

nation [ˈneɪʃən] *n* : nación *f*

national[1] [ˈnæʃənəl] *adj* : nacional

national[2] *n* : ciudadano *m,* -na *f;* nacional *mf*

nationalism [ˈnæʃənə,lɪzəm] *n* : nacionalismo *m*

nationalist[1] [ˈnæʃənəlɪst] *adj* : nacionalista

nationalist[2] *n* : nacionalista *mf*

nationalistic [,næʃənəˈlɪstɪk] *adj* : nacionalista

nationality [,næʃəˈnæləţi] *n, pl* **-ties** : nacionalidad *f*

nationalization [,næʃənələˈzeɪʃən] *n* : nacionalización *f*

nationalize [ˈnæʃənə,laɪz] *vt* **-ized; -izing** : nacionalizar

nationally [ˈnæʃənəli] *adv* : a escala nacional, a nivel nacional

nationwide [ˈneɪʃənˈwaɪd] *adj* : en toda la nación, por todo el país

native[1] [ˈneɪt̬ɪv] *adj* **1** INNATE : innato **2** : natal <her native city : su ciudad natal> **3** INDIGENOUS : indígeno, autóctono

native[2] *n* **1** ABORIGINE : nativo *m,* -va *f;* indígena *mf* **2** : natural *m* <he's a native of Mexico : es natural de México>

Native American → **American Indian**

nativity [nəˈtɪvəţi, neɪ-] *n, pl* **-ties 1** BIRTH : navidad *f* **2 the Nativity** : la Natividad, la Navidad

natty [ˈnæţi] *adj* **-tier; -est** : elegante, garboso

natural[1] [ˈnætʃərəl] *adj* **1** : natural, de la naturaleza <natural woodlands : bosques naturales> <natural childbirth : parto natural> **2** INNATE : innato, natural **3** UNAFFECTED : natural, sin afectación **4** LIFELIKE : natural, vivo

natural[2] *n* **to be a natural** : tener un talento innato (para algo)

natural gas *n* : gas *m* natural

natural history *n* : historia *f* natural

naturalist [ˈnætʃərəlɪst] *n* : naturalista *mf*
naturalization [ˌnætʃərələˈzeɪʃən] *n* : naturalización *f*
naturalize [ˈnætʃərəˌlaɪz] *vt* **-ized; -izing** : naturalizar
naturally [ˈnætʃərəli] *adv* **1** INHERENTLY : naturalmente, intrínsecamente **2** UNAFFECTEDLY : de manera natural **3** OF COURSE : por supuesto, naturalmente
naturalness [ˈnætʃərəlnəs] *n* : naturalidad *f*
natural science *n* : ciencias *fpl* naturales
nature [ˈneɪtʃər] *n* **1** : naturaleza *f* <the laws of nature : las leyes de la naturaleza> **2** KIND, SORT : índole *f,* clase *f* <things of this nature : cosas de esta índole> **3** DISPOSITION : carácter *m,* natural *m,* naturaleza *f* <it is his nature to be friendly : es de natural simpático> <human nature : la naturaleza humana>
naught [ˈnɔt] *n* **1** : nada *f* <to come to naught : reducirse a nada, fracasar> **2** ZERO : cero *m*
naughtily [ˈnɔt̬əli] *adv* : traviesamente, con malicia
naughtiness [ˈnɔt̬inəs] *n* : mala conducta *f,* travesuras *fpl,* malicia *f*
naughty [ˈnɔt̬i] *adj* **-tier; -est 1** MISCHIEVOUS : travieso, pícaro **2** RISQUÉ : picante, subido de tono
nausea [ˈnɔziə, ˈnɔʃə] *n* **1** SICKNESS : náuseas *fpl* **2** DISGUST : asco *m*
nauseate [ˈnɔziˌeɪt, -ʒi-, -si-, -ʃi-] *vt* **-ated; -ating 1** SICKEN : darle náuseas (a alguien) **2** DISGUST : asquear, darle asco (a alguien)
nauseating *adj* : nauseabundo, repugnante
nauseatingly [ˈnɔziˌeɪt̬ɪŋli, -ʒi-, -si-, -ʃi-] *adv* : hasta el punto de dar asco <nauseatingly sweet : tan dulce que da asco>
nauseous [ˈnɔʃəs, -ziəs] *adj* **1** SICK : mareado, con náuseas **2** SICKENING : nauseabundo
nautical [ˈnɔt̬ɪkəl] *adj* : náutico
nautilus [ˈnɔt̬ələs] *n, pl* **-luses** *or* **-li** [-ˌlaɪ, -ˌliː] : nautilo *m*
naval [ˈneɪvəl] *adj* : naval
nave [ˈneɪv] *n* : nave *f*
navel [ˈneɪvəl] *n* : ombligo *m*
navigability [ˌnævɪgəˈbɪlət̬i] *n* : navegabilidad *f*
navigable [ˈnævɪgəbəl] *adj* : navegable
navigate [ˈnævəˌgeɪt] *v* **-gated; -gating** *vi* : navegar — *vt* **1** STEER : gobernar (un barco), pilotar (un avión) **2** : navegar por (un río, etc.)
navigation [ˌnævəˈgeɪʃən] *n* : navegación *f*
navigator [ˈnævəˌgeɪt̬ər] *n* : navegante *mf*
navy [ˈneɪvi] *n, pl* **-vies 1** FLEET : flota *f* **2** : marina *f* de guerra, armada *f* <the United States Navy : la armada de los Estados Unidos> **3** *or* **navy blue** : azul *m* marino
nay[1] [ˈneɪ] *adv* : no
nay[2] *n* : no *m,* voto *m* en contra
Nazi [ˈnɑtsi, ˈnæt-] *n* : nazi *mf*
Nazism [ˈnɑtˌsɪzəm, ˈnæt-] *or* **Naziism** [ˈnɑtsiˌɪzəm, ˈnæt-] *n* : nazismo *m*
Neanderthal man [niˈændərˌθɔl, -ˌtɔl] *n* : hombre *m* de Neanderthal
near[1] [ˈnɪr] *vt* **1** : acercarse a <the ship is nearing port : el barco se está acercando al puerto> **2** : estar a punto de <she is nearing graduation : está a punto de graduarse>
near[2] *adv* **1** CLOSE : cerca <my family lives quite near : mi familia vive muy cerca> **2** NEARLY : casi <I came near to finishing : casi terminé>
near[3] *adj* **1** CLOSE : cercano, próximo **2** SIMILAR : parecido, semejante
near[4] *prep* : cerca de
nearby[1] [nɪrˈbaɪ, ˈnɪrˌbaɪ] *adv* : cerca
nearby[2] *adj* : cercano
nearly [ˈnɪrli] *adv* **1** ALMOST : casi <nearly asleep : casi dormido> **2 not nearly** : ni con mucho, ni mucho menos <it was not nearly so bad as I had expected : no fue ni con mucho tan malo como esperaba>
nearness [ˈnɪrnəs] *n* : proximidad *f*
nearsighted [ˈnɪrˌsaɪt̬əd] *adj* : miope, corto de vista
nearsightedly [ˈnɪrˌsaɪt̬ədli] *adv* : con miopía
nearsightedness [ˈnɪrˌsaɪt̬ədnəs] *n* : miopía *f*
neat [ˈniːt] *adj* **1** CLEAN, ORDERLY : ordenado, pulcro, limpio **2** UNDILUTED : solo, sin diluir **3** SIMPLE, TASTEFUL : sencillo y de buen gusto **4** CLEVER : hábil, ingenioso <a neat trick : un truco ingenioso>
neatly [ˈniːtli] *adv* **1** TIDILY : ordenadamente **2** CLEVERLY : ingeniosamente
neatness [ˈniːtnəs] *n* : pulcritud *f,* limpieza *f,* orden *m*
nebula [ˈnɛbjʊlə] *n, pl* **-lae** [-ˌliː, -ˌlaɪ] : nebulosa *f*
nebulous [ˈnɛbjʊləs] *adj* : nebuloso, vago
necessarily [ˌnɛsəˈsɛrəli] *adv* : necesariamente, forzosamente
necessary[1] [ˈnɛsəˌsɛri] *adj* **1** INEVITABLE : inevitable **2** COMPULSORY : necesario, obligatorio **3** ESSENTIAL : imprescindible, preciso, necesario
necessary[2] *n, pl* **-saries** : lo esencial, lo necesario
necessitate [nɪˈsɛsəˌteɪt] *vt* **-tated; -tating** : necesitar, requerir
necessity [nɪˈsɛsət̬i] *n, pl* **-ties 1** NEED : necesidad *f* **2** REQUIREMENT : requisito *m* indispensable **3** POVERTY : indigencia *f,* necesidad *f* **4** INEVITABILITY : inevitabilitad *f*
neck[1] [ˈnɛk] *vi* : besuquearse

neck[2] *n* **1 :** cuello *m* (de una persona), pescuezo *m* (de un animal) **2** COLLAR **:** cuello *m* **3 :** cuello *m* (de una botella), mástil *m* (de una guitarra)

neckerchief [ˈnɛkərtʃəf, -ˌtʃiːf] *n, pl* **-chiefs** [-tʃəfs, -ˌtʃiːfs] **:** pañuelo *m* (para el cuello), mascada *f Mex*

necklace [ˈnɛkləs] *n* **:** collar *m*

neckline [ˈnɛkˌlaɪn] *n* **:** escote *m*

necktie [ˈnɛkˌtaɪ] *n* **:** corbata *f*

nectar [ˈnɛktər] *n* **:** néctar *m*

nectarine [ˌnɛktəˈriːn] *n* **:** nectarina *f*

née *or* **nee** [ˈneɪ] *adj* **:** de soltera <Mrs. Smith, née Whitman : la señora Smith, de soltera Whitman>

need[1] [ˈniːd] *vt* **1 :** necesitar <I need your help : necesito su ayuda> <I need money : me falta dinero> **2** REQUIRE **:** requerir, exigir <that job needs patience : ese trabajo exige paciencia> **3 to need to :** tener que <he needs to study : tiene que estudiar> <they need to be scolded : hay que reprenderlos> — *v aux* **1** MUST **:** tener que, deber <need you shout? : ¿tienes que gritar?> **2 to be needed :** hacer falta <you needn't worry : no hace falta que te preocupes, no hay por qué preocuparse>

need[2] *n* **1** NECESSITY **:** necesidad *f* <in case of need : en caso de necesidad> **2** LACK **:** falta *f* <the need for better training : la falta de mejor capacitación> <to be in need : necesitar> **3** POVERTY **:** necesidad *f,* indigencia *f* **4 needs** *npl* **:** requisitos *mpl,* carencias *fpl*

needful [ˈniːdfəl] *adj* **:** necesario

needle[1] [ˈniːdəl] *vt* **-dled; -dling :** pinchar

needle[2] *n* **1 :** aguja *f* <to thread a needle : enhebrar una aguja> <knitting needle : aguja de tejer> **2** POINTER **:** aguja *f,* indicador *m*

needlepoint [ˈniːdəlˌpɔint] *n* **1** LACE **:** encaje *m* de mano **2** EMBROIDERY **:** bordado *m* en cañamazo

needless [ˈniːdləs] *adj* **:** innecesario

needlessly [ˈniːdləsli] *adv* **:** sin ninguna necesidad, innecesariamente

needlework [ˈniːdəlˌwərk] *n* **:** bordado *m*

needn't [ˈniːdənt] (*contraction of* **need not**) → **need**

needy[1] [ˈniːdi] **needier; -est** *adj* **:** necesitado

needy[2] *n* **the needy :** los necesitados *mpl*

nefarious [nɪˈfæriəs] *adj* **:** nefario, nefando, infame

negate [nɪˈgeɪt] *vt* **-gated; -gating 1** DENY **:** negar **2** NULLIFY **:** invalidar, anular

negation [nɪˈgeɪʃən] *n* **:** negación *f*

negative[1] [ˈnɛgət̬ɪv] *adj* **:** negativo

negative[2] *n* **1 :** negación *f* (en lingüística) **2 :** negativa *f* <to answer in the negative : contestar con una negativa> **3 :** término *m* negativo (en matemáticas) **4 :** negativo *m,* imagen *f* en negativo (en fotografía)

negatively [ˈnɛgət̬ɪvli] *adv* **:** negativamente

neglect[1] [nɪˈglɛkt] *vt* **1 :** desatender, descuidar <to neglect one's health : descuidar la salud> **2 :** no cumplir con, faltar a <to neglect one's obligations : faltar uno a sus obligaciones> <he neglected to tell me : omitió decírmelo>

neglect[2] *n* **1 :** negligencia *f,* descuido *m,* incumplimiento *m* <through neglect : por negligencia> <neglect of duty : incumplimiento del deber> **2 in a state of neglect :** abandonado, descuidado

neglectful [nɪˈglɛktfəl] *adj* **:** descuidado *m*

negligee [ˌnɛgləˈʒeɪ] *n* **:** negligé *m*

negligence [ˈnɛglɪdʒən*t*s] *n* **:** descuido *m,* negligencia *f*

negligent [ˈnɛglɪdʒənt] *adj* **:** negligente, descuidado — **negligently** *adv*

negligible [ˈnɛglɪdʒəbəl] *adj* **:** insignificante, despreciable

negotiable [nɪˈgoːʃəbəl, -ʃiə-] *adj* **:** negociable

negotiate [nɪˈgoːʃiˌeɪt] *v* **-ated; -ating** *vi* **:** negociar — *vt* **1 :** negociar, gestionar <to negotiate a treaty : negociar un trato> **2 :** salvar, franquear <they negotiated the obstacles : salvaron los obstáculos> <to negotiate a turn : tomar una curva>

negotiation [nɪˌgoːʃiˈeɪʃən, -siˈeɪ-] *n* **:** negociación *f*

negotiator [nɪˈgoːʃiˌeɪtər, -siˌeɪ-] *n* **:** negociador *m,* -dora *f*

Negro [ˈniːˌgroː] *n, pl* **-groes :** negro *m,* -gra *f*

neigh[1] [ˈneɪ] *vi* **:** relinchar

neigh[2] *n* **:** relincho *m*

neighbor[1] [ˈneɪbər] *vt* **:** ser vecino de, estar junto a <her house neighbors mine : su casa está junto a la mía> — *vi* **:** estar cercano, lindar, colindar <her land neighbors on mine : sus tierras lindan con las mías>

neighbor[2] *n* **1 :** vecino *m,* -na *f* **2 love thy neighbor :** ama a tu prójimo

neighborhood [ˈneɪbərˌhʊd] *n* **1 :** barrio *m,* vecindad *f,* vecindario *m* **2 in the neighborhood of :** alrededor de, cerca de

neighborly [ˈneɪbərli] *adv* **:** amable, de buena vecindad

neither[1] [ˈniːðər, ˈnaɪ-] *adj* **:** ninguno (de los dos)

neither[2] *conj* **1 :** ni <neither asleep nor awake : ni dormido ni despierto> **2** NOR **:** ni (tampoco) <I'm not asleep — neither am I : no estoy dormido — ni yo tampoco>

neither[3] *pron* **:** ninguno

nemesis [ˈnɛməsɪs] *n, pl* **-eses** [-ˌsiːz] **1** RIVAL **:** rival *mf* **2** RETRIBUTION **:** justo castigo *m*

neologism [ni'ɑlə,dʒɪzəm] *n* : neologismo *m*
neon[1] ['ni:,ɑn] *adj* : de neón <neon sign : letrero de neón>
neon[2] *n* : neón *m*
Nepali [nə'pɔli, -'pɑ-, -'pæ-] *n* : nepalés *m*, -lesa *f* — **Nepali** *adj*
neophyte ['ni:ə,faɪt] *n* : neófito *m*, -ta *f*
nephew ['nɛ,fju:, *chiefly British* 'nɛ,vju:] *n* : sobrino *m*
nepotism ['nɛpə,tɪzəm] *n* : nepotismo *m*
Neptune ['nɛp,tu:n, -,tju:n] *n* : Neptuno *m*
nerd ['nərd] *n* : ganso *m*, -sa *f*
nerve ['nərv] *n* **1** : nervio *m* **2** COURAGE : coraje *m*, valor *m*, fuerza *f* de la voluntad <to lose one's nerve : perder el valor> **3** AUDACITY, GALL : atrevimiento *m*, descaro *m* <of all the nerve! : ¡qué descaro!> **4 nerves** *npl* : nervios *mpl* <a fit of nerves : un ataque de nervios>
nervous ['nərvəs] *adj* **1** : nervioso <the nervous system : el sistema nervioso> **2** EXCITABLE : nervioso, excitable <to get nervous : excitarse, ponerse nervioso> **3** FEARFUL : miedoso, temeroso
nervously ['nərvəsli] *adv* : nerviosamente
nervousness ['nərvəsnəs] *n* : nerviosismo *m*, nerviosidad *f*, ansiedad *f*
nervy ['nərvi] *adj* **nervier; -est 1** COURAGEOUS : valiente **2** IMPUDENT : atrevido, descarado, fresco *fam* **3** NERVOUS : nervioso
nest[1] ['nɛst] *vi* : anidar
nest[2] *n* **1** : nido *m* (de un ave), avispero *m* (de una avispa), madriguera *f* (de un animal) **2** REFUGE : nido *m*, refugio *m* **3** SET : juego *m* <a nest of tables : un juego de mesitas>
nestle ['nɛsəl] *vi* **-tled; -tling** : acurrucarse, arrimarse cómodamente
net[1] ['nɛt] *vt* **netted; netting 1** CATCH : pescar, atrapar con una red **2** CLEAR : ganar neto <they netted $5000 : ganaron $5000 netos> **3** YIELD : producir neto
net[2] *adj* : neto <net weight : peso neto> <net gain : ganancia neta>
net[3] *n* : red *f*, malla *f*
nether ['nɛðər] *adj* **1** : inferior, más bajo **2 the nether regions** : el infierno
nettle[1] ['nɛṭəl] *vt* **-tled; -tling** : irritar, provocar, molestar
nettle[2] *n* : ortiga *f*
network ['nɛt,wərk] *n* **1** SYSTEM : red *f* **2** CHAIN : cadena *f* <a network of supermarkets : una cadena de supermercados>
neural ['nʊrəl, 'njʊr-] *adj* : neural
neuralgia [nʊ'rældʒə, njʊ-] *n* : neuralgia *f*
neuritis [nʊ'raɪṭəs, njʊ-] *n, pl* **-ritides** [-'rɪṭə,di:z] *or* **-ritises** : neuritis *f*
neurological [,nʊrə'lɑdʒɪkəl, ,njʊr-] *or* **neurologic** [,nʊrə'lɑdʒɪk, ,njʊr-] *adj* : neurológico
neurologist [nʊ'rɑlədʒɪst, njʊ-] *n* : neurólogo *m*, -ga *f*
neurology [nʊ'rɑlədʒi, njʊ-] *n* : neurología *f*
neurosis [nʊ'ro:sɪs, njʊ-] *n, pl* **-roses** [-,si:z] : neurosis *f*
neurotic[1] [nʊ'rɑṭɪk, njʊ-] *adj* : neurótico
neurotic[2] *n* : neurótico *m*, -ca *f*
neuter[1] ['nu:ṭər, 'nju:-] *vt* : castrar
neuter[2] *adj* : neutro
neutral[1] ['nu:trəl, 'nju:-] *adj* **1** IMPARTIAL : neutral, imparcial <to remain neutral : permanecer neutral> **2** : neutro <a neutral color : un color neutro> **3** : neutro (en la química o la electricidad)
neutral[2] *n* : punto *m* muerto (de un automóvil)
neutrality [nu:'træləṭi:, nju:-] *n* : neutralidad *f*
neutralization [,nu:trələ'zeɪʃən, ,nju:-] *n* : neutralización *f*
neutralize ['nu:trə,laɪz, 'nju:-] *vt* **-ized; -izing** : neutralizar
neutron ['nu:,trɑn, 'nju:-] *n* : neutrón *m*
never ['nɛvər] *adv* **1** : nunca, jamás <he never studies : nunca estudia> **2 never again** : nunca más, nunca jamás **3 never mind** : no importa
nevermore [,nɛvər'mor] *adv* : nunca más
nevertheless [,nɛvərðə'lɛs] *adv* : sin embargo, no obstante
new ['nu:, 'nju:] *adj* **1** : nuevo <a new dress : un vestido nuevo> **2** RECENT : nuevo, reciente <what's new? : ¿qué hay de nuevo?> <a new arrival : un recién llegado> **3** DIFFERENT : nuevo, distinto <this problem is new : este problema es distinto> <new ideas : ideas nuevas> **4 like new** : como nuevo
newborn ['nu:,bɔrn, 'nju:-] *adj* : recién nacido
newcomer ['nu:,kʌmər, 'nju:-] *n* : recién llegado *m*, recién llegada *f*
newfangled ['nu:'fæŋgəld, 'nju:-] *adj* : novedoso
newfound ['nu:'faʊnd, 'nju:-] *adj* : recién descubierto
newly ['nu:li, 'nju:-] *adv* : recién, recientemente
newlywed ['nu:li,wɛd, 'nju:-] *n* : recién casado *m*, -da *f*
new moon *n* : luna *f* nueva
newness ['nu:nəs, 'nju:-] *n* : novedad *f*
news ['nu:z, 'nju:z] *n* : noticias *fpl*
newscast ['nu:z,kæst, 'nju:z-] *n* : noticiero *m*, informativo *m*
newscaster ['nu:z,kæstər, 'nju:z-] *n* : presentador *m*, -dora *f*; locutor *m*, -tora *f*

newsletter [ˈnuːzˌlɛt̬ər, ˈnjuːz-] *n* : boletín *m* informativo

newsman [ˈnuːzmən, ˈnjuːz-, -ˌmæn] *n, pl* **-men** [-mən, -ˌmɛn] : periodista *m,* reportero *m*

newspaper [ˈnuːzˌpeɪpər, ˈnjuːz-] *n* : periódico *m,* diario *m*

newspaperman [ˈnuːzˌpeɪpərˌmæn, ˈnjuːz-] *n, pl* **-men** [-mən, -ˌmɛn] **1** REPORTER : periodista *m,* reportero *m* **2** : dueño *m* de un periódico

newsprint [ˈnuːzˌprɪnt, ˈnjuːz-] *n* : papel *m* de prensa

newsstand [ˈnuːzˌstænd, ˈnjuːz-] *n* : quiosco *m,* puesto *m* de periódicos

newswoman [ˈnuːzˌwʊmən, ˈnjuːz-] *n, pl* **-women** [-ˌwɪmən] : periodista *f,* reportera *f*

newsworthy [ˈnuːzˌwərði, ˈnjuːz-] *adj* : de interés periodístico

newsy [ˈnuːziː, ˈnjuː-] *adj* **newsier; -est** : lleno de noticias

newt [ˈnuːt, ˈnjuːt] *n* : tritón *m*

New Year *n* : Año *m* Nuevo

New Year's Day *n* : día *m* del Año Nuevo

New Yorker [nuːˈjɔrkər, njuː-] *n* : neoyorquino *m,* -na *f*

New Zealander [nuːˈziːləndər, njuː-] *n* : neozelandés *m,* -desa *f*

next[1] [ˈnɛkst] *adv* **1** AFTERWARD : después, luego <what will you do next? : ¿qué harás después?> **2** NOW : después, ahora, entonces <next I will sing a song : ahora voy a cantar una canción> **3** : la próxima vez <when next we meet : la próxima vez que nos encontremos>

next[2] *adj* **1** ADJACENT : contiguo, de al lado **2** COMING : que viene, próximo <next Friday : el viernes que viene> **3** FOLLOWING : siguiente <the next year : el año siguiente>

next–door [ˈnɛkstˈdor] *adj* : de al lado

next to[1] *adv* ALMOST : casi, prácticamente <next to impossible : casi imposible>

next to[2] *prep* : junto a, al lado de

nib [ˈnɪb] *n* : plumilla *f*

nibble[1] [ˈnɪbəl] *v* **-bled; -bling** *vt* : pellizcar, mordisquear, picar — *vi* : picar

nibble[2] *n* : mordisco *m*

Nicaraguan [ˌnɪkəˈrɑgwən] *n* : nicaragüense *mf* — **Nicaraguan** *adj*

nice [ˈnaɪs] *adj* **nicer; nicest 1** REFINED : pulido, refinado **2** SUBTLE : fino, sutil **3** PLEASING : agradable, bueno, lindo <nice weather : buen tiempo> **4** RESPECTABLE : bueno, decente **5 nice and** : bien, muy <nice and hot : bien caliente> <nice and slow : despacito>

nicely [ˈnaɪsli] *adv* **1** KINDLY : amablemente **2** POLITELY : con buenos modales **3** ATTRACTIVELY : de buen gusto

niceness [ˈnaɪsnəs] *n* : simpatía *f,* amabilidad *f*

nicety [ˈnaɪsət̬i] *n, pl* **-ties 1** DETAIL, SUBTLETY : sutileza *f,* detalle *m* **2 niceties** *npl* : lujos *mpl,* detalles *mpl*

niche [ˈnɪtʃ] *n* **1** RECESS : nicho *m,* hornacina *f* **2** : nicho *m,* hueco *m* <to make a niche for oneself : hacerse un hueco, encontrarse una buena posición>

nick[1] [ˈnɪk] *vt* : cortar, hacer una muesca en

nick[2] *n* **1** CUT : corte *m,* muesca *f* **2 in the nick of time** : en el momento crítico, justo a tiempo

nickel [ˈnɪkəl] *n* **1** : níquel *m* **2** : moneda *f* de cinco centavos

nickname[1] [ˈnɪkˌneɪm] *vt* **-named; -naming** : apodar

nickname[2] *n* : apodo *m,* mote *m,* sobrenombre *m*

nicotine [ˈnɪkəˌtiːn] *n* : nicotina *f*

niece [ˈniːs] *n* : sobrina *f*

Nigerian [naɪˈdʒɪriən] *n* : nigeriano *m,* -na *f* — **Nigerian** *adj*

niggardly [ˈnɪgərdli] *adj* : mezquino, tacaño

niggling [ˈnɪgəlɪŋ] *adj* **1** PETTY : insignificante **2** PERSISTENT : constante, persistente <a niggling doubt : una duda constante>

nigh[1] [ˈnaɪ] *adv* **1** NEARLY : casi **2 to draw nigh** : acercarse, avecinarse

nigh[2] *adj* : cercano, próximo

night[1] [ˈnaɪt] *adj* : nocturno, de la noche <the night sky : el cielo nocturno> <night shift : turno de la noche>

night[2] *n* **1** EVENING : noche *f* <at night : de noche> <last night : anoche> <tomorrow night : mañana por la noche> **2** DARKNESS : noche *f,* oscuridad *f* <night fell : cayó la noche>

nightclothes [ˈnaɪtˌkloːðz, -ˌkloːz] *npl* : ropa *f* de dormir

nightclub [ˈnaɪtˌklʌb] *n* : cabaret *m,* club *m* nocturno

night crawler [ˈnaɪtˌkrɔlər] *n* EARTHWORM : lombriz *f* (de tierra)

nightfall [ˈnaɪtˌfɔl] *n* : anochecer *m*

nightgown [ˈnaɪtˌgaʊn] *n* : camisón *m* (de noche)

nightingale [ˈnaɪtənˌgeɪl, ˈnaɪt̬ɪŋ-] *n* : ruiseñor *m*

nightly[1] [ˈnaɪtli] *adv* : cada noche, todas las noches

nightly[2] *adj* : de todas las noches

nightmare [ˈnaɪtˌmær] *n* : pesadilla *f*

nightmarish [ˈnaɪtˌmærɪʃ] *adj* : de pesadilla

night owl *n* : noctámbulo *m,* -la *f*

nightshade [ˈnaɪtˌʃeɪd] *n* : hierba *f* mora

nightshirt [ˈnaɪtˌʃərt] *n* : camisa *f* de dormir

nightstick [ˈnaɪtˌstɪk] *n* : porra *f*

nighttime [ˈnaɪtˌtaɪm] *n* : noche *f*

nil [ˈnɪl] *n* : nada *f,* cero *m*

nimble [ˈnɪmbəl] *adj* **-bler; -blest 1** AGILE : ágil **2** CLEVER : hábil, ingenioso

nimbleness [ˈnɪmbəlnəs] *n* : agilidad *f*

nimbly [ˈnɪmbli] *adv* : con agilidad, ágilmente

nincompoop [ˈnɪnkəm,puːp, ˈnɪŋ-] *n* FOOL : tonto *m*, -ta *f*; bobo *m*, -ba *f*

nine[1] [ˈnaɪn] *adj* **1** : nueve **2 nine times out of ten** : casi siempre

nine[2] *n* : nueve *m*

nine hundred[1] *adj* : novecientos

nine hundred[2] *n* : novecientos *m*

ninepins [ˈnaɪn,pɪnz] *n* : bolos *mpl*

nineteen[1] [naɪnˈtiːn] *adj* : diecinueve

nineteen[2] *n* : diecinueve *m*

nineteenth[1] [naɪnˈtiːnθ] *adj* : decimonoveno, decimonono <the nineteenth century : el siglo diecinueve>

nineteenth[2] *n* : decimonoveno *m*, -na *f*; decimonono *m*, -na *f* (en una serie) **2** : diecinueveavo *m*, diecinueveava parte *f*

ninetieth[1] [ˈnaɪntiəθ] *adj* : nonagésimo

ninetieth[2] *n* **1** : nonagésimo *m*, -ma *f* (en una serie) **2** : noventavo *m*, noventava parte *f*

ninety[1] [ˈnaɪnti] *adj* : noventa

ninety[2] *n, pl* **-ties** : noventa *m*

ninth[1] [ˈnaɪnθ] *adj* : noveno

ninth[2] *n* **1** : noveno *m*, -na *f* (en una serie) **2** : noveno *m*, novena parte *f*

ninny [ˈnɪni] *n, pl* **ninnies** FOOL : tonto *m*, -ta *f*; bobo *m*, -ba *f*

nip[1] [ˈnɪp] *vt* **nipped; nipping 1** PINCH : pellizcar **2** BITE : morder, mordisquear **3 to nip in the bud** : cortar de raíz

nip[2] *n* **1** TANG : sabor *m* fuerte **2** PINCH : pellizco *m* **3** NIBBLE : mordisco *m* **4** SWALLOW : trago *m*, traguito *m* **5 there's a nip in the air** : hace fresco

nipple [ˈnɪpəl] *n* : pezón *m* (de una mujer), tetilla *f* (de un hombre)

nippy [ˈnɪpi] *adj* **-pier; -est 1** SHARP : fuerte, picante **2** CHILLY : frío <it's nippy today : hoy hace frío>

nit [ˈnɪt] *n* : liendre *f*

nitrate [ˈnaɪ,treɪt] *n* : nitrato *m*

nitric acid [ˈnaɪtrɪk] *n* : ácido *m* nítrico

nitrite [ˈnaɪ,traɪt] *n* : nitrito *m*

nitrogen [ˈnaɪtrədʒən] *n* : nitrógen *m*

nitroglycerin *or* **nitroglycerine** [,naɪtroˈglɪsərən] *n* : nitroglicerina *f*

nitwit [ˈnɪt,wɪt] *n* : zonzo *m*, -za *f*; bobo *m*, -ba *f*

no[1] [ˈnoː] *adv* : no <are you leaving?—no : ¿te vas?—no> <no less than : no menos de> <to say no : decir que no> <like it or no : quieras o no quieras>

no[2] *adj* **1** : ninguno <it's no trouble : no es ningún problema> <she has no money : no tiene dinero> **2** (*indicating a small amount*) <we'll be there in no time : llegamos dentro de poco, no tardamos nada> **3** (*expressing a negation*) <he's no liar : no es mentiroso>

no[3] *n, pl* **noes** *or* **nos** [ˈnoːz] **1** DENIAL : no *m* <I won't take no for an answer : no aceptaré un no por respuesta> **2** : vota *f* en contra <the noes have it : se ha rechazado la moción>

nobility [noˈbɪləti] *n* : nobleza *f*

noble[1] [ˈnoːbəl] *adj* **-bler; -blest 1** ILLUSTRIOUS : noble, glorioso **2** ARISTOCRATIC : noble **3** STATELY : majestuoso, magnífico **4** LOFTY : noble, elevado <noble sentiments : sentimientos elevados>

noble[2] *n* : noble *mf*, aristócrata *mf*

nobleman [ˈnoːbəlmən] *n, pl* **-men** [-mən, -,mɛn] : noble *m*, aristócrata *m*

nobleness [ˈnoːbəlnəs] *n* : nobleza *f*

noblewoman [ˈnoːbəl,wʊmən] *n, pl* **-women** [-,wɪmən] : noble *f*, aristócrata *f*

nobly [ˈnoːbli] *adv* : noblemente

nobody[1] [ˈnoːbədi, -,bɑdi] *n, pl* **-bodies** : don nadie *m* <he's a mere nobody : es un don nadie>

nobody[2] *pron* : nadie

nocturnal [nɑkˈtərnəl] *adj* : nocturno

nocturne [ˈnɑk,tərn] *n* : nocturno *m*

nod[1] [ˈnɑd] *v* **nodded; nodding** *vi* **1** : saludar con la cabeza, asentir con la cabeza **2 to nod off** : dormirse, quedarse dormido — *vt* : inclinar (la cabeza) <to nod one's head in agreement : asentir con la cabeza>

nod[2] *n* : saludo *m* con la cabeza, señal *m* con la cabeza, señal *m* de asentimiento

node [ˈnoːd] *n* : nudo *m* (de una planta)

nodule [ˈnɑ,dʒuːl] *n* : nódulo *m*

noel [noˈɛl] *n* **1** CAROL : villancico *m* de Navidad **2 Noel** CHRISTMAS : Navidad *f*

noes → **no[3]**

noise[1] [ˈnɔɪz] *vt* **noised; noising** : rumorear, publicar

noise[2] *n* : ruido *m*

noiseless [ˈnɔɪzləs] *adj* : silencioso, sin ruido

noiselessly [ˈnɔɪzləsli] *adv* : silenciosamente

noisemaker [ˈnɔɪz,meɪkər] *n* : matraca *f*

noisiness [ˈnɔɪzinəs] *n* : ruido *m*

noisome [ˈnɔɪsəm] *adj* : maloliente, fétido

noisy [ˈnɔɪzi] *adj* **noisier; -est** : ruidoso — **noisily** [ˈnɔɪzəli] *adv*

nomad[1] [ˈnoː,mæd] → **nomadic**

nomad[2] *n* : nómada *mf*

nomadic [noˈmædɪk] *adj* : nómada

nomenclature [ˈnoːmən,kleɪtʃər] *n* : nomenclatura *f*

nominal [ˈnɑmənəl] *adj* **1** : nominal <the nominal head of his party : el jefe nominal de su partido> **2** TRIFLING : insignificante

nominally [ˈnɑmənəli] *adv* : sólo de nombre, nominalmente

nominate [ˈnɑmə,neɪt] *vt* **-nated; -nating 1** PROPOSE : proponer (como candidato), nominar **2** APPOINT : nombrar

nomination [ˌnɑməˈneɪʃən] *n* **1** PROPOSAL : propuesta *f*, postulación *f* **2** APPOINTMENT : nombramiento *m*
nominative[1] [ˈnɑmənəṯɪv] *adj* : nominativo
nominative[2] *n or* **nominative case** : nominativo *m*
nominee [ˌnɑməˈniː] *n* : candidato *m*, -ta *f*
nonaddictive [ˌnɑnəˈdɪktɪv] *adj* : que no crea dependencia
nonalcoholic [ˌnɑnˌælkəˈhɔlɪk] *adj* : sin alcohol, no alcohólico
nonaligned [ˌnɑnəˈlaɪnd] *adj* : no alineado
nonbeliever [ˌnɑnbəˈliːvər] *n* : no creyente *mf*
nonbreakable [ˌnɑnˈbreɪkəbəl] *adj* : irrompible
nonce [ˈnɑnts] *n* **for the nonce** : por el momento
nonchalance [ˌnɑnʃəˈlɑnts] *n* : indiferencia *f*, despreocupación *f*
nonchalant [ˌnɑnʃəˈlɑnt] *adj* : indiferente, despreocupado, impasible
nonchalantly [ˌnɑnʃəˈlɑntli] *adv* : con aire despreocupado, con indiferencia
noncombatant [ˌnɑnkəmˈbætənt, -ˈkɑmbə-] *adj* : no combatiente *mf*
noncommissioned officer [ˌnɑnkəˈmɪʃənd] *n* : suboficial *mf*
noncommittal [ˌnɑnkəˈmɪṯəl] *adj* : evasivo, que no se compromete
nonconductor [ˌnɑnkənˈdʌktər] *n* : aislante *m*
nonconformist [ˌnɑnkənˈfɔrmɪst] *n* : inconformista *mf*, inconforme *mf*
nonconformity [ˌnɑnkənˈfɔrməṯi] *n* : inconformidad *f*, no conformidad *f*
noncontagious [ˌnɑnkənˈteɪdʒəs] *adj* : no contagioso
nondenominational [ˌnɑndɪˌnɑməˈneɪʃənəl] *adj* : no sectario
nondescript [ˌnɑndɪˈskrɪpt] *adj* : anodino, soso
nondiscriminatory [ˌnɑndɪˈskrɪmənəˌtori] *adj* : no discriminatorio
nondrinker [ˌnɑnˈdrɪŋkər] *n* : abstemio *m*, -mia *f*
none[1] [ˈnʌn] *adv* : de ninguna manera, de ningún modo, nada <he was none too happy : no se sintió nada contento> <I'm none the worse for it : no estoy peor por ello> <none too soon : a buena hora>
none[2] *pron* : ninguno, ninguna
nonentity [ˌnɑnˈɛntəṯi] *n, pl* **-ties** : persona *f* insignificante, nulidad *f*
nonessential [ˌnɑnɪˈsɛntʃəl] *adj* : secundario, no esencial
nonessentials [ˌnɑnɪˈsɛntʃəlz] *npl* : cosas *fpl* secundarias, cosas *fpl* accesorias
nonetheless [ˌnʌnðəˈlɛs] *adv* : sin embargo, no obstante
nonexistence [ˌnɑnɪgˈzɪstənts] *n* : inexistencia *f*
nonexistent [ˌnɑnɪgˈzɪstənt] *adj* : inexistente
nonfat [ˌnɑnˈfæt] *adj* : sin grasa
nonfattening [ˌnɑnˈfætənɪŋ] *adj* : que no engorda
nonfiction [ˌnɑnˈfɪkʃən] *n* : no ficción *f*
nonflammable [ˌnɑnˈflæməbəl] *adj* : no inflamable
nonintervention [ˌnɑnˌɪntərˈvɛntʃən] *n* : no intervención *f*
nonmalignant [ˌnɑnməˈlɪgnənt] *adj* : no maligno, benigno
nonnegotiable [ˌnɑnnɪˈgoːʃəbəl, -ʃiə-] *adj* : no negociable
nonpareil[1] [ˌnɑnpəˈrɛl] *adj* : sin parangón, sin par
nonpareil[2] *n* : persona *f* sin igual, cosa *f* sin par
nonpartisan [ˌnɑnˈpɑrṯəzən, -sən] *adj* : imparcial
nonpaying [ˌnɑnˈpeɪɪŋ] *adj* : que no paga
nonpayment [ˌnɑnˈpeɪmənt] *n* : impago *m*, falta *f* de pago
nonperson [ˌnɑnˈpərsən] *n* : persona *f* sin derechos
nonplus [ˌnɑnˈplʌs] *vt* **-plussed; -plussing** : confundir, desconcertar, dejar perplejo
nonprescription [ˌnɑnprɪˈskrɪpʃən] *adj* : disponible sin receta del médico
nonproductive [ˌnɑnprəˈdʌktɪv] *adj* : improductivo
nonprofit [ˌnɑnˈprɑfət] *adj* : sin fines lucrativos
nonproliferation [ˌnɑnprəˌlɪfəˈreɪʃən] *adj* : no proliferación
nonresident [ˌnɑnˈrɛzədənt, -ˌdɛnt] *n* : no residente *mf*
nonscheduled [ˌnɑnˈskɛˌdʒuːld] *adj* : no programado, no regular
nonsectarian [ˌnɑnˌsɛkˈtæriən] *adj* : no sectario
nonsense [ˈnɑnˌsɛnts, ˈnɑntsənts] *n* : tonterías *fpl*, disparates *mpl*
nonsensical [nɑnˈsɛntsɪkəl] *adj* ABSURD : absurdo, disparatado — **nonsensically** [-kli] *adv*
nonsmoker [ˌnɑnˈsmoːkər] *n* : no fumador *m*, -dora *f*; persona *f* que no fuma
nonstandard [ˌnɑnˈstændərd] *adj* : no regular, no estándar
nonstick [ˌnɑnˈstɪk] *adj* : antiadherente
nonstop[1] [ˌnɑnˈstɑp] *adv* : sin parar <he talked nonstop : habló sin parar>
nonstop[2] *adj* : directo, sin escalas <nonstop flight : vuelo directo>
nonsupport [ˌnɑnsəˈpɔrt] *n* : falta *f* de manutención
nontaxable [ˌnɑnˈtæksəbəl] *adj* : exento de impuestos
nontoxic [ˌnɑnˈtɑksɪk] *adj* : no tóxico
nonviolence [ˌnɑnˈvaɪlənts, -ˈvaɪə-] *n* : no violencia *f*
nonviolent [ˌnɑnˈvaɪlənt, -ˈvaɪə-] *adj* : pacífico, no violento
noodle [ˈnuːdəl] *n* : fideo *m*, tallarín *m*

nook [ˈnʊk] *n* : rincón *m,* recoveco *m,* escondrijo *m* <in every nook and cranny : en todos los rincones>
noon [ˈnuːn] *n* : mediodía *m*
noonday [ˈnuːnˌdeɪ] *n* : mediodía *m* <the noonday sun : el sol de mediodía>
no one *pron* NOBODY : nadie
noontime [ˈnuːnˌtaɪm] *n* : mediodía *m*
noose [ˈnuːs] *n* **1** LASSO : lazo *m* **2 hangman's noose:** dogal *m,* soga *f*
nor [ˈnɔr] *conj* : ni <neither good nor bad : ni bueno ni malo> <nor I! : ¡ni yo tampoco!>
Nordic [ˈnɔrdɪk] *adj* : nórdico
norm [ˈnɔrm] *n* **1** STANDARD : norma *f,* modelo *m* **2** CUSTOM, RULE : regla *f* general, lo normal
normal [ˈnɔrməl] *adj* : normal — **normally** *adv*
normalcy [ˈnɔrməlsi] *n* : normalidad *f*
normality [nɔrˈmæləṭi] *n* : normalidad *f*
normalize [ˈnɔrməˌlaɪz] *vt* : normalizar
Norse [ˈnɔrs] *adj* : nórdico
north¹ [ˈnɔrθ] *adv* : al norte
north² *adj* : norte, del norte <the north coast : la costa del norte>
north³ *n* **1** : norte *m* **2 the North** : el Norte *m*
northbound [ˈnɔrθˌbaʊnd] *adv* : con rumbo al norte
North American *n* : norteamericano *m,* -na *f* — **North American** *adj*
northeast¹ [nɔrθˈiːst] *adv* : hacia el nordeste
northeast² *adj* : nordeste, del nordeste
northeast³ *n* : nordeste *m,* noreste *m*
northeasterly¹ [nɔrθˈiːstərli] *adv* : hacia el nordeste
northeasterly² *adj* : nordeste, del nordeste
northeastern [nɔrθˈiːstərn] *adj* : nordeste, del nordeste
northerly¹ [ˈnɔrðərli] *adv* : hacia el norte
northerly² *adj* : del norte <a northerly wind : un viento del norte>
northern [ˈnɔrðərn] *adj* : norte, norteño, septentrional
Northerner [ˈnɔrðərnər] *n* : norteño *m,* -ña *f*
northern lights → aurora borealis
North Pole : Polo *m* Norte
North Star *n* : estrella *f* polar
northward [ˈnɔrθwərd] *adv & adj* : hacia el norte
northwest¹ [nɔrθˈwɛst] *adv* : hacia el noroeste
northwest² *adj* : del noroeste
northwest³ *n* : noroeste *m*
northwesterly¹ [nɔrθˈwɛstərli] *adv* : hacia el noroeste
northwesterly² *adj* : del noroeste
northwestern [nɔrθˈwɛstərn] *adj* : noroeste, del noroeste
Norwegian [nɔrˈwiːdʒən] *n* **1** : noruego *m,* -ga *f* **2** : noruego *m* (idioma) — **Norwegian** *adj*
nose¹ [ˈnoːz] *v* **nosed; nosing** *vt* **1** SMELL : olfatear **2** : empujar con el hocico <the dog nosed open the bag : el perro abrió el saco con el hocico> **3** EDGE, MOVE : mover poco a poco — *vi* **1** PRY : entrometerse, meter las narices **2** EDGE : avanzar poco a poco
nose² *n* **1** : nariz *f* (de una persona), hocico *m* (de un animal) <to blow one's nose : sonarse las narices> **2** SMELL : olfato *m,* sentido *m* del olfato **3** FRONT : parte *f* delantera, nariz *f* (de un avión), proa *f* (de un barco) **4 to follow one's nose** : dejarse guiar por el instinto
nosebleed [ˈnoːzˌbliːd] *n* : hemorragia *f* nasal
nosedive [ˈnoːzˌdaɪv] *n* **1** : descenso *m* en picada (de un avión) **2** : caída *f* súbita (de precios, etc.)
nose–dive [ˈnoːzˌdaɪv] *vi* : descender en picada, caer en picada
nostalgia [nɑˈstældʒə, nə-] *n* : nostalgia *f*
nostalgic [nɑˈstældʒɪk, nə-] *adj* : nostálgico
nostril [ˈnɑstrəl] *n* : ventana *f* de la nariz
nostrum [ˈnɑstrəm] *n* : panacea *f*
nosy *or* **nosey** [ˈnoːzi] *adj* **nosier; -est** : entrometido
not [ˈnɑt] *adv* **1** (*used to form a negative*) : no <she is not tired : no está cansada> <not to say something would be wrong : no decir nada sería injusto> **2** (*used to replace a negative clause*) : no <are we going or not? : ¿vamos a ir o no?> <of course not! : ¡claro que no!>
notable¹ [ˈnoːṭəbəl] *adj* **1** NOTEWORTHY : notable, de notar **2** DISTINGUISHED, PROMINENT : distinguido, destacado
notable² *n* : persona *f* importante, personaje *m*
notably [ˈnoːṭəbli] *adv* : notablemente, particularmente
notarize [ˈnoːṭəˌraɪz] *vt* **-rized; -rizing** : autenticar, autorizar
notary public [ˈnoːṭəri] *n, pl* **-ries public** *or* **-ry publics** : notario *m,* -ria *f;* escribano *m,* -na *f*
notation [noˈteɪʃən] *n* **1** NOTE : anotación *f,* nota *f* **2** : notación *f* <musical notation : notación musical>
notch¹ [ˈnɑtʃ] *vt* : hacer una muesca en, cortar
notch² *n* : muesca *f,* corte *m*
note¹ [ˈnoːt] *vt* **noted; noting 1** NOTICE : notar, observar, tomar nota de **2** RECORD : anotar, apuntar
note² *n* **1** : nota *f* (musical) **2** COMMENT : nota *f,* comentario *m* **3** LETTER : nota *f,* cartita *f* **4** PROMINENCE : prestigio *m* <a musician of note : un músico destacado> **5** ATTENTION : atención *f* <to take note of : prestar atención a>

notebook [ˈnoːt͵bʊk] *n* : libreta *f,* cuaderno *m*

noted [ˈnoːṭəd] *adj* EMINENT : renombrado, eminente, celebrado

noteworthy [ˈnoːt͵wərðiː] *adj* : notable, de notar, de interés

nothing[1] [ˈnʌθɪŋ] *adv* **1** : de ninguna manera <nothing daunted, we carried on : sin amilanarnos, seguimos adelante> **2 nothing like** : no...en nada <he's nothing like his brother : no se parece en nada a su hermano>

nothing[2] *n* **1** NOTHINGNESS : nada *f* **2** ZERO : cero *m* **3** : persona *f* de poca importancia, cero *m* **4** TRIFLE : nimiedad *f*

nothing[3] *pron* : nada <there's nothing better : no hay nada mejor> <nothing else : nada más> <nothing but : solamente> <they mean nothing to me : ellos me son indiferentes>

nothingness [ˈnʌθɪŋnəs] *n* **1** VOID : vacío *m,* nada *f* **2** NONEXISTENCE : inexistencia *f* **3** TRIFLE : nimiedad *f*

notice[1] [ˈnoːṭɪs] *vt* **-ticed; -ticing** : notar, observar, advertir, darse cuenta de

notice[2] *n* **1** NOTIFICATION : aviso *m,* notificación *f* **2** ATTENTION : atención *f* <to take notice of : prestar atención a>

noticeable [ˈnoːṭɪsəbəl] *adj* : evidente, perceptible — **noticeably** [-bli] *adv*

notification [͵noːṭəfəˈkeɪʃən] *n* : notificación *f,* aviso *m*

notify [ˈnoːṭə͵faɪ] *vt* **-fied; -fying** : notificar, avisar

notion [ˈnoːʃən] *n* **1** IDEA : idea *f,* noción *f* **2** WHIM : capricho *m,* antojo *m* **3 notions** *npl* : artículos *mpl* de mercería

notoriety [͵noːṭəˈraɪəṭi] *n* : mala fama *f,* notoriedad *f*

notorious [noˈtoːriəs] *adj* : de mala fama, célebre, bien conocido

notwithstanding[1] [͵nɑtwɪθˈstændɪŋ, -wɪð-] *adv* NEVERTHELESS : no obstante, sin embargo

notwithstanding[2] *conj* : a pesar de que

notwithstanding[3] *prep* : a pesar de, no obstante

nougat [ˈnuːgət] *n* : turrón *m*

nought [ˈnɔt, ˈnɑt] → **naught**

noun [ˈnaʊn] *n* : nombre *m,* sustantivo *m*

nourish [ˈnərɪʃ] *vt* **1** FEED : alimentar, nutrir, sustentar **2** FOSTER : fomentar, alentar

nourishing [ˈnərɪʃɪŋ] *adj* : alimenticio, nutritivo

nourishment [ˈnərɪʃmənt] *n* : nutrición *f,* alimento *m,* sustento *m*

novel[1] [ˈnɑvəl] *adj* : original, novedoso

novel[2] *n* : novela *f*

novelist [ˈnɑvəlɪst] *n* : novelista *mf*

novelty [ˈnɑvəlṭi] *n, pl* **-ties 1** : novedad *f* **2 novelties** *npl* TRINKETS : baratijas *fpl,* chucherías *fpl*

November [noˈvɛmbər] *n* : noviembre *m*

novice [ˈnɑvɪs] *n* : novato *m,* -ta *f;* principiante *mf;* novicio *m,* -cia *f*

now[1] [ˈnaʊ] *adv* **1** PRESENTLY : ahora, ya, actualmente <from now on : de ahora en adelante> <long before now : ya hace tiempo> <now and then : de vez en cuando> **2** IMMEDIATELY : ahora (mismo), inmediatamente <do it right now! : ¡hazlo ahora mismo!> **3** THEN : ya, entonces <now they were ready : ya estaban listos> **4** (*used to introduce a statement, a question, a command, or a transition*) <now hear this! : ¡presten atención!> <now what do you think of that? : ¿qué piensas de eso?>

now[2] *n* (*indicating the present time*) <until now : hasta ahora> <by now : ya> <ten years from now : dentro de 10 años>

now[3] *conj* **now that** : ahora que, ya que

nowadays [ˈnaʊə͵deɪz] *adv* : hoy en día, actualmente, en la actualidad

nowhere[1] [ˈnoː͵*h*wɛr] *adv* **1** : en ninguna parte, a ningún lado <nowhere to be found : en ninguna parte, por ningún lado> <you're going nowhere : no estás yendo a ningún lado, no estás yendo a ninguna parte> **2 nowhere near** : ni con mucho, nada cerca <it's nowhere near here : no está nada cerca de aquí>

nowhere[2] *n* **1** : ninguna parte *f* **2 out of nowhere** : de la nada

noxious [ˈnɑkʃəs] *adj* : nocivo, dañino, tóxico

nozzle [ˈnɑzəl] *n* : boca *f*

nuance [ˈnuː͵ɑn*t*s, ˈnjuː-] *n* : matiz *m*

nub [ˈnʌb] *n* **1** KNOB, LUMP : protuberancia *f,* nudo *m* **2** GIST : quid *m,* meollo *m*

nuclear [ˈnuːkliər, ˈnjuː-] *adj* : nuclear

nucleus [ˈnuːkliəs, ˈnjuː-] *n, pl* **-clei** [-kli͵aɪ] : núcleo *m*

nude[1] [ˈnuːd, ˈnjuːd] *adj* **nuder; nudest** : desnudo

nude[2] *n* : desnudo *m*

nudge[1] [ˈnʌdʒ] *vt* **nudged; nudging** : darle con el codo (a alguien)

nudge[2] *n* : toque *m* que se da con el codo

nudism [ˈnuː͵dɪzəm, ˈnjuː-] *n* : nudismo *m*

nudist [ˈnuːdɪst, ˈnjuː-] *n* : nudista *mf*

nudity [ˈnuːdəṭi, ˈnjuː-] *n* : desnudez *f*

nugget [ˈnʌgət] *n* : pepita *f*

nuisance [ˈnuːsən*t*s, ˈnjuː-] *n* **1** BOTHER : fastidio *m,* molestia *f,* lata *f* **2** PEST : peste *f;* pesado *m,* -da *f fam*

null [ˈnʌl] *adj* : nulo <null and void : nulo y sin efecto>

nullify [ˈnʌlə͵faɪ] *vt* **-fied; -fying** : invalidar, anular

numb[1] [ˈnʌm] *vt* : entumecer, adormecer

numb[2] *adj* : entumecido, dormido <numb with fear : paralizado de miedo>
number[1] ['nʌmbər] *vt* **1** COUNT, INCLUDE : contar, incluir **2** : numerar <number the pages : numera las páginas> **3** TOTAL : ascender a, sumar
number[2] *n* **1** : número *m* <in round numbers : en números redondos> <telephone number : número de teléfono> **2 a number of** : varios, unos pocos, unos cuantos
numberless ['nʌmbərləs] *adj* : innumerable, sin número
numbness ['nʌmnəs] *n* : entumecimiento *m*
numeral ['nuːmərəl, 'njuː-] *n* : número *m* <Roman numeral : número romano>
numerator ['nuːmə,reɪt̬ər, 'njuː-] *n* : numerador *m*
numeric [nʊ'mɛrɪk, njʊ-] *adj* : numérico
numerical [nʊ'mɛrɪkəl, njʊ-] *adj* : numérico — **numerically** [-kli] *adv*
numerous ['nuːmərəs, 'njuː-] *adj* : numeroso
numismatics [,nuːməz'mæt̬ɪks, ,njuː-] *n* : numismática *f*
numskull ['nʌm,skʌl] *n* : tonto *m*, -ta *f*; mentecato *m*, -ta *f*; zoquete *m fam*
nun ['nʌn] *n* : monja *f*
nuptial ['nʌpʃəl] *adj* : nupcial
nuptials ['nʌpʃəlz] *npl* WEDDING : nupcias *fpl*, boda *f*
nurse[1] ['nərs] *vt* **nursed; nursing 1** SUCKLE : amamantar **2** : cuidar (de), atender <to nurse the sick : cuidar a los enfermos> <to nurse a cold : curarse de un resfriado>
nurse[2] *n* **1** : enfermero *m*, -ra *f* **2** → **nursemaid**
nursemaid ['nərs,meɪd] *n* : niñera *f*
nursery ['nərsəri] *n*, *pl* **-eries 1** *or* **day nursery** : guardería *f* **2** : vivero *m* (de plantas)
nursing home *n* : hogar *m* de ancianos, clínica *f* de reposo
nurture[1] ['nərtʃər] *vt* **-tured; -turing 1** FEED, NOURISH : nutrir, alimentar **2** EDUCATE : criar, educar **3** FOSTER : alimentar, fomentar
nurture[2] *n* **1** UPBRINGING : crianza *f*, educación *f* **2** FOOD : alimento *m*
nut ['nʌt] *n* **1** : nuez *f* **2** : tuerca *f* <nuts and bolts : tuercas y tornillos> **3** LUNATIC : loco *m*, -ca *f*; chiflado *m*, -da *f fam* **4** ENTHUSIAST : fanático *m*, -ca *f*; entusiasta *mf*
nutcracker ['nʌt,krækər] *n* : cascanueces *m*
nuthatch ['nʌt,hætʃ] *n* : trepador *m*
nutmeg ['nʌt,mɛg] *n* : nuez *f* moscada
nutrient ['nuːtriənt, 'njuː-] *n* : nutriente *m*, alimento *m* nutritivo
nutriment ['nuːtrəmənt, 'njuː-] *n* : nutrimento *m*
nutrition [nʊ'trɪʃən, njʊ-] *n* : nutrición *f*
nutritional [nʊ'trɪʃənəl, njʊ-] *adj* : alimenticio
nutritious [nʊ'trɪʃəs, njʊ-] *adj* : nutritivo, alimenticio
nuts ['nʌts] *adj* **1** FANATICAL : fanático **2** CRAZY : loco, chiflado *fam*
nutshell ['nʌt,ʃɛl] *n* **1** : cáscara *f* de nuez **2 in a nutshell** : en pocas palabras
nutty ['nʌti] *adj* **-tier; -tiest** : loco, chiflado *fam*
nuzzle ['nʌzəl] *v* **-zled; -zling** *vi* NESTLE : acurrucarse, arrimarse — *vt* : acariciar con el hocico
nylon ['naɪ,lɑn] *n* **1** : nilón *m* **2 nylons** *npl* : medias *fpl* de nilón
nymph ['nɪmpf] *n* : ninfa *f*

O

o ['oː] *n*, *pl* **o's** *or* **os** ['oːz] **1** : decimoquinta letra del alfabeto inglés **2** ZERO : cero *m*
O ['oː] → **oh**
oaf ['oːf] *n* : zoquete *m*; bruto *m*, -ta *f*
oafish ['oːfɪʃ] *adj* : torpe, lerdo
oak ['oːk] *n*, *pl* **oaks** *or* **oak** : roble *m*
oaken ['oːkən] *adj* : de roble
oar ['or] *n* : remo *m*
oarlock ['or,lɑk] *n* : tolete *m*, escálamo *m*
oasis [o'eɪsɪs] *n*, *pl* **oases** [-,siːz] : oasis *m*
oat ['oːt] *n* : avena *f*
oath ['oːθ] *n*, *pl* **oaths** ['oːðz, 'oːθs] **1** : juramento *m* <to take an oath : prestar juramento> **2** SWEARWORD : mala palabra *f*, palabrota *f*
oatmeal ['oːt,miːl] *n* : avena *f* <instant oatmeal : avena instantánea>
obdurate ['ɑbdʊrət, -djʊ-] *adj* : inflexible, firme, obstinado
obedience [o'biːdiənts] *n* : obediencia *f*
obedient [o'biːdiənt] *adj* : obediente — **obediently** *adv*
obelisk ['ɑbə,lɪsk] *n* : obelisco *m*
obese [o'biːs] *adj* : obeso
obesity [o'biːsəti] *n* : obesidad *f*
obey [o'beɪ] *v* **obeyed; obeying** : obedecer <to obey the law : cumplir la ley>
obfuscate ['ɑbfə,skeɪt] *vt* **-cated; -cating** : ofuscar, confundir
obituary [ə'bɪtʃʊ,ɛri] *n*, *pl* **-aries** : obituario *m*, necrología *f*
object[1] [əb'dʒɛkt] *vt* : objetar — *vi* : oponerse, poner reparos, hacer objeciones
object[2] ['ɑbdʒɪkt] *n* **1** : objeto *m* **2** OBJECTIVE, PURPOSE : objetivo *m*, pro-

pósito *m* **3** : complemento *m* (en gramática)

objection [əbˈdʒɛkʃən] *n* : objeción *f*

objectionable [əbˈdʒɛkʃənəbəl] *adj* : ofensivo, indeseable — **objectionably** [-bli] *adv*

objective[1] [əbˈdʒɛktɪv] *adj* **1** IMPARTIAL : objetivo, imparcial **2** : de complemento, directo (en gramática)

objective[2] *n* **1** : objetivo *m* **2** *or* **objective case** : acusativo *m*

objectively [əbˈdʒɛktɪvli] *adv* : objetivamente

objectivity [ˌɑbˌdʒɛkˈtɪvət̬i] *n, pl* **-ties** : objetividad *f*

obligate [ˈɑbləˌgeɪt] *vt* **-gated; -gating** : obligar

obligation [ˌɑbləˈgeɪʃən] *n* : obligación *f*

obligatory [əˈblɪgəˌtori] *adj* : obligatorio

oblige [əˈblaɪdʒ] *vt* **obliged; obliging** **1** COMPEL : obligar **2** : hacerle un favor (a alguien), complacer <to oblige a friend : hacerle un favor a un amigo> **3 to be much obliged** : estar muy agradecido

obliging [əˈblaɪdʒɪŋ] *adj* : servicial, complaciente — **obligingly** *adv*

oblique [oˈbliːk] *adj* **1** SLANTING : oblicuo **2** INDIRECT : indirecto — **obliquely** *adv*

obliterate [əˈblɪt̬əˌreɪt] *vt* **-ated; -ating** **1** ERASE : obliterar, borrar **2** DESTROY : destruir, eliminar

obliteration [əˌblɪt̬əˈreɪʃən] *n* : obliteración *f*

oblivion [əˈblɪviən] *n* : olvido *m*

oblivious [əˈblɪviəs] *adj* : inconsciente — **obliviously** *adv*

oblong[1] [ˈɑˌblɔŋ] *adj* : oblongo

oblong[2] *n* : figura *f* oblonga, rectángulo *m*

obnoxious [ɑbˈnɑkʃəs, əb-] *adj* : repugnante, odioso — **obnoxiously** *adv*

oboe [ˈoːˌboː] *n* : oboe *m*

oboist [ˈoˌboɪst] *n* : oboe *mf*

obscene [ɑbˈsiːn, əb-] *adj* : obsceno, indecente — **obscenely** *adv*

obscenity [ɑbˈsɛnət̬i, əb-] *n, pl* **-ties** : obscenidad *f*

obscure[1] [ɑbˈskjʊr, əb-] *vt* **-scured; -scuring** **1** CLOUD, DIM : oscurecer, nublar **2** HIDE : ocultar

obscure[2] *adj* **1** DIM : oscuro **2** REMOTE, SECLUDED : recóndito **3** VAGUE : oscuro, confuso, vago **4** UNKNOWN : desconocido <an obscure poet : un poeta desconocido> — **obscurely** *adv*

obscurity [ɑbˈskjʊrət̬i, əb-] *n, pl* **-ties** : oscuridad *f*

obsequious [əbˈsiːkwiəs] *adj* : servil, excesivamente atento

observable [əbˈzərvəbəl] *adj* : observable, perceptible

observance [əbˈzərvənts] *n* **1** FULFILLMENT : observancia *f,* cumplimiento *m* **2** PRACTICE : práctica *f*

observant [əbˈzərvənt] *adj* : observador

observation [ˌɑbsərˈveɪʃən, -zər-] *n* : observación *f*

observatory [əbˈzərvəˌtori] *n, pl* **-ries** : observatorio *m*

observe [əbˈzərv] *v* **-served; -serving** *vt* **1** OBEY : observar, obedecer **2** CELEBRATE : celebrar, guardar (una práctica religiosa) **3** WATCH : observar, mirar **4** REMARK : observar, comentar — *vi* LOOK : mirar

obsess [əbˈsɛs] *vt* : obsesionar

obsession [ɑbˈsɛʃən, əb-] *n* : obsesión *f*

obsessive [ɑbˈsɛsɪv, əb-] *adj* : obsesivo — **obsessively** *adv*

obsolescence [ˌɑbsəˈlɛsənts] *n* : obsolescencia *f*

obsolescent [ˌɑbsəˈlɛsənt] *adj* : obsolescente <to become obsolescent : caer en desuso>

obsolete [ˌɑbsəˈliːt, ˈɑbsəˌ-] *adj* : obsoleto, anticuado

obstacle [ˈɑbstɪkəl] *n* : obstáculo *m,* impedimento *m*

obstetric [əbˈstɛtrɪk] *or* **obstetrical** [-trɪkəl] *adj* : obstétrico

obstetrician [ˌɑbstəˈtrɪʃən] *n* : obstetra *mf;* tocólogo *m,* -ga *f*

obstetrics [əbˈstɛtrɪks] *ns & pl* : obstetricia *f,* tocología *f*

obstinacy [ˈɑbstənəsi] *n, pl* **-cies** : obstinación *f,* terquedad *f*

obstinate [ˈɑbstənət] *adj* : obstinado, terco — **obstinately** *adv*

obstreperous [əbˈstrɛpərəs] *adj* **1** CLAMOROUS : ruidoso, clamoroso **2** UNRULY : rebelde, indisciplinado

obstruct [əbˈstrʌkt] *vt* : obstruir, bloquear

obstruction [əbˈstrʌkʃən] *n* : obstrucción *f,* bloqueo *m*

obstructive [əbˈstrəktɪv] *adj* : obstructor

obtain [əbˈteɪn] *vt* : obtener, conseguir — *vi* PREVAIL : imperar, prevalecer

obtainable [əbˈteɪnəbəl] *adj* : obtenible, asequible

obtrude [əbˈtruːd] *v* **-truded; -truding** *vt* **1** EXTRUDE : expulsar **2** IMPOSE : imponer — *vi* INTRUDE : inmiscuirse, entrometerse

obtrusive [əbˈtruːsɪv] *adj* **1** IMPERTINENT, MEDDLESOME : impertinente, entrometido **2** PROTRUDING : prominente

obtuse [ɑbˈtuːs, əb-, -ˈtjuːs] *adj* : obtuso, torpe

obtuse angle *n* : ángulo obtuso

obviate [ˈɑbviˌeɪt] *vt* **-ated; -ating** : obviar, evitar

obvious [ˈɑbviəs] *adj* : obvio, evidente, manifiesto

obviously [ˈɑbviəsli] *adv* **1** CLEARLY : obviamente, evidentemente **2** OF COURSE : claro, por supuesto

occasion[1] [əˈkeɪʒən] *vt* : ocasionar, causar

occasion² *n* **1** OPPORTUNITY : oportunidad *f,* ocasión *f* **2** CAUSE : motivo *m,* razón *f* **3** INSTANCE : ocasión *f* **4** EVENT : ocasión *f,* acontecimiento *m* **5 on ~** : de vez en cuando, ocasionalmente

occasional [əˈkeɪʒənəl] *adj* : ocasional

occasionally [əˈkeɪʒənəli] *adv* : de vez en cuando, ocasionalmente

occidental [ˌɑksəˈdɛntəl] *adj* : oeste, del oeste, occidental

occult¹ [əˈkʌlt, ˈɑˌkʌlt] *adj* **1** HIDDEN, SECRET : oculto, secreto **2** ARCANE : arcano, esotérico

occult² *n* **the occult** : las ciencias ocultas

occupancy [ˈɑkjəpəntsi] *n, pl* **-cies** : ocupación *f,* habitación *f*

occupant [ˈɑkjəpənt] *n* : ocupante *mf*

occupation [ˌɑkjəˈpeɪʃən] *n* : ocupación *f,* profesión *f,* oficio *m*

occupational [ˌɑkjəˈpeɪʃənəl] *adj* : ocupacional

occupy [ˈɑkjəˌpaɪ] *vt* **-pied; -pying** : ocupar

occur [əˈkər] *vi* **occurred; occurring** **1** EXIST : encontrarse, existir **2** HAPPEN : ocurrir, acontecer, suceder, tener lugar **3** : ocurrirse <it occurred to him that. . . : se le ocurrió que. . .>

occurrence [əˈkərənts] *n* : acontecimiento *m,* suceso *m,* ocurrencia *f*

ocean [ˈoːʃən] *n* : océano *m*

oceanic [ˌoːʃiˈænɪk] *adj* : oceánico

oceanography [ˌoːʃəˈnɑgrəfi] *n* : oceanografía *f*

ocelot [ˈɑsəˌlɑt, ˈoː-] *n* : ocelote *m*

ocher *or* **ochre** [ˈoːkər] *n* : ocre *m*

o'clock [əˈklɑk] *adv* (*used in telling time*) <it's ten o'clock : son las diez> <at six o'clock : a las seis>

octagon [ˈɑktəˌgɑn] *n* : octágono *m*

octagonal [ɑkˈtægənəl] *adj* : octagonal

octave [ˈɑktɪv] *n* : octava *f*

October [ɑkˈtoːbər] *n* : octubre *m*

octopus [ˈɑktəˌpʊs, -pəs] *n, pl* **-puses** *or* **-pi** [-ˌpaɪ] : pulpo *m*

ocular [ˈɑkjələr] *adj* : ocular

oculist [ˈɑkjəlɪst] *n* **1** OPHTHALMOLOGIST : oftalmólogo *m,* -ga *f;* oculista *mf* **2** OPTOMETRIST : optometrista *mf*

odd [ˈɑd] *adj* **1** : sin pareja, suelto <an odd sock : un calcetín sin pareja> **2** UNEVEN : impar <odd numbers : números impares> **3** : y pico, y tantos <forty odd years ago : hace cuarenta y pico años> **4** : alguno, uno que otro <odd jobs : algunos trabajos> **5** STRANGE : extraño, raro

oddball [ˈɑdˌbɔl] *n* : excéntrico *m,* -ca *f;* persona *f* rara

oddity [ˈɑdət̬i] *n, pl* **-ties** : rareza *f,* cosa *f* rara

oddly [ˈɑdli] *adv* : de manera extraña

oddness [ˈɑdnəs] *n* : rareza *f,* excentricidad *f*

odds [ˈɑdz] *npl* **1** CHANCES : probabilidades *fpl* **2** : puntos *mpl* de ventaja (de una apuesta) **3 to be at odds** : estar en desacuerdo

odds and ends *npl* : costillas *fpl,* cosas *fpl* sueltas, cachivaches *mpl*

ode [ˈoːd] *n* : oda *f*

odious [ˈoːdiəs] *adj* : odioso — **odiously** *adv*

odor [ˈoːdər] *n* : olor *m*

odorless [ˈoːdərləs] *adj* : inodoro, sin olor

odorous [ˈoːdərəs] *adj* : oloroso

odyssey [ˈɑdəsi] *n, pl* **-seys** : odisea *f*

o'er [ˈor] → **over**

of [ˈʌv, ˈɑv] *prep* **1** FROM : de <a man of the city : un hombre de la ciudad> **2** (*indicating character or background*) : de <a woman of great ability : una mujer de gran capacidad> **3** (*indicating cause*) : de <he died of the flu : murió de la gripe> **4** BY : de <the works of Shakespeare : las obras de Shakespeare> **5** (*indicating contents, material or quantity*) : de <a house of wood : una casa de madera> <a glass of water : un vaso de agua> **6** (*indicating belonging or connection*) : de <the front of the house : el frente de la casa> **7** ABOUT : sobre, de <tales of the West : los cuentos del Oeste> **8** (*indicating a particular example*) : de <the city of Caracas : la ciudad de Caracas> **9** FOR : por, a <love of country : amor por la patria> **10** (*indicating time or date*) <five minutes of ten : las diez menos cinco> <the eighth of April : el ocho de abril>

off¹ [ˈɔf] *adv* **1** (*indicating change of position or state*) <to march off : marcharse> <he dozed off : se puso a dormir> **2** (*indicating distance in space or time*) <some miles off : a varias millas> <the holiday is three weeks off : faltan tres semanas para la fiesta> **3** (*indicating removal*) <the knob came off : se le cayó el pomo> **4** (*indicating termination*) <shut the television off : apaga la televisión> **5** (*indicating suspension of work*) <to take a day off : tomarse un día de descanso> **6 off and on** : de vez en cuando

off² *adj* **1** FARTHER : más remoto, distante <the off side of the building : el lado distante del edificio> **2** STARTED : empezado <to be off on a spree : irse de juerga> **3** OUT : apagado <the light is off : la luz está apagada> **4** CANCELED : cancelado, suspendido **5** INCORRECT : erróneo, incorrecto **6** REMOTE : remoto, lejano <an off chance : una posibilidad remota> **7** FREE : libre <I'm off today : hoy estoy libre> **8 to be well off** : vivir con desahogo, tener bastante dinero

off³ *prep* **1** (*indicating physical separation*) : de <she took it off the table : lo tomó de la mesa> <a shop off the main street : una tienda al lado de la calle principal> **2** : a la costa de, a expensas de <he lives off his sister : vive a expensas de su hermana> **3** (*indicating the suspension of an activity*) <to be off duty : estar libre> <he's off liquor : ha dejado el alcohol> **4** BELOW : por debajo de <he's off his game : está por debajo de su juego normal>

offal [ˈɔfəl] *n* **1** RUBBISH, WASTE : desechos *mpl*, desperdicios *mpl* **2** VISCERA : vísceras *fpl*, asaduras *fpl*

offend [əˈfɛnd] *vt* **1** VIOLATE : violar, atentar contra **2** HURT : ofender <to be easily offended : ser muy susceptible>

offender [əˈfɛndər] *n* : delincuente *mf;* infractor *m,* -tora *f*

offense *or* **offence** [əˈfɛnts, ˈɔˌfɛnts] *n* **1** INSULT : ofensa *f,* injuria *f,* agravio *m* <to take offense : ofenderse> **2** ASSAULT : ataque *m* **3** : ofensiva *f* (en deportes) **4** CRIME, INFRACTION : infracción *f,* delito *m*

offensive[1] [əˈfɛntsɪv, ˈɔˌfɛnt-] *adj* : ofensivo — **offensively** *adv*

offensive[2] *n* : ofensiva *f*

offer[1] [ˈɔfər] *vt* **1** : ofrecer <they offered him the job : le ofrecieron el puesto> **2** PROPOSE : proponer, sugerir **3** SHOW : ofrecer, mostrar <to offer resistance : ofrecer resistencia>

offer[2] *n* : oferta *f,* ofrecimiento *m,* propuesta *f*

offering [ˈɔfərɪŋ] *n* : ofrenda *f*

offhand[1] [ˈɔfˈhænd] *adv* : sin preparación, sin pensarlo

offhand[2] *adj* **1** IMPROMPTU : improvisado **2** ABRUPT : brusco

office [ˈɔfəs] *n* **1** : cargo *m* <to run for office : presentarse como candidato> **2** : oficina *f,* despacho *m,* gabinete *m* (en la casa) <office hours : horas de oficina>

officeholder [ˈɔfəsˌhoːldər] *n* : titular *mf*

officer [ˈɔfəsər] *n* **1** *or* **police officer** : policía *mf,* agente *mf* de policía **2** OFFICIAL : oficial *mf;* funcionario *m,* -ria *f;* director *m,* -tora *f* (en una empresa) **3** COMMISSIONED OFFICER : oficial *mf*

official[1] [əˈfɪʃəl] *adj* : oficial — **officially** *adv*

official[2] *n* : funcionario *m,* -ria *f;* oficial *mf*

officiate [əˈfɪʃiˌeɪt] *v* **-ated; -ating** *vi* **1** : arbitrar (en deportes) **2 to officiate at** : oficiar, celebrar — *vt* : arbitrar

officious [əˈfɪʃəs] *adj* : oficioso

offing [ˈɔfɪŋ] *n* **in the offing** : en perspectiva

offset [ˈɔfˌsɛt] *vt* **-set; -setting** : compensar

offshoot [ˈɔfˌʃuːt] *n* **1** OUTGROWTH : producto *m,* resultado *m* **2** BRANCH, SHOOT : retoño *m,* rama *f,* vástago *m* (de una planta)

offshore[1] [ˈɔfˈʃor] *adv* : a una distancia de la costa

offshore[2] *adj* **1** : de (la) tierra <an offshore wind : un viento que sopla de tierra> **2** : (de) costa afuera, cercano a la costa <an offshore island : una isla costera>

offspring [ˈɔfˌsprɪŋ] *ns & pl* **1** YOUNG : crías *fpl* (de los animales) **2** PROGENY : prole *f,* progenie *f*

off-the-road [ˈɔfðəˈroːd] *adj* : extraoficial

often [ˈɔfən, ˈɔftən] *adv* : muchas veces, a menudo, seguido

oftentimes [ˈɔfənˌtaɪmz, ˈɔftən-] *or* **ofttimes** [ˈɔftˌtaɪms] → **often**

ogle [ˈoːgəl] *vt* **ogled; ogling** : comerse con los ojos, quedarse mirando a

ogre [ˈoːgər] *n* : ogro *m*

oh [ˈoː] *interj* : ¡oh!, ¡ah!, ¡ay! <oh, of course : ah, por supuesto> <oh no! : ¡ay no!> <oh really? : ¿de veras?>

ohm [ˈoːm] *n* : ohm *m,* ohmio *m*

oil[1] [ˈɔɪl] *vt* : lubricar, engrasar, aceitar

oil[2] *n* **1** : aceite *m* **2** PETROLEUM : petróleo *m* **3** *or* **oil painting** : óleo *m,* pintura *f* al óleo **4** *or* **oil paint(s)** : óleo *m*

oilcloth [ˈɔɪlˌklɔθ] *n* : hule *m*

oiliness [ˈɔɪlinəs] *n* : lo aceitoso

oilskin [ˈɔɪlˌskɪn] *n* **1** : hule *m* **2 oilskins** *npl* : impermeable *m*

oily [ˈɔɪli] *adj* **oilier; -est** : aceitoso, grasiento, grasoso <oily fingers : dedos grasientos>

ointment [ˈɔɪntmənt] *n* : ungüento *m,* pomada *f*

OK[1] [ˌoːˈkeɪ] *vt* **OK'd** *or* **okayed** [ˌoːˈkeɪd]; **OK'ing** *or* **okaying** APPROVE, AUTHORIZE : dar el visto bueno a, autorizar, aprobar

OK[2] *or* **okay** [ˌoːˈkeɪ] *adv* **1** WELL : bien **2** YES : sí, por supuesto

OK[3] *adj* : bien <he's OK : está bien> <it's OK with me : estoy de acuerdo>

OK[4] *n* : autorización *f,* visto *m* bueno

okra [ˈoːkrə, *South also* -kri] *n* : quingombó *m*

old[1] [ˈoːld] *adj* **1** ANCIENT : antiguo <old civilizations : civilizaciones antiguas> **2** FAMILIAR : viejo <old friends : viejos amigos> <the same old story : el mismo cuento> **3** (*indicating a certain age*) <he's ten years old : tiene diez años (de edad)> **4** AGED : viejo, anciano <an old woman : una anciana> **5** FORMER : antiguo <her old neighborhood : su antiguo barrio> **6** WORN-OUT : viejo, gastado

old[2] *n* **1 the old** : los viejos, los ancianos **2 in the days of old** : antaño, en los tiempos antiguos

olden [ˈoːldən] *adj* : de antaño, de antigüedad

old–fashioned [ˈoːldˈfæʃənd] *adj* : anticuado, pasado de moda

old maid *n* **1** SPINSTER : soltera *f* **2** FUSSBUDGET : maniático *m,* -ca *f;* melindroso *m,* -sa *f*

old–time [ˈoːldˈtaɪm] *adj* : antiguo

old–timer [ˈoːldˈtaɪmər] *n* **1** VETERAN : veterano *m,* -na *f* **2** *or* **oldster** : anciano *m,* -na *f*

old–world [ˈoːldˈwərld] *adj* : pintoresco (de antaño)

oleander [ˈoːliˌændər] *n* : adelfa *f*

oleomargarine [ˌoːlioˈmɑrdʒərən] → **margarine**

olfactory [ɑlˈfæktəri,ol-] *adj* : olfativo

oligarchy [ˈɑləˌgɑrki, ˈoːlə-] *n, pl* **-chies** : oligarquía *f*

olive [ˈɑlɪv, -ləv] *n* **1** : aceituna *f,* oliva *f* (fruta) **2** : olivo *m* (árbol) **3** *or* **olive green** : color *m* aceituna, verde *m* oliva

Olympic Games [oˈlɪmpɪk] *npl* : Juegos *mpl* Olímpicos

Omani [oˈmɑni, -ˈmæ-] *n* : omaní *mf* — **Omani** *adj*

ombudsman [ˈɑmˌbʊdzmən, ɑmˈbʊdz-] *n, pl* **-men** [-mən, -ˌmɛn] : ombudsman *m*

omelet *or* **omelette** [ˈɑmlət, ˈɑmə-] *n* : omelette *mf,* tortilla *f* de huevo

omen [ˈoːmən] *n* : presagio *m,* augurio *m,* agüero *m*

ominous [ˈɑmənəs] *adj* : ominoso, agorero, de mal agüero

ominously [ˈɑmənəsli] *adv* : de manera amenazadora

omission [oˈmɪʃən] *n* : omisión *f*

omit [oˈmɪt] *vt* **omitted; omitting 1** LEAVE OUT : omitir, excluir **2** NEGLECT : omitir <they omitted to tell us : omitieron decírnoslo>

omnipotence [ɑmˈnɪpət̮ən*t*s] *n* : omnipotencia *f* — **omnipotent** [ɑmˈnɪpət̮ənt] *adj*

omnipresent [ˌɑmnɪˈprɛzənt] *adj* : omnipresente

omniscient [ɑmˈnɪʃənt] *adj* : omnisciente

omnivorous [ɑmˈnɪvərəs] *adj* **1** : omnívoro **2** AVID : ávido, voraz

on[1] [ˈɑn, ˈɔn] *adv* **1** (*indicating contact with a surface*) <put the top on : pon la tapa> <he has a hat on : lleva un sombrero puesto> **2** (*indicating forward movement*) <from that moment on : a partir de ese momento> <farther on : más adelante> **3** (*indicating operation or an operating position*) <turn the light on : prende la luz>

on[2] *adj* **1** (*being in operation*) <the radio is on : el radio está prendido> **2** (*taking place*) <the game is on : el juego ha comenzado> **3 to be on to** : estar enterado de

on[3] *prep* **1** (*indicating position*) : en, sobre, encima de <on the table : en (sobre, encima de) la mesa> <shadows on the wall : sombras en la pared> <on horseback : a caballo> **2** AT, TO : a <on the right : a la derecha> **3** ABOARD, IN : en, a <on the plane : en el avión> <he got on the train : subió al tren> **4** (*indicating time*) <she worked on Saturdays : trabajaba los sábados> <every hour on the hour : a la hora en punto> **5** (*indicating means or agency*) : por <he cut himself on a tin can : se cortó con una lata> <to talk on the telephone : hablar por teléfono> **6** (*indicating a state or process*) : en <on fire : en llamas> <on the increase : en aumento> **7** (*indicating connection or membership*) : en <on a committee : en una comisión> **8** (*indicating an activity*) <on vacation : de vacaciones> <on a diet : a dieta> **9** ABOUT, CONCERNING : sobre <a book on insects : un libro sobre insectos> <reflect on that : reflexiona sobre eso>

once[1] [ˈwʌn*t*s] *adv* **1** : una vez <once a month : una vez al mes> <once and for all : de una vez por todas> **2** EVER : alguna vez **3** FORMERLY : antes, anteriormente

once[2] *adj* FORMER : antiguo

once[3] *n* **1** : una vez **2 at ~** SIMULTANEOUSLY : al mismo tiempo, simultáneamente **3 at ~** IMMEDIATELY : inmediatamente, en seguida

once[4] *conj* : una vez que, tan pronto como

once–over [ˌwʌn*t*sˈoːvər, ˈwʌn*t*sˌ-] *n* **to give someone the once–over** : echarle un vistazo a alguien

oncoming [ˈɑnˌkʌmɪŋ, ˈɔn-] *adj* : que viene

one[1] [ˈwʌn] *adj* **1** (*being a single unit*) : un, una <he only wants one apple : sólo quiere una manzana> **2** (*being a particular one*) : un, una <he arrived early one morning : llegó temprano una mañana> **3** (*being the same*) : mismo, misma <they're all members of one team : todos son miembros del mismo equipo> <one and the same thing : la misma cosa> **4** SOME : alguno, alguna; un, una <I'll see you again one day : algún día te veré otra vez> <at one time or another : en una u otra ocasión>

one[2] *n* **1** : uno *m* (número) **2** (*indicating the first of a set or series*) <from day one : desde el primer momento> **3** (*indicating a single person or thing*) <the one (girl) on the right : la de la derecha> <he has the one but needs the other : tiene uno pero necesita el otro>

one[3] *pron* **1** : uno, una <one of his friends : una de sus amigas> <one never knows : uno nunca sabe, nunca se sabe> <to cut one's finger : cortarse el dedo> **2 one and all** : todos, todo el mundo **3 one another** : el uno al otro, se <they loved one another : se amaban> **4 that one** : aquél, aquella **5 which one?** : ¿cuál?

onerous [ˈɑnərəs, ˈoːnə-] *adj* : oneroso, gravoso

oneself [ˌwʌnˈsɛlf] *pron* **1** (*used reflexively or for emphasis*) : se, sí mismo, uno mismo <to control oneself : controlarse> <to talk to oneself

: hablarse a sí mismo> <to do it oneself : hacérselo uno mismo> **2 by ~** : solo

one–sided [ˈwʌnˈsaɪdəd] *adj* **1** : de un solo lado **2** LOPSIDED : asimétrico **3** BIASED : parcial, tendencioso **4** UNILATERAL : unilateral

onetime [ˈwʌnˈtaɪm] *adj* FORMER : antiguo

one–way [ˈwʌnˈweɪ] *adj* **1** : de sentido único, de una sola dirección <a one-way street : una calle de sentido único> **2** : de ida, sencillo <a one-way ticket : un boleto de ida>

ongoing [ˈɑnˌgoːɪŋ] *adj* **1** CONTINUING : en curso, corriente **2** DEVELOPING : en desarrollo

onion [ˈʌnjən] *n* : cebolla *f*

only[1] [ˈoːnli] *adv* **1** MERELY : sólo, solamente, nomás <for only two dollars : por tan sólo dos dólares> <only once : sólo una vez, no más de una vez> <I only did it to help : lo hice por ayudar nomás> **2** SOLELY : únicamente, sólo, solamente <only he knows it : solamente él lo sabe> **3** (*indicating a result*) <it will only cause him problems : no hará más que crearle problemas> **4 if only** : ojalá, por lo menos <if only it were true! : ¡ojalá sea cierto!> <if he could only dance : si por lo menos pudiera bailar>

only[2] *adj* : único <an only child : un hijo único> <the only chance : la única oportunidad>

only[3] *conj* BUT : pero <I would go, only I'm sick : iría, pero estoy enfermo>

onset [ˈɑnˌsɛt] *n* : comienzo *m,* llegada *f*

onslaught [ˈɑnˌslɔt, ˈɔn-] *n* : arremetida *f,* embestida *f,* embate *m*

onto [ˈɑnˌtuː, ˈɔn-] *prep* : sobre

onus [ˈoːnəs] *n* : responsabilidad *f,* carga *f*

onward[1] [ˈɑnwərd, ˈɔn-] *or* **onwards** *adv* FORWARD : adelante, hacia adelante

onward[2] *adj* : hacia adelante

onyx [ˈɑnɪks] *n* : ónix *m*

ooze[1] [ˈuːz] *v* **oozed; oozing** *vi* : rezumar — *vt* **1** : rezumar **2** EXUDE : irradiar, rebosar <to ooze confidence : irradiar confianza>

ooze[2] *n* SLIME : cieno *m,* limo *m*

opal [ˈoːpəl] *n* : ópalo *m*

opaque [oˈpeɪk] *adj* **1** : opaco **2** UNCLEAR : poco claro

open[1] [ˈoːpən] *vt* **1** : abrir <open the door : abre la puerta> **2** UNCOVER : destapar **3** UNFOLD : desplegar, abrir **4** CLEAR : abrir (un camino, etc.) **5** INAUGURATE : abrir (una tienda), inaugurar (una exposición, etc.) **6** INITIATE : initiar, entablar, abrir <to open the meeting : abrir la sesión> <to open a discussion : entablar un debate> — *vi* **1** : abrirse **2** BEGIN : empezar, comenzar

open[2] *adj* **1** : abierto <an open window : una ventana abierta> **2** FRANK : abierto, franco, directo **3** UNCOVERED : descubierto, abierto **4** EXTENDED : extendido, abierto <with open arms : con los brazos abiertos> **5** UNRESTRICTED : libre, abierto **6** UNDECIDED : pendiente, por decidir, sin resolver <an open question : una cuestión pendiente> **7** AVAILABLE : vacante, libre <the job is open : el puesto está vacante>

open[3] *n* **in the open 1** OUTDOORS : al aire libre **2** KNOWN : conocido, sacado a la luz

open-air [ˈoːpənˈær] *adj* OUTDOOR : al aire libre

open-and-shut [ˈoːpənəndˈʃʌt] *adj* : claro, evidente <an open-and-shut case : un caso muy claro>

opener [ˈoːpənər] *n* : destapador *m,* abrelatas *m,* abridor *m*

openhanded [ˌoːpənˈhændəd] *adj* : generoso, liberal

openhearted [ˌoːpənˈhɑrtəd] *adj* **1** FRANK : franco, sincero **2** : generoso, de gran corazón

opening [ˈoːpənɪŋ] *n* **1** BEGINNING : comienzo *m,* principio *m,* apertura *f* **2** APERTURE : abertura *f,* brecha *f,* claro *m* (en el bosque) **3** OPPORTUNITY : oportunidad *f*

openly [ˈoːpənli] *adv* **1** FRANKLY : abiertamente, francamente **2** PUBLICLY : públicamente, declaradamente

openness [ˈoːpənnəs] *n* : franqueza *f*

opera [ˈɑprə, ˈɑpərə] *n* **1** : ópera *f* **2** → **opus**

opera glasses *npl* : gemelos *mpl* de teatro

operate [ˈɑpəˌreɪt] *v* **-ated; -ating** *vi* **1** ACT, FUNCTION : operar, funcionar, actuar **2 to operate on (someone)** : operar a (alguien) — *vt* **1** WORK : operar, manejar, hacer funcionar (una máquina) **2** MANAGE : manejar, administrar (un negocio)

operatic [ˌɑpəˈrætɪk] *adj* : operístico

operation [ˌɑpəˈreɪʃən] *n* **1** FUNCTIONING : funcionamiento *m* **2** USE : uso *m,* manejo *m* (de máquinas) **3** SURGERY : operación *f,* intervención *f* quirúrgica

operational [ˌɑpəˈreɪʃənəl] *adj* : operacional, de operación

operative [ˈɑpərətɪv, -ˌreɪ-] *adj* **1** OPERATING : vigente, en vigor **2** WORKING : operativo **3** SURGICAL : quirúrgico

operator [ˈɑpəˌreɪtər] *n* : operador *m,* -dora *f*

operetta [ˌɑpəˈrɛtə] *n* : opereta *f*

ophthalmologist [ˌɑfˌθælˈmɑlədʒɪst, -θəˈmɑ-] *n* : oftalmólogo *m,* -ga *f*

ophthalmology [ˌɑfˌθælˈmɑlədʒi, -θəˈmɑ-] *n* : oftalmología *f*

opiate [ˈoːpiət, -piˌeɪt] *n* : opiato *m*

opinion [əˈpɪnjən] *n* : opinión *f*

opinionated [əˈpɪnjəˌneɪtəd] *adj* : testarudo, dogmático

opium [ˈoːpiəm] *n* **:** opio *m*
opossum [əˈpɑsəm] *n* **:** zarigüeya *f,* oposum *m*
opponent [əˈpoːnənt] *n* **:** oponente *mf;* opositor *m,* -tora *f;* contrincante *mf* (en deportes)
opportune [ˌɑpərˈtuːn, -ˈtjuːn] *adj* **:** oportuno — **opportunely** *adv*
opportunist [ˌɑpərˈtuːnɪst, -ˈtjuː-] *n* **:** oportunista *mf*
opportunity [ˌɑpərˈtuːnəti, -ˈtjuː-] *n, pl* **-ties :** oportunidad *f,* ocasión *f,* chance *m,* posibilidades *fpl*
oppose [əˈpoːz] *vt* **-posed; -posing 1 :** ir en contra de, oponerse a <good opposes evil : el bien se opone al mal> **2** COMBAT **:** luchar contra, combatir, resistir
opposite[1] [ˈɑpəzət] *adv* **:** enfrente
opposite[2] *adj* **1** FACING **:** de enfrente <the opposite side : el lado de enfrente> **2** CONTRARY **:** opuesto, contrario <in opposite directions : en direcciones contrarias> <the opposite sex : el sexo opuesto, el otro sexo>
opposite[3] *n* **:** lo contrario, lo opuesto
opposite[4] *prep* **:** enfrente de, frente a
opposition [ˌɑpəˈzɪʃən] *n* **1 :** oposición *f,* resistencia *f* **2 in opposition to** AGAINST **:** en contra de
oppress [əˈprɛs] *vt* **1** PERSECUTE **:** oprimir, perseguir **2** BURDEN **:** oprimir, agobiar
oppression [əˈprɛʃən] *n* **:** opresión *f*
oppressive [əˈprɛsɪv] *adj* **1** HARSH **:** opresivo, severo **2** STIFLING **:** agobiante, sofocante <oppressive heat : calor sofocante>
oppressor [əˈprɛsər] *n* **:** opresor *m,* -sora *f*
opprobrium [əˈproːbriəm] *n* **:** oprobio *m*
opt [ˈɑpt] *vi* **:** optar
optic [ˈɑptɪk] *or* **optical** [-tɪkəl] *adj* **:** óptico
optician [ɑpˈtɪʃən] *n* **:** óptico *m,* -ca *f*
optics [ˈɑptɪks] *npl* **:** óptica *f*
optimal [ˈɑptəməl] *adj* **:** óptimo
optimism [ˈɑptəˌmɪzəm] *n* **:** optimismo *m*
optimist [ˈɑptəmɪst] *n* **:** optimista *mf*
optimistic [ˌɑptəˈmɪstɪk] *adj* **:** optimista
optimistically [ˌɑptəˈmɪstɪkli] *adv* **:** con optimismo, positivamente
optimum[1] [ˈɑptəməm] *adj* → **optimal**
optimum[2] *n, pl* **-ma** [ˈɑptəmə] **:** lo óptimo, lo ideal
option [ˈɑpʃən] *n* **:** opción *f* <she has no option : no tiene más remedio>
optional [ˈɑpʃənəl] *adj* **:** facultativo, optativo
optometrist [ɑpˈtɑmətrɪst] *n* **:** optometrista *mf*
optometry [ɑpˈtɑmətri] *n* **:** optometría *f*
opulence [ˈɑpjələnts] *n* **:** opulencia *f*
opulent [ˈɑpjələnt] *adj* **:** opulento
opus [ˈoːpəs] *n, pl* **opera** [ˈoːpərə, ˈɑpə-] **:** opus *m,* obra *f* (de música)
or [ˈɔr] *conj* **1** (*indicating an alternative*) **:** o (u *before words beginning with* o *or* ho) <coffee or tea : café o té> <one day or another : un día u otro> **2** (*following a negative*) **:** ni <he didn't have his keys or his wallet : no llevaba ni sus llaves ni su billetera>
oracle [ˈɔrəkəl] *n* **:** oráculo *m*
oral [ˈorəl] *adj* **:** oral — **orally** *adv*
orange [ˈɔrɪndʒ] *n* **1 :** naranja *f,* china *f PRi* (fruto) **2 :** naranja *m* (color), color *m* de china *PRi*
orangeade [ˌɔrɪndʒˈeɪd] *n* **:** naranjada *f*
orangutan [əˈræŋəˌtæŋ, -ˈræŋgə-, -ˌtæn] *n* **:** orangután *m*
oration [əˈreɪʃən] *n* **:** oración *f,* discurso *m*
orator [ˈɔrəṭər] *n* **:** orador *m,* -dora *f*
oratorio [ˌɔrəˈtoriˌoː] *n, pl* **-rios :** oratorio *m*
oratory [ˈɔrəˌtori] *n, pl* **-ries :** oratoria *f*
orb [ˈɔrb] *n* **:** orbe *m*
orbit[1] [ˈɔrbət] *vt* **1** CIRCLE **:** girar alrededor de **2 :** poner en órbita (un satélite, etc.) — *vi* **:** orbitar
orbit[2] *n* **:** órbita *f*
orbital [ˈɔrbəṭəl] *adj* **:** orbital
orchard [ˈɔrtʃərd] *n* **:** huerto *m*
orchestra [ˈɔrkəstrə] *n* **:** orquesta *f*
orchestral [ɔrˈkɛstrəl] *adj* **:** orquestal
orchestrate [ˈɔrkəˌstreɪt] *vt* **-trated; -trating 1 :** orquestar, instrumentar (en música) **2** ORGANIZE **:** arreglar, organizar
orchestration [ˌɔrkəˈstreɪʃən] *n* **:** orquestación *f*
orchid [ˈɔrkɪd] *n* **:** orquídea *f*
ordain [ɔrˈdeɪn] *vt* **1 :** ordenar (en religión) **2** DECREE **:** decretar, ordenar
ordeal [ɔrˈdiːl, ˈɔrˌdiːl] *n* **:** prueba *f* dura, experiencia *f* terrible
order[1] [ˈɔrdər] *vt* **1** ORGANIZE **:** arreglar, ordenar, poner en orden **2** COMMAND **:** ordenar, mandar **3** REQUEST **:** pedir, encargar <to order a meal : pedir algo de comer> — *vi* **:** hacer un pedido
order[2] *n* **1 :** orden *f* <a religious order : una orden religiosa> **2** COMMAND **:** orden *f,* mandato *m* <to give an order : dar una orden> **3** REQUEST **:** orden *f,* pedido *m* <purchase order : orden de compra> **4** ARRANGEMENT **:** orden *m* <in chronological order : por orden cronológico> **5** DISCIPLINE **:** orden *m* <law and order : el orden público> **6 in order to :** para **7 out of order :** descompuesto, averiado **8 orders** *npl or* **holy orders :** órdenes *fpl* sagradas
orderliness [ˈɔrdərlinəs] *n* **:** orden *m*
orderly[1] [ˈɔrdərli] *adj* **1** METHODICAL **:** ordenado, metódico **2** PEACEFUL **:** pacífico, disciplinado
orderly[2] *n, pl* **-lies 1 :** ordenanza *m* (en el ejército) **2 :** camillero *m* (en un hospital)

ordinal [ˈɔrdənəl] *n or* **ordinal number :** ordinal *m,* número *m* ordinal

ordinance [ˈɔrdənənts] *n* **:** ordenanza *f,* reglamento *m*

ordinarily [ˌɔrdənˈɛrəli] *adv* **:** ordinariamente, por lo general

ordinary [ˈɔrdənˌɛri] *adj* **1** NORMAL, USUAL **:** normal, usual **2** AVERAGE **:** común y corriente, normal **3** MEDIOCRE **:** mediocre, ordinario

ordination [ˌɔrdənˈeɪʃən] *n* **:** ordenación *f*

ordnance [ˈɔrdnənts] *n* **:** artillería *f*

ore [ˈor] *n* **:** mineral *m* (metalífero), mena *f*

oregano [əˈrɛgəˌnoː] *n* **:** orégano *m*

organ [ˈɔrgən] *n* **1 :** órgano *m* (instrumento) **2 :** órgano *m* (del cuerpo) **3** PERIODICAL **:** publicación *f* periódica, órgano *m*

organic [ɔrˈgænɪk] *adj* **:** orgánico — **organically** *adv*

organism [ˈɔrgəˌnɪzəm] *n* **:** organismo *m*

organist [ˈɔrgənɪst] *n* **:** organista *mf*

organization [ˌɔrgənəˈzeɪʃən] *n* **1** ORGANIZING **:** organización *f* **2** BODY **:** organización *f,* organismo *m*

organizational [ˌɔrgənəˈzeɪʃənəl] *adj* **:** organizativo

organize [ˈɔrgəˌnaɪz] *vt* **-nized; -nizing :** organizar, arreglar, poner en orden

organizer [ˈɔrgəˌnaɪzər] *n* **:** organizador *m,* -dora *f*

orgasm [ˈɔrˌgæzəm] *n* **:** orgasmo *m*

orgy [ˈɔrdʒi] *n, pl* **-gies :** orgía *f*

orient [ˈoriˌɛnt] *vt* **:** orientar

Orient *n* **the Orient :** el Oriente

oriental [ˌoriˈɛntəl] *adj* **:** del Oriente, oriental

Oriental *n* **:** oriental *mf*

orientation [ˌoriənˈteɪʃən] *n* **:** orientación *f*

orifice [ˈɔrəfəs] *n* **:** orificio *m*

origin [ˈɔrədʒən] *n* **1** ANCESTRY **:** origen *m,* ascendencia *f* **2** SOURCE **:** origen *m,* raíz *f,* fuente *f*

original[1] [əˈrɪdʒənəl] *adj* **:** original

original[2] *n* **:** original *m*

originality [əˌrɪdʒəˈnæləṭi] *n* **:** originalidad *f*

originally [əˈrɪdʒənəli] *adv* **1** AT FIRST **:** al principio, originariamente **2** CREATIVELY **:** originalmente, con originalidad

originate [əˈrɪdʒəˌneɪt] *v* **-nated; -nating** *vt* **:** originar, iniciar, crear — *vi* **1** BEGIN **:** originarse, empezar **2** COME **:** provenir, proceder, derivarse

originator [əˈrɪdʒəˌneɪṭər] *n* **:** creador *m,* -dora *f;* inventor *m,* -tora *f*

oriole [ˈoriˌoːl, -iəl] *n* **:** oropéndola *f*

ornament[1] [ˈɔrnəmənt] *vt* **:** adornar, decorar, ornamentar

ornament[2] *n* **:** ornamento *m,* adorno *m,* decoración *f*

ornamental [ˌɔrnəˈmɛntəl] *adj* **:** ornamental, de adorno, decorativo

ornamentation [ˌɔrnəmənˈteɪʃən, -mɛn-] *n* **:** ornamentación *f*

ornate [ɔrˈneɪt] *adj* **:** elaborado, recargado

ornery [ˈɔrnəri, ˈɑrnəri] *adj* **ornerier; -est :** de mal genio, malhumorado

ornithologist [ˌɔrnəˈθɑlədʒɪst] *n* **:** ornitólogo *m,* -ga *f*

ornithology [ˌɔrnəˈθɑlədʒi] *n, pl* **-gies :** ornitología *f*

orphan[1] [ˈɔrfən] *vt* **:** dejar huérfano

orphan[2] *n* **:** huérfano *m,* -na *f*

orphanage [ˈɔrfənɪdʒ] *n* **:** orfelinato *m,* orfanato *m*

orthodontics [ˌɔrθəˈdɑntɪks] *n* **:** ortodoncia *f*

orthodontist [ˌɔrθəˈdɑntɪst] *n* **:** ortodoncista *mf*

orthodox [ˈɔrθəˌdɑks] *adj* **:** ortodoxo

orthodoxy [ˈɔrθəˌdɑksi] *n, pl* **-doxies :** ortodoxia *f*

orthographic [ˌɔrθəˈgræfɪk] *adj* **:** ortográfico

orthography [ɔrˈθɑgrəfi] *n, pl* **-phies** SPELLING **:** ortografía *f*

orthopedic [ˌɔrθəˈpiːdɪk] *adj* **:** ortopédico

orthopedics [ˌɔrθəˈpiːdɪks] *ns & pl* **:** ortopedia *f*

orthopedist [ˌɔrθəˈpiːdɪst] *n* **:** ortopedista *mf*

oscillate [ˈɑsəˌleɪt] *vi* **-lated; -lating :** oscilar

oscillation [ˌɑsəˈleɪʃən] *n* **:** oscilación *f*

osmosis [ɑzˈmoːsɪs, ɑs-] *n* **:** ósmosis *f,* osmosis *f*

ostensible [ɑˈstɛntsəbəl] *adj* APPARENT **:** aparente, ostensible — **ostensibly** [-bli] *adv*

ostentation [ˌɑstənˈteɪʃən] *n* **:** ostentación *f,* boato *m*

ostentatious [ˌɑstənˈteɪʃəs] *adj* **:** ostentoso — **ostentatiously** *adv*

osteopath [ˈɑstiəˌpæθ] *n* **:** osteópata *f*

osteopathy [ˌɑstiˈɑpəθi] *n* **:** osteopatía *f*

osteoporosis [ˌɑstiopəˈroːsɪs] *n, pl* **-roses** [-ˌsiːz] **:** osteoporosis *f*

ostracism [ˈɑstrəˌsɪzəm] *n* **:** ostracismo *m*

ostracize [ˈɑstrəˌsaɪz] *vt* **-cized; -cizing :** condenar al ostracismo, marginar, aislar

ostrich [ˈɑstrɪtʃ, ˈɔs-] *n* **:** avestruz *m*

other[1] [ˈʌðər] *adv* **other than :** aparte de, fuera de

other[2] *adj* **:** otro <the other boys : los otros muchachos> <smarter than other people : más inteligente que los demás> <on the other hand : por otra parte, por otro lado> <every other day : cada dos días>

other[3] *pron* **:** otro, otra <one in front of the other : uno tras otro> <myself and three others : yo y tres otros, yo y tres más> <somewhere or other : en alguna parte>

otherwise[1] [ˈʌðər,waɪz] *adv* **1** DIFFERENTLY **:** de otro modo, de manera distinta <he could not act otherwise : no pudo actuar de manera distinta> **2** **:** eso aparte, por lo demás <I'm dizzy, but otherwise I'm fine : estoy mareado pero, por lo demás, estoy bien> **3** OR ELSE **:** de lo contario, si no <do what I tell you, otherwise you'll be sorry : haz lo que te digo, de lo contario, te arrepentirás>

otherwise[2] *adj* **:** diferente, distinto <the facts are otherwise : la realidad es diferente>

otter [ˈɑtər] *n* **:** nutria *f*

ought [ˈɔ̌t] *v aux* **:** deber <you ought to take care of yourself : deberías cuidarte>

oughtn't [ˈɔtənt] (*contraction of* **ought not**) → **ought**

ounce [ˈaʊnts] *n* **:** onza *f*

our [ˈɑr, ˈaʊr] *adj* **:** nuestro

ours [ˈaʊrz, ˈɑrz] *pron* **:** nuestro, nuestra <a cousin of ours : un primo nuestro>

ourselves [ɑrˈsɛlvz, aʊr-] *pron* **1** (*used reflexively*) **:** nos, nosotros <we amused ourselves : nos divertimos> <we were always thinking of ourselves : siempre pensábamos en nosotros> **2** (*used for emphasis*) **:** nosotros mismos, nosotras mismas <we did it ourselves : lo hicimos nosotros mismos>

oust [ˈaʊst] *vt* **:** desbancar, expulsar

ouster [ˈaʊstər] *n* **:** expulsión *f* (de un país, etc.), destitución *f* (de un puesto)

out[1] [ˈaʊt] *vi* **:** revelarse, hacerse conocido

out[2] *adv* **1** (*indicating direction or movement*) **:** para afuera <she opened the door and looked out : abrió la puerta y miró para afuera> **2** (*indicating a location away from home or work*) **:** fuera, afuera <to eat out : comer afuera> **3** (*indicating loss of control or possession*) <they let the secret out : sacaron el secreto a la luz> **4** (*indicating completion or discontinuance*) <his money ran out : se le acabó el dinero> <to turn out the light : apagar la luz> **5** OUTSIDE **:** fuera, afuera <out in the garden : afuera en el jardín> **6** ALOUD **:** en voz alta, en alto <to cry out : gritar>

out[3] *adj* **1** EXTERNAL **:** externo, exterior **2** OUTLYING **:** alejado, distante <the out islands : las islas distantes> **3** ABSENT **:** ausente **4** UNFASHIONABLE **:** fuera de moda **5** EXTINGUISHED **:** apagado

out[4] *prep* **1** (*used to indicate an outward movement*) **:** por <I looked out the window : miré por la ventana> <she ran out the door : corrió por la puerta> **2** → **out of**

out-and-out [ˈaʊtənˈaʊt] *adj* UTTER **:** redomado, absoluto

outboard motor [ˈaʊt,bord] *n* **:** motor *m* fuera de borde

outbound [ˈaʊt,baʊnd] *adj* **:** que sale, de salida

outbreak [ˈaʊt,breɪk] *n* **:** brote *m* (de una enfermedad), comienzo *m* (de guerra), ola *f* (de violencia), erupción *f* (de granos)

outbuilding [ˈaʊt,bɪldɪŋ] *n* **:** edificio *m* anexo

outburst [ˈaʊt,bərst] *n* **:** arranque *m,* arrebato *m*

outcast [ˈaʊt,kæst] *n* **:** marginado *m,* -da *f;* paria *mf*

outcome [ˈaʊt,kʌm] *n* **:** resultado *m,* desenlace *m,* consecuencia *f*

outcrop [ˈaʊt,krɑp] *n* **:** afloramiento *m*

outcry [ˈaʊt,kraɪ] *n, pl* **-cries :** clamor *m,* protesta *f*

outdated [,aʊtˈdeɪtəd] *adj* **:** anticuado, fuera de moda

outdistance [,aʊtˈdɪstənts] *vt* **-tanced; -tancing :** aventajar, dejar atrás

outdo [,aʊtˈduː] *vt* **-did** [-ˈdɪd]; **-done** [-ˈdʌn]; **-doing**; **-does** [-ˈdʌz] **:** superar

outdoor [ˈaʊtˈdor] *adj* **:** al aire libre <outdoor sports : deportes al aire libre> <outdoor clothing : ropa de calle>

outdoors[1] [ˈaʊtˈdorz] *adv* **:** afuera, al aire libre

outdoors[2] *n* **:** aire *m* libre

outer [ˈaʊtər] *adj* **1 :** exterior, externo **2 outer space :** espacio *m* exterior

outermost [ˈaʊtər,moːst] *adj* **:** más remoto, más exterior, extremo

outfield [ˈaʊt,fiːld] *n* **the outfield :** los jardines

outfielder [ˈaʊt,fiːldər] *n* **:** jardinero *m,* -ra *f*

outfit[1] [ˈaʊt,fɪt] *vt* **-fitted; -fitting** EQUIP **:** equipar

outfit[2] *n* **1** EQUIPMENT **:** equipo *m* **2** COSTUME, ENSEMBLE **:** traje *m,* conjunto *m* **3** GROUP **:** conjunto *m*

outgo [ˈaʊt,goː] *n, pl* **outgoes :** gasto *m*

outgoing [ˈaʊt,goːɪŋ] *adj* **1** OUTBOUND **:** que sale **2** DEPARTING **:** saliente <an outgoing president : un presidente saliente> **3** EXTROVERTED **:** extrovertido, expansivo

outgrow [,aʊtˈgroː] *vt* **-grew** [-ˈgruː]; **-grown** [-ˈgroːn]; **-growing 1 :** crecer más que <that tree outgrew all the others : ese árbol creció más que todos los otros> **2 to outgrow one's clothes :** quedarle pequeña la ropa a uno

outgrowth [ˈaʊt,groːθ] *n* **1** OFFSHOOT **:** brote *m,* vástago *m* (de una planta) **2** CONSEQUENCE **:** consecuencia *f,* producto *m,* resultado *m*

outing [ˈaʊtɪŋ] *n* **:** excursión *f*

outlandish [aʊtˈlændɪʃ] *adj* **:** descabellado, muy extraño

outlast [,aʊtˈlæst] *vt* **:** durar más que

outlaw[1] [ˈaʊt,lɔ] *vt* **:** hacerse ilegal, declarar fuera de la ley, prohibir

outlaw[2] *n* : bandido *m,* -da *f;* bandolero *m,* -ra *f;* forajido *m,* -da *f*

outlay [ˈaʊt,leɪ] *n* : gasto *m,* desembolso *m*

outlet [ˈaʊt,lɛt, -lət] *n* **1** EXIT : salida *f,* escape *m* <electrical outlet : toma de corriente> **2** RELIEF : desahogo *m* **3** MARKET : mercado *m,* salida *f*

outline[1] [ˈaʊt,laɪn] *vt* **-lined; -lining 1** SKETCH : diseñar, esbozar, bosquejar **2** DEFINE, EXPLAIN : perfilar, delinear, explicar <she outlined our responsibilities : delineó nuestras responsabilidades>

outline[2] *n* **1** PROFILE : perfil *m,* silueta *f,* contorno *m* **2** SKETCH : bosquejo *m,* boceto *m* **3** SUMMARY : esquema *m,* resumen *m,* sinopsis *m* <an outline of world history : un esquema de la historia mundial>

outlive [,aʊtˈlɪv] *vt* **-lived; -living** : sobrevivir a

outlook [ˈaʊt,lʊk] *n* **1** VIEW : vista *f,* panorama *f* **2** POINT OF VIEW : punto *m* de vista **3** PROSPECTS : perspectivas *fpl*

outlying [ˈaʊt,laɪɪŋ] *adj* : alejado, distante, remoto <the outlying areas : las afueras>

outmoded [,aʊtˈmoːdəd] *adj* : pasado de moda, anticuado

outnumber [,aʊtˈnʌmbər] *vt* : superar en número a, ser más numeroso de

out of *prep* **1** (*indicating direction or movement from within*) : de, por <we ran out of the house : salimos corriendo de la casa> <to look out of the window : mirar por la ventana> **2** (*being beyond the limits of*) <out of control : fuera de control> <to be out of sight : desaparecer de vista> **3** OF : de <one out of four : uno de cada cuatro> **4** (*indicating absence or loss*) : sin <out of money : sin dinero> <we're out of matches : nos hemos quedado sin fósforos> **5** BECAUSE OF : por <out of curiosity : por curiosidad> **6** FROM : de <made out of plastic : hecho de plástico>

out–of–date [,aʊt̬əvˈdeɪt] *adj* : anticuado, obsoleto, pasado de moda

out-of-door [,aʊt̬əvˈdor] *or* **out-of-doors** [-ˈdorz] *adj* → **outdoor**

out-of-doors *n* → **outdoors**

outpatient [ˈaʊt,peɪʃənt] *n* : paciente *m* externo, paciente *f* externa

outpost [ˈaʊt,poːst] *n* : puesto *m* avanzado

output[1] [ˈaʊt,pʊt] *vt* **-putted** *or* **-put; -putting** : producir

output[2] *n* : producción *f* (de una fábrica), rendimiento *m* (de una máquina), productividad *f* (de una persona)

outrage[1] [ˈaʊt,reɪdʒ] *vt* **-raged; -raging 1** INSULT : ultrajar, injuriar **2** INFURIATE : indignar, enfurecer

outrage[2] *n* **1** ATROCITY : atropello *m,* atrocidad *f,* atentado *m* **2** SCANDAL : escándalo *m* **3** ANGER : ira *f,* furia *f*

outrageous [,aʊtˈreɪdʒəs] *adj* **1** SCANDALOUS : escandaloso, ofensivo, atroz **2** UNCONVENTIONAL : poco convencional, extravagante **3** EXORBITANT : exorbitante, excesivo (dícese de los precios, etc.)

outright[1] [,aʊtˈraɪt] *adv* **1** COMPLETELY : por completo, totalmente <to sell outright : vender por completo> <he refused it outright : lo rechazó rotundamente> **2** DIRECTLY : directamente, sin reserva **3** INSTANTLY : al instante, en el acto

outright[2] [ˈaʊt,raɪt] *adj* **1** COMPLETE : completo, absoluto, categórico <an outright lie : una mentira absoluta> **2** : sin reservas <an outright gift : un regalo sin reservas>

outset [ˈaʊt,sɛt] *n* : comienzo *m,* principio *m*

outshine [,aʊtˈʃaɪn] *vt* **-shone** [-ˈʃoːn, -ˈʃɒn] *or* **-shined; -shining** : eclipsar

outside[1] [,aʊtˈsaɪd, ˈaʊt,-] *adv* : fuera, afuera

outside[2] *adj* **1** : exterior, externo <the outside edge : el borde exterior> <outside influences : influencias externas> **2** REMOTE : remoto <an outside chance : una posibilidad remota>

outside[3] *n* **1** EXTERIOR : parte *f* de afuera, exterior *m* **2** MOST : máximo *m* <three weeks at the outside : tres semanas como máximo> **3 from the outside** : desde afuera, desde fuera

outside[4] *prep* : fuera de, afuera de <outside my window : fuera de mi ventana> <outside regular hours : fuera del horario normal> <outside the law : afuera de la ley>

outside of *prep* **1** → **outside**[4] **2** → **besides**[2]

outsider [,aʊtˈsaɪdər] *n* : forastero *m,* -ra *f*

outskirts [ˈaʊt,skərts] *npl* : afueras *fpl,* alrededores *mpl*

outsmart [,aʊtˈsmɑrt] → **outwit**

outspoken [,aʊtˈspoːkən] *adj* : franco, directo

outstanding [,aʊtˈstændɪŋ] *adj* **1** UNPAID : pendiente **2** NOTABLE : destacado, notable, excepcional, sobresaliente

outstandingly [,aʊtˈstændɪŋli] *adv* : excepcionalmente

outstrip [,aʊtˈstrɪp] *vt* **-stripped** *or* **-stript** [-ˈstrɪpt]; **-stripping 1** : aventajar, dejar atrás <he outstripped the other runners : aventajó a los otros corredores> **2** SURPASS : aventajar, sobrepasar

outward[1] [ˈaʊtwərd] *or* **outwards** [-wərdz] *adv* : hacia afuera, hacia el exterior

outward[2] *adj* **1** : hacia afuera <an outward flow : un flujo hacia afuera> **2** : externo, external <outward beauty : belleza externa>

outwardly [ˈaʊtwərdli] *adv* **1** EXTERNALLY : externalmente **2** APPARENTLY : aparentemente <outwardly friendly : aparentemente simpático>
outwit [ˌaʊtˈwɪt] *vt* **-witted; -witting** : ser más listo que
ova → **ovum**
oval[1] [ˈoːvəl] *adj* : ovalado, oval
oval[2] *n* : óvalo *m*
ovary [ˈoːvəri] *n, pl* **-ries** : ovario *m*
ovation [oˈveɪʃən] *n* : ovación *f*
oven [ˈʌvən] *n* : horno *m*
over[1] [ˈoːvər] *adv* **1** (*indicating movement across*) <he flew over to London : voló a Londres> <come on over! : ¡ven acá!> **2** (*indicating an additional amount*) <the show ran 10 minutes over : el espectáculo terminó 10 minutos de tarde> **3** ABOVE, OVERHEAD : por encima **4** AGAIN : otra vez, de nuevo <over and over : una y otra vez> <to start over : volver a empezar> **5 all over** EVERYWHERE : por todas partes **6 to fall over** : caerse **7 to turn over** : poner boca abajo, voltear
over[2] *adj* **1** HIGHER, UPPER : superior **2** REMAINING : sobrante, que sobra **3** ENDED : terminado, acabado <the work is over : el trabajo está terminado>
over[3] *prep* **1** ABOVE : encima de, arriba de, sobre <over the fireplace : encima de la chimenea> <the hawk flew over the hills : el halcón voló sobre los cerros> **2** : más de <over $50 : más de $50> **3** ALONG : por, sobre <to glide over the ice : deslizarse sobre el hielo> **4** (*indicating motion through a place or thing*) <they showed me over the house : me mostraron la casa> **5** ACROSS : por encima de, sobre <he jumped over the ditch : saltó por encima de la zanja> **6** UPON : sobre <a cape over my shoulders : una capa sobre los hombros> **7** ON : por <to speak over the telephone : hablar por teléfono> **8** DURING : en, durante <over the past 25 years : durante los últimos 25 años> **9** BECAUSE OF : por <they fought over the money : se pelearon por el dinero>
overabundance [ˌoːvərəˈbʌndəntk] *n* : superabundancia *f*
overabundant [ˌoːvərəˈbʌndənt] *adj* : superabundante
overactive [ˌoːvərˈæktɪv] *adj* : hiperactivo
overall [ˌoːvərˈɔl] *adj* : total, global, de conjunto
overalls [ˈoːvərˌɔlz] *npl* : overol *m*
overawe [ˌoːvərˈɔ] *vt* **-awed; -awing** : intimidar, impresionar
overbearing [ˌoːvərˈbærɪŋ] *adj* : dominante, imperioso, prepotente
overboard [ˈoːvərˌbord] *adv* : por la borda, al agua
overburden [ˌoːvərˈbərdən] *vt* : sobrecargar, agobiar
overcast [ˈoːvərˌkæst] *adj* CLOUDY : nublado
overcharge [ˌoːvərˈtʃɑrdʒ] *vt* **-charged; -charging** : cobrarle de más (a alguien)
overcoat [ˈoːvərˌkoːt] *n* : abrigo *m*
overcome [ˌoːvərˈkʌm] *v* **-came** [-ˈkeɪm]; **-come; -coming** *vt* **1** CONQUER : vencer, derrotar, superar **2** OVERWHELM : abrumar, agobiar — *vi* : vencer
overconfidence [ˌoːvərˈkɑnfədənts] *n* : exceso *m* de confianza
overconfident [ˌoːvərˈkɑnfədənt] *adj* : demasiado confiado
overcook [ˌoːvərˈkʊk] *vt* : recocer, cocer demasiado
overcrowded [ˌoːvərˈkraʊdəd] *adj* **1** PACKED : abarrotado, atestado de gente **2** OVERPOPULATED : superpoblado
overdo [ˌoːvərˈduː] *vt* **-did** [-ˈdɪd]; **-done** [-ˈdʌn]; **-doing; -does** [-ˈdʌz] **1** : hacer demasiado **2** EXAGGERATE : exagerar **3** OVERCOOK : recocer
overdose [ˈoːvərˌdoːs] *n* : sobredosis *f*
overdraft [ˈoːvərˌdræft] *n* : sobregiro *m*, descubierto *m*
overdraw [ˌoːvərˈdrɔ] *vt* **-drew** [-ˈdruː]; **-drawn** [-ˈdrɔn]; **-drawing 1** : sobregirar <my account is overdrawn : tengo la cuenta en descubierto> **2** EXAGGERATE : exagerar
overdue [ˌoːvərˈduː] *adj* **1** UNPAID : vencido y sin pagar **2** TARDY : de retraso, tardío
overeat [ˌoːvərˈiːt] *vi* **-ate** [-ˈeɪt]; **-eaten** [-ˈiːtən]; **-eating** : comer demasiado
overelaborate [ˌoːvərɪˈlæbərət] *adj* : recargado
overestimate [ˌoːvərˈɛstəˌmeɪt] *vt* **-mated; -mating** : sobreestimar
overexcited [ˌoːvərɪkˈsaɪtəd] *adj* : sobreexcitado
overexpose [ˌoːvərɪkˈspoːz] *vt* **-posed; -posing** : sobreexponer
overfeed [ˌoːvərˈfiːd] *vt* **-fed** [-ˈfɛd]; **-feeding** : sobrealimentar
overflow[1] [ˌoːvərˈfloː] *vt* **1** : desbordar **2** INUNDATE : inundar — *vi* : desbordarse, rebosar
overflow[2] [ˈoːvərˌfloː] *n* **1** : derrame *m*, desbordamiento *m* (de un río) **2** SURPLUS : exceso *m*, excedente *m*
overfly [ˌoːvərˈflaɪ] *vt* **-flew** [-ˈfluː]; **-flown** [-ˈfloːn]; **-flying** : sobrevolar
overgrown [ˌoːvərˈgroːn] *adj* **1** : cubierto <overgrown with weeds : cubierto de malas hierbas> **2** : demasiado grande
overhand[1] [ˈoːvərˌhænd] *adv* : por encima de la cabeza
overhand[2] *adj* : por lo alto (tirada)
overhang[1] [ˌoːvərˈhæŋ] *v* **-hung** [-ˈhʌŋ]; **-hanging** *vt* **1** : sobresalir por encima de **2** THREATEN : amenazar — *vi* : sobresalir
overhang[2] [ˈoːvərˌhæŋ] *n* : saliente *mf*

overhaul [ˌoːvərˈhɔl] *vt* **1 :** revisar <to overhaul an engine : revisar un motor> **2** OVERTAKE : adelantar
overhead[1] [ˌoːvərˈhɛd] *adv* : por encima, arriba, por lo alto
overhead[2] [ˈoːvərˌhɛd] *adj* : de arriba
overhead[3] [ˈoːvərˌhɛd] *n* : gastos *mpl* generales
overhear [ˌoːvərˈhɪr] *vt* **-heard; -hearing :** oír por casualidad
overheat [ˌoːvərˈhiːt] *vt* : recalentar, sobrecalentar, calentar demasiado
overjoyed [ˌoːvərˈdʒɔɪd] *adj* : rebosante de alegría
overkill [ˈoːvərˌkɪl] *n* : exceso *m,* excedente *m*
overland[1] [ˈoːvərˌlænd, -lənd] *adv* : por tierra
overland[2] *adj* : terrestre, por tierra
overlap[1] [ˌoːvərˈlæp] *v* **-lapped; -lapping** *vt* : traslapar — *vi* : traslaparse, solaparse
overlap[2] [ˈoːvərˌlæp] *n* : traslapo *m*
overlay[1] [ˌoːvərˈleɪ] *vt* **-laid** [-ˈleɪd]; **-laying :** recubrir, revestir
overlay[2] [ˈoːvərˌleɪ] *n* : revestimiento *m*
overload [ˌoːvərˈloːd] *vt* : sobrecargar
overlong [ˌoːvərˈlɔŋ] *adj* : excesivamente largo, largo y pesado
overlook [ˌoːvərˈlʊk] *vt* **1** INSPECT : inspeccionar, revisar **2 :** tener vista a, dar a <a house overlooking the valley : una casa que tiene vista al valle> **3** MISS : pasar por alto **4** EXCUSE : dejar pasar, disculpar
overly [ˈoːvərli] *adv* : demasiado
overnight[1] [ˌoːvərˈnaɪt] *adv* **1 :** por la noche, durante la noche **2 :** de la noche a la mañana <we can't do it overnight : no podemos hacerlo de la noche a la mañana>
overnight[2] [ˈoːvərˈnaɪt] *adj* **1 :** de noche <an overnight stay : una estancia de una noche> <an overnight bag : una bolsa de viaje> **2** SUDDEN : repentino
overpass [ˈoːvərˌpæs] *n* : paso *m* elevado, paso *m* a desnivel *Mex*
overpopulated [ˌoːvərˈpɑpjəˌleɪṱəd] *adj* : sobrepoblado
overpower [ˌoːvərˈpaʊər] *vt* **1** CONQUER, SUBDUE : vencer, superar **2** OVERWHELM : abrumar, agobiar <overpowered by the heat : sofocado por el calor>
overpraise [ˌoːvərˈpreɪz] *vt* **-praised; -praising :** adular
overrate [ˌoːvərˈreɪt] *vt* **-rated; -rating :** sobrevalorar, sobrevaluar
override [ˌoːvərˈraɪd] *vt* **-rode** [-ˈroːd]; **-ridden** [-ˈrɪdən]; **-riding 1 :** predominar sobre, contar más que <hunger overrode our manners : el hambre predominó sobre los modales> **2** ANNUL : anular, invalidar <to override a veto : anular un veto>
overrule [ˌoːvərˈruːl] *vt* **-ruled; -ruling :** anular (una decisión), desautorizar (una persona), denegar (un pedido)
overrun [ˌoːvərˈrʌn] *v* **-ran** [-ˈræn]; **-running** *vt* **1** INVADE : invadir **2** INFEST : infestar, plagar **3** EXCEED : exceder, rebasar — *vi* : rebasar el tiempo previsto
overseas[1] [ˌoːvərˈsiːz] *adv* : en el extranjero <to travel overseas : viajar al extranjero>
overseas[2] [ˈoːvərˌsiːz] *adj* : extranjero, exterior
oversee [ˌoːvərˈsiː] *vt* **-saw** [-ˈsɔ]; **-seen** [-ˈsiːn]; **-seeing** SUPERVISE : supervisar
overseer [ˈoːvərˌsiːər] *n* : supervisor *m,* -sora *f;* capataz *mf*
overshadow [ˌoːvərˈʃæˌdoː] *vt* **1** DARKEN : oscurecer, ensombrecer **2** ECLIPSE, OUTSHINE : eclipsar
overshoe [ˈoːvərˌʃuː] *n* : chanclo *m*
overshoot [ˌoːvərˈʃuːt] *vt* **-shot** [-ˈʃɑt]; **-shooting :** pasarse de <to overshoot the mark : pasarse de la raya>
oversight [ˈoːvərˌsaɪt] *n* : descuido *m,* inadvertencia *f*
oversleep [ˌoːvərˈsliːp] *vi* **-slept** [-ˈslɛpt]; **-sleeping :** no despertarse a tiempo, quedarse dormido
overspread [ˌoːvərˈsprɛd] *vt* **-spread; -spreading :** extenderse sobre
overstaffed [ˌoːvərˈstæft] *adj* : con exceso de personal
overstate [ˌoːvərˈsteɪt] *vt* **-stated; -stating** EXAGGERATE : exagerar
overstatement [ˌoːvərˈsteɪtmənt] *n* : exageración *f*
overstep [ˌoːvərˈstɛp] *vt* **-stepped; -stepping** EXCEED : sobrepasar, traspasar, exceder
overt [oˈvərt, ˈoːˌvərt] *adj* : evidente, manifiesto, patente
overtake [ˌoːvərˈteɪk] *vt* **-took** [-ˈtʊk]; **-taken** [-ˈteɪkən]; **-taking :** pasar, adelantar, rebasar *Mex*
overthrow[1] [ˌoːvərˈθroː] *vt* **-threw** [-ˈθruː]; **-thrown** [-ˈθroːn]; **-throwing 1** OVERTURN : dar la vuelta a, volcar **2** DEFEAT, TOPPLE : derrocar, derribar, deponer
overthrow[2] [ˈoːvərˌθroː] *n* : derrocamiento *m,* caída *f*
overtime [ˈoːvərˌtaɪm] *n* **1 :** horas *fpl* extras (de trabajo) **2 :** prórroga *f* (en deportes)
overtly [oˈvərtli, ˈoːˌvərt-] *adv* OPENLY : abiertamente
overtone [ˈoːvərˌtoːn] *n* **1 :** armónico *m* (en música) **2** HINT, SUGGESTION : tinte *m,* insinuación *f*
overture [ˈoːvərˌtʃʊr, -tʃər] *n* **1** PROPOSAL : propuesta *f* **2 :** obertura *f* (en música)
overturn [ˌoːvərˈtərn] *vt* **1** UPSET : dar la vuelta a, volcar **2** NULLIFY : anular, invalidar — *vi* TURN OVER : volcar, dar un vuelco

overuse [ˌoːvərˈjuːz] *vt* **-used; -using** : abusar de

overview [ˈoːvərˌvjuː] *n* : resumen *m,* visión *f* general

overweening [ˌoːvərˈwiːnɪŋ] *adj* **1** ARROGANT : arrogante, soberbio **2** IMMODERATE : desmesurado

overweight [ˌoːvərˈweɪt] *adj* : demasiado gordo, demasiado pesado

overwhelm [ˌoːvərˈ*h*wɛlm] *vt* **1** CRUSH, DEFEAT : aplastar, arrollar **2** SUBMERGE : inundar, sumergir **3** OVERPOWER : abrumar, agobiar <overwhelmed by remorse : abrumado de remordimiento>

overwhelming [ˌoːvərˈ*h*wɛlmɪŋ] *adj* **1** CRUSHING : abrumador, apabullante **2** SWEEPING : arrollador, aplastante <an overwhelming majority : una mayoría aplastante>

overwork [ˌoːvərˈwərk] *vt* **1** : hacer trabajar demasiado **2** OVERUSE : abusar de — *vi* : trabajar demasiado

overwrought [ˌoːvərˈrɔt] *adj* : alterado, sobreexcitado

ovoid [ˈoːˌvɔɪd] *or* **ovoidal** [oˈvɔɪdəl] *adj* : ovoide

ovulate [ˈɑvjəˌleɪt, ˈoː-] *vi* **-lated; -lating** : ovular

ovulation [ˌɑvjəˈleɪʃən, ˌoː-] *n* : ovulación *f*

ovum [ˈoːvəm] *n, pl* **ova** [-və] : óvulo *m*

owe [ˈoː] *vt* **owed; owing** : deber <you owe me $10 : me debes $10> <he owes his wealth to his father : le debe su riqueza a su padre>

owing to *prep* : debido a

owl [ˈaʊl] *n* : búho *m,* lechuza *f,* tecolote *m Mex*

own[1] *v* [ˈoːn] *vt* **1** POSSESS : poseer, tener, ser dueño de **2** ADMIT : reconocer, admitir — *vi* **to own up** : reconocer (algo), admitir (algo)

own[2] *adj* : propio, personal, particular <his own car : su propio coche>

own[3] *pron* **my** (**your, his/her, our, their**) **own** : el mío, la mía; el tuyo, la tuya; el suyo, la suya; el nuestro, la nuestra <to each his own : cada uno a lo suyo> <money of my own : mi propio dinero> <to be on one's own : estar solo>

owner [ˈoːnər] *n* : dueño *m,* -ña *f;* propietario *m,* -ria *f*

ownership [ˈoːnərˌʃɪp] *n* : propiedad *f*

ox [ˈɑks] *n, pl* **oxen** [ˈɑksən] : buey *m*

oxidation [ˌɑksəˈdeɪʃən] *n* : oxidación *f*

oxide [ˈɑkˌsaɪd] *n* : óxido *m*

oxidize [ˈɑksəˌdaɪz] *vt* **-dized; -dizing** : oxidar

oxygen [ˈɑksɪdʒən] *n* : oxígeno *m*

oyster [ˈɔɪstər] *n* : ostra *f,* ostión *m Mex*

ozone [ˈoːˌzoːn] *n* : ozono *m*

P

p [ˈpiː] *n, pl* **p's** *or* **ps** [ˈpiːz] : decimosexta letra del alfabeto inglés

pace[1] [ˈpeɪs] *v* **paced; pacing** *vi* : caminar, ir y venir — *vt* **1** : caminar por <she paced the floor : caminaba de un lado a otro del cuarto> **2 to pace a runner** : marcarle el ritmo a un corredor

pace[2] *n* **1** STEP : paso *m* **2** RATE : paso *m,* ritmo *m* <to set the pace : marcar el paso, marcar la pauta>

pacemaker [ˈpeɪsˌmeɪkər] *n* : marcapasos *m*

pacific [pəˈsɪfɪk] *adj* : pacífico

pacifier [ˈpæsəˌfaɪər] *n* : chupete *m,* chupón *m,* mamila *f Mex*

pacifism [ˈpæsəˌfɪzəm] *n* : pacifismo *m*

pacifist [ˈpæsəfɪst] *n* : pacifista *mf*

pacify [ˈpæsəˌfaɪ] *vt* **-fied; -fying 1** SOOTHE : apaciguar, pacificar **2** : pacificar (un país, una región, etc.)

pack[1] [ˈpæk] *vt* **1** PACKAGE : empaquetar, embalar, envasar **2** : empacar, meter (en una maleta) <to pack one's bag : hacer la maleta> **3** FILL : llenar, abarrotar <a packed theater : un teatro abarrotado> **4 to pack off** SEND : mandar — *vi* : empacar, hacer las maletas

pack[2] *n* **1** BUNDLE : bulto *m,* fardo *m* **2** BACKPACK : mochila *f* **3** PACKAGE : paquete *m,* cajetilla *f* (de cigarillos, etc.) **4** : manada *f* (de lobos, etc.), jauría *f* (de perros) <a pack of thieves : una pandilla de ladrones>

package[1] [ˈpækɪdʒ] *vt* **-aged; -aging** : empaquetar, embalar

package[2] *n* : paquete *m,* bulto *m*

packer [ˈpækər] *n* : empacador *m,* -dora *f*

packet [ˈpækət] *n* : paquete *m*

pact [ˈpækt] *n* : pacto *m,* acuerdo *m*

pad[1] [ˈpæd] *vt* **padded; padding 1** FILL, STUFF : rellenar, acolchar (una silla, una pared) **2** : meter paja en, rellenar <to pad a speech : rellenar un discurso>

pad[2] *n* **1** CUSHION : almohadilla *f* <a shoulder pad : una hombrera> **2** TABLET : bloc *m* (de papel) **3** *or* **lily pad** : hoja *f* grande (de un nenúfar) **4 ink pad** : tampón *m* **5 launching pad** : plataforma *f* (de lanzamiento)

padding [ˈpædɪŋ] *n* **1** FILLING : relleno *m* **2** : paja *f* (en un discurso, etc.)

paddle[1] [ˈpædəl] *v* **-dled; -dling** *vt* **1** : hacer avanzar (una canoa) con canalete **2** HIT : azotar, darle nalgadas a (con una pala o paleta) — *vi* **1** : remar (en una canoa) **2** SPLASH : chapotear, mojarse los pies

paddle[2] *n* **1 :** canalete *m,* zagual *m* (de una canoa, etc.) **2 :** pala *f,* paleta *f* (en deportes)

paddock [ˈpædək] *n* **1** PASTURE **:** potrero *m* **2 :** paddock *m,* cercado *m* (en un hipódromo)

paddy [ˈpædi] *n, pl* **-dies :** arrozal *m*

padlock[1] [ˈpædˌlɑk] *vt* **:** cerrar con candado

padlock[2] *n* **:** candado *m*

pagan[1] [ˈpeɪgən] *adj* **:** pagano

pagan[2] *n* **:** pagano *m,* -na *f*

paganism [ˈpeɪgənˌɪzəm] *n* **:** paganismo *m*

page[1] [ˈpeɪdʒ] *vt* **paged; paging :** llamar por altavoz

page[2] *n* **1** BELLHOP **:** botones *m* **2 :** página *f* (de un libro, etc.)

pageant [ˈpædʒənt] *n* **1** SPECTACLE **:** espectáculo *m* **2** PROCESSION **:** desfile *m*

pageantry [ˈpædʒəntri] *n* **:** pompa *f,* fausto *m*

pagoda [pəˈgoːdə] *n* **:** pagoda *f*

paid → **pay**

pail [ˈpeɪl] *n* **:** balde *m,* cubo *m,* cubeta *f Mex*

pailful [ˈpeɪlˌfʊl] *n* **:** balde *m,* cubo *m,* cubeta *f Mex*

pain[1] [ˈpeɪn] *vt* **:** doler

pain[2] *n* **1** PENALTY **:** pena *f* <under pain of death **:** so pena de muerte> **2** SUFFERING **:** dolor *m,* malestar *m,* pena *f* (mental) **3 pains** *npl* EFFORT **:** esmero *m,* esfuerzo *m* <to take pains **:** esmerarse>

painful [ˈpeɪnfəl] *adj* **:** doloroso — **painfully** *adv*

painkiller [ˈpeɪnˌkɪlər] *n* **:** analgésico *m*

painless [ˈpeɪnləs] *adj* **:** indoloro, sin dolor

painlessly [ˈpeɪnləsli] *adv* **:** sin dolor

painstaking [ˈpeɪnˌsteɪkɪŋ] *adj* **:** esmerado, cuidadoso, meticuloso — **painstakingly** *adv*

paint[1] [ˈpeɪnt] *v* **:** pintar

paint[2] *n* **:** pintura *f*

paintbrush [ˈpeɪntˌbrʌʃ] *n* **:** pincel *m* (de un artista), brocha *f* (para pintar casas, etc.)

painter [ˈpeɪntər] *n* **:** pintor *m,* -tora *f*

painting [ˈpeɪntɪŋ] *n* **:** pintura *f*

pair[1] [ˈpær] *vt* **:** emparejar, poner en parejas — *vi* **:** emparejarse

pair[2] *n* **:** par *m* (de objetos), pareja *f* (de personas o animales) <a pair of scissors **:** unas tijeras>

pajamas [pəˈdʒɑməz, -ˈdʒæ-] *npl* **:** pijama *m,* piyama *mf*

Pakistani [ˌpækɪˈstæni, ˌpɑkɪˈstɑni] *n* **:** paquistaní *mf* — **Pakistani** *adj*

pal [ˈpæl] *n* **:** amigo *m,* -ga *f;* compinche *mf fam;* chamo *m,* -ma *f Ven fam;* cuate *m,* -ta *f Mex*

palace [ˈpæləs] *n* **:** palacio *m*

palatable [ˈpælət̬əbəl] *adj* **:** sabroso

palate [ˈpælət] *n* **1 :** paladar *m* (de la boca) **2** TASTE **:** paladar *m,* gusto *m*

palatial [pəˈleɪʃəl] *adj* **:** suntuoso, espléndido

palaver [pəˈlævər, -ˈlɑ-] *n* **:** palabrería *f*

pale[1] [ˈpeɪl] *v* **paled; paling** *vi* **:** palidecer — *vt* **:** hacer pálido

pale[2] *adj* **paler; palest 1 :** pálido <to turn pale **:** palidecer, ponerse pálido> **2 :** claro (dícese de los colores)

paleness [ˈpeɪlnəs] *n* **:** palidez *f*

Palestinian [ˌpæləˈstɪniən] *n* **:** palestino *m,* -na *f* — **Palestinian** *adj*

palette [ˈpælət] *n* **:** paleta *f* (para mezclar pigmentos)

palisade [ˌpæləˈseɪd] *n* **1** FENCE **:** empalizada *f,* estacada *f* **2** CLIFFS **:** acantilado *m*

pall[1] [ˈpɔl] *vi* **:** perder su sabor, dejar de gustar

pall[2] *n* **1 :** paño *m* mortuario (sobre un ataúd) **2** COVER **:** cortina *f* (de humo, etc.) **3 to cast a pall over :** ensombrecer

pallbearer [ˈpɔlˌbɛrər] *n* **:** portador *m,* -dora *f* del féretro

pallet [ˈpælət] *n* **1** BED **:** camastro *m* **2** PLATFORM **:** plataforma *f* de carga

palliative [ˈpæliˌeɪt̬ɪv, ˈpæljət̬ɪv] *adj* **:** paliativo

pallid [ˈpæləd] *adj* **:** pálido

pallor [ˈpælər] *n* **:** palidez *f*

palm[1] [ˈpɑm, ˈpɑlm] *vt* **1** CONCEAL **:** escamotear (un naipe, etc.) **2 to palm off :** encajar, endilgar *fam* <he palmed it off on me **:** me lo endilgó>

palm[2] *n* **1** *or* **palm tree :** palmera *f* **2 :** palma *f* (de la mano)

Palm Sunday *n* **:** Domingo *m* de Ramos

palomino [ˌpæləˈmiːˌnoː] *n, pl* **-nos :** caballo *m* de color dorado

palpable [ˈpælpəbəl] *adj* **:** palpable — **palpably** [-bli] *adv*

palpitate [ˈpælpəˌteɪt] *vi* **-tated; -tating :** palpitar

palpitation [ˌpælpəˈteɪʃən] *n* **:** palpitación *f*

palsy [ˈpɔlzi] *n, pl* **-sies 1 :** parálisis *f* **2** → **cerebral palsy**

paltry [ˈpɔltri] *adj* **-trier; -est :** mísero, mezquino, insignificante <a paltry excuse **:** una mala excusa>

pampas [ˈpæmpəz, ˈpɑmpəs] *npl* **:** pampa *f*

pamper [ˈpæmpər] *vt* **:** mimar, consentir, chiquear *Mex*

pamphlet [ˈpæmpflət] *n* **:** panfleto *m,* folleto *m*

pan[1] [ˈpæn] *vt* **panned; panning** CRITICIZE **:** poner por los suelos — *vi* **to pan for gold :** cribar el oro con batea, lavar oro

pan[2] *n* **1 :** cacerola *f,* cazuela *f* **2 frying pan :** sartén *mf,* freidera *f Mex*

panacea [ˌpænəˈsiːə] *n* **:** panacea *f*

Panamanian [ˌpænəˈmeɪniən] *n* **:** panameño *m,* -ña *f* — **Panamanian** *adj*

pancake [ˈpænˌkeɪk] *n* **:** panqueque *m*

pancreas [ˈpæŋkriəs, ˈpæn-] *n* : páncreas *m*
panda [ˈpændə] *n* : panda *mf*
pandemonium [ˌpændəˈmoːniəm] *n* : pandemonio *m,* pandemónium *m*
pander [ˈpændər] *vi* **to pander to** : satisfacer, complacer (a alguien) <to pander to popular taste : satisfacer el gusto popular>
pane [ˈpeɪn] *n* : cristal *m,* vidrio *m*
panel[1] [ˈpænəl] *vt* **-eled** *or* **-elled; -eling** *or* **-elling** : adornar con paneles
panel[2] *n* **1** : lista *f* de nombres (de un jurado, etc.) **2** GROUP : panel *m,* grupo *m* <discussion panel : panel de discusión> **3** : panel *m* (de una pared, etc.) **4 instrument panel** : tablero *m* de instrumentos
paneling [ˈpænəlɪŋ] *n* : paneles *mpl*
pang [ˈpæŋ] *n* : puntada *f,* punzada *f*
panic[1] [ˈpænɪk] *v* **-icked; -icking** *vt* : llenar de pánico — *vi* : ser presa de pánico
panic[2] *n* : pánico *m*
panicky [ˈpænɪki] *adj* : presa de pánico
panorama [ˌpænəˈræmə, -ˈrɑ-] *n* : panorama *m*
panoramic [ˌpænəˈræmɪk, -ˈrɑ-] *adj* : panorámico
pansy [ˈpænzi] *n, pl* **-sies** : pensamiento *m*
pant[1] [ˈpænt] *vi* : jadear, resoplar
pant[2] *n* : jadeo *m,* resoplo *m*
pantaloons [ˌpæntəˈluːnz] → **pants**
panther [ˈpænθər] *n* : pantera *f*
panties [ˈpæntiz] *npl* : calzones *mpl,* pantaletas *fpl*
pantomime[1] [ˈpæntəˌmaɪm] *v* **-mimed; -miming** *vt* : representar mediante la pantomima — *vi* : hacer la mímica
pantomime[2] *n* : pantomima *f*
pantry [ˈpæntri] *n, pl* **-tries** : despensa *f*
pants [ˈpænts] *npl* **1** TROUSERS : pantalón *m,* pantalones *mpl* **2** → **panties**
pap [ˈpæp] *n* : papilla *f* (para bebés, etc.)
papal [ˈpeɪpəl] *adj* : papal
papaya [pəˈpaɪə] *n* : papaya *f* (fruta)
paper[1] [ˈpeɪpər] *vt* WALLPAPER : empapelar
paper[2] *adj* : de papel
paper[3] *n* **1** : papel *m* <a piece of paper : un papel> **2** DOCUMENT : papel *m,* documento *m* **3** NEWSPAPER : periódico *m,* diario *m*
paperback [ˈpeɪpərˌbæk] *n* : libro *m* en rústica
paper clip *n* : clip *m,* sujetapapeles *m*
paperweight [ˈpeɪpərˌweɪt] *n* : pisapapeles *m*
papery [ˈpeɪpəri] *adj* : parecido al papel
papier-mâché [ˌpeɪpərməˈʃeɪ, ˌpæˌpjeɪmæˈʃeɪ] *n* : papel *m* maché
papoose [pæˈpuːs, pə-] *n* : niño *m,* -ña *f* de los indios norteamericanos
paprika [pəˈpriːkə, pæ-] *n* : pimentón *m,* paprika *f*
papyrus [pəˈpaɪrəs] *n, pl* **-ruses** *or* **-ri** [-ri, -ˌraɪ] : papiro *m*
par [ˈpɑr] *n* **1** VALUE : valor *m* (nominal), par *f* <below par : debajo de la par> **2** EQUALITY : igualdad *f* <to be on a par with : estar al mismo nivel que> **3** : par *m* (en golf)
parable [ˈpærəbəl] *n* : parábola *f*
parachute[1] [ˈpærəˌʃuːt] *vi* **-chuted; -chuting** : lanzarse en paracaídas
parachute[2] *n* : paracaídas *m*
parachutist [ˈpærəˌʃuːtɪst] *n* : paracaidista *mf*
parade[1] [pəˈreɪd] *vi* **-raded; -rading 1** MARCH : desfilar **2** SHOW OFF : pavonearse, lucirse
parade[2] *n* **1** PROCESSION : desfile *m* **2** DISPLAY : alarde *m*
paradigm [ˈpærəˌdaɪm] *n* : paradigma *m*
paradise [ˈpærəˌdaɪs, -ˌdaɪz] *n* : paraíso *m*
paradox [ˈpærəˌdɑks] *n* : paradoja *f*
paradoxical [ˌpærəˈdɑksɪkəl] *adj* : paradójico — **paradoxically** *adv*
paraffin [ˈpærəfən] *n* : parafina *f*
paragraph[1] [ˈpærəˌgræf] *vt* : dividir en párrafos
paragraph[2] *n* : párrafo *m,* acápite *m*
Paraguayan [ˌpærəˈgwaɪən, -ˈgweɪ-] *n* : paraguayo *m,* -ya *f* — **Paraguayan** *adj*
parakeet [ˈpærəˌkiːt] *n* : periquito *m*
parallel[1] [ˈpærəˌlɛl, -ləl] *vt* **1** MATCH, RESEMBLE : ser paralelo a, ser análogo a, corresponder con **2** : extenderse en línea paralela con <the road parallels the river : el camino se extiende a lo largo del río>
parallel[2] *adj* : paralelo
parallel[3] *n* **1** : línea *f* paralela, superficie *f* paralela **2** : paralelo *m* (en geografía) **3** SIMILARITY : paralelismo *m,* semejanza *f*
parallelogram [ˌpærəˈlɛləˌgræm] *n* : paralelogramo *m*
paralysis [pəˈræləsɪs] *n, pl* **-yses** [-ˌsiːz] : parálisis *f*
paralyze [ˈpærəˌlaɪz] *vt* **-lyzed; -lyzing** : paralizar
parameter [pəˈræmətər] *n* : parámetro *m*
paramount [ˈpærəˌmaʊnt] *adj* : supremo <of paramount importance : de suma importancia>
paranoia [ˌpærəˈnɔɪə] *n* : paranoia *f*
paranoid [ˈpærəˌnɔɪd] *adj* : paranoico
parapet [ˈpærəpət, -ˌpɛt] *n* : parapeto *m*
paraphernalia [ˌpærəfəˈneɪljə, -fər-] *ns & pl* : parafernalia *f*
paraphrase[1] [ˈpærəˌfreɪz] *vt* **-phrased; -phrasing** : parafrasear
paraphrase[2] *n* : paráfrasis *f*
paraplegic[1] [ˌpærəˈpliːdʒɪk] *adj* : parapléjico
paraplegic[2] *n* : parapléjico *m,* -ca *f*

parasite ['pærəˌsaɪt] *n* : parásito *m*

parasitic [ˌpærə'sɪt̬ɪk] *adj* : parasitario

parasol ['pærəˌsɔl] *n* : sombrilla *f,* quitasol *m,* parasol *m*

paratrooper ['pærəˌtru:pər] *n* : paracaidista *mf* (militar)

parboil ['parˌbɔɪl] *vt* : sancochar, cocer a medias

parcel[1] ['parsəl] *vt* **-celed** *or* **-celled; -celing** *or* **-celling** *or* **to parcel out** : repartir, parcelar (tierras)

parcel[2] *n* **1** LOT : parcela *f,* lote *m* **2** PACKAGE : paquete *m,* bulto *m*

parch ['partʃ] *vt* : resecar

parchment ['partʃmənt] *n* : pergamino *m*

pardon[1] ['pardən] *vt* **1** FORGIVE : perdonar, disculpar <pardon me! : ¡perdone!, ¡disculpe la molestia!> **2** REPRIEVE : indultar (a un delincuente)

pardon[2] *n* **1** FORGIVENESS : perdón *m* **2** REPRIEVE : indulto *m*

pardonable ['pardənəbəl] *adj* : perdonable, disculpable

pare ['pær] *vt* **pared; paring 1** PEEL : pelar **2** TRIM : recortar **3** REDUCE : reducir <he pared it (down) to 50 pages : lo redujo a 50 páginas>

parent ['pærənt] *n* **1** : madre *f,* padre *m* **2 parents** *npl* : padres *mpl*

parentage ['pærəntɪdʒ] *n* : linaje *m,* abolengo *m,* origen *m*

parental [pə'rɛntəl] *adj* : de los padres

parenthesis [pə'rɛnθəsɪs] *n, pl* **-theses** [-ˌsi:z] : paréntesis *m*

parenthetic [ˌpærən'θɛt̬ɪk] *or* **parenthetical** [-t̬ɪkəl] *adj* : parentético — **parenthetically** [-t̬ɪkli] *adv*

parenthood ['pærəntˌhʊd] *n* : paternidad *f*

parfait [par'feɪ] *n* : postre *m* elaborado con frutas y helado

pariah [pə'raɪə] *n* : paria *mf*

parish ['pærɪʃ] *n* : parroquia *f*

parishioner [pə'rɪʃənər] *n* : feligrés *m,* -gresa *f*

parity ['pærət̬i] *n, pl* **-ties** : paridad *f*

park[1] ['park] *vt* : estacionar, parquear, aparcar *Spain* — *vi* : estacionarse, parquearse, aparcar *Spain*

park[2] *n* : parque *m*

parka ['parkə] *n* : parka *f*

parkway ['parkˌweɪ] *n* : carretera *f* ajardinada, bulevar *m*

parley[1] ['parli] *vi* : parlamentar, negociar

parley[2] *n, pl* **-leys** : negociación *f,* parlamento *m*

parliament ['parləmənt, 'parljə-] *n* : parlamento *m*

parliamentary [ˌparlə'mɛntəri, ˌparljə-] *adj* : parlamentario

parlor ['parlər] *n* **1** : sala *f,* salón *m* (en una casa) **2** : salón *m* <beauty parlor : salón de belleza> **3 funeral parlor** : funeraria *f*

parochial [pə'ro:kiəl] *adj* **1** : parroquial **2** PROVINCIAL : pueblerino, de miras estrechas

parody[1] ['pærədi] *vt* **-died; -dying** : parodiar

parody[2] *n, pl* **-dies** : parodia *f*

parole [pə'ro:l] *n* : libertad *f* condicional

paroxysm ['pærəkˌsɪzəm, pə'rak-] *n* : paroxismo *m*

parquet ['parˌkeɪ, par'keɪ] *n* : parquet *m,* parqué *m*

parrakeet → **parakeet**

parrot ['pærət] *n* : loro *m,* papagayo *m*

parry[1] ['pæri] *v* **-ried; -rying** *vi* : parar un golpe — *vt* EVADE : esquivar (una pregunta, etc.)

parry[2] *n, pl* **-ries** : parada *f*

parsimonious [ˌparsə'mo:niəs] *adj* : tacaño, mezquino

parsley ['parsli] *n* : perejil *m*

parsnip ['parsnɪp] *n* : chirivía *f*

parson ['parsən] *n* : pastor *m,* -tora *f;* clérigo *m*

parsonage ['parsənɪdʒ] *n* : rectoría *f,* casa *f* del párroco

part[1] ['part] *vi* **1** SEPARATE : separarse, despedirse <we should part as friends : debemos separarnos amistosamente> **2** OPEN : abrirse <the curtains parted : las cortinas se abrieron> **3 to part with** : dehacerse de — *vt* **1** SEPARATE : separar **2 to part one's hair** : hacerse la raya, peinarse con raya

part[2] *n* **1** SECTION, SEGMENT : parte *f,* sección *f* **2** PIECE : pieza *f* (de una máquina, etc.) **3** ROLE : papel *m* **4** : raya *f* (del pelo)

partake [par'teɪk, pər-] *vi* **-took** [-'tʊk]; **-taken** [-'teɪkən]; **-taking 1 to partake of** CONSUME : comer, beber, tomar **2 to partake in** : participar en (una actividad, etc.)

partial ['parʃəl] *adj* **1** BIASED : parcial, tendencioso **2** INCOMPLETE : parcial, incompleto **3 to be partial to** : ser aficionado a

partiality [ˌparʃi'ælət̬i] *n, pl* **-ties** : parcialidad *f*

partially ['parʃəli] *adv* : parcialmente

participant [pər'tɪsəpənt, par-] *n* : participante *mf*

participate [pər'tɪsəˌpeɪt, par-] *vi* **-pated; -pating** : participar

participation [pərˌtɪsə'peɪʃən, par-] *n* : participación *f*

participle ['part̬əˌsɪpəl] *n* : participio *m*

particle ['part̬ɪkəl] *n* : partícula *f*

particular[1] [par'tɪkjələr] *adj* **1** SPECIFIC : particular, en particular <this particular person : esta persona en particular> **2** SPECIAL : particular, especial <with particular emphasis : con un énfasis especial> **3** FUSSY : exigente, maniático <to be very particular : ser muy especial> <I'm not particular : me da igual>

particular[2] *n* **1** DETAIL : detalle *m,* sentido *m* **2 in particular** : en particular, en especial

particularly [pɑr'tɪkjələrli] *adv* **1** ESPECIALLY : particularmente, especialmente **2** SPECIFICALLY : específicamente, en especial

partisan ['pɑrt̬əzən, -sən] *n* **1** ADHERENT : partidario *m,* -ria *f* **2** GUERRILLA : partisano *m,* -na *f;* guerrillero *m,* -ra *f*

partition[1] [pər'tɪʃən, pɑr-] *vt* : dividir <to partition off (a room) : dividir con un tabique>

partition[2] *n* **1** DISTRIBUTION : partición *f,* división *f,* reparto *m* **2** DIVIDER : tabique *m,* mampara *f,* biombo *m*

partly ['pɑrtli] *adv* : en parte, parcialmente

partner ['pɑrtnər] *n* **1** COMPANION : compañero *m,* -ra *f* **2** : pareja *f* (en un juego, etc.) <dancing partner : pareja de baile> **3** SPOUSE : cónyuge *mf* **4** *or* **business partner** : socio *m,* -cia *f;* asociado *m,* -da *f*

partnership ['pɑrtnər,ʃɪp] *n* **1** ASSOCIATION : asociación *f,* compañerismo *m* **2** : sociedad *f* (de negociantes) <to form a partnership : asociarse>

part of speech : categoría *f* gramatical

partridge ['pɑrtrɪdʒ] *n, pl* **-tridge** *or* **-tridges** : perdiz *f*

party ['pɑrti] *n, pl* **-ties 1** : partido *m* (político) **2** PARTICIPANT : parte *f,* participante *mf* **3** GROUP : grupo *m* (de personas) **4** GATHERING : fiesta *f* <to throw a party : dar una fiesta>

parvenu ['pɑrvə,nuː, -,njuː] *n* : advenedizo *m,* -za *f*

pass[1] ['pæs] *vi* **1** : pasar, cruzarse <a car passed by : pasó un coche> <we passed in the hallway : nos cruzamos en el pasillo> **2** CEASE : pasarse <the pain passed : se pasó el dolor> **3** ELAPSE : pasar, transcurrir **4** PROCEED : pasar <let me pass : déjame pasar> **5** HAPPEN : pasar, ocurrir **6** : pasar, aprobar (en un examen) **7** RULE : fallar <the jury passed on the case : el jurado falló en el caso> **8** *or* **to pass down** : pasar <the throne passed to his son : el trono pasó a su hijo> **9 to let pass** OVERLOOK : pasar por alto **10 to pass as** : pasar por **11 to pass away** *or* **to pass on** DIE : fallecer, morir — *vt* **1** : pasar por <they passed the house : pasaron por la casa> **2** OVERTAKE : pasar, adelantar **3** SPEND : pasar (tiempo) **4** HAND : pasar <pass me the salt : pásame la sal> **5** : aprobar (un examen, una ley)

pass[2] *n* **1** CROSSING, GAP : paso *m,* desfiladero *m,* puerto *m* <mountain pass : puerto de montaña> **2** PERMIT : pase *m,* permiso *m* **3** : pase *m* (en deportes) **4** SITUATION : situación *f* (difícil) <things have come to a pretty pass! : ¡hasta dónde hemos llegado!>

passable ['pæsəbəl] *adj* **1** ADEQUATE : adecuado, pasable **2** : transitable (dícese de un camino, etc.)

passably ['pæsəbli] *adv* : pasablemente

passage ['pæsɪdʒ] *n* **1** PASSING : paso *m* <the passage of time : el paso del tiempo> **2** PASSAGEWAY : pasillo *m* (dentro de un edificio), pasaje *m* (entre edificios) **3** VOYAGE : travesía *f* (por el mar), viaje *m* <to grant safe passage : dar un salvoconducto> **4** SECTION : pasaje *m* (en música o literatura)

passageway ['pæsɪdʒ,weɪ] *n* : pasillo *m,* pasadizo *m,* corredor *m*

passbook ['pæs,bʊk] *n* BANKBOOK : libreta *f* de ahorros

passé [pæ'seɪ] *adj* : pasado de moda

passenger ['pæsəndʒər] *n* : pasajero *m,* -ra *f*

passerby [,pæsər'baɪ, 'pæsər,-] *n, pl* **passersby** : transeúnte *mf*

passing ['pæsɪŋ] *n* DEATH : fallecimiento *m*

passion ['pæʃən] *n* : pasión *f,* ardor *m*

passionate ['pæʃənət] *adj* **1** IRASCIBLE : irascible, iracundo **2** ARDENT : apasionado, ardiente, ferviente, fogoso

passionately ['pæʃənətli] *adv* : apasionadamente, fervientemente, con pasión

passive[1] ['pæsɪv] *adj* : pasivo — **passively** *adv*

passive[2] *n* : voz *f* pasiva (en gramática)

Passover ['pæs,oːvər] *n* : Pascua *f* (en el judaísmo)

passport ['pæs,port] *n* : pasaporte *m*

password ['pæs,wərd] *n* : contraseña *f*

past[1] ['pæst] *adv* : por delante <he drove past : pasamos en coche>

past[2] *adj* **1** AGO : hace <10 years past : hace 10 años> **2** LAST : último <the past few months : los últimos meses> **3** BYGONE : pasado <in past times : en tiempos pasados> **4** : pasado (en gramática)

past[3] *n* : pasado *m*

past[4] *prep* **1** BY : por, por delante de <he ran past the house : pasó por la casa corriendo> **2** BEYOND : más allá de <just past the corner : un poco más allá de la esquina> <we went past the exit : pasamos la salida> **3** AFTER : despúes de <past noon : después del mediodía> <half past two : las dos y media>

pasta ['pɑstə, 'pæs-] *n* : pasta *f*

paste[1] ['peɪst] *vt* **pasted; pasting** : pegar (con engrudo)

paste[2] *n* **1** : pasta *f* <tomato paste : pasta de tomate> **2** : engrudo *m* (para pegar)

pasteboard ['peɪst,bord] *n* : cartón *m,* cartulina *f*

pastel [pæ'stɛl] *n* : pastel *m* — **pastel** *adj*

pasteurization [,pæstʃərə'zeɪʃən, ,pæstjə-] *n* : pasteurización *f*

pasteurize ['pæstʃə,raɪz, 'pæstjə-] *vt* **-ized; -izing** : pasteurizar

pastime ['pæs,taɪm] *n* : pasatiempo *m*

pastor ['pæstər] *n* : pastor *m,* -tora *f*

pastoral [ˈpæstərəl] *adj* **:** pastoral

past participle *n* **:** participio *m* pasado

pastry [ˈpeɪstri] *n, pl* **-ries 1** DOUGH **:** pasta *f,* masa *f* **2 pastries** *npl* **:** pasteles *mpl*

pasture[1] [ˈpæstʃər] *v* **-tured; -turing** *vi* GRAZE **:** pacer, pastar — *vt* **:** apacentar, pastar

pasture[2] *n* **:** pastizal *m,* potrero *m,* pasto *m*

pasty [ˈpeɪsti] *adj* **pastier; -est 1 :** pastoso (en consistencia) **2** PALLID **:** pálido

pat[1] [ˈpæt] *vt* **patted; patting :** dar palmaditas a, tocar

pat[2] *adv* **:** de memoria <to have down pat : saberse de memoria>

pat[3] *adj* **1** APT **:** apto, apropiado **2** GLIB **:** fácil **3** UNYIELDING **:** firme <to stand pat : mantenerse firme>

pat[4] *n* **1** TAP **:** golpecito *m,* palmadita *f* <a pat on the back : una palmadita en la espalda> **2** CARESS **:** caricia *f* **3 :** porción *f* <a pat of butter : una porción de mantequilla>

patch[1] [ˈpætʃ] *vt* **1** MEND, REPAIR **:** remender, parchar, ponerle un parche a **2 to patch together** IMPROVISE **:** confeccionar, improvisar **3 to patch up :** arreglar <they patched things up : hicieron las paces>

patch[2] *n* **1 :** parche *m,* remiendo *m* (para la ropa) <eye patch : parche para el ojo> **2** PIECE **:** mancha *f,* trozo *m* <a patch of sky : un trozo de cielo> **3** PLOT **:** parcela *f,* terreno *m* <cabbage patch : parcela de repollos>

patchwork [ˈpætʃˌwərk] *n* **:** labor *f* de retazos

patchy [ˈpætʃi] *adj* **patchier; -est 1** IRREGULAR **:** irregular, desigual **2** INCOMPLETE **:** parcial, incompleto

patent[1] [ˈpætənt] *vt* **:** patentar

patent[2] *adj* [ˈpætənt, ˈpeɪt-] **1** OBVIOUS **:** patente, evidente **2** [ˈpæt-] PATENTED **:** patentado

patent[3] [ˈpætənt] *n* **:** patente *f*

patently [ˈpætəntli] *adv* **:** patentemente, evidentemente

paternal [pəˈtərnəl] *adj* **1** FATHERLY **:** paternal **2 :** paterno <paternal grandfather : abuelo paterno>

paternity [pəˈtərnəti] *n* **:** paternidad *f*

path [ˈpæθ, ˈpaθ] *n* **1** TRACK, TRAIL **:** camino *m,* sendero *m,* senda *f* **2** COURSE, ROUTE **:** recorrido *m,* trayecto *m,* trayectoria *f*

pathetic [pəˈθɛtɪk] *adj* **:** patético — **pathetically** [-tɪkli] *adv*

pathological [ˌpæθəˈlɑdʒɪkəl] *adj* **:** patológico

pathologist [pəˈθɑlədʒɪst] *n* **:** patólogo *m,* -ga *f*

pathology [pəˈθɑlədʒi] *n, pl* **-gies :** patología *f*

pathos [ˈpeɪˌθɑs, ˈpæ-, -ˌθɔs] *n* **:** patetismo *m*

pathway [ˈpæθˌweɪ] *n* **:** camino *m,* sendero *m,* senda *f,* vereda *f*

patience [ˈpeɪʃənts] *n* **:** paciencia *f*

patient[1] [ˈpeɪʃənt] *adj* **:** paciente — **patiently** *adv*

patient[2] *n* **:** paciente *mf*

patio [ˈpætiˌoː] *n, pl* **-tios :** patio *m*

patriarch [ˈpeɪtriˌɑrk] *n* **:** patriarca *m*

patrimony [ˈpætrəˌmoːni] *n, pl* **-nies :** patrimonio *m*

patriot [ˈpeɪtriət] *n* **:** patriota *mf*

patriotic [ˌpeɪtriˈɑtɪk] *adj* **:** patriótico — **patriotically** *adv*

patriotism [ˈpeɪtriəˌtɪzəm] *n* **:** patriotismo *m*

patrol[1] [pəˈtroːl] *v* **-trolled; -trolling :** patrullar

patrol[2] *n* **:** patrulla *f*

patrolman [pəˈtroːlmən] *n, pl* **-men** [-mən, -ˌmɛn] **:** policía *mf,* guardia *mf*

patron [ˈpeɪtrən] *n* **1** SPONSOR **:** patrocinador *m,* -dora *f* **2** CUSTOMER **:** cliente *m,* -ta *f* **3** *or* **patron saint :** patrono *m,* -na *f*

patronage [ˈpeɪtrənɪdʒ, ˈpæ-] *n* **1** SPONSORSHIP **:** patrocinio *m* **2** CLIENTELE **:** clientela *f* **3 :** influencia *f* (política)

patronize [ˈpeɪtrəˌnaɪz, ˈpæ-] *vt* **-ized; -izing 1** SPONSOR **:** patrocinar **2 :** ser cliente de (un negocio) **3 :** tratar con condescendencia

patter[1] [ˈpætər] *vi* **1** TAP **:** golpetear, tamborilear (dícese de la lluvia) **2 to patter about :** corretear (con pasos ligeros)

patter[2] *n* **1** TAPPING **:** golpeteo *m,* tamborileo *m* (de la lluvia), correteo *m* (de pies) **2** CHATTER **:** palabrería *f,* parloteo *m fam*

pattern[1] [ˈpætərn] *vt* **1** BASE **:** basar (en un modelo) **2 to pattern after :** hacer imitación de

pattern[2] *n* **1** MODEL **:** modelo *m,* patrón *m* (de costura) **2** DESIGN **:** diseño *m,* dibujo *m,* estampado *m* (de tela) **3** NORM, STANDARD **:** pauta *f,* norma *f,* patrón *m*

patty [ˈpæti] *n, pl* **-ties :** porción *f* de carne picada (u otro alimento) en forma de ruedita <a hamburger patty : una hamburguesa>

paucity [ˈpɔsəti] *n* **:** escasez *f*

paunch [ˈpɔntʃ] *n* **:** panza *f,* barriga *f*

pauper [ˈpɔpər] *n* **:** pobre *mf,* indigente *mf*

pause[1] [ˈpɔz] *vi* **paused; pausing :** hacer una pausa, pararse (brevemente)

pause[2] *n* **:** pausa *f*

pave [ˈpeɪv] *vt* **paved; paving :** pavimentar <to pave with stones : empedrar>

pavement [ˈpeɪvmənt] *n* **:** pavimento *m,* empedrado *m*

pavilion [pəˈvɪljən] *n* **:** pabellón *m*

paving [ˈpeɪvɪŋ] → **pavement**

paw[1] [ˈpɔ] *vt* **:** tocar, manosear, sobar

paw[2] *n* **:** pata *f,* garra *f,* zarpa *f*

pawn[1] [ˈpɔn] *vt* **:** empeñar, prendar

pawn[2] *n* **1** PLEDGE, SECURITY **:** prenda *f* **2** PAWNING **:** empeño *m* **3 :** peón *m* (en ajedrez)

pawnbroker [ˈpɔn,broːkər] *n* **:** prestamista *mf*

pawnshop [ˈpɔn,ʃɑp] *n* **:** casa *f* de empeños, monte *m* de piedad

pay[1] [ˈpeɪ] *v* **paid** [ˈpeɪd]; **paying** *vt* **1 :** pagar (una cuenta, a un empleado, etc.) **2 to pay attention :** poner atención, prestar atención, hacer caso **3 to pay back :** pagar, devolver <she paid them back : les devolvió el dinero> <I'll pay you back for what you did! : ¡me las pagarás!> **4 to pay off** SETTLE **:** saldar, cancelar (una deuda, etc.) **5 to pay one's respects :** presentar uno sus respetos **6 to pay a visit :** hacer una visita — *vi* **:** valer la pena <crime doesn't pay : no hay crimen sin castigo>

pay[2] *n* **:** paga *f*

payable [ˈpeɪəbəl] *adj* DUE **:** pagadero

paycheck [ˈpeɪ,tʃɛk] *n* **:** sueldo *m*, cheque *m* del sueldo

payee [peɪˈiː] *n* **:** beneficiario *m*, -ria *f* (de un cheque, etc.)

payment [ˈpeɪmənt] *n* **1 :** pago *m* **2** INSTALLMENT **:** plazo *m*, cuota *f* **3** REWARD **:** recompensa *f*

payroll [ˈpeɪ,roːl] *n* **:** nómina *f*

PC [,piːˈsiː] *n, pl* **PCs** *or* **PC's :** PC *mf*, computadora *f* personal

pea [ˈpiː] *n* **:** chícharo *m*, guisante *m*, arveja *f*

peace [ˈpiːs] *n* **1 :** paz *f* <peace treaty : tratado de paz> <peace and tranquillity : paz y tranquilidad> **2** ORDER **:** orden *m* (público)

peaceable [ˈpiːsəbəl] *adj* **:** pacífico — **peaceably** [-bli] *adv*

peaceful [ˈpiːsfəl] *adj* **1** PEACEABLE **:** pacífico **2** CALM, QUIET **:** tranquilo, sosegado — **peacefully** *adv*

peacemaker [ˈpiːs,meɪkər] *n* **:** conciliador *m*, -dora *f*; mediador *m*, -dora *f*

peach [ˈpiːtʃ] *n* **:** durazno *m*, melocotón *m*

peacock [ˈpiː,kɑk] *n* **:** pavo *m* real

peak[1] [ˈpiːk] *vi* **:** alcanzar su nivel máximo

peak[2] *adj* **:** máximo

peak[3] *n* **1** POINT **:** punta *f* **2** CREST, SUMMIT **:** cima *f*, cumbre *f* **3** APEX **:** cúspide *f*, apogeo *m*, nivel *m* máximo

peaked [ˈpiːkəd] *adj* SICKLY **:** pálido

peal[1] [ˈpiːl] *vi* **:** repicar

peal[2] *n* **:** repique *m*, tañido *m* (de campanada) <peals of laughter : carcajadas>

peanut [ˈpiː,nʌt] *n* **:** maní *m*, cacahuate *m Mex*, cacahuete *m Spain*

pear [ˈpær] *n* **:** pera *f*

pearl [ˈpərl] *n* **:** perla *f*

pearly [ˈpərli] *adj* **pearlier; -est :** nacarado

peasant [ˈpɛzənt] *n* **:** campesino *m*, -na *f*

peat [ˈpiːt] *n* **:** turba *f*

pebble [ˈpɛbəl] *n* **:** piedrita *f*, piedrecita *f*, guijarro *m*

pecan [pɪˈkɑn, -ˈkæn, ˈpiː,kæn] *n* **:** pacana *f*, nuez *f Mex*

peccadillo [,pɛkəˈdɪlo] *n, pl* **-loes** *or* **-los :** pecadillo *m*

peccary [ˈpɛkəri] *n, pl* **-ries :** pécari *m*, pecarí *m*

peck[1] [ˈpɛk] *vt* **:** picar, picotear

peck[2] *n* **1 :** medida *f* de áridos equivalente a 8.810 litros **2 :** picotazo *m* (de un pájaro) <a peck on the cheek : un besito en la mejilla>

pectoral [ˈpɛktərəl] *adj* **:** pectoral

peculiar [pɪˈkjuːljər] *adj* **1** DISTINCTIVE **:** propio, peculiar, característico <peculiar to this area : propio de esta zona> **2** STRANGE **:** extraño, raro — **peculiarly** *adv*

peculiarity [pɪ,kjuːlˈjærət̬i, -,kjuːliˈær-] *n, pl* **-ties 1** DISTINCTIVENESS **:** peculiaridad *f* **2** ODDITY, QUIRK **:** rareza *f*, idiosincrasia *f*, excentricidad *f*

pecuniary [pɪˈkjuːni,ɛri] *adj* **:** pecuniario

pedagogical [,pɛdəˈgɑdʒɪkəl, -ˈgoː-] *adj* **:** pedagógico

pedagogy [ˈpɛdə,goːdʒi, -,gɑ-] *n* **:** pedagogía *f*

pedal[1] [ˈpɛdəl] *v* **-aled** *or* **-alled; -aling** *or* **-alling** *vi* **:** pedalear — *vt* **:** darle a los pedales de

pedal[2] *n* **:** pedal *m*

pedant [ˈpɛdənt] *n* **:** pedante *mf*

pedantic [pɪˈdæntɪk] *adj* **:** pedante

pedantry [ˈpɛdəntri] *n, pl* **-ries :** pedantería *f*

peddle [ˈpɛdəl] *vt* **-dled; -dling :** vender (en las calles)

peddler [ˈpɛdlər] *n* **:** vendedor *m*, -dora *f* ambulante; mercachifle *m*

pedestal [ˈpɛdəstəl] *n* **:** pedestal *m*

pedestrian[1] [pəˈdɛstriən] *adj* **1** COMMONPLACE **:** pedestre, ordinario **2 :** de peatón <pedestrian crossing : paso de peatones>

pedestrian[2] *n* **:** peatón *m*, -tona *f*

pediatric [,piːdiˈætrɪk] *adj* **:** pediátrico

pediatrician [,piːdiəˈtrɪʃən] *n* **:** pediatra *mf*

pediatrics [,piːdiˈætrɪks] *ns & pl* **:** pediatría *f*

pedigree [ˈpɛdə,griː] *n* **1** FAMILY TREE **:** árbol *m* genealógico **2** LINEAGE **:** pedigrí *m* (de un animal), linaje *m* (de una persona)

peek[1] [ˈpiːk] *vi* **1** PEEP **:** espiar, mirar furtivamente **2** GLANCE **:** echar un vistazo

peek[2] *n* **1 :** miradita *f* (furtiva) **2** GLANCE **:** vistazo *m*, ojeada *f*

peel[1] [ˈpiːl] *vt* **1 :** pelar (fruta, etc.) **2** *or* **to peel away :** quitar — *vi* **:** pelarse (dícese de la piel), desconcharse (dícese de la pintura)

peel[2] *n* **:** cáscara *f*

peep[1] ['piːp] *vi* **1** PEEK : espiar, mirar furtivamente **2** CHEEP : piar **3 to peep out** SHOW : asomarse

peep[2] *n* **1** CHEEP : pío *m* (de un pajarito) **2** GLANCE : vistazo *m,* ojeada *f*

peer[1] ['pɪr] *vi* : mirar detenidamente, mirar con atención

peer[2] *n* **1** EQUAL : par *m,* igual *mf* **2** NOBLE : noble *mf*

peerage ['pɪrɪdʒ] *n* : nobleza *f*

peerless ['pɪrləs] *adj* : sin par, incomparable

peeve[1] ['piːv] *vt* **peeved; peeving** : fastidiar, irritar, molestar

peeve[2] *n* : queja *f*

peevish ['piːvɪʃ] *adj* : quejoso, fastidioso — **peevishly** *adv*

peevishness ['piːvɪʃnəs] *n* : irritabilidad *f*

peg[1] ['pɛg] *vt* **pegged; pegging 1** PLUG : tapar (con una clavija) **2** FASTEN, FIX : sujetar (con estaquillas) **3 to peg out** MARK : marcar (con estaquillas)

peg[2] *n* : estaquilla *f* (para clavar), clavija *f* (para tapar)

pejorative [pɪ'dʒɔrət̬ɪv] *adj* : peyorativo — **pejoratively** *adv*

pelican ['pɛlɪkən] *n* : pelícano *m*

pellagra [pə'lægrə, -'leɪ-] *n* : pelagra *f*

pellet ['pɛlət] *n* **1** BALL : bolita *f* <food pellet : bolita de comida> **2** SHOT : perdigón *m*

pell–mell ['pɛl'mɛl] *adv* : desordenadamente, atropelladamente

pelt[1] ['pɛlt] *vt* **1** THROW : lanzar, tirar (algo a alguien) **2 to pelt with stones** : apedrear — *vi* BEAT : golpear con fuerza <the rain was pelting down : llovía a cántaros>

pelt[2] *n* : piel *f,* pellejo *m*

pelvic ['pɛlvɪk] *adj* : pélvico

pelvis ['pɛlvɪs] *n, pl* **-vises** *or* **-ves** ['pɛl,viːz] : pelvis *f*

pen[1] ['pɛn] *vt* **penned; penning 1** *or* **pen in** : encerrar (animales) **2** WRITE : escribir

pen[2] *n* **1** CORRAL : corral *m,* redil *m* (para ovejas) **2** : pluma *f* <fountain pen : pluma fuente> <ballpoint pen : bolígrafo>

penal ['piːnəl] *adj* : penal

penalize ['piːnəl,aɪz, 'pɛn-] *vt* **-ized; -izing** : penalizar, sancionar, penar

penalty ['pɛnəlti] *n, pl* **-ties 1** PUNISHMENT : pena *f,* castigo *m* **2** DISADVANTAGE : desventaja *f,* castigo *m,* penalty *m* (en deportes) **3** FINE : multa *f*

penance ['pɛnənts] *n* : penitencia *f*

pence → **penny**

penchant ['pɛntʃənt] *n* : inclinación *f,* afición *f*

pencil[1] ['pɛntsəl] *vt* **-ciled** *or* **-cilled; -ciling** *or* **-cilling** : escribir con lápiz, dibujar con lápiz

pencil[2] *n* : lápiz *m*

pendant ['pɛndənt] *n* : colgante *m*

pending[1] ['pɛndɪŋ] *adj* : pendiente

pending[2] *prep* **1** DURING : durante **2** AWAITING : en espera de

pendulum ['pɛndʒələm, -djʊləm] *n* : péndulo *m*

penetrate ['pɛnə,treɪt] *vt* **-trated; -trating** : penetrar

penetrating ['pɛnə,treɪt̬ɪŋ] *adj* : penetrante, cortante

penetration [,pɛnə'treɪʃən] *n* : penetración *f*

penguin ['pɛŋgwɪn, 'pɛn-] *n* : pingüino *m*

penicillin [,pɛnə'sɪlən] *n* : penicilina *f*

peninsula [pə'nɪntsələ, -'nɪntʃʊlə] *n* : península *f*

penis ['piːnəs] *n, pl* **-nes** [-,niːz] *or* **-nises** : pene *m*

penitence ['pɛnət̬ənts] *n* : arrepentimiento *m,* penitencia *f*

penitent[1] ['pɛnət̬ənt] *adj* : arrepentido, penitente

penitent[2] *n* : penitente *mf*

penitentiary [,pɛnə'tɛntʃəri] *n, pl* **-ries** : penitenciaría *f,* prisión *m,* presidio *m*

penmanship ['pɛnmən,ʃɪp] *n* : escritura *f,* caligrafía *f*

pen name *n* : seudónimo *m*

pennant ['pɛnənt] *n* : gallardete *m* (de un barco), banderín *m*

penniless ['pɛniləs] *adj* : sin un centavo

penny ['pɛni] *n, pl* **-nies** *or* **pence** ['pɛnts] **1** : penique *m* (del Reino Unido) **2** *pl* **-nies** CENT : centavo *m* (de los Estados Unidos)

pension[1] ['pɛntʃən] *vt or* **to pension off** : jubilar

pension[2] *n* : pensión *m,* jubilación *f*

pensive ['pɛntsɪv] *adj* : pensativo, meditabundo — **pensively** *adv*

pent ['pɛnt] *adj* : encerrado <pent-up feelings : emociones reprimidas>

pentagon ['pɛntə,gɑn] *n* : pentágono *m*

pentagonal [pɛn'tægənəl] *adj* : pentagonal

penthouse ['pɛnt,haʊs] *n* : ático *m,* penthouse *m*

penury ['pɛnjəri] *n* : penuria *f,* miseria *f*

peon ['piː,ɑn, -ən] *n, pl* **-ons** *or* **-ones** [peɪ'oːniːz] : peón *m*

peony ['piːəni] *n, pl* **-nies** : peonía *f*

people[1] ['piːpəl] *vt* **-pled; -pling** : poblar

people[2] *ns & pl* **1 people** *npl* : gente *f,* personas *fpl* <people like him : él le cae bien a la gente> <many people : mucha gente, muchas personas> **2** *pl* **peoples** : pueblo *m* <the Cuban people : el pueblo cubano>

pep[1] ['pɛp] *vt* **pepped; pepping** *or* **to pep up** : animar

pep[2] *n* : energía *f,* vigor *m*

pepper[1] ['pɛpər] *vt* **1** : añadir pimienta a **2** RIDDLE : acribillar (a balazos) **3** SPRINKLE : salpicar <peppered with quotations : salpicado de citas>

pepper[2] *n* **1 :** pimienta *f* (condimento) **2 :** pimiento *m,* pimentón *m* (fruta) **3** → **chili**
peppermint [ˈpɛpərˌmɪnt] *n* **:** menta *f*
peppery [ˈpɛpəri] *adj* **:** picante
peppy [ˈpɛpi] *adj* **peppier; -est :** lleno de energía, vivaz
peptic [ˈpɛptɪk] *adj* **peptic ulcer :** úlcera *f* estomacal
per [ˈpər] *prep* **1 :** por <miles per hour : millas por hora> **2** ACCORDING TO **:** según <per his specifications : según sus especificaciones>
per annum [pərˈænəm] *adv* **:** al año, por año
percale [ˌpərˈkeɪl, ˈpər-ˌ; ˌpərˈkæl] *n* **:** percal *m*
per capita [pərˈkæpɪt̬ə] *adv & adj* **:** per cápita
perceive [pərˈsiːv] *vt* **-ceived; -ceiving 1** REALIZE **:** percatarse de, concientizarse de, darse cuenta de **2** NOTE **:** percibir, notar
percent[1] [pərˈsɛnt] *adv* **:** por ciento
percent[2] *n, pl* **-cent** *or* **-cents 1 :** por ciento <10 percent of the population : el 10 por ciento de la población> **2** → **percentage**
percentage [pərˈsɛntɪdʒ] *n* **:** porcentaje *m*
perceptible [pərˈsɛptəbəl] *adj* **:** perceptible — **perceptibly** [-bli] *adv*
perception [pərˈsɛpʃən] *n* **1 :** percepción *f* <color perception : la percepción de los colores> **2** INSIGHT **:** perspicacia *f* **3** IDEA **:** idea *f,* imagen *f*
perceptive [pərˈsɛptɪv] *adj* **:** perspicaz
perceptively [pərˈsɛptɪvli] *adv* **:** con perspicacia
perch[1] [ˈpərtʃ] *vi* **1** ROOST **:** posarse **2** SIT **:** sentarse (en un sitio elevado) — *vt* PLACE **:** posar, colocar
perch[2] *n* **1** ROOST **:** percha *f* (para los pájaros) **2** *pl* **perch** *or* **perches :** perca *f* (pez)
percolate [ˈpərkəˌleɪt] *vi* **-lated; -lating :** colarse, filtrarse <percolated coffee : café filtrado>
percolator [ˈpərkəˌleɪt̬ər] *n* **:** cafetera *f* de filtro
percussion [pərˈkʌʃən] *n* **1** STRIKING **:** percusión *f* **2** *or* **percussion instruments :** instrumentos *mpl* de percusión
peremptory [pəˈrɛmptəri] *adj* **:** perentorio
perennial[1] [pəˈrɛniəl] *adj* **1 :** perenne, vivaz <perennial flowers : flores perennes> **2** RECURRENT **:** perenne, continuo <a perennial problem : un problema eterno>
perennial[2] *n* **:** planta *f* perenne, planta *f* vivaz
perfect[1] [pərˈfɛkt] *vt* **:** perfeccionar
perfect[2] [ˈpərfɪkt] *adj* **:** perfecto — **perfectly** *adv*
perfection [pərˈfɛkʃən] *n* **:** perfección *f*
perfectionist [pərˈfɛkʃənɪst] *n* **:** perfeccionista *mf*
perfidious [pərˈfɪdiəs] *adj* **:** pérfido
perforate [ˈpərfəˌreɪt] *vt* **-rated; -rating :** perforar
perforation [ˌpərfəˈreɪʃən] *n* **:** perforación *f*
perform [pərˈfɔrm] *vt* **1** CARRY OUT **:** realizar, hacer, desempeñar **2** PRESENT **:** representar, dar (una obra teatral, etc.) — *vi* **:** actuar (en una obra teatral), cantar (en una ópera, etc.), tocar (en un concierto, etc.), bailar (en un ballet, etc.)
performance [pərˈfɔrmən*t*s] *n* **1** EXECUTION **:** ejecución *f,* realización *f,* desempeño *m,* rendimiento *m* **2** INTERPRETATION **:** interpretación *f* <his performance of Hamlet : su interpretación de Hamlet> **3** PRESENTATION **:** representación *f* (de una obra teatral), función *f*
performer [pərˈfɔrmər] *n* **:** artista *mf;* actor *m,* -triz *f;* intérprete *mf* (de música)
perfume[1] [pərˈfjuːm, ˈpərˌ-] *vt* **-fumed; -fuming :** perfumar
perfume[2] [ˈpərˌfjuːm, pərˈ-] *n* **:** perfume *m*
perfunctory [pərˈfʌŋktəri] *adj* **:** mecánico, superficial, somero
perhaps [pərˈhæps] *adv* **:** tal vez, quizá, quizás
peril [ˈpɛrəl] *n* **:** peligro *m*
perilous [ˈpɛrələs] *adj* **:** peligroso — **perilously** *adv*
perimeter [pəˈrɪmət̬ər] *n* **:** perímetro *m*
period [ˈpɪriəd] *n* **1 :** punto *m* (en puntuación) **2 :** período *m* <a two-hour period : un período de dos horas> **3** STAGE **:** época *f* (histórica), fase *f,* etapa *f*
periodic [ˌpɪriˈɑdɪk] *or* **periodical** [-dɪkəl] *adj* **:** periódico — **periodically** [-dɪkli] *adv*
periodical [ˌpɪriˈɑdɪkəl] *n* **:** publicación *f* periódica, revista *f*
peripheral [pəˈrɪfərəl] *adj* **:** periférico
periphery [pəˈrɪfəri] *n, pl* **-eries :** periferia *f*
periscope [ˈpɛrəˌskoːp] *n* **:** periscopio *m*
perish [ˈpɛrɪʃ] *vi* DIE **:** perecer, morirse
perishable[1] [ˈpɛrɪʃəbəl] *adj* **:** perecedero
perishable[2] *n* **:** producto *m* perecedero
perjure [ˈpərdʒər] *vt* **-jured; -juring** (*used in law*) **to perjure oneself :** perjurar, perjurarse
perjury [ˈpərdʒəri] *n* **:** perjurio *m*
perk[1] [ˈpərk] *vt* **1 :** levantar (las orejas, etc.) **2** *or* **to perk up** FRESHEN **:** arreglar — *vi* **to perk up :** animarse, reanimarse
perk[2] *n* **:** extra *m*
perky [ˈpərki] *adj* **perkier; -est :** animado, alegre, lleno de vida
permanence [ˈpərmənən*t*s] *n* **:** permanencia *f*

permanent[1] ['pərmənənt] *adj* : permanente — **permanently** *adv*
permanent[2] *n* : permanente *f*
permeable ['pərmiəbəl] *adj* : permeable
permeate ['pərmi,eɪt] *v* **-ated; -ating** *vt* **1** PENETRATE : penetrar, impregnar **2** PERVADE : penetrar, difundirse por — *vi* : penetrar
permissible [pər'mɪsəbəl] *adj* : permisible, lícito
permission [pər'mɪʃən] *n* : permiso *m*
permissive [pər'mɪsɪv] *adj* : permisivo
permit[1] [pər'mɪt] *vt* **-mitted; -mitting** : permitir, dejar <weather permitting : si el tiempo lo permite>
permit[2] ['pər,mɪt, pər'-] *n* : permiso *m,* licencia *f*
pernicious [pər'nɪʃəs] *adj* : pernicioso
peroxide [pə'rɑk,saɪd] *n* **1** : peróxido *m* **2** → **hydrogen peroxide**
perpendicular[1] [,pərpən'dɪkjələr] *adj* **1** VERTICAL : vertical **2** : perpendicular <perpendicular lines : líneas perpendiculares> — **perpendicularly** *adv*
perpendicular[2] *n* : perpendicular *f*
perpetrate ['pərpə,treɪt] *vt* **-trated; -trating** : perpetrar, cometer (un delito)
perpetrator ['pərpə,treɪtər] *n* : autor *m,* -tora *f* (de un delito)
perpetual [pər'pɛtʃʊəl] *adj* **1** EVERLASTING : perpetuo, eterno **2** CONTINUAL : perpetuo, continuo, constante
perpetually [pər'pɛtʃʊəli, -tʃəli] *adv* : para siempre, eternamente
perpetuate [pər'pɛtʃʊ,eɪt] *vt* **-ated; -ating** : perpetuar
perpetuity [,pərpə'tu:əti, -'tju:-] *n, pl* **-ties** : perpetuidad *f*
perplex [pər'plɛks] *vt* : dejar perplejo, confundir
perplexed [pər'plɛkst] *adj* : perplejo
perplexity [pər'plɛksəti] *n, pl* **-ties** : perplejidad *f,* confusión *f*
persecute ['pərsɪ,kju:t] *vt* **-cuted; -cuting** : perseguir
persecution [,pərsɪ'kju:ʃən] *n* : persecución *f*
perseverance [,pərsə'vɪrənts] *n* : perseverancia *f*
persevere [,pərsə'vɪr] *vi* **-vered; -vering** : perseverar
Persian ['pərʒən] *n* **1** : persa *mf* **2** : persa *m* (idioma) — **Persian** *adj*
persist [pər'sɪst] *vi* : persistir
persistence [pər'sɪstənts] *n* **1** CONTINUATION : persistencia *f* **2** TENACITY : perseverancia *f,* tenacidad *f*
persistent [pər'sɪstənt] *adj* : persistente — **persistently** *adv*
person ['pərsən] *n* **1** HUMAN, INDIVIDUAL : persona *f,* individuo *m,* ser *m* humano **2** : persona *f* (en gramática) **3 in person** : en persona
personable ['pərsənəbəl] *adj* : agradable
personage ['pərsənɪdʒ] *n* : personaje *m*
personal ['pərsənəl] *adj* **1** OWN, PRIVATE : personal, particular, privado <for personal reasons : por razones personales> **2** : en persona <to make a personal appearance : presentarse en persona, hacerse acto de presencia> **3** : íntimo, personal <personal hygiene : higiene personal> **4** INDISCREET, PRYING : indiscreto, personal
personality [,pərsən'æləti] *n, pl* **-ties** **1** DISPOSITION : personalidad *f,* temperamento *m* **2** CELEBRITY : personalidad *f,* personaje *m,* celebridad *f*
personalize ['pərsənə,laɪz] *vt* **-ized; -izing** : personalizar
personally ['pərsənəli] *adv* **1** : personalmente, en persona <I'll do it personally : lo haré personalmente> **2** : como persona <personally she's very amiable : como persona es muy amable> **3** : personalmente <personally, I don't believe it : yo, personalmente, no me lo creo>
personification [pər,sɑnəfə'keɪʃən] *n* : personificación *f*
personify [pər'sɑnə,faɪ] *vt* **-fied; -fying** : personificar
personnel [,pərsən'ɛl] *n* : personal *m*
perspective [pər'spɛktɪv] *n* : perspectiva *f*
perspicacious [,pərspə'keɪʃəs] *adj* : perspicaz
perspiration [,pərspə'reɪʃən] *n* : transpiración *f,* sudor *m*
perspire [pər'spaɪr] *vi* **-spired; -spiring** : transpirar, sudar
persuade [pər'sweɪd] *vt* **-suaded; -suading** : persuadir, convencer
persuasion [pər'sweɪʒən] *n* : persuasión *f*
persuasive [pər'sweɪsɪv, -zɪv] *adj* : persuasivo — **persuasively** *adv*
persuasiveness [pər'sweɪsɪvnəs, -zɪv-] *n* : persuasión *f*
pert ['pərt] *adj* **1** SAUCY : descarado, impertinente **2** JAUNTY : alegre, animado <a pert little hat : un sombrero coqueto>
pertain [pər'teɪn] *vi* **1** BELONG : pertenecer (a) **2** RELATE : estar relacionado (con)
pertinence ['pərtənənts] *n* : pertinencia *f*
pertinent ['pərtənənt] *adj* : pertinente
perturb [pər'tərb] *vt* : perturbar
perusal [pə'ru:zəl] *n* : lectura *f* cuidadosa
peruse [pə'ru:z] *vt* **-rused; -rusing** **1** READ : leer con cuidado **2** SCAN : recorrer con la vista <he perused the newspaper : echó un vistazo al periódico>
Peruvian [pə'ru:viən] *n* : peruano *m,* -na *f* — **Peruvian** *adj*
pervade [pər'veɪd] *vt* **-vaded; -vading** : penetrar, difundirse por
pervasive [pər'veɪsɪv, -zɪv] *adj* : penetrante

perverse [pər'vərs] *adj* **1** CORRUPT : perverso, corrompido **2** STUBBORN : obstinado, porfiado, terco (sin razón) — **perversely** *adv*

perversion [pər'vərʒən] *n* : perversión *f*

perversity [pər'vərsəṭi] *n, pl* **-ties 1** CORRUPTION : corrupción *f* **2** STUBBORNNESS : obstinación *f,* terquedad *f*

pervert[1] [pər'vərt] *vt* **1** DISTORT : pervertir, distorsionar **2** CORRUPT : pervertir, corromper

pervert[2] ['pər,vərt] *n* : pervertido *m,* -da *f*

peso ['peɪ,soː] *n, pl* **-sos** : peso *m*

pessimism ['pɛsə,mɪzəm] *n* : pesimismo *m*

pessimist ['pɛsəmɪst] *n* : pesimista *mf*

pessimistic [,pɛsə'mɪstɪk] *adj* : pesimista

pest ['pɛst] *n* **1** NUISANCE : peste *f;* latoso *m,* -sa *f fam* <to be a pest : dar (la) lata> **2** : insecto *m* nocivo, animal *m* nocivo <the squirrels were pests : las ardillas eran una plaga>

pester ['pɛstər] *vt* **-tered; -tering** : molestar, fastidiar

pesticide ['pɛstə,saɪd] *n* : pesticida *m*

pestilence ['pɛstələnts] *n* : pestilencia *f,* peste *f*

pestle ['pɛsəl, 'pɛstəl] *n* : mano *f* de mortero, mazo *m,* maja *f*

pet[1] ['pɛt] *vt* **petted; petting** : acariciar

pet[2] *n* **1** : animal *m* doméstico **2** FAVORITE : favorito *m,* -ta *f*

petal ['pɛṭəl] *n* : pétalo *m*

petite [pə'tiːt] *adj* : pequeña, menuda, chiquita

petition[1] [pə'tɪʃən] *vt* : peticionar

petition[2] *n* : petición *f*

petitioner [pə'tɪʃənər] *n* : peticionario *m,* -ria *f*

petrify ['pɛtrə,faɪ] *vt* **-fied; -fying** : petrificar

petroleum [pə'troːliəm] *n* : petróleo *m*

petticoat ['pɛṭi,koːt] *n* : enagua *f,* fondo *m Mex*

pettiness ['pɛṭinəs] *n* **1** INSIGNIFICANCE : insignificancia *f* **2** MEANNESS : mezquindad *f*

petty ['pɛṭi] *adj* **-tier; -est 1** MINOR : menor <petty cash : dinero para gastos menores> **2** INSIGNIFICANT : insignificante, trivial, nimio **3** MEAN : mezquino

petty officer *n* : suboficial *mf*

petulance ['pɛtʃələnts] *n* : irritabilidad *f,* mal genio *m*

petulant ['pɛtʃələnt] *adj* : irritable, de mal genio

petunia [pɪ'tuːnjə, -'tjuː-] *n* : petunia *f*

pew ['pjuː] *n* : banco *m* (de iglesia)

pewter ['pjuːṭər] *n* : peltre *m*

pH [,piː'eɪtʃ] *n* : pH *m*

phallic ['fælɪk] *adj* : fálico

phallus ['fæləs] *n, pl* **-li** ['fæ,laɪ] *or* **-luses** : falo *m*

phantasy ['fæntəsi] → **fantasy**

phantom ['fæntəm] *n* : fantasma *m*

pharaoh ['fɛr,oː, 'feɪ,roː] *n* : faraón *m*

pharmaceutical [,fɑrmə'suːṭɪkəl] *adj* : farmacéutico

pharmacist ['fɑrməsɪst] *n* : farmacéutico *m,* -ca *f*

pharmacology [,fɑrmə'kɑlədʒi] *n* : farmacología *f*

pharmacy ['fɑrməsi] *n, pl* **-cies** : farmacia *f*

pharynx ['færɪŋks] *n, pl* **pharynges** [fə'rɪn,dʒiːz] : faringe *f*

phase[1] ['feɪz] *vt* **phased; phasing 1** SYNCHRONIZE : sincronizar, poner en fase **2** STAGGER : escalonar **3 to phase in** : introducir progresivamente **4 to phase out** : retirar progresivamente, dejar de producir

phase[2] *n* **1** : fase *f* (de la luna, etc.) **2** STAGE : fase *f,* etapa *f*

pheasant ['fɛzənt] *n, pl* **-ant** *or* **-ants** : faisán *m*

phenomenal [fɪ'nɑmənəl] *adj* : extraordinario, excepcional

phenomenon [fɪ'nɑmə,nɑn, -nən] *n, pl* **-na** [-nə] *or* **-nons 1** : fenómeno *m* **2** *pl* **-nons** PRODIGY : fenómeno *m,* prodigio *m*

philanthropic [,fɪlən'θrɑpɪk] *adj* : filantrópico

philanthropist [fə'læntθrəpɪst] *n* : filántropo *m,* -pa *f*

philanthropy [fə'læntθrəpi] *n, pl* **-pies** : filantropía *f*

philately [fə'læṭəli] *n* : filatelia *f*

philodendron [,fɪlə'dɛndrən] *n, pl* **-drons** *or* **-dra** [-drə] : arácea *f*

philosopher [fə'lɑsəfər] *n* : filósofo *m,* -fa *f*

philosophic [,fɪlə'sɑfɪk] *or* **philosophical** [-fɪkəl] *adj* : filosófico — **philosophically** [-kli] *adv*

philosophize [fə'lɑsə,faɪz] *vi* **-phized; -phizing** : filosofar

philosophy [fə'lɑsəfi] *n, pl* **-phies** : filosofía *f*

phlebitis [flɪ'baɪṭəs] *n* : flebitis *f*

phlegm ['flɛm] *n* : flema *f*

phlox ['flɑks] *n, pl* **phlox** *or* **phloxes** : polemonio *m*

phobia ['foːbiə] *n* : fobia *f*

phoenix ['fiːnɪks] *n* : fénix *m*

phone[1] ['foːn] *v* → **telephone**[1]

phone[2] *n* → **telephone**[2]

phoneme ['foː,niːm] *n* : fonema *m*

phonetic [fə'nɛṭɪk] *adj* : fonético

phonetics [fə'nɛṭɪks] *n* : fonética *f*

phonics ['fɑnɪks] *n* : método *m* fonético de aprender a leer

phonograph ['foːnə,græf] *n* : fonógrafo *m,* tocadiscos *m*

phony[1] *or* **phoney** ['foːni] *adj* **-nier; -est** : falso

phony[2] *or* **phoney** *n, pl* **-nies** : farsante *mf;* charlatán *m,* -tana *f*

phosphate ['fɑs,feɪt] *n* : fosfato *m*

phosphorescence [,fɑsfə'rɛsənts] *n* : fosforescencia *f*

phosphorescent [ˌfɑsfəˈrɛsənt] *adj* : fosforescente — **phosphorescently** *adv*

phosphorus [ˈfɑsfərəs] *n* : fósforo *m*

photo [ˈfoːˌtoː] *n, pl* **-tos** : foto *f*

photocopier [ˈfoːt̬oˌkɑpiər] *n* : fotocopiadora *f*

photocopy[1] [ˈfoːt̬oˌkɑpi] *vt* **-copied; -copying** : fotocopiar

photocopy[2] *n, pl* **-copies** : fotocopia *f*

photoelectric [ˌfoːt̬oɪˈlɛktrɪk] *adj* : fotoeléctrico

photogenic [ˌfoːt̬əˈdʒɛnɪk] *adj* : fotogénico

photograph[1] [ˈfoːt̬əˌgræf] *vt* : fotografiar

photograph[2] *n* : fotografía *f,* foto *f* <to take a photograph of : tomarle una fotografía a, tomar una fotografía de>

photographer [fəˈtɑgrəfər] *n* : fotógrafo *m,* -fa *f*

photographic [ˌfoːt̬əˈgræfɪk] *adj* : fotográfico — **photographically** [-fɪkli] *adv*

photography [fəˈtɑgrəfi] *n* : fotografía *f*

photosynthesis [ˌfoːt̬oˈsɪnθəsɪs] *n* : fotosíntesis *f*

photosynthetic [ˌfoːt̬osɪnˈθɛt̬ɪk] *adj* : fotosintético, de fotosíntesis

phrase[1] [ˈfreɪz] *vt* **phrased; phrasing** : expresar

phrase[2] *n* : frase *f,* locución *f* <to coin a phrase : para decirlo así>

phylum [ˈfaɪləm] *n, pl* **-la** [-lə] : phylum *m*

physical[1] [ˈfɪzɪkəl] *adj* **1** : físico <physical laws : leyes físicas> **2** MATERIAL : material, físico **3** BODILY : físico, corpóreo — **physically** [-kli] *adv*

physical[2] *n* CHECKUP : chequeo *m,* reconocimiento *m* médico

physician [fəˈzɪʃən] *n* : médico *m,* -ca *f*

physicist [ˈfɪzəsɪst] *n* : físico *m,* -ca *f*

physics [ˈfɪzɪks] *ns & pl* : física *f*

physiognomy [ˌfɪziˈɑgnəmi] *n, pl* **-mies** : fisonomía *f*

physiological [ˈfɪziəˈlɑdʒɪkəl] *or* **physiologic** [-dʒɪk] *adj* : fisiológico

physiologist [ˌfɪziˈɑlədʒɪst] *n* : fisiólogo *m,* -ga *f*

physiology [ˌfɪziˈɑlədʒi] *n* : fisiología *f*

physique [fəˈziːk] *n* : físico *m*

pi [ˈpaɪ] *n, pl* **pis** [ˈpaɪz] : pi *f*

pianist [piˈænɪst, ˈpiːənɪst] *n* : pianista *mf*

piano [piˈænoː] *n, pl* **-anos** : piano *m*

piazza [piˈæzə, -ˈɑtsə] *n, pl* **-zas** *or* **-ze** [-ˈɑtˌseɪ] : plaza *f*

picayune [ˌpɪkiˈjuːn] *adj* : trivial, nimio, insignificante

piccolo [ˈpɪkəˌloː] *n, pl* **-los** : flautín *m*

pick[1] [ˈpɪk] *vt* **1** : picar, labrar (con un pico) <he picked the hard soil : picó la tierra dura> **2** : quitar, sacar (poco a poco) <to pick meat off the bones : quitar pedazos de carne de los huesos> **3** : recoger, arrancar (frutas, flores, etc.) **4** SELECT : escoger, elegir **5** PROVOKE : provocar <to pick a quarrel : buscar pleito, buscar pelea> **6 to pick a lock** : forzar una cerradura **7 to pick someone's pocket** : robarle algo del bolsillo de alguien <someone picked my pocket! : ¡me robaron la cartera del bolsillo!> — *vi* **1** NIBBLE : picar, picotear **2 to pick and choose** : ser exigente **3 to pick at** : tocar, rascarse (una herida, etc.) **4 to pick on** TEASE : mofarse de, atormentar

pick[2] *n* **1** CHOICE : selección *f* **2** BEST : lo mejor <the pick of the crop : la crema y nata> **3** → **pickax**

pickax [ˈpɪkˌæks] *n* : pico *m,* zapapico *m,* piqueta *f*

pickerel [ˈpɪkərəl] *n, pl* **-el** *or* **-els** : lucio *m* pequeño

picket[1] [ˈpɪkət] *v* : piquetear

picket[2] *n* **1** STAKE : estaca *f* **2** STRIKER : huelguista *mf,* integrante *mf* de un piquete

pickle[1] [ˈpɪkəl] *vt* **-led; -ling** : encurtir, escabechar

pickle[2] *n* **1** BRINE : escabeche *m* **2** GHERKIN : pepinillo *m* (encurtido) **3** JAM, TROUBLE : lío *m,* apuro *m*

pickpocket [ˈpɪkˌpɑkət] *n* : carterista *mf*

pickup [ˈpɪkˌəp] *n* **1** IMPROVEMENT : mejora *f* **2** *or* **pickup truck** : camioneta *f*

pick up *vt* **1** LIFT : levantar **2** TIDY : arreglar, ordenar — *vi* IMPROVE : mejorar

picnic[1] [ˈpɪkˌnɪk] *vi* **-nicked; -nicking** : ir de picnic

picnic[2] *n* : picnic *m*

pictorial [pɪkˈtoriəl] *adj* : pictórico

picture[1] [ˈpɪktʃər] *vt* **-tured; -turing** **1** DEPICT : representar **2** IMAGINE : imaginarse <can you picture it? : ¿te lo puedes imaginar?>

picture[2] *n* **1** : cuadro *m* (pintado o dibujado), ilustración *f,* fotografía *f* **2** DESCRIPTION : descripción *f* **3** IMAGE : imagen *f* <he's the picture of his father : es la viva imagen de su padre> **4** MOVIE : película *f*

picturesque [ˌpɪktʃəˈrɛsk] *adj* : pintoresco

pie [ˈpaɪ] *n* : pastel *m* (con fruta o carne), empanada *f* (con carne)

piebald [ˈpaɪˌbɔld] *adj* : picazo, pío

piece[1] [ˈpiːs] *vt* **pieced; piecing** **1** PATCH : parchar, arreglar **2 to piece together** : construir pieza por pieza

piece[2] *n* **1** FRAGMENT : trozo *m,* pedazo *m* **2** COMPONENT : pieza *f* <a three-piece suit : un traje de tres piezas> **3** UNIT : pieza *f* <a piece of fruit : una (pieza de) fruta> **4** WORK : obra *f,* pieza *f* (de música, etc.) **5** (*in board games*) : ficha *f,* pieza *f,* figura *f* (en ajedrez)

piecemeal[1] [ˈpiːsˌmiːl] *adv* : poco a poco, por partes

piecemeal[2] *adj* : hecho poco a poco, poco sistemático

pied [ˈpaɪd] *adj* : pío

pier [ˈpɪr] *n* **1** : pila *f* (de un puente) **2** WHARF : muelle *m,* atracadero *m,* embarcadero *m* **3** PILLAR : pilar *m*

pierce [ˈpɪrs] *vt* **pierced; piercing 1** PENETRATE : atravesar, traspasar, penetrar (en) <the bullet pierced his leg : la bala le atravesó la pierna> <to pierce one's heart : traspasarle el corazón a uno> **2** PERFORATE : perforar, agujerear (las orejas, etc.) **3 to pierce the silence** : desgarrar el silencio

piety [ˈpaɪəti] *n, pl* **-eties** : piedad *f*

pig [ˈpɪg] *n* **1** HOG, SWINE : cerdo *m,* -da *f;* puerco *m,* -ca *f* **2** SLOB : persona *f* desaliñada; cerdo *m,* -da *f* **3** GLUTTON : glotón *m,* -tona *f* **4** *or* **pig iron** : lingote *m* de hierro

pigeon [ˈpɪdʒən] *n* : paloma *f*

pigeonhole [ˈpɪdʒənˌhoːl] *n* : casilla *f*

pigeon–toed [ˈpɪdʒənˌtoːd] *adj* : patituerto

piggish [ˈpɪgɪʃ] *adj* **1** GREEDY : glotón **2** DIRTY : cochino, sucio

piggyback [ˈpɪgiˌbæk] *adv & adj* : a cuestas

pigheaded [ˈpɪgˌhɛdəd] *adj* : terco, obstinado

piglet [ˈpɪglət] *n* : cochinillo *m;* lechón *m,* -chona *f*

pigment [ˈpɪgmənt] *n* : pigmento *m*

pigmentation [ˌpɪgmənˈteɪʃən] *n* : pigmentación *f*

pigmy → **pygmy**

pigpen [ˈpɪgˌpɛn] *n* : chiquero *m,* pocilga *f*

pigsty [ˈpɪgˌstaɪ] → **pigpen**

pigtail [ˈpɪgˌteɪl] *n* : coleta *f,* trenza *f*

pike [ˈpaɪk] *n, pl* **pike** *or* **pikes 1** : lucio *m* (pez) **2** LANCE : pica *f* **3** → **turnpike**

pile[1] [ˈpaɪl] *v* **piled; piling** *vt* : amontonar, apilar — *vi* **to pile up** : amontonarse, acumularse

pile[2] *n* **1** STAKE : pilote *m* **2** HEAP : montón *m,* pila *f* **3** NAP : pelo *m* (de telas)

piles [ˈpaɪlz] *npl* HEMORRHOIDS : hemorroides *fpl,* almorranas *fpl*

pilfer [ˈpɪlfər] *vt* : robar (cosas pequeñas), ratear

pilgrim [ˈpɪlgrəm] *n* : peregrino *m,* -na *f*

pilgrimage [ˈpɪlgrəmɪdʒ] *n* : peregrinación *f*

pill [ˈpɪl] *n* : pastilla *f,* píldora *f*

pillage[1] [ˈpɪlɪdʒ] *vt* **-laged; -laging** : saquear

pillage[2] *n* : saqueo *m*

pillar [ˈpɪlər] *n* : pilar *m,* columna *f*

pillory [ˈpɪləri] *n, pl* **-ries** : picota *f*

pillow [ˈpɪˌloː] *n* : almohada *f*

pillowcase [ˈpɪˌloːˌkeɪs] *n* : funda *f*

pilot[1] [ˈpaɪlət] *vt* : pilotar, pilotear

pilot[2] *n* : piloto *mf*

pilot light *n* : piloto *m*

pimento [pəˈmɛnˌtoː] → **pimiento**

pimiento [pəˈmɛnˌtoː, -ˈmjɛn-] *n, pl* **-tos** : pimiento *m* morrón

pimp [ˈpɪmp] *n* : proxeneta *m*

pimple [ˈpɪmpəl] *n* : grano *m*

pimply [ˈpɪmpəli] *adj* **-plier; -est** : cubierto de granos

pin[1] [ˈpɪn] *vt* **pinned; pinning 1** FASTEN : prender, sujetar (con alfileres) **2** HOLD, IMMOBILIZE : inmovilizar, sujetar **3 to pin one's hopes on** : poner sus esperanzas en

pin[2] *n* **1** : alfiler *m* <safety pin : alfiler de gancho> <a bobby pin : una horquilla> **2** BROOCH : alfiler *m,* broche *m,* prendedor *m* **3** *or* **bowling pin** : bolo *m*

pinafore [ˈpɪnəˌfor] *n* : delantal *m*

pincer [ˈpɪntsər] *n* **1** CLAW : pinza *f* (de una langosta, etc.) **2 pincers** *npl* : pinzas *fpl,* tenazas *fpl,* tenaza *f*

pinch[1] [ˈpɪntʃ] *vt* **1** : pellizcar <she pinched my cheek : me pellizcó el cachete> **2** STEAL : robar — *vi* : apretar <my shoes pinch : me aprietan los zapatos>

pinch[2] *n* **1** EMERGENCY : emergencia *f* <in a pinch : en caso necesario> **2** PAIN : dolor *m,* tormento *m* **3** SQUEEZE : pellizco *m* (con los dedos) **4** BIT : pizca *f,* pellizco *m* <a pinch of cinnamon : una pizca de canela>

pinch hitter *n* **1** SUBSTITUTE : sustituto *m,* -ta *f* **2** : bateador *m* emergente (en beisbol)

pincushion [ˈpɪnˌkʊʃən] *n* : acerico *m,* alfiletero *m*

pine[1] [ˈpaɪn] *vi* **pined; pining 1 to pine away** : languidecer, consumirse **2 to pine for** : añorar, suspirar por

pine[2] *n* **1** : pino *m* (árbol) **2** : madera *f* de pino

pineapple [ˈpaɪnˌæpəl] *n* : piña *f,* ananá *m,* ananás *m*

pinion[1] [ˈpɪnjən] *vt* : sujetar los brazos de, inmovilizar

pinion[2] *n* : piñón *m*

pink[1] [ˈpɪŋk] *adj* : rosa, rosado

pink[2] *n* **1** : clavelito *m* (flor) **2** : rosa *m,* rosado *m* (color) **3 to be in the pink** : estar en plena forma, rebosar de salud

pinkeye [ˈpɪŋkˌaɪ] *n* : conjuntivitis *f* aguda

pinkish [ˈpɪŋkɪʃ] *adj* : rosáceo

pinnacle [ˈpɪnɪkəl] *n* **1** : pináculo *m* (de un edificio) **2** PEAK : cima *f,* cumbre *f* (de una montaña) **3** ACME : pináculo *m,* cúspide *f,* apogeo *m*

pinpoint [ˈpɪnˌpɔɪnt] *vt* : precisar, localizar con precisión

pint [ˈpaɪnt] *n* : pinta *f*

pinto [ˈpɪnˌtoː] *n, pl* **pintos** : caballo *m* pinto

pinworm [ˈpɪnˌwərm] *n* : oxiuro *m*

pioneer[1] [ˌpaɪəˈnɪr] *vt* : promover, iniciar, introducir

pioneer[2] *n* : pionero *m,* -ra *f*

pious [ˈpaɪəs] *adj* **1** DEVOUT **:** piadoso, devoto **2** SANCTIMONIOUS **:** beato

piously [ˈpaɪəsli] *adv* **1** DEVOUTLY **:** piadosamente **2** SANCTIMONIOUSLY **:** santurronamente

pipe[1] [ˈpaɪp] *v* **piped; piping** *vi* **:** hablar en voz chillona — *vt* **1** PLAY **:** tocar (el caramillo o la flauta) **2 :** conducir por tuberías <to pipe water : transportar el agua por tubería>

pipe[2] *n* **1 :** caramillo *m* (instrumento musical) **2** BAGPIPE **:** gaita *f* **3 :** tubo *m,* caño *m* <gas pipes : tubería de gas> **4 :** pipa *f* (para fumar)

pipeline [ˈpaɪpˌlaɪn] *n* **1 :** conducto *m,* oleoducto *m* (para petróleo), gasoducto *m* (para gas) **2** CONDUIT **:** vía *f* (de información, etc.)

piper [ˈpaɪpər] *n* **:** músico *m,* -ca *f* que toca el caramillo o la gaita

piping [ˈpaɪpɪŋ] *n* **1 :** música *f* del caramillo o de la gaita **2** TRIM **:** cordoncillo *m,* ribete *m* con cordón

piquant [ˈpiːkənt, ˈpɪkwənt] *adj* **1** SPICY **:** picante **2** INTRIGUING **:** intrigante, estimulante

pique[1] [ˈpiːk] *vt* **piqued; piquing 1** IRRITATE **:** picar, irritar **2** AROUSE **:** despertar (la curiosidad, etc.)

pique[2] *n* **:** pique *m,* resentimiento *m*

piracy [ˈpaɪrəsi] *n, pl* **-cies :** piratería *f*

piranha [pəˈrɑnə, -ˈrɑnjə, -ˈrænjə] *n* **:** piraña *f*

pirate [ˈpaɪrət] *n* **:** pirata *mf*

pirouette [ˌpɪrəˈwɛt] *n* **:** pirueta *f*

pis → **pi**

Pisces [ˈpaɪˌsiːz, ˈpɪ-; ˈpɪsˌkeɪs] *n* **:** Piscis *mf*

pistachio [pəˈstæʃiˌoː, -ˈstɑ-] *n, pl* **-chios :** pistacho *m*

pistil [ˈpɪstəl] *n* **:** pistilo *m*

pistol [ˈpɪstəl] *n* **:** pistola *f*

piston [ˈpɪstən] *n* **:** pistón *m,* émbolo *m*

pit[1] [ˈpɪt] *v* **pitted; pitting** *vt* **1 :** marcar de hoyos, picar (una superficie) **2 :** deshuesar (una fruta) **3 to pit against :** enfrentar a, oponer a — *vi* **:** quedar marcado

pit[2] *n* **1** HOLE **:** fosa *f,* hoyo *m* <a bottomless pit : un pozo sin fondo> **2** MINE **:** mina *f* **3 :** foso *m* <orchestra pit : foso orquestal> **4** POCKMARK **:** marca *f* (en la cara), cicatriz *f* de viruela **5** STONE **:** hueso *m,* pepa *f* (de una fruta) **6 pit of the stomach :** boca *f* del estómago

pitch[1] [ˈpɪtʃ] *vt* **1** SET UP **:** montar, armar (una tienda) **2** THROW **:** lanzar, arrojar **3** ADJUST, SET **:** dar el tono de (un discurso, un instrumento musical) — *vi* **1** *or* **pitch forward** FALL **:** caerse **2** LURCH **:** cabecear (dícese de un barco o un avión), dar bandazos

pitch[2] *n* **1** LURCHING **:** cabezada *f,* cabeceo *m* (de un barco o un avión) **2** SLOPE **:** (grado de) inclinación *f,* pendiente *f* **3 :** tono *m* (en música) <perfect pitch : oído absoluto> **4** THROW **:** lanzamiento *m* **5** DEGREE **:** grado *m,* nivel *m,* punto *m* <the excitement reached a high pitch : la excitación llegó a un punto culminante> **6** *or* **sales pitch :** presentación *f* (de un vendedor) **7** TAR **:** pez *f,* brea *f*

pitcher [ˈpɪtʃər] *n* **1** JUG **:** jarra *f,* jarro *m,* cántaro *m,* pichel *m* **2 :** lanzador *m,* -dora *f* (en béisbol, etc.)

pitchfork [ˈpɪtʃˌfɔrk] *n* **:** horquilla *f,* horca *f*

piteous [ˈpɪtiəs] *adj* **:** lastimoso, lastimero — **piteously** *adv*

pitfall [ˈpɪtˌfɔl] *n* **:** peligro *m* (poco obvio), dificultad *f*

pith [ˈpɪθ] *n* **1 :** médula *f* (de una planta) **2** CORE **:** meollo *m,* entraña *f*

pithy [ˈpɪθi] *adj* **pithier; -est :** conciso y sustancioso <pithy comments : comentarios sucintos>

pitiable [ˈpɪt̬iəbəl] → **pitiful**

pitiful [ˈpɪt̬ɪfəl] *adj* **1** LAMENTABLE **:** lastimero, lastimoso, lamentable **2** CONTEMPTIBLE **:** despreciable, lamentable — **pitifully** [-fli] *adv*

pitiless [ˈpɪt̬ɪləs] *adj* **:** despiadado — **pitilessly** *adv*

pittance [ˈpɪtənts] *n* **:** miseria *f*

pituitary [pəˈtuːəˌtɛri, -ˈtjuː-] *adj* **:** pituitario

pity[1] [ˈpɪt̬i] *vt* **pitied; pitying :** compadecer, compadecerse de

pity[2] *n, pl* **pities 1** COMPASSION **:** compasión *f,* piedad *f* **2** SHAME **:** lástima *f,* pena *f* <what a pity! : ¡qué lástima!>

pivot[1] [ˈpɪvət] *vi* **1 :** girar sobre un eje **2 to pivot on :** girar sobre, depender de

pivot[2] *n* **:** pivote *m*

pivotal [ˈpɪvət̬əl] *adj* **:** fundamental, central

pixie *or* **pixy** [ˈpɪksi] *n, pl* **pixies :** elfo *m,* hada *f*

pizza [ˈpiːtsə] *n* **:** pizza *f*

pizzazz *or* **pizazz** [pəˈzæz] *n* **1** GLAMOR **:** encanto *m* **2** VITALITY **:** animación *f,* vitalidad *f*

placard [ˈplækərd, -ˌkɑrd] *n* POSTER **:** cartel *m,* póster *m,* afiche *m*

placate [ˈpleɪˌkeɪt, ˈplæ-] *vt* **-cated; -cating :** aplacar, apaciguar

place[1] [ˈpleɪs] *vt* **placed; placing 1** PUT, SET **:** poner, colocar **2** SITUATE **:** situar, ubicar, emplazar <to be well placed : estar bien situado> <to place in a job : colocar en un trabajo> **3** IDENTIFY, RECALL **:** identificar, ubicar, recordar <I can't place him : no lo ubico> **4 to place an order :** hacer un pedido

place[2] *n* **1** SPACE **:** sitio *m,* lugar *m* <there's no place to sit : no hay sitio para sentarse> **2** LOCATION, SPOT **:** lugar *m,* sitio *m,* parte *f* <place of work : lugar de trabajo> <our summer place : nuestra casa de verano> <all over the place : por todas partes> **3** RANK **:** lugar *m,* puesto *m* <he took first place : ganó el primer lugar> **4**

POSITION : lugar *m* <everything in its place : todo en su debido lugar> <to feel out of place : sentirse fuera de lugar> **5** SEAT : asiento *m,* cubierto *m* (a la mesa) **6** JOB : puesto *m* **7** ROLE : papel *m,* lugar *m* <to change places : cambiarse los papeles> **8 to take place :** tener lugar **9 to take the place of :** sustituir a

placebo [plə'siːˌboː] *n, pl* **-bos :** placebo *m*

placement ['pleɪsmənt] *n* **:** colocación *f*

placenta [plə'sɛntə] *n, pl* **-tas** *or* **-tae** [-ti, -ˌtaɪ] **:** placenta *f*

placid ['plæsəd] *adj* **:** plácido, tranquilo — **placidly** *adv*

plagiarism ['pleɪdʒəˌrɪzəm] *n* **:** plagio *m*

plagiarist ['pleɪdʒərɪst] *n* **:** plagiario *m,* -ria *f*

plagiarize ['pleɪdʒəˌraɪz] *vt* **-rized; -rizing :** plagiar

plague¹ ['pleɪg] *vt* **plagued; plaguing 1** AFFLICT **:** plagar, afligir **2** HARASS **:** acosar, atormentar

plague² *n* **1 :** plaga *f* (de insectos, etc.) **2 :** peste *f* (en medicina)

plaid¹ ['plæd] *adj* **:** escocés, de cuadros <a plaid skirt : una falda escocesa>

plaid² *n* TARTAN **:** tela *f* escocesa, tartán *m*

plain¹ ['pleɪn] *adj* **1** SIMPLE, UNADORNED **:** liso, sencillo, sin adornos **2** CLEAR **:** claro <in plain language : en palabras claras> **3** FRANK **:** franco, puro <the plain truth : la pura verdad> **4** HOMELY **:** ordinario, poco atractivo **5 in plain sight :** a la vista de todos

plain² *n* **:** llanura *f,* llano *m,* planicie *f*

plainly ['pleɪnli] *adv* **1** CLEARLY **:** claramente **2** FRANKLY **:** francamente, con franqueza **3** SIMPLY **:** sencillamente

plaintiff ['pleɪntɪf] *n* **:** demandante *mf*

plaintive ['pleɪntɪv] *adj* MOURNFUL **:** lastimero, plañidero

plait¹ ['pleɪt, 'plæt] *vt* **1** PLEAT **:** plisar **2** BRAID **:** trenzar

plait² *n* **1** PLEAT **:** pliegue *m* **2** BRAID **:** trenza *f*

plan¹ ['plæn] *v* **planned; planning** *vt* **1 :** planear, proyectar, planificar <to plan a trip : planear un viaje> <to plan a city : planificar una ciudad> **2** INTEND **:** tener planeado, proyectar — *vi* **:** hacer planes

plan² *n* **1** DIAGRAM **:** plano *m,* esquema *m* **2** SCHEME **:** plan *m,* proyecto *m,* programa *m* <to draw up a plan : elaborar un proyecto>

plane¹ ['pleɪn] *vt* **planed; planing :** cepillar (madera)

plane² *adj* **:** plano

plane³ *n* **1 :** plano *m* (en matemáticas, etc.) **2** LEVEL **:** nivel *m* **3 :** cepillo *m* (de carpintero) **4** → **airplane**

planet ['plænət] *n* **:** planeta *f*

planetarium [ˌplænə'tɛriəm] *n, pl* **-iums** *or* **-ia** [-iə] **:** planetario *m*

planetary ['plænəˌtɛri] *adj* **:** planetario

plank ['plæŋk] *n* **1** BOARD **:** tablón *m,* tabla *f* **2 :** artículo *m,* punto *m* (de una plataforma política)

plankton ['plæŋktən] *n* **:** plancton *m*

plant¹ ['plænt] *vt* **1 :** plantar (flores, árboles), sembrar (semillas) **2** PLACE **:** plantar, colocar <to plant an idea : inculcar una idea>

plant² *n* **1 :** planta *f* <leafy plants : plantas frondosas> **2** FACTORY **:** planta *f,* fábrica *f* <hydroelectric plant : planta hidroeléctrica> **3** MACHINERY **:** maquinaria *f,* equipo *m*

plantain ['plæntən] *n* **1 :** llantén *m* (mala hierba) **2 :** plátano *m,* plátano *m* macho *Mex* (fruta)

plantation [plæn'teɪʃən] *n* **:** plantación *f,* hacienda *f* <a coffee plantation : un cafetal>

planter ['plæntər] *n* **1 :** hacendado *m,* -da *f* (de una hacienda) **2** FLOWERPOT **:** tiesto *m,* maceta *f*

plaque ['plæk] *n* **1** TABLET **:** placa *f* **2 :** placa *f* (dental)

plasma ['plæzmə] *n* **:** plasma *m*

plaster¹ ['plæstər] *vt* **1 :** enyesar, revocar (con yeso) **2** COVER **:** cubrir, llenar <a wall plastered with notices : una pared cubierta de avisos>

plaster² *n* **1 :** yeso *m,* revoque *m* (para paredes, etc.) **2 :** escayola *f,* yeso *m* (en medicina) **3 plaster of Paris** ['pærɪs] **:** yeso *m* mate

plaster cast *n* **:** vaciado *m* de yeso

plasterer ['plæstərər] *n* **:** revocador *m,* -dora *f*

plastic¹ ['plæstɪk] *adj* **1 :** de plástico **2** PLIABLE **:** plástico, flexible **3 plastic surgery :** cirugía *f* plástica

plastic² *n* **:** plástico *m*

plate¹ ['pleɪt] *vt* **plated; plating :** chapar (en metal)

plate² *n* **1** PLAQUE, SHEET **:** placa *f* <a steel plate : una placa de acero> **2** UTENSILS **:** vajilla *f* (de metal) <silver plate : vajilla de plata> **3** DISH **:** plato *m* **4** DENTURES **:** dentadura *f* postiza **5** ILLUSTRATION **:** lámina *f* (en un libro) **6 license plate :** matrícula *f,* placa *f* de matrícula

plateau [plæ'toː] *n, pl* **-teaus** *or* **-teaux** [-'toːz] **:** meseta *f*

platform ['plætˌfɔrm] *n* **1** STAGE **:** plataforma *f,* estrado *m,* tribuna *f* **2 :** andén *m* (de una estación de ferrocarril) **3 political platform :** plataforma *f* política, programa *m* electoral

plating ['pleɪṭɪŋ] *n* **1 :** enchapado *m* **2 silver plating :** plateado *m*

platinum ['plætənəm] *n* **:** platino *m*

platitude ['plæṭəˌtuːd, -ˌtjuːd] *n* **:** lugar *m* común, perogrullada *f*

platoon [plə'tuːn] *n* **:** sección *f* (en el ejército)

platter ['plæṭər] *n* **:** fuente *f*

platypus [ˈplætɪpəs, -ˌpʊs] *n, pl* **platypuses** *or* **platypi** [-ˌpaɪ, -ˌpiː] : ornitorrinco *m*

plausibility [ˌplɔzəˈbɪləti] *n, pl* **-ties** : credibilidad *f,* verosimilitud *f*

plausible [ˈplɔzəbəl] *adj* : creíble, convincente, verosímil — **plausibly** [-bli] *adv*

play[1] [ˈpleɪ] *vi* **1** : jugar <to play with a doll : jugar con una muñeca> <to play with an idea : darle vueltas a una idea> **2** FIDDLE, TOY : jugar, juguetear <don't play with your food : no juegues con la comida> **3** : tocar <to play in a band : tocar en un grupo> **4** : actuar (en una obra de teatro) — *vt* **1** : jugar (un deporte, etc.), jugar a (un juego), jugar contra (un contrincante) **2** : tocar (música o un instrumento) **3** PERFORM : interpretar, hacer el papel de (un carácter), representar (una obra de teatro) <she plays the lead : hace el papel principal>

play[2] *n* **1** GAME, RECREATION : juego *m* <children at play : niños jugando> <a play on words : un juego de palabras> **2** ACTION : juego *m* <the ball is in play : la pelota está en juego> <to bring into play : poner en juego> **3** DRAMA : obra *f* de teatro, pieza *f* (de teatro) **4** MOVEMENT : juego *m* (de la luz, una brisa, etc.) **5** SLACK : juego *m* <there's not enough play in the wheel : la rueda no da lo suficiente>

playacting [ˈpleɪˌæktɪŋ] *n* : actuación *f,* teatro *m*

player [ˈpleɪər] *n* **1** : jugador *m,* -dora *f* (en un juego) **2** ACTOR : actor *m,* actriz *f* **3** MUSICIAN : músico *m,* -ca *f*

playful [ˈpleɪfəl] *adj* **1** FROLICSOME : juguetón **2** JOCULAR : jocoso — **playfully** *adv*

playfulness [ˈpleɪfəlnəs] *n* : lo juguetón, jocosidad *f,* alegría *f*

playground [ˈpleɪˌgraʊnd] *n* : patio *m* de recreo, jardín *m* para jugar

playhouse [ˈpleɪˌhaʊs] *n* **1** THEATER : teatro *m* **2** : casita *f* de juguete

playing card *n* : naipe *m,* carta *f*

playmate [ˈpleɪˌmeɪt] *n* : compañero *m,* -ra *f* de juego

play–off [ˈpleɪˌɔf] *n* : desempate *m*

playpen [ˈpleɪˌpɛn] *n* : corral *m* (para niños)

plaything [ˈpleɪˌθɪŋ] *n* : juguete *m*

playwright [ˈpleɪˌraɪt] *n* : dramaturgo *m,* -ga *f*

plaza [ˈplæzə, ˈplɑ-] *n* **1** SQUARE : plaza *f* **2 shopping plaza** MALL : centro *m* comercial

plea [ˈpliː] *n* **1** : acto *m* de declararse <he entered a plea of guilty : se declaró culpable> **2** APPEAL : ruego *m,* súplica *f*

plead [ˈpliːd] *v* **pleaded** *or* **pled** [ˈplɛd]; **pleading** *vi* **1** : declararse (culpable o inocente) **2 to plead for** : suplicar, implorar — *vt* **1** : alegar, pretextar <he pleaded illness : pretextó la enfermedad> **2 to plead a case** : defender un caso

pleasant [ˈplɛzənt] *adj* : agradable, grato, bueno — **pleasantly** *adv*

pleasantness [ˈplɛzəntnəs] *n* : lo agradable, amenidad *f*

pleasantries [ˈplɛzəntriz] *npl* : cumplidos *mpl,* cortesías *fpl* <to exchange pleasantries : intercambiar cumplidos>

please[1] [ˈpliːz] *v* **pleased; pleasing** *vt* **1** GRATIFY : complacer <please yourself! : ¡cómo quieras!> **2** SATISFY : contentar, satisfacer — *vi* **1** SATISFY : complacer, agradar <anxious to please : deseoso de complacer> **2** LIKE : querer <do as you please : haz lo que quieras, haz lo que te parezca>

please[2] *adv* : por favor

pleased [ˈpliːzd] *adj* : contento, satisfecho, alegre

pleasing [ˈpliːzɪŋ] *adj* : agradable — **pleasingly** *adv*

pleasurable [ˈplɛʒərəbəl] *adj* PLEASANT : agradable

pleasure [ˈplɛʒər] *n* **1** WISH : deseo *m,* voluntad *f* <at your pleasure : cuando guste> **2** ENJOYMENT : placer *m,* disfrute *m,* goce *m* <with pleasure : con mucho gusto> **3** : placer *m,* gusto *m* <it's a pleasure to be here : me da gusto estar aquí> <the pleasures of reading : los placeres de leer>

pleat[1] [ˈpliːt] *vt* : plisar

pleat[2] *n* : pliegue *m*

plebeian [plɪˈbiən] *adj* : ordinario, plebeyo

pledge[1] [ˈplɛdʒ] *vt* **pledged; pledging** **1** PAWN : empeñar, prendar **2** PROMISE : prometer, jurar

pledge[2] *n* **1** SECURITY : garantía *f,* prenda *f* **2** PROMISE : promesa *f*

plenteous [ˈplɛntiəs] *adj* : copioso, abundante

plentiful [ˈplɛntɪfəl] *adj* : abundante — **plentifully** [-fli] *adv*

plenty [ˈplɛnti] *n* : abundancia *f* <plenty of time : tiempo de sobra> <plenty of visitors : muchos visitantes>

plethora [ˈplɛθərə] *n* : plétora *f*

pleurisy [ˈplʊrəsi] *n* : pleuresía *f*

pliable [ˈplaɪəbəl] *adj* : flexible, maleable

pliant [ˈplaɪənt] → **pliable**

pliers [ˈplaɪərz] *npl* : alicates *mpl,* pinzas *fpl*

plight [ˈplaɪt] *n* : situación *f* difícil, apuro *m*

plod [ˈplɑd] *vi* **plodded; plodding** **1** TRUDGE : caminar pesadamente y lentamente **2** DRUDGE : trabajar laboriosamente

plot[1] [ˈplɑt] *v* **plotted; plotting** *vt* **1** DEVISE : tramar **2 to plot out** : trazar, determinar (una posición, etc.) — *vi* CONSPIRE : conspirar

plot[2] *n* **1** LOT : terreno *m,* parcela *f,* lote *m* **2** STORY : argumento *m* (en el teatro), trama *f* (en un libro, etc.) **3** CONSPIRACY, INTRIGUE **:** complot *m,* intriga *f*

plotter [ˈplɑt̬ər] *n* **:** conspirador *m,* -dora *f;* intrigante *mf*

plow[1] *or* **plough** [ˈplaʊ] *vt* **1 :** arar (la tierra) **2 to plow the seas :** surcar los mares

plow[2] *or* **plough** *n* **1 :** arado *m* **2** → **snowplow**

plowshare [ˈplaʊˌʃɛr] *n* **:** reja *f* del arado

ploy [ˈplɔɪ] *n* **:** estratagema *f,* maniobra *f*

pluck[1] [ˈplʌk] *vt* **1** PICK **:** arrancar **2 :** desplumar (un pollo, etc.) — *vi* **to pluck at :** tirar de

pluck[2] *n* **1** TUG **:** tirón *m* **2** COURAGE, SPIRIT **:** valor *m,* ánimo *m*

plucky [ˈplʌki] *adj* **pluckier; -est :** valiente, animoso

plug[1] [ˈplʌg] *vt* **plugged; plugging 1** BLOCK **:** tapar **2** PROMOTE **:** hacerle publicidad a, promocionar **3 to plug in :** enchufar

plug[2] *n* **1** STOPPER **:** tapón *m* **2 :** enchufe *m* (eléctrico) **3** ADVERTISEMENT **:** publicidad *f,* propaganda *f*

plum [ˈplʌm] *n* **1 :** ciruela *f* (fruta) **2 :** color *m* ciruela **3** PRIZE **:** premio *m,* algo muy atractivo

plumage [ˈplu:mɪdʒ] *n* **:** plumaje *m*

plumb[1] [ˈplʌm] *vt* **1 :** aplomar <to plumb a wall : aplomar una pared> **2** SOUND **:** sondear, sondar

plumb[2] *adv* **1** VERTICALLY **:** a plomo, verticalmente **2** EXACTLY **:** justo, exactamente **3** COMPLETELY **:** completamente, absolutamente <plumb crazy : loco de remate>

plumb[3] *adj* **:** a plomo

plumb[4] *n or* **plumb line :** plomada *f*

plumber [ˈplʌmər] *n* **:** plomero *m,* -ra *f;* fontanero *m,* -ra *f*

plumbing [ˈplʌmɪŋ] *n* **1 :** plomería *f,* fontanería *f* (trabajo del plomero) **2** PIPES **:** cañería *f,* tubería *f*

plume [ˈplu:m] *n* **1** FEATHER **:** pluma *f* **2** TUFT **:** penacho *m* (en un sombrero, etc.)

plumed [ˈplu:md] *adj* **:** con plumas <white-plumed birds : aves de plumaje blanco>

plummet [ˈplʌmət] *vi* **:** caer en picada, desplomarse

plump[1] [ˈplʌmp] *vi or* **to plump down :** dejarse caer (pesadamente)

plump[2] *adv* **1** STRAIGHT **:** a plomo **2** DIRECTLY **:** directamente, sin rodeos <he ran plump into the door : dio de cara con la puerta>

plump[3] *adj* **:** llenito *fam,* regordete *fam,* rechoncho *fam*

plumpness [ˈplʌmpnəs] *n* **:** gordura *f*

plunder[1] [ˈplʌndər] *vi* **:** saquear, robar

plunder[2] *n* **:** botín *m*

plunderer [ˈplʌndərər] *n* **:** saqueador *m,* -dora *f*

plunge[1] [ˈplʌndʒ] *v* **plunged; plunging** *vt* **1** IMMERSE **:** sumergir **2** THRUST **:** hundir, clavar — *vi* **1** DIVE **:** zambullirse (en el agua) **2 :** meterse precipitadamente o violentamente <they plunged into war : se enfrascaron en una guerra> <he plunged into depression : cayó en la depresión> **3** DESCEND **:** descender en picada <the road plunges dizzily : la calle desciende vertiginosamente>

plunge[2] *n* **1** DIVE **:** zambullida *f* **2** DROP **:** descenso *m* abrupto <the plunge in prices : el desplome de los precios>

plural[1] [ˈplʊrəl] *adj* **:** plural

plural[2] *n* **:** plural *m*

plurality [plʊˈræləṭi] *n, pl* **-ties :** pluralidad *f*

pluralize [ˈplʊrəˌlaɪz] *vt* **-ized; -izing :** pluralizar

plus[1] [ˈplʌs] *adj* **1** POSITIVE **:** positivo <a plus factor : un factor positivo> **2** (*indicating a quantity in addition*) <a grade of C plus : una calificación entre C y B> <a salary of $30,000 plus : un sueldo de más de $30,000>

plus[2] *n* **1** *or* **plus sign :** más *m,* signo *m* de más **2** ADVANTAGE **:** ventaja *f*

plus[3] *prep* **:** más (en matemáticas)

plus[4] *conj* AND **:** y

plush[1] [ˈplʌʃ] *adj* **1 :** afelpado **2** LUXURIOUS **:** lujoso

plush[2] *n* **:** felpa *f,* peluche *m*

plushy [ˈplʌʃi] *adj* **plushier; -est :** lujoso

Pluto [ˈplu:to:] *n* **:** Plutón *m*

plutocracy [plu:ˈtɑkrəsi] *n, pl* **-cies :** plutocracia *f*

plutonium [plu:ˈto:niəm] *n* **:** plutonio *m*

ply[1] [ˈplaɪ] *v* **plied; plying** *vt* **1** USE, WIELD **:** manejar <to ply an ax : manejar un hacha> **2** PRACTICE **:** ejercer <to ply a trade : ejercer un oficio> **3 to ply with questions :** acosar con preguntas

ply[2] *n, pl* **plies 1** LAYER **:** chapa *f* (de madera), capa *f* (de papel) **2** STRAND **:** cabo *m* (de hilo, etc.)

plywood [ˈplaɪˌwʊd] *n* **:** contrachapado *m*

pneumatic [nʊˈmæṭɪk, njʊ-] *adj* **:** neumático

pneumonia [nʊˈmo:njə, njʊ-] *n* **:** pulmonía *f,* neumonía *f*

poach [ˈpo:tʃ] *vt* **1 :** cocer a fuego lento <to poach an egg : escalfar un huevo> **2 to poach game :** cazar ilegalmente — *vi* **:** cazar ilegalmente

poacher [ˈpo:tʃər] *n* **:** cazador *m* furtivo, cazadora *f* furtiva

pock [ˈpɑk] *n* **1** PUSTULE **:** pústula *f* **2** → **pockmark**

pocket[1] [ˈpɑkət] *vt* **1 :** meterse en el bolsillo <he pocketed the pen : se metió la pluma en el bolsillo> **2** STEAL **:** embolsarse

pocket[2] *n* **1 :** bolsillo *m,* bolsa *f Mex* <a coat pocket : el bolsillo de un abrigo>

<air pockets : bolsas de aire> **2** CENTER : foco *m,* centro *m* <a pocket of resistance : un foco de resistencia>

pocketbook [ˈpɑkətˌbʊk] *n* **1** PURSE : cartera *f,* bolso *m,* bolsa *f Mex* **2** MEANS : recursos *mpl*

pocketknife [ˈpɑkətˌnaɪf] *n, pl* **-knives** : navaja *f*

pocket-size [ˈpɑkətˈsaɪz] *adj* : de bolsillo

pockmark [ˈpɑkˌmɑrk] *n* : cicatriz *f* de viruela, viruela *f*

pod [ˈpɑd] *n* : vaina *f* <pea pod : vaina de guisantes>

podiatrist [pəˈdaɪətrɪst, po-] *n* : podólogo *m,* -ga *f*

podiatry [pəˈdaɪətri, po-] *n* : podología *f,* podiatría *f*

podium [ˈpoːdiəm] *n, pl* **-diums** *or* **-dia** [-diə] : podio *m,* estrado *m,* tarima *f*

poem [ˈpoːəm] *n* : poema *m,* poesía *f*

poet [ˈpoːət] *n* : poeta *mf*

poetic [poˈɛtɪk] *or* **poetical** [-t̬ɪkəl] *adj* : poético

poetry [ˈpoːətri] *n* : poesía *f*

pogrom [ˈpoːgrəm, pəˈgrɑm, ˈpɑgrəm] *n* : pogrom *m*

poignancy [ˈpɔɪnjəntsi] *n, pl* **-cies** : lo conmovedor

poignant [ˈpɔɪnjənt] *adj* **1** PAINFUL : penoso, doloroso <poignant grief : profundo dolor> **2** TOUCHING : conmovedor, emocionante

poinsettia [pɔɪnˈsɛt̬iə, -ˈsɛt̬ə] *n* : flor *f* de Nochebuena

point[1] [ˈpɔɪnt] *vt* **1** SHARPEN : afilar (la punta de) **2** INDICATE : señalar, indicar <to point the way : señalar el camino> **3** AIM : apuntar **4 to point out** : señalar, indicar — *vi* **1 to point at** : señalar (con el dedo) **2 to point to** INDICATE : señalar, indicar

point[2] *n* **1** ITEM : punto *m* <the main points : los puntos principales> **2** QUALITY : cualidad *f* <her good points : sus buenas cualidades> <it's not his strong point : no es su (punto) fuerte> **3** (*indicating a chief idea or meaning*) <it's beside the point : no viene al caso> <to get to the point : ir al grano> <to stick to the point : no salirse del tema> **4** PURPOSE : fin *m,* propósito *m* <there's no point to it : no vale la pena, no sirve para nada> **5** PLACE : punto *m,* lugar *m* <points of interest : puntos interesantes> **6** : punto *m* (en una escala) <boiling point : punto de ebullición> **7** MOMENT : momento *m,* coyuntura *f* <at this point : en este momento> **8** TIP : punta *f* **9** HEADLAND : punta *f,* cabo *m* **10** PERIOD : punto *m* (marca de puntuación) **11** UNIT : punto *m* <he scored 15 points : ganó 15 puntos> <shares fell 10 points : las acciones bajaron 10 enteros> **12 compass points** : puntos *mpl* cardinales **13 decimal point** : punto *m* decimal, coma *f*

point-blank[1] [ˈpɔɪntˈblæŋk] *adv* **1** : a quemarropa <to shoot point-blank : disparar a quemarropa> **2** BLUNTLY, DIRECTLY : a bocajarro, sin rodeos, francamente

point-blank[2] *adj* **1** : a quemarropa <point-blank shots : disparos a quemarropa> **2** BLUNT, DIRECT : directo, franco

pointedly [ˈpɔɪntədli] *adv* : intencionadamente, directamente

pointer [ˈpɔɪntər] *n* **1** STICK : puntero *m* (para maestros, etc.) **2** INDICATOR, NEEDLE : indicador *m,* aguja *f* **3** : perro *m* de muestra **4** HINT, TIP : consejo *m*

pointless [ˈpɔɪntləs] *adj* : inútil, ocioso, vano <it's pointless to continue : no tiene sentido continuar>

point of view *n* : perspectiva *f,* punto *m* de vista

poise[1] [ˈpɔɪz] *vt* **poised; poising** BALANCE : equilibrar, balancear

poise[2] *n* : aplomo *m,* compostura *f*

poison[1] [ˈpɔɪzən] *vt* **1** : envenenar, intoxicar **2** CORRUPT : corromper

poison[2] *n* : veneno *m*

poison ivy *n* : hiedra *f* venenosa

poisonous [ˈpɔɪzənəs] *adj* : venenoso, tóxico, ponzoñoso

poke[1] [ˈpoːk] *v* **poked; poking** *vt* **1** JAB : golpear (con la punta de algo), dar <he poked me with his finger : me dio con el dedo> **2** THRUST : introducir, asomar <I poked my head out the window : asomé la cabeza por la ventana> — *vi* **1 to poke around** RUMMAGE : hurgar **2 to poke along** DAWDLE : demorarse, entretenerse

poke[2] *n* : golpe *m* abrupto (con la punta de algo)

poker [ˈpoːkər] *n* **1** : atizador *m* (para el fuego) **2** : póker *m,* poker *m* (juego de naipes)

polar [ˈpoːlər] *adj* : polar

polar bear *n* : oso *m* blanco

Polaris [poˈlærɪs, -ˈlɑr-] → **North Star**

polarize [ˈpoːləˌraɪz] *vt* **-ized; -izing** : polarizar

pole [ˈpoːl] *n* **1** : palo *m,* poste *m,* vara *f* <telephone pole : poste de teléfonos> **2** : polo *m* <the South Pole : el Polo Sur> **3** : polo *m* (eléctrico o magnético)

Pole [ˈpoːl] *n* : polaco *m,* -ca *f*

polecat [ˈpoːlˌkæt] *n, pl* **polecats** *or* **polecat 1** : turón *m* (de Europa) **2** SKUNK : mofeta *f,* zorrillo *m*

polemical [pəˈlɛmɪkəl] *adj* : polémico

polemics [pəˈlɛmɪks] *ns & pl* : polémica *f*

polestar [ˈpoːlˌstɑr] → **North Star**

police[1] [pəˈliːs] *vt* **-liced; -licing** : mantener el orden en <to police the streets : patrullar las calles>

police[2] *ns & pl* **1** : policía *f* (organización) **2** POLICE OFFICERS : policías *mfpl*

policeman [pəˈliːsmən] *n, pl* **-men** [-mən, -ˌmɛn] : policía *m*

police officer *n* : policía *mf,* agente *mf* de policía

policewoman [pə'liːs,wʊmən] *n, pl* **-women** [-,wɪmən] : policía *f,* mujer *f* policía

policy ['pɑləsi] *n, pl* **-cies 1** : política *f* <foreign policy : política exterior> **2** *or* **insurance policy** : póliza *f* de seguros, seguro *m*

polio[1] ['poːli,oː] *adj* : de polio <polio vaccine : vacuna contra la polio>

polio[2] *n* → **poliomyelitis**

poliomyelitis [,poːli,oː,maɪə'laɪtəs] *n* : poliomielitis *f,* polio *f*

polish[1] ['pɑlɪʃ] *vt* **1** : pulir, lustrar, sacar brillo a <to polish one's nails : pintarse las uñas> **2** REFINE : pulir, perfeccionar

polish[2] *n* **1** LUSTER : brillo *m,* lustre *m* **2** REFINEMENT : refinamiento *m* **3** : betún *m* (para zapatos), cera *f* (para suelos y muebles), esmalte *m* (para las uñas)

Polish[1] ['poːlɪʃ] *adj* : polaco

Polish[2] *n* : polaco *m* (idioma)

polite [pə'laɪt] *adj* **-liter; -est** : cortés, correcto, educado

politely [pə'laɪtli] *adv* : cortésmente, correctamente, con buenos modales

politeness [pə'laɪtnəs] *n* : cortesía *f*

politic ['pɑlə,tɪk] *adj* : diplomático, prudente

political [pə'lɪtɪkəl] *adj* : político — **politically** [-tɪkli] *adv*

politician [,pɑlə'tɪʃən] *n* : político *m,* -ca *f*

politics ['pɑlə,tɪks] *ns & pl* : política *f*

polka ['poːlkə, 'poːkə] *n* : polka *f*

polka dot ['poːkə,dɑt] *n* : lunar *m* (en un diseño)

poll[1] ['poːl] *vt* **1** : obtener (votos) <she polled over 1000 votes : obtuvo más de 1000 votos> **2** CANVASS : encuestar, sondear — *vi* : obtener votos

poll[2] *n* **1** SURVEY : encuesta *f,* sondeo *m* **2 polls** *npl* : urnas *fpl* <to go to the polls : acudir a las urnas, ir a votar>

pollen ['pɑlən] *n* : polen *m*

pollinate ['pɑlə,neɪt] *vt* **-nated; -nating** : polinizar

pollination [,pɑlə'neɪʃən] *n* : polinización *f*

pollster ['poːlstər] *n* : encuestador *m,* -dora *f*

pollutant [pə'luːtənt] *n* : contaminante *m*

pollute [pə'luːt] *vt* **-luted; -luting** : contaminar

pollution [pə'luːʃən] *n* : contaminación *f*

pollywog *or* **polliwog** ['pɑli,wɔg] *n* TADPOLE : renacuajo *m*

polo ['poː,loː] *n* : polo *m*

poltergeist ['poːltər,gaɪst] *n* : poltergeist *m,* fantasma *m* travieso

polyester ['pɑli,ɛstər, ,pɑli'-] *n* : poliéster *m*

polygamous [pə'lɪgəməs] *adj* : polígamo

polygamy [pə'lɪgəmi] *n* : poligamia *f*

polygon ['pɑli,gɑn] *n* : polígono *m*

polymer ['pɑləmər] *n* : polímero *m*

polyunsaturated [,pɑli,ʌn'sætʃə,reɪtəd] *adj* : poliinsaturado

pomegranate ['pɑmə,grænət, 'pɑm,grænət] *n* : granada *f* (fruta)

pommel[1] ['pʌməl] *vt* → **pummel**

pommel[2] ['pʌməl, 'pɑ-] *n* **1** : pomo *m* (de una espada) **2** : perilla *f* (de una silla de montar)

pomp ['pɑmp] *n* **1** SPLENDOR : pompa *f,* esplendor *m* **2** OSTENTATION : boato *m,* ostentación *f*

pom-pom ['pɑm,pɑm] *n* : borla *f,* pompón *m*

pomposity [pɑm'pɑsəti] *n, pl* **-ties** : pomposidad *f*

pompous ['pɑmpəs] *adj* : pomposo — **pompously** *adv*

poncho ['pɑn,tʃoː] *n, pl* **-chos** : poncho *m*

pond ['pɑnd] *n* : charca *f* (natural), estanque *m* (artificial)

ponder ['pɑndər] *vt* : reflexionar, considerar — *vi* **to ponder over** : reflexionar sobre, sopesar

ponderous ['pɑndərəs] *adj* : pesado

pontiff ['pɑntɪf] *n* POPE : pontífice *m*

pontificate [pɑn'tɪfə,keɪt] *vi* **-cated; -cating** : pontificar

pontoon [pɑn'tuːn] *n* : pontón *m*

pony ['poːni] *n, pl* **-nies** : poni *m,* poney *m,* jaca *f*

ponytail ['poːni,teɪl] *n* : cola *f* de caballo, coleta *f*

poodle ['puːdəl] *n* : caniche *m*

pool[1] ['puːl] *vt* : mancomunar, hacer un fondo común de

pool[2] *n* **1** : charca *f* <a swimming pool : una piscina> **2** PUDDLE : charco *m* **3** RESERVE, SUPPLY : fondo *m* común (de recursos), reserva *f* **4** : billar *m* (juego)

poor ['pʊr, 'por] *adj* **1** : pobre <poor people : los pobres> **2** SCANTY : pobre, escaso <poor attendance : baja asistencia> **3** UNFORTUNATE : pobre <poor thing! : ¡pobrecito!> **4** BAD : malo <to be in poor health : estar mal de salud>

poorly ['pʊrli, 'por-] *adv* : mal

pop[1] ['pɑp] *v* **popped; popping** *vi* **1** BURST : reventarse, estallar **2** : ir, venir, o aparecer abruptamente <he popped into the house : se metió en la casa> <a menu pops up : aparece un menú> **3 to pop out** PROTRUDE : salirse, saltarse <my eyes popped out of my head : se me saltaban los ojos> — *vt* **1** BURST : reventar **2** : hacer o meter abruptamente <he popped it into his mouth : se lo metió en la boca>

pop[2] *adj* : popular <pop music : música popular>

pop[3] *n* **1** : estallido *m* pequeño (de un globo, etc.) **2** SODA : refresco *m,* gaseosa *f*

popcorn [ˈpɑpˌkɔrn] *n* **:** palomitas *fpl* (de maíz)

pope [ˈpoːp] *n* **:** papa *m* <Pope John : el Papa Juan>

poplar [ˈpɑplər] *n* **:** álamo *m*

poplin [ˈpɑplɪn] *n* **:** popelín *m,* popelina *f*

poppy [ˈpɑpi] *n, pl* **-pies :** amapola *f*

populace [ˈpɑpjələs] *n* **1** MASSES **:** pueblo *m* **2** POPULATION **:** población *f*

popular [ˈpɑpjələr] *adj* **1 :** popular <the popular vote : el voto popular> **2** COMMON **:** generalizado, común <popular beliefs : creencias generalizadas> **3 :** popular, de gran popularidad <a popular singer : un cantante popular>

popularity [ˌpɑpjəˈlærət̬i] *n* **:** popularidad *f*

popularize [ˈpɑpjələˌraɪz] *vt* **-ized; -izing :** popularizar

popularly [ˈpɑpjələrli] *adv* **:** popularmente, vulgarmente

populate [ˈpɑpjəˌleɪt] *vt* **-lated; -lating :** poblar

population [ˌpɑpjəˈleɪʃən] *n* **:** población *f*

populous [ˈpɑpjələs] *adj* **:** populoso

porcelain [ˈporsələn] *n* **:** porcelana *f*

porch [ˈportʃ] *n* **:** porche *m*

porcupine [ˈpɔrkjəˌpaɪn] *n* **:** puerco *m* espín

pore[1] [ˈpor] *vi* **pored; poring 1** GAZE **:** mirar (con atención) **2 to pore over :** leer detenidamente, estudiar

pore[2] *n* **:** poro *m*

pork [ˈpork] *n* **:** carne *f* de cerdo, carne *f* de puerco

pornographic [ˌpɔrnəˈgræfɪk] *adj* **:** pornográfico

pornography [pɔrˈnɑgrəfi] *n* **:** pornografía *f*

porous [ˈporəs] *adj* **:** poroso

porpoise [ˈpɔrpəs] *n* **1 :** marsopa *f* **2** DOLPHIN **:** delfín *m*

porridge [ˈpɔrɪdʒ] *n* **:** sopa *f* espesa de harina, gachas *fpl*

port[1] [ˈport] *adj* **:** de babor <on the port side : a babor>

port[2] *n* **1** HARBOR **:** puerto *m* **2** ORIFICE **:** orificio *m* (de una válvula, etc.) **3 :** puerto *m* (de una computadora) **4** PORTHOLE **:** portilla *f* **5** *or* **port side :** babor *m* (de un barco) **6 :** oporto *m* (vino)

portable [ˈport̬əbəl] *adj* **:** portátil

portal [ˈport̬əl] *n* **:** portal *m*

portend [pɔrˈtɛnd] *vt* **:** presagiar, augurar

portent [ˈpɔrˌtɛnt] *n* **:** presagio *m,* augurio *m*

portentous [pɔrˈtɛntəs] *adj* **:** profético, que presagia

porter [ˈport̬ər] *n* **:** maletero *m,* mozo *m* (de estación)

portfolio [portˈfoːliˌo] *n, pl* **-lios 1** FOLDER **:** cartera *f* (para llevar papeles), carpeta *f* **2 :** cartera *f* (diplomática) **3 investment portfolio :** cartera de inversiones

porthole [ˈportˌhoːl] *n* **:** portilla *f* (de un barco), ventanilla *f* (de un avión)

portico [ˈport̬ɪˌko] *n, pl* **-coes** *or* **-cos :** pórtico *m*

portion[1] [ˈporʃən] *vt* DISTRIBUTE **:** repartir

portion[2] *n* PART, SHARE **:** porción *f,* parte *f*

portly [ˈportli] *adj* **-lier; -est :** corpulento

portrait [ˈportrət, -ˌtreɪt] *n* **:** retrato *m*

portray [porˈtreɪ] *vt* **1** DEPICT **:** representar, retratar **2** DESCRIBE **:** describir **3** PLAY **:** interpretar (un personaje)

portrayal [porˈtreɪəl] *n* **1** REPRESENTATION **:** representación *f* **2** PORTRAIT **:** retrato *m*

Portuguese [ˌportʃəˈgiːz, -ˈgiːs] *n* **1 :** portugués *m,* -guesa *f* (persona) **2 :** portugués *m* (idioma) — **Portuguese** *adj*

pose[1] [ˈpoːz] *v* **posed; posing** *vt* PRESENT **:** plantear (una pregunta, etc.), representar (una amenaza) — *vi* **1 :** posar (para una foto, etc.) **2 to pose as :** hacerse pasar por

pose[2] *n* **1 :** pose *f* <to strike a pose : asumir una pose> **2** PRETENSE **:** pose *f,* afectación *f*

posh [ˈpɑʃ] *adj* **:** elegante, de lujo

position[1] [pəˈzɪʃən] *vt* **:** colocar, situar, ubicar

position[2] *n* **1** APPROACH, STANCE **:** posición *f,* postura *f,* planteamiento *m* **2** LOCATION **:** posición *f,* ubicación *f* **3** STATUS **:** posición *f* (en una jerarquía) **4** JOB **:** puesto *m*

positive [ˈpɑzət̬ɪv] *adj* **1** DEFINITE **:** incuestionable, inequívoco <positive evidence : pruebas irrefutables> **2** CONFIDENT **:** seguro **3 :** positivo (en gramática, matemáticas, y física) **4** AFFIRMATIVE **:** positivo, afirmativo <a positive response : una respuesta positiva>

positively [ˈpɑzət̬ɪvli] *adv* **1** FAVORABLY **:** favorablemente **2** OPTIMISTICALLY **:** positivamente **3** DEFINITELY **:** definitivamente, en forma concluyente **4** (*used for emphasis*) **:** realmente, verdaderamente <it's positively awful! : ¡es verdaderamente malo!>

possess [pəˈzɛs] *vt* **1** HAVE, OWN **:** poseer, tener **2** SEIZE **:** apoderarse de <he was possessed by fear : el miedo se apoderó de él>

possession [pəˈzɛʃən] *n* **1** POSSESSING **:** posesión *f* **2 :** posesión *f* (por un demonio, etc.) **3 possessions** *npl* PROPERTY **:** bienes *mpl,* propiedad *f*

possessive[1] [pəˈzɛsɪv] *adj* **1 :** posesivo (en gramática) **2** JEALOUS **:** posesivo, celoso

possessive[2] *n or* **possessive case :** posesivo *m*

possessor [pə'zɛsər] *n* : poseedor *m,* -dora *f*
possibility [,pɑsə'bɪləṭi] *n, pl* **-ties** : posibilidad *f*
possible ['pɑsəbəl] *adj* : posible
possibly ['pɑsəbli] *adv* **1** CONCEIVABLY : posiblemente <it can't possibly be true! : ¡no puede ser!> **2** PERHAPS : quizás, posiblemente
possum ['pɑsəm] → **opossum**
post[1] ['po:st] *vt* **1** MAIL : echar al correo, mandar por correo **2** ANNOUNCE : anunciar <they've posted the grades : han anunciado las notas> **3** AFFIX : fijar, poner (noticias, etc.) **4** STATION : apostar **5 to keep (someone) posted** : tener al corriente (a alguien)
post[2] *n* **1** POLE : poste *m,* palo *m* **2** STATION : puesto *m* **3** CAMP : puesto *m* (militar) **4** JOB, POSITION : puesto *m,* empleo *m,* cargo *m*
postage ['po:stɪdʒ] *n* : franqueo *m*
postal ['po:stəl] *adj* : postal
postcard ['po:st,kɑrd] *n* : postal *f,* tarjeta *f* postal
poster ['po:stər] *n* : póster *m,* cartel *m,* afiche *m*
posterior[1] [pɑ'stɪriər, po-] *adj* : posterior
posterior[2] *n* BUTTOCKS : trasero *m,* nalgas *fpl,* asentaderas *fpl*
posterity [pɑ'stɛrəṭi] *n* : posteridad *f*
postgraduate[1] [,po:st'grædʒʊət] *adj* : de postgrado
postgraduate[2] *n* : postgraduado *m,* -da *f*
posthaste ['po:st'heɪst] *adv* : a toda prisa
posthumous ['pɑstʃəməs] *adj* : póstumo — **posthumously** *adv*
postman ['po:stmən, -,mæn] → **mailman**
postmark[1] ['po:st,mɑrk] *vt* : matasellar
postmark[2] *n* : matasellos *m*
postmaster ['po:st,mæstər] *n* : administrador *m,* -dora *f* de correos
postmortem [,po:st'mɔrṭəm] *n* : autopsia *f*
postnatal [,po:st'neɪṭəl] *adj* : postnatal <postnatal depression : depresión posparto>
post office *n* : correo *m,* oficina *f* de correos
postoperative [,po:st'ɑpərəṭɪv, -,reɪ-] *adj* : posoperatorio
postpaid [,po:st'peɪd] *adv* : con franqueo pagado
postpone [,po:st'po:n] *vt* **-poned; -poning** : postergar, aplazar, posponer
postponement [,po:st'po:nmənt] *n* : postergación *f,* aplazamiento *m*
postscript ['po:st,skrɪpt] *n* : postdata *f,* posdata *f*
postulate ['pɑstʃə,leɪt] *vt* **-lated; -lating** : postular
posture[1] ['pɑstʃər] *vi* **-tured; -turing** : posar, asumir una pose
posture[2] *n* : postura *f*
postwar [,po:st'wɔr] *adj* : de (la) posguerra
posy ['po:zi] *n, pl* **-sies 1** FLOWER : flor *f* **2** BOUQUET : ramo *m,* ramillete *m*
pot[1] ['pɑt] *vt* **potted; potting** : plantar (en una maceta)
pot[2] *n* **1** : olla *f* (de cocina) **2 pots and pans** : cacharros *mpl*
potable ['po:ṭəbəl] *adj* : potable
potash ['pɑt,æʃ] *n* : potasa *f*
potassium [pə'tæsiəm] *n* : potasio *m*
potato [pə'teɪṭo] *n, pl* **-toes** : papa *f,* patata *f Spain*
potato chips *npl* : papas *fpl* fritas (de bolsa)
potbellied ['pɑt,bɛlid] *adj* : panzón, barrigón *fam*
potbelly ['pɑt,bɛli] *n* : panza *f,* barriga *f*
potency ['po:tən*t*si] *n, pl* **-cies 1** POWER : fuerza *f,* potencia *f* **2** EFFECTIVENESS : eficacia *f*
potent ['po:tənt] *adj* **1** POWERFUL : potente, poderoso **2** EFFECTIVE : eficaz <a potent medicine : una medicina bien fuerte>
potential[1] [pə'tɛntʃəl] *adj* : potencial, posible
potential[2] *n* **1** : potencial *m* <growth potential : potencial de crecimiento> <a child with potential : un niño que promete> **2** : potencial *m* (eléctrico) — **potentially** *adv*
potful ['pɑt,fʊl] *n* : contenido *m* de una olla <a potful of water : una olla de agua>
pothole ['pɑt,ho:l] *n* : bache *m*
potion ['po:ʃən] *n* : brebaje *m,* poción *f*
potluck ['pɑt,lʌk] *n* **to take potluck** : tomar lo que haya
potpourri [,po:pʊ'ri:] *n* : popurrí *m*
potshot ['pɑt,ʃɑt] *n* **1** : tiro *m* al azar <to take potshots at : disparar al azar a> **2** CRITICISM : crítica *f* (hecha al azar)
potter ['pɑṭər] *n* : alfarero *m,* -ra *f*
pottery ['pɑṭəri] *n, pl* **-teries** : cerámica *f*
pouch ['paʊtʃ] *n* **1** BAG : bolsa *f* pequeña **2** : bolsa *f* (de un animal)
poultice ['po:ltəs] *n* : emplasto *m,* cataplasma *f*
poultry ['po:ltri] *n* : aves *fpl* de corral
pounce ['paʊn*t*s] *vi* **pounced; pouncing** : abalanzarse
pound[1] ['paʊnd] *vt* **1** CRUSH : machacar, machucar, majar **2** BEAT : golpear, machacar <she pounded the lessons into them : les machacaba las lecciones> <he pounded home his point : les hizo entender su razonamiento> — *vi* **1** BEAT : palpitar (dícese del corazón) **2** RESOUND : retumbar, resonar **3** : andar con paso pesado <we pounded through the mud : caminamos pesadamente por el barro>

pound[2] *n* **1 :** libra *f* (unidad de peso) **2 :** libra *f* (unidad monetaria) **3 dog pound :** perrera *f*

pour [ˈpor] *vt* **1 :** echar, verter, servir (bebidas) <pour it into a pot : viértalo en una olla> **2 :** proveer con abundancia <they poured money into it : le invirtieron mucho dinero> **3 to pour out :** dar salida a <he poured out his feelings to her : se desahogó con ella> — *vi* **1** FLOW **:** manar, fluir, salir <blood was pouring from the wound : la sangre le salía de la herida> **2 it's pouring (outside) :** está lloviendo a cántaros

pout[1] [ˈpaʊt] *vi* **:** hacer pucheros

pout[2] *n* **:** puchero *m*

poverty [ˈpɑvərt̬i] *n* **:** pobreza *f,* indigencia *f*

powder[1] [ˈpaʊdər] *vt* **1 :** empolvar <to powder one's face : empolvarse la cara> **2** PULVERIZE **:** pulverizar

powder[2] *n* **:** polvo *m,* polvos *mpl*

powdery [ˈpaʊdəri] *adj* **:** polvoriento, como polvo

power[1] [ˈpaʊər] *vt* **:** impulsar, propulsar

power[2] *n* **1** AUTHORITY **:** poder *m,* autoridad *f* <executive powers : poderes ejecutivos> **2** ABILITY **:** capacidad *f,* poder *m* **3 :** potencia *f* (política) <foreign powers : potencias extranjeras> **4** STRENGTH **:** fuerza *f* **5 :** potencia *f* (en física y matemáticas)

powerful [ˈpaʊərfəl] *adj* **:** poderoso, potente — **powerfully** *adv*

powerhouse [ˈpaʊərˌhaʊs] *n* **:** persona *f* dinámica

powerless [ˈpaʊərləs] *adj* **:** impotente

power plant *n* **:** central *f* eléctrica

powwow [ˈpaʊˌwaʊ] *n* **:** conferencia *f*

pox [ˈpɑks] *n, pl* **pox** *or* **poxes 1** CHICKEN POX **:** varicela *f* **2** SYPHILIS **:** sífilis *f*

practicable [ˈpræktɪkəbəl] *adj* **:** practicable, viable, factible

practical [ˈpræktɪkəl] *adj* **:** práctico

practicality [ˌpræktɪˈkæləti] *n, pl* **-ties :** factibilidad *f,* viabilidad *f*

practical joke *n* **:** broma *f* (pesada)

practically [ˈpræktɪkli] *adv* **1 :** de manera práctica **2** ALMOST **:** casi, prácticamente

practice[1] *or* **practise** [ˈpræktəs] *vt* **-ticed** *or* **-tised; -ticing** *or* **-tising 1 :** practicar <he practiced his German on us : practicó el alemán con nosotros> <to practice politeness : practicar la cortesía> **2 :** ejercer <to practice medicine : ejercer la medicina>

practice[2] *n* **1** USE **:** práctica *f* <to put into practice : poner en práctica> **2** CUSTOM **:** costumbre *f* <it's a common practice here : por aquí se acostumbra hacerlo> **3** TRAINING **:** práctica *f* **4 :** ejercicio *m* (de una profesión)

practitioner [prækˈtɪʃənər] *n* **1 :** profesional *mf* **2 general practitioner :** médico *m,* -ca *f*

pragmatic [prægˈmæt̬ɪk] *adj* **:** pragmático — **pragmatically** *adv*

pragmatism [ˈprægməˌtɪzəm] *n* **:** pragmatismo

prairie [ˈprɛri] *n* **:** pradera *f,* llanura *f*

praise[1] [ˈpreɪz] *vt* **praised; praising :** elogiar, alabar <to praise God : alabar a Dios>

praise[2] *n* **:** elogio *m,* alabanza *f*

praiseworthy [ˈpreɪzˌwərði] *adj* **:** digno de alabanza, loable

prance[1] [ˈprænts] *vi* **pranced; prancing 1 :** hacer cabriolas, cabriolar <a prancing horse : un caballo haciendo cabriolas> **2** SWAGGER **:** pavonearse

prance[2] *n* **:** cabriola *f*

prank [ˈpræŋk] *n* **:** broma *f,* travesura *f*

prankster [ˈpræŋkstər] *n* **:** bromista *mf*

prattle[1] [ˈprætəl] *vt* **-tled; -tling :** parlotear *fam,* cotorrear *fam,* balbucear (como un niño)

prattle[2] *n* **:** parloteo *m fam,* cotorreo *m fam,* cháchara *f fam*

prawn [ˈprɔn] *n* **:** langostino *m,* camarón *m,* gamba *f*

pray [ˈpreɪ] *vt* ENTREAT **:** rogar, suplicar — *vi* **:** rezar

prayer [ˈprɛr] *n* **1 :** plegaria *f,* oración *f* <to say one's prayers : orar, rezar> <the Lord's Prayer : el Padrenuestro> **2** PRAYING **:** rezo *m,* oración *f* <to kneel in prayer : arrodillarse para rezar>

praying mantis → **mantis**

preach [ˈpriːtʃ] *vi* **:** predicar — *vt* ADVOCATE **:** abogar por <to preach cooperation : promover la cooperación>

preacher [ˈpriːtʃər] *n* **1 :** predicador *m,* -dora *f* **2** MINISTER **:** pastor *m,* -tora *f*

preamble [ˈpriːˌæmbəl] *n* **:** preámbulo *m*

prearrange [ˌpriːəˈreɪndʒ] *vt* **-ranged; -ranging :** arreglar de antemano

precarious [priˈkæriəs] *adj* **:** precario — **precariously** *adv*

precariousness [priˈkæriəsnəs] *n* **:** precariedad *f*

precaution [priˈkɔʃən] *n* **:** precaución *f*

precautionary [priˈkɔʃəˌnɛri] *adj* **:** preventivo, cautelar, precautorio

precede [priˈsiːd] *v* **-ceded; -ceding :** preceder a

precedence [ˈprɛsədənts, prɪˈsiːdənts] *n* **:** precedencia *f*

precedent [ˈprɛsədənt] *n* **:** precedente *m*

precept [ˈpriːˌsɛpt] *n* **:** precepto *m*

precinct [ˈpriːˌsɪŋkt] *n* **1** DISTRICT **:** distrito *m* (policial, electoral, etc.) **2 precincts** *npl* PREMISES **:** recinto *m,* predio *m,* límites *mpl* (de una ciudad)

precious [ˈprɛʃəs] *adj* **1 :** precioso <precious gems : piedras preciosas> **2** DEAR **:** querido **3** AFFECTED **:** afectado

precipice [ˈprɛsəpəs] *n* **:** precipicio *m*

precipitate [priˈsɪpəˌteɪt] *v* **-tated; -tating** *vt* **1** HASTEN, PROVOKE **:** precipitar, provocar **2** HURL **:** arrojar **3**

: precipitar (en química) — *vi* : precipitarse (en química), condensarse (en meteorología)

precipitation [pri͵sɪpəˈteɪʃən] *n* **1** HASTE : precipitación *f,* prisa *f* **2** : precipitaciones *fpl* (en meteorología)

precipitous [priˈsɪpət̬əs] *adj* **1** HASTY, RASH : precipitado **2** STEEP : escarpado, empinado <a precipitous drop : una caída vertiginosa>

précis [preɪˈsiː] *n, pl* **précis** [-ˈsiːz] : resumen *m*

precise [priˈsaɪs] *adj* **1** DEFINITE : preciso, explícito **2** EXACT : exacto, preciso <precise calculations : cálculos precisos> — **precisely** *adv*

preciseness [priˈsaɪsnəs] *n* : precisión *f,* exactitud *f*

precision [priˈsɪʒən] *n* : precisión *f*

preclude [priˈkluːd] *vt* **-cluded; -cluding** : evitar, impedir, excluir (una posibilidad, etc.)

precocious [priˈkoːʃəs] *adj* : precoz — **precociously** *adv*

precocity [priˈkɑsət̬i] *n* : precocidad *f*

preconceive [͵priːkənˈsiːv] *vt* **-ceived; -ceiving** : preconcebir

preconception [͵priːkənˈsɛpʃən] *n* : idea *f* preconcebida

precondition [͵priːkənˈdɪʃən] *n* : precondición *f,* condición *f* previa

precook [͵priːˈkʊk] *vt* : precocinar

precursor [priˈkərsər] *n* : precursor *m,* -sora *f*

predator [ˈprɛdət̬ər] *n* : depredador *m,* -dora *f*

predatory [ˈprɛdə͵tori] *adj* : depredador

predecessor [ˈprɛdə͵sɛsər, ˈpriː-] *n* : antecesor *m,* -sora *f;* predecesor *m,* -sora *f*

predestination [pri͵dɛstəˈneɪʃən] *n* : predestinación *f*

predestine [priˈdɛstən] *vt* **-tined; -tining** : predestinar

predetermine [͵priːdɪˈtərmən] *vt* **-mined; -mining** : predeterminar

predicament [priˈdɪkəmənt] *n* : apuro *m,* aprieto *m*

predicate¹ [ˈprɛdə͵keɪt] *vt* **-cated; -cating 1** AFFIRM : afirmar, aseverar **2 to be predicated on** : estar basado en

predicate² [ˈprɛdɪkət] *n* : predicado *m*

predict [priˈdɪkt] *vt* : pronosticar, predecir

predictable [priˈdɪktəbəl] *adj* : previsible — **predictably** [-bli] *adv*

prediction [priˈdɪkʃən] *n* : pronóstico *m,* predicción *f*

predilection [͵prɛdəlˈɛkʃən, ͵priː-] *n* : predilección *f*

predispose [͵priːdɪˈspoːz] *vt* **-posed; -posing** : predisponer

predominance [priˈdɑmənənts] *n* : predominio *m*

predominant [priˈdɑmənənt] *adj* : predominante — **predominantly** *adv*

predominate [priˈdɑmə͵neɪt] *vi* **-nated; -nating 1** : predominar (en cantidad) **2** PREVAIL : prevalecer

preeminence [priˈɛmənənts] *n* : preeminencia *f*

preeminent [priˈɛmənənt] *adj* : preeminente

preeminently [priˈɛmənəntli] *adv* : especialmente

preempt [priˈɛmpt] *vt* **1** APPROPRIATE : apoderarse de, apropriarse de **2** : reemplazar (un programa de televisión, etc.) **3** FORESTALL : adelantarse a (un ataque, etc.)

preen [ˈpriːn] *vt* : arreglarse (el pelo, las plumas, etc.)

prefabricated [͵priːˈfæbrə͵keɪt̬əd] *adj* : prefabricado

preface [ˈprɛfəs] *n* : prefacio *m,* prólogo *m*

prefatory [ˈprɛfə͵tori] *adj* : preliminar

prefer [priˈfər] *vt* **-ferred; -ferring 1** : preferir <I prefer coffee : prefiero café> **2 to prefer charges against** : presentar cargos contra

preferable [ˈprɛfərəbəl] *adj* : preferible

preferably [ˈprɛfərəbli] *adv* : preferentemente, de preferencia

preference [ˈprɛfrənts, ˈprɛfər-] *n* : preferencia *f,* gusto *m*

preferential [͵prɛfəˈrɛntʃəl] *adj* : preferencial, preferente

prefigure [priˈfɪgjər] *vt* **-ured; -uring** FORESHADOW : prefigurar, anunciar

prefix [ˈpriː͵fɪks] *n* : prefijo *m*

pregnancy [ˈprɛgnəntsi] *n, pl* **-cies** : embarazo *m,* preñez *f*

pregnant [ˈprɛgnənt] *adj* **1** : embarazada (dícese de una mujer), preñada (dícese de un animal) **2** MEANINGFUL : significativo

preheat [͵priːˈhiːt] *vt* : precalentar

prehensile [priˈhɛntsəl, -ˈhɛn͵saɪl] *adj* : prensil

prehistoric [͵priːhɪsˈtɔrɪk] *or* **prehistorical** [-ɪkəl] *adj* : prehistórico

prejudge [͵priːˈdʒʌdʒ] *vt* **-judged; -judging** : prejuzgar

prejudice¹ [ˈprɛdʒədəs] *vt* **-diced; -dicing 1** DAMAGE : perjudicar **2** BIAS : predisponer, influir en

prejudice² *n* **1** DAMAGE : perjuicio *m* (en derecho) **2** BIAS : prejuicio *m*

prelate [ˈprɛlət] *n* : prelado *m*

preliminary¹ [priˈlɪmə͵nɛri] *adj* : preliminar

preliminary² *n, pl* **-naries 1** : preámbulo *m,* preludio *m* **2 preliminaries** *npl* : preliminares *mpl*

prelude [ˈprɛ͵luːd, ˈprɛl͵juːd; ˈpreɪ͵luːd, ˈpriː-] *n* : preludio *m*

premarital [͵priːˈmærət̬əl] *adj* : prematrimonial

premature [͵priːməˈtʊr, -ˈtjʊr, -ˈtʃʊr] *adj* : prematuro — **prematurely** *adv*

premeditate [priˈmɛdə͵teɪt] *vt* **-tated; -tating** : premeditar

premeditation [priˌmɛdəˈteɪʃən] *n* : premeditación *f*
premenstrual [priˈmɛntstrʊəl] *adj* : premenstrual
premier[1] [priˈmɪr, -ˈmjɪr; ˈpriːmiər] *adj* : principal
premier[2] *n* PRIME MINISTER : primer ministro *m,* primera ministra *f*
premiere[1] [prɪˈmjɛr, -ˈmɪr] *vt* **-miered; -miering** : estrenar
premiere[2] *n* : estreno *m*
premise [ˈprɛmɪs] *n* **1** : premisa *f* <the premise of his arguments : la premisa de sus argumentos> **2 premises** *npl* : recinto *m,* local *m*
premium [ˈpriːmiəm] *n* **1** BONUS : prima *f* **2** SURCHARGE : recargo *m* <to sell at a premium : vender (algo) muy caro> **3 insurance premium** : prima *f* (de seguros) **4 to set a premium on** : darle un gran valor (a algo)
premonition [ˌpriːməˈnɪʃən, ˌprɛmə-] *n* : presentimiento *m,* premonición *f*
prenatal [ˌpriːˈneɪtəl] *adj* : prenatal
preoccupation [priˌɑkjəˈpeɪʃən] *n* : preocupación *f*
preoccupied [priˈɑkjəˌpaɪd] *adj* : abstraído, ensimismado, preocupado
preoccupy [priˈɑkjəˌpaɪ] *vt* **-pied; -pying** : preocupar
preparation [ˌprɛpəˈreɪʃən] *n* **1** PREPARING : preparación *f* **2** MIXTURE : preparado *m* <a preparation for burns : un preparado para quemaduras> **3 preparations** *npl* ARRANGEMENTS : preparativos *mpl*
preparatory [priˈpærəˌtori] *adj* : preparatorio
prepare [priˈpær] *v* **-pared; -paring** *vt* : preparar — *vi* : prepararse
prepay [ˌpriːˈpeɪ] *vt* **-paid; -paying** : pagar por adelantado
preponderance [priˈpɑndərənts] *n* : preponderancia *f*
preponderant [priˈpɑndərənt] *adj* : preponderante — **preponderantly** *adv*
preposition [ˌprɛpəˈzɪʃən] *n* : preposición *f*
prepositional [ˌprɛpəˈzɪʃənəl] *adj* : preposicional
prepossessing [ˌpriːpəˈzɛsɪŋ] *adj* : atractivo, agradable
preposterous [priˈpɑstərəs] *adj* : absurdo, ridículo
prerequisite[1] [priˈrɛkwəzət] *adj* : necesario, esencial
prerequisite[2] *n* : condición *f* necesario, requisito *m* previo
prerogative [priˈrɑgət̬ɪv] *n* : prerrogativa *f*
presage [ˈprɛsɪdʒ, priˈseɪdʒ] *vt* **-saged; -saging** : presagiar
preschool [ˈpriːˌskuːl] *adj* : preescolar <preschool students : estudiantes de preescolar>
prescribe [priˈskraɪb] *vt* **-scribed; -scribing 1** ORDAIN : prescribir, ordenar **2** : recetar (medicinas, etc.)
prescription [priˈskrɪpʃən] *n* : receta *f*
presence [ˈprɛzənts] *n* : presencia *f*
present[1] [priˈzɛnt] *vt* **1** INTRODUCE : presentar <to present oneself : presentarse> **2** : presentar (una obra de teatro, etc.) **3** GIVE : entregar (un regalo, etc.), regalar, obsequiar **4** SHOW : presentar, ofrecer <it presents a lovely view : ofrece una vista muy linda>
present[2] [ˈprɛzənt] *adj* **1** : actual <present conditions : condiciones actuales> **2** : presente <all the students were present : todos los estudiantes estaban presentes>
present[3] [ˈprɛzənt] *n* **1** GIFT : regalo *m,* obsequio *m* **2** : presente *m* <at present : en este momento> **3** *or* **present tense** : presente *m*
presentation [ˌpriːˌzɛnˈteɪʃən, ˌprɛzən-] *n* : presentación *f* <presentation ceremony : ceremonia de entrega>
presentiment [priˈzɛntəmənt] *n* : presentimiento *m,* premonición *f*
presently [ˈprɛzəntli] *adv* **1** SOON : pronto, dentro de poco **2** NOW : actualmente, ahora
present participle *n* : participio *m* presente, participio *m* activo
preservation [ˌprɛzərˈveɪʃən] *n* : conservación *f,* preservación *f*
preservative [priˈzərvət̬ɪv] *n* : conservante *m*
preserve[1] [priˈzərv] *vt* **-served; -serving 1** PROTECT : proteger, preservar **2** : conservar (los alimentos, etc.) **3** MAINTAIN : conservar, mantener
preserve[2] *n* **1** *or* **preserves** *npl* : conserva *f* <peach preserves : duraznos en conserva> **2** : coto *m* <game preserve : coto de caza>
preside [priˈzaɪd] *vi* **-sided; -siding 1 to preside over** : presidir <he presided over the meeting : presidió la reunión> **2 to preside over** : supervisar <she presides over the department : dirige el departamento>
presidency [ˈprɛzədəntsi] *n, pl* **-cies** : presidencia *f*
president [ˈprɛzədənt] *n* : presidente *m,* -ta *f*
presidential [ˌprɛzəˈdɛntʃəl] *adj* : presidencial
press[1] [ˈprɛs] *vt* **1** PUSH : apretar **2** SQUEEZE : apretar, prensar (frutas, flores, etc.) **3** IRON : planchar (ropa) **4** URGE : instar, apremiar <he pressed me to come : insistió en que viniera> — *vi* **1** PUSH : apretar <press hard : aprieta con fuerza> **2** CROWD : apiñarse **3** : abrirse paso <I pressed through the crowd : me abrí paso entre el gentío> **4** URGE : presionar
press[2] *n* **1** CROWD : multitud *f* **2** : imprenta *f,* prensa *f* <to go to press : entrar en prensa> **3** URGENCY : urgencia *f,* prisa *f* **4** PRINTER, PUBLISHER : imprenta *f,* editorial *f* **5 the press** : la

prensa <freedom of the press : libertad de prensa>

pressing [ˈprɛsɪŋ] *adj* URGENT : urgente

pressure[1] [ˈprɛʃər] *vt* **-sured; -suring** : presionar, apremiar

pressure[2] *n* **1** : presión *f* <to be under pressure : estar bajo presión> **2** → **blood pressure**

pressurize [ˈprɛʃəˌraɪz] *vt* **-ized; -izing** : presurizar

prestige [prɛˈstiːʒ, -ˈstiːdʒ] *n* : prestigio *m*

prestigious [prɛˈstɪdʒəs] *adj* : prestigioso

presto [ˈprɛsˌtoː] *adv* : de pronto

presumably [priˈzuːməbli] *adv* : es de suponer, supuestamente <presumably, he's guilty : supone que es culpable>

presume [priˈzuːm] *vt* **-sumed; -suming 1** ASSUME, SUPPOSE : suponer, asumir, presumir **2 to presume to** : atreverse a, osar

presumption [priˈzʌmpʃən] *n* **1** AUDACITY : atrevimiento *m,* osadía *f* **2** ASSUMPTION : presunción *f,* suposición *f*

presumptuous [priˈzʌmptʃʊəs] *adj* : descarado, atrevido

presuppose [ˌpriːsəˈpoːz] *vt* **-posed; -posing** : presuponer

pretend [priˈtɛnd] *vt* **1** CLAIM : pretender **2** FEIGN : fingir, simular — *vi* : fingir

pretense *or* **pretence** [ˈpriːˌtɛnts, priˈtɛnts] *n* **1** CLAIM : afirmación *f* (falsa), pretensión *f* **2** FEIGNING : fingimiento *m,* simulación *f* <to make a pretense of doing something : fingir hacer algo> <a pretense of order : una apariencia de orden> **3** PRETEXT : pretexto *m* <under false pretenses : con pretextos falsos, de manera fraudulenta>

pretension [priˈtɛntʃən] *n* **1** CLAIM : pretensión *f,* afirmación *f* **2** ASPIRATION : aspiración *f,* ambición *f* **3** PRETENTIOUSNESS : pretensiones *fpl*, presunción *f*

pretentious [priˈtɛntʃəs] *adj* : pretencioso

pretentiousness [priˈtɛntʃəsnəs] *n* : presunción *f,* pretenciones *fpl*

pretext [ˈpriːˌtɛkst] *n* : pretexto *m,* excusa *f*

prettily [ˈprɪtəli] *adv* : atractivamente

prettiness [ˈprɪtinəs] *n* : lindeza *f*

pretty[1] [ˈprɪti] *adv* : bastante, bien <it's pretty obvious : está bien claro> <it's pretty much the same : es más o menos igual>

pretty[2] *adj* **-tier; -est** : bonito, lindo, guapo <a pretty girl : una muchacha guapa> <what a pretty dress! : ¡qué vestido más lindo!>

pretzel [ˈprɛtsəl] *n* : galleta *f* salada (en forma de nudo)

prevail [priˈveɪl] *vi* **1** TRIUMPH : prevalecer **2** PREDOMINATE : predominar **3 to prevail upon** : persuadir, convencer <I prevailed upon her to sing : la convencí para que cantara>

prevalence [ˈprɛvələnts] *n* : preponderancia *f,* predominio *m*

prevalent [ˈprɛvələnt] *adj* **1** COMMON : común y corriente, general **2** WIDESPREAD : extendido

prevaricate [priˈværəˌkeɪt] *vi* **-cated; -cating** LIE : mentir

prevarication [priˌværəˈkeɪʃən] *n* : mentira *f*

prevent [priˈvɛnt] *vt* **1** AVOID : prevenir, evitar <steps to prevent war : medidas para evitar la guerra> **2** HINDER : impedir

preventable [priˈvɛntəbəl] *adj* : evitable

preventative [priˈvɛntətɪv] → **preventive**

prevention [priˈvɛntʃən] *n* : prevención *f*

preventive [priˈvɛntɪv] *adj* : preventivo

preview [ˈpriːˌvju] *n* : preestreno *m*

previous [ˈpriːviəs] *adj* : previo, anterior <previous knowledge : conocimientos previos> <the previous day : el día anterior> <in the previous year : en el año pasado>

previously [ˈpriːviəsli] *adv* : antes

prewar [ˌpriːˈwɔr] *adj* : de antes de la guerra

prey [ˈpreɪ] *n, pl* **preys** : presa *f*

prey on *vt* **1** : cazar, alimentarse de <it preys on fish : se alimenta de peces> **2 to prey on one's mind** : hacer presa en alguien, atormentar a alguien

price[1] [ˈpraɪs] *vt* **priced; pricing** : poner un precio a

price[2] *n* : precio *m* <peace at any price : la paz a toda costa>

priceless [ˈpraɪsləs] *adj* : inestimable, inapreciable

prick[1] [ˈprɪk] *vt* **1** : pinchar **2 to prick up one's ears** : levantar las orejas — *vi* : pinchar

prick[2] *n* **1** STAB : pinchazo *m* <a prick of conscience : un remordimiento> **2** → **pricker**

pricker [ˈprɪkər] *n* THORN : espina *f*

prickle[1] [ˈprɪkəl] *vi* **-led; -ling** : sentir un cosquilleo, tener un hormigueo

prickle[2] *n* **1** : espina *f* (de una planta) **2** TINGLE : cosquilleo *m,* hormigueo *m*

prickly [ˈprɪkəli] *adj* **1** THORNY : espinoso **2** : que pica <a prickly sensation : un hormigueo>

prickly pear *n* : tuna *f*

pride[1] [ˈpraɪd] *vt* **prided; priding** : estar orgulloso de <to pride oneself on : preciarse de, enorgullecerse de>

pride[2] *n* : orgullo *m*

priest [ˈpriːst] *n* : sacerdote *m,* cura *m*

priestess [ˈpriːstɪs] *n* : sacerdotisa *f*

priesthood [ˈpriːstˌhʊd] *n* : sacerdocio *m*

priestly [ˈpriːstli] *adj* : sacerdotal

prig [ˈprɪg] *n* : mojigato *m,* -ta *f;* gazmoño *m,* -ña *f*

prim [ˈprɪm] *adj* **primmer; primmest** **1** PRISSY : remilgado **2** PRUDISH : mojigato, gazmoño

primarily [praɪˈmɛrəli] *adv* : principalmente, fundamentalmente

primary[1] [ˈpraɪˌmɛri, ˈpraɪməri] *adj* **1** FIRST : primario **2** PRINCIPAL : principal **3** BASIC : fundamental

primary[2] *n, pl* **-ries** : elección *f* primaria

primary color *n* : color *m* primario

primary school → **elementary school**

primate *n* **1** [ˈpraɪˌmeɪt, -mət] : primado *m* (obispo) **2** [-ˌmeɪt] : primate *m* (animal)

prime[1] [ˈpraɪm] *vt* **primed; priming** **1** : cebar <to prime a pump : cebar una bomba> **2** PREPARE : preparar (una superficie para pintar) **3** COACH : preparar (a un testigo, etc.)

prime[2] *adj* **1** CHIEF, MAIN : principal, primero **2** EXCELLENT : de primera (categoría), excelente

prime[3] *n* **the prime of one's life** : la flor de la vida

prime minister *n* : primer ministro *m*, primera ministra *f*

primer[1] [ˈprɪmər] *n* **1** READER : cartilla *f* **2** MANUAL : manual *m*

primer[2] [ˈpraɪmər] *n* **1** : cebo *m* (para explosivos) **2** : base *f* (de pintura)

primeval [praɪˈmiːvəl] *adj* : primitivo, primigenio

primitive [ˈprɪmət̬ɪv] *adj* : primitivo

primly [ˈprɪmli] *adv* : mojigatamente

primness [ˈprɪmnəs] *n* : mojigatería *f*, gazmoñería *f*

primordial [praɪˈmɔrdiəl] *adj* : primordial, fundamental

primp [ˈprɪmp] *vi* : arreglarse, acicalarse

primrose [ˈprɪmˌroːz] *n* : primavera *f*, prímula *f*

prince [ˈprɪnts] *n* : príncipe *m*

princely [ˈprɪntsli] *adj* : principesco

princess [ˈprɪntsəs, ˈprɪnˌsɛs] *n* : princesa *f*

principal[1] [ˈprɪntsəpəl] *adj* : principal — **principally** *adv*

principal[2] *n* **1** PROTAGONIST : protagonista *mf* **2** : director *m*, -tora *f* (de una escuela) **3** CAPITAL : principal *m*, capital *m* (en finanzas)

principality [ˌprɪntsəˈpæləṯi] *n, pl* **-ties** : principado *m*

principle [ˈprɪntsəpəl] *n* : principio *m*

print[1] [ˈprɪnt] *vt* : imprimir (libros, etc.) — *vi* : escribir con letra de molde

print[2] *n* **1** IMPRESSION : marca *f*, huella *f*, impresión *f* **2** : texto *m* impreso <to be out of print : estar agotado> **3** LETTERING : letra *f* **4** ENGRAVING : grabado *m* **5** : copia *f* (en fotografía) **6** : estampado *m* (de tela)

printer [ˈprɪntər] *n* **1** : impresor *m*, -sora *f* (persona) **2** : impresora *f* (máquina)

printing [ˈprɪntɪŋ] *n* **1** : impresión *f* (acto) <the third printing : la tercera tirada> **2** : imprenta *f* (profesión) **3** LETTERING : letras *fpl* de molde

printing press *n* : prensa *f*

print out *vt* : imprimir (de una computadora)

printout [ˈprɪntˌaʊt] *n* : copia *f* impresa (de una computadora)

prior [ˈpraɪər] *adj* **1** : previo **2 prior to** : antes de

priority [praɪˈɔrəṯi] *n, pl* **-ties** : prioridad *f*

priory [ˈpraɪəri] *n, pl* **-ries** : priorato *m*

prism [ˈprɪzəm] *n* : prisma *m*

prison [ˈprɪzən] *n* : prisión *f*, cárcel *f*

prisoner [ˈprɪzənər] *n* : preso *m*, -sa *f*; recluso *m*, -sa *f* <prisoner of war : prisionero de guerra>

prissy [ˈprɪsi] *adj* **-sier; -est** : remilgado, melindroso

pristine [ˈprɪsˌtiːn, prɪsˈ-] *adj* : puro, prístino

privacy [ˈpraɪvəsi] *n, pl* **-cies** : privacidad *f*

private[1] [ˈpraɪvət] *adj* **1** PERSONAL : privado, particular <private property : propiedad privada> **2** INDEPENDENT : privado, independiente <private studies : estudios privados> **3** SECRET : secreto **4** SECLUDED : aislado, privado — **privately** *adv*

private[2] *n* : soldado *m* raso

privateer [ˌpraɪvəˈtɪr] *n* : corsario *m*

privation [praɪˈveɪʃən] *n* : privación *f*

privilege [ˈprɪvlɪdʒ, ˈprɪvə-] *n* : privilegio *m*

privileged [ˈprɪvlɪdʒd, ˈprɪvə-] *adj* : privilegiado

privy[1] [ˈprɪvi] *adj* **to be privy to** : estar enterado de

privy[2] *n, pl* **privies** : excusado *m*, retrete *m* (exterior)

prize[1] [ˈpraɪz] *vt* **prized; prizing** : valorar, apreciar

prize[2] *adj* **1** : premiado <a prize stallion : un semental premiado> **2** OUTSTANDING : de primera, excepcional

prize[3] *n* **1** AWARD : premio *m* <third prize : el tercer premio> **2** : joya *f*, tesoro *m* <he's a real prize : es un tesoro>

prizefighter [ˈpraɪzˌfaɪṯər] *n* : boxeador *m*, -dora *f* profesional

prizewinning [ˈpraɪzˌwɪnɪŋ] *adj* : premiado

pro[1] [ˈproː] *adv* : a favor

pro[2] *adj* → **professional[1]**

pro[3] *n* **1** : pro *m* <the pros and cons : los pros y los contras> **2** → **professional[2]**

probability [ˌprɑbəˈbɪləṯi] *n, pl* **-ties** : probabilidad *f*

probable [ˈprɑbəbəl] *adj* : probable — **probably** [-bli] *adv*

probate[1] [ˈproːˌbeɪt] *vt* **-bated; -bating** : autenticar (un testamento)

probate[2] *n* : autenticación *f* (de un testamento)

probation [pro'beɪʃən] *n* **1 :** período *m* de prueba (para un empleado, etc.) **2 :** libertad *f* condicional (para un preso)
probationary [pro'beɪʃə,nɛri] *adj* **:** de prueba
probe[1] ['pro:b] *vt* **probed; probing 1 :** sondar (en medicina y tecnología) **2** INVESTIGATE **:** investigar, sondear
probe[2] *n* **1 :** sonda *f* (en medicina, etc.) <space probe : sonda espacial> **2** INVESTIGATION **:** investigación *f,* sondeo *m*
probity ['pro:bəṭi] *n* **:** probidad *f*
problem[1] ['prɑbləm] *adj* **:** difícil
problem[2] *n* **:** problema *m*
problematic [,prɑblə'mæṭɪk] *or* **problematical** [-ṭɪkəl] *adj* **:** problemático
proboscis [prə'bɑsɪs] *n, pl* **-cises** *also* **-cides** [-sə,di:z] **:** probóscide *f*
procedural [prə'si:dʒərəl] *adj* **:** de procedimiento
procedure [prə'si:dʒər] *n* **:** procedimiento *m* <administrative procedures : trámites administrativos>
proceed [pro'si:d] *vi* **1 :** proceder <to proceed to do something : proceder a hacer algo> **2** CONTINUE **:** continuar, proseguir, seguir <he proceeded to the next phase : pasó a la segunda fase> **3** ADVANCE **:** avanzar <as the conference proceeded : mientras seguía avanzando la conferencia> <the road proceeds south : la calle sigue hacia el sur>
proceeding [pro'si:dɪŋ] *n* **1** PROCEDURE **:** procedimiento *m* **2 proceedings** *npl* EVENTS **:** acontecimientos *mpl* **3 proceedings** *npl* MINUTES **:** actas *fpl* (de una reunión, etc.)
proceeds ['pro:,si:dz] *npl* **:** ganancias *fpl*
process[1] ['prɑ,sɛs, 'pro:-] *vt* **:** procesar, tratar
process[2] *n, pl* **-cesses** ['prɑ,sɛsəz, 'pro:-, -səsəz, -sə,si:z] **1 :** proceso *m* <the process of elimination : el proceso de eliminación> **2** METHOD **:** proceso *m,* método *m* <manufacturing processes : procesos industriales> **3 :** acción *f* judicial <due process of law : el debido proceso (de la ley)> **4** SUMMONS **:** citación *f* **5** PROJECTION **:** protuberancia *f* (anatómica) **6 in the process of :** en vías de <in the process of repair : en reparaciones>
procession [prə'sɛʃən] *n* **:** procesión *f,* desfile *m* <a funeral procession : un cortejo fúnebre>
processional [prə'sɛʃənəl] *n* **:** himno *m* para una procesión
processor ['prɑ,sɛsər, 'pro:-, -səsər] *n* **1 :** procesador *m* (de una computadora) **2 food processor :** procesador *m* de alimentos
proclaim [pro'kleɪm] *vt* **:** proclamar
proclamation [,prɑklə'meɪʃən] *n* **:** proclamación *f*
proclivity [pro'klɪvəṭi] *n, pl* **-ties :** proclividad *f*
procrastinate [prə'kræstə,neɪt] *vi* **-nated; -nating :** demorar, aplazar las responsabilidades
procrastination [prə,kræstə'neɪʃən] *n* **:** aplazamiento *m,* demora *f,* dilación *f*
procreate ['pro:kri,eɪt] *vi* **-ated; -ating :** procrear
procreation [,pro:kri'eɪʃən] *n* **:** procreación *f*
proctor[1] ['prɑktər] *vt* **:** supervisar (un examen)
proctor[2] *n* **:** supervisor *m,* -sora *f* (de un examen)
procure [prə'kjʊr] *vt* **-cured; -curing 1** OBTAIN **:** procurar, obtener **2** BRING ABOUT **:** provocar, lograr, conseguir
procurement [prə'kjʊrmənt] *n* **:** obtención *f*
prod[1] ['prɑd] *vt* **prodded; prodding 1** JAB, POKE **:** pinchar, golpear (con la punta de algo) **2** GOAD **:** incitar, estimular
prod[2] *n* **1** JAB, POKE **:** golpe *m* (con la punta de algo), pinchazo *m* **2** STIMULUS **:** estímulo *m* **3 cattle prod :** picana *f,* aguijón *m*
prodigal[1] ['prɑdɪgəl] *adj* SPENDTHRIFT **:** pródigo, despilfarrador, derrochador
prodigal[2] *n* **:** pródigo *m,* -ga *f;* derrochador *m,* -dora *f*
prodigious [prə'dɪdʒəs] *adj* **1** MARVELOUS **:** prodigioso, maravilloso **2** HUGE **:** enorme, vasto <prodigious sums : muchísimo dinero> **— prodigiously** *adv*
prodigy ['prɑdədʒi] *n, pl* **-gies :** prodigio *m* <child prodigy : niño prodigio>
produce[1] [prə'du:s, -'dju:s] *vt* **-duced; -ducing 1** EXHIBIT **:** presentar, mostrar **2** YIELD **:** producir **3** CAUSE **:** producir, causar **4** CREATE **:** producir <to produce a poem : escribir un poema> **5 :** poner en escena (una obra de teatro), producir (una película)
produce[2] ['prɑ,du:s, 'pro:-, -,dju:s] *n* **:** productos *mpl* agrícolas
producer [prə'du:sər, -'dju:-] *n* **:** productor *m,* -tora *f*
product ['prɑ,dʌkt] *n* **:** producto *m*
production [prə'dʌkʃən] *n* **:** producción *f*
productive [prə'dʌktɪv] *adj* **:** productivo
productivity [,pro:,dʌk'tɪvəṭi, ,prɑ-] *n* **:** productividad *f*
profane[1] [pro'feɪn] *vt* **-faned; -faning :** profanar
profane[2] *adj* **1** SECULAR **:** profano **2** IRREVERENT **:** irreverente, impío
profanity [pro'fænəṭi] *n, pl* **-ties 1** IRREVERENCE **:** irreverencia *f,* impiedad *f* **2 :** blasfemias *fpl,* obscenidades *fpl* <don't use profanity : no digas blasfemias>
profess [prə'fɛs] *vt* **1** DECLARE **:** declarar, manifestar **2** CLAIM **:** pretender **3 :** profesar (una religión, etc.)

professedly [prə'fɛsədli] *adv* **1** OPENLY : declaradamente **2** ALLEGEDLY : supuestamente

profession [prə'fɛʃən] *n* : profesión *f*

professional[1] [prə'fɛʃənəl] *adj* : profesional — **professionally** *adv*

professional[2] *n* : profesional *mf*

professionalism [prə'fɛʃənəˌlizəm] *n* : profesionalismo *m*

professor [prə'fɛsər] *n* : profesor *m* (universitario), profesora *f* (universitaria); catedrático *m*, -ca *f*

proffer ['prɑfər] *vt* **-fered; -fering** : ofrecer, dar

proficiency [prə'fɪʃən*t*si] *n* : competencia *f*, capacidad *f*

proficient [prə'fɪʃənt] *adj* : competente, experto — **proficiently** *adv*

profile ['proːˌfaɪl] *n* : perfil *m* <a portrait in profile : un retrato de perfil> <to keep a low profile : no llamar la atención, hacerse pasar desapercibido>

profit[1] ['prɑfət] *vi* : sacar provecho (de), beneficiarse (de)

profit[2] *n* **1** ADVANTAGE : provecho *m*, partido *m*, beneficio *m* **2** GAIN : beneficio *m*, utilidad *f*, ganancia *f* <to make a profit : sacar beneficios>

profitable ['prɑfət̬əbəl] *adj* : rentable, lucrativo — **profitably** [-bli] *adv*

profitless ['prɑfətləs] *adj* : infructuoso, inútil

profligate ['prɑflɪgət, -ˌgeɪt] *adj* **1** DISSOLUTE : disoluto, licencioso **2** SPENDTHRIFT : despilfarrador, derrochador, pródigo

profound [prə'faʊnd] *adj* : profundo

profoundly [prə'faʊndli] *adv* : profundamente, en profundidad

profundity [prə'fʌndət̬i] *n, pl* **-ties** : profundidad *f*

profuse [prə'fjuːs] *adj* **1** COPIOUS : profuso, copioso **2** LAVISH : pródigo — **profusely** *adv*

profusion [prə'fjuːʒən] *n* : abundancia *f*, profusión *f*

progeny ['prɑdʒəni] *n, pl* **-nies** : progenie *f*

progesterone [pro'dʒɛstəˌroːn] *n* : progesterona *f*

prognosis [prɑg'noːsɪs] *n, pl* **-noses** [-ˌsiːz] : pronóstico *m* (médico)

program[1] ['proːˌgræm, -grəm] *vt* **-grammed** *or* **-gramed; -gramming** *or* **-graming** : programar

program[2] *n* : programa *m*

programmer ['proːˌgræmər] *n* : programador *m*, -dora *f*

programming ['proːˌgræmɪŋ] *n* : programación *f*

progress[1] [prə'grɛs] *vi* **1** PROCEED : progresar, adelantar **2** IMPROVE : mejorar

progress[2] ['prɑgrəs, -ˌgrɛs] *n* **1** ADVANCE : progreso *m*, adelanto *m*, avance *m* <to make progress : hacer progresos> **2** BETTERMENT : mejora *f*, mejoramiento *m*

progression [prə'grɛʃən] *n* **1** ADVANCE : avance *m* **2** SEQUENCE : desarrollo *m* (de eventos)

progressive [prə'grɛsɪv] *adj* **1** : progresista <a progressive society : una sociedad progresista> **2** : progresivo <a progressive disease : una enfermedad progresiva> **3** *or* **Progressive** : progresista (en política) **4** : progresivo (en gramática)

progressively [prə'grɛsɪvli] *adv* : progresivamente, poco a poco

prohibit [pro'hɪbət] *vt* : prohibir

prohibition [ˌproːə'bɪʃən, ˌproːhə-] *n* : prohibición *f*

prohibitive [pro'hɪbət̬ɪv] *adj* : prohibitivo

project[1] [prə'dʒɛkt] *vt* **1** PLAN : proyectar, planear **2** : proyectar (imágenes, misiles, etc.) — *vi* PROTRUDE : sobresalir, salir

project[2] ['prɑˌdʒɛkt, -dʒɪkt] *n* : proyecto *m*, trabajo *m* (de un estudiante) <research project : proyecto de investigación>

projectile [prə'dʒɛktəl, -ˌtaɪl] *n* : proyectil *m*

projection [prə'dʒɛkʃən] *n* **1** PLAN : plan *m*, proyección *f* **2** : proyección *f* (de imágenes, misiles, etc.) **3** PROTRUSION : saliente *m*

projector [prə'dʒɛktər] *n* : proyector *m*

proletarian[1] [ˌproːlə'tɛriən] *adj* : proletario

proletarian[2] *n* : proletario *m*, -ria *f*

proletariat [ˌproːlə'tɛriət] *n* : proletariado *m*

proliferate [prə'lɪfəˌreɪt] *vi* **-ated; -ating** : proliferar

proliferation [prəˌlɪfə'reɪʃən] *n* : proliferación *f*

prolific [prə'lɪfɪk] *adj* : prolífico

prologue ['proːˌlɔg] *n* : prólogo *m*

prolong [prə'lɔŋ] *vt* : prolongar

prolongation [ˌproːˌlɔŋ'geɪʃən] *n* : prolongación *f*

prom ['prɑm] *n* : baile *m* formal (de un colegio)

promenade[1] [ˌprɑmə'neɪd, -'nɑd] *vi* **-naded; -nading** : pasear, pasearse, dar un paseo

promenade[2] *n* : paseo *m*

prominence ['prɑmənən*t*s] *n* **1** PROJECTION : prominencia *f* **2** EMINENCE : eminencia *f*, prestigio *m*

prominent ['prɑmənənt] *adj* **1** OUTSTANDING : prominente, destacado **2** PROJECTING : prominente, saliente

prominently ['prɑmənəntli] *adv* : destacadamente, prominentemente

promiscuity [ˌprɑmɪs'kjuːət̬i] *n, pl* **-ties** : promiscuidad *f*

promiscuous [prə'mɪskjʊəs] *adj* : promiscuo — **promiscuously** *adv*

promise[1] ['prɑməs] *v* **-ised; -ising** : prometer

promise[2] *n* **1 :** promesa *f* <he kept his promise : cumplió su promesa> **2 to show promise :** prometer

promising ['prɑməsɪŋ] *adj* **:** prometedor

promissory ['prɑmə,sori] *adj* **:** que promete <a promissory note : un pagaré>

promontory ['prɑmən,tori] *n, pl* **-ries :** promontorio *m*

promote [prə'mo:t] *vt* **-moted; -moting 1 :** ascender (a un alumno o un empleado) **2** ADVERTISE **:** promocionar, hacerle publicidad a **3** FURTHER **:** promover, fomentar

promoter [prə'mo:t̬ər] *n* **:** promotor *m,* -tora *f;* empresario *m,* -ria *f* (en deportes)

promotion [prə'mo:ʃən] *n* **1 :** ascenso *m* (de un alumno o un empleado) **2** FURTHERING **:** promoción *f,* fomento *m* **3** ADVERTISING **:** publicidad *f,* propaganda *f*

promotional [prə'mo:ʃənəl] *adj* **:** promocional

prompt[1] ['prɑmpt] *vt* **1** INDUCE **:** provocar (una cosa), inducir (a una persona) <curiosity prompted me to ask you : la curiosidad me indujo a preguntarle> **2 :** apuntar (a un actor, etc.)

prompt[2] *adj* **:** pronto, rápido <prompt payment : pago puntual>

prompter ['prɑmptər] *n* **:** apuntador *m,* -dora *f* (en teatro)

promptly ['prɑmptli] *adv* **:** inmediatamente, rápidamente

promptness ['prɑmptnəs] *n* **:** prontitud *f,* rapidez *f*

prone ['pro:n] *adj* **1** LIABLE **:** propenso, proclive <accident-prone : propenso a los accidentes> **2 :** boca abajo, decúbito prono <in a prone position : en decúbito prono>

prong ['prɔŋ] *n* **:** punta *f,* diente *m*

pronoun ['pro:,naʊn] *n* **:** pronombre *m*

pronounce [prə'naʊnts] *vt* **-nounced; -nouncing 1 :** pronunciar <how do you pronounce your name? : ¿cómo se pronuncia su nombre?> **2** DECLARE **:** declarar **3 to pronounce sentence :** dictar sentencia, pronunciar un fallo

pronounced [prə'naʊntst] *adj* MARKED **:** pronunciado, marcado

pronouncement [prə'naʊntsmənt] *n* **:** declaración *f*

pronunciation [prə,nʌntsi'eɪʃən] *n* **:** pronunciación *f*

proof[1] ['pru:f] *adj* **:** a prueba <proof against tampering : a prueba de manipulación>

proof[2] *n* **:** prueba *f*

proofread ['pru:f,ri:d] *v* **-read; -reading** *vt* **:** corregir — *vi* **:** corregir pruebas

proofreader ['pru:f,ri:dər] *n* **:** corrector *m,* -tora *f* (de pruebas)

prop[1] ['prɑp] *vt* **propped; propping 1 to prop against :** apoyar contra **2 to prop up** SUPPORT **:** apoyar, apuntalar, sostener **3 to prop up** SUSTAIN **:** alentar (a alguien), darle ánimo (a alguien)

prop[2] *n* **1** SUPPORT **:** puntal *m,* apoyo *m,* soporte *m* **2 :** accesorio *m* (en teatro)

propaganda [,prɑpə'gændə, ,pro:-] *n* **:** propaganda *f*

propagandize [,prɑpə'gæn,daɪz, ,pro:-] *v* **-dized; -dizing** *vt* **:** someter a propaganda — *vi* **:** hacer propaganda

propagate ['prɑpə,geɪt] *v* **-gated; -gating** *vi* **:** propagarse — *vt* **:** propagar

propagation [,prɑpə'geɪʃən] *n* **:** propagación *f*

propane ['pro:,peɪn] *n* **:** propano *m*

propel [prə'pɛl] *vt* **-pelled; -pelling :** impulsar, propulsar, impeler

propellant *or* **propellent** [prə'pɛlənt] *n* **:** propulsor *m*

propeller [prə'pɛlər] *n* **:** hélice *f*

propensity [prə'pɛntsət̬i] *n, pl* **-ties :** propensión *f,* tendencia *f,* inclinación *f*

proper ['prɑpər] *adj* **1** RIGHT, SUITABLE **:** apropiado, adecuado **2 :** propio, mismo <the city proper : la propia ciudad> **3** CORRECT **:** correcto **4** GENTEEL **:** fino, refinado, cortés **5** OWN, SPECIAL **:** propio <proper name : nombre propio> — **properly** *adv*

property ['prɑpərti] *n, pl* **-ties 1** CHARACTERISTIC **:** característica *f,* propiedad *f* **2** POSSESSIONS **:** propiedad *f* **3** BUILDING **:** inmueble *m* **4** LAND, LOT **:** terreno *m,* lote *m,* parcela *f* **5** PROP **:** accesorio *m* (en teatro)

prophecy ['prɑfəsi] *n, pl* **-cies :** profecía *f,* vaticinio *m*

prophesy ['prɑfə,saɪ] *v* **-sied; -sying** *vt* **1** FORETELL **:** profetizar (como profeta) **2** PREDICT **:** profetizar, predecir, vaticinar — *vi* **:** hacer profecías

prophet ['prɑfət] *n* **:** profeta *m,* profetisa *f*

prophetic [prə'fɛt̬ɪk] *or* **prophetical** [-t̬ɪkəl] *adj* **:** profético — **prophetically** [-tɪkli] *adv*

propitiate [pro'pɪʃi,eɪt] *vt* **-ated; -ating :** propiciar

propitious [prə'pɪʃəs] *adj* **:** propicio

proponent [prə'po:nənt] *n* **:** defensor *m,* -sora *f;* partidario *m,* -ria *f*

proportion[1] [prə'porʃən] *vt* **:** proporcionar <well-proportioned : de buenas proporciones>

proportion[2] *n* **1** RATIO **:** proporción *f* **2** SYMMETRY **:** proporción *f,* simetría *f* <out of proportion : desproporcionado> **3** SHARE **:** parte *f* **4 proportions** *npl* SIZE **:** dimensiones *fpl*

proportional [prə'porʃənəl] *adj* **:** proporcional — **proportionally** *adv*

proportionate [prə'porʃənət] *adj* **:** proporcional — **proportionately** *adv*

proposal [prə'po:zəl] *n* **1** PROPOSITION **:** propuesta *f,* proposición *f* <marriage

proposal : propuesta de matrimonio> 2 PLAN : proyecto *m,* propuesta *f*
propose [prə'po:z] *v* **-posed; -posing** *vi* : proponer matrimonio — *vt* **1** INTEND : pensar, proponerse **2** SUGGEST : proponer
proposition [ˌprɑpə'zɪʃən] *n* **1** PROPOSAL : proposición *f,* propuesta *f* **2** STATEMENT : proposición *f*
propound [prə'paʊnd] *vt* : proponer, exponer
proprietary [prə'praɪəˌtɛri] *adj* : propietario, patentado
proprietor [prə'praɪət̬ər] *n* : propietario *m,* -ria *f*
propriety [prə'praɪət̬i] *n, pl* **-eties 1** DECORUM : decencia *f,* decoro *m* **2 proprieties** *npl* CONVENTIONS : convenciones *fpl,* cánones *mpl* sociales
propulsion [prə'pʌlʃən] *n* : propulsión *f*
prosaic [pro'zeɪɪk] *adj* : prosaico
proscribe [pro'skraɪb] *vt* **-scribed; -scribing** : proscribir
prose ['pro:z] *n* : prosa *f*
prosecute ['prɑsɪˌkju:t] *vt* **-cuted; -cuting 1** CARRY OUT : llevar a cabo **2** : procesar, enjuiciar <prosecuted for fraud : procesado por fraude>
prosecution [ˌprɑsɪ'kju:ʃən] *n* **1** : procesamiento *m* <the prosecution of forgers : el procesamiento de falsificadores> **2** PROSECUTORS : acusación *f* <witness for the prosecution : testigo de cargo>
prosecutor ['prɑsɪˌkju:t̬ər] *n* : acusador *m,* -dora *f;* fiscal *mf*
prospect[1] ['prɑˌspɛkt] *vi* : prospectar (el terreno) <to prospect for gold : buscar oro>
prospect[2] *n* **1** VISTA : vista *f,* panorama *m* **2** POSSIBILITY : posibilidad *f* **3** OUTLOOK : perspectiva *f* **4** : posible cliente *m,* -ta *f* <a salesman looking for prospects : un vendedor buscando nuevos clientes>
prospective [prə'spɛktɪv, 'prɑˌspɛk-] *adj* **1** EXPECTANT : futuro <prospective mother : futura madre> **2** POTENTIAL : potencial, posible <prospective employee : posible empleado>
prospector ['prɑˌspɛktər, prɑ'spɛk-] *n* : prospector *m,* -tora *f;* explorador *m,* -dora *f*
prospectus [prə'spɛktəs] *n* : prospecto *m*
prosper ['prɑspər] *vi* : prosperar
prosperity [prɑ'spɛrət̬i] *n* : prosperidad *f*
prosperous ['prɑspərəs] *adj* : próspero
prostate ['prɑˌsteɪt] *n* : próstata *f*
prosthesis [prɑs'θi:sɪs, 'prɑsθə-] *n, pl* **-theses** [-ˌsi:z] : prótesis *f*
prostitute[1] ['prɑstəˌtu:t, -ˌtju:t] *vt* **-tuted; -tuting 1** : prostituir **2 to prostitute oneself** : prostituirse
prostitute[2] *n* : prostituto *m,* -ta *f*
prostitution [ˌprɑstə'tu:ʃən, -'tju:-] *n* : prostitución *f*
prostrate[1] ['prɑˌstreɪt] *vt* **-trated; -trating 1** : postrar **2 to prostrate oneself** : postrarse
prostrate[2] *adj* : postrado
prostration [prɑ'streɪʃən] *n* : postración *f*
protagonist [pro'tægənɪst] *n* : protagonista *mf*
protect [prə'tɛkt] *vt* : proteger
protection [prə'tɛkʃən] *n* : protección *f*
protective [prə'tɛktɪv] *adj* : protector
protector [prə'tɛktər] *n* **1** : protector *m,* -tora *f* (persona) **2** GUARD : protector *m* (aparato)
protectorate [prə'tɛktərət] *n* : protectorado *m*
protégé ['pro:t̬əˌʒeɪ] *n* : protegido *m,* -da *f*
protein ['pro:ˌti:n] *n* : proteína *f*
protest[1] [pro'tɛst] *vt* **1** ASSERT : afirmar, declarar **2** : protestar <they protested the decision : protestaron (por) la decisión> — *vi* **to protest against** : protestar contra
protest[2] ['pro:ˌtɛst] *n* **1** DEMONSTRATION : manifestación *f* (de protesta) <a public protest : una manifestación pública> **2** COMPLAINT : queja *f,* protesta *f*
Protestant ['prɑt̬əstənt] *n* : protestante *mf*
Protestantism ['prɑt̬əstənˌtɪzəm] *n* : protestantismo *m*
protocol ['pro:t̬əˌkɔl] *n* : protocolo *m*
proton ['proˌtɑn] *n* : protón *m*
protoplasm ['pro:t̬əˌplæzəm] *n* : protoplasma *m*
prototype ['pro:t̬əˌtaɪp] *n* : prototipo *m*
protozoan [ˌpro:t̬ə'zo:ən] *n* : protozoario *m,* protozoo *m*
protract [pro'trækt] *vt* : prolongar
protractor [pro'træktər] *n* : transportador *m* (instrumento)
protrude [pro'tru:d] *vi* **-truded; -truding** : salir, sobresalir
protrusion [pro'tru:ʒən] *n* : protuberancia *f,* saliente *m*
protuberance [pro'tu:bərən*t*s, -'tju:-] *n* : protuberancia *f*
proud ['praʊd] *adj* **1** HAUGHTY : altanero, orgulloso, arrogante **2** : orgulloso <she was proud of her work : estaba orgullosa de su trabajo> <too proud to beg : demasiado orgulloso para rogar> **3** GLORIOUS : glorioso — **proudly** *adv*
prove ['pru:v] *v* **proved; proved** *or* **proven** ['pru:vən]; **proving** *vt* **1** TEST : probar **2** DEMONSTRATE : probar, demostrar — *vi* : resultar <it proved effective : resultó efectivo>
Provençal [ˌpro:vɑn'sɑl, ˌprɑvən-] *n* **1** : provenzal *mf* **2** : provenzal *m* (idioma) — **Provençal** *adj*

proverb ['prɑ,vərb] *n* : proverbio *m,* refrán *m*

proverbial [prə'vərbiəl] *adj* : proverbial

provide [prə'vaɪd] *v* **-vided; -viding** *vt* **1** STIPULATE : estipular **2 to provide with** : proveer de, proporcionar — *vi* **1** : proveer <the Lord will provide : el Señor proveerá> **2 to provide for** SUPPORT : mantener **3 to provide for** ANTICIPATE : hacer previsiones para, prever

provided [prə'vaɪdəd] *or* **provided that** *conj* : con tal (de) que, siempre que

providence ['prɑvədənts] *n* **1** PRUDENCE : previsión *f,* prudencia *f* **2** *or* **Providence** : providencia *f* <divine providence : la Divina Providencia> **3 Providence** GOD : Providencia *f*

provident ['prɑvədənt] *adj* **1** PRUDENT : previsor, prudente **2** FRUGAL : frugal, ahorrativo

providential [,prɑvə'dɛntʃəl] *adj* : providencial

providing that → **provided**

province ['prɑvɪnts] *n* **1** : provincia *f* (de un país) <to live in the provinces : vivir en las provincias> **2** FIELD, SPHERE : campo *m,* competencia *f* <it's not in my province : no es de mi competencia>

provincial [prə'vɪntʃəl] *adj* **1** : provincial <provincial government : gobierno provincial> **2** : provinciano, pueblerino <a provincial mentality : una mentalidad provinciana>

provision[1] [prə'vɪʒən] *vt* : aprovisionar, abastecer

provision[2] *n* **1** PROVIDING : provisión *f,* suministro *m* **2** STIPULATION : condición *f,* salvedad *f,* estipulación *f* **3 provisions** *npl* : despensa *f,* víveres *mpl,* provisiones *fpl*

provisional [prə'vɪʒənəl] *adj* : provisional, provisorio — **provisionally** *adv*

proviso [prə'vaɪ,zo:] *n, pl* **-sos** *or* **-soes** : condición *f,* salvedad *f,* estipulación *f*

provocation [,prɑvə'keɪʃən] *n* : provocación *f*

provocative [prə'vɑkət̬ɪv] *adj* : provocador, provocativo <a provocative article : un artículo que hace pensar>

provoke [prə'vo:k] *vt* **-voked; -voking** : provocar

prow ['praʊ] *n* : proa *f*

prowess ['praʊəs] *n* **1** VALOR : valor *m,* valentía *f* **2** SKILL : habilidad *f,* destreza *f*

prowl ['praʊl] *vi* : merodear, rondar — *vt* : rondar por

prowler ['praʊlər] *n* : merodeador *m,* -dora *f*

proximity [prɑk'sɪmət̬i] *n* : proximidad *f*

proxy ['prɑksi] *n, pl* **proxies 1** : poder *m* (de actuar en nombre de alguien) <by proxy : por poder> **2** AGENT : apoderado *m,* -da *f;* representante *mf*

prude ['pru:d] *n* : mojigato *m,* -ta *f;* gazmoño *m,* -ña *f*

prudence ['pru:dənts] *n* **1** SHREWDNESS : prudencia *f,* sagacidad *f* **2** CAUTION : prudencia *f,* cautela *f* **3** THRIFTINESS : frugalidad *f*

prudent ['pru:dənt] *adj* **1** SHREWD : prudente, sagaz **2** CAUTIOUS, FARSIGHTED : prudente, previsor, precavido **3** THRIFTY : frugal, ahorrativo — **prudently** *adv*

prudery ['pru:dəri] *n, pl* **-eries** : mojigatería *f,* gazmoñería *f*

prudish ['pru:dɪʃ] *adj* : mojigato, gazmoño

prune[1] ['pru:n] *vt* **pruned; pruning** : podar (arbustos, etc.), acortar (un texto), recortar (gastos, etc.)

prune[2] *n* : ciruela *f* pasa

prurient ['prʊriənt] *adj* : lascivo

pry ['praɪ] *v* **pried; prying** *vi* : curiosear, huronear <to pry into other people's business : meterse uno en lo que no le importa> — *vt or* **to pry open** : abrir (con una palanca), apalancar

psalm ['sɑm, 'sɑlm] *n* : salmo *m*

pseudonym ['su:də,nɪm] *n* : seudónimo *m*

psoriasis [sə'raɪəsɪs] *n* : soriasis *f,* psoriasis *f*

psyche ['saɪki] *n* : psique *f,* psiquis *f*

psychiatric [,saɪki'ætrɪk] *adj* : psiquiátrico, siquiátrico

psychiatrist [sə'kaɪətrɪst, saɪ-] *n* : psiquiatra *mf,* siquiatra *mf*

psychiatry [sə'kaɪətri, saɪ-] *n* : psiquiatría *f,* siquiatría *f*

psychic[1] ['saɪkɪk] *adj* **1** : psíquico, síquico (en psicología) **2** CLAIRVOYANT : clarividente

psychic[2] *n* : vidente *mf,* clarividente *mf*

psychoanalysis [,saɪkoə'næləsɪs] *n, pl* **-yses** : psicoanálisis *m,* sicoanálisis *m*

psychoanalyst [,saɪko'ænəlɪst] *n* : psicoanalista *mf,* sicoanalista *mf*

psychoanalytic [,saɪko,ænəl'ɪt̬ɪk] *adj* : psicoanalítico, sicoanalítico

psychoanalyze [,saɪko'ænəl,aɪz] *vt* **-lyzed; -lyzing** : psicoanalizar, sicoanalizar

psychological [,saɪkə'lɑdʒɪkəl] *adj* : psicológico, sicológico — **psychologically** *adv*

psychologist [saɪ'kɑlədʒɪst] *n* : psicólogo *m,* -ga *f;* sicólogo *m,* -ga *f*

psychology [saɪ'kɑlədʒi] *n, pl* **-gies** : psicología *f,* sicología *f*

psychopath ['saɪkə,pæθ] *n* : psicópata *mf,* sicópata *mf*

psychopathic [,saɪkə'pæθɪk] *adj* : psicopático, sicopático

psychosis [saɪ'ko:sɪs] *n, pl* **-choses** [-'ko:,si:z] : psicosis *f,* sicosis *f*

psychosomatic [,saɪkəsə'mæt̬ɪk] *adj* : psicosomático, sicosomático

psychotherapist [,saɪko'θɛrəpɪst] *n* : psicoterapeuta *mf,* sicoterapeuta *mf*

psychotherapy [ˌsaɪkoˈθɛrəpi] *n, pl* **-pies :** psicoterapia *f,* sicoterapia *f*

psychotic[1] [saɪˈkɑtɪk] *adj* **:** psicótico, sicótico

psychotic[2] *n* **:** psicótico *m,* -ca *f;* sicótico *m,* -ca *f*

puberty [ˈpjuːbərti] *n* **:** pubertad *f*

pubic [ˈpjuːbɪk] *adj* **:** pubiano, púbico

public[1] [ˈpʌblɪk] *adj* **:** público — **publicly** *adv*

public[2] *n* **:** público *m*

publication [ˌpʌbləˈkeɪʃən] *n* **:** publicación *f*

publicist [ˈpʌbləsɪst] *n* **:** publicista *mf*

publicity [pəˈblɪsəti] *n* **:** publicidad *f*

publicize [ˈpʌbləˌsaɪz] *vt* **-cized; -cizing :** publicitar

public school *n* **:** escuela *f* pública

publish [ˈpʌblɪʃ] *vt* **:** publicar

publisher [ˈpʌblɪʃər] *n* **:** casa *f* editorial (compañía); editor *m,* -tora *f* (persona)

pucker[1] [ˈpʌkər] *vt* **:** fruncir, arrugar — *vi* **:** arrugarse

pucker[2] *n* **:** arruga *f,* frunce *m,* fruncido *m*

pudding [ˈpʊdɪŋ] *n* **:** budín *m,* pudín *m*

puddle [ˈpʌdəl] *n* **:** charco *m*

pudgy [ˈpʌdʒi] *adj* **pudgier; -est :** regordete *fam,* rechoncho *fam,* gordinflón *fam*

puerile [ˈpjʊrəl] *adj* **:** pueril

Puerto Rican[1] [ˌpwɛrtəˈriːkən, ˌportə-] *adj* **:** puertorriqueño

Puerto Rican[2] *n* **:** puertorriqueño *m,* -ña *f*

puff[1] [ˈpʌf] *vi* **1** BLOW **:** soplar **2** PANT **:** resoplar, jadear **3 to puff up** SWELL **:** hincharse — *vt* **1** BLOW **:** soplar <to puff smoke : echar humo> **2** INFLATE **:** inflar, hinchar <to puff out one's cheeks : inflar las mejillas>

puff[2] *n* **1** GUST **:** soplo *m,* ráfaga *f,* bocanada *f* (de humo) **2** DRAW **:** chupada *f* (a un cigarrillo) **3** SWELLING **:** hinchazón *f* **4 cream puff :** pastelito *m* de crema **5 powder puff :** borla *f*

puffy [ˈpʌfi] *adj* **puffier; -est 1** SWOLLEN **:** hinchado, inflado **2** SPONGY **:** esponjoso, suave

pug [ˈpʌg] *n* **1 :** doguillo *m* (perro) **2** *or* **pug nose :** nariz *f* achatada

pugnacious [ˌpʌgˈneɪʃəs] *adj* **:** pugnaz, agresivo

puke [ˈpjuːk] *vi* **puked; puking :** vomitar, devolver

pull[1] [ˈpʊl, ˈpʌl] *vt* **1** DRAW, TUG **:** tirar de, jalar **2** EXTRACT **:** sacar, extraer <to pull teeth : sacar muelas> <to pull a gun on : amenazar a (alguien) con pistola> **3** TEAR **:** desgarrarse (un músculo, etc.) **4 to pull down :** bajar, echar abajo, derribar (un edificio) **5 to pull in** ATTRACT **:** atraer (una muchedumbre, etc.) <to pull in votes : conseguir votos> **6 to pull off** REMOVE **:** sacar, quitar **7 to pull oneself together :** calmarse, tranquilizarse **8 to pull up** RAISE **:** levantar, subir — *vi* **1** DRAW, TUG **:** tirar, jalar **2** (*indicating movement in a specific direction*) <they pulled in front of us : se nos metieron delante> <to pull to a stop : pararse> **3 to pull through** RECOVER **:** recobrarse, reponerse **4 to pull together** COOPERATE **:** trabajar juntos, cooperar

pull[2] *n* **1** TUG **:** tirón *m,* jalón *m* <he gave it a pull : le dio un tirón> **2** ATTRACTION **:** atracción *f,* fuerza *f* <the pull of gravity : la fuerza de la gravedad> **3** INFLUENCE **:** influencia *f* **4** HANDLE **:** tirador *m* (de un cajón, etc.) **5 bell pull :** cuerda *f*

pullet [ˈpʊlət] *n* **:** polla *f,* gallina *f* (joven)

pulley [ˈpʊli] *n, pl* **-leys :** polea *f*

pullover [ˈpʊlˌoːvər] *n* **:** suéter *m*

pulmonary [ˈpʊlməˌnɛri, ˈpʌl-] *adj* **:** pulmonar

pulp [ˈpʌlp] *n* **1 :** pulpa *f* (de una fruta, etc.) **2** MASH **:** papilla *f,* pasta *f* <wood pulp : pasta de papel, pulpa de papel> <to beat to a pulp : hacer papilla (a alguien)> **3 :** pulpa *f* (de los dientes)

pulpit [ˈpʊlˌpɪt] *n* **:** púlpito *m*

pulsate [ˈpʌlˌseɪt] *vi* **-sated; -sating 1** BEAT **:** latir, palpitar **2** VIBRATE **:** vibrar

pulsation [ˌpʌlˈseɪʃən] *n* **:** pulsación *f*

pulse [ˈpʌls] *n* **:** pulso *m*

pulverize [ˈpʌlvəˌraɪz] *vt* **-ized; -izing :** pulverizar

puma [ˈpuːmə, ˈpjuː-] *n* **:** puma *m;* león *m,* leona *f* (in various countries)

pumice [ˈpʌməs] *n* **:** piedra *f* pómez

pummel [ˈpʌməl] *vt* **-meled; -meling :** aporrear, apalear

pump[1] [ˈpʌmp] *vt* **1 :** bombear <to pump water : bombear agua> <to pump (up) a tire : inflar una llanta> **2 :** mover (una manivela, un pedal, etc.) de arriba abajo <to pump someone's hand : darle un fuerte apretón de manos (a alguien)> **3 to pump out :** sacar, vaciar (con una bomba)

pump[2] *n* **1 :** bomba *f* <water pump : bomba de agua> **2** SHOE **:** zapato *m* de tacón

pumpernickel [ˈpʌmpərˌnɪkəl] *n* **:** pan *m* negro de centeno

pumpkin [ˈpʌmpkɪn, ˈpʌŋkən] *n* **:** calabaza *f,* zapallo *m Arg, Chile, Peru, Uru*

pun[1] [ˈpʌn] *vi* **punned; punning :** hacer juegos de palabras

pun[2] *n* **:** juego *m* de palabras, albur *m Mex*

punch[1] [ˈpʌntʃ] *vt* **1** HIT **:** darle un puñetazo (a alguien), golpear <she punched him in the nose : le dio un puñetazo en la nariz> **2** PERFORATE **:** perforar (papel, etc.), picar (un boleto)

punch[2] *n* **1 :** perforadora *f* <paper punch : perforadora de papel> **2** BLOW **:** golpe *m,* puñetazo *m* **3 :** ponche *m* <fruit punch : ponche de frutas>

punctilious [pəŋk'tɪliəs] *adj* : puntilloso
punctual ['pʌŋktʃʊəl] *adj* : puntual
punctuality [ˌpʌŋktʃʊ'æləṭi] *n* : puntualidad *f*
punctually ['pʌŋktʃʊəli] *adv* : puntualmente, a tiempo
punctuate ['pʌŋktʃʊˌeɪt] *vt* **-ated; -ating** : puntuar
punctuation [ˌpʌŋktʃʊ'eɪʃən] *n* : puntuación *f*
puncture[1] ['pʌŋktʃər] *vt* **-tured; -turing** : pinchar, punzar, perforar, ponchar *Mex*
puncture[2] *n* : pinchazo *m*, ponchadura *f Mex*
pundit ['pʌndɪt] *n* : experto *m*, -ta *f*
pungency ['pʌndʒəntsi] *n* : acritud *f*, acrimonia *f*
pungent ['pʌndʒənt] *adj* : acre
punish ['pʌnɪʃ] *vt* : castigar
punishable ['pʌnɪʃəbəl] *adj* : punible
punishment ['pʌnɪʃmənt] *n* : castigo *m*
punitive ['pju:nəṭɪv] *adj* : punitivo
punt[1] ['pʌnt] *vt* : impulsar (un barco) con una pértiga — *vi* : despejar (en deportes)
punt[2] *n* **1** : batea *f* (barco) **2** : patada *f* de despeje (en deportes)
puny ['pju:ni] *adj* **-nier; -est** : enclenque, endeble
pup ['pʌp] *n* : cachorro *m*, -rra *f* (de un perro); cría *f* (de otros animales)
pupa ['pju:pə] *n, pl* **-pae** [-pi, -ˌpaɪ] *or* **-pas** : crisálida *f*, pupa *f*
pupil ['pju:pəl] *n* **1** : alumno *m*, -na *f* (de colegio) **2** : pupila *f* (del ojo)
puppet ['pʌpət] *n* : títere *m*, marioneta *f*
puppy ['pʌpi] *n, pl* **-pies** : cachorro *m*, -rra *f*
purchase[1] ['pərtʃəs] *vt* **-chased; -chasing** : comprar
purchase[2] *n* **1** PURCHASING : compra *f*, adquisición *f* **2** : compra *f* <last-minute purchases : compras de última hora> **3** GRIP : agarre *m*, asidero *m* <she got a firm purchase on the wheel : se agarró bien del volante>
purchase order *n* : orden *f* de compra
pure ['pjʊr] *adj* **purer; purest** : puro
puree[1] [pjʊ'reɪ, -'ri:] *vt* **-reed; -reeing** : hacer un puré con
puree[2] *n* : puré *m*
purely ['pjʊrli] *adv* **1** WHOLLY : puramente, completamente <purely by chance : por pura casualidad> **2** SIMPLY : sencillamente, meramente
purgative ['pərgəṭɪv] *n* : purgante *m*
purgatory ['pərgəˌtori] *n, pl* **-ries** : purgatorio *m*
purge[1] ['pərdʒ] *vt* **purged; purging** : purgar
purge[2] *n* : purga *f*
purification [ˌpjʊrəfə'keɪʃən] *n* : purificación *f*
purify ['pjʊrəˌfaɪ] *vt* **-fied; -fying** : purificar
puritan ['pjʊrətən] *n* : puritano *m*, -na *f*
puritanical [ˌpju:rə'tænɪkəl] *adj* : puritano
purity ['pjʊrəṭi] *n* : pureza *f*
purl[1] ['pərl] *v* : tejer al revés, tejer del revés
purl[2] *n* : punto *m* del revés
purloin [pər'lɔɪn, 'pərˌlɔɪn] *vt* : hurtar, robar
purple ['pərpəl] *n* : morado *m*, color *m* púrpura
purport [pər'port] *vt* : pretender <to purport to be : pretender ser>
purpose ['pərpəs] *n* **1** INTENTION : propósito *m*, intención *f* <on purpose : a propósito, adrede> **2** FUNCTION : función *f* **3** RESOLUTION : resolución *f*, determinación *f*
purposeful ['pərpəsfəl] *adj* : determinado, decidido, resuelto
purposefully ['pərpəsfəli] *adv* : decididamente, resueltamente
purposely ['pərpəsli] *adv* : intencionadamente, a propósito, adrede
purr[1] ['pər] *vi* : ronronear
purr[2] *n* : ronroneo *m*
purse[1] ['pərs] *vt* **pursed; pursing** : fruncir <to purse one's lips : fruncir la boca>
purse[2] *n* **1** HANDBAG : cartera *f*, bolso *m*, bolsa *f Mex* <a change purse : un monedero> **2** FUNDS : fondos *mpl* **3** PRIZE : premio *m*
pursue [pər'su:] *vt* **-sued; -suing** **1** CHASE : perseguir **2** SEEK : buscar, tratar de encontrar <to pursue pleasure : buscar el placer> **3** FOLLOW : seguir <the road pursues a northerly course : el camino sigue hacia el norte> **4** : dedicarse a <to pursue a hobby : dedicarse a un pasatiempo>
pursuer [pər'su:ər] *n* : perseguidor *m*, -dora *f*
pursuit [pər'su:t] *n* **1** CHASE : persecución *f* **2** SEARCH : búsqueda *f*, busca *f* **3** ACTIVITY : actividad *f*, pasatiempo *m*
purveyor [pər'veɪər] *n* : proveedor *m*, -dora *f*
pus ['pʌs] *n* : pus *m*
push[1] ['pʊʃ] *vt* **1** SHOVE : empujar **2** PRESS : apretar, pulsar <push that button : aprieta ese botón> **3** PRESSURE, URGE : presionar **4 to push around** BULLY : intimidar, mangonear — *vi* **1** SHOVE : empujar **2** INSIST : insistir, presionar **3 to push off** LEAVE : marcharse, irse, largarse *fam* **4 to push on** PROCEED : seguir
push[2] *n* **1** SHOVE : empujón *m* **2** DRIVE : empuje *m*, energía *f*, dinamismo *m* **3** EFFORT : esfuerzo *m*
push-button ['pʊʃ'bʌtən] *adj* : de botones
pushcart ['pʊʃˌkɑrt] *n* : carretilla *f* de mano
pushy ['pʊʃi] *adj* **pushier; -est** : mandón, prepotente

pussy [ˈpʊsi] *n, pl* **pussies** : gatito *m,* -ta *f;* minino *m,* -na *f*
pussy willow *n* : sauce *m* blanco
pustule [ˈpʌsˌtʃuːl] *n* : pústula *f*
put [ˈpʊt] *v* **put; putting** *vt* **1** PLACE : poner, colocar <put it on the table : ponlo en la mesa> **2** INSERT : meter **3** (*indicating causation of a state or feeling*) : poner <it put her in a good mood : la puso de buen humor> <to put into effect : poner en práctica> **4** IMPOSE : imponer <they put a tax on it : lo gravaron con un impuesto> **5** SUBJECT : someter, poner <to put to the test : poner a prueba> <to put to death : ejecutar> **6** EXPRESS : expresar, decir <he put it simply : lo dijo sencillamente> **7** APPLY : aplicar <to put one's mind to something : proponerse hacer algo> 8 SET : poner <I put him to work : lo puse a trabajar> **9** ATTACH : dar <to put a high value on : dar gran valor a> **10** PRESENT : presentar, exponer <to put a question to someone : hacer una pregunta a alguien> — *vi* **1 to put to sea** : hacerse a la mar **2 to put up with** : aguantar, soportar
put away *vt* **1** KEEP : guardar **2** *or* **to put aside** : dejar a un lado
put by *vt* SAVE : ahorrar
put down *vt* **1** SUPPRESS : aplastar, suprimir **2** ATTRIBUTE : atribuir <she put it down to luck : lo atribuyó a la suerte>
put in *vi* : presentarse <I've put in for the position : me presenté para el puesto> — *vt* DEVOTE : dedicar (unas horas, etc.)
put off *vt* DEFER : aplazar, posponer
put on *vt* **1** ASSUME : afectar, adoptar **2** PRODUCE : presentar (una obra de teatro, etc.) **3** WEAR : ponerse
put out *vt* INCONVENIENCE : importunar, incomodar
putrefy [ˈpjuːtrəˌfaɪ] *v* **-fied; -fying** *vt* : pudrir — *vi* : pudrirse
putrid [ˈpjuːtrɪd] *adj* : putrefacto, pútrido
putter [ˈpʌtər] *vi or* **to putter around** : entretenerse
putty[1] [ˈpʌti] *vt* **-tied; -tying** : poner masilla en
putty[2] *n, pl* **-ties** : masilla *f*
put up *vt* **1** LODGE : alojar **2** CONTRIBUTE : contribuir, pagar
puzzle[1] [ˈpʌzəl] *vt* **-zled; -zling 1** CONFUSE : confundir, dejar perplejo **2 to puzzle out** : dar vueltas a, tratar de resolver
puzzle[2] *n* **1** : rompecabezas *m* <a crossword puzzle : un crucigrama> **2** MYSTERY : misterio *m,* enigma *m*
puzzlement [ˈpʌzəlmənt] *n* : desconcierto *m,* perplejidad *f*
pygmy[1] [ˈpɪgmi] *adj* : enano, pigmeo
pygmy[2] *n, pl* **-mies 1** DWARF : enano *m,* -na *f* **2 Pygmy** : pigmeo *m,* -mea *f*
pylon [ˈpaɪˌlɑn, -lən] *n* **1** : torre *f* de conducta eléctrica **2** : pilón *m* (de un puente)
pyramid [ˈpɪrəˌmɪd] *n* : pirámide *f*
pyre [ˈpaɪr] *n* : pira *f*
pyromania [ˌpaɪroˈmeɪniə] *n* : piromanía *f*
pyromaniac [ˌpaɪroˈmeɪniˌæk] *n* : pirómano *m,* -na *f*
pyrotechnics [ˌpaɪrəˈtɛknɪks] *npl* **1** FIREWORKS : fuegos *mpl* artificiales **2** DISPLAY, SHOW : espectáculo *m,* muestra *f* de virtuosismo <computer pyrotechnics : efectos especiales hechos por computadora>
python [ˈpaɪˌθɑn, -θən] *n* : pitón *f,* serpiente *f* pitón

Q

q [ˈkjuː] *n, pl* **q's** *or* **qs** [ˈkjuːz] : decimoséptima letra del alfabeto inglés
quack[1] [ˈkwæk] *vi* : graznar
quack[2] *n* **1** : graznido *m* (de pato) **2** CHARLATAN : curandero *m,* -ra *f;* matasanos *m fam*
quadrangle [ˈkwɑˌdræŋgəl] *n* **1** COURTYARD : patio *m* interior **2** → **quadrilateral**
quadrant [ˈkwɑdrənt] *n* : cuadrante *m*
quadrilateral [ˌkwɑdrəˈlæt̬ərəl] *n* : cuadrilátero *m*
quadruped [ˈkwɑdrəˌpɛd] *n* : cuadrúpedo *m*
quadruple [kwɑˈdruːpəl, -ˈdrʌ-; ˈkwɑdrə-] *v* **-pled; -pling** *vt* : cuadruplicar — *vi* : cuadruplicarse
quadruplet [kwɑˈdruːplət, -ˈdrʌ-; ˈkwɑdrə-] *n* : cuatrillizo *m,* -za *f*
quagmire [ˈkwægˌmaɪr, ˈkwɑg-] *n* : cenagal *m,* lodazal *m*
quail[1] [ˈkweɪl] *vi* : encogerse, acobardarse
quail[2] *n, pl* **quail** *or* **quails** : codorniz *f*
quaint [ˈkweɪnt] *adj* **1** ODD : extraño, curioso **2** PICTURESQUE : pintoresco — **quaintly** *adv*
quaintness [ˈkweɪntnəs] *n* : rareza *f,* lo curioso
quake[1] [ˈkweɪk] *vi* **quaked; quaking** : temblar
quake[2] *n* : temblor *m,* terremoto *m*
qualification [ˌkwɑləfəˈkeɪʃən] *n* **1** LIMITATION, RESERVATION : reserva *f,* limitación *f* <without qualification : sin reservas> **2** REQUIREMENT : requisito *m* **3 qualifications** *npl* ABILITY : aptitud *f,* capacidad *f*
qualified [ˈkwɑləˌfaɪd] *adj* : competente, capacitado
qualify [ˈkwɑləˌfaɪ] *v* **-fied; -fying** *vt* **1** : matizar <to qualify a statement

: matizar una declaración> **2** MODIFY : calificar (en gramática) **3** : habilitar <the certificate qualified her to teach : el certificado la habilitó para enseñar> — *vi* **1** : obtener el título, recibirse <to qualify as an engineer : recibirse de ingeniero> **2** : clasificarse (en deportes)

quality [ˈkwɑləṭi] *n, pl* **-ties 1** NATURE : carácter *m* **2** ATTRIBUTE : cualidad *f* **3** GRADE : calidad *f* <of good quality : de buena calidad>

qualm [ˈkwɑm, ˈkwɑlm, ˈkwɔm] *n* **1** MISGIVING : duda *f,* aprensión *f* **2** RESERVATION, SCRUPLE : escrúpulo *m,* reparo *m*

quandary [ˈkwɑndri] *n, pl* **-ries** : dilema *m*

quantity [ˈkwɑntəṭi] *n, pl* **-ties** : cantidad *f*

quantum theory [ˈkwɑntəm] *n* : teoría *f* cuántica

quarantine[1] [ˈkwɔrənˌtiːn] *vt* **-tined; -tining** : poner en cuarentena

quarantine[2] *n* : cuarentena *f*

quarrel[1] [ˈkwɔrəl] *vi* **-reled** *or* **-relled; -reling** *or* **-relling** : pelearse, reñir, discutir

quarrel[2] *n* : pelea *f,* riña *f,* disputa *f*

quarrelsome [ˈkwɔrəlsəm] *adj* : pendenciero, discutidor

quarry[1] [ˈkwɔri] *vt* **quarried; quarrying 1** EXTRACT : extraer, sacar <to quarry marble : extraer mármol> **2** EXCAVATE : excavar <to quarry a hill : excavar un cerro>

quarry[2] *n, pl* **quarries 1** PREY : presa *f* **2** *or* **stone quarry** : cantera *f*

quart [ˈkwɔrt] *n* : cuarto *m* de galón

quarter[1] [ˈkwɔrṭər] *vt* **1** : dividir en cuatro partes **2** LODGE : alojar, acuartelar (tropas)

quarter[2] *n* **1** : cuarto *m,* cuarta parte *f* <a foot and a quarter : un pie y cuarto> <a quarter after three : las tres y cuarto> **2** : moneda *f* de 25 centavos, cuarto *m* de dólar **3** DISTRICT : barrio *m* <business quarter : barrio comercial> **4** PLACE : parte *f* <from all quarters : de todas partes> <at close quarters : de muy cerca> **5** MERCY : clemencia *f,* cuartel *m* <to give no quarter : no dar cuartel> **6 quarters** *npl* LODGING : alojamiento *m,* cuartel *m* (militar)

quarterly[1] [ˈkwɔrṭərli] *adv* : cada tres meses, trimestralmente

quarterly[2] *adj* : trimestral

quarterly[3] *n, pl* **-lies** : publicación *f* trimestral

quartermaster [ˈkwɔrṭərˌmæstər] *n* : intendente *mf*

quartet [kwɔrˈtɛt] *n* : cuarteto *m*

quartz [ˈkwɔrts] *n* : cuarzo *m*

quash [ˈkwɑʃ, ˈkwɔʃ] *vt* **1** ANNUL : anular **2** QUELL : sofocar, aplastar

quaver[1] [ˈkweɪvər] *vi* **1** SHAKE : temblar <her voice was quavering : su voz temblaba> **2** TRILL : trinar

quaver[2] *n* : temblor *m* (de la voz)

quay [ˈkiː, ˈkeɪ, ˈkweɪ] *n* : muelle *m*

queasiness [ˈkwiːzinəs] *n* : mareo *m,* náusea *f*

queasy [ˈkwiːzi] *adj* **-sier; -est** : mareado

queen [ˈkwiːn] *n* : reina *f*

queenly [ˈkwiːnli] *adj* **-lier; -est** : de reina, regio

queer [ˈkwɪr] *adj* : extraño, raro, curioso — **queerly** *adv*

quell [ˈkwɛl] *vt* : aplastar, sofocar

quench [ˈkwɛntʃ] *vt* **1** EXTINGUISH : apagar, sofocar **2** SATISFY : saciar, satisfacer (la sed)

querulous [ˈkwɛrələs, ˈkwɛrjələs, ˈkwɪr-] *adj* : quejumbroso, quejoso — **querulously** *adv*

query[1] [ˈkwɪri, ˈkwɛr-] *vt* **-ried; -rying 1** ASK : preguntar, interrogar <we queried the professor : preguntamos al profesor> **2** QUESTION : cuestionar, poner en duda <to query a matter : cuestionar un asunto>

query[2] *n, pl* **-ries 1** QUESTION : pregunta *f* **2** DOUBT : duda *f*

quest[1] [ˈkwɛst] *v* : buscar

quest[2] *n* : búsqueda *f*

question[1] [ˈkwɛstʃən] *vt* **1** ASK : preguntar **2** DOUBT : poner en duda, cuestionar **3** INTERROGATE : interrogar — *vi* INQUIRE : inquirir, preguntar

question[2] *n* **1** QUERY : pregunta *f* **2** ISSUE : asunto *m,* problema *f,* cuestión *f* **3** POSSIBILITY : posibilidad *f* <it's out of the question : es indiscutible> **4** DOUBT : duda *f* <to call into question : poner en duda>

questionable [ˈkwɛstʃənəbəl] *adj* : dudoso, discutible, cuestionable <questionable results : resultados discutibles> <questionable motives : motivos sospechosos>

questioner [ˈkwɛstʃənər] *n* : interrogador *m,* -dora *f*

question mark *n* : signo *m* de interrogación

questionnaire [ˌkwɛstʃəˈnær] *n* : cuestionario *m*

queue[1] [ˈkjuː] *vi* **queued; queuing** *or* **queueing** : hacer cola

queue[2] *n* **1** PIGTAIL : coleta *f,* trenza *f* **2** LINE : cola *f,* fila *f*

quibble[1] [ˈkwɪbəl] *vi* **-bled; -bling** : quejarse por nimiedades, andar con sutilezas

quibble[2] *n* : objeción *f* de poca monta, queja *f* insignificante

quick[1] [ˈkwɪk] *adv* : rápidamente

quick[2] *adj* **1** RAPID : rápido **2** ALERT, CLEVER : listo, vivo, agudo **3 a quick temper** : un genio vivo

quick[3] *n* **1** FLESH : carne *f* viva **2 to cut someone to the quick** : herir a alguien en lo más vivo

quicken [ˈkwɪkən] *vt* **1** REVIVE : resucitar **2** AROUSE : estimular, despertar **3** HASTEN : acelerar <she quickened her pace : aceleró el paso>

quickly [ˈkwɪkli] *adv* **:** rápidamente, rápido, de prisa
quickness [ˈkwɪknəs] *n* **:** rapidez *f*
quicksand [ˈkwɪkˌsænd] *n* **:** arena *f* movediza
quicksilver [ˈkwɪkˌsɪlvər] *n* **:** mercurio *m,* azogue *m*
quick-tempered [ˈkwɪkˈtɛmpərd] *adj* **:** irascible, de genio vivo
quick-witted [ˈkwɪkˈwɪt̬əd] *adj* **:** agudo
quiet[1] *v* [ˈkwaɪət] *vt* **1** SILENCE **:** hacer callar, acallar **2** CALM **:** calmar, tranquilizar — *vi* **to quiet down :** calmarse, tranquilizarse
quiet[2] *adv* **:** silenciosamente <a quiet-running engine : un motor silencioso>
quiet[3] *adj* **1** CALM **:** tranquilo, calmoso **2** MILD **:** sosegado, suave <a quiet disposition : un temperamento sosegado> **3** SILENT **:** silencioso **4** UNOBTRUSIVE **:** discreto **5** SECLUDED **:** aislado <a quiet nook : un rincón aislado> — **quietly** *adv*
quiet[4] *n* **1** CALM **:** calma *f,* tranquilidad *f* **2** SILENCE **:** silencio *m*
quietness [ˈkwaɪətnəs] *n* **:** suavidad *f,* tranquilidad *f,* quietud *f*
quietude [ˈkwaɪəˌtuːd, -ˌtjuːd] *n* **:** quietud *f,* reposo *m*
quill [ˈkwɪl] *n* **1** SPINE **:** púa *f* (de un puerco espín) **2 :** pluma *f* (para escribir)
quilt[1] [ˈkwɪlt] *vt* **:** acolchar
quilt[2] *n* **:** colcha *f,* edredón *m*
quince [ˈkwɪnts] *n* **:** membrillo *m*
quinine [ˈkwaɪˌnaɪn] *n* **:** quinina *f*
quintessence [kwɪnˈtɛsənts] *n* **:** quintaesencia *f*
quintet [kwɪnˈtɛt] *n* **:** quinteto *m*
quintuple [kwɪnˈtuːpəl, -ˈtjuː-, -ˈtʌ-; ˈkwɪntə-] *adj* **:** quíntuplo
quintuplet [kwɪnˈtʌplət, -ˈtuː-, -ˈtjuː-; ˈkwɪntə-] *n* **:** quintillizo *m,* -za *f*
quip[1] [ˈkwɪp] *vi* **quipped; quipping :** bromear
quip[2] *n* **:** ocurrencia *f,* salida *f*
quirk [ˈkwərk] *n* **:** peculiaridad *f,* rareza *f* <a quirk of fate : un capricho del destino>
quirky [ˈkwərki] *adj* **-kier; -est :** peculiar, raro
quit [ˈkwɪt] *v* **quit; quitting** *vt* **:** dejar, abandonar <to quit smoking : dejar de fumar> — *vi* **1** STOP **:** parar **2** RESIGN **:** dimitir, renunciar
quite [ˈkwaɪt] *adv* **1** COMPLETELY **:** completamente, totalmente **2** RATHER **:** bastante <quite near : bastante cerca>
quits [ˈkwɪts] *adj* **to call it quits :** quedar en paz
quitter [ˈkwɪt̬ər] *n* **:** derrotista *mf*
quiver[1] [ˈkwɪvər] *vi* **:** temblar, estremecerse, vibrar
quiver[2] *n* **1 :** carcaj *m,* aljaba *f* (para flechas) **2** TREMBLING **:** temblor *m,* estremecimiento *m*
quixotic [kwɪkˈsɑt̬ɪk] *adj* **:** quijotesco
quiz[1] [ˈkwɪz] *vt* **quizzed; quizzing :** interrogar, hacer una prueba a (en el colegio)
quiz[2] *n, pl* **quizzes :** examen *m* corto, prueba *f*
quizzical [ˈkwɪzɪkəl] *adj* **1** TEASING **:** burlón **2** CURIOUS **:** curioso, interrogativo
quorum [ˈkworəm] *n* **:** quórum *m*
quota [ˈkwoːt̬ə] *n* **:** cuota *f,* cupo *m*
quotable [ˈkwoːt̬əbəl] *adj* **:** citable
quotation [kwoˈteɪʃən] *n* **1** CITATION **:** cita *f* **2** ESTIMATE **:** presupuesto *m,* estimación *f* **3** PRICE **:** cotización *f*
quotation marks *npl* **:** comillas *fpl*
quote[1] [ˈkwoːt] *vt* **quoted; quoting 1** CITE **:** citar **2** VALUE **:** cotizar (en finanzas)
quote[2] *n* **1** → **quotation 2 quotes** *npl* → **quotation marks**
quotient [ˈkwoːʃənt] *n* **:** cociente *m*

R

r [ˈɑr] *n, pl* **r's** *or* **rs** [ˈɑrz] **:** decimoctava letra del alfabeto inglés
rabbi [ˈræˌbaɪ] *n* **:** rabino *m,* -na *f*
rabbit [ˈræbət] *n, pl* **-bit** *or* **-bits :** conejo *m,* -ja *f*
rabble [ˈræbəl] *n* **1** MASSES **:** populacho *m* **2** RIFFRAFF **:** chusma *f,* gentuza *f*
rabid [ˈræbɪd] *adj* **1 :** rabioso, afectado con la rabia **2** FURIOUS **:** furioso **3** FANATIC **:** fanático
rabies [ˈreɪbiːz] *ns & pl* **:** rabia *f*
raccoon [ræˈkuːn] *n, pl* **-coon** *or* **-coons :** mapache *m*
race[1] [ˈreɪs] *vi* **raced; racing 1 :** correr, competir (en una carrera) **2** RUSH **:** ir a toda prisa, ir corriendo
race[2] *n* **1** CURRENT **:** corriente *f* (de agua) **2 :** carrera *f* <dog race : carrera de perros> <the presidential race : la carrera presidential> **3 :** raza *f* <the black race : la raza negra> <the human race : el género humano>
racecourse [ˈreɪsˌkors] *n* **:** pista *f* (de carreras)
racehorse [ˈreɪsˌhors] *n* **:** caballo *m* de carreras
racer [ˈreɪsər] *n* **:** corredor *m,* -dora *f*
racetrack [ˈreɪsˌtræk] *n* **:** pista *f* (de carreras)
racial [ˈreɪʃəl] *adj* **:** racial — **racially** *adv*
racism [ˈreɪˌsɪzəm] *n* **:** racismo *m*
racist [ˈreɪsɪst] *n* **:** racista *mf*

rack[1] ['ræk] *vt* **1 :** atormentar <racked with pain : atormentado por el dolor> **2 to rack one's brains :** devanarse los sesos

rack[2] *n* **1** SHELF, STAND **:** estante *m* <a luggage rack : un portaequipajes> <a coatrack : un perchero, una percha> **2 :** potro *m* (instrumento de la tortura)

racket ['rækət] *n* **1 :** raqueta *f* (en deportes) **2** DIN **:** estruendo *m,* bulla *f,* jaleo *m fam* **3** SWINDLE **:** estafa *f,* timo *m fam*

racketeer [ˌrækə'tɪr] *n* **:** estafador *m,* -dora *f*

raconteur [ˌræˌkɑn'tər] *n* **:** anecdotista *mf*

racy ['reɪsi] *adj* **racier; -est :** subido de tono, picante

radar ['reɪˌdɑr] *n* **:** radar *m*

radial ['reɪdiəl] *adj* **:** radial

radiance ['reɪdiənts] *n* **:** resplandor *m*

radiant ['reɪdiənt] *adj* **:** radiante — **radiantly** *adv*

radiate ['reɪdiˌeɪt] *v* **-ated; -ating** *vt* **:** irradiar, emitir <to radiate heat : irradiar el calor> <to radiate happiness : rebosar de alegría> — *vi* **1 :** irradiar **2** SPREAD **:** salir, extenderse <to radiate (out) from the center : salir del centro>

radiation [ˌreɪdi'eɪʃən] *n* **:** radiación *f*

radiator ['reɪdiˌeɪtər] *n* **:** radiador *m*

radical[1] ['rædɪkəl] *adj* **:** radical — **radically** [-kli] *adv*

radical[2] *n* **:** radical *mf*

radii → **radius**

radio[1] ['reɪdiˌoː] *v* **:** llamar por radio, transmitir por radio

radio[2] *n, pl* **-dios :** radio *m* (aparato), radio *f* (emisora, radiodifusión)

radioactive ['reɪdio'æktɪv] *adj* **:** radiactivo, radioactivo

radioactivity [ˌreɪdioˌæk'tɪvət̬i] *n, pl* **-ties :** radiactividad *f,* radioactividad *f*

radiologist [ˌreɪdi'ɑləd͡ʒɪst] *n* **:** radiólogo *m,* -ga *f*

radiology [ˌreɪdi'ɑləd͡ʒi] *n* **:** radiología *f*

radish ['rædɪʃ] *n* **:** rábano *m*

radium ['reɪdiəm] *n* **:** radio *m*

radius ['reɪdiəs] *n, pl* **radii** [-diˌaɪ] **:** radio *m*

radon ['reɪˌdɑn] *n* **:** radón *m*

raffle[1] ['ræfəl] *vt* **-fled; -fling :** rifar, sortear

raffle[2] *n* **:** rifa *f,* sorteo *m*

raft ['ræft] *n* **1 :** balsa *f* <rubber rafts : balsas de goma> **2** LOT, SLEW **:** montón *m* <a raft of documents : un montón de documentos>

rafter ['ræftər] *n* **:** par *m,* viga *f*

rag ['ræg] *n* **1** CLOTH **:** trapo *m* **2 rags** *npl* TATTERS **:** harapos *mpl,* andrapos *mpl*

ragamuffin ['rægəˌmʌfən] *n* **:** pilluelo *m,* -la *f*

rage[1] ['reɪd͡ʒ] *vi* **raged; raging 1 :** estar furioso, rabiar <to fly into a rage : enfurecerse> **2 :** bramar, hacer estragos <the wind was raging : el viento bramaba> <flu raged through the school : la gripe hizo estragos por el colegio>

rage[2] *n* **1** ANGER **:** furia *f,* ira *f,* cólera *f* **2** FAD **:** moda *f,* furor *m*

ragged ['rægəd] *adj* **1** UNEVEN **:** irregular, desigual **2** TORN **:** hecho jirones **3** TATTERED **:** andrajoso, harapiento

ragout [ræ'guː] *n* **:** ragú *m,* estofado *m*

ragtime ['rægˌtaɪm] *n* **:** ragtime *m*

ragweed ['rægˌwiːd] *n* **:** ambrosía *f*

raid[1] ['reɪd] *vt* **1 :** invadir, hacer una incursión en <raided by enemy troops : invadido por tropas enemigas> **2 :** asaltar, atracar <the gang raided the warehouse : la pandilla asaltó el almacén> **3 :** allanar, hacer una redada en <police raided the house : la policía allanó la vivienda>

raid[2] *n* **1 :** invasión *f* (militar) **2 :** asalto *m* (por delincuentes) **3 :** redada *f,* allanamiento *m* (por la policía)

raider ['reɪdər] *n* **1** ATTACKER **:** asaltante *mf;* invasor *m,* -sora *f* **2 corporate raider :** tiburón *m*

rail[1] ['reɪl] *vi* **1 to rail against** REVILE **:** denostar contra **2 to rail at** SCOLD **:** regañar, reprender

rail[2] *n* **1** BAR **:** barra *f,* barrera *f* **2** HANDRAIL **:** pasamanos *m,* barandilla *f* **3** TRACK **:** riel *m* (para ferrocarriles) **4** RAILROAD **:** ferrocarril *m*

railing ['reɪlɪŋ] *n* **1 :** baranda *f* (de un balcón, etc.) **2** RAILS **:** verja *f*

raillery ['reɪləri] *n, pl* **-leries :** bromas *fpl*

railroad ['reɪlˌroːd] *n* **:** ferrocarril *m*

railway ['reɪlˌweɪ] → **railroad**

raiment ['reɪmənt] *n* **:** vestiduras *fpl*

rain[1] ['reɪn] *vi* **1 :** llover <it's raining : está lloviendo> **2 to rain down** SHOWER **:** llover <insults rained down on him : le llovieron los insultos>

rain[2] *n* **:** lluvia *f*

rainbow ['reɪnˌboː] *n* **:** arco *m* iris

raincoat ['reɪnˌkoːt] *n* **:** impermeable *m*

raindrop ['reɪnˌdrɑp] *n* **:** gota *f* de lluvia

rainfall ['reɪnˌfɔl] *n* **:** lluvia *f,* precipitación *f*

rainstorm ['reɪnˌstɔrm] *n* **:** temporal *m* (de lluvia)

rainwater ['reɪnˌwɔt̬ər] *n* **:** agua *f* de lluvia

rainy ['reɪni] *adj* **rainier; -est :** lluvioso

raise[1] ['reɪz] *vt* **raised; raising 1** LIFT **:** levantar, subir, alzar <to raise one's spirits : levantarle el ánimo a alguien> **2** ERECT **:** levantar, erigir **3** COLLECT **:** recaudar <to raise money : recaudar dinero> **4** REAR **:** criar <to raise one's children : criar uno a sus niños> **5** GROW **:** cultivar **6** INCREASE **:** aumentar, subir **7** PROMOTE **:** ascender **8** PROVOKE **:** provocar <it raised

a laugh : provocó una risa> **9** BRING UP : sacar (temas, objeciones, etc.)

raise[2] *n* : aumento *m*

raisin ['reɪzən] *n* : pasa *f*

raja *or* **rajah** ['rɑdʒə, -ˌdʒɑ, -ˌʒɑ] *n* : rajá *m*

rake[1] ['reɪk] *v* **raked; raking** *vt* **1** : rastrillar <to rake leaves : rastrillar las hojas> **2** SWEEP : barrer <raked with gunfire : barrido con metralla> — *vi* **to rake through** : revolver, hurgar en

rake[2] *n* **1** : rastrillo *m* **2** LIBERTINE : libertino *m*, -na *f;* calavera *m*

rakish ['reɪkɪʃ] *adj* **1** JAUNTY : desenvuelto, desenfadado **2** DISSOLUTE : libertino, disoluto

rally[1] ['ræli] *v* **-lied; -lying** *vi* **1** MEET, UNITE : reunirse, congregarse **2** RECOVER : recuperarse — *vt* **1** ASSEMBLE : reunir (tropas, etc.) **2** RECOVER : recobrar (la fuerza, el ánimo, etc.)

rally[2] *n, pl* **-lies** : reunión *f,* mitin *m,* manifestación *f*

ram[1] ['ræm] *v* **rammed; ramming** *vt* **1** DRIVE : hincar, clavar <he rammed it into the ground : lo hincó en la tierra> **2** SMASH : estrellar, embestir — *vi* COLLIDE : chocar (contra), estrellarse

ram[2] *n* **1** : carnero *m* (animal) **2 battering ram** : ariete *m*

RAM ['ræm] *n* : RAM *f*

ramble[1] ['ræmbəl] *vi* **-bled; -bling 1** WANDER : pasear, deambular **2 to ramble on** : divagar, perder el hilo **3** SPREAD : trepar (dícese de una planta)

ramble[2] *n* : paseo *m,* excursión *f*

rambler ['ræmblər] *n* **1** WALKER : excursionista *mf* **2** ROSE : rosa *f* trepadora

rambunctious [ræm'bʌŋkʃəs] *adj* UNRULY : alborotado

ramification [ˌræməfə'keɪʃən] *n* : ramificación *f*

ramify ['ræməˌfaɪ] *vi* **-fied; -fying** : ramificarse

ramp ['ræmp] *n* : rampa *f*

rampage[1] ['ræmˌpeɪdʒ, ræm'peɪdʒ] *vi* **-paged; -paging** : andar arrasando todo, correr destrozando

rampage[2] ['ræmˌpeɪdʒ] *n* : alboroto *m,* frenesí *m* (de violencia)

rampant ['ræmpənt] *adj* : desenfrenado

rampart ['ræmˌpɑrt] *n* : terraplén *m,* muralla *f*

ramrod ['ræmˌrɑd] *n* : baqueta *f*

ramshackle ['ræmˌʃækəl] *adj* : destartalado

ran → **run**

ranch ['ræntʃ] *n* **1** : hacienda *f,* rancho *m,* finca *f* ganadera **2** FARM : granja *f* <fruit ranch : granja de frutas>

rancher ['ræntʃər] *n* : estanciero *m,* -ra *f;* ranchero *m,* -ra *f*

rancid ['ræntsɪd] *adj* : rancio

rancor ['ræŋkər] *n* : rencor *m*

random ['rændəm] *adj* **1** : fortuito, aleatorio **2 at ~** : al azar — **randomly** *adv*

rang → **ring**

range[1] ['reɪndʒ] *v* **ranged; ranging** *vt* ARRANGE : alinear, ordenar, arreglar — *vi* **1** ROAM : deambular <to range through the town : deambular por el pueblo> **2** EXTEND : extenderse <the results range widely : los resultados se extienden mucho> **3** VARY : variar <discounts range from 20% to 40% : los descuentos varían entre 20% y 40%>

range[2] *n* **1** ROW : fila *f,* hilera *f* <a mountain range : una cordillera> **2** GRASSLAND : pradera *f,* pampa *f* **3** STOVE : cocina *f* **4** VARIETY : variedad *f,* gama *f* **5** SPHERE : ámbito *m,* esfera *f,* campo *m* **6** REACH : registro *m* (de la voz), alcance *m* (de un arma de fuego) **7 shooting range** : campo *m* de tiro

ranger ['reɪndʒər] *n or* **forest ranger** : guardabosque *mf*

rangy ['reɪndʒi] *adj* **rangier; -est** : alto y delgado

rank[1] ['ræŋk] *vt* **1** RANGE : alinear, ordenar, poner en fila **2** CLASSIFY : clasificar — *vi* **1 to rank above** : ser superior a **2 to rank among** : encontrarse entre, figurar entre

rank[2] *adj* **1** LUXURIANT : lozano, exuberante (dícese de una planta) **2** SMELLY : fétido, maloliente **3** OUTRIGHT : completo, absoluto <a rank injustice : una injusticia manifiesta>

rank[3] *n* **1** LINE, ROW : fila *f* <to close ranks : cerrar filas> **2** GRADE, POSITION : grado *m,* rango *m* (militar) <to pull rank : abusar de su autoridad> **3** CLASS : categoría *f,* clase *f* **4 ranks** *npl* : soldados *mpl* rasos

rank and file *n* **1** RANKS : soldados *mpl* rasos **2** : bases *fpl* (de un partido, etc.)

rankle ['ræŋkəl] *v* **-kled; -kling** *vi* : doler — *vt* : irritar, herir

ransack ['rænˌsæk] *vt* : revolver, desvalijar, registrar de arriba abajo

ransom[1] ['ræntsəm] *vt* : rescatar, pagar un rescate por

ransom[2] *n* : rescate *m*

rant ['rænt] *vi or* **to rant and rave** : despotricar, desvariar

rap[1] ['ræp] *v* **rapped; rapping** *vt* **1** KNOCK : golpetear, dar un golpe en **2** CRITICIZE : criticar — *vi* **1** CHAT : charlar, cotorrear *fam* **2** KNOCK : dar un golpe

rap[2] *n* **1** BLOW, KNOCK : golpe *m,* golpecito *m* **2** CHAT : charla *f* **3** *or* **rap music** : rap *m* **4 to take the rap** : pagar el pato *fam*

rapacious [rə'peɪʃəs] *adj* **1** GREEDY : avaricioso, codicioso **2** PREDATORY : rapaz, de rapiña **3** RAVENOUS : voraz

rape[1] ['reɪp] *vt* **raped; raping** : violar

rape[2] *n* **1** : colza *f* (planta) **2** : violación *f* (de una persona)

rapid [ˈræpɪd] *adj* : rápido — **rapidly** *adv*
rapidity [rəˈpɪdəṭi] *n* : rapidez *f*
rapids [ˈræpɪdz] *npl* : rápidos *mpl*
rapier [ˈreɪpiər] *n* : estoque *m*
rapist [ˈreɪpɪst] *n* : violador *m*, -dora *f*
rapport [ræˈpor] *n* : relación *f* armoniosa, entendimiento *m*
rapt [ˈræpt] *adj* : absorto, embelesado
rapture [ˈræptʃər] *n* : éxtasis *m*
rapturous [ˈræptʃərəs] *adj* : extasiado, embelesado
rare [ˈrær] *adj* **rarer; rarest 1** RAREFIED : enrarecido **2** FINE : excelente, excepcional <a rare talent : un talento excepcional> **3** UNCOMMON : raro, poco común **4** : poco cocido (dícese de la carne)
rarefy [ˈrærəˌfaɪ] *vt* **-fied; -fying** : rarificar, enrarecer
rarely [ˈrærli] *adv* SELDOM : pocas veces, rara vez
raring [ˈrærən, -ɪŋ] *adj* : lleno de entusiasmo, con muchas ganas
rarity [ˈrærəṭi] *n, pl* **-ties** : rareza *f*
rascal [ˈræskəl] *n* : pillo *m*, -lla *f*; pícaro *m*, -ra *f*
rash[1] [ˈræʃ] *adj* : imprudente, precipitado — **rashly** *adv*
rash[2] *n* : sarpullido *m*, erupción *f*
rashness [ˈræʃnəs] *n* : precipitación *f*, impetuosidad *f*
rasp[1] [ˈræsp] *vt* **1** SCRAPE : raspar, escofinar **2 to rasp out** : decir en voz áspera
rasp[2] *n* : escofina *f*
raspberry [ˈræzˌbɛri] *n, pl* **-ries** : frambuesa *f*
rat [ˈræt] *n* : rata *f*
ratchet [ˈrætʃət] *n* : trinquete *m*
rate[1] [ˈreɪt] *vt* **rated; rating 1** CONSIDER, REGARD : considerar, estimar **2** DESERVE : merecer
rate[2] *n* **1** PACE, SPEED : velocidad *f*, ritmo *m* <at this rate : a este paso> **2** : índice *m*, tasa *f* <birth rate : índice de natalidad> <interest rate : tasa de interés> **3** CHARGE, PRICE : precio *m*, tarifa *f*
rather [ˈræðər, ˈrʌ-, ˈrɑ-] *adv* **1** (*indicating preference*) <she would rather stay in the house : preferiría quedarse en casa> <I'd rather not : mejor que no> **2** (*indicating preciseness*) <my father, or rather my stepfather : mi padre, o mejor dicho mi padrastro> **3** INSTEAD : sino que, más que, al contrario <I'm not pleased; rather I'm disappointed : no estoy satisfecho, sino desilusionado> **4** SOMEWHAT : algo, un tanto <rather strange : un poco extraño> **5** QUITE : bastante <rather difficult : bastante difícil>
ratification [ˌræṭəfəˈkeɪʃən] *n* : ratificación *f*
ratify [ˈræṭəˌfaɪ] *vt* **-fied; -fying** : ratificar
rating [ˈreɪṭɪŋ] *n* **1** STANDING : clasificación *f*, posición *f* **2 ratings** *npl* : índice *m* de audiencia
ratio [ˈreɪʃio] *n, pl* **-tios** : proporción *f*, relación *f*
ration[1] [ˈræʃən, ˈreɪʃən] *vt* : racionar
ration[2] *n* **1** : ración *f* **2 rations** *npl* PROVISIONS : víveres *mpl*
rational [ˈræʃənəl] *adj* : racional, razonable, lógico — **rationally** *adv*
rationale [ˌræʃəˈnæl] *n* **1** EXPLANATION : explicación *f* **2** BASIS : base *f*, razones *fpl*
rationalization [ˌræʃənələˈzeɪʃən] *n* : racionalización *f*
rationalize [ˈræʃənəˌlaɪz] *vt* **-ized; -izing** : racionalizar
rattle[1] [ˈræṭəl] *v* **-tled; -tling** *vi* **1** CLATTER : traquetear, hacer ruido **2 to rattle on** CHATTER : parlotear *fam* — *vt* **1** : hacer sonar, agitar <the wind rattled the door : el viento sacudió la puerta> **2** DISCONCERT, WORRY : desconcertar, poner nervioso **3 to rattle off** : despachar, recitar, decir de corrido
rattle[2] *n* **1** CLATTER : traqueteo *m*, ruido *m* **2** *or* **baby's rattle** : sonajero *m* **3** : cascabel *m* (de una culebra)
rattler [ˈræṭələr] → **rattlesnake**
rattlesnake [ˈræṭəlˌsneɪk] *n* : serpiente *f* de cascabel
ratty [ˈræṭi] *adj* **rattier; -est** : raído, andrajoso
raucous [ˈrɔkəs] *adj* **1** HOARSE : ronco **2** BOISTEROUS : escandaloso, bullicioso — **raucously** *adv*
ravage[1] [ˈrævɪdʒ] *vt* **-aged; -aging** : devastar, arrasar, hacer estragos
ravage[2] *n* : destrozo *m*, destrucción *f* <the ravages of war : los estragos de la guerra>
rave [ˈreɪv] *vi* **raved; raving 1** : delirar, desvariar <to rave like a maniac : desvariar como un loco> **2 to rave about** : hablar con entusiasmo sobre, entusiasmarse por
ravel [ˈrævəl] *v* **-eled** *or* **-elled; -eling** *or* **-elling** *vt* UNRAVEL : desenredar, desenmarañar — *vi* FRAY : deshilacharse
raven [ˈreɪvən] *n* : cuervo *m*
ravenous [ˈrævənəs] *adj* : hambriento, voraz — **ravenously** *adv*
ravine [rəˈviːn] *n* : barranco *m*, quebrada *f*
ravish [ˈrævɪʃ] *vt* **1** PLUNDER : saquear **2** ENCHANT : embelesar, cautivar, encantar
raw [ˈrɔ] *adj* **rawer; rawest 1** UNCOOKED : crudo **2** UNTREATED : sin tratar, sin refinar, puro <raw data : datos en bruto> <raw materials : materias primas> **3** INEXPERIENCED : novato, inexperto **4** OPEN : abierto, en carne viva <a raw sore : una llaga abierta> **5** : frío y húmedo <a raw day : un día crudo> **6** UNFAIR : injusto <a raw deal : un trato injusto, una injusticia>

rawhide [ˈrɔˌhaɪd] *n* **:** cuero *m* sin curtir

ray [ˈreɪ] *n* **1 :** rayo *m* (de la luz, etc.) <a ray of hope : un resquicio de esperanza> **2 :** raya *f* (pez)

rayon [ˈreɪˌɑn] *n* **:** rayón *m*

raze [ˈreɪz] *vt* **razed; razing :** arrasar, demoler

razor [ˈreɪzər] *n* **1 straight razor :** navaja *f* (de afeitar) **2 safety razor :** maquinilla *f* de afeitar, rastrillo *m Mex*

reach[1] [ˈriːtʃ] *vt* **1** EXTEND **:** extender, alargar <to reach out one's hand : extender la mano> **2 :** alcanzar <I couldn't reach the apple : no pude alcanzar la manzana> **3 :** llegar a, llegar hasta <the shadow reached the wall : la sombra llegó hasta la pared> **4** CONTACT **:** contactar, ponerse en contacto con — *vi* **1** *or* **to reach out :** extender la mano **2** STRETCH **:** extenderse **3 to reach for :** tratar de agarrar

reach[2] *n* **:** alcance *m*, extensión *f*

react [riˈækt] *vi* **:** reaccionar

reaction [riˈækʃən] *n* **:** reacción *f*

reactionary[1] [riˈækʃəˌnɛri] *adj* **:** reaccionario

reactionary[2] *n, pl* **-ries :** reaccionario *m*, -ria *f*

reactor [riˈæktər] *n* **:** reactor *m* <nuclear reactor : reactor nuclear>

read[1] [ˈriːd] *v* **read** [ˈrɛd]; **reading** *vt* **1 :** leer <to read a story : leer un cuento> **2** INTERPRET **:** interpretar <it can be read two ways : se puede interpretar de dos maneras> **3 :** decir, poner <the sign read "No smoking" : el letrero decía "No Fumar"> **4 :** marcar <the thermometer reads 70° : el termómetro marca 70°> — *vi* **1 :** leer <he can read : sabe leer> **2** SAY **:** decir <the list reads as follows : la lista dice lo siguiente>

read[2] *n* **to be a good read :** ser una lectura amena

readable [ˈriːdəbəl] *adj* **:** legible — **readably** [-bli] *adv*

reader [ˈriːdər] *n* **:** lector *m*, -tora *f*

readily [ˈrɛdəli] *adv* **1** WILLINGLY **:** de buena gana, con gusto **2** EASILY **:** fácilmente, con facilidad

readiness [ˈrɛdinəs] *n* **1** WILLINGNESS **:** buena disposición *f* **2 to be in readiness :** estar preparado

reading [ˈriːdɪŋ] *n* **:** lectura *f*

readjust [ˌriːəˈdʒʌst] *vt* **:** reajustar — *vi* **:** volverse a adaptar

readjustment [ˌriːəˈdʒʌstmənt] *n* **:** reajuste *m*

ready[1] [ˈrɛdi] *vt* **readied; readying :** preparar

ready[2] *adj* **readier; -est 1** PREPARED **:** listo, preparado **2** WILLING **:** dispuesto **3 :** a punto de <ready to cry : a punto de llorar> **4** AVAILABLE **:** disponible <ready cash : efectivo> **5** QUICK **:** vivo, agudo <a ready wit : un ingenio agudo>

ready–made [ˈrɛdiˈmeɪd] *adj* **:** preparado, confeccionado

reaffirm [ˌriːəˈfərm] *vt* **:** reafirmar

real[1] [ˈriːl] *adv* VERY **:** muy <we had a real good time : lo pasamos muy bien>

real[2] *adj* **1 :** inmobilario <real property : bien inmueble, bien raíz> **2** GENUINE **:** auténtico, genuino **3** ACTUAL, TRUE **:** real, verdadero <a real friend : un verdadero amigo> **4 for real** SERIOUSLY **:** de veras, de verdad

real estate *n* **:** propiedad *f* inmobiliaria, bienes *mpl* raíces

realign [ˌriːəˈlaɪn] *vt* **:** realinear

realignment [ˌriːəˈlaɪnmənt] *n* **:** realineamiento *m*

realism [ˈriːəˌlɪzəm] *n* **:** realismo *m*

realist [ˈriːəlɪst] *n* **:** realista *mf*

realistic [ˌriːəˈlɪstɪk] *adj* **:** realista

realistically [ˌriːəˈlɪstɪkli] *adv* **:** de manera realista

reality [riˈæləti] *n, pl* **-ties :** realidad *f*

realization [ˌriːələˈzeɪʃən] *n* **:** realización *f*

realize [ˈriːəˌlaɪz] *vt* **-ized; -izing 1** ACCOMPLISH **:** realizar, llevar a cabo **2** GAIN **:** obtener, realizar, sacar <to realize a profit : realizar beneficios> **3** UNDERSTAND **:** darse cuenta de, saber

really [ˈrɪli, ˈriː-] *adv* **1** ACTUALLY **:** de verdad, en realidad **2** TRULY **:** verdaderamente, realmente **3** FRANKLY **:** francamente, en serio

realm [ˈrɛlm] *n* **1** KINGDOM **:** reino *m* **2** SPHERE **:** esfera *f*, campo *m*

ream[1] [ˈriːm] *vt* **:** escariar

ream[2] *n* **1 :** resma *f* (de papel) **2 reams** *npl* LOADS **:** montones *mpl*

reap [ˈriːp] *v* **:** cosechar

reaper [ˈriːpər] *n* **1 :** cosechador *m*, -dora *f* (persona) **2 :** cosechadora *f* (máquina)

reappear [ˌriːəˈpɪr] *vi* **:** reaparecer

reappearance [ˌriːəˈpɪrənts] *n* **:** reaparición *f*

rear[1] [ˈrɪr] *vt* **1** LIFT, RAISE **:** levantar **2** BREED, BRING UP **:** criar — *vi or* **to rear up :** encabritarse

rear[2] *adj* **:** trasero, posterior, de atrás

rear[3] *n* **1** BACK **:** parte *f* de atrás <to bring up the rear : cerrar la marcha> **2** *or* **rear end :** trasero *m*

rear admiral *n* **:** contraalmirante *mf*

rearrange [ˌriːəˈreɪndʒ] *vt* **-ranged; -ranging :** colocar de otra manera, volver a arreglar, reorganizar

reason[1] [ˈriːzən] *vt* THINK **:** pensar — *vi* **:** razonar <I can't reason with her : no puedo razonar con ella>

reason[2] *n* **1** CAUSE, GROUND **:** razón *f*, motivo *m* <the reason for his trip : el motivo de su viaje> <for this reason : por esta razón, por lo cual> <the reason why : la razón por la cual, el porqué> **2** SENSE **:** razón *f* <to lose

one's reason : perder los sesos> <to listen to reason : avenirse a razones>
reasonable ['riːzənəbəl] *adj* **1** SENSIBLE : razonable **2** INEXPENSIVE : barato, económico
reasonably ['riːzənəbli] *adv* **1** SENSIBLY : razonablemente **2** FAIRLY : bastante
reasoning ['riːzənɪŋ] *n* : razonamiento *m,* raciocinio *m,* argumentos *mpl*
reassess [ˌriːə'sɛs] *vt* : revaluar, reconsiderar
reassurance [ˌriːə'ʃʊrən*t*s] *n* : consuelo *m,* palabras *fpl* alentadoras
reassure [ˌriːə'ʃʊr] *vt* **-sured; -suring** : tranquilizar
reawaken [ˌriːə'weɪkən] *vt* : volver a despertar, reavivar
rebate ['riːˌbeɪt] *n* : reembolso *m,* devolución *f*
rebel[1] [rɪ'bɛl] *vi* **-belled; -belling** : rebelarse, sublevarse
rebel[2] ['rɛbəl] *adj* : rebelde
rebel[3] ['rɛbəl] *n* : rebelde *mf*
rebellion [rɪ'bɛljən] *n* : rebelión *f*
rebellious [rɪ'bɛljəs] *adj* : rebelde
rebelliousness [rɪ'bɛljəsnəs] *n* : rebeldía *f*
rebirth [ˌriː'bərθ] *n* : renacimiento *m*
rebound[1] ['riːˌbaʊnd, ˌriː'baʊnd] *vi* : rebotar
rebound[2] ['riːˌbaʊnd] *n* : rebote *m*
rebuff[1] [ri'bʌf] *vt* : desairar, rechazar
rebuff[2] *n* : desaire *m,* rechazo *m*
rebuild [ˌriː'bɪld] *vt* **-built** [-'bɪlt]; **-building** : reconstruir
rebuke[1] [ri'bjuːk] *vt* **-buked; -buking** : reprender, regañar
rebuke[2] *n* : reprimenda *f,* reproche *m*
rebut [ri'bʌt] *vt* **-butted; -butting** : rebatir, refutar
rebuttal [ri'bʌtəl] *n* : refutación *f*
recalcitrant [ri'kælsətrənt] *adj* : recalcitrante
recall[1] [ri'kɔl] *vt* **1** : llamar, retirar <recalled to active duty : llamado al servicio activo> **2** REMEMBER : recordar, acordarse de **3** REVOKE : revocar
recall[2] [ri'kɔl, 'riːˌkɔl] *n* **1** : retirada *f* (de personas o mercancías) **2** MEMORY : memoria *f* <to have total recall : poder recordar todo>
recant [ri'kænt] *vt* : retractarse de — *vi* : retractarse, renegar
recapitulate [ˌriːkə'pɪtʃəˌleɪt] *v* **-lated; -lating** : resumir, recapitular
recapture [ˌriː'kæptʃər] *vt* **-tured; -turing 1** REGAIN : volver a tomar, reconquistar **2** RELIVE : revivir (la juventud, etc.)
recede [ri'siːd] *vi* **-ceded; -ceding 1** WITHDRAW : retirarse, retroceder **2** FADE : desvanecerse, alejarse **3** SLANT : inclinarse **4 to have a receding hairline** : tener entradas
receipt [ri'siːt] *n* **1** : recibo *m* **2 receipts** *npl* : ingresos *mpl,* entradas *fpl*
receivable [ri'siːvəbəl] *adj* **accounts receivable** : cuentas por cobrar
receive [ri'siːv] *vt* **-ceived; -ceiving 1** GET : recibir <to receive a letter : recibir una carta> <to receive a blow : recibir un golpe> **2** WELCOME : acoger, recibir <to receive guests : tener invitados> **3** : recibir, captar (señales de radio)
receiver [ri'siːvər] *n* **1** : receptor *m,* -tora *f* (en futbol americano) **2** : receptor *m* (de radio o televisión) **3 telephone receiver** : auricular *m*
recent ['riːsənt] *adj* : reciente — **recently** *adv*
receptacle [ri'sɛptɪkəl] *n* : receptáculo *m,* recipiente *m*
reception [ri'sɛpʃən] *n* : recepción *f*
receptionist [ri'sɛpʃənɪst] *n* : recepcionista *mf*
receptive [ri'sɛptɪv] *adj* : receptivo
receptivity [ˌriːˌsɛp'tɪvəṭi] *n* : receptividad *f*
recess[1] ['riːˌsɛs, rɪ'sɛs] *vt* **1** : poner en un hueco <recessed lighting : iluminación empotrada> **2** ADJOURN : suspender, levantar
recess[2] *n* **1** ALCOVE : hueco *m,* nicho *m* **2** BREAK : receso *m,* descanso *m,* recreo *m* (en el colegio)
recession [ri'sɛʃən] *n* : recesión *f,* depresión *f* económica
recessive [ri'sɛsɪv] *adj* : recesivo
recharge [ˌriː'tʃɑrdʒ] *vt* **-charged; -charging** : recargar
rechargeable [ˌriː'tʃɑrdʒəbəl] *adj* : recargable
recipe ['rɛsəˌpiː] *n* : receta *f*
recipient [ri'sɪpiənt] *n* : recipiente *mf*
reciprocal [ri'sɪprəkəl] *adj* : recíproco
reciprocate [ri'sɪprəˌkeɪt] *vi* **-cated; -cating** : reciprocar
reciprocity [ˌrɛsə'prɑsəṭi] *n, pl* **-ties** : reciprocidad *f*
recital [ri'saɪṭəl] *n* **1** PERFORMANCE : recital *m* **2** ENUMERATION : relato *m,* enumeración *f*
recitation [ˌrɛsə'teɪʃən] *n* : recitación *f*
recite [ri'saɪt] *vt* **-cited; -citing 1** : recitar (un poema, etc.) **2** RECOUNT : narrar, relatar, enumerar
reckless ['rɛkləs] *adj* : imprudente, temerario — **recklessly** *adv*
recklessness ['rɛkləsnəs] *n* : imprudencia *f,* temeridad *f*
reckon ['rɛkən] *vt* **1** CALCULATE : calcular, contar **2** CONSIDER : considerar
reckoning ['rɛkənɪŋ] *n* **1** CALCULATION : cálculo *m* **2** SETTLEMENT : ajuste *m* de cuentas <day of reckoning : día del juicio final>
reclaim [ri'kleɪm] *vt* **1** : ganar, sanear <to reclaim marshy land : sanear las tierras pantanosas> **2** RECOVER : recobrar, reciclar <to reclaim old tires : reciclar llantas desechadas> **3** REGAIN : reclamar, recuperar <to reclaim one's rights : reclamar uno sus derechos>

recline [ri'klaɪn] *vi* **-clined; -clining 1** LEAN : reclinarse **2** REPOSE : recostarse
recluse ['rɛ,klu:s, ri'klu:s] *n* : solitario *m*, -ria *f*
recognition [,rɛkɪg'nɪʃən] *n* : reconocimiento *m*
recognizable ['rɛkəg,naɪzəbəl] *adj* : reconocible
recognize ['rɛkɪg,naɪz] *vt* **-nized; -nizing** : reconocer
recoil[1] [ri'kɔɪl] *vi* : retroceder, dar un culatazo
recoil[2] ['ri:,kɔɪl, ri'-] *n* : retroceso *m*, culatazo *m*
recollect [,rɛkə'lɛkt] *v* : recordar
recollection [,rɛkə'lɛkʃən] *n* : recuerdo *m*
recommend [,rɛkə'mɛnd] *vt* **1** : recomendar <she recommended the medicine : recomendó la medicina> **2** ADVISE, COUNSEL : aconsejar, recomendar
recommendation [,rɛkəmən'deɪʃən] *n* : recomendación *f*
recompense[1] ['rɛkəm,pɛnts] *vt* **-pensed; -pensing** : indemnizar, recompensar
recompense[2] *n* : indemnización *f*, compensación *f*
reconcile ['rɛkən,saɪl] *v* **-ciled; -ciling** *vt* **1** : reconciliar (personas), conciliar (ideas, etc.) **2 to reconcile oneself to** : resignarse a — *vi* MAKE UP : reconciliarse, hacer las paces
reconciliation [,rɛkən,sɪli'eɪʃən] *n* : reconciliación *f* (con personas), conciliación *f* (con ideas, etc.)
recondite ['rɛkən,daɪt, ri'kɑn-] *adj* : recóndito, abstruso
recondition [,ri:kən'dɪʃən] *vt* : reacondicionar
reconnaissance [ri'kɑnəzənts, -sənts] *n* : reconocimiento *m*
reconnoiter *or* **reconnoitre** [,ri:kə'nɔɪtər, ,rɛkə-] *v* **-tered** *or* **-tred; -tering** *or* **-tring** *vt* : reconocer — *vi* : hacer un reconocimiento
reconsider [,ri:kən'sɪdər] *vt* : reconsiderar, repensar
reconsideration [,ri:kən,sɪdə'reɪʃən] *n* : reconsideración *f*
reconstruct [,ri:kən'strʌkt] *vt* : reconstruir
record[1] [ri'kɔrd] *vt* **1** WRITE DOWN : anotar, apuntar **2** REGISTER : registrar, hacer constar **3** INDICATE : marcar (una temperatura, etc.) **4** TAPE : grabar
record[2] ['rɛkərd] *n* **1** DOCUMENT : registro *m*, documento *m* oficial **2** HISTORY : historial *m* <a good academic record : un buen historial académico> <criminal record : antecedentes penales> **3** : récord *m* <the world record : el récord mundial> **4** : disco *m* (de música, etc.) <to make a record : grabar un disco>
recorder [ri'kɔrdər] *n* **1** : flauta *f* dulce (instrumento de viento) **2 tape recorder** : grabadora *f*
recount[1] [ri'kaʊnt] *vt* **1** NARRATE : narrar, relatar **2** : volver a contar (votos, etc.)
recount[2] ['ri:,kaʊnt, ,ri'-] *n* : recuento *m*
recoup [ri'ku:p] *vt* : recuperar, recobrar
recourse ['ri:,kors, ri'-] *n* : recurso *m* <to have recourse to : recurrir a>
recover [ri'kʌvər] *vt* REGAIN : recobrar — *vi* RECUPERATE : recuperarse
recovery [ri'kʌvəri] *n, pl* **-eries** : recuperación *f*
re–create [,ri:kri'eɪt] *vt* **-ated; -ating** : recrear
recreation [,rɛkri'eɪʃən] *n* : recreo *m*, esparcimiento *m*, diversión *f*
recreational [,rɛkri'eɪʃənəl] *adj* : recreativo, de recreo
recrimination [ri,krɪmə'neɪʃən] *n* : recriminación *f*
recruit[1] [ri'kru:t] *vt* : reclutar
recruit[2] *n* : recluta *mf*
recruitment [ri'kru:tmənt] *n* : reclutamiento *m*, alistamiento *m*
rectal ['rɛktəl] *adj* : rectal
rectangle ['rɛk,tæŋgəl] *n* : rectángulo *m*
rectangular [rɛk'tæŋgjələr] *adj* : rectangular
rectify ['rɛktə,faɪ] *vt* **-fied; -fying** : rectificar
rectitude ['rɛktə,tu:d, -,tju:d] *n* : rectitud *f*
rector ['rɛktər] *n* : rector *m*, -tora *f*
rectory ['rɛktəri] *n, pl* **-ries** : rectoría *f*
rectum ['rɛktəm] *n, pl* **-tums** *or* **-ta** [-tə] : recto *m*
recuperate [ri'ku:pə,reɪt, -'kju:-] *v* **-ated; -ating** *vt* : recuperar — *vi* : recuperarse, restablecerse
recuperation [ri,ku:pə'reɪʃən, -,kju:-] *n* : recuperación *f*
recur [ri'kər] *vi* **-curred; -curring** : volver a ocurrir, volver a producirse, repetirse
recurrence [ri'kərənts] *n* : repetición *f*, reaparición *f*
recurrent [ri'kərənt] *adj* : recurrente, que se repite
recycle [ri'saɪkəl] *vt* **-cled; -cling** : reciclar
red[1] ['rɛd] *adj* **1** : rojo, colorado <to be red in the face : ponerse colorado> <to have red hair : ser pelirrojo> **2** COMMUNIST : rojo, comunista
red[2] *n* **1** : rojo *m*, colorado *m* **2 Red** COMMUNIST : comunista *mf*
red blood cell *n* : glóbulo *m* rojo
red–blooded ['rɛd'blʌdəd] *adj* : vigoroso
redcap ['rɛd,kæp] → **porter**
redden ['rɛdən] *vt* : enrojecer — *vi* BLUSH : enrojecerse, ruborizarse
reddish ['rɛdɪʃ] *adj* : rojizo
redecorate [,ri:'dɛkə,reɪt] *vt* **-rated; -rating** : renovar, pintar de nuevo

redeem [ri'di:m] *vt* **1** RESCUE, SAVE : rescatar, salvar **2** : desempeñar <she redeemed it from the pawnshop : lo desempeñó de la casa de empeños> **3** : redimir (en religión) **4** : canjear, vender <to redeem coupons : canjear cupones>

redeemer [ri'di:mər] *n* : redentor *m*, -tora *f*

redemption [ri'dɛmpʃən] *n* : redención *f*

redesign [ˌri:di'zaɪn] *vt* : rediseñar

red–handed ['rɛd'hændəd] *adj* : con las manos en la masa

redhead ['rɛdˌhɛd] *n* : pelirrojo *m*, -ja *f*

red–hot ['rɛd'hɑt] *adj* **1** : candente **2** ARDENT : ardiente, fervoroso

rediscover [ˌri:di'skʌvər] *vt* : redescubrir

redistribute [ˌri:di'strɪˌbju:t] *vt* **-uted; -uting** : redistribuir

red–letter ['rɛd'lɛt̬ər] *adj* **red–letter day** : día *m* memorable

redness ['rɛdnəs] *n* : rojez *f*

redo [ˌri:'du:] *vt* **-did** [-dɪd]; **-done** [-'dʌn]; **-doing 1** : hacer de nuevo **2** → **redecorate**

redolence ['rɛdələnts] *n* : fragancia *f*

redolent ['rɛdələnt] *adj* **1** FRAGRANT : fragante, oloroso **2** SUGGESTIVE : evocador

redouble [ri'dʌbəl] *vt* **-bled; -bling** : redoblar, intensificar (esfuerzos, etc.)

redoubtable [rɛ'daʊt̬əbəl] *adj* : temible

redress [ri'drɛs] *vt* : reparar, remediar, enmendar

red snapper *n* : pargo *m*, huachinango *m Mex*

red tape *n* : papeleo *m*

reduce [ri'du:s, -'dju:s] *v* **-duced; -ducing** *vt* **1** LESSEN : reducir, disminuir, rebajar (precios) **2** DEMOTE : bajar de categoría, degradar **3 to be reduced to** : verse rebajado a, verse forzado a **4 to reduce someone to tears** : hacer llorar a alguien — *vi* SLIM : adelgazar

reduction [ri'dʌkʃən] *n* : reducción *f*, rebaja *f*

redundant [ri'dʌndənt] *adj* : superfluo, redundante

redwood ['rɛdˌwʊd] *n* : secoya *f*

reed ['ri:d] *n* **1** : caña *f*, carrizo *m*, junco *m* **2** : lengüeta *f* (para instrumentos de viento)

reef ['ri:f] *n* : arrecife *m*, escollo *m*

reek[1] ['ri:k] *vi* : apestar

reek[2] *n* : hedor *m*

reel ['ri:l] *vt* **1 to reel in** : enrollar, sacar (un pez) del agua **2 to reel off** : recitar de un tirón — *vi* **1** SPIN, WHIRL : girar, dar vueltas **2** STAGGER : tambalearse

reel[2] *n* **1** : carrete *m* (de pescar etc.), rollo *m* (de fotos) **2** : baile *m* escocés **3** STAGGER : tambaleo *m*

reelect [ˌri:ɪ'lɛkt] *vt* : reelegir

reenact [ˌri:ɪ'nækt] *vt* : representar de nuevo, reconstruir

reenter [ˌri:'ɛntər] *vt* : volver a entrar

reestablish [ˌri:ɪ'stæblɪʃ] *vt* : restablecer

reevaluate [ˌri:ɪ'væljʊˌeɪt] *vt* **-ated; -ating** : revaluar

reevaluation [ˌri:ɪˌvæljʊ'eɪʃən] *n* : revaluación *f*

reexamine [ˌri:ɪg'zæmən, -ɛg-] *vt* **-ined; -ining** : volver a examinar, reexaminar

refer [ri'fər] *v* **-ferred; -ferring** *vt* DIRECT, SEND : remitir, enviar <to refer a patient to a specialist : enviar a un paciente a un especialista> — *vi* **to refer to** MENTION : referirse a, aludir a

referee[1] [ˌrɛfə'ri:] *v* **-eed; -eeing** : arbitrar

referee[2] *n* : árbitro *m*, -tra *f*; réferi *mf*

reference ['rɛfrənts, 'rɛfə-] *n* **1** ALLUSION : referencia *f*, alusión *f* <to make reference to : hacer referencia a> **2** CONSULTATION : consulta *f* <for future reference : para futuras consultas> **3** *or* **reference book** : libro *m* de consulta **4** TESTIMONIAL : informe *m*, referencia *f*, recomendación *f*

referendum [ˌrɛfə'rɛndəm] *n*, *pl* **-da** [-də] *or* **-dums** : referéndum *m*

refill[1] [ˌri:'fɪl] *vt* : rellenar

refill[2] ['ri:ˌfɪl] *n* : recambio *m*

refinance [ˌri:'faɪˌnænts] *vt* **-nanced; -nancing** : refinanciar

refine [ri'faɪn] *vt* **-fined; -fining 1** : refinar (azúcar, petróleo, etc.) **2** PERFECT : perfeccionar, pulir

refined [ri'faɪnd] *adj* **1** : refinado (dícese del azúcar, etc.) **2** CULTURED : culto, educado, refinado

refinement [ri'faɪnmənt] *n* : refinamiento *m*, fineza *f*, finura *f*

refinery [ri'faɪnəri] *n*, *pl* **-eries** : refinería *f*

reflect [ri'flɛkt] *vt* **1** : reflejar <to reflect light : reflejar la luz> <happiness is reflected in her face : la felicidad se refleja en su cara> **2 to reflect that** : pensar que, considerar que — *vi* **1 to reflect on** : reflexionar sobre **2 to reflect badly on** : desacreditar, perjudicar

reflection [ri'flɛkʃən] *n* **1** : reflexión *f*, reflejo *m* (de la luz, de imágenes, etc.) **2** THOUGHT : reflexión *f*, meditación *f*

reflective [ri'flɛktɪv] *adj* **1** THOUGHTFUL : reflexivo, pensativo **2** : reflectante (en física)

reflector [ri'flɛktər] *n* : reflector *m*

reflex ['ri:ˌflɛks] *n* : reflejo *m*

reflexive [ri'flɛksɪv] *adj* : reflexivo <a reflexive verb : un verbo reflexivo>

reform[1] [ri'fɔrm] *vt* : reformar — *vi* : reformarse

reform[2] *n* : reforma *f*

reformation [ˌrɛfər'meɪʃən] *n* : reforma *f* <the Reformation : la Reforma>

reformatory [ri'fɔrmə,tori] *n, pl* **-ries** : reformatorio *m*
reformer [ri'fɔrmər] *n* : reformador *m*, -dora *f*
refract [ri'frækt] *vt* : refractar — *vi* : refractarse
refraction [ri'frækʃən] *n* : refracción *f*
refractory [ri'fræktəri] *adj* OBSTINATE : refractario, obstinado
refrain[1] [ri'freɪn] *vi* **to refrain from** : abstenerse de
refrain[2] *n* : estribillo *m* (en música)
refresh [ri'frɛʃ] *vt* : refrescar <to refresh one's memory : refrescarle la memoria a uno>
refreshment [ri'frɛʃmənt] *n* **1** : refresco *m* **2 refreshments** *npl* : refrigerio *m*
refrigerate [ri'frɪdʒə,reɪt] *vt* **-ated; -ating** : refrigerar
refrigeration [ri,frɪdʒə'reɪʃən] *n* : refrigeración *f*
refrigerator [ri'frɪdʒə,reɪtər] *n* : refrigerador *mf*, nevera *f*
refuel [ri:'fju:əl] *v* **-eled** *or* **-elled; -eling** *or* **-elling** *vi* : repostar — *vt* : llenar de combustible
refuge ['rɛ,fju:dʒ] *n* : refugio *m*
refugee [,rɛfjʊ'dʒi:] *n* : refugiado *m*, -da *f*
refund[1] [ri'fʌnd, 'ri:,fʌnd] *vt* : reembolsar, devolver
refund[2] ['ri:,fʌnd] *n* : reembolso *m*, devolución *f*
refundable [ri'fʌndəbəl] *adj* : reembolsable
refurbish [ri'fərbɪʃ] *vt* : renovar, restaurar
refusal [ri'fju:zəl] *n* : negativa *f*, rechazo *m*, denegación *f* (de una petición)
refuse[1] [ri'fju:z] *vt* **-fused; -fusing 1** REJECT : rechazar, rehusar **2** DENY : negar, rehusar, denegar <to refuse permission : negar el permiso> **3 to refuse to** : negarse a
refuse[2] ['rɛ,fju:s, -,fju:z] *n* : basura *f*, desechos *mpl*, desperdicios *m*
refutation [,rɛfjʊ'teɪʃən] *n* : refutación *f*
refute [ri'fju:t] *vt* **-futed; -futing 1** DENY : desmentir, negar **2** DISPROVE : refutar, rebatir
regain [ri:'geɪn] *vt* **1** RECOVER : recuperar, recobrar **2** REACH : alcanzar <to regain the shore : llegar a la tierra>
regal ['ri:gəl] *adj* : real, regio
regale [ri'geɪl] *vt* **-galed; -galing 1** ENTERTAIN : agasajar, entretener **2** AMUSE, DELIGHT : deleitar, divertir
regalia [ri'geɪljə] *npl* : ropaje *m*, vestiduras *fpl*, adornos *mpl*
regard[1] [ri'gɑrd] *vt* **1** OBSERVE : observar, mirar **2** HEED : tener en cuenta, hacer caso de **3** CONSIDER : considerar **4** RESPECT : respetar <highly regarded : muy estimado> **5 as regards** : en cuanto a, en lo que se refiere a
regard[2] *n* **1** CONSIDERATION : consideración *f* **2** ESTEEM : respeto *m*, estima *f* **3** PARTICULAR : aspecto *m*, sentido *m* <in this regard : en este sentido> **4 regards** *npl* : saludos *mpl*, recuerdos *mpl* **5 with regard to** : con relación a, con respecto a
regarding [ri'gɑrdɪŋ] *prep* : con respecto a, en cuanto a
regardless [ri'gɑrdləs] *adv* : a pesar de todo
regardless of *prep* : a pesar de, sin tener en cuenta <regardless of our mistakes : a pesar de nuestros errores> <regardless of age : sin tener en cuenta la edad>
regenerate [ri'dʒɛnə,reɪt] *v* **-ated; -ating** *vt* : regenerar — *vi* : regenerarse
regeneration [ri,dʒɛnə'reɪʃən] *n* : regeneración *f*
regent ['ri:dʒənt] *n* **1** RULER : regente *mf* **2** : miembro *m* de la junta directiva (de una universidad, etc.)
regime [reɪ'ʒi:m, rɪ-] *n* : régimen *m*
regimen ['rɛdʒəmən] *n* : régimen *m*
regiment[1] ['rɛdʒə,mɛnt] *vt* : reglamentar
regiment[2] ['rɛdʒəmənt] *n* : regimiento *m*
region ['ri:dʒən] *n* **1** : región *f* **2 in the region of** : alrededor de
regional ['ri:dʒənəl] *adj* : regional — **regionally** *adv*
register[1] ['rɛdʒəstər] *vt* **1** RECORD : registrar, inscribir **2** INDICATE : marcar (temperatura, medidas, etc.) **3** REVEAL : manifestar, acusar <to register surprise : acusar sorpresa> **4** : certificar (correo) — *vi* ENROLL : inscribirse, matricularse
register[2] *n* : registro *m*
registrar ['rɛdʒə,strɑr] *n* : registrador *m*, -dora *f* oficial
registration [,rɛdʒə'streɪʃən] *n* **1** REGISTERING : inscripción *f*, matriculación *f*, registro *m* **2** *or* **registration number** : matrícula *f*, número *m* de matrícula
registry ['rɛdʒəstri] *n, pl* **-tries** : registro *m*
regress [ri'grɛs] *vi* : retroceder
regression [ri'grɛʃən] *n* : retroceso *m*, regresión *f*
regressive [ri'grɛsɪv] *adj* : regresivo
regret[1] [ri'grɛt] *vt* **-gretted; -gretting** : arrepentirse de, lamentar <he regrets nothing : no se arrepiente de nada> <I regret to tell you : lamento decirle>
regret[2] *n* **1** REMORSE : arrepentimiento *m*, remordimientos *mpl* **2** SADNESS : pesar *m*, dolor *m* **3 regrets** *npl* : excusas *fpl* <to send one's regrets : excusarse>
regretful [ri'grɛtfəl] *adj* : arrepentido, pesaroso
regretfully [ri'grɛtfəli] *adv* : con pesar
regrettable [ri'grɛtəbəl] *adj* : lamentable — **regrettably** [-bli] *adv*

regular[1] [ˈrɛgjələr] *adj* **1** NORMAL : regular, normal, usual **2** STEADY : uniforme, regular <a regular pace : un paso regular> **3** CUSTOMARY, HABITUAL : habitual, de costumbre

regular[2] *n* : cliente *mf* habitual

regularity [ˌrɛgjəˈlærət̬i] *n, pl* **-ties** : regularidad *f*

regularly [ˈrɛgjələrli] *adv* : regularmente, con regularidad

regulate [ˈrɛgjəˌleɪt] *vt* **-lated; -lating** : regular

regulation [ˌrɛgjəˈleɪʃən] *n* **1** REGULATING : regulación *f* **2** RULE : regla *f,* reglamento *m,* norma *f* <safety regulations : reglas de seguridad>

regurgitate [riˈgərdʒəˌteɪt] *v* **-tated; -tating** : regurgitar, vomitar

rehabilitate [ˌriːhəˈbɪləˌteɪt, ˌriːə-] *vt* **-tated; -tating** : rehabilitar

rehabilitation [ˌriːhəˌbɪləˈteɪʃən, ˌriːə-] *n* : rehabilitación *f*

rehearsal [riˈhərsəl] *n* : ensayo *m*

rehearse [riˈhərs] *v* **-hearsed; -hearsing** : ensayar

reheat [ˌriːˈhiːt] *vt* : recalentar

reign[1] [ˈreɪn] *vi* **1** RULE : reinar **2** PREVAIL : reinar, predominar

reign[2] *n* : reinado *m*

reimburse [ˌriːəmˈbərs] *vt* **-bursed; -bursing** : reembolsar

reimbursement [ˌriːəmˈbərsmənt] *n* : reembolso *m*

rein[1] [ˈreɪn] *vt* : refrenar (un caballo)

rein[2] *n* **1** : rienda *f* <to give free rein to : dar rienda suelta a> **2** CHECK : control *m* <to keep a tight rein on : llevar un estricto control de>

reincarnation [ˌriːɪnˌkɑrˈneɪʃən] *n* : reencarnación *f*

reindeer [ˈreɪnˌdɪr] *n* : reno *m*

reinforce [ˌriːənˈfors] *vt* **-forced; -forcing** : reforzar

reinforcement [ˌriːənˈforsmənt] *n* : refuerzo *m*

reinstate [ˌriːənˈsteɪt] *vt* **-stated; -stating 1** : reintegrar, restituir (una persona) **2** RESTORE : restablecer (un servicio, etc.)

reinstatement [ˌriːənˈsteɪtmənt] *n* : reintegración *f,* restitución *f,* restablecimiento *m*

reiterate [riˈɪt̬əˌreɪt] *vt* **-ated; -ating** : reiterar, repetir

reiteration [riˌɪt̬əˈreɪʃən] *n* : reiteración *f,* repetición *f*

reject[1] [riˈdʒɛkt] *vt* : rechazar

reject[2] [ˈriːˌdʒɛkt] *n* : desecho *m* (cosa), persona *f* rechazada

rejection [riˈdʒɛkʃən] *n* : rechazo *m*

rejoice [riˈdʒɔɪs] *vi* **-joiced; -joicing** : alegrarse, regocijarse

rejoin *vt* [ˌriːˈdʒɔɪn] **1** : reincorporarse a, reintegrarse a <he rejoined the firm : se reincorporó a la firma> **2** [riˈ-] REPLY, RETORT : replicar

rejoinder [riˈdʒɔɪndər] *n* : réplica *f*

rejuvenate [riˈdʒuːvəˌneɪt] *vt* **-nated; -nating** : rejuvenecer

rejuvenation [riˌdʒuːvəˈneɪʃən] *n* : rejuvenecimiento *m*

rekindle [ˌriːˈkɪndəl] *vt* **-dled; -dling** : reavivar

relapse[1] [riˈlæps] *vi* **-lapsed; -lapsing** : recaer, volver a caer

relapse[2] [ˈriːˌlæps, riˈlæps] *n* : recaída *f*

relate [riˈleɪt] *v* **-lated; -lating** *vt* **1** TELL : relatar, contar **2** ASSOCIATE : relacionar, asociar <to relate crime to poverty : relacionar la delincuencia a la pobreza> — *vi* **1** CONNECT : conectar, estar relacionado (con) **2** INTERACT : relacionarse (con), llevarse bien (con) **3 to relate to** UNDERSTAND : identificarse con, simpatizar con

related [riˈleɪt̬əd] *adj* : emparentado <to be related to : ser pariente de>

relation [riˈleɪʃən] *n* **1** NARRATION : relato *m,* narración *f* **2** RELATIVE : pariente *mf,* familiar *mf* **3** RELATIONSHIP : relación *f* <in relation to : en relación con, con relación a> **4 relations** *npl* : relaciones *fpl* <public relations : relaciones públicas>

relationship [riˈleɪʃənˌʃɪp] *n* **1** CONNECTION : relación *f* **2** KINSHIP : parentesco *m*

relative[1] [ˈrɛlət̬ɪv] *adj* : relativo — **relatively** *adv*

relative[2] *n* : pariente *mf,* familiar *mf*

relativity [ˌrɛləˈtɪvət̬i] *n, pl* **-ties** : relatividad *f*

relax [riˈlæks] *vt* : relajar, aflojar — *vi* : relajarse

relaxation [ˌriːˌlækˈseɪʃən] *n* **1** RELAXING : relajación *f,* aflojamiento *m* **2** DIVERSION : esparcimiento *m,* distracción *f*

relay[1] [ˈriːˌleɪ, riˈleɪ] *vt* **-layed; -laying** : transmitir

relay[2] [ˈriːˌleɪ] *n* **1** : relevo *m* **2** *or* **relay race** : carrera de relevos

release[1] [riˈliːs] *vt* **-leased; -leasing 1** FREE : liberar, poner en libertad **2** LOOSEN : soltar, aflojar <to release the brake : soltar el freno> **3** RELINQUISH : renunciar a, ceder **4** ISSUE : publicar (un libro), estrenar (una película), sacar (un disco)

release[2] *n* **1** LIBERATION : liberación *f,* puesta *f* en libertad **2** RELINQUISHMENT : cesión *f* (de propiedad, etc.) **3** ISSUE : estreno *m* (de una película), puesta *f* en venta (de un disco), publicación *f* (de un libro) **4** ESCAPE : escape *m,* fuga *f* (de un gas)

relegate [ˈrɛləˌgeɪt] *vt* **-gated; -gating** : relegar

relent [riˈlɛnt] *vi* : ablandarse, ceder

relentless [riˈlɛntləs] *adj* : implacable, sin tregua

relentlessly [riˈlɛntləsli] *adv* : implacablemente

relevance [ˈrɛləvən*t*s] *n* : pertinencia *f,* relación *f*

relevant [ˈrɛləvənt] *adj* : pertinente — **relevantly** *adv*

reliability [riˌlaɪəˈbɪləti] *n, pl* **-ties 1** : fiabilidad *f,* seguridad *f* (de una cosa) **2** : formalidad *f,* seriedad *f* (de una persona)

reliable [riˈlaɪəbəl] *adj* : confiable, fiable, fidedigno, seguro

reliably [riˈlaɪəbli] *adv* : sin fallar <to be reliably informed : saber (algo) de fuentes fidedignas>

reliance [riˈlaɪənts] *n* **1** DEPENDENCE : dependencia *f* **2** CONFIDENCE : confianza *f*

reliant [riˈlaɪənt] *adj* : confiable, dependente

relic [ˈrɛlɪk] *n* **1** : reliquia *f* **2** VESTIGE : vestigio *m*

relief [riˈliːf] *n* **1** : alivio *m,* desahogo *m* <relief from pain : alivio del dolor> **2** AID, WELFARE : ayuda *f* (benéfica), asistencia *f* social **3** : relieve *m* (en la escultura) <relief map : mapa en relieve> **4** REPLACEMENT : relevo *m*

relieve [riˈliːv] *vt* **-lieved; -lieving 1** ALLEVIATE : aliviar, mitigar <to feel relieved : sentirse aliviado> **2** FREE : liberar, eximir <to relieve someone of responsibility for : eximir a alguien de la responsabilidad de> **3** REPLACE : relevar (a un centinela, etc.) **4** BREAK : romper <to relieve the monotony : romper la monotonía>

religion [riˈlɪdʒən] *n* : religión *f*

religious [riˈlɪdʒəs] *adj* : religioso — **religiously** *adv*

relinquish [riˈlɪŋkwɪʃ, -ˈlɪn-] *vt* **1** GIVE UP : renunciar a, abandonar **2** RELEASE : soltar

relish[1] [ˈrɛlɪʃ] *vt* : saborear (comida), disfrutar con (una idea, una perspectiva, etc.)

relish[2] *n* **1** ENJOYMENT : gusto *m,* deleite *m* **2** : salsa *f* (condimento)

relive [ˌriːˈlɪv] *vt* **-lived; -living** : revivir

relocate [ˌriːˈloːˌkeɪt, ˌriːloˈkeɪt] *v* **-cated; -cating** *vt* : reubicar, trasladar — *vi* : trasladarse

relocation [ˌriːloˈkeɪʃən] *n* : reubicación *f,* traslado *m*

reluctance [riˈlʌktənts] *n* : renuencia *f,* reticencia *f,* desgana *f*

reluctant [riˈlʌktənt] *adj* : renuente, reacio, reticente

reluctantly [riˈlʌktəntli] *adv* : a regañadientes

rely [riˈlaɪ] *vi* **-lied; -lying 1** DEPEND : depender (de), contar (con) **2** TRUST : confiar (en)

remain [riˈmeɪn] *vi* **1** : quedar <very little remains : queda muy poco> <the remaining 10 minutes : los 10 minutos que quedan> **2** STAY : quedarse, permanecer **3** CONTINUE : continuar, seguir <to remain the same : continuar siendo igual> **4 to remain to** : quedar por <to remain to be done : quedar por hacer> <it remains to be seen : está por ver>

remainder [riˈmeɪndər] *n* : resto *m,* remanente *m*

remains [riˈmeɪnz] *npl* : restos *mpl* <mortal remains : restos mortales>

remark[1] [riˈmɑrk] *vt* **1** NOTICE : observar **2** SAY : comentar, observar — *vi* **to remark on** : hacer observaciones sobre

remark[2] *n* : comentario *m,* observación *f*

remarkable [riˈmɑrkəbəl] *adj* : extraordinario, notable — **remarkably** [-bli] *adv*

rematch [ˈriːˌmætʃ] *n* : revancha *f*

remedial [riˈmiːdiəl] *adj* : correctivo <remedial classes : clases para alumnos atrasados>

remedy[1] [ˈrɛmədi] *vt* **-died; -dying** : remediar

remedy[2] *n, pl* **-dies** : remedio *m,* medicamento *m*

remember [riˈmɛmbər] *vt* **1** RECOLLECT : acordarse de, recordar **2** : no olvidar <remember my words : no olvides mis palabras> <to remember to : acordarse de> **3** : dar saludos, dar recuerdos <remember me to her : dale saludos de mi parte> **4** COMMEMORATE : recordar, conmemorar

remembrance [riˈmɛmbrənts] *n* **1** RECOLLECTION : recuerdo *m* <in remembrance of : en conmemoración de> **2** MEMENTO : recuerdo *m*

remind [riˈmaɪnd] *vt* : recordar <remind me to do it : recuérdame que lo haga> <she reminds me of Clara : me recuerda de Clara>

reminder [riˈmaɪndər] *n* : recuerdo *m*

reminisce [ˌrɛməˈnɪs] *vi* **-nisced; -niscing** : rememorar los viejos tiempos

reminiscence [ˌrɛməˈnɪsənts] *n* : recuerdo *m,* reminiscencia *f*

reminiscent [ˌrɛməˈnɪsənt] *adj* **1** NOSTALGIC : reminiscente, nostálgico **2** SUGGESTIVE : evocador, que recuerda — **reminiscently** *adv*

remiss [riˈmɪs] *adj* : negligente, descuidado, remiso

remission [riˈmɪʃən] *n* : remisión *f*

remit [riˈmɪt] *vt* **-mitted; -mitting 1** PARDON : perdonar **2** SEND : remitir, enviar (dinero)

remittance [riˈmɪtənts] *n* : remesa *f*

remnant [ˈrɛmnənt] *n* : restos *mpl,* vestigio *m*

remodel [riˈmɑdəl] *vt* **-eled** *or* **-elled; -eling** *or* **-elling** : remodelar, reformar

remonstrate [riˈmɑnˌstreɪt] *vi* **-strated; -strating** : protestar <to remonstrate with someone : quejarse a alguien>

remorse [riˈmɔrs] *n* : remordimiento *m*

remorseful [riˈmɔrsfəl] *adj* : arrepentido, lleno de remordimiento

remorseless [riˈmɔrsləs] *adj* **1** PITILESS : despiadado **2** RELENTLESS : implacable

remote [ri'mo:t] *adj* **-moter; -est 1** FAR-OFF : lejano, remoto <remote countries : países remotos> <in the remote past : en el pasado lejano> **2** SECLUDED : recóndito **3** : a distancia, remoto <remote control : control remoto> **4** SLIGHT : remoto **5** ALOOF : distante

remotely [ri'mo:tli] *adv* **1** SLIGHTLY : remotamente **2** DISTANTLY : en un lugar remoto, muy lejos

remoteness [ri'mo:tnəs] *n* : lejanía *f*

removable [ri'mu:vəbəl] *adj* : movible, separable

removal [ri'mu:vəl] *n* : separación *f,* extracción *f,* supresión *f* (en algo escrito), eliminación *f* (de problemas, etc.)

remove [ri'mu:v] *vt* **-moved; -moving 1** : quitar, quitarse <remove the lid : quite la tapa> <to remove one's hat : quitarse el sombrero> **2** EXTRACT : sacar, extraer <to remove the contents of : sacar el contenido de> **3** ELIMINATE : eliminar, disipar

remunerate [ri'mju:nə,reɪt] *vt* **-ated; -ating** : remunerar

remuneration [ri,mju:nə'reɪʃən] *n* : remuneración *f*

remunerative [ri'mju:nərət̬ɪv, -,reɪ-] *adj* : remunerativo

renaissance [,rɛnə'sɑnts, -'zɑnts; 'rɛnə,-] *n* : renacimiento *m* <the Renaissance : el Renacimiento>

renal ['ri:nəl] *adj* : renal

rename [,ri:'neɪm] *vt* **-named; -naming** : ponerle un nombre nuevo a

rend ['rɛnd] *vt* **rent** ['rɛnt]; **rending** : desgarrar

render ['rɛndər] *vt* **1** : derretir <to render lard : derretir la manteca> **2** GIVE : prestar, dar <to render aid : prestar ayuda> **3** MAKE : hacer, volver, dejar <it rendered him helpless : lo dejó incapacitado> **4** TRANSLATE : traducir, verter <to render into English : traducir al inglés>

rendezvous ['rɑndɪ,vu:, -deɪ-] *ns & pl* : encuentro *m,* cita *f*

rendition [rɛn'dɪʃən] *n* : interpretación *f*

renegade ['rɛnɪ,geɪd] *n* : renegado *m,* -da *f*

renege [ri'nɪg, -'nɛg] *vi* **-neged; -neging** : no cumplir con (una promesa, etc.)

renew [ri'nu:, -'nju:] *vt* **1** REVIVE : renovar, reavivar <to renew the sentiments of youth : renovar los sentimientos de la juventud> **2** RESUME : reanudar **3** EXTEND : renovar <to renew a subscription : renovar una suscripción>

renewable [ri'nu:əbəl, -'nju:-] *adj* : renovable

renewal [ri'nu:əl, -'nju:-] *n* : renovación *f*

renounce [ri'naʊnts] *vt* **-nounced; -nouncing** : renunciar a

renovate ['rɛnə,veɪt] *vt* **-vated; -vating** : restaurar, renovar

renovation [,rɛnə'veɪʃən] *n* : restauración *f,* renovación *f*

renown [ri'naʊn] *n* : renombre *m,* fama *f,* celebridad *f*

renowned [ri'naʊnd] *adj* : renombrado, célebre, famoso

rent[1] ['rɛnt] *vt* : rentar, alquilar

rent[2] *n* **1** : renta *f,* alquiler *m* <for rent : se alquila> **2** RIP : rasgadura *f*

rental[1] ['rɛntəl] *adj* RENT : de alquiler

rental[2] *n* : alquiler *m*

renter ['rɛntər] *n* : arrendatario *m,* -ria *f*

renunciation [ri,nʌntsi'eɪʃən] *n* : renuncia *f*

reopen [,ri:'o:pən] *vt* : volver a abrir

reorganization [,ri:,ɔrgənə'zeɪʃən] *n* : reorganización *f*

reorganize [,ri:'ɔrgən,aɪz] *vt* **-nized; -nizing** : reorganizar

repair[1] [ri'pær] *vt* : reparar, arreglar, refaccionar

repair[2] *n* **1** : reparación *f,* arreglo *m* **2** CONDITION : estado *m* <in bad repair : en mal estado>

reparation [,rɛpə'reɪʃən] *n* **1** AMENDS : reparación *f* **2 reparations** *npl* COMPENSATION : indemnización *f*

repartee [,rɛpər'ti:, -,pɑr-, -'teɪ] *n* : intercambio *m* de réplicas ingeniosas

repast [ri'pæst, 'ri:,pæst] *n* : comida *f*

repatriate [ri'peɪtri,eɪt] *vt* **-ated; -ating** : repatriar

repay [ri'peɪ] *vt* **-paid; -paying** : pagar, devolver, reembolsar

repeal[1] [ri'pi:l] *vt* : abrogar, revocar

repeal[2] *n* : abrogación *f,* revocación *f*

repeat[1] [ri'pi:t] *vt* : repetir

repeat[2] *n* : repetición *f*

repeatedly [ri'pi:t̬ədli] *adv* : repetidamente, repetidas veces

repel [ri'pɛl] *vt* **-pelled; -pelling 1** REPULSE : repeler (un enemigo, etc.) **2** RESIST : repeler **3** REJECT : rechazar, repeler **4** DISGUST : repugnar, darle asco (a alguien)

repellent *or* **repellant** [ri'pɛlənt] *n* : repelente *m*

repent [ri'pɛnt] *vi* : arrepentirse

repentance [ri'pɛntənts] *n* : arrepentimiento *m*

repentant [ri'pɛntənt] *adj* : arrepentido

repercussion [,ri:pər'kʌʃən, ,rɛpər-] *n* : repercusión *f*

repertoire ['rɛpər,twɑr] *n* : repertorio *m*

repertory ['rɛpər,tori] *n, pl* **-ries** : repertorio *m*

repetition [,rɛpə'tɪʃən] *n* : repetición *f*

repetitious [,rɛpə'tɪʃəs] *adj* : repetitivo, reiterativo — **repetitiously** *adv*

repetitive [ri'pɛt̬ət̬ɪv] *adj* **:** repetitivo, reiterativo

replace [ri'pleɪs] *vt* **-placed; -placing** **1 :** volver a poner <replace it in the drawer : vuelve a ponerlo en el cajón> **2** SUBSTITUTE **:** reemplazar, sustituir **3 :** reponer <to replace the worn carpet : reponer la alfombra raída>

replaceable [ri'pleɪsəbəl] *adj* **:** reemplazable

replacement [ri'pleɪsmənt] *n* **1** SUBSTITUTION **:** reemplazo *m,* sustitución *f* **2** SUBSTITUTE **:** sustituto *m,* -ta *f;* suplente *mf* (persona) **3 replacement part :** repuesto *m,* pieza *f* de recambio

replenish [ri'plɛnɪʃ] *vt* **:** rellenar, llenar de nuevo

replenishment [ri'plɛnɪʃmənt] *n* **:** reabastecimiento *m*

replete [ri'pli:t] *adj* **:** repleto, lleno

replica ['rɛplɪkə] *n* **:** réplica *f,* reproducción *f*

reply[1] [ri'plaɪ] *vi* **-plied; -plying :** contestar, responder

reply[2] *n, pl* **-plies :** respuesta *f,* contestación *f*

report[1] [ri'port] *vt* **1** ANNOUNCE **:** relatar, anunciar **2 :** dar parte de, informar de, reportar <he reported an accident : dio parte de un accidente> <to report a crime : denunciar un delito> **3 :** informar acerca de (en un periódico, la televisión, etc.) — *vi* **1 :** hacer un informe, informar **2 to report for duty :** presentarse, reportarse

report[2] *n* **1** RUMOR **:** rumor *m* **2** REPUTATION **:** reputación *f* <people of evil report : personas de mala fama> **3** ACCOUNT **:** informe *m,* reportaje *m* (en un periódico, etc.) **4** BANG **:** estallido *m* (de un arma de fuego)

report card *n* **:** boletín *m* de calificaciones, boletín *m* de notas

reportedly [ri'portədli] *adv* **:** según se dice, según se informa

reporter [ri'port̬ər] *n* **:** periodista *mf;* reportero *m,* -ra *f*

repose[1] [ri'po:z] *vi* **-posed; -posing :** reposar, descansar

repose[2] *n* **1 :** reposo *m,* descanso *m* **2** CALM **:** calma *f,* tranquilidad *f*

repository [ri'pɑzə,tori] *n, pl* **-ries :** depósito *m*

repossess [,ri:pə'zɛs] *vt* **:** recuperar, recobrar la posesión de

reprehensible [,rɛpri'hɛntsəbəl] *adj* **:** reprensible — **reprehensibly** *adv*

represent [,rɛprɪ'zɛnt] *vt* **1** SYMBOLIZE **:** representar <the flag represents our country : la bandera representa a nuestro país> **2 :** representar, ser un representante de <an attorney who represents his client : un abogado que representa su cliente> **3** PORTRAY **:** presentar <he represents himself as a friend : se presenta como amigo>

representation [,rɛprɪ,zɛn'teɪʃən, -zən-] *n* **:** representación *f*

representative[1] [,rɛprɪ'zɛntət̬ɪv] *adj* **:** representativo

representative[2] *n* **1 :** representante *mf* **2 :** diputado *m,* -da *f* (en la política)

repress [ri'prɛs] *vt* **:** reprimir

repression [ri'prɛʃən] *n* **:** represión *f*

repressive [ri'prɛsɪv] *adj* **:** represivo

reprieve[1] [ri'pri:v] *vt* **-prieved; -prieving :** indultar

reprieve[2] *n* **:** indulto *m*

reprimand[1] ['rɛprə,mænd] *vt* **:** reprender

reprimand[2] *n* **:** reprimenda *f*

reprint[1] [ri'prɪnt] *vt* **:** reimprimir

reprint[2] ['ri:,prɪnt, ri'prɪnt] *n* **:** reedición *f*

reprisal [ri'praɪzəl] *n* **:** represalia *f*

reproach[1] [ri'pro:tʃ] *vt* **:** reprochar

reproach[2] *n* **1** DISGRACE **:** deshonra *f* **2** REBUKE **:** reproche *m,* recriminación *f*

reproachful [ri'pro:tʃfəl] *adj* **:** de reproche

reproduce [,ri:prə'du:s, -'dju:s] *v* **-duced; -ducing** *vt* **:** reproducir — *vi* BREED **:** reproducirse

reproduction [,ri:prə'dʌkʃən] *n* **:** reproducción *f*

reproductive [,ri:prə'dʌktɪv] *adj* **:** reproductor

reproof [ri'pru:f] *n* **:** reprobación *f,* reprimenda *f,* reproche *m*

reprove [ri'pru:v] *vt* **-proved; -proving :** reprender, censurar

reptile ['rɛp,taɪl] *n* **:** reptil *m*

republic [ri'pʌblɪk] *n* **:** república *f*

republican[1] [ri'pʌblɪkən] *adj* **:** republicano

republican[2] *n* **:** republicano *m,* -na *f*

repudiate [ri'pju:di,eɪt] *vt* **-ated; -ating** **1** REJECT **:** rechazar **2** DISOWN **:** repudiar, renegar de

repudiation [ri,pju:di'eɪʃən] *n* **:** rechazo *m,* repudio *m*

repugnance [ri'pʌgnənts] *n* **:** repugnancia *f*

repugnant [ri'pʌgnənt] *adj* **:** repugnante, asqueroso

repulse[1] [ri'pʌls] *vt* **-pulsed; -pulsing** **1** REPEL **:** repeler **2** REBUFF **:** desairar, rechazar

repulse[2] *n* **:** rechazo *m*

repulsive [ri'pʌlsɪv] *adj* **:** repulsivo, repugnante, asqueroso — **repulsively** *adv*

reputable ['rɛpjət̬əbəl] *adj* **:** acreditado, de buena reputación

reputation [,rɛpjə'teɪʃən] *n* **:** reputación *f,* fama *f*

repute [ri'pju:t] *n* **:** reputación *f,* fama *f*

reputed [ri'pju:t̬əd] *adj* **:** reputado, supuesto <she's reputed to be the best : tiene fama de ser la mejor>

reputedly [ri'pju:t̬ədli] *adv* **:** supuestamente, según se dice

request[1] [ri'kwɛst] *vt* **:** pedir, solicitar, rogar <to request assistance : solicitar asistencia, pedir ayuda> <I requested him to do it : le pedí que lo hiciera>

request[2] *n* : petición *f,* solicitud *f,* pedido *m*
requiem [ˈrɛkwiəm, ˈreɪ-] *n* : réquiem *m*
require [riˈkwaɪr] *vt* **-quired; -quiring** **1** CALL FOR, DEMAND : requerir, exigir <if required : si se requiere> <to require that something be done : exigir que algo se haga> **2** NEED : necesitar, requerir
requirement [riˈkwaɪrmənt] *n* **1** NECESSITY : necesidad *f* **2** DEMAND : requisito *m,* demanda *f*
requisite[1] [ˈrɛkwəzɪt] *adj* : esencial, necesario
requisite[2] *n* : requisito *m,* necesidad *f*
requisition[1] [ˌrɛkwəˈzɪʃən] *vt* : requisar
requisition[2] *n* : requisición *f,* requisa *f*
reread [ˌriːˈriːd] *vt* **-read; -reading** : releer
reroute [ˌriːˈruːt, -ˈraʊt] *vt* **-routed; -routing** : desviar
resale [ˈriːˌseɪl, ˌriːˈseɪl] *n* : reventa *f* <resale price : precio de venta>
rescind [riˈsɪnd] *vt* **1** CANCEL : rescindir, cancelar **2** REPEAL : abrogar, revocar
rescue[1] [ˈrɛsˌkjuː] *vt* **-cued; -cuing** : rescatar, salvar
rescue[2] *n* : rescate *m*
rescuer [ˈrɛskjuər] *n* : salvador *m,* -dora *f*
research[1] [riˈsərtʃ, ˈriːˌsərtʃ] *v* : investigar
research[2] *n* : investigación *f*
researcher [riˈsərtʃər, ˈriːˌ-] *n* : investigador *m,* -dora *f*
resemblance [riˈzɛmbləntś] *n* : semejanza *f,* parecido *m*
resemble [riˈzɛmbəl] *vt* **-sembled; -sembling** : parecerse a, asemejarse a
resent [riˈzɛnt] *vt* : resentirse de, ofenderse por
resentful [riˈzɛntfəl] *adj* : resentido, rencoroso — **resentfully** *adv*
resentment [riˈzɛntmənt] *n* : resentimiento *m*
reservation [ˌrɛzərˈveɪʃən] *n* **1** : reservación *f,* reserva *f* <to make a reservation : hacer una reservación> **2** DOUBT, MISGIVING : reserva *f,* duda *f* <without reservations : sin reservas> **3** : reserva *f* (de indios americanos)
reserve[1] [riˈzərv] *vt* **-served; -serving** : reservar
reserve[2] *n* **1** STOCK : reserva *f* <to keep in reserve : guardar en reserva> **2** RESTRAINT : reserva *f,* moderación *f* **3 reserves** *npl* : reservas *fpl* (militares)
reserved [riˈzərvd] *adj* : reservado
reservoir [ˈrɛzərˌvwɑr, -ˌvwɔr, -ˌvɔr] *n* : embalse *m*
reset [ˌriːˈsɛt] *vt* **-set; -setting** : reajustar, poner en hora (un reloj), reinicializar (una computadora)
reside [riˈzaɪd] *vi* **-sided; -siding** **1** DWELL : residir **2** LIE : radicar, residir <the power resides in the presidency : el poder radica en la presidencia>
residence [ˈrɛzədənts] *n* : residencia *f*
resident[1] [ˈrɛzədənt] *adj* : residente
resident[2] *n* : residente *mf*
residential [ˌrɛzəˈdɛntʃəl] *adj* : residencial
residual [riˈzɪdʒʊəl] *adj* : residual
residue [ˈrɛzəˌduː, -ˌdjuː] *n* : residuo *m,* resto *m*
resign [riˈzaɪn] *vt* **1** QUIT : dimitir, renunciar **2 to resign oneself** : aguantarse, resignarse
resignation [ˌrɛzɪgˈneɪʃən] *n* : resignación *f*
resignedly [riˈzaɪnədli] *adv* : con resignación
resilience [riˈzɪljənts] *n* **1** : capacidad *f* de recuperación, adaptabilidad *f* **2** ELASTICITY : elasticidad *f*
resiliency [riˈzɪljəntsi] → **resilience**
resilient [riˈzɪljənt] *adj* **1** STRONG : resistente, fuerte **2** ELASTIC : elástico
resin [ˈrɛzən] *n* : resina *f*
resist [riˈzɪst] *vt* **1** WITHSTAND : resistir <to resist heat : resistir el calor> **2** OPPOSE : oponerse a
resistance [riˈzɪstənts] *n* : resistencia *f*
resistant [riˈzɪstənt] *adj* : resistente
resolute [ˈrɛzəˌluːt] *adj* : firme, resuelto, decidido
resolutely [ˈrɛzəˌluːtli, ˌrɛzəˈ-] *adv* : resueltamente, firmemente
resolution [ˌrɛzəˈluːʃən] *n* **1** SOLUTION : solución *f* **2** RESOLVE : resolución *f,* determinación *f* **3** DECISION : propósito *m,* decisión *f* <New Year's resolutions : propósitos para el Año Nuevo> **4** MOTION, PROPOSAL : moción *f,* resolución *f* (legislativa)
resolve[1] [riˈzɑlv] *vt* **-solved; -solving** **1** SOLVE : resolver, solucionar **2** DECIDE : resolver <she resolved to get more sleep : resolvió dormir más>
resolve[2] *n* : resolución *f,* determinación *f*
resonance [ˈrɛzənənts] *n* : resonancia *f*
resonant [ˈrɛzənənt] *adj* : resonante, retumbante
resort[1] [riˈzɔrt] *vi* **to resort to** : recurrir <to resort to force : recurrir a la fuerza>
resort[2] *n* **1** RECOURSE : recurso *m* <as a last resort : como último recurso> **2** HANGOUT : lugar *m* popular, lugar *m* muy frecuentado **3** : lugar *m* de vacaciones <tourist resort : centro turístico>
resound [riˈzaʊnd] *vi* : retumbar, resonar
resounding [riˈzaʊndɪŋ] *adj* **1** RESONANT : retumbante, resonante **2** ABSOLUTE, CATEGORICAL : rotundo, tremendo <a resounding success : un éxito rotundo>
resource [ˈriːˌsors, riˈsors] *n* **1** RESOURCEFULNESS : ingenio *m,* recursos *mpl* **2 resources** *npl* : recursos *mpl*

<natural resources : recursos naturales> **3 resources** *npl* MEANS : recursos *mpl*, medios *mpl*, fondos *mpl*
resourceful [ri'sorsfəl, -'zors-] *adj* : ingenioso
resourcefulness [ri'sorsfəlnəs, -'zors-] *n* : ingenio *m*, recursos *mpl*, inventiva *f*
respect[1] [ri'spɛkt] *vt* : respetar, estimar
respect[2] *n* **1** REFERENCE : relación *f*, respeto *m* <with respect to : en lo que respecta a> **2** ESTEEM : respeto *m*, estima *f* **3** DETAIL, PARTICULAR : detalle *m*, sentido *m*, respeto *m* <in some respects : en algunos sentidos> **4 respects** *npl* : respetos *mpl* <to pay one's respects : presentar uno sus respetos>
respectability [ri,spɛktə'bɪləti] *n* : respetabilidad *f*
respectable [ri'spɛktəbəl] *adj* **1** PROPER : respetable, decente **2** CONSIDERABLE : considerable, respetable <a respectable amount : una cantidad respetable> — **respectably** [-bli] *adv*
respectful [ri'spɛktfəl] *adj* : respetuoso — **respectfully** *adv*
respectfulness [ri'spɛktfəlnəs] *n* : respetuosidad *f*
respective [ri'spɛktɪv] *adj* : respectivo <their respective homes : sus casas respectivas> — **respectively** *adv*
respiration [,rɛspə'reɪʃən] *n* : respiración *f*
respirator ['rɛspə,reɪtər] *n* : respirador *m*
respiratory ['rɛspərə,tori, rɪ'spaɪrə-] *adj* : respiratorio
respite ['rɛspɪt, rɪ'spaɪt] *n* : respiro *m*, tregua *f*
resplendent [ri'splɛndənt] *adj* : resplandeciente — **resplendently** *adv*
respond [ri'spɑnd] *vi* **1** ANSWER : contestar, responder **2** REACT : responder, reaccionar <to respond to treatment : responder al tratamiento>
response [ri'spɑnts] *n* : respuesta *f*
responsibility [ri,spɑntsə'bɪləti] *n, pl* **-ties** : responsabilidad *f*
responsible [ri'spɑntsəbəl] *adj* : responsable — **responsibly** [-bli] *adv*
responsive [ri'spɑntsɪv] *adj* **1** ANSWERING : que responde **2** SENSITIVE : sensible, receptivo
responsiveness [ri'spɑntsɪvnəs] *n* : receptividad *f*, sensibilidad *f*
rest[1] ['rɛst] *vi* **1** REPOSE : reposar, descansar **2** RELAX : quedarse tranquilo **3** STOP : pararse, detenerse **4** DEPEND : basarse (en), descansar (sobre), depender (de) <the decision rests with her : la decisión pesa sobre ella> **5 to rest on :** apoyarse en, descansar sobre <to rest on one's arm : apoyarse en el brazo> — *vt* **1** RELAX : descansar **2** SUPPORT : apoyar **3 to rest one's eyes on :** fijar la mirada en
rest[2] *n* **1** RELAXATION, REPOSE : reposo *m*, descanso *m* **2** SUPPORT : soporte *m*, apoyo *m* **3** : silencio *m* (en música) **4** REMAINDER : resto *m* **5 to come to rest** : pararse
restatement [,ri:'steɪtmənt] *n* : repetición *f*
restaurant ['rɛstə,rɑnt, -rənt] *n* : restaurante *m*
restful ['rɛstfəl] *adj* **1** RELAXING : relajante **2** PEACEFUL : tranquilo, sosegado
restitution [,rɛstə'tu:ʃən, -'tju:-] *n* : restitución *f*
restive ['rɛstɪv] *adj* : inquieto, nervioso
restless ['rɛstləs] *adj* **1** FIDGETY : inquieto, agitado **2** IMPATIENT : impaciente **3** SLEEPLESS : desvelado <a restless night : una noche en blanco>
restlessly ['rɛstləsli] *adv* : nerviosamente
restlessness ['rɛstləsnəs] *n* : inquietud *f*, agitación *f*
restoration [,rɛstə'reɪʃən] *n* : restauración *f*, restablecimiento *m*
restore [ri'stor] *vt* **-stored; -storing 1** RETURN : volver **2** REESTABLISH : restablecer **3** REPAIR : restaurar
restrain [ri'streɪn] *vt* **1** : refrenar, contener **2 to restrain oneself** : contenerse
restrained [ri'streɪnd] *adj* : comedido, templado, contenido
restraint [ri'streɪnt] *n* **1** RESTRICTION : restricción *f*, limitación *f*, control *m* **2** CONFINEMENT : encierro *m* **3** RESERVE : reserva *f*, control *m* de sí mismo
restrict [ri'strɪkt] *vt* : restringir, limitar, constreñir
restricted [ri'strɪktəd] *adj* **1** LIMITED : limitado, restringido **2** CLASSIFIED : secreto, confidencial
restriction [ri'strɪkʃən] *n* : restricción *f*
restrictive [ri'strɪktɪv] *adj* : restrictivo — **restrictively** *adv*
restructure [ri'strʌktʃər] *vt* **-tured; -turing** : reestructurar
result[1] [ri'zʌlt] *vi* : resultar <to result in : resultar en, tener por resultado>
result[2] *n* : resultado *m*, consecuencia *f* <as a result of : como consecuencia de>
resultant [ri'zʌltənt] *adj* : resultante
resume [ri'zu:m] *v* **-sumed; -suming** *vt* : reanudar — *vi* : reanudarse
résumé *or* **resume** *or* **resumé** ['rɛzə,meɪ, ,rɛzə'-] *n* **1** SUMMARY : resumen *m* **2** CURRICULUM VITAE : currículum *m*, currículo *m*
resumption [ri'zʌmpʃən] *n* : reanudación *f*
resurface [,ri:'sərfəs] *v* **-faced; -facing** *vt* : pavimentar (una carretera) de nuevo — *vi* : volver a salir en la superficie
resurgence [ri'sərdʒənts] *n* : resurgimiento *m*

resurrect [ˌrɛzəˈrɛkt] *vt* : resucitar, desempolvar
resurrection [ˌrɛzəˈrɛkʃən] *n* : resurrección *f*
resuscitate [riˈsʌsəˌteɪt] *vt* **-tated; -tating** : resucitar, revivir
retail¹ [ˈriːˌteɪl] *vt* : vender al por menor, vender al detalle
retail² *adv* : al por menor, al detalle
retail³ *adj* : detallista, minorista
retail⁴ *n* : venta *f* al detalle, venta *f* al por menor
retailer [ˈriːˌteɪlər] *n* : detallista *mf*, minorista *mf*
retain [riˈteɪn] *vt* : retener, conservar, guardar
retainer [riˈteɪnər] *n* **1** SERVANT : criado *m*, -da *f* **2** ADVANCE : anticipo *m*
retaliate [riˈtæliˌeɪt] *vi* **-ated; -ating** : responder, contraatacar, tomar represalias
retaliation [riˌtæliˈeɪʃən] *n* : represalia *f*, retaliación *f*
retard [riˈtɑrd] *vt* : retardar, retrasar
retarded [riˈtɑrdəd] *adj* : retrasado
retch [ˈrɛtʃ] *vi* : hacer arcadas
retention [riˈtɛntʃən] *n* : retención *f*
retentive [riˈtɛntɪv] *adj* : retentivo
reticence [ˈrɛtəsənts] *n* : reticencia *f*
reticent [ˈrɛtəsənt] *adj* : reticente
retina [ˈrɛtənə] *n, pl* **-nas** *or* **-nae** [-əni, -ənˌaɪ] : retina *f*
retinue [ˈrɛtənˌuː, -ˌjuː] *n* : séquito *m*, comitiva *f*, cortejo *m*
retire [riˈtaɪr] *vi* **-tired; -tiring 1** RETREAT, WITHDRAW : retirarse, retraerse **2** : retirarse, jubilarse (de su trabajo) **3** : acostarse, irse a dormir
retiree [riˌtaɪˈriː] *n* : jubilado *m*, -da *f*
retirement [riˈtaɪrmənt] *n* : jubilación *f*
retiring [riˈtaɪrɪŋ] *adj* SHY : retraído
retort¹ [riˈtɔrt] *vt* : replicar
retort² *n* : réplica *f*
retrace [ˌriːˈtreɪs] *vt* **-traced; -tracing** : volver sobre, desandar <to retrace one's steps : volver uno sobre sus pasos>
retract [riˈtrækt] *vt* **1** TAKE BACK, WITHDRAW : retirar, retractarse de **2** : retraer (las garras) — *vi* : retractarse
retractable [riˈtræktəbəl] *adj* : retractable
retrain [ˌriːˈtreɪn] *vt* : reciclar, reconvertir
retreat¹ [riˈtriːt] *vi* : retirarse
retreat² *n* **1** WITHDRAWAL : retirada *f*, repliegue *m*, retiro *m* <to beat a retreat : batirse en retirada> **2** REFUGE : retiro *m*, refugio *m*
retrench [riˈtrɛntʃ] *vt* : reducir (gastos) — *vi* : economizar
retribution [ˌrɛtrəˈbjuːʃən] *n* PUNISHMENT : castigo *m*, pena *f* merecida
retrieval [riˈtriːvəl] *n* : recuperación *f* <beyond retrieval : irrecuperable> <data retrieval : recuperación de datos>
retrieve [riˈtriːv] *vt* **-trieved; -trieving 1** : cobrar <to retrieve game : cobrar la caza> **2** RECOVER : recuperar
retriever [riˈtriːvər] *n* : perro *m* cobrador
retroactive [ˌrɛtroˈæktɪv] *adj* : retroactivo — **retroactively** *adv*
retrograde [ˈrɛtrəˌgreɪd] *adj* : retrógrado
retrospect [ˈrɛtrəˌspɛkt] *n* **in retrospect** : mirando hacia atrás, retrospectivamente
retrospective [ˌrɛtrəˈspɛktɪv] *adj* : retrospectivo
return¹ [riˈtərn] *vi* **1** : volver, regresar <to return home : regresar a casa> **2** REAPPEAR : reaparecer, resurgir **3** ANSWER : responder — *vt* **1** REPLACE, RESTORE : devolver, volver (a poner), restituir <to return something to its place : volver a poner algo en su lugar> **2** YIELD : producir, redituar, rendir **3** REPAY : pagar, devolver <to return a compliment : devolver un cumplido>
return² *adj* : de vuelta
return³ *n* **1** RETURNING : regreso *m*, vuelta *f*, retorno *m* **2** *or* **tax return** : declaración *f* de impuestos **3** YIELD : rédito *m*, rendimiento *m*, ganancia *f* **4 returns** *npl* DATA, RESULTS : resultados *mpl*, datos *mpl*
reunion [riˈjuːnjən] *n* : reunión *f*, reencuentro *m*
reunite [ˌriːjʊˈnaɪt] *v* **-nited; -niting** *vt* : (volver a) reunir — *vi* : (volver a) reunirse
reusable [riˈjuːzəbəl] *adj* : reutilizable
reuse [riˈjuːz] *vt* **-used; -using** : reutilizar, usar de nuevo
revamp [ˌriˈvæmp] *vt* : renovar
reveal [riˈviːl] *vt* **1** DIVULGE : revelar, divulgar <to reveal a secret : revelar un secreto> **2** SHOW : manifestar, mostrar, dejar ver
reveille [ˈrɛvəli] *n* : toque *m* de diana
revel¹ [ˈrɛvəl] *vi* **-eled** *or* **-elled; -eling** *or* **-elling 1** CAROUSE : ir de juerga **2 to revel in** : deleitarse en
revel² *n* : juerga *f*, parranda *f fam*
revelation [ˌrɛvəˈleɪʃən] *n* : revelación *f*
reveler *or* **reveller** [ˈrɛvələr] *n* : juerguista *mf*
revelry [ˈrɛvəlri] *n, pl* **–ries** : juerga *f*, parranda *f fam*, jarana *f fam*
revenge¹ [riˈvɛndʒ] *vt* **-venged; -venging** : vengar <to revenge oneself on : vengarse de>
revenge² *n* : venganza *f*
revenue [ˈrɛvəˌnuː, -ˌnjuː] *n* : ingresos *mpl*, rentas *fpl*
reverberate [riˈvərbəˌreɪt] *vi* **-ated; -ating** : reverberar
reverberation [riˌvərbəˈreɪʃən] *n* : reverberación *f*
revere [riˈvɪr] *vt* **-vered; -vering** : reverenciar, venerar

reverence [ˈrɛvərənts] *n* **:** reverencia *f,* veneración *f*
reverend [ˈrɛvərənd] *adj* **:** reverendo <the Reverend John Chapin : el reverendo John Chapin>
reverent [ˈrɛvərənt] *adj* **:** reverente — **reverently** *adv*
reverie [ˈrɛvəri] *n, pl* **-eries :** ensueño *m*
reversal [ˈrɛvərsəl] *n* **1** INVERSION **:** inversión *f* (del orden normal) **2** CHANGE **:** cambio *m* total **3** SETBACK **:** revés *m,* contratiempo *m*
reverse[1] [riˈvərs] *v* **-versed; -versing** *vt* **1** INVERT **:** invertir **2** CHANGE **:** cambiar totalmente **3** ANNUL **:** anular, revocar — *vi* **:** dar marcha atrás
reverse[2] *adj* **1 :** inverso <in reverse order : en orden inverso> <the reverse side : el reverso> **2** OPPOSITE **:** contrario, opuesto
reverse[3] *n* **1** OPPOSITE **:** lo contrario, lo opuesto **2** SETBACK **:** revés *m,* contratiempo *m* **3** BACK **:** reverso *m,* dorso *m,* revés *m* **4** *or* **reverse gear :** marcha *f* atrás, reversa *f Col, Mex*
reversible [riˈvərsəbəl] *adj* **:** reversible
reversion [riˈvərʒən] *n* **:** reversión *f,* vuelta *f*
revert [riˈvərt] *vi* **:** revertir
review[1] [riˈvjuː] *vt* **1** REEXAMINE **:** volver a examinar, repasar (una lección) **2** CRITICIZE **:** reseñar, hacer una crítica de **3** EXAMINE **:** examinar, analizar <to review one's life : examinar su vida> **4 to review the troops :** pasar revista a las tropas
review[2] *n* **1** INSPECTION **:** revista *f* (de tropas) **2** ANALYSIS, OVERVIEW **:** resumen *m,* análisis *m* <a review of current affairs : un análisis de las actualidades> **3** CRITICISM **:** reseña *f,* crítica *f* (de un libro, etc.) **4 :** repaso *m* (para un examen) **5** REVUE **:** revista *f* (musical)
reviewer [riˈvjuːər] *n* **:** crítico *m,* -ca *f*
revile [riˈvaɪl] *vt* **-viled; -viling :** injuriar, denostar
revise [riˈvaɪz] *vt* **-vised; -vising :** revisar, corregir, refundir <to revise a dictionary : corregir un diccionario>
revision [riˈvɪʒən] *n* **:** revisión *f*
revival [riˈvaɪvəl] *n* **1 :** renacimiento *m* (de ideas, etc.), restablecimiento *m* (de costumbres, etc.), reactivación *f* (de la economía) **2 :** reanimación *f,* resucitación *f* (en medicina) **3** *or* **revival meeting :** asamblea *f* evangelista
revive [riˈvaɪv] *v* **-vived; -viving** *vt* **1** REAWAKEN **:** reavivar, reanimar, reactivar (la economía), resucitar (a un paciente) **2** REESTABLISH **:** restablecer — *vi* **1 :** renacer, reanimarse, reactivarse **2** COME TO **:** recobrar el sentido, volver en sí
revoke [riˈvoːk] *vt* **-voked; -voking :** revocar
revolt[1] [riˈvoːlt] *vi* **1** REBEL **:** rebelarse, sublevarse **2 to revolt at :** sentir repugnancia por — *vt* DISGUST **:** darle asco (a alguien), repugnar
revolt[2] *n* REBELLION **:** rebelión *f,* revuelta *f,* sublevación *f*
revolting [riˈvoːltɪŋ] *adj* **:** asqueroso, repugnante
revolution [ˌrɛvəˈluːʃən] *n* **:** revolución *f*
revolutionary[1] [ˌrɛvəˈluːʃənˌɛri] *adj* **:** revolucionario
revolutionary[2] *n, pl* **-aries :** revolucionario *m,* -ria *f*
revolutionize [ˌrɛvəˈluːʃənˌaɪz] *vt* **-ized; -izing :** cambiar radicalmente, revolucionar
revolve [riˈvɑlv] *v* **-volved; -volving** *vt* ROTATE **:** hacer girar — *vi* **1** ROTATE **:** girar <to revolve around : girar alrededor de> **2 to revolve in one's mind :** darle vueltas en la cabeza a alguien
revolver [riˈvɑlvər] *n* **:** revólver *m*
revue [riˈvjuː] *n* **:** revista *f* (musical)
revulsion [riˈvʌlʃən] *n* **:** repugnancia *f*
reward[1] [riˈwɔrd] *vt* **:** recompensar, premiar
reward[2] *n* **:** recompensa *f*
rewrite [ˌriːˈraɪt] *vt* **-wrote; -written; -writing :** escribir de nuevo, volver a escribir
rhapsody [ˈræpsədi] *n, pl* **-dies 1 :** elogio *m* excesivo <to go into rhapsodies over : extasiarse por> **2 :** rapsodia *f* (en música)
rhetoric [ˈrɛt̬ərɪk] *n* **:** retórica *f*
rhetorical [rɪˈtɔrɪkəl] *adj* **:** retórico
rheumatic [rʊˈmæt̬ɪk] *adj* **:** reumático
rheumatism [ˈruːməˌtɪzəm, ˈrʊ-] *n* **:** reumatismo *m*
rhinestone [ˈraɪnˌstoːn] *n* **:** diamante *m* de imitación
rhino [ˈraɪˌnoː] *n, pl* **rhino** *or* **rhinos** → **rhinoceros**
rhinoceros [raɪˈnɑsərəs] *n, pl* **-eroses** *or* **-eros** *or* **-eri** [-ˌraɪ] **:** rinoceronte *m*
rhododendron [ˌroːdəˈdɛndrən] *n* **:** rododendro *m*
rhombus [ˈrɑmbəs] *n, pl* **-buses** *or* **-bi** [-ˌbaɪ, -bi] **:** rombo *m*
rhubarb [ˈruːˌbɑrb] *n* **:** ruibarbo *m*
rhyme[1] [ˈraɪm] *vi* **rhymed; rhyming :** rimar
rhyme[2] *n* **1 :** rima *f* **2** VERSE **:** verso *m* (en rima)
rhythm [ˈrɪðəm] *n* **:** ritmo *m*
rhythmic [ˈrɪðmɪk] *or* **rhythmical** [-mɪkəl] *adj* **:** rítmico — **rhythmically** [-mɪkli] *adv*
rib[1] [ˈrɪb] *vt* **ribbed; ribbing 1 :** hacer en canalé <a ribbed sweater : un suéter en canalé> **2** TEASE **:** tomarle el pelo (a alguien)
rib[2] *n* **1 :** costilla *f* (de una persona o un animal) **2 :** nervio *m* (de una bóveda o una hoja), varilla *f* (de un

paraguas), canalé *m* (de una prenda tejida)
ribald [ˈrɪbəld] *adj* : escabroso, procaz
ribbon [ˈrɪbən] *n* **1** : cinta *f* **2 to tear to ribbons** : hacer jirones
rice [ˈraɪs] *n* : arroz *m*
rich [ˈrɪtʃ] *adj* **1** WEALTHY : rico **2** SUMPTUOUS : suntuoso, lujoso **3** : pesado <rich foods : comida pesada> **4** ABUNDANT : abundante **5** : vivo, intenso <rich colors : colores vivos> **6** FERTILE : fértil, rico
riches [ˈrɪtʃəz] *npl* : riquezas *fpl*
richly [ˈrɪtʃli] *adv* **1** SUMPTUOUSLY : suntuosamente, ricamente **2** ABUNDANTLY : abundantemente **3 richly deserved** : bien merecido
richness [ˈrɪtʃnəs] *n* : riqueza *f*
rickets [ˈrɪkəts] *n* : raquitismo *m*
rickety [ˈrɪkət̬i] *adj* : desvencijado, destartalado
ricksha *or* **rickshaw** [ˈrɪkˌʃɔ] *n* : cochecillo *m* tirado por un hombre
ricochet[1] [ˈrɪkəˌʃeɪ] *vi* **-cheted** [-ˌʃeɪd] *or* **-chetted** [-ˌʃɛt̬əd]; **-cheting** [-ˌʃeɪɪŋ] *or* **-chetting** [-ˌʃɛt̬ɪŋ] : rebotar
ricochet[2] *n* : rebote *m*
rid [ˈrɪd] *vt* **rid; ridding 1** FREE : librar <to rid the city of thieves : librar la ciudad de ladrones> **2 to rid oneself of** : desembarazarse de
riddance [ˈrɪdənts] *n* : libramiento *m* <good riddance! : ¡adiós y buen viaje!, ¡vete con viento fresco!>
riddle[1] [ˈrɪdəl] *vt* **-dled; -dling** : acribillar <riddled with bullets : acribillado a balazos> <riddled with errors : lleno de errores>
riddle[2] *n* : acertijo *m*, adivinanza *f*
ride[1] [ˈraɪd] *v* **rode** [ˈroːd]; **ridden** [ˈrɪdən]; **riding** *vt* **1** : montar, ir, andar <to ride a horse : montar a caballo> <to ride a bicycle : montar en bicicleta, andar en bicicleta> <to ride the bus : ir en autobús> **2** TRAVERSE : recorrer <he rode 5 miles : recorrió 5 millas> **3** TEASE : burlarse de, ridiculizar **4** CARRY : llevar **5** WEATHER : capear <they rode out the storm : capearon el temporal> **6 to ride the waves** : surcar los mares — *vi* **1** : montar a caballo, cabalgar **2** TRAVEL : ir, viajar (en coche, en bicicleta, etc.) **3** RUN : andar, marchar <the car rides well : el coche anda bien> **4 to ride at anchor** : estar fondeado **5 to let things ride** : dejar pasar las cosas
ride[2] *n* **1** : paseo *m*, vuelta *f* (en coche, en bicicleta, a caballo) <to go for a ride : dar una vuelta> <to give someone a ride : llevar en coche a alguien> **2** : aparato *m* (en un parque de diversiones)
rider [ˈraɪdər] *n* **1** : jinete *mf* <the rider fell off his horse : el jinete se cayó de su caballo> **2** CYCLIST : ciclista *mf* **3** MOTORCYCLIST : motociclista *mf* **4** CLAUSE : cláusula *f* añadida
ridge [ˈrɪdʒ] *n* **1** CHAIN : cadena *f* (de montañas o cerros) **2** : caballete *m* (de un techo), cresta *f* (de una ola o una montaña), cordoncillo *m* (de telas)
ridicule[1] [ˈrɪdəˌkjuːl] *vt* **-culed; -culing** : burlarse de, mofarse de, ridiculizar
ridicule[2] *n* : burlas *fpl*
ridiculous [rəˈdɪkjələs] *adj* : ridículo, absurdo
ridiculously [rəˈdɪkjələsli] *adv* : de forma ridícula
rife [ˈraɪf] *adj* : abundante, común <to be rife with : estar plagado de>
riffraff [ˈrɪfˌræf] *n* : chusma *f*, gentuza *f*
rifle[1] [ˈraɪfəl] *v* **-fled; -fling** *vt* RANSACK : desvalijar, saquear — *vi* : **to rifle through** : revolver
rifle[2] *n* : rifle *m*, fusil *m*
rift [ˈrɪft] *n* **1** FISSURE : grieta *f*, fisura *f* **2** BREAK : ruptura *f* (entre personas), división *f* (dentro de un grupo)
rig[1] [ˈrɪg] *vt* **rigged; rigging 1** : aparejar (un barco) **2** EQUIP : equipar **3** FIX : amañar (una elección, etc.) **4 to rig up** CONSTRUCT : construir, erigir **5 to rig oneself out as** : vestirse de
rig[2] *n* **1** : aparejo *m* (de un barco) **2** *or* **oil rig** : torre *f* de perforación, plataforma *f* petrolífera
rigging [ˈrɪgɪŋ, -gən] *n* : jarcia *f*, aparejo *m*
right[1] [ˈraɪt] *vt* **1** FIX, RESTORE : reparar <to right the economy : reparar la economía> **2** STRAIGHTEN : enderezar
right[2] *adv* **1** : bien <to live right : vivir bien> **2** PRECISELY : precisamente, justo <right in the middle : justo en medio> **3** DIRECTLY, STRAIGHT : derecho, directamente <he went right home : fue derecho a casa> **4** IMMEDIATELY : inmediatamente <right after lunch : inmediatamente después del almuerzo> **5** COMPLETELY : completamente <he felt right at home : se sintió completamente cómodo> **6** : a la derecha <to look left and right : mirar a la izquierda y a la derecha>
right[3] *adj* **1** UPRIGHT : bueno, honrado <right conduct : conducta honrada> **2** CORRECT : correcto <the right answer : la respuesta correcta> **3** APPROPRIATE : apropiado, adecuado, debido <the right man for the job : el hombre perfecto para el trabajo> **4** STRAIGHT : recto <a right line : una línea recta> **5** : derecho <the right hand : la mano derecha> **6** SOUND : bien <he's not in his right mind : no está bien de la cabeza>
right[4] *n* **1** GOOD : bien *m* <to do right : hacer el bien> **2** : derecha *f* <on the right : a la derecha> **3** *or* **right hand** : mano *f* derecha **4** ENTITLEMENT : derecho *m* <the right to vote : el derecho a votar> <women's rights : los derechos de la mujer> **5 the Right** : la derecha (en la política)

right angle *n* : ángulo *m* recto

right–angled [ˈraɪtˈæŋgəld] *or* **right–angle** [-gəl] *adj* **1** : en ángulo recto **2 right–angled triangle** : triángulo *m* rectángulo

righteous [ˈraɪtʃəs] *adj* : recto, honrado — **righteously** *adv*

righteousness [ˈraɪtʃəsnəs] *n* : rectitud *f*, honradez *f*

rightful [ˈraɪtfəl] *adj* **1** JUST : justo **2** LAWFUL : legítimo — **rightfully** *adv*

right–hand [ˈraɪtˈhænd] *adj* **1** : situado a la derecha **2** RIGHT-HANDED : para la mano derecha, con la mano derecha **3 right–hand man** : brazo *m* derecho

right–handed [ˈraɪtˈhændəd] *adj* **1** : diestro <a right-handed pitcher : un lanzador diestro> **2** : para la mano derecha, con la mano derecha **3** CLOCKWISE : en la dirección de las manecillas del reloj

rightly [ˈraɪtli] *adv* **1** JUSTLY : justamente, con razón **2** PROPERLY : debidamente, apropiadamente **3** CORRECTLY : correctamente

right–of–way [ˈraɪt̬əˈweɪ, -əv-] *n, pl* **rights–of–way 1** : preferencia (del tráfico) **2** ACCESS : derecho *m* de paso

rightward [ˈraɪtwərd] *adj* : a la derecha, hacia la derecha

right–wing [ˈraɪtˈwɪŋ] *adj* : derechista

right wing *n* **the right wing** : la derecha

right–winger [ˈraɪtˈwɪŋər] *n* : derechista *mf*

rigid [ˈrɪdʒɪd] *adj* : rígido — **rigidly** *adv*

rigidity [rɪˈdʒɪdət̬i] *n, pl* **-ties** : rigidez *f*

rigmarole [ˈrɪgməˌroːl, ˈrɪgə-] *n* **1** NONSENSE : galimatías *m*, disparates *mpl* **2** PROCEDURES : trámites *mpl*

rigor [ˈrɪgər] *n* : rigor *m*

rigor mortis [ˌrɪgərˈmɔrt̬əs] *n* : rigidez *f* cadavérica

rigorous [ˈrɪgərəs] *adj* : rigoroso — **rigorously** *adv*

rile [ˈraɪl] *vt* **riled; riling** : irritar

rill [ˈrɪl] *n* : riachuelo *m*

rim [ˈrɪm] *n* **1** EDGE : borde *m* **2** : llanta *f*, rin *m Col, Mex* (de una rueda) **3** FRAME : montura *f* (de anteojos)

rime [ˈraɪm] *n* : escarcha *f*

rind [ˈraɪnd] *n* : corteza *f*

ring[1] [ˈrɪŋ] *v* **rang** [ˈræŋ]; **rung** [ˈrʌŋ]; **ringing** *vi* **1** : sonar <the doorbell rang : el timbre sonó> <to ring for : llamar> **2** RESOUND : resonar **3** SEEM : parecer <to ring true : parecer cierto> — *vt* **1** : tocar, hacer sonar (un timbre, una alarma, etc.) **2** SURROUND : cercar, rodear

ring[2] *n* **1** : anillo *m*, sortija *f* <wedding ring : anillo de matrimonio> **2** BAND : aro *m*, anillo *m* <piston ring : aro de émbolo> **3** CIRCLE : círculo *m* **4** ARENA : arena *f*, ruedo *m* <a boxing ring : un cuadrilátero, un ring> **5** GANG : banda *f* (de ladrones, etc.) **6** SOUND : timbre *m*, sonido *m* **7** CALL : llamada *f* (por teléfono)

ringer [ˈrɪŋər] *n* **to be a dead ringer for** : ser un vivo retrato de

ringleader [ˈrɪŋˌliːdər] *n* : cabecilla *mf*

ringlet [ˈrɪŋlət] *n* : sortija *f*, rizo *m*

ringworm [ˈrɪŋˌwərm] *n* : tiña *f*

rink [ˈrɪŋk] *n* : pista *f* <skating rink : pista de patinaje>

rinse[1] [ˈrɪnts] *vt* **rinsed; rinsing** : enjuagar <to rinse out one's mouth : enjuagarse la boca>

rinse[2] *n* : enjuague *m*

riot[1] [ˈraɪət] *vi* : amotinarse

riot[2] *n* : motín *m*, tumulto *m*, alboroto *m*

rioter [ˈraɪət̬ər] *n* : alborotador *m*, -dora *f*

riotous [ˈraɪət̬əs] *adj* **1** UNRULY, WILD : desenfrenado, alborotado **2** ABUNDANT : abundante

rip[1] [ˈrɪp] *v* **ripped; ripping** *vt* : rasgar, arrancar, desgarrar — *vi* : rasgarse, desgarrarse

rip[2] *n* : rasgón *m*, desgarrón *m*

ripe [ˈraɪp] *adj* **riper; ripest 1** MATURE : maduro <ripe fruit : fruta madura> **2** READY : listo, preparado

ripen [ˈraɪpən] *v* : madurar

ripeness [ˈraɪpnəs] *n* : madurez *f*

rip–off [ˈrɪpˌɔf] *n* **1** THEFT : robo *m* **2** SWINDLE : estafa *f*, timo *m fam*

ripple[1] [ˈrɪpəl] *v* **-pled; -pling** *vi* : rizarse, ondear, ondular — *vt* : rizar

ripple[2] *n* : onda *f*, ondulación *f*

rise[1] [ˈraɪz] *vi* **rose** [ˈroːz]; **risen** [ˈrɪzən]; **rising 1** GET UP : levantarse <to rise to one's feet : ponerse de pie> **2** : elevarse, alzarse <the mountains rose to the west : las montañas se elevaron al oeste> **3** : salir (dícese del sol y de la luna) **4** : subir (dícese de las aguas, del humo, etc.) <the river rose : las aguas subieron de nivel> **5** INCREASE : aumentar, subir **6** ORIGINATE : nacer, proceder **7 to rise in rank** : ascender **8 to rise up** REBEL : sublevarse, rebelarse

rise[2] *n* **1** ASCENT : ascensión *f*, subida *f* **2** ORIGIN : origen *m* **3** ELEVATION : elevación *f* **4** INCREASE : subida *f*, aumento *m*, alzamiento *m* **5** SLOPE : pendiente *f*, cuesta *f*

riser [ˈraɪzər] *n* **1** : contrahuella *f* (de una escalera) **2 early riser** : madrugador *m*, -dora *f* **3 late riser** : dormilón *m*, -lona *f*

risk[1] [ˈrɪsk] *vt* : arriesgar

risk[2] *n* : riesgo *m*, peligro *m* <at risk : en peligro> <at your own risk : por su cuenta y riesgo>

risky [ˈrɪski] *adj* **riskier; -est** : arriesgado, peligroso, riesgoso

risqué [rɪˈskeɪ] *adj* : escabroso, picante, subido de tono

rite [ˈraɪt] *n* : rito *m*

ritual[1] [ˈrɪtʃʊəl] *adj* : ritual — **ritually** *adv*
ritual[2] *n* : ritual *m*
rival[1] [ˈraɪvəl] *vt* **-valed** *or* **-valled; -valing** *or* **-valling** : rivalizar con, competir con
rival[2] *adj* : competidor, rival
rival[3] *n* : rival *mf;* competidor *m,* -dora *f*
rivalry [ˈraɪvəlri] *n, pl* **-ries** : rivalidad *f,* competencia *f*
river [ˈrɪvər] *n* : río *m*
riverbank [ˈrɪvər,bæŋk] *n* : ribera *f,* orilla *f*
riverbed [ˈrɪvər,bɛd] *n* : cauce *m,* lecho *m*
riverside [ˈrɪvər,saɪd] *n* : ribera *f,* orilla *f*
rivet[1] [ˈrɪvət] *vt* **1** : remachar **2** FIX : fijar (los ojos, etc.) **3** FASCINATE : fascinar, cautivar
rivet[2] *n* : remache *m*
rivulet [ˈrɪvjələt] *n* : arroyo *m,* riachuelo *m* <rivulets of sweat : gotas de sudor>
roach [ˈroːtʃ] → **cockroach**
road [ˈroːd] *n* **1** : carretera *f,* calle *f,* camino *m* **2** PATH : camino *m,* sendero *m,* vía *f* <on the road to a solution : en vías de una solución>
roadblock [ˈroːd,blɑk] *n* : control *m*
roadrunner [ˈroːd,rʌnər] *n* : correcaminos *m*
roadside [ˈroːd,saɪd] *n* : borde *m* de la carretera
roadway [ˈroːd,weɪ] *n* : carretera *f,* calzada *f*
roam [ˈroːm] *vi* : vagar, deambular, errar — *vt* : vagar por
roan[1] [ˈroːn] *adj* : ruano
roan[2] *n* : caballo *m* ruano
roar[1] [ˈror] *vi* : rugir, bramar <to roar with laughter : reírse a carcajadas> — *vt* : decir a gritos
roar[2] *n* **1** : rugido *m,* bramido *m* (de un animal) **2** DIN : clamor *m* (de gente), fragor *m* (del trueno), estruendo *m* (del tráfico, etc.)
roast[1] [ˈroːst] *vt* : asar (carne, papas), tostar (café, nueces) — *vi* : asarse
roast[2] *adj* **1** : asado <roast chicken : pollo asado> **2 roast beef** : rosbif *m*
roast[3] *n* : asado *m*
rob [ˈrɑb] *v* **robbed; robbing** *vt* **1** STEAL : robar **2** DEPRIVE : privar, quitar — *vi* : robar
robber [ˈrɑbər] *n* : ladrón *m,* -drona *f*
robbery [ˈrɑbəri] *n, pl* **-beries** : robo *m*
robe[1] [ˈroːb] *vt* **robed; robing** : vestirse
robe[2] *n* **1** : toga *f* (de magistrados, etc.), sotana *f* (de eclesiásticos) <robe of office : traje de ceremonias> **2** BATHROBE : bata *f*
robin [ˈrɑbən] *n* : petirrojo *m*
robot [ˈroː,bɑt, -bət] *n* : robot *m*
robust [roˈbʌst, ˈroː,bʌst] *adj* : robusto, fuerte — **robustly** *adv*
rock[1] [ˈrɑk] *vt* **1** : acunar (a un niño), mecer (una cuna) **2** SHAKE : sacudir — *vi* SWAY : mecerse, balancearse
rock[2] *adj* : de rock
rock[3] *n* **1** ROCKING : balanceo *m* **2** *or* **rock music** : rock *m,* música *f* rock **3** : roca *f* (substancia) **4** STONE : piedra *f*
rock and roll *n* : rock and roll *m*
rocker [ˈrɑkər] *n* **1** : balancín *m* **2** *or* **rocking chair** : mecedora *f,* balancín *m* **3 to be off one's rocker** : estar chiflado, estar loco
rocket[1] [ˈrɑkət] *vi* : dispararse, subir rápidamente
rocket[2] *n* : cohete *m*
rocking horse *n* : caballito *m* (de balancín)
rock salt *n* : sal *f* gema
rocky [ˈrɑki] *adj* **rockier; -est 1** : rocoso, pedregoso **2** UNSTEADY : inestable
rod [ˈrɑd] *n* **1** BAR : barra *f,* varilla *f,* vara *f* (de madera) <a fishing rod : una caña (de pescar)> **2** : medida *f* de longitud equivalente a 5.03 metros (5 yardas)
rode → **ride**[1]
rodent [ˈroːdənt] *n* : roedor *m*
rodeo [ˈroːdi,oː, roˈdeɪ,oː] *n, pl* **-deos** : rodeo *m*
roe [ˈroː] *n* : hueva *f*
roe deer *n* : corzo *m*
rogue [ˈroːg] *n* SCOUNDREL : pícaro *m,* -ra *f;* pillo *m,* -lla *f*
roguish [ˈroːgɪʃ] *adj* : pícaro, travieso
role [ˈroːl] *n* : papel *m,* función *f,* rol *m*
roll[1] [ˈroːl] *vt* **1** : hacer rodar <to roll the ball : hacer rodar la pelota> <to roll one's eyes : poner los ojos en blanco> **2** : liar (un cigarillo) **3** *or* **to roll up** : enrollar <to roll (oneself) up into a ball : hacerse una bola> **4** FLATTEN : estirar (masa), laminar (metales), pasar el rodillo por (el césped) **5 to roll up one's sleeves** : arremangarse — *vi* **1** : rodar <the ball kept on rolling : la pelota siguió rodando> **2** SWAY : balancearse <the ship rolled in the waves : el barco se balanceó en las olas> **3** REVERBERATE, SOUND : tronar (dícese del trueno), redoblar (dícese de un tambor) **4 to roll along** PROCEED : ponerse en marcha **5 to roll around** : revolcarse **6 to roll by** : pasar **7 to roll over** : dar una vuelta
roll[2] *n* **1** LIST : lista *f* <to call the roll : pasar lista> <to have on the roll : tener inscrito> **2** *or* **bread roll** : panecito *m,* bolillo *m Mex* **3** : rollo *m* (de papel, de tela, etc.) <a roll of film : un carrete> <a roll of bills : un fajo> **4** : redoble *m* (de tambores), retumbo *m* (del trueno, etc.) **5** ROLLING, SWAYING : balanceo *m*
roller [ˈroːlər] *n* **1** : rodillo *m* **2** CURLER : rulo *m*
roller coaster [ˈroːlər,koːstər] *n* : montaña *f* rusa

roller–skate ['ro:lər,skeɪt] *vi* **-skated; -skating :** patinar (sobre ruedas)
roller skate *n* **:** patín *m* (de ruedas)
rollicking ['rɑlɪkɪŋ] *adj* **:** animado, alegre
rolling pin *n* **:** rodillo *m*
Roman[1] ['ro:mən] *adj* **:** romano
Roman[2] *n* **:** romano *m,* -na *f*
Roman Catholic *n* **:** católico *m,* -ca *f* — **Roman Catholic** *adj*
Roman Catholicism *n* **:** catolicismo *m*
romance[1] [ro'mænts, 'ro:,mænts] *vi* **-manced; -mancing** FANTASIZE **:** fantasear
romance[2] *n* **1 :** romance *m,* novela *f* de caballerías **2 :** novela *f* de amor, novela *f* romántica **3** AFFAIR **:** romance *m,* amorío *m*
Romanian [rʊ'meɪniən, ro-] *n* **1 :** rumano *m,* -na *f* **2 :** rumano *m* (idioma) — **Romanian** *adj*
Roman numeral *n* **:** número *m* romano
romantic [ro'mæntɪk] *adj* **:** romántico — **romantically** [-tɪkli] *adv*
romp[1] ['rɑmp] *vi* FROLIC **:** retozar, jugetear
romp[2] *n* **:** retozo *m*
roof[1] ['ru:f, 'rʊf] *vt* **:** techar
roof[2] *n, pl* **roofs** ['ru:fs, 'rʊfs; 'ru:vz, 'rʊvz] **1 :** techo *m,* tejado *m,* techado *m* **2 roof of the mouth :** paladar *m*
roofing ['ru:fɪŋ, 'rʊfɪŋ] *n* **:** techumbre *f*
rooftop ['ru:f,tɑp, 'rʊf-] *n* ROOF **:** tejado *m*
rook[1] ['rʊk] *vt* CHEAT **:** defraudar, estafar, timar
rook[2] *n* **1 :** grajo *m* (ave) **2 :** torre *f* (en ajedrez)
rookie ['rʊki] *n* **:** novato *m,* -ta *f*
room[1] ['ru:m, 'rʊm] *vi* LODGE **:** alojarse, hospedarse
room[2] *n* **1** SPACE **:** espacio *m,* sitio *m,* lugar *m* <to make room for **:** hacer lugar para> **2 :** cuarto *m,* habitación *f* (en una casa), sala *f* (para reuniones, etc.) **3** BEDROOM **:** dormitorio *m,* habitación *f,* pieza *f* **4** (*indicating possibility or opportunity*) <room for improvement **:** posibilidad de mejorar> <there's no room for error **:** no hay lugar para errores>
roomer ['ru:mər, 'rʊmər] *n* **:** inquilino *m,* -na *f*
rooming house *n* **:** pensión *f*
roommate ['ru:m,meɪt, 'rʊm-] *n* **:** compañero *m,* -ra *f* de cuarto
roomy ['ru:mi, 'rʊmi] *adj* **roomier; -est 1** SPACIOUS **:** espacioso, amplio **2** LOOSE **:** suelto, holgado <a roomy blouse **:** una blusa holgada>
roost[1] ['ru:st] *vi* **:** posarse, dormir (en una percha)
roost[2] *n* **:** percha *f*
rooster ['ru:stər, 'rʊs-] *n* **:** gallo *m*
root[1] ['ru:t, 'rʊt] *vi* **1 :** arraigar <the plant rooted easily **:** la planta arraigó con facilidad> <deeply rooted traditions **:** tradiciones profundamente arraigadas> **2 :** hozar (dícese de los cerdos) <to root around in **:** hurgar en> **3 to root for :** apoyar a, alentar — *vt* **to root out** *or* **to root up :** desarraigar (plantas), extirpar (problemas, etc.)
root[2] *n* **1 :** raíz *f* (de una planta) **2** ORIGIN **:** origen *m,* raíz *f* **3** CORE **:** centro *m,* núcleo *m* <to get to the root of the matter **:** ir al centro del asunto>
rootless ['ru:tləs, 'rʊt-] *adj* **:** desarraigado
rope[1] ['ro:p] *vt* **roped; roping 1** TIE **:** amarrar, atar **2** LASSO **:** lazar **3 to rope off :** acordonar
rope[2] *n* **:** soga *f,* cuerda *f*
rosary ['ro:zəri] *n, pl* **-ries :** rosario *m*
rose[1] → **rise**[1]
rose[2] ['ro:z] *adj* **:** rosa, color de rosa
rose[3] *n* **1 :** rosal *m* (planta), rosa *f* (flor) **2 :** rosa *m* (color)
rosebush ['ro:z,bʊʃ] *n* **:** rosal *m*
rosemary ['ro:z,mɛri] *n, pl* **-maries :** romero *m*
rosette [ro'zɛt] *n* **:** escarapela *f* (hecho de cintas), roseta *f* (en arquitectura)
Rosh Hashanah [,rɑʃhɑ'ʃɑnə, ,ro:ʃ-] *n* **:** el Año Nuevo judío
rosin ['rɑzən] *n* **:** colofonia *f*
roster ['rɑstər] *n* **:** lista *f*
rostrum ['rɑstrəm] *n, pl* **-trums** *or* **-tra** [-trə] **:** tribuna *f,* estrado *m*
rosy ['ro:zi] *adj* **rosier; -est 1 :** sonrosado, de color rosa **2** PROMISING **:** prometedor, halagüeno
rot[1] ['rɑt] *v* **rotted; rotting** *vi* **:** pudrirse, descomponerse — *vt* **:** pudrir, descomponer
rot[2] *n* **:** putrefacción *f,* descomposición *f,* podredumbre *f*
rotary[1] ['ro:t̬əri] *adj* **:** rotativo, rotatorio
rotary[2] *n, pl* **-ries 1 :** máquina *f* rotativa **2** TRAFFIC CIRCLE **:** rotonda *f,* glorieta *f*
rotate ['ro:,teɪt] *v* **-tated; -tating** *vi* REVOLVE **:** girar, rotar — *vt* **1** TURN **:** hacer girar, darle vueltas a **2** ALTERNATE **:** alternar
rotation [ro'teɪʃən] *n* **:** rotación *f*
rote ['ro:t] *n* **to learn by rote :** aprender de memoria
rotor ['ro:t̬ər] *n* **:** rotor *m*
rotten ['rɑtən] *adj* **1** PUTRID **:** podrido, putrefacto **2** CORRUPT **:** corrompido **3** BAD **:** malo <a rotten day **:** un día malísimo>
rottenness ['rɑtənnəs] *n* **:** podredumbre *f*
rotund [ro'tʌnd] *adj* **1** ROUNDED **:** redondeado **2** PLUMP **:** regordete *fam,* llenito *fam*
rouge ['ru:ʒ, 'ru:dʒ] *n* **:** colorete *m*
rough[1] ['rʌf] *vt* **1** ROUGHEN **:** poner áspero **2 to rough out** SKETCH **:** esbozar, bosquejar **3 to rough up** BEAT **:** darle una paliza (a alguien) **4 to rough it :** vivir sin comodidades

rough[2] *adj* **1** COARSE **:** áspero, basto **2** UNEVEN **:** desigual, escabroso, accidentado (dícese del terreno) **3 :** agitado (dícese del mar), tempestuoso (dícese del tiempo), violento (dícese del viento) **4** VIOLENT **:** violento, brutal <a rough neighborhood : un barrio peligroso> **5** DIFFICULT **:** duro, difícil **6** CRUDE **:** rudo, tosco, burdo <a rough cottage : una casita tosca> <a rough draft : un borrador> <a rough sketch : un bosquejo> **7** APPROXIMATE **:** aproximado <a rough idea : una idea aproximada>

rough[3] *n* **1 the rough :** el rough (en golf) **2 in the rough :** en borrador

roughage [ˈrʌfɪdʒ] *n* **:** fibra *f*

roughen [ˈrʌfən] *vt* **:** poner áspero — *vi* **:** ponerse áspero

roughly [ˈrʌfli] *adv* **1 :** bruscamente <to treat roughly : maltratar> **2** CRUDELY **:** burdamente **3** APPROXIMATELY **:** aproximadamente, más o menos

roughneck [ˈrʌfˌnɛk] *n* **:** matón *m*

roughness [ˈrʌfnəs] *n* **:** rudeza *f,* aspereza *f*

roulette [ruːˈlɛt] *n* **:** ruleta *f*

round[1] [ˈraʊnd] *vt* **1 :** redondear <she rounded the edges : redondeó los bordes> **2** TURN **:** doblar <to round the corner : dar la vuelta a la esquina> **3 to round off :** redondear (un número) **4 to round off** *or* **to round out** COMPLETE **:** rematar, terminar **5 to round up** GATHER **:** reunir

round[2] *adv* → **around[1]**

round[3] *adj* **1 :** redondo <a round table : una mesa redonda> <in round numbers : en números redondos> <round shoulders : espaldas cargadas> **2 round trip :** viaje *m* de ida y vuelta

round[4] *n* **1** CIRCLE **:** círculo *m* **2** SERIES **:** serie *f,* sucesión *f* <a round of talks : una ronda de negociaciones> <the daily round : la rutina cotidiana> **3 :** asalto *m* (en boxeo), recorrido *m* (en golf), vuelta *f* (en varios juegos) **4 :** salva *f* (de aplausos) **5 round of drinks :** ronda *f* **6 round of ammunition :** disparo *m,* cartucho *m* **7 rounds** *npl* **:** recorridos *mpl* (de un cartero), rondas *fpl* (de un vigilante), visitas *fpl* (de un médico) <to make the rounds : hacer visitas>

round[5] *prep* → **around[2]**

roundabout [ˈraʊndəˌbaʊt] *adj* **:** indirecto <to speak in a roundabout way : hablar con rodeos>

roundly [ˈraʊndli] *adv* **1** THOROUGHLY **:** completamente **2** BLUNTLY **:** francamente, rotundamente **3** VIGOROUSLY **:** con vigor

roundness [ˈraʊndnəs] *n* **:** redondez *f*

roundup [ˈraʊndˌʌp] *n* **1 :** rodeo *m* (de animales), redada *f* (de delincuentes, etc.) **2** SUMMARY **:** resumen *m*

round up *vt* **1 :** rodear (ganado), reunir (personas) **2** SUMMARIZE **:** hacer un resumen de

roundworm [ˈraʊndˌwərm] *n* **:** lombriz *f* intestinal

rouse [ˈraʊz] *vt* **roused; rousing 1** AWAKE **:** despertar **2** EXCITE **:** excitar <it roused him to fury : lo enfureció>

rout[1] [ˈraʊt] *vt* **1** DEFEAT **:** derrotar, aplastar **2 to rout out :** hacer salir

rout[2] *n* **1** DISPERSAL **:** desbandada *f,* dispersión *f* **2** DEFEAT **:** derrota *f* aplastante

route[1] [ˈruːt, ˈraʊt] *vt* **routed; routing :** dirigir, enviar, encaminar

route[2] *n* **:** camino *m,* ruta *f,* recorrido *m*

routine[1] [ruːˈtiːn] *adj* **:** rutinario — **routinely** *adv*

routine[2] *n* **:** rutina *f*

rove [ˈroːv] *v* **roved; roving** *vi* **:** vagar, errar — *vt* **:** errar por

rover [ˈroːvər] *n* **:** vagabundo *m,* -da *f*

row[1] [ˈroː] *vt* **1 :** avanzar a remo <to row a boat : remar> **2 :** llevar a remo <he rowed me to shore : me llevó hasta la orilla> — *vi* **:** remar

row[2] [ˈraʊ] *n* **1 :** paseo *m* en barca <to go for a row : salir a remar> **2** LINE, RANK **:** fila *f,* hilera *f* **3** SERIES **:** serie *f* <three days in a row : tres días seguidos> **4** RACKET **:** estruendo *m,* bulla *f* **5** QUARREL **:** pelea *f,* riña *f*

rowboat [ˈroːˌboːt] *n* **:** bote *m* de remos

rowdiness [ˈraʊdinəs] *n* **:** bulla *f*

rowdy[1] [ˈraʊdi] *adj* **-dier; -est :** escandaloso, alborotador

rowdy[2] *n, pl* **-dies :** alborotador *m,* -dora *f*

royal[1] [ˈrɔɪəl] *adj* **:** real — **royally** *adv*

royal[2] *n* **:** persona de linaje real, miembro de la familia real

royalty [ˈrɔɪəlti] *n, pl* **-ties 1 :** realeza *f* (posición) **2 :** miembros *mpl* de la familia real **3 royalties** *npl* **:** derechos *mpl* de autor

rub[1] [ˈrʌb] *v* **rubbed; rubbing** *vt* **1 :** frotar, restregar <to rub one's hands together : frotarse las manos> **2** MASSAGE **:** friccionar, masajear **3** CHAFE **:** rozar **4** POLISH **:** frotar, pulir **5** SCRUB **:** fregar **6 to rub elbows with :** codearse con **7 to rub someone the wrong way :** sacar de quicio a alguien, caerle mal a alguien — *vi* **to rub against :** rozar

rub[2] *n* **1** RUBBING **:** frotamiento *m,* fricción *f* **2** DIFFICULTY **:** problema *m*

rubber [ˈrʌbər] *n* **1 :** goma *f,* caucho *m,* hule *m Mex* **2 rubbers** *npl* OVERSHOES **:** chanclos *mpl*

rubber band *n* **:** goma *f* (elástica), gomita *f*

rubber–stamp [ˈrʌbərˈstæmp] *vt* **1** APPROVE **:** aprobar, autorizar **2** STAMP **:** sellar

rubber stamp *n* **:** sello *m* (de goma)

rubbery [ˈrʌbəri] *adj* **:** gomoso

rubbish [ˈrʌbɪʃ] *n* : basura *f,* desechos *mpl,* desperdicios *mpl*
rubble [ˈrʌbəl] *n* : escombros *mpl,* ripio *m*
ruble [ˈruːbəl] *n* : rublo *m*
ruby [ˈruːbi] *n, pl* **-bies 1** : rubí *m* (gema) **2** : color *m* de rubí
rudder [ˈrʌdər] *n* : timón *m*
ruddy [ˈrʌdi] *adj* **-dier; -est** : rubicundo (dícese de la cara, etc.), rojizo (dícese del cielo)
rude [ˈruːd] *adj* **ruder; rudest 1** CRUDE : tosco, rústico **2** IMPOLITE : grosero, descortés, maleducado **3** ABRUPT : brusco <a rude awakening : una sorpresa desagradable>
rudely [ˈruːdli] *adv* : groseramente
rudeness [ˈruːdnəs] *n* **1** IMPOLITENESS : grosería *f,* descortesía *f,* falta *f* de educación **2** ROUGHNESS : tosquedad *f* **3** SUDDENNESS : brusquedad *f*
rudiment [ˈruːdəmənt] *n* : rudimento *m,* noción *f* básica <the rudiments of Spanish : los rudimentos del español>
rudimentary [ˌruːdəˈmɛntəri] *adj* : rudimentario, básico
rue [ˈruː] *vt* **rued; ruing** : lamentar, arrepentirse de
rueful [ˈruːfəl] *adj* **1** PITIFUL : lastimoso **2** REGRETFUL : arrepentido, pesaroso
ruffian [ˈrʌfiən] *n* : matón *m*
ruffle[1] [ˈrʌfəl] *vt* **-fled; -fling 1** AGITATE : agitar, rizar (agua) **2** RUMPLE : arrugar (ropa), despeinar (pelo) **3** ERECT : erizar (plumas) **4** VEX : alterar, irritar, perturbar **5** : fruncir volantes en (tela)
ruffle[2] *n* FLOUNCE : volante *m*
ruffly [ˈrʌfəli] *adj* : con volantes
rug [ˈrʌg] *n* : alfombra *f,* tapete *m*
rugged [ˈrʌgəd] *adj* **1** ROUGH, UNEVEN : accidentado, escabroso <rugged mountains : montañas accidentadas> **2** HARSH : duro, severo **3** ROBUST, STURDY : robusto, fuerte
ruin[1] [ˈruːən] *vt* **1** DESTROY : destruir, arruinar **2** BANKRUPT : arruinar, hacer quebrar
ruin[2] *n* **1** : ruina *f* <to fall into ruin : caer en ruinas> **2** : ruina *f,* perdición *f* <to be the ruin of : ser la perdición de> **3 ruins** *npl* : ruinas *fpl,* restos *mpl* <the ruins of the ancient temple : las ruinas del templo antiguo>
ruinous [ˈruːənəs] *adj* : ruinoso
rule[1] [ˈruːl] *v* **ruled; ruling** *vt* **1** CONTROL, GOVERN : gobernar (un país), controlar (las emociones) **2** DECIDE : decidir, fallar <the judge ruled that... : el juez falló que...> **3** DRAW : trazar con una regla — *vi* **1** GOVERN : gobernar, reinar **2** PREVAIL : prevalecer, imperar **3 to rule against** : fallar en contra de
rule[2] *n* **1** REGULATION : regla *f,* norma *f* **2** CUSTOM, HABIT : regla *f* general <as a rule : por lo general> **3** GOVERNMENT : gobierno *m,* dominio *m* **4** RULER : regla *f* (para medir)
ruler [ˈruːlər] *n* **1** LEADER, SOVEREIGN : gobernante *mf;* soberano *m,* -na *f* **2** : regla *f* (para medir)
ruling [ˈruːlɪŋ] *n* : resolución *f,* fallo *m*
rum [ˈrʌm] *n* : ron *m*
Rumanian [rʊˈmeɪniən] → **Romanian**
rumble[1] [ˈrʌmbəl] *vi* **-bled; -bling** : retumbar, hacer ruidos (dícese del estómago)
rumble[2] *n* : estruendo *m,* ruido *m* sordo, retumbo *m*
ruminant[1] [ˈruːmənənt] *adj* : rumiante
ruminant[2] *n* : rumiante *m*
ruminate [ˈruːməˌneɪt] *vi* **-nated; -nating 1** : rumiar (en zoología) **2** REFLECT : reflexionar, rumiar
rummage [ˈrʌmɪdʒ] *v* **-maged; -maging** *vi* : hurgar — *vt* RANSACK : revolver <they rummaged the attic : revolvieron el ático>
rummy [ˈrʌmi] *n* : rummy *m* (juego de naipes)
rumor[1] [ˈruːmər] *vt* : rumorear <it is rumored that. . . : se rumorea que. . . , se dice que. . .>
rumor[2] *n* : rumor *m*
rump [ˈrʌmp] *n* **1** : ancas *fpl,* grupa *f* (de un animal) **2** : cadera *f* <rump steak : filete de cadera>
rumple [ˈrʌmpəl] *vt* **-pled; -pling** : arrugar (ropa, etc.), despeinar (pelo)
rumpus [ˈrʌmpəs] *n* : lío *m,* jaleo *m fam*
run[1] [ˈrʌn] *v* **ran** [ˈræn]; **run; running** *vi* **1** : correr <she ran to catch the bus : corrió para alcanzar el autobús> <run and fetch the doctor : corre a buscar al médico> **2** : circular, correr <the train runs between Detroit and Chicago : el tren circula entre Detroit y Chicago> <to run on time : ser puntual> **3** FUNCTION : funcionar, ir <the engine runs on gasoline : el motor funciona con gasolina> <to run smoothly : ir bien> **4** FLOW : correr, ir **5** LAST : durar <the movie runs for two hours : la película dura dos horas> <the contract runs for three years : el contrato es válido por tres años> **6** : desteñir, despintar (dícese de los colores) **7** EXTEND : correr, extenderse **8 to run for office** : postularse, presentarse — *vt* **1** : correr <to run 10 miles : correr 10 millas> <to run errands : hacer los mandados> <to run out of town : hacer salir del pueblo> **2** PASS : pasar **3** DRIVE : llevar en coche **4** OPERATE : hacer funcionar (un motor, etc.) **5** : echar <to run water : echar agua> **6** MANAGE : dirigir, llevar (un negocio, etc.) **7** EXTEND : tender (un cable, etc.) **8 to run a risk** : correr un riesgo
run[2] *n* **1** : carrera *f* <at a run : a la carrera, corriendo> <to go for a run : ir a correr> **2** TRIP : vuelta *f,* paseo *m* (en coche), viaje *m* (en avión) **3** SERIES : serie *f* <a run of disappointments : una serie de desilusiones> <in

the long run : a la larga> <in the short run : a corto plazo> 4 DEMAND : gran demanda *f* <a run on the banks : una corrida bancaria> **5** (*used for theatrical productions and films*) <to have a long run : mantenerse mucho tiempo en la cartelera> **6** TYPE : tipo *m* <the average run of students : el tipo más común de estudiante> **7** : carrera *f* (en béisbol) **8** : carrera *f* (en una media) **9 to have the run of** : tener libre acceso de (una casa, etc.) **10 ski run** : pista *f* (de esquí)

runaway[1] [ˈrʌnəˌweɪ] *adj* **1** FUGITIVE : fugitivo **2** UNCONTROLLABLE : incontrolable, fuera de control <runaway inflation : inflación desenfrenada> <a runaway success : un éxito aplastante>

runaway[2] *n* : fugitivo *m*, -va *f*

rundown [ˈrʌnˌdaʊn] *n* SUMMARY : resumen *m*

run–down [ˈrʌnˈdaʊn] *adj* **1** DILAPIDATED : ruinoso, destartalado **2** SICKLY, TIRED : cansado, débil

rung[1] → **ring**[1]

rung[2] [ˈrʌŋ] *n* : peldaño *m*, escalón *m*

run–in [ˈrʌnˌɪn] *n* : disputa *f*, altercado *m*

runner [ˈrʌnər] *n* **1** RACER : corredor *m*, -dora *f* **2** MESSENGER : mensajero *m*, -ra *f* **3** TRACK : riel *m* (de un cajón, etc.) **4** : patín *m* (de un trineo), cuchilla *f* (de un patín) **5** : estolón *m* (planta)

runner–up [ˌrʌnərˈʌp] *n, pl* **runners–up** : subcampeón *m*, -peona *f*

running [ˈrʌnɪŋ] *adj* **1** FLOWING : corriente <running water : agua corriente> **2** CONTINUOUS : continuo <a running battle : una lucha continua> **3** CONSECUTIVE : seguido <six days running : por seis días seguidos>

run over *vt* : atropellar — *vi* OVERFLOW : rebosar

runt [ˈrʌnt] *n* : animal *m* pequeño <the runt of the litter : el más pequeño de la camada>

runway [ˈrʌnˌweɪ] *n* : pista *f* de aterrizaje

rupee [ruːˈpiː, ˈruːˌ-] *n* : rupia *f*

rupture[1] [ˈrʌptʃər] *v* **-tured; -turing** *vt* **1** BREAK, BURST : romper, reventar **2** : causar una hernia en — *vi* : reventarse

rupture[2] *n* **1** BREAK : ruptura *f* **2** HERNIA : hernia *f*

rural [ˈrʊrəl] *adj* : rural, campestre

ruse [ˈruːs, ˈruːz] *n* : treta *f*, ardid *m*, estratagema *f*

rush[1] [ˈrʌʃ] *vi* : correr, ir de prisa <to rush around : correr de un lado a otro> <to rush off : irse corriendo> — *vt* **1** HURRY : apresurar, apurar **2** ATTACK : abalanzarse sobre, asaltar

rush[2] *adj* : urgente

rush[3] *n* **1** HASTE : prisa *f*, apuro *m* **2** SURGE : ráfaga *f* (de aire), torrente *m* (de aguas), avalancha *f* (de gente) **3** DEMAND : demanda *f* <a rush on sugar : una gran demanda para el azúcar> **4** : carga *f* (en futbol americano) **5** : junco *m* (planta)

russet [ˈrʌsət] *n* : color *m* rojizo

Russian [ˈrʌʃən] *n* **1** : ruso *m*, -sa *f* **2** : ruso *m* (idioma) — **Russian** *adj*

rust[1] [ˈrʌst] *vi* : oxidarse — *vt* : oxidar

rust[2] *n* **1** : herrumbre *f*, orín *m*, óxido *m* (en los metales) **2** : roya *f* (en las plantas)

rustic[1] [ˈrʌstɪk] *adj* : rústico, campestre — **rustically** [-tɪkli] *adv*

rustic[2] *n* : rústico *m*, -ca *f*; campesino *m*, -na *f*

rustle[1] [ˈrʌsəl] *v* **-tled; -tling** *vt* **1** : hacer susurrar, hacer crujir <to rustle a newspaper : hacer crujir un periódico> **2** STEAL : robar (ganado) — *vi* : susurrar, crujir

rustle[2] *n* : murmullo *m*, susurro *m*, crujido *m*

rustler [ˈrʌsələr] *n* : ladrón *m*, -drona *f* de ganado

rusty [ˈrʌsti] *adj* **rustier; -est** : oxidado, herrumbroso

rut [ˈrʌt] *n* **1** GROOVE, TRACK : rodada *f*, surco *m* **2 to be in a rut** : ser esclavo de la rutina

ruthless [ˈruːθləs] *adj* : despiadado, cruel — **ruthlessly** *adv*

ruthlessness [ˈruːθləsnəs] *n* : crueldad *f*, falta *f* de piedad

Rwandan [rʊˈɑndən] *n* : ruandés *m*, -desa *f* — **Rwandan** *adj*

rye [ˈraɪ] *n* **1** : centeno *m* **2** *or* **rye whiskey** : whisky *m* de centeno

S

s [ˈɛs] *n, pl* **s's** *or* **ss** [ˈɛsəz] : decimonovena letra del alfabeto inglés

Sabbath [ˈsæbəθ] *n* **1** : sábado *m* (en el judaísmo) **2** : domingo *m* (en el cristianismo)

saber [ˈseɪbər] *n* : sable *m*

sable [ˈseɪbəl] *n* **1** BLACK : negro *m* **2** : marta *f* cebellina (animal)

sabotage[1] [ˈsæbəˌtɑʒ] *vt* **-taged; -taging** : sabotear

sabotage[2] *n* : sabotaje *m*

sac [ˈsæk] *n* : saco *m* (anatómico)

saccharin [ˈsækərən] *n* : sacarina *f*

saccharine *adj* [ˈsækərən, -ˌriːn, -ˌraɪn] : meloso, empalagoso

sachet [sæˈʃeɪ] *n* : bolsita *f* (perfumada)

sack[1] [ˈsæk] *vt* **1** FIRE : echar (del trabajo), despedir **2** PLUNDER : saquear

sack[2] *n* BAG : saco *m*

sacrament [ˈsækrəmənt] *n* : sacramento *m*

sacramental [ˌsækrəˈmɛntəl] *adj* : sacramental

sacred [ˈseɪkrəd] *adj* **1** RELIGIOUS : sagrado, sacro <sacred texts : textos sagrados> **2** HOLY : sagrado **3 sacred to** : consagrado a

sacrifice[1] [ˈsækrəˌfaɪs] *vt* **-ficed; -ficing 1** : sacrificar **2 to sacrifice oneself** : sacrificarse

sacrifice[2] *n* : sacrificio *m*

sacrilege [ˈsækrəlɪdʒ] *n* : sacrilegio *m*

sacrilegious [ˌsækrəˈlɪdʒəs, -ˈliː-] *adj* : sacrílego

sacrosanct [ˈsækroˌsæŋkt] *adj* : sacrosanto

sad [ˈsæd] *adj* **sadder; saddest** : triste — **sadly** *adv*

sadden [ˈsædən] *vt* : entristecer

saddle[1] [ˈsædəl] *vt* **-dled; -dling** : ensillar

saddle[2] *n* : silla *f* (de montar)

sadism [ˈseɪˌdɪzəm, ˈsæ-] *n* : sadismo *m*

sadist [ˈseɪdɪst, ˈsæ-] *n* : sádico *m*, -ca *f*

sadistic [səˈdɪstɪk] *adj* : sádico — **sadistically** [-tɪkli] *adv*

sadness [ˈsædnəs] *n* : tristeza *f*

safari [səˈfɑri, -ˈfær-] *n* : safari *m*

safe[1] [ˈseɪf] *adj* **safer; safest 1** UNHARMED : ileso <safe and sound : sano y salvo> **2** SECURE : seguro **3 to be on the safe side** : para mayor seguridad **4 to play it safe** : ir a la segura

safe[2] *n* : caja *f* fuerte

safeguard[1] [ˈseɪfˌgɑrd] *vt* : salvaguardar, proteger

safeguard[2] *n* : salvaguarda *f*, protección *f*

safekeeping [ˈseɪfˈkiːpɪŋ] *n* : custodia *f*, protección *f* <to put into safekeeping : poner en buen recaudo>

safely [ˈseɪfli] *adv* **1** UNHARMED : sin incidentes, sin novedades <they landed safely : aterrizaron sin novedades> **2** SECURELY : con toda seguridad, sin peligro

safety [ˈseɪfti] *n, pl* **-ties** : seguridad *f*

safety belt *n* : cinturón *m* de seguridad

safety pin *n* : alfiler *m* de gancho, alfiler *m* de seguridad, imperdible *m Spain*

saffron [ˈsæfrən] *n* : azafrán *m*

sag[1] [ˈsæg] *vi* **sagged; sagging 1** DROOP, SINK : combarse, hundirse, inclinarse **2** : colgar, caer <his jowls sagged : le colgaban las mejillas> **3** FLAG : flaquear, decaer <his spirits sagged : se le flaqueó el ánimo>

sag[2] *n* : combadura *f*

saga [ˈsɑgə, ˈsæ-] *n* : saga *f*

sagacious [səˈgeɪʃəs] *adj* : sagaz

sage[1] [ˈseɪdʒ] *adj* **sager; -est** : sabio — **sagely** *adv*

sage[2] *n* **1** : sabio *m*, -bia *f* **2** : salvia *f* (planta)

sagebrush [ˈseɪdʒˌbrʌʃ] *n* : artemisa *f*

Sagittarius [ˌsædʒəˈtɛriəs] *n* : Sagitario *mf*

said → **say**

sail[1] [ˈseɪl] *vi* **1** : navegar (en un barco) **2** : ir fácilmente <we sailed right in : entramos sin ningún problema> — *vt* **1** : gobernar (un barco) **2 to sail the seas** : cruzar los mares

sail[2] *n* **1** : vela *f* (de un barco) **2** : viaje *m* en velero <to go for a sail : salir a navegar>

sailboat [ˈseɪlˌboːt] *n* : velero *m*, barco *m* de vela

sailfish [ˈseɪlˌfɪʃ] *n* : pez *m* vela

sailor [ˈseɪlər] *n* : marinero *m*

saint [ˈseɪnt, *before a name* ˌseɪnt *or* sənt] *n* : santo *m*, -ta *f* <Saint Francis : San Francisco> <Saint Rose : Santa Rosa>

saintliness [ˈseɪntlinəs] *n* : santidad *f*

saintly [ˈseɪntli] *adj* **saintlier; -est** : santo

sake [ˈseɪk] *n* **1** BENEFIT : bien *m* <for the children's sake : por el bien de los niños> **2** (*indicating an end or a purpose*) <art for art's sake : el arte por el arte> <let's say, for argument's sake, that he's wrong : pongamos que está equivocado> **3 for goodness' sake!** : ¡por (el amor de) Dios!

salable *or* **saleable** [ˈseɪləbəl] *adj* : vendible

salacious [səˈleɪʃəs] *adj* : salaz — **salaciously** *adv*

salad [ˈsæləd] *n* : ensalada *f*

salamander [ˈsæləˌmændər] *n* : salamandra *f*

salami [səˈlɑmi] *n* : salami *m*

salary [ˈsæləri] *n, pl* **-ries** : sueldo *m*

sale [ˈseɪl] *n* **1** SELLING : venta *f* **2** : liquidación *f*, rebajas *fpl* <on sale : de rebaja> **3 sales** *npl* : ventas *fpl* <to work in sales : trabajar en ventas>

salesman [ˈseɪlzmən] *n, pl* **-men** [-mən, -ˌmɛn] **1** : vendedor *m*, dependiente *m* (en una tienda) **2 traveling salesman** : viajante *m*, representante *m*

salesperson [ˈseɪlzˌpərsən] *n* : vendedor *m*, -dora *f*; dependiente *m*, -ta *f* (en una tienda)

saleswoman [ˈseɪlzˌwʊmən] *n, pl* **-women** [-ˌwɪmən] **1** : vendedora *f*, dependienta *f* (en una tienda) **2 traveling saleswoman** : viajante *f*, representante *f*

salient [ˈseɪljənt] *adj* : saliente, sobresaliente

saline [ˈseɪˌliːn, -ˌlaɪn] *adj* : salino

saliva [səˈlaɪvə] *n* : saliva *f*

salivary [ˈsæləˌvɛri] *adj* : salival <salivary gland : glándula salival>

salivate [ˈsæləˌveɪt] *vi* **-vated; -vating** : salivar

sallow [ˈsæloː] *adj* : amarillento, cetrino

sally[1] [ˈsæli] *vi* **-lied; -lying** SET OUT : salir, hacer una salida

sally[2] *n, pl* **-lies 1** : salida *f* (militar), misión *f* **2** QUIP : salida *f*, ocurrencia *f*

salmon ['sæmən] *ns & pl* **1 :** salmón *m* (pez) **2 :** color *m* salmón

salon [sə'lɑn, 'sæˌlɑn, sæ'lɔ̃] *n* **:** salón *m* <beauty salon : salón de belleza>

saloon [sə'lu:n] *n* **1** HALL **:** salón *m* (en un barco) **2** BARROOM **:** bar *m*

salsa ['sɔlsə, 'sɑl-] *n* **:** salsa *f* mexicana, salsa *f* picante

salt[1] ['sɔlt] *vt* **:** salar, echarle sal a

salt[2] *adj* **:** salado

salt[3] *n* **:** sal *f*

saltwater ['sɔltˌwɔt̬ər, -ˌwɑ-] *adj* **:** de agua salada

salty ['sɔlt̬i] *adj* **saltier; -est :** salado

salubrious [sə'lu:briəs] *adj* **:** salubre

salutary ['sæljəˌtɛri] *adj* **:** saludable, salubre

salutation [ˌsæljə'teɪʃən] *n* **:** saludo *m,* salutación *f*

salute[1] [sə'lu:t] *v* **-luted; -luting** *vt* **1 :** saludar (con gestos o ceremonias) **2** ACCLAIM **:** reconocer, aclamar — *vi* **:** hacer un saludo

salute[2] *n* **1 :** saludo *m* (gesto), salva *f* (de cañonazos) **2** TRIBUTE **:** reconocimiento *m,* homenaje *m*

salvage[1] ['sælvɪdʒ] *vt* **-vaged; -vaging :** salvar, rescatar

salvage[2] *n* **1** SALVAGING **:** salvamento *m,* rescate *m* **2 :** objetos *mpl* salvados

salvation [sæl'veɪʃən] *n* **:** salvación *f*

salve[1] ['sæv, 'sav] *vt* **salved; salving :** calmar, apaciguar <to salve one's conscience : aliviarse la conciencia>

salve[2] *n* **:** ungüento *m*

salvo ['sælˌvo:] *n, pl* **-vos** *or* **-voes :** salva *f*

same[1] ['seɪm] *adj* **:** mismo, igual <the results are the same : los resultados son iguales> <he said the same thing as you : dijo lo mismo que tú>

same[2] *pron* **:** mismo <it's all the same to me : me da lo mismo> <the same to you! : ¡igualmente!>

sameness ['seɪmnəs] *n* **1** SIMILARITY **:** identidad *f,* semejanza *f* **2** MONOTONY **:** monotonía *f*

sample[1] ['sæmpəl] *vt* **-pled; -pling :** probar

sample[2] *n* **:** muestra *f,* prueba *f*

sampler ['sæmplər] *n* **:** dechado *m* (en bordado)

sanatorium [ˌsænə'toriəm] *n, pl* **-riums** *or* **-ria** [-iə] **:** sanatorio *m*

sanctify ['sæŋktəˌfaɪ] *vt* **-fied; -fying :** santificar

sanctimonious [ˌsæŋktə'mo:niəs] *adj* **:** beato, santurrón

sanction[1] ['sæŋkʃən] *vt* **:** sancionar, aprobar

sanction[2] *n* **1** AUTHORIZATION **:** sanción *f,* autorización *f* **2 sanctions** *npl* **:** sanciones *fpl* <to impose sanctions on : imponer sanciones a>

sanctity ['sæŋktət̬i] *n, pl* **-ties :** santidad *f*

sanctuary ['sæŋktʃʊˌɛri] *n, pl* **-aries 1 :** presbiterio *m* (en una iglesia) **2** REFUGE **:** refugio *m,* asilo *m*

sand[1] ['sænd] *vt* **:** lijar (madera)

sand[2] *n* **:** arena *f*

sandal ['sændəl] *n* **:** sandalia *f*

sandbank ['sændˌbæŋk] *n* **:** banco *m* de arena

sandpaper *n* **:** papel *m* de lija

sandpiper ['sændˌpaɪpər] *n* **:** andarríos *m*

sandstone ['sændˌsto:n] *n* **:** arenisca *f*

sandstorm ['sændˌstɔrm] *n* **:** tormenta *f* de arena

sandwich[1] ['sændˌwɪtʃ] *vt* **:** intercalar, encajonar, meter (entre dos cosas)

sandwich[2] *n* **:** sandwich *m,* emparedado *m,* bocadillo *m Spain*

sandy ['sændi] *adj* **sandier; -est :** arenoso

sane ['seɪn] *adj* **saner; sanest 1 :** cuerdo **2** SENSIBLE **:** sensato, razonable

sang → **sing**

sanguine ['sæŋgwən] *adj* **1** RUDDY **:** sanguíneo, rubicundo **2** HOPEFUL **:** optimista

sanitarium [ˌsænə'tɛriəm] *n, pl* **-iums** *or* **-ia** [-iə] → **sanatorium**

sanitary ['sænətɛri] *adj* **1 :** sanitario <sanitary measures : medidas sanitarias> **2** HYGIENIC **:** higiénico **3 sanitary napkin :** compresa *f,* paño *m* higiénico

sanitation [ˌsænə'teɪʃən] *n* **:** sanidad *f*

sanity ['sænət̬i] *n* **:** cordura *f,* razón *f* <to lose one's sanity : perder el juicio>

sank → **sink**

Santa Claus ['sæntəˌklɔz] *n* **:** Papá Noel, San Nicolás

sap[1] ['sæp] *vt* **sapped; sapping 1** UNDERMINE **:** socavar **2** WEAKEN **:** minar, debilitar

sap[2] *n* **1 :** savia *f* (de una planta) **2** SUCKER **:** inocentón *m,* -tona *f*

sapling ['sæplɪŋ] *n* **:** árbol *m* joven

sapphire ['sæˌfaɪr] *n* **:** zafiro *m*

sarcasm ['sɑrˌkæzəm] *n* **:** sarcasmo *m*

sarcastic [sɑr'kæstɪk] *adj* **:** sarcástico — **sarcastically** [-tɪkli] *adv*

sarcophagus [sɑr'kɑfəgəs] *n, pl* **-gi** [-ˌgaɪ, -ˌdʒaɪ] **:** sarcófago *m*

sardine [sɑr'di:n] *n* **:** sardina *f*

sardonic [sɑr'dɑnɪk] *adj* **:** sardónico — **sardonically** [-nɪkli] *adv*

sarsaparilla [ˌsæspə'rɪlə, ˌsɑrs-] *n* **:** zarzaparrilla *f*

sash ['sæʃ] *n* **1 :** faja *f* (de un vestido), fajín *m* (de un uniforme) **2** *pl* **sash :** marco *m* (de una ventana)

sassafras ['sæsəˌfræs] *n* **:** sasafrás *m*

sassy ['sæsi] *adj* **sassier; -est** → **saucy**

sat → **sit**

Satan ['seɪtən] *n* **:** Satanás *m,* Satán *m*

satanic [sə'tænɪk, seɪ-] *adj* **:** satánico — **satanically** [-nɪkli] *adv*

satchel ['sætʃəl] *n* **:** cartera *f,* saco *m*

sate ['seɪt] *vt* **sated; sating :** saciar

satellite ['sætə,laɪt] *n* **:** satélite *m* <spy satellite **:** satélite espía>
satiate ['seɪʃi,eɪt] *vt* **-ated; -ating :** saciar, hartar
satin ['sætən] *n* **:** raso *m,* satín *m,* satén *m*
satire ['sæ,taɪr] *n* **:** sátira *f*
satiric [sə'tɪrɪk] *or* **satirical** [-ɪkəl] *adj* **:** satírico
satirize ['sætə,raɪz] *vt* **-rized; -rizing :** satirizar
satisfaction [,sætəs'fækʃən] *n* **:** satisfacción *f*
satisfactory [,sætəs'fæktəri] *adj* **:** satisfactorio, bueno — **satisfactorily** [-rəli] *adv*
satisfy ['sætəs,faɪ] *v* **-fied; -fying** *vt* **1** PLEASE **:** satisfacer, contentar **2** CONVINCE **:** convencer **3** FULFILL **:** satisfacer, cumplir con, llenar **4** SETTLE **:** pagar, saldar (una cuenta) — *vi* SUFFICE **:** bastar
saturate ['sætʃə,reɪt] *vt* **-rated; -rating 1** SOAK **:** empapar **2** FILL **:** saturar
saturation [,sætʃə'reɪʃən] *n* **:** saturación *f*
Saturday ['sætər,deɪ, -di] *n* **:** sábado *m*
Saturn ['sætərn] *n* **:** Saturno *m*
satyr ['seɪtər, 'sæ-] *n* **:** sátiro *m*
sauce ['sɔs] *n* **:** salsa *f*
saucepan ['sɔs,pæn] *n* **:** cacerola *f,* cazo *m,* cazuela *f*
saucer ['sɔsər] *n* **:** platillo *m*
sauciness ['sɔsinəs] *n* **:** descaro *m,* frescura *f*
saucy ['sɔsi] *adj* **saucier; -est** IMPUDENT **:** descarado, fresco *fam* — **saucily** *adv*
sauna ['sɔnə, 'saʊnə] *n* **:** sauna *mf*
saunter ['sɔntər, 'sɑn-] *vi* **:** pasear, parsearse
sausage ['sɔsɪdʒ] *n* **:** salchicha *f,* embutido *m*
sauté [sɔ'teɪ, soː-] *vt* **-téed** *or* **-téd; -téing :** saltear, sofreír
savage[1] ['sævɪdʒ] *adj* **:** salvaje, feroz — **savagely** *adv*
savage[2] *n* **:** salvaje *mf*
savagery ['sævɪdʒri, -dʒəri] *n, pl* **-ries 1** FEROCITY **:** ferocidad *f* **2** WILDNESS **:** salvajismo *m*
save[1] ['seɪv] *vt* **saved; saving 1** RESCUE **:** salvar, rescatar **2** PRESERVE **:** preservar, conservar **3** KEEP **:** guardar, ahorrar (dinero), almacenar (alimentos)
save[2] *prep* EXCEPT **:** salvo, excepto, menos
savior ['seɪvjər] *n* **1 :** salvador *m,* -dora *f* **2 the Savior :** el Salvador *m*
savor[1] ['seɪvər] *vt* **:** saborear
savor[2] *n* **:** sabor *m*
savory ['seɪvəri] *adj* **:** sabroso
saw[1] → **see**
saw[2] ['sɔ] *vt* **sawed; sawed** *or* **sawn** ['sɔn]; **sawing :** serrar, cortar (con sierra)
saw[3] *n* **:** sierra *f*
sawdust ['sɔ,dʌst] *n* **:** aserrín *m,* serrín *m*
sawhorse ['sɔ,hɔrs] *n* **:** caballete *m,* burro *m* (en carpintería)
sawmill ['sɔ,mɪl] *n* **:** aserradero *m*
saxophone ['sæksə,foːn] *n* **:** saxofón *m*
say[1] ['seɪ] *v* **said** ['sɛd]; **saying; says** ['sɛz] *vt* **1** EXPRESS, UTTER **:** decir, expresar <to say no **:** decir que no> <that goes without saying **:** ni que decir tiene> <no sooner said than done **:** dicho y hecho> <to say again **:** repetir> <to say one's prayers **:** rezar> **2** INDICATE **:** marcar, poner <my watch says three o'clock **:** mi reloj marca las tres> <what does the sign say? **:** ¿qué pone el letrero?> **3** ALLEGE **:** decir <it's said that she's pretty **:** se dice que es bonita> — *vi* **:** decir
say[2] *n, pl* **says** ['seɪz] **:** voz *f,* opinión *f* <to have no say **:** no tener ni voz ni voto> <to have one's say **:** dar uno su opinión>
saying ['seɪɪŋ] *n* **:** dicho *m,* refrán *m*
scab ['skæb] *n* **1 :** costra *f,* postilla *f* (en una herida) **2** STRIKEBREAKER **:** rompehuelgas *mf,* esquirol *mf*
scabbard ['skæbərd] *n* **:** vaina *f* (de una espada), funda *f* (de un puñal, etc.)
scabby ['skæbi] *adj* **scabbier; -est :** lleno de costras
scaffold ['skæfəld, -,foːld] *n* **1** *or* **scaffolding :** andamio *m* (para obreros, etc.) **2 :** patíbulo *m,* cadalso *m* (para ejecuciones)
scald ['skɔld] *vt* **1** BURN **:** escaldar **2** HEAT **:** calentar (hasta el punto de ebullición)
scale[1] ['skeɪl] *v* **scaled; scaling** *vt* **1 :** escamar (un pescado) **2** CLIMB **:** escalar (un muro, etc.) **3 to scale down :** reducir — *vi* WEIGH **:** pesar <he scaled in at 200 pounds **:** pesó 200 libras>
scale[2] *n* **1** *or* **scales :** balanza *f,* báscula *f* (para pesar) **2 :** escama *f* (de un pez, etc.) **3** EXTENT **:** escala *f,* proporción *f* <wage scale **:** escala salarial> **4 :** escala *f* (en música, en cartografía, etc.) <to draw to scale **:** dibujar a escala>
scallion ['skæljən] *n* **:** cebollino *m,* cebolleta *f*
scallop ['skɑləp, 'skæ-] *n* **1 :** vieira *f* (molusco) **2 :** festón *m* (decoración)
scalp[1] ['skælp] *vt* **:** arrancar la cabellera a
scalp[2] *n* **:** cuero *m* cabelludo
scalpel ['skælpəl] *n* **:** bisturí *m,* escalpelo *m*
scaly ['skeɪli] *adj* **scalier; -est :** escamoso
scam ['skæm] *n* **:** estafa *f,* timo *m fam,* chanchullo *m fam*
scamp ['skæmp] *n* **:** bribón *m,* -bona *f;* granuja *mf;* travieso *m,* -sa *f*
scamper ['skæmpər] *vi* **:** corretear

scan[1] [ˈskæn] *vt* **scanned; scanning 1** : escandir (versos) **2** SCRUTINIZE : escudriñar, escrutar <to scan the horizon : escudriñar el horizonte> **3** PERUSE : echarle un vistazo a (un periódico, etc.) **4** EXPLORE : explorar (con radar), hacer un escáner de (en ecografía) **5** : escanear (una imagen)
scan[2] *n* **1** : ecografía *f*, examen *m* ultrasónico (en medicina) **2** : imagen *f* escaneada (en una computadora)
scandal [ˈskændəl] *n* **1** DISGRACE, OUTRAGE : escándalo *m* **2** GOSSIP : habladurías *fpl*, chismes *mpl*
scandalize [ˈskændəlˌaɪz] *vt* **-ized; -izing** : escandalizar
scandalous [ˈskændələs] *adj* : de escándalo
Scandinavian[1] [ˌskændəˈneɪviən] *adj* : escandinavo
Scandinavian[2] *n* : escandinavo *m*, -va *f*
scanner [ˈskænər] *n* : escáner *m*, scanner *m*
scant [ˈskænt] *adj* : escaso
scanty [ˈskænti] *adj* **scantier; -est** : exiguo, escaso <a scanty meal : una comida insuficiente> — **scantily** [-təli] *adv*
scapegoat [ˈskeɪpˌgoːt] *n* : chivo *m* expiatorio, cabeza *f* de turco
scapula [ˈskæpjələ] *n, pl* **-lae** [-ˌliː, -ˌlaɪ] *or* **-las** → **shoulder blade**
scar[1] [ˈskɑr] *v* **scarred; scarring** *vt* : dejar una cicatriz en — *vi* : cicatrizar
scar[2] *n* : cicatriz *f*, marca *f*
scarab [ˈskærəb] *n* : escarabajo *m*
scarce [ˈskɛrs] *adj* **scarcer; -est** : escaso
scarcely [ˈskɛrsli] *adv* **1** BARELY : apenas **2** : ni mucho menos, ni nada que se le parezca <he's scarcely an expert : ciertamente no es experto>
scarcity [ˈskɛrsəṭi] *n, pl* **-ties** : escasez *f*
scare[1] [ˈskɛr] *vt* **scared; scaring** : asustar, espantar
scare[2] *n* **1** FRIGHT : susto *m*, sobresalto *m* **2** ALARM : pánico *m*
scarecrow [ˈskɛrˌkroː] *n* : espantapájaros *m*, espantajo *m*
scarf [ˈskɑrf] *n, pl* **scarves** [ˈskɑrvz] *or* **scarfs 1** MUFFLER : bufanda *f* **2** KERCHIEF : pañuelo *m*
scarlet [ˈskɑrlət] *n* : escarlata *f* — **scarlet** *adj*
scarlet fever *n* : escarlatina *f*
scary [ˈskɛri] *adj* **scarier; -est** : espantoso, pavoroso
scathing [ˈskeɪðɪŋ] *adj* : mordaz, cáustico
scatter [ˈskæṭər] *vt* : esparcir, desparramar — *vi* DISPERSE : dispersarse
scavenge [ˈskævəndʒ] *v* **-venged; -venging** *vt* : rescatar (de la basura), pepenar *CA, Mex* — *vi* : rebuscar, hurgar en la basura <to scavenge for food : andar buscando comida>
scavenger [ˈskævəndʒər] *n* **1** : persona *f* que rebusca en las basuras; pepenador *m*, -dora *f CA, Mex* **2** : carroñero *m*, -ra *f* (animal)
scenario [səˈnæriˌoː, -ˈnɑr-] *n, pl* **-ios 1** PLOT : argumento *m* (en teatro), guión *m* (en cine) **2** SITUATION : situación *f* hipotética <in the worst-case scenario : en el peor de los casos>
scene [ˈsiːn] *n* **1** : escena *f* (en una obra de teatro) **2** SCENERY : decorado *m* (en el teatro) **3** VIEW : escena *f* **4** LOCALE : escenario *m* **5** COMMOTION, FUSS : escándalo *m*, escena *f* <to make a scene : armar un escándalo>
scenery [ˈsiːnəri] *n, pl* **-eries 1** : decorado *m* (en el teatro) **2** LANDSCAPE : paisaje *m*
scenic [ˈsiːnɪk] *adj* : pintoresco
scent[1] [ˈsɛnt] *vt* **1** SMELL : oler, olfatear **2** PERFUME : perfumar **3** SENSE : sentir, percibir
scent[2] *n* **1** ODOR : olor *m*, aroma *m* **2** : olfato *m* <a dog with a keen scent : un perro con un buen olfato> **3** PERFUME : perfume *m*
scented [ˈsɛntəd] *adj* : perfumado
scepter [ˈsɛptər] *n* : cetro *m*
sceptic [ˈskɛptɪk] → **skeptic**
schedule[1] [ˈskɛˌdʒuːl, -dʒəl, *esp Brit* ˈʃɛdˌjuːl] *vt* **-uled; -uling** : planear, programar
schedule[2] *n* **1** PLAN : programa *m*, plan *m* <on schedule : según lo previsto> <behind schedule : atrasado, con retraso> **2** TIMETABLE : horario *m*
scheme[1] [ˈskiːm] *vi* **schemed; scheming** : intrigar, conspirar
scheme[2] *n* **1** PLAN : plan *m*, proyecto *m* **2** PLOT, TRICK : intriga *f*, ardid *m* **3** FRAMEWORK : esquema *f* <a color scheme : una combinación de colores>
schemer [ˈskiːmər] *n* : intrigante *mf*
schism [ˈsɪzəm, ˈskɪ-] *n* : cisma *m*
schizophrenia [ˌskɪtsəˈfriːniə, ˌskɪzə-, -ˈfrɛ-] *n* : esquizofrenia *f*
schizophrenic [ˌskɪtsəˈfrɛnɪk, ˌskɪzə-] *n* : esquizofrénico *m*, -ca *f* — **schizophrenic** *adj*
scholar [ˈskɑlər] *n* **1** STUDENT : escolar *mf*; alumno *m*, -na *f* **2** EXPERT : especialista *mf*
scholarly [ˈskɑlərli] *adj* : erudito
scholarship [ˈskɑlərˌʃɪp] *n* **1** LEARNING : erudición *f* **2** GRANT : beca *f*
scholastic [skəˈlæstɪk] *adj* : académico
school[1] [ˈskuːl] *vt* : instruir, enseñar
school[2] *n* **1** : escuela *f*, colegio *m* (institución) **2** : estudiantes *mfpl* y profesores *mpl* (de una escuela) **3** : escuela *f* (en pintura, etc.) <the Flemish school : la escuela flamenca> **4 school of fish** : banco *m*, cardumen *m*
schoolboy [ˈskuːlˌbɔɪ] *n* : escolar *m*, colegial *m*
schoolgirl [ˈskuːlˌgərl] *n* : escolar *f*, colegiala *f*

schoolhouse ['skuːl,haʊs] *n* : escuela *f*
schoolmate ['skuːl,meɪt] *n* : compañero *m*, -ra *f* de escuela
schoolroom ['skuːl,ruːm, -,rʊm] → **classroom**
schoolteacher ['skuːl,tiːtʃər] *n* : maestro *m*, -tra *f*; profesor *m*, -sora *f*
schooner ['skuːnər] *n* : goleta *f*
science ['saɪən*t*s] *n* : ciencia *f*
scientific [,saɪən'tɪfɪk] *adj* : científico — **scientifically** [-fɪkli] *adv*
scientist ['saɪəntɪst] *n* : científico *m*, -ca *f*
scintillating ['sɪntə,leɪt̬ɪŋ] *adj* : chispeante, brillante
scissors ['sɪzərz] *npl* : tijeras *fpl*
scoff ['skɑf] *vi* **to scoff at** : burlarse de, mofarse de
scold ['skoːld] *vt* : regañar, reprender, reñir
scoop[1] ['skuːp] *vt* **1** : sacar (con pala o cucharón) **2 to scoop out** HOLLOW : vaciar, ahuecar
scoop[2] *n* : pala *f* (para harina, etc.), cucharón *m* (para helado, etc.)
scoot ['skuːt] *vi* : ir rápidamente <she scooted around the corner : volvió la esquina a toda prisa>
scooter ['skuːt̬ər] *n* : patineta *f*, monopatín *m*, patinete *m*
scope ['skoːp] *n* **1** RANGE : alcance *m*, ámbito *m*, extensión *f* **2** OPPORTUNITY : posibilidades *fpl*, libertad *f*
scorch ['skɔrtʃ] *vt* : chamuscar, quemar
score[1] ['skor] *v* **scored; scoring** *vt* **1** RECORD : anotar **2** MARK, SCRATCH : marcar, rayar **3** : marcar, meter (en deportes) **4** GAIN : ganar, apuntarse **5** GRADE : calificar (exámenes, etc.) **6** : instrumentar, orquestar (música) — *vi* **1** : marcar (en deportes) **2** : obtener una puntuación (en un examen)
score[2] *n, pl* **scores 1** *or pl* **score** TWENTY : veintena *f* **2** LINE, SCRATCH : línea *f*, marca *f* **3** : resultado *m* (en deportes) <what's the score? : ¿cómo va el marcador?> **4** GRADE, POINTS : calificación *f* (en un examen), puntuación *f* (en un concurso) **5** ACCOUNT : cuenta *f* <to settle a score : ajustar una cuenta> <on that score : a ese respecto> **6** : partitura *f* (musical)
scorn[1] ['skɔrn] *vt* : despreciar, menospreciar, desdeñar
scorn[2] *n* : desprecio *m*, menosprecio *m*, desdén *m*
scornful ['skɔrnfəl] *adj* : desdeñoso, despreciativo — **scornfully** *adv*
Scorpio ['skɔrpi,oː] *n* : Escorpio *mf*, Escorpión *mf*
scorpion ['skɔrpiən] *n* : alacrán *m*, escorpión *m*
Scot ['skɑt] *n* : escocés *m*, -cesa *f*
Scotch[1] ['skɑtʃ] *adj* → **Scottish**[1]
Scotch[2] *npl* **the Scotch** : los escoceses
scot–free ['skɑt'friː] *adj* **to get off scot–free** : salir impune, quedar sin castigo
Scots ['skɑts] *n* : escocés *m* (idioma)
Scottish[1] ['skɑtɪʃ] *adj* : escocés
Scottish[2] *n* → **Scots**
scoundrel ['skaʊndrəl] *n* : sinvergüenza *mf;* bellaco *m*, -ca *f*
scour ['skaʊər] *vt* **1** EXAMINE, SEARCH : registrar (un área), revisar (documentos, etc.) **2** SCRUB : fregar, restregar
scourge[1] ['skərdʒ] *vt* **scourged; scourging** : azotar
scourge[2] *n* : azote *m*
scout[1] ['skaʊt] *vi* **1** RECONNOITER : reconocer **2 to scout around for** : explorar en busca de
scout[2] *n* **1** : explorador *m*, -dora *f* **2** *or* **talent scout** : cazatalentos *mf*
scow ['skaʊ] *n* : barcaza *f*, gabarra *f*
scowl[1] ['skaʊl] *vi* : fruncir el ceño
scowl[2] *n* : ceño *m* fruncido
scram ['skræm] *vi* **scrammed; scramming** : largarse
scramble[1] ['skræmbəl] *v* **-bled; -bling** *vi* **1** : trepar, gatear (con torpeza) <he scrambled over the fence : se trepó a la cerca con dificultad> **2** STRUGGLE : pelearse (por) <they scrambled for seats : se pelearon por los asientos> — *vt* **1** JUMBLE : mezclar **2 to scramble eggs** : hacer huevos revueltos
scramble[2] *n* : rebatiña *f*, pelea *f*
scrap[1] ['skræp] *v* **scrapped; scrapping** *vt* DISCARD : desechar — *vi* FIGHT : pelearse
scrap[2] *n* **1** FRAGMENT : pedazo *m*, trozo *m* **2** FIGHT : pelea *f* **3** *or* **scrap metal** : chatarra *f* **4 scraps** *npl* LEFTOVERS : restos *mpl*, sobras *fpl*
scrapbook ['skræp,bʊk] *n* : álbum *m* de recortes
scrape[1] ['skreɪp] *v* **scraped; scraping** *vt* **1** GRAZE, SCRATCH : rozar, rascar <to scrape one's knee : rasparse la rodilla> **2** CLEAN : raspar <to scrape carrots : raspar zanahorias> **3 to scrape off** : raspar (pintura, etc.) **4 to scrape up** *or* **to scrape together** : juntar, reunir poco a poco — *vi* **1** RUB : rozar **2 to scrape by** : arreglárselas, ir tirando
scrape[2] *n* **1** SCRAPING : raspadura *f* **2** SCRATCH : rasguño *m* **3** PREDICAMENT : apuro *m*, aprieto *m*
scratch[1] ['skrætʃ] *vt* **1** : arañar, rasguñar <to scratch an itch : rascarse> **2** MARK : rayar, marcar **3 to scratch out** : tachar
scratch[2] *n* **1** : rasguño *m*, arañazo *m* (en la piel), rayón *m* (en un mueble, etc.) **2** : sonido *m* rasposo <I heard a scratch at the door : oí como que raspaban a la puerta>
scratchy ['skrætʃi] *adj* **scratchier; -est** : áspero, que pica <a scratchy sweater : un suéter que pica>
scrawl[1] ['skrɔl] *v* : garabatear
scrawl[2] *n* : garabato *m*

scrawny [ˈskrɔni] *adj* **scrawnier; -est** : flaco, escuálido
scream[1] [ˈskriːm] *vi* : chillar, gritar
scream[2] *n* : chillido *m,* grito *m*
screech[1] [ˈskriːtʃ] *vi* : chillar (dícese de las personas o de los animales), chirriar (dícese de los frenos, etc.)
screech[2] *n* 1 : chillido *m,* grito *m* (de una persona o un animal) 2 : chirrido *m* (de frenos, etc.)
screen[1] [ˈskriːn] *vt* **1** SHIELD : proteger **2** CONCEAL : tapar, ocultar **3** EXAMINE : someter a una revisión, hacerle un chequeo (a un paciente) **4** SIEVE : cribar
screen[2] *n* **1** PARTITION : biombo *m,* pantalla *f* **2** SIEVE : criba *f* **3** : pantalla *f* (de un televisor, una computadora, etc.) **4** MOVIES : cine *m* **5** *or* **window screen** : ventana *f* de tela metálica
screw[1] [ˈskruː] *vt* : atornillar — *vi* **to screw in** : atornillarse
screw[2] *n* **1** : tornillo *m* (para fijar algo) **2** TWIST : vuelta *f* **3** PROPELLER : hélice *f*
screwdriver [ˈskruːˌdraɪvər] *n* : destornillador *m,* desarmador *m Mex*
scribble[1] [ˈskrɪbəl] *v* **-bled; -bling** : garabatear
scribble[2] *n* : garabato *m*
scribe [ˈskraɪb] *n* : escriba *m*
scrimp [ˈskrɪmp] *vi* **1 to scrimp on** : escatimar **2 to scrimp and save** : hacer economías
script [ˈskrɪpt] *n* **1** HANDWRITING : letra *f,* escritura *f* **2** : guión *m* (de una película, etc.)
scriptural [ˈskrɪptʃərəl] *adj* : bíblico
scripture [ˈskrɪptʃər] *n* **1** : escritos *mpl* sagrados (de una religión) **2 the Scriptures** *npl* : las Sagradas Escrituras
scroll [ˈskroːl] *n* **1** : rollo *m* (de pergamino, etc.) **2** : voluta *f* (adorno en arquitectura)
scrotum [ˈskroːtəm] *n, pl* **scrota** [-tə] *or* **scrotums** : escroto *m*
scrounge [ˈskraʊndʒ] *v* **scrounged; scrounging** *vt* **1** BUM : gorrear *fam,* sablear *fam* (dinero) **2 to scrounge around for** : buscar, andar a la busca de — *vi* **to scrounge off someone** : vivir a costa de alguien
scrub[1] [ˈskrʌb] *vt* **scrubbed; scrubbing** : restregar, fregar
scrub[2] *n* **1** THICKET, UNDERBRUSH : maleza *f,* matorral *m,* matorrales *mpl* **2** SCRUBBING : fregado *m,* restregadura *f*
scrubby [ˈskrʌbi] *adj* **-bier; -est 1** STUNTED : achaparrado **2** : cubierto de maleza
scruff [ˈskrʌf] *n* **by the scruff of the neck** : por el cogote, por el pescuezo
scrumptious [ˈskrʌmpʃəs] *adj* : delicioso, muy rico
scruple [ˈskruːpəl] *n* : escrúpulo *m*
scrupulous [ˈskruːpjələs] *adj* : escrupuloso — **scrupulously** *adv*
scrutinize [ˈskruːtənˌaɪz] *vt* **-nized; -nizing** : escrutar, escudriñar
scrutiny [ˈskruːtəni] *n, pl* **-nies** : escrutinio *m,* inspección *f*
scuff [ˈskʌf] *vt* : rayar, raspar <to scuff one's feet : arrastrar los pies>
scuffle[1] [ˈskʌfəl] *vi* **-fled; -fling 1** TUSSLE : pelearse **2** SHUFFLE : caminar arrastrando los pies
scuffle[2] *n* **1** TUSSLE : refriega *f,* pelea *f* **2** SHUFFLE : arrastre *m* de los pies
scull[1] [ˈskʌl] *vi* : remar (con espadilla)
scull[2] *n* OAR : espadilla *f*
sculpt [ˈskʌlpt] *v* : esculpir
sculptor [ˈskʌlptər] *n* : escultor *m,* -tora *f*
sculpture[1] [ˈskʌlptʃər] *vt* **-tured; -turing** : esculpir
sculpture[2] *n* : escultura *f*
scum [ˈskʌm] *n* **1** FROTH : espuma *f,* nata *f* **2** : verdín *m* (encima de un líquido)
scurrilous [ˈskərələs] *adj* : difamatorio, calumnioso, injurioso
scurry [ˈskəri] *vi* **-ried; -rying** : corretear
scurvy [ˈskərvi] *n* : escorbuto *m*
scuttle[1] [ˈskʌtəl] *v* **-tled; -tling** *vt* : hundir (un barco) — *vi* SCAMPER : corretear
scuttle[2] *n* : cubo *m* (para carbón)
scythe [ˈsaɪð] *n* : guadaña *f*
sea[1] [ˈsiː] *adj* : del mar
sea[2] *n* **1** : mar *mf* <the Black Sea : el Mar Negro> <on the high seas : en alta mar> <heavy seas : mar gruesa, mar agitada> **2** MASS : mar *m,* multitud *f* <a sea of faces : un mar de rostros>
seabird [ˈsiːˌbərd] *n* : ave *f* marina
seacoast [ˈsiːˌkoːst] *n* : costa *f,* litoral *m*
seafarer [ˈsiːˌfærər] *n* : marinero *m*
seafaring[1] [ˈsiːˌfærɪŋ] *adj* : marinero
seafaring[2] *n* : navegación *f*
seafood [ˈsiːˌfuːd] *n* : mariscos *mpl*
seagull [ˈsiːˌgʌl] *n* : gaviota *f*
sea horse [ˈsiːˌhɔrs] *n* : hipocampo *m,* caballito *m* de mar
seal[1] [ˈsiːl] *vt* **1** CLOSE : sellar, cerrar <to seal a letter : cerrar una carta> <to seal an agreement : sellar un acuerdo> **2 to seal up** : tapar, rellenar (una grieta, etc.)
seal[2] *n* **1** : foca *f* (animal) **2** : sello *m* <seal of approval : sello de aprobación> **3** CLOSURE : cierre *m,* precinto *m*
sea level *n* : nivel *m* del mar
sea lion *n* : león *m* marino
sealskin [ˈsiːlˌskɪn] *n* : piel *f* de foca
seam[1] [ˈsiːm] *vt* **1** STITCH : unir con costuras **2** MARK : marcar
seam[2] *n* **1** STITCHING : costura *f* **2** LODE, VEIN : veta *f,* filón *m*
seaman [ˈsiːmən] *n, pl* **-men** [-mən, -ˌmɛn] **1** SAILOR : marinero *m* **2** : marino *m* (en la armada)
seamless [ˈsiːmləs] *adj* **1** : sin costuras, de una pieza **2** : perfecto <a seamless transition : una transición fluida>

seamstress ['siːmpstrəs] *n* : costurera *f*
seamy ['siːmi] *adj* **seamier; -est** : sórdido
séance ['seɪ‚ɑnts] *n* : sesión *f* de espiritismo
seaplane ['siː‚pleɪn] *n* : hidroavión *m*
seaport ['siː‚port] *n* : puerto *m* marítimo
sear ['sɪr] *vt* **1** PARCH, WITHER : secar, resecar **2** SCORCH : chamuscar, quemar
search¹ ['sərtʃ] *vt* : registrar (un edificio, un área), cachear (a una persona), buscar en — *vi* **to search for** : buscar
search² *n* : búsqueda *f,* registro *m* (de un edificio, etc.), cacheo *m* (de una persona)
searchlight ['sərtʃ‚laɪt] *n* : reflector *m*
seashell ['siː‚ʃɛl] *n* : concha *f* (marina)
seashore ['siː‚ʃor] *n* : orilla *f* del mar
seasick ['siː‚sɪk] *adj* : mareado <to get seasick : marearse>
seasickness ['siː‚sɪknəs] *n* : mareo *m*
seaside → **seacoast**
season¹ ['siːzən] *vt* **1** FLAVOR, SPICE : sazonar, condimentar **2** CURE : curar, secar <seasoned wood : madera seca> <a seasoned veteran : un veterano avezado>
season² *n* **1** : estación *f* (del año) **2** : temporada *f* (en deportes, etc.) <baseball season : temporada de beisbol>
seasonable ['siːzənəbəl] *adj* **1** : propio de la estación (dícese del tiempo, de las temperaturas, etc.) **2** TIMELY : oportuno
seasonal ['siːzənəl] *adj* : estacional — **seasonally** *adv*
seasoning ['siːzənɪŋ] *n* : condimento *m,* sazón *f*
seat¹ ['siːt] *vt* **1** SIT : sentar <please be seated : siéntense, por favor> **2** HOLD : tener cabida para <the stadium seats 40,000 : el estadio tiene 40,000 asientos>
seat² *n* **1** : asiento *m,* plaza *f* (en un vehículo) <take a seat : tome asiento> **2** BOTTOM : fondillos *mpl* (de la ropa), trasero *m* (del cuerpo) **3** : sede *f* (de un gobierno, etc.)
seat belt *n* : cinturón *m* de seguridad
sea urchin *n* : erizo *m* de mar
seawall ['siː‚wɑl] *n* : rompeolas *m,* dique *m* marítimo
seawater ['siː‚wɔt̬ər, -‚wɑ-] *n* : agua *f* de mar
seaweed ['siː‚wiːd] *n* : alga *f* marina
seaworthy ['siː‚wərði] *adj* : en condiciones de navegar
secede [sɪ'siːd] *vi* **-ceded; -ceding** : separarse (de una nación, etc.)
seclude [sɪ'kluːd] *vt* **-cluded; -cluding** : aislar
seclusion [sɪ'kluːʒən] *n* : aislamiento *m*
second¹ ['sɛkənd] *vt* : secundar, apoyar (una moción)
second² *or* **secondly** ['sɛkəndli] *adv* : en segundo lugar
second³ *adj* : segundo
second⁴ *n* **1** : segundo *m,* -da *f* (en una serie) **2** : segundo *m,* segunda parte *f* **3** : segundo *m,* ayudante *m* (en deportes) **4** MOMENT : segundo *m,* momento *m*
secondary ['sɛkən‚dɛri] *adj* : secundario
secondhand ['sɛkənd'hænd] *adj* : de segunda mano
second lieutenant *n* : alférez *mf,* subteniente *mf*
second–rate ['sɛkənd'reɪt] *adj* : mediocre, de segunda categoría
secrecy ['siːkrəsi] *n, pl* **-cies** : secreto *m*
secret¹ ['siːkrət] *adj* : secreto — **secretly** *adv*
secret² *n* : secreto *m*
secretarial [‚sɛkrə'tɛriəl] *adj* : de secretario, de oficina
secretariat [‚sɛkrə'tɛriət] *n* : secretaría *f,* secretariado *m*
secretary ['sɛkrə‚tɛri] *n, pl* **-taries 1** : secretario *m,* -ria *f* (en una oficina, etc.) **2** : ministro *m,* -tra *f;* secretario *m,* -ria *f* <Secretary of State : Secretario de Estado>
secrete [sɪ'kriːt] *vt* **-creted; -creting 1** : secretar, segregar (en fisiología) **2** HIDE : ocultar
secretion [sɪ'kriːʃən] *n* : secreción *f*
secretive ['siːkrət̬ɪv, sɪ'kriːt̬ɪv] *adj* : reservado, callado, secreto
sect ['sɛkt] *n* : secta *f*
sectarian [sɛk'tɛriən] *adj* : sectario
section ['sɛkʃən] *n* : sección *f,* parte *f* (de un mueble, etc.), sector *m* (de la población), barrio *m* (de una ciudad)
sectional ['sɛkʃənəl] *adj* **1** : en sección, en corte <a sectional diagram : un gráfico en corte> **2** FACTIONAL : de grupo, entre facciones **3** : modular <sectional furniture : muebles modulares>
sector ['sɛktər] *n* : sector *m*
secular ['sɛkjələr] *adj* **1** : secular, laico <secular life : la vida secular> **2** : seglar (dícese de los sacerdotes, etc.)
secure¹ [sɪ'kjʊr] *vt* **-cured; -curing 1** FASTEN : asegurar (una puerta, etc.), sujetar **2** GET : conseguir
secure² *adj* **-curer; -est** : seguro — **securely** *adv*
security [sɪ'kjʊrət̬i] *n, pl* **-ties 1** SAFETY : seguridad *f* **2** GUARANTEE : garantía *f* **3 securities** *npl* : valores *mpl*
sedan [sɪ'dæn] *n* **1** *or* **sedan chair** : silla *f* de manos **2** : sedán *m* (automóvil)
sedate¹ [sɪ'deɪt] *vt* **-dated; -dating** : sedar
sedate² *adj* : sosegado — **sedately** *adv*
sedation [sɪ'deɪʃən] *n* : sedación *f*
sedative¹ ['sɛdət̬ɪv] *adj* : sedante
sedative² *n* : sedante *m,* calmante *m*

sedentary [ˈsɛdənˌtɛri] *adj* : sedentario

sedge [ˈsɛʤ] *n* : juncia *f*

sediment [ˈsɛdəmənt] *n* : sedimento *m* (geológico), poso *m* (en un líquido)

sedimentary [ˌsɛdəˈmɛntəri] *adj* : sedimentario

sedition [sɪˈdɪʃən] *n* : sedición *f*

seditious [sɪˈdɪʃəs] *adj* : sedicioso

seduce [sɪˈduːs, -ˈdjuːs] *vt* **-duced; -ducing** : seducir

seduction [sɪˈdʌkʃən] *n* : seducción *f*

seductive [sɪˈdʌktɪv] *adj* : seductor, seductivo

see[1] [ˈsiː] *v* **saw** [ˈsɔ]; **seen** [ˈsiːn]; **seeing** *vt* **1** : ver <I saw a dog : vi un perro> <see you later! : ¡hasta luego!> **2** EXPERIENCE : ver, conocer **3** UNDERSTAND : ver, entender **4** ENSURE : asegurarse <see that it's correct : asegúrese de que sea correcto> **5** ACCOMPANY : acompañar **6 to see off** : despedir, despedirse de — *vi* **1** : ver <seeing is believing : ver para creer> **2** UNDERSTAND : entender, ver <now I see! : ¡ya entiendo!> **3** CONSIDER : ver <let's see : vamos a ver> **4 to see to** : ocuparse de

see[2] *n* : sede *f* <the Holy See : la Santa Sede>

seed[1] [ˈsiːd] *vt* **1** SOW : sembrar **2** : despepitar, quitarle las semillas a

seed[2] *n, pl* **seed** *or* **seeds 1** : semilla *f*, pepita *f* (de una fruta) **2** SOURCE : germen *m*, semilla *f*

seedless [ˈsiːdləs] *adj* : sin semillas

seedling [ˈsiːdlɪŋ] *n* : plantón *m*

seedpod [ˈsiːdˌpɑd] → **pod**

seedy [ˈsiːdi] *adj* **seedier; -est 1** : lleno de semillas **2** SHABBY : raído (dícese de la ropa) **3** RUN-DOWN : ruinoso (dícese de los edificios, etc.), sórdido

seek [ˈsiːk] *v* **sought** [ˈsɔt]; **seeking** *vt* **1** : buscar <to seek an answer : buscar una solución> **2** REQUEST : solicitar, pedir **3 to seek to** : tratar de, intentar de — *vi* SEARCH : buscar

seem [ˈsiːm] *vi* : parecer

seeming [ˈsiːmɪŋ] *adj* : aparente, ostensible

seemingly [ˈsiːmɪŋli] *adv* : aparentemente, según parece

seemly [ˈsiːmli] *adj* **seemlier; -est** : apropiado, decoroso

seep [ˈsiːp] *vi* : filtrarse

seer [ˈsiːər] *n* : vidente *mf*, clarividente *mf*

seesaw[1] [ˈsiːˌsɔ] *vi* **1** : jugar en un subibaja **2** VACILLATE : vacilar, oscilar

seesaw[2] *n* : balancín *m*, subibaja *m*

seethe [ˈsiːð] *vi* **seethed; seething 1** : bullir, hervir **2 to seethe with anger** : rabiar, estar furioso

segment [ˈsɛgmənt] *n* : segmento *m*

segmented [ˈsɛgˌmɛntəd, sɛgˈmɛn-] *adj* : segmentado

segregate [ˈsɛgrɪˌgeɪt] *vt* **-gated; -gating** : segregar

segregation [ˌsɛgrɪˈgeɪʃən] *n* : segregación *f*

seismic [ˈsaɪzmɪk, ˈsaɪs-] *adj* : sísmico

seize [ˈsiːz] *v* **seized; seizing** *vt* **1** CAPTURE : capturar, tomar, apoderarse de **2** ARREST : detener **3** CLUTCH, GRAB : agarrar, coger, aprovechar (una oportunidad) **4 to be seized with** : estar sobrecogido por — *vi or* **to seize up** : agarrotarse

seizure [ˈsiːʒər] *n* **1** CAPTURE : toma *f*, captura *f* **2** ARREST : detención *f* **3** : ataque *m* <an epileptic seizure : un ataque epiléptico>

seldom [ˈsɛldəm] *adv* : pocas veces, rara vez, casi nunca

select[1] [səˈlɛkt] *vt* : escoger, elegir, seleccionar (a un candidato, etc.)

select[2] *adj* : selecto

selection [səˈlɛkʃən] *n* : selección *f*, elección *f*

selective [səˈlɛktɪv] *adj* : selectivo

selenium [səˈliːniəm] *n* : selenio *m*

self [ˈsɛlf] *n, pl* **selves** [ˈsɛlvz] **1** : ser *m*, persona *f* <the self : el yo> <with his whole self : con todo su ser> <her own self : su propia persona> **2** SIDE : lado (de la personalidad) <his better self : su lado bueno>

self–addressed [ˌsɛlfəˈdrɛst] *adj* : con la dirección del remitente <include a self-addressed envelope : incluya un sobre con su nombre y dirección>

self–appointed [ˌsɛlfəˈpɔɪntəd] *adj* : autoproclamado, autonombrado

self–assurance [ˌsɛlfəˈʃʊrənts] *n* : seguridad *f* en sí mismo

self–assured [ˌsɛlfəˈʃʊrd] *adj* : seguro de sí mismo

self–centered [ˌsɛlfˈsɛntərd] *adj* : egocéntrico

self–confidence [ˌsɛlfˈkɑnfədənts] *n* : confianza *f* en sí mismo

self–confident [ˌsɛlfˈkɑnfədənt] *adj* : seguro de sí mismo

self–conscious [ˌsɛlfˈkɑntʃəs] *adj* : cohibido, tímido

self–consciously [ˌsɛlfˈkɑntʃəsli] *adv* : de manera cohibida

self–consciousness [ˌsɛlfˈkɑntʃəsnəs] *n* : vergüenza *f*, timidez *f*

self–contained [ˌsɛlfkənˈteɪnd] *adj* **1** INDEPENDENT : independiente **2** RESERVED : reservado

self–control [ˌsɛlfkənˈtroːl] *n* : autocontrol *m*, control *m* de sí mismo

self–defense [ˌsɛlfdɪˈfɛnts] *n* : defensa *f* propia, defensa *f* personal <to act in self-defense : actuar en defensa propia> <self-defense class : clase de defensa personal>

self–denial [ˌsɛlfdɪˈnaɪəl] *n* : abnegación *f*

self–destructive [ˌsɛlfdɪˈstrʌktɪv] *adj* : autodestructivo

self–determination [ˌsɛlfdɪˌtərməˈneɪʃən] *n* : autodeterminación *f*

self–discipline [ˌsɛlfˈdɪsəplən] *n* : autodisciplina *f*

self-employed [ˌsɛlfɪmˈplɔɪd] *adj* : que trabaja por cuenta propia, autónomo
self-esteem [ˌsɛlfɪˈstiːm] *n* : autoestima *f,* amor *m* propio
self-evident [ˌsɛlfˈɛvədənt] *adj* : evidente, manifiesto
self-explanatory [ˌsɛlfɪkˈsplænəˌtori] *adj* : fácil de entender, evidente
self-expression [ˌsɛlfɪkˈsprɛʃən] *n* : expresión *f* personal
self-government [ˌsɛlfˈgʌvərmənt, -vərn-] *n* : autogobierno *m*
self-help [ˌsɛlfˈhɛlp] *n* : autoayuda *f*
self-important [ˌsɛlfɪmˈpɔrtənt] *adj* **1** VAIN : vanidoso, presumido **2** ARROGANT : arrogante
self-indulgent [ˌsɛlfɪnˈdʌldʒənt] *adj* : que se permite excesos
self-inflicted [ˌsɛlfɪnˈflɪktəd] *adj* : autoinfligido
self-interest [ˌsɛlfˈɪntrəst, -təˌrɛst] *n* : interés *m* personal
selfish [ˈsɛlfɪʃ] *adj* : egoísta
selfishly [ˈsɛlfɪʃli] *adv* : de manera egoísta
selfishness [ˈsɛlfɪʃnəs] *n* : egoísmo *m*
selfless [ˈsɛlfləs] *adj* UNSELFISH : desinteresado
self-made [ˌsɛlfˈmeɪd] *adj* : próspero gracias a sus propios esfuerzos
self-pity [ˌsɛlfˈpɪti] *n, pl* **-ties** : autocompasión *f*
self-portrait [ˌsɛlfˈpɔrtrət] *n* : autorretrato *m*
self-propelled [ˌsɛlfproˈpɛld] *adj* : autopropulsado
self-reliance [ˌsɛlfriˈlaɪənts] *n* : independencia *f,* autosuficiencia *f*
self-respect [ˌsɛlfriˈspɛkt] *n* : autoestima *f,* amor *m* propio
self-restraint [ˌsɛlfriˈstreɪnt] *n* : autocontrol *m,* moderación *f*
self-righteous [ˌsɛlfˈraɪtʃəs] *adj* : santurrón, moralista
self-sacrifice [ˌsɛlfˈsækrəˌfaɪs] *n* : abnegación *f*
selfsame [ˈsɛlfˌseɪm] *adj* : mismo
self-service [ˌsɛlfˈsərvɪs] *adj* **1** : de autoservicio **2 self-service restaurant** : autoservicio *m*
self-sufficiency [ˌsɛlfsəˈfɪʃəntsi] *n* : autosuficiencia *f*
self-sufficient [ˌsɛlfsəˈfɪʃənt] *adj* : autosuficiente
self-taught [ˌsɛlfˈtɔt] *adj* : autodidacto
sell [ˈsɛl] *v* **sold** [ˈsoːld]; **selling** *vt* : vender — *vi* : venderse
seller [ˈsɛlər] *n* : vendedor *m,* -dora *f*
selves → **self**
semantics [sɪˈmæntɪks] *ns & pl* : semántica *f*
semaphore [ˈsɛməˌfor] *n* : semáforo *m*
semblance [ˈsɛmbləntsˌ] *n* : apariencia *f*
semen [ˈsiːmən] *n* : semen *m*
semester [səˈmɛstər] *n* : semestre *m*
semicolon [ˈsɛmiˌkoːlən, ˈsɛˌmaɪ-] *n* : punto y coma *m*
semiconductor [ˈsɛmikənˌdʌktər, ˈsɛˌmaɪ-] *n* : semiconductor *m*
semifinal [ˈsɛmiˌfaɪnəl, ˈsɛˌmaɪ-] *n* : semifinal *f*
seminar [ˈsɛməˌnɑr] *n* : seminario *m*
seminary [ˈsɛməˌnɛri] *n, pl* **-naries** : seminario *m*
senate [ˈsɛnət] *n* : senado *m*
senator [ˈsɛnətər] *n* : senador *m,* -dora *f*
send [ˈsɛnd] *vt* **sent** [ˈsɛnt]; **sending 1** : mandar, enviar <to send a letter : mandar una carta> <to send word : avisar, mandar decir> **2** PROPEL : mandar, lanzar <he sent it into left field : lo mandó al jardín izquierdo> <to send up dust : alzar polvo> **3 to send into a rage** : poner furioso
sender [ˈsɛndər] *n* : remitente *mf* (de una carta, etc.)
Senegalese [ˌsɛnəgəˈliːz, -ˈliːs] *n* : senegalés *m,* -lesa *f* — **Senegalese** *adj*
senile [ˈsiːˌnaɪl] *adj* : senil
senility [sɪˈnɪləti] *n* : senilidad *f*
senior[1] [ˈsiːnjər] *adj* **1** ELDER : mayor <John Doe, Senior : John Doe, padre> **2** : superior (en rango), más antiguo (en años de servicio) <a senior official : un alto oficial>
senior[2] *n* **1** : superior *m* (en rango) **2 to be someone's senior** : ser mayor que alguien <she's two years my senior : me lleva dos años>
seniority [ˌsiːˈnjɔrəti] *n* : antigüedad *f* (en años de servicio)
sensation [sɛnˈseɪʃən] *n* : sensación *f*
sensational [sɛnˈseɪʃənəl] *adj* : que causa sensación <sensational stories : historias sensacionalistas>
sense[1] [ˈsɛnts] *vt* **sensed; sensing** : sentir <he sensed danger : se dio cuenta del peligro>
sense[2] *n* **1** MEANING : sentido *m,* significado *m* **2** : sentido *m* <the sense of smell : el sentido del olfato> **3 to make sense** : tener sentido
senseless [ˈsɛntsləs] *adj* **1** MEANINGLESS : sin sentido, sin razón **2** UNCONSCIOUS : inconsciente
senselessly [ˈsɛntsləsli] *adv* : sin sentido
sensibility [ˌsɛntsəˈbɪləti] *n, pl* **-ties** : sensibilidad *f*
sensible [ˈsɛntsəbəl] *adj* **1** PERCEPTIBLE : sensible, perceptible **2** AWARE : consciente **3** REASONABLE : sensato <a sensible man : un hombre sensato> <sensible shoes : zapatos prácticos> — **sensibly** [-bli] *adv*
sensibleness [ˈsɛntsəbəlnəs] *n* : sensatez *f,* solidez *f*
sensitive [ˈsɛntsətɪv] *adj* **1** : sensible, delicado <sensitive skin : piel sensible> **2** IMPRESSIONABLE : sensible, impresionable **3** TOUCHY : susceptible

sensitiveness [ˈsɛntsət̬ɪvnəs] → **sensitivity**

sensitivity [ˌsɛntsəˈtɪvət̬i] *n, pl* **-ties** : sensibilidad *f*

sensor [ˈsɛnˌsɔr, ˈsɛntsər] *n* : sensor *m*

sensory [ˈsɛntsəri] *adj* : sensorial

sensual [ˈsɛntʃʊəl] *adj* : sensual — **sensually** *adv*

sensuous [ˈsɛntʃʊəs] *adj* : sensual

sent → **send**

sentence¹ [ˈsɛntənts, -ənz] *vt* **-tenced; -tencing** : sentenciar

sentence² *n* **1** JUDGMENT : sentencia *f* **2** : oración *f*, frase *f* (en gramática)

sentiment [ˈsɛntəmənt] *n* **1** BELIEF : opinión *f* **2** FEELING : sentimiento *m* **3** → **sentimentality**

sentimental [ˌsɛntəˈmɛntəl] *adj* : sentimental

sentimentality [ˌsɛntəˌmɛnˈtæləti] *n, pl* **-ties** : sentimentalismo *m*, sensiblería *f*

sentinel [ˈsɛntənəl] *n* : centinela *mf*, guardia *mf*

sentry [ˈsɛntri] *n, pl* **-tries** : centinela *mf*

sepal [ˈsiːpəl, ˈsɛ-] *n* : sépalo *m*

separable [ˈsɛpərəbəl] *adj* : separable

separate¹ [ˈsɛpəˌreɪt] *v* **-rated; -rating** *vt* **1** DETACH, SEVER : separar **2** DISTINGUISH : diferenciar, distinguir — *vi* PART : separarse

separate² [ˈsɛprət, ˈsɛpə-] *adj* **1** INDIVIDUAL : separado, aparte <a separate state : un estado separado> <in a separate envelope : en un sobre aparte> **2** DISTINCT : distinto

separately [ˈsɛprətli, ˈsɛpə-] *adv* : por separado, separadamente, aparte

separation [ˌsɛpəˈreɪʃən] *n* : separación *f*

sepia [ˈsiːpiə] *n* : color *m* sepia

September [sɛpˈtɛmbər] *n* : septiembre *m*, setiembre *m*

sepulchre [ˈsɛpəlkər] *n* : sepulcro *m*

sequel [ˈsiːkwəl] *n* **1** CONSEQUENCE : secuela *f*, consecuencia *f* **2** : continuación *f* (de una película, etc.)

sequence [ˈsiːkwənts] *n* **1** SERIES : serie *f*, sucesión *f*, secuencia *f* (matemática o musical) **2** ORDER : orden *m*

sequester [sɪˈkwɛstər] *vt* : aislar

sequin [ˈsiːkwən] *n* : lentejuela *f*

sequoia [sɪˈkwɔɪə] *n* : secoya *f*, secuoya *f*

sera → **serum**

Serb [ˈsərb] *or* **Serbian** [ˈsərbiən] *n* : serbio *m*, -bia *f* — **Serb** *or* **Serbian** *adj*

Serbo–Croatian [ˌsərbokroˈeɪʃən] *n* : serbocroata *m* (idioma) — **Serbo–Croatian** *adj*

serenade¹ [ˌsɛrəˈneɪd] *vt* **-naded; -nading** : darle una serenata (a alguien)

serenade² *n* : serenata *f*

serene [səˈriːn] *adj* : sereno — **serenely** *adv*

serenity [səˈrɛnət̬i] *n* : serenidad *f*

serf [ˈsərf] *n* : siervo *m*, -va *f*

serge [ˈsərdʒ] *n* : sarga *f*

sergeant [ˈsɑrdʒənt] *n* : sargento *mf*

serial¹ [ˈsɪriəl] *adj* : seriado

serial² *n* : serie *f*, serial *m* (de radio o televisión), publicación *f* por entregas

serially [ˈsɪriəli] *adv* : en serie

series [ˈsɪrˌiːz] *n, pl* **series** : serie *f*, sucesión *f*

serious [ˈsɪriəs] *adj* **1** SOBER : serio **2** DEDICATED, EARNEST : serio, dedicado <to be serious about something : tomar algo en serio> **3** GRAVE : serio, grave <serious problems : problemas graves>

seriously [ˈsɪriəsli] *adv* **1** EARNESTLY : seriamente, con seriedad, en serio **2** SEVERELY : gravemente

seriousness [ˈsɪriəsnəs] *n* : seriedad *f*, gravedad *f*

sermon [ˈsərmən] *n* : sermón *m*

serpent [ˈsərpənt] *n* : serpiente *f*

serrated [səˈreɪt̬əd, ˈsɛrˌeɪt̬əd] *adj* : dentado, serrado

serum [ˈsɪrəm] *n, pl* **serums** *or* **sera** [ˈsɪrə] : suero *m*

servant [ˈsərvənt] *n* : criado *m*, -da *f*; sirviente *m*, -ta *f*

serve [ˈsərv] *v* **served; serving** *vi* **1** : servir <to serve in the navy : servir en la armada> <to serve on a jury : ser miembro de un jurado> **2** DO, FUNCTION : servir <to serve as : servir de, servir como> **3** : sacar (en deportes) — *vt* **1** : servir <to serve God : servir a Dios> **2** HELP : servir <it serves no purpose : no sirve para nada> **3** : servir (comida o bebida) <dinner is served : la cena está servida> **4** SUPPLY : abastecer **5** CARRY OUT : cumplir, hacer <to serve time : servir una pena> **6 to serve a summons** : entregar una citación

server [ˈsərvər] *n* **1** : camarero *m*, -ra *f*; mesero *m*, -ra *f* (en un restaurante) **2** *or* **serving dish** : fuente *f* (para servir comida)

service¹ [ˈsərvəs] *vt* **-viced; -vicing** **1** MAINTAIN : darle mantenimiento a (una máquina), revisar **2** REPAIR : arreglar, reparar

service² *n* **1** HELP, USE : servicio *m* <to do someone a service : hacerle un servicio a alguien> <at your service : a sus órdenes> <to be out of service : no funcionar> **2** CEREMONY : oficio *m* (religioso) **3** DEPARTMENT, SYSTEM : servicio *m* <social services : servicios sociales> <train service : servicio de trenes> **4** SET : juego *m*, servicio *m* <tea service : juego de té> **5** MAINTENANCE : mantenimiento *m*, revisión *f*, servicio *m* **6** : saque *m* (en deportes) **7 armed services** : fuerzas *fpl* armadas

serviceable [ˈsərvəsəbəl] *adj* **1** USEFUL : útil **2** DURABLE : duradero

serviceman [ˈsərvəsˌmæn, -mən] *n, pl* **-men** [-mən, -ˌmɛn] : militar *m*

service station *n* **:** estación *f* de servicio
servicewoman [ˈsərvəsˌwʊmən] *n, pl* **-women** [-ˌwɪmən] **:** militar *f*
servile [ˈsərvəl, -ˌvaɪl] *adj* **:** servil
serving [ˈsərvɪŋ] *n* HELPING **:** porción *f,* ración *f*
servitude [ˈsərvəˌtuːd, -ˌtjuːd] *n* **:** servidumbre *f*
sesame [ˈsɛsəmi] *n* **:** ajonjolí *m,* sésamo *m*
session [ˈsɛʃən] *n* **:** sesión *f*
set[1] [ˈsɛt] *v* **set; setting** *vt* **1** SEAT **:** sentar **2** *or* **to set down** PLACE **:** poner, colocar **3** ARRANGE **:** fijar, establecer <to set the date : poner la fecha> <he set the agenda : estableció la agenda> **4** ADJUST **:** poner (un reloj, etc.) **5** (*indicating the causing of a certain condition*) <to set fire to : prenderle fuego a> <she set it free : lo soltó> **6** MAKE, START **:** poner, hacer <I set them working : los puse a trabajar> — *vi* **1** SOLIDIFY **:** fraguar (dícese del cemento, etc.), cuajar (dícese de la gelatina, etc.) **2 :** ponerse (dícese del sol o de la luna)
set[2] *adj* **1** ESTABLISHED, FIXED **:** fijo, establecido **2** RIGID **:** inflexible <to be set in one's ways : tener costumbres muy arraigadas> **3** READY **:** listo, preparado
set[3] *n* **1** COLLECTION **:** juego *m* <a set of dishes : un juego de platos, una vajilla> <a tool set : una caja de herramientas> **2** *or* **stage set :** decorado *m* (en el teatro), plató *m* (en el cine) **3** APPARATUS **:** aparato *m* <a television set : un televisor> **4 :** conjunto *m* (en matemáticas)
setback [ˈsɛtˌbæk] *n* **:** revés *m,* contratiempo *m*
set in *vi* BEGIN **:** comenzar, empezar
set off *vt* **1** PROVOKE **:** provocar **2** EXPLODE **:** hacer estallar (una bomba, etc.) — *vi or* **to set forth :** salir
set out *vi* **:** salir (de viaje) — *vt* INTEND **:** proponerse
settee [sɛˈtiː] *n* **:** sofá *m*
setter [ˈsɛtər] *n* **:** setter *mf* <Irish setter : setter irlandés>
setting [ˈsɛtɪŋ] *n* **1 :** posición *f,* ajuste *m* (de un control) **2 :** engaste *m,* montura *f* (de una gema) **3** SCENE **:** escenario *m* (de una novela, etc.) **4** SURROUNDINGS **:** ambiente *m,* entorno *m,* marco *m*
settle [ˈsɛtəl] *v* **settled; settling** *vi* **1** ALIGHT, LAND **:** posarse (dícese de las aves), depositarse (dícese del polvo) **2** SINK **:** asentarse (dícese de los edificios) <he settled into the chair : se arrellanó en la silla> **3 :** instalarse (en una casa), establecerse (en una ciudad o región) **4 to settle down :** calmarse, tranquilizarse <settle down! : ¡tranquilízate!, ¡cálmate!> **5 to settle down :** sentar cabeza, hacerse sensato <to marry and settle down : casarse y sentar cabeza> — *vt* **1** ARRANGE, DECIDE **:** fijar, decidir, acordar (planes, etc.) **2** RESOLVE **:** resolver, solucionar <to settle an argument : resolver una discusión> **3** PAY **:** pagar <to settle an account : saldar una cuenta> **4** CALM **:** calmar (los nervios), asentar (el estómago) **5** COLONIZE **:** colonizar **6 to settle oneself :** acomodarse, hacerse cómodo
settlement [ˈsɛtəlmənt] *n* **1** PAYMENT **:** pago *m,* liquidación *f* **2** COLONY **:** asentamiento *m* **3** RESOLUTION **:** acuerdo *m*
settler [ˈsɛtələr] *n* **:** poblador *m,* -dora *f;* colono *m,* -na *f*
set up *vt* **1** ASSEMBLE **:** montar, armar **2** ERECT **:** levantar, erigir **3** ESTABLISH **:** establecer, fundar, montar (un negocio) **4** CAUSE **:** armar <they set up a clamor : armaron un alboroto>
seven[1] [ˈsɛvən] *adj* **:** siete
seven[2] *n* **:** siete *m*
seven hundred[1] *adj* **:** setecientos
seven hundred[2] *n* **:** setecientos *m*
seventeen[1] [ˌsɛvənˈtiːn] *adj* **:** diecisiete
seventeen[2] *n* **:** diecisiete *m*
seventeenth[1] [ˌsɛvənˈtiːnθ] *adj* **:** decimoséptimo
seventeenth[2] *n* **1 :** decimoséptimo *m,* -ma *f* (en una serie) **2 :** diecisieteavo *m,* diecisieteava parte *f*
seventh[1] [ˈsɛvənθ] *adj* **:** séptimo
seventh[2] *n* **1 :** séptimo *m,* -ma *f* (en una serie) **2 :** séptimo *m,* séptima parte *f*
seventieth[1] [ˈsɛvəntiəθ] *adj* **:** septuagésimo
seventieth[2] *n* **1 :** septuagésimo *m,* -ma *f* (en una serie) **2 :** setentavo *m,* setentava parte *f,* septuagésima parte *f*
seventy[1] [ˈsɛvənti] *adj* **:** setenta
seventy[2] *n, pl* **-ties :** setenta *m*
sever [ˈsɛvər] *vt* **-ered; -ering :** cortar, romper
several[1] [ˈsɛvrəl, ˈsɛvə-] *adj* **1** DISTINCT **:** distinto **2** SOME **:** varios <several weeks : varias semanas>
several[2] *pron* **:** varios, varias
severance [ˈsɛvrənts, sɛvə-] *n* **1 :** ruptura *f* (de relaciones, etc.) **2 severance pay :** indemnización *f* (por despido)
severe [səˈvɪr] *adj* **severer; -est 1** STRICT **:** severo **2** AUSTERE **:** sobrio, austero **3** SERIOUS **:** grave <a severe wound : una herida grave> <severe aches : dolores fuertes> **4** DIFFICULT **:** duro, difícil — **severely** *adv*
severity [səˈvɛrəti] *n* **1** HARSHNESS **:** severidad *f* **2** AUSTERITY **:** sobriedad *f,* austeridad *f* **3** SERIOUSNESS **:** gravedad *f* (de una herida, etc.)
sew [ˈsoː] *v* **sewed; sewn** [ˈsoːn] *or* **sewed; sewing :** coser
sewage [ˈsuːɪdʒ] *n* **:** aguas *fpl* negras, aguas *fpl* residuales
sewer[1] [ˈsoːər] *n* **:** uno que cose
sewer[2] [ˈsuːər] *n* **:** alcantarilla *f,* cloaca *f*

sewing [ˈsoːɪŋ] *n* **:** costura *f*

sex [ˈsɛks] *n* **1 :** sexo *m* <the opposite sex : el sexo opuesto> **2** COPULATION **:** relaciones *fpl* sexuales

sexism [ˈsɛkˌsɪzəm] *n* **:** sexismo *m*

sexist[1] [ˈsɛksɪst] *adj* **:** sexista

sexist[2] *n* **:** sexista *mf*

sextant [ˈsɛkstənt] *n* **:** sextante *m*

sextet [sɛkˈstɛt] *n* **:** sexteto *m*

sexton [ˈsɛkstən] *n* **:** sacristán *m*

sexual [ˈsɛkʃuəl] *adj* **:** sexual — **sexually** *adv*

sexuality [ˌsɛkʃuˈæləti] *n* **:** sexualidad *f*

sexy [ˈsɛksi] *adj* **sexier; -est :** sexy

shabbily [ˈʃæbəli] *adv* **1 :** pobremente <shabbily dressed : pobremente vestido> **2** UNFAIRLY **:** mal, injustamente

shabbiness [ˈʃæbinəs] *n* **1 :** lo gastado (de ropa, etc.) **2 :** lo mal vestido (de personas) **3** UNFAIRNESS **:** injusticia *f*

shabby [ˈʃæbi] *adj* **shabbier; -est 1 :** gastado (dícese de la ropa, etc.) **2 :** mal vestido (dícese de las personas) **3** UNFAIR **:** malo, injusto <shabby treatment : mal trato>

shack [ˈʃæk] *n* **:** choza *f,* rancho *m*

shackle[1] [ˈʃækəl] *vt* **-led; -ling :** ponerle grilletes (a alguien)

shackle[2] *n* **:** grillete *m*

shad [ˈʃæd] *n* **:** sábalo *m*

shade[1] [ˈʃeɪd] *v* **shaded; shading** *vt* **1** SHELTER **:** proteger (del sol o de la luz) **2** *or* **to shade in :** matizar los colores de — *vi* **:** convertirse gradualmente <his irritation shaded into rage : su irritación iba convirtiéndose en furia>

shade[2] *n* **1 :** sombra *f* <to give shade : dar sombra> **2 :** tono *m* (de un color) **3** NUANCE **:** matiz *m* **4 :** pantalla *f* (de una lámpara), persiana *f* (de una ventana)

shadow[1] [ˈʃædoː] *vt* **1** DARKEN **:** ensombrecer **2** TRAIL **:** seguir de cerca, seguirle la pista (a alguien)

shadow[2] *n* **1 :** sombra *f* **2** DARKNESS **:** oscuridad *f* **3** TRACE **:** sombra *f,* atisbo *m,* indicio *m* <without a shadow of a doubt : sin sombra de duda, sin lugar a dudas> **4 to cast a shadow over :** ensombrecer

shadowy [ˈʃædowi] *adj* **1** INDISTINCT **:** vago, indistinto **2** DARK **:** oscuro

shady [ˈʃeɪdi] *adj* **shadier; -est 1 :** sombreado (dícese de un lugar), que da sombra (dícese de un árbol) **2** DISREPUTABLE **:** sospechoso (dícese de una persona), turbio (dícese de un negocio, etc.)

shaft [ˈʃæft] *n* **1 :** asta *f* (de una lanza), astil *m* (de una flecha), mango *m* (de una herramienta) **2** *or* **mine shaft :** pozo *m*

shaggy [ˈʃægi] *adj* **shaggier; -est 1** HAIRY **:** peludo <a shaggy dog : un perro peludo> **2** UNKEMPT **:** enmarañado, despeinado (dícese del pelo, de las barbas, etc.)

shake[1] [ˈʃeɪk] *v* **shook** [ˈʃʊk]; **shaken** [ˈʃeɪkən]; **shaking** *vt* **1 :** sacudir, agitar, hacer temblar <he shook his head : negó con la cabeza> **2** WEAKEN **:** debilitar, hacer flaquear <it shook her faith : debilitó su confianza> **3** UPSET **:** afectar, alterar **4 to shake hands with someone :** darle la mano a alguien, estrecharle la mano a alguien — *vi* **:** temblar, sacudirse

shake[2] *n* **:** sacudida *f,* apretón *m* (de manos)

shaker [ˈʃeɪkər] *n* **1 salt shaker :** salero *m* **2 pepper shaker :** pimentero *m* **3 cocktail shaker :** coctelera *f*

shake–up [ˈʃeɪkˌʌp] *n* **:** reorganización *f*

shakily [ˈʃeɪkəli] *adv* **:** temblorosamente

shaky [ˈʃeɪki] *adj* **shakier; -est 1** SHAKING **:** tembloroso **2** UNSTABLE **:** poco firme, inestable **3** PRECARIOUS **:** precario, incierto **4** QUESTIONABLE **:** dudoso, cuestionable <shaky arguments : argumentos discutibles>

shale [ˈʃeɪl] *n* **:** esquisto *m*

shall [ˈʃæl] *v aux, past* **should** [ˈʃʊd]; *present s & pl* **shall 1** (*used to express a command*) <you shall do as I say : harás lo que te digo> **2** (*used to express futurity*) <we shall see : ya veremos> <when shall we expect you? : ¿cuándo te podemos esperar?> **3** (*used to express determination*) <you shall have the money : tendrás el dinero> **4** (*used to express a condition*) <if he should die : si muriera> <if they should call, tell me : si llaman, dímelo> **5** (*used to express obligation*) <he should have said it : debería haberlo dicho> **6** (*used to express probability*) <they should arrive soon : deben (de) llegar pronto> <why should he lie? : ¿porqué ha de mentir?>

shallow [ˈʃæloː] *adj* **1 :** poco profundo (dícese del agua, etc.) **2** SUPERFICIAL **:** superficial

shallows [ˈʃæloːz] *npl* **:** bajío *m,* bajos *mpl*

sham[1] [ˈʃæm] *v* **shammed; shamming :** fingir

sham[2] *adj* **:** falso, fingido

sham[3] *n* **1** FAKE, PRETENSE **:** farsa *f,* simulación *f,* imitación *f* **2** FAKER **:** impostor *m,* -tora *f;* farsante *mf*

shamble [ˈʃæmbəl] *vi* **-bled; -bling :** caminar arrastrando los pies

shambles [ˈʃæmbəlz] *ns & pl* **:** caos *m,* desorden *m,* confusión *f*

shame[1] [ˈʃeɪm] *vt* **shamed; shaming 1 :** avergonzar <he was shamed by their words : sus palabras le dieron vergüenza> **2** DISGRACE **:** deshonrar

shame[2] *n* **1 :** vergüenza *f* <to have no shame : no tener vergüenza> **2** DISGRACE **:** vergüenza *f,* deshonra *f* **3** PITY **:** lástima *f,* pena *f* <what a shame! : ¡qué pena!>

shamefaced [ˈʃeɪmˌfeɪst] *adj* : avergonzado

shameful [ˈʃeɪmfəl] *adj* : vergonzoso — **shamefully** *adv*

shameless [ˈʃeɪmləs] *adj* : descarado, desvergonzado — **shamelessly** *adv*

shampoo[1] [ʃæmˈpuː] *vt* : lavar (el pelo)

shampoo[2] *n, pl* **-poos** : champú *m*

shamrock [ˈʃæmˌrɑk] *n* : trébol *m*

shank [ˈʃæŋk] *n* : parte *f* baja de la pierna

shan't [ˈʃænt] (*contraction of* **shall not**) → **shall**

shanty [ˈʃænti] *n, pl* **-ties** : choza *f,* rancho *m*

shape[1] [ˈʃeɪp] *v* **shaped; shaping** *vt* **1** : dar forma a, modelar (arcilla, etc.), tallar (madera, piedra), formar (carácter) <to be shaped like : tener forma de> **2** DETERMINE : decidir, determinar — *vi or* **to shape up** : tomar forma

shape[2] *n* **1** : forma *f,* figura *f* <in the shape of a circle : en forma de círculo> **2** CONDITION : estado *m,* condiciones *fpl,* forma *f* (física) <to get in shape : ponerse en forma>

shapeless [ˈʃeɪpləs] *adj* : informe

shapely [ˈʃeɪpli] *adj* **shapelier; -est** : curvilíneo, bien proporcionado

shard [ˈʃɑrd] *n* : fragmento *m,* casco *m* (de cerámica, etc.)

share[1] [ˈʃɛr] *v* **shared; sharing** *vt* **1** APPORTION : dividir, repartir **2** : compartir <they share a room : comparten una habitación> — *vi* : compartir

share[2] *n* **1** PORTION : parte *f,* porción *f* <one's fair share : lo que le corresponde a uno> **2** : acción *f* (en una compañía) <to hold shares : tener acciones>

sharecropper [ˈʃɛrˌkrɑpər] *n* : aparcero *m,* -ra *f*

shareholder [ˈʃɛrˌhoːldər] *n* : accionista *mf*

shark [ˈʃɑrk] *n* : tiburón *m*

sharp[1] [ˈʃɑrp] *adv* : en punto <at two o'clock sharp : a las dos en punto>

sharp[2] *adj* **1** : afilado, filoso <a sharp knife : un cuchillo afilado> **2** PENETRATING : cortante, fuerte **3** CLEVER : agudo, listo, perspicaz **4** ACUTE : agudo <sharp eyesight : vista aguda> **5** HARSH, SEVERE : duro, severo, agudo <a sharp rebuke : una reprimenda mordaz> **6** STRONG : fuerte <sharp cheese : queso fuerte> **7** ABRUPT : brusco, repentino **8** DISTINCT : nítido, definido <a sharp image : una imagen bien definida> **9** ANGULAR : anguloso (dícese de la cara) **10** : sostenido (en música)

sharp[3] *n* : sostenido *m* (en música)

sharpen [ˈʃɑrpən] *vt* : afilar, aguzar <to sharpen a pencil : sacarle punta a un lápiz> <to sharpen one's wits : aguzar el ingenio>

sharpener [ˈʃɑrpənər] *n* : afilador *m* (para cuchillos, etc.), sacapuntas *m* (para lápices)

sharply [ˈʃɑrpli] *adv* **1** ABRUPTLY : bruscamente **2** DISTINCTLY : claramente, marcadamente

sharpness [ˈʃɑrpnəs] *n* **1** : lo afilado (de un cuchillo, etc.) **2** ACUTENESS : agudeza *f* (de los sentidos o de la mente) **3** INTENSITY : intensidad *f,* agudeza *f* (de dolores, etc.) **4** HARSHNESS : dureza *f,* severidad *f* **5** ABRUPTNESS : brusquedad *f* **6** CLARITY : nitidez *f*

sharpshooter [ˈʃɑrpˌʃuːt̬ər] *n* : tirador *m,* -dora *f* de primera

shatter [ˈʃæt̬ər] *vt* **1** : hacer añicos <to shatter the silence : romper el silencio> **2 to be shattered by** : quedar destrozado por — *vi* : hacerse añicos, romperse en pedazos

shave[1] [ˈʃeɪv] *v* **shaved; shaved** *or* **shaven** [ˈʃeɪvən]; **shaving** *vt* **1** : afeitar, rasurar <she shaved her legs : se rasuró las piernas> <they shaved (off) his beard : le afeitaron la barba> **2** SLICE : cortar (en pedazos finos) — *vi* : afeitarse, rasurarse

shave[2] *n* : afeitada *f,* rasurada *f*

shaver [ˈʃeɪvər] *n* : afeitadora *f,* máquina *f* de afeitar, rasuradora *f*

shawl [ˈʃɔl] *n* : chal *m,* mantón *m,* rebozo *m*

she [ˈʃiː] *pron* : ella

sheaf [ˈʃiːf] *n, pl* **sheaves** [ˈʃiːvz] : gavilla *f* (de cereales), haz *m* (de flechas), fajo *m* (de papeles)

shear [ˈʃɪr] *vt* **sheared; sheared** *or* **shorn** [ˈʃorn]; **shearing 1** : esquilar, trasquilar <to shear sheep : trasquilar ovejas> **2** CUT : cortar (el pelo, etc.)

shears [ˈʃɪrz] *npl* : tijeras *fpl* (grandes)

sheath [ˈʃiːθ] *n, pl* **sheaths** [ˈʃiːðz, ˈʃiːθs] : funda *f,* vaina *f*

sheathe [ˈʃiːð] *vt* **sheathed; sheathing** : envainar, enfundar

shed[1] [ˈʃɛd] *vt* **shed; shedding 1** : derramar (sangre o lágrimas) **2** EMIT : emitir (luz) <to shed light on : aclarar> **3** DISCARD : mudar (la piel, etc.) <to shed one's clothes : quitarse uno la ropa>

shed[2] *n* : cobertizo *m*

she'd [ˈʃiːd] (*contraction of* **she had** *or* **she would**) → **have, would**

sheen [ˈʃiːn] *n* : brillo *m,* lustre *m*

sheep [ˈʃiːp] *ns & pl* : oveja *f*

sheepfold [ˈʃiːpˌfoːld] *n* : redil *m*

sheepish [ˈʃiːpɪʃ] *adj* : avergonzado

sheepskin [ˈʃiːpˌskɪn] *n* : piel *f* de oveja, piel *f* de borrego

sheer[1] [ˈʃɪr] *adv* **1** COMPLETELY : completamente, totalmente **2** VERTICALLY : verticalmente

sheer[2] *adj* **1** TRANSPARENT : vaporoso, transparente **2** ABSOLUTE, UTTER : puro <by sheer luck : por pura suerte> **3** STEEP : escarpado, vertical

sheet [ˈʃiːt] *n* **1** *or* **bedsheet** [ˈbɛdˌʃiːt] : sábana *f* **2** : hoja *f* (de papel) **3**

: capa *f* (de hielo, etc.) **4** : lámina *f,* placa *f* (de vidrio, metal, etc.), plancha *f* (de metal, madera, etc.) <baking sheet : placa de horno>

sheikh *or* **sheik** [ˈʃiːk, ˈʃeɪk] *n* : jeque *m*

shelf [ˈʃɛlf] *n, pl* **shelves** [ˈʃɛlvz] **1** : estante *m,* anaquel *m* (en una pared) **2** : banco *m,* arrecife *m* (en geología) <continental shelf : plataforma continental>

shell[1] [ˈʃɛl] *vt* **1** : desvainar (chícharos), pelar (nueces, etc.) **2** BOMBARD : bombardear

shell[2] *n* **1** SEASHELL : concha *f* **2** : cáscara *f* (de huevos, nueces, etc.), vaina *f* (de chícharos, etc.), caparazón *m* (de crustáceos, tortugas, etc.) **3** : cartucho *m,* casquillo *m* <a .45 caliber shell : un cartucho calibre .45> **4** *or* **racing shell** : bote *m* (para hacer regatas de remos)

she'll [ˈʃiːl, ˈʃɪl] (*contraction of* **she shall** *or* **she will**) → **shall, will**

shellac[1] [ʃəˈlæk] *vt* **-lacked; -lacking** **1** : laquear (madera, etc.) **2** DEFEAT : darle una paliza (a alguien), derrotar

shellac[2] *n* : laca *f*

shellfish [ˈʃɛl,fɪʃ] *n* : marisco *m*

shelter[1] [ˈʃɛltər] *vt* **1** PROTECT : proteger, abrigar **2** HARBOR : dar refugio a, albergar

shelter[2] *n* : refugio *m,* abrigo *m* <to take shelter : refugiarse>

shelve [ˈʃɛlv] *vt* **shelved; shelving** **1** : poner en estantes **2** DEFER : dar carpetazo a

shenanigans [ʃəˈnænɪgənz] *npl* **1** TRICKERY : artimañas *fpl* **2** MISCHIEF : travesuras *fpl*

shepherd[1] [ˈʃɛpərd] *vt* **1** : cuidar (ovejas, etc.) **2** GUIDE : conducir, guiar

shepherd[2] *n* : pastor *m*

shepherdess [ˈʃɛpərdəs] *n* : pastora *f*

sherbet [ˈʃərbət] *or* **sherbert** [-bərt] *n* : sorbete *m,* nieve *f Cuba, Mex, PRi*

sheriff [ˈʃɛrɪf] *n* : sheriff *mf*

sherry [ˈʃɛri] *n, pl* **-ries** : jerez *m*

she's [ˈʃiːz] (*contraction of* **she is** *or* **she has**) → **be, have**

shield[1] [ˈʃiːld] *vt* **1** PROTECT : proteger **2** CONCEAL : ocultar <to shield one's eyes : taparse los ojos>

shield[2] *n* **1** : escudo *m* (armadura) **2** PROTECTION : protección *f,* blindaje *m* (de un cable)

shier, shiest → **shy**

shift[1] [ˈʃɪft] *vt* **1** CHANGE : cambiar <to shift gears : cambiar de velocidad> **2** MOVE : mover **3** TRANSFER : transferir <to shift the blame : echarle la culpa (a otro)> — *vi* **1** CHANGE : cambiar **2** MOVE : moverse **3 to shift for oneself** : arreglárselas solo

shift[2] *n* **1** CHANGE, TRANSFER : cambio *m* <a shift in priorities : un cambio de prioridades> **2** : turno *m* <night shift : turno de noche> **3** DRESS : vestido *m* (suelto) **4** → **gearshift**

shiftless [ˈʃɪftləs] *adj* : perezoso, vago, holgazán

shifty [ˈʃɪfti] *adj* **shiftier; -est** : taimado, artero <a shifty look : una mirada huidiza>

shilling [ˈʃɪlɪŋ] *n* : chelín *m*

shimmer [ˈʃɪmər] *vi* GLIMMER : brillar con luz trémula

shin[1] [ˈʃɪn] *vi* **shinned; shinning** : trepar, subir <she shinned up the pole : subió al poste>

shin[2] *n* : espinilla *f,* canilla *f*

shine[1] [ˈʃaɪn] *v* **shone** [ˈʃoːn, *esp Brit and Canadian* ˈʃɒn] *or* **shined; shining** *vi* **1** : brillar, relucir <the stars were shining : las estrellas brillaban> **2** EXCEL : brillar, lucirse — *vt* **1** : alumbrar <he shined the flashlight at it : lo alumbró con la linterna> **2** POLISH : sacarle brillo a, lustrar

shine[2] *n* : brillo *m,* lustre *m*

shingle[1] [ˈʃɪŋgəl] *vt* **-gled; -gling** : techar

shingle[2] *n* : tablilla *f* (para techar)

shingles [ˈʃɪŋgəlz] *npl* : herpes *m*

shinny [ˈʃɪni] *vi* **-nied; -nying** → **shin**[1]

shiny [ˈʃaɪni] *adj* **shinier; -est** : brillante

ship[1] [ˈʃɪp] *vt* **shipped; shipping** **1** LOAD : embarcar (en un barco) **2** SEND : transportar (en barco), enviar <to ship by air : enviar por avión>

ship[2] *n* **1** : barco *m,* buque *m* **2** → **spaceship**

shipboard [ˈʃɪp,bord] *n* **on ~** : a bordo

shipbuilder [ˈʃɪp,bɪldər] *n* : constructor *m,* -tora *f* naval

shipment [ˈʃɪpmənt] *n* **1** SHIPPING : transporte *m,* embarque *m* **2** : envío *m,* remesa *f* <a shipment of medicine : un envío de medicina>

shipping [ˈʃɪpɪŋ] *n* **1** SHIPS : barcos *mpl,* embarcaciones *fpl* **2** TRANSPORTATION : transporte *m* (de mercancías)

shipshape [ˈʃɪpˈʃeɪp] *adj* : ordenado

shipwreck[1] [ˈʃɪp,rɛk] *vt* **to be shipwrecked** : naufragar

shipwreck[2] *n* : naufragio *m*

shipyard [ˈʃɪp,jɑrd] *n* : astillero *m*

shirk [ˈʃərk] *vt* : eludir, rehuir <to shirk one's responsibilities : esquivar uno sus responsabilidades>

shirt [ˈʃərt] *n* : camisa *f*

shiver[1] [ˈʃɪvər] *vi* **1** : tiritar (de frío) **2** TREMBLE : estremecerse, temblar

shiver[2] *n* : escalofrío *m,* estremecimiento *m*

shoal [ˈʃoːl] *n* : banco *m,* bajío *m*

shock[1] [ˈʃɑk] *vt* **1** UPSET : conmover, conmocionar **2** STARTLE : asustar, sobresaltar **3** SCANDALIZE : escandalizar **4** : darle una descarga eléctrica a

shock[2] *n* **1** COLLISION, JOLT : choque *m,* sacudida *f* **2** UPSET : conmoción *f,* golpe *m* emocional **3** : shock *m* (en medicina) **4** *or* **electric shock** : descarga *f* eléctrica **5** SHEAVES : gavillas *fpl* **6** **shock of hair** : mata *f* de pelo

shock absorber *n* **:** amortiguador *m*

shoddy [ˈʃɑdi] *adj* **shoddier; -est :** de mala calidad <a shoddy piece of work : un trabajo chapucero>

shoe[1] [ˈʃuː] *vt* **shod** [ˈʃɑd]; **shoeing :** herrar (un caballo)

shoe[2] *n* **1 :** zapato *m* <the shoe industry : la industria del calzado> **2** HORSESHOE **:** herradura *f* **3 brake shoe :** zapata *f*

shoelace [ˈʃuːˌleɪs] *n* **:** cordón *m* (de zapatos)

shoemaker [ˈʃuːˌmeɪkər] *n* **:** zapatero *m,* -ra *f*

shone → **shine**

shook → **shake**

shoot[1] [ˈʃuːt] *v* **shot** [ˈʃɑt]; **shooting** *vt* **1 :** disparar, tirar <to shoot a bullet : tirar una bala> **2 :** pegarle un tiro a, darle un balazo a <he shot her : le pegó un tiro> <they shot and killed him : lo mataron a balazos> **3** THROW **:** lanzar (una pelota, etc.), echar (una mirada) **4** PHOTOGRAPH **:** fotografiar **5** FILM **:** filmar — *vi* **1 :** disparar (con un arma de fuego) **2** DART **:** ir rápidamente <it shot past : pasó como una bala>

shoot[2] *n* **:** brote *m,* retoño *m,* vástago *m*

shooting star *n* **:** estrella *f* fugaz

shop[1] [ˈʃɑp] *vi* **shopped; shopping :** hacer compras <to go shopping : ir de compras>

shop[2] *n* **1** WORKSHOP **:** taller *m* **2** STORE **:** tienda *f*

shopkeeper [ˈʃɑpˌkiːpər] *n* **:** tendero *m,* -ra *f*

shoplift [ˈʃɑpˌlɪft] *vi* **:** hurtar mercancía (de una tienda) — *vt* **:** hurtar (de una tienda)

shoplifter [ˈʃɑpˌlɪftər] *n* **:** ladrón *m,* -drona *f* (que roba en una tienda)

shopper [ˈʃɑpər] *n* **:** comprador *m,* -dora *f*

shore[1] [ˈʃor] *vt* **shored; shoring :** apuntalar <they shored up the wall : apuntalaron la pared>

shore[2] *n* **1 :** orilla *f* (del mar, etc.) **2** PROP **:** puntal *m*

shoreline [ˈʃorˌlaɪn] *n* **:** orilla *f*

shorn → **shear**

short[1] [ˈʃɔrt] *adv* **1** ABRUPTLY **:** repentinamente, súbitamente <the car stopped short : el carro se paró en seco> **2 to fall short :** no alcanzar, quedarse corto

short[2] *adj* **1 :** corto (de medida), bajo (de estatura) **2** BRIEF **:** corto <short and sweet : corto y bueno> <a short time ago : hace poco> **3** CURT **:** brusco, cortante, seco **4 :** corto (de tiempo, de dinero) <I'm one dollar short : me falta un dólar>

short[3] *n* **1 shorts** *npl* **:** shorts *mpl,* pantalones *mpl* cortos **2** → **short circuit**

shortage [ˈʃɔrtɪdʒ] *n* **:** falta *f,* escasez *f,* carencia *f*

shortcake [ˈʃɔrtˌkeɪk] *n* **:** tarta *f* de fruta

shortchange [ˈʃɔrtˈtʃeɪndʒ] *vt* **-changed; -changing :** darle mal el cambio (a alguien)

short circuit *n* **:** cortocircuito *m,* corto *m* (eléctrico)

shortcoming [ˈʃɔrtˌkʌmɪŋ] *n* **:** defecto *m*

shortcut [ˈʃɔrtˌkʌt] *n* **1 :** atajo *m* <to take a shortcut : cortar camino> **2 :** alternativa *f* fácil, método *m* rápido

shorten [ˈʃɔrtən] *vt* **:** acortar — *vi* **:** acortarse

shorthand [ˈʃɔrtˌhænd] *n* **:** taquigrafía *f*

short–lived [ˈʃɔrtˈlɪvd, -ˈlaɪvd] *adj* **:** efímero

shortly [ˈʃɔrtli] *adv* **1** BRIEFLY **:** brevemente <to put it shortly : para decirlo en pocas palabras> **2** SOON **:** dentro de poco

shortness [ˈʃɔrtnəs] *n* **1 :** lo corto <shortness of stature : estatura baja> **2** BREVITY **:** brevedad *f* **3** CURTNESS **:** brusquedad *f* **4** SHORTAGE **:** falta *f,* escasez *f,* carencia *f*

shortsighted [ˈʃɔrtˌsaɪt̬əd] → **nearsighted**

shot [ˈʃɑt] *n* **1 :** disparo *m,* tiro *m* <to fire a shot : disparar> **2** PELLETS **:** perdigones *mpl* **3 :** tiro *m* (en deportes) **4** ATTEMPT **:** intento *m,* tentativa *f* <to have a shot at : hacer un intento por> **5** RANGE **:** alcance *m* <a long shot : una posibilidad remota> **6** PHOTOGRAPH **:** foto *f* **7** INJECTION **:** inyección *f* **8 :** trago *m* (de licor)

shotgun [ˈʃɑtˌɡʌn] *n* **:** escopeta *f*

should → **shall**

shoulder[1] [ˈʃoːldər] *vt* **1** JOSTLE **:** empujar (con el hombro) **2 :** ponerse al hombro (una mochila, etc.) **3 :** cargar con (la responsabilidad, etc.)

shoulder[2] *n* **1 :** hombro *m* <to shrug one's shoulders : encogerse los hombros> **2 :** arcén *m* (de una carretera)

shoulder blade *n* **:** omóplato *m,* omoplato *m,* escápula *f*

shouldn't [ˈʃʊdənt] (*contraction of* **should not**) → **should**

shout[1] [ˈʃaʊt] *v* **:** gritar, vocear

shout[2] *n* **:** grito *m*

shove[1] [ˈʃʌv] *v* **shoved; shoving :** empujar bruscamente

shove[2] *n* **:** empujón *m,* empellón *m*

shovel[1] [ˈʃʌvəl] *vt* **-veled** *or* **-velled; -veling** *or* **-velling 1 :** mover con (una) pala <they shoveled the dirt out : sacaron la tierra con palas> **2** DIG **:** cavar (con una pala)

shovel[2] *n* **:** pala *f*

show[1] [ˈʃoː] *v* **showed; shown** [ˈʃoːn] *or* **showed; showing** *vt* **1** DISPLAY **:** mostrar, enseñar **2** REVEAL **:** demostrar, manifestar, revelar <he showed himself to be a coward : se reveló como cobarde> **3** TEACH **:** enseñar **4** PROVE **:** demostrar, probar **5** CON-

DUCT, DIRECT : llevar, acompañar <to show someone the way : indicarle el camino a alguien> **6** : proyectar (una película), dar (un programa de televisión) — *vi* **1** : notarse, verse <the stain doesn't show : la mancha no se ve> **2** APPEAR : aparecer, dejarse ver

show[2] *n* **1** : demostración *f* <a show of force : una demostración de fuerza> **2** EXHIBITION : exposición *f,* exhibición *f* <flower show : exposición de flores> <to be on show : estar expuesto> **3** : espectáculo *m* (teatral), programa *m* (de televisión, etc.) <to go to a show : ir al teatro>

showcase [ˈʃoːˌkeɪs] *n* : vitrina *f*

showdown [ˈʃoːˌdaʊn] *n* : confrontación *f* (decisiva)

shower[1] [ˈʃaʊər] *vt* **1** SPRAY : regar, mojar **2** HEAP : colmar <they showered him with gifts : lo colmaron de regalos, le llovieron los regalos> — *vi* **1** BATHE : ducharse, darse una ducha **2** RAIN : llover

shower[2] *n* **1** : chaparrón *m,* chubasco *m* <a chance of showers : una posibilidad de chaparrones> **2** : ducha *f* <to take a shower : ducharse> **3** PARTY : fiesta *f* <a bridal shower : una despedida de soltera>

show off *vt* : hacer alarde de, ostentar — *vi* : lucirse

show up *vi* APPEAR : aparecer — *vt* EXPOSE : revelar

showy [ˈʃoːi] *adj* **showier; -est** : llamativo, ostentoso — **showily** *adv*

shrank → **shrink**

shrapnel [ˈʃræpnəl] *ns & pl* : metralla *f*

shred[1] [ˈʃrɛd] *vt* **shredded; shredding** : hacer trizas, desmenuzar (con las manos), triturar (con una máquina) <to shred vegetables : cortar verduras en tiras>

shred[2] *n* **1** STRIP : tira *f,* jirón *m* (de tela) **2** BIT : pizca *f* <not a shred of evidence : ni la mínima prueba>

shrew [ˈʃruː] *n* **1** : musaraña *f* (animal) **2** : mujer *f* regañona, arpía *f*

shrewd [ˈʃruːd] *adj* : astuto, inteligente, sagaz — **shrewdly** *adv*

shrewdness [ˈʃruːdnəs] *n* : astucia *f*

shriek[1] [ˈʃriːk] *vi* : chillar, gritar

shriek[2] *n* : chillido *m,* alarido *m,* grito *m*

shrill [ˈʃrɪl] *adj* : agudo, estridente

shrilly [ˈʃrɪli] *adv* : agudamente

shrimp [ˈʃrɪmp] *n* : camarón *m,* langostino *m*

shrine [ˈʃraɪn] *n* **1** TOMB : sepulcro *m* (de un santo) **2** SANCTUARY : lugar *m* sagrado, santuario *m*

shrink [ˈʃrɪŋk] *vi* **shrank** [ˈʃræŋk]; **shrunk** [ˈʃrʌŋk] *or* **shrunken** [ˈʃrʌŋkən]; **shrinking 1** RECOIL : retroceder <he shrank back : se echó para atrás> **2** : encogerse (dícese de la ropa)

shrinkage [ˈʃrɪŋkɪdʒ] *n* : encogimiento *m* (de ropa, etc.), contracción *f,* reducción *f*

shrivel [ˈʃrɪvəl] *vi* **-veled** *or* **-velled; -veling** *or* **-velling** : arrugarse, marchitarse

shroud[1] [ˈʃraʊd] *vt* : envolver

shroud[2] *n* **1** : sudario *m,* mortaja *f* **2** VEIL : velo *m* <wrapped in a shroud of mystery : envuelto en un aura de misterio>

shrub [ˈʃrʌb] *n* : arbusto *m,* mata *f*

shrubbery [ˈʃrʌbəri] *n, pl* **-beries** : arbustos *mpl,* matas *fpl*

shrug [ˈʃrʌg] *vi* **shrugged; shrugging** : encogerse de hombros

shrunk → **shrink**

shuck[1] [ˈʃʌk] *vt* : pelar (mazorcas, etc.), abrir (almejas, etc.)

shuck[2] *n* **1** HUSK : cascarilla *f,* cáscara *f* (de una nuez, etc.), hojas *fpl* (de una mazorca) **2** SHELL : concha *f* (de una almeja, etc.)

shudder[1] [ˈʃʌdər] *vi* : estremecerse

shudder[2] *n* : estremecimiento *m,* escalofrío *m*

shuffle[1] [ˈʃʌfəl] *v* **-fled; -fling** *vt* MIX : mezclar, revolver, barajar (naipes) — *vi* : caminar arrastrando los pies

shuffle[2] *n* **1** : acto *m* de revolver <each player gets a shuffle : a cada jugador le toca barajar> **2** JUMBLE : revoltijo *m* **3** : arrastramiento *m* de los pies

shun [ˈʃʌn] *vt* **shunned; shunning** : evitar, esquivar, eludir

shunt [ˈʃʌnt] *vt* : desviar, cambiar de vía (un tren)

shut [ˈʃʌt] *v* **shut; shutting** *vt* **1** CLOSE : cerrar <shut the lid : tápalo> **2 to shut out** EXCLUDE : excluir, dejar fuera a (personas), no dejar que entre (luz, ruido, etc.) **3 to shut up** CONFINE : encerrar — *vi* : cerrarse <the factory shut down : la fábrica cerró sus puertas>

shut–in [ˈʃʌtˌɪn] *n* : inválido *m,* -da *f* (que no puede salir de casa)

shutter [ˈʃʌtər] *n* **1** : contraventana *f,* postigo *m* (de una ventana o puerta) **2** : obturador *m* (de una cámara)

shuttle[1] [ˈʃʌt̬əl] *v* **-tled; -tling** *vt* : transportar <she shuttled him back and forth : lo llevaba de acá para allá> — *vi* : ir y venir

shuttle[2] *n* **1** : lanzadera *f* (para tejer) **2** : vehículo *m* que hace recorridos cortos **3** → **space shuttle**

shuttlecock [ˈʃʌt̬əlˌkɑk] *n* : volante *m*

shut up *vi* : callarse <shut up! : ¡cállate (la boca)!>

shy[1] [ˈʃaɪ] *vi* **shied; shying** : retroceder, asustarse

shy[2] *adj* **shier** *or* **shyer** [ˈʃaɪər]; **shiest** *or* **shyest** [ˈʃaɪəst] **1** TIMID : tímido **2** WARY : cauteloso <he's not shy about asking : no vacila en preguntar> **3** SHORT : corto (de dinero, etc.) <I'm two dollars shy : me faltan dos dólares>

shyly ['ʃaɪli] *adv* **:** tímidamente

shyness ['ʃaɪnəs] *n* **:** timidez *f*

sibling ['sɪblɪŋ] *n* **:** hermano *m,* hermana *f*

Sicilian [sə'sɪljən] *n* **:** siciliano *m,* -na *f* — **Sicilian** *adj*

sick ['sɪk] *adj* **1 :** enfermo **2** NAUSEOUS **:** mareado, con náuseas <to get sick : vomitar> **3 :** para uso de enfermos <sick day : día de permiso (por enfermedad)>

sickbed ['sɪk,bɛd] *n* **:** lecho *m* de enfermo

sicken ['sɪkən] *vt* **1 :** poner enfermo **2** REVOLT **:** darle asco (a alguien) — *vi* **:** enfermar(se), caer enfermo

sickening ['sɪkənɪŋ] *adj* **:** asqueroso, repugnante, nauseabundo

sickle ['sɪkəl] *n* **:** hoz *f*

sickly ['sɪkli] *adj* **sicklier; -est 1 :** enfermizo **2** → **sickening**

sickness ['sɪknəs] *n* **1 :** enfermedad *f* **2** NAUSEA **:** náuseas *fpl*

side ['saɪd] *n* **1 :** lado *m,* costado *m* (de una persona), ijada *f* (de un animal) **2 :** lado *m,* cara *f* (de una moneda, etc.) **3 :** lado *m,* parte *f* <he's on my side : está de mi parte> <to take sides : tomar partido>

sideboard ['saɪd,bord] *n* **:** aparador *m*

sideburns ['saɪd,bərnz] *npl* **:** patillas *fpl*

sided ['saɪdəd] *adj* **:** que tiene lados <one-sided : de un lado>

side effect *n* **:** efecto *m* secundario

sideline ['saɪd,laɪn] *n* **1 :** línea *f* de banda (en deportes) **2 :** actividad *f* suplementaria (en negocios) **3 to be on the sidelines :** estar al margen

sidelong ['saɪd,lɔŋ] *adj* **:** de reojo, de soslayo

sideshow ['saɪd,ʃo:] *n* **:** espectáculo *m* secundario, atracción *f* secundaria

sidestep ['saɪd,stɛp] *v* **-stepped; -stepping** *vi* **:** dar un paso hacia un lado — *vt* AVOID **:** esquivar, eludir

sidetrack ['saɪd,træk] *vt* **:** desviar (una conversación, etc.), distraer (a una persona)

sidewalk ['saɪd,wɔk] *n* **:** acera *f,* vereda *f,* andén *m CA, Col,* banqueta *f Mex*

sideways[1] ['saɪd,weɪz] *adv* **1 :** hacia un lado <it leaned sideways : se inclinaba hacia un lado> **2 :** de lado, de costado <lie sideways : acuéstese de costado>

sideways[2] *adj* **:** hacia un lado <a sideways glance : una mirada de reojo>

siding ['saɪdɪŋ] *n* **1 :** apartadero *m* (para trenes) **2 :** revestimiento *m* exterior (de un edificio)

sidle ['saɪdəl] *vi* **-dled; -dling :** moverse furtivamente

siege ['si:dʒ, 'si:ʒ] *n* **:** sitio *m* <to be under siege : estar sitiado>

siesta [si:'ɛstə] *n* **:** siesta *f*

sieve ['sɪv] *n* **:** tamiz *m,* cedazo *m,* criba *f* (en minerología)

sift ['sɪft] *vt* **1 :** tamizar, cerner <sift the flour : tamice la harina> **2** *or* **sift through :** examinar cuidadosamente, pasar por el tamiz

sifter ['sɪftər] *n* **:** tamiz *m,* cedazo *m*

sigh[1] ['saɪ] *vi* **:** suspirar

sigh[2] *n* **:** suspiro *m*

sight[1] ['saɪt] *vt* **:** ver (a una persona), divisar (la tierra, un barco)

sight[2] *n* **1 :** vista *f* (facultad) <out of sight : fuera de vista> **2 :** algo visto <it's a familiar sight : se ve con frecuencia> <she's a sight for sore eyes : da gusto verla> **3 :** lugar *m* de interés (para turistas, etc.) **4 :** mira *f* (de un rifle, etc.) **5** GLIMPSE **:** mirada *f* breve <I caught sight of her : la divisé, alcancé a verla>

sightless ['saɪtləs] *adj* **:** invidente, ciego

sightseer ['saɪt,si:ər] *n* **:** turista *mf*

sign[1] ['saɪn] *vt* **1 :** firmar <to sign a check : firmar un cheque> **2** *or* **to sign on** HIRE **:** contratar (a un empleado), fichar (a un jugador) — *vi* **1 :** hacer una seña <she signed for him to stop : le hizo una seña para que se parara> **2 :** comunicarse por señas

sign[2] *n* **1** SYMBOL **:** símbolo *m,* signo *m* <minus sign : signo de menos> **2** GESTURE **:** seña *f,* señal *f,* gesto *m* **3 :** letrero *m,* cartel *m* <neon sign : letrero de neón> **4** TRACE **:** señal *f,* indicio *m*

signal[1] ['sɪgnəl] *vt* **-naled** *or* **-nalled; -naling** *or* **-nalling 1 :** hacerle señas (a alguien) <she signaled me to leave : me hizo señas para que saliera> **2** INDICATE **:** señalar, indicar — *vi* **:** hacer señas, comunicar por señas

signal[2] *adj* NOTABLE **:** señalado, notable

signal[3] *n* **:** señal *f*

signature ['sɪgnə,tʃʊr] *n* **:** firma *f*

signet ['sɪgnət] *n* **:** sello *m*

significance [sɪg'nɪfɪkənts] *n* **1** MEANING **:** significado *m* **2** IMPORTANCE **:** importancia *f*

significant [sɪg'nɪfɪkənt] *adj* **1** IMPORTANT **:** importante **2** MEANINGFUL **:** significativo — **significantly** *adv*

signify ['sɪgnə,faɪ] *vt* **-fied; -fying 1 :** indicar <he signified his desire for more : haciendo señas indicó que quería más> **2** MEAN **:** significar

sign language *n* **:** lenguaje *m* por señas

signpost ['saɪn,po:st] *n* **:** poste *m* indicador

silence[1] ['saɪlənts] *vt* **-lenced; -lencing :** silenciar, acallar

silence[2] *n* **:** silencio *m*

silent ['saɪlənt] *adj* **1 :** callado <to remain silent : quedarse callado, guardar silencio> **2** QUIET, STILL **:** silencioso **3** MUTE **:** mudo <a silent letter : una letra muda>

silently ['saɪləntli] *adv* **:** silenciosamente, calladamente

silhouette[1] [,sɪlə'wɛt] *vt* **-etted; -etting :** destacar la silueta de <it was

silhouetted against the sky : se perfilaba contra el cielo>

silhouette[2] *n* : silueta *f*

silica [ˈsɪlɪkə] *n* : sílice *f*

silicon [ˈsɪlɪkən, -ˌkɑn] *n* : silicio *m*

silk [ˈsɪlk] *n* : seda *f*

silken [ˈsɪlkən] *adj* **1** : de seda <a silken veil : un velo de seda> **2** SILKY : sedoso <silken hair : cabellos sedosos>

silkworm [ˈsɪlkˌwərm] *n* : gusano *m* de seda

silky [ˈsɪlki] *adj* **silkier; -est** : sedoso

sill [ˈsɪl] *n* : alféizar *m* (de una ventana), umbral *m* (de una puerta)

silliness [ˈsɪlinəs] *n* : tontería *f*, estupidez *f*

silly [ˈsɪli] *adj* **sillier; -est** : tonto, estúpido, ridículo

silo [ˈsaɪˌloː] *n, pl* **silos** : silo *m*

silt [ˈsɪlt] *n* : cieno *m*

silver[1] [ˈsɪlvər] *adj* **1** : de plata <a silver spoon : una cuchara de plata> **2** → **silvery**

silver[2] *n* **1** : plata *f* **2** COINS : monedas *fpl* **3** → **silverware 4** : color *m* plata

silverware [ˈsɪlvərˌwær] *n* **1** : artículos *mpl* de plata, platería *f* **2** FLATWARE : cubertería *f*

silvery [ˈsɪlvəri] *adj* : plateado

similar [ˈsɪmələr] *adj* : similar, parecido, semejante

similarity [ˌsɪməˈlærət̬i] *n, pl* **-ties** : semejanza *f*, parecido *m*

similarly [ˈsɪmələrli] *adv* : de manera similar

simile [ˈsɪməˌliː] *n* : símil *m*

simmer [ˈsɪmər] *v* : hervir a fuego lento

simper[1] [ˈsɪmpər] *vi* : sonreír como un tonto

simper[2] *n* : sonrisa *f* tonta

simple [ˈsɪmpəl] *adj* **simpler; -plest 1** INNOCENT : inocente **2** PLAIN : sencillo, simple **3** EASY : simple, sencillo, fácil **4** STRAIGHTFORWARD : puro, simple <the simple truth : la pura verdad> **5** NAIVE : ingenuo, simple

simpleton [ˈsɪmpəltən] *n* : bobo *m*, -ba *f*; tonto *m*, -ta *f*

simplicity [sɪmˈplɪsət̬i] *n* : simplicidad *f*, sencillez *f*

simplification [ˌsɪmpləfəˈkeɪʃən] *n* : simplificación *f*

simplify [ˈsɪmpləˌfaɪ] *vt* **-fied; -fying** : simplificar

simply [ˈsɪmpli] *adv* **1** PLAINLY : sencillamente **2** SOLELY : simplemente, sólo **3** REALLY : absolutamente

simulate [ˈsɪmjəˌleɪt] *vt* **-lated; -lating** : simular

simultaneous [ˌsaɪməlˈteɪniəs] *adj* : simultáneo — **simultaneously** *adv*

sin[1] [ˈsɪn] *vi* **sinned; sinning** : pecar

sin[2] *n* : pecado *m*

since[1] [ˈsɪnts] *adv* **1** : desde entonces <they've been friends ever since : desde entonces han sido amigos> <she's since become mayor : más tarde se hizo alcalde> **2** AGO : hace <he's long since dead : murió hace mucho>

since[2] *conj* **1** : desde que <since he was born : desde que nació> **2** INASMUCH AS : ya que, puesto que, dado que

since[3] *prep* : desde

sincere [sɪnˈsɪr] *adj* **-cerer; -est** : sincero — **sincerely** *adv*

sincerity [sɪnˈsɛrət̬i] *n* : sinceridad *f*

sinew [ˈsɪnˌjuː, ˈsɪˌnuː] *n* **1** TENDON : tendón *m*, nervio *m* (en la carne) **2** POWER : fuerza *f*

sinewy [ˈsɪnjʊi, ˈsɪnʊi] *adj* **1** STRINGY : fibroso **2** STRONG, WIRY : fuerte, nervudo

sinful [ˈsɪnfəl] *adj* : pecador (dícese de las personas), pecaminoso

sing [ˈsɪŋ] *v* **sang** [ˈsæŋ] *or* **sung** [ˈsʌŋ]; **sung; singing** : cantar

singe [ˈsɪndʒ] *vt* **singed; singeing** : chamuscar, quemar

singer [ˈsɪŋər] *n* : cantante *mf*

single[1] [ˈsɪŋgəl] *vt* **-gled; -gling** *or* **to single out 1** SELECT : escoger **2** DISTINGUISH : señalar

single[2] *adj* **1** UNMARRIED : soltero **2** SOLE : solo <a single survivor : un solo sobreviviente> <every single one : cada uno, todos>

single[3] *n* **1** : soltero *m*, -ra *f* <for married couples and singles : para los matrimonios y los solteros> **2** *or* **single room** : habitación *f* individual **3** DOLLAR : billete *m* de un dólar

single–handed [ˈsɪŋgəlˈhændəd] *adj* : sin ayuda, solo

singly [ˈsɪŋgli] *adv* : individualmente, uno por uno

singular[1] [ˈsɪŋgjələr] *adj* **1** : singular (en gramática) **2** OUTSTANDING : singular, sobresaliente **3** STRANGE : singular, extraño

singular[2] *n* : singular *m*

singularly [ˈsɪŋgjələrli] *adv* : singularmente

sinister [ˈsɪnəstər] *adj* : siniestro

sink[1] [ˈsɪŋk] *v* **sank** [ˈsæŋk] *or* **sunk** [ˈsʌŋk]; **sunk; sinking** *vi* **1** : hundirse (dícese de un barco) **2** DROP, FALL : descender, caer <to sink into a chair : dejarse caer en una silla> <her heart sank : se le cayó el alma a los pies> **3** DECREASE : bajar — *vt* **1** : hundir (un barco, etc.) **2** EXCAVATE : excavar (un pozo para minar), perforar (un pozo de agua) **3** PLUNGE, STICK : clavar, hincar **4** INVEST : invertir (fondos)

sink[2] *n* **1 kitchen sink** : fregadero *m*, lavaplatos *m Chile, Col, Mex* **2 bathroom sink** : lavabo *m*, lavamanos *m*

sinner [ˈsɪnər] *n* : pecador *m*, -dora *f*

sinuous [ˈsɪnjʊəs] *adj* : sinuoso — **sinuously** *adv*

sinus [ˈsaɪnəs] *n* : seno *m*

sip[1] [ˈsɪp] *v* **sipped; sipping** *vt* : sorber — *vi* : beber a sorbos

sip[2] *n* : sorbo *m*

siphon[1] [ˈsaɪfən] *vt* : sacar con sifón

siphon[2] *n* : sifón *m*
sir [ˈsər] *n* **1** (*in titles*) : sir *m* **2** (*as a form of address*) : señor *m* <Dear Sir : Muy señor mío> <yes sir! : ¡sí, señor!>
sire[1] [ˈsaɪr] *vt* **sired; siring** : engendrar, ser el padre de
sire[2] *n* : padre *m*
siren [ˈsaɪrən] *n* : sirena *f*
sirloin [ˈsərˌlɔɪn] *n* : solomillo *m*
sirup → **syrup**
sisal [ˈsaɪsəl, -zəl] *n* : sisal *m*
sissy [ˈsɪsi] *n, pl* **-sies** : mariquita *f fam*
sister [ˈsɪstər] *n* : hermana *f*
sisterhood [ˈsɪstərˌhʊd] *n* **1** : condición *f* de ser hermana **2** : sociedad *f* de mujeres
sister–in–law [ˈsɪstərɪnˌlɔ] *n, pl* **sisters–in–law** : cuñada *f*
sisterly [ˈsɪstərli] *adj* : de hermana
sit [ˈsɪt] *v* **sat** [ˈsæt]; **sitting** *vi* **1** : sentarse, estar sentado <he sat down : se sentó> **2** ROOST : posarse **3** : sesionar <the legislature is sitting : la legislatura está en sesión> **4** POSE : posar (para un retrato) **5** LIE, REST : estar (ubicado) <the house sits on a hill : la casa está en una colina> — *vt* SEAT : sentar, colocar <I sat him on the sofa : lo senté en el sofá>
site [ˈsaɪt] *n* 1 PLACE : sitio *m,* lugar *m* **2** LOCATION : emplazamiento *m,* ubicación *f*
sitting room → **living room**
sitter [ˈsɪtər] → **baby–sitter**
situated [ˈsɪtʃʊˌeɪtəd] *adj* LOCATED : ubicado, situado
situation [ˌsɪtʃʊˈeɪʃən] *n* **1** LOCATION : situación *f,* ubicación *f,* emplazamiento *m* **2** CIRCUMSTANCES : situación *f* **3** JOB : empleo *m*
six[1] [ˈsɪks] *adj* : seis
six[2] *n* : seis *m*
six–gun [ˈsɪksˌgʌn] *n* : revólver *m* (con seis cámaras)
six hundred[1] *adj* : seiscientos
six hundred[2] *n* : seiscientos *m*
six–shooter [ˈsɪksˌʃuːtər] → **six–gun**
sixteen[1] [sɪksˈtiːn] *adj* : dieciséis
sixteen[2] *n* : dieciséis *m*
sixteenth[1] [sɪksˈtiːnθ] *adj* : decimosexto
sixteenth[2] *n* **1** : decimosexto *m,* -ta *f* (en una serie) **2** : dieciseisavo *m,* dieciseisava parte *f*
sixth[1] [ˈsɪksθ, ˈsɪkst] *adj* : sexto
sixth[2] *n* **1** : sexto *m,* -ta *f* (en una serie) **2** : sexto *m,* sexta parte *f*
sixtieth[1] [ˈsɪkstiəθ] *adj* : sexagésimo
sixtieth[2] *n* **1** : sexagésimo *m,* -ma *f* (en una serie) **2** : sesentavo *m,* sesentava parte *f*
sixty[1] [ˈsɪksti] *adj* : sesenta
sixty[2] *n, pl* **-ties** : sesenta *m*
sizable *or* **sizeable** [ˈsaɪzəbəl] *adj* : considerable
size[1] [ˈsaɪz] *vt* **sized; sizing 1** : clasificar según el tamaño **2 to size up** : evaluar, apreciar
size[2] *n* **1** DIMENSIONS : tamaño *m,* talla *f* (de ropa), número *m* (de zapatos) **2** MAGNITUDE : magnitud *f*
sizzle [ˈsɪzəl] *vi* **-zled; -zling** : chisporrotear
skate[1] [ˈskeɪt] *vi* **skated; skating** : patinar
skate[2] *n* **1** : patín *m* <roller skate : patín de ruedas> **2** : raya *f* (pez)
skateboard [ˈskeɪtˌbord] *n* : monopatín *m*
skater [ˈskeɪtər] *n* : patinador *m,* -dora *f*
skein [ˈskeɪn] *n* : madeja *f*
skeletal [ˈskɛlətəl] *adj* **1** : óseo (en anatomía) **2** EMACIATED : esquelético
skeleton [ˈskɛlətən] *n* **1** : esqueleto *m* (anatómico) **2** FRAMEWORK : armazón *mf*
skeptic [ˈskɛptɪk] *n* : escéptico *m,* -ca *f*
skeptical [ˈskɛptɪkəl] *adj* : escéptico
skepticism [ˈskɛptəˌsɪzəm] *n* : escepticismo *m*
sketch[1] [ˈskɛtʃ] *vt* : bosquejar — *vi* : hacer bosquejos
sketch[2] *n* **1** DRAWING, OUTLINE : esbozo *m,* bosquejo *m* **2** ESSAY : ensayo *m*
sketchy [ˈskɛtʃi] *adj* **sketchier; -est** : incompleto, poco detallado
skewer[1] [ˈskjuːər] *vt* : ensartar (carne, etc.)
skewer[2] *n* : brocheta *f,* broqueta *f*
ski[1] [ˈskiː] *vi* **skied; skiing** : esquiar
ski[2] *n, pl* **skis** : esquí *m*
skid[1] [ˈskɪd] *vi* **skidded; skidding** : derrapar, patinar
skid[2] *n* : derrape *m,* patinazo *m*
skier [ˈskiːər] *n* : esquiador *m,* -dora *f*
skiff [ˈskɪf] *n* : esquife *m*
skill [ˈskɪl] *n* **1** DEXTERITY : habilidad *f,* destreza *f* **2** CAPABILITY : capacidad *f,* arte *m,* técnica *f* <organizational skills : la capacidad para organizar>
skilled [ˈskɪld] *adj* : hábil, experto
skillet [ˈskɪlət] *n* : sartén *mf*
skillful [ˈskɪlfəl] *adj* : hábil, diestro
skillfully [ˈskɪlfəli] *adv* : con habilidad, con destreza
skim[1] [ˈskɪm] *vt* **skimmed; skimming 1** *or* **to skim off** : espumar, descremar (leche) **2** : echarle un vistazo a (un libro, etc.), pasar rozando (un superficie)
skim[2] *adj* : descremado <skim milk : leche descremada>
skimp [ˈskɪmp] *vi* **to skimp on** : escatimar
skimpy [ˈskɪmpi] *adj* **skimpier; -est** : exiguo, escaso, raquítico
skin[1] [ˈskɪn] *vt* **skinned; skinning** : despellejar, desollar
skin[2] *n* **1** : piel *f,* cutis *m* (de la cara) <dark skin : piel morena> **2** RIND : piel *f*
skin diving *n* : buceo *m,* submarinismo *m*
skinflint [ˈskɪnˌflɪnt] *n* : tacaño *m,* -ña *f*

skinned ['skɪnd] *adj* **:** de piel <tough-skinned : de piel dura>
skinny ['skɪni] *adj* **skinnier; -est** **:** flaco
skip[1] ['skɪp] *v* **skipped; skipping** *vi* **:** ir dando brincos — *vt* **:** saltarse
skip[2] *n* **:** brinco *m,* salto *m*
skipper ['skɪpər] *n* **:** capitán *m,* -tana *f*
skirmish[1] ['skərmɪʃ] *vi* **:** escaramuzar
skirmish[2] *n* **:** escaramuza *f,* refriega *f*
skirt[1] ['skərt] *vt* **1** BORDER **:** bordear **2** EVADE **:** evadir, esquivar
skirt[2] *n* **:** falda *f,* pollera *f*
skit ['skɪt] *n* **:** sketch *m* (teatral)
skittish ['skɪt̬ɪʃ] *adj* **:** asustadizo, nervioso
skulk ['skʌlk] *vi* **:** merodear
skull ['skʌl] *n* **1 :** cráneo *m,* calavera *f* **2 skull and crossbones :** calavera *f* (bandera pirata)
skunk ['skʌŋk] *n* **:** zorrillo *m,* mofeta *f*
sky ['skaɪ] *n, pl* **skies :** cielo *m*
skylark ['skaɪˌlɑrk] *n* **:** alondra *f*
skylight ['skaɪˌlaɪt] *n* **:** claraboya *f,* tragaluz *m*
skyline ['skaɪˌlaɪn] *n* **:** horizonte *m*
skyrocket ['skaɪˌrɑkət] *vi* **:** dispararse
skyscraper ['skaɪˌskreɪpər] *n* **:** rascacielos *m*
slab ['slæb] *n* **:** losa *f* (de piedra), tabla *f* (de madera), pedazo *m* grueso (de pan, etc.)
slack[1] ['slæk] *adj* **1** CARELESS **:** descuidado, negligente **2** LOOSE **:** flojo **3** SLOW **:** de poco movimiento
slack[2] *n* **1 :** parte *f* floja <to take up the slack : tensar (una cuerda, etc.)> **2 slacks** *npl* **:** pantalones *mpl*
slacken ['slækən] *vt* **:** aflojar — *vi* **:** aflojarse
slag ['slæg] *n* **:** escoria *f*
slain → **slay**
slake ['sleɪk] *vt* **slaked; slaking :** saciar (la sed), satisfacer (la curiosidad)
slam[1] ['slæm] *v* **slammed; slamming** *vt* **1 :** cerrar de golpe <he slammed the door : dio un portazo> **2 :** tirar o dejar caer de golpe <he slammed down the book : dejó caer el libro de un golpe> — *vi* **1 :** cerrarse de golpe **2 to slam into :** chocar contra
slam[2] *n* **:** golpe *m,* portazo *m* (de una puerta)
slander[1] ['slændər] *vt* **:** calumniar, difamar
slander[2] *n* **:** calumnia *f,* difamación *f*
slanderous ['slændərəs] *adj* **:** difamatorio, calumnioso
slang ['slæŋ] *n* **:** argot *m,* jerga *f*
slant[1] ['slænt] *vi* **:** inclinarse, ladearse — *vt* **1** SLOPE **:** inclinar **2** ANGLE **:** sesgar, orientar, dirigir <a story slanted towards youth : un artículo dirigido a los jóvenes>
slant[2] *n* **1** INCLINE **:** inclinación *f* **2** PERSPECTIVE **:** perspectiva *f,* enfoque *m*
slap[1] ['slæp] *vt* **slapped; slapping :** bofetear, cachetear, dar una palmada (en la espalda, etc.)
slap[2] *n* **:** bofetada *f,* cachetada *f,* palmada *f*
slash[1] ['slæʃ] *vt* **1** GASH **:** cortar, hacer un tajo en **2** REDUCE **:** reducir, rebajar (precios)
slash[2] *n* **:** tajo *m,* corte *m*
slat ['slæt] *n* **:** tablilla *f,* listón *m*
slate ['sleɪt] *n* **1 :** pizarra *f* <a slate roof : un techo de pizarra> **2 :** lista *f* de candidatos (políticos)
slaughter[1] ['slɔt̬ər] *vt* **1** BUTCHER **:** matar (animales) **2** MASSACRE **:** masacrar (personas)
slaughter[2] *n* **1 :** matanza *f* (de animales) **2** MASSACRE **:** masacre *f,* carnicería *f*
slaughterhouse ['slɔt̬ərˌhaʊs] *n* **:** matadero *m*
Slav ['slɑv, 'slæv] *n* **:** eslavo *m,* -va *f*
slave[1] ['sleɪv] *vi* **slaved; slaving :** trabajar como un burro
slave[2] *n* **:** esclavo *m,* -va *f*
slaver ['slævər, 'sleɪ-] *vi* **:** babear
slavery ['sleɪvəri] *n* **:** esclavitud *f*
Slavic ['slɑvɪk, 'slæ-] *adj* **:** eslavo
slavish ['sleɪvɪʃ] *adj* **1** SERVILE **:** servil **2** IMITATIVE **:** poco original
slay ['sleɪ] *vt* **slew** ['slu:]; **slain** ['sleɪn]; **slaying :** asesinar, matar
slayer ['sleɪər] *n* **:** asesino *m,* -na *f*
sleazy ['sli:zi] *adj* **sleazier; -est 1** SHODDY **:** chapucero, de mala calidad **2** DILAPIDATED **:** ruinoso **3** DISREPUTABLE **:** de mala fama
sled[1] ['slɛd] *v* **sledded; sledding** *vi* **:** ir en trineo — *vt* **:** transportar en trineo
sled[2] *n* **:** trineo *m*
sledge ['slɛdʒ] *n* **1 :** trineo *m* (grande) **2** → **sledgehammer**
sledgehammer ['slɛdʒˌhæmər] *n* **:** almádena *f,* combo *m Chile, Peru*
sleek[1] ['sli:k] *vt* SLICK **:** alisar
sleek[2] *adj* **:** liso y brillante
sleep[1] ['sli:p] *vi* **slept** ['slɛpt]; **sleeping :** dormir
sleep[2] *n* **1 :** sueño *m* **2 to go to sleep :** dormirse
sleeper ['sli:pər] *n* **1 :** durmiente *mf* <to be a light sleeper : tener el sueño ligero> **2** *or* **sleeping car :** coche *m* cama, coche *m* dormitorio
sleepily ['sli:pəli] *adv* **:** de manera somnolienta
sleepiness ['sli:pinəs] *n* **:** somnolencia *f*
sleepless ['sli:pləs] *adj* **:** sin dormir, desvelado <to have a sleepless night : pasar la noche en blanco>
sleepwalker ['sli:pˌwɔkər] *n* **:** sonámbulo *m,* -la *f*
sleepy ['sli:pi] *adj* **sleepier; -est 1** DROWSY **:** somnoliento, soñoliento <to be sleepy : tener sueño> **2** LETHARGIC **:** aletargado, letárgico
sleet[1] ['sli:t] *vi* **to be sleeting :** caer aguanieve

sleet[2] *n* : aguanieve *f*

sleeve ['sliːv] *n* : manga *f* (de una camisa, etc.)

sleeveless ['sliːvləs] *adj* : sin mangas

sleigh[1] ['sleɪ] *vi* : ir en trineo

sleigh[2] *n* : trineo *m* (tirado por caballos)

sleight of hand [ˌslaɪṭəv'hænd] : prestidigitación *f*, juegos *mpl* de manos

slender ['slɛndər] *adj* **1** SLIM : esbelto, delgado **2** SCANTY : exiguo, escaso <a slender hope : una esperanza lejana>

sleuth ['sluːθ] *n* : detective *mf*; sabueso *m*, -sa *f*

slew → **slay**

slice[1] ['slaɪs] *vt* **sliced; slicing** : cortar

slice[2] *n* : rebanada *f*, tajada *f*, lonja *f* (de carne, etc.), rodaja *f* (de una verdura, fruta, etc.), trozo *m* (de pastel, etc.)

slick[1] ['slɪk] *vt* : alisar

slick[2] *adj* **1** SLIPPERY : resbaladizo, resbaloso **2** CRAFTY : astuto, taimado

slicker ['slɪkər] *n* : impermeable *m*

slide[1] ['slaɪd] *v* **slid** ['slɪd]; **sliding** ['slaɪdɪŋ] *vi* **1** SLIP : resbalar **2** GLIDE : deslizarse **3** DECLINE : bajar <to let things slide : dejar pasar las cosas> — *vt* : correr, deslizar

slide[2] *n* **1** SLIDING : deslizamiento *m* **2** SLIP : resbalón *m* **3** : tobogán *m* (para niños) **4** : TRANSPARENCY : diapositiva *f* (fotográfica) **5** DECLINE : descenso *m*

slier, sliest → **sly**

slight[1] ['slaɪt] *vt* : desairar, despreciar

slight[2] *adj* **1** SLENDER : esbelto, delgado **2** FLIMSY : endeble **3** TRIFLING : leve, insignificante <a slight pain : un leve dolor> **4** SMALL : pequeño, ligero <not in the slightest : en absoluto>

slight[3] *n* SNUB : desaire *m*

slightly ['slaɪtli] *adv* : ligeramente, un poco

slim[1] ['slɪm] *v* **slimmed; slimming** : adelgazar

slim[2] *adj* **slimmer; slimmest 1** SLENDER : esbelto, delgado **2** SCANTY : exiguo, escaso

slime ['slaɪm] *n* **1** : baba *f* (secretado por un animal) **2** MUD, SILT : fango *m*, cieno *m*

slimy ['slaɪmi] *adj* **slimier; -est** : viscoso

sling[1] ['slɪŋ] *vt* **slung** ['slʌŋ]; **slinging 1** THROW : lanzar, tirar **2** HANG : colgar

sling[2] *n* **1** : honda *f* (arma) **2** : cabestrillo *m* <my arm is in a sling : llevo el brazo en cabestrillo>

slingshot ['slɪŋˌʃɑt] *n* : tiragomas *m*, resortera *f Mex*

slink ['slɪŋk] *vi* **slunk** ['slʌŋk]; **slinking** : caminar furtivamente

slip[1] ['slɪp] *v* **slipped; slipping** *vi* **1** STEAL : ir sigilosamente <to slip away : escabullirse> <to slip out the door : escaparse por la puerta> **2** SLIDE : resbalarse, deslizarse **3** LAPSE : caer <to slip into error : equivocarse> **4 to let slip** : dejar escapar **5 to slip into** PUT ON : ponerse — *vt* **1** PUT : meter, poner **2** PASS : pasar <she slipped me a note : me pasó una nota> **3 to slip one's mind** : olvidársele a uno

slip[2] *n* **1** PIER : atracadero *m* **2** MISHAP : percance *m*, contratiempo *m* **3** MISTAKE : error *m*, desliz *m* <a slip of the tongue : un lapsus> **4** PETTICOAT : enagua *f* **5** : injerto *m*, esqueje *m* (de una planta) **6 slip of paper** : papelito *m*

slipper ['slɪpər] *n* : zapatilla *f*, pantufla *f*

slipperiness ['slɪpərinəs] *n* **1** : lo resbaloso, lo resbaladizo **2** TRICKINESS : astucia *f*

slippery ['slɪpəri] *adj* **slipperier; -est 1** : resbaloso, resbaladizo <a slippery road : un camino resbaloso> **2** TRICKY : artero, astuto, taimado **3** ELUSIVE : huidizo, escurridizo

slipshod ['slɪpˌʃɑd] *adj* : descuidado, chapucero

slip up *vi* : equivocarse

slit[1] ['slɪt] *vt* **slit; slitting** : cortar, abrir por lo largo

slit[2] *n* **1** OPENING : abertura *f*, rendija *f* **2** CUT : corte *m*, raja *f*, tajo *m*

slither ['slɪðər] *vi* : deslizarse

sliver ['slɪvər] *n* : astilla *f*

slob ['slɑb] *n* : persona *f* desaliñada <what a slob! : ¡qué cerdo!>

slobber[1] ['slɑbər] *vi* : babear

slobber[2] *n* : baba *f*

slogan ['sloːgən] *n* : lema *m*, eslogan *m*

sloop ['sluːp] *n* : balandra *f*

slop[1] ['slɑp] *v* **slopped; slopping** *vt* : derramar — *vi* : derramarse

slop[2] *n* : bazofia *f*

slope[1] ['sloːp] *vi* **sloped; sloping** : inclinarse <the road slopes upward : el camino sube (en pendiente)>

slope[2] *n* : inclinación *f*, pendiente *f*, declive *m*

sloppy ['slɑpi] *adj* **sloppier; -est 1** MUDDY, SLUSHY : lodoso, fangoso **2** UNTIDY : descuidado (en el trabajo, etc.), desaliñado (de aspecto)

slot ['slɑt] *n* : ranura *f*

sloth ['slɔθ, 'sloːθ] *n* **1** LAZINESS : pereza *f* **2** : perezoso *m* (animal)

slouch[1] ['slaʊtʃ] *vi* : andar con los hombros caídos, repantigarse (en un sillón)

slouch[2] *n* **1** SLUMPING : mala postura *f* **2** BUNGLER, IDLER : haragán *m*, -gana *f*; inepto *m*, -ta *f* <to be no slouch : no quedarse atrás>

slough[1] ['slʌf] *vt* : mudar de (piel)

slough[2] ['sluː, 'slaʊ] *n* SWAMP : ciénaga *f*

Slovak ['sloːˌvɑk, -ˌvæk] *or* **Slovakian** [sloː'vɑkiən, -'væ-] *n* : eslovaco *m*, -ca *f* — **Slovak** *or* **Slovakian** *adj*

Slovene ['sloːˌviːn] *or* **Slovenian** [sloː'viːniən] *n* : esloveno *m*, -na *f* — **Slovene** *or* **Slovenian** *adj*

slovenly ['slɑvənli, 'slʌv-] *adj* : descuidado (en el trabajo, etc.), desaliñado (de aspecto)

slow[1] [slo:] *vt* : retrasar, reducir la marcha de — *vi* : ir más despacio

slow[2] *adv* : despacio, lentamente

slow[3] *adj* **1** : lento <a slow process : un proceso lento> **2** : atrasado <my watch is slow : mi reloj está atrasado, mi reloj se atrasa> **3** SLUGGISH : lento, poco activo **4** STUPID : lento, torpe, corto de alcances

slowly [slo:li] *adv* : lentamente, despacio

slowness [slo:nəs] *n* : lentitud *f,* torpeza *f*

sludge ['slʌdʒ] *n* : aguas *fpl* negras, aguas *fpl* residuales

slug[1] ['slʌg] *vt* **slugged; slugging** : pegarle un porrazo (a alguien)

slug[2] *n* **1** : babosa *f* (molusco) **2** BULLET : bala *f* **3** TOKEN : ficha *f* **4** BLOW : porrazo *m,* puñetazo *m*

sluggish ['slʌgɪʃ] *adj* : aletargado, lento

sluice[1] ['slu:s] *vt* **sluiced; sluicing** : lavar en agua corriente

sluice[2] *n* : canal *m*

slum ['slʌm] *n* : barriada *f,* barrio *m* bajo

slumber[1] ['slʌmbər] *vi* : dormir

slumber[2] *n* : sueño *m*

slump[1] ['slʌmp] *vi* **1** DECLINE, DROP : disminuir, bajar **2** SLOUCH : encorvarse, dejarse caer (en una silla, etc.)

slump[2] *n* : bajón *m,* declive *m* (económico)

slung → **sling**

slunk → **slink**

slur[1] ['slər] *vt* **slurred; slurring** : ligar (notas musicales), tragarse (las palabras)

slur[2] *n* **1** : ligado *m* (en música), mala pronunciación *f* (de las palabras) **2** ASPERSION : calumnia *f,* difamación *f*

slurp[1] ['slərp] *vi* : beber o comer haciendo ruido — *vt* : sorber ruidosamente

slurp[2] *n* : sorbo *m* (ruidoso)

slush ['slʌʃ] *n* : nieve *f* medio derretida

slut ['slʌt] *n* PROSTITUTE : ramera *f,* fulana *f*

sly ['slaɪ] *adj* **slier** ['slaɪər]; **sliest** ['slaɪəst] **1** CUNNING : astuto, taimado **2** UNDERHANDED : soplado — **slyly** *adv*

slyness ['slaɪnəs] *n* : astucia *f*

smack[1] ['smæk] *vi* **to smack of** : oler a, saber a — *vt* **1** KISS : besar, plantarle un beso (a alguien) **2** SLAP : pegarle una bofetada (a alguien) **3 to smack one's lips** : relamerse

smack[2] *adv* : justo, exactamente <smack in the face : en plena cara>

smack[3] *n* **1** TASTE, TRACE : sabor *m,* indicio *m* **2** : chasquido *m* (de los labios) **3** SLAP : bofetada *f* **4** KISS : beso *m*

small ['smɔl] *adj* **1** : pequeño, chico <a small house : una casa pequeña> <small change : monedas de poco valor> **2** TRIVIAL : pequeño, insignificante

smallness ['smɔlnəs] *n* : pequeñez *f*

smallpox ['smɔl,pɑks] *n* : viruela *f*

smart[1] ['smɑrt] *vi* **1** STING : escocer, picar, arder **2** HURT : dolerse, resentirse <to smart under a rejection : dolerse ante un rechazo>

smart[2] *adj* **1** BRIGHT : listo, vivo, inteligente **2** STYLISH : elegante — **smartly** *adv*

smart[3] *n* : escozor *m,* dolor *m*

smartness ['smɑrtnəs] *n* **1** INTELLIGENCE : inteligencia *f* **2** ELEGANCE : elegancia *f*

smash[1] ['smæʃ] *vt* **1** BREAK : romper, quebrar, hacer pedazos **2** WRECK : destrozar, arruinar **3** CRASH : estrellar, chocar — *vi* **1** SHATTER : hacerse pedazos, hacerse añicos **2** COLLIDE, CRASH : estrellarse, chocar

smash[2] *n* **1** BLOW : golpe *m* **2** COLLISION : choque *m* **3** BANG, CRASH : estrépito *m*

smattering ['smætərɪŋ] *n* **1** : nociones *fpl* <she has a smattering of programming : tiene nociones de programación> **2** : un poco, unos cuantos <a smattering of spectators : unos cuantos espectadores>

smear[1] ['smɪr] *vt* **1** DAUB : embadurnar, untar (mantequilla, etc.) **2** SMUDGE : emborronar **3** SLANDER : calumniar, difamar

smear[2] *n* **1** SMUDGE : mancha *f* **2** SLANDER : calumnia *f*

smell[1] ['smɛl] *v* **smelled** *or* **smelt** ['smɛlt]; **smelling** *vt* : oler, olfatear <to smell danger : olfatear el peligro> — *vi* : oler <to smell good : oler bien>

smell[2] *n* **1** : olfato *m,* sentido *m* del olfato **2** ODOR : olor *m*

smelly ['smɛli] *adj* **smellier; -est** : maloliente

smelt[1] ['smɛlt] *vt* : fundir

smelt[2] *n, pl* **smelts** *or* **smelt** : eperlano *m* (pez)

smile[1] ['smaɪl] *vi* **smiled; smiling** : sonreír

smile[2] *n* : sonrisa *f*

smirk[1] ['smərk] *vi* : sonreír con suficiencia

smirk[2] *n* : sonrisa *f* satisfecha

smite ['smaɪt] *vt* **smote** ['smo:t]; **smitten** ['smɪtən] *or* **smote; smiting 1** STRIKE : golpear **2** AFFLICT : afligir

smith ['smɪθ] *n* : herrero *m,* -ra *f*

smithy ['smɪθi] *n, pl* **smithies** : herrería *f*

smock ['smɑk] *n* : bata *f,* blusón *m*

smog ['smɑg, 'smɔg] *n* : smog *m*

smoke[1] ['smo:k] *v* **smoked; smoking** *vi* **1** : echar humo, humear <a smoking chimney : una chimenea que echa humo> **2** : fumar <I don't smoke : no fumo> — *vt* : ahumar (carne, etc.)

smoke[2] *n* : humo *m*

smoke detector [dɪˈtɛktər] *n* : detector *m* de humo
smoker [ˈsmoːkər] *n* : fumador *m,* -dora *f*
smokestack [ˈsmoːkˌstæk] *n* : chimenea *f*
smoky [ˈsmoːki] *adj* **smokier; -est 1** SMOKING : humeante **2** : a humo <a smoky flavor : un sabor a humo> **3** : lleno de humo <a smoky room : un cuarto lleno de humo>
smolder [ˈsmoːldər] *vi* **1** : arder sin llama **2** : arder (en el corazón) <his anger smoldered : su rabia ardía>
smooth[1] [ˈsmuːð] *vt* : alisar
smooth[2] *adj* **1** : liso (dícese de una superficie) <smooth skin : piel lisa> **2** : suave (dícese de un movimiento) <a smooth landing : un aterrizaje suave> **3** : sin grumos <a smooth sauce : una salsa sin grumos> **4** : fluido <smooth writing : escritura fluida>
smoothly [ˈsmuːðli] *adv* **1** GENTLY, SOFTLY : suavemente **2** EASILY : con facilidad, sin problemas
smoothness [ˈsmuːðnəs] *n* : suavidad *f*
smother [ˈsmʌðər] *vt* **1** SUFFOCATE : ahogar, sofocar **2** COVER : cubrir **3** SUPPRESS : contener — *vi* : asfixiarse
smudge[1] [ˈsmʌdʒ] *v* **smudged; smudging** *vt* : emborronar — *vi* : correrse
smudge[2] *n* : mancha *f,* borrón *m*
smug [ˈsmʌg] *adj* **smugger; smuggest** : suficiente, pagado de sí mismo
smuggle [ˈsmʌgəl] *vt* **-gled; -gling** : contrabandear, pasar de contrabando
smuggler [ˈsmʌgələr] *n* : contrabandista *mf*
smugly [ˈsmʌgli] *adv* : con suficiencia
smut [ˈsmʌt] *n* **1** SOOT : tizne *m,* hollín *m* **2** FUNGUS : tizón *m* **3** OBSCENITY : obscenidad *f,* inmundicia *f*
smutty [ˈsmʌti] *adj* **smuttier; -est 1** SOOTY : tiznado **2** OBSCENE : obsceno, indecente
snack [ˈsnæk] *n* : refrigerio *m,* bocado *m,* tentempié *m fam* <an afternoon snack : una merienda>
snag[1] [ˈsnæg] *v* **snagged; snagging** *vt* : enganchar — *vi* : engancharse
snag[2] *n* : problema *m,* inconveniente *m*
snail [ˈsneɪl] *n* : caracol *m*
snake [ˈsneɪk] *n* : culebra *f,* serpiente *f*
snakebite [ˈsneɪkˌbaɪt] *n* : mordedura *f* de serpiente
snap[1] [ˈsnæp] *v* **snapped; snapping** *vi* **1** : intentar morder (dícese de un perro, etc.), picar (dícese de un pez) **2** : hablar con severidad <he snapped at me! : ¡me gritó!> **3** BREAK : romperse, quebrarse (haciendo un chasquido) — *vt* **1** BREAK : partir (en dos), quebrar **2** : hacer (algo) de un golpe <to snap open : abrir de golpe> **3** RETORT : decir bruscamente **4** CLICK : chasquear <to snap one's fingers : chasquear los dedos>
snap[2] *n* **1** CLICK, CRACK : chasquido *m* **2** FASTENER : broche *m* **3** CINCH : cosa *f* fácil <it's a snap : es facilísimo>
snapdragon [ˈsnæpˌdrægən] *n* : dragón *m* (flor)
snapper [ˈsnæpər] → **red snapper**
snappy [ˈsnæpi] *adj* **snappier; -est 1** FAST : rápido <make it snappy! : ¡date prisa!> **2** LIVELY : vivaz **3** CHILLY : frío **4** STYLISH : elegante
snapshot [ˈsnæpˌʃɑt] *n* : instantánea *f*
snare[1] [ˈsnær] *vt* **snared; snaring** : atrapar
snare[2] *n* : trampa *f,* red *f*
snare drum *n* : tambor *m* con bordón
snarl[1] [ˈsnɑrl] *vi* **1** TANGLE : enmarañar, enredar **2** GROWL : gruñir
snarl[2] *n* **1** TANGLE : enredo *m,* maraña *f* **2** GROWL : gruñido *m*
snatch[1] [ˈsnætʃ] *vt* : arrebatar
snatch[2] *n* : fragmento *m*
sneak[1] [ˈsniːk] *vi* : ir a hurtadillas — *vt* : hacer furtivamente <to sneak a look : mirar con disimulo> <he sneaked a smoke : fumó un cigarrillo a escondidas>
sneak[2] *n* : soplón *m,* -plona *f*
sneakers [ˈsniːkərz] *npl* : tenis *mpl,* zapatillas *fpl*
sneaky [ˈsniːki] *adj* **sneakier; -est** : solapado
sneer[1] [ˈsnɪr] *vi* : sonreír con desprecio
sneer[2] *n* : sonrisa *f* de desprecio
sneeze[1] [ˈsniːz] *vi* **sneezed; sneezing** : estornudar
sneeze[2] *n* : estornudo *m*
snicker[1] [ˈsnɪkər] *vi* : reírse disimuladamente
snicker[2] *n* : risita *f*
snide [ˈsnaɪd] *adj* : sarcástico
sniff[1] [ˈsnɪf] *vi* **1** SMELL : oler, husmear (dícese de los animales) **2 to sniff at** : despreciar, desdeñar — *vt* **1** SMELL : oler **2 to sniff out** : olerse, husmear
sniff[2] *n* **1** SNIFFING : aspiración *f* por la nariz **2** SMELL : olor *m*
sniffle [ˈsnɪfəl] *vi* **-fled; -fling** : respirar con la nariz congestionada
sniffles [ˈsnɪfəlz] *npl* : resfriado *m*
snip[1] [ˈsnɪp] *vt* **snipped; snipping** : cortar (con tijeras)
snip[2] *n* : tijeretada *f,* recorte *m*
snipe[1] [ˈsnaɪp] *vi* **sniped; sniping** : disparar
snipe[2] *n, pl* **snipes** *or* **snipe** : agachadiza *f*
sniper [ˈsnaɪpər] *n* : francotirador *m,* -dora *f*
snivel [ˈsnɪvəl] *vi* **-veled** *or* **-velled; -veling** *or* **-velling 1** → **snuffle 2** WHINE : lloriquear
snob [ˈsnɑb] *n* : esnob *mf,* snob *mf*
snobbery [ˈsnɑbəri] *n, pl* **-beries** : esnobismo *m*
snobbish [ˈsnɑbɪʃ] *adj* : esnob, snob
snobbishness [ˈsnɑbɪʃnəs] *n* : esnobismo *m*
snoop[1] [ˈsnuːp] *vi* : husmear, curiosear
snoop[2] *n* : fisgón *m,* -gona *f*

snooze[1] ['snuːz] *vi* **snoozed; snoozing** : dormitar
snooze[2] *n* : siestecita *f,* siestita *f*
snore[1] ['snor] *vi* **snored; snoring** : roncar
snore[2] *n* : ronquido *m*
snort[1] ['snɔrt] *vi* : bufar, resoplar
snort[2] *n* : bufido *m,* resoplo *m*
snout ['snaʊt] *n* : hocico *m,* morro *m*
snow[1] ['snoː] *vi* **1** : nevar <I'm snowed in : estoy aislado por la nieve> **2 to be snowed under** : estar inundado
snow[2] *n* : nieve *f*
snowball ['snoːˌbɔl] *n* : bola *f* de nieve
snowdrift ['snoːˌdrɪft] *n* : ventisquero *m*
snowfall ['snoːˌfɔl] *n* : nevada *f*
snowplow ['snoːˌplaʊ] *n* : quitanieves *m*
snowshoe ['snoːˌʃuː] *n* : raqueta *f* (para nieve)
snowstorm ['snoːˌstɔrm] *n* : tormenta *f* de nieve, ventisca *f*
snowy ['snoːi] *adj* **snowier; -est** : nevoso <a snowy road : un camino nevado>
snub[1] ['snʌb] *vi* **snubbed; snubbing** : desairar
snub[2] *n* : desaire *m*
snub–nosed ['snʌbˌnoːzd] *adj* : de nariz respingada
snuff[1] ['snʌf] *vt* **1** : apagar (una vela) **2** : sorber (algo) por la nariz
snuff[2] *n* : rapé *m*
snuffle ['snʌfəl] *vi* **-fled; -fling** : respirar con la nariz congestionada
snug ['snʌg] *adj* **snugger; snuggest 1** COMFORTABLE : cómodo **2** TIGHT : ajustado, ceñido <snug pants : pantalones ajustados>
snuggle ['snʌgəl] *vi* **-gled; -gling** : acurrucarse <to snuggle up to someone : arrimársele a alguien>
snugly ['snʌgli] *adv* **1** COMFORTABLY : cómodamente **2** : de manera ajustada <the shirt fits snugly : la camisa queda ajustada>
so[1] ['soː] *adv* **1** (*referring to something indicated or suggested*) <do you think so? : ¿tú crees?> <so it would seem : eso parece> <I told her so : se lo dije> <he's ready, or so he says : según dice, está listo> <it so happened that. . . : resultó que. . .> <do it like so : hazlo así> <so be it : así sea> **2** ALSO : también <so do I : yo también> **3** THUS : así, de esta manera **4** : tan <he'd never been so happy : nunca había estado tan contento> **5** CONSEQUENTLY : por lo tanto
so[2] *conj* **1** THEREFORE : así que **2** *or* **so that** : para que, así que, de manera que **3 so what?** : ¿y qué?
soak[1] ['soːk] *vi* : estar en remojo — *vt* **1** : poner en remojo **2 to soak up** ABSORB : absorber
soak[2] *n* : remojo *m*
soap[1] ['soːp] *vt* : enjabonar
soap[2] *n* : jabón *m*
soapsuds ['soːpˌsʌdz] → **suds**
soapy ['soːpi] **soapier; -est** *adj* : jabonoso <a soapy taste : un gusto a jabón> <a soapy texture : una textura de jabón>
soar ['sor] *vi* **1** FLY : volar **2** RISE : remontar el vuelo (dícese de las aves) <her hopes soared : su esperanza renació> <prices are soaring : los precios están subiendo vertiginosamente>
sob[1] ['sɑb] *vi* **sobbed; sobbing** : sollozar
sob[2] *n* : sollozo *m*
sober ['soːbər] *adj* **1** : sobrio <he's not sober enough to drive : está demasiado borracho para manejar> **2** SERIOUS : serio
soberly ['soːbərli] *adv* **1** : sobriamente **2** SERIOUSLY : seriamente
sobriety [sə'braɪəṭi, so-] *n* **1** : sobriedad *f* <sobriety test : prueba de alcoholemia> **2** SERIOUSNESS : seriedad *f*
so–called ['soː'kɔld] *adj* : supuesto, presunto <the so-called experts : los expertos, así llamados>
soccer ['sɑkər] *n* : futbol *m,* fútbol *m*
sociable ['soːʃəbəl] *adj* : sociable
social[1] ['soːʃəl] *adj* : social — **socially** *adv*
social[2] *n* : reunión *f* social
socialism ['soːʃəˌlɪzəm] *n* : socialismo *m*
socialist[1] ['soːʃəlɪst] *adj* : socialista
socialist[2] *n* : socialista *mf*
socialize ['soːʃəˌlaɪz] *v* **-ized; -izing** *vt* **1** NATIONALIZE : nacionalizar **2** : socializar (en psicología) — *vi* : alternar, circular <to socialize with friends : alternar con amigos>
social work *n* : asistencia *f* social
society [sə'saɪəṭi] *n, pl* **-eties 1** COMPANIONSHIP : compañía *f* **2** : sociedad *f* <a democratic society : una sociedad democrática> <high society : alta sociedad> **3** ASSOCIATION : sociedad *f,* asociación *f*
sociology [ˌsoːsi'ɑləʤi] *n* : sociología *f*
sociological [ˌsoːsiə'lɑʤɪkəl] *adj* : sociológico
sociologist [ˌsoːsi'ɑləʤɪst] *n* : sociólogo *m,* -ga *f*
sock[1] ['sɑk] *vt* : pegar, golpear, darle un puñetazo a
sock[2] *n* **1** *pl* **socks** *or* **sox** ['sɑks] : calcetín *m,* media *f* <shoes and socks : zapatos y calcetines> **2** *pl* **socks** ['sɑks] PUNCH : puñetazo *m*
socket ['sɑkət] *n* **1** *or* **electric socket** : enchufe *m,* toma *f* de corriente **2** : glena *f* (de una articulación) <shoulder socket : glena del hombro> **3 eye socket** : órbita *f,* cuenca *f*
sod[1] ['sɑd] *vt* **sodded; sodding** : cubrir de césped
sod[2] *n* TURF : césped *m,* tepe *m*

soda [ˈsoːdə] *n* **1** *or* **soda water** : soda *f* **2** *or* **soda pop** : gaseosa *f,* refresco *m* **3** *or* **ice–cream soda** : refresco *m* con helado

sodden [ˈsɑdən] *adj* SOGGY : empapado

sodium [ˈsoːdiəm] *n* : sodio *m*

sodium bicarbonate *n* : bicarbonato *m* de soda

sodium chloride → **salt**

sofa [ˈsoːfə] *n* : sofá *m*

soft [ˈsɔft] *adj* **1** : blando <a soft pillow : una almohada blanda> **2** SMOOTH : suave (dícese de las texturas, de los sonidos, etc.) **3** NONALCOHOLIC : no alcohólico <a soft drink : un refresco>

softball [ˈsɔftˌbɔl] *n* : softbol *m*

soften [ˈsɔfən] *vt* : ablandar (algo sólido), suavizar (la piel, un golpe, etc.), amortiguar (un impacto) — *vi* : ablandarse, suavizarse

softly [ˈsɔftli] *adv* : suavemente <she spoke softly : habló en voz baja>

softness [ˈsɔftnəs] *n* **1** : blandura *f,* lo blando (de una almohada, de la mantequilla, etc.) **2** SMOOTHNESS : suavidad *f*

software [ˈsɔftˌwær] *n* : software *m*

soggy [ˈsɑgi] *adj* **soggier; -est** : empapado

soil[1] [ˈsɔɪl] *vt* : ensuciar — *vi* : ensuciarse

soil[2] *n* **1** DIRTINESS : suciedad *f* **2** DIRT, EARTH : suelo *m,* tierra *f* **3** COUNTRY : patria *f* <her native soil : su tierra natal>

sojourn[1] [ˈsoːˌdʒərn, soːˈdʒərn] *vi* : pasar una temporada

sojourn[2] *n* : estadía *f,* estancia *f,* permanencia *f*

solace [ˈsɑləs] *n* : consuelo *m*

solar [ˈsoːlər] *adj* : solar <the solar system : el sistema solar>

sold → **sell**

solder[1] [ˈsɑdər, ˈsɔ-] *vt* : soldar

solder[2] *n* : soldadura *f*

soldier[1] [ˈsoːldʒər] *vi* : servir como soldado

soldier[2] *n* : soldado *mf*

sole[1] [ˈsoːl] *adj* : único

sole[2] *n* **1** : suela *f* (de un zapato) **2** : lenguado *m* (pez)

solely [ˈsoːli] *adv* : únicamente, sólo

solemn [ˈsɑləm] *adj* : solemne, serio — **solemnly** *adv*

solemnity [səˈlɛmnət̬i] *n, pl* **-ties** : solemnidad *f*

solicit [səˈlɪsət] *vt* : solicitar

solicitous [səˈlɪsət̬əs] *adj* : solícito

solicitude [səˈlɪsəˌtuːd, -ˌtjuːd] *n* : solicitud *f*

solid[1] [ˈsɑləd] *adj* **1** : macizo <a solid rubber ball : una bola maciza de caucho> **2** CUBIC : tridimensional **3** COMPACT : compacto, denso **4** STURDY : sólido **5** CONTINUOUS : seguido, continuo <two solid hours : dos horas seguidas> <a solid line : una línea continua> **6** UNANIMOUS : unánime **7** DEPENDABLE : serio, fiable **8** PURE : macizo, puro <solid gold : oro macizo>

solid[2] *n* : sólido *m*

solidarity [ˌsɑləˈdærət̬i] *n* : solidaridad *f*

solidify [səˈlɪdəˌfaɪ] *v* **-fied; -fying** *vt* : solidificar — *vi* : solidificarse

solidity [səˈlɪdət̬i] *n, pl* **-ties** : solidez *f*

solidly [ˈsɑlədli] *adv* **1** : sólidamente **2** UNANIMOUSLY : unánimemente

soliloquy [səˈlɪləkwi] *n, pl* **-quies** : soliloquio *m*

solitaire [ˈsɑləˌtɛr] *n* : solitario *m*

solitary [ˈsɑləˌtɛri] *adj* **1** ALONE : solitario **2** SECLUDED : apartado, retirado **3** SINGLE : solo

solitude [ˈsɑləˌtuːd, -ˌtjuːd] *n* : soledad *f*

solo[1] [ˈsoːˌloː] *vi* : volar en solitario (dícese de un piloto)

solo[2] *adv & adj* : en solitario, a solas

solo[3] *n, pl* **solos** : solo *m*

soloist [ˈsoːloɪst] *n* : solista *mf*

solstice [ˈsɑlstɪs] *n* : solsticio *m*

soluble [ˈsɑljəbəl] *adj* : soluble

solution [səˈluːʃən] *n* : solución *f*

solve [ˈsɑlv] *vt* **solved; solving** : resolver, solucionar

solvency [ˈsɑlvəntsi] *n* : solvencia *f*

solvent [ˈsɑlvənt] *n* : solvente *m*

Somali [soˈmɑli, sə-] *n* : somalí *mf* — **Somali** *adj*

somber [ˈsɑmbər] *adj* **1** DARK : sombrío, oscuro <somber colors : colores oscuros> **2** GRAVE : sombrío, serio **3** MELANCHOLY : sombrío, lúgubre

sombrero [səmˈbrɛrˌoː] *n, pl* **-ros** : sombrero *m* (mexicano)

some[1] [ˈsʌm] *adj* **1** : un, algún <some lady stopped me : una mujer me detuvo> <some distant galaxy : alguna galaxia lejana> **2** : algo de, un poco de <he drank some water : tomó (un poco de) agua> **3** : unos <do you want some apples? : ¿quieres unas manzanas?> <some years ago : hace varios años>

some[2] *pron* **1** : algunos <some went, others stayed : algunos se fueron, otros se quedaron> **2** : un poco, algo <there's some left : queda un poco> <I have gum; do you want some? : tengo chicle, ¿quieres?>

somebody [ˈsʌmbədi, -ˌbɑdi] *pron* : alguien

someday [ˈsʌmˌdeɪ] *adv* : algún día

somehow [ˈsʌmˌhaʊ] *adv* **1** : de alguna manera, de algún modo <I'll do it somehow : lo haré de alguna manera> **2** : por alguna rázon <somehow I don't trust her : por alguna razón no me fío de ella>

someone [ˈsʌmˌwʌn] *pron* : alguien

somersault[1] [ˈsʌmərˌsɔlt] *vi* : dar volteretas, dar un salto mortal

somersault[2] *n* : voltereta *f,* salto *m* mortal

something [ˈsʌmθɪŋ] *pron* : algo <I want something else : quiero otra cosa> <she's writing a novel or something : está escribiendo una novela o no sé qué>
sometime [ˈsʌmˌtaɪm] *adv* : algún día, en algún momento <sometime next month : durante el mes que viene>
sometimes [ˈsʌmˌtaɪmz] *adv* : a veces, algunas veces, de vez en cuando
somewhat [ˈsʌmˌhwʌt, -ˌhwɑt] *adv* : algo, un tanto
somewhere [ˈsʌmˌ*h*wɛr] *adv* **1** : en alguna parte, a algún lugar **2 somewhere else** : en otro sitio
son [ˈsʌn] *n* : hijo *m*
sonar [ˈsoːˌnɑr] *n* : sonar *m*
sonata [səˈnɑtə] *n* : sonata *f*
song [ˈsɔŋ] *n* : canción *f,* canto *m* (de un pájaro)
songbird [ˈsɔŋˌbərd] *n* : pájaro *m* cantor
sonic [ˈsɑnɪk] *adj* **1** : sónico **2 sonic boom** : estampido *m* sónico
son–in–law [ˈsʌnɪnˌlɔ] *n, pl* **sons–in–law** : yerno *m,* hijo *m* político
sonnet [ˈsɑnət] *n* : soneto *m*
sonorous [ˈsɑnərəs, səˈnorəs] *adj* : sonoro
soon [ˈsuːn] *adv* **1** : pronto, dentro de poco <he'll arrive soon : llegará pronto> **2** QUICKLY : pronto <as soon as possible : lo más pronto posible> <the sooner the better : cuanto antes mejor>
soot [ˈsʊt, ˈsuːt, ˈsʌt] *n* : hollín *m,* tizne *m*
soothe [ˈsuːð] *vt* **soothed; soothing 1** CALM : calmar, tranquilizar **2** RELIEVE : aliviar
soothsayer [ˈsuːθˌseɪər] *n* : adivino *m,* -na *f*
sooty [ˈsʊti, ˈsuː-, ˈsʌ-] *adj* **sootier; -est** : cubierto de hollín, tiznado
sop¹ [ˈsɑp] *vt* **sopped; sopping 1** DIP : mojar **2** SOAK : empapar **3 to sop up** : rebañar, absorber
sop² *n* **1** CONCESSION : concesión *f* **2** BRIBE : soborno *m*
sophisticated [səˈfɪstəˌkeɪt̬əd] *adj* **1** COMPLEX : complejo **2** WORLDLY-WISE : sofisticado
sophistication [səˌfɪstəˈkeɪʃən] *n* **1** COMPLEXITY : complejidad *f* **2** URBANITY : sofisticación *f*
sophomore [ˈsɑfˌmor, ˈsɑfəˌmor] *n* : estudiante *mf* de segundo año
soporific [ˌsɑpəˈrɪfɪk, ˌsoː-] *adj* : soporífero
soprano [səˈpræˌnoː] *n, pl* **-nos** : soprano *mf*
sorcerer [ˈsɔrsərər] *n* : hechicero *m,* brujo *m,* mago *m*
sorceress [ˈsɔrsərəs] *n* : hechicera *f,* bruja *f,* maga *f*
sorcery [ˈsɔrsəri] *n* : hechicería *f,* brujería *f*
sordid [ˈsɔrdɪd] *adj* : sórdido
sore¹ [ˈsor] *adj* **sorer; sorest 1** PAINFUL : dolorido, doloroso <I have a sore throat : me duele la garganta> **2** ACUTE, SEVERE : extremo, grande <in sore straits : en grandes apuros> **3** ANGRY : enojado, enfadado
sore² *n* : llaga *f*
sorely [ˈsorli] *adv* : muchísimo <it was sorely needed : se necesitaba urgentemente> <she was sorely missed : la echaban mucho de menos>
soreness [ˈsornəs] *n* : dolor *m*
sorghum [ˈsɔrgəm] *n* : sorgo *m*
sorority [səˈrɔrət̬i] *n, pl* **-ties** : hermandad *f* (de estudiantes femeninas)
sorrel [ˈsɔrəl] *n* **1** : alazán *m* (color o animal) **2** : acedera *f* (hierba)
sorrow [ˈsɑrˌoː] *n* : pesar *m,* dolor *m,* pena *f*
sorrowful [ˈsɑrofəl] *adj* : triste, afligido, apenado
sorrowfully [ˈsɑrofəli] *adv* : con tristeza
sorry [ˈsɑri] *adj* **sorrier; -est 1** PITIFUL : lastimero, lastimoso **2 to be sorry** : sentir, lamentar <I'm sorry : lo siento> **3 to feel sorry for** : compadecer <I feel sorry for him : me da pena>
sort¹ [ˈsɔrt] *vt* : clasificar
sort² *n* **1** KIND : tipo *m,* clase *f* <a sort of writer : una especie de escritor> **2** NATURE : índole *f* **3 out of sorts** : de mal humor
sortie [ˈsɔrti, sɔrˈtiː] *n* : salida *f*
SOS [ˌɛsˌoːˈɛs] *n* : SOS *m*
so–so [ˈsoːˈsoː] *adj & adv* : así así, de modo regular
soufflé [suːˈfleɪ] *n* : suflé *m*
sought → **seek**
soul [ˈsoːl] *n* **1** SPIRIT : alma *f* **2** ESSENCE : esencia *f* **3** PERSON : persona *f,* alma *f*
soulful [ˈsoːlfəl] *adj* : conmovedor, lleno de emoción
sound¹ [ˈsaʊnd] *vt* **1** : sondar (en navegación) **2** *or* **to sound out** PROBE : sondear **3** : hacer sonar, tocar (una trompeta, etc.) — *vi* **1** : sonar <the alarm sounded : la alarma sonó> **2** SEEM : parecer
sound² *adj* **1** HEALTHY : sano <safe and sound : sano y salvo> <of sound mind and body : en pleno uso de sus facultades> **2** FIRM, SOLID : sólido **3** SENSIBLE : lógico, sensato **4** DEEP : profundo <a sound sleep : un sueño profundo>
sound³ *n* **1** : sonido *m* <the speed of sound : la velocidad del sonido> **2** NOISE : sonido *m,* ruido *m* <I heard a sound : oí un sonido> **3** CHANNEL : brazo *m* de mar, canal *m* (ancho)
soundless [ˈsaʊndləs] *adj* : sordo
soundlessly [ˈsaʊndləsli] *adv* : silenciosamente
soundly [ˈsaʊndli] *adv* **1** SOLIDLY : sólidamente **2** SENSIBLY : lógicamente, sensatamente **3** DEEPLY : profunda-

mente <sleeping soundly : durmiendo profundamente>

soundness ['saʊndnəs] *n* **1** SOLIDITY : solidez *f* **2** SENSIBLENESS : sensatez *f,* solidez *f*

soundproof ['saʊnd,pruːf] *adj* : insonorizado

sound wave *n* : onda *f* sonora

soup ['suːp] *n* : sopa *f*

sour[1] ['saʊər] *vi* : agriarse, cortarse (dícese de la leche) — *vt* : agriar, cortar (leche)

sour[2] *adj* **1** ACID : agrio, ácido (dícese de la fruta, etc.), cortado (dícese de la leche) **2** DISAGREEABLE : desagradable, agrio

source ['sors] *n* : fuente *f,* origen *m,* nacimiento *m* (de un río)

sourness ['saʊərnəs] *n* : acidez *f*

south[1] ['saʊθ] *adv* : al sur, hacia el sur <the window looks south : la ventana mira al sur> <she continued south : continuó hacia el sur>

south[2] *adj* : sur, del sur <the south entrance : la entrada sur> <South America : Sudamérica, América del Sur>

south[3] *n* : sur *m*

South African *n* : sudafricano *m,* -na *f* — **South African** *adj*

South American[1] *adj* : sudamericano, suramericano

South American[2] *n* : sudamericano *m,* -na *f;* suramericano *m,* -na *f*

southbound ['saʊθ,baʊnd] *adj* : con rumbo al sur

southeast[1] [saʊ'θiːst] *adj* : sureste, sudeste, del sureste

southeast[2] *n* : sureste *m,* sudeste *m*

southeasterly [saʊ'θiːstərli] *adv & adj* **1** : del sureste (dícese del viento) **2** : hacia el sureste

southeastern [saʊ'θiːstərn] → **southeast**[1]

southerly ['sʌðərli] *adv & adj* : del sur

southern ['sʌðərn] *adj* : sur, sureño, meridional, austral <a southern city : una ciudad del sur del país, una ciudad meridional> <the southern side : el lado sur>

Southerner ['sʌðərnər] *n* : sureño *m,* -ña *f*

South Pole : Polo *m* Sur

southward ['saʊθwərd] *or* **southwards** [-wərdz] *adv & adj* : hacia el sur

southwest[1] [saʊθ'wɛst, *as a nautical term often* saʊ'wɛst] *adj* : suroeste, sudoeste, del suroeste

southwest[2] *n* : suroeste *m,* sudoeste *m*

southwesterly [saʊθ'wɛstərli] *adv & adj* **1** : del suroeste (dícese del viento) **2** : hacia el suroeste

southwestern [saʊθ'wɛstərn] → **southwest**[1]

souvenir [,suːvə'nɪr, 'suːvə,-] *n* : recuerdo *m,* souvenir *m*

sovereign[1] ['sɑvərən] *adj* : soberano

sovereign[2] *n* **1** : soberano *m,* -na *f* (monarca) **2** : soberano *m* (moneda)

sovereignty ['sɑvərənti] *n, pl* **-ties** : soberanía *f*

Soviet ['soːvi,ɛt, 'sɑ-, -viət] *adj* : soviético

sow[1] ['soː] *vt* **sowed; sown** ['soːn] *or* **sowed; sowing 1** PLANT : sembrar **2** SCATTER : esparcir

sow[2] ['saʊ] *n* : cerda *f*

sox → **sock**

soybean ['sɔɪ,biːn] *n* : soya *f,* soja *f*

spa ['spɑ] *n* : balneario *m*

space[1] ['speɪs] *vt* **spaced; spacing** : espaciar

space[2] *n* **1** PERIOD : espacio *m,* lapso *m,* período *m* **2** ROOM : espacio *m,* sitio *m,* lugar *m* <is there space for me? : ¿hay sitio para mí?> **3** : espacio *m* <blank space : espacio en blanco> **4** : espacio *m* (en física) **5** PLACE : plaza *f,* sitio *m* <to reserve space : reservar plazas> <parking space : sitio para estacionarse>

spacecraft ['speɪs,kræft] *n* : nave *f* espacial

spaceflight ['speɪs,flaɪt] *n* : vuelo *m* espacial

spaceman ['speɪsmən, -,mæn] *n, pl* **-men** [-mən, -,mɛn] : astronauta *m,* cosmonauta *m*

spaceship ['speɪs,ʃɪp] *n* : nave *f* espacial

space shuttle *n* : transbordador *m* espacial

space suit *n* : traje *m* espacial

spacious ['speɪʃəs] *adj* : espacioso, amplio

spade[1] ['speɪd] *v* **spaded; spading** *vt* : palear — *vi* : usar una pala

spade[2] *n* **1** SHOVEL : pala *f* **2** : pica *f* (naipe)

spaghetti [spə'gɛti] *n* : espagueti *m,* espaguetis *mpl,* spaghetti *mpl*

span[1] ['spæn] *vt* **spanned; spanning** : abarcar (un período de tiempo), extenderse sobre (un espacio)

span[2] *n* **1** : lapso *m,* espacio *m* (de tiempo) <life span : duración de la vida> **2** : luz *f* (entre dos soportes)

spangle ['spæŋgəl] *n* : lentejuela *f*

Spaniard ['spænjərd] *n* : español *m,* -ñola *f*

spaniel ['spænjəl] *n* : spaniel *m*

Spanish[1] ['spænɪʃ] *adj* : español

Spanish[2] *n* **1** : español *m* (idioma) **2 the Spanish** *npl* : los españoles

spank ['spæŋk] *vt* : darle nalgadas (a alguien)

spar[1] ['spɑr] *vi* **sparred; sparring** : entrenarse (en boxeo)

spar[2] *n* : palo *m,* verga *f* (de un barco)

spare[1] ['spær] *vt* **spared; sparing 1** : perdonar <to spare someone's life : perdonarle la vida a alguien> **2** SAVE : ahorrar, evitar <I'll spare you the trouble : le evitaré la molestia> **3** : prescindir de <I can't spare her : no puedo prescindir de ella> <can you

spare a dollar? : ¿me das un dólar?> **4** STINT : escatimar <they spared no expense : no repararon en gastos> **5 to spare** : de sobra
spare² *adj* **1** : de repuesto, de recambio <spare tire : llanta de repuesto> **2** EXCESS : de más, de sobra <spare time : tiempo libre> **3** LEAN : delgado
spare³ *n or* **spare part** : repuesto *m,* recambio *m*
sparing [ˈspærɪŋ] *adj* : parco, económico — **sparingly** *adv*
spark¹ [ˈspɑrk] *vi* : chispear, echar chispas — *vt* PROVOKE : despertar, provocar <to spark interest : despertar interés>
spark² *n* **1** : chispa *f* <to throw off sparks : echar chispas> **2** GLIMMER, TRACE : destello *m,* pizca *f*
sparkle¹ [ˈspɑrkəl] *vi* **-kled; -kling 1** FLASH, SHINE : destellar, centellear, brillar **2** : estar muy animado (dícese de una conversación, etc.)
sparkle² *n* : destello *m,* centelleo *m*
sparkler [ˈspɑrklər] *n* : luz *f* de bengala
spark plug *n* : bujía *f*
sparrow [ˈspæroː] *n* : gorrión *m*
sparse [ˈspɑrs] *adj* **sparser; -est** : escaso — **sparsely** *adv*
spasm [ˈspæzəm] *n* **1** : espasmo *m* (muscular) **2** BURST, FIT : arrebato *m*
spasmodic [spæzˈmɑdɪk] *adj* **1** : espasmódico **2** SPORADIC : irregular, esporádico — **spasmodically** [-dɪkli] *adv*
spastic [ˈspæstɪk] *adj* : espástico
spat¹ → **spit¹**
spat² [ˈspæt] *n* : discusión *f,* disputa *f,* pelea *f*
spatial [ˈspeɪʃəl] *adj* : espacial
spatter¹ [ˈspæt̬ər] *v* : salpicar
spatter² *n* : salpicadura *f*
spatula [ˈspætʃələ] *n* : espátula *f,* paleta *f* (para servir)
spawn¹ [ˈspɔn] *vi* : desovar, frezar — *vt* GENERATE : generar, producir
spawn² *n* : hueva *f,* freza *f*
spay [ˈspeɪ] *vt* : esterilizar (una perra, etc.)
speak [ˈspiːk] *v* **spoke** [ˈspoːk]; **spoken** [ˈspoːkən]; **speaking** *vi* **1** TALK : hablar <to speak to someone : hablar con alguien> <who's speaking? : ¿de parte de quien?> <so to speak : por así decirlo> **2 to speak out** : hablar claramente **3 to speak out against** : denunciar **4 to speak up** : hablar en voz alta **5 to speak up for** : defender — *vt* **1** SAY : decir <she spoke her mind : habló con franqueza> **2** : hablar (un idioma)
speaker [ˈspiːkər] *n* **1** : hablante *mf* <a native speaker : un hablante nativo> **2** : orador *m,* -dora *f* <the keynote speaker : el orador principal> **3** LOUDSPEAKER : altavoz *m,* altoparlante *m*
spear¹ [ˈspɪr] *vt* : atravesar con una lanza
spear² *n* : lanza *f*
spearhead¹ [ˈspɪrˌhɛd] *vt* : encabezar
spearhead² *n* : punta *f* de lanza
spearmint [ˈspɪrmɪnt] *n* : menta *f* verde
special [ˈspɛʃəl] *adj* : especial <nothing special : nada en especial, nada en particular> — **specially** *adv*
specialist [ˈspɛʃəlɪst] *n* : especialista *mf*
specialization [ˌspɛʃələˈzeɪʃən] *n* : especialización *f*
specialize [ˈspɛʃəˌlaɪz] *vi* **-ized; -izing** : especializarse
specialty [ˈspɛʃəlt̬i] *n, pl* **-ties** : especialidad *f*
species [ˈspiːˌʃiːz, -ˌsiːz] *ns & pl* : especie *f*
specific [spɪˈsɪfɪk] *adj* : específico, determinado — **specifically** [-fɪkli] *adv*
specification [ˌspɛsəfəˈkeɪʃən] *n* : especificación *f*
specify [ˈspɛsəˌfaɪ] *vt* **-fied; -fying** : especificar
specimen [ˈspɛsəmən] *n* **1** SAMPLE : espécimen *m,* muestra *f* **2** EXAMPLE : espécimen *m,* ejemplar *m*
speck [ˈspɛk] *n* **1** SPOT : manchita *f* **2** BIT, TRACE : mota *f,* pizca *f,* ápice *m*
speckled [ˈspɛkəld] *adj* : moteado
spectacle [ˈspɛktɪkəl] *n* **1** : espectáculo *m* **2 spectacles** *npl* GLASSES : lentes *fpl,* gafas *fpl,* anteojos *mpl,* espejuelos *mpl*
spectacular [spɛkˈtækjələr] *adj* : espectacular
spectator [ˈspɛkˌteɪt̬ər] *n* : espectador *m,* -dora *f*
specter *or* **spectre** [ˈspɛktər] *n* : espectro *m,* fantasma *m*
spectrum [ˈspɛktrəm] *n, pl* **spectra** [-trə] *or* **spectrums 1** : espectro *m* (de colores, etc.) **2** RANGE : gama *f,* abanico *m*
speculate [ˈspɛkjəˌleɪt] *vi* **-lated; -lating 1** : especular (en finanza) **2** WONDER : preguntarse, hacer conjeturas
speculation [ˌspɛkjəˈleɪʃən] *n* : especulación *f*
speculative [ˈspɛkjəˌleɪt̬ɪv] *adj* : especulativo
speculator [ˈspɛkjəˌleɪt̬ər] *n* : especulador *m,* -dora *f*
speech [ˈspiːtʃ] *n* **1** : habla *f,* modo *m* de hablar, expresión *f* **2** ADDRESS : discurso *m*
speechless [ˈspiːtʃləs] *adj* : enmudecido, estupefacto
speed¹ [ˈspiːd] *v* **sped** [ˈspɛd] *or* **speeded; speeding** *vi* **1** : ir a toda velocidad, correr a toda prisa <he sped off : se fue a toda velocidad> **2** : conducir a exceso de velocidad <a ticket for speeding : una multa por exceso de velocidad> — *vt* **to speed up** : acelerar
speed² *n* **1** SWIFTNESS : rapidez *f* **2** VELOCITY : velocidad *f*

speedboat [ˈspiːd,boːt] *n* : lancha *f* motora
speed bump *n* : badén *m*
speed limit *n* : velocidad *f* máxima, límite *m* de velocidad
speedometer [spɪˈdɑmət̬ər] *n* : velocímetro *m*
speedup [ˈspiːd,ʌp] *n* : aceleracion *f*
speedy [ˈspiːdi] *adj* **speedier, -est** : rápido — **speedily** [-dəli] *adv*
spell[1] [ˈspɛl] *vt* **1** : escribir, deletrear (verbalmente) <how do you spell it? : ¿cómo se escribe?, ¿cómo se deletrea?> **2** MEAN : significar <that could spell trouble : eso puede significar problemas> **3** RELIEVE : relevar
spell[2] *n* **1** TURN : turno *m* **2** PERIOD, TIME : período *m* (de tiempo) **3** ENCHANTMENT : encanto *m,* hechizo *m,* maleficio *m*
spellbound [ˈspɛl,baʊnd] *adj* : embelesado
speller [ˈspɛlər] *n* : persona *f* que escribe <she's a good speller : tiene buena ortografía>
spelling [ˈspɛlɪŋ] *n* : ortografía *f*
spend [ˈspɛnd] *vt* **spent** [ˈspɛnt]; **spending 1** : gastar (dinero, etc.) **2** PASS : pasar (el tiempo) <to spend time on : dedicar tiempo a>
spendthrift [ˈspɛnd,θrɪft] *n* : derrochador *m,* -dora *f;* despilfarrador *m,* -dora *f*
sperm [ˈspərm] *n, pl* **sperm** *or* **sperms** : esperma *mf*
spew [ˈspjuː] *vi* : salir a chorros — *vt* : vomitar, arrojar (lava, etc.)
sphere [ˈsfɪr] *n* : esfera *f*
spherical [ˈsfɪrɪkəl, ˈsfɛr-] *adj* : esférico
spice[1] [ˈspaɪs] *vt* **spiced; spicing 1** SEASON : condimentar, sazonar **2** *or* **to spice up** : salpimentar, hacer más interesante
spice[2] *n* **1** : especia *f* **2** FLAVOR, INTEREST : sabor *m* <the spice of life : la sal de la vida>
spick–and–span [ˈspɪkənˈspæn] *adj* : limpio y ordenado
spicy [ˈspaɪsi] *adj* **spicier; -est 1** SPICED : condimentado, sazonado **2** HOT : picante **3** RACY : picante
spider [ˈspaɪdər] *n* : araña *f*
spigot [ˈspɪgət, -kət] *n* : llave *f,* grifo *m,* canilla *Arg, Uru*
spike[1] [ˈspaɪk] *vt* **spiked; spiking 1** FASTEN : clavar (con clavos grandes) **2** PIERCE : atravesar **3** : añadir alcohol a <he spiked her drink with rum : le puso ron a la bebida>
spike[2] *n* : clavo *m* grande
spill[1] [ˈspɪl] *vt* **1** SHED : derramar, verter <to spill blood : derrame sangre> **2** DIVULGE : revelar, divulgar — *vi* : derramarse
spill[2] *n* **1** SPILLING : derrame *m,* vertido *m* <oil spill : derrame de petróleo> **2** FALL : caída *f*
spin[1] [ˈspɪn] *v* **spun** [ˈspʌn]; **spinning** *vi* **1** : hilar **2** TURN : girar **3** REEL : dar vueltas <my head is spinning : la cabeza me está dando vueltas> — *vt* **1** : hilar (hilo, etc.) **2** : tejer <to spin a web : tejer una telaraña> **3** TWIRL : hacer girar
spin[2] *n* : vuelta *f,* giro *m* <to go for a spin : dar una vuelta (en coche)>
spinach [ˈspɪnɪtʃ] *n* : espinacas *fpl,* espinaca *f*
spinal column [ˈspaɪnəl] *n* BACKBONE : columna *f* vertebral
spinal cord *n* : médula *f* espinal
spindle [ˈspɪndəl] *n* **1** : huso *m* (para hilar) **2** : eje *m* (de un mecanismo)
spindly [ˈspɪndli] *adj* : larguirucho *fam,* largo y débil (dícese de una planta)
spine [ˈspaɪn] *n* **1** BACKBONE : columna *f* vertebral, espina *f* dorsal **2** QUILL : púa *f* (de un animal) **3** THORN : espina *f* **4** : lomo *m* (de un libro)
spineless [ˈspaɪnləs] *adj* **1** : sin púas, sin espinas **2** INVERTEBRATE : invertebrado **3** WEAK : débil (de carácter)
spinet [ˈspɪnət] *n* : espineta *f*
spinster [ˈspɪntstər] *n* : soltera *f*
spiny [ˈspaɪni] *adj* **spinier; -est** : con púas (dícese de los animales), espinoso (dícese de las plantas)
spiral[1] [ˈspaɪrəl] *vi* **-raled** *or* **-ralled; -raling** *or* **-ralling** : ir en espiral
spiral[2] *adj* : espiral, en espiral <a spiral staircase : una escalera de caracol>
spiral[3] *n* : espiral *f*
spire [ˈspaɪr] *n* : aguja *f*
spirit[1] [ˈspɪrət] *vt* **to spirit away** : hacer desaparecer
spirit[2] *n* **1** : espíritu *m* <body and spirit : cuerpo y espíritu> **2** GHOST : espíritu *m,* fantasma *m* **3** MOOD : espíritu *m,* humor *m* <in the spirit of friendship : en el espíritu de amistad> <to be in good spirits : estar de buen humor> **4** ENTHUSIASM, VIVACITY : espíritu *m,* ánimo *m,* brío *m* **5 spirits** *npl* : licores *mpl*
spirited [ˈspɪrət̬əd] *adj* : animado, energético
spiritless [ˈspɪrətləs] *adj* : desanimado
spiritual[1] [ˈspɪrɪtʃʊəl, -tʃəl] *adj* : espiritual — **spiritually** *adv*
spiritual[2] *n* : espiritual *m* (canción)
spiritualism [ˈspɪrɪtʃʊə,lɪzəm, -tʃə-] *n* : espiritismo *m*
spirituality [,spɪrɪtʃʊˈælət̬i] *n, pl* **-ties** : espiritualidad *f*
spit[1] [ˈspɪt] *v* **spit** *or* **spat** [ˈspæt]; **spitting** : escupir
spit[2] *n* **1** SALIVA : saliva *f* **2** ROTISSERIE : asador *m* **3** POINT : lengua *f* (de tierra)
spite[1] [ˈspaɪt] *vt* **spited; spiting** : fastidiar, molestar
spite[2] *n* **1** : despecho *m,* rencor *m* **2 in spite of** : a pesar de (que), pese a (que)

spiteful [ˈspaɪtfəl] *adj* : malicioso, rencoroso
spitting image *n* **to be the spitting image of** : ser el vivo retrato de
spittle [ˈspɪtəl] *n* : saliva *f*
splash[1] [ˈsplæʃ] *vt* : salpicar — *vi* **1** : salpicar **2 to splash around** : chapotear
splash[2] *n* **1** SPLASHING : salpicadura *f* **2** SQUIRT : chorrito *m* **3** SPOT : mancha *f*
splatter [ˈsplætər] → **spatter**
splay [ˈspleɪ] *vt* : extender (hacia afuera) <to splay one's fingers : abrir los dedos> — *vi* : extenderse (hacia afuera)
spleen [ˈspliːn] *n* **1** : bazo *m* (órgano) **2** ANGER, SPITE : ira *f*, rencor *m*
splendid [ˈsplɛndəd] *adj* : espléndido — **splendidly** *adv*
splendor [ˈsplɛndər] *n* : esplendor *m*
splice[1] [ˈsplaɪs] *vt* **spliced; splicing** : empalmar, unir
splice[2] *n* : empalme *m*, unión *f*
splint [ˈsplɪnt] *n* : tablilla *f*
splinter[1] [ˈsplɪntər] *vt* : astillar — *vi* : astillarse
splinter[2] *n* : astilla *f*
split[1] [ˈsplɪt] *v* **split; splitting** *vt* **1** CLEAVE : partir, hender <to split wood : partir madera> **2** BURST : romper, rajar <to split open : abrir> **3** DIVIDE, SHARE : dividir, repartir — *vi* **1** : partirse (dícese de la madera, etc.) **2** BURST, CRACK : romperse, rajarse **3** *or* **to split up** : dividirse
split[2] *n* **1** CRACK : rajadura *f* **2** TEAR : rotura *f* **3** DIVISION : división *f*, escisión *f*
splurge[1] [ˈsplərdʒ] *v* **splurged; splurging** *vt* : derrochar — *vi* : derrochar dinero
splurge[2] *n* : derroche *m*
spoil[1] [ˈspɔɪl] *v* **spoiled** *or* **spoilt** [ˈspɔɪlt]; **spoiling** *vt* **1** PILLAGE : saquear **2** RUIN : estropear, arruinar **3** PAMPER : consentir, mimar — *vi* : estropearse, echarse a perder
spoil[2] *n* PLUNDER : botín *m*
spoke[1] → **speak**
spoke[2] [ˈspoːk] *n* : rayo *m* (de una rueda)
spoken → **speak**
spokesman [ˈspoːksmən] *n, pl* **-men** [-mən, -ˌmɛn] : portavoz *mf*; vocero *m*, -ra *f*
spokeswoman [ˈspoːksˌwʊmən] *n, pl* **-women** [-ˌwɪmən] : portavoz *f*, vocera *f*
sponge[1] [ˈspʌndʒ] *vt* **sponged; sponging** : limpiar con una esponja
sponge[2] *n* : esponja *f*
spongy [ˈspʌndʒi] *adj* **spongier; -est** : esponjoso
sponsor[1] [ˈspɑntsər] *vt* : patrocinar, auspiciar, apadrinar (a una persona)
sponsor[2] *n* : patrocinador *m*, -dora *f*; padrino *m*, madrina *f*
sponsorship [ˈspɑntsərˌʃɪp] *n* : patrocinio *m*, apadrinamiento *m*
spontaneity [ˌspɑntəˈniːəti, -ˈneɪ-] *n* : espontaneidad *f*
spontaneous [spɑnˈteɪniəs] *adj* : espontáneo — **spontaneously** *adv*
spoof [ˈspuːf] *n* : burla *f*, parodia *f*
spook[1] [ˈspuːk] *vt* : asustar
spook[2] *n* : fantasma *m*, espíritu *m*, espectro *m*
spooky [ˈspuːki] *adj* **spookier; -est** : que da miedo, espeluzante
spool [ˈspuːl] *n* : carrete *m*
spoon[1] [ˈspuːn] *vt* : comer, servir, o echar con cuchara
spoon[2] *n* : cuchara *f*
spoonful [ˈspuːnˌfʊl] *n* : cucharada *f* <by the spoonful : a cucharadas>
spoor [ˈspʊr, ˈspor] *n* : rastro *m*, pista *f*
sporadic [spəˈrædɪk] *adj* : esporádico — **sporadically** [-dɪkli] *adv*
spore [ˈspor] *n* : espora *f*
sport[1] [ˈsport] *vi* FROLIC : retozar, juguetear — *vt* SHOW OFF : lucir, ostentar
sport[2] *n* **1** : deporte *m* <outdoor sports : deportes al aire libre> **2** JEST : broma *f* **3 to be a good sport** : tener espíritu deportivo
sportsman [ˈsportsmən] *n, pl* **-men** [-mən, -ˌmɛn] : deportista *m*
sportsmanship [ˈsportsmənˌʃɪp] *n* : espíritu *m* deportivo, deportividad *f Spain*
sportswoman [ˈsportsˌwʊmən] *n, pl* **-women** [-ˌwɪmən] : deportista *f*
sporty [ˈsporti] *adj* **sportier; -est** : deportivo
spot[1] [ˈspɑt] *v* **spotted; spotting** *vt* **1** STAIN : manchar **2** RECOGNIZE, SEE : ver, reconocer <to spot an error : descubrir un error> — *vi* : mancharse
spot[2] *adj* : hecho al azar <a spot check : un vistazo, un control aleatorio>
spot[3] *n* **1** STAIN : mancha *f* **2** DOT : punto *m* **3** PIMPLE : grano *m* <to break out in spots : salirle granos a alguien> **4** PREDICAMENT : apuro *m*, aprieto *m*, lío *m* <in a tight spot : en apuros> **5** PLACE : lugar *m*, sitio *m* <to be on the spot : estar en el lugar>
spotless [ˈspɑtləs] *adj* : impecable, inmaculado — **spotlessly** *adv*
spotlight[1] [ˈspɑtˌlaɪt] *vt* **-lighted** *or* **-lit** [-ˌlɪt]; **-lighting 1** LIGHT : iluminar (con un reflector) **2** HIGHLIGHT : destacar, poner en relieve
spotlight[2] *n* **1** : reflector *m*, foco *m* **2 to be in the spotlight** : ser el centro de atención
spotty [ˈspɑti] *adj* **spottier; -est** : irregular, desigual
spouse [ˈspaʊs] *n* : cónyuge *mf*
spout[1] [ˈspaʊt] *vt* **1** : lanzar chorros de **2** DECLAIM : declamar — *vi* : salir a chorros
spout[2] *n* **1** : pico *m* (de una jarra, etc.) **2** STREAM : chorro *m*
sprain[1] [ˈspreɪn] *vt* : sufrir un esguince en

sprain[2] *n* : esguince *m,* torcedura *f*

sprawl[1] ['sprɔl] *vi* **1** LIE : tumbarse, echarse, despatarrarse **2** EXTEND : extenderse

sprawl[2] *n* **1** : postura *f* despatarrada **2** SPREAD : extensión *f,* expansión *f*

spray[1] ['spreɪ] *vt* : rociar (una superficie), pulverizar (un líquido)

spray[2] *n* **1** BOUQUET : ramillete *m* **2** MIST : rocío *m* **3** ATOMIZER : atomizador *m,* pulverizador *m*

spray gun *n* : pistola *f*

spread[1] ['sprɛd] *v* **spread; spreading** *vt* **1** *or* **to spread out** : desplegar, extender **2** SCATTER, STREW : esparcir **3** SMEAR : untar (mantequilla, etc.) **4** DISSEMINATE : difundir, sembrar, propagar — *vi* **1** : difundirse, correr, propagarse **2** EXTEND : extenderse

spread[2] *n* **1** EXTENSION : extensión *f,* difusión *f* (de noticias, etc.), propagación *f* (de enfermedades, etc.) **2** : colcha *f* (para una cama), mantel *m* (para una mesa) **3** PASTE : pasta *f* <cheese spread : pasta de queso>

spreadsheet ['sprɛd,ʃiːt] *n* : hoja *f* de cálculo

spree ['spri] *n* **1** : acción *f* desenfrenada <to go on a shopping spree : comprar como loco> **2** BINGE : parranda *f,* juerga *f* <on a spree : de parranda, de juerga>

sprig ['sprɪg] *n* : ramita *f,* ramito *m*

sprightly ['spraɪtli] *adj* **sprightlier; -est** : vivo, animado <with a sprightly step : con paso ligero>

spring[1] ['sprɪŋ] *v* **sprang** ['spræŋ] *or* **sprung** ['sprʌŋ]; **sprung; springing** *vi* **1** LEAP : saltar **2** : mover rápidamente <the lid sprang shut : la tapa se cerró de un golpe> <he sprang to his feet : se paró de un salto> **3 to spring up** : brotar (dícese de las plantas), surgir **4 to spring from** : surgir de — *vt* **1** RELEASE : soltar (de repente) <to spring the news on someone : sorprender a alguien con las noticias> <to spring a trap : hacer saltar una trampa> **2** ACTIVATE : accionar (un mecanismo) **3 to spring a leak** : hacer agua

spring[2] *n* **1** SOURCE : fuente *f,* origen *m* **2** : manantial *m,* fuente *f* <hot spring : fuente termal> **3** : primavera *f* <spring and summer : la primavera y el verano> **4** : resorte *m,* muelle *m* (de metal, etc.) **5** LEAP : salto *m,* brinco *m* **6** RESILIENCE : elasticidad *f*

springboard ['sprɪŋ,bord] *n* : trampolín *m*

springtime ['sprɪŋ,taɪm] *n* : primavera *f*

springy ['sprɪŋi] *adj* **springier; -est 1** RESILIENT : elástico **2** LIVELY : enérgico

sprinkle[1] ['sprɪŋkəl] *vt* **-kled; -kling** : rociar (con agua), espolvorear (con azúcar, etc.), salpicar

sprinkle[2] *n* : llovizna *f*

sprinkler ['sprɪŋkələr] *n* : rociador *m,* aspersor *m*

sprint[1] ['sprɪnt] *vi* : echar la carrera, esprintar (en deportes)

sprint[2] *n* : esprint *m* (en deportes)

sprite ['spraɪt] *n* : hada *f,* elfo *m*

sprocket ['sprɑkət] *n* : diente *m* (de una rueda dentada)

sprout[1] ['spraʊt] *vi* : brotar

sprout[2] *n* : brote *m,* retoño *m,* vástago *m*

spruce[1] ['spruːs] *v* **spruced; sprucing** *vt* : arreglar — *vi or* **to spruce up** : arreglarse, acicalarse

spruce[2] *adj* **sprucer; sprucest** : pulcro, arreglado

spruce[3] *n* : picea *f* (árbol)

spry ['spraɪ] *adj* **sprier** *or* **spryer** ['spraɪər]; **spriest** *or* **spryest** ['spraɪəst] : ágil, activo

spun → **spin**

spunk ['spʌŋk] *n* : valor *m,* coraje *m,* agallas *fpl fam*

spunky ['spʌŋki] *adj* **spunkier; -est** : animoso, corajudo

spur[1] ['spər] *vt* **spurred; spurring** *or* **to spur on** : espolear (un caballo), motivar (a una persona, etc.)

spur[2] *n* **1** : espuela *f,* acicate *m* **2** STIMULUS : acicate *m* **3** : espolón *m* (de aves gallináceas)

spurious ['spjʊriəs] *adj* : espurio

spurn ['spərn] *vt* : desdeñar, rechazar

spurt[1] ['spərt] *vt* SQUIRT : lanzar un chorro de — *vi* SPOUT : salir a chorros

spurt[2] *n* **1** : actividad *f* repentina <a spurt of energy : una explosión de energía> <to do in spurts : hacer por rachas> **2** JET : chorro *m* (de agua, etc.)

sputter[1] ['spʌtər] *vi* **1** JABBER : farfullar **2** : chisporrotear (dícese de la grasa, etc.), petardear (dícese de un motor)

sputter[2] *n* **1** JABBER : farfulla *f* **2** : chisporroteo *m* (de grasa, etc.), petardeo *m* (de un motor)

spy[1] ['spaɪ] *v* **spied; spying** *vt* SEE : ver, divisar — *vi* : espiar <to spy on someone : espiar a alguien>

spy[2] *n* : espía *mf*

squab ['skwɑb] *n, pl* **squabs** *or* **squab** : pichón *m*

squabble[1] ['skwɑbəl] *vi* **-bled; -bling** : reñir, pelearse, discutir

squabble[2] *n* : riña *f,* pelea *f,* discusión *f*

squad ['skwɑd] *n* : pelotón *m* (militar), brigada *f* (de policías), cuadrilla *f* (de obreros, etc.)

squadron ['skwɑdrən] *n* : escuadrón *m* (de militares), escuadrilla *f* (de aviones), escuadra *f* (de naves)

squalid ['skwɑlɪd] *adj* : miserable

squall ['skwɔl] *n* **1** : aguacero *m* tormentoso, chubasco *m* tormentoso **2 snow squall** : tormenta *f* de nieve

squalor ['skwɑlər] *n* : miseria *f*

squander ['skwɑndər] *vt* : derrochar (dinero, etc.), desaprovechar (una oportunidad, etc.), desperdiciar (talentos, energías, etc.)

square[1] ['skwær] *vt* **squared; squaring 1 :** cuadrar **2 :** elevar al cuadrado (en matemáticas) **3** CONFORM **:** conciliar (con), ajustar (con) **4** SETTLE **:** saldar (una cuenta) <I squared it with him : lo arreglé con él>

square[2] *adj* **squarer; -est 1 :** cuadrado <a square house : una casa cuadrada> **2** RIGHT-ANGLED **:** a escuadra, en ángulo recto **3 :** cuadrado (en matemáticas) <a square mile : una milla cuadrada> **4** HONEST **:** justo <a square deal : un buen acuerdo> <fair and square : en buena lid>

square[3] *n* **1 :** escuadra *f* (instrumento) **2 :** cuadrado *m,* cuadro *m* <to fold into squares : plegar en cuadrados> **3 :** plaza *f* (de una ciudad) **4 :** cuadrado *m* (en matemáticas)

squarely ['skwærli] *adv* **1** EXACTLY **:** exactamente, directamente, justo **2** HONESTLY **:** honradamente, justamente

square root *n* **:** raíz *f* cuadrada

squash[1] ['skwɑʃ, 'skwɔʃ] *vt* **1** CRUSH **:** aplastar **2** SUPPRESS **:** acallar (protestas), sofocar (una rebelión)

squash[2] *n* **1** *pl* **squashes** *or* **squash :** calabaza *f* (vegetal) **2** *or* **squash racquets :** squash *m* (deporte)

squat[1] ['skwɑt] *vi* **squatted; squatting 1** CROUCH **:** agacharse, ponerse en cuclillas **2 :** ocupar un lugar sin derecho

squat[2] *adj* **squatter; squattest :** bajo y ancho, rechoncho *fam* (dícese de una persona)

squat[3] *n* **1 :** posición *f* en cuclillas **2 :** ocupación *f* ilegal (de un lugar)

squaw ['skwɔ] *n* **:** india *f* (norteamericana)

squawk[1] ['skwɔk] *vi* **:** graznar (dícese de las aves), chillar

squawk[2] *n* **:** graznido *m* (de un ave), chillido *m*

squeak[1] ['skwi:k] *vi* **:** chillar (dícese de un animal), chirriar (dícese de un objeto)

squeak[2] *n* **:** chillido *m,* chirrido *m*

squeaky ['skwi:ki] *adj* **squeakier; -est :** chirriante <a squeaky voice : una voz chillona>

squeal[1] ['skwi:l] *vi* **1 :** chillar (dícese de las personas o los animales), chirriar (dícese de los frenos, etc.) **2** PROTEST **:** quejarse

squeal[2] *n* **1 :** chillido *m* (de una persona o un animal) **2** SCREECH **:** chirrido *m* (de frenos, etc.)

squeamish ['skwi:mɪʃ] *adj* **:** impresionable, sensible <he's squeamish about cockroaches : las cucarachas le dan asco>

squeeze[1] ['skwi:z] *vt* **squeezed; squeezing 1** PRESS **:** apretar, exprimir (naranjas, etc.) **2** EXTRACT **:** extraer (jugo, etc.)

squeeze[2] *n* **:** apretón *m*

squelch ['skwɛltʃ] *vt* **:** aplastar (una rebelión, etc.)

squid ['skwɪd] *n, pl* **squid** *or* **squids :** calamar *m*

squint[1] ['skwɪnt] *vi* **:** mirar con los ojos entornados

squint[2] *adj* *or* **squint-eyed** ['skwɪnt,aɪd] **:** bizco

squint[3] *n* **:** ojos *mpl* bizcos, bizquera *f*

squire ['skwaɪr] *n* **:** hacendado *m,* -da *f;* terrateniente *mf*

squirm ['skwərm] *vi* **:** retorcerse

squirrel ['skwərəl] *n* **:** ardilla *f*

squirt[1] ['skwərt] *vt* **:** lanzar un chorro de — *vi* SPURT **:** salir a chorros

squirt[2] *n* **:** chorrito *m*

stab[1] [stæb] *vt* **stabbed; stabbing 1** KNIFE **:** acuchillar, apuñalar **2** STICK **:** clavar (con una aguja, etc.), golpear (con el dedo, etc.)

stab[2] *n* **1 :** puñalada *f,* cuchillada *f* **2** JAB **:** pinchazo *m* (con una aguja, etc.), golpe *m* (con un dedo, etc.) **3 to take a stab at :** intentar

stability [stə'bɪləti] *n, pl* **-ties :** estabilidad *f*

stabilize ['steɪbə,laɪz] *v* **-lized; -lizing** *vt* **:** estabilizar — *vi* **:** estabilizarse

stable[1] ['steɪbəl] *vt* **-bled; -bling :** poner (ganado) en un establo, poner (caballos) en una caballeriza

stable[2] *adj* **-bler; -blest 1** FIXED, STEADY **:** fijo, sólido, estable **2** LASTING **:** estable, perdurable <a stable government : un gobierno estable> **3 :** estacionario (en medicina), equilibrado (en psicología)

stable[3] *n* **:** establo *m* (para ganado), caballeriza *f* o cuadra *f* (para caballos)

staccato [stə'kɑto:] *adj* **:** staccato

stack[1] ['stæk] *vt* **1** PILE **:** amontonar, apilar **2** COVER **:** cubrir, llenar <he stacked the table with books : cubrió la mesa de libros>

stack[2] *n* **1** PILE **:** montón *m,* pila *f* **2** SMOKESTACK **:** chimenea *f*

stadium ['steɪdiəm] *n, pl* **-dia** [-diə] *or* **-diums :** estadio *m*

staff[1] ['stæf] *vt* **:** proveer de personal

staff[2] *n, pl* **staffs** ['stæfs, stævz] *or* **staves** ['stævz, 'steɪvz] **1 :** bastón *m* (de mando), báculo *m* (de obispo) **2** *pl* **staffs** PERSONNEL **:** personal *m* **3** *pl* **staffs :** pentagrama *m* (en música)

stag[1] ['stæg] *adv* **:** solo, sin pareja <to go stag : ir solo>

stag[2] *adj* **:** sólo para hombres

stag[3] *n, pl* **stags** *or* **stag :** ciervo *m,* venado *m*

stage[1] ['steɪdʒ] *vt* **staged; staging :** poner en escena (una obra de teatro)

stage[2] *n* **1** PLATFORM **:** estrado *m,* tablado *m,* escenario *m* (de un teatro) **2** PHASE, STEP **:** fase *f,* etapa *f* <stage of development : fase de desarrollo> <in stages : por etapas> **3 the stage :** el teatro *m*

stagecoach ['steɪdʒ,ko:tʃ] *n* **:** diligencia *f*

stagger[1] ['stægər] *vi* TOTTER : tambalearse — *vt* **1** ALTERNATE : alternar, escalonar (turnos de trabajo) **2** : hacer tambalear <to be staggered by : quedarse estupefacto por>
stagger[2] *n* : tambaleo *m*
staggering ['stægərɪŋli] *adj* : asombroso
stagnant ['stægnənt] *adj* : estancado
stagnate ['stæg͵neɪt] *vi* **-nated; -nating** : estancarse
staid ['steɪd] *adj* : serio, sobrio
stain[1] ['steɪn] *vt* **1** DISCOLOR : manchar **2** DYE : teñir (madera, etc.) **3** SULLY : manchar, empañar
stain[2] *n* **1** SPOT : mancha *f* **2** DYE : tinte *m,* tintura *f* **3** BLEMISH : mancha *f,* mácula *f*
stainless ['steɪnləs] *adj* : sin mancha <stainless steel : acero inoxidable>
stair ['stær] *n* **1** STEP : escalón *m,* peldaño *m* **2 stairs** *npl* : escalera *f,* escaleras *fpl*
staircase ['stær͵keɪs] *n* : escalera *f,* escaleras *fpl*
stairway ['stær͵weɪ] *n* : escalera *f,* escaleras *fpl*
stake[1] ['steɪk] *vt* **staked; staking 1** : estacar, marcar con estacas (una propiedad) **2** BET : jugarse, apostar **3 to stake a claim to** : reclamar, reivindicar
stake[2] *n* **1** POST : estaca *f* **2** BET : apuesta *f* <to be at stake : estar en juego> **3** INTEREST, SHARE : interés *m,* participación *f*
stalactite [stə'læk͵taɪt] *n* : estalactita *f*
stalagmite [stə'læg͵maɪt] *n* : estalagmita *f*
stale ['steɪl] *adj* **staler; stalest** : viejo <stale bread : pan duro> <stale news : viejas noticias>
stalemate ['steɪl͵meɪt] *n* : punto *m* muerto, impasse *m*
stalk[1] ['stɔk] *vt* : acechar — *vi* : caminar rígidamente (por orgullo, ira, etc.)
stalk[2] *n* : tallo *m* (de una planta)
stall[1] ['stɔl] *vt* **1** : parar (un motor) **2** DELAY : entretener (a una persona), demorar — *vi* **1** : pararse (dícese de un motor) **2** DELAY : demorar, andar con rodeos
stall[2] *n* **1** : compartimiento *m* (de un establo) **2** : puesto *m* (en un mercado, etc.)
stallion ['stæljən] *n* : caballo *m* semental
stalwart ['stɔlwərt] *adj* **1** STRONG : fuerte <a stalwart supporter : un firme partidario> **2** BRAVE : valiente, valeroso
stamen ['steɪmən] *n* : estambre *m*
stamina ['stæmənə] *n* : resistencia *f*
stammer[1] ['stæmər] *vi* : tartamudear, titubear
stammer[2] *n* : tartamudeo *m,* titubeo *m*
stamp[1] ['stæmp] *vt* **1** : pisotear (con los pies) <to stamp one's feet : patear, dar una patada> **2** IMPRESS, IMPRINT : sellar (una factura, etc.), acuñar (monedas) **3** : franquear, ponerle estampillas a (correo)
stamp[2] *n* **1** : sello *m* (para documentos, etc.) **2** DIE : cuño *m* (para monedas) **3** *or* **postage stamp** : sello *m,* estampilla *f,* timbre *m CA, Mex*
stampede[1] [stæm'piːd] *vi* **-peded; -peding** : salir en estampida
stampede[2] *n* : estampida *f*
stance ['stæn*t*s] *n* : postura *f*
stanch ['stɔntʃ, 'stɑntʃ] *vt* : detener, estancar (un líquido)
stand[1] ['stænd] *v* **stood** ['stʊd]; **standing** *vi* **1** : estar de pie, estar parado <I was standing on the corner : estaba parada en la esquina> **2** *or* **to stand up** : levantarse, pararse, ponerse de pie **3** *(indicating a specified position or location)* <they stand third in the country : ocupan el tercer lugar en el país> <the machines are standing idle : las máquinas están paradas> **4** *(referring to an opinion)* <how does he stand on the matter ? : ¿cuál es su postura respecto al asunto?> **5** BE : estar <the house stands on a hill : la casa está en una colina> **6** CONTINUE : seguir <the order still stands : el mandato sigue vigente> — *vt* **1** PLACE, SET : poner, colocar <he stood them in a row : los colocó en hilera> **2** TOLERATE : aguantar, soportar <he can't stand her : no la puede tragar> **3 to stand firm** : mantenerse firme **4 to stand guard** : hacer la guardia
stand[2] *n* **1** RESISTANCE : resistencia *f* <to make a stand against : resistir a> **2** BOOTH, STALL : stand *m,* puesto *m,* kiosko *m* (para vender periódicos, etc.) **3** BASE : pie *m,* base *f* **4** : grupo *m* (de árboles, etc.) **5** POSITION : posición *f,* postura *f* **6 stands** *npl* GRANDSTAND : tribuna *f*
standard[1] ['stændərd] *adj* **1** ESTABLISHED : estándar, oficial <standard measures : medidas oficiales> <standard English : el inglés estándar> **2** NORMAL : normal, estándar, común **3** CLASSIC : estándar, clásico <a standard work : una obra clásica>
standard[2] *n* **1** BANNER : estandarte *m* **2** CRITERION : criterio *m* **3** RULE : estándar *m,* norma *f,* regla *f* **4** LEVEL : nivel *m* <standard of living : nivel de vida> **5** SUPPORT : poste *m,* soporte *m*
standardize ['stændər͵daɪz] *vt* **-ized; -izing** : estandarizar
standard time *n* : hora *f* oficial
stand by *vt* : atenerse a, cumplir con (una promesa, etc.) — *vi* **1** : mantenerse aparte <to stand by and do nothing : mirar sin hacer nada> **2** : estar preparado, estar listo (para un anuncio, un ataque, etc.)
stand for *vt* **1** REPRESENT : significar **2** PERMIT, TOLERATE : permitir, tolerar
standing ['stændɪŋ] *n* **1** POSITION, RANK : posición *f* **2** DURATION : duración *f*

stand out *vi* **1** : destacar(se) <she stands out from the rest : se destaca entre los otros> **2 to stand out against** RESIST : oponerse a

standpoint ['stænd,pɔint] *n* : punto *m* de vista

standstill ['stænd,stɪl] *n* **1** STOP : detención *f,* paro *m* <to come to a standstill : pararse> **2** DEADLOCK : punto *m* muerto, impasse *m*

stand up *vt* : dejar plantado <he stood me up again : otra vez me dejó plantado> — *vi* **1** ENDURE : durar, resistir **2 to stand up for** : defender **3 to stand up to** : hacerle frente (a alguien)

stank → **stink**

stanza ['stænzə] *n* : estrofa *f*

staple[1] ['steɪpəl] *vt* **-pled; -pling** : engrapar, grapar

staple[2] *adj* : principal, básico <a staple food : un alimento básico>

staple[3] *n* **1** : producto *m* principal **2** : grapa *f* (para engrapar papeles)

stapler ['steɪplər] *n* : engrapadora *f,* grapadora *f*

star[1] ['stɑr] *v* **starred; starring** *vt* **1** : marcar con una estrella o un asterisco **2** FEATURE : ser protagonizado por — *vi* : tener el papel principal <to star in : protagonizar>

star[2] *n* : estrella *f*

starboard ['stɑrbərd] *n* : estribor *m*

starch[1] ['stɑrtʃ] *vt* : almidonar

starch[2] *n* : almidón *m,* fécula *f* (comida)

starchy ['stɑrtʃi] *adj* **starchier; -est** : lleno de almidón <a starchy diet : una dieta feculenta>

stardom ['stɑrdəm] *n* : estrellato *m*

stare[1] ['stær] *vi* **stared; staring** : mirar fijamente

stare[2] *n* : mirada *f* fija

starfish ['stɑr,fɪʃ] *n* : estrella *f* de mar

stark[1] ['stɑrk] *adv* : completamente <stark raving mad : loco de remate> <stark naked : completamente desnudo>

stark[2] *adj* **1** ABSOLUTE : absoluto **2** BARREN, DESOLATE : desolado, desierto **3** BARE : desnudo **4** HARSH : severo, duro

starlight ['stɑr,laɪt] *n* : luz *f* de las estrellas

starling ['stɑrlɪŋ] *n* : estornino *m*

starry ['stɑri] *adj* **starrier; -est** : estrellado

start[1] ['stɑrt] *vi* **1** JUMP : levantarse de un salto, sobresaltarse, dar un respingo **2** BEGIN : empezar, comenzar **3** SET OUT : salir (de viaje, etc.) **4** : arrancar (dícese de un motor) — *vt* **1** BEGIN : empezar, comenzar, iniciar **2** CAUSE : provocar, causar **3** ESTABLISH : fundar, montar, establecer <to start a business : montar un negocio> **4** : arrancar, poner en marcha, encender <to start the car : arrancar el motor>

start[2] *n* **1** JUMP : sobresalto *m,* respingo *m* **2** BEGINNING : principio *m,* comienzo *m* <to get an early start : salir temprano>

starter ['stɑrt̬ər] *n* **1** ENTRANT : participante *mf* (en deportes) **2** APPETIZER : entremés *m,* aperitivo *m* **3** : motor *m* de arranque (de un vehículo)

startle ['stɑrtəl] *vt* **-tled; -tling** : asustar, sobresaltar

starvation [stɑr'veɪʃən] *n* : inanición *f,* hambre *f*

starve ['stɑrv] *v* **starved; starving** *vi* : morirse de hambre — *vt* : privar de comida

stash ['stæʃ] *vt* : esconder, guardar (en un lugar secreto)

state[1] ['steɪt] *vt* **stated; stating 1** REPORT : puntualizar, exponer (los hechos, etc.) <state your name : diga su nombre> **2** ESTABLISH, FIX : establecer, fijar

state[2] *n* **1** CONDITION : estado *m,* condición *f* <a liquid state : un estado líquido> <state of mind : estado de ánimo> <in a bad state : en malas condiciones> **2** NATION : estado *m,* nación *f* **3** : estado *m* (dentro de un país) <the States : los Estados Unidos>

stateliness ['steɪtlinəs] *n* : majestuosidad *f*

stately ['steɪtli] *adj* **statelier; -est** : majestuoso

statement ['steɪtmənt] *n* **1** DECLARATION : declaración *f,* afirmación *f* **2** *or* **bank statement** : estado *m* de cuenta

stateroom ['steɪt,ru:m, -,rʊm] *n* : camarote *m*

statesman ['steɪtsmən] *n, pl* **-men** [-mən, -,mɛn] : estadista *mf*

static[1] ['stæt̬ɪk] *adj* : estático

static[2] *n* : estática *f,* interferencia *f*

station[1] ['steɪʃən] *vt* : apostar, estacionar

station[2] *n* **1** : estación *f* (de trenes, etc.) **2** RANK, STANDING : condición *f* (social) **3** : canal *m* (de televisión), estación *f* o emisora *f* (de radio) **4 police station** : comisaría *f* **5 fire station** : estación *f* de bomberos, cuartel *m* de bomberos

stationary ['steɪʃə,nɛri] *adj* **1** IMMOBILE : estacionario, inmovible **2** UNCHANGING : inmutable, inalterable

stationery ['steɪʃə,nɛri] *n* : papel *m* y sobres *mpl* (para correspondencia)

station wagon *n* : camioneta *f* guayín, camioneta *f* ranchera

statistic [stə'tɪstɪk] *n* : estadística *f* <according to statistics : según las estadísticas>

statistical [stə'tɪstɪkəl] *adj* : estadístico

statue ['stæ,tʃu:] *n* : estatua *f*

statuesque [,stætʃʊ'ɛsk] *adj* : escultural

statuette [,stætʃʊ'ɛt] *n* : estatuilla *f*

stature ['stætʃər] *n* **1** HEIGHT : estatura *f,* talla *f* **2** PRESTIGE : talla *f,* prestigio *m*

status [ˈsteɪtəs, ˈstæ-] *n* **:** condición *f,* situación *f,* estatus *m* (social) <marital status : estado civil>
statute [ˈstæˌtʃuːt] *n* **:** ley *f,* estatuto *m*
staunch [ˈstɔntʃ] *adj* **:** acérrimo, incondicional, leal <a staunch supporter : un partidario incondicional> — **staunchly** *adv*
stave[1] [ˈsteɪv] *vt* **staved** *or* **stove** [ˈstoːv]; **staving 1 to stave in :** romper **2 to stave off :** evitar (un ataque), prevenir (un problema)
stave[2] *n* **:** duela *f* (de un barril)
staves → **staff**
stay[1] [ˈsteɪ] *vi* **1** REMAIN **:** quedarse, permanecer <to stay in : quedarse en casa> <he stayed in the city : permaneció en la ciudad> **2** CONTINUE **:** seguir, quedarse <it stayed cloudy : siguió nublado> <to stay awake : mantenerse despierto> **3** LODGE **:** hospedarse, alojarse (en un hotel, etc.) — *vt* **1** HALT **:** detener, suspender (una ejecución, etc.) **2 to stay the course :** aguantar hasta el final
stay[2] *n* **1** SOJOURN **:** estadía *f,* estancia *f,* permanencia *f* **2** SUSPENSION **:** suspensión *f* (de una sentencia) **3** SUPPORT **:** soporte *m*
stead [ˈstɛd] *n* **1 :** lugar *m* <she went in his stead : fue en su lugar> **2 to stand (someone) in good stead :** ser muy útil a, servir de mucho a
steadfast [ˈstɛdˌfæst] *adj* **:** firme, resuelto <a steadfast friend : un fiel amigo> <a steadfast refusal : una negativa categórica>
steadily [ˈstɛdəli] *adv* **1** CONSTANTLY **:** continuamente, sin parar **2** FIRMLY **:** con firmeza **3** FIXEDLY **:** fijamente
steady[1] [ˈstɛdi] *v* **steadied; steadying** *vt* **:** sujetar <she steadied herself : recobró el equilibrio> — *vi* **:** estabilizarse
steady[2] *adj* **steadier; -est 1** FIRM, SURE **:** seguro, firme <to have a steady hand : tener buen pulso> **2** FIXED, REGULAR **:** fijo <a steady income : ingresos fijos> **3** CALM **:** tranquilo, ecuánime <she has steady nerves : es imperturbable> **4** DEPENDABLE **:** responsable, fiable **5** CONSTANT **:** constante
steak [ˈsteɪk] *n* **:** bistec *m,* filete *m,* churrasco *m,* bife *m Arg, Chile, Uru*
steal [ˈstiːl] *v* **stole** [ˈstoːl]; **stolen** [ˈstoːlən]; **stealing** *vt* **:** robar, hurtar — *vi* **1 :** robar, hurtar **2 :** ir sigilosamente <to steal away : escabullirse>
stealth [ˈstɛlθ] *n* **:** sigilo *m*
stealthily [ˈstɛlθəli] *adv* **:** furtivamente
stealthy [ˈstɛlθi] *adj* **stealthier; -est :** furtivo, sigiloso
steam[1] [ˈstiːm] *vi* **:** echar vapor <to steam away : moverse echando vapor> — *vt* **1 :** cocer al vapor (en cocina) **2 to steam open :** abrir con vapor
steam[2] *n* **1 :** vapor *m* **2 to let off steam :** desahogarse
steamboat [ˈstiːmˌboːt] → **steamship**
steam engine *n* **:** motor *m* de vapor
steamroller [ˈstiːmˌroːlər] *n* **:** apisonadora *f*
steamship [ˈstiːmˌʃɪp] *n* **:** vapor *m,* barco *m* de vapor
steamy [ˈstiːmi] *adj* **steamier; -est 1 :** lleno de vapor **2** EROTIC **:** erótico <a steamy romance : un tórrido romance>
steed [ˈstiːd] *n* **:** corcel *m*
steel[1] [ˈstiːl] *vt* **to steel oneself :** armarse de valor
steel[2] *adj* **:** de acero
steel[3] *n* **:** acero *m*
steely [ˈstiːli] *adj* **steelier; -est :** como acero <a steely gaze : una mirada fría> <steely determination : determinación férrea>
steep[1] [ˈstiːp] *vt* **:** remojar, dejar (té, etc.) en infusión
steep[2] *adj* **1 :** empinado, escarpado <a steep cliff : un precipicio escarpado> **2** CONSIDERABLE **:** considerable, marcado **3** EXCESSIVE **:** excesivo <steep prices : precios muy altos>
steeple [ˈstiːpəl] *n* **:** aguja *f,* campanario *m*
steeplechase [ˈstiːpəlˌtʃeɪs] *n* **:** carrera *f* de obstáculos
steeply [ˈstiːpli] *adv* **:** abruptamente
steer[1] [ˈstɪr] *vt* **1 :** conducir (un coche), gobernar (un barco) **2** GUIDE **:** dirigir, guiar
steer[2] *n* **:** buey *m*
steering wheel *n* **:** volante *m*
stein [ˈstaɪn] *n* **:** jarra *f* (para cerveza)
stellar [ˈstɛlər] *adj* **:** estelar
stem[1] [ˈstɛm] *v* **stemmed; stemming** *vt* **:** detener, contener, parar <to stem the tide : detener el curso> — *vi* **to stem from :** provenir de, ser el resultado de
stem[2] *n* **:** tallo *m* (de una planta)
stench [ˈstɛntʃ] *n* **:** hedor *m,* mal olor *m*
stencil[1] [ˈstɛntsəl] *vt* **-ciled** *or* **-cilled; -ciling** *or* **-cilling :** marcar utilizando una plantilla
stencil[2] *n* **:** plantilla *f* (para marcar)
stenographer [stəˈnɑgrəfər] *n* **:** taquígrafo *m,* -fa *f*
stenographic [ˌstɛnəˈgræfɪk] *adj* **:** taquigráfico
stenography [stəˈnɑgrəfi] *n* **:** taquigrafía *f*
step[1] [ˈstɛp] *vi* **stepped; stepping 1 :** dar un paso <step this way, please : pase por aquí, por favor> <he stepped outside : salió> **2 to step on :** pisar
step[2] *n* **1 :** paso *m* <step by step : paso por paso> **2** STAIR **:** escalón *m,* peldaño *m* **3** RUNG **:** escalón *m,* travesaño *m* **4** MEASURE, MOVE **:** medida *f,* paso *m* <to take steps : tomar medidas> **5** STRIDE **:** paso *m* <with a quick step : con paso rápido>

stepbrother ['stɛp,brʌðər] *n* **:** hermanastro *m*

stepdaughter ['stɛp,dɔt̬ər] *n* **:** hijastra *f*

stepfather ['stɛp,fɑðər, -,fa-] *n* **:** padrastro *m*

stepladder ['stɛp,lædər] *n* **:** escalera *f* de tijera

stepmother ['stɛp,mʌðər] *n* **:** madrastra *f*

steppe ['stɛp] *n* **:** estepa *f*

stepping–stone ['stɛpɪŋ,sto:n] *n* **:** pasadera *f* (en un río, etc.), trampolín *m* (al éxito)

stepsister ['stɛp,sɪstər] *n* **:** hermanastra *f*

stepson ['stɛp,sʌn] *n* **:** hijastro *m*

step up *vt* INCREASE **:** aumentar

stereo[1] ['stɛri,o:, 'stɪr-] *adj* **:** estéreo

stereo[2] *n, pl* **stereos :** estéreo *m*

stereophonic [,stɛrio'fɑnɪk, ,stɪr-] *adj* **:** estereofónico

stereotype[1] ['stɛrio,taɪp, 'stɪr-] *vt* **-typed; -typing :** estereotipar

stereotype[2] *n* **:** estereotipo *m*

sterile ['stɛrəl] *adj* **:** estéril

sterility [stə'rɪlət̬i] *n* **:** esterilidad *f*

sterilization [,stɛrələ'zeɪʃən] *n* **:** esterilización *f*

sterilize ['stɛrə,laɪz] *vt* **-ized; -izing :** esterilizar

sterling ['stərlɪŋ] *adj* **1 :** de ley <sterling silver : plata de ley> **2** EXCELLENT **:** excelente

stern[1] ['stərn] *adj* **:** severo, adusto — **sternly** *adv*

stern[2] *n* **:** popa *f*

sternness ['stərnnəs] *n* **:** severidad *f*

sternum ['stərnəm] *n, pl* **sternums** *or* **sterna** [-nə] **:** esternón *m*

stethoscope ['stɛθə,sko:p] *n* **:** estetoscopio *m*

stevedore ['sti:və,dor] *n* **:** estibador *m,* -dora *f*

stew[1] ['stu:, 'stju:] *vt* **:** estofar, guisar — *vi* **1 :** cocer (dícese de la carne, etc.) **2** FRET **:** preocuparse

stew[2] *n* **1 :** estofado *m,* guiso *m* **2 to be in a stew :** estar agitado

steward ['stu:ərd, 'stju:-] *n* **1** MANAGER **:** administrador *m* **2 :** auxiliar *m* de vuelo (en un avión), camarero *m* (en un barco)

stewardess ['stu:ərdəs, 'stju:-] *n* **1** MANAGER **:** administradora *f* **2 :** camarera *f* (en un barco) **3 :** auxiliar *f* de vuelo, azafata *f,* aeromoza *f* (en un avión)

stick[1] ['stɪk] *v* **stuck** ['stʌk]; **sticking** *vt* **1** STAB **:** clavar **2** ATTACH **:** pegar **3** PUT **:** poner **4 to stick out :** sacar (la lengua, etc.), extender (la mano) — *vi* **1** ADHERE **:** pegarse, adherirse **2** JAM **:** atascarse **3 to stick around :** quedarse **4 to stick out** PROJECT **:** sobresalir (de una superficie), asomar (por detrás o debajo de algo) **5 to stick to :** no abandonar <stick to your guns : manténgase firme> **6 to stick up :** estar parado (dícese del pelo, etc.), sobresalir (de una superficie) **7 to stick with :** serle fiel a (una persona), seguir con (una cosa) <I'll stick with what I know : prefiero lo conocido>

stick[2] *n* **1** BRANCH, TWIG **:** ramita *f* **2 :** palo *m,* vara *f* <a walking stick : un bastón>

sticker ['stɪkər] *n* **:** etiqueta *f* adhesiva

stickler ['stɪklər] *n* **:** persona *f* exigente <to be a stickler for : insistir mucho en>

sticky ['stɪki] *adj* **stickier; -est 1** ADHESIVE **:** pegajoso, adhesivo **2** MUGGY **:** bochornoso **3** DIFFICULT **:** difícil

stiff ['stɪf] *adj* **1** RIGID **:** rígido, tieso <a stiff dough : una masa firme> **2 :** agarrotado, entumecido <stiff muscles : músculos entumecidos> **3** STILTED **:** acartonado, poco natural **4** STRONG **:** fuerte (dícese del viento, etc.) **5** DIFFICULT, SEVERE **:** severo, difícil, duro

stiffen ['stɪfən] *vt* **1** STRENGTHEN **:** fortalecer, reforzar (tela, etc.) **2 :** hacer más duro (un castigo, etc.) — *vi* **1** HARDEN **:** endurecerse **2 :** entumecerse (dícese de los músculos)

stiffly ['stɪfli] *adv* **1** RIGIDLY **:** rígidamente **2** COLDLY **:** con frialdad

stiffness ['stɪfnəs] *n* **1** RIGIDITY **:** rigidez *f* **2** COLDNESS **:** frialdad *f* **3** SEVERITY **:** severidad *f*

stifle ['staɪfəl] *vt* **-fled; -fling** SMOTHER, SUPPRESS **:** sofocar, reprimir, contener <to stifle a yawn : reprimir un bostezo>

stigma ['stɪgmə] *n, pl* **stigmata** [stɪg'mɑt̬ə, 'stɪgmət̬ə] *or* **stigmas :** estigma *m*

stigmatize ['stɪgmə,taɪz] *vt* **-tized; -tizing :** estigmatizar

stile ['staɪl] *n* **:** escalones *mpl* para cruzar un cerco

stiletto [stə'lɛ,t̬o:] *n, pl* **-tos** *or* **-toes :** estilete *m*

still[1] ['stɪl] *vt* CALM **:** pacificar, apaciguar — *vi* **:** pacificarse, apaciguarse

still[2] *adv* **1** QUIETLY **:** quieto <sit still! : ¡quédate quieto!> **2 :** de todos modos, aún, todavía <she still lives there : aún vive allí> <it's still the same : sigue siendo lo mismo> **3** IN ANY CASE **:** de todos modos, aún así <he still has doubts : aún así le quedan dudas> <I still prefer that you stay : de todos modos prefiero que te quedes>

still[3] *adj* **1** MOTIONLESS **:** quieto, inmóvil **2** SILENT **:** callado

still[4] *n* **1** SILENCE **:** quietud *f,* calma *f* **2 :** alambique *m* (para destilar alcohol)

stillborn ['stɪl,bɔrn] *adj* **:** nacido muerto

stillness ['stɪlnəs] *n* **:** calma *f,* silencio *m*

stilt ['stɪlt] *n* **:** zanco *m*

stilted ['stɪltəd] *adj* **:** afectado, poco natural

stimulant ['stɪmjələnt] *n* : estimulante *m* — **stimulant** *adj*
stimulate ['stɪmjə,leɪt] *vt* **-lated; -lating** : estimular
stimulation [,stɪmjə'leɪʃən] *n* **1** STIMULATING : estimulación *f* **2** STIMULUS : estímulo *m*
stimulus ['stɪmjələs] *n, pl* **-li** [-,laɪ] **1** : estímulo *m* **2** INCENTIVE : acicate *m*
sting[1] ['stɪŋ] *v* **stung** ['stʌŋ]; **stinging** *vt* **1** : picar <a bee stung him : le picó una abeja> **2** HURT : hacer escocer (físicamente), herir (emocionalmente) — *vi* **1** : picar (dícese de las abejas, etc.) **2** SMART : escocer, arder
sting[2] *n* : picadura *f* (herida), escozor *m* (sensación)
stinger ['stɪŋər] *n* : aguijón *m* (de una abeja, etc.)
stinginess ['stɪndʒinəs] *n* : tacañería *f*
stingy ['stɪndʒi] *adj* **stingier; -est 1** MISERLY : tacaño, avaro **2** PALTRY : mezquino, mísero
stink[1] ['stɪŋk] *vi* **stank** ['stæŋk] *or* **stunk** ['stʌŋk]; **stunk; stinking** : apestar, oler mal
stink[2] *n* : hedor *m,* mal olor *m,* peste *f*
stint[1] ['stɪnt] *vt* : escatimar <to stint oneself of : privarse de> — *vi* **to stint on** : escatimar
stint[2] *n* : período *m*
stipend ['staɪ,pɛnd, -pənd] *n* : estipendio *m*
stipulate ['stɪpjə,leɪt] *vt* **-lated; -lating** : estipular
stipulation [,stɪpjə'leɪʃən] *n* : estipulación *f*
stir[1] ['stər] *v* **stirred; stirring** *vt* **1** AGITATE : mover, agitar **2** MIX : revolver, remover **3** INCITE : incitar, impulsar, motivar **4** *or* **to stir up** AROUSE : despertar (memorias, etc.), provocar (ira, etc.) — *vi* : moverse, agitarse
stir[2] *n* **1** MOTION : movimiento *m* **2** COMMOTION : revuelo *m*
stirrup ['stərəp, 'stɪr-] *n* : estribo *m*
stitch[1] ['stɪtʃ] *vt* : coser, bordar (para decorar) — *vi* : coser
stitch[2] *n* **1** : puntada *f* **2** TWINGE : punzada *f,* puntada *f*
stock[1] ['stɑk] *vt* : surtir, abastecer, vender — *vi* **to stock up** : abastecerse
stock[2] *n* **1** SUPPLY : reserva *f,* existencias *fpl* (en comercio) <to be out of stock : estar agotadas las existencias> **2** SECURITIES : acciones *fpl,* valores *mpl* **3** LIVESTOCK : ganado *m* **4** ANCESTRY : linaje *m,* estirpe *f* **5** BROTH : caldo *m* **6 to take stock** : evaluar
stockade [stɑ'keɪd] *n* : estacada *f*
stockbroker ['stɑk,bro:kər] *n* : corredor *m,* -dora *f* de bolsa
stockholder ['stɑk,ho:ldər] *n* : accionista *mf*
stocking ['stɑkɪŋ] *n* : media *f* <a pair of stockings : unas medias>
stock market *n* : bolsa *f*
stockpile[1] ['stɑk,paɪl] *vt* **-piled; -piling** : acumular, almacenar
stockpile[2] *n* : reservas *fpl*
stocky ['stɑki] *adj* **stockier; -est** : robusto, fornido
stockyard ['stɑk,jɑrd] *n* : corral *m*
stodgy ['stɑdʒi] *adj* **stodgier; -est 1** DULL : aburrido, pesado **2** OLD-FASHIONED : anticuado
stoic[1] ['sto:ɪk] *or* **stoical** [-ɪkəl] *adj* : estoico — **stoically** [-ɪkli] *adv*
stoic[2] *n* : estoico *m,* -ca *f*
stoicism ['sto:ə,sɪzəm] *n* : estoicismo *m*
stoke ['sto:k] *vt* **stoked; stoking** : atizar (un fuego), echarle carbón a (un horno)
stole[1] → **steal**
stole[2] ['sto:l] *n* : estola *f*
stolen → **steal**
stolid ['stɑlɪd] *adj* : impasible, imperturbable — **stolidly** *adv*
stomach[1] ['stʌmɪk] *vt* : aguantar, soportar
stomach[2] *n* **1** : estómago *m* **2** BELLY : vientre *m,* barriga *f,* panza *f* **3** DESIRE : ganas *fpl* <he had no stomach for a fight : no quería pelea>
stomachache ['stʌmɪk,eɪk] *n* : dolor *m* de estómago
stomp ['stɑmp, 'stɔmp] *vt* : pisotear — *vi* : pisar fuerte
stone[1] ['sto:n] *vt* **stoned; stoning** : apedrear, lapidar
stone[2] *n* **1** : piedra *f* **2** PIT : hueso *m,* pepa *f* (de una fruta)
Stone Age *n* : Edad *f* de Piedra
stony ['sto:ni] *adj* **stonier; -est 1** ROCKY : pedregoso **2** UNFEELING : insensible, frío <a stony stare : una mirada glacial>
stood → **stand**
stool ['stu:l] *n* **1** SEAT : taburete *m,* banco *m* **2** FOOTSTOOL : escabel *m* **3** FECES : deposición *f* de heces
stoop[1] ['stu:p] *vi* **1** CROUCH : agacharse **2 to stoop to** : rebajarse a
stoop[2] *n* **1** : espaldas *fpl* encorvadas <to have a stoop : ser encorvado> **2** : entrada *f* (de una casa)
stop[1] ['stɑp] *v* **stopped; stopping** *vt* **1** PLUG : tapar **2** PREVENT : impedir, evitar <she stopped me from leaving : me impidió que saliera> **3** HALT : parar, detener **4** CEASE : dejar de <he stopped talking : dejó de hablar> — *vi* **1** HALT : detenerse, parar **2** CEASE : cesar, terminar <the rain won't stop : no deja de llover> **3** STAY : quedarse <she stopped with friends : se quedó en casa de unos amigos> **4 to stop by** : visitar
stop[2] *n* **1** STOPPER : tapón *m* **2** HALT : parada *f,* alto *m* <to come to a stop : pararse, detenerse> <to put a stop to : poner fin a> **3** : parada *f* <bus stop : parada de autobús>
stopgap ['stɑp,gæp] *n* : arreglo *m* provisorio
stoplight ['stɑp,laɪt] *n* : semáforo *m*

stoppage [ˈstɑpɪdʒ] *n* **:** acto *m* de parar <a work stoppage : un paro>
stopper [ˈstɑpər] *n* **:** tapón *m*
storage [ˈstorɪdʒ] *n* **:** almacenamiento *m,* almacenaje *m*
storage battery *n* **:** acumulador *m*
store[1] [ˈstor] *vt* **stored; storing :** guardar, almacenar
store[2] *n* **1** RESERVE, SUPPLY **:** reserva *f* **2** SHOP **:** tienda *f* <grocery store : tienda de comestibles>
storehouse [ˈstorˌhaʊs] *n* **:** almacén *m,* depósito *m*
storekeeper [ˈstorˌkiːpər] *n* **:** tendero *m,* -ra *f*
storeroom [ˈstorˌruːm, -ˌrʊm] *n* **:** almacén *m,* depósito *m*
stork [ˈstɔrk] *n* **:** cigüeña *f*
storm[1] [ˈstɔrm] *vi* **1 :** llover o nevar tormentosamente **2** RAGE **:** ponerse furioso, vociferar **3 to storm out :** salir echando pestes — *vt* ATTACK **:** asaltar
storm[2] *n* **1 :** tormenta *f,* tempestad *f* **2** UPROAR **:** alboroto *m,* revuelo *m,* escándalo *m* <a storm of abuse : un torrente de abusos>
stormy [ˈstɔrmi] *adj* **stormier; -est :** tormentoso
story [ˈstori] *n, pl* **stories 1** NARRATIVE **:** cuento *m,* relato *m* **2** ACCOUNT **:** historia *f,* relato *m* **3 :** piso *m,* planta *f* (de un edificio) <first story : planta baja>
stout [ˈstaʊt] *adj* **1** FIRM, RESOLUTE **:** firme, resuelto **2** STURDY **:** fuerte, robusto, sólido **3** FAT **:** corpulento, gordo
stove[1] [ˈstoːv] *n* **:** cocina *f* (para cocinar), estufa *f* (para calentar)
stove[2] → **stave[1]**
stow [ˈstoː] *vt* **1** STORE **:** poner, meter, guardar **2** LOAD **:** cargar — *vi* **to stow away :** viajar de polizón
stowaway [ˈstoːəˌweɪ] *n* **:** polizón *m*
straddle [ˈstrædəl] *vt* **-dled; -dling :** sentarse a horcajadas sobre
straggle [ˈstrægəl] *vi* **-gled; -gling :** rezagarse, quedarse atrás
straggler [ˈstrægələr] *n* **:** rezagado *m,* -da *f*
straight[1] [ˈstreɪt] *adv* **1 :** derecho, directamente <go straight, then turn right : sigue derecho, luego gira a la derecha> **2** HONESTLY **:** honestamente <to go straight : enmendarse> **3** CLEARLY **:** con claridad **4** FRANKLY **:** francamente, con franqueza
straight[2] *adj* **1 :** recto (dícese de las líneas, etc.), derecho (dícese de algo vertical), lacio (dícese del pelo) **2** HONEST, JUST **:** honesto, justo **3** NEAT, ORDERLY **:** arreglado, ordenado
straighten [ˈstreɪtən] *vt* **1 :** enderezar, poner derecho **2 to straighten up :** arreglar, ordenar <he straightened up the house : arregló la casa>
straightforward [streɪtˈfɔrwərd] *adj* **1** FRANK **:** franco, sincero **2** CLEAR, PRECISE **:** puro, simple, claro
straightway [ˈstreɪtˈweɪ, -ˌweɪ] *adv* **:** inmediatamente
strain[1] [ˈstreɪn] *vt* **1** EXERT **:** forzar (la vista, la voz) <to strain oneself : hacer un gran esfuerzo> **2** FILTER **:** colar, filtrar **3** INJURE **:** lastimarse, hacerse daño en <to strain a muscle : sufrir un esguince>
strain[2] *n* **1** LINEAGE **:** linaje *m,* abolengo *m* **2** STREAK, TRACE **:** veta *f* **3** VARIETY **:** tipo *m,* variedad *f* **4** STRESS **:** tensión *f,* presión *f* **5** SPRAIN **:** esguince *m,* torcedura *f* (del tobillo, etc.) **6 strains** *npl* TUNE **:** melodía *f,* acordes *mpl,* compases *fpl*
strainer [ˈstreɪnər] *n* **:** colador *m*
strait [ˈstreɪt] *n* **1 :** estrecho *m* **2 straits** *npl* DISTRESS **:** aprietos *mpl,* apuros *mpl* <in dire straits : en serios aprietos>
straitened [ˈstreɪtənd] *adj* **in straitened circumstances :** en apuros económicos
strand[1] [ˈstrænd] *vt* **1 :** varar **2 to be left stranded :** quedar(se) varado, quedar colgado <they left me stranded : me dejaron abandonado>
strand[2] *n* **1 :** hebra *f* (de hilo, etc.) <a strand of hair : un pelo> **2** BEACH **:** playa *f*
strange [ˈstreɪndʒ] *adj* **stranger; -est 1** QUEER, UNUSUAL **:** extraño, raro **2** UNFAMILIAR **:** desconocido, nuevo
strangely [ˈstreɪndʒli] *adv* ODDLY **:** de manera extraña <to behave strangely : portarse de una manera rara> <strangely, he didn't call : curiosamente, no llamó>
strangeness [ˈstreɪndʒnəs] *n* **1** ODDNESS **:** rareza *f* **2** UNFAMILIARITY **:** lo desconocido
stranger [ˈstreɪndʒər] *n* **:** desconocido *m,* -da *f;* extraño *m,* -ña *f*
strangle [ˈstræŋgəl] *vt* **-gled; -gling :** estrangular
strangler [ˈstræŋglər] *n* **:** estrangulador *m,* -dora *f*
strap[1] [ˈstræp] *vt* **strapped; strapping 1** FASTEN **:** sujetar con una correa **2** FLOG **:** azotar (con una correa)
strap[2] *n* **1 :** correa *f* **2 shoulder strap :** tirante *m*
strapless [ˈstræpləs] *n* **:** sin tirantes
strapping [ˈstræpɪŋ] *adj* **:** robusto, fornido
stratagem [ˈstræṭədʒəm, -ˌdʒɛm] *n* **:** estratagema *f,* artimaña *f*
strategic [strəˈtiːdʒɪk] *adj* **:** estratégico
strategy [ˈstræṭədʒi] *n, pl* **-gies :** estrategia *f*
stratified [ˈstræṭəˌfaɪd] *adj* **:** estratificado
stratosphere [ˈstræṭəˌsfɪr] *n* **:** estratosfera *f*
stratum [ˈstreɪṭəm, ˈstræ-] *n, pl* **strata** [-ṭə] **:** estrato *m,* capa *f*
straw *n* **1 :** paja *f* <the last straw : el colmo> **2** *or* **drinking straw :** pajita *f,* popote *m Mex*

strawberry [ˈstrɔˌbɛri] *n, pl* **-ries** : fresa *f*

stray[1] [ˈstreɪ] *vi* **1** WANDER : alejarse, extraviarse <the cattle strayed away : el ganado se descarrió> **2** DIGRESS : desviarse, divagar

stray[2] *adj* : perdido, callejero (dícese de un perro o un gato), descarriado (dícese del ganado)

stray[3] *n* : animal *m* perdido, animal *m* callejero

streak[1] [ˈstriːk] *vt* : hacer rayas en <blue streaked with grey : azul veteado con gris> — *vi* : ir como una flecha

streak[2] *n* **1** : raya *f,* veta *f* (en mármol, queso, etc.), mechón *m* (en el pelo) **2** : rayo *m* (de luz) **3** TRACE : veta *f* **4** : racha *f* <a streak of luck : una racha de suerte>

stream[1] [ˈstriːm] *vi* : correr, salir a chorros <tears streamed from his eyes : las lágrimas brotaban de sus ojos> — *vt* : derramar, dejar correr <to stream blood : derramar sangre>

stream[2] *n* **1** BROOK : arroyo *m,* riachuelo *m* **2** RIVER : río *m* **3** FLOW : corriente *f,* chorro *m*

streamer [ˈstriːmər] *n* **1** PENNANT : banderín *m* **2** RIBBON : serpentina *f* (de papel), cinta *f* (de tela)

streamlined [ˈstriːmˌlaɪnd] *adj* **1** : aerodinámico (dícese de los automóviles, etc.) **2** EFFICIENT : eficiente, racionalizado

street [ˈstriːt] *n* : calle *f*

streetcar [ˈstriːtˌkɑr] *n* : tranvía *m*

strength [ˈstrɛŋkθ] *n* **1** POWER : fuerza *f* **2** SOLIDITY, TOUGHNESS : solidez *f,* resistencia *f,* dureza *f* **3** INTENSITY : intensidad *f* (de emociones, etc.), lo fuerte (de un sabor, etc.) **4** : punto *m* fuerte <strengths and weaknesses : virtudes y defectos> **5** NUMBER : número *m,* complemento *m* <in full strength : en gran número>

strengthen [ˈstrɛŋkθən] *vt* **1** : fortalecer (los músculos, el espíritu, etc.) **2** REINFORCE : reforzar **3** INTENSIFY : intensificar, redoblar (esfuerzos, etc.) — *vi* **1** : fortalecerse, hacerse más fuerte **2** INTENSIFY : intensificarse

strenuous [ˈstrɛnjʊəs] *adj* **1** VIGOROUS : vigoroso, enérgico **2** ARDUOUS : duro, riguroso

strenuously [ˈstrɛnjʊəsli] *adv* : vigorosamente, duro

stress[1] [ˈstrɛs] *vt* **1** : someter a tensión (física) **2** EMPHASIZE : enfatizar, recalcar **3** **to stress out** : estresar

stress[2] *n* **1** : tensión *f* (en un material) **2** EMPHASIS : énfasis *m,* acento *m* (en lingüística) **3** TENSION : tensión *f* (nerviosa), estrés *m*

stressful [ˈstrɛsfəl] *adj* : estresante

stretch[1] [ˈstrɛtʃ] *vt* **1** EXTEND : estirar, extender, desplegar (alas) **2** **to stretch the truth** : forzar la verdad, exagerar — *vi* : estirarse

stretch[2] *n* **1** STRETCHING : extensión *f,* estiramiento *m* (de músculos) **2** ELASTICITY : elasticidad *f* **3** EXPANSE : tramo *m,* trecho *m* <the home stretch : la recta final> **4** PERIOD : período *m* (de tiempo)

stretcher [ˈstrɛtʃər] *n* : camilla *f*

strew [ˈstruː] *vt* **strewed; strewed** *or* **strewn** [ˈstruːn]; **strewing** **1** SCATTER : esparcir (semillas, etc.), desparramar (papeles, etc.) **2** **to strew with** : cubrir de

stricken [ˈstrɪkən] *adj* **stricken with** : aquejado de (una enfermedad), afligido por (tristeza, etc.)

strict [ˈstrɪkt] *adj* : estricto — **strictly** *adv*

strictness [ˈstrɪktnəs] *n* : severidad *f,* lo estricto

stricture [ˈstrɪktʃər] *n* : crítica *f,* censura *f*

stride[1] [ˈstraɪd] *vi* **strode** [ˈstroːd]; **stridden** [ˈstrɪdən]; **striding** : ir dando trancos, ir dando zancadas

stride[2] *n* : tranco *m,* zancada *f*

strident [ˈstraɪdənt] *adj* : estridente

strife [ˈstraɪf] *n* : conflictos *mpl,* disensión *f*

strike[1] [ˈstraɪk] *v* **struck** [ˈstrʌk]; **struck; striking** *vt* **1** HIT : golpear (a una persona) <to strike a blow : pegar un golpe> **2** DELETE : suprimir, tachar **3** COIN, MINT : acuñar (monedas) **4** : dar (la hora) **5** AFFLICT : sobrevenir <he was stricken with a fever : le sobrevino una fiebre> **6** IMPRESS : impresionar, parecer <her voice struck me : su voz me impresionó> <it struck him as funny : le pareció chistoso> **7** : encender (un fósforo) **8** FIND : descubrir (oro, petróleo) **9** ADOPT : adoptar (una pose, etc.) — *vi* **1** HIT : golpear <to strike against : chocar contra> **2** ATTACK : atacar **3** : declararse en huelga

strike[2] *n* **1** BLOW : golpe *m* **2** : huelga *f,* paro *m* <to be on strike : estar en huelga> **3** ATTACK : ataque *m*

strikebreaker [ˈstraɪkˌbreɪkər] *n* : rompehuelgas *mf,* esquirol *mf*

strike out *vi* **1** HEAD : salir (para) **2** : ser ponchado (en béisbol) <the batter struck out : poncharon al bateador>

striker [ˈstraɪkər] *n* : huelgista *mf*

strike up *vt* START : entablar, empezar

striking [ˈstraɪkɪŋ] *adj* : notable, sorprendente, llamativo <a striking beauty : una belleza imponente> — **strikingly** *adv*

string[1] [ˈstrɪŋ] *vt* **strung** [ˈstrʌŋ]; **stringing** **1** THREAD : ensartar <to string beads : ensartar cuentas> **2** HANG : colgar (con un cordel)

string[2] *n* **1** : cordel *m,* cuerda *f* **2** SERIES : serie *f,* sarta *f* (de insultos, etc.) **3** **strings** *npl* : cuerdas *fpl* (en música)

string bean *n* : judía *f,* ejote *m Mex*

stringent [ˈstrɪndʒənt] *adj* : estricto, severo

stringy ['strɪŋi] *adj* **stringier; -est** : fibroso
strip¹ ['strɪp] *v* **stripped; stripping** *vt* : quitar (ropa, pintura, etc.), desnudar, despojar — *vi* UNDRESS : desnudarse
strip² *n* : tira *f* <a strip of land : una faja>
stripe¹ ['straɪp] *vt* **striped** ['straɪpt]; **striping** : marcar con rayas o listas
stripe² *n* **1** : raya *f*, lista *f* **2** BAND : franja *f*
striped ['straɪpt, 'straɪpəd] *adj* : a rayas, de rayas, rayado, listado
strive ['straɪv] *vi* **strove** ['stro:v]; **striven** ['strɪvən] *or* **strived; striving 1 to strive for** : luchar por lograr **2 to strive to** : esforzarse por
strode → **stride**
stroke¹ ['stro:k] *vt* **stroked; stroking** : acariciar
stroke² *n* : golpe *m* <a stroke of luck : un golpe de suerte>
stroll¹ ['stro:l] *vi* : pasear, pasearse, dar un paseo
stroll² *n* : paseo *m*
stroller ['stro:lər] *n* : cochecito *m* (para niños)
strong ['strɔŋ] *adj* **1** : fuerte **2** HEALTHY : sano **3** ZEALOUS : ferviente
stronghold ['strɔŋˌho:ld] *n* : fortaleza *f*, fuerte *m*, bastión *m* <a cultural stronghold : un baluarte de la cultura>
strongly ['strɔŋli] *adv* **1** POWERFULLY : fuerte, con fuerza **2** STURDILY : fuertemente, sólidamente **3** INTENSELY : intensamente, profundamente **4** WHOLEHEARTEDLY : totalmente
struck → **strike¹**
structural ['strʌktʃərəl] *adj* : estructural
structure¹ ['strʌktʃər] *vt* **-tured; -turing** : estructurar
structure² *n* **1** BUILDING : construcción *f* **2** ARRANGEMENT, FRAMEWORK : estructura *f*
struggle¹ ['strʌgəl] *vi* **-gled; -gling 1** CONTEND : forcejear (físicamente), luchar, contender **2** : hacer con dificultad <she struggled forward : avanzó con dificultad>
struggle² *n* : lucha *f*, pelea *f* (física)
strum ['strʌm] *vt* **strummed; strumming** : rasguear
strung → **string¹**
strut¹ ['strʌt] *vi* **strutted; strutting** : pavonearse
strut² *n* **1** : pavoneo *m* <he walked with a strut : se pavoneaba> **2** : puntal *m* (en construcción, etc.)
strychnine ['strɪkˌnaɪn, -nən, -ˌni:n] *n* : estricnina *f*
stub¹ ['stʌb] *vt* **stubbed; stubbing 1 to stub one's toe** : darse en el dedo (del pie) **2 to stub out** : apagarse
stub² *n* : colilla *f* (de un cigarrillo), cabo *m* (de un lápiz, etc.), talón *m* (de un cheque)
stubble ['stʌbəl] *n* **1** : rastrojo *m* (de plantas) **2** BEARD : barba *f*
stubborn ['stʌbərn] *adj* **1** OBSTINATE : terco, obstinado, empecinado **2** PERSISTENT : pertinaz, persistente — **stubbornly** *adv*
stubbornness ['stʌbərnnəs] *n* **1** OBSTINACY : terquedad *f*, obstinación *f* **2** PERSISTENCE : persistencia *f*
stubby ['stʌbi] *adj* **stubbier; -est** : corto y grueso <stubby fingers : dedos regordetes>
stucco ['stʌko:] *n, pl* **stuccos** *or* **stuccoes** : estuco *m*
stuck → **stick¹**
stuck–up ['stʌk'ʌp] *adj* : engreído, creído *fam*
stud¹ ['stʌd] *vt* **studded; studding** : tachonar, salpicar
stud² *n* **1** *or* **stud horse** : semental *m* **2** : montante *m* (en construcción) **3** HOBNAIL : tachuela *f*, tachón *m*
student ['stu:dənt, 'stju:-] *n* : estudiante *mf;* alumno *m*, -na *f* (de un colegio)
studied ['stʌdid] *adj* : intencionado, premeditado
studio ['stu:diˌo:, 'stju:-] *n, pl* **studios** : estudio *m*
studious ['stu:diəs, 'stju:-] *adj* : estudioso — **studiously** *adv*
study¹ ['stʌdi] *v* **studied; studying 1** : estudiar **2** EXAMINE : examinar, estudiar
study² *n, pl* **studies 1** STUDYING : estudio *m* **2** OFFICE : estudio *m*, gabinete *m* (en una casa) **3** RESEARCH : investigación *f*, estudio *m*
stuff¹ ['stʌf] *vt* : rellenar, llenar, atiborrar
stuff² *n* **1** POSSESSIONS : cosas *fpl* **2** ESSENCE : esencia *f* **3** SUBSTANCE : cosa *f*, cosas *fpl* <some sticky stuff : una cosa pegajosa> <she knows her stuff : es experta>
stuffing ['stʌfɪŋ] *n* : relleno *m*
stuffy ['stʌfi] *adj* **stuffier; -est 1** CLOSE : viciado, cargado <a stuffy room : una sala mal ventilada> <stuffy weather : tiempo bochornoso> **2** : tapado (dícese de la nariz) **3** STODGY : pesado, aburrido
stumble¹ ['stʌmbəl] *vi* **-bled; -bling 1** TRIP : tropezar, dar un traspié **2** FLOUNDER : quedarse sin saber qué hacer o decir **3 to stumble across** *or* **to stumble upon** : dar con, tropezar con
stumble² *n* : tropezón *m*, traspié *m*
stump¹ ['stʌmp] *vt* : dejar perplejo <to be stumped : no tener respuesta>
stump² *n* **1** : muñón *m* (de un brazo o una pierna) **2** *or* **tree stump** : cepa *f*, tocón *m* **3** STUB : cabo *m*
stun ['stʌn] *vt* **stunned; stunning 1** : aturdir (con un golpe) **2** ASTONISH, SHOCK : dejar estupefacto, dejar atónito, aturdir
stung → **sting¹**
stunk → **stink¹**

stunning [ˈstʌnɪŋ] *adj* **1** ASTONISHING : asombroso, pasmoso, increíble **2** STRIKING : imponente, impresionante (dícese de la belleza)

stunt[1] [ˈstʌnt] *vt* : atrofiar

stunt[2] *n* : proeza *f* (acrobática)

stupefy [ˈstuːpəˌfaɪ, ˈstjuː-] *vt* **-fied; -fying 1** : aturdir, atontar (con drogas, etc.) **2** AMAZE : dejar estupefacto, dejar atónito

stupendous [stʊˈpɛndəs, stjʊ-] *adj* **1** MARVELOUS : estupendo, maravilloso **2** TREMENDOUS : tremendo — **stupendously** *adv*

stupid [ˈstuːpəd, ˈstjuː-] *adj* **1** IDIOTIC, SILLY : tonto, bobo, estúpido **2** DULL, OBTUSE : lento, torpe, lerdo

stupidity [stʊˈpɪdət̬i, stjʊ-] *n* : tontería *f*, estupidez *f*

stupidly [ˈstuːpədli, ˈstjuː-] *adv* **1** IDIOTICALLY : estúpidamente, tontamente **2** DENSELY : torpemente

stupor [ˈstuːpər, ˈstjuː-] *n* : estupor *m*

sturdily [ˈstərdəli] *adv* : sólidamente

sturdiness [ˈstərdinəs] *n* : solidez *f* (de muebles, etc.), robustez *f* (de una persona)

sturdy [ˈstərdi] *adj* **sturdier; -est** : fuerte, robusto, sólido

sturgeon [ˈstərdʒən] *n* : esturión *m*

stutter[1] [ˈstʌt̬ər] *vi* : tartamudear

stutter[2] *n* STAMMER : tartamudeo *m*

sty [ˈstaɪ] *n* **1** *pl* **sties** PIGPEN : chiquero *m*, pocilga *f* **2** *pl* **sties** *or* **styes** : orzuelo *m* (en el ojo)

style[1] [ˈstaɪl] *vt* **styled; styling 1** NAME : llamar **2** : peinar (pelo), diseñar (vestidos, etc.) <carefully styled prose : prosa escrita con gran esmero>

style[2] *n* **1** : estilo *m* <that's just his style : él es así> <to live in style : vivir a lo grande> **2** FASHION : moda *f*

stylish [ˈstaɪlɪʃ] *adj* : de moda, elegante, chic

stylishly [ˈstaɪlɪʃli] *adv* : con estilo

stylishness [ˈstaɪlɪʃnəs] *n* : estilo *m*

stylize [ˈstaɪˌlaɪz, ˈstaɪə-] *vt* : estilizar

stylus [ˈstaɪləs] *n, pl* **styli** [ˈstaɪˌlaɪ] **1** PEN : estilo *m* **2** NEEDLE : aguja *f* (de un tocadiscos)

stymie [ˈstaɪmi] *vt* **-mied; -mieing** : obstaculizar

suave [ˈswɑv] *adj* : fino, urbano

sub[1] [ˈsʌb] *vi* **subbed; subbing** → **substitute**[1]

sub[2] *n* **1** → **substitute**[2] **2** → **submarine**

subcommittee [ˈsʌbkəˌmɪt̬i] *n* : subcomité *m*

subconscious[1] [səbˈkɑntʃəs] *adj* : subconsciente — **subconsciously** *adv*

subconscious[2] *n* : subconsciente *m*

subcontract [ˌsʌbˈkɑnˌtrækt] *vt* : subcontratar

subdivide [ˌsʌbdəˈvaɪd, ˈsʌbdəˌvaɪd] *vt* **-vided; -viding** : subdividir

subdivision [ˈsʌbdəˌvɪʒən] *n* : subdivisión *f*

subdue [səbˈduː, -ˈdjuː] *vt* **-dued; -duing 1** OVERCOME : sojuzgar (a un enemigo), vencer, superar **2** CONTROL : dominar **3** SOFTEN : suavizar, atenuar (luz, etc.), moderar (lenguaje)

subhead [ˈsʌbˌhɛd] *or* **subheading** [-ˌhɛdɪŋ] *n* : subtítulo *m*

subject[1] [səbˈdʒɛkt] *vt* **1** CONTROL, DOMINATE : controlar, dominar **2** : someter <they subjected him to pressure : lo sometieron a presiones>

subject[2] [ˈsʌbdʒɪkt] *adj* **1** : subyugado, sometido <a subject nation : una nación subyugada> **2** PRONE : sujeto, propenso <subject to colds : sujeto a resfriarse> **3 subject to** : sujeto a <subject to congressional approval : sujeto a la aprobación del congreso>

subject[3] [ˈsʌbdʒɪkt] *n* **1** : súbdito *m*, -ta *f* (de un gobierno) **2** TOPIC : tema *m* **3** : sujeto *m* (en gramática)

subjection [səbˈdʒɛkʃən] *n* : sometimiento *m*

subjective [səbˈdʒɛktɪv] *adj* : subjetivo — **subjectively** *adv*

subjectivity [ˌsʌbˌdʒɛkˈtɪvət̬i] *n* : subjetividad *f*

subjugate [ˈsʌbdʒɪˌgeɪt] *vt* **-gated; -gating** : subyugar, someter, sojuzgar

subjunctive [səbˈdʒʌŋktɪv] *n* : subjuntivo *m* — **subjunctive** *adj*

sublet [ˈsʌbˌlɛt] *vt* **-let; -letting** : subarrendar

sublime [səˈblaɪm] *adj* : sublime

sublimely [səˈblaɪmli] *adv* **1** : de manera sublime **2** UTTERLY : absolutamente, completamente

submarine[1] [ˈsʌbməˌriːn, ˌsʌbməˈ-] *adj* : submarino

submarine[2] *n* : submarino *m*

submerge [səbˈmərdʒ] *v* **-merged; -merging** *vt* : sumergir — *vi* : sumergirse

submission [səbˈmɪʃən] *n* **1** YIELDING : sumisión *f* **2** PRESENTATION : presentación *f*

submissive [səbˈmɪsɪv] *adj* : sumiso, dócil

submit [səbˈmɪt] *v* **-mitted; -mitting** *vi* YIELD : rendirse <to submit to : someterse a> — *vt* PRESENT : presentar

subnormal [ˌsʌbˈnɔrməl] *adj* : por debajo de lo normal

subordinate[1] [səˈbɔrdənˌeɪt] *vt* **-nated; -nating** : subordinar

subordinate[2] [səˈbɔrdənət] *adj* : subordinado <a subordinate clause : una oración subordinada>

subordinate[3] *n* : subordinado *m*, -da *f*; subalterno *m*, -na *f*

subordination [səˌbɔrdənˈeɪʃən] *n* : subordinación *f*

subpoena[1] [səˈpiːnə] *vt* **-naed; -naing** : citar

subpoena[2] *n* : citación *f*, citatorio *m*

subscribe [səbˈskraɪb] *vi* **-scribed; -scribing 1** : suscribirse (a una revista, etc.) **2 to subscribe to** : sus-

cribir (una opinión, etc.), estar de acuerdo con
subscriber [səb'skraɪbər] *n* : suscriptor *m*, -tora *f* (de una revista, etc.); abonado *m*, -da *f* (de un servicio)
subscription [səb'skrɪpʃən] *n* : suscripción *f*
subsequent ['sʌbsɪkwənt, -sə,kwɛnt] *adj* : subsiguiente <subsequent to : posterior a>
subsequently ['sʌb,kwɛntli, -kwənt-] *adv* : posteriormente
subservient [səb'sərviənt] *adj* : servil
subside [səb'saɪd] *vi* **-sided; -siding 1** SINK : hundirse, descender **2** ABATE : calmarse (dícese de las emociones), amainar (dícese del viento, etc.)
subsidiary[1] [səb'sɪdi,ɛri] *adj* : secundario
subsidiary[2] *n, pl* **-ries** : filial *f*, subsidiaria *f*
subsidize ['sʌbsə,daɪz] *vt* **-dized; -dizing** : subvencionar, subsidiar
subsidy ['sʌbsədi] *n, pl* **-dies** : subvención *f*, subsidio *m*
subsist [səb'sɪst] *vi* : subsistir, mantenerse, vivir
subsistence [səb'sɪstənts] *n* : subsistencia *f*
substance ['sʌbstənts] *n* **1** ESSENCE : sustancia *f*, esencia *f* **2** : sustancia *f* <a toxic substance : una sustancia tóxica> **3** WEALTH : riqueza *f* <a woman of substance : una mujer acaudalada>
substandard [,sʌb'stændərd] *adj* : inferior, deficiente
substantial [səb'stæntʃəl] *adj* **1** ABUNDANT : sustancioso <a substantial meal : una comida sustanciosa> **2** CONSIDERABLE : considerable, apreciable **3** SOLID, STURDY : sólido
substantially [səb'stæntʃəli] *adv* : considerablemente
substantiate [səb'stæntʃi,eɪt] *vt* **-ated; -ating** : confirmar, probar, justificar
substitute[1] ['sʌbstə,tu:t, -,tju:t] *v* **-tuted; -tuting** *vt* : sustituir — *vi* **to substitute for** : sustituir
substitute[2] *n* **1** : sustituto *m*, -ta *f*; suplente *mf* (persona) **2** : sucedáneo *m* <sugar substitute : sucedáneo de azúcar>
substitute teacher *n* : profesor *m*, -sora *f* suplente
substitution [,sʌbstə'tu:ʃən, -'tju:-] *n* : sustitución *f*
subterfuge ['sʌbtər,fju:dʒ] *n* : subterfugio *m*
subterranean [,sʌbtə'reɪniən] *adj* : subterráneo
subtitle ['sʌb,taɪtəl] *n* : subtítulo *m*
subtle ['sʌtəl] *adj* **-tler; -tlest 1** DELICATE, ELUSIVE : sutil, delicado **2** CLEVER : sutil, ingenioso
subtlety ['sʌtəlti] *n, pl* **-ties** : sutileza *f*
subtly ['sʌtəli] *adv* : sutilmente
subtotal ['sʌb,to:təl] *n* : subtotal *m*
subtract [səb'trækt] *vt* : restar, sustraer
subtraction [səb'trækʃən] *n* : resta *f*, sustracción *f*
suburb ['sʌ,bərb] *n* : municipio *m* periférico, suburbio *m*
suburban [sə'bərbən] *adj* : de las afueras (de una ciudad), suburbano
subversion [səb'vərʒən] *n* : subversión *f*
subversive [səb'vərsɪv] *adj* : subversivo
subway ['sʌb,weɪ] *n* : metro *m*, subterráneo *m Arg, Uru*
succeed [sək'si:d] *vt* FOLLOW : suceder a — *vi* : tener éxito (dícese de las personas), dar resultado (dícese de los planes, etc.) <she succeeded in finishing : logró terminar>
success [sək'sɛs] *n* : éxito *m*
successful [sək'sɛsfəl] *adj* : exitoso, logrado — **successfully** *adv*
succession [sək'sɛʃən] *n* : sucesión *f* <in succesion : sucesivamente>
successive [sək'sɛsɪv] *adj* : sucesivo, consecutivo — **successively** *adv*
successor [sək'sɛsər] *n* : sucesor *m*, -sora *f*
succinct [sək'sɪŋkt, sə'sɪŋkt] *adj* : sucinto — **succinctly** *adv*
succor[1] ['sʌkər] *vt* : socorrer
succor[2] *n* : socorro *m*
succotash ['sʌkə,tæʃ] *n* : guiso *m* de maíz y frijoles
succulent[1] ['sʌkjələnt] *adj* : suculento, jugoso
succulent[2] *n* : suculenta *f* (planta)
succumb [sə'kʌm] *vi* : sucumbir
such[1] ['sʌtʃ] *adv* **1** SO : tan <such tall buildings : edificios tan grandes> **2** VERY : muy <he's not in such good shape : anda un poco mal> **3 such that** : de tal manera que
such[2] *adj* : tal <there's no such thing : no existe tal cosa> <in such cases : en tales casos> <animals such as cows and sheep : animales como vacas y ovejas>
such[3] *pron* **1** : tal <such was the result : tal fue el resultado> <he's a child, and acts as such : es un niño, y se porta como tal> **2** : algo o alguien semejante <books, papers and such : libros, papeles y cosas por el estilo>
suck ['sʌk] *vi* **1** : chupar (por la boca), aspirar (dícese de las máquinas) **2** SUCKLE : mamar — *vt* : sorber (bebidas), chupar (dulces, etc.)
sucker ['sʌkər] *n* **1** : ventosa *f* (de un insecto, etc.) **2** : chupón *m* (de una planta) **3** → **lollipop 4** FOOL : tonto *m*, -ta *f*; idiota *mf*
suckle ['sʌkəl] *v* **-led; -ling** *vt* : amamantar — *vi* : mamar
suckling ['sʌklɪŋ] *n* : lactante *mf*
sucrose ['su:,kro:s, -,kro:z] *n* : sacarosa *f*
suction ['sʌkʃən] *n* : succión *f*

Sudanese [ˌsuːdənˈiːz, -ˈiːs] *n* : sudanés *m*, -nesa *f* — **Sudanese** *adj*
sudden [ˈsʌdən] *adj* **1** : repentino, súbito <all of a sudden : de pronto, de repente> **2** UNEXPECTED : inesperado, improvisto **3** ABRUPT, HASTY : precipitado, brusco
suddenly [ˈsʌdənli] *adv* **1** : de repente, de pronto **2** ABRUPTLY : bruscamente
suddenness [ˈsʌdənnəs] *n* **1** : lo repentino **2** ABRUPTNESS : brusquedad *f* **3** HASTINESS : lo precipitado
suds [ˈsʌdz] *npl* : espuma *f* (de jabón)
sue [ˈsuː] *v* **sued; suing** *vt* : demandar — *vi* **to sue for** : demandar por (daños, etc.)
suede [ˈsweɪd] *n* : ante *m*, gamuza *f*
suet [ˈsuːət] *n* : sebo *m*
suffer [ˈsʌfər] *vi* : sufrir — *vt* **1** : sufrir, padecer (dolores, etc.) **2** PERMIT : permitir, dejar
sufferer [ˈsʌfərər] *n* : persona que padece (una enfermedad, etc.)
suffering [ˈsʌfərɪŋ] *n* : sufrimiento *m*
suffice [səˈfaɪs] *vi* **-ficed; -ficing** : ser suficiente, bastar
sufficient [səˈfɪʃənt] *adj* : suficiente
sufficiently [səˈfɪʃəntli] *adv* : (lo) suficientemente, bastante
suffix [ˈsʌˌfɪks] *n* : sufijo *m*
suffocate [ˈsʌfəˌkeɪt] *v* **-cated; -cating** *vt* : asfixiar, ahogar — *vi* : asfixiarse, ahogarse
suffocation [ˌsʌfəˈkeɪʃən] *n* : asfixia *f*, ahogo *m*
suffrage [ˈsʌfrɪdʒ] *n* : sufragio *m*, derecho *m* al voto
suffuse [səˈfjuːz] *vt* **-fused; -fusing** : impregnar (de olores, etc.), bañar (de luz), teñir (de colores), llenar (de emociones)
sugar¹ [ˈʃʊgər] *vt* : azucarar
sugar² *n* : azúcar *mf*
sugarcane [ˈʃʊgərˌkeɪn] *n* : caña *f* de azúcar
sugary [ˈʃʊgəri] *adj* **1** : azucarado <sugary desserts : postres azucarados> **2** SACCHARINE : empalagoso
suggest [səgˈdʒɛst, sə-] *vt* **1** PROPOSE : sugerir **2** IMPLY : indicar, dar a entender
suggestible [səgˈdʒɛstəbəl, sə-] *adj* : influenciable
suggestion [səgˈdʒɛstʃən, sə-] *n* **1** PROPOSAL : sugerencia *f* **2** INDICATION : indicio *m* **3** INSINUATION : insinuación *f*
suggestive [səgˈdʒɛstɪv, sə-] *adj* : insinuante — **suggestively** *adv*
suicidal [ˌsuːəˈsaɪdəl] *adj* : suicida
suicide [ˈsuːəˌsaɪd] *n* **1** : suicidio *m* (acto) **2** : suicida *mf* (persona)
suit¹ [ˈsuːt] *vt* **1** ADAPT : adaptar **2** BEFIT : convenir a, ser apropiado a **3** BECOME : favorecer, quedarle bien (a alguien) <the dress suits you : el vestido te queda bien> **4** PLEASE : agradecer, satisfacer, convenirle bien (a alguien) <does Friday suit you? : ¿le conviene el viernes?> <suit yourself! : ¡como quieras!>
suit² *n* **1** LAWSUIT : pleito *m*, litigio *m* **2** : traje *m* (ropa) **3** : palo *m* (de naipes)
suitability [ˌsuːtəˈbɪləti] *n* : idoneidad *f*, lo apropiado
suitable [ˈsuːtəbəl] *adj* : apropiado, idóneo — **suitably** [-bli] *adv*
suitcase [ˈsuːtˌkeɪs] *n* : maleta *f*, valija *f*, petaca *f Mex*
suite [ˈswiːt, *for 2 also* ˈsuːt] *n* **1** : suite *f* (de habitaciones) **2** SET : juego *m* (de muebles)
suitor [ˈsuːtər] *n* : pretendiente *m*
sulfur [ˈsʌlfər] *n* : azufre *m*
sulfuric acid [ˌsʌlˈfjʊrɪk] *adj* : ácido *m* sulfúrico
sulfurous [ˌsʌlˈfjʊrəs, ˈsʌlfərəs, ˈsʌlfjə-] *adj* : sulfuroso
sulk¹ [ˈsʌlk] *vi* : estar de mal humor, enfurruñarse *fam*
sulk² *n* : mal humor *m*
sulky [ˈsʌlki] *adj* **sulkier; -est** : malhumorado, taimado *Chile*
sullen [ˈsʌlən] *adj* **1** MOROSE : hosco, taciturno **2** DREARY : sombrío, deprimente
sullenly [ˈsʌlənli] *adv* **1** MOROSELY : hoscamente **2** GLOOMILY : sombríamente
sully [ˈsʌli] *vt* **sullied; sullying** : manchar, empañar
sultan [ˈsʌltən] *n* : sultán *m*
sultry [ˈsʌltri] *adj* **sultrier; -est** **1** : bochornoso <sultry weather : tiempo sofocante, tiempo bochornoso> **2** SENSUAL : sensual, seductor
sum¹ [ˈsʌm] *vt* **summed; summing** **1** : sumar (números) **2** → **sum up**
sum² *n* **1** AMOUNT : suma *f*, cantidad *f* **2** TOTAL : suma *f*, total *f* **3** : suma *f*, adición *f* (en matemáticas)
sumac [ˈʃuːˌmæk, ˈsuː-] *n* : zumaque *m*
summarize [ˈsʌməˌraɪz] *v* **-rized; -rizing** : resumir, compendiar
summary¹ [ˈsʌməri] *adj* **1** CONCISE : breve, conciso **2** IMMEDIATE : inmediato <a summary dismissal : un despido inmediato>
summary² *n, pl* **-ries** : resumen *m*, compendio *m*
summer [ˈsʌmər] *n* : verano *m*
summery [ˈsʌməri] *adj* : veraniego
summit [ˈsʌmət] *n* **1** : cumbre *f*, cima *f* (de una montaña) **2** *or* **summit conference** : cumbre *f*
summon [ˈsʌmən] *vt* **1** CALL : convocar (una reunión, etc.), llamar (a una persona) **2** : citar (en derecho) **3** **to summon up** : armarse de (valor, etc.) <to summon up one's strength : reunir fuerzas>
summons [ˈsʌmənz] *n, pl* **summonses** **1** SUBPOENA : citación *f*, citatorio *m Mex* **2** CALL : llamada *f*, llamamiento *m*
sumptuous [ˈsʌmptʃʊəs] *adj* : suntuoso

sum up *vt* **1** SUMMARIZE : resumir **2** EVALUATE : evaluar — *vi* : recapitular
sun[1] [ˈsʌn] *vt* **sunned; sunning 1** : poner al sol **2 to sun oneself** : asolearse, tomar el sol
sun[2] *n* **1** : sol *m* **2** SUNSHINE : luz *f* del sol
sunbeam [ˈsʌn,biːm] *n* : rayo *m* de sol
sunblock [ˈsʌn,blɑk] *n* : filtro *m* solar
sunburn[1] [ˈsʌn,bərn] *vi* **-burned** [-,bərnd] *or* **-burnt** [-,bərnt]; **-burning** : quemarse por el sol
sunburn[2] [ˈsʌn,bərn] *n* : quemadura *f* de sol
sundae [ˈsʌndi] *n* : sundae *m*
Sunday [ˈsʌn,deɪ, -di] *n* : domingo *m*
sundial [ˈsʌn,daɪl] *n* : reloj *m* de sol
sundown [ˈsʌn,daʊn] → **sunset**
sundries [ˈsʌndriz] *npl* : artículos *mpl* diversos
sundry [ˈsʌndri] *adj* : varios, diversos
sunflower [ˈsʌn,flaʊər] *n* : girasol *m*, mirasol *m*
sung → **sing**
sunglasses [ˈsʌn,glæsəz] *npl* : gafas *fpl* de sol, lentes *mpl* de sol
sunk → **sink**[1]
sunken [ˈsʌŋkən] *adj* : hundido
sunlight [ˈsʌn,laɪt] *n* : sol *m*, luz *f* del sol
sunny [ˈsʌni] *adj* **sunnier; -est** : soleado
sunrise [ˈsʌn,raɪz] *n* : salida *f* del sol
sunset [ˈsʌn,sɛt] *n* : puesta *f* del sol
sunshine [ˈsʌn,ʃaɪn] *n* : sol *m*, luz *f* del sol
sunspot [ˈsʌn,spɑt] *n* : mancha *f* solar
sunstroke [ˈsʌn,stroːk] *n* : insolación *f*
suntan [ˈsʌn,tæn] *n* : bronceado *m*
sup [ˈsʌp] *vi* **supped; supping** : cenar
super [ˈsuːpər] *adj* : súper <super! : ¡fantástico!>
superabundance [,suːpərəˈbʌndənts] *n* : superabundancia *f*
superb [sʊˈpərb] *adj* : magnífico, espléndido — **superbly** *adv*
supercilious [,suːpərˈsɪliəs] *adj* : altivo, altanero, desdeñoso
supercomputer [ˈsuːpərkəm,pjuːtər] *n* : supercomputadora *f*
superficial [,suːpərˈfɪʃəl] *adj* : superficial — **superficially** *adv*
superfluous [sʊˈpərflʊəs] *adj* : superfluo
superhighway [ˈsuːpər,haɪ,weɪ, ,suːpərˈ-] *n* : autopista *f*
superhuman [,suːpərˈhjuːmən] *adj* **1** SUPERNATURAL : sobrenatural **2** HERCULEAN : sobrehumano
superimpose [,suːpərɪmˈpoːz] *vt* **-posed; -posing** : superponer, sobreponer
superintend [,suːpərɪnˈtɛnd] *vt* : supervisar
superintendent [,suːpərɪnˈtɛndənt] *n* : portero *m*, -ra *f* (de un edificio); director *m*, -tora *f* (de una escuela, etc.); superintendente *mf* (de policía)
superior[1] [sʊˈpɪriər] *adj* **1** BETTER : superior **2** HAUGHTY : altivo, altanero
superior[2] *n* : superior *m*
superiority [sʊ,pɪriˈɔrəti] *n, pl* **-ties** : superioridad *f*
superlative[1] [sʊˈpərlətɪv] *adj* **1** : superlativo (en gramática) **2** SUPREME : supremo **3** EXCELLENT : excelente, excepcional
superlative[2] *n* : superlativo *m*
supermarket [ˈsuːpər,mɑrkət] *n* : supermercado *m*
supernatural [,suːpərˈnætʃərəl] *adj* : sobrenatural
supernaturally [,suːpərˈnætʃərəli] *adv* : de manera sobrenatural
superpower [ˈsuːpər,paʊər] *n* : superpotencia *f*
supersede [,suːpərˈsiːd] *vt* **-seded; -seding** : suplantar, reemplazar, sustituir
supersonic [,suːpərˈsɑnɪk] *adj* : supersónico
superstition [,suːpərˈstɪʃən] *n* : superstición *f*
superstitious [,suːpərˈstɪʃəs] *adj* : supersticioso
superstructure [ˈsuːpər,strʌktʃər] *n* : superestructura *f*
supervise [ˈsuːpər,vaɪz] *vt* **-vised; -vising** : supervisar, dirigir
supervision [,suːpərˈvɪʒən] *n* : supervisión *f*, dirección *f*
supervisor [ˈsuːpər,vaɪzər] *n* : supervisor *m*, -sora *f*
supervisory [,suːpərˈvaɪzəri] *adj* : de supervisor
supine [sʊˈpaɪn] *adj* **1** : en decúbito supino, en decúbito dorsal **2** ABJECT, INDIFFERENT : indiferente, apático
supper [ˈsʌpər] *n* : cena *f*, comida *f*
supplant [səˈplænt] *vt* : suplantar
supple [ˈsʌpəl] *adj* **-pler; -plest** : flexible
supplement[1] [ˈsʌplə,mɛnt] *vt* : complementar, completar
supplement[2] [ˈsʌpləmənt] *n* **1** : complemento *m* <dietary supplement : complemento alimenticio> **2** : suplemento *m* (de un libro o periódico)
supplementary [,sʌpləˈmɛntəri] *adj* : suplementario
supplicate [ˈsʌplə,keɪt] *v* **-cated; -cating** *vi* : rezar — *vt* : suplicar
supplier [səˈplaɪər] *n* : proveedor *m*, -dora *f*; abastecedor *m*, -dora *f*
supply[1] [səˈplaɪ] *vt* **-plied; -plying** : suministrar, proveer de, proporcionar
supply[2] *n, pl* **-plies 1** PROVISION : provisión *f*, suministro *m* <supply and demand : la oferta y la demanda> **2** STOCK : reserva *f*, existencias *fpl* (de un negocio) **3 supplies** *npl* PROVISIONS : provisiones *fpl*, víveres *mpl*, despensa *f*
support[1] [səˈport] *vt* **1** BACK : apoyar, respaldar **2** MAINTAIN : mantener, sos-

tener, sustentar **3** PROP UP **:** sostener, apoyar, apuntalar, soportar
support[2] *n* **1 :** apoyo *m* (moral), ayuda *f* (económica) **2** PROP **:** soporte *m,* apoyo *m*
supporter [sə'portər] *n* **:** partidario *m,* -ria *f*
suppose [sə'po:z] *vt* **-posed; -posing 1** ASSUME **:** suponer, imaginarse **2** BELIEVE **:** suponer, creer **3 to be supposed to :** tener que, deber
supposition [ˌsʌpə'zɪʃən] *n* **:** suposición *f*
suppository [sə'pɑzəˌtori] *n, pl* **-ries :** supositorio *m*
suppress [sə'prɛs] *vt* **1** SUBDUE **:** sofocar, suprimir, reprimir (una rebelión, etc.) **2 :** suprimir, ocultar (información) **3** REPRESS **:** reprimir, contener <to suppress a yawn : reprimir un bostezo>
suppression [sə'prɛʃən] *n* **1** SUBDUING **:** represión *f* **2 :** supresión *f* (de información) **3** REPRESSION **:** represión *f,* inhibición *f*
supremacy [sʊ'prɛməsi] *n, pl* **-cies :** supremacía *f*
supreme [sʊ'pri:m] *adj* **:** supremo
Supreme Being *n* **:** Ser *m* Supremo
supremely [sʊ'pri:mli] *adv* **:** totalmente, sumamente
surcharge ['sərˌtʃɑrdʒ] *n* **:** recargo *m*
sure[1] ['ʃʊr] *adv* **1** ALL RIGHT **:** por supuesto, claro **2** *(used as an intensifier)* <it sure is hot! : ¡hace tanto calor!> <she sure is pretty! : ¡qué linda es!>
sure[2] *adj* **surer; -est :** seguro <to be sure about something : estar seguro de algo> <a sure sign : una clara señal> <for sure : seguro, con seguridad>
surely ['ʃʊrli] *adv* **1** CERTAINLY **:** seguramente **2** *(used as an intensifier)* <you surely don't mean that! : ¡no me digas que estás hablando en serio!>
sureness ['ʃʊrnəs] *n* **:** certeza *f,* seguridad *f*
surety ['ʃʊrəṯi] *n, pl* **-ties :** fianza *f,* garantía *f*
surf ['sərf] *n* **1** WAVES **:** oleaje *m* **2** FOAM **:** espuma *f*
surface[1] ['sərfəs] *v* **-faced; -facing** *vi* **:** salir a la superficie — *vt* **:** revestir (una carretera)
surface[2] *n* **1 :** superficie *f* **2 on the surface :** en apariencia
surfboard ['sərfˌbord] *n* **:** tabla *f* de surf, tabla *f* de surfing
surfeit ['sərfət] *n* **:** exceso *m*
surfing ['sərfɪŋ] *n* **:** surf *m,* surfing *m*
surge[1] ['sərdʒ] *vi* **surged; surging 1 :** hincharse (dícese del mar), levantarse (dícese de las olas) **2** SWARM **:** salir en tropel (dícese de la gente, etc.)
surge[2] *n* **1 :** oleaje *m* (del mar), oleada *f* (de gente) **2** FLUSH **:** arranque *m,* arrebato *m* (de ira, etc.) **3** INCREASE **:** aumento *m* (súbito)
surgeon ['sərdʒən] *n* **:** cirujano *m,* -na *f*
surgery ['sərdʒəri] *n, pl* **-geries :** cirugía *f*
surgical ['sərdʒɪkəl] *adj* **:** quirúrgico — **surgically** [-kli] *adv*
surly ['sərli] *adj* **surlier; -est :** hosco, arisco
surmise[1] [sər'maɪz] *vt* **-mised; -mising :** conjeturar, suponer, concluir
surmise[2] *n* **:** conjetura *f*
surmount [sər'maʊnt] *vt* **1** OVERCOME **:** superar, vencer, salvar **2** CLIMB **:** escalar **3** CAP, TOP **:** coronar
surname ['sərˌneɪm] *n* **:** apellido *m*
surpass [sər'pæs] *vt* **:** superar, exceder, rebasar, sobrepasar
surplus ['sərˌplʌs] *n* **:** excedente *m,* sobrante *m,* superávit *m* (de dinero)
surprise[1] [sə'praɪz, sər-] *vt* **-prised; -prising :** sorprender
surprise[2] *n* **:** sorpresa *f* <to take by surprise : sorprender>
surprising [sə'praɪzɪŋ, sər-] *adj* **:** sorprendente — **surprisingly** *adv*
surrender[1] [sə'rɛndər] *vt* **1 :** entregar, rendir **2 to surrender oneself :** entregarse — *vi* **:** rendirse
surrender[2] *n* **:** rendición *m* (de una ciudad, etc.), entrega *f* (de posesiones)
surreptitious [ˌsərəp'tɪʃəs] *adj* **:** subrepticio — **surreptitiously** *adv*
surrogate ['sərəgət, -ˌgeɪt] *n* **:** sustituto *m*
surround [sə'raʊnd] *vt* **:** rodear
surroundings [sə'raʊndɪŋz] *npl* **:** ambiente *m,* entorno *m*
surveillance [sər'veɪlən*t*s, -'veɪljən*t*s, -'veɪən*t*s] *n* **:** vigilancia *f*
survey[1] [sər'veɪ] *vt* **-veyed; -veying 1 :** medir (un terreno) **2** EXAMINE **:** inspeccionar, examinar, revisar **3** POLL **:** hacer una encuesta de, sondear
survey[2] ['sərˌveɪ] *n, pl* **-veys 1** INSPECTION **:** inspección *f,* revisión *f* **2 :** medición *f* (de un terreno) **3** POLL **:** encuesta *f,* sondeo *m*
surveyor [sər'veɪər] *n* **:** agrimensor *m,* -sora *f*
survival [sər'vaɪvəl] *n* **:** supervivencia *f,* sobrevivencia *f*
survive [sər'vaɪv] *v* **-vived; -viving** *vi* **:** sobrevivir — *vt* OUTLIVE **:** sobrevivir a
survivor [sər'vaɪvər] *n* **:** superviviente *mf,* sobreviviente *mf*
susceptibility [səˌsɛptə'bɪləṯi] *n, pl* **-ties :** vulnerabilidad *f,* propensión *f* (a enfermedades, etc.)
susceptible [sə'sɛptəbəl] *adj* **1** VULNERABLE **:** vulnerable, sensible <susceptible to flattery : sensible a halagos> **2** PRONE **:** propenso <susceptible to colds : propenso a resfriarse>
suspect[1] [sə'spɛkt] *vt* **1** DISTRUST **:** dudar de **2 :** sospechar (algo), sospechar de (una persona) **3** IMAGINE, THINK **:** imaginarse, creer

suspect² ['sʌs,pɛkt, sə'spɛkt] *adj* : sospechoso, dudoso, cuestionable
suspect³ ['sʌs,pɛkt] *n* : sospechoso *m*, -sa *f*
suspend [sə'spɛnd] *vt* : suspender
suspenders [sə'spɛndərz] *npl* : tirantes *mpl*
suspense [sə'spɛnts] *n* : incertidumbre *f*, suspenso *m* (en una película, etc.)
suspenseful [sə'spɛntsfəl] *adj* : de suspenso
suspension [sə'spɛntʃən] *n* : suspensión *f*
suspicion [sə'spɪʃən] *n* **1** : sospecha *f* **2** TRACE : pizca *f*, atisbo *m*
suspicious [sə'spɪʃəs] *adj* **1** QUESTIONABLE : sospechoso, dudoso **2** DISTRUSTFUL : suspicaz, desconfiado
suspiciously [sə'spɪʃəsli] *adv* : de modo sospechoso, con recelo
sustain [sə'steɪn] *vt* **1** NOURISH : sustentar **2** PROLONG : sostener **3** SUFFER : sufrir **4** SUPPORT, UPHOLD : apoyar, respaldar, sostentar
sustenance ['sʌstənənts] *n* **1** NOURISHMENT : sustento *m* **2** SUPPORT : sostén *m*
svelte ['sfɛlt] *adj* : esbelto
swab¹ ['swɑb] *vt* **swabbed; swabbing** **1** CLEAN : lavar, limpiar **2** : aplicar a (con hisopo)
swab² *n or* **cotton swab** : hisopo *m* (para aplicar medicinas, etc.)
swaddle ['swɑdəl] *vt* **-dled; -dling** ['swɑdəlɪŋ] : envolver (en pañales)
swagger¹ ['swægər] *vi* : pavonearse
swagger² *n* : pavoneo *m*
swallow¹ ['swɑloː] *vt* **1** : tragar (comida, etc.) **2** ENGULF : tragarse, envolver **3** REPRESS : tragarse (insultos, etc.) — *vi* : tragar
swallow² *n* **1** : golondrina *f* (pájaro) **2** GULP : trago *m*
swam → **swim¹**
swamp¹ ['swɑmp] *vt* : inundar
swamp² *n* : pantano *m*, ciénaga *f*
swampy ['swɑmpi] *adj* **swampier; -est** : pantanoso, cenagoso
swan ['swɑn] *n* : cisne *f*
swap¹ ['swɑp] *vt* **swapped; swapping** : cambiar, intercambiar <to swap places : cambiarse de sitio>
swap² *n* : cambio *m*, intercambio *m*
swarm¹ ['swɔrm] *vi* : enjambrar
swarm² *n* : enjambre *m*
swarthy ['swɔrði, -θi] *adj* **swarthier; -est** : moreno
swashbuckling ['swɑʃ,bʌklɪŋ] *adj* : de aventurero
swat¹ ['swɑt] *vt* **swatted; swatting** : aplastar (un insecto), darle una palmada (a alguien)
swat² *n* : palmada *f* (con la mano), golpe *m* (con un objeto)
swatch ['swɑtʃ] *n* : muestra *f*
swath ['swɑθ, 'swɔθ] *or* **swathe** ['swɑð, 'swɔð, 'sweɪð] *n* : franja *f* (de grano segado)
swathe ['swɑð, 'swɔð, 'sweɪð] *vt* **swathed; swathing** : envolver
swatter ['swɑtər] → **flyswatter**
sway¹ ['sweɪ] *vi* : balancearse, mecerse — *vt* INFLUENCE : influir en, convencer
sway² *n* **1** SWINGING : balanceo *m* **2** INFLUENCE : influjo *m*
swear ['swær] *v* **swore** ['swor]; **sworn** ['sworn]; **swearing** *vi* **1** VOW : jurar **2** CURSE : decir palabrotas — *vt* : jurar
swearword ['swær,wərd] *n* : mala palabra *f*, palabrota *f*
sweat¹ ['swɛt] *vi* **sweat** *or* **sweated; sweating** **1** PERSPIRE : sudar, transpirar **2** OOZE : rezumar **3 to sweat over** : sudar la gota gorda por
sweat² *n* : sudor *m*, transpiración *f*
sweater ['swɛtər] *n* : suéter *m*
sweatshirt ['swɛt,ʃərt] *n* : sudadera *f*
sweaty ['swɛti] *adj* **sweatier; -est** : sudoroso, sudado, transpirado
Swede ['swiːd] *n* : sueco *m*, -ca *f*
Swedish¹ ['swiːdɪʃ] *adj* : sueco
Swedish² *n* **1** : sueco *m* (idioma) **2 the Swedish** *npl* : los suecos
sweep¹ ['swiːp] *v* **swept** ['swɛpt]; **sweeping** *vt* **1** : barrer (el suelo, etc.), limpiar (suciedad, etc.) <he swept the books aside : apartó los libros de un manotazo> **2** *or* **to sweep through** : extenderse por (dícese del fuego, etc.), azotar (dícese de una tormenta) — *vi* **1** : barrer, limpiar **2** : extenderse (en una curva), describir una curva <the sun swept across the sky : el sol describía una curva en el cielo>
sweep² *n* **1** : barrido *m*, barrida *f* (con una escoba) **2** : movimiento *m* circular **3** SCOPE : alcance *m*
sweeper ['swiːpər] *n* : barrendero *m*, -ra *f*
sweeping ['swiːpɪŋ] *adj* **1** WIDE : amplio (dícese de un movimiento) **2** EXTENSIVE : extenso, radical **3** INDISCRIMINATE : indiscriminado, demasiado general **4** OVERWHELMING : arrollador, aplastante
sweepstakes ['swiːp,steɪks] *ns & pl* **1** : carrera *f* (en que el ganador se lleva el premio entero) **2** LOTTERY : lotería *f*
sweet¹ ['swiːt] *adj* **1** : dulce <sweet desserts : postres dulces> **2** FRESH : fresco **3** : sin sal (dícese de la mantequilla, etc.) **4** PLEASANT : dulce, agradable **5** DEAR : querido
sweet² *n* : dulce *m*
sweeten ['swiːtən] *vt* : endulzar
sweetener ['swiːtənər] *n* : endulzante *m*
sweetheart ['swiːt,hɑrt] *n* : novio *m*, -via *f* <thanks, sweetheart : gracias, cariño>
sweetly ['swiːtli] *adv* : dulcemente
sweetness ['swiːtnəs] *n* : dulzura *f*
sweet potato *n* : batata *f*, boniato *m*
swell¹ ['swɛl] *vi* **swelled; swelled** *or* **swollen** ['swoːlən, 'swʌl-]; **swelling** **1** *or* **to swell up** : hincharse <her

ankle swelled : se le hinchó el tobillo> **2** *or* **to swell out** : inflarse, hincharse (dícese de las velas, etc.) **3** INCREASE : aumentar, crecer
swell[2] *n* **1** : oleaje *m* (del mar) **2** → **swelling**
swelling [ˈswɛlɪŋ] *n* : hinchazón *f*
swelter [ˈswɛltər] *vi* : sofocarse de calor
swept → **sweep**[1]
swerve[1] [ˈswərv] *vi* **swerved; swerving** : virar bruscamente
swerve[2] *n* : viraje *m* brusco
swift[1] [ˈswɪft] *adj* **1** FAST : rápido, veloz **2** SUDDEN : repentino, súbito — **swiftly** *adv*
swift[2] *n* : vencejo *m* (pájaro)
swiftness [ˈswɪftnəs] *n* : rapidez *f,* velocidad *f*
swig[1] [ˈswɪg] *vi* **swigged; swigging** : tomar a tragos, beber a tragos
swig[2] *n* : trago *m*
swill[1] [ˈswɪl] *vt* : chupar, beber a tragos grandes
swill[2] *n* **1** SLOP : bazofia *f* **2** GARBAGE : basura *f*
swim[1] [ˈswɪm] *vi* **swam** [ˈswæm]; **swum** [ˈswʌm]; **swimming 1** : nadar **2** FLOAT : flotar **3** REEL : dar vueltas <his head was swimming : la cabeza le daba vueltas>
swim[2] *n* : baño *m,* chapuzón *m* <to go for a swim : ir a nadar>
swimmer [ˈswɪmər] *n* : nadador *m,* -dora *f*
swindle[1] [ˈswɪndəl] *vt* **-dled; -dling** : estafar, timar
swindle[2] *n* : estafa *f,* timo *m fam*
swindler [ˈswɪndələr] *n* : estafador *m,* -dora *f;* timador *m,* -dora *f*
swine [ˈswaɪn] *ns & pl* : cerdo *m,* -da *f*
swing[1] [ˈswɪŋ] *v* **swung** [ˈswʌŋ]; **swinging** *vt* **1** : describir una curva con <he swung the ax at the tree : le dio al arbol con el hacha> **2** : balancear (los brazos, etc.), hacer oscilar **3** SUSPEND : colgar — *vi* **1** SWAY : balancearse (dícese de los brazos, etc.), oscilar (dícese de un objeto), columpiarse, mecerse (en un columpio) **2** SWIVEL : girar (en un pivote) <the door swung shut : la puerta se cerró> **3** CHANGE : virar, cambiar (dícese de las opiniones, etc.)
swing[2] *n* **1** SWINGING : vaivén *m,* balanceo *m* **2** CHANGE, SHIFT : viraje *m,* movimiento *m* **3** : columpio *m* (para niños) **4 to take a swing at someone** : intentar pegarle a alguien
swipe[1] [ˈswaɪp] *vt* **swiped; swiping 1** STRIKE : dar, pegar (con un movimiento amplio) **2** WIPE : limpiar **3** STEAL : birlar *fam,* robar
swipe[2] *n* BLOW : golpe *m*
swirl[1] [ˈswərl] *vi* : arremolinarse
swirl[2] *n* **1** EDDY : remolino *m* **2** SPIRAL : espiral *f*
swish[1] [ˈswɪʃ] *vt* : mover (produciendo un sonido) <she swished her skirt : movía la falda> — *vi* : moverse (produciendo un sonido) <the cars swished by : se oían pasar los coches>
swish[2] *n* : silbido *m* (de un látigo, etc.), susurro *m* (de agua), crujido *m* (de ropa, etc.)
Swiss [ˈswɪs] *n* : suizo *m,* -za *f* — **Swiss** *adj*
swiss chard *n* : acelga *f*
switch[1] [ˈswɪtʃ] *vt* **1** LASH, WHIP : azotar **2** CHANGE : cambiar de **3** EXCHANGE : intercambiar **4 to switch on** : encender, prender **5 to switch off** : apagar — *vi* **1** : moverse de un lado al otro **2** CHANGE : cambiar **3** SWAP : intercambiarse
switch[2] *n* **1** WHIP : vara *f* **2** CHANGE, SHIFT : cambio *m* **3** : interruptor *m,* llave *f* (de la luz, etc.)
switchboard [ˈswɪtʃˌbord] *n* : conmutador *m,* centralita *f*
swivel[1] [ˈswɪvəl] *vi* **-veled** *or* **-velled; -veling** *or* **-velling** : girar (sobre un pivote)
swivel[2] *n* : base *f* giratoria
swollen → **swell**[1]
swoon[1] [ˈswuːn] *vi* : desvanecerse, desmayarse
swoon[2] *n* : desvanecimiento *m,* desmayo *m*
swoop[1] [ˈswuːp] *vi* : abatirse (dícese de las aves), descender en picada (dícese de un avión)
swoop[2] *n* : descenso *m* en picada
sword [ˈsɔrd] *n* : espada *f*
swordfish [ˈsɔrdˌfɪʃ] *n* : pez *m* espada
swore, sworn → **swear**
swum → **swim**[1]
swung → **swing**[1]
sycamore [ˈsɪkəˌmor] *n* : sicomoro *m*
sycophant [ˈsɪkəfənt, -ˌfænt] *n* : adulador *m,* -dora *f*
syllabic [səˈlæbɪk] *adj* : silábico
syllable [ˈsɪləbəl] *n* : sílaba *f*
syllabus [ˈsɪləbəs] *n, pl* **-bi** [-ˌbaɪ] *or* **-buses** : programa *m* (de estudios)
symbol [ˈsɪmbəl] *n* : símbolo *m*
symbolic [sɪmˈbɑlɪk] *adj* : simbólico — **symbolically** [-kli] *adv*
symbolism [ˈsɪmbəˌlɪzəm] *n* : simbolismo *m*
symbolize [ˈsɪmbəˌlaɪz] *vt* **-ized; -izing** : simbolizar
symmetrical [səˈmɛtrɪəl] *or* **symmetric** [-trɪk] *adj* : simétrico — **symmetrically** [-trɪkli] *adv*
symmetry [ˈsɪmətri] *n, pl* **-tries** : simetría *f*
sympathetic [ˌsɪmpəˈθɛt̬ɪk] *adj* **1** PLEASING : agradable **2** RECEPTIVE : receptivo, favorable **3** COMPASSIONATE, UNDERSTANDING : comprensivo, compasivo
sympathetically [ˌsɪmpəˈθɛt̬ɪkli] *adv* : con compasión, con comprensión

sympathize [ˈsɪmpəˌθaɪz] *vi* **-thized; -thizing :** compadecer <I sympathize with you : te compadezco>
sympathy [ˈsɪmpəθi] *n, pl* **-thies 1** COMPASSION **:** compasión *f* **2** UNDERSTANDING **:** comprensión *f* **3** AGREEMENT **:** solidaridad *f* <in sympathy with : de acuerdo con> **4** CONDOLENCES **:** pésame *m,* condolencias *fpl*
symphonic [sɪmˈfɑnɪk] *adj* **:** sinfónico
symphony [ˈsɪmpfəni] *n, pl* **-nies :** sinfonía *f*
symposium [sɪmˈpoːziəm] *n, pl* **-sia** [-ziə] *or* **-siums :** simposio *m*
symptom [ˈsɪmptəm] *n* **:** síntoma *m*
symptomatic [ˌsɪmptəˈmæt̬ɪk] *adj* **:** sintomático
synagogue [ˈsɪnəˌgɑg, -ˌgɔg] *n* **:** sinagoga *f*
synchronize [ˈsɪŋkrəˌnaɪz, ˈsɪn-] *v* **-nized; -nizing** *vi* **:** estar sincronizado — *vt* **:** sincronizar
syncopate [ˈsɪŋkəˌpeɪt, ˈsɪn-] *vt* **-pated; -pating :** sincopar
syncopation [ˌsɪŋkəˈpeɪʃən, ˌsɪn-] *n* **:** síncopa *f*
syndicate[1] [ˈsɪndəˌkeɪt] *vi* **-cated; -cating :** formar una asociación
syndicate[2] [ˈsɪndɪkət] *n* **:** asociación *f,* agrupación *f*
syndrome [ˈsɪnˌdroːm] *n* **:** síndrome *m*
synonym [ˈsɪnəˌnɪm] *n* **:** sinónimo *m*
synonymous [səˈnɑnəməs] *adj* **:** sinónimo
synopsis [səˈnɑpsɪs] *n, pl* **-opses** [-ˌsiːz] **:** sinopsis *f*
syntax [ˈsɪnˌtæks] *n* **:** sintaxis *f*
synthesis [ˈsɪnθəsɪs] *n, pl* **-theses** [-ˌsiːz] **:** síntesis *f*
synthesize [ˈsɪnθəˌsaɪz] *vt* **-sized; -sizing :** sintetizar
synthetic[1] [sɪnˈθɛt̬ɪk] *adj* **:** sintético, artificial — **synthetically** [-t̬ɪkli] *adv*
synthetic[2] *n* **:** producto *m* sintético
syphilis [ˈsɪfələs] *n* **:** sífilis *f*
Syrian [ˈsɪriən] *n* **:** sirio *m,* -ria *f* — **Syrian** *adj*
syringe [səˈrɪndʒ, ˈsɪrɪndʒ] *n* **:** jeringa *f,* jeringuilla *f*
syrup [ˈsərəp, ˈsɪrəp] *n* **:** jarabe *m,* almíbar *m* (de azúcar y agua)
system [ˈsɪstəm] *n* **1** METHOD **:** sistema *m,* método *m* **2** APPARATUS **:** sistema *m,* instalación *f,* aparato *m* <electrical system : instalación eléctrica> <digestive system : aparato digestivo> **3** BODY **:** organismo *m,* cuerpo *m* <diseases that affect the whole system : enfermedades que afectan el organismo entero> **4** NETWORK **:** red *f*
systematic [ˌsɪstəˈmæt̬ɪk] *adj* **:** sistemático — **systematically** [-t̬ɪkli] *adv*
systematize [ˈsɪstəməˌtaɪz] *vt* **-tized; -tizing :** sistematizar
systemic [sɪsˈtɛmɪk] *adj* **:** sistémico

T

t [ˈtiː] *n, pl* **t's** *or* **ts** [ˈtiːz] **:** vigésima letra del alfabeto inglés
tab [ˈtæb] *n* **1** FLAP, TAG **:** lengüeta *f* (de un sobre, una caja, etc.), etiqueta *f* (de ropa) **2** → **tabulator 3** BILL, CHECK **:** cuenta *f* **4 to keep tabs on :** tener bajo vigilancia
tabby [ˈtæbi] *n, pl* **-bies 1** *or* **tabby cat :** gato *m* atigrado **2 :** gata *f*
tabernacle [ˈtæbərˌnækəl] *n* **:** tabernáculo *m*
table [ˈteɪbəl] *n* **1 :** mesa *f* <a table for two : una mesa para dos> **2** LIST **:** tabla *f* <multiplication table : tabla de multiplicar> **3 table of contents :** índice *m* de materias
tableau [tæˈbloː, ˈtæˌ-] *n, pl* **-leaux** [-ˈbloːz, -ˌbloːz] **:** retablo *m,* cuadro *m* vivo (en teatro)
tablecloth [ˈteɪbəlˌklɔθ] *n* **:** mantel *m*
tablespoon [ˈteɪbəlˌspuːn] *n* **1 :** cuchara *f* (de mesa) **2** → **tablespoonful**
tablespoonful [ˈteɪbəlˌspuːnˌfʊl] *n* **:** cucharada *f*
tablet [ˈtæblət] *n* **1** PLAQUE **:** placa *f* **2** PAD **:** bloc *m* (de papel) **3** PILL **:** tableta *f,* pastilla *f,* píldora *f* <an aspirin tablet : una tableta de aspirina>
table tennis *n* **:** tenis *m* de mesa
tableware [ˈteɪbəlˌwær] *n* **:** vajillas *fpl,* cubiertos *mpl* (de mesa)
tabloid [ˈtæˌblɔɪd] *n* **:** tabloide *m*
taboo[1] [təˈbuː, tæ-] *adj* **:** tabú
taboo[2] *n* **:** tabú *m*
tabular [ˈtæbjələr] *adj* **:** tabular
tabulate [ˈtæbjəˌleɪt] *vt* **-lated; -lating :** tabular
tabulator [ˈtæbjəˌleɪt̬ər] *n* **:** tabulador *m*
tacit [ˈtæsɪt] *adj* **:** tácito, implícito — **tacitly** *adv*
taciturn [ˈtæsɪˌtərn] *adj* **:** taciturno
tack[1] [ˈtæk] *vt* **1 :** sujetar con tachuelas **2 to tack on** ADD **:** añadir, agregar
tack[2] *n* **1 :** tachuela *f* **2** COURSE **:** rumbo *m* <to change tack : cambiar de rumbo>
tackle[1] [ˈtækəl] *vt* **-led; -ling 1 :** taclear (en futbol americano) **2** CONFRONT **:** abordar, enfrentar, emprender (un problema, un trabajo, etc.)
tackle[2] *n* **1** EQUIPMENT, GEAR **:** equipo *m,* aparejo *m* **2 :** aparejo *m* (de un buque) **3 :** tacleada *f* (en futbol americano)
tacky [ˈtæki] *adj* **tackier; -est 1** STICKY **:** pegajoso **2** CHEAP, GAUDY **:** de mal gusto, naco *Mex*
tact [ˈtækt] *n* **:** tacto *m,* delicadeza *f,* discreción *f*

tactful [ˈtæktfəl] *adj* **:** discreto, diplomático, de mucho tacto
tactfully [ˈtæktfəli] *adv* **:** discretamente, con mucho tacto
tactic [ˈtæktɪk] *n* **:** táctica *f*
tactical [ˈtæktɪkəl] *adj* **:** táctico, estratégico
tactics [ˈtæktɪks] *ns & pl* **:** táctica *f*, estrategia *f*
tactile [ˈtæktəl, -ˌtaɪl] *adj* **:** táctil
tactless [ˈtæktləs] *adj* **:** indiscreto, poco delicado
tactlessly [ˈtæktləsli] *adv* **:** rudamente, sin tacto
tadpole [ˈtædˌpoːl] *n* **:** renacuajo *m*
taffeta [ˈtæfətə] *n* **:** tafetán *m*, tafeta *f Arg, Mex, Uru*
taffy [ˈtæfi] *n, pl* **-fies :** caramelo *m* de melaza, chicloso *m Mex*
tag[1] [ˈtæg] *v* **tagged; tagging** *vt* **1** LABEL **:** etiquetar **2** TAIL **:** seguir de cerca **3** TOUCH **:** tocar (en varios juegos) — *vi* **to tag along :** pegarse, acompañar
tag[2] *n* **1** LABEL **:** etiqueta *f* **2** SAYING **:** dicho *m*, refrán *m*
tail[1] [ˈteɪl] *vt* FOLLOW **:** seguir de cerca, pegarse
tail[2] *n* **1 :** cola *f*, rabo *m* (de un animal) **2 :** cola *f*, parte *f* posterior <a comet's tail : la cola de un cometa> **3 tails** *npl* **:** cruz *f* (de una moneda) <heads or tails : cara o cruz>
tailed [ˈteɪld] *adj* **:** que tiene cola
tailgate[1] [ˈteɪlˌgeɪt] *vi* **-gated; -gating :** seguir a un vehículo demasiado de cerca
tailgate[2] *n* **:** puerta *f* trasera (de un vehículo)
taillight [ˈteɪlˌlaɪt] *n* **:** luz *f* trasera (de un vehículo), calavera *f Mex*
tailor[1] [ˈteɪlər] *vt* **1 :** confeccionar o alterar (ropa) **2** ADAPT **:** adaptar, ajustar
tailor[2] *n* **:** sastre *m*, -tra *f*
tailpipe [ˈteɪlˌpaɪp] *n* **:** tubo *m* de escape
tailspin [ˈteɪlˌspɪn] *n* **:** barrena *f*
taint[1] [ˈteɪnt] *vt* **:** contaminar, corromper
taint[2] *n* **:** corrupción *f*, impureza *f*
take[1] [ˈteɪk] *v* **took** [ˈtʊk]; **taken** [ˈteɪkən]; **taking** *vt* **1** CAPTURE **:** capturar, apresar **2** GRASP **:** tomar, agarrar <to take the bull by the horns : tomar al toro por los cuernos> **3** CATCH **:** tomar, agarrar <taken by surprise : tomado por sorpresa> **4** CAPTIVATE **:** encantar, fascinar **5** INGEST **:** tomar, ingerir <take two pills : tome dos píldoras> **6** REMOVE **:** sacar, extraer <take an orange : saca una naranja> **7 :** tomar, coger (un tren, un autobús, etc.) **8** NEED, REQUIRE **:** tomar, requirir <these things take time : estas cosas toman tiempo> **9** BRING, CARRY **:** llevar, sacar, cargar <take them with you : llévalos contigo> <take the trash out : saca la basura> **10** BEAR, ENDURE **:** soportar, aguantar (dolores, etc.) **11** ACCEPT **:** aceptar (un cheque, etc.), seguir (consejos), asumir (la responsabilidad) **12** SUPPOSE **:** suponer <I take it that... : supongo que...> **13** (*indicating an action or an undertaking*) <to take a walk : dar un paseo> <to take a class : tomar una clase> **14 to take place** HAPPEN **:** tener lugar, suceder, ocurrir — *vi* **:** agarrar (dícese de un tinte), prender (dícese de una vacuna)
take[2] *n* **1** PROCEEDS **:** recaudación *f*, ingresos *mpl*, ganancias *fpl* **2 :** toma *f* (de un rodaje o una grabación)
take back *vt* **:** retirar (palabras, etc.)
take in *vt* **1 :** tomarle a, achicar (un vestido, etc.) **2** INCLUDE **:** incluir, abarcar **3** ATTEND **:** ir a <to take in a movie : ir al cine> **4** GRASP, UNDERSTAND **:** captar, entender **5** DECEIVE **:** engañar
takeoff [ˈteɪkˌɔf] *n* **1** PARODY **:** parodia *f* **2 :** despegue *m* (de un avión o cohete)
take off *vt* REMOVE **:** quitar <take off your hat : quítate el sombrero> — *vi* **1 :** despegar (dícese de un avión o un cohete) **2** LEAVE **:** irse, partir
take on *vt* **1** TACKLE **:** abordar, emprender (problemas, etc.) **2** ACCEPT **:** aceptar, encargarse de, asumir (una responsabilidad) **3** CONTRACT **:** contratar (trabajadores) **4** ASSUME **:** adoptar, asumir, adquirir <the neighborhood took on a dingy look : el barrio asumió una apariencia deprimente>
takeover [ˈteɪkˌoːvər] *n* **:** toma *f* (de poder o de control), adquisición *f* (de una empresa por otra)
take over *vt* **:** tomar el poder de, tomar las riendas de — *vi* **:** asumir el mando
taker [ˈteɪkər] *n* **:** persona *f* interesada <available to all takers : disponible a cuantos estén interesados>
take up *vt* **1** LIFT **:** levantar **2** SHORTEN **:** acortar (una falda, etc.) **3** BEGIN **:** empezar, dedicarse a (un pasatiempo, etc.) **4** OCCUPY **:** ocupar, llevar (tiempo, espacio) **5** PURSUE **:** volver a (una cuestión, un asunto) **6** CONTINUE **:** seguir con
talc [ˈtælk] *n* **:** talco *m*
talcum powder [ˈtælkəm] *n* **:** talco *m*, polvos *mpl* de talco
tale [ˈteɪl] *n* **1** ANECDOTE, STORY **:** cuento *m*, relato *m*, anécdota *f* **2** FALSEHOOD **:** cuento *m*, mentira *f*
talent [ˈtælənt] *n* **:** talento *m*, don *m*
talented [ˈtæləntəd] *adj* **:** talentoso
talisman [ˈtælɪsmən, -lɪz-] *n, pl* **-mans :** talismán *m*
talk[1] [ˈtɔk] *vi* **1 :** hablar <he talks for hours : se pasa horas hablando> **2** CHAT **:** charlar, platicar — *vt* **1** SPEAK **:** hablar <to talk French : hablar francés> <to talk business : hablar de negocios> **2** PERSUADE **:** influenciar, convencer <she talked me out of it : me convenció que no lo hiciera> **3**

to talk over DISCUSS : hablar de, discutir

talk[2] *n* **1** CONVERSATION : charla *f,* plática *f,* conversación *f* **2** GOSSIP, RUMOR : chisme *m,* rumores *mpl*

talkative [ˈtɔkət̬ɪv] *adj* : locuaz, parlanchín, charlatán

talker [ˈtɔkər] *n* : conversador *m,* -dora *f;* hablador *m,* -dora *f*

tall [ˈtɔl] *adj* : alto <how tall is he? : ¿cuánto mide?>

tallness [ˈtɔlnəs] *n* HEIGHT : estatura *f* (de una persona), altura *f* (de un objeto)

tallow [ˈtæloː] *n* : sebo *m*

tally[1] [ˈtæli] *v* **-lied; -lying** *vt* RECKON : contar, hacer una cuenta de — *vi* MATCH : concordar, corresponder, cuadrar

tally[2] *n, pl* **-lies** : cuenta *f* <to keep a tally : llevar la cuenta>

talon [ˈtælən] *n* : garra *f* (de un ave de rapiña)

tambourine [ˌtæmbəˈriːn] *n* : pandero *m,* pandereta *f*

tame[1] [ˈteɪm] *vt* **tamed; taming** : domar, amansar, domesticar

tame[2] *adj* **tamer; -est 1** DOMESTICATED : domesticado, manso **2** DOCILE : manso, dócil **3** DULL : aburrido, soso

tamely [ˈteɪmli] *adv* : mansamente, dócilmente

tamer [ˈteɪmər] *n* : domador *m,* -dora *f*

tamp [ˈtæmp] *vt* : apisonar

tamper [ˈtæmpər] *vi* **to tamper with** : adulterar (una sustancia), forzar (un sello, una cerradura), falsear (documentos), manipular (una máquina)

tampon [ˈtæmˌpɑn] *n* : tampón *m*

tan[1] [ˈtæn] *v* **tanned; tanning** *vt* **1** : curtir (pieles) **2** : broncear — *vi* : broncearse

tan[2] *n* **1** SUNTAN : bronceado *m* <to get a tan : broncearse> **2** : color *m* canela, color *m* café con leche

tandem[1] [ˈtændəm] *adv or* **in tandem** : en tándem

tandem[2] *n* : tándem *m* (bicicleta)

tang [ˈtæŋ] *n* : sabor *m* fuerte

tangent [ˈtændʒənt] *n* : tangente *f* <to go off on a tangent : irse por la tangente>

tangerine [ˈtændʒəˌriːn, ˌtændʒəˈ-] *n* : mandarina *f*

tangible [ˈtændʒəbəl] *adj* : tangible, palpable — **tangibly** [-bli] *adv*

tangle[1] [ˈtæŋgəl] *v* **-gled; -gling** *vt* : enredar, enmarañar — *vi* : enredarse

tangle[2] *n* : enredo *m,* maraña *f*

tango[1] [ˈtæŋˌgoː] *vi* : bailar el tango

tango[2] *n, pl* **-gos** : tango *m*

tangy [ˈtæŋi] *adj* **tangier; -est** : que tiene un sabor fuerte

tank [ˈtæŋk] *n* : tanque *m,* depósito *m* <fuel tank : depósito de combustibles>

tankard [ˈtæŋkərd] *n* : jarra *f*

tanker [ˈtæŋkər] *n* : buque *m* cisterna, camión *m* cisterna, avión *m* cisterna <an oil tanker : un petrolero>

tanner [ˈtænər] *n* : curtidor *m,* -dora *f*

tannery [ˈtænəri] *n, pl* **-neries** : curtiduría *f,* tenería *f*

tannin [ˈtænən] *n* : tanino *m*

tantalize [ˈtæntəˌlaɪz] *vt* **-lized; -lizing** : tentar, atormentar (con algo inasequible)

tantalizing [ˈtæntəˌlaɪzɪŋ] *adj* : tentador, seductor

tantamount [ˈtæntəˌmaʊnt] *adj* : equivalente

tantrum [ˈtæntrəm] *n* : rabieta *f,* berrinche *m* <to throw a tantrum : hacer un berrinche>

tap[1] [ˈtæp] *vt* **tapped; tapping 1** : ponerle una espita a, sacar líquido de (un barril, un tanque, etc.) **2** : intervenir (una línea telefónica) **3** PAT, TOUCH : tocar, golpear ligeramente <he tapped me on the shoulder : me tocó en el hombro>

tap[2] *n* **1** FAUCET : llave *f,* grifo *m* <beer on tap : cerveza de barril> **2** : extracción *f* (de líquido) <a spinal tap : una punción lumbar> **3** PAT, TOUCH : golpecito *m,* toque *m*

tape[1] [ˈteɪp] *vt* **taped; taping 1** : sujetar o mendar con cinta adhesiva **2** RECORD : grabar

tape[2] *n* **1** : cinta *f* (adhesiva, magnética, etc.) **2** → **tape measure**

tape measure *n* : cinta *f* métrica

taper[1] [ˈteɪpər] *vi* **1** : estrecharse gradualmente <its tail tapers towards the tip : su cola va estrechándose hacia la punta> **2** *or* **to taper off** : disminuir gradualmente

taper[2] *n* **1** CANDLE : vela *f* larga y delgada **2** TAPERING : estrechamiento *m* gradual

tapestry [ˈtæpəstri] *n, pl* **-tries** : tapiz *m*

tapeworm [ˈteɪpˌwərm] *n* : solitaria *f,* tenia *f*

tapioca [ˌtæpiˈoːkə] *n* : tapioca *f*

tar[1] [ˈtɑr] *vt* **tarred; tarring** : alquitranar

tar[2] *n* : alquitrán *m,* brea *f,* chapopote *m Mex*

tarantula [təˈræntʃələ, -ˈræntələ] *n* : tarántula *f*

tardiness [ˈtɑrdinəs] *n* : tardanza *f,* retraso *m*

tardy [ˈtɑrdi] *adj* **-dier; -est** LATE : tardío, de retraso

target[1] [ˈtɑrgət] *vt* : fijar como objetivo, dirigir, destinar

target[2] *n* **1** : blanco *m* <target practice : tiro al blanco> **2** GOAL, OBJECTIVE : meta *f,* objetivo *m*

tariff [ˈtærɪf] *n* DUTY : tarifa *f,* arancel *m*

tarnish[1] [ˈtɑrnɪʃ] *vt* **1** DULL : deslustrar **2** SULLY : empañar, manchar (una reputación, etc.) — *vi* : deslustrarse

tarnish[2] *n* : deslustre *m*

tarpaulin [tɑr'pɔlən, 'tɑrpə-] *n* : lona *f* (impermeable)

tarry[1] ['tæri] *vi* **-ried; -rying** : demorarse, entretenerse

tarry[2] ['tɑri] *adj* **1** : parecido al alquitrán **2** : cubierto de alquitrán

tart[1] ['tɑrt] *adj* **1** SOUR : ácido, agrio **2** CAUSTIC : mordaz, acrimonioso — **tartly** *adv*

tart[2] *n* : tartaleta *f*

tartan ['tɑrtən] *n* : tartán *m*

tartar ['tɑrt̬ər] *n* **1** : tártaro *m* <tartar sauce : salsa tártara> **2** : sarro *m* (dental)

tartness ['tɑrtnəs] *n* **1** SOURNESS : acidez *f* **2** ACRIMONY, SHARPNESS : mordacidad *f*, acrimonia *f*, acritud *f*

task ['tæsk] *n* : tarea *f*, trabajo *m*

taskmaster ['tæsk,mæstər] *n* **to be a hard taskmaster** : ser exigente, ser muy estricto

tassel ['tæsəl] *n* : borla *f*

taste[1] ['teɪst] *v* **tasted; tasting** *vt* : probar (alimentos), degustar, catar (vinos) <taste this soup : prueba esta sopa> — *vi* : saber <this tastes good : esto sabe bueno>

taste[2] *n* **1** SAMPLE : prueba *f*, bocado *m* (de comida), trago *m* (de bebidas) **2** FLAVOR : gusto *m*, sabor *m* **3** : gusto *m* <she has good taste : tiene buen gusto> <in bad taste : de mal gusto>

taste bud *n* : papila *f* gustativa

tasteful ['teɪstfəl] *adj* : de buen gusto

tastefully ['teɪstfəli] *adv* : con buen gusto

tasteless ['teɪstləs] *adj* **1** FLAVORLESS : sin sabor, soso, insípido **2** : de mal gusto <a tasteless joke : un chiste de mal gusto>

taster ['teɪstər] *n* : degustador *m*, -dora *f*; catador *m*, -dora *f* (de vinos)

tastiness ['teɪstinəs] *n* : lo sabroso

tasty ['teɪsti] *adj* **tastier; -est** : sabroso, gustoso

tatter ['tæt̬ər] *n* **1** SHRED : tira *f*, jirón *m* (de tela) **2 tatters** *npl* : andrajos *mpl*, harapos *mpl* <to be in tatters : estar por los suelos>

tattered ['tæt̬ərd] *adj* : andrajoso, en jirones

tattle ['tæt̬əl] *vi* **-tled; -tling 1** CHATTER : parlotear *fam*, cotorrear *fam* **2 to tattle on someone** : acusar a alguien

tattletale ['tæt̬əl,teɪl] *n* : soplón *m*, -plona *f fam*

tattoo[1] [tæ'tu:] *vt* : tatuar

tattoo[2] *n* : tatuaje *m* <to get a tattoo : tatuarse>

taught → **teach**

taunt[1] ['tɔnt] *vt* MOCK : mofarse de, burlarse de

taunt[2] *n* : mofa *f*, burla *f*

Taurus ['tɔrəs] *n* : Tauro *mf*

taut ['tɔt] *adj* : tirante, tenso — **tautly** *adv*

tautness ['tɔtnəs] *n* : tirantez *f*, tensión *f*

tavern ['tævərn] *n* : taberna *f*

tawdry ['tɔdri] *adj* **-drier; -est** : chabacano, vulgar

tawny ['tɔni] *adj* **-nier; -est** : leonado

tax[1] ['tæks] *vt* **1** : gravar, cobrar un impuesto sobre **2** CHARGE : acusar <they taxed him with neglect : fue acusado de incumplimiento> **3 to tax someone's strength** : ponerle a prueba las fuerzas (a alguien)

tax[2] *n* **1** : impuesto *m*, tributo *m* **2** BURDEN : carga *f*

taxable ['tæksəbəl] *adj* : sujeto a un impuesto

taxation [tæk'seɪʃən] *n* : impuestos *mpl*

tax–exempt ['tæksɪg'zɛmpt, -ɛg-] *adj* : libre de impuestos

taxi[1] ['tæksi] *vi* **taxied; taxiing** *or* **taxying; taxis** *or* **taxies 1** : ir en taxi **2** : rodar sobre la pista de aterrizaje (dícese de un avión)

taxi[2] *n, pl* **taxis** : taxi *m*, libre *m Mex*

taxicab ['tæksi,kæb] → **taxi**[2]

taxidermist ['tæksə,dərmɪst] *n* : taxidermista *mf*

taxidermy ['tæksə,dərmi] *n* : taxidermia *f*

taxpayer ['tæks,peɪər] *n* : contribuyente *mf*, causante *mf Mex*

TB [,ti:'bi:] → **tuberculosis**

tea ['ti:] *n* **1** : té *m* (planta y bebida) **2** : merienda *f*, té *m* (comida)

teach ['ti:tʃ] *v* **taught** ['tɔt]; **teaching** *vt* : enseñar, dar clases de <she teaches math : da clases de matemáticas> <she taught me everything I know : me enseñó todo lo que sé> — *vi* : enseñar, dar clases

teacher ['ti:tʃər] *n* : maestro *m*, -tra *f* (de enseñanza primaria); profesor *m*, -sora *f* (de enseñanza secundaria)

teaching ['ti:tʃɪŋ] *n* : enseñanza *f*

teacup ['ti:,kʌp] *n* : taza *f* para té

teak ['ti:k] *n* : teca *f*

teakettle ['ti:,kɛtəl] *n* : tetera *f*

teal ['ti:l] *n, pl* **teal** *or* **teals** : cerceta *f* (pato)

team[1] ['ti:m] *vi or* **to team up 1** : formar un equipo (en deportes) **2** COLLABORATE : asociarse, juntarse, unirse

team[2] *adj* : de equipo

team[3] *n* **1** : tiro *m* (de caballos), yunta *f* (de bueyes o mulas) **2** : equipo *m* (en deportes, etc.)

teammate ['ti:m,meɪt] *n* : compañero *m*, -ra *f* de equipo

teamster ['ti:mstər] *n* : camionero *m*, -ra *f*

teamwork ['ti:m,wərk] *n* : trabajo *m* en equipo, cooperación *f*

teapot ['ti:,pɑt] *n* : tetera *f*

tear[1] ['tær] *v* **tore** ['tor]; **torn** ['torn]; **tearing** *vt* **1** RIP : desgarrar, romper, rasgar (tela) <to tear to pieces : hacer pedazos> **2** *or* **to tear apart** DIVIDE : dividir **3** REMOVE : arrancar <torn from his family : arrancado de su familia> **4 to tear down** : derribar — *vi* **1** RIP : desgarrarse, romperse **2** RUSH

: ir a gran velocidad <she went tearing down the street : se fue como rayo por la calle>

tear[2] *n* : desgarradura *f,* rotura *f,* desgarro *m* (muscular)

tear[3] [ˈtɪr] *n* : lágrima *f*

teardrop [ˈtɪr,drɑp] → **tear**[3]

tearful [ˈtɪrfəl] *adj* : lloroso, triste — **tearfully** *adv*

tease[1] [ˈtiːz] *vt* **teased; teasing 1** MOCK : burlarse de, mofarse de **2** ANNOY : irritar, fastidiar

tease[2] *n* **1** TEASING : burla *f,* mofa *f* **2** : bromista *mf;* guasón *m,* -sona *f*

teaspoon [ˈtiː,spuːn] *n* **1** : cucharita *f* **2** → **teaspoonful**

teaspoonful [ˈtiː,spuːn,fʊl] *n, pl* **-spoonfuls** [-,fʊlz] *or* **-spoonsful** [-,spuːnz,fʊl] : cucharadita *f*

teat [ˈtiːt] *n* : tetilla *f*

technical [ˈtɛknɪkəl] *adj* : técnico — **technically** [-kli] *adv*

technicality [,tɛknəˈkæləṭi] *n, pl* **-ties** : detalle *m* técnico

technician [tɛkˈnɪʃən] *n* : técnico *m,* -ca *f*

technique [tɛkˈniːk] *n* : técnica *f*

technological [,tɛknəˈlɑdʒɪkəl] *adj* : tecnológico

technology [tɛkˈnɑlədʒi] *n, pl* **-gies** : tecnología *f*

teddy bear [ˈtɛdi] *n* : oso *m* de peluche

tedious [ˈtiːdiəs] *adj* : aburrido, pesado, monótono — **tediously** *adv*

tediousness [ˈtiːdiəsnəs] *n* : lo aburrido, lo pesado

tedium [ˈtiːdiəm] *n* : tedio *m,* pesadez *f*

tee [ˈtiː] *n* : tee *mf*

teem [ˈtiːm] *vi* **to teem with** : estar repleto de, estar lleno de

teenage [ˈtiːn,eɪdʒ] *or* **teenaged** [-eɪdʒd] *adj* : adolescente, de adolescencia

teenager [ˈtiːn,eɪdʒər] *n* : adolescente *mf*

teens [ˈtiːnz] *npl* : adolescencia *f*

teepee → **tepee**

teeter[1] [ˈtiːṭər] *vi* : balancearse, tambalearse

teeter[2] *n or* **teeter–totter** [ˈtiːṭər-,tɑṭər] → **seesaw**

teeth → **tooth**

teethe [ˈtiːð] *vi* **teethed; teething** : formársele a uno los dientes <the baby's teething : le están saliendo los dientes al niño>

telecast[1] [ˈtɛlə,kæst] *vt* **-cast; -casting** : televisar, transmitir por televisión

telecast[2] *n* : transmisión *f* por televisión

telecommunication [ˈtɛləkə,mjuːnəˈkeɪʃən] *n* : telecomunicación *f*

telegram [ˈtɛlə,græm] *n* : telegrama *m*

telegraph[1] [ˈtɛlə,græf] *v* : telegrafiar

telegraph[2] *n* : telégrafo *m*

telepathic [,tɛləˈpæθɪk] *adj* : telepático — **telepathically** [-θɪkli] *adv*

telepathy [təˈlɛpəθi] *n* : telepatía *f*

telephone[1] [ˈtɛlə,foːn] *v* **-phoned; -phoning** *vt* : llamar por teléfono a, telefonear — *vi* : telefonear

telephone[2] *n* : teléfono *m*

telescope[1] [ˈtɛlə,skoːp] *vi* **-scoped; -scoping** : plegarse (como un telescopio)

telescope[2] *n* : telescopio *m*

telescopic [,tɛləˈskɑpɪk] *adj* : telescópico

televise [ˈtɛlə,vaɪz] *vt* **-vised; -vising** : televisar

television [ˈtɛlə,vɪʒən] *n* : televisión *f*

tell [ˈtɛl] *v* **told** [ˈtoːld]; **telling** *vt* **1** COUNT : contar, enumerar <all told : en total> **2** INSTRUCT : decir <he told me how to fix it : me dijo cómo arreglarlo> <they told her to wait : le dijeron que esperara> **3** RELATE : contar, relatar, narrar <to tell a story : contar una historia> **4** DIVULGE, REVEAL : revelar, divulgar <he told me everything about her : me contó todo acerca de ella> **5** DISCERN : discernir, notar <I can't tell the difference : no noto la diferencia> — *vi* **1** SAY : decir <I won't tell : no voy a decírselo a nadie> **2** KNOW : saber <you never can tell : nunca se sabe> **3** SHOW : notarse, hacerse sentir <the strain is beginning to tell : la tensión se empieza a notar>

teller [ˈtɛlər] *n* **1** NARRATOR : narrador *m,* -dora *f* **2** *or* **bank teller** : cajero *m,* -ra *f*

temerity [təˈmɛrəṭi] *n, pl* **-ties** : temeridad *f*

temp [ˈtɛmp] *n* : empleado *m,* -da *f* temporal

temper[1] [ˈtɛmpər] *vt* **1** MODERATE : moderar, temperar **2** ANNEAL : templar (acero, etc.)

temper[2] *n* **1** DISPOSITION : carácter *m,* genio *m* **2** HARDNESS : temple *m,* dureza *f* (de un metal) **3** COMPOSURE : calma *f,* serenidad *f* <to lose one's temper : perder los estribos> **4** RAGE : furia *f* <to fly into a temper : ponerse furioso>

temperament [ˈtɛmpərmənt, -prə-, -pərə-] *n* : temperamento *m*

temperamental [,tɛmpərˈmɛntəl, -prə-, -pərə-] *adj* : temperamental

temperance [ˈtɛmprən*t*s] *n* : templanza *f,* temperancia *f*

temperate [ˈtɛmpərət] *adj* : templado (dícese del clima, etc.), moderado

temperature [ˈtɛmpər,tʃʊr, -prə-, -pərə-, -tʃər] *n* **1** : temperatura *f* **2** FEVER : calentura *f,* fiebre *f*

tempest [ˈtɛmpəst] *n* : tempestad *f*

tempestuous [tɛmˈpɛstʃʊəs] *adj* : tempestuoso

temple [ˈtɛmpəl] *n* **1** : templo *m* (en religión) **2** : sien *f* (en anatomía)

tempo [ˈtɛm,poː] *n, pl* **-pi** [-,piː] *or* **-pos** : ritmo *m,* tempo *m* (en música)

temporal [ˈtɛmpərəl] *adj* : temporal

temporarily [,tɛmpəˈrɛrəli] *adv* : temporalmente, provisionalmente

temporary [ˈtɛmpəˌrɛri] *adj* : temporal, provisional, provisorio
tempt [ˈtɛmpt] *vt* : tentar
temptation [tɛmpˈteɪʃən] *n* : tentación *f*
tempter [ˈtɛmptər] *n* : tentador *m*
temptress [ˈtɛmptrəs] *n* : tentadora *f*
ten[1] [ˈtɛn] *adj* : diez
ten[2] *n* **1** : diez *m* (número) **2** : decena *f* <tens of thousands : decenas de millares>
tenable [ˈtɛnəbəl] *adj* : sostenible, defendible
tenacious [təˈneɪʃəs] *adj* : tenaz
tenacity [təˈnæsət̬i] *n* : tenacidad *f*
tenancy [ˈtɛnəntsi] *n, pl* **-cies** : tenencia *f,* inquilinato *m* (de un inmueble)
tenant [ˈtɛnənt] *n* : inquilino *m,* -na *f;* arrendatario *m,* -ria *f*
tend [ˈtɛnd] *vt* : atender, cuidar (de), ocuparse de — *vi* : tender <it tends to benefit the consumer : tiende a beneficiar al consumidor>
tendency [ˈtɛndəntsi] *n, pl* **-cies** : tendencia *f,* proclividad *f,* inclinación *f*
tender[1] [ˈtɛndər] *vt* : entregar, presentar <I tendered my resignation : presenté mi renuncia>
tender[2] *adj* **1** : tierno, blando <tender steak : bistec tierno> **2** AFFECTIONATE, LOVING : tierno, cariñoso, afectuoso **3** DELICATE : tierno, sensible, delicado
tender[3] *n* **1** OFFER : propuesta *f,* oferta *f* (en negocios) **2 legal tender** : moneda *f* de curso legal
tenderize [ˈtɛndəˌraɪz] *vt* **-ized; -izing** : ablandar (carnes)
tenderloin [ˈtɛndɛrˌlɔɪn] *n* : lomo *f* (de res o de puerco)
tenderly [ˈtɛndərli] *adv* : tiernamente, con ternura
tenderness [ˈtɛndərnəs] *n* : ternura *f*
tendon [ˈtɛndən] *n* : tendón *m*
tendril [ˈtɛndrɪl] *n* : zarcillo *m*
tenement [ˈtɛnəmənt] *n* : casa *f* de vecindad
tenet [ˈtɛnət] *n* : principio *m*
tennis [ˈtɛnəs] *n* : tenis *m*
tenor [ˈtɛnər] *n* **1** PURPORT : tenor *m,* significado *m* **2** : tenor *m* (en música)
tenpins [ˈtɛnˌpɪnz] *npl* : bolos *mpl,* boliche *m*
tense[1] [ˈtɛnts] *v* **tensed; tensing** *vt* : tensar — *vi* : tensarse, ponerse tenso
tense[2] *adj* **tenser; tensest 1** TAUT : tenso, tirante **2** NERVOUS : tenso, nervioso
tense[3] *n* : tiempo *m* (de un verbo)
tensely [ˈtɛntsli] *adv* : tensamente
tenseness [ˈtɛntsnəs] → **tension**
tension [ˈtɛntʃən] *n* **1** TAUTNESS : tensión *f,* tirantez *f* **2** STRESS : tensión *f,* nerviosismo *m,* estrés *m*
tent [ˈtɛnt] *n* : tienda *f* de campaña
tentacle [ˈtɛntɪkəl] *n* : tentáculo *m*
tentative [ˈtɛntət̬ɪv] *adj* **1** HESITANT : indeciso, vacilante **2** PROVISIONAL : sujeto a cambios, provisional
tentatively [ˈtɛntət̬ɪvli] *adv* : provisionalmente
tenth[1] [ˈtɛnθ] *adj* : décimo
tenth[2] *n* **1** : décimo *m,* -ma *f* (en una serie) **2** : décimo *m,* décima parte *f*
tenuous [ˈtɛnjʊəs] *adj* : tenue, débil <tenuous reasons : razones poco convincentes>
tenuously [ˈtɛnjʊəsli] *adv* : tenuemente, ligeramente
tenure [ˈtɛnjər] *n* : tenencia *f* (de un cargo o una propiedad), titularidad *f* (de un puesto académico)
tepee [ˈtiːˌpiː] *n* : tipi *m*
tepid [ˈtɛpɪd] *adj* : tibio
term[1] [ˈtərm] *vt* : calificar de, llamar, nombrar
term[2] *n* **1** PERIOD : término *m,* plazo *m,* período *m* **2** : término *m* (en matemáticas) **3** WORD : término *m,* vocablo *m* <legal terms : términos legales> **4 terms** *npl* CONDITIONS : términos *mpl,* condiciones *fpl* **5 terms** *npl* RELATIONS : relaciones *fpl* <to be on good terms with : tener buenas relaciones con> **6 in terms of** : con respecto a, en cuanto a
terminal[1] [ˈtərmənəl] *adj* : terminal
terminal[2] *n* **1** : terminal *m,* polo *m* (en electricidad) **2** : terminal *m* (de una computadora) **3** STATION : terminal *f,* estación *f* (de transporte público)
terminate [ˈtərməˌneɪt] *v* **-nated; -nating** *vi* : terminar(se), concluirse — *vt* : terminar, poner fin a
termination [ˌtərməˈneɪʃən] *n* : cese *m,* terminación *f*
terminology [ˌtərməˈnɑlədʒi] *n, pl* **-gies** : terminología *f*
terminus [ˈtərmənəs] *n, pl* **-ni** [-ˌnaɪ] *or* **-nuses 1** END : término *m,* fin *m* **2** : terminal *f* (de transporte público)
termite [ˈtərˌmaɪt] *n* : termita *f*
tern [ˈtərn] *n* : golondrina *f* de mar
terrace[1] [ˈtɛrəs] *vt* **-raced; -racing** : formar en terrazas, disponer en bancales
terrace[2] *n* **1** PATIO : terraza *f,* patio *m* **2** : terraplén *m,* terraza *f,* bancal *m* (en agricultura)
terra–cotta [ˌtɛrəˈkɑt̬ə] *n* : terracota *f*
terrain [təˈreɪn] *n* : terreno *m*
terrapin [ˈtɛrəpɪn] *n* : galápago *m* norteamericano
terrarium [təˈræriəm] *n, pl* **-ia** [-iə] *or* **-iums** : terrario *m*
terrestrial [təˈrɛstriəl] *adj* : terrestre
terrible [ˈtɛrəbəl] *adj* : atroz, horrible, terrible
terribly [ˈtɛrəbli] *adv* **1** BADLY : muy mal **2** EXTREMELY : terriblemente, extremadamente
terrier [ˈtɛriər] *n* : terrier *mf*
terrific [təˈrɪfɪk] *adj* **1** FRIGHTFUL : aterrador **2** EXTRAORDINARY : extraordinario, excepcional **3** EXCELLENT : excelente, estupendo
terrify [ˈtɛrəˌfaɪ] *vt* **-fied; -fying** : aterrorizar, aterrar, espantar

terrifying [ˈtɛrəˌfaɪɪŋ] *adj* : espantoso, aterrador
territory [ˈtɛrəˌtori] *n, pl* **-ries** : territorio *m* — **territorial** [ˌtɛrəˈtoriəl] *adj*
terror [ˈtɛrər] *n* : terror *m*
terrorism [ˈtɛrərˌɪzəm] *n* : terrorismo *m*
terrorist[1] [ˈtɛrərɪst] *adj* : terrorista
terrorist[2] *n* : terrorista *mf*
terrorize [ˈtɛrərˌaɪz] *vt* **-ized; -izing** : aterrorizar
terry [ˈtɛri] *n, pl* **-ries** *or* **terry cloth** : (tela de) toalla *f*
terse [ˈtərs] *adj* **terser; tersest** : lacónico, conciso, seco — **tersely** *adv*
tertiary [ˈtərʃiˌɛri] *adj* : terciario
test[1] [ˈtɛst] *vt* : examinar, evaluar — *vi* : hacer pruebas
test[2] *n* : prueba *f,* examen *m,* test *m* <to put to the test : poner a prueba>
testament [ˈtɛstəmənt] *n* **1** WILL : testamento *m* **2** : Testamento *m* (en la Biblia) <the Old Testament : el Antiguo Testamento>
testicle [ˈtɛstɪkəl] *n* : testículo *m*
testify [ˈtɛstəˌfaɪ] *v* **-fied; -fying** *vi* : testificar, atestar, testimoniar — *vt* : testificar
testimonial [ˌtɛstəˈmoːniəl] *n* **1** REFERENCE : recomendación *f* **2** TRIBUTE : homenaje *m,* tributo *m*
testimony [ˈtɛstəˌmoːni] *n, pl* **-nies** : testimonio *m,* declaración *f*
test tube *n* : probeta *f,* tubo *m* de ensayo
testy [ˈtɛsti] *adj* **-tier; -est** : irritable
tetanus [ˈtɛtənəs] *n* : tétano *m,* tétanos *m*
tête–à–tête [ˌtɛtəˈtɛt, ˌteɪtəˈteɪt] *n* : conversación *f* en privado
tether[1] [ˈtɛðər] *vt* : atar (con una cuerda), amarrar
tether[2] *n* : atadura *f,* cadena *f,* correa *f*
text [ˈtɛkst] *n* **1** : texto *m* **2** TOPIC : tema *m* **3** → **textbook**
textbook [ˈtɛkstˌbʊk] *n* : libro *m* de texto
textile [ˈtɛkˌstaɪl, ˈtɛkstəl] *n* : textil *m,* tela *f* <the textile industry : la industria textil>
textual [ˈtɛkstʃʊəl] *adj* : textual
texture [ˈtɛkstʃər] *n* : textura *f*
than[1] [ˈðæn] *conj* : que, de <it's worth more than that : vale más que eso> <more than you think : más de lo que piensas>
than[2] *prep* : que, de <you're better than he is : eres mejor que él> <more than once : más de una vez>
thank [ˈθæŋk] *vt* : agradecer, darle (las) gracias (a alguien) <thank you! : ¡gracias!> <I thanked her for the present : le di las gracias por el regalo> <I thank you for your help : le agradezco su ayuda>
thankful [ˈθæŋkfəl] *adj* : agradecido
thankfully [ˈθæŋkfəli] *adv* **1** GRATEFULLY : con agradecimiento **2** FORTUNATELY : afortunadamente, por suerte <thankfully, it's over : se acabó, gracias a Dios>
thankfulness [ˈθæŋkfəlnəs] *n* : agradecimiento *m,* gratitud *f*
thankless [ˈθæŋkləs] *adj* : ingrato <a thankless task : un trabajo ingrato>
thanks [ˈθæŋks] *npl* **1** : agradecimiento *m* **2 thanks!** : ¡gracias!
Thanksgiving [θæŋksˈgɪvɪŋ, ˈθæŋksˌ-] *n* : el día de Acción de Gracias (fiesta estadounidense)
that[1] [ˈðæt] *adv (in negative constructions)* : tan <it's not that expensive : no es tan caro> <not that much : no tanto>
that[2] *adj, pl* **those** : ese, esa, aquel, aquella <do you see those children? : ¿ves a aquellos niños?>
that[3] *conj & pron* : que <he said that he was afraid : dijo que tenía miedo> <the book that he wrote : el libro que escribió>
that[4] *pron, pl* **those** [ˈðoːz] **1** : ése, ésa, eso <that's my father : ése es mi padre> <those are the ones he likes : ésos son los que le gustan> <what's that? : ¿qué es eso?> **2** (*referring to more distant objects or time*) : aquél, aquélla, aquello <those are maples and these are elms : aquéllos son arces y éstos son olmos> <that came to an end : aquello se acabó>
thatch[1] [ˈθætʃ] *vt* : cubrir o techar con paja
thatch[2] *n* : paja *f* (usada para techos)
thaw[1] [ˈθɔ] *vt* : descongelar — *vi* : derretirse (dícese de la nieve), descongelarse (dícese de los alimentos)
thaw[2] *n* : deshielo *m*
the[1] [ðə, *before vowel sounds usu* ðiː] *adv* **1** (*used to indicate comparison*) <the sooner the better : cuanto más pronto, mejor> <she likes this one the best : éste es el que más le gusta> **2** (*used as a conjunction*) : cuanto <the more I learn, the less I understand : cuanto más aprendo, menos entiendo>
the[2] *art* : el, la, los, las <the gloves : los guantes> <the suitcase : la maleta> <forty cookies to the box : cuarenta galletas por caja>
theater *or* **theatre** [ˈθiːətər] *n* **1** : teatro *m* (edificio) **2** DRAMA : teatro *m,* drama *m*
theatrical [θiˈætrɪkəl] *adj* : teatral, dramático
thee [ˈðiː] *pron* : te, ti
theft [ˈθɛft] *n* : robo *m,* hurto *m*
their [ˈðɛr] *adj* : su <their friends : sus amigos>
theirs [ˈðɛrz] *pron* : (el) suyo, (la) suya, (los) suyos, (las) suyas <they came for theirs : vinieron por el suyo> <theirs is bigger : la suya es más grande, la de ellos es más grande> <a brother of theirs : un hermano suyo, un hermano de ellos>

them [ˈðɛm] *pron* **1** (*as a direct object*) : los (*Spain sometimes* les), las <I know them : los conozco> **2** (*as indirect object*) : les, se <I sent them a letter : les mandé una carta> <give it to them : dáselo (a ellos)> **3** (*as object of a preposition*) : ellos, ellas <go with them : ve con ellos> **4** (*for emphasis*) : ellos, ellas <I wasn't expecting them : no los esperaba a ellos>

theme [ˈθiːm] *n* **1** SUBJECT, TOPIC : tema *m* **2** COMPOSITION : composición *f*, trabajo *m* (escrito) **3** : tema *m* (en música)

themselves [ðəmˈsɛlvz, ðɛm-] *pron* **1** (*as a reflexive*) : se, sí <they enjoyed themselves : se divirtieron> <they divided it among themselves : lo repartieron entre sí, se lo repartieron> **2** (*for emphasis*) : ellos mismos, ellas mismas <they built it themselves : ellas mismas lo construyeron>

then[1] [ˈðɛn] *adv* **1** : entonces, en ese tiempo <I was sixteen then : tenía entonces dieciséis años> <since then : desde entonces> **2** NEXT : después, luego <we'll go to Toronto, then to Winnipeg : iremos a Toronto, y luego a Winnipeg> **3** BESIDES : además, aparte <then there's the tax : y aparte está el impuesto> **4** : entonces, en ese caso <if you like music, then you should attend : si te gusta la música, entonces deberías asistir>

then[2] *adj* : entonces <the then governor of Georgia : el entonces gobernador de Georgia>

thence [ˈðɛnts, ˈθɛnts] *adv* : de ahí, de ahí en adelante

theologian [ˌθiːəˈloːdʒən] *n* : teólogo *m*, -ga *f*

theological [ˌθiːəˈlɑdʒɪkəl] *adj* : teológico

theology [θiˈɑlədʒi] *n, pl* **-gies** : teología *f*

theorem [ˈθiːərəm, ˈθɪrəm] *n* : teorema *m*

theoretical [ˌθiːəˈrɛtɪkəl] *adj* : teórico — **theoretically** *adv*

theorize [ˈθiːəˌraɪz] *vi* **-rized; -rizing** : teorizar

theory [ˈθiːəri, ˈθɪri] *n, pl* **-ries** : teoría *f*

therapeutic [ˌθɛrəˈpjuːtɪk] *adj* : terapéutico — **therapeutically** *adv*

therapist [ˈθɛrəpɪst] *n* : terapeuta *mf*

therapy [ˈθɛrəpi] *n, pl* **-pies** : terapia *f*

there[1] [ˈðær] *adv* **1** : ahí, allí, allá <stand over there : párate ahí> <over there : por allí, por allá> <who's there? : ¿quién es?> **2** : ahí, en esto, en eso <there is where we disagree : en eso es donde no estamos de acuerdo>

there[2] *pron* **1** (*introducing a sentence or clause*) <there comes a time to decide : llega un momento en que tiene uno que decidir> **2 there is, there are** : hay <there are many children here : aquí hay muchos niños> <there's a good hotel downtown : hay un buen hotel en el centro>

thereabouts [ðærəˈbaʊts, ˈðærəˌ-] *or* **thereabout** [-ˈbaʊt, -ˌbaʊt] *adv* **or thereabouts** : por ahí, más o menos <at five o'clock or thereabouts : por ahí de las cinco>

thereafter [ðærˈæftər] *adv* : después <shortly thereafter : poco después>

thereby [ðærˈbaɪ, ˈðærˌbaɪ] *adv* : de tal modo, de ese manera, así

therefore [ˈðærˌfor] *adv* : por lo tanto, por consiguiente

therein [ðærˈɪn] *adv* **1** : allí adentro, ahí adentro <the contents therein : lo que allí se contiene> **2** : allí, en ese aspecto <therein lies the problem : allí está el problema>

thereof [ðærˈʌv, -ˈɑv] *adv* : de eso, de esto

thereupon [ˈðærəˌpɑn, -ˌpɔn; ˌðærəˈpɑn, -ˈpɔn] *adv* : acto seguido, inmediatamente (después)

therewith [ðærˈwɪð, -ˈwɪθ] *adv* : con eso, con ello

thermal [ˈθərməl] *adj* **1** : térmico (en física) **2** HOT : termal

thermodynamics [ˌθərmodaɪˈnæmɪks] *ns & pl* : termodinámica *f*

thermometer [θərˈmɑmət̬ər] *n* : termómetro *m*

thermos [ˈθərməs] *n* : termo *m*

thermostat [ˈθərməˌstæt] *n* : termostato *m*

thesaurus [θɪˈsɔrəs] *n, pl* **-sauri** [-ˈsɔrˌaɪ] *or* **-sauruses** [-ˈsɔrəsəz] : diccionario *m* de sinónimos

these → **this**

thesis [ˈθiːsɪs] *n, pl* **theses** [ˈθiːˌsiːz] : tesis *f*

they [ˈðeɪ] *pron* : ellos, ellas <they are here : están aquí> <they don't know : ellos no saben>

they'd [ˈðeɪd] (*contraction of* **they had** *or* **they would**) → **have, would**

they'll [ˈðeɪl, ˈðɛl] (*contraction of* **they shall** *or* **they will**) → **shall, will**

they're [ˈðɛr] (*contraction of* **they are**) → **be**

they've [ˈðeɪv] (*contraction of* **they have**) → **have**

thiamine [ˈθaɪəmɪn, -ˌmiːn] *n* : tiamina *f*

thick[1] [ˈθɪk] *adj* **1** : grueso <a thick plank : una tabla gruesa> **2** : espeso, denso <thick syrup : jarabe espeso> — **thickly** *adv*

thick[2] *n* **1 in the thick of** : en medio de <in the thick of the battle : en lo más reñido de la batalla> **2 through thick and thin** : a las duras y a las maduras

thicken [ˈθɪkən] *vt* : espesar (un líquido) — *vi* : espesarse

thickener [ˈθɪkənər] *n* : espesante *m*

thicket [ˈθɪkət] *n* : matorral *m*, maleza *f*, espesura *f*

thickness [ˈθɪknəs] *n* : grosor *m,* grueso *m,* espesor *m*
thickset [ˈθɪkˈsɛt] *adj* STOCKY : robusto, fornido
thick–skinned [ˈθɪkˈskɪnd] *adj* : poco sensible, que no se ofende fácilmente
thief [ˈθiːf] *n, pl* **thieves** [ˈθiːvz] : ladrón *m,* -drona *f*
thieve [ˈθiːv] *v* **thieved; thieving** : hurtar, robar
thievery [ˈθiːvəri] *n* : hurto *m,* robo *m,* latrocinio *m*
thigh [ˈθaɪ] *n* : muslo *m*
thighbone [ˈθaɪˌboːn] *n* : fémur *m*
thimble [ˈθɪmbəl] *n* : dedal *m*
thin[1] [ˈθɪn] *v* **thinned; thinning** *vt* : hacer menos denso, diluir, aguar (un líquido), enrarecer (un gas) — *vi* : diluirse, aguarse (dícese de un líquido), enrarecerse (dícese de un gas)
thin[2] *adj* **thinner; -est 1** LEAN, SLIM : delgado, esbelto, flaco **2** SPARSE : ralo, escaso <a thin beard : una barba rala> **3** WATERY : claro, aguado, diluido **4** FINE : delgado, fino <thin slices : rebanadas finas>
thing [ˈθɪŋ] *n* **1** AFFAIR, MATTER : cosa *f,* asunto *m* <don't talk about those things : no hables de esas cosas> <how are things? : ¿cómo van las cosas?> **2** ACT, EVENT : cosa *f,* suceso *m,* evento *m* <the flood was a terrible thing : la inundación fue una cosa terrible> **3** OBJECT : cosa *f,* objeto *m* <don't forget your things : no olvides tus cosas>
think [ˈθɪŋk] *v* **thought** [ˈθɔt]; **thinking** *vt* **1** : pensar <I thought to return early : pensaba regresar temprano> **2** BELIEVE : pensar, creer, opinar **3** PONDER : pensar, reflexionar **4** CONCEIVE : ocurrirse, concebir <we've thought up a plan : se nos ha ocurrido un plan> — *vi* **1** REASON : pensar, razonar **2** CONSIDER : pensar, considerar <think of your family first : primero piensa en tu familia>
thinker [ˈθɪŋkər] *n* : pensador *m,* -dora *f*
thinly [ˈθɪnli] *adv* **1** LIGHTLY : ligeramente **2** SPARSELY : escasamente <thinly populated : poco populado> **3** BARELY : apenas
thinness [ˈθɪnnəs] *n* : delgadez *f*
thin–skinned [ˈθɪnˈskɪnd] *adj* : susceptible, muy sensible
third[1] [ˈθərd] *or* **thirdly** [-li] *adv* : en tercer lugar <she came in third : llegó en tercer lugar>
third[2] *adj* : tercero <the third day : el tercer día>
third[3] *n* **1** : tercero *m,* -ra *f* (en una serie) **2** : tercero *m,* tercera parte *f*
third world *n* **the Third World** : el Tercer Mundo *m*
thirst[1] [ˈθərst] *vi* **1** : tener sed **2 to thirst for** DESIRE : tener sed de, estar sediento de
thirst[2] *n* : sed *f*
thirsty [ˈθərsti] *adj* **thirstier; -est** : sediento, que tiene sed <I'm thirsty : tengo sed>
thirteen[1] [ˌθərˈtiːn] *adj* : trece
thirteen[2] *n* : trece *m*
thirteenth[1] [ˌθərˈtiːnθ] *adj* : décimo tercero
thirteenth[2] *n* **1** : decimotercero *m,* -ra *f* (en una serie) **2** : treceavo *m,* treceava parte *f*
thirtieth[1] [ˈθərtiəθ] *adj* : trigésimo
thirtieth[2] *n* **1** : trigésimo *m,* -ma *f* (en una serie) **2** : treintavo *m,* treintava parte *f*
thirty[1] [ˈθərti] *adj* : treinta
thirty[2] *n, pl* **thirties** : treinta *m*
this[1] [ˈðɪs] *adv* : así, a tal punto <this big : así de grande>
this[2] *adj, pl* **these** [ˈðiːz] : este <these things : estas cosas> <read this book : lee este libro>
this[3] *pron, pl* **these** : esto <what's this? : ¿qué es esto?> <this wasn't here yesterday : esto no estaba aquí ayer>
thistle [ˈθɪsəl] *n* : cardo *m*
thong [ˈθɔŋ] *n* **1** STRAP : correa *f,* tira *f* **2** *or* **thong sandal** : chancla *f,* chancleta *f*
thorax [ˈθorˌæks] *n, pl* **-raxes** *or* **-races** [ˈθorəˌsiːz] : tórax *m*
thorn [ˈθɔrn] *n* : espina *f*
thorny [ˈθɔrni] *adj* **thornier; -est** : espinoso
thorough [ˈθəroː] *adj* **1** CONSCIENTIOUS : concienzudo, meticuloso **2** COMPLETE : absoluto, completo — **thoroughly** *adv*
thoroughbred [ˈθəroˌbrɛd] *adj* : de pura sangre (dícese de un caballo)
Thoroughbred *n or* **Thoroughbred horse** : pura sangre *mf*
thoroughfare [ˈθəroˌfær] *n* : vía *f* pública, carretera *f*
thoroughness [ˈθəronəs] *n* : esmero *m,* meticulosidad *f*
those → **that**
thou [ˈðaʊ] *pron* : tú
though[1] [ˈðoː] *adv* **1** HOWEVER, NEVERTHELESS : sin embargo, no obstante **2 as ~** : como si <as though nothing had happened : como si nada hubiera pasado>
though[2] *conj* : aunque, a pesar de <though it was raining, we went out : salimos a pesar de la lluvia>
thought[1] → **think**
thought[2] [ˈθɔt] *n* **1** THINKING : pensamiento *m,* ideas *fpl* <Western thought : el pensamiento occidental> **2** COGITATION : pensamiento *m,* reflexión *f,* raciocinio *m* **3** IDEA : idea *f,* ocurrencia *f* <it was just a thought : fue sólo una idea>
thoughtful [ˈθɔtfəl] *adj* **1** PENSIVE : pensativo, meditabundo **2** CONSIDERATE : considerado, atento, cortés — **thoughtfully** *adv*
thoughtfulness [ˈθɔtfəlnəs] *n* : consideración *f,* atención *f,* cortesía *f*

thoughtless ['θɔtləs] *adj* **1** CARELESS : descuidado, negligente **2** INCONSIDERATE : desconsiderado — **thoughtlessly** *adv*

thousand1 ['θaʊzənd] *adj* : mil

thousand2 *n, pl* **-sands** *or* **-sand** : mil *m*

thousandth1 ['θaʊzəntθ] *adj* : milésimo

thousandth2 *n* **1** : milésimo *m*, -ma *f* (en una serie) **2** : milésimo *m*, milésima parte *f*

thrash ['θræʃ] *vt* **1** → **thresh 2** BEAT : golpear, azotar, darle una paliza (a alguien) **3** FLAIL : sacudir, agitar bruscamente

thread1 ['θrɛd] *vt* **1** : enhilar, enhebrar (una aguja) **2** STRING : ensartar (cuentas en un hilo) **3 to thread one's way** : abrirse paso

thread2 *n* **1** : hilo *m*, hebra *f* <needle and thread : aguja e hilo> <the thread of an argument : el hilo de un debate> **2** : rosca *f*, filete *m* (de un tornillo)

threadbare ['θrɛd'bær] *adj* **1** SHABBY, WORN : raído, gastado **2** TRITE : trillado, tópico, manido

threat ['θrɛt] *n* : amenaza *f*

threaten ['θrɛtən] *v* : amenazar

threatening ['θrɛtənɪŋ] *adj* : amenazador — **threateningly** *adv*

three1 ['θriː] *adj* : tres

three2 *n* : tres *m*

threefold ['θriːˌfoːld] *adj* TRIPLE : triple

three hundred1 *adj* : trescientos

three hundred2 *n* : trescientos *m*

threescore ['θriː'skor] *adj* SIXTY : sesenta

thresh ['θrɛʃ] *vt* : trillar (grano)

thresher ['θrɛʃər] *n* : trilladora *f*

threshold ['θrɛʃˌhoːld, -ˌoːld] *n* : umbral *m*

threw → **throw**1

thrice ['θraɪs] *adv* : tres veces

thrift ['θrɪft] *n* : economía *f*, frugalidad *f*

thriftless ['θrɪftləs] *adj* : despilfarrador, manirroto

thrifty ['θrɪfti] *adj* **thriftier; -est** : económico, frugal — **thriftily** ['θrɪftəli] *adv*

thrill1 ['θrɪl] *vt* : emocionar — *vi* **to thrill to** : dejarse conmover por, estremecerse con

thrill2 *n* : emoción *f*

thriller ['θrɪlər] *n* **1** : evento *m* emocionante **2** : obra *f* de suspenso

thrilling ['θrɪlɪŋ] *adj* : emocionante, excitante

thrive ['θraɪv] *vi* **throve** ['θroːv] *or* **thrived; thriven** ['θrɪvən] **1** FLOURISH : florecer, crecer abundantemente **2** PROSPER : prosperar

throat ['θroːt] *n* : garganta *f*

throaty ['θroːti] *adj* **throatier; -est** : ronco (dícese de la voz)

throb1 ['θrab] *vi* **throbbed; throbbing** : palpitar, latir (dícese del corazón), vibrar (dícese de un motor, etc.)

throb2 *n* : palpitación *f*, latido *m*, vibración *f*

throe ['θroː] *n* **1** PAIN, SPASM : espasmo *m*, dolor *m* <the throes of childbirth : los dolores de parto> **2 throes** *npl* : lucha *f* larga y ardua <in the throes of : en el medio de>

throne ['θroːn] *n* : trono *m*

throng1 ['θrɔŋ] *vt* CROWD : atestar, atiborrar, llenar — *vi* : aglomerarse, amontonarse

throng2 *n* : muchedumbre *f*, gentío *m*, multitud *f*

throttle1 ['θratəl] *vt* **-tled; -tling 1** STRANGLE : estrangular, ahogar **2 to throttle down** : desacelerar (un motor)

throttle2 *n* **1** : válvula *f* reguladora **2 at full throttle** : a toda máquina

through1 ['θruː] *adv* **1** : a través, de un lado a otro <let them through : déjenlos pasar> **2** : de principio a fin <she read the book through : leyó el libro de principio a fin> **3** COMPLETELY : completamente <soaked through : completamente empapado>

through2 *adj* **1** DIRECT : directo <a through train : un tren directo> **2** FINISHED : terminado, acabado <we're through : hemos terminado>

through3 *prep* **1** : a través de, por <through the door : por la puerta> <a road through the woods : un camino que atraviesa el bosque> **2** BETWEEN : entre <a path through the trees : un sendero entre los árboles> **3** BECAUSE OF : a causa de, como consecuencia de **4** (*in expressions of time*) <through the night : durante la noche> <to go through an experience : pasar por una experiencia> **5** : a, hasta <from Monday through Friday : de lunes a viernes>

throughout1 [θruː'aʊt] *adv* **1** EVERYWHERE : por todas partes **2** THROUGH : desde el principio hasta el fin de (algo)

throughout2 *prep* **1** : en todas partes de, a través de <throughout the United States : en todo Estados Unidos> **2** : de principio a fin de, durante <throughout the winter : durante todo el invierno>

throve → **thrive**

throw1 ['θroː] *vt* **threw** ['θruː]; **thrown** ['θroːn]; **throwing 1** TOSS : tirar, lanzar, echar, arrojar, aventar *Col, Mex* <to throw a ball : tirar una pelota> **2** UNSEAT : desmontar (a un jinete) **3** CAST : proyectar <it threw a long shadow : proyectó una sombra larga> **4 to throw a party** : dar una fiesta **5 to throw into confusion** : desconcertar **6 to throw out** DISCARD : botar, tirar (en la basura)

throw[2] *n* TOSS : tiro *m,* tirada *f,* lanzamiento *m,* lance *m* (de dados)
thrower ['θroːər] *n* : lanzador *m,* -dora *f*
throw up *v* VOMIT : vomitar, devolver
thrush ['θrʌʃ] *n* : tordo *m,* zorzal *m*
thrust[1] ['θrʌst] *vt* **thrust; thrusting 1** SHOVE : empujar bruscamente **2** PLUNGE, STAB : apuñalar, clavar <he thrust a dagger into her heart : la apuñaló en el corazón> **3 to thrust one's way** : abrirse paso **4 to thrust upon** : imponer a
thrust[2] *n* **1** PUSH, SHOVE : empujón *m,* empellón *m* **2** LUNGE : estocada *f* (en esgrima) **3** IMPETUS : ímpetu *m,* impulso *m,* propulsión *f* (de un motor)
thud[1] ['θʌd] *vi* **thudded; thudding** : producir un ruido sordo
thud[2] *n* : ruido *m* sordo (que produce un objeto al caer)
thug ['θʌg] *n* : matón *m*
thumb[1] ['θʌm] *vt* : hojear (con el pulgar)
thumb[2] *n* : pulgar *m,* dedo *m* pulgar
thumbnail ['θʌm,neɪl] *n* : uña *f* del pulgar
thumbtack ['θʌm,tæk] *n* : tachuela *f,* chinche *f*
thump[1] ['θʌmp] *vt* POUND : golpear, aporrear — *vi* : latir con vehemencia (dícese del corazón)
thump[2] *n* THUD : ruido *m* sordo
thunder[1] ['θʌndər] *vi* **1** : tronar <it rained and thundered all night : llovió y tronó durante la noche> **2** BOOM : retumbar, bramar, resonar — *vt* ROAR, SHOUT : decir a gritos, vociferar
thunder[2] *n* : truenos *mpl*
thunderbolt ['θʌndər,boːlt] *n* : rayo *m*
thunderclap ['θʌndər,klæp] *n* : trueno *m*
thunderous ['θʌndərəs] *adj* : atronador, ensordecedor, estruendoso
thundershower ['θʌndər,ʃaʊər] *n* : lluvia *f* con truenos y relámpagos
thunderstorm ['θʌndər,stɔrm] *n* : tormenta *f* con truenos y relámpagos
thunderstruck ['θʌndər,strʌk] *adj* : atónito
Thursday ['θərz,deɪ, -di] *n* : jueves *m*
thus ['ðʌs] *adv* **1** : así, de esta manera **2** SO : hasta (cierto punto) <the weather's been nice thus far : hasta ahora ha hecho buen tiempo> **3** HENCE : por consiguiente, por lo tanto
thwart ['θwɔrt] *vt* : frustrar
thy ['ðaɪ] *adj* : tu
thyme ['taɪm, 'θaɪm] *n* : tomillo *m*
thyroid ['θaɪ,rɔɪd] *n or* **thyroid gland** : tiroides *mf,* glándula *f* tiroidea
thyself [ðaɪ'sɛlf] *pron* : ti, ti mismo
tiara [ti'ærə, -'ɑr-] *n* : diadema *f*
tibia ['tɪbiə] *n, pl* **-iae** [-bi,iː] : tibia *f*
tic ['tɪk] *n* : tic *m*
tick[1] ['tɪk] *vi* **1** : hacer tictac **2** OPERATE, RUN : operar, andar (dícese de un mecanismo) <what makes him tick? : ¿qué es lo que lo mueve?> — *vt or* **to tick off** CHECK : marcar
tick[2] *n* **1** : tictac *m* (de un reloj) **2** CHECK : marca *f* **3** : garrapata *f* (insecto)
ticket[1] ['tɪkət] *vt* LABEL : etiquetar
ticket[2] *n* **1** : boleto *m,* entrada *f* (de un espectáculo), pasaje *m* (de avión, tren, etc.) **2** SLATE : lista *f* de candidatos
tickle[1] ['tɪkəl] *v* **-led; -ling** *vt* **1** AMUSE : divertir, hacerle gracia (a alguien) **2** : hacerle cosquillas (a alguien) <don't tickle me! : ¡no me hagas cosquillas!> — *vi* : picar
tickle[2] *n* : cosquilla *f*
ticklish ['tɪkəlɪʃ] *adj* **1** : cosquilloso (dícese de una persona) **2** DELICATE, TRICKY : delicado, peliagudo
tidal ['taɪdəl] *adj* : de marea, relativo a la marea
tidal wave *n* : maremoto *m*
tidbit ['tɪd,bɪt] *n* **1** BITE, SNACK : bocado *m,* golosina *f* **2** : dato *m* o noticia *f* interesante <useful tidbits of information : informaciones útiles>
tide[1] ['taɪd] *vt* **tided; tiding** *or* **to tide over** : proveer lo necesario para aguantar una dificultad <this money will tide you over until you find work : este dinero te mantendrá hasta que encuentres empleo>
tide[2] *n* **1** : marea *f* **2** CURRENT : corriente *f* (de eventos, opiniones, etc.)
tidily ['taɪdəli] *adv* : ordenadamente
tidiness ['taɪdinəs] *n* : aseo *m,* limpieza *f,* orden *m*
tidings ['taɪdɪŋz] *npl* : nuevas *fpl*
tidy[1] ['taɪdi] *vt* **-died; -dying** : asear, limpiar, poner en orden
tidy[2] *adj* **-dier; -est 1** CLEAN, NEAT : limpio, aseado, en orden **2** SUBSTANTIAL : grande, considerable <a tidy sum : una suma considerable>
tie[1] ['taɪ] *v* **tied; tying** *or* **tieing** *vt* **1** : atar, amarrar <to tie a knot : atar un nudo> <to tie one's shoelaces : atarse los cordones> **2** BIND, UNITE : ligar, atar **3** : empatar <they tied the score : empataron el marcador> — *vi* : empatar <the two teams were tied : los dos equipos empataron>
tie[2] *n* **1** : ligadura *f,* cuerda *f,* cordón *m* (para atar algo) **2** BOND, LINK : atadura *f,* ligadura *f,* vínculo *m,* lazo *m* <family ties : lazos familiares> **3** *or* **railroad tie** : traviesa *f* **4** DRAW : empate *m* (en deportes) **5** NECKTIE : corbata *f*
tier ['tɪr] *n* : hilera *f,* escalón *m*
tiff ['tɪf] *n* : disgusto *m,* disputa *f*
tiger ['taɪgər] *n* : tigre *m*
tight[1] ['taɪt] *adv* TIGHTLY : bien, fuerte <shut it tight : ciérralo bien>
tight[2] *adj* **1** : bien cerrado, hermético <a tight seal : un cierre hermético> **2** STRICT : estricto, severo **3** TAUT : tirante, tenso **4** SNUG : apretado, ajustado, ceñido <a tight dress : un vestido ceñido> **5** DIFFICULT : difícil <to be in a tight spot : estar en un aprieto> **6** STINGY : apretado, avaro, agarrado

fam **7** CLOSE **:** reñido <a tight game : un juego reñido> **8** SCARCE **:** escaso <money is tight : escasea el dinero>

tighten [ˈtaɪtən] *vt* **:** tensar (una cuerda, etc.), apretar (un nudo, un tornillo, etc.), apretarse (el cinturón), reforzar (las reglas)

tightly [ˈtaɪtli] *adv* **:** bien, fuerte

tightness [ˈtaɪtnəs] *n* **:** lo apretado, lo tenso, tensión *f*

tightrope [ˈtaɪtˌroːp] *n* **:** cuerda *f* floja

tights [ˈtaɪts] *npl* **:** leotardo *m,* malla *f*

tightwad [ˈtaɪtˌwɑd] *n* **:** avaro *m,* -ra *f;* tacaño *m,* -ña *f*

tigress [ˈtaɪgrəs] *n* **:** tigresa *f*

tile[1] [ˈtaɪl] *vt* **tiled; tiling :** embaldosar (un piso), revestir de azulejos (una pared), tejar (un techo)

tile[2] *n* **1** *or* **floor tile :** losa *f,* baldosa *f,* mosaico *m Mex* (de un piso) **2 :** azulejo *m* (de una pared) **3 :** teja *f* (de un techo)

till[1] [ˈtɪl] *vt* **:** cultivar, labrar

till[2] *n* **:** caja *f,* caja *f* registradora

till[3] *prep & conj* → **until**

tiller [ˈtɪlər] *n* **1 :** cultivador *m,* -dora *f* (de la tierra) **2 :** caña *f* del timón (de un barco)

tilt[1] [ˈtɪlt] *vt* **:** ladear, inclinar — *vi* **:** ladearse, inclinarse

tilt[2] *n* **1** SLANT **:** inclinación *f* **2 at full tilt :** a toda velocidad

timber [ˈtɪmbər] *n* **1 :** madera *f* (para construcción) **2** BEAM **:** viga *f*

timberland [ˈtɪmbərˌlænd] *n* **:** bosque *m* maderero

timbre [ˈtæmbər, ˈtɪm-] *n* **:** timbre *m*

time[1] [ˈtaɪm] *vt* **timed; timing 1** SCHEDULE **:** fijar la hora de, calcular el momento oportuno para **2** CLOCK **:** cronometrar, medir el tiempo de (una competencia, etc.)

time[2] *n* **1 :** tiempo *m* <the passing of time : el paso del tiempo> <she doesn't have time : no tiene tiempo> **2** MOMENT **:** tiempo *m,* momento *m* <this is not the time to bring it up : no es el momento de sacar el tema> **3 :** vez *f* <she called you three times : te llamó tres veces> <three times greater : tres veces mayor> **4** AGE **:** tiempo *m,* era *f* <in your grandparents' time : en el tiempo de tus abuelos> **5** TEMPO **:** tiempo *m,* ritmo *m* (en música) **6 :** hora *f* <what time is it? : ¿qué hora es?> <at the usual time : a la hora acostumbrada> <to keep time : ir a la hora> <to lose time : atrasar> **7** EXPERIENCE **:** rato *m,* experiencia *f* <we had a nice time together : pasamos juntos un rato agradable> <to have a rough time : pasarlo mal> <have a good time! : ¡que se diviertan!> **8 at times** SOMETIMES **:** a veces **9 for the time being :** por el momento, de momento **10 from time to time** OCCASIONALLY **:** de vez en cuando **11 in time** PUNCTUALLY **:** a tiempo **12 in time** EVENTUALLY **:** con el tiempo **13 time after time :** una y otra vez

timekeeper [ˈtaɪmˌkiːpər] *n* **:** cronometrador *m,* -dora *f*

timeless [ˈtaɪmləs] *adj* **:** eterno

timely [ˈtaɪmli] *adj* **-lier; -est :** oportuno

timepiece [ˈtaɪmˌpiːs] *n* **:** reloj *m*

timer [ˈtaɪmər] *n* **:** temporizador *m,* cronómetro *m*

times [ˈtaɪmz] *prep* **:** por <3 times 4 is 12 : 3 por 4 son 12>

timetable [ˈtaɪmˌteɪbəl] *n* **:** horario *m*

timid [ˈtɪmɪd] *adj* **:** tímido — **timidly** *adv*

timidity [təˈmɪdət̬i] *n* **:** timidez *f*

timorous [ˈtɪmərəs] *adj* **:** timorato, miedoso

timpani [ˈtɪmpəni] *npl* **:** timbales *mpl*

tin [ˈtɪn] *n* **1 :** estaño *m,* hojalata *f* (metal) **2** CAN **:** lata *f,* bote *m,* envase *m*

tincture [ˈtɪŋktʃər] *n* **:** tintura *f*

tinder [ˈtɪndər] *n* **:** yesca *f*

tine [ˈtaɪn] *n* **:** diente *m* (de un tenedor, etc.)

tinfoil [ˈtɪnˌfɔɪl] *n* **:** papel *m* (de) aluminio

tinge[1] [ˈtɪndʒ] *vt* **tinged; tingeing** *or* **tinging** [ˈtɪndʒɪŋ] TINT **:** matizar, teñir ligeramente

tinge[2] *n* **1** TINT **:** matiz *m,* tinte *m* sutil **2** TOUCH **:** dejo *m,* sensación *f* ligera

tingle[1] [ˈtɪŋgəl] *vi* **-gled; -gling :** sentir (un) hormigueo, sentir (un) cosquilleo

tingle[2] *n* **:** hormigueo *m,* cosquilleo *m*

tinker [ˈtɪŋkər] *vi* **to tinker with :** arreglar con pequeños ajustes, toquetear (con intento de arreglar)

tinkle[1] [ˈtɪŋkəl] *vi* **-kled; -kling :** tintinear

tinkle[2] *n* **:** tintineo *m*

tinsel [ˈtɪntsəl] *n* **:** oropel *m*

tint[1] [ˈtɪnt] *vt* **:** teñir, colorar

tint[2] *n* **:** tinte *m*

tiny [ˈtaɪni] *adj* **-nier; -est :** diminuto, minúsculo

tip[1] [ˈtɪp] *v* **tipped; tipping** *vt* **1** *or* **to tip over :** volcar, voltear, hacer caer **2** TILT **:** ladear, inclinar <to tip one's hat : saludar con el sombrero> **3** TAP **:** tocar, golpear ligeramente **4 :** darle una propina (a un mesero, etc.) <I tipped him $5 : le di $5 de propina> **5 :** adornar o cubrir la punta de <wings tipped in red : alas que tienen las puntas rojas> **6 to tip off :** dar información a — *vi* TILT **:** ladearse, inclinarse

tip[2] *n* **1** END, POINT **:** punta *f,* extremo *m* <on the tip of one's tongue : en la punta de la lengua> **2** GRATUITY **:** propina *f* **3** ADVICE, INFORMATION **:** consejo *m,* información *f* (confidencial)

tip–off [ˈtɪpˌɔf] *n* **1** SIGN **:** indicación *f,* señal *f* **2** TIP **:** información *f* (confidencial)

tipple [ˈtɪpəl] *vi* **-pled; -pling** : tomarse unas copas
tipsy [ˈtɪpsi] *adj* **-sier; -est** : achispado
tiptoe[1] [ˈtɪpˌtoː] *vi* **-toed; -toeing** : caminar de puntillas
tiptoe[2] *adv* : de puntillas
tiptoe[3] *n* : punta *f* del pie
tip–top[1] [ˈtɪpˈtɑp, -ˌtɑp] *adj* EXCELLENT : excelente
tip–top[2] *n* SUMMIT : cumbre *f,* cima *f*
tirade [ˈtaɪˌreɪd] *n* : diatriba *f*
tire[1] [ˈtaɪr] *v* **tired; tiring** *vt* : cansar, agotar, fatigar — *vi* : cansarse
tire[2] *n* : llanta *f,* neumático *m,* goma *f*
tired [ˈtaɪrd] *adj* : cansado, agotado, fatigado <to get tired : cansarse>
tireless [ˈtaɪrləs] *adj* : incansable, infatigable — **tirelessly** *adv*
tiresome [ˈtaɪrsəm] *adj* : fastidioso, pesado, tedioso — **tiresomely** *adv*
tissue [ˈtɪˌʃuː] *n* **1** : pañuelo *m* de papel **2** : tejido *m* <lung tissue : tejido pulmonar>
titanic [taɪˈtænɪk, tə-] *adj* GIGANTIC : titánico, gigantesco
titanium [taɪˈteɪniəm, tə-] *n* : titanio *m*
titillate [ˈtɪtəlˌeɪt] *vt* **-lated; -lating** : excitar, estimular placenteramente
title[1] [ˈtaɪtəl] *vt* **-tled; -tling** : titular, intitular
title[2] *n* : título *m*
titter[1] [ˈtɪtər] *vi* GIGGLE : reírse tontamente
titter[2] *n* : risita *f,* risa *f* tonta
tizzy [ˈtɪzi] *n, pl* **tizzies** : estado *m* agitado o nervioso <I'm all in a tizzy : estoy todo alterado>
TNT [ˌtiːˌɛnˈtiː] *n* : TNT *m*
to[1] [ˈtuː] *adv* **1** : a un estado consciente <to come to : volver en sí> **2 to and fro** : de aquí para allá, de un lado para otro
to[2] *prep* **1** (*indicating a place*) : a <to go to the doctor : ir al médico> <I'm going to John's : voy a la casa de John> **2** TOWARD : a, hacia <two miles to the south : dos millas hacia el sur> **3** ON : en, sobre <apply salve to the wound : póngale ungüento a la herida> **4** UP TO : hasta, a <to a degree : hasta cierto grado> <from head to toe : de pies a cabeza> **5** (*in expressions of time*) <it's quarter to seven : son las siete menos cuarto> **6** UNTIL : a, hasta <from May to December : de mayo a diciembre> **7** (*indicating belonging or possession*) : de, a <the key to the lock : la llave del candado> **8** (*indicating response*) : a <dancing to the rhythm : bailando al compás> **9** (*indicating comparison or proportion*) : a <it's similar to mine : es parecido al mío> <they won 4 to 2 : ganaron 4 a 2> **10** (*indicating agreement or conformity*) : a, de acuerdo con <made to order : hecho a la orden> <to my knowledge : a mi saber> **11** (*indicating inclusion*) : en cada, por <twenty to the box : veinte por caja> **12** (*used to form the infinitive*) <to understand : entender> <to go away : irse>
toad [ˈtoːd] *n* : sapo *m*
toadstool [ˈtoːdˌstuːl] *n* : hongo *m* (no comestible)
toady [ˈtoːdi] *n, pl* **toadies** : adulador *m,* -dora *f*
toast[1] [ˈtoːst] *vt* **1** : tostar (pan) **2** : brindar por <to toast the victors : brindar por los vencedores> **3** WARM : calentar <to toast oneself : calentarse>
toast[2] *n* **1** : pan *m* tostado, tostadas *fpl* **2** : brindis *m* <to propose a toast : proponer un brindis>
toaster [ˈtoːstər] *n* : tostador *m*
tobacco [təˈbækoː] *n, pl* **-cos** : tabaco *m*
toboggan[1] [təˈbɑgən] *vi* : deslizarse en tobogán
toboggan[2] *n* : tobogán *m*
today[1] [təˈdeɪ] *adv* **1** : hoy <she arrives today : hoy llega> **2** NOWADAYS : hoy en día
today[2] *n* : hoy *m* <today is a holiday : hoy es día de fiesta>
toddle [ˈtɑdəl] *vi* **-dled; -dling** : hacer pininos, hacer pinitos
toddler [ˈtɑdələr] *n* : niño *m* pequeño, niña *f* pequeña (que comienza a caminar)
to–do [təˈduː] *n, pl* **to–dos** [-ˈduːz] FUSS : lío *m,* alboroto *m*
toe [ˈtoː] *n* : dedo *m* del pie
toenail [ˈtoːˌneɪl] *n* : uña *f* del pie
toffee *or* **toffy** [ˈtɔfi, ˈtɑ-] *n, pl* **toffees** *or* **toffies** : caramelo *m* elaborado con azúcar y mantequilla
toga [ˈtoːgə] *n* : toga *f*
together [təˈgɛðər] *adv* **1** : juntamente, juntos (el uno con el otro) <Susan and Sarah work together : Susan y Sarah trabajan juntas> **2 ~ with** : junto con
togetherness [təˈgɛðərnəs] *n* : unión *f,* compañerismo *m*
togs [ˈtɑgz, ˈtɔgz] *npl* : ropa *f*
toil[1] [ˈtɔɪl] *vi* : trabajar arduamente
toil[2] *n* : trabajo *m* arduo
toilet [ˈtɔɪlət] *n* **1** : arreglo *m* personal **2** BATHROOM : (cuarto de) baño *m,* servicios *mpl* (públicos), sanitario *m Col, Mex, Ven* **3** : inodoro *m* <to flush the toilet : jalar la cadena>
toilet paper *n* : papel *m* higiénico
toiletries [ˈtɔɪlətriz] *npl* : artículos *mpl* de tocador
token [ˈtoːkən] *n* **1** PROOF, SIGN : prueba *f,* muestra *f,* señal *m* **2** SYMBOL : símbolo *m* **3** SOUVENIR : recuerdo *m* **4** : ficha *f* (para transporte público, etc.)
told → **tell**
tolerable [ˈtɑlərəbəl] *adj* : tolerable — **tolerably** [-bli] *adv*
tolerance [ˈtɑlərənts] *n* : tolerancia *f*
tolerant [ˈtɑlərənt] *adj* : tolerante — **tolerantly** *adv*

tolerate ['tɑlə,reɪt] *vt* **-ated; -ating 1** ACCEPT : tolerar, aceptar **2** BEAR, ENDURE : tolerar, aguantar, soportar
toleration [,tɑlə'reɪʃən] *n* : tolerancia *f*
toll[1] ['to:l] *vt* : tañer, sonar (una campana) — *vi* : sonar, doblar (dícese de las campanas)
toll[2] *n* **1** : peaje *m* (de una carretera, un puente, etc.) **2** CASUALTIES : pérdida *f*, número *m* de víctimas **3** TOLLING : tañido *m* (de campanas)
tollbooth ['to:l,bu:θ] *n* : caseta *f* de peaje
tollgate ['to:l,geɪt] *n* : barrera *f* de peaje
tomahawk ['tɑmə,hɔk] *n* : hacha *f* de guerra (de los indígenas norteamericanos)
tomato [tə'meɪto, -'mɑ-] *n, pl* **-toes** : tomate *m*
tomb ['tu:m] *n* : sepulcro *m*, tumba *f*
tomboy ['tɑm,bɔɪ] *n* : marimacho *mf*; niña *f* que se porta como muchacho
tombstone ['tu:m,sto:n] *n* : lápida *f*
tomcat ['tɑm,kæt] *n* : gato *m* (macho)
tome ['to:m] *n* : tomo *m*
tomorrow[1] [tə'mɑro] *adv* : mañana
tomorrow[2] *n* : mañana *m*
tom–tom ['tɑm,tɑm] *n* : tam-tam *m*
ton ['tən] *n* : tonelada *f*
tone[1] ['to:n] *vt* **toned; toning 1** *or* **to tone down** : atenuar, suavizar, moderar **2** *or* **to tone up** STRENGTHEN : tonificar, vigorizar
tone[2] *n* : tono *m* <in a friendly tone : en tono amistoso> <a greyish tone : un tono grisáceo>
tongs ['tɑŋz, 'tɔŋz] *npl* : tenazas *fpl*
tongue ['tʌŋ] *n* **1** : lengua *f* **2** LANGUAGE : lengua *f*, idioma *m*
tongue–tied ['tʌŋ,taɪd] *adj* **to get tongue–tied** : trabársele la lengua a uno
tonic[1] ['tɑnɪk] *adj* : tónico
tonic[2] *n* **1** : tónico *m* **2** *or* **tonic water** : tónica *f*
tonight[1] [tə'naɪt] *adv* : esta noche
tonight[2] *n* : esta noche *f*
tonsil ['tɑntsəl] *n* : amígdala *f*, angina *f Mex*
tonsillitis [,tɑntsə'laɪtəs] *n* : amigdalitis *f*, anginas *fpl Mex*
too ['tu:] *adv* **1** ALSO : también **2** EXCESSIVELY : demasiado <it's too hot in here : aquí hace demasiado calor>
took → **take**[1]
tool[1] ['tu:l] *vt* **1** : fabricar, confeccionar (con herramientas) **2** EQUIP : instalar maquinaria en (una fábrica)
tool[2] *n* : herramienta *f*
toolbox ['tu:l,bɑks] *n* : caja *f* de herramientas
toot[1] ['tu:t] *vt* : sonar (un claxon o un pito)
toot[2] *n* : pitido *m*, bocinazo *m* (de un claxon)
tooth ['tu:θ] *n, pl* **teeth** ['ti:θ] : diente *m*
toothache ['tu:θ,eɪk] *n* : dolor *m* de muelas
toothbrush ['tu:θ,brʌʃ] *n* : cepillo *m* de dientes
toothless ['tu:θləs] *adj* : desdentado
toothpaste ['tu:θ,peɪst] *n* : pasta *f* de dientes, crema *f* dental, dentífrico *m*
toothpick ['tu:θ,pɪk] *n* : palillo *m* (de dientes), mondadientes *m*
top[1] ['tɑp] *vt* **topped; topping 1** COVER : cubrir, coronar **2** SURPASS : sobrepasar, superar **3** CLEAR : pasar por encima de
top[2] *adj* : superior <the top shelf : la repisa superior> <one of the top lawyers : uno de los mejores abogados>
top[3] *n* **1** : parte *f* superior, cumbre *f*, cima *f* (de un monte, etc.) <to climb to the top : subir a la cumbre> **2** COVER : tapa *f*, cubierta *f* **3** : trompo *m* (juguete) **4 on top of** : encima de
topaz ['to:,pæz] *n* : topacio *m*
topcoat ['tɑp,ko:t] *n* : sobretodo *m*, abrigo *m*
topic ['tɑpɪk] *n* : tema *f*, tópico *m*
topical ['tɑpɪkəl] *adj* : de interés actual
topmost ['tɑp,mo:st] *adj* : más alto
top–notch ['tɑp'nɑtʃ] *adj* : de lo mejor, de primera categoría
topographic [,tɑpə'græfɪk,] *or* **topographical** [-fɪkəl] *adj* : topográfico
topography [tə'pɑgrəfi] *n, pl* **-phies** : topografía *f*
topple ['tɑpəl] *v* **-pled; -pling** *vi* : caerse, venirse abajo — *vt* : volcar, derrocar (un gobierno, etc.)
topsoil ['tɑp,sɔɪl] *n* : capa *f* superior del suelo
topsy–turvy [,tɑpsi'tərvi] *adv & adj* : patas arriba, al revés
torch ['tɔrtʃ] *n* : antorcha *f*
tore → **tear**[1]
torment[1] [tɔr'mɛnt, 'tɔr,-] *vt* : atormentar, torturar, martirizar
torment[2] ['tɔr,mɛnt] *n* : tormento *m*, suplicio *m*, martirio *m*
tormentor [tɔr'mɛntər] *n* : atormentador *m*, -dora *f*
torn → **tear**[1]
tornado [tɔr'neɪdo] *n, pl* **-does** *or* **-dos** : tornado *m*
torpedo[1] [tɔr'pi:do] *vt* : torpedear
torpedo[2] *n, pl* **-does** : torpedo *m*
torpid ['tɔrpɪd] *adj* **1** SLUGGISH : aletargado **2** APATHETIC : apático
torpor ['tɔrpər] *n* : letargo *m*, apatía *f*
torrent ['tɔrənt] *n* : torrente *m*
torrential [tɔ'rɛntʃəl, tə-] *adj* : torrencial
torrid ['tɔrɪd] *adj* : tórrido
torso ['tɔr,so:] *n, pl* **-sos** *or* **-si** [-,si:] : torso *m*
tortilla [tɔr'ti:jə] *n* : tortilla *f*
tortoise ['tɔrtəs] *n* : tortuga *f* (terrestre)
tortoiseshell ['tɔrtəs,ʃɛl] *n* : carey *m*, concha *f*
tortuous ['tɔrtʃʊəs] *adj* : tortuoso

torture[1] [ˈtɔrtʃər] *vt* **-tured; -turing** : torturar, atormentar

torture[2] *n* : tortura *f,* tormento *m* <it was sheer torture! : ¡fue un verdadero suplicio!>

torturer [ˈtɔrtʃərər] *n* : torturador *m,* -dora *f*

toss[1] [ˈtɔs, ˈtɑs] *vt* **1** AGITATE, SHAKE : sacudir, agitar, mezclar (una ensalada) **2** THROW : tirar, echar, lanzar — *vi* : sacudirse, moverse agitadamente <to toss and turn : dar vueltas>

toss[2] *n* THROW : lanzamiento *m,* tiro *m,* tirada *f,* lance *m* (de dados, etc.)

toss–up [ˈtɔs,ʌp] *n* : posibilidad *f* igual <it's a toss-up : quizá sí, quizá no>

tot [ˈtɑt] *n* : pequeño *m,* -ña *f*

total[1] [ˈtoːtəl] *vt* **-taled** *or* **-talled; -taling** *or* **-talling 1** *or* **to total up** ADD : sumar, totalizar **2** AMOUNT TO : ascender a, llegar a

total[2] *adj* : total, completo, absoluto — **totally** *adv*

total[3] *n* : total *m*

totalitarian [toː,tæləˈtɛriən] *adj* : totalitario

totalitarianism [toː,tæləˈtɛriə,nɪzəm] *n* : totalitarismo *m*

totality [toːˈtæləṭi] *n, pl* **-ties** : totalidad *f*

tote [ˈtoːt] *vt* **toted; toting** : cargar, llevar

totem [ˈtoːtəm] *n* : tótem *m*

totter [ˈtɑtər] *vi* : tambalearse

touch[1] [ˈtʌtʃ] *vt* **1** FEEL, HANDLE : tocar, tentar **2** AFFECT, MOVE : conmover, afectar, tocar <his gesture touched our hearts : su gesto nos tocó el corazón> — *vi* : tocarse

touch[2] *n* **1** : tacto *m* (sentido) **2** DETAIL : toque *m,* detalle *m* <a touch of color : un toque de color> **3** BIT : pizca *f,* gota *f,* poco *m* **4** ABILITY : habilidad *f* <to lose one's touch : perder la habilidad> **5** CONTACT : contacto *m,* comunicación *f* <to keep in touch : mantenerse en contacto>

touchdown [ˈtʌtʃ,daʊn] *n* : touchdown *m* (en futbol americano)

touch up *vt* : retocar

touchy [ˈtʌtʃi] *adj* **touchier; -est 1** : sensible, susceptible (dícese de una persona) **2** : delicado <a touchy subject : un tema delicado>

tough[1] [ˈtʌf] *adj* **1** STRONG : fuerte, resistente (dícese de materiales) **2** LEATHERY : correoso <a tough steak : un bistec duro> **3** HARDY : fuerte, robusto (dícese de una persona) **4** STRICT : severo, exigente **5** DIFFICULT : difícil **6** STUBBORN : terco, obstinado

tough[2] *n* : matón *m,* persona *f* ruda y brusca

toughen [ˈtʌfən] *vt* : fortalecer, endurecer — *vi* : endurecerse, hacerse más fuerte

toughness [ˈtʌfnəs] *n* : dureza *f*

toupee [tuːˈpeɪ] *n* : peluquín *m,* bisoñé *m*

tour[1] [ˈtʊr] *vi* : tomar una excursión, viajar — *vt* : recorrer, hacer una gira por

tour[2] *n* **1** : gira *f,* tour *m,* excursión *f* **2 tour of duty** : período *m* de servicio

tourist [ˈtʊrɪst, ˈtər-] *n* : turista *mf*

tournament [ˈtərnəmənt, ˈtʊr-] *n* : torneo *m*

tourniquet [ˈtərnɪkət, ˈtʊr-] *n* : torniquete *m*

tousle [ˈtaʊzəl] *vt* **-sled; -sling** : desarreglar, despeinar (el cabello)

tout [ˈtaʊt] *vt* : promocionar, elogiar (con exageración)

tow[1] [ˈtoː] *vt* : remolcar

tow[2] *n* : remolque *m*

toward [ˈtord, təˈwɔrd] *or* **towards** [ˈtordz, təˈwɔrdz] *prep* **1** (*indicating direction*) : hacia, rumbo a <heading toward town : dirigiéndose rumbo al pueblo> <efforts towards peace : esfuerzos hacia la paz> **2** (*indicating time*) : alrededor de <toward midnight : alrededor de la medianoche> **3** REGARDING : hacia, con respecto a <his attitude toward life : su actitud hacia la vida> **4** FOR : para, como pago parcial de (una compra o deuda)

towel [ˈtaʊəl] *n* : toalla *f*

tower[1] [ˈtaʊər] *vi* **to tower over** : descollar sobre, elevarse sobre, dominar

tower[2] *n* : torre *f*

towering [ˈtaʊərɪŋ] *adj* : altísimo, imponente

town [ˈtaʊn] *n* : pueblo *m,* ciudad *f* (pequeña)

township [ˈtaʊn,ʃɪp] *n* : municipio *m*

tow truck [ˈtoː,trʌk] *n* : grúa *f*

toxic [ˈtɑksɪk] *adj* : tóxico

toxicity [tɑkˈsɪsəṭi] *n, pl* **-ties** : toxicidad *f*

toxin [ˈtɑksɪn] *n* : toxina *f*

toy[1] [ˈtɔɪ] *vi* : juguetear, jugar

toy[2] *adj* : de juguete <a toy rifle : un rifle de juguete>

toy[3] *n* : juguete *m*

trace[1] [ˈtreɪs] *vt* **traced; tracing 1** : calcar (un dibujo, etc.) **2** OUTLINE : delinear, trazar (planes, etc.) **3** TRACK : describir (un curso, una historia) **4** FIND : localizar, ubicar

trace[2] *n* **1** SIGN, TRACK : huella *f,* rastro *m,* indicio *m,* vestigio *m* <he disappeared without a trace : desapareció sin dejar rastro> **2** BIT, HINT : pizca *f,* ápice *m,* dejo *m*

trachea [ˈtreɪkiə] *n, pl* **-cheae** [-ki,iː] : tráquea *f*

tracing paper *n* : papel *m* de calcar

track[1] [ˈtræk] *vt* **1** TRAIL : seguir la pista de, rastrear **2** : dejar huellas de <he tracked mud all over : dejó huellas de lodo por todas partes>

track[2] *n* **1** : rastro *m,* huella *f* (de animales), pista *f* (de personas) **2** PATH : pista *f,* sendero *m,* camino *m* **3** *or* **railroad track** : vía *f* (férrea) **4** → **racetrack 5** : oruga *f* (de un tanque,

etc.) **6** : pista *f* (deporte) **7 to keep track of** : llevar la cuenta de
track–and–field [ˈtrækənd'fiːld] *adj* : de pista y campo
tract [ˈtrækt] *n* **1** AREA : terreno *m*, extensión *f*, área *f* **2** : tracto *m* <digestive tract : tracto digestivo> **3** PAMPHLET : panfleto *m*, folleto *m*
traction [ˈtrækʃən] *n* : tracción *f*
tractor [ˈtræktər] *n* **1** : tractor *m* (vehículo agrícola) **2** TRUCK : camión *m* (con remolque)
trade[1] [ˈtreɪd] *v* **traded; trading** *vi* : comerciar, negociar — *vt* EXCHANGE : intercambiar, canjear
trade[2] *n* **1** OCCUPATION : oficio *m*, profesión *f*, ocupación *f* <a carpenter by trade : carpintero de oficio> **2** COMMERCE : comercio *m*, industria *f* <free trade : libre comercio> <the book trade : la industria del libro> **3** EXCHANGE : intercambio *m*, canje *m*
trade–in [ˈtreɪd,ɪn] *n* : artículo *m* que se canjea por otro
trademark [ˈtreɪd,mɑrk] *n* **1** : marca *f* registrada **2** CHARACTERISTIC : sello *m* característico (de un grupo, una persona, etc.)
trader [ˈtreɪdər] *n* : negociante *mf*, tratante *mf*, comerciante *mf*
tradesman [ˈtreɪdzmən] *n*, *pl* **-men** [-mən, -,mɛn] **1** CRAFTSMAN : artesano *m*, -na *f* **2** SHOPKEEPER : tendero *m*, -ra *f*; comerciante *mf*
trade wind *n* : viento *m* alisio
tradition [trəˈdɪʃən] *n* : tradición *f*
traditional [trəˈdɪʃənəl] *adj* : tradicional — **traditionally** *adv*
traffic[1] [ˈtræfɪk] *vi* **trafficked; trafficking** : traficar (en)
traffic[2] *n* **1** COMMERCE : tráfico *m*, comercio *m* <the drug traffic : el narcotráfico> **2** : tráfico *m*, tránsito *m*, circulación *f* (de vehículos, etc.)
traffic circle *n* : rotonda *f*, glorieta *f*
trafficker [ˈtræfɪkər] *n* : traficante *mf*
traffic light *n* : semáforo *m*, luz *f* (de tránsito)
tragedy [ˈtrædʒədi] *n*, *pl* **-dies** : tragedia *f*
tragic [ˈtrædʒɪk] *adj* : trágico — **tragically** *adv*
trail[1] [ˈtreɪl] *vi* **1** DRAG : arrastrarse **2** LAG : quedarse atrás, retrasarse **3 to trail away** *or* **to trail off** : disminuir, menguar, desvanecerse — *vt* **1** DRAG : arrastrar **2** PURSUE : perseguir, seguir la pista de
trail[2] *n* **1** TRACK : rastro *m*, huella *f*, pista *f* <a trail of blood : un rastro de sangre> **2** : cola *f*, estela *f* (de un meteoro) **3** PATH : sendero *m*, camino *m*, vereda *f*
trailer [ˈtreɪlər] *n* **1** : remolque *m*, tráiler *m* (de un camión) **2** : caravana *f* (vivienda ambulante)
train[1] [ˈtreɪn] *vt* **1** : entrenar (atletas), capacitar (empleados), adiestrar, amaestrar (animales) **2** POINT : apuntar (un arma, etc.) — *vi* : entrenar(se) (físicamente), prepararse (profesionalmente) <she's training at the gym : se está entrenando en el gimnasio>
train[2] *n* **1** : cola *f* (de un vestido) **2** RETINUE : cortejo *m*, séquito *m* **3** SERIES : serie *f* (de eventos) **4** : tren *m* <passenger train : tren de pasajeros>
trainee [treɪˈniː] *n* : aprendiz *m*, -diza *f*
trainer [ˈtreɪnər] *n* : entrenador *m*, -dora *f*
traipse [ˈtreɪps] *vi* **traipsed; traipsing** : andar de un lado para otro, vagar
trait [ˈtreɪt] *n* : rasgo *m*, característica *f*
traitor [ˈtreɪtər] *n* : traidor *m*, -dora *f*
traitorous [ˈtreɪtərəs] *adj* : traidor
trajectory [trəˈdʒɛktəri] *n*, *pl* **-ries** : trayectoria *f*
tramp[1] [ˈtræmp] *vi* : caminar (a paso pesado) — *vt* : deambular por, vagar por <to tramp the streets : vagar por las calles>
tramp[2] *n* **1** VAGRANT : vagabundo *m*, -da *f* **2** HIKE : caminata *f*
trample [ˈtræmpəl] *vt* **-pled; -pling** : pisotear, hollar
trampoline [,træmpəˈliːn, ˈtræmpə,-] *n* : trampolín *m*, cama *f* elástica
trance [ˈtrænts] *n* : trance *m*
tranquil [ˈtræŋkwəl] *adj* : calmo, tranquilo, sereno — **tranquilly** *adv*
tranquilize [ˈtræŋkwə,laɪz] *vt* **-ized; -izing** : tranquilizar
tranquilizer [ˈtræŋkwə,laɪzər] *n* : tranquilizante *m*
tranquillity *or* **tranquility** [træŋˈkwɪləti] *n* : sosiego *m*, tranquilidad *f*
transact [trænˈzækt] *vt* : negociar, gestionar, hacer (negocios)
transaction [trænˈzækʃən] *n* **1** : transacción *f*, negocio *m*, operación *f* **2 transactions** *npl* RECORDS : actas *fpl*
transatlantic [,træntsətˈlæntɪk, ,trænz-] *adj* : transatlántico
transcend [trænˈsɛnd] *vt* : trascender, sobrepasar
transcribe [trænˈskraɪb] *vt* **-scribed; -scribing** : transcribir
transcript [ˈtræn,skrɪpt] *n* : copia *f* oficial
transcription [trænˈskrɪpʃən] *n* : transcripción *f*
transfer[1] [træntsˈfər, ˈtrænts,fər] *v* **-ferred; -ferring** *vt* **1** : trasladar (a una persona), transferir (fondos) **2** : transferir, traspasar, ceder (propiedad) **3** PRINT : imprimir (un diseño) — *vi* **1** MOVE : trasladarse, cambiarse **2** CHANGE : transbordar, cambiar (de un transporte a otro) <she transferred at E Street : hizo un transborde a la calle E>
transfer[2] [ˈtrænts,fər] *n* **1** TRANSFERRING : transferencia *f* (de fondos, de

propiedad, etc.), traslado *m* (de una persona) **2** DECAL : calcomanía *f* **3** : boleto *m* (para cambiar de un avión, etc., a otro)
transferable [træn*t*s'fərəbəl] *adj* : transferible
transference [træn*t*s'fərən*t*s] *n* : transferencia *f*
transfigure [træn*t*s'fɪgjər] *vt* **-ured; -uring** : transfigurar, transformar
transfix [træn*t*s'fɪks] *vt* **1** PIERCE : traspasar, atravesar **2** IMMOBILIZE : paralizar
transform [træn*t*s'fɔrm] *vt* : transformar
transformation [,træn*t*sfər'meɪʃən] *n* : transformación *f*
transformer [træn*t*s'fɔrmər] *n* : transformador *m*
transfusion [træn*t*s'fju:ʒən] *n* : transfusión *f*
transgress [træn*t*s'grɛs, trænz-] *vt* : transgredir, infringir
transgression [træn*t*s'grɛʃən, trænz-] *n* : transgresión *f*
transient¹ ['træntʃənt, 'trænsiənt] *adj* : pasajero, transitorio — **transiently** *adv*
transient² *n* : transeúnte *mf*
transistor [træn'zɪstər, -'sɪs-] *n* : transistor *m*
transit ['træn*t*sɪt, 'trænzɪt] *n* **1** PASSAGE : pasaje *m,* tránsito *m* <in transit : en tránsito> **2** TRANSPORTATION : transporte *m* (público) **3** : teodolito *m* (instrumento topográfico)
transition [træn'sɪʃən, -'zɪʃ-] *n* : transición *f*
transitional [træn'sɪʃənəl, -'zɪʃ-] *adj* : de transición
transitive ['træn*t*səṭɪv, 'trænzə-] *adj* : transitivo
transitory ['træn*t*sə,tori, 'trænzə-] *adj* : transitorio
translate [træn*t*s'leɪt, trænz-; 'træn*t*s,-, 'træns,-] *vt* **-lated; -lating** : traducir
translation [træn*t*s'leɪʃən, trænz-] *n* : traducción *f*
translator [træn*t*s'leɪṭər, trænz-; 'træn*t*s,-, 'træns,-] *n* : traductor *m,* -tora *f*
translucent [træn*t*s'lu:sənt, trænz-] *adj* : translúcido
transmission [træn*t*s'mɪʃən, trænz-] *n* : transmisión *f*
transmit [træn*t*s'mɪt, trænz-] *vt* **-mitted; -mitting** : transmitir
transmitter [træn*t*s'mɪṭər, trænz-; 'træn*t*s,-, 'træns,-] *n* : transmisor *m,* emisor *m*
transom ['træn*t*səm] *n* : montante *m* (de una puerta), travesaño *m* (de una ventana)
transparency [træn*t*s'pærən*t*si] *n, pl* **-cies** : transparencia *f*
transparent [træn*t*s'pærənt] *adj* **1** : transparente, traslúcido <a transparent fabric : una tela transparente> **2** OBVIOUS : transparente, obvio, claro — **transparently** *adv*
transpiration [,træn*t*spə'reɪʃən] *n* : transpiración *f*
transpire [træn*t*s'paɪr] *vi* **-spired; -spiring 1** : transpirar (en biología y botanía) **2** TURN OUT : resultar **3** HAPPEN : suceder, ocurrir, tener lugar
transplant¹ [træn*t*s'plænt] *vt* : trasplantar
transplant² ['træn*t*s,plænt] *n* : trasplante *m*
transport¹ [træn*t*s'port, 'træn*t*s,-] *vt* **1** CARRY : transportar, acarrear **2** ENRAPTURE : transportar, extasiar
transport² ['træn*t*s,port] *n* **1** TRANSPORTATION : transporte *m,* transportación *f* **2** RAPTURE : éxtasis *m* **3** *or* **transport ship** : buque *m* de transporte (de personal militar)
transportation [,træn*t*spər'teɪʃən] *n* : transporte *m,* transportación *f*
transpose [træn*t*s'po:z] *vt* **-posed; -posing** : trasponer, trasladar, transportar (una composición musical)
transverse [træn*t*s'vərs, trænz-] *adj* : transversal, transverso, oblicuo — **transversely** *adv*
trap¹ ['træp] *vt* **trapped; trapping** : atrapar, apresar (en una trampa)
trap² *n* : trampa *f* <to set a trap : tender una trampa>
trapdoor ['træp'dor] *n* : trampilla *f,* escotillón *m*
trapeze [træ'pi:z] *n* : trapecio *m*
trapezoid ['træpə,zɔɪd] *n* : trapezoide *m,* trapecio *m*
trapper ['træpər] *n* : trampero *m,* -ra *f;* cazador *m,* -dora *f* (que usa trampas)
trappings ['træpɪŋz] *npl* **1** : arreos *mpl,* jaeces *mpl* (de un caballo) **2** ADORNMENTS : adornos *mpl,* pompa *f*
trash ['træʃ] *n* : basura *f*
trauma ['trɔmə, 'traʊ-] *n* : trauma *m*
traumatic [trə'mæṭɪk, trɔ-, traʊ-] *adj* : traumático
travel¹ ['trævəl] *vi* **-eled** *or* **-elled; -eling** *or* **-elling 1** JOURNEY : viajar **2** GO, MOVE : desplazarse, moverse, ir <the waves travel at uniform speed : las ondas se desplazan a una velocidad uniforme>
travel² *n* : viajes *mpl*
traveler *or* **traveller** ['trævələr] *n* : viajero *m,* -ra *f*
traverse [trə'vərs, træ'vərs, 'trævərs] *vt* **-versed; -versing** CROSS : atravesar, extenderse a través de, cruzar
travesty ['trævəsti] *n, pl* **-ties** : parodia *f*
trawl¹ ['trɔl] *vi* : pescar con red de arrastre, rastrear
trawl² *n or* **trawl net** : red *f* de arrastre
trawler ['trɔlər] *n* : barco *m* de pesca (utilizado para rastrear)
tray ['treɪ] *n* : bandeja *f,* charola *f Bol, Mex, Peru*

treacherous ['trɛtʃərəs] *adj* **1** TRAITOROUS : traicionero, traidor **2** DANGEROUS : peligroso

treacherously ['trɛtʃərəsli] *adv* : a traición

treachery ['trɛtʃəri] *n, pl* **-eries** : traición *f*

tread[1] ['trɛd] *v* **trod** ['trɑd]; **trodden** ['trɑdən] *or* **trod; treading** *vt* TRAMPLE : pisotear, hollar — *vi* **1** WALK : caminar, andar **2 to tread on** : pisar

tread[2] *n* **1** STEP : paso *m,* andar *m* **2** : banda *f* de rodadura (de un neumático, etc.) **3** : escalón *m* (de una escalera)

treadle ['trɛdəl] *n* : pedal *m* (de una máquina)

treadmill ['trɛd,mɪl] *n* **1** : rueda *f* de andar **2** ROUTINE : rutina *f*

treason ['tri:zən] *n* : traición *f* (a la patria, etc.)

treasure[1] ['trɛʒər, 'treɪ-] *vt* **-sured; -suring** : apreciar, valorar

treasure[2] *n* : tesoro *m*

treasurer ['trɛʒərər, 'treɪ-] *n* : tesorero *m,* -ra *f*

treasury ['trɛʒəri, 'treɪ-] *n, pl* **-suries** : tesorería *f,* tesoro *m*

treat[1] ['tri:t] *vt* **1** DEAL WITH : tratar (un asunto) <the article treats of poverty : el artículo trata de la pobreza> **2** HANDLE : tratar (a una persona), manejar (un objeto) <to treat something as a joke : tomar(se) algo a broma> **3** INVITE : invitar, convidar <he treated me to a meal : me invitó a comer> **4** : tratar, atender (en medicina) **5** PROCESS : tratar <to treat sewage : tratar las aguas negras>

treat[2] *n* : gusto *m,* placer *m* <it was a treat to see you : fue un placer verte> <it's my treat : yo invito>

treatise ['tri:tɪs] *n* : tratado *m,* estudio *m*

treatment ['tri:tmənt] *n* : trato *m,* tratamiento *m* (médico)

treaty ['tri:ti] *n, pl* **-ties** : tratado *m,* convenio *m*

treble[1] ['trɛbəl] *vt* **-bled; -bling** : triplicar

treble[2] *adj* **1** → **triple 2** : de tiple, soprano (en música) **3 treble clef** : clave *f* de sol

treble[3] *n* : tiple *m,* parte *f* soprana

tree ['tri:] *n* : árbol *m*

treeless ['tri:ləs] *adj* : carente de árboles

trek[1] ['trɛk] *vi* **trekked; trekking** : hacer un viaje largo y difícil

trek[2] *n* : viaje *m* largo y difícil

trellis ['trɛlɪs] *n* : enrejado *m,* espaldera *f,* celosía *f*

tremble ['trɛmbəl] *vi* **-bled; -bling** : temblar

tremendous [trɪ'mɛndəs] *adj* : tremendo — **tremendously** *adv*

tremor ['trɛmər] *n* : temblor *m*

tremulous ['trɛmjələs] *adj* : trémulo, tembloroso

trench ['trɛntʃ] *n* **1** DITCH : zanja *f* **2** : trinchera *f* (militar)

trenchant ['trɛntʃənt] *adj* : cortante, mordaz

trend[1] ['trɛnd] *vi* : tender, inclinarse

trend[2] *n* **1** TENDENCY : tendencia *f* **2** FASHION : moda *f*

trendy ['trɛndi] *adj* **trendier; -est** : de moda

trepidation [,trɛpə'deɪʃən] *n* : inquietud *f,* ansiedad *f*

trespass[1] ['trɛspəs, -,pæs] *vi* **1** SIN : pecar, transgredir **2** : entrar ilegalmente (en propiedad ajena)

trespass[2] *n* **1** SIN : pecado *m,* transgresión *f* <forgive us our trespasses : perdónanos nuestras deudas> **2** : entrada *f* ilegal (en propiedad ajena)

tress ['trɛs] *n* : mechón *m*

trestle ['trɛsəl] *n* **1** : caballete *m* (armazón) **2** *or* **trestle bridge** : puente *m* de caballete

triad ['traɪ,æd] *n* : tríada *f*

trial[1] ['traɪəl] *adj* : de prueba <trial period : período de prueba>

trial[2] *n* **1** : juicio *m,* proceso *m* <to stand trial : ser sometido a juicio> **2** AFFLICTION : aflicción *f,* tribulación *f* **3** TEST : prueba *f,* ensayo *m*

triangle ['traɪ,æŋgəl] *n* : triángulo *m*

triangular [traɪ'æŋgjələr] *adj* : triangular

tribal ['traɪbəl] *adj* : tribal

tribe ['traɪb] *n* : tribu *f*

tribesman ['traɪbzmən] *n, pl* **-men** [-mən, -,mɛn] : miembro *m* de una tribu

tribulation [,trɪbjə'leɪʃən] *n* : tribulación *f*

tribunal [traɪ'bju:nəl, trɪ-] *n* : tribunal *m,* corte *f*

tributary ['trɪbjə,tɛri] *n, pl* **-taries** : afluente *m*

tribute ['trɪb,ju:t] *n* : tributo *m*

trick[1] ['trɪk] *vt* : engañar, embaucar

trick[2] *n* **1** RUSE : trampa *f,* treta *f,* artimaña *f* **2** PRANK : broma *f* <we played a trick on her : le gastamos una broma> **3** : truco *m* <magic tricks : trucos de magia> <the trick is to wait five minutes : el truco está en esperar cinco minutos> **4** MANNERISM : peculiaridad *f,* manía *f* **5** : baza *f* (en juegos de naipes)

trickery ['trɪkəri] *n* : engaños *mpl,* trampas *fpl*

trickle[1] ['trɪkəl] *vi* **-led; -ling** : gotear, chorrear

trickle[2] *n* : goteo *m,* hilo *m*

trickster ['trɪkstər] *n* : estafador *m,* -dora *f;* embaucador *m,* -dora *f*

tricky ['trɪki] *adj* **trickier; -est 1** SLY : astuto, taimado **2** DIFFICULT : delicado, peliagudo, difícil

tricycle ['traɪsəkəl, -,sɪkəl] *n* : triciclo *m*

trident ['traɪdənt] *n* : tridente *m*

triennial [traɪ'ɛniəl] *adj* : trienal

trifle[1] ['traɪfəl] *vi* **-fled; -fling** : jugar, juguetear

trifle[2] *n* : nimiedad *f,* insignificancia *f*
trifling [ˈtraɪflɪŋ] *adj* : trivial, insignificante
trigger[1] [ˈtrɪgər] *vt* : causar, provocar
trigger[2] *n* : gatillo *m*
trigonometry [ˌtrɪgəˈnɑmətri] *n* : trigonometría *f*
trill[1] [ˈtrɪl] *vi* QUAVER : trinar, gorjear — *vt* : vibrar <to trill the *r* : vibrar la *r*>
trill[2] *n* **1** QUAVER : trino *m,* gorjeo *m* **2** : vibración *f* (en fonología)
trillion [ˈtrɪljən] *n* : billón *m*
trilogy [ˈtrɪlədʒi] *n, pl* **-gies** : trilogía *f*
trim[1] [ˈtrɪm] *vt* **trimmed; trimming 1** DECORATE : adornar, decorar **2** CUT : recortar **3** REDUCE : recortar, reducir <to trim the excess : recortar el exceso>
trim[2] *adj* **trimmer; trimmest 1** SLIM : esbelto **2** NEAT : limpio y arreglado, bien cuidado
trim[3] *n* **1** CONDITION : condición *f,* estado *m* <to keep in trim : mantenerse en buena forma> **2** CUT : recorte *m* **3** TRIMMING : adornos *mpl*
trimming [ˈtrɪmɪŋ] *n* : adornos *mpl,* accesorios *mpl*
Trinity [ˈtrɪnət̬i] *n* : Trinidad *f*
trinket [ˈtrɪŋkət] *n* : chuchería *f,* baratija *f*
trio [ˈtriːˌoː] *n, pl* **trios** : trío *m*
trip[1] [ˈtrɪp] *v* **tripped; tripping** *vi* **1** : caminar (a paso ligero) **2** STUMBLE : tropezar **3 to trip up** ERR : equivocarse, cometer un error — *vt* **1** : hacerle una zancadilla (a alguien) <you tripped me on purpose! : ¡me hiciste la zancadilla a propósito!> **2** ACTIVATE : activar (un mecanismo) **3 to trip up** : hacer equivocar (a alguien)
trip[2] *n* **1** JOURNEY : viaje *m* <to take a trip : hacer un viaje> **2** STUMBLE : tropiezo *m,* traspié *m*
tripartite [traɪˈpɑrˌtaɪt] *adj* : tripartito
tripe [ˈtraɪp] *n* **1** : mondongo *m,* callos *mpl,* pancita *f Mex* **2** TRASH : porquería *f*
triple[1] [ˈtrɪpəl] *vt* **-pled; -pling** : triplicar
triple[2] *adj* : triple
triple[3] *n* : triple *m*
triplet [ˈtrɪplət] *n* **1** : terceto *m* (en poesía, música, etc.) **2** : trillizo *m,* -za *f* (persona)
triplicate [ˈtrɪplɪkət] *n* : triplicado *m*
tripod [ˈtraɪˌpɑd] *n* : trípode *m*
trite [ˈtraɪt] *adj* **triter; tritest** : trillado, tópico, manido
triumph[1] [ˈtraɪəmpf] *vi* : triunfar
triumph[2] *n* : triunfo *m*
triumphal [traɪˈʌmpfəl] *adj* : triunfal
triumphant [traɪˈʌmpfənt] *adj* : triunfante, triunfal — **triumphantly** *adv*
trivia [ˈtrɪviə] *ns & pl* : trivialidades *fpl,* nimiedades *fpl*
trivial [ˈtrɪviəl] *adj* : trivial, intrascendente, insignificante
triviality [ˌtrɪviˈæləti] *n, pl* **-ties** : trivialidad *f*
trod, trodden → **tread**[1]
troll [ˈtroːl] *n* : duende *m* o gigante *m* de cuentos folklóricos
trolley [ˈtrɑli] *n, pl* **-leys** : tranvía *m*
trombone [trɑmˈboːn] *n* : trombón *m*
trombonist [trɑmˈboːnɪst] *n* : trombón *m*
troop[1] [ˈtruːp] *vi* : desfilar, ir en tropel
troop[2] *n* **1** : escuadrón *m* (de caballería) **2** GROUP : grupo *m,* banda *f* (de personas) **3 troops** *npl* SOLDIERS : tropas *fpl,* soldados *mpl*
trooper [ˈtruːpər] *n* **1** : soldado *m* (de caballería) **2** : policía *m* montado **3** : policía *m* (estatal)
trophy [ˈtroːfi] *n, pl* **-phies** : trofeo *m*
tropic[1] [ˈtrɑpɪk] *or* **tropical** [-pɪkəl] *adj* : tropical
tropic[2] *n* **1** : trópico *m* <tropic of Cancer : trópico de Cáncer> **2 the tropics** : el trópico
trot[1] [ˈtrɑt] *vi* **trotted; trotting** : trotar
trot[2] *n* : trote *m*
trouble[1] [ˈtrʌbəl] *v* **-bled; -bling** *vt* **1** DISTURB, WORRY : molestar, perturbar, inquietar **2** AFFLICT : afligir, afectar — *vi* : molestarse, hacer un esfuerzo <they didn't trouble to come : no se molestaron en venir>
trouble[2] *n* **1** PROBLEMS : problemas *mpl,* dificultades *fpl* <to be in trouble : estar en un aprieto> <heart trouble : problemas de corazón> **2** EFFORT : molestia *f,* esfuerzo *m* <to take the trouble : tomarse la molestia> <it's not worth the trouble : no vale la pena>
troublemaker [ˈtrʌbəlˌmeɪkər] *n* : agitador *m,* -dora *f;* alborotador *m,* -dora *f*
troublesome [ˈtrʌbəlsəm] *adj* : problemático, dificultoso — **troublesomely** *adv*
trough [ˈtrɔf] *n, pl* **troughs** [ˈtrɔfs, ˈtrɔvz] **1** : comedero *m,* bebedero *m* (de animales) **2** CHANNEL, HOLLOW : depresión *f* (en el suelo), seno *m* (de olas)
trounce [ˈtraʊnts] *vt* **trounced; trouncing 1** THRASH : apalear, darle una paliza (a alguien) **2** DEFEAT : derrotar contundentemente
troupe [ˈtruːp] *n* : troupe *f*
trousers [ˈtraʊzərz] *npl* : pantalón *m,* pantalones *mpl*
trout [ˈtraʊt] *n, pl* **trout** : trucha *f*
trowel [ˈtraʊəl] *n* **1** : llana *f,* paleta *f* (de albañil) **2** : desplantador *m* (de jardinero)
truant [ˈtruːənt] *n* : alumno *m,* -na *f* que falta a clase sin permiso
truce [ˈtruːs] *n* : tregua *f,* armisticio *m*
truck[1] [ˈtrʌk] *vt* : transportar en camión
truck[2] *n* **1** : camión *m* (vehículo automóvil), carro *m* (manual) **2** DEAL-

INGS : tratos *mpl* <to have no truck with : no tener nada que ver con>

trucker [ˈtrʌkər] *n* : camionero *m,* -ra *f*

truculent [ˈtrʌkjələnt] *adj* : agresivo, beligerante

trudge [ˈtrʌdʒ] *vi* **trudged; trudging** : caminar a paso pesado

true[1] [ˈtruː] *vt* **trued; trueing** : aplomar (algo vertical), nivelar (algo horizontal), centrar (una rueda)

true[2] *adv* **1** TRUTHFULLY : lealmente, sinceramente **2** ACCURATELY : exactamente, certeramente

true[3] *adj* **truer; truest 1** LOYAL : fiel, leal **2** : cierto, verdadero, verídico <it's true : es cierto, es la verdad> <a true story : una historia verídica> **3** GENUINE : auténtico, genuino — **truly** *adv*

true–blue [ˈtruːˈbluː] *adj* LOYAL : leal, fiel

truffle [ˈtrʌfəl] *n* : trufa *f*

truism [ˈtruːˌɪzəm] *n* : perogrullada *f,* verdad *f* obvia

trump[1] [ˈtrʌmp] *vt* : matar (en juegos de naipes)

trump[2] *n* : triunfo *m* (en juegos de naipes)

trumped–up [ˈtrʌmptˈʌp] *adj* : inventado, fabricado <trumped-up charges : falsas acusaciones>

trumpet[1] [ˈtrʌmpət] *vi* **1** : sonar una trompeta **2** : berrear, bramar (dícese de un animal) — *vt* : proclamar a los cuatro vientos

trumpet[2] *n* : trompeta *f*

trumpeter [ˈtrʌmpət̬ər] *n* : trompetista *mf*

truncate [ˈtrʌŋˌkeɪt, ˈtrʌn-] *vt* **-cated; -cating** : truncar

trundle [ˈtrʌndəl] *v* **-dled; -dling** *vi* : rodar lentamente — *vt* : hacer rodar, empujar lentamente

trunk [ˈtrʌŋk] *n* **1** : tronco *m* (de un árbol o del cuerpo) **2** : trompa *f* (de un elefante) **3** CHEST : baúl *m* **4** : maletero *m,* cajuela *f Mex* (de un auto) **5 trunks** *npl* : traje *m* de baño (de caballero)

truss[1] [ˈtrʌs] *vt* : atar (con fuerza)

truss[2] *n* **1** FRAMEWORK : armazón *m* (de una estructura) **2** : braguero *m* (en medicina)

trust[1] [ˈtrʌst] *vi* : confiar, esperar <to trust in God : confiar en Dios> — *vt* **1** ENTRUST : confiar, encomendar **2** : confiar en, tenerle confianza a <I trust you : te tengo confianza>

trust[2] *n* **1** CONFIDENCE : confianza *f* **2** HOPE : esperanza *f,* fe *f* **3** CREDIT : crédito *m* <to sell on trust : fiar> **4** : fideicomiso *m* <to hold in trust : guardar en fideicomiso> **5** : trust *m* (consorcio empresarial) **6** CUSTODY : responsabilidad *f,* custodia *f*

trustee [ˌtrʌsˈtiː] *n* : fideicomisario *m,* -ria *f;* fiduciario *m,* -ria *f*

trustful [ˈtrʌstfəl] *adj* : confiado — **trustfully** *adv*

trustworthiness [ˈtrəstˌwərðinəs] *n* : integridad *f,* honradez *f*

trustworthy [ˈtrəstˌwərði] *adj* : digno de confianza, confiable

trusty [ˈtrəsti] *adj* **trustier; -est** : fiel, confiable

truth [ˈtruːθ] *n, pl* **truths** [ˈtruːðz, ˈtruːθs] : verdad *f*

truthful [ˈtruːθfəl] *adj* : sincero, veraz — **truthfully** *adv*

truthfulness [ˈtruːθfəlnəs] *n* : sinceridad *f,* veracidad *f*

try[1] [ˈtraɪ] *v* **tried; trying** *vt* **1** : enjuiciar, juzgar, procesar <he was tried for murder : fue procesado por homicidio> **2** : probar <did you try the salad? : ¿probaste la ensalada?> **3** TEST : tentar, poner a prueba <to try one's patience : tentarle la paciencia a uno> **4** ATTEMPT : tratar (de), intentar **5** *or* **to try on** : probarse (ropa) — *vi* : tratar, intentar

try[2] *n, pl* **tries** : intento *m,* tentativa *f*

tryout [ˈtraɪˌaʊt] *n* : prueba *f*

tsar [ˈzɑr, ˈtsɑr, ˈsɑr] → **czar**

T–shirt [ˈtiːˌʃərt] *n* : camiseta *f*

tub [ˈtʌb] *n* **1** CASK : cuba *f,* barril *m,* tonel *m* **2** CONTAINER : envase *m* (de plástico, etc.) <a tub of margarine : un envase de margarina> **3** BATHTUB : tina *f* (de baño), bañera *f*

tuba [ˈtuːbə, ˈtjuː-] *n* : tuba *f*

tube [ˈtuːb, ˈtjuːb] *n* **1** PIPE : tubo *m* **2** : tubo *m* (de dentífrico, etc.) **3** *or* **inner tube** : cámara *f* **4** : tubo *m* (de un aparato electrónico) **5** : trompa *f* (en anatomía)

tubeless [ˈtuːbləs, ˈtjuːb-] *adj* : sin cámara (dícese de una llanta)

tuber [ˈtuːbər, ˈtjuː-] *n* : tubérculo *m*

tubercular [tʊˈbərkjələr, tjʊ-] → **tuberculous**

tuberculosis [tʊˌbərkjəˈloːsɪs, tjʊ-] *n, pl* **-loses** [-ˌsiːz] : tuberculosis *f*

tuberculous [tʊˈbərkjələs, tjʊ-] *adj* : tuberculoso

tuberous [ˈtuːbərəs, ˈtjuː-] *adj* : tuberoso

tubing [ˈtuːbɪŋ, ˈtjuː-] *n* : tubería *f*

tubular [ˈtuːbjələr, ˈtjuː-] *adj* : tubular

tuck[1] [ˈtʌk] *vt* **1** PLACE, PUT : meter, colocar <tuck in your shirt : métete la camisa> **2** : guardar, esconder <to tuck away one's money : guardar uno bien su dinero> **3** COVER : arropar (a un niño en la cama)

tuck[2] *n* : pliegue *m,* alforza *f*

Tuesday [ˈtuːzˌdeɪ, ˈtjuːz-, -di] *n* : martes *m*

tuft [ˈtʌft] *n* : penacho *m* (de plumas), copete *m* (de pelo)

tug[1] [ˈtʌg] *v* **tugged; tugging** *vi* : tirar, jalar, dar un tirón — *vt* : jalar, arrastrar, remolcar (con un barco)

tug[2] *n* **1** : tirón *m,* jalón *m* **2** → **tugboat**

tugboat [ˈtʌgˌboːt] *n* : remolcador *m*

tug–of–war [ˌtʌgəˈwɔr] *n, pl* **tugs–of–war** : tira y afloja *m*

tulip [ˈtuːlɪp, ˈtjuː-] *n* : tulipán *m*

tumble[1] [ˈtʌmbəl] *v* **-bled; -bling** *vi* **1** : dar volteretas (en acrobacia) **2** FALL : caerse, venirse abajo — *vt* **1** TOPPLE : volcar **2** TOSS : hacer girar
tumble[2] *n* : voltereta *f,* caída *f*
tumbler [ˈtʌmblər] *n* **1** ACROBAT : acróbata *mf,* saltimbanqui *mf* **2** GLASS : vaso *m* (de mesa) **3** : clavija *f* (de una cerradura)
tummy [ˈtʌmi] *n, pl* **-mies** BELLY : panza *f,* vientre *m*
tumor [ˈtuːmər ˈtjuː-] *n* : tumor *m*
tumult [ˈtuːˌmʌlt ˈtjuː-] *n* : tumulto *m,* alboroto *m*
tumultuous [tʊˈmʌltʃʊəs, tjuː-] *adj* : tumultuoso
tuna [ˈtuːnə ˈtjuː-] *n, pl* **-na** *or* **-nas** : atún *m*
tundra [ˈtʌndrə] *n* : tundra *f*
tune[1] [ˈtuːn, ˈtjuːn] *v* **tuned; tuning** *vt* **1** ADJUST : ajustar, hacer más preciso, afinar (un motor) **2** : afinar (un instrumento musical) **3** : sintonizar (un radio o televisor) — *vi* **to tune in** : sintonizar (con una emisora)
tune[2] *n* **1** MELODY : tonada *f,* canción *f,* melodía *f* **2 in tune** : afinado (dícese de un instrumento o de la voz), sintonizado, en sintonía
tuneful [ˈtuːnfəl, ˈtjuːn-] *adj* : armonioso, melódico
tuner [ˈtuːnər, ˈtjuː-] *n* : afinador *m,* -dora *f* (de instrumentos); sintonizador *m* (de un radio o un televisior)
tungsten [ˈtʌŋkstən] *n* : tungsteno *m*
tunic [ˈtuːnɪk, ˈtjuː-] *n* : túnica *f*
tuning fork *n* : diapasón *m*
Tunisian [tuːˈniːʒən, tjuːˈnɪziən] *n* : tunecino *m,* -na *f* — **Tunisian** *adj*
tunnel[1] [ˈtʌnəl] *vi* **-neled** *or* **-nelled; -neling** *or* **-nelling** : hacer un túnel
tunnel[2] *n* : túnel *m*
turban [ˈtərbən] *n* : turbante *m*
turbid [ˈtərbɪd] *adj* : turbio
turbine [ˈtərbən, -ˌbaɪn] *n* : turbina *f*
turboprop [ˈtərboːˌprɑp] *n* : turbopropulsor *m* (motor), avión *m* turbopropulsado
turbulence [ˈtərbjələnts] *n* : turbulencia *f*
turbulent [ˈtərbjələnt] *adj* : turbulento — **turbulently** *adv*
tureen [təˈriːn, tjʊ-] *n* : sopera *f*
turf [ˈtərf] *n* SOD : tepe *m*
turgid [ˈtərdʒɪd] *adj* **1** SWOLLEN : turgente **2** : ampuloso, hinchado <turgid style : estilo ampuloso>
turkey [ˈtərki] *n, pl* **-keys** : pavo *m*
turmoil [ˈtərˌmɔɪl] *n* : agitación *f,* desorden *m,* confusión *f*
turn[1] [ˈtərn] *vt* **1** : girar, voltear, volver <to turn one's head : voltear la cabeza> <she turned her chair toward the fire : giró su asiento hacia la hoguera> **2** ROTATE : darle vuelta a, hacer girar <turn the handle : dale vuelta a la manivela> **3** SPRAIN, WRENCH : dislocar, torcer **4** UPSET : revolver (el estómago) **5** TRANSFORM : convertir <to turn water into wine : convertir el agua en vino> **6** SHAPE : tornear (en carpintería) — *vi* **1** ROTATE : girar, dar vueltas **2** : girar, doblar, dar una vuelta <turn left : doble a la izquierda> <to turn around : dar la media vuelta> **3** BECOME : hacerse, volverse, ponerse **4** SOUR : agriarse, cortarse (dícese de la leche) **5 to turn to** : recurrir a <they have no one to turn to : no tienen quien les ayude>
turn[2] *n* **1** : vuelta *f,* giro *m* <a sudden turn : una vuelta repentina> **2** CHANGE : cambio *m* **3** CURVE : curva *f* (en un camino) **4** : turno *m* <they're awaiting their turn : están esperando su turno> <whose turn is it? : ¿a quién le toca?>
turncoat [ˈtərnˌkoːt] *n* : traidor *m,* -dora *f*
turn down *vt* **1** REFUSE : rehusar, rechazar <they turned down our invitation : rehusaron nuestra invitación> **2** LOWER : bajar (el volumen)
turn in *vt* : entregar <to turn in one's work : entregar uno su trabajo> <they turned in the suspect : entregaron al sospechoso> — *vi* : acostarse, irse a la cama
turnip [ˈtərnəp] *n* : nabo *m*
turn off *vt* : apagar (la luz, la radio, etc.)
turn on *vt* : prender (la luz, etc.), encender (un motor, etc.)
turnout [ˈtərnˌaʊt] *n* : concurrencia *f*
turn out *vt* **1** EVICT, EXPEL : expulsar, echar, desalojar **2** PRODUCE : producir **3** → **turn off** — *vi* **1** : concurrir, presentarse <many turned out to vote : muchos concurrieron a votar> **2** PROVE, RESULT : resultar
turnover [ˈtərnˌoːvər] *n* **1** : tarta *f* (rellena de fruta) **2** : volumen *m* (de ventas) **3** : rotación *f* (de personal) <a high turnover : un alto nivel de rotación>
turn over *vt* **1** TRANSFER : entregar, transferir (un cargo o una responsabilidad) **2** : voltear, darle la vuelta a <turn the cassette over : voltea el cassette>
turnpike [ˈtərnˌpaɪk] *n* : carretera *f* de peaje
turnstile [ˈtərnˌstaɪl] *n* : torniquete *m* (de acceso)
turntable [ˈtərnˌteɪbəl] *n* : tornamesa *mf*
turn up *vi* **1** APPEAR : aparecer, presentarse **2** HAPPEN : ocurrir, suceder (inesperadamente) — *vt* : subir (el volumen)
turpentine [ˈtərpənˌtaɪn] *n* : aguarrás *m,* trementina *f*
turquoise [ˈtərˌkɔɪz, -ˌkwɔɪz] *n* : turquesa *f*
turret [ˈtərət] *n* **1** TOWER : torre *f* pequeña **2** : torreta *f* (de un tanque, un avión, etc.)
turtle [ˈtərtəl] *n* : tortuga *f* (marina)

turtledove [ˈtərtəl,dʌv] *n* : tórtola *f*
turtleneck [ˈtərtəl,nɛk] *n* : cuello *m* de tortuga, cuello *m* alto
tusk [ˈtʌsk] *n* : colmillo *m*
tussle[1] [ˈtʌsəl] *vi* **-sled; -sling** SCUFFLE : pelearse, reñir
tussle[2] *n* : riña *f,* pelea *f*
tutor[1] [ˈtuːtər, ˈtjuː-] *vt* : darle clases particulares (a alguien)
tutor[2] *n* : tutor *m,* -tora *f;* maestro *m,* -tra *f* (particular)
tuxedo [,tək'siː,doː] *n, pl* **-dos** *or* **-does** : esmoquin *m,* smoking *m*
TV [,tiːˈviː, ˈtiː,viː] → **television**
twain [ˈtweɪn] *n* : dos *m*
twang[1] [ˈtwæŋ] *vt* : pulsar la cuerda de (una guitarra) — *vi* : hablar en tono nasal
twang[2] *n* **1** : tañido *m* (de una cuerda de guitarra) **2** : tono *m* nasal (de voz)
tweak[1] [ˈtwiːk] *vt* : pellizcar
tweak[2] *n* : pellizco *m*
tweed [ˈtwiːd] *n* : tweed *m*
tweet[1] [ˈtwiːt] *vi* : piar
tweet[2] *n* : gorjeo *m,* pío *m*
tweezers [ˈtwiːzərz] *npl* : pinzas *fpl*
twelfth[1] [ˈtwɛlfθ] *adj* : duodécimo
twelfth[2] *n* **1** : duodécimo *m,* -ma *f* (en una serie) **2** : doceavo *m,* doceava parte *f*
twelve[1] [ˈtwɛlv] *adj* : doce
twelve[2] *n* : doce *m*
twentieth[1] [ˈtwʌntiəθ, ˈtwɛn-] *adj* : vigésimo
twentieth[2] *n* **1** : vigésimo *m,* -ma *f* (en una serie) **2** : veinteavo *m,* veinteava parte *f*
twenty[1] [ˈtwʌnti, ˈtwɛn-] *adj* : veinte
twenty[2] *n, pl* **-ties** : veinte *m*
twice [ˈtwaɪs] *adv* : dos veces <twice a day : dos veces al día> <it costs twice as much : cuesta el doble>
twig [ˈtwɪg] *n* : ramita *f*
twilight [ˈtwaɪ,laɪt] *n* : crepúsculo *m*
twill [ˈtwɪl] *n* : sarga *f,* tela *f* cruzada
twin[1] [ˈtwɪn] *adj* : gemelo, mellizo
twin[2] *n* : gemelo *m,* -la *f;* mellizo *m,* -za *f*
twine[1] [ˈtwaɪn] *v* **twined; twining** *vt* : entrelazar, entrecruzar — *vi* : enroscarse (alrededor de algo)
twine[2] *n* : cordel *m,* cuerda *f,* mecate *m CA, Mex, Ven*
twinge[1] [ˈtwɪndʒ] *vi* **twinged; twinging** *or* **twingeing** : sentir punzadas
twinge[2] *n* : punzada *f,* dolor *m* agudo
twinkle[1] [ˈtwɪŋkəl] *vi* **-kled; -kling 1** : centellear, titilar (dícese de las estrellas o de la luz) **2** : chispear, brillar (dícese de los ojos)
twinkle[2] *n* : centelleo *m* (de las estrellas), brillo *m* (de los ojos)
twirl[1] [ˈtwərl] *vt* : girar, darle vueltas a — *vi* : girar, dar vueltas (rápidamente)
twirl[2] *n* : giro *m,* vuelta *f*
twist[1] [ˈtwɪst] *vt* : torcer, retorcer <he twisted my arm : me torció el brazo> — *vi* : retorcerse, enroscarse, serpentear (dícese de un río, un camino, etc.)
twist[2] *n* **1** BEND : vuelta *f,* recodo *m* (en el camino, el río, etc.) **2** TURN : giro *m* <give it a twist : hazlo girar> **3** SPIRAL : espiral *f* <a twist of lemon : una rodajita de limón> **4** : giro *m* inesperado (de eventos, etc.)
twister [ˈtwɪstər] **1** → **tornado 2** → **waterspout**
twitch[1] [ˈtwɪtʃ] *vi* : moverse nerviosamente, contraerse espasmódicamente (dícese de un músculo)
twitch[2] *n* : espasmo *m,* sacudida *f* <a nervous twitch : un tic nervioso>
twitter[1] [ˈtwɪtər] *vi* CHIRP : gorjear, cantar (dícese de los pájaros)
twitter[2] *n* : gorjeo *m*
two[1] [ˈtuː] *adj* : dos
two[2] *n, pl* **twos** : dos *m*
twofold[1] [ˈtuːˈfoːld] *adv* : al doble
twofold[2] [ˈtuː,foːld] *adj* : doble
two hundred[1] *adj* : doscientos
two hundred[2] *n* : doscientos *m*
twosome [ˈtuːsəm] *n* COUPLE : pareja *f*
tycoon [taɪˈkuːn] *n* : magnate *mf*
tying → **tie[1]**
type[1] [ˈtaɪp] *v* **typed; typing** *vt* **1** TYPEWRITE : escribir a máquina, pasar (un texto) a máquina **2** CATEGORIZE : categorizar, identificar — *vi* : escribir a máquina
type[2] *n* **1** KIND : tipo *m,* clase *f,* categoría *f* **2** *or* **printing type** : tipo *m*
typewrite [ˈtaɪp,raɪt] *v* **-wrote; -written** : escribir a máquina
typewriter [ˈtaɪp,raɪtər] *n* : máquina *f* de escribir
typhoid[1] [ˈtaɪ,fɔɪd, taɪˈ-] *adj* : relativo al tifus o a la tifoidea
typhoid[2] *n or* **typhoid fever** : tifoidea *f*
typhoon [taɪˈfuːn] *n* : tifón *m*
typhus [ˈtaɪfəs] *n* : tifus *m,* tifo *m*
typical [ˈtɪpɪkəl] *adj* : típico, característico — **typically** *adv*
typify [ˈtɪpə,faɪ] *vt* **-fied; -fying** : ser típico o representativo de (un grupo, una clase, etc.)
typist [ˈtaɪpɪst] *n* : mecanógrafo *m,* -fa *f*
typographic [,taɪpəˈgræfɪk] *or* **typographical** [-fɪkəl] *adj* : tipográfico — **typographically** [-fɪkli] *adv*
typography [taɪˈpɑgrəfi] *n* : tipografía *f*
tyrannical [təˈrænɪkəl, taɪ-] *adj* : tiránico — **tyrannically** [-nɪkli] *adv*
tyrannize [ˈtɪrə,naɪz] *vt* **-nized; -nizing** : tiranizar
tyranny [ˈtɪrəni] *n, pl* **-nies** : tiranía *f*
tyrant [ˈtaɪrənt] *n* : tirano *m,* -na *f*
tzar [ˈzɑr, ˈtsɑr, ˈsɑr] → **czar**

U

u [ˈjuː] *n, pl* **u's** *or* **us** [ˈjuːz] : vigésima primera letra del alfabeto inglés
ubiquitous [juːˈbɪkwət̬əs] *adj* : ubicuo, omnipresente
udder [ˈʌdər] *n* : ubre *f*
UFO [ˌjuːˌɛfˈoː, ˈjuːˌfoː] *n, pl* **UFO's** *or* **UFOs** (*unidentified flying object*) : ovni *m,* OVNI *m*
Ugandan [juːˈgændən, -ˈgɑn-; uːˈgɑn-] *n* : ugandés *m,* -desa *f* — **Ugandan** *adj*
ugliness [ˈʌglinəs] *n* : fealdad *f*
ugly [ˈʌgli] *adj* **uglier; -est 1** UNATTRACTIVE : feo **2** DISAGREEABLE : desagradable, feo <ugly weather : tiempo feo> <to have an ugly temper : tener mal genio>
Ukrainian [juːˈkreɪniən, -ˈkraɪ-] *n* : ucraniano *m,* -na *f* — **Ukrainian** *adj*
ukulele [ˌjuːkəˈleɪli] *n* : ukelele *m*
ulcer [ˈʌlsər] *n* : úlcera *f* (interna), llaga *f* (externa)
ulcerate [ˈʌlsəˌreɪt] *vi* **-ated; -ating** : ulcerarse
ulceration [ˌʌlsəˈreɪʃən] *n* **1** : ulceración *f* **2** ULCER : úlcera *f,* llaga *f*
ulcerous [ˈʌlsərəs] *adj* : ulceroso
ulna [ˈʌlnə] *n* : cúbito *m*
ulterior [ˌʌlˈtɪriər] *adj* : oculto <ulterior motive : motivo oculto, segunda intención>
ultimate [ˈʌltəmət] *adj* **1** FINAL : último, final **2** SUPREME : supremo, máximo **3** FUNDAMENTAL : fundamental, esencial
ultimately [ˈʌltəmətli] *adv* **1** FINALLY : por último, finalmente **2** EVENTUALLY : a la larga, con el tiempo
ultimatum [ˌʌltəˈmeɪt̬əm, -ˈmɑ-] *n, pl* **-tums** *or* **-ta** [-t̬ə] : ultimátum *m*
ultraviolet [ˌʌltrəˈvaɪələt] *adj* : ultravioleta
umbilical cord [ˌʌmˈbɪlɪkəl] *adj* : cordón umbilical
umbrage [ˈʌmbrɪdʒ] *n* **to take umbrage at** : ofenderse por
umbrella [ˌʌmˈbrɛlə] *n* **1** : paraguas *m* **2 beach umbrella** : sombrilla *f*
umpire[1] [ˈʌmˌpaɪr] *v* **-pired; -piring** : arbitrar
umpire[2] *n* : árbitro *m,* -tra *f*
umpteenth [ˌʌmpˈtiːnθ] *adj* : enésimo
unable [ˌʌnˈeɪbəl] *adj* : incapaz <to be unable to : no poder>
unabridged [ˌʌnəˈbrɪdʒd] *adj* : íntegro
unacceptable [ˌʌnɪkˈsɛptəbəl] *adj* : inaceptable
unaccompanied [ˌʌnəˈkʌmpənid] *adj* : solo, sin acompañamiento (en música)
unaccountable [ˌʌnəˈkaʊntəbəl] *adj* : inexplicable, incomprensible — **unaccountably** [-bli] *adv*
unaccustomed [ˌʌnəˈkʌstəmd] *adj* **1** UNUSUAL : desacostumbrado, inusual **2** UNUSED : inhabituado <unaccustomed to noise : inhabituado al ruido>
unacquainted [ˌʌnəˈkweɪnt̬əd] *adj* **to be unacquainted with** : desconocer, ignorar
unadorned [ˌʌnəˈdɔrnd] *adj* : sin adornos, puro y simple
unadulterated [ˌʌnəˈdʌltəˌreɪt̬əd] *adj* **1** PURE : puro <unadulterated food : comida pura> **2** ABSOLUTE : completo, absoluto
unaffected [ˌʌnəˈfɛktəd] *adj* **1** : no afectado, indiferente **2** NATURAL : sin afectación, natural
unaffectedly [ˌʌnəˈfɛktədli] *adv* : de manera natural
unafraid [ˌʌnəˈfreɪd] *adj* : sin miedo
unaided [ˌʌnˈeɪdəd] *adj* : sin ayuda, solo
unambiguous [ˌʌnæmˈbɪgjʊəs] *adj* : inequívoco
unanimity [ˌjuːnəˈnɪmət̬i] *n* : unanimidad *f*
unanimous [jʊˈnænəməs] *adj* : unánime — **unanimously** *adv*
unannounced [ˌʌnəˈnaʊnst] *adj* : sin dar aviso
unanswered [ˌʌnˈæntsərd] *adj* : sin contestar
unappealing [ˌʌnəˈpiːlɪŋ] *adj* : desagradable
unappetizing [ˌʌnˈæpəˌtaɪzɪŋ] *adj* : poco apetitoso, poco apetecible
unarmed [ˌʌnˈɑrmd] *adj* : sin armas, desarmado
unassisted [ˌʌnəˈsɪstəd] *adj* : sin ayuda
unassuming [ˌʌnəˈsuːmɪŋ] *adj* : modesto, sin pretensiones
unattached [ˌʌnəˈtætʃt] *adj* **1** LOOSE : suelto **2** INDEPENDENT : independiente **3** : solo (ni casado ni prometido)
unattractive [ˌʌnəˈtræktɪv] *adj* : poco atractivo
unauthorized [ˌʌnˈɔθəˌraɪzd] *adj* : sin autorización, no autorizado
unavailable [ˌʌnəˈveɪləbəl] *adj* : no disponible
unavoidable [ˌʌnəˈvɔɪdəbəl] *adj* : inevitable, ineludible
unaware[1] [ˌʌnəˈwær] *adv* → **unawares**
unaware[2] *adj* : inconsciente
unawares [ˌʌnəˈwærz] *adv* **1** : por sorpresa <to catch someone unawares : agarrar a alguien desprevenido> **2** UNINTENTIONALLY : inconscientemente, inadvertidamente
unbalanced [ˌʌnˈbælәntst] *adj* : desequilibrado
unbearable [ˌʌnˈbærəbəl] *adj* : insoportable, inaguantable — **unbearably** [-bli] *adv*
unbecoming [ˌʌnbɪˈkʌmɪŋ] *adj* **1** UNSEEMLY : impropio, indecoroso **2** UNFLATTERING : poco favorecedor

unbelievable [ˌʌnbəˈliːvəbəl] *adj* : increíble — **unbelievably** [-bli] *adv*
unbend [ˌʌnˈbɛnd] *vi* **-bent** [-ˈbɛnt]; **-bending** RELAX : relajarse
unbending [ˌʌnˈbɛndɪŋ] *adj* : inflexible
unbiased [ˌʌnˈbaɪəst] *adj* : imparcial, objetivo
unbind [ˌʌnˈbaɪnd] *vt* **-bound** [-ˈbaʊnd]; **-binding 1** UNFASTEN, UNTIE : desatar, desamarrar **2** RELEASE : liberar
unbolt [ˌʌnˈboːlt] *vt* : abrir el cerrojo de, descorrer el pestillo de
unborn [ˌʌnˈbɔrn] *adj* : aún no nacido, que va a nacer
unbosom [ˌʌnˈbʊzəm, -ˈbuː-] *vt* : revelar, divulgar
unbreakable [ˌʌnˈbreɪkəbəl] *adj* : irrompible
unbridled [ˌʌnˈbraɪdəld] *adj* : desenfrenado
unbroken [ˌʌnˈbroːkən] *adj* **1** INTACT : intacto, sano **2** CONTINUOUS : continuo, ininterrumpido
unbuckle [ˌʌnˈbʌkəl] *vt* **-led; -ling** : desabrochar
unburden [ˌʌnˈbərdən] *vt* **1** UNLOAD : descargar **2 to unburden oneself** : desahogarse
unbutton [ˌʌnˈbʌtən] *vt* : desabrochar, desabotonar
uncalled-for [ˌʌnˈkɔldˌfɔr] *adj* : inapropiado, innecesario
uncanny [ənˈkæni] *adj* **-nier; -est 1** STRANGE : extraño **2** EXTRAORDINARY : raro, extraordinario — **uncannily** [-ˈkænəli] *adv*
unceasing [ˌʌnˈsiːsɪŋ] *adj* : incesante, continuo — **unceasingly** *adv*
unceremonious [ˌʌnˌsɛrəˈmoːniəs] *adj* **1** INFORMAL : sin ceremonia, sin pompa **2** ABRUPT : abrupto, brusco — **unceremoniously** *adv*
uncertain [ˌʌnˈsərtən] *adj* **1** INDEFINITE : indeterminado **2** UNSURE : incierto, dudoso **3** CHANGEABLE : inestable, variable <uncertain weather : tiempo inestable> **4** HESITANT : indeciso **5** VAGUE : poco claro
uncertainly [ˌʌnˈsərtənli] *adv* : dudosamente, con desconfianza
uncertainty [ˌʌnˈərtənti] *n, pl* **-ties** : duda *f*, incertidumbre *f*
unchangeable [ˌʌnˈtʃeɪndʒəbəl] *adj* : inalterable, inmutable
unchanged [ˌʌnˈtʃeɪndʒd] *adj* : sin cambiar
unchanging [ˌʌnˈtʃeɪdʒɪŋ] *adj* : inalterable, inmutable, firme
uncharacteristic [ˌʌnˌkærɪktəˈrɪstɪk] *adj* : inusual, desacostumbrado
uncharged [ˌʌnˈtʃɑrdʒd] *adj* : sin carga (eléctrica)
uncivilized [ˌʌnˈsɪvəˌlaɪzd] *adj* **1** BARBAROUS : incivilizado, bárbaro **2** WILD : salvaje
uncle [ˈʌŋkəl] *n* : tío *m*
unclean [ˌʌnˈkliːn] *adj* **1** IMPURE : impuro **2** DIRTY : sucio
unclear [ˌʌnˈklɪr] *adj* : confuso, borroso, poco claro
Uncle Sam [ˈsæm] *n* : el Tío Sam
unclog [ˌʌnˈklɑg] *vt* **-clogged; -clogging** : desatascar, destapar
unclothed [ˌʌnˈkloːðd] *adj* : desnudo
uncomfortable [ˌʌnˈkʌmpfərtəbəl] *adj* **1** : incómodo (dícese de una silla, etc.) **2** UNEASY : inquieto, incómodo
uncommitted [ˌʌnkəˈmɪtəd] *adj* : sin compromisos
uncommon [ˌʌnˈkɑmən] *adj* **1** UNUSUAL : raro, poco común **2** REMARKABLE : excepcional, extraordinario
uncommonly [ˌʌnˈkɑmənli] *adv* : extraordinariamente
uncompromising [ˌʌnˈkɑmprəˌmaɪzɪŋ] *adj* : inflexible, intransigente
unconcerned [ˌʌnkənˈsərnd] *adj* : indiferente — **unconcernedly** [-ˈsərnədli] *adv*
unconditional [ˌʌnkənˈdɪʃənəl] *adj* : incondicional — **unconditionally** *adv*
unconscious[1] [ˌʌnˈkɑntʃəs] *adj* : inconsciente — **unconsciously** *adv*
unconscious[2] *n* : inconsciente *m*
unconsciousness [ˌʌnˈkɑntʃəsnəs] *n* : inconsciencia *f*
unconstitutional [ˌʌnˌkɑntstəˈtuːʃənəl, -ˈtjuː-] *adj* : inconstitucional
uncontrollable [ˌʌnkənˈtroːləbəl] *adj* : incontrolable, incontenible — **uncontrollably** [-bli] *adv*
uncontrolled [ˌʌnkənˈtroːld] *adj* : incontrolado
unconventional [ˌʌnkənˈvɛntʃənəl] *adj* : poco convencional
unconvincing [ˌʌnkənˈvɪntsɪŋ] *adj* : poco convincente
uncouth [ˌʌnˈkuːθ] *adj* CRUDE, ROUGH : grosero, rudo
uncover [ˌʌnˈkʌvər] *vt* **1** : destapar (un objeto), dejar al descubierto **2** EXPOSE, REVEAL : descubrir, revelar, exponer
uncultivated [ˌʌnˈkʌltəˌveɪtəd] *adj* : inculto
uncurl [ˌʌnˈkərl] *vt* UNROLL : desenrollar — *vi* : desenrollarse, desrizarse (dícese del pelo)
uncut [ˌʌnˈkʌt] *adj* **1** : sin cortar <uncut grass : hierba sin cortar> **2** : sin tallar, en bruto <an uncut diamond : un diamante en bruto> **3** UNABRIDGED : completo, íntegro
undaunted [ˌʌnˈdɔntəd] *adj* : impávido
undecided [ˌʌndiˈsaɪdəd] *adj* **1** IRRESOLUTE : indeciso, irresoluto **2** UNRESOLVED : pendiente, no resuelto
undefeated [ˌʌndiˈfiːtəd] *adj* : invicto
undeniable [ˌʌndiˈnaɪəbəl] *adj* : innegable — **undeniably** [-bli] *adv*
under[1] [ˈʌndər] *adv* **1** LESS : menos <$10 or under : $10 o menos> **2** UNDERWATER : debajo del agua **3** : bajo los efectos de la anestesia

under[2] *adj* **1** LOWER : (más) bajo, inferior **2** SUBORDINATE : inferior **3** : insuficiente <an under dose of medicine : una dosis insuficiente de medicina>

under[3] *prep* **1** BELOW, BENEATH : debajo de, abajo de <under the table : abajo de la mesa> <we walked under the arch : pasamos por debajo del arco> <under the sun : bajo el sol> **2** : menos de <in under 20 minutes : en menos de 20 minutos> **3** (*indicating rank or authority*) : bajo <under the command of : bajo las órdenes de> **4** SUBJECT TO : bajo <under suspicion : bajo sospecha> <under the circumstances : dadas las circunstancias> **5** ACCORDING TO : según, de acuerdo con, conforme a <under the present laws : según las leyes actuales>

underage [ˌʌndərˈeɪdʒ] *adj* : menor de edad

underbrush [ˈʌndərˌbrəʃ] *n* : maleza *f*

underclothes [ˈʌndərˌkloːz, -ˌkloːðz] → **underwear**

underclothing [ˈʌndərˌkloːðɪŋ] → **underwear**

undercover [ˌʌndərˈkʌvər] *adj* : secreto, clandestino

undercurrent [ˈʌndərˌkərənt] *n* **1** : corriente *f* submarina **2** UNDERTONE : corriente *f* oculta, trasfondo *m*

undercut [ˌʌndərˈkʌt] *vt* **-cut; -cutting** : vender más barato que

underdeveloped [ˌʌndərdɪˈvɛləpt] *adj* : subdesarrollado, atrasado

underdog [ˈʌndərˌdɔg] *n* : persona *f* que tiene menos posibilidades

underdone [ˌʌndərˈdʌn] *adj* RARE : poco cocido

underestimate [ˌʌndərˈɛstəˌmeɪt] *vt* **-mated; -mating** : subestimar, menospreciar

underexposed [ˌʌndərɪkˈspoːzd] *adj* : subexpuesto (en fotografía)

underfoot [ˌʌndərˈfʊt] *adv* **1** : bajo los pies <to trample underfoot : pisotear> **2 to be underfoot** : estorbar <they're always underfoot : están siempre estorbando>

undergarment [ˈʌndərˌgɑrmənt] *n* : prenda *f* íntima

undergo [ˌʌndərˈgoː] *vt* **-went** [-ˈwɛnt;]; **-gone** [-ˈgɔn]; **-going** : sufrir, experimentar <to undergo an operation : someterse a una intervención quirúrgica>

undergraduate [ˌʌndərˈgrædʒʊət] *n* : estudiante *m* universitario, estudiante *f* universitaria

underground[1] [ˌʌndərˈgraʊnd] *adv* **1** : bajo tierra **2** SECRETLY : clandestinamente, en secreto <to go underground : pasar a la clandestinidad>

underground[2] [ˈʌndərˌgraʊnd] *adj* **1** SUBTERRANEAN : subterráneo **2** SECRET : secreto, clandestino

underground[3] [ˈʌndərˌgraʊnd] *n* : movimiento *m* o grupo *m* clandestino

undergrowth [ˈʌndərˈgroːθ] *n* : maleza *f*, broza *f*

underhand[1] [ˈʌndərˌhænd] *adv* **1** SECRETLY : de manera clandestina **2** *or* **underhanded** : sin levantar el brazo por encima del hombro (en deportes)

underhand[2] *adj* **1** SLY : solapado **2** : por debajo del hombro (en deportes)

underhanded [ˌʌndərˈhændəd] *adj* **1** SLY : solapado **2** SHADY : turbio, poco limpio

underline [ˈʌndərˌlaɪn] *vt* **-lined; -lining 1** : subrayar **2** EMPHASIZE : subrayar, acentuar, hacer hincapié en

underlying [ˌʌndərˈlaɪɪŋ] *adj* **1** : subyacente <the underlying rock : la roca subyacente> **2** FUNDAMENTAL : fundamental, esencial

undermine [ˌʌndərˈmaɪn] *vt* **-mined; -mining 1** : socavar (una estructura, etc.) **2** SAP, WEAKEN : minar, debilitar

underneath[1] [ˌʌndərˈniːθ] *adv* : debajo, abajo <the part underneath : la parte de abajo>

underneath[2] *prep* : debajo de, abajo de

undernourished [ˌʌndərˈnərɪʃt] *adj* : desnutrido

underpants [ˈʌndərˌpænts] *npl* : calzoncillos *mpl*, calzones *mpl*

underpass [ˈʌndərˌpæs] *n* : paso *m* a desnivel

underprivileged [ˌʌndərˈprɪvlɪdʒd] *adj* : desfavorecido

underrate [ˌʌndərˈreɪt] *vt* **-rated; -rating** : subestimar, menospreciar

underscore [ˈʌndərˌskor] *vt* **-scored; -scoring** → **underline**

undersea[1] [ˌʌndərˈsiː] *or* **underseas** [-ˈsiːz] *adv* : bajo la superficie del mar

undersea[2] *adj* : submarino

undersecretary [ˌʌndərˈsɛkrəˌtɛri] *n, pl* **-ries** : subsecretario *m*, -ria *f*

undersell [ˌʌndərˈsɛl] *vt* **-sold; -selling** : vender más barato que

undershirt [ˈʌndərˌʃərt] *n* : camiseta *f*

undershorts [ˈʌndərˌʃɔrts] *npl* : calzoncillos *mpl*

underside [ˈʌndərˌsaɪd, ˌʌndərˈsaɪd] *n* : parte *f* de abajo

undersized [ˌʌndərˈsaɪzd] *adj* : más pequeño de lo normal

understand [ˌʌndərˈstænd] *v* **-stood** [-ˈstʊd;]; **-standing** *vt* **1** COMPREHEND : comprender, entender <I don't understand it : no lo entiendo> <that's understood : eso se comprende> <to make oneself understood : hacerse entender> **2** BELIEVE : entender <to give someone to understand : dar a alguien a entender> **3** INFER : tener entendido <I understand that she's leaving : tengo entendido que se va> — *vi* : comprender, entender

understandable [ˌʌndərˈstændəbəl] *adj* : comprensible

understanding[1] [ˌʌndərˈstændɪŋ] *adj* : comprensivo, compasivo

understanding[2] *n* **1** GRASP : comprensión *f,* entendimiento *m* **2** SYMPATHY : comprensión *f* (mutua) **3** INTERPRETATION : interpretación *f* <it's my understanding that... : tengo la impresión de que..., tengo entendido que...> **4** AGREEMENT : acuerdo *m,* arreglo *m*

understate [ˌʌndərˈsteɪt] *vt* **-stated; -stating** : minimizar, subestimar

understatement [ˌʌndərˈsteɪtmənt] *n* : atenuación *f* <that's an understatement : decir sólo eso es quedarse corto>

understudy [ˈʌndərˌstʌdi] *n, pl* **-dies** : sobresaliente *mf,* suplente *mf* (en el teatro)

undertake [ˌʌndərˈteɪk] *vt* **-took** [-ˈtʊk]; **-taken** [-ˈteɪkən]; **-taking 1** : emprender (una tarea), asumir (una responsabilidad) **2** PROMISE : comprometerse (a hacer algo)

undertaker [ˈʌndərˌteɪkər] *n* : director *m,* -tora *f* de funeraria

undertaking [ˈʌndərˌteɪkɪŋ, ˌʌndərˈ-] *n* **1** ENTERPRISE, TASK : empresa *f,* tarea *f* **2** PLEDGE : promesa *f,* garantía *f*

undertone [ˈʌndərˌtoːn] *n* **1** : voz *f* baja <to speak in an undertone : hablar en voz baja> **2** HINT, UNDERCURRENT : trasfondo *m,* matiz *m*

undertow [ˈʌndərˌtoː] *n* : resaca *f*

undervalue [ˌʌndərˈvælˌjuː] *vt* **-ued; -uing** : menospreciar, subestimar

underwater[1] [ˌʌndərˈwɔt̬ər, -ˈwɑ-] *adv* : debajo (del agua)

underwater[2] *adj* : submarino

under way [ˌʌndərˈweɪ] *adv* : en marcha, en camino <to get under way : ponerse en marcha>

underwear [ˈʌndərˌwær] *n* : ropa *f* interior, ropa *f* íntima

underworld [ˈʌndərˌwərld] *n* **1** HELL : infierno *m* **2 the underworld** CRIMINALS : la hampa, los bajos fondos

underwrite [ˈʌndərˌraɪt, ˌʌndərˈ-] *vt* **-wrote** [-ˌroːt, -ˈroːt]; **-written** [-ˌrɪtən, -ˈrɪtən]; **-writing 1** INSURE : asegurar **2** FINANCE : financiar **3** BACK, ENDORSE : suscribir, respaldar

underwriter [ˈʌndərˌraɪt̬ər, ˌʌndərˈ-] *n* INSURER : asegurador *m,* -dora *f*

undeserving [ˌʌndiˈzərvɪŋ] *adj* : indigno

undesirable[1] [ˌʌndiˈzaɪrəbəl] *adj* : indeseable

undesirable[2] *n* : indeseable *mf*

undeveloped [ˌʌndiˈvɛləpt] *adj* : sin desarrollar, sin revelar (dícese de una película)

undies [ˈʌndiːz] → **underwear**

undignified [ˌʌnˈdɪgnəfaɪd] *adj* : indecoroso

undiluted [ˌʌndaɪˈluːtəd, -də-] *adj* : sin diluir, concentrado

undiscovered [ˌʌndɪˈskʌvərd] *adj* : no descubierto

undisputed [ˌʌndɪˈspjuːt̬əd] *adj* : indiscutible

undisturbed [ˌʌndɪˈstərbd] *adj* : tranquilo (dícese de una persona), sin tocar (dícese de un objeto)

undivided [ˌʌndɪˈvaɪdəd] *adj* : íntegro, completo

undo [ˌʌnˈduː] *vt* **-did** [-ˈdɪd]; **-done** [-ˈdʌn]; **-doing 1** UNFASTEN : desabrochar, desatar, abrir **2** ANNUL : anular **3** REVERSE : deshacer, reparar (daños, etc.) **4** RUIN : arruinar, destruir

undoing [ˌʌnˈduːɪŋ] *n* : ruina *f,* perdición *f*

undoubted [ˌʌnˈdaʊt̬əd] *adj* : cierto, indudable — **undoubtedly** *adv*

undress [ˌʌnˈdrɛs] *vt* : desvestir, desabrigar, desnudar — *vi* : desvestirse, desnudarse

undrinkable [ˌʌnˈdrɪŋkəbəl] *adj* : no potable

undue [ˌʌnˈduː, -ˈdjuː] *adj* : excesivo, indebido — **unduly** *adv*

undulate [ˈʌndʒəˌleɪt] *vi* **-lated; -lating** : ondular

undulation [ˌʌndʒəˈleɪʃən] *n* : ondulación *f*

undying [ˌʌnˈdaɪɪŋ] *adj* : perpetuo, imperecedero

unearth [ˌʌnˈərθ] *vt* **1** EXHUME : desenterrar, exhumar **2** DISCOVER : descubrir

unearthly [ˌʌnˈərθli] *adj* **-lier; -est** : sobrenatural, de otro mundo

uneasily [ˌʌnˈiːzəli] *adv* : inquietamente, con inquietud

uneasiness [ˌʌnˈiːzinəs] *n* : inquietud *f*

uneasy [ˌʌnˈiːzi] *adj* **-easier; -est 1** AWKWARD : incómodo **2** WORRIED : preocupado, inquieto **3** RESTLESS : inquieto, agitado

uneducated [ˌʌnˈɛdʒəˌkeɪt̬əd] *adj* : inculto, sin educación

unemployed [ˌʌnɪmˈplɔɪd] *adj* : desempleado

unemployment [ˌʌnɪmˈplɔɪmənt] *n* : desempleo *m*

unending [ˌʌnˈɛndɪŋ] *adj* : sin fin, interminable

unendurable [ˌʌnɪnˈdʊrəbəl, -ɛn-, -ˈdjʊr-] *adj* : insoportable, intolerable

unequal [ˌʌnˈiːkwəl] *adj* **1** : desigual **2** INADEQUATE : incapaz, incompetente <to be unequal to a task : no estar a la altura de una tarea>

unequaled *or* **unequalled** [ˌʌnˈiːkwəld] *adj* : sin igual

unequivocal [ˌʌnɪˈkwɪvəkəl] *adj* : inequívoco, claro — **unequivocally** *adv*

unerring [ˌʌnˈɛrɪŋ, -ˈər-] *adj* : infalible

unethical [ˌʌnˈɛθɪkəl] *adj* : poco ético

uneven [ˌʌnˈiːvən] *adj* **1** ODD : impar (dícese de un número) **2** : desigual, desnivelado (dícese de una superficie) <uneven terrain : terreno accidentado> **3** IRREGULAR : irregular, poco uniforme **4** UNEQUAL : desigual

unevenly [ˌʌnˈiːvənli] *adv* : desigualmente, irregularmente
uneventful [ˌʌnɪˈvɛntfəl] *adj* : sin incidentes, tranquilo
unexpected [ˌʌnɪkˈspɛktəd] *adj* : imprevisto, inesperado — **unexpectedly** *adv*
unfailing [ˌʌnˈfeɪlɪŋ] *adj* **1** CONSTANT : constante **2** INEXHAUSTIBLE : inagotable **3** SURE : a toda prueba, indefectible
unfair [ˌʌnˈfær] *adj* : injusto — **unfairly** *adv*
unfairness [ˌʌnˈfærnəs] *n* : injusticia *f*
unfaithful [ˌʌnˈfeɪθfəl] *adj* : desleal, infiel — **unfaithfully** *adv*
unfaithfulness [ˌʌnˈfeɪθfəlnəs] *n* : infidelidad *f*, deslealtad *f*
unfamiliar [ˌʌnfəˈmɪljər] *adj* **1** STRANGE : desconocido, extraño <an unfamiliar place : un lugar nuevo> **2 to be unfamiliar with** : no estar familiarizado con, desconocer
unfamiliarity [ˌʌnfəˌmɪliˈærət̬i] *n* : falta *f* de familiaridad
unfashionable [ˌʌnˈfæʃənəbəl] *adj* : fuera de moda
unfasten [ˌʌnˈfæsən] *vt* : desabrochar, desatar (una cuerda, etc.), abrir (una puerta)
unfavorable [ˌʌnˈfeɪvərəbəl] *adj* : desfavorable, mal — **unfavorably** [-bli] *adv*
unfeeling [ˌʌnˈfiːlɪŋ] *adj* : insensible — **unfeelingly** *adv*
unfinished [ˌʌnˈfɪnɪʃd] *adj* : inacabado, incompleto
unfit [ˌʌnˈfɪt] *adj* **1** UNSUITABLE : inadecuado, impropio **2** UNSUITED : no apto, incapaz **3** : incapacitado (físicamente) <to be unfit : no estar en forma>
unflappable [ˌʌnˈflæpəbəl] *adj* : imperturbable
unflattering [ˌʌnˈflæt̬ərɪŋ] *adj* : poco favorecedor
unfold [ˌʌnˈfoːld] *vt* **1** EXPAND : desplegar, desdoblar, extender <to unfold a map : desplegar un mapa> **2** DISCLOSE, REVEAL : revelar, exponer (un plan, etc.) — *vi* **1** DEVELOP : desarrollarse, desenvolverse <the story unfolded : el cuento se desarrollaba> **2** EXPAND : extenderse, desplegarse
unforeseeable [ˌʌnforˈsiːəbəl] *adj* : imprevisible
unforeseen [ˌʌnforˈsiːn] *adj* : imprevisto
unforgettable [ˌʌnfərˈgɛt̬əbəl] *adj* : inolvidable, memorable — **unforgettably** [-bli] *adv*
unforgivable [ˌʌnfərˈgɪvəbəl] *adj* : imperdonable
unfortunate[1] [ˌʌnˈfɔrtʃənət] *adj* **1** UNLUCKY : desgraciado, infortunado, desafortunado <how unfortunate! : ¡qué mala suerte!> **2** INAPPROPRIATE : inoportuno <an unfortunate comment : un comentario poco feliz>
unfortunate[2] *n* : desgraciado *m*, -da *f*
unfortunately [ˌʌnˈfɔrtʃənətli] *adv* : desafortunadamente
unfounded [ˌʌnˈfaʊndəd] *adj* : infundado
unfreeze [ˌʌnˈfriːz] *v* **-froze** [-ˈfroːz]; **-frozen** [-ˈfroːzən]; **-freezing** *vt* : descongelar — *vi* : descongelarse
unfriendliness [ˌʌnˈfrɛndlinəs] *n* : hostilidad *f*, antipatía *f*
unfriendly [ˌʌnˈfrɛndli] *adj* **-lier; -est** : poco amistoso, hostil
unfurl [ˌʌnˈfərl] *vt* : desplegar, desdoblar — *vi* : desplegarse
unfurnished [ˌʌnˈfərnɪʃt] *adj* : desamueblado
ungainly [ˌʌnˈgeɪnli] *adj* : desgarbado
ungodly [ˌʌnˈgɔdli, -ˈgɑd-] *adj* **1** IMPIOUS : impío **2** OUTRAGEOUS : atroz, terrible <at an ungodly hour : a una hora intempestiva>
ungrateful [ˌʌnˈgreɪtfəl] *adj* : desagradecido, ingrato — **ungratefully** *adv*
ungratefulness [ˌʌnˈgreɪtfəlnəs] *n* : ingratitud *f*
unhappily [ˌʌnˈhæpəli] *adv* **1** SADLY : tristemente **2** UNFORTUNATELY : desafortunadamente, lamentablemente
unhappiness [ˌʌnˈhæpinəs] *n* : infelicidad *f*, tristeza *f*, desdicha *f*
unhappy [ˌʌnˈhæpi] *adj* **-pier; -est 1** UNFORTUNATE : desafortunado, desventurado **2** MISERABLE, SAD : infeliz, triste, desdichado **3** INOPPORTUNE : inoportuno, poco feliz
unharmed [ˌʌnˈhɑrmd] *adj* : salvo, ileso
unhealthy [ˌʌnˈhɛlθi] *adj* **-thier; -est 1** UNWHOLESOME : insalubre, malsano, nocivo a la salud <an unhealthy climate : un clima insalubre> **2** SICKLY : de mala salud, enfermizo
unheard–of [ˌʌnˈhərdəv] *adj* : sin precedente, inaudito, insólito
unhinge [ˌʌnˈhɪndʒ] *vt* **-hinged; -hinging 1** : desquiciar (una puerta, etc.) **2** DISRUPT, UNSETTLE : trastornar, perturbar
unholy [ˌʌnˈhoːli] *adj* **-lier; -est 1** : profano, impío **2** UNGODLY : atroz, terrible
unhook [ˌʌnˈhʊk] *vt* **1** : desenganchar, descolgar (de algo) **2** UNDO : desabrochar
unhurt [ˌʌnˈhərt] *adj* : ileso
unicorn [ˈjuːnəˌkɔrn] *n* : unicornio *m*
unidentified [ˌʌnaɪˈdɛntəˌfaɪd] *adj* : no identificado <unidentified flying object : objeto volador no identificado>
unification [ˌjuːnəfəˈkeɪʃən] *n* : unificación *f*
uniform[1] [ˈjuːnəˌfɔrm] *adj* : uniforme, homogéneo, constante
uniform[2] *n* : uniforme *m*
uniformity [ˌjuːnəˈfɔrmət̬i] *n, pl* **-ties** : uniformidad *f*

unify [ˈjuːnə,faɪ] *vt* **-fied; -fying** : unificar, unir
unilateral [,juːnəˈlætərəl] *adj* : unilateral — **unilaterally** *adv*
unimaginable [,ʌnɪˈmædʒənəbəl] *adj* : inimaginable, inconcebible
unimportant [,ʌnɪmˈpɔrtənt] *adj* : intrascendente, insignificante, sin importancia
uninhabited [,ʌnɪnˈhæbətəd] *adj* : deshabitado, desierto, despoblado
uninhibited [,ʌnɪnˈhɪbətəd] *adj* : desenfadado, desinhibido, sin reservas
uninjured [,ʌnˈindʒərd] *adj* : ileso
unintelligent [,ʌnɪnˈtɛlədʒənt] *adj* : poco inteligente
unintelligible [,ʌnɪnˈtɛlədʒəbəl] *adj* : ininteligible, incomprensible
unintentional [,ʌnɪnˈtɛntʃənəl] *adj* : no deliberado, involuntario
unintentionally [,ʌnɪnˈtɛntʃənəli] *adv* : involuntariamente, sin querer
uninterested [,ʌnˈɪntə,rɛstəd, -trəstəd] *adj* : indiferente
uninteresting [,ʌnˈɪntə,rɛstɪŋ, -trəstɪŋ] *adj* : poco interesante, sin interés
uninterrupted [,ʌn,ɪntəˈrʌptəd] *adj* : ininterrumpido, continuo
union [ˈjuːnjən] *n* **1** : unión *f* **2** *or* **labor union** : sindicato *m,* gremio *m*
unionize [ˈjuːnjə,naɪz] *v* **-ized; -izing** *vt* : sindicalizar, sindicar — *vi* : sindicalizarse
unique [jʊˈniːk] *adj* **1** SOLE : único, solo **2** UNUSUAL : extraordinario
uniquely [jʊˈniːkli] *adv* **1** EXCLUSIVELY : exclusivamente **2** EXCEPTIONALLY : excepcionalmente
unison [ˈjuːnəsən, -zən] *n* **1** : unísono *m* (en música) **2** CONCORD : acuerdo *m,* armonía *f,* concordia *f* **3 in ~** SIMULTANEOUSLY : simultáneamente, al unísono
unit [ˈjuːnɪt] *n* **1** : unidad *f* **2** : módulo *m* (de un mobiliario)
unite [jʊˈnaɪt] *v* **united; uniting** *vt* : unir, juntar, combinar — *vi* : unirse, juntarse
unity [ˈjuːnəti] *n, pl* **-ties 1** UNION : unidad *f,* unión *f* **2** HARMONY : armonía *f,* acuerdo *m*
universal [,juːnəˈvərsəl] *adj* **1** GENERAL : general, universal <a universal rule : una regla universal> **2** WORLDWIDE : universal, mundial — **universally** *adv*
universe [ˈjuːnə,vərs] *n* : universo *m*
university [,juːnəˈvərsəti] *n, pl* **-ties** : universidad *f*
unjust [,ʌnˈdʒʌst] *adj* : injusto — **unjustly** *adv*
unjustifiable [,ʌn,dʒʌstəˈfaɪəbəl] *adj* : injustificable
unjustified [,ʌnˈdʒʌstə,faɪd] *adj* : injustificado
unkempt [,ʌnˈkɛmpt] *adj* : descuidado, desaliñado, despeinado (dícese del pelo)
unkind [,ʌnˈkaɪnd] *adj* : poco amable, cruel — **unkindly** *adv*
unkindness [,ʌnˈkaɪndnəs] *n* : crueldad *f,* falta *f* de amabilidad
unknowing [,ʌnˈnoːɪŋ] *adj* : inconsciente, ignorante — **unknowingly** *adv*
unknown [,ʌnˈnoːn] *adj* : desconocido
unlawful [,ʌnˈlɔfəl] *adj* : ilícito, ilegal — **unlawfully** *adv*
unleash [,ʌnˈliːʃ] *vt* : soltar, desatar
unless [ənˈlɛs] *conj* : a menos que, salvo que, a no ser que
unlike[1] [,ʌnˈlaɪk] *adj* **1** DIFFERENT : diferente, distinto **2** UNEQUAL : desigual
unlike[2] *prep* **1** : diferente de, distinto de <unlike the others : distinto a los demás> **2** : a diferencia de <unlike her sister, she is shy : a diferencia de su hermana, es tímida>
unlikelihood [,ʌnˈlaɪkli,hʊd] *n* : improbabilidad *f*
unlikely [,ʌnˈlaɪkli] *adj* **-lier; -est 1** IMPROBABLE : improbable, poco probable **2** UNPROMISING : poco prometedor
unlimited [,ʌnˈlɪmətəd] *adj* : ilimitado
unload [,ʌnˈloːd] *vt* **1** REMOVE : descargar, desembarcar (mercancías o pasajeros) **2** : descargar (un avión, un camión, etc.) **3** DUMP : deshacerse de — *vi* : descargar (dícese de un avión, un camión, etc.)
unlock [,ʌnˈlɑk] *vt* **1** : abrir (con llave) **2** DISCLOSE, REVEAL : revelar
unluckily [,ʌnˈlʌkəli] *adv* : desgraciadamente
unlucky [,ʌnˈlʌki] *adj* **-luckier; -est 1** : de mala suerte, desgraciado, desafortunado <an unlucky year : un año de mala suerte> **2** INAUSPICIOUS : desfavorable, poco propicio **3** REGRETTABLE : lamentable
unmanageable [,ʌnˈmænɪdʒəbəl] *adj* : difícil de controlar, poco manejable, ingobernable
unmarried [,ʌnˈmærid] *adj* : soltero
unmask [,ʌnˈmæsk] *vt* EXPOSE : desenmascarar
unmerciful [,ʌnˈmərsɪfəl] *adj* MERCILESS : despiadado — **unmercifully** *adv*
unmistakable [,ʌnmɪˈsteɪkəbəl] *adj* : evidente, inconfundible, obvio — **unmistakably** [-bli] *adv*
unmoved [,ʌnˈmuːvd] *adj* : impasible <to be unmoved by : permanecer impasible ante>
unnatural [,ʌnˈnætʃərəl] *adj* **1** ABNORMAL, UNUSUAL : anormal, poco natural, poco normal **2** AFFECTED : afectado, forzado <an unnatural smile : una sonrisa forzada> **3** PERVERSE : perverso, antinatural
unnecessary [,ʌnˈnɛsə,sɛri] *adj* : innecesario — **unnecessarily** [-,nɛsəˈsɛrəli] *adv*

unnerve [ˌʌnˈnərv] *vt* **-nerved; -nerving** : turbar, desconcertar, poner nervioso
unnoticed [ˌʌnˈnoːtəst] *adj* : inadvertido <to go unnoticed : pasar inadvertido>
unobstructed [ˌʌnəbˈstrʌktəd] *adj* : libre, despejado
unobtainable [ˌʌnəbˈteɪnəbəl] *adj* : inasequible
unobtrusive [ˌʌnəbˈstruːsɪv] *adj* : discreto
unoccupied [ˌʌnˈɑkjəˌpaɪd] *adj* **1** IDLE : desempleado, desocupado **2** EMPTY : desocupado, libre, deshabitado
unofficial [ˌʌnəˈfɪʃəl] *adj* : extraoficial, oficioso, no oficial
unorganized [ˌʌnˈɔrgəˌnaɪzd] *adj* : desorganizado
unorthodox [ˌʌnˈɔrθəˌdɑks] *adj* : poco ortodoxo, poco convencional
unpack [ˌʌnˈpæk] *vt* : desempacar — *vi* : desempacar, deshacer las maletas
unpaid [ˌʌnˈpeɪd] *adj* : no remunerado, no retribuido <an unpaid bill : una cuenta pendiente>
unparalleled [ˌʌnˈpærəˌlɛld] *adj* : sin igual
unpatriotic [ˌʌnˌpeɪtriˈɑt̬ɪk] *adj* : antipatriótico
unpleasant [ˌʌnˈplɛzənt] *adj* : desagradable — **unpleasantly** *adv*
unplug [ˌʌnˈplʌg] *vt* **-plugged; -plugging 1** UNCLOG : destapar, desatascar **2** DISCONNECT : desconectar, desenchufar
unpopular [ˌʌnˈpɑpjələr] *adj* : impopular, poco popular
unpopularity [ˌʌnˌpɑpjəˈlærət̬i] *n* : impopularidad *f*
unprecedented [ˌʌnˈprɛsəˌdɛntəd] *adj* : sin precedentes, inaudito, nuevo
unpredictable [ˌʌnpriˈdɪktəbəl] *adj* : impredecible
unprejudiced [ˌʌnˈprɛdʒədəst] *adj* : imparcial, objetivo
unprepared [ˌʌnpriˈpærd] *adj* : no preparado <an unprepared speech : un discurso improvisado>
unpretentious [ˌʌnpriˈtɛntʃəs] *adj* : modesto, sin pretensiones
unprincipled [ˌʌnˈprɪntsəpəld] *adj* : sin principios, carente de escrúpulos
unproductive [ˌʌnprəˈdʌktɪv] *adj* : improductivo
unprofitable [ˌʌnˈprɑfət̬əbəl] *adj* : no rentable, poco provechoso
unpromising [ˌʌnˈprɑməsɪŋ] *adj* : poco prometedor
unprotected [ˌʌnprəˈtɛktəd] *adj* : sin protección, desprotegido
unprovoked [ˌʌnprəˈvoːkt] *adj* : no provocado
unpunished [ˌʌnˈpʌnɪʃt] *adj* : impune <to go unpunished : escapar sin castigo>
unqualified [ˌʌnˈkwɑləˌfaɪd] *adj* **1** : no calificado, sin título **2** COMPLETE : completo, absoluto <an unqualified denial : una negación incondicional>
unquestionable [ˌʌnˈkwɛstʃənəbəl] *adj* : incuestionable, indudable, indiscutible — **unquestionably** [-bli] *adv*
unquestioning [ˌʌnˈkwɛstʃənɪŋ] *adj* : incondicional, absoluto, ciego
unravel [ˌʌnˈrævəl] *v* **-eled** *or* **-elled; -eling** *or* **-elling** *vt* **1** DISENTANGLE : desenmarañar, desenredar **2** SOLVE : aclarar, desenmarañar, desentrañar — *vi* : deshacerse
unreal [ˌʌnˈriːl] *adj* : irreal
unrealistic [ˌʌnˌriːəˈlɪstɪk] *adj* : poco realista
unreasonable [ˌʌnˈriːzənəbəl] *adj* **1** IRRATIONAL : poco razonable, irrazonable, irracional **2** EXCESSIVE : excesivo <unreasonable prices : precios excesivos>
unreasonably [ˌʌnˈriːzənəbli] *adv* **1** IRRATIONALLY : irracionalmente, de manera irrazonable **2** EXCESSIVELY : excesivamente
unrefined [ˌʌnriˈfaɪnd] *adj* **1** : no refinado, sin refinar (dícese del azúcar, de la harina, etc.) **2** : poco refinado, inculto (dícese de una persona)
unrelated [ˌʌnriˈleɪt̬əd] *adj* : no relacionado, inconexo
unrelenting [ˌʌnriˈlɛntɪŋ] *adj* **1** STERN : severo, inexorable **2** CONSTANT, RELENTLESS : constante, implacable
unreliable [ˌʌnriˈlaɪəbəl] *adj* : que no es de fiar, de poca confianza, inestable (dícese del tiempo)
unrepentant [ˌʌnriˈpɛntənt] *adj* : impenitente
unresolved [ˌʌnriˈzɑlvd] *adj* : pendiente, no resuelto
unrest [ˌʌnˈrɛst] *n* : inquietud *f,* malestar *m* <political unrest : disturbios políticos>
unrestrained [ˌʌnriˈstreɪnd] *adj* : desenfrenado, incontrolado
unrestricted [ˌʌnriˈstrɪktəd] *adj* : sin restricción <unrestricted access : libre acceso>
unrewarding [ˌʌnriˈwɔrdɪŋ] *adj* THANKLESS : ingrato
unripe [ˌʌnˈraɪp] *adj* : inmaduro, verde
unrivaled *or* **unrivalled** [ˌʌnˈraɪvəld] *adj* : incomparable
unroll [ˌʌnˈroːl] *vt* : desenrollar — *vi* : desenrollarse
unruffled [ˌʌnˈrʌfəld] *adj* **1** SERENE : sereno, tranquilo **2** SMOOTH : tranquilo, liso <unruffled waters : aguas tranquilas>
unruliness [ˌʌnˈruːlinəs] *n* : indisciplina *f*
unruly [ˌʌnˈruːli] *adj* : indisciplinado, díscolo, rebelde
unsafe [ˌʌnˈseɪf] *adj* : inseguro
unsaid [ˌʌnˈsɛd] *adj* : sin decir <to leave unsaid : quedar por decir>
unsanitary [ˌʌnˈsænəˌtɛri] *adj* : antihigiénico

unsatisfactory [ˌʌnˌsæt̬əsˈfæktəri] *adj* : insatisfactorio
unsatisfied [ˌʌnˈsæt̬əsˌfaɪd] *adj* : insatisfecho
unscathed [ˌʌnˈskeɪðd] *adj* UNHARMED : ileso
unscheduled [ˌʌnˈskɛˌdʒuːld] *adj* : no programado, imprevisto
unscientific [ˌʌnˌsaɪənˈtɪfɪk] *adj* : poco científico
unscrupulous [ˌʌnˈskruːpjələs] *adj* : inescrupuloso, sin escrúpulos — **unscrupulously** *adv*
unseal [ˌʌnˈsiːl] *vt* : abrir, quitarle el sello a
unseasonable [ˌʌnˈsiːzənəbəl] *adj* **1** : extemporáneo <unseasonable rain : lluvia extemporánea> **2** UNTIMELY : extemporáneo, inoportuno
unseemly [ˌʌnˈsiːmli] *adj* **-lier; -est 1** INDECOROUS : indecoroso **2** INAPPROPRIATE : impropio, inapropiado
unseen [ˌʌnˈsiːn] *adj* **1** UNNOTICED : inadvertido **2** INVISIBLE : oculto, invisible
unselfish [ˌʌnˈsɛlfɪʃ] *adj* : generoso, desinteresado — **unselfishly** *adv*
unselfishness [ˌʌnˈsɛlfɪʃnəs] *n* : generosidad *f*, desinterés *m*
unsettle [ˌʌnˈsɛt̬əl] *vt* **-tled; -tling** DISTURB : trastornar, alterar, perturbar
unsettled [ˌʌnˈsɛt̬əld] *adj* **1** CHANGEABLE : inestable, variable <unsettled weather : tiempo inestable> **2** DISTURBED : agitado, inquieto <unsettled waters : aguas agitadas> **3** UNDECIDED : pendiente (dícese de un asunto), indeciso (dícese de una persona) **4** UNPAID : sin saldar, pendiente **5** UNINHABITED : despoblado, no colonizado
unshaped [ˌʌnˈʃeɪpt] *adj* : sin forma, informe
unsightly [ˌʌnˈsaɪtli] *adj* UGLY : feo, de aspecto malo
unskilled [ˌʌnˈskɪld] *adj* : no calificado
unskillful [ˌʌnˈskɪlfəl] *adj* : inexperto, poco hábil
unsnap [ˌʌnˈsnæp] *vt* **-snapped; -snapping** : desabrochar
unsociable *adj* : poco sociable
unsolved [ˌʌnˈsɔlvd] *adj* : no resuelto, sin resolver
unsophisticated [ˌʌnsəˈfɪstəˌkeɪt̬əd] *adj* **1** NAIVE, UNWORLDLY : ingenuo, de poco mundo **2** SIMPLE : simple, poco sofisticado, rudimentario
unsound [ˌʌnˈsaʊnd] *adj* **1** UNHEALTHY : enfermizo, de mala salud **2** : poco sólido, defectuoso (dícese de una estructura, etc.) **3** INVALID : inválido, erróneo **4 of unsound mind** : mentalmente incapacitado
unspeakable [ˌʌnˈspiːkəbəl] *adj* **1** INDESCRIBABLE : indecible, inexpresable, incalificable **2** HEINOUS : atroz, nefando, abominable — **unspeakably** [-bli] *adv*
unspecified [ˌʌnˈspɛsəˌfaɪd] *adj* : indeterminado, sin especificar
unspoiled [ˌʌnˈspɔɪld] *adj* **1** : conservado, sin estropear (dícese de un lugar) **2** : que no está mimado (dícese de un niño)
unstable [ˌʌnˈsteɪbəl] *adj* **1** CHANGEABLE : variable, inestable, cambiable <an unstable pulse : un pulso irregular> **2** UNSTEADY : inestable, poco sólido (dícese de una estructura)
unsteadily [ˌʌnˈstɛdəli] *adv* : de modo inestable
unsteadiness [ˌʌnˈstɛdinəs] *n* : inestabilidad *f*, inseguridad *f*
unsteady [ˌʌnˈstɛdi] *adj* **1** UNSTABLE : inestable, variable **2** SHAKY : tembloroso
unstoppable [ˌʌnˈstɑpəbəl] *adj* : irrefrenable, incontenible
unsubstantiated [ˌʌnsəbˈstæntʃiˌeɪt̬əd] *adj* : no corroborado, no demostrado
unsuccessful [ˌʌnsəkˈsɛsfəl] *adj* : fracasado, infructuoso
unsuitable [ˌʌnˈsuːt̬əbəl] *adj* : inadecuado, impropio, inapropiado <an unsuitable time : una hora inconveniente>
unsuited [ˌʌnˈsuːt̬əd] *adj* : inadecuado, inepto
unsung [ˌʌnˈsʌŋ] *adj* : olvidado
unsure [ˌʌnˈʃʊr] *adj* : incierto, dudoso
unsurpassed [ˌʌnsərˈpæst] *adj* : sin par, sin igual
unsuspecting [ˌʌnsəˈspɛktɪŋ] *adj* : desprevenido, desapercibido, confiado
unsympathetic [ˌʌnˌsɪmpəˈθɛt̬ɪk] *adj* : poco comprensivo, indiferente
untangle [ˌʌnˈteɪŋgəl] *vt* **-gled; -gling** : desenmarañar, desenredar
unthinkable [ˌʌnˈθɪŋkəbəl] *adj* : inconcebible, impensable
unthinking [ˌʌnˈθɪŋkɪŋ] *adj* : irreflexivo, inconsciente — **unthinkingly** *adv*
untidy [ˌʌnˈtaɪdi] *adj* **1** SLOVENLY : desaliñado **2** DISORDERLY : desordenado, desarreglado
untie [ˌʌnˈtaɪ] *vt* **-tied; -tying** *or* **-tieing** : desatar, deshacer
until[1] [ˌʌnˈtɪl] *prep* : hasta <until now : hasta ahora>
until[2] *conj* : hasta que <until they left : hasta que salieron> <don't answer until you're sure : no contestes hasta que (no) estés seguro>
untimely [ˌʌnˈtaɪmli] *adj* **1** PREMATURE : prematuro <an untimely death : una muerte prematura> **2** INOPPORTUNE : inoportuno, intempestivo
untold [ˌʌnˈtoːld] *adj* **1** : nunca dicho <the untold secret : el secreto sin contar> **2** INCALCULABLE : incalculable, indecible
untouched [ˌʌnˈtʌtʃt] *adj* **1** INTACT : intacto, sin tocar, sin probar (dícese de la comida) **2** UNAFFECTED : insensible, indiferente

untoward [ˌʌnˈtɔrd, -ˈtoːərd, -təˈwɔrd] *adj* **1** : indecoroso, impropio (dícese del comportamiento) **2** ADVERSE, UNFORTUNATE : desafortunado, adverso <untoward effects : efectos perjudiciales> **3** UNSEEMLY : indecoroso

untrained [ˌʌnˈtreɪnd] *adj* : inexperto, no capacitado

untreated [ˌʌnˈtriːtəd] *adj* : no tratado (dícese de una enfermedad, etc.), sin tratar (dícese de un material)

untroubled [ˌʌnˈtrʌbəld] *adj* : tranquilo <to be untroubled by : no estar afectado por>

untrue [ˌʌnˈtruː] *adj* **1** UNFAITHFUL : infiel **2** FALSE : falso

untrustworthy [ˌʌnˈtrʌstˌwərði] *adj* : de poca confianza (dícese de una persona), no fidedigno (dícese de la información)

untruth [ˌʌnˈtruːθ, ˈʌnˌ-] *n* : mentira *f,* falsedad *f*

untruthful [ˌʌnˈtruːθfəl] *adj* : mentiroso, falso

unusable [ˌʌnˈjuːzəbəl] *adj* : inútil, inservible

unused [ˌʌnˈjuːzd, *in sense 1 usually* -ˈjuːst] *adj* **1** UNACCUSTOMED : inhabituado **2** NEW : nuevo **3** IDLE : no utilizado (dícese de la tierra) **4** REMAINING : restante <the unused portion : la porción restante>

unusual [ˌʌnˈjuːʒʊəl] *adj* : inusual, poco común, raro

unusually [ˌʌnˈjuːʒʊəli, -ˈjuːʒəli] *adv* : excepcionalmente, extraordinariamente, fuera de lo común

unwanted [ˌʌnˈwɑntəd] *adj* : superfluo, de sobre

unwarranted [ˌʌnˈwɔrəntəd] *adj* : injustificado

unwary [ˌʌnˈwæri] *adj* : incauto

unwavering [ˌʌnˈweɪvərɪŋ] *adj* : firme, inquebrantable <an unwavering gaze : una mirada fija>

unwelcome [ˌʌnˈwɛlkəm] *adj* : importuno, molesto

unwell [ˌʌnˈwɛl] *adj* : enfermo, mal

unwholesome [ˌʌnˈhoːlsəm] *adj* **1** UNHEALTHY : malsano, insalubre **2** PERNICIOUS : pernicioso **3** LOATHSOME : repugnante, muy desagradable

unwieldy [ˌʌnˈwiːldi] *adj* CUMBERSOME : difícil de manejar, torpe y pesado

unwilling [ˌʌnˈwɪlɪŋ] *adj* : poco dispuesto <to be unwilling to : no estar dispuesto a>

unwillingly [ˌʌnˈwɪlɪŋli] *adv* : a regañadientes, de mala gana

unwind [ˌʌnˈwaɪnd] *v* **-wound** [-ˈwaʊnd]; **-winding** *vt* **1** UNROLL : desenrollar **2** RELAX : relajar — *vi* : desenrollarse

unwise [ˌʌnˈwaɪz] *adj* : imprudente, desacertado, poco aconsejable

unwisely [ˌʌnˈwaɪzli] *adv* : imprudentemente

unwitting [ˌʌnˈwɪṭɪŋ] *adj* **1** UNAWARE : inconsciente **2** INADVERTENT : involuntario, inadvertido <an unwitting mistake : un error inadvertido> — **unwittingly** *adv*

unworthiness [ˌʌnˈwərðinəs] *n* : falta *f* de valía

unworthy [ˌʌnˈwərði] *adj* **1** UNDESERVING : indigno <to be unworthy of : no ser digno de> **2** UNMERITED : inmerecido

unwrap [ˌʌnˈræp] *vt* **-wrapped; -wrapping** : desenvolver, deshacer

unwritten [ˌʌnˈrɪtən] *adj* : no escrito

unyielding [ˌʌnˈjiːldɪŋ] *adj* : firme, inflexible, rígido

unzip [ˌʌnˈzɪp] *vt* **-zipped; -zipping** : abrir el cierre de

up¹ [ˈʌp] *v* **upped** [ˈʌpt]; **upping; ups** *vt* INCREASE : aumentar, subir <they upped the prices : aumentaron los precios> — *vi* **to up and** : agarrar y *fam* <she up and left : agarró y se fue>

up² *adv* **1** ABOVE : arriba, en lo alto <up in the mountains : arriba en las montañas> **2** UPWARDS : hacia arriba <push it up : empújalo hacia arriba> <the sun came up : el sol salió> <prices went up : los precios subieron> **3** (*indicating an upright position or waking state*) <to sit up : ponerse derecho> <they got up late : se levantaron tarde> <I stayed up all night : pasé toda la noche sin dormir> **4** (*indicating volume or intensity*) <to speak up : hablar más fuerte> **5** (*indicating a northerly direction*) <the climate up north : el clima del norte> <I'm going up to Canada : voy para Canadá> **6** (*indicating the appearance or existence of something*) <the book turned up : el libro apareció> **7** (*indicating consideration*) <she brought the matter up : mencionó el asunto> **8** COMPLETELY : completamente <eat it up : cómetelo todo> **9** : en pedazos <he tore it up : lo rompió en pedazos> **10** (*indicating a stopping*) <the car pulled up to the curb : el carro paró al borde de la acera> **11** (*indicating an even score*) <the game was 10 up : empataron a 10>

up³ *adj* **1** (*risen above the horizon*) <the sun is up : ha salido el sol> **2** (*being above a normal or former level*) <prices are up : los precios han aumentado> <the river is up : las aguas están altas> **3** : despierto, levantado <up all night : despierto toda la noche> **4** BUILT : construido <the house is up : la casa está construida> **5** OPEN : abierto <the windows are up : las ventanas están abiertas> **6** (*moving or going upward*) <the up staircase : la escalera para subir> **7** ABREAST : enterado, al día, al corriente <to be up on the news : estar al corriente de las noticias> **8** PREPARED : preparado <we were up for the test

: estuvimos preparados para el examen> **9** FINISHED : terminado, acabado <time is up : se ha terminado el tiempo permitido> **10 to be up** : pasar <what's up? : ¿qué pasa?>

up[4] *prep* **1** (*to, toward, or at a higher point of*) <he went up the stairs : subió la escalera> **2** (*to or toward the source of*) <to go up the river : ir río arriba> **3** ALONG : a lo largo, por <up the coast : a lo largo de la costa> <just up the way : un poco más adelante> <up and down the city : por toda la ciudad>

upbraid [ˌʌpˈbreɪd] *vt* : reprender, regañar

upbringing [ˈʌpˌbrɪŋɪŋ] *n* : crianza *f,* educación *f*

upcoming [ˌʌpˈkʌmɪŋ] *adj* : próximo

update[1] [ˌʌpˈdeɪt] *vt* **-dated; -dating** : poner al día, poner al corriente, actualizar

update[2] [ˈʌpˌdeɪt] *n* : actualización *f,* puesta *f* al día

upend [ˌʌpˈɛnd] *vt* **1** : poner vertical **2** OVERTURN : volcar

upgrade[1] [ˈʌpˌgreɪd, ˌʌpˈ-] *vt* **-graded; -grading** : elevar la categoría de (un puesto, etc.), implementar mejoras a (una facilidad, etc.)

upgrade[2] [ˈʌpˌgreɪd] *n* **1** SLOPE : cuesta *f,* pendiente *f* **2** RISE : aumento *m* de categoría (de un puesto), ascenso *m* (de un empleado)

upheaval [ˌʌpˈhiːvəl] *n* **1** : levantamiento *m* (en geología) **2** DISTURBANCE, UPSET : trastorno *m,* agitación *f,* conmoción *f*

uphill[1] [ˌʌpˈhɪl] *adv* : cuesta arriba

uphill[2] [ˈʌpˌhɪl] *adj* **1** ASCENDING : en subida **2** DIFFICULT : difícil, arduo

uphold [ˌʌpˈhoːld] *vt* **-held; -holding 1** SUPPORT : sostener, apoyar, mantener **2** RAISE : levantar **3** CONFIRM : confirmar (una decisión judicial)

upholster [ˌʌpˈhoːlstər] *vt* : tapizar

upholsterer [ˌʌpˈhoːlstərər] *n* : tapicero *m,* -ra *f*

upholstery [ˌʌpˈhoːlstəri] *n, pl* **-steries** : tapicería *f*

upkeep [ˈʌpˌkiːp] *n* : mantenimiento *m*

upland [ˈʌplənd, -ˌlænd] *n* : altiplanicie *f,* altiplano *m*

uplift[1] [ˌʌpˈlɪft] *vt* **1** RAISE : elevar, levantar **2** ELEVATE : elevar, animar (el espíritu, la mente, etc.)

uplift[2] [ˈʌpˌlɪft] *n* : elevación *f*

upon [əˈpɔn, əˈpɑn] *prep* : en, sobre <upon the desk : sobre el escritorio> <upon leaving : al salir> <questions upon questions : pregunta tras pregunta>

upper[1] [ˈʌpər] *adj* **1** HIGHER : superior <the upper classes : las clases altas> **2** : alto (en geografía) <the upper Mississippi : el alto Mississippi>

upper[2] *n* : parte *f* superior (del calzado, etc.)

uppercase [ˌʌpərˈkeɪs] *adj* : mayúsculo

upper hand *n* : ventaja *f,* dominio *m*

uppermost [ˈʌpərˌmoːst] *adj* : más alto <it was uppermost in his mind : era lo que más le preocupaba>

upright[1] [ˈʌpˌraɪt] *adj* **1** VERTICAL : vertical **2** ERECT : erguido, derecho <to sit upright : sentarse derecho> **3** JUST : recto, honesto, justo

upright[2] *n* : montante *m,* poste *m,* soporte *m*

uprising [ˈʌpˌraɪzɪŋ] *n* : insurrección *f,* revuelta *f,* alzamiento *m*

uproar [ˈʌpˌror] *n* COMMOTION : alboroto *m,* jaleo *m,* escándalo *m*

uproarious [ˌʌpˈroriəs] *adj* **1** CLAMOROUS : estrepitoso, clamoroso **2** HILARIOUS : muy divertido, hilarante — **uproariously** *adv*

uproot [ˌʌpˈruːt, -ˈrʊt] *vt* : desarraigar

upset[1] [ˌʌpˈsɛt] *vt* **-set; -setting 1** OVERTURN : volcar **2** SPILL : derramar **3** DISTURB : perturbar, disgustar, inquietar, alterar **4** SICKEN : sentar mal a <it upsets my stomach : me sienta mal al estómago> **5** DISRUPT : trastornar, desbaratar (planes, etc.) **6** DEFEAT : derrotar (en deportes)

upset[2] *adj* **1** DISPLEASED, DISTRESSED : disgustado, alterado **2 to have an upset stomach** : estar mal del estómago, estar descompuesto (de estómago)

upset[3] [ˈʌpˌsɛt] *n* **1** OVERTURNING : vuelco *m* **2** DISRUPTION : trastorno *m* (de planes, etc.) **3** DEFEAT : derrota *f* (en deportes)

upshot [ˈʌpˌʃɑt] *n* : resultado *m* final

upside–down [ˌʌpˌsaɪdˈdaʊn] *adj* : al revés

upside down [ˌʌpˌsaɪdˈdaʊn] *adv* **1** : al revés **2** : en confusión, en desorden

upstairs[1] [ˌʌpˈstærz] *adv* : arriba, en el piso superior

upstairs[2] [ˈʌpˌstærz, ˌʌpˈ-] *adj* : de arriba

upstairs[3] [ˈʌpˌstærz, ˌʌpˈ-] *ns & pl* : piso *m* de arriba, planta *f* de arriba

upstanding [ˌʌpˈstændɪŋ, ˈʌpˌ-] *adj* HONEST, UPRIGHT : honesto, íntegro, recto

upstart [ˈʌpˌstɑrt] *n* : advenedizo *m,* -za *f*

upswing [ˈʌpˌswɪŋ] *n* : alza *f,* mejora *f* notable <to be on the upswing : estar mejorándose>

uptight [ˌʌpˈtaɪt] *adj* : tenso, nervioso

up to *prep* **1** : hasta <up to a year : hasta un año> <in mud up to my ankles : en barro hasta los tobillos> **2 to be up to** : estar a la altura de <I'm not up to going : no estoy en condiciones de ir> **3 to be up to** : depender de <it's up to the director : depende del director>

up–to–date [ˌʌptəˈdeɪt] *adj* **1** CURRENT : corriente, al día <to keep up-to-date

: mantenerse al corriente> **2** MODERN : moderno

uptown [ˈʌpˈtaʊn] *adv* : hacia la parte alta de la ciudad, hacia el distrito residencial

upturn [ˈʌpˌtərn] *n* : mejora *f,* auge *m* (económico)

upward[1] [ˈʌpwərd] *or* **upwards** [-wərdz] *adv* : hacia arriba

upward[2] *adj* : ascendente, hacia arriba

upwind [ˌʌpˈwɪnd] *adv & adj* : contra el viento

uranium [jʊˈreɪniəm] *n* : uranio *m*

Uranus [jʊˈreɪnəs, ˈjʊrənəs] *n* : Urano *m*

urban [ˈərbən] *adj* : urbano

urbane [ˌərˈbeɪn] *adj* : urbano, cortés

urchin [ˈərtʃən] *n* **1** SCAMP : granuja *mf;* pillo *m,* -lla *f* **2 sea urchin** : erizo *m* de mar

urethra [jʊˈriːθrə] *n, pl* **-thras** *or* **-thrae** [-ˌθriː] : uretra *f*

urge[1] [ˈərdʒ] *vt* **urged; urging 1** PRESS : instar, apremiar, insistir <we urged him to come : insistimos en que viniera> **2** ADVOCATE : recomendar, abogar por **3 to urge on** : animar, alentar

urge[2] *n* : impulso *m,* ganas *fpl,* compulsión *f*

urgency [ˈərdʒəntsi] *n, pl* **-cies** : urgencia *f*

urgent [ˈərdʒənt] *adj* **1** PRESSING : urgente, apremiante **2** INSISTENT : insistente **3 to be urgent** : urgir

urgently [ˈərdʒəntli] *adv* : urgentemente

urinal [ˈjʊrənəl, *esp Brit* jʊˈraɪnəl] *n* : orinal *m* (recipiente), urinario *m* (lugar)

urinary [ˈjʊrəˌnɛri] *adj* : urinario

urinate [ˈjʊrəˌneɪt] *vi* **-nated; -nating** : orinar

urination [ˌjʊrəˈneɪʃən] *n* : orinación *f*

urine [ˈjʊrən] *n* : orina *f*

urn [ˈərn] *n* **1** VASE : urna *f* **2** : recipiente *m* (para servir café, etc.)

Uruguayan [ˌʊrəˈgwaɪən, ˌjʊr-, -ˈgweɪ-] *n* : uruguayo *m,* -ya *f* — **Uruguayan** *adj*

us [ˈʌs] *pron* **1** (*as direct object*) : nos <they were visiting us : nos visitaban> **2** (*as indirect object*) : nos <he gave us a present : nos dio un regalo> **3** (*as object of preposition*) : nosotros, nosotras <stay with us : quédese con nosotros> <both of us : nosotros dos> **4** (*for emphasis*) : nosotros <it's us! : ¡somos nosotros!>

usable [ˈjuːzəbəl] *adj* : utilizable

usage [ˈjuːsɪdʒ, -zɪdʒ] *n* **1** HABIT : costumbre *f,* hábito *m* **2** USE : uso *m*

use[1] [ˈjuːz] *v* **used** [ˈjuːzd, *in phrase "used to" usually* ˈjuːstuː]; **using** *vt* **1** EMPLOY : emplear, usar **2** CONSUME : consumir, tomar (drogas, etc.) **3** UTILIZE : usar, utilizar <to use tact : usar tacto> <he used his friends to get ahead : usó a sus amigos para mejorar su posición> **4** TREAT : tratar <they used the horse cruelly : maltrataron al caballo> **5 to use up** : agotar, consumir, gastar — *vi* (*used in the past with* **to** *to indicate a former fact or state*) : soler, acostumbrar <winters used to be colder : los inviernos solían ser más fríos, los inviernos eran más fríos> <she used to dance : acostumbraba bailar>

use[2] [ˈjuːs] *n* **1** APPLICATION, EMPLOYMENT : uso *m,* empleo *m,* utilización *f* <out of use : en desuso> <ready for use : listo para usar> <to be in use : usarse, estar funcionando> <to make use of : servirse de, aprovechar> **2** USEFULNESS : utilidad *f* <to be of no use : no servir (para nada)> <it's no use! : ¡es inútil!> **3 to have the use of** : poder usar, tener acceso a **4 to have no use for** : no necesitar <she has no use for poetry : a ella no le gusta la poesía>

used [ˈjuːzd] *adj* **1** SECONDHAND : usado, de segunda mano <used cars : coches usados> **2 used to** ACCUSTOMED : acostumbrado <used to the heat : acostumbrado al calor>

useful [ˈjuːsfəl] *adj* : útil, práctico — **usefully** *adv*

usefulness [ˈjuːsfəlnəs] *n* : utilidad *f*

useless [ˈjuːsləs] *adj* : inútil — **uselessly** *adv*

uselessness [ˈjuːsləsnəs] *n* : inutilidad *f*

user [ˈjuːzər] *n* : usuario *m,* -ria *f*

usher[1] [ˈʌʃər] *vt* **1** ESCORT : acompañar, conducir **2 to usher in** : hacer pasar (a alguien) <to usher in a new era : anunciar una nueva época>

usher[2] *n* : acomodador *m,* -dora *f*

usherette [ˌʌʃəˈrɛt] *n* : acomodadora *f*

usual [ˈjuːʒʊəl] *adj* **1** NORMAL : usual, normal **2** CUSTOMARY : acostumbrado, habitual, de costumbre **3** ORDINARY : ordinario, típico

usually [ˈjuːʒʊəli, ˈjuːʒəli] *adv* : usualmente, normalmente

usurp [jʊˈsərp, -ˈzərp] *vt* : usurpar

usurper [jʊˈsərpər, -ˈzər-] *n* : usurpador *m,* -dora *f*

utensil [jʊˈtɛntsəl] *n* **1** : utensilio *m* (de cocina) **2** IMPLEMENT : implemento *m,* útil *m* (de labranza, etc.)

uterus [ˈjuːtərəs] *n, pl* **uteri** [-ˌraɪ] : útero *m,* matriz *f*

utilitarian [juːˌtɪləˈtɛriən] *adj* : utilitario

utility [juːˈtɪləti] *n, pl* **-ties 1** USEFULNESS : utilidad *f* **2 public utility** : empresa *f* de servicio público

utilization [ˌjuːtələˈzeɪʃən] *n* : utilización *f*

utilize [ˈjuːtəlˌaɪz] *vt* **-lized; -lizing** : utilizar, hacer uso de

utmost[1] [ˈʌtˌmoːst] *adj* **1** FARTHEST : extremo, más lejano **2** GREATEST : sumo, mayor <of the utmost importance : de suma importancia>

utmost[2] *n* : lo más posible <to the utmost : al máximo>

utopia [jʊˈtoːpiə] *n* : utopía *f*

utopian [jʊˈtoːpiən] *adj* : utópico

utter[1] [ˈʌtər] *vt* : decir, articular, pronunciar (palabras)
utter[2] *adj* : absoluto — **utterly** *adv*
utterance [ˈʌtərənts] *n* : declaración *f*, articulación *f*

V

v [ˈviː] *n, pl* **v's** *or* **vs** [ˈviːz] : vigésima segunda letra del alfabeto inglés
vacancy [ˈveɪkəntsi] *n, pl* **-cies 1** EMPTINESS : vacío *m*, vacuidad *f* **2** : vacante *f*, puesto *m* vacante <to fill a vacancy : ocupar un puesto> **3** : habitación *f* libre (en un hotel) <no vacancies : completo>
vacant [ˈveɪkənt] *adj* **1** EMPTY : libre, desocupado (dícese de los edificios, etc.) **2** : vacante (dícese de los puestos) **3** BLANK : vacío, ausente <a vacant stare : una mirada ausente>
vacate [ˈveɪˌkeɪt] *vt* **-cated; -cating** : desalojar, desocupar
vacation[1] [veɪˈkeɪʃən, və-] *vi* : pasar las vacaciones, vacacionar *Mex*
vacation[2] *n* : vacaciones *fpl* <to be on vacation : estar de vacaciones>
vacationer [veɪˈkeɪʃənər, və-] *n* : turista *mf*, veraneante *mf*, vacacionista *mf CA, Mex*
vaccinate [ˈvæksəˌneɪt] *vt* **-nated; -nating** : vacunar
vaccination [ˌvæksəˈneɪʃən] *n* : vacunación *f*
vaccine [vækˈsiːn, ˈvækˌ-] *n* : vacuna *f*
vacillate [ˈvæsəˌleɪt] *vi* **-lated; -lating 1** HESITATE : vacilar **2** SWAY : oscilar
vacillation [ˌvæsəˈleɪʃən] *n* : indecisión *f*, vacilación *f*
vacuous [ˈvækjʊəs] *adj* **1** EMPTY : vacío **2** INANE : vacuo, necio, estúpido
vacuum[1] [ˈvæˌkjuːm, -kjəm] *vt* : limpiar con aspiradora, pasar la aspiradora por
vacuum[2] *n, pl* **vacuums** *or* **vacua** [ˈvækjʊə] : vacío *m*
vacuum cleaner *n* : aspiradora *f*
vagabond[1] [ˈvægəˌbɑnd] *adj* : vagabundo
vagabond[2] *n* : vagabundo *m*, -da *f*
vagary [ˈveɪgəri, vəˈgɛri] *n, pl* **-ries** : capricho *m*
vagina [vəˈdʒaɪnə] *n, pl* **-nae** [-ˌniː, -ˌnaɪ] *or* **-nas** : vagina *f*
vagrancy [ˈveɪgrəntsi] *n* : vagancia *f*
vagrant[1] [ˈveɪgrənt] *adj* : vagabundo
vagrant[2] *n* : vagabundo *m*, -da *f*
vague [ˈveɪg] *adj* **vaguer; -est 1** IMPRECISE : vago, impreciso <a vague feeling : una sensación indefinida> <I haven't the vaguest idea : no tengo la más remota idea> **2** UNCLEAR : borroso, poco claro <a vague outline : un perfil indistinto> **3** ABSENTMINDED : distraído
vaguely [ˈveɪgli] *adv* : vagamente, de manera imprecisa
vagueness [ˈveɪgnəs] *n* : vaguedad *f*, imprecisión *f*
vain [ˈveɪn] *adj* **1** WORTHLESS : vano **2** FUTILE : vano, inútil <in vain : en vano> **3** CONCEITED : vanidoso, presumido
vainly [ˈveɪnli] *adv* : en vano, vanamente, inútilmente
valance [ˈvælənts, ˈveɪ-] *n* **1** FLOUNCE : volante *m* (de una cama, etc.) **2** : galería *f* de cortina (sobre una ventana)
vale [ˈveɪl] *n* : valle *m*
valedictorian [ˌvæləˌdɪkˈtoriən] *n* : estudiante *mf* que pronuncia el discurso de despedida en ceremonia de graduación
valedictory [ˌvæləˈdɪktəri] *adj* : de despedida
valentine [ˈvælənˌtaɪn] *n* : tarjeta *f* que se manda el Día de los Enamorados (el 14 de febrero)
Valentine's Day *n* : Día *m* de los Enamorados
valet [ˈvæˌleɪ, væˈleɪ, ˈvælət] *n* : ayuda *m* de cámara
valiant [ˈvæljənt] *adj* : valiente, valeroso
valiantly [ˈvæljəntli] *adv* : con valor, valientemente
valid [ˈvæləd] *adj* : válido
validate [ˈvæləˌdeɪt] *vt* **-dated; -dating** : validar, dar validez a
validity [vəˈlɪdəti, væ-] *n* : validez *f*
valise [vəˈliːs] *n* : maleta *f* (de mano)
valley [ˈvæli] *n, pl* **-leys** : valle *m*
valor [ˈvælər] *n* : valor *m*, valentía *f*
valorous [ˈvælərəs] *adj* : valeroso, valiente
valuable[1] [ˈvæljʊəbəl, ˈvæljəbəl] *adj* **1** EXPENSIVE : valioso, de valor **2** WORTHWHILE : valioso, apreciable
valuable[2] *n* : objeto *m* de valor
valuation [ˌvæljʊˈeɪʃən] *n* **1** APPRAISAL : valoración *f*, tasación *f* **2** VALUE : valuación *f*
value[1] [ˈvælˌjuː] *vt* **-ued; -uing 1** APPRAISE : valorar, avaluar, tasar **2** APPRECIATE : valorar, apreciar
value[2] *n* **1** : valor *m* <of little value : de poco valor> <to be a good value : estar bien de precio, tener buen precio> <at face value : en su sentido literal>

2 values *npl* : valores *mpl* (morales), principios *mpl*
valueless ['væljuːləs] *adj* : sin valor
valve ['vælv] *n* : válvula *f*
vampire ['væm,paɪr] *n* **1** : vampiro *m* **2** *or* **vampire bat** : vampiro *m*
van[1] ['væn] → **vanguard**
van[2] *n* : furgoneta *f,* camioneta *f*
vanadium [və'neɪdiəm] *n* : vanadio *m*
vandal ['vændəl] *n* : vándalo *m*
vandalism ['vændəl,ɪzəm] *n* : vandalismo *m*
vandalize ['vændəl,aɪz] *vt* : destrozar, destruir, estropear
vane ['veɪn] *n or* **weather vane** : veleta *f*
vanguard ['væn,gɑrd] *n* : vanguardia *f*
vanilla [və'nɪlə, -'nɛ-] *n* : vainilla *f*
vanish ['vænɪʃ] *vi* : desaparecer, disiparse, desvanecerse
vanity ['vænət̬i] *n, pl* **-ties 1** : vanidad *f* **2** *or* **vanity table** : tocador *m*
vanquish ['væŋkwɪʃ, 'væn-] *vt* : vencer, conquistar
vantage point ['væntɪdʒ] *n* : posición *f* ventajosa
vapid ['væpəd, 'veɪ-] *adj* : insípido, insulso
vapor ['veɪpər] *n* : vapor *m*
vaporize ['veɪpə,raɪz] *v* **-rized; -rizing** *vt* : vaporizar — *vi* : vaporizarse, evaporarse
vaporizer ['veɪpə,raɪzər] *n* : vaporizador *m*
variability [,vɛriə'bɪlət̬i] *n, pl* **-ties** : variabilidad *f*
variable[1] ['vɛriəbəl] *adj* : variable <variable cloudiness : nubosidad variable>
variable[2] *n* : variable *f,* factor *m*
variance ['vɛriən*t*s] *n* **1** DISCREPANCY : varianza *f,* discrepancia *f* **2** DISAGREEMENT : desacuerdo *m* <at variance with : en desacuerdo con>
variant[1] ['vɛriənt] *adj* : variante, divergente
variant[2] *n* : variante *f*
variation [,vɛri'eɪʃən] *n* : variación *f,* diferencias *fpl*
varicose ['værə,koːs] *adj* : varicoso
varicose veins *npl* : varices *fpl*, várices *fpl*
varied ['vɛrid] *adj* : variado, dispar, diferente
variegated ['vɛriə,geɪt̬ɛd] *adj* : abigarrado, multicolor
variety [və'raɪət̬i] *n, pl* **-ties 1** DIVERSITY : diversidad *f,* variedad *f* **2** ASSORTMENT : surtido *m* <for a variety of reasons : por diversas razones> **3** SORT : clase *f* **4** BREED : variedad *f* (de plantas)
various ['vɛriəs] *adj* : varios, diversos
varnish[1] ['vɑrnɪʃ] *vt* : barnizar
varnish[2] *n* : barniz *f*
varsity ['vɑrsət̬i] *n, pl* **-ties** : equipo *m* universitario
vary ['vɛri] *v* **varied; varying** *vt* : variar, diversificar — *vi* **1** CHANGE : variar, cambiar **2** DEVIATE : desviarse
vascular ['væskjələr] *adj* : vascular
vase ['veɪs, 'veɪz, 'vɑz] *n* : jarrón *m,* florero *m*
vassal ['væsəl] *n* : vasallo *m,* -lla *f*
vast ['væst] *adj* : inmenso, enorme, vasto
vastly ['væstli] *adv* : enormemente
vastness ['væstnəs] *n* : vastedad *f,* inmensidad *f*
vat ['væt] *n* : cuba *f,* tina *f*
vaudeville ['vɔdvəl, -,vɪl; 'vɔdə,vɪl] *n* : vodevil *m*
vault[1] ['vɔlt] *vi* LEAP : saltar
vault[2] *n* **1** JUMP : salto *m* <pole vault : salto de pértiga, salto con garrocha> **2** DOME : bóveda *f* **3** : bodega *f* (para vino), bóveda *f* de seguridad (de un banco) **4** CRYPT : cripta *f*
vaulted ['vɔltəd] *adj* : abovedado
vaunted ['vɔntəd] *adj* : cacareado, alardeado <a much vaunted wine : un vino muy alardeado>
VCR [,viː,siː'ɑr] *n* : video *m,* videocasetera *f*
veal ['viːl] *n* : ternera *f,* carne *f* de ternera
veer ['vɪr] *vi* : virar (dícese de un barco), girar (dícese de un coche), torcer (dícese de un camino)
vegetable[1] ['vɛdʒtəbəl, 'vɛdʒət̬ə-] *adj* : vegetal
vegetable[2] *n* **1** : vegetal *m* <the vegetable kingdom : el reino vegetal> **2** : verdura *f,* hortaliza *f* (para comer)
vegetarian [,vɛdʒə'tɛriən] *n* : vegetariano *mf*
vegetarianism [,vɛdʒə'tɛriə,nɪzəm] *n* : vegetarianismo *m*
vegetate ['vɛdʒə,teɪt] *vi* **-tated; -tating** : vegetar
vegetation [,vɛdʒə'teɪʃən] *n* : vegetación *f*
vehemence ['viːəmən*t*s] *n* : intensidad *f,* vehemencia *f*
vehement ['viːəmənt] *adj* : intenso, vehemente
vehemently ['viːəməntli] *adv* : vehementemente, con vehemencia
vehicle ['viːəkəl, 'viː,hɪkəl] *n* **1** *or* **motor vehicle** : vehículo *m* **2** MEDIUM : vehículo *m,* medio *m*
vehicular [vi'hɪkjələr, və-] *adj* : vehicular <vehicular homicide : muerte por atropello>
veil[1] ['veɪl] *vt* **1** CONCEAL : velar, disimular **2** : cubrir con un velo <to veil one's face : cubrirse con un velo>
veil[2] *n* : velo *m* <bridal veil : velo de novia>
vein ['veɪn] *n* **1** : vena *f* (en anatomía, botánica, etc.) **2** LODE : veta *f,* vena *f,* filón *m* **3** STYLE : vena *f* <in a humorous vein : en vena humorística>
veined ['veɪnd] *adj* : veteado (dícese del queso, de los minerales, etc.)

velocity [vəˈlɑsət̬i] *n, pl* **-ties** : velocidad *f*
velour [vəˈlʊr] *or* **velours** [-ˈlʊrz] *n* : velour *m*
velvet[1] [ˈvɛlvət] *adj* **1** : de terciopelo **2** → **velvety**
velvet[2] *n* : terciopelo *m*
velvety [ˈvɛlvət̬i] *adj* : aterciopelado
venal [ˈviːnəl] *adj* : venal, sobornable
vend [ˈvɛnd] *vt* : vender
vendetta [vɛnˈdɛt̬ə] *n* : vendetta *f*
vendor [ˈvɛndər] *n* : vendedor *m*, -dora *f*; puestero *m*, -ra *f*
veneer[1] [vəˈnɪr] *vt* : enchapar, chapar
veneer[2] *n* **1** : enchapado *m*, chapa *f* **2** APPEARANCE : apariencia *f*, barniz *m* <a veneer of culture : un barniz de cultura>
venerable [ˈvɛnərəbəl] *adj* : venerable
venerate [ˈvɛnəˌreɪt] *vt* **-ated; -ating** : venerar
veneration [ˌvɛnəˈreɪʃən] *n* : veneración *f*
venereal disease [vəˈnɪriəl] *n* : enfermedad *f* venérea
venetian blind [vəˈniːʃən] *n* : persiana *f* veneciana
Venezuelan [ˌvɛnəˈzweɪlən, -zʊˈeɪ-] *n* : venezolano *m*, -na *f* — **Venezuelan** *adj*
vengeance [ˈvɛndʒənts] *n* : venganza *f* <to take vengeance on : vengarse de>
vengeful [ˈvɛndʒfəl] *adj* : vengativo
venial [ˈviːniəl] *adj* : venial <a venial sin : un pecado venial>
venison [ˈvɛnəsən, -zən] *n* : venado *m*, carne *f* de venado
venom [ˈvɛnəm] *n* **1** : veneno *m* **2** MALICE : veneno *m*, malevolencia *f*
venomous [ˈvɛnəməs] *adj* : venenoso
vent[1] [ˈvɛnt] *vt* : desahogar, dar salida a <to vent one's feelings : desahogarse>
vent[2] *n* **1** OPENING : abertura *f* (de escape), orificio *m* **2** *or* **air vent** : respiradero *m*, rejilla *f* de ventilación **3** OUTLET : desahogo *m* <to give vent to one's anger : desahogar la ira>
ventilate [ˈvɛntəlˌeɪt] *vt* **-lated; -lating** : ventilar
ventilation [ˌvɛntəlˈeɪʃən] *n* : ventilación *f*
ventilator [ˈvɛntəlˌeɪt̬ər] *n* : ventilador *m*
ventricle [ˈvɛntrɪkəl] *n* : ventrículo *m*
ventriloquism [vɛnˈtrɪləˌkwɪzəm] *n* : ventriloquia *f*
ventriloquist [vɛnˈtrɪləˌkwɪst] *n* : ventrílocuo *m*, -cua *f*
venture[1] [ˈvɛntʃər] *v* **-tured; -turing** *vt* **1** RISK : arriesgar **2** OFFER : aventurar <to venture an opinion : aventurar una opinión> — *vi* : arriesgarse, atreverse, aventurarse
venture[2] *n* **1** UNDERTAKING : empresa *f* **2** GAMBLE, RISK : aventura *f*, riesgo *m*
venturesome [ˈvɛntʃərsəm] *adj* **1** ADVENTUROUS : audaz, atrevido **2** RISKY : arriesgado
venue [ˈvɛnˌjuː] *n* **1** PLACE : lugar *m* **2** : jurisdicción *f* (en derecho)
Venus [ˈviːnəs] *n* : Venus *m*
veracity [vəˈræsət̬i] *n, pl* **-ties** : veracidad *f*
veranda *or* **verandah** [vəˈrændə] *n* : terraza *f*, veranda *f*
verb [ˈvərb] *n* : verbo *m*
verbal [ˈvərbəl] *adj* : verbal
verbalize [ˈvərbəˌlaɪz] *vt* **-ized; -izing** : expresar con palabras, verbalizar
verbally [ˈvərbəli] *adv* : verbalmente, de palabra
verbatim[1] [vərˈbeɪt̬əm] *adv* : palabra por palabra, textualmente
verbatim[2] *adj* : literal, textual
verbose [vərˈboːs] *adj* : verboso, prolijo
verdant [ˈvərdənt] *adj* : verde, verdeante
verdict [ˈvərdɪkt] *n* **1** : veredicto *m* (de un jurado) **2** JUDGMENT, OPINION : juicio *m*, opinión *f*
verge[1] [ˈvərdʒ] *vi* **verged; verging** : estar al borde, rayar <it verges on madness : raya en la locura>
verge[2] *n* **1** EDGE : borde *m* **2 to be on the verge of** : estar a pique de, estar al borde de, estar a punto de
verification [ˌvɛrəfəˈkeɪʃən] *n* : verificación *f*
verify [ˈvɛrəˌfaɪ] *vt* **-fied; -fying** : verificar, comprobar, confirmar
veritable [ˈvɛrət̬əbəl] *adj* : verdadero — **veritably** *adv*
vermicelli [ˌvərməˈtʃɛli, -ˈsɛli] *n* : fideos *mpl* finos
vermin [ˈvərmən] *ns & pl* : alimañas *fpl*, bichos *mpl*, sabandijas *fpl*
vermouth [vərˈmuːth] *n* : vermut *m*
vernacular[1] [vərˈnækjələr] *adj* : vernáculo
vernacular[2] *n* : lengua *f* vernácula
versatile [ˈvərsət̬əl] *adj* : versátil
versatility [ˌvərsəˈtɪlət̬i] *n* : versatilidad *f*
verse [ˈvərs] *n* **1** LINE, STANZA : verso *m*, estrofa *f* **2** POETRY : poesía *f* **3** : versículo *m* (en la Biblia)
versed [ˈvərst] *adj* : versado <to be well versed in : ser muy versado en>
version [ˈvərʒən] *n* : versión *f*
versus [ˈvərsəs] *prep* : versus
vertebra [ˈvərt̬əbrə] *n, pl* **-brae** [-ˌbreɪ, -ˌbriː] *or* **-bras** : vértebra *f*
vertebrate[1] [ˈvərt̬əbrət, -ˌbreɪt] *adj* : vertebrado
vertebrate[2] *n* : vertebrado *m*
vertex [ˈvərˌtɛks] *n, pl* **vertices** [ˈvərt̬əˌsiːz] **1** : vértice *m* (en matemáticas y anatomía) **2** SUMMIT, TOP : ápice *m*, cumbre *f*, cima *f*
vertical[1] [ˈvərt̬ɪkəl] *adj* : vertical — **verticalmente** *adv*
vertical[2] *n* : vertical *f*
vertigo [ˈvərt̬ɪˌgoː] *n, pl* **-goes** *or* **-gos** : vértigo *m*
verve [ˈvərv] *n* : brío *m*

very[1] [ˈvɛri] *adv* **1** EXTREMELY : muy, sumamente <very few : muy pocos> <I am very sorry : lo siento mucho> **2** (*used for emphasis*) <at the very least : por lo menos, como mínimo> <the same dress : el mismo vestido>

very[2] *adj* **verier; -est 1** EXACT, PRECISE : mismo, exacto <at that very moment : en ese mismo momento> <it's the very thing : es justo lo que hacía falta> **2** BARE, MERE : solo, mero <the very thought of it : sólo pensarlo> **3** EXTREME : extremo, de todo <at the very top : arriba de todo>

vespers [ˈvɛspərz] *npl* : vísperas *fpl*

vessel [ˈvɛsəl] *n* **1** CONTAINER : vasija *f*, recipiente *m* **2** BOAT, CRAFT : nave *f*, barco *m*, buque *m* **3** : vaso *m* <blood vessel : vaso sanguíneo>

vest[1] [ˈvɛst] *vt* **1** CONFER : conferir <to vest authority in : conferirle la autoridad a> **2** CLOTHE : vestir

vest[2] *n* **1** : chaleco *m* **2** UNDERSHIRT : camiseta *f*

vestibule [ˈvɛstəˌbjuːl] *n* : vestíbulo *m*

vestige [ˈvɛstɪdʒ] *n* : vestigio *m*, rastro *m*

vestment [ˈvɛstmənt] *n* : vestidura *f*

vestry [ˈvɛstri] *n, pl* **-tries** : sacristía *f*

vet [ˈvɛt] *n* **1** → **veterinarian 2** → **veteran**[2]

veteran[1] [ˈvɛt̬ərən, ˈvɛtrən] *adj* : veterano

veteran[2] *n* : veterano *m*, -na *f*

Veterans Day *n* : día *m* del Armisticio (celebrado el 11 de noviembre en los Estados Unidos)

veterinarian [ˌvɛt̬ərəˈnɛriən, ˌvɛtəˈnɛr-] *n* : veterinario *m*, -ria *f*

veterinary [ˈvɛt̬ərəˌnɛri] *adj* : veterinario

veto[1] [ˈviːto] *vt* **1** FORBID : prohibir **2** : vetar <to veto a bill : vetar un proyecto de ley>

veto[2] *n, pl* **-toes 1** : veto *m* <the power of veto : el derecho de veto> **2** BAN : veto *m*, prohibición *f*

vex [ˈvɛks] *vt* : contrariar, molestar, irritar

vexation [vɛkˈseɪʃən] *n* : contrariedad *f*, irritación *f*

via [ˈvaɪə, ˈviːə] *prep* : por, vía

viability [ˌvaɪəˈbɪlət̬i] *n* : viabilidad *f*

viable [ˈvaɪəbəl] *adj* : viable

viaduct [ˈvaɪəˌdʌkt] *n* : viaducto *m*

vial [ˈvaɪəl] *n* : frasco *m*

vibrant [ˈvaɪbrənt] *adj* **1** LIVELY : vibrante, animado, dinámico **2** BRIGHT : fuerte, vivo (dícese de los colores)

vibrate [ˈvaɪˌbreɪt] *vi* **-brated; -brating 1** OSCILLATE : vibrar, oscilar **2** THRILL : bullir <to vibrate with excitement : bullir de emoción>

vibration [vaɪˈbreɪʃən] *n* : vibración *f*

vicar [ˈvɪkər] *n* : vicario *m*, -ria *f*

vicarious [vaɪˈkæriːəs, vɪ-] *adj* : indirecto — **vicariously** *adv*

vice [ˈvaɪs] *n* : vicio *m*

vice admiral *n* : vicealmirante *mf*

vice president *n* : vicepresidente *m*, -ta *f*

viceroy [ˈvaɪsˌrɔɪ] *n* : virrey *m*, -rreina *f*

vice versa [ˌvaɪsɪˈvərsə, ˌvaɪsˈvər-] *adv* : viceversa

vicinity [vəˈsɪnət̬i] *n, pl* **-ties 1** NEIGHBORHOOD : vecindad *f*, inmediaciones *fpl* **2** NEARNESS : proximidad *f*

vicious [ˈvɪʃəs] *adj* **1** DEPRAVED : depravado, malo **2** SAVAGE : malo, fiero, salvaje <a vicious dog : un perro feroz> **3** MALICIOUS : malicioso

viciously [ˈvɪʃəsli] *adv* : con saña, brutalmente

viciousness [ˈvɪʃəsnəs] *n* : brutalidad *f*, ferocidad *f* (de un animal), malevolencia *f* (de un comentario, etc.)

vicissitudes [vəˈsɪsəˌtuːdz, vaɪ-, -ˌtjuːdz] *npl* : vicisitudes *fpl*

victim [ˈvɪktəm] *n* : víctima *f*

victimize [ˈvɪktəˌmaɪz] *vt* **-mized; -mizing** : tomar como víctima, perseguir, victimizar *Arg, Mex*

victor [ˈvɪktər] *n* : vencedor *m*, -dora *f*

Victorian [vɪkˈtoːriən] *adj* : victoriano

victorious [vɪkˈtoːriəs] *adj* : victorioso — **victoriously** *adv*

victory [ˈvɪktəri] *n, pl* **-ries** : victoria *f*, triunfo *m*

victuals [ˈvɪt̬əlz] *npl* : víveres *mpl*, provisiones *fpl*

video[1] [ˈvɪdiˌoː] *adj* : de video <video recording : grabación de video>

video[2] *n* **1** : video *m* (medio o grabación) **2** → **videotape**[2]

videocassette [ˌvɪdiokəˈsɛt] *n* : videocasete *m*, videocassette *m*

videocassette recorder → **VCR**

videotape[1] [ˈvɪdioˌteɪp] *vt* **-taped; -taping** : grabar en video, videograbar

videotape[2] *n* : videocinta *f*

vie [ˈvaɪ] *vi* **vied; vying** [ˈvaɪɪŋ] : competir, rivalizar

Vietnamese [viˌɛtnəˈmiːz, -ˈmiːs] *n* : vietnamita *mf* — **Vietnamese** *adj*

view[1] [ˈvjuː] *vt* **1** OBSERVE : mirar, ver, observar **2** CONSIDER : considerar, contemplar

view[2] *n* **1** SIGHT : vista *f* <to come into view : aparecer> **2** ATTITUDE, OPINION : opinión *f*, parecer *m*, actitud *f* <in my view : en mi opinión> **3** SCENE : vista *f*, panorama *f* **4** INTENTION : idea *f*, vista *f* <with a view to : con vistas a, con la idea de> **5 in view of** : dado que, en vista de (que)

viewer [ˈvjuːər] *n or* **television viewer** : telespectador *m*, -dora *f*; televidente *mf*

viewpoint [ˈvjuːˌpɔɪnt] *n* : punto *m* de vista

vigil [ˈvɪdʒəl] *n* **1** : vigilia *f*, vela *f* **2 to keep vigil** : velar

vigilance [ˈvɪdʒələnts] *n* : vigilancia *f*

vigilant [ˈvɪdʒələnt] *adj* : vigilante

vigilante [ˌvɪdʒəˈlænˌtiː] *n* : integrante *mf* de un comité de vigilancia (que actúa como policía)
vigilantly [ˈvɪdʒələntli] *adv* : con vigilancia
vigor [ˈvɪgər] *n* : vigor *m*, energía *f*, fuerza *f*
vigorous [ˈvɪgərəs] *adj* : vigoroso, enérgico — **vigorously** *adv*
Viking [ˈvaɪkɪŋ] *n* : vikingo *m*, -ga *f*
vile [ˈvaɪl] *adj* **viler; vilest 1** WICKED : vil, infame **2** REVOLTING : asqueroso, repugnante **3** TERRIBLE : horrible, atroz <vile weather : tiempo horrible> <to be in a vile mood : estar de un humor de perros>
vilify [ˈvɪləˌfaɪ] *vt* **-fied; -fying** : vilipendiar, denigrar, difamar
villa [ˈvɪlə] *n* : casa *f* de campo, quinta *f*
village [ˈvɪlɪdʒ] *n* : pueblo *m* (grande), aldea *f* (pequeña)
villager [ˈvɪlɪdʒər] *n* : vecino *m*, -na *f* (de un pueblo); aldeano *m*, -na *f* (de una aldea)
villain [ˈvɪlən] *n* : villano *m*, -na *f*; malo *m*, -la *f* (en ficción, películas, etc.)
villainess [ˈvɪlənɪs, -nəs] *n* : villana *f*
villainous [ˈvɪlənəs] *adj* : infame, malvado
villainy [ˈvɪləni] *n, pl* **-lainies** : vileza *f*, maldad *f*
vim [ˈvɪm] *n* : brío *m*, vigor *m*, energía *f*
vindicate [ˈvɪndəˌkeɪt] *vt* **-cated; -cating 1** EXONERATE : vindicar, disculpar **2** JUSTIFY : justificar
vindication [ˌvɪndəˈkeɪʃən] *n* : vindicación *f*, justificación *f*
vindictive [vɪnˈdɪktɪv] *adj* : vengativo
vine [ˈvaɪn] *n* **1** GRAPEVINE : vid *f*, parra *f* **2** : planta *f* trepadora, enredadera *f*
vinegar [ˈvɪnɪgər] *n* : vinagre *m*
vinegary [ˈvɪnɪgəri] *adj* : avinagrado
vineyard [ˈvɪnjərd] *n* : viña *f*, viñedo *m*
vintage[1] [ˈvɪntɪdʒ] *adj* **1** : añejo (dícese de un vino) **2** CLASSIC : clásico, de época
vintage[2] *n* **1** : cosecha *f* <the 1947 vintage : la cosecha de 1947> **2** ERA : época *f*, era *f* <slang of recent vintage : argot de la época reciente>
vinyl [ˈvaɪnəl] *n* : vinilo
viola [viːˈoːlə] *n* : viola *f*
violate [ˈvaɪəˌleɪt] *vt* **-lated; -lating 1** BREAK : infringir, violar, quebrantar <to violate the rules : violar las reglas> **2** RAPE : violar **3** DESECRATE : profanar
violation [ˌvaɪəˈleɪʃən] *n* **1** : violación *f*, infracción *f* (de una ley) **2** DESECRATION : profanación *f*
violence [ˈvaɪlənts, ˈvaɪə-] *n* : violencia *f*
violent [ˈvaɪlənt, ˈvaɪə-] *adj* : violento
violently [ˈvaɪləntli, ˈvaɪə-] *adv* : violentamente, con violencia
violet [ˈvaɪlət, ˈvaɪə-] *n* : violeta *f*
violin [ˌvaɪəˈlɪn] *n* : violín *m*
violinist [ˌvaɪəˈlɪnɪst] *n* : violinista *mf*
violoncello [ˌvaɪələnˈtʃɛloː, ˌviː-] → **cello**
VIP [ˌviːˌaɪˈpiː] *n, pl* **VIPs** [-ˈpiːz] : VIP *mf*, persona *f* de categoría
viper [ˈvaɪpər] *n* : víbora *f*
viral [ˈvaɪrəl] *adj* : viral, vírico <viral pneumonia : pulmonía viral>
virgin[1] [ˈvərdʒən] *adj* **1** CHASTE : virginal <the virgin birth : el alumbramiento virginal> **2** : virgen, intacto <a virgin forest : una selva virgen> <virgin wool : lana virgen>
virgin[2] *n* : virgen *mf*
virginity [vərˈdʒɪnət̬i] *n* : virginidad *f*
Virgo [ˈvərˌgoː, ˈvɪr-] *n* : Virgo *mf*
virile [ˈvɪrəl, -ˌaɪl] *adj* : viril, varonil
virility [vəˈrɪlət̬i] *n* : virilidad *f*
virtual [ˈvərtʃʊəl] *adj* : virtual <a virtual dictator : un virtual dictador> <virtual reality : realidad virtual>
virtually [ˈvərtʃʊəli, ˈvərtʃəli] *adv* : en realidad, de hecho, casi
virtue [ˈvərˌtʃuː] *n* **1** : virtud *f* **2 by virtue of** : en virtud de, debido a
virtuosity [ˌvərtʃʊˈɑsət̬i] *n, pl* **-ties** : virtuosismo *m*
virtuoso [ˌvərtʃʊˈoːsoː, -zoː] *n, pl* **-sos** *or* **-si** [-ˌsiː, -ˌziː] : virtuoso *m*, -sa *f*
virtuous [ˈvərtʃʊəs] *adj* : virtuoso, bueno — **virtuously** *adv*
virulence [ˈvɪrələnts, ˈvɪrjə-] *n* : virulencia *f*
virulent [ˈvɪrələnt, ˈvɪrjə-] *adj* : virulento
virus [ˈvaɪrəs] *n* : virus *m*
visa [ˈviːzə, -sə] *n* : visa *f*
vis–à–vis [ˌviːzəˈviː, -sə-] *prep* : con relación a, con respecto a
viscera [ˈvɪsərə] *npl* : vísceras *fpl*
visceral [ˈvɪsərəl] *adj* : visceral
viscosity [vɪsˈkɑsət̬i] *n, pl* **-ties** : viscosidad *f*
viscount [ˈvaɪˌkæʊnt] *n* : vizconde *m*
viscountess [ˈvaɪˌkæʊntɪs] *n* : vizcondesa *f*
viscous [ˈvɪskəs] *adj* : viscoso
vise [ˈvaɪs] *n* : torno *m* de banco, tornillo *m* de banco
visibility [ˌvɪzəˈbɪlət̬i] *n, pl* **-ties** : visibilidad *f*
visible [ˈvɪzəbəl] *adj* **1** : visible <the visible stars : las estrellas visibles> **2** OBVIOUS : evidente, patente
visibly [ˈvɪzəbli] *adv* : visiblemente
vision [ˈvɪʒən] *n* **1** EYESIGHT : vista *f*, visión *f* **2** APPARITION : visión *f*, aparición *f* **3** FORESIGHT : visión *f* (del futuro), previsión *f* **4** IMAGE : imagen *f* <she had visions of a disaster : se imaginaba un desastre>
visionary[1] [ˈvɪʒəˌnɛri] *adj* **1** FARSIGHTED : visionario, con visión de futuro **2** UTOPIAN : utópico, poco realista
visionary[2] *n, pl* **-ries** : visionario *m*, -ria *f*

visit[1] [ˈvɪzət] *vt* **1** : visitar, ir a ver **2** AFFLICT : azotar, afligir <visited by troubles : afligido con problemas> — *vi* : hacer (una) visita
visit[2] *n* : visita *f*
visitor [ˈvɪzətər] *n* : visitante *mf* (a una ciudad, etc.), visita *f* (a una casa)
visor [ˈvaɪzər] *n* : visera *f*
vista [ˈvɪstə] *n* : vista *f*
visual [ˈvɪʒʊəl] *adj* : visual <the visual arts : las artes visuales> — **visually** *adv*
visualize [ˈvɪʒʊəˌlaɪz] *vt* **-ized; -izing** : visualizar, imaginarse, hacerse una idea de
vital [ˈvaɪtəl] *adj* **1** : vital <vital organs : órganos vitales> **2** CRUCIAL : esencial, crucial, decisivo <of vital importance : de suma importancia> **3** LIVELY : enérgico, lleno de vida, vital
vitality [vaɪˈtæləti] *n, pl* **-ties** : vitalidad *f,* energía *f*
vitally [ˈvaɪtəli] *adv* : sumamente
vital statistics *npl* : estadísticas *fpl* demográficas
vitamin [ˈvaɪtəmən] *n* : vitamina *f* <vitamin deficiency : carencia vitamínica>
vitreous [ˈvɪtriəs] *adj* : vítreo
vitriolic [ˌvɪtriˈɑlɪk] *adj* : mordaz, virulento
vituperation [vaɪˌtuːpəˈreɪʃən, -ˌtjuː-] *n* : vituperio *m*
vivacious [vəˈveɪʃəs, vaɪ-] *adj* : vivaz, animado, lleno de vida
vivaciously [vəˈveɪʃəsli, vaɪ-] *adv* : con vivacidad, animadamente
vivacity [vəˈvæsəti, vaɪ-] *n* : vivacidad *f*
vivid [ˈvɪvəd] *adj* **1** LIVELY : lleno de vitalidad **2** BRILLIANT : vivo, intenso <vivid colors : colores vivos> **3** INTENSE, SHARP : vívido, gráfico <a vivid dream : un sueño vívido>
vividly [ˈvɪvədli] *adv* **1** BRIGHTLY : con colores vivos **2** SHARPLY : vívidamente
vividness [ˈvɪvədnəs] *n* **1** BRIGHTNESS : intensidad *f,* viveza *f* **2** SHARPNESS : lo gráfico, nitidez *f*
vivisection [ˌvɪvəˈsɛkʃən, ˈvɪvəˌ-] *n* : vivisección *f*
vixen [ˈvɪksən] *n* : zorra *f,* raposa *f*
vocabulary [voːˈkæbjəˌlɛri] *n, pl* **-laries 1** : vocabulario *m* **2** LEXICON : léxico *m*
vocal [ˈvoːkəl] *adj* **1** : vocal **2** LOUD, OUTSPOKEN : ruidoso, muy franco
vocal cords *npl* : cuerdas *fpl* vocales
vocalist [ˈvoːkəlɪst] *n* : cantante *mf,* vocalista *mf*
vocalize [ˈvoːkəlˌaɪz] *vt* **-ized; -izing** : vocalizar
vocation [voˈkeɪʃən] *n* : vocación *f* <to have a vocation for : tener vocación de>
vocational [voˈkeɪʃənəl] *adj* : profesional <vocational guidance : orientación profesional>
vociferous [voˈsɪfərəs] *adj* : ruidoso, vociferante
vodka [ˈvɑdkə] *n* : vodka *m*
vogue [ˈvoːg] *n* : moda *f,* boga *f* <to be in vogue : estar de moda, estar en boga>
voice[1] [ˈvɔɪs] *vt* **voiced; voicing** : expresar
voice[2] *n* **1** : voz *f* <in a low voice : en voz baja> <to lose one's voice : quedarse sin voz> <the voice of the people : la voz del pueblo> **2 to make one's voice heard** : hacerse oír
voice box → **larynx**
voiced [ˈvɔɪst] *adj* : sonoro
void[1] [ˈvɔɪd] *vt* : anular, invalidar <to void a contract : anular un contrato>
void[2] *adj* **1** EMPTY : vacío, desprovisto <void of content : desprovisto de contenido> **2** INVALID : inválido, nulo
void[3] *n* : vacío *m*
volatile [ˈvɑlətəl] *adj* : volátil, inestable
volatility [ˌvɑləˈtɪləti] *n* : volatilidad *f,* inestabilidad *f*
volcanic [vɑlˈkænɪk] *adj* : volcánico
volcano [vɑlˈkeɪˌnoː] *n, pl* **-noes** *or* **-nos** : volcán *m*
vole [ˈvoːl] *n* : campañol *m*
volition [voˈlɪʃən] *n* : volición *f,* voluntad *f* <of one's own volition : por voluntad propia>
volley [ˈvɑli] *n, pl* **-leys 1** : descarga *f* (de tiros) **2** : torrente *m,* lluvia *f* (de insultos, etc.) **3** : salva *f* (de aplausos) **4** : volea *f* (en deportes)
volleyball [ˈvɑliˌbɔl] *n* : voleibol *m*
volt [ˈvoːlt] *n* : voltio *m*
voltage [ˈvoːltɪdʒ] *n* : voltaje *m*
volubility [ˌvɑljəˈbɪləti] *n* : locuacidad *f*
voluble [ˈvɑljəbəl] *adj* : locuaz
volume [ˈvɑljəm, -ˌjuːm] *n* **1** BOOK : volumen *m,* tomo *m* **2** SPACE : capacidad *f,* volumen *m* (en física) **3** AMOUNT : cantidad *f,* volumen *m* **4** LOUDNESS : volumen *m*
voluminous [vəˈluːmənəs] *adj* : voluminoso
voluntary [ˈvɑlənˌtɛri] *adj* : voluntario — **voluntarily** [ˌvɑlənˈtɛrəli] *adv*
volunteer[1] [ˌvɑlənˈtɪr] *vt* : ofrecer, dar <to volunteer one's assistance : ofrecer la ayuda> — *vi* : ofrecerse, alistarse como voluntario
volunteer[2] *n* : voluntario *m,* -ria *f*
voluptuous [vəˈlʌptʃʊəs] *adj* : voluptuoso
vomit[1] [ˈvɑmət] *v* : vomitar
vomit[2] *n* : vómito *m*
voodoo [ˈvuːˌduː] *n, pl* **voodoos** : vudú *m*
voracious [vɔˈreɪʃəs, və-] *adj* : voraz
voraciously [vɔˈreɪʃəsli, və-] *adv* : vorazmente, con voracidad
vortex [ˈvɔrˌtɛks] *n, pl* **vortices** [ˈvɔrtəˌsiːz] : vórtice *m*

vote[1] [ˈvoːt] *vi* **voted; voting :** votar <to vote Democratic : votar por los demócratas>

vote[2] *n* **1 :** voto *m* **2** SUFFRAGE **:** sufragio *m,* derecho *m* al voto

voter [ˈvoːtər] *n* **:** votante *mf*

voting [ˈvoːt̬ɪŋ] *n* **:** votación *f*

vouch [ˈvæʊtʃ] *vi* **to vouch for :** garantizar (algo), responder de (algo), responder por (alguien)

voucher [ˈvæʊtʃər] *n* **1** RECEIPT **:** comprobante *m* **2 :** vale *m* <travel voucher : vale de viajar>

vow[1] [væʊ] *vt* **:** jurar, prometer, hacer voto de

vow[2] *n* **:** promesa *f,* voto *m* (en la religión) <a vow of poverty : un voto de pobreza>

vowel [ˈvæʊəl] *n* **:** vocal *m*

voyage[1] [ˈvɔɪɪdʒ] *vi* **-aged; -aging :** viajar

voyage[2] *n* **:** viaje *m*

voyager [ˈvɔɪɪdʒər] *n* **:** viajero *m,* -ra *f*

vulcanize [ˈvʌlkəˌnaɪz] *vt* **-nized; -nizing :** vulcanizar

vulgar [ˈvʌlgər] *adj* **1** COMMON, PLEBIAN **:** ordinario, populachero, del vulgo **2** COARSE, CRUDE **:** grosero, de mal gusto, majadero *Mex* **3** INDECENT **:** indecente, colorado (dícese de un chiste, etc.)

vulgarity [ˌvʌlˈgærət̬i] *n, pl* **-ties :** grosería *f,* vulgaridad *f*

vulgarly [ˈvʌlgərli] *adv* **:** vulgarmente, groseramente

vulnerability [ˌvʌlnərəˈbɪlət̬i] *n, pl* **-ties :** vulnerabilidad *f*

vulnerable [ˈvʌlnərəbəl] *adj* **:** vulnerable

vulture [ˈvʌltʃər] *n* **:** buitre *m,* zopilote *m CA, Mex*

vying → **vie**

W

w [ˈdʌbəlˌjuː] *n, pl* **w's** *or* **ws** [-ˌjuːz] **:** vigésima tercera letra del alfabeto inglés

wad[1] [ˈwɑd] *vt* **wadded; wadding 1 :** hacer un taco con, formar en una masa **2** STUFF **:** rellenar

wad[2] *n* **:** taco *m* (de papel), bola *f* (de algodón, etc.), fajo *m* (de billetes)

waddle[1] [ˈwɑdəl] *vi* **-dled; -dling :** andar como un pato

waddle[2] *n* **:** andar *m* de pato

wade [ˈweɪd] *v* **waded; wading** *vi* **1 :** caminar por el agua **2 to wade through :** leer (algo) con dificultad — *vt or* **to wade across :** vadear

wading bird *n* **:** zancuda *f,* ave *f* zancuda

wafer [ˈweɪfər] *n* **:** barquillo *m,* galleta *f* de barquillo

waffle [ˈwɑfəl] *n* **1 :** wafle *m* **2 waffle iron :** waflera *f*

waft [ˈwɑft, ˈwæft] *vt* **:** llevar por el aire — *vi* **:** flotar

wag[1] [ˈwæg] *v* **wagged; wagging** *vt* **:** menear — *vi* **:** menearse, moverse

wag[2] *n* **1 :** meneo *m* (de la cola) **2** JOKER, WIT **:** bromista *mf*

wage[1] [ˈweɪdʒ] *vt* **waged; waging :** hacer, librar <to wage war : hacer la guerra>

wage[2] *n or* **wages** *npl* **:** sueldo *m,* salario *m* <minimum wage : salario mínimo>

wager[1] [ˈweɪdʒər] *v* **:** apostar

wager[2] *n* **:** apuesta *f*

waggish [ˈwægɪʃ] *adj* **:** burlón, bromista (dícese de una persona), chistoso (dícese de un comentario)

waggle [ˈwægəl] *vt* **-gled; -gling :** menear, mover (de un lado a otro)

wagon [ˈwægən] *n* **1 :** carro *m* (tirado por caballos) **2** CART **:** carrito *m* **3** → **station wagon**

waif [ˈweɪf] *n* **:** niño *m* abandonado, animal *m* sin hogar

wail[1] [ˈweɪl] *vi* **:** gemir, lamentarse

wail[2] *n* **:** gemido *m,* lamento *m*

wainscot [ˈweɪnskət, -ˌskɑt, -ˌskoːt] *or* **wainscoting** [-skət̬ɪŋ, -ˌskɑ-, -ˌskoː-] *n* **:** boiserie *f,* revestimiento *m* de paneles de madera

waist [ˈweɪst] *n* **:** cintura *f* (del cuerpo humano), talle *m* (de ropa)

waistline [ˈweɪstˌlaɪn] → **waist**

wait[1] [ˈweɪt] *vi* **:** esperar <to wait for something : esperar algo> <wait and see! : ¡espera y verás!> <I can't wait : me muero de ganas> — *vt* **1** AWAIT **:** esperar **2** DELAY **:** retrasar <don't wait lunch : no retrase el almuerzo> **3** SERVE **:** servir, atender <to wait tables : servir (a la mesa)>

wait[2] *n* **1 :** espera *f* **2 to lie in wait :** estar al acecho

waiter [ˈweɪt̬ər] *n* **:** mesero *m,* camarero *m,* mozo *m Arg, Chile, Col, Peru*

waiting room *n* **:** sala *f* de espera

waitress [ˈweɪtrəs] *n* **:** mesera *f,* camarera *f,* moza *f Arg, Chile, Col, Peru*

waive [ˈweɪv] *vt* **waived; waiving :** renunciar a <to waive one's rights : renunciar a sus derechos> <to waive the rules : no aplicar las reglas>

waiver [ˈweɪvər] *n* **:** renuncia *f*

wake[1] [ˈweɪk] *v* **woke** [ˈwoːk]; **woken** [ˈwoːkən] *or* **waked; waking** *vi or* **to wake up :** despertar(se) <he woke at noon : se despertó al mediodía> <wake up! : ¡despiértate!> — *vt* **:** despertar

wake[2] *n* **1** VIGIL **:** velatorio *m,* velorio *m* (de un difunto) **2** TRAIL **:** estela *f* (de un barco, un huracán, etc.) **3** AFTERMATH **:** consecuencias *fpl* <in the wake of : tras, como consecuencia de>

wakeful ['weɪkfəl] *adj* **1** SLEEPLESS **:** desvelado **2** VIGILANT **:** alerta, vigilante

waken ['weɪkən] → **awake**

walk[1] ['wɔk] *vi* **1 :** caminar, andar, pasear <you're walking too fast : estás caminando demasiado rápido> <to walk around the city : pasearse por la ciudad> **2 :** ir andando, ir a pie <we had to walk home : tuvimos que ir a casa a pie> **3 :** darle base por bolas (a un bateador) — *vt* **1 :** recorrer, caminar <she walked two miles : caminó dos millas> **2** ACCOMPANY **:** acompañar **3 :** sacar a pasear (a un perro)

walk[2] *n* **1 :** paseo *m,* caminata *f* <to go for a walk : ir a caminar, dar un paseo> **2** PATH **:** camino *m* **3** GAIT **:** andar *m* **4 :** marcha *f* (en beisbol) **5 walk of life :** esfera *f,* condición *f*

walker ['wɔkər] *n* **1 :** paseante *mf;* andador *m,* -dora *f* **2** HIKER **:** excursionista *mf* **3** *or* **baby walker :** andador *m*

walking stick *n* **:** bastón *m*

walkout ['wɔk,aʊt] *n* STRIKE **:** huelga *f*

walk out *vi* **1** STRIKE **:** declararse en huelga **2** LEAVE **:** salir, irse **3 to walk out on :** abandonar, dejar

wall[1] ['wɔl] *vt* **1 to wall in :** cercar con una pared o un muro, tapiar, amurallar **2 to wall off :** separar con una pared o un muro **3 to wall up :** tapiar, condenar (una ventana, etc.)

wall[2] *n* **1 :** muro *m* (exterior) <the walls of the city : las murallas de la ciudad> **2 :** pared *f* (interior) **3** BARRIER **:** barrera *f* <a wall of mountains : una barrera de montañas> **4 :** pared *f* (en anatomía)

wallaby ['wɑləbi] *n, pl* **-bies :** ualabí *m*

walled ['wɔld] *adj* **:** amurallado

wallet ['wɑlət] *n* **:** billetera *f,* cartera *f*

wallflower ['wɔl,flaʊər] *n* **1 :** alhelí *m* (flor) **2 to be a wallflower :** comer pavo

wallop[1] ['wɑləp] *vt* **1** TROUNCE **:** darle una paliza (a alguien) **2** SOCK **:** pegar fuerte

wallop[2] *n* **:** golpe *m* fuerte, golpazo *m*

wallow[1] ['wɑ,loː] *vi* **1 :** revolcarse <to wallow in the mud : revolcarse en el lodo> **2** DELIGHT **:** deleitarse <to wallow in luxury : nadar en lujos>

wallow[2] *n* **:** revolcadero *m* (para animales)

wallpaper[1] ['wɔl,peɪpər] *vt* **:** empapelar

wallpaper[2] *n* **:** papel *m* pintado

walnut ['wɔl,nʌt] *n* **1 :** nuez *f* (fruta) **2 :** nogal *m* (árbol y madera)

walrus ['wɔlrəs, 'wɑl-] *n, pl* **-rus** *or* **-ruses :** morsa *f*

waltz[1] ['wɔlts] *vi* **1 :** valsar, bailar el vals **2** BREEZE **:** pasar con ligereza <to waltz in : entrar tan campante>

waltz[2] *n* **:** vals *m*

wan ['wɑn] *adj* **wanner; -est 1** PALLID **:** pálido **2** DIM **:** tenue <wan light : luz tenue> **3** LANGUID **:** lánguido <a wan smile : una sonrisa lánguida> — **wanly** *adv*

wand ['wɑnd] *n* **:** varita *f* (mágica)

wander ['wɑndər] *vi* **1** RAMBLE **:** deambular, vagar, vagabundear **2** STRAY **:** alejarse, desviarse, divagar <she let her mind wander : dejó vagar la imaginación> — *vt* **:** recorrer <to wander the streets : vagar por las calles>

wanderer ['wɑndərər] *n* **:** vagabundo *m,* -da *f;* viajero *m,* -ra *f*

wanderlust ['wɑndər,lʌst] *n* **:** pasión *f* por viajar

wane[1] ['weɪn] *vi* **waned; waning 1 :** menguar (dícese de la luna) **2** DECLINE **:** disminuir, decaer, menguar

wane[2] *n* **on the wane :** decayendo, en decadencia

wangle ['wæŋgəl] *vt* **-gled; -gling** FINAGLE **:** arreglárselas para conseguir

want[1] ['wɑnt, 'wɔnt] *vt* **1** LACK **:** faltar **2** REQUIRE **:** requerir, necesitar **3** DESIRE **:** querer, desear

want[2] *n* **1** LACK **:** falta *f* **2** DESTITUTION **:** indigencia *f,* miseria *f* **3** DESIRE, NEED **:** deseo *m,* necesidad *f*

wanting ['wɑntɪŋ, 'wɔn-] *adj* **1** ABSENT **:** ausente **2** DEFICIENT **:** deficiente <he's wanting in common sense : le falta sentido común>

wanton ['wɑntən, 'wɔn-] *adj* **1** LEWD, LUSTFUL **:** lascivo, lujurioso, licencioso **2** INHUMANE, MERCILESS **:** despiadado <wanton cruelty : crueldad despiadada>

wapiti ['wɑpəti] *n, pl* **-ti** *or* **-tis :** uapití *m*

war[1] ['wɔr] *vi* **warred; warring :** combatir, batallar, hacer la guerra

war[2] *n* **:** guerra *f* <to go to war : entrar en guerra>

warble[1] ['wɔrbəl] *vi* **-bled; -bling :** gorjear, trinar

warble[2] *n* **:** trino *m,* gorjeo *m*

warbler ['wɔrblər] *n* **:** pájaro *m* gorjeador, curruca *f*

ward[1] ['wɔrd] *vt* **to ward off :** desviar, protegerse contra

ward[2] *n* **1 :** sala *f* (de un hospital, etc.) <maternity ward : sala de maternidad> **2 :** distrito *m* electoral o administrativo (de una ciudad) **3 :** pupilo *m,* -la *f* (de un tutor, etc.)

warden ['wɔrdən] *n* **1** KEEPER **:** guarda *mf;* guardián *m,* -diana *f* <game warden : guardabosque> **2** *or* **prison warden :** alcaide *m*

wardrobe ['wɔrd,roːb] *n* **1** CLOSET **:** armario *m* **2** CLOTHES **:** vestuario *m,* guardarropa *f*

ware ['wær] *n* **1** POTTERY **:** cerámica *f* **2 wares** *npl* GOODS **:** mercancía *f,* mercadería *f*

warehouse ['wær,haʊs] *n* **:** depósito *m,* almacén *m,* bodega *f Chile, Col, Mex*

warfare [ˈwɔrˌfær] *n* **1** WAR : guerra *f* **2** STRUGGLE : lucha *f* <the warfare against drugs : la lucha contra las drogas>
warhead [ˈwɔrˌhɛd] *n* : ojiva *f,* cabeza *f* (de un misil)
warily [ˈwærəli] *adv* : cautelosamente, con cautela
wariness [ˈwærinəs] *n* : cautela *f*
warlike [ˈwærˌlaɪk] *adj* : belicoso, guerrero
warm[1] [ˈwɔrm] *vt* **1** HEAT : calentar, recalentar **2 to warm one's heart** : reconfortar a uno, alegrar el corazón **3 to warm up** : calentar (los músculos, un automóvil, etc.) — *vi* **1** : calentarse **2 to warm to** : tomarle simpatía (a alguien), entusiasmarse con (algo)
warm[2] *adj* **1** LUKEWARM : tibio, templado **2** : caliente, cálido, caluroso <a warm wind : un viento cálido> <a warm day : un día caluroso, un día de calor> <warm hands : manos calientes> **3** : caliente, que abriga <warm clothes : ropa de abrigo> <I feel warm : tengo calor> **4** CARING, CORDIAL : cariñoso, cordial **5** : cálido (dícese de colores) **6** FRESH : fresco, reciente <a warm trail : un rastro reciente> **7** (*used for riddles*) : caliente
warm–blooded [ˈwɔrmˈblʌdəd] *adj* : de sangre caliente
warmhearted [ˈwɔrmˈhɑrt̬əd] *adj* : cariñoso
warmly [ˈwɔrmli] *adv* **1** AFFECTIONATELY : calurosamente, afectuosamente **2 to dress warmly** : abrigarse
warmonger [ˈwɔrˌmɑŋgər, -ˌmʌŋ-] *n* : belicista *mf*
warmth [ˈwɔrm*p*θ] *n* **1** : calor *m* **2** AFFECTION : cariño *m,* afecto *m* **3** ENTHUSIASM : ardor *m,* entusiasmo *m*
warm–up [ˈwɔrmˌʌp] *n* : calentamiento *m*
warn [ˈwɔrn] *vt* **1** CAUTION : advertir, alertar **2** INFORM : avisar, informar
warning [ˈwɔrnɪŋ] *n* **1** ADVICE : advertencia *f,* aviso *m* **2** ALERT : alerta *f,* alarma *f*
warp[1] [ˈwɔrp] *vt* **1** : alabear, combar **2** PERVERT : pervertir, deformar — *vi* : pandearse, alabearse, combarse
warp[2] *n* **1** : urdimbre *f* <the warp and the weft : la urdimbre y la trama> **2** : alabeo *m* (en la madera, etc.)
warrant[1] [ˈwɔrənt] *vt* **1** ASSURE : asegurar, garantizar **2** GUARANTEE : garantizar **3** JUSTIFY, MERIT : justificar, merecer
warrant[2] *n* **1** AUTHORIZATION : autorización *f,* permiso *m* <an arrest warrant : una orden de detención> **2** JUSTIFICATION : justificación *f*
warranty [ˈwɔrənti, ˌwɔrənˈtiː] *n, pl* **-ties** : garantía *f*
warren [ˈwɔrən] *n* : madriguera *f* (de conejos)
warrior [ˈwɔriər] *n* : guerrero *m,* -ra *f*
warship [ˈwɔrˌʃɪp] *n* : buque *m* de guerra
wart [ˈwɔrt] *n* : verruga *f*
wartime [ˈwɔrˌtaɪm] *n* : tiempo *m* de guerra
wary [ˈwæri] *adj* **warier; -est** : cauteloso, receloso <to be wary of : desconfiar de>
was → **be**
wash[1] [ˈwɔʃ, ˈwɑʃ] *vt* **1** CLEAN : lavar(se), limpiar, fregar <to wash the dishes : lavar los platos> <to wash one's hands : lavarse las manos> **2** DRENCH : mojar **3** LAP : bañar <waves were washing the shore : las olas bañaban la orilla> **4** CARRY, DRAG : arrastrar **5 to wash away** : llevarse (un puente, etc.) — *vi* **1** : lavarse (dícese de una persona o la ropa) <the dress washes well : el vestido se lava bien> **2 to wash against** *or* **to wash over** : bañar
wash[2] *n* **1** : lavado *m* <to give something a wash : lavar algo> **2** LAUNDRY : artículos *mpl* para lavar, ropa *f* sucia **3** : estela *f* (de un barco)
washable [ˈwɔʃəbəl, ˈwɑ-] *adj* : lavable
washboard [ˈwɔʃˌbord, ˈwɑʃ-] *n* : tabla *f* de lavar
washbowl [ˈwɔʃˌboːl, ˈwɑʃ-] *n* : lavabo *m,* lavamanos *m*
washcloth [ˈwɔʃˌklɔθ, ˈwɑʃ-] *n* : toallita *f* (para lavarse)
washed–out [ˈwɔʃtˈaʊt, ˈwɑʃt-] *adj* **1** : desvaído (dícese de colores) **2** EXHAUSTED : agotado, desanimado
washed–up [ˈwɔʃtˈʌp, ˈwɑʃt-] *adj* : acabado (dícese de una persona), fracasado (dícese de un negocio, etc.)
washer [ˈwɔʃər, ˈwɑ-] *n* **1** → **washing machine 2** : arandela *f* (de una llave, etc.)
washing [ˈwɔʃɪŋ, ˈwɑ-] *n* WASH : ropa *f* para lavar
washing machine *n* : máquina *f* de lavar, lavadora *f*
washout [ˈwɔʃˌaʊt, ˈwɑʃ-] *n* **1** : erosión *f* (de la tierra) **2** FAILURE : fracaso *m* <she's a washout : es un desastre>
washroom [ˈwɔʃˌruːm, ˈwɑʃ-, -ˌrʊm] *n* : servicios *mpl* (públicos), baño *m,* sanitario *m Col, Mex, Ven*
wasn't [ˈwʌzənt] (*contraction of* **was not**) → **be**
wasp [ˈwɑsp] *n* : avispa *f*
waspish [ˈwɑspɪʃ] *adj* **1** IRRITABLE : irritable, irascible **2** CAUSTIC : cáustico, mordaz
waste[1] [ˈweɪst] *v* **wasted; wasting** *vt* **1** DEVASTATE : arrasar, arruinar, devastar **2** SQUANDER : desperdiciar, despilfarrar, malgastar <to waste time : perder tiempo> — *vi or* **to waste away** : consumirse, chuparse
waste[2] *adj* **1** BARREN : yermo, baldío **2** DISCARDED : de desecho **3** EXCESS : sobrante

waste[3] *n* **1** → **wasteland 2** MISUSE : derroche *m,* desperdicio *m,* despilfarro *m* <a waste of time : una pérdida de tiempo> **3** RUBBISH : basura *f,* desechos *mpl,* desperdicios *mpl* **4** EXCREMENT : excremento *m*

wastebasket [ˈweɪstˌbæskət] *n* : cesto *m* (de basura), papelera *f,* zafacón *m Car*

wasteful [ˈweɪstfəl] *adj* : despilfarrador, derrochador, pródigo

wastefulness [ˈweɪstfəlnəs] *n* : derroche *m,* despilfarro *m*

wasteland [ˈweɪstˌlænd, -lənd] *n* : baldío *m,* yermo *m,* desierto *m*

watch[1] [ˈwɑtʃ] *vi* **1** *or* **to keep watch** : velar **2** OBSERVE : mirar, ver, observar **3 to watch for** AWAIT : esperar, quedar a la espera de **4 to watch out** : tener cuidado <watch out! : ¡ten cuidado!, ¡ojo!> — *vt* **1** OBSERVE : mirar, observar **2** *or* **to watch over** : vigilar, cuidar **3** : tener cuidado de <watch what you do : ten cuidado con lo que haces>

watch[2] *n* **1** : guardia *f* <to be on watch : estar de guardia> **2** SURVEILLANCE : vigilancia *f* **3** LOOKOUT : guardia *mf,* centinela *f,* vigía *mf* **4** TIMEPIECE : reloj *m*

watchdog [ˈwɑtʃˌdɔg] *n* : perro *m* guardián

watcher [ˈwɑtʃər] *n* : observador *m,* -dora *f*

watchful [ˈwɑtʃfəl] *adj* : alerta, vigilante, atento

watchfulness [ˈwɑtʃfəlnəs] *n* : vigilancia *f*

watchman [ˈwɑtʃmən] *n, pl* **-men** [-mən, -ˌmɛn] : vigilante *m,* guarda *m*

watchword [ˈwɑtʃˌwərd] *n* **1** PASSWORD : contraseña *f* **2** SLOGAN : lema *m,* eslogan *m*

water[1] [ˈwɔt̬ər, ˈwɑ-] *vt* **1** : regar (el jardín, etc.) **2 to water down** DILUTE : diluir, aguar — *vi* : lagrimar (dícese de los ojos), hacérsele agua la boca a uno <my mouth is watering : se me hace agua la boca>

water[2] *n* : agua *f*

water buffalo *n* : búfalo *m* de agua

watercolor [ˈwɔt̬ərˌkʌlər, ˈwɑ-] *n* : acuarela *f*

watercourse [ˈwɔt̬ərˌkors, ˈwɑ-] *n* : curso *m* de agua

watercress [ˈwɔt̬ərˌkrɛs, ˈwɑ-] *n* : berro *m*

waterfall [ˈwɔt̬ərˌfɔl, ˈwɑ-] *n* : cascada *f,* salto *m* de agua, catarata *f*

waterfowl [ˈwɔt̬ərˌfaʊl, ˈwɑ-] *n* : ave *f* acuática

waterfront [ˈwɔt̬ərˌfrʌnt, ˈwɑ-] *n* **1** : tierra *f* que bordea un río, un lago, o un mar **2** WHARF : muelle *m*

water lily *n* : nenúfar *m*

waterlogged [ˈwɔt̬ərˌlɔgd, ˈwɑt̬ərˌlɑgd] *adj* : lleno de agua, empapado, inundado (dícese del suelo)

watermark [ˈwɔt̬ərˌmɑrk, ˈwɑ-] *n* **1** : marca *f* del nivel de agua **2** : filigrana *f* (en el papel)

watermelon [ˈwɔt̬ərˌmɛlən, ˈwɑ-] *n* : sandía *f*

water moccasin → **moccasin**

waterpower [ˈwɔt̬ərˌpaʊər, ˈwɑ-] *n* : energía *f* hidráulica

waterproof[1] [ˈwɔt̬ərˌpruːf, ˈwɑ-] *vt* : hacer impermeable, impermeabilizar

waterproof[2] *adj* : impermeable, a prueba de agua

watershed [ˈwɔt̬ərˌʃɛd, ˈwɑ-] *n* **1** : línea *f* divisoria de aguas **2** BASIN : cuenca *f* (de un río)

waterskiing [ˈwɔt̬ərˌskiːɪŋ, ˈwɑ-] *n* : esquí *m* acuático

waterspout [ˈwɔt̬ərˌspaʊt, ˈwɑ-] *n* WHIRLWIND : tromba *f* marina

watertight [ˈwɔt̬ərˌtaɪt, ˈwɑ-] *adj* **1** : hermético **2** IRREFUTABLE : irrebatible, irrefutable <a watertight contract : un contrato sin lagunas>

waterway [ˈwɔt̬ərˌweɪ, ˈwɑ-] *n* : vía *f* navegable

waterworks [ˈwɔt̬ərˌwərks, ˈwɑ-] *npl* : central *f* de abastecimiento de agua

watery [ˈwɔt̬əri, ˈwɑ-] *adj* **1** : acuoso, como agua **2** : aguado, diluido <watery soup : sopa aguada> **3** : lloroso <watery eyes : ojos llorosos> **4** WASHED-OUT : desvaído (dícese de colores)

watt [ˈwɑt] *n* : vatio *m*

wattage [ˈwɑt̬ɪdʒ] *n* : vataje *m*

wattle [ˈwɑt̬əl] *n* : carúncula *f* (de un ave, etc.)

wave[1] [ˈweɪv] *v* **waved; waving** *vi* **1** : saludar con la mano, hacer señas con la mano <she waved at him : lo saludó con la mano> **2** FLUTTER, SHAKE : ondear, agitarse **3** UNDULATE : ondular — *vt* **1** SHAKE : agitar **2** BRANDISH : blandir **3** CURL : ondular, marcar (el pelo) **4** SIGNAL : hacerle señas a (con la mano) <he waved farewell : se despidió con la mano>

wave[2] *n* **1** : ola *f* (de agua) **2** CURL : onda *f* (en el pelo) **3** : onda *f* (en física) **4** SURGE : oleada *f* <a wave of enthusiasm : una oleada de entusiasmo> **5** GESTURE : señal *f* con la mano, saludo *m* con la mano

wavelength [ˈweɪvˌlɛŋkθ] *n* : longitud *f* de onda

waver [ˈweɪvər] *vi* **1** VACILLATE : vacilar, fluctuar **2** FLICKER : parpadear, titilar, oscilar **3** FALTER : flaquear, tambalearse

wavy [ˈweɪvi] *adj* **wavier; -est** : ondulado

wax[1] [ˈwæks] *vi* **1** : crecer (dícese de la luna) **2** BECOME : volverse, ponerse <to wax indignant : indignarse> — *vt* : encerar

wax[2] *n* **1** BEESWAX : cera *f* de abejas **2** : cera *f* <floor wax : cera para el piso>

3 *or* **earwax** [ˈɪrˌwæks] : cerilla *f,* cerumen *m*

waxen [ˈwæksən] *adj* : de cera

waxy [ˈwæksi] *adj* **waxier; -est** : ceroso

way [ˈweɪ] *n* **1** PATH, ROAD : camino *m,* vía *f* **2** ROUTE : camino *m,* ruta *f* <to go the wrong way : equivocarse de camino> <I'm on my way : estoy de camino> **3** : línea *f* de conducta, camino *m* <he chose the easy way : optó por el camino fácil> **4** MANNER, MEANS : manera *f,* modo *m,* forma *f* <in the same way : del mismo modo, igualmente> <there are no two ways about it : no cabe la menor duda> **5** (*indicating a wish*) <have it your way : como tú quieras> <to get one's own way : salirse uno con la suya> **6** STATE : estado *m* <things are in a bad way : las cosas marchan mal> **7** RESPECT : aspecto *m,* sentido *m* **8** CUSTOM : costumbre *f* <to mend one's ways : dejar las malas costumbres> **9** PASSAGE : camino *m* <to get in the way : meterse en el camino> **10** DISTANCE : distancia *f* <to come a long way : hacer grandes progresos> **11** DIRECTION : dirección *f* <come this way : venga por aquí> <which way did he go? : ¿por dónde fue?> **12 by the way** : a propósito, por cierto **13 by way of** VIA : vía, pasando por **14 out of the way** REMOTE : remoto, recóndito **15** → **under way**

wayfarer [ˈweɪˌfærər] *n* : caminante *mf*

waylay [ˈweɪˌleɪ] *vt* **-laid** [-ˌleɪd]; **-laying** ACCOST : abordar

wayside [ˈweɪˌsaɪd] *n* : borde *m* del camino

wayward [ˈweɪwərd] *adj* **1** UNRULY : díscolo, rebelde **2** UNTOWARD : adverso

we [ˈwiː] *pron* : nosotros, nosotras

weak [ˈwiːk] *adj* **1** FEEBLE : débil, endeble **2** : flojo, pobre <a weak excuse : una excusa poco convincente> **3** DILUTED : aguado, diluido <weak tea : té poco cargado> **4** FAINT : tenue (dícese de los colores, las luces, los sonidos, etc.)

weaken [ˈwiːkən] *vt* : debilitar — *vi* : debilitarse, flaquear

weakling [ˈwiːklɪŋ] *n* : alfeñique *m fam;* debilucho *m,* -cha *f*

weakly[1] [ˈwiːkli] *adv* : débilmente

weakly[2] *adj* **weaklier; -est** : débil, enclenque

weakness [ˈwiːknəs] *n* **1** FEEBLENESS : debilidad *f* **2** FAULT, FLAW : flaqueza *f,* punto *m* débil

wealth [ˈwɛlθ] *n* **1** RICHES : riqueza *f* **2** PROFUSION : abundancia *f,* profusión *f*

wealthy [ˈwɛlθi] *adj* **wealthier; -est** : rico, acaudalado, adinerado

wean [ˈwiːn] *vt* **1** : destetar (a los niños o las crías) **2 to wean someone away from** : quitarle a alguien la costumbre de

weapon [ˈwɛpən] *n* : arma *f*

weaponless [ˈwɛpənləs] *adj* : desarmado

wear[1] [ˈwær] *v* **wore** [ˈwor]; **worn** [ˈworn]; **wearing** *vt* **1** : llevar (ropa, un reloj, etc.), calzar (zapatos) <to wear a happy smile : sonreír alegremente> **2** *or* **to wear away** : desgastar, erosionar (rocas, etc.) **3 to wear out** : gastar <he wore out his shoes : gastó sus zapatos> **4 to wear out** EXHAUST : agotar, fatigar <to wear oneself out : agotarse> — *vi* **1** LAST : durar **2 to wear off** DIMINISH : disminuir **3 to wear out** : gastarse

wear[2] *n* **1** USE : uso *m* <for everyday wear : para todos los días> **2** CLOTHING : ropa *f* <children's wear : ropa de niños> **3** DETERIORATION : desgaste *m* <to be the worse for wear : estar deteriorado>

wearable [ˈwærəbəl] *adj* : que puede ponerse (dícese de una prenda)

wear and tear *n* : desgaste *m*

weariness [ˈwɪrinəs] *n* : fatiga *f,* cansancio *m*

wearisome [ˈwɪrisəm] *adj* : aburrido, pesado, cansado

weary[1] [ˈwɪri] *v* **-ried; -rying** *vt* **1** TIRE : cansar, fatigar **2** BORE : hastiar, aburrir — *vi* : cansarse

weary[2] *adj* **-rier; -est 1** TIRED : cansado **2** FED UP : harto **3** BORED : aburrido

weasel [ˈwiːzəl] *n* : comadreja *f*

weather[1] [ˈwɛðər] *vt* **1** WEAR : erosionar, desgastar **2** ENDURE : aguantar, sobrellevar, capear <to weather the storm : capear el temporal>

weather[2] *n* : tiempo *m*

weather–beaten [ˈwɛðərˌbiːtən] *adj* : curtido

weatherman [ˈwɛðərˌmæn] *n, pl* **-men** [-mən, -ˌmɛn] METEOROLOGIST : meteorólogo *m,* -ga *f*

weatherproof [ˈwɛðərˌpruːf] *adj* : que resiste a la intemperie, impermeable

weather vane → **vane**

weave[1] [ˈwiːv] *v* **wove** [ˈwoːv] *or* **weaved; woven** [ˈwoːvən] *or* **weaved; weaving** *vt* **1** : tejer (tela) **2** INTERLACE : entretejer, entrelazar **3 to weave one's way through** : abrirse camino por — *vi* **1** : tejer **2** WIND : serpentear, zigzaguear

weave[2] *n* : tejido *m,* trama *f*

weaver [ˈwiːvər] *n* : tejedor *m,* -dora *f*

web[1] [ˈwɛb] *vt* **webbed; webbing** : cubrir o proveer con una red

web[2] *n* **1** COBWEB, SPIDERWEB : telaraña *f,* tela *f* de araña **2** ENTANGLEMENT, SNARE : red *f,* enredo *m* <a web of intrigue : una red de intriga> **3** : membrana *f* interdigital (de aves) **4** NETWORK : red *f* <a web of highways : una red de carreteras>

webbed [ˈwɛbd] *adj* : palmeado <webbed feet : patas palmeadas>

wed [ˈwɛd] *vt* **wedded; wedding 1** MARRY : casarse con **2** UNITE : ligar, unir

we'd [ˈwiːd] (*contraction of* **we had, we should,** *or* **we would**) → **have, should, would**

wedding [ˈwɛdɪŋ] *n* : boda *f,* casamiento *m*

wedge[1] [ˈwɛdʒ] *vt* **wedged; wedging 1** : apretar (con una cuña) <to wedge open : mantener abierto con una cuña> **2** CRAM : meter, embutir

wedge[2] *n* **1** : cuña *f* **2** PIECE : porción *f,* trozo *m*

wedlock [ˈwɛdˌlɑk] → **marriage**

Wednesday [ˈwɛnzˌdeɪ, -di] *n* : miércoles *m*

wee [ˈwiː] *adj* : pequeño, minúsculo <in the wee hours : a las altas horas>

weed[1] [ˈwiːd] *vt* **1** : desherbar, desyerbar **2 to weed out** : eliminar, quitar

weed[2] *n* : mala hierba *f*

weedy [ˈwiːdi] *adj* **weedier; -est 1** : cubierto de malas hierbas **2** LANKY, SKINNY : flaco, larguirucho *fam*

week [ˈwiːk] *n* : semana *f*

weekday [ˈwiːkˌdeɪ] *n* : día *m* laborable

weekend [ˈwiːkˌɛnd] *n* : fin *m* de semana

weekly[1] [ˈwiːkli] *adv* : semanalmente

weekly[2] *adj* : semanal

weekly[3] *n, pl* **-lies** : semanario *m*

weep [ˈwiːp] *v* **wept** [ˈwɛpt]; **weeping** : llorar

weeping willow *n* : sauce *m* llorón

weepy [ˈwiːpi] *adj* **weepier; -est** : lloroso, triste

weevil [ˈwiːvəl] *n* : gorgojo *m*

weft [ˈwɛft] *n* : trama *f*

weigh [ˈweɪ] *vt* **1** : pesar **2** CONSIDER : considerar, sopesar **3 to weigh anchor** : levar anclas **4 to weigh down** : sobrecargar (con una carga), abrumar (con preocupaciones, etc.) — *vi* **1** : pesar <it weighs 10 pounds : pesa 10 libras> **2** COUNT : tener importancia, contar **3 to weigh on one's mind** : preocuparle a uno

weight[1] [ˈweɪt] *vt* **1** : poner peso en, sujetar con un peso **2** BURDEN : cargar, oprimir

weight[2] *n* **1** HEAVINESS : peso *m* <to lose weight : bajar de peso, adelgazar> **2** : peso *m* <weights and measures : pesos y medidas> **3** : pesa *f* <to lift weights : levantar pesas> **4** BURDEN : peso *m,* carga *f* <to take a weight off one's mind : quitarle un peso de encima a uno> **5** IMPORTANCE : peso *m* **6** INFLUENCE : influencia *f,* autoridad *f* <to throw one's weight around : hacer sentir su influencia>

weighty [ˈweɪṭi] *adj* **weightier; -est 1** HEAVY : pesado **2** IMPORTANT : importante, de peso

weird [ˈwɪrd] *adj* **1** MYSTERIOUS : misterioso **2** STRANGE : extraño, raro — **weirdly** *adv*

welcome[1] [ˈwɛlkəm] *vt* **-comed; -coming** : darle la bienvenida a, recibir

welcome[2] *adj* : bienvenido <to make someone welcome : acoger bien a alguien> <you're welcome! : ¡de nada!, ¡no hay de qué!>

welcome[3] *n* : bienvenida *f,* recibimiento *m,* acojida *f*

weld[1] [ˈwɛld] *v* : soldar

weld[2] *n* : soldadura *f*

welder [ˈwɛldər] *n* : soldador *m,* -dora *f*

welfare [ˈwɛlˌfær] *n* **1** WELL-BEING : bienestar *m* **2** : asistencia *f* social

well[1] [ˈwɛl] *vi or* **to well up** : brotar, manar

well[2] *adv* **better** [ˈbɛṭər]; **best** [ˈbɛst] **1** RIGHTLY : bien, correctamente **2** SATISFACTORILY : bien <to turn out well : resultar bien, salir bien> **3** COMPLETELY : completamente <well-hidden : completamente escondido> **4** INTIMATELY : bien <I knew him well : lo conocía bien> **5** CONSIDERABLY, FAR : muy, bastante <well ahead : muy adelante> <well before the deadline : bastante antes de la fecha> **6 as well** ALSO : también **7** → **as well as**

well[3] *adj* **1** SATISFACTORY : bien <all is well : todo está bien> **2** DESIRABLE : conveniente <it would be well if you left : sería conveniente que te fueras> **3** HEALTHY : bien, sano

well[4] *n* **1** : pozo *m* (de agua, petróleo, gas, etc.), aljibe *m* (de agua) **2** SOURCE : fuente *f* <a well of information : una fuente de información> **3** *or* **stairwell** : caja *f,* hueco *m* (de la escalera)

well[5] *interj* **1** (*used to introduce a remark*) : bueno **2** (*used to express surprise*) : ¡vaya!

we'll [ˈwiːl, wɪl] (*contraction of* **we shall** *or* **we will**) → **shall, will**

well–balanced [ˈwɛlˈbælənst] *adj* : equilibrado

well–being [ˈwɛlˈbiːɪŋ] *n* : bienestar *m*

well–bred [ˈwɛlˈbrɛd] *adj* : fino, bien educado

well–done [ˈwɛlˈdʌn] *adj* **1** : bien hecho <well-done! : ¡bravo!> **2** : bien cocido

well–known [ˈwɛlˈnoːn] *adj* : famoso, bien conocido

well–meaning [ˈwɛlˈmiːnɪŋ] *adj* : bienintencionado, que tiene buenas intenciones

well–nigh [ˈwɛlˈnaɪ] *adv* : casi <well-nigh impossible : casi imposible>

well–off [ˈwɛlˈɔf] → **well–to–do**

well–rounded [ˈwɛlˈraʊndəd] *adj* : completo, equilibrado

well–to–do [ˌwɛltəˈduː] *adj* : próspero, adinerado, rico

welt [ˈwɛlt] *n* **1 :** vira *f* (de un zapato) **2** WHEAL **:** verdugón *m*

welter [ˈwɛltər] *n* **:** fárrago *m,* revoltijo *m* <a welter of data : un fárrago de datos>

wend [ˈwɛnd] *vi* **to wend one's way :** ponerse en camino, encaminar sus pasos

went → go

wept → weep

were → be

we're [ˈwɪr, ˈwər, ˈwiːər] (*contraction of* **we are**) **→ be**

werewolf [ˈwɪrˌwʊlf, ˈwɛr-, ˈwər-, -ˌwʌlf] *n, pl* **-wolves** [-ˌwʊlvz, -ˌwʌlvz] **:** hombre *m* lobo

west[1] [ˈwɛst] *adv* **:** al oeste

west[2] *adj* **:** oeste, del oeste, occidental <west winds : vientos del oeste>

west[3] *n* **1 :** oeste *m* **2 the West :** el Oeste, el Occidente

westerly [ˈwɛstərli] *adv & adj* **:** del oeste

western [ˈwɛstərn] *adj* **1 :** Occidental, del Oeste **2 :** occidental, oeste

Westerner [ˈwɛstərnər] *n* **:** habitante *mf* del oeste

West Indian *n* **:** antillano *m,* -na *f* — **West Indian** *adj*

westward [ˈwɛstwərd] *adv & adj* **:** hacia el oeste

wet[1] [ˈwɛt] *vt* **wet** *or* **wetted; wetting :** mojar, humedecer

wet[2] *adj* **wetter; wettest 1 :** mojado, húmedo <wet clothes : ropa mojada> **2** RAINY **:** lluvioso **3 wet paint :** pintura *f* fresca

wet[3] *n* **1** MOISTURE **:** humedad *f* **2** RAIN **:** lluvia *f*

we've [ˈwiːv] (*contraction of* **we have**) **→ have**

whack[1] [ˈhwæk] *vt* **:** golpear (fuertemente), aporrear

whack[2] *n* **1 :** golpe *m* fuerte, porrazo *m* **2** ATTEMPT **:** intento *m,* tentativa *f*

whale[1] [ˈhweɪl] *vi* **whaled; whaling :** cazar ballenas

whale[2] *n, pl* **whales** *or* **whale :** ballena *f*

whaleboat [ˈhweɪlˌboːt] *n* **:** ballenero *m*

whalebone [ˈhweɪlˌboːn] *n* **:** barba *f* de ballena

whaler [ˈhweɪlər] *n* **1 :** ballenero *m,* -ra *f* **2 → whaleboat**

wharf [ˈhwɔrf] *n, pl* **wharves** [ˈhwɔrvz] **:** muelle *m,* embarcadero *m*

what[1] [ˈhwɑt, ˈhwʌt] *adv* **1** HOW **:** cómo, cúanto <what he suffered! : ¡cómo sufría!> **2 what with :** entre <what with one thing and another : entre una cosa y otra>

what[2] *adj* **1** (*used in questions*) **:** qué <what more do you want? : ¿qué más quieres?> <what color is it? : ¿de qué color es?> **2** (*used in exclamations*) **:** qué <what an idea! : ¡qué idea!> **3** ANY, WHATEVER **:** cualquier <give what help you can : da cualquier contribución que puedas>

what[3] *pron* **1** (*used in direct questions*) **:** qué <what happened? : ¿qué pasó?> <what does it cost? : ¿cuánto cuesta?> **2** (*used in indirect statements*) **:** lo que, que <I don't know what to do : no sé que hacer> <do what I tell you : haz lo que te digo> **3 what for** WHY **:** porqué **4 what if :** y si <what if he knows? : ¿y si lo sabe?>

whatever[1] [hwɑtˈɛvər, ˌhwʌt-] *adj* **1** ANY **:** cualquier, cualquier...que <whatever way you prefer : de cualquier manera que prefiera, como prefiera> **2** (*in negative constructions*) <there's no chance whatever : no hay ninguna posibilidad> <nothing whatever : nada en absoluto>

whatever[2] *pron* **1** ANYTHING **:** (todo) lo que <I'll do whatever I want : haré lo que quiera> **2** (*no matter what*) <whatever it may be : sea lo que sea> **3** WHAT **:** qué <whatever do you mean? : ¿qué quieres decir?>

whatsoever[1] [ˌhwɑtsoˈɛvər, ˌhwʌt-] *adj* **→ whatever**[1]

whatsoever[2] *pron* **→ whatever**[2]

wheal [ˈhwiːl] *n* **:** verdugón *m*

wheat [ˈhwiːt] *n* **:** trigo *m*

wheaten [ˈhwiːtən] *adj* **:** de trigo

wheedle [ˈhwiːdəl] *vt* **-dled; -dling** CAJOLE **:** engatusar <to wheedle something out of someone : sonsacarle algo a alguien>

wheel[1] [ˈhwiːl] *vt* **:** empujar (una bicicleta, etc.), mover (algo sobre ruedas) — *vi* **1** ROTATE **:** girar, rotar **2 to wheel around** TURN **:** darse la vuelta

wheel[2] *n* **1 :** rueda *f* **2** *or* **steering wheel :** volante *m* (de automóviles, etc.), timón *m* (de barcos o aviones) **3 wheels** *npl* **:** maquinaria *f,* fuerza *f* impulsora <the wheels of government : la maquinaria del gobierno>

wheelbarrow [ˈhwiːlˌbærˌoː] *n* **:** carretilla *f*

wheelchair [ˈhwiːlˌtʃær] *n* **:** silla *f* de ruedas

wheeze[1] [ˈhwiːz] *vi* **wheezed; wheezing :** resollar, respirar con dificultad

wheeze[2] *n* **:** resuello *m*

whelk [ˈhwɛlk] *n* **:** buccino *m*

whelp[1] [ˈhwɛlp] *vi* **:** parir

whelp[2] *n* **:** cachorro *m,* -rra *f*

when[1] [ˈhwɛn] *adv* **:** cuándo <when will you return? : ¿cuándo volverás?> <he asked me when I would be home : me preguntó cuándo estaría en casa>

when[2] *conj* **1** (*referring to a particular time*) **:** cuando, en que <when you are ready : cuando estés listo> <the days when I clean the house : los días en que limpio la casa> **2** IF **:** cuando, si <how can I go when I have no money? : ¿cómo voy a ir si no tengo dinero?> **3** ALTHOUGH **:** cuando <you said it was big when actually it's

small : dijiste que era grande cuando en realidad es pequeño>

when[3] *pron* : cuándo <since when are you the boss? : ¿desde cuándo eres el jefe?>

whence ['*h*wɛnts] *adv* : de donde

whenever[1] [*h*wɛn'ɛvər] *adv* **1** : cuando sea <tomorrow or whenever : manaña o cuando sea> **2** (*in questions*) : cuándo

whenever[2] *conj* **1** : siempre que, cada vez que <whenever I go, I'm disappointed : siempre que voy, quedo desilusionado> **2** WHEN : cuando <whenever you like : cuando quieras>

where[1] ['*h*wɛr] *adv* : dónde, adónde <where is he? : ¿dónde está?> <where did they go? : ¿adónde fueron?>

where[2] *conj* : donde, adonde <she knows where the house is : sabe donde está la casa> <she goes where she likes : va adonde quiera>

where[3] *pron* : donde <Chicago is where I live : Chicago es donde vivo>

whereabouts[1] ['*h*wɛrə,baʊts] *adv* : dónde, por dónde <whereabouts is the house? : ¿dónde está la casa?>

whereabouts[2] *ns & pl* : paradero *m*

whereas [*h*wɛr'æz] *conj* **1** : considerando que (usado en documentos legales) **2** : mientras que <I like the white one whereas she prefers the black : me gusta el blanco mientras que ella prefiere el negro>

whereby [*h*wɛr'baɪ] *adv* : por lo cual

wherefore ['*h*wɛr,for] *adv* : por qué

wherein [*h*wɛr'ɪn] *adv* : en el cual, en el que

whereof [*h*wɛr'ʌv, -ɑv] *conj* : de lo cual

whereupon ['*h*wɛrə,pɑn, -,pɔn] *conj* : con lo cual, después de lo cual

wherever[1] [*h*wɛr'ɛvər] *adv* **1** WHERE : dónde, adónde **2** : en cualquier parte <or wherever : o donde sea>

wherever[2] *conj* : dondequiera que, donde sea <wherever you go : dondequiera que vayas>

wherewithal ['*h*wɛrwɪ,ðɔl, -,θɔl] *n* : medios *mpl*, recursos *mpl*

whet ['*h*wɛt] *vt* **whetted; whetting** **1** SHARPEN : afilar **2** STIMULATE : estimular <to whet the appetite : estimular el apetito>

whether ['*h*wɛðər] *conj* **1** : si <I don't know whether it is finished : no sé si está acabado> <we doubt whether he'll show up : dudamos que aparezca> **2** (*used in comparisons*) <whether I like it or not : tanto si quiero como si no> <whether he comes or he doesn't : venga o no>

whetstone ['*h*wɛt,sto:n] *n* : piedra *f* de afilar

whey ['*h*weɪ] *n* : suero *m* (de la leche)

which[1] ['*h*wɪtʃ] *adj* : qué, cuál <which tie do you prefer? : ¿cuál corbata prefieres?> <which ones? : ¿cuáles?> <tell me which house is yours : dime qué casa es la tuya>

which[2] *pron* **1** : cuál <which is the right answer? : ¿cuál es la respuesta correcta?> **2** : que, el (la) cual <the cup which broke : la taza que se quebró> <the house, which is made of brick : la casa, la cual es de ladrillo>

whichever[1] [*h*wɪtʃ'ɛvər] *adj* : el (la) que, cualquiera que <whichever book you like : cualquier libro que te guste>

whichever[2] *pron* : el (la) que, cualquiera que <take whichever you want : toma el que quieras> <whichever I choose : cualquiera que elija>

whiff[1] ['*h*wɪf] *v* PUFF : soplar

whiff[2] *n* **1** PUFF : soplo *m*, ráfaga *f* **2** SNIFF : olor *m* **3** HINT : dejo *m*, pizca *f*

while[1] ['*h*waɪl] *vt* **whiled; whiling** : pasar <to while away the time : matar el tiempo>

while[2] *n* **1** TIME : rato *m*, tiempo *m* <after a while : después de un rato> <in a while : dentro de poco> **2 to be worth one's while** : valer la pena

while[3] *conj* **1** : mientras <whistle while you work : silba mientras trabajas> **2** WHEREAS : mientras que **3** ALTHOUGH : aunque <while it's very good, it's not perfect : aunque es muy bueno, no es perfecto>

whim ['*h*wɪm] *n* : capricho *m*, antojo *m*

whimper[1] ['*h*wɪmpər] *vi* : lloriquear, gimotear

whimper[2] *n* : quejido *m*

whimsical ['*h*wɪmzɪkəl] *adj* **1** CAPRICIOUS : caprichoso, fantasioso **2** ERRATIC : errático — **whimsically** *adv*

whine[1] ['*h*waɪn] *vi* **whined; whining** **1** : lloriquear, gimotear, gemir **2** COMPLAIN : quejarse

whine[2] *n* : quejido *m*, gemido *m*

whinny[1] ['*h*wɪni] *vi* **-nied; -nying** : relinchar

whinny[2] *n, pl* **-nies** : relincho *m*

whip[1] ['*h*wɪp] *v* **whipped; whipping** *vt* **1** SNATCH : sacar (rápidamente), arrebatar <she whipped the cloth off the table : arrebató el mantel de la mesa> **2** LASH : azotar **3** DEFEAT : vencer, derrotar **4** INCITE : incitar, despertar <to whip up enthusiasm : despertar el entusiasmo> **5** BEAT : batir (huevos, crema, etc.) — *vi* FLAP : agitarse

whip[2] *n* **1** : látigo *m*, azote *m*, fusta *f* (de jinete) **2** : miembro *m* de un cuerpo legislativo encargado de disciplina

whiplash ['*h*wɪp,læʃ] *n or* **whiplash injury** : traumatismo *m* cervical

whippet ['*h*wɪpət] *n* : galgo *m* pequeño, galgo *m* inglés

whippoorwill ['*h*wɪpər,wɪl] *n* : chotacabras *mf*

whir[1] ['*h*wər] *vi* **whirred; whirring** : zumbar

whir[2] *n* : zumbido *m*

whirl[1] [ˈhwərl] *vi* **1** SPIN **:** dar vueltas, girar <my head is whirling **:** la cabeza me está dando vueltas> **2 to whirl about :** arremolinarse, moverse rápidamente

whirl[2] *n* **1** SPIN **:** giro *m,* vuelta *f,* remolino *m* (dícese del polvo, etc.) **2** BUSTLE **:** bullicio *m,* torbellino *m* (de actividad, etc.) **3 to give it a whirl :** intentar hacer, probar

whirlpool [ˈhwərl,puːl] *n* **:** vorágine *f,* remolino *m*

whirlwind [ˈhwərl,wɪnd] *n* **:** remolino *m,* torbellino *m,* tromba *f*

whisk[1] [ˈhwɪsk] *vt* **1 :** llevar <she whisked the children off to bed **:** llevó a los niños a la cama> **2 :** batir <to whisk eggs **:** batir huevos> **3 to whisk away** *or* **to whisk off :** sacudir

whisk[2] *n* **1** WHISKING **:** sacudida *f* (movimiento) **2 :** batidor *m* (para batir huevos, etc.)

whisk broom *n* **:** escobilla *f*

whisker [ˈhwɪskər] *n* **1 :** pelo *m* (de la barba o el bigote) **2 whiskers** *npl* **:** bigotes *mpl* (de animales)

whiskey *or* **whisky** [ˈhwɪski] *n, pl* **-keys** *or* **-kies :** whisky *m*

whisper[1] [ˈhwɪspər] *vi* **:** cuchichear, susurrar — *vt* **:** decir en voz baja, susurrar

whisper[2] *n* **1** WHISPERING **:** susurro *m,* cuchicheo *m* **2** RUMOR **:** rumor *m* **3** TRACE **:** dejo *m,* pizca *f*

whistle[1] [ˈhwɪsəl] *v* **-tled; -tling** *vi* **:** silbar, chiflar, pitar (dícese de un tren, etc.) — *vt* **:** silbar <to whistle a tune **:** silbar una melodía>

whistle[2] *n* **1** WHISTLING **:** chiflido *m,* silbido *m* **2 :** silbato *m,* pito *m* (instrumento)

whit [ˈhwɪt] *n* BIT **:** ápice *m,* pizca *f*

white[1] [ˈhwaɪt] *adj* **whiter; -est :** blanco

white[2] *n* **1 :** blanco *m* (color) **2 :** clara *f* (de huevos) **3** *or* **white person :** blanco *m,* -ca *f*

white blood cell *n* **:** glóbulo *m* blanco

whitecaps [ˈhwaɪt,kæps] *npl* **:** cabrillas *fpl*

white–collar [ˈhwaɪtˈkɑlər] *adj* **1 :** de oficina **2 white–collar worker :** oficinista *mf*

whitefish [ˈhwaɪt,fɪʃ] *n* **:** pescado *m* blanco

whiten [ˈhwaɪtən] *vt* **:** blanquear — *vi* **:** ponerse blanco

whiteness [ˈhwaɪtnəs] *n* **:** blancura *f*

white–tailed deer [ˈhwaɪtˈteɪld] *n* **:** ciervo *f* de Virginia

whitewash[1] [ˈhwaɪt,wɔʃ] *vt* **1 :** enjalbegar, blanquear <to whitewash a fence **:** enjalbegar una valla> **2** CONCEAL **:** encubrir (un escándalo, etc.)

whitewash[2] *n* **1 :** jalbegue *m,* lechada *f* **2** COVER-UP **:** encubrimiento *m*

whither [ˈhwɪðər] *adv* **:** adónde

whiting [ˈhwaɪtɪŋ] *n* **:** merluza *f,* pescadilla *f* (pez)

whitish [ˈhwaɪtɪʃ] *adj* **:** blancuzco

whittle [ˈhwɪtəl] *vt* **-tled; -tling 1 :** tallar (madera) **2 to whittle down :** reducir, recortar <to whittle down expenses **:** reducir los gastos>

whiz[1] *or* **whizz** [ˈhwɪz] *vi* **whizzed; whizzing 1** BUZZ **:** zumbar **2 to whiz by :** pasar muy rápido, pasar volando

whiz[2] *or* **whizz** *n, pl* **whizzes 1** BUZZ **:** zumbido *m* **2 to be a whiz :** ser un prodigio, ser muy hábil

who [ˈhuː] *pron* **1** (*used in direct and indirect questions*) **:** quién <who is that? **:** ¿quién es ése?> <who did it? **:** ¿quién lo hizo?> <we know who they are **:** sabemos quiénes son> **2** (*used in relative clauses*) **:** que, quien <the lady who lives there **:** la señora que vive allí> <for those who wait **:** para los que esperan, para quienes esperan>

whodunit [huːˈdʌnɪt] *n* **:** novela *f* policíaca

whoever [huːˈɛvər] *pron* **1 :** quienquiera que, quien <whoever did it **:** quienquiera que lo hizo> <give it to whoever you want **:** dalo a quien quieras> **2** (*used in questions*) **:** quién <whoever could that be? **:** ¿quién podría ser?>

whole[1] [ˈhoːl] *adj* **1** UNHURT **:** ileso **2** INTACT **:** intacto, sano **3** ENTIRE **:** entero, íntegro <the whole island **:** toda la isla> <whole milk **:** leche entera> **4 a whole lot :** muchísimo

whole[2] *n* **1 :** todo *m* **2 as a whole :** en conjunto **3 on the whole :** en general

wholehearted [ˈhoːlˈhɑrtəd] *adj* **:** sin reservas, incondicional

whole number *n* **:** entero *m*

wholesale[1] [ˈhoːl,seɪl] *v* **-saled; -saling** *vt* **:** vender al por mayor — *vi* **:** venderse al por mayor

wholesale[2] *adv* **:** al por mayor

wholesale[3] *adj* **1 :** al por mayor <wholesale grocer **:** tendero al por mayor> **2** TOTAL **:** total, absoluto <wholesale slaughter **:** matanza sistemática>

wholesale[4] *n* **:** mayoreo *m*

wholesaler [ˈhoːl,seɪlər] *n* **:** mayorista *mf*

wholesome [ˈhoːlsəm] *adj* **1 :** sano <wholesome advice **:** consejo sano> **2** HEALTHY **:** sano, saludable

whole wheat *adj* **:** de trigo integral

wholly [ˈhoːli] *adv* **1** COMPLETELY **:** completamente **2** SOLELY **:** exclusivamente, únicamente

whom [ˈhuːm] *pron* **1** (*used in direct questions*) **:** a quién <whom did you choose? **:** ¿a quién elegiste?> **2** (*used in indirect questions*) **:** de quién, con quién, en quién <I don't know whom to consult **:** no sé con quién consultar> **3** (*used in relative clauses*) **:** que, a quien <the lawyer whom I recommended to you **:** el abogado que te recomendé>

whomever [huːmˈɛvər] *pron* : a quienquiera que, a quien

whoop[1] [ˈ*h*wuːp, ˈ*h*wʊp] *vi* : gritar, chillar

whoop[2] *n* : grito *m*

whooping cough *n* : tos *f* ferina

whopper [ˈ*h*wɑpər] *n* **1** : cosa *f* enorme **2** LIE : mentira *f* colosal

whopping [ˈ*h*wɑpɪŋ] *adj* : enorme

whore [ˈhor] *n* : puta *f*, ramera *f*

whorl [ˈ*h*wɔrl, ˈ*h*wərl] *n* : espiral *f*, espira *f* (de una concha), línea *f* (de una huella digital)

whose[1] [ˈhuːz] *adj* **1** (*used in questions*) : de quién <whose truck is that? : ¿de quién es ese camión?> **2** (*used in relative clauses*) : cuyo <the person whose work is finished : la persona cuyo trabajo está terminado>

whose[2] *pron* : de quién <tell me whose it was : dime de quién era>

why[1] [ˈ*h*waɪ] *adv* : por qué <why did you do it? : ¿por qué lo hizo?>

why[2] *n, pl* **whys** REASON : porqué *m*, razón *f*

why[3] *conj* : por qué <I know why he left : yo sé por qué salió> <there's no reason why it should exist : no hay razón para que exista>

why[4] *interj* (*used to express surprise*) : ¡vaya!, ¡mira!

wick [ˈwɪk] *n* : mecha *f*

wicked [ˈwɪkəd] *adj* **1** EVIL : malo, malvado **2** MISCHIEVOUS : travieso, pícaro <a wicked grin : una sonrisa traviesa> **3** TERRIBLE : terrible, horrible <a wicked storm : una tormenta horrible>

wickedly [ˈwɪkədli] *adv* : con maldad

wickedness [ˈwɪkədnəs] *n* : maldad *f*

wicker[1] [ˈwɪkər] *adj* : de mimbre

wicker[2] *n* **1** : mimbre *m* **2** → **wickerwork**

wickerwork [ˈwɪkərˌwərk] *n* : artículos *mpl* de mimbre

wicket [ˈwɪkət] *n* **1** WINDOW : ventanilla *f* **2** *or* **wicket gate** : postigo *m* **3** : aro *m* (en croquet), palos *mpl* (en críquet)

wide[1] [ˈwaɪd] *adv* **wider; widest 1** WIDELY : por todas partes <to travel far and wide : viajar por todas partes> **2** COMPLETELY : completamente, totalmente <wide open : abierto de par en par> **3 wide apart** : muy separados

wide[2] *adj* **wider; widest 1** VAST : vasto, extensivo <a wide area : una área extensiva> **2** : ancho <three meters wide : tres metros de ancho> **3** BROAD : ancho, amplio **4** *or* **wide–open** : muy abierto **5 wide of the mark** : desviado, lejos del blanco

wide–awake [ˈwaɪdəˈweɪk] *adj* : (completamente) despierto

wide–eyed [ˈwaɪdˈaɪd] *adj* **1** : con los ojos muy abiertos **2** NAIVE : inocente, ingenuo

widely [ˈwaɪdli] *adv* : extensivamente, por todas partes

widen [ˈwaɪdən] *vt* : ampliar, ensanchar — *vi* : ampliarse, ensancharse

widespread [ˈwaɪdˈsprɛd] *adj* : extendido, extenso, difuso

widow[1] [ˈwɪˌdoː] *vt* : dejar viuda <to be widowed : enviudar>

widow[2] *n* : viuda *f*

widower [ˈwɪdowər] *n* : viudo *m*

width [ˈwɪdθ] *n* : ancho *m*, anchura *f*

wield [ˈwiːld] *vt* **1** USE : usar, manejar <to wield a broom : usar una escoba> **2** EXERCISE : ejercer <to wield influence : influir>

wiener [ˈwiːnər] → **frankfurter**

wife [ˈwaɪf] *n, pl* **wives** [ˈwaɪvz] : esposa *f*, mujer *f*

wifely [ˈwaɪfli] *adj* : de esposa, conyugal

wig [ˈwɪg] *n* : peluca *f*

wiggle[1] [ˈwɪgəl] *v* **-gled; -gling** *vt* : menear, contonear <to wiggle one's hips : contonearse> — *vi* : menearse

wiggle[2] *n* : meneo *m*, contoneo *m*

wiggly [ˈwɪgəli] *adj* **-glier; -est 1** : que se menea **2** WAVY : ondulado

wigwag [ˈwɪgˌwæg] *vi* **-wagged; -wagging** : comunicar por señales

wigwam [ˈwɪgˌwɑm] *n* : wigwam *m*

wild[1] [ˈwaɪld] *adv* **1** → **wildly 2 to run wild** : descontrolarse

wild[2] *adj* **1** : salvaje, silvestre, cimarrón <wild horses : caballos salvajes> <wild rice : arroz silvestre> **2** DESOLATE : yermo, agreste **3** UNRULY : desenfrenado **4** CRAZY : loco, fantástico <wild ideas : ideas locas> **5** BARBAROUS : salvaje, bárbaro **6** ERRATIC : errático <a wild throw : un tiro errático>

wild[3] *n* → **wilderness**

wildcat [ˈwaɪldˌkæt] *n* **1** : gato *m* montés **2** BOBCAT : lince *m* rojo

wilderness [ˈwɪldərnəs] *n* : yermo *m*, desierto *m*

wildfire [ˈwaɪldˌfaɪr] *n* **1** : fuego *m* descontrolado **2 to spread like wildfire** : propagarse como un reguero de pólvora

wildflower [ˈwaɪldˌflaʊər] *n* : flor *f* silvestre

wildfowl [ˈwaɪldˌfaʊl] *n* : ave *f* de caza

wildlife [ˈwaɪldˌlaɪf] *n* : fauna *f*

wildly [ˈwaɪldli] *adv* **1** FRANTICALLY : frenéticamente, como un loco **2** EXTREMELY : extremadamente <wildly happy : loco de felicidad>

wile[1] [ˈwaɪl] *vt* **wiled; wiling** LURE : atraer

wile[2] *n* : ardid *m*, artimaña *f*

will[1] [ˈwɪl] *v past* **would** [ˈwʊd]; *pres sing & pl* **will** *vi* WISH : querer <do what you will : haz lo que quieras> — *v aux* **1** (*expressing willingness*) <no one would take the job : nadie aceptaría el trabajo> <I won't do it : no lo haré> **2** (*expressing habitual action*) <he will get angry over nothing : se pone furioso por cualquier cosa> **3** (*forming the future tense*)

<tomorrow we will go shopping : mañana iremos de compras> **4** (*expressing capacity*) <the couch will hold three people : en el sofá cabrán tres personas> **5** (*expressing determination*) <I will go despite them : iré a pesar de ellos> **6** (*expressing probability*) <that will be the mailman : eso ha de ser el cartero> **7** (*expressing inevitability*) <accidents will happen : los accidentes ocurrirán> **8** (*expressing a command*) <you will do as I say : harás lo que digo>

will[2] *vt* **1** ORDAIN **:** disponer, decretar <if God wills it : si Dios lo dispone, si Dios quiere> **2 :** lograr a fuerza de voluntad <they were willing him to succeed : estaban deseando que tuviera éxito> **3** BEQUEATH **:** legar

will[3] *n* **1** DESIRE **:** deseo *m,* voluntad *f* **2** VOLITION **:** voluntad *f* <free will : libre albedrío> **3** WILLPOWER **:** voluntad *f,* fuerza *f* de voluntad <a will of iron : una voluntad férrea> **4 :** testamento *m* <to make a will : hacer testamento>

willful *or* **wilful** [ˈwɪlfəl] *adj* **1** OBSTINATE **:** obstinado, terco **2** INTENTIONAL **:** intencionado, deliberado **— willfully** *adv*

willing [ˈwɪlɪŋ] *adj* **1** INCLINED, READY **:** listo, dispuesto **2** OBLIGING **:** servicial, complaciente

willingly [ˈwɪlɪŋli] *adv* **:** con gusto

willingness [ˈwɪlɪŋnəs] *n* **:** buena voluntad *f*

willow [ˈwɪˌloː] *n* **:** sauce *m*

willowy [ˈwɪlowi] *adj* **:** esbelto

willpower [ˈwɪlˌpaʊər] *n* **:** voluntad *f,* fuerza *f* de voluntad

wilt [ˈwɪlt] *vi* **1 :** marchitarse (dícese de las flores) **2** LANGUISH **:** debilitarse, languidecer

wily [ˈwaɪli] *adj* **wilier; -est :** artero, astuto

win[1] [ˈwɪn] *v* **won** [ˈwʌn]; **winning** *vi* **:** ganar **—** *vt* **1 :** ganar, conseguir **2 to win over :** ganarse a **3 to win someone's heart :** conquistar a alguien

win[2] *n* **:** triunfo *m,* victoria *f*

wince[1] [ˈwɪnts] *vi* **winced; wincing :** estremecerse, hacer una mueca de dolor

wince[2] *n* **:** mueca *f* de dolor

winch [ˈwɪntʃ] *n* **:** torno *m*

wind[1] [ˈwɪnd] *vt* **:** dejar sin aliento <to be winded : quedarse sin aliento>

wind[2] [ˈwaɪnd] *v* **wound** [ˈwaʊnd]; **winding** *vi* MEANDER **:** serpentear **—** *vt* **1** COIL, ROLL **:** envolver, enrollar **2** TURN **:** hacer girar <to wind a clock : darle cuerda a un reloj>

wind[3] [ˈwɪnd] *n* **1 :** viento *m* <against the wind : contra el viento> **2** BREATH **:** aliento *m* **3** FLATULENCE **:** flatulencia *f,* ventosidad *f* **4 to get wind of :** enterarse de

wind[4] [ˈwaɪnd] *n* **1** TURN **:** vuelta *f* **2** BEND **:** recodo *m,* curva *f*

windbreak [ˈwɪndˌbreɪk] *n* **:** barrera *f* contra el viento, abrigadero *m*

windfall [ˈwɪndˌfɔl] *n* **1 :** fruta *f* caída **2 :** beneficio *m* imprevisto

wind instrument *n* **:** instrumento *m* de viento

windlass [ˈwɪndləs] *n* **:** cabrestante *m*

windmill [ˈwɪndˌmɪl] *n* **:** molino *m* de viento

window [ˈwɪnˌdoː] *n* **1 :** ventana *f* (de un edificio o una computadora), ventanilla *f* (de un vehículo o avión), vitrina *f* (de una tienda) **2 → windowpane**

windowpane [ˈwɪnˌdoːˌpeɪn] *n* **:** vidrio *m*

window–shop [ˈwɪndoˌʃɑp] *vi* **-shopped; -shopping :** mirar las vitrinas

windpipe [ˈwɪndˌpaɪp] *n* **:** tráquea *f*

windshield [ˈwɪndˌʃiːld] *n* **1 :** parabrisas *m* **2 windshield wiper :** limpiaparabrisas *m*

windup [ˈwaɪndˌʌp] *n* **:** conclusión *f*

wind up *vt* END **:** terminar, concluir **—** *vi* **:** terminar, acabar

windward[1] [ˈwɪndwərd] *adj* **:** de barlovento

windward[2] *n* **:** barlovento *m*

windy [ˈwɪndi] *adj* **windier; -est 1 :** ventoso <it's windy : hace viento> **2** VERBOSE **:** verboso, prolijo

wine[1] [ˈwaɪn] *v* **wined; wining** *vi* **:** beber vino **—** *vt* **to wine and dine :** agasajar

wine[2] *n* **:** vino *m*

wing[1] [ˈwɪŋ] *vi* FLY **:** volar

wing[2] *n* **1 :** ala *f* (de un ave, un avión, o un edificio) **2** FACTION **:** ala *f* <the right wing of the party : el ala derecha del partido> **3 wings** *npl* **:** bastidores *mpl* (de un teatro) **4 on the wing :** al vuelo, volando **5 under one's wing :** bajo el cargo de uno

winged [ˈwɪŋd, ˈwɪŋəd] *adj* **:** alado

wink[1] [ˈwɪŋk] *vi* **1 :** guiñar el ojo **2** BLINK **:** pestañear, parpadear **3** FLICKER **:** parpadear, titilar

wink[2] *n* **1 :** guiño *m* (del ojo) **2** NAP **:** siesta *f* <not to sleep a wink : no pegar el ojo>

winner [ˈwɪnər] *n* **:** ganador *m,* -dora *f*

winning [ˈwɪnɪŋ] *adj* **1** VICTORIOUS **:** ganador **2** CHARMING **:** encantador

winnings [ˈwɪnɪŋz] *npl* **:** ganancias *fpl*

winnow [ˈwɪˌnoː] *vt* **:** aventar (el grano, etc.)

winsome [ˈwɪnsəm] *adj* CHARMING **:** encantador

winter[1] [ˈwɪntər] *adj* **:** invernal, de invierno

winter[2] *n* **:** invierno *m*

wintergreen [ˈwɪntərˌgriːn] *n* **:** gaulteria *f*

wintertime [ˈwɪntərˌtaɪm] *n* **:** invierno *m*

wintry [ˈwɪntri] *adj* **wintrier; -est 1** WINTER **:** invernal, de invierno **2** COLD

: frío <she gave us a wintry greeting : nos saludó fríamente>

wipe[1] [ˈwaɪp] *vt* **wiped; wiping 1** : limpiar, pasarle un trapo a <to wipe one's feet : limpiarse los pies> **2 to wipe away** : enjugar (lágrimas), borrar (una memoria) **3 to wipe out** ANNIHILATE : aniquilar, destruir

wipe[2] *n* : pasada *f* (con un trapo, etc.)

wire[1] [ˈwaɪr] *vt* **-wired; wiring 1** : instalar el cableado en (una casa, etc.) **2** BIND : atar con alambre **3** TELEGRAPH : telegrafiar, mandarle un telegrama (a alguien)

wire[2] *n* **1** : alambre *m* <barbed wire : alambre de púas> **2** : cable *m* (eléctrico o telefónico) **3** CABLEGRAM, TELEGRAM : telegrama *m,* cable *m*

wireless [ˈwaɪrləs] *adj* : inalámbrico

wiretapping [ˈwaɪr,tæpɪŋ] *n* : intervención *f* electrónica

wiring [ˈwaɪrɪŋ] *n* : cableado *m*

wiry [ˈwaɪri] *adj* **wirier; -est 1** : hirsuto, tieso (dícese del pelo) **2** : esbelto y musculoso (dícese del cuerpo)

wisdom [ˈwɪzdəm] *n* **1** KNOWLEDGE : sabiduría *f* **2** JUDGMENT, SENSE : sensatez *f*

wisdom tooth *n* : muela *f* de juicio

wise[1] [ˈwaɪz] *adj* **wiser; wisest 1** LEARNED : sabio **2** SENSIBLE : sabio, sensato, prudente **3** KNOWLEDGEABLE : entendido, enterado <they're wise to his tricks : conocen muy bien sus mañas>

wise[2] *n* : manera *f,* modo *m* <in no wise : de ninguna manera>

wisecrack [ˈwaɪz,kræk] *n* : broma *f,* chiste *m*

wisely [ˈwaɪzli] *adv* : sabiamente, sensatamente

wish[1] [ˈwɪʃ] *vt* **1** WANT : desear, querer **2 to wish (something) for** : desear <they wished me well : me desearon lo mejor> — *vi* **1** : pedir (como deseo) **2** : querer <as you wish : como quieras>

wish[2] *n* **1** : deseo *m* <to grant a wish : conceder un deseo> **2 wishes** *npl* : saludos *mpl*, recuerdos *mpl* <to send best wishes : mandar muchos recuerdos>

wishbone [ˈwɪʃ,boːn] *n* : espoleta *f*

wishful [ˈwɪʃfəl] *adj* **1** HOPEFUL : deseoso, lleno de esperanza **2 wishful thinking** : ilusiones *fpl*

wishy-washy [ˈwɪʃi,wɔʃi, -,wɑʃi] *adj* : insípido, soso

wisp [ˈwɪsp] *n* **1** BUNCH : manojo *m* (de paja) **2** STRAND : mechón *m* (de pelo) **3** : voluta *f* (de humo)

wispy [ˈwɪspi] *adj* **wispier; -est** : tenue, ralo (dícese del pelo)

wisteria [wɪsˈtɪriə] *n* : glicinia *f*

wistful [ˈwɪstfəl] *adj* : añorante, anhelante, melancólico — **wistfully** *adv*

wistfulness [ˈwɪstfəlnəs] *n* : añoranza *f,* melancolía *f*

wit [ˈwɪt] *n* **1** INTELLIGENCE : inteligencia *f* **2** CLEVERNESS : ingenio *m,* gracia *f,* agudeza *f* **3** HUMOR : humorismo *m* **4** JOKER : chistoso *m,* -sa *f* **5 wits** *npl* : razón *f,* buen juicio *m* <scared out of one's wits : muerto de miedo> <to be at one's wits' end : estar desesperado>

witch [ˈwɪtʃ] *n* : bruja *f*

witchcraft [ˈwɪtʃ,kræft] *n* : brujería *f,* hechicería *f*

witch doctor *n* : hechicero *m,* -ra *f*

witchery [ˈwɪtʃəri] *n, pl* **-eries 1** → **witchcraft 2** CHARM : encanto *m*

witch–hunt [ˈwɪtʃ,hʌnt] *n* : caza *f* de brujas

with [ˈwɪð, ˈwɪθ] *prep* **1** : con <I'm going with you : voy contigo> <coffee with milk : café con leche> **2** AGAINST : con <to argue with someone : discutir con alguien> **3** (*used in descriptions*) : con, de <the girl with red hair : la muchacha de pelo rojo> **4** (*indicating manner, means, or cause*) : con <to cut with a knife : cortar con un cuchillo> <fix it with tape : arréglalo con cinta> <with luck : con suerte> **5** DESPITE : a pesar de, aún con <with all his work, the business failed : a pesar de su trabajo, el negocio fracasó> **6** REGARDING : con respecto a, con <the trouble with your plan : el problema con su plan> **7** ACCORDING TO : según <it varies with the season : varía según la estación> **8** (*indicating support or understanding*) : con <I'm with you all the way : estoy contigo hasta el fin>

withdraw [wɪðˈdrɔ, wɪθ-] *v* **-drew** [-ˈdruː]; **-drawn** [-ˈdrɔn]; **-drawing** *vt* **1** REMOVE : retirar, apartar, sacar (dinero) **2** RETRACT : retractarse de — *vi* : retirarse, recluirse (de la sociedad)

withdrawal [wɪðˈdrɔəl, wɪθ-] *n* **1** : retirada *f,* retiro *m* (de fondos, etc.), retraimiento *m* (social) **2** RETRACTION : retractación *f* **3 withdrawal symptoms** : síndrome *m* de abstinencia

withdrawn [wɪðˈdrɔn, wɪθ-] *adj* : retraído, reservado, introvertido

wither [ˈwɪðər] *vt* : marchitar, agostar — *vi* **1** WILT : marchitarse **2** WEAKEN : decaer, debilitarse

withhold [wɪθˈhoːld, wɪð-] *vt* **-held** [-ˈhɛld]; **-holding** : retener (fondos), aplazar (una decisión), negar (permiso, etc.)

within[1] [wɪðˈɪn, wɪθ-] *adv* : dentro

within[2] *prep* **1** : dentro de <within the limits : dentro de los límites> **2** (*in expressions of distance*) : a menos de <within 10 miles of the ocean : a menos de 10 millas del mar> **3** (*in expressions of time*) : dentro de <within an hour : dentro de una hora> <within a month of her birthday : a poco menos de un mes de su cumpleaños>

without[1] [wɪð'aʊt, wɪθ-] *adv* **1** OUTSIDE : fuera **2 to do without** : pasar sin algo

without[2] *prep* **1** OUTSIDE : fuera de **2** : sin <without fear : sin temor> <he left without his briefcase : se fue sin su portafolios>

withstand [wɪθ'stænd, wɪð-] *vt* **-stood** [-'stʊd]; **-standing 1** BEAR : aguantar, soportar **2** RESIST : resistir, resistirse a

witless ['wɪtləs] *adj* : estúpido, tonto

witness[1] ['wɪtnəs] *vt* **1** SEE : presenciar, ver, ser testigo de **2** : atestiguar (una firma, etc.) — *vi* TESTIFY : atestiguar, testimoniar

witness[2] *n* **1** TESTIMONY : testimonio *m* <to bear witness : atestiguar, testimoniar> **2** : testigo *mf* <witness for the prosecution : testigo de cargo>

witticism ['wɪṭə,sɪzəm] *n* : agudeza *f*, ocurrencia *f*

witty ['wɪṭi] *adj* **-tier; -est** : ingenioso, ocurrente, gracioso

wives → **wife**

wizard ['wɪzərd] *n* **1** SORCERER : mago *m*, brujo *m*, hechicero *m* **2** : genio *m* <a math wizard : un genio en matemáticas>

wizened ['wɪzənd, 'wiː-] *adj* : arrugado, marchito

wobble[1] ['wɑbəl] *vi* **-bled; -bling** : bambolearse, tambalearse, temblar (dícese de la voz)

wobble[2] *n* : tambaleo *m*, bamboleo *m*

wobbly ['wɑbəli] *adj* : bamboleante, tambaleante, inestable

woe ['woː] *n* **1** GRIEF, MISFORTUNE : desgracia *f*, infortunio *m*, aflicción *f* **2 woes** *npl* TROUBLES : penas *fpl*, males *mpl*

woeful ['woːfəl] *adj* **1** SORROWFUL : afligido, apenado, triste **2** UNFORTUNATE : desgraciado, infortunado **3** DEPLORABLE : lamentable

woke, woken → **wake**[1]

wolf[1] ['wʊlf] *vt or* **to wolf down** : engullir

wolf[2] *n, pl* **wolves** ['wʊlvz] : lobo *m*, -ba *f*

wolfram ['wʊlfrəm] → **tungsten**

wolverine [,wʊlvə'riːn] *n* : glotón *m* (animal)

woman ['wʊmən] *n, pl* **women** ['wɪmən] : mujer *f*

womanhood ['wʊmən,hʊd] *n* **1** : condición *f* de mujer **2** WOMEN : mujeres *fpl*

womanly ['wʊmənli] *adj* : femenino

womb ['wuːm] *n* : útero *m*, matriz *f*

won → **win**

wonder[1] ['wʌndər] *vi* **1** SPECULATE : preguntarse, pensar <to wonder about : preguntarse por> **2** MARVEL : asombrarse, maravillarse — *vt* : preguntarse <I wonder if they're coming : me pregunto si vendrán>

wonder[2] *n* **1** MARVEL : maravilla *f*, milagro *m* <to work wonders : hacer maravillas> **2** AMAZEMENT : asombro *m*

wonderful ['wʌndərfəl] *adj* : maravilloso, estupendo

wonderfully ['wʌndərfəli] *adv* : maravillosamente, de maravilla

wonderland ['wʌndər,lænd, -lənd] *n* : país *m* de las maravillas

wonderment ['wʌndərmənt] *n* : asombro *m*

wondrous ['wʌndrəs] → **wonderful**

wont[1] ['wɔnt, 'woːnt, 'wɑnt] *adj* : acostumbrado, habituado

wont[2] *n* : hábito *m*, costumbre *f*

won't ['woːnt] (*contraction of* **will not**) → **will**[1]

woo ['wuː] *vt* **1** COURT : cortejar **2** : buscar el apoyo de (clientes, votantes, etc.)

wood[1] ['wʊd] *adj* : de madera

wood[2] *n* **1** *or* **woods** *npl* FOREST : bosque *m* **2** : madera *f* (materia) **3** FIREWOOD : leña *f*

woodchuck ['wʊd,tʃʌk] *n* : marmota *f* de América

woodcut ['wʊd,kʌt] *n* **1** : plancha *f* de madera (para imprimir imágenes) **2** : grabado *m* en madera

woodcutter ['wʊd,kʌṭər] *n* : leñador *m*, -dora *f*

wooded ['wʊdəd] *adj* : arbolado, boscoso

wooden ['wʊdən] *adj* **1** : de madera <a wooden cross : una cruz de madera> **2** STIFF : rígido, inexpresivo (dícese del estilo, de la cara, etc.)

woodland ['wʊdlənd, -,lænd] *n* : bosque *m*

woodpecker ['wʊd,pɛkər] *n* : pájaro *m* carpintero

woodshed ['wʊd,ʃɛd] *n* : leñera *f*

woodsman ['wʊdzmən] → **woodcutter**

woodwind ['wʊd,wɪnd] *n* : instrumento *m* de viento de madera

woodworking ['wʊd,wərkɪŋ] *n* : carpintería *f*

woody ['wʊdi] *adj* **woodier; -est 1** → **wooded 2** : leñoso <woody plants : plantas leñosas> **3** : leñoso (dícese de la textura), a madera (dícese del aroma, etc.)

woof ['wʊf] → **weft**

wool ['wʊl] *n* : lana *f*

woolen[1] *or* **woollen** ['wʊlən] *adj* : de lana

woolen[2] *or* **woollen** *n* **1** : lana *f* (tela) **2 woolens** *npl* : prendas *fpl* de lana

woolly ['wʊli] *adj* **-lier; -est 1** : lanudo **2** CONFUSED : confuso, vago

woozy ['wuːzi] *adj* **-zier; -est** : mareado

word[1] ['wərd] *vt* : expresar, formular, redactar

word[2] *n* **1** : palabra *f*, vocablo *m*, voz *f* <word for word : palabra por palabra> <in one's own words : en sus

propias palabras> <words fail me : me quedo sin habla> **2** REMARK : palabra *f* <by word of mouth : de palabra> <to have a word with : hablar (dos palabras) con> **3** COMMAND : orden *f* <to give the word : dar la orden> <just say the word : no tienes que decirlo> **4** MESSAGE, NEWS : noticias *fpl* <is there any word from her? : ¿hay noticias de ella?> <to send word : mandar un recado> **5** PROMISE : palabra *f* <to keep one's word : cumplir uno su palabra> **6 words** *npl* QUARREL : palabra *f,* riña *f* <to have words with : tener unas palabras con, reñir con> **7 words** *npl* TEXT : letra *f* (de una canción, etc.)

wordiness [ˈwərdinəs] *n* : verbosidad *f*

wording [ˈwərdɪŋ] *n* : redacción *f,* lenguaje *m* (de un documento)

word processing *n* : procesamiento *m* de textos

word processor *n* : procesador *m* de textos

wordy [ˈwərdi] *adj* **wordier; -est** : verboso, prolijo

wore → **wear**[1]

work[1] [ˈwərk] *v* **worked** [ˈwərkt] *or* **wrought** [ˈrɔt]; **working** *vt* **1** OPERATE : trabajar, operar <to work a machine : operar una máquina> **2** : lograr, conseguir (algo) con esfuerzo <to work one's way up : lograr subir por sus propios esfuerzos> **3** EFFECT : efectuar, llevar a cabo, obrar (milagros) **4** MAKE, SHAPE : elaborar, fabricar, formar <a beautifully wrought vase : un florero bellamente elaborado> **5 to work up** : estimular, excitar <don't get worked up : no te agites> — *vi* **1** LABOR : trabajar <to work full-time : trabajar a tiempo completo> **2** FUNCTION : funcionar, servir

work[2] *adj* : laboral

work[3] *n* **1** LABOR : trabajo *m,* labor *f* **2** EMPLOYMENT : trabajo *m,* empleo *m* **3** TASK : tarea *f,* faena *f* **4** DEED : obra *f,* labor *f* <works of charity : obras de caridad> **5** : obra *f* (de arte o literatura) **6** → **workmanship 7 works** *npl* FACTORY : fábrica *f* **8 works** *npl* MECHANISM : mecanismo *m*

workable [ˈwərkəbəl] *adj* **1** : explotable (dícese de una mina, etc.) **2** FEASIBLE : factible, realizable

workaday [ˈwərkəˌdeɪ] *adj* : ordinario, banal

workbench [ˈwərkˌbɛntʃ] *n* : mesa *f* de trabajo

workday [ˈwərkˌdeɪ] *n* **1** : jornada *f* laboral **2** WEEKDAY : día *m* hábil, día *m* laborable

worker [ˈwərkər] *n* : trabajador *m,* -dora *f;* obrero *m,* -ra *f*

working [ˈwərkɪŋ] *adj* **1** : que trabaja <working mothers : madres que trabajan> <the working class : la clase obrera> **2** : de trabajo <working hours : horas de trabajo> **3** FUNCTIONING : que funciona, operativo **4** SUFFICIENT : suficiente <a working majority : una mayoría suficiente> <working knowledge : conocimientos básicos>

workingman [ˈwərkɪŋˌmæn] *n, pl* **-men** [-mən, -ˌmɛn] : obrero *m*

workman [ˈwərkmən] *n, pl* **-men** [-mən, -ˌmɛn] **1** → **workingman 2** ARTISAN : artesano *m*

workmanlike [ˈwərkmənˌlaɪk] *adj* : bien hecho, competente

workmanship [ˈwərkmənˌʃɪp] *n* **1** WORK : ejecución *f,* trabajo *m* **2** CRAFTSMANSHIP : artesanía *f,* destreza *f*

workout [ˈwərkˌaʊt] *n* : ejercicios *mpl* físicos, entrenamiento *m*

work out *vt* **1** DEVELOP, PLAN : idear, planear, desarrollar **2** RESOLVE : solucionar, resolver <to work out the answer : calcular la solución> — *vi* **1** TURN OUT : resultar **2** SUCCEED : lograr, dar resultado, salir bien **3** EXERCISE : hacer ejercicio

workroom [ˈwərkˌruːm, -ˌrʊm] *n* : taller *m*

workshop [ˈwərkˌʃɑp] *n* : taller *m* <ceramics workshop : taller de cerámica>

world[1] [ˈwərld] *adj* : mundial, del mundo <world championship : campeonato mundial>

world[2] *n* : mundo *m* <around the world : alrededor del mundo> <a world of possibilities : un mundo de posibilidades> <to think the world of someone : tener a alguien en alta estima> <to be worlds apart : no tener nada que ver (uno con otro)>

worldly [ˈwərldli] *adj* **1** : mundano <wordly goods : bienes materiales> **2** SOPHISTICATED : sofisticado, de mundo

worldwide[1] [ˈwərldˈwaɪd] *adv* : mundialmente, en todo el mundo

worldwide[2] *adj* : global, mundial

worm[1] [ˈwərm] *vi* **1** CRAWL : arrastrarse, deslizarse (como gusano) <to worm one's way into someone's confidence : ganarse la confianza de alguien> **2 to worm something out of someone** : sonsacarle algo a alguien — *vt* : desparasitar (un animal)

worm[2] *n* **1** : gusano *m,* lombriz *f* **2 worms** *npl* : lombrices *fpl* (parásitos)

wormy [ˈwərmi] *adj* **wormier; -est** : infestado de gusanos

worn → **wear**[1]

worn–out [ˈwornˈaʊt] *adj* **1** USED : gastado, desgastado **2** TIRED : agotado

worried [ˈwərid] *adj* : inquieto, preocupado

worrier [ˈwəriər] *n* : persona *f* que se preocupa mucho

worrisome [ˈwərisəm] *adj* **1** DISTURBING : preocupante, inquietante **2** : que se preocupa mucho (dícese de una persona)

worry[1] [ˈwəri] *v* **-ried; -rying** *vt* : preocupar, inquietar — *vi* : preocuparse, inquietarse, angustiarse

worry[2] *n, pl* **-ries** : preocupación *f,* inquietud *f,* angustia *f*

worse[1] [ˈwərs] *adv* (*comparative of* **bad** *or of* **ill**) : peor <to feel worse : sentirse peor>

worse[2] *adj* (*comparative of* **bad** *or of* **ill**) : peor <from bad to worse : de mal en peor> <to get worse : empeorar>

worse[3] *n* : estado *m* peor <to take a turn for the worse : ponerse peor> <so much the worse : tanto peor>

worsen [ˈwərsən] *vt* : empeorar — *vi* : empeorar(se)

worship[1] [ˈwərʃəp] *v* **-shiped** *or* **-shipped; -shiping** *or* **-shipping** *vt* : adorar, venerar <to worship God : adorar a Dios> — *vi* : practicar una religión

worship[2] *n* : adoración *f,* culto *m*

worshiper *or* **worshipper** [ˈwərʃəpər] *n* : devoto *m,* -ta *f;* adorador *m,* -dora *f*

worst[1] [ˈwərst] *vt* DEFEAT : derrotar

worst[2] *adv* (*superlative of* **ill** *or of* **bad** *or* **badly**) : peor <the worst dressed of all : el peor vestido de todos>

worst[3] *adj* (*superlative of* **bad** *or of* **ill**) : peor <the worst movie : la peor película>

worst[4] *n* **the worst** : lo peor, el (la) peor <the worst is over : ya ha pasado lo peor>

worsted [ˈwʊstəd, ˈwərstəd] *n* : estambre *m*

worth[1] [ˈwərθ] *n* **1** : valor *m* (monetario) <ten dollars' worth of gas : diez dólares de gasolina> **2** MERIT : valor *m,* mérito *m,* valía *f* <an employee of great worth : un empleado de gran valía>

worth[2] *prep* **to be worth** : valer <her holdings are worth a fortune : sus propiedades valen una fortuna> <it's not worth it : no vale la pena>

worthiness [ˈwərðinəs] *n* : mérito *m*

worthless [ˈwərθləs] *adj* **1** : sin valor <worthless trinkets : chucherías sin valor> **2** USELESS : inútil

worthwhile [wərθˈhwaɪl] *adj* : que vale la pena

worthy [ˈwərði] *adj* **-thier; -est 1** : digno <worthy of promotion : digno de un ascenso> **2** COMMENDABLE : meritorio, encomiable

would [ˈwʊd] *past of* **will 1** (*expressing preference*) <I would rather go alone than with her : preferiría ir sola que con ella> **2** (*expressing intent*) <those who would ban certain books : aquellos que prohibirían ciertos libros> **3** (*expressing habitual action*) <he would often take his kids to the park : solía llevar a sus hijos al parque> **4** (*expressing contingency*) <I would go if I had the money : iría yo si tuviera el dinero> **5** (*expressing probability*) <she would have won if she hadn't tripped : habría ganado si no hubiera tropezado> **6** (*expressing a request*) <would you kindly help me with this? : ¿tendría la bondad de ayudarme con esto?>

would–be [ˈwʊdˈbiː] *adj* : potencial <a would-be celebrity : un aspirante a celebridad>

wouldn't [ˈwʊdˈənt] (*contraction of* **would not**) → **would**

wound[1] [ˈwuːnd] *vt* : herir

wound[2] *n* : herida *f*

wound[3] [ˈwaʊnd] → **wind**[2]

wove, woven → **weave**[1]

wrangle[1] [ˈræŋgəl] *vi* **-gled; -gling** : discutir, reñir <to wrangle over : discutir por>

wrangle[2] *n* : riña *f,* disputa *f*

wrap[1] [ˈræp] *v* **wrapped; wrapping** *vt* **1** COVER : envolver, cubrir <to wrap a package : envolver un paquete> <wrapped in mystery : envuelto en misterio> **2** ENCIRCLE : rodear, ceñir <to wrap one's arms around someone : estrechar a alguien> **3 to wrap up** FINISH : darle fin a (algo) — *vi* **1** COIL : envolverse, enroscarse **2 to wrap up** DRESS : abrigarse <wrap up warmly : abrígate bien>

wrap[2] *n* **1** WRAPPER : envoltura *f* **2** : prenda *f* que envuelve (como un chal, una bata, etc.)

wrapper [ˈræpər] *n* : envoltura *f,* envoltorio *m*

wrapping [ˈræpɪŋ] *n* : envoltura *f,* envoltorio *m*

wrath [ˈræθ] *n* : ira *f,* cólera *f*

wrathful [ˈræθfəl] *adj* : iracundo

wreak [ˈriːk] *vt* : infligir, causar <to wreak havoc : crear caos, causar estragos>

wreath [ˈriːθ] *n, pl* **wreaths** [ˈriːðz, ˈriːθs] : corona *f* (de flores, etc.)

wreathe [ˈriːð] *vt* **wreathed; wreathing 1** ADORN : coronar (de flores, etc.) **2** ENVELOP : envolver <wreathed in mist : envuelto en niebla>

wreck[1] [ˈrɛk] *vt* : destruir, arruinar, estrellar (un automóvil), naufragar (un barco)

wreck[2] *n* **1** WRECKAGE : restos *mpl* (de un buque naufragado, un avión siniestrado, etc.) **2** RUIN : ruina *f,* desastre *m* <this place is a wreck! : ¡este lugar está hecho un desastre!> <to be a nervous wreck : tener los nervios destrozados>

wreckage [ˈrɛkɪdʒ] *n* : restos *mpl* (de un buque naufragado, un avión siniestrado, etc.), ruinas *fpl* (de un edificio)

wrecker [ˈrɛkər] *n* **1** TOW TRUCK : grúa *f* **2** : desguazador *m* (de autos, barcos, etc.), demoledor *m* (de edificios)

wren [ˈrɛn] *n* : chochín *m*

wrench[1] [ˈrɛntʃ] *vt* **1** PULL : arrancar (de un tirón) **2** SPRAIN, TWIST : torcerse (un tobillo, un músculo, etc.)

wrench[2] *n* **1** TUG : tirón *m,* jalón *m* **2** SPRAIN : torcedura *f* **3** *or* **monkey wrench** : llave *f* inglesa

wrest [ˈrɛst] *vt* : arrancar
wrestle¹ [ˈrɛsəl] *v* **-tled; -tling** *vi* **1** : luchar, practicar la lucha (en deportes) **2** STRUGGLE : luchar <to wrestle with a dilemma : lidiar con un dilema> — *vt* : luchar contra
wrestle² *n* STRUGGLE : lucha *f*
wrestler [ˈrɛsələr] *n* : luchador *m*, -dora *f*
wrestling [ˈrɛsəlɪŋ] *n* : lucha *f*
wretch [ˈrɛtʃ] *n* : infeliz *mf;* desgraciado *m*, -da *f*
wretched [ˈrɛtʃəd] *adj* **1** MISERABLE, UNHAPPY : desdichado, afligido <I feel wretched : me siento muy mal> **2** UNFORTUNATE : miserable, desgraciado, lastimoso <wretched weather : tiempo espantoso> **3** INFERIOR : inferior, malo
wretchedly [ˈrɛtʃədli] *adv* : miserablemente, lamentablemente
wriggle [ˈrɪgəl] *vi* **-gled; -gling** : retorcerse, menearse
wring [ˈrɪŋ] *vt* **wrung** [ˈrʌŋ]; **wringing 1** *or* **to wring out** : escurrir, exprimir (el lavado) **2** EXTRACT : arrancar, sacar (por la fuerza) **3** TWIST : torcer, retorcer **4 to wring someone's heart** : partirle el corazón a alguien
wringer [ˈrɪŋər] *n* : escurridor *m*
wrinkle¹ [ˈrɪŋkəl] *v* **-kled; -kling** *vt* : arrugar — *vi* : arrugarse
wrinkle² *n* : arruga *f*
wrinkly [ˈrɪŋkəli] *adj* **wrinklier; -est** : arrugado
wrist [ˈrɪst] *n* **1** : muñeca *f* (en anatomía) **2** *or* **wristband** [ˈrɪstˌbænd] CUFF : puño *m*
writ [ˈrɪt] *n* : orden *f* (judicial)
write [ˈraɪt] *v* **wrote** [ˈroːt]; **written** [ˈrɪtən]; **writing** : escribir
write down *vt* : apuntar, anotar
write off *vt* CANCEL : cancelar
writer [ˈraɪṭər] *n* : escritor *m*, -tora *f*
writhe [ˈraɪð] *vi* **writhed; writhing** : retorcerse
writing [ˈraɪṭɪŋ] *n* : escritura *f*
wrong¹ [ˈrɔŋ] *vt* **wronged; wronging** : ofender, ser injusto con
wrong² *adv* : mal, incorrectamente
wrong³ *adj* **wronger** [ˈrɔŋər]; **wrongest** [ˈrɔŋəst] **1** EVIL, SINFUL : malo, injusto, inmoral **2** IMPROPER, UNSUITABLE : inadecuado, inapropiado, malo **3** INCORRECT : incorrecto, erróneo, malo <a wrong answer : una mala respuesta> **4 to be wrong** : equivocarse, estar equivocado
wrong⁴ *n* **1** INJUSTICE : injusticia *f*, mal *m* **2** OFFENSE : ofensa *f*, agravio *m* (en derecho) **3 to be in the wrong** : haber hecho mal, estar equivocado
wrongdoer [ˈrɔŋˌduːər] *n* : malhechor *m*, -chora *f*
wrongdoing [ˈrɔŋˌduːɪŋ] *n* : fechoría *f*, maldad *f*
wrongful [ˈrɔŋfəl] *adj* **1** UNJUST : injusto **2** UNLAWFUL : ilegal
wrongly [ˈrɔŋli] *adv* **1** : injustamente **2** INCORRECTLY : erróneamente, incorrectamente
wrote → **write**
wrought [ˈrɔt] *adj* **1** SHAPED : formado, forjado <wrought iron : hierro forjado> **2** *or* **wrought up** : agitado, excitado
wrung → **wring**
wry [ˈraɪ] *adj* **wrier** [ˈraɪər]; **wriest** [ˈraɪəst] **1** TWISTED : torcido <a wry neck : un cuello torcido> **2** : irónico, sardónico (dícese del humor)

X

x¹ *n, pl* **x's** *or* **xs** [ˈɛksəz] **1** : vigésima cuarta letra del alfabeto inglés **2** : incógnita *f* (en matemáticas)
x² [ˈɛks] *vt* **x–ed** [ˈɛkst]; **x–ing** *or* **x'ing** [ˈɛksiŋ] DELETE : tachar
xenon [ˈziːˌnɑn, ˈzɛ-] *n* : xenón *m*
xenophobia [ˌzɛnəˈfoːbiə, ˌziː-] *n* : xenofobia *f*
Xmas [ˈkrɪsməs] *n* : Navidad *f*
x–ray [ˈɛksˌreɪ] *vt* : radiografiar
X ray [ˈɛksˌreɪ] *n* **1** : rayo *m* X **2** *or* **X–ray photograph** : radiografía *f*
xylophone [ˈzaɪləˌfoːn] *n* : xilófono *m*

Y

y [ˈwaɪ] *n, pl* **y's** *or* **ys** [ˈwaɪz] : vigésima quinta letra del alfabeto inglés
yacht¹ [ˈjɑt] *vi* : navegar (a vela), ir en yate <to go yachting : irse a navegar>
yacht² *n* : yate *m*
yak [ˈjæk] *n* : yac *m*
yam [ˈjæm] *n* **1** : ñame *m* **2** SWEET POTATO : batata *f*, boniato *m*
yank¹ [ˈjæŋk] *vt* : tirar de, jalar, darle un tirón a
yank² *n* : tirón *m*
Yankee [ˈjæŋki] *n* : yanqui *mf*
yap¹ [ˈjæp] *vi* **yapped; yapping 1** BARK, YELP : ladrar, gañir **2** CHATTER : cotorrear *fam*, parlotear *fam*
yap² *n* : ladrido *m*, gañido *m*

yard [ˈjɑrd] *n* **1 :** yarda *f* (medida) **2** SPAR **:** verga *f* (de un barco) **3** COURTYARD **:** patio *m* **4 :** jardín *m* (de una casa) **5 :** depósito *m* (de mercancías, etc.)

yardage [ˈjɑrdɪdʒ] *n* **:** medida *f* en yardas

yardarm [ˈjɑrd,ɑrm] *n* **:** penol *m*

yardstick [ˈjɑrd,stɪk] *n* **1 :** vara *f* **2** CRITERION **:** criterio *m,* norma *f*

yarn [ˈjɑrn] *n* **1 :** hilado *m* **2** TALE **:** historia *f,* cuento *m* <to spin a yarn **:** inventar una historia>

yawl [ˈjɔl] *n* **:** yola *f*

yawn[1] [ˈjɔn] *vi* **1 :** bostezar **2** OPEN **:** abrirse

yawn[2] *n* **:** bostezo *m*

ye [ˈjiː] *pron* **:** vosotros, vosotras

yea[1] [ˈjeɪ] *adv* YES **:** sí

yea[2] *n* **:** voto *m* a favor

year [ˈjɪr] *n* **1 :** año *m* <last year **:** el año pasado> <he's ten years old **:** tiene diez años> **2 :** curso *m,* año *m* (escolar) **3 years** *npl* AGES **:** siglos *mpl,* años *mpl* <I haven't seen them in years **:** hace siglos que no los veo>

yearbook [ˈjɪr,bʊk] *n* **:** anuario *m*

yearling [ˈjɪrlɪŋ, ˈjərlən] *n* **:** animal *m* menor de dos año

yearly[1] [ˈjɪrli] *adv* **:** cada año, anualmente

yearly[2] *adj* **:** anual

yearn [ˈjərn] *vi* **:** anhelar, ansiar

yearning [ˈjərnɪŋ] *n* **:** anhelo *m*

yeast [ˈjiːst] *n* **:** levadura *f*

yell[1] [ˈjɛl] *vi* **:** gritar, chillar — *vt* **:** gritar

yell[2] *n* **:** grito *m,* alarido *m* <to let out a yell **:** dar un grito>

yellow[1] [ˈjɛlo] *vi* **:** ponerse amarillo, volverse amarillo

yellow[2] *adj* **1 :** amarillo **2** COWARDLY **:** cobarde

yellow[3] *n* **:** amarillo *m*

yellow fever *n* **:** fiebre *f* amarilla

yellowish [ˈjɛloɪʃ] *adj* **:** amarillento

yellow jacket *n* **:** avispa *f* (con rayas amarillas)

yelp[1] [ˈjɛlp] *vi* **:** dar un gañido (dícese de un animal), dar un grito (dícese de una persona)

yelp[2] *n* **:** gañido *m* (de un animal), grito *m* (de una persona)

yen [ˈjɛn] *n* **1** DESIRE **:** deseo *m,* ganas *fpl* **2 :** yen *m* (moneda japonesa)

yeoman [ˈjoːmən] *n, pl* **-men** [-mən, -mɛn] **:** suboficial *mf* de marina

yes[1] [ˈjɛs] *adv* **:** sí <to say yes **:** decir que sí>

yes[2] *n* **:** sí *m*

yesterday[1] [ˈjɛstər,deɪ, -di] *adv* **:** ayer

yesterday[2] *n* **1 :** ayer *m* **2 the day before yesterday :** anteayer

yet[1] [ˈjɛt] *adv* **1** BESIDES, EVEN **:** aún <yet more problems **:** más problemas aún> <yet again **:** otra vez> **2** SO FAR **:** aún, todavía <not yet **:** todavía no> <as yet **:** hasta ahora, todavía> **3 :** ya <has he come yet? **:** ¿ya ha venido?> **4** EVENTUALLY **:** todavía, algún día **5** NEVERTHELESS **:** sin embargo

yet[2] *conj* **:** pero

yew [ˈjuː] *n* **:** tejo *m*

yield[1] [ˈjiːld] *vt* **1** SURRENDER **:** ceder <to yield the right of way **:** ceder el paso> **2** PRODUCE **:** producir, dar, rendir (en finanzas) — *vi* **1** GIVE **:** ceder <to yield under pressure **:** ceder por la presión> **2** GIVE IN, SURRENDER **:** ceder, rendirse, entregarse

yield[2] *n* **:** rendimiento *m,* rédito *m* (en finanzas)

yodel[1] [ˈjoːdəl] *vi* **-deled** *or* **-delled; -deling** *or* **-delling :** cantar al estilo tirolés

yodel[2] *n* **:** canción *f* al estilo tirolés

yoga [ˈjoːgə] *n* **:** yoga *m*

yogurt [ˈjoːgərt] *n* **:** yogur *m,* yogurt *m*

yoke[1] [ˈjoːk] *vt* **yoked; yoking :** uncir (animales)

yoke[2] *n* **1 :** yugo *m* (para uncir animales) <the yoke of oppression **:** el yugo de la opresión> **2** TEAM **:** yunta *f* (de bueyes) **3 :** canesú *m* (de ropa)

yokel [ˈjoːkəl] *n* **:** palurdo *m,* -da *f*

yolk [ˈjoːk] *n* **:** yema *f* (de un huevo)

Yom Kippur [,joːmkɪˈpʊr, ,jɑm-, -ˈkɪpər] *n* **:** el Día *m* del Perdón, Yom Kippur

yon [ˈjɑn] → **yonder**

yonder[1] [ˈjɑndər] *adv* **:** allá <over yonder **:** allá lejos>

yonder[2] *adj* **:** aquel <yonder hill **:** aquella colina>

yore [ˈjoːr] *n* **in days of yore :** antaño

you [ˈjuː] *pron* **1** (*used as subject — familiar*) **:** tú; vos (*in some Latin American countries*); ustedes *pl;* vosotros, vosotras *pl Spain* **2** (*used as subject — formal*) **:** usted, ustedes *pl* **3** (*used as indirect object — familiar*) **:** te, les *pl* (se *before lo, la, los, las*), os *pl Spain* <he told it to you **:** te lo contó> <I gave them to (all of, both of) you **:** se los di> **4** (*used as indirect object — formal*) **:** lo (*Spain sometimes* le), la; los (*Spain sometimes* les), las *pl* **5** (*used after a preposition — familiar*) **:** ti; vos (*in some Latin American countries*); ustedes *pl;* vosotros, vosotras *pl Spain* **6** (*used after a preposition — formal*) **:** usted, ustedes *pl* **7** (*used as an impersonal subject*) <you never know **:** nunca se sabe> <you have to be aware **:** hay que ser consciente> <you mustn't do that **:** eso no se hace> **8 with you** (*familiar*) **:** contigo; con ustedes *pl;* con vosotros, con vosotras *pl Spain* **9 with you** (*formal*) **:** con usted, con ustedes *pl*

you'd [ˈjuːd, ˈjʊd] (*contraction of* **you had** *or* **you would**) → **have, would**

you'll [ˈjuːl, ˈjʊl] (*contraction of* **you shall** *or* **you will**) → **shall, will**

young[1] [ˈjʌŋ] *adj* **younger** [ˈjʌŋgər]; **youngest** [-gəst] **1 :** joven, pequeño, menor <young people **:** los jóvenes>

<my younger brother : mi hermano menor> <she is the youngest : es la más pequeña> **2** FRESH, NEW : tierno (dícese de las verduras), joven (dícese del vino) **3** YOUTHFUL : joven, juvenil
young[2] *npl* : jóvenes *mfpl* (de los humanos), crías *fpl* (de los animales)
youngster [ˈjʌŋkstər] *n* **1** YOUTH : joven *mf* **2** CHILD : chico *m*, -ca *f;* niño *m*, -ña *f*
your [ˈjʊr, ˈjoːr, jər] *adj* **1** (*familiar singular*) : tu <your cat : tu gato> <your books : tus libros> <wash your hands : lávate las manos> **2** (*familiar plural*) su, vuestro *Spain* <your car : su coche, el coche de ustedes> **3** (*formal*) : su <your houses : sus casas> **4** (*impersonal*) : el, la, los, las <on your left : a la izquierda>
you're [ˈjʊr, ˈjoːr, ˈjər, ˈjuːər] (*contraction of* **you are**) → **be**
yours [ˈjʊrz, ˈjoːrz] *pron* **1** (*belonging to one person — familiar*) : (el) tuyo, (la) tuya, (los) tuyos, (las) tuyas <those are mine; yours are there : ésas son mías; las tuyas están allí> <is this one yours? : ¿éste es tuyo?> **2** (*belonging to more than one person — familiar*) : (el) suyo, (la) suya, (los) suyos, (las) suyas; (el) vuestro, (la) vuestra, (los) vuestros, (las) vuestras *Spain* <our house and yours : nuestra casa y la suya> **3** (*formal*) : (el) suyo, (la) suya, (los) suyos, (las) suyas
yourself [jərˈsɛlf] *pron, pl* **yourselves** [-ˈsɛlvz] **1** (*used reflexively — familiar*) : te, se *pl,* os *pl Spain* <wash yourself : lávate> <you dressed yourselves : se vistieron, os vestisteis> **2** (*used reflexively — formal*) : se <did you hurt yourself? : ¿se hizo daño?> <you've gotten yourselves dirty : se ensuciaron> **3** (*used for emphasis*) : tú mismo, tú misma; usted mismo, usted misma; ustedes mismos, ustedes mismas *pl;* vosotros mismos, vosotras mismas *pl Spain* <you did it yourselves? : ¿lo hicieron ustedes mismos?, ¿lo hicieron por sí solos?>
youth [ˈjuːθ] *n, pl* **youths** [ˈjuːðz, ˈjuːθs] **1** : juventud *f* <in her youth : en su juventud> **2** BOY : joven *m* **3** : jóvenes *mfpl,* juventud *f* <the youth of our city : los jóvenes de nuestra ciudad>
youthful [ˈjuːθfəl] *adj* **1** : de juventud **2** YOUNG : joven **3** JUVENILE : juvenil
youthfulness [ˈjuːθfəlnəs] *n* : juventud *f*
you've [ˈjuːv] (*contraction of* **you have**) → **have**
yowl[1] [ˈjæʊl] *vi* : aullar
yowl[2] *n* : aullido *m*
yo–yo [ˈjoːˌjoː] *n, pl* **-yos** : yoyo *m,* yoyó *m*
yucca [ˈjʌkə] *n* : yuca *f*
Yugoslavian [ˌjuːgoˈslɑviən] *n* : yugoslavo *m*, -va *f* — **Yugoslavian** *adj*
yule [ˈjuːl] *n* CHRISTMAS : Navidad *f*
yuletide [ˈjuːlˌtaɪd] *n* : Navidades *fpl*

Z

z [ˈziː] *n, pl* **z's** *or* **zs** : vigésima sexta letra del alfabeto inglés
Zambian [ˈzæmbiən] *n* : zambiano *m*, -na *f* — **Zambian** *adj*
zany[1] [ˈzeɪni] *adj* **-nier; -est** : alocado, disparatado
zany[2] *n, pl* **-nies** : bufón *m*, -fona *f*
zeal [ˈziːl] *n* : fervor *m,* celo *m,* entusiasmo *m*
zealot [ˈzɛlət] *n* : fanático *m*, -ca *f*
zealous [ˈzɛləs] *adj* : celoso — **zealously** *adv*
zebra [ˈziːbrə] *n* : cebra *f*
zenith [ˈziːnəθ] *n* **1** : cenit *m* (en astronomía) **2** PEAK : apogeo *m,* cenit *m* <at the zenith of his career : en el apogeo de su carrera>
zephyr [ˈzɛfər] *n* : céfiro *m*
zeppelin [ˈzɛplən, -pəlɪn] *n* : zepelín *m*
zero[1] [ˈziːro, ˈzɪro] *vi* **to zero in on** : apuntar hacia, centrarse en (un problema, etc.)
zero[2] *adj* : cero, nulo <zero degrees : cero grados> <zero opportunities : oportunidades nulas>
zero[3] *n, pl* **-ros** : cero *m* <below zero : bajo cero>
zest [ˈzɛst] *n* **1** GUSTO : entusiasmo *m,* brío *m* **2** FLAVOR : sabor *m,* sazón *f*
zestful [ˈzɛstfəl] *adj* : brioso
zigzag[1] [ˈzɪgˌzæg] *vi* **-zagged; -zagging** : zigzaguear
zigzag[2] *adv & adj* : en zigzag
zigzag[3] *n* : zigzag *m*
Zimbabwean [zɪmˈbɑbwiən, -bweɪ-] *n* : zimbabuense *mf* — **Zimbabwean** *adj*
zinc [ˈzɪŋk] *n* : cinc *m,* zinc *m*
zing [ˈzɪŋ] *n* **1** HISS, HUM : zumbido *m,* silbido *m* **2** ENERGY : brío *m*
zinnia [ˈzɪniə, ˈziː-, -njə] *n* : zinnia *f*
Zionism [ˈzaɪəˌnɪzəm] *n* : sionismo *m*
Zionist [ˈzaɪənɪst] *n* : sionista *mf*
zip[1] [ˈzɪp] *v* **zipped; zipping** *vt or* **to zip up** : cerrar el cierre de — *vi* **1** SPEED : pasarse volando <the day zipped by : el día se pasó volando> **2** HISS, HUM : silbar, zumbar
zip[2] *n* **1** ZING : zumbido *m,* silbido *m* **2** ENERGY : brío *m*
zip code *n* : código *m* postal
zipper [ˈzɪpər] *n* : cierre *m,* cremallera *f,* zíper *m CA, Mex*
zippy [ˈzɪpi] *adj* **-pier; -est** : brioso

zircon ['zər,kɑn] *n* : circón *m,* zircón *m*
zirconium [,zər'ko:niəm] *n* : circonio *m*
zither ['zɪðər, -θər] *n* : cítara *f*
zodiac ['zo:di,æk] *n* : zodíaco *m*
zombie ['zɑmbi] *n* : zombi *mf,* zombie *mf*
zone[1] ['zo:n] *vt* **zoned; zoning 1** : dividir en zonas **2** DESIGNATE : declarar <to zone for business : declarar como zona comercial>
zone[2] *n* : zona *f*
zoo ['zu:] *n, pl* **zoos** : zoológico *m,* zoo *m*
zoological [,zo:ə'lɑdʒɪkəl, ,zu:ə-] *adj* : zoológico
zoologist [zo'ɑlədʒɪst, zu:-] *n* : zoólogo *m,* -ga *f*
zoology [zo'ɑlədʒi, zu:-] *n* : zoología *f*
zoom[1] ['zu:m] *vi* **1** : zumbar, ir volando <to zoom past : pasar volando> **2** CLIMB : elevarse <the plane zoomed up : el avión se elevó>
zoom[2] *n* **1** : zumbido *m* <the zoom of an engine : el zumbido de un motor> **2** : subida *f* vertical (de un avión, etc.) **3** *or* **zoom lens** : zoom *m*
zucchini [zʊ'ki:ni] *n, pl* **-ni** *or* **-nis** : calabacín *m,* calabacita *f Mex*
zygote ['zaɪ,go:t] *n* : zigoto *m,* cigoto *m*

Common Spanish Abbreviations
Abreviaturas comunes en español

SPANISH ABBREVIATION AND EXPANSION		ENGLISH EQUIVALENT	
abr.	abril	**Apr.**	April
A.C., a.C.	antes de Cristo	**BC**	before Christ
a. de J.C.	antes de Jesucristo	**BC**	before Christ
admon., admón.	administración	—	administration
a/f	a favor	—	in favor
ago.	agosto	**Aug.**	August
Apdo.	apartado (de correos)	—	P.O. box
aprox.	aproximadamente	**approx.**	approximately
Aptdo.	apartado (de correos)	—	P.O. box
Arq.	arquitecto	**arch.**	architect
A.T.	Antiguo Testamento	**O. T.**	Old Testament
atte.	atentamente	—	sincerely
atto., atta.	atento, atenta	—	kind, courteous
av., avda.	avenida	**ave.**	avenue
a/v.	a vista	—	on receipt
BID	Banco Interamericano de Desarrollo	**IDB**	Interamerican Development Bank
B^{o}	banco	—	bank
BM	Banco Mundial		World Bank
c/, C/	calle	**st.**	street
C	centígrado, Celsius	**C**	centigrade, Celsius
C.	compañía	**Co.**	company
CA	corriente alterna	**AC**	alternating current
cap.	capítulo	**ch., chap.**	chapter
c/c	cuenta corriente	—	current account, checking account
c.c.	centímetros cúbicos	**cu. cm**	cubic centimeters
CC	corriente continua	**DC**	direct current
c/d	con descuento	—	with discount
Cd.	ciudad	—	city
CE	Comunidad Europea	**EC**	European Community
CEE	Comunidad Económica Europea	**EEC**	European Economic Community
cf.	confróntese	**cf.**	compare
cg.	centígramo	**cg**	centigram
CGT	Confederación General de Trabajadores *or* del Trabajo	—	confederation of workers, workers' union
CI	coeficiente intelectual *or* de inteligencia	**IQ**	intelligence quotient
Cía.	compañía	**Co.**	company
cm.	centímetro	**cm**	centimeter

SPANISH ABBREVIATION AND EXPANSION		ENGLISH EQUIVALENT	
Cnel.	coronel	**Col.**	colonel
col.	columna	**col.**	column
Col. *Mex*	Colonia	—	—
Com.	comandante	**Cmdr.**	commander
comp.	compárese	**comp.**	compare
Cor.	coronel	**Col.**	colonel
C.P.	código postal	—	zip code
CSF, c.s.f.	coste, seguro y flete	**c.i.f.**	cost, insurance, and freight
cta.	cuenta	**ac., acct.**	account
cte.	corriente	**cur.**	current
c/u	cada uno, cada una	**ea.**	each
CV	caballo de vapor	**hp**	horsepower
D.	Don	—	—
Da., D.ª	Doña	—	—
d.C.	después de Cristo	**AD**	anno Domini (in the year of our Lord)
dcha.	derecha	—	right
d. de J.C.	después de Jesucristo	**AD**	anno Domini (in the year of our Lord)
dep.	departamento	**dept.**	department
DF, D.F.	Distrito Federal	—	Federal District
dic.	diciembre	**Dec.**	December
dir.	director, directora	**dir.**	director
dir.	dirección	—	address
Dña.	Doña	—	—
do.	domingo	**Sun.**	Sunday
dpto.	departamento	**dept.**	department
Dr.	doctor	**Dr.**	doctor
Dra.	doctora	**Dr.**	doctor
dto.	descuento	—	discount
E, E.	Este, este	**E**	East, east
Ed.	editorial	—	publishing house
Ed., ed.	edición	**ed.**	edition
edif.	edificio	**bldg.**	building
edo.	estado	**st.**	state
EEUU, EE.UU.	Estados Unidos	**US, U.S.**	United States
ej.	por ejemplo	**e.g.**	for example
E.M.	esclerosis multiple	**MS**	multiple sclerosis
ene.	enero	**Jan.**	January
etc.	etcétera	**etc.**	et cetera
ext.	extensión	**ext.**	extension
F	Fahrenheit	**F**	Fahrenheit
f.a.b.	franco a bordo	**f.o.b.**	free on board
FC	ferrocarril	**RR**	railroad
feb.	febrero	**Feb.**	February
FF AA, FF.AA.	Fuerzas Armadas	—	armed forces
FMI	Fondo Monetario Internacional	**IMF**	International Monetary Fund
g.	gramo	**g., gm, gr.**	gram
G.P.	giro postal	**M.O.**	money order
gr.	gramo	**g., gm, gr.**	gram

SPANISH ABBREVIATION AND EXPANSION		ENGLISH EQUIVALENT	
Gral.	general	**Gen.**	general
h.	hora	**hr.**	hour
Hnos.	hermanos	**Bros.**	brothers
I + D, I & D, I y D	investigación y desarrollo	**R & D**	research and development
i.e.	esto es, es decir	**i.e.**	that is
incl.	inclusive	**incl.**	inclusive, inclusively
Ing.	ingeniero, ingeniera	**eng.**	engineer
IPC	indice de precios al consumo	**CPI**	consumer price index
IVA	impuesto al valor agregado	**VAT**	value-added tax
izq.	izquierda	**l.**	left
juev.	jueves	**Thurs.**	Thursday
jul.	julio	**Jul.**	July
jun.	junio	**Jun.**	June
kg.	kilogramo	**kg**	kilogram
km.	kilómetro	**km**	kilometer
km/h	kilómetros por hora	**kph**	kilometers per hour
kv, kV	kilovatio	**kw, kW**	kilowatt
l.	litro	**l, lit.**	liter
Lic.	licenciado, licenciada	—	*usually indicates a college graduate*
Ltda.	limitada	**Ltd.**	limited
lun.	lunes	**Mon.**	Monday
m	masculino	**m**	masculine
m	metro	**m**	meter
m	minuto	**m**	minute
mar.	marzo	**Mar.**	March
mart.	martes	**Tues.**	Tuesday
mg.	miligramo	**mg**	milligram
miérc.	miércoles	**Wednes.**	Wednesday
min	minuto	**min.**	minute
mm.	milímetro	**mm**	millimeter
M-N, m/n	moneda nacional	—	national currency
Mons.	monseñor	**Msgr.**	monsignor
Mtro.	maestro	—	teacher
Mtra.	maestra	—	teacher
N, N.	Norte, norte	**N, no.**	North, north
n/	nuestro	—	our
n.º	número	**no.**	number
N. de (la) R.	nota de (la) redacción	—	editor's note
NE	nordeste	**NE**	northeast
NN.UU.	Naciones Unidas	**UN**	United Nations
NO	noroeste	**NW**	northwest
nov.	noviembre	**Nov.**	November
N.T.	Nuevo Testamento	**N.T.**	New Testament
ntra., ntro.	nuestra, nuestro	—	our
NU	Naciones Unidas	**UN**	United Nations
núm.	número	**num.**	number
O, O.	Oeste, oeste	**W**	West, west
oct.	octubre	**Oct.**	October
OEA, O.E.A.	Organización de Estados Americanos	**OAS**	Organization of American States

SPANISH ABBREVIATION AND EXPANSION		ENGLISH EQUIVALENT	
OMS	Organización Mundial de la Salud	**WHO**	World Health Organization
ONG	organización no gubernamental	**NGO**	non-governmental organization
ONU	Organización de las Naciones Unidas	**UN**	United Nations
OTAN	Organización del Tratado del Atlántico Norte	**NATO**	North Atlantic Treaty Organization
p.	página	**p.**	page
P, P.	padre (*in religion*)	**Fr.**	father
pág.	página	**pg.**	page
pat.	patente	**pat.**	patent
PCL	pantalla de cristal líquido	**LCD**	liquid crystal display
P.D.	postdata	**P.S.**	postscript
p. ej.	por ejemplo	**e.g.**	for example
PNB	Producto Nacional Bruto	**GNP**	gross national product
P°	paseo	**Ave.**	avenue
p.p.	porte pagado	**ppd.**	postpaid
PP, p.p.	por poder, por poderes	**p.p.**	by proxy
prom.	promedio	**av., avg.**	average
ptas., pts.	pesetas	—	—
q.e.p.d.	que en paz descanse	**R.I.P.**	may he/she rest in peace
R, R/	remite	—	sender
RAE	Real Academia Española	—	—
ref., ref.ª	referencia	**ref.**	reference
rep.	república	**rep.**	republic
r.p.m.	revoluciones por minuto	**rpm.**	revolutions per minute
rte.	remite, remitente	—	sender
s.	siglo	**c., cent.**	century
s/	su, sus	—	his, her, your, their
S, S.	Sur, sur	**S, so.**	South, south
S.	san, santo	**St.**	saint
S.A.	sociedad anónima	**Inc.**	incorporated (company)
sáb.	sábado	**Sat.**	Saturday
s/c	su cuenta	—	your account
SE	sudeste, sureste	**SE**	southeast
seg.	segundo, segundos	**sec.**	second, seconds
sep., sept.	septiembre	**Sept.**	September
s.e.u.o.	salvo error u omisión	—	errors and omissions excepted
Sgto.	sargento	**Sgt.**	sergeant
S.L.	sociedad limitada	**Ltd.**	limited (corporation)
S.M.	Su Majestad	**HM**	His Majesty, Her Majesty
s/n	sin número	—	no (street) number
s.n.m.	sobre el nivel de mar	**a.s.l.**	above sea level
SO	sudoeste/suroeste	**SW**	southwest

SPANISH ABBREVIATION AND EXPANSION		ENGLISH EQUIVALENT	
S.R.C.	se ruega contestación	**R.S.V.P.**	please reply
ss.	siguientes	—	the following ones
SS, S.S.	Su Santidad	**H.H.**	His Holiness
Sta.	santa	**St.**	saint
Sto.	santo	**St.**	saint
t, t.	tonelada	**t., tn.**	ton
TAE	tasa anual efectiva	**APR**	annual percentage rate
tb.	también	—	also
tel., Tel.	teléfono	**tel.**	telephone
Tm.	tonelada métrica	**MT**	metric ton
Tn.	tonelada	**t., tn.**	ton
trad.	traducido	**tr., trans., transl.**	translated
UE	Unión Europea	**EU**	European Union
Univ.	universidad	**Univ., U.**	university
UPC	unidad procesadora central	**CPU**	central processing unit
Urb.	urbanización	—	residential area
v	versus	**v., vs.**	versus
v	verso	**v., ver., vs.**	verse
v.	véase	**vid.**	see
Vda.	viuda	—	widow
v.g., v.gr.	verbigracia	**e.g.**	for example
vier., viern.	viernes	**Fri.**	Friday
V.M.	Vuestra Majestad	—	Your Majesty
V^{0}B^0, V.^{0}B.^{0}	visto bueno	—	OK, approved
vol, vol.	volumen	**vol.**	volume
vra., vro.	vuestra, vuestro	—	your

Common English Abbreviations
Abreviaturas comunes en inglés

ENGLISH ABBREVIATION AND EXPANSION		SPANISH EQUIVALENT	
AAA	American Automobile Association	—	—
AD	anno Domini (in the year of our Lord)	**d.C., d. de J.C.**	después de Cristo, después de Jesucristo
AK	Alaska	—	Alaska
AL, Ala.	Alabama	—	Alabama
Alas.	Alaska	—	Alaska
a.m., AM	ante meridiem (before noon)	**a.m.**	ante meridiem (de la mañana)
Am., Amer.	America, American	—	América, americano
amt.	amount	—	cantidad
anon.	anonymous	—	anónimo
ans.	answer	—	respuesta
Apr.	April	**abr.**	abril
AR	Arkansas	—	Arkansas
Ariz.	Arizona	—	Arizona
Ark.	Arkansas	—	Arkansas
asst.	assistant	**ayte.**	ayudante
atty.	attorney	—	abogado, -da
Aug.	August	**ago.**	agosto
ave.	avenue	**av., avda.**	avenida
AZ	Arizona	—	Arizona
BA	Bachelor of Arts	**Lic.**	Licenciado, -da en Filosofía y Letras
BA	Bachelor of Arts (degree)	—	Licenciatura en Filosofía y Letras
BC	before Christ	**a.C., A.C., a. de J.C.**	antes de Cristo, antes de Jesucristo
BCE	before the Christian Era, before the Common Era	—	antes de la era cristiana, antes de la era común
bet.	between	—	entre
bldg.	building	**edif.**	edificio
blvd.	boulevard	**blvar., br.**	bulevar
Br., Brit.	Britain, British	—	Gran Bretaña, británico
Bro(s).	brother(s)	**Hno(s),**	hermano(s)
BS	Bachelor of Science	**Lic.**	Licenciado, -da en Ciencias
BS	Bachelor of Science (degree)	—	Licenciatura en Ciencias
c	carat	—	quilate
c	cent	—	centavo

ENGLISH ABBREVIATION AND EXPANSION		SPANISH EQUIVALENT	
c	centimeter	**cm.**	centímetro
c	century	**s.**	siglo
c	cup	—	taza
C	Celsius, centigrade	**C**	Celsius, centígrado
CA, Cal., Calif.	California	—	California
Can., Canad.	Canada, Canadian	—	Canadá, canadiense
cap.	capital	—	capital
cap.	capital	—	mayúscula
Capt.	captain	—	capitán
cent.	century	**s.**	siglo
CEO	chief executive officer	—	presidente, -ta (de una corporación)
ch., chap.	chapter	**cap.**	capítulo
CIA	Central Intelligence Agency	—	—
cm	centimeter	**cm.**	centímetro
Co.	company	**C., Cía.**	compañía
co.	county	—	condado
CO	Colorado	—	Colorado
c/o	care of	**a/c**	a cargo de
COD	cash on delivery, collect on delivery	—	(pago) contra reembolso
col.	column	**col.**	columna
Col., Colo.	Colorado	—	Colorado
Conn.	Connecticut	—	Connecticut
corp.	corporation	—	corporación
CPR	cardiopulmonary resuscitation	**RCP**	reanimación cardiopulmonar, resucitación cardiopulmonar
ct.	cent	—	centavo
CT	Connecticut	—	Connecticut
D.A.	district attorney	—	fiscal (del distrito)
DC	District of Columbia	—	—
DDS	Doctor of Dental Surgery	—	doctor de cirugía dental
DE	Delaware	—	Delaware
Dec.	December	**dic.**	diciembre
Del.	Delaware	—	Delaware
DJ	disc jockey		disc-jockey
dept.	department	**dep., dpto.**	departamento
DMD	Doctor of Dental Medicine	—	doctor de medicina dental
doz.	dozen	—	docena
Dr.	doctor	**Dr., Dra.**	doctor, doctora
DST	daylight saving time	—	—
DVM	Doctor of Veterinary Medicine	—	doctor de medicina veterinaria
E	East, east	**E, E.**	Este, este
ea.	each	**c/u**	cada uno, cada una
e.g.	for example	**v.g., v.gr.**	verbigracia

ENGLISH ABBREVIATION AND EXPANSION		SPANISH EQUIVALENT	
EMT	emergency medical technician	—	técnico, -ca en urgencias médicas
Eng.	England, English	—	Inglaterra, inglés
esp.	especially	—	especialmente
EST	eastern standard time	—	—
etc.	et cetera	**etc.**	etcétera
f	false	—	falso
f	female	**f**	femenino
F	Fahrenheit	**F**	Fahrenheit
FBI	Federal Bureau of Investigation	—	—
Feb.	February	**feb.**	febrero
fem.	feminine	—	femenino
FL, Fla.	Florida	—	Florida
Fri.	Friday	**vier., viern.**	viernes
ft.	feet, foot	—	pie(s)
g	gram	**g., gr.**	gramo
Ga., GA	Georgia	—	Georgia
gal.	gallon	—	galón
Gen.	general	**Gral.**	general
gm	gram	**g., gr.**	gramo
gov.	governor	—	gobernador, -dora
govt.	government	—	gobierno
gr.	gram	**g., gr.**	gramo
HI	Hawaii	—	Hawai, Hawaii
hr.	hour	**h.**	hora
HS	high school	—	colegio secundario
ht.	height	—	altura
Ia., IA	Iowa	—	Iowa
ID	Idaho	—	Idaho
i.e.	id est (that is)	**i.e.**	id est (esto es, es decir)
IL, Ill	Illinois	—	Illinois
in.	inch	—	pulgada
IN	Indiana	—	Indiana
Inc.	incorporated (company)	**S.A.**	sociedad anónima
Ind.	Indian, Indiana	—	Indiana
Jan.	January	**ene.**	enero
Jul.	July	**jul.**	julio
Jun.	June	**jun.**	junio
Jr., Jun.	Junior	**Jr.**	Júnior
Kan., Kans.	Kansas	—	Kansas
kg	kilogram	**kg.**	kilogramo
km	kilometer	**km.**	kilómetro
KS	Kansas	—	Kansas
Ky., KY	Kentucky	—	Kentucky
l	liter	**l.**	litro
l.	left	**izq.**	izquierda
L	large	**G**	(talla) grande
La, LA	Louisiana	—	Luisiana, Louisiana
lb.	pound	—	libra

ENGLISH ABBREVIATION AND EXPANSION		SPANISH EQUIVALENT	
Ltd.	limited (corporation)	**S.L.**	sociedad limitada
m	male	**m**	masculino
m	meter	**m**	metro
m	mile	—	milla
M	medium	**M**	(talla) mediana
MA	Massachusetts	—	Massachusetts
Maj.	major	—	mayor
Mar.	March	**mar.**	marzo
masc.	masculine	—	masculino
Mass.	Massachusetts	—	Massachusetts
Md., MD	Maryland	—	Maryland
M.D.	Doctor of Medicine	—	doctor de medicina
Me., ME	Maine	—	Maine
Mex.	Mexican, Mexico	**Méx.**	mexicano, México
mg	milligram	**mg.**	miligramo
mi.	mile	—	milla
MI, Mich.	Michigan	—	Michigan
min.	minute	**min**	minuto
Minn.	Minnesota	—	Minnesota
Miss.	Mississippi	—	Mississippi, Misisipí
ml	mililiter	**ml.**	mililitro
mm	millimeter	**mm.**	milímetro
MN	Minnesota	—	Minnesota
mo.	month	—	mes
Mo., MO	Missouri	—	Missouri
Mon.	Monday	**lun.**	lunes
Mont.	Montana	—	Montana
mpg	miles per gallon	—	millas por galón
mph	miles per hour	—	millas por hora
MS	Mississippi	—	Mississippi, Misisipí
mt.	mount, mountain	—	monte, montaña
MT	Montana	—	Montana
mtn.	mountain	—	montaña
N	North, north	**N**	Norte, norte
NASA	National Aeronautics and Space Administration	—	—
NC	North Carolina	—	Carolina del Norte, North Carolina
ND, N. Dak.	North Dakota	—	Dakota del Norte, North Dakota
NE	northeast	**NE**	nordeste
NE, Neb., Nebr.	Nebraska	—	Nebraska
Nev.	Nevada	—	Nevada
NH	New Hampshire	—	New Hampshire
NJ	New Jersey	—	Nueva Jersey, New Jersey
NM., N. Mex.	New Mexico	—	Nuevo México, New Mexico
no.	north	**N**	norte
no.	number	**n.º**	número
Nov.	November	**nov.**	noviembre
N.T.	New Testament	**N.T.**	Nuevo Testamento

ENGLISH ABBREVIATION AND EXPANSION		SPANISH EQUIVALENT	
NV	Nevada	—	Nevada
NW	northwest	**NO**	noroeste
NY	New York	**NY**	Nueva York, New York
O	Ohio	—	Ohio
Oct.	October	**oct.**	octubre
OH	Ohio	—	Ohio
OK, Okla.	Oklahoma	—	Oklahoma
OR, Ore., Oreg.	Oregon	—	Oregon
O.T.	Old Testament	**A.T.**	Antiguo Testamento
oz.	ounce, ounces	—	onza, onzas
p.	page	**p.**	página
Pa., PA	Pennsylvania	—	Pennsylvania, Pensilvania
pat.	patent	**pat.**	patente
PD	police department	—	departamento de policía
PE	physical education	—	educación física
Penn., Penna.	Pennsylvania	—	Pennsylvania, Pensilvania
pg.	page	**pág.**	página
PhD	Doctor of Philosophy	—	doctor, -tora (en filosofía)
pkg.	package	—	paquete
p.m., PM	post meridiem (afternoon)	**p.m.**	post meridiem (de la tarde)
P.O.	post office	—	oficina de correos, correo
pp.	pages	**págs.**	páginas
PR	Puerto Rico	**PR**	Puerto Rico
pres.	present	—	presente
pres.	president		presidente, -ta
prof.	professor	—	profesor, -sora
P.S.	postscript	**P.D.**	postdata
P.S.	public school	—	escuela pública
pt.	pint	—	pinta
pt.	point	**pto.**	punto
PTA	Parent-Teacher Association	—	—
PTO	Parent-Teacher Organization	—	—
q, qt.	quart	—	cuarto de galón
r.	right	**dcha.**	derecha
rd.	road	**c/, C/**	calle
RDA	recommended daily allowance	—	consumo diario recomendado
recd.	received	—	recibido
Rev.	reverend	**Rdo.**	reverendo
RI	Rhode Island	—	Rhode Island
rpm	revolutions per minute	**r.p.m.**	revoluciones por minuto
RR	railroad	**FC**	ferrocarril

ENGLISH ABBREVIATION AND EXPANSION		SPANISH EQUIVALENT	
R.S.V.P	please reply (répondez s'il vous plaît)	**S.R.C.**	se ruega contestación
rt.	right	**dcha.**	derecha
rte.	route	—	ruta
S	small	**P**	(talla) pequeña
S	South, south	**S**	Sur, sur
S.A.	South America	—	Sudamérica, América del Sur
Sat.	Saturday	**sáb.**	sábado
SC	South Carolina	—	Carolina del Sur, South Carolina
SD, S. Dak.	South Dakota	—	Dakota del Sur, South Dakota
SE	southeast	**SE**	sudeste, sureste
Sept.	September	**sep., sept.**	septiembre
so.	south	**S**	sur
sq.	square		cuadrado
Sr.	Senior	**Sr.**	Sénior
Sr.	sister (*in religion*)	—	sor
st.	state	—	estado
st.	street	**c/, C/**	calle
St.	saint	**S., Sto., Sta.**	santo, santa
Sun.	Sunday	**dom.**	domingo
SW	southwest	**SO**	sudoeste, suroeste
t.	teaspoon	—	cucharadita
T, tb., tbsp.	tablespoon	—	cucharada (grande)
Tenn.	Tennessee	—	Tennessee
Tex.	Texas	—	Texas
Thu., Thur., Thurs.	Thursday	**juev.**	jueves
TM	trademark	—	marca (de un producto)
TN	Tennessee	—	Tennessee
tsp.	teaspoon	—	cucharadita
Tue., Tues.	Tuesday	**mart.**	martes
TX	Texas	—	Texas
UN	United Nations	**NU, NN.UU.**	Naciones Unidas
US	United States	**EEUU, EE.UU.**	Estados Unidos
USA	United States of America	**EEUU, EE.UU.**	Estados Unidos de América
usu.	usually	—	usualmente
UT	Utah	—	Utah
v.	versus	**v**	versus
Va., VA	Virginia	—	Virginia
vol.	volume	**vol.**	volumen
VP	vice president	—	vicepresidente, -ta
vs.	versus	**v**	versus
Vt., VT	Vermont	—	Vermont

ENGLISH ABBREVIATION AND EXPANSION		SPANISH EQUIVALENT	
W	West, west	**O**	Oeste, oeste
WA, Wash.	Washington (state)	—	Washington
Wed.	Wednesday	**miérc.**	miércoles
WI, Wis., Wisc.	Wisconsin	—	Wisconsin
wt.	weight	—	peso
WV, W. Va.	West Virginia	—	Virginia del Oeste, West Virginia
WY, Wyo.	Wyoming	—	Wyoming
yd.	yard	—	yarda
yr.	year	—	año

Metric System : Conversions
Sistema métrico : conversiones

Length

unit	number of meters	approximate U.S. equivalents	
millimeter	0.001	0.039	inch
centimeter	0.01	0.39	inch
meter	1	39.37	inches
kilometer	1,000	0.62	mile

Longitud

unidad	número de metros	equivalentes aproximados de los EE.UU.	
milímetro	0.001	0.039	pulgada
centímetro	0.01	0.39	pulgada
metro	1	39.37	pulgadas
kilómetro	1,000	0.62	milla

Area

unit	number of square meters	approximate U.S. equivalents	
square centimeter	0.0001	0.155	square inch
square meter	1	10.764	square feet
hectare	10,000	2.47	acres
square kilometer	1,000,000	0.3861	square mile

Superficie

unidad	número de metros cuadrados	equivalentes aproximados de los EE.UU.	
centímetro cuadrado	0.0001	0.155	pulgada cuadrada
metro cuadrado	1	10.764	pies cuadrados
hectárea	10,000	2.47	acres
kilómetro cuadrado	1,000,000	0.3861	milla cuadrada

Volume

unit	number of cubic meters	approximate U.S. equivalents	
cubic centimeter	0.000001	0.061	cubic inch
cubic meter	1	1.307	cubic yards

Volumen

unidad	número de metros cúbicos	equivalentes aproximados de los EE.UU	
centímetro cúbico	0.000001	0.061	pulgada cúbica
metro cúbico	1	1.307	yardas cúbicas

Capacity

unit	number of liters	approximate U.S. equivalents		
		CUBIC	DRY	LIQUID
liter	1	61.02 cubic inches	0.908 quart	1.057 quarts

Capacidad

unidad	número de litros	equivalentes aproximados de los EE.UU.		
		CÚBICO	SECO	LIQUIDO
litro	1	61.02 pulgadas cúbicas	0.908 cuarto	1.057 cuartos

Mass and Weight

unit	number of grams	approximate U.S. equivalents	
milligram	0.001	0.015	grain
centigram	0.01	0.154	grain
gram	1	0.035	ounce
kilogram	1,000	2.2046	pounds
metric ton	1,000,000	1.102	short tons

Masa y peso

unidad	número de gramos	equivalentes aproximados de los EE.UU.	
miligramo	0.001	0.015	grano
centigramo	0.01	0.154	grano
gramo	1	0.035	onza
kilogramo	1.000	2.2046	libras
tonelada métrica	1,000,000	1.102	toneladas cortas

Nations of the World
Naciones del mundo

Africa/África

ENGLISH	SPANISH
Algeria	Argelia
Angola	Angola
Benin	Benin
Botswana	Botswana, Botsuana
Burkina Faso	Burkina Faso
Burundi	Burundi
Cameroon	Camerún
Cape Verde	Cabo Verde
Central African Republic	República Centroafricana
Chad	Chad
Comoro Islands	Islas Comores, Comoras
Congo	Congo
Democratic Republic of Congo	República Democrática del Congo
Djibouti	Djibouti, Djibuti
Egypt	Egipto
Equatorial Guinea	Guinea Ecuatorial
Eritrea	Eritrea
Ethiopia	Etiopía
Gabon	Gabón
Gambia	Gambia
Ghana	Ghana
Guinea	Guinea
Guinea-Bissau	Guinea-Bissau
Ivory Coast	Costa de Marfil
Kenya	Kenya, Kenia
Lesotho	Lesotho, Lesoto
Liberia	Liberia
Libya	Libia
Madagascar	Madagascar
Malawi	Malawi, Malaui
Mali	Malí
Mauritania	Mauritania
Mauritius	Mauricio
Morocco	Marruecos
Mozambique	Mozambique
Namibia	Namibia
Niger	Níger
Nigeria	Nigeria
Rwanda	Ruanda, Rwanda
São Tomé and Principe	Santo Tomé y Príncipe
Senegal	Senegal
Seychelles	Seychelles
Sierra Leone	Sierra Leona
Somalia	Somalia
South Africa, Republic of	Sudáfrica, República de
Sudan	Sudán
Swaziland	Suazilandia, Swazilandia
Tanzania	Tanzanía, Tanzania
Togo	Togo

ENGLISH	SPANISH
Tunisia	Túnez
Uganda	Uganda
Zambia	Zambia
Zimbabwe	Zimbabwe, Zimbábue

Antarctica/Antártida

No independent countries
No tiene países independientes

Asia/Asia

Afghanistan	Afganistán
Armenia	Armenia
Azerbaijan	Azerbaiyán, Azerbaiján
Bahrain	Bahrein
Bangladesh	Bangladesh
Bhutan	Bhután, Bután
Brunei	Brunei
Cambodia	Camboya
China	China
Cyprus	Chipre
Georgia, Republic of	Georgia
India	India
Indonesia	Indonesia
Iran	Irán
Iraq	Iraq, Irak
Israel	Israel
Japan	Japón
Jordan	Jordania
Kazakhstan	Kazajstán
Korea, North	Corea del Norte
Korea, South	Corea del Sur
Kuwait	Kuwait
Kyrgyzstan	Kirguistán, Kirguizistán
Laos	Laos
Lebanon	Líbano
Malaysia	Malasia
Maldive Islands	Maldivas
Mongolia	Mongolia
Myanmar	Myanmar
Nepal	Nepal
Oman	Omán
Pakistan	Pakistán
Philippines	Filipinas
Qatar	Qatar
Saudi Arabia	Arabia Saudita, Arabia Saudí
Singapore	Singapur
Sri Lanka	Sri Lanka
Syria	Siria
Taiwan	Taiwán
Tajikistan	Tayikistán
Thailand	Tailandia
Turkey	Turquía
Turkmenistan	Turkmenistán
United Arab Emirates	Emiratos Árabes Unidos
Uzbekistan	Uzbekistán
Vietnam	Vietnam
Yemen	Yemen

Europe/Europa

ENGLISH	SPANISH
Albania	Albania
Andorra	Andorra
Austria	Austria
Belarus	Belarús
Belgium	Bélgica
Bosnia and Herzegovina	Bosnia y Hercegovina, Bosnia y Herzegovina
Bulgaria	Bulgaria
Croatia	Croacia
Czech Republic	República Checa
Denmark	Dinamarca
Estonia	Estonia
Finland	Finlandia
France	Francia
Germany	Alemania
Greece	Grecia
Hungary	Hungría
Iceland	Islandia
Ireland	Irlanda
Italy	Italia
Latvia	Letonia
Liechtenstein	Liechtenstein
Lithuania	Lituania
Luxembourg	Luxemburgo
Macedonia	Macedonia
Malta	Malta
Moldavia	Moldavia
Monaco	Mónaco
Netherlands	Países Bajos
Norway	Noruega
Poland	Polonia
Portugal	Portugal
Romania	Rumania, Rumanía
Russian Federation	Federación de Rusia
San Marino	San Marino
Slovakia	Eslovaquia
Slovenia	Eslovenia
Spain	España
Sweden	Suecia
Switzerland	Suiza
Ukraine	Ucrania
United Kingdom	Reino Unido
Vatican City	Ciudad del Vaticano
Yugoslavia	Yugoslavia

North America/Norteamérica

ENGLISH	SPANISH
Antigua and Barbuda	Antigua y Barbuda
Bahamas	Bahamas
Barbados	Barbados
Belize	Belice
Bermuda	Bermudas
Canada	Canadá
Costa Rica	Costa Rica
Cuba	Cuba
Dominica	Dominica
Dominican Republic	República Dominicana

ENGLISH	SPANISH
El Salvador	El Salvador
Grenada	Granada
Guatemala	Guatemala
Haiti	Haití
Honduras	Honduras
Jamaica	Jamaica
Mexico	México, Méjico
Nicaragua	Nicaragua
Panama	Panamá
Saint Kitts-Nevis	Saint Kitts y Nevis
Saint Lucia	Santa Lucía
Saint Vincent and the Grenadines	San Vicente y las Granadinas
Trinidad and Tobago	Trinidad y Tobago
United States of America	Estados Unidos de América

Oceania/Oceanía

ENGLISH	SPANISH
Australia	Australia
Fiji	Fiji
Kiribati	Kiribati
Marshall Islands	Islas Marshall
Nauru	Nauru
New Zealand	Nueva Zelanda, Nueva Zelandia
Papua New Guinea	Papua Nueva Guinea
Soloman Islands	Islas Salomón
Tonga	Tonga
Tuvalu	Tuvalu
Vanuatu	Vanuatu
Western Samoa	Samoa del Oeste

South America/Sudamérica

ENGLISH	SPANISH
Argentina	Argentina
Bolivia	Bolivia
Brazil	Brasil
Chile	Chile
Colombia	Colombia
Ecuador	Ecuador
Guyana	Guyana
Paraguay	Paraguay
Peru	Perú
Suriname	Surinam
Uruguay	Uruguay
Venezuela	Venezuela

Sample Correspondence
Ejemplos de correspondencia

1. Correspondence in Spanish

a. Appointment Confirmation

Western Booksellers, Inc.
One Maywell Street
Beverly, MA 01915
Telephone: 617-414-5252

12 de enero de 19--

Sr. Francisco Pérez Martínez
Editores Internacionales S.A. de C.V.
Independencia No. 322
Col. Juárez
06050 MEXICO D.F.

Estimado Sr. Pérez:

De acuerdo con lo convenido en nuestra conversación teléfonica, quisiera mediante la presente confirmar nuestra próxima reunión, fijada para el jueves, 29 de enero, a las diez de la mañana. Nuestra oficina en Maywell está ubicada en la zona comercial principal, así que le será relativamente fácil de encontrar. Si tuviera alguna dificultad no dude en ponerse en contacto con nosotros.

A la espera de sus prontas noticias, lo saluda atentamente

James Michaels
Chief Executive Officer

b. Order

LaPrade Industries
42 Grove Street
Rockland, IL 61107
815-327-0605

8 de noviembre de 19--

Figueroa e Hijos S.A.
Calle San Bernardo, 15 - 3º- C
33204 GIJON

Estimados señores:

Les rogamos remitan urgentemente los siguientes productos a cargo de la cuenta 570:

Cantidad:	*Concepto:*	*Precio-Unidad:*	*Importe:*
4	No. 47 mesita de noche	295	1.180
2	No. 115 estantería	1.050	2.200
		Total	3.380

Rogándoles que se sirvan acusar recibo, los saluda atentamente

Roger Westfield

Roger Westfield

c. Request for Information

Pine Hill Gourmet Foods, Inc.
608 South Street
Shreveport, LA 71118
Telephone (123) 123-4567

22 de junio de 19--

Antonio Valle y Cía
Calle 29 No. 2867
Casilla de Correos 238
7600 MAR DEL PLATA
Pcia. de Buenos Aires

Estimados señores:

Les rogamos que se sirvan remitirnos información completa sobre su surtido de cafés y productos de confitería. Tenemos interés en vender sus productos a través de nuestro catálogo, así que les agradeceríamos que incluyeran una lista de precios al por mayor.

Los saluda atentamente

Jane Conner

d. Job Application

Inés Ruiz G.
Calle 89, 14A-22
MARACAIBO 4001, Edo. Zulia

10 de marzo de 19--

Sra. María Suárez
Productos Estrella
Edif. Bolívar, Piso 7, Of. 3-A
Av. Madrid No. 322
Urb. Las Mercedes
CARACAS 0160, D.F.

Estimada Sra. Suárez

Respondiendo a su anuncio que apareció en *El Sol* del 7 de marzo en el cual solicitan un agente comercial bilingüe, tengo el placer de ofrecerle mis servicios.

Como puede apreciarse en el currículum vitae adjunto, tengo cuatro años de experiencia como agente comercial. Además, hablo tanto inglés como español con fluidez, y tengo conocimientos básicos de japonés y alemán.

Quedo a su entera disposición para proveer más información y referencias si así fuera necesario.

Muy atentamente

Inés Ruiz G.

Inés Ruiz G.

e. Thank-you

Productos Vásquez, S.A.
Sarmiento 1337, 8º P. "C"
1041 BUENOS AIRES

8 de octubre de 19--

Sr. Juan Pérez García
Av. Providencia Nº 920, Of. 12
Las Condes
SANTIAGO 10

Estimado Sr. Pérez:

Fue un placer comunicarme con usted la semana pasada para solicitarle información. Su cortesía y seriedad me causaron muy buena impresión, y me sorprendió muy gratamente la celeridad con la que me envió la información solicitada.

Agradeciéndole la prontitud de sus gestiones queda de usted su servidor.

Muy atentamente,

Ramón Vásquez

2. Correspondencia en inglés

a. Confirmación de una cita

CSC BUSINESS SOFTWARE
666 Fifth Avenue, Suite 1810
New York, NY 10036
212-876-5432

April 17, 19--

Dr. Arne Grondahl
Internasjonalt Forlag A/S
Postboks 19—Sentrum
0101 Oslo 1

Dear Dr. Grondahl:

Charles St. Cyr has asked me to confirm your luncheon meeting with him and a representative of Third Millennium at 12:30 on Friday, May 2. The Thai Monsoon Restaurant, located in the Metropolis Hotel at 29 West 49th Street, is convenient to numerous midtown offices and the prime shopping and entertainment districts, and you should have no trouble finding it. You will be Mr. St. Cyr's guest for lunch.

I am enclosing a map of the New York City area for your convenience.

Sincerely,

Jan Jordan
Secretary to Mr. St. Cyr

Enclosure

b. Pedido

Rodriguez Manufacturers, Inc.
333 West 145th Street
New York, NY 10031
Telephone: 212-598-1534

December 3, 19--

Mr. Ted Munson, Manager
Allen & Allen, Inc.
44 Hudson Drive
Elizabeth, NJ 07202

Dear Mr. Munson:

Please accept this order for immediate shipment to our Wood Products Division, 2255 West 189th Street, New York, NY, and charge to our account no. 8189:

Quantity:	*Description:*	*Unit Price:*	*Total:*
1800	No. 202 T Hinges, Brass Plate	$1.50 pr	$2,700
600	No. 78 Corner Braces, Brass Plate	1.75 ea	1,050
		Total	$3,750

Any assistance you can give in expediting this order will be greatly appreciated, as a recent flurry or orders has depleted our stock.

Sincerely,

Adrienne Barstow

Adrienne Barstow
Purchasing Agent

c. Solicitud de información

Acme Equipment Company
42 Grove Street
Rockford, IL 61107
815-327-0605

February 17, 19--

Ms. Linda Thomas
Laprade Industries
1525 State Street
Cleveland, OH 44140

Dear Ms. Thomas:

We are currently planning to add yard and garden tractors to our line of leased equipment. It is my pleasure to announce that we shall feature Harris Tractors.

Would you please send us a complete list of models and specifications for Harris Tractors. It would be helpful to have the following data by April 30:

1. Horsepower
2. Range of job function
3. Commercial or homeowner equipment
4. Contract samples
5. Sales terms

Since the publication date for our catalog is slated for May, your early reply will be appreciated.

Sincerely yours,

Thomas Domizio
Marketing Manager

d. Solicitud de trabajo

Albert Conner
3 Ternure Avenue
Suffern, NY 10901

August 8, 19--

Ms. Jane Atkins
Barnham & Riley, Inc.
5 Astor Place
New York, NY 10003

Dear Ms. Atkins:

Your advertisement in *The New York Times* for an administrative assistant is of great interest to me. I have spent five years as Executive Secretary to the Vice President for Marketing at Marc Bros. and have all the qualifications you're seeking.

As you can see from the enclosed resume, my background includes strong computer skills. I have worked extensively with several popular word-processing programs, and have had the primary responsibility for producing newsletters and overhead slide presentations. I have a working knowledge of several spreadsheet programs, as well as basic bookkeeping skills.

Should you find my background meets your needs, I would appreciate the opportunity for a personal interview to discuss the contribution I can make to your company.

Sincerely,

Albert Conner

Albert Conner

Enc.

e. Carta de agradecimiento

Fairfield Textiles Company
71 Santa Maria Blvd.
Los Angeles, CA 90027
Tel: (213) 455-5222

January 2, 19--

Ms. Barbara Raycroft
Fairfield Textiles Company
4860 South Beach Drive
Palo Alto, CA 94303

Dear Barbara:

Thank you very much for all the kind hospitality that you showed to me during my stay in Palo Alto. I thoroughly enjoyed the tour of our Palo Alto plant, and I was glad to finally have the opportunity to meet you and your staff in person.

I certainly hope to see you again at this year's sales meeting. And again, many thanks for making my trip such a pleasant one.

Sincerely,

Michelle Sharma